# The Complete
# Directory for
# People with Disabilities

# 2007

## Fifteenth Edition

# The Complete
# Directory for
# People with Disabilities

A Comprehensive
Source Book for
Individuals and Professionals

A SEDGWICK PRESS Book

Grey House
Publishing

| | |
|---|---|
| PUBLISHER: | Leslie Mackenzie |
| EDITORIAL DIRECTOR: | Laura Mars-Proietti |
| PRODUCTION MANAGER: | Karen Stevens |
| PRODUCTION ASSISTANT: | Stephanie Capozzi, Karynn, Kettinq, Sharon Moskiewicz, Erica Schneider |
| EDITORIAL ASSISTANT: | Jane Murphy |
| MARKETING DIRECTOR: | Jessica Moody |

A Sedgwick Press Book
Grey House Publishing, Inc.
185 Millerton Road
Millerton, NY 12546
518.789.8700
FAX 518.789.0545
www.greyhouse.com
e-mail: books @greyhouse.com

First edition published 1991
Fifteenth edition published 2006

The complete directory for people with disabilities : products, resources, books, services.—1992-2005
1022p.; 29cm

Other title: Directory for people with disabilities
Title varies.
Annual

1. People with disabilities—Services for—United States—Directories. 2. People with disabilities—Services for—United States—Periodicals. 3. Disabled Persons—United States—Bibliography. 4. Disabled Persons—United States—Directory. 5. Information Services—United States—Bibliography. 6. Information Services—United States—Directory. 7. Mental Retardation—Rehabilitation—United States—Bibliography. 8. Mental Retardation—Rehabilitation—United States—Directory. 9. Rehabilitation—United States—Bibliography. 10. Rehabilitation—United States—Directory. I. Title: Directory for people with disabilities.
HV1553.C58
362.4/048/02573                                                                                    92-658843
Printed in the USA
ISBN 10: 1-59237-147-7    ISBN 13: 978-1-59237-147-1    softcover

# Table of Contents

**Introduction**

*It's Your Career: Work-Based Learning Opportunities for College Students with Disabilities*
*Taking Charge: Stories of Success and Self-Determination*
*Glossary of Disability-Related Terms*

# Introduction

Welcome to the fifteenth edition of *The Complete Directory for People with Disabilities*. Since the first edition in 1991, the number of disabled Americans has increased dramatically. The 1990 US census estimated between 35 and 45 million disabled Americans. The 2000 US Census estimates nearly 50 million. Studies suggest several reasons for this growth, including an aging population, improved survival rate for many conditions, growing awareness of new syndromes, and the ADA's broad definition of the disabled population.

On the other hand, the strengthened commitment of physicians, healthcare workers, and disabled individuals and their families that enables this community to participate as fully as possible in school, work and social settings, suggests to some that the number of disabled individuals has actually decreased in the last decade.

Whichever side of the fence you're on, the widely acclaimed *Complete Directory for People with Disabilities* is an invaluable resource for all those committed to empowering disabled individuals. It contains thousands of resources, products and services for people with vision and hearing impairments, learning difficulties, and physical conditions. Coverage extends from Associations to Publications to Products that enable and enhance the lifestyle of people with disabilities. Listings include Camps, Living Facilities, Print and Electronic Resources and much more. The comprehensive Table of Contents is your guide through the 27 chapters and more than 100 subchapters contained in this rich resource.

We utilized many resources to update these listings, including fax campaigns, the Internet and telephone research. This 2007 edition contains 6,795 listings with descriptions and key contacts, 6,102 fax numbers, 5,254 e-mail addresses and 6,049 web sites. This detailed directory includes ways for people with disabilities to successfully live side by side with the non-disabled population, in school, at work and in social settings.

In addition to the 6,795 listings, this edition includes valuable educational articles for the disabled community and all who support them. Following this Introduction you'll find the following documents from DO-IT at the University of Washington:

1. *It's Your Career: Work-Based Learning Opportunities for College Students with Disabilities*
2. *Taking Charge: Stories of Success and Self-Determination*
3. *Glossary of Disability-Related Terms.*

*The Complete Directory for People with Disabilities* was developed, as stated in the first edition, "to provide a single information resource for people with disabilities, their families, friends, and the professionals that help them." Our mission has not changed, and our success is due in large part to the educators, librarians and the disability community who have come to depend on this directory, and who continue to send us new information and editorial feedback. Their cooperation and support are largely responsible for the strength of this directory.

We are confident that this resource will save hours of research time. Information on disabilities continues to be scattered, and searching the Internet is time consuming with results that are often overwhelming and unedited. *The Complete Directory for People with Disabilities* provides comprehensive, critical and immediate information in just one source that can be accessed quickly and easily.

This edition includes three indexes to provide quick, easy access to its 6,795 listings:

**Disability & Subject Index**: Organized alphabetically by hundreds of topics relevant to people with disabilities, this index groups together all listings on a particular subject (i.e., autism or language disorders), regardless of type.

**Entry Index**: This alphabetical list of all entries saves time searching for an organization or group that may be repeated in several chapters.

**Geographic Index:** Organizes listings alphabetically by state.

*The Complete Directory for People with Disabilities* is also available as an Online Database, as well as in a customized, downloadable database.

Other health resource titles by Grey House include *The Complete Learning Disabilities Directory, The Complete Directory for People with Chronic Illness* and *The Complete Mental Health Directory.* Available soon is *The Grey House Rare Disorders Directory,* with comprehensive data on more than 700 rare health disorders.

As always, we welcome your comments, and look forward to another year of serving the disability community.

# It's Your Career:  Work-Based Learning Opportunities for College Students With Disabilities

**DO·IT** | **How Students can Prepare for Career Success**

Most students expect to work after college graduation. However, your job search shouldn't begin when you graduate. Career planning and preparation should occur throughout your college studies. You do not need to settle on one area to pursue right away, and you can change directions. But, be sure to prepare for the long run – for your lifelong career or multiple careers.

There is a myth that if you have a college degree, you have a job. The fact is that approximately twenty percent of college graduates are unemployed. It takes the average college graduate three to six months to secure employment after graduation. You need a career seeking strategy and a little experience. Otherwise, you're likely to be just another résumé in a stack of hundreds.

As a future employee, a college student with a disability faces unique challenges. Like other students, you need to find a way to meet the specific qualifications of the desired job. You also need to demonstrate that you have transferable skills – in other words, skills you've acquired through education and previous work experiences that can transfer to a new employment situation. Transferable skills include communication, trouble-shooting, decision-making, leadership, and problem-solving. These are some of the skills that cross jobs, careers, and industries. Opportunities to acquire these skills are available at campuses nationwide.

## Why Participate in Work-Based Learning?

Work-based learning experiences can help a student choose careers, network with potential employers, select courses of study, and develop job skills directly relevant to future employment. Through the interaction of study and work experience, you can enhance your academic knowledge, personal development, and professional preparation. Specifically, work-based learning opportunities can help you:

- Clarify academic and career interests.
- Pay for your education.
- Gain academic credit.
- Apply practical theories from classroom work.
- Develop human relations skills through interaction with co-workers.
- Gain exposure to specialized facilities not available on campus.
- Develop job-search skills.
- Develop résumés and cover letters.
- Identify career assistance programs.
- Develop contacts for employment after graduation.

As a student with a disability, work-based learning can also give you a chance to practice disclosing your disability and requesting accommodations from potential employers while determining which accommodations work best for you.

Many colleges offer programs that help students gain work experience before graduation. Programs vary from campus to campus. You will

## CAREERS

**C**areers,

**A**cademics,

**R**esearch,

**E**xperiential

**E**ducation, and

**R**elevant

**S**kills

need to do some research to find those best suited to you. Work-based learning options found at many postsecondary institutions include internships, cooperative education, job shadowing, service learning, independent study, informational interviews, and career services. Below are descriptions of typical services these programs offer.

## What is an Internship?

An internship is a time-limited intensive learning experience outside of the traditional classroom. You are placed in a supervised work-based learning situation with employers for planned learning activities. Internships give you broad overviews of occupational fields, while providing opportunities to experience work responsibilities and develop work-readiness skills. College credit may be provided depending on your academic program.

## What is Cooperative Education?

Cooperative education programs work with students, faculty, staff, and employers to help students clarify career and academic goals, and expand classroom study by participating in paid, practical work experiences. These programs provide opportunities to work in trainee positions in your fields of interest and to gain career-related experience as a part of your academic programs. Academic credit may be arranged.

## What is Job Shadowing?

Job shadowing, where you visit a business to observe one or more positions, provides you with a realistic view of one or more occupations. You observe essential functions of occupational areas of interest. Experiences vary in time from one hour to a full day depending on the amount of time employers can provide as well as your level of interest. Job shadowing experiences offer opportunities for career exploration. However, they do not typically generate academic credit.

## What is Service Learning?

Service learning programs offer students opportunities to become concerned, informed and productive citizens by providing community service in non-paid, volunteer positions. These programs increase the relevancy of academic learning by giving you opportunities to apply knowledge and skills while making contributions to your local community. Academic credit may or may not be arranged depending on your field of study.

## What is an Independent Study?

It is often possible for students to earn academic credit for work experiences outside of a structured career-based program. Many academic programs allow independent studies as optional program components. If you choose to take this option, you would work one-on-one with an individual faculty member to develop projects for credit. Projects can range from research papers to work experience within your field of study. Work experience, coupled with documentation, such as a journal or paper, is an excellent way to practice and demonstrate the skills you've learned in college.

## What is an Informational Interview?

Informational interviews, where you meet with people working in your chosen careers to ask questions about particular occupations or companies, allow you to gain personal perspectives on your career interests. Through informational interviews you can learn more about your career interests from the people who work in the field every day. Those experiences do not typically generate academic credit.

## What is Career Services?

A career services office provides a variety of career and job search services to students and alumni. It acts as a liaison between students, alumni, faculty, staff, and prospective employers by organizing campus interviews, employer information and career fairs. Many career services offices also provide job listings and job lines for students and alumni to access in their search for employment. Some help students develop career plans and job search skills through individual counseling and job search workshops.

## Which Employers Participate?

Federal and state agencies and public, private and nonprofit businesses seek college students for placements across the country and overseas. The majority of opportunities are for sophomores and above, but some employers also offer opportunities to freshmen and high school students as well. Microsoft, Boeing, USDA Forest Service,

Weyerhaeuser, IBM, NASA, U.S. Department of Energy, U.S. Central Intelligence Agency and the President's Committee on Employment of People with Disabilities are just a few of the thousands of employers nationwide who offer valuable work-based learning opportunities to students.

## Who are the Team Players?

Many work-based learning opportunity providers are committed to assisting all students, including students with disabilities, as they prepare to enter the professional world. If you are...

**A college student with a disability:**
- Register with campus work-based learning programs, such as career services and cooperative education, so they can notify you of work-based learning opportunities.
- Participate in available orientations, seminars, workshops, and individual counseling sessions to effectively enhance your job search skills.
- Let the work-based learning and disabled student services coordinators know what types of accommodations you may need to effectively perform in a work setting.
- Access local support networks and disability services organizations that may be able to aid you in your job search.

**An employer:**
- Update your position announcements and notify work-based learning coordinators of new positions.
- Work in partnership with work-based learning centers to proactively develop strategies to encourage students with disabilities to participate in your work environment.
- Educate your staff regarding diversity.

**A faculty member, staff, teacher, or counselor:**
- Encourage students with disabilities to gain work experiences.
- Invite staff members from cooperative education, career services and other campus programs to speak to your classes.
- Encourage employers to recruit students with disabilities for work opportunities.

**Disabled Student Services:**
- Encourage students to register and participate in work-based learning programs on campus.
- Be proactive in students' academic and career plans. Let them know how accommodations are provided in the workplace.
- Help campus work-based learning programs recruit and accommodate students with disabilities.

## Resources

You can learn more about work-based learning opportunities, job search skills, employers, legal issues of employment, and career planning at the following Web sites.

- DO-IT CAREERS
  *http://www.washington.edu/doit/Careers/*
- ADA Technical Assistance
  *http://www.adata.org/*
- Career Builder
  *http://www.careerbuilder.com/*
- Career Resource Center
  *http://www.careers.org/*
- Careerfile
  *http://www.careerfile.com/*
- Entry Point
  *http://www.entrypoint.org/*
- Job Access
  *http://www.jobaccess.org/*
- Job Accommodation Network
  *http://janweb.icdi.wvu.edu/*
- Job Net
  *http://www.westga.edu/~coop/index.html*
- Monster.com
  *http://www.monster.com/*
- Occupational Outlook Handbook
  *http://stats.bls.gov/oco/*
- The Riley Guide
  *http://www.dbm.com/jobguide/*

# Taking Charge: Stories of Success and Self-Determination

**DO·IT**    By Sheryl Burgstahler, Ph.D.

We often hear about the problems young people with disabilities face – physical obstacles, social rejection, academic failure, and medical crises. Yet some people do overcome significant challenges and lead successful lives. What does "success" mean to them and how do they achieve it? What internal characteristics do these individuals possess and what external factors have been present in their lives? What advice do they have to help young people build personal strengths to overcome the challenges they no doubt will face?

Included in this brochure are insights from successful young people and adults with disabilities associated with the DO-IT project. These insights may help young people learn to lead self-determined lives. But, what is self-determination? There are many definitions to choose from. The following definition is concise and incorporates a number of common themes found in other definitions.

> *Self-determination is a combination of skills, knowledge, and beliefs that enable a person to engage in goal-directed, self-regulated, autonomous behavior. An understanding of one's strengths and limitations together with a belief in oneself as capable and effective are essential to self-determination. When acting on the basis of these skills and attitudes, individuals have greater ability to take control of their lives and assume the role of successful adults.* (Field et al., 1998, p. 115)

Gaining control over your life involves learning and then successfully applying a number of self-determination skills, such as goal-setting, understanding your abilities and disabilities, problem-solving, and self-advocacy. The personal process of learning, using, and self-evaluating these skills in a variety of settings is at the heart of self-determination.

The content of this publication is organized around the following advice synthesized from hundreds of responses of the successful young people and adults with disabilities who contributed:

1) Define success for yourself.
2) Set personal, academic, and career goals. Keep your expectations high.
3) Understand your abilities and disabilities. Play to your strengths.
4) Develop strategies to meet your goals.
5) Use technology as an empowering tool.
6) Work hard. Persevere. Be flexible.
7) Develop a support network. Look to family, friends, and teachers.

Perhaps young people with disabilities will find the experiences of others useful as they set their course toward successful, self-determined lives.

## Define success for yourself.

People define success in many ways. Several successful people with disabilities use these words:

- *Success is defined by who we are, what we believe in, and what we think it means to be "successful." For some it is money; for others, relationships; for others, it's family; for others, it's jobs, for some it is religion, and for others it is education. I believe that success is reaching my own personal dreams. I'm not done with my dreams, but know that I have been successful so far because I've worked toward my goals regardless of my disability. (college student who is deaf)*

- *Success is possessing the capability for self-determination. Self determination is the ability to decide what I want to do with my life, and then to act on that decision. (high school student who is blind)*

- *A successful life is one where I can be actively engaged in creative activities that make a contribution to the lives of others. Success is a kind of bi-product and NOT an end in itself!* (professor who is blind)
- *To me, having a successful life is being able to do things independently for myself, and not always have someone there to do things for me. It's achieving my goals on my own terms and at my own pace.* (high school student with mobility/orthopedic impairment)

## Set personal, academic, and career goals. Keep your expectations high.

Successful young people and adults share their views below about how they set goals and maintain high expectations:

- *A combination of people and events has helped me maintain high standards. This all started during the summer months when my mother and neighbor friend pushed me to improve my academic skills. At the time it wasn't high standards that I was working for, but rather escaping embarrassment. For me, I wanted no one to know I had a disability and would have done most anything to hide it. These summer study sessions provided a stepping stone for future success in high school and college. Success builds upon itself. This was my start to expecting to do well in school.*
- *I'm just stubborn and I refuse to lower my expectations.* (college student with a mobility/orthopedic impairment)
- *My parents helped me maintain high expectations for myself. They taught me never to say "I can't" at anything I try.* (high school student with cerebral palsy)
- *My mobility teacher made me confident in my ability to learn, which has helped me maintain high expectations.* (college student who is blind)
- *My parents expected me to do as well as other students without disabilities, if not better. My parents actively sought help for my hearing impairment in the forms of speech therapists,* audiologists, *and teachers to make sure that I had an equal chance in public schools. Before choosing a new house, my parents did a lot of research on the local schools.* (college student who is deaf)
- *My brother and sister had one single expectation that determined my success: I was not treated differently in any way because I could not see.* (computer scientist who is blind)
- *I am still in the process of learning to "stretch" but I start by identifying what I can already do - what I am comfortable doing and feel good at. Then I say to myself (sometimes in writing) I can do more. I can do better, what is it BEYOND what I already can do that I want to be able to do? Then I write down goals or ideas and make efforts to "stretch" myself.* (adult with hearing and mobility impairments)
- *Very early on, I became the stubborn guy I am today. "Can't" wasn't in my vocabulary, which, of course, was helped by a set of parents who offered me opportunities to do most of the things everyone else did and encouraged me to set very high standards. By now, I do realize that everyone has a path in life that their unique set of talents and lack thereof gives them. I will never be mistaken for an athlete. However, knowing what talents I do have, I press myself to be the best historian/philosopher/writer that I can be.* (college student with a mobility impairment)
- *I set personal, academic, and/or career goals by knowing where my limits are and working around them. If someone says I can't do something, and I haven't tried it before, that just makes me more determined to prove that someone wrong. If I fail, at least I tried. That's what counts.* (college students with mobility impairments)
- *One of the main reasons people do not set high expectations is fear of failure.... start by having achievable goals that are not long-term. Instead, develop week long, achievable goals that lead to success. Build on each success and make each goal a little higher. Think of it as a metaphorical high jump. You cannot set the bar too high in the beginning or you just set yourself up for failure.* (adult with hearing and mobility impairments)

## Understand your abilities and disabilities. Play to your strengths.

People with disabilities who consider themselves successful generally accept their disabilities as one aspect of who they are, do not define themselves by their disabilities, recognize that they are not responsible for their disabilities, and know that they are not inherently impaired. They recognize their responsibility for their own happiness and future. Below are insights from successful people with disabilities:

- *My personal opinion about disabilities is that everyone is disabled. It just so happens that there is a certain group whose disabilities are more obvious than others. (high school student with mobility and visual impairments)*

- *My parents helped me learn to accept responsibility for myself by treating me the same as my siblings. They gave me the same punishments and chores, and they expected me to do well in school. (high school student with speech, hearing and mobility/orthopedic impairments)*

- *Do not make people feel sorry for you or pity you. Get people to view you as an able person who is capable of anything within your reach if the doors of opportunity are open. (graduate student with a hearing impairment)*

- *Clearly disabilities can be obstacles. However, they ought to be focused on as obstacles which problem solving can surmount. Sometimes, trade-offs do exist. I once wanted to go into biochemistry, but my lack of fine-motor skills and general distrust of lab partners made me realize that I wanted something I could do on my own - hence, history-philosophy. Perhaps I could have found adaptive technology to help me in biology and chemistry, but I had other loves as well, so I went for them. Admittedly, I rerouted, but for those who are determined to be biochemists and such, most obstacles can be overcome by abilities. (college student with mobility impairment)*

- *Focus on the ABILITY in disability more than the dis. If we can do that, then we are more apt to succeed. Also, know your limits. If you don't know what you can or can't do, how do you expect other people to know? Plan for success by using more of the cans than the can'ts. (college student with mobility impairment)*

## Develop strategies to meet your goals.

Successful people use creative strategies to reach their goals. They look at options and make informed decisions. Successful planning requires that you know your rights and responsibilities and strengths and challenges; set goals; work toward those goals; and use tools and resources available to you. One key skill for success is self-advocacy. Being able to self-advocate requires that a young person become an expert on their disability, know what specific services and help they need, and be able to use strategies to obtain this help and support. One's life should not be defined by the assumptions of others. Insights by successful people with disabilities are shared below.

- *There is a difference between being the recipient of an act ("victimized") and allowing yourself to become overly affected by that act - i.e., to become a "victim." (adult with mobility/orthopedic impairment)*

- *We don't have to be "victims" of other people's assumptions. We are only victims if we choose not to take charge of a situation. If you are blind and someone grabs your arm and pushes you across the street and you don't say anything, but would like to, then you are letting the other person force the result of his assumptions on you. If you, on the other hand, either say, "thank you, but I'll be fine" or "let me take your arm," depending on what you would like to do, then you are taking charge and aren't a victim. (adult who is blind)*

- *I could never achieve anything without writing things down. Sometimes I use a calendar, sometimes a blank sheet of paper or my notebook, and sometimes the computer. But without putting my plans on paper, I am not able to get things done. I use a prioritization process. I write out everything that I need to do - including the small things like getting dressed, taking medications, and riding the bus. Then I mark the things that must get done today or tomorrow as opposed to later, and I prioritize in order of importance. The list I make is constantly changing but I get a lot of satisfaction crossing off accomplished steps. It also helps me to break down larger tasks into smaller ones. I make lists, plan how to do the things on the lists, then use the lists to motivate me to get things done. Never leave home without it! (adult with mobility and hearing impairments)*

- *The more often I express my needs and preferences, the easier it becomes, and the easier it becomes, the more comfortable I am, and that makes people more comfortable, and on and on and on... and somewhere in the midst of this is the need to be both polite and clear. (adult who is deaf)*

- *The way to preempt or erase assumptions is to tell people what you need rather than let them "act out" what they think you need. It is okay to say what you need help with. I think that is part of being independent. And just by being out and about and going about your normal business you also show people what you don't need help with. (adult who is blind)*

## Use technology as an empowering tool.

Being technologically competent has become an avenue to academic and career success. Computer technology is one of the most powerful tools available to individuals with disabilities. Technology, including computers, adaptive technology and the Internet, can help maximize independence, productivity and participation. It can lead to high levels of success – personally, socially, academically, and professionally. As reported by successful individuals with disabilities:

- *The computer helps me organize my thoughts. I can read and make improvements with ease. I can check all of my papers for spelling errors before I*

*send them. I am a really BAD speller. (high school student with a learning disability)*

- *I use a combination of a palmtop note-taker computer and a desktop computer to write. Without them I'd be lost. (college student with mobility/health impairment)*

- *Without computers or the Net I would not be doing many things that I'm doing today. For instance, I am involved in a writing forum on the Net that lets writers talk about writing and share their pieces of literature with each other. Since I want to be a writer this has been VERY helpful. (high school student with a Dyslexia and Attention Deficit Disorder)*

- *One of my two or three best friends – maybe best next to my wife – and I met on the Internet, and we are not only friends but close working colleagues. (professor who is blind)*

- *Technology is not a nicety; it is a necessity. Get it, learn it and use it. (college student who is blind)*

## Work hard. Persevere. Be flexible.

Knowing and valuing yourself, setting goals, and planning help build important foundations, but action is required to make your dreams come true. To take control of your life, it is necessary to choose and take appropriate action. Take charge. Move forward. Sometimes students with disabilities need to work harder to achieve the same level of success as their peers. As reported by one student who is blind:

*I accepted the fact that I must work harder than other students to get the same grade.*

But, learning to work hard has a positive side:

*Sometimes I think that all of us with disabilities have an advantage over those who have things come easier to them. Whatever it is we want, we have to want it and then work for it. That necessary desire promotes drive to accomplish, succeed, or achieve. Others around us may be content to float, or do the minimum most of the* time, but not for us. For us, having what everybody else has is an accomplishment, and having tasted success we want to keep succeeding.

The willingness to take risks is critical to achieving success. As reported by one young person with a mobility impairment:

*I keep going when people tell me I can't. I am not afraid to try things and I don't give up. My parents took me everywhere and I did everything like a normal kid. I have a good friend from kindergarten who is able bodied, and she knows me so well that we do all sorts of stuff that people might not think I could do, but we come up with a flexible plan and we do it.*

Advice about risk taking from successful people with disabilities includes:

- *Nothing worthwhile comes without risk. Without risk, success cannot be achieved.*
- *Never give up.*
- *Do not pity yourself for what cards you have been dealt. It happened… now move on.*
- *That moment of insecurity is worth the achievement in the end. It is important to keep that in mind throughout life.*

## Develop a support network. Look to family, friends, and teachers.

Successful adults with disabilities report that they were supported in youth by opportunities for inclusion, high expectations from adults, disability-related accommodations that de-emphasized their differences, promotion of autonomy, encouragement of friendships, and support from caring adults. On the other hand, their progress was inhibited by segregation, treatment that highlighted their differences, restricted opportunities for independence, social isolation and social rejection.

Below, successful individuals with disabilities share examples of how they stay actively involved.

- *I am in my school's band and on our Youth Leadership Team. In the past, I was part of the speech team and Student Council. I think being a part of clubs has given me confidence and boosted my self-esteem. I enjoy music, and think it is an awesome feeling to be able to go out and be a part of my school's band to cheer on the sports teams and to contribute to a music concert. (college student who is blind)*
- *I have been involved in the drama club at my school. (high school student who uses a wheelchair for mobility)*
- *I have been involved in internships. They give me experiences that are needed for jobs. I've also been part of a city hall committee. This will help me know how professional life is. (college student with mobility/health impairment)*

No one achieves success alone. The comments below provide examples of how successful individuals with disabilities have found, accessed, and used resources to help them achieve success personally, socially, academically, and professionally.

- *Most of the resources I use I either found through word of mouth (from parents, friends, and others I know), from newsletters, or from the Internet. Sometimes, I find out about something useful by accident, and at other times I ask around or look on the Internet for a specific resource. I often ask others whose opinion I respect for advice, especially when I am making a making a major decision. I subscribe to a few newsletters and magazines that provide information on topics that interest me and keep lists of useful Web sites on my home page. (Ph.D. Candidate who is blind)*
- *I ask questions. (high school student with a brain injury)*
- *One of my resources is my best friend. When I take her along with me, I can tell that people who don't know me feel comfortable being around me. My friend and I think that there isn't a way that I can't be a part of what she is doing. Being with her is one of the ways I use a natural resource. (high school student with mobility/orthopedic and speech impairments)*

## Video

This brochure summarizes content that is covered in the DO-IT video, *Taking Charge: Stories of Success and Self-Determination.* The 17-minute videotape can be purchased from DO-IT. They may be freely viewed at *http://www.washington.edu/doit/Video/taking_charge.html.* Permission is granted to reproduce DO-IT videos for educational, noncommercial purposes as long as the source is acknowledged.

Grants and gifts fund DO-IT publications, videotapes, and programs to support the academic and career success of people with disabilities. Contribute today by sending a check to DO-IT, Box 355670, University of Washington, Seattle, WA 98195-5670.

*Your gift is tax deductible as specified in IRS regulations. Pursuant to RCW 19.09, the University of Washington is registered as a charitable organization with the Secretary of State, State of Washington. For more information, call the Office of the Secretary of State, 800-322-4483.*

## About DO-IT

Primary funding for DO-IT is provided by the National Science Foundation, the State of Washington, and the U.S. Department of Education. Additional grants and gifts have been received from the AOL Foundation, the Boeing Company, the Braitmayer Foundation, the Jeld-Wen Foundation, Microsoft, Mitsubishi Electric America Foundation, NEC Foundation of America, the Samuel S. Johnson Foundation, the Seattle Foundation, the Telecommunications Funding Partnership, US WEST Communications, Visio Corporation, and the Washington State Office of Superintendent of Public Instruction. Funding for the creation of this publication was provided by Mitsubishi Electric America Foundation, a non-profit foundation jointly funded by Mitsubishi Electric Corporation of Japan and its American affiliates wit the mission of contributing to a better world for us all by helping young people with disabilities, through technology, to maximize their potential and participation in society.

For more information, to be placed on the mailing list, or to request materials in an alternate format, contact:

## DO-IT

University of Washington
Box 355670
Seattle, WA 98195-5670
*doit@u.washington.edu*
*http://www.washington.edu/doit/*
206-221-4171 (FAX)
206-685-DOIT (3648) (voice/TTY)
888-972-DOIT (3648) (voice/TTY) WA, outside Seattle
509-328-9331 (voice/TTY) Spokane
Director: Sheryl Burgstahler, Ph.D.

**University of Washington**
College of Engineering
Computing & Communications
College of Education

# Glossary of Disability-Related Terms

**Accessible:** In the case of a facility, readily usable by a particular individual; in the case of a program or activity, presented or provided in such a way that a particular individual can participate, with or without auxiliary aid(s); in the case of electronic resources, accessible with or without adaptive computer technology.

**Access barriers:** Any obstruction that prevents people with disabilities from using standard facilities, equipment and resources.

**Accessible Web design:** Creating World Wide Web pages according to universal design principles to eliminate or reduce barriers, including those that affect people with disabilities.

**Accommodation:** An adjustment to make a program, facility, or resource accessible to a person with a disability.

**Adaptive technology:** Hardware or software products that provide access to a computer that is otherwise inaccessible to an individual with a disability.

**ALT attribute:** HTML code that works in combination with graphical tags to provide alternative text for graphical elements.

**Alternative keyboard:** A keyboard that is different from a standard computer keyboard in its size or layout of keys.

**Americans with Disabilities Act of 1990 (ADA):** A comprehensive federal law that prohibits discrimination on the basis of disability in employment, public services, public accommodations and services operated by private entities, and telecommunications .

**American Standard Code for Information Interchange (ASCII):** Standard for unformatted plain text which enables transfer of data between platforms and computer systems.

**Applet:** Computer program that runs from within another application.

**Assistive technology:** Technology used to assist a person with a disability, e.g., wheelchair, handsplints, computer-based equipment.

**Binary files:** Electronic files with formatting information that is software dependent.

**Braille:** System of embossed characters formed by using a Braille cell, a combination of six dots consisting of two vertical columns of three dots each. Each simple Braille character is formed by one or more of these dots and occupies a full cell or space. Some Braille may use eight dots.

**Browser:** Software designed to access and display information available on the World Wide Web. Browsers may be graphical or text-based. Text-only browsers cannot display images, sound clips, video and plug-in features that graphical browsers can. Talking browsers are also available for use by people who have difficulty reading text due to a learning disability or visual impairment.

**Captioned film or videos:** Transcription of the verbal portion of films or videos displayed to make them accessible to people who are deaf.

**Captioning:** Text that is included with video presentations or broadcasts that enables people with hearing impairments to have access to the audio portion of the material.

**Closed Circuit TV Magnifier (CCTV):** Camera used to magnify books or other materials to a monitor or television.

**Communication device:** Hardware that allows a person who has difficulty using their voice clearly to use words or symbols for communication. May range in complexity from a simple picture board to complex electronic devices that allow personalized, unique construction of ideas.

**Compensatory tools:** Adaptive computing systems that allow people with disabilities to use computers to complete tasks that they would have difficulty doing without a computer, e.g., reading, writing, communicating, accessing information.

**Digital:** Computer formatted data or information.

**Disability:** Physical or mental impairment that substantially limits one or more major life activities; a record of such an impairment; or being regarded as having such an impairment (Americans with Disabilities Act of 1990).

**Discrimination:** Act of making a difference in treatment or favor on a basis other than individual merit.

**Electronic information:** Any digital data for use with computers or computer networks including disks, CD-ROMs, World Wide Web resources.

**Facility:** All or any portion of a physical complex, including buildings, structures, equipment, grounds, roads, and parking lots.

**FM Sound Amplification System:** Electronic amplification system consisting of three components: a microphone/transmitter, monaural FM receiver and a combination charger/carrying case. It provides wireless FM broadcast from a speaker to a listener who has a hearing impairment.

**Graphical User Interface (GUI):** Program interface that presents digital information and software programs in an image-based format as compared to a character-based format.

**Hardware:** Physical equipment related to computers.

**Hearing impairments:** Complete or partial loss of ability to hear caused by a variety of injuries or diseases including congenital defects.

**Helper:** An external program that can be called up by a Web browser to display specially formatted material, such as word processed documents, spreadsheet documents or video/sound pieces. The Helper program is launched by the Web browser as a separate application to view or play the file.

**Host:** Any computer which holds Internet resources for access by others, or the computer that maintains your Internet access and electronic mail account.

**HTML validation:** Process that analyzes HTML documents identifies HTML errors and non-standard codes.

**HyperText Transfer Protocol (HTTP):** Communication protocol used by the World Wide Web to transfer text, graphics, audio, and video.

**Hyperlink, hypertext:** Highlighted word or graphic on a Web page that when selected allows the user to jump to another part of the document or another Web page.

**Hypertext Markup Language (HTML):** Programming language or code used to create World Wide Web pages.

**Image map:** Picture or graphic on a Web page in which hyperlinks are embedded.

**Input:** Any method by which information is entered into a computer.

**Internet:** Computer network connecting government, education, commercial, other organization and individual computer systems.

**Interpreter:** Professional person who assists a deaf person in communicating with hearing people.

**Java:** Programming language used to create programs or applets that work with some World Wide Web browsers to include features with animation or other characteristics not available through standard HTML.

**Joystick:** A device consisting of a lever that allows a pointer to move up, right, left, or down and serves as an alternative to a mouse. It usually includes buttons to enable mouse clicks.

**Keyboard emulation:** A method of having an alternative device and/or software, such as a switch-based system, serve the role of a keyboard.

**Keyguard:** A plastic or metal shield that covers a keyboard with holes over the keys. It allows use of a keyboard without undesired activation of surrounding keys.

**Large print books:** Most ordinary print is six to ten points in height (about 1/16 to 1/8 of an inch). Large type is 14 to 18 points (about 1/8 to 1/4 of an inch) and sometimes larger. The format of large print books is also proportionately larger (usually 8 1/2 x 11 inches).

**Lynx:** Text-based World Wide Web browser.

**Mainstreaming, inclusion:** The inclusion of people with disabilities, with or without special accommodations, in programs, activities, and facilities with their non-disabled peers.

**Major life activities:** Functions such as caring for oneself, performing manual tasks, walking, seeing, hearing, speaking, breathing, learning, working, and participating in community activities (Americans with Disabilities Act of 1990).

**Mobility impairment:** Disability that affects movement ranging from gross motor skills such as walking to fine motor movement involving manipulation of objects by hand.

**Mouse emulation:** A method of having an alternative device and/or software, such a switch based system, serve the role of a mouse.

**Multimedia:** In terms of electronic information, any data which is presented through several formats including text, graphics, moving pictures and sound.

**Onscreen keyboard:** See *Virtual Keyboard.*

**Optical character recognition (OCR):** Technology system that scans and converts printed materials into electronic text.

**Output:** Any method of displaying or presenting electronic information to the user through a computer monitor or other device.

**Peripheral Neuropathy:** A condition caused by damage to the nerves in the peripheral nervous system which includes nerves that run from the brain and spinal cord to the rest of the body.

**Physical or mental impairment:** Any physiological disorder or condition, cosmetic disfigurement, or anatomical loss affecting one or more of the following body systems: neurological; musculoskeletal; special sense organs; respiratory, including speech organs; cardiovascular; reproductive; digestive; genitourinary; hemic and lymphatic; skin; and endocrine; or any mental or psychological disorder, such as mental retardation, organic brain syndrome, emotional or mental illness, and specific learning disabilities (Americans with Disabilities Act of 1990).

**Plug-in:** Separate program written to be launched by a specific Web browser to display or run special elements in Web pages, such as animation, video, or audio.

**Qualified individual with a disability:** An individual with a disability who, with or without reasonable modification to rules, policies, or practices, the removal of architectural, communication, or transportation barriers, or the provision of auxiliary aids and services, meets the essential eligibility requirements for the receipt of services or the participation in programs or activities provided by a public entity (Americans with Disabilities Act of 1990).

**Reader:** Volunteer or employee of an individual with a disability (e.g., visual impairment, learning disability) who reads printed material in person or records to audio-tape.

**Reading system:** Hardware and software designed to provide access to printed text for people with visual impairments, mobility impairments, or learning disabilities. Character recognition software controls a scanner that takes an image of a printed page, converts it to computer text using recognition software and then reads the text using a synthesized voice.

**Refreshable Braille Display:** Hardware connected to a computer that echoes screen text on a box that has cells consisting of pins that move up and down to create Braille characters.

**Repetitive Stress Injury (RSI):** This disability may be chronic or acute and usually is described as pain caused by overuse of extremities, usually hands and wrists.

**Scanning input:** A switch-based method of controlling a computer. Activations of a switch will, in order, bring up a control panel that upon subsequent switch activations, allow a user to focus in on a desired control or keystroke. Custom scanning layouts can be created for a variety of purposes and programs and may also be used in a communication device.

**Screen enlargement:** Hardware and/or software that increases the size of characters and text on a computer screen.

**Screen reader:** Software used to echo text on a computer screen to audio output, often used by people who are blind, with visual impairments, or with learning disabilities.

**Screen resolution:** Refers to the clarity or sharpness of an image. For computer monitors, this term indicates the number of dots on the screen used to create text and graphics. Higher resolution means more dots, indicating increased sharpness and potentially smaller text.

**Section 508 of the Rehabilitation Act:** Legislation that requires Federal Agencies to develop, procure, and use accessible electronic and information technology.

**Sensory impairment:** A disability that affects touch, sight and/or hearing.

**Server:** Any computer that stores information that is available to other users, often over the Internet.

**Sign language:** Manual communication commonly used by deaf. The gestures or symbols in sign language are organized in a linguistic way. Each individual gesture is called a sign. Each sign has three distinct parts; the handshape, the position of the hands, and the movement of the hands. American Sign Language (ASL) is the most commonly used sign language in the United States. Deaf people from different countries speak different sign languages.

**Specific Learning Disability:** Disorder in one or more of the basic psychological processes involved in understanding or in using language, spoken or written, which may manifest itself in difficulties listening, thinking, speaking, reading, writing, spelling, or doing mathematical calculations. Frequent limitations include hyperactivity, distractibility, emotional instability, visual and/or auditory perception difficulties and/or motor limitations, depending on the type(s) of learning disability.

**Speech impairment:** Problems in communication and related areas such as oral motor function, ranging from simple sound substitutions to the inability to understand or use language or use the oral-motor mechanism for functional speech.

**Speech input or speech recognition:** A method of controlling a computer and creating text by dictation. Speech input software is combined with a microphone.

**Standard HTML:** Version of HTML accessible by all browsers.

**Streaming multimedia:** A method of transferring audio and/or video via a network from a server to an end user's computer. During the transmission, the material is displayed or played on the target computer.

**Switch input:** A method of controlling a computer or communication device. It is most often used with Morse code or scanning methods, but may also be used for controlling household appliances and related controls. Switches are available in a nearly endless array of sizes, shapes, and activation methods.

**Tag:** HTML code that prescribes the structure and formatting of Web pages.

**Telecommunications Device for the Deaf (TDD) or Teletypewriter (TTY):** A device which enables someone who has a speech or hearing impairment to use a telephone when communicating with someone else who has a TDD/TTY. TDD/TTYs can be used with any telephone, and one needs only a basic typing ability to use them.

**Trackball:** A mouse alternative that is basically an upside-down mouse. Useful for some people with mobility impairments because it isolates pointer movement from button clicking.

**Traumatic Brain Injury (TBI):** Open and closed head injuries resulting in impairments in one or more areas, including cognition; language; memory; attention; reasoning; abstract thinking; judgment; problem-solving; sensory, perceptual, and motor abilities; psychosocial behavior; physical functions; information processing; and speech. The term does not apply to brain injuries that are congenital, degenerative, or induced by birth trauma.

**Universal design:** Designing programs, services, tools, and facilities so that they are useable, without modification, by the widest range of users possible, taking into account a variety of abilities and disabilities.

**Universal design of instruction:** The design of instructional materials and activities that make learning achievable by students with a wide variety of abilities and disabilities.

**Universal Resource Locator (URL):** Address used to locate a specific resource on the Internet. DO-IT's URL is *http://www.washington.edu/doit/*.

**Vocational Rehabilitation Act of 1973:** Act prohibiting discrimination on the basis of disability which applies to any program that receives federal financial support. Section 504 of the Act is aimed at making educational programs and facilities accessible to all students. Section 508 of the Act requires that electronic office equipment purchased through federal procurement meets disability access guidelines.

**Virtual keyboard:** Software used to emulate a keyboard. A picture of a keyboard is displayed on a computer screen and the user points and clicks on the pictures of keys to enter text.

**Vision impairments:** Complete or partial loss of ability to see, caused by a variety of injuries or diseases including congenital defects. Legal blindness is defined as visual acuity of 20/200 or less in the better eye with correcting lenses, or widest diameter of visual field subtending an angular distance no greater than 20 degrees.

**Word prediction:** Software that reduces the number of keystrokes needed to type words and sentences. As characters are entered on either a standard, alternative or virtual keyboard, suggested completions of the word that has been started are provided to the user.

**World Wide Web (WWW, W3, or Web):** Hypertext and multimedia gateway to the Internet.

## About DO-IT

DO-IT (Disabilities, Opportunities, Internetworking, and Technology) helps individuals with disabilities transition to college and careers. Primary funding for DO-IT is provided by the National Science Foundation, the U.S. Department of Education, and the State of Washington. For more information, to be placed on the mailing list, or to request materials in an alternate format, contact:

**DO-IT**
University of Washington
Box 355670
Seattle, WA 98195-5670
*doit@u.washington.edu*
*http://www.washington.edu/doit/*
206-221-4171 (FAX)
206-685-DOIT (voice/TTY)
888-972-DOIT (voice/TTY) WA, outside Seattle
509-328-9331 (voice/TTY) Spokane
Director: Sheryl Burgstahler, Ph.D.

Grants and gifts funds DO-IT publications, videotapes, and programs to support the academic and career success of people with disabilities. Contribute today by sending a check to DO-IT, Box 355670, University of Washington, Seattle, WA 98195-5670.

*Your gift is tax deductible as specified in IRS regulations. Pursuant to RCW 19.09, the University of Washington is registered as a charitable organization with the Secretary of State, State of Washington. For more information, call the Office of the Secretary of State, 800-322-4483.*

**University of Washington**
College of Engineering
Computing & Communications
College of Education

# User Guide

Descriptive listings in *The Complete Directory for People with Disabilities* are organized into 27 chapters, by resource type. You will find the following types of listings throughout the book:

- National Agencies & Associations
- State Agencies & Associations
- Camps & Exchanges Programs
- Manufacturers of Assistive Devices, Clothing, Computer Equipment & Supplies
- Print & Electronic Media
- Living Centers & Facilities
- Libraries & Research Centers
- Conferences & Trade Shows

Below is a sample listing illustrating the kind of information that is or might be included in an Association entry. Each numbered item of information is described in the paragraphs on the following page.

---

1 ➤ 1234

2 ➤ **Advocacy Center for Seniors with Disabilities**

3 ➤ 1762 South Major Drive
New Orleans, LA 98087

4 ➤ **800-000-0000**

5 ➤ **058-884-0709**

6 ➤ **Fax: 058-884-0568**

7 ➤ **TDD: 800-000-0001**

8 ➤ **email: info@sadvoc.com**

9 ➤ **www.sadvoc.com**

10 ➤ Barbara Pierce, Executive Director
Diane Watkins, Marketing Director
Robert Goldfarb, Administrative Assistant

11 ➤ The mission of the Center is to advance the dignity, equality, self-determination and choices of senior citizens with disabilities. It provides referrals, publishes information, including a monthly newsletter, offers workshops and consultation on legal, social, travel, and medical issues. The Center works with various local organizations to help seniors with disabilities stay active in their community.

12 ➤ Founded 1964

13 ➤ 18 pages

14 ➤ Monthly

# User Key

1 ➤ **Record Number**: Entries are listed alphabetically within each category and numbered sequentially. The entry numbers, rather than page numbers, are used in the indexes to refer to listings.

2 ➤ **Organization Name**: Formal name of company or organization. Where organization names are completely capitalized, the listing will appear at the beginning of the alphabetized section. In the case of publications, the title of the publication will appear first, followed by the publisher.

3 ➤ **Address**: Location or permanent address of the organization.

4 ➤ **Toll Free Number**: This is listed when provided by the organization.

5 ➤ **Phone Number**: The listed phone number is usually for the main office of the organization, but may also be for the sales, marketing, or public relations office as provided by the organization.

6 ➤ **Fax Number**: This is listed when provided by the organization.

7 ➤ **TDD Number**: This is listed when provided. It refers to Telephone Device for the Deaf.

8 ➤ **E-Mail**: This is listed when provided by the organization and is generally the main office e-mail.

9 ➤ **Web Site**: This is also referred to as an URL address. These web sites are accessed through the Internet by typing *http://* before the URL address.

10 ➤ **Key Personnel**: Name and titles of department heads of the organization.

11 ➤ **Organization Description**: This paragraph contains a brief description of the organization and their services.

12 ➤ **Year Founded:** The year in which the organization was established or founded. If the organization has changed its name, the founding date is usually for the earliest name under which it was known.

13 ➤ **Number of Pages**: Number of pages if the listing is a publication.

14 ➤ **Frequency**: The frequency of the listing if it is a publication.

## Resources for the Disabled

**1** **American Art Therapy Association (AATA)**
5999 Stevenson Avenue
Alexandria, VA 22304
703-212-2238
888-290-0878
FAX: 703-212-2238
www.arttherapy.org

*Edward J Stygar Jr, Executive Director*

Organization of professionals who believe the art process is a beneficial and healing process.

**2** **American Dance Therapy Association (ADTA)**
2000 Century Plaza
Suite 108
Columbia, MD 21044
410-997-4040
FAX: 410-997-4048
e-mail: info@adta.org
www.adta.org

*Patricia Gardner, Office Manager*
*Elissa Q White, President of the Board*

Dance-movement therapy is a psychotherapeutic use of movement as a process which furthers the emotional, cognitive and physical integration of the individual.

**3** **American Music Therapy Association (AMTA)**
8455 Colesville Road
Suite 1000
Silver Spring, MD 20910
301-589-3300
FAX: 301-589-5175
e-mail: info@musictherapy.org
www.musictherapy.org

*Andrea H Farbman, Executive Director*
*Judy Simpson, Director Government Relations*

AMTA's purpose is the progressive development of the therapeutic use of music in rehabilitation, special education and community settings. Predecessors to the American Music Therapy Association included the National Association for Music Therapy founded in 1950 and the American Association for Music Therapy founded in 1971. AMTA is committed to the advancement of education, training, professional standards, credentials and research in support of the music therapy profession.

**4** **Arena Stage**
11101 Sixth Street
Washington, DC 20024
202-554-9066
FAX: 202-484-6279
e-mail: info@arenastage.org
www.arenastage.org

*Thomas C Fichandler, Founding Executive Director*
*Stephen Richard, Chief Executive Officer*

A pioneer in providing access to theater for people with disabilities and the birthplace of Audio Description. Offers infrared assistive listening devices (both loop and headset), program books in Braille, large print and wheelchair accessible seating with adjacent companion seating. Audio cassette format available upon request. Sign Interpretation and Audio Description are offered at selected performances. Cafe menus and shop lists in Braille. Wheelchair-accessible with lifts and ramps.

**5** **Art and Disabilities**
Brookline Books
39 University Road
Brookline, MA 02445
617-734-6772
800-666-2665
FAX: 617-734-3952
e-mail: brooklinebooks@brooklinebooks.com
www.brooklinebooks.com

*William H Walters, Author*
*Esther Isabe Wilder, Author*

A step-by-step guide to establishing creative arts centers for people with disabilities. Includes philosophy and making creative arts centers happen.

**6** **Art for All the Children: Approaches to Art Therapy for Children with Disabilities**
2600 South 1st Street
Springfield, IL 62704
217-789-8980
800-258-8980
FAX: 217-789-9130
e-mail: books@ccthomas.com
www.ccthomas.com

*Frances E Anderson, author*
*Michael Thomas, President*

This second edition is for art therapists in training and for in-service professionals in art therapy, art education and special education who have children with disabilities as a part of their case/class load. *$56.95*
*398 pages Paperback*
*ISBN 0-398060-07-X*

**7** **Association for Theatre and Accessibility**
300 UCLA Medical Plaza
Suite 3330
Los Angeles, CA 90095
310-794-1141

e-mail: oraynor@mednet.ucla.edu
www.npi.ucla.edu/ata

*Olivia Raynor, Executive Director*
*Beth Sotffmacher, Technical Coordinator*
*John Clare, President*

A nonprofit with the purpose of fostering the full participation and involvement of individuals with all types of disabilities in drama and theater. Newsletters and annual conferences.

**8** **Deaf Artists of America**
302 Goodman Street N
Suite 205
Rochester, NY 14607
716-244-3460
800-421-1220
FAX: 716-244-3690
TTY: 716-244-3460

*Tom Willard, Executive Director*

Organized to bring support and recognition to deaf and hard of hearing artists. Goals are to publish information about deaf artists, provide cultural and educational opportunities, exhibit and market deaf artists' work, and collect and disseminate information about deaf artists.

**9** **Deaf Entertainment Foundation (DEF)**
Deaf Entertainment Guild (Deg)
8306 Wilshire Boulevard
Suite 906
Beverly Hills, CA 90211
323-782-1344
FAX: 213-782-1344
TTY:323-782-1797
e-mail: deafent@aol.com
www.deo.org

*Mark Brudney, Marketing and Public Relations*
*Eldon Greenfield, DEOnline Webmaster*
*Dan McClintock, DEOnline Editor*

Provides information to promote and accelerate the presence of deaf and hard of hearing talents in motion pictures, television, theater, and the performing arts.

**10    Disability and Social Performance: Using Drama to Achieve Successful Acts**
Brookline Books
39 University Road
Brookline, MA  02445                    617-734-6772
                                         800-666-2665
                                    FAX: 617-734-3952
                e-mail: brooklinebks@delphi.com
                        www.brooklinebooks.com

*William H Walters, Author*
*Esther Wilder, Author*

This book makes a major contribution to the understanding of disability, people with disabilities and the creative power they possess which can be unleashed through performance. *$17.95*

**11    Freedom to Create**
National Institute of Art and Disabilities
551 23rd Street
Richmond, CA  94804                     510-620-0290
                                    FAX: 510-620-0326
                      e-mail: admin@niadart.org

*Elias Katz, Author*
*Patricia Coleman, President*

Presents philosophy and practical experiences enabling teachers to stimulate creativity in the visual arts for students with and without disabilities.

**12    Friends-In-Art**
American Council of the Blind
1155 15th Street NW
Suite 1004
Washington, DC  20005                   202-467-5081
                                        800-424-8666
                                    FAX: 202-467-5085
                          e-mail: info@acb.org
                                www.acb.org

*Melanie Brunson, Executive Director*
*Chris Grey, President*

Aims to enlarge the art experience of blind people, encourages blind people to visit museums, galleries, concerts, the theater and other enjoyable public places, offers consultation to program planners in establishing accessible art and museum exhibits and presents Performing Arts Showcases at the American Council of the Blinds' national convention.

**13    Institute for Therapy Throughout the Arts**
Division 3 of Oakton College
7701 Lincoln Avenue
Skokie, IL  60077                       847-635-1654
                                    FAX: 847-446-8458
                                       www.oakton.edu

In its twentieth year of service, ITA provides creative arts therapies for adults and children with special needs through the use of music, art, drama and or dance. Services include: assessment, treatment planning, one-to-one services and group therapy. ITA also offers adaptive lessons to students with special needs and workshops on topics related to the expressive arts therapies.

**14    Manual of Sequential Art Activities for Classified Children and Adolescents**
Charles C Thomas
2600 S 1st Street
Springfield, IL  62704                  217-789-8980
                                        800-258-8980
                                    FAX: 217-789-9130
                     e-mail: books@ccthomas.com
                            www.ccthomas.com

*Charles C Thomas, Publisher*
*Michael Thomas, President*

Offers information to the special education professional on art therapy and management. *$41.95*

*246 pages Softcover*
*ISBN 0-39805 -85-6*

**15    Music for Developing Speech & Language Skills in Children**
MMB Music
3526 Washington Avenue
Saint Louis, MO  63103                  314-531-9635
                                        800-543-3771
                                    FAX: 314-531-8384
                     e-mail: info@mmbmusic.com
                            www.mmbmusic.com

*Dr Michel, J Jones, author*
*Marcia Goldberg, President*

Designed to promote awareness of learning potential in creative abilities for young children who have moderate to severe disabilities. *$18.95*
        *49 pages*
        *ISBN 0-918812-69-0*

**16    National Arts and Disability Center (NADC)**
Tarjan Center for Developmental Disabilities
300 UCLA Medical Plaza
Suite 3310
Los Angeles, CA  90095                  310-794-1141
                                    FAX: 310-794-1143
              e-mail: oraynor@mednet.ucla.edu
                            nadc.ucla.edu

*Olivia Raynor MD, Executive Director*
*Beth Stoffmacher, Technical Assistance Coordinator*

NADC has a database and website which deals with access to and participation in the arts by people with disabilities.

**17    National Association for Drama Therapy**
15 Post Side Lane
Pittsford, NY  14534                    585-381-5618
                                    FAX: 585-383-1474
                      e-mail: nadt@mgmtsol.com
                                www.nadt.org

*Sherry Diamond, President*
*Kate Hurd, Vice President*

**18    National Theatre Workshop of the Handicapped (NTWH)**
535 Greenwich Street
New York, NY  10013                     212-206-7789
                                    FAX: 212-206-0200
                   e-mail: admissions@ntwh.org
                                www.ntwh.org

*Jason Matthews, Director Admissions*
*Rick Curry, Executive Director*

**19    National Theatre of the Deaf**
139 North Main Street
West Hartford, CT  06107                860-236-4193
                                    FAX: 860-236-4163
                                    TTY:860-236-4193
                          e-mail: info@ntd.org
                                www.ntd.org

*Paul Winters, Executive Director*

Professional development of deaf actors, national theatrical touring company of deaf and hearing actors.

**20    Non-Traditional Casting Project**
1560 Broadway
Suite 1600
New York, NY  10036                     212-730-4750
                                    FAX: 212-730-4820
                          e-mail: info@ntcp.org
                                www.ntcp.org

*Sharon Jensen, Executive Director*
*Nancy Kim, Program Manager*

**21**   **VSA Arts**
JFK Center for the Performing Arts
818 Connecticut Avenue NW
Suite 600
Washington, DC  20006

202-628-2800
800-933-8721
FAX: 202-737-0725
TTY: 202-737-0645
e-mail: info@vsarts.com
www.vsarts.org

*Soula Antoniou, Executive Director*
*Tanya L Travers, Marketing Manager*

VSA Arts is an international nonprofit agency that promotes education and lifelong learning opportunities in the arts for people with disabilities. We promote the arts for children and adults with disabilities, strengthening the human spirit and improving quality of life for everyone.

## Automobile

**22    Ability Center**
Contact Technologies
11600 Western Avenue
Stanton, CA  90680

714-890-8262
877-938-8267
FAX: 714-901-1492
e-mail: terry@abilitycenter.com
www.abilitycenter.com

*Terry Barton, Manager*

Offers rear or side entry designed with painstaking craftsmanship using steel.

**23    Acc-u-trol**
Ahnafield Corporation
2444 Production Drive
Indianapolis, IN  46241

317-241-2444
800-636-8060
FAX: 317-636-8098
www.ahnafield.com

*Bruce Ahnafield, President*
*Jeff Ahnafield, Sales Manager*

Computer-controlled device that operates all secondary accessory functions. These functions may include ignition, lift and door operation, windows, wipers, lights and flashers.

**24    Adaptive Vans for the Physically Challenged**
Mobility Works
810 Moe Drive
Akron, OH  44310

330-633-1118
800-638-8267
FAX: 330-633-0330
e-mail: bkoeblitz@mobility-works.com
www.mobility-works.com

*Bill Koeblitz, President*
*Taylor F Clark, VP/General Manager*

Mobility Works builds adaptive vans for the disabled and their special needs. Adaptations include lowered floors, raised roofs, wheelchair lifts, custom interiors, custom exteriors, driving systems, power transfer seats, wheelchair tie-downs, wheelchair ramps, remote entry systems and rooftop wheelchair carriers for cars.

**25    Aeroquip Wheelchair Securement System**
Aeroquip Corporation
300 S East Avenue
Jackson, MI  49203

517-789-4144
FAX: 517-789-4716

Wheelchair users can have adaptable, safe, easily attached securement during transportation.

**26    Arcola Mobility**
51 Kero Road
Carlstadt, NJ  07072

201-507-8500
800-ARC-OLA1
FAX: 201-507-5372
e-mail: brianp@arcolasales.com
www.arcolasales.com

*Tony Perez, Sales Represen/Mobility Vehicle*
*Brian Pruiksma, Lifts/Ramps/Etc Sales Rep*

Arcola sells new and used accessible vehicles and adaptive driving equipment including hand controls, wheelchair lifts and securement systems. Daily, weekly and monthly vehicle rentals available. Stairway lift, porch elevators and ramps for the home sold and rented.

**27    Automobile Lifts for Scooters, Wheelchairs and Powerchairs**
Bruno Independent Living Aids
PO Box 84
Oconomowoc, WI  53066

262-567-4990
800-882-8183
FAX: 262-953-5501
e-mail: webmaster@bruno.com
www.bruno.com

*Patrick Foy, National Sales Manager*
*Karla Branham Shaw, Marketing*
*Michael Bruno, Owner*

Over 18 different styles of automobile lifts for scooters, wheelchairs and powerchairs for nearly any car, van, truck or sport utility vehicle that can raise most scooters or wheelchiars under 200 pounds and powerchairs up to 300 pounds. All Bruno lifts are eligible for reimbursement of up to $1000.00 from GM, Saturn, Ford, and Chrysler under the terms of their Mobility Programs.

**28    Ball Bearing Spinner**
Kroepke Kontrols
PO Box 288
Ellicottville, NY  14731

718-885-1100
FAX: 718-885-1110
e-mail: kkontrols@aol.com
www.kroepkekontrols.com

One-lever-fingertip control which is custom designed for each car but does not interfere with normal operation of your car and ball joints for perfect alignment. Can be installed by any car dealer or mechanic in 2 hours. *$44.00*

**29    Blinker Buddy II Electronic Turn Signal**
HARC Mercantile
1111 W Centre Avenue
Portage, MI  49024

269-324-1615
800-445-9968
FAX: 269-324-2387
e-mail: home@harcmercantile.com
www.harcmercantile.com

*Ronald Slager, President*

Sounds a loud tone and flashes a light when the turn signal is on. *$79.95*

**30    Braun Corporation**
PO Box 310
Winamac, IN  46996

574-946-6153
800-843-5438
FAX: 574-946-4670
www.braunlift.com

*Jeff Ruff, Executive VP Sales*
*William Roth, President*

Manufactures wheelchair lifts and lowered floor minivans as well as many other mobility products.

**31    Chevy Lowered Floor**
Ahnafield Corporation
2444 Production Drive
Indianapolis, IN  46241

317-241-2444
800-636-8060
FAX: 317-636-8098
www.ahnafield.com

*Jeff Ahnafield, Sales Manager*
*Bruce Ahanfield, President*

Full size Chevy van lowered floor from 4 to 12 depths.

**32** **Classic**
Ricon
7900 Nelson Road
Panorama City, CA 91402

818-267-3000
800-322-2884
FAX: 818-267-3001
e-mail: sales@riconcorp.com
www.riconcorp.com

*William Baldwin, Chief Executive Officer*

Deluxe van conversion with equipment and accessories to offer freedom to the physically challenged.

**33** **Classic Coach Interiors**
Classic Coach Interiors
1935 Burlington Avenue
Kewanee, IL 61443

309-852-4656
800-209-7225
FAX: 309-852-3463

*George Giesenhagen, Manager*

Offers van conversions with state-of-the-art equipment for the physically challenged.

**34** **DW Auto & Home Mobility**
1208 N Garth Avenue
Columbia, MO 65203

573-449-3859
800-568-2271
FAX: 573-449-4187
e-mail: info@dwauto.com
www.dwauto.com

*Sheila Lynch, Business Manager*
*Shawn Bright, Owner*

Paratransit conversions and personalized conversions for the physically challenged. Home elevators and lifts. Scooter, wheelchairs and DME.

**35** **Dodge Lowered Floor**
Ahnafield Corporation
2444 Production Drive
Indianapolis, IN 46241

317-241-2444
800-636-8060
FAX: 317-636-8098
www.ahnafield.com

*Jeff Ahnafield, Sales Manager*
*Bruce Ahanfield, President*

Full size Dodge van lowered floor from 4 to 12 depths.

**36** **Drive Master Company**
37 Daniel Road W
Fairfield, NJ 07004

973-808-9709
FAX: 973-808-9713
e-mail: sales@drivemaster.net
www.drivemaster.net

*Peter B Ruprecht, President*
*Tina Knapik, VP Operations Manager*

Full service mobility center, raised tops/doors, drop floors, custom driving equipment, distributor of name brand devices and systems for full sized and mini vans. Sister company Van Master rents mobility equipped vans.

**37** **Dual Brake Control**
Kroepke Kontrols
PO Box 288
Ellicottville, NY 14731

718-885-1100
FAX: 718-885-1110
e-mail: kkontrols@aol.com
www.kroepkekontrols.com

One lever fingertip brake controls, precision machines of the finest quality steel, are inconspicuous and do not take up lots of leg room. *$105.00*

**38** **Entervan**
Braun Corporation
PO Box 310
Winamac, IN 46996

574-946-6153
800-THE-LIFT
www.entervan.com

*William Roth, President*

The Entervan accessible features are designed to blend seamlessly into the original design of the Chrysler minivan. In fact, you'll find the Entervan to be virtually indistinguishable from other minivans on the road, with the only differences being the easily accessible qualities of the van.

**39** **Escort II XL**
Worldwide Mobility Products
720 N Golden Street
Suite B6
Gilbert, AZ 85233

480-497-4692
800-848-3433
FAX: 480-497-3834
e-mail: www.mobliftl@msn.com
www.worldwide-mobility.com

*Greg Maloy, Owner*

Automatically lifts and secures for transportation a fully assembled, three-wheel, electric scooter. *$1625.00*

**40** **Foot Steering**
Drive Master Company
37 Daniel Road W
Fairfield, NJ 07004

973-808-9709
FAX: 973-808-9713
e-mail: sales@drivemaster.net
www.drivemaster.net

*Peter Ruprecht, President*

Custom installed system to steer a vehicle with your foot.

**41** **Foot Steering System**
Ahnafield Corporation
2444 Production Drive
Indianapolis, IN 46241

317-241-2444
800-636-8060
FAX: 317-636-8098
www.ahnafield.com

*Jeff Ahnafield, Sales Manager*
*Bruce Ahanfield, President*

**42** **Ford Lowered Floor**
Ahnafield Corporation
2444 Production Drive
Indianapolis, IN 46241

317-241-2444
800-636-8060
FAX: 317-636-8098
www.ahnafield.com

*Jeff Ahnafield, Sales Manager*
*Bruce Ahanfield, President*

Full size Ford van lowered floor from 4 to 12 depths.

**43** **Gresham Driving Aids**
30800 S Wixom Road
Wixom, MI 48393

248-624-1533
800-521-8930
FAX: 248-624-6358
www.greshamdrivingaids.com

*Larry Pratt, Sales Manager*
*Bill Dillon, Owner*

Offers a full-service package to physically challenged individuals including lowered floors, raised roofs and doors and high-quad driver control systems. Dealer for Braun, Ricon, Crow River and Bruno wheelchair lifts.

**44    Hand Brake Control Only**
Kroepke Kontrols
PO Box 288
Ellicottville, NY  14731                       718-885-1100
                                          FAX: 718-885-1110
                                    e-mail: kkontrols@aol.com
                                    www.kroepkekontrols.com
One lever, fingertip brake controls that are custom designed to
fit each car, completely adjustable and offer positioning opera-
tion at your fingertips. *$130.00*

**45    Hand Control Systems**
Wright-Way
175 E Interstate 30
Garland, TX  75043                            972-240-8839
                                              800-241-8839
                                         FAX: 972-240-0412
                            e-mail: mobility@wrightwayinc.com
                                      www.wrightwayinc.com

*Thomas Wright, President*

Various automobile control systems that use hand, foot and
steering aids for the disabled, including complete vehicle modifications.

**46    Hand Dimmer Switch**
Gresham Driving Aids
30800 S Wixom Road
Wixom, MI  48393                              248-624-1533
                                              800-521-8930
                                         FAX: 248-624-6358
                               www.greshamdrivingaids.com

*Bill Dillon, Owner*

This switch is recommended for left leg handicaps or when a
right leg handicap uses a left foot throttle. *$36.25*

**47    Hand Dimmer Switch with Horn Button**
Gresham Driving Aids
30800 S Wixom Road
Wixom, MI  48393                              248-624-1533
                                              800-521-8930
                                         FAX: 248-624-6358
                               www.greshamdrivingaids.com

*Bill Dillon, Owner*

Attaches to the handle of control with a chrome plated steel insulated switch box, giving an instant warning without removing
your hand from the steering wheel. *$28.75*

**48    Hand Gas & Brake Control**
Kroepke Kontrols
PO Box 288
Ellicottville, NY  14731                       718-885-1100
                                          FAX: 718-885-1110
                                    e-mail: kkontrols@aol.com
                                    www.kroepkekontrols.com
Driving controls that are attached by a control level right on to
the gas and brake pedals for easy maneuvering and convenience.
*$220.00*

**49    Hand Operated Parking Brake**
Gresham Driving Aids
30800 S Wixom Road
Wixom, MI  48393                              248-624-1533
                                              800-521-8930
                                         FAX: 248-624-6358
                               www.greshamdrivingaids.com

*Bill Dillon, Owner*

Converts foot parking brake to a hand operation for easy access
and maneuverability. *$30.20*

**50    Hand Parking Brake**
Kroepke Kontrols
PO Box 288
Ellicottville, NY  14731                       718-885-1100
                                          FAX: 718-885-1110
                                    e-mail: kkontrols@aol.com
                                    www.kroepkekontrols.com

One lever fingertip brake controls for your car that offer easy installment, complete adjustability, complete independence and
more. *$25.00*

**51    Handicapped Driving Aids**
Handicapped Driving Aids of Michigan
4020 2nd Street
Suite 30
Wayne, MI  48184                              734-595-4400
                                         FAX: 734-595-4520

*Jeff Stys, Manager*

Automobiles and vans customized, modified and equipped with
industry approved handicapped equipment for ease of operation.

**52    Headlight Dimmer Switch**
Kroepke Kontrols
PO Box 288
Ellicottville, NY  14731                       718-885-1100
                                          FAX: 718-885-1110
                                    e-mail: kkontrols@aol.com
                                    www.kroepkekontrols.com
One lever, fingertip controls for the disabled driver. *$23.00*

**53    Horizontal Steering**
Drive Master Company
37 Daniel Road W
Fairfield, NJ  07004                           973-808-9709
                                          FAX: 973-808-9713
                              e-mail: sales@drivemaster.net
                                       www.drivemaster.net

*Peter Ruprecht, President*
*Christina Ruprecht, VP*
*Shelby Wells, Sales Manager*

Horizontal steering system is customized to meet the needs of
the high-level, spinally injured and all others who experience
limited arm strength and range of motion.

**54    Horn Control Switch**
Kroepke Kontrols
PO Box 288
Ellicottville, NY  14731                       718-885-1100
                                          FAX: 212-885-1110
                                    e-mail: kkontrols@aol.com
                                    www.kroepkekontrols.com
One lever, fingertip controls that do not interfere with the nor-
mal operation of your car. *$23.00*

**55    Institute for Driver Rehabilitation**
156 E Commodore Boulevard
Jackson, NJ  08527                            609-734-8000
                                              800-866-1529
                                         FAX: 732-928-2449

*Debra Jackrel, President*
*Ted Jackrel, Program Director*
*Peter Goddard, Executive Director*

Driver evaluation training for the physically/mentally challenged offering state certified driving instructors. Door-to-door
pickup at home, work or rehab centers.

**56    Joystick Driving Control**
Ahnafield Corporation
2444 Production Drive
Indianapolis, IN  46241                       317-241-2444
                                              800-636-8060
                                         FAX: 317-636-8098
                                          www.ahnafield.com

*Jeff Ahnafield, Sales Manager*
*Bruce Ahnafield, President*

Single lever, two axis, remote control system for steering,
brakes, and accelerator.

**57  Key Holders, Ignition & Door Keys**
Gresham Driving Aids
30800 S Wixom Road
Wixom, MI 48393
248-624-1533
800-521-8930
FAX: 248-624-6358
www.greshamdrivingaids.com

*Bill Dillon, Owner*
Easy for arthritic hands to handle. Easily installed. *$18.70*

**58  Kneelkar**
Mednet
555 Industrial Park Drive
Battle Creek, MI 49015
269-964-7920
FAX: 269-962-8841

*Anthony Vandillin, Owner*
Offers the ultimate van conversions with equipment that is easily installed and accessible for the physically challenged.

**59  Latchloc Automatic Wheelchair Tiedown**
Ahnafield Corporation
2444 Production Drive
Indianapolis, IN 46241
317-241-2444
800-636-8060
FAX: 317-636-8098
www.ahnafield.com

*Jeff Ahnafield, Sales Manager*
*Bruce Ahanfield, President*
An independent wheelchair tiedown system utilized primarily by individuals who drive from their wheelchairs.

**60  Left Foot Accelerator**
Gresham Driving Aids
30800 S Wixom Road
Wixom, MI 48393
248-624-1533
800-521-8930
FAX: 248-624-6358
www.greshamdrivingaids.com

*Bill Dillon, Owner*
A custom pedal designed for left-foot usage. Stainless steel cross bar attaches above the throttle pedal and leaves right pedal free for right foot use. *$80.50*

**61  Left Foot Gas Pedal**
Kroepke Kontrols
PO Box 288
Ellicottville, NY 14731
718-885-1100
FAX: 212-885-1110
e-mail: kkontrols@aol.com
www.kroepkekontrols.com
One lever, fingertip controls that offer custom design, easy installment and complete freedom for the disabled driver. *$90.00*

**62  Left Hand Shift Lever**
Gresham Driving Aids
PO Box 930334
Wixom, MI 48393
248-624-1533
800-521-8930
FAX: 248-624-6358
www.greshamdrivingaids.com

*Bill Dillon, Owner*
Converts steering wheel lever or automatic transmission selector lever to left hand usage for right arm handicaps. *$34.50*

**63  Low Effort and No Effort Steering**
Drive Master Company
37 Daniel Road
Fairfield, NJ 07004
973-808-9709
FAX: 973-808-9713
e-mail: sales@drivemaster.net
www.drivemaster.net

*Peter B Ruprecht, President*
*Christina M Ruprecht, General Manager*
*J Shelby Wells, Sales Manager*
Reduced effort steering modifications available for nearly all vehicles. Additional products are pedal extensions which are 1 inch to 4 inch clamp-on aluminum blocks and 6 inch to 12 inch adjustable fold-down pedals.

**64  Mini-Bus and Mini-Vans**
Arcola Bus Sales
51 Kero Road
Carlstadt, NJ 07072
201-507-8500
800-ARC-OLA1
FAX: 201-507-5372
e-mail: tonyp@arcolamobility.com
www.arcolamobility.com

*Tony Perez, Mobility Sales Representative*
*Brian Pruiksma, Sales Representative*
*Andrew Rolfe, Owner*
Offers a virtually unlimited choice of chassis size, body style, floor plan and optional features. We provide transporters for almost every use, including school buses, vans, mini-coaches, medium-duty buses and personalized vans for the disabled.

**65  Mini-Rider**
Ricon
7900 Nelson Road
Panorama City, CA 91402
818-267-3000
800-322-2884
FAX: 818-267-3001
e-mail: sales@riconcorp.com
www.riconcorp.com

*William Baldwin, Chief Executive Officer*
Deluxe van conversions.

**66  Mitsubishi Truck: FE434**
Mitsubishi Fuso Truck of America
2015 Center Square Road
Swedesboro, NJ 08085
856-467-4500
FAX: 856-467-4695

*Robert Dowell, Manager*
A cab-over, turbo-charged diesel with optional four-speed automatic transmission, has wide angle front and side windows for improved visibility.

**67  Mobility Vehicle Stairlifts and Ramps**
Arcola Bus Sales
51 Kero Road
Carlstadt, NJ 07072
201-507-8500
800-ARC-OLA1
FAX: 201-507-5372
e-mail: tonyp@arcolamobility.com
www.arcolamobility.com

*Tony Perez, Mobility Sales Representative*
*Brian Pruiksma, Accessibility Products*
*Andrew Rolfe, Owner*
Arcola Mobility is a leading dealer of personal, accessible mini and full-size vans with custom conversions and modifications available. We offer a complete line of adaptive driving equipment, including wheelchair lifts, ramps, hand controls, steering devices, scooter lifters, car top wheelchair carriers and power transfer seats. In addition to new custom vehicles, we also have an extensive selection of used vehicles for the physically challenged.

**68    Monarch Mark 1-A**
Access Mobility Systems
21104 70th Avenue W
Edmonds, WA 98026

425-771-4659
800-854-4176
FAX: 425-771-3946
e-mail: info@accessams.com
www.accessams.com

*Jennifer Richardson, Owner*

System of hand controls which incorporates a popular method of operation by pushing the control handles directly toward the brakes.

**69    Monmouth Vans, Access and Mobility**
5105 Route 33
34
Wall Township, NJ 07727

732-919-1444
800-221-0034
FAX: 732-919-0256
e-mail: info@monmouthvans.com
www.monmouthvans.com

*Eugene Morton, President*
*Raymond Morton, VP*
*Arthur Smith, Sales Manager*

Full vehicle modifications for driving and for transport of people with disabilities. Access equipment for buildings, e.g. ramps, stair lifts, pool lifts, automatic door openers and patient transfer lifts, pride jazzy portable and modular wheelchairs and scooters. Large selection of modified vans in stock.

**70    New Quad Grip**
Gresham Driving Aids
30800 S Wixom Road
Wixom, MI 48393

248-624-1533
800-521-8930
FAX: 248-624-6358
www.greshamdrivingaids.com

*Bill Dillon, Owner*

Automobile aids for the disabled. $40.25

**71    PAC Unit**
Ahnafield Corporation
2444 Production Drive
Indianapolis, IN 46241

317-241-2444
800-636-8060
FAX: 317-636-8098
www.ahnafield.com

*Jeff Ahnafield, Sales Manager*
*Bruce Ahnafield, President*

Low effort accelerator and brake remote serves hand control.

**72    Pedal Ease**
Ahnafield Corporation
2444 Production Drive
Indianapolis, IN 46241

317-241-2444
800-636-8060
FAX: 317-636-8098
www.ahnafield.com

*Jeff Ahnafield, Sales Manager*
*Bruce Ahnafield, President*

Low effort accelerator and brake remote serves foot control.

**73    Portable Hand Controls**
Ahnafield Corporation
2444 Production Drive
Indianapolis, IN 46241

317-241-2444
800-636-8060
FAX: 317-636-8098
www.ahnafield.com

*Jeff Ahnafield, Sales Manager*
*Bruce Ahanfield, President*

**74    Portable Vehicle Controls**
Contact Technologies
1033 Business Center Circle
Newbury Park, CA 91320

805-498-8157
FAX: 805-498-2747

Fully portable, integrated, automotive hand control unit.

**75    Power Seat Base (6-Way)**
Ricon
7900 Nelson Road
Panorama City, CA 91402

818-267-3000
800-322-2884
FAX: 818-267-3001
www.riconcorp.com

*William Baldwin, Chief Executive Officer*

Facilitates a driver's self-transfer from a wheelchair to the driving seat and allows optimal driving positioning.

**76    Quad Grip with Pin**
Gresham Driving Aids
30800 S Wixom Road
Wixom, MI 48393

248-624-1533
800-521-8930
FAX: 248-624-6358
www.greshamdrivingaids.com

*Bill Dillon, Owner*

Automobile aids for the disabled. $40.25

**77    Rampvan**
Independent Mobility Systems
4100 W Piedras Street
Farmington, NM 87401

505-326-4538
800-467-8267
FAX: 505-326-4846
e-mail: info@imsvans.com
www.ims-vans.com

*Greg Anesi, President*

Fully accessible minivan conversions with automatic doors and ramps, manufactured by Toyota, Chrysler, Dodge and Ford minivans.

**78    Recreation Vehicles**
Lazy Days RV Center
6130 Lazy Days Boulevard
Seffner, FL 33584

813-246-4777
800-626-7800
FAX: 813-246-4408
www.lazydays.com

*Jack Graham*
*Don Wallace, President*

Customized recreational vehicles for people with disabilities. Specializing in wheelchair accessible bathrooms.

**79    Reduced Effort Steering**
Ahnafield Corporation
2444 Production Drive
Indianapolis, IN 46241

317-241-2444
800-636-8060
FAX: 317-636-8098
www.ahnafield.com

*Jeff Ahnafield, Sales Manager*
*Bruce Ahanfield, President*

**80    Right Hand Turn Signal Switch Lever**
Gresham Driving Aids
30800 S Wixom Road
Wixom, MI 48393

248-624-1533
800-521-8930
FAX: 248-624-6358
www.greshamdrivingaids.com

*Bill Dillon, Owner*

Converts signal switch to right hand usage for left arm handicaps. $34.50

**81**   **Slim Line Brake Only**
Gresham Driving Aids
30800 S Wixom Road
Wixom, MI 48393
248-624-1533
800-521-8930
FAX: 248-624-6358
www.greshamdrivingaids.com

*Bill Dillon, Owner*

A chrome plated steel handle, contour shaped, with a left hand or right hand unit available. *$155.25*

**82**   **Slim Line Control**
Gresham Driving Aids
30800 S Wixom Road
Wixom, MI 48393
248-624-1533
800-521-8930
FAX: 248-624-6358
www.greshamdrivingaids.com

*Bill Dillon, Owner*

A plated, strong, compact unit designed to be easily transferred from car to car. Built of heavy steel tubing, welded and chrome plated and contour-shaped for maximum driving room. *$201.25*

**83**   **Slim Line Control: Brake and Throttle**
Gresham Driving Aids
30800 S Wixom Road
Wixom, MI 48393
248-624-1533
800-521-8930
FAX: 248-624-6358
www.greshamdrivingaids.com

*Bill Dillon, Owner*

Brake is actuated by pushing the control lever directly towards the brake. Throttle is actuated by moving the lever at right angles to the brake movement, toward the seat. The weight of the operator's hand is sufficient to hold the throttle at any designed speed. *$300.00*

**84**   **Steering Backup System**
Ahnafield Corporation
2444 Production Drive
Indianapolis, IN 46241
317-241-2444
800-636-8060
FAX: 317-636-8098
www.ahnafield.com

*Jeff Ahnafield, Sales Manager*
*Bruce Ahanfield, President*

**85**   **Superarm Lift**
Handicaps
4335 S Santa Fe Drive
Englewood, CO 80110
303-781-2062
800-782-4335
FAX: 303-761-6811
e-mail: Forest77@earthlink.com
www.handicapsinc.com

*Geraldine O'Dell, Owner*

Made for vans and motor homes. No platform is necessary and no doorways are blocked by lift that is simple and safe to use.

**86**   **Tim's Trim**
25 Bermar Park
Rochester, NY 14624
585-429-6270
888-468-6784
FAX: 585-429-6355
e-mail: timstriminc@yahoo.com
www.theoptionstore.com

*Timothy A Miller, President*

Offers vehicle modifications, drop floors, raised tops/doors, driving equipment, touch pads and lifts. Also is a member of NEMDA and QAP certified

**87**   **Transportation Equipment for People with Disabilities**
Drive Master Company
37 Daniel Road W
Fairfield, NJ 07004
973-808-9709
877-282-8267
FAX: 973-808-9713
e-mail: sales@drivemaster.net
www.drivemaster.net

*Peter Ruprecht, President*

Wheelchair lifts and ramps, hand and foot controls, steering and braking modifications, complete van conversions, home modifications, wheelchairs and scooters and wheelchair accessible van rentals.

**88**   **Tri-Post Steering Wheel Spinner**
Gresham Driving Aids
30800 S Wixom Road
Wixom, MI 48393
248-624-1533
800-521-8930
FAX: 248-624-6358
www.greshamdrivingaids.com

*Bill Dillon, Owner*

Three nylon posts, adjustable for proper fit to drivers hand, to control the wheel, for use by persons with weak or limp wrists. *$40.25*

**89**   **Trunk Lift**
Fortress
PO Box 489
Clovis, CA 93613
559-322-5437
FAX: 559-323-0299

Scooters trunk lifts.

**90**   **Ultra-Lite XL Hand Control**
Drive Master Company
37 Daniel Road W
Fairfield, NJ 07004
973-808-9709
FAX: 973-808-9713
e-mail: sales@drivemaster.net
www.drivemaster.net

*Peter Ruprecht, President*

Allows the driver to operate gas and brake by hand— push for brake— pull for gas. Can be installed in nearly every vehicle.

**91**   **Vantage Mini-Vans**
Vantage Mini-Vans
5202 S 28th Place
Phoenix, AZ 85040
602-243-2700
FAX: 602-304-2804
e-mail: info@vantagemobility.com
www.vantagemobility.com

*Doug Eaton, Sales Executive*

Personalized vehicles with lowered floors and swing-away ramps.

**92**   **Voice Choice**
Ahnafield Corporation
2444 Production Drive
Indianapolis, IN 46241
317-241-2444
800-636-8060
FAX: 317-636-8098
www.ahnafield.com

*Jeff Ahnafield, Sales Manager*
*Bruce Ahnafield, President*

Voice recognition system for accessories.

**93** **Voice Scan**
Ahnafield Corporation
2444 Production Drive
Indianapolis, IN 46241
317-241-2444
800-636-8060
FAX: 317-636-8098
www.ahnafield.com

*Jeff Ahnafield, Sales Manager*
*Bruce Ahnafield, President*

Voice feedback control for accessories.

**94** **Warp Drive**
Ahnafield Corporation
2444 Production Drive
Indianapolis, IN 46241
317-241-2444
800-636-8060
FAX: 317-636-8098
www.ahnafield.com

*Jeff Ahnafield, Sales Manager*
*Bruce Ahnafield, President*

Low effort steering wheel attachment accelerator and brake hand control serves system.

**95** **Wheelers Accessible Van Rentals**
6614 W Sweetwater Avenue
Glendale, AZ 85304
623-776-8830
800-456-1371
FAX: 623-412-9920
e-mail: info@wheelersvanrentals.com
www.wheelersvanrentals.com

*Tammy Smith, Manager*

Daily, weekly and monthly rentals. Locations throughout the US.

**96** **XL Steering**
Ahnafield Corporation
2444 Production Drive
Indianapolis, IN 46241
317-241-2444
800-636-8060
FAX: 317-636-8098

*Jeff Ahnafield, Sales Manager*
*Bruce Ahnafield, President*

Extra light, small diameter, remote steering system.

# Bath

**97** **ARJO**
50 Gary Avenue
Roselle, IL 60172
630-307-2756
800-323-1245
FAX: 888-594-2756
e-mail: info@arjousa.com
www.arjo.com

*Lorena Chevrie, Marketing Communications*
*Ross Scavuzzo, President*

Concerto shower and procedure trolley allows patients to be cleansed and changed while laying in a supine position.

**98** **Adaptive Design Shop**
12847 Point Pleasant Drive
Fairfax, VA 22033
703-631-1585
800-351-2327
FAX: 775-256-2556
e-mail: info@email.com
www.adaptivedesignshop.com

*Joe Rickerson, Marketing Director*

Offers various adjustable models of bath and shower chairs, as well as adjustable toilet and commode supports for toddlers through adults. Call for a free brochure. Prices range from $200 to $800.

**99** **Adjustable Bath Seat**
Arista Surgical Supply Company/AliMed
297 High Street
Dedham, MA 02026
781-329-2900
800-223-1984
FAX: 781-329-8392
e-mail: arista@alimed.com
www.aristasurgical.com

*Julian Cherubini, President*

Bath seat that fits easily in any size tub. Easily adjustable to any height for easier maneuverability. *$44.00*

**100** **Adjustable Raised Toilet Seat & Guard**
Frohock-Stewart
39400 Taylor Parkway
N Ridgeville, OH 44035
440-329-6000
800-343-6059
FAX: 800-329-6270

*A Mixon Iii, Chief Executive Officer*

The seat features an exclusive pivot locking system so it won't slip or tip and the adjustable guard rail fits all toilets.

**101** **AirLift Toileting System from Mobility**
5726 La Jolla Boulevard
Suite 104
La Jolla, CA 92037
858-456-8121
866-456-8121
FAX: 858-456-8139
e-mail: info@mobilityinc.net
www.mobilityinc.net

*Steve Winston, VP Sales*
*Eric Proffitt, VP Marketing*

The Mobility AirLift toileting system makes it easy and painless to get on and off the toilet with or without an assistant. The Air-Lift absorbs the user's weight, providing gentle lowering to a sitting position and smooth lifting to a standing position.

**102** **BIT Talking Scale Bathroom Scale**
Sense-Sations
919 Walnut Street
Philadelphia, PA 19107
215-627-0600
800-876-5456
FAX: 215-922-0692

*Patricia Johnson, Chief Executive Officer*

Push the on button and the scale will invite you to jump on and discover how much weight you have lost or gained. *$91.50*

**103** **Bath Fixtures**
Crane Plumbing/Fiat Products
1000 Industrial Drive
Suite 2a
Bensenville, IL 60106
630-350-7575
FAX: 630-350-7775
www.craneplumbing.com

*Dave Pardue, Owner*

Manufacturers plumbing fixtures for the disabled. Products include toilets, lavatories, showers and tub/shower units.

**104** **Bath Products**
Snug Seat
PO Box 1739
Matthews, NC 28106
704-882-0666
800-336-7684
FAX: 704-882-0751
e-mail: information@snugseat.com
www.snugseat.com

*Steve Scribner, VP*
*Kirk MacKenzie, President*

Offers a wide range of products to meet the transportation, mobility, seating and bath aid needs for people of all ages. From car seats and standers for children with special needs to versatile wheelchairs that offer adults customized options and the freedom to go anywhere with confidence.

**105 Bath Shower & Commode Chair**
Clarke Health Care Products
1003 International Drive
Oakdale, PA 15071
724-695-2122
888-347-4537
FAX: 724-695-2922
e-mail: info@clarkehealthcare.com
www.clarkehealthcare.com

*Susan Grabel, Marketing*
*Gerard Clarke, Owner*

Posterior and anterior tilt, fits over most toilets. Includes soft seat, collection pan, adjustable foot rest and head rest. Portable and self propel model also available.

**106 Bath Supports**
Columbia Medical Manufacturing
13577 Larwin Circle
Santa Fe Springs, CA 90670
562-282-0264
800-454-6612
FAX: 310-305-1718
e-mail: cmedonline@aol.com
www.columbiamedical.com

*Gary Werschmidt, President*

Offers a full line of toilet supports, positioning commodes, wrap-around bath supports, reclining chairs and car seats for children from 20 to 102 pounds.

**107 Bath and Shower Bench 3301B**
Mada Medical Products
625 Washington Avenue
Carlstadt, NJ 07072
201-460-0454
800-526-6370
FAX: 201-460-3509
e-mail: sales@madamedical.com
www.madainternational.com

*Diane Lind, Operations Manager*
*Jeffrey Adam, Vice President*

The bath and shower bench is corrosion resistent, has a cross brace design and angled legs to prevent tipping, and seat height adjustments.

**108 BathEase**
3815 Darston Street
Palm Harbor, FL 34685
727-786-2604
888-747-7845
FAX: 727-786-2604
e-mail: bathease@aol.com
www.bathease.com

*Thomas Fitz Gerald, President/CEO*
*Terry Stickler, Director R&D*
*Gerry Grondin, Production Manager*

BathEase is the original, standard size, residential style, acrylic bathtub with a door. Ideal for use in private homes by all who are ambulatory, the award winning design was specially created as an aid to daily living for the elderly and physically challenged. *$1897.00*

**109 Bathtub Safety Rail**
Arista Surgical Supply Company/AliMed
297 High Street
Dedham, MA 02026
212-679-3694
800-223-1984
FAX: 212-696-9046
e-mail: arista@alimed.com
www.aristasurgical.com
Made of stainless steel, this safety rail fits in any size bathtub and offers safety and independence at bathing time. *$55.00*

**110 Braun Corporation**
Braun Corporation
PO Box 310
Winamac, IN 46996
574-946-6153
800-843-5438
FAX: 574-946-4670
www.braunlift.com

*Carolyn Watts, Public Affairs Contact*
*William Roth, President*

Offers a variety of assistive devices for the bath and surrounding environment.

**111 Can-Do Products Catalog**
Independent Living Aids
PO Box 9022
Hicksville, NY 11802
516-937-1848
800-537-2118
FAX: 516-937-3906

*Marvin Sandler, President*
*Fran Hennelly, Sales Director*
*84 pages Quarterly*

**112 Commode**
Maxi Aids
42 Executive Boulevard
Suite 3209
Farmingdale, NY 11735
631-752-0521
800-522-6294
FAX: 631-752-0689
e-mail: sales@maxiaids.com
www.maxiaids.com
Adjustable seat height for patient comfort. *$65.95*

**113 DSI**
16141 Runnymede Street
Van Nuys, CA 91406
818-782-6793
FAX: 818-782-6485
e-mail: info@wavegrip.com
www.wavegrip.com

*Greg Paquin, Marketing Manager*
*Bill Butt, Vice President*

Designer grab bars with ergonomic grip. Available in colors and custom shapes. New fold down shower seat. Support grips extend out from the wall 24 or 30. Concealed fastener and modular components for many design possibilities. Price ranges from $30.00 to $280.00.

**114 Deluxe Bath Bench with Adjustable Legs**
Maxi Aids
42 Executive Boulevard
Suite 3209
Farmingdale, NY 11735
631-752-0521
800-522-6294
FAX: 631-752-0689
e-mail: sales@maxiaids.com
www.maxiaids.com
Bath bench with back support and adjustable legs. *$49.95*

**115 Electric Leg Bag Emptier and Tub Slide Shower Chair**
RD Equipment
230 Percival Drive
West Barnstable, MA 02668
508-362-7498
FAX: 508-362-7498
e-mail: info@rdequipment.com
www.rdequipment.com

*Richard J Dagostino, Inventor/President*
*Diana M Pontieri, Sales Manager*

Designed for independence, this small, lightweight, battery-operated valve attaches to the bottom of the leg bag. A simple flip of the switch empties the leg bag, allowing the user to take in unlimited amounts of fluids. Tub Slide Shower Chair is a complete bathroom care system, with no need of costly renovations. Eliminates all transfers in the bathroom. *$200.00*

**116 Freedom Bath**
Arjo
50 Gary Avenue
Roselle, IL 60172
630-307-2756
800-323-1245
FAX: 888-594-2756
e-mail: lchevrie@arjousa.com
www.arjo.com

*Lorena Chevrie, Marketing Communications*
*Ross Scavuzzo, President*

Residents can relax on a semi-reclining seat and enjoy the soothing deluxe whirlpool system. Freedom Bath offers a revolutionary solution with its unique Roll-Door.

**117 Great Big Safety Tub Mat**
Maxi Aids
42 Executive Boulevard
Suite 3209
Farmingdale, NY 11735
631-752-0521
800-522-6294
FAX: 631-752-0689
e-mail: sales@maxiaids.com
www.maxiaids.com

Tub mat provides security against falls in the bath and shower. *$16.95*

**118 Long Handled Bath Sponges**
Therapro
225 Arlington Street
Framingham, MA 01702
508-872-9494
800-257-5376
FAX: 508-875-2062
e-mail: info@theraproducts.com
www.theraproducts.com

*Karen Conrad, Owner*

Plastic-handled, 18-inch bath sponge. Handle may be heated and bent for easy reach. *$2.50*

**119 Modular Wall Grab Bars**
Frohock-Stewart
39400 Taylor Parkway
N Ridgeville, OH 44035
440-329-6000
FAX: 440-365-7483

*A Mixon Iii, Chief Executive Officer*

Engineered for strength and beauty, these bars can be assembled in various combinations to fit any bath or shower.

**120 Pik Stik**
Mobilelectrics Company
4014 Bardstown Road
Louisville, KY 40218
800-URM-OVIN
FAX: 502-495-2476

Provides reaching and grasping power with accuracy and ease.

**121 Portable Shampoo Bowl**
Ambulatory Cosmetology Technicians
12762 Brookhurst Street
Suite 532
Garden Grove, CA 92840
949-833-1432

*Shirley D Smith*

A bowl designed to allow a person who is in a wheelchair or sitting on a regular chair to shampoo hair.

**122 Prelude**
Arjo
50 Gary Avenue
Roselle, IL 60172
630-307-2756
800-323-1245
FAX: 888-594-2756
e-mail: lchevrie@arjousa.com
www.arjo.com

*Lorena Chevrie, Marketing Communications*
*Ross Scavuzzo, President*

Prelude shower cabinet allows patients to be showered in comfort and privacy, at the same time as protecting staff from excessive splashing.

**123 SLIDER Bathing System**
Assistive Technology
21279 Protecta Drive
Elkhart, IN 46516
574-522-7201
800-478-2363
FAX: 574-293-0202
e-mail: info@pvcdme.com
www.pvcdme.com

The SLIDER bathing system eliminates costly roll-in shower renovations, bathroom transfers and other family members don't lose access to a bathtub. The SLIDER works with any standard built-in tub and rolls directly over any commode. The SLIDER utilizes 5 inch lock casters and has two swing-away arm rests for lateral transfers. Sliding gear functions in either direction. The SLIDER bathing system...a cost effective alternative to bathroom renovation.

**124 Suregrip Bathtub Rail**
Frohock-Stewart
39400 Taylor Parkway
N Ridgeville, OH 44035
440-329-6000
FAX: 440-365-7483

*A Mixon Iii, Chief Executive Officer*

Compact and versatile, the bars have a soft-touch, contoured, white vinyl gripping area for added safety.

**125 Talking Bathroom Scale**
Independent Living Aids
PO Box 9022
Hicksville, NY 11802
516-937-1848
800-537-2118
FAX: 516-937-3906
e-mail: can-do@independentliving.com
www.independentliving.com

*Marvin Sandler, President*

Talking scale. *$59.95*

**126 Terry-Wash Mitt: Medium Size**
Therapro
225 Arlington Street
Framingham, MA 01702
508-872-9494
800-257-5376
FAX: 508-875-2062
e-mail: info@theraproducts.com
www.theraproducts.com

*Karen Conrad, Owner*

Includes a thumb socket and a palm pocket to hold a bar of soap. *$8.00*

**127 Toilet Guard Rail**
Maxi Aids
42 Executive Boulevard
Suite 3209
Farmingdale, NY 11735
631-752-0521
800-522-6294
FAX: 631-752-0689
e-mail: sales@maxiaids.com
www.maxiaids.com

Made of chrome-plated, heavy gauge steel. Fits securely to the toilet for maximum sturdiness. *$43.95*

**128 Transfer Tub Bench**
Arista Surgical Supply Company/AliMed
297 High Street
Dedham, MA 02026
781-329-2900
800-223-1984
FAX: 781-329-8392
e-mail: aristasurgical@juno.com
www.aristasurgical.com

*Julian Cherubini, President*

Curved padded backrest for comfortable support. Backrest also assists patient during lateral transfer. *$64.00*

**129 Tri-Grip Bathtub Rail**
Maxi Aids
42 Executive Boulevard
Suite 3209
Farmingdale, NY 11735
631-752-0521
800-522-6294
FAX: 631-752-0689
e-mail: sales@maxiaids.com
www.maxiaids.com
Two gripping heights for easy bathtub entrance or exit. *$36.95*

**130 Tub Slide Shower Chair**
RD Equipment
230 Percival Drive
West Barnstable, MA 02668
508-362-7498
FAX: 508-362-7498
e-mail: info@rdequipment.com
www.rdequipment.com

*Richard J Dagostino, Proprietor/Inventor*
*Diana M Pontieri, Sales Manager*

The tub slide shower chair was designed for the elderly and disabled to make any bathroom (at home or when travelling) accessible with little or no renovations. Go from the bed, to the commode and over to the bathtub for a shower using one product. No transfers in the bathroom whatsoever. *$2000.00*

# Bed

**131 ASSISTECH**
2738 N Campbell Avenue
Tucson, AZ 85719
520-883-8600
FAX: 520-883-3172
e-mail: info@azhearing.com
www.azhearing.com

*Oliver Simoes, Owner*
Sells hearing, visual and mobility aid devices. *$39.00*

**132 Adjustable Bed**
Golden Technologies
401 Bridge Street
Old Forge, PA 18518
570-451-7477
800-624-6374
FAX: 570-451-7494
e-mail: info@goldentech.com
www.goldentech.com

*Rich Golden, CEO*
*Fred Kiwax, VP*
*Bob Golden, President*

Trouble-free gear motor, safety features, dual massage, variable speed timer and more, for the ultimate sleep experience.

**133 Bye-Bye Decubiti Air Mattress Overlay**
Ken McRight Supplies
7456 S Oswego Avenue
Tulsa, OK 74136
918-492-9657
FAX: 918-492-9694

*Ken McRight, President*
Originally designed for hospital beds, converts any bed into an exceptionally therapeutic, flotation unit when used between the conventional mattress and pad. The complete overlay is comprised of five individually inflatable, 100 percent natural rubber, ventilated sections enclosed within separate pockets of a soft fleece cover. Conforms to any configuration of electric or manual beds. *$731.50*

**134 Cervical Support Pillow**
Wise Enterprises
5017 El Don Drive
Rocklin, CA 95677
916-624-3848
888-947-3368
FAX: 916-624-3848
e-mail: wisent@pacbell.net
www.wisent.com/pillows.htm

*Tom Wise, Owner*
These hypoallergenic, antimicrobial fiber pillows support the neck in a natural position. Standard, midsize and petite pillows support the neck while sleeping on the back or side. The compact travel pillow offers support while sitting or lying down. The cervical roll has a gentle center and firm ends to ensure maximum comfort and proper support. Position the roll under the neck, back or knees. Standard and midsize fits adults, petite fits children and small adults.

**135 Foam Decubitus Bed Pads**
Profex Medical Products
PO Box 140188
Memphis, TN 38114
800-325-0196
FAX: 901-454-9850
e-mail: info@profexmed.com
www.profexmed.com
Convoluted foam provides extra back support and comfort for wheelchair users.

**136 Hard Manufacturing Company**
230 Grider Street
Buffalo, NY 14215
716-893-1800
800-873-4273
FAX: 716-896-2579
e-mail: currier@hardmfg.com
www.hardmfg.com

*Kevin Currier, Corporate Sales*
*William Godin, President*
Manufacturer of pediatric cribs and age appropriate youth beds. Free catalog.

**137 Jackson Cervipillo**
Wise Enterprises
5017 El Don Drive
Rocklin, CA 95677
916-624-3848
888-947-3368
FAX: 916-624-3848
e-mail: wisent@pacbell.net
www.wisent.com/pillows.htm

*Tom Wise, Owner*
The Jackson Cervipillo confortably supports the neck vertebrae when sleeping on the side or on the back. Pillow measures 7 in diameter and is 17 long. A machine-washable cover is available separately.

**138 Med Covers**
Med Covers
PO Box 1527e
Garner, NC 27529
919-779-3555
800-948-8917
FAX: 919-779-3540
e-mail: medteam@medcovers.com
www.medcovers.com

*Jeanie Falkie, Sales Counsultant Med Division*
Manufactures cases and covers for the medical and data capture industries. Specializing in oxygen cylinder, scooter and wheelchairs covers, and accessories.

**139 NeckEase**
Wise Enterprises
5017 El Don Drive
Rocklin, CA 95677

916-624-3848
888-947-3368
FAX: 916-624-3848
e-mail: wisent@pacbell.net
www.wisent.com/pillows.htm

*Tom Wise, Owner*

Microwave NeckEase for penetrating heat that sooths stiff necks and shoulders, easing tension. NeckEase features a unique filling of organic, long grain rice and aromatic herbs and spices. When heated, this filling provides soothing, moist aromatherapy. Heat lasts about 30-45 minutes. Available in two sizes: small fits snugly around the neck, applying gentle pressure at the base of the skull; Large may be worn for a snug fit, or loosely for application on the shoulder and upper back.

**140 Permaflex Home Care Mattress**
BG Industries
8550 Balboa Boulevard
Suite 214
Northridge, CA 91325

818-894-0744
800-822-8288
www.bgind.com

*Larry Lankard, President*

Mattress with flame retardant upholstery material, water-repellant, anti-microbial and tear-resistant cover, for extra comfort.

**141 Priva**
PO Box 448
Champlain, NY 12919

514-356-8881
800-761-8881
FAX: 514-356-0055
e-mail: piv@priva-inc.com
www.priva-inc.com

*David Horowitz, President*
*Natasha Pietramala, Director HHC Division*

Reusable incontinence care products including briefs, liners, inserts and sheet protectors. Manufacturers of Quorum Zip & Block anti-allergen bedding.

**142 SleepSafe Beds**
3135 Dillons Mill Road
Callaway, VA 24067

540-334-1600
866-852-2337
FAX: 540-334-2100
www.sleepsafebed.com

Perfect for adult home or home care use. Offering twin or full size bed frames in classic style, these beds offer an attractive alternative to a hospital bed. Keeps the user safe during rest and electrically adjusts smoothly for user comfort and caregiver ease of use.

**143 Sonic Alert Bed Shaker**
ASSISTECH
2738 N Campbell Avenue
Tucson, AZ 85719

520-883-8600
FAX: 520-883-3172
www.azhearing.com

*Oliver Simoes, Owner*
*$49.00*

**144 Vibes Bed Shaker**
ASSISTECH
2738 N Campbell Avenue
Tucson, AZ 85719

520-883-8600
FAX: 520-883-3172
www.azhearing.com

*Oliver Simoes, Owner*

**145 Vibration Watch/Countdown Timer**
Global Assistive Devices
4950 N Dixie Highway
Oakland Park, FL 33334

954-776-1373
FAX: 954-776-8136
TTY:954-776-1373
e-mail: info@globalassistive.com
www.globalassistive.com

*Peggy Hewitt, Marketing Manager*

This useful innovation reminds you and alerts you. Use for medical conditions. It can even be used as a travel alarm. Unique Auto Repeat Countdown Timer resets itself each time it reaches zero.

**146 Waterproof Sheet-Topper Mattress and Chair Pad**
Pillow Talk
348 Pond Road
Freehold, NJ 07728

732-780-9483
FAX: 732-780-0279
e-mail: info@pillowtalkusa.com
www.pillowtalkusa.com

*Jack Fajerman, President*
*Dorothy Faferman, Owner*

This soft pad lies on the top sheet, absorbing accidents from incontinence, pregnancy or medical problems. Waterproof barrier locks out moisture, soiling and stains and eliminates midnight linen changes and the resulting laundry. Available in bed sizes W/4 Anchor, twin, full, queen, king, and crib.

# Communication

**147 ACS Wireless: Advanced Cyber Solutions**
3744 Civic Center Drive
North Las Vegas, NV 89030

702-364-1114
FAX: 702-364-1718
e-mail: info@advancedcyber.com
www.advancedcyber.com

This company makes a telephone headset.

**148 ADA Hotel Built-In Alerting System**
HARC Mercantile
1111 W Centre Avenue
Portage, MI 49024

269-324-1615
800-445-9968
FAX: 269-324-2387
e-mail: home@harcmercantile.com
www.harcmercantile.com

*Ronald Slager, President*
*Ronald Damstra, Technical Sales Manager*

Visual alerting system for ADA compliance for multihousing/rooms facilities, like hospitals, dorms, senior housing for persons who are hard of hearing or deaf. Alerts to five conditions: smoke, door bell, telephone ring, wake up and House central alarm.

**149 Able-Phone 110**
DQP
14167 Meadow Drive
Grass Valley, CA 95945

916-477-1234
800-456-4979
FAX: 530-477-7122

Cordless headset telephone with keypad.

**150 Able-Phone 2500**
DQP
14167 Meadow Drive
Grass Valley, CA 95945

916-477-1234
800-456-4979
FAX: 530-477-7122

Remote control emergency message telephone.

**151    Able-Switch 300**
DQP
14167 Meadow Drive
Grass Valley, CA  95945                    916-477-1234
                                           800-456-4979
                                    FAX: 530-477-7122

Wireless remote control.

**152    Able-Switch 500**
DQP
14167 Meadow Drive
Grass Valley, CA  95945                    916-477-1234
                                           800-456-4979
                                    FAX: 530-477-7122

Wireless remote receiver/controller.

**153    Able-Switch SW-1**
DQP
14167 Meadow Drive
Grass Valley, CA  95945                    916-477-1234
                                           800-456-4979
                                    FAX: 530-477-7122

Touch switch.

**154    Access Control Systems: NHX Nurse Call System**
Aiphone Corporation
1700 130th Avenue NE
Bellevue, WA  98005                        425-455-0510
                                           800-692-0200
                                    FAX: 425-455-0071
                              e-mail: info@aiphone.com
                                      www.aiphone.com

*Tak Kanie, President*

AIPHONE manufactures audio and video intercom systems for home or business to help the physically disabled answer doors and communicate through physical barriers; also ADA-compliant emergency call intercom stations for use in public facilities and an Environmental Control System for persons with limited mobility.

**155    Adaptek Systems**
2320 Brighton Henrietta Town Line R
Rochester, NY  14623
                                           800-685-4566
                                    FAX: 585-475-9889

Developers of a voice output module designed to work with the Kurzweil voice-recognition system. The device provides voice output of what the computer hears for persons with visual impairments.

**156    Akron Resources**
20 La Porte Street
Arcadia, CA  91006                         626-254-9005
                                    FAX: 626-254-9266
                                          www.akron.com

*Lisa Avalos, Operations Manager*
*Paul Brassard, Owner*

Manufacturers of infrared amplification systems for televisions or stereos. $29-$69.00.

**157    Ameriphone**
12082 Western Avenue
Garden Grove, CA  92841
                                           800-874-3005
                                    FAX: 714-897-4703
                        e-mail: ameriphone@ameriphone.com
                                    www.ameriphone.com

*Lisa DeLeuil, Sales Manager*
*Michael Hartberger, President*
*John Koste, Product Manager*

The Ameriphone Dialogue RC is a remote-controlled speakerphone that can be activated up to 40 feet away. It features up to 20 memory buttons that you scan and select by gently pressing the remote control or blowing in the optional Airswitch or squeezing the optional pillow switch. Features voice activated answering for complete independence and access to telephone company services such as call waiting. Phones $299.00-$399.00. Accessories $39-$99.

**158    Ameriphone Hearing Assistance Telephone**
12082 Western Avenue
Garden Grove, CA  92841
                                           800-874-3005
                                    FAX: 714-897-4703
                        e-mail: ameriphone@ameriphone.com
                                    www.ameriphone.com

*Lisa DeLeuil, Sales Manager*
*Michael Hartberger, President*
*John Koste, Product Manager*

A communication-enhanced telephone with a large button and contrasting graphics for optimum visibility and dialing ease. Amplifies incoming voice by 30 db gain and has a frequency screening feature that permits user to identify sound frequencies. *$119.95*

**159    Amplified Handsets**
HARC Mercantile
1111 W Centre Avenue
Portage, MI  49024                         269-324-1615
                                           800-445-9968
                                    FAX: 269-324-2387
                        e-mail: home@harcmercantile.com
                                    www.harcmercantile.com

*Ronald Slager, President*

Choices of touch activated, electronic control, rotary (thumb wheel) volume control, that can directly replace old handset, stocked in round and square styles. This also includes an electric transmitter with variable settings. *$39.95*

**160    Amplified Phones**
HARC Mercantile
1111 W Centre Avenue
Portage, MI  49024                         269-324-1615
                                           800-445-9968
                                    FAX: 269-324-2387
                        e-mail: home@harcmercantile.com
                                    www.harcmercantile.com

*Ronald Slager, President*

Low frequency ringer, indicator light, enhances or amplifies sound, some that automatically return to normal dial tone when phone receiver is hung up, lighted easy to read dial pad and volume control boosts incoming sound. *$95.00*

**161    Amplified Portable Phone**
HARC Mercantile
1111 W Centre Avenue
Portage, MI  49024                         269-324-1615
                                           800-445-9968
                                    FAX: 269-324-2387
                        e-mail: home@harcmercantile.com
                                    www.harcmercantile.com

*Ronald Slager, President*
Portable amplified phones. *$199.00*

**162    Answerall 100**
DQP
14167 Meadow Drive
Grass Valley, CA  95945                    916-477-1234
                                           800-456-4979
                                    FAX: 530-477-7122

Answering machine for TDD and voice.

**163    Artificial Larynx**
HARC Mercantile
1111 W Centre Avenue
Portage, MI 49024

269-324-1615
800-445-9968
FAX: 269-324-2387
e-mail: home@harcmercantile.com
www.harcmercantile.com

*Ronald Slager, President*

For people unable to use their larynx, a hand-held speaking aid
that simulates the natural vibrations of voice. *$220.00*

**164    Assistive Technology**
333 Elm Street
Dedham, MA 02026

781-461-8200
800-793-9227
FAX: 781-461-8213
e-mail: customercare@assistivetech.com
www.assistivetech.com

*Jane Oles, Customer Service Manager*
*Roxanne Varteressian, Marketing Specialist*
*James Lewis, President*

A premiere developer of innovative technology solutions for
people with physical and learning disabilities. Breakthrough
products enable people of all ages and abilities to live and learn
independently. Supportive material for teachers, clinicians and
those with disabilities.

**165    BESTspeech**
Berkeley Speech Technologies
2246 6th Street
Berkeley, CA 94710

510-841-5083
FAX: 510-841-5093
e-mail: webmaster@bst.com
www.bestspeech.com

This text-to-speech facility is useful to persons who are blind or
vision impaired and may be used by those with speech, hearing
and learning difficulties.

**166    Big Red Switch**
AbleNet
2808 Fairview Avenue N
Saint Paul, MN 55113

800-322-0956
FAX: 651-294-2259
e-mail: customerservice@ablenetinc.com
www.ablenetinc.com

*Mary Kay Walch*

Five inches across the top and activates no matter where on its
surface it is touched. It is made of shatterproof plastic and contains a cord storage compartment. Also available in green, yellow and blue. *$42.00*

**167    Cornell Communications**
7915 N 81st Street
Milwaukee, WI 53223

414-351-4660
800-558-8957
FAX: 414-351-4657
e-mail: sales@cornell.com
www.cornell.com

*David D Thompson, Account Executive*
*Pauline Haack, Customer Service*
*Randy Stell, Account Executive*

Cornell's Rescue Assistance Systems allow personnel to request
emergency assistance. Applications include handicapped evac-
uations, parking garages and elevators. Voice, intercom and visual only signaling systems are available.

**168    Davis Center**
1 Mannino Drive
Rockaway, NJ 07866

973-347-7662
FAX: 973-691-0611
e-mail: info@thedaviscenter.net
www.thedaviscenter.com

*Dorinne S Davis, President*

Sound-based therapies that help hearing, learning, speech and
well-being. Complete hearing, speech and CAP testing.

**169    Flashing Lamp Telephone Ring Alerter**
Independent Living Aids
PO Box 9022
Hicksville, NY 11802

516-937-1848
800-537-2118
FAX: 516-937-3906
e-mail: can-do@independentliving.com
www.independentliving.com

*Marvin Sandler, President*

Once your phone is plugged into the Telephone Ring Alerter, the
lamp light will flash with each ring, alerting you that there is a
phone call. *$62.00*

**170    Gabbi Talk Phone**
Sense-Sations
919 Walnut Street
Philadelphia, PA 19107

215-627-0600
FAX: 215-922-0692

*Patricia Johnson, Chief Executive Officer*

The talking telephone for mistake-free dialing lets the individual know what numbers they have dialed. *$28.50*

**171    Genesis One**
2827b Cleveland Road
Wooster, OH 44691

330-263-0015
888-221-5032
FAX: 775-252-4834
e-mail: info@apt-technology.com
www.apt-technology.com

*Larry Shirer, President*

Dedicated to sales and manufacturing of user friendly, and reliable, assistive technology products and systems. These products
are designed to increase independence and improve the quality
of life for persons with disabilities.
*c pages*

**172    Headmaster Plus**
Prentke Romich Company
1022 Heyl Road
Wooster, OH 44691

330-262-1984
800-262-1984
FAX: 330-263-4829
e-mail: info@prentrom.com
www.prentrom.com

*Dave Moffatt, President*

A headpointing system that takes the place of a mouse and allows individuals who cannot use their hands but have good head
control access to the computer. A transmitting unit sits atop the
monitor and sends signals to the user's headset. The user puffs
into a tube connected to the headset to make selections. Typing
can be done with optional on-screen keyboards. *$1195.00*

**173    Ideal-Phone**
IDEAMATICS
1364 Beverly Road
Suite 101
McLean, VA 22101

703-903-4972
800-247-IDEA
FAX: 703-903-8949
e-mail: ideamatics@ideamatics.net
www.ideamatics.org

*David L Danner, President*
*Pamela Danner, Owner*

Integrates the personal computer and the telephone into a single, efficient workstation. It is ideal for mobility-impaired persons and others who need a hands-free operation of the phone. The Ideal-Phone includes one PC Board, a Plantronics headset, software for access and logging and complete documentation. It can be integrated into programs or pops-up over any application. MS-DOS based, version 3.0 or higher are available. *$195.00*

**174    IntelliKeys**
IntelliTools
1720 Corporate Circle
Petaluma, CA  94954                      707-773-2000
                                         800-889-6687
                                    FAX: 707-773-2001
                          e-mail: tech@intellitools.com
                                   www.intellitools.com

*Arjan Khalsa, Chief Executive Officer*

Card and cable to create keyboard port on Apple IIe computer to allow use of IntelliKeys alternative keyboard.

**175    LPB Communications**
960 Brook Road
Norristown, PA  19401                    856-365-8080
                                    FAX: 856-365-8999
                        e-mail: lpbsales@lpbinc.com
                                       www.lpbinc.com

*John Devecka, VP Sales*

Limited area AM and FM broadcast systems for hearing assistance and language translation manufacturing since 1960. Systems for small conference halls, churches and Olympic stadiums. Components or complete system. *$400.00*

**176    Language, Learning & Living**
Prentke Romich Company
1022 Heyl Road
Wooster, OH  44691                       330-262-1984
                                         800-262-1984
                                    FAX: 330-263-4829
                           e-mail: info@prentrom.com
                                      www.prentrom.com

*Dave Moffatt, President*

A Minspeak application program designed for adolescent and adult individuals with developmental disabilities and associated learning difficulties. The software is used with Prentke Romich Company augmentative communication devices. *$355.00*

**177    Large Button Speaker Phone**
HARC Mercantile
1111 W Centre Avenue
Portage, MI  49024                       269-324-1615
                                         800-445-9968
                                    FAX: 269-324-2387
                     e-mail: home@harcmercantile.com
                               www.harcmercantile.com

*Ronald Slager, President*

Speakerphone with or without remote control. *$395.00*

**178    Large Print Telephone Dial**
Maxi Aids
42 Executive Boulevard
Suite 3209
Farmingdale, NY  11735                   631-752-0521
                                         800-522-6294
                                    FAX: 631-752-0689
                        e-mail: sales@maxiaids.com
                                      www.maxiaids.com
Pressure sensitive dial with numbers that are easy to see for the disabled. *$69.00*

**179    Large Print Touch-Telephone Overlays**
Maxi Aids
42 Executive Boulevard
Suite 3209
Farmingdale, NY  11735                   631-752-0521
                                         800-522-6294
                                    FAX: 631-752-0689
                        e-mail: sales@maxiaids.com
                                      www.maxiaids.com

Pressure-sensitive and easy to apply overlays that make everyday phones accessible. *$49.00*

**180    Liberator**
Prentke Romich Company
1022 Heyl Road
Wooster, OH  44691                       330-262-1984
                                         800-262-1984
                                    FAX: 330-263-4829
                           e-mail: info@prentrom.com
                                      www.prentrom.com

*Dave Moffatt, President*

A portable electronic communication device that uses Minspeak so that symbols are used to represent words, sentences or phrases. Liberator can be accessed by pressing keys, optical headpointing and a wide variety of switch activated scans. It can be configured with 8, 32 or 128 locations. It offers a variety of unique features to permit the most effective communication possible. *$7,345-$8,575.*

**181    Meroni Premiapri Press-Button Door Knob**
Meroni Locks of America
8012 NW 75th Avenue
Tamarac, FL  33321
                                         800-749-5625
                                    FAX: 305-556-2405

*Michael Knight, Director*
*P Carlo Cau, VP*

Door lock used in environments where barrier free access is required.

**182    Metropolitan Washington Ear**
35 University Boulevard E
Silver Spring, MD  20901                 301-681-6636
                                    FAX: 301-681-5227
                          e-mail: info@washear.org
                                      www.washear.org

*Nancy Knauss, Executive Director*

Multi-media reading service for blind and visually impaired. Offering 24 hour audio radio reading, dial-in newspapers and web casting, as well as audio description at theaters, museums and films.

**183    Micro IntroVoice III**
Voice Connexion
10522 Covington Circle
Villa Park, CA  92861                    714-685-1066
                                    FAX: 714-628-1321
                          e-mail: voicecnx@aol.com
                               www.voicecnx.com/miv3.htm?
Voice activated interface unit that can be installed on most existing and all new wheelchairs; occupants are then able to speak commands to control the motion of the chair. *$2495.00*

**184    Mini Teleloop**
HARC Mercantile
1111 W Centre Avenue
Portage, MI  49024                       269-324-1615
                                         800-445-9968
                                    FAX: 269-324-2387
                     e-mail: home@harcmercantile.com
                               www.harcmercantile.com

*Ronald Slager, President*

Home induction loop amplifier for use with hearing aids equipped with T-Coil. *$159.95*

**185  Multiple Phone/Device Switch**
HARC Mercantile
1111 W Centre Avenue
Portage, MI 49024

269-324-1615
800-445-9968
FAX: 269-324-2387
e-mail: home@harcmercantile.com
www.harcmercantile.com

*Ronald Slager, President*
Used to switch phone lines between two devices. *$34.95*

**186  Oticon Portable Telephone Amplifier**
Hear You Are
4 Musconetcong Avenue
Stanhope, NJ 07874

800-287-EARS
FAX: 973-347-7662
Attaches to any sound source, picks up sound, amplifies it and induces it onto hearing aid telecoils. *$93.00*

**187  Outdoor Loud Bell**
Hear You Are
4 Musconetcong Avenue
Stanhope, NJ 07874

800-287-EARS
FAX: 973-347-7662
This outdoor bell with a loud mechanical ringer features an easy, plug-in installation to either a modular or hook-up. *$79.16*

**188  Personal FM Systems**
HARC Mercantile
1111 W Centre Avenue
Portage, MI 49024

269-324-1615
800-445-9968
FAX: 269-324-2387
e-mail: home@harcmercantile.com
www.harcmercantile.com

*Ronald Slager, President*
Wireless FM systems transmit sound via a radio carrier wave. *$599.95*

**189  Personal Infrared Listening System**
HARC Mercantile
1111 W Centre Avenue
Portage, MI 49024

269-324-1615
800-445-9968
FAX: 269-324-2387
e-mail: home@harcmercantile.com
www.harcmercantile.com

*Ronald Slager, President*
Wireless method of listening to TV and radio with individually controlled amplification. *$199.00*

**190  Phone-TTY**
1246 Route 46 W
Parsippany, NJ 07054

973-299-6627
888-332-3889
FAX: 973-299-7768
e-mail: phonetty@aol.com
www.phone-tty.com

*Anna M Terrazzino, Executive Director*
Develops and promotes better communications for the deaf using ordinary telephone equipment and current technology. Installs computerized phone-television equipment in the homes of individuals who are deaf, enabling these individuals to communicate with local police, hospitals, answering services and news services.

**191  Plantronics SP-04**
DQP
14167 Meadow Drive
Grass Valley, CA 95945

800-456-4979
FAX: 530-477-7122

Headset telephone for people who have a hard time grasping the telephone.

**192  Prentke Romich Company**
1022 Heyl Road
Wooster, OH 44691

330-262-1984
800-262-1984
FAX: 330-263-4829
e-mail: info@prentrom.com
www.prentrom.com

*Barry Romich, Chairman*
*Joe Durbin, President*
*Cherie Weaver, Marketing Coordinator*

The Prentke Romich Company is a full service company offering easy, yet powerful communication aids. The company believes in supporting customers before and after the sale by offering funding assistance, distance learning training, extended warranty, service assistance and much more. Visit our website to view our full line catalog, read about our success stories and to sign up for our online newsletter.

**193  Push to Talk Amplified Handset**
HARC Mercantile
1111 W Centre Avenue
Portage, MI 49024

269-324-1615
800-445-9968
FAX: 269-324-2387
e-mail: home@harcmercantile.com
www.harcmercantile.com

*Ronald Slager, President*
Replacement receiver which is hearing aid compatible and is designed for high noise conditions. *$79.95*

**194  Remote Control Speakerphone**
Ameriphone
12082 Western Avenue
Garden Grove, CA 92841

800-874-3005
FAX: 714-897-4703
e-mail: ameriphone@ameriphone.com
www.ameriphone.com

*Lisa DeLeuil, Sales Manager*
*Michael Hartberger, President*
*John Koste, Product Manager*

A multi-functional speaker phone specially designed to meet the needs of motion-impaired persons who are unable to use a conventional phone without assistance.

**195  Ring-a-Lite**
Tellus Business Services
1120 SW Sampson Road
Lees Summit, MO 64081

816-554-3777
FAX: 816-765-3301
e-mail: telus@birch.net
www.birch.net/~telus/ring.htm

*Ralph Taylor, Partner*
*Ron Toles, Owner*

Allows persons to see a telephone ringing, eliminating missing calls. This easy to use unit connects directly to existing telephone connections and also works to signal incoming TDD messages. *$39.95*

**196  Room Valet Visual-Tactile Alerting System**
HARC Mercantile
1111 W Centre Avenue
Portage, MI 49024

269-324-1615
800-445-9968
FAX: 269-324-2387
e-mail: home@harcmercantile.com
www.harcmercantile.com

*Ronald Slager, President*

ADA compliant built-in visual-tactile alerting system. The Room Valet is fully supervised and has power failure back up. Alerts to in-room smoke, building alarm, door, phone and alarm clock. Designed for permanent installation.

**197  Scanning Director II**
APT Technology
236a N Main Street
Shreve, OH  44676

330-567-2001
800-549-2001
FAX: 330-567-3073
e-mail: sales@apt-technology.com
www.apt-technology.com

*Grace Miller, Office Manager*

Controls all features of a TV, VCR, satellite system, etc. by means of scanning controlled by a single or dual switch. Operates also as an accessory to an ECU, also controls 16 lamps/appliances using X-10. *$795.00*

**198  Silent Call Communications**
5095 Williams Lake Road
Waterford, MI  48329

800-572-5227
FAX: 248-377-4168
e-mail: silentcall@ameritech.net
www.silentcall.com

*George Elwell, President*
*Suzie Wright, Office Manager*

Alerting devices such as paging systems and smoke detectors for deaf and deaf-blind people.

**199  Silent Call: Portable Visual and/or Vibratory Alerting System**
Hear You Are
4 Musconetcong Avenue
Stanhope, NJ  07874

800-278-EARS
FAX: 973-347-7662

Small portable alerting device strobe light and vibrator announcer. Alerts to doorbell, telephone, smoke detector or sound monitors activations. Each alert is identified by a different colored light indicator. *$249.95*

**200  Sonic Alert**
Harris Communications
15155 Technology Drive
Eden Prairie, MN  55344

952-906-1180
800-825-6758
FAX: 952-906-1099
e-mail: info@harriscomm.com
www.harriscomm.com

*Bill Williams, National Sales Manager*
*Lori Foss, Marketing Director*
*Robert Harris, Owner*

Offers visual alerting devices that provide safety and convenience by turning vital sound into flashing light: telephone ring signalers, doorbell signalers, baby cry signalers and wake up alarms. Free catalog available.

**201  Sonic Alert: Visual and Vibratory Alarm Clock**
Hear You Are
4 Musconetcong Avenue
Stanhope, NJ  07874

800-284-EARS
FAX: 973-347-7662

Clock features a large green LED display with extremely loud pulsating alarm. The tone and volume is adjustable so users can select their individual needs. Outlets are provided for a table lamp and a bed shaker. *$52.45*

**202  Sound Induction Receiver**
HARC Mercantile
1111 W Centre Avenue
Portage, MI  49024

269-324-1615
800-445-9968
FAX: 269-324-2387
e-mail: home@harcmercantile.com
www.harcmercantile.com

*Ronald Slager, President*

Sound induction receiver to be used with any loop system. *$67.00*

**203  SpeakEasy Communication Aid**
AbleNet
2808 Fairview Avenue N
Saint Paul, MN  55113

800-322-0956
FAX: 612-379-9143
e-mail: customerservice@ablenetinc.com
www.ablenetinc.com

SpeakEasy is a digitalized voice output communication Aid that is ideal for anyone who is beginning to develop communication skills such as making choices and identifying symbols. It holds 12 messages totaling four minutes and 20 seconds of recording time. It measures 7 1/2 inch by 1 3/4 inch and weighs only one pound. Activate messages using the built-in keyboard or via external switch. *$399.00*

**204  Speakwriter 2000**
HumanWare
6140 Horseshoe Bar Road
Suite P
Loomis, CA  95650

916-652-7253

Talking typewriter.

**205  Speech Discrimination Unit**
HARC Mercantile
1111 W Centre Avenue
Portage, MI  49024

269-324-1615
800-445-9968
FAX: 269-324-2387
e-mail: home@harcmercantile.com
www.harcmercantile.com

*Ronald Slager, President*

Speech Adjust-A-Tone improves speech discrimination for use with telephone and/or TV and radio. *$189.95*

**206  Speechmaker-Personal Speech Amplifier**
HARC Mercantile
1111 W Centre Avenue
Portage, MI  49024

269-324-1615
800-445-9968
FAX: 269-324-2387
e-mail: home@harcmercantile.com
www.harcmercantile.com

*Ronald Slager, President*

Portable, body worn, personal speech amplifier for people with a weak voice. *$316.00*

**207  Standard Touch Turner Sip & Puff Switch**
Access to Recreation
8 Sandra Court
Newbury Park, CA  91320

805-498-7535
800-634-4351
FAX: 805-498-8186
e-mail: dkrebs@accesstr.com
www.accesstr.com

*Don Krebs, President*

A page turning device.

**208 Step-by-Step Communicator**
AbleNet
2808 Fairview Avenue N
Saint Paul, MN 55113

800-322-0956
FAX: 612-379-9143
e-mail: customerservice@ablenetinc.com
www.ablenetinc.com

Allows you to record a series of messages (as many as you want up to the 75 second limit). It has a 2 1/2 inches diameter switch surface and is 3 inches at its tallest point. Angled switch surface makes it easy to see and access. *$129.00*

**209 Strobe Light Signalers**
HARC Mercantile
1111 W Centre Avenue
Portage, MI 49024

269-324-1615
800-445-9968
FAX: 269-324-2387
e-mail: home@harcmercantile.com
www.harcmercantile.com

*Ronald Slager, President*

Strobe alerts. Plugs into receivers for signaling systems. *$39.95*

**210 TTY's: Telephone Device for the Deaf**
HARC Mercantile
1111 W Centre Avenue
Portage, MI 49024

269-324-1615
800-445-9968
FAX: 269-324-2387
e-mail: home@harcmercantile.com
www.harcmercantile.com

*Ronald Slager, President*

With or without printer. *$239.00*

**211 TalkTrac Wearable Communicator**
Ablenet
2808 Fairview Avenue N
Saint Paul, MN 55113

800-322-0956
FAX: 612-379-9143
e-mail: customerservice@ablenetinc.com
www.ablenetinc.com

The TalkTrac Wearable Communicator is a personal, portable communication aid that is wearable on the wrist. TalkTrac features: simple to use, 75 seconds of recording time, four 3/4 x 1/2 message locations, rechargeable, water resistant, adjustable 9" band, Boardmaker compatible.

**212 Talkback Wireless Doorbell Intercom**
Rice International Corporation
7952 Pines Boulevard
Pembroke Pines, FL 33024

954-983-6464
FAX: 305-895-7660

*Donald Van Der Laan, General Manager*
*Suzanne Minnick, Advertising Manager*

Wireless radio frequency combined with doorbell and intercom. Outside unit uses 9 volt battery and features hands free operation. This device automatically turns off after one minute. *$99.95*

**213 Talking Calculators**
ASSISTECH
2738 N Campbell Avenue
Tucson, AZ 85719

520-883-8600
FAX: 520-883-3172
e-mail: info@assistivedevices.net
www.azhearing.com

*Oliver Simoes, Owner*

**214 Talking Clocks**
HARC Mercantile
1111 W Centre Avenue
Portage, MI 49024

269-324-1615
800-445-9968
FAX: 269-324-2387
e-mail: home@harcmercantile.com
www.harcmercantile.com

*Ronald Slager, President*

Talking clocks with loud alarms, high and low volume control, choices of sound effects, hourly report options. Other languages are available. *$20.50*

**215 Talking Watches**
HARC Mercantile
1111 W Centre Avenue
Portage, MI 49024

269-324-1615
800-445-9968
FAX: 269-324-2387
e-mail: home@harcmercantile.com
www.harcmercantile.com

*Ronald Slager, President*

Digital display, hourly reports, alarm with rooster crow, in English or Spanish. *$20.25*

**216 Telecaption Adapter**
HARC Mercantile
1111 W Centre Avenue
Portage, MI 49024

269-324-1615
800-445-9968
FAX: 269-324-2387
e-mail: home@harcmercantile.com
www.harcmercantile.com

*Ronald Slager, President*

Caption opens up the world of television to hearing impaired people. Viewers can read on the screen what they may not be able to hear. Closed captions are the dialogue and sound effects of a TV program or home video printed on the screen, similar to subtitles. *$159.95*

**217 Touch Turner-Page Turning Devices**
Touch Turner Company
13621 103rd Avenue NE
Arlington, WA 98223

360-651-1962
FAX: 360-658-9380
e-mail: touchturner@worldnet.att.net
www.touchturner.com

*Karen Rieger, President*

Turns pages in either direction powered by flashlight batteries and holds the reading at the proper angle for sitting or reclining.

**218 Ultratec: Auto Answer TTY**
Hear You Are
4 Musconetcong Avenue
Stanhope, NJ 07874

800-278-EARS
FAX: 973-347-7662

Full featured, primitive TTY with auto answering features for business or emergency services. Has direct connect or acoustic coupling with turbo communications mode, equipped with auto ID and relay Voice Announcer. Large memory buffer supports storing of conversation, memory message and directories. *$549.00*

**219 Unity**
Prentke Romich Company
1022 Heyl Road
Wooster, OH 44691

330-262-1984
800-262-1984
FAX: 330-263-4829
e-mail: info@prentrom.com
www.prentrom.com

*Dave Moffatt, President*

A Minspeak application program available for the Liberator and Delta Talker communication devices. Provides single word vocabulary to people of all ages at varying stages of language development, who may be either cognitively intact or challenged. *$355.00*

**220    Vantage**
Prentke Romich Company
1022 Heyl Road
Wooster, OH  44691                              330-262-1984
                                                800-262-1984
                                           FAX: 330-263-4829
                                       e-mail: info@prentrom.com
                                            www.prentrom.com

*Dave Moffatt, President*

Vantage is a portable communication aid that features the Unity Enhanced vocabulary software and a large high quality dynamic display. Vantage also employs the recently upgraded 4.0 operating system that makes system settings quick and easy. Vantage has synthesized speech powered by DECtalk Software, Spelling and Word Protection software, built-in visor (flip-up protective cover), digitized speech capability and built-in computer access and ECU controls. 15 and 45 location keyguards available. *$6295.00*

**221    Vibrotactile Personal Alerting System**
HARC Mercantile
1111 W Centre Avenue
Portage, MI  49024                              269-324-1615
                                                800-445-9968
                                           FAX: 269-324-2387
                                    e-mail: home@harcmercantile.com
                                          www.harcmercantile.com

*Ronald Slager, President*

Composed of a small wireless personal device that receives coded signals and a group of transmitters that send them. *$195.95*

**222    Viewstar**
Viewstar
15303 Ventura Boulevard
Sherman Oaks, CA  91403                         818-382-4104

*Leonard Weinstein, Technical Director*

A stand-alone CCTV system for single view reading, writing and examining small objects. *$1545.00*

**223    Voice Amplified Handsets**
HARC Mercantile
1111 W Centre Avenue
Portage, MI  49024                              269-324-1615
                                                800-445-9968
                                           FAX: 269-324-2387
                                    e-mail: home@harcmercantile.com
                                          www.harcmercantile.com

*Ronald Slager, President*

Designed for the person who has a weak speaking voice. Control increases the level of the user's voice and can increase as much as 30%. *$65.00*

**224    WalkerTalker**
Prentke Romich Company
1022 Heyl Road
Wooster, OH  44691                              330-262-1984
                                                800-262-1984
                                           FAX: 330-263-4829
                                       e-mail: info@prentrom.com
                                            www.prentrom.com

*Dave Moffatt, President*

A portable direct selection communication device for active persons. The 16 location keyboard and speakers are carried in a belt that straps comfortably around the waist. The keyboard can be removed from its pouch to use by activating keys. Two versions are available, standard memory and expanded memory. *$1195.00*

**225    Whisper 2000**
DQP
14167 Meadow Drive
Grass Valley, CA  95945
                                                800-456-4979
                                           FAX: 530-477-7122
Personal sound amplification system that features a transmitter, phone and relay system for the hard-of-hearing.

# Chairs

**226    Adjustable Chair**
Bailey Manufacturing Company
PO Box 130
Lodi, OH  44254                                 330-948-2655
                                                800-321-8372
                                           FAX: 800-224-5390
                                    e-mail: baileymfg@baileymfg.com
                                            www.baileymfg.com

*Adelle McClendon, Customer Service*
*Sandy Mooney, Customer Service*
*Judie Butler, Dealer Contact*

The seat and footboard of this versatile chair can be adjusted to accommodate children of various sizes. A classroom-suitable variation of this model is also available.

**227    Adjustable Clear Acrylic Tray**
Bailey Manufacturing Company
118 Lee Street
Suite 130
Lodi, OH  44254                                 330-948-1080
                                                800-321-8372
                                           FAX: 800-224-5390
                                    e-mail: baileymfg@attmail.com
                                            www.baileymfg.com

*Larry Strimple, President*

Adjusts for height and depth and is equipped with a spill rim for easy to clean edges.

**228    Adjustable Rigid Chair**
Kuschall North America
1811 Lefthand Circle
Suite B
Longmont, CO  80501                             303-682-2571
                                                888-682-2571
                                           FAX: 866-651-6973
                                            www.kuschallna.com

*Terry Mulkey, Owner*

The Champion 3000 is a fully adjustable rigid frame chair weighing only 21 pounds with a new clamping system that adjusts seat height and angle without tools.

**229    Adjustable Tee Stool**
Bailey Manufacturing Company
118 Lee Street
Suite 130
Lodi, OH  44254                                 330-948-1080
                                                800-321-8372
                                           FAX: 800-224-5390
                                    e-mail: baileymfg@attmail.com
                                            www.baileymfg.com

*Larry Strimple, President*

May be used to encourage balance as well as develop integrative and perceptual motor skills.

**230  AirLift Toileting System**
Mobility
5726 La Jolla Boulevard
Suite 104
La Jolla, CA  92037

858-456-8121
866-456-8121
FAX: 858-456-8139
e-mail: info@mobilityinc.net
www.mobilityinc.net

*Steve Winston, VP Sales*
*Eric Proffitt, VP Marketing*

The Mobility AirLift toileting system makes it easy and painless to get on and off the toilet. With or without an assistant, the Air-Lift absorbs the user's weight, providing gentle lowering to a sitting position and smooth lifting to a standing position.

**231  BackSaver**
BackSaver Products Company
53 Jeffrey Avenue
Holliston, MA  01746

508-429-5940
800-251-2225
FAX: 508-429-8698
e-mail: stevek@backsaver.com
www.backsavercorp.com

*Steven Kusmin, Sales Director*

Eliminates slouching and extra pressure on your back and thighs which impairs circulation.

**232  Better Back**
Orthopedic Products Corporation
4100 1/2 Glencoe Avenue
Marina Del Rey, CA  90292

323-584-6977
FAX: 310-306-0177

An orthopedic multi-purpose seat.

**233  Carendo**
Arjo
50 Gary Avenue
Roselle, IL  60172

630-307-2756
800-323-1245
FAX: 888-594-2756
e-mail: lchevrie@arjousa.com
www.arjo.com

*Lorena Cherie, Marketing Communications*
*Ross Scavuzzo, President*

The Carendo hygiene chair has been designed for caregivers.

**234  Century 50/60XR Sit**
Arjo
50 Gary Avenue
Roselle, IL  60172

630-307-2756
800-323-1245
FAX: 888-594-2756
e-mail: lchevrie@arjousa.com
www.arjo.com

*Lorena Cherie, Marketing Communications*
*Ross Scavuzzo, President*

This bathing system has a built-in cleaning/disinfectant injection system with adjustable flowmeter. The incorporation of an automatic hot water alarm/shut-off system, and digital temperature monitors, helps to assure resident safety and comfort.

**235  Convert-Able Table**
Rehab and Educational Aids for Living
187 S Main Street
Dolgeville, NY  13329

800-696-7041
FAX: 315-429-3071
e-mail: rdesign@tweny.rr.com
www.realdesigninc.com

*Kris Wohnsen, Sales*

This table has push button height adjustment and interchangeable tops so it can become a desk, art easel or a sensory stimulation bowl.

**236  Evac + Chair Emergency Wheelchair**
Evac + Chair Corporation
PO Box 2396
New York, NY  10021

212-369-4094
FAX: 212-369-3710
e-mail: sales@evac-chair.com
www.evac-chair.com

*Robert McLean, Sales Manager*

Gravity driven evaluation chair allows one nondisabled person to smoothly glide a seated passenger down fire stairs and across landings to exit on a combination of wheels and track belts. Pivots in own width for tight landing turns. Aluminum; weight 18 pounds. Compactly stores on wall mount, 38 by 20 by 9 inches. Maximum capacity 300 pounds. Self braking features. No installation, works on all fire exit stairs. *$950.00*

**237  Golden Technologies**
401 Bridge Street
Old Forge, PA  18518

570-451-7477
800-624-6374
FAX: 800-628-5165

*Bob Golden, President*

**238  High-Low Chair**
Rehab and Educational Aids for Living
187 S Main Street
Dolgeville, NY  13329

800-696-7041
FAX: 315-429-3071

*Kris Wohnsen, Sales*

A high chair and mobile floor sitter in one. The high-low chair comes with colorful upholstered wipe clean seat and height adjustable tray. The chair has a single lever adjustment to change the seat height. Lateral and head supports are available as options. *$1199.00*

**239  Hygea-Chair**
TRIAID
PO Box 1364
Cumberland, MD  21501

301-759-3525
800-306-6777
FAX: 301-759-3525
e-mail: sales@triaid.com
www.triaid.com

*Iain A MacDonald, Sales Director*
*Ann M Hutter, Sales Executive/Manager*

Available in four sizes, the Hygea-Chair is an all purpose hygiene chair for children. It is supplied complete with a range of accessories fitted as standard to enhance the flexibility of the system: braked wheels, harness, footrest and seat insert comfort cover. It can be used in the shower, over the toilet or as a commode. *$950.00*

**240  Ladybug Corner Chair**
Rehab and Educational Aids for Living
187 S Main Street
Dolgeville, NY  13329

800-696-7041
FAX: 315-429-3071

For children 0-3 years. This chair is adjustable for long legs for conventional sitting.

**241  Lumex Recliner**
Graham-Field Health Products
2935 Northeast Parkway
Atlanta, GA  30360

770-447-1609
800-347-5678
FAX: 800-726-0601
e-mail: cs@grahamfield.com
www.grahamfield.com

*Irwin Selinger, Chief Executive Officer*

Combines therapeutic benefits of position change with attractive appearance.

**242  Mulholland Positioning Systems**
PO Box 391
Santa Paula, CA 93061
805-525-7165
800-543-4769
FAX: 805-933-1082
e-mail: info@mulhollandinc.com
www.mulhollandinc.com

*John Oderkirk, Marketing*
*Larry Mulholland, Owner*

Provides a full line of standing aids, seating systems, adaptive components and bath aids.

**243  Prime Engineering**
Prime Engineering
4202 W Sierra Madre Avenue
Fresno, CA 93722
559-276-0991
800-827-8263
FAX: 800-800-3355
e-mail: info@primeengineering.com
www.primeengineering.com

*Peggy Woodward, Sales*
*Bruce Boegel, Manager*

Prime Engineering is a leading manufacturer of adult and pediatric standing devices and patient transfer equipment. Products include the all-new Support Standing System, Granstand III MSS Standing System Kidstand III MSS Standing System Superstand Multi-Position Pediatric Stander, the Lift, the CindyLift and the Original Lift Walker.

**244  Quality Lift Chair**
Mobilelectrics Company
4014 Bardstown Road
Louisville, KY 40218
800-876-6846
FAX: 502-495-2476

Come and go as you please, sit and stand when you want, without help from anyone.

**245  Roll Chair**
Bailey Manufacturing Company
118 Lee Street
Suite 130
Lodi, OH 44254
330-948-1080
800-321-8372
FAX: 800-224-5390
e-mail: baileymfg@attmail.com
www.baileymfg.com

*Larry Strimple, President*

The padded roll helps maintain proper hip abduction and prevents scissoring of the legs.

**246  Safari Tilt**
Convaid Products
PO Box 4209
Palos Verdes Peninsula, CA 90274
310-618-0111
888-266-8243
FAX: 310-618-8811
e-mail: custservice@convaid.com
www.convaid.com

*Mervyn Watkins, President*

A semi-contour seat provides positioning with 5-45 degree tilt adjustment. One step design folds compactly into a lightweight chair.

**247  Spatial Tilt Custom Chair**
Redman Powerchair
1660 S Research Loop
Suite 126
Tucson, AZ 85710
520-546-6002
800-727-6684
FAX: 520-546-5530

*Don Redman, Owner*

Custom chair designed for comfort with a solid seat and back with modifications available for seat depth, height or width.

**248  Special Needs 5**
Baby Jogger Company
8575 Magellan Parkway
Suite 1000
Richmond, VA 23227
804-726-1327
800-241-1848
FAX: 804-262-6277
e-mail: bfetzer@babyjogger.com
www.babyjogger.com/p6.asp

*Billy Fetzer, Sales Representative*
*David Boardman, President*

Special need mobility devices give passengers smooth rides indoors and outdoors. The light weight, aluminum frame supports up to 200 pounds. Modifications available.

**249  Transfer Bench with Back**
Frohock-Stewart
39400 Taylor Parkway
North Ridgeville, OH 44035
440-329-6000
FAX: 440-365-7483

*A Mixon Iii, Chief Executive Officer*

This bench with air-cushioned seat sections has a full, reversible backrest for safety and comfort.

## Cushions & Wedges

**250  ACU Massage Cushion**
Massage Relaxation Products
PO Box 7243
Alhambra, CA 91802
800-999-1089

Hundreds of tiny massaging beads which help relieve lower back pain through massaging your own acupressure points.

**251  Action Products**
22 N Mulberry Street
Hagerstown, MD 21740
301-797-1414
800-228-7763
FAX: 301-733-2073
e-mail: service@actionproducts.com
www.actionproducts.com

*Dee Price, Customer Service Manager*
*Troy McKnight, President*
*Michael Bredal, VP Sales North America*

Wheelchair pads, mattress pads, positioning cushions and insoles that aid in the prevention and cure of pressure sores by reducing pressure. All products are made of Akton viscoelastic polymer that does not leak, flow or bottom out. Manufacturer of the Xact line of positioning cushions for patients with high risk of skin breakdown.

**252  Adjustable Wedge**
Bailey Manufacturing Company
118 Lee Street
Suite 130
Lodi, OH 44254
330-948-1080
800-321-8372
FAX: 800-224-5390
e-mail: baileymfg@attmail.com
www.baileymfg.com

*Larry Strimple, President*

Orthopedically and neurologically disabled children can freely move arms and hands while lying on this adjustable wedge.

**253  Back Machine**
Kingstar International America
PO Box 10157
Chicago, IL  60610
312-951-1115
FAX: 312-943-1727
www.kingstar.com

*Robin Morgenstern, President*
*Musa Hammad, Manager*

A nine position adjustable lumbar support that is compact and lightweight, portable and able to fit most chairs, adaptable for different body sizes and will not lose its shape. The inner spring design will give the spinal column over-all support to compensate for stress, fatigue and improper posture.

**254  Back-Huggar Pillow**
Bodyline Comfort Systems
3730 Kori Road
Jacksonville, FL  32257
904-262-4068
800-874-7715
FAX: 904-262-2225
e-mail: info@bodyline.com
www.bodyline.com

*John Fiore, Owner*

Exclusive design makes almost any seat more comfortable by exerting soothing pressure against back muscles and discs.

**255  BetaBed Pressure Pad**
Huntleigh Healthcare
40 Christopher Way
Eatontown, NJ  07724
732-935-0975
800-223-1218
FAX: 732-578-9889
www.huntleigh-healthcare.com

*Robert Angel, President/CEO*

Alternating pressure pad system automatically relieves tissue damaging pressure every 2 minutes.

**256  Bye-Bye Decubiti (BBD)**
Ken McRight Supplies
7456 S Oswego Avenue
Tulsa, OK  74136
918-492-9657
FAX: 918-492-9694

*Ken McRight, President*

The BBD therapeutic wheelchair cushions have been market-proven since 1951 — in the prevention and cure of pressure sores (decubiti). These natural rubber inflatable products have recently been expanded to include pediatric, sports and double-valve models. Moderately priced, they offer a viable and cost-effective alternative in the market. $84.00-$112.00

**257  Dynamic Systems**
235 Sunlight Drive
Leicester, NC  28748
828-683-3523
FAX: 828-683-3511
e-mail: dsi@sunmatecushions.com
www.sunmatecushions.com

*Pamela Price, Customer Service*
*Ellie Brown, Executive Officer Manufacturing*
*Charles Yost, Chief Executive Officer*

SunMate orthopedic foam sheets and cushions, pudgee pads for pressure relief and skin breakdown prevention, laminar wheelchair cushions and Foam-in-Place Seating for custom molding seat inserts. Sample packs and literature available upon request.

**258  Econo-Float Water Flotation Cushion**
Jefferson Industries
1985 Rutgers University Boulevard
Lakewood, NJ  08701
732-905-9001
800-257-5145
FAX: 732-905-9899

*Charles Landa, General Manager*

An inexpensive, yet effective approach to the problem of pressure ulcers for patients confined to wheelchairs, geriatric chairs, etc. *$15.00*

**259  Econo-Float Water Flotation Mattress**
Jefferson Industries
1985 Rutgers University Boulevard
Lakewood, NJ  08701
732-905-9001
800-257-5145
FAX: 732-905-9899

*Charles Landa, General Manager*

Helps prevent and treat pressure ulcers by reducing and distributing pressure over the patient's bony prominences while supporting the body evenly over a greater surface area. *$39.00*

**260  Enhancer Cushion**
ROHO Group
100 N Florida Avenue
Belleville, IL  62221
618-277-9150
800-851-3449
FAX: 618-277-9561
e-mail: mail@therohogroup.com
www.therohogroup.com

*Jackie Wiegert, Corporate Marketing*
*Tom Olesky, Chief Executive Officer*

Uses AIR IN PLACE progressive positioning for enhanced midline channeling of the femurs, lateral stability and tissue protection.

**261  Flex-Air Pressure Relief System**
Relax-A-Flex
211 River Street
Bennington, VT  05201
802-447-1166
800-782-8889
FAX: 802-442-6875

*Jeff Wilkinson, Owner*
Solves mattress problems.

**262  Functional Forms**
Consumer Care Products
1446 Pilgrim Road
Plymouth, WI  53073
920-893-4614
FAX: 800-977-2256
e-mail: ccpi@consumercareinc.com
www.consumercareinc.com

*Terry Grall, Owner*

These blocks, wedges, rolls, cervical pillows, head and leg supports and barrel rolls in resilient high density foam covered with durable antibacterial, antistatic, flame resistant, nonabsorbent vinyl are used to attain individualized support for the most difficult positioning needs for children and adults. Unique sizes allow fitting for almost any person. Use during exercise, feeding, therapy, recreation and rest at home, school and health care facilities. Packages available.

**263  GT Wheelchair Cushion**
Relax-A-Flex
211 River Street
Bennington, VT  05201
802-447-1166
800-782-8889
FAX: 802-442-6875

*Jeff Wilkinson, Owner*

The specially designed gel pads in this cushion help relieve pressure on the back.

**264    Gaymar Industries**
Gaymar Industries
10 Centre Drive
Orchard Park, NY  14127
716-662-2551
800-828-7341
FAX: 800-993-7890
e-mail: pmatteliano@gaymar.com
www.gaymar.com

*Steve Snyder, VP Marketing*
*Peggy Matteliano, Communications Specialist*
*Thomas Stewart, Chief Executive Officer*

Gaymar offers a complete line of support surfaces, including low-air-loss mattresses, specialty foam mattresses, turning mattresses, air overlays and fluid therapy beds. These products economically prevent and treat bedsores. Clinical and reimbursement professionals are available to answer any question related to bedsores (decubitus ulcers). Also offers a complete line of temperature control devices. The T-Pump delivers warm therapy to effectively dilate vessels and increase blood flow.

**265    Geo-Matt for High Risk Patients**
Span-America Medical Systems
70 Commerce Center
Greenville, SC  29615
864-288-8877
800-888-6752
FAX: 864-288-8692
www.spanamerica.com

*James Ferguson, Chief Executive Officer*

Helps prevent pressure sores in high risk patients.

**266    High Profile Single Compartment Cushion**
ROHO Group
100 N Florida Avenue
Belleville, IL  62221
618-277-9150
800-851-3449
FAX: 618-277-9561
e-mail: mail@therohogroup.com
www.therohogroup.com

*Jackie Wiegert, Corporate Marketing*
*Tom Olesky, Chief Executive Officer*

With 4 inch cells, the HIGH PROFILE is the cushion of choice for individuals who suffer from ischemic ulcers (pressure sores) or who have a history of tissue breakdown.

**267    Inflatable Back Pillow**
Corflex
669 East Industrial Park Drive
Manchester, NH  03109
603-623-3344
800-426-7353
FAX: 603-623-4111
e-mail: sales@corflex.com
www.corflex.com

*Paul Lorenzetti, Owner*

Folds flat to fit into its own carrying case, this inflatable back pillow ensures comfort while at home or traveling.

**268    Jobri**
520 N Division Street
Konawa, OK  74849
580-925-4100
800-432-2225
FAX: 800-769-0520
e-mail: support@jobri.com
www.jobri.com

*Mike Deaton, Customer Service Manager*
*Brian Gourley, Chief Executive Officer*

**269    Lumbo-Posture Back Support**
Ken McRight Supplies
7456 S Oswego Avenue
Tulsa, OK  74136
918-492-9657
FAX: 918-492-9694

*Ken McRight, President*

Rubber inflatable back support that offers therapeutic relief to all who must sit for lengthy periods of time, whether used in a wheelchair, auto or bed. *$97.65*

**270    Lumex Cushions and Mattresses**
Graham-Field Health Products
2935 Northeast Parkway
Atlanta, GA  30360
770-447-1609
800-347-5678
FAX: 800-726-0601
www.grahamfield.com

*Irwin Selinger, Chief Executive Officer*

Line of cushions and pillows give comfort and independence to the physically challenged.

**271    Medpro Static Air Chair Cushion**
Medpro
1950 Rutgers University Boulevard
Lakewood, NJ  08701
800-257-5145
FAX: 732-905-9899

*Jody Gorran, President*

Provides a protective layer of air beneath the patient helping prevent and treat pressure ulcers. *$94.95*

**272    Medpro Static Air Mattress Overlay**
Medpro
1950 Rutgers University Boulevard
Lakewood, NJ  08701
800-257-5145
FAX: 732-905-9899

*Jody Gorran, President*

Supports the patient on a cushioned network of air designed to redistribute the patient's weight reducing tissue interface pressure. Medpro's design incorporates a series of 65 air-breather vents that maintain air circulation. Medpro effectively reduces pressure and helps prevent and treat pressure ulcers. *$164.95*

**273    Mini-Max Cushion**
ROHO
100 N Florida Avenue
Belleville, IL  62221
618-277-9150
800-850-7646
FAX: 618-277-6518
e-mail: mail@rohogroup.com
www.therohogroup.com

*Julie Petry, Corporate Marketing*
*Tom Olesky, Chief Executive Officer*

Designed for the active individual with low risk of skin breakdown. The unique air cells of the MINI-MAX provide significant shock and impact absorption, skin protection and stability.

**274    NEXUS Wheelchair Cushioning System**
ROHO
100 N Florida Avenue
Belleville, IL  62221
618-277-9150
800-850-7646
FAX: 618-277-6518
e-mail: mail@rohogroup.com
www.therohogroup.com

*Julie Petry, Corporate Marketing*
*Tom Olesky, Chief Executive Officer*

A unique modular cushion that mates a contoured polyurethane foam base with a dry flotation support pad. It is designed to give the user positioning and stability, while offering maximum protection to the ischia, sacrum and coccyx.

**275  Nek-Lo, Nek-Lo Hot and Cold Pillow-Perfect, Body Buddy, Hugg-L-O Pillow**
Rinz-L-O Pillow Company
340 W Maplehurst Street
Ferndale, MI 48220
248-548-3993
800-594-9093
FAX: 248-548-0447
e-mail: rinzlo@netzero.net

*G Rick Rinz, President*
*Ken Mack, Office Manager*
*Phill McAllister, Sales Manager*

Nek-Lo a U-shaped cervical pillow; Nek-Lo Hot and Cold - U-shaped pillow with hot/cold pack; Pillow-Perfect - uses your conventional pillow to insert cover that has cervical support form piece; Magne-Aid and Magne-Systems - magnetic therapy braces, Hugg-L-O pillow V shaped body positioning, Hugg-L-O Extra pillow is 4 inches longer than original Hugg-L-O pillow. *$12.98*

**276  Pediatric Seating System**
ROHO
100 N Florida Avenue
Belleville, IL 62221
618-277-9150
800-850-7646
FAX: 618-277-6518
e-mail: rohoinc@rohoinc.com
www.rohoinc.com

*Julie Petry, Corporate Marketing*
*Tom Olesky, Chief Executive Officer*

ROHO Cushions for kids use individual air cells, creating the most versatile and dynamic cushioning products available. These cushions are designed to specifically fit pediatric wheelchairs.

**277  Quadtro Cushion**
ROHO
100 N Florida Avenue
Belleville, IL 62221
618-277-9150
800-851-3499
FAX: 618-277-9561
e-mail: mail@therohogroup.com
www.therohogroup.com

*Julie Petry, Corporate Marketing*
*Tom Olesky, Chief Executive Officer*

For individuals who require special positioning of the pelvis or thighs and are at risk of skin breakdown, the Quadtro, with 4 inch cell height and air in place, progressive positioning is the cushion of choice.

**278  Silicone Padding**
Spenco Medical Group
PO Box 2501
Waco, TX 76702
254-772-6000
800-433-3334

*Steven Smith, Chief Executive Officer*

For the management of pressure sores, this padding provides a special support system which allows even distribution of pressure and cool, comfortable, well-ventilated support.

**279  Soft-Touch Convertible Flotation Mattress**
Medpro
1950 Rutgers University Boulevard
Lakewood, NJ 08701
800-257-5145
FAX: 732-905-9899

*Jody Gorran, President*

Gives the patient the option to choose between water and gel flotation depending on the needs of the patient. The mattress helps prevent and treat pressure ulcers by spreading the patient's weight over a greater surface area. $164.95-$239.95.

**280  Soft-Touch Gel Flotation Cushion**
Medpro
1940 Rutgers University Boulevard
Lakewood, NJ 08701
732-905-9001
800-257-5145
FAX: 732-905-9899

*Jody Gorran, President*

Acts like an additional layer of fatty tissue beneath the patient to help prevent and treat pressure sores. *$99.95*

**281  Spenco Medical Group**
PO Box 2501
Waco, TX 76702
254-772-6000
800-433-3334
e-mail: spenco@spenco.com
www.spenco.com

*Mark B Connors, VP Sales/Marketing*
*Patty Smith, Controller*
*Steven B Smith, CEO*

Wheel chair cushions, silicore mattress pads, wound dressings, second skin blister and burn pads, polysorb insoles, elbow, knee and wrist supports and walking shoes.

**282  Stop-Leak Gel Flotation Mattress**
Jefferson Industries
1989 Rutgers University Boulevard
Lakewood, NJ 08701
732-905-9001
800-257-5145
FAX: 732-905-9899

*Charles Landa, General Manager*

Protects persons from messy leaks while it protects from pressure ulcers. *$54.00*

**283  Sun-Mate Seat Cushions**
Dynamic Systems
235 Sunlight Drive
Leicester, NC 28748
828-683-3523
FAX: 828-683-3511
e-mail: dsi@sunmatecushions.com
www.sunmatecushions.com

*Pamela Price, Customer Service*
*Ellie Brown, Executive Officer Manufacturing*
*Charles Yost, Chief Executive Officer*

Line of cushions, pads and accessory items for personal comfort of the disabled. SunMate Orthopedic foam cushions and sheets that contours slowly to give uniform pressure distribution and soft spring back. Liquid SunMate for Foam-in-Place Seating (FIPS) to make custom molded seat inserts.

**284  Twin-Rest Seat Cushion & Glamour Pillow**
Better Sleep
57 Industrial Road
Berkeley Heights, NJ 07922
908-464-2200
FAX: 908-464-0058

*William Emery Jr, President*

Makes any seat more comfortable because it is ingeniously designed to soothe sensitive areas while at work, in the car or at home.

# Dressing Aids

**285  Button Aid**
Maxi Aids
42 Executive Boulevard
Suite 3209
Farmingdale, NY 11735
631-752-0521
800-522-6294
FAX: 631-752-0689
e-mail: sales@maxiaids.com
www.maxiaids.com
Makes buttoning possible with the use of only one hand. *$9.95*

**286  Clothing Identification Kit**
Sense-Sations
919 Walnut Street
Philadelphia, PA  19107                215-627-0600
                                    FAX: 215-922-0692

*Patricia Johnson, Chief Executive Officer*
This kit contains labels and tells you what is on the hanger. *$7.75*

**287  Deluxe Sock and Stocking Aid**
Therapro
225 Arlington Street
Framingham, MA  01702                508-872-9494
                                     800-257-5376
                                 FAX: 508-875-2062
                          e-mail: info@theraproducts.com
                                www.theraproducts.com

*Karen Conrad, Owner*
Flexible plastic, lined with blue nylon to reduce friction and outside with beige terry cloth to hold sock firmly until it is on the foot. *$12.95*

**288  Dressing Stick**
Maxi Aids
42 Executive Boulevard
Suite 3209
Farmingdale, NY  11735                631-752-0521
                                     800-522-6294
                                 FAX: 631-752-0689
                          e-mail: sales@maxiaids.com
                                www.maxiaids.com
Helps put on coats, sweaters and garments even when arm and shoulder movement is limited. *$7.95*

**289  Elastic Shoelaces**
Therapro
225 Arlington Street
Framingham, MA  01702                508-872-9494
                                     800-257-5376
                                 FAX: 508-875-2062
                          e-mail: info@theraproducts.com
                                www.theraproducts.com

*Karen Conrad, Owner*
The elastic laces allow the wearer to slip tied shoes on and off. *$4.25*

**290  Featherweight Reachers**
Therapro
225 Arlington Street
Framingham, MA  01702                508-872-9494
                                     800-257-5376
                                 FAX: 508-875-2062
                          e-mail: info@theraproducts.com
                                www.theraproducts.com

*Karen Conrad, Owner*
Useful in dressing or retrieving objects. *$17.95*

**291  Folding Dressing Stick**
Access with Ease
PO Box 1150
Chino Valley, AZ  86323              928-636-9469
                                     800-531-9479
                                 FAX: 928-636-0292
                          e-mail: KMJC@northlink.com
Helps the physically-challenged user put on shirts, coats and jackets easily. The dressing sticks are available 12 to 28 inches long. Folds for easy storage. *$16.95*

**292  Heavy Duty Sock Tuckers**
Sense-Sations
919 Walnut Street
Philadelphia, PA  19107                215-627-0600
                                    FAX: 215-922-0692

*Patricia Johnson, Chief Executive Officer*

This device keeps socks and hosiery paired throughout the laundering cycles. *$1.50*

**293  Mirror Go Lightly**
AbleNet
2808 Fairview Avenue N
Saint Paul, MN  55113
                                     800-322-0956
                                 FAX: 612-379-9143
                    e-mail: customerservice@ablenetinc.com
                                www.ablenetinc.com
Framed in plastic, the mirror can be tilted to provide either a normal or magnified image or to direct its lights at, or away from, the user. *$22.00*

**294  Molded Sock and Stocking Aid**
Therapro
225 Arlington Street
Framingham, MA  01702                508-872-9494
                                     800-257-5376
                                 FAX: 508-875-2062
                          e-mail: info@theraproducts.com
                                www.theraproducts.com

*Karen Conrad, Owner*
Sock or stocking is pulled over the molded plastic and then can be put on more easily. *$13.25*

**295  Say What**
Maxi Aids
42 Executive Boulevard
Suite 3209
Farmingdale, NY  11735                631-752-0521
                                     800-522-6294
                                 FAX: 631-752-0689
                          e-mail: sales@maxiaids.com
                                www.maxiaids.com
Braille the tag with information that the wearer wants on the tag and place the tag on a hanger. The custom-identification program makes it easier for the user to remember and identify just the right clothes. *$4.95*

## Health Aids

**296  AMI**
PO Box 808
Groton, CT  06340                    860-536-3735
                                     800-248-4031
                                 FAX: 860-536-4362
                          e-mail: sales@aquamassage.com
                                www.amiaqua.com

*David Cote, President*
*Dow Cote, Domestic Sales Manager*

The Aqua PT provides the major benefits of Hydrotherapy, Massage Therapy and Dry Heat Therapy. 36 water jets provide continuous full body or localized massage while the client remains CLOTHED AND DRY! Adjustable water pressure, temperature and pulsation frequency can massage in either a two direction travel mode for musculoskeletal pain management or a one direction mode, flowing water from head to foot for a contrast massage-relax therapy. $25,000 to $30,000.

**297  Absorbent Dressing Powder**
Baxter Healthcare Corporation
1 Baxter Parkway
Deerfield, IL  60015                 847-948-2000
                                 FAX: 847-948-3948
                                www.baxter.com

*Robert Parkinson Jr, Chief Executive Officer*
Powder dressing for the treatment of pressure sores and other skin ulcers.

**298    American Medical Industries**
330 E 3rd Street
Suite 2
Dell Rapids, SD  57022                605-428-5501
                                  FAX: 605-428-5502
        e-mail: sales@americanmedicalindustries.com
                                  www.ezhealthcare.com

*Dan Anderson, CEO*

EZ-Swallow, EZ-Health, EZ-Home Care, Kleen-Handz,
Kleen-Scent, EZ-Irrigator, EZ-VU, Pureshark, Gobot and AMI
are all trademarks of American Medical Industries. Healthcare
products made easy.

**299    Aud-A-Mometer**
Maxi Aids
42 Executive Boulevard
Suite 3209
Farmingdale, NY  11735                631-752-0521
                                      800-522-6294
                                  FAX: 631-752-0689
                          e-mail: sales@maxiaids.com
                                      www.maxiaids.com

Audible clinical thermometer. *$199.95*

**300    BIPAP S/T Ventilatory Support System**
Respironics
1010 Murry Ridge Lane
Murrysville, PA  15668                724-387-5200
                                  FAX: 724-387-5012
        e-mail: customerservice@respironics.com
                                  www.respironics.com

*John Miclot, Chief Executive Officer*
*Gerald McGinnis, Chairman*
*Daniel Bevevino, VP/CFO*

Respironics, a recognized resource in the medical device market, provides innovative products and unique designs to the
health care provider while helping them to grow and manage
their business efficiently.

**301    Bed Rails**
Mada Medical Products
625 Washington Avenue
Carlstadt, NJ  07072                  201-460-0454
                                      800-526-6370
                                  FAX: 201-460-3509
              e-mail: sales@madamedical.com
                          www.madainternational.com

*Jeffrey Adam, Vice President*

Chrome plated steel rails and crossbars, all welded construction,
telescopic side rail length adjustable, and a standard rail height
of 16 inches.

**302    Coast to Coast Home Medical**
3381 Fairlane Farms Road
Suite 4d
Wellington, FL  33414                 561-792-4009
                                      800-330-6316

*Keri Suess, Owner*

Home-delivered medical supplies for diabetes, respiratory, arthritis and impotence supplies.

**303    Drew Karol Industries**
PO Box 1066
Greenville, MS  38702                 662-378-2188
                                  FAX: 601-378-3188
                      e-mail: dki@techinfo.com

*Andrew Hoszowski, President*

Orally operated toothbrush and dental care system for persons
with limited or complete loss of hand or arm use - wheelchair accessible. *$600.00*

**304    Duraline Medical Products**
PO Box 67
Leipsic, OH  45856                    419-943-2044
                                      800-654-3376
                                  FAX: 419-943-3637
                      e-mail: duraline@q1.net
                                  www.dmponline.com

*Robert Freier, Owner*

An assortment of quality incontinence products for adults and
children.

**305    Duro-Med Industries**
1778 W Cherry Street
Jesup, GA  31545                      912-427-7358
                                      800-526-4753
                                  FAX: 800-479-7968

*Mike Mazza, President*

Manufacturers of a complete line of home health care products.
Featured products are patient gowns, back and seat cushions,
pillows and a complete line of aids for daily living.

**306    Easy Ply**
BioMedical Life Systems
PO Box 1360
Vista, CA  92085
                                      800-726-8367
                                  FAX: 760-727-4220
              e-mail: information@bmls.com
                                      www.bmls.com

This disposable electrode has a cloth backing of a super-breath-
able medical tape that allows for comfort and a longer life.

**307    Electronic Stethoscopes**
HARC Mercantile
1111 W Centre Avenue
Portage, MI  49024                    269-324-1615
                                      800-445-9968
                                  FAX: 269-324-2387
              e-mail: home@harcmercantile.com
                              www.harcmercantile.com

*Ronald Slager, President*

High production fidelity with a number volume control wheels.
*$454.95*

**308    Emergency Medical Identification with Free Fax**
Merion Station Mail Order Company
PO Box 11
Jenkintown, PA  19046                 800-333-8247
                                      800-333-TAGS
                                  FAX: 877-738-2500

*Linda R Katz, President*
*Alex Katz, Secretary/Treasurer*

Emergency medical identification tags, pendants and bracelets.
*$24.95*

**309    Fold-Down 3-in-1 Commode**
Mada Medical Products
625 Washington Avenue
Carlstadt, NJ  07072                  201-460-0454
                                      800-526-6370
                                  FAX: 201-460-3509
              e-mail: sales@madamedical.com
                          www.madainternational.com

*Jeffrey Adam, Vice President*

The Fold-Down commode is constructed of heavy duty, 1 inch
diameter, steel tubing with X frame, has folding features convenient for storage and transport, easily removable back rest, and
full length armrests.

**310    Grab Bars and Tub Rails**
Mada Medical Products
625 Washington Avenue
Carlstadt, NJ 07072
201-460-0454
800-526-6370
FAX: 201-460-3509
e-mail: sales@madamedical.com
www.madainternational.com

*Jeffrey Adam, Vice President*

Several models made of heavy walled steel, available in knurled steel or white epoxy paint, various lengths and round flanges for either vertical or horizontal mounting.

**311    Healing Dressing for Pressure Sores**
Baxter Healthcare Corporation
1 Baxter Parkway
Deerfield, IL 60015
847-948-2000
FAX: 847-948-3948
www.baxter.com

*Robert Parkinson Jr, Chief Executive Officer*

A dressing specifically designed to promote healing of pressure sores and other dermal ulcers.

**312    Invacare Corporation**
1 Invacare Way
Elyria, OH 44035
440-329-6000
800-333-6900
FAX: 440-329-6568
e-mail: selder@invacare.com
www.invacare.com

*Susan Elder, Dir. Marketing/Communications*
*A Mixon Iii, Chief Executive Officer*

The world's leading manufacturer and distributor of medical products which promote recovery and active lifestyles through more than 25,000 providers worldwide.

**313    MADAMIST 50/50 PSI Air Compressor**
Mada Medical Products
625 Washington Avenue
Carlstadt, NJ 07072
201-460-0454
800-526-6370
FAX: 201-460-3509
e-mail: sales@madamedical.com
www.madainternational.com

*Jeffrey Adam, Vice President*

The new compressor rated at 50 PSI is designed to drive humidifiers, nebulizers, mist tents and is ideal to administer pentamidine aerosol therapy.

**314    MedDev Corporation**
730 N Pastoria Avenue
Sunnyvale, CA 94085
408-730-9702
800-543-2789
FAX: 408-730-9732
e-mail: info@meddev-corp.com
www.meddev-corp.com

*Suzanne Gray, Owner*

Aids to rehabilitate hands following injury or illness, including patented complementary FingerHelper, ThumbHelper and Iso HandHelper models. Med Dev also manufactures Soft Touch foam exercisers and the FiddlLink exerciser for digital dexterity. The Ultimate Hand Helper, an ergonomically designed hand excerciser, is curved to conform to the shape of the hand.

**315    Medi-Grip**
Therapro
225 Arlington Street
Framingham, MA 01702
508-872-9494
800-257-5376
FAX: 508-875-2062
e-mail: info@theraproducts.com
www.theraproducts.com

*Karen Conrad, Owner*

Reasonably priced, nonskid material. This nonslip material is available in marine blue, desert sand and burgundy rolls 12 inches x 144 inches. *$11.95*

**316    Pocket Otoscope**
HARC Mercantile
1111 W Centre Avenue
Portage, MI 49024
269-324-1615
800-445-9968
FAX: 269-324-2387
e-mail: home@harcmercantile.com
www.harcmercantile.com

*Ronald Slager, President*

Simple, durable and dependable pocket otoscope uses standard replaceable parts. *$24.00*

**317    Standard 3-in-1 Commode**
Mada Medical Products
625 Washington Avenue
Carlstadt, NJ 07072
201-460-0454
800-526-6370
FAX: 201-460-3509
e-mail: sales@madamedical.com
www.madainternational.com

*Jeffrey Adam, Vice President*

The standard commode is constructed of a heavy duty anodized aluminum frame, seat adjustment and an easily removable back rest.

**318    Strider**
Osborn Medical Corporation
PO Box 324
Utica, MN 55979
507-287-6554
800-535-5865
FAX: 507-932-5044
www.osbornmedical.com

*Bill Davis, President*

Strider allows you to exercise in most chairs found in your home. No more small, uncomfortable bicycle seats to sit on while exercising. With Strider, your hands are free to read the paper or your favorite book while you exercise.

**319    Talking Thermometers**
Maxi Aids
42 Executive Boulevard
Suite 3209
Farmingdale, NY 11735
631-752-0521
800-522-6294
FAX: 631-752-0689
e-mail: sales@maxiaids.com
www.maxiaids.com

Clearly announces temperature in Fahrenheit or Celcius. *$17.95*

**320    Transfer Bench**
Mada Medical Products
625 Washington Avenue
Carlstadt, NJ 07072
201-460-0454
800-526-6370
FAX: 201-460-3509
e-mail: sales@madamedical.com
www.madainternational.com

*Jeffrey Adam, Vice President*

The transfer bench is a one piece bench with a wide base for stability, 1" diameter aluminum framework, corrosion resistant, and an adjustable seat.

## Hearing Aids

**321  Auditech: DirectEar Transmitter and Headset**
PO Box 821105
Vicksburg, MS 39182

800-229-8293
FAX: 800-221-8639
e-mail: info@auditechusa.com
www.auditechusa.com

Turn up the volume when watching TV. The headset can also be used separately in public theaters and cinemas, that have infrared transmission. Additional headset receivers can be purchased. A neckloop can also be added to the headset. *$219.00*

**322  Auditech: Personal PA Value Pack System**
PO Box 821105
Vicksburg, MS 39182

800-229-8293
FAX: 800-221-8639
e-mail: info@auditechusa.com
www.auditechusa.com

Reliable hearing assistance. This wireless FM system broadcasts to listeners with a hearing assistance system, helping them overcome background noise at a distance from the sound source. *$899.00*

**323  Auditech: Pocketalker Pro**
PO Box 821105
Vicksburg, MS 39182

800-229-8293
FAX: 800-221-8639
e-mail: info@auditechusa.com
www.auditechusa.com

Pocketalker Pro can help you hear virtually anywhere whether in a car, crowded restaurant or at a noisy gathering. It can work to reduce background noise and easily converts to the Telelink. *$140.00*

**324  Battery Device Adapter**
AbleNet
2808 Fairview Avenue N
Roseville, MN 55113

651-294-2200
800-322-0956
FAX: 651-294-2259
e-mail: customerservice@ablenetinc.com
www.ablenetinc.com

*Mary Kay Walch*

A cable which connects to and adapts battery-operated devices for external switch control. Two sizes are available to adapt devices with either AA or C and D size batteries. *$8.00*

**325  Custom Earmolds**
Lloyd Hearing Aid Corporation
PO Box 1645
Rockford, IL 61110

815-964-4191
800-323-4212
FAX: 815-964-8378
e-mail: hearingaids@inwave.com
www.lloydhearingaid.com

*Andrew Palmquist, President*

Hearing aid molds, custom built to the exact fit of the customer. *$29.95*

**326  Digital Hearing Aids**
Lloyd Hearing Aid Corporation
128 Kishwaukee Street
Rockford, IL 61104

815-964-4191
800-323-4212
FAX: 815-964-8378
e-mail: hearingaids@inwave.com

*Andrew Palmquist, President*

Latest hearing technology. Huge discounts on most makes. *$7.50*

**327  Doorbell Signalers**
HARC Mercantile
1111 W Centre Avenue
Portage, MI 49024

269-324-1615
800-445-9968
FAX: 269-324-2387
e-mail: home@harcmercantile.com
www.harcmercantile.com

*Ronald Slager, President*

Doorbell signalers to alert with either louder chime or flashing light. *$29.99*

**328  Double Gong Indoor/Outdoor Ringer**
HARC Mercantile
1111 W Centre Avenue
Portage, MI 49024

269-324-1615
800-445-9968
FAX: 269-324-2387
e-mail: home@harcmercantile.com
www.harcmercantile.com

*Ronald Slager, President*

Loud outdoor ringer that attaches to the wall for outside applications. *$50.00*

**329  Duracell & Rayovac Hearing Aid Batteries**
Lloyd Hearing Aid Corporation
128 Kishwaukee Street
Rockford, IL 61104

815-964-4191
800-323-4212
FAX: 815-964-8378
e-mail: hearingaids@inwave.com

*Andrew Palmquist, President*

Batteries for hearing aids at discounted prices. As low as 70 cents each.

**330  Harris Communications**
Harris Communications
15155 Technology Drive
Eden Prairie, MN 55344

952-906-1180
800-825-6758
FAX: 952-906-1099
e-mail: info@harriscomm.com
www.harriscomm.com

*Bill Williams, National Sales Manager*
*Robert Harris, Owner*

A national distributor of assistive devices for the deaf and hard-of-hearing with many manufacturers represented. Catalog includes a wide range of assistive devices as well as a variety of books and video tapes related to deaf and hard-of-hearing issues. Products available for children, teachers, hearing professionals, interpreters and anyone interested in deaf culture, hearing loss and sign language.
*180 pages Yearly*

**331  Hearing Aid Batteries**
HARC Mercantile
1111 W Centre Avenue
Portage, MI 49024

269-324-1615
800-445-9968
FAX: 269-324-2387
e-mail: home@harcmercantile.com
www.harcmercantile.com

*Ronald Slager, President*

Hearing aid batteries in all popular sizes in mercury, zinc air, silver as well as Nicad and Varta and batteries for electrolarynx and infrared systems. *$3.95-$25.00*

**332  Hearing Aid Battery Testers**
HARC Mercantile
1111 W Centre Avenue
Portage, MI 49024

269-324-1615
800-445-9968
FAX: 269-324-2387
e-mail: home@harcmercantile.com
www.harcmercantile.com

*Ronald Slager, President*

From pocket size to professional type battery testers which test mercury, zinc air, silver, specialty and general usage batteries. *$11.95*

**333  Hearing Aid Dehumidifier**
HARC Mercantile
1111 W Centre Avenue
Portage, MI 49024

269-324-1615
800-445-9968
FAX: 269-324-2387
e-mail: home@harcmercantile.com
www.harcmercantile.com

*Ronald Slager, President*

Removes moisture from hearing aids and valuables. Contains desiccant pack and humidity guide, all in a rugged, vinyl case which provides protection and is water resistant. *$6.00*

**334  In the Ear Hearing Aid Battery Extractor**
HARC Mercantile
1111 W Centre Avenue
Portage, MI 49024

269-324-1615
800-445-9968
FAX: 269-324-2387
e-mail: home@harcmercantile.com
www.harcmercantile.com

*Ronald Slager, President*

Ideal tool to use when battery is stuck in battery compartment in ITE and canal hearing aids. *$3.00*

**335  Micro Audiometrics Corporation**
655 Keller Road
Murphy, NC 28906

828-644-0771
800-729-9509
866-327-7226
FAX: 828-644-0772
e-mail: sales@microaud.com
www.microaud.com

*Jason Keller, VP*
*Lance Ralph, Marketing*
*James Keller, Owner*

Manufacturer and distributor of hearing testing instruments, including the complete line of Earscan.

**336  Model E-90W Hearing Aid**
Rhodes Hearing
PO Box 358
Brookport, IL 62910

618-564-2026

*Mary Rhodes, President*

This hearing aid slips directly into the ear. *$327.00*

**337  Model F-188T Hearing Aid**
Rhodes Hearing
PO Box 358
Brookport, IL 62910

618-564-2026

*Mary Rhodes, President*

Designed to fit behind your ear at the most natural hearing level for detecting both distance and sound direction. *$329.00*

**338  Mushroom Inserts**
Lloyd Hearing Aid Corporation
PO Box 1645
Rockford, IL 61110

815-964-4191
800-323-4212
FAX: 815-964-8378
e-mail: hearingaids@inwave.com

*Andrew Palmquist, President*

A universal earplug useful in wearing behind the ear type hearing instruments. *$2.50*

**339  Oval Window Audio**
33 Wildflower Court
Nederland, CO 80466

303-447-3607
FAX: 303-447-3607
e-mail: info@ovalwindowaudio.com
www.ovalwindowaudio.com

*Norman Lederman, Director R&D/Owner*
*Paula Hendricks, Educational Director*

Manufacturer of induction loop hearing assistance technologies compatible with hearing aids already used by many hard of hearing people. Also multisensory sound systems for use in speech and music therapy and science classes.

# Kitchen & Eating Aids

**340  Bagel Holder**
Maxi Aids
42 Executive Boulevard
Suite 3209
Farmingdale, NY 11735

631-752-0521
800-522-6294
FAX: 631-752-0689
e-mail: sales@maxiaids.com
www.maxiaids.com

Holds bagels in place for easy slicing. *$3.95*

**341  Big Bold Timer Low Vision**
Maxi Aids
42 Executive Boulevard
Suite 3209
Farmingdale, NY 11735

631-752-0521
800-522-6294
FAX: 631-752-0689
e-mail: sales@maxiaids.com
www.maxiaids.com

Sixty-minute mechanical timer with large, easy-to-read numbers for the vision impaired. *$9.95*

**342  Box Top Opener**
Sammons Preston Rolyan
W68n158 Evergreen Boulevard
Cedarburg, WI 53012

800-323-5547
FAX: 262-387-8748
e-mail: customersupport@sammonspreston.com
www.sammonspreston.com

This handy device exerts the pressure on those hard-to-open boxes of laundry/dishwasher soap, rice and prepared dinners. *$2.95*

**343  Capscrew**
Access with Ease
PO Box 1150
Chino Valley, AZ 86323

928-636-9469
800-531-9479
FAX: 928-636-0292
e-mail: KMJC@northlink.com

Remove lids and caps easily. Can be mounted on walls or cupboards. Non-slip surface grips small and large jars. *$7.95*

**344   Cool Handle**
Maxi Aids
42 Executive Boulevard
Suite 3209
Farmingdale, NY  11735                631-752-0521
                                      800-522-6294
                              FAX: 631-752-0689
                       e-mail: sales@maxiaids.com
                              www.maxiaids.com
A specially designed, heat-resistant handle, available in three
sizes which can be affixed to the handles of most fry, sauce and
saute pans. *$7.95*

**345   Cordless Receiver**
AbleNet
2808 Fairview Avenue N
Saint Paul, MN  55113
                                      800-322-0956
                              FAX: 651-294-2259
            e-mail: customerservice@ablenetinc.com
                              www.ablenetinc.com
The Cordless Receiver in conjunction with the Cordless Big Red
Switch, can be used anywhere a switch is currently used to control battery or electrically-operated toys, games or appliances;
augmentative communication systems; and computers (through
a computer switch interface). *$79.00*

**346   Deluxe Long Ring Low Vision Timer**
Maxi Aids
42 Executive Boulevard
Suite 3209
Farmingdale, NY  11735                631-752-0521
                              FAX: 631-752-0689
                       e-mail: sales@maxiaids.com
                              www.maxiaids.com
Bold black numerals on white background allows for easy read-
ing at any distance. *$17.95*

**347   Deluxe Roller Knife**
Sammons Preston Rolyan
4 Sammons Court
Bolingbrook, IL  60440                630-226-1300
                                      800-228-3693
                              FAX: 262-387-9748
        e-mail: customerservice@sammonspreston.com
                              www.sammonspreston.com
Stainless steel blade rolls smoothly, cutting food cleanly.
*$10.95*

**348   Dual Brush with Suction Base**
Sammons Preston Rolyan
4 Sammons Court
Bolingbrook, IL  60440                630-226-1300
                                      800-228-3693
                              FAX: 262-387-8748
        e-mail: customerservice@sammonspreston.com
                              www.sammonspreston.com
Two brushes clean the inside and outside of bottles and glasses at
the same time using just one hand. *$14.50*

**349   Easy Pour Locking Lid Pot**
Maxi Aids
42 Executive Boulevard
Suite 3209
Farmingdale, NY  11735                631-752-0521
                                      800-522-6294
                              FAX: 631-752-0689
                       e-mail: sales@maxiaids.com
                              www.maxiaids.com
Baked enamel and dishwasher safe, the pot comes with an easy
lid that locks in place for extra safety. *$24.95*

**350   Electric Can Opener & Knife Sharpener**
Maxi Aids
42 Executive Boulevard
Suite 3209
Farmingdale, NY  11735                631-752-0521
                                      800-522-6294
                              FAX: 631-752-0689
                       e-mail: sales@maxiaids.com
                              www.maxiaids.com

Features include a powerful magnetic lid holder, the ability to
open odd-shaped cans, and easy operation for the physically
challenged. *$19.95*

**351   Evio Plastics**
PO Box 2295
Sandusky, OH  44871                   419-621-1105
                              FAX: 419-626-2183

*Doug Didion, Administrator Director*
*Danny Thomas, Owner*
Handi Holder is a plastic holder for 1/2 gallon paper cartons of
milk or juice. It is used to pour milk or juice without spills by using the handle.

**352   Food Markers/Rubberbands**
Maxi Aids
42 Executive Boulevard
Suite 3209
Farmingdale, NY  11735                631-752-0521
                                      800-522-6294
                              FAX: 631-752-0689
                       e-mail: sales@maxiaids.com
                              www.maxiaids.com
These are durable plastic markers, easily identified by touch,
texture, shape and form which help the visually impaired orient
themselves to food location on the plate. *$11.95*

**353   Funnel**
Sense-Sations
919 Walnut Street
Philadelphia, PA  19107               215-627-0600
                              FAX: 215-922-0692

*Patricia Johnson, Chief Executive Officer*
Wide mouth funnel aids in pouring liquids or dry goods from
container to container. *$1.25*

**354   Good Grips Cutlery**
Therapro
225 Arlington Street
Framingham, MA  01702                 508-872-9494
                                      800-257-5376
                              FAX: 508-875-2062
                       e-mail: info@theraproducts.com
                              www.theraproducts.com

*Karen Conrad, Owner*
Stainless steel utensils have a special twist built into the metal to
facilitate bending of a spoon or fork at any angle for right or left
handed people. *$7.50*

**355   Granberg Superior Systems**
Saskatoon
Saskatchewan, Canada, S7L5Y          306-374-9440
                              FAX: 306-373-8715
Height adjustable cabinets for easy reach to food and other ne-
cessities.

**356   Guide A Knife**
Maxi Aids
42 Executive Boulevard
Suite 3209
Farmingdale, NY  11735                631-752-0521
                                      800-522-6294
                              FAX: 631-752-0689
                       e-mail: sales@maxiaids.com
                              www.maxiaids.com
Adjustable food slicing system guides the knife for even, uni-
form slices while protecting the user. *$11.95*

**357 Handy-Helper Cutting Board**
Maxi Aids
42 Executive Boulevard
Suite 3209
Farmingdale, NY 11735
631-752-0521
800-522-6294
FAX: 631-752-0689
e-mail: sales@maxiaids.com
www.maxiaids.com
Laminated cutting board with unique features to hold food in place with corner ledge for cutting and spreading. *$19.95*

**358 Innerlip Plates**
Therapro
225 Arlington Street
Framingham, MA 01702
508-872-9494
800-257-5376
FAX: 508-875-2062
e-mail: info@theraproducts.com
www.theraproducts.com

*Karen Conrad, Owner*
Food may be pushed to the side of the plate, then scooped up with a fork and spoon. Available in beige or blue. *$5.00*

**359 Jordan's Motility Solutions: Adapt-Able Utensils**
PO Box 132772
Tyler, TX 75713
903-526-2100
FAX: 903-526-2103
e-mail: info@disabilityaccessories.com
www.disabilityaccessories.com

*Gene Howland, President*
Adapt-Able eating utensils encourage independent eating for individuals with limited mobility. Angle and reach of utensils can be adjusted to address specific needs.

**360 Long Oven Mitts**
Sammons Preston Rolyan
4 Sammons Court
Bolingbrook, IL 60440
630-226-1300
800-228-3693
FAX: 262-387-8748
e-mail: customerservice@sammonspreston.com
www.sammonspreston.com
Protect hands and forearms from heat, flames and oven grates with these practical mitts that allow a longer reach and less bending. *$8.95*

**361 Magnetic Card Reader**
Maxi Aids
42 Executive Boulevard
Suite 3209
Farmingdale, NY 11735
631-752-0521
800-522-6294
FAX: 631-752-0689
e-mail: sales@maxiaids.com
www.maxiaids.com
Produces audible labels so a recorded card can be taped on cans of food or a box of cake mix; even adding instructions for baking. *$159.95*

**362 Make-and-Shake Ice Tray**
Sense-Sations
919 Walnut Street
Philadelphia, PA 19107
215-627-0600
FAX: 215-922-0692

*Patricia Johnson, Chief Executive Officer*
A covered ice tray that can be filled with water and then safely transported to the freezer without spilling. *$2.00*

**363 Maxi Aid Braille Timer**
Maxi Aids
PO Box 3209
Farmingdale, NY 11735
631-752-0521
800-522-6294
FAX: 631-752-0689
e-mail: sales@maxiaids.com
www.maxiaids.com

Three raised dots at 15, 30 and 45, two raised dots at remaining five minute intervals and one raised dot at remaining two and a half minute intervals, offers ease of operation to make this a helpful aid for the visually impaired. *$12.95*

**364 Nosey Cup**
Therapro
225 Arlington Street
Framingham, MA 01702
508-872-9494
800-257-5376
FAX: 508-875-2062
e-mail: info@theraproducts.com
www.theraproducts.com

*Karen Conrad, Owner*
For those with a stiff neck or persons who can't tip their head back while drinking. *$6.00*

**365 Paring Boards**
Therapro
225 Arlington Street
Framingham, MA 01702
508-872-9494
800-257-5376
FAX: 508-875-2062
e-mail: info@theraproducts.com
www.theraproducts.com

*Karen Conrad, Owner*
Suction feet stabilize board and stainless steel prongs hold food in place for easy, one-handed cutting. *$32.50*

**366 PowerLink 2 Control Unit**
AbleNet
2808 Fairview Avenue N
Saint Paul, MN 55113
800-322-0956
FAX: 651-294-2259
e-mail: customerservice@ablenetinc.com
www.ablenetinc.com
The PowerLink 2 Control Unit allows switch operation of electrical appliances. It can be used to activate 1 or 2 appliances (up to 1700 watts combined). If 2 appliances are used, they will activate simultaneously. There are four modes of control on the PowerLink 2; direct mode, timed (seconds) mode, timed (minutes) mode and latch mode. Meets safety standards from Underwriters Laboratory (UL) and Canadian Standards Association (CSA) for electrical appliances. *$159.00*

**367 Sammons Preston Rolyan**
4 Sammons Court
Bolingbrook, IL 60440
630-226-1300
800-228-3693
FAX: 262-387-8748
e-mail: customerservice@sammonspreston.com
www.sammonspreston.com
Sammons Preston Rolyan is a leading provider of rehabilitation and assistive devices to help those with disabilities meet daily physical challenges and achieve their greatest level of independence. With one of the industry's largest catalogs, Sammons Preston Rolyan offers a wide range of products available.
*Annually*

**368 Slicing Aid**
Snug Seat
PO Box 1739
Matthews, NC 28106
704-882-0666
800-336-7684
FAX: 704-882-0751
e-mail: sales@snugseat.com
www.snugseat.com

*Earlene Hucks, Marketing Coordinator*
*Kirk Mackenzie, Owner*
The design of these knives allows a better working posture and makes optimal use of strength in the arms and hands.

**369  Small Appliance Receiver**
AbleNet
2808 Fairview Avenue N
Saint Paul, MN  55113

800-322-0956
FAX: 651-294-2259
e-mail: customerservice@ablenetinc.com
www.ablenetinc.com

The Small Appliance Receiver, in conjunction with the Cordless Big Red Switch, allows you to control small electrical appliances in the environment without a cord. It should only be used with low-wattage appliances (under 500 watts) which have two prong plugs (ie, radios, fans, lamps, blenders, etc.). It should not be used with heat generating appliances. *$32.00*

**370  Steel Food Guard**
Maxi Aids
42 Executive Boulevard
Suite 3209
Farmingdale, NY  11735

631-752-0521
800-522-6294
FAX: 631-752-0689
e-mail: sales@maxiaids.com
www.maxiaids.com

Provides stable area to push against while eating. *$ 10.95*

**371  Thick-n-Easy**
Therapro
225 Arlington Street
Framingham, MA  01702

508-872-9494
800-257-5376
FAX: 508-875-2062
e-mail: info@theraproducts.com
www.theraproducts.com

*Karen Conrad, Owner*

Instant food thickener that sets in 30 seconds and will not become thicker even after refrigeration. *$6.50*

**372  Thumbs Up Cup**
Therapro
225 Arlington Street
Framingham, MA  01702

508-872-9494
800-257-5376
FAX: 508-875-2062
e-mail: info@theraproducts.com
www.theraproducts.com

*Karen Conrad, Owner*

This cup is designed for those with limited strength or coordination or arthritis. The two backward-tilt handles and thumb rests allow finger joints to be used to their greatest mechanical advantage. *$9.50*

**373  Un-Skru**
Multi-Marketing & Manufacturers
PO Box 1070
Littleton, CO  80160

303-794-5955
800-506-0248
e-mail: penlane@xpert.net
www.seniorshops.com/unskru.html

*Janet Lane, President*

This jar and bottle opener mounts permanently to the underside of a cabinet, shelf, table or counter so it is out of sight yet always ready to use. Opens all sizes of jar lids — easily and with little strength. *$7.95*

**374  Undercounter Lid Opener**
Sammons Preston Rolyan
4 Sammons Court
Bolingbrook, IL  60440

630-226-1300
800-228-3693
FAX: 262-387-8748
e-mail: customerservice@sammonspreston.com
www.sammonspreston.com

The gripper of this unit which installs under the counter can help unscrew any cap. *$5.75*

**375  Uni-Turner**
Sammons Preston Rolyan
4 Sammons Court
Bolingbrook, IL  60440

630-226-1300
800-228-3693
FAX: 262-387-8748
e-mail: customerservice@sammonspreston.com
www.sammonspreston.com

Odd shaped handles can be turned easily with one-handed, L-shaped Uni-Turner. *$16.50*

**376  Universal Hand Cuff**
Therapro
225 Arlington Street
Framingham, MA  01702

508-872-9494
800-257-5376
FAX: 508-875-2062
e-mail: info@theraproducts.com
www.theraproducts.com

*Karen Conrad, Owner*

Comfortable cuff with Velcro strap holds utensils, toothbrushes, etc. *$9.95*

# Lifts, Ramps & Elevators

**377  Accessibility Lift**
Inclinator Company of America
601 Gibson Boulevard
Harrisburg, PA  17104

717-939-8420
800-343-9007
FAX: 717-234-0941
e-mail: isaks@inclinator.com
www.inclinator.com

*Dotty Keith, Sales Manager*
*Stephen Nock, President*

An economical lift for restricted usage that provides barrier-free access that can be used by churches, schools, lodging halls and meeting halls to meet compliance requirements, with the dignified convenience and freedom they deserve.

**378  Adjustable Incline Board**
Bailey Manufacturing Company
118 Lee Street
Suite 130
Lodi, OH  44254

330-948-1080
800-321-8372
FAX: 330-948-4439
e-mail: baileymfg@attmail.com
www.baileymfg.com

*Larry Strimple, President*

Incline board for the physically challenged with a foot board with non-slip tread.

**379  AlumiRamp**
855 E Chicago Road
Quincy, MI  49082

517-639-8777
800-800-3864
FAX: 517-639-4314
e-mail: ramps@alumiramp.com
www.alumiramp.com

*Linda Burke, President*
*Doug Cannon, Customer Service*
*Pam Kelley, Customer Service*

Complete line of modular and portable ramps for both home and vehicle use. Welded construction and non-skid extruded surfaces are featured on all our ramps.

**380    Area Access**
8117 Ransell Road
Falls Church, VA  22042                703-573-2111
                                       800-333-2732
                                  FAX: 703-207-0446
                           e-mail: c_wenn@hotmail.com
                                   www.areaaccess.com

*Cliff Wenn, Sales Manager*
*Barbara Spellman, Mobility Consultant*
*Scott Hobson, Owner*

Serving the entire Mid-Atlantic with scooters, stairway lifts and
elevators. Large inventory and fully stocked showrooms.

**381    Barrier Free Lifts**
9230 Prince William Street
Manassas, VA  20110                    703-361-6531

**382    Bruno Independent Living Aids**
Bruno Independent Living Aids
PO Box 84
Oconomowoc, WI  53066                  262-567-4990
                                       800-882-8183
                                  FAX: 262-567-4341
                          e-mail: webmaster@bruno.com
                                       www.bruno.com

*Patrick Foy, National Sales Manager*
*Karla Branham Shaw, Marketing*
*Michael Bruno, Owner*

An ISO 9001 Certified Manufacturer of automotive lifts for
scooter, wheelchairs, and powerchairs, three and four wheel
scooters, and straight and custom curve stairlifts.

**383    Butlers Wheelchair Lifts**
Flinchbaugh Company
390 Eberts Lane
York, PA  17403                        717-848-2418
                                       800-326-2418
                                  FAX: 717-843-7385

*Gregg Kenkins, President*
*Brian McMaster, President Sales*
*Greg E Ness, Sales Manager*

This wheelchair lift can be equipped with an end ramp and guard.
Automatically retractable, it locks firmly into place when the lift
is in operation.

**384    Cheney's Liberty II**
Handi-Lift
730 Garden Street
Carlstadt, NJ  07072                   201-933-0111
                                       800-503-2003
                                  FAX: 845-947-4522
                                   www.handilift.com

*Douglas Boydston, Owner*

Economical lift for straight stairways.

**385    Classique**
Handi-Lift
730 Garden Street
Carlstadt, NJ  07072                   201-933-0111
                                       800-503-2003
                                  FAX: 845-947-4522
                                   www.handilift.com

*Douglas Boydston, Owner*

The Classique elevator answers access problems in churches,
schools and small offices.

**386    Columbus McKinnon Corporation**
140 John James Audubon Parkway
Amherst, NY  14228                     716-689-5400
                                       800-888-0985
                                  FAX: 716-696-3220

*Larry Smith, Manager*
*Timothy Tevens, Chief Executive Officer*

Supplies various lift and transfer systems for independent or attended applications including ceiling mounted or freestanding
overhead track lifts and mobile floorbase units for homes,
schools and healthcare facilities. Lift Systems for transferring
between bed, chair, commode or bath are available with a variety of slings, scales and accessories.

**387    Curb-Sider Super XL**
Bruno Independent Living Aids
PO Box 84
Oconomowoc, WI  53066                  262-567-4990
                                       800-882-8183
                                  FAX: 262-953-5501
                                       www.bruno.com

*Michael R Bruno, Chairman/CEO/Owner*

The lift of choice for storing your fully or partially assembled
scooter or power chair weighing up to 400 pounds in the rear of
your van or minivan, SUV, pickup truck or some station wagon
applications.

**388    Custom Lift Residential Elevators**
Waupaca Elevator Company
1726 N Ballard Road
Appleton, WI  54911                    920-991-9082
                                       800-238-8739
                                  FAX: 920-991-9087
                        e-mail: csr@waupacaelevator.com
                                www.waupacaelevator.com

*Bill Michael, Owner*

Waupaca Elevator residential elevators and dumbwaiters add
value, convenience and reliability to today's homes.

**389    Deluxe Convertible Exercise Staircase**
Sammons Preston Rolyan
4 Sammons Court
Bolingbrook, IL  60440                 630-226-1300
                                       800-228-3693
                                  FAX: 262-387-8748
                  e-mail: customerservice@sammonspreston.com
                                www.sammonspreston.com

Here's an exercise staircase to fit any department configuration.
Just reposition a few nuts and bolts to change from a straight to a
corner type staircase.

**390    Easy Pivot Transfer Machine**
Rand-Scot
401 Linden Center Drive
Fort Collins, CO  80524                970-484-7967
                                       800-467-7967
                                  FAX: 970-467-7967
                          e-mail: randscot@webaccess.net
                                   www.easypivot.com

*Joel Lerich, President*

The Easy Pivot Patient Lifting System allows for strain-free,
one-caregiver transfers of the disabled individual.

**391    Easy Stand**
Altimate Medical
PO Box 180
Morton, MN  56270                      507-697-6393
                                       800-342-8969
                                  FAX: 507-637-3024

*Alan Tholkes, Chief Executive Officer*

Designed to make standing fast and simple. The easy to operate, hydraulic lift system provides a controlled lifting and lowering. With the convenience of simply transferring to the chair and reaching a standing position in seconds with no straps to struggle with.

**392  Econol Elevator Lift Corporation**
2513 Center Street
Suite 854
Cedar Falls, IA  50613

800-328-2560
FAX: 319-277-4778

*Sharon R Martin, President*
*Adrian L Martin, Sales*

Offers a full line of lifts, dumbwaiters, stair riders and elevators for persons with disabilities.

**393  Econol Stairway Chair Ride**
Econol Stairway Lift Corporation
2513 Center Street
Cedar Falls, IA  50613

This chair ride unit is of sturdy steel construction and rides sideways, not backwards.

**394  Economical Liberty**
Handi-Lift
730 Garden Street
Carlstadt, NJ  07072

201-933-0111
800-503-2003
FAX: 845-947-4522

*Douglas Boydston, Owner*

Installs quickly and easily on most straight stairways. It uses regular household current and mounts over the carpet or directly to the stairs without marring.

**395  Electra-Ride Elite**
Bruno Independent Living Aids
PO Box 84
Oconomowoc, WI  53066

262-567-4990
800-882-8183
FAX: 262-953-5501
www.bruno.com

*Michael R Bruno, Chairman/CEO/Owner*

The new Electra-Ride Elite installs to within 5 inches of the wall and has a 350 pound weight capacity. Bruno stairlifts can fit almost any custom curve or straight rail application and require no structural modification to the stairway. Plus, battery power allows for uninterupted operation even during a power outage.

**396  Electra-Ride III**
Bruno Independent Living Aids
PO Box 84
Oconomowoc, WI  53066

262-567-4990
800-882-8183
FAX: 262-953-5501
www.bruno.com

*Michael R Bruno, Chairman/CEO/Owner*

Bruno stairlifts can fit almost any custom curve or straight rail application and require no structural modification to the stairway. Plus, battery power allows for uninterupted operation even during a power outage.

**397  Excel Stairway Lift**
Access Industries
4001 E 138th Street
Grandview, MO  64030

800-829-9760
FAX: 816-763-4467
e-mail: marketing@accessind.com
www.accessind.com

Installs easily on either side of a straight stairway for independent, step-free living. The lift fastens securely to the stairs without marring walls and is adjustable to match any stairway slope with an incline angle up to 45 degrees. Available with battery back up.

**398  Freedom Wheelchair Lifts**
580 Tc Jester Boulevard
Houston, TX  77007

713-864-1460

*Carlos Saez, Owner*

**399  Freedom Wheels**
580 TC Jester Boulevard
Houston, TX  77007

713-864-1460
FAX: 713-864-1469
e-mail: info@freedomwheels.com
www.freedomwheels.com/index.html

*N Donnelly*

Freedom Wheels, Inc. is committed to people with disabilities and personal transportation options for an independent lifestyle.

**400  Golden-Glide Stairway Lift**
Access Industries
4001 E 138th Street
Grandview, MO  64030

800-829-9760
FAX: 816-763-4467
e-mail: marketing@accessind.com
www.accessind.com

Model 95 monorail track design can be custom-made to fit virtually any stairway. The unit can carry a side rider around stairway curves and corners with 90 to 180 degree turns and one or more landings. The lift can carry a maximum of 300 pounds up to 6 feet on its roomy 17-1/2 inch seat. Call and send controls are available at top or bottom landings. A four point safety sensor is a standard security feature.

**401  Handi Home Lift**
Handi-Lift
730 Garden Street
Carlstadt, NJ  07072

201-933-0111
800-503-2003
FAX: 845-947-4522

*Douglas Boydston, Owner*

An outdoor lift designed to provide access over porch stairs or other steps that impede movement.

**402  Handi Prolift**
Handi-Lift
730 Garden Street
Carlstadt, NJ  07072

201-933-0111
800-503-2003
FAX: 845-947-4522

*Douglas Boydston, Owner*

Provides dependable vertical transportation for multi-level buildings.

**403  Handi-Ramp**
Handi-Ramp
510 North Avenue
Libertyville, IL  60048

847-680-7700
800-876-7267
FAX: 847-816-8866
e-mail: rampmarketing@aol.com
www.handiramp.com

*Thomas Disch, President/CEO*
*Mike Smith, Production Manager*
*Cheryl Machnich, Sales/Marketing Manager*

Provides a complete line of economical, ADA Compliant access ramping products. Line includes van attachable and wheelchair tie downs; aluminum or expanded metal folding portables; aluminum channels; portable, sectional ramp systems; semi-permanent ramps, platforms and systems. All ramp series are available in varied lengths and widths in combination with platforms and optional hand railing, single or double bar construction with return ends. Special Order ramps and ramp systems. Valued at $100.

**404    Homecare Products EZ-Access Portable Ramps**

15824 SE 296th Street
Kent, WA  98042

800-451-1903
FAX: 800-630-2350
e-mail: ezaccess@homecareproducts.com
www.homecareproducts.com

*Don Everard, VP Marketing*
*Deanne Sandvold, VP Sales*

EZ-ACCESS Ramps bridge gaps over curbs and steps, allowing scooters and wheelchairs to continue on a smooth, safe course. Available in several different styles and sizes, ranging from a two-foot curb ramp to a 10-foot multi-purpose ramp. All ramps are made of anodized aluminum.

**405    Homewaiter**

Inclinator Company of America
601 Gibson Boulevard
Harrisburg, PA  17104

717-939-8420
800-343-9007
FAX: 717-234-0941
e-mail: isaks@inclinator.com
www.inclinator.com

*Dotty Keith, Sales Manager*
*Stephen Nock, President*

With its roller truck riding in a specially formed monorail, it is easy to install and highly adaptable to existing conditions. It can travel up to 35 feet, opening on any or all three sides at different stations, whether at counter level or floor level.

**406    Horcher Lifting Systems**

324 Cypress Road
Ocala, FL  34472

352-687-8020
800-582-8732
FAX: 866-378-3318
e-mail: us-office@horcher.com
www.horcher.com

*David Schultz, General Manager*
*Sharon Harbert, Administrative Assistant*

Barrier Free Lifts by Horcher leads the industry for excellence in patient transfers and technology for over 18 years. They offer state of the art ceiling track systems, floor base lifts and bathing systems such as the Unilift, PC-2, Diana, Lexa, and Raisa to achieve greater mobility.

**407    Inclinette**

Inclinator Company of America
601 Gibson Boulevard
Harrisburg, PA  17104

717-939-8420
800-343-9007
FAX: 717-234-0941
e-mail: isaks@inclinator.com
www.inclinator.com

*Stephen Nock, President*

Inclinette provides comfort and convenience in providing multi-floor access to persons who have difficulty climbing stairs.

**408    Lectra-Lift**

La-Z-Boy
1284 N Telegraph Road
Monroe, MI  48162

734-242-1444
FAX: 734-457-2005
www.lazboy.com

*Gerald L Kiser, President*
*David M Risley, SVP/CFO*
*Patrick H Norton, Chairman*

This power recliner has a single motor drive that operates three distinct cycles: lifting, leg elevation and full power recline.

**409    Liberty LT**

Handi-Lift
730 Garden Street
Carlstadt, NJ  07072

201-933-0111
800-503-2003
FAX: 845-947-4522

*Douglas Boydston, Owner*

Stair lift with dual armrests that lock into position. The comfortable, contoured seat is designed to swivel and move forward at the bottom or top landings to facilitate transfer.

**410    LiftUp**

15 Highland Road
Eastham, MA  02642

508-255-5394

*Richard C Peterson, Publisher*

Plans for electric transfer device, especially suitable for bathroom use, lifts user erect with unique upper-body sling. Developed by an engineer to help cope with his multiple sclerosis quadriplegia, there are many now in use. Low-cost and simple make-it-yourself. *$ 19.00*

**411    Lifts for Swimming Pools and Spas**

Aquatic Access
417 Dorsey Way
Louisville, KY  40223

502-425-5817
800-325-5438
FAX: 502-425-9607
e-mail: info@AquaticAccess.com
www.AquaticAccess.com

*Linda Nolan, President*
*Liz Waters, Advertising*
*Ann Bryant, Customer Service/Sales*

Aquatic Access manufacturers and sells water-powered lifts providing access to in-ground and above-ground swimming pools, spas, boats and docks. *$2310.00*

**412    Lizzie Lift**

Handicap Helpers
604 W Main Street
Appalachia, VA  24216

276-565-1889
FAX: 276-565-3623
e-mail: JBlevins@me.vcos.edu
www.hurtback.org

*James W Blevins, President*

A stable patient lift that provides independence for the disabled by allowing one caregiver to move them from bed to upright position more easily and effectively. The Lizzie Lift which can be used as a gurney bed, lounge chair or wheelchair, not only decreases back injury for caregivers but also alleviates the fear of being moved. Can be used in hospitals, nursing homes and homes. FDA listing, Patent pending. $7,000-$8,000.

**413    Mecalift Sling Lifter**

50 Gary Avenue
Roselle, IL  60172

630-307-2756

*Ross Scavuzzo, President*

**414    Minivator Residential Elevator**
Access Industries
4001 E 138th Street
Grandview, MO  64030

800-829-9760
FAX: 816-763-4467
e-mail: marketing@accessind.com
www.accessind.com

The perfect choice for a person who is contemplating moving from their multi-storied home because they cannot get up and down the stairs. The low cost, compact Minivator elevator can help these people live independently. The Minivator can be installed in the corner of a room without a shaft or hoistway, so the elevator doesn't have to disfigure the structure. The Minivator elevator can take a person or persons between floors in less than a minute and can accommodate a standard size wheelchair.

**415    One for All Lift All**
Amigo Mobility International
6693 Dixie Highway
Bridgeport, MI  48722

989-777-0910
800-692-6446
FAX: 989-777-8184
www.myamigo.com

*Mike Galen, Controller*
*Shirley Beebe, Order/Sales Operations*
*Mike LeBrake, Product Manager*

The Lift-All transports your wheelchair easily into the trunk of an automobile and neatly stores it for easy access.

**416    Ortho Kinetics**
W220n507 Springdale Road
Waukesha, WI  53186

800-824-1068
FAX: 262-542-4258

*Anne Tyler, Director Marketing*

Products to enhance people's lives through mobility. These electric three and four wheel vehicles are designed to surpass consumer expectations by providing total comfort, convenience and performance features found nowhere else. Ortho-Kinetics has a full line of vehicles for any application.

**417    Out-Sider III**
Bruno Independent Living Aids
PO Box 84
Oconomowoc, WI  53066

262-567-4990
800-882-8183
FAX: 262-953-5501
www.bruno.com

*Michael R Bruno, Chairman/CEO/Owner*

Lets you carry your scooter fully assembled and keeps your trunk space available for other things.

**418    Parker Bath**
Arjo
50 Gary Avenue
Roselle, IL  60172

630-307-2756
800-323-1245
FAX: 888-594-2756
e-mail: lchevrie@arjousa.com
www.arjo.com

*Lorena Chevrie, Marketing Communications*
*Ross Scavuzzo, President*

This involves no manual lifting, strain or stress for the caregiver.

**419    Patient Lifting & Injury Prevention**
ARJO
50 N Gary Avenue
Roselle, IL  60172

630-307-2756
800-323-1245
FAX: 888-594-2756
e-mail: info@arjousa.com
www.arjo.com

*Alexis LaSalvia, Marketing Communications*

Aids in patient lifting while protecting the caregiver from the risk of backstrain.

**420    Pool Lifts for In-Ground Pools**
Aquatic Access
417 Dorsey Way
Louisville, KY  40223

502-425-5817
800-325-5438
FAX: 502-425-9607
e-mail: info@AquaticAccess.com
www.AquaticAccess.com

*Liz Waters, Marketing*
*Linda Nolan, President*

Provide independent or assisted access to in-ground pools. Lifts are powered with water pressure from a garden hose and are portable. Some lifts have a three-hundred pound lift capacity and others have a four-hundred pound capacity, perfect for commercial installations or home use. ADA compliant. *$3245.00*

**421    Porch-Lift Vertical Platform Lift**
Access Industries
4001 E 138th Street
Grandview, MO  64030

800-829-9760
FAX: 816-763-4467
e-mail: marketing@accessind.com
www.accessind.com

Provide stairway access indoors and out for people who use wheelchairs. Lifting heights range from 1 to 144 feet and are available for both commercial and residential applications. Easy to install and operate, the units are space and cost efficient solutions to ADA compliance.

**422    Ramplette Telescoping Ramp**
Graham-Field Health Products
2935 Northeast Parkway
Atlanta, GA  30360

770-447-1609
800-347-5678
FAX: 800-726-0601
www.grahamfield.com

*Irwin Selinger, Chief Executive Officer*

A multi-functional, easily moved, economical ramp weighing 25 pounds.

**423    Ricon Corporation**
12450 Montague Street
Pacoima, CA  91331

818-899-7588
800-322-2884
FAX: 818-890-3354
www.riconcorp.com

Ricon corporation is a world leader in the manufacture of lifts and other mobility products for people with disabilities. The Ricon product line features the Activan(R) a lowered floor minivan conversion, wheelchair lifts power seat base and automatic door openers.

**424    Silver Glide Stairway Lift**
Access Industries
4001 E 138th Street
Grandview, MO  64030

800-829-9760
FAX: 816-763-4467
e-mail: marketing@accessind.com
www.accessind.com

The economical Silver-Glide easily installs on either side of a straight stairway. The seat, armrest and footrest can be folded to save stairway space when the unit is not in use. The unit plugs into an outlet at the top or bottom of the stairs and uses regular household current. Also available with battery operated system. Heavy duty steel cable drive system permits the rider to travel up to 20 feet.

**425  Smart Leg**
Invacare Corporation
899 Cleveland Street
Elyria, OH 44035                     440-329-6000

e-mail: info@invacare.com
www.invacare.com

*A Malachi Mixon III, CEO*
*Gerald B Blouch, President/COO*
*Thomas R Miklich, CFO*

An ingenious elevating leg rest that automatically extends to correctly fit every outstretched leg.

**426  Smooth Mover**
Dixie EMS
385 Union Avenue
Brooklyn, NY 11211                   718-387-9305
                                     800-347-3494
                                 FAX: 718-387-9310
e-mail: customerSVC@dixieems.com
www.dixieems.com

*Eva Silverstein, President*

Patient mover is a board designed to transfer patients from bed to stretcher or table with one or two people. *$199.95*

**427  SpectraLift**
Inclinator Company of America
601 Gibson Boulevard
Harrisburg, PA 17104                 717-939-8420
                                     800-343-9007
                                 FAX: 717-234-0941
e-mail: isaks@inclinator.com
www.inclinator.com

*Dotty Keith, Sales Manager*
*Stephen Nock, President*

A newly designed hydraulic wheelchair lift made of fiberglass construction suitable for commercial and residential use.

**428  Spectrum Aquatics**
7100 Spectrum Lane
Missoula, MT 59808                   406-543-5309

*Dave Murray, President*

**429  Spectrum Products**
7100 Spectrum Lane
Missoula, MT 59808                   406-542-9781
                                     800-791-8056
                                 FAX: 406-542-1158
e-mail: info@spectrumproducts.com
www.spectrumproducts.com

*Gerry McConnell, President*

Manufacturers of swimming pool disabled access products such as lifts, ramps, railings, ladders, and stainless steel hydrotherapy tanks for the swimming pool and medical therapy markets.

**430  Stair & Glide Stairway Lift**
Access Industries
4001 E 138th Street
Grandview, MO 64030
                                     800-829-9760
                                 FAX: 816-763-4467
e-mail: marketing@accessind.com
www.accessind.com

Solves many multi-level accessibility problems in home. Lifts easily to install on straight or curved stairways. The rail attaches directly to steps without disturbing walls or staircase. The heavy duty drive mechanism means reliable, trouble-free operation. Public building and outdoor packages available.

**431  StairLIFT SC & SL**
Inclinator Company of America
601 Gibson Boulevard
Harrisburg, PA 17104                 717-939-8420
                                     800-343-9007
                                 FAX: 717-234-0941
e-mail: isaks@inclinator.com
www.inclinator.com

*Stephen Nock, President*
Simple, self-contained and efficient stair units.

**432  Stairway Elevators**
Bruno Independent Living Aids
1780 Executive Drive
Suite 84
Oconomowoc, WI 53066                 262-567-4990
                                     800-882-8183
                                 FAX: 262-567-4341
e-mail: webmaster@bruno.com

*Michael Bruno, Owner*

Bruno offers a full line of stairway elevators, including the Electra-Ride II featuring access during power interruptions, convenient installation, comfort and a powerful drive system. The Electra-Ride which features battery-powered technology, a rail width of 25 inches and seat rotation for easy transfers. The Comfort-Ride AC stair lift which is battery operated, has a rail width of 7.25 inches and folded width of less than 14.5 inches.

**433  Stand Aid**
Stand Aid Enterprises
PO Box 386
Sheldon, IA 51201
                                 FAX: 305-933-5210
e-mail: standaid@reconnect.com
www.standaid.com

Stand Aid can help you achieve independence and mobility safely and easily. Lifts you from a chair or bed with the flick of a switch, securing the user in an upright standing position.

**434  Straight and Custom Curved Stairlifts**
Bruno Independent Living Aids
PO Box 84
Oconomowoc, WI 53066                 262-567-4990
                                     800-882-8183
                                 FAX: 262-953-5501
e-mail: webmaster@bruno.com
www.bruno.com

*Patrick Foy, National Sales Manager*
*Karla Branham Shaw, Marketing*
*Michael Bruno, Owner*

Bruno stairlifts can fit almost any curve or straight rail application and requires little or no structural modification to the stairway. Normal rail position for a Bruno inside turn is 7 to 8 inches from the wall or obstruction which is the tightest radius of any stairlift manufacturing company in the world. The Bruno inside turn is ideal for bi-level homes or staircases with mid-level doors. Bruno's unique battery power allows for uninterrupted operation even during a power outage.

**435  SureHands Lift & Care Systems**
982 County Route 1
Pine Island, NY 10969                845-258-6500
                                     800-724-5305
                                 FAX: 845-258-6634
e-mail: info@surehands.com
www.surehands.com

*Thomas Herceg, President*
*Joyce Moraczewski, Marketing Coordinator*
*Carol Colegrove, Sales Coordinator*

SureHands Lift & Care Systems offer a unique, patented and exlusive range of lift and transfer systems to meet private and institutional needs of individuals with motor disabilties. Includes permanent and portable models for homes, workplaces and recreation. The SureHands Body Support offers safe, easy and secure transfers for user and the opportunity for independent transfers for some. They are a back-saver for caregivers. All lifts are easily maintained and operated with mininum assistance.

**436 Swing-A-Way**
Braun Corporation
PO Box 310
Winamac, IN 46996

574-946-6153
800-THE-LIFT
FAX: 574-946-4670

*William Roth, President*

A swing lift for transporting patients from bed to bath and more. It features a gravity-down operation made possible by a newly designed pump module package. The new, quieter module features a built-in hand pump and a plastic reservoir for easy fluid checking. This is a vehicle lift not bath lift.

**437 Thyssen Krupp Access**
4001 E 138th Street
Grandview, MO 64030

816-763-3100
800-829-9760
FAX: 816-763-4467
e-mail: marketing@tkaccess.com
www.tkaccess.com

*Michael Bolton, Marketing Supervisor*
*Bill Koch, VP Sales*
*Pat Schmidt, Business Development Specialist*

Whether you want to open your facility or stay in the home you love, Thyssen Krupp Access has the perfect wheelchair lift, stair lift or elevator to suit your budget and needs. Our lifts have the best warranties. Our nationwide network of dealers are close by and ready to help.

**438 Turning Automotive Seating (TAS)**
Bruno Independent Living Aids
PO Box 84
Oconomowoc, WI 53066

262-567-4990
800-882-8183
FAX: 262-953-5501
www.bruno.com

*Michael R Bruno, Chairman/CEO/Owner*

Transfer in and out of a car, minivan, pickup truck and full size van without any lifting!

**439 VPL Series Vertical Wheelchair Lift**
Access Industries
4001 E 138th Street
Grandview, MO 64030

800-829-9760
FAX: 816-763-4467
e-mail: marketing@accessind.com
www.accessind.com

Provide stairway access indoors and out for people who use wheelchairs. Lifting heights from 1 to 144 feet for loads up to 750 pounds are available for both commercial and residential applications. Easy to install and operate, the units are space and cost efficient solutions to ADA access compliance. Attendant operation, toe-guard enclosure and restricted access hoistway enclosure options are available.

**440 Vangater, Vangater II, Mini-Vangater**
PO Box 310
Winamac, IN 46996

800-THE-LIFT
FAX: 574-946-7935
www.braunlift.com

Tri-fold and fold-in-half lifts represent a major innovation in the field of adapted van transportation.

**441 Vertical Home Lift Sales**
2715 Seaboard Lane
Long Beach, CA 90805

562-634-5962
800-795-6227
FAX: 562-634-4120

*Rick Pierce, Vertical Home Lift Sales*
*Betty Haskings, Office Manager*
*Jerry MacDonald, President*

Sales and service of van and truck lifts. Sales and service of wheel chair lifts for vans and automobiles. Sales, installation and service of vertical home lifts, scooter lifts and pool lifts. Sales of scooters.

**442 Vestibular Board**
Bailey Manufacturing Company
118 Lee Street
Suite 130
Lodi, OH 44254

330-948-1080
800-321-8372
FAX: 330-948-4439
e-mail: baileymfg@attmail.com
www.baileymfg.com

*Larry Strimple, President*

Creates tilting in a rolling motion for reclining patients who need help developing balance.

**443 Wecolator Stairway Lift**
Access Industries
4001 E 138th Street
Grandview, MO 64030

800-829-9760
FAX: 816-763-4467
e-mail: marketing@accessind.com
www.accessind.com

Solves many multi-level accessibility problems in home. Lifts easily to install on straight or curved stairways. The rail attaches directly to steps without disturbing walls or staircase. The heavy duty drive mechanism means reliable, trouble-free operation. Public building and outdoor packages available.

**444 Wheelchair Carrier**
203 Matzinger Road
Toledo, OH 43612

419-478-4423
800-541-3213
FAX: 419-476-1324
e-mail: davidm@wheelchaircarrier.com
www.wheelchaircarrier.com

*Mark Makulinsky, President*
*Mike Siler, Engineer*

Wheelchair, scooter and powerchair carriers for hitch mount on vehicles, priced from $199 to $999.

**445 Ziggy Medi-Chair**
Laszlo Corporation
PO Box 1182
Florissant, MO 63031

314-830-3222
FAX: 314-830-3222
e-mail: suhayda@aol.com
mc-usa.com

*Les Suhayda, President*
*Dale Bibko, Secretary*

A lift and transfer system that maximizes time and safety for disabled and bedridden patients. A multifunctional product that benefits patients with disabilities and caregivers in a home or institutional government. A motorized system that lifts patients and saves caregivers from injury and workman's compensation claims.

## Major Catalogs

**446 AMI: Accessories for Mobile Independence**
5235 Mission Oaks Boulevard
Suite 381
Camarillo, CA 93012          805-987-8653

*Gay Dawson, Owner*

Ponchos, tote bags, gloves, and sweat pants for wheelchair-using consumers.

**447 AbleNet**
2808 Fairview Avenue N
Saint Paul, MN 55113          612-379-0956
800-322-0956
FAX: 651-294-2259
e-mail: customerservice@ablenetinc.com
www.ablenetinc.com

*Allison Locey, Administrative Assistant*
*Kara Hans O'Brien, Marketing Coordinator*

Creates and markets simple technology and educational services that enhance the quality of life for people with disabilities. By developing, and supporting easy-to-use, affordable and durable assistive technology to an individual's needs, capabilities, and interests, AbleNet's products foster independence, participation, inclusion and fun throughout a lifetime.

**448 Access Store Products for Barrier Free Environments**
Access Store.Com
820 W 7th Street
Chico, CA 95928          530-879-5600
800-497-2003
FAX: 530-893-1560
e-mail: sales@accessstore.com
www.accessstore.com

*Timothy Vander Heiden, President*
*Lisa Bantum, Sales Administrator*

One of the largest online ADA Compliance Catalogs available. Offers everything from innovative barrier removal products to survey equipment, to unique specialty products.

**449 Achievement Products**
PO Box 9033
Canton, OH 44711          800-373-4699
FAX: 800-766-4303
e-mail: info@specialkidszone.com
www.specialkidszone.com

*Teresa Cardon, VP*

Offer a wide range of pediatric rehabilitation equipment and special education products including foam and weights, weighted vests, positioning equipment, sensory integration products and ADL. Call for your free catalog.

**450 Adaptive Clothing: Adults**
Special Clothes
PO Box 333
E Harwich, MA 02645          508-896-7939
FAX: 508-896-7939
e-mail: SPECIALCLO@aol.com
www.special-clothes.com

*Judith Sweeney, President*

Special Clothes produces a catalogue of garments for adults with disabilities and/or incontinence. Offerings include: undergarments, snap-crotch tee shirts, sleepwear, jumpsuits, bibs and some footwear. The catalogue is available without charge. Comparable to department store prices. Special Clothes produces a catalog of adaptive clothing for children in sizes from toddler through young adults. A full line of clothing is included from undergarments through wheelchair jackets and ponchos.

**451 Adaptive Technology Catalog**
Synapse Adaptive
3095 Kerner Boulevard
Suite S
San Rafael, CA 94901          415-455-9700
800-317-9611
FAX: 415-455-9801
e-mail: info@synapseadaptive.com
www.synapseadaptive.com

*Martin Tibor, Owner*

Speech recognition and adaptive technology for individuals with disabilities.

**452 Adrian's Closet**
PO Box 9506
Rancho Santa Fe, CA 92067          800-831-2577
FAX: 714-364-4380
e-mail: adrians@electriciti.com
Fashions for the physically challenged child. Clothing offers Velcro closures, front pockets, concealed back openings and fashions for seated posture.

**453 Adult Long Jumpsuit with Feet**
Special Clothes
PO Box 333
E Harwich, MA 02645          508-896-7939
FAX: 508-896-7939
e-mail: specialclo@aol.com
www.special-clothes.com

*Judith Sweeney, President*

Line of clothing for people with disabilities. Child and adult catalog available.

**454 Adult Short Jumpsuit**
Special Clothes
PO Box 333
E Harwich, MA 02645          508-896-7939
FAX: 508-896-7939
e-mail: specialclo@aol.com
www.special-clothes.com

*Judith Sweeney, President*

This pull-on jumpsuit provides comfort and full coverage without bulk. Wide leg ribbing ends at mid-thigh, with snaps at the crotch. We use fine quality, comfortable cotton knit. 100% cotton knit. Made in USA. Option: long sleeves - add $3.00. Colors: white, navy, teal, light blue, light pink, red, burgundy, royal blue and black. Sm & Med: $36.50/3 for $104.00; L & XL: $39.00/3 for $111.25; and XXL: $42.00/3 for $119.25.

**455 American Discount Medical**
11124 NE Halsey Street
# 677
Portland, OR 97220          503-257-0820
800-877-9100
FAX: 503-258-8197
e-mail: adm@information44.com
www.americandiscountmed.com

*Tom Ruf, General Manager*

Deeply discounts every major brand medical product available.

**456 Apria Healthcare**
26220 Enterprise Court
Lake Forest, CA 92630          949-639-2000
800-277-4288
e-mail: contact_us@apria.com
www.apria.com

*Lawrence Higby, Chief Executive Officer*

Lifts, chairs, bathroom aids, bedroom aids, eating utensils and independent living aids for the physically challenged.

**457    Armstrong Medical**
575 Knightsbridge Parkway
Lincolnshire, IL  60069                    847-913-0101
                                          800-323-4220
                                     FAX: 847-913-0138
                                www.armstrongmedical.com

*Warren Armstrong, President*
Training aids, anatomical models, medical equipment, pediatrics equipment and rehabilitation equipment.

**458    Assistive Technology Journal**
1700 N Moore Street
Suite 1540
Arlington, VA  22209                       703-524-6686
                                     FAX: 703-524-6630
*$32.50*
   *Bi-Annually*

**459    Assistive Technology Sourcebook**
Special Needs Project
324 State Street
Suite H
Santa Barbara, CA  93101                   805-962-8087
                                          800-333-6867
                                     FAX: 805-962-5087
                          e-mail: books@specialneeds.com
                                www.specialneeds.com

*Alexandra Enders, Editor*
*Marian Hall, Editor*
Provides you with 18 chapters of practical information on all aspects of assistive technology for individuals with functional limitations. *$60.00*
   *576 pages*

**460    Bailey**
Bailey Manufacturing
PO Box 130
Lodi, OH  44254                            330-948-2655
                                          800-321-8372
                                     FAX: 330-948-4439
                         e-mail: baileymfg@attmail.com
                                www.baileymfg.com

*Dave Bailey, Owner*
Ambulation aids, balance aids, benches, chairs, exercise devices, tables, stools, rehabilitation and physical therapy equipment for the physically challenged.
   *70 pages*

**461    Best 25 Catalog Resources for Making Life Easier**
Meeting Life's Challenges
9042 Aspen Grove Lane
Madison, WI  53717                         608-824-0402
                                     FAX: 608-824-0403
              e-mail: help@MeetingLifesChallenges.com
                    www.MeetingLifesChallenges.com
Unique reference guide to locate thousands of useful and hard-to-find adaptive devices to make dressing, eating, cooking, grooming, communicating, playing, exercising, etc. easier, safer and less frustrating for people of all ages and disabilities. A comprehensive, up-do-date reference for people with disabilities, caregivers and healthcare professionals. *$8.95*
   *36 pages*
   *ISBN 1-891854-03-8*

**462    Body Suits**
Special Clothes
PO Box 333
E Harwich, MA  02645                       508-896-7939
                                     FAX: 508-430-2410
                          e-mail: specialclo@aol.com
                                www.special-clothes.com

*Judith Sweeney, President*
These are one piece garments that can be used to protect skin under braces, to add warmth and to shield incisions. Prices range from $18.25-22.50.

**463    Carolyn's Low Vision Products**
1415 57th Avenue W
Bradenton, FL  34207                       800-648-2266
                                     FAX: 941-739-5503
                        e-mail: sales@carolynscatalog.com
                                www.carolynscatalog.com

*Carolyn Tojek, President*
Free mail-order catalog of items for visually impaired people. We also have a retail store.

**464    Communication Aids for Children and Adults**
Crestwood Communication Aids
6625 N Sidney Place
Milwaukee, WI  53209                       414-352-5678
                                     FAX: 414-352-5679
                          e-mail: crestcomm@aol.com
                                www.communicationaids.com

*Ruth B Leff MS CCC, President/Language Pathologist*
A free catalog of communication aids for children and adults with disabilities. Over 300 light and high tech switches and aids, and a large selection of adapted and voice-activated toys. Talking Pictures and Passports communication boards, easy to use and moderately priced talking aids.
   *32 pages Yearly*

**465    Danmar Products**
221 Jackson Industrial Drive
Ann Arbor, MI  48103                       734-761-1990
                                          800-783-1998
                                     FAX: 734-761-8977
                       e-mail: sales@danmarproducts.com
                                www.danmarproducts.com

*Dan Russo, President*
*Suzanne Gubachy, Sales Manager*
*Amy Belleau, Sales Marketing*
Manufactures adaptive equipment for persons with physical and mental disabilities, from seating and positioning equipment, flotation devices, toileting aids to hard and soft shell helmets.

**466    Enrichments Catalog**
Sammons Preston Rolyan
4 Sammons Court
Bolingbrook, IL  60440                     630-226-1300
                                          800-323-5547
                                     FAX: 630-226-1389
                         e-mail: spr@abilityone.com
                      www.sammonsprestonrolyan.com
Provides people with physical challenges with the products they need to help live their lives to the fullest. Includes items for everyday tasks and personal care; assistive products for home use; toileting and bathing aids; grooming and dressing devices; kitchen and dining aids. Also items for range of motion, mobility and exercise such as weights, therapy putty and exercise equipment; ergonomic gloves and supports; canes, crutches, walkers and wheelchair accessories. 36-page catalog.

**467    Equipment Shop**
PO Box 33
Bedford, MA  01730                         781-275-7681
                                          800-525-7681
                                     FAX: 781-275-4094
                         e-mail: info@equipmentshop.com
                                www.equipmentshop.com

*Kenneth D Larson, Owner*
Pediatric therapy equipment including pezzi Gymnastik balls, Tripp Trapp chair, airex mats, tricycle accessories, sensory integration equipment and adaptive devices.

**468    Everest & Jennings**
Division of Graham-Field
2935 Northeast Parkway
Atlanta, GA  30360

770-368-4724
800-347-5678
FAX: 800-726-0601
e-mail: cs@everestjennings.com
www.everestjennings.com

Manufactures more than 200 items for persons with physical disabilities, including wheelchairs, seat cushions, shower chairs, grab bars and more.

**469    Express Medical Supply**
28 Seebold Spur
Fenton, MO  63026

636-349-8448
800-633-2139
FAX: 800-633-9188
e-mail: sales@exmed.net
www.exmed.net

*Chris Winston, Manager*
*Bill Nahm, Manager*

Offers a full line of medical and ostomy supplies. at discounted prices. Order by phone or online.

**470    FlagHouse Rehab Resources**
601 Flaghouse Drive
Hasbrouck Heights, NJ  07604

201-288-7600

*George Carmel, President*

**471    FlagHouse Special Populations**
601 FlagHouse Drive
Hasbrouck Heights, NJ  07604

201-288-7600
800-793-7900
FAX: 800-793-7922
e-mail: sales@flaghouse.com
www.flaghouse.com

*Brigid de Lime, Sr Brand Manager*
*Diana Hohman, Brand Manager*

Contains over 2,000 products of interest to therapy professionals.
*Bi-Annually*

**472    HAC Hearing Aid Centers of America: HARC Mercantile**
Hearing Center
1111 W Centre Avenue
Portage, MI  49024

269-324-0301
800-445-9968
FAX: 800-413-5248
TTY: 800-445-9968
e-mail: home@harcmercantile.com
www.harcmercantile.com

*Ronald Slager, President*

Specializes in products for the hard of hearing and deaf as required under ADA including visual alerting products for fire, phone, door, wake up, phone amplification, TTY, FM and infrared listening systems.

**473    Harris Communications**
Harris Communications
15155 Technology Drive
Eden Prairie, MN  55344

952-906-1180
800-825-6758
FAX: 952-906-1099
e-mail: mail@harriscomm.com
www.harriscomm.com

*Bill Williams, National Sales Manager*
*Robert Harris, Owner*

A national distributor of assistive devices for the deaf and hard of hearing with many manufacturers represented. Catalog includes a wide range of assistive devices as well as a variety of books and videotapes related to deaf and hard-of-hearing issues. Products available for children, teachers, hearing professionals, interpreters and anyone interested in deaf culture, hearing loss and sign language.
*180 pages Yearly*

**474    Health and Rehabilitation Products**
Luminaud
8688 Tyler Boulevard
Mentor, OH  44060

440-255-9082
800-255-3408
FAX: 440-255-2250
e-mail: info@luminaud.com
www.luminaud.com

*Thomas Lennox, President*
*Dorothy Lennox, VP*

Switches for limited capability, stoma and trach covers, shower protectors and thermo-stim oral motor stimulator. Personal voice amplifiers for people with weak voices. Artificial larynges for people with no voices. Small electronic communication boards. Books for laryngectomies and speech pathologists.

**475    HealthCare Solutions**
Blue Chip II
3478 Hauck Road
Cincinnati, OH  45241

513-271-5115
800-417-5115
FAX: 513-527-3686

*LK Barker, Director*

Quality rehabilitation equipment sales and rental. Available equipment includes manual and powered mobility, positioning/seating equipment, vehicle modification, environmental controls, augmentative and alternative communication devices, adaptive computer access, ambulance aids and aids for daily living. Equipment provision is carried out through a total team approach.

**476    Hear You Are**
98 Us Highway 46
Budd Lake, NJ  07828

973-347-7662
FAX: 973-691-0611

*Dorinne S Davis, President*

A large catalog of various assistive and communication devices for people who are hearing impaired. *$3.00*
*42 pages*

**477    Hig's Manufacturing**
2917 Anthony Lane
Minneapolis, MN  55418

612-788-1183
FAX: 612-638-1341

*James Murphy, Owner*

Factory direct, lightweight aluminum, portable, 2 & 4-way folding, telescoping tracks, threshold, van, scooter and approach ramps.

**478    Huntleigh Healthcare**
40 Christopher Way
Eatontown, NJ  07724

732-935-0975
800-223-1218
FAX: 732-578-9889
www.huntleigh-healthcare.com

*Robert Angel, President/CEO*

Offers quality products including support surfaces, seating surfaces and intermittent pneumatic compression devices.

**479**    **Kleinert's**
3968 194th Trail
Golden Beach, FL  33160          305-937-0824
                                 800-463-7337
                                 FAX: 305-937-0825
                                 e-mail: mbrier1930@aol.com
                                 www.hygienics.com

*Michael Brier, President/CEO*

Offers a complete line of incontinence products and skin care products consisting of disposable and reuseable panties for women and pants for men. Also disposable liners.
        *16 pages Bi-Annual*

**480**    **LS&S**
PO Box 673
Northbrook, IL  60065            847-498-9777
                                 800-468-4789
                                 FAX: 847-498-1482
                                 TTY: 800-317-8533
                                 e-mail: info@LSSproducts.com
                                 www.LSSproducts.com

*Melissa Balbach, Owner*

Specializes in products for the blind, visually impaired, hearing impaired, and deaf. Free catalog upon request.

**481**    **Lighthouse Low Vision Products**
Lighthouse International
111 E 59th Street
New York, NY  10022              212-821-9200
                                 800-829-0500
                                 FAX: 212-821-9707
                                 e-mail: info@lighthouse.org
                                 www.lighthouse.org

*Tara Cortes, President*

This supplier provides vision-related products.

**482**    **Luminaud**
8688 Tyler Boulevard
Mentor, OH  44060                440-255-9082
                                 800-255-3408
                                 FAX: 440-255-2250
                                 e-mail: info@luminaud.com
                                 www.luminaud.com

*Thomas Lennox, President*
*Dorothy Lennox, VP*

Offers a line of artificial larynx, personal voice amplifiers, special switches, stoma covers and other communication, health and safety items.

**483**    **MOMS Catalog**
24700 Avenue Rockefeller
Valencia, CA  91355
                                 800-232-7443
                                 FAX: 888-874-4347
                                 e-mail: moms@hdis.com
                                 www.momscatalog.com

MOMS catalog features high quality, incontinence supplies, mobility products, bath safety products urological products, aids for daily living products, ostomy supplies and many other adpative items. MOMS offers low prices, excellent customer service and convenient home delivery to your doorstep.
        *52 pages*

**484**    **Maxi Aids**
PO Box 3209
Farmingdale, NY  11735           631-752-0521
                                 800-522-6294
                                 FAX: 631-752-0689
                                 e-mail: sales@maxiaids.com
                                 www.maxiaids.com

Products specially designed for the blind, low vision, visually impaired, deaf, deaf-blind, hard of hearing, arthritic, diabetic and individuals with special needs.

**485**    **New Vision Store**
919 Walnut Street
Philadelphia, PA  19107          215-627-0600

                                 e-mail: webmaster@thenewvisionstore.com
                                 www.thenewvisionstore.com

*Patricia Johnson, Chief Executive Officer*

Catalog for individuals with visual impairments, listing visual aids, magnifiers, large print books and more.
        *30 pages*

**486**    **Nurion-Raycal**
2 Station Square
Paoli, PA  19301                 610-647-2435
                                 FAX: 610-647-2216

*Nazir A Ali, President*

Electronic travel aids for the blind, deaf-blind, visually impaired persons, and those with hemispatial neglect. Devices detect obstacles, find clear paths, landmarks. Lase Cane incorporates lasers to detect drop-offs, obstacles at different heights and distances. Polaron, a hand-held or chest-mounted unit, utilizes ultrasound to detect obstacles at various distances. Wheelchair Pathfinders incorporate ultrasound and lasers to detect drop-offs and obstacles on the sides and forward.

**487**    **Pearson Performance Solutions**
1 North Deerborne Street
16th Floor
Chicago, IL  60602               312-938-9200
                                 800-922-7343
                                 FAX: 312-242-4400
                                 e-mail: pearsonreidlondonhouse@pearson.com
                                 www.pearsonreidlondonhouse.com

Publishes human resource assessment instruments for employment settings. The instruments include job analysis procedures to identify important characteristics for job success and objective assessment procedures to evaluate applicants and employees on these characteristics.

**488**    **Pearson Reid London House**
1 N Dearborn Street
Floor 16
Chicago, IL  60602               312-938-9200

*Adrea Allen, Manager*

**489**    **Potomac Technology**
1 Church Street
Suite 101
Rockville, MD  20850             301-762-4005
                                 800-433-2838
                                 FAX: 301-762-1892
                                 e-mail: info@potomactech.com
                                 www.potomactech.com

*Patricia Relidan, VP/Manager*

This catalog offers a variety of products for the deaf and hard of hearing, such as: wake-up devices, alarm clocks, alerting systems, assistive listening devices, signalers, smoke detectors, TTY, telephones and telephone amplifiers. We also carry novelties, and educational books and videos.
        *24 pages*

**490**    **Prentke Romich Company Product Catalog**
1022 Heyl Road
Wooster, OH  44691               330-262-1984
                                 800-262-1984
                                 FAX: 330-263-4829
                                 e-mail: info@prentrom.com
                                 www.prentrom.com

*Cherie Weaver, Marketing Coordinator*
*Dave Moffatt, President*

A full line, product catalog containing information on speech-output communication devices, environmental controls and computer access products.

**491  Products for People with Disabilities**
LS&S
PO Box 673
Northbrook, IL 60065

847-498-9777
800-468-4789
FAX: 847-498-1482
TTY: 800-317-8533
e-mail: info@LSSproducts.com
www.LSSproducts.com

*Melissa Balbach, Owner*

LS&S, LLC has a free catalog of products for the blind, deaf, visually and hearing impaired including: TTYs, computer adaptive devices, CCTVs, talking blood pressure, blood glucose and talking scales.

**492  Rehabilitation Engineering and Assistive Technology Society of North America (RESNA)**
1700 N Moore Street
Suite 1540
Arlington, VA 22209

703-524-6686
FAX: 703-524-6630
TTY:703-524-6639
e-mail: info@resna.org
www.resna.org

*Thomas A Gorski, Executive Director*

RESNA improves the potential of people with disabilities to achieve their goals through the use of technology. RESNA promotes research, development, education, advocacy and provision of technology; and by supporting the people engaged in these activities.

**493  Sammons Preston Enrichments Catalog**
Sammons Preston Rolyan
4 Sammons Court
Bolingbrook, IL 60440

630-226-1300
800-228-3693
FAX: 262-387-8748
e-mail: customerservice@sammonspreston.com
www.sammonspreston.com

*Tony Napolitano, Director Marketing Services*

Our Enrichnments Catalog offers products that make the tasks and challenges of living at home— bathing, getting dressed, getting around— a little easier. Choose from personal care items to kitchen and dining aids, household helpers to mobility devices, plus a complete selection of pain-reducing products, exercise items, health monitoring equipment and more.
*40 pages Yearly*

**494  Special Edition for Disabled People**
Lawrence Research Group
PO Box 31039
San Francisco, CA 94131

415-981-3650
800-242-2823
FAX: 415-468-3912
e-mail: info@xandria.com
www.xandria.com

*Marcia Jackson, Marketing Director*
*B Lawrence, Owner*

Sexual aids for the handicapped. A catalog of product and informational resources and quotes from the top professionals in this field. *$4.00*

*32 pages*

**495  Sportaid**
78 Bay Creek Road
Loganville, GA 30052

770-554-5033
800-743-7203
FAX: 770-554-5944
e-mail: info@sportaid.com
www.sportaid.com

*Jimmy Green*
*Stacy Green, Owner*

Offers an assortment of wheelchairs (everyday and racing), wheelchair sports equipment, replacement tires, hubs, spokes, pushrims, cushions and more. Call for free catalog.
*68 pages Yearly*

**496  Ultratec**
450 Science Drive
Madison, WI 53711

608-238-5400
800-482-2424
FAX: 608-238-3008
e-mail: service@ultratec.com
www.ultratec.com

*Jackie Morgan, Director Marketing*
*Robert Engel, President*

The world's largest manufacturer of text telephones and amplified telephones. Products include desktop TTYs with built-in printer, memory capabilities, as well as compact portable units for cellular and cordless use. Ultratec also manufactures public TTYs for pay phone accessibility.
*Yearly*

**497  WCI/Weitbrecht Communications**
2716 Ocean Park Boulevard
Suite 1007
Santa Monica, CA 90405

310-452-8613
800-233-9130
FAX: 310-450-9918
e-mail: sales@weitbrecht.com
www.weitbrecht.com

*Donna Barwald, Sales Manager*

Catalog featuring a wide range of assistive devices for the deaf, hard of hearing, mobility and speech impaired.
*24 pages*

**498  Walgreens Home Medical Center**
7173 Cermak Road
Berwyn, IL 60402

708-795-1295
800-323-2828
FAX: 708-795-1308

*Paul Pankros RPh, Director*
*Stan Kozlowski, Manager*

Hospital supplies and home medical equipment with nationwide direct mail delivery.

**499  Walton Way Medical**
1225 Walton Way
Augusta, GA 30901

706-722-0276
FAX: 706-722-0279

*Michael Bower, President*

Offers medical, therapeutic, urological, hygiene and skin care products for disabled persons.

## Miscellaneous

**500  BeOK Key Lever**
Sammons Preston Rolyan
4 Sammons Court
Bolingbrook, IL  60440
630-226-1300
800-228-3693
FAX: 262-387-8748
e-mail: customerservice@sammonspreston.com
www.sammonspreston.com
Handy accessory helps position key to provide maximum leverage enabling the user to work the most stubborn lock. *$11.50*

**501  Big Lamp Switch**
Maxi Aids
42 Executive Boulevard
Suite 3209
Farmingdale, NY  11735
631-752-0521
800-522-6294
FAX: 631-752-0689
e-mail: sales@maxiaids.com
www.maxiaids.com
This big, three-spoked knob replaces small rotating knobs which are a problem for those with arthritis or other limitations of the fingers. *$6.75*

**502  Book Holder**
Access with Ease
PO Box 1150
Chino Valley, AZ  86323
928-636-9469
800-531-9479
FAX: 928-636-0292
e-mail: KMJC@northlink.com
This hands free reading book holder enables the user to read hands free. Moveable pegs prevent slipping, yet allow easy turning. Folds flat and has built in handle for easy carrying. *$16.95*

**503  Bookholder: Roberts**
Therapro
225 Arlington Street
Framingham, MA  01702
508-872-9494
800-257-5376
FAX: 508-875-2062
e-mail: info@theraproducts.com
www.theraproducts.com

*Karen Conrad, Owner*

Gray plastic, ideal for hand free reading, adjusts to all sizes of books and prevents pages from flipping for the physically challenged. *$27.50*

**504  Brandt Industries**
4461 Bronx Boulevard
Bronx, NY  10470
718-994-0800
800-221-8031
FAX: 718-325-7995
e-mail: info@brandtind.com
www.brandtind.com

*Neil Brandt, President*
*Kathy Rice, Order Expediter*

**505  Bus and Taxi Sign**
Maxi Aids
42 Executive Boulevard
Suite 3209
Farmingdale, NY  11735
631-752-0521
800-522-6294
FAX: 631-752-0689
e-mail: sales@maxiaids.com
www.maxiaids.com
Signs that the individual with a disability can use to attract the attention of bus or taxi drivers. *$3.75*

**506  Call Alarm/Switch Delay Unit**
Words+
40015 Sierra Highway
Suite B145
Palmdale, CA  93550
800-869-8521
FAX: 661-266-8969

*Ginger Woltosz, VP*
*Tim Ross, Manager*

For use with any single system. Provides loud audible attention-getting alarm that can be either a steady or pulsating tone. Once activated, the alarm must be turned off by pressing a reset button. *$299.00*

**507  Care Electronics**
4700 Sterling Drive
Suite D
Boulder, CO  80301
303-444-2273
888-444-8284
FAX: 303-447-3502
e-mail: tmoody@riveraisland.com
www.medicalshoponline.com

*Donna Lewis, Sales Manager*
*Tom Moody, President*

Care Electronics manufactures safety monitoring systems for caregivers, home-health care, and nursing homes. WanderCARE monitors loved ones who tend to wander away from home. Care Deluxe Occupancy systems monitor patients in bed and in wheelchairs to help prevent falls. WetSENSE provides incontinence monitors.

**508  Center for Assistive Technology and Environmental Access**
GA Institute Of Technology College of Architecture
490 10th Street NW
Atlanta, GA  30332
404-894-4960
FAX: 404-894-9320
www.catea.org

*Barbara Christopher, Administrative Coordinator*
*Elizabeth Bryant, Project Director II*

The Center for Assistive Technology and Environmental Access (CATEA) promotes independence and participation of people with disabilities through a cariety of projects that focus on research, developmental, education and technology improvement.

**509  Child Convertible Balance Beam Set**
Bailey Manufacturing Company
118 Lee Street
Suite 130
Lodi, OH  44254
330-948-1080
800-321-8372
FAX: 330-948-4439
e-mail: baileymfg@attmail.com
www.baileymfg.com

*Larry Strimple, President*

This convertible set is used to develop balance in two stages.

**510  Child Variable Balance Beam**
Bailey Manufacturing Company
135 S Mount Zion Road
Lebanon, IN  46052
765-482-7775
800-321-8372
FAX: 800-224-5390
e-mail: baileymfg@attmail.com
www.baileymfg.com

*Jaqueline Bailey, Owner*

The four walking beams can be arranged in several different ways for variable balance training.

**511  Child's Mobility Crawler**
Bailey Manufacturing Company
118 Lee Street
Suite 130
Lodi, OH  44254

330-948-1080
800-321-8372
FAX: 330-948-4439
e-mail: baileymfg@attmail.com
www.baileymfg.com

*Larry Strimple, President*

Neurologically delayed or orthopedically impaired small children can perform crawling and coordination exercises while being comfortably supported by the crawler.

**512  Choice Switch Latch and Timer**
AbleNet
2808 Fairview Avenue N
Saint Paul, MN  55113

800-322-0956
FAX: 651-294-2259
e-mail: customerservice@ablenetinc.com
www.ablenetinc.com

A Choice Switch Latch and Timer allows one user to learn to make choices. It has two switch inputs and can control two devices. Once one device has been activated, the other will not function until the first one is turned off or completes its timed cycle. *$83.00*

**513  Cordless Big Red Switch**
AbleNet
2808 Fairview Avenue N
Saint Paul, MN  55113

800-322-0956
FAX: 651-294-2259
e-mail: customerservice@ablenetinc.com
www.ablenetinc.com

The Cordless Big Red Switch, when used in conjunction with either the Cordless Receiver or the Small Appliance Receiver, gives you cordless control of toys, games, and appliances in your environment. *$89.00*

**514  DEUCE Environmental Control Unit**
APT Technology
236a N Main Street
Shreve, OH  44676

330-567-2001
888-549-2001
FAX: 330-567-3073
e-mail: sales@apt-technology.com
www.apt-technology.com

*Grace Miller, Office Manager*

Allows a severely disabled person to control a variety of useful devices via a dual switch. DEUCE controls phone, 4 AC powered devices such as a radio, 4 switch controlled devices such as a page turner and up to 16 lights and or appliances distributed around the environment. Starts at $1,500.

**515  Dazor Manufacturing Corporation**
4483 Duncan Avenue
Saint Louis, MO  63110

314-652-2400
800-345-9103
FAX: 314-652-2069
e-mail: info@dazor.com
www.dazor.com

*Kirk Cressey, Marketing Director*
*Bob Smith, National Sales Manager*
*Mark Hogrebe, President*

Dazor is a US manufacturer of quality task lighting. Products include fluorescent, incandescent and halogen lighting fixtures. Illuminated magnifiers combine light and magnification to greatly enhance activities such as reading and make hobbies more enjoyable. All lamps come in a variety of mounting options to include desk bases, clamp on, floor stands and wall tracks. $95 - $450.

**516  Digi-Flex**
Therapro
225 Arlington Street
Framingham, MA  01702

508-872-9494
800-257-5376
FAX: 508-875-2062
e-mail: info@theraproducts.com
www.theraproducts.com

*Karen Conrad, Owner*

This is a unique hand and finger exercise unit. Recommended for use of individuation of fingers, web space and general strengthening of work hands. Available in a variety of resistances. *$17.50*

**517  Dorma Architectural Hardware**
PO Box Ac
Reamstown, PA  17567

800-523-8483
FAX: 717-336-2106
e-mail: archdw@dorma-usa.com
www.dorma-usa.com

*Paul Kosakowski, President/CEO*
*Gary Phillips AHC, VP Regional Sales, East*
*Ken Theaker, VP Regional Sales, West*

DORMA provides a complete line of door controls, including barrier-free units that comply with the Americans with Disabilities Act. A wide variety of surface applied and concealed closers, low energy operators, exit devices and electronic access control systems are available to address these equipments.

**518  Dual Switch Latch and Timer**
AbleNet
2808 Fairview Avenue N
Saint Paul, MN  55113

800-322-0956
FAX: 651-294-2259
e-mail: customerservice@ablenetinc.com
www.ablenetinc.com

A Dual Switch Latch and Timer allows two users to activate two devices at a time in the latch. Timed seconds or timed minutes mode of control. *$88.00*

**519  Folding Reacher**
Accent Books & Products
PO Box 700
Bloomington, IL  61702

309-378-2961
800-787-8444
FAX: 309-378-4420
e-mail: acmtlvng@aol.com

Lightweight, adjustable, foldable reachers allowing one-handed operation. *$13.95*

**520  Foot Inversion Tread**
Bailey Manufacturing Company
118 Lee Street
Suite 130
Lodi, OH  44254

330-948-1080
800-321-8372
FAX: 330-948-4439
e-mail: baileymfg@attmail.com
www.baileymfg.com

*Larry Strimple, President*

Effective for correcting flat feet. These angled boards require the patient to walk on the outside of the foot instead of the arch.

**521  Foot Placement Ladder**
Bailey Manufacturing Company
118 Lee Street
Suite 130
Lodi, OH  44254

330-948-1080
800-321-8372
FAX: 330-948-4439
e-mail: baileymfg@attmail.com
www.baileymfg.com

*Larry Strimple, President*

Adjustable cross bars for different length steps. Reinforced metal crosses for easier climbing for the physically-disabled.

**522 Handy Reacher**
Access with Ease
PO Box 1150
Chino Valley, AZ 86323
    928-636-9469
    800-531-9479
    FAX: 928-636-0292
    e-mail: KMJC@northlink.com
Long handled reacher works for retrieving items off shelves, picking fruit in the garden, dusting high places, getting objects behind the couch and lots of uses. Rubber jaws that open 5 inches wide with a magnet on one tip, wooden arm that extends the reach 30 inches to a metal handle. Other model reachers are available. *$7.95*

**523 Hospital Environmental Control System**
Prentke Romich Company
1022 Heyl Road
Wooster, OH 44691
    330-262-1984
    800-262-1984
    FAX: 330-263-4829
    e-mail: info@prentrom.com
    www.prentrom.com

*Dave Moffatt, President*
Permits the non-ambulatory patient to operate a variety of electrical items in a single room. A large liquid crystal display is mounted in front of the user and they scan through the menu of operations and make a selection using a sip-puff switch. Options include nurse call, standard telephone functions, electric bed control, hospital television operation and electrical appliance on and off. *$3860.00*

**524 Knock Light**
HARC Mercantile
1111 W Centre Avenue
Portage, MI 49024
    269-324-1615
    800-445-9968
    FAX: 269-324-2387
    e-mail: home@harcmercantile.com
    www.harcmercantile.com

*Ronald Slager, President*
Easily attaches to a door with velcro, portable. *$ 29.95*

**525 Leg Elevation Board**
Bailey Manufacturing Company
118 Lee Street
Suite 130
Lodi, OH 44254
    330-948-1080
    800-321-8372
    FAX: 330-948-4439
    e-mail: baileymfg@attmail.com
    www.baileymfg.com

*Larry Strimple, President*
Includes seven positions to a 30 degree incline, three pillows with Velcro, easy carry hand slot and a natural finish.

**526 Leveron**
Lindustries
21 Shady Hill Road
Weston, MA 02493
    781-237-8177

*Willard H Lind, President/Owner*
*Louise T Lind, VP*
Leveron is a doorknob lever handle for ease of operation. Leveron converts standard doorknobs to lever action without removing existing hardware. No gripping, twisting or pinching when hands are wet, arthritic or arms are full. Leveron provides convenience. Available in five colors: almond, satin brass, silver metallic, dark bronze and Hi-Glow (glows in the dark) at low cost to comply with ADA access requirements in public and private places. *$16.95*

**527 Location Finder**
Maxi Aids
42 Executive Boulevard
Suite 3209
Farmingdale, NY 11735
    631-752-0521
    800-522-6294
    FAX: 631-752-0689
    e-mail: sales@maxiaids.com
    www.maxiaids.com
Helps find house, apartment, car or office. Just press the transmitter and sound will be emitted indicating the location. *$99.95*

**528 Longreach Reacher**
Therapro
225 Arlington Street
Framingham, MA 01702
    508-872-9494
    800-257-5376
    FAX: 508-875-2062
    e-mail: info@theraproducts.com
    www.theraproducts.com

*Karen Conrad, Owner*
Reacher is useful when reaching, sitting or when standing. *$18.95*

**529 Loop Scissors**
Therapro
225 Arlington Street
Framingham, MA 01702
    508-872-9494
    800-257-5376
    FAX: 508-875-2062
    e-mail: info@theraproducts.com
    www.theraproducts.com

*Karen Conrad, Owner*
Pliable, plastic handles that allow for easy and controlled cutting. *$14.25*

**530 Plastic Card Holder**
Therapro
225 Arlington Street
Framingham, MA 01702
    508-872-9494
    800-257-5376
    FAX: 508-875-2062
    e-mail: info@theraproducts.com
    www.theraproducts.com

*Karen Conrad, Owner*
For those with reduced finger control. *$4.00*

**531 Power Door**
11240 Gemini Lane
Dallas, TX 75229
    800-688-1758
    FAX: 972-620-9875
    e-mail: info@powerdoor.com
    www.powerdoor.com

*Jim Goldthwaite, National Sales Manager*
Power door, low energy door operators.

**532 ProtectaCap, ProtectaCap+PLUS, ProtectaChin Guard and ProtectaHip**
Plum Enterprises
PO Box 85
Valley Forge, PA 19481
    610-783-7377
    800-321-PLUM
    FAX: 610-783-7577
    www.plument.com

*Janice Carrington, President*
Plum Enterprises award winning, exquiste, ergonomic protective wear keeps you safe from the dangers of falls. ProtectCap+Plus and ProtectHips are engineered for superior shock-absorption and designed for exquiste simplicity and amazing lightweight comfort. The perfect blend of style and function.

**533  Rocker Balance Square**
Bailey Manufacturing Company
118 Lee Street
Suite 130
Lodi, OH  44254

330-948-1080
800-321-8372
FAX: 330-948-4439
e-mail: baileymfg@attmail.com
www.baileymfg.com

*Larry Strimple, President*

The rocker is used in developing activity, balance control and coordination.

**534  Scott Sign Systems**
PO Box 1047
Tallevast, FL  34270

941-355-5171
800-237-9447
FAX: 941-351-1787
e-mail: mail@scottsigns.com
www.scottsigns.com

*Kathy Hannon, President*

Call for a brochure.

**535  Series Adapter**
AbleNet
2808 Fairview Avenue N
Saint Paul, MN  55113

800-322-0956
FAX: 651-294-2259
e-mail: customerservice@ablenetinc.com
www.ablenetinc.com

Allows two-switch operation of any battery-operated device or electrical devices. *$13.00*

**536  Signaling Wake-Up Devices**
HARC Mercantile
1111 W Centre Avenue
Portage, MI  49024

269-324-1615
800-445-9968
FAX: 269-324-2387
e-mail: home@harcmercantile.com
www.harcmercantile.com

*Ronald Slager, President*

Wake up devices. Vibrating alarm clocks, available with flashing lights, louder alarm noises and more. *$29.50*

**537  Smoke Detector with Strobe**
HARC Mercantile
1111 W Centre Avenue
Portage, MI  49024

269-324-1615
800-445-9968
FAX: 269-324-2387
e-mail: home@harcmercantile.com
www.harcmercantile.com

*Ronald Slager, President*

Most of the smoke alarms are twice as loud, and have a 120+ candela strobe that will wake a person from a sound sleep. Mounting hardware for ceiling or wall. *$165.95*

**538  SteeleVest**
Steele
PO Box 7304
Kingston, WA  98346

360-297-4555
888-783-3538
FAX: 360-297-2816
e-mail: info@steelevest.com
www.steelevest.com

*Sandra Steele, Manager*

Vest developed by NASA provides an external cooling system.

**539  TV & VCR Remote**
AbleNet
2808 Fairview Avenue N
Saint Paul, MN  55113

800-322-0956
FAX: 651-294-2259
e-mail: customerservice@ablenetinc.com
www.ablenetinc.com

Controls a TV, a VCR or a TV that is connected through a VCR tuner. It may be programmed to control functions such as on and off, channel up, preprogrammed TV channels and, if desired, other TV functions such as mute and pause. *$82.00*

**540  Tactile Thermostat**
Sense-Sations
919 Walnut Street
Philadelphia, PA  19107

215-627-0600
FAX: 215-922-0692

*Patricia Johnson, Chief Executive Officer*

Large embossed numbers on cover ring and raised temperature setting knob. *$31.50*

**541  Therapy Putty**
Therapro
225 Arlington Street
Framingham, MA  01702

508-872-9494
800-257-5376
FAX: 508-875-2062
e-mail: info@theraproducts.com
www.theraproducts.com

*Karen Conrad, Owner*

Designed to exercise and strengthen hands, ranging from soft to firm for developing a stronger grasp. Available in two, four and six ounce sizes. Three ounce putty in unique clear fist shaped container.

**542  Transcription Services**
Access-USA
PO Box 160
Clayton, NY  13624

800-263-2750
FAX: 800-563-1687
e-mail: info@access-usa.com
www.access-usa.com

*Deborah Haight, PICOE*

Access-USA provides one-stop alternate format transcription services for almost any type of document-reports, schedules, menus, monthly statements, brochures, reports, etc. Items may be submitted on computer disk, hard copy or email. Alternate formats include Braille, large print, Braille and print, audio recordings, adapted disks as well as video services-open/closed captioning and video descriptions. Accessible products Braille Business Cards and ADA signage. Braille and print stickers.

**543  Visual Alerting Guest Room Kit**
HARC Mercantile
1111 W Centre Avenue
Portage, MI  49024

269-324-1615
800-445-9968
FAX: 269-324-2387
e-mail: home@harcmercantile.com
www.harcmercantile.com

*Ronald Slager, President*

ADA compliant visual alerting guest room kit for the hard of hearing and deaf. Includes visual smoke detector, phone alert, door knock sensor, tactile alarm clock and telephone amplifier. Variations include TTY.

**544    Window-Ease**
A-Solution
1332 Cobo Place NE
Albuquerque, NM 87106                    505-256-0115
                                  FAX: 505-256-3756
                                  www.windowease.com

*Robert Gorrell, President*
*Jeff Dodd, Sales*

Device adapts horizontally and vertically sliding windows to
ANSI A117.1 standards. 10:1 mechanical advantage at the crank
arm opens a 50lb window with 5lbs force. Price ranges from
$350.00-$450.00.

---

## Office Devices & Workstations

**545    Auditech: Audioport Personal Amplifier**
PO Box 821105
Vicksburg, MS 39182
                                     800-229-8293
                                FAX: 800-221-8639
                             e-mail: info@auditechusa.com
                                  www.auditechusa.com
Make everyday conversations more comfortable and easy to
hear with the Audioport. This all-in-one unit has a powerful
built-in microphone and amplifer, so no wires or separate transmitters are needed. Designed for one-on-one or small group conversations, it amplies up to eight feet away. It automatically
adjusts for sharp sudden noises and allows user's voice to sound
natural. All in one small, durable unit. *$189.00*

**546    Combination File/Reference Carousel**
Center for Rehabilitation Technology
490 10th Street NW
Suite 118
Atlanta, GA 30318                    404-712-5667
                                     800-457-9555
                                FAX: 404-875-9409
                             e-mail: rerc-br@scsn.net

*TW Gannaway, Executive VP*
*Anthony Stringer PhD*

Offers two reading platforms and file holders joined on one easily rotated carousel. The carousel is easily rotated by head,
mouth or handstick. Page retainer adjusts to hold open a variety
of books and magazines. *$299.00*

**547    Don Johnston**
26799 W Commerce Drive
Volo, IL 60073                       847-740-0749
                                     800-999-4660
                                FAX: 847-740-7326
                           e-mail: info@donjohnston.com
                                  www.donjohnston.com

*Ruth Ziolkowski, President*

A provider of quality products and services that enable people
with special needs to discover their potential and experience
success. Products are developed for the areas of Physical Access, Augmentative Communication and for those who struggle
with reading and writing.

**548    Extensions for Independence**
555 Saturn Boulevard
Suite B-368
San Diego, CA 92154                  619-423-7709
                                FAX: 619-423-7709
                           e-mail: info@mouthstick.net
                                  www.mouthstick.net

*Arthur Heyer, President*

Develops, manufactures and markets special vocational equipment for the physically handicapped. Products: mouthsticks,
computer mechanical aids: key locks and diskette loaders. Also,
turntable desks, wheelchair portable desks, filing trays with
slanted sides, telephone adapters, and motorized artist easel. All
these products have been designed to solve the functional limitations of people with little or no use of hands and/or arms.

**549    Infogrip: AdjustaCart**
1794 E Main Street
Ventura, CA 93001                    805-652-0770
                                     800-397-0921
                             e-mail: sales@infogrip.com

*Liza Jacobs, President*

Sit or stand while working with this easily adjustable desk. With
a simple squeeze of a paddle the front surface travel range of 12
3/4. The front surface tilts 9 degrees toward and 15 degrees away
from you. Anthro carts are made of 1" thick industrial grade
particleboard shelves with high-pressure laminated 16 gauge
steel tube legs that safely hold 150 pounds. Spring assisted
mechanism. There are holes in 1: increment in the legs so that
you can put the shelves and accessories where needed. *$629.00*

**550    Infogrip: BAT Personal Keyboard**
1794 E Main Street
Ventura, CA 93001                    805-652-0770
                                     800-397-0921
                                FAX: 805-652-0880
                             e-mail: sales@infogrip.com

*Liza Jacobs, President*

One handed, compact input device that replicates all the functions of a full size keyboard, but with greater efficiency and convenience. Bat is easy to learn and use. Letters, numbers,
commands and macros are simple key combinations, chords,
that you can master in no time. BAT's unique ergonomic design
reduces hand strain and fatigue for greater comfort and productivity. *$200.00*

**551    Maxi Marks**
Maxi Aids
42 Executive Boulevard
Suite 3209
Farmingdale, NY 11735                631-752-0521
                                     800-522-6294
                                FAX: 631-752-0689
                             e-mail: sales@maxiaids.com
                                  www.maxiaids.com
Braille writing and identification products. *$2.50*

**552    Pencil/Pen Weighted Holders**
Therapro
225 Arlington Street
Framingham, MA 01702                 508-872-9494
                                     800-257-5376
                                FAX: 508-875-2062
                           e-mail: info@theraproducts.com
                                  www.theraproducts.com

*Karen Conrad, Owner*

Securely hold any pencil or pen. These weighted holders allow
for more control along with proprioceptive feedback to encourage better writing skills.

**553    PhoneMax Amplified Telephone**
Assistive Devices Network
2241 S Triangle X Lane
Tucson, AZ 85713                     866-674-3549
                                FAX: 520-883-3172
                           e-mail: info@assistivedevices.net
                                  www.assistivedevices.net

**554 Raised Line Drawing Kit**
Maxi Aids
42 Executive Boulevard
Suite 3209
Farmingdale, NY 11735
631-752-0521
800-522-6294
FAX: 631-752-0689
e-mail: sales@maxiaids.com
www.maxiaids.com

For writing script or drawing graphs by the use of special plastic paper. *$24.45*

**555 Sharp Calculator with Illuminated Numbers**
Independent Living Aids
PO Box 9022
Hicksville, NY 11802
516-937-1848
800-537-2118
FAX: 516-937-3906
e-mail: can-do@independentliving.com
www.independentliving.com

*Marvin Sandler, President*

A trim desktop calculator with large illuminated numbers that can be carried anywhere. *$34.95*

**556 Signature and Address Self-Inking Stamps**
Independent Living Aids
PO Box 9022
Hicksville, NY 11802
516-937-1848
800-537-2118
FAX: 516-937-3906
e-mail: can-do@independentliving.com
www.independentliving.com

*Marvin Sandler, President*

Gives thousands of impressions before requiring re-inking. *$11.95*

**557 Steady Write**
Maxi Aids
42 Executive Boulevard
Suite 3209
Farmingdale, NY 11735
631-752-0521
800-522-6294
FAX: 631-752-0689
e-mail: sales@maxiaids.com
www.maxiaids.com

Furnishes the writer with increased holding capacity and stabilizes the hand. *$6.95*

**558 TAJ Braille Typewriter**
Maxi Aids
42 Executive Boulevard
Suite 3209
Farmingdale, NY 11735
631-752-0521
800-522-6294
FAX: 631-752-0689
e-mail: sales@maxiaids.com
www.maxiaids.com

Smooth edged, simple and sturdy construction. Creates braille on 8 1/2 x 11 paper. *$495.00*

**559 Talking Desktop Calculators**
Maxi Aids
42 Executive Boulevard
Suite 3209
Farmingdale, NY 11735
631-752-0521
800-522-6294
FAX: 631-752-0689
e-mail: sales@maxiaids.com
www.maxiaids.com

Unique voice synthesizers call out numerals and functions as they are keyed in or read out data stored in memory. *$467.95*

**560 Talking Electronic Organizers**
Independent Living Aids
PO Box 9022
Hicksville, NY 11802
516-937-1848
800-537-2118
FAX: 516-937-3906
e-mail: can-do@independentliving.com
www.independentliving.com

*Marvin Sandler, President*

Electronic, portable, personal organizers that talk the user through all the functions and are totally voice interactive. *$199.95* and up.

**561 Television Remote Controls with Large Numbers**
Independent Living Aids
PO Box 9022
Hicksville, NY 11802
516-937-1848
800-537-2118
FAX: 516-937-3906
e-mail: can-do@independentliving.com
www.independentliving.com

*Marvin Sandler, President*

Large 5 1/2 inch x 8 1/2 inch unit that has easy to see and use buttons. Can be used on nearly every TV, VCR and cable boxes. *$39.95*

**562 Three M Brailler**
Maxi Aids
42 Executive Boulevard
Suite 3209
Farmingdale, NY 11735
631-752-0521
800-522-6294
FAX: 631-752-0689
e-mail: sales@maxiaids.com
www.maxiaids.com

For visually impaired, blind and sighted persons, produces braille on 3/8 and 1/2 inch vinyl tape. The dial has braille and regular characters. *$47.95*

# Scooters

**563 Alante**
Golden Technologies
401 Bridge Street
Old Forge, PA 18518
570-451-7477
800-624-6374
FAX: 570-451-7494
e-mail: info@goldentech.com
www.goldentech.com

*Rich Golden, CEO*
*Bob Golden, President*
*Bob Smith, VP Sales*

Rear-wheel-drive vehicle that represents the best in powered mobility.

**564 Amigo Mobility International**
Amigo Mobility International
6693 Dixie Highway
Bridgeport, MI 48722
989-777-0910
800-692-6446
FAX: 800-334-7274
e-mail: info@myamigo.com
www.myamigo.com

*Alison Newkirk, Sales Rep*
*Sandy Roth, Sales Rep*
*Allan Thieme, Chief Executive Officer*

An industry leader in the power operated scooters, Amigo provides innovative, durable, and customized mobility solutions for the disabled, injured, and seniors worldwide. *$2495.00*

**565  Amphibious ATV Distributors**
Amphibious ATV Distributors
2760 Greendale Drive
Sarasota, FL  34232
                              941-379-6186
                              800-843-2811
                         FAX: 941-377-8979
                    e-mail: CBeach1419@aol.com
                         www.maxsixwheel.com

*Clay Beach, Owner*

A two and four passenger, all-terrain vehicle that can provide
you with year round activities the whole family can enjoy. Accessible and drivable for the physically disabled. Used in hunting, fishing and outdoor activities on land and in the water. Many
options and accessories available. Delivery anywhere in the US
and worldwide. $5,000-$9,000.

**566  Avant Walker**
ETAC USA
PO Box 1739
Matthews, NC  28106
                              800-678-7684
                         FAX: 704-882-0751
                    e-mail: info@snugseat.com
                      www.snugseat.com/avant.html
Elegant styling makes the Avant an attractive companion. The
adjustable height seat and backrest offer comfort and security
whenever or wherever you choose to stop and rest. Pressure sensitive brakes require little strength to operate. Folds easily with
one hand. Lifetime warranty on frame and brake straps for original owner. $395-$50.

**567  Bravo! + Three-Wheel Scooter**
EZ-International
3275 Intertech Drive
Suite 500
Brookfield, WI  53045
                              262-790-5200
                              800-824-1068
                         FAX: 262-542-3990

*Anne Tyler, Marketing Director*
*Richard Lang, Owner*

Designed to increase your mobility indoors. The Bravo! plus has
extendible rear wheels for outdoor use and comes with easy to
use finger tip controls and a maintenance free gel-cell battery.
Available in red, blue, green or light sand gray with an optional
power seat lift. Call for complete line of 3 and 4-wheel electronic
vehicles.

**568  Cruiser Bus Buggy 4MB**
Convaid Products
PO Box 2458
Palos Verdes Peninsula, CA  90274
                              310-618-0111
                         FAX: 310-618-8811
                         www.convaid.com

*Mervyn Watkins, President*

In sizes from infant through young adult, this positioning buggy
is crash-tested.

**569  Cub, SuperCub and Special Edition Scooters**
Bruno Independent Living Aids
PO Box 84
Oconomowoc, WI  53066
                              262-567-4990
                              800-882-8183
                         FAX: 262-953-5501
                    e-mail: webmaster@bruno.com
                         www.bruno.com

*Patrick Foy, National Sales Manager*
*Karla Branham Shaw, Marketing*
*Michael Bruno, Owner*

Bruno Independent Living Aids, Inc. has over 12 different
scooter models. Bruno Cub and SuperCub scooters, has front or
rear-wheel drive, in both 3 and 4-wheel versions and comes in
four different colors plus a pediatric version. Each scooter can
handle up to 300 pounds. Bruno Special Edition scooters resem-
ble a fire engine, police car, Humvee and motorcycle.
$2,000-$5,000

**570  Electric Mobility Corporation**
PO Box 156
Sewell, NJ  08080
                              856-468-1000
                              800-257-7955
                         FAX: 856-468-3426
                         www.emobility.com

*Scott Patrick, Manager*
Manufactures Rascal Scooters.

**571  Explorer+ 4-Wheel Scooter**
EZ-International
3275 Intertech Drive
Brookfield, WI  53045
                              262-790-5200
                              800-824-1068
                         FAX: 262-790-5204
                         www.orthokinetics.com

*Anne Tyler, Director Marketing*
*Richard Lang, Owner*

A tough and rugged 4-wheel, rear-wheel drive, transaxle scooter
designed to take you just about anywhere you want to go. Easy to
use finger-tip controls and maintenance free gel-cell batteries
and an extendible, take-apart frame, make the Explorer+ a perfect fit for people seeking greater mobility. Available in red,
blue, green and gray, with an optional power seat lift.
$3,499-$3,999.

**572  Featherlite**
No Boundaries
12882 Valley View Street
Suite 5
Garden Grove, CA  92845
                              714-891-5899
                              800-926-8637
                         FAX: 714-891-0658
                         www.noboundaries.tv

*Norman Stein, Owner*

Lightweight scooter folds in seconds without tools or bending
down for hassle free travel on airplanes, cruise ships, trains,
RVs, buses and more! Heaviest component weighs 27 pounds.
Fits easily in almost any vehicle trunk.

**573  Invacare Fulfillment Center**
Invacare Corporation
1 Invacare Way
Elyria, OH  44035
                              440-329-6000
                              800-333-6900
                         FAX: 440-329-6568
                    e-mail: info@invacare.com
                         www.invacare.com

*Susan Elder, Dir Marketing/Communications*
*A Mixon Iii, Chief Executive Officer*

Invacare Corporation is the world's leading manufacturer and
distributor of non-acute medical products which promote recovery and active lifestyles for people requiring home and other
non-acute health care.

**574  Leisure Lift**
Leisure Lift
1800 Merriam Lane
Kansas City, KS  66106
                              800-255-0285
                         FAX: 913-722-2614
                    e-mail: leisure-lift@kc.rr.com
                         www.pacesaver.com

*DuWayne E Kramer Jr, President*

Leisure Lift offers light three wheel scooter models and seven
power wheelchair models. *$2695.00*

**575  MVP+ 3-Wheel Scooter**
EZ-International
3275 Intertech Drive
Suite 500
Brookfield, WI 53045                              262-790-5200
                                                  800-824-1068
                                                  FAX: 262-790-5204

*Richard Land, Owner*

The MVP+ is the rugged 3-wheel rear-wheel drive, transaxle scooter with finger tip controls, and featuring an extendible, take-apart frame for a perfect fit. The MVP+ comes with maintenance free gel-cell batteries and is available in red, blue, green or light sand gray, with an optional power seat lift. $2,599-$3,099.

**576  Motorized Stander**
Advanced Technology Corporation
1601 Charlotte Street
Kansas City, MO 64108                             816-421-6688
                                                  800-785-9108
                                                  FAX: 816-221-8371
                                                  e-mail: advancedtech@prodigy.net

*Joel Poindexter, Marketing Executive*

Occupant-operated motorized vehicle that offers independence, increased mobility and ease of movement to disabled people.

**577  Motovator Three-Wheel Scooter**
Motovator
22626 Normandie Avenue
Suite E
Torrance, CA 90502                                310-320-5941

                           e-mail: gene.massey@motovator.com
                                   www.motovator.com

This three-wheel electric wheelchair is a very maneuverable scooter with a turning radius that will get you around furniture, around a corner, through a doorway and more.

**578  Moxie**
No Boundaries
12882 Valley View Street
Suite 5
Garden Grove, CA 92845                            714-891-5899
                                                  800-926-8637
                                                  FAX: 714-891-0658
                                                  www.noboundaries.tv

*Norman Stein, Owner*

Disassembles into three parts in less than a minute. Heaviest component weighs 41 pounds. Portable, affordable and downright snazzy!

**579  Nova Rollators**
ETAC USA
2325 Parklawn Drive
Suite J
Waukesha, WI 53186
                                                  800-678-3822
                                                  FAX: 262-796-4605
                           e-mail: etac1usa@execpc.com
Light and easy to handle, fully adjustable for individual needs. Large cushioned tires allow the Nova to roll outdoors and indoors. $498-$637.
                           *$498 - $637*

**580  Outdoor Independence**
Palmer Industries
PO Box 5707
Endicott, NY 13763                                607-754-2957
                                                  800-847-1304
                                                  FAX: 607-754-1954
                           e-mail: palmer@palmerind.com
                                   www.palmerind.com

*Joanne Martone, Information Specialist*
*Lisa Carter, Sales Manager*
*Jack Palmer, President*

The futuristic, electric three-wheeler designed to take you almost anywhere.

**581  Pace Saver Plus II**
Leisure-Lift
1800 Merriam Lane
Kansas City, KS 66106                             800-255-0285

                           e-mail: leisure-lift@kc.rr.com
                                   www.pacesaver.com
The scooter combines outdoor ruggedness with indoor maneuverability at a low price.

**582  Palmer Independence**
Palmer Industries
PO Box 5707
Endicott, NY 13763                                607-754-2957
                                                  800-847-1304
                                                  FAX: 607-754-1954
                                                  www.palmerind.com

*Lisa Carter, Manager*
*Jack Palmer, President*

Futuristic electric outdoor three wheeler designed to take the rider almost anywhere.

**583  Palmer Twosome**
Palmer Industries
PO Box 5707
Endicott, NY 13763                                607-754-2957
                                                  800-847-1304
                                                  FAX: 607-754-1954
                           e-mail: palmer@palmerind.com
                                   www.palmerind.com

*Joanne Martone, Information Specialist*
*Lisa Carter, Sales Manager*
*Jack Palmer, President*

All electric two seat vehicle for those who can't pedal.

**584  Polaris Trail Blazer**
Polaris Industries
2100 Highway 55
Medina, MN 55340                                  763-542-0500
                                                  800-765-2747
                           www.polarisindustries.com

*Bennett J Morgan, President/COO*
*Thomas Tiller, CEO*
*Michael Malone, VP*

A four-wheeler that has many engineered innovations, features such as: full floorboards for full comfort, single lever breaking with auxiliary foot brake, electronic throttle control, parking brake and adjustable handlebars.

**585  Quickie 2**
Sunrise Medical/Quickie Designs
2382 Faraday Avenue
Suite 200
Carlsbad, CA 92008                                760-930-1500
                                                  FAX: 760-930-1585
                           www.sunrisemedical.com

*Michael Hammes, Chief Executive Officer*

This custom, ultralight, folding, everyday scooter offers portability and performance plus modular flexibility.

**586  Rascal 3-Wheeler**
Electric Mobility Corporation
PO Box 156
Sewell, NJ 08080                                  856-468-1000
                                                  800-257-7955
                                                  FAX: 856-468-3426
                                                  www.emobility.com

*Scott Patrick, Manager*

For primarily outdoor use, this three wheeler provides extra strength, durability and reliability.

**587 Rascal ConvertAble**
Electric Mobility Corporation
PO Box 156
Sewell, NJ 08080
856-468-1000
800-257-7955
FAX: 856-468-3426
www.emobility.com

*Scott Patrick, Manager*

An electric vehicle that's a compact mobile chair one minute and a rugged outdoor scooter the next. Use both indoors and outdoors. Also available with joystick controls.

**588 Regal Scooters**
Bruno Independent Living Aids
1780 Executive Drive
Suite 84
Oconomowoc, WI 53066
262-567-4990
800-882-8183
FAX: 262-567-4341
e-mail: webmaster@bruno.com
www.bruno.com

*Michael Bruno, Owner*

This line includes the Regal Standard, the Regal Large Adult, the Regal Small Adult, the Regal Pediatric, The Regal Ten models 65 and 75, and The Regal Four. These scooters offer adjustable flip-up armrests, pneumatic tires front and rear, and more.

**589 Regent**
Golden Technologies
401 Bridge Street
Old Forge, PA 18518
570-451-7477
800-624-6324
FAX: 570-451-7974
e-mail: info@goldentech.com
www.goldentech.com

*Bob Golden, President*

Top-rated performance scooter, with extra features and economically priced.

**590 Roadster 20**
ATV Solutions
4700 W 60th Avenue
Unit 4
Arvada, CO 80003
303-450-2881
866-777-9727
888-867-1159
FAX: 303-450-2880
e-mail: sales@atvsolutions.com
www.atvsolutions.com

*Andrew Miro, Owner*

Great for indoor or outdoor use. The powerful, quiet drive system, independent front suspension and fully reclining high-back seat make for a smooth, quiet ride. The Roadster is loaded with great features at a bargain price.

**591 Safari Scooter**
Ranger All Seasons Corporation
PO Box 132
George, IA 51237
712-475-2811
800-225-3811
FAX: 712-475-3320
e-mail: sales@rangerallseason.com
www.rangerallseason.com

*Randy Riecks, Sales Manager*
*Larry Kruse, Owner*

Safari is Ranger's most popular scooter. Available in either a 40 inch or 43 inch frame length with an ultra-quiet, totally enclosed transacle drive. The Safari has some of the same features as the SOLO, the user-friendly take-apart and tiller adjustment, color impregnated— not painted— ABS plastic body. The most versatile Ranger Scooter, the Safari is an excellent choice for indoor use, and can take the place of most front wheel drive scooters. It is also an excellent outdoor scooter.

**592 Scoota Bug**
Golden Technologies
401 Bridge Street
Old Forge, PA 18518
570-451-7477
800-624-6324
FAX: 570-451-7974
e-mail: info@goldentech.com
www.goldentech.com

*Bob Golden, President*

A lightweight, completely modular scooter, that disassembles and fits into most auto trunks.

**593 Scooter Discounters**
1945 Winterhaven Drive
Virginia Beach, VA 23456
757-430-2664
800-229-1317
e-mail: sales@scooterone.com
www.scooterone.com

Offers electric scooters, scooter lifts, ramps, batteries and more at excellent value without sacrificing quality or service.

**594 Shuttle**
Mobilelectrics Company
4014 Bardstown Road
Louisville, KY 40218
800-876-6846
FAX: 502-495-2476

A three wheel scooter with safety features for ease of handling, comfort and maximum pleasure.

**595 Sidekick Scooter**
Mobilelectrics Company
4014 Bardstown Road
Louisville, KY 40218
800-876-6846
FAX: 502-495-2476

The seat and foot space provides ample comfort for the average person and the length of the scooter gives it indoor maneuverability.

**596 Sierra 3000/4000**
EZ-International
3275 Intertech Drive
Suite 500
Brookfield, WI 53045
262-790-5200
800-824-1068
FAX: 262-790-5204
e-mail: info@ez-international.com
www.ez-international.com

*Richard Lang, Owner*

Look to the Sierra 3000/4000 series vehicles for comfort, convenience and performance. Increased leg and foot room, adjustable seat height and arm width, as well as adjustable tiller angle provide maximum comfort. For convenience, the Sierra is equipped with integrated cargo and cup holders and thumb/finger controls with built in wrist rest. Advanced safety features such as stall and free-wheeling situation identification and correction, anti roll-back sensory device and audio/visual feedback.

**597 Solo Scooter**
Ranger All Seasons Corporation
PO Box 132
George, IA 51237
712-475-2811
800-225-3811
FAX: 712-475-3320
e-mail: sales@rangerallseason.com
www.rangerallseason.com

*Randy Riecks, Sales Manager*
*Larry Kruse, Owner*

The SOLO is Ranger's flagship model. Introduction of the SOLO 1991 set the standard for easy disassembly of a scooter. The SOLO has a long list of user friendly features including patented take-apart and tiller adjustment mechanisms, non-rusting aluminum frame, comfortable contoured seats as standard, color impregnated-not painted-ABS plastic bodies, charger plug conveniently located on the Accelerator box and many more. Available in ultra-quiet drive and four wheel models.

**598    SoloRider Industries**
7315 S Revere Parkway
Suite 604
Centennial, CO  80112
303-858-0505
800-898-3353
FAX: 303-858-0707
e-mail: info@solorider.com
www.solorider.com

*Roger Pretekin, President*
*Don Conty, Sr VP/Marketing*
*Tom Durbin, VP Sales*

Manufactures and distributes the AteeA- the revolutionary single rider specifically designed to meet the needs of individuals with disabilities.

**599    Sportster 10**
ATV Solutions
4700 W 60th Avenue
Unit 4
Arvada, CO  80003
303-450-2881
866-777-9727
888-867-1159
FAX: 303-450-2880
e-mail: sales@atvsolutions.com
www.atvsolutions.com

*Andrew Miro, Owner*

Sportster 10 is our most maneuverable scooter, ideal for riders who must operate in tight spaces. Equipped with all of the great features of the Roadster 20, this three-wheeler is an exceptional buy.

**600    Surry Tricycloped**
National Manufacturing Company
PO Box 577
Sterling, ID  83210
208-343-3639

The Surry has a sleek, aerodynamic design with canted side rails and simple hand controls for gas and brakes.

**601    Systems 2000**
BioMedical Life Systems
PO Box 1360
Vista, CA  92085
760-727-5600
800-726-8367
FAX: 760-727-4220
e-mail: information@bmls.com
www.bmls.com

*Richard Saxon, Chief Executive Officer*

This five-mode TENS device has four adjustable modulations, plus conventional settings and comes with a five-year warranty.

**602    Terra-Jet: Utility Vehicle**
TERRA-JET USA
PO Box 918
Innis, LA  70747
225-492-2249
800-864-5000
FAX: 225-492-2249
e-mail: terra.jet@terra.jet.com
terra.jet.com

*Larry Rabalaus, President*
*Michelle Radalais, Secretary/Treasurer*

TERRA-JET utility vehicles are unique in their ability to traverse many different types of terrain in remote areas otherwise inaccessible. It has a multitude of uses for industry, sportsmen or the whole family. Uniquely designed, industrial duty construction of low maintenance and low fuel consumption. $8,675-$21,995.

**603    Terrier Tricycle**
TRIAID
PO Box 1364
Cumberland, MD  21501
301-759-3525
800-306-6777
FAX: 301-759-3525
e-mail: sales@triaid.com
www.triaid.com

*Iain A MacDonald, Sales Director*
*Ann M Hutter, Sales Executive/Manager*

Provides fun therapy and actively encourages participation, awareness and the building of self confidence. Designed for children from about five years it features ATB styling, 16 inch wheels, adjustable steering stop and a supportive saddle. Handlebar and seat adjustments combine with a broad wheelbase to ensure the rider is in the optimum position to pedal and the tricycle gives good stability and confident handling. Support accessories are available.

**604    Trekker 40**
ATV Solutions
4700 W 60th Avenue
Unit 4
Arvada, CO  80003
303-450-2881
866-777-9727
888-867-1159
FAX: 303-450-2880
e-mail: sales@atvsolutions.com
www.atvsolutions.com

*Andrew Miro, Owner*

Our biggest, toughest scooter. With a huge 450 pound capacity and five inches of ground clearance, this machine is ideal for the daily outdoor user. The high top speed means you get there fast and the four-wheel suspension makes the ride smooth and comfortable.

**605    Tri-Lo's**
TRIAID
PO Box 1364
Cumberland, MD  21501
301-759-3525
800-306-6777
FAX: 301-759-3525
e-mail: sales@triaid.com
www.triaid.com

*Iain A MacDonald, Sales Director*
*Ann M Hutter, Sales Executive/Manager*

Available in three sizes, these tricycles provide fun therapy for children from 2-15 years. Propelled by hand cranks, the Tri-Lo's are highly recommended by therapists for spina bifida children and any other child where the use of the lower limbs is restricted. The Tri-Lo's feature a robust frame with allowance for growth, low foot platform for ease of transfer, padded seat and back cushion, padded armrests, two forms of braking and an anti-tipping device. *$740.00*

**606    Tri-Wheelers**
Braun Corporation
PO Box 310
Winamac, IN  46996
574-946-6153
800-843-5438
FAX: 574-946-4670

*William Roth, President*

Provides convenience features, producing a high efficiency performance with ultra-smooth operation.

**607 Triumph 3000/4000**
EZ-International
3275 Intertech Drive
Suite 500
Brookfield, WI 53045      262-790-5200
800-824-1068
FAX: 262-790-5204

*Richard Lang, Owner*

The Triumph 3000/4000 series vehicles provide unique comfort and convenience features found nowhere else. Digital Dash with soft touch keypad, deluxe seat with suspension and integral cargo and cup holders are just a few of these features. Equipped with TOPS 24 (Total Ortho Power System) ensuring maximum power, performance and reliability. Luxurious options such as velour or allante seat fabrics, stylized wheels, metallic or pearl color options and digital controls are all standard. $2,899-$3,39

**608 Triumph Scooter**
EZ-International
3275 Intertech Drive
Suite 500
Brookfield, WI 53045      262-790-5200
800-824-1068
FAX: 262-790-5204
e-mail: info@ez-international.com
www.ez-international.com

*Richard Lang, Owner*

The sleek, rugged, three-wheel, rear-wheel drive, transaxle scooter with up-top controls, designed to help increase mobility and become more active. The Triumph is designed for both indoor and outdoor use. Available in red, blue, green or gray, with an optional power seat lift. $2,899-$3,399.

**609 Uno Walker**
ETAC USA
2325 Parklawn Drive
Suite J
Waukesha, WI 53186
800-678-3822
FAX: 262-796-4605
e-mail: etac1usa@execpc.com
www.execpc.com/~etac1usa
A number one in any language. Elegantly designed with height adjustable handles, seat mudguards, and adjustable wheel locks are standard. Accessories include tray assemble, basket, crutch/cane holder, backrest and oxygen holder. $299-$400.

**610 X10 Powerhouse**
Words+
40015 Sierra Highway
Suite B145
Palmdale, CA 93550      661-266-8500
800-869-8521
FAX: 661-266-8969

*Ginger Woltosz, VP*
*Tim Ross, Manager*

Controls AC-powered appliances with a control unit and appliance modules. Plug the appliance modules into the outlets, then plug the appliances into the modules. *$199.00*

## Stationery

**611 Address Book**
Sense-Sations
919 Walnut Street
Philadelphia, PA 19107      215-627-0600
FAX: 215-922-0692

*Patricia Johnson, Chief Executive Officer*

The big print address book is the first personal book to provide enlarged writing spaces, making it easier to write down and retrieve information. *$12.50*

**612 Big Print Address Book**
Access with Ease
PO Box 1150
Chino Valley, AZ 86323      928-636-9469
800-531-9479
FAX: 928-636-0292
e-mail: KMJC@northlink.com

*Karen Clymer, President*

Oversized organizer makes locating information easier for those with limited vision. The 7 1/2 inch by 9 1/2 inch plastic coil bound book has more than 500 listings with laminated alphabet tabs. *$16.95*

**613 Bold Line Paper**
Sense-Sations
919 Walnut Street
Philadelphia, PA 19107      215-627-0600
FAX: 215-922-0692

*Patricia Johnson, Chief Executive Officer*

This pad consists of 100 sheets of paper with bold lines to help guide the writing of an individual with limited vision. *$2.50*

**614 Braille Notebook**
Maxi Aids
42 Executive Boulevard
Suite 3209
Farmingdale, NY 11735      631-752-0521
800-522-6294
FAX: 631-752-0689
e-mail: sales@maxiaids.com
www.maxiaids.com
Made of heavy-duty board, covered with waterproof imitation leather and three rings for binding, including braille paper and titles. *$12.95*

**615 Braille: Greeting Cards**
Sense-Sations
919 Walnut Street
Philadelphia, PA 19107      215-627-0600
FAX: 215-922-0692

*Patricia Johnson, Chief Executive Officer*

Birthday, anniversary, get well, sympathy and Christmas cards offering braille print for the blind. *$.95*

**616 Brailled Desk Calendar**
Maxi Aids
42 Executive Boulevard
Suite 3209
Farmingdale, NY 11735      631-752-0521
800-522-6294
FAX: 631-752-0689
e-mail: sales@maxiaids.com
www.maxiaids.com
Schedule appointments, remember birthdays or write messages for a particular day. *$39.95*

**617 Clip Board Notebook**
Sense-Sations
919 Walnut Street
Philadelphia, PA 19107      215-627-0600
FAX: 215-922-0692

*Patricia Johnson, Chief Executive Officer*

Kit includes a pack of Bold Line paper and black ink pen. *$5.95*

**618 Deluxe Signature Guide**
Maxi Aids
42 Executive Boulevard
Suite 3209
Farmingdale, NY 11735      631-752-0521
800-522-6294
FAX: 631-752-0689
e-mail: sales@maxiaids.com
www.maxiaids.com
Rods supported by two rubber blocks facilitate writing. *$1.25*

**619** **Highlighter and Note Tape**
Therapro
225 Arlington Street
Framingham, MA 01702
508-872-9494
800-257-5376
FAX: 508-875-2062
e-mail: info@theraproducts.com
www.theraproducts.com

*Karen Conrad, Owner*

A great way to highlight and draw attention to words without damaging original. Price ranges from $4.00-$7.00.

**620** **Letter Writing Guide**
Independent Living Aids
PO Box 9022
Hicksville, NY 11802
516-937-1848
800-537-2118
FAX: 516-937-3906
e-mail: can-do@independentliving.com
www.independentliving.com

*Marvin Sandler, President*

Sturdy plastic sheet with 13 apertures corresponding to standard line spacing. *$3.49*

**621** **Lettering Guide Value Pack**
Independent Living Aids
PO Box 9022
Hicksville, NY 11802
516-937-1848
800-537-2118
FAX: 516-937-3906
e-mail: can-do@independentliving.com
www.independentliving.com

*Marvin Sandler, President*

Included in this useful pack are four durable plastic lettering and number guides for tracing letters when the individual is unable to write letters unassisted. *$6.29*

**622** **Wings & Wheels Greeting Cards**
Wings & Wheels
5 Cleveland Avenue
Dover, NJ 07801
800-422-5309
FAX: 973-989-9072
e-mail: flyingspiritedmsn.com
www.wings-wheels.com

*Nanette Courtine, Owner*

Offer inclusive greeting cards. Depicts people with disabilities on the cards.

# Visual Aids

**623** **Aluminum Adjustable Support Canes for the Blind**
Maxi Aids
42 Executive Boulevard
Suite 3209
Farmingdale, NY 11735
631-752-0521
800-522-6294
FAX: 631-752-0689
e-mail: sales@maxiaids.com
www.maxiaids.com
Adjustable canes for the visually impaired. *$17.95*

**624** **Audio Book Contractors**
PO Box 40115
Washington, DC 20016
202-363-3429
FAX: 202-363-3429
e-mail: flogibsonABC@aol.com
www.audiobookcontractors.com

*Flo Gibson, President*

Over 950 titles of unabridged classic books on audio cassettes in sturdy vinyl covers with picture and spine windows. Discounted prices for disabled patrons.

**625** **Beyond Sight**
5650 S Windermere Street
Littleton, CO 80120
303-795-6455
FAX: 303-795-6425
e-mail: bsistore@beyondsite.com
www.beyondsight.com

*Jim Misener, President*

Products for the blind and visually impaired including talking clocks, watches and calculators. They also carry a large selection of braille products, magnifiers, reading machines and computer equipment. New products include: Accucheck Voicemate and PureFocus vision spray and GPS Talk, the first talking GPS system for the blind.

**626** **Big Number Pocket Sized Calculator**
Independent Living Aids
PO Box 9022
Hicksville, NY 11802
516-937-1848
800-537-2118
FAX: 516-937-3906
e-mail: can-do@independentliving.com
www.independentliving.com

*Marvin Sandler, President*

A handy pocket size calculator with big numbers that fits easily into purse or pocket. *$14.95*

**627** **Braille Compass**
Maxi Aids
42 Executive Boulevard
Suite 3209
Farmingdale, NY 11735
631-752-0521
800-522-6294
FAX: 631-752-0689
e-mail: sales@maxiaids.com
www.maxiaids.com
The visually impaired can tell the direction by using this compass. *$42.95*

**628** **Braille Plates for Elevator**
Maxi Aids
42 Executive Boulevard
Suite 3209
Farmingdale, NY 11735
631-752-0521
800-522-6294
FAX: 631-752-0689
e-mail: sales@maxiaids.com
www.maxiaids.com
The plates have curing type pressure sensitive material applied for metal to metal bonding. *$79.95*

**629** **Braille Touch-Time Watches**
Independent Living Aids
PO Box 9022
Hicksville, NY 11802
516-937-1848
800-537-2118
FAX: 516-937-3906
e-mail: can-do@independentliving.com
www.independentliving.com

*Marvin Sandler, President*

White dial with black numerals and hands makes telling time possible quickly and easily for the visually impaired. *$44.95*

**630** **Circline Illuminated Magnifer**
Dazor Manufacturing Corporation
11721 Dunlap Industrial Drive
Maryland Heights, MO 63043
314-652-2400
800-345-9103
FAX: 314-652-2069
e-mail: info@dazor.com
www.dazor.com

*Kirk Cressey, Marketing Director*
*Bob Smith, National Sales Manager*

Provides even, shadow free light under the magnifying lens with a 22-watt circline fluorescent. The magnifier is mounted on a floating arm that allows you to position the light source and lens with the touch of a finger.

**631 Extra Loud Alarm with Lighter Plug**
HARC Mercantile
1111 W Centre Avenue
Portage, MI 49024

269-324-1615
800-445-9968
FAX: 269-324-2387
e-mail: home@harcmercantile.com
www.harcmercantile.com

*Ronald Slager, President*

Battery operated, easy to read, digital clock with extra loud alarm. *$45.00*

**632 Low Vision Telephones**
2241 S Triangle X Lane
Tucson, AZ 85713

520-299-7900
FAX: 520-883-3172
e-mail: info@assistivedevices.net
assistivedevices.net/about.htm

*Lynn Lowe, President*

**633 Magni-Cam & Primer**
Innoventions
9593 Corsair Drive
Conifer, CO 80433

303-797-6554
800-854-6554
FAX: 303-727-4940
e-mail: magnicam@magnicam.com
www.magnicam.com/

*Charleen Freeman, Sales Manager*
*Mark Freeman, President*

Magni-Cam and Primer are hand-held, light weight, inexpensive auto-focus electronic magnification systems designed to meet the reading and writing needs of those with low vision. The systems present the image in black and white or in color with three different view modes. Connects to any TV monitor in minutes. Systems read any surface with no distortion. A battery powered system is available, providing total portability and flexibility.

**634 Magnifier Bookweight**
Levenger
420 South Congress Avenuenue
Delray Beach, FL 33445

561-276-4141
800-667-8034
FAX: 800-544-6910
e-mail: cservice@levenger.com
www.levenger.com

The Magnifier Bookweight features an optical quality magnifier and is long enough to enlarge the full width of most book pages while holing the pages open. This magnifier is encased in embossed leather and enlarges approximately four lines of text at a time to twice the original size.

**635 Man's Low-Vision Quartz Watches**
Independent Living Aids
PO Box 9022
Hicksville, NY 11802

516-937-1848
800-537-2118
FAX: 516-937-3906
e-mail: can-do@independentliving.com
www.independentliving.com

*Marvin Sandler, President*

An inexpensive, easy-to-read watch with chrome case. *$27.95*

**636 Men's/Women's Low Vision Watches & Clocks**
Maxi Aids
42 Executive Boulevard
Suite 3209
Farmingdale, NY 11735

631-752-0521
800-522-6294
FAX: 631-752-0689
e-mail: sales@maxiaids.com
www.maxiaids.com

Choose from a wide range of watches from braille automatic to quartz pocket watches.

**637 Rigid Aluminum Cane with Golf Grip**
Maxi Aids
42 Executive Boulevard
Suite 3209
Farmingdale, NY 11735

631-752-0521
800-522-6294
FAX: 631-752-0689
e-mail: sales@maxiaids.com
www.maxiaids.com

A straight, tubular, heavy gauge aluminum rigid cane for blind and visually impaired persons. *$12.95*

**638 Stretch-View Wide-View Rectangular Illuminated Magnifier**
Dazor Manufacturing Corporation
11721 Dunlap Industrial Drive
Maryland Heights, MO 63043

314-652-2400
800-345-9103
FAX: 314-652-2069
e-mail: info@dazor.com
www.dazor.com

*Kirk Cressey, Marketing Director*
*Bob Smith, National Sales Manager*

Provides shadow-free illumination or a highlighting effect under the magnifying lens with an 18-watt compact fluorescent light source. The magnifier is mounted on a floating arm that allows you to position the light source and lens with the touch of a finger.

**639 Three M Large Printed Labeler**
Maxi Aids
42 Executive Boulevard
Suite 3209
Farmingdale, NY 11735

631-752-0521
800-522-6294
FAX: 631-752-0689
e-mail: sales@maxiaids.com
www.maxiaids.com

Ideal for persons with low vision. Can also be read tactually by blind persons with a knowledge of the print alphabet. *$133.95*

**640 Timex Easy Reader**
Independent Living Aids
PO Box 9022
Hicksville, NY 11802

516-937-1848
800-537-2118
FAX: 516-937-3906
e-mail: can-do@independentliving.com
www.independentliving.com

*Marvin Sandler, President*

An easy-to-read large face watch that's water resistant. *$29.95*

**641 Unisex Low Vision Watch**
Independent Living Aids
PO Box 9022
Hicksville, NY 11802

516-937-1848
800-537-2118
FAX: 516-937-3906
e-mail: can-do@independentliving.com
www.independentliving.com

*Marvin Sandler, President*

Unisex watch with large numbers and wide hands. Gold-toned case with either expansion or leather band. *$31.95*

# Walking Aids: Canes, Crutches & Walkers

**642  Air Lift Oxygen Carriers**
Air Lift Unlimited
1212 Kerr Gulch Road
Evergreen, CO 80439
303-526-4700
800-776-6771
FAX: 303-526-4774
e-mail: info@airlift.com
www.airlift.com

*Lori Fortier, Office Manager*
*Michael Moore, President*

Air Lift offers a full line of carriers for portable liquid and cylinder oxygen systems. These versatile carriers meet the needs of oxygen-dependent individuals and parents with oxygen-dependent children seeking more comfortable and convenient ways to transport oxygen. Carriers include backpacks, fanny packs, shoulder/hand bags and carriers for wheelchairs, scooters and walkers. All carriers feature non-flammable, washable fabric and adjustable straps; liquid carriers feature mesh pouches.

**643  Aluminum Crutches**
Arista Surgical Supply Company
297 High Street
Dedham, MA 02026
781-329-2900
800-223-1984
FAX: 781-329-8392
e-mail: arista@alimed.com
www.aristasurgical.com

*Julian Cherubini, President*

Lightweight aluminum crutches with wood underarms and handgrips. *$25.00*

**644  Aluminum Walking Canes**
Maxi Aids
42 Executive Boulevard
Suite 3209
Farmingdale, NY 11735
631-752-0521
800-522-6294
FAX: 631-752-0689
e-mail: sales@maxiaids.com
www.maxiaids.com

Lightweight but strong, these walking canes are made of a heavy gauge aluminum tube with safety locknuts and heavy-duty rubber tips. *$10.75*

**645  Arrow Walker**
TRIAID
PO Box 1364
Cumberland, MD 21501
301-759-3525
800-306-6777
FAX: 301-759-3525
e-mail: sales@triaid.com
www.triaid.com

*Iain A MacDonald, Sales Director*
*Ann M Hutter, Sales Executive/Manager*

A weight supportive walker designed for children with cerebral palsy or other neuromuscular handicaps. Its comprehensive range of accessories and adjustments allow the Arrow Walker to be tailored to each individual user's needs. The innovative design allows these alterations to be made quickly and easily, enabling multiple daily therapy sessions to take place. The low profile shape allows easier access through doorways and around obstacles. *$957.00*

**646  Crutches**
Mada Medical Products
625 Washington Avenue
Carlstadt, NJ 07072
201-460-0454
800-526-6370
FAX: 201-460-3509
e-mail: sales@madamedical.com
www.madainternational.com

*Jeffrey Adam, Vice President*

All aluminum construction, underarm crutch with double pushbutton height adjustment.

**647  Deluxe Nova Wheeled Walker & Avant Wheeled Walker**
Sammons Preston Rolyan
W68n158 Evergreen Boulevard
Cedarburg, WI 53012
800-323-5547
FAX: 262-387-8748
e-mail: customersupport@sammonspreston.com
www.sammonspreston.com

Lightweight and simple to handle with an easy-to-operate braking system. *$425.40*

**648  Deluxe Standard Wood Cane**
Arista Surgical Supply Company/AliMed
297 High Street
Dedham, MA 02026
781-329-2900
800-223-1984
FAX: 781-329-8392
e-mail: arista@alimed.com
www.aristasurgical.com

*Julian Cherubini, President*

A standard old-fashioned wooden cane for the physically challenged. *$10.00*

**649  Freedom Three Wheel Walker**
Mada Medical Products
625 Washington Avenue
Carlstadt, NJ 07072
201-460-0454
800-526-6370
FAX: 201-460-3509
e-mail: sales@madamedical.com
www.madainternational.com

*Jeffrey Adam, Vice President*

The freedom walker has ultra light touch, locking loop brakes and sure grip hand grips.

**650  Liberty Lightweight Aluminum Stroll Walker**
Mada Medical Products
625 Washington Avenue
Carlstadt, NJ 07072
201-460-0454
800-526-6370
FAX: 201-460-3509
e-mail: sales@madamedical.com
www.madainternational.com

*Jeffrey Adam, Vice President*

The Liberty walker has a spring loaded push down braking system, adjustable handle height with locking system, a 12" wide fully padded seat, and a removable shopping basket.

**651  Maxi Superior Cane**
Maxi Aids
42 Executive Boulevard
Suite 3209
Farmingdale, NY 11735
631-752-0521
800-522-6294
FAX: 631-752-0689
e-mail: sales@maxiaids.com
www.maxiaids.com

Convenient folding cane designed for optimum balance. Tapered joints provide rigidity when open, and are made of heavy gauge aluminum. *$17.50*

**652    Minova Walker**
ETAC USA
2325 Parklawn Drive
Suite J
Waukesha, WI 53186

800-678-3822
FAX: 262-796-4605
e-mail: etac1usa@execpc.com
www.execpc.com/~etac1usa

Childrens Walker shares the same basic principles as Adult Nova. The handles are adjustable for both width and height. The walker is easy to fold with a remarkable safety braking system. $498-$525.

**653    Nova Walker**
ETAC USA
2325 Parklawn Drive
Suite J
Waukesha, WI 53186

800-678-3822
FAX: 262-796-4605
e-mail: etac1usa@execpc.com
www.execpc.com/~etac1usa

Elegant design that provides a comfortable, natural walking style. The seat offers security and stability wherever you go. Folds easily with one hand. Offers lifetime warranty on frame and brake straps for original user.

**654    Out-N-About American Walker**
742 Market Street
Oregon, WI 53575

608-835-9255
FAX: 608-835-5234

*Luann Smith, President*

The lightweight Out-N-About is easy to handle. The four wheel design provides greater support and stability than any other walking aids. Its large rubber tires move effortlessly over most surfaces, indoors and out. The small turning radius makes it ideal for getting through confined spaces and narrow doorways. The attractive, burgundy colored, tubular steel frame is extremely durable. The Out-N-About folds flat and stands alone for easy storage. Made in USA.

**655    Patriot Extra Wide Folding Walkers**
Mada Medical Products
625 Washington Avenue
Carlstadt, NJ 07072

201-460-0454
800-526-6370
FAX: 201-460-3509
e-mail: sales@madamedical.com
www.madainternational.com

*Jeffrey Adam, Vice President*

The extra wide walkers have padded foam hand grips, two-stage push button folding mechanism, dual width adjustment, height adjustment, and nonskid tips.

**656    Patriot Folding Walker Series**
Mada Medical Products
625 Washington Avenue
Carlstadt, NJ 07072

201-460-0454
800-526-6370
FAX: 201-460-3509
e-mail: sales@madamedical.com
www.madainternational.com

*Jeffrey Adam, Vice President*

The patriot walker has high density, padded foam hand grips, high strength 1" lightweight, anodized, dull silver aluminum tube construction, adjustable height with push-button lock security, nonskid tips, and a single button folding mechanism.

**657    Patriot Reciprocal Folding Walkers**
Mada Medical Products
625 Washington Avenue
Carlstadt, NJ 07072

201-460-0454
800-526-6370
FAX: 201-460-3509
e-mail: sales@madamedical.com
www.madainternational.com

*Jeffrey Adam, Vice President*

The reciprocal folding walkers have padded foam hand grips, adjustable height with snap-in security, double front cross brace, and nonskid tips.

**658    Prone Support Walker**
Consumer Care Products
PO Box 684
Sheboygan, WI 53082

920-893-4614
FAX: 920-459-9070

*Terry Grall, President*
*Alice Maffongelli, Customer Service*

This walker, in five sizes for children to adults, facilitates semi-prone to full upright mobility and dynamic weight bearing. The walker requires the user to push off the floor teaching the user to work with the floor and achieving a more efficient gait. Options such as tray, back support, and hip pads allow adaptation to most needs. $750-$1,300.

**659    Push-Button Quad Cane**
Arista Surgical Supply Company/AliMed
297 High Street
Dedham, MA 02026

781-329-2900
800-223-1984
FAX: 781-329-8392
e-mail: arista@alimed.com
www.aristasurgical.com

*Julian Cherubini, President*

A reliable walking cane offering independence to the physically challenged user. *$25.00*

**660    Quad Canes**
Mada Medical Products
625 Washington Avenue
Carlstadt, NJ 07072

201-460-0454
800-526-6370
FAX: 201-460-3509
e-mail: sales@madamedical.com
www.madainternational.com

*Jeffrey Adam, Vice President*

There are large and small base quad canes with high density foam grips.

**661    Rand-Scot**
401 Linden Center Drive
Fort Collins, CO 80524

970-484-7967
800-467-7967
FAX: 970-484-3800
TTY: 800-467-7967
e-mail: info@randscot.com
www.randscot.com

*Joel Lerich, President*
*Joellen Sarmast, Business Manager*

Manufactures the Easy Pivot patient lift, the BBD wheelchair cushion line and Saratoga Exercise products for the disabled. Offers a line of patient lifts and standers for the disabled. Manufactures the EasyPivot patient lift for 1 person transfers. A video is available at no charge for potential users. $800.-$3,000.

**662    Secret Agent Walking Stick**
Gold Violin
1717-2B Allied Streetreet
Suite I
Charlottesville, VA 22903

434-923-3277
877-648-8400
www.goldviolin.com

The Secret Agent Walking Stick features a built-in flashlight, a red reflector and a built-in secret pill compartment. this folding aluminum cane is height adjustable and has a derby-style handle and a non-skid rubber tip. A nylon carrying case is included. The walking stick comes in a choich of gold, bronze, or black shaft with a faux burled walnut handle.

**663  StairClimber**
Martin Technology
29 N Main Street
Gloversville, NY  12078          518-725-1837
                                 800-800-1410
                            FAX: 518-725-9522

*Michael Lewy, Owner*
A walker-capable person can climb and descend stairs with this walker-designed StairClimber.

**664  Standing Aid Frame with Rear Entry**
Consumer Care Products
PO Box 684
Sheboygan, WI  53082          920-893-4614
                         FAX: 920-459-9070

*Terry Grall, President*
*Alice Maffongelli, Customer Service*
This rugged stander, made of natural hardwood in sizes for one to twelve year olds, allows weight bearing in an upright position. Table, upper trunk and/or head support, hip pads and casters allow individualized fitting. The new hinged rear entry option makes entry into this stander easy and quick for parents, teachers and therapists. $572-$1,800.

**665  Stick Canes**
Mada Medical Products
625 Washington Avenue
Carlstadt, NJ  07072          201-460-0454
                              800-526-6370
                         FAX: 201-460-3509
              e-mail: sales@madamedical.com
                      www.madainternational.com

*Jeffrey Adam, Vice President*
Mada's stick canes are adjustable with a locking security system.

**666  Torso Support**
Grandmar
5675-C Landregan Street
Emeryville, CA  94608          510-428-0441

*John Cains, President*
An aid for people who are unable to maintain an upright position in an automobile or a wheelchair.

**667  Ventura Enterprises**
35 Lawton Avenue
Danville, IN  46122          317-745-2989
                        FAX: 317-745-3179
              www.venturaenterprises.com

*Linda Plunkett, President*
Manufacturer of everyday living mobility aids. Products include carrying aids for walkers and wheelchairs and also wheelchair cushions.

**668  WCIB Heavy-Duty Folding Cane**
Maxi Aids
42 Executive Boulevard
Suite 3209
Farmingdale, NY  11735          631-752-0521
                                800-522-6294
                           FAX: 631-752-0689
                e-mail: sales@maxiaids.com
                        www.maxiaids.com
A four section aluminum folding cane with a golf-type grip handle and flexible wrist loop. #1749015, 34-60 *$17.95*

**669  Walker Leg Support**
Sammons Preston Rolyan
W68n158 Evergreen Boulevard
Cedarburg, WI  53012
                                800-228-3693
                           FAX: 262-387-8748
      e-mail: customerservice@sammonspreston.com
                      www.sammonspreston.com
For lower extremity trauma. An alternative to crutches that allows safe, stable ambulation and frees hands and arms for daily tasks. *$11.50*

## Wheelchairs: Accessories

**670  Advantage Wheelchair & Walker Bags**
Laurel Designs
1805 Mar West Street
Apt A
Belvedere Tiburon, CA  94920
                           FAX: 415-435-1451
                e-mail: laureld@ncal.verio.com

*Janet Sawyer, Co-Owner*
*Lynn Montoya, Co-Owner*
Wheelchair sport packs include: long, short, neon, multi-color and blowin' in the wind socks. Prices range from $20.00 to $60.00.

**671  Automatic Wheelchair Anti-Rollback Device**
Alzheimer's Store
Ageless Design
12633 159th Court N
Jupiter, FL  33478          561-744-0210
                            800-752-3238
                       FAX: 561-745-9572
              e-mail: cs@alzstore.com
                      www.alzstore.com
As a wheelchair user transfers to and from the chair, a pair of brake arms grabs the tires to prevent the chair from rolling backwards. Once the individual is seated, the device switches to stand-by modeand the wheelchair returns to standard funcion.

**672  Battery Operated Cushion**
DA Schulman
7701 Newton Avenue N
Brooklyn Park, MN  55444          763-561-2908

Battery-operated, dynamic cushion for wheelchairs.

**673  Dual-Mode Charger**
Lester Electrical
625 W a Street
Lincoln, NE  68522          402-477-8988
                       FAX: 402-474-1769
              e-mail: sales@lesterelectrical.com
                      www.lesterelectrical.com

*Ken Jeffcoat, Director Sales/Marketing*
*Bob Haahr, Cust Service Manager*
*James Carrier, President*
Fully automatic battery charger.

**674  Ezback Recline Control**
APT Technology
236a N Main Street
Shreve, OH  44676          330-567-2001
                           888-549-2001
                      FAX: 330-567-3073
              e-mail: sales@apt-technology.com
                      www.apt-technology.com

*Helen L Thompson, Marketing Manager*
*David M Bayer, Rehab Engineer*

A versatile, easy to install and operate motor controller intended to control power recline and similar machinery on a power wheelchair. Optional EDMA permits control of 2 motors via a single or dual switch. Accommodates limit switches, various configurations and is rugged and reliable. *$685.00*

**675  Featherspring**
712 N 34th Street
Seattle, WA  98103                    206-545-8585
                                     FAX: 206-547-8589
                                     www.featherspring.com

*Peter Rothschild, President*

Foot supports for wheelchair users to prevent and treat cold feet, sore heels, swollen feet and weak ankles. *$199.95*

**676  George H Snyder Enterprises**
5809 NE 21st Avenue
Fort Lauderdale, FL  33308
                                     FAX: 954-491-2886

*George Snyder, President*

Attachments for wheelchairs.

**677  Lifestand**
Frank Mobility Systems
1003 International Drive
Oakdale, PA  15071                   724-695-7822
                                     888-426-8581
                                     FAX: 724-695-3710
                                     e-mail: Dallery@msn.com
                                     www.lifestandusa.com

*Jacques A Dallery, President*
*Werner Frank, Owner*

Lifestand offers a full line of standing wheelchairs for manual operation. Power assisted are fully motorized. *$7000.00*

**678  Mat Factory**
760 W 16th Street
Suite E
Costa Mesa, CA  92627                949-645-3122
                                     800-628-7626
                                     FAX: 949-645-0966
                                     e-mail: info@matfactoryinc.com
                                     www.matfactoryinc.com

*Roger Maloney, President*
*Peggy Maloney, Owner*

The Safety Deck II is an interlocking grid system made from re-cycled rubber tires and recycled PVC. The tiles are set directly on top of the ground and permit grass to grow through the holes and cover the surface. The system provides safe, non-barrier access for wheelchairs over grass. Once the grass has covered the tiles the only maintenance required is watering and mowing. Safety Deck II also allows for beach and sand access.

**679  One Thousand FS**
Fortress
PO Box 489
Clovis, CA  93613                    559-322-5437
                                     FAX: 559-323-0299
Add-on power system installs in minutes, enabling the driver to relax and drive anywhere with smooth, silent electric power.

**680  Pac-All Wheelchair Carrier**
Pac-All Carriers
2321 Carolton Road
Maitland, FL  32751                  407-830-6604
                                     800-628-6672
                                     FAX: 407-339-2847

*LE Angel*

No more lifting and no more pain wheelchair carrier. VA ap-proved. Made in USA.

*$158 - $226.40*

**681  Scooter & Wheelchair Battery Fuel Gauges and Motor Speed Controllers**
Curtis Instruments
200 Kisco Avenue
Mount Kisco, NY  10549               914-666-2971
                                     FAX: 914-666-2188
                                     e-mail: mikolaya@curtisinst.com
                                     www.curtisinstruments.com

*Stuart Marwell, Chief Executive Officer*

Provides a readable, accurate indication of battery in easy to read type of display. Innovative, efficient motor speed control-lers for single or dual PM motor vehicles.

**682  Thomas Hardware, Parts & Fasteners**
1001 Rockland Street
Reading, PA  19604
                                     800-634-4293
                                     FAX: 800-634-3099

*Bob Ruhe, Marketing Manager*

Wheelchair restraint kits.

**683  Tilt-N-Table**
Osterguard Enterprises c/o Jim's Shop
3228 W Olive Avenue
Fresno, CA  93722                    559-275-4695

*Jim Ii, Owner*

These are lightweight tables for wheelchairs that are angle and height adjustable to your changing needs.

**684  Wheel Life News**
University of Virginia, Rehab Engineering Centers
3363 University Station
Charlottesville, VA  22903           434-924-0311

*John Casteen Iii, President*

Features tie downs and other adaptive technology for persons with disabilities.

**685  Wheelchair Accessories**
Diestco Manufacturing Company
PO Box 6504
Chico, CA  95927                     530-893-3136
                                     800-795-2392
                                     FAX: 530-893-2635
                                     e-mail: info@diestco.com
                                     www.diestco.com

*Chris Cawthon, VP Sales/Marketing*
*Dan Diestel, Owner*

Diestco makes innovative accessories for wheelchairs, scooters and walkers. Products include canopies, backpacks, cupholders, pouches, threshhold ramps, laptrays and others.

**686  Wheelchair Aide**
Graham-Field
400 Rabro Drive
Hauppauge, NY  11788                 631-348-1364

This is a heavy-duty wheelchair comfort tray which surrounds the wheelchair user and provides a large, smooth surface for din-ing, writing, hobbies or work. The heavy gauge plastic tray is easy to clean and attaches with two Velcro straps.

**687  Wheelchair Back Pack and Tote Bag**
Med Covers
1639 Green Street
Suite D
Raleigh, NC  27603                   919-829-5777

Accessories are specifically designed with the wheelchair user in mind. The Back Pack has a main roomy pouch for larger items and has a full length zipper with four sliders for convenient access.

**688  Wheelchair Rocker**
Artec
PO Box 25103a
Greenville, SC  29616                    864-288-2111

*Randy Crew, President*
The Carolina Rocker turns a wheelchair into a rocking chair for fun, relaxation and therapy for children and adults. $499

**689  Wheelchair Work Table**
Bailey Manufacturing Company
118 Lee Street
Lodi, OH  44254                         330-948-1080
                                        800-321-8372
                                   FAX: 330-948-4439
                         e-mail: baileymfg@attmail.com
                                   www.baileymfg.com

*Larry Strimple, President*
An adjustable height, functional, individual cut-out work table featuring a wood-grain laminate, scratch resistant top with chrome plated steel legs.

## Wheelchairs: General

**690  Act Wheelchair**
Etac USA
2325 Parklawn Drive
Suite J
Waukesha, WI  53186
                                        800-678-3822
                                   FAX: 262-796-4605
                         e-mail: etac1usa@execpc.com
                               www.execpc.com/~etac1usa
A carefully designed Swedish wheelchair made of lightweight titanium for active users. Seat frame and upholstery are adjustable to fit each individual. Available in Frame widths from 15.5 to 18 inches. The colors available are: black, red plum teal, blue and silver. Lifetime warranty on frame for original user.

**691  Bariatric Wheelchairs Regency FL**
Gendron
Lugbill Road
Archbold, OH  43502                      419-445-6060
                                        800-537-2521
                                   www.gendroninc.com

*Steven Cotter, VP Sales/President*
Bariatric wheelchairs, for users weighing up to seven hundred pounds. Manual and power styles built to order for specific needs.

**692  Basic Wheelchair**
ETAC USA
2325 Parklawn Drive
Suite J
Waukesha, WI  53186
                                        800-678-3822
                                   FAX: 262-796-4605
                         e-mail: etac1usa@execpc.com
                               www.execpc.com/~etac1usa
A carefully designed crossfolding wheelchair made from extruded aluminum, the Basic is designed with the caregiver in mind and easily folds for transportation or storage. Available in widths of 14 to 20 inches, has incontinence upholstery which is easily washable with mild soap and water. Swing away, detachable leg rests and foot rests are standard with fixed hub rear wheels. $1,000 - $2,000

**693  Big Bounder Power Wheelchair**
21st Century Scientific
4915 Industrial Way
Coeur D Alene, ID  83815                 208-667-8800
                                        800-448-3680
                                   FAX: 208-667-6600
                         e-mail: 21st@wheelchairs.com
                                   www.wheelchairs.com

*RD Davidson, Sales/Marketing Director*
*Ron Prior, Owner*
Manufactured for the bariatric in virtually any dimension. Its powerful motors and rugged frame can accommodate users up to 1000 lb. 21st Century Scientific, Inc's unique construction can reduce the overall width of the chair. This may make the difference between using normal doorways or remodeling a home. $10,495.

**694  Breezy**
Sunrise Medical/Quickie Designs
2382 Faraday Avenue
Carlsbad, CA  92008                      760-930-1500
                                   FAX: 760-930-1585
                                   www.sunrisemedical.com

*Michael Hammes, Chief Executive Officer*
This lightweight chair is durable, comfortable and flexible enough to meet the needs of a wide range of wheelchair users.

**695  Champion 1000**
Kuschall of America
3601 Rider Trail S
Earth City, MO  63045                    314-512-7000
                                        800-654-4768
                                   FAX: 800-542-3567
Ultralight wheelchair designed to improve mobility. $1,689

**696  Champion 2000**
Kuschall of America
3601 Rider Trail S
Earth City, MO  63045                    314-512-7000
                                        800-654-4768
                                   FAX: 800-542-3567
Rigid chair that folds side-to-side. $1,765

**697  Champion 3000**
Kuschall of America
3601 Rider Trail S
Earth City, MO  63045                    314-512-7000
                                        800-654-4768
                                   FAX: 800-542-3567
The high-performance chair built for perfectionists. $1,695

**698  Choosing a Wheelchair: A Guide for Optimal Independence**
Patient-Centered Guides
101 Morris Street
Sebastopol, CA  95472                    707-829-0515
                                        800-294-4747
                                   FAX: 800-997-9901
                         e-mail: order@oreilly.com
                                   www.patientcenters.com

*Linda Lamb, Editor*
*Shawnde Paull, Marketing*
*Tim O'Reilly, Chief Executive Officer*
With the right wheelchair, quality of life increases dramatically and even people with severe disabilities can have a considerable degree of independence and activity. Choosing the wrong chair can indeed the tantamount to confinement. This book describes technology, options, and the selection process to help you identify the chair than can provide you with optimal independence. *$9.95*

*186 pages Paperback*
*ISBN 1-565924-11-8*

**699**  **Convaid**
PO Box 4209
Palos Verdes Peninsula, CA  90274     310-618-0111
                                      888-266-8243
                                      FAX: 310-618-2166
                                      e-mail: convaid@convaid.com
                                      www.convaid.com

*Merv Watkins, Owner*

Five different styles of wheelchairs.

**700**  **Cross Wheelchair**
ETAC USA
2325 Parklawn Drive
Suite J
Waukesha, WI  53186
                                      800-678-3822
                                      FAX: 262-796-4605
                                      e-mail: etac1usa@execpc.com
                                      www.execpc.com/~etac1usa
A carefully designed crossfolding Swedish wheelchair made of
aluminum. The cross has a contouring back rest upholstery that
can be adjusted as the user needs to change. Frame widths available in 14 -20 inches. Seat frame and upholstery are adjustable to
fit each individual. Lifetime warranty on frame for original user.
$1,295 -$2,500

**701**  **Custom**
Fortress
PO Box 489
Clovis, CA  93613                     559-322-5437
                                      FAX: 559-323-0299
Ultralight aluminum wheelchair that can be customized to cus-
tomer's requests. Fifteen frame colors, eight seat widths and
depths, along with thirteen rear wheel combinations are just a
few of the features offered at the standard package price.

**702**  **Custom Durable**
21279 Protecta Drive
Elkhart, IN  46516                    574-522-7199
                                      800-933-0256
                                      FAX: 574-293-0202

*Dawn Slabach, President*

Wheelchairs; accessories.

**703**  **Edge**
Fortress
PO Box 489
Clovis, CA  93613                     559-322-5437
                                      FAX: 559-323-0299
An ultra lightweight aircraft aluminum wheelchair that is suit-
able for sports, school or the workplace.

**704**  **Etac USA: F3 Wheelchair**
2325 Parklawn Drive
Suite J
Waukesha, WI  53186
                                      800-678-3822
                                      FAX: 262-796-4605
                                      e-mail: etac1usa@execpc.com
                                      www.execpc.com/~etac1usa
A swedish wheelchair designed to provide function, comfort and
flexibility. Seat frame and upholstery are adjustable to fit each
individual. Swing away, detachable footrests are standard.
Available in frame widths from 14, 18 and 20 inch. Numerous
accessories are available in order to individualize each chair.
Lifetime warranty on frame for original user.

**705**  **Evacu-Trac**
Garaventa Canada
PO Box L-1
Blaine, WA  98230                     360-332-2231
                                      800-663-6556
This emergency evacuation chair is designed for safety and fast
operation.

**706**  **Folding Chair with a Rigid Feel**
Kuschall of America
3601 Rider Trail S
Earth City, MO  63045                 314-512-7000
                                      800-654-4768
                                      FAX: 800-542-3567
The Champion 1000 is a new concept in folding chairs. Even
though it's ultra light, it has the feel and performance of a rigid
chair.

**707**  **Formula Series Active Mobility Wheelchairs**
Everest & Jennings
3233 Mission Oaks Boulevard
Camarillo, CA  93012                  805-389-7450

This is a new series of lightweight wheelchairs designed for the
active user.

**708**  **Freestyle II**
Fortress
PO Box 489
Clovis, CA  93613                     559-322-5437
                                      FAX: 559-323-0299
Effort-sparing, ultra-lightweight aircraft aluminum construc-
tion and design allow for easy propelling over various rolling
surfaces.

**709**  **Gadabout Wheelchairs**
Gadabout Wheelchairs
1165 Portland Avenue
Rochester, NY  14621                  585-338-1000
                                      800-828-4242

*Michael Fonte, Owner*

Enjoy independence with the wheelchair that is lightweight,
portable, convenient, comfortable and sturdy.

**710**  **Gem Wheelchair & Scooter Service: Mobility &
Homecare**
17639 Union Tpke
Flushing, NY  11366                   718-463-3800
                                      800-943-3578
                                      FAX: 718-969-8300
                                      e-mail: wheelsus@aol.com
                                      www.wheelchairsusa.com

*Jeff Bochner, President*

GEM sells and services all makes and models of manual and motorized wheelchairs, power scooters, ramps, stairway lifts, and
homecare products including diapers, chux, and bathroom
safety equipment. Clients are in all five New York City Boroughs and Nassau County. Medicare and Medicaid accepted,
pick-up and delivery, loaner equipment, and while-u-wait repair
services available. Gem also buys and sells used equipment.

**711**  **Gendron**
Lugbill Road
Archbold, OH  43502                   419-445-6060
                                      800-537-2521
                                      FAX: 419-446-2631

*Steven Cotter, VP Sales/President*

Manufacturer of wheelchairs for a variety of other applications,
specializing in bariatric mobility products.

**712**  **HiRider**
Gaymar Industries
10 Centre Drive
Orchard Park, NY  14127               716-662-2551
                                      800-828-7341

*Thomas Stewart, Chief Executive Officer*

A wheelchair that provides mobility in both sitting and standing
positions.

**713  Innovative Products**
4351 W College Avenue
Appleton, WI 54914
920-738-9090
800-424-3369
FAX: 920-738-9050

*Art Fochs, Vice President*
Wheelchairs; accessories.

**714  Liberty**
Fortress
PO Box 489
Clovis, CA 93613
559-322-5437
FAX: 559-323-0299
Ultra lightweight wheelchair provides a comfortable fit and leaves people able to function as normally as possible in daily activities.

**715  Lightweight Breezy**
Motion Design
2382 Faraday Avenue
Suite 200
Carlsbad, CA 92008
760-930-1500
FAX: 760-930-1585
www.sunrisemedical.com

*Michael Hammes, Chief Executive Officer*
A lightweight wheelchair. *$750.00*

**716  Majors Medical Equipment**
14601 Old Lima Road
Suite 100
Fort Wayne, IN 46818
260-637-8586
800-611-5552
e-mail: majorsmedical@majorsmedical.com

*Larry Bobay, Owner*
America's largest selection of wheelchairs and homecare equipment.

**717  Natural Access**
PO Box 5729
Santa Monica, CA 90409
310-392-9864
800-411-7789
FAX: 310-392-3874
e-mail: national@superlink.net
www.landeez.com

*John Egan, Owner*
Provides the Landeez all-terrain wheelchair, that can roll easily on sand, gravel and snow for outdoor fun. The entire chair can fit inside a travel bag!

**718  Patient Transport Chair**
Mada Medical Products
625 Washington Avenue
Carlstadt, NJ 07072
201-460-0454
800-526-6370
FAX: 201-460-3509
e-mail: sales@madamedical.com
www.madainternational.com

*Jeffrey Adam, Vice President*
Mada's lightweight design transport chair is constructed of heavy gauge chrome-plated, steel tubing with reinforced cross braces.

**719  Posture-Glide Lounger**
Graham-Field Health Products
2935 Northeast Parkway
Atlanta, GA 30360
770-447-1609
800-347-5678
FAX: 800-726-0601
www.grahamfield.com

*Irwin Selinger, Chief Executive Officer*

Provides all day comfort and safe, independent mobilization with feet or hands. The ergonomically engineered seat back provides correct support.

**720  Prairie Cruiser**
Wheelchairs of Kansas
PO Box 32
Ellis, KS 67637
785-726-4950
800-537-6454
FAX: 800-337-2447
e-mail: workinfo@go2wok.com
www.wheelchairsofkansas.com
A large-frame powerchair constructed of high quality, stress tested stainless steel to insure durability and peak performance.

**721  Redman Apache**
Redman Powerchair
3840 S Palo Verde Road
Tucson, AZ 85714
520-546-6002
800-727-6684
FAX: 520-546-5530

*Don Redman, Owner*
These ultralight, active use wheelchairs offer quick release rear wheels, adjustable arm height and detachable arm swing-away.

**722  Redman Crow Line**
Redman Powerchair
3840 S Palo Verde Road
Tucson, AZ 85714
520-546-6002
800-727-6684
FAX: 520-546-5530

*Don Redman, Owner*
Reclining wheelchair that reclines a full 90 degrees to flat and can be stopped anywhere on the axis.

**723  Rolls 2000 Series**
Invacare Corporation
899 Cleveland Street
Elyria, OH 44035
440-329-6000
800-333-6900
e-mail: info@invacare.com
These wheelchairs are the first light-weight wheelchairs designed for rental use.

**724  Skyway**
Skyway Machine
4451 Caterpillar Road
Redding, CA 96003
530-243-5151
800-332-3357
FAX: 530-243-5104
e-mail: sales@skywaywheels.com
www.skywaytuffwheels.com

*Parrey Cremeans, Sales Manager*
*Bart Weems, Sales/Customer Service*
*Ken Coster, President*

For over 20 years Skyway has been the world leader in composite wheels. Supplying over 650 different wheel combinations for wheelchairs, lawn and garden products, bicycles and a large assortment of wheeled devices. Wheel sizes range from 4 inch to 24 inch diameter.

**725  Stand-Up Wheelchairs**
Lifestand
PO Box 232171
Encinitas, CA 92023
800-782-6324
FAX: 610-586-0847
e-mail: dallery@msn.com

*Jacques A Dallery, President*
Offers a complete line of manual, electric and stand-up wheelchairs for the disabled.

**726 Standard Wheelchair**
Mada Medical Products
625 Washington Avenue
Carlstadt, NJ 07072 — 201-460-0454
800-526-6370
FAX: 201-460-3509
e-mail: sales@madamedical.com
www.madainternational.com

*Jeffrey Adam, Vice President*

Mada's standard wheelchairs are designed and built for long-lasting, reliable operation. Each wheelchair is constructed of heavy gauge, chrome plated, steel framework and tube in tube construction at stress points. Mada's state-of-the art engineering uses the most modern components to provide the strength needed while keeping the chair's weight down.

**727 Surf Chair**
2052 S Peninsula Drive
Daytona Beach, FL 32118 — 386-253-0986
800-841-6610
FAX: 386-253-7600
Wheelchairs; accessories.

**728 Swede Elite**
ETAC USA
2325 Parklawn Drive
Suite J
Waukesha, WI 53186 — 800-678-3822
FAX: 262-796-4605
e-mail: etac1usa@execpc.com
A carefully designed Swedish wheelchair made of lightweight titanium for the active user. Available in frame widths from 14-18 inches and colors available are: black, red, plum, teal-blue, and Silver. Custom colors available at additional cost and there is a lifetime warranty on the frame for original user. $1,740-$2,500

**729 Vista Wheelchair**
Arista Surgical Supply Company/AliMed
297 High Street
Dedham, MA 02026 — 781-329-2900
800-223-1984
FAX: 800-437-2966
e-mail: aristasurgical@juno.com
www.aristasurgical.com

*Julian Cherubini, President*

Vista has a rugged cold-rolled steel frame, durable vinyl upholstery and steel bearings to assure a smooth ride. $220.00

**730 Wheelchair with Shock Absorbers**
Iron Horse Productions
3114 Strawberry Lane
Port Huron, MI 48060 — 810-987-6700
800-426-0354
The Iron Horse is a revolutionary concept in wheelchair design that offers comfort, indoors and outdoors. $2375.00

## Wheelchairs: Pediatric

**731 Commuter & Kid's Commuter**
Fortress
PO Box 489
Clovis, CA 93613 — 559-322-5437
FAX: 559-323-0299
The first of a new generation of power wheelchairs. These chairs feature direct drive power yet are foldable, transportable and affordable.

**732 Convaid**
2830 California Street
Torrance, CA 90503 — 310-618-0111
888-266-8243
FAX: 310-539-3670
e-mail: convaid@earthlink.net
www.convaid.com

*Merv Watkins, President*
*Rodolfo Restelli, Controller*
*Nathan Watkins, Executive VP*

Convaid manufactures Mobile Positioning Systems for children. The Expedition, Safari Tilt, Cruiser, EZ Rider and Metro offer a noninstitutional styling and are lightweight and compact-folding. The steel/aluminum structure is engineered for maximum comfort and durability. The mobile positioning lines come with more than 20 positioning features and a full range of positioning adaptations. All chairs have been successfully crash-tested and offer a limited lifetime warranty (except the Metro).

**733 Etac USA: Sting Wheelchair**
2325 Parklawn Drive
Suite J
Waukesha, WI 53186 — 800-678-3822
FAX: 262-796-4605
e-mail: etac1usa@execpc.com
www.execpc.com/~etac1usa
A swedish wheelchair designed to adjust to meet the growing child's every need. Both the seat and the backrest are width, height, and angle adjustable. Foot rest, adjustable in height, depth and angle, swings back under the seat. Numerous accessories available. Lifetime warranty on frame for the original user.

**734 Imp Tricycle**
TRIAID
PO Box 1364
Cumberland, MD 21501 — 301-759-3525
800-306-6777
FAX: 301-759-3525
e-mail: sales@triaid.com
www.triaid.com

*Iain A MacDonald, Sales Director*
*Ann M Hutter, Sales Executive/Manager*

Provides fun therapy and actively encourages participation, awareness and the building of self confidence. Designed for children from about 3 years, it features ATB styling, 12 inch wheels, adjustable steering stop and a supportive saddle. Handlebar and seat adjustments combine with a broad wheelbase to ensure the rider is in the optimum position to pedal and the tricycle gives good stability and confident handling. Support accessories are available. $590.00

**735 Kid's Custom**
Fortress
PO Box 489
Clovis, CA 93613 — 559-322-5437
FAX: 559-323-0299
Custom pediatric mobility needs. This ultra light-weight chair is tailored fit to each child, to make wheeling fun and encourages kids to be active because they feel free, safe and secure.

**736 Kid's Edge**
Fortress
PO Box 489
Clovis, CA 93613 — 559-322-5437
FAX: 559-323-0299
This wheelchair offers multiple options, features and modifications at no upcharge.

**737 Kid's Liberty**
Fortress
PO Box 489
Clovis, CA 93613 — 559-322-5437
FAX: 559-323-0299

Offers a broad range of seat heights, widths and depths, back heights and numerous other modifications to accommodate the specific and unique requirements of children.

**738  Kid-Friendly Chairs**
Vector Mobility
5030 E Jensen Avenue
Fresno, CA  93725

800-441-0358
FAX: 559-441-0359

Manual base offers the lowest available floor to seat height, growth capability, one-third the parts of a conventional chair and no welds to break. The power unit features standard shapes and personality designs from elephants to inch worms and autos to rainbows, lowest seat height, and smallest turning radius on the market.

**739  Seven Fifty-Five FS**
Fortress
PO Box 489
Clovis, CA  93613

559-322-5437
FAX: 559-323-0299

Unharness the curiosity of childhood with the modular power/base seating system that sets kids free. This device is engineered and built especially for children.

**740  TMX Tricycle**
TRIAID
PO Box 1364
Cumberland, MD  21501

301-759-3525
800-306-6777
FAX: 301-759-3525
e-mail: sales@triaid.com
www.triaid.com

*Iain A MacDonald, Sales Director*
*Ann M Hutter, Sales Executive/Manager*

Provides fun therapy and actively encourages participation, awareness and the building of self confidence. Designed for children from about eight years, it features ATB styling, 20 inch wheels, adjustable steering stop and a supportive saddle. Handlebar and seat adjustments combine with a broad wheelbase to ensure the rider is in the optimum position to pedal and the tricycle gives good stability and confident handling. Support accessories are available. *$795.00*

# Wheelchairs: Powered

**741  Bounder Plus Power Wheelchair**
21st Century Scientific
4915 Industrial Way
Coeur D Alene, ID  83815

208-667-8800
800-448-3680
FAX: 208-667-6600
e-mail: 21st@wheelchairs.com
www.wheelchairs.com

*RD Davidson, Sales/Marketing Director*
*Jeanie L Saville, Sales Associate*
*Ron Prior, Owner*

Available in widths of 16 to 20 inches for users up to 500 pounds with a 2 year warranty on the entire chair. It offers all the standard features of a BOUNDER, plus reinforced rear wheel mounts, reinforced caster barrels, and super duty upholstery (with double liner and web straps under every screw). The BOUNDER Plus also features tandem cross struts, middle vertical support strut, seat rails supported at five points and back upholstery attached with machine screws.

**742  Bounder Power Wheelchair**
21st Century Scientific
4915 Industrial Way
Coeur D Alene, ID  83815

208-667-8800
800-448-3680
FAX: 208-667-6600
e-mail: 21st@wheelchairs.com
www.wheelchairs.com

*RD Davidson, Sales/Marketing Director*
*Jeanie L Saville, Sales Associate*
*Ron Prior, Owner*

Available in a variety of widths from 16 to 18 inches for users up to 250 pounds. The rugged frame is constructed with steel tubing. The standard 12 position Adjustable Front Forks, made of 1/4 inch thick steel, provides impact dampening and seat tilt adjustment. A Dual Group 27 Sliding Battery Box provides extended range and easy battery maintenance. *$8695.00*

**743  Damaco D90**
Damaco
20542 Plummer Street
Chatsworth, CA  91311

800-432-2434
FAX: 818-709-5282

Portable power unit that fits manual wheelchairs with large rear wheels. Weighing just 22 pounds, the power system can be removed and stored in a matter of seconds. *$2495.00*

**744  Geronimo**
Redman Powerchair
3840 S Palo Verde Road
Suite 202
Tucson, AZ  85714

520-546-6002
800-727-6684
FAX: 520-546-5530

*Don Redman, Owner*

Wheelchair offering direct drive, two year electronic guarantee and micro controls.

**745  One Thousand FS**
Fortress
PO Box 489
Clovis, CA  93613

559-322-5437
FAX: 559-323-0299

Add-on power system installs in minutes, enabling the driver to relax and drive anywhere with smooth, silent electric power.

**746  Permobil Max 90**
Permobil
30 Ray Avenue
Burlington, MA  01803

781-272-7410
FAX: 781-229-9841

The power wheelchair for those needing an easily maneuverable and quiet indoor chair but who also need to use their chair outdoors.

**747  Permobil Super 90**
Permobil
30 Ray Avenue
Burlington, MA  01803

781-272-7410
FAX: 781-229-9841

The power wheelchair is designed for travel over uneven and hilly terrain outdoors and indoors.

**748  Power for Off-Pavement**
Redman Powerchair
3840 S Palo Verde Road
Suite 202
Tucson, AZ  85714

520-546-6002
800-727-6684
FAX: 520-546-5530

*Don Redman, Owner*

Power-drive wheelchair has a solid seat and can handle safely and securely knolls and off-pavement terrain.

**749 Reclining Power Wheelchairs**
LaBac Systems
4965 Kingston Street
Denver, CO 80239
303-914-9914
800-445-4402

*Josh Barnum, President*
Power recline seating systems for wheelchairs, offering more comfort and dependability for the physically challenged.

**750 Roll-Aid**
Stand Aid of Iowa
PO Box 386
Sheldon, IA 51201
800-831-8580
FAX: 712-324-5210
e-mail: standaid@connect.com
Adapts to fit all standard collapsible wheelchairs. It is convenient, portable and provides electric rollator mobility instantly.
*$1748.00*

## Wheelchairs: Racing

**751 Aeroedge**
Fortress
PO Box 489
Clovis, CA 93613
559-322-5437
FAX: 559-323-0299
The ultimate in racing wheelchair design. Two innovative and exclusive Fortress features make this the fastest machine on three wheels.

**752 Eagle Sportschairs**
2351 Parkwood Road
Snellville, GA 30039
770-972-0763
800-932-9380
FAX: 770-985-4885
e-mail: bewing@bellsouth.net
www.eaglesportschairs.com

*Barry Ewing, Owner*
*Marty Frierson, Sales*

The Eagle line of custom lightweight performance chairs includes a range of options to fit all racing and sport needs including; track, baseball, quad-rugby, tennis, field events and waterskiing. Also popular for daily use. We are able to customize any chair to accommodate size and disability and all frames have a full five year warranty.

**753 East Penn Manufacturing Company**
East Penn Manufacturing Company
PO Box 147
Lyon Station, PA 19536
610-682-6361
FAX: 610-682-4781
e-mail: eastpenn@eastpenn-delu.com

*Harold Eberly, VP Sales*
*Daniel Langdon, President*

Specially engineered for demanding deep-cycle applications Gelled electrolyte Deka Dominator Batteries provides maintenance-free operation, longer battery life and hours of reliable performance. Their excellent recharge characteristics provide quick turn around time.

**754 Invacare Top End**
4501 63rd Circle
Pinellas Park, FL 33781
727-522-8677
800-532-8677
FAX: 727-522-1007
www.invacare.com

*Mary Carol Peterson, Marketing*
*Al Crisp, Manager*

Manufacturers of light weight, rigid, sport-specific wheelchairs such as the Eliminator line of racing chairs, T-3 tennis and softball chairs, and the Terminator for quad rugby and basketball. The Excelerator, XLT three-wheel hand cycle for adults and juniors. Check out our full line of wheelchairs to fit every need. $1,895-$2,495

# Aging

**755    Aging in America**
1500 Pelham Parkway S
Bronx, NY 10461                        718-824-4004

*Linda Martin, Executive VP*
*Julie Dalton, Vice President*

Research and services organization for professionals in gerontology. Objectives are: to produce, implement and share effective and affordable programs and services that improve the quality of life for the elderly community; to better prepare professionals and students interested in or currently involved with, aging and the aged. Conducts research projects, educational and training seminars, and in-service curricula for long-term and acute care facilities.

**756    Alabama Association of Homes and Services for the Aging**
1520 Cooper Hill Road
Birmingham, AL 35210                   205-951-2442
                                       FAX: 205-956-5001
                                       e-mail: alahsa@ala-net.com

*Wray Tomlin, President*

**757    American Association of Homes and Services for the Aging**
2519 Connecticut Avenue NW
Washington, DC 20008                   202-783-2242
                                       FAX: 202-783-2255
                                       e-mail: info@aahsa.org
                                       www.aahsa.org

*Doug Eadie, Founder*
*William Minnix Jr, President*

The American Association of Homes and Services for the Aging (AAHS) represents not-for-profit organizations dedicated to providing high-quality health care, housing and services to the nation's elderly. AAHSA organizations serve more than one million older persons af all income levels, creeds and races.

**758    Arizona Association of Homes and Housing for the Aging**
3839 N 3rd Street
Suite 201
Phoenix, AZ 85012                      602-230-0026
                                       FAX: 602-230-0563
                                       e-mail: azaha@azaha.org
                                       azaha.org

*Lindsey Norris, Executive Director*

The Arizona Association of Homes and Houses for the Aging is a not-for-profit trade association representing more than 100 facilities dedicated to providing quality health care, housing and services to over 12,000 elderly Arizona citizens. AzAHA is the only association in Arizona representing the full continuum of long term care, housing and services including: retirement communities, HUD subsidized senior housing, assisted living and nursing facilities.

**759    Association of Ohio Philanthropic Homes and Housing for Aging**
855 S Wall Street
Columbus, OH 43206                     614-444-2882
                                       FAX: 614-444-2974
                                       e-mail: info@aopha.org
                                       www.aopha.org

*John Alfano, President/CEO*
*George M Evans, Jr., President/CEO*

Founded in 1937, AOPHA, the advocate of not-for-profit services for older Ohioans, is a statewide nonprofit trade association representing over 335 not-for-profit senior housing apartments, home and community-based service providers, assisted living facilities, nursing homes and continuing care retirement communities (CCRCs).

**760    California Association of Homes and Services for the Aging**
1315 i Street
Suite 100
Sacramento, CA 95814                   916-392-5111
                                       FAX: 916-428-4250
                                       e-mail: aburnsjohnson@aging.org
                                       www.aging.org

*Anne Johnson, CEO and President*

The California Association of Homes and Services for the Aging (CAHSA) is the primary statewide association for not-for-profit organizations providing health care, housing and community services to older adults.

**761    Center for Understanding Aging**
200 Executive Boulevard
Suite 201
Southington, CT 06489                  718-824-4004
                                       FAX: 718-824-4242
                                       e-mail: coer.natal@snet.net

*Anita Porco, Chairperson*
*Duncan Wyeth, Vice Chairman*

Seeks to dispel myths about aging and old age, encourages communication among generations and works to create a social environment where people of all ages can live together. Also serves as a clearinghouse of information on issues of aging and intergenerational programs. Provides professional speakers and workshop leaders.

**762    Children of Aging Parents**
PO Box 167
Richboro, PA 18954                     215-945-6900
                                       800-227-7294
                                       FAX: 215-945-8720
                                       e-mail: info@caps4caregivers.org
                                       www.caps4caregivers.org
A national clearinghouse for caregivers of the elderly. It provides information and referral, educational programs and materials and caregiver support groups. CAPS also produces a quarterly newsletter which is available through the organization. Individuals: $25.00. Organizational/Professional: $100.00.

**763    Colorado Association of Homes and Services for the Aging (CAHSA)**
1888 Sherman Street
Suite 610
Denver, CO 80203                       303-837-8834
                                       FAX: 303-837-8836
                                       www.cahsa.org

*Laura Landwirth, Executive Director*

The American Association of Homes and Services for the Aging (AAHS) represents nonprofit organizations dedicated to providing high quality health care, housing and services to the nation's elderly. AAHSA organizations serve more than one million older persons af all income levels, creeds and races.

**764    Connecticut Association of Not-for-Profit Providers for the Aging**
1340 Worthington Ridge
Berlin, CT 06037                       860-828-2903
                                       FAX: 860-828-8694
                                       e-mail: canpfa@canpfa.org
                                       www.canpfa.org

CANPFA promotes a vision of the world in which every community offers an integrated and coordinated continuum of high quality, affordable health care, housing and community based services. CANPFA members are all mission-driven, not-for-profits. Not-for-profits focus on caring and providing services for their residents and clients. They re-invest their income into their facilities, resident programs and staff development. They are rooted in their communities.

**765    Delaware Association of Nonprofit Homes for the Aging**

1175 McKee Road
Dover, DE  19904                     302-674-8030
                                   FAX: 302-674-8650

**766    Georgia Association of Homes and Services for the
Aging**

607 Peachtree Street NE
Atlanta, GA  30308                   404-572-6170
                                   FAX: 404-872-1737
                              e-mail: gahsa@gahsa.org
                                      www.gahsa.org

*Normer Adams, Executive Director*

The Georgia Association of Homes and Services for the Aging (GAHSA) is an affiliated partner of the American Association of Homes and Services of the Aging (AASHA), which represents over 5,600 nonprofit facilities, over one million older adults in the United States and maintains an impressive staff of 80 professionals at its headquarters in Washington, D.C.

**767    Indiana Association of Homes for the Aging**

PO Box 68829
Indianapolis, IN  46268              317-733-2380
                                   FAX: 317-733-2385
                            e-mail: jimleich@iahsa.com
                                       www.iahsa.com

*Jim Leich, President*
*Susan Darwent, VP of Operations*
*Linda Woolley, VP of Health Policy*

Indiana Association of Homes and Services for the Aging (IAHSA) members are non-profit organizations, providing hgh quality health care, services and housing for over 25,000 seniors in Indiana.

**768    Iowa Association of Homes and Services for the Aging**

1701 48th Street
Suite 203
West Des Moines, IA  50266           515-440-4630
                                   FAX: 515-440-4631
                              e-mail: iahsa@ageiowa.org
                                      www.ageiowa.org

*Dana Petrowsky, President/CEO*
*Mark Tiegland, VP Member Services*
*Kristie Oliver, VP Government Relations*

IAHSA inspires leadership and benevolence in its members through networking education, information and advocacy.

**769    Kansas Association of Homes for the Aging**

217 SE 8th Avenue
2
Topeka, KS  66603                    785-233-7443
                                   FAX: 785-233-9471
                                      www.kahsa.org

*John Grace, President and CEO*
*Kevin McFarland, Executive VP*
*Debra Harmon Zehr, Executive VP*

KAHSA represents 160 not-for-profit nursing homes, retirement communities, hospital long-term care units, assisted living facilities, senior housing and community based service programs for the elderly.

**770    Kentucky Association of Not-for-Profit Homes and Services for the Aging**

2501 Nelson Miller Parkway
Louisville, KY  40223                502-992-4380
                                   FAX: 502-992-4390
                               e-mail: info@kahsa.com
                                      www.kahsanet.org

*Timothy L Veno, President*

**771    Life Service Network of Illinois: Springfi eld**

2 Lawrence Square
Springfield, IL  62704               217-789-1677
                                   FAX: 217-789-1778
                                e-mail: info@lsni.org
                                        www.lsni.org

*Kirk Riva, Vice President*
*Jennifer Pickett, Director Marketing*

The American Association of Homes and Services for the Aging (AAHS) represents not-for-profit organizations dedicated to providing high-quality health care, housing and services to the nation's elderly. AAHSA organizations serve more than one million older persons af all income levels, creeds and races.

**772    Life Services Network of Illinois**

911 N Elm Street
Suite 228
Hinsdale, IL  60521                  630-325-6170
                                   FAX: 630-325-0749
                                e-mail: info@lsni.org
                                        www.lsni.org

*Dennis Bozzi, President*

For nearly 75 years, Life Services Network of Illinois, a state-wide trade association, has represented providers of the complete contiuum of services for older adults, including nursing facilities, assisted living, senior housing and home and community based services. Our success as an association is founded in our commitment to helping our members overcome obstacles while identifying future opportunities for their success.

**773    Lighthouse International**

Lighthouse International
111 E 59th Street
New York, NY  10022                  212-821-9200
                                     800-829-0500
                                   FAX: 212-821-9707
                             e-mail: info@lighthouse.org
                                     www.lighthouse.org

*Tara A Cortes, President and CEO*

**774    Louisiana Association of Homes and Service for the
Aging**

PO Box 1748
Marrero, LA  70073                   225-757-1350
                                   FAX: 504-689-3982
                          e-mail: gulfstatesahsa@aol.com
                                   www.gulfstatesahsa.org

*Karen Contrenchis, President*

**775    Massachusetts Aging Services Association**

60 Seminary Avenue
Auburndale, MA  02466                617-224-2999
                                   FAX: 617-663-7046
                          e-mail: office@MassAging.org
                                    www.massaging.org

The Massachusetts Aging Services Association (MassAging) is the only Massachusetts membership association representing the full continuum of not-for-profit providers of aging services. MassAging works to achieve a system of healthy, affordable, and ethical aging services for older persons in Massachusetts. MassAging is proudly affiliated with the American Association of Homes and Services for the Aging (AAHSA), a national associaton of not-for-profit homes and services for he aging.

**776    Michigan Association of Homes and Serivces for the Aging**
6512 Centurion Drive
Suite 380
Lansing, MI 48917                     517-323-3687
                                  FAX: 517-323-4569
                          e-mail: dherbel@mahsahome.org
                                     www.mahsahome.org

*David E Herbel, CEO and President*

The Michigan Association of Homes and Services for the Aging represents and promotes the common interests of its members through leadership, advocacy, education and other services in order to enhance members' ability to serve their constituencies.

**777    Mid-Atlantic LifeSpan**
2 Uite 220
Columbia, MD 21046                    410-381-1176
                                  FAX: 410-381-0240
                           e-mail: admin@manpha.org
                                       www.manpha.org

*Isabella Firth, President*

LifeSpan is the newest, largest and most powerful senior care provider association in the Mid-Atlantic, representing more than 300 senior care provider organizations in Maryland and the District of Columbia. LifeSpan's members include non-profits and proprietary assisted living, contiuing care retirement communities, nursing facilities, subsidized senior housing and community and hospital based programs.

**778    Minnesota Health and Housing Alliance**
2 Uite 350 S
Saint Paul, MN 55114                  651-645-4545
                                      800-462-5368
                                  FAX: 651-645-0002
                             e-mail: info@mhha.com
                                         www.mhha.com

*Gayle Kvenvold, President/CEO*

Minnesota's largest statewide trade association for providers of older adult services, MHHA represents the complete continuum of care, including nursing home care, senior housing with supportive services, independent senior housing and community-based services.

**779    Mississippi Association of Homes and Services for the Aging**
Naval Home
1800 Beach Drive
Gulfport, MS 39507                    601-896-3110
                                  FAX: 601-897-4013

**780    Missouri Association of Homes for the Aging**
308a Monroe Street
2
Jefferson City, MO 65101              573-635-6244
                                  FAX: 573-635-6618

*Denise Clemonds, Executive Director*

**781    National Voluntary Organizations for Independent Living for the Aging**
300 D Street SW
Suite 801
Washington, DC 20024                  202-479-1200
                                  FAX: 202-479-6674
                               e-mail: info@ncoa.org
                                          www.ncoa.org

*James Firman, President and CEO*

The National Council on the Aging is a national network of organizations and individuals dedicated to improving the health and independence of older persons and increasing their continuing contributions to communities, society and future generations.

**782    Nebraska Association of Homes for the Aging**
625 S 14th Street
Lincoln, NE 68508                     402-489-1117
                                  FAX: 402-434-5685

*Kimberle Hall, Executive Director*

**783    New Jersey Association of Nonprofit Homes for the Aging**
13 Roszel Road
Suite A104
Princeton, NJ 08540                   609-452-1161
                                  FAX: 609-452-2907
                          e-mail: jduggan@njanpha.org
                                      www.njanpha.org

*June Duggan, CEO and President*
*Francis Byrne, VP*

The New Jersey Association of Non-Profit Homes for the Aging (NJANPHA) is the statewide association of not-for-profit organizations which are dedicated to providing and enhancing quality of life services to the diverse aging population. The Association encourages cooperaton with communities and ther entities, both public and private, interested in aging.

**784    New York Association of Homes and Services for the Aging**
194 Washington Avenue
4th Floor
Albany, NY 12210                      518-436-5697
                                  FAX: 518-455-8908
                                       www.nyahsa.org

*Carl Young, President*

NYAHSA is a statewide organization of socially responsible, community-benefit organizations dedicated to providing high quality health care, housing, and community services to the elderly and people with special needs.

**785    North Carolina Association of Nonprofits for the Aging**
3700 National Drive
Suite 218
Raleigh, NC 27612                     919-571-8333
                                  FAX: 919-571-1297
                      e-mail: swilliamson@ncanpha.org
                                      www.ncanpha.org

*Susan Williamson, Executive Director*
*John Syria, Director*

The North Carolina Association of Non-Profit Homes for the Aging (NCANPHA) is the state association of not-for-profit providers dedicated to providing quality health care, housing, health, community and related services to the elderly.

**786    Northern New England Association of Homes and Services for the Aging**
75 Pearl Street
Portland, ME 04101                    207-773-4822
                                  FAX: 207-773-0101

*Sheila Deringis, Member Services Director*

NNEAHSA's mission is to promote the interests of its not-for-profit members in Maine, New Hampshire, and Vermont which provide healthy, affordable and ethical long-term care to our older citizens through education, advocacy, representation and collaboration.

**787    Oklahoma Association of Homes and Services for the Aging**
PO Box 1383
El Reno, OK 73036                     405-262-5262

                                e-mail: info@okahsa.org
                                       www.okahsa.org

*Karen Stanhope, President*
*Mary Brinkley, Executive Director*

The Oklahoma Association of Homes and Services for the Aging is the Oklahoma state association of not-for-profit organizations dedicated to establishing the highest standards of excellence for services to the aging in Oklanhoma. OKAHSA's purpose is to be supportive of each member organization's quest for excellence.

**788   Oregon Association of Homes for the Aging**
7340 SW Hunziker Street
Suite 104
Tigard, OR  97223                         503-598-9689
                                 FAX: 503-624-0870
                           e-mail: rgulyas@oashs.org
                                    www.oashs.org

*Mark King, President*
*Ruth Gulyas, Executive Director*
*Michael Morgan, Manager*

The Oregon Alliance of Senior & Health Services is the state association of not-for-profit, mission-directed organizations dedicated to providing quality housing, health, community and related services to the elderly and disabled.

**789   Pennsylvania Association of Nonprofit Homes for the Aging**
1100 Bent Creek Boulevard
Mechanicsburg, PA  17050                  717-795-9684
                                 FAX: 717-763-1057
                           e-mail: info@panpha.org
                                    www.panpha.org

*Ron Barth, President and CEO*
*W M Russ McDaid, VP*
*Holly Rosini, VP and COO*

PANPHA represents over 320 nonprofit providers of long-term care and housing services for 65,000 elderly residents across Pennsylvania. The Association is committed to helping its members provide quality care efficiently and effectively for the individuals and families they serve. In the age of impersonal care, PANPHA members put people before profits.

**790   Quality Health Care Foundation of Wyoming**
520 Randall Avenue
Cheyenne, WY  82001                       307-637-7575
                                 FAX: 307-634-0804
The American Association of Homes and Services for the Aging (AAHS) represents not-for-profit organizations dedicated to providing high-quality health care, housing and services to the nation's elderly. AAHSA organizations serve more than one million older persons af all income levels, creeds and races.

**791   Rhode Island Association of Facilities for the Aging**
225 Chapman Street
Providence, RI  02905                     401-490-7612
                                          866-883-1631
                                 FAX: 401-490-7614
                                 TTY: 401-490-4597
                           e-mail: info@riafsa.org
                                    www.riafsa.org

*Julie Richard, President*
*Paul Barrette, Secretary*
*Christopher Novak, Manager*

RIAFSA was formally organized in 1989 as an associaton of non-profit facilities and services primarily for the elderly. RIAFSA members include senior housing, assisted living, nursing homes and home and community based services.

**792   Shiloh Senior Citizens Center**
1510 9th Street NW
Washington, DC  20001                     202-232-1425

Offers daily programs, activities, counseling, noon meals, and transportation for deaf and hard of hearing seniors, 60 and older, living in the District of Columbia.

**793   South Carolina Association of Nonprofit Homes for the Aging**
1110 Marshall Road
Greenwood, SC  29646                      864-455-6800
                                 FAX: 803-227-7161

*Danny Satterfield, Manager*

The American Association of Homes and Services for the Aging (AAHS) represents not-for-profit organizations dedicated to providing high-quality health care, housing and services to the nation's elderly. AAHSA organizations serve more than one million older persons af all income levels, creeds and races.

**794   Tennessee Association of Homes for the Aging**
500 Interstate Boulevard S
Suite 325
Nashville, TN  37210                      615-256-1800
                                 FAX: 615-726-3082
                           e-mail: cermshar@tha.com
                                    www.tha.com/tnahsa/

*Carrie Ermshar, President*

TNAHSA is an association of faclities and professionals providing quality housing, health, community and related services for the elderly. TNAHSA represents and promotes the common interest of its members through leadership, advocacy, education, communication and other services in order to enhance members' ability to serve their constituencies.

**795   Texas Association of Homes and Services for the Aging**
2205 Hancock Drive
Austin, TX  78756                         512-467-2242
                                 FAX: 512-467-2275
                                    www.tahsa.org

*George Linial, CEO and President*
*Donna Loflin, VP of Education*

The American Association of Homes and Services for the Aging (AAHS) represents not-for-profit organizations dedicated to providing high-quality health care, housing and services to the nation's elderly. AAHSA organizations serve more than one million older persons af all income levels, creeds and races.

**796   Washington Association of Housing and Services for the Aging**
1570 Wilmington Drive
Suite 220
Dupont, WA  98327                         253-964-8870
                                 FAX: 253-964-8876
                           e-mail: wahsa@wahsa.com
                                    www.wahsa.com

*Deb Murphy, CEO*

Washington Association of Housing and Services for the Aging (WASHA) is the state association serving primarily not-for-profit organizations dedicated to providing quality housing, health, community and related services to older persons.

**797   West Virginia Hospital Association**
100 Association Drive
Charleston, WV  25311                     304-344-9744
                                 FAX: 304-344-9745
                                    www.wvha.com

*Steven J Summer, President and CEO*
*Kathy L Watts, Director*
*Joan K Morton, Executive Assistant*

For 80 years, the West Virginia Hospital Association, a not-for-profit statewide organization, has represented our member hospitals and health systems across the contiuum of care.

**798** **Wisconsin Association of Homes & Services for the Aging**
204 S Hamilton Street
Madison, WI 53703                     608-255-7060
FAX: 608-255-7064
e-mail: jsauer@wahsa.org
www.wahsa.org

*Steve Jaberg, President*
*Craig Ubbelohde, VP*
*Miriam Ownby, VP*

The Wisconsin Association of Homes and Services for the Aging (WAHSA) is a statewide membership organization of not-for-profit corporations principally serving the elderly and disabled.

## Business Support

**799** **Abilities!**
201 I U Willets Road
Albertson, NY 11507                    516-465-1400
FAX: 516-747-5400
www.ncds.org

*Kevin McGilloway, CEO*
*Stephen V Murphy, President*
*Ralph F Palleschi, President and COO*

Helps the business community develop effective, low-cost corporate policies and practices for integrating people with disabilities in the workplace.

**800** **Council of Better Business Bureaus Foundat ion**
4200 Wilson Boulevard
Suite 800
Arlington, VA 22203                    703-276-0100
FAX: 703-525-8277
e-mail: media@cbbb.bbb.org
www.bbb.org

*Candy McIlhenny, Executive Director*
*Warren Clark, President*
*Thomas J Ryan, Senior VP*

Seven Title III compliance guides are available for: car sales and service; restaurants and bars; recreation and fitness centers; grocery stores; retail stores; professional offices; and travel and tour agents. *$2.50*

**801** **Disability Community Small Business Development Center**
2568 Packard Street
Ann Arbor, MI 48104                    734-971-0277
FAX: 734-971-0826
TTY:734-971-0277
e-mail: cilstaff@aacil.org
www.aacil.org

*James Magyar, Executive Director*

The Ann Arbor Center for Independent Living utilizes the independent living model, a well-demonstrated and effective four-pronged advocacy and service delivery strategy. Fueled by a consumer-driven philosophy, we provide four core services required of all Centers for Independent Living along with several other servies. The four core services are: Information and Referral, Peer Support, Advocacy, and Independent Living Skill Development.

**802** **Fedcap Rehabilitation Services**
211 W 14th Street
New York, NY 10011                     212-727-4200
FAX: 212-727-4374
TTY:212-727-4384
e-mail: info@fedcap.org
www.fedcap.org

*Susan Fonsa, Executive Director*
*Michael Brenner, President*
*Mark O'Donoghue, VP*

Fedcap helps NYC work. Since 1935, we have helped people with all types of disabilities and barriers to employment join the workforce, while providing vital services to business and government.

**803** **Independent Visually Impaired Enterprisers**
American Council Of The Blind
1155 15th Street NW
Suite 1004
Washington, DC 20005                   202-467-5081
800-424-8666
FAX: 202-467-5085
e-mail: terrypach@aol.com
www.acb.org

*Mary Susan Orester, President*
*James Radcliff, VP*
*Terry Pacheco, Membership Services Coordinator*

Strives to broaden vocational opportunities in business for the visually impaired. Works to improve rehabilitation facilities for all types of business enterprises and publicizes the capabilities of blind and visually impaired business persons.

**804** **International Association of Machinists**
9000 Machinists Place
Upper Marlboro, MD 20772               301-967-4500
FAX: 316-522-7989
e-mail: websteward@goiam.org
www.goiam.org

*Steve Rayni, President*
*R Buffenbarger, Chief Executive Officer*

Placement programs for persons with disabilities.

**805** **Job Accommodation Network**
PO Box 6080
Morgantown, WV 26506                   304-293-7186
800-526-7234
FAX: 304-293-5407
e-mail: jan@jan.wvu.edu
www.jan.wvu.edu

*DJ Hendricks, Director*

JAN's mission is to facilitate the employment and retention of workers with disabilities by providing employers, employment providers, people with disabilities, their family members and other interested parties with information on job accomodations, self-employment and small business opportunities and related subjects. JAN's efforts are in support of the employment, including self-employment and small business ownership, of people with disabilities.

**806** **Life Development Institute**
18001 N 79th Avenue
Suite E71
Glendale, AZ 85308                     623-773-2774
FAX: 623-773-2788
www.life-development-inst.org

*Veronica Crawford, President*
*Robert Crawford, Chief Executive Officer*

Serves older adolescents and adults with learning disabilities, ADD and related disorders. The purpose of the training is to enable program participants to pursue responsible independent living, enhance academic/workplace literacy skills and facilitate placement in educational/employment opportunities, commensurate with individual capabilities. Includes a stand alone, regionally accredited 2-year college.

**807  Opportunity Plus of NC**
PO Box 35481
Charlotte, NC  28235                              704-519-0600
                                            FAX: 704-519-0699
                              e-mail: info@opportunity-plus.org
                                      www.opportunity-plus.org

*Don Olin, President*
*Dallas Bolan, Executive Director*

Opportunity Plus of North Carolina was founded 25 years ago to serve the needs of people with disabilities in the Charlotte metropolitan area and its contiguous counties. Our goal is to treat each person as an individual. Customized career paths are developed by discovering hidden potentials, addressing specific needs and removing hurdles.

## General Disabilities

**808  ARC**
1010 Wayne Avenue
Suite 650
Silver Spring, MD  20910                         301-565-3842
                                            FAX: 301-565-3843
                                     e-mail: info@thearc.org
                                             www.thearc.org

*Martha Hulse, CFO*
*Steven M Eidelman, Chief Executive Officer*
*Chris Privett, Director Communications*

National organization of people and for people with mental retardation and related developmental disabilities and their families. Devoted to promoting supports and services for people with mental retardation and their families. Also fosters research and education regarding the prevention of mental retardation in infants and young children.

**809  Academy of Dentistry for Persons with Disabilities**
401 N Michigan Avenue
Chicago, IL  60611                               312-527-6764
                                            FAX: 312-673-6663
                                  e-mail: scd@scdonline.org
                                           www.scdonline.org

*Roseann Mulligan DDS MS, VP*
*Kristen Smith, Executive Director*

Special Care Dentistry (SCD) is headquartered in Chicago and has a wide ranging membership that includes: dentists, dental hygienists; dental assistants; non-dental health care providers; health program administrators; and others who share our mission. There is also a participating membership category for hospitals, agencies that serve people with special needs and other advocacy and heath care organizations.

**810  Access Unlimited**
570 Hance Road
Binghamton, NY  13903                            607-669-4822
                                                 800-849-2143
                                            FAX: 607-669-4595
                                        www.accessunlimited.com

*Sherry Sinai, Administrative Coordinator*
*Sherry Lowry, Director*
*Thomas Egan, Owner*

At Access Unlimited, we believe that mobility, like people, comes in all shapes and colors. We celebrate the rich diversity of our customers' needs by creating products that alow easy access to any vehicle, from cars and vans to trucks and SUVs. We believe that adaptive equipment should be unobtrusive and should meet the needs of its user with a minimum of modifications to vehicle and lifestyle.

**811  Accu-Chem Laboratories**
990 N Bowser Road
Suite 800-880
Richardson, TX  75081                            972-234-5412
                                                 800-451-0116
                                            FAX: 972-234-5707
                             e-mail: newsletter@accuchem.com
                                             www.accuchem.com

*John Laseter, President*

Accu-Chem provides analytical and consulting services in forensic and postmortem toxicology. Our staff routinely provides qualitative and quantitative analyses of body fluids and tissues for drugs, poisons and recognized toxic chemicals. Additionally, full characterization of seized drugs and residues are also provided.

**812  Acupressure Institute**
1533 Shattuck Avenue
Berkeley, CA  94709                              510-845-1059
                                                 800-442-2232
                                            FAX: 510-845-1496
                                 e-mail: info@acupressure.com
                                          www.acupressure.com

*Michael Reed Gach, Executive Director*

Information, career training and mail order catalog.

**813  Advocacy Center**
590 South Avenue
Rochester, NY  14620                             585-546-1700
                                                 800-650-4967
                                            FAX: 585-546-7069
                                            TTY: 585-546-1700
                             e-mail: info@advocacycenter.com
                                       www.advocacycenter.com

*Steven Voellinger, President*
*Paul Shew, Executive Director*
*Joyce Steel, Program Coordinator*

Is a non profit organization located in New York State that educates, supports, and advocates with people who have disabilities, their families and circles of support.

**814  Advocacy Center for Persons with Disabilities**
2671 W Executive Center Circle
Suite 100
Tallahassee, FL 32301                            850-488-9071
                                                 800-342-0823
                                            FAX: 850-488-8640
                                            TTY: 800-346-4127
                             e-mail: info@advocacycenter.org
                                       www.advocacycenter.org

*Gary Weston, Executive Director*
*Hubert Grisson, President*

The Advocacy Center for Persons with Disabilites Inc., is a non-profit organization providing protection and advocacy services in the State of Florida. The Center's mission is to advance the dignity, equality, self-determination and expressed choices of individuals with disabilities.

**815    Advocates for Children of New York**
151 W 30th Street
Floor 5
New York, NY 10001                    212-947-9779

e-mail: info@advocatesforchildren.org
www.advocatesforchildren.org

*Jill Chaifetz, Executive Director*

AFC works on behalf of children from infancy to age 21 who are at greatest risk for school-based discrimination and/or academic failure. These include children wirh disabilities, ethnic minorities, immigrants, homeless children, foster care children, limited English proficient children and those living in poverty.

**816    Alliance for Technology Access**
1304 Southpoint Boulevard
Suite 240
Petaluma, CA 94954                    707-765-2080
FAX: 707-765-2080
TTY:707-778-3015
e-mail: atainfo@ataccess.org
www.ataccess.org

*Mary Lester, Executive Director*
*Russ Holland, Program Director*

The ATA is a growing national network of technology resource centers, organizations, individuals and companies. ATA encourages and facilitates the empowerment of people with disabilities to participate fully in their communities. Through public education, information and referral, capacity building in community organizations, and advocacy/policy efforts, the ATA enables millions of people to live, learn, work, define their futures, and achieve their dreams.

**817    American Academy of Pediatrics**
141 Northwest Point Boulevard
Elk Grove Village, IL 60007           847-434-4000
FAX: 847-434-8000
www.aap.org

*Carol Berkowitz MD, President*
*Joann Barbour, Manager*

Organization of 60,000 pediatricians committed to the attainment of optimal physical, mental, and social health and well-being for all infants, children, adolescents and young adults.

**818    American Association for the Advancement of Science**
Project On Science, Technology and Disability
1200 New York Avenue NW
Washington, DC 20005                  202-326-6400
FAX: 202-289-4021
e-mail: sjackson@aaas.org
www.aaas.org

*Gilbert S Omenn MD, President*
*Shirley Jackson, Chair*
*Alan Leshner, Chief Executive Officer*

The American Association for the Advancement of Science (AAAS) is an international non-profit organization dedicated to advancing science around the world by serving as an educator, leader, spokesperson and professional association.

**819    American Association of Music Therapy**
8455 Colesville Road
Suite 1000
Silver Spring, MD 20910               301-589-3300
FAX: 301-589-5175
e-mail: info@musictherapy.org
www.musictherapy.org

*Andrea Farbman Ed D, Executive Director*

Music Therapy is an established healthcare profession that uses music to address physical, emotional, cognitive, and social needs of individuals of all ages. Music therapy improves the quality of life for persons who are well and meets the needs of children and adults with disabilities or illnesses.

**820    American Association of People with Disabilities**
1629 K Street NW
Suite 503
Washington, DC 20006                  202-457-0046
800-840-8844
FAX: 202-457-0473
e-mail: aapd@aol.com
www.aapd-dc.org

The largest national nonprofit cross-disability member organization in the United States, dedicated to ensuring economic self-sufficiency and political empowerment for he more than 56 million Americans with disabilities.

**821    American Board of Chelation Therapy**
1407 N Wells Street
# B
Chicago, IL 60610                     312-266-3688
FAX: 312-266-3685

*Jack Hank, Executive Director*
Certification Board.

**822    American Botanical Council**
6200 Manor Road
Austin, TX 78723                      512-926-4900
FAX: 512-926-2345
e-mail: abc@herbalgram.org
www.herbalgram.org

*Mark Blumenthal, Founder/Executive Director*

The American Botanical Council (ABC) is the leading independent, nonprofit, international member-based organization providing education using science-based ad traditional information to promote the responsible use of herbal medicine.

**823    American Camping Association**
5000 State Road 67 N
Martinsville, IN 46151                765-342-8456
800-428-2267
FAX: 765-342-2065
www.acacamps.org

*Ann Sheets, President*
*Dawn Ewing, VP*
*Peg Smith, CEO*

The American Camp Association is a community of camp professionals who, for nearly 100 years, have joined together to share our knowledge and experience and to ensure the quality of camp programs. Because of our diverse 7,000 plus emmbership and exceptional programs, children and adults have the opportunity to learn powerful lessons in cmmunity, character-building, skill development, and healthy-living—-lessons that can be learned nowhere else.

**824    American Chiropractic Association**
1701 Clarendon Boulevard
Arlington, VA 22209                   703-276-8800
FAX: 703-243-2593
e-mail: memberinfo@acatoday.org
www.acatoday.org

*Kevin Corcoran, Executive VP*
*Janet Ridgely, VP Administration*

The ACA is a professional organization representing Doctors of Chiropratic. Its mission is to preserve, protect, improve, and promote the chiropractic profession and the services of Doctors of Chiropratic for the benefit of the patients they serve. The purpose of the ACA is to provide leadership in health care and a positive vision for the chiropractic profession and its natural approach to health and wellness.

**825    American Counseling Association**
5999 Stevenson Avenue
Alexandria, VA 22304                703-823-9800
                                    800-473-2329
                                FAX: 703-823-6862
                                TTY: 703-823-6862
        e-mail: webmaster@counseling.org
                     www.counseling.org

*Sam Gladding, President*
*Richard Yep, Executive Director*

The American Counseling Association is a not-for-profit, professional and educational organization that is dedicated to the growth and enhancement of the counseling profession.

**826    American Herbalists Guild**
141 Nob Hill Road
Cheshire, CT 06410                  770-751-6021
                                FAX: 770-751-7472
        e-mail: ahgoffice@earthlink.net
        www.americanherbalistsguild.com

*Aviva Jill Romm, President*
*Roy Upton, VP*

Information on herbal therapies and a directory of schools and teachers.

**827    American Massage Therapy Association**
500 Davis Street
Suite 900
Evanston, IL 60201                  847-864-0123
                                    877-905-2700
                                FAX: 847-864-1178
        e-mail: info@amtamassage.org
                     www.amtamassage.org

*Mary Beth Braun, President*
*M K Brennan, VP*
*Liz Lucas, Executive Director*

AMTA works to establish massage therapy as integral to the maintenance of good health and complementary to other therapeudic processes; to advance the profession through ethics and standards, certification, school accreditation, continuing education, professional publications, legislative efforts, public education, and fostering the development of members.

**828    American Organization for Bodywork Therapies of Asia**
1010 Haddonfield Berlin Road
Suite 408
Voorhees, NJ 08043                  856-782-1616
                                FAX: 856-782-1653
        e-mail: office@aobta.org
                     www.aobta.org

*Debra Howard, President*
*Julie Kaplan, VP*
*Angela Pflugfelder, Manager*

The American Organization for Bodywork Therapies of Asia (AOBTA) is a professional membership organizaton which promotes Asian Bodywork Therapy and its practitioners while honoring a diversity of disciplines. AOBTA serves its community of members by supporting appropriate credentialing; defining scope of practice and educational standards; and providing resources for training, professional development and networking. AOBTA advocates public policy to protect its members.

**829    American Pacific University**
615 Piikoi Street
Suite 501
Honolulu, HI 96814                  808-596-7765
                                    888-577-9278
                                    577-927-8
                                FAX: 808-596-7764
        e-mail: matt@ampac.edu
                     www.ampac.edu

*Matthew James, President*
*Alex Docker, Program Director*
*Todd Levinson, Director*

Provides a large variety of media resources.

**830    American Public Health Association**
800 i Street NW
Washington, DC 20001                202-777-2742
                                FAX: 202-777-2534
        e-mail: comments@apha.org
                     www.apha.org

*Georges C Benjamin, Executive Director*

Organization of public health professionals that represents more than 50,000 members from over 50 occupations of public health.

**831    American Red Cross: National Headquarters**
2025 E Street NW
Washington, DC 20006                202-639-3685
                                FAX: 202-303-4498
        e-mail: usa@redcross.org
                     www.redcross.org

*Arthur Howard, Chairman*
*Linda Mathes, CEO*
*Jack McGuire, President*

Today, in addition to domestic disaster relief, the American Red Cross offers compassionate services in five other areas: community services that help the needy; support and comfort for military members and their families; the collection, processing and distribution of lifesaving blood and blood products; educational programs that promote health and safety; and international relief and development programs.

**832    American Self-Help Clearinghouse**
Saint Clares Hospital
St Clares Health Services
Denville, NJ 07834                  973-586-5000
                                    800-367-6274
                                FAX: 973-326-9467
        e-mail: info@selfhelpgroups.org
                     www.selfhelpgroups.org

*Edward J Madara MS, Director*

Provides information on national self-help groups and offers training and technical assistance to exisiting and new self-help groups and clearinghouses. It has compiled a national database of over 800 of these model groups. Provides information on resource groups such as Violence Anonymous, Batterers Anonymous, and Stalkers' Victims Support Groups.

**833    American Social Health Association**
PO Box 13827
Research Triangle Park, NC 27709    919-361-8400
                                FAX: 919-361-8425
                     www.ashastd.org

*Jim Allen, President*

The American Social Health Association is recognized by the public, patients, providers and policy makers for developing and delivering accurate, medically reliable information about STDs. Public and college health clinics across the US order ASHA educational pamphlets and books to give to clients and students. Community-based organizations depend on ASHA, too, to help communicate about risk, transmission, prevention, testing, and treatment.

**834    American Society for the Alexander Techniq ue**
PO Box 60008
Florence, MA  01062                413-584-2359
                                   800-473-0620
                              FAX: 413-584-3097
                            e-mail: info@amsat.ws
                                    www.amsat.ws

*Ralph Zito, Chair*
*Indrani Gallagher, Administrator*

The Alexander Technique is a proven, effective self help method
for improving balance and coordination and increasing movement awareness by eliminating habitual reactions of misuse in
every day activities. AmSats mission is to define, maintain and
promote the Alexander Technique at its highest standard of professional practice and conduct.

**835    Association for Applied Psychophysiology and Biofeed-
back**
10200 West Avenue
Wheat Ridge, CO  80033             303-422-8436
                                   800-477-8892
                              FAX: 303-422-8894
                    e-mail: aapb@resourcenter.com
                                     www.aapb.org

*Steven M Baskin PhD BCIAC, President*
*Francine Butler, Executive Director*

Provides names and phone numbers of local chapters. Mission is
to advance the development, dissemination and utilization of
knowledge about applied psychophysiology and biofeedback to
improve health and the quality of life through research, education, and practice.

**836    Association for Network Care**
444 Main Street
Longmont, CO  80501                303-678-8101
                              FAX: 303-678-8089
          e-mail: info@associationfornetworkcare.com
                   www.associationfornetworkcare.com

*Richard Kaye, VP*
*John Michael, Manager*

Supports the consciousness, advances the practice of, and promotes the public availability of Network Spinal Analysis. Supports the advancement and understanding of the relationship of
the spine and nervous system to consciousness, the expression of
innate intelligence, self-organization, and healing. Encourages
the support of the science, art, and philosophically similar and
compatible models in various healing arts through workshops,
seminars, journals, newsletters and research projects.

**837    Association for Neurologically Impaired Brain Injured
Children**
21212 26th Avenue
Bayside, NY  11360                 718-423-9550
                              FAX: 718-423-9838
                           e-mail: info@anibic.org

*Alvin Clotkin, President*
*Gerard Smith, Executive Director*
*Christine Fisher, Intake Coordinator*

ANIBIc is a voluntary, multi-service organization that is dedicated to serving individuals with severe learning disabilities,
neurological impairments and other developmental disabilities.
Services include: residential, vocational, family support services, recreation (children and adults), respite (adult), in home
support services, counseling and tramatic brain injury services
(adults).

**838    Association for Persons in Supported Employment**
1627 Monument Avenue
Richmond, VA  23220                804-278-9187
                              FAX: 804-278-9377
                           e-mail: apse@apse.org
                                     www.apse.org

*Teresa Grossi, VP*
*Suzanne Hutcheson, President*
*Celane Whorter, Executive Director*

Supported employment enables people with disabilities who
have not been successfully employed to work and contribute to
society. Focuses on a person's abiliities and provides the supports the individual needs to be successful on a long-term basis.

**839    Association for Persons with Severe Handicaps (TASH)**
29 W Susquehanna Avenue
Suite 210
Baltimore, MD  21204               410-821-9632
                                   800-482-8274
                              FAX: 410-828-6706
                           e-mail: info@tash.org
                                     www.tash.org

*Nancy Weiss, Executive Director*
*John Austin*

International association of people with disabilities, their family members, other advocates and professionals, fighting for a
society in which inclusion of all people in all aspects of society
is the norm.

**840    Association of University Centers on Disabilities**
AUCD
1010 Wayne Avenue
Suite 920
Silver Spring, MD  20910           301-588-8252
                              FAX: 301-588-2842
                      e-mail: kmusheno@aucd.org
                                     www.aucd.org

*George Jesien, Executive Director*
*Frederick B Palmer, MD, President*
*Royal P Walker, Secretary*

The central office for the 61 University Centers for Excellence
programs and 21 Mental Retardation and Developmental Disabilities Research Centers and is their representative to the federal government. UCEDD's are located at major universities
and teaching hospitals in all 50 states, the District of Columbia
and many US territories. UCCED's target their activities to support the independence, productivity and integration into the
community of individuals with developmental disabilities.

**841    Association on Higher Education and Disability
(AHEAD)**
University Of Massachusetts, Boston
PO Box 540666
Waltham, MA  02454                 781-788-0003
                              FAX: 781-788-0033
                         e-mail: ahead@ahead.org
                                     www.ahead.org

*Jim Kessler, President*
*Stephan J Smith, Executive Director*
*Caroline Forsberg, Director of Communication*

International, multicultural organization of proessionals committed to full participation in higher education for persons with
disabilities. Plans and develops training programs, workshops,
publications and conferences. Founded in 1977 to address the
need and concern for upgrading the quality of services and support available to persons with disabilities in higher education.

**842    Bastyr University Natural Health Clinic**
1307 N 45th Street
Suite 200
Seattle, WA  98103                 206-834-4100
                              FAX: 206-834-4107
                                www.bastyrcenter.org

Offers naturopathic medicine visits, nutrition consultations, counseling, acupuncture treatments and Chinese herbal medicine services.

**843   Beach Center on Families and Disability**
University of Kansas
1200 Sunnyside Avenue
Room 3136
Lawrence, KS 66045
                          785-864-2700
                          FAX: 785-864-7605
                          TTY:785-864-3434
                          e-mail: beachcenter@ku.edu
                          www.beachcenter.org

*Ann Turnbull, Co-Founder, Co-Director*
*Rud Turnbull, Co-Founder, Co-Director*
*Robert Hemenway, Chief Executive Officer*

A federally funded center that conducts research and training in the factors that contribute to the successful functioning of families with members who have disabilities.

**844   Bio-Electro-Magnetics Institute**
2490 W Moana Lane
Reno, NV 89509
                          775-786-5768
                          FAX: 775-827-9099

*Pang Bai, Owner*

**845   Bonnie Prudden Myotherapy**
PO Box 65240
Tucson, AZ 85728
                          520-529-3979
                          800-221-4634
                          FAX: 520-529-6679
                          e-mail: info@bonnieprudden.com
                          www.bonnieprudden.com

*Enid Whittaker, Associate Director*

Provides a list of Certified Myotherapists, clinics where Myotherapy is offered, as well as informational brochures on Myotherapy workshops and products.

**846   CAPP National Parent Resource Center Federation for Children with Special Needs**
59 Temple Place
Suite 664
Boston, MA 02111
                          617-542-7860
                          866-815-8122
                          FAX: 617-542-7832
                          e-mail: info@ppal.net
                          www.ppal.net

*Donna Welles, Executive Director*
*Lisa Lambert, Assistant Director*
*Diane Haynes, Director Operations*

A parent-run resource system designed to further the needs and goals of family-centered, community-based coordinated care for children with special health needs and their families. Offers written materials, training packages, workshops and presentations for parents and professionals on special education, health care financing and other topics.

**847   CARF Rehabilitation Accreditation Commission**
4891 E Grant Road
Tucson, AZ 85712
                          520-325-1044
                          888-281-6531
                          FAX: 520-318-1129
                          www.carf.org

*Brian Boon PhD, President/CEO*

CARF serves as the standards-setting and accrediting body for rehabilitation and life enhancement programs and services. The independent, not-for-profit commission promotes quality, value, and optimal outcomes of services through a consultative accreditation process that centers on enhancing the lives of the persons served. At present, CARD has accredited more than 19,000 programs and services in the US, Canada, and Sweden in the areas of adult day services, behavioral health, and medical rehab.

**848   California State Oriental Medical Association (CSOMA)**
703 Market Street
Suite 250
San Francisco, CA 94103
                          800-477-4564
                          FAX: 415-357-1940
                          e-mail: info@csomaonline.org
                          www.csomaonline.org

*Bill Mosca LAc, Executive Director*

A professional organization of licensed acupuncturists and supporters of Oriental medicine dedicated to the preservation and advancement of the art, science, and practice of Oriental medicine in a caring and ethical manner, thereby enhancing the health and well-being of the general public.

**849   Canine Companions for Independence**
National Offices
PO Box 446
Santa Rosa, CA 95402
                          707-577-1700
                          800-572-2275
                          FAX: 707-577-1711
                          TTY: 707-577-1756
                          e-mail: info@caninecompanions.org
                          www.caninecompanions.org

*Ted Rogahn, President*
*Anne Gittinger, VP*

A nonprofit organization that provides highly trained assistance dogs for people with disabilities, helping them to achieve greater independence.

**850   Canine Helpers for the Handicapped**
5699 Ridge Road
Lockport, NY 14094
                          716-433-4035
                          FAX: 716-439-0822
                          e-mail: chhdogs@aol.com
                          www.caninehelpers.netfirms.com

*Beverly Underwood, Executive Director/Founder*

A nonprofit organization devoted to training dogs to assist people with disabilities to lead more independent, secure lives.
*1983*

**851   Center Academy**
6710 86th Avenue
Pinellas Park, FL 33782
                          727-541-5716
                          FAX: 727-544-8186
                          e-mail: infopp@centerccademy.com
                          www.centeracademy.com

*Mack Hicks, Founder*
*Eric V Larson, PhD, President/COO*
*Patricia Lambert, Principal*

Provides day programs for students grades 4-12 who have learning disabilities or who need motivation.

**852   Center for Assistive Technology**
University at Buffalo
322 Stockton Kimball Tower
Buffalo, NY 14214
                          716-829-3141
                          800-628-2281
                          FAX: 716-829-3217
                          TTY: 716-829-3141
                          e-mail: cat-webmaster@buffalo.edu
                          www.cat.buffalo.edu

*Joseph P Lane, Director*
*Michael Noe, MD*

The Center for Assistive Technology (CAT) was established within the School of Health Related Professions in 1988. CAT conducts research, education and service programs in assistive technology for persons with disabilities and the elderly, in four related areas: Research, development and communications, education programs, client assessment and training services and dissemination.

**853 Center for Assistive Technology and Environmental Access**
490 Tenth Street NW
Atlanta, GA 30332
404-894-4960
FAX: 404-894-9320
e-mail: catea@coa.gatech.edu
www.catea.org

*Robert G Bingham-Roy, Associate Director*
*Deborah Bursa, Project Director II*
*Elizabeth Bryant, Project Director II*

CATEA supports individuals with disabilities of any age within the State of Georgia and beyond through expert services, research, design and technological development, information dissemination, and educational programs.

**854 Center for Disability Resources**
University of South Carolina
8301 Farrow Road
Columbia, SC 29208
803-935-5231
FAX: 803-935-5059
www.uscm.med.sc.edu/cdrhome

*Dr Richard Ferrante, Executive Director*
*Donald Wuori, MD*

Information on early intervention and the elderly.

**855 Center for Mind/Body Studies**
5225 Connecticut Avenue NW
Washington, DC 20015
202-966-7338
FAX: 202-966-2589
e-mail: center@cmbm.org
www.cmbm.org

*Troy Centazzo, Associate Director*
*Michelle Clermont, Administrative Director*
*Jim Gordon, Manager*

The Center for Mind-Body Medicine is a non-profit educational organization dedicated to reviving the spirit and transforming the practice of medicine. The Center is working to create a more effective, comprehensive and compassionate model of healthcare and education. The Center's model combines the precision of modern science with the best of the world's healing traditions. This model is based on self-awareness and relies on "self-care" as its core.

**856 Center for Universal Design**
NC State University
Campus
Box 8613
Raleigh, NC 27695
919-515-5091
800-647-6777
FAX: 919-515-8951
e-mail: cud@ncsu.edu
www.design.ncsu.edu/cud

*Nilda Cosco, Director*
*H Trussell, Manager*
*Dick Duncan, Director Training*

A federally funded resource center that works toward improving housing for people with disabilities. Provides technical assistance, training and publications on accessible housing and universal design.

**857 Change**
1413 Park Road NW
Washington, DC 20010
202-387-3725
FAX: 202-387-3729

*Gracie Rolling, Executive Director*

Offers counseling/assessment, emergency food and clothing referrals, rental assistance and job assistance to disabled persons in the District of Columbia area.

**858 Children's Alliance**
420 Capitol Avenue
Frankfort, KY 40601
502-875-3399
FAX: 502-223-4200
www.childrensallianceky.org

*Bart Baldwin, President*

An association of individuals and human services organizations committed to being a voice for at-risk children and families. Interacts with the legislative and executive branches of government and assists members in developing services that most effectively meet the needs of at-risk children and families.

**859 Children's National Medical Center**
111 Michigan Avenue NW
Washington, DC 20010
202-884-5000
FAX: 202-884-4492
e-mail: cnmc.org
www.cnmc.org

*Donald Brown, President*
*Edwin Zechman Jr, Chief Executive Officer*

Our mission is to be preeminent in providing health care services that enhance the health and well-being of children regionally, nationally and internationally. Through leadership and innovation, Children's will create solutions to pediatric health care problems. To meet the unique health care needs of children, adolescents and their families, Children's will excel in Care, Advocacy, Research and Education.

**860 Childrens Alliance**
420 Capitol Avenue
Frankfort, KY 40601
502-875-3399
FAX: 502-223-4200
e-mail: melissa.lawson@childrensallianceky.org
www.childrensallianceky.org

*Bart Baldwin, President*
*Melissa Lawson, Director Member Services*
*Nannette Lenington, Business Manager*

The Children's Alliance is a not-for-profit association of children and family service agencies throughout Kentucky, who serve abused, neglected and abandoned children and their families.

**861 College of Maharishi Vedic Medicine Health Center**
1000 N 4th Street
Fairfield, IA 52557
641-472-1148
800-369-6480
FAX: 641-472-1179
e-mail: admissions@mum.edu
www.mum.edu

*Maharishi Mahesh Yogi, Founder*

Provides referrals consultations to the Fairfield community and to visitors from around the world at its clinic on the Maharishi University of Management campus. Staff physicians are medical doctors with years of experience practicing Maharishi Vedic Medicine.

**862 Department of Physical Medicine & Rehabilitation at Sinai Hospital**
2401 W Belvedere Avenue
Baltimore, MD 21215
410-601-5584
FAX: 410-601-9692
lifebridgehealth.org

*Scott E Brown MD, Chief Physical Med/Rehab Dept*
*Gerald Felsenthal MD*

**863 Disabled Children's Relief Fund**
PO Box 89
Freeport, NY 11520
516-377-1605
FAX: 516-377-3978
e-mail: dc1605@aol.com
www.dcrf.com

*Jerome H Blue PhD, President*

National not-for-profit organization that provides modest grants for disabled children with preference given to those with no health insurance. Grants are provided for assistive devices, equipment and rehabilitative services.

**864 Disabled and Alone/Life Services for the Handicapped**
352 Park Avenue S
11th Floor
New York, NY 10010
212-532-6740
800-995-0066
FAX: 212-532-3588
e-mail: info@disabledandalone.org
www.disabledandalone.org

*Leslie Park, Chairman*
*Roslyn Brilliant, MBA, Executive Director*
*Peter Van Nuys, VP*

A national nonprofit humanitarian organization whose primary concern is the well-being of handicapped persons, particularly when their families can no longer care for them. Disabled and Alone 1) Helps families do sensible planning for and with their disabled children; 2) Provides advocacy and oversight when the parents cannot do so; 3) Advises families, attorneys and financial planners about life planning for a family member with a disability.

**865 Distance Education and Training Council**
1601 18th Street NW
Washington, DC 20009
202-234-5100
FAX: 202-332-1386
e-mail: detc@detc.org
www.detc.org

*Michael P Lambert, Executive Director*

Advocates quality distance education in America. Serves as a clearinghouse of information about the field and sponsors a nationally recognized accrediting agency for distance education.

**866 Division for Physical and Health Disabilities**
1110 N Glebe Road
Suite 300
Arlington, VA 22201
888-232-7733
FAX: 703-624-9494
www.cec.sped.org

*Kathy Segers, President*
*Pamela DeLoach, VP*

Advocates for quality education for individuals with physical disabilities, multiple disabilities, and special health care needs served in schools, hospitals, or home settings. DPHD's members include classroom teachers, administrators, related service personnel, hospital/homebound teachers, and parents.

**867 Dynamic Learning Center**
PO Box 112
Ben Lomond, CA 95005
831-336-3457
FAX: 831-336-5854

**868 ERIC Clearinghouse on Disabilities and Special Education**
Council for Exceptional Children
1110 N Glebe Road
Suite 300
Arlington, VA 22201
888-232-7733
FAX: 703-264-9494
TTY:866-915-5000
www.ericec.org

*Drew Allbritten MD, Executive Director*

ERIC Clearinghouse on Disabilities and Gifted Education gathers and disseminates educational information on all disabilities and on giftedness across all age levels. As part of the ERIC network, the clearinghouse acquires, selects, abstracts, and indexes the professional literature on disabilities and giftedness for the ERIC database. The Clearinghouse also develops publications, including digests, research syntheses, and bibliographies

**869 Easter Seals**
230 W Monroe Street
Suite 1800
Chicago, IL 60606
312-726-6800
800-221-6827
FAX: 312-726-1494
TTY: 312-726-4258
www.easterseals.com

*James Williams Jr, Chief Executive Officer*

Easter Seals has been helping individuals with disabilities and special needs, and their families, live better lives for over 80 years. From child development centers to physical rehabilitation and job training for people with disabilities, Easter Seals offers a variety of services to help people with disabilities address life's challenges and achieve personal goals.

**870 Educational Accessibility Services**
Wayne State University
5221 Gullen Mall
Detroit, MI 48202
313-577-2116
FAX: 313-577-4898
TTY:313 577-3365
e-mail: eas@teadmin.sa.wayne.edu
www.eas.wayne.edu

*Denise Torres, Executive Director*

A powerful advocating force for students with disabilities at the university. Our purpose is to provide students with the resources they need to succeed and to support their participation in all University programs and activities with dignity and independence.

**871 Electro Medical**
18433 Amistad Street
Fountain Valley, CA 92708
714-964-6776
800-422-8726
FAX: 714-428-4599
www.accuwavesources.com

*Cherie Fisher, President*

**872 Environmental Health Center: Dallas**
8345 Walnut Hill Lane
Suite 220
Dallas, TX 75231
214-368-4132
FAX: 214-691-8432
e-mail: contact@ehcd.com
www.ehcd.com

*William J Rea, Director*
*David Hicks, Manager*

Clinic providing patient care in the areas of Immunotherapy, Nutrition, Physical Therapy, Chemical Depuration, Energy Balancing, Electromagnetic Sensitivity Testing, Psychological Support Services, Family Practice Medicine and Internal Medicine.

**873 Esalen Institute**
55000 Highway 1
Big Sur, CA 93920
831-667-3000
FAX: 831-667-2724
e-mail: info@esalen.org
www.esalen.org

*Michael Murphy, Chairman*
*Gordon Wheeler, Manager*

Founded in 1962 as an alternative education center devoted to the exploration of the world of unrealized human capacities that lies beyond the imagination. Blends East/West philosophies, experiential/didactic workshops, and a steady influx of philosophers, psychologists, artists, and religious thinkers.
*1962*

**874    Estate Planning for the Disabled**

3100 Arapahoe Avenue
Suite 112
Boulder, CO  80303
800-683-4607
www.ability.org.uk/estate_planning.html
Counsels and assists parents of children with special needs to develop viable estate plans, letters of intent, wills and special needs trusts. EPD will work with the appropriate professionals and agencies to help put together an effective comprehensive plan.

**875    Family Resource Center on Disabilities**

20 E Jackson Boulevard
Suite 300
Chicago, IL  60604
312-939-3513
800-952-4199
FAX: 312-939-7297
TTY: 312-939-3519
e-mail: that-user-name@frcd.org
www.frcd.org

*Gail Jones, President*
*Charlotte Jardins, Executive Director*

Not-for-profit advocacy organization dedicated to improving services for all children with disabilities by providing support and services to affected families, informing parents of their rights, and helping parents become advocates for their children. Offers family support services, training, seminars and information and referral services. Publishes monthly newsletter.

**876    Family Voices**

2340 Alamo Avenue SE
Suite 102
Albuquerque, NM  87106
505-872-4774
888-835-5669
888-835-5669
FAX: 505-872-4780
e-mail: kidshealth@familyvoices.org
www.familyvoices.org

*Jennifer Cernoch, Executive Director*
*Julie Beckett, Director of National Policy*

Not-for-profit voluntary organization dedicated to ensuring that children's health issues are addressed as public and private healthcare systems undero change in communities, states and the nation. National grassroots clearinghouse for information and education in ways to assure and improve health care for children with disabilities and chronic conditions. Provides materials including pamphlets, a newsletter and one-page papers on important topics.

**877    Favarh/Farmington Valley ARC**

PO Box 1099
Canton, CT  06019
860-693-6662
FAX: 860-693-8662
e-mail: favarh@favarh.org
www.favarh.org

*Lyn Fierri, President*
*Tom Thompson, Executive Director*

Provides a variety of programs and services to adults with developmental, physical or mental disabilities and their families throughout the Farmington Valley communities of Avon, Burlington and more. Favarh's programs are designed to enhance the personal, social, emotional, vocational and living capabilities of persons with disabilities.

**878    Federation for Children with Special Needs**

1135 Tremont Street
Suite 420
Roxbury Crossing, MA  02120
617-236-7210
800-331-0688
FAX: 617-572-2094
e-mail: fcsninfo@fcsn.org
www.fcsn.org

*Daniel Heffernan Esq, President Board of Directors*
*Jane Wolfson, Director of Development*
*Rich Robison, President*

Provides information, support and assistance to parents of children with disabilities, their professional partners and their communities.

**879    Focus Alternative Learning Center**

PO Box 452
Canton, CT  06019
860-693-8809
FAX: 860-693-0141
e-mail: info@focus-alternatice.org
www.focus-alternative.org

*Donna Swanson, Executive Director*
*Yvonne Gardner, Program Coordinator*

A private non profit, licensed clinical and learning center specialized in the treatment of creatively wired and socially challenged kids. We treat kids on the autism spectrum who suffer from high anxiety, experience processing difficulties and learning problems.

**880    Fragrance and Health**

Human Ecology Action League (Heal)
PO Box 509
Stockbridge, GA  30281
404-248-1898
FAX: 404-248-0162
e-mail: healnatnl@aol.com
www.ecolivingcenter.com

*Katherine P Collier, Membership Coordinator/Manager*

**881    Friends of Disabled Adults and Children**

4900 Lewis Road
Stone Mountain, GA  30083
770-491-9014
FAX: 770-491-0026
e-mail: chrisbrand@fodac.org
www.fodac.org

*Chris Brand, CEO and President*
*Ed Butchart, Founder*

Not-for-profit organization dedicated to providing necessary services and support to physically and mobility impaired people of all ages. Provides free mobility impairment, rehabilitative, and home healthcare equipment. Provides variety of brochures and pamphlets. Community reentering program.

**882    George Washington University Health Resource Center**

2121 K Street NW
Suite 220
Washington, DC  20037
202-741-2412
800-544-3284
FAX: 202-973-0908
e-mail: askheath@gwu.edu
www.heath.gwu.edu

*Dr Pamela Ekpone, Director*
*Zavolia Willis, Assistant Director*
*Dan Gardner, Publications Manager*

National clearinghouse for information about education after high school for people with disabilities. Also serves as an information exchange about educational support services, policies, procedures, adaptations and opportunities on American campuses, vocational-technical schools, adult education programs, independent living centers and other training entities after high school.

**883 Goodwill Industries International**
15810 Indianola Drive
Rockville, MD 20855
301-530-6500
800-741-0186
FAX: 301-530-1516
e-mail: Contactus@goodwill.org
www.goodwill.org

*George W Kessinger, President and CEO*
*Edward A Osborne, Chair, Board of Directors*

Strives to achieve the full participation in society of disabled persons and other individuals with special needs by expanding their opportunities and occupational capabilities through a network of 179 autonomous, nonprofit, community-based organizations providing services throughout the world in response to local needs.

**884 Great Lakes Association of Clinical Medicine**
70 W Huron Street
Chicago, IL 60610
312-266-7246

Members practice chelation therapy.

**885 Health Action**
243 Pebble Beach Drive
Goleta, CA 93117
805-685-4670
FAX: 805-685-4710
www.healthaction.net
Our mission is to foster innovation in health care that will increase health status, increase customer satisfaction, increase profitability, increase clinical efficacy and eliminate error, support provider efficiency and enhance clinical outcomes, and empower consumer self-managed care.

**886 Health Resource Center for Women with Disabilities**
Rehabilitation Institute Of Chicago
345 E Superior Street
Chicago, IL 60611
312-238-1000
800-354-7342
FAX: 312-238-1205
e-mail: webmaster@ric.org
www.rehabchicago.org

*Wayne M Lerner, President/CEO*

RIC has earned a worldwide reputation as being a leader in patient health care, advocacy, research and educating health professionals in physical medicine and rehabilitation. People from around the globe choose RIC because of our expertise in treating a range of conditions, from the most complex conditions including cerebral palsy, spinal cord injury, stroke and traumatic brain injury, to the more common, such as arthritis, chronic pain, and sports injuries.

**887 Homeopathic Educational Services**
2124 Kittredge Street
Berkeley, CA 94704
510-649-0294
800-359-9051
e-mail: mail@homeopathic.com
www.homeopathic.com

*Dana Ullman, Director and Owner*

Resource center for homeopathic products and services including books, tapes, research, medicines, medicine kits, software for the general public and the health professional and correspondence courses.

**888 Human Ecology Action League (HEAL)**
PO Box 509
Stockbridge, GA 30281
404-248-1898
FAX: 404-248-0162
e-mail: healnatnl@aol.com
members.aol.com

*Katherine P Collier, Membership Coordinator/Manager*

HEAL is a nonprofit education and information organization. It is primarily a member service organization. It is overseen by a volunteer Governing Board, and has its business office in Atlanta Georgia. HEAL is solely funded by memberships and by donations.

**889 IL Center: Cape Organization for Rights of the Disabled**
1019 Iyannough Road
Suite 4
Hyannis, MA 02601
508-775-8300
800-541-0282
FAX: 508-775-7022
TTY: 800-541-0282
e-mail: pburkley@cape.com
www.cordonline.org

*Pamela Burkley, Executive Director*

The Cape Organization for the Rights of the Disabled (CORD) has been aggresively working since 1984 to advance the independence, productivity, and integration of people with disabilities including deaf and hard of hearing people, into mainstream society.
*1984*

**890 Informed Birth and Parenting**
PO Box 3675
Ann Arbor, MI 48106
313-662-6857

www.thelaboroflove.com
Resources on pregnancy, childbirth, and parenting; refers midwives; certifies educators and assistants.

**891 Institute for Health and Disability**
University of Minnesota
420 Delaware Street SE
Minneapolis, MN 55455
612-624-1412
TTY:612-624-3939
e-mail: umnpeds@umn.edu
www.peds.umn.edu

*Marty Smith, Executive Director*
*Deborah Roman, Manager*

The mission of the Department of Pediatrics is to advance the state of knowledge in child health and disease; to educate medical students and physicians in training and practice; to educate other health professionals and the public in childhood disease prevention, treatment, research, and advocacy; and to provide standards for the highest quality of child health care.

**892 Institute for Music, Health and Education**
PO Box 4179
Boulder, CO 80306
303-443-8484

**893 Institute for Scientific Research**
PO Box 2720
Fairmont, WV 26555
304-368-9300
866-725-9300
FAX: 304-368-9313
e-mail: info@isr.us
www.isr.us

*James Estep, President*

Institute for Scientific Research, Inc. performs cutting-edge research across a variety of scientific and engineering disciplines. Our people participate in world-class projects from concept through development, in some of today's most fascinating scientific fields.

**894    Institute of Transpersonal Psychology**
1069 E Meadow Circle
Palo Alto, CA  94303                    650-493-4430
                              FAX: 650-493-6835
                         e-mail: itpinfo@itp.edu
                                    www.itp.edu

*John Axtell, Chief Communications Officer*
*Pat Luce, President*

The Institute of Transpersonal Psychology is a private, non-sec-
tarian graduate school accredited by the Western Association of
Schools and Colleges. For over twenty-five years the Institute
has remained a leader at the forefront of psychological research
and education, probing the mind, body, spirit connection. The
Institute's challenging and transformative educational paradigm has attracted students from all over the world.

**895    InterNatural**
PO Box 489
Twin Lakes, WI  53181              262-889-8581
                                   800-643-4221
                              FAX: 800-905-6887
       e-mail: webmaster_internat@lotuspress.com
                              www.internatural.com
InterNatural is a retailer of natural health, beauty aid, herbal and
other alternative health products. We provide products with a
"purpose" to aid people in both understanding and implementing
true choices in their life. The products we carry can be generally
classified as "products that promote consciousness". We present
choices in terms of natural ingredients, cruelty free products and
ecologically sound choices.

**896    International Academy of Oral Medicine and Toxicol-
ogy**
8297 Champions Gate Boulevard
# 193
Champions Gate, FL 33896           863-420-6373
                              FAX: 863-420-6394
                         e-mail: info@iaomt.org
                                    www.iaomt.org

*Kim Smith, Executive Director*

Nonprofit organization dedicated to funding solid peer-reviewed scientific research in the area of toxic substances used in
dentistry as well as providing continuing education and carefully reviewed procedures, protocols, and methodologies to reduce the risk for patients and professionals.

**897    International Association of Professional Natural
Hygientists**
2000 S Ocean Drive
Hallandale Beach, FL  33009         954-454-2220

*Nick Jnega, Owner*

Members are physicians who specialize in therapeutic fasting.

**898    International Chiropractors Association**
1110 N Glebe Road
Suite 1000
Arlington, VA  22201               703-528-5000
                                   800-423-4690
                              FAX: 703-528-5023
                    e-mail: chiro@chiropractic.org
                              www.chiropractic.org

*C J Mertz, President*
*Ronald Hendrickson, Executive Director*

Established in 1926 to empower humanity in the expression of
maximum health, wellness and human potential through the universal chiropractic expression and utilization. Strives to advance chiropractics throughout the world as a distinct health
care profession predicated upon its unique philosophy, science
and art.

*1926*

**899    International Clinic of Biological Regeneration**
PO Box 509
Florissant, MO  63032              314-921-3997
                                   800-826-5366
                              FAX: 314-921-8485
                         e-mail: info@icbr.com
                                    www.icbr.com

*C Tom Smith, President*
International cell therapy center since 1981.
*1981*

**900    International College of Applied Kinesiology**
6405 Metcalf Avenue
Suite 503
Shawnee Mission, KS  66202         913-384-5336
                              FAX: 913-384-5112
                         e-mail: info@icak.com
                                    www.icak.com

*Eric Pierotti, President*
*Michael D Allan, VP*
*Terry Underwood, Executive Director*
Referral service for applied kinesiologists.

**901    International Institute of Reflexology**
PO Box 12462
St Petersburg, FL  33733           727-343-4811
                              FAX: 727-381-2807
                    e-mail: iir@tampabay.rr.com
                              www.reflexology-usa.net

*Nancy Byers, Manager*
Information, seminars, publications and referrals. Also holds
Reflexology Training workshops throughout the United States.

**902    International Medical and Dental Hypnotherapy Asso-
ciation**
4110 Edgeland Avenue
Suite 800
Royal Oak, MI  48073               248-549-5594
                                   800-257-5467
                              www\.imdha.com

**903    International Ozone Association**
PO Box 28873
Scottsdale, AZ  85255              480-529-3787
                              FAX: 480-361-7725
                    e-mail: RonCaron@io3a.org
                              www.int-ozone-assoc.org
The IOA is a not-for-profit educational association which performs its information-sharing functions through sponsorship of
international symposia, seminars, publications, and the development of personal relationships among ozone specialists
throughout the world.

**904    International Women's Health Coalition**
333 7th Avenue
6th Floor
New York, NY  10001                212-979-8500
                              FAX: 212-979-9009
                         e-mail: info@iwhc.org
                                    www.iwhc.org

*Adrienne Germain, President*
*Patricia Moser, Executive VP*

Information and pamphlets on sexually transmitted diseases and
other health concerns.

**905    Invincible Athletics**
PO Box 541
Lancaster, MA  01523               508-368-1818

Teaches how to incorporate Ayurvedic training principles into
athletic conditioning.

**906    Kessler Institute for Rehabilitation**
1199 Pleasant Valley Way
West Orange, NJ 07052
973-731-3600
800-248-3221
FAX: 973-243-6819
www.kessler-rehab.com

*Robert Brehm, President*
*Bonnie Evans, Manager*

Kessler Institute for Rehabilitation is world renowned for treating individuals with physical disabilities, resulting from spinal cord and brain injuries, stroke and amputee, sports and work-related, and other illnesses and injuries. Kessler offers comprehensive programs designed to meet each person's individual needs.

**907    Mainstream**
300 S Rodney Parham Road
Suite 5
Little Rock, AR 72205
501-280-0012
FAX: 501-280-9267
TTY:501-280-9262
e-mail: mainstreamlr@earthlink.net
www.mainstreamilrc.com

*Rita Byers, Executive Director*

Non-profit organization that works with employers and service providers around the country to increase employment opportunities for persons with disabilities.

**908    Matheny School and Hospital**
PO Box 339
Peapack, NJ 07977
908-234-0011
FAX: 908-719-2137
e-mail: info@matheny.org
www.matheny.org

*Steven Proctor, President*

A residential and outpatient facility for children and adults with physical disabilities such as Cerebral Palsy, Spina Bifida, Muscular Dystrophy and Lesch-Nyhan disease. Matheny offers medical and dental care, therapies, augmentative communication, and other allied health services as well as special education, respite care and adult medical day care.

**909    MedEscort International**
PO Box 8766
Allentown, PA 18105
610-791-3111
800-255-7182
FAX: 610-791-9189
e-mail: medescort@fast.net
www.medescort.com

*David M Stein, Medical Director*
*Sherrye L Sefcik, Senior Flight Nurse*
*Craig Poliner, President*

MedEscort International was founded over a decade ago with these basic principles and philosophies as its foundation. MedEscort has served the health care community, throughout the world, and has strived to perfect the techniques of moving patients from one place to another. Our medical staff includes registered nurses, respiratory therapists, paramedics, and physicians. MedEscort has developed comprehensive, individual aeromedical services to meet each patient's needs with a personal touch.

**910    Metametrix Clinical Laboratory**
4855 Peachtree Industrial Boulevard
Suite 201
Norcross, GA 30092
770-446-5483
800-221-4640
FAX: 770-441-2237
e-mail: inquiries@metametrix.com
www.metametrix.com/

*J Alexander Bralley, CEO*

Metametrix Clinical Laboratory has been a pioneer and leader in the development of nutritional, metabolic, and toxicant analyses since 1984. Metametrix is committed to helping health care professionals identify nutritional influences on health and disease, and is recognized internationally for its laboratory procedures in nutritional and biochemical testing.

**911    Mind-Body Clinic**
824 Boylston Street
Chestnut Hill, MA 02467
617-991-0102
FAX: 617-991-0112
e-mail: mbmi@bidmc.harvard.edu

*Francis Meaney, Chairman*
*Herbert Benson, Chairman*
*Lisa Teague, Manager*

**912    Mind/Body Health Services**
393 Dixon Road
Boulder, CO 80302
303-440-8460
FAX: 303-440-7580

*Joan Borysenko, President*

**913    Mobility International USA**
PO Box 10767
Eugene, OR 97440
541-343-1284
FAX: 541-343-6812
e-mail: info@miusa.org
www.miusa.org

*Susan Sygall, Executive Director*
*Cerise Roth-Vinson, Director of Administration*
*Cindy Lewis, Director Programs*

A US based national nonprofit organization dedicated to empowering people with disabilities around the world through leadership development, training and international exchange to ensure inclusion of people with disabilities in international exchange and development programs. The National Clearinghouse on Disability & Exchange, a joint project managed by MIUSA provides free information and referrals.

**914    NLP Comprehensive**
19336 Goddard Ranch Court
Unit 120
Morrison, CO 80465
303-987-2224
800-233-1657
FAX: 303-987-2228
e-mail: learn@nlpco.com
www.nlpco.com

*Tom Dotz, Manager*

NLP, or Neuro-Linguistic Programming, is the science of how the brain codes learning and experience. This coding affects all communication and behavior. NLP Comprehensive helps individuals and businesses make the fullest use of their talents and resources. We teach the thought processes and communication strategies of exceptional performers through workshops, books, and tapes.

**915    National Association for Holistic Aromatherapy**
3327 W Indian Trail Road
Pmb 144
Spokane, WA 99208
509-325-3419
FAX: 509-325-3479
e-mail: info@naha.org
www.naha.org

*Kelly Holland Azzaro, VP*
*Michele Miller, President*

The NAHA is an educational, nonprofit organization dedicated to enhancing public awareness of the benefits of true aromatherapy. It offers aromatherapy courses and acts as a referral service.

**916 National Association of Developmental Disabilities Councils**
225 Reinekers Lane
Suite 650b
Alexandria, VA 22314 703-739-4400
FAX: 703-739-6030
e-mail: info@nacdd.org
www.nacdd.org

*Karen Flippo, CEO*
*Anne Rohall, Director*

The National Association of Councils on Developmental Disabilities (NACDD) is a national, member-driven organization consisting of 55 State and Territorial Councils. NACDD places high value on meaningful participation and contribution by Council members and staff of all Member Councils, and we advocate and continually work towards positive system change on behalf of individuals with developmental disabilities and their families.

**917 National Association of Protection and Advocacy Systems**
900 2nd Street NE
Suite 211
Washington, DC 20002 202-408-8362
FAX: 202-408-9520
e-mail: info@napas.org
www.napas.org

*Ross Capon, Executive Director*

Voluntary national membership association of protection and advocacy systems and client assistance programs. Promoting and strengthening the role and performance of its members in providing quality legally based advocacy services.

**918 National Association of Retired Volunteer Program Directors**
703 Main Street
Paterson, NJ 07503 973-754-2675

*Maureen Mulligan, President*

Seeks to provide national visibility and advocacy to facilitate communications among membership and to act as representative for those served by RSVP before national governmental bodies. Bestows grants and awards, compiles statistics and conducts workshops.

**919 National Association of the Physically Handicapped**
754 Staeger Street
Akron, OH 44306 330-724-1994
800-743-5008
e-mail: trumanjm@aol.com
www.naph.net

*Jim Truman, National President*

The NAPH advances the social, economic, and physical welfare of the physically handicapped in the United States. NAPH proposes and supports legislation to provide more educational and rehabilitation opportunities, tax relief, employment, and other benefits for the physically handicapped. Data and information relating to the physically handicapped are collected and studied and reported to members. NAPH supports efforts to make all public buildings accessible to the physically handicapped.
*1958*

**920 National Center for Education in Maternal and Child Health**
Georgetown University
PO Box 571272
Washington, DC 20057 202-687-0100
FAX: 202-784-9777
e-mail: info@ncemch.org
www.ncemch.org

*Rochelle Mayer, Research Professor and Director*

Provides information on children with special health needs, child health and development, adolescent health, nutrition, violence and injury prevention and other issues of maternal and child health for health professionals and the public.

**921 National Clearinghouse on Women and Girls with Disabilities**
Educational Equity Concepts
100 5th Avenue
Floor 8
New York, NY 10011 212-243-1110
FAX: 212-627-0407
TTY:212-243-1110
e-mail: information@edequity.org
www.edequity.org

*Holly Delany Cole, President*
*Edward Greene, VP*
*Cindy Weinbaum, Vice President*

Provides information, resources and referrals. Publishes Bridging the Gap, a national directory which lists organizations that serve women and girls with disabilities and gives resource information. Also publishes curriculum on children with disabilities and programs in science for children with disabilties.

**922 National College of Naturopathic Medicine**
049 SW Porter Street
Portland, OR 97201 503-552-1555
FAX: 503-499-0022
www.ncnm.edu

*William Keppler, President*
*Pauline Baumannn, Chair of the Board*

NCNM offers two graduate professional degrees in accredited and recognized programs that prepare you for licensed practice in many states and provinces: Doctor of Naturopathic Medicine, a four-year program of clinical sciences and holistic methods of healing and disease prevention, instilled with the ancient principle of the healing power of nature. Master of Science in Oriental Medicine, a four-year program that delves deeply into thousands of years of classical Chinese methods of diagnostics.

**923 National Council for Community Behavioral Healthcare**
12300 Twinbrook Parkway
Suite 320
Rockville, MD 20852 301-984-6200
FAX: 301-881-7159
e-mail: membership@nccbh.org
www.nccbh.org

*Linda Rosenberg, President/CEO*
*Jeannie Campbell, Executive VP*

The National Council for Community Behavioral Healthcare is the oldest and largest trade association respresenting the nation's providers of mental health, substance abuse and developmental disability services. Members include community mental health centers, hospitals, state associations of providers, and local behavioral health authorities. Individual practicioners, consultants, and senior behavioral health administrators are members of the National Council's individual membership section.

**924 National Council on Disability**
1331 F Street NW
Suite 850
Washington, DC 20004 202-272-2004
FAX: 202-272-2022
TTY:202-272-2074
e-mail: info@ncd.gov
www.ncd.gov

*Sandra S Parrino, Chairperson*
*Ethel Briggs, Executive Director*

Federal agency led by 15 members appointed by the President of the United States and confirmed by the United States Senate. The overall purpose of the National Council is to promote policies, programs, practices and procedures that guarantee equal opportunities to persons with disabilities.

**925  National Council on Independent Living**
1916 Wilson Boulevard
Suite 209
Arlington, VA  22201
703-525-3406
877-525-3400
FAX: 703-525-3409
TTY: 703-525-4153
e-mail: ncil@ncil.org
www.ncil.org

*John Lancaster, Executive Director*

Advances the independent living philosophy and advocates for the human rights of and services for people with disabilities to further their full integration and participation in society. The National Council on Independent Living (NCIL) is the oldest cross disability, grassroots organization run by and for people with disabilities.

**926  National Dissemination Center for Children and Youth with Disabilities (NICHCY)**
PO Box 1492
Washington, DC  20013
202-884-8200
800-695-0285
FAX: 202-884-8441
e-mail: nichcy@aed.org
www.nichcy.org

*Suzanne Ripley, Director*

Provides free information to assist parents, educators, caregivers, advocates and others in helping children and youth with disabilities become participating members of the community. In addition to a wealth of printed materials, the Center disseminates materials on cassette, computer disc and in Spanish. The Center can also provide personal responses to specific questions.

**927  National Early Childhood Technical Assistance Center**
8040 Unc-Ch
Chapel Hill, NC  27599
919-962-2001
FAX: 919-966-7463
TTY:919-843-3269
e-mail: nectac@unc.edu
www.nectac.org

*Pascal Trohanis, Director*
*Lynne Kahn, Associate Director*
*Shelley deFosset, Associate Director*

Assists states and other designated governing jurisdictions as they develop multidisciplinary, coordinated and comprehensive services for children with special needs.

**928  National Easter Seal Society**
230 W Monroe Street
Floor 18
Chicago, IL  60606
312-726-6800
FAX: 312-726-1494
www.easterseal.com

*Janet D Jamieson, Communications Manager*
*James Williams Jr, Chief Executive Officer*

The mission of the Society is to help people with disabilities achieve independence. Easter Seals provides quality rehabilitation services, technological assistance and disability prevention, advocacy and public education programs. A nationwide network of affiliate societies serving each of the 50 United States, the District of Columbia and Puerto Rico, all of which work together to serve more than 1 million people each year. There are 160 chapters offering more than 400 programs nationwide.

**929  National Endowment for the Arts: Office for AccessAbility**
1100 Pennsylvania Avenue NW
Washington, DC  20506
202-682-5485

*Dana Gioia, Chairman*
*Joy Kiser, Manager*

Offers technical assistance on making programs accessible to older adults and individuals with various disabilities.

**930  National Guild of Hypnotists**
PO Box 308
Merrimack, NH  03054
603-429-9438
FAX: 603-424-8066
e-mail: ngh@ngh.net
www.ngh.net

*Dwight Damon, President*

The National Guild of Hypnotists, Inc. is a not-for-profit, educational corporation in the State of New Hampshire. Founded in Boston, Massachusetts in 1951, the Guild is a professional organization comprised of dedicated individuals committed to advancing the field of hypnotism. We provide an open forum for the free exchange of ideas concerning hypnotism. The Guild is a resource for members and a vehicle for legal and legislative action.
*1951*

**931  National Information Center for Children**
PO Box 1492
Washington, DC  20013
202-884-8200

*Susan Ripley, Manager*

**932  National Information Clearinghouse**
Association for the Care of Childrens Health
7910 Woodmont Avenue
Suite 300
Bethesda, MD  20814
301-654-6549
800-922-9224
FAX: 301-986-4553

A national information and referral system providing assistance to meet the information needs of caregivers and to protect the rights of infants with disabilities and life-threatening conditions.

**933  National Institute on Disability and Rehabilitation Research**
400 Maryland Avenue SW
Washington, DC  20202
202-401-0689
800-872-5327
FAX: 202-401-0689
TTY: 800-437-0833
e-mail: customerservice@inet.ed.gov
www.ed.gov

*Lacy B Ward Jr, VP*
*Daniel Holt, Director*

Conducts comprehensive and coordinated programs of extramural research and related activities to maximize the full inclusion, social integration, employment and independent living of disabled individuals of all ages. Provides funding for programs to assist ADA compliance, including Regional Disability and Business Technical Assistance Centers, Materials Development Projects, and Peer Training Projects.

**934  National Maternal and Child Health Bureau**
5600 Fishers Lane
Rockville, MD  20857
301-443-2170
800-275-4772
FAX: 301-443-1797
e-mail: ctibbs@hrsa.gov
www.ask.hrsa.gov

*Michael A Mucci, Director*
*Peter C Van Dyck MD, Associate Administrator*

Offers information, books and pamphlets to professionals, parents and children facing health issues or disabilities.

**935 National Mental Health Association**

2001 N Beauregard Street
12th Floor
Alexandria, VA 22311

703-684-7722
800-969-6642
FAX: 703-684-5968
TTY: 800-433-5959
e-mail: infoctr@nmha.org
www.nmha.org

*Michael Faenza, President and CEO*

Nonprofit organization addressing all issues related to mental health and mental illness. With more than 340 affiliates nationwide, NMHA works to improve the mental health of all Americans, especially the 54 million individuals with mental disorders, through advocacy, education, research and service.
*1909*

**936 National Organization on Disability**

910 16th Street NW
Suite 600
Washington, DC 20006

202-293-5960
FAX: 202-293-7999
TTY:202-293-5968
e-mail: ability@nod.org
www.nod.org

*Michael R Deland, President/Chairman*
*Christopher Reeve, Vice Chairman*

The National Organization on Disability promotes the full and equal participation of men, women and children with disabilities in all aspects of American life. Founded in 1982, NOD is the leading national disability organization concerned with all disabilites, all age groups and all disability issues.
*1982*

**937 National Parent Network on Disabilities**

1130 17th Street NW
Suite 400
Washington, DC 20036

202-463-2299

e-mail: npnd@cs.net
Network of parents to promote mutual support and advocacy for children, youth, and adults with disabilities.

**938 National Rehabilitation Association (NRA)**

633 South Washington Street
Alexandria, VA 22314

703-836-0850
FAX: 703-836-0848
TTY:703-836-0849
e-mail: info@nationalrehab.org
www.nationalrehab.org

*Linda Winslow, Executive Director*

Dedicated to advocating, supporting, and enhancing the lives of individuals with disabilities and their families. disseminates up-to-date information, conducts educational seminars, and provides opportunities through knowledge and diversity for professionals in the field of rehabilitation. Produces educational materials and sponsors an annual training conference with exhibits displaying the latest in rehabilitation technologies, awards, and provides access to a nationwide employment network.

**939 National Rehabilitation Information Center (NARIC)**

4200 Forbes Boulevard
Suite 202
Lanham, MD 20706

301-459-5900
FAX: 301-459-4263
e-mail: naricinfo@heitechservices.com
www.naric.com

*Mark X Odum, Director*

For 20 years, the staff of the NARIC has collected and disseminated the results of federally funded research projects. NARIC's literature collection, which also includes commercially published books, journal articles and audiovisuals, averages around 200 new documents per month. Funded by the National Institute on Disability and Rehabilitation Research to serve anyone, professional or lay person, who is interested in disability and rehabilitation.

**940 National Respite Locator Service**

800 Eastowne Drive
Suite 105
Chapel Hill, NC 27514

919-490-5577
FAX: 919-490-4905
e-mail: awilcow@chtop.org
www.respitelocator.org

*Angela Wilcox, Director*
*Michael Mathers, Executive Director*

Dedicated to assisting parents, caregivers and professionals find temporary relief services in their state and local area. Provides appropriate referrals for further assistance and has a leaflet describing the organization.

**941 National Vaccine Information Center**

204 Mill Street
56B1
Vienna, VA 22180

703-938-0342
FAX: 703-938-5768
www.nvic.org

*Barbara Fisher, President*
*Kathryn Williams, Vice President*

A national nonprofit educational organization dedicated to preventing, through public education, vaccine injuries and deaths. NVIC represents vaccine consumers and health care providers, including parents whose children suffered illness or died following vaccination. NVIC supports the right of vaccine consumers to have access to the safest and most effective vaccine as well as the right to make informed, independent vaccination decisions.

**942 National Women's Health Network**

514 10th Street NW
Suite 400
Washington, DC 20004

202-347-1140
FAX: 202-347-1168
e-mail: nwhn@nwhn.org
www.womenshealthnetwork.org

*Cynthia Pearson, Executive Director*
*Kristen Suthers, Program Coordinator*

The National Women's Health Network improves the health of all women by developing and promoting a critical analysis of health issues in order to affect policy and support consumer decision-making. The Network aspires to a health care system that is guided by social justice and reflects the needs of diverse women.

**943 Native American Protection and Advocacy**

3535 E 30th Street
Suite 201
Farmington, NM 87402

505-566-5880
800-862-7271
FAX: 505-566-5889
www.nativelegalnet.org

*Therese Yanan, Executive Director*

The Native American Protection & Advocacy which helps protect, promote, and expand the legal and human rights of Native Americans with disabilities. There are several goals for this organization, including quality legal representation for individuals with disabilities in various areas such as abuse and neglect, special education, civil rights and discrimination and employment.

**944    North America Riding for the Handicapped Association**

PO Box 33150
Denver, CO  80233                            303-452-1212
                                             800-369-7433
                                        FAX: 303-252-4610
                                   e-mail: narha@narha.org
                                             www.narha.org

*Sheila Kemperdietrich, Chief Executive Officer*
*Jean Kavanaugh, Executive Assistant*

National nonprofit equestrian organization dedicated to serving individuals with disability by giving disabled individuals the opportunity to ride horses. Establishes safety standards, provides continuing education and offers networking opportunities for both its individuals and center members. Produces educational materials including fact sheets, brochures, booklets, audio-visual tapes, a directory and NARHA's magazine Strides.

**945    Nurse Healers: Professional Associates International**

PO Box 158
Warnerville, NY  12187                       518-325-1185
                                             877-326-4774
                                        FAX: 509-693-3537
                        e-mail: nh-pai@therapeutic-touch.org
                                   www.therapeutic-touch.org

*Dolores Krieger, Founder*

Cooperative among health professionals interested in healing. Sets the standards for the practice and teaching of Therapeutic Touch. Voluntary, not-for-profit organization.

**946    Pacific Institute of Aromatherapy**

PO Box 6723
San Rafael, CA  94903                        415-479-9120
                                        FAX: 415-479-0614
                                 e-mail: Monika@osapia.com
                        www.pacificinstituteofaromatherapy.com

*Kurt Schnaubelt, Owner*

Offers courses in the practice of aromatherapy.

**947    Parent Professional Advocacy League**

59 Temple Place
Suite 664
Boston, MA  02111                            617-542-7860
                                             866-815-8122
                                        FAX: 617-542-7832
                                     e-mail: info@ppal.net
                                             www.ppal.net

*Donna Welles, Executive Director*
*Lisa Lambert, Assistant Director*
*Rina Cavallini, Director*

Promotes a strong voice for families of children and adolescents with mental health needs. Advocates for supports, treatments and policies that enable families to live in their communities in an environment of stability and respect.

**948    Parent to Parent**

3805 Presidential Parkway
Suite 207
Atlanta, GA  30340                           770-451-5484
                                             800-229-2038
                                        FAX: 770-458-4091
                         e-mail: info@parenttoparentofga.org
                                   www.parenttoparentga.org

*Esther Sherberger, Director*
*Debra Tucker, Executive Director*

Dedicated to strengthening, supporting, and empowering families by establishing one to one parent to parent contacts. Enhances the ability of parents to access services and resources for children with special needs by providing information, resources, and referrals to appropriate services; supports and empowers families to participate in parent programs and disability issues. Educational materials consist of a quarterly newsletter and a fact sheet containing managed care information.

**949    Parents Helping Parents (PHP)**

3041 Olcott Street
Santa Clara, CA  95054                       408-727-5775
                                        FAX: 408-727-0182
                                      e-mail: info@php.com
                                             www.php.com

*Mary Ellen Peterson, CEO*
*Joanna Jagger, Board Chair*

Dedicated to assisting children with any type of special need: mental, physical, emotional, or learning disability. Mission is to help children with special needs receive love, hope, respect, and services needed to achieve their full potential by strengthening their families and the professionals who serve them. Developed and implemented numerous programs; produce a variety of educational and support materials, including information packets, brochures, database and a quarterly newletter.

**950    Parents for Residential Reform**

Federation For Children With Special Needs
1135 Tremont Street
Suite 420
Roxbury Crossing, MA  02120                  617-236-7210
                                             800-672-7084
                                        FAX: 617-572-2094
                                      e-mail: pfrr@fcsn.org
                                             www.pfrr.org

*Andrea Watson, Founder and Project Coordinator*
*Rich Robison, President*

Parents of children with special needs, whose children require intensive residential education settings, face a myriad of unique circumstances in their efforts to provide ongoing support to their children. PFRR provides information on placement, restraint medication, IEP, standardized testing, transition, parent/peer connections, workshops, trainings and the maze of state and federal agencies. We educate on the rights of parents, and their young people who are receiving services.

**951    People First International**

PO Box 12642
Salem, OR  97309                             503-362-0336
                                        FAX: 503-585-4718
                                e-mail: people1@people1.org
                                             www.people1.org

*Steven Kramer, President*
*Ruth Morris, VP*
*Rodney Carver, VP*

Self-advocacy organization of developmentally disabled people who have joined together to learn how to speak for themselves.

**952    People-to-People Committee for the Handicapped**

PO Box 18131
Washington, DC  20036                        301-493-5883
                                        FAX: 301-493-0510
                               e-mail: ngvb096@prodigy.com

*David Brigham, Chairman*

Individuals concerned about that circumstances of handicapped people throughout the world. Disseminates information, acts as a consultant in promoting exchange activities, coordinates special assistance in developing countries and more.

**953    People-to-People Committee on Disability**

501 E Armour Boulevard
Kansas City, MO  64109                       816-531-4701
                                        FAX: 816-561-7502
                                    e-mail: marcb@ptpi.org
                        www.ptpi.org/programs/disability.jsp

*Mary Eisenhower, President/CEO*
*Marc L Bright, Exec VP/Program Director*

Individuals concerned about the circumstances of handicapped people throughout the world. Disseminates information, acts as a consultant in promoting exchange activities, coordinates special assistance projects in developing countries and more.

**954 People-to-People International: Committee for the Handicapped**
501 E Armour Boulevard
Kansas City, MO 64109
816-531-7231
800-676-7874
FAX: 816-561-7502
e-mail: ptpi@ptpi.org
www.ptpi.org

*Marc L Bright, Deputy CEO/Executive VP*
*Mary Eisenhower, Chief Executive Officer*
*Rosanne Rosen, Senior VP of Operations*

Goals of this committee include: betterment of the handicapped through international unity; educating those with and without handicaps through technical assistance; opening access doors through sensory aids, prosthetic devices and travel tips; and co-ordination of major international cultural exchanges.

**955 Polarity Wellness Center**
10 Leonard Street
Suite A
New York, NY 10013
212-334-8392
FAX: 212-925-5675
www.acsu.buffalo.edu
Information, publications and referral directories.

**956 Portland Naturopathic Clinic: NCNM National Health Centers Eastside Clinic**
National College of Naturopathic Medicine
049 SW Porter Street
Portland, OR 97201
503-552-1555
FAX: 503-827-8460
www.ncnm.edu

*William J Keppler, President*

Outpatient clinic in naturopathic medicine with diagnostic services, naturopathic treatments and a natural pharmacy.

**957 Quan Yin Healing Arts Center**
455 Valencia Street
San Francisco, CA 94103
415-861-4964
FAX: 415-861-0579
e-mail: qyhacinfo@aol.com
www.quanyinhealingarts.com

*Carla Wilson, Executive Director*

Acupuncture, herbal medicine, yoga and massage therapy, lectures, discussion groups and nutritional information.

**958 Rehabilitation International**
25 E 21st Street
4th Floor
New York, NY 10010
212-420-1500
FAX: 212-505-0871
e-mail: RI@riglobal.org
www.rehab-international.org

*Michael Fox, President*
*Tomas Lagerwall, Manager*

Worldwide network of people with disabilities, service providers and government agencies working together to improve the quality of life for the dosabled people and their families, has more than 200 member organizations in 90 nations.

**959 Rehabilitation Services**
1490 E Beltline Avenue SE
Grand Rapids, MI 49506
616-940-0040
FAX: 616-940-8151
e-mail: dcrsal@msn.com
www.hopenetworkrehab.org

*Margaret Kroese, Executive Director*
*Mary Baily, Admissions Manager*
*Amanda Lake, Admissions Manager*

An office of Hope Netowrk, one of the largest, private, nonprofit organization of its kind in Michigan. The purpose is to assist people with brain injuries and/or physical disabilities in achieving an optimal level of self determinations, dignity, and independence as they develop and attain goals to overcome environmental barriers and mobilize adaptive skills.

**960 Rehabilitation Services Administration of the District of Columbia**
810 1st Street NE
Washington, DC 20002
202-442-8663
FAX: 202-442-8742
e-mail: dcrsal@msn.com

*Elizabeth B Parker, Administrator*

Provides comprehensive vocational and independent living services to persons with disabilities to promote their opportunities for employment, economic self-sufficiency and independence. RSA works with communities, businesses and organizations in an effort to ensure that individuals attain integrated employment in the mainstream of society.

**961 Rocky Mountain Resource & Training Institute**
3630 Sinton Road
Suite 103
Colorado Springs, CO 80907
800-949-4262
FAX: 719-444-0269
TTY:800-949-4232

Serves people with disabilities and provides training to the agencies that assist them. Facilitates disabled individuals' transition from school to adult life; provides information and resources concerning assistive technology, devices, and services; promotes and ensures compliance with the federal Americans with Disabilities Act (ADA) and other legislation promoting the rights and inclusion of people with disabilities; promotes supported employment, strategic planning and development.

**962 Ronald McDonald House**
1500 17th Street
Huntington, WV 25701
304-529-1122
FAX: 304-529-2970
e-mail: margaret@mchouse.org
www.mchouse.org

*Margaret Wilson, Manager*

A home-away-from-home, a temporary lodging facility for the families of seriously ill children being treated at nearby hospitals. Each house is run by a local nonprofit agency comprised of members of the medical community, McDonald's owners, businesses and civic organizations and parent volunteers.

**963 Scientific Health Solutions**
1621 N Circle Drive
Colorado Springs, CO 80909
719-548-1600
800-331-2303
FAX: 719-572-8081
www.tomlevymd.com/serumtest.htm

*Thomas Levy, Founder*

SHS seeks to help those who are looking to avoid new dental toxicity by offering serum biocompatibility testing to help guide the choice of replacement dental materials.

**964 St. John Valley Associates**
10c 11th Avenue
Madawaska, ME 04756
207-728-7197
FAX: 207-728-7550
e-mail: sjva@nci1.net

*Stephen Richard, Administrator*

A nonprofit association with the mission of empowering adult citizens with mental retardation to dignify themselves. Three broad-based programs and services (Independence Plus, Job Involvements, People Now) are designed to allow each individual to upgrade learning skills, assert rights, increase independence and accept new responsibilities. *$75.00*

**965 TEACCH**
University of North Carolina at Chapel Hill
100 Renee Lynne Court
Chapel Hill, NC 27599          919-966-5296
                    FAX: 919-966-4003
                    e-mail: teacch@unc.edu
                    www.teacch.com

*Gary Mesibov, Director*
*Ricky Bass, Manager*

Focus on the person with autism and the development of a program around this person's skills, interests and needs.

**966 Teacher Preparation and Special Education**
2134 G Street NW
Suite 416
Washington, DC 20052          202-994-6160
                    800-449-7343
                    FAX: 202-994-7207
                    gsehd.gwu.edu

*Jay Shotel, Professor of Special Education*

Administers the Education of the Handicapped Act and related programs for the education of handicapped children, including grants to institutions of higher learning and fellowships to train educational personnel. Grants to states for the education of handicapped children, research and demonstration.

**967 Technology and Media Division**
Council For Exceptional Children
1110 N Glebe Road
Suite 300
Arlington, VA 22201          703-245-0600
                    888-CEC-SPED
                    FAX: 703-264-9494
                    TTY: 866-915-5000
                    e-mail: service@cec.sped.org
                    www.cec.sped.org

*Drew Allbritten MD, Executive Director*
*Bruce Ramirez, Manager*

Promotes the availability and effective use of technolgy and media for individuals with disabilities and/or who are gifted. Members include special education teachers, speech and language therapists, rehabilitation therapists, counselors, researchers, teacher educators and others.

**968 Thresholds Psychiatric Rehabilitation Centers**
4101 N Ravenswood Avenue
Chicago, IL 60613          773-880-6260
                    888-99R-EHAB
                    888-997-3422
                    FAX: 773-880-6279
                    TTY:773-880-6263
                    e-mail: thresholds@thresholds.org
                    www.thresholds.org

*Susan Bottum, President*
*Margot Anderson, VP*
*Mark Furlong, Administrator*

A nationally-recognized psychosocial rehabilitation agency serving persons with severe and persistent mental illness. The agency offers its programming at 22 service locations and more than 40 residential facilities throughout Chicago and Northern Illinois. Also offers specialized programming for older adults, young adults, parents, the homeless and the hearing impaired and mentally ill.
                    *Sliding scale*

**969 Trager International**
13801 W Center Street
Burton, OH 44021          440-834-0308
                    FAX: 440-834-0365
                    e-mail: info@trager-us.org
                    www.trager-us.org

*Anna Bowers, Executive Director*

Represents and supports Trager psychophysical integration and Mentastics movement education.

**970 Upledger Institute**
11211 Prosperity Farms Road
Suite D325
Palm Beach Gardens, FL 33410          561-622-4334
                    800-233-5880
                    FAX: 561-622-4771
                    e-mail: edsrv@upledger.com
                    www.upledger.com

*John Upledger, President*

Health resource center dedicated to the advancement of complementary and innovative techniques.

**971 Visiting Nurse Association of America**
99 Summer Street
Suite 1700
Boston, MA 02110          617-737-3200
                    888-866-8773
                    FAX: 617-737-1144
                    e-mail: vnaa@vnaa.org
                    www.vnaa.org

*Carolyn Markey, President and CEO*
*Jean Ellis, VP*
*Pat Bernard, VP*

Serve our members through work in promoting community based home health care, through business development, national puble imaging, member services and government advocacy.

**972 Vocational Rehabilitation Center**
1875 New Hope Street
Norristown, PA 19401          484-250-4340
                    800-221-1042
                    FAX: 610-520-0935
OVR is the Pennsylvania Office of Vocational Rehabilitation, a state agency that helps persons with disabilities help themselves to prepare for, start and maintain a career. OVR has fifteen offices located around the state with over 400 professional vocational rehabilitation counselors. These counselors work every year with thousands of persons who have physical, mental and emotional disabilities.

**973 Wheelchair Access**
PO Box 12
Glenmoore, PA 19343          610-942-0282
                    FAX: 610-942-0282
                    e-mail: frankgomez@waccess.org
                    www.waccess.org

*Frank Gomez, Contact*

Dedicated to providing comprehensive information to individuals with disabilities concerning wheelchair accessible homes for sale or rent, vans, wheelchairs, and any other equipment they require. Produces a variety of educational materials including a regular newsletter.

**974 Women to Women**
PO Box 306
Portland, ME 04112          800-798-7902
                    800-448-4919
                    FAX: 207-791-7869
                    e-mail: personalprogram@womentowomen.com
                    www.womentowomen.com
Combination of alternative and conventional medicine in women's health, bring science and disipline to natural and preventative methods. Publishes the Creating Health Guide, a quarterly collection of articles written by the health care professionals at Women to Women.

**975  World Institute on Disability**
510 16th Street
Suite 100
Oakland, CA 94612
510-763-4100
FAX: 510-763-4109
TTY:510-208-9496
e-mail: wid@wid.org
www.wid.org

*Kathy Martinez, Executive Director*

A public policy center that is run by persons with disabilities. Research, training and public policy center promoting the civil rights and the full societal inclusion of people with disabilities.

**976  Wyoming Institute for Disabilities (WIND)**
1000 E University Avenue
Dept 4298
Laramie, WY 82071
307-766-2761
FAX: 307-766-9463
TTY:3077662720
e-mail: wind.uwyo.edu
wind.uwyo.edu

*Keith Miller, Executive Director*

Provides teaching, research, information services, and technical assistance to both the University and Wyoming at large.

# Hearing Impaired

**977  Academy of Dispensing Audiologists**
401 N Michigan Avenue
Suite 2200
Chicago, IL 60611
866-493-5544
FAX: 312-673-6725
e-mail: info@audiologist.org
www.audiologist.org

*Craig Johnson AuD, President*

The ADA is dedicated to leadership in advancing practitioner excellence, high ethical standards, professional autonomy, hearing technology, and sound business practices in the provision of quality audiological care.

**978  Academy of Rehabilitative Audiology**
PO Box 26532
Minneapolis, MN 55426
952-920-0484
FAX: 952-920-6098
e-mail: ara@incnet.com
www.audrehab.org

*Jill E Preminger, President*
*Frances Laven, Manager*

Provides professional education, research and interest in programs for hearing handicapped persons.

**979  Advocates for Hearing Impaired Youth**
PO Box 75949
Washington, DC 20013
301-589-8444
FAX: 301-547-1103
Information on deafness, hearing impairments, child welfare and advocacy.

**980  Alexander Graham Bell Association for the Deaf and Hard of Hearing**
3417 Volta Place NW
Washington, DC 20007
202-337-5220
FAX: 202-337-8314
TTY:202-337-5221
e-mail: info@agbell.org
www.agbell.org

*K Todd Houston, Executive Director and CEO*
*Jessica Ripper, Sr Dir Marketing/Communications*

The Alexander Graham Bell Association for the Deaf and Hard of Hearing (AG Bell) is the world's oldest and largest membership organization promoting the use of spoken language by children and adults who are hearing impaired. Members include parents of children with hearing loss, adults who are deaf or hard of hearing, educators, audiologists, speech-language pathologists, physicians and other professionals in fields related to hearing loss and deafness.

**981  American Academy of Environmental Medicine**
7701 E Kellogg Drive
Suite 625
Wichita, KS 67207
316-684-5500
FAX: 316-684-5709
e-mail: centraloffice@aaem.com
www.aaem.com

*James F Coyimo, President*
*Bobbie Hinshaw, Executive Director*

Environmental Medicine is the comprehensive, proactive and preventive strategic approach to medical care dedicated to the evaluation, management, and prevention of the adverse consequences resulting from Environmentally Triggered Illnesses.

**982  American Academy of Otolaryngology: Head and Neck Surgery**
1 Prince Street
Alexandria, VA 22314
703-836-4444
FAX: 703-683-5100
TTY:703-519-1585
www.entnet.org

*Jennifer Derebery, President*
*Tom Harlow, Finance Executive*

Promotes the art and science of medicine related to otolaryngology-head and neck surgery, including providing continuing medical education courses and publications.

**983  American Association of Oriental Medicine**
PO Box 162340
Sacramento, CA 95816
916-443-4770
866-455-7999
FAX: 916-443-4766
e-mail: execdir@aaom.org
www.aaom.org

*William Morris, President of the Board*

The AAOM represents and advocates on behalf of the professional Oriental Medicine provider in order to ensure that the well-being of the public is protected, and to ensure that Oriental Medicine providers are given their rightful place in the healthcare system.

**984  American Association of the Deaf-Blind**
8630 Fenton Street
Suite 121
Silver Spring, MD 20910
301-495-4403
800-735-2258
FAX: 301-495-4404
TTY: 301-495-4402
e-mail: info@aadb.org
www.aadb.org

*Jamie Pope, Executive Director*
*Arthur Roehrig, President*

A national consumer organization of, by and for deaf-blind americans. The mission of this association is to endeavor to enable deaf-blind persons to achieve their maximum potential through increased independence, productivity and integration into the community. *$15.00*

*Membership dues*

**985    American Hearing Research Foundation**

8 S Michigan Avenue
Suite 814
Chicago, IL  60603                                  312-726-9670
                                              FAX: 312-726-9695
                               e-mail: lkoch@american-hearing.org
                                         www.american-hearing.org

*Richard G Muench, Chairman of the Board*
*Timothy C Hain, MD, Vice President*
*William L Lederer, Executive Director*

The purposes of the Foundation are to promote, conduct and furnish financial assistance for medical research into the cause, prevention and cure of deafness, impaired hearing and balance disorders; encourage the collaboration of clinical and laboratory research; encourage and improve teaching in the medical aspects of hearing problems; and disseminate the most reliable scientific knowledge to physicians, hearing professionals and the public.

**986    American Society for Deaf Children**

3820 Hartzdale Drive
Camp Hill, PA  17011                                717-761-2595
                                                    800-942-2732
                                              FAX: 717-334-8808
                                              TTY: 916-641-6084
                                          e-mail: asdc1@aol.com
                                           www.deafchildren.org

*Natalie Long, President*

ASDC was founded in 1967 as a parent-helping-parents organization. Today, ASDC is a national, independent non-profit organization whose purpose is providing support, encouragement, and information to families raising children who are deaf or hard of hearing.
                     *1967*

**987    American Society of Deaf Social Workers**

11300 Us Highway 19 N
Clearwater, FL  33764                               727-541-2646
                                                    800-288-4673
                                              FAX: 727-541-4402

*C Brett, President*

**988    American Speech-Language-Hearing Association**

10801 Rockville Pike
Rockville, MD  20852                                301-897-5700
                                                    800-638-8255
                                              FAX: 301-571-0457
                                              TTY: 301-897-5700
                                          e-mail: leader@asha.org
                                                   www.asha.org

*Lawrence W Higdon, President*
*Arlene Pietranton, Executive Director*
*Roberta B Aungst, VP*

Provides information for both the general public and physicians in an easy-to-access manner, on speech, hearing and language disorders. Exhibits by companies specializing in alternative and augmentative communications products, publishers, software and hardware companies, and hearing aid testing equipment manufacturers.

**989    American Tinnitus Association**

PO Box 5
Portland, OR  97207                                 503-248-9985
                                                    800-634-8978
                                              FAX: 503-248-0024
                                          e-mail: tinnitus@ata.org
                                                    www.ata.org

*Cheryl Ginnis, Executive Director*
*Barbara Sanders, Director Education*
*Rachel Wray, Director Advocacy and Support*

The American Tinnitus Association (ATA) is the national champion of tinnitus awareness, prevention, and treatment. Under its guiding principles—Education, Advocacy, Research and Support—the ATA offers prevention programs in schools, urges governmental and private organizations to support hearing conservation, funds the nation's brightest researchers, and facilitates self-help groups around the country.

**990    Arkansas Rehabilitation Research and Training Center
for the Deaf and Hard of Hearing**

University Of Arkansas
26 Corporate Hill Drive
Little Rock, AR  72205                              501-686-9691
                                              FAX: 501-686-9698
                                              TTY:501-686-9691
                              e-mail: rehabres@cavern.uark.edu
                                           www.uark.edu/deafrtc

*Douglas Watson, Executive Director*
*Glenn Anderson, Director*
*Steven Boone, Director*

Focuses on issues affecting the employability of deaf and hard of hearing rehabilitation clients; career assessment, career mobility, and advancement. Provides information and/or databases related to the rehabilitation of deaf and hard of hearing people served by the Federal/State Vocational Rehabilitation Program.

**991    Association of Late-Deafened Adults**

8038 Macintosh Lane
Rockford, IL  61107                                 815-332-1515
                                                    866-402-2532
                                       e-mail: JaneS256@aol.com
                                                   www.alda.org

*Jane Schlau, Regional Director*

Provides resources, information, and advocacy of the needs of deafened adults. Publishes ALDA News.

**992    Auditory-Verbal International**

1390 Chain Bridge Road
# 100
McLean, VA  22101                                   703-739-1049
                                              FAX: 703-739-0395
                                              TTY:703-739-0874
                                         e-mail: audiverb@aol.com
                                          www.auditory-verbal.org

*Steven Rech, President*
*Anne Ackerman, Executive Director*

The goal of the Auditory-Verbal approach is for children who are dead or hard of hearing to grow up in a typical learning environment and to become independent, participating citizens in mainstream society. The Auditory-Verbal philosophy supports the option for children with all degrees of hearing impairment to develop the ability to listen and use verbal communication within their own family and community constellations.

**993    Better Hearing Institute**

515 King Street
Suite 420
Alexandria, VA  22314                               703-684-3391
                                                    888-432-7453
                                              FAX: 703-684-6048
                                        e-mail: mail@betterhearing.org
                                               www.betterhearing.org

*Sergei Kochkin PhD, Executive Director*
*Renee La Mura, Administrative Director*

Implements national public information programs on hearing loss and medical, surgical, hearing aid, and rehabilitation assistance.

**994**    **Boys Town National Research Hospital**
555 N 30th Street
Omaha, NE 68131                                    402-498-6511
                                              FAX: 402-498-6638
                                       e-mail: peb@boystown.org
                                       www.boystownhospital.org

*Patrick E Brookhouser, President*

State-of-the-art research, diagnosis and treatment of individuals
with ear diseases, hearing and balance disorders, cleft lip and
palate, and speech/language problems.

**995**    **Caption Center**
125 Western Avenue
Boston, MA 02134                                   617-927-9225
                                              FAX: 617-300-1020
                                              TTY:617-300-3600
                                       e-mail: access@wgbh.org
                                       www.wgbh.org/caption

*Lori Kay, Director*

Has been pioneering and delivering accessible media to disabled
adults, students and their families, teachers and friends for over
30 years. Each year, the Center captions more than 10,000 hours
worth of broadcast and cable programs, feature films, large-format and IMAX films, home videos, music videos, DVDs,
teleconferences and CD-Roms.

**996**    **Captioned Media Program**
National Association of the Deaf
1447 E Main Street
Spartanburg, SC 29307                              864-585-1778
                                                   864-585-2617
                                              FAX: 864-585-2611
                                              TTY: 800-237-6819
                                          e-mail: info@cfv.org
                                          www.cfv.org

*Bill Stark, Project Director*

Provides open-captioned media on a free-loan basis to deaf and
hard of hearing persons, parents and teachers of hard of hearing
children and groups/organizations that serve deaf and hard of
hearing persons. Over 4,000 titles in our collection and media is
available via mail (postage paid both ways) and through Internet
streaming via our website.

**997**    **Center on Employment**
National Technical Institute For The Deaf (NTID)
52 Lomb Memorial Drive
Rochester, NY 14623                                585-475-6426
                                              FAX: 585-475-7570
                                       e-mail: ntidcoe@rit.edu
                                       www.rit.edu/ntid/coop/jobs

*Allen Vaala, Director*

The NTID Center on Employment is a resource for employers
seeking qualified, technically trained college graduates and
coops/interns who are deaf. Some 1,100 students from all over
the U.S. study at NTID, and the seven other colleges of Rochester Institute of Technology, in programs at various degree levels
in Business. Computing and Information Sciences, the Graphic
Arts and Science and Engineering.

**998**    **Cochlear Implant Club International**
5335 Wisconsin Avenue NW
Suite 440
Washington, DC 20015                               202-895-2781
                                              FAX: 202-895-2782
                                          e-mail: info@cici.org
                                          www.cici.org

*John McCelland, President*

Not-for-profit voluntary organization dedicated to serving implant users, candidates, their families and professional supporters. Purposes are to promote opportunities afforded by the use of
cochlear implants through mutual sharing of ideas and personal
experiences; enhance community awareness of hearing impairment and to promote better understanding of implants; and to
promote improved financial support. Publishes educational materials including a newsletter, brochures, and audiovisual aids.

**999**    **Communication Service for the Deaf: Sioux Falls**
102 N Krohn Place
Sioux Falls, SD 57103                              605-367-5760
                                                   800-642-6410
                                              FAX: 605-367-5958
                                              TTY: 605-367-5761
                                       e-mail: rnorris@c-s-d.org
                                       www.c-s-d.org

*Benjamin Soukup, President/CEO*

Since 1975, CSD has provided a variety of services to deaf and
hard of hearing individuals. From relay services to community
interpreting, advocacy to education, CSD promotes self-actual-
ization, professional growth, independence and greater access
for our consumers across the country.
   *1975*

**1000**   **Conference of Educational Administrators Serving the Deaf**
PO Box 1778
St Augustine, FL 32085                             904-810-5200
                                              FAX: 904-810-5525
                                       e-mail: email@ceasd.org
                                       www.ceasd.org

*Joe Finnegan, Executive Director*

CEASD provides an opportunity for professional educators to
work together for the improvement of schools and educational
programs for individuals who are deaf or hard of hearing. The
organization brings together a rich composite of resources and
reaches out to both enhance educational programs and influence
educational policy makers.

**1001**   **Council of American Instructors of the Dea f**
PO Box 377
Bedford, TX 76095                                  817-354-8414
                                              TTY:817-354-8414
                                       e-mail: caid@swbell.net
                                       www.caid.org

*Robert Hill, President*
*Helen Lovato, Office Manager*

Focuses on an organization of teachers and other education related personnel to promote student learning and development by
bringing together local, state, regional and national interest organizations.

**1002**   **Davis Center for Hearing, Speech and Learning: Hearing Therapy**
98 Us Highway 46
Budd Lake, NJ 07828                                973-347-7662
                                              FAX: 973-691-0611
                                       e-mail: info@daviscenter.net
                                       www.thedaviscenter.com

*Dorinne S Davis, Director*
*Eric S Kalugin, Senior VP*

The Davis Center's Sound Therapy Programs make positive
changes for children and adults with Autism, ADD/ADHD, Auditory Processing Issues, Dyslexia, Learning Disabilities and
other learning challenges. Our programs adress issues such as:
phonics, spelling, writing, reading comprehension, hearing
only parts of words, following directions, discriminating between sounds, sound sensitivity, behavioral responses, focus,
attention and more.

**1003  Deaf Artists of America**
302 Goodman Street N
Suite 205
Rochester, NY  14607            716-244-3460
                                800-421-1220
                           FAX: 716-244-3690
                           TTY: 716-244-3460

*Tom Willard, Executive Director*

Organized to bring support and recognition to deaf and hard of hearing artists. Goals are to publish information about deaf artists, provide cultural and educational opportunities, exhibit and market deaf artists' work, and collect and disseminate information about deaf artists.

**1004  Deaf Entertainment Foundation (DEF)**
Deaf Entertainment Guild (Deg)
8306 Wilshire Boulevard
Suite 906
Beverly Hills, CA 90211         323-782-1344
                           FAX: 213-782-1344
                           TTY:323-782-1797
                  e-mail: deafent@aol.com
                            www.deo.org

*Mark Brudney, Marketing and Public Relations*
*Eldon Greenfield, DEOnline Webmaster*
*Dan McClintock, DEOnline Editor*

Provides information to promote and accelerate the presence of deaf and hard of hearing talents in motion pictures, television, theater, and the performing arts.

**1005  Deaf REACH**
3521 12th Street NE
Washington, DC  20017           202-832-6681
                           FAX: 202-832-8454
                 e-mail: info@deaf-reach.org
                         www.deaf-reach.org

*Rudy Gawlik, President*
*Peter Goodman, VP*
*Sarah Brown, Executive Director*

Offers referral, education, advocacy, counseling, and housing services for deaf mentally ill, multihandicapped and/or low income deaf people in the metro District of Columbia area.

**1006  Deaf and Hard of Hearing Entrepreneurs Council**
814 Thayer Avenue
Suite 303
Silver Spring, MD  20910
                           FAX: 301-588-0390
                e-mail: jmcfadden@macf.com

*Jim McFadden, President*

Encourages, recognizes, and promotes entrepreneurship by people who are deaf and hard of hearing. Publishes Deaf and Hard of Hearing Entrepreneurs Council (newsletter).

**1007  Deafness Research Foundation**
2801 M Street NW
Washington, DC  20007           703-610-9025
                                800-829-5934
                           FAX: 202-293-1805
                       e-mail: info@drf.org
                            www.drf.org

*Ryan Dryden, Executive Director*

Founded in 1958, the Deafness Research Foundation is the leading source of private funding for basic and clinical research in the hearing science. The DRF is committed to making lifelong hearing health a national priority by funding research and implementing education projects in both the government and private sectors.

*1958*

**1008  Deafness and Communicative Disorders Branch of Rehab Services Administration Office**
Special Education And Rehab Services
400 Maryland Avenue SW
Washington, DC  20202           202-245-7489
                                800-872-5327
                           FAX: 202-205-9340
                           TTY: 800-437-0833
             e-mail: customerservice@inet.ed.gov
                            www.ed.gov

*Clare Cotton, Chairperson*

Promotes improved rehabilitation services for deaf and hard of hearing people and individuals with speech or language impairments. Provides technical assistance to public and private agencies and individuals.

**1009  Dogs for the Deaf**
10175 Wheeler Road
Central Point, OR  97502        541-826-9220
                           FAX: 541-826-6696
                           TTY:541-826-9220
             e-mail: info@dogsforthedeaf.org
                      www.dogsforthedeaf.org

*Robin Dickson, CEO and President*

Trains hearing dogs to alert deaf persons to certain sounds. Dogs are chosen from pet adoption shelters and assigned on the basis of a prioritized waiting list. Five to six months of training teaches them to alert their masters to the sounds of alarm clocks, smoke alarms, doorbells, oven timers, telephones, etc.

**1010  Ear Foundation**
955 Woodland Street
Nashville, TN  37206            615-627-2724
                                800-545-4327
                           FAX: 615-627-2728
                           TTY: 615-284-7807
             e-mail: amy@earfoundation.org
                      www.earfoundation.org

*Amy Nielsen, Associate Director*
*Suzanne Wyatt, Executive Director*
*Michael Glasscock III, President Emeritus*

National, nonprofit organization committed to integrating the hearing and balance impaired into the mainstream of society through public awareness and medical education. Also administers The Meniere's Network, a national network of patient support groups providing people with the opportunity to share experiences and coping strategies.

**1011  Episcopal Conference of the Deaf**
475 N 5th Street
Philadelphia, PA  19123         215-247-1059
                           FAX: 215-247-1059
                           TTY:610-408-9747
                  e-mail: bmose@aol.com
                            www.ecdeaf.com

*Rev Jay Croft, President*
*Rev Bill Mosier, VP*
*Rev Barbara Allen, VP*

Promotes ministry for deaf people throughout the Episcopal Church. Affiliated with approximately 65 congregations in the United States. Publishes The Deaf Episcopalian. *$10.00*
              *8-12 pages Quarterly*

**1012  Gallaudet University Alumni Association**
Gallaudet University
800 Florida Avenue NE
Washington, DC  20002           202-651-5000
                           FAX: 202-651-5000
                           TTY:202-651-5000
        e-mail: admissions.office@gallaudet.edu
                          www.gallaudet.edu

*Erving Jordan, President*

Represents more than 14,000 alumni of Gallaudet University across the United States and around the world. A liberal arts university for students who are deaf or hard of hearing. Publishes Gallaudet Today.

**1013    Georgiana Institute**

PO Box 10
Roxbury, CT  06783                    860-355-1545

e-mail: georgianainstitute@snet.net
www.georgianainstitute.org

*Annabel Stehli*
*Peter Stehli, Manager*

Organization promoting Auditory Integration Training in the USA.

**1014    HEAR Center**

301 E Del Mar Boulevard
Pasadena, CA  91101                    626-796-2016
FAX: 626-796-2320
e-mail: auditory@hearcenter.org
www.hearcenter.org

*Josephine Wilson, Executive Director*

Auditory and verbal program designed to help hearing impaired children, infants and adults lead normal and productive lives. Seeks to develop auditory techniques to aid people who have communication problems due to deafness. Offers diagnostic evaluations for speech and hearing. Individual auditory, verbal training and speech-language therapy.

**1015    Hands Organization**

2501 W 103rd Street
Chicago, IL  60655                    773-239-6662
FAX: 773-239-2565
TTY:773-239-6662
e-mail: handsorg@aol.com
www.handsdeaf.org

*Kate Kubey, Executive Director*

A nonprofit organization of both deaf and hearing persons working together to address the needs and concerns of the deaf community. The organization is working to raise the consciousness of the hearing world to the realities of deafness, and to bridge the gap between services already in place for the deaf and the large number of deaf people who have never been reached by those services. Offers a monthly publication.

**1016    Health Resource Center**

American Council On Education
1 Dupont Circle NW
Suite 800
Washington, DC  20036                    202-939-9300
800-544-3284
FAX: 202-833-4760
e-mail: comments@ace.nche.edu
www.acenet.edu

*David Ward, President*

Offers publications and a telephone service of use to administrators, service providers, teachers, instructors, rehabilitation counselors, health professionals and individuals with disabilities and their families.

**1017    Hear Now**

9745 E Hampden Avenue
Suite 300
Denver, CO  80231
800-648-4327
Committed to making technology accessible to deaf and hard of hearing individuals throughout the United States. Provides hearing aids and cochlear implants for very low income, hard of hearing and deaf individuals.

**1018    Hearing Education and Awareness for Rockers**

PO Box 760847
San Francisco, CA  94146                    415-409-3277
FAX: 415-409-5683
e-mail: orders@hearnet.com
www.hearnet.com

*Kathy Peck, Executive Director*

H.E.A.R. is a non-profit volunteer organization dedicated to raising awarenss of the real dangers of repeated exposure to excessive noise levels from music which can lead to permanent, and sometimes debilitating, hearing loss and tinnitus.

**1019    House Ear Institute**

2100 W 3rd Street
Los Angeles, CA  90057                    213-483-4431
FAX: 213-483-8789
TTY:213-484-2642
e-mail: webmaster@hei.org
www.hei.org

*Jim Boswell, CEO*
*Howard House, MD*

Offers pediatric hearing tests, otologic and audiologic evaluation and treatment, rehabilitation, hearing aid dispensing, and cochlear implant services. Outreach programs focus on families with hearing impaired children.

**1020    International Catholic Deaf Association**

7202 Buchanan Street
Landover Hills, MD  20784                    301-429-0697
FAX: 301-429-0697
TTY:301429069817
e-mail: homeoffice@icda-us.org
www.icda-us.org

*Peter Un, President*
*Brian Swatek, VP*

Responds to spiritual-related requests worldwide from deaf or hard of hearing Catholics.

**1021    International Hearing Dog**

5901 E 89th Avenue
Henderson, CO  80640                    303-287-3277
FAX: 303-287-3425
TTY:303-287-3277
e-mail: ihdi@aol.com
www.ihdi.org

*Valerie Foss-Brugger, President and Director*

Trains dogs to assist deaf and hearing impaired persons by alerting to smoke alarms, alarm clocks, telephones, doorbells, babies, etc.

**1022    International Hearing Society**

16880 Middlebelt Road
Suite 4
Livonia, MI  48154                    734-522-7200
800-521-5247
FAX: 734-522-0200

*Cindy Helms, Manager*

Professional association of specialists who test hearing and select, fit and dispense hearing instruments. The society conducts programs of competence qualifications, education and training.

**1023    International Lutheran Deaf Association**

1333 S Kirkwood Road
Saint Louis, MO  63122                    314-965-9917
FAX: 314-965-9000
www.lcmsdeaf.org/ilda

*Pam Kane, President*
*Greg Desrosiers, President-Elect*

An organization that is committed to spreading the gospel of Jesus Christ among deaf and hard of hearing people through mission work in the United States and around the world. The main focus of ILDA is to support Lutheran mission work with deaf people in other countries.
*1971*

### 1024 John Tracy Clinic

806 W Adams Boulevard
Los Angeles, CA 90007

213-748-5481
800-522-4582
FAX: 213-749-1651
TTY: 213-747-2924
e-mail: mmartindale@jtc.org
www.jtc.org

*Barbara Hecht PhD, Executive Director*
*Maura Martindale, VP, Educational Services*

Educational facility for infants and preschool-aged children who have hearing losses and their families. In addition to on-site services, worldwide correspondence courses in English and Spanish are offered to parents whose children are preschool age and are hard of hearing, deaf, or deaf-blind. All services of JTC are free of charge to the families. The Clinic also offers on site and online Master's Degrees in Deaf Education with USC.

### 1025 Junior National Association of the Deaf

814 Thayer Avenue
Silver Spring, MD 20910

301-587-1788
FAX: 301-587-1791
TTY:301-587-1789
e-mail: nadinfo@nad.org
www.nad.org

*Kelby Brick, Director of Law and Advocacy*
*Anita B Farb, Director of Outreach*
*Nancy Bloch, CEO*

Develops and promotes citizenship, scholarship, and leadership skills in deaf and hard of hearing students of grades 7 through 12.

### 1026 League for the Hard of Hearing

50 Broadway
Floor 6
New York, NY 10004

917-305-7700
FAX: 954-485-6336
e-mail: inf@lhh.org
www.lhh.org

*Nancy Nadler, Executive Director*
*Kim Schur, Director*

National diagnostic rehabilitation, human services agency founded in 1910. Offers comprehensive services for infants, children and adults with hearing loss regardless of age or mode of communication. Clinical programs iclude Tinnitus Center and Cochlear Implant evaluation, consultation, auditory training. LHH also offers extensive public education programs, advocacy, support and publications.
*1910*

### 1027 Lexington School for the Deaf: Center for the Deaf

30th Avenue and 75th Street
Jackson Heights, NY 11372

718-899-8800
FAX: 718-899-9846
e-mail: generalinfo@lexnyc.org
www.lexnyc.org

*Gerard J Buckley, President*

Offers a comprehensive range of services to deaf, hard of hearing and speech impaired persons from infancy to elderly through its affiliate agencies: The Center for Mental Health Services; The Lexington Hearing and Speech Center, Lexington Vocational Services, and the Lexington School for the Deaf. The Lexington Center also provides services through its research division which houses the only federally funded Rehabilitation Engineering Center.

### 1028 Michigan Association for Deaf and Hard of Hearing

2929 Covington Court
Unit 200
Lansing, MI 48912

517-487-0066
800-968-7327
FAX: 517-487-0202
TTY: 517-487-2586
e-mail: yourear@madhh.org
www.madhh.org

*Nancy Asher, Executive Director*
*L'Tonya Felder, Program Coordinator*
*SaDonna White, Interpreter/Project Coordinator*

Substance abuse and anti violence prevention videos for deaf and hard of hearing students (alcohol, marijuana, inhalants) acted in sign language, voicing and captioning. HIV/AIDS prevention and information for the deaf and hard of hearing. Lending library books, videos and audio tapes. Accessibility to courts video and information. TTY distribution program.

### 1029 National Association of the Deaf

814 Thayer Avenue
Suite 250
Silver Spring, MD 20910

301-587-1788
FAX: 301-587-1791
TTY:301-587-1789
e-mail: NADinfo@nad.org
www.nad.org

*Nancy J Bloch, CEO*
*Kelby Brick, Director Law and Advocacy*
*Anita B Farb, Director Communications*

Nation's largest organization safeguarding the accessability and civil rights of 28 million deaf and hard of hearing Americans in education, employment, health care, and telecommunications. Focuses on grassroots advocacy and empowerment, captioned media deafness-related information and publications, legal assistance, and policy development.

### 1030 National Black Deaf Advocates

PO Box 22846
Rochester, NY 14692

585-475-2411
800-421-1220
FAX: 585-475-6500
e-mail: president@nbda.org
www.nbda.org

*Albert Simone, President*
*Claudia Gordon, VP*

The Mission of the National Black Deaf Advocate is to promote the leadership development, economic and educational opportunities, social equality, and to safeguard the general health and welfare of Black deaf and hard of hearing people.

### 1031 National Captioning Institute

1900 Gallows Road
Suite 3000
Vienna, VA 22182

703-917-7600
FAX: 703-917-9853
TTY:703-917-7600
e-mail: mail@ncicap.org
www.ncicap.org

*Gene Chao, President*
*Karen O'Connor, National Director Sales*
*Jack Gates, CEO*

Formed in 1979, the nonprofit National Captioning Institute is the global captioning leader, supplying the highest quality closed-captioning services to the television, cable, and home video industries.

*1979*

**1032    National Catholic Office of the Deaf**
7202 Buchanan Street
Landover Hills, MD  20784                301-577-1684
                                                                FAX: 301-577-1690
                                                                TTY:301-577-4184
                                                        e-mail: ncod@erols.com
                                                                www.ncod.org

*Arvilla Rank, Executive Director*

Helps coordinate efforts of deaf or hard of hearing people who
are involved in the ministry, acts as a resource center, assists
bishops and pastors become available to the deaf and hard of
hearing.

**1033    National Center for Accessible Media**
Wgbh Educational Foundation
125 Western Avenue
Boston, MA  02134                        617-300-2000
                                                            FAX: 617-300-1035
                                                            TTY:617-300-2489
                                                    e-mail: ncam@wgbh.org
                                                            ncam.wgbh.org

*Larry Goldberg, Director*
*Brad Botkin, Director*
*Henry Becton, Chief Executive Officer*

Aims to increase access to public mass media (television, radio,
print, movies, multimedia) for unserved customers, such as disabled people or speakers of other languages.

**1034    National Cued Speech Association**
Information Service
23970 Hermitage Road
Shaker Heights, OH  44122                216-292-6213
                                                            TTY:800-459-3529
                                                        www.cuedspeech.org

*Sarina Roffe, President*
*Carolyn Ostrander, VP*
*Pamela Beck, Owner*

Membership organization that provides advocacy and support
regarding use of Cued Speech. Information available.

**1035    National Deaf Education Network and Clearinghouse**
Gallaudet University
800 Florida Avenue NE
Washington, DC  20002                    202-651-5000
                                                            FAX: 202-651-5101
                                                            TTY:202-651-5101

*Erving Jordan, President*

Responds to inquiries about a diverse range of topics related to
deaf and hard of hearing children in the age group of 0 to 21.

**1036    National Family Association for Deaf-Blind**
141 Middle Neck Road
Sands Point, NY  11050                   516-944-8900
                                                            800-225-0411
                                                            FAX: 516-883-9060
                                                    e-mail: nfadb@aol.com
                                                            www.nfadb.org

*Sheri Stanger, President*
*Pearl Veesart, VP*
*Joseph Nulty, Executive Director*

A membership organization which provides resources, education, advocacy, referrals and support for families with children
who are deaf-blind; professionals in the field and individuals
who are deaf-blind.

**1037    National Fraternal Society of the Deaf**
1118 S 6th Street
Springfield, IL  62703                   217-789-7429
                                                        FAX: 217-789-7489
                                                        TTY:217-789-7438
                                                e-mail: thefrat@nfsd.com
                                                        www.nfsd.com

*Al Nevel, President*
*Christopher McQuaid, Chairman*

Work in the area of life insurance and advocacy for deaf people.
Has 75 divisions across the country.

**1038    National Information Center for Children and Youth
with Disabilities (NICHCY)**
PO Box 1492
Washington, DC  20013                    202-884-8200
                                                            800-695-0285
                                                        FAX: 202-884-8441
                                                e-mail: nichcy@aed.org
                                                        www.nichcy.org

*Susan Ripley, Manager*

Provides fact sheets, state resource sheets and general information to assist parents, educators, caregivers, advocates and others in helping children and youth with disabilities participate as
fully as possible in their communities.

**1039    National Information Clearinghouse on Children who
are Deaf-Blind**
Teaching Research
345 Monmouth Avenue
Monmouth, OR  97361                      503-838-8391
                                                        FAX: 503-838-8150
                                                        TTY:800-854-7013
                                                e-mail: dblink@tr.wou.edu
                                                        www.tr.wou.edu/dblink

*John Reiman, Director*
*Meredith Brodsky, Executive Director*

Collects, organizes, and disseminates information related to
children and youth of ages 0 to 21 who are deaf-blind and connects consumers of deaf-blind information to the appropriate resources. Publishes a number of topical papers and publishes
Deaf-Blind Perspective.

**1040    National Institute on Deafness and Other Communica-
tion Disorders (NIDCD)**
31 Center Drive
Bethesda, MD  20892                      301-496-7243
                                                        800-241-1044
                                                        FAX: 301-402-0018
                                                        TTY: 800-241-1055
                                                e-mail: nidcdinfo@nidcd.nih.gov
                                                        www.nidcd.nih.gov

*Patricia Blessing, Chief OHCPL/NIDCD*

The NIDCD Information Clearinghouse is a national resource
center for health information about hearing, balance, smell,
taste, voice, speech and language for health professionals, patients, industry and the public.

**1041    National Rehabilitation Information Center (NARIC)**
4200 Forbes Boulevard
Suite 202
Lanham, MD  20706                        301-459-5900
                                                        800-346-2742
                                                        FAX: 301-459-4263
                                                e-mail: naricinfo@heitechservices.com
                                                        www.naric.com

*Mark Odum, Director*

Provides information and referral services on disability and rehabilitation, including quick information and referral, database
searches of the bibliographic database REHABDATA, and document delivery.

**1042 National Technical Institute for the Deaf**
52 Lomb Memorial Drive
Rochester, NY 14623                        585-475-6426
                                      FAX: 585-475-5978
                                      TTY:585-475-6400
                                      e-mail: ntidmc@rit.edu
                                      www.rit.edu/ntid

*T Alan Hurwitz, VP and Dean*
*Allen Vaala, Manager*

Provides technological postsecondary education to deaf and
hard-of-hearing students. One of eight colleges of Rochester Institute of Technology.

**1043 National Theatre of the Deaf**
139 North Main Street
West Hartford, CT 06107                    860-236-4193
                                      FAX: 860-236-4163
                                      TTY:860-236-4193
                                      e-mail: info@ntd.org
                                      www.ntd.org

*Paul Winters, Executive Director*

Professional development of deaf actors, national theatrical
touring company of deaf and hearing actors.

**1044 Okada Specialty Guide Dogs**
543 Esteppe Road
Front Royal, VA 22630                      352-344-2212
                                      FAX: 352-344-0210
                                      e-mail: okada@hitter.net
                                      www.okadadogs.com

*Pat Putnam, Director*

Trains dogs to aid deaf, hearing-impaired, Alzheimer's, seizure,
amnesia and residential companion guide dogs.

**1045 Registry of Interpreters for the Deaf**
333 Commerce Street
Alexandria, VA 22314                       703-838-0030
                                      FAX: 703-838-0454
                                      TTY:703-838-0459
                                      e-mail: info@rid.org
                                      www.rid.org

*Clay Nettles, Executive Director*
*Melissa Bowhay, Membership Services Coordinator*

A membership organization with over 7,000 members, including professional interpreters and translators, individuals who
are deaf or hard of hearing, and professionals in related fields.

**1046 Rehabilitation Engineering Research Center on Hearing
Enhancement and Assistive Devices**
Lexington School for the Deaf/Center for the Deaf
800 Florida Avenue NE
Washington, DC 20002                       202-651-5335
                                      FAX: 202-651-5324
                                      TTY:202-651-5335
                                      e-mail: matthew.bakke@gallaudet.edu
                                      www.hearingresearch.org

*Matthew Bakke, Director*
*Kelly Crain, Program Manager*

The Rehabilitation Engineering Center (RERC) on Hearing Enhancement is a national project funded by the United States Department of Education, National Institute on Disability and
Rehabilitation Research (NIDRR) in the Office of Special Education and Rehabilitation Services (OSERS). The objective of
the project is to conduct research programs that promote technological solutions to problems confronting people who are hard of
hearing.

**1047 Rehabilitation Research & Training Center for Persons
Who Are Hard of Hearing or Deafened**
California School Of Professional Psychology
6160 Cornerstone Ct E
San Diego, CA 92121                        858-623-2777
                                      FAX: 858-642-0266

Focuses on conducting research and developing training programs related to employment and personal adjustment of individuals who are hard of hearing or late deafened.

**1048 SEE Center for the Advancement of Deaf Children**
PO Box 1181
Los Alamitos, CA 90720                     562-430-1467
                                      FAX: 562-795-6614
                                      e-mail: seecenter@seecenter.org
                                      www.seecenter.org

*Esther Zawolkow, Executive Director*

Information and referral for parents and educators of deafness-related topics and Signing Exact English (SEE).

**1049 Scottish Rite Center for Childhood Language Disorders**

Childrens Hospital
1630 Columbia Road NW
Washington, DC 20009                       202-939-4703
                                      FAX: 202-939-4717

*T Robinson, Executive Director*

Offers speech-language evaluations and treatment, hearing
screening and consultations to children ages birth through adolescence. Bilingual services are also available.

**1050 Self Help for Hard of Hearing People**
7910 Woodmont Avenue
Suite 1200
Bethesda, MD 20814                         301-657-2248
                                      FAX: 301-913-9413
                                      TTY:301-657-2249
                                      e-mail: info@hearingloss.org
                                      www.shhh.org

*Terry Portis, Executive Director*
*Toni Barrient, Director Member Services*
*Brenda Battat, Senior Director*

A nonprofit, educational organization that is dedicated to the
well-being of people of all ages and communication styles who
do not hear well. SHHH is the largest international consumer organization of its kind.

**1051 Sound, Listening, and Learning Center**
301 E Bethany Home Road
Suite A107
Phoenix, AZ 85012                          602-381-0086
                                      FAX: 602-957-6741
                                      e-mail: info@soundlistening.com
                                      www.soundlistening.com

Sound Listening & Learning Center provides the Tomatis
Method, a truly transformative program of sound stimulation,
audio-vocal activities, and consultation using patented equipment. The Method focuses on our most basic skill—listening.
How we listen to ourselves and others profoundly affects our
learning, speech/language, communication, thoughts, feelings,
and relationships.

**1052 Tele-Consumer Hotline**
PO Box 27279
Washington, DC 20038
                                      800-332-1124
                                      FAX: 800-332-1124

Impartial consumer information service about residential telecommunication concerns.

**1053** **Telecommunications for the Deaf (TDI)**
8630 Fenton Street
Suite 604
Silver Spring, MD 20910
301-589-3786
FAX: 301-589-3797
TTY:301-589-3006
e-mail: info@tdi-online.org
www.tdi-online.org

*Roy Miller, President*
*Joseph Duarte, VP*
*Claude L Stout, Executive Director*

Promoting equal access to telecommunications and media for people who are deaf, late-deafened, hard of hearing or deaf-blind through consumer education and involvement; technical assistance and consulting; applications of exisiting and emerging technologies; networking and collaboration; uniformity of standards; and national policy development and advocacy.

**1054** **Tripod**
1727 W Burbank Boulevard
Burbank, CA 91506
818-972-2080
FAX: 818-972-2090
e-mail: info@tripod.org
www.tripod.org

An educational program for deaf and hard-of-hearing students in conjunction with Burbank Unified School District. The program offers educational services from birth through 12th grade. This partnership features co-enrollment and co-teaching models.

**1055** **USA Deaf Sports Federation**
102 N Krohn Place
Sioux Falls, SD 57103
605-367-5760
FAX: 605-367-5760
e-mail: homeoffice@usadeafsports.org
www.usdeafsports.org

*Bobbie Beth Scoggins, President*

The USA Deaf Sports Federation's purpose was to foster and regulate uniform rules of competition and provide social outlets for deaf members and their friends; serve as a parent organization for regional sports organizations; conduct annual athletic competitions; and assist in the participation of U.S. teams in international competition.

**1056** **Vestibular Disorders Association**
Vestibular Disorders Association
PO Box 13305
Portland, OR 97213
503-229-7705
800-837-8428
FAX: 503-229-8064
e-mail: veda@vestibular.org
www.vestibular.org

*Lisa Haven Ph D, Executive Director*
*Elizabeth A Commerford MSW, President*
*Al Bowman DPT, VP*

Provides information and support for people with inner-ear vestibular disorders and the professionals who treat them, and develops awareness of the issues surrounding these disorders.
*1987*

**1057** **WRAD**
PO Box 3211
Quartz Hill, CA 93586
FAX: 805-943-6112
TTY:805-943-8879
e-mail: Brucegross@aol.com

*Bruce Gross, President*

WRAD represents the community of persons that are deaf or hard of hearing and all of its subgroups. People who were formerly greatly restricted by deafness, and who believed there was no possible remediation for deafness or way for inclusion into general society, now have laws, technologies, and better opportunities for success and achievement. WRAD provides the needed advocacy and resources for this community.

## Professional

**1058** **ACB Government Employees**
American Council Of The Blind
1155 15th Street NW
Suite 1004
Washington, DC 20005
202-467-5081
800-424-8666
FAX: 202-467-5085
e-mail: tpacheco@acb.org
www.acb.org

*Terry Pacheko, Membership Services Coordinator*
*Melanie Brunson, Executive Director*

Members are present, former and retired employees of federal, state and local government agencies. Concerns of the organization include recruitment, placement and advancement of blind and visually impaired employees.

**1059** **ACB Social Service Providers**
American Council Of The Blind
1155 15th Street NW
Suite 1004
Washington, DC 20005
202-467-5081
800-424-8666
FAX: 202-467-5085
e-mail: info@acb.org
www.acb.org

*Melanie Brunson, Executive Director*

Blind and visually impaired social workers, social service professionals, students pursuing careers in social work and other interested persons are members of this organization. ACBSSP works to promote full participation by visually impaired social services professionals in the field of social welfare.

**1060** **ACS Federal Healthcare**
5270 Shawnee Road
Alexandria, VA 22312
703-941-5798

Project RSVP supports the SSA's initiative to expand operations vocational rehabilitation services through a national network of private providers. Rehabilitation companies interested in gaining access to a new client base, acquiring a new funding stream, and developing creative service delivery and entrepreneurial partnerships, may benefit from such a program.

**1061** **AHEAD Association**
PO Box 540666
Waltham, MA 02454
781-788-0003
FAX: 781-788-0033
TTY:781-788-0003
e-mail: ahead@ahead.org
www.ahead.org

*Stephen J Smith, Executive Director*

This is a national association of professionals working on college campuses with disabled students.

**1062** **American Academy of Biological Dentistry**
PO Box 856
Carmel Valley, CA 93924
831-659-5385
e-mail: mail@biologicaldentistry.org
www.biologicaldentistry.org

*William Glaros, President*

Promotes non-toxic diagnostic and therapeutic approaches in dentistry; hosts seminars on biological diagnosis and therapy.

# Associations /Professional

**1063  American Academy of Environmental Medicine**
7701 E Kellogg Drive
Suite 625
Wichita, KS  67207
316-684-5500
FAX: 316-684-5709
e-mail: administrator@aaem.com
www.aaem.com

*James M Willoughby II DO, President*
*Bobbie Hinshaw, Executive Director*

Training for physicians in environmental medicine.

**1064  American Academy of Orthomolecular Medicine**
Huxley Institute For Biosocial Research
900 N Federal Highway
Boca Raton, FL  33432
800-847-3802

Provides information and referrals to orthomolecular physicians.

**1065  American Academy of Osteopathy**
3500 Depauw Boulevard
Suite 1080
Indianapolis, IN  46268
317-879-1881
FAX: 317-879-0563
e-mail: snoone@academyofosteopathy.org
www.academyofosteopathy.org

*Stephen J Noone, Executive Director*
*Diana Finley, Associate Executive Director*

The mission of the American Academy of Osteopathy is to teach, advocate, and research the science, art and philosophy of osteopathic medicine, emphasizing the integration of osteopathic principles, practice and manipulative treatment in patient care.

**1066  American Academy of Physical Medicine and Rehabilitation**
1 Ibm Plaza
Suite 2500
Chicago, IL  60611
312-464-9700
FAX: 312-464-0227
e-mail: info@aapmr.org
www.aapmr.org

*Bruce M Gans, President*
*Joel M Press, VP*
*Ronald Henrichs, Executive Director*

This national medical specialty society represents more than 6,500 physical medicine and rehabilitation physicians, whose patients include people with physical disabilities and chronic, disabling illnesses. The academy's mission is to maximize quality of life, minimize the incidence and prevalence of impairments and disability, promote societal health and enhance the understanding and development of the specialty. The organization offers information, referrals, and patient materials.

**1067  American Association of Children's Residential Centers**

11700 W Lake Park Drive
Milwaukee, WI  53224
877-33A-ACRC
FAX: 877-36A-ACRC
e-mail: info@aacrc-dc.org
www.aacrc-dc.org

*William P Martone, President*

The American Association of Children's Residential Centers believes that children and adolescents, and their families, are entitled to treatment which offers the maximum opportunity for growth and change. AACRC believes that clinically crafted residential treatment options, ranging from community based homes through institutional environments, are essential components in a comprehensive system of behavioral health care.

**1068  American Association of Childrens Residential Centers**
11700 W Lake Park Drive
Milwaukee, WI  53224
877-33A-ACRC
FAX: 877-36A-ACRC
e-mail: info@aacrc-dc.org
www.aacrc-dc.org

*William P Martone, President*

Brings professionals together to advance the frontiers of knowledge pertaining to the spectrum of therapeudic living environments for children and adolescents with behavioral health disorders.

**1069  American Association of Naturopathic Physicians**
3201 New Mexico Avenue NW
Suite 350
Washington, DC  20016
202-895-1392
866-538-2267
FAX: 202-274-1992
e-mail: member.services@naturopathic.org
www.naturopathic.org
Founded in 1985, the American Association of Naturopathic Physicians (AANP) is the national professional society representing naturopathic physicians who are licensed or eligible for licensing as primary care providers. Policy is established through a House of Delegates, which consists of representatives from 34 state naturopathic associations, four naturopathic specialty societies and the four recognized naturopathic medical programs.
*1985*

**1070  American College of Advancement in Medicine**
24411 Ridge Route Drive
Suite 115
Laguna Hills, CA  92653
949-309-3520
800-532-3688
FAX: 949-309-3538
e-mail: info@acam.org
www.acam.org

*Sharon Urch, Executive Director*
*Marcus McGee, Member Services Director*
*Drew McGray, Exhibitor Director*

Provides training and education to physicians and scientists. Also provides physician referrals and informational material.

**1071  American College of Nurse Midwives**
8403 Colesville Road
Suite 1550
Silver Spring, MD  20910
240-485-1800
FAX: 240-485-1818
e-mail: info@acnm.org
www.acnm.org

*Katherine Camacho Carr, President*
*Gwendolyn Spears, VP*

The American College of Nurse-Midwives (ACNM) is the oldest women's health care organization in the U.S. ACNM provides research, accredits midwifery education programs, administers and promotes continuing education programs, establishes clinical practice standards, creates liasons with state and federal agencies and members of Congress.

**1072  American Group Psychotherapy Association**
25 E 21st Street
6th Floor
New York, NY  10010
212-477-2677
877-668-2472
FAX: 212-979-6627
e-mail: info@agpa.org
www.agpa.org

*Robert H Klein PhD, President*
*Elizabeth B Knight, President-Elect*
*Marsha Block, Chief Executive Officer*

AGPA serves as the national voice specific to the interests of group psychotherapy. Its 4,100 members and 31 affiliate societies provide a wealth of professional, educational and social support for group psychotherapists in the United States and around the world.

**1073    American Holistic Medical Association**

12101 Menaul Boulevard NE
Suite C
Albuquerque, NM  87112                505-292-7788
                                       888-500-7999
                             FAX: 505-293-7582
         e-mail: ksummers@holisticmedicine.org
                  www.holisticmedicine.org

*Amy Driggs, Associate Director*
*Ken Jacobson, Executive Director*
*Kimberly Summers, Membership Services*

The mission of the AMHA is to support practitioners in their evolving personal and professional development as healers and to educate physicians about holistic medicine.

**1074    American Occupational Therapy Association**

PO Box 31220
Bethesda, MD  20824                   301-652-2682
                                       800-789-2682
                             FAX: 301-652-7711
                             TTY: 800-377-8555
                      e-mail: praota@aota.org
                               www.aota.org

*M Carolyn Baum, President*
*Charles Christiansen, VP*
 *Mary Binderman, Manager*

Settings include schools, hospitals, skilled nursing facilities, home health, outpatient rehabilitation clinicss, psychiatric facilities and community health programs.

**1075    American Psychiatric Association**

Psychiatric Services
1000 Wilson Boulevard
Suite 1825
Arlington, VA  22209                  703-907-7300
                             FAX: 703-907-1095
                   e-mail: psjournal@psych.org
                          ps.psychiatryonline.org

*Constance Gartner, Managing Editor*
*Andrew Prugar, Editorial Assistant*
*James Scully, Manager*

The American Psychiatric Association is a medical specialty society recognized worldwide. Its over 35,000 U.S. and international member physicians work together to ensure humane care and effective treatment for all persons with mental disorder, including mental retardation and substance-related disorders. It is the voice and conscience of modern psychiatry. Its vision is a society that has avaliable, accessible quality psychiatric diagnosis and treatment.

**1076    American Society of Bariatric Physicians**

2821 S Parker Road
Suite 625
Aurora, CO  80014                     303-770-2526
                             FAX: 303-779-4834
                      e-mail: info@asbp.org
                               www.asbp.org

*G Michael Steelman, President*
*John Kelly, VP*
*Beth A Little, Executive Director*

The American Society of Bariatric Physicians is an international association and allied health care professionals with special interest and experience in the comprehensive treatment of overweight, obesity and related disorders.

**1077    American Society of Clinical Hypnosis**

140 N Bloomingdale Road
Bloomingdale, IL  60108               630-980-4740
                             FAX: 630-351-8490
                        e-mail: info@asch.net
                               www.asch.net

*Catherine Kasper, Executive Director*

Physicians and dentists trained in hypnosis for treating health conditions.

**1078    American Society of Teachers of the Alexander Technique**

PO Box 60008
Florence, MA  01062                   413-584-2359
                                       800-473-0620
                             FAX: 413-584-3097
                        e-mail: info@amsat.ws
                               www.amsat.ws

*Claire Creese, Chairman*
*Indrani Gallagher, Administrator*

The AmSAT Mission: To define, maintain and promote the Alexander Technique at its highest standard of professional practice and conduct.

**1079    Association for the Care of Children's Health**

19 Mantua Road
Mount Royal, NJ  08061                609-224-1742
                             FAX: 609-423-3420
         e-mail: amkent@tmg.smarthub.com
                               www.acch.org

The Association for the Care of Children's Health (ACCH) is an international, multidisciplinary membership organization of healthcare providers, parents, educators, researchers, chaplains, facility designers, social service professionals, corporations, institutions, and policy makers.

**1080    Behavior Therapy and Research Society**

Temple University Medical School
3420 N Broad Street
Philadelphia, PA  19140               215-707-4019
                                       800-331-2839
                             FAX: 215-707-4086
                          www.medschool.temple.edu

*John M Daly MD, Dean*
*Judith Russo, Manager*

This organization promotes behavior therapy by conducting and facilitating research in behavioral interventions and providing information through consultations, conferences and publications, about the use of these methods.

**1081    Blind Information Technology Specialists**

American Council of the Blind
1155 15th Street NW
Suite 1004
Washington, DC  20005                 202-467-5081
                                       800-424-8666
                                       202-467-5085
         e-mail: earlene@earlenehughes.com
                               www.acb.org/bits

*Earlene Hughes, President*
*Melanie Brunson, Executive Director*

Formerly the Visually Impaired Data Processors, BITS is a non profit organization which fosters the career development of blind computer professionals, promotes the use of computer technology by blind persons to improve the wualtiy of their personal and professional lives, and advocare for improved information access for all visually impaired people.

**1082 Case Management Society of America**
8201 Cantrell Road
Suite 230
Little Rock, AR 72227      501-225-2229
FAX: 501-221-9068
e-mail: cmsa@cmsa.org
www.cmsa.org

*Jeanne Boling, Executive Director/Owner*
*Cathy Crowell, Senior Director*

The Case Management Society of America is an international, non-profit organization founded in 1990 dedicated to the support and development of the profession of case management through educational forums, networking opportunities and legislative involvement.
*1990*

**1083 College of Optometrists in Vision Development**
215 W Garfield Road
Suite 210
Aurora, OH 44202      330-995-0718
888-268-3770
FAX: 330-995-0719
e-mail: info@covd.org
www.covd.org

*Pamela R Happ, Executive Director*

The College of Optometrists in Vision Development (COVD) is an international membership association of eye care professionals including optometrists, optometry students, and vision therapists. Members of COVD provide developmental vision care, vision therapy and vision rehabilitation services for children and adults.

**1084 Community Enterprises**
PO Box 598
Northampton, MA 01061      413-584-1460

www.communityenterprises.com

*Richard Benne, President*

Provide supported education services in a community college setting; supported employment including job training, placement and follow-up; transitional services from group homes and other settings to supported living within the community.

**1085 Council for Exceptional Children: Teacher Education Division**
1110 N Glebe Road
Suite 300
Arlington, VA 22201      703-245-0600
FAX: 703-264-9494
www.cec.sped.org

*Drew Allbritten, Executive Director*
*Bruce Ramirez, Manager*

Promotes the preparation and continuing professional development of effective professionals in special education and related fields. TED's members include persons involved in the education and continuing development of professionals in special education and related fields, such as general education, allied health, speech and language pathology, rehabilitation, legal services and more.

**1086 Environmental Dental Association**
285 N El Camino Real
Suite 102
Encinitas, CA 92024      858-586-1208

e-mail: info@enviromentaldental.com
Organization of alternative dentists concerned about the toxic effects of dental materials and procedures.

**1087 Feldenkrais Guild of North America (FGNA)**
3611 SW Hood Avenue
Suite 100
Portland, OR 97239      503-221-6612
866-333-6248
FAX: 503-221-6616
e-mail: guild@feldenkrais.com
www.feldenkrais.com

*Barbara Greenfield, Executive Director*

This is the organization which sets the standards for and certifies all FELDENKRAIS practitioners in North America. In order to practice, a practitioner must be a graduate of an FGNA accredited program (a minimum of 800 instruction hours over a three to four year period), and agree to follow both the Code of Professional Conduct and the Standards of Practice. FGNA may be contacted for further information about the FELDENKRAIS METHOD or for a list of FELDENKRAIS practitioners sorted by region.

**1088 International Association of Yoga Therapists**
115 South McCormick Street
#3
Prescott, AZ 86303      928-541-0004
FAX: 928-541-0182
e-mail: mail@iayt.org
www.iayt.org

*John Kepner, Director*
*Veronica Zador, President*
*Amber Elliot, Membership Coordinator*

Champions the cause of yoga through annual conferences, annual journals and newsletters. Serves the growing number of yoga teachers, especially those who use yoga therapeutically.

**1089 Job Accommodation Network**
PO Box 6080
Morgantown, WV 26506      304-293-7186
800-526-7234
FAX: 304-293-5407
e-mail: jan@jan.wvu.edu
www.jan.wvu.edu

*Kathern Willard, Information Assistant*
*Kim Kerns, Information Assistant*

JAN's mission is to facilitate the employment and retention of workers with disabilities by providing employers, employment providers, people with disabilities, their family members and other interested parties with information on job accomodations, self-employment and small business opportunities and related subjects. JAN's efforts are in support of the employment, including self-employment and small business ownership, of people with disabilities.

**1090 Maharishi Ayur-Veda Medical Center**
1734 Jasmine Avenue
Fairfield, IA 52556      641-469-6706
800-248-9050
FAX: 641-472-2496
e-mail: theraj@theraj.com
www.theraj.com

The RAJ opened its doors in April 1993 and soon gained a reputation as America's premier Ayurveda Health Center. It is the only such facility outside of India specifically built to offer traditional Ayurveda rejuvenation treatments.
*1993*

**1091 National Association of Blind Educators**
National Federation Of The Blind
1800 Johnson Street
Baltimore, MD 21230      410-659-9314
FAX: 410-685-5653
e-mail: nfb@nfb.org
www.nfb.org

*Marc Maurer, President*
*Joyce Scanlan, Director*
*Peggy Elliott, Director*

Membership organization of blind teachers, professors and instructors in all levels of education. Provides support and information regarding professional responsibilities, classroom techniques, national testing methods and career obstacles. Publishes The Blind Educator, national magazine specifically for blind educators.

## 1092  National Association of Blind Lawyers
National Federation Of The Blind
1800 Johnson Street
Baltimore, MD  21230
410-659-9314
FAX: 410-685-5653
e-mail: nfb@nfb.org
www.nfb.org

*Joyce Scanlan, Program Director*
*Pam Allen, Director*
*Marc Maurer, President*

Membership organization of blind attorneys, law students, judges and others in the law field. Provides support and information regarding employment, techniques used by the blind, advocacy, laws affecting the blind, current information about the American Bar Association and other issues for blind lawyers.

## 1093  National Association of Blind Secretaries and Transcribers
National Federation Of The Blind
1800 Johnson Street
Baltimore, MD  21230
410-659-9314
FAX: 410-685-5653
e-mail: nfb@nfb.org
www.nfb.org

*Marc Maurer, President*

Membership organization of blind secretaries and transcribers at all levels, including medical and paralegal transcription, office workers, customer-service personnel and many other similar fields. Addresses issues such as technology, accomodation, career planning and job training.

## 1094  National Association of Blind Teachers
American Council Of The Blind
1155 15th Street NW
Suite 1004
Washington, DC  20005
202-467-5081
800-424-8666
FAX: 202-467-5085
e-mail: info@acb.org
www.acb.org

*Melanie Brunson, Executive Director*

Works to advance the teaching profession for blind and visually impaired people, protects the interest of teachers, presents discussions and solutions for special problems encountered by blind teachers and publishes a directory of blind teachers in the US.

## 1095  National Association of Protection and Advocacy Systems
900 2nd Street NE
Suite 211
Washington, DC  20002
202-408-8362
FAX: 202-408-9520
TTY:202-408-9521
e-mail: info@napas.org
www.napas.org

*Ross Capon, Executive Director*

The National Association of Protection and Advocacy Systems, Inc. (NAPAS) is the voluntary national membership association of protection and advocacy systems and client assistance programs. It assumes leadership in promoting and strenghening the role and performance of its members in providing quality legally based advocacy services. NAPAS has a vision of society where people with disabilities exercise self-determination and choice and have equality of opportunity and full participation.

## 1096  National Association of State Directors of Developmental Disabilities Services (NASDDDS)
113 Oronoco Street
Alexandria, VA  22314
703-683-4202
FAX: 703-683-8773
e-mail: ksnyder@nasddds.org
www.nasddds.org

*Robert Gettings, Executive Director*
*Charles R Moseley, Director*
*Robin Cooper, Director*

A nonprofit organization devoted to improving and expanding services to persons with developmental disabilities. The primary aims of the association are to: facilitate an exchange of information regarding the most advanced and efficacious methods of providing care and training to this population and represent the interests of state programs for persons with mental retardation/developmental disabilities in the development and implementation of federal programs.

## 1097  National Clearinghouse of Rehabilitation Training Materials
Oklahoma State University
206 W Sixth Street
Stillwater, OK  74078
405-744-7213
800-223-5219
FAX: 405-744-2001
TTY: 405-744-2002
e-mail: info@www.nchrtm.okstate.edu
www.nchrtm.okstate.edu

*Jennifer Ahlert, PR Coordiantor*
*Carolyn Cail, Information Coordinator*
*Charles Feasley, Director*

For over 40 years, the National Clearinghouse of Rehabilitation Training Materials (NCRTM) has been providing educational materials to the rehabilitation community. Whether you are an educator, student, individual with disabilities or family member of an individual with disabilities, we provide a full range of services.

## 1098  National Deaf Education Network and Clearinghouse
Gallaudet University
800 Florida Avenue NE
Washington, DC  20002
202-651-5000
FAX: 202-651-5101
TTY:202-651-5101
e-mail: michael.wynne@gallaudet.edu
clerccenter.gallaudet.edu

*Michael Wynne, Admissions Contact*
*Katherine Jankowski, Schools Programs Contact*
*Erving Jordan, President*

Gallaudet University's Laurent Clerc National Deaf Education Center shares the concerns of parents and professionals about the achievement of deaf and hard of hearing students in different learning environments across the country. We all know that deaf and hard of hearing students can and do excel, but we also know that not all deaf and hard of hearing students are achieving their full potential.

## 1099  National Federation of the Blind: Merchants Division
National Federation of the Blind
1800 Johnson Street
Baltimore, MD  21230
410-659-9314
FAX: 410-685-5653
e-mail: nfb@nfb.org
www.nfb.org

*Marc Maurer, President*
*Joyce Scanlan, Director*
*Peggy Elliott, Director*

Membership organization of blind persons employed in either self-employment work or the Randolph-Sheppard vending program. Provides information regarding rehabilitation, social security, tax and other issues which directly affect blind merchants. Serves as advocacy and support group.

**1100    National Federation of the Blind: Blind Industrial Workers Division**
National Federation of the Blind
1800 Johnson Street
Baltimore, MD 21230                      410-659-9314
                                    FAX: 410-685-5653
                                    e-mail: nfb@nfb.org
                                         www.nfb.org

*Marc Maurer, President*

Membership organization of blind persons employed in industrial and manufacturing work or in government job programs for the blind. Dedicated to protecting the rights of blind workers in salary, job stability, advancement, and labor issues.

**1101    National Federation of the Blind: Computer Science Division**
National Federation of the Blind
1800 Johnson Street
Baltimore, MD 21230                      410-659-9314
                                    FAX: 410-685-5653
                                    e-mail: nfb@nfb.org
                                         www.nfb.org

*Marc Maurer, President*

National organization of blind persons knowledgeable in the computer science and technology fields. Works to develop new technologies, to secure access to current technology and to develop new ways of using current or new technologies by the blind.

**1102    National Federation of the Blind: Public Employees Division**
National Federation of the Blind
4792 Parkhurst Drive NE
Apt 230
Bremerton, WA 98310                      410-659-9314
                                    FAX: 410-685-5653
                       e-mail: ieweich@worldnet.att.net
                                         www.nfb.org

*Ivan Weich, President*

Organization of blind persons holding local, state or federal jobs. Focuses on issues such as changes in governmental hiring and retention practices, new job skills needed for the future, government employment downsizing, new electronic means of finding public sector jobs, self-advocacy and career planning strategies.

**1103    National Federation of the Blind: Science and Engineering Division**
National Federation of the Blind
1800 Johnson Street
Baltimore, MD 21230                      410-659-9314
                                    FAX: 410-685-5653
                                    e-mail: nfb@nfb.org
                                         www.nfb.org

*Marc Maurer, President*
*Joyce Scanlan, Program Director*

Blind persons with expertise and experience in fields such as genetics, telecommunications, biology, chemistry, physics and nuclear physics or mechanical, electronic and chemical engineering. This is a strong support group to encourage blind persons in pursuit of these careers, many of which have been considered not possible for the blind in the past.

**1104    National Federation of the Blind: Writers Division**
National Federation of the Blind
1800 Johnson Street
Baltimore, MD 21230                      410-659-9314
                                    FAX: 410-685-5653
                                    e-mail: nfb@nfb.org
                                         www.nfb.org

*Marc Maurer, President*
*Pam Allen, Director*
*Diane McGeorge, Director*

Blind writers in all styles, including poetry, short story, fiction, non-fiction, magazine writing and theatrical work offer encouragement and support to blind writers and authors. Issues cover various aspects of this business, including selling your work, publishing, technology, motivation and discovering writing and publishing resources.

**1105    National Mobility Equipment Dealers Association**
6
3327 W Bearss Avenue
Tampa, FL 33618                          813-264-2697
                                         800-833-0427
                                    FAX: 813-962-8970
                                    e-mail: nmeda@aol.com
                                         www.nmeda.org

*Dana Roeling, Executive Director*

NMEDA is a non-profit trade association of mobility equipment dealers, driver rehabilitation specialists, and other professionals dedicated to broadening the opportunities for people with disabilities to drive or be transported in vehicles modified with mobility equipment. All members work together to improve transportation options of people with disabilities.

**1106    Rolf Institute**
5055 Chaparral Court
Suite 103
Boulder, CO 80301                        303-449-5903
                                         800-530-8875
                                    FAX: 303-449-5978
                                    e-mail: seecof@aol.com
                                         www.rolf.org

*Ida P Rolf, Founder*

Established in 1971, The Rolf Institute is a nonprofit corporation, organized and existing under the laws of California and Colorado. It is recognized by the US Government as a tax-exempt educational and scientific research organization.
        *1971*

**1107    United Educational Services**
PO Box 1099
Buffalo, NY 14224
                                         800-458-7900
                                    FAX: 716-668-7875

*David L Slosson, VP*
*Cathy A Rajca, Customer Service*

Publisher and distributor of Curricular Materials, Tests, Developmental Resource and Collaborative Materials for Speech-Language Pathologists, special educators, and classroom teachers. United also sponsors professional workshops for special educators, classroom teachers, counselors, administrators and parents.

**1108    Universal Institute: Rehab & Fitness Center**
15-17 Microlab Road
Suite 101
Livingston, NJ 07039                     973-992-8181
                                    FAX: 973-992-9797
                       e-mail: chesney12@comcast.net
                                         www.d2motion.com

*Scott Chesney, Director*
*Jaymee Bernstein, Executive Director*

Universal institute is a 15,000 square foot, state of the art rehabilitation facility that specializes in neurological disorders such as brain injuries, spinal cord injury, strokes, etc. We offer PT, OT, speech pathology, cognitive remediation, aqua therapy and EMG biofeedback.

**1109    Universal Pediatric Services**
1115 N Warrior Lane
Waukee, IA 50263                         515-987-3436
                                         800-383-0303
                                    FAX: 515-224-0630
                                    e-mail: hrjay123@aol.com

Universal Pediatric Services, provides high tech care to medically fragile children and adults in the home setting. Emphasis is placed on the provision of services in the rural areas, the ability to service high tech needs and the promotion of primary nurse concept.

**1110    Victorian Acres Premier**
1427 34th Avenue SW
Altoona, IA  50009                          515-967-0103
FAX: 515-967-0101

*Staci Bell, Manager*

VAP is a quality provider of rehabilitation, vocational, residential and community-based treatment programs for persons with acquired brain injury. Services are offered to a broad range of ages, acquities and funding resources. Res-Care Premier currently operates programs in Illinois, Missouri, Iowa, Texas and Florida, with plans for program development across the US.

**1111    World Chiropractic Alliance**
2950 N Dobson Road
Suite 1
Chandler, AZ  85224                         480-786-9235
                                            800-347-1011
                                       FAX: 480-732-9313
e-mail: comments@worldchiropracticalliance.org
www.worldchiropracticalliance.org

*Matthew McCoy, Chairman*

Dedicated to protecting and strengthening chiropractic around the world. Serving as a watchdog and advocacy organization, we place our emphasis on education and political action.
*1989*

## Specific Disabilities

**1112    ARRISE**
Oak Leyden Developmental
9238 Parklane Avenue
Franklin Park, IL  60131                    847-451-2740
FAX: 847-451-4008

*Jayna Sullivan, Manager*
Provides information about autism.

**1113    Acid Maltase Deficiency Association (AMDA)**
PO Box 700248
San Antonio, TX  78270                      210-494-6144
                                       FAX: 210-490-7161
e-mail: tianrama@aol.com
www.amda-pompe.org
Offers a newletter, informational materials, networking, referrals to local resources, national advocacy efforts, and also maintains a research registry.
*1994*

**1114    Alzheimer's Disease Education and Referral Center (ADEAR)**
PO Box 8250
Silver Spring, MD  20907
                                            800-438-4380
                                       FAX: 301-495-3334
e-mail: adear@nia.nih.gov
www.alzheimers.nia.nih.gov
The Alzheimer's Disease Education and Referral (ADEAR) center provides information about Alzheimer's disease and related disorders to health professionals, patients and their families and the public. Most of the publications are provided at no charge as a service of the National Institute on Aging (NIA), one of the Federal Government's National Institutes of Health.

*1990*

**1115    American Academy for Cerebral Palsy and Developmental Medicine**
555 E Wells Street
Suite 1100
Milwaukee, WI  53202                        414-918-3014
                                       FAX: 414-276-2146
e-mail: woppenhe@ucla.edu
www.aacpdm.org

*William Oppenheim MD, VP*
*Luciano Dias MD, President*
*Barry Russman MD, VP*

Multidisciplinary scientific society devoted to the study of cerebral palsy and other childhood onset disabilities, to promoting professional education for the treatment and management of these conditions and to improving the quality of life for people with these disabilities.
*September*

**1116    American Academy of Allergy, Asthma and Immunology**
555 E Wells Street
Suite 1100
Milwaukee, WI  53202                        414-272-6071
                                            800-822-2762
                                       FAX: 414-272-6070
e-mail: info@aaaai.org
www.aaaai.org

*Sandra Gawchik, Co-Director*
*Stanley Goldstein, Director*
*Kay Whalen, Executive Vice President*

Nonprofit association representing allergists, clinical immunologists, asthma specialists, allied health professionals, and others with a special interest in allergy and asthma. The AAAAI's mission is to advance the knowledge, education and practice of allergy, asthma and immunology.

**1117    American Academy of Child and Adolescent Psychiatry**

3615 Wisconsin Avenue NW
Washington, DC  20016                       202-966-7300
                                       FAX: 202-966-2891
e-mail: webthing@aacap.org
www.aacap.org

*Greg Fritz MD, Secretary*
*Thomas F Anders MD, President*
*Virginia Q Anthony, Executive Director*

A 501 (C)(3) nonprofit membership organization composed of over 6,500 child and adolescent psychiatrists. Members actively research, evaluate, diagnose and treat psychiatric disorders and pride themselves on giving direction to and responding quickly to new developments in addressing the health care needs of children and their families.
*53 pages*

**1118    American Amputee Foundation**
PO Box 250218
Little Rock, AR  72225                      501-666-2523
                                       FAX: 501-666-8367
e-mail: info@americanamputee.org
www.americanamputee.org

*Kathy Heshman, Info Specialist*
*Cathrine Walden, Executive Director*

Serves primarily as a national information clearinghouse and referral center assisting mainly amputees and their families. AAF researches and gathers information including studies, product information, services, self-help publications and review articles written within the field. AAF has helped with claims, justification letters to payers, testimony and life care planning. Free information packet for phone or letter inquiries.

*1975*

## 1119 American Association of Naturopathic Physicians

3201 New Mexico Avenue NW
Suite 350
Washington, DC 20016      202-895-1392
866-538-2267
FAX: 202-274-1992
e-mail: member.services@naturopathic.org
www.naturopathic.org

*Nancy Dunne, President*

Founded in 1985, the American Association of Naturopathic Physicians (AANP) is the national professional society representing naturopathic physicians who are licensed or eligible for licensing as primary care providers. Policy is established through a House of Delegates, which consists of representatives from 34 state naturopathic associations, four naturopathic specialty societies and the four recognized naturopathic medical programs.
*1985*

## 1120 American Association of Naturopathic Physicians

3201 New Mexico Avenue NW
Suite 350
Washington, DC 20016      202-895-1392
866-538-2267
FAX: 202-274-1992
e-mail: member.services@naturopathic.org
www.naturopathic.org

*Nancy Dunne, President*

Founded in 1985, the American Association of Naturopathic Physicians (AANP) is the national professional society representing naturopathic physicians who are licensed or eligible for licensing as primary care providers. Policy is established through a House of Delegates, which consists of representatives from 34 state naturopathic associations, four naturopathic specialty societies and the four recognized naturopathic medical programs.
*1985*

## 1121 American Association of Spinal Cord Injury Nurses

7520 Astoria Boulevard
East Elmhurst, NY 11370      718-803-3782
FAX: 718-803-0414
e-mail: aascin@unitedspinal.org
www.aascin.org

*Vivian Beyda PhD, Associate Executive Director*
*Stephen Sofer PhD, Program Manager*
*Sara Lerman MPH, Program Manager*

A nonprofit organization dedicated to promoting quality care for individuals with spinal cord impairment. The AASCIN is a membership organization of registered and licensed practical nurses in the US and Canada who practice in diverse SCI settings. The AASCIN Nursing Research Program funds research in the area of spinal cord impairment and nursing practice. There is an annual educational conference sponsored by AASCIN. In addition, 'SCI Nursing' is published by AASCIN.
*1983*

## 1122 American Association of Spinal Cord Injury Psychologists & Social Workers

7520 Astoria Boulevard
East Elmhurst, NY 11370      718-803-3782
FAX: 718-803-0414
e-mail: aascipsw@unitedspinal.org
www.aascipsw.org

*Peter Addesso, President*
*J Scott Richards, President*

Organized and operated for scientific and educational purposes to advance and improve the psychosocial care of persons with spinal cord impairment, develop and promote education and research related to the psychosocial care of persons with spinal cord injury, recognize psychologists and social workers whose careers are devoted to the problems of spinal cord impairment.

## 1123 American Back Society

2647 International Boulevard
Suite 401
Oakland, CA 94601      510-536-9929
FAX: 510-536-1812
e-mail: info@americanbacksoc.org
www.americanbacksoc.org

*Scott Haldeman MD PhD, President*
*Aubrey Swartz, Executive Director*
*Ronald Donelson MD MS, VP*

The American Back Society was founded in Oakland, California in 1982 as a nonprofit organization dedicated to providing an interdisciplinary forum for health care professionals and scientists interested in relieving pain and diminishing impairment through proper diagnosis and treatment of patients suffering from spinal pathology.
*1982*

## 1124 American Board for Certification in Orthotics & Prosthetics

330 John Carlyle Street
Suite 210
Alexandria, VA 22314      703-836-7114
FAX: 703-836-0838
e-mail: info@abcop.org
www.abcop.org

*William W DeToro, President*
*Kathy Carter, Executive Director*

The American Board for Certification in Orthotics and Prosthetics (ABC) is the national certifying and accrediting body for the orthotic and prosthetic professions. The public requires and deserves assurance that the persons providing orthotic and prosthetic services and care are qualified to provide the appropriate services, and it was on this basis that the ABC was established as a credentialing organization.

## 1125 American Cancer Society

1599 Clifton Road
Atlanta, GA 30329      404-320-3333
800-ACS-2345
FAX: 404-325-2217
www.cancer.org

*Gary J Streit, Chair*
*John B Seffrin PhD, CEO*
*Ralph B Vance MD, President*

The American Cancer Society is the nationwide community-based voluntary health organization dedicated to eliminating cancer as a major health problem by preventing cancer, saving lives, and diminishing suffering from cancer, through research, education, advocacy, and service.

## 1126 American Chemical Society Committee on Chemists with Disabilities

1155 16th Street NW
Washington, DC 20036      202-872-4600
800-227-5558
FAX: 202-776-8258
e-mail: webmaster@acs.org
www.acs.org

*William F Carroll Jr, President*
*James D Burke, Chair of the Board*
*John Crum, Chief Executive Officer*

Strives to inform chemistry educators and employers of scientific and technical personnel about the capabilities and contributions of chemical professionals who happen to have physical, sensory or learning disabilities. Mission is to promote opportunities—educational and professional—for persons with disabilities interested in pursuing careers in chemistry and in fields requiring knowledge of chemistry, and to demonstrate the capabilities of those persons to educators, employers and peers.

**1127  American Cleft Palate/Craniofacial Association**
1504 E Franklin Street
Suite 102
Chapel Hill, NC 27514                              919-933-9044
                                                   800-24C-LEFT
                                              FAX: 919-933-9604
                                        e-mail: info@acpa-cpf.org
                                               www.cleftline.org

*Earl J Seaver PhD, President*
*Kerry F Callahan MA, Secretary*
*Nancy C Smythe, Executive Director*

International nonprofit medical society of health care professionals who treat and/or perform research on birth defects of the head and face. Publishes Cleft Palate-Craniofacial Journal. Affiliated with Cleft Palate Foundation.

**1128  American Diabetes Association**
National Call Center
1701 N Beauregard Street
Alexandria, VA 22311
                                                   800-342-2383
                                     e-mail: webmaster@diabetes.org
                                                www.diabetes.org

*Lawrence T Smith, Chair of the Board*
*Robert A Rizza, President*
*Karmeen Kulkarni, President*

Mission is to prevent and cure diabetes, and to improve the lives of all people affected by diabetes.

**1129  American Heart Association: National Center**
7272 Greenville Avenue
Dallas, TX 75231                                   214-373-6300
                                                   800-242-8721
                                              FAX: 214-706-5233
                                             www.americanheart.org

*M Wheeler, Chief Executive Officer*

Fifty-five state affiliates monitoring local chapters offering educational materials, seminars, conferences and transportation for members nationwide. Maintains a listing of over 1,000 stroke support groups across the nation for referral to stroke survivors, their families, caregivers and interested professionals.

**1130  American Juvenile Arthritis Organization (AJAO)**
Arthritis Foundation
PO Box 7669
Atlanta, GA 30357                                  404-872-7100
                                                   800-568-4045
                                                 www.arthritis.org

*Laura Robbins, Chair*
*John H Klippel, CEO and President*

Arthritis Foundation efforts center on the three-fold mission of the organization: research, prevention and quality of life. The Arthritis Foundation currently provides nearly $20 million in grants to nearly 300 researchers to help find a cure, prevention or better treatment for arthritis. The Arthritis Foundation's sponsorship of research for more than 50 years has resulted in major treatment advances for most arthritis diseases.

**1131  American Lung Association**
61 Broadway
Floor 6
New York, NY 10006                                 212-315-8700
                                                   800-586-4872
                                              FAX: 212-315-8870
                                          e-mail: info@lungusa.org
                                                  www.lungusa.org

*John Kirkwood, Chief Executive Officer*

Voluntary health organization with a national office and constituent and affiliate associations around the country. Fights lung disease in all its forms, with special emphasis on asthma, tobacco control and environmental health.

**1132  American Network of Community Options and Resources**
1101 King Street
Suite 380
Alexandria, VA 22314                               703-535-7850
                                              FAX: 703-535-7860
                                         e-mail: ancor@ancor.org
                                                  www.ancor.org

*Renee L Pietrangelo, CEO*
*Fred Romkema, President*
*Patti Manus, Secretary*

Nonprofit trade association representing private providers who provide supports and services to people with disabilities.

**1133  American Orthotic and Prosthetic Association**
1666 K Street NW
Suite 440
Washington, DC 20006                               571-431-0876
                                              FAX: 571-431-0899
                                          e-mail: info@aopanet.org
                                                  www.aopanet.org

*Tyler J Wilson, Executive Director*

A national trade association representing patient care facilities and manufacturers of prosthetic and orthotic devices. A major focus is to provide industry companies with information about reimbursement, insurance and government regulations and other business management issues.
                                                        *1917*

**1134  American Osteopathic Association**
142 E Ontario Street
Chicago, IL 60611                                  312-202-8000
                                                   800-621-1773
                                              FAX: 312-202-8200
                                          e-mail: info@osteotech.org
                                                 www.osteopathic.org

*George Thomas, President*
*John Crosby J D, Executive Director*

National organization for the advancement of osteopathic medicine in the US, and the professional association for over 48,000 physicians. The AOA accredits the Colleges of Osteopathic Medicine, osteopathic internship and residency programs and health care facilities.

**1135  American Paraplegia Society**
Journal Of Spinal Cord Medicine
7520 Astoria Boulevard
East Elmhurst, NY 11370                            718-803-3782
                                              FAX: 718-803-0414
                                        e-mail: aps@unitedspinal.org
                                                   www.apssci.org

*Todd A Linsenmeyer, Chair*
*Joel Delisa, Director*
*Mario Balmaseda, Director*

Organized and operated for scientific and educational purposes to advance and improve health care of persons with spinal cord impairment, develop and promote education and research related to spinal cord impairment, recognize physicians and doctoral level researchers whose careers are devoted to the problems of spinal cord impairment.

**1136  American Sleep Disorders Association**
1 Westbrook Corporate Center
Suite 920
Westchester, IL 60154                              708-492-0930
                                              FAX: 708-492-0943
                                         e-mail: paldrich@aasmnet.org
                                                  www.aasmnet.org

*Jerome Barrett, Executive Director*
*Richard Rosenberg, Director*
*Pat Aldrich, Assistant Executive Director*

Dedicated to improving sleep health and promoting the highest quality education and research within the field of sleep medicine.

**1137  American Spinal Injury Association**

2020 Peachtree Road NW
Atlanta, GA  30309                         404-355-9772
                                       FAX: 404-355-1826
                                    www.asia-spinalinjury.org

*Marcia L Sipski MD, President and Director*
*Glenn Rechtine MD, President and Director*

Professional association for physicans and other health professionals working in all aspects of spinal cord injury. Conducts annual scientific meeting to survey latest advancements in the field. See website for full details.
                    *1973*

**1138  American Stroke Association**

American Heart Association
7272 Greenville Avenue
Dallas, TX  75231                          214-373-6300
                                            888-478-7653
                                       FAX: 214-706-5231
                           e-mail: strokeconnection@heart.org
                                    www.strokeassociation.org

*M Wheeler, Chief Executive Officer*

Fifty-five state affiliates monitoring local chapters offering educational materials, seminars, conferences and transportation for members nationwide. Maintains a listing of over 1,000 stroke support groups across the nation for referral to stroke survivors, their families, caregivers and interested professionals.

**1139  American Urological Association Foundation**

1000 Corporate Boulevard
Suite 410
Linthicum, MD  21090                       410-689-3990
                                            800-828-7866
                                       FAX: 410-689-3998
                              e-mail: admin@afud.org
                                         www.afud.org

*Donald Lee, Chairman*
*Brian Walsh, Vice Chairman*
*Richard Williams, President*

The AFUD is a 501(c)(3) organization dedicated to the prevention of urologic diseases through the expansion of patient education, research, public awareness and advocacy.

**1140  Amytrophic Lateral Sclerosis Association**

27001 Agoura Road
Suite 150
Calabasas Hills, CA  91301                 818-880-9007
                                            800-782-4747
                                       FAX: 818-880-9006
                          e-mail: alsinfo@alsa-national.org
                                          www.alsa.org

*Gary Leo, CEO and President*
*Jeff Snyder, Vice President/Communications*

National not-for-profit voluntary health organization dedicated solely to the fight against ALS. Purpose is to encourage, identify and fund quality research into the cause, means of prevention and possible cures of ALS and improve living with ALS.

**1141  Angelman Syndrome Foundation**

3015 E New York Street
Suite A2265
Aurora, IL  60504                          630-978-4245
                                            800-432-6435
                                            630-978-7408
                              e-mail: info@angelman.org
                                       www.angelman.org

*Jay Vogelsang, President*
*Eileen Braun, Executive Director*

To advance the awareness and treatment of Angelman Syndrome through education, information exchange and research.

**1142  Arthritis Consulting Services**

2787 E Oakland Park Boulevard
Suite 204
Fort Lauderdale, FL  33306                 954-739-3202
                                            800-327-3027
                                       FAX: 954-337-2887
                          e-mail: acs@stoparthritis.com
                                    www.stoparthritis.com

*Donna K Pinorsky RN BA, Administrator*
*Pat Rothblatt, Office Manager*

For over 40 years Arthritis Consulting Services has been committed to the treatment and elimination fo symptoms commonly associated with arthritis. Through the use of natural hormones/compounds and ingredients we have successfully alleviated arthritic symptoms in our patients.

**1143  Arthritis Foundation**

1330 W Peachtree Street NW
Suite 100
Atlanta, GA  30309                         404-872-7100
                                            800-283-7800
                                       FAX: 404-872-9559
                              e-mail: help@arthritis.org
                                        www.arthritis.org

*John H Klippel, CEO and President*

Offers information and referrals regarding educational materials and programs, fund-raising, support groups, seminars and conferences offered by 55 local chapters across the United States.

**1144  Association for Children with Down Syndrome**

4 Fern Place
Plainview, NY  11803                       516-933-4700
                                       FAX: 516-933-9524
                          e-mail: information@acds.org
                                          www.acds.org

*Sebastian Musio, Executive Director*

ACDS provides a continuum of year-round programs and services that include diagnostic evaluations and treatment, early intervention, day care/nursery, preschool, special education and clinical services for children, from infancy to age 5; individualized residential services for adults, age 21 and over; and evening and weekend recreation and socialization services for children, age 5 and over. The agency also provides nursery/day care programs in an integrated setting.
                    *1966*

**1145  Association of Birth Defect Children**

930 Woodcock Road
Suite 225
Orlando, FL  32803                         407-895-0802
                                            800-313-2232
                          e-mail: staff@birthdefects.org
                                      www.birthdefects.org

*Betty Mekdeci, Manager*

National not-for-profit organization that functinos as a clearinghouse, providing parents and professionals with information about birth defects and services for children with disabilities. Studies the links between drugs, radiation, alcohol, chemicals, lead, mercury, dioxin, and birth defects. Publishes newsletters and publications for parents, professionals, and interested organizations.

**1146  Association of Children's Prosthetic/Orthotic Clinics**

6300 N River Road
Suite 727
Rosemont, IL  60018                        847-698-1694
                                    FAX: 847-823-0536
                                 e-mail: king@aaos.org
                                        www.acpoc.org

*Sheril King, Executive Director*

Established for the purpose of supporting clinical teams that treat children with prosthetic or orthotic devices. Goals are achieved through programs of professional education and clinical research.

**1147  Asthma and Allergy Foundation of America**

1233 20th Street NW
Suite 402
Washington, DC  20036                      202-466-7643
                                           800-727-8462
                                    FAX: 202-466-8940
                                 e-mail: info@aafa.org
                                        www.aafa.org

*Chris Ward, President*
*Bill Lin, Executive Director*

Not-for-profit organization dedicated to improving the quality of life for people with asthma and allergies and their caregivers through education, advocacy and research. Provides practical information, community based services, support and referrals through a national network of chapters and educational support groups. Also raises funds for asthma care and research.
*1953*

**1148  Ataxia-Telangiectasia Children's Project (A-T Children's Project)**

668 S Military Trail
Deerfield Beach, FL  33442                 954-481-6611
                                           800-543-5728
                                    FAX: 954-725-1153
                                 e-mail: info@atcp.org
                                        www.atcp.org

*Brad A Margus, President*
*Jennifer Thornton, Executive Director*
*Rosa Fernandez, Family Support/Communications*

A public, tax-exempt, nonprofit organization formed to raise funds through events and contributions from corporations, foundations and friends. Funds are used to accelerate first-rate, international scientific research aimed at finding a cure and improving the lives of all children with ataxia-telangiectasia.

**1149  Attention Deficit Disorder Association**

12345 Jones Road
Suite 287-7
Houston, TX  77070                         281-897-0982
                                    FAX: 281-894-6883
                              e-mail: addaoffice@pdq.net
                                        www.adda-sr.org

*Pam Esser, President*

Mission is to help people with AD/HD lead happier, more successful lives through education, research and public advocacy. Whether you have AD/HD yourself, someone special in your life does, or you treat, counsel or teach those who do, ADDA is an organization for you. ADDA focuses especially on the needs of AD/HD adults and young adults with AD/HD. Parents of children with AD/HD are also welcome.

**1150  Attention Deficit Information Network**

58 Prince Street
Needham, MA  02492                         781-455-9895
                                    FAX: 781-449-1332
                                 e-mail: adin@gis.net
                               www.addinfonetwork.org

A nonprofit volunteer organization that offers support and information to families of children and adults with ADD, and to professionals through a network of AD-IN chapters. AD-IN was founded in 1988 by several parent support group leaders on the premise of parents helping parents deal with their children with ADD. Network has parent and adult support group chapters throughout the country.

**1151  Autism Services Center**

PO Box 507
Huntington, WV  25710                      304-525-8014
                                    FAX: 304-525-8026
                                 www.autismservices.com

*Ruth C Sullivan, Executive Director*
*Jodi Fields, Director Office Administration*

Service agency for individuals with autism and other developmental disabilities and their families. Assists families and agencies attempting to meet the unique needs of individuals with autism and other developmental disabilities: makes available technical assistance in designing programs. Provides supervised apartments, groups homes, respite services, independent living programs and job-coached employment. Provides case management services for a four-county area in West Virginia.

**1152  Autism Society of America**

7910 Woodmont Avenue
Suite 300
Bethesda, MD  20814                        301-657-0881
                                           800-328-8476
                                    FAX: 301-657-0869
                              e-mail: info@autism-society.org
                                   www.autism-society.org

*Lee Grossman, President and CEO*
*Ann Pulley, Manager*

ASA is the largest and oldest grassroots organization within the autism community, with chapters in nearly every state and over 60,000 members and supporters nationwide. ASA is the leading source of education, information and referral about autism spectrum disorders and has been the leader in advocacy and legislative initiatives for more than four decades.

**1153  Autism Treatment Center of America**

2080 S Undermountain Road
Sheffield, MA  01257                       413-229-2100
                                           877-766-7473
                                    FAX: 413-229-3202
                              e-mail: info@optioninstitute.com
                                 www.autismtreatmentcenter.org

*Barry Kaufman, Director and Founder*
*Samahria Kaufman, Director*
*Bryn Hogan, Director*

Since 1983, the Autism Treatment Center of America has provided innovative training programs for parents and professionals caring for children challenged by Autism, Autism Spectrum Disorders, Pervasive Developmental Disorder (PDD) and other developmental difficulties. The Son-Rise Program teaches a specific yet comprehensive system of treatment and education designed to help families and caregivers enable their children to dramatically improve in all areas of learning.
*1983*

**1154  Batten Disease Support and Research Association**

120 Humphries Drive
Suite 2
Reynoldsburg, OH  43068                    740-927-4298
                                           800-448-4570
                                 e-mail: bdsra1@bdsra.org
                                        www.bdsra.org

*George Maxim, President*
*Lance Johnston, Executive Director*

An international support and research networking organization for families of children and young adults with an inherited neurological degenerative disorder known as Batten Disease.

*1986*

**1155 Bell**
National Mental Health Association
2001 N Beauregard Street
12th Floor
Alexandria, VA 22311
703-684-7722
800-969-NMHA
FAX: 703-684-5968
TTY: 800-433-5959
www.nmha.org

*Michael Faenza, Chief Executive Officer*

Targets public and private mental health organizations as well as interested corporations, agencies and individuals. The Bell contains information about a variety of issues pertaining to mental health, including: the effects of managed care on mental health care; the implications of Congressional decisions for mental health; prevention efforts on the local, state and national levels; national anti-stigma efforts and national public education campaigns. *$24.00*
*Monthly*

**1156 Birth Defect Research for Children**
930 Woodcock Road
Suite 225
Orlando, FL 32803
407-895-0802
800-313-2232
FAX: 407-245-7087
e-mail: staff@birthdefects.org
www.birthdefects.org

*Betty Mekdeci, Manager*

A nonprofit organization that provides information about birth defects of all kinds to parents and professionals. Offers a library of medical books and files of information on less common categories of birth defects and is involved in research to discover possible links between environmental exposures and birth defects.

**1157 Brain Injury Association of America**
8201 Greensboro Drive
Suite 611
McLean, VA 22102
703-761-0750
800-444-6443
FAX: 703-761-0755
e-mail: shconnors@biausa.org
www.biausa.org

*Susan H Connors, President/CEO*
*Roxanne Dean, I&R Manager*

Creating a better future through brain injury prevention, research, education and advocacy.

**1158 Brain Injury Association of New York State**
10 Colvin Avenue
Albany, NY 12206
518-459-7911
800-228-8201
FAX: 518-482-5285
e-mail: info@bianys.org
www.bianys.org

*Michael Kaplen, President*
*Judith Avner, Executive Director*
*Judith Sandman, Director Membership and Developm*

Statewide nonprofit membership organization that advocates on behalf of individuals with brain injury and their families and promotes prevention.

*1982*

**1159 Brain Injury Association of Texas**
1339 Lamar Square Drive
Suite C
Austin, TX 78704
512-326-1212
800-392-0040
512-326-8088
FAX: 512-326-8088
e-mail: info@biatx.org
www.biatx.org

*Margaret Struchen, President*

The Brain Injury Association of Texas is an organization which arose from the mutual frustration and sense of helplessness experienced by families in their search for appropriate facilities and support to return loved ones who had sustained brain injuries to maximum functioning potential. It was organized in 1982 as the Texas Head Injury Association by a group of family members and health care professionals in an effort to meet the needs of the survivors of brain injury.
*1982*

**1160 Breast Cancer Action**
55 New Montgomery Street
Suite 323
San Francisco, AR 94105
415-243-9301
877-278-6722
FAX: 415-243-3996
e-mail: info@bcaction.org
www.bcaction.org

*Barbara Brenner, Executive Director*
*Alex Momtchiloff, Development Director*
*Brenda Salgado, Program Manager*

Carries the voices of people affected by breast cancer to inspire and compel the changes necessary to end the breast cancer epidemic. Holds monthly meetings and publishes a bimonthly newsletter on topics related to breast cancer. Works closely with California Breast Cancer Organization and the National Cancer Coalition.
*1990*

**1161 Cancer Care: National Office**
275 7th Avenue
New York, NY 10001
212-712-6120
800-813-HOPE
FAX: 212-712-8495
e-mail: info@cancercare.org
www.cancercare.org

*Paul Friedman, President*
*Diana Blum, Executive Director*

Cancer Care is a national nonprofit organization whose mission is to provide free professional help to people with all cancers through counseling, education, information and referral and direct financial assistance.

**1162 Cancer Control Society**
2043 N Berendo Street
Los Angeles, CA 90027
323-663-7801
FAX: 323-663-7757
e-mail: cancercontrol@cox.net
www.cancercontrolsociety.com

*Frank Cousineau, VP*
*Norman Fritz, President*
*Lorraine Rosenthal, Co-Founder*

To prevent and control cancer and other degenerative diseases through nutrition and nontoxic alternative therapies.

**1163 Cerebral Palsy Associations of New York State**
90 State Street
Suite 929
Albany, NY 12207       518-436-0178
FAX: 518-436-8619
e-mail: info@cerebralpalsynys.org
www.cerebralpalsynys.org

*Susan Constantino, Executive Director*
*Cheryl Bradway, Administrative Assistant*
*Barbara Crosier, Legislative Affairs Director*

Mission is to advocate and provide direct services with and for individuals with cerebral palsy and other significant disabilities, and their families, throughout New York State, in order to promote lifelong opportunities and choices for independence, inclusion and enhanced quality of life. Provides services and programs for more than 40,000 individuals with cerebral palsy and developmental disabilities and their families.

**1164 Child Neurology Service**
Inova Fairfax Hospital For Children
3300 Gallows Road
Falls Church, VA 22042       703-776-4001

www.inova.org

*John Singleton, President*

Offers infants and children to age 21 with neurological problems diagnosis, consultation, recommendations for therapy and more services. We also care for adults with cerebral palsy.

**1165 Children and Adults with Attention Deficit Disorders (CHADD)**
8181 Professional Place
Suite 150
Landover, MD 20785       301-306-7070
800-233-4050
FAX: 301-306-7090
www.chadd.org

*Mary Durheim, President*

National nonprofit organization founded in 1987 in response to the frustration and sense of isolation experienced by parents and their children with AD/HD.

**1166 Christopher Reeve Paralysis Foundation**
636 Morris Tpke
Suite 3a
Short Hills, NJ 07078       973-379-2690
800-225-0292
FAX: 973-912-9433
e-mail: info@paralysis.org
www.crpf.org

*Kathy Lewis, President*
*Joel Faden, Chairman*
*John Hughes, Vice Chairman*

Committed to funding research that develops treatments and cures for paralysis caused by spinal cord injury and other central nervous system disorders. The Foundation also vigorously works to improve the quality of life for people living with disabilities through its grants program, paralysis resource center and advocacy efforts.

**1167 Citizens Alliance for Venereal Disease Awareness**
Mount Prospect Community Center
1000 W Central Road
Mt Prospect, IL 60056       847-255-5380

*Walter Cook, Chief Executive Officer*

Offers information on symptoms, treatment and prevention of STDs.

**1168 Cleft Palate Foundation**
1504 E Franklin Street
Suite 102
Chapel Hill, NC 27514       919-933-9044
800-24 -LEFT
FAX: 919-933-9604
e-mail: info@cleftline.org
www.cleftline.org

*Earl J Seaver, President*
*Nancy Smythe, Executive Director*
*Louis Argenta, Director*

A nonprofit organization dedicated to optimizing the quality of life for individuals affected by facial birth defects. It was founded by the American Cleft Palate-Craniofacial Association to be the public service arm of the professional Association. Produces free publications.
*1973*

**1169 College of Syntonic Optometry**
322 N Aurora Street
Ithaca, NY 14850       607-277-4749
FAX: 607-277-5216
www.syntonicphototherapy.com

*Larry Wallace, President*
*Cathy Stern, VP*
*Larry Od*

An active and growing post-graduate educational organization.

**1170 Community Services for Autistic Adults and Children**
751 Twinbrook Parkway
Rockville, MD 20851       301-762-1650
FAX: 301-762-5230
TTY:800-735-2258
e-mail: csaac@csaac.com
www.csaac.org

*Peter Donaghy, Executive Director*

CSAAC is a private, nonprofit agency dedicated to serving persons disabled by autism.

**1171 Connecticut Association for Children and Adults with Learning Disabilities (CACLD)**
25 Van Zant Street
Suite 15-5
Norwalk, CT 06855       203-838-5010
FAX: 203-866-6108
e-mail: cacld@optonline.net
www.cacld.org

*Beryl Kaufman, Executive Director*

CACLD is a regional nonprofit organization providing information and support to benefit children and adults with LD and ADD. CACLD is a resource for families and professionals.

**1172 Cranial Academy**
8202 Clearvista Parkway
Suite 9d
Indianapolis, IN 46256       317-594-0411

www.cranialacademy.com

*Theresa S Crampton, President*
*Harold I Magoum, VP*
*Patricia S Crampton, Executive Director*

Not-for-profit group comprised of physicians dedicated to promote and safeguard the health of their patients. Since the not-for-profit group was founded in 1947, its members have carried on the traditions of their founders, who placed the welfare of their patients above all other considerations.

*1947*

**1173  DB-Link**
Teaching Research
345 Monmouth Avenue N
Monmouth, OR 97361
503-838-8391
FAX: 503-838-8150
e-mail: kenyond@wou.edu
www.tr.wou.edu/dblink

*John Reiman, Director*
*Meredith Brodsky, Executive Director*

TRI has nearly 70 staff members in its main office in Monmouth and a branch office in Eugene, Oregon. Specific areas of work include studies examining the relationship between teaching and learning, model development and training in early childhood education, technical assistance in special education, research and development work in the area of traumatic brain injury and national technical assistance and information dissemination for deaf-blind individuals and their families.

**1174  Dental Amalgam Mercury Syndrome (DAMS)**
1079 Summit Avenue
Saint Paul, MN 55105
800-311-6265
e-mail: dentaltruth@yahoo.com
Offers information dedicated to enlightening the public on the potential risks of mercury in dental amalgam fillings.

**1175  Epilepsy Foundation**
4351 Garden City Drive
Landover, MD 20785
301-459-3700
800-332-1000
FAX: 301-459-3700
e-mail: epilepsy@peaknet.net
www.epilepsyfoundation.org

*Eric R Hargis, President*
*S. Tyrone Alexander, Member of the Board*
*Gregory L Barkley, MD, Member of the Board*

The Epilepsy Foundation is the national voluntary agency solely dedicated to the welfare of the 2.7 million people with epilepsy in the U.S. and their families. The organization works to ensure that people with seizures are able to participate in all life experiences; and to prevent, control and cure epilepsy through research, education, advocacy and services.
*1968*

**1176  Exceptional Cancer Patients**
522 Jackson Park Drive
Meadville, PA 16335
814-337-8192
FAX: 814-337-0699
e-mail: info@mind-body.org
www.ecap-online.org

*Barry Bittman, CEO/Medical Director/Owner*

Provides exceptional resources, comprehensive professional training programs and extraordinary interdisciplinary retreats that help people facing the challenges of cancer and other chronic illnesses discover their inner healing resources.

**1177  Families Together in NYS: Children with Mental Needs and Developmental Disabilities**
16 Elk Street
Albany, NY 12207
518-432-0333
888-326-8644
FAX: 518-434-6478
e-mail: info@ftnys.org
www.ftnys.org

*Diane Kopitowsky, President*
*Davin Robinson, VP*

Families Together in NYS, is a non profit parent-run organization that strives to establish a unified voice for families of children with special emotional, behavioral, social, and mental health needs. Our mission is to ensre that every family has access to needed information, support, and services. Family Together offers support, advocacy and education to parents and family memebers through its quarterly newsletters, annual conference, legislative luncheon, toll-free information and much more.

**1178  Families of Spinal Muscular Atrophy**
PO Box 196
Libertyville, IL 60048
847-367-7620
800-886-1762
FAX: 847-367-7623
e-mail: sma@fsma.org
www.fsma.org

*Audrey Lewis, Executive Director*
*Colleen McCarthy O'Toole, Office Manager*

Families of Spinal Muscular Atrophy is the largest international organization dedicated solely to: eradicating spinal muscular atrophy (SMA) by promoting and supporting research, helping families cope with SMA through informational programs and support, and educating the public and professional community about SMA.
*1984*

**1179  Federation of Families for Children's Mental Health**
1101 King Street
Suite 420
Alexandria, VA 22314
703-684-7710
FAX: 703-836-1040
e-mail: ffcmh@ffcmh.org
www.ffcmh.com

*Wendy Luckenbill, President*
*Arthur Penn, VP*
*Sandra Spencer, Executive Director*

A national parent-run organization focused on the needs of children with emotional, behavioral or mental disorders and their families. Call national office for local chapter referral. Sliding scale membership.

**1180  Feingold Association of the US**
554 E Main Street
Suite 301
Riverhead, NY 11901
631-369-9340
800-321-3287
FAX: 631-369-2988
e-mail: flifer@aol.com
www.feingold.org

*Debbie Lehner, Manager*

An organization of families and professionals, the Feingold Association of the United States is dedicated to helping children and adults apply proven dietary techniques for better behavior, learning and health.

**1181  Health Education AIDS Liason (HEAL)**
PO Box 1103
New York, NY 10113
212-873-0780
FAX: 212-873-0891
www.healaids.com

*Michael Ellner, President*
*Roberto Giraldo, Member of the Board*
*Barnett J Weiss, Member of the Board*

Nonprofit, community-based educational organization providing information, hope, and support to people who are HIV positive or living with AIDS. The men and women at HEAL are health professionals, people living with life threatening diseases, and concerned volunteers.

**1182 Herpes Resource Center**
American Social Health Association
PO Box 13827
Research Triangle Park, NC 27709
919-361-8400
FAX: 919-361-8425
www.ashastd.org

*James R Allen MD MPH, President*
*Deborah Arrindell, VP, Health Policy*

The Herpes Resource Center (HRC) focuses on increasing education, public awareness, and support to anyone concerned about herpes. Since its formation in 1979, the HRC has helped over five million people. The work of the HRC is funded primarily through individual gifts, subscriptions and product sales, with additional support in the form of corporate contributions. Today, people continue to depend on ASHA and the HRC for educational information about herpes.

**1183 International Association for Cancer Victors: Northern California Chapter**
5336 Harwood Road
San Jose, CA 95124
408-249-4516
FAX: 408-264-9659
e-mail: cavictor@ix.netcom.com
www.cancervictors.org
Volunteer community service organization to inform and support interested persons who want to learn more about natural, nontoxic remedies and practices.
*1962*

**1184 International Resource Center for Down Syndrome**
1621 Euclid Avenue
Cleveland, OH 44115
216-621-5858
FAX: 216-621-0221

**1185 International Rett Syndrome Association**
9121 Piscataway Road
#2B
Clinton, MD 20735
301-856-3334
800-818-7388
FAX: 301-856-3336
e-mail: irsa@rettsyndrome.org
www.rettsyndrome.org

*Kathy Hunter, President*
*Barry Rinehart, CEO*

Nonprofit voluntary organization dedicated to serving as an information and referral center for physicians and families of children with Rett Syndrome. The Association's mission includes supporting and promoting research into the prevention, control, and cure of the disorder; increasing public awareness; and providing emotional support for affected families. Engages in patient advocacy; promotes family and professional education; and provides referrals to support groups.
*1985*

**1186 Joni and Friends**
PO Box 3333
Agoura Hills, CA 91376
818-707-5664
800-523-5777
FAX: 818-707-2391
TTY: 818-707-9707
e-mail: jafmin@joniandfriends.org
www.joniandfriends.org

*Joni Eareckson Tada, Founder*
*Tina Beeson, Dir Correspondence & Resources*

A nonprofit organization seeking to accelerate Christian ministry with people affected by disabilities. JAF educates churches and the community worldwide concerning the needs of the disabled and how those needs can be met. We sponsor family retreats for families with disabled members. Wheels for the World collects, restores and distributes used wheelchairs to disadvantaged populations around the world.

*1979*

**1187 Judge David L Bazelon Center for Mental Health Law**
1101 15th Street NW
Suite 1212
Washington, DC 20005
202-467-5730
FAX: 202-223-0409
TTY:202-467-4232
e-mail: info@bazelon.org
www.bazelon.org

*Robert Bernstein, Executive Director*
*Ira Burnim, Legal Director*
*Clay Braswell, Development Director*

The mission of the Judge David L. Bazelon Center for Mental Health Law is to protect and advance the rights of adults and children who have mental disabilities. The Center envisions an America where people who have mental illnesses or developmental disabilities exercise their own life choices and have access to the resources that enable them to participate fully in their communities.

**1188 Juvenile Diabetes Foundation International**
120 Wall Street
New York, NY 10005
212-785-9500
800-533-CURE
FAX: 212-785-9595
e-mail: info@jdrf.org
www.jdf.org

*Larry Soler, Vice President*
*Laura Whitton, Manager*
*Ronnie Tepp, National Manager*

The world's leading nonprofit, nongovernmental funder of diabetes research. It was founded in 1970 by parents of children with diabetes. JDF's mission is to find a cure for diabetes and its complications through the support of research. JDF also sponsors international workshops and conferences for biomedical researchers, individual chapters offer support groups and other activities for families affected by diabetes. JDF has more than 110 chapters and affiliates worldwide. Quarterly newsletter.
*1970*

**1189 Learning Disabilities Association of America (LDA)**
4156 Library Road
Pittsburgh, PA 15234
412-341-1515
FAX: 412-344-0224
e-mail: info@LDAAmerica.org
www.ldanatl.org

*Suzanne Fornaro, President*
*Ken Warlick, Secretary*

Our purpose is to advance the education and general welfare of children and adults of normal or potentially normal intelligence who manifest disabilities of a perceptual, conceptual, or coordinative nature.

**1190 Leukemia & Lymphoma Society**
1311 Mamaroneck Avenue
White Plains, NY 10605
914-949-5213
800-955-4572
FAX: 914-949-6691
www.leukemia.org

*Dwayne Howell, CEO and President*
*Cynthia Gardner, Executive VP*
*Richard Geswell, Executive VP*

The Leukemia and Lymphoma Society is the world's largest voluntary health organization dedicated to funding blood cancer research, education and patient services.

*1949*

#### 1191 Leukemia Society of America
600 3rd Avenue
4th Floor
New York, NY 10016     212-573-8484
800-955-4572
www.leukemia.org

*Dwayne Howell PhD, President/CEO*

National voluntary health agency dedicated to curing leukemia, lymphoma, Hodkin's disease and myeloma and to improving the quality of life and their families.

#### 1192 Lighthouse International
The Sol and Lillian Goldman Building
111 E 59th Street
New York, NY 10022     212-821-9200
800-829-0500
888-222-9320
FAX: 212-821-9707
TTY:212-821-9173
e-mail: info@lighthouse.org
www.lighthouse.org

*William B Follett, Chairman*
*Tara A Cortes, President/CEO*

A leading resource worldwide on vision impairment and rehabilitation. Through its pioneering work in vision rehabilitation services, education, research and advocacy, Lighthouse International enables people of all ages who are blind or partially sighted to lead independent and productive lives. Founded in 1905 and headquartered in New York, Lighthouse International is a not-for-profit organization, depending on the support of individuals, foundations and corporations.
*1905*

#### 1193 Little People of America
5289 NE Elam
Suite F-700
Hillsboro, OR 97124     503-846-1562
888-572-2001
FAX: 503-846-1590
e-mail: info@lpaonline.org
www.lpaonline.org

*Tricia Mason, National President*
*Matt Roloff, Manager*

Assists dwarfs with their physical and developmental concerns resulting from short stature, usually no taller then 4' 10". Provides medical, environmental, educational, vocational, and parental guidance, so that short-statured individuals and their families may enhance their lives and lifestyles with minimal limitations.
*1957*

#### 1194 March of Dimes Birth Defects Foundation
1275 Mamaroneck Avenue
White Plains, NY 10605     914-949-7166
800-996-2724
FAX: 914-997-4763
www.modimes.org
The mission of the March of Dimes is to improve the health of babies by preventing birth defects and infant mortality. The MOD Resource Center provides information and referral services to the public from 9:00 am to 8:00 pm EST.

#### 1195 Mississippi Society for Disabilities
PO Box 4958
Jackson, MS 39296     601-362-2585
800-962-2400
FAX: 601-982-1951
www.mississippicap.com

*Presley Posey, Executive Director*

Provides a broad spectrum of programs and services to meet the needs of Mississippi children and adults with disabilities, thus enabling them to achieve maximum independence and gain the greatest possible quality of life.

#### 1196 Multiple Sclerosis Center of Oregon
Oregon Health & Sciences University
3181 SW Sam Jackson Park Road
Portland, OR 97239     503-494-3460

www.ohsu.edu

*Peter O Kohler MD, President*
*Steven D Stadum JD, Chief Administrative Officer*
*James Morgan, Executive Director*

Committed to Multiple Sclerosis research and patient and community education.

#### 1197 Multiple Sclerosis Foundation
6350 N Andrews Avenue
Fort Lauderdale, FL 33309     954-776-6805
800-225-6495
FAX: 954-938-8708
e-mail: admin@msfocus.org
www.msfocus.org

*Jules Kuperberg, Administrator*

Contemporary national, nonprofit organization that provides free support services and public education for persons with Multiple Sclerosis, newsletters, toll-free phone support, information, referrals, home care, assitive technology, and support groups.

#### 1198 Muscular Dystrophy Association
3300 E Sunrise Drive
Tucson, AZ 85718     520-529-2000
800-572-1717
FAX: 520-529-5383
e-mail: mda@mdausa.org
www.mdausa.org

*Robert Ross, Chief Executive Officer*
*Chris Rosa, PhD, Member of the Board*

MDA provides comprehensive medical services to tens of thousands of people with neuromuscular diseases at some 230 hospital-affiliated clinics across the country. The Association's worldwide research program, which funds over 400 individual scientific investigations annually, represents the largest single effort to advance knowledge of neuromuscular diseases and to find cures and treatments for them. In addition, MDA conducts far-reaching educational programs for the public and professionals.

#### 1199 Myositis Association
1233 20th Street NW
Suite 402
Washington, DC 20036     202-887-0082
FAX: 202-466-8940
e-mail: tma@myositis.org
www.myositis.org

*Bob Goldberg, Executive Director*
*Theresa Reynolds Curry, Communications Manager*
*Jami Latham, Member Services/Operations Coord*

The Myositis Association is dedicated to finding a cure for inflammatory and other related myopathies, while serving those affected by these diseases.
*1993*

#### 1200 NIH Osteoporosis and Related Bone Diseases National Resource Center
2 Ams Circle
Bethesda, MD 20892     202-223-0344
800-624-BONE
FAX: 202-293-2356
TTY: 202-466-4315
e-mail: naimsboneinfo@mail.nih.gov
www.naims.nih.gov/bone
Distributes information to patients, health professionals and the public on osteoporosis, Paget's disease of bone, osteogenesis imperfecta, and other metabolic bone diseases. Information on prevention, early detection and treatment of these diseases is available.

**1201 National AIDS Fund**

729 15th Street NW
Floor 9
Washington, DC 20005     202-408-4848
FAX: 202-408-1818
e-mail: info@aidsfund.org
www.aidsfund.org

*Kandy Ferree, President and CEO*
*Krista Bradley, Program Officer*
*Lissa Gilden, Development Officer*

Dedicated to eliminating HIV/AIDS as a major health and social problem.

**1202 National Alliance on Mental Illness (NAMI)**

Colonial Place Three
2107 Wilson Boulevard, Suite 300
Arlington, VA 22201     703-524-7600
800-950-NAMI
FAX: 703-524-9094
TTY: 703-516-7227
www.nami.org

*Suzanne Vogel-Scibilia MD, President*
*Fredrick R Sandoval, First Vice President*
*Anand Pandya MD, Second Vice President*

NAMI is a nonprofit, grassroots, self-help, support and advocacy organization of consumers, families, and friends of people with severe mental illnesses, such as schizophrenia, schizoaffective disorder, bipolar disorder, major depressive disorder, obsessive-compulsive disorder, panic and other severe anxiety disorders, autism and pervasive developmental disorders, attention deficit/hyperactivity disorder, and other severe and persistent mental illnesses that affect the brain.

**1203 National Amputation Foundation**

40 Church Street
Malverne, NY 11565     516-887-3600
FAX: 516-887-3667
e-mail: amps76@aol.com
www.nationalamputation.org

*Alfred Pennacchia, President*

Helps people who have had amputations to adjust to society. Members are military veterans with service connected amputations, as well as civilian amputees, who help show new amputees how to cope. Publishes a veteran newsletter for amputees. Donated medical equipment give-a-way program to anyone in need. Items must be picked up.
*Quarterly 1919*

**1204 National Association for Continence**

PO Box 1019
Charleston, SC 29402     843-377-0900
800-252-3337
FAX: 843-377-0905
e-mail: memberservices@nafc.org
www.nafc.org

*Katherine Jeter, Founder*
*Nancy Muller, Executive Director*
*Jeff Irwin, Financial Reporting*

NAFC is the world's largest and most prolific consumer advocacy organization dedicated to helping people who struggle with incontinence and related voiding dysfunction.

**1205 National Association for Down Syndrome**

PO Box 206
Wilmette, IL 60091     630-325-9112
FAX: 630-325-8842
e-mail: info@nads.org
www.nads.org

*Diane Gomboz, President*
*Jackie Rotondi, First VP*
*M Sheila Hebein, Executive Director*

Works for a strong network of support systems within their own organization and with medical, educational and school service professionals who work with children and adults with Down Syndrome. NADS serves the Chicago Metropolitan area.

**1206 National Association to Aid Fat Americans**

PO Box 188620
Sacramento, CA 95818     916-443-0303

*Patrick Vujovich, President*

Support and education for overweight people.

**1207 National Ataxia Foundation**

2600 Fernbrook Lane N
Suite 119
Minneapolis, MN 55447     763-553-0020
FAX: 763-553-0167
e-mail: naf@ataxia.org
www.ataxia.org

*Becky Kowalkowski, Patient Services Director*
*Mike Parent, Executive Director*

The National Ataxia Foundation is a nonprofit, membership-supported organization established in 1957 to help ataxia families. The Foundation is dedicated to improving the lives of persons affected by ataxia through support, education, and research.
*1957*

**1208 National Brachial Plexus/Erb's Palsy Association**

PO Box 23
Larsen, WI 54947     920-836-2151
FAX: 209-644-5813
e-mail: info@nbpepa.org
www.nbpepa.org

*Brenda Copeland-Moore, President*
*Kris Kiesow, Treasurer*
*Cheryl Pratt, VP*

To educate, inform, and assist those affected by Brachial Plexus Palsy by offering information, contacts, resources, parent matching, and assistance developing chapters or support groups throughout the United States.

**1209 National Center for Learning Disabilities**

381 Park Avenue S
Room 1401
New York, NY 10016     212-545-7510
888-575-7373
888-575-7373
FAX: 212-545-9665
www.ncld.org

*Frederic Poses, Chairman*
*James Wendorf, Executive Director*
*Sheldon Horowitz, Director, Professional Services*

National, nonprofit organization dedicated to increasing opportunities for all individuals with learning disabilities to achieve their potential. Services include national information and resources, public outreach and communications and legislative advocacy and public policy. Free online newsletters available through the website.
*1977*

**1210 National Council for Community Behavioral Healthcare**

12300 Twinbrook Parkway
Suite 320
Rockville, MD 20852     301-984-6200
FAX: 301-881-7159
e-mail: membership@nccbh.org
www.nccbh.org

*Linda Rosenberg, Chief Executive Officer*

National organization of community-based providers of behavioral health services. Mission is to champion opportunities that advance our members' ability to deliver proactive and holistic health care services.

**1211    National Council on Spinal Cord Injury**

151 Tremont Street
Boston, MA  02111                    617-451-5757
                                FAX: 617-338-4266
                            e-mail: neuro@jiac.net
                            www.asia-spinalinjury.org

*Arthur D Ullian, Chairman*
*Robert Kargman, Owner*

A membership organization for agencies and individuals. Fosters communication among members of the spinal cord injury community and the general public. Supports research and works for the integration of individuals with spinal cord injury into the general community.

**1212    National Diabetes Information Clearinghouse**

1 Information Way
Bethesda, MD  20892                  301-654-3327
                                     800-860-8747
                                FAX: 703-738-4929
                          e-mail: ndic@info.niddk.nih.gov
                          www.diabetes.niddk.nih.gov

An information and referral service of the National Institute of Diabetes and Digestive and Kidney Diseases, one of the National Institutes of Health. The clearinghouse responds to written inquiries, develops and distributes publications about diabetes, and provides referrals to diabetes organizations, including support groups. The NDIC maintains a database of patient and professional education materials, from which literature searches are generated.
*1978*

**1213    National Digestive Diseases Information Clearinghouse**

2 Information Way
Bethesda, MD  20892                  301-654-3810
                                     800-891-5389
                                FAX: 703-738-4929
                          e-mail: nddic@info.niddk.nih.gov
                          www.digestive.niddk.nih.gov

Information and referral service of the National Institute of Diabetes and Digestive and Kidney Diseases. A central information resource on the prevention and management of digestive diseases, the clearinghouse responds to written inquiries, develops and distributes publications about digestive diseases, provides referrals to digestive disease organizations and support groups, and maintains a database of patient and professional education materials from which literature searches are generated.
*1980*

**1214    National Down Syndrome Congress**

1307 Center Drive
Suite 102
Atlanta, GA  30338                   770-604-9500
                                     800-232-6372
                          e-mail: info@ndsccenter.org
                          www.ndsccenter.org

*David Tolleson, Executive Director*
*Betty Totten, Manager*

To provide leadership in all areas of concern related to persons with Down syndrome.

**1215    National Down Syndrome Society**

666 Broadway
New York, NY  10012                  212-460-9330
                                     800-221-4602
                                FAX: 212-979-2873
                          e-mail: info@ndss.org
                          www.ndss.org

*Alan P Brownstein, President*

Not-for-profit organization increases public awareness about Down syndrome and works to discover its underlying causes through research, education and advocacy. Distributes timely and informative materials, encourages and supports the activities of local parent support groups, sponsors sonferences and scientific symposia and undertakes major advocacy efforts—all to increase awareness and acceptance of people with Down syndrome.
*1979*

**1216    National Fragile X Foundation**

PO Box 190488
San Francisco, CA  94119             925-938-9300
                                     800-688-8765
                                FAX: 925-938-9315
                          e-mail: NATLFX@FragileX.org
                          www.fragilex.org

*Robert Miller, Executive Director*

Unites the fragile X community to enrich lives through educational and emotional support, promote public and professional awareness and advance research toward improvement treatments and cure for fragile X syndrome.

**1217    National Hemophilia Foundation**

116 W 32nd Street
Floor 11
New York, NY  10001                  212-328-3700
                                     800-424-2634
                                FAX: 212-328-3777
                          e-mail: info@hemophilia.org
                          www.hemophilia.org

*Paul Haas, President*
*Alan Kinniburgh, CEO*

The mission of the National Hemophilia Foundation is education, research and advocacy on behalf of people with bleeding disorders.

**1218    National Institute of Arthritis and Musculoskeletal and Skin Diseases**

1 Ams Circle
Bethesda, MD  20892                  301-495-4484
                                     877-226-4267
                                FAX: 301-718-6366
                                TTY: 301-565-2966
                          e-mail: niamsinfo@mail.nih.gov
                          www.nih.gov/niams

*Dr Stephen I Katz, Director*
*Kelly Collins, Manager*

Mission is to support research into the causes, treatment and prevention of arthritis and musculoskeletal and skin diseases, the training of basic and clinical scientists to carry out this research, and the dissemination of information on research progress in these diseases.

**1219    National Institute of Neurological Disorders and Stroke**

PO Box 5801
Bethesda, MD  20824                  301-496-5751
                                     800-352-9424
                                FAX: 301-402-2186
                                TTY: 301-468-5981
                          www.ninds.nih.gov

*Audrey Penn, Executive Officer*

America's focal point for support of research on brain and nervous system disorders. Its active public information program provides physicians, patients and the public with educational materials and research highlights. Materials provided by the public information program include brochures, fact sheets, information packets and special reports. All publications are free of charge.

**1220  National Kidney and Urologic Diseases Information Clearinghouse**
3 Information Way
Bethesda, MD  20892                   301-654-4415
                                       800-891-5390
                                  FAX: 703-738-4929
                    e-mail: nkudic@info.niddk.nih.org
                                    www.niddk.nih.gov

*Mel Eagle, Manager*

NKUDIC was established in 1987 to increase knowledge and understanding about diseases of the kidneys and urologic system among people with these conditions and their families, health care professionals, and the general public.
*1987*

**1221  National Library Services for the Blind & Physically Handicapped**
Library of Congress
1291 Taylor Street NW
Washington, DC  20011                 202-707-5100
                                       888-657-7323
                                  FAX: 202-707-0712
                                  TTY:202-707-0744
                             e-mail: nls@loc.gov
                                     www.loc.gov.nls

*Frank Kurt Cylke, Director*

Administers a free library program of braille and audio materials circulated to eligible borrowers in the United States by postage-free mail.

**1222  National Mental Health Association**
2001 N Beauregard Street
12th Floor
Alexandria, VA  22311                 703-684-7722
                                       800-433-5959
                                  FAX: 703-684-5968
                                  TTY: 800-433-5959
                         e-mail: infoctr@nmha.org
                                       www.nmha.org

*Michael Faenza, President and CEO*

Nonprofit organization addressing all issues related to mental health and mental illness. With more than 340 affiliates nationwide, NMHA works to improve the mental health of all Americans, especially the 54 million individuals with mental disorders, through advocacy, education, research and service.
*1909*

**1223  National Mental Health Consumers Self-Help Clearinghouse**
1211 Chestnut Street
Suite 1207
Philadelphia, PA  19107               215-751-1810
                                       800-553-4539
                                  FAX: 215-636-6312
                      e-mail: info@mhselfhelp.org
                                   www.mhselfhelp.org

*Karena Bayruns, Information/Referral*
*Mimi Rose, Program Director*
*Shannon Flannagan, Manager*

Consumer-run national technical assistance center serving the mental health consumer movement. We help connect individuals to self-help and advocacy resources, and we offer expertise to self-help groups and other peer-run services for mental health consumers.

**1224  National Multiple Sclerosis Society**
733 3rd Avenue
New York, NY  10017                   212-986-3240
                                       800-344-4867
                                  FAX: 314-781-1440
                     e-mail: info@gatewaymssociety.org
                                  www.nationalmssociety.org

*Edward A Kangas, Chairman/CEO*
*Susan Locke Wilkey, Secretary*
*Joyce M Nelson, President/CEO*

Mission is to end the devastating effects of MS. Provides professional and public education; information and referral; and supports research. One hundred and forty local chapters and branches offer counseling services, advocacy, discount prescription and health care products program, and assistance in obtaining adaptive equipment.

**1225  National Organization for Rare Disorders**
PO Box 1968
Danbury, CT  06813                    203-744-0100
                                       800-999-6673
                                  FAX: 203-797-9590
                                  TTY: 203-797-9590
                     e-mail: orphan@rarediseases.org
                                     www.rarediseases.org

*Abbey Meyers, President*
*Karen Ball, CEO/Founder*

Unique federation of voluntary health organizations dedicated to helping people with rare orphan diseases and assisting the organizations that serve them. NORD is committed to the identification, treatment and cure of rare disorders through programs of education, advocacy, research and service.

**1226  National Parkinson Foundation**
1501 NW 9th Avenue Bob Hope Road
Miami, FL  33136                      305-547-6666
                                       800-327-4545
                                  FAX: 305-243-5595
                      e-mail: contact@parkinson.org
                                      www.parkinson.org

*Daniel Arty, President*
*Paul F Oreffice, Chairman*
*Alan M Slewett, Secretary*

The purpose of this Foundation is to find the cause and cure for Parkinson's Disease and related neurodegenerative disorders through research, to educate general medical practitioners to detect the early warning signs of Parkinson's Disease and to improve the quality of life for both patients and their caregivers. Provides current information to patients, caregivers and families. Publishes quarterly newsletter.
*1957*

**1227  National Stroke Association**
9707 E Easter Lane
Centennial, CO  80112                 303-649-9299
                                       800-878-6537
                                  FAX: 303-649-1328
                         e-mail: cgriffin@stroke.org
                                        www.stroke.org

*George L Davis, Chairman of the Board*
*James Baranski, Chief Executive Officer*

The only national health organization solely committed to stroke prevention, treatment, rehabilitation and community reintegration. Provides packaged training programs, on-site assistance, physician, patient and family education materials to acute and rehab hospitals. Develops workshops; operates the Stroke Information & Referral Center and produces professional publications such as Stroke: Clinical Updates and the Journal of Stroke and Cerebrovascular Diseases.

**1228 Overeaters Anonymous World Service Office**
PO Box 44020
Rio Rancho, NM 87174
505-891-2664
FAX: 505-891-4320
e-mail: info@oa.org
www.oa.org

*Naomi Lippel, Executive Director*

OA is not just about weight loss, obesity or diets; it addresses physical, emotional and spiritual well-being. It is not a religious organization and does not promote any particular diet. To address weight loss, OA encourages members to develop a food plan with a health care professional and a sponsor.

**1229 PACER Center (Parent Advocacy Coalition for Educational Rights)**
8161 Normandale Boulevard
Minneapolis, MN 55437
952-838-9000
800-537-2237
FAX: 952-838-0199
TTY: 952-838-0190
e-mail: pacer@pacer.org
www.pacer.org

*Paula F Goldberg, Executive Director*

Mission is to expand opportunities and enhance the quality of life of children and young adults with disabilities and their families based on the concept of parents helping parents. Offers workshops, individual assistance and written information. Provides programs and materials that assist multicultural families, programs for students, schools and professionals with disability awareness puppet and child abuse prevention programs. Computer Resource Center/Software Lending Library available.
*1977*

**1230 Paralyzed Veterans of America**
801 18th Street NW
Washington, DC 20006
202-872-1300
800-424-8200
e-mail: info@pva.org
www.pva.org

*Randy Pleza, President*

A congressionally chartered veterans service organization, has developed a unique expertise on a wide variety of issues involving the special needs of our members— veterans of the armed forces who have experienced spinal cord injury or dysfunction.
*1946*

**1231 Parents of Children with Down Syndrome**
11600 Nebel Street
Rockville, MD 20852
301-984-5781
FAX: 301-816-2429

*Fred Beughmen, Executive Director*

Activities include formal and informal meetings; parent-to-parent counseling; contacting new parents of Down Syndrome children to offer support and information on community resources; providing information on doctors, hospitals and professionals.

**1232 People Against Cancer**
PO Box 10
Otho, IA 50569
515-972-4444
FAX: 515-972-4415
e-mail: info@peopleagainstcancer.net
www.peopleagainstcancer.com

*Frank Wiewel, Executive Director*

A nonprofit, grassroots public benefit organization dedicated to 'New Directions in the War on Cancer.' We are a democratic organization of people with cancer, their loved ones and citizens working together to protect and enhance medical freedom of choice.

**1233 Polio Connection of America**
PO Box 182
Howard Beach, NY 11414
607-962-9806
FAX: 718-738-1509
e-mail: w1066polio@hotmail.com
www.geocities.com

*George Cook, Executive Director*

This is a voluntary nonprofit organization dedicated to locating polio survivors and providing them with information concerning Post-Polio Syndrome. Committed to locating, informing and supporting polio survivors affected with Post-Polio Syndrome to help them receive appropriate treatment. Provides appropriate referrals, as well as educational materials including a newsletter, brochures and booklets. Also an advocate for Post-Polio Syndrome research.
*8 pages Quarterly*

**1234 Polio Health International**
4207 Lindell Boulevard
Suite 110
Saint Louis, MO 63108
314-534-0475
FAX: 314-534-5070
e-mail: info@post-polio.org
www.post-polio.org

Enhances the lives and independence of polio survivors and home ventilator users through education, advocacy, research and networking.

**1235 Polio Society**
4200 Wisconsin Avenue
#106273
Washington, DC 20016
301-897-8180
FAX: 202-994-3153

*Jessica Scheer, Executive Director*

Provides educational resources and support group services to people who had polio and are now experiencing the late effects of polio.

**1236 Post-Polio Health International**
4207 Lindell Boulevard
Suite 110
Saint Louis, MO 63108
314-534-0475
FAX: 314-534-5070
e-mail: info@post-polio.org
www.post-polio.org

*Frederick Maynard, President and Chairperson*
*Lawrence Becker, VP*
*John L Headly, Executive Director*

Post-Polio Health International's mission is to enhance the lives and independence of polio survivors and home ventilator users through education, advocacy, research and networking.

**1237 Prader-Willi Alliance of New York**
PO Box 1114
Niagara Falls, NY 14304
800-442-1655
FAX: 716-271-2782
e-mail: alliance@prader-willi.org
www.prader-willi.org

*Daniel Angiolillo, President*
*Daniel Maillet, VP*
*Volena Howe, VP*

The Prader-Willi Foundation is a national, nonprofit, public charity that works for the benefit of individuals with Prader-Willi syndrome and their families.

**1238  Prader-Willi Syndrome Association USA**

5700 Midnight Pass Road
Suite 6
Sarasota, FL 34242                                   941-312-0400
                                                     800-926-4797
                                              FAX: 941-312-0142
                                  e-mail: national@pwsausa.org
                                               www.pwsausa.org

*Janalee Heinemann, Executive Director*

National, nonprofit public charity that works for the benefit of
individuals with Prader-Willi syndrome and their families.

**1239  Providence Speech and Hearing Center**

1301 W Providence Avenue
Orange, CA 92868                                     714-639-4990
                                              FAX: 714-744-3841
                                      e-mail: pshc@pshc.org
                                                 www.pshc.org

*Mary Jo Hooper, Executive Director*
*Laurie Stratford, Administrative Services Manager*

Mission is to provide the highest quality services available in the
identification, diagnosis, treatment and prevention of speech,
language and hearing disorders for persons of all ages.

**1240  Rasmussen's Syndrome and Hemispherectomy Support
Network**

8235 Lethbridge Road
Millersville, MD 21108                               410-987-5221
                                              FAX: 410-987-521
                                      e-mail: rssnlynn@aol.com

*Al & Lynn Miller, Founders*

National not-for-profit organization dedicated to providing information and support to individuals affected by Rasmussen's
Syndrome and Hemispherectomy. Publishes a periodic newsletter and disseminates reprints of medical journal articles concerning Rasmussen's Syndrome and its treatments. Maintains a
support network that provides encouragement and information
to individuals affected by Rasmussen's Syndrome and their families.

**1241  Shake-A-Leg**

PO Box 1264
Newport, RI 02840                                    401-849-8898
                                              FAX: 401-848-9072
                                  e-mail: shakealeg@shakealeg.org
                                               www.shakealeg.org

*Paul Callahan, President*

Nonprofit charitable organization founded to serve people with
disabilities, with an emphasis placed on spinal cord and related
nervous system impairments. Mission is to provide mainstream,
complimentary and recreational therapeutic services that develop independent living skills for individuals who have experienced spinal cord injury and related nervous system disorders.
                                                              *1982*

**1242  Simonton Cancer Center**

PO Box 6607
Malibu, CA 90264                                     818-879-7904
                                                     800-459-3424
                                              FAX: 310-457-0421
                          e-mail: simontoncancercenter@msn.com
                                             www.simontoncenter.com

*O Carl Simonton, Medical Director*

The Simonton Cancer Center offers a "New Patient Program"
for cancer patients and their support person. In these sessions,
Dr. Simonton presents the refined specific information for increasing survival, decreasing tumor growth and most important,
improving the quality of life of the individual.

**1243  Society for Progressive Supranuclear Palsy (SPSP)**

11350 McCormick Road
Suite 906
Hunt Valley, MD 21031                                410-771-6220
                                                     800-457-4777
                                              FAX: 410-785-7009
                                      e-mail: speca@curepsp.org
                                                  www.psp.org

*John Scally, Owner*
*Richard Zyne, Executive Director*
*Kathleen M Speca, Director Development/PR*

The Society for PSP is dedicated to increasing awareness of Progressive Supranuclear Palsy, advancing research towards a
cure, and providing hope, support and education for persons
with PSP, their families and healthcare professionals.

**1244  Spina Bifida Association of America**

4590 Macarthur Boulevard NW
Suite 250
Washington, DC 20007                                 202-944-3285
                                                     800-621-3141
                                              FAX: 202-944-3295
                                      e-mail: sbaa@sbaa.org
                                                 www.sbaa.org

*Douglas Sorocco, President*
*Cindy Brownstein, Chief Executive Officer*

Nonprofit organization. Mission is to promote the prevention of
spina bifida and to enhance the lives of all affected. Addresses
the specific needs of the spina bifida community and serves as
the national representative of almost 60 chapters. Toll free 800
information and referral service. Legislative updates.
                                                              *1973*

**1245  Spinal Cord Society (SCS)**

19051 County Highway 1
Fergus Falls, MN 56537                               218-739-5252
                                              FAX: 218-739-5262
                                     www.members.aol.com/scsweb

*Charles Carson, President*

SCS is a large grass roots organization linked by over 200 chapters, a monthly Newsletter, and thousands of members throughout North America and 24 other countries. Its goal is cure of
spinal cord injury paralysis. It is an organization of the spinal
cord injured, their families and friends, and dedicated scientists
and physicians who are aiming at the ultimate goal of cure
through improved treatment and research.
                                                              *1978*

**1246  Support Group for Brachial Plexus Injury**

18 Staci Lane
Webster, NY 14580                                    585-787-0197
                                              FAX: 585-872-6158

The Support Group for Brachial Plexus Injury was established
to provide resources and emotional support to families impacted
by Erb's Palsy and other brachial plexus injuries by advising on
how best to receive and obtain insurance and treatment for this
disorder.

**1247  Texas Speech-Language-Hearing Association**

918 Congress Avenue
Suite 200
Austin, TX 78701                                     512-452-4636
                                                     888-729-8742
                                              FAX: 512-454-3036
                                  e-mail: tsha@assnmgmt.com
                                                 www.txsha.org

*Lynn Flahive, President*
*Roy Bohrer, Executive Director*

Mission is to encourage and promote the role of the speech-language pathologist and audiologist as a professional in the delivery of clinical services to persons with communications
disorders. Encourages basic scientific study of processes of individual human communication with reference to speech, hearing and language.

**1248  Tourette Syndrome Association**
4240 Bell Boulevard
Bayside, NY  11361
718-224-2999
888-486-8738
FAX: 718-224-9596
e-mail: ts@tsa-usa.org
www.tsa-usa.org

*Fred Cook, Director*
*Judit Ungar, President*

National, nonprofit membership organization. Mission is to identify the cause of, find the cure for, and control the effects of this disorder. A growing number of local chapters nationwide provide educational materials, seminars, conferences and support groups for over 35,000 members. Publishes brochures, flyers, educational materials and papers on treatment and research. Offers videos for purchase through a catalog of publications.
*1972*

**1249  United Cerebral Palsy Association**
1660 L Street NW
Suite 700
Washington, DC  20036
202-776-0406
800-872-5827
FAX: 202-776-0414
TTY: 202-973-7197
e-mail: webmaster@ucp.org
www.ucpa.org

*Thomas O'Donnell, Chair*
*Stephen Bennett, CEO and President*
*Duncan Wyeth, Vice Chair*

National not-for-profit self-help organization dedicated to providing information and support to individuals with Cerebral Palsy and other disabilities, and their families. Supports more than 160 local affiliates; these affiliates provide a variety of programs and services for affected families, including support groups. Offers several educational and support materials, including a quarterly magazine, regular newsletters, and research reports.

**1250  United Cerebral Palsy Association of New York State**
330 W 34th Street
Floor 15
New York, NY  10001
212-947-5770
FAX: 212-594-4538
e-mail: info@cerebralpalsynys.org
www.cerebralpalsynys.org

*Susan Constantino, Executive Director*
*Barbara Crosier, Director Legislative Affairs*
*Michael Alvaro, Associate Executive Director*

Mission is to advocate and provide direct services with and for individuals with cerebral palsy and other significant disabilities, and their families, throughout New York State, in order to promote lifelong opportunities and choices for independence, inclusion and enhanced quality of life. Provides services and programs for more than 40,000 individuals with cerebral palsy and developmental disabilities and their families.

**1251  Vermont Back Research Center**
1 S Prospect Street
Burlington, VT  05401
802-656-4582
800-527-7320
FAX: 802-660-9243
Conducts research aimed at reducing back-related disability following injury or acute pain episodes. Current research includes studies of posture, seating, vibration, materials handling, and exercise. The Center develops and tests assistive devices, and promotes employment of people with back disorders and rapid return to work after injury. The staff provides a variety of information services, including bibliographic searches and fact finding.

**1252  YAI: National Institute for People with Disabilities**
460 W 34th Street
New York, NY  10001
212-273-6100

www.yai.org

*Joel M Levy, CEO*
*Philip H Levy, President/COO*
*Stephen E Freeman, Associate Executive Director*

Committed to improving the lives of people with mental retardation and developmental and learning disabilities, and to assist them in maximizing their potential as productive, self sufficient citizens.
*1957*

# Visually Impaired

**1253   Blind Childrens Center**
4120 Marathon Street
Los Angeles, CA  90029
323-664-2153
800-222-3567
FAX: 323-665-3828
e-mail: info@blindchildrenscenter.org
www.blindchildrenscenter.org

*Lillian Ray Titcomb, Founder*
*Midge Horton, Executive Director*

A family centered agency which serves children with visual impairmetns from birth to school age. The center based and home based programs and services help the children aquire skills and build their independence. The center utilizes its experience and expertise to serve families and professionals worlwide through support services, education and research.
*1938*

**1254  ACB Radio Amateurs**
American Council of the Blind
4911 Old Canton Road
Jackson, MS  39211
601-432-6293
FAX: 601-982-6746
www.acb.org

*Mike Duke, President*

ACBRA is an organization of blind and sighted licensed radio amateurs who work together to make the hobby more accessible to people who are blind

**1255  Achromatopsia Network**
PO Box 214
Berkeley, CA  94701
510-540-4700
FAX: 510-540-4767
e-mail: oscar@sinewave.com
www.achromat.org

*Frances Futterman, President*

The Achromatopsia Network is a nonprofit organization for individuals concerned with achromatopsia. It is committed to sharing information about achromatopsia and providing resources to meet the special needs of those affected by this eye condition; helping individuals and families concerned with achromatopsia to connect with one another; and promoting awareness and educating with a special emphasis on accomplishing this goal among those who provides services to the visually impaired.

**1256  American Academy of Ophthalmology**
PO Box 7424
San Francisco, CA  94120
415-561-8500
FAX: 415-561-8533
e-mail: aaoe@aao.org
www.aao.org

*Susan Day, President*
*Dunbar Hoskins, Executive Vice President*

Founded in 1896, but was incorporated as an independent organization in 1979 when the AAOO was divided into separate academies. The American Academy of Ophthalmology is the largest national membership association of Eye MDs. Eye MDs are ophthalmologists, medical doctors who provide comprehensive eye care, including medical, surgical and optical care. More than 90 percent of practicing US Eye MDs are Acadmey members, and the Academy has more than 7,000 international members.
*1979*

**1257  American Action Fund for Blind Children and Adults**
1800 Johnson Street
Suite 100
Baltimore, MD  21230  410-659-9315
FAX: 410-685-5653
e-mail: actionfund@nfb.org
www.actionfund.org

*Jean Dyon Norris, Director*
*Marc Mauer, President*

A service agency which specializes in providing to blind people help which is not readily available to them from government programs or other existing service systems. The services are planned especially to meet the needs of blind children, the elderly blind, and the deaf-blind.
*1919*

**1258  American Association of the Deaf-Blind**
8630 Fenton Street
Suite 121
Silver Spring, MD  20910  301-495-4403
FAX: 301-495-4404
TTY:301-495-4402
e-mail: info@aadb.org
www.aadb.org

*Harry Anderson, President*
*Arthur Roehrig, VP*

National consumer organization, of, by and for deaf-blind Americans. Deaf-blind does not necessarily mean totally deaf and totally blind. It is a broad term that describes people who have varying degrees and types of both vision and hearing loss together. Mission is to endeavor to enable deaf-blind persons to achieve their maximum potential through increased independence, productivity and integration into the community.

**1259  American Council of Blind Lions**
PO Box 2312
Fort Collins, CO  80522  970-484-2598

e-mail: info@acb.org
www.acb.org/acbl/

*Alan Beatty, Contact*

A wonderful combination of Lionism and visual impairment nurtures the American Council of Blind Lions. ACBL's mission is awareness and highlights the great activities of the Knights of the Blind. The goals are to assist all clubs in their understanding of issues surrounding blind and visually impaired individuals.
*1971*

**1260  American Council of the Blind**
1155 15th Street NW
Suite 720
Washington, DC  20005  202-467-5081
800-424-8666
FAX: 202-467-5085
e-mail: info@acb.org
www.acb.org

*Melanie Brunson, Executive Director*

A national membership organization whose members are visually impaired and fully sighted individuals who are concerned about the dignity and well-being of blind people throughout America. Formed in 1961, the Council has become the largest organization of blind people in the US with over 70 state affiliates and special interest chapters.

*1961*

**1261  American Foundation for the Blind**
11 Penn Plaza
Suite 300
New York, NY  10001  212-502-7600
800-232-5463
FAX: 212-502-7777
e-mail: afbinfo@afb.net
www.afb.org

*Carl R Augusto, President/CEO*

The organizaton to which Helen Keller devoted her life, is a national nonprofit organization whose mission is to ensure that the ten million Americans who are blind or visually impaired enjoy the same rights and opportunities as other citizens.
*1921*

**1262  American Optometric Association**
243 N Lindbergh Boulevard
1st Floor
St Louis, MS  63141  800-365-2219
FAX: 314-991-4101
e-mail: MDJones@aoa.org
www.aoanet.org

*Michael D Jones, Executive Director*

Founded in 1898, the premier authority in the optometric industry. With more than 32,000 members and 6,600 US and foreign communities, the AOA leads the way in its mission of imporving the quality and availability of eye and vision care everywhere.
*1998*

**1263  American Printing House for the Blind**
PO Box 6085
Louisville, KY  40206  502-895-2405
800-223-1839
FAX: 502-899-2274
e-mail: info@aph.org
www.aph.org

*Tuck Tinsley, President*
*Bob Brasher, VP Advisory Services/Research*

The world's largest nonprofit organization creating educational, workplace and independent living products and services for people who are visually impaired. Also promotes independence of the blind and visually impaired persons by providing specialized materials, products, and services needed for educationand life.
*1958*

**1264  Associated Blind**
315 5th Avenue
Room 807
New York, NY  10016  212-683-4950
FAX: 212-683-4975
e-mail: memberservices@esightcareers.net
www.tabinc.org

*Herbert R Brinberg, Chairman*
*Nancy O'Connell, Executive Director*
*Theodore S Francavilla, Treasurer*

Privately funded, non-profit agency, that was founded by a group of blind individuals as an organization promoting autonomy and self-determination. The mission is to assist individuals who are blind, visually impaired or who have physical disabilities to become self-reliant and achieve financial independence through mainstream employment.

*1938*

**1265  Associated Services for the Blind**
919 Walnut Street
Philadelphia, PA  19107                215-627-0600
FAX: 215-922-0692
e-mail: dfgodzieba@asb.org
www.asb.org

*Patricia C Johnson, CEO*
*Dolores Ferrara-Godzieba, Director*

Non profit organization established to promote self-esteem, independence and self-determination in people who are blind or visually impaired. This is accomplished by providing support through education, training and resources, as well as through community action and public education, serving as a voice and advocate for the rights of all people who are blind or visually impaired.
*1983*

**1266  Association for Education & Rehabilitation of the Blind & Visually Impaired**
1703 N Beauregard Street
Suite 440
Alexandria, VA  22311                 703-671-4500
877-492-2708
FAX: 703-671-6391
e-mail: aer@aerbvi.org
www.aerbvi.org

*Sandra Ruconich, President*
*Jim Gandorf, Executive Director*
*Mark Richard, Owner*

The only international organization dedicated to rendering all possible support and assistance to the professionals who work in all phases of education and rehabilitation of blind and visually impaired children and adults.
*1984*

**1267  Association for Macular Diseases**
210 E 64th Street
8th Floor
New York, NY  10021                   212-605-3719
800-622-8524
FAX: 212-605-3795
e-mail: association@retinal-research.org
www.macula.org

*Nikolai Stevenson, President*
*Joan Daly RN, Treasurer*

Today this association acts as a nationwide support group for individuals and their families endeavoring to adjust to the restrictions and changes brought about by macualr disease.
*1978*

**1268  Blind Childrens Center**
4120 Marathon Street
Los Angeles, CA  90029                323-664-2153
800-222-3566
FAX: 323-665-3828
e-mail: info@blindchildrenscenter.org
www.blindchildrenscenter.org

*Midge Horton, Executive Director*

A family centered agency which serves children with visual impairments from birth to school-age. The center-based and home-based programs and services help the children aquire skills and build their independence. The center utilizes its expertise and experience to serve families and professionals worldwide through support services, education, and research.

*1938*

**1269  Blinded Veterans Association**
477 H Street NW
Washington, DC  20001                 202-371-8880
800-669-7079
FAX: 202-371-8258
e-mail: bva@bva.org
www.bva.org

*Thomas H Miller, Executive Director*
*Brigitte Jones, Administrative Director*

Helps veterans and their families meet the challenges of blindness.Offers two main service programs without cost to blinded veterans. Field service program provides counseling to veterans and families and information on benefits and rehabilitation.
*1945*

**1270  Books for Blind and Physically Handicapped Individuals**
Library of Congress
1291 Taylor Street NW
Washington, DC  20011                 202-707-5100
888-657-7323
FAX: 202-707-0712
TTY:202-707-0744
e-mail: nls@loc.gov
www.loc.gov/nls

*Frank Kurt Cylke, Director*
*Marvine Wanamaker, Assistant Director*

Administers a national library service that provides braille and recorded books and magazines on free loan to anyone who cannot read standard print because of visual of physical disabilities who are eligible residents of the Unites States of America citizens living abroad.
*1931*

**1271  Braille Institute of America**
741 N Vermont Avenue
Los Angeles, CA  90029                323-660-3880
800-272-4553
FAX: 323-663-0867
e-mail: info@brailleinstitute.org
www.brailleinstitute.org

*Thomas W Burton, Chairman*
*Leslie E Stocker, President*

Provides an environment of hope and encouragement for people who are blind and visually impaired through integrated educational, social and recreational programs and services.
*1929*

**1272  Braille Revival League**
1102 W International Airport Road
Anchorage, AK  99518
800-424-8666
e-mail: abilink@ak.net
www.acb.org

*Lynne Koral, President*

Encourages blind people to read and write in braille, advocates for mandatory braille instruction in educational facilities for the blind, strives to make available a supply of braille materials from libraries and printing houses and more.

**1273  California State Library Braille and Talki ng Book Library**
PO Box 942837
Sacramento, CA  94237                 916-634-0640
800-952-5666
FAX: 916-654-1119
e-mail: btbl@library.ca.gov
www.library.ca.gov/html/pubser05.cfm

*Aimee Sqourakis, Sr Librarian*

The State Library stands as one of California's great public research institutions with a five-fold mission:serving the needs of elected officials and state agency employees;preserving the state's cultural heritage by collecting historic materials on California and the West;assisting public libraries through financial aid and consulting services;offering special services to disadvantaged and handicapped clients;ensuring that the general public has convenient and consistent access to resources.
*1950*

**1274   Canine Helpers for the Handicapped**
5699 Ridge Road
Lockport, NY 14094                     716-433-4035
FAX: 716-439-0822
e-mail: chhdogs@aol.com
www.caninehelpers.netfirms.com

*Beverly Underwood, Executive Director*

Designed to unite deserving people with highly trained, disability specific dogs. The ultimate goal of this non-profit organization is to achieve a high degree of independence for the clients who have various physical and emotional challenges. Whether the need be for hearing, service, mobility (multi-service), seizure alert or therapy dogs, we are equipped to match a person with the right dog and train both to become an efficient team.
*1983*

**1275   Caption Center**
125 Western Avenue
Boston, MA 02134                       617-927-9225
FAX: 617-300-1020
TTY:617-300-3600
e-mail: access@wgbh.org
www.icdri.org/dhhi/ccowgbh

*Lori Kay, Director*
*Larry Goldberg, Director*

Has been pioneering and delivering accessible media to disabled adults, students and their families, teachers and friends for over 30 years. Each year, the Center captions more than 10,000 hours worth of broadcast and cable programs, feature films, large-format and IMAX films, home videos, music videos, DVDs, teleconferences and CD-Roms.

**1276   Chicago Lighthouse for People who are Blind and Visually Impaired**
1850 W Roosevelt Road
Chicago, IL 60608                      312-666-1331
FAX: 312-243-8539
TTY:312-666-8874
e-mail: support@chicagolighthouse.org
www.thechicagolighthouse.org

*James Kesteloot, Executive Director*

A non profit agency committed to providing the highest quality educational, clinical, vocational, and rehabilitation services for children, youth and adults who are blind or visually impaired, including deaf blind and multi disabled. Also respects personal dignity and partners with individuals to enhance independent living and self sufficiency. This agency is a leader, innovator and advocate for people who are blind or visually impaired, enhancing the quality of life for all individuals.
*1906*

**1277   Columbia Lighthouse for the Blind**
1120 20th Street NW
Suite 750s
Washington, DC 20036                   202-454-6400
877-324-5252
FAX: 202-454-6401
e-mail: info@clb.org
www.clb.org

*Dale Otto, CEO*
*Kim Zimmer, COO*
*Peter Mayo, President*

Offer programs that enable individuals who are blind or visually impaired to obtain and maintain independence at home, school, work and in the community. The programs and services include asistive technology training, career services, rehabilitation services, comprehensive low vision care and a wide range of children's programs.
*2000*

**1278   Council of Families with Visual Impairments**
American Council of the Blind
6686 NE Capricorn Lane
Bremerton, WA 98311                    202-467-5081
800-424-8666
FAX: 202-467-5085
e-mail: cindybur@comcast.net
www.acb.org

*Cindy Burgett, President*

A network of parents with blind or visually impaired children that offers support and outreach, shares experiences in parent/child relationships, exchanges educational, cultural and medical information about child development and more.

**1279   Deaf-Blind Division of the National Federation of the Blind**
National Federation of the Blind
1800 Johnson Street
Baltimore, MD 21230                    410-659-9314
FAX: 410-685-5653
e-mail: nfb@nfb.org
www.nfb.org

*Marc Maurer, President*

The nation's largest and most influential membership organization of blind persons, with a two-fold purpose: to help blind persons achieve self-confidence and self respect and to act as a vehicle for collective self-expression by the blind.
*1940*

**1280   Eye Bank Association of America**
1015 18th Street NW
Suite 1010
Washington, DC 20036                   202-775-4999
FAX: 202-429-6036
e-mail: info@restoresight.org
www.restoresight.org

*Patricia Acken-Oneil, President/CEO*
*Joseph Kelly, COO/Managing Director*

Established in 1961 by the American Academy of Ophthalmology's Committee on Eye Banks, the EBAA is a not-for-profit organization of eye banks dedicated to the restoration of sight through the promotion and advancement of eye banking.
*1961*

**1281   Fidelco Guide Dog Foundation**
103 Old Iron Ore Road
Bloomfield, CT 06002                   860-243-5200
FAX: 860-243-7215
e-mail: apply@fidelco.org
www.fidelco.org

*Roberta C Kaman, Chairman*
*Anthony G Alessi, President*
*George J Salpietro, Executive Director*

More than just New England's only guide dog school, it is a family, a group of people tied together by their mission to help bring increased freedom and independence to men and women who are visually impaired. Also breeds, trains, and places the highest quality German Shepards with men and women across the Northeast.

*1961*

**1282  Fight for Sight**
381 Park Avenue S
Room 809
New York, NY 10016

212-679-6060
FAX: 212-679-4466
e-mail: info@fightforsight.com
www.fightforsight.com

*Kenneth R Barasch, President*
*George W Feld, Vice President*
*Mary Prudden, Executive Director*

The mission is to support vision research, to find causes and cures for blindness, and to help save the sight of children through support of pediatric eye centers.
*1946*

**1283  Guide Dog Users**
14311 Astrodome Drive
Silver Spring, MD 20906

301-598-5771
888-858-1008
FAX: 301-871-7591
e-mail: info@gdui.org
www.gdui.org

*Jane Sheehan, Office Manager*

An international organization dedicated to advocacy, peer support, public education and all aspects of training, working and living with dogs specially trained to guide blind and visually impaired people.
*1972*

**1284  Guide Dogs for the Blind**
PO Box 151200
San Rafael, CA 94915

415-499-4000
800-295-4050
FAX: 415-499-4035
e-mail: information@guidedogs.com
www.guidedogs.com

*Robert Phillips, CEO/President*

A nonprofit, charitable organization with a mission to provide Guide Dogs and training in their use to visually impaired people throughout the United States and Canada.
*1942*

**1285  Guiding Eyes for the Blind**
611 Granite Springs Road
Yorktown Heights, NY 10598

914-245-4024
800-942-0149
FAX: 914-245-1609
e-mail: info@guidingeyes.org
www.guidingeyes.org

*William Badger, President/CEO*
*Carolyn Kihm, Director of Human Resources*
*Bev Klayman, Manager of Admissions Services*

An internationally recognized guide dog school that is dedicated to enriching the lives of blind and visually impaired men and women by providing them with the freedom to travel safely, thereby assuring greater independence, dignity and new horizons of opportunity
*1954*

**1286  Guiding Eyes for the Blind: Breeding and Placement Center**
Guiding Eyes for the Blind
361 Route 164
Patterson, NY 12563

845-878-3330

e-mail: jrussenberger@guidingeyes.org
www.guidingeyes.org

*Jane Russenberger, Executive Director*
*Janine Haughney, Director*
*Lee Nordin, Program Director*

Provides the means for blind and visually impaired individuals to achieve mobility, independence and companionship through the use of our professionally bred and trained guide dogs. Each month Guiding Eyes graduates approximately 12 guide dog/student teams from all over the US, Canada, and internationally. The guide dogs, 26 day residential training program, special needs program and lifetime follow-up services are offered at no cost to the students. Also provides at home training at no cost.
*1954*

**1287  Helen Keller National Center for Deaf-Blin d Youths and Adults**
141 Middle Neck Road
Sands Point, NY 11050

516-944-8900
FAX: 516-944-7302
e-mail: hkncinfo@hknc.org
www.hknc.org

*Joseph Nulty, Executive Director*
*Nancy O'Donnell, Information Services*

A national rehabilitation program serving youth and adults who are deaf-blind. Also provides services to youths and adults who are deaf-blin daccording to the definition of deaf-blindness in the Helen Keller Act.
*1967*

**1288  Horizons for the Blind**
2 N Williams Street
Crystal Lake, IL 60014

815-444-8800
FAX: 815-444-8830
e-mail: mail@horizons-blind.org
www.horizons-blind.org

*Camille Cafarelli, Executive Director*

A not for profit organization whose mission is to improve the quality of life for individuals who are blind and visually impaired, many who are senior citizens, by increasing accessibility to culture, education, recreation, employment and consumer information.
*1977*

**1289  Information Access Project: National Federation of the Blind**
1800 Johnson Street
Baltimore, MD 21230

410-659-9314
FAX: 410-685-5653
e-mail: nfb@nfb.org
www.nfb.org

*Marc Maurer, President*
*Joyce Scanlan, Program Director*

The nation's largest and most influential membership organization of blind persons. The purpose of the federation is to help blind persons achieve self confidence and self respect and to act as a vehicle for collective self expression by the blind. Members of the NFB strive to educate the public that the blind are normal individuals who can compete on terms of equality.
*1940*

**1290  Institute for Families of Blind Children**
4650 Sunset Boulevard
Mail Stop 111
Los Angeles, CA 90027

323-669-4649
FAX: 323-665-7869
e-mail: info@instituteforfamilies.org
www.instituteforfamilies.org

*Nancy Mansfield, Executive Director*

A non profit organization and all services are provided at no cost to families and professionals. Offers counseling and support to families facing the devastating diagnosis of visual impairment in their child and is there for every family member of the family during the many difficult days, weeks, and months of treatment.

*1987*

**1291  International Association of Audio Information Services (IAAIS)**
1102 W International Airport Road
Anchorage, AK  99518
412-434-6023
800-280-5325
e-mail: aiblink@ak.net
www.iaais.org

*Heather Lusignan, President*
*Lori Kesigner, Administrative Assistant*

A volunteer driven membership organization of services that turn text into speech for people who cannot see, hold or comprehend the printed word and who may be unable to access information due to a disability or health condition. IAAIS shall encourage and support the establishment and maintenance of audio information services that provide access to printed information for individuals who cannot read conventional print because of blindess or any other visual, physical or learning disability.
*1977*

**1292  Jewish Braille Institute International**
110 E 30th Street
New York, NY  10016
212-889-2525
800-433-1531
FAX: 212-689-3692
e-mail: admin@jbilibrary.org
www.jbilibrary.org

*Ellen Isler, President*
*Israel Taub, Vice President/CFO*

Formerly the Jewish Braille Institute of America seeks the integration of Jews who are blind, visually impaired, reading disabled and physically handicapped in the Jewish community and society in general.
*1931*

**1293  John Milton Society for the Blind**
370 Lexington Avenue
Room 1007
New York, NY  10017
212-870-3335
FAX: 212-870-3229
e-mail: care@careministries.org
www.jmsblind.org

*Darcy Quigley, Executive Director*

Publishes free magazines and Bible studies in Braille, cassette and large print for blind and visually impaired youth and adults.

**1294  Library Users of America**
American Council of the Blind
13532 W Choctaw Trail
Homer Glen, IL  60491
800-424-8666
FAX: 202-467-5085
e-mail: info@visionww.org
libraryusers.tripod.com/

*Barry Levine, President*
*Paul Edwards, Vice President*
*Pat Price, Treasurer*

Dedicated to the improvement of information access for blind and visually impaired people. Special emphasis is placed upon the development, acquisition and use of technology which enables those with vision loss to use printed materials independently in local library settings and elsewhere. Efforts are also made to eliminate service inequities arising from geographical, technological, attitudinal or informational barriers.

**1295  Lighthouse International**
111 E 59th Street
New York, NY  10022
212-821-9200
800-829-0500
FAX: 212-821-9707
e-mail: info@lighthouse.org
www.lighthouse.org

*Tara A Cortes, President*

The leader worldwide in helping people who are blind or partially sighted overcome the challenges of vision loss. Is also dedicated to preventing the disabling effects of uncorrectable vision loss from conditions such as macular degeneration, diabetes related eye disease, cataracts and glaucoma.
*1905*

**1296  Lions Clubs International**
300 W 22nd Street
Oak Brook, IL  60523
630-571-5466
FAX: 630-571-8890
e-mail: it@lionsclubs.org
www.lionsclubs.org

*Clement Kusiak, International President*
*Gary Lapentina, Chief Executive Officer*

Lions are known for their service to persons who are blind and visually impaired
*1917*

**1297  National Alliance of Blind Students NABS Liaison**
American Council of the Blind
62 Marshall Road
Ridgefield, CT  06877
800-424-8666
e-mail: info@acb.org
www.blindstudents.org

*Jennifer Barrow, President*

A student affiliate of the American Council of the Blind which is a national organization of blind and visually impaired high school and college students who believe that every blind and visually impaired student has the right to an equal and accessible education. Also encourages blind and visually impaired students to challenge their limits and reach their potential.
*1974*

**1298  National Association for Parents of Children with Visual Impairments (NAPVI)**
PO Box 317
Watertown, MA  02471
617-972-7441
800-562-6265
FAX: 617-972-7444
e-mail: napvi@perkins.org
www.spedex.com/napvi

*Mary Zabelski, President*
*Susan Laventure, Executive Director*

A non profit organization of, by and for parents committed to providing support to the parents of children who have visual impairments . Also a national organization that enables parents to find information and resources for their children who are blind or visually impaired including those with additional disabilities. NAPVI also provides leadership, support, and training to assist parents in helping children reach their potential.

**1299  National Association for Visually Handicapped**
22 W 21st Street
Floor 6
New York, NY  10010
212-889-3141
FAX: 212-727-2931
e-mail: staff@navh.org
www.navh.org

*Lorianie Marchi, CEO*

The only nonprofit health organization in the world solely dedicated to providing assistance to the partially sighted whose mission is to help the hard of seeing worldwide cope with the psychological effects of visual impairment and to provide low vision services, visual aids and training to anyone in need of these services.

**1300    National Association of Blind Students**
National Federation of the Blind
1800 Johnson Street
Baltimore, MD  21230                           410-659-9314
                                          FAX: 410-685-5653
                                   e-mail: sassywolf@ev1.net
                                          www.nfbstudents.org

*Marc Maurer, President*
*Joyce Scanlan, Program Director*

An organization comprimised of blind high school and college
students and is dedicated to changing the negative attitudes and
stereotypes that exist about blindness in order to secure equality and opportunity for all blind students.
*1967*

**1301    National Association of Guide Dog Users**
National Federation of the Blind
55 Delaware Avenue
Somerset, MA  02726                            508-679-8543

                                   e-mail: nfbmass@earthlink.net
                                          www.nfb-nagdu.org

*Priscilla Ferris, President*
*Marion Gwizdala, VP*

Provides information and support for guide dog users and works
to secure high standards in guide dog training. Addresses issues
of discrimination of guide dog users and offers public education
about guide dog use.

**1302    National Association to Promote the Use of Braille**
National Federation of the Blind
5805 Kellogg Avenue
Edina, MN  55424                               952-927-7694

                                   e-mail: nadine.jacobson@visi.com
                                          www.nfbcal.org

*Nadine Jacobson, President*

Dedicated to securing improved Braille instruction, increasing
the number of braille materials available to the blind and providing information of braille in securing independence, education
and employment for the blind.

**1303    National Braille Association**
3 Townline Circle
Rochester, NY  14623                           585-427-8260
                                          FAX: 585-427-0263
                              e-mail: nbaoffice@nationalbraille.org
                                          www.nationalbraille.org

*Angela Coffaro, Executive Director*
*Mary Archer, President*
*Jean Simpson, VP*

Providing continuing education to those who prepare braille,
and provides braille materials to persons who are visually impaired. Maintains collection of Braille textbooks, music, technical tables, and general interest items. Catalogs of the Braille
collection in print or Braille are available on request.

**1304    National Braille Press**
88 Saint Stephen Street
Boston, MA  02115                              617-266-6160
                                               888-965-8965
                                               888-965-8965
                                          FAX: 617-437-0456
                                   e-mail: orders@nbp.org
                                          www.nbp.org

*Paul V McLaughlin, Chairman*
*William Kilimanjaro, President*

The guiding purposes of National Braille Press are to promote
the literacy of blind children through braille, and to provide access to information that empowers blind people to actively engage in work, family, /and commuity affairs.

*1927*

**1305    National Camp for Blind Children**
Christian Record Services
1300 King Street E
Suite 119
Oshawa Ontario, Canada, L1H                    905-436-6938
                                          FAX: 905-436-7102
                       e-mail: ppage@christianrecordservices.ca
                                          www.crsblindservices.ca

*Daniel Jackson, Chairman*
*Pat Page, Director*

To enrich lives of those who are blind, visually impaired or
physically challenged regardless of race, creed, economic status
or gender. Also encourages each camper to achieve greater
self-esteem and self confidence while seeking to excel in the use
of his/her physical , mental, and spiritual capacities. Provides
fee Christian publications and programs for people with visual
impairments.
*Monthly 1999*

**1306    National Center for Vision and Child Development**
Lighthouse International
111 E 59th Street
New York, NY  10022                            212-821-9200
                                               800-829-0500
                                          FAX: 212-821-9707
                                   e-mail: info@lighthouse.org
                                          www.lighthouse.org

*Tara A Cortes, President/CEO*

The worldwide leader in helping people of all ages who are blind
or partially sighted overcome the challenges of vision loss.

**1307    National Diabetes Action Network for the Blind**
National Federation of the Blind
1412 i 70 Drive SW
Suite C
Columbia, MO  65203                            573-875-8911

                                   e-mail: ebryant@socket.net
                                          www.nfb.org/diabetes.htm

*Paul Price, President*
*Ericie Woods, First VP*
*Ed Bryant, Manager*

Leading support and information organization of persons losing
vision due to diabetes. Provides personal contact and resource
information with other blind diabetics about non-visual techniques of independently managing diabetes, monitoring glucose
levels, measuring insulin and other matters concerning diabetes.
Publishes Voice of the Diabetic, the leading publication about
diabetes and blindness.

**1308    National Federation of the Blind**
1800 Johnson Street
Baltimore, MD  21230                           410-659-9314
                                          FAX: 410-685-5653
                                   e-mail: nfb@nfb.org
                                          www.nfb.org

*Marc Maurer, President*
*Joyce Scanlan, Training Program Director*

The largest membership organization of blind people in the nation, with chapters in every state and approximately 50,000 individual members. It seeks to integrate the blind into society on
the basis of equality with the sighted so that the blind are seen as
normal, participating citizens. Has 700 local chapters.

*1940*

**1309 National Federation of the Blind: Human Services Division**
1026 E 36th Street
Baltimore, MD 21218          410-659-9314

e-mail: maricco@uwalumni.com
www.nfb.org/nfbdvlst.htm

*Marc Maurer, President*

Membership organization of blind persons working in counseling, personnel, psychology, social work, psychiatry, rehabilitation, and other social science and human resource fields. Dedicated to improving employment opportunities and advancement for blind persons and provides resources regarding blindness-related techniques and methods used in these fields.

**1310 National Federation of the Blind: Masonic Square Club**
358 Orange Street
Apt 409
New Haven, CT 06511          203-787-0287

www.nfb.org

*Ben Snow, President*

Blind individuals committed to sharing of Masonic experiences, goals and history.

**1311 National Federation of the Blind: Music Division**
National Association of Blind Musicians
1740 Tamarack Lane
Janesville, WI 53545          608-752-8749

e-mail: lmentink@tds.net
www.nfb.org

*Linda Mentink, President*

Blind persons dedicated to advancing employment and entertainment opportunities in various music fields. Offers support and information regarding copyright, publishing, promotion and other career details.

**1312 National Industries for the Blind**
1310 Braddock Place
Alexandria, VA 22314          703-998-0770
FAX: 703-998-8268
e-mail: info@nib.org
www.nib.org

*Jim Gibbons, President/CEO*
*Angela Jackson, Vice President*

A nonprofit organization that represents over 100 associated industries serving people who are blind in thirty-six states. These agencies serve people who are blind or visually impaired and help them to reach their full potential. Services include job and family counseling, job skills training, instruction in Braille and other communication skills, children's programs and more.

**1313 National Library Services for the Blind & Physically Handicapped**
Library of Congress
1291 Taylor Street NW
Washington, DC 20011          202-707-5100
888-657-7323
FAX: 202-707-0712
TTY:202-707-0744
www.loc.gov.nls

*Frank Kurt Cylke, Director*

Administers the free program that loans recorded and braille books and magazines, music scores in braille and large print, and especially designed playback equipment to residents of the United States who are unable to read or use standard print materials because of visual or physical impairment.

**1314 National Organization of Parents of Blind Children**
National Federation of the Blind
1800 Johnson Street
Baltimore, MD 21230          410-659-9314
FAX: 410-685-5653
e-mail: nfb@nfb.org
www.nfb.org/nopbc.htm

*Marc Maurer, President*

Support information and advocacy organization of parents of blind or visually impaired children. Addresses issues ranging from help to parents of a newborn blind infant, mobility and braille instruction, education, social and community participation, development of self confidence and other vital factors involved in growth of a blind child.

**1315 National Organization of the Senior Blind**
111 Marquette Avenue
Apt 503
Minneapolis, MN 55401          612-375-1625

e-mail: judysanders@usfamily.net
www.nfb.org

*Judy Sanders, President*

Membership organization of elderly blind persons providing support and information to other blind seniors. Issues include concerns such as remaining active in community and social life, maintaining private homes or living in retirement communities or nursing homes, learning the techniques used by the blind, independently caring for oneself and maintaining a positive apporach to vision loss.

**1316 New Eyes for the Needy**
PO Box 332
Short Hills, NJ 07078          973-376-4903
FAX: 973-376-3807

*Alyce Twomey, Executive Director*

Non profit organization founded to improve the vision of the less fortunate throughout the world by providing assistance for the purchase of new eyeglasses in the United States and recycling used eyeglasses for distribution overseas.
*1932*

**1317 Prevent Blindness America**
211 W Wacker Drive
Suite 1700
Chicago, IL 60606          312-363-6001
800-331-2020
FAX: 847-843-8458
e-mail: info@preventblindness.org
www.preventblindness.org

*R Rick Hart, Chairman*
*Joanne Angle, Executive Director*
*Hugh Parry, Chief Executive Officer*

The nation's leading volunteer eye health and safety organization dedicated to fighting blindness and saving sight. Also touches the lives of millions of people each year through public and professional education, advocacy, certified vision screening training, community and patient service programs and research.
*1908*

**1318 Recording for the Blind & Dyslexic**
20 Roszel Road
Princeton, NJ 08540          609-452-0606
866-732-3585
FAX: 609-750-1838
e-mail: custserv@rfbd.org
www.rfbd.org

*Stephanie Campbell, Executive Director*
*John Kelly, Chief Executive Officer*

Provides recorded and computerized textbooks, library services and other educational resources to people who cannot effectively read standard print because of visual impairment, dyslexia or other physical disability.

### 1319 Seeing Eye

PO Box 375
Morristown, NJ 07963
973-539-4425
FAX: 973-539-0922
e-mail: info@seeingeye.org
www.seeingeye.org

*Kenneth Rosenthal, President*

An organization that concentrates on its mission to enhance the independence, dignity, and self confidence of blind people through the use of seeing eye dogs, and on improving its ability to fulfill this mission. Will also continue to be, as it is in the present, the best organization of its kind in the world.
*1929*

### 1320 Services for the Visually Impaired

8720 Georgia Avenue
Suite 210
Silver Spring, MD 20910
301-589-0894
FAX: 301-589-7281
e-mail: info@servicesvi.org
www.servicesvi.org

*Ann Cook, Executive Director*
*Joel R Kahn, Business Manager*
*Gail Snider, Volunteer Coordinator*

Provides skills and resources to DC area residents who are blind or experiencing vision loss, and are also committed to helping people regain their indepence and maintaining it.
*1973*

### 1321 Special Technologies Alternative Resources

210 McMorran Boulevard
Port Huron, MI 48060
810-982-3600
800-272-8570
FAX: 810-987-6768
TTY: 810-455-0200
e-mail: star@sccl.lib.mi.us
www.sccl.lib.mi.us/star.html

*Stan Arnett Ii, Assistant Library Director*
*Mary Koch, Manager*

Addresses the needs of a very unique diverse group of people by offering a full range of library services for people who cannot read standard print. Provides reading material in specialized formats that permit individuals with disabilities to have access to the written word, delivering to customer's mailboxes free of charge. Talking Book Machines, recorded books and magazines, descriptive videos, large print editions and braille books and magazines.

### 1322 Taping for the Blind

3935 Essex Lane
Houston, TX 77027
713-622-2767
FAX: 713-622-2772
e-mail: taping@hal-pc.org
www.tapingfortheblind.org

*Randy De La Garza, President*
*Cynthia Franzetti, Executive Director*
*Janet Parisi, Secretary*

An independent non profit educational organization funded by corporations, listeners and individuals, with a mission to turn sight into sound, enriching the lives of individuals with visual, physical and learning disabilities.

*1967*

### 1323 United States Association of Blind Athletes

33 N Institute Street
Colorado Springs, CO 80903
719-630-0422
FAX: 719-630-0616
e-mail: mlucas@usaba.org
www.usaba.org

*Mark Lucas, Executive Director*
*Nicole Jamentas, Communications Director*
*Ryan Ortiz, Development Director*

The mission is to increase the number and quality of grassroots through competitive, world class athletic opportunities for Americans who are blind or visually impaired. Also value the life enhancing aspects of sports and the opportunity to demonstrate the abilities of people who are blind and visually impaired.
*1976*

### 1324 Vermont Association for the Blind and Visually Impaired

37 Elmwood Avenue
Burlington, VT 05401
802-863-1358
800-639-5861
FAX: 802-863-1481
e-mail: general@vabvi.org
www.vabvi.org

*Steven Pouliot, Executive Director*

Founded from assistance with the Helen Keller and the American Foundation for the Blind with the mission to enable Vermonters with vision problems, whether blindness or impairment, to achieve and maintain independence. Also promotes self advocacy, independence, and coping skills through our education programsand adult services.
*1926*

### 1325 Vision World Wide

5707 Brockton Drive
Apt 302
Indianapolis, IN 46220
317-254-1332
800-431-1739
FAX: 317-251-6588
e-mail: info@visionww.org
www.visionww.org

*William Corbin, Chairman*
*Patricia L Price, Founder/President*

A non profit organization dedicated to improving the lives of the vision impaired through direct interaction and indirectly through the caregiving community. Also serve both the totally blind and those with various degrees and forms of vision loss.
*1995*

### 1326 Visions/Services for the Blind & Visually Impaired

135 W 23rd Street
New York, NY 10011
646-486-4444
FAX: 646-486-4343
e-mail: info@visionsvcb.org
www.visionsvcb.org

*Nancy Jones, President*
*David Koch, VP*
*Burton M Strauss Jr, Treasurer*

Non profit rehabilitation and social service organization whose purpose is to develop and implement programs to assist blind and visually impaired people of all ages to lead independent and active lives in their homes and communities; and to educate the public to understand the capabilities and needs of people who are blind or visually impaired so that they might be integrated into all aspects of community life.

**1327  Visually Impaired Veterans of America**
American Council of the Blind
1075 N Rancho Avenue
Colton, CA  92324                           909-825-3067
                                          FAX: 909-213-8570
                       e-mail: bj2kiowa@worldnet.att.net
                                            www.acb.org

*John Fleming, President*

Maintain, promote and foster the well bring and rehabilitation of
all visually Impaired Veterans of the Armed Forces of the United
States of America who are eligible to receive from the Veterans
Administration; develops and encourages the practice of high
standards of personal professional conduct among Visually Impaired Veterans; maintain, promote, and foster public confidence and awareness In Visually Impaired Veterans.

**1328  Washington Ear**
35 University Boulevard E
Silver Spring, MD  20901                     301-681-6636
                                          FAX: 301-681-5227
                       e-mail: information@washear.org
                                          www.washear.org

*Brother Hilary Mettes, Chairman*
*Margaret Pfanstiehl, President*
*Nancy Knauss, Executive Director*

A non profit organization providing reading and information
services for blind, visually impaired and physically disabled
people who cannot effectively read print, see plays, watch television programs and films, or view museum exhibits. Ear free
services strive to substitute hearing for seeing, improving the
lives of people with limited or no vision by enabling them to be
well-informed, fully productive members of their families, their
communities and the working world.
                       *1974*

## Alabama

**1329  ASCCA**
Alabama Easter Seal Society
PO Box 21
Jacksons Gap, AL  36861
256-825-9226
800-843-2267
FAX: 256-825-8332
e-mail: info@campascca.org
www.campascca.org

*Matt Rickman, Camp Director*
*Josh Rhodes, Program Director*
*John Stephenson, Administrator*

Programs for campers with asthma/respiratory ailments, blood disorders, diabetes, epilepsy and spina bifida. Coed, ages 6-99. One-week sessions June-August.

**1330  Adventure Program**
Lakeshore Foundation
4000 Ridgeway Drive
Birmingham, AL  35209
205-313-7400
888-868-2303
FAX: 205-313-7475
e-mail: information@lakeshore.org
www.lakeshore.org

*Jeffrey Underwood, President*
*Jill Collins, Director of Recreation/Athletics*
*Wynna Harris, Director of Aquatics/Fitness*

The Lakeshore Foundation Adverture Program is a community resource, not only for individuals, but also for other organizations that serve people with disabilities. They organize adventures, assist with equipment, and make every effort to increase the accessibility of the outdoors. Certified Therapeutic recreation specialists coordinate the program.

**1331  Basketball School**
PO Box 698
Talladega, AL  35161
256-761-3259

*Carl Ponder, Principal*

**1332  Camp Seale Harris Southeastern Diabetes Education Services**
500 Chase Park S
Suite 104
Hoover, AL  35244
205-402-0415
FAX: 205-402-0416
e-mail: info@southeasterndiabetes.org
www.southeasterndiabetes.org

*Terry Ackley, Executive Director*

A summer residential program that is located at Camp ASCCA (Alabama's Special Camp for Children and Adults), that encourages and motivates youth to reach their full potential despite diabetes, and teaches families how to serve as the primary educators and supporters for children and adolescents living with this illness.

**1333  Camp Candlelight**
Epillepsy Foundation North and Central Alabama
701 37th Street S
Suite 2
Birmingham, AL  35222
205-324-4222
800-950-6662
FAX: 205-324-4338
e-mail: epilepsy@aol.com
www.epilepsyfoundation.org/ncalabama/

*Judith Adamson, Executive Director*
*Heather Hill, Program Director*
*Angel Burgett, Program Assistant*

Every summer, the Epilepsy Foundation offers a week-long camp for children ages 6 to 18. Activities are held on the 230 wooded acres of Camp ASCCA. Trained counselors, program staff and three registered nurses supervise the campers.

**1334  Camp Rap-A-Hope Medical Society and the Alliance to the Medical**
Society State of Alabama
2701 Airport Boulevard
Mobile, AL  36606
251-476-9494
FAX: 251-476-9495
e-mail: rapahope@earthlink.net
www.camprapahope.org

*Kathy Simpson, President*
*Melissa McNichol, Camp Director*
*Nell Gustavson, Administrative Assisant*

Camp Rap-A-Hope is a one-week summer camp for children and teenagers who are battling cancer or have ever been diagnosed with cancer and are 7 to 17 years of age. It is free of charge. Camp Rap-A-Hope strives to make sure every camper gets the opportunity to develop new skills and self-confidence. Camp activities are appropriate for our campers' ages and abilities and include, but are not limited to: swimming, music, arts and crafts, archery, fishing, canoeing and horseback riding.

**1335  Camp Seale Harris**
South Eastern Diabetes Education Services
500 Chase Park South
Suite 104
Hoover, AL  35244
205-402-0415
FAX: 205-402-0416
e-mail: info@southeasterndiabetes.org
www.southeasterndiabetes.org/

*Terry Ackley, Executive Director*
*Sara Latimer, Counselor/Camp Activities Drctr*
*Miranda Springer, Fund Development Director*

Offers education and day camps providing activities and structured diabetes education. With the assistance of a host of volunteer staff to include physicians, nurses, diabetes educators, dieticians, pharmacists, camp counselors, teachers, and friends, youth living with diabetes can engage in the typical camp activities that all children love and expect from camp-swimming, fishing, boating, hiking, and horseback riding.

**1336  Camp Smile-A-Mile**
PO Box 550155
Birmingham, AL  35255
205-323-8427
888-500-7920
FAX: 205-323-6220
e-mail: campsam@mindspring.com
www.campsam.org

*Jennifer Queen, Program Director*
*Lynn Thompson, Executive Director*
*Stephanie C Wilkins, Community Relations Manager*

Camp Smile-A-Mile is a non-profit organization for children who have or had cancer in Alabama. Camp Smile-A-Mile's mission is to provide challenging, unforgettable recreational and educational experiences for young cancer patients from across Alabama at no cost to their families. Our purpose is to provide these children with avenues for fellowship, to help them cope with their disease, and to prepare them for life.

**1337  Camp Wheezeaway American Lung Association of Alabama**
3125 Independence Drive
Suite 325
Birmingham, AL  35209
205-933-8821
251-456-1115
FAX: 251-456-1116
e-mail: Lungcs1@aol.com
www.alabamalung.org

*Connie Sullivan, Camp Director*
*Margaret Jakes MD, Medical Director*
*Joseph LaRussa MD, Co-Medical Director*

Camp WheezeAway is a 5 day overnight camp for 8-12 with moderate to severe asthma in Alabama held at Camp ASCCA in Jackson's Gap, AL and is sponsored by the American Lung Association. Children are monitered while enjoying all the normal camp activities including ropes courses, canoeing, swimming, arts & crafts, horseback riding, fishing, tubing & more and above all learn to manage their asthma.

## 1338 Liz Moore Low Vision Center

Low Vision Center
50 Medical Park Drive E
Birmingham, AL 35235
205-956-3276
FAX: 205-838-3515
e-mail: mcjones@ehs.com
www.ehs.com

Madelyn Jones, Director
Pat Lowe, Manager

## 1339 Summer Camp for Children with Muscular Dystrophy

Muscular Dystrophy Association
700 Century Park S
Suite 129
Birmingham, AL 35226
205-823-8191
800-525-6793
FAX: 205-823-1057
e-mail: birminghamdistrict@mdausa.org
www.mdausa.org

Robert Ross, President/CEO
Debbie Sutton, Manager
Michael A Blishak, Director Community Programs

Offers a wide range of activities specially designed for young people who have limited mobility or use wheelchairs.

## 1340 Summer Enrichment Camp

Alabama School for Deaf
P O Box 698
205 East South Street
Talladega, AL 35160
205-761-3328
FAX: 205-761-3378
e-mail: graham.terry@aidb.aidb.state.al.us
www.aidb.state.al.us/aidb

Terry Graham Ed.D, President
Teresa Caudle, Director Audiology
Walter Ripley, Director Athletic Programs

The Alabama School for the Deaf Summer Enrichment Camp is designed especially for deaf and hard of hearing children ages 6-15. Recreation activities include swimming, skating, outdoor games, horseback riding, field trips, arts and craft. Tuition is free.

# Alaska

## 1341 American Diabetes Summer Camp

American Diabetes Association
801 W Fireweed Lane
Suite 103
Anchorage, AK 99503
907-272-1424
800-342-2383
FAX: 907-272-1428
e-mail: estankavish@diabetes.org
www.diabetes.org

Eileen Stankavich, Program Director
Michelle Cassano, Executive Director

A residential camp for children with diabetes, ages 7 to 17.

## 1342 Camp Alpine

Alpine Alternatives
2217 E Tudor Road
Suite 1
Anchorage, AK 99507
907-562-7372
800-361-4174
FAX: 907-563-9232
e-mail: info@alpinealternatives.org
www.alpinealternatives.org/getinvolved.HTML

Gayla Valle, President
Kris Johnston, Vice President
Margaret Webber, Director

Our programs are designed to help people expand their horizons, master new skills, make new friends, and increase motor coordination. Most importantly, participants experience growth in self-confidence and independence that affects all aspects of an individual's life. Our services are open to all, regardless of type of disability or age. Activities include canoeing, hiking, swimming, outdoor games, sports, nature identification and much more.

## 1343 Camp Birchwood

Muscular Dystrophy Association (MDA)
121 West Fireweed Lane
Anchorage, AK 99507
907-276-2131

www.mdausa.org/clinics/camp/faq.aspx

Sara Gaar, Director
Chris Robinson, Director
Ramona Jobe, Health Care Services Director

A summer camp at Birchwood Camp in Chugiak, Alaska for individuals ages 6-21 who are affected by any of the 40-plus neuromuscular diseases in MDA's program. Common activities include: swimming, hockey, baseball, soccer, football, boating, horseback riding, fishing, music, cooking, arts and crafts, movies, dancing, talent shows, Harley-Davidson motorcycle sidecar or three-wheeled cycle rides, a visit from fire fighters and time for socializing and laughing.

## 1344 Camp Kushtaka American Diabetes Summer Camp

American Diabetes Association
801 West Fireweed Lane
Suite 103
Anchorage, AK 99503
907-272-1424
888-DIA-ETES
FAX: 907-272-1428
e-mail: estankavich@diabetes.org
www.diabetes.org

Eileen Stankavich, Program Director
Lynn B Nicholas FACHE, Chief Executive Officer
Richard Kah Ph.D, Chief Medical/Scientfic Officer

Camp is located in Cooper Landing, Alaska. Specializes in programs for campers with asthma/respiratory ailments and diabetes. Coed, ages 7-17. The camp combines ongoing and informal diabetes management and education along with the fun of outdoor activities such as hiking, canoeing, crafts and swimming. There is even an overnight campout for the older campers. Resident physicians, nurses and dieticians round out the regular Camp Fire staff.

## 1345 Camp Wheeze Away

American Lung Association
2217 E Tudor Road
Suite 1
Anchorage, AK 99507
907-562-7372
FAX: 907-562-0545
TTY:907-563-8284
e-mail: sesa@sesa.org
www.sesa.org

Galya Valle, President
Kris Johnson, Vice President
Chris Robinson, Executive Director

Offers support to campers with disabilities ranging from Spina Bifida, Multiple Sclerosis, Paraplegia and Quadriplegia to Downs Syndrome, Autism, and other mental disabilities.

**1346 Champ Camp American Lung Association of Alaska**
PO Box B
Indianapolis, IN 46240                    317-679-1860

e-mail: mferreira@aklung.org
www.aklung.org/asthma/champcamp/

*Michelle Ferreira, Lung Health Progam Coordinator*
*Kathy Case MD, Medical Director*
*Marge Larson, Chief Executive Officer*

Champ Camp is a week long summer recreation and asthma education program at Camp Kushtaka on the beautiful shores of Kenai Lake. Campers are able to explore their skills in outdoor activities including canoeing, hiking, swimming, archery, and arts and crafts. More importantly, Champ Camp boosts self-confidence and instills a sense of responsibility. It teaches preventive measures to improve asthma management, and avoid asthmatic episodes as well as increases a camper's sense of independence.

**1347 Kushtaka**
801 W Fireweed Lane
Suite 103
Anchorage, AK 99503                    907-272-1424

*Michelle Casssano, Executive Director*

**1348 Muscular Dystrophy Association Free Camp**
2217 E Tudor Road
Suite 1
Anchorage, AK 99507                    907-562-7372

*Chris Robinson, Executive Director*

**1349 Outdoor Recreation and Community Accesss**
Special Education Service Agency
3501 Denali Street
Suite 101
Anchorage, AK 99503                    907-562-7372
                                   FAX: 907-562-0545
                                   TTY:907-563-8284
                                   e-mail: sesa@sesa.org
                                   www.sesa.org

*Gayla Valle, President*
*Kris Johnston, VP*
*Chris Robinson, Executive Director*

Is a public agency which provides assistance to Alaskan school districts and early intervention programs serving students with low incidence disabilities.

# Arizona

**1350 Arizona Camp Sunrise**
American Cancer Society
2929 E Thomas Road
Phoenix, AZ 85016                    602-553-7129
                                   800-865-1582
                              FAX: 602-381-1582
                    e-mail: barb@azcampsunrise.org
                    www.azcampsunrise.org/prog_sunrise.htmL

*Barbara Nicholas, Program Director*
*Steve Slaughter, President*
*Mike Kaczocha, Camp Director*

Camp is in Payson, Arizona. Provides one-week summer camping sessions at no charge to children aged 8-18 who have had, or currently have, cancer.

**1351 Camp Civitan**
Civitan Foundation
PO Box 643
Williams, AZ 86046                    602-989-2095
                              FAX: 602-953-2946
                    e-mail: info@campcivitan.com
                    www.campcivitan.org

*Marianne Beram, Camp Director*
*Mike Beram, Assitant Director*
*Felicia Parker, Director Health Services*

Camp for the physically and/or mentally challenged. Ages 12 and up. Week long summer sessions offered near Williams, Arizona. Activities include arts and crafts, hikes, sports, sing-a-longs, dances etc. $250 per week.

**1352 Camp Honor**
Hemophilia Association
4001 N 24th Street
Phoenix, AZ 85016                    602-955-3947
                                   888-754-7017
                              FAX: 602-955-1962
                    e-mail: mike@hemophiliaz.org
                    www.hemophiliaz.org

*Richard Traulsen, President*
*Neil Frick MS, VP Medical/Research Information*
*Howard A Balasm, Chief Operating Officer*

Camp is located in Payson, Arizona at the Whispering Hope Ranch. One-week sessions for children with hemophilia or HIV and their siblings, as well as children of hemophiliacs. Coed, ages 7-17. Activities include swimming, canoeing, sports, archery and arts and crafts (to name a few fun things).

**1353 Camp Not-A-Wheeze American Lung Association**
102 West McDowell Road
Phoenix, AZ 85003                    602-258-7507
                                   602-258-7507
                    e-mail: infophoenix@lungaz.org
                    www.lungusa2.org/arizonanewmexico/

*Rhonda Follman, Health Services/Camp Director*
*John L Kirkwood, ALA President/CEO*
*Joseph Bergen, Chief Operating Officer/EVP*

Camp Not-A-Wheeze is designed especially for kids ages 7-14 with moderate to severe asthma and was created to provide a traditional residential camp experience and teach children how to manage their asthma.

**1354 Camp Rainbow**
Phoenix Childrens Hospital (PCH)
1919 E Thomas Road
Phoenix, AZ 85016                    602-546-1000
                              FAX: 602-546-0276
                    www.phxchildrens.com/about/services/

*Kathy Nord, Director*
*Robert Meyer, President/CEO PCH*
*David Notrica MD, President Medical Staff PCH*

Camp is located in Prescott, Arizona. Offers one-week sessions for children who have had, or currently have, cancer. Boys and girls ages 7-17. Camp activities include swimming, horseback riding, arts and crafts, canoeing, performing arts, archery, rollerskating, fishing, an overnight camping trip and much more! It's a week filled with laughter, new experiences and new friends.

**1355 Easter Seals Arizona**
2075 S Cottonwood Drive
Tempe, AZ 85282                    480-222-4104
                                   800-626-6061
                              FAX: 480-222-4123
                              TTY: 480-222-4100
                    e-mail: mmedoro@azseals.org
                    www.az.easterseals.com

*Michael Medoro, VP/COO*
*Michael Fitzgerald, President/CEO*

Provides services to children and adults with disabilities and other special needs, and supportto their families.

## 1356 Lake Powell Summer Adventure Camp
Easter Seals Arizona
2075 South Cottonwoon Drive
Tempe, AZ 85282

480-222-4100
800-626-6061
FAX: 480-222-4123
e-mail: mmedoro@azseals.org
www.eastersealsarizona.org

Michael Medoro, Adapted Respite/Recreation Drtr
Scott Johnson, Development Director
Jessica Magdaleno, Head Start Therapy Program

Offers a variety of services to help people with disabilities address life's challenges and achieve personal goals. Camp features alternative, high-adventure, camping experiences for children ages 13-23. Daily activities include environmental awareness presentations from a National Park guide, archery, wave runners, swimming, art & crafts, kayaking, hiking, and fishing.

## 1357 Lions Camp Tatiyee
PO Box 6910
Mesa, AZ 85216

480-380-4254
800-246-9771
FAX: 602-244-8667
e-mail: lionscamp@cableaz.com
www.lionscampt.org

Pamela Swanson, Executive Director

Camp is located in Lakeside, Arizona. Provides one-week sessions for campers with a wide variety of disabilities. May-August. Coed, ages 7-17 and seniors. Featured activities include arts and crafts, ceramics/pottery, climbing/rappelling, counselor training (CIT), drama, fishing, football, hiking, nature/environmental studies and team building.

# California

## 1358 Bar 717 Ranch/Camp Trinity
PO Box 150
Hayfork, CA 96041

530-628-5992
FAX: 530-628-9392
e-mail: camptrinity@bar717.com
www.bar717.com

Kent Collard, Director

Offers two, three and four-week camping sessions May-September. Accepts campers with diabetes and mobility limitation. Coed, ages 8-16. Also families, single adults and seniors.

## 1359 Camp Paivika
Ability First
1300 E Green Street
Pasadena, CA 91106

626-396-1010
877-768-4600
FAX: 626-396-1021
e-mail: contactus@abilityfirst.org
www.abilityfirst.org

Patricia Vick, Chairman
Lori E Gangeni, President
Kelly Kunsak, Director

Residential camping program activities of which include aquatics and infant through adult recreational and enrichment programs, adapted sports, martial arts and work force services.

## 1360 Camp Bloomfield and Foundation for the Jun
5300 Angeles Vista Boulevard
Los Angeles, CA 90043

323-295-4555

## 1361 Camp Bloomfield and the Junior Blind of Am erica Foundation
5300 Angeles Vista Boulevard
Los Angeles, CA 90043

323-295-4555
FAX: 323-296-0424
e-mail: info@juniorblind.org
www.juniorblind.org/

Frank Cardenas, Director Recreation Services
Debra Adams, Director Children's Programs
Robert Ralls, President

Camp is located in Malibu. Offers one and two-week camping sessions June-August for blind and visually impaired campers. Coed, ages 5-18. Also families and single adults.

## 1362 Camp Conrad Chinnock
Diabetic Youth Services
501 W Walnut Street
Compton, CA 90220

310-604-2473
888-800-4010
FAX: 888-800-4010
e-mail: programs@dys.org
www.dys.org

Rocky Wilson, Executive Director
Ryan Martz, Program Director
Tom Jenkins, Chief Administrator

Offers one and two-week sessions for campers with diabetes. Coed, ages 7-16. Also families.

## 1363 Camp Del Corazon
11615 Hesby Street
North Hollywood, CA 91601

818-754-0312
888-621-4800
FAX: 818-754-0842
e-mail: information@campdelcorazon.org
www.campdelcorazon.org

Lisa Knight RN, Executive Director/Co-Founder
Kevin Shannon MD, Medical Director/Co-Founder
Glenn Knight, CEO/Board Member

Active program for campers with heart disease, Camp del Corazon provides summer activities free of charge that include hiking and archery, arts and crafts, court and field games, waterfront activities and a beach barbecue.

## 1364 Camp El Camino Pines
Lutheran Retreats
1300 E Colorado Street
Glendale, CA 91205

818-243-8700
800-464-2417
FAX: 818-243-2700
e-mail: infor@lrccsca.org
www.lrccsca.org

Anthony Briggs, Executive Director
Glen Egertson, Camp Director
Chris Smith, Program Director

Camp is located in Frazier Park, California. Christian camp offering half-week and one-week sessions for hearing impaired campers. Coed, ages 8-18. Also families.

## 1365 Camp Esperanza Arthritis Foundation
Southern California Chapter
4311 Wilshire Boulevard
Suite 530
Los Angeles, CA 90010

323-954-5760
FAX: 323-954-5790
e-mail: kquinn@arthritis.org
www.arthritis.org/communities/

Kristie Quinn, Camp Director
John H Klippel MD, President/CEO
Laura Robbins, Chair

A one-week camp in August that allows children suffering from arthritis to participate in such activities as horseback riding, swimming, etc. in a fun-filled environment.

**1366 Camp Forrest**
Angel View Crippled Children's Foundation
12379 Miracle Hill Road
Desert Hot Springs, CA 92240           760-329-6471
FAX: 760-324-9024
e-mail: angelviewcamp@aol.com
www.angelview.org

*Mel Haber, President*
*David Thornton, Administrator*
*Howard Gordon, Director*

Camp is located in Joshua Tree, California. Offers to one-week sessions June-August to both able-bodied campers and those with a wide variety of disabilities. Coed, ages 10-25. Activities include archery, arts and crafts, cookouts, swimming, sports and games, hiking and star study.

**1367 Camp Joan Mier**
Ability First
11777 Ellice Street
Malibu, CA 90265                      310-457-9863
FAX: 310-457-6374
e-mail: contactus@abilityfirst.org
www.abilityfirst.org

*Kelly Privitt, Camp Director*
*Stuart M Wilkinson, Chair*
*Richard Greening, Chief Executive Officer*

Camp is located in Malibu. Offers one-week sessions June-August to campers with a wide variety of disabilities.

**1368 Camp Krem**
Camping Unlimited
4610 Whitesands Court
El Sobrante, CA 94803                 510-222-6662
FAX: 510-223-3046
e-mail: campkrem@campingunlimited.com
www.campingunlimited.com

*Teresa Tucker, Executive Director*

Camp Krem offers a traditional camping program for children and adults with developmental disabilities, encouraging choice and decision-making. Activities include swimming, hiking, and joint programs with camps for normal campers. Six travel camps that enables campers to experience adventure and self-sufficiency for any teens and adults is also available. Tuition $585 per 1 week session. Longer sessions also available.

**1369 Camp Laurel**
PO Box 661
Alpine, NJ 07620                      201-750-0515
800-327-3509
FAX: 201-750-0665
e-mail: info@camplaurel.com
www.camplaurel.com
Tanya Dansky, Director
Provides half-week to one-week sessions for children with HIV/AIDS. Coed, ages 6-16. Also families.

**1370 Camp Okizu**
Okizu Foundation
16 Digital Drive
Novato, CA 94949                      415-382-9083
FAX: 415-382-8384
e-mail: info@okizu.org
www.okizu.org

*Suzanne Randall, Executive Director*

Camp is located in Berry Creek, California. Offers one-week sessions June-August for children who have cancer. Coed, ages 6-17. Also siblings.

**1371 Camp Paivika**
Ability First
1300 E Green Street
Pasadena, CA 91106                    626-396-1010
877-768-4800
FAX: 626-396-1021
e-mail: contactus@abilityfirst.org
www.abilityfirst.org

*Kelly Kunsak, Camp Director*
*Lori E Gangini, President*
*Patricia Vick, Chairman*

Camp is located in Crestline, California. A nonprofit camp owned and operated by Ability First to provide outdoor, recreational camping services for children and adults with physical and/or developmental disabilities. Located in the San Bernadino mountains, the camp has a dining lodge and rec room, four cabins, infirmary, program building and pool that are all fully accessible. Camp is available to rent during winter/spring for up to 80 people. Coed, ages 7-70.

**1372 Camp Rainbow**
Phoenix Childrens Hospital
1919 E Thomas Road
Phoenix, AZ 85016                     602-546-1000

www.phxchildrens.com

*Robert Meyer, President/CEO*
*Larry Smith, Chief Financial Officer*

Camp is located in Glendale, California. One-week sessions in August for campers with HIV and cancer. Coed, ages 7-17.

**1373 Camp Ronald McDonald at Eagle Lake**
Eagle Lake Children's Charities
PO Box 172
Susanville, CA 96130                  530-825-3158
916-734-4230
FAX: 530-825-3158
e-mail: vicky@campronald.org
www.campronald.org

*Vicky Flaig MEd/RD, Camp Director*

Is a fully accessible residential camp for kids with special needs. The goal of the camp is to provide confidence building experiences to children who are at risk, disadvantaged and/or living with physical or emotional disabilities.

**1374 Camp Ronald McDonald for Good Times**
Ronald McDonald House of California
1954 Cotner Avenue
Los Angeles, CA 90025                 310-268-8488
800-625-7295
FAX: 310-473-3338
e-mail: info@campronaldmcdonald.org
www.campronaldmcdonald.org

*Carol Horvitz, Executive Director*
*Chadwick Edwards, Program Director*
*Ken Mortensen, Facilities Director*

Camp is located in Mountain Center, California. Year-round camping sessions at no charge for children who have cancer. Coed, ages 7-18. Also families.

**1375 Camp-A-Lot**
Arc Of San Diego
3030 Market Street
Suite B
San Diego, CA 92102                   619-685-1100
800-748-5575
FAX: 619-234-3759
e-mail: pals@arc-sd.com
www.arc-sd.com

*Lin Taylor, Camp Director*

Offers one-week sessions for children and adults with attention deficit disorder, autism, mobility limitation and developmental disabilities.

**1376 Camping Unlimited**
Camping Unlimited for Children
4610 Whitesands Court
El Sobrante, CA 94803
510-222-6662
FAX: 510-223-3046
e-mail: campkrem@campingunlimited.com
www.campingunlimited.com

*Teresa Tucker, Executive Director*

Camp is located in Boulder Creek, California. Offers one and two-week sessions June-August to campers with a variety of disabilities. Coed, ages 5-50. Camping unlimited also weekend programs and travel camps, year round progams and recreation.

**1377 Camps for Children & Teens with Diabetes**
Diabetes Society of Santa Clara Valley
1165 Lincoln Avenue
Suite 300
San Jose, CA 95125
408-287-3785
800-989-1165
FAX: 408-287-2701
e-mail: camp@diabetesscv.org
www.diabetesscv.org

*Sharon Ogbor, Executive Director*
*Stephanie Demos, Development Director*

Since 1974, sponsors up to 20 day camps, family camps and resident camps for children 4 through 17. These camps provide an opportunity for children with diabetes to go to camp, meet other children and gain a better understanding of their diabetes. The total experience can help campers develop more confidence in their abilities to control their diabetes effectively while enjoying the traditional camp experience. Camps are located throughout CA and parts of Nevada.

**1378 Costanoan**
Via Rehabilitation Services
2851 Park Avenue
Santa Clara, CA 95050
408-243-7861
FAX: 408-243-0452
e-mail: camp@viaservices.org
www.viaservices.org

*Richard Frazier, Camp Director*
*Liya Murphy, Camp Registrar*
*Kay Walker, Chief Executive Officer*

Camp Costanoan is a residential, respite and recreational camp for children and adults, ages 5 and older, with physical and/or developmental disabilities. Camp Costanoan enhances camper self-esteem, improves socialization skills and provides hands-on learning and therapeutic recreation opportunities. Additionally, Camp Costanoan provides respite for families of individuals with disabilities.

**1379 Diabetic Youth Foundation**
5167 Clayton Road
Suite F
Concord, CA 94521
925-680-4994
FAX: 925-680-4863
e-mail: info@dyf.org
www.dyf.org

*Mats Wallin, Executive Director*
*Janet Cooper, Camp Director*
*Jeff Heiser, Program Director*

We offer summer residential camp programs (Bearskin Meadow Camp) and year-round educational and recreational programs for children, teens and families affected by diabetes.

**1380 Easter Seal Camp Harmon**
9010 Soquel Drive
Aptos, CA 95003
831-684-2166

*Bruce Hinman, President*

**1381 Easter Seals Camp Harmon**
Easter Seals Central California
9010 Soquel Drive
Aptos, CA 95003
831-684-2380
FAX: 831-684-1018
TTY:831-684-1054
e-mail: jennifer@es-cc.org
www.centralcal.easterseals.com

*Jennifer Johnson, Camping Services Coordinator*

Camp is located in Boulder Creek, California. 6-10 day sessions for children and adults with physical and developmental disabilities. Coed, ages 8-65.

**1382 Easter Seals Summer Camp Programs**
180 Grand Avenue
Suite 300
Oakland, CA 94568
510-835-2131
FAX: 510-835-1847
e-mail: edolan@esba.org
www.bayarea.easterseals.com

*Maureen K Kavalar, VP Program/Provider Services*
*Maureen Haller, VP Development Services*
*James E Williams, President/CEO*

Offers education, adventure and the experience and enjoyment of living-out-of-doors in a striking and challenging wilderness environment. Serves ages 6 to 60, male and female.

**1383 Enchanted Hills Camp for the Blind**
Lighthouse for the Blind
214 Van Ness Avenue
San Francisco, CA 94102
415-431-1481
FAX: 415-863-7568
TTY:415-431-4572
e-mail: executive@lighthouse-sf.org
www.lighthouse-sf.org

*Anita S Aaron, Executive Director*
*Anthony Fletcher, Director Community Services*
*Julie McCarthy, Facilities Manager*

Camp is located in Napa, California. Half-week, one and two-week sessions for blind, deaf/blind children and adults, ages 5 and up. This program offers a basic camping experience. Activities include music, art, dance, hiking and riding. Camperships are available to California residents.

**1384 Gloriana Opera Company**
PO Box 273
Fort Bragg, CA 95437
707-964-7469
e-mail: gloriana@mcn.org
www.gloriana.org

*Diane Larson, President*
*Jerry Greenberg, VP/Director*
*Ana Lucas, Artistic Director*

Since 1977 superlative music theater productions all year long, plus concert, childrens workshops and classes.

**1385 Junior Blind of America**
5300 Angeles Vista Boulevard
Los Angeles, CA 90043
323-295-4555
FAX: 323-296-0424
e-mail: info@juniorblind.org
www.juniorblind.org

*Miki Jordan, President/CEO*

Provides unique programs and services to help blind or visually impaired individuals maximize their potential and achieve their highest possible level of independence.

**1386   Junior Wheelchair Sports Camp**
Santa Barbara Parks and Recreation Department
PO Box 1990
Santa Barbara, CA 93102          805-564-5418
                                FAX: 805-564-5480
                         www.sbparksandrecreation.org

*Nancy Rapp, Executive Director*
*Sarah Clayton, Recreation Manager*
*Antonio Velasquez, Community Services Supervisor*

This five-day camp is for children 5-19 years old that are physically disabled. Sports instruction in aquatics, tennis, track and field, basketball, archery and new sports activities introduced each year. The camp counselors and instructors are also physically disabled to provide the children with a role model. Fee based on fundraising efforts.

**1387   Lazy J Ranch Camp**
12220 Cotharin Road
Malibu, CA 90265               310-457-5572
                              FAX: 310-457-8882
                      e-mail: crazzycraig@earthlink.net
                           www.LazyJRanchCamp.com

*Craig Johnson, Executive Director*

Offers 1 or 2 week sessions for campers. Coed, ages 6-13.

**1388   Pilgrim Pines Camp**
United Church Of Christ
39570 Glen Road
Yucaipa, CA 92399              909-797-1821
                               800-616-6612
                             FAX: 909-797-2691
                        e-mail: info@pilgrimpinescamp.org
                           www.pilgrimpinescamp.org

*Gail Benson, Executive Director*
*Kirsten Sumpter, Summer Camp Director*
*Shelley Wallace, Guest Services Manager*

Christian camp offering one-week sessions for campers with developmental disabilities. Coed, ages 10-Adult. Also families.

**1389   Quest Camp**
2333 San Ramon Valley Boulevard
Suite 125
San Ramon, CA 94583           925-743-1370
                              FAX: 925-743-1937
                         e-mail: bfield12@aol.com
                            www.questcamps.com

*Robert Field Phd, Director*

Camp is located in Alamo, California. Day camp offering three to eight-week sessions including psychological treatment for children with ADD and other mild to moderate psychological disorders. Coed, ages 6-15.

**1390   Quickie Sports Camps**
Quickie Designs
2382 Faraday Ave
Suite 200
Carlsbad, CA 92008            760-930-1500
                               800-456-8168
                             FAX: 760-930-1585
                        e-mail: Webmaster@Sunmed.com
                           www.sunrisemedical.com

*Michael N Hammes, President/CEO*

Tennis and basketball camps for the wheelchair bound.

**1391   Reach for the Sky**
American Cancer Society
2655 Camino Del Rio North
Suite 100
San Diego, CA 92108           619-299-4200
                               800-227-2345
                             FAX: 619-296-0928
                      e-mail: robby.medina@cancer.org
                                www.cancer.org

*Stephen Sener, President*
*Richard Wender, Vice President*
*Robby Medina, Camp Administrator*

One-week sessions for children who have had, or currently have, cancer. Coed, ages 8-18.

**1392   Reach for the Sky Day Camp**
American Cancer Society
2655 Camino Del Rio North
Suite 100
San Diego, CA 92108           619-299-4200
                             FAX: 619-296-0928
                                www.cancer.org

*John R Kelly, Chairman*
*Stephen Browning, Vice President*

One-week sessions for children who have cancer and their siblings. Coed, ages 4-10.

**1393   San Gabriel Valley Family YMCA Camping Ser vices**
PO Box 1958
Wrightwood, CA 92397          760-249-3822
                             FAX: 760-249-4492
                        e-mail: jemery@sgvymca.org
                     www.sgvymca.org/Campingservices.html

*Jim Emery, Director Camping Services*
*Toby Hettler, Program Director*
*Lynn Werhan, Maintenance Director*

Summer residential camp situated in the heart of the Angeles National Forest in California's San Gabriel Mountains for children with disabilities, ages 8 to 18. Outdoor activities encourage campers to expand their sense of their own capabilities, while also helping them participate in the achievements of the group.

**1394   Summer Day Camp**
Yorba Linda Placentia Farm YMCA
13821 Newport Avenue
Tustin, CA 92780              714-549-9622
                             FAX: 714-777-1903
                                www.ymcaoc.org

*Clare Kenna, Executive Director*
*Alfred Herzing, Board Chair*
*Dave Gruchow, Board of Governors*

One-week sessions for children with ADD and speech/communication impairment. Coed, ages 5-14.

# Colorado

**1395   Breckenridge Outdoor Education Center**
PO Box 697
Breckenridge, CO 80424        970-453-6422
                             FAX: 970-453-4676
                          e-mail: boec@boec.org
                                www.boec.org

*Bruce Fitch, Executive Director*
*Bob Bond, Wilderness Program Director*
*Cindy Wetherald, Associate Program Director*

Provides year-round adventure based wilderness and adaptive ski programs for people with disabilities. The Center excels in offering challenging, rewarding outdoor experiences individually designed to the abilities and needs of participants.

**1396  Camp Paha**
City of Lakewood
480 South Allison Parkway
Lakewood, CO  80226

303-987-2490
FAX: 303-987-4863
TTY:303-987-7716
e-mail: joabur@lakewood.org
www.lakewood.org

*Jo Burns, Executive Director*
*Zane Devan, Manager*

Camp Paha is a day camp for children ages 6-17 and young adults ages 18-25 with disabilities. We provide programs for campers with all disability types: developmental, physical, emotional, behavioral, and learning. Camp Paha offers safe, quality, fun and challenging activities. Camp provides campers and opportunity to participate in aquatics, sports, games, nature, music, drama, hiking, arts and crafts, and field trips into the community.

**1397  Camp Shady Brook**
YMCA of the Pikes Peak Region (PPYMCA)
207 North Nevada Avenue
Colorado Springs, CO  80903

719-329-7266
FAX: 719-272-7026
e-mail: campinfo@ppymca.org
www.ppymca.org

*Clint Knox, Executive Director*
*Tish Johnston, Program Director*
*Karstin Knutson, Officer Manager*

Camp is located in Sedalia, Colorado. One-week sessions for campers with HIV. Boys and girls 7-16. Also families, seniors and single adults.

**1398  Challenge Aspen**
PO Box M
Aspen, CO  81612

970-923-0578
800-530-3907
FAX: 970-923-7338
e-mail: possibilities@challengeaspen.com
www.challengeaspen.com

*Houston Cowan, Executive Director*
*Amanda Boxtel, Special Projects Mgr/Co-Founder*
*Sarah Williams, Program Director*

Challenge Aspen provides recreational and cultural experiences for individuals who have mental or physical disabilities. Challenge Aspen offers a variety of recreational programs to fit a diversity of needs and interests. We offer both summer, winter and special events for both adults and children.

**1399  Colorado Lions Camp**
PO Box 9043
Woodland Park, CO  80866

719-687-2087
FAX: 719-687-7435
e-mail: lionscampco@aol.com
www.lionscampco.org/

*Dan Smith, President*
*Sheri Sherve, Vice President*
*Bruce Wadman, Treasurer*

Outdoor recreational camping for the handicapped. All normal camp activities offered. 1 to 4 staff supervision with a nurse or doctor in attendance.

**1400  Easter Seals Colorado Rocky Mountain Villa**
PO Box 115
Empire, CO  80043

303-569-2333
FAX: 303-569-3857
e-mail: campinfo@cess.org
co.easterseals.com/

*Lynn Robinson, President*
*Shirley Barenberg, Vice President*
*Nancy Hanson, VP*

Camp is located in Empire, Colorado. One-week sessions June-August for children and adults with a wide variety of disabilities. Coed, ages 7-70. Single adults, families.

**1401  Glacier View Ranch**
Rocky Mountain Conference of the
Seventh Day Adventist Church
2520 South Downing Street
Denver, CO  80210

303-733-3771
FAX: 303-733-1843
e-mail: webmaster@rmcsda.com
www.rmcsda.org

*Dorothy Opp, President*
*James Brauer, Religious Leader*
*Marlene Perry, Youth Coordinator*

Camp is located in Ward, Colorado. One-week sessions June and July. Programs for campers with asthma/respiratory aliments. Coed, ages 7-17.

**1402  Magic of Music and Dance**
PO Box M
Aspen, CO  81612

970-923-0578
800-530-3901
FAX: 970-923-7338
e-mail: possibilities@challengeaspen.com
www.challengeaspen.com

*Amanda Boxtel, Director of Special Projects*
*Houston Cowan, Executive Director*

Camp activities focus on music and performing arts for children with disabilities.

**1403  Rocky Mountain Village**
Easter Seals Colorado
PO Box 115
Empire, CO  80438

303-569-2333
FAX: 303-569-3857
e-mail: campinfo@cess.org
www.eastersealsco.org

*Roman Kratczyk, Director*

Sessions are conducted for both developmentally and physically disabled children and adults. Activities include swimming, horseback riding, outdoor education, zigline challenge course elements.

**1404  Sky Ranch Lutheran Camp**
805 S Shields Street
Fort Collins, CO  80521

970-493-5258
FAX: 970-493-7960
e-mail: info@skyranch.us
www.fortnet.org/skyranch

*Ralph Yernberg, Executive Director*
*Joel Abenth, Director Program Ministries*
*Stephanie Dugger, Development Assistant*

Daily Bible study and worship for disabled campers.

# Connecticut

**1405  Camp Harkness**
301 Great Neck Road
Route 213
Waterford, CT  06385

860-443-7818
866-284-1595
FAX: 860-236-6205
TTY: 860-859-5493
e-mail: info@ciboakhill.org
www.campharkness.com/Default.htm

*Vicki Severin, Camp Director*
*Scott Walls, Program Manager*
*Trish Hesslein, Director Community Relations*

In 1991 a group of parents and adults with spina bifida, were brought together with the mission to educate the public about spina bifida and issues affecting people who have this disability in addition To providing support and information and promoting programs that will help people with spina bifida. Since then SBAC has worked hard to support parents, adults with spina bifida and families

## 1406 Camp Horizons

PO Box 323
South Windham, CT 06266          860-456-1032
                              FAX: 860-456-4721
      e-mail: lauren.perrotti@camphorizons.org
                    www.camphorizons.org

*Lauren Perrotti, Director Operations*
*Chris Naboe, Executive Director*

Two, four, six and eight-week sessions June-August for campers with developmental disabilities and autism. Coed, ages 8-40.

## 1407 Camp Isola Bella

American School For The Deaf
139 N Main Street
West Hartford, CT 06107          860-570-2300
                                 860-570-2222
                              FAX: 860-824-4276
                              TTY: 860-824-5558
      e-mail: Steve.Borsotti@asd-1817.org
                    www.asd-1817.org

*Harvey J Corson, Executive Director*
*Steve Borsotti, Director*

Hearing-impaired children, ages 6-19, blend educational instruction in communications with recreational activities. Qualified deaf and hearing staff members with experience in education, child care and counseling are employed at the camp.

## 1408 Camp Jewell YMCA Outdoor Center

YMCA of Greater Hartford
6 Prock Hill Road
PO Box 8
Colebrook, CT 06021          860-379-4679
                             888-412-2267
                          FAX: 860-397-8715
                          TTY: 888-412-2267
      e-mail: camp.jewell@ghymca.org
                    www.ghymca.org

*Brian Rupe, Executive Director*
*Eric Tucker, Associate Executive*
*Jodi Gove, Ranch Program Coordinator*

Camp is located in Colebrook, Connecticut. Two-week sessions for children with cancer. Coed, ages 8-16. Also families.

## 1409 Easter Seal Camp Hemlocks

85 Jones Street
PO Box 198
Hebron, CT 06248          860-228-9496
                          800-832-4409
                       FAX: 860-228-2091
                       TTY: 312-726-4258
      e-mail: info@eastersealscamphemlocks.org
            www.eastersealscamphemlocks.org/

*Denise Hornbecker, Vice President*
*Sunny Ku, Camp Director*

Camp is located in Hebron, Connecticut. One and two-week sessions June-August for campers with a variety of disabilities. Coed, ages 6-80. Families, seniors, single adults.

## 1410 Hole in the Wall Gang Camp

565 Ashford Center Road
Ashford, CT 06278          860-429-3444
                        FAX: 860-429-7295
      e-mail: ashford@holeinthewallgang.org
                www.holeinthewallgang.org

*James Canton, Executive Director*
*Padraig Barry, Assistant Camp Director*
*Matthew Cook, Manager*

Low-cost eight-week sessions June-August for children with cancer and HIV. Coed, ages 7-15.

## 1411 Mansfield's Holiday Hill Camp

Holiday Recreation Center
41 Chaffeeville Road
Mansfield Center, CT 06250          860-423-1375
                                 FAX: 860-456-2444
      e-mail: dudley.hamlin@snet.net
                www.holidayrecreation.com

*Dudley Hamlin, Executive Director*
*Wendy Duff-Hamlin, Director*
*Shannon Cartier, Assistant Director*

A home not far from home where beautiful fields, forests, facilities and a caring staff support the activities and relationships of our camp families. The camp offers many programs such as: Outdoor Adventure; Tumbling; Dance; Adventure Ropes Course; Swimming; Arts & Crafts; Archery; Tennis and more to thirty boys and girls.

## 1412 Mansfields Holiday Hill

41 Chaffeeville Road
Mansfield Center, CT 06250          860-423-1375
                                 FAX: 860-456-2444
      e-mail: dudley.hamlin@snet.net
                www.bunk1.com

*Dudley Hamlin, Executive Director*

Is a positive, enjoyable, child-centered community, promoting the healthy development of children while meeting families needs for safety and convenience.

## 1413 Marvelwood Summer

Marvelwood School
PO Box 3001
Kent, CT 06757          860-927-0047
                     FAX: 860-927-0021
      e-mail: summerschool@marvelwood.org
                www.themarvelwoodschool.net

*Scott E Pottbecker, Headmaster of School*
*Anne Scott, Principal*

The emphasis in this summer program is on diagnosis and remediation of individual reading, spelling, writing, mathematics and study problems. Offered to ages 12-16.

## 1414 Shadybrook Learning Center

PO Box 365
Moodus, CT 06469          860-873-8800
                          800-666-4752
                       FAX: 860-873-1849
      e-mail: info@shadybrook.com
            www.kidscamps.com/specialty/shadybrook

Up to seven week summer residential, individualized program incorporating educational, recreational and vocational programs. This disguised learning environment promotes independence, friendships, and social appropriateness where learning is fun and fun is learning.

**1415  TSA CT Kid's Summer Event**
Tourette Syndrome Association of Connecticut (TSA)
915 Brickyard Road
Woodstock, CT  06281                203-912-7310

e-mail: ts@tsact.org
www.tsact.org

*Donna Blain, President/Chairperson*
*Andrew Vogel, Executive Director*
*Stefanie Fuller, Director*

TSA of Connecticut sponsors summer events for children with TS/Tourette Syndrome activities of which include minature golf in addition to an Annual Conference. The kids' program at this annual conference provides children who have TS a unique opportunity to meet other children like them who also struggle with TS. Entertainment includes puppeteers, magicians, learning karate from the experts, getting face paintings and more.
*uniqu pages*

## Delaware

**1416  Childrens Beach House**
100 W 10th Street
Suite 411
Wilmington, DE  19801              302-655-4288
FAX: 302-655-4216
e-mail: inquiry@cbhinc.org
www.cbhinc.org

*Teresa Tipton, Program Coordinator*
*Richard Garrett, Director*
*Elizabeth Christopher, Director*

Camp is located in Lewes, Delaware. Four-week sessions June-August for Delaware children with hearing impairment or speech/communication impairment. Coed, ages 6-12.

## District of Columbia

**1417  Columbia Lighthouse for the Blind Summer Camp**
Columbia Lighthouse for the Blind
1120 20th Street NW
Suite 750
Washington, DC  20036              202-454-6400
877-324-5252
FAX: 202-454-6401
e-mail: info@clb.org
www.clb.org

*Peter Mayo, President*
*Antoine Johnson, Camp Programs Director*
*Michelle Tatro, Public Relations/Media*

Helps enable the blind or visually impaired to obtain and maintain independence at home, school, work and in the community. Programs and services include early intervention services, training and consultation in assistive technology, career placement services, comprehensive low vision care and a wide range of rehabilitation services. Highly acclaimed summer camp, picnics and holiday activities encourage blind and visualy impaired children to make new friends and experience the joys of childhood.

**1418  Lab School of Washington**
4759 Reservoir Road Northwest
Washington, DC  20007              202-965-6600
FAX: 202-965-5106
e-mail: labschool@webmail.org
www.labschool.org

*Sally Smith, Founder/Manager*

The Lab School six week summer session includes individualized reading, spelling, writing, study skills and math programs. A multisensory approach addresses the needs of bright learning disabled children. Related services such as speech/language therapy and occupational therapy are integrated into the curriculum. Elementary/Intermediate; Junior High/High School.

## Florida

**1419  Boggy Creek Gang Camp**
30500 Brantley Branch Road
Eustis, FL  32736                  352-483-4200
866-468-6443
FAX: 352-483-0589
e-mail: info@boggycreek.org
www.boggycreek.org

*Dorcas Tomasek, Camp Director*
*June Clark, President/COO*
*James R Ellis Lt General, CEO/Chairman*

Year-round sessions for children with a variety of chronic or life-threatening illnesses including cancer, hemophila, epilepsy, heart defects, HIV, spina bifida and asthma/respiratory ailments. Coed, ages 7-16.

**1420  Camp Thunderbird**
Florida Fund For Special Children
380 Semoran Commerce Place
Suite B-204 PO Box 1300
Apopka, FL  32704                  407-889-4503
FAX: 407-889-5710
e-mail: contact@questinc.org
www.questinc.org

*Katie Porta, President*
*Shirley O'Brien, Executive Director*
*Rob Hungate, Chairman*

Residential summer camping program for children and adults with a developmental disability. Campers enjoy swimming, sports, nature hikes, canoeing, etc. One and two-week sessions June-August. Coed, ages 8-80.

**1421  Camp World Light**
Florida Baptist Convention
1230 Hendricks Avenue
Jacksonville, FL  32207            904-396-2351
800-226-8584
FAX: 904-396-6470
e-mail: bluesprings@flbaptist.org.
www.flbaptist.org

*Sharon Thompson PhD, Executive Director*
*John Sullivan, Religious Leader*
*Bob Bumgarner, Director Leadership Development*

Camp is located in Marianna, Florida. One-week sessions June-July for girls with ADD. Ages 8-18. Activities include arts/crafts, challenge/rope courses, clowning, community service, dance, drama, drawing/painting, leadership development, performing arts and sailing.

**1422  Center Academy at Pinellas Park**
6710 86th Avenue
Pinellas Park, FL  33782           727-541-5716
FAX: 727-544-8186
e-mail: infopp@centeracademy.com
www.centeracademy.com/PinellasPark.htm

*John Porter MD, Academy Director*
*Mack R Hicks PhD, Founder/Chairman of the Board*
*Andrew P Hicks PhD, CEO/Clinical Director*

Specifically designed for the learning disabled child and other children with difficulties in concentration, strategy, social skills, impulsivity, distractibility and study strategies. Programs offered include: attention training, visual-motor remediation, socialization skills training, relaxation training, horseback riding and more. The day camp meets weekdays from 9-3 for 3,4 or 5 week sessions.

### 1423 Florida Camp for Children and Youth with Diabetes

PO Box 14136
Gainesville, FL 32604 352-334-1323
FAX: 352-334-1325

*Rosalie Bandyopadhyay, Director*

An adventure camp for children and youth with diabetes.

### 1424 Florida Diabetes Camp

PO Box 14136
Gainesville, FL 32604 352-334-1321
FAX: 352-334-1326
e-mail: fccyd@hotmail.com
www.floridadiabetescamp.org

*Rosalie Bandyopadhyay, Executive Director*
*Al Avendano, Program Director*
*Gary Cornwell, Volunteer Program Director*

Camp is located in De Leon Springs, Florida. One and two-week sessions June-August for children with diabetes. Coed, ages 6-18 and families.

### 1425 Florida Lions Camp

Lions of Multiple District 35
2819 Tiger Lake Road
Lake Wales, FL 33898 863-696-1948
FAX: 863-696-2398
e-mail: flc@gtc.net
www.lionscampfl.org

*Rob Cage, Camp Program Director*
*Carissa Moen, Co-Summer Director*
*Hugo Paleaz, Aquatics Director*

One-week sessions June-August for children with a variety of disabilities. Coed, ages 5-21. A variety of traditional summer camp activities which include: swimming, canoeing, fishing, hiking, camping out and cooking over a fire, games, arts & crafts, singing & dancing, hay-wagon rides, challenge course and much more. Activities are adapted to the age and ability of each camper to ensure maximum participation, safety and fun.

### 1426 Florida School for the Deaf and Blind

207 North San Marco Avenue
Saint Augustine, FL 32084 904-827-2200
800-344-3732
FAX: 904-827-2222
e-mail: dillinghame@fsdb.k12.fl.us
www.fsdb.k12.fl.us

*Elmer Dillingham, President/Administrator*
*Kathy Gillespie, Director Public Information*
*Margaret W Van Ormer, Director Instructional Services*

There is no cost to families for tuition for eligible Florida residents to enroll their children in this program which includes such activities as swimming, walking club, yoga, in addition to arts/crafts, game nights and much more.

### 1427 Florida Sheriffs Caruth Camp

Florida Sheriffs Youth Ranches
PO Box 2000
Boys Ranch, FL 32064 386-842-5501
800-765-3797
FAX: 386-842-2429
e-mail: fsyr@youthranches.org
www.youthranches.org

*Sheriff Bill Farmer, Chairman of the Board*
*Roger Bouchard, President*
*Dan Hager, Vice Chairman*

Camp is located in Inglis, Florida. One-week sessions for children with ADD. Coed, ages 10-15.

### 1428 Indian Acres Camp for Boys

4452 Rainbow Avenue
Weston, FL 33332 954-385-3545
FAX: 954-349-7812
e-mail: geoff@indianacres.com
www.indianacres.com

*Lisa Newman, Director/Co-Owner*
*Jeffrey Newman, Director/Co-Owner*
*Michael Burness, Asistant Director*

Camp is located in Fryeburg, Florida. Four and seven-week sessions June-August for boys with ADD ages 7-16.

### 1429 VACC Camp

Miami Childrens Hospital
3200 SW 60th Court
Suite 203
Miami, FL 33155 305-666-4113
FAX: 305-663-8417
e-mail: bela.florentin@mch.com
www.vacccamp.com

*Moises Simpser MD, Director*
*Bela Florentin, VACC Camp Coordinator*

Free week-long overnight camp for ventilation assisted children and their families.

# Georgia

### 1430 Camp Breathe Easy

American Lung Association
2452 Spring Road
Smyrna, GA 30080 770-434-5864
800-LUN- USA
FAX: 770-319-0349
e-mail: mail@alaga.org
www.alaga.org/CBE1.html

*Chanda Mobley PhD, Executive Director*
*Starla Hairston, Program Director*
*Donna Brazzell, Director Special Projects*

Camp Breathe Easy is a seven-day, six-night overnight camp for children, ages 7-13, with asthma who need medication and are limited in summer camping opportunities. The children learn asthma self-management techniques and coping strategies to better handle their illness. Campers swim, repel off trees, fish, canoe, play soccer, basketball and miniature golf, and participate in ceramics and arts and crafts.

### 1431 Camp Independence

2951 Flowers Road South
Suite 211
Atlanta, GA 30341 770-452-1539
800-633-2339
e-mail: tracy@kidneyga.org
www.nkfg.org/services/campind.htm

*Tracy Jenny, Camp Director*
*Christopher Starr, Executive Director*
*Charles C Starr, Chief Executive Officer*

Camp Independence is Georgia's a overnight, week-long summer camp providing essential medical care, treatment & fun for kids with kidney disease and transplants. Camp Independence recognizes that campers are normal children but have special needs providing these children with opportunities for development & individual growth, peer support & normal life experiences. Activities include swimming, arts & crafts, fishing and horsebackriding, in addition to archery, games and sports, and ceramics.

**1432 Camp Lookout**
Holston Conference Camping
3130 Highway 157
Rising Fawn, GA 30738
706-820-1163
FAX: 706-820-9911
e-mail: info@camplookout.com
www.camplookout.com

*Don Washburn, Executive Director*
*Jackie Washburn, Assistant Director*

Offering a variety of educational opportunities for students in
1st through 12th grades. Offerings of 1/2 to 5 day programs are
available

**1433 Camp Twin Lakes**
5909 Peachtree Dunwoody Road NE
Suite 802
Atlanta, GA 30328
404-231-9887
FAX: 770-351-0475
e-mail: info@camptwinlakes.org
www.camptwinlakes.org

*Eric M Robbins, Executive Director*
*Daniel Matthews, Camp Director*
*Frank Beall, Special Projects Coordinator*

One-week sessions June-August for children with a variety of
medical problems. Coed, ages 8-18.

**1434 Squirrel Hollow Summer Camp**
The Bedford School
5665 Milam Road
Fairburn, GA 30213
770-774-8001
FAX: 770-774-8005
e-mail: bbox@thebedfordschool.org
www.thebedfordschool.org

*Betsy Box, Founder/Executive Director*

A remedial summer program for children with academic needs
held on the campus of The Bedford School in Fairburn, Georgia.
It is a five week day camp held from June 19 to July 21 and serves
ages 6-16. For mor information contact Betsy Box at (770)
774-8001.

# Hawaii

**1435 Camp Erdman YMCA**
YMCA Camp H R Erdman
69-385 Farrington Highway
Waialua, HI 96791
808-637-4615
FAX: 808-637-8874
e-mail: jheimowitz@ymcahonolulu.org
www.camperdman.net

*Josh Heimowitz, Executive Director*
*Elizabeth Staib-King, Senior Program Director*
*Mandy MacMahan, Resident/Family Program Director*

Traditional Resident Camp program is five nights and six days
of fun-filled activities that will create positive lifetime memories. Camp activitiesinclude: arts & crafts, swimming,
kayaking, hiking, challenge course, snorkeling, athletics, nature, dance & drama, beach writing and archery . Traditional
Resident Camp Experience (Ages 6-15) serving the needs of the
disabled.

**1436 Camp Mokuleia**
Episcopal Church Of Hawaii
68-729 Farrington Highway
Waialua, HI 96791
808-637-6241
FAX: 808-637-5505
e-mail: info@campmokuleia.com
www.campmokuleia.com/main.php

*Laurie Schlegel, General Manager*
*Mandy McMahan, Camp Director*
*Nani Lowery, Business Manager*

One and two-week sessions for children with cancer. Boys and
girls, ages 7-17.

# Idaho

**1437 Camp Hodia**
1701 North 12th Avenue
Boise, ID 83702
208-336-6829
FAX: 208-322-0402
e-mail: info@hodia.com
www.hodia.com

*Don Scott RN, Summer Camp Director*
*Lynn Wilson RN, Assistant Camp Director*
*Barb Scott RN, Secretary*

Camp is located in Alturas Lake, Idaho. One-week sessions for
children with diabetes. Coed, ages 8-18. Ski Camp in Sun Valley
in January, ages 12-18.

# Illinois

**1438 ADA Triangle D Camp**
American Diabetes Association
30 North Michigan Avenue
Suite 2015
Chicago, IL 60602
312-346-1805
888-342-2383
FAX: 312-346-5342
e-mail: sapsey@diabetes.org
www.diabetes.org

*Suzanne Apsey, Program Director*
*Sara Wichman, Program Assistant*
*Nancy Harris, Executive Director*

A special camp program combining summer activities, diabetes
education and medical supervision with one week sessions during July. Coed, ages from 9 to 13. Featured activities include: archery, arts and crafts, baseball/softball, boating, challenge/rope
courses, soccer and recreational swimming.

**1439 American Diabetes Association: Camp Grenada**
American Diabetes Association
2580 East Federal Drive
Suite 403
Decatur, IL 62526
217-875-9011
888-342-2383
FAX: 217-875-6849
e-mail: dscott@diabetes.org
www.diabetes.org

*Donna Scott, Executive Director*

Camp is located in Monticello, Illinois. One-week sessions for
children with diabetes. Boys and girls 8-17.

**1440 Camp Little Giant**
Southern Illinois University
206 Touch of Nature Road
Makanda, IL 62958
618-453-1121
FAX: 618-453-1188
e-mail: tonec@tonec.siu.edu
www.pso.siu.edu/tonec

*Vicki Lang, Therapuetic Rec Specialist*
*David Geneme, Manager*

One and two week sessions for campers with a variety of disabilities. Coed, ages 8-80.

**1441 Camp New Hope**
PO Box 764
Mattoon, IL 61938
217-895-2341
FAX: 217-895-3658
e-mail: cnhinc@rr1.net
www.rr1.net/users/cnhinc/

*Kim Carmack, Executive Director*
*Terri Taylor, Program Coordinator*

Advocacy services, social and recreational services and a summer camp for the disabled. The camp accommodates people of widely diverse needs and abilities including access for wheelchair users. Co-ed, for those 8 years and older, including adults. Facilities include a mini golf area; pontoon boat; fishing deck; playground; trails; swimmming pool; and sleeping cabins with air conditioning.

**1442 Easter Seals Camp: Illinois**
11285a Fox Road
Yorkville, IL 60560
630-553-7361
FAX: 630-896-6257
www2.kidscamps.com

**1443 Easter Seals of Bartholomew County**
Easter Seals
230 W Monroe Street
Suite 1800
Chicago, IL 60606
312-726-6200
800-221-6827
FAX: 312-726-1494
TTY: 312-726-4258
e-mail: info@easterseals.com
www.easterseals.com

*James E Williams Jr, President/CEO*
*Joanne Cloonan, Project Manager Executive Office*

Serves the needs of disabled persons and allows them to experience the joys and challenges unique to summer camp. Activities include: campfire sing-a-longs to boating, nature walks, swimming, and arts and crafts.

**1444 Easter Seals: UCP Timber Pointe Outdoor Center**
Easter Seals
230 W Monroe Street
Suite 1800
Chicago, IL 60606
312-726-6200
FAX: 312-726-1494
e-mail: kpodeszw@easterseals-ucp.org
www.easterseals.com

*Kurt Podeszwa, Director of Camping/VP*
*Wayne Baum, President*

One and two-week sessions for campers with a wide variety of disabilities. Coed, ages 6-99. Campers experience different activities each day such as arts and crafts, music, horses, field sports, outdoor nature, swimming, canoeingand fishing. Every night there is a different activity: skit night, casino night, boat night (campers go out on the lake on pontoon boats), night swim, camp fires, and of course, everyone's favorite - a dance on the last night.

**1445 JCYS Camp Red Leaf**
26710 West Nippersink Road
Ingleside, IL 60041
847-740-5010
FAX: 847-740-5014
e-mail: awarner@jcys.org
www.jcys.org

*Anthony Warner, Director*
*Chuck Kahalnik, President*

For campers with developmental disabilities and mobility limitation.

**1446 Jewish Council for Youth Services**
JCYS Camp Red Leaf
26710 West Nippersink Road
Ingleside, IL 60041
847-740-5010
FAX: 847-740-5014
e-mail: info@jcys.org
www.jcys.org/northshore/

*Danielle Weinstein, Director*
*Valerie Ravenna, Assistant Director*
*Joe Knudsen, Coach*

Overnight summer camp for youth and adults with developmental disabilites. Family Camps, respite weekends, trips, and other special events are offered throughout the year.

**1447 Olympia**
Southern Illinois University Carbondale
Southern Illinois University
Carbondale, IL 62901
618-536-2431
FAX: 618-453-2230
TTY:618-453-2276
e-mail: siucnews@siu.edu
www.siuc.edu

*Ben Dziegielewski, Executive Director*
*Elaine Blinde, Manager*

Located on 6,500 acres of forests and meadows on the shores of Little Grassy Lake, Olympia Camp is for mentally and physically handicapped children and adults. Among the activities offered are arts and crafts, hay wagon rides, canoeing and swimming.

**1448 Rimland Services for Autistic Citizens**
1265 Harney Avenue
Evanston, IL 60202
847-328-4090
877-395-6937
FAX: 847-328-8364
e-mail: dwork@rimland.org
www.rimland.org

*Pamela Watson, Chief Executive Officer*
*Edna Adams, Operations Assoc Exec Director*
*Dave Work, Programs Assoc Exec Director*

An accessible camp facility that can be utilized by groups for day use or overnight camping experiences. Six winterized cabins, a meeting facility, indoor pool, full food service, and an excellent staff are available. Educational programs can be arranged or you can utilize the facility to manage your own programs.

**1449 Shady Oaks Camp**
16300 South Parker Road
Homer Glen, IL 60491
708-301-0816
FAX: 708-301-5091
e-mail: soc16300@aol.com
www.shadyoakscamp.org

*Scott Steele, Executive Director*

Shady Oaks Camp provides outdoor fun and recreation for children and adults with cerebral palsy and similar disabilities. Our camp is organized with the goal of providing stimulating life experiences that our campers may not have the opportunity to engage in elsewhere.

**1450 Summer Wheelchair Sports Camp**
University of Illinois/Division of Rehab Education
1207 S Oak Street
Champaign, IL 61820
217-333-4607
FAX: 217-333-0248
e-mail: sportscamp@uiuc.edu
www.disability.uiuc.edu/athletics/

*Maureen Gilbert, Director*
*Karen Wold, Learning Disability Specialist*
*Theresa Rear, Hearing Impaired Interpreter*

Rigorous camps designed for individuals with lower extremity physical disabilities. Camp attndees will spend an average of 8-9 hours a day, focusing on development and refinement of fitness, techniques and strategies. Strength training, nutrition and mental training sessions will also be included in all camps. The camp staff is comprised of athletic staff and faculty front, the Division of Rehabilitation Education Services and local wheelchair athletes with coaching experience.

**1451 Touch of Nature Environmental Center**
Mail Code 6888
Carbondale, IL 62901
618-453-1121
FAX: 618-453-1188
e-mail: tonec@tonec.siu.edu
www.pso.siu.edu/tonec

*Vicki Lang, Camp Director*
*Chilang Lawless, Camp Registrant*
*David Gename, Manager*

Providing a traditional camping experience for non-traditional campers, including recreational and outdoor programs for adults and children with various developmental, mental and physical disabilities as well as learning and behavioral disorders.

**1452 Triangle D Camp for Children with Diabetes**
Northern Illinois A DA
30 N Michigan Avenue
Suite 2015
Chicago, IL 60602
312-346-1805
888-342-2383
FAX: 312-346-5342
e-mail: info@diabetes123.com
www.childrenwithdiabetes.com

*Sue Apsey, Director*
*Nancy Harris, Executive Director*

Camp is located in Ingleside, Illinois. One-week sessions in August. Coed, ages 8-13.

**1453 YMCA Camp Duncan**
Tourette Syndrome Camp Organization
6933 North Kedzie
Suite 816
Chicago, IL 60645
773-465-7536
847-546-8086
FAX: 847-546-3550
e-mail: info@ymcacampduncan.org
www.tourettecamp.com/

*Rona Roffey, Camp Director*
*Tammy Welninski, Day Camp Director*
*Addie Smits, Director Group Services*

The Tourette Syndrome/TS Camp USA, founded in 1994, is a residential camping program designed for girls and boys ages 8 - 16+ whose primary diagnosis is TS, and to a lesser degree, OCD and ADD/ADHD. The TS Camp is held at YMCA Camp Duncan which is located 30 miles north of Chicago. The goal of the camp is to allow children with TS an opportunity to meet other children, share similar experiences and coping mechanisms in a fun, safe and positive environment.

## Indiana

**1454 Bradford Woods/Camp Riley**
Indiana University
5040 State Road 67 N
Martinsville, IN 46151
765-342-2915
FAX: 765-349-1086
TTY:765-349-5117
e-mail: bradwood@indiana.edu
www.bradwoods.org

*John Koenig, Executive Director*

One and two-week sessions for children with a variety of disabilities. Coed, ages 8-18.

**1455 CHAMP Camp**
St Vincent Children s Specialty Hospital
PO Box 40306
Indianapolis, IN 46240
317-679-1860
e-mail: admin@champcamp.org
www.champcamp.org

*David Carter, Co-Founder*
*Nancy Mccurdy, Camp Director*
*Deb Wagner, Manager*

Camp in Cleveland, Ohio for children with hearing impairment, developmental disabilities, speech/communication impairment and visual impairment/blindness.

**1456 Camp Challenge**
8914 US Highway 50 East
Bedford, IN 47421
812-834-5159
e-mail: camp@hpcisp.com
www.campc.org

*Ralph Price, Director*
*Lyn Price, Assistant Director*
*Mike Corrence, Camp Director*

One and two-week sessions for campers with developmental and or physical disabilities, hearing impairment and the blind/visually impaired. Ages 6-99 and families.

**1457 Camp Crosley YMCA**
Muncie Family YMCA
165 EMS T2 Lane
North Webster, IN 46555
574-834-2331
FAX: 574-834-3313
e-mail: info@campcrosley.org
www.campcrosley.org

*Richard Armstrong, Executive Director*
*Larry McCullin, Program Director*
*Randle Cassady, Summer Camp Director*

Camp is located in North Webster, Indiana. Half-week, one, two and three-week sessions for campers with asthma/respiratory ailments and diabetes. Coed, ages 7-17. Also families and seniors.

**1458 Camp John Warvel**
American Diabetes Association
6415 Castleway West Drive
Indianapolis, IN 46250
317-352-9226
800-228-2897
FAX: 317-594-0748
www.diabetes.com

*Elaine McClane, Director Programs*
*Renea Marsh, Executive Director*

Camp is located in North Webster, Indiana. Provides an enjoyable, safe and educational out-of-doors experience for children with insulin-dependent diabetes. A unique learning atmosphere for children to acquire new skills in caring for their disease. The camp experience instills confidence for the child's self-management of diabetes. Offers one-week sessions and can accommodate 200 campers, boys and girls aged 7-16.

**1459 Camp Millhouse**
25600 Kelly Road
South Bend, IN 46614
574-233-2202
FAX: 574-233-2511
e-mail: leabee37@comcast.net
www.campmillhouse.org

*Lea Anne Pitcher, Director*

Nestled in a rustic clearing surrounded by 45 acres of woods, Camp Millhouse is a retreat for children and young adults with mental and physical disabilities. Hiking trails, nature studies, crafts, swimming, and stories around the bonfire make up activities campers long remember. One-week session. Co-ed, ages 4 to 30.

# Camps /Iowa

**1460 Easter Seal Crossroads Rehabilitation Cent er**
4740 Kingsway Drive
Indianapolis, IN 46205          317-466-1000
                              FAX: 317-466-2000
                              TTY:317-479-3232
www.eastersealcrossroad.org

David Brandt, Chairman of the Board
James Vento, President
David Bussard, Director

A community resource working in partnership with children and adults with disabilities or special needs and their families to promote growth, independence and dignity.

**1461 Easter Seals ARC of Northeast Indiana**
4919 Coldwater Road
Fort Wayne, IN 46825          260-456-4534
                              800-234-7811
                              FAX: 260-482-7875
                    e-mail: shinkle@arc-nei.org
                    www.easersealsarcnein.org/

F. Gil Perry, Chairperson
Nikki Holm, Senior Vice Chairperson
R Green, Vice Chairperson

Offers camp respite for adults, camp respite for children, day camping for adults, recreational services for adults, and vacation get-away program.

**1462 Easter Seals of Wayne & Union Counties**
National Easter Seals
PO Box 86
Centerville, IN 47330          765-855-2482
                               FAX: 765-855-2482
                    e-mail: easterseals@juno.com
                    eastersealswu.tripad.com

Pat Bowers, Executive Director

Providing programs and services for youth and adults with disabilities in Wayne and Union Counties, Indiana. Limited to our service area.

**1463 Englishton Park Academic Remediation**
Englishton Park Presbyterian
PO Box 228
Lexington, IN 47138          812-889-2681

                    e-mail: tbarnet@venus.net
                    www.englishtonpark.org

Lisa Barnett, Co-Director
Thomas Barnett, Co-Director

Camp is located in Lexington, Indiana. Two-week sessions for children with ADD. Boys and girls, ages 7-12.

**1464 Happiness Bag**
3833 Union Road
Terre Haute, IN 47802          812-234-8867
                               FAX: 812-238-0728
                    e-mail: jmexdir@aol
                    www.happinessbag.org

Richard Shagley, President of the Board
Jodi Moan, Executive Director

Serves developmentally disabled age 5-adult; day and residential camp program; after school program; scouting; Special Olympic anticipation (basketball, athletics, bowling, softball and aquatics); and a bowling league.

**1465 Happy Hollow Childrens Camp**
615 N Alabama Streeet
Suite 228
Indianapolis, IN 46204          317-638-0195

                    e-mail: hhvdir@aol.com
                    www.happyhollowcamp.net

Robert Stephens, Vice President
Richard Von Der Haar, President/Chairman
Bernard Schrader, Executive Director

Is a non profit residential summer camp that was founded to give low income, inner city children a week of fresh air, outdoor adventure and unique education at little or no cost. Age range of participants (8 to 14).

**1466 Isanogel Center**
7601 W Isanogel Road
50
Muncie, IN 47304          765-288-1073
                          FAX: 765-288-3103
                          TTY:765-288-1073
                    e-mail: isanogel@iquest.net
                    www.isanogelcenter.org

Tanner Underwood, President of the Board
Karen Kovac, Executive Director

One and two-week sessions June-August for special needs children through adults. Coed, ages 5-99.

**1467 Twin Lakes Camp**
1451 East Twin Lakes Road
Hillsboro, IN 47949          765-798-4000
                             FAX: 765-798-4010
                    e-mail: outdoors@twinlakescamp.com
                    www.twinlakescamp.com

Jon Beight, Executive Director
Brad Carter, Director
Walter Payne, Director

Provides a summer camp program for special needs children and young adults. Campers suffer from a wide range of maladies including crippling accidents, Spina Bifida, epilepsy, Cerebral Palsy, Muscular Dystrophy, Quadriplegia, Paraplegia, and other disabling diseases. Campers range in age from 8 to 27.

# Iowa

**1468 Camp Courageous of Iowa**
PO Box 418
Monticello, IA 52310          319-465-5916
                              FAX: 319-465-5919
                    e-mail: info@campcourageous.org
                    www.campcourageous.org

Charlie Becker, Executive Director
Jeanne Muellerleile, Camp Director

A year round residential and respite care facility for individuals with special needs. Campers range in age from 1-99 years old. Activities include traditional activities like canoeing, hiking, swimming, nature and crafts plus adventure activities like caving, rock climbing, etc. Campers with disabilities have opportunities to succeed at challenging activities. This feeling of self-worth can transfer to home, work or school environments.

144

**1469 Camp Hertko Hollow**
101 Locust Street
Des Moines, IA 50309
515-276-2237
800-DIA-ETES
888-437-8652
FAX: 515-251-5831
e-mail: a.wolf@camphertkohollow.com
www.CampHertkoHollow.com

*Ann Wolf, Exeuctive Director*
*Vivian Murry, Camp Director*

Camp Hertko Hollow is a resident camp held at the Des Moines YMCA Camp site, located along the Des Moines River north of Boone, Iowa. Activities include horseback riding, swimming, canoeing, rappelling, crafts, ropes course, archery and riflery to name a few, plus special activities for different ages. Half-week and one-week sessions for children with diabetes. Coed, ages 6-16.

**1470 Camp L-Kee-Ta**
Girl Scouts of Shining Trail
1308 Broadway Street
PO Box 190
West Burlington, IA 52655
319-752-3639
FAX: 319-753-1410
e-mail: info@girlscoutsofstc.org
www.girlscoutsofstc.org

*Donna Logan, Chief Executive Officer*
*Becky Godfrey, Camp Director*
*Kim Hull, Associate Executive Director*

Camp is located in Danville, Iowa. Half-week and one-week sessions June-August for children with asthma/respiratory ailments. Girls, ages 7-18 and families.

**1471 Camp Tanager**
1614 West Mount Vernon Road
Mount Vernon, IA 52314
319-363-0681
FAX: 319-365-6411
e-mail: dpirrie@tanagerplace.org
www.camptanager.org

*Donald Pirrie, Director*

Offers camp experiences for children 7 to 12 whose special social, economic or medical needs might not otherwise allow them to enjoy a summer camp experience. This private, non-profit camp serves over 600 children each summer with the staff-camper ratio being 1:6.

**1472 Camp Wyoming**
9106 42nd Avenue
Wyoming, IA 52362
563-488-3893
FAX: 563-488-3895
e-mail: campwyo@netins.net
www.campwyoming.net

*Kevin Cullum, Executive Director*
*Robyn Meyers, Assistant Director*
*Paul Scott, Maintenance Director*

Mainstreaming available June through August. Youth and adults with mild to moderate mental and physical disabilities can take part in a one week experience of fun and fellowship in early July.

**1473 Des Moines YMCA Camp**
YMCA Of Greater Des Moines
1192 166th Drive
Boone, IA 50036
515-432-7558
866-902-9622
FAX: 515-432-5414
e-mail: ycamp@dmymca.org
www.y-camp.org

*David Sherry, Director*
*Tom Hamilton, Chief Volunteer Officer*
*Vernon Delpesce, President/CEO*

Camp is located in Boone, Iowa. Year-round one and two-week sessions for boys and girls with cancer, diabetes, asthma, cystic fibrosis, hearing impaired and other disabilities. Coed, ages 6-16 and families.

**1474 Easter Seals Camp Sunnyside**
Easter Seals Iowa
401 Northeast 66th Avenue
PO Box 4002
Des Moines, IA 50333
515-274-1529
800-211-9273
FAX: 515-289-1281
TTY: 515-289-4069
e-mail: mtope@eastersealsia.org
www.ia.easterseals.org

*Marcia Tope, Camp Director*
*Donna Elbrecht, President*

Each summer from June through August, campers with disabilities ages five and up, take part in one week camping sessions, gaining skills and independence by participating in activities like swimming, horseback riding, canoeing, fishing, camping and more. Coed, ages 4-95. Accepts seniors and single adults. Financial assistance available.

**1475 Riverside Lutheran Bible Camp**
3001 Riverside Road
Story City, IA 50248
515-733-5271
800-372-7748
FAX: 515-733-4096
e-mail: RLBC@storycity.net
www.riversidelbc.org

*Dave McDermott, Director*
*Jan McDermott, Associate Director*
*Dan Scharnhorst, Program Coordinator*

Helps disabled people to develop, renew and nurture their relationship with Jesus Christ in a unique Christian environment.

**1476 University of Iowa: Wendell Johnson Speech and Hearing Clinic**
250 Hawkins Drive
Iowa City, IA 52242
319-335-1845
FAX: 319-335-8851
e-mail: wendy-fick@uiowa.edu
www.shc.uiowa.edu

*Linda Louko, Clinic Director*
*Marlea O'Brien, Child Language Research Center*
*Dorothy Albright, Department Administration*

The clinic offers assessment and remediation for communication disorders in adults and children. The clinic also offers a Intensive Summer Residential Clinic for school age children needing intervention services because of speech, language, hearing and/or reading problems.

**1477 Wesley Woods Camp & Retired Center**
Iowa United Methodist Conference Center
10896 Nixon Street
Des Moines, IA 50125
515-961-4523
866-684-7753
FAX: 515-974-8950
e-mail: WESLEYWOODS.CAMP@IAUMC.ORG
www.gbgm-umc.org/wesleywoods/

*Dick Faris, Director Camp/Retreat Ministries*
*Kathy Potter, Camps Registrar*
*Deke Rider, Program Coordinator*

Camp is located in Indianola, Iowa. Half-week and one-week sessions June-August for campers with developmental disabilities. Coed, ages 18-99.

# Kansas

**1478 Camp Discovery**
American Diabetes Association
837 S Hillside Street
Wichita, KS 67211

316-684-6091
800-362-1355
888-342-2838
FAX: 316-684-5675
e-mail: cwalter@diabetes.org
www.diabetes.org

*Crystal Walter, Camp Director*
*Lawrence T Smith, Chair*
*Lynn B Nicholas FACHE, Chief Executive Officer*

Camp is located in Junction City, Kansas. Offers young people with diabetes a week of fun at rock springs 4-H Center. Special attention to diabetes makes Camp Discovery a safe environment for active youth while providing valuable diabetes managment education. Call the American Diabetes Association Kansas area office for more information. Coed, ages 8-17.

**1479 Kansas Jaycees Cerebral Palsy Ranch**

PO Box 267
Augusta, KS 67010

316-775-2421
FAX: 316-775-2421
e-mail: execdirector@cpranch.org
www.cpranch.org

*Cheryl Schmeidler, Executive Director*
*Jana Allar, Program Coordinator*
*Sarah Walker, Camp Director*

Our mission is to provide a program which will allow individuals to enjoy their highest level of functioning and independence, consistant with their abilities, in a summer camp setting.

**1480 Kansas Jaycees' Cerebral Palsy Ranch**

6411 SW 50th Street
El Dorado, KS 67042

316-775-1146
FAX: 316-775-2421
e-mail: execdirector.cpranch.org
www.cpranch.org

*Cheryl Schmeidler, Executive Director*
*Diane Carswell, President*

Our mission is to provide a program which will allow individuals to enjoy their highest level of functioning and independence, consistant with their abilities, in a summer camp setting.

# Kentucky

**1481 Bethel Mennonite Camp**
2773 Bethel Church Road
Clayhole, KY 41317

606-666-4911
FAX: 606-666-4216
e-mail: grow@bethelcamp.org
www.bethelcamp.org

*Roger Voth, Director*
*Ruth Voth, Director*

A non profit ministry that reaches out to God to meet a wider variety of needs.

**1482 Cedar Ridge Camp**
4010 Routt Road
Louisville, KY 40299

502-267-5848
FAX: 502-267-0116
e-mail: andrew@cedarridgecamp.com
www.cedarridgecamp.com/

*Andrew Hartmans, Executive Director*

Half-week, one and two-week sessions for children with diabetes, developmental disabilities and muscular dystrophy. Coed, ages 6-17.

**1483 Easter Seal Camp KYSOC**
Kentucky Easter Sales Society
1902 Easter Day Road
Carrollton, KY 41008

502-732-5333
800-888-5377
FAX: 502-732-0783
e-mail: fun@kysoc.org
www.cardinalhill.org

*Karry Gillihan, President*
*Beth Monarch, Vice President*
*Sallie Price, Director*

Our services include: Adult day care services; audiology services; developmental intervention; medical day hospital; nursing; occupational therapy; physical therapy; psychological counseling; social services/case management and speech-language therapy.

**1484 Life Adventure Camp**
Life Adventure Camp of the Bluegrass
570 Milner Road
Versailles, KY 40383

859-873-3271
FAX: 859-873-2410
e-mail: info@clevelandhome.org
www.lifeadventurecamp.org

*Claudeca Clark, President*
*Essie Rogers, Equine Center Director*

Wilderness camp for children, male and female, ages 9-18, with emotional and behavioral problems. Half week and one week sessions June-August.

# Louisiana

**1485 Camp Bon Coeur**
The Heart Camp
PO Box 53765
Lafayette, LA 70505

337-233-8437
FAX: 337-233-4160
e-mail: info@heartcamp.com
www.heartcamp.com

*Calvin Guidry, President*
*Claire Foret, Vice President*
*Susannah Craig, Executive Director*

Two-week sessions June-July for children with heart defects. Coed, ages 8-16.

**1486 Camp Challenge**
PO Box 641253
Kenner, LA 70064

504-347-2267

e-mail: info@campc.org
www.campchallenge.org

*Carl Klutz, Director*
*Cecil Klutz, Director*

Camp Challenge is a grass roots non-profit organization dedicated to giving ill children and their siblings ages 6 through 18 a summer camp experience. Camp is open to all children who reside in Louisiana and have a form of cancer and chronic hematological disorders. These children do not have to pay for camp, it is free for all campers.

**1487 LA Lions Camp for Disabled/Diabetic Youth**
LA Lions League Crippled Child
PO Box 171
Leesville, LA 71496 337-239-6567
FAX: 337-239-9975
e-mail: lalions@lionscamp.org
lionscamp.org/index.html

*Raymond E Cecil III, Director*
*Carol Laughlin, Executive Director*

One-week sessions June-August for disabled children. Coed, ages 7-19.

**1488 LA Lions LPDCI Camp Pelican**
1835 Saint Roch Avenue
New Orleans, LA 70117 504-944-0166
FAX: 504-948-9555
e-mail: mlandry@tulane.edu
www.lionscamp.org/

*R Tony Ricard, President/CEO*
*Cathy Allain, Assistant Camp Director*
*Michael Landry MD, Medical Director*

Camp Pelican is an overnight residential camp for children with moderate to severe asthma or other pulmonary problems. Founded in 1977, Camp Pelican is jointly sponsored by the Louisiana Pulmonary Disease Camp Inc and the Louisiana Lions Camp. Over 100 children attend annually and participate in education, sports, arts and crafts, swimming and other camping activities. Medical staff including physicians, nurses, respiratory therapists and social workers participate in camp. Coed, ages 5-17.

**1489 Med-Camps of Louisiana**
102 Thomas Road
Suite 615
West Monroe, LA 71291 318-329-8405
877-282-0802
FAX: 318-329-8407
e-mail: medcamps@hotmail.com
www.medcamps.com

*Mike Epler, President*
*Caleb Seney, Executive Director*

Serves children with severe asthma and allergies and many more.

# Maine

**1490 AH! Asthma Camp**
YMCA Camp of Maine
305 Winthrop Center Road
Winthrop, ME 04364 207-395-4200
207-395-7230
FAX: 207-395-7230
e-mail: info@maineycamp.org
www.maineycamp.org/htm/

*Rhonda Vosmus RRT-AE-C, Camp Director*
*Jon Musmand MD, Medical Director*

AH! Asthma camp is an overnight camp. It is held at the State YMCA Camp in Winthrop, Maine, for one week during the month of August. Children participate in canoeing, swimming, arts and crafts, and other activities alongside Y-Campers. Asthma Camp is a great way for kids to have fun while learning more about their asthma and how to keep it under control. Doctors, Nurses, and Respiratory Therapists provide medical care around the clock to AH! Campers. Coed, ages of 8 and 13.

**1491 Bishopswood**
Diocese of Maine Episcopal
143 State Street
Portland, ME 04101 207-772-6923
800-244-6062
FAX: 207-773-0095
e-mail: gkoch@diomaine.org
www.diomaine.org

*Georgia L Koch, Director*
*Heidi Shott, Press Officer/Communications*
*Elizabeth Ring, Director Resource Center*

Camp is located in Hope, Maine. One to seven-week sessions for hearing impaired children June-August. Coed, ages 7-16.

**1492 Camp Capella**
United Cerebral Palsy of Maine
700 Mount Hope Avenue
Suite 320
Bangor, ME 04401 207-941-2952
FAX: 207-941-2955
e-mail: ucp2@midmaine.org
www.ucp.org

*Tricia Kail, Director of Services*
*Bobbi Jo Yeager, Executive Director*
*Stephanie Cote, Public Relations/Development*

Provides an opportunity for children with disabilities to engage in various recreational and social experiences.

**1493 Camp Lawroweld**
Northern New England Conference
228 West Side Road
Weld, ME 04285 207-585-2984
FAX: 207-585-2895
www.lawroweld.org

*Joseph Stagg Lawrence, Founder*
*Clarence Well, Founder*
*Harry Sabnani, Executive Director*

Camp is located in Weld, Maine. Week sessions July for campers who are blind or visually impaired, all ages. Other camps coed, ages 9-16 and families, single adults, June - September.

**1494 Camp Waban**
5 Dunaway Drive
Sanford, ME 04073 207-324-7955
FAX: 207-324-6050
e-mail: waban@gwi.netn.org
www.waban.org

*Neal Meltzer, Executive Director*
*Gervaise Flynn, Assistant Executive Director*
*Paula Leavitt, Clinical Director*

Camp is a non profit corporation organized to develop and operate programs which promote the general welfare and education of children and adults with developmental disabilities.

**1495 Pine Tree Camp**
Pine Tree Society
149 Front Street
PO Box 518
Bath, ME 04530 207-397-4101
FAX: 207-397-5324
e-mail: info@pinetreesociety.org
www.pinetreesociety.org

*Kenneth Textor, President*
*Anne Marsh, Executive Director*
*Dawn Willard-Robinson, Program Management Director*

Provides direct service programs statewide to people with disabilities.

## Maryland

**1496 Camp Glyndon**
American Diabetes Association
800 Wyman Park Drive
Suite 110
Baltimore, MD 21211     410-265-0075
   800-342-2383
FAX: 410-235-4048
e-mail: askada@diabetes.org
www.diabetes.org

*Larry K Ellingson, Chairman*
*Lynn B Nicholas, Chief Executive Officer*
*Alan D Cherrington, President*

Camp is located in Nanjemoy, Maryland. ne and two-week sessions July-August for children with diabetes and their families. Coed, ages 8-16.

**1497 Camp Greentop**
League Serving People With Disabilities
1111 East Cold Spring Lane
Baltimore, MD 21239    410-323-0500
FAX: 410-323-3298
e-mail: leaguelink@leagueforpeople.org
www.campgreentop.org

*Janice Frey-Angel, Chief Executive Officer*
*Toni Carter, Medical Day Program Director*
*Stephen Freeman, Wellness Director*

Camp is located in Sabillasville, Maryland. Summer residential camp located in the Catoctin Mountain National Park. Since 1937, Greentop has been serving children and adults with physical and multiple disabilities in a completely accessible camp setting. Campers enjoy a traditional camping program. Medical facilities staffed 24 hours a day. Half-week/one/two-week sessions June-August. ACA/MD Youth Camp.

**1498 Camp JCC**
Jewish Community Center of Greater Washington JCC
6125 Montrose Road
Rockville, MD 20852    301-230-3704
FAX: 301-881-6549
e-mail: campjcc@jccgw.org
www.jccgw.org

*Diane Kendall, Camp Director*

Camp JCC serves children with disabilities alongside their neighbors anf friends. The American Camping Association has presented a National award to Camp JCC for its extraordinary model inclusion program. We also offer a program designed especially for 13-21 year olds with severe to profound disabilities. In order for us to afford to do these things, we count on contributions to our Inclusion Fund. Four and eight-week sessions general day camp program offering June-August for children.

**1499 Camp Merrick**
PO Box 56
Nanjemoy, MD 20662    301-870-5858
FAX: 301-246-9108
e-mail: administrator@lionscampmerrick.org
www.lionscampmerrick.org

*Robert Rainey, Administrator*

Programs offered April-January for children who are blind/visually impaired, hearing impaired or diabetic. Coed, ages 6-15.

**1500 Camp Sunrise**
American Cancer Society Maryland
8219 Town Center Drive
Baltimore, MD 21236    410-931-6850
888-670-0472
FAX: 410-931-6875
e-mail: sherryce.robinson@cancer.org
www.cancer.org

*Sherryce Robinson, Mission Delivery Manager*
*Kira Elring, Regional Mission Director*
*Gloria Jetter, Regional Executive Director*

Camp is located in Whitehall, Maryland. One-week sessions free of charge to children who have had, or currently have, cancer. Coed, ages 4-18.

**1501 Camp Superkids**
American Lung Association of Maryland
11350 McCormick Road
Executive Plaza 1, Suite 600
Hunt Valley, MD 21031    410-560-2120

e-mail: hdougherty@marylandlung.org
www.marylandlung.org

*Heather Dougherty, Camp Director*
*Marianne Hiteshew, Medical Director*
*Ceal Curry, Medical Director*

Overnight asthma camp for children 7 1/2 to 12 years of age. During the week of camp the kids will participate in arts and crafts, nature hikes, karate, swimming, sport activities and much more. Along with these activities there are 2 sessions a day of asthma education.

**1502 Capital Camps**
Jewish Camp and Conference Services
133 Rollins Avenue
Suite 4
Rockville, MD 20852    301-468-2267
FAX: 301-468-1719
TTY:717-794-2177
e-mail: info@capitalcamps.org
www.capitalcamps.org

*David M Phillips, Executive Director*
*Rebecca Glass, Camp Director*

Capital Camps is a Jewish Community Centers Association (JCCA) and American Camping Association (ACA) accredited camp for young people grades 3 through 12 in the greater Washington, Maryland and Northern Virginia regions. Coed, ages 7 to 17.

**1503 Easter Seals Camp Fairlee Manor**
Easter Seals DE/ MD Eastern Shore
22242 Bay Shore Road
Chestertown, MD 21620    410-778-0566
FAX: 410-778-0567
e-mail: fairlee@esdeo.org
www.de.easters.com

*Dan Tabacheck, Director*

One-week sessions June-August for campers with disabilities. Coed, ages 8-99, families, seniors, single adults.

**1504 Kamp A-Komp-Plish**
9035 Ironsides Road
Nanjemoy, MD 20622    301-870-3226
FAX: 301-870-2620
e-mail: kampakomplish@melwood.org
www.kamakomplish.org/

*Heidi Aldous, Camp Director*
*Doria Fleisher, Equestrian Manager*
*Earl Copus, Owner*

Camp is located in Nanjemoy, Maryland. Half-week, one-week and two-week sessions for blind/visually impaired children and those with developmental disabilities and mobility limitation. Coed, ages 8-16.

**1505  Lions Camp Merrick**
PO Box 375
Waldorf, MD  20604
301-893-8898
FAX: 301-374-2282
e-mail: cmpmerrick@aol.com
www.lionscampmerrick.org

*Gregory V Floberg, Executive Director*
*Kevin V Rupert, Camp Administrator*
*Pat Moffat, Administrative Assistant*

This recreational camp for special needs children offers a complete waterfront program including swimming, canoeing and fishing for ages 6-16. Designed for children who are deaf and hard of hearing, children of deaf parents, and children with diabetes. Also helps children to learn to deal with their special conditions.

**1506  Maryland National Capital Park and Planning Commission**
Special Populations Division
6611 Kenilworth Avenue
Riverdale, MD  20737
301-454-1740
FAX: 301-454-1750
e-mail: webmanager@mncppc.org
www.mncppc.org

*Elizabette M Hewlett, Chairman*
*William M Eley Jr, Vice Chairman*
*Laurie Verge, Program Director*

Offers year round and seasonal activities and programs for individuals with disabilities and families including day camps, horseback riding, beep ball, aquatics, special events and much more.

**1507  Milldale Camp**
J CC Of Baltimore
3506 Gwynnbrook Avenue
Owings Mills, MD  21117
410-429-4900
FAX: 410-578-0102
e-mail: milldale@jcc.org
www.campmilldale.org

*Jodi Fishman, Camp Director*
*Jessica Witenstein-Weaver, Special Needs Coordinator*

Camp is located in Reisterstown, MD. Four and eight week sessions, June - August. Inclusion program for children entering grades 5-13 with learning, developmental, social, emotional and physical disabilities. Self-contained program for teenagers with disabilities ages 14-21 focusing on recreational and vocational activities, including weekly field trips.

**1508  Raven Rock Lutheran Camp**
17912 Harbaugh Valley Road
PO Box 136
Sabillasville, MD  21780
410-303-2108
800-321-5824
e-mail: ravenrock@innernet.net
www.ravenrock.org

*Brenda Minnich, Executive Director*
*Stephen Demik, Program Director*
*John Corkal, Director*

Christ-centered program for youth and mentally retarded adults.

**1509  Youth Leadership Camp**
National Association of the Deaf
8630 Fenton Street
Suite 820
Silver Spring, MD  20910
301-587-1788
FAX: 301-587-1791
TTY:301-587-1789
e-mail: infor@nad.org
www.nad.org

*Bill Stark, Camp Director*
*Jennifer Yost Ortiz, Youth Programs Coordinator*

Sponsored by the National Association of the Deaf, this camp emphasizes leadership training for deaf teenagers and young adults. In addition to many recreational activities and sports, there are academic offerings and camp projects.

# Massachusetts

**1510  AU Kamp for Kids**
Abilities Unlimited
61 Union Street
PO Box 219
Westfield, MA  01086
413-562-5678
FAX: 413-562-1239
e-mail: info@abilitiesunlimited.org
www.abilitiesunlimited.org

*C. David Scanlin PhD, Executive Director*

Two-week sessions July-August for children and young adults with a variety of disabilities. Coed, ages 3-22.

**1511  Agassiz Village**
238 Bedford Street
Suite 8
Lexington, MA  02420
781-860-0200
FAX: 781-860-0352
www.agassizvillage.com

*Lisa M Gillis, Executive Director/Camp Director*
*Sarah Dodd, Program Director*
*Denise Donellan, Health Director*

Camp is located in Poland, Maine. Camp is located in Poland, Maine. Offers two and three-week sessions June-August for children with cerebral palsy, mobility limitation and spina bifida. Coed, ages 7-14.

**1512  Becket Chimney Corners YMCA Outdoor Center**
748 Hamilton Road
Becket, MA  01223
413-623-8991
FAX: 413-623-5890
e-mail: bccymca@bccymca.org
www.bccymca.org

*Philip Connor, Executive Director*
*Steve Hammil, Outdoor Camp Director*
*Sasha Armstrong, Officer Manager*

Half-week and one-week sessions for campers with asthma/respiratory ailments. Coed, ages 1-99, families, seniors, single adults.

**1513  CNS Camp New Connections**
Mclean Hospital
115 Mill Street
Belmont, MA  02478
617-855-2000
800-333-0338
FAX: 617-855-3691
e-mail: info@mclean.harvard.edu
www.mcleanhospital.org

*Roya Ostovar PhD, Center Director*
*Brandi Henson PsyD, Camp Coordinator*
*Joseph Gold MD, Clinical Director*

Six-week sessions June-August for children with autism. Coed, ages 6-14.

**1514  Camp Joslin**
One Joslin Place
Boston, MA  02215
617-732-2400
FAX: 617-735-1925
e-mail: camp@joslin.harvard.edu
www.joslin.org

*C Ronald Kahn, President/Director*
*Stephanie Holloway, Camp Coordinator*
*Martin J Abrahamson MD, SVP Medical Director*

Camp is located in Charlton, Massachusetts. For boys, ages 7-16, with diabetes. This program offers active summer sports and activities, supplemented by medical treatment and diabetes education. Coed Winter Camp and Coed Weekend Retreats are offered during the school year.

## 1515 Camp Ramah in New England (Summer)

39 Bennett Street
Palmer, MA 01069
413-283-9771
FAX: 413-283-6661
www.campramahNE.org

*Howard Blas, Director*
*Rabbi Ed Gelb, Camp Director*

8 week sleep-away camp for Jewish adolescents with developmental disabilities. Full camping program includes swimming, Hebrew singing and dancing, sports, arts and crafts, daily services, Kosher food and Jewish studies classes. Some mainstreaming and vocational opportunities.

## 1516 Camp Ramah in New England (Winter)

35 Highland Circle
Needham, MA 02494
781-449-7090
FAX: 781-449-6331
e-mail: joels@campramahne.org
www.campramahne.org

*Joel Stavsky, Director*

8 week sleep-away camp for Jewish adolescents with developmental disabilities. Full camping program includes swimming, Hebrew singing and dancing, sports, arts and crafts, daily services, Kosher food and Jewish studies classes. Vocational program for select group of former campers.

## 1517 Camp Waziyatah

19 Vose Lane
East Walpole, MA 02032
508-668-9758
FAX: 508-668-2665
e-mail: info@wazi.com
www.wazi.com

*Penny Kerns, Director*

Camp is located in Waterford, Massachusetts. Three, four and seven-week sessions June-August for campers with cancer and diabetes. Coed, ages 8-15 and families, single adults.

## 1518 Carroll School Summer Programs

25 Baker Bridge Road
Lincoln, MA 01773
781-259-8342
FAX: 781-259-8852
e-mail: info@carrollscholl.org
www.carrollschool.org

*Philip Burling, Chairman*
*Stephen Wilkins, Principal*

Academic and recreational programs designed to improve learning skills and build self-confidence. The school is a tutorial program for students not achieving their potential due to poor skills in reading, writing and math. The summer camp complements the summer school offering outdoor activities in a supportive, non-competitive environment.

## 1519 Clara Barton Diabetes Camp

Clara Barton For Girls With Diabetes
30 Enis Road
PO Box 356
North Oxford, MA 01537
508-987-2056
FAX: 508-987-2002
e-mail: info@bartoncenter.org
www.bartoncenter.org

*John Maconga, President*
*Kerry Packard, Program Coordinator*
*Martha Houlihan, Finance/Technology Coordinator*

Girls, ages 3-17, with diabetes participate in a well-rounded camp program with special education in diabetes, health and safety. Activities include swimming, boating, sports, dance, music and arts and crafts. Two week adventure camp for high school girls offering camping, hiking, canoeing, etc. Also a minicamp (one week) for girls 6-12. Day camps are offered in Worcester, Boston, and New York City.

## 1520 Eagle Hill School: Summer Program

242 Old Petersham Road
Hardwick, MA 01037
413-477-6000
FAX: 413-477-6837
e-mail: admission@ehs1.org
www.ehs1.org

*Peter J Donald, Headmaster*

For children ages 9-19 with specific learning (dis)abilities and/or Attention Deficit Disorder, this summer program is designed to remediate academic and social deficits while maintaining progress achieved during the school year. Electives and sports activities are combined with the academic courses to address the needs of the whole person in a camp-like atmosphere.

## 1521 Easter Seals Massachusetts-Agassiz Village

484 Main Street
6th Floor
Worcester, MA 01608
508-757-2756
800-922-8290
FAX: 508-831-9768
e-mail: camp@eastersealsma.org
www.eastersealsma.org

*Kirk Joslin, Chief Executive Officer*
*Stefanie Morissette, Camp Manager*

Mission is to help children and adults with disabilities expand their independence.

## 1522 Four-H Camp Howe

PO Box 326
Goshen, MA 01032
413-549-3969
FAX: 413-577-0760
e-mail: office@camphowe.com
www.camphowe.com

*Terrie Campbell, Camp Director*

One and two-week sessions June-August for children with a variety of disabilities. Coed, ages 7-17.

## 1523 Handi-Kids

470 Pine Street
Bridgewater, MA 02324
508-697-7557
FAX: 508-697-1529
e-mail: info@handikids.org
www.handikids.org

*Ginny Pitts, Executive Director*
*Mary Gallant, Program Director*
*Jane Pariseau, Theraputic Riding Director*

A therapeutic recreational facility in Bridgewater, Massachusetts offering after-school programs, special events, school vacation full-week and summer day camp programs. Every individual is welcome. Two-week sessions July-August.
*Sliding Scale*

## 1524 Madden Open Hearts Camp

250 Monument Valley Road
Great Barrington, MA 01230
413-528-2229
888-611-1113
FAX: 413-528-6553
e-mail: info@openheartscamp.org
www.openheartscamp.org

*David Zaleon, Camp Director*

Eight week program for children who have had and are fully recovered from open heart surgery or a heart transplant. Four two week sessions by age group. Small camp - 25 campers per session.

**1525 Riverview School**
551 Route 6a
East Sandwich, MA 02537
508-888-0489
FAX: 508-833-7001
e-mail: admissions@riverviewschool.org
www.riverviewschool.org

*Jeanne M Pacheco, Director Admissions/Placement*
*Maureen B Brenner, Head of School/Principal*

An independent, residential school of interntaional reputation and service enrolling approximately 180 male and female students in its sencondary and post sencondary programs. Students share a common history of lifelong difficulty with academic achievement and the development of friendships. On measures of intellectual ability, most students score within the 70-100 range and have primary diagnosis of learning disability and/or complex language or learning disorder.

**1526 Tower Program at Regis College**
Regis College
235 Wellesley Street
Weston, MA 02493
781-768-7000
FAX: 781-768-8339
e-mail: admission@regiscollege.edu
www.regiscollege.edu

*Mary England, President*
*Pamela Menke, Vice Prsident*

Helps average and above average college-bound students, ages 16-17, having a diagnosed dyslexic learning disability, to adjust to a college setting. Emphasis is on instruction and academic reinforcement, affective support, awareness of support services available on most college campuses and strategy training.

**1527 Winnekeag**
34 Sawyer Street
PO Box 1169
South Lancaster, MA 01561
978-365-4551
FAX: 978-365-3838
e-mail: sneconference@sneconline.org
www.sneconline.org

*Frank Tochterman, President/Religious Leader*

Camp is located in Ashburnham, Massachusetts. Camping sessions for blind/visually impaired children. Coed, ages 8-16.

---

# Michigan

**1528 ADA Teen Camp at Covenant Point**
American Diabetes Association
30 North Michigan Avenue
Suite 2015
Chicago, IL 60602
312-346-1805
888-342-2383
FAX: 312-346-5342
e-mail: sapsey@diabetes.org
www.diabetes.org/

*Loynn Nicholas, CEO*
*Nancy Harris, Executive Director*
*Suzanne Aspey, Program Director*

One-week sessions for children and teenagers with diabetes. Coed, ages 4 to 9. Camp season runs from June through August and is located in Iron River, Michigan. Featured activities include: arts and crafts, nature/environmental studies, recreational swimming and team building.

**1529 Adventure Learning Center at Eagle Village**
4507 170th Avenue
Hersey, MI 49639
231-832-2234
800-748-0061
FAX: 231-832-0385
e-mail: info@eaglevillage.org
www.eaglevillage.org

*Jon Lauderbach, Chairman*
*Gary Bennett, President/CEO*
*Anne Soczawa, Director of Finance*

This program accepts youth, ages 5-17, who are high risk or special needs - behavioral problems, emotionally unstable or Attention Deficit. The camping experience includes canoeing, hiking, swimming and high adventure activities. Half-week, one-week, and two-week sessions June-August. Coed.

**1530 Camp Barakel**
PO Box 159
Fairview, MI 48621
989-848-2279
FAX: 989-848-2280
e-mail: info@campbarakel.org
www.campbarakel.org

*Lee Brown, Program Director*

Five-day Christian camp experience in mid-August for campers ages 13-55 who are physically disabled, visually impaired, upper trainable mentally impaired or educable mentally impaired, bus transportation provided from locations in Lansing, Flint and Bay City, Michigan.

**1531 Camp Catch-a-Rainbow**
American Cancer Society
1755 Abbey Road East
Lansing, MI 48823
517-332-2222
800-ACS-2345
FAX: 517-664-1497
e-mail: deb.dillingham@cancer.org
www.cancer.org

*Debra Dillingham, Director*
*Greg Bontrager, Chief Executive Officer*

Camp is located in Montague, Michigan. One-week sessions for children with cancer. Co-ed ages 7-15.

**1532 Camp Nissokone**
YMCA Camping Services
7300 Hickory Ridge Road
Holly, MI 48442
248-887-4533
248-887-5203
e-mail: office@ycampingservices.org
www.ycampingservices.org/

*Jennifer Buckelew, Director*
*David Marks, Director*

A six week summer resident camp program for boys and girls whose learning and behavior styles have made successful participation in the traditional camp program difficult. All camp activities have a special emphasis on building self-esteem and peer relationships. Strong in waterfront, nature, campcrafts and a special arts program.

**1533 Camp O'Fair Winds**
Girl Scouts Fair Winds Council
2300 Austins Parkway
Flint, MI 48507
810-230-0244
800-482-6734
FAX: 810-230-0955
e-mail: tplotz@gsfwc.org
www.gsfwc.org

*Therese Plotz, Camp Director*
*Dawn Reha, Executive Director*

Accepts diabetic and learning disabled girls ages 6-12. Also accepts girls with other physical disabilities. Please call for more information.

**1534  Camp O'Fair Winds**
Girl Scouts Fair Winds Council
2300 Austins Parkway
Flint, MI  48507
810-230-0244
800-482-6734
FAX: 810-230-0955
e-mail: dreha@gsfwc.org
www.gsfwc.org

*Therese Plotz, Chief Executive Camp Director*
*Dawn Reha, Executive Director*
*Ellen Metler, Program Director*

Provides a rustic environment to facilitate and appreciate the outdoors. To further enhance this appreciation and to teach teamwork and self-reliance, every group of campers, fourth grade and older, will plan and carry out a primitive overnight camping trip. All of our programs are designed to encourage risk-taking in a safe and supportive environment. Girls develop self confidence and group communication skills as they plan their own activities and set goals for themselves.

**1535  Camp Roger**
The American Camping Association
8356 Belding Road
Rockford, MI  49341
616-874-7286
FAX: 616-874-5734
e-mail: office@camproger.org
www.camproger.org

*Doug Vanderwell, Executive Director*
*Phil Warners, Director Outdoor Education*
*Kathy Collins, Executive Assistant*

Camp Roger provides a fun top-notch summer program for disabled campers. Campers learn to love the woods, the water and the trails, getting to enjoy a wide variety of activities all designed to be fun, to build friendships, and develop self confidence.

**1536  Camp Tall Turf**
Christian Camps and Inner City Youth
935 Baxter Street Southeast
Grand Rapids, MI  49506
616-459-7206
FAX: 616-988-4596
e-mail: tallturf@iserv.net
www.tallturf.org

*Steve Farber, Chairman*
*Jack Kooyman, President*
*Denise Fase, Program Administrator*

Camp is located in Walkerville, Michigan. Summer camping sessions for youth with asthma/respiratory ailments and ADD. Coed, ages 8-16.

**1537  Central Michigan University Summer Clinics**
Health Professions, Building 1165
Central Michigan University
Mount Pleasant, MI  48859
989-774-3803
FAX: 989-744-1891
e-mail: churc1g@cmich.edu
www.chp.cmich.edu

*Dan Konkle, Director*
*Gerald Church, Audiology Division Director*
*Laurie Bahlke, Speech/Language Supervisor*

Designed for children, ages 6 and up, with speech, language and hearing disorders who can benefit from intensive clinical work. A wide range of recreational and social activities form part of the clinical program and promote the social use of skills learned in class.

**1538  Echo Grove Camp**
The Salvation Army
1101 Camp Road
(248) 628-3108
Leonard, MI  48367
248-628-3108
FAX: 248-628-7055
e-mail: info@echogrove.org
www.echogrove.org/

*Dale Johnson, Camp Director*

Since 1921, the Army's Echo Grove Camp has offered a structured camping program for children, adults and seniors referred through Corps Community Centers. During the course of Echo Grove's 12 week season, the camp includes programs geared for every need and interest. In addition to outdoor recreation, camps may include religious, musical and skill-building instruction.

**1539  Fowler Center**
2315 Harmon Lake Road
Mayfield, MI  48744
989-673-2050
FAX: 989-673-6355
e-mail: info@thefowlercenter.org
www.thefowlercenter.org/

*John S Fowler, Chairman and Founder*

Half-week, one-week and two-week sessions. June-August for campers with disabilities. Coed, ages 6-99, families, seniors.

**1540  Indian Trails Camp**
0-1859 Lake Michigan Drive Northwes
Grand Rapids, MI  49504
616-677-5251
FAX: 616-677-2955
e-mail: lynnyntema@indiantrailscamp.org
www.indiantrailscamp.org

*Lynn Gust, Executive Director*

Year round residential camping program for children and adults with physical disabilities. One and two-week sessions. Coed, ages 6-70.

**1541  Sherman Lake YMCA Outdoor Center**
6225 North 39th Street
Augusta, MI  49012
269-731-3000
FAX: 269-731-3020
e-mail: shermanlakeymca@ymcasl.org
www.shermanlakeymca.org

*Luke Austenfeld, Executive Director*
*Jeff Brown, Program Manager*
*Lorrie Syverson, Director Camping Services*

Summer camping sessions for campers with ADD and spina bifida. Coed, ages 6-15 and families, seniors.

**1542  YMCA Camp Copneconic**
Flint Michigan YMCA
10407 North Fenton Road
Fenton, MI  48430
810-629-9622
FAX: 810-629-2128
e-mail: fritzcheek@campcopneconic.org
www.campcopneconic.org

*John Carlson, Executive Director*
*Matt Langdon, Associate Executive Director*
*Shelly Hilton, Director School Programs*

Camp is located in Fenton, Michigan. Summer sessions for campers with diabetes. Coed, ages 3-16 and seniors.

# Minnesota

## 1543 Camp Buckskin
PO Box 389
Ely, MN 55731
218-365-2121
FAX: 218-365-2880
e-mail: buckskin@spacestar.net
www.campbuckskin.com

*Thomas R Bauer CCD, Camp Director*

Camp is located in Ely, Minnesota. Buckskin assists LD and ADD/ADHD individuals to realize and develop the potentials and abilities which they possess. Teaches a combination of traditional camp, academic activities and social skills so the campers experience success in many areas. 1:3 staff ratio ensures the program is individualized to meet each camper's needs.

## 1544 Camp Courage
Courage Center Headquarters
3915 Golden Valley Road
Minneapolis, MN 55422
763-520-0520
FAX: 763-520-0577
www.courage.org

*Jan Malcolm, Chief Executive Officer*
*Nancy Larkin, Chief Operating Officer*
*Alice Johnson, Chief Financial Officer*

Camp is located in Maple Lake, Minnesota. Summer sessions for campers with a variety of disabilities. Coed, ages 6-99, families, seniors.

## 1545 Camp Courage North
PO Box 1626
Lake George, MN 56458
218-266-3658
FAX: 231-826-6345
e-mail: camping@courage.org
www.couragecamps.org

*Tom Fogarty, Director*
*Mary Jensen, Manager*

Camp is located in Lake George, Minnesota. Summer sessions for campers who have blood disorders, hearing impairment, mobility limitation or are blind/visually impaired. Coed, ages 7-70.

## 1546 Camp Eden Wood
Friendship Ventures
6350 Indian Chief Road
Eden Prairie, MN 55346
952-852-0101
800-450-8376
FAX: 952-852-0123
e-mail: fv@friendshipventures.org
www.friendshipventures.org

*Georgann Rumsey, President/CEO*
*Laurie Tschetter, Program Director*
*Ed Stracke, President*

Camp is located in Eden Prairie, Minnesota. Offers resident camp programs for children, teenagers and adults with developmental, physical or multiple disabilities, Down Syndrome, special medical conditions, Williams Syndrome, autism and/or other conditions. Fishing, creative arts, golf, sports and other activities are available. Respite care weekend camps year round for children, teenagers and adults. Guided vacations for teens and adults with developmental disabilities or other unique needs.

## 1547 Camp Friendship
Friendship Ventures
10509 108th Street Northwest
Annandale, MN 55302
952-852-0101
800-450-8376
FAX: 952-852-0123
e-mail: fv@friendshipventures.org
www.friendshipventures.org

*Laurie Tschetter, Program Director*

Camp Friendship offers resident camp programs for children, teenagers and adults with developmental, physical or multiple disabilities, special medical conditions, Down Syndrome, Williams Syndrome, autism or other conditions. Summer camp offers archery, sailing, horseback riding, biking, fishing, creative arts, adventure challenge programs and other activities. Weekend camps and longer available. Other services available throughout the year. Coed, ages 5-90, families, seniors.

## 1548 Camp Knutson
11169 Whitefish Avenue
Crosslake, MN 56442
218-543-4232

e-mail: rlarson@lssmn.org
www.lssmn.org

*Mark Peterson, President/CEO*
*Mary Kay Williams, Program Manager*
*Rob Larson, Executive Director*

Provides a camping program for mentally and physically disabled and emotionally disturbed children and adults. Campers must come with an established group that brings its own counselors. Swimming, sailing, archery, nature study and hiking are among the non-competitive activities.

## 1549 Camp New Hope
10509 108th Street Northwest
Annandale, MN 55302
952-852-0101
800-450-8376
FAX: 952-852-0123
e-mail: fv@friendshipventures.org
www.campnewhopemn.org

*Lori Bittner, Director*

CNH is a private, non-profit organization which provides quality educational, recreational and leisure opportunities to children and adults with mental, physical and other developmental disabilities. Stimulating programs and quality care. Half-week and one-week sessions June-September. Coed, ages 6-99, families, seniors, single adults.

## 1550 Camp Winnebago
19708 Camp Winnebago Road
Caledonia, MN 55921
507-724-2351
FAX: 507-724-3786
e-mail: director@CampWinnebago.org
www.campwinnebago.org

*Theresa Burroughs, Executive Director*
*Al Fravert, President*
*Mike Werner, Vice President*

Offers one week summer sessions for children and adults with developmental disabilities. Also, integrated youth sessions to allow friends and siblings to attend with traditional campers. Respite week-ends are offered monthly throughout the year. Travel vacations are also offered as an option. Publishes a newsletter and makes a video available. Coed, ages 6-99, families, seniors, singles adults.

## 1551 Courage Center II
3915 Golden Valley Road
Minneapolis, MN 55422
763-520-0312
FAX: 763-520-0577
e-mail: camping@mtn.org
www.courage.org

*Richard Lund, Chairman*
*Jeff Bangsberg, Vice Chairman*
*Mary Jensen, Manager*

Summer camping sessions for children who have cerebral palsy, hearing impairment, mobility limitation, speech/comminication impairment or are blind/visually impaired. Coed, ages 5-14.

**1552 Needlepoint Daypoint**
American Diabetes Association
715 Florida Avenue South
Florida West Bldg, Suite 307
Minneapolis, MN 54426
763-593-5333
FAX: 763-593-1520
e-mail: rmartin@diabetes.org
www.diabetes.org

Becky Martin, Program Director
Carol Holten, Program Assistant
Diane Fave, Manager

Camping for children who have type 1 diabetes. Coed, ages 5-16.

**1553 Search Beyond Adventures**
4603 Bloomington Avenue
Minneapolis, MN 55407
612-721-2800
800-800-9979
FAX: 877-721-3409
e-mail: travel@searchbeyond.com
www.searchbeyond.com

Kailash Dhaksinamurthi, Camp Director
Chuck Johnson, Camp Director

Offers a wide variety of tours for adults with mental retardation. Programs vary from 4 to 12 days throughout North America and international. Offices in Minneapolis, Boston, Orlando, and Los Angeles areas. Bus, rail, cruise, air tours offered.

**1554 St Paul Academy and Summit School**
1712 Randolph Avenue
Saint Paul, MN 55105
651-698-2451
FAX: 651-698-6787
e-mail: info@spa.edu
www.spa.edu

Bryn Roberts, Head of School
Ned Smith, Principal
Byron E Starns, Secretary

In pursuit of excellence in teaching and learning, St Paul Academy and Summit School educates a diverse and motivated group of young people for leadership and service, inspires in them an enduring love of learning, and helps them lead productive, ethical and joyful lives.

**1555 St. Paul Academy and Summit School**
1712 Randolph Avenue
Saint Paul, MN 55105
651-698-2451
FAX: 651-698-6787
e-mail: info@spa.edu
www.spa.edu

Pamela Clarke, Head of School
Marlene Odahlen-Hinz, Assistant Director
Ned Smith, Principal

Individualized instruction in basic skills, reading, math, composition, and study skills.

**1556 Wilderness Canoe Base**
Lake Wapogasset Lutheran Bible Camp
12477 Gunflint Trail
Grand Marais, MN 55604
218-388-2241
800-454-2922
FAX: 218-388-9400
e-mail: paddle@wildernesscanoebase.org
www.wildernesscanoebase.org

Jedidiah Scharmer, Director
Andrea Scharmer, Program/Community Coordinator
Jacob Calvert, Facilities Manager

Camp is located in Grand Marais, Minnesota. Summer sessions for campers with substance abuse problems. Coed to age 99, families, seniors, single adults.

**1557 YMCA Camp Ihduhapi**
Minneapolis YMCA Camping Services
4 West Rustic Lodge
Minneapolis, MN 55419
612-822-2267
FAX: 612-823-2482
e-mail: info@campicaghowan.org
www.campicaghowan.org

Bryan Burns, Executive Director
Matt Saari, Assistant Executive Director

Camp is located in Loretto, Minnesota. Summer sessions for campers with asthma/respiratory ailments and epilepsy. Coed, ages 7-16.

# Mississippi

**1558 Tik-A-Witha**
PO Box B
Tupelo, MS 38802
662-844-7577
800-624-4185
FAX: 662-680-3164
e-mail: board@girlscoutsnems.org
www.girlscoutsnems.org/camp.html

Jenny H Jones, Camp Director
Sarah Edwards, Chief Executive Officer
Rebecca Cook, President

Resident camp, camp season begins in June and ends in July sessions are one week, two weeks. Campers include girls ages 6 to 17. Capacity is 100. Financial aid is available. Activities include Arts/Crafts, Camping Skills/Outdoor Living, Canoeing/Rope Courses, Counselor Training, Drama, Hiking, Horseback Western, Kayaking, Leadership Development, Nature/Eviroment Studies, Swimming-Recreational, Team Building.

# Missouri

**1559 Camp Black Hawk**
Bear River Ranch
16795 Highway East
Rolla, MO 65401
573-458-2125
FAX: 573-458-2126
e-mail: director@bearriverranch.com
www.bearriverranch.com

Lori Martin, Executive Director
Scott Martin, Owner
Rachel Martin, Assistant Program Director

Coed summer camp for children and adults with developmental disabilites.

**1560 Camp Carpe Diem**
Bear River Ranch
16795 Highway East
Rolla, MO 65401
573-458-2125
FAX: 573-458-2126
e-mail: director@bearriverranch.com
www.bearriverranch.com

Lori Martin, Director
Scott Martin, Owner
Rachel Martin, Assistant Program Director

Coed summer camp for children and adults with developmental disablitites who need high support.

**1561 Camp Hickory Hill**
Central Missouri Diabetic Childrens Camp
PO Box 1942
Columbia, MO 65205
573-445-9146
FAX: 573-445-5196
e-mail: camphickoryhill@yahoo.com
www.camphickoryhill.com

Pamela Marquis, Camp Director

Educates diabetic children concerning diabetes and its care. In addition to daily educational sessions on some aspects of diabetes, campers participate in swimming, sailing, arts and crafts and overnight camping. Coed, ages 8-17.

### 1562 Camp Lakewood

YMCA of the Ozarks
13528 State Highway AA
Potosi, MO 63664
573-438-2154
FAX: 573-438-5752
e-mail: camplakewood@ymcastlouis.org
www.ymcaoftheozarks.org/CampLakewood/

*Shawn Moriarty, Camp Director*
*Libby Staley, Program Director*
*Nicholas Beheler, Assistant Program Director*

The YMCA day camp for children ages 6-8. Children are under the direction and supervision of their counselors and engage in small group and camp-wide activities and work on developing their skills and self-confidence.

### 1563 Camp MITIOG

Share
10015 Northwest Ambassador Drive
Kansas City, MO 64153
816-221-6268
FAX: 816-221-1420

*Brenda O'Dell, Director*

Camp is located in Excelsior Springs, Missouri. One-week summer sessions for children with spina bifida. Coed, ages 6-16.

### 1564 Concerned Care Recreation Day Camp

Clayton County Developmental Disabilities Board
920 South Kent Street
Suite B
Liberty, MO 64068
816-474-3026
FAX: 816-474-3029
e-mail: ccareinc@crn.org
www.macdds.org/Counties/clay.html

*John Whalen, Director*
*Jim Humpman, Assistant Director*
*Karl Morris, Executive Director*

Summer sessions for campers with developmental disabilities. Coed, ages 7-16.

### 1565 Council for Extended Care of Mentally Retarded Citizens

5257 Shaw Avenue
Suite 305
Saint Louis, MO 63110
314-781-4950
FAX: 314-771-8880
e-mail: cecmrc@aol.com
cecstl.org

*Cynthia Compton, Executive Director*
*Marge Lindhorst, Supported Living Director*

Services are provided to adults and children with developmental disabilities. Supported living arrangements are located in St. Louis city, St. Louis county and St. Charles County. Group home and camp services are located in Dittmer, MO. Travel program also available.

### 1566 EDI Camp

Wyman Center
600 Kiwanis Drive
Eureka, MO 63025
636-938-5245
FAX: 636-938-5289
e-mail: info@wymancenter.org
www.wymancenter.org

*David Hilliard, President*
*Kristine Ramsey, Chief Development Officer*
*Carl Hill, Chief Operating Officer*

Youngsters with diabetes learn how to care for themselves while participating in a wide variety of outdoor activities and trips. The camp, managed and financed by the American Diabetes Association Greater St. Louis Affiliate, offers camperships to children from the Greater St. Louis area, ages 7-16, but nonresidents may also apply.

### 1567 Kiwanis Camp Wyman

Wyman Center
600 Kiwanis Drive
Eureka, MO 63025
636-938-5245
FAX: 636-938-5289
e-mail: info@wymancenter.org
www.wymancenter.org

*David A Hilliard, President*
*Claire Wyneken, Chief Programs Officer*
*Kristine Ramsey, Chief Development Officer*

Summer sessions for youth with diabetes. Coed, ages 8-16, run in conjunction with the American Diabetes Association. Call for program description.

### 1568 Lions Den Outdoor Learning Center

3602 Lions Den Road
Imperial, MO 63052
636-296-4480
FAX: 636-296-4476
e-mail: info@wymancenter.org
www.wymancenter.org

*Mia Olmer, Director*

Varied programs for mentally retarded children, ages 6 and up, includes daily living, socialization and language skills. Sports, tent camping, crafts, and nature study are also offered. Sliding scale tuition for 2 weeks.

### 1569 Sidney R Baer Day Camp

2 Millstone Drive
Saint Louis, MO 63146
314-442-3423
FAX: 314-432-5825
TTY:314-442-3225
e-mail: jboime@jccstl.org
www.jccstl.org

*Ken Weintraub, President*
*Joey Boime, Camp Director*

Co-ed day camp serving campers ages 5-12 years old.

### 1570 Sunnyhill Adventure Center

Council for Extended Care
6555 Sunlit Way
Dittmer, MO 63023
636-274-9044
FAX: 636-285-1305
e-mail: cecmrc@aol.com
www.sunnyhilladventures.org

*Rob Darroch, Executive Director*
*Kim Smallacombe, Program Director*

Camp is located in Dittmer, Missouri. Summer sessions for campers with developmental disabilities and autism. Coed, ages 8-99. Sunnyhill Adventures is program that offers campers fun, exciting, educational experiences in a beautiful outdoor setting. Our residential summer camp combines traditional camping activities plus specially selected and adapted events to meet the needs of each camper group.

### 1571 Wonderland Camp Foundation

18591 Miller Circle
Rocky Mount, MO 65072
573-392-1000
FAX: 573-392-3605
e-mail: wondcamp@advertisnet.com
www.wonderlandcamp.org

*Allen Moore, Chief Executive Officer*
*Marcela Trujillo, Program Director*

One-week sessions May-January for mentally/physically challenged campers and respite care. Coed, ages 6-80, families, seniors, single adults.

**1572  YMCA Camp Lakewood**
Ymca Of The Ozarks
13528 State Highway A
Potosi, MO  63664

573-438-2154
888-386-9622
888-386-9622
FAX: 573-438-3913
e-mail: ozarkhr@ymcastlouis.org
www.ymcastlouis.org

*Shawn Moriarty, Director*
*Jeff Clay, Director*

Summer sessions for campers with asthma/respiratory ailments.
Coed, ages 6-18.

# Nebraska

**1573  Camp Comeca**
Overlook Lodge
75670 Road 417
Cozad, NE  69130

308-784-2808
FAX: 308-784-4208
e-mail: comeca@cozadtel.net
www.campcomeca.com

*Mary Garner, Director*
*Chic Garner, Directors*
*Charles Garner, Manager*

Camp is located in Cozad, Nebraska. Summer sessions for campers with diabetes and hearing impairment. Coed, ages 6-19, families, seniors, single adults.

**1574  Camp Easter Seals**
Easter Seals Nebraska
638 North 109th Plaza
Omaha, NE  68154

402-345-2200
800-650-9880
FAX: 402-345-2500
e-mail: mtufte@ne.easterseals.com
www.ne.easterseals.com

*Karen Ginder, President/CEO*
*Val Mcpherson, Development Director*
*Mike Tufte, Camp Respite/Recreation Director*

Offers a variety of services to help people with disabilities address life's challenges and achieve personal goals.

**1575  Camp Floyd Rogers**
Floyd Rogers Foundation
PO Box 31536
Omaha, NE  68131

402-341-0866
FAX: 402-341-0866
www.campfloydrogers.com

*Kelly Krambeck, Camp Director*

A camp for diabetic children. Coed, ages 8-18. 100 children come to Camp Floyd Rogers each summer. They come to enjoy activities, participate in special events, engage in innovative evening programs, and they meet other children their own age with diabetes. Camp Floyd Rogers offers young people an opportunity to share some of life's adventures with others who also happen to have diabetes.

**1576  Christian Record Services/National Camps for Blind Children**
4444 South 52nd Street
Lincoln, NE  68516

402-488-0981
FAX: 402-488-7582
e-mail: info@christianrecord.org
www.christianrecord.org

*Lawrence Pitcher, President*
*Ronald Welch, District Director*
*Dorothy Marston, District Director*

Provides free Christian publications and programs, as well as new opportunities for people with visual impairments. Free services include subscription magazines available in braille, large print and audio cassette, full-vision books combining braille and print, lending library, gift bibles and study guides in braille, large print and audio cassette, national camps for blind children and scholarship assistance for blind young people trying to obtain a college education.

**1577  Eastern Nebraska 4-H Camps and Centers**
University of Nebraska
21520 West Highway 31
Gretna, NE  68028

402-332-4496
FAX: 402-332-2580
e-mail: 4hcampea@unl.edu
4h.unl.edu

*Buzz Wheeler, Eastern NE 4H Center Director*
*Brad Mellema, State 4H Camp Director*
*Barb Votaw, South Central 4H Center Director*

Beautiful modern facilities overlooking Platte River for the disabled campers.

**1578  Kamp Kaleo**
46872 Willow Springs Road
Burwell, NE  68823

402-477-4131
FAX: 402-476-8100
e-mail: kamp@micrord.com
www.kampkaleo.com/html/kampkaleo.html

*Judie L Luther, Program Manager*
*Roddy Dunkerson, Religious Leader*

Camp is located in Burwell, Nebraska. Summer sessions for campers who are blind/visually impaired or have developmental disabilities. Coed, ages 9-18 and families, seniors, single adults.

**1579  National Camps for Blind Children**
Christian Record
4444 S 52nd Street
Lincoln, NE  68516

402-488-0981
FAX: 402-488-7582
e-mail: info@christianrecord.org
www.christianrecord.org

*Arturo Grayman, National Director*
*Lawrence Pitcher, President*

Over 50 camps throughout the US and Canada are offered at no cost to legally blind children, ages 9-19. Activities include archery, beeper basketball, water sports, hiking and rock climbing and horseback riding.

**1580  YMCA Camp Kitaki**
Lincoln YMCA
216 North 11th Street
Suite 400
Lincoln, NE  68508

402-434-9205
FAX: 402-434-9208
www.ymcalincoln.org

*Ron Navratil, Chief Voltuneer Officer*
*Chris Klingenberg, Branch Excutive Director*
*Barbara A Bettin, President/CEO*

Camp is located in Louisville, Nebraska. Summer sessions for children with cystic fibrosis. Coed, ages 7-17 and families.

## New Hampshire

**1581  Camp Allen**
56 Camp Allen Road
Bedford, NH  03110

603-622-8471
FAX: 603-626-4295
e-mail: mary@campallennh.org
www.campallennh.org/

*Mary Constance, Executive Director*
*Debra Schulte, Office Manager*

A residential summer camp for individuals with disabilities. All of the activities are conducted by individual coordinators under the supervision of Program Director. Some of the activities include, aquatics, arts, crafts, games and nature programs. All camp events, special events, evening programs, and field trips are scheduled throughout the summer and are structured to meet the individual abilities and needs of each camper.

**1582  Camp Dartmouth-Hitchcock**
Dartmouth-Hitchcock Medical Center Pediatrics
1 Medical Center Drive
Lebanon, NH  03756

603-650-1070
FAX: 603-653-6050
e-mail: pediatric.residency.program@hitchcock.org
www.hitchcock.org

*John F Modlin, Chairman*
*Jody Stygles, Manager*

To provide high quality health care and comfort to the ill, to prevent illness among the well, and to advance health care through education, research, community service and the improvement of clinical practice.

**1583  Camp Fatima**
32 Fatima Road
PO Box 206
Gilmanton Iron Works, NH  03837

603-569-5851
FAX: 603-569-5038
e-mail: info@ diocamps.org
www.diocamps.org

*Gus Planchett, Executive Director*
*Michael Drumm, Marketing Director*
*Joanne Towle, Business Manager/Registrar*

Summer sessions for children with developmental disabilities, mobility limitation and speech/communication impairment.

**1584  Camp Kaleidoscope**
City of Lebanon New Hampshire
51 North Park Street
Lebanon, NH  03766

603-448-5121
FAX: 603-448-1496
e-mail: recreation@lebcity.com
www.lebcity.com

*Cindy Heath, Executive Director*
*Kevin Talcott, Assistant Director*
*Paul Coats, Program Coordinator*

Summer sessions for campers with ADD. Coed, ages 5-12.

**1585  Easter Seal Camp: New Hampshire**
555 Auburn Street
Manchester, NH  03103

603-623-8863
800-870-8728
FAX: 603-625-1148
e-mail: dgordon@eastersealsnh.org
nh.easterseals.com

*Robert Kelly, Camp Director*
*Larry Gammon, President*

Mission is to create solutions that change the lives of children and adults with disabilities or special needs or their families. From campfire sing-a-longs and late night ghost stories, to boating, nature walks, swimming, and arts and crafts, Easter Seals camps provide the same excitement and activity available at other summer camp programs. Easter Seals campers experience the joys and challenges of camp in a fully-accessible setting.

**1586  Easter Seals NH Camp Sno-Mo**
Easter Seals NH Camping Programs
200 Zachary Road
Building 2
Manchester, NH  03103

603-623-8863

e-mail: dgordon@eastersealsnh.org
www.eastersealsnh.org/services/camping

*Robert Kelly, Camp Director*
*Van Davis, President*
*Douglas Gordon, Director Recreation*

Easteer Seals Camp Sno-Mo is an intergrated camp, bringing together disabled invidual ages (1-24) with able bodied boy scouts. Our emphasis is on positive social interaction while finding an individual level of sucess in all passes of the camping process.

## New Jersey

**1587  Aldersgate Center**
PO Box 122
Swartswood, NJ  07877

973-383-5978
FAX: 973-383-4428
e-mail: aldersgate@tellurian.net
www.aldersgatenj.com

*Declan Thompson, Director*
*Richard Thompson, Grounds/Facilities Manager*
*Dale Card, Finance*

Camp is located in Newton, New Jersey. Summer sessions for campers with developmental disabilities. Coed, ages 6-18 and families, single adults.

**1588  Camp Carefree**
The American Diabetes Association
1846 West Seventh Street
Piscataway, NJ  08850

732-752-5847
603-859-0410
e-mail: carefreecamp@aol
www.campcarefreekids.org

*Phyllis Woestemeyer, Camp Director*

Camp is located in Wolfeboro, New Hampshire. Sessions for campers with diabetes.

**1589  Camp Chatterbox**
150 New Providence Road
Mountainside, NJ  07092

908-301-5451

e-mail: campchatterbox@earthlink.net
www.campchatterbox.org

*Joan Bruno, Director*

Is an intensive therapy camp for children ages 5-16, who use augmentative and alternative communications (AAC) devices and a training program for their parents. A unique feature of Camp Chatterbox is that a parent attends the program with his or her child. This not only widens the scope of training opportunities for the parents, but it helps siblings become an integral part of the training program. Parents, siblings and campers stay together in the cabins with campers of similar ages.

**1590   Camp Jotoni**
ARC of Somerset County
141 South Main Street
Manville, NJ 08835                    908-725-8544
                              FAX: 908-753-7868
                    e-mail: bonnies@thearcofsomerset.org
                         www.thearcofsomerset.org

*Judy Miao, Executive Director*
*Bonnie C Sovinee, Development Director*
*Chris Gunning, Residential Director*

Sponsored by the Arc of Somerset County, Camp Jotoni is a day and residential camp for children and adults with developmental disabilities. Campers are ages five to adult. Set on 15 acres in Somerset County, the camp features a junior Olympic size pool, cabins, dining hall, playgrounds, open air pavilions, unspoiled woods, and wildlife. Coed, ages 5-99.

**1591   Camp Lou Henry Hoover**
Girl Scouts of Washington Rock Council
201 Grove Street East
Westfield, NJ 07090                    908-232-3236
                              FAX: 908-232-4508
                       e-mail: dhooker@gswrc.com.
                           www.camphoover.org

*Deb Hooker, Camp Director*
*Coleen Hay, Camp Registrar*
*John Shabatura, Camp Ranger*

Camp is located in Middleville, New Jersey. Sessions for girls who are blind/visually impaired, ages 7-18.

**1592   Camp Merry Heart**
Easter Seals New Jersey
21 O'Brien Road
Hackettstown, NJ 07840                 908-852-3896
                              FAX: 908-852-9263
                              TTY:732-257-4442
                    e-mail: ahumanick@njeasterseals.com
                          www.njeasterseals.com

*Brian J Fitzgerald, President*
*Alexander Humanick, Executive Director*
*Daniel Tabacheck, Camping Coordinator*

An organized program of swimming, arts and crafts, boating, nature study and travel offered to campers with a variety of disabilities. Coed, ages 5-80, families, seniors. Fall and spring travel programs for adults.

**1593   Camp Sun'N Fun**
The Arc of Gloucester
1555 Gateway Boulevard
Woodbury, NJ 08096                     856-848-8648
                              FAX: 856-848-7753
                    e-mail: webmaster@thearcgloucester.org
                         www.thearcgloucester.org

*Ana Rivera, Executive Director*

Camp is located in Williamstown, New Jersey. Summer sessions for campers with developmental disabilities. Coed, ages 8-88. Activities include swimming, arts & crafts, nature, sports, games, music, dance and drama.

**1594   Camp Vacamas**
Vacamas Program for Youth
256 Macopin Road
West Milford, NJ 07480                 973-838-1394
                                       877-428-8222
                              FAX: 973-838-7534
                         e-mail: info@vacamas.org
                            www.vacamas.com

*Michael Friedman, Executive Director*
*Sandi Friedman, Associate Executive Director*

Disadvantaged children with asthma or sickle cell anemia, ages 8-16, are offered special programs in canoeing, backpacking, camping, music and leadership training. Sliding scale tuition. Year round programs for youth at risk groups. Conference center facility open for group rentals.

**1595   Cerebral Palsy Center Summer Program**
Cerebral Palsy of New Jersey
354 South Broad Street
Trenton, NJ 08608                      888-322-1918
                              FAX: 609-392-3505
                              TTY:609-392-7044
                         e-mail: info@cpofnj.org
                            www.cpofnj.org/

*Patrick Colligan, Executive Director*
*Raymond Freeman, Manager of Housing*
*Kristina Callender, Residential Services NJ/North*

Cerebral Palsy of New Jersey offers a wide array of services and support to children and adults with disabilities and to their families. Whether they're offering assistance in school or the workplace or helping out at home, CP of New Jersey's staff is trained and knowledgeable. Together they form a network that allows people with disabilities to achieve their goals.

**1596   Cross Roads Outdoor Ministries**
29 Pleasant Grove Road
Port Murray, NJ 07865                  908-832-7264
                              FAX: 908-832-6593
                    e-mail: crossroadsom@yahoo.com
                         www.crossroadsretreat.com/

*Andrew Molnar, Director*
*Marie Skweir, Religious Leader*

Program for ages 6-15 offers Bible study, worship, swimming, crafts, hiking, canoeing and campfires. Special education program for those with developmental disabilities.

**1597   Easter Seals Camp Merry Heart**
Easter Seals
21 O Brien Road
Hackettstown, NJ 07840                 908-852-3896
                              FAX: 908-852-9263

*Alexander Humanick, Executive Director*

An organized program of swimming, arts and crafts, boating, nature study and travel offered to the physically disabled, developmentally disabled, cerebral palsied, brain damaged and head injured children, ages 5-18, adults 19-75+. Fall and spring travel programs for adults, Respite Weekends, call for rates.

**1598   Nejeda**
Camp Nejeda Foundation
PO Box 156
Stillwater, NJ 07875                   973-383-2611
                              FAX: 973-383-9891
                       e-mail: info@campnejeda.org
                           www.campnejeda.org

*James Daschbach, Director*
*Philip Rea, Executive Director*

For children with diabetes, ages 7-15. Provides an active and safe camping experience which enables the children to learn about and understand diabetes. Activities include boating, swimming, fishing, archery, as well as camping skills.

**1599   New Jersey Camp Jaycee**
The Arc of New Jersey
985 Livingston Avenue
North Brunswick, NJ 08902              732-246-2525
                              FAX: 732-214-1834
                       e-mail: info@campjaycee.org
                           www.campjaycee.org

*Thomas Baffuto, Executive Director*
*Victor M Mankoski, Coordinator of Camping Services*

Camp Jaycee is located on 185 acres of forests, fields and streams located in the lovely Pocono Mountains, a short distance from the New Jersey border. Sessions for children and adults with autism and developmental disabilities. Goals of Camp Jaycee are centered around developing social skills, improving self esteem, increasing confidence, learning in a fun environment, developing physical fitness, and establishing meaningful relationships with new friends. Coed, ages 7-85.

**1600    New Jersey YMHA/YWHA Camps Milford**
21 Plymouth Street
Fairfield, NJ 07004                     973-575-3333
                                        800-776-5657
                                   FAX: 973-575-4188
                          e-mail: info@njycamps.org
                                    www.njycamps.org

*Leonard M Robinson, Camp Director*

Camp is located in Milford, Pennsylvania. Summer sessions for children with ADD. Coed, ages 6-17 and families.

**1601    Oak Spring Program**
Girl Scouts of Delaware-Raritan
108 Church Lane
East Brunswick, NJ 08816                732-821-9090
                                        800-572-2656
                                   FAX: 732-821-4211
                            e-mail: info@gsofdr.org
                                      www.gsofdr.org

*Allen Vicky, Facilities Director*
*Ginger Haithcox, Oak Spring Daycamp Director*
*Mark Timari, Oak Spring Camp Ranger*

Camp is located in Somerset, New Jersey. Sessions for girls with mobility limitation, ages 6-16.

**1602    Round Lake Camp**
21 Plymouth Street
Fairfield, NJ 07004                     973-575-3333
                                        800-776-5657
                                   FAX: 973-575-4188
                           e-mail: rlc@njycamps.org
                                    www.njycamps.org

*Karen Rubin Brand, Director Alumni Association*
*Bruce Nussman, Scholarship Chairman*

For ages 7-18, this camp provides individualized academics in reading, language development and math for children with mild learning disabilities, Round Lake also offers therapeutic recreation and Jewish cultural values to its participants.

## New Mexico

**1603    ADA Camp for Kids**
American Diabetes Association
2625 Pennsylvania Street Northeast
Suite 225
Albuquerque, NM 87110                   505-266-5716
                                        888-342-2383
                                   FAX: 505-268-4533
                         e-mail: askada@diabetes.org
                                      www.diabetes.org

*Cyndy Ankiewicz, Executive Director*

One-week camping session for children with diabetes. Coed, ages 8-13. Camp will be held at Manzano Mountain Retreat, one hour from Albuquerque, New Mexico. Please call for exact dates.

**1604    Camp Enchantment**
American Cancer Society
10501 Montgomery Boulevard NE
Suite 300
Albuquerque, NM 87111                   505-262-2333
                                        800-227-2345
                                   FAX: 505-266-9513
                         e-mail: gesquive@cancer.org
                                        www.cancer.org

*Geraldine Esquivel, Director*

Camp Enchantment offers an exciting opportunity for children with cancer to have fun and celebrate life through friendships and discoveries in a safe and respectful atmosphere. Held in June of each year, this one-week camp session is designed especially for kids with cancer and provides opportunities to celebrate life, enhance one's emotional well-being, increase decision-making and coping skills, and to deal with the impact of cancer. Coed, ages 7-17.

**1605    Santa Fe Mountain Center**
PO Box 449
Tesuque, NM 87574                       505-983-6158
                                   FAX: 505-983-0460
                          e-mail: info@santafemc.org
                                       www.sf-mc.com

*Sky Gray, Executive Director*
*Marge Kelley, Associate Director*
*Jenn Jevertson, Adventure Program Manager*

Camp sessions offered to disabled campers from the ages of 1-20.

## New York

**1606    American Diabetes Association Summer Camp**
American Diabetes Association
595 Blossom Road
Suite 208
Rochester, NY 14610                     585-458-3040
                                        888-342-3472
                                   FAX: 585-458-3138
                         e-mail: bkoch@diabetes.org
                                  www.diabetescamps.org

*Brandi Koch, Program Coordinator*
*Travis Heider, Manager*

Camp is located in Rush, New York. Sessions for children with diabetes. Coed, ages 8-16.

**1607    Camp Aldersgate**
Med Camps Coordinator
PO Box 367
Brantingham, NY 13312                   315-348-8833
                                   FAX: 315-348-4279
                        e-mail: info@aldersgateny.org
                                   www.aldersgateny.org

*Sarah M Spencer, Director*
*Nick Bufano, Executive Director*

A private nonprofit social service agency allied with the United Methodist Church which co-sponsors a series of summer medical camps with Med Camps of Arkansas, Inc., and thirteen various health agencies. The camps allow children and youth, ages 6-16, who have various medical conditions and physical disabilities to enjoy traditional camping experiences adapted to their abilities. The Camp also offers respite care, senior citizens programs, West Side Clinic and the Children's Center. Coed.

**1608 Camp Glengarra**
Girl Scouts - Foothills Council
33 Jewett Place
Utica, NY 13501
315-733-2391
FAX: 315-733-1909
e-mail: nbrown@girlscoutsfoothills.org
www.girlscoutsfoothills.org

*Natalie Brown, Executive Director*
*Karen Lubecki, Camp Director*
*Kristi Brennan, Development/Communications Mgr*

Camp Glengarra is located on 500+ acres of fields and forests, about eight miles west of Camden. This Girl Scout Camp hosts a myriad of programs throughout the year as well as summer day and resident camp. Summer sessions for girls 5-17 with ADD or asthma/respiratory ailments.

**1609 Camp Huntington**
56 Bruceville Road
High Falls, NY 12440
845-687-7840
FAX: 845-687-7211
e-mail: camphtgtn@aol.com
www.camphuntington.com

*Bruria Bodek Falik, Executive Director*
*Daniel Falk, Director*
*Harvey Goodman, Operation/Program Supervisor*

A co-ed residential camp for the learning disabled, ADD, neurologically impaired and mild-moderate mental retardation.

**1610 Camp Jened**
United Cerebral Palsy Association New York
Adams Road
PO Box 483
Rock Hill, NY 12775
845-434-2220
FAX: 845-434-2253
e-mail: jened@catskill.net
www.campjened.org

*Michael Branam, Executive Director*

Camp is located in Rock Hill, New York. Sessions for adults with severe developmental and physical disabilities. Coed, ages 18-99.

**1611 Camp Mark Seven**
Mark Seven Deaf Foundation
144 Mohawk Hotel Road
Old Forge, NY 13420
315-357-6089
FAX: 315-357-6403
e-mail: execdir@campmark7.org
www.campmark7.org

*Dave Staehle, Executive Director*
*Jane Fluman, Program Director*
*Ursula Smith, Deaf Youth Program Director*

Adirondack Mountain camp for hard-of-hearing, deaf and hearing people. Coed, ages 1-99, families, seniors and single adults.

**1612 Camp Northwood**
132 State Route 365
Remsen, NY 13438
315-831-3621
FAX: 315-831-5867
e-mail: campinfo@nwood.com
www.nwood.com

*Gordon W Felt, President*
*Donna Felt, International Counselor*

Summer sessions for children with ADD. Coed, ages 8-18.

**1613 Camp Oakhurst**
New York Service for the Handicapped
853 Broadway
Suite 605
New York, NY 10003
212-533-4020
FAX: 212-533-4023
e-mail: oakhurst06@aol.com
www.campchannel.com/campoakhurst/

*Marvin A Raps, Executive Director*

Camp is located in Oakhurst, New Jersey. Summer sessions for campers with cerebral palsy, mobility limitation and spina bifida. Coed, age 8-18.

**1614 Camp Ramapo**
Route 52 Salisbury Turnpike
PO Box 266
Rhinebeck, NY 12572
845-876-8403
FAX: 845-876-8414
e-mail: office@ramapoforchildren.org
www.ramapoforchildren.org

*Bernie Kosberg, Executive Director*
*Mike Kunin, Associate Director*

Residential program which serves children, ages 4-16, with a wide range of emotional, behavioral and learning problems. A one-to-one ratio of counselors-to-campers enables children to build healthy relationships, increase self-esteem and improve learning skills. Character values such as honesty, concern for others, responsibility and the courage to do one's best are encouraged. Campers demonstrate significant gains in their ability to maintain relationships, control impulses and adjust.

**1615 Camp Sisol**
Jewish Community Center of Greater Rochester/JCC
1200 Edgewood Avenue
Rochester, NY 14618
585-461-2000
FAX: 585-461-0805
TTY:585-461-2000
e-mail: rrosner@jccrochester.org
www.jccrochester.org

*Jane Glazer, President*
*Leslie Berkowitz, Director*

Camp is located in Honeoye Falls, New York. Summer sessions for children with autism. Coed, ages 5-16.

**1616 Camp Venture**
100 Convent Road
PO Box 402
Nanuet, NY 10954
845-624-3862
FAX: 845-624-7064
e-mail: jenkahn@campventure.org
www.campventure.org

*Daniel Lukens, Executive Director*

In more than a dozen Rockland neighborhoods, residential, employment, rehabilitation or recreation programs have arisen to help people with disabilities contribute to the life of the community. There are, for instance, more than a dozen Community Residential Facilities, Venture Industries, Venture Day Treatment, Day Habilitation, Venture Chorus, after school programs and more.

**1617 Camp Whitman on Seneca Lake**
150 Whitman Road
PO Box 278
Dresden, NY 14441
315-536-7753
FAX: 315-536-2128
e-mail: camp@campwhitman.org
www.campwhitman.org

*Thomas D Montgomery, Executive Director*
*Sam Edwards, Camp Operator*
*Chris Ruthven, Property Manager*

Summer sessions for young people and adults with developmental disabilities. Coed, ages 10-adult.

**1618 Casowasco Camp, Conference and Retreat Center**
158 Casowasco Drive
Moravia, NY 13118
315-364-8756
FAX: 315-364-7636
e-mail: info@casowasco.org
www.casowasco.org

*Michael D Huber, Executive Director*
*Roger Marshall, Property Manager*
*Robbin Hunsberger, Food Service Manager*

Camp is located in Moravia, New York. Summer sessions for children with ADD. Coed, ages 6-18 and families.

## 1619 Client Assistance Program

401 State Street
Schenectady, NY 12305      518-388-2892
800-624-4143
FAX: 518-388-2860
e-mail: webmaster@cqcapd.state.ny.us
www.cqcapd.state.ny.us

*Gary O'Brien, Chairman/Manager*
*Lisa Rosano-Naczkowski, Program Director*

## 1620 Clover Patch Camp

Center for the Disabled
55 Helping Hand Lane
Glenville, NY 12302      518-384-3081
FAX: 518-384-3001
e-mail: cloverpatchcamp@cftd.org
www.cloverpatchcamp.org

*Christopher Schelin, Program Administrator*
*Laura Taylor, Camp Director*

Camp is located in Scotia, NY. Summer sessions for campers with a variety of disabilities. Coed, ages 5-85.

## 1621 Deaf or Hard of Hearing Services New York State Education Department

Vocational-Educational Services for Individuals
with Disabilities
1 Commerce Plaza, Room 1601
Albany, NY 12234      518-474-5652
800-222-5627
FAX: 518-473-5769
TTY: 518-474-5652
e-mail: dsteele@mail.nysed.gov
www.vesid.nysed.gov

*Dorothy Steele, Program Coordinator*
*Rebecca Cort, Deputy Commisioner*
*Richard Mills, Commisioner*

A non-profit community that has a mission to empower clients to overcome barriers facing individuals experiencing deafness and hearing loss and to give them full access to opportunities that are readily available to persons who hear.

## 1622 Early Intervention Program

New York State Department of Health
Corning Tower Building
Empire State Plaza
Albany, NY 12237      518-473-7016
800-522-5006
FAX: 518-486-1090
e-mail: blm01@health.state.ny.us
www.health.state.ny.us/nysdoh/eip

*Barbara Nctague, Director*

Mission is to identify and evaluate as early as possible those infants and toddlers who healthy development is compromised and provide for appropriate intervention to improve child and family development.

## 1623 Father Drumgoole Connelly Summer Camp

Catholic Youth Organization
6581 Hylan Boulevard
Staten Island, NY 10309      718-317-2600
FAX: 718-317-2830
www.mountloretto.org

*Frank Minotti, Camp Director*

Summer sessions for children with epilepsy, hearing impairment and developmental disabilities. Coed, ages 5-13.

## 1624 Freedom Camp

199 Franklin Street
Suite 204
Auburn, NY 13021      315-253-1038
FAX: 315-253-1135
e-mail: aa@aaa.com
www.cayuganet.org

*Edward Herrling, Director*

A summer day camp for youths with disabilities sponsored by Freedom Recreational Services. Freedom Camp is offered in two-week sessions at Casey Park in Auburn, New York.

## 1625 Friends Academy Summer Camps

Duck Pond Road
Locust Valley, NY 11560      516-676-0393
FAX: 516-465-1720
e-mail: info@fa.org
www.fa.org

*Patty Ziplow, Director of Admissions*
*Richard Mack, Executive Director*
*Carl Pozzi, Development Director*

Summer sessions for children with diabetes. Coed, ages 3-14, families.

## 1626 Gow School Summer Programs

2491 Emery Road
PO Box 85
South Wales, NY 14139      716-652-3450
FAX: 716-652-3457
e-mail: summer@gow.org
www.gow.org

*David Mendlewski, Director of Summer Program*
*Bradley Rogers, Principal/Headmaster*
*Gayle Hutton, Development Director*

Co-ed summer programs for students ages 8-16 with dyslexia or similar learning disabilities offer a balanced blend of morning academics, afternoon/evening traditional camp activities and weekend overnights. The primary purpose of these programs is to provide a positive experience while balancing these three elements. Committed to the creation of a positive and enjoyable experience for each participant by defining and merging the goals of the camp and the school, with those of camper students.

## 1627 Happiness is Camping

2169 Grand Concourse
Bronx, NY 10453      718-295-3100
FAX: 718-295-0406
e-mail: hicoffice@happinessiscamping.org
www.happinessiscamping.org

*Murray Struver, Founder/CEO*
*Kurt Struver, Director*
*John Thaxton, Member of the Board*

Camp is located in Blairstown, New Jersey. Camping sessions for children with cancer. Coed, ages 7-15.

## 1628 Henry Kaufmann Campgrounds Staten Island

667 Blauvelt Road
Pearl River, NY 10965      845-735-2718
FAX: 845-735-3544

*Jeffrey Alan Coopersmith, Director*
*Morris W Offit, President*
*Susan K Stern, Chair*

Disabled campers.

**1629 Huntington**
58 Bruceville Road
High Falls, NY 12440 845-687-7840
FAX: 845-687-7211
e-mail: camphtgtn@aol.com
www.camphuntington.com

*Bruria Bodek Falik, Executive Director*
*Daniel Falk, Director*

Camp is located in High Falls, New York. Summer sessions for children and young adults with a variety of disabilities. Coed, ages 6-21.

**1630 Kamp Kiwanis**
New York District Kiwanis
9020 Kiwanis Road
Taberg, NY 13471 315-336-4568
FAX: 315-336-3845
e-mail: kampkiwanis@mybizz.net
www.kiwanis-ny.org/kamp

*Orlando Marrazzo Jr, President*
*Rebecca Lopez, Executive Director/CEO*
*Donald Herring, Foundation Secretary*

Kamp Kiwanis is a mainstream camp for underprivileged youth with and without special needs. 20 campers with disabilities are integrated into weekly sessions. Coed, ages 8-14, seniors and single adults.

**1631 Maplebrook School**
5142 Route 22
Amenia, NY 12501 845-373-9511
FAX: 845-373-8368
e-mail: mbsecho@aol.com
www.maplebrookschool.org

*Donna Konkolics, Headmaster*
*Jerome I Rossman Jr, President*
*Mark J Metzger, Vice President*

A coeductional boarding school which offers a six week camp for children with learning differences and ADD.

**1632 Marist Brothers Mid-Hudson Valley Camp**
PO Box 197
Esopus, NY 12429 845-384-6620
FAX: 845-384-6479
www.esopuscamps.com

*Bro Don Nugent, Administrator*
*Bro Damian Novello, Director*
*Michelle Fleming, Director Special Children*

Serves special people: children who have cancer or who are HIV positive, deaf or mentally retarded.

**1633 Ninety-Second Street Y Camps Nesher Program**
1395 Lexington Avenue
New York, NY 10128 212-415-5626
FAX: 212-415-5637
e-mail: mmandel@92y.org
www.92y.org

*Melanie S Mandel, Director Of Program*
*Sol Adler, Executive Director*

After-school recreation programs for children ages 4-20 with developmental disabilities.

**1634 Presbyterian Center at Holmes**
60 Denton Lake Road
Holmes, NY 12531 845-878-6383
FAX: 845-878-7824
e-mail: holmespca@aol.com
www.presbyteriancenter.org

*Peter D Surgenor, Executive Director*
*Robin Garzoni, Program Director*
*Diane Ball, Office Manager*

Provides programmed events, as well as rental facilities for self-directed conferences and individual retreats.

**1635 Programs for Children 3 to 5 with Disabili lities**
New York State Education Department
1 Commerce Plaza
Suite 1624
Albany, NY 12234 518-473-2878
FAX: 518-486-7693
e-mail: schyer@mail.nysed.gov
www.vesid.nysed.gov/specialized

*Micheal Plotvker, Manager*
*Richard Mills, Commissioner of Education*
*James DeLorenzo, State Coordinator Special Ed*

The Mission of the Office of Vocational and Educational Services for Individuals with Disabilities (VESID) is to promote educational equity and excellence for students with disabilities and provide the highest quality vocational rehabilitation and independent living services to all eligible persons as quickly as those services are required to enable them to work and live independent, self-directed lives.

**1636 Programs for Children Birth to 2 with Disa abilities**
New York State Department of Health
Empire State Plaza
Corning Tower Bldg, Room 287
Albany, NY 12237 518-473-7016
FAX: 518-486-1090
e-mail: blm01@health.state.ny.us
www.nichcy.org/stateshe/ny.htm

*Barbara McTeague, Acting Director*

The Early Intervention Program offers a variety of therapeutic and support services to eligible infants and toddlers with disabilities and their families.

**1637 Programs for Children with Special Health Care Needs**
New York State Department of Health
ESP Corning Tower Building
Room 208
Albany, NY 12237 518-474-2001
FAX: 518-474-5445
e-mail: sjs11@health.state.ny.us
www.health.state.ny.us/nysdoh/child/

*Susan Slade, Director*
*Patricia Hess, Manager*

The Children with Special Health Care Needs Program (CSHCN) is a statewide public health program that provides information and referral services for health and related areas for families of CSHCN. This program is a referral linkage system to provide for those children ages birth to 21 who have, or are suspected of having, a serious or chronic physical, developmental, behavioral, or emotional condition who require a health or related service of a type or amount beyond what is generally required.

**1638 Radalbek**
RR1
Box 28K
Hancock, NY 13783 607-467-2159
FAX: 607-467-2159

*Grace Kinzer, Director*

A year-round residential program, for ages 14-18, to educate and train the mentally retarded, emotionally disturbed and learning disabled in self-help skills. The program curriculum is educational, vocational and recreational, with special workshops and programs for all ages.

**1639 Rochester Rotary Sunshine Camp**
Rochester Rotary Club
100 Meridian Centre
Suite 304
Rochester, NY 14618
585-546-7435
FAX: 585-546-8675
e-mail: sknipper@rochester.com
www.rochester.com

*Tracey Dreisbach, Executive Director*
*Stacy Morabito, Accounting Manager*
*Linda Garland, Executive Assistant*

Camp is located in Rush, New York. Camping sessions for children and young adults with a variety of disabilities. Ages 7-21.

**1640 Rolling Hills Country Day Camp**
14 Dittmar Road
PO Box 6623
Freehold, NJ 07728
732-308-0405
FAX: 732-780-4726
e-mail: info@rollinghillsdaycamp.com
www.rollinghillsdaycamp.com

*Billy Breitner, Director/Owner*
*Stan Breitner, Director/Owner*
*Dustin Breitner, Director/Owner*

Summer sessions for children with ADD. Coed, ages 3-12.

**1641 Summit Camp**
18 East 41st Street
Suite 402
New York, NY 10017
212-689-3880
800-323-9908
FAX: 212-689-3880
e-mail: summitcamp@aol.com
www.summitcamp.com

*Mayer and Ninette Stiskin, Executive Directors/Co-Founders*
*Regina Skyer, Clinical Social Worker*
*Tim Kedge, Head Counselor/Program Director*

Camp is located in Honesdale, Pennsylvania. Summer sessions for children with ADD. Coed, ages 8-17.

**1642 VISIONS Vacation Camp for the Blind**
VISIONS/Services for the Blind & Visually Impaired
500 Greenwich Street
3rd Floor
New York, NY 10013
212-625-1616
888-245-8333
e-mail: nnowak@visionsvcb.org
www.visionsvcb.org/camp.asp

*Nancy T Jones, President*
*David Koch, Vice President*
*Burton M Strauss Jr, Treasurer*

Is a non profit agency that promotes the independence of people of all ages who are blind or visually imparied.

**1643 Wagon Road Camp**
Children's Aid Society Summer Camps
105 East 22nd Street
New York, NY 10010
212-949-4800
914-238-4761
FAX: 212-477-3705
e-mail: ellenl@childrensaidsociety.org
www.childrensaidsociety.org

*Yahaira Jimenez, Camp Director*
*Ellen Lubel, Public Relations Director*
*C Warren Moses, Chief Executive Officer*

Wagon Road Day Camp is a co-ed program for children ages 6-13 with a variety of disabilities held within Chappaqua, New York. Uniquely qualified specialists in Project Adventure activities, athletics, horsemanship, theater arts, nature/ecology studies and arts/crafts complement the day camp staff. Special events including Carnival, Olympics, Crazy Hat Day, Western Day, and optional sleepovers add to the summer excitement providing children with an enriching multicultural experience.

**1644 YMCA Camp Chingachgook on Lake George**
Capital District YMCA
1872 Pilot Knob Road
Kattskill Bay, NY 12844
518-656-9462
FAX: 518-656-9362
e-mail: chingachgook@cdymca.org
www.chingachgook.org

*George Painter, Executive Director*
*John F Flynn, President/CEO*
*David Brown, VP Operations*

Sailing programs for people with disabilities. Sessions for campers who are blind/visually impaired. Coed, ages 7-16, families, seniors and single adults.

**1645 YMCA Camp Weona**
YMCA of Greater Buffalo
280 Cayuga Road
Buffalo, NY 14225
716-565-6008
FAX: 716-565-6007
e-mail: dschaefer@buffaloymca.org
www.wnybiz.com.campweona/

*Jennifer Schubert, Executive Director*
*Shauna Parkinson, Program Director*

Camp is located in Gainesville, New York. Camping sessions for children and adults with epilepsy. Coed, ages 7-16, families and single adults. Nestled in 1,000 acres of hardwood and pine forests, Weona has miles of picturesque hiking trails, brooks, a heated outdoor pool and a world class adventure ropes course. Our indoor facilities include arts and crafts studios, environmental classrooms and a challenging rock climbing wall. It is the ideal setting for hands-on fun, adventure and learning.

# North Carolina

**1646 Camp Carolina Trails for Children**
American Diabetes Association
1701 N Beauregard Street
Alexandria, VA 22311
800-342-2383
888-342-2383
e-mail: AskADA@diabetes.org
www.diabetes.org/

*Emily Nivens, Director*
*Mona Tucker, Principal*
*Richard Kahn PhD, Chief Scientific/Medical Officer*

The American Diabetes Association Camp Carolina Trails is an exciting week of summer fun for boys and girls entering grades 4 through 11. Camp includes many sports and activities such as swimming, hiking, canoeing and arts and crafts. It is held at YMCA Camp Hanes on 400 acres next to hanging Rock State Park which is located at the base of Sauratown Mountain, just 30 minutes north of Winston-Salem, North Carolina. Camp for ages 10-17. Use address given in Virginia for more information.

**1647 Camp Royall**
Autism Society of North Carolina
505 Oberlin Road
Suite 230
Raleigh, NC 27605
919-743-0204
FAX: 919-542-1033
e-mail: info@autismsociety-nc.org
www.autismsociety-nc.org

*Ann Palmer, President*
*Jill Hinton-Keel, Executive Director*

Camping sessions for children and adults with autism. Coed, ages 4-99.

**1648 Camp Sky Ranch**
634 Sky Ranch Road
Blowing Rock, NC 28605
828-264-8600
FAX: 828-265-2339
e-mail: jsharp1@triad.rr.com
www.campskyranch.com

*Jack Sharp, Director*
*Betty Sharp, Director*

A private, residential camp for the developmentally delayed. This season is the camp's 56th year of providing a real camping experience for the handicapped. Camp Sky Ranch was the first private camp for the handicapped in the Southeast. Activities include: swimming, boating, horseback riding, and more. Campers must be able to walk, dress and feed themselves, and take care of their toilet needs.

**1649 Camp Tekoa UMC**
Western NC Conference/United Methodist Church
211 Thomas Road
PO Box 160
Hendersonville, NC 28793
828-692-6516
FAX: 828-697-3699
e-mail: director@camptekoa.org
www.camptekoa.org

*Karen Rohrer, Business Manager*
*James S Johnson, Director*
*Mike Pruett, Program Manager*

Camping for children with asthma/respiratory ailments, hearing impairment and developmental disabilities. Coed, ages 6-17.

**1650 Cullowhee Experience**
Western Carolina University
152 University Outreach Center
Cullowhee, NC 28723
828-227-7211
FAX: 828-227-7424
e-mail: mramsey@email.wcu.edu
www.wcu.edu

*Marty Ramsey, Director*
*John Bardo, President*

Mission is to provide students with the opportunity to learn, live, and have fun exercising their minds and bodies with kindred spirits in a safe and beautiful environment.

**1651 Mount Shepherd Retreat Center**
1045 Mount Shepherd Road Ext
Asheboro, NC 27205
336-629-4085
FAX: 336-629-4880
e-mail: mtsheph@asheboro.com
www.mtshepherd.org/directions.php

*Kent L Shrader, Executive Director*
*Vicky Matthew, Administrator*

Camping for children with developmental disabilities. Coed, ages 14 to Adults. Mount Shepherd Retreat Center offers a year-round camping program. Our summer program attracts children and youth from around the region and across the state. We also offer facilities for you or your group to get away from it all and enjoy a weekend retreat on the grounds.

**1652 SOAR Summer Adventures**
PO Box 388
Balsam, NC 28707
828-456-3435
FAX: 828-456-3449
e-mail: jonathan@soarnc.org
www.soarnc.org/html/

*Jonathan Jones, Executive Director*
*John Willson, LD and AD/HD Services Director*
*Ed Parker, Admissions Director*

A nonprofit adventure program working with disadvantaged youth diagnosed with learning disabilities in an outdoor, challenge based environment. Focuses on esteem building and social skills development through rock climbing, backpacking, whitewater rafting, mountaineering, sailing, snorkeling, and much more. Offers two week, one month, and semester programs available. SOAR programs utilize North Carolina, Florida, Colorado, American Southwest, Alaska, and Jamaica as program areas.

**1653 Stone Mountain School**
126 Camp Elliott Road
Black Mountain, NC 28711
828-669-8639
FAX: 828-669-2521
e-mail: info@stonemountainschool.com
www.stonemountainschool.com

*Sam Moore, Executive Director*
*Sue Miller, Public Relations*

Year round therapeutic wilderness school for emotionally disturbed boys grades 6-12. Certified mental health program, licensed by the department of facility services and certified special education school.

**1654 Talisman Summer Camp**
126 Camp Elliott Road
Black Mountain, NC 28711
828-669-8639
FAX: 828-669-2521
e-mail: summer@stonemountainschool.com
www.talismansummercamp.com

*Linda Tatsapaugh, Director*
*Charlie Talley, Executive Director*
*Emily Darby, Sight Program Manager*

Camp is located in Black Mountain, North Carolina. Offers a program of hiking, rafting, climbing, and caving for learning disabled ADD/ADHD and autistic young people. Coed, ages 9-18.

# North Dakota

**1655 American Diabetes Association**
1323 23rd Street S
Suite C
Fargo, ND 58103
701-234-0123
888-342-2383
FAX: 701-235-3080
e-mail: schristensen@diabetes.org
www.diabetes.org

*Sheila Christensen, Executive Director*

**1656 Camp Sioux**
American Diabetes Association
1323 23rd Street South
Suite C
Grand Forks, ND 58103
701-234-0123
800-676-4065
FAX: 701-235-3080
e-mail: AskADA@diabetes.org
www.diabetes.org/

*Becky Martin, Camp Director*

Camp Sioux, located in Park River, ND, is a week-long residential summer camp for children ages 8-14 who are living with diabetes. Programs encourage independence and self management with appropriate medical supervision to ensure the best possible experience for every camper. Nutrition activities, blood glucose monitoring, and injections/medications are integrated into the camp program.

# Ohio

## 1657 Akron Rotary Camp
4460 Rex Lake Drive
Akron, OH 44319 330-644-4512
FAX: 330-644-1013
e-mail: rotarycamp@akronymca.org
www.akronymca.com/camp/rotary/

Dan Reynolds, Executive Director
Alexander Kuzmetsov, Camp Counselor
Amanda Grobler, Office Administrator

The Rotary Camp for Children with Special Needs, in cooperation with the Akron Area YMCA, offers camping experiences for children and adults with disabilities. Rotary Camp is American Camping Association (ACA) accredited and provides a nurturing and enriching atmosphere where campers develop friendships, skills and memories that will last a lifetime. Coed, ages 6-17.

## 1658 Beech Brook
3737 Lander Road
Pepper Pike, OH 44124 216-831-2255
FAX: 216-831-0638
e-mail: debra_rex@beechbrook.org
www.beechbrook.org

Debra Rex, President
Renita Allen, Vice President
Mario Tonti, Executive Director

Residential and day treatment center. Treatment center for emotionally disturbed children, including residential and day treatment; foster care; adoption; adn community based programs.

## 1659 Breezewood Acres United Way of Central Ohio
Franklin County Council for Retarded Citizens
2344 East Fifth Avenue
Columbus, OH 43219 614-252-4900
FAX: 614-252-4901

Garnett L Steele, Executive Director

Camp is located Sunbury, Ohio. Camping sessions for children and adults with mobility limitation or speech/communication impairment. Ages 6-99.

## 1660 Camp Allyn
Stepping Stones Center
5650 Given Road
Cincinnati, OH 45243 513-831-4660
FAX: 513-831-5918
e-mail: ssc@steppingstonescenter.org
www.steppingstonescenter.org

Susan Radabaugh, Executive Director
Dennis Carter, Associate Director

A camp in Batavia, Ohio for children and adults with disabilities. Coed, ages 7-60. Campers participate in crafts, swimming, hiking, nature, sports and motor activities. Camp sessions range from 3 to 10 days, are theme oriented, and geared to individual abilities and interests.

## 1661 Camp Cheerful
Achievement Centers For Children
15000 Cheerful Lane
Strongsville, OH 44136 440-238-6200
FAX: 440-238-1858
e-mail: tim.fox@achievementctrs.org
www.achievementcenters.org

Patricia W Nobili, Executive Director
Tim Fox, Director Camp Services
Susan Hyman, Manager Rehabilitation Services

Sessions for campers with developmental disabilities, mobility limitation and speech/communication impairment. Coed, ages 7-99.

## 1662 Camp Courageous
12701 Waterville Swanton Road
Whitehouse, OH 43571 419-380-4002
866-740-8117
FAX: 419-381-8304
e-mail: cherylt@campcourageous.com
www.campcourageous.com

Cheryl Tresnan, Camp Director
Kalli Hintz, Assistant Camp Director
Jenny Nowak, Camp Coordinator

Camp Courageous provides residential camping services for people with developmental disabilities from ages 7-75 years old. Our six day, 5 night programs give campers a chance to experience activities such as: aquatics, arts and crafts, animal programs, sports skills, hiking, recreational and leisure education programs, nature studies, drama, cookouts and campfires.

## 1663 Camp Emanuel
P O Box 2146
Dayton, OH 45401 937-274-9908

e-mail: Info@CampEmanuel.org
www.campemanuel.org/

Nan Crawford, Executive Director
Douglas Lehrer, MD, President
James Brink, Vice President/Treasurer

Camp for hearing impaired and normal hearing youth.

## 1664 Camp Ho Mita Koda
Diabetes Association Of Greater Cleveland
3601 Green Road
Suite 100
Cleveland, OH 44122 216-591-0800
FAX: 216-591-0320
e-mail: camp@dagc.org
www.camphomitakoda.org

Liberty A Wright, Camp Administrator
Jackquie Dickinson, President

Camp is located in Newbury, Ohio. Summer sessions for children with type 1 diabetes. Coed, ages 6-15. Type 2 diabetes, coed, ages 12-17. Bicycle adventure, coed, ages 13-19. Mini-day camp, ages 4-7, coed.

## 1665 Camp Libbey
Maumee Valley GSC
2244 Collingwood Boulevard
Toledo, OH 43620 419-243-8216
800-860-4516
FAX: 419-245-5357
e-mail: lbowerman@mvgsc.org
www.gsmvc.org/contact.htm

Bowerman Laura, Executive Director
Jeff Baldwin, Camp Ranger
Christine Gustin, Camp Manager

Camp for girls 7-18 with asthma/respiratory ailments, diabetes, epilepsy and muscular dystrophy is located in Defiance, Ohio.

## 1666 Camp Nuhop
404 Hillcrest Drive
Ashland, OH 44805 419-289-2227
FAX: 419-289-2227
e-mail: campnuhop@zoominternet.net
www.campnuhop.org

Jerry Dunlap, Executive Director
Ann Bell, Co-Director Summer Program
Mark Sommer, Director Support Services

A summer residential program for any youngster from 6 to 18 with a learning disability, behavior disorder or Attention Deficit Disorder. 84 campers and 41 staff members live on site in groups of to seven campers to every three counselors. Activities focus on positive self-concept and behaviors and teaches children to learn how to find their strengths, abilities and talents from a positive, yet realistic viewpoint.

# Camps /Ohio

**1667 Camp Stepping Stone**
Stepping Stones Center
5650 Given Road
Cincinnati, OH 45243
513-831-4660
FAX: 513-831-5918
e-mail: ssc@steppingstonescenter.org
www.steppingstonescenter.org

*Susan Radabaugh, Executive Director*
*Clifford Dornette, President*
*Fred Fischer, Vice President*

Nonprofit United Way affiliated camp serving all disabilities and charging on a sliding scale.

**1668 Day Happiness Camp**
Catholic Charities Services
7911 Detroit Avenue
Cleveland, OH 44102
216-334-2945
FAX: 216-334-2905

*Molly Worthington, Program Director*
*Tom Mullen, President*

Camping for children and adults with various disabilities. Coed, ages 21-75.

**1669 Echoing Hills**
36272 CR 79
Warsaw, OH 43844
740-327-2311
800-419-6513
FAX: 740-327-6371
e-mail: info@campechoinghills.org
www.campechoinghillsvillages.org

*Christy Kuhns, Camp Program Director*
*Larry Stitt, Camp Administrator*
*Jimmy McNutt, Camp Activities Coordinator*

Summer camp for children and adults with cerebral palsy. Coed, ages 7-70.

**1670 Happiness Day at Parmadale**
Catholic Charities Services
7911 Detroit Avenue
Cleveland, OH 44102
216-334-2963
800-869-6525
FAX: 216-334-2905
TTY: 440-845-7700
e-mail: mjscott@clevelandcatholiccharities.org
www.clevelandcatholiccharities.org/camping/

*Marilyn Scott, Camp Program Administrator*
*Dennis McNulty, Disability Services Director*

Camp is located in Parma, Ohio. Summer sessions for children and young adults with developmental disabilities. Coed, ages 6-21.

**1671 Happiness Day at St. Augustine Academy**
Cleveland Catholic Charities
14808 Lake Avenue
Lakewood, OH 44107
216-221-4227
FAX: 216-221-7453
e-mail: gwanous@st-aug-academy.org
www.clevelandcatholiccharities.org/camping/

*Georgianne Wanous, Executive Director*
*Fr. Joseph McNulty, Disability Ministry Director*
*Sr. Corita Ambro, Program Director*

Serves mentally retarded campers with multiple handicaps.

**1672 Happiness Day at the Center for Pastoral Leadership**
Catholic Charities Services
7911 Detroit Avenue
Cleveland, OH 44102
216-334-2958
FAX: 216-334-2983
e-mail: lbtaylor@clevelandcatholiccharities.org
www.clevelandcatholiccharities.o rg/camping/

*Tana Minneti, Camp Director*
*Eilean Klear, Camping Programs Director*
*Lynette Taylor, Camp Registrar*

Camp is located in Wickliffe, Ohio. Summer sessions for children and young adults with developmental disabilities. Coed, ages 6-21.

**1673 Highbrook Lodge**
Cleveland Sight Center
1909 East 101st Street
PO Box 1988
Cleveland, OH 44106
216-791-8118
FAX: 216-791-1101
www.clevelandsightcenter.org/camp

*Michael Grady, President/Executive Director*
*John Saada Sr., Chair*
*Andrew Sikorovsky, Treasurer*

Camp is located in Chardon, Ohio. Summer sessions for blind and disabled children, adults and families. There are seven sessions held annually during June, July and August with an entire range of outdoor camp activities. Camp activities focus on learning through play. Weekly rate: $100-$260 per week.

**1674 Ko-Man-She**
American Diabetes Association
1 Elizabeth Place
Suite 180
Dayton, OH 45408
937-220-6611
FAX: 937-224-0240
e-mail: info@diabetesdayton.org
www.diabetesdayton.org

*Peggy White, Executive Director*
*Susan McGovern, Program Director*
*Sally Kattau, President*

Camp is located in Bellefontaine, Ohio. Summer sessions for children with diabetes. Coed, ages 8-17. Held in July.

**1675 Leo Yassenoff JCC Day Camps**
1125 College Avenue
Columbus, OH 43209
614-231-2731
FAX: 614-231-8222
e-mail: rfox@columbusjcc.org
www.columbusjcc.org

*Rachel Fox, Camping Services Director*
*Jeanna Brownlee, Sports Camps Director*

Summer camping sessions for children and young adults with developmental, physical, emotional, mental and learning disabilities. Coed, ages 3-25.

**1676 Recreation Unlimited**
7700 Piper Road
Ashley, OH 43003
740-548-7006
FAX: 740-747-2640
e-mail: info@recreationunlimited.org
www.recreationunlimited.org

*Laura Smith, Program Director*
*Paul Huttlin, Executive Director/CEO*

Camping sessions for children and adults with a variety of disabilities. Coed, ages 5-99, families, seniors and single adults.

**1677 YMCA Camp Fitch**
Youngstown YMCA
17 North Champion Street
Youngstown, OH 44503
330-744-8411
FAX: 330-744-8416
www.campfitch.com

*Mike Shaffer, Executive Director*
*Kathy Portman, Assistant Director*

Camp is located in North Springfield, Pennsylvania. Camping sessions for children and adults with diabetes, hearing impairment, developmental disabilities, mobility limitation and speech/communication impairment. Ages 8-16, families and seniors.

166

**1678  YMCA Outdoor Center Campbell Gard**
4803 Augspurger Road
Hamilton, OH  45055
513-867-0600
877-224-9622
FAX: 513-867-0127
e-mail: pruby@gmvymca.org
www.ccgymca.org

*Rick Taylor, Executive Director*
*Vicky Williams, Senior Program Director*
*Curt Wright, Program Director*

Camp is located in Hamilton, Ohio. Camping sessions for children with ADD, autism, developmental disabilities and blindness/visual impairment. Coed, ages 6-17 and families.

## Oklahoma

**1679  Camp Classen YMCA**
YMCA of Greater Oklahoma City
500 North Broadway Avenue
Suite 150
Oklahoma City, OK 73102
405-297-7740
FAX: 405-297-7745
e-mail: amcwhort@ymcaokc.org
www.campclassenymca.org

*Albert P McWhorter, Executive Director*

Camp is located in Davis, Oklahoma. Sessions for children and adults with diabetes. Coed, ages 8-17, families, seniors and single adults.

**1680  Easter Seals Oklahoma**
Easter Seals America
701 Northeast 13th Street
Oklahoma City, OK  73104
405-239-2525
FAX: 405-239-2278
e-mail: esok1@coxinet.net
www.easterealsoklahoma.org

*Patricia Filer, Executive Director*

Providing services such as adult day services, child development center, OTIPT, speech therapy, reading/tutoring, vision and hearing screening.

## Oregon

**1681  Camp Christmas Seal**
American Lung Association of Oregon
7420 Southwest Bridgeport Road
Suite 200
Tigard, OR 97224
503-924-4094
800-LUN- USA
FAX: 503-924-4120
e-mail: info@lungoregon.org
www.lungoregon.org

*Beverly Stewart, Camp Director*
*Scott Hill, Chairman*
*Jennifer Baldwin, Development/Communications*

Camp is located in Sisterhood, Oregon. Sessions for children with asthma/respiratory ailments. Coed, ages 8-15.

**1682  Camp Latgawa**
United Methodist Camp & Retreat Ministries
1505 Southwest 18th Avenue
Portland, OR  97201
503-226-7931
800-593-7539
FAX: 532-283-196
e-mail: latgawa@gocamping.orgf
www.gocamping.org/latgawa.html

*Lisa Jean Hoefner, Reverend, Executive Director*
*Eva LaBonty, Director*
*Greg Clensy, Director*

Camp Latgawa offers activities for all ages, some favorites include: natural waterfall slide, hiking and backpacking trails, archery, volleyball, ping pong, basketball, fishing, horseshoes, swimming in solar heated pool and a new meditation labyrinth. We pride ourselves on healthy and delicious food and bake fresh bread twice daily!

**1683  Camp Magruder**
Conference of United Methodists
1505 Southwest 18th Avenue
Portland, OR  97201
503-226-7931
800-593-7539
FAX: 503-226-4158
e-mail: magruder@gocamping.org
www.campmagruder.org/

*Roy Quist, Camp Director*
*Nicole Robbins, Program Director*
*Pat Ryan, Facilities Manager*

Camp is located in Rockaway Beach, Oregon. Sessions for children and adults with cancer and developmental disabilities. Coed, ages 9-18, families, seniors and single adults.

**1684  Camp Taloali**
D Sipp
15934 N Santiam Highway
Stayton, OR  97383
503-769-6415
TTY:503-769-6415
e-mail: info@taloali.org
www.taloali.org

*Sarah Hafer, Camp Director*

Summer sessions for children with hearing impairment. Coed, ages 9-17.

**1685  Easter Seals Oregon Camping Program**
5757 SW Macadam Avenue
Portland, OR  97239
503-228-5108
800-556-6020
FAX: 503-228-1352
e-mail: info@or.easterseals.com
or.easterseals.com

*David Cheveallier, CEO and President*

Camp is located in Corbett, Oregon. Summer sessions for children and adults with a variety of disabilities. Coed, ages 6-90.

**1686  Gales Creek Diabetes Camp**
Gales Creek Camp Foundation
6975 SW Sandburg Street
Suite 150
Portland, OR  97223
503-968-2267
FAX: 503-443-2313
e-mail: info@galescreekcamp.org
www.galescreekcamp.org

*Ted Gwin, Chairman*
*Bruce Boston, President*

Camp is located in Forest Grove, Oregon. Summer sessions for children with diabetes. Coed, ages 6-16, family and pre-school family camps also available.

**1687  Meadowood Springs Speech and Hearing Camp**
Institute for Rehabilitation Research
PO Box 1025
Pendleton, OR  97801
541-276-2752
FAX: 541-276-7227
e-mail: meadowoodcamp@uci.net
www.meadowoodsprings.com

*Irene Willard, Administrator*
*Marie Story, Assistant*

On 143 acres in the Blue Mountains of Eastern Oregon, this camp is designed to help young people who have diagnosed clinical disorders of speech, hearing or language. A full range of activities in recreational and clinical areas is available.

**1688 Mt Hood Kiwanis Camp**
Kiwanis Club of Montavilla
9320 SW Barbur Boulevard
Suite 165
Portland, OR  97219
503-452-7416
FAX: 503-452-0062
e-mail: information@mhkc.org
www.mhkc.org

*Gene Nudelman, Executive Director*
*Charlene Dickinson, Administrator*

Camp is located in Government Camp, Oregon. Summer sessions for children and adults with a variety of disabilities. Coed, ages 9-35.

**1689 Strength for the Journey**
OR/ID Conference of United Methodist Church
1505 S W 18th Avenue
Portland, OR  97201
503-226-7931
800-593-7539
FAX: 503-226-4158
e-mail: info@gocamping.org
www.gocamping.org

*Lisa Hoefner, Executive Director*

Camp is located near Sisters, Oregon. For adults living with HIV/AIDS.

**1690 Suttle Lake United Methodist Camp**
Conference of United Methodists
1505 SW 18th Avenue
Portland, OR  97201
503-226-7931
800-593-7539
FAX: 503-226-4158
e-mail: camping@gocamping.org
www.gocamping.org

*Lisa Jean Hoefner, Director*
*Jane Petke, Program Director*
*Bob Meyers, Religious Leader*

Camp is located in Sisters, Oregon. Camping sessions for children and adults with HIV. Coed, ages 6-18, families, seniors and single adults.

**1691 Upward Bound Camp: Evans Creek**
American Camping Association
PO Box C
Stayton, OR  97383
503-897-2447
FAX: 503-897-4116
e-mail: ubc@open.org
www.upwardboundcamp.org

*Jerry Pierce, Executive Director*
*Laura Pierce, Director*

Camping Christian for children and adults with a variety of disabilities. Ages 12-99, seniors and single adults.

**1692 YWCA Camp Westwind**
Y W C A of Greater Portland
1111 SW 10th Avenue
Portland, OR  97205
503-294-7400
FAX: 503-294-7399
e-mail: LindaD@ymca-pox.org
www.ywca-pdx.org

*Erika Silver, Director Operations*

Camp is located in Neotsu, Oregon. Sessions for children with hearing impairment. Coed, ages 7-17 and families.

**1693 Achieva**
711 Bingham Street
Pittsburgh, PA  15203
412-995-5000
888-272-7229
FAX: 412-995-5001
e-mail: contact@achieva.info
www.achieva.info

*Marsha Blanco, CEO/President*
*Ray Rykaceski, Executive Vice President*
*Gary Horner, CFO*

Life-long services for people with disabilities.

**1694 Briarwood Day Camp**
1380 Creek Road
Furlong, PA  18925
215-598-7143
FAX: 215-602-1060
www.briarwood-camp.com

*Ted Levine, Owner*

A comprehensive day camp providing lunch and transportation for children with disabilities.

**1695 Camp AIM Lloyd Institute**
2 Chatham Center
Suite 1500
Pittsburgh, PA  15219
412-454-0200
FAX: 412-281-6622
e-mail: mlloyd@lloydinstitute.com
www.lloydinstitute.com

*Michael E Lloyd, Founder*

Is a solid six week summer day program of adaptive aquatics, physical education, music expression, crafts, songs, special events, self-help, and socialization skills learning.

**1696 Camp ARC Spencer**
A RC of Beaver county
3582 Brodhead Road
Suite 202
Monaca, PA  15061
724-774-6600
800-272-0567
FAX: 724-775-2905
e-mail: arcbeaver@achieva.info

*Jacqueline Finney, Executive Director*

Camp is located in Fombell, Pennsylvania. Summer sessions for children and adults with developmental disabilities. Coed, ages 5-99.

**1697 Camp Can Do**
Easter Seals Southeastern PA
468 N Middletown Road
Media, PA  19063
610-565-2353
FAX: 610-565-5256
www.easterseals-sepa.org

*Carl Webster, Chief Executive Officer*
*Lexy Chapel, Assistant Director*
*Donna Keiths, Executive Director*

Camp is located in Kulpsville, Pennsylvania. Summer sessions for children and young adults with a variety of disabilities. Coed, ages 5-21

**1698 Camp Carefree**
Easter Seals Southeastern PA
797 E Lancaster Avenue
Suite 2
Downingtown, PA 19335
610-873-3990
800-221-6827
FAX: 610-565-5256
www.easterseals-sepa.org

*Kendr Brooks, Recreation Director*
*Donna Keiths, Executive Director*

Camp is located in Coatesville, Pennsylvania. Summer sessions for children and young adults with a variety of disabilities. Coed, ages 5-21.

**1699   Camp Dunmore**
Easter Seals Southeastern PA
468 N Middletown Road
Media, PA  19063

610-565-2353
FAX: 610-565-5256
www.easterseals-sepa.org

*Carl Webster, Chief Executive Officer*
*Lexy Chapel, Assistant Director*
*Donna Keiths, Executive Director*

Summer sessions for children and young adults with a variety of disabilities. Coed, ages 5-21.

**1700   Camp Joy**
3325 Swamp Creek Road
Schwenksville, PA  19473

610-754-6878
FAX: 610-754-7880
e-mail: campjoy@fast.net
www.campjoy.com

*Angus Murray, Camp Director*

A special needs camp for kids and adults (ages 4-80+) with developmental disabilities such as: mental retardation, autism, brain injury, neurological disorder, visual and/or hearing impairments, Angelman and Down syndromes, and other developmental disabilities.

**1701   Camp Keystone**
Rr 1
Box 1515
Clifton, PA  18424

570-842-4521
FAX: 570-842-2158
e-mail: glance@keycommresp.com
www.campkey.com

*Gloria J Lance, Director*
*Joy Smith, Executive Director*

Keystone serves both children and adults with a variety of disabilities in various residential settings. Support services include 24 hour supervision, on site nursing services, special and therapeutic recreation programs and psychological and psychiatric services. Ages 6-66, seniors and single adults.

**1702   Camp Lee Mar**
805 Redgate Road
Dresher, PA  19025

215-658-1708
FAX: 215-658-1710
e-mail: gtour400@aol.com
www.leemar.com

*Ariel J Segal, Executive Director*
*Lee Morone, Director*

Seven week summer camp for children and young adults with mild to moderate developmental disabilities. 5-21 years of age

**1703   Camp Setebaid**
Setebaid Services
PO Box 196
Winfield, PA  17889

570-524-9090
FAX: 570-523-0769
e-mail: info@setebaidservices.org
www.setebaidservices.org

*Mark Moyer, Executive Director*
*Diane Facer, Office Assistant*

Camping sessions for children with diabetes. Coed, ages 3-13 years. Family retreat for children with diabetes and their families.

**1704   Camp Surefoot**
Easter Seals Southeastern PA
468 N Middletown Road
Media, PA  19063

610-565-2353
FAX: 215-945-4073
www.easterseals-sepa.org

*Carl Webster, Director*
*Donna Keiths, Executive Director*

Camp is located in Levittown, Pennsylvania. Sessions for children and young adults with a variety of disabilities. Coed, ages 5-21.

**1705   Crestfield Camp**
Pittsburgh Presbytery
195 Taggert Road
Slippery Rock, PA  16057

724-794-4022
800-794-1948
FAX: 724-794-1665
e-mail: programs@crestfield.net
www.childrenwithdiabetes.com/camps

*Ida Eckstein, Executive Director*
*Kevin Starchaer, Program Director*

Camp is located at 195 Taggart Road, Slippery Rock, Pennsylvania. Summer sessions for children with diabetes. Coed, ages 9-18 and families.

**1706   Elling Camps**
Rr 1
Box 54
Thompson, PA  18465

717-756-2706
FAX: 717-756-3306

*Lloyd E Elling, Director*

For youth ages 6-21 with learning disabilities and accompanying difficulties. This camp allows them to learn to adjust socially in a community atmosphere. The structured camp program includes land and water sports, nature and forestry, industrial arts, construction and work programs, and arts and crafts.

**1707   Handi Camp**
Handi Vangelism Ministries International
PO Box 122
Akron, PA  17501

717-859-4777
FAX: 717-859-4505
e-mail: info@hvmi.org
wwww.hvmi.org

*Brian Robinson, Handi Camp Director*

Christian, overnight camping program for people with disabilities, ages 7-50, in Eastern PA and Southern NJ. Sponsored by Handi Vangelism Ministries International.

**1708   Helping Hands**
415 Hoffmansville Road
Bechtelsville, PA  19505

610-754-6491
FAX: 610-754-7157
e-mail: hhandsinc@comcast.net
www.helpinghands.com

*Bruce Waters, Executive Director*

Provides vocational and recreational programs for individuals with developmental disabilities. Offers support and information to parents, caregivers, and individuals impacted by disabilities.

**1709   Innabah**
712 Pughtown Road
Spring City, PA  19475

610-469-6111
877-UMC-CAMP
FAX: 610-469-0330
e-mail: camp@innabah.org
www.innabah.org

*Christy Heflin, Executive Director*

Sessions for children and young adults with developmental disabilities. Ages 4-18, families and seniors.

# Camps /Pennsylvania

**1710 Ken-Crest Services**
502 W Germantown Pike
Suite 200
Plymouth Meeting, PA 19462
610-825-9360
FAX: 610-825-4127
e-mail: kencrest@kencrest.org
www.kencrest.org

*William Nolan, Chief Executive Officer*
*Mary Ellen Caffrey, Director Childrens Services*

Ken-Crest provides services and supports for people who have developmental disability or who are at risk for disability across southeastern Pennsylvania and Delaware. Ken-Crest's community-based programs span the entire age continuum. Services for children include assessment, early intervention, therapies and parent education. For adults, Ken-Crest provides a full range of residential, employment, healthcare and therapy services.

**1711 Kweebec**
PO Box 511
Narberth, PA 19072
800-543-9830
FAX: 610-667-6376
e-mail: ckweebec@aol.com
www.kweebec.com

*Les Weiser, Director*

Camp is located in Schwenksville, Pennsylvania. Sessions for children and adults with diabetes. Coed, ages 6-16, families, seniors and single adults.

**1712 Living Waters**
Penn West Conference Ucc
320 S Maple Avenue
Greensburg, PA 15601
724-834-0344
FAX: 724-834-0324
www.pennwest.org

*Alan McLarty, Conference Minister/Manager*
*Linda Miller, Associate Conference Minister*

Camp is located in Schellsburg, Pennsylvania. Sessions for children and adults with developmental disabilities, ages 6-96 and families.

**1713 Make-a-Friend**
3975 Conshohocken Avenue
Philadelphia, PA 19131
215-879-1001
FAX: 215-879-8424
sepa.easterseals.com
Mission is to create solutions that change lives of children and adults with disabilities or other special needs and their families.

**1714 Outside in School**
PO Box 639
Greensburg, PA 15601
724-837-1518
FAX: 724-837-0801
e-mail: outside@icubed.com
www.outsideinschool.com

*Michael C Henkel, Executive Director*

Camp is located in Bolivar, Pennsylvania. Sessions for children with ADD and substance abuse problems. Boys 11-18 and girls 13-18.

**1715 Phelps School Summer School**
583 Sugartown Road
Malvern, PA 19355
610-644-1754
FAX: 610-644-6679
e-mail: admis@thephelpsschool.org
www.thephelpsschool.org

*Mike Reardon, Director of Admissions*
*Emily Shaker, Admissions Representative*
*Norman Phelps Jr, Principal*

Open for grades 7-11 to make up academic deficiencies or complete studies in English, math and reading. Sports include riding, tennis and swimming. A program is also available to a limited number of international students in English as a Second Language.

**1716 Ramah in the Poconos**
261 Old York Road
Suite 734
Jenkintown, PA 19046
215-885-8903
FAX: 215-885-8905
e-mail: info@ramahpoconos.org
www.ramahpoconos.org &campramah.org

*Marla Berkowits, Kesher Director*
*Todd Zeff, Executive Director*

Camp is located in Lake Como, Pennsylvania. Summer sessions for children and adults with hearing impairment. Coed, ages 10-16, families and seniors.

**1717 Sequanota**
PO Box 245
Jennerstown, PA 15547
814-629-6627
FAX: 814-629-0128
e-mail: campsequanota@foodcity.net
www.sequanota.net

*Bob Williams, Executive Director*

Summer sessions for adults with developmental disabilities and speech/communication impairment.

**1718 Souderton Special Needs Day Camp**
149 E Cherry Lane
Souderton, PA 18964
215-723-6061

*Donna Huff*
*Charles Amuso, Administrator*

Field trips and special events for disabled campers.

**1719 Variety Club Camp**
PO Box 609
Worcester, PA 19490
610-584-4366
FAX: 610-584-5586
e-mail: varietyclubcamp@hotmail.com

*Ralph Townsend, Director*
*Jen Tanzola, Manager*

Year-round camping and recreation facility for children with special needs and their families. Includes summer camping, aquatics, weekend retreats and other specialty programs. Coed, ages 5-21.

**1720 Wesley Woods**
Rr 1
Box 155
Grand Valley, PA 16420
814-436-7802
FAX: 814-436-7669
e-mail: wesleywoods@tbscc.com
www.wesleywoods.com

*Fred Hunt, President*
*Alice Rentz, Vice President*
*Harold Burns, Director*

Exceptional children's camp for children with emotional and intellectual handicaps.

**1721 Woodlands**
134 Shenot Road
Wexford, PA 15090
724-935-6533
FAX: 724-934-9610
e-mail: info@woodlandsfoundation.org
www.woodlandsfoundation.org

*Peter Clakeley, Executive Director*
*Jessica Schlie, Program Director*

Summer camping sessions and collaborative opportunities with charities serving individuals with disability and chronic illness. Year-round weekend retreats and aquatic programs for children and young adults with a variety of disabilities. Coed, ages 7-21.

Project adventure includes swimming, fishing, music and art and more in which disabled campers participate. Enjoy the fun and adventure of exploring a river in a canoe in the new canoe program.

## Rhode Island

**1722  Aldersgate Center**
1043 Snake Hill Road
North Scituate, RI  02857                    401-568-4350
                                        FAX: 401-568-1840
                         e-mail: aldersgate@juno.com
                              www.campaldersgate.com

*Jeffrey Thomas, Executive Director*

Summer sessions for children and adults with asthma/respiratory ailments. Coed, ages 7-99 and families.

**1723  Camp Ruggles**
133 Stone Dam Road
North Scituate, RI  02857                    401-647-5508

                              e-mail: info@ricamps.org
                                       www.ricamps.org

*John Jacques, President*

Camp Ruggles is located in Glocester, RI, and is a summer day camp for emotionally handicapped children. The Camp offers a 6 week co-ed summer session for 60 children ages 6-12.

**1724  Canonicus Camp**
American Baptist Churches Rhode Island
PO Box 330
Exeter, RI  02822                            401-294-6318
                                             800-294-6318
                                        FAX: 401-294-7780
                         e-mail: camp@canonicus.org
                                      www.canonicus.org

*Elizabeth Lussiern, Director of Administration*
*Linda Martin, Conferencing Coordinator*
*Colleen Tolhurst, Registrar*

Summer sessions for children with asthma/respiratory ailments. Coed, ages 4-18.

## South Carolina

**1725  Burnt Gin Camp**
SC Department of Health and Environmental Control
PO Box 101106
Columbia, SC  29211                          803-737-0400
                                        FAX: 803-898-0613
                  www.scdhec.net/hs/mch/burntgin/hsbgin1.hpm

*Marie Aimone, Camp Director*
*Charles Way, Manager*

A residental camp for children who have physical disabilities and/or chronic illnesses. Camper/staff ratio is 2:1. Five seven-day sessions for 7-15 year olds and one six-day sesssion for 16-19 year olds. Limited to residents of South Carolina.

**1726  Camp Gravatt**
1006 Camp Gravatt Road
Aiken, SC  29805                             803-648-1817
                                        FAX: 803-648-7453
                         e-mail: gravatt@mindspring.com
                                    www.bishopgravatt.org

*Duncan C Ely, Executive Director*

## South Dakota

**1727  NeSoDak Bible Camp/Klein Ranch**
Lutherans Outdoors South Dakota
3285 Camp Dakota Drive
Waubay, SD  57273                            605-947-4440
                                        FAX: 605-947-4370
                  e-mail: nesodak@lutheransoutdoors.org
                              www.lutheransoutdoors.org

*Tricia Larson, Director*
*Lando Anderson, Program Director*
*Teri Gaier, Executive Director*

Camp is located in Waubay, South Dakota. Sessions for children with diabetes. Coed, ages 8-18.

## Tennessee

**1728  Camp Discovery**
Tennessee Jaycee Fund
PO Box 10206
Knoxville, TN  37939                          615-331-6345
                                        FAX: 615-293-4497
                         e-mail: directorjayceecamp.org
                                      www.jayceecap.org

*Dawn Hickman, Director*
*Paula Petty, Camp Caretaker*

Serves children with skin conditions including: Epidermolysis Bullosa, Psoriasis, Alopecia, Vitiligo, Eczema, Scleroderma, Congential Nevus, Ehlers-Danlos, Ichthyosis, Ectodermal Dysplasia and more. The Camp is located at 400 Camp Discovery Lane in Gainsboro, TN.

**1729  Easter Seals Camp**
6300 Benders Ferry Road
Mount Juliet, TN  37122                       615-444-2829
                                        FAX: 615-444-8576
                  e-mail: camp@eastersealstn.com
                              www.eastersealstn.com

*Leslie Sohls, Executive Director*
*Penny Williams, Office Manager*

Summer sessions for children and adults with various disabilities, ages 6-99.

**1730  Indian Creek Camp**
Kentucky Tennessee Conference
PO Box 1088
Goodlettsville, TN  37070                     615-859-1391
                                        FAX: 615-859-2120
                  e-mail: info@indiancreekcamp.com
                              www.indiancreekcamp.com

*Jerry Mahn, Director*
*Aaron Raines, Assistant Director*
*Richard Hallock, President*

Camp is located in Liberty, Tennessee. Summer sessions for children and adults who are blind/visually impaired. Coed, ages 7-17, families and seniors.

## Texas

**1731   Camp CAMP**
PO Box 27086
San Antonio, TX 78227                     210-292-3566
                                     FAX: 210-292-3577
                      e-mail: campmail@campcamp.org
                               www.campcamp.org

*Susan Osborne, Family Services Director*
*Janice Bob, Development Director*
*Suzanne Reily, Training Director*

Camping for children and young adults with a variety of disabilities. Coed, ages 5-21. Respite services throughout calendar year. Adult camp ages 22-45.

**1732   Camp John Marc**
Special Camps for Special Kids
2824 Swiss Avenue
Dallas, TX 75204                          214-360-0056
                                     FAX: 214-368-2003
                      e-mail: mail@campjohnmarc.org
                             www.campjohnmarc.org

*Brooks Cullum, Chairman*
*Vance C Gilmore, Executive Director*

Camp is located in Meridian, Texas. Year-round camping for children with a variety of disabilities. Coed, ages 6-16 and families.

**1733   Camp Summit**
2915 L B J Fwy
Suite 185
Dallas, TX 75234                          972-484-8900
                                     FAX: 972-620-1945
                               www.campsummittx.org

*Lisa Braziel, Camp Director*
*Carla Weiland, Chief Executive Officer*

Camp is located in Argyle, Texas. Camping for children and adults with a variety of disabilities. Coed, ages 6-99.

**1734   Camp Sweeney**
Southwestern Diabetic Fund
PO Box 918
Gainesville, TX 76241                     940-665-2011
                                     FAX: 940-665-9467
                      e-mail: info@campsweeney.org
                               www.campsweeney.org

*Milton Dixon, Chairman*
*Ernie Fernandez, Executive Director*

Teaches self-care and self-reliance to children ages 7-18 with diabetes. Campers participate in such activities such as swimming, fishing, horseback riding and arts and crafts while learning about how to self manage their diabetes.

**1735   Camp for All**
Vicki La Rue
10500 Northwest Fwy
Suite 220
Houston, TX 77092                         713-686-5666
                                     FAX: 713-686-1242
                  e-mail: houstonoffice@campforall.org
                               www.campforall.org

*Vicki Rue, Executive Director*
*Janet Johnson, Camp Director*
*Teri Todd, Operations Manager*

Fully-accessible year round camp facility is located in Burton, Texas. Camping for children and adults with a variety of disabilities. Coed, ages 5-35 and up and families.

**1736   Dallas Academy**
950 Tiffany Way
Dallas, TX 75218                          214-324-1481
                                     FAX: 214-327-8537
                  e-mail: mail@dallas-academy.com
                             www.dallas-academy.com

*Jim Richardson, Executive Director*
*Miscy Stockton, Director of the Lower School*

7-week summer session for students who are having difficulty in regular school classes.

**1737   Growing Together Diabetes Camp**
PO Box 6400
Tyler, TX 75711                           903-596-3645
                                          800-648-8141
                                     FAX: 903-535-6783
                                          www.etmc.org

*Stella Hecker, Director*
*Marie Taylor, Director*

A summer camp for youths ages 6 to 15 with Type 1 or Type 2 diabetes.

**1738   Hill School of Fort Worth**
4817 Odessa Avenue
Fort Worth, TX 76133                      817-923-9482
                                     FAX: 817-923-4894
                  e-mail: hillschool@hillschool.org
                               www.hillschool.org

*Mitch Weatherly, Chairman*
*Mark Jackson, Senior Vice President*
*Greg Owens, Principal*

Provides an alternative learning environment for students having average or above-average intelligence with learning differences. Hill school is an established leader in North Texas with a 25 year history of effectively serving LD children. Beginning in 1961 as a tutorial service, Hill became a formal school in 1973. Our mission is to help those who learn differently develop skills and strategies to succeed. We do this by developing academic/study skills, and self-discipline.

**1739   Hughen Center**
2849 9th Avenue
Port Arthur, TX 77642                     409-983-6659
                                     FAX: 409-983-6408
                  e-mail: hughencenter@yahoo.com

*Rita Morston, Administrator*

The Center provides a therapeutic, educational, and recreational program for children with physical disabilities. Physical and occupational therapy are featured. Day and residential.

**1740   Texas 4-H Center**
5600 FM 3021
Brownwood, TX 76801                       325-784-5482
                                     FAX: 325-784-6486
                      e-mail: cross@tamu.edu
                               texas4h-ctr.tamu.edu

*Scott Cross, Director*
*Darlene Locke, Program Director*

Leadership activities and personal growth.

**1741   Texas Lions Camp**
PO Box 290247
Kerrville, TX 78029                       830-896-8500
                                     FAX: 830-896-3666
                      e-mail: tlc@ktc.com
                               www.lionscamp.com

*Stephen S Mabry, Executive Director*

The primary purpose of the League shall be to provide, without charge, a camp for physically disabled, hearing/vision impaired and diabetic children from the State of Texas, regardless of race, religion, or national origin. Our goal is to create an atmosphere wherein campers will learn the can do philosophy and be allowed to achieve maximum personal growth and self-esteem. The camp welcomes boys and girls ages 7-16.

## Utah

**1742  Camp Kostopulos**
Kostopulos Dream Foundation
2500 Emigration Cyn
Salt Lake City, UT  84108          801-582-0700
                                   FAX: 801-583-5176
                                   e-mail: kdf@campk.org
                                   www.campk.org

*Gary Ethington, Executive Director*

Summer camping for children and adults ages 7-65 with a variety of disabilities. Year round recreation on site and community based activities.

**1743  FCYD Camp**
Foundation for Children and Youth
1995 W 9000 S
West Jordan, UT  84088             801-566-6913

                    e-mail: fcydwebstaff@networld.com
                                   www.fcyd-inc.org

*Dave Okubo, President*
*Elizabeth Elmer, Vice President*
*Sherrie Hardy, Director*

Camping for children with diabetes. Coed, ages 1-18 and families.

## Vermont

**1744  Bennington School Summer Program**
192 Fairview Street
Bennington, VT  05201              802-447-1557
                                   800-639-3156
                                   FAX: 802-442-1118
          e-mail: admissions@benningtonschoolinc.org
                                   www.benningtonschoolinc.org

*Patrick Ramsay, Director Admissions*
*Jeffrey LaBonte, Executive Director*

A 115 bed residential treatment center serving emotionally and behaviorally disordered adolescent male and female students. Offers fully accredited on-grounds educational and summer programs in a beautiful rural setting with many recreational and cultural opportunities.

**1745  Camp Betsey Cox**
140 Betsey Cox Lane
Pittsfield, VT  05763              802-483-6611

                                   e-mail: betcoxvt@aol.com
                                   www.campbetseycox.com

*Lorrie Byrom, Camp Director*
*Devri Byrom, Winter Office Director*

Camp is located in Pittsford, Vermont. Summer sessions for girls aged 9-15 with ADD.

**1746  Camp Thorpe**
680 Capen Hill Road
Goshen, VT  05733                  802-247-6611

                                   e-mail: cthorpe@sover.net
                                   www.campthorpe.org

*Lyle Jepson, Director*

Focuses on meeting the needs of each individual camper; showing each of them that they have the ability and potential. Also provides positive camping experience for children challenged with handicapping conditions.

**1747  Farm and Wilderness Camps**
263 Farm and Wilderness Road
Plymouth, VT  05056                802-422-3761
                                   FAX: 802-422-8660
                                   e-mail: fandw@fandw.org
                                   www.fandw.org

*Robert Schultz, President*

Gives people the opportunity to emphasize the building of community through the values of cooperation, simplicity, responsibility, empathy, spirituality, and services.

**1748  Silver Towers Camp**
1116 Us Route 5
E Dummerston, VT  05346            800-385-8524
                                   FAX: 802-442-4675
                                   e-mail: graymgt@sover.net
                                   www.silvertowerscamp.org

*Dr Valeri Allen, Camp Director*
*Brenda Metcalf, Office Manager*

Programs are tailored to the abilities and interests of each individual and a staff which provides encouragement and guidance.

## Virginia

**1749  Adventure Day Camp**
Early Years Academy
13817 Spriggs Road
Manassas, VA  20112                703-590-3659
                                   FAX: 703-491-0836
                         www.princewilliamacademy.com

*Samia Harris, Principal*

Camping for children with asthma/respiratory ailments and cancer. Coed, ages 2-13.

**1750  American Diabetes Summer Camp**
American Diabetes Association
1701 N Beauregard Street
Alexandria, VA  22311              703-549-1500
                                   800-342-2383
                                   e-mail: webmaster@diabetes.org
                                   www.diabetes.org

*Lynn B Nicholas, Chief Executive Officer*
*Alan Cherrington, President*
*Catherine Tibbetts, President*

The American Diabetes Association is the nation's leading non-profit health organization providing diabetes research, information, advocacy and year round programs for children with diabetes.

**1751  Camp Baker**
Greater Richmond ARC
7600 Beach Road
Chesterfield, VA  23838            804-748-4789
                                   FAX: 804-496-9657
                         e-mail: campbaker@RichmondARC.org
                                   www.richmondarc.org

Supports children from age 6 through adulthood with mental retardation and similar developmental disabilities.

**1752 Camp Dickenson**
Holsten Conference Camping
801 Camp Dickson Lane
Fries, VA 24330
276-744-7241
FAX: 276-744-7241
e-mail: cdickenson@tcia.net

*Chuck Jones, Director*
*Heather Jones, Director*

Camp is located in Fries, Virginia. Camping for children and adults with developmental disabilities. Coed, ages 5-18, families, seniors and single adults.

**1753 Camp Easter Seal: East/West**
Easter Seals Virginia
201 E Main Street
Salem, VA 24153
540-777-2267
800-365-1656
FAX: 540-777-2194
www.va.easter-seals.org

*Kim Hutchinson, President*
*Tristan Robertson, Director*

Summer camp sessions for children and adults ages 5-99 with physical disabilities, cognitive disabilities and sensory impairments. Therapeutic recreation activities including swimming, fishing, sports, horseback riding, rock climbing, and more. Twenty-six-day speech therapy camp children with disabilities ages 8-16. Twelve-day Spina Bifida Self Help Skills Camp.

**1754 Camp Holiday Trails**
400 Holiday Trails Lane
Charlottesville, VA 22903
434-977-3781
FAX: 434-977-8814
e-mail: holidaytrails@nexet.net
avenue.org/cht

*Tina LaRoche, Director*

Private, nonprofit camp for children with special health needs and various chronic illnesses. Residential, 2-week sessions are open June - August; camperships are available. Coed 7-17, nationwide and international. Canoeing, swimming, horseback riding, arts and crafts, drama, ropes course, etc. 24-hr. medical supervision by doctor and nursing staff. Air conditioned cabins.

**1755 Camp Virginia Jaycee**
2494 Camp Jaycee Road
Blue Ridge, VA 24064
540-947-2972
800-865-0092
FAX: 540-947-2043
e-mail: ewerness@campvirginiajaycee.com
www.campvirginiajaycee.com

*Everett M Werness, President*
*Cindy Rinker, Camp Director*

Summer camping for children and adults with developmental disabilities. Coed, ages 7-70. Weekend respite camps for children and adults with mental retardation.

**1756 Civitan Acres**
Eggleston Services
1161 Ingleside Road
Norfolk, VA 23502
757-858-8011
FAX: 757-627-4760
e-mail: info@egglestonservices.org
www.egglestonservices.org/programs_ca.html

*John Rynearson, Vice President*
*David Bledsoe, Director*

Camping for children and adults with developmental disabilities. Coed, ages 5-99.

**1757 Loudoun County Special Recreation Programs**
Loudoun County Local Government
215 Depot Ct SE
Leesburg, VA 20175
703-777-0343
FAX: 703-771-5354
e-mail: prcs@loudoun.gov
www.loudoun.gov

*Diane Ryburn, Director*
*Cynthia Welsh, Executive Director*

Offers and promotes integration opportunities for individuals with disabilities. Coordinates ADA issues and Very Special Arts and Special Olympics for Loudoun County. Summer camps, sports, socials and community trips.

**1758 Makemie Woods Camp**
Presbytery of Eastern Virginia
PO Box 39
Lanexa, VA 23089
757-566-1496
800-566-1496
e-mail: makwoods@makwoods.org
www.makwoods.org

*Mike Burcher, Director*
*Jenny Mcdevitt, Program Director*
*Michelle Burcher, Administrator*

Residential Christian camp that tailors each group and individual goals. Counselors serve as teachers, friends and activity leaders. For children 8-18 with diabetes.

**1759 Makemie Woods Camp/Conference Retreat**
Presbytery of Eastern Virginia
801 Loudoun Avenue
Portsmouth, VA 23707
757-397-7063
800-989-2193
FAX: 757-397-7246
e-mail: info@pcusa-peva.org
www.makwoods.org

*Michelle Burcher, Director*
*Richard J Short, Religious Leader*

Counselors serve as teachers, friends and activity leaders. The individual is important within the small group. No camper is lost in the crowd, but is an integral partner in the group process. Residential Christian Camp and conference center. Summer camp for children 8-18 and special camp for children with diabetes.

**1760 Oakland School & Camp**
Boyd Tavern
Keswick, VA 22947
434-293-9059
FAX: 434-296-8930
e-mail: oaklandschool@earthlink.net
www.oaklandschool.net

*Joanne Dondero, President*
*Carol Smieciuch, Executive Director*

A highly individualized program stresses improving reading ability. Subjects taught are reading, English composition, math and word analysis. Recreational activities include horseback riding, sports, swimming, tennis, crafts, archery and camping. For girls and boys, ages 8-14.

**1761 Oakland School and Camp**
Boyd Tavern
Keswick, VA 22947
434-293-9059
FAX: 434-296-8930
e-mail: oaklandschool@earthlink.net
www.oaklandschool.net

*Carol Smieciuch, Executive Director*
*Beth Clttone, Assistant Director*

For children of average to above average ability who have learning disabilities or have been unable to learn in a traditional classroom.

**1762 Overlook Camp**
3014 Camp Overlook Lane
Keezletown, VA 22832
540-269-2267
FAX: 540-269-2267
e-mail: overlookum@aol.com
www.gbgm-umc.org

*Ronald Robey, Executive Director*

A Christian life experience for youth and children, located at the base of the scenic Massanutten Mountains.

# Washington

**1763 Camp Fun in the Sun**
Inland North West Health Services
157 S Howard Street
Suite 500
Spokane, WA 99201
509-232-8138
FAX: 509-232-8151
e-mail: randalll@cherspokane.org
www.campfuninthesun.org

*Lisa Randall, Director*
*Diane Lenier, Executive Director*

Summer camping for children with diabetes. Coed, ages 6-18.

**1764 Camp Killoqua**
Camp Fire U SA
4312 Rucker Avenue
Everett, WA 98203
425-258-5437
FAX: 425-252-2267
e-mail: info@campfireusasnohoneish.org
www.campfireusasnohomish.org/killoqua

*Carol Johnson, Director*
*Dave Surface, Executive Director*

Camp is located in Stanwood, Washington. Camping for children with developmental disabilities. Coed, ages 6-17.

**1765 Easter Seals Camp Stand by Me**
Easter Seal Society of Washington
17809 S Vaughan Road
Vaughn, WA 98394
253-884-2722
FAX: 253-884-0200
e-mail: camp@wa.easterseals.com
www.seals.org

*Cathy Bisaillon, Chief Executive Officer*

Camp is located in Vaughn, Washington. Summer camping for adults and children with developmental disabilities and mobility limitation. Coed, ages 7-65, seniors. Respite weekends October thru May.

**1766 Northwest Kiwanis Camp**
PO Box 1227
Port Hadlock, WA 98339
360-732-7222

e-mail: info@kiwaniscamp.com
kiwaniscamp.com

*Charise Diamond, Director*

Campers range from 6-60 in age, and includes those with developmental disabilities, cerebral palsy, autism, downs syndrome, and other physical and/or mental handicaps.

**1767 Volasuca Volunteers of America**
Volunteers of America
2802 Broadway
Everett, WA 98201
425-259-3191
FAX: 425-258-2838
e-mail: info@voaww.org
www.voaww.org

*Chris Shroy, Program Director*
*Chris Robinson, Chief Executive Officer*

Camp is located in Sultan, Washington. Summer sessions for children and adults with a variety of disabilities. Coed, ages 6-13, families and single adults.

**1768 YMCA Camp Orkila**
Y MC A of Greater Seattle
909 4th Avenue
Seattle, WA 98104
206-382-5003
FAX: 206-382-4920
www.seattleymca.org

*Dimitri Stankevich, Program Director*

Camping for children with blood disorders and diabetes, ages 8-18.

# West Virginia

**1769 Mountaineer Spina Bifida Camp**
350 Capitol Street
Suite 427
Charleston, WV 25301
304-558-7098
800-642-9704
FAX: 304-558-2866
www2.kidscamps.com

*Nancy Dunst, Camp Director*
*Tonya Brown-Stobble, RN*

Is a non profit organization which pursues education and training and focuses on activities that promote independence and those that facilitate everyday life. The objectives are to build self esteem, promote independence and enhance the development of social skills.

**1770 Stepping Stones**
400 Mylan Park Lane
Morgantown, WV 26501
304-296-0150
800-982-8799
FAX: 304-983-8031
www.steppingstonescenter.net

*Missy Weimer, Director*
*Bob Pirner, Manager*

Non-profit organization that serves individuals with disabilities. Programs include recreation, summer camps, technology and speech therapy.

**1771 YMCA Camp Horseshoe**
Ohio and W Virginia Y MC A
Rr 2
Box 138
Saint George, WV 26287
304-478-2481
FAX: 304-478-4446
e-mail: horseshoe@hi-y.org
www.hi-y.org

*David King, Executive Director*
*Sharon Cassidy, Camp Horseshoe Secretary*

Summer camping for children with cancer, ages 7-18.

# Camps /Wisconsin

## Wisconsin

**1772  Bright Horizons Summer Camp**
Sickle Cell Disease Association of Illinois
200 North Michigan Avenue
Suite 605
Chicago, IL  60601
312-345-1100
866-798-1097
FAX: 312-803-1953
e-mail: support@sicklecelldisease-il.org
www.sicklecelldisease-il.org

*Howard Anderson, President*
*Valeria C Beckley, Director*
*Dorothy C Moore MD, Chief Medical Officer*

Camp is located in Williams Bay, Wisconsin. Camping for children with blood disorders, ages 7-13.

**1773  Easter Seal Camp Wawbeek**
Easter Seals Wisconsin
101 Nob Hill Road
Room 301
Madison, WI  53713
608-277-8288
800-422-2324
FAX: 608-277-8333
TTY: 608-277-8031
e-mail: wawbeek@wi-easterseals.org
www.eastersealswisconsin.com

*Kelly Housman, Program Director*
*Nance Roepke, Executive Director*
*Christine Fessler, Chief Executive Officer*

Disabled campers. Offers adventure programs, camp sessions for other health agencies, family camp opportunities and year round respite sessions. Coed, ages 8-99.

**1774  Lutherdale Bible Camp**
N7891 Us Highway 12
Elkhorn, WI  53121
262-742-2352
FAX: 262-742-3169
e-mail: lutherdale@lutherdale.org
www.lutherdale.org

*Jeffrey Bluhm, Executive Director*
*Casey Rohee, Assistant Director*

Summer camping for people with developmental disabilities. Coed, ages 9-18 and families, seniors.

**1775  Phantom Lake YMCA Camp**
S110w30240 Ymca Camp Road
Mukwonago, WI  53149
262-363-4386
FAX: 262-363-4351
e-mail: office@phantomlakeymca.com
www.phantomlakeymca.com

*Ted Anderson, Member of the Board*
*Riley Cooper, Member of the Board*
*Kathy Jensen, Member of the Board*

Summer camping for children with epilepsy, ages 7-15.

**1776  Timbertop Nature Adventure Camp**
YMCA Camp Glacier Hollow
1000 Division Street
Stevens Point, WI  54481
715-342-2980
FAX: 715-342-2987
e-mail: pmatthai@spymca.org
www.spymca.org

*Peter Matthai, Camp Director*
*Dave Morgan, Executive Director*

For children who can benefit from an individualized program of learning in a non-competitive outdoor setting under the skilled leadership of people who understand the environment and the unique potential of these children.

**1777  Triangle Y Ranch YMCA**
Y MC A of Tri- County mtero mil
5535 S Church Road
West Bend, WI  53095
262-675-9622
FAX: 262-675-4982
e-mail: kwilliams@ymcamke.org
www.ymcamke.org

*Cathy Palmer, Executive Director*
*Cliss Clauer, Executive Director*

Camp is located in West Bend, Wisconsin. Summer camping for children with ADD. Coed, ages 5-14.

**1778  Wisconsin Badger Camp**
PO Box 723
Platteville, WI  53818
608-348-9689
FAX: 608-348-9737
e-mail: wiscbadgercamp@centurytel.net
www.badgercamp.org

*Brent Bowers, Executive Director*
*Carissa Miller, Camp Director*

Mission is to serve people with developmental disabilities by providing quality outdoor recreational experience. All developmentally disabled individuals, regardless of the severity of their disability or inability to pay are welcome.

**1779  Wisconsin Lions Camp**
Wisconsin Lions Foundation
3834 County Road A
Rosholt, WI  54473
715-677-4969
877-463-6953
FAX: 715-677-3297
TTY: 715-677-6999
e-mail: ifno@wisconsinlionscamp.com
www.wisconsinlionscamp.com

*Andrea Yenter, Camp Operations Manager*
*Evett Hartvig, Executive Director*

Serves children who have either a visual, hearing or mild cognitive disability, as well as diabetes types I and II. Program activities include sailing, ropes course, hiking and canoe trips, environmental education, swimming, camping, canoeing, outdoor living skills and handicrafts. ACA accredited, located in central Wisconsin, near Stevens Point.

## Dresses & Skirts

**1780 Budget Cotton/Poly Open Back Gown**
Buck & Buck
3111 27th Avenue S
Seattle, WA 98144
206-722-4196
800-458-0600
FAX: 800-317-2182
e-mail: info@buckandbuck.com
www.buckandbuck.com

*Julie Buck, Owner*
Short raglan sleeves, lace at neck and bodice over lapping snapback closure. *$11.00*

**1781 Budget Flannel Open Back Gown**
Buck & Buck
3111 27th Avenue S
Seattle, WA 98144
206-722-4196
800-458-0600
FAX: 800-317-2182
e-mail: info@buckandbuck.com
www.buckandbuck.com

*Julie Buck, Owner*
3/4 raglan sleeve, lace at neck and bodice. *$13.00*

**1782 Cotton/Poly Nancy Frocks**
Buck & Buck
3111 27th Avenue S
Seattle, WA 98144
206-722-4196
800-458-0600
FAX: 800-317-2182
e-mail: info@buckandbuck.com
www.buckandbuck.com

*Julie Buck, Owner*
Comes in short and long sleeves, assorted florals and plaids. *$35.00*

**1783 Dusters**
Buck & Buck
3111 27th Avenue S
Seattle, WA 98144
206-722-4196
800-458-0600
FAX: 800-317-2182
e-mail: info@buckandbuck.com
www.buckandbuck.com

*Julie Buck, Owner*
Three types: Floral, Budget Better. Snap front styles and gathered yokes, flannel *$16.00-$24.00*.

**1784 Flannel Gowns**
Buck & Buck
3111 27th Avenue S
Seattle, WA 98144
206-722-4196
800-458-0600
FAX: 800-317-2182
e-mail: info@buckandbuck.com
www.buckandbuck.com

*Julie Buck, Owner*
Comes in long or short with a deep button-front opening for ease of slipping on. Shorter long length. *$16.50*

**1785 Fleece Cape/Poncho**
Laurel Designs
1805 Mar West Street
Apt A
Belvedere Tiburon, CA 94920
FAX: 415-435-1451
e-mail: laureld@ncal.verio.com

*Janet Sawyer, Co-Owner*
*Lynn Montoya, Co-Owner*
Warm and cozy high insulated cape with hood for wheelchair users, zip front, velcro side closure, self belt. All sizes and a variety of colors. *$53.00*

**1786 Float Dress**
Buck & Buck
3111 27th Avenue S
Seattle, WA 98144
206-722-4196
800-458-0600
FAX: 800-317-2182
e-mail: info@buckandbuck.com
www.buckandbuck.com

*Julie Buck, Owner*
A safe bet for everyone from a size medium to a 6X. Gathered yoke front and back and literally yards of fabric for fullness. Comes in cotton or polyester. *$34.00*

**1787 Muu Muu**
Buck & Buck
3111 27th Avenue S
Seattle, WA 98144
206-722-4196
800-458-0600
FAX: 800-317-2182
e-mail: info@buckandbuck.com
www.buckandbuck.com

*Julie Buck, Owner*
Comes in long and short styles, assorted bright floral prints. *$20.00-$22.00*.

**1788 Polyester Nancy Frocks**
Buck & Buck
3111 27th Avenue S
Seattle, WA 98144
206-722-4196
800-458-0600
FAX: 800-317-2182
e-mail: info@buckandbuck.com
www.buckandbuck.com

*Julie Buck, Owner*
Comes in short and long sleeves, assorted florals. *$ 35.00*

## Footwear

**1789 Acrylic Leg Warmers**
Buck & Buck
3111 27th Avenue S
Seattle, WA 98144
206-722-4196
800-458-0600
FAX: 800-317-2182
e-mail: info@buckandbuck.com
www.buckandbuck.com

*Julie Buck, Owner*
Recommended for large or swollen legs where knee socks are too restrictive. *$7.00*

**1790 Adult Acorn Polartec Socks**
Special Clothes
PO Box 333
E Harwich, MA 02645
508-430-2410
FAX: 508-430-2410
e-mail: specialclo@aol.com
www.special-clothes.com

*Judith Sweeney, President*
These plush socks are made of Polartec fleece for unparalleled softness and comfort. The mid-calf length keeps feet and lower legs warmer than any conventional sock and the fabric has 2 way stretch to minimize binding. Polartec fleece is a remarkable light-weight fabric which breathes and insulates. Machine washable, of course. 100% Polartec fleece. Made in USA. Colors: solid black or charcoal print. *$18.00*

*Per pair*

**1791  Adult Acorn Slippers**
Special Clothes
PO Box 333
E Harwich, MA  02645

508-430-2410
FAX: 508-430-2410
e-mail: specialclo@aol.com
www.special-clothes.com

*Judith Sweeney, President*

These great looking, beautifully made slipper shoes keep chilly feet warm and comfortable. The sole is cut of fine suede leather, and the uppers and insoles are soft, plush polartec fleece. The knit cuff at the ankle opens wide to slip on easily, yet is snug enough to keep the slippers in place. Machine washable. Polartec fleece, suede sole, acrylic cuff. Made in USA. Colors: burgundy with navy cuff or dark green with navy cuff. *$30.00*
*Per pair*

**1792  Booties with Non-Skid Soles**
Buck & Buck
3111 27th Avenue S
Seattle, WA  98144

206-722-4196
800-458-0600
FAX: 800-317-2182
e-mail: info@buckandbuck.com
www.buckandbuck.com

*Julie Buck, Owner*

Acrylic knit or quilted cotton/poly and shearling inner. *$17.00*

**1793  Foot Snugglers**
Buck & Buck
3111 27th Avenue S
Seattle, WA  98144

206-722-4196
800-458-0600
FAX: 800-317-2182
e-mail: info@buckandbuck.com
www.buckandbuck.com

*Julie Buck, Owner*

Quilted poly/cotton outers lined with plush shearling pile, provide a thick, comfortable cushion which helps minimize the pressure points on tender areas. *$23.00*

**1794  Lok-Tie Shoe Laces**
Laurel Designs
1805 Mar West Street
Apt A
Belvedere Tiburon, CA  94920

FAX: 415-435-1451
e-mail: laureld@ncal.verio.com

*Janet Sawyer, Co-Owner*
*Lynn Montoya, Co-Owner*

Specially designed slide locks laces in place. Can be used with one hand. Stretch laces allow maximum comfort. *$4.00*

**1795  TRU-Mold Shoes**
42 Breckenridge Street
Buffalo, NY  14213

716-881-4484
800-843-6653
FAX: 716-881-0406

*Husain Syed, Production Manager*

Custom made, fully molded shoes, relieve pressure in sensitive areas by taking all of the weight off the painful areas.

**1796  Terrycloth Slippers**
Buck & Buck
3111 27th Avenue S
Seattle, WA  98144

206-722-4196
800-458-0600
FAX: 800-317-2182
e-mail: info@buckandbuck.com
www.buckandbuck.com

*Julie Buck, Owner*

Lined cotton/poly terrycloth upper with sewn-on, non-skid sole. *$18.00*

**1797  Velcro Booties**
Buck & Buck
3111 27th Avenue S
Seattle, WA  98144

206-722-4196
800-458-0600
FAX: 800-317-2182
e-mail: info@buckandbuck.com
www.buckandbuck.com

*Julie Buck, Owner*

The high-domed toe, and extra-wide, non-skid sole design accommodates virtually every foot related problem. *$18.00*

**1798  Velcro Sneaker**
Buck & Buck
3111 27th Avenue S
Seattle, WA  98144

206-722-4196
800-458-0600
FAX: 800-317-2182
e-mail: info@buckandbuck.com
www.buckandbuck.com

*Julie Buck, Owner*

Two velcro straps, nylon upper, rubber sole. *$22.00*

**1799  Washable Shoes**
Buck & Buck
3111 27th Avenue S
Seattle, WA  98144

206-722-4196
800-458-0600
FAX: 800-317-2182
e-mail: info@buckandbuck.com
www.buckandbuck.com

*Julie Buck, Owner*

Vinyl upper with velcro closure, nonskid sole. *$18.00*

## Jackets

**1800  Fleece Bed Jacket**
Buck & Buck
3111 27th Avenue S
Seattle, WA  98144

206-722-4196
800-458-0600
FAX: 800-317-2182
e-mail: info@buckandbuck.com
www.buckandbuck.com

*Julie Buck, Owner*

Full snap front opening and collar. Assorted bright colors and pastel prints. *$22.00*

**1801  Jackets**
Special Clothes
PO Box 333
E Harwich, MA  02645

508-430-2410
FAX: 508-430-2410
e-mail: specialclo@aol.com
www.special-clothes.com

*Judith Sweeney, President*

Available styles include a unique, back opening jacket designed to fit easily over contractures and for wheelchair comfort. Prices range from $72.00-$89.00.

**1802 Rain Poncho**
Laurel Designs
1805 Mar West Street
Apt A
Belvedere Tiburon, CA 94920
FAX: 415-435-1451
e-mail: laureld@ncal.verio.com

*Janet Sawyer, Co-Owner*
*Lynn Montoya, Co-Owner*

A favorite, this rain poncho slips on in a hurry to keep you dry. All sizes and a variety of colors. *$39.00*

**1803 Wheelchair Ponchos**
Special Clothes
PO Box 333
E Harwich, MA 02645
508-430-2410
FAX: 580-430-2410
e-mail: specialclo@aol.com
www.special-clothes.com

*Judith Sweeney, President*

These ponchos are cut shorter in the back for wheelchair comfort. Prices range from $76.00-$95.00.

## Miscellaneous & Catalogs

**1804 AMI: Accessories for Mobile Independence**
5235 Mission Oaks Boulevard
Suite 381
Camarillo, CA 93012
FAX: 805-987-8653

*Gay Dawson, Owner*

Ponchos, tote bags, gloves, and sweat pants for wheelchair-using consumers.

**1805 Adaptive Clothing: Adults**
Special Clothes
PO Box 333
E Harwich, MA 02645
508-430-2410
FAX: 508-430-2410
e-mail: specialslo@aol.com
www.special-clothes.com

*Judith Sweeney, President*

Special Clothes produces a catalogue of garments for adults with disabilities and/or incontinence. Offerings include: undergarments, snap-crotch tee shirts, sleepwear, jumpsuits, bibs and some footwear. The catalogue is available without charge. Comparable to department store prices. Special Clothes produces a catalog of adaptive clothing for children in sizes from toddler through young adults. A full line of clothing is included from undergarments through wheelchair jackets and ponchos.

**1806 Adrian's Closet**
PO Box 9506
Rancho Santa Fe, CA 92067
800-831-2577
e-mail: adrians@electriciti.com
Fashions for the physically challenged child. Clothing offers Velcro closures, front pockets, concealed back openings and fashions for seated posture.

**1807 Adult Long Jumpsuit with Feet**
Special Clothes
PO Box 333
E Harwich, MA 02645
508-430-2410
FAX: 580-430-2410
e-mail: specialclo@aol.com
www.special-clothes.com

*Judith Sweeney, President*

A full, snap crotch for full access. For safety, feet have non-skid bottoms. 100% cotton knit. Made in USA. Also, identical in style, but are made of fleece for extra warmth. Fleece fabric is soft 100% cotton, and is available in medium blue only. Made in USA. Options on fleece jumpsuits available for additional charge. Long knit jumpsuit with feet: #A2051; long fleece jumpsuit: #A2032; long fleece jumpsuit with feet: #A2052.

**1808 Adult Short Jumpsuit**
Special Clothes
PO Box 333
E Harwich, MA 02645
508-430-2410
FAX: 508-430-2410
e-mail: specialclo@aol.com
www.special-clothes.com

*Judith Sweeney, President*

This pull-on jumpsuit provides comfort and full coverage without bulk. Wide leg ribbing ends at mid-thigh, with snaps at the crotch. We use fine quality, comfortable cotton knit. 100% cotton knit. Made in USA. Option: long sleeves - add $3.00. Colors: white, navy, teal, light blue, light pink, red, burgundy, royal blue and black. Sm & Med: $36.50/3 for $104.00; L & XL: $39.00/3 for $111.25; and XXL: $42.00/3 for $119.25.

**1809 Bibs**
Special Clothes
PO Box 333
E Harwich, MA 02645
508-430-2410
FAX: 580-430-2410
e-mail: specialclo@aol.com
www.special-clothes.com

*Judith Sweeney, President*

A variety of bib styles are available to protect clothing inconspicuously.

**1810 Body Suits**
Special Clothes
PO Box 333
E Harwich, MA 02645
508-430-2410
FAX: 508-430-2410
e-mail: specialclo@aol.com
www.special-clothes.com

*Judith Sweeney, President*

These are one piece garments that can be used to protect skin under braces, to add warmth and to shield incisions. Prices range from $18.25-22.50.

**1811 Buck and Buck Clothing**
3111 27th Avenue S
Seattle, WA 98144
206-722-4196
800-458-0600
FAX: 206-722-1144
e-mail: julie@buckandbuck.com
www.buckandbuck.com

*Julie & Bill Buck, Co-Owners*

Clothing for the disabled and elderly.
*88 pages Yearly 1981*

**1812 Carolyn's Catalog**
3938 S Tamiami Trail
Sarasota, FL 34207
941-373-9100
800-648-2266
e-mail: sales@carolynscatalog.com
www.carolynscatalog.com

*Carolyn Tojek, President*

Free, mail-order catalog of items for visually impaired people.

**1813    Clothing Solutions**
1525 W Alton Avenue
Santa Ana, CA  92704
714-427-0781
800-336-2660
FAX: 800-683-6510
e-mail: info@clothingsolutions.com
www.clothingsolutions.com

*Jim Lechner, Owner*

The nation's leading designer and manufacturer of assistive clothing for men and women. Free 56 page catalog available by calling 800-500-0260. 100% guarantee on all products.

**1814    Cotton Stockings**
Buck & Buck
3111 27th Avenue S
Seattle, WA  98144
206-722-4196
800-458-0600
FAX: 800-317-2182
e-mail: info@buckandbuck.com
www.buckandbuck.com

*Julie Buck, Owner*

Come in regular and snug-fit, cover leg to mid-thigh and work well for swollen legs.

**1815    Easy Dressing Fashions: JC Penney**
6501 Legacy Drive
Plano, TX  75024
972-431-8676
FAX: 972-431-9103

*Natalie Torre, Marketing Manager*

This is an entire collection of women's and men's fashions that are designed for easy wear, easy care and complete comfort. Plus, a selection of women's apparel with velcro brand wavelock fasteners.

**1816    Exquisite Egronomic Protective Wear**
Plum Enterprises
PO Box 85
Valley Forge, PA  19481
610-783-7377
FAX: 610-783-7577
e-mail: lynn@plument.com
www.plument.com

*Janice Carrington, President*

Egronomic Protective Wear; ProtectaCap custom-fitting head-gear has earned an unparalleled reputation for quality, safety, and comfort. ProtectaCap+Plus technologically-advanced protective headgear closes the gap between hard and soft helmets. Comes with optional ProtectaChin Guard and new sporty design. Protecthip protective undergarment is the intelligent, innovative solution to the problem of hip injuries for both men and women. Ladies' styles are covered with attractive stretch lace.

**1817    Fashion Ease**
1541 60th Street
Brooklyn, NY  11219
718-853-6376
800-221-8929
FAX: 718-436-2067
e-mail: fashionease.com@aol
www.fashionease.com

*Stacey Samuels, Customer Service Agent*
*Abraham Klein, Owner*

Adaptive apparel and footwear for people who require ease in dressing. Free catalogue.

*64 pages Yearly*

**1818    Forde's Functional Fashions**
8020 East Drive
Suite #137
North Bay Village, FL  33141
305-754-4457
800-531-7705
FAX: 305-757-5447
e-mail: fashions@fordes.com
www.fordes.com

*Patricia Forde MA RN CEAC, President*

A fashion forward line of easy to wear clothing and accessories for men, women and children. Items include, sportswear, outerwear, ponchos, robes, sleepwear, dresses, wheelchair bags, walker bags and more. Hard to find specialty items for many special needs. Designs for people who use wheelchairs. Velcro closures if buttons are a problem. Fun clothing protectors too. Choose from our terrific assortment of fabrics and colors to suit all your fashion needs in simply functional style.

**1819    Headliner**
Designs for Comfort
4310 Highborne Drive NE
Marietta, GA  30066
770-565-8246
800-443-9226
FAX: 877-350-0501
e-mail: headliner@mindspring.com

*Curt Maurer, President*

A patented cap and hairpiece combination, the Headliner is both a quick, stylish coverup and an upbeat wig alternative for women experiencing hair care problems or hair loss. Ideal for social gatherings and outdoor activities as well as for sleeping and hospital stays. *$ 25.00*

**1820    Knee Socks**
Buck & Buck
3111 27th Avenue S
Seattle, WA  98144
206-722-4196
800-458-0600
FAX: 800-317-2182
e-mail: info@buckandbuck.com
www.buckandbuck.com

*Julie Buck, Owner*

Comes in regular and large size. *$3.50*

**1821    Laurel Designs Catalog**
Laurel Designs
1805 Mar W Street
Apt A
Belvedere Tiburon, CA  94920
415-435-1891
FAX: 415-435-1451
e-mail: laureld@ncal.verio.com

*Janet Sawyer, Owner*
*Lynn Montoya, Owner*

Clothing for wheelchair users including rain wear, panchos and fleece capes. Other items include quality carrying bags for wheelchairs, walkers, crutches, accessories, and cookbooks of four ingredients only recipes. Home remodeling video 'Building & Remodeling for Accessibility', reacher and large print dictionary.
*8 pages BiAnnual*

**1822    M&M Health Care Apparel Company**
Fashion Collection
1541 60th Street
Brooklyn, NY  11219
718-871-8188
800-221-8929
FAX: 718-436-2067
e-mail: fashionease@aol.com

*Stacey Samuels, Customer Service Agent*
*Abraham Klein, Owner*

Specialized clothing for disabled people.

## 1823 No-Run Nylon Stockings
Buck & Buck
3111 27th Avenue S
Seattle, WA 98144
206-722-4196
800-458-0600
FAX: 800-317-2182
e-mail: info@buckandbuck.com
www.buckandbuck.com

*Julie Buck, Owner*

A full-length, heavy-weight stocking. *$2.25*

## 1824 Professional Fit Clothing
831 N Lake Street
Suite 1
Burbank, CA 91502
818-563-1975
800-422-2348
FAX: 818-563-1834
e-mail: kurt@professionalfit.com
www.professionalfit.com

*Tom Pirruccello, President*
*Kurt Rieback, Owner*

Professional fit clothing caters to homes that care for people with developmental disabilities and individuals who are physically challenged. Our clothing is fashionable, affordable and can be adapted to each person's special needs. There is a free catalog.
*20 pages*

## 1825 Quilted Waterproof Bib
Buck & Buck
3111 27th Avenue S
Seattle, WA 98144
206-722-4196
800-458-0600
FAX: 800-317-2182
e-mail: info@buckandbuck.com
www.buckandbuck.com

*Julie Buck, Owner*

Made with a nylon backing, these attractive bibs will not soak through like most others, protecting clothing from stains. *$15.00*

## 1826 Rolli Moden Catalog
12225 World Trade Drive
Suite T
San Diego, CA 92128
858-676-1825
800-707-2395
FAX: 858-676-0820
e-mail: rm@rolli-moden.com
www.rolli-moden.com

*Karen Turley, General Manager*
*Douglas Buddenhagen, President*

A line of fashionable clothing and accessories for adult wheelchair users available.
*16-24 pages Quarterly*

## 1827 Special Clothes Adult Catalogue
Special Clothes
PO Box 333
E Harwich, MA 02645
508-430-2410
FAX: 508-430-2410
e-mail: specialclo@aol.com
www.special-clothes.com

*Judith Sweeney, President*

Produces a catalogue of adaptive clothing for adults with disabilities. Offers include undergarments, casual bottoms, jumpsuits, sleepwear, swimwear, footwear and bibs. Prices are comparable to deparment store prices. The catalogue is free.

*1-14 pages*

## 1828 Special Clothes for Special Children
Special Clothes
PO Box 333
E Harwich, MA 02645
508-430-2410
FAX: 508-430-2410
e-mail: specialclo@aol.com
www.special-clothes.com

*Judith Sweeney, President*

Offers a variety of clothes for disabled children ranging from casual unisex clothes to undergarments. Clothing offers velcro closures, adjustable waistbands, drop-front briefs, wheelchair ponchos and more.

## 1829 Specialty Care Shoppe
16126 E 161st Street S
Bixby, OK 74008
918-366-1208
FAX: 918-366-9445
e-mail: deb@specialtycareshoppe.com
www.specialtycareshoppe.com

*Deb Marshall, Owner*

Catalog of attractive, affordable clothing and accessories for adults with special needs. Includes items for edema, incontinence, alzheimers, limited mobility, and hand impairment.

## 1830 Super Stretch Socks
Buck & Buck
3111 27th Avenue S
Seattle, WA 98144
206-722-4196
800-458-0600
FAX: 800-317-2182
e-mail: info@buckandbuck.com
www.buckandbuck.com

*Julie Buck, Owner*

This sock has been improved to stretch laterally throughout the foot area as well as at the top. *$3.75*

## 1831 Swimwear
Special Clothes
PO Box 333
E Harwich, MA 02645
508-430-2410
FAX: 508-430-2410
e-mail: specialclo@aol.com
www.special-clothes.com

*Judith Sweeney, President*

Cotton lycra swimsuits are available in boys and girls styles from size toddler-teen. One piece, designed to completely cover a diaper.

## 1832 Trisha's of Acton
PO Box 599
Acton, MA 01720
978-263-9318
877-955-5551
FAX: 978-263-4555
e-mail: trishas@tiac.net
www.trishasofacton.com

*K Julie McCarthy, President*

Clothing and accessories that provide dignity, freedom of movement and independence for the physically challenged.

## 1833 Wishing Wells Clothing Collection
11684 Ventura Boulevard
Suite 965
Studio City, CA 91604
818-840-6919
FAX: 818-760-3878
e-mail: FABC@dawnwells.com
www.dawnwells.com

*Dawn Wells, Owner*
*Lorraine Parker, General Manager*

Features designs full of back overlap construction and all velcro closures clothing.

## Robes & Sleepwear

**1834 Adult Snap Front Sleeper**
Special Clothes
PO Box 333
E Harwich, MA 02645

508-430-2410
FAX: 508-430-2410
e-mail: specialclo@aol.com
www.special-clothes.com

*Judith Sweeney, President*

This soft, comfortable one piece garment is designed for easy dressing and full access. The top fastens down the front with snaps. The bottom section folds up from the back, and snaps to the waist. 100% cotton knit. Made in USA. Option, short sleeves - add $1.00. Colors: white, navy, teal, light blue, light pink, red, burgudy, royal blue and black. Sm & Med: $36.50/ 3 for $104.00; L & XL: $39.00/ 3 for $111.25; XXL: $42.00/3 for $119.75.

**1835 Chamois Shower Robe**
Buck & Buck
3111 27th Avenue S
Seattle, WA 98144

206-722-4196
800-458-0600
FAX: 800-317-2182
e-mail: info@buckandbuck.com
www.buckandbuck.com

*Julie Buck, Owner*

Totally covers a man or woman being wheeled to and from the shower or bath. Having test washed several fabrics, the chamois beat terry cloth for comfort, durability and faster drying time in the laundry. *$34.00*

**1836 Creative Designs**
Barbara Arnold
3704 Carlisle Court
Modesto, CA 95356

209-523-3166
800-335-4852
FAX: 209-523-5893
e-mail: robes4you@aol.com
www.robes4you.com

*Barbara Arnold, Owner*

Designer of the original Change-A-Robe and the new Handi-Robe, which allows the wearer to put it on without having to stand up. Robes are designed especially for physically challenged, disabled individuals, and wheelchair users.

**1837 Flannel Pajamas**
Buck & Buck
3111 27th Avenue S
Seattle, WA 98144

206-722-4196
800-458-0600
FAX: 800-317-2182
e-mail: info@buckandbuck.com
www.buckandbuck.com

*Julie Buck, Owner*
*$18.00*

**1838 Fleece Robe**
Buck & Buck
3111 27th Avenue S
Seattle, WA 98144

206-722-4196
800-458-0600
FAX: 800-317-2182
e-mail: info@buckandbuck.com
www.buckandbuck.com

*Julie Buck, Owner*

All with full-length, snap-front openings, patch pockets, short and long. Short: $39.00.

**1839 His & Hers**
Wishing Wells Collection
11684 Ventura Boulevard
Suite 965
Studio City, CA 91604

818-840-6919
FAX: 818-760-3878
e-mail: FABC@dawnwells.com
www.dawnwells.com

*Dawn Wells, Owner*

This sleep shirt is designed for him or her.

**1840 Nightshirts**
Buck & Buck
3111 27th Avenue S
Seattle, WA 98144

206-722-4196
800-458-0600
FAX: 800-317-2182
e-mail: info@buckandbuck.com
www.buckandbuck.com

*Julie Buck, Owner*

Come in flannel or cotton patterns and prints in sizes S-XL, for men. *$16.00*

**1841 Open Back Nightshirts**
Buck & Buck
3111 27th Avenue S
Seattle, WA 98144

206-722-4196
800-458-0600
FAX: 800-317-2182
e-mail: info@buckandbuck.com
www.buckandbuck.com

*Julie Buck, Owner*

Come in cotton or flannel (sizes S-XL). *$18.00*

**1842 Terrycloth Robes**
Buck & Buck
3111 27th Avenue S
Seattle, WA 98144

206-722-4196
800-458-0600
FAX: 800-317-2182
e-mail: info@buckandbuck.com
www.buckandbuck.com

*Julie Buck, Owner*

Two pockets, sash belts, assorted colors. *$36.00*

## Shirts & Tops

**1843 Adult Pull-On Feeding Bib**
Special Clothes
PO Box 333
E Harwich, MA 02645

508-430-2410
FAX: 508-430-2410
e-mail: specialclo@aol.com
www.special-clothes.com

*Judith Sweeney, President*

This basic bib does a great job of protecting clothing from messy food and drink spills. It is constructed of sturdy, rib knit neckband which slips on comfortably. The front pocket catches food particles and is fastened at both sides with velcro for easy cleaning. 100% nylon with neckband of 100% cotton rib. Made in USA. Colors: white or light blue. One size: 17 inches wide, & 23 inches from shoulder to bottom. *$15.00*

**1844 Avoid Eye Strain, Feel it T-Shirt**
Sense-Sations
919 Walnut Street
Philadelphia, PA 19107

215-627-0600
FAX: 215-922-0692

*Patricia Johnson, Chief Executive Officer*

This slogan is printed in raised writing boldly across the front of our T-shirt. *$5.95*

**1845 Basic Rear Closure Sweat Top**
Buck & Buck
3111 27th Avenue S
Seattle, WA 98144
206-722-4196
800-458-0600
FAX: 800-317-2182
e-mail: info@buckandbuck.com
www.buckandbuck.com

*Julie Buck, Owner*

Top opens completely down the back for ease of dressing with velcro tab closures. *$20.50*

**1846 Cotton Full-Back Vest**
Buck & Buck
3111 27th Avenue S
Seattle, WA 98144
206-722-4196
800-458-0600
FAX: 800-317-2182
e-mail: info@buckandbuck.com
www.buckandbuck.com

*Julie Buck, Owner*

Wide shoulder straps that don't slide off shoulders. *$4.50*

**1847 Dutch Neck T-Shirt**
Buck & Buck
3111 27th Avenue S
Seattle, WA 98144
206-722-4196
800-458-0600
FAX: 800-317-2182
e-mail: info@buckandbuck.com
www.buckandbuck.com

*Julie Buck, Owner*

Stretchy neck makes it easy to get over the head. *$ 5.50*

**1848 Open Back T-Shirts**
Buck & Buck
3111 27th Avenue S
Seattle, WA 98144
206-722-4196
800-458-0600
FAX: 800-317-2182
e-mail: info@buckandbuck.com
www.buckandbuck.com

*Julie Buck, Owner*

Velcro tabs down the back. *$8.00*

**1849 Printed Rear Closure Sweat Top**
Buck & Buck
3111 27th Avenue S
Seattle, WA 98144
206-722-4196
800-458-0600
FAX: 800-317-2182
e-mail: info@buckandbuck.com
www.buckandbuck.com

*Julie Buck, Owner*

Comes in assorted colors, plain or with animal motifs. *$33.00*

**1850 Rear Closure Shirts**
Buck & Buck
3111 27th Avenue S
Seattle, WA 98144
206-722-4196
800-458-0600
FAX: 800-317-2182
e-mail: info@buckandbuck.com
www.buckandbuck.com

*Julie Buck, Owner*

Velcro tabs down the back on T-shirts and dress shirts. *$24.00*

**1851 Rear Closure T-Shirt**
Buck & Buck
3111 27th Avenue S
Seattle, WA 98144
206-722-4196
800-458-0600
FAX: 800-317-2182
e-mail: info@buckandbuck.com
www.buckandbuck.com

*Julie Buck, Owner*

Closes down the back with velcro tabs. *$8.50*

**1852 Serape**
Laurel Designs
1805 Mar West Street
Apt A
Belvedere Tiburon, CA 94920
FAX: 415-435-1451
e-mail: laureld@ncal.verio.com

*Janet Sawyer, Co-Owner*
*Lynn Montoyo, Co-Owner*

This unique sleeveless thermal vest is designed for active wheelchair persons. Multi-colored, one size fits all. *$30.00*

**1853 T Shirt is Done in Braille: Read Gently**
Sense-Sations
919 Walnut Street
Philadelphia, PA 19107
215-627-0600
FAX: 215-922-0692

*Patricia Johnson, Chief Executive Officer*

This slogan is printed in raised writing and braille dots. *$5.95*

---

# Slacks & Pants

**1854 Comanche Pants**
Wheelies Manufacturing
33 NE Main Street
PO Box 97496
Winston, OR 97496
541-679-2318
FAX: 541-673-8719

*Alice King, Store Manager*
*Leslie Bozovich, Customer Service*

An innovative answer to dressing a person who cannot stand. These pants are sculptured to provide total coverage. A new freedom in dressing; easy for attendant or for self-dressing. They can be put on a seated person right in the chair with no lifting or standing. *$35.00*

**1855 Jumpsuits**
Special Clothes
PO Box 333
E Harwich, MA 02645
508-430-2410
FAX: 508-430-2410
e-mail: specialclo@aol.com
www.special-clothes.com

*Judith Sweeney, President*

Several styles of one-piece garments are available for dressing ease. Front opening styles are designed for easy access. Prices range from $32.20–$44.00.

**1856 Knit Pants**
Special Clothes
PO Box 333
E Harwich, MA 02645
508-430-2410
FAX: 508-430-2410
TTY:508-430-2410
e-mail: specialclo@aol.com
www.special-clothes.com

*Judith Sweeney, President*

Offers the best in comfort and convenience. Designed with a longer crotch and wider seat for a great fit. The elasticized waistband contains a hidden drawstring for size adjustments, and pockets are placed low for easy access while sitting. Order a full snap crotch (Option #1), for full access. Available in soft, 100% cotton knit. Made in USA. Colors: Light blue, teal, light pink, burgundy, navy and black. Sm & Med: $41.00; L & XL $45.00; XXL $48.00. Add full snap crotch.

## 1857 Pants & Slacks
Special Clothes
PO Box 333
E Harwich, MA  02645

508-430-2410
FAX: 508-430-2410
e-mail: specialclo@aol.com
www.special-clothes.com

*Judith Sweeney, President*

A variety of pant and skirt styles is available in sizes 2 toddler - 18 teen. These include straight leg and baggy jeans, drop front pleated dress pants, knit pants, shorts and skirted leggings. Prices range from $16.50-$44.00.

## 1858 Side Velcro Slacks
Buck & Buck
3111 27th Avenue S
Seattle, WA  98144

206-722-4196
800-458-0600
FAX: 800-317-2182
e-mail: info@buckandbuck.com
www.buckandbuck.com

*Julie Buck, Owner*

Slacks open down both sides from waist to hip with velcro tab closures at sides. *$25.00*

## 1859 Side-Zip Sweat Pants
Buck & Buck
3111 27th Avenue S
Seattle, WA  98144

206-722-4196
800-458-0600
FAX: 800-317-2182
e-mail: info@buckandbuck.com
www.buckandbuck.com

*Julie Buck, Owner*

Out-seam zippers un-zip 3/4 of the way down the sides to enable dressing a resident with severe leg contractures. *$32.00*

## 1860 Trunks
Buck & Buck
3111 27th Avenue S
Seattle, WA  98144

206-722-4196
800-458-0600
FAX: 800-317-2182
e-mail: info@buckandbuck.com
www.buckandbuck.com

*Julie Buck, Owner*

Come in cotton or nylon, flare leg, full cut. *$4.00*

# Undergarments

## 1861 Adult Absorbent Briefs
Special Clothes
PO Box 333
E Harwich, MA  02645

508-430-2410
FAX: 508-430-2410
e-mail: specialclo@aol.com
www.special-clothes.com

*Judith Sweeney, President*

Soft, comfortable, 100% cotton knit brief is seven layers thick at the crotch. Sides of the brief are a non-bulky single layer. The waistband elastic is enclosed in a soft cotton knit casing and does not touch the skin. Comfortable cotton rib knit bands circle the leg. This brief will not replace a diaper, but provides absorbency for light incontinence.

## 1862 Adult Lap Shoulder Bodysuit
Special Clothes
PO Box 333
E Harwich, MA  02645

508-430-2410
FAX: 508-430-2410
TTY:508-430-2410
e-mail: specialclo@aol.com
www.special-clothes.com

Bodysuit styles fasten at the crotch with sturdy snaps to stay neatly tucked. All are made of soft, absorbent 100% cotton knit for maximum comfort. They are cut wide at the hip and seat for full coverage, and will accomodate a diaper if necessary. Soft knit rib circles the neck and leg. This cool tank style slips on easily. Deep armholes are banded with rib knit. all styles: Small/Medium $33.00/3 for $94.00; Large/X Large $38.00/3 for $108.00; XX Large $41.00/3 for $116.00. A choice of 9 colors.

## 1863 Adult Sleeveless Bodysuit
Special Clothes
PO Box 333
E Harwich, MA  02645

508-430-2410
FAX: 508-430-2410
e-mail: specialclo@aol.com
www.special-clothes.com

*Judith Sweeney, President*

Bodysuit styles fasten at the crotch with sturdy snaps to stay neatly tucked. All are made of soft, absorbent 100% cotton knit for maximum comfort. They are cut wide at the hip and seat for full coverage, and will accomodate a diaper if necessary. Soft knit rib circles the neck and leg. This cool tank style slips on easily. Deep armholes are banded with rib knit. All styles: Small/Medium $33.00/3 for $94.00; Large/X-Large $38.00/3 for $108.00; XX Large $41.00/3 for $116.00. A choice of 9 colors.

## 1864 Adult Swim Diaper
Special Clothes
PO Box 333
E Harwich, MA  02645

508-430-2410
FAX: 508-430-2410
e-mail: specialclo@aol.com
www.special-clothes.com

*Judith Sweeney, President*

This pant is made of soft, silent, light-weight, impermeable fabric- waterproof and secure. It is a containment brief, designed to be used in the pool in place of cloth or disposable diapers, which can become waterlogged or disintegrate in the water. Waist and legbands should be snug for proper fit, so please consult sizing chart before ordering. Darlex with lining of 100% cotton knit. Lycra waist and legbands. Made in USA.

## 1865 Adult Tee Shoulder Bodysuit
Special Clothes
PO Box 333
E Harwich, MA  02645

508-430-2410
FAX: 508-430-2410
TTY:508-430-2410
e-mail: specialclo@aol.com
www.special-clothes.com

Styles fasten at the crotch with sturdy snaps to stay neatly tucked. All are made of soft, absorbent 100% cotton knit for maximum comfort. They are cut wide at the hip and seat for full coverage, and will accommodate a diaper if necessary. Soft knit rib circles the neck and leg. This bodysuit looks like a regular tee shirt, but snaps at the crotch for a neat appearance. Small/Medium $33.00/3 for $94.00; Large/X Large $38.00/3 fpr $108.00; XX Large $41.00/3 for $116.00. Choice of 9 colors.

**1866 Adult Waterproof Overpant**
Special Clothes
PO Box 333
E Harwich, MA 02645
508-430-2410
FAX: 508-430-2410
e-mail: specialclo@aol.com
www.special-clothes.com

*Judith Sweeney, President*

Overpants are made of a soft, silent, lightweight fabric which is waterproof and very secure. It is designed to be used over our Adult Absorbent Brief, or cloth diapers. It is completely latex-free and is an excellent non-allergenic substitute for rubber or vinyl pants. Waist and legbands should be snug to minimize leakage, so please consult the sizing chart before ordering. Darlex with lining of 100% cotton. Lycra waist and legbands. Made in USA.

**1867 Adult Wet Wrap Swim Vest**
Special Clothes
PO Box 333
E Harwich, MA 02645
508-430-2410
FAX: 508-430-2410
e-mail: specialclo@aol.com
www.special-clothes.com

*Judith Sweeney, President*

This vest is made of neoprene - the same material used in wet suits - and it effectively insulates the torso to retain body heat. Muscles relax, enhancing the quality of recreational swimming or water therapy. The wrap design allows full freedom of movement. Made of Neoprene in the USA. Note: Vest provides warmth ony. It is not a flotation device. Wet wrap sizes: Adult small, adult medium and adult large.

**1868 Briefs**
Special Clothes
PO Box 333
E Harwich, MA 02645
508-430-2410
FAX: 508-430-2410
e-mail: specialclo@aol.com
www.special-clothes.com

*Judith Sweeney, President*

A variety of unique brief styles available for easy access and practicality.

**1869 Cloth Diapers**
Angel Fluff Diaper Company
PO Box 1131
Lewisburg, TN 37091
931-359-9604
800-996-2644
FAX: 931-359-8420
e-mail: custserv@angelfluff.com
www.angelfluff.com

Top quality cloth diapers.

**1870 Nylon Snip Slip**
Buck & Buck
3111 27th Avenue S
Seattle, WA 98144
206-722-4196
800-458-0600
FAX: 800-317-2182
e-mail: info@buckandbuck.com
www.buckandbuck.com

*Julie Buck, Owner*

Just snip with scissors at the appropriate hem length and it's ready to wear. *$12.00*

**1871 Nylon Stretch Bra**
Buck & Buck
3111 27th Avenue S
Seattle, WA 98144
206-722-4196
800-458-0600
FAX: 800-317-2182
e-mail: info@buckandbuck.com
www.buckandbuck.com

*Julie Buck, Owner*

Front hook closure with built-up shoulder straps. *$ 16.00*

**1872 Panties**
Buck & Buck
3111 27th Avenue S
Seattle, WA 98144
206-722-4196
800-458-0600
FAX: 800-317-2182
e-mail: info@buckandbuck.com
www.buckandbuck.com

*Julie Buck, Owner*

Come in nylon or cotton, band leg for comfort. *$4.00*

**1873 Safe and Dry-Feel and Sure-Toddler Dry**
Hygienics Direct Company
3968 194th Trail
Golden Beach, FL 33160
305-937-0824
888-463-7337
e-mail: mbrier1930@aol.com
www.hygenics.com

*Michael Brier, President*

A variety of stress incontinence disposable liners which absorb 8-10 oz. of fluid packaged in 20 and 40 counts. Also available are patented knit nylon panties in medium, large and extra large sizes. All products are priced for the mass market.

**1874 Support Plus**
99 West Street
Suite 500
Medfield, MA 02052
508-359-2910
800-229-2910
FAX: 508-359-0139
www.supportplus.com

*Ed Janos, President*

Offers a selection of support undergarments, braces and shoes for the physically challenged and medical professionals.

## Assistive Devices

**1875 Ability Research**
PO Box 1721
Minnetonka, MN 55343          952-939-0121
                              FAX: 952-890-8393
                    e-mail: ability@skypoint.com
                        www.abilityresearch.com

*John Severson, President*

Manufacturers and marketers of assistive technology equipment.

**1876 Adaptivation**
2225 W 50th Street
Suite 100
Sioux Falls, SD 57105          605-335-4445
                               800-723-2783
                         FAX: 605-335-4446
                  e-mail: info@adaptivation.com
                         www.adaptivation.com

*Amy Koch, Marketing Director*
*Jonathan Eckrich, President*

Manufacturers of environmental control switches, auditory paging systems, a mouse emulator program, and communication devices.

**1877 Adaptive Device Locator System**
Academic Software
3504 Tates Creek Road
Lexington, KY 40517          859-552-1020
                       FAX: 253-799-4012
                  e-mail: asistaff@acsw.com
                         www.acsw.com

*Warren E Lacefield PhD, President*
*Penelope Ellis, Marketing Director*
*Sylvia P Lacefield, Graphic Artist*

Employs a unique, goal-oriented approach to aid individuals in identifying adaptive devices with potential to support various physical limitations. Devices are categorized in seven databases: Existence, Travel, In-situ Motion, Environmental Adaptation, Communication, and Sports & recreation. ADLS provides its users with device descriptions, pictures and lists of sources for locating products and product information. *$200.00*

**1878 Analog Switch Pad**
Academic Software
331 W 2nd Street
Lexington, KY 40507          859-233-2332
                             800-842-2357
                        FAX: 859-231-0725

*Warren E Lacefield PhD, President*
*Penelope Ellis, Marketing Director*

A touch-activated, force-adjustable, low-voltage DC, electronic switch designed to control battery-operated toys, environmental controls, and computer access interfaces. This device features a large activation area that is soft and compliant to the touch. Force sensitivity is adjusted by a small dial from approximately 1 ounce to 32 ounces activation pressure, applied over an area ranging from the size of a fingertip to the size of the entire switch surface. *$149.00*

**1879 Arkenstone: The Benetech Initiative**
480 S California Avenue
Palo Alto, CA 94306          650-475-5440
                        FAX: 650-475-1067
              e-mail: wynn@freedomscientific.com
                      www.freedomscentific.com

*Lee Hamilton, President/CEO*
*Roberta G Brosnaha, General Manager/VP*

Offers various models of ready-to-read personal computers for the disabled.

**1880 Augmentative Communication Systems (AAC)**
Z YG O Industries
PO Box 1008
Portland, OR 97207          503-598-7531
                            800-234-6006
                       FAX: 503-684-6011
              e-mail: zygo@zygo-usa.com
                      www.zygo-usa.com

*Lawrence Weiss, President*

Full range of AAC systems and assistive technology including computer-based systems and computer access programs and devices.

**1881 Away We Ride IntelliKeys Overlay**
Soft Touch
4300 Stine Road
Suite 401
Bakersfield, CA 93313          661-396-8676
                               877-763-8868
                          FAX: 661-396-8760
                e-mail: softtouch@funsoftware.com
                        www.funsoftware.com

*Roxanne Butterfield*
*Joyce Meyer, President*

Four full color preprinted overlays to use with Away We Ride. Just put them on an IntelliKeys keyboard and you are ready to go.

**1882 BIGmack Communication Aid**
AbleNet
2808 Fairview Avenue N
Roseville, MN 55113          651-294-2200
                             800-322-0956
                        FAX: 651-294-2222
            e-mail: customerservice@ablenetinc.com
                       www.ablenetinc.com

*Dave Binziazk, Director*

A single message communication aid, BIGmack has 75 seconds of memory and has a 5 inches in diameter switch surface. *$86.00*

**1883 C2ILMAX**
Image Systems
12975 16th Avenue N
Suite 300
Minneapolis, MN 55441          952-935-1171
                               800-462-4370
                          FAX: 952-935-1386
             e-mail: custserv@imagesystemscorp.com
                      www.imagesystemscorp.com

*Dennis Stollenwerk, General Sales*

LCD or CRT displays designed for applications requiring a larger viewing area and high to ultrahigh resolution.

**1884 Close-Up 6.5**
Norton- Lambert Corporation
PO Box 4085
Santa Barbara, CA 93140          805-964-6767
                            FAX: 805-683-5679
                e-mail: sales@norton-lambert.com
                        www.norton-lambert.com

*Jeannie Vesely, Marketing Coordinator*

Remotely controls PC's via modem. Telecommute from your home or laptop PC to your office PC. Run applications, update spreadsheets, print documents remotely and access networks on remote PCs. Features: fast screen and file transfers, synchronize files, unattended transfers, multi-level security, transaction logs, automated installation. *$199.00*

**1885    Computer Switch Interface**
AbleNet
2808 Fairview Avenue N
Roseville, MN  55113                     651-294-2200
                                         800-322-0956
                              FAX: 651-294-2259
        e-mail: customerservice@ablenetinc.com
                              www.ablenetinc.com

*Cheryl Volkman, Director*
*Peter Lytle, Executive Committee*
Allows single switch access to an Apple computer. *$ 36.00*

**1886    Concepts on the Move Advanced Overlay CD**
Soft Touch
4300 Stine Road
Suite 401
Bakersfield, CA  93313                   661-396-8676
                                         877-763-8868
                              FAX: 661-396-8760
              e-mail: softtouch@softtouch.com
                              www.softtouch.com

*Jo Myer, President*
*Joyce Meyer, President*
Use this overlay CD with Concepts on the Move Advanced Preacademics. Overlays match the concepts and graphics in the program. Includes standard overlays with all the choices and SoftTouch's changeable format overlays. Print and laminate the blank templates. Then print and laminate the picture keys in all three sizes - small, medium and large. Includes Overlay Printer by IntelliTools for easy printing.

**1887    Concepts on the Move Basic Overlay CD**
Soft Touch
4300 Stine Road
Suite 401
Bakersfield, CA  93313                   661-396-8676
                                         877-763-8868
                              FAX: 661-396-8760
          e-mail: softtouch@softtouch.com.com
                              www.softtouch.com

*Roxanne Butterfield, Marketing*
*Joyce Meyer, President*
Use this Overlay CD with Concepts on the Move Basic Preacademics. Overlays match the concepts and graphics in the program. Includes standard overlays with all the choices and SoftTouch's changeable format overlays. Print and laminate the blank templates. Then print and laminate the picture keys in all three sizes - small, medium and large. It is easy and fast to place the images on the blank templates.

**1888    Darci Too**
WesTest Engineering Corporation
810 Shepard Lane
Farmington, UT  84025                    801-451-9191
                              FAX: 801-457-9393
                  e-mail: mary@westest.com
                              www.westest.com

*Mary L Lynds, Manager*
*Robert Lessman, President*
A universal device which allows people with physical disabilities to replace the keyboard and mouse on a personal computer with a device that matches their physical capabilities. DARCI TOO works with almost any personal computer and provides access to all computer functions. *$995.00*

**1889    EZ Touch Panel**
1120 W Avenue J
Lancaster, CA  93534                     661-723-6523
                                         800-869-8521
                              FAX: 661-723-2114
                              www.words-tlus.com

*Jess Dahlan, President*
*Momoko Deran, Chief Executive Director*
*Walt Wolosz, Manager*

Touch screen input is the most direct and intuitive method for picture-based communication for those with the required motor skills. *$399.00*

**1890    Expanded Keyboard Emulator**
Words Plus
1220 W Avenue J
Lancaster, CA  93534                     661-723-6523
                                         800-869-8521
                              FAX: 661-723-2114
                  e-mail: info@words-plus.com
                              www.words-plus.com

*Jeff Dalhen, President*
*Janet Aviles, Customer Service Supervisor*
*Walt Wolosz, Manager*
Provides DUA1 word prediction, abbreviation expansion (macrocapability), five different methods of voice output, keyboard control, RAM-resident and the ability to run in graphics mode and access to commercial software applications.

**1891    Eyegaze Computer System**
LC Technologies
3955 Pender Drive
Suite 120
Fairfax, VA  22030                       703-385-7133
                                         800-393-4293
                              FAX: 703-385-1737
                              www.eyegaze.com

*Nancy Cleveland, Medical Coordinator*
Enables people with physical disabilities to do many things with their eyes that they would otherwise do with their hands.

**1892    Fall Fun IntelliKeys Overlay**
Soft Touch
4300 Stine Road
Suite 401
Bakersfield, CA  93313                   661-396-8676
                                         877-763-8868
                              FAX: 661-396-8760
              e-mail: softtouch@funsoftware.com
                              www.funsoftware.com

*Roxanne Butterfield, Marketing*
*Joyce Meyer, President*
Seven full color preprinted overlays to use with Fall Fun. Just put them on an IntelliKeys keyboard and you are ready to go.

**1893    FingerFoniks**
Words- Plus
1220 W Avenue J
Lancaster, CA  93534                     661-723-6523
                                         800-869-8521
                              FAX: 661-723-2114
                  e-mail: info@words-plus.com
                              www.words-plus.com

*Ginger Woltosz, Vice President*
*Tim Ross, Manager*
*Walt Wolosz, Manager*
One-pound, hand-held, communicator incorporating synthesized and recorded speech. The user makes words and sentences by pressing sound (phoneme) keys on a membrane keyboard. *$995.00*

**1894    Five Green & Speckled Frogs IntelliKeys Overlay**
Soft Touch
4300 Stine Road
Suite 401
Bakersfield, CA  93313                   661-396-8676
                                         877-763-8868
                              FAX: 661-396-8760
              e-mail: softtouch@funsoftware.com
                              www.funsoftware.com

*Roxanne Butterfield, Marketing*
*Joyce Meyer, President*

Seven full color preprinted overlays to use with Five Green and Speckled Frogs. Just put them on an IntelliKeys keyboard and you are ready to go.

**1895 Florida New Concepts Marketing**
Florida New Concepts Marketing
PO Box 261
Port Richey, FL 34673
                        813-842-3231
                        800-456-7097
                    FAX: 813-845-7544
                    e-mail: compulenz@ate.net
                    www.gulfside.com/compulenz

*Alan Lezark, Market Representative*

Compu-Lenz, a combination fresnel magnifier and glass glare filter in an adjustable hood. When placed on the front of a PC monitor it magnifies the character size, reduces glare and enhances contrast. *$204.95*

**1896 GW Micro**
725 Airport North Office Park
Fort Wayne, IN 46825
                        260-489-3671
                    FAX: 260-489-2608
                    e-mail: sales@gwmicro.com
                    www.gwmicro.com

*Dan Weirich, Owner*
*Chris Park, Sales Manager*

Computer hardware and software products for people with disabilities.

**1897 Infogrip: ErgoPOD Model 500**
1794 E Main Street
Ventura, CA 93001
                        805-652-0770
                        800-397-0921
                    FAX: 805-652-0880
                    e-mail: sales@infogrip.com
                    www.infogrip.com

*Liza Jacobs, President*
*Aaron Gaston, Vice President*

ErgoPOD Model 500 provides a workstation solution to computer users who work from a reclining position. Model 500 straddles a bed or recliner and can hold up to 21" monitors anywhere on its surface, and will securely position the monitor at angles up to 60 degrees. The adjustable keyboard mechanism and motorized height adjustment make ergonomic configuration easy — even for the most demanding cases. *$1895.00*

**1898 IntelliKeys IIe**
Intelli Tools
1720 Corporate Circle
Petaluma, CA 94954
                        707-773-2000
                        800-899-6687
                    FAX: 707-773-2001
                    e-mail: info@intellitools.com
                    www.intellitools.com

*Caroline Van Howe, Marketing Director*
*Ed Koenit, Chief Financial Officer*
*Arjan Khalsa, Chief Executive Officer*

Card and cable to create keyboard port on Apple IIe computer to allow use of IntelliKeys alternative keyboard. *$129.95*

**1899 Internal I/O Port Adapter**
AbleNet
2808 Fairview Avenue N
Roseville, MN 55113
                        651-294-2200
                        800-322-0956
                    FAX: 651-294-2259
                    e-mail: customerservice@ablenetinc.com
                    www.ablenetinc.com

*Mary Kay Walch, Executive Director*

A converting cable designed to provide a 9-pin joystick port for Apple II+ and older model computers. *$18.00*

**1900 Jelly Bean Switch**
AbleNet
2808 Fairview Avenue N
Roseville, MN 55113
                        651-294-2200
                        800-322-0956
                    FAX: 612-379-9143
                    e-mail: customerservice@ablenetinc.com
                    www.ablenetinc.com

*Cheryl Volkman, Chairman of the Board*

A momentary touch switch made of shatterproof plastic, small and sensitive to 2-3 ounces of pressure, this switch is provided audible feedback when activated and is a compact version of the Big Red Switch. *$42.00*

**1901 KeyWiz**
Words+
42505 10th Street W
Suite 109
Lancaster, CA 93534
                        800-869-8521
                    FAX: 661-266-8969

*Phil Lawrence, Vice President*
*Rachel Nielsen, Customer Support*

A software and hardware product designed to operate on an IBM compatible PC. The software provides word prediction, abbreviation expansion and access to commercial software applications. *$695.00*

**1902 Keyguards for IntelliKeys**
Intelli Tools
1720 Corporate Circle
Petaluma, CA 94954
                        707-773-2000
                        800-899-6687
                    FAX: 707-773-2001
                    e-mail: info@intellitools.com
                    www.intellitools.com

*Beta Davis, Director Sales Operations*
*Lari Castle, Supervisor*
*Arjan Khalsa, Chief Executive Officer*

Acrylic keyguards for each of IntelliKeys six standard overlays. *$250.00*

**1903 Large Print Keyboard Labels**
Hooleon Corp
PO Box 589
Melrose, NM 88124
                        505-253-4503
                        800-937-1337
                    FAX: 505-253-4299
                    e-mail: sales@hooleon.com
                    www.hooleon.com

*Barry Green, Sales Manager*
*Joan Crozier, President/Sales*

Pressure sensitive labels for computer keyboards.

**1904 LinkPower 50**
Words+
1220 W Avenue J Lancaster
Palmdale, CA 93543
                        661-723-6523
                        800-869-8521
                    FAX: 661-723-2114
                    e-mail: ifo@words-plus.com
                    www.words-plus.org

*Ginger Woltosz, Vice President*
*Tim Ross, Manager*
*Walt Wolosz, Manager*

AC-to-DC switching power converter provides a continuous, independent multi-output, multi-voltage power supply to any augcom device, laptop computer, pointing device, voice synthesizer, cellular phone, or other battery-operated device directly from a wheelchair. *$449.00*

**1905  MessageMate**
Words+
42505 10th Street W
Suite 109
Lancaster, CA  93534

661-723-2114
800-869-8521
FAX: 661-266-8969
e-mail: info@words-plus.com
www.words-plus.com

*Ginger Woltosz, Vice President*
*Tim Ross, Manager*

Lightweight, hand-held communicator providing high-quality analog recording capability using either direct select keyboards or 1 to 2 switch access. Price ranges from $549.00 to $999.00.

**1906  Monkeys Jumping on the Bed IntelliKeys Overlay**
Soft Touch
4300 Stine Road
Suite 401
Bakersfield, CA  93313

661-396-8676
877-763-8868
FAX: 661-396-8760
e-mail: softtouch@funsoftware.com
www.funsoftware.com

*Roxanne Butterfield, Marketing*
*Joyce Meyer, President*

Seven full color preprinted overlays to use with Monkeys Jumping. Just put them on an IntelliKeys keyboard and you are ready to go.

**1907  Morse Code Equalizer**
Words+
42505 10th Street W
Suite 109
Lancaster, CA  93534

661-723-6523
800-869-8521
FAX: 661-723-2114
e-mail: info@words-plus.com
www.words-plus.com

*Ginger Woltosz, Vice President*
*Tim Ross, Manager*
*Walt Wolosz, Manager*

Provides complete word processing and voice output communications with single or dual switch Morse code inputs. Originally designed for a blind user with only eyelid movement. The system can be used by both sighted and visually impaired persons. *$1395.00*

**1908  Mouthsticks**
Sammons Preston Rolyan
4 Sammons Court
Bolingbrook, IL  60440

630-226-1300
800-323-5547
FAX: 630-226-1389
e-mail: spr@abilityone.com
www.sammonsprestonrolyan.com

*Steve Brown, Director*

Wide offering of mouthsticks featuring various functions (BK 5380, 5381, 5383, 5385, 6002, or BK 5370 series).

**1909  Old MacDonald's Farm IntelliKeys Overlay**
Soft Touch
4300 Stine Road
Suite 401
Bakersfield, CA  93313

661-396-8676
877-763-8868
FAX: 661-396-8760
e-mail: softtouch@funsoftware.com
www.funsoftware.com

*Roxanne Butterfield, Marketing*
*Joyce Meyer, President*

Extend your students' learning with more than 45 pre-made overlays that support all of the skills learned at the farm. Use with the IntelliKeys keyboard. Simply print and use. Print an extra set to make off computer activities, too. Note: Requires Overlay Maker or Overlay Printer by IntelliTools.

**1910  Perfect Solutions**
10513 Versailles Boulevard
Wellington, FL  33467

561-790-1070
800-726-7086
FAX: 561-790-0108
e-mail: perfect@gate.net
www.perfectsolutions.com

*Andrew Kramer, President*
*Peter Flanagan, Owner*

A computer for every student and it speaks! Wireless laptop computers starting at $290.00 are ideal for students to carry with them all day. Text-to-speech and web browsing are available. *$290.00*

**1911  Phillip Roy**
PO Box 130
Indian Rocks Beach, FL  33785

727-593-2700
800-255-9085
FAX: 727-595-2685
e-mail: info@philliproy.com
www.philliproy.com

*Ruth Bragman PhD, President*
*Phil Padol, Vice President*
*Phillip Roy, Manager*

Offers multimedia materials appropriate for use with individuals with disabilities. Programs range from preschool through the adult level. Many of the programs are high interest topics/low vocabulary, ideal for transition and employability skills. Materials are also available which focus on social and personal development. Call for a free catalog.

**1912  Rodeo IntelliKeys Overlay**
Soft Touch
4300 Stine Road
Suite 401
Bakersfield, CA  93313

661-396-8676
877-763-8868
FAX: 661-396-8760
e-mail: softtouch@funsoftware.com
www.funsoftware.com

*Roxanne Butterfield, Marketing*
*Joyce Meyer, President*

Four full color preprinted overlays to use with The Rodeo. Just put them on an IntelliKeys keyboard and you are ready to go.

**1913  SS-Access Single Switch Interface for PC's with MS-DOS**
Academic Software
331 W 2nd Street
Lexington, KY  40507

859-233-2332
800-842-2357
FAX: 859-231-0725

*Warren E Lacefield PhD, President*
*Penelope Ellis, Marketing Director*

A general purpose single switch hardware and software interface for DOS and the IBM and compatible PC family. It is designed to be easy to install, simple to use, and compatible with the widest possible range of computers and application software programs. SS-ACCESS! connects to one of the PC serial ports and provides a jack to connect an external switch. The DOS version of the software works by sending a user defined keystroke to the PC keyboard buffer whenever the switch is pressed. *$90.00*

**1914  Simplicity**
Words+
42505 10th Street W
Suite 109
Lancaster, CA  93534                    661-266-8500
                                        800-869-8521
                              FAX: 661-266-8969

*Phil Lawrence, VP*
*Rachel Nielsen, Customer Support*

Swing-down mount for portable computers and other devices is
made from high-quality aircraft aluminum. Simplicity contains
very few moving parts and installs in minutes, providing a positive, secure support for computer/device in both the stored and
overlap position. *$595.00*

**1915  Slim Armstrong Mounting System**
AbleNet
2808 Fairview Avenue N
Roseville, MN  55113                    651-294-2200
                                        800-322-0956
                              FAX: 651-294-2259
            e-mail: customerservice@ablenetinc.com
                        www.ablenetinc.com
Slim Armstrong is a mounting system strong enough to hold up
to five pounds in any position. Mix and match parts to create the
system length you desire. *$188.00*

**1916  Smart Modem**
H AR C Mercantile
1111 West Center
Portage, MI  49024                      269-324-1615
                                        800-445-9968
                              FAX: 269-324-2387
            e-mail: home@harcmercantile.com
                        www.harcmercantile.com

*Ronald Slager, President*

Smart modem makes your computer accessible to a TTY.
*$349.00*

**1917  SoftTouch Favorites IntelliKeys Overlay**
Soft Touch
4300 Stine Road
Suite 401
Bakersfield, CA  93313                  661-396-8676
                                        877-763-8868
                              FAX: 661-396-8760
            e-mail: softtouch@softtouch.com
                        www.softtouch.com

*Roxanne Butterfield, Marketing*
*Joyce Meyer, President*

Four full color preprinted overlays to use with SoftTouch Favorites. Just put them on an IntelliKeys keyboard and you are ready
to go.

**1918  Songs I Sing at Preschool IntelliKeys Over lay**
Soft Touch
4300 Stine Road
Suite 401
Bakersfield, CA  93313                  661-396-8676
                                        877-763-8868
                              FAX: 661-396-8760
            e-mail: support@softtouch.com
                        www.softtouch.com

*Joyce Meyer, Director*
*Roxanne Butterfield, Marketing*

Pre-made overlays for use with Songs I Sing at Preschool. Simply print and use with an IntelliKeys keyboard. Print an extra set
to make off computer activities, too.

**1919  String Switch**
AbleNet
2808 Fairview Avenue N
Roseville, MN  55113                    651-294-2200
                                        800-322-0956
                              FAX: 651-294-2259
            e-mail: customerservice@ablenetinc.com
                        www.ablenetinc.com
Ideal for students who have limited finger and hand mobility, as
well as those with minimal strength. *$28.00*

**1920  Switch Basics IntelliKeys Overlay**
Soft Touch
4300 Stine Road
Suite 401
Bakersfield, CA  93313                  661-396-8676
                                        877-763-8868
                              FAX: 661-396-8760
            e-mail: softtouch@softtouch.com
                        www.softtouch.com

*Joyce Meyer, President*
*Roxanne Butterfield, Marketing*

Four preprinted overlays to use with Switch Basics. Just put
them on an IntelliKeys keyboard and you're ready to go.

**1921  Symbi-Key Computer Switch Interface**
AbleNet
1081 10th Avenue SE
Minneapolis, MN  55414
                                        800-322-0956
                              FAX: 651-294-2254
            e-mail: hresources@ablenetinc.com
                        www.ablenetinc.com

*Cheryl Volkam, President/CEO*

The Symbi-Key can be programmed to simulate any key stroke
or a series of keystrokes ( up to 5 per key) for single switch access to software programs whether or not it was designed for
switch access. Works well in DOS and all versions of Windows
providing access to any IBM program. *$299.00*

**1922  Teach Me Phonemics Blends Overlay CD**
Soft Touch
4300 Stine Road
Suite 401
Bakersfield, CA  93313                  661-396-8676
                                        877-763-8868
                              FAX: 661-396-8760
            e-mail: softtouch@softtouch.com
                        www.softtouch.com

*Roxanne Butterfield, Marketing*
*Joyce Meyer, President*

Teach Me Phonemics Blends Overlay CD contains over 40
IntelliKeys overlays for use with Teach Me Phonemics - Blends
program. Choose either 4-item or 9-item layout to match the presentation you use in the program. Print extra copies of the overlays for off computer activites, too.

**1923  Teach Me Phonemics Medial Overlay CD**
Soft Touch Incorporated
4300 Stine Road
Suite 401
Bakersfield, CA  93313                  661-396-8676
                                        877-763-8868
                              FAX: 661-396-8676
            e-mail: softtouch@funsoftware.com
                        www.softtouch.com

*Joyce Meyer, President*
*Roxanne Butterfield, Marketing*

Teach Me Phonemics Medial Overlay CD contains over 40
IntelliKeys overlays for use with Teach Me Phonemics - Medial
program. Choose either 4-item or 9-item layout to match the presentation you use in the program. Print extra copies of the overlays for off computer activites, too.

**1924 Teach Me Phonemics Overlay Series Bundle**
Soft Touch
4300 Stine Road
Suite 401
Bakersfield, CA 93313              661-396-8676
                                    877-763-8868
                              FAX: 661-396-8760
                e-mail: softtouch@funsoftware.com
                              www.softtouch.com

*Roxanne Butterfield, Marketing*
*Joyce Meyer, President*

Teach Me Phonemics Overlay Series Bundle includes one copy of each Teach Me Phonemics Overlay CD - Initial, Medial, Final and - four CD's in all.

**1925 Teach Me to Talk Overlay CD**
Soft Touch
4300 Stine Road
Suite 401
Bakersfield, CA 93313              661-396-8676
                                    877-763-8868
                              FAX: 661-396-8760
                e-mail: softtouch@softtouch.com
                              www.softtouch.com

*Roxanne Butterfield, Marketing*
*Joyce Meyer, President*

For older version of Teach Me to Talk. Mac only version with red label and PC only version with yellow label. More than 48 pre-made overlays that match the activities on Teach Me to Talk. Simply print and use with an IntelliKeys keyboard. Print an extra set to make off computer activities, too.

**1926 Teach Me to Talk: USB-Overlay CD**
Soft Touch
4300 Stine Road
Suite 401
Bakersfield, CA 93313              661-396-8676
                              FAX: 661-396-8676
                e-mail: softtouch@softtouch.com
                              www.softtouch.com

*Joyce Meyer, President*
*Roxanne Butterfiled, Marketing*

Revised version of Teach Me to Talk Overlays for the newest version that is USB IntelliKeys compatible. This CD contains more than 48 overlays that match the activities and updated graphics of Teach Me to Talk. Includes Overlay Printer by IntelliTools for easy printing.

**1927 Teen Tunes Plus IntelliKeys Overlay**
Soft Touch
4300 Stine Road
Suite 401
Bakersfield, CA 93313              661-396-8676
                                    877-763-8868
                              FAX: 661-396-8760
                e-mail: softtouch@softtouch.com
                              www.softtouch.com

*Roxanne Butterfield, Marketing*
*Joyce Meyer, President*

Seven full color, preprinted overlays to use with Teen Tunes Plus. Just put them on an IntelliKeys keyboard and you're ready to go.

**1928 TouchCorders Holder**
Soft Touch
4300 Stine Road
Suite 401
Bakersfield, CA 93313              661-396-8676
                                    877-763-8868
                              FAX: 661-396-8760
                e-mail: support@softtouch.com
                              www.softtouch.com

*Roxanne Butterfield, Marketing*
*Joyce Meyer, President*

The TouchCorders Holder enables you to position up to 4 TouchCorders for sequencing, spelling, communication, story telling and more. The TouchCorders Holder holds TouchCorders snugly and keeps them in place even when you are offering multiple choices to students in a group setting. The sturdy triangular shape presents TouchCorders at a 30-degree angle for better visual and physical access.

**1929 Turtle Teasers IntelliKeys Overlay**
Soft Touch
4300 Stine Road
Suite 401
Bakersfield, CA 93313              661-396-8676
                                    877-763-8868
                              FAX: 661-396-8760
                e-mail: softtouch@funsoftware.com
                              www.funsoftware.com

*Roxanne Butterfield, Marketing*
*Joyce Meyer, President*

Seven full color preprinted overlays to use with Turtle Teasers. Just put them on the IntelliKeys keyboard and you're ready to go.

**1930 U-Control II**
Words+
42505 10th Street W
Suite 109
Lancaster, CA 93534
                                    800-869-8521
                              FAX: 661-266-8969
                     e-mail: info@word+.com
                              www.words+.us.com

*Jeff Dhalan, President*
*Janet Aviles, Customer Support*

Works with the Words+ system (EX Keys, Morse WSKE, Scanning WSKE, Talking Screen) to provide wireless, portable control of items which are already infrared-controlled such as a TV, VCR, CD player, etc. *$395.00*

**1931 Universal Switch Mounting System**
AbleNet
2808 Fairview Avenue N
Roseville, MN 55113              651-294-2200
                                    800-322-0956
                              FAX: 651-294-2259
            e-mail: customerservice@ablenetinc.com
                              www.ablenetinc.com

*Mary Kate Walch, Director*

Mounting system that allows switch placement in any position. A single lever locks all joints securely in place. Extends to 20 1/2 inches and holds up to five pounds. A mounting system for quick and easy positioning. *$210.00*

**1932 VISION**
Artic Technologies
1000 John R Roadrive
Suite 108
Troy, MI 48083                    248-588-7370
                              FAX: 248-588-2650
                     e-mail: info@artictech.com
                              www.artictech.com
The premier access system for blind users of IBM personal computers.

**1933 WinSCAN: The Single Switch Interface for PC's with Windows**
Academic Software
3504 Tates Creek Road
Lexington, KY 40517              859-522-1020
                              FAX: 253-799-4012
                     e-mail: asistaff@acsw.com
                              www.acsw.com

*Warren E Lacefield, President*
*Penelope Ellis, Marketing Director/COO*

A general purpose single-switch control interface for Windows. It provides single-switch users independent control access to educational and productivity software, multimedia programs, and recreational activities that run under Windows 3.1 and higher versions on IBM and compatible PC's. The user can navigate through Windows; choose program icons and run programs, games, and CD's; even surf the Internet with WinSCAN and his or her adaptive switch. *$349.00*

**1934 Words+ Equalizer**
Words Plus
1220 W Avenue J
Lancaster, CA 93534

661-723-6523
800-869-8521
FAX: 661-723-2114
e-mail: info@words-plus.com
www.words-plus.org

*Ginger Woltosz, Vice President*
*Walt Wolosz, Manager*

A hardware/software product designed to operate on an IBM compatible PC. The software provides an intelligent word prediction scheme, a calculator, music, plus the ability to draw and play games. Equalizer is a dedicated augmentative communication system designed for use by individuals with severe motor disability. *$1395.00*

**1935 Words+ IST (Infrared, Sound, Touch)**
Words+
42505 10th Street W
Suite 109
Lancaster, CA 93534

661-723-6523
800-869-8521
FAX: 661-723-2114
e-mail: info@words-plus.com
www.words-plus

*Phil Lawrence, VP*
*Rachel Nielsen, Customer Support*
*Walt Wolosz, Manager*

A unique switch that is activated by slight movement or faint sound. The switch provides user control when connected to a device driven by a single switch. Individuals are currently accessing a wide variety of communication and computer systems with movement using the IST switch. Price ranges from $295.00 to $495.00.

## Braille Products

**1936 Access Systems International**
415 English Avenue
Monterey, CA 93940

831-373-6291
FAX: 831-375-5313

Developers of Braille printers.

**1937 Braille Blazer**
Blazie Engineering
11800 31st Court N
St Petersburg, FL 33716

800-444-4443
FAX: 727-803-8001

Braille printer.

**1938 Braille Keyboard Labels**
Hooleon Corporation
PO Box 589
Melrose, NM 88124

928-634-7515
800-937-1337
FAX: 505-253-4299
e-mail: sales@hooleon.com
www.hooleon.com

*Barry Green, Sales Manager*
*Joan Crozier, President/Sales*

Also large print keyboard labels and large print with Braille.

**1939 Braille N' Speak**
Blazie Engineering
11800 31st Court N
St Petersburg, FL 33716

800-444-4443
FAX: 727-803-8001

A compact, portable talking device with a seven-key braille keyboard, may be used as a talking computer terminal, a braille to print transcriber and a word processor.

**1940 Brailon Thermoform Duplicator**
American Thermoform Corporation
1758 Brackett Street
La Verne, CA 91750

909-593-6711
FAX: 909-593-8001
e-mail: atc@atcbrleqp.com
www.atcbrleqp.com

*Ruth Haggen, Vice President*
*Gary Nunnelly, Owner*

This copy machine, for producing tactile images, copies any brailled or embossed original, by a vacuum forming process. This model is for the reproduction of teaching aids and mobility maps.

**1941 Computer Paper for Brailling**
Maxi Aids
42 Executive Boulevard
Suite 3209
Farmingdale, NY 11735

631-752-0521
800-522-6294
FAX: 631-752-0689
e-mail: sales@maxiaids.com
www.maxiaids.com

*Elliot Zaretsky, Contact*

Specially made paper for braille printing. 1,000 sheets/case *$69.95*

**1942 Duxbury Braille Translator**
Duxbury Systems
270 Littleton Road
Suite 6
Westford, MA 01886

978-692-3000
FAX: 978-692-7912
e-mail: info@duxsys.com
www.duxburysystems.com

*Dan Thibert, Operation Manager*
*Joe Sullivan, President*

A complete line of easy to use word processing and Braille translation software available for Windows (including NT) and Macintosh. Applications for anyone wanting to produce or communicate with Braille; signs, note cards, textbooks, business communications and forms, telephone bills, etc. Simple to use, FREE technical support. Free one year upgrades. DBT is for producing Braille in English, Spanish, French, Portuguese, Italian, Latin, Greek, German and other languages. *$600.00*

**1943 Enabling Technologies Company**
1601 NE Braille Place
Jensen Beach, FL 34957

772-225-3687
800-777-3687
FAX: 772-225-3299
e-mail: enabling@brailler.com
www.brailler.com

*Dede Haskins, Vice President*
*Greg Schenk, Marketing Executive*

Manufactures the most complete line of American made Braille embossers, including desktop or portable models capable of producing high quality single sided or interpoint Braille. Also carries a complete line of adaptive technology aids for the blind community at affordable prices.

**1944 Freedom Scientific Blind/ Low Vision Group**
11800 31st Court N
Saint Petersburg, FL 33716          727-803-8000
                                     800-444-4443
                               FAX: 727-803-8001
                               www.freedomscientific.com

*Lee Hamilton, President*

Developer and manufacturer of assistive technology products for blind and visually impaired individuals. Software: JANS for Windows, ScreenReader, Magic Screen Magnifier, Open Book Scanning and Reading Software. Hardware: Braille Wireless, personal note takers: Braille 'n Speak, BrailleLite, Type 'n Speak, Type Lite, Braille Embossers, Computer Braille Displays. Training and tutorials available. *$16.95*

**1945 Hooleon Corporation**
PO Box 589
Melrose, NM 88124                   928-634-7515
                                     800-937-1337
                               FAX: 928-634-4620
                          e-mail: sales@hooleon.com
                                     www.hooleon.com

*Barry Green, Sales Manager*
*Joan Crozier, President/Sales*

Large print and combination Braille adhesive keytop labels for computer keyboards. Helps visually impaired computer users access correct key strokes either by sight or by touch. Raised Braille meets ADA specifications and large print fills key top surface.

**1946 Infogrip: Large Print/Braille Keyboard Labels**
1794 E Main Street
Ventura, CA 93001                   805-652-0770
                                     800-397-0921
                               FAX: 805-652-0880
                          e-mail: sales@infogrip.com
                                     www.infogrip.com

*Liza Jacobs, President*

Makes a standard keyboard more accessible for visually impaired individuals with large print or Braille keyboard labels. Characters on the large print labels are .5" by .25", about 3 times larger than standard keyboard characters. Braille labels are available as clear labels with Braille dots or large print with Braille. Each set includes all the keys used on a standard Windows keyboard. *$29.00*

**1947 MegaDots**
Raised Dot Computing
408 S Baldwin Street
Madison, WI 53703                   608-257-9595
                                     800-347-9594
                               FAX: 608-257-4143
                          e-mail: info@rdcbraille.com
                                     www.rdcbraille.com

*Theresa Wantuch, Sales Manager*
*Caryn Navy, VP Technical Support*
*David Holladay, President*

A revolutionary new braille translator for the PC that lets you finish projects quickly and easily. Intelligent document importation recognizes what word processor your text is from, and guesses that appropriate format for each paragraph, yielding high quality braille. *$540.00*

**1948 Raised Dot Computing**
Duxbury Systems Incorporated
270 Littleton Road
Suite 6
Westford, MA 01886                  978-692-3000
                               FAX: 978-692-7912
                          e-mail: info@duxsys.com
                                     www.duxburysystems.com

*Joe Sullivan, President*
*Peter Sullivan, VP/Software Development*

Software for the visually impaired.

**1949 Touchdown Keytop/Keyfront Kits**
Hooleon Corporation
PO Box 589
Melrose, NM 88124                   505-253-4503
                                     800-937-1337
                               FAX: 505-253-4299
                                     www.hooleon.com

*Barry Green, Sales Manager*
*Joan Crozier, President*

These kits enlarge the key legends of a computer and include Braille for easy recognition.

# Information Centers & Databases

**1950 ABLEDATA**
8630 Fenton Street
Suite 930
Silver Spring, MD 20910             301-608-8998
                                     800-227-0216
                               FAX: 301-608-8958
                               TTY: 301-608-8912
                          e-mail: abledata@orcmacro.com
                                     www.abledata.com

*Katherine Belknap, Project Director*
*David Johnson, Publications Director*
*Carolyn Johnson, Information Specialist*

ABLEDATA is an electronic database of assistive technology and rehabilitation equipment products for children and adults with physical, cognitive and sensory disabilities. ABLEDATA staff can perform database searches or the database can be searched on the ABLEDATA website database printouts, informer consumer guides and fact website sheets are available at cost from the office or free from the website.

**1951 ATTAIN**
Division of Disability Aging & Rehab Services
32 E Washington Street
Suite 1400
Indianapolis, IN 46204              317-232-1147
                                     800-528-8246
                               FAX: 317-486-8809
                          e-mail: attain@attaininc.org
                                     www.attaininc.org

*Gary R Hand, Executive Director*
*Peter Bisbecos, Manager*

Nonprofit organization that creates system change by expanding the availability of community-based technology-related activities, outreach services, empowerment and advocacy activities through the development of a comprehensive, consumer-responsive, statewide program to serve individuals with disabilities, of all ages and all disabilities, their families, caregivers, educators and service providers. Provides trainings, information and referrals, system change and assessments for equipment needs.

**1952 Aloha Special Technology Access Center**
710 Green Street
Honolulu, HI 96813                  808-523-5547
                               FAX: 808-536-3765
                          e-mail: astachi@yahoo.com
                                     www.geocities.com/astachi

*Ali Sildert, President*

Computer technology center.

**1953  Audiogram/Clinical Records Manager**
98 Us Highway 46
Budd Lake, NJ 07828                           973-347-7662
                                        FAX: 973-691-0611
                                        www.daviscenter.com

*Torine Davis, Director*

Keeps track of client audiogram history and can print or view client with audiogram. The company no longer works with hearing aids. *$414.75*

**1954  Birmingham Alliance for Technology Access Center**
Birmingham Independent Living Center
206 13th Street S
Birmingham, AL 35233                      205-251-2223
                                    FAX: 205-251-0605
                                    TTY:205-251-2223
                                 e-mail: bilc@bellsouth.net
                                    www.birminghamilc.org

*Phil Klebine, President*
*Graham Sisson, Vice President*
*Daniel Kessler, Executive Director*

Computer technology center.

**1955  Bluegrass Technology Center**
961 Beasley Street
Suite 103a
Lexington, KY 40509                       859-294-4343
                                         800-209-7767
                                    FAX: 859-255-0059
                                    TTY: 606-491-8700
                              e-mail: office@bluegrass-tech.org
                                   www.bluegrass-tech.org

*Jennifer Bell, President*
*Angie Youngs Jayarante, Vice President*
*Jean Isaacs, Executive Director*

Provides assistive technology information, consulting and training for education, health professionals, consumers and parents of consumers. Maintains extensive lending library of assistive devices and adapted toys. Statewide training such as; AAC, how to obtain funding for assistive technology, augmentative and alternate communication, equipment implementation strategies, specific to hardware and software, etc.

**1956  CHID Combined Health Information Database**
National Institute of Health
PO Box C
Rockville, MD                             301-402-8714
                                    FAX: 301-770-5164

*Richard Pike*

A computerized bibliographic database, developed and managed by health-related agencies of the Federal Government.

**1957  CITE: Lighthouse for Central Florida**
215 E New Hampshire Street
Orlando, FL 32804                         407-898-9243
                                    FAX: 407-898-0672
                                 e-mail: info@cite-fl.com
                                www.centralflordilighthouse.org

*Lee Masehi, Executive Director*

CITE promotes the independence of adults and children with blindness, low vision and other disabilities through technology, education, support and advocacy.

**1958  Carolina Computer Access Center**
401 Night E 2nd Street
Charlotte, NC 28202                       704-342-3004
                                    FAX: 704-342-1513
                                 e-mail: bellsluth.net
                                    ccac.ataccess.org

*Linda Schilling, Executive Director*

Nonprofit, community-based technology resource center for people with disabilities, providing information about and demonstration of the technology tools that enable individuals with disabilities to control and direct their own lives. Services and programs include: assessments, demonstrations, resource information, lending library, workshops and outreach.

**1959  Center for Accessible Technology**
2547 8th Street
Suite 12a
Berkeley, CA 94710                        510-841-3224
                                    FAX: 510-841-7956
                                 e-mail: info@cforat.org
                                       www.cforat.org

*Dmitri Belser, Executive Director*
*Eric Smith, Administrative Director*

The Center is a grassroots, consumer-based agency with programs that connect people with all types of disabilities, family members, educators, therapists and others with computer-based tools. Services include assessment, ongoing training, curriculum adaption, classes, demonstrations and a newsletter.

**1960  Center for Applied Special Technology**
40 Harvard Mill Square
Suite 3
Wakefield, MA 01880                       781-245-2212
                                         781-245-9320
                                    FAX: 781-245-5212
                                 e-mail: cast@cast.org
                                       www.cast.org

*Stephen P Crosby, Chairman*
*Sally Bowles, Director*
*David Rose, Executive Director*

Expands opportunities for individuals with special needs through innovative use of computers and related technology. We pursue this mission through research and product development that further universal design for learning.

**1961  Center for Assistive Technology & Inclusive Education Studies**
PO Box 7718
Ewing, NJ 08628                           609-771-3016
                                    FAX: 609-637-5179
                                 e-mail: caties@tcnj.edu
                                       caties.tcnj.edu

*Amy G Dell, Executive Director*

Computer technology center offering resource time, workshops, technology, training and evaluations.

**1962  Center on Evaluation of Assistive Technology**
National Rehabilitation Hospital
102 Irving Street NW
Washington, DC 20010                      202-877-1000
                                    FAX: 202-723-0628
                                    TTY:202-726-3996
                              e-mail: justin.m.carter@medstar.net
                                      www.nrhrehab.org

*Thomas J Collamore, Director*
*Edward B Healton, Senior Vice President*
*Edward Eckenhoff, Chief Executive Officer*

The center develops ways of collecting, producing and distributing information to help users, prescribers and third-party payers make intelligent selections of devices.

**1963  Compuserve: Handicapped Users' Database**
5000 Arlington Centre Boulevard
Columbus, OH 43220                        614-457-8600
                                    FAX: 614-538-4023

*Audrey Weil, General Manager*
*John Miller, Chief Executive Officer*

This nationwide database with bulletin boards provides information for persons with disabilities and the issues and technologies that are of interest to them.

**1964 Computer & Web Resources for People With Disabilities**
Alliance for Technology Access
1304 Southpoint Boulevard
Suite 240
Petaluma, CA 94954
707-765-2080
800-455-7970
FAX: 415-455-0654
e-mail: atainfo@ataaccess.org
www.ataccess.org

*Mary Lester, Executive Director*

A guide to maneuvering the growing world of computers, both the mainstream and the assistive technology.

*ISBN 0-897933-00-1*

**1965 Computer Access Center**
6234 W 87th Street
Los Angeles, CA 90045
310-338-1597
FAX: 310-338-9318
e-mail: info@cac.org
www.cac.org

*Mary Ann Glicksman, Executive Director*
*Joanne Orenski, Financial Administrator*
Computer technology center.

**1966 Computer Center for Visually Impaired People: Division of Continuing Studies**
Baruch College
1 Bernard Baruch Way
New York, NY 10010
646-312-1000
FAX: 646-312-5101
e-mail: caps@baruch.cuny.edu
www.baruch.cuny.edu/ccvip

*Karen Gourgey, Director*
*Judith Gerber, Manager*
Offers courses, tutors, equipment and assistance.

**1967 Computer and Web Resources for People with Disabilities**
Hunter House Publishers
PO Box 2914
Alameda, CA 94501
510-865-5282
800-266-5592
FAX: 510-865-4295
e-mail: ordering@hunterhouse.com
www.hunterhouse.com

*Kiran S Rana, Publisher*

Part One describes conventional and assistive technologies and gives strategies for accessing the Internet. Part Two features easy-to-use charts organized by key access concerns, and provides detailed descriptions of software, hardware, and communication aids. Part Three is a gold mine of Web resources, publications, support organizations, government programs, and technology vendors. *$27.95*

*ISBN 0-897933-01-X*

**1968 Computer-Enabling Drafting for People with Physical Disabilities**
County College of Morris
214 Center Grove Road
Randolph, NJ 07869
973-328-5000
888-226-8001
FAX: 973-328-5286
www.ccm.edu

*Edward Yaw, President*
*Brandi Robinson, Vice President*
Computer service.

**1969 Computers to Help People**
913 Acewood Boulevard
Apt 109
Madison, WI 53714
608-257-5917
FAX: 608-257-3480
e-mail: techorlochpi.org
www.chpi.org

*Carl Durocher, Assistive Technologies Manager*
*Johnny R Lee, Operations Manager*
*John J Boyer, Executive Director*

A center for assistive technology, assessment, consulting and training, specializing in computer access products for persons with sensory or mobility impairments. Also provides a print-to-braille service with a specialty in technical writing.

**1970 DIRLINE**
National Library of Medicine
8600 Rockville Pike
Bethesda, MD 20894
301-496-6308
888-346-3656
FAX: 301-496-4450
e-mail: custserv@nml.nih.gov
www.nlm.nih.gov/

*Robert Mehnert, Manager*

18,000 listings of organizations that serve as information resources, including libraries, professional associations and government agencies.

**1971 Developmental Disabilities Council**
647 Main Street
70802
Baton Rouge, LA 70801
225-342-6804
800-922-3425
FAX: 225-342-1970
www.ladc.org

*Sandee Winchell, Executive Director*
Computer technology center.

**1972 Employment Resources Program**
330 South Grand Avenue W
Springfield, IL 62704
217-523-2587
800-447-4221
FAX: 217-523-0427

*Ceceila Haasis, Employment Resource Program Mgr*

An information and referral service that encourages inquiries from professionals, individuals with disabilities, family members, organizations or anyone requesting information pertaining to disabilities. The staff at DRN uses both computer listings and in-house library files to provide the programs services. The DRN program is funded by a grant from the Illinois Department of Rehabilitation Services.

**1973 Functional Skills Screening Inventory**
Functional Resources
3905 Huntington Drive
Amarillo, TX 79109
806-353-1114
FAX: 806-353-1114
e-mail: webmaster@winfssi.comnhsc.edu
www.winfssi.com

*Ed Hammer PhD, Owner*
*Heather Becker PhD, Owner*

Assesses the individual's level of functional skills and identifies supports needed by educational, rehabilitation and residential programs serving moderately and severely disabled persons. Includes enviromental assessments as well as profiles of jobs and training sites.

**1974  High Tech Center**
Sacremento State
6000 J Street
Sacramento, CA  95819           916-278-7915
                                FAX: 916-278-3660
                                e-mail: sswd@csus.edu
                                www.csus.edu/sswd/services
The Center offers assesment and training in adaptive hardware/software for eligible students with disabilities at Sacremento State upon referral from the Office of Services to Students with Disabilities.

**1975  Increasing Capabilities Access Network**
26 Corporate Hill Drive
Little Rock, AR  72205          501-666-8868
                                800-828-2799
                                FAX: 501-666-5319
                                www.arkansas-ican.org

*Barry Valetich, Project Director*
*Barbara Gullett, Executive Director*

A consumer responsive statewide systems change program promoting assistive technology for persons of all ages with disabilities. The program provides information on new and existing technology and maintains an equipment exchange free of charge. Training on assistive technology is also provided.

**1976  International Center for the Disabled**
340 E 24th Street
New York, NY  10010             212-585-6000
                                FAX: 212-585-6161
                                e-mail: info@icdrehab.org
                                www.icdrehab.org

*Michael Burks, Chairman*
*Wen Lu, Secretary/Treasurer*
*Les Halpert, Chief Executive Officer*

The ICD is a comprehensive outpatient rehabilitation facility, providing medical rehabilitation, behavioral health and vocational services to children and adults with a broad range of physical, communication, emotional and cognitive disabilities.

**1977  Kentucky Assistive Technology Service Network**
8412 Westport Road
Louisville, KY  40242           502-429-4484
                                800-327-5287
                                FAX: 502-429-7114
                                e-mail: katsnet@iglow.com
                                www.katsnet.org

*Ronji Dearborn, Information/Referral Specialist*

Statewide network of four regional assistive technology centers with a central coordinating office in Louisville and two regional centers in eastern Kentucky. Network services include but are not limited to assistive technology of services, loan of assistive devices, funding information and referral, assessment and evaluations, consultations on appropriate technologies, training, and technical assistance.

**1978  Learning Independence Through Computers**
1001 Eastern Avenue
Baltimore, MD  21202            410-659-5462
                                FAX: 410-659-5472
                                e-mail: lincmd@aol.com
                                www.linc.org

*Susan Pompa, Associate Director*
*Mary Salkever, Executive Director*

Computer technology center.

**1979  MEDLINE**
Dialog Corporation
800 W California Avenue
Suite 100
Sunnyvale, CA  94086            408-524-4600
                                800-334-2564
                                FAX: 650-254-7070
                                www.dialog.com

*David Brown, General Manager*
*Mike Eastwood, Vice President*

Bibliographic citations to biomedical literature.

**1980  Maine CITE**
University of Maine at Augusta
46 University Drive
Augusta, ME  04330              207-621-3000
                                877-862-1234
                                FAX: 207-621-3293
                                e-mail: umaweb@maine.edu
                                www.uma.maine.edu/cs/

*Robert Stewart, Telecommunications Manager*
*Lauren Dubois, Director Computer Services*
*Pat Lynch, Manager*

Computer technology center.

**1981  Maryland Technology Assistance Program**
Maryland Department of Disabilities
2301 Argonne Drive
Suite T-17
Baltimore, MD  21218            410-554-9230
                                800-832-4827
                                FAX: 410-554-9237
                                e-mail: mdtap@mdtap.org
                                www.mdtap.org

*Jessica Voilmer, Office Manager*

Assistive technology center. Information and referral, equipment display loans and demonstration, funding sources, alternative media, training, workshops and seminars. Rural outreach for individuals with disability in Maryland.

**1982  Minnesota STAR Program**
50 Sherburne Avenue
Room 309
Saint Paul, MN  55155           651-201-2640
                                888-234-1267
                                FAX: 651-282-6671
                                e-mail: star.program@state.mn.us
                                www.admin.state.mn.us/assistivetechnology

*Chuck Rassbach, Executive Director*

STAR's mission is to help all Minnesotans with disabilities gain access to and acquire the assistive technology they eed to live, learn, work and lay. The Minnesota STAR program is federally funded by the Rehabilitation Services Administration.

**1983  Mississippi Project START**
PO Box 1698
Jackson, MS  39215              601-987-4872
                                800-852-8328
                                FAX: 601-364-2349
                                e-mail: contactus@msprojectstart.org
                                www.msprojectstart.org

*Steve Powers, Project Director*

Project START is a Tech Act project established to bring about systems change in the field of assistive technology in the State of Mississippi. Activities include providing training opportunities for consumers and service providers on subjects such as state-of-the-art AT devices, their application and funding resources; referral information on AT evaluation centers; technical assistance to AT users; establishment of an AT equipment loan program and an Information and Referral Service.

**1984** **National Technology Database**
American Foundation for the Blind/ AF B Press
11 Penn Plaza
Suite 300
New York, NY 10001
212-502-7600
800-232-5463
FAX: 412-741-0609
e-mail: afbinfo@afb.net
www.afb.org

*Carl Augusto, President*

This database includes resources for visually impaired persons.
*$99.00*

**1985** **New Jersey Department of Labor & Workforce Development**
Office of the Commissioner
PO Box 110
Trenton, NJ 08625
609-292-2323
FAX: 609-633-9271
e-mail: cmycoff@dol.state.nj.us
www.state.nj.us/labor

*David J Socolow, Commissioner-Designate*
*Marilyn D Davis, Deputy Commissioner*
*Kevin D Jarvis, Chief Of Staff*

Oversees various federal and state vocational rehabilitation services including sheltered workshops and independent living centers; adjudication of permanent disability claims filed with the Social Security Administration; oversees New Jesey's temporary disability program covering non-work related illnesses and injuries

**1986** **New Mexico Technology Assistance Program**
New Mexico State Department of Education
435 Saint Michaels Drive
Suite D
Santa Fe, NM 87505
800-866-2253
FAX: 505-954-8608
TTY:800-659-4915
e-mail: aklaus@state.nm.us
www.nmtap.com

*Andy Winnegar, Director*

Examines and works to eliminate barriers to obtaining assistive technology in New Mexico. Has established a statewide program for coordinating assistive technology services; is designed to assist people with disabilities to locate, secure, and maintain assistive technology.

**1987** **Northern Illinois Center for Adaptive Technology**
3615 Louisiana Road
Rockford, IL 61108
815-229-2163

e-mail: davegrass@eartlink.net
nicat.ataccess.org

*Dave Grass, President*
Computer technology center.

**1988** **OCCK**
1710 W Schilling Road
Salina, KS 67401
785-827-9383
800-526-9731
FAX: 785-823-2015
e-mail: occk@occk.com
www.occk.com

*Phyllis Anderson, Director Community Resource Dev.*
*Kathy Reed, Director Personal Supports*
*Carolee Miner, Chief Executive Officer*

Computer technology center; training center for employment and independent living for people with disabilities; family support center. Kansas AgrAbility program coordinator, Kansas equipment exchange site.

**1989** **Parents, Let's Unite for Kids**
560 32nd Street W
Billings, MT 59102
406-255-0540
800-222-7585
FAX: 255-052-
TTY: 406-657-2055
e-mail: pluk@info.org
www.pluk.org

*Dennis Moore, Executive Director*

Computer technology center. Parents, Let's Unite for Kids offers an assistive technology lab that is open to people of all ages. The lab is a computer and assistive technology demonstration site. There is no charge for services.

**1990** **Pathfinder Parent Training and Information Center**
Pathfinder
1600 2nd Avenue NW
Minot, ND 58701
701-837-7500
800-245-5840
FAX: 701-837-7458
e-mail: ndpass1@minot.com
www.pathfinder.minot.com

*Kathryn Erickson, Executive Director*

A member of the National Parent Training and Information Program which helps parents to better understand their child's disability and to obtain information about the programs, services and resources available. The center provides referrals through their program, support for educational programs for children with disabilities and helps parents learn to communicate more effectively with those involved in their child's program.

**1991** **Pennsylvania's Initiative on Assistive Technology**
Temple University Institute on Disabilities
423 Ritter Annex
1301 Cecil B Moore Avenue
Philadelphia, PA 19122
215-204-3862
800-204-7428
FAX: 215-204-9371
TTY: 800-750-7428
e-mail: piat@temple.edu
www.disabilities.temple.edu

*Amy Goldman, Project Director*
*Alex Holzman, Executive Director*

Assistive technology related information and advocacy for Pennsylvanians with disabilities; assistance with funding; short-term equipment loan and used equipment exchange programs.

**1992** **Rehabilitation Engineering & Assistive Technology Society of North America (RESNA)**
1700 N Moore Street
Suite 1540
Arlington, VA 22209
703-524-6686
FAX: 703-524-6630
TTY:703-524-6639
e-mail: info@resna.org
www.resna.org

*Thomas A Gorski, Executive Director*
*Rosina Romano, Meetings/Membership Coordinator*

Improves the potential of people with disabilities to achieve their goals through the use of technology and disability. Promotes research, development, education, advocacy and provision of technology, and by supporting the people engaged in theses activities.

**1993** **Resource Center for Independent Living**
PO Box 210
Utica, NY 13503
315-797-4642
FAX: 315-797-4747
e-mail: burt.danovitz@rcil.com
www.rcil.com

*Burton Danovitz, Executive Director*
Services and advocacy for indiviuals with disabilities.

**1994** **SACC Assistive Technoloy Center**
PO Box 1325
Simi Valley, CA 93062
805-582-1881
FAX: 805-582-2855
e-mail: dssaccca@aol.com

*Debi Schultze, CEO*
SACC connects children, adults and seniors with special needs to computers, technologies and resources. We provide information and referral, assessments, tutoring, presentations and outreach awareness.

**1995** **South Dakota Department of Human Services: Computer Technology Services**
500 E Capitol Avenue
Pierre, SD 57501
605-000-1111
800-265-9684
FAX: 605-773-5483
TTY: 605-773-3195
e-mail: gary.goeden@state.sd.us

*Gary Goeden*
*Jeff Pierce, Manager*
Computer technology center.

**1996** **Star Center**
1119 Old Humboldt Road
Jackson, TN 38305
731-668-3888
800-464-5619
FAX: 731-668-1666
e-mail: infostar@starcenter.tn.org
www.starcenter.tn.org

*Judy Duke, Outreach Manager*
*Margaret Doumitt, Chief Executive Officer*

Nation's largest assistive technology center dedicated to helping children and adults with disabilities achieve their goals for competitive employment, effective learning, returning to or starting school and independent living. Programs include: high-tech training, music therapy, art therapy, low vision evaluation, orientation and mobility evaluation and training, augmentative communication evaluation, vocational evaluations, assistive technology, job placement services and job skills training.

**1997** **Students with Disabilities Office**
University of Texas at Austin
1 University Station
A5800
Austin, TX 78712
512-471-3434
FAX: 512-475-7730
www.utexas.edu/depts/dos/ssd

*Jennifer Maedgen, Assistant Dean of Students*
*Sheldon Ekland-Olson, Chief Executive Officer*

**1998** **TASK Team of Advocates for Special Kids**
100 W Cerritos Avenue
Anaheim, CA 92805
714-533-8275
FAX: 714-533-2533
e-mail: taskca@aol.com

*Marta Anchondo, Executive Director*
Computer technology center.

**1999** **Tech Connection**
35 Haddon Avenue
Shrewsbury, NJ 07702
732-747-5310
FAX: 732-747-1896
e-mail: tecconn@aol.com
www.techconnection.org

*Joanne Castellano, Director*

Offers a noncommercial center to examine and try computers, adapted equipment, alternative input devices, and a variety of software. Program of Family Resource Associates and a member of the Alliance for Technology Access (ATA), a growing national coalition of computer resource centers, professionals, technology developers and vendors, interacting with new technology to enrich the lives of people with disabilities. Tech Connection offers evaluations, for computer technology.

**2000** **Tech-Able**
1114 Brett Drive SW
Suite 100
Conyers, GA 30094
770-922-6768
FAX: 770-922-6769
e-mail: techable@techable.org
www.techable.org

*Carolyn Gonagill, Executive Director*
*Pat Hanus, Executive Assistant*
*Joe Tedesco, Assistive Tech Practitioner*

Provide assistive technology to individuals with disabilities, toy-lending and software libraries, product demonstration, access to technology devices and fabrication of keyguards for keyboards. Low vision consultant on Thursdays; computer training for persons with disabilities.

**2001** **Technical Aids & Assistance for the Disabled Center**
1950 W Roosevelt Road
Chicago, IL 60608
708-867-6060
800-346-2939
FAX: 312-421-3464
TTY: 312-421-3373

*Andres Hernandez, Executive Director*
*Robert Kaige, Technologist*

Provides consultation and technical advice on adaptive aids, software and hardware.

**2002** **Technology Access Center of Tucson**
PO Box 13178
Tucson, AZ 85732
520-745-5588
FAX: 520-745-1265
e-mail: tactaz@aol.com
www.ed.arizona.edu/tact

*Linda Bishop, Director Services*
*Sonia Rameriez, Service Coordinator*
*Linda Gonzalez, Manager*

A resource center that provides assistive technology services for people with disabilities. Center personnel develop, provide and coordinate those services in communities throughout Middle Tennessee. Services are designed to assist people with disabilities to learn about, choose, acquire and use assistive technology devices. Services are offered to any child or adult with sensory, motor or cognitive disabilities, their family members, and professionals who serve them and employ them.

**2003** **Technology Assistance for Special Consumers**
PO Box 443
Huntsville, AL 35804
256-532-5336
FAX: 256-532-2355
e-mail: tasc@hiwaay.net
www.ataccess.org

*Linda Rags, Executive Director*

T.A.S.C. is a computer resource center with 10 computers, which are equipped with special adaptations for those who are blind, visually impaired, or severely physically disabled. Our staff demonstrates and trains individuals on this equipment so that they can become more independent at home, school, and work. Over 2,500 pieces of educational software are available for individuals who are learning disabled, mentally retarded or who have developmental delays.

**2004 Tenessee Technology Access Project Department of Human Services**
400 Deadrick Street
Nashville, TN 37248
615-313-5183
800-732-5059
FAX: 615-532-4685
TTY: 615-741-4566
e-mail: tn.ttap@state.tn.us
www.state.tn.us/humanserv/ttap_index.htm

*Gina Lodge, Commissioner*
*Kevin Wright, Executive Director TTAP*
*Laura Wilson, Administrative Assistant TTAP*

Provides Tennesseans who have disabilities with comprehensive information related to assistive technology including resources for assistive technology devices and services, information about the funding of devices and services, resources for advocacy services, statewide systems change initiatives/activities, and assistive technology centers.

**2005 Tidewater Center for Technology Access Special Education Annex**
1415 Laskin Road
Virginia Beach, VA 23451
757-437-6542
FAX: 757-263-2801
e-mail: tcta@aol.com
tcta.access.org

*Jane DeBord, Director*
*Myra Jessie Flint, Designee*

Nonprofit organization providing persons with disabilities access, support, and knowledge—re: technology; organization contracts for consultations, workshops and training, or conventional and assistive technologies including computers, augmented communication devices and software; resources: extensive lending library of educational software; books and videotape library; yearly individual membership and corporate membership fees; working/presentation and evaluation fees available upon request.

**2006 University of Idaho Center on Disabilities and Human Development**
University of Idaho
129 W 3rd Street
Moscow, ID 83843
208-885-6466
800-IDA-TECH
FAX: 208-885-3628
www.educ.uidaho.edu/idatech

*Ron Seiler, Director*
*Bob Hieronymus, Executive Director*
*Sue House, Information and Referral*

A University affiliated project (UAP) dedicated to the implementation of a comprehensive system for the delivery of assistive technology devices and services to Idaho citizens with disabilities, their families or representatives in a timely, cost efficient manner. Our goals are to: provide training and technical assistance; to promote public awareness of assistive technology and to increase the capacity of public agencies and private entities to serve people with disabilities.

**2007 Vermont Assistive Technology Project: Department of Aging & Disabilities**
Agency of Human Services
103 S Main Street
Weeks Building
Waterbury, VT 05671
802-241-2620
800-750-6355
FAX: 802-241-2174
TTY: 802-241-1464
e-mail: atinfo@dail.state.vt.us
www.dad.state.vt.us/atp

*Julie L Tucker, Project Director*
*Betsy Ross, Administration*
*Dan Gilman, AT Access Specialist*

Increase the awareness and change policies to insure assistive technology is available to all Vermonters with disabilities.

**2008 Washington Technology Access Center**
8705 232nd Place SW
Edmonds, WA 98026
425-883-4141
FAX: 425-776-3663

*Grant Lord, Founder*

The center was formed as a nonprofit organization to demonstrate how computer technology can transform limitations into opportunities for those with special needs. WTAC's mission is to increase the awareness, understanding and implementation of computer technology for persons with special needs, their friends, families, educators, rehabilitation and health professionals, public officials and employees.

**2009 Xerox Imaging Systems/Adaptive Products Department**

Personal Reader Department
9 Centennial Drive
Peabody, MA 01960
978-977-2000
800-248-6550
FAX: 978-977-2409

Offers information on new services, assistive devices and technology for blind, visually impaired, learning disabled and other print disabled individuals.

**2010 Your Voice Village**
171 River Drive
Hadley, MA 01035
800-637-8720
FAX: 413-585-1137

*Michael Oestreicher, Director*

A politically and socially interactive full-service computer on line service serving 43,000,000 people with disabilities. Make a difference. Be involved. Take part in polls. Let Washington know how you feel. The database also allows participants to make air line reservations, car rentals and more. *$19.95*

# Keyboards, Mouses & Joysticks

**2011 A4 Tech (USA) Corporation**
5585 Brooks Street
Montclair, CA 91763
909-986-0966
FAX: 909-986-0626
e-mail: info@a4tech.com
www.a4tech.com

Manufacturers of a cordless mouse, trackballs and joysticks that emulate mouse controls, flatbed scanners, modified keyboards, and other specialty mouses.

**2012 Abacus**
3150 Patterson Avenue SE
Grand Rapids, MI 49512
616-698-0330
800-451-4319
FAX: 616-698-0325
e-mail: info@abacuspub.com
www.abacuspub.com

*Arnie Lee, President*

Designs a mouse software program that permits programs written for one computer to be run on another computer.

**2013 Ability Center of Greater Toledo**
5605 Monroe Street
Sylvania, OH 43560
419-885-5733
FAX: 419-882-4813
ww.abilitycenter.org

*Tim Harrington, President*

Manufactures keyboard wrist supports to help prevent repetitive motion disorders.

**2014 Dreamer**
TS Micro Tech
17109 Gale Avenue
City of Industry, CA  91745
626-839-8998
FAX: 626-839-8516
e-mail: sales@fancard.com
www.fancard.com

*Steve Heung, Owner*

An intelligent, add-on function keyboard providing single-keystroke access to multiple-keystroke functions.

**2015 FlexShield Keyboard Protectors**
Hooleon Corporation
PO Box 589
Melrose, NM  88124
928-634-7515
800-937-1337
FAX: 928-634-4620
e-mail: sales@hooleon.com
www.hooleon.com

*Barry Green, Sales Manager*
*Joan Crozier, President*

Transparent keyboard protectors allowing instant recognition of keytop legends. They have a matte finish to reduce glare.

**2016 Infogrip: King Keyboard**
1794 E Main Street
Ventura, CA  93001
805-652-0770
800-397-0921
FAX: 805-652-0880
e-mail: sales@infogrip.com
www.infogrip.com

*Liza Jacobs, President*
*Aaron Gaston, Vice President*

Giant alternative keyboard that plugs directly into a computer—no special interface is required. The keys are 1.25 inches in diameter, slightly recessed, and provide both tactile and auditory feedback. The King has a built-in keyboard so that you can rest on its surface without activating keys. This keyboard allows you to control both keyboard and mouse functions, so it's great for people who have difficulty maneuvering a standard mouse. *$130.00*

**2017 Infogrip: Large Print Keyboard**
1794 E Main Street
Ventura, CA  93001
805-652-0770
800-397-0921
FAX: 805-652-0880
e-mail: sales@infogrip.com
www.infogrip.com

*Liza Jacobs, President*
*Aaron Gaston, Vice President*

Standard Windows keyboard with large print keys. The keyboard and its keys are the same size as a standard keyboard; however, the print has been enhanced. The characters measure .5" by .25", about 3 times larger than standard keyboard characters. *$130.00*

**2018 Infogrip: OnScreen**
1794 E Main Street
Ventura, CA  93001
805-652-0770
800-397-0921
FAX: 805-652-0880
e-mail: sales@infogrip.com
www.infogrip.com

*Liza Jacobs, President*

OnScreen features word prediction/completion (with an editable dictionary), Key Dwell Timer (a timer that selects a key under the cursor), integrated Verbal Keys Feedback, Show and Hide Keys (turns on/off keys to prevent access and minimize confusion) a Smart Window (automatically re-positions the keyboard or panels off of the area in use). On Screen also offers edit, numeric, macro, calculator and Windows enhancement capabilities. *$200.00*

**2019 IntelliKeys**
Intelli Tools
1720 Corporate Circle
Petaluma, CA  94954
707-773-2000
800-899-6687
FAX: 707-773-2001
e-mail: info@intellitools.com
www.intellitools.com

*Beth Davis, Director Sales Operation*
*Lari Castle, Supervisor*
*Arjan Khalsa, Chief Executive Officer*

Alternative, touch-sensitive keyboards; plugs into any Macintosh or Windows computer. *$395.00*

**2020 IntelliKeys USB**
Intelli Tools
1720 Corporate Circle
Petaluma, CA  94954
707-773-2000
800-899-6687
FAX: 707-773-2001
e-mail: info@intellitools.com
www.intellitools.com

*Paula Irons, Director Marketing/Communication*
*Arjan Khalsa, Chief Executive Officer*

IntelliKeys alternative keyboard for USB computers and Windows 2000, Mac OSX. *$69.95*

**2021 Jouse**
Prentke Romich Company
1022 Heyl Road
Wooster, OH  44691
330-262-1984
800-262-1984
FAX: 330-263-4829
e-mail: info@prentrom.com
www.prentrom.com

*Jennifer Monahan, Specialized Speech Technologist*
*Dave Moffatt, President*

A joystick-operated mouse that is controlled with the mouth. Moving the joystick moves the cursor. Mouse button activations can be made with the sip and puff switch that is built into the joystick. Typing can be achieved through an on-screen keyboard. Nothing is attached to the operator. The adjustable Jouse arm mounts on a table or desktop and swings away when bumped. *$995.00*

**2022 Key Tronic KB 5153 Touch Pad Keyboard**
KeyTronic
PO Box 14687
Spokane Valley, WA  99214
800-262-6006

Integrates a regular full-function keyboard, a numeric keypad with a cursor key capability and a touch pad into one unit.

**2023 Liaison Computer Work Station**
Genesis One Technologies
343 W Milltown Road
Wooster, OH  44691
330-259-1304
888-221-5032
FAX: 775-252-4834
e-mail: sales@genesis.net
www.genesisone.net

*Grace Miller, Office Manager*

A full function computer work station for high level (C-2 to C-5) spinal cord injured users. It transparently emulates both keyboard and mouse, using rapid direct selection which commonly yields letter by letter typing rates of 15 to 20 words per minute. The user controls it via proportional IR remote control from the DU-IT controlled power wheelchair and chin or tongue/lip controller or via a desk-mounted proportional controller as a stand alone device. Full ECU features included. *$ 4685.00*

**2024  Magic Wand Keyboard**
In Touch Systems
11 Westview Road
Spring Valley, NY  10977                    845-354-7431
                                            800-332-6244
                                   www.magicwandkeyboard.com

*Jerry Crouch, President*
*Susan Crouch, Vice President*

The magic wand keyboard allows your child to use a keyboard and mouse easily-no light beams, microphones, or sensors to wear of position. This miniature computer keyboard has zero-force keys that work with the slightest touch of a wand (hand-held of mouthstick). No strength required.

**2025  McKey Mouse**
In Touch Systems
11 Westview Road
Spring Valley, NY  10977                    845-354-7431

                                        www.prop.or.jp

*Jerry Crouch, President*

Microsoft compatible mouse for persons with little or no hand/arm movement; it's an option for the Magic Wand Keyboard and adds full mouse function without adding any extra devices.

**2026  PortaPower Plus**
Words+
42505 10th Street W
Suite 109
Lancaster, CA  93534                        661-266-8500
                                            800-869-8521
                                       FAX: 661-266-8969

*Phil Lawrence, VP*
*Rachel Nielsen, Customer Support*

Rechargeable battery pack designed to give longer life and remote usage time to laptop computers and other portable battery-operated devices and accessories. Requires a 12 volt auto adapter. *$149.00*

**2027  Step on It! Computer Control Pedals**
1290 Carmead Parkway
Suite 118
Sunnyvale, CA  94086                        408-736-6086
                                       FAX: 408-736-6083
                                         www.bilbo.com

*Sergei Burkov, President*
*Katie Sheinin, Manager*

BILBO Innovations, Inc. manufactures and sells Step On It keyboard control pedals. Ergonomic foot switches to emulate keystrokes and mouse clicks. Designed for victims of Repetitive Strain Injury (RSI), Carpal Tunnel Syndrome (CTS), handicapped and disabled. *$99.00*

**2028  Unicorn Keyboards**
Intelli Tools
1720 Corporate Circle
Petaluma, CA  94954                         707-773-2000
                                            800-899-6687
                                       FAX: 707-773-2001
                              e-mail: info@intellitools.com
                                     www.intellitools.com

*Paula Irons, Marketing Director*
*Arjan Khalsa, Chief Executive Officer*

Alternative keyboards with membrane surface and large, user-defined keys. Large and small sizes are available. *$250.00*

## Scanners

**2029  Scanmaster**
4 Townsend W
Suite 17
Nashua, NH  03063                           603-882-5200
                                       FAX: 603-880-3843

*W Parr, Chief Executive Officer*

A digital color scanner for desktop scanning. It allows the user to digitalize, modify, enhance and store images in color or black and white.

**2030  Scanning WSKE**
Words+
42505 10th Street W
Suite 109
Lancaster, CA  93534                        661-723-6523
                                            800-869-8521
                                       FAX: 661-723-2114
                                       www.words-plus.com

*Ginger Woltosz, VP*
*Jeff Dahlen, Manager*
*Walt Wolosz, Manager*

A software and a hardware product designed to operate on an IBM compatible PC. The software provides dual word prediction, abbreviation expansion, five different methods of voice output, and access to commercial software applications.

**2031  System 2000/Versa**
Words+
40015 Sierra Highway
Suite B145
Palmdale, CA  93550
                                            800-869-8521
                                       FAX: 661-266-8969

*Ginger Woltosz, VP*
*Tim Ross, Manager*

Provides all of the strategies currently being used in AAC, from dynamic display color pictographic language, to dual-word prediction text language, in a single system.

**2032  Zygo Industries**
ZYGO Industries
PO Box 1008
Portland, OR  97207                         503-598-7531
                                            800-234-6006
                                       FAX: 503-684-6011
                               e-mail: zygo@zygo-usa.com
                                       www.zygo-usa.com

*Lawrence Weiss, President/Owner*

## Screen Enhancement

**2033  Beamscope II**
Florida New Concepts Marketing
PO Box 261
Port Richey, FL  34673                      727-842-3231
                                            800-456-7097
                                       FAX: 727-845-7544
                               e-mail: compulnz@gte.net

*Alan Lezark, President*

Meets the needs of low vision individuals in the recreational area. All models utilize a diamond cut freznel lens that can double the size of a TV screen.

# Computers /Speech Synthesizers

*$25 - $74*

**2034 Boxlight**
Boxlight Corporation
19472 Powder Hill Place NE
Suite 100
Poulsbo, WA 98370
360-779-7901
800-884-6464
e-mail: sales@boxlight.com
www.boxlight.com

*Joanne Luttrell, Marketing*
*Herb Myers, President*

BOXLIGHT is a global presentation solutions partner for trainers, educators and professional speakers. Solutions include projector sales, national rental service, technical support, repair, and presentation peripherals. For more information visit us online.

**2035 FDR Series of Low Vision Reading Aids**
Optelec U S
3030 Enterprise Court
Suite C
Vista, CA 92081
800-828-1056
FAX: 978-692-6073
e-mail: chrish@optelec.com
www.optelec.com

*Annette Fasnacht, President*
*James Bailey, Vice President*

The Low Vision Reading Aids features; high resolution, positive and negative display, a high-quality zoom lens, versatile swivel and a 12 inch or 19 inch high-resolution monitor, color or black and white, computer compatible, or portable.

**2036 InFocus**
AI Squared
PO Box 669
Manchester Center, VT 05255
802-362-3612
FAX: 802-362-1670
e-mail: zoomtext@alsquared.com

*Benjermin Weiss, President*

A memory-resident program that magnifies text and graphics - the entire screen, a single line or a portion of the screen.

**2037 Portable Large Print Computer**
Human Ware
175 Mason Circle
Concord, CA 94520
925-680-7100
800-722-3393
FAX: 925-681-4630
e-mail: us.info@humanware.com
www.humanware.com

*Jim Halliday, President/Chief Executive Office*
*Sharon Spiker, Administrator*

A portable large print computer which magnifies up to 64 times. It is linked to a PC and has a hand-held camera.

**2038 ZoomText**
A I Squared
PO Box 669
Manchester Center, VT 05255
802-362-3612
800-859-3612
FAX: 802-362-1670
e-mail: zoomtext@alsquared.com
www.aisquared.com

*Benjermin Weiss, President*

A RAM-resident program that enlarges screen characters up to eight times. It runs on IBM PC, XT, AT and PS/2.

## Speech Synthesizers

**2039 Artic Business Vision (for DOS) and Artic WinVision (for Windows 95)**
Artic Technologies
55 Park Drive
Troy, MI 48083
248-588-7370
FAX: 248-588-2650
e-mail: info@artictech.com
www.artictech.com

*Dale McDaniel, Vice President Marketing*
*Kathy Gargagliano, VP Operations*

A speech processor for blind computer users featuring true interactive speech with spread sheets, word processors, database managers, etc. Now available with both Windows 3.1 and Windows 95 access. *$ 495.00*

**2040 Audapter Speech System**
Personal Data Systems
638 Sobrato Lane
Campbell, CA 95008
408-866-1126
FAX: 408-866-1128
e-mail: info@personaldatasystems.com
www.personaldatasystems.com

*Robert Gallati, Director*
*Noel Runyan, President*

A speech synthesizer. Its features include: intelligibility over 93 percent on the industry standard MRT test, fast response, 700-word-per-minute speech rate, speech halt control, compact unit with built-in speaker and serial interface.

**2041 Computerized Speech Lab**
Kay Elemetrics Corporation
2 Bridgewater Lane
Lincoln Park, NJ 07035
973-628-6200
800-289-5297
FAX: 973-628-6363
www.kayelemetrics.com

*John Crump, President*

Hardware/software for the acquisition, analysis/display, playback and storage of speech signals.

**2042 Digital Voice for Talking Database**
Hy-Tek Manufacturing Company
1980 W Us Highway 30
Sugar Grove, IL 60554
630-466-7664
FAX: 630-466-7678

*William Bastian, Owner*

This product adds speech to PC files. Uses include personnel identification and security, multilingual training, assembly instructions and reminders.

**2043 DynaVox Devices & Software**
Dyna Vox Systems
2100 Wharton Street
Suite 400
Pittsburgh, PA 15203
412-381-4883
800-344-1778
FAX: 412-381-5241
e-mail: sales@dynavoxsys.com
www.dynavoxsys.com

*Joe Swenson, President*

Allow non-speaking individuals to communicate their thoughts, ideas and feelings easily. The devices' built-in infrared technology also provides users with more independence, allowing them to access TVs, VCRs, and computers. DynaVox software helps turn Macintosh and Windows and computers into communication devices so clinicians can use their computers to conduct training and assessments.

202

# Computers /Speech Synthesizers

**2044  Electronic Speech Assistance Devices**
Luminaud
8688 Tyler Boulevard
Mentor, OH 44060                                440-255-9082
                                                800-255-3408
                                           FAX: 440-255-2250
                                    e-mail: info@luminaud.com
                                           www.luminaud.com

*Thomas Lennox, President*
*Dorothy Lennox, Vice President*

Offers a full line of speech aids, voice amplifiers, mini-vox amplifiers, laryngectomec products.

**2045  Hawk Communication Device**
Wayne County Regional Educational Service Agency
33500 Van Born Road
Wayne, MI 48184                                 734-334-1300
                                           FAX: 734-334-1494
                                                   rvhs.net

*Marlene Davis, Chief Executive Officer*

The Hawk employs digital voice technology for high quality, natural voice output. The touch panel is divided into a three by three matrix for a total of nine selection areas. A bulletin microphone allows the recording of up to five seconds worth of digital speech into each of the nine selection areas. *$250.00*

**2046  In Cube Pro Voice Command**
Command Corporation
11080 Old Roswell Road
Suite 200
Alpharetta, GA 30004                            770-360-1230

                          e-mail: webmaster@commandcorp.com
                                        www.commandcorp.com
Continuous speech recognition system which can be used by people with disabilities. IN CUBE provides greatly increased capability, enhanced computer control and access. Blind and low-vision users gain voice access to the graphic user interface. Mobility-impaired people, including quadriplegics, benefit from voice window navigation and voice macro command input. Victims of various repetitive strain injuries RSI use IN CUBE to replace and eliminate repetitive keyboard and mouse operations. *$395.00*

**2047  Keywi**
Consultants for Communication Technology
35 Bell Avenue
Pittsburgh, PA 15205                            412-761-6062
                                           FAX: 412-761-7336
                                    e-mail: cct@concommtech.com
                                          www.concommtech.com

*Kathleen H Miller, President/Owner*

Keywi enables a laptop computer to become a complete communication device. Create entire conversations, call a friend on the telephone, manage your business or personal affairs. Requires minimal training. Multiple access methods-switch, mouse, joystick, keyboard. Custom vocabulary. Powerful word prediction abilities. *$495.00*

**2048  Laptalker**
Automated Functions
7700 Leesburg Pike
Suite 420
Falls Church, VA 22043                          703-883-9797
                                           FAX: 703-883-9798

*R Morford, Owner*

A portable talking computer that gives visually impaired people complete desk top PC compatibility.

**2049  Mega Wolf Communication Device**
Wayne County Regional Educational Service Agency
33500 Van Born Road
Wayne, MI 48184                                 734-334-1300
                                           FAX: 734-334-1432
                                                 www.resa.net

*Kimberly Kaminski, Assistant Operations*
*Marlene E Davis, Administrator*

A low cost voice output communication device which is primarily intended to provide the power of speech to those individuals who are most severely challenged mentally and/or physically. The WOLF device is User programmable and uses the Texas Instruments' Touch and Tell case and touch panel; ADAMLAB electronics with synthesized (robotic) voice. For users able to point with approximately 6 ounces of pressure. *$400.00*

**2050  One-Step Communicator**
AbleNet
2808 Fairview Avenue N
Roseville, MN 55113                             651-294-2200
                                                800-322-0956
                                           FAX: 651-294-2259
                              e-mail: customerservice@ablenetinc.com
                                           www.ablenetinc.com

*Dave Dinckik, Director*

The One-Step Communicator has 20 seconds of memory and has an angled switch surface making it easy to see and access. The switch surface is 2 1/2 inches in diameter. Detachable mounting base makes it easy to position a single unit in a variety of locations. *$129.00*

**2051  Phone Manager**
Consultants for Communication Technology
508 Bellevue Ter
Pittsburgh, PA 15202                            412-761-6062
                                           FAX: 412-761-7336
                                    e-mail: cct@concommtech.com
                                          www.concommtech.com

*Kathleen H Miller Phd, Partner*
*Jaime Oliva, Partner*

Software that allows the user to dial an outgoing call directly from the computer, even with a single switch. Synthesized speech is sent through the phone line. The synthesizer then turns into a speaker phone enabling hands free, two way conversations. *$300.00*

**2052  Talking Screen**
Words+
42505 10th Street W
Suite 109
Lancaster, CA 93534                             661-723-6523
                                                800-869-8521
                                           FAX: 661-723-2114
                                    e-mail: info@words-plus.com
                                           www.words-pous.com

*Ginger Woltosz, Vice President*
*Tim Ross, Manager*
*Walt Wolosz, Manager*

An augmentative communication program that allows the user to select graphic symbols on the display to produce speech output. Symbols can be used either singly or in sequence as picture abbreviations. *$1395.00*

**2053  Turnkey Computer Systems for the Visually, Physically, and Hearing Impaired**
E V A S
39 Canal Street
Westerly, RI 02891                              401-596-3155
                                                800-872-3827
                                           FAX: 401-596-3979
                                     e-mail: contact@evas.com
                                                www.evas.com

*Sara Swerdlick, Customer Service Manager*
*Gerald Swerdlick, Owner*

203

Offers clear speech with pleasant inflection and tonal quality as well as variable pitch, intonation and voices.

**2054  Voice-It**
V XI Corporation Incorporated
1 Front Street
Rollinsford, NH  03869                        603-742-2888
                                              800-742-8588
                                         FAX: 603-742-5065
                              e-mail: info@vxicorp.com
                                        www.vxicorp.com

*Richard Hale, President*
*Cheryl Keene, Senior Telecommunications Analys*

Adds voice to popular spreadsheet and word processing applications on IBM PCs and compatibles, turning spreadsheets and word processing documents into talking documents.

**2055  Window-Eyes**
G W Micro
725 Airport North Office Park
Fort Wayne, IN  46825                         260-489-3671
                                         FAX: 260-489-2608
                            e-mail: sales@gwmicro.com
                                        www.gwmicro.com

*Daniel Weirich, Owner*
*Doug Geoffray, Owner*

Provides access to available software automatically reading information important to the user while ignoring the rest. A screen reader for the windows operative system.

## Software: Math

**2056  AIMS Multimedia**
Discovery Education
8145 Holton Drive
Florence, KY  41042                           859-342-7200
                                         FAX: 877-324-6830
                           e-mail: info@multimedia.com
                                    www.aimsmultimedia.com

*Mike Wright, Director*
*Lynn Fassett, Administrative Assistant*
*Cindy Vogt, Human Resources Executive*

AIMS Multimedia is a leader in the production and distribution of trinaing and educational programs for the business and K-12 communities via YHS, interactive CD-ROM, DVD and Internet streaming video.

**2057  Access to Math**
Don Johnston
26799 W Commerce Drive
Volo, IL  60073                               847-740-0749
                                              800-999-4660
                                         FAX: 847-740-7326
                          e-mail: info@donjohnston.com
                                      www.donjohnston.com

*Ruth Ziolkowski, President*

This Macintosh Math Worksheet program is two products in one. For teachers, it makes customized worksheets in a snap. For students who struggle, it provides individualized on-screen lessons that contribute to success. *$79.00*

**2058  Basic Math Competency Skill Building**
Educational Activities Software
PO Box 754
Baldwin, NY  11510                            516-867-7878
                                              800-645-2796
                                         FAX: 516-379-7429
                       e-mail: achieve@ea-software.com
                                       www.ea-software.com

*Alan Stern, Sales Director/Manager*

Comprehensive MATH SKILLS software tutorials teach concepts ranging from rounding and tables to measuring area. MAC/WIN compatible. *$369.00*
                   *Per Unit*

**2059  Basic Math: Detecting Special Needs**
Allyn & Bacon
75 Arlington Street
Suite 300
Boston, MA  02116                             617-848-6000
                                              800-852-8024
                                         FAX: 617-848-7490
                                        www.adlongman.com

*Thomas Longman, Founder*

Describes special mathematics needs of special learners.
            *180 pages 1989*
            *ISBN 0-205116-35-3*

**2060  Campaign Math**
Mindplay
3130 N Dodge Boulevard
Tucson, AZ  85716                             520-323-1303
                                              800-221-7911
                                         FAX: 520-322-0363

A complete program on the electoral process as well as a math package which teaches ratios, fractions and percentages.

**2061  Fraction Factory**
Queue
1450 Barnum Avenue
Suite 207
Bridgeport, CT  06610                         203-335-0906
                                              800-232-2224
                                         FAX: 203-336-2481
                            e-mail: queueinc@aol.com
                                        www.queueinc.com

**2062  Information & Referral Services**
Information and Referral Services
3130 N Dodge Boulevard
Tucson, AZ  85716                             520-881-1794
                                              800-632-3474
                                         FAX: 520-323-2110
                            e-mail: inform@azinfo.org
                                         www.azinfo.org

*Leslie Ann Williams, Executive Director*

Provides information about health and human services for people in Arizona over the telephone. Information specialists help callers clarify their needs, and provide referrals to the appropriate service agency.

**2063  King's Rule**
WINGS for Learning
1600 Green Hills Road
Scotts Valley, CA  95066                      831-464-3600
                                         FAX: 831-464-3600

*Ani Stocks, Owner*

A software mathematical problem solving game. Students discover mathematical rules as they work their way through a castle and generate and test a working hypothesis by asking questions.

**2064  Learning About Numbers**
C&C Software
5713 Kentford Circle
Wichita, KS  67220                            316-683-6056
                                              800-752-2086

*Carol Clark, President*

Three programs use the power of computer graphics to provide young children with a variety of experiences in working with numbers. *$50.00*

**2065  Math Rabbit**
Learning Company
100 Pine Street
Suite 1900
San Francisco, CA  94111                510-490-7311
                                        800-825-4420
                              FAX: 408-263-3358
www.learningcompanyschool.com
Teaches early math concepts by matching objects to numbers,
then adding and subtracting up to 18.

**2066  Math for Everyday Living**
Educational Activities Software
PO Box 754
Baldwin, NY  11510                      516-867-7878
                                        800-645-2796
                              FAX: 516-379-7429
e-mail: astearn@ea-software.com
www.ea-software.com

*Alan Stern, Director of Sales*
Real life math skills are taught with this tutorial and practice
software program. Examples include Paying for a Meal (addition and subtraction), Working with Sales Slips (multiplication), Unit Pricing (division), Sales Tax (percent), Earning with
Overtime (fractions) plus more. Software: CD-Rom, Windows,
MAC, and DOS. *$159.00*

**2067  Math for Successful Living**
Siboney Learning Group
PO Box 220520
Saint Louis, MO  63122                  314-909-1670
                                        888-726-8100
                              FAX: 314-984-8063
e-mail: crichter@sibneylg.com
www.ea-software.com

*Carrie Richter, Sales Coordinator*
*Bill Edwards, President*
These programs include managing a checking account, budget-
ing, shopping strategies and buying on credit.

**2068  Optimum Resource Educational Software**
Optimum Resource
18 Hunter Road
Hilton Head Island, SC  29926           843-689-8000
                              FAX: 843-689-8008
e-mail: sticky@stickybear.com
www.stickybear.com

*Chris Gintz, Chief Executive Officer*
A complete topical curriculum of reading, math, keyboard skills
and science programs that are age and skill specific. *$59.95*

**2069  Piece of Cake Math**
Queue Inc.
1 Control Drive
Shelton, CT  06484                      203-446-8100
                                        800-232-2224
                              FAX: 800-775-2729
e-mail: jdk@queueinc.com
www.queueinc.com

*Jonathan Kantrowitz, Owner*
Color, sound and animation combine forces in a program of five
games focusing on basic mathematical operations.

**2070  Puzzle Tanks**
WINGS for Learning
1600 Green Hills Road
Scotts Valley, CA  95066                831-464-3600
                              FAX: 831-464-3600

*Ani Stocks, Owner*
A mathematical problem solving game that involves multi-step
problems.

**2071  Right Turn**
WINGS for Learning
1600 Green Hills Road
Scotts Valley, CA  95066                831-464-3600
                              FAX: 831-464-3600

*Ani Stocks, Owner*
Requires students to predict, experiment and learn about the
mathematical concepts of rotation and transformation.

**2072  RoboMath**
3130 N Dodge Boulevard
Tucson, AZ  85716                       520-881-1794

*Leslie Williams, Executive Director*

**2073  Stickybear Math**
Optimum Resource
18 Hunter Road
Hilton Head Island, SC  29926           843-689-8000
                              FAX: 843-689-8008
e-mail: stickyb@stickybear.com
www.stickybear.com

*Chris Gintz, Chief Executive Officer*
Sharpen basic addition and subtraction skills with this captivat-
ing series of math exercises. *$59.95*

**2074  Stickybear Numbers**
Optimum Resource
18 Hunter Road
Hilton Head Island, SC  29926           843-689-8000
                              FAX: 843-689-8008
e-mail: sticky@stickybear.com
www.stickybear.com

*Chris Gintz, Chief Executive Officer*
Counting and number recognition are as easy as 1-2-3 with this
award-winning program. *$59.95*

**2075  Stickybear Word Problems**
Optimum Resource
18 Hunter Road
Hilton Head Island, SC  29926           843-689-8000
                              FAX: 843-689-8008
e-mail: sticky@stickybear.com
www.stickybear.com

*Chris Gintz, Chief Executive Officer*
Hundreds of different word problems make it easy for students
to practice basic math skills. *$59.95*

**2076  Stickybear's Math Splash**
Optimum Resource
18 Hunter Road
Hilton Head Island, SC  29926           843-689-8000
                              FAX: 843-689-8008
e-mail: sticky@stickybear.com
www.stickybear.com

*Chris Gintz, Chief Executive Officer*
Unique multiple activities keep the learning level high while
children acquire skills in addition, subtraction, multiplication
and division. *$59.95*

**2077  Stickybear's Math Town**
Optimum Resource
18 Hunter Road
Hilton Head Island, SC  29926           843-689-8000
                              FAX: 843-689-8008
e-mail: sticky@stickybear.com
www.stickybear.com

*Chris Gintz, Chief Executive Officer*

Children ages 5-10 gain proficiency in addition, subtraction, multiplication and division, as well as life skills and word problems. In English and Spanish, children sharpen skills both vertically and horizontally, clear crisp graphics and sound enable teachers to monitor and access skills and development. *$59.95*

**2078** **Tomorrow's Promise: Mathematics**
Compass Learning
9920 Pacific Heights Boulevard
San Diego, CA 92121     858-587-0087
800-247-1380
FAX: 619-622-7873
www.compasslearning.com

*Rajeev Turi, President*

By integrating interdisciplinary content and real-world application of skills, this product emphasizes the practical value of fundamental math skills. It helps your students develop a problem-solving aptitude for ongoing mathematics achievement.

## Software: Miscellaneous

**2079** **Adventures in Musicland**
Electronic Courseware Systems
1713 S State Street
Champaign, IL 61820     217-359-7099
800-832-4965
FAX: 217-359-6578
e-mail: support@ecsmedia.com
www.ecsmedia.com

*G Peters, President*
*Jodie Varner, Marketing Manager*

This unique set of music games features characters from Lewis Carroll's, Alice in Wonderland. Players learn through pictures, sounds, and animation which help develop understanding of musical tones, composers, and musical symbols. Games include MusicMatch, Melody Mixup, Picture Perfect and Sound Concentration. *$49.95*

**2080** **Ai Squared**
PO Box 669
Manchester Center, VT 05255     802-362-3612
800-859-0270
FAX: 802-362-1670
e-mail: zoomtext@aisquared.com
www.aisquared.com

*Marilyn Petty, Director*
*Benjermin Weiss, President*

Developers of software for the visually impaired.

**2081** **All About You: Appropriate Special Interactions and Self-Esteem**
P CI Educational Publishing
PO Box 34270
San Antonio, TX 78265     210-377-1999
800-594-4263
FAX: 888-259-8284
www.pcicatalog.com

*Jeff Clain, Chief Executive Officer*
*Janie McLane, Senior Vice President*

This game offers parents and game players a new line of communication when discussing various issues such as learning to be thoughtful, respecting the rights and feelings of others, how to make and keep friends and more. *$49.95*

**2082** **All Star Review**
Tom Snyder Productions
100 Talcott Avenue
# 6
Watertown, MA 02472     617-926-6000
800-342-0236
FAX: 800-304-1254
e-mail: ask@tomsnyder.com
www.tomsnyder.com

*Rick Abrahams, Manager*

This package turns group review into a baseball game for small and large groups.

**2083** **Assistive Software Products**
Innovation Management Group
21350 N Huff Street
Suite 112
Chatsworth, CA 91311     818-346-3581
800-889-0987
FAX: 818-701-1581
e-mail: cs@imgpresents.com
www.imgpresents.com

*Jerry Hussong, Vice President*
*Kermit Komm, Owner*

IMG is the leading provider of programmable, infinitely sizeable, Onscreen Keyboards with Macro Panels, Text to Speech, Network Logon, and Word Prediction. CrossScanner adds switch scanning capabilities to Onscreen. Other products include: SmartClick for Hover and Dwell; Joystick-to-Mouse for Joystick/Game devices; and The Magnifier for screen magnification and cursor tracking.

**2084** **At Home with Stickybear**
Optimum Resource
18 Hunter Road
Hilton Head Island, SC 29926     843-689-8000
FAX: 843-689-8008
e-mail: sticky@stickybear.com
www.stickybear.com

*Chris Gintz, Chief Executive Officer*

This dynamic new multifaceted program covers a wide range of preschool skills that go far beyond the strictly academic! At Stickybear's house, children discover the alphabet, numbers, shapes, colors; plus social skills, important safety messages and delightful off-screen activities that foster creativity. *$59.95*

**2085** **Attainment Company**
I ET Resources
504 Commerce Parkway
PO Box 930160
Verona, WI 53593     608-845-7880
800-327-4269
FAX: 800-942-3865
e-mail: info@attainmentcompany.com
www.attainmentcompany.com

*Brent Denu, Marketing Coordinator*
*Julie Denu, Technical Support*
*Theresa O'Connor, Office Manager*

Augmentative/alternative communication, software, videos, print and hands-on materials for developmental and cognitive disabilities.

**2086** **Attention Getter**
Soft Touch
4300 Stine Road
Suite 401
Bakersfield, CA 93313     661-396-8676
877-763-8868
FAX: 661-396-8760
e-mail: support @softtouch.com
www.funsoftware.com

*Joyce Meyer, President*
*Roxanne Butterfield, Marketing*

The whimsical photos morph to another photo and then to a third photo in categories. Paired with interesting sounds and music, the photo animations are so engaging that the student is motivated to activate the computer to see and hear the next one. This is a perfect vehicle to achieve goals aimed at attention getting, activating a switch or intentionality. Compatible with USB IntelliKeys keyboards.

**2087 Attention Teens**
Soft Touch
4300 Stine Road
Suite 401
Bakersfield, CA 93313

661-396-8676
877-763-8868
FAX: 661-396-8760
e-mail: support@softtouch.com
www.softtouch.com

*Roxanne Butterfield, Marketing*
*Joyce Meyer, President*

Attention Teens (formerly known as Loony Teens) is a program for teens with disabilities who need powerful input to get their attention. Attention Teens is a computer program to do just this. Paired with interesting sounds and music, the photo animations are so engaging that the student is motivated to activate the computer to see and hear the next one. Compatible with USB IntelliKeys keyboards.

**2088 Away We Ride**
Soft Touch
4300 Stine Road
Suite 401
Bakersfield, CA 93313

661-396-8676
877-763-8868
FAX: 661-396-8760
e-mail: support@softtouch.com
www.softtouch.com

*Roxanne Butterfield, Marketing*
*Joyce Meyer, President*

Software for children and teens. For Macintosh and PC.

**2089 Bailey's Book House**
Edmark Corporation
PO Box 97021
Redmond, WA 98073

425-556-8400
800-691-2986
www.edmark.com

Software for children.

**2090 Battenberg & Associates**
11135 Rolling Springs Drive
Carmel, IN 46033

317-843-2208

Offers various software programs that develop the user's visual memory, sequencing skills, word recognition, hand-eye coordination and more.

**2091 Behavior Skills: Learning How People Should Act**
Programming Concepts
PO Box 34270
San Antonio, TX 78265

210-377-1999
800-594-4263
FAX: 888-828-
www.pcieducation.com

*Jeff Clain, Chief Executive Officer*
*Janie Haugen, Program Director*

Helps players learn what behavior is acceptable and what behavior is not acceptable in the real world. *$49.95*

**2092 Blocks in Motion**
Don Johnston
26799 W Commerce Drive
Volo, IL 60073

847-740-0749
800-999-4660
FAX: 847-740-7326
e-mail: info@donjohnston.com
www.donjohnston.com

*Ruth Ziolkowski, President*

This unique art and motion program makes drawing, creating and animating fun and educational for all users. Based on the Piagetian Theory for motor-sensory development, this program promotes the concept that the process is as educational and as much fun as the end result. *$79.00*

**2093 CINTEX: Speak to Your Appliances**
NanoPac
4823 S Sheridan Road
Suite 302
Tulsa, OK 74145

918-665-0329
800-580-6086
FAX: 918-665-0361
e-mail: info@nanopac.com
www.nanopac.com

*Silvio V Cianfrone CCSP, President*

CINTEX, with a voice recognition program, will control up to 256 off/on appliances, dial and answer the phone, flash for call waiting, dial from a directory, control TV's, VCR's, stereos and more — all with your voice. CINTEX2 includes the necessary hardware and voice macros which you can use to immediately control your environment. You can tailor these macros to your personal needs and add new macros. Pops-up over current application allowing instant access. $695-$2,000.

**2094 Car Builder**
Optimum Resource
18 Hunter Road
Hilton Head Island, SC 29926

843-689-8000
FAX: 843-689-8008
e-mail: sticky@stickybear.com
www.stickybear.com

*Chris Gintz, Chief Executive Officer*
*Richard Hefter, President*

As design engineers, users build cars on screen, specifying chassis length, wheelbase, engine type, transmission, fuel tank size, suspension, steering, tires and brakes. All functional choices are interrelated and will affect the performance of the final design. *$59.99*

**2095 Center for Best Practices in Early Childhood**
32 Horrabin Hall
Macomb, IL 61455

309-298-1634
FAX: 309-298-2305
e-mail: l-robinson1@wiu.edu
www.wiu.edu/thecenter/

*Linda Robinson, Assistant Director*

A group of early childhood projects which focus on assistive technology for children ages birth to 8 with disabilities and their families. Services include technology training, curricula, books, software and online workshops.

**2096 Clock**
Compass Learning
203 Colorado Street
Austin, TX 78701

858-587-0087
800-247-1380
FAX: 619-622-7873
www.compasslearning.com

*Rajeev Turi, President*

An extremely simple, easy-to-use program for children who are learning how to read the time of day from clocks and digital displays. Apple and MS-DOS and Mac available. *$39.95*

**2097  Co:Writer**
Don Johnston
26799 W Commerce Drive
Volo, IL  60073
847-740-0749
800-999-4660
FAX: 847-740-7326
e-mail: info@donjohnston.com
www.donjohnston.com

*Ketan Kothari, Chief Executive Officer*
*Ruth Ziolkowski, President*

A writing description program that helps construct sentences. This is an easy-to-use, intelligent word prediction program that works in conjunction with any word processor or text application program to reduce the number of keystrokes necessary to complete an intended word or sentence. This invaluable program can help make the writing process easier, faster and even better for writers of all ages and ability levels. *$290.00*

**2098  Community Skills: Learning to Function in Your Neighborhood**
Programming Concepts
PO Box 34270
San Antonio, TX  78265
800-594-4263
FAX: 888-259-8284
e-mail: pciinfo@pcieducation.com
www.pcieducation.com

*Janie Haugen, Program Director*
*Jeff McLean, President/CEO*

Offers parents and educators a functional way to teach community life skills. *$49.95*

**2099  Companion Activities**
Soft Touch
4300 Stine Road
Suite 401
Bakersfield, CA  93313
661-396-8676
877-763-8868
FAX: 661-396-8760
e-mail: support@softtouch.com
www.softouch.com

*Joyce Meyer, President*
*Roxanne Butterfield, Marketing*

Print your own books, worksheets, flash cards, board games, matching games, bingo games, card games and many more. This CD offers numerous companion activities to different SoftTouch software titles. Activities range from very easy to difficult. Companion activities are great tools to reinforce learning. Use the work sheets - black and white and color - in the inclusion class for students with special needs.

**2100  Concepts on the Move Advanced Preacademics**
Soft Touch
4300 Stine Road
Suite 401
Bakersfield, CA  93313
661-396-8676
877-763-8868
FAX: 661-396-8760
e-mail: softtouch@funsoftware.com
www.funsoftware.com

*Roxanne Butterfield, Marketing*
*Joyce Meyer, President*

Choose from five concepts groups: categories, occupations, functions, goes with and prepositions. Use our Steps to Learning Design to choose how many concepts to present at one time and where to place each one in the scan array, on screen keyboard or IntelliKeys keyboard. Watch and listen as the concept morphs or changes and music plays. The words are also shown to reinforce emerging literacy skills. Compatible with USB IntelliKeys.

**2101  Cooking Class: Learning About Food Preparation**
Programming Concepts
PO Box B
San Antonio, TX  78265
800-594-4263
FAX: 218-480-5
e-mail: tciinfo@tcieducatio.com
www.tcieducation.com

*Janie Haugen, Program Director*
*Jeff McLane, President/CEO*

This game offers parents and educators a new way to teach basic preparation skills. Kitchen safety and sanitation are stressed throughout the game. *$49.95*

**2102  Dilemma**
Educational Activities Software
PO Box 754
Baldwin, NY  11510
516-867-7878
800-645-2796
FAX: 516-379-7429
e-mail: achieve@ea-software.com

*Alan Stern, Sales Director/Manager*

Realistic stories with a choice of different gripping endings, color graphics, a built-in dictionary and a user controlled reading rate make these computer programs compelling enough to interest all students. Comprehension and vocabulary questions follow each story. *$159.00*

**2103  Dino-Games**
Academic Software
331 W 2nd Street
Lexington, KY  40507
859-233-2332
800-842-2357
FAX: 859-231-0725

*Warren E Lacefield PhD, President*
*Penelope Ellis, Marketing Director*

Dino-Games are single switch software programs for early switch practice. Dinosaur games provide practice in pattern recognition, cause and effect demonstration, directionality training, number concepts and problem solving. They are compatible with most popular switch interfaces and alternate keyboards. For Macintosh, IBM and compatibles. DINO-LINK is a matching game; DINO-MAZE is a series of maze games; DINO-FIND is a game of concentration; and DINO-DOT is a collection of dot-to-dot games.
*$39.95 per game*

**2104  Directions: Technology in Special Education**
DREAMMS for Kids
273 Ringwood Road
Freeville, NY  13068
607-539-3027
FAX: 607-539-9930
www.dreamms.org

A CD containing all of 'Directions' past articles and information gathered from their newsletter which lists resources for assistive and adaptive computer tehnologies in the home, school and community. *$24.95*

**2105  ESI Master Resource Guide**
Educational Software Institute
4213 S 94th Street
Omaha, NE  68127
402-592-3300
800-955-5570
FAX: 402-592-2017
e-mail: info@edsoft.com
www.edsoft.com

*Lee Myers, President*
*Kathy Cavanaugh, Catalog Manager*

Educational Software Institute (ESI) provides a one-stop shop to purchase software titles by all of the best publishers. The ESI Master Gold Book catalog and CD-ROM represents more than 400 software publishers, with information on more than 8,000 software titles. Take the confusion out of software selection by calling ESI for all of your software needs - including competitive prices, software previews, knowledgeable assistance, and the largest selection available all in one place.
*Yearly*

**2106    EZ Keys**
Words+
42505 10th Street W
Suite 109
Lancaster, CA  93534                    661-266-5800
                                        800-869-8521
                                    FAX: 661-266-8969
                            e-mail: info@words-plus.com
                                    www.words-plus.com

*Ginger Woltosz, Vice President*
*Tim Ross, Manager*

A software and hardware product designed to operate on an IBM compatible PC. The software provides dual word prediction, abbreviation expansion, five different methods of voice output and access to commercial software applications. *$1395.00*

**2107    Early Games for Young Children**
Queue Incorporated
1 Control Drive
Shelton, CT  06484                      203-446-8100
                                        800-232-2224
                                    FAX: 203-336-2481
                            e-mail: jdk@queueinc.com
                                    www.queueinc.com

*Jonathan Kantrowitz, Owner*

Software that includes nine activities that entertain preschoolers in honing basic math and language skills.

**2108    Early Music Skills**
Electronic Courseware Systems
1713 S State Street
Champaign, IL  61820                    217-359-7099
                                        800-832-4965
                                    FAX: 217-359-6578
                            e-mail: support@ecsmedia.com
                                    www.ecsmedia.com

*G Peters, President*
*Jodie Varner, Marketing Manager*

A tutorial and drill program designed for the beginning music student. It covers four basic music reading skills: recognition of line and space notes; comprehension of the numbering system for the musical staff; visual and aural identification of notes moving up and down; and recognition of notes stepping and skipping up and down. *$ 39.95*

**2109    Eating Skills: Learning Basic Table Manners**
P CI Education Publishing
PO Box 34270
San Antonio, TX  78265                  210-377-1999
                                        800-594-4263
                                    FAX: 210-377-1121
                            e-mail: pciinfo@pcieducation.com
                                    www.pcieducation.com

*Janie Haugen, Program Director*
*Jeff Clain, Chief Executive Officer*

Offers parents and educators a functional way to teach and reinforce basic table manners. *$49.95*

**2110    Electronic Courseware Systems**
1713 S State Street
Champaign, IL  61820                    217-359-7099
                                        800-832-4965
                                    FAX: 217-359-6578
                            e-mail: sales@ecsmedia.com
                                    www.ecsmedia.com

*Jodie Varner, Manager*
*G Peters, President*

Offers a complete library of instructional software for music, math, science and social studies.

**2111    Fall Fun**
Soft Touch
4300 Stine Road
Suite 401
Bakersfield, CA  93313                  661-396-8676
                                        877-763-8868
                                    FAX: 661-396-8760
                            e-mail: softtouch@fsofttouch.com
                                    www.softtouch.com

*Joyce Meyer, President*
*Roxanne Butterfield, Marketing*

Your students can begin their day with the Pledge of Allegiance, Pumpkins, Owls, and Cats. Witches adorn Five Pumpkins Sitting on the Gate. Five Fat Turkeys out smart the pilgrims with song and antics. The owl and cat have songs of their own. A variety of activities reinforce concepts such as short, tall, first, second, third, same and different. Fall Fun includes cause and effect and easy to more difficult levels. Eight songs in all.

**2112    Five Green & Speckled Frogs**
Soft Touch
4300 Stine Road
Suite 401
Bakersfield, CA  93313                  661-396-8676
                                        877-763-8868
                                    FAX: 661-396-8760
                            e-mail: softtouch@softtouch.com
                                    www.softtouch.com

*Roxanne Butterfield, Marketing*
*Joyce Meyer, President*

Laugh, learn and sing with Five Humorous Frogs. Activities start with cause and effect and progress to teach directionality and simple subtraction. This classic song makes learning numbers and number worlds easy. Selections can be set to 2, 3, 4, 5, or 6 on-screen choices. Two games are included. One teaches direction on a number line. If the child moves the frog in the correct direction, the frog gets a point. The other game teaches beginning subtraction.

**2113    Free and User Supported Software for the IBM PC: A Resource Guide**
McFarland & Company
960 NC Highway 88 W
PO Box 677
Jefferson, NC  28640                    336-246-4460
                                        800-253-2187
                                    FAX: 336-246-5018
                            e-mail: info@mcfarlandpub.com
                                    www.mcfarlandpub.com

A selection of word processing, database management, spreadsheets, and graphics programs are described and evaluated. Describes how the program works and its strengths and weaknesses. Rating charts cover such aspects as ease of use, ease of learning, documentation, and general utility. *$27.50*

*224 pages Paperback*
*ISBN 0-89950 -99-0*

**2114 GoalView Performance Information System for Special Education**
Learning Tools International
2391 Circadian Way
Santa Rosa, CA  95407

707-521-3530
800-333-9954
FAX: 707-521-3535
e-mail: info@Ltools.com
www.goalview.com

*Cathy Zier, Vice President*
*Kirk Wilson, Owner*

An Internet information system for students, educators and parents that enables accountability and achievement tracking; prepares IDEA compliant IEP's in minutes; provides over 250,000 education standards and special education goals and objectives in English and Spanish; generates Federal compliance reports; and creates IDEA GoalCard progress reports for students, schools and districts for every reporting period.

**2115 HELP**
V OR T Corporation
PO Box 60132
Palo Alto, CA  94306

650-322-8282
888-757-VORT
FAX: 650-327-0747
e-mail: sales@vort.com
www.vort.com

*Tom Holt, Founder/Owner*

A software version of HELP, covers over 650 skills in 6 developmental areas; cognitive, motor skills, language, gross motor, social and self-help.

**2116 Handbook of Adaptive Switches and Augmentative Communication Devices**
Academic Software
331 W 2nd Street
Lexington, KY  40507

859-233-2332
800-842-2357
FAX: 859-231-0725

*Warren E Lacefield PhD, President/Author*
*Penelope Ellis, Marketing Director*
*Cindy L George, Author*

This second edition contains physical descriptions and laboratory test data for a variety of commercially available pressure switches and augmentative communication devices and chapters on physical interaction, seating and positioning, and control access. It is an essential tool for assistive technology professionals and therapists who make decisions concerning physical access. *$60.00*
*300 pages Hardcover*

**2117 HandiWARE**
Microsystems Software
600 Worcester Road
Framingham, MA  01702

508-626-8511
800-828-2600
FAX: 508-879-1069
e-mail: infor@microsys.com
www.handiware.com

*Terri McGrath, Sales/Marketing*
*Bill Kilroy, Product Manager*

Adapted access software, assists persons with physical, hearing and visual impairments in accessing computers running DOS and Windows. HandiWARE is a suite of 8 software programs which provide users with screen magnification, alternate keyboard access, word prediction, augmentative communication, hands free telephone access, a visual beep. $20.00-$595.00.

**2118 How to Write for Everyday Living**
Educational Activities Software
PO Box 754
Baldwin, NY  11510

516-867-7878
800-645-2796
FAX: 516-379-7429
e-mail: achieve@ea-software.com

*Alan Stern, Manager*

An individualized Life Skills WRITING Software program emphasizing the reading, writing, communication and reference skills needed for real-life tasks: preparing a resume, an employment form, a business letter and envelope, a learner's permit, a social security application and banking forms. *$159.00*

**2119 I KNOW American History**
Soft Touch
4300 Stine Road
Suite 401
Bakersfield, CA  93313

661-396-8676
877-763-8868
FAX: 661-396-8760
e-mail: support@softtouch.com
www.softtouch.com

*Joyce Meyer, President*
*Roxanne Butterfield, Marketing*

The new I KNOW programs is the way students practice attending, choice making and turn-taking while uncovering learning puzzles. Each press reveals more of the image while the narrator reads the text on the screen. Offers three levels of language: short phrases, short sentences and longer sentences to match the student's learning level. Choose from the five topic areas: American Symbols, Westward Movement, Early Colonial Americans, Industrial Revolution and Biographies.

**2120 I KNOW American History Overlay CD**
Soft Touch
4300 Stine Road
Suite 401
Bakersfield, CA  93313

661-396-8676
877-763-8868
FAX: 661-396-8760
e-mail: softtouch@softtouch.com
www.softtouch.com

*Roxanne Butterfield, Marketing*
*Joyce Meyer, President*

Use this Overlay CD with I KNOW American History program. Includes standard overlays and SoftTouch's changeable overlays. Includes Overlay Printer by IntelliTools. Use Overlay Maker by IntelliTools (not included) to modify the overlays or to make additional learning materials.

**2121 IntelliPics Studio 3**
Intelli Tools
1720 Corporate Circle
Petaluma, CA  94954

707-773-2000
800-899-6687
FAX: 707-773-2001
e-mail: info@intellitools.com
www.intellitools.com

*Beth Davis, Director Sales & Operations*
*Lori Castle, Supervisor*
*Arjan Khalsa, Chief Executive Officer*

Multimedia authoring tool for both students and teachers to create activities, games, quizzes, slide shows, reports and presentations. *$395.00*

**2122 KIDS (Keyboard Introductory Development Series)**
Electronic Courseware Systems
1713 S State Street
Champaign, IL 61820
217-359-7099
800-832-4965
FAX: 217-359-6578
e-mail: sales@ecsmedia.com
www.ecsmedia.com

*G Peters, President*
*Jodie Varner, Marketing Manager*

A four disk series for the very young. Zoo Puppet Theater reinforces learning correct finger numbers for piano playing; Race Car Keys teaches keyboard geography by recognizing syllables or note names; Dinosaurs Lunch teaches placement of the notes on the treble staff; and Follow Me asks the student to play notes that have been presented aurally. *$49.95*

**2123 Katie's Farm**
Lawrence Productions
1800 S 53th Street
Galesburg, MI 49053
269-665-7075
800-421-4157
FAX: 269-665-7060
e-mail: sales@lpi.com
www.lpi.com

*John W Lawrence, Chairman/Owner*

Software for children ages four through eight.

**2124 Keyboard Tutor, Music Software**
Electronic Courseware Systems
1713 S State Street
Champaign, IL 61820
217-359-7099
800-832-4965
FAX: 217-359-6578
e-mail: sales@ecsmedia.com
www.ecsmedia.com

*G Peters, President*
*Jodie Varner, Marketing Manager*

Presents exercises for learning elementary keyboard skills including knowledge of names of the keys, piano keys matched to notes, notes matched to piano keys, whole steps and half steps. Each lesson allows unlimited practice of the skills. The program may be used with or without a midi keyboard attached to the computer. *$39.95*

**2125 Keyboarding by Ability**
Teachers Institute for Special Education
9933 NW 45th Street
Sunrise, FL 33351
954-572-6220
FAX: 954-572-6220
e-mail: tise@special-education-soft.com
www.special-education-soft.com

*Gary Byowitz, Director*

Allows the learning diabled or dyslexic student to acquire keyboarding skills through visually cued alphabetical approach designed and tested to meet the specific learning style needs of this unique population at every grade level. Package contains: IBM software, a set of lesson plans and instructional goals; supplamental graded data input exercises. *$148.95*

**2126 Keyboarding for the Physically Handicapped**
Teachers Institute for Special Education
4 Gabalin Court
Huntington Station, NY 11746
631-549-1715
FAX: 516-549-1715
e-mail: jackheller@aol.com
www.users.aol.com/jackheller

*Jack Heller, Director/Owner*

Customed designed touch typing programs for any student. A person needs order by the number of usable fingers on each hand (not counting the thumb), and whether or not a one finger or a head-pointer edition is wanted. Package includes IBM software; a complete set of lesson plans and instructional goals. *$149.95*

**2127 Keyboarding with One Hand**
Teachers Institute for Special Education
PO Box 2300
Wantagh, NY 11793
FAX: 516-781-4070
e-mail: jackheller@aol.com
www.users.aol.com/jackheller

*Jack Heller, Director*

This 22 lesson tutorial developed through 25 years of research, testing and teaching allows a student with one hand to aqure employable keyboarding skills using a touch system designed for the standard IBM PC keyboard. *$79.95*

**2128 LPDOS Deluxe**
Optelec U S
3030 Enterprise Court
Suite C
Vista, CA 92081
800-828-1056
FAX: 978-692-6073
e-mail: chrish@optelec.com
www.optelec.com

*Annette Z Fasnacht, President*
*Robert Auger, General Manager*

Large print software programs. *$595.00*

**2129 Large Print DOS**
Optelec U S
PO Box 796
Westford, MA 01886
978-692-9496
800-828-1056
FAX: 978-692-6073
www.optelec.com

*Annette Fasnacht, President*
*James Bailey, Vice President*

**2130 Laureate Learning Systems**
110 E Spring Street
Winooski, VT 05404
802-655-4755
800-562-6801
FAX: 802-655-4757
e-mail: info@llsys.com
www.laureatelearning.com

*Michelle L Oakes, Administrative Assistant*
*Kathy Hollandsworth, Office Manager*
*Mary Wilson, Owner*

Laureate publishes award-winning talking software for children and adults with disabilities. Programs cover cause and effect, language development, cognitive processing, and reading. High-quality speech, colorful graphics and amusing animation make learning fun. Accessible with touchscreen, single switch, keyboard and mouse. No reading required. Available on a hybrid CD-ROM for Windows and Macintosh. Visit our website for more information or call for a free catalog.

**2131 Learning Company**
222 3rd Avenue SE
Suite 400
Cedar Rapids, IA 52401
319-395-9626
888-242-6747
FAX: 319-395-0217
www.learningcompany.com

*Barry O'Callaghan, Chief Executive Officer*
*Simon Calver, Chief Operating Officer*

Software for children. For Macintosh or Windows (3.1 DOS or Windows 95, Windows 98 required).

**2132    Little Red Hen**
Compass Learning
9920 Pacific Heights Boulevard
San Diego, CA  92121                                858-587-0087
                                                    800-247-1380
                                             FAX: 619-622-7873
                                             www.compasslearning.com

*Rajeev Paulate, President*
*Eric Loeffel, Executive Vice President/COO*

Children learn about the rewards of hard work when they discover who the Little Red Hen's friends miss out on freshly baked bread. Puzzles, rhymes, story writing and other interactive exercises enhance the creative learning process. *$34.95*

**2133    Looking Good: Learning to Improve Your Appearance**
Programming Concepts
PO Box 12428
San Antonio, TX  78212
                                                    800-594-4263
                                             FAX: 218-480-5

*Janie Haugen, Program Director*
*Jeff Mclane, President/CEO*

This game offers a creative way to discuss all areas of grooming. *$49.95*

**2134    Monkeys Jumping on the Bed**
Soft Touch
4300 Stine Road
Suite 401
Bakersfield, CA  93313                             661-396-8676
                                                   877-763-8868
                                             FAX: 661-396-8760
                                    e-mail: support@softtouch.com
                                             www.softouch.com

*Roxanne Butterfield, Marketing*
*Joyce Meyer, President*

This program combines a favorite preschool song with number and color activities. Children and adults will enjoy engaging music and delightful animation. Students with cognitive delays respond to upbeat music and interesting sounds. Large graphics help learners focus on the action. Several important concepts are presented in enjoyable activity formats. Students learn cause and effect in Let's Play and Just for Fun.

**2135    Morse Code WSKE**
Words+
42505 10th Street W
Suite 109
Lancaster, CA  93534                               661-723-6523
                                                   800-869-8521
                                             FAX: 661-266-8969
                                    e-mail: info@words-plus.com
                                             www.words-plus.org

*Ginger Woltosz, Vice President*
*Walt Wolosz, Manager*

A software and hardware product designed to operate on an IBM compatible PC.

**2136    Multi-Scan Single Switch Activity Center**
Academic Software
331 W 2nd Street
Lexington, KY  40507                               859-233-2332
                                                   800-842-2357
                                             FAX: 859-231-0725

*Warren E Lacefield PhD, President*
*Penelope Ellis, Marketing Director*

A single switch activity center containing four educational games: Match, Maze, Dot-to-Dot, and Concentration, along with six graphics libraries; Dinosaurs, Sports, Animals, Independent Living, Vocations, and Cosmetology. MULTI-SCAN allows you to select a graphic library, choose games for each user, and adjust the difficulty level and other settings for each game. Other features allow you to save the game setups under each user's name and print out individual performance reports after sessions. *$154.00*

**2137    Muppet Learning Keys**
WINGS for Learning
1600 Green Hills Road
Scotts Valley, CA  95066                           831-464-3600
                                             FAX: 831-464-3600

*Ani Stocks, Owner*

Designed to introduce children to the world of the computer as they become familiar with letters, numbers and colors.

**2138    My Own Pain**
Soft Touch
4300 Stine Road
Suite 401
Bakersfield, CA  93313                             661-396-8676
                                                   877-763-8868
                                             FAX: 661-396-8760
                                             www.softtouch.com

*Roxanne Butterfield, Marketing Director*
*Joyce Meyer, President*

Three activities - three levels. Press the switch and the paint brush chooses the color and paints the vehicle. Music reinforces the sounds when the picture is complete. A second activity allows the student to choose the color and paint the vehicle parts any color he or she wants. The third activity is a blueprint. Print the color that matches the one in the wire drawing. Color the drawing to complete the picture.

**2139    Old MacDonald's Farm Deluxe**
Soft Touch
4300 Stine Road
Suite 401
Bakersfield, CA  93313                             661-396-8676
                                                   877-763-8868
                                             FAX: 661-396-8760
                                    e-mail: support@softtouch.com
                                             www.softtouch.com

*Roxanne Butterfield, Marketing*
*Joyce Meyer, President*

Toddlers, preschoolers and early elementary students will be entertained and captivated by the six major activities and animations in the delightful program. Includes 18 real animation images or 9 cartoon like characters. The teacher or child can choose which animals they want to sing about. Some activities are designed for children within the normal population, others are designed for students with moderate and severe disabilities.

**2140    Please Understand Me: Software Program and Books**
Cambridge Educational
PO Box 931
Monmouth Junction, NJ  08852                       609-671-1000
                                                   800-468-4227
                                             FAX: 800-329-6687
                                    e-mail: stesrv@films.com
                                             www.cambridgeeducational.com
Promotes self-understanding while helping each student understand they are different from others. *$69.00*
                      *209 pages BiAnnual*
                      *ISBN 0-927368-56-x*

**2141    Pond**
WINGS for Learning
1600 Green Hills Road
Scotts Valley, CA  95066                           831-464-3600
                                             FAX: 831-464-3600

*Ani Stocks, Owner*

Software game that teaches pattern recognition and encourages observation, trial and error and the interpretation of data.

## 2142  Print, Play & Learn #1 Old Mac's Farm

Soft Touch Incorporated
4300 Stine Road
Suite 401
Bakersfield, CA  93313                    661-396-8676
                                          877-763-8868
                                    FAX: 661-396-8760
                        e-mail: softtouch@software.com
                                     www.softtouch.com

*Roxanne Butterfield, Marketing Director*
*Joyce Meyer, President*

Once your students have completed Old Mac's Farm, let them use the fun off-computer activities to continue learning. Over 25 activites with 250 sheets you print. Board games, dot-to-dot drawings, word puzzles, make a scene, flash cards. Concentration, sentence strips, worksheets and much more are availablefor techers to expand their teaching goals. This CD is full of activites to print and use.

## 2143  Print, Play & Learn #7: Sampler

Soft Touch
4300 Stine Road
Suite 401
Bakersfield, CA  93313                    661-396-8676
                                          877-763-8868
                                    FAX: 661-396-8760
                        e-mail: support@softtouch.com
                                     www.softtouch.com

*Roxanne Butterfield, Marketing*
*Joyce Meyer, President*

Print, Play and Learn Sampler gives you over 200 activites organized by training, easy, medium and hard levels so you can ready to help your student advance. Activites cover a wide range of basic knowledge, including colors, shapes, numbers, letters and much, much more. Note: Requires Overlay Maker or Overlay Printer by IntelliTools and a color printer.

## 2144  Puzzle Power: Sampler

Soft Touch
4300 Stine Road
Suite 401
Bakersfield, CA  93313                    661-396-8676
                                          877-763-8868
                                    FAX: 661-396-8760
                        e-mail: support@softtouch.com
                                     www.funsoftware.com

*Joyce Meyer, President*
*Roxanne Butterfield, Marketing*

Puzzle Power - Sampler offers a variety of puzzles in different themes. Each theme puzzle is followed by a puzzle of one item in this category. For example, first solve a puzzle for occupations. Then, solve a puzzle that is a baker. The pictures are large, clear and easily identifiable.

## 2145  Puzzle Power: Zoo & School Days

Soft Touch
4300 Stine Road
Suite 401
Bakersfield, CA  93313                    661-396-8676
                                          877-763-8868
                                    FAX: 661-396-8760
                        e-mail: support@softtouch.com
                                     www.softtouch.com

*Roxanne Butterfield, Marketing Director*
*Joyce Meyer, President*

Here is a program for all of our students who need puzzle skills, but cannot access commercial puzzles. Puzzle Power puzzles start with just two pieces and progress to 16 pieces. The pictures are large, clear and easily identifiable. Four different activites enable all students to be successful. Automatic Placement: the student just presses the switch or keyboard to place the pieces. Magnet Mouse: all the student needs to do is move the mouse and it drops into place.

## 2146  Rodeo

Soft Touch
4300 Stine Road
Suite 401
Bakersfield, CA  93313                    661-396-8676
                                          877-763-8868
                                    FAX: 661-396-8760
                     e-mail: softtouch@funsoftware.com
                                    www.funsoftware.com

*Roxanne Butterfield, Marketing*
*Joyce Meyer, President*

Rodeo action and familiar tunes for teens and preteens. Four activities invite students to learn, laugh, and sing as they go to the rodeo with up to six age-peer friends. Age-appropriate graphics with surprising animations reinforce the learning. The graphics are large and coorful, the melodies familiar, and the words descriptive of the action on the screen.

## 2147  Shop Til You Drop

Soft Touch
4300 Stine Road
Suite 401
Bakersfield, CA  93313                    661-396-8676
                                          877-763-8868
                                    FAX: 661-396-8760
                        e-mail: softtouch@softtouch.com
                                     www.softtouch.com

*Roxanne Butterfield, Marketing*
*Joyce Meyer, President*

Designed specifically for preteens and teens with moderate and severe disabilities, this program will become a staple for the classroom. The student goes shopping and can choose which outfits to put together. They may choose to purchase the outfit - of course, with mom's credit card. Another activity is a video arcade game about money. Shop 'Til You Drop can be adjusted from a single switch cause-and-effect program to row-and-column scanning to direct choice.

## 2148  Songs I Sing at Preschool

Soft Touch
4300 Stine Road
Suite 401
Bakersfield, CA  93313                    661-396-8676
                                          877-763-8868
                                    FAX: 661-396-8760
                     e-mail: softtouch@funsoftware.com
                                    www.funsoftware.com

*Roxanne Butterfield, Marketing*
*Joyce Meyer, President*

Songs I Sing at Preschool offers many options for the teacher and the student. Over the years, our software has used music because our students really respond to the sounds and rhythms of songs. Teachers select which songs to present, how many to present at one time and where to place each song on the overlay, keyboard or scan array.

## 2149  Stickybear Town Builder

Optimum Resource
18 Hunter Road
Hilton Head Island, SC  29926             843-689-8000
                                    FAX: 843-689-8008
                        e-mail: stickyb@stickybear.com
                                     www.stickybear.com

*Chris Gintz, Chief Executive Officer*

Children learn to read maps, build towns, take trips and use a compass in this simulation program. *$59.95*

## 2150  Stickybear Typing

Optimum Resource
18 Hunter Road
Hilton Head Island, SC  29926             843-689-8000
                                    FAX: 843-689-8008
                        e-mail: stickyb@stickybear.com
                                     www.stickybear.com

*Chris Gintz, Chief Executive Officer*

Sharpen typing skills with three challenging activities: Stickybear Keypress, Stickybear Thump and Stickybear Stories. *$59.95*

**2151 Stickybear's Early Learning Activities**
Optimum Resource
18 Hunter Road
Hilton Head Island, SC 29926
843-689-8000
FAX: 843-689-8008
e-mail: sticky@stickybear.com
www.stickybear.com

*Chris Gintz, Chief Executive Officer*

Two modes of play, structure and non-structured, allow youngsters to learn through prompted direction or by the discovery method. Lively animation and sound keep attention levels high and Stickybear's Early Learning Activities is bilingual, so youngsters can build skills in both English and Spanish. *$59.95*

**2152 Stickybear's Kindergarden Activities**
Optimum Resource
18 Hunter Road
Hilton Head Island, SC 29926
843-689-8000
FAX: 843-689-8008
e-mail: sticky@stickybear.com
www.stickybear.com

*Chris Gintz, Chief Executive Officer*

This dynamic new multifaceted program covers a wide range of preschool skills that go far beyond the stricktly academic! At Stickybear's house, children discover the alphabet, numbers, shapes, colors, plus - social skills, important safety messages and delightful off-screen activities that foster creativity. Over three hours of original music can be compose by a chid and saved for future use. *$59.95*

**2153 Stickybear's Science Fair: Light**
Optimum Resource
18 Hunter Road
Hilton Head Island, SC 29926
843-689-8000
FAX: 843-689-8008
e-mail: stickyb@stickybear.com
www.stickybear.com

*Chris Gintz, Chief Executive Officer*

The first in the new series of science-based programs Stickybear Science Fair: Light presents a content rich environment which allows students, ages 7-12 to explore, experiment with and understand light and it's properties. The program presents experiments, both structured and free-form, which allow users to work with prisms, lenses, color mixing, optical illusions and more. *$59.95*

**2154 Storybook Maker Deluxe**
Compass Learning
Evening Creek Drive N
Suite 200
San Diego, CA 92128
858-587-0087
800-247-1380
FAX: 619-622-7873
www.compasslearning.com

*Rajeev Puri, President*
*Eric Loeffel, Chief Operating Officer*
*Martin Kenney Jr, Chief Executive Officer*

Using Storybook Maker Deluxe and their imaginations, students can create and publish stories filled with exciting graphics. Students can write stories and watch as the text appears in the setting they've chosen. Engaging sounds and music, plus lively animations, provide positive learning reinforcement throughout the program. *$44.95*

**2155 Super Challenger**
Electronic Courseware Systems
1713 S State Street
Champaign, IL 61820
217-359-7099
800-832-4965
FAX: 217-359-6578
e-mail: support@ecsmedia.com
www.ecsmedia.com

*Jodie Varner, Manager*
*G Peters, President*

An aural-visual musical game that increases the player's ability to remember a series of pitches as they are played by the computer. The game is based on a 12-note chromatic scale, a major scale, and a minor scale. Each pitch is reinforced visually with a color representation of a keyboard on the display screen. Computer/software. *$39.95*

**2156 Switch Basics**
Soft Touch
4300 Stine Road
Suite 401
Bakersfield, CA 93313
661-396-8676
877-763-8868
FAX: 661-396-8760
e-mail: softtouch@funsoftware.com
www.funsoftware.com

*Roxanne Butterfield, Marketing Director*
*Joyce Meyer, President*

Discover whimsical animations and real life pictures while learning switch operations. Intriguing and humorous, nine different programs offer a multitude of learning experiences for all ages. Program options include: cause and effect, scanning, step scanning, row and column activites for one or two players. Watch the clouds roll away revealing African animals; visit the beauty salon or barber shop; work two to sixteen piece puzzles; or add swimming fish to a huge aquarium.

**2157 Teach Me Phonemics Series Bundle**
Soft Touch
4300 Stine Road
Suite 401
Bakersfield, CA 93313
661-396-8676
877-763-8868
FAX: 661-396-8760
e-mail: support@softtouch.com
www.funsoftware.com

*Joyce Meyer, President*
*Roxanne Butterfield, Marketing*

The Teach Me Phonemics Series Bundle includes one copy of each Teach Me Phonemics program - Initial, Medial, Final and Blends - four CD's in all.

**2158 Teach Me Phonemics Super Bundle**
Soft Touch
4300 Stine Road
Suite 401
Bakersfield, CA 93313
661-396-8676
877-763-8868
FAX: 661-396-8760
e-mail: softtouch@funsoftware.com
www.funsoftware.com

*Roxanne Butterfield, Marketing*
*Joyce Meyer, President*

Teach Me Phonemics Super Bundle includes all 4 Teach Me Phonemics programs and all 4 Teach Me Phonemics overlay CD's - eight CD's in all.

**2159    Teach Me Phonemics: Blends**
Soft Touch
4300 Stine Road
Suite 401
Bakersfield, CA  93313                661-396-8676
                                      877-763-8868
                         FAX: 661-396-8760
               e-mail: softtouch@funsoftware.com
                          www.funsoftware.com

*Roxanne Butterfield, Marketing*
*Joyce Meyer, President*

Teach Me Phonemics - Blends helps students explore words and
hear the initial blend sounds. It features musical interludes and
movement to engage the student. Teachers select the best combination options to motivate and engage the student. Options turn
off and on the fly so you can quickly make changes to keep the
student engaged.

**2160    Teach Me Phonemics: Final**
Soft Touch
4300 Stine Road
Suite 401
Bakersfield, CA  93313                661-396-8676
                                      877-763-8868
                         FAX: 661-396-8760
               e-mail: softtouch@funsoftware.com
                          www.funsoftware.com

*Roxanne Butterfield*
*Joyce Meyer, President*

Teach me Phonemics - Final helps students explore words and
hear the final sounds. It features musical interludes and movement to engage the student. Options turn off and on the fly so you
can quickly make changes to keep the student engaged.

**2161    Teach Me Phonemics: Initial**
Soft Touch
4300 Stine Road
Suite 401
Bakersfield, CA  93313                661-396-8676
                                      877-763-8868
                         FAX: 661-396-8760
               e-mail: softtouch@softtouch.com
                          www.softtouch.com

*Roxanne Butterfield, Marketing*
*Joyce Meyer, President*

Teach Me Phonemics - Initial helps students explore the words
and hear the initial sounds. It features musical interludes and
movement to engage the student. Teachers select the best combination options to motivate and engage the student. Options turn
off and on the fly so you can quickly make changes to keep the
student engaged.

**2162    Teach Me Phonemics: Medial**
Soft Touch
4300 Stine Road
Suite 401
Bakersfield, CA  93313                661-396-8676
                                      877-763-8868
                         FAX: 661-396-8760
               e-mail: softtouch@softtouch.com
                          www.softtouch.com

*Roxanne Butterfield, Marketing*
*Joyce Meyer, President*

Teach Me Phonemics - Medial helps students explore the words
and hear the medial sounds. It features musical interludes and
movement to engage the student. Teachers select the best combination options to motivate and engage the student. Options turn
off and on the fly so you can quickly make changes to keep the
student engaged.

**2163    Teach Me to Talk**
Soft Touch
4300 Stine Road
Suite 401
Bakersfield, CA  93313                661-396-8676
                                      877-763-8868
                         FAX: 661-396-8760
               e-mail: softtouch@softtouch.com
                          www.softtouch.com

*Roxanne Butterfield, Marketing*
*Joyce Meyer, President*

The first activity Teach Me to Talk is used as a springboard for
the student to learn to speak the word. There are 150 real pictures. When a picture is chosen, it appears on a clear background
with musical interludes, movement, written word and spoken
word. It culminates by morphing to the corresponding black and
white Mayer-Johnson symbol. The second activity Story Time,
takes some of these nouns and puts them in four line poetry. This
helps students hear the word in the midst of a sentence.

**2164    Teen Tunes Plus**
Soft Touch
4300 Stine Road
Suite 401
Bakersfield, CA  93313                661-396-8676
                                      877-763-8868
                         FAX: 661-396-8760
               e-mail: softtouch@softtouch.com
                          www.funsoftware.com

*Joyce Meyer, President*
*Roxanne Butterfield, Marketing*

Introduce switch use to older students with disabilities. Large
intersting graphics, a variety of musical interludes, and surprising animations are combined with calm soothing music and
beautiful pictures in the software specifically designed for preteens and teens with severe cognitive delays and/or physical disabilities, and older students learning to use a switch.

**2165    There are Tyrannosaurs Trying on Pants in My Bed-
room**
Compass Learning
203 Colorado Street
Austin, TX  78701                     858-587-0087
                                      800-247-1380
                         FAX: 619-622-7873
                    www.compasslearning.com

*Rajeev Puri, President*
*Eric Loeffel, Executive Vice President*

In this popular story, Saturday chores turn into fun-filled frol-
icking when dinosaurs come for a visit. Sounds, music and animation make learning about phonics and vocabulary dyno-mite.
*$34.95*

**2166    Three Billy Goats Gruff**
Compass Learning
203 Colorado Street
Austin, TX  78701                     858-587-0087
                                      800-247-1380
                         FAX: 619-622-7873
                    www.compasslearning.com

*Rajeev Puri, President*
*Eric Loeffer, Executive Vice President/ OO*

Motivating exercises and creative activities provide hours of
learning fun while young students follow the adventure of The
Three Billy Goats Gruff in this animated version of the timeless
tale. *$ 34.95*

**2167 Three Little Pigs**
Compass Learning
203 Colorado Street
Austin, TX 78701
858-587-0087
800-247-1380
FAX: 619-622-7873
www.compasslearning.com

*Rajeev Puri, President*
*Eric Loeffel, Executive Vice President*

Help young students build reading comprehension and writing skills with this interactive version of the children's classic, The Three Little Pigs. Animated storytelling and creative activities inspire children to read, write and rhyme. *$34.95*

**2168 TouchCorders**
Soft Touch
4300 Stine Road
Suite 401
Bakersfield, CA 93313
661-396-8676
877-763-8868
FAX: 661-396-8760
e-mail: softtouch@funsoftware.com
www.funsoftware.com

*Roxanne Butterfield, Marketing*
*Joyce Meyer, President*

TouchCorders are the flexible and easty-to-use communicator designed by Jo Meyer and Linda Bidabe for reach classroom use. TouchCorders are sensitive to touch at every angle and give the student kinesthetic feedback. With the unique Add 'n Touch system, Jo connects the puzzles bases of 2 or more TouchCorders on the fly to present vocabulary, sequencing, story telling, social stories, concepts and other curriculum and communication opportunities.

**2169 TouchWindow Touch Screen**
Riverdeep Incorporated
100 Pine Street
Suite 1900
San Francisco, CA 94111
415-659-2000
800-542-4222
e-mail: edmarkteam@edmark.com
www.edmark.com

*Barry Callaghan, Chairman/CEO*
*Simon Calver, Chief Executive Officer*
*Robert Kilgarriff, Sales Executive*

Software for children. *$335.00*

**2170 Turtle Teasers**
Soft Touch
4300 Stine Road
Suite 401
Bakersfield, CA 93313
661-396-8676
877-763-8868
FAX: 661-396-8760
e-mail: softtouch@softtouch.com
www.softtouch.com

*Joyce Meyer, President*
*Roxanne Butterfield, Marketing*

Three Games, Three Levels from Easy, Medium to Hard. The Shell Game - easy: Watch one of the three turles get the tomato. Then watch carefully as they switch positions and pop shut. Choose incorrectly and the frog disappears until the correct one is displayed. The Pond - medium: Watch the tomato disappear somewhere in the pond scene. Tomato Dump - hard: Hit the shell and it turns into the tomato, giving a score. There are different difficulty levels to equalize all students.

**2171 Volcanoes**
Earthware Computer Services
2386 Spring Boulevard
Eugene, OR 97403
FAX: 541-342-3416
Simulation of volcano in which children play the role of the scientists. *$49.50*

**2172 What Was That!**
Compass Learning
203 Colorado Street
Austin, TX 78701
858-587-0087
800-247-1380
FAX: 619-622-7873
www.compasslearning.com

*Rajeev Puri, President*
*Eric Loeffel, CEO*

In this bedtime story, noises in the night send three brother bears scurrying out of bed. Thoughtful questions test young readers' comprehension, while games, voice recording, writing practice and other playful activities stimulate their creativity.

**2173 Wivik 3**
Prentke Romich Company
1022 Heyl Road
Wooster, OH 44691
330-262-1984
800-262-1984
FAX: 330-263-4829
e-mail: info@prentrom.com
www.prentrom.com

*Dave Moffatt, President*

On-screen keyboard provides access to any application in the latest Windows operating systems. Selections are made by clicking, dwelling or switch scanning. Enhancements include word prediction and abbreviation expansion.

**2174 You Tell Me: Learning Basic Information**
Programming Concepts
PO Box 34270
San Antonio, TX 78265
800-594-4263
FAX: 888-259-8284
e-mail: pciinfo@pcieducation.com
www.pcieducation.com

*Janie Haugen, Program Director*
*Jeff McLane, President/CEO*

This game teaches and reinforces basic information all individuals need to know. Questions asked in this game help prepare people to communicate personal identification information important to community survival. *$49.95*

## Software: Professional

**2175 Acrontech International**
5500 Main Street
Williamsville, NY 14221
FAX: 716-854-4014
This company supplies software, audio mixers, and closed-caption televisions.

**2176 DME VI**
Dezine Associates
2625 Cumberland Parkway SE
Suite 310
Atlanta, GA 30339
678-264-4400
800-447-7370
800-254-9872
www.carecentric.com

*Don Decorte, Director*
*John Festa, Chief Executive Officer*

This full-featured software package specific to the health care industry includes accounts receivable, order entry, inventory control and sale management in an easy-to-use format.

**2177 DPS with BCP**
V OR T Corporation
PO Box 60132
Palo Alto, CA 94306

650-322-8282
FAX: 650-327-0747
e-mail: sales@vort.com
www.vort.com

*Tom Holt, Owner*

This program uses unique DPS branching techniques to access goals and objectives.

**2178 Diagnostic Report Writer**
Parrot Software
190 Sandy Ridge Road
State College, PA 16803

800-727-7681
FAX: 814-237-7282

*Fred Weiner, Owner*

Creates a three page single-spaced diagnostic report for a child with a communication disorder from a list of questions; sections of the report include developmental and background history, oral peripheral exam, speech and language analysis, summary and recommendations.

**2179 Discriptive Language Arts Development**
Educational Activities Software
PO Box 754
Baldwin, NY 11510

516-867-7878
800-645-2796
FAX: 516-379-7429
e-mail: achieve@ea-software.com
www.ea-software.com

*Alan Stern, Manager*

This multimedia language arts development program provides instruction and application of fundamental English skills and concepts. *$395.00*

**2180 EZ Dot**
CAPCO Capability Corporation
1522 N Washington Street
Suite 200
Spokane, WA 99201

FAX: 509-535-1011

A critical software tool used in vocational counseling, job restructuring, recruitment and placement, better utilization of workers, and safety issues. This software offers occupational data by title, code, industry, GEO, DPT, or OGA. *$295.00*

**2181 EZ Keys for Windows**
Words+
42505 10th Street W
Suite 109
Lancaster, CA 93534

661-723-6523
800-869-8521
FAX: 661-266-8969
e-mail: info@words-plus.com
www.words-plus.com

*Phil Lawrence, Vice President*
*Rachel Nielsen, Customer Support*
*Walt Wolosz, Manager*

A software and hardware product designed to operate on an IBM compatible PC. The software provides dual word prediction, abbreviation expansion, five different methods of voice output and access to commercial software applications. *$1395.00*

**2182 Goals and Objectives**
JE Stewart Teaching Tools
PO Box 15308
Seattle, WA 98115

206-262-9538
FAX: 206-262-9538

*J E Stewart, Owner*

Goals and Objectives software helps teachers make student plans including IEP's, IPP's and IHP's. The system provides curricula for all students and programs to develop and evaluate plans, print reports and make data forms. Systems are available for Windows and Macintosh for $139.

**2183 Goals and Objectives IEP Program**
Curriculum Associates
PO Box 2001
N Billerica, MA 01862

978-667-8000
800-225-0248
FAX: 800-366-1158
e-mail: info@curriculumassociates.com
www.curriculumassociates.com

*Frank Ferguson, President/Owner*
*Katherine Harvey, Vice President*

BRIGANCE CIBS-R standardized scoring conversion software, is a teacher's tool that prints goal and objective pages of the IEP. In less than two minutes per student, a teacher types student data into the computer.

**2184 Nasometer**
Kay Elemetrics Corporation
2 Bridgewater Lane
Lincoln Park, NJ 07035

973-628-6200
800-289-5297
FAX: 973-628-6363
e-mail: sales@kaypentax.com
www.kaypentax.com

*John Crump, President*
*Steve Crump, Direct Sales*

Measures the ratio of acoustic energy for the nasal and real-time visual cueing during therapy. Used clinically in the areas of cleft palate, motor speach disorders, hearing impairment and palatal prosthetic fittings.

**2185 PSS CogRehab Software**
Psychological Software Services
6555 Carrollton Avenue
Indianapolis, IN 46220

317-257-9672
FAX: 317-257-9674
e-mail: nsc@netdirect.net
www.neuroscience.cnter.com

*Nancy Bracy, Sales/Production*
*Odie Bracy, Executive Director*

PSS CogRehab Software is a comprehensive and easy-to-use multimedia cognitive rehabilitation software available, for clinical and educational use with head injury, stroke LD/ADD and other brain compromises. The packages include 64 computerized therapy tasks which contain modifiable parameters that will accommodate most requirements. Exercises include attention and executive skills, multiple modalities of visuosatial and memory skills, simple, complex, proble-solving skills.
*$260 - $2500*

**2186 Parrot Easy Language Simple Anaylsis**
Parrot Software
PO Box 250755
W Bloomfield, MI 48325

248-788-8360
800-727-7681
www.parrotsoftware.com

*Fred Weiner, Owner*

Designed for grammatical analysis of language samples. The user types and translates language samples of up to 100 utterances.

**2187 TOVA**
Universal Attention Disorders
4281 Katella Avenue
Suite 215
Los Alamitos, CA 90720

714-821-9611
800-PAY-ATTN
FAX: 714-229-8782

*Lawrence Greenberg, Developer*

A computerized assessment which, in conjunction with classroom behavior ratings, is a highly effective screening tool for ADD. TOVA includes software, complete instructions, and supporting data including norms.

**2188 TTAP Outreach: Technology Team Assessment Process**
27 Horrabin Hall
Macomb, IL 61455

309-298-1634
FAX: 309-298-2305
e-mail: l_robinsonl@wiu.edu
www.mprojects.wiu.edu

*Linda Robinson, Coordinator*

Provides training to early childhood personnel and families on a team-based model for technology assessment. TTAP's procedures are designed to assess children's ability to use technology as a tool for achieving IEP/IFSP goals. Training and written materials are available.

**2189 Visi-Pitch III**
Kayelemetrics Corporation
2 Bridgewater Lane
Lincoln Park, NJ 07035

973-628-6200
FAX: 973-628-6363
e-mail: info@kayepentax.com
www.kayepentax.com

*Robert McClurkin, Marketing Director*
*Steve Crump, Sales*
*John Crump, President*

Assists the speech/voice clinician in assessment and treatment tasks across an expansive range of disorders.

# Software: Reading & Language Arts

**2190 Choices, Choices 5.0**
Tom Snyder Productions
100 Talcott Avenue
# 6
Watertown, MA 02472

617-926-6000
800-342-0236
FAX: 800-304-1254
e-mail: ask@tomsnyder.com
www.tomsnyder.com

*Rick Abrahams, Manager*

Teaches students to take responsibility for their behavior. Helps students develop the skills and awareness they need to make wise choices and to think through the consequences of their actions.

**2191 Circletime Tales Deluxe**
Don Johnston
26799 W Commerce Drive
Volo, IL 60073

847-740-0749
800-999-4660
FAX: 847-740-7326
e-mail: info@donjohnston.com
www.donjohnston.com

*Ruth Ziolkowski, President*

This interactive CD-ROM introduces and reinforces pre-literacy concepts using nursery rhymes and songs familiar to many children. This English/Spanish program emphasizes listening to and learning basic concepts such as opposites, directionality, colors and counting. *$59.00*

**2192 Community Exploration**
Compass Learning
203 Colorado Street
Austin, TX 78701

858-587-0087
800-247-1380
FAX: 619-622-7873
www.compasslearning.com

*Rajeev Puri, President*
*Eric Loeffel, Executive Vice President*

An award-winning learning adventure takes students who are learning English as a second language on a field trip to the make-believe town of Cornerstone. More than 50 community locations come to life with sound and animation. While exploring places in this typical American community where people live, work and play, students also enhance important English language skills. Offers an exciting approach for any age student who needs to improve their English language proficiency. 4-12. *$19.95*

**2193 Conversations**
Educational Activities Software
PO Box 754
Baldwin, NY 11510

516-867-7878
800-645-2796
FAX: 516-379-7429
e-mail: achieve@ea-software.com
www.ea-software.com

*Alan Stern, Manager*

Using American digitalized voices, CONVERSATIONS provides 14 different dialogues in which the student can participate. The topics offer learners important information about American culture and the workplace. Available for DOS. *$195.00*

**2194 Core-Reading and Vocabulary Development**
Educational Activities
PO Box 87
Baldwin, NY 11510

516-223-4666
800-645-3739
FAX: 516-623-9282
e-mail: learn@edact.com
www.edact.com

*Alfred Harris, President*
*Carol Stern, VP*

Students begin with 36 basic words and progress to more than 200. Reading and writing activities are coordinated and integrated throughout the program for more substantial permanent learning. Five units covering readability levels from pre-primer to grade three.
*Full Program*

**2195 Day at Play: A IKanDu Little Book**
Don Johnston
26799 W Commerce Drive
Volo, IL 60073

847-740-0749
800-999-4660
FAX: 847-740-7323
e-mail: info@donjohnston.com
www.donjohnston.com

*Ketan Kothari, Chief Executive Officer*
*Ruth Ziolkowski, President*

One of the products in the UKanDu Little Book Series. This early literacy program consists of several four-page animated stories that help build language experience for emergent and early readers. Children fill-in-the-blank to complete a sentence on each page and then watch the page come alive with animation and sound. After completion, it can be printed to make a book. All children can be successful as there are no wrong answers. *$45.00*

**2196  Friday Afternoon**
13500 Evening Creek Drive N
Suite 200
San Diego, CA 92128

858-587-0087
800-247-1380
FAX: 619-622-7873
www.compasslearning.com

*Rajeev Puri, President*
*Eric Loeffel, Chief Operating Officer*
*Martin Kenney Jr, Chief Executive Officer*

Save hours of preparation time and dazzle your students with interesting new activities to supplement their classroom learning. With Friday afternoon, you'll produce flash cards, word puzzles, even customized bingo cards and more, all at the click of a mouse. MacIntosh diskette. *$99.95*

**2197  How to Read for Everyday Living**
Educational Activities Software
PO Box 754
Baldwin, NY  11510

516-867-7878
800-645-2796
FAX: 516-379-7429
e-mail: achieve@ea-software.com
www.ea-software.com

*Alan Stern, Manager*

Basic vocabulary and key words are taught and, when need, retaught using alternative teaching strategies. Passages that students read help put the vocabulary into context. Each lesson is followed by crossword and other puzzles check comprehension.

**2198  Learning English: Primary**
13500 Evening Creek Drive N
Suite 200
San Diego, CA 92128

858-587-0087
800-247-1380
FAX: 619-622-7873
www.compasslearning.com

*Rajeev Puri, President*
*Eric Loeffel, Executive Vice President*
*Martin Kenney Jr, Chief Executive Officer*

Four stories and rhymes help students familiarize themselves with essential English language concepts, recognize patterns in language and associate words with objects. *$49.95*

**2199  Learning English: Rhyme Time**
Compass Learning
13500 Evening Creek Drive N
San Diego, CA  92128

858-587-0087
800-247-1380
FAX: 619-622-7873
www.compasslearning.com

*Rajeev Turi, President*
*Martin Kenney Jr, Chief Executive Officer*

Using classic children's rhymes in an animated multimedia program, students work on language skills, vocabulary and comprehension.

**2200  Lexia I, II and III Reading Series**
Lexia Learning Systems
PO Box 466
Lincoln, MA  01773

781-259-8752
800-435-3942
FAX: 781-259-1349
e-mail: info@lexialearning.com
www.lexialearning.com

*Henry Morgan, Director*
*Jonathan Bower, Chief Executive Officer*

Lexia's software helps children and adults with learning disabilities master their core reading skills. Based on the Orton Gillingham method, Lexia Early Reading, Phonics Based Reading and SOS (Strategies for Older Students) apply phonics principles to help students learn essential sound-symbol correspondence and decoding skills. The Quick Reading Tests generate detailed skill reports in only 5-8 minutes per student to provide data for further instruction. Price: $40-400 per workstation.

**2201  Memory Castle**
WINGS for Learning
1600 Green Hills Road
Scotts Valley, CA  95066

831-464-3600
FAX: 831-464-3600

*Ani Stocks, Owner*

Introduces a strategy to increase memory skills via an adventure game. Set in a castle, the game requires memory, reading, spelling skills and more to win.

**2202  On a Green Bus: A UKanDu Little Book**
Don Johnston
26799 W Commerce Drive
Volo, IL  60073

847-740-0749
800-889-5242
FAX: 847-740-7326
e-mail: support@donjohnston.com
www.donjohnston.com

*Ruth Ziolkowski, President*

This early literacy program that consists of several create-your-own 4-page animated stories that help build language experience on each page and then watch the page come alive with animation and sound. After completing the story, students can print it out to make a book which can be read over and over again. Because there are no wrong answers, all children can have a successful literacy experience. *$ 45.00*

**2203  Open Book**
Freedom Scientific
11800 31st Court N
St Petersburg, FL  33716

727-803-8000
800-444-4443
FAX: 727-803-8001
e-mail: info@freedomscientific.com
www.freedomscientific.com

*Lee Hamilton, Director*

Software that reads scanned text allowed and includes other features that aid the vision-impaired. *$995.00*

**2204  Optimum Resource Software**
18 Hunter Road
Hilton Head, SC  29926

843-689-8000
FAX: 843-689-8008
e-mail: stickyb@stickybear.com
www.optimumlearning.com

*Chris Gintz, Chief Executive Officer*
*Maureen Richards, Administration*

Optimum Resource publishes over 100 K-12 education curriculum software titles under its varietal brands, StickyBear, MiddleWare, High School and Tools for Teachers.

**2205  Out and About: A UKanDu Little Book**
Don Johnston
26799 W Commerce Drive
Volo, IL  60073

847-740-0749
800-999-4660
FAX: 847-740-7326
e-mail: info@donjohnston.com
www.donjohnston.com

*Ruth Ziolkowski, President*

One of the products in the UKanDu Little Book Series. This early literacy program consists of several four-page animated stories that help build language experience for emergent and early readers. Children fill-in-the-blank to complete a sentence on each page and then watch the page come alive with animation and sound. After completion, it can be printed to make a book. *$45.00*

**2206 Programs for Aphasia and Cognitive Disorders**
Parrot Software
PO Box 250755
W Bloomfield, MI 48325          248-788-8360
                                800-727-7681
                      wwww.parrotsoftware.com

*Fred Weiner, Owner*

Over 50 different computer programs that facilitate language, memory and attention training. Programs are available for MS DOS, WINDOWS and Apple II.

**2207 Punctuation Rules**
Optimum Resource
18 Hunter Road
Hilton Head Island, SC 29926          843-689-8000
                            FAX: 843-689-8008
                      e-mail: sticky@stickybear.com
                            www.stickybear.com

*Chris Gintz, Chief Executive Officer*

Punctuation Rules is designed to help students improve their punctuation skills. Students work with appropriate level sentences which follow common rules of punctuation. The program covers material ranging from categories of sentences to forming possessives and allows students to gain strength in their ability to correctly use periods, commas, apostrophes, question marks, colons, hyphens, quotation marks, exclamation points and more. *$59.95*

**2208 Quick Reading Test, Phonics Based Reading, Reading SOS (Strategies for Older Students)**
Lexia Learning Systems
PO Box 466
Lincoln, MA 01773          781-259-8752
                          800-435-3942
                     FAX: 781-259-1349
               e-mail: info@lexialearning.com
                     www.lexialearning.com

*Jonathan Bower, Chief Executive Officer*
*Bob Baker, Sales Representative*

Lexia's software helps children and adults with learning disabilities master their core reading skills. Based on the Orton Gillingham method, Phonics Based Reading and S.O.S. (Strategies for the Older Student) apply phonics principles to help students learn essential sound-symbol correspondence and decoding skills. The Quick Reading Tests generate detailed phonemic skills reports in only 5-8 minutes per student to provide teachers with accurate data to focus their instruction. Price: $67-$500.

**2209 Quick Talk**
Educational Activities Software
PO Box 754
Baldwin, NY 11510          516-867-7878
                          800-645-2796
                     FAX: 516-379-7429
               e-mail: achieve@ea-software.com
                     www.ea-software.com

*Alan Stern, Manager*

Students will learn and use new vocabulary immediately: high-frequency, everyday vocabulary words are introduced and used contextually using human speech, graphics and text. Voice-interactive program (MS-DOS). *$65.00*

**2210 Race the Clock**
Mindplay
4440 S Williams Boulevard
Suite 206
Tucson, AZ 85716          520-888-0
                          800-888-7904
                     FAX: 520-322-0363
               e-mail: mail@mindplay.com
                     www.mindplay.com
A matching game, uses the animation capabilities to teach verbs. The player chooses a matching game from a menu.

**2211 Reader Rabbit**
Learning Company
100 Pine Street
Suite 1900
San Francisco, CA 94111          800-825-4420
                         FAX: 877-278-7456
          e-mail: SchoolCustomerService@riverdeep.net
                    www.learningcompanyschool.com
Supports young students in building fundamental reading readiness skills in a playful, multi-sensory environment.

**2212 Reading Comprehension Series**
Optimum Resource
18 Hunter Road
Hilton Head Island, SC 29926          843-689-8000
                            FAX: 843-689-8008
                      e-mail: sticky@stickybear.com
                            www.stickybear.com

*Chris Gintz, Chief Executive Officer*

The Reading Comprehension Series, includes six volumes for Windows, MacIntosh, DOS or Apple II computers. Packed with intriguing multi-level stories, each volume will capture the interest of children ages 8-14 while teaching them crucial reading comprehension skills. These open-ended programs are versatile and easy to use. *$59.95*

**2213 Simon Sounds it Out**
Don Johnston
26799 W Commerce Drive
Volo, IL 60073          847-740-0749
                        800-999-4660
                   FAX: 847-740-7326
             e-mail: info@donjohnston.com
                   www.donjohnston.com

*Don Johnston, Chief Executive Officer*
*Ruth Ziolkowski, President*

This interactive phonics program enables students to learn and practice letter sounds with an instructional and nonthreatening on-screen tutor. This phonics program was designed by leading learning authorities and extensively tested in classrooms. Colorful graphics, digitalized sound and amusing animations reward students and motivate them to continue learning. *$59.00 1998*

**2214 Simon Spells**
Don Johnston
26799 W Commerce Drive
Volo, IL 60073          847-740-0749
                        800-999-4660
                   FAX: 847-740-7326
             e-mail: info@donjohnston.com
                   www.donjohnston.com

*Don Johnston, Founder*
*Ruth Ziolkowski, President*

This innovative spelling program guides students through individualized instruction presented in a way that enables them to work at their own pace. Words are phonemically presented, as well as placed in the context of sentences so as to help increase vocabulary comprehension and spelling skills. Student progress is tracked and results are stored. *$59.00*

**2215 Sound Sentences**
Educational Activities Software
PO Box 754
Baldwin, NY 11510                        516-867-7878
                                         800-645-2796
                                   FAX: 516-379-7429
                    e-mail: achieve@ea-software.com
                              www.ea-software.com

*Alan Stern, Manager*

This sound-interactive program breaks away from traditional language instruction. Instead of formal concentration on verb and basic vocabulary, students meet everyday English with colloquialisms they will hear in real life situations. They reinforce their knowledge of sentence structure while acquiring the ability to communicate in daily settings. (For MAC, MS-DOS and Windows). *$65.00*

**2216 Spelling Rules**
Optimum Resource
18 Hunter Road
Hilton Head Island, SC 29926            843-689-8000
                                   FAX: 843-689-8008
                     e-mail: sticky@stickybear.com
                               www.stickybear.com

*Chris Gintz, Chief Executive Officer*

A curriculum based, easy-to-use program that provides students with the practice they need to build strong spelling skills. *$59.95*

**2217 Spelling Test Generator**
Optimum Resource
18 Hunter Road
Hilton Head Island, SC 29926            843-689-8000
                                   FAX: 843-689-8008
                    e-mail: stickyb@stickybear.com
                               www.stickybear.com

*Chris Gintz, Chief Executive Officer*

Using more than 3000 of the most commonly encountered words in the English language, the Spelling Test Generator prepares spelling lists on the basis of difficulty, grade level, vowels, diphthongs, word origins and starting/ending letters or sounds. *$59.95*

**2218 Stickybear Parts of Speech**
Optimum Resource
18 Hunter Road
Hilton Head Island, SC 29926            843-689-8000
                                   FAX: 843-689-8008
                    e-mail: stickyb@stickybear.com
                               www.stickybear.com

*Chris Gintz, Chief Executive Officer*

Children learn parts of speech with this exciting new program. *$59.95*

**2219 Stickybear Reading**
Optimum Resource
18 Hunter Road
Hilton Head Island, SC 29926            843-689-8000
                                   FAX: 843-689-8008
                    e-mail: stickyb@stickybear.com
                               www.stickybear.com

*Chris Gintz, Chief Executive Officer*

Children build vocabulary and reading comprehension skills using hundreds of word/picture sets and thousands of put-together sentence parts. *$49.95*

**2220 Stickybear Reading Comprehension**
Optimum Resource
18 Hunter Road
Hilton Head Island, SC 29926            843-689-8000
                                   FAX: 843-689-8008
                    e-mail: stickyb@stickybear.com
                               www.stickybear.com

*Chris Gintz, Chief Executive Officer*

This multi-level reading comprehension program helps children improve reading skills with 30 high-interest stories and question sets created by the Weekly Reader editors. *$59.95*

**2221 Stickybear Spellgrabber**
Optimum Resource
18 Hunter Road
Hilton Head Island, SC 29926            843-689-8000
                                   FAX: 843-689-8008
                    e-mail: stickyb@stickybear.com
                               www.stickybear.com

*Chris Gintz, Chief Executive Officer*

Build spelling and vocabulary skills with three different activities: Picture Spell, Word Spell and Bear Dunk. *$59.95*

**2222 Stickybear Spelling**
Optimum Resource
18 Hunter Road
Hilton Head Island, SC 29926            843-689-8000
                                   FAX: 843-689-8008
                     e-mail: sticky@stickybear.com
                               www.stickybear.com

*Chris Gintz, Chief Executive Officer*

Children ages 6 and up discover and practice critical spelling skills as they work with three unique action-packed activities, each with four graded levels of difficulty. The program is open-ended and teachers may add, change and modify the word lists for each individual. Stickybear Spelling contains more than 2000 recorded words. Levels may be set to allow students of different ages or abilities to compete effectively. *$59.95*

**2223 Stickybear Spelling Rules**
Optimum Resource
18 Hunter Road
Hilton Head Island, SC 29926            843-689-8000
                                   FAX: 843-689-8008
                    e-mail: stickyb@stickybear.com
                               www.stickybear.com

*Chris Gintz, Chief Executive Officer*

Spelling Rules is designed to help students improve spelling accuracy and master the fundamentals - forming plurals (adding s, adding es, f, fe, to ves) and compound words, I before E rule, capitalization and many others. *$59.95*

**2224 Stickybear's Reading Fun Park**
Optimum Resource
18 Hunter Road
Hilton Head Island, SC 29926            843-689-8000
                                   FAX: 843-689-8008
                    e-mail: stickyb@stickybear.com
                               www.stickybear.com

*Chris Gintz, Chief Executive Officer*

Children ages 4-8 discover and practice critical reading skills as the famous stickybear family guides users through unique, action-packed activities, each with multiple levels of difficulty and skills that address both the auditory and visual needs of budding readers. *$59.95*

**2225 Stickybear's Reading Room**
Optimum Resource
18 Hunter Road
Hilton Head Island, SC 29926                843-689-8000
                                   FAX: 843-689-8008
                         e-mail: stickyb@stickybear.com
                                   www.stickybear.com

*Chris Gintz, Chief Executive Officer*

The perfect combination of learning and fun, our award winning Stickybear's Reading Room provides colorful motivating thinking skills practice for children ages 4-8 with four unique bilingual learning activities. *$59.95*

**2226 Tomorrow's Promise: Language Arts**
Compass Learning
13500 Evening Creek Drive N
San Diego, CA 92128                         858-587-0087
                                            800-521-8538
                                   FAX: 619-622-7873
                              www.compasslearning.com

*Steve Allen, Alternate Channels Manager*
*Martin Kenney Jr, Chief Executive Officer*

You'll strengthen students' grammar, usage and vocabulary skills and promote higher order thinking skills with this comprehensive Language Arts curriculum. It utilizes cross-curricular, thematic instruction engaging multimedia learning exercises that encourage writing, speaking and listening proficiency. Promotes higher order thinking skills. *$279.95*

**2227 Tomorrow's Promise: Reading**
Compass Learning
203 Colorado Street
Austin, TX 78701                            858-587-0087
                                            800-521-8538
                                   FAX: 619-622-7873
                              www.compasslearning.com

*Steve Allen, Alternate Channels Manager*

This multimedia curriculum balances thematic, interactive exploration with core skills development, increasing your students' early reading proficiency, building a solid literacy foundation and fostering a lifelong love for reading. *$279.95*

**2228 Tomorrow's Promise: Spelling**
Compass Learning
203 Colorado Street
Austin, TX 78701                            858-587-0087
                                            800-678-1412
                                   FAX: 858-622-7877
                   e-mail: support@compasslearning.com
                              www.compasslearning.com

*Steve Allen, Alternate Channels Manager*

Lovable characters and engaging multimedia effects put young students on a fast-track to early spelling proficiency with fourteen activities and three games. A full year's instruction on each CD includes 30 world lists per grade, in story context, or create word lists to suit your needs. This program addresses students' multiple learning styles and rewards students as they progress through each stage of spelling skill acquisition. *$99.95*

**2229 Vocabulary Development**
Optimum Resource
18 Hunter Road
Hilton Head Island, SC 29926                843-689-8000
                                   FAX: 843-689-8008
                         e-mail: stickyb@stickybear.com
                                   www.stickybear.com

*Chris Gintz, Chief Executive Officer*

A featured program in the middle school series. Vocabulary Development is designed to help students increase vocabulary as they strengthen reading skills. Students relate their current knowledge of vocabulary to the context in which they discover an unfamiliar word. Utilizing a variety of contextual aids, this program illustrates synonyms, antonyms, prefixes, suffixes, homophones, multiple meanings and context clues, allowing students to apply experience and context. *$59.95*

**2230 Whoops**
Cornucopia Software
PO Box 6111
Albany, CA 94706                            510-528-7000

                    e-mail: supportstaff@practicemagic.com
                                   www.practicemagic.com

*Christina Morua, Manager*

Checks spelling three ways. It checks words as they are typed, it checks an entire screen and highlights the errors and it reads ASCII text files from a disk and lists errors.

## Software: Vocational

**2231 Functional Literacy System**
Conover Company
2926 Hidden Hollow Road
Oshkosh, WI 54904                           920-231-4667
                                            800-933-1933
                                   FAX: 920-231-4809
                            e-mail: conover@execpc.com
                              www.conovercompany.com

*Terry Schmitz, President*

Assessment and skill building for basic functional literacy. This multimedia software program is adult in format and uses live action video taken in actual community settings to help learners become more capable of functioning independently. Twenty different programs are currently available. *$99.00*

**2232 Learning Activity Packets**
2926 Hidden Hollow Road
Oshkosh, WI 54904                           920-231-4667
                                            800-933-1933
                                   FAX: 920-231-4809
                            e-mail: conover@execpc.com
                              www.conovercompany.com

*Terry Schmitz, President*
*Bechky Schmitz, Vice President*

Demonstrates how basic academic skills relate to 30 major career areas. LAPs provide valuable diagnostics in applied academic applications and demonstrates to users the importance of academics as they relate to the workplace. Software. *$99.00*

**2233 Microcomputer Evaluation of Careers & Academics (MECA)**
Conover Company
2926 Hidden Hollow Road
Oshkosh, WI 54904                           920-231-4667
                                            800-933-1933
                                   FAX: 920-231-4809
                            e-mail: conover@execpc.com
                              www.conovercompany.com

*Terry Schmitz, President*

A cost-effective, technology-based, career development system which provides users with opportunities to get their hands dirty. The MECA system utilizes work simulations and is built around common occupational clusters. Each cluster, or career area, consists of hands-on WORK SAMPLES which provide a variety of career exploration and assessment experiences, linked to LEARNING ACTIVITY PACKETS, which integrate basic academic skills into the career planning and placement process. $580-$1,070.

**2234 OASYS**
Vertek
12835 Bel Red Road
Suite 112
Bellevue, WA 98005          425-455-9921
                            800-220-4409
                        FAX: 425-454-7264
            e-mail: marketing@vertekinc.com
                        www.vertekinc.com

*Gale Gibson, President*
*Jack Rosenoss, Vice President*

A software system that matches a person's skills and abilities to occupations and employers.

**2235 Reading in the Workplace**
Educational Activities Software
PO Box 754
Baldwin, NY 11510          516-867-7878
                            800-645-2796
                        FAX: 516-379-7429
            e-mail: achieve@ea-software.com
                        www.ea-software.com

*Alan Stern, Manager*

A job-based, reading software program using real-life problems and solutions to capture students' attention and improve their vocabulary and comprehension skills. Units include: automotive, clerical, health care and construction. *$295.00*

**2236 Stickybear Typing**
Optimum Resource
18 Hunter Road
Hilton Head Island, SC 29926     843-689-8000
                             FAX: 843-689-8008
            e-mail: stickyb@stickybear.com
                        www.stickybear.com

*Chris Gintz, Chief Executive Officer*

The award winning Stickybear Typing program allows users to sharpen typing skills and achieve keyboard mastery with three engaging and amusing multi-level activities. *$59.95*

**2237 Vocational Interest Profile Report**
Cambridge Educational
90 Maccorkle Avenue SW
South Charleston, WV 25303     304-744-2055
                            800-468-4227
                        FAX: 800-329-6687
            e-mail: melindab@citynet.net
                        www.cambridgeol.com

*Melinda Ball, Marketing Director*

Software that is designed to allow students to systematically define broad work categories that are of most interest. *$64.86*

ISBN 0-927368-59-5

**2238 Work-Related Vocational Assessment Systems**
Valpar International
12778 W North Avenue
Building A
Brookfield, WI 53005          262-797-0840
                            800-633-3321
                        FAX: 262-797-8488
            e-mail: sales@valparint.com
                        www.valparint.com

*Neal Gunderson, President*
*Patricia L Rastatter, VP Operations*

Criterion-referenced to Department of Labor standards. Evaluate academic levels for reading, spelling, math and language, and various other aptitudes.

**2239 Workplace Skills: Learning How to Function on the Job**

Programming Concepts
PO Box 12428
San Antonio, TX 78212          800-594-4263
                            FAX: 218-480-5

*Janie Haugen, Program Director*
*Jeff Mclane, President/CEO*

Offers parents and educators a functional means by which to discuss all aspects of finding and keeping a job. *$49.95*

## Word Processors

**2240 DARCI**
Wes Test Engineering Corporation
810 Shepard Lane
Farmington, UT 84025          801-451-9191
                            FAX: 801-451-9393
                        www.westest.com

*Mary Lynds, Purchasing*
*Pam Burns, Office Manager*
*Robert Lessman, President*

Provides transparent access to all computer functions by replacing the computer's keyboard with a smart joystick. *$975.00*

**2241 Eye Relief Word Processing Software**
SkiSoft Publishing Corporation
PO Box 364
Lexington, MA 02420          781-863-1876
                            FAX: 781-861-0086
            e-mail: info@skisoft.com
                        www.skisoft.com

*Ken Skier, President*
*Cynthia Skier, CFO*

Large-type word processing program for visually-impaired PC users. *$295.00*

**2242 IntelliTalk**
Intelli Tools
1720 Corporate Circle
Petaluma, CA 94954          707-773-2000
                            800-899-6687
                        FAX: 707-773-2001
            e-mail: tech@intellitools.com
                        www.intellitools.com

*Beth Davis, Director Sales Operator*
*Lori Castle, Supervisor*
*Arjan Khalsa, Chief Executive Officer*

Talking word-processing program available for MacIntosh, Apple IIe, IBM compatible and Windows computers. *$39.95*

**2243 Large Type**
PO Box 1088
Hewitt, NJ 07421          973-853-6585
                            800-736-2216
                        FAX: 928-832-2894

*Donald Selwyn, Director*

Display enlargement programs for visually impaired users. Consist of a variety of programs for different needs, ranging from basic to full-featured.

**2244  Pegasus LITE**
Words+
42505 10th Street W
Suite 109
Lancaster, CA  93534

661-723-6523
800-869-8521
FAX: 661-723-2114
e-mail: info@words-plus.com
www.words-plus.com

*Phil Lawrence, Vice President*
*Rachel Nielsen, Customer Support*
*Walt Wolosz, Manager*

Provides all of the strategies currently being used in AAC, from dynamic display color pictographic language, to dual-word prediction text language, in a single system. *$6995.00*

**2245  Up and Running**
Intelli Tools
5221 Central Avenue
Suite 205
Richmond, CA  94804

800-899-6687
e-mail: info@intellitools.com
www.intellitools.com

*Beth Davis, Director Sales & Operations*
*Lori Castle, Supervisor*

Instantly use hundreds of popular commercial software programs with this custom collection of setups and overlays. *$69.95*

**2246  Write This Way**
Compass Learning Incorporated
203 Colorado Street
Austin, TX  78701

512-447-8828
800-521-8538
FAX: 619-622-7873
www.compasslearning.com

*Steve Allen, Alternate Channels Manager*
*Mike Campasso, Owner*

An easy-to-use, versatile word processor designed with learning disabled or hearing-impaired individuals in mind. Apple or Mac available. *$99.95*

**2247  Write: OutLoud**
Don Johnston
26799 W Commerce Drive
Volo, IL  60073

847-740-0749
800-999-4660
FAX: 847-740-7326
e-mail: info@donjohnston.com
www.donjohnston.com

*Don Johnston, Founder*
*Ruth Ziolkowski, President*

The award-winning feasible and user friendly talking word processor with talking spell checker. Text-to-speech technology provides multi-sensory learning and positive reinforcements for writers of all ages and ability levels. *$99.00*

## General

**2248  APSE Conference: Revitalizing Supported Employment, Climbing to the Future**
Association for Persons in Supported Employment
1627 Monument Avenue
Richmond, VA  23220                          804-278-9187
                                        FAX: 804-278-9377
                              e-mail: apse@apse.com
                                        www.apse.org

*Suzanne Hutcheson, President*
*Teresa Grossi, Vice President*
*Celane Whorter, Executive Director*

A major conference on Supported Employment. The conference includes 130 sessions presented by nationally recognized leaders in the field. Conference attendees come from all 50 states, Canada and several foreign countries and include professionals in supported employment, occupational therapy, rehabilitation technology and other related fields.
*July*

**2249  Abilities Expo**
Advanstar Communications
440 Wheelers Farms Road
Suite 101
Milford, CT  06461                           203-882-1300
                                        FAX: 203-882-1800
                      e-mail: abilities@advanstar.com
                                  www.abilitiesexpo.com

*Diane Waltersdorf, Show Director*

The one show for assisted and independent living products and services in the US.

**2250  Alexander Graham Bell Association for the Deaf and Hard of Hearing Annual Conference**
3417 Volta Place NW
Washington, DC  20007                        202-337-5220
                                        FAX: 202-337-8314
                              e-mail: info@agbell.org
                                        www.agbell.org

*K Todd Houston, Executive Director/CEO*
*Wendy Will, Executive Assistant*
*Garrett W Yates, Advertising/Exhibitor Sales*

Over 60 booths offering information on resources and technology for the deaf and hard of hearing.
*June*

**2251  American Academy for Cerebral Palsy and Developmental Medicine Annual Conference**
555 E Wells Street
Suite 1100
Milwaukee, IL  53202                         414-918-3014
                                        FAX: 414-276-2146
                              e-mail: king@aaos.org
                                        www.aacpdm.org

*Sheril King, Executive Director*

Holds annual conference in September with instructional courses such as: the fundamentals of normal walking, management of drooling in the developmentally disabled, technology dependent children, evaluation and treatment of feeding, nutritional and growth problems in the child with disabilities, Spina Bifida care, spasticity, measurement, sexual behavior and problems of the young disabled adult, grant seeking programs that care for the special needs child, etc.

*September*

**2252  American Academy of Ophthalmology Annual Meeting**
655 Beach Street
San Francisco, CA  94109                     415-561-8500
                                        FAX: 415-561-8575
                              e-mail: meetings@aao.org
                                        www.aao.org

*Dunbar Hoskins, Executive Vice President*

Offers the most comprehensive program with more than 2000 scientific presentations and six subspecialty day programs
*October*

**2253  American Association of the Deaf-Blind National Conference**
8630 Fenton Street
Suite 121
Silver Spring, MD  20910                     301-495-4403
                                        FAX: 301-495-4404
                                        TTY:301-495-4402
                           e-mail: aadb-info@aadb.org
                                        www.aadb.org

*Jamie Pope, Executive Director*

A week of general meetings, workshops, tours and evening recreational activities.
*June*

**2254  American Association on Mental Retardation AAMR Annual Meeting**
444 N Capitol Street NW
Washington, DC  20001                        202-387-1968
                                             800-424-3688
                                        FAX: 202-387-2193
                              e-mail: maria@aamr.org
                                        www.aamr.org

*M Doreen Croser, Executive Director*
*Maria A Alfaro, Meeting Planner/Web Associate*

At The Crossroads: Ethics, Genetics, Leadership and Self-Determination, the annual meeting offers a full compliment of workshops, symposia, and multiperspective sessions that fill four days including social events.
*May/June*

**2255  American Board of Disability Analysts**
Disability Analyst
345 24th Avenue N
Suite 200
Nashville, TN  37203                         615-327-2984
                                        FAX: 615-327-9235
                        e-mail: americanbd@aol.com

*Alexander E Horwitz MD, Executive Officer*
*Kenneth N Anchor PhD, President/Editor*
*Gabriel Sella MD, Continuing Education Coordinator*

**2256  American Council of the Blind Annual Convention**
1155 15th Street NW
Suite 1004
Washington, DC  20005                        202-467-5081
                                             800-424-8666
                                        FAX: 202-467-5085
                              e-mail: info@acb.org
                                        www.acb.org

*Melanie Brunson, Executive Director*
*Cynthia Towers, Convention Coordinator*

Offers 50-75 booths of information for the blind.

# Conferences & Shows /General

*June/July*

**2257  American Diabetes Association Annual Conference**
National Call Center
1701 N Beauregard Street
Alexandria, VA  22311                703-379-7755
                                     800-342-2383
www.diabetes.org/main/application/commercewf

*Christina Pappas, Marketing Planner*

Trade show featuring exhibits of equipment and supplies used by professionals involved in the treatment of diabetes.

**2258  American Physical Therapy Association Annual Conference & Exposition**
1111 N Fairfax Street
Alexandria, VA  22314                703-684-2782
                                     800-999-2782
                              FAX: 703-684-7343
                              TTY: 703-683-6748
                     e-mail: benmassey@apta.org
                                     www.apta.org

*Ben F Massey Jr, President*
*Frank Mallon, Chief Executive Officer*

The national event for physical therapy. Features advanced programming presented by 3000 top physical therapy professionals.

**2259  American Rehabilitation Counseling Association**
American Counseling Association
5999 Stevenson Avenue
Alexandria, VA  22304                703-823-9800
                                     800-347-6647
                              FAX: 703-823-0252
                              TTY: 703-823-6862
                e-mail: webmaster@counseling.org
                               www.counseling.org

*Richard Yep, Executive Director*
*Robin Hayes, Conventions/Meetings*
*March/April*

**2260  American Speech-Language-Hearing Association**
10801 Rockville Pike
Rockville, MD  20852                 301-897-5700
                                     800-638-8255
                              FAX: 301-571-0457
                              TTY: 301-897-5700
                  e-mail: convention@asha.org
                                     www.asha.org

*Lawrence Higdon, President*
*Arlene A Pietranton, Executive Director*
*Joanne Jessen, Publications Director*

Exhibits by companies specializing in alternative and augmentative communication products, publishers, software and hardware companies, and hearing aid testing equipment manufacturers. Speech-Language Pathologist Professionals who identify, asses, and treat speech and language problems. Audiologists are hearing health care professionals who specialize in preventing, identifying and assesing hearing disorders as well as providing audiologic treatment including hearing aids and more. *$.80*

**2261  American Spinal Injury Association Annual Scientific Meeting**
2020 Peachtree Road NW
Atlanta, GA  30309                   404-355-9772
                              FAX: 404-355-1826
                e-mail: asia-office@shepherd.org
                           www.asia-spinalinjury.org

*Marca L Sipski-Alexander MD, President*
*Glenn Rechtine MD, Preseident Elect*
*Amie Jackson, Secretary-Treasurer*

Professional association for physicans and other health professionals working in all aspects of spinal cord injury. Also holds an annual scientific that surveys the latest advancements in the field.
*May*

**2262  Annual Santa Barbara Sports Festival**
PO Box 50001
Santa Barbara, CA  93150             805-897-2680

                   e-mail: RHanna@SantaBarbaraCA.gov
                               www.semananautica.com
Includes activities such as ocean competition, swimming, masters swimming, kayaking, water polo, volleyball tournaments, biathlon, running, triathlon, racquetball, softball tournament, outrigger, and regatta. Participants of all ages and abilities are welcome.
*June/July*

**2263  Association for Education & Rehabilitation of the Blind & Visually Impaired Intl Conference**
1703 N Beauregard Street
Suite 440
Alexandria, VA  22311                703-671-4500
                                     877-492-2708
                              FAX: 703-671-6391
                     e-mail: aer@aerbvi.org
                                     www.aerbvi.org

*Gregory L Goodrich, President*
*Barbara Sherr, Acting Director*
*Mark Richert, Owner*

Dedicated to rendering support and assistance to the professionals who work in all phases of education and rehabilitation of blind and visually impaired children and adults.
*July*

**2264  Attention Deficit Disorders Association, Southern Region: Annual Conference**
12345 Jones Road
Suite 287-7
Houston, TX  77070                   281-897-0982
                              FAX: 281-894-6883
                     e-mail: addaoffice@pdq.net
                                     www.adda-sr.org

*Pam Esser, President*

Mission is to: provide a resource network; to support individuals impacted by attention deficit disorders; to advocate for the development of community resources and services that meet the educational, social, and health care needs of all individuals with ADD/ADHD.
*February*

**2265  Blazing Toward a Cure Annual Conference**
National Parkinson Foundation
1501 NW 9th Avenue
Miami, FL  33136                     305-547-6666
                                     800-327-4545
                              FAX: 305-243-5595
                  e-mail: contact@parkinson.org
                                     www.parkinson.org

*Daniel Arty, President*
*Alan M Slewett, Secretary*
*Jose Garcia-Pedrosa, Executive Director*

Purpose is to find the cause and cure for Parkinson's Disease and related neurodegenerative disorders through research, education and dissemination of current information to patients, caregivers and families.

*July/August*

**2266   Blind Childrens Center Annual Meeting**
4120 Marathon Street
Los Angeles, CA  90029
323-664-2153
800-222-3567
FAX: 323-665-3828
e-mail: info@blindchildrenscenter.org
www.blindchildrenscenter.org

*Laurie Headley, Contact*
*Midge Horton, Executive Director*

A family-centered agency which serves children with visual impairments from birth to school-age. The center-based and home-based services help the children to acquire skills and build their independence. The Center utilizes its expertise and experience to serve families and professionals worldwide through support services, education and research.
*September*

**2267   Blinded Veterans Association National Convention**
477 H St NW
Washington, DC  20001
202-371-8880
800-669-7079
FAX: 202-371-8258
e-mail: bva@bva.org
www.bva.org

*Thomas H Miller, Executive Director*
*Annette Mongelli, Conventions Coordinator*

Helps veterans and their families meet the challenges of blindness.Offers two main service programs without cost to blinded veterans. Field service program provides counseling to veterans and families and information on benefits and rehabilitation.
*August*

**2268   Children and Adolescents with Emotional and Behavioral Disorders**
Virginia Commonwealth University, Medical College
PO Box 980489
Richmond, VA  23298
804-828-1831
FAX: 804-828-2645

*Cynthia R Eillis MD, Program Chair*
*Catherine Howard, Executive Director*
*October*

**2269   Closing the Gap's Annual Conference**
PO Box 68
Henderson, MN  56044
507-248-3294
FAX: 507-248-3810
e-mail: info@closingthegap.com
www.closingthegap.com

*Dolores Hagen, President*

Topics will cover a broad spectrum of technology as it is being applied to all disabilities and age groups in education, rehabilitation, vocation and independent living. People with disabilities, special educators, rehabilitation professionals, administrators, service/care providers, personnel managers, government officials, and hardware/software developers will share their experiences and insights at what has become known as the most significant networking experience of the year.
*October*

**2270   Contemporary Issues in Behavioral Health Care**
American Assn. of Children's Residential Centers
11700 W Lake Park Drive
Milwaukee, WI  53224
877-332-2272
FAX: 877-362-2272
e-mail: mskarich@alliance1.org
www.aacrc-dc.org

*William P Marton, President*
*Maggie Skarich, National Coordinator*

One-day program that will address accreditation as it relates to current behavioral health care challenges held in Pasadena, CA.

*October*

**2271   Council for Exceptional Children Annual Convention and Expo**
1110 N Glebe Road
Suite 300
Arlington, VA  22201
703-245-0600
888-232-7733
FAX: 703-264-9494
TTY:866-915-5000
e-mail: service@cec.sped.org
www.cec.sped.org

*Jim McCormick, President*
*Drew Allbritten, Executive Director*
*Bruce Ramirez, Manager*

Works to improve the educational success of children with disabilities and/or gifts and talents.
*April*

**2272   Eye Bank Association of America Annual Meeting**
1015 18th Street NW
Suite 1010
Washington, DC  20036
202-775-4999
FAX: 202-429-6036
e-mail: malene@restoresight.org
www.restoresight.org

*Patricia Acken-O'Neill Esq, President/CEO*
*Patricia Hardy, Meetingds Assistant*

A four day program, which includes a series or presentations in administrative, hospital development, scientific and technical fields that are relative to eye banking.
*June*

**2273   Handicapped Student Program Postsecondary Education Association**
PO Box 21192
Columbus, OH  43221
614-488-4972
FAX: 614-488-1774
e-mail: ahead@postbox.acs.ohio-state.edu
www.ahead.org

*Ed Suddeth, Executive Director*
*July*

**2274   Joint Conference with ABMPP Annual Conference**
American Board of Disability Analysts
345 24th Avenue N
Suite 200
Nashville, TN  37203
615-327-2984
FAX: 615-327-9235
e-mail: americanbd@aol.com

*Kenneth Anchor, President*

Joint Conference with ABMPP Annual Conference Charleston, South Carolina.
*May*

**2275   Journal of Rehabilitation and Annual Conference**
National Rehabilitation Association (NRA)
633 S Washington Street
Alexandria, VA  22314
703-836-0850
FAX: 703-836-0848
TTY:703-836-0849
e-mail: info@nationalrehab.org
www.nationalrehab.org

*Linda Winslow, Executive Director*

Includes exhinits of companies that prodive services and products to rehab professionals and persons with disabilities. Journal of Rehabilitation articles are written by professionals in the fields of rehabilitation and are peer reviewed. Editorial Content reflects the broad perspectives of the associations membership.

**2276  Lowe's Syndrome Association Conference**
18919 Voss Road
Dallas, TX  75287
612-869-5693
FAX: 612-866-3222
e-mail: info@lowesyndrome.org
www.lowesyndrome.org

*Jane Gallery, President*

An international conference held approximately every two years where family, friends, medical and other professionals gather to exchange ideas and information. Next Conference held in 2008.
*June*

**2277  MedTrade/Comtrade, FutureShow**
SEMCO Productions
1130 Hightower Trail
Atlanta, GA  30350
770-998-9800
FAX: 770-642-4715
e-mail: info@semcopro.com
wwww.semcopro.com

*Mark Simmering, Executive VP/COO*
*Beth Lange*
*Tracy Conrad, Owner*

A showplace for more than 25,000 healthcare products and services, including respiratory, rehab, home healthcare, long-term care/alternate site, wound care/skin care, med/surg, sports medicine, IV therapy, computer and automation technology, and telecommunications.
*October*

**2278  National Council on the Aging Conference**
Conference Department
409 3rd St SW
Washington, DC  20024
202-362-1464
800-424-9046
FAX: 202-479-0735
e-mail: info@ncoa.org
www.ncoa.com

*James P Firman, President*

Offers ideas and programs to increase your program and administrative skills through NCOA's professional development tracks and offering of continuing education units.
*May*

**2279  National Managed Health Care Congress**
71 2nd Avenue
3rd Floor
Waltham, MA  02451
781-663-6000
FAX: 781-663-6422
e-mail: SMeehan@iirusa.com
www.nmhcc.com

*Megan Antonelli, Event Director*
*Shawn Meehan, Exhibit/Underwriter Sales*

Attracts nearly 7,000 delegates, thereby reinforcing its status as the nation's largest conferences for all managed care constituencies.
*April*

**2280  Prader-Willi Alliance of New York Annual Conference**
PO Box 1114
Niagara Falls, NY  14304
585-442-1655
800-442-1655
FAX: 585-271-2782
e-mail: alliance@prader-willi.org
www.prader-willi.org

*Daniel D Angiolillo, President*
*Elinor G Baller, Secretary*

Through conferences, publications, electronic communication and networking (parent-to-parent, parent-to professional, and professional-to-professional), the Prader-Willi Alliance provides a valuable resource for individuals and families sharing the same concerns.

*July*

**2281  RESNA Annual Conference**
1700 N Moore Street
Suite 1540
Arlington, VA  22209
703-524-6686
FAX: 703-524-6630
TTY:703-524-6639
e-mail: conference@resna.org
www.resna.org

*Thomas A Gorski, Executive Director*
*Rosina Romano, Meetings/Membership Coordinator*

A multidisciplinary association for the advancement of rehabilitation and assistive technologies, holds an annual conference in June. The conference brings together a large number of rehabilitation professionals, products and services from around the world and has something to offer for both professionals and consumers. The conference provides an informative and thought provoking forum for anyone with interests in rehabilitation technology.
*June*

**2282  Rehabilitation International**
25 E 21st Street
4th Floor
New York, NY  10010
212-420-1500
FAX: 212-505-0871
e-mail: Rehabintl@rehab-international.org
www.rehab-international.org

*Michael Fox, President*
*Tomas Lagerwall, Manager*
*Michele Morgan, Program Coordinator*

Worldwide network of people with disabilities, service providers and government agencies working together to improve the quality of life for the disabled people and their families, has more than 200 member organizations in 90 nations.

**2283  Rehabilitation Technology Association Conference**
PO Box 1004
Institute, WV  25112
304-766-4602
800-624-8284
FAX: 304-766-2689

*Betty Jo Tyler, RTA Coordinator*
*Dave Whipp, Information Manager*

Holds annual conference in the spring. Publishes a quarterly newsletter and houses the Project Enable computerized bulletin board system.

**2284  Santa Barbara Wheelchair Sports Conference**
Santa Barbara Parks and Recreation Department
PO Box 1990
Santa Barbara, CA  93102
805-564-5421
FAX: 805-564-5480

*Mariana de Sena RT CTRS, Recreation Supervisor*
*Richard Johns, Manager*

Offers a yearly conference, offers programs and services for individuals with a physically disabling condition, head injured individuals that may be visually and hearing impaired. Offers excursions, outings, competition, recreation, etc.

**2285  SubAcute Care: American SubAcute Care Association Annual Convention/Expo**
PO Box 17413
Washington, DC  20041
FAX: 703-318-7568

*Sherlyn Remley, Exhibit Sales*
*Jim Wasson, Exhibit Sales*

Totally dedicated to servicing the subacute arena and its major entities. Features 100+ booths and over 75 exhibitors.

**2286  Tourette Syndrome Association Conference**
4240 Bell Boulevard
Bayside, NY  11361
718-224-2999
800-237-0717
FAX: 718-279-9596
e-mail: ts@tsa-usa.org
www.tsa-usa.org

*Judit Ungar, President*
*Gary Frank, Executive Vice President*

More than 400 attendees coming together for this biennial conference that brings together members of the TS community and their families, educators, TS advocates, physicians, researchers, allied professionals, and TSA staff member to interact, socialize, share ideas, discuss issues of concern, learn from experts, and in many instances meet face to face for the first time.
*Spring*

**2287  United Cerebral Palsy Association Development Conference**
1660 L St NW
Suite 700
Washington, DC  20036
202-776-0406
800-872-5827
FAX: 202-776-0414
TTY: 202-973-7197
e-mail: webmaster@ucp.org
www.ucpa.org

*Stephen Bennett, President/CEO*

National, not-for-profit self-help organization dedicated to providing information and support to individuals with cerebral palsy and other disabilities, and their families. Supports more than 160 local affiliates; these affiliates provide a variety of programs and services for affected families, including support groups. Offers several educational and support materials, including a quarterly magazine, regular newsletters, and research reports.

**2288  United Cerebral Palsy Association of New York State Annual Conference**
90 State Street
Suite 929
Albany, NY  12207
518-436-0178
FAX: 518-436-8619
e-mail: info@cerebralpalsynys.org
www.cpofnys.org

*Susan Constantino, Executive Director*
*Michael Alvaro, Associate Executive Director*
*Marie Colbert, Executive Secretary*

Offers 50 sessions and features many outstanding presenters in areas such as assitive technology, education, health care, clinical services, public relations and development, and finance and management.
*October*

**2289  Winter Conference**
American Board of Disability Analysts
345 24th Avenue N
Suite 200
Nashville, TN  37203
615-327-2984
FAX: 615-327-9235
e-mail: americanbd@aol.com

*Kenneth Anchor, President*

Joint Conference: American Board of Disability.

**2290  Young Onset Parkinson Conference**
National Parkinson Foundation
1501 NW 9th Avenue
Miami, FL  33136
305-547-6666
800-327-4545
FAX: 305-243-4403
e-mail: contact@parkinson.org
www.parkinson.org

*Daniel Arty, President*
*Alan M Slewett Esq, Secretary*
*Jose Garcia-Pedrosa, Executive Director*

Purpose is to find the cause and cure for Parkinson's Disease and related neurodegenerative disorders through research, education and dissemination of current information to patients, care-givers and families.
*Annual*

## Associations

**2291  Adaptive Environments Center**

374 Congress Street
Suite 301
Boston, MA  02210                        617-695-1225
                                    FAX: 617-482-8099
                     e-mail: info@adaptiveenvironments.org
                                      www.adaptenv.org

*Allen Crocker, President*
*Andy Washburn, Information Specialist*
*Kathy Gips, Director Training*

Develops educational programs and materials on universal design, Americans with Disabilities Act, home adaptation, and more. Central Adaptive Environments publication list also available.

**2292  Building Owners and Managers Association International**

1201 New York Avenue NW
Suite 300
Washington, DC  20005                    202-408-2662
                                    FAX: 202-371-0181
                                       www.boma.org

*Dave Johnston, Director Codes/Standards*
*Henry Chamberlain, President*

Conducts seminars nationwide and publishes resource guidebooks for building owners and managers on ADA requirements for commercial facilities and places of public accommodation.

**2293  Challenges Unlimited**

171 River Drive
Hadley, MA  01035
                                         800-637-8720
                                    FAX: 413-585-1137

*Michael Oestreicher, President*

A multi-disciplined design firm founded in 1984 by concerned design professionals. The team includes architects, engineers, designers and landscape architects specializing in accessible corporate, municipal and private facilities.

**2294  Mark Elmore Associates Architects**

42 East Street
Suite 104
Crystal Lake, IL  60014                  815-455-7260
                                         800-801-7766
                                    FAX: 815-455-2238
                      e-mail: mark@elmore-architects.com
                               www.elmore-architects.com

*Mark Elmore, President*

Architectural designs for accessible residential and commercial buildings. ADA compliance reviews.

**2295  National Conference on Building Codes and Standards**

505 Huntmar Park Drive
Suite 210
Herndon, VA  20170                       703-437-0100
                                    FAX: 703-481-3596
                        e-mail: membership@ncsbcs.org
                                     www.ncsbcs.org

*Debbie Becker, Administrative Assistant*

Serves as a forum in the interchange of information and provides technical services, education and training to our members to enhance the public's social and economic well being through safe, durable, affordable, accessible and efficient buildings.

**2296  National Council of Architectural Registration Boards (NCARB)**

1801 K Street NW
Suite 1100-K
Washington, DC  20006                    202-783-6500
                                    FAX: 202-783-0290
                     e-mail: customerservice@ncarb.org
                                      www.ncarb.org

*Lenore M Lucey, Executive Vice President*

Research service in print and online information. Large collection of books and periodicals on the building/architectural environments.

**2297  Overcoming Mobility Barriers International**

1022 S 4st Street
Omaha, NE  68105                         402-342-5731
                                    FAX: 402-342-5731

*Kay Neil, Executive Director*

Members are government officials, service consumers and providers, and other persons interested in removing mobility barriers for elderly, handicapped and disadvantaged persons. Advises and works in conjunction with other groups and government agencies to establish safety standards for special equipment used in retrofitting vehicles and works to retrain drivers in the use of nonconventional driving controls. Addresses such problems as possible allocation of fuel to social service agencies.

**2298  Paradigm Design Group**

Paralyzed Veterans of America
801 18th Street NW
Washington, DC  20006                    202-872-1300
                                         800-424-8200
                                    FAX: 202-416-7647
                                  e-mail: info@pva.org
                                       www.pva.org

*Carol Lopez, Director of Architecture*
*Del Mcneal, Executive Director*
*Randy Pleza, President*

Specialized firm providing architectural consulting services related to accessible designs. Experience includes product design and building codes and standards.

**2299  United States Access Board**

1331 F Street NW
Suite 1000
Washington, DC  20004                    202-628-3100
                                         800-872-2253
                                    FAX: 202-272-0081
                       e-mail: info@access-board.gov
                                   www.access-board.gov

*Dave Yanchulis, Public Affairs Specialist*
*Leland Schwartz, Owner*

Offers information and referrals on architectural accessibility for architects, designers, government agencies, building owners and consumers. A list of free publications is available on request. The Access Board also enforces the Architectural Barriers Act, which covers buildings and facilities designed, built or altered since 1968 with certain federal funds or leased by federal agencies. Publications: Access Currents, bi-monthly newsletter.

## Publications & Videos

**2300  Access Currents**
United States Access Board
1331 F Street NW
Suite 1000
Washington, DC  20004
202-628-3100
800-872-2253
FAX: 202-272-0081
e-mail: info@access-board.gov
www.access-board.gov

*Jan Tuck, Chair*
*David L Bibb, Vice Chair*
*Leland Schwartz, Owner*

Offers information and referrals on architectural accessibility for architects, designers, government agencies, building owners and consumers. A list of free publications is available on request.
*bi-monthly*

**2301  Access Equals Opportunity**
Council of B BB s Foundation
4200 Wilson Boulevard
Suite 800
Arlington, VA  22203
703-276-0100
FAX: 703-525-8277
e-mail: media@cbbb.bbb.org
www.bbb.org

*Charlie Underhill, Chief Operating Officer*
*Steven J Cole, Chief Executive Officer*

These six Title III compliance guides for existing small businesses offer creative cheap and easy suggestions for complying with the public accommodations section of the ADA. Each guide is industry specific for: retail stores, car sales/service, restaurants/bars, medical offices and fun/fitness centers. They include suggestions for readily achievable removal of architectural barriers; effective communication; and guidance for nondiscriminatory policies or procedures. *$2.50*

**2302  Access House**
Northside Mental Health Center
1109 E 139th Avenue
Tampa, FL  33613
813-972-2289

*Cecil Woodside, Director*
Barrier free regulations for design and construction.

**2303  Access for All**
Hospital Audiences
220 W 42nd Street
Frnt 3
New York, NY  10036
212-575-7660
FAX: 212-575-7669
e-mail: info@hostau.org
www.hospitalaudiences.org

*Tricia Hennessey, Access Director*
*Max Daniels, Manager*

Provides physical and program accessibility information for people with disabilities to New York City cultural institutions including theaters, museums, galleries, etc.

**2304  Accessible Home of Your Own**
Accent Books & Products
PO Box 700
Bloomington, IL  61702
309-378-2961
800-787-8444
FAX: 309-378-4420
e-mail: acmtlvng@aol.com
www.accentonliving.com

*Raymond C Cheever, Publisher*
*Betty Garee, Editor*

This guide includes 14 articles that have appeared in the magazine on the popular subject of how to make a disabled persons home more accessible. *$5.95*
*52 pages Paperback*
*ISBN 0-91570 -29-9*

**2305  Adaptable Housing: A Technical Manual for Implementing Adaptable Dwelling**
H UD U SE R
PO Box 23268
Washington, DC  20026
202-708-3178
800-245-2691
FAX: 202-708-9981
TTY: 800-927-7589
e-mail: helpdesk@huduser.org
www.huduser.org

*Patrick J Tewey, Director*
*William Reeder, Director*

An illustrated manual describing methods for implementing adaptability in housing. *$3.00*

**2306  Adaptive Environments Center Home Assessment Form**

374 Congress Street
Suite 301
Boston, MA  02210
617-695-1225
FAX: 617-482-8099
e-mail: info@adaptiveenvironment.org
www.adaptenv.org

*Allen Crocker, President*
*Valerie Fletcher, Executive Director*

A handy checklist for evaluating a disabled person's abilities and his/her home limitations to determine what accessibility modifications will be most effective. *$5.00*

**2307  Consumer's Guide to Home Adaptation**
Adaptive Environments Center
374 Congress Street
Suite 301
Boston, MA  02210
617-695-1225
FAX: 617-482-8099
e-mail: info@AdaptiveEnvironments.org
www.adaptiveEnvironments.org

*Valerie Fletcher, Executive Director*
*Ana Gomez, Coordinator Design/Communication*
*Mike DiLorenzo, Publications Coordinator*

A workbook that enables people with disabilities to plan the modifications necessary to adapt their homes. Describes how to widen doorways, lower countertops, etc. *$12.00*
*52 pages Paperback*

**2308  Design for Acessibility**
National Endowment for the Arts Office
1100 Pennsylvania Avenue NW
Washington, DC  20506
202-682-5485
FAX: 202-682-5715
e-mail: webmgr@arts.endow.gov
www.arts.gov

*Paula Terry, Director*
*Joy Kiser, Manager*

A handbook for compliance with Section 504 of the Rehabilitation Act of 1973 and the Americans with Disablities Act of 1990 including technical assistance on making arts programs accessible to staff, performers and audience.

*101 pages 1987*
*ISBN 0-160042-83-6*

**2309  Directory of Accessible Building Products**
N AH B Research Center
400 Prince Georges Boulevard
Upper Marlboro, MD  20774
301-249-4000
800-638-8556
FAX: 301-430-6180
www.nahbrc.org

*Pamela Eggleston, Program Manager*
*Mike Luzier, President*

Contains descriptions of more than 200 commercially available products designed for use by people with disabilities and age-related limitations. Paperback. *$5.00*
*104 pages Yearly*

**2310  Do-Able Renewable Home**
A AR P Fulfillment
601 East Street NW
Washington, DC  20049
202-434-2277
800-424-3410
FAX: 202-434-3443
e-mail: member@aarp.org
www.aarp.org

*William Novelli, Chief Executive Officer*
*Marie Smith, President*

Describes how individuals with disabilities can modify their homes for independent living. Room-by-room modifications are accompanied by illustrations.

**2311  ECHO Housing: Recommended Construction and Installation Standards**
601 East Street NW
Washington, DC  20049
888-687-2277
www.aarp.org

*William Bill Novelli, Chief Executive Officer*
*Marie Smith, President*

Illustrated design, construction, and installation standards for temporary dwelling units for elderly people on single family residential property.

**2312  Electronic House: Enhanced Lifestyles with Electronics**
Electronic House
111 Speen Street
Suite 989
Framingham, MA  01701
508-820-1515
800-375-8015
FAX: 508-663-1599
e-mail: kmoyes@ehpub.com
www.electronichouse.com

*Kenneth Moyes, Owner/Chief Executive Officer*
*Julie Jacobson, Vice President*

Dedicated to home automation. Featuring both extravagant and affordable smart homes that can be controlled with one touch. EH covers electronic systems that give homeowners more security, entertainment, convenience, and fun. Articles cover whole house control and subsystems like residential lighting, security, home theater, energy management and telecommunications. *$23.95*
*84 pages BiMonthly*
*ISSN 0886-66 3*

**2313  Fair Housing Design Guide for Accessibility**
National Council on Multifamily Housing Industry
1201 15th & M Street NW
Washington, DC  20005
202-266-8200
800-368-5242
FAX: 202-266-8400
www.nahb.com

*David F Wilson, President*
*David L Pressly Jr, Vice President*

Specifically tailored to address the needs of architects and builders. The book includes a detailed technical analysis of the legislation's impact on multifamily design, highlights potential construction problems, and identifies possible solutions. *$29.95*

**2314  Ideas for Making Your Home Accessible**
Accent Books & Products
PO Box 700
Bloomington, IL  61702
309-378-2961
800-787-8444
FAX: 309-378-4420
e-mail: acmtlvng@aol.com
www.accentonliving.com

*Raymond C Cheever, Publisher*
*Betty Garee, Editor*

Offers over 100 pages of tips and ideas to help build or remodel a home. Includes many special devices and where to get them. *$7.50*
*94 pages Paperback*
*ISBN 0-91570 -08-6*

**2315  North Carolina Accessibility Code**
North Carolina Department of Insurance
PO Box 26387
Raleigh, NC  27611
919-661-5880

e-mail: lwright@ncdoi.net

*Laurel W Wright, Chief Acessiability Section*

Making buildings and facilities accessible to and usable by the physically handicapped. *$20.00*
*678 pages Triannually*

**2316  Removing the Barriers: Accessibility Guidelines and Specifications**
A PP A
1643 Prince Street
Alexandria, VA  22314
703-684-1446
FAX: 703-549-2772
e-mail: webmaster@appa.org
www.appa.org

*Wayne Leroy, Vice President*
*Steve Glazner, Communications Director*
*E Medlin, Executive Vice President*

Offers site accessibility, building entrances, doors, interior circulation, restrooms and bathing facilities, drinking fountains and additional resources. *$45.00*
*125 pages*
*ISBN 0-91335 -59-9*

**2317  Smart Kitchen/How to Design a Comfortable, Safe & Friendly Workplace**
Ceres Press
PO Box 87
Woodstock, NY  12498
845-679-5573
888-804-8848
FAX: 845-679-5573
e-mail: cem620@aol.com
www.healthyhighways.com

*David Goldbeck, Director/Owner*

This book provides information about designing kitchens that may be helpful to people with disabilities as well as safe and energy efficient. *$16.95*
*132 pages Paperback*

**2318  United Spinal Association**
7520 Astoria Boulevard
East Elmhurst, NY  11370
718-803-3782
800-444-0120
FAX: 718-803-0414
e-mail: info@unitedspinal.org
www.unitedspinal.org

*Peter F Addesso, President*

Association news and articles on architecture and barrier-free design, legislation and other current events affecting veterans.
   *Monthly*

## General

**2319  Accessibility Consultants**
12542 Riva Ridge Lane
Houston, TX  77071
713-728-0924
FAX: 713-728-4857
www.accesibiltycheck.com

*Doug Teresa Darr, President*
*Joe Bontke, VP*

Focuses on the integration of people with disabilities into everyday life. Areas of concentration include adaptation of public facilities, preconstruction planning, corporate policies and
training, job description seminars and workplace modifications.

**2320  American Board of Professional Disability Consultants**
1350 Beverly Road
Suite 115-327
Mc Lean, VA  22101
703-952-0024
FAX: 703-952-0028

*Taras Cerkevitch, Operations Director*
*Mark Long, Development Director*
*Bashar Islam, Owner*

Certifies physicians, psychologists, attorneys, and counselors
as specialists in disability and personal injury.

**2321  Augmentative Communication Consultants (ACCI)**
PO Box 731
Moon Township, PA  15108
412-264-6121
800-982-2248
FAX: 412-269-0923
e-mail: accil@earthlink.net
www.acciinc.com

*Millie Telega, President/Owner*

ACCI is owned by the mother of a multiple handicapped son who
is non-verbal. ACCI specializes in communication devices, educational software, provocational training materials, computer
access, environmental controls, switches, resource books and
in-service training. Offers a wide range of products, so that
ACCI can help one make the right choice. Price Range $24 -
$6,500.

**2322  Behavior Service Consultants**
PO Box 97
Greenbelt, MD  20768
301-474-2146
301-474-1544
FAX: 301-474-1544

*Leopold Walder, Director*
*Marcella Walder, Clinical Social Worker*

Offers consultative services regarding behavior modification
techniques, neurological testing, therapy for individuals, families and groups.

**2323  Community Alternatives Unlimited**
8700 W Bryn Mawr Avenue
Suite 500
Chicago, IL  60631
708-867-4000
FAX: 773-867-4168

*Joanell Voigt, Executive Director*
*Steve Zider PhD, Associate Director*

Provides freestanding case management to individuals with developmental disabilities and mental illness. Provides services
throughout the North Side of Chicago, and additionally, the
Northern Suburbs of Cook and Lake counties.

**2324  Getting the Most Out of Consultation Services**
Independent Living Research Utilization I LR U
2323 S Shepherd Drive
Suite 1000
Houston, TX  77019
713-520-0232
FAX: 713-520-5785
e-mail: ilru@ilru.org
www.ilru.org

*Laurie Redd, Executive Director*

A practical, nuts-and-bolts approach to help make working with
a consultant a positive, helpful experience for independent living centers.
*10 pages*

**2325  National Business & Disability Council**
201 I U Willets Road
Albertson, NY  11507
516-465-1516
FAX: 516-465-3730
e-mail: info@business-disability.com
www.nbdc.com

*Michael J McGowan*
*Laura M Francis*

Dedicated to increasing the employment of people with disabilities through a coordinated effort of N America's largest employers. Believing that people with disabilities bring value to the
workplace. Provides the leadership necessary to infuse effective
employment practices for workers with disabilities in our global
economy.

**2326  Rehab Assist**
Case Management Company
6250 N River Road
Suite 3000
Rosemont, IL  60018
847-292-4444
FAX: 847-292-7424

*Henry P Brennan MS, Director*
*Thomas J Kleinhenz RN, Director*

Medical and catastrophic intervention consultants providing
objective, independent evaluations and recommendations. Services include assessments, on-site evaluations, life care planning, file and chart review, billing audits, medical and worker's
compensation case management, and medical/legal consultations.

**2327  RehabTech Associates**
122 Ridge Drive
Valatie, NY  12184
518-758-7887
FAX: 518-758-8505

*Juergen Babirad, Interim Chair/Partner*

A disability consulting firm that conducts research and other
projects related to disability. It also publishes and distributes
publications on disability.

## Aids for the Classroom

**2328  AEPS Child Progress Record: For Children Ages Three to Six**
Brookes Publishing
PO Box 10624
Baltimore, MD 21285
410-337-9580
800-638-3775
FAX: 410-337-8539
e-mail: custserv@brookespublishing.com
www.brookespublishing.com

*Anastasia Worchester, Publicity Manager*
*Tracy Gray, Educational Sales Manager*
*Paul Brooks, Owner*

This chart helps monitor change by visually displaying current abilities, intervention targets, and child progress. In packages of 30. *$21.00*
*8 pages Gate-fold*
*ISBN 1-557662-51-7*

**2329  AEPS Curriculum for Three to Six Years**
Brookes Publishing
PO Box 10624
Baltimore, MD 21285
410-337-9580
800-638-3775
FAX: 410-337-8539
e-mail: custserv@brookespublishing.com
www.brookespublishing.com

*Jeff Brookes, Exhibits Coordinator*
*Tracy Gray, Educational Sales Manager*
*Dante Washington, Account Sales Manager*

*$49.00*
*304 pages Spiral-bound*
*ISBN 1-557661-88-X*

**2330  AEPS Data Recording Forms: For Children Ages Three to Six**
Brookes Publishing
PO Box 10624
Baltimore, MD 21285
410-337-9580
800-638-3775
FAX: 410-337-8539
e-mail: custserv@brookespublishing.com
www.brookespublishing.com

*Paul Brooks, Owner*

These forms can be used by child development professionals on four separate occasions to pinpoint and then monitor a child's strengths and needs in the six key areas of skill development measured by the AEPS Test. Packages of 10. *$24.00*
*36 pages Saddle-stiched*
*ISBN 1-557662-49-5*

**2331  AEPS Family Interest Survey**
Brookes Publishing
PO Box 10624
Baltimore, MD 21285
410-337-9580
800-638-3775
FAX: 410-337-8539
e-mail: custserv@brookespublishing.com
www.brookespublishing.com

*Clary Creighton, Exhibits Coordinator*
*Tracy Gracy, Educational Sales Manager*
*Paul Brooks, Owner*

This is a 30-item checklist that helps families to identify interests and concerns to address in a child's IEP/IFSP. Comes in packages of 30. *$15.00*

*8 pages Saddle-stiched*
*ISBN 1-557660-98-0*

**2332  AEPS Family Report: For Children Ages Birth to Three**
Brookes Publishing
PO Box 10624
Baltimore, MD 21285
410-337-9580
800-638-3775
FAX: 410-337-8539
e-mail: custserv@brookespublishing.com
www.brookespublishing.com

*Clary Creighton, Exhibits Coordinator*
*Tracy Gray, Educational Sales Manager*
*Paul Brooks, Owner*

This is a 64-item questionnaire that asks parents to rank their child's abilities on specific skills. In packages of 10. *$17.00*
*20 pages Saddle-stiched*
*ISBN 1-557660-99-9*

**2333  Advanced Language Tool Kit**
Educators Publishing Service
625 Mount Auburn Street
Suite 3
Cambridge, MA 02138
617-547-6706
800-225-5750
FAX: 888-440-2665
e-mail: feedback@epsbooks.com
www.epsbooks.com

*Charles Heinle, Vice President*
*Alexandra S Bigelow, Author*
*Gunnar Voltz, President*

Provides an overview of the structure, organization, and sound units that are needed to develop skills for advanced reading and spelling. The kit contains a teacher's manual and threee packs of cards. *$60.00*

*ISBN 0-838885-48-9*

**2334  Affix & Root Cards**
Educators Publishing Service
625 Mount Auburn Street
Suite 3
Cambridge, MA 02138
617-547-6706
800-225-5750
FAX: 888-440-2665
e-mail: feedback@epsbooks.com
www.epsbooks.com

*Charles H Heinle, Vice President*
*Alexandra S Bigelow, Author*
*Gunnar Voltz, President*

These cards are specially designed to reinforce the adolescent's knowledge of reading, spelling and vocabulary and should be used in conjunction with language-training materials found in the Alphabetic Phonics and Gillingham curricula. Color-coded cards present word parts, definitions, and example words. *$29.70*
*140 Cards*
*ISBN 0-838803-24-5*

**2335  All Kinds of Minds**
Educators Publishing Service
PO Box 9031
Cambridge, MA 02139
617-547-6706
800-225-5750
FAX: 888-440-2665
e-mail: feedback@epsbooks.com
www.epsbooks.com

*Charles H Heinle, Vice President*
*Alexandra S Bigelow, Author*
*Gunnar Voltz, President*

A Young Student's Book about Learning Abilities and Learning Disorders is mainly a fictitious account of five appealing and realistic characters, each of whom has one or more learning disorders. Young readers will easily identify with the experiences of the characters as they appear in a variety of situations, and, at the level, there are suggestions for overcoming the effects of learning disorders. *$24.75*
> *296 pages*
> *ISBN 0-838820-90-5*

**2336 American Sign Language Handshape Cards**
T J Publishers, Distributor
817 Silver Spring Avenue
Suite 206
Silver Spring, MD 20910
301-585-4440
800-999-1168
FAX: 301-585-5930
e-mail: tjpubinc@aol.com

*Angela K Thames, President*
*Jerald A Murphy, Vice President*

Durable flashcards illustrate basic handshapes, classifiers and the American manual alphabet. An instructional booklet describes games for differing skill levels to improve vocabulary, increase hand and eye coordination, sign recognition and usage. *$16.95*

**2337 Assistive Technology in the Schools: A Guide for Idaho Educators**
Idaho Assistive Technology Project
129 West 3rd Street
Moscow, ID 83843
208-885-3559
800-432-8324
FAX: 208-885-3628
e-mail: rseiler@uidaho.edu
www.educ.uidaho.edu/idatech

*Jill Iris, Training Coordinator*
*Ron Seiler, Project Coordinator*
*$15.00*

**2338 Asthma Action Cards: Child Care Asthma/Allergy Action Card**
Asthma and Allergy Foundation of America
1125 20th Street NW
Suite 402
Washington, DC 20036
202-466-7643
FAX: 202-466-8940
e-mail: info@aafa.org
www.aafa.org

*Bill Lin, Executive Director*

Includes necessary information a provider needs to care for a young child who has asthma and allergies. The card includes a medication plan, a list of the child's specific signs and symptoms that indicate the child is having trouble breathing, and steps on how to handle an emergency situation.

**2339 Asthma Action Cards: Student Asthma Action Card**
Asthma and Allergy Foundation of America
1233 20th Street NW
Suite 402
Washington, DC 20036
202-466-7643
800-727-8462
e-mail: info@aafa.org
www.aafa.org

*Chris Ward, President*
*Ben C Hadden, VP Finance & Treasurer*
*Bill Lin, Executive Director*

Tool for communicating school aged children's and teen's asthma managment plan to school personnel. Includes sections for asthma triggers, daily medications, and emergency directions.

**2340 Auditech: Classroom Amplification System Focus CFM802**
PO Box 821105
Vicksburg, MS 39182
800-229-8293
FAX: 800-221-8639
e-mail: info@auditechusa.com
www.auditechusa.com
The SOUNDFOCUS FM System is designed to cover background noise and compensate for distance. Students find it easier to focus their attention and not strain to be heard. Two speaker system. *$1052.00*

**2341 Auditech: Personal FM Educational System**
PO Box 821105
Vicksburg, MS 39182
800-229-8293
FAX: 800-221-8639
e-mail: info@auditechusa.com
www.auditechusa.com
Personal FM Educational System is a portable system for classroom use. The teacher wears a microphone. Students use a portable receiver which works clearly and easily. For users who have a hearing problem, a switch, a necklooop telecoil coupler is available. *$679.00*

**2342 Auditory-Verbal Therapy for Parents and Professionals**
Alexander Graham Bell Association
3417 Volta Place NW
Washington, DC 20007
202-337-5220
FAX: 202-337-8314
e-mail: info@agbell.org
www.agbell.org

*Jessica Ripper, Senior Director Marketing/Commun*
*Todd Houston, Executive Director*

To teach children to listen, process spoken language and talk, auditory-verbal therapy develops language and speech through listening with effective use of hearing aids and partnership of parents, children and professionals. *$39.95*
> *313 pages Paperback*

**2343 Barrier Free Education**
Center for Assistive Technology & Env Access
490 10th Street NW
Atlanta, GA 30332
404-894-4960
800-726-9119
FAX: 404-894-9320
www.catea.org

*Elizabeth Bryant, Project Director*

Math and science activities pose unique accommodation challenges for students with disabilities. The Barrier Free Education resource on accessible science experiments was developed for high school chemistry and physics students with physical or visual disabilities under the National Science Foundation's Program for Persons with Disabilities.

**2344 Basic Course in American Sign Language Package**
T J Publishers
2544 Tarpley Road
Suite 108
Carrollton, TX 75006
972-416-0800
800-999-1168
FAX: 301-585-5930
e-mail: TJPubinc@aol.com

*Angela K Thames, President*
*Jerald A Murphy, VP*

Accompanying videotapes and textbooks will include voice translations. Hearing students can analyze sound for initial instruction, or opt to turn off the sound to sharpen visual acuity. Package includes the A Basic Course in American Sign Language text, Student Study Guide, the original four 1-hour videotapes plus the ABCASL Vocabulary Videotape. *$139.95*

*280 pages*

**2345    Beginning Reasoning and Reading**
Educators Publishing Service
625 Mount Auburn Street
Suite 3
Cambridge, MA  02138                    617-547-6706
                                        800-225-5750
                                FAX: 888-440-2665
                    e-mail: feedback@epsbooks.com
                                www.epsbooks.com

*Charles H Heinle, Vice President*
*Alexandra S Bigelow, Author*
*Gunnar Volta, President*

This workbook develops basic language and thinkink skills that build the foundation for reading comprehension. Workbook exercises reinforce reading as a critical activity. *$10.45*

*ISBN 0-838830-01-3*

**2346    Board Games for Play and Say**
Pro- Ed
8700 Shoal Creek Boulevard
Austin, TX  78757                       512-451-3246
                                        800-897-3202
                                FAX: 512-451-8542
                    e-mail: info@proedinc.com
                                www.proedinc.com

*Peggy Kipping, Senior Editor*
*Kathy Synatschk, Executive Editor*
*Donald Hammill, Owner*

Designed to make therapy more fun and enhance simple words and the production of speech sounds in isolation, phrases and sentences. *$59.00*
                        *8 Games*

**2347    Book of Possibilities: Elementary Edition**
AbleNet
2808 Fairview Avenue N
Roseville, MN  55113                    651-294-2200
                                        800-322-0956
                                FAX: 651-294-2259
                    e-mail: customerservice@ablenetinc.com
                                www.ablenetinc.com

*Cheryl Volkan, President/CEO*

Activity ideas for all elementary age switch users to be included in a variety of math, science, language arts, social studies, spelling and reading activities. A valuable how to resource for every educator that serves students with severe disabilities. *$27.00*

**2348    Book of Possibilities: Secondary Edition**
AbleNet
2808 Fairview Avenue N
Roseville, MN  55113                    651-294-2200
                                        800-322-0956
                                FAX: 651-294-2222
                    e-mail: customerservice@ablenetinc.com
                                www.ablenetinc.com

*Cheryl Volkam, President/CEOr*

Suggestions for including secondary age switch users in a variety of school experiences throughout the day. Includes sections on secondary academics, general classroom activities like giving tests or reports and noncurricular activities like school plays and sports events. A valuable how to resource for educators that serve students with severe disabilities. *$27.00*

**2349    Buy!**
JE Stewart Teaching Tools
PO Box 15308
Seattle, WA  98115                      206-262-9538
                                FAX: 206-262-9538

*J E Stewart, Owner*

Teaches 50 words as they appear in commercial and community situations such as clinic, sale, receipt, price and cleaner. These words are functional at school, on the job and shopping. *$32.50*

*116 pages*
*ISBN 1-877866-05-9*

**2350    Catalog for Teaching Life Skills to Persons with Development Disability**
P CI Educational Publishing
PO Box 34270
San Antonio, TX  78265                  210-377-1999
                                        800-594-4263
                                www.pcicatalog.com

*Jeff Clain, Chief Executive Officer*
*Janie Haugen Mclane, Senior Vice President/Founder*
*Leslie Boulet, Senior Marketing Manager*

Over 200 educational products that help individuals learn and maintain the life skills they need to succeed in an inclusive society.

**2351    Childs Spelling System: The Rules**
Educators Publishing Service
PO Box 9031
Cambridge, MA  02139                    617-547-6706
                                        800-225-5750
                                FAX: 888-440-2665
                    e-mail: feedback@epsbooks.com
                                www.epsbooks.com

*Charles H Heinle, Vice President*
*Alexandra S Bigelow, Author*
*Gunnar Voltz, President*

This book presents reasonable explanations of spelling rules, makes suggestions for more effective teaching and provides lists of examples and exceptions. Basic spelling rules are listed on inside front cover. *$7.15*
                *32 pages*
                *ISBN 0-838801-12-9*

**2352    Classroom GOAL: Guide for Optimizing Auditory Learning Skills**
Alexander Graham Bell Association
3417 Volta Place NW
Washington, DC  20007                   202-337-5220
                                FAX: 202-337-8314
                    e-mail: info@agbell.org
                                www.agbell.org

*Todd Houston, Executive Director*

This reader-friendly teacher's guide filled with tips, source materials and sample charts and plans is designed for educators who have yearned for a resource that explains how to incorporate auditory goals into academic learning for students with different degrees of hearing loss. *$34.95*
                *Paperback*

**2353    Classroom Notetaker: How to Organize a Program Serving Students with Hearing Impairments**
Alexander Graham Bell Association
3417 Volta Place NW
Washington, DC  20007                   202-337-5220
                                FAX: 202-337-8314
                    e-mail: info@agbell.org
                                www.agbell.org

*Todd Houston, Executive Director*

This detailed manual for instructors, administrators and staff notetakers promotes classroom notetaking within long-term educational programs as absolutely vital for students who are deaf and hard of hearing from elementary school to college. *$24.95*

*127 pages Paperback*

**2354 Community Services for the Blind and Partially Sighted Store: Sight Connection**
Community Service for the Blind
9709 3rd Avenue NE
Suite 100
Seattle, WA 98115
206-525-5556
800-458-4888
FAX: 206-525-0422
e-mail: csbstore@csbps.com
www.sightconnection.com

*June Mansfield, Chief Executive Officer*

Over 300 practical products for living with vision loss selected by certified vision rehabilitation specialists from Community Services for the Blind and Partially Sighted. Easy-to-use online store features large print, large photos, secure transactions, and links to other vision-related resources. Free store catalog available by mail in large print, Braille, audiotape or PC disk. Phone and mail orders welcome. Store open 9-5, M-F, Pacific Time.

**2355 Community Signs**
JE Stewart Teaching Tools
PO Box 15308
Seattle, WA 98115
206-262-9538
FAX: 206-262-9538

*J E Stewart, Owner*

Teaches 50 words like go, fire, rest room, men, women, danger and walk needed to successfully navigate our environment. *$ 32.50*

**2356 Comprehensive Assessment of Spoken Language (CASL)**
AGS
PO Box 99
Circle Pines, MN 55014
800-328-2560
FAX: 800-471-8457
e-mail: agsmail@agsnet.com
www.agsnet.com

*Kevin Brueggeman, President*
*Robert Zaske, Market Manager*

CASL is an individually and orally administered research-based, theory-drive oral language assessment battery for ages 3 through 21. Fifteen tests measure language processing skills - comprehension, expression, and retrieval - in four language structure categories: lexical/semantic, syntactic, supralinguistic and pragmatic. *$299.95*

**2357 Creative Arts Therapy Catalogs**
MMB Music
3526 Washington Avenue
Saint Louis, MO 63103
314-531-9635
800-543-3771
FAX: 314-531-8384
e-mail: info@mmbmusic.com
www.mmbmusic.com

*Marcia Lee Goldberg, President*

Catalogs of books, videos, recordings for the creative arts and wellness (music, art, dance, poetry, drama, therapies, photography).

**2358 Cursive Writing Skills**
Educators Publishing Service
625 Mount Auburn Street
Suite 3
Cambridge, MA 02138
617-547-6706
800-225-5750
FAX: 888-440-2665
e-mail: feedback@epsbooks.com
www.epsbooks.com

*Charles H Heinle, Vice President*
*Alexandra S Bigelow, Author*
*Gunnar Volta, President*

These two books, written by Diana King, for grades 7-adult for right and left-handed students. Books include exercises to establish good posture; pencil grip and paper position for both lower case and upper case letters, students also practice joining letters and copying. *$ 7.15*

*ISBN 0-83881 -05-*

**2359 Don Johnston**
26799 West Commerce Drive
Volo, IL 60073
847-740-0749
800-999-4660
FAX: 847-740-7326
e-mail: info@donjohnston.com
www.donjohnston.com

*Don Johnston, Leader*
*Ruth Ziolkowski, President*

A provider of quality products and services that enable people with special needs to discover their potential and experience success. Products are developed for the areas of Physical Access, Augmentative Communication and for those who struggle with reading and writing.

**2360 Dyslexia Training Program**
Educators Publishing Service
PO Box 9031
Cambridge, MA 02139
617-547-6706
800-225-5750
FAX: 888-440-2665
e-mail: feedback@epsbooks.com
www.epsbooks.com

*Charles H Heinle, Vice President*
*Alexandra S Bigelow, Author*
*Gunnar Voltz, President*

This program from the Texas Scottish Rite Hospital for grades 2-8 introduces reading and writing through a two-year, cumulative series of daily one-hour videotaped lessons and accompanying student's books and teacher's guides. It is presented in a structured multi-sensory sequence of alphabet, reading, spelling, cursive handwriting, listening, language history and review activities. Students are in a class of nor more than six who work with instructional tapes as teacher's guides are available.
*$6.75 - $15*

**2361 Exceptional Teaching Aids**
5673 West Las Positas Boulevard
Suite 207
Pleasanton, CA 94588
925-598-0082
800-549-6999
FAX: 925-598-0086
e-mail: info@exceptionalteaching.com
www.exceptionalteaching.com

*Helene Holman, Owner/manager*
*Susan Taylor, Order Information*
*Kelli Cooney, Order Information*

Providing educational teaching aids for the blind and visually impaired via catalog. Price range $2-600.

**2362 Explode the Code Books 1-8**
Educators Publishing Service
PO Box 9031
Cambridge, MA 02139
617-547-6706
800-225-5750
FAX: 888-440-BOOK
e-mail: feedback@epsbooks.com
www.epsbooks.com

*Alexandra S Bigelow, Author*
*Gunnar Voltz, President*

A program of workbooks helps children learn to read by teaching them to use the sounds of letters. This carefully sequenced program provides experience recognizing and combining sounds in order to read words, phrases, sentences and stories, as well as to build vocabulary. A set of fifty-four illustrated cards to practice the sounds taught in books 1-3 is now available. *$6.20*

*Grades K-4, 1-3*
*ISBN 0-83881 -60-*

**2363  First Course in Phonic Reading**
Educators Publishing Service
PO Box 9031
Cambridge, MA  02139      617-547-6706
800-225-5750
FAX: 888-440-2665
e-mail: feedback@epsbooks.com
www.epsbooks.com

*Charles H Heinle, Vice President*
*Alexandra S Bigelow, Author*
*Gunnar Voltz, President*

This book provides students with a basic foundation in phonics beginning with common consonants and short vowels, syllabication and spelling rules are also taught. There is a special emphasis on auditory and kinesthetic involvement. *$10.65*
*Grades 2-3*
*ISBN 0-838801-24-2*

**2364  Food!**
JE Stewart Teaching Tools
PO Box 15308
Seattle, WA  98115      206-262-9538
FAX: 206-262-9538

*J E Stewart, Owner*

Teaches 50 words like salt, pepper, hamburger, fruit, milk and soup, seen commonly on menus, packages and in directions used at home and at play. *$32.50*

**2365  Fun for Everyone**
AbleNet
2808 Fairview Avenue N
Roseville, MN  55113      800-322-0956
FAX: 651-294-2254
e-mail: hresources@ablenetinc.com
www.ablenetinc.com

*Cheryl Volkam, President/CEO*

Today, simple technology allows children and adults with disabilities to participate in leisure activities they were limited or excluded from in the past. *$20.00*

**2366  Fundamentals of Autism**
Slosson Educational Publications
PO Box 280
East Aurora, NY  14052      716-652-0930
888-756-7766
888-756-7760
FAX: 800-655-3840
e-mail: slosson@slosson.com
www.slosson.com

*Steven Slosson, President*
*John Slosson, VP*
*David Slosson, VP*

The Fundamentals of Autism handbook provides a quick, user friendly, effective and accurate approach to help in identifying and developing educationally related program objectives for children diagnosed as autistic. These materials have been designed to be easily and functionally used by teachers, therapists, special education/learning disability resource specialists, psychologists and others who work with children diagnosed as autistic. *$56.00*

*72 pages*

**2367  GO-MO Articulation Cards**
Pro-Ed Publications
8700 Shoal Creek Boulevard
Austin, TX  78757      512-451-3246
800-897-3202
FAX: 800-397-7633
e-mail: feedback@proedinc.com
www.proedinc.com

*Donald Hammill, Owner*
*Courtney King, Marketing Coordinator*

The most popular system used for remedying defective speech articulation in children and adults. This popular card set was the first and is still the best therapy tool of its kind, as it continues to produce results and maintains the interest of students of all ages.

**2368  Get Ready/Get Set/Go for the Code**
Educators Publishing Service
PO Box 9031
Cambridge, MA  02139      617-547-6706
800-225-5750
FAX: 888-440-2665
e-mail: feedback@epsbooks.com
www.epsbooks.com

*Charles H Heinle, Vice President*
*Alexandra S Bigelow, Author*
*Gunnar Voltz, President*

Primers for the Explode the Code series teaches consonants through engaging activities which includes: tracking, tracing, matching, copying, and following directions. The Activities progress is difficulty, and the three-book series for grades K-1 is cumulative. A set of picture letter cards are available.
*80-96 pages $4.50 - $5.50*
*ISBN 0-83881 -80-*

**2369  Gillingham Manaual**
Educators Publishing Service
PO Box 9031
Cambridge, MA  02139      617-547-6706
800-225-5750
FAX: 888-440-2665
e-mail: feedback@epsbooks.com
www.epsbooks.com

*Charles H Heinle, Vice President*
*Alexandra S Bigelow, Author*
*Gunnar Voltz, President*

Basic hardcover instructional manual for multisensory, phonetic technique of teaching reading to children with specific language disability. A classic. Many associated teaching materials, including drill cards, and stories.
*352 pages $17.55 - $69*
*ISBN 0-83880 -00-*

**2370  Guide to Teaching Phonics**
Educators Publishing Service
625 Mount Auburn Street
Suite 3
Cambridge, MA  02138      617-547-6706
800-225-5750
FAX: 888-440-2665
e-mail: feedback@epsbooks.com
www.epsbooks.com

*Charles H Heinle, Vice President*
*Alexandra S Bigelow, Author*
*Gunnar Voltz, President*

This flexible teacher's guide presents multisensory procedures developed in association with the late Dr. Samuel Orton. They consist of 100 phonograms for teaching phonetic elements and their sequences in words for reading, writing and spelling. Also contains coordinated Phonics Cards. *$13.50*

*96 pages*
*ISBN 0-838802-41-9*

**2371  Homemade Battery-Powered Toys**
Special Needs Project
324 State Street
Suite H
Santa Barbara, CA  93101

805-962-8087
800-333-6867
FAX: 805-962-5087
e-mail: books@specialneeds.com
www.specialneeds.com

*Hod Gray, Administrator/Owner*
*Laraine Gray, Coordinator*

Describes how to make simple switches and educational devices for severely handicapped children. *$7.50*

**2372  How the Student with Hearing Loss Can Succeed in College, Second Edition**
Alexander Graham Bell Association
3417 Volta Place NW
Washington, DC  20007

202-337-5220
FAX: 202-337-8314
e-mail: info@agbell.org
www.agbell.org

*Jim Reisler, President*
*Todd Houston, Executive Director*

This revised book informs student who are deaf and hard of hearing about the mutual and co-equal effort that students and professionals must exert together to achieve success for students to be successful. *$28.95*
*278 pages Paperback*

**2373  If it is to Be, it is Up to Me**
AVKO Dyslexia Research Foundation
3084 West Willard Road
Clio, MI  48420

810-686-9283
866-285-6612
FAX: 810-686-1101
e-mail: avkoemail@aol.com
www.avko.org

*Don Cabe, Executive Research Director*

This book is designed for parents to use. It will prove to the student that he isn't dumb. It builds self-confidence as the student learns he can learn without studying. *$9.95*
*112 pages*
*ISBN 1-56400 -42-1*

**2374  Implementing Cognitive Strategy Instruction Across the School**
Brookline Books
39 University Road
Brookline, MA  02445

617-734-6772
800-666-2665
FAX: 617-734-3952
e-mail: milt@brooklinebooks.com
www.brooklinebooks.com

*William H Walters, Author*
*Esther Isabe Wilder, Author*

Describes basic classroom based programs planned and executed by teachers to focus and guide students with serious reading problems to be goal oriented, strategic and self-assessing. *$24.95*

*ISBN 0-914797-75-1*

**2375  Inclusive Play People**
Educational Equity Concepts
114 East 32nd Street
New York, NY  10016

212-725-1803
FAX: 212-725-0947
TTY:212-725-1803
e-mail: information@edequity.org
www.edequity.org

Six sturdy multiracial wooden figures that provide a unique variety of nonstereotyped work and family roles and are inclusive of disabled and nondisabled people of various ages. For block building and dramatic play. *$25.00*

**2376  Instruction of Persons with Severe Handicaps**
McGraw-Hill School Publishing
220 East Danieldale Road
Desoto, TX  75115

972-224-1111
800-442-9685
FAX: 972-228-1982
www.mhschool.com

*Joseph Gavigan, President*

A complete introduction to the status of education as it pertains to people with severe handicaps.

**2377  Integrating Transition Planning Into the IEP Process**
Council for Exceptional Children
1110 North Glebe Road
Suite 300
Arlington, VA  22201

703-245-0600
888-232-7733
FAX: 703-264-9494
e-mail: president@cec.sped.org
www.cec.sped.org

*Janice Burdick, President*
*Suzanne Martin, Immediate Past President*
*Bruce Ramirez, Manager*

Helps students with disabilities make a smooth transition from school to adult life. *$15.70*
*78 pages*

**2378  Keeping Ahead in School**
Educators Publishing Service
PO Box 9031
Cambridge, MA  02139

617-547-6706
800-225-5750
FAX: 888-440-2665
e-mail: feedback@epsbooks.com
www.epsbooks.com

*Charles H Heinle, Vice President*
*Alexandra S Bigelow, Author*
*Gunnar Voltz, President*

This book helps students not only understand their own strengths and weaknesses but also more fully appreciate their individuality. He suggests specific ways to approach work, bypass or overcome learning disorders, and manage other struggles that may beset students in school. *$24.75*
*320 pages Paperback*
*ISBN 0-838820-69-7*

**2379  KeyMath Teach and Practice**
AGS
PO Box 99
Circle Pines, MN  55014

800-328-2560
FAX: 800-471-8457
e-mail: agsmail@agsnet.com
www.agsnet.com

*Kevin Brueggeman, President*
*Robert Zaske, Market Manager*

This set of materials provides all the tools needed to assess students' math skills...and the strategies to deal with problem areas. Three sets are available: Basic Concepts Package; Operations Package; and Applications Package. $219.95 each or $599.95 for whole set.

**2380  Kim Marshall Series in English**
Educators Publishing Service
625 Mount Auburn Street
Suite 3
Cambridge, MA  02138
617-547-6706
800-225-5750
FAX: 888-440-2665
e-mail: feedback@epsbooks.com
www.epsbooks.com

*Charles H Heinle, Vice President*
*Alexandra S Bigelow, Author*
*Gunnar Voltz, President*

These two books for grades 4-8 contain a total of 36 cumulative units in grammar, writing skills and word analysis. English-Part A reviews writing skills and usage, while English-Part B reviews word analysis and parts of speech. There is a teacher's manual designed to accompany each book.
*104 pages $8 - $8.95*

**2381  Kim Marshall Series in Math**
Educators Publishing Service
625 Mount Auburn Street
Suite 3
Cambridge, MA  02138
617-547-6706
800-225-5750
FAX: 888-440-2665
e-mail: feedback@epsbooks.com
www.epsbooks.com

*Charles H Heinle, Vice President*
*Alexandra S Bigelow, Author*
*Gunnar Voltz, President*

These two books for grades 4-8 contain 35 units that cover basic computation skills, Roman numerals, English and metric measurements, graphing, fractions and basic geometry. There is a teacher's manual designed to accompany each book.
*104 pages $10.45 - $11.60*

**2382  Kim Marshall Series in Reading**
Educators Publishing Service
PO Box 9031
Cambridge, MA  02139
617-547-6706
800-225-5750
FAX: 888-440-2665
e-mail: feedback@epsbooks.com
www.epsbooks.com

*Charles H Heinle, Vice President*
*Alexandra S Bigelow, Author*

These two books for grades 4-6 contain 186 interesting stories with comprehension questions that encourage careful reading and stimulate thinking. Because of the wide appeal of the stories, these books can be used to meet the needs of a variety of students. *$8.00*
*104 pages Grades 4-6*

**2383  Kim Marshall Series in Vocabulary**
Educators Publishing Service
625 Mount Auburn Street
Suite 3
Cambridge, MA  02138
617-547-6706
800-225-5750
FAX: 888-440-2665
e-mail: feedback@epsbooks.com
www.epsbooks.com

*Charles H Heinle, Vice President*
*Alexandra S Bigelow, Author*
*Gunnar Voltz, President*

This approachable vocabulary program for grades 4-8 consists of 900 words chosen to be interesting and useful and to broaden vocabulary and improve spelling. The two books in the series each contain 18 units, and every one of these units introduces 25 words followed by 5 pages of exercises and a weekly test. A teacher's manual is available for each book. *$9.75*

*128 pages*

**2384  Lakeshore Learning Materials**
2695 East Dominguez Street
Carson, CA  90895
310-537-8600
800-421-5354
FAX: 800-537-5403
e-mail: lakeshore@lakeshorelearning.com
www.lakeshorelearning.com

*Michael Kaplan, Chief Executive Officer*

Offers books, resources, testing materials, assessment information and special education materials for the professional in the field of special education.
*190 pages*

**2385  Language Parts Catalog**
Educators Publishing Service
PO Box 9031
Cambridge, MA  02139
617-547-6706
800-225-5750
FAX: 888-440-2665
e-mail: feedback@epsbooks.com
www.epsbooks.com

*Charles H Heinle, Vice President*
*Alexandra S Bigelow, Author*
*Gunnar Voltz, President*

Informatively and humorously explains the various aspects of language and how they operate, asking students to imagine that they are reading a catalog featuring different parts to order that can help them improve their language abilities. *$9.00*

*ISBN 0-838819-80-X*

**2386  Language Tool Kit**
Educators Publishing Service
625 Mount Auburn Street
Suite 3
Cambridge, MA  02138
617-547-6706
800-225-5750
FAX: 888-440-2665
e-mail: feedback@epsbooks.com
www.epsbooks.com

*Charles H Heinle, Vice President*
*Alexandra S Bigelow, Author*
*Gunnar Voltz, President*

This kit teaches reading and spelling to students in grades 1-3 with specific language disability. It contains 163-426 cards and a comprehensive 32-page teacher's manual. Also available in Spanish. *$30.00*
*32 pages English Edition*
*ISBN 0-838885-20-3*

**2387  Language, Speech and Hearing Services in School**
American Speech-Language-Hearing Association
10801 Rockville Pike
Rockville, MD  20852
301-897-5700
800-638-8255
FAX: 301-571-0457
e-mail: actioncenter@asha.org
www.asha.org

*John E Bernthal, President*
*Arlene Peitranton, Executive Director*
*Joanne Jessen, Publications Director*

Professional journal for clinicians, audiologists and speech-language pathologists. *$30.00*

**2388  Learning American Sign Language**
Harris Communications
15155 Technology Drive
Eden Prairie, MN  55344
952-906-1180
800-825-6758
FAX: 952-906-1180
e-mail: info@harriscomm.com
www.harriscomm.com

*Robert Harris, President/CEO/Owner*

Offers over 700 titles on ASL including books, videotapes, CDs & DVDs. Free catalog available. *$78.95*
*350 pages Video & Book*

**2389 Learning to Listen**
Educators Publishing Service
PO Box 9031
Cambridge, MA 02139
617-547-6706
800-225-5750
FAX: 888-440-2665
e-mail: feedback@epsbooks.com
www.epsbooks.com

*Charles H Heinle, Vice President*
*Alexandra S Bigelow, Author*
*Gunnar Voltz, President*

A program to improve classroom listening skills in a variety of situations. Presents students in grades 7-9 with instruction and 33 exercises on eight basic listening skills. After reading about a particular skill, students practice it by listening to a selection and then answering questions about the selection in writing. A teachers manual is available to accompany the student book. *$6.20*
*48 pages*
*ISBN 0-838820-61-1*

**2390 Learning to Sign in My Neighborhood**
T J Publishers
2544 Tarpley Road
Suite 108
Carrollton, TX 75006
972-416-0800
800-999-1168
FAX: 301-585-5930
e-mail: tjpubinc@aol.com

*Angela K Thames, President*
*Jerald A Murphy, Vice President*

Beautifully illustrated coloring book lets children learn signs from kids just like themselves! Recommended for ages 4 and up, let children have fun while they learn signs for words typically used in day-to-day activities. *$3.50*
*32 pages Softcover*
*ISBN 0-93266-36-1*

**2391 Learning to Use Cursive Handwriting**
Educators Publishing Service
625 Mount Auburn Street
Suite 3
Cambridge, MA 02138
617-547-6706
800-225-5750
FAX: 888-440-2665
e-mail: feedback@epsbooks.com
www.epsbooks.com

*Charles H Heinle, Vice President*
*Alexandra S Bigelow, Author*
*Gunnar Voltz, President*

This multisensory program with instructions for introducing, teaching, practicing and reviewing lower- and upper-case cursive letters; masters, with letter forms and lined and patterned writing paper; and wall cards, for lower- and upper-case letters. *$ 10.60*
*96 pages Manual*
*ISBN 0-838802-53-2*

**2392 Learning to Use Manuscript Handwriting**
Educators Publishing Service
625 Mount Auburn Street
Suite 3
Cambridge, MA 02138
617-547-6706
800-225-5750
FAX: 888-440-2665
e-mail: feedback@epsbooks.com
www.epsbooks.com

*Charles H Heinle, Vice President*
*Alexandra S Bigelow, Author*
*Gunnar Voltz, President*

This multisensory program contains a manual with instructions for introducing, teaching, practicing and reviewing lower- and upper-case manuscript letters; masters with letter forms and lined and patterned writing paper; and wall cards for lower- and upper-case letters. *$10.30*
*76 pages Paperback*
*ISBN 0-838802-50-8*

**2393 Let's Read: A Linguistic Reading Program**
Educators Publishing Service
625 Mount Auburn Street
Suite 3
Cambridge, MA 02138
617-547-6706
800-225-5750
FAX: 888-440-2665
e-mail: feedback@epsbooks.com
www.epsbooks.com

*Charles H Heinle, Vice President*
*Alexandra S Bigelow, Author*
*Gunnar Volta, President*

This linguistic approach to teaching reading emphasizes the basic relationship of spelling to sound, presenting like concepts together, providing reading materials for practice, and building on previously mastered skills for grades 1-3. Word lists and teacher's manuals are available for Let's Read books 1-4, and Let's Look workbooks accompany the texts.
*$10.35 - $19.15*

**2394 Literacy Program**
Educators Publishing Service
PO Box 9031
Cambridge, MA 02139
617-547-6706
800-225-5750
FAX: 888-440-2665
e-mail: feedback@epsbooks.com
www.epsbooks.com

*Charles H Heinle, Vice President*
*Alexandra S Bigelow, Author*
*Gunnar Voltz, President*

This one year course, developed by the Scottish Rite Hospital, consists of 160 one hour videotaped lessons accompanied by student workbooks, designed for high schoolers and adults who read below a sixth grade level. This program uses multisensory applications to teach alphabet, reading, cursive writing, spelling, math and listening comprehension with frequent new activities. This is an ideal series for a community adult reading program. Grades 1-4.
*$2.25 -$18*

**2395 Literature Based Reading**
Oryx Press
4041 North Central Avenue
Suite 700
Phoenix, AZ 85012
602-265-2651
800-279-6799
FAX: 800-279-4663
Series offering children's books and activities to enrich the K-5 curriculum.

**2396 Living an Idea: Empowerment and the Evolution of an Alternative School**
Brookline Books
39 University Road
Brookline, MA 02445
617-734-6772
800-666-2665
FAX: 617-734-3952
e-mail: brooklinebks@delphi.com
www.brooklinebooks.com

*William H Walters, Author*
*Esther Isabe Wilder, Author*

This book is about the creation and 14 year evolution of a public alternative inner-city high school. The school lived an idea - empowerment. Students were encouraged to participate in shaping many aspects of their education, teachers were responsible for running the school, and parents invited to help govern. *$27.95*

ISBN 0-91479-68-9

**2397 Low Tech Assistive Devices: A Handbook for the School Setting**
Therapro Inc.
225 Arlington Street
Framingham, MA 01702
508-872-9494
800-257-5376
FAX: 508-875-2062
e-mail: info@theraproducts.com
www.theraproducts.com

*Karen Conrad, Founder/Owner*

A how-to book with step by step directions and detailed illustrations for fabrication of frequently requested low-tech assistive devices. *$45.00*
*320 pages Paperback*

**2398 MTA Readers**
Educators Publishing Service
625 Mount Auburn Street
Suite 3
Cambridge, MA 02138
617-547-6706
800-225-5750
FAX: 888-440-2665
e-mail: feedback@epsbooks.com
www.epsbooks.com

*Charles H Heinle, Vice President*
*Alexandra S Bigelow, Author*
*Gunnar Voltz, President*

Illustrated readers for grades 1-3 that accompany the MTA Reading and Spelling Program (Multisensory Teaching Approach). Phonetic elements in a structured, but entertaining context.
*48+ pages $4.65 - $11.65*
*ISBN 0-83882-33-3*

**2399 Making School Inclusion Work: A Guide to Everyday Practice**
Brookline Books
39 University Road
Brookline, MA 02445
617-734-6772
800-666-2665
FAX: 617-734-3952
www.brooklinebooks.com

*William H Walters, Author*
*Esther Isabe Wilder, Author*

This book tells the reader how to conduct a truly inclusive program, regardless of ethnic or racial background, economic level and physical or cognitive ability. *$24.95*
*254 pages*
*ISBN 0-914791-96-4*

**2400 Making the Writing Process Work: Strategie s for Composition and Self-Regulation**
Brookline Books
PO Box 1047
Cambridge, MA 02139
617-734-6772
800-666-2665
FAX: 617-734-3952
e-mail: brooklinebks@delphi.com
www.brooklinebooks.com

*William H Walters, Author*
*Esther Isabe Wilder, Author*

This book is geared toward students who have difficulty organizing their thoughts and developing their writing. The specific stategies teach students how to approach, organize, and produce a final written product.. *$24.95*

240 pages Paperback
ISBN 1-571290-10-9

**2401 Manual Alphabet Poster**
TJ Publishers
2544 Tarpley Road
Suite 108
Carrollton, TX 75006
972-416-0800
800-999-1168
FAX: 972-416-0944
e-mail: TJPubinc@aol.com
www.TJpublishers.com

*Pat O'Rourke, President*
Poster presents the manual alphabet. *$4.50*

**2402 Many Faces of Dyslexia**
International Dyslexia Association
8600 Lasalle Road
Suite 382
Baltimore, MD 21286
410-296-0232
FAX: 410-296-5069
www.interdys.org

*Megan Cohen, Executive Director*
Gives information on the teaching and rehabilitation techniques for people with dyslexia. *$16.50*
*Paperback*

**2403 Match-Sort-Assemble Job Cards**
Exceptional Education
PO Box 15308
Seattle, WA 98115
206-262-9538

*Jeff Stewart, Owner*
Teaches workers to use a series of symbolic cues to control their own production cycles. *$565.00*
*Class Set*

**2404 Match-Sort-Assemble Pictures**
Exceptional Education
PO Box 15308
Seattle, WA 98115
206-262-9538

*Jeff Stewart, Owner*
People with profound, severe and moderate mental retardation have immediate access with MSA Pictures. Students work with pictures (and if necessary a template) to match, sort, assemble and disassemble parts that vary in shape, length and diameter. *$426.00*
*Class Set*

**2405 Match-Sort-Assemble SCHEMATICS**
Exceptional Education
PO Box 15308
Seattle, WA 98115
206-262-9538

*Jeff Stewart, Owner*
Students with moderate and mild mental retardation and those who have completed MSA Pictures are ready for MSA Schematics. It increases abstraction and displacement of instruction from the work clearly and simply. *$495.00*
*Class Set*

**2406 Match-Sort-Assemble TOOLS**
Exceptional Education
PO Box 15308
Seattle, WA 98115
206-262-9538
FAX: 475-486-4510

*JE Stewart, Owner*

Students and clients learn to use the tools required for many jobs in light industry. Mastery of the production cycle with independence, endurance and the ability to learn new tasks through pictures and schematics and basic hand functions will help clients acquire and maintain employment in a competitive field. *$595.00*
*Class Set*

## 2407 Meeting-in-a-Box
Asthma and Allergy Foundation of America
1233 20th Street NW
Suite 402
Washington, DC 20036    202-466-7643
800-7AS-THMA
FAX: 202-466-8940
e-mail: info@aafa.org
www.aafa.org

*Chris Ward, President*
*Bill Mclin, Executive Director*
A series of self-contained, comprehensive kits that contain all the necessary components for a successful asthma presentation.

## 2408 More Food!
JE Stewart Teaching Tools
PO Box 15308
Seattle, WA 98115    206-262-9538
FAX: 206-262-9538

*J E Stewart, Owner*
Teaches 50 more words found in restaurants, grocery stores, cookbooks such as pizza, carrot, tacos, oysters and pineapple. These words are functional at home, going shopping and during leisure. *$32.50*

## 2409 More Work!
J E Stewart Teaching Tools
PO Box 15308
Seattle, WA 98115    206-262-9538
FAX: 206-262-9538

*J E Stewart, Owner*
Teaches 50 words as they appear on parts, tools, job instructions, signs and labels, such as fill, grasp, release, lock, search, position and select. These words are functional in school and on-the-job. *$32.50*

## 2410 Multisensory Teaching Approach
Educators Publishing Service
PO Box 9031
Cambridge, MA 02139    617-367-2700
800-225-5750
FAX: 617-547-0412
www.epsbooks.com
Comprehensive multisensory program in reading, writing, spelling, alphabet and dictionary skills for remedial and regular instruction. Based on Orton-Gillingham and Alphabetic Phonics. A complete program organized in kits, with additional classroom materials, supplementary materials, and handwriting programs.
*$110 - $140*
*ISBN 0-83888 -10-9*

## 2411 Peabody Articulation Decks
AGS
PO Box 99
Circle Pines, MN 55014    651-287-7220
800-328-2560
FAX: 763-786-9007
e-mail: agsmail@agsnet.com
www.agsnet.com

*Keith Powel, Special Education Transition Coo*
*Robert Zaske, Marketing Manager*
Complete kit of playing-card sized PAD decks let students focus on the 18 most commonly misarticulated English consonants and blends. *$115.95*

*ISBN 0-88671 -75-4*

## 2412 Phonemic Awareness in Young Children: A Classroom Curriculum
Brookes Publishing
PO Box 10624
Baltimore, MD 21285    410-337-9580
800-638-3775
FAX: 410-337-8539
e-mail: custserv@brookespublishing.com
www.brookespublishing.com

*Clary Creighton, Exhibits Coordinator*
*Tracy Gray, Educational Sales Manager*
*Paul Brooks, Owner*
This is a supplemental, whole-class curriculum for improving pre-literacy listening skills. It contains activities that are fun, easy to use, and proven to work in any kindergarten classroom - general, bilingual, inclusive, or special education. This program takes only 15-20 minutes a day. *$24.95*
*208 pages Spiral-bound 1997*
*ISBN 1-557663-21-1*

## 2413 Phonics for Thought
Educators Publishing Service
PO Box 9031
Cambridge, MA 02139    617-367-2700
800-225-5750
FAX: 617-547-0412
www.epsbooks.com
*$8.00*
*Paperback*

## 2414 Phonological Awareness Training for Reading
Pro-Ed Publications
8700 Shoal Creek Boulevard
Austin, TX 78757    512-451-3246
800-897-3202
FAX: 800-397-7633
e-mail: feedback@proedinc.com
www.proedinc.com

*Joshua Jeffrey, Marketing Custodian*
*Courtney King, Marketing Coordinator*
*Donald Hammill, Owner*
Designed to increase the level of phonological awareness in young children. Can be taught individually or in small groups and takes about 12 to 14 weeks to complete if children are taught in short sessions three or four times a week. *$129.00*

## 2415 Play and Say Cards
Pro-Ed Publications
8700 Shoal Creek Boulevard
Austin, TX 78757    512-451-3246
800-897-3202
FAX: 512-451-8542
e-mail: info@proedinc.com
www.proedinc.com

*Donald Hammill, Owner*
*Courtney King, Marketing Coordinator*
16 decks of bright, full-color playing cards, each of which carriers a frequently misarticulated speech sound. *$89.00*

## 2416 Play!
JE Stewart Teaching Tools
PO Box 15308
Seattle, WA 98115    206-262-9538
FAX: 206-262-9538

*J E Stewart, Owner*
Teaches 50 more words as they appear at recreation sites, on signs and labels and in newspapers and magazines, such as movie, visitor, ticket, gallery and zoo. These words are functional in school and at leisure. *$32.50*

**2417  Power Breathing Program**
Asthma and Allergy Foundation of America
1125 15th Street NW
Suite 502
Washington, DC 20005                         202-466-7643
                                        FAX: 202-466-8940
                                        e-mail: info@aafa.org
                                             www.aafa.org

*Bill McLin, Executive Director*

Devoloped the only asthma education program specifically designed for and pre-tested with teens. Teens with asthma have
special challenges. This interactive program covers everything
from the basics of asthma to dealing with their asthma in social
situations, in college, and on the job. Includes everything you
need to present this three-four session program. *$295.00*

**2418  Primary Phonics**
Educators Publishing Service
625 Mount Auburn Street
Suite 3
Cambridge, MA 02138                         617-547-6706
                                             800-225-5750
                                        FAX: 888-440-2665
                                e-mail: feedback@epsbooks.com
                                             www.epsbooks.com

*Charles H Heinie, Vice President*
*Alexandra S Bigelow, Author*
*Gunnar Voltz, President*

A program of storybooks and coordinated workbooks that
teaches reading for grades K-2. A structured phonetic approach.
Contains 8 student workbooks, with 8 sets of 10 coordinated
storybooks; consonant workbooks; initial consonant blend
workbooks; picture dictionary, and coloring book. *$3.65*
            *$3.65 - $26.35*
            *ISSN 0838-83 0*

**2419  Programmed Phonics Books 1-2 & Cassettes**
Educators Publishing Service
625 Mount Auburn Street
Suite 3
Cambridge, MA 02138                         617-547-6706
                                             800-225-5750
                                        FAX: 888-440-2665
                                e-mail: feedback@epsbooks.com
                                             www.epsbooks.com

*Charles H Heinle, Vice President*
*Gunnar Voltz, President*

This self-instructing program is for children who are having difficulty with the word recognition phase of reading vocabulary
that exceeds their reading vocabulary. The books review consonants and all consonant blends. A teacher's guide and script includes dictation, which is also available on cassettes. *$7.70*
            *88 pages $7.50 - $45*
            *ISSN 0838-83 0*

**2420  Programming Concepts**
PCI
PO Box 34270
San Antonio, TX 78265                       210-377-1999
                                             800-594-4263
                                        FAX: 210-377-1121
                                e-mail: pciinfo@pcieducation.com
                                        wwww.pcieducations.com

*Jeff Clain, Chief Executive Officer*

**2421  Reading for Content**
Educators Publishing Service
PO Box 9031
Cambridge, MA 02139                         617-547-6706
                                             800-225-5750
                                        FAX: 888-440-2665
                                e-mail: feedback@epsbooks.com
                                             www.epsbooks.com

*Charles H Heinle, Vice President*
*Alexandra S Bigelow, Author*
*Gunnar Voltz, President*

This four book series for grades 3-6 has been completely revised
and updated so that the reading passages are more current and interesting. Each book contains 43 one-page reading questions. A
detachable answer sheet and progress graph are involved in each
book.
            *96 pages $7.75 each*

**2422  Reading from Scratch**
Educators Publishing Service
PO Box 9031
Cambridge, MA 02139                         617-367-2700
                                             800-225-5750
                                        FAX: 617-547-0412
                                             www.epsbooks.com

Contains multisensory reading and spelling material and oral
and written lessons and exercises in syntax, grammar, and
precomposition topics. Complete set.
            *$6.25 - $49.30*
            *ISBN 0-83888 -75-5*

**2423  Reasoning and Reading Levels I and II**
Educators Publishing Service
625 Mount Auburn Street
Suite 3
Cambridge, MA 02138                         617-547-6706
                                             800-225-5750
                                        FAX: 888-440-2665
                                e-mail: feedback@epsbooks.com
                                             www.epsbooks.com

*Charles H Heinle, Vice President*
*Alexandra S Bigelow, Author*
*Gunnar Voltz, President*

Three four-unit workbooks are based on the belief that reasoning, language, and reading comprehension go hand in hand. The
four units are word meaning, sentence menaing, paragraph
meaning and reasoning skills. Completely revised.
            *$10.45 each*

**2424  Recipe for Reading**
Educators Publishing Service
PO Box 9031
Cambridge, MA 02139                         617-367-2700
                                             800-435-7728
                                        FAX: 888-440-2665
                                e-mail: feedback@epsbooks.com
                                             www.epsbooks.com

*Alexandra S Bigelow, Author*
*Charles Heinle, Vice President*

A basic reading manual with 21 storybooks and 7 workbooks for
grades K-3. For remedial work. Multisensory, phonetically
structured. program also includes sequence chart, a record progress, and writing paper of assorted sizes.
            *$4.50 - $56.25*
            *ISSN 0838-84 1*

**2425  Resourcing: Handbook for Special Education Resource
Teachers**
Council for Exceptional Children
1110 North Glebe Road
Suite 300
Arlington, VA 22201                         703-245-0600
                                             888-cec-sped
                                        FAX: 703-264-9494
                                e-mail: service@cec.sped.org
                                             www.cec.sped.org

*Jim McCormick, President*
*Jamie Hopkins, Vice President*
*Bruce Ramirez, Manager*

Everything you need to know to be a resource for other teachers
and support personnel who work with special education students. *$12.00*

*64 pages*

**2426  Rewarding Speech**
Speech Bin
1965 25th Avenue
Vero Beach, FL  32960

772-770-0007
800-477-3324
FAX: 772-770-0006
e-mail: thespeechbin@aol.com
www.speechbin.com

*Jan J Binney, Senior Editor*

Reproducible reward certificates for children. *$12.95*
*32 pages*

**2427  Rule-ette**
Educators Publishing Service
31 Smith Place
Cambridge, MA  02138

617-547-6706
800-225-5750
FAX: 888-440-2665
e-mail: feedback@epsbooks.com
www.epsbooks.com

*Charles H Heinle, Vice President*
*Alexandra S Bigelow, Author*
*Gunnar Voltz, President*

A spelling card game that teaches basic spelling rules. The game was developed for grades 3-Adult. *$14.65*
*Ages 3-Adult*
*ISBN 0-838806-72-*

**2428  SAYdee Posters**
Speech Bin
1965 25th Avenue
Vero Beach, FL  32960

772-770-0007
800-477-3324
FAX: 772-770-0006
e-mail: info@speechbin.com
www.speechbin.com

*Jan J Binney, Senior Editor*

Colorful speech and language posters. *$20.00*
*24 pages*
*ISBN 0-93785 -47-5*

**2429  Second Course in Phonic Reading**
Educators Publishing Service
625 Mount Auburn Street
Suite 3
Cambridge, MA  02138

617-547-6706
800-225-5750
FAX: 888-440-2665
e-mail: feedback@epsbooks.com
www.epsbooks.com

*Charles H Heinle, Vice President*
*Alexandra S Bigelow, Author*
*Gunnar Voltz, President*

Two structured phonetic workbooks to teach reading for grades 2-3 and 4-5. Book 1 focuses on sounds of the letters, phonogram combinations, word families, and spelling rules. Book 2 develops comprehension and vocabulary skills. *$10.65*
*Per Book*
*ISSN 0838-81 6*

**2430  Sequential Spelling I-VII**
AVKO Educational Research Foundation
3084 West Willard Road
Clio, MI  48420

810-686-9283
FAX: 810-686-1101
www.avko.org

*Don McCabe, Executive Research Director*

Spelling books for individuals to classrooms. Builds from easier words of a word family to important power words that build self-confidence. Each of the seven levels contains 180 spelling lessons that teach phonics through the backdoor of spelling. Students learn the patterns without having to learn rules or studying. Teachers have no papers to correct.

*72 pages $8.95 each*
*ISBN 1-56400 -11-6*

**2431  Signing Naturally Curriculum**
Harris Communications
15155 Technology Drive
Eden Prairie, MN  55344

952-906-1180
800-825-6758
FAX: 952-906-1099
e-mail: info@harriscomm.com
www.harriscomm.com

*Robert Harris, President/Owner*
*Bill Williams, National Sales*

A series based on the functional approach that is the most popular and widely used sign language curriculum designed for teaching American Sign Language. Book and videotape set for level 1 & 2. Teacher's curriculum is also available.

**2432  Small Wonder**
AGS
PO Box 99
Circle Pines, MN  55014

800-328-2560
FAX: 800-471-8457
e-mail: agsmail@agsnet.com
www.agsnet.com

*Robert Zaske, Marketing Manager*
*Kevin Brueggeman, President*

This infant through toddler program offers a delightful array of activities to teach babies about themselves, others, their surroundings and the world outside. Level One - zero to 18 months; Level Two 18-36 months. Discount price of $389.95 when both levels ordered. *$229.95*

*ISBN 0-91347 -62-5*

**2433  Solving Language Difficulties: Remedial Routines**
Educators Publishing Service
625 Mount Auburn Street
Suite 3
Cambridge, MA  02138

617-547-6706
800-225-5750
FAX: 888-440-2665
e-mail: feedback@epsbooks.com
www.epsbooks.com

*Charles H Heinle, Vice President*
*Alexandra S Bigelow, Author*
*Gunnar Voltz, President*

A basic workbook for children in grades 4-6 who have a specific language disability. It can be used in any corrective reading program. It deals extensively with syllables, syllable division, prefixes, suffixes, accent and other important topics. *$9.75*
*176 pages*
*ISBN 0-838803-26-1*

**2434  Sound Workbook**
Educators Publishing Service
PO Box 9031
Cambridge, MA  02139

617-547-6706
800-225-5750
FAX: 888-440-2665
e-mail: feedback@epsbooks.com
www.epsbooks.com

*Charles H Heinle, Vice President*
*Alexandra S Bigelow, Author*
*Gunnar Voltz, President*

This workbook for grades 1-2 reinforces the teaching of specific vowel combinations. *$5.50*

*44 pages*
*ISBN 0-838817-08-4*

**2435 Sound-Off 1-5**
Educators Publishing Service
625 Mount Auburn Street
Suite 3
Cambridge, MA  02138
617-547-6706
800-225-5750
FAX: 888-440-2665
e-mail: feedback@epsbooks.com
www.epsbooks.com

*Charles H Heinle, Vice President*
*Alexandra S Bigelow, Author*
*Gunnar Voltz, President*

These five workbooks for grades K-2 cover the introduction of consonants and final consonant blends and consonant diagraphs, vowel-consonant-e combinations, and vowel + r combinations. There is a teacher's guide for each book. *$5.50*
*32-48 pages Per Book*
*ISBN 0-83885 -34-*

**2436 Speech Bin**
Abilitations
3155 Northwoods Parkway
Norcross, GA  30071
800-850-8602
FAX: 800-845-1535
e-mail: orders@sportime.com
www.speechbin.com

*Cecilia Cruse MS OTR/L, Education Director*
*Debbie Kissel, New Product Development*

Activities, worksheets and games to encourage practice of speech and language skills. *$25.00*
*128 pages*
*ISBN 0-93785 -42-4*

**2437 Speech-Language Delights**
1965 25th Avenue
Vero Beach, FL  32960
772-770-0007

**2438 Spell of Words**
Educators Publishing Service
625 Mount Auburn Street
Suite 3
Cambridge, MA  02138
617-547-6706
800-225-5750
FAX: 888-440-2665
e-mail: feedback@epsbooks.com
www.epsbooks.com

*Charles H Heinle, Vice President*
*Gunnar Voltz, President*

This book can be used with any student, from grade 7-adult, who needs help in spelling. It covers syllabication, word building with prefixes, word patterns, phonograms, suffixes, plurals and possessives. Chapters contain explanations of spelling rules, exercises and suggestions for short compositions. *$9.25*
*128 pages Grades 7-Adult*
*ISBN 0-838801-55-2*

**2439 Spellbinding 2**
Educators Publishing Service
625 Mount Auburn Street
Suite 3
Cambridge, MA  02138
617-547-6706
800-225-5750
FAX: 888-440-2665
e-mail: feedback@epsbooks.com
www.epsbooks.com

*Charles H Heinle, Vice President*
*Alexandra S Bigelow, Author*
*Gunnar Voltz, President*

Spellbinding 2 adds practice exercises with more complicated spelling problems and introduces new areas of study. The manuals give answers to exercises and include a large number of new dictations. *$11.55*

*96+ pages Each*
*ISBN 0-838814-75-1*

**2440 Spellbound**
Educators Publishing Service
PO Box 9031
Cambridge, MA  02139
617-547-6706
800-225-5750
FAX: 888-440-2665
e-mail: feedback@epsbooks.com
www.epsbooks.com

*Charles H Heinle, Vice President*
*Alexandra S Bigelow, Author*
*Gunnar Voltz, President*

This workbook begins with teaching simple, consistent rules and then moves on to those that are more difficult. By an inductive process, students use their own observations to confirm the spelling rules they learn. Each portion of the text is followed by exercises for drill and kinesthetic reinforcement. *$8.65*
*144 pages Grades 7-Adult*
*ISBN 0-838801-65-X*

**2441 Spelling Dictionary**
Educators Publishing Service
625 Mount Auburn Street
Suite 3
Cambridge, MA  02138
617-547-6706
800-225-5750
FAX: 888-440-2665
e-mail: feedback@epsbooks.com
www.epsbooks.com

*Charles H Heinle, Vice President*
*Alexandra S Bigelow, Author*
*Gunnar Voltz, President*

This handy reference is a dictionary/thesaurus of words most frequently used by student writers in the elementary grades. Words are listed without definitions, and synonyms are offered for commonly used words like said, big, good, etc. Children can add their own words at the bottom of each page. *$4.50*
*52 pages*
*ISBN 0-838820-56-5*

**2442 Spelling Workbooks Emphasizing Rules and Generalization for Corrective Drill**
Educators Publishing Service
625 Mount Auburn Street
Suite 3
Cambridge, MA  02138
617-547-6706
800-225-5750
FAX: 888-440-2665
e-mail: feedback@epsbooks.com
www.epsbooks.com

*Charles H Heinle, Vice President*
*Alexandra S Bigelow, Author*
*Gunnar Voltz, President*

Includes exercises for children in grades 7-12 who have reading difficulties and closely associated spelling weaknesses. The material is divided into phonetic drills, spelling rules and generalizations, syllable concepts, and punctuation symbols. There are frequent review exercises. Similar programs are available for grades 4-6 ($11.70). *$12.25*
*144 pages Grades 7-12*
*ISBN 0-838800-90-4*

**2443 Starting Over**
Educators Publishing Service
625 Auburn Street
3rd Floor
Cambridge, MA  02138
617-547-6706
800-225-5750
FAX: 888-440-2665
e-mail: feedback@epsbooks.com
www.epsbooks.com

*Charles H Heinle, Vice President*
*Alexandra S Bigelow, Author*
*Gunnar Voltz, President*

This comprehensive program is for a student who is ready to try to learn to read again, or for those who are learning English as a second language. Employs multisensory phonics, whole words, and language experience techniques to teach the building of words, vocabulary, and sentences. *$24.00*

*ISBN 0-838881-65-5*

**2444    Structure of Words**
Educators Publishing Service
PO Box 9031
Cambridge, MA  02139          617-547-6706
                              800-225-5750
                    FAX: 888-440-2665
            e-mail: feedback@epsbooks.com
                    www.epsbooks.com

*Charles H Heinle, Vice President*
*Alexandra S Bigelow, Author*
*Gunnar Voltz, President*

Designed to help students in grades 7-12 learn to spell by using logic as well as memorization and drill, and to help them pronounce and arrive at the meanings of unfamiliar words. The consistent theme throughout is that of spelling, gradually shifting into the analysis of word structure and the development of a rich vocabulary. *$21.15*
        *96 pages Grades 7-12*
        *ISBN 0-838801-35-8*

**2445    Studio 49 Catalog**
MMB Music
3526 Washington Avenue
Saint Louis, MO  63103          314-531-9635
                                800-543-3771
                      FAX: 314-531-8384
              e-mail: info@mmbmusic.com
                      www.mmbmusic.com

*Marcia Lee Goldberg, President*
*Michelle Greenlaw, Vice President*

Percussion instruments for school, therapy, church and family.

**2446    Study Power: Study Skills to Improve Your Learning and Your Grades**
Brookline Books
39 University Road
Brookline, MA  02445          617-558-8010
                              800-666-2665
                    FAX: 617-558-8011
            e-mail: milt@brooklinebooks.com
                    www.brooklinebooks.com
The techniques in the easy-to-use, self-teaching manual have yielded remarkable success for students from elementary to medical school, at all levels of intelligence and achievement. Key skills covered include: listening, note taking, concentration, summarizing, reading comprehension, memorization, test taking, preparing papers and reports, time management and more. These abilities are vital to success throughout every stage of learning; the benefits will last a lifetime. *$15.95*

*ISBN 1-571290-46-X*

**2447    Syracuse Community-Referenced Curriculum Guide for Students with Disabilties**
Brookes Publishing
PO Box 10624
Baltimore, MD  21285          410-337-9580
                              800-638-3775
                    FAX: 410-337-8539
        e-mail: custserv@brookespublishing.com
                www.brookespublishing.com

*Paul Brooks, Owner*

Serving learners from kindergarten through age 21, this field-tested curriculum is a for professionals and parents devoted to directly preparing a student to function in the world. it examines the role of community living domains, functional academics, and embedded skills and includes practical implementation strategies and information for preparing students whose learning needs go beyond the scope of traditional academic programs. *$54.95*
        *416 pages Spiral-bound*
        *ISBN 1-557660-27-1*

**2448    Teaching Individuals with Physical and Multiple Disabilities**
McGraw-Hill, School Publishing
220 East Danieldale Road
Desoto, TX  75115          972-224-1111
                          800-442-9685
                FAX: 972-228-1061
                www.mhschool.com

*Joseph Gavigan, President*

Focuses on the functional needs of the handicapped and the teaching skills of background teachers that they need to help them reach the highest possible level of self-sufficiency.
        *410 pages*

**2449    Teaching Students Ways to Remember**
Brookline Books
39 University Road
Brookline, MA  02445          617-558-8010
                              800-666-2665
                    FAX: 617-558-8011
            e-mail: milt@brooklinebooks.com
                    www.brooklinebooks.com
Teaches techniques for improving or strengthening memory.
*$21.95*

*ISBN 0-914797-67-0*

**2450    Teaching Test-Taking Skills: Helping Students Show What They Know**
Brookline Books
39 University Road
Brookline, MA  02445          617-558-8010
                              800-666-2665
                    FAX: 617-558-8011
            e-mail: milt@brooklinebooks.com
                    www.brooklinebooks.com
Test-taking skills that, when used effectively, contribute to test-wise performance and help students work productively with test materials. *$21.95*

*ISBN 0-914797-76-X*

**2451    Tools for Transition**
AGS
PO Box 99
Circle Pines, MN  55014          800-328-2560
                        FAX: 800-471-8457
              e-mail: agsmail@agsnet.com
                      www.agsnet.com

*Robert Zaske, Marketing Manager*

This program prepares students with learning disabilities for postsecondary education. *$129.95*

**2452    VAK Tasks Workbook: Visual, Auditory and Kinesthetic**
Educational Tutorial Consortium
4400 South 44th Street
Lincoln, NE  68516          402-489-8133
                    FAX: 402-489-8160
              e-mail: etc@altel.net
                      www.etc-ne.com

*T Cross, Owner*

A workbook emphasizing the multisensory approach to teaching vocabulary and spelling. It is intended for middle-grade and older students working with prefixes, roots, suffixes, homonyms, and the spelling of easily confused endings. Includes spelling posters. *$7.00*
*96 pages Paperback*

**2453    Volunteer Transcribing Services**
205 East 3rd Avenue
Suite 200
San Mateo, CA  94401                      650-344-8664
                                          FAX: 650-632-3510

*Alanah Hoffman, Coordinator*

VTS is a nonprofit California corporation that produces large print school books for visually impaired students in grades K-12.

**2454    Word Attack Manual**
Educators Publishing Service
625 Auburn Street
3rd Floor
Cambridge, MA  02138                      617-547-6706
                                          800-225-5750
                                          FAX: 888-440-2665
                          e-mail: feedback@epsbooks.com
                                          www.epsbooks.com

*Charles H Heinle, Vice President*
*Alexandra S Bigelow, Author*
*Gunnar Voltz, President*

This manual and test booklet are designed to develop word recognition and spelling skills for students in grades 6-10. Contents include lessons on syllables, syllabication and accent, consonants and consonant blends, diagraphs, diphthongs, prefixes, suffixes, and compound words, and using the dictionary. *$21.15*
*176 pages Grades 6-10*
*ISBN 0-838881-00-5*

**2455    Word Demons**
Educators Publishing Service
625 Mount Auburn Street
Suite 3
Cambridge, MA  02138                      617-547-6706
                                          800-225-5750
                                          FAX: 888-440-2665
                          e-mail: feedback@epsbooks.com
                                          www.epsbooks.com

*Charles H Heinle, Vice President*
*Alexandra S Bigelow, Author*
*Gunnar Voltz, President*

This spelling game helps students master the 86 non-phonetic words that are demons for the child in grades 2-4 with a language disability. *$14.40*
*Grades 2-4*
*ISBN 0-838803-28-8*

**2456    Word Elements: How They Work Together**
Educators Publishing Service
625 Mount Auburn Street
Suite 3
Cambridge, MA  02138                      617-547-6706
                                          800-225-5750
                                          FAX: 888-440-2665
                          e-mail: feedback@epsbooks.com
                                          www.epsbooks.com

*Charles H Heinle, Vice President*
*Alexandra S Bigelow, Author*
*Gunnar Voltz, President*

This vocabulary workbook teaches common word elements - prefixes, suffixes, and roots and their meanings for grades 6-8. *$ 10.65*

*112 pages Grades 6-8*
*ISBN 0-838815-50-2*

**2457    Word Mastery**
Educators Publishing Service
625 Mount Auburn Street
Suite 3
Cambridge, MA  02138                      617-547-6706
                                          800-225-5750
                                          FAX: 888-440-2665
                          e-mail: feedback@epsbooks.com
                                          www.epsbooks.com

*Charles H Heinle, Vice President*
*Alexandra S Bigelow, Author*
*Gunnar Voltz, President*

This phonics classic introduces over 3,500 words and supplements any reading program with its straightforward phonics instruction. It teaches students in grades 1-3 the letters of the alphabet with key words, and follows with vowels, consonants, vowel combinations, consonant diagraphs and blends, and phonetic rules. *$8.95*
*124 pages Grades 1-3*
*ISBN 0-838820-00-X*

**2458    Wordly Wise A,B,C**
Educators Publishing Service
PO Box 9031
Cambridge, MA  02139                      617-547-6706
                                          800-225-5750
                                          FAX: 888-440-2665
                          e-mail: feedback@epsbooks.com
                                          www.epsbooks.com

*Charles H Heinle, Vice President*
*Alexandra S Bigelow, Author*
*Gunnar Voltz, President*

This series of three vocabulary books for grades 2-4 presents 8-12 words in each lesson with brief definitions, illustrations and sentences using each word in context. Exercises reinforce learning by teaching students to use words precisely in a variety of situations. Keys and tests are available for each book.
*64 pages $5.50 each*
*ISSN 0838-84 8*

**2459    Work!**
JE Stewart Teaching Tools
PO Box 15308
Seattle, WA  98115                        206-262-9538
                                          FAX: 206-262-9538

*J E Stewart, Owner*

Teaches 50 words as they appear on parts, tools, job instructions, signs, labels such as: hard hat, assembly, clamp, cut, drill, package and schedule. These words are functional in school and on-the-job. *$32.50*

**2460    Working Together & Taking Part**
A GS
PO Box 99
Circle Pines, MN  55014
                                          800-328-2560
                                          FAX: 800-471-8457
                          e-mail: agsmail@agsnet.com
                                          www.agsnet.com

*Kevin Brueggeman, President*
*Robert Zaske, Market Manager*

Two programs to build children's social skills in grades 3-6 through folk literature. Has 31 activity-rich lessons, teaching skills like: following rules, accepting differences, speaking assertively and helping others. Discount price of $279.00 when ordering both. *$149.95*

### 2461 Writing Skills 1 and 2
Educators Publishing Service
625 Mount Auburn Street
Suite 3
Cambridge, MA 02138
617-547-6706
800-225-5750
FAX: 888-440-2665
e-mail: feedback@epsbooks.com
www.epsbooks.com

*Charles H Heinle, Vice President*
*Alexandra S Bigelow, Author*
*Gunnar Voltz, President*

Students practice writing sentences and developing paragraphs through writing about their ideas and personal experiences. A logical sequence takes students from individual sentences to basic paragraphs of 5 sentences, expanded paragraphs, and essays. *$7.50*
*64 pages Grades 4-6, 7-9*
*ISBN 0-83882 -50-*

### 2462 Writing Skills for the Adolescent
Educators Publishing Service
PO Box 9031
Cambridge, MA 02139
617-547-6706
800-225-5750
FAX: 888-440-2665
e-mail: feedback@epsbooks.com
www.epsbooks.com

*Charles H Heinle, Vice President*
*Alexandra S Bigelow, Author*
*Gunnar Voltz, President*

Teaches the writing process in a series of logical steps as students learn to write and improve sentences, they work on grammar, which is taught in terms of writing. Meanwhile, they learn to generate ideas to compose topic sentences and to use transitional words. They gradually progress from paragraph writing to essay writing. *$10.65*
*96 pages Paperback*
*ISBN 0-838817-04-1*

## Associations

### 2463 AVKO Dyslexia Research Foundation
3084 West Willard Road
Clio, MI 48420
810-686-9283
FAX: 810-686-1101
e-mail: avkoemail@aol.com
www.avko.org

*Don McCabe, Executive Research Director*

Comprised of individuals interested in helping others learn to read and spell. Develops and sells materials for teaching dyslexics or others with learning disabilities using a method involving audio, visual, kinesthetic and oral (multi-sensory) techniques.

### 2464 Alliance for Parental Involvement in Education
PO Box 59
East Chatham, NY 12060
518-392-6900
FAX: 518-392-6900
e-mail: allpie@taconic.net
www.croton.com/allpie

A nonprofit organization to encourage and assist parental involvement in education, public, private and home. Offers a newsletter, a book catolog, retreats, workshops, and a lending library.

### 2465 Alternative Work Concepts
PO Box 11452
Eugene, OR 97440
541-345-3043
FAX: 541-345-9669
e-mail: awc@teleport.com
www.teleport.com

*Liz Fox, Executive Director*

To promote individualized, integrated, and meaningful employment opportunities in the community for adults with multiple disabilities; to improve the quality of life and provide continuous opportunities for personal growth for these individuals; and to assist businesses with workforce diversification.

### 2466 American Council for Headache Education (ACHE)
19 Mantua Road
Mount Royal, NJ 08061
856-423-0043
800-255-2243
FAX: 856-423-0082
e-mail: achehq@talley.com
www.achenet.org

*Linda McGillicuddy, Executive Director*

Nonprofit, patient-health, professional partnership dedicated to advancing the treatment and management of headaches and to raising the public awareness of headache as valid, biologically based illness.

### 2467 American School Counselor Association
American Counselling Association
1101 King Street
Suite 625
Alexandria, VA 22314
703-683-2722
800-306-4722
FAX: 703-683-1619
e-mail: asca@schoolcounselor.org
www.schoolcounselor.org

*Richard Wong, Executive Director*
*Kathleen Rakestraw, Director of Communications*

ASCA focuses on providing professional devleopment, enhancing school counseling programs, and research effective school counseling practices. Mission is to promote excellence in professional school counseling and the development of all students.

### 2468 Association on Higher Education and Disability
1200 Spa
Waltham, MA 54066
781-788-0003
FAX: 781-788-0033
TTY:617-287-3882
e-mail: ahead@ahead.org
www.ahead.org

*Ethan Smith, President*

Higher education for people with disabilities. A vital resource, promoting excellence through education, communication and training.

### 2469 CARF Rehabilitation Accreditation Commission
CARF International
4891 East Grant Road
Tucson, AZ 85712
520-325-1044
888-816-5321
FAX: 520-318-1129
e-mail: postmaster@carf.org
www.carf.org

*Brian Boon PhD, President/CEO*

Independent, nonprofit commission promotes quality services for people with disabilities and others in need of rehabilitation. CARF establishes customer-focused standards to help organizations measure and improve the quality of their rehabilitation programs and services. When reviewing a rehabilitation program or service, CARF applies standards that have been developed and accepted by peers in the field.

**2470    CEC-Division for Early Childhood**
Council for Exceptional Children
1110 North Glebe Road
Suite 300
Arlington, VA  22201                   703-245-0600
                                       888-232-7733
                                  FAX: 703-264-9494
                        e-mail: service@cec.sped.org
                                     www.cec.sped.org

*Jim McCormick, President*
*Drew Allbritten, Executive Director*
*Bruce Ramirez, Manager*

A division of The Council for Exceptional Children. Promotes education for young children and infants with special needs, initiates programs that cooperatively involve parents in their children's education, stimulates communication and joint activity among early childhood organizations, sponsors professional development and disseminates research findings and information addressing issues of early childhood education and more.

**2471    Clearinghouse for Specialized Media and Technology**
California Department of Education
1430 North Street
Room 3207
Sacramento, CA  95814                  916-324-4244
                                  FAX: 916-323-9732
                                   www.cde.ca.gov/re/pn/sm

*David Supkofl, Manager*

Assists schools and students in the identification and acquisition of textbooks, reference books and study materials in aural media, braille, large print and electronic media access technology.

**2472    Council for Exceptional Children**
1110 North Glebe Road
Suite 300
Arlington, VA  22201                   703-245-0600
                                       888-232-7733
                                  FAX: 703-264-9494
                      e-mail: president@cec.sped.org
                                     www.cec.sped.org

*Janice Burdick, President*
*Suzanne Martin, Immediate Past President*
*Bruce Ramirez, Manager*

The largest international organization dedicated to improving educational success for individuals with exceptionalities. CEC sets professional standards, advocates for appropriate government policies, provides continual professional development and advocates for newly and historically underserved individuals with exceptionalities. Helps professionals obtain conditions and resources necessary for effective practice.

**2473    Educational Referral Service**
Doctor Yvonne Jones and Associates
2222 Eastlake Avenue E
Seattle, WA  98102                     206-325-2600
                                  FAX: 206-328-9172

*Yvonne Jones*

Specializes in matching children with the learning environments that are best for them and works with families to help them identify concerns and establish priorities about their child's education.

**2474    Institute on Disability/UCED**
University of New Hampshire
10 West Edge Drive
Suite 101
Durham, NH  03824                      603-862-2110
                                  FAX: 603-862-0555
                     e-mail: institutedisability@unh.edu
                                     www.iod.unh.edu

*Jan Nisbet, Director*
*Nancy Cicolini, Office Manager*
*Janice Mutschler, Manager*

This mission of the Institute is to improve the knowledge, policy and practice related to the economic and social participation of persons with disabilities. The Institute provides a blend of programs that address the needs of local schools, community services and state and federal agencies. The Institute's goal is to increase the ability of the State of New Hampshire to foster inclusion of persons with disabilities into their communities.

**2475    International Association of Parents and Professionals for Safe Alternatives in Childbirth**
RR 4
Box 646
Marble Hill, MO  63764                 573-238-2010
                                  FAX: 573-238-2010
                         e-mail: napsac@clas.net
                                     www.napsac.org

*Lee Stewart, President*
*David Stewart, Executive Director*

Dedicated to exploring, implementing, and establishing safe, family-centered childbirth programs that meet the social and emotional needs of families as well as provide the safe, appropriate aspects of medical science.

**2476    International Childbirth Education Association**
PO Box 20048
Minneapolis, MN  55420                 952-854-8660
                                       800-624-4934
                                  FAX: 952-854-8772
                            e-mail: info@icea.org
                                     www.icea.org

*Doris Olson, President*
*Sandra Anderson, Educator*

Offer teaching certificates, seminars, continuing education workshops, and a mail order center.

**2477    International Dyslexia Association**
1500 Hallbrook Drive
Columbia, SC  29209                    803-695-1400
                                       800-722-1213
                                  FAX: 803-695-1214
                         e-mail: info@interdys.org
                                     www.interdys.org

*Anne Vickers, Executive Director*
*Thrace Mears, Admissions Director*
*John W Weaver, Advancement Director*

Provides free information and referral services for diagnosis and tutoring for parents, educators, physicians, and individuals with dyslexia. 48 countries. Membership includes yearly journal and quarterly newsletter. Call for conference dates.

**2478    International Organization for the Education of the Hearing Impaired**
Alexander Graham Bell Association
3417 Volta Place NW
Washington, DC  20007                  202-337-5220
                                       866-337-5220
                                  FAX: 202-337-8314
                          e-mail: info@agbell.org
                                     www.agbell.org

*Todd Houston, Executive Director*

Professional educators of the hearing impaired make up the members of this organization which promotes the excellence in teaching the hearing impaired child.

# Education /Associations

**2479 Jewish Guild for the Blind**
JGB Audio Library
15 West 65th Street
New York, NY 10023
212-769-6200
800-284-4422
FAX: 212-769-6266
e-mail: info@jgb.org
www.JGB.org

*Alan Morse, President*
*James M Dubin, President/CEO*
*Victoria Kella, Public Relations Manager*

Tape recordings of best-selling books in 28 subject categories for blind, visually impaired and disabled persons.

**2480 Job Accommodation Network**
Office of Disability and Employment Policy
PO Box 6080
Morgantown, WV 26506
800-232-9675
800-526-7234
FAX: 304-093-5407
e-mail: jan@jan.wvu.edu
www.jan.wvu.edu

*DJ Hendricks, Director*

International toll-free consulting service that provides information about job accommodations and the employability of people with disabilities. Also provides information regarding the Americans with Disabilities Act (ADA).

**2481 Michigan Psychological Association**
2105 University Park Drive
Suite C1
Okemos, MI 48864
517-347-1885
800-270-9070
FAX: 517-347-1896
e-mail: mpa@acd.net
www.michpsych.org

*Judith Kovach, Executive Director*

Nonprofit organization of over 1000 psychologists, working to advance psychology as a science and a profession and to promote the public welfare by encouraging the highest professional standards, offering public education and providing a public service, and by participating in the public policy process on behalf of the profession and health care consumers.

**2482 National Association of Colleges and Employers**
62 Highland Avenue
Bethlehem, PA 18017
610-868-1421
800-544-5272
FAX: 610-868-0208
www.naceweb.org

*Vanessa Strauss, President*
*Shawn Vanderziel, Director Human Resources*
*Sandra Dalious, Human Resources Manager*

A national association with services for career planning, placement and recruitment professionals.

**2483 National Association of Private Special Education Centers**
1522 K St NW
Suite 1032
Washington, DC 20005
202-408-3338
FAX: 202-408-3340
e-mail: napsec@aol.com
www.napsec.org

*Sherry L Kolbe, Executive Director*
*Jonathan Cartagena, Communications Coordinator*
*Rebecca Kantz, Membership Services Coordinator*

Membership directory offering information on NAPSEC member schools nationwide available.

**2484 National Center for Homeopathy**
801 North Fairfax Street
Suite 306
Alexandria, VA 22314
703-548-7790
877-624-0613
FAX: 703-548-7792
e-mail: info@homeopathic.org
www.homeopathic.org

*Jean Hoagland, President*
*Shirley Grassflower, Vice President*
*Sharon Stevenson, Executive Director*

Provides information, referral lists, and courses to professionals.

**2485 National Clearinghouse for Professions in Special Education**
Council for Exceptional Children
1110 North Glebe Road
Suite 300
Arlington, VA 22201
703-245-0600
FAX: 703-264-9494
www.cec.sped.org

*Janice Burdick, President*
*Bruce Ramirez, Manager*

Designed to encourage individuals to seek careers in the various fields related to the education of children and youth with disabilities.

**2486 National Council on Rehabilitation Education**
California State University, Fresno
5005 North Maple Avenue Ms3
Fresno, CA 93740
559-278-4240
FAX: 559-278-0045
www.rehabeducators.org

*Charles Arokiasamy MD, Administrative Secretary*
*Brooke Beckege, Assistant Administrative Secreta*
*John Welty, Chief Executive Officer*

Members include academic institutions and organizations, professional educators, researchers, and students. Assists in the documentation of the effect of education in improving services to persons with disabilities; determines the skills and training necessary for effective rehabilitation services; develops role models, standards and uniform licensure and certification requirements for rehabilitation personnel.

**2487 National Education Association of the United States**
1201 16th Street NW
Washington, DC 20036
202-833-4000
www.nea.org

*John Wilson, Chief Executive Officer*
Offers information to educational professionals.

**2488 National Society for Experiential Education**
515 King Street
Suite 420
Alexandria, VA 22314
703-706-9552
FAX: 703-684-6048
www.nsee.org

*Karen Roloff, President*
*Albert Cabral, Vice President*

National nonprofit organization which advocates experiential learning and works with college administrators and high school and college internship programs.

**2489 President's Committee for People with Intellectual Disabilities**
Administration for Children & Families
370 L Enfant Promenade SW
Washington, DC 20447

202-619-0634
FAX: 202-205-9519
www.acf.hhs.gov/programs/pcpid

*Sally Atwater, Executive Director*
*George Bouthilet PhD, Research Director*
*Lauerdia Roach, Special Assistant*

Prepares an annual report to the president of the United States addressing issues concerning citizens with intellectual disabilities.

**2490 Rifin Family/Daughters of Israel**
JGB Audio Library for the Blind
15 West 65th Street
New York, NY 10023

212-769-6200
800-284-4422
FAX: 212-769-6266
e-mail: info@JGB.org
www.JGB.org

*Peter Wiliamson, Director*
*Wanda Figueroa-Kilroy, Executive Vice President*
*Alan Morse, Manager*

**2491 SSD (Services for Students with Disabilities)**
College Board
45 Columbus Avenue
New York, NY 10023

212-713-8000
FAX: 212-713-8277
www.collegeboard.com

*Gaston Caperton, President*

National, nonprofit membership association dedicated to preparing, inspiring and connecting students to college and opportunity. Founded in 1900, the association is composed of more than 3,800 schools, colleges, universities and other educational organizations. Services for Students with Disabilities (SSD) provides special arrangements to minimize the possible effects of disabilities on test performance through it's Admissions Testing Program (ATP).

**2492 Target Teach**
Evans Newton
15941 North 77th Street
Scottsdale, AZ 85260

480-998-2777
800-443-0544
FAX: 480-951-2895
e-mail: info@evansnewton.com
www.evansnewton.com

*Jocklyn Smith, Director*
*Gary Davis, Director of Curriculum and Instr*
*Jamie Piotti, Chief Executive Officer*

Aligns and monitors Special Education Instructional Materials to tests that are used to measure the effectiveness of Special Education Instructional Programs.

**2493 United Cerebral Palsy Research and Educational Foundation**
1660 L Street NW
Suite 700
Washington, DC 20036

202-776-0406
800-872-5827
FAX: 202-776-0414
e-mail: webmaster@ucp.org
www.ucpa.org

*William H Macy, UUCP Ambassador*
*Stephen Bennett, Chief Executive Officer*

Grants are awarded to institutions or organizations on behalf of a principal investigator in support of biomedical and bioengineering research in areas which have a significant relationship to cerebral palsy. While most research on central nervous system structure, function and disorder may be useful, the Foundation requires that research proposals address issues of relevance to cerebral palsy.

# Directories

**2494 BOSC: Directory of Facilities for People with Learning Disabilities**
Books on Special Children
PO Box 3378
Amherst, MA 01004

413-256-8164
FAX: 413-256-8896
e-mail: irene@boscbooks.com
www.boscbooks.com

*Michael Young, President*

Directory of schools, independent living programs, clinics and centers, colleges and vocational programs, agencies and commercial products. Five sections in special post binder that can be updated annually. Hardcover. *$70.00*
*300+ pages Yearly*
*ISSN 0961-3888*

**2495 Complete Directory for Pediatric Disorders**
Sedgwick Press/Grey House Publishing
PO Box 860
Millerton, NY 12546

518-789-8700
800-562-2139
FAX: 518-789-0556
e-mail: books@greyhouse.com
www.greyhouse.com

*Leslie Mackenzie, Publisher*
*Laura Mars, Editorial Director*
*Jessica Moody, Marketing Director*

An annual directory for professionals, parents and caregivers. Provides valuable information on more than 200 pediatric conditions, disorders, diseases and disabilities, including informative descriptions and a wide variety of resources, from associations to publications. *$145.00*
*702 pages Annual*
*ISBN 1-891482-41-6*

**2496 Complete Directory for People with Chronic Illness**
Sedgwick Press/Grey House Publishing
PO Box 860
Millerton, NY 12546

518-789-8700
800-562-2139
FAX: 518-789-0556
e-mail: books@greyhouse.com
www.greyhouse.com

*Leslie Mackenzie, Publisher*
*Laura Mars, Editorial Director*
*Jessica Moody, Marketing Director*

This directory is structured around the ninety most prevalent chronic illnesses. Each chronic illness chapter includes an informative description, plus a comprehensive listing of resources and support services available for people diagnosed with chronic illness and their network of supportive individuals. *$165.00*

*Annual*

**2497  Complete Learning Disabilities Directory**
Sedgwick Press/Grey House Publishing
PO Box 860
Millerton, NY  12546
                                518-789-8700
                                800-562-2139
                        FAX: 518-789-0556
            e-mail: books@greyhouse.com
                    www.greyhouse.com

*Leslie Mackenzie, Publisher*
*Laura Mars, Editorial Director*
*Jessica Moody, Marketing Director*

A comprehensive educational guide offering over 6,500 listings on associations and organizations, schools, government agencies, testing materials, camps, products, books, newsletters, legal information, classroom materials and more. Includes separate chapters on ADD and Literacy, as well as informative articles. *$145.00*
        *702 pages Annual*
        *ISBN 1-891482-41-6*

**2498  Complete Mental Health Directory**
Sedgwick Press/Grey House Publishing
PO Box 860
Millerton, NY  12546
                                518-789-8700
                                800-562-2139
                        FAX: 518-789-0556
            e-mail: books@greyhouse.com
                    www.greyhouse.com

*Leslie Mackenzie, Publisher*
*Laura Mars, Editorial Director*
*Jessica Moody, Marketing Director*

This directory offers comprehensive information covering the field of behavioral health, with critical information for both the layman and the mental health professional. It covers, in depth, 25 specific mental disorders, and includes informative descriptions and a complete list of resources.
        *Annual*

**2499  Diabetes: Caring for Your Emotions as Well as Your Health**
Harper Collins Publishers/ Basic Books
10 East 53rd Street
New York, NY  10022
                                212-207-7000
                                800-242-7737
                        FAX: 212-207-7203

*Jane Friedman, Chief Executive Officer*

This book offers suggestions for adaptation, relationships with medical personnel, family strategies, employment questions, technology and support groups. *$15.00*

        *ISBN 1-852300-47-7*

**2500  Dictionary of Special Education and Rehabilitation**
Love Publishing Company
9101 East Kenyon Avenue
Suite 2200
Denver, CO  80237
                                303-221-7333
                        FAX: 303-221-7444
            e-mail: lpc@lovepyblishing.com
                    www.lovepublishing.com

*Ann Vernon, Author*
*Stan Love, Owner*

A valuable basic resource in the field. It incorporates hundreds of additions and changes. *$39.95*

*Paperback*
*ISBN 0-891082-43-3*

**2501  Directory for Exceptional Children**
Porter Sargent Publishers
11 Beacon Street
Suite 1400
Boston, MA  02108
                                617-523-1670
                                800-342-7470
                        FAX: 617-523-1021
            e-mail: orders@portersargent.com
                    www.portersargent.com

*Porter Sergent Steft, author*
*John Yonce, General Manager*
*Daniel Mckeever, Senior Editor*
*Leslie A Weston, Production Manager*

A comprehensive, objective survey of 3000 schools, facilities and organizations across the country serving children and young adults with developmental, emotional, physical and mental disabilities. *$75.00*
        *1120 pages Trienniel*
        *ISBN 0-875581-50-1*

**2502  Educators Resource Directory**
Sedgwick Press/Grey House Publishing
PO Box 860
Millerton, NY  12546
                                518-789-8700
                                800-562-2139
                        FAX: 518-789-0545
            e-mail: books@greyhouse.com
                    www.greyhouse.com

*Leslie Mackenzie, Publisher*
*Laura Mars, Editorial Director*
*Jessica Moody, Marketing Director*

Gives education professionals immediate access to Associations and Organizations, Conferences and Trade Shows, Educational Research Centers, Employment Opportunities and Teaching Abroad, School Library Services, Scholarships, Financial Resources and much more. *$ 145.00*
        *591 pages Annual*
        *ISBN 1-930956-48-7*

**2503  Enhancing Children's Communication: Research & Foundations**
Enhancing Childrens Communication Research & Found
PO Box 10624
Baltimore, MD  21285
                                410-337-9580
                                800-638-3775
                        FAX: 410-337-8539
        e-mail: custserv@brookespublishing.com
                www.brookespublishing.com

*Jeff Brookes, Director*
*Paul Brooks, Owner*

This groundbreaking book provides helpful insights, unique perspectives, and innovative strategies that are needed to intervene successfully with children whose developmental disabilities affect their use of communication and language. *$43.00*
        *448 pages 1992*
        *ISBN 1-557660-76-X*

**2504  Exceptional Children: An Introductory Survey of Special Education**
McGraw-Hill School Publishing
220 East Danieldale Road
Desoto, TX  75115
                                972-224-1111
                                800-442-9685
                        FAX: 972-228-1982
                    www.mhschool.com

*Joseph Gavigan, President*

The focus of this survey is on observable characteristics of exceptional persons, and the instructional practices which foster their fullest development.

*704 pages*

**2505 Increasing and Decreasing Behaviors of Persons with Severe Retardation and Autism**
Research Press
PO Box 9177
Champaign, IL 61826
217-352-3273
800-519-2707
FAX: 217-352-1221
e-mail: rp@researchpress.com
www.researchpress.com

*Russell Pence, President*

These well-organized manuals are written for teachers, aides and persons responsible for designing or evaluating behavioral programs. Offers specific guidelines for arranging and managing the learning environment as well as standards for evaluating and maintaining success. In Volume Two of this series, chapters address more restrictive procedures including physical restraint, punishment, time-out and overcorrection. Set of two volumes. *$32.95*
*428 pages Item 2650*
*ISBN 0-878222-65-0*

**2506 Teaching Special Students in Mainstream**
Books on Special Children
PO Box 305
Congers, NY 10920
845-638-1236
FAX: 845-638-0847
e-mail: irene@boscbooks.com
Overview of mainstream, team of professionals managing classroom behavior, tips for teachers, social acceptance and handling of specific differences. *$33.00*
*515 pages Softcover*

**2507 Young Children with Special Needs**
McGraw-Hill School Publishing
220 East Danieldale Road
Desoto, TX 75115
972-224-1111
800-442-9685
FAX: 972-228-1982
www.mhschool.com

*Glenn Evans, Chief Executive Officer*
*Phyllis Hsiao Hillwig, Chief Operating Officer*
*Joseph Gavigan, President*

This text examines development in the critical areas of motor, self-help, cognitive, language, social, emotional and play skills.
*526 pages*

## Educational Publishers

**2508 AFB Press**
American Foundation for the Blind / AFB Press
11 Penn Plaza
New York, NY 10001
212-502-7600
FAX: 212-502-7772
e-mail: afborders@abdintl.com
www.afb.org

*Carl R Augusto, President/CEO*
*Maureen Fox, Assistant Director*

Develops, publishes, and sells a wide variety of informative books, pamphlets, periodicals, and videos for students, professionals, and researchers in the blindness and visual impairment fields, for people professionally involved in making the mainstream community accessible, and for blind and visually impaired people and their families; publication and video orders.

**2509 American Association for Counseling & Development**
American Counseling Association
5999 Stevenson Avenue
Alexandria, VA 22304
703-823-9800
800-347-6647
FAX: 800-473-2329
e-mail: webmaster@counseling.org
www.counseling.org

*Marie Wakefield, President*
*Richard Yep, Executive Director*
Offers tools and books for the professional.

**2510 Brookes Publishing Company**
PO Box 10624
Baltimore, MD 21285
410-337-9580
800-638-3775
FAX: 410-337-8539
www.brookespublishing.com

*Paul H Brooks, President/Owner*

**2511 Brookline Books**
39 University Road
Brookline, MA 02445
617-734-6772
800-666-2665
FAX: 617-734-3952
e-mail: brooklinebks@delphi.com
www.brooklinebooks.com

*William H Walters, Author*
*Esther Isabe Wilder, Author*

Offers books for teachers and parents on law and legislation, education, integration and mainstreaming for the disabled, their families, caregivers and teachers.

**2512 Brooks/Cole Publishing Company**
511 Forest Lodge Road
Pacific Grove, CA 93950
831-373-0728
800-354-9706
FAX: 831-375-6414
Offers books in Special Education for those preparing to be special educators and for in-service professionals.

**2513 Charles C Thomas Publisher**
2600 South 1st Street
Springfield, IL 62704
217-789-8980
800-258-8980
FAX: 217-789-9130
e-mail: books@ccthomas.com
www.ccthomas.com

*Michael Thomas, President*

Publishes specialty titles and textbooks in medicine, dentistry, nursing, and veterinary medicine, as well as a complete line in the behavioral sciences, criminal justice, education, special education, and rehabilitation. Aims to accommodate the current needs for information.

**2514 Eric Clearinghouse on Disabilities and Gifted Education**
Council for Exceptional Children
1110 N Glebe Road
Suite 300
Arlington, VA 22201
703-245-0600
FAX: 703-264-9494
www.cec.sped.org

*Janice Burdick, President*
*Bruce Ramirez, Manager*

Provides information on special and gifted education. Provides referrals, offers patient networking services and provides information on current research programs. Focuses its efforts on prevention, identification, assessment, intervention and enrichment both in special settings and within mainstream communities. Offers a variety of materials including brochures and Spanish language matereials.

**2515 Gallaudet University Bookstore**
Gallaudet University
800 Florida Avenue NE
Washington, DC 20002

202-651-5000
800-621-2736
FAX: 202-651-5489
e-mail: bookstore.mailorder@gallaudet.edu
www.gallaudet.edu

*Angelu Jorge-Quinones, Board of Trustees*
*Erving Jordan, President*

Offers informational resources for the deaf, parents of the deaf, professionals, special educators and more. Produces a yearly catalog of materials on sign language and deafness.

**2516 Greenwood Publishing Group**
88 Post Road W
Westport, CT 06880

203-226-3571
FAX: 203-222-1502
e-mail: webmaster@greenwood.com
www.greenwood.com

*David A Copeland, Author*
*Kirstin Olsen, Author*
*Wayne Smith, President*

**2517 Grey House Publishing**
185 Millerton Road
Millerton, NY 12546

518-789-8700
800-562-2139
FAX: 518-789-0545
e-mail: books@greyhouse.com
www.greyhouse.com

*Richard Gottlieb, President*
*Leslie Mackenzie, Publisher*
*Laura Mars, Editorial Director*

Grey House Publishing publishes directories, handbooks and reference works for public, high school and academic libraries and the business and health communities. Most titles are available as online databases.

**2518 Information from HEATH Resource Center**
National Clearinghouse on Postsecondary Education
1 Dupont Circle NW
Suite 800
Washington, DC 20036

202-939-9320
800-544-3284
FAX: 202-833-5696
e-mail: heath@ace.nche.edu
www.HEATH-resource-center.org

The HEATH Resource Center operates the national clearinghouse on postsecondary education for individuals with disabilities. Support from the US Department of Education enables the Center, a program of the America Council on Education, to serve as an information exchange on educational support services; adaptations; and opportunities at American campuses, vocational-technical schools, adult education programs, independent living centers, and other postsecondary training entities.

**2519 McGraw-Hill Company**
2460 Kerper Boulevard
Dubuque, IA 52001

563-588-1451
800-553-4920
www.mcgraw-hill.com

*Dana Kramer, Director*
*Kurt Strand, Vice President*

Offers a catalog of testing resources and materials for the special educator.

**2520 National Association of School Psychologists**
4340 East West Highway
Suite 402
Bethesda, MD 20814

301-657-0270
FAX: 301-657-0275
e-mail: lnealis@naspweb.org
www.nasponline.org

*Libby Kuffner Nealis, Director Public Policy*
*Susan Gorin, Executive Director*

Represents over 22,500 school psychologists and related professionals. It serves its members and society by advancing the profession of school psychology and advocating for the rights, welfare, education and mental health of children, youth and their families.

**2521 Oryx Press**
4041 North Central Avenue
Suite 700
Phoenix, AZ 85012

602-265-2651
800-279-6799
FAX: 800-279-4663

**2522 Pro-Ed**
8700 Shoal Creek Boulevard
Austin, TX 78757

512-451-3246
800-897-3202
FAX: 800-397-7633
e-mail: feedback@proedinc.com
www.proedinc.com

*Donald Hammill, Owner*
*Courtney King, Marketing Coordinator*

Publishes, produces and sells books, curricular therapy materials and journals dedicated to psychology, special education and speech, language and hearing.

**2523 Ragged Edge Reader**
Advocado Press
PO Box 145
Louisville, KY 40201

888-739-1920
FAX: 502-899-9562
e-mail: office@advocadopress.org
www.raggededgemagazine.com

*T Smith, Circulation Manager*

A print compilation of articles that have appeared on our Ragged Edge online website. *$12.50*
*36 pages*

**2524 Research Press**
PO Box 9177
Champaign, IL 61826

217-352-3273
800-519-2707
FAX: 217-352-1221
e-mail: rp@researchpress.com
www.researchpress.com

*Dennis Wiziecki, Marketing Department*
*Mark Amendola, Author*
*Russell Pence, President*

**2525 Special Needs Project**
324 State Street
Suite H
Santa Barbara, CA 93101

805-962-8087
800-333-6867
FAX: 805-962-5087
www.specialneeds.com

*Hod Gray, Founder*

**2526  Waterfront Books Publishing Company**
85 Crescent Road
Burlington, VT  05401
802-658-7477
800-639-6063
FAX: 802-860-1368
e-mail: helpkids@waterfrontbooks.com
www.waterfrontbooks.com

*Sherrill N Musty, Owner*

## State Agencies: Alabama

**2527  Alabama Department of Education: Division of Special Education Services**
Alabama Department of Education
PO Box 302101
Montgomery, AL  36104
334-242-4363
FAX: 205-242-9192
www.alsde.edu

*Bill East, Assistant Director*

**2528  Getting Ready for the Outside World (G.R.O.W.)**
River View School
551 Route 6a
East Sandwich, MA  02537
508-888-0489
FAX: 508-833-7001
www.riverviewschool.org

*Jeanne Pacheco, Director Admissions/Placement*
*Maureen Brenner, Principal*

The G.R.O.W. Program is a unique ten month transitional prgoram (1-3 years) for high school graduates with diagnosed learning disabilities who share a common hisotry of lifelong difficulty with academic achievement and the development of friendships. This post secondary program is designed to further develop academic, vocational and life skills, to enable students to function as independently as possible.

## State Agencies: Alaska

**2529  Alaska Department of Education: Office of Special Education**
801 West 10th Street
Suite 200
Juneau, AK  99801
907-465-2880
FAX: 907-465-3396
www.eed.state.ak.us

*Myrna Howe, State Director*
*Karen Rehfeld, Executive Director*

Administers special educational programs through the Division of Education Program Support to the disabled residing in the Alaska area.

## State Agencies: Arkansas

**2530  Arkansas Department of Special Education**
4 Capitol Mall
Suite 105-C
Little Rock, AR  72201
501-682-1121
800-NAT-URAL
FAX: 501-682-4313
www.arkansas.com

*Diane Sydoriak MD, Associate Director Special Educa*
*Barbara Pardue, Executive Director*

Provides oversight of all educational programs for children and youth with disabilities, ages 3 to 21. Provides technical assistance to all public agencies providing educational services to this population.

## State Agencies: Arizona

**2531  Arizona Department of Education**
State of Arizona
1535 West Jefferson Street
Phoenix, AZ  85007
602-271-0945
800-352-4558
FAX: 602-542-5404
e-mail: essdesk@ade.az.gov
www.ade.az.gov

*Joanne Phillips, State Director Special Education*
*Joe Sambo, Office Manager*
*Robert Plummer, Manager*

## State Agencies: California

**2532  California Department of Education: Special Education Division**
721 Capitol Mall
Sacramento, CA  95814
916-324-4244
FAX: 916-657-4770

*Jack O'Connell, Superintendent*
*Leo Sandoval, Director Special Education*
*David Supkofl, Manager*

Through consultants, coordinates the establishment and operations of special public school programs for blind and partially sighted pupils. The staff includes two regionally based consultant specialists in the education of visually impaired children, and the eligible age for help is 3-21.

## State Agencies: Colorado

**2533  Colorado Department of Education: Special Education Service Unit**
Colorado Department of Education
201 East Colfax Avenue
Denver, CO  80203
303-698-2121
FAX: 303-866-6811
www.cde.state.co.us

*William Maloney, Commissioner*
*Laura Reilly, Chief Executive Officer*

Provides consultation on materials and educational services for visually handicapped children, supervises volunteer services, transcribes textbooks for visually handicapped students.

## State Agencies: Connecticut

**2534  Connecticut Department of Education: Bureau of Special Education**
Connecticut Department of Education
25 Industrial Park Road
Middletown, CT  06457
860-632-1485
FAX: 860-632-8870
www.ctserc.org

*Marianne Kirner, Executive Director*
*Carol Sullivan, Assistant Director*

Commitment is to serve as a centralized resource for professionals, families, and community members regarding education and early intervention/prevention for all of Connecticut's children and their families, particularly children with special needs, at-risk learners, and diverse learners. SERC strives for the highest possible level of excellence assistance initiatives, family education and support, and information and materials dissemination.

**2535 Connecticut State Board of Education and Services for the Blind**
State of Connecticut Agency
184 Windsor Avenue
Windsor, CT 06095       860-602-4000
800-842-4510
FAX: 860-602-4030
e-mail: brian.sigman@po.state.ct.us
www.besb.state.ct.us

*Brian Sigman, Executive Director*
*Keith Maynard, Plant Manager*

Provides consultation for the education of visually disabled children, provides Braille instruction, independent living skills training, vocational rehabilitation services and community outreach and advocacy.

## State Agencies: Delaware

**2536 Department of Public Instruction: Exceptional Children & Special Programs Division**
Department of Education
401 Federal Street
Suite 2
Dover, DE 19903       302-735-4210
FAX: 302-739-2388

*Martha Toomey, Director*

## State Agencies: DC

**2537 District of Columbia Public Schools: Special Education Division**
825 North Capitol Street NE
7th Floor
Washington, DC 20002       202-442-4800
202-442-5517

*Paul L Vance MD, Superintendent*

Committed to providing a continuum of services that offers students with disabilities the opportunity to actively participate in the learning environment of their neighborhood school.

**2538 National Clearinghouse on Family Support and Children's Mental Health**
1 Dupont Circle NW
Suite 800
Washington, DC 20036       202-939-9320
800-544-3284
FAX: 202-833-4760
e-mail: heatah@ace.nche.edu

## State Agencies: Florida

**2539 Florida Department of Education: Bureau of Education for Exceptional Students**
325 West Gaines Street
Suite 614
Tallahassee, FL 32399       850-414-4615
FAX: 850-245-0953
www.fldoe.org

*John Winn, Commissioner*
*Bambi Lockman, Bureau Chief*
*Sandra Bell, Manager*

The Department of Education strives to improve educational services for students with special needs.

## State Agencies: Georgia

**2540 Georgia State Department of Education: Program for Exceptional Children**
Georgia Department Of Education
1870 Twin Towers East
Suite 1970
Atlanta, GA 30334       770-980-5100
FAX: 404-651-6457
www.doe.k12.da.us

*Kathy Cox, State Superintendent*
*Marlene Bryar, Director*
*Frank Koues, Auditor*

Provides consultation on educational services for local schools, offers psychological testing and evaluation, maintains resource rooms in district schools and more for the blind and handicapped throughout the state.

## State Agencies: Hawaii

**2541 Hawaii Department of Education: Special Needs**
Hawaii Department of Education
3430 Leahi Avenue
Honolulu, HI 96815       808-941-3894
FAX: 808-732-3701

*Margaret Donovan MD, State Administrator*

Provides consultation on educational services for local schools, offers psychological testing and evaluation, maintains resource rooms in district schools and more for the blind and handicapped throughout the state.

## State Agencies: Illinois

**2542 Activities for Developing Pre-Skill Concepts In Children with Autism**
Autism Society of North Carolina Bookstore
505 Oberlin Road
Suite 230
Raleigh, NC 27605       919-743-0204
800-442-2762
FAX: 919-743-0208
e-mail: dcoffey@autismsociety-nc.org
www.autismsociety-nc.org

*Darla Coffey, Bookstore Manager*
*Jill Keel, Executive Director*

Chapters include auditory development, concept development, social development and visual-motor integration. *$36.00*

**2543 Illinois State Board of Education: Department of Special Education**
100 North 1st Street
Springfield, IL 62777          217-782-6601
                        FAX: 217-782-0372
            e-mail: pstadeke@spr6.isbe.il.us
                              www.isbe.net

*Gail Lieberman, Policy Advisor*

Mission is to advance the human and civil rights of people with disabilities in Illinois. Statewide advocacy organization providing self-advocacy assistance, legal services, education and public policy initiatives. Designated to implement the federal protection and advocacy system; has broad statutory power to enforce the rights of people with physical and mental disabilities, including developmental disabilities and mental illnesses.

## State Agencies: Indiana

**2544 Indiana Department of Education: Special Education Division**
Indiana Department of Education
229 State House
Indianapolis, IN 46204          317-232-0570
                        FAX: 317-233-0586
                 www.ideanet.doe.state.in.us

*Robert Marra, Assistant State Director*

Provides consultation on educational services for local schools, offers psychological testing and evaluation, maintains resource rooms in district schools and more for the blind and handicapped throughout the state.

## State Agencies: Iowa

**2545 Iowa Department of Public Instruction: Bureau of Special Education**
Grimes State Office Building
Des Moines, IA 50319          515-281-3176
                        FAX: 515-242-6019
                 www.state.ia.us/educate/

*Lana Michelson, Bureau Chief*

## State Agencies: Kansas

**2546 Kansas State Board of Education: Special Education Outcomes Team**
Kansas State Board of Education
120 SE 10th Avenue
Topeka, KS 66612          785-291-3097
                         785-296-3201
                   FAX: 913-296-7933
                       www.kansped.org

*Zoann Torrey, Director Team Leader*
*Carol Dermyer, Assitant Director*

Provides consultation on educational services for local schools, offers psychological testing and evaluation, maintains resource rooms in district schools and more for the blind and handicapped throughout the state.

## State Agencies: Kentucky

**2547 Kentucky Department of Education: Division of Exceptional Children's Services**
500 Mero Street
Room 805
Frankfort, KY 40601          502-564-4970
                        FAX: 502-564-6721
            e-mail: marmstro@kde.state.ky.us
                          www.kde.state.ky.us

*Johnny Grissom, Associate Commissioner*
*Judy Mallory, Executive Director*

Provides consultation on educational services for local schools, offers psychological testing and evaluation, maintains resource rooms in district schools and more for the blind and handicapped throughout the state.

## State Agencies: Louisiana

**2548 Louisiana Department of Education: Office of Special Education Services**
Louisiana Department of Education
PO Box 94064
Baton Rouge, LA 70804          225-383-4761
                           877-453-2721
                     FAX: 504-342-5880
                        www.doe.state.la.us

*Cecil J Picard, State Superintendent*
*Kim Fitch, Director Human Resources*
*George Nelson, President*

## State Agencies: Massachusetts

**2549 Massachusetts Department of Education: Program Quality Assurance**
Massachusetts Department of Education
350 Main Street
Malden, MA 02148          781-388-3300
                      FAX: 617-388-3476

*Pamela Kaufamann, Administrator*

## State Agencies: Maryland

**2550 Maryland State Department of Education: Division of Special Education**
200 West Baltimore Street
Baltimore, MD 21201          410-333-2490
                        FAX: 410-333-8165
                      www.msde.state.md.us

*Richard Steinke, State Director*

Provides consultation on educational services for local schools, offers psychological testing and evaluation, maintains resource rooms in district schools and more for the blind and handicapped throughout the state.

## State Agencies: Michigan

**2551 Michigan Department of Education: Special Education Services**
Michigan Department of Education
PO Box 30008
Lansing, MI 48909                      517-373-3654
                                  FAX: 517-373-7504
                        e-mail: mdeweb@michigan.gov
                                 www.michigan.gov/mde

*Jeremy Hughes, Superintendent*
*Bobbie Butler, Manager*

Provides consultation on educational services for local schools, offers psychological testing and evaluation, maintains resource rooms in district schools and more for the blind and handicapped throughout the state.

**2552 Services for Students with Disabilities**
University of Michigan
6-664 Haven Hall
Ann Arbor, MI 48109                    734-763-9259
                                  FAX: 734-936-3947
                         e-mail: sgoodin@umich.edu
                              www.umich.edu/~sswd/

*Sam Goodin, Director*
*Carl Pierson Manager*

Offers information to parents and students.

## State Agencies: Minnesota

**2553 Community Supports for People with Disabilities (CSP)**
South Central Technical College (SCTC)
1920 Lee Boulevard
North Mankato, MN 56003                507-389-7200
                                       800-722-9359
                                 www.southcentral.edu

*Christensen Tami, Executive Director*
*Keith Stover, President*

Human services program available as a physical or online program, designed for those wanting to earn a certificate, diploma or associate degree as a Direct Support Professional for use in the health and human services industries. The program comprises eight courses relating to professional services and support for people with disabilities.

**2554 Professional Development Programs**
14524 61st Street North
Stillwater, MN 55082                   651-439-8865
                                  FAX: 651-439-0421
                        e-mail: programs@pdppro.com
                                     www.pdppro.com

*Eileen Richter, Director*
*Alexis Richter, Administrator*

Sponsors cutting edge and popular continuing education workshops and symposia of interest to professionals who provide services to children and adults with special needs.

## State Agencies: Missouri

**2555 Missouri Department of Elementary and Secondary Education: Special Education Programs**
Missouri Department of Elementary and Secondary Ed
PO Box 480
Jefferson City, MO 65102               573-751-5739
                                  FAX: 573-526-4404
                       e-mail: doug.roach@dese.mo.gov
                               www.dese.mo.gov/divspeced

*Pam Williams, Director*

The Division of Special Education provides assistance to public school districts in the supervision, establishment, and improvement of programs of instruction for children with disabilities. The division operates the Missouri School for the Deaf, School for the Blind and State Schools for the Severely Handicapped. The division also supports a statewide system of sheltered workshops for adults with disabilities.

## State Agencies: Mississippi

**2556 Mississippi Department of Education: Office of Special Services**
Mississippi Department of Education
PO Box 771
Jackson, MS 39205                      601-432-1200
                                  FAX: 601-359-2198
                     e-mail: sthompson@mde.k12.ms.us
                                   www.mde.k12.ms.us

*Carolyn Black, Director*

Key priorities are: reading, early literacy, student achievement, teachers/teaching, leadership/principals, safe and orderly schools, parent relations/community involvement, and technology.

## State Agencies: Montana

**2557 Department of Public Health Human Services**
PO. Box 202501
Helena, MT 59620                       406-444-4429
                                       888-231-9393
                                  FAX: 406-444-3921
                                     www.opi.mt.gov.

*Robert Runkel, Executive Director*
*Linda Mcculloch, Superintendent*

Provides consultation on educational services for local schools, offers psychological testing and evaluation, maintains resource rooms in district schools and more for the blind and handicapped throughout the state.

## State Agencies: North Carolina

**2558 North Carolina Department of Public Instruction: Exceptional Children Division**
301 North Wilmington Street
Raleigh, NC 27601                      919-715-1565
                                  FAX: 919-715-1569
                       e-mail: lharris@dpi.state.nc.us
                                  www.publicschools.org

*Lowell Harris, Director*

Provides consultation on educational services for local schools, offers psychological testing and evaluation, maintains a continuum of educational sources in local schools for disabled children.

## State Agencies: North Dakota

**2559   North Dakota Department of Education: Special Education**
600 East Boulevard Avenue
Bismarck, ND 58505
701-328-2455
FAX: 701-328-4149
www.dpi.state.nd.us

*Robert Rutten, Director*
*Jeanette Kolberg, Assistant Director*
*Bryan Klipfel, Manager*

Provides consultation on educational services for local schools, offers psychological testing and evaluation, maintains resource rooms in district schools and more for the blind and handicapped throughout the state.

## State Agencies: Nebraska

**2560   Nebraska Department of Education: Special Populations Office**
Department of Education
PO Box 94987
Lincoln, NE 68509
402-471-2471
FAX: 402-471-5022
www.nde.state.ne.us/SPED/sped.html

*Gary Sherman, Executive Director*

Assists school districts in establishing and maintaining effective special education programs for children with disabilities (date of diagnosis through the school year when a child reaches 21). Major function: provide technical assistance to school districts and to parents of children with disabilities, assist programs in meeting state and federal special education regulations. Also responsible for assuring that the rights of children with disabilities and their parents are protected.

## State Agencies: New Hampshire

**2561   New Hampshire Department of Education: Bureau for Special Education Services**
New Hampshire Department of Education
101 Pleasant Street
Concord, NH 03301
603-271-3494
FAX: 603-271-1953
www.ed.state.nh.us

*Lyonel Tracy, Commissioner*
*Paul Ezen, Deputy Commissioner*

Provides educational leadership and services which promote equal educational opportunites, quality practices and programs that enable NH residents to become fully productive members of society.

**2562   New Hampshire Technology Partnership Project: Institute on Disability**
Institute of Disability of the University of NH
Concord Center Ferry Street
Concord, NH 03301
603-228-2084
800-238-2048
FAX: 603-228-3270
TTY: 603-224-0630
e-mail: sd@cisunix.unh.edu
www.nhassistivetechnology.org

*Jan Nisbet, Director*
*Mary Schuh, Executive Director*
*Eve Fralick, Associate Director*

The goal of the New Hampshire Assistive Technology Partnership Project is to increase access to assistive technology through the creation and support of consumer driven systems for the provision of state-of-the-art assistive techology products and services for citizens in the state of New Hampshire.

## State Agencies: New Jersey

**2563   New Jersey Department of Education: Office of Special Education Program**
New Jersey Department of Education
PO Box 500
Trenton, NJ 08625
609-292-8853
FAX: 609-984-8422
www.nj.gov/njded/specialed/

*Barbara Gantwerk, Director*
*Alfred Murray, Executive Director*

## State Agencies: New Mexico

**2564   New Mexico State Department of Education**
300 Don Gaspar Avenue
Santa Fe, NM 87501
505-827-6508
FAX: 505-827-6696
www.sde.state.nm.us

*Bill Trant, Assistant Director*
*Judy Parks, Assistant Director*

Provides consultation on educational services for local schools, offers psychological testing and evaluation, maintains resource rooms in district schools and more for the blind and handicapped throughout the state.

## State Agencies: Nevada

**2565   Nevada Department of Education: Special Eduction Branch**
700 East 5th Street
Suite 113
Carson City, NV 89701
775-884-6125
FAX: 775-687-9123
www.doe.nv.gov

*Frankie McCabe, Director Office for Special Ed.*

The Office of Special Ed and School Improvement Program of the Nevada State Department of Education is responsible for management of state and federal programs providing educational opportunities for students with diverse learning needs. Included are such programs as: special education/disabled (IDEA); disadvantaged/at-risk programs (Title I/IASA); early childhood programs (Title I/ESEA); early childhood programs; migrant education; English language learners; NRS 395 student placement program.

## State Agencies: New York

**2566   New York State Education Department**
1606 One Commerce Plaza
Albany, NY 12234
518-474-5548
FAX: 518-473-5387
e-mail: nysed@mail.gov
www.nysed.gov

*Tom Neveldine, Assistant Commissioner*

Provides vocational rehabilitation and educational services for eligible individuals with disabilities throughout New York State. Services include evaluation, counseling, job placement, and referral to other agencies.

## State Agencies: Ohio

**2567 Ohio Department of Education: Division of Special Education**
Ohio Department of Education
25 South Front Street
Columbus, OH 43215
614-466-2650
877-644-6338
FAX: 614-387-0964
www.ode.state.oh.us

*Mike Armstrong, Director*

Provides technical assistance to educational agencies for the development and implementation of educational services to meet the needs of students with disabilities and/or those who are gifted. Provides information to parents. Administers state and federal funds allocated to educational agencies for the provision of services to students with disabilities and/or those who are gifted.

## State Agencies: Oklahoma

**2568 Oklahoma State Department of Education**
2500 North Lincoln Boulevard
Suite 411
Oklahoma City, OK 73105
405-521-3301
FAX: 405-522-3503
www.sde.state.ok.us

*Misty Kimbrough, Executive Director*
*Sandy Garrett, Administrator*

Provides consultation on educational services for local schools, offers psychological testing and evaluation, maintains resource rooms in district schools and more for the blind and handicapped throughout the state.

## State Agencies: Oregon

**2569 Oregon Department of Education: Office of Special Education**
Oregon Department of Education:
255 Capitol St NE
Salem, OR 97310
503-986-4614
FAX: 503-378-5156
www.ode.state.or.us/sped/index/htm

*Nancy Latini, Assistant Superintendent*
*Heidi Cockrell, Executive Assistant*
*Katy Coba, Executive Director*

State agency ensuring provision of special education services to children with disabilities from birth to age 21.

## State Agencies: Pennsylvania

**2570 Pennsylvania Department of Education: Bureau of Special Education**
333 Market Street
7th Floor
Harrisburg, PA 17126
717-783-6913
FAX: 717-783-6139
e-mail: 00specialed@psupen.psu.edu
www.pde.state.pa.us

*Linda Rhen, Administrator*
*John Tommasini, Assistant Director*

Provides effective and efficient administration of the Commonwealth of Pennsylvania's resources dedicated to enabling school districts to maintain high standards in the delivery of special education services and programs for all exceptional students.

## State Agencies: Rhode Island

**2571 Rhode Island Department of Education: Office of Special Needs**
265 Westminster Street
Providence, RI 02903
401-784-9500
FAX: 401-222-6030
www.ride.ri.gov

*Thomas Dipaola, Director*
*Alfred Moscola, Manager*

Provides consultation on educational services for local schools, offers psychological testing and evaluation, maintains resource rooms in district schools and more for the blind and handicapped throughout the state.

## State Agencies: South Carolina

**2572 South Carolina Assistive Technology Program (SCATP)**

Center for Disability Resources
Midlands Center
8301 Farrow Road
Columbia, SC 29203
803-935-5263
800-915-4522
FAX: 803-935-5342
e-mail: evelyne@cdd.sc.edu
www.sc.edu/scatp

*Evelyn Evans, Project Director*
*Janet Jendron, Program Coordinator*
*Marie Queen, Executive Director*

SCATP is a federally funded project concerned with getting technology into th hands of people with disabilities so that they might live, work, learn and be a more independent part of the community.

**2573 South Carolina Department of Education: Office of Exceptional Children**
1429 Senate Street
Columbia, SC 29201
803-734-8806
FAX: 803-734-4824
e-mail: sdurant@sde.state.sc.us
www.scschools.com

*Susan Durant, State Director*

Provides consultation on educational services for local schools, offers psychological testing and evaluation, maintains resource rooms in district schools and more for the blind and handicapped throughout the state.

## State Agencies: South Dakota

**2574  South Dakota Department of Education & Cultural Affairs: Office of Special Education**
700 Governors Drive
Pierre, SD  57501                              605-773-3131
                                          FAX: 605-773-6139

*Deboarh Barnett, State Director*
*Dorothy Liegl, Manager*

## State Agencies: Tennessee

**2575  Tennessee Department of Education**
710 James Robertson Parkway
Nashville, TN  37243                           615-741-2851
                                               888-212-3162
                                          FAX: 615-532-9412
                                      www.state.tn.us/education

*Joseph Fisher, Executive Director*

Provides consultation on educational services for local schools, offers psychological testing and evaluation, maintains resource rooms in district schools and more for the blind and handicapped throughout the state.

## State Agencies: Texas

**2576  Texas Education Agency**
1701 North Congress Avenue
Austin, TX  78701                              512-463-8532
                                          FAX: 512-463-9434
                                          www.tea.state.tx.us

*Shirley J Neeley, Commissioner of Education*

Provides consultation on educational services for local schools, offers psychological testing and evaluation, maintains resource rooms in district schools and more for the blind and handicapped throughout the state.

**2577  Texas Education Agency: Special Education Unit**
1701 Congress Avenue
Austin, TX  78701                              512-463-8532
                                          FAX: 512-463-9434
                          e-mail: wmccain@tmail.tea.state.tx.us
                                     www.tea.state.tx.us/Cate

*Gene Lenz, Deputy Associate Commissioner*
*Shirley Neeley, Administrator*

**2578  Texas School of the Deaf**
1102 South Congress Avenue
Austin, TX  78704                              512-462-5353
                                               800-332-3873
                                          www.tsd.state.tx.us

*Claire Bugen, Administrator*
*Betty Bounds, Assistant Superintendent*

Promote quality educational opportunities and achievement for the deaf students of Texas by providing a comprehensive educational and residential program and a complete array of consultative services for parents and professionals throughout the state.

## State Agencies: Utah

**2579  Utah State Office of Education: At-Risk and Special Education Service Unit**
Utah State Office of Education
250 East 500 South
Salt Lake City, UT  84111                      801-538-7500
                                          FAX: 801-538-7881
                                          www.usoe.k12.ut.us

*Patti Harrington, Manager*

Provides consultation on educational services for local schools, offers psychological testing and evaluation, maintains resource rooms in district schools and more for the blind and handicapped throughout the state.

## State Agencies: Vermont

**2580  Vermont Special Education: Division of Special Education**
Vermont Department of Education
120 State Street
Montpelier, VT  05620                          802-828-3273
                                          FAX: 802-828-3140
                               e-mail: edinfo@educ.state.vt.us
                       www.state.vt.us/educ/new/html/pgm_sped.html

*Richard H Cate, Education Commissioner*
*Francis Woods, Manager*

Provides technical assistance to schools and other organizations to help ensure that schools understand and comply with federal and state laws and regulations related to providing special education services. In addition, the special education division offers a due process procedure to parents who have concerns about services offered to their children.

## State Agencies: Virginia

**2581  Virginia Department of Education: Division of Pre & Early Adolescent Education**
PO Box 2120
Richmond, VA  23218                            804-340-0072
                                          FAX: 804-371-2456
                                          www.pen.k12.va.us

*Austin Tuning, Lead Specialist Special Educatio*

Provides consultation on educational services for local schools, offers psychological testing and evaluation, maintains resource rooms in district schools and more for the blind and handicapped throughout the state.

## State Agencies: Washington

**2582  Superintendent of Public Instruction: Special Education Section**
PO Box 47200
Olympia, WA  98504                             360-725-6000
                                          FAX: 360-586-0247
                                          www.k12.wa.us

*Douglas Gill, Executive Director*

Provides leadership, service and support for the development and implementation of research-based curriculum to assure that all learners achieve at all levels.

## State Agencies: West Virginia

**2583 West Virginia Department of Education: Office of Special Education**
1900 Kanawha Boulevard East
Room 6
Charleston, WV 25305
304-558-0549
FAX: 304-558-3741
wvde.state.wv.us

*Katherine Boyer, Director*
*Mary Nunn, Assistant Director*
*Sarah Hamrick, Executive Director*

Provides consultation on educational services for local schools, offers psychological testing and evaluation, maintains resource rooms in district schools and more for the blind and handicapped throughout the state.

## State Agencies: Wyoming

**2584 Wyoming Department of Education**
2300 Capitol Avenue
Cheyenne, WY 82002
307-777-7690
FAX: 307-777-6234
www.k12.wy.us

*Sharon Davarno, State Director*
*Trent Blankenship, State Superintendent*

Mission is to lead, model, and support continuous improvement of education for everyone in Wyoming.

## Magazines & Journals

**2585 Academic Acceptance of ASL**
Gallaudet University Press
11030 South Langley Avenue
Chicago, IL 60628
202-651-5488
800-621-2736
FAX: 202-651-5489
This monograph presents a dozen articles that demonstrate clearly and convincingly that the study of ASL affords the same educational values and the same intellectual rewards as the study of any other foreign language. *$15.95*
*196 pages*

**2586 Adapted Physical Activity Quarterly**
Human Kinetics
PO Box 5076
Champaign, IL 61825
217-351-5076
800-747-4457
FAX: 217-351-2674
e-mail: humank@hkusa.com
www.humankinetics.com

*Brian Holding, Chief Executive Officer*
*Donna Loyle, Journals Director*
*Rainer Martens, President*

This quarterly journal contains information on current opinions, legislation, regulatory concerns, and trends. It also reports on research and investigations of case studies, programming, techniques, design of equipment and facilities. *$24.00*
*Quarterly*
*ISSN 0736-58 9*

**2587 Advance for Providers of Post-Acute Care**
Merion Publications
PO Box 61556
King of Prussia, PA 19406
610-278-1400
800-355-5627
FAX: 610-278-1421
www.advanceweb.com
A free magazine for providers of post-acute care.

**2588 CEC Catalog**
Council for Exceptional Children
1110 North Glebe Road
Suite 300
Arlington, VA 22201
703-245-0600
888-232-7733
FAX: 703-264-9494
e-mail: president@cec.sped.org
www.cec.sped.org

*Janice Burdick, President*
*Bruce Ramirez, Manager*

Semi-annual catalog from the Council for Exceptional Children offering books, guides, materials, products and services for the special educator.
*18 pages*

**2589 Case Manager Magazine**
Elsevier Health
360 Park Avenue South
New York, NY 10010
212-989-5800

journals.elsevierhealth.com

*Catherine M Mullahy, Editor in Chief*
*John Ragazzi, President*

This national magazine is for medical case managers, social workers, counselors and home health professionals who work with people with serious injury or illness. It is a membership benefit of CMSA, the national association for case managers.
*$55.00*
*84 pages BiMonthly*

**2590 Catalyst**
The Catalyst
1259 El Camino Real
Suite 275
Menlo Park, CA 94025
800-647-0314
e-mail: info@thecatalyst.us
www.thecatalyst.us

*Sue Swezey, Editor*

Digest of news and information on the use of computers in special education. *$15.00*
*20 pages Quarterly*

**2591 Clinical Connection**
American Advertising Dist of Northern Virginia
708 Pendleton Street
Alexandria, VA 22314
703-549-5126
FAX: 703-548-5563

*Georgina Ruley, Publisher*
*Roger Parks, Owner*

Covers speech language pathology.

**2592 College and University**
AACRAO
1 Dupont Circle NW
Suite 520
Washington, DC 20036
202-293-9161
FAX: 202-872-8857
e-mail: info@aacrao.com
www.aacrao.org

*Joseph Roof, President*
*Luz Barreras, Vice President*

Scholarly research journal. American Association of Collegiate Registrars and Admissions Offers (AACRAO) is a nonprofit, voluntary, professional, educational association of degree-granting, postsecondary institutions, government agencies, private educational organizations and education-oriented businesses in the United States and abroad. $50 per year US; $60 per year international.

*30 pages Quarterly*
*ISSN 0010-0889*

**2593  Continuing Care**
Stevens Publishing Corporation
5151 Belt Line Road
10th Floor
Dallas, TX  75254                   972-687-6700
                          FAX: 972-687-6769
            e-mail: custserv@stevenspublishing.com
                 www.stevenspublishing.com

*Craig Stevens, President/CEO*

A national magazine for case management and discharge planning professionals published monthly except for December. *$119.00*
                   *34 pages Monthly*

**2594  Counseling Psychologist**
American Psychological Association
2455 Teller Road
Thousand Oaks, CA  91320            805-499-9734
                                     800-818-7243
                          FAX: 805-499-0871
                 e-mail: info@sagepub.com
                      www.sagepub.com
Thematic issues in the theory, research and practice of counseling psychology. *$78.00*
              *Bi-Monthly*

**2595  Counseling and Values**
American Counseling Association
5999 Stevenson Avenue
Alexandria, VA  22304               703-823-9800
                                     800-347-6647
                          FAX: 800-823-0252
                   www.counseling.org

*Dennis Engels, Editor*
*Richard Yep, Executive Director*

Counseling and Values is the official journal of the Association for Spiritual, Ethical, and Religious Values in Counseling (ASERVIC), a member association of the American Counseling Association. Counseling and Values s a professional journal of theory, research, and informed opinion concerned with the relationships among psychology, philosophy, religion, social values, and counseling. *$12.00*
                   *TriAnnual*

**2596  Directions: Technology in Special Education**
DREAMMS for Kids
273 Ringwood Road
Freeville, NY  13068                607-539-3027
                          FAX: 607-539-9930
                      www.dreamms.org

*Janet P Hosmer, Contact*

Provides technology tips to ease home instruction and use; describes and reviews adaptive educational software and hardware; reviews pertinent literature and audio and videotapes; describes adaptive and assistive technology devices; provides on-line service information for the disabled; announces upcoming educational and technology conference; and reports on new Department of Education legislation. *$14.95*
                   *Monthly*

**2597  Disability Studies Quarterly**
Department of Public Management
Suffolk University
Boston, MA  02108                   617-725-8483
                          FAX: 617-573-8711
            e-mail: per00906@acad.suffolk.edu

*David Pfeiffer, Editor*
*Monique Perrier, Administrative Assistant*

Contains articles on aspects of disability, often focusing on one topic, such as gender and sexuality, communication technology and measurement in disability. Also includes information on books and resources available for persons with disabilities. *$35.00*

*75 pages Quarterly*

**2598  Early Intervention**
Early Childhood Intervention Clearinghouse
830 South Spring Street
Springfield, IL  62704              217-522-4340
                                     800-852-4302
                          FAX: 217-522-4670
            e-mail: clearinghouse@eosinc.com
                 www.eiclearinghouse.org

*Chet Brandt, Executive Director*
*Patricia Taylor, Project Associate*

Features articles, conference calendar, material reviews and news concerning early childhood intervention and disability.
                   *4 pages Quarterly*

**2599  Exceptional Children**
Council for Exceptional Children
1110 North Glebe Road
Suite 300
Arlington, VA  22201                703-245-0600
                          FAX: 703-264-9494
                 e-mail: service@cec.sped.org
                      www.cec.sped.org

*Jim McCormick, President*
*Drew Allbritten, Executive Director*
*Bruce Ramirez, Manager*

Articles include research, literature surveys and position papers concerning exceptional children, special education and mainstreaming. *$58.00*
                   *96 pages BiMonthly*

**2600  Focus on Autism and Other Developmental Disabilities**
Pro-Ed Publications
8700 Shoal Creek Boulevard
Austin, TX  78757                   512-451-3246
                                     800-897-3202
                          FAX: 800-397-7633
            e-mail: feedback@proedinc.com
                      www.proedinc.com

*Donald Hammill, Owner*
*Courtney King, Marketing Coordinator*

Practical management, treatment and planning strategies; a must for persons working with individuals with autism and other developmental disabilities. *$43.00*
                   *64 pages Quarterly*

**2601  Focus on Exceptional Children**
Love Publishing Company
9101 East Kenyon Avenue
Suite 2200
Denver, CO  80237                   303-221-7333
                          FAX: 303-221-7444
            e-mail: lpc@lovepublishing.com
                 www.lovepublishing.com

*Scott Thomas, Manager*
*Stan Love, Owner*

Contains research and theory-based articles on special education topics, with an emphasis on application and intervention, of interest to teachers, professors and administrators. *$36.00*
                   *Monthly 1969*

**2602  HomeCare Magazine**
Trimedia Publications
Stuart Ranch Road
Malibu, CA  90265                   866-212-1154
                                     800-543-4116
                          FAX: 402-505-7173
            e-mail: kcavallo@interec.com
                 www.homecaremag.com

*Stacy Branning, Publisher*

The business magazine of the home medical equipment industry offering information on legislation and regulations affecting the homecare industry, monthly profiles of suppliers, operational tips, newest products in the industry, advice on sales, government regulations. *$ 65.00*
*120 pages Monthly*

### 2603 Horizons

Haras & Trebor
PO Box 985
Gambrills, MD 21054

301-621-9332
FAX: 410-767-5850
TTY:301-621-9332
e-mail: storrsjh@aol.com

*James Storrs, Publisher*

Monthly newspaper for people with disabilities serving Maryland, Virginia, and Washington DC *$17.00*
*20 pages Monthly*
*ISSN 1064-64 4*

### 2604 I Wonder Who Else Can Help

AARP
601 East Street NW
Washington, DC 20049

202-434-2277
800-687-2277
FAX: 202-434-3443
e-mail: member@aarp.org
www.aarp.org

*William Novelli, Chief Executive Officer*

Contains information about crisis counseling, needs and resources, written in lay terms.

### 2605 International Rehabilitation Review

Rehabilitation International
25 East 21st Street
New York, NY 10010

212-420-1500
FAX: 212-505-0871
e-mail: rehabintal@aol.com

*Barbara Duncan, Editor*
*Kathy Marchael, Editorial Assistant*
*Tomas Lagerwall, Manager*

International overview of activities and programs in vocational and medical rehabilitation, prosthesis and orthotics and special education. *$30.00*
*TriAnnual*

### 2606 Intervention in School and Clinic

Pro-Ed Publications
8700 Shoal Creek Boulevard
Austin, TX 78757

512-451-3246
800-897-3202
FAX: 512-451-8542
e-mail: info@proedinc.com
www.proedinc.com

*Donald Hammill, Owner*

A hands-on, how-to resource for teachers and clinicians working with students for whom minor curriculum and environmental modifications are ineffective. *$35.00*
*64 pages*

### 2607 Journal for Vocational Special Needs Education

University of Wisconsin
1025 West Johnson Street
Madison, WI 53706

608-263-9250
FAX: 608-262-3050
e-mail: jgugerty@education.wisc.edu
www.cew.wisc.edu/jvsne/

*John Gugerty, Co-Editor*

Articles on vocational education for special needs population, including persons with physical and mental disabilities. *$16.00*

### 2608 Journal of Applied School Psychology

Haworth Press
10 Alice Street
Binghamton, NY 13904

607-722-5857
800-429-6784
FAX: 607-722-6362
e-mail: orders@haworthpress.com
www.haworthpress.com

*Charles Maher, Editor*
*Roger Hall, Director*
*William Cohen, Owner*

This journal disseminates the latest and the highest quality information to all professionals who provide special services in the schools and related educational settings. *$60.00*
*BiAnnually*

### 2609 Journal of Counseling & Development

American Counseling Association
5999 Stevenson Avenue
Alexandria, VA 22304

703-823-9800
800-633-4931
FAX: 703-823-8052
www.counseling.org

*A Scott McGowan, Editor*
*Carolyn Baker, Publications Director*
*Richard Yep, Executive Director*

Publishes archival material, also publishes articles that have broad interest for a readership composed mostly of counselors and other mental health professionals who work in private practice, schools, colleges, community agencies, hospitals, and government. An appropriate outlet for articles that: critcally intergrate published research; examine current professional and scientific issues; report research, new techniques, innovatetive programs and practices; and examine ACA as an organization. *$140.00*
*128 pages Quarterly*

### 2610 Journal of Emotional and Behavioral Disorders

Pro-Ed Publications
8700 Shoal Creek Boulevard
Austin, TX 78757

512-451-3246
800-897-3202
FAX: 800-397-7633
e-mail: feedback@proedinc.com
www.proedinc.com

*Donald Hammill, Owner*
*Courtney King, Marketing Coordinator*

An international, multidisciplinary journal featuring articles on research, practice and theory related to individuals with emotional and behavioral disorders and to the professionals who serve them. *$39.00*
*64 pages Quarterly*

### 2611 Journal of Learning Disabilities

Pro-Ed
8700 Shoal Creek Boulevard
Austin, TX 78757

512-451-3246
800-897-3202
FAX: 800-397-7633
e-mail: feedback@proedinc.com
www.proedinc.com

*Joshua Jeffrey, Marketing Custodian*
*Courtney King, Marketing Coordinator*
*Donald Hammill, Owner*

An international, multidisciplinary publication containing articles on practice, research and theory related to learning disabilities. Published bi-monthly. *$49.00*

*Magazine*

**2612  Journal of Motor Behavior**
Heldref Publications
1319 18th Street NW
Washington, DC  20036                     202-296-6267
                                          800-365-9753
                                    FAX: 202-293-6130
                          e-mail: subscribe@heldref.org
                                          www.heldref.org

*Emilli Pawlowsky, Marketing Manager*
*Laura Rosse, Assistant Marketing Manager*
*Douglas Kirkpatrick, Publisher*

A professional journal aimed at psychologists, therapists and educators who work in the areas of motor behavior, psychology, neurophysiology, kinesiology, and biomechanics. Offers up-to-date information on the latest techniques, theories and developments concerning motor control. *$77.00*
*115 pages Quarterly 1969*

**2613  Journal of Musculoskeletal Pain**
Haworth Press
10 Alice Street
Binghamton, NY  13904                     607-722-5857
                                          800-429-6784
                                    FAX: 607-722-6362
                      e-mail: orders@haworthpress.com
                                   www.haworthpress.com

*Sandy Sickels, Vice President*
*Becky Minerbaum, Advertising Manager*
*S Harrington-Miller, Advertising*

This journal serves as a central resource for the dissemination of information about musculoskeletal pain. *$75.00*
*110 pages Quarterly*

**2614  Journal of Postsecondary Education & Disability**
AHEAD
PO Box 540666
Waltham, MA  02454                        781-788-0003
                                    FAX: 781-788-0033
                                    TTY:617-287-3882
                              e-mail: ahead@ahead.org
                                          www.ahead.org

*Jim Kessler, President*
*Stephan J Smith, Executive Director*

Provides in-depth examination of research, issues, policies and programs in postsecondary education.

**2615  Journal of Prosthetics and Orthotics**
330 John Carlyle Street
Suite 210
Alexandria, VA  22314                     703-836-7116
                                    FAX: 703-836-0838
                               e-mail: info@abcop.org
                                          www.abcop.org

*William Detoro, President*
*Stephen Fletcher, Secretary Treasurer*
*Tyler Wilson, Executive Director*

Provides the latest research and clinical thinking in orthotics and prosthetics, including information on new devices, fitting techniques and patient management experiences. Each issue contains research-based information and articles reviewed and approved by a highly qualified editorial board. *$60.00*
*64 pages Quarterly*
*ISSN 1040-88 0*

**2616  Journal of Reading, Writing and Learning Disabled International**
Hemisphere Publishing Corporation
1900 Frost Road
Suite 101
Bristol, PA  19007                        215-785-5800
                                    FAX: 215-785-6616
Articles on reading, writing and learning disabilities, including mainstreaming issues. *$9.00*

**2617  Journal of School Health Association**
PO Box 708
Kent, OH  44240                           330-678-1601
                                    FAX: 330-678-4526
                              e-mail: asha@ashaweb.org
                                          www.ashaweb.org

*Susan Wooley, Executive Director*
*Thomas Reed, Manager*

This is a monthly journal which offers information to professionals and parents on school health. Membership dues, $95.00.

**2618  Journal of Special Education**
Pro-Ed
8700 Shoal Creek Boulevard
Austin, TX  78757                         512-451-3246
                                          800-897-3202
                                    FAX: 800-397-7633
                         e-mail: feedback@proedinc.com
                                          www.proedinc.com

*Donald Hammill, Owner*
*Courtney King, Marketing Coordinator*

Internationally known as the prime research journal in special education. JSE provides research articles of special education for individuals with disabilities, ranging from mild to severe. Published quarterly. *$39.00*
*Magazine*

**2619  Journal of Vocational Behavior**
Academic Press, Journals Division
525 B Street
Suite 1900
San Diego, CA  92101                      619-231-0926
                                    FAX: 619-231-0928
                              www.academicpress.com/jvb

*Jasna Markovac, Vice President*

The Journal of Vocational Behavior publishes empirical and theoretical articles that expand knowledge of vocational behavior and career development across the life span. Research presented in the journal encompasses the general categories of career choice, implementation, and vocational adjustment and adaptation. The articles are also valuable for applications in counseling and career development programs in colleges and universities, business and industry, government, and the military. *$7.00*

**2620  MDA Newsmagazine**
Muscular Dystrophy Association
3275 West Ina Road
Suite 155
Tucson, AZ  85741                         520-795-3434
                                    FAX: 520-795-3989
                       e-mail: tusconservices@mdausa.org

*Kelly Larkin, Executive Director*

Presents news related to muscular dystrophy and other neuromuscular diseases including research, personal profiles, fundraising activities and patient services.

**2621  Measurement and Evaluation in Counseling and Development**
American Association for Counseling & Development
5999 Stevenson Avenue
Alexandria, VA  22304                     800-347-6647
                                          800-473-2329
                                    FAX: 703-823-6862
                                          www.counseling.org

*William D Schafer, Editor*

Journal with professional articles on testing and evaluation. *$23.00*

*Quarterly*

**2622 Our World**
National Center for Learning Disabilities
381 Park Avenue S
Room 1401
New York, NY 10016
212-545-7510
800-575-7373
888-575-7373
FAX: 212-545-9665
e-mail: help@ncld.org
www.ld.org

*James H Wendorf, Executive Director*
*Marica Griffith, Marketing Executive*

Contains features, articles, human interest news and information and information, and other practical material to benefit the
millions of children and adults with learning disabilities and
their families, as well as educators and other helping professionals. Magazine.
*Quarterly*

**2623 Psychiatric Staffing Crisis in Community Mental Health**

Nat l Council for Community Behavioral Healthcare
12300 Twinbrook Parkway
Suite 320
Rockville, MD 20852
301-984-6200
FAX: 301-881-7159
www.nccbh.org

*Dale Klatszaer, Board Chair*
*Linda Rosenberg, Chief Executive Officer*

Find out some of the simple, low-cost ways you can increase
workplace satisfaction among staff psychiatrists and compete
successfully for their talents. *$20.00*

**2624 Readings: A Journal of Reviews and Commentary in
Mental Health**
American Orthopsychiatric Association
PO Box 110
Tempe, AZ 85280
480-727-7518
FAX: 480-727-7518
e-mail: americanortho@asu.edu
www.americanortho.com

*Gary Melton, President*
*Rosario Ceballo, Director*

Reviews of recent books in mental health and allied disciplines.
Includes essay reviews and brief reviews. *$25.00*
*32 pages Quarterly*

**2625 Rehab Pro**
3540 Soquel Avenue
Suite A
Santa Cruz, CA 95062
831-464-4892
800-240-9059
FAX: 831-576-1417
e-mail: glenn@btfenterprises.com
www.rehabpro.org

*Glenn Zimmerman, Executive Director*
*Alan Gale, Executive Manager*

The magazine is to promote the profession and to inform the public about the activities of the national organization, its state
chapter affiliates, and the work of its special interest sections.
*38 pages BiMonthly*

**2626 Remedial and Special Education**
Pro-Ed Publications
8700 Shoal Creek Boulevard
Austin, TX 78757
512-451-3246
800-897-3202
FAX: 800-397-7633
e-mail: feedback@proedinc.com
www.proedinc.com

*Donald Hammill, Owner*
*Courtney King, Marketing Coordinator*

A professional journal that bridges the gap between theory and
practice. Emphasis is on topical reviews, syntheses of research,
field evaluation studies and recommendations for the practice of
remedial and special education. Published six times a year.
*$39.00*
*64 pages*

**2627 Teaching Exceptional Children**
Council for Exceptional Children
1110 North Glebe Road
Suite 300
Arlington, VA 22201
703-245-0600
FAX: 703-264-9494
www.cec.sped.org

*Janice Burdick, President*
*Bruce Ramirez, Manager*

Journal designed for teachers of gifted students and students
with disabilities, featuring practical methods and materials for
classroom use. *$58.00*
*96 pages BiMonthly*

**2628 Topics in Language Disorders**
Aspen Publishers
200 Orchard Ridge Drive
Gaithersburg, MD 20878
301-698-7100
800-234-1660
FAX: 301-695-7931
www.aspenpublishers.com

*Jack Bruggeman, Publisher*

Peer review journal for professionals in the field of language
disorders. Published quarterly. *$86.00*
*104 pages*

# Newsletters

**2629 Alert**
Association on Handicapped Student Service Program
PO Box 21192
Columbus, OH 43221
614-365-5216
FAX: 614-365-6718

Keeps members informed about Association activities, current
legislative issues, innovative programs, and more. *$30.00*

**2630 Camp Virginia Jaycee Newsletter**
Dare Care Charity
2494 Camp Jaycee Road
Blue Ridge, VA 24064
540-947-2972
800-865-0092
FAX: 540-947-2043
e-mail: ewerness@campvirginiajaycee.com
www.campvirginiajaycee.com

*Everett M Werness, President*
*Cindy Rinker, Camp Director*

Summer camping for children and adults with developmental
disabilities. Coed, ages 7-70. Weekend respite camps for children and adults with mental retardation.
*8 pages quarterly*

**2631 Counseling Today**
American Counseling Association
5999 Stevenson Avenue
Alexandria, VA 22304
703-823-9800
800-473-2329
FAX: 703-823-0252
www.counseling.org

*Richard Yep, Executive Director*
*Jonathan Rollins, Editor*

Aims to serve individuals active in porfessional counseling, in
the school and university, in the workplace and the marketplace,
as well as other citizens, community leaders and policy makers
who appreciate the importance of the role of professional counselors in today's society.

*Monthly*

**2632**   **Counselor Education and Supervision**
American Counseling Association
5999 Stevenson Avenue
Alexandria, VA  22304                            703-823-9800
                                            FAX: 800-473-2329
                    e-mail: webmaster@counseling.org
                                            www.counseling.org

*Margaret L Fong, Editor*
*Richard Yep, Executive Director*

Dedicated to the growth and development of the counseling profession and those who are served. *$18.00*
                    *Quarterly*

**2633**   **Counterpoint**
National Association of State Directors of Special
10860 Hampton Road
Fairfax Station, VA  22039                       703-519-3800
                                            FAX: 703-503-8627
Newspaper designed for teachers of disabled and gifted students, featuring practical methods and materials for classroom use. *$36.00*
                    *Quarterly*

**2634**   **Disability Compliance for Higher Education**
LRP Publications
PO Box 24668
West Palm Beach, FL  33416                       561-622-6520
                                                 800-341-7874
                                            FAX: 215-784-9639
                    e-mail: custserve@lrp.com
                                            www.lrp.com

*Kenneth Kahn, Chief Executive Officer*
*Jim Nartini, Vice President*

The only newsletter that is dedicated to the exclusive coverage of disability issues that affect colleges and universities. *$195.00*
                    *8 pages Monthly*

**2635**   **Disability Resources Monthly**
Disability Resources
4 Glatter Lane
South Setauket, NY  11720                        631-585-0290
                                            FAX: 631-585-0290
                    e-mail: pubs@disabilityresources.org
                                    www.disabilityresources.org

*Avery Klauber, Director*

A newsletter that monitors, reviews and reports on resources for independent living. A monthly newsletter that features short topical articles, news items and reviews of books, pamphlets, periodicals, videotapes, on-line services, organizations and other resources for and about people with disabilities. It is intended primarily for librarians, social workers, educators, rehabilitation specialists, disability advocates, ADA coordinators and other health and social service professionals. *$33.00*
                    *4 pages Monthly 1993*
                    *ISSN 1070-72 0*

**2636**   **Early Childhood Reporter**
LRP Publications
747 Dresher Road
Horsham, PA  19044                               215-784-0912
                                                 800-341-7874
                                            FAX: 215-784-9014
                    e-mail: custserve@lrp.com
                                            www.lrp.com

*Kenneth Kahn, Founder/President*

Monthly reports with information on federal, state, and local legislation affecting the implementation of early intervention and preschool programs for children with disabilities. *$145.00*

*12-16 pages $10 shipping*

**2637**   **Fact Sheets**
University of NH: Institute on Disability
10 W West H Drive
Suite 101
Durham, NH  03824                                603-862-4320
                                            FAX: 603-862-0555
                    e-mail: institutedisability@unh.edu
                                            www.iod.unh.edu

*Jan Nisbet, Executive Director*

The Institute on Disability provides information to family consumers, community personnel and professionals through books articles, videos, newsletters, internet and press coverage, including TV, radio and consumers forums.

**2638**   **Healthline**
CV Mosby Company
11830 Westline Industrial Drive
Saint Louis, MO  63146                           314-872-8370
                                                 800-325-4177
                                            FAX: 314-432-1380
                    e-mail: journal.service@mosby.com
                                            www.mosby.com

*Paul Insel, Editor*

Health and fitness information for healthcare professionals and the general public alike.
                    *Monthly*

**2639**   **Help Newsletter**
Learning Disabilities Association of Arkansas
7509 Cantrell Road
Suite 103c
Little Rock, AR  72207                           501-666-8777
                                            FAX: 501-666-8777
                    e-mail: info@ldaarkansas.org
                                            www.ldaarkansas.org

*Dana Jackson, Executive Director*
*Kristen Joyner, Director Development*

Information on how to overcome obstacles and to achieve in spite of learning disabilities. *$30.00*
                    *8 pages Quarterly*

**2640**   **International Rolf Institute**
5055 Chaparral Court
Suite 103
Boulder, CO  80301                               303-449-5903
                                                 800-530-8875
                                            FAX: 503-444-5978
                                            www.rolf.org

Information, practitioner training and certification.

**2641**   **Learning Disabilities Consultants Newsletter**
Learning Disabilities Consultants
PO Box 716
Bryn Mawr, PA  19010                             610-668-2225
                                                 800-869-8336
                                            FAX: 610-446-6129

*Richard Cooper, Director*
*Lawrence Singer, Owner*

Newsletter providing information about learning disabilities and differences. It contains both local and national news items and includes in each issue articles about various aspects of learning problems encountered in both children and adults. *$10.00*
                    *6 pages 5x Year*

**2642**   **MA Report**
National Allergy and Asthma Network
3554 Chain Bridge Road
Suite 200
Fairfax, VA  22030                               703-385-4403
                                            FAX: 703-352-4354

Offers information on medical breakthroughs, patient care, public awareness, activities and events focusing on the allergy and asthma patient. This newsletter is the only Monthly Asthma Report that a patient will need to keep fully informed with medical articles written by experts in the field.
*Monthly*

**2643 NYALD News**
New York Association for the Learning Disabled
90 South Swan Street
Albany, NY 12210                                 518-465-6115

*Kelly Jarrard, Executive Director*
*Michael Vacek, Manager*

Newsletter offering information on the learning disabled in the New York area.
*Monthly*

**2644 National Institute of Dental and Craniofac ial Research**
National Oral Health Information Clearinghouse
1 NOHIC Way
Bethesda, MD 20892                              301-402-7364
                                          FAX: 301-480-4098
                              e-mail: niderinfo@mail.nih.gov
                                            www.nider.nih.gov

*Julianna Harris, Senior Information Specialist*

Professional/consumer fact sheets, brochures, information packets and reports.

**2645 O&P Almanac**
American Orthotic & Prosthetic Association
1666 K Street NW
Suite 440
Washington, DC 20006                           571-431-0876
                                          FAX: 571-431-0899
                                 e-mail: info@aopanet.org
                                            www.aopanet.org

*Lisa Gough, Editor-in-Chief*
*Carrie Parsons, Managing Editor*

Offers in-depth coverage on orthotics and prosthetics to current professional, government, business and reimbursement activities affecting the orthotics and prosthetics industry. *$59.00*
*80 pages Monthly*

**2646 Occupational Therapy in Health Care**
Haworth Press
10 Alice Street
Binghamton, NY 13904                           607-722-5857
                                               800-429-6784
                                          FAX: 607-771-0021
                          e-mail: getinfo@haworthpress.com
                                         www.haworthpress.com

*Bill Palmer, VP/Publications Director*
*Rebecca Browne, Administrative Manager*
*William Cohen, Owner*

Each issue focuses on significant practices and concerns involving occupational therapy and therapists. *$75.00*

**2647 Ohio Coalition for the Education of Children with Disabilities**
165 West Center Street
Suite 302
Marion, OH 43302                               740-382-5452
                                               800-374-2806
                                          FAX: 740-383-6421
                                    e-mail: ocecd@gte.net
                                               www.ocecd.org

*Margret Burley, Executive Director*
*Lee Ann Derugen, Co-Director*
*Martha Lause, Librarian*

Forum is a newsletter reporting on educational, legislative and other developments affecting persons with disabilities.

*8 pages*

**2648 SAMHSA News**
U S Department of Health and Human Services
200 Independence Avenue SW
Washington, DC 20201                           202-690-7650
                                               877-696-6775
                                            www.samhsa.gov

*Mark Weber, Associate Administrator*
*Deborah Goodmad, Public Affairs Specialist*

This quarterly agency newsletter reports on information on substance abuse, mental health treatment and prevention programs of the Substance Abuse and Mental Health Services Administration.
*Quarterly*

**2649 Sibling Information Network Newsletter**
AJ Pappanikou Center
253 Farmington Avenue
Suite 262
Farmington, CT 06030                           860-679-1500
                                               866-623-1315
                                          FAX: 860-679-1571
                                          www.uconnucedd.org

*Mary Beth Bruder, Director*

Contains information aimed at the varying interested of our membership. Program descriptions, requests for assistance, conference announcements, literature summaries and research reports. *$8.50*

**2650 Sibpage**
AJ Pappanikou Center
263 Farmington Avenue
Suite 262
Farmington, CT 06030                           860-679-1500
                                               866-623-1315
                                          FAX: 860-679-1571
                                          www.uconnucedd.org

*Mary Beth Bruder, Director*
*Jill Cotter, Instructor*

Developed specifically for children containing games, recipes, pen pals, and articles written by siblings relating to developmental disabilities.
*4 pages*

**2651 Sower**
Beatrice State Development Center
3000 Lincoln Boulevard
Beatrice, NE 68310                             402-223-6002
                                          FAX: 402-223-6073

Current programs, objectives and goals, needs and actual happenings at the institution.
*12 pages*

**2652 Special Edge**
Resources in Special Education
1107 9th Street
4th Floor
Sacramento, CA 95814                           916-492-9990
                                               877-493-7833
                                          FAX: 415-565-3012
                                    e-mail: rise@wested.org

Provides education news, collaborative programs, amendments to the laws, tools for accommodations, resource information, a calendar of events, and more.
*BiMonthly*

**2653 Special Education Report**
LRP Publications
1901 North Moore Street
Suite 1106
Arlington, VA 22209                            703-516-7002
                                          FAX: 703-516-9313
                                               www.lrp.com

*Patrick Harden, Manager*

Current, pertinent information about federal legislation, regulations, programs and funding for educating children with disabilities. Covers federal and state litigation on the Individuals with Disabilities Education Act and other relevant laws. Looks at innovations and research in the field. *$266.00*
*8 pages BiWeekly*
*ISSN 0194-22 5*

**2654 Topics in Early Childhood Special Education**
Pro-Ed Publication
8700 Shoal Creek Boulevard
Austin, TX 78757
512-451-3246
800-897-3202
FAX: 800-397-7633
e-mail: info@proedinc.com
www.proedinc.com

*Donald Hammill, Owner*
*Courtney King, Marketing Coordinator*

Designed for professionals helping young children with special needs in areas such as assessment, special programs, social policies and developmental aids. *$43.00*
*Quarterly*

**2655 Treatment Review**
AIDS Treatment Data Network
611 Broadway
Room 613
New York, NY 10012
212-253-7922
800-734-7104
FAX: 212-260-8869
e-mail: network@atdn.org
www.atdn.org

*Mark Harrington, Executive Director*
*Max Setulveda, Financing Manager*

Individual members recieve treatment education, counseling, referrals and case management support. Services are available in both English and Spanish. The Treatment Review newsletter includes descriptions of approved, alternative and experimental treatments, as well as announcements of seminars and forums on treatments and clinical trials.
*Quarterly*

**2656 VIP Newsletter**
311 W Broadway St
Suite 1
Mt Pleasant, MI 48858
989-779-9966
FAX: 989-779-0015
e-mail: bcf@blindchildrensfund.org
www.blindchildrensfund.org

*Blind Children's Fund, author*
*Karla Storrer, Executive Director*
*Didi Duncan, Outreach Director*

Provides parents and professionals with information, materials and resources that help them succesfullly teach and nurture blind, visually and multi-impaired infants and preschoolers. *$10.00*
194

## Professional Texts

**2657 A Teacher's Guide to HCU**
Arizona Department of Health Services
150 North 18th Avenue
Suite 310
Phoenix, AZ 85007
602-271-0945
FAX: 602-542-1235
e-mail: piowebmaster@azdhs.gov
www.azdhs.gov

*Susan Gerard, Director*
*Robert Plummer, Manager*

Resource book for preschool teachers and school staff on homocysteinuria basics and classroom activities. *$2.50*

**2658 A Teacher's Guide to Isovaleric Acidemia**
150 North 18th Avenue
Phoenix, AZ 85007
602-542-1000
FAX: 602-542-0883
www.azdhs.gov

*Susan Gered, Director*

Resource book for preschool teachers and school staff on isovaleric acidemia basics and classroom activities. *$2.50*

**2659 A Teacher's Guide to MSUD**
Arizona Department of Health Services
1740 West Adams Street
Phoenix, AZ 85007
602-271-0945
FAX: 602-542-1235
e-mail: piowebmaster@azdhs.gov
www.azdhs.gov

*Susan Gerard, Director*
*Susan Gerard, Director*

Resource book for preschool teachers and school staff on MSUD basics and classroom activities. *$2.50*

**2660 A Teacher's Guide to Methylmalonic Acidemia**
Arizona State Department of Health Services
1740 West Adams Street
Phoenix, AZ 85007
602-542-1073
FAX: 602-542-1235
e-mail: piowebmaster@azdhs.gov
www.azdhs.gov

*Susan Gerard, Director*

Resource book for preschool teachers and school staff on methylmalonic acidemia basics and classroom activities. *$2.50*

**2661 A Teacher's Guide to PKU**
Arizona Department of Health Services
1740 West Adams Street
Phoenix, AZ 85007
602-542-1886
FAX: 602-542-1890
e-mail: piowebmaster@azdhs.gov
www.azdhs.gov

*Susan Gerard, Director*
*Margaret Tate, Manager*

Resource book for preschool teachers and school staff on PKU basics, NutraSweet warning, and classroom activities. *$2.50*
*13 pages*

**2662 A Teacher's Guide to Propionic Acidemia**
Arizona Department of Health Services
1740 West Adams Street
Phoenix, AZ 85007
602-271-0945
FAX: 602-542-1235
e-mail: piowebmaster@azdhs.gov
www.azdhs.gov

*Susan Gerard, Director*
*Robert Plummer, Manager*

Resource book for preschool teachers and school staff on propionic acidemia basics and classroom activities. *$2.50*

**2663 ADD Challenge: A Practical Guide for Teachers**
Research Press
PO Box 9177
Champaign, IL 61826
217-352-3273
800-519-2707
FAX: 217-352-1221
e-mail: rp@researchpress.com
www.researchpress.com

*Russell Tence, President*
*$15.95*

*196 pages*
*ISBN 0-878223-45-2*

**2664 ADHD in the Classroom: Strategies for Teachers**
Guilford Publication
72 Spring Street
New York, NY 10012
212-431-9800
800-365-7006
FAX: 212-966-6708
e-mail: info@guilford.com

*Bob Matloff, President*

Designed specifically to help teachers with their ADHD students, thereby providing a better learning environment for the entire class. *$95.00*

*ISBN 0-898629-85-3*

**2665 ADHD in the Schools: Assessment and Intervention Strategies**
72 Spring Street
New York, NY 10012
212-431-9800
800-365-7006
FAX: 212-966-6708
e-mail: info@guilford.com
www.guilford.com

*Seymour Weingarten, Editor-in-Chief*
*Judith Grauman, Managing Editor*
*Bob Matloff, President*

The landmark volume emphasizes the need for a team effort among parents, community-based professionals, and educators. Provides practical information for educators that is based on empirical findings. Chapters Focus on how to identify and assess students who might have ADHD, the relationship between ADHD and learning disabilities; how to develop and supplement classroom-based programs. Communication strategies to assist physicians and the need for community-based treatments *$36.00*

*269 pages Paperback*
*ISBN 0-898622-45-X*

**2666 AEPS Curriculum for Birth to Three Years**
Brookes Publishing
PO Box 10624
Baltimore, MD 21285
410-337-9580
800-638-3775
FAX: 410-337-8539
e-mail: custserv@brookespublishing.com
www.brookespublishing.com

*Paul Brooks, Owner*

Directly linked to IEP/IFSP goals developed for a child from the AEPS test measure, the AEPS curriculum provides a complete set of learning activities to facilitate children's acquisition of functional skills. *$59.95*
*496 pages*
*ISBN 1-557660-96-4*

**2667 Access to Health Care: Number 1&2**
World Institute on Disability
510 16th Street
Suite 100
Oakland, CA 94612
510-763-4100
510-209-9493
FAX: 510-763-4109
e-mail: wid@wid.org
www.wid.org

*Stanley K Yarnell, Chairman*
*Martin B Schulter, Vice Chairman*

These health policy bulletins analyze health care needs. Volume 1 focuses on a wide range of information relevant to addressing the adequacy of the health care system for persons with disabilities or chronic illness. *$6.50*

*63 pages Paperback*

**2668 Access to Health Care: Number 3&4**
World Institute on Disability
510 16th Street
Suite 100
Oakland, CA 94612
510-763-4100
FAX: 510-763-4109
e-mail: wid@wid.org
www.wid.org

*Stanley K Yarnell, Chairman*
*Martin B Schulter, Vice Chairman*

These policy bulletins focus on the capacity of the private and public health insurance systems to respond to the health care needs of persons with disabilities or chronic illness. *$6.50*
*91 pages Paperback*

**2669 Activity-Based Approach to Early Intervention, 2nd Edition**
Brookes Publishing
PO Box 10624
Baltimore, MD 21285
410-337-9580
800-638-3775
FAX: 410-337-8539
e-mail: custserv@brookespublishing.com
www.brookespublishing.com

*Clary Creighton, Exhibits Coordinator*
*Tracy Gray, Educational Sales Manager*
*Paul Brooks, Owner*

Activity-based intervention shows how to use natural and relevant events to teach infants and young children, of all abilities, effectively and efficiently. *$24.00*
*240 pages*
*ISBN 1-55766 -87-5*

**2670 Adapted Physical Education for Students with Autism**
Charles C Thomas Publisher
2600 South 1st Street
Springfield, IL 62704
217-789-8980
800-258-8980
FAX: 217-789-9130
e-mail: books@ccthomas.com
www.ccthomas.com

*Michael Thomas, President*

Focuses on the physical education needs and curriculum for autistic children. Available in cloth, paperback and hardcover. *$23.95*
*142 pages Paper*
*ISBN 0-398060-85-1*

**2671 Adapting Early Childhood Curricula for Children with Special Needs**
McGraw-Hill School Publishing
220 East Danieldale Road
Desoto, TX 75115
972-224-1111
800-442-9685
FAX: 972-228-1982
www.mhschool.com

*Joseph Gavigan, President*

Offers information on educating the disabled.

**2672 Adapting Instruction for the Mainstream: A Sequential Approach to Teaching**
McGraw-Hill School Publishing
220 East Danieldale Road
Desoto, TX 75115
972-224-1111
800-442-9685
FAX: 972-228-1982
www.mcgrawhill.com

*Joseph Gavigan, President.*
*Todd Painter, Assistant Director*

This text gives both regular and special education teachers everything they need to help mildly handicapped students succeed in the mainstream.

*226 pages*

**2673  Adaptive Education Strategies Building on Diversity**
Brookes Publishing Company
PO Box 10624
Baltimore, MD  21285                          410-337-9580
                                             800-638-3775
                                        FAX: 410-337-8539
        e-mail: custserv@brookespublishing.com
                www.brookespublishing.com

*Tracy Gray, Educational Sales Manager*
*Paul Brooks, Owner*

Based on more than two decades of systematic research, this comprehensive manual provides a road map to the effective implementation of adaptive education. *$35.00*
        *304 pages Paperback 1992*
        *ISBN 1-557880-84-0*

**2674  Advanced Sign Language Vocabulary: A Resource Text for Educators**
Charles C Thomas Publisher
2600 South 1st Street
Springfield, IL  62704                         217-789-8980
                                              800-258-8980
                                         FAX: 217-789-9130
                e-mail: books@ccthomas.com
                        www.ccthomas.com

*Janice Ahmad, Author*
*Edward Allen, Author*
*Michael Thomas, President*

This book is a collection of advanced sign language vocabulary for use by educators, interpreters, parents or anyone wishing to enlarge their sign vocabulary. *$48.95*
        *202 pages Paperback 1991*
        *ISBN 0-398057-22-2*

**2675  Advances in Cardiac and Pulmonary Rehabilitation**
Haworth Press
10 Alice Street
Binghamton, NY  13904                          607-722-5857
                                              800-429-6784
                                         FAX: 607-722-6362
        e-mail: orders@haworthpress.com
                www.haworthpress.com

*Sandy Sickels, Vice President*
*Becky Minerbaum, Advertising Manager*
*William Cohen, Owner*

Enhance your rehabilitation program with this authoritative volume. *$34.95*
        *74 pages Hardcover*
        *ISBN 0-866869-86-3*

**2676  Aging Brain**
Taylor & Francis Group
325 Chestnut Street
Suite 800
Philadelphia, PA  19106                        215-625-8900
                                              800-354-1420
                                         FAX: 215-625-8914
                www.taylorandfrancisgroup.com

*Kevin Bradley, Chief Executive Officer*
Elderly treatment.

*225 pages Paperback*
*ISBN 0-85066 -78-0*

**2677  Aging and Rehabilitation II**
Springer Publishing Company
11 West 42nd Street
15th Floor
New York, NY  10036                            212-431-4370
                                              877-687-7476
                                         FAX: 212-941-7842
        e-mail: Contactus@springerpub.com
                www.springerpub.com

*Sheri Sussman, Vice President*
*Anette Imperati, Marketing/Sales Director*
*Ursula Springer, President*

Current, multidisciplinary investigations of various practice issues. Leading experts in the field use a practical perspective to provide specific comments on interventions. The scope of this work encompasses the autonomy of elderly disabled, mobility, mental health and value issues, as well as basic aspects in rehabilitation of the elderly. *$41.95*
        *367 pages Hardcover*
        *ISBN 0-82617 -80-3*

**2678  Alphabetic Phonics Curriculum**
Educators Publishing Service
625 Mount Auburn Street
Suite 3
Cambridge, MA  02138                           617-547-6706
                                              800-225-5750
                                         FAX: 888-440-2665
        e-mail: feedback@epsbooks.com
                www.epsbooks.com

*Charles H Heinle, Vice President*
*Alexandra S Bigelow, Author*
*Gunnar Voltz, President*

Ungraded multisensory curriculum for teaching phonics and the structure of language. Uses Orton-Gillingham approach to teach handwriting, spelling, reading, reading comprehension, and oral and written expression. program includes basic manual, workbooks, tests, teachers' guides, drill cards and all cards. *$28.15*

        *ISSN 8388-42*

**2679  Alternative Educational Delivery Systems**
National Association of School Psychologists
4340 E West Highway
Suite 402
Bethesda, MD  20814                            301-657-0270
                                         FAX: 301-657-0275

*Susan Gorin, Executive Director*

A book offering information to the professional on how to enhance educational options for all students.

**2680  Alternative Teaching Strategies**
Special Needs Project
324 State Street
Suite H
Santa Barbara, CA  93101                       805-962-8087
                                              800-333-6867
                                         FAX: 805-962-5087
                www.specialneeds.com

*Hod Gray, Founder*

Offers help for teachers who teach behaviorally troubled students.

**2681 Antecedent Control: Innovative Approaches to Behavioral Support**
Brookes Publishing
PO Box 10624
Baltimore, MD 21285              410-337-9585
800-638-3775
FAX: 410-337-8539
e-mail: custserv@brookespublishing.com
www.brookespublishing.com

*Melissa Behm, President*

This book explains the theory and methodology of antecedent control. The treatment techniques in this book are effective for both children and adults.
*416 pages Paperback 1998*
*ISBN 1-55766 -34-3*

**2682 Applied Rehabilitation Counseling**
Springer Publishing Company
11 West 42nd Street
15th Floor
New York, NY 10036             212-431-4370
877-687-7476
FAX: 212-941-7842
e-mail: contactus@springerpub.com
www.springerpub.com

*Annette Imperati, Marketing/Sales Director*
*Sheri Sussman, Vice President*
*Ursula Springer, President*

This comprehensive text describes current theories, techniques, and their applications to specific disabled populations. Perspectives on varying counseling approaches such as psychodynamic, existential, gestalt, behavioral and psychoeducational orientations are systematically outlined in an easy-to-follow format. Practical applications for counseling are emphasized with attention given to strategies, goal-setting and on-going evaluations. *$29.95*
*400 pages Softcover*
*ISBN 0-82615 -70-4*

**2683 Art-Centered Education and Therapy for Children with Disabilities**
Charles C Thomas
2600 South 1st Street
Springfield, IL 62704           217-789-8980
800-258-8980
FAX: 217-789-9130
e-mail: books@ccthomas.com
www.ccthomas.com

*Michael Thomas, President*

This book has been written to help both the regular education, and art and special education teachers, both pre- and in-service, better understand some of the issues and realities of providing education and remediation to children with disabilities. The book is also offered as model concept that has govern the author's personal and professional career of over thirty years. *$35.95*
*284 pages Paperback*
*ISBN 0-398060-06-1*

**2684 Assessing the Handicaps/Needs of Children**
Books on Special Children
PO Box 3378
Amherst, MA 01004           413-256-8164
FAX: 413-256-8896
e-mail: irene@boscbooks.com
www.boscbooks.com
Papers on treatment, rehab and social support in assessing the needs of mentally retarded children. *$66.00*

*260 pages Hardcover*
*ISBN 0-12218 -02-0*

**2685 Assessment & Management of Mainstreamed Hearing-Impaired Children**
Pro-Ed Publications
8700 Shoal Creek Boulevard
Austin, TX 78757             512-451-3246
800-897-3202
FAX: 800-397-7633
e-mail: feedback@proedinc.com
www.proedinc.com

*Donald Hammill, Owner*
*Courtney King, Marketing Coordinator*

The theoretical and practical considerations of developing appropriate programming for hearing-impaired children who are being educated in mainstream educational settings are presented in this book.

**2686 Assessment Log & Developmental Progress Charts for the Carolina Curriculum**
Brookes Publishing
PO Box 10624
Baltimore, MD 21285             410-337-9580
800-638-3775
FAX: 410-337-8539
e-mail: custserv@brookespublishing.com
www.brookespublishing.com

*Clary Creighton, Exhibits Coordinator*
*Tracy Gray, Educational Sales Manager*
*Paul Brooks, Owner*

This 28-page booklet allows the progress of children with skills in the 12-36 month development range to be easily recorded. Available in packages of 10. *$23.00*
*28 pages Saddle-stiched*
*ISBN 1-557662-21-5*

**2687 Assessment and Remediation of Articulatory and Phonological Disorders**
McGraw-Hill School Publishing
220 East Danieldale Road
Desoto, TX 75115             972-224-1111
800-442-9685
FAX: 972-228-1982
www.mhschool.com

*Joseph Gavigan, President*
Offers comprehensive coverage of articulation disorders.

**2688 Assessment in Mental Handicap: A Guide to Assessment Practices & Tests**
Brookline Books
39 University Road
Brookline, MA 02445           617-734-6772
800-666-BOOK
FAX: 617-734-3952
e-mail: brooklinebks@delphi.com
www.brooklinebooks.com

*William H Walters, Author*
*Esther Isabe Wilder, Author*

Helps professionals understand the rationale and uses for assessment practices, and provides details of appropriate instruments within each type: adaptive behavior scales, assessment of behavioral disturbances, early development and Plagetian tests. *$20.00*
*Hardcover*
*ISBN 0-91479 -31-X*

**2689 Assessment of Children and Youth**
Longman Education/Addison Wesley
1185 Avenue of the Americas
New York, NY 10036           212-782-3300
800-322-1377
FAX: 800-333-3328
www.longman.awl.com

*Ginny Blanford, Editor*

Introductory text for preservice and in-service special educators on assessment, based on the principle that every child is unique. Comprehensive coverage of both formal and informal assessment instruments. *$50.00*
*640 pages Paperback*
*ISBN 0-80131-02-5*

## 2690 Assessment of Individuals with Severe Disabilities

Brookes Publishing Company
PO Box 10624
Baltimore, MD 21285

410-337-9580
800-638-3775
FAX: 410-337-8539
e-mail: custserv@brookespublishing.com
www.brookespublishing.com

*Clary Creighton, Exhibits Coordinator*
*Tracy Gray, Educational Sales Manager*
*Paul Brooks, Owner*

This expanded text offers instructors guidelines to design a comprehensive educational assessment for individuals with severe disabilities. *$34.00*
*432 pages Paperback 1991*
*ISBN 1-557660-67-0*

## 2691 Assessment of the Technology Needs of Vending Facilitiy Managers In Tennessee

Mississippi State University
PO Box 6189
Mississippi State, MS 39762

662-325-8122
800-675-7782
FAX: 662-325-8989
www.blind.msstate.edu/

*Moore, Maxson, Cavenugh, Johnson, Pearson, author*
*Kelly Schaefer, Publications Manager*
*Thomas Adkins, Executive Director*

This report summarizes the results and recommendations of a survey conducted of vending facility managers throughout the state of Tennessee who participate in the Randolph-Sheppard program. *$15.00*
*39 pages Paperback*

## 2692 Assessment: The Special Educator's Role

Brooks Publishing Company
511 Forest Lodge Road
Pacific Grove, CA 93950

831-373-0728
FAX: 831-375-6414
e-mail: bc-info@brookscole.com
www.brookespublishing.com

Aimed at students with little or no classroom experience in assessment, the book focuses on the integration of dynamic, curriculum-based and norm-referenced data for diagnostic decisions and program planning.
*580 pages Casebound*
*ISBN 0-53421-32-1*

## 2693 Asthma Management and Education

Asthma and Allergy Foundation of America
1125 15th Street NW
Suite 502
Washington, DC 20005

202-466-7643
FAX: 202-466-8940
e-mail: info@aafa.org
www.aafa.org

*Todd Houston, Director*
*Bill McLin, Executive Director*

One session, two hour program developed to educate allied health professionals about up-to-date asthma care and patient education, information and materials. Includes hands on experience with peak flow meters and demonstrations of medical devices.

## 2694 Aston-Patterning

PO Box 3568
Incline Village, NV 89450

775-831-8228
FAX: 775-831-8955
e-mail: info@astonenterprises.com
www.astonenterprises.com

*Jane Davis, Administrative Assistant*
*J Aston, Owner*

Integrated system of movement education, body assessment, environmental modification and fitness training.

## 2695 Attention Deficit Disorder in Children and Adolescents

Charles C Thomas
2600 South 1st Street
Springfield, IL 62704

217-789-8980
800-258-8980
FAX: 217-789-9130
e-mail: books@ccthomas.com
www.ccthomas.com

*Mikal Aasved, Author*
*Howard Earle, Author*
*Michael Thomas, President*

Presents an analysis of case studies of children and adolescents with attentional deficits and hyperactivity, demonstrating causal factors in these disorders and suggesting treatment strategies both in psychological and medical practice. Written as a review and summary of twenty years of private practice. *$35.95*
*292 pages Paperback*
*ISBN 0-39806-12-2*

## 2696 Aural Habilitation

Alexander Graham Bell Association
3417 Volta Place NW
Washington, DC 20007

202-337-5220
FAX: 202-337-8314
e-mail: info@agbell.org
www.agbell.org

*Gayla Hutsell, Chief Programs Officer*
*Todd Houston, Executive Director*

This classic text for professionals, educators and parents discusses verbal learning and aural habilitation of young children with hearing losses to ensure that each child is educated in the best setting. It discusses communication, normal development of spoken language, speech audiologic assessment, hearing aids and use of residual hearing, and program designs for individualized needs, including the assessment and planning of IEPs. *$26.95*
*324 pages*

## 2697 Behavior Analysis in Education: Focus on Measurably Superior Instruction

Brooks Publishing Company
PO Box 10624
Baltimore, MD 21285

410-337-9580
800-638-3775
FAX: 410-337-8539
e-mail: custserv@brookespublishing.com
www.brookespublishing.com

*Clary Creighton, Exhibits Coordinator*
*Tracy Gray, Educational Sales Manager*
*Paul Brooks, Owner*

Designed to disseminate measurably superior instructional strategies to those interested in advancing sound, pedagogically effective, field-tested educational practices, this book is intended for graduate-level courses and seminars in special education and/or psychology focusing on behavior analysis and instruction.

*512 pages Casebound*
*ISBN 0-53422 -60-9*

**2698  Behavior Modification**
Sage Publications
2455 Teller Road
Thousand Oaks, CA  91320
805-499-0721
800-818-7243
FAX: 805-499-0871
www.sagepublications.com

*Blaise R Simqu, Chief Executive Officer*
*Stephen Barr, Senior Vice President*

Describes in detail for replication purposes assessment and modification techniques for problems in psychiatric, clinical, educational and rehabilitation settings. *$53.00*
*640 pages Quarterly*

**2699  Behavior Therapy for Developmentally Disabled**
Books on Special Children
PO Box 3378
Amherst, MA  01004
413-256-8164
FAX: 413-256-8896
e-mail: irene@boscbooks.com
www.boscbooks.com
Definitions, treatments, and behavioral approaches for language deficits, visually impaired, autistic children and adults. *$47.50*
*416 pages Softcover*

**2700  Behavioral Disorders**
Council for Exceptional Children
1110 North Glebe Road
Suite 300
Arlington, VA  22201
703-245-0600
866-915-5000
FAX: 703-264-1637
e-mail: services@cec.sped.org
www.cec.sped.org

*Jamie Hopkins, President*
*Drew Allbirtten, Executive Director*
*Bruce Ramirez, Manager*

Provides professionals with a means to exchange information and share ideas related to research, empirically tested educational innovations and issues and concerns relevant to students with behavioral disorders. Individual, $20; Institution, $50.
*Quarterly*

**2701  Behind Special Education**
Love Publishing Company
9101 East Kenyon Avenue
Suite 2200
Denver, CO  80237
303-221-7333
FAX: 303-221-7444
e-mail: lpc@lovepub.com
www.lovepublishing.com

*Ann Vernon, Author*
*Stan Love, Owner*

This new work is a critical analysis of the nature of disability, special education, school organization and reform progress. *$24.95*

*ISBN 0-89108 -17-4*

**2702  Beyond Drill & Practice: Expanding the Computer Mainstream**
Council for Exceptional Children
1110 North Glebe Road
Suite 300
Arlington, VA  22201
703-245-0600
866-915-5000
FAX: 703-264-9494
e-mail: servcie@cec.sped.org
www.cec.sped.org

*Drew Allbritten, Executive Director*
*Jim Mccormick, President*
*Bruce Ramirez, Manager*

Explore the use of the computer for teaching and motivating children with disabilities and other problem learners. Let teachers use these programs and strategies that show you how it works. *$10.00*
*120 pages*

**2703  Biomedical Concerns in Persons with Down's Syndrome**
Paul H Brookes Publishing Company
PO Box 10624
Baltimore, MD  21285
410-337-9580
800-638-3775
FAX: 410-337-8539
e-mail: custserv@brookespublishing.com
www.brookespublishing.com

*Karen G Radke, Marketing Director*
*Clary Creighton, Exhibits Coordinator*
*Paul Brooks, Owner*

Written by leading authorities and spanning many disciplines and specialties, this comprehensive resource provides vital information on biomedical issues concerning individuals with Down's Syndrome. *$45.00*
*336 pages Hardcover 1992*
*ISBN 1-557660-89-1*

**2704  Breaking Barriers**
AbleNet
2008 Fairview Avenue N
Roseville, MN  55113
800-322-0956
FAX: 651-294-2259
e-mail: customerservice@ablenetinc.com
www.ablenetinc.com

*Cheryl Volkam, President/Chief Executive Office*

A practical resource for parents, caregivers, teachers and therapists. *$15.00*

**2705  Building the Healing Partnership: Parents, Professionals and Children**
Brookline Books
39 University Road
Brookline, MA  02445
617-734-6772
800-666-BOOK
FAX: 617-734-3952
e-mail: brooklinebks@delphi.com
www.brooklinebooks.com

*William H Walters, Author*
*Esther Isabe Wilder, Author*

Successful programs understand that the disabled child's needs must be considered in the context of a family. This book was specifically written for practitioner's who must work with families but who have insufficient training in family systems assessment and intervention. It is a valuable blend of theory and practice with pointers for applying the principles. *$24.95*
*Paperback*
*ISBN 0-91479 -63-8*

**2706  Career Assessment Inventories Learning Disabled**
C FK R Career Materials
11860 Kemper Road
Suite 7
Auburn, CA  95603
530-889-2357
800-525-5626
FAX: 530-889-0433
e-mail: ffrerry@cfkr.com
www.cfkr.com

*Francis Ferry, Operation Manager*

Takes personality, ability and interest into account in pointing learning disabled students of all ages toward intelligent and realistic career choices. Contains binder with paperback teaching guide plus 50 interest inventories and 50 abilities inventories. *$50.00*

**2707  Caring for Children with Chronic Illness**
11 West 42nd Street
New York, NY  10036                      212-431-4370
                                        877-687-7476
                                   FAX: 212-941-7842
e-mail: marketing@springerpub.com
                          www.springerpub.com

*Annette Imperati, Marketing/Sales Director*
*Ursula Springer, President*

A critical look at the current medical, social, and psychological framework for providing care to children with chronic illnesses. Emphasizing the need to create integrated, interdisciplinary approaches, it discusses issues such as the roles of families, professionals, and institutions in providing health care, the impact of a child's illness on various family structures, financing care, the special problems of chronically ill children as they become adolescents and more. *$36.95*
          *320 pages Hardcover*
          *ISBN 0-82615 -00-1*

**2708  Carolina Curriculum for Infants and Toddlers with Special Needs, 2nd Edition**
Brookes Publishing
PO Box 10624
Baltimore, MD  21285                     410-337-9580
                                        800-638-3775
                                   FAX: 410-337-8539
e-mail: custserv@brookespublishing.com
                       www.brookespublishing.com

*Clary Creighton, Exhibits Coordinator*
*Tracy Gray, Educational Sales Manager*
*Paul Brooks, Owner*

This book includes detailed assessment and intervention sequences, daily routine integration strategies, sensorimotor adaptations, and a sample 24-page assessment log that shows readers how to chart a child's individual progress. *$40.00*
          *384 pages Spiral-bound*
          *ISBN 1-55766 -74-3*

**2709  Carolina Curriculum for Preschoolers with Special Needs**
Brookes Publishing
PO Box 10624
Baltimore, MD  21285                     410-337-9580
                                        800-638-3775
                                   FAX: 410-337-8539
e-mail: custserv@brookespublishing.com
                       www.brookespublishing.com

*Clary Creighton, Exhibits Coordinator*
*Tracy Gray, Educational Sales Manager*
*Paul Brooks, Owner*

This curriculum provides detailed teaching and assessment techniques, plus a sample 28-page assessment log that shows readers how to chart a child's individual progress. This guide is for children between 2 and 5 in their developmental stages who are considered at risk for developmental delay or who exhibit special needs. *$34.00*
          *352 pages Spiral-bound*
          *ISBN 1-55766 -32-8*

**2710  Challenge of Educating Together Deaf and Hearing Youth: Making Manistreaming Work**
Charles C Thomas
2600 South 1st Street
Springfield, IL  62704                   217-789-8980
                                        800-258-8980
                                   FAX: 217-789-9130
e-mail: books@ccthomas.com
                           www.ccthomas.com

*Michael Thomas, President*

Those who have this challenge of education: teachers, administrators, other professionals, parents, and concerned individuals will benefit from this book. Also available in cloth. *$28.95*

          *198 pages Softcover*
          *ISBN 0-398063-91-5*

**2711  Challenged Scientists: Disabilities and the Triumph of Excellence**
Greenwood Publishing Group
88 Post Road West
Suite 5007
Westport, CT  06880                      203-226-3571
                                        800-225-5800
                                   FAX: 203-222-1502
                          www.greenwood.com

*Wayne Smith, President*

This volume points out how the increasing need for scientists in this country can be lessened by utilizing a long overlooked pool of scientific talent in those persons who are scientifically oriented but who happen to have physical or sensory disabilities. Hardcover. $49.95-$55.00.
          *208 pages*
          *ISBN 0-275938-73-5*

**2712  Child Care and the ADA: A Handbook for Inclusive Programs**
Brookes Publishing
PO Box 10624
Baltimore, MD  21285                     410-337-9580
                                        800-638-3775
                                   FAX: 410-337-8539
e-mail: custserv@brookespublishing.com
                       www.brookespublishing.com

*Clary Creighton, Exhibits Coordinator*
*Tracy Gray, Educational Sales Manager*
*Paul Brooks, Owner*

This book is designed for educators and administrators in child care settings. It offers a straightforward discussion of the Americans with Disabilities Act including children with disabilities in community programs. *$25.95*
          *240 pages Paperback*
          *ISBN 1-55766 -85-5*

**2713  Child with Disabling Illness**
Lippincott, Williams & Wilkins
227 East Washington Square
Philadelphia, PA  19106                  215-521-8300
                                        800-777-2295
                                   FAX: 301-824-7390
                                www.lpub.com

*J Lippincott, Chief Executive Officer*

*$108.50*
          *700 pages*

**2714  Childhood Behavior Disorders: Applied Research & Educational Practice**
Pro-Ed Publications
8700 Shoal Creek Boulevard
Austin, TX  78757                        512-451-3246
                                        800-897-3202
                                   FAX: 800-397-7633
e-mail: feedback@proedinc.com
                             www.proedinc.com

*Donald Hammill, Owner*
*Courtney King, Marketing Coordinator*

The only comprehensive overview of childhood behavior disorders. This book gives you the how and why for helping children with behavior disorders.

# Education /Professional Texts

**2715 Childhood Disablity and Family Systems**
Haworth Press
10 Alice Street
Binghamton, NY 13904          607-722-5857
                              800-429-6784
                         FAX: 607-722-6362
            e-mail: orders@haworthpress.com
                      www.haworthpress.com

*William Cohen, President/Owner*
*Maevin B Sussman PhD, Co-Editor*
*S Harrington-Miller, Advertising*

Focuses on what the presence of a disabled child means to a family. Those professionals involved in teaching, research, and direct care with families having disabled children will value the coverage of such topics as the contemporary context of disability, ethical issues, family effects, and care systems. *$74.95*
            *246 pages Hardcover*
            *ISBN 0-866566-71-6*

**2716 Children and Youth Assisted by Medical Technology in Educational Settings, 2nd Edition**
Brookes Publishing
PO Box 10624
Baltimore, MD 21285          410-337-9580
                              800-638-3775
                         FAX: 410-337-8539
        e-mail: custserv@brookespublishing.com
                    www.brookespublishing.com

*Clary Creighton, Exhibits Coordinator*
*Tracy Gray, Educational Sales Manager*
*Paul Brooks, Owner*

Contains detailed daily care guidelines and emergency-response techniques, including information on working with a range of students who have the HIV infection, that rely on ventilators, that utilize tube feeding, or require catheterization. Also covers every aspect of planning for inclusive classrooms, including information on personnel training, entrance planning and transition, legal requirements, and transportation issues. *$52.00*
            *432 pages Spiral-bound 1997*
            *ISBN 1-55766 -36-3*

**2717 Children with ADD: A Shared Responsibility**
Council for Exceptional Children
1110 North Glebe Road
Suite 300
Arlington, VA 22201          703-245-0600
                              888-232-7733
                         FAX: 703-264-9494
          e-mail: president@cec.sped.org
                        www.cec.sped.org

*Jim Mccormick, President*
*Suzanne Martin, Immediate Past President*
*Bruce Ramirez, Manager*

This book represents a consensus of what professionals and parents believe ADD is all about and how children with ADD may best be served. Reviews the evaluation process under IDEA and 504 and presents effective classroom strategies. *$8.90*
            *35 pages*
            *ISBN 0-865862-33-8*

**2718 Children's Needs Psychological Perspective**
National Association of School Psychologists
8455 Colesville Road
Suite 1000
Silver Spring, MD 20910          301-681-3223
                            FAX: 301-608-2514
This very popular monograph was developed with the recognition that many factors beyond the classroom and the child's own personal characteristics influence school success.

*637 pages*

**2719 Choices: A Guide to Sex Counseling for the Physically Disabled Adult**
Krieger Publishing Company
PO Box 9542
Melbourne, FL 32902          321-724-9542
                              800-724-0025
                         FAX: 321-951-3671
        e-mail: info@krieger-publishing.com
                    www.krieger-publishing.com

*R Krieger, Owner*

Provides rehabilitation professionals with the basic information necessary for limited sexuality counseling of physically disabled adults. *$14.50*
            *132 pages*
            *ISBN 0-898749-03-4*

**2720 Choosing Options and Accommodations for Children**
Brookes Publishing
PO Box 10624
Baltimore, MD 21285          410-337-9580
                              800-638-3775
                         FAX: 410-337-8539
        e-mail: custserv@brookespublishing.com
                    www.brookespublishing.com

*Clary Creighton, Exhibits Coordinator*
*Tracy Gray, Educational Sales Manager*
*Paul Brooks, Owner*

Bridging the gap between the philosophy and practice of inclusive education, this important manual provides a practical assessment and planning process for the inclusion of students with disabilities in general education classrooms. *$29.00*
            *192 pages*
            *ISBN 1-55766 -06-5*

**2721 Classroom Success for the LD and ADHD Child**
John F Blair Publishing
1406 Plaza Drive
Winston Salem, NC 27103          336-768-1374
                                  800-222-9796
                             FAX: 336-768-9194
            e-mail: sakowski@blairpub.com
                          www.blairpub.com

*Suzanne Stevens, author*
*Carolyn Sakowski, President*

This book offers suggestions on teaching techniques, adapting texts, recognition of children with disabilities and testing, grading and mainstreaming the learning disabled and ADHD child. *$12.95*
            *314 pages Paperback*
            *ISBN 0-895871-42-4*

**2722 Clinical Management of Childhood Stuttering, 2nd Edition**
Pro-Ed Publications
8700 Shoal Creek Boulevard
Austin, TX 78757          512-451-3246
                           800-897-3202
                      FAX: 800-397-7633
          e-mail: feedback@proedinc.com
                        www.proedinc.com

*Donald Hammill, Owner*
*Courtney King, Marketing Coordinator*

Updates and integrates recent findings in childhood stuttering into a broad range of therapeutic strategies for assessing and treating the young dysfluent child. *$38.00*

*336 pages*

**2723  Cognitive Approaches to Learning Disabilities**
Pro-Ed Publications
8700 Shoal Creek Boulevard
Austin, TX  78757
512-451-3246
800-897-3202
FAX: 800-397-7633
e-mail: feedback@proedinc.com
www.proedinc.com

*Joshua Jeffrey, Marketing Custodian*
*Courtney King, Marketing Coordinator*
*Donald Hammill, Owner*

The first to bridge the gap between cognitive psychology and information processing theory in understanding learning disabilities. *$39.00*
*495 pages Hardcover*

**2724  Cognitive Strategy Instruction That Really Improves Children's Academic Skills**
Brookline Books
39 University Road
Brookline, MA  02445
617-743-6772
800-666-BOOK
FAX: 617-734-3952
www.brooklinebooks.com

*William H Walters, Author*
*Esther Isabe Wilder, Author*

A concise and focused work that summarily presents the few procedures for teaching strategies that aid academic subject matter learning: decoding reading comprehension, vocabulary, math, spelling and writing. Learning unrelated facts and science. Completely revised in 1995. *$27.95*
*Paperback*
*ISBN 1-571290-07-9*

**2725  Collaborating for Comprehensive Services for Young Children and Families**
Brookes Publishing Company
PO Box 10624
Baltimore, MD  21285
410-337-9580
800-638-3775
FAX: 410-337-8539
e-mail: cutserv@brookespublishing.com
www.brookespublishing.com

*Clary Creighton, Exhibits Coordinator*
*Tracy Gray, Educational Sales Manager*
*Paul Brooks, Owner*

Taking collaboration a step beyond basic implementation, this useful book shows agency and school leaders how to coordinate their efforts to stretch human services dollars while still providing quality programs. Provides the building blocks needed to establish a local interagency coordinating council. *$37.00*
*272 pages 1992*
*ISBN 1-557661-03-0*

**2726  Collaborative Teams for Students with Severe Disabilities**
Brookes Publishing
PO Box 10624
Baltimore, MD  21285
410-337-9580
800-638-3775
FAX: 410-337-8539
e-mail: custserv@brookespublishing.com
www.brookespublishing.com

*Clary Creighton, Exhibits Coordinator*
*Tracy Gray, Educational Sales Manager*
*Paul Brooks, Owner*

How can educators, parents and therapists work together to ensure the best possible educational experience for students with severe disabilities? This resource describes how a collaborative team can successfully create exciting learning opportunities for students, while teaching them to participate fully at home, school, work and play. *$30.00*

*304 pages*
*ISBN 1-55766-88-3*

**2727  Communicating with Parents of Exceptional Children**
Love Publishing Company
PO Box 22353
Denver, CO  80222
303-221-7333
FAX: 303-221-7444
www.lovepublishing.com

*Stan Love, Owner*

This book shows how teachers can facilitate parent involvement with children's education. It presents the mirror model of parent involvement, family, dynamics, how to listen actively to parents, values and perceptions, problem-solving, parent conferences and training groups. *$19.95*

*ISBN 0-89108-67-4*

**2728  Communication & Language Acquisition: Discoveries from Atypical Development**
Brookes Publishing
PO Box 10624
Baltimore, MD  21285
410-337-9580
800-638-3775
FAX: 410-337-8539
e-mail: custserv@brookespublishing.com
www.brookespublishing.com

*Clary Creighton, Exhibits Coordinator*
*Tracy Gray, Educational Sales Manager*
*Paul Brooks, Owner*

This text demonstrates how the study of language acquisition in children with atypical development promotes advances in basic theory. *$44.00*
*352 pages Hardcover 1997*
*ISBN 1-557662-79-7*

**2729  Communication Skills for Working with Elders**
Springer Publishing Company
11 West 42nd Street
New York, NY  10036
212-431-4370
877-687-7476
FAX: 212-941-7842
e-mail: marketing@springerpub.com
www.springerpub.com

*Annette Imperati, Marketing/Sales Director*
*Ursula Springer, President*

How aging and illness affects communication. *$17.95*
*160 pages Softcover*
*ISBN 0-82615-20-7*

**2730  Communication Unbound**
Teachers College Press
PO Box 20
Williston, VT  05495
800-575-6566
800-575-6566
FAX: 802-864-7622
e-mail: tcc.orders@aidcvt.com
www.tcp.com

*Michael Mcgann, Administrator*

Complete title is 'Communication Unbound: How Facilitated Communication is Challenging the Traditional Views of Autism and Ability/Disablity'. Reveals the wonder of expression by people who have been trapped in silence and diminished by presumptions of their incompetence. *$18.95*

*240 pages Paperback*
*ISBN 0-087737-21-4*

**2731 Complete Handbook of Children's Reading Disorders: You Can Prevent or Correct LDs**
Gallery Bookshop
PO Box 270
Mendocino, CA 95460

707-937-2665
FAX: 707-937-3737
e-mail: info@gallerybooks.com
www.gallerybooks.com

*Linda Pack, Manager*
*Tony Miksak, Owner*

The complete handbook of children's reading disorders. *$34.95*
*732 pages Paperback*
*ISBN 0-80772 -83-3*

**2732 Comprehensive Assessment in Special Education**
Charles C Thomas
2600 South 1st Street
Springfield, IL 62704

217-789-8980
800-258-8980
FAX: 217-789-9130
e-mail: books@ccthomas.com
www.ccthomas.com

*Michael Thomas, President*
*D Sexton, Author*

The purpose of this book is to incorporate (1) detailed approaches to assessment, (2) assessment fundamentals, (3) traditional and emerging assessment, (4) today's special assessment concerns. *$104.95*
*578 pages Hardcover*
*ISBN 0-398056-45-5*

**2733 Computer Access/Computer Learning**
Special Needs Project
324 State Street
Suite H
Santa Barbara, CA 93101

805-962-8087
800-333-6867
FAX: 805-962-5087
www.specialneeds.com

*Hod Gray, Founder*

A resource manual in adaptive technology and computer training. *$22.50*

**2734 Consulting Psychologists Press**
PO Box 10096
Palo Alto, CA 94303

650-964-3722
800-624-1765
FAX: 650-969-8608
www.cpp-db.com

Catalog offering job assessment software, career development reports, educational assessment information and books for the professional.

**2735 Counseling Persons with Communication Disorders and Their Families**
Pro-Ed Publications
8700 Shoal Creek Boulevard
Austin, TX 78757

512-451-3246
800-897-3202
FAX: 800-397-7633
e-mail: feedback@proedinc.com
www.proedinc.com

*Donald Hammill, Owner*
*Courtney King, Marketing Coordinator*

A learning manual for speech-language pathologists and audiologists on how to deal with the emotional issues facing them in their work with clients with communication disorders and their families. *$ 29.00*

*187 pages*

**2736 Creating Positive Classroom Environments: Strategies for Behavior Management**
Brooks / Cole Publishing Company
511 Forest Lodge Road
Pacific Grove, CA 93950

831-373-0728
800-354-9706
FAX: 831-375-6414
e-mail: bc-info@brookscole.com
www.brookescole.com

A hands-on text that offers an approach to classroom management that encourages situation-specific decision making. Presenting research-based information on how to establish an effective behavior management system in both regular and special education settings, the book centers on ways to help students manage their own behavior, rather than on ways their behavior can be managed by teachers, peers, parents or other adults.
*448 pages Paperbound*
*ISBN 0-53422 -54-4*

**2737 Critical Voices on Special Education**
State University of New York Press
194 Washington Avenue
Suite 305
Albany, NY 12210

518-472-5000
800-666-2211
FAX: 518-472-5038
e-mail: info@sunypress.edu
www.sunypress.edu

*James Peltz, Interim Director*
*Janice Vunk, Assistant Director*
*Elizabeth Capaldi, Chief Executive Officer*

Problems and progress concerning the mildly handicapped. *$21.95*
*265 pages Paperback*
*ISBN 0-79140 -20-3*

**2738 Cultural Diversity, Families and the Special Education System**
Teachers College Press
1234 Amsterdam Avenue
New York, NY 10027

212-678-3929
800-575-6566
FAX: 212-678-4149
e-mail: tcpress@tc.columbia.edu
www.teacherscollegepress.com

*Mary Lynch, Manager*

This timely and thought-provoking book explores the quadruple disadvantage faced by the parents of poor, minority, handicapped children whose first language is not that of the school they attend. *$22.95*
*296 pages Paperback*
*ISBN 0-807731-19-6*

**2739 Curriculum Decision Making for Students with Severe Handicaps**
Teachers College Press
Columbia University
New York, NY 10027

212-678-3929
800-575-6566
FAX: 212-678-4149
e-mail: tspress@ts.columbia.edu.
www.teacherscollegepress.com

*Brian Ellerbeck, Executive Acquisitions Editor*
*Susan Liddicoat, Acquisitions Editor*
*Mary Lynch, Manager*

The inclusion of severely handicapped students within the scope of public education has brought about many changes for teachers in special education, this book helps the professional to distinguish which avenues are the best to take. *$17.95*

*192 pages Paperback*
*ISBN 0-807728-61-6*

**2740  Deciphering the System: A Guide for Families of Young Disabled Children**
Brookline Books
39 University Road
Brookline, MA  02445

617-734-6772
800-666-BOOK
FAX: 617-734-3952
e-mail: brooklinebooks@brooklinebooks.com
www.brooklinebooks.com

*William H Walters, Author*
*Esther Isabe Wilder, Author*

This book informs parents of disabled children (0-5) of their rights and the service system, e.g., ways to manage the cumulating information, tips on IEP and IFSP meetings and the educational assessment process, and how parents can work with multiple service providers. It includes contributions from both parents and professionals who have experience with the service system. *$21.95*

*ISBN 0-914797-87-5*

**2741  Defining Rehabilitation Agency Types**
Mississippi State University
PO Box 6189
Mississippi State, MS  39762

662-325-2001
800-675-7782
FAX: 662-325-8989
www.blind.msstate.edu

*Kelly Schaefer, Dissemination Specialist*
*Elton Moore, Executive Director*

Relationships of participant selection and cost factors of service delivery across rehabilitation agency types. A national survey of state agencies for the blind was conducted to examine factors that define the characteristics of different agencies; similar programs were grouped together. Classification criteria were developed to distinguish agencies into logical groups based on line of authority, funding and operating procedures. *$10.00*
*15 pages Paperback*

**2742  Designing and Using Assistive Technology: The Human Perspective**
Brookes Publishing
PO Box 10624
Baltimore, MD  21285

410-337-9580
800-638-3775
FAX: 410-337-8539
e-mail: custserv@brookespublishing.com
www.brookespublishing.com

*Clary Creighton, Exhibits Coordinator*
*Tracy Gray, Educational Sales Manager*
*Paul Brooks, Owner*

Presented here is a holistic perspective on how and why people choose and use AT. Features personal insights and the latest research on design and development. *$31.00*
*352 pages Paperback 1998*
*ISBN 1-55766 -14-9*

**2743  Developing Cross-Cultural Competence:Guide to Working with Young Children & Their Families**
Brookes Publishing
PO Box 10624
Baltimore, MD  21285

410-337-9580
800-638-3775
FAX: 410-337-8539
e-mail: custserv@brookespublishing.com
www.brookespublishing.com

*Clary Creighton, Exhibits Coordinator*
*Tracy Gray, Educational Sales Manager*
*Paul Brooks, Owner*

This enlightening book perceptively and sensitively explores cultural, ethnic, and language diversity in human services. For those who work with families whose infants and young children may have or be at risk for a disability or chronic illness. (Second Edition) *$ 32.00*
*448 pages Paperback*
*ISBN 1-55766 -31-9*

**2744  Developing Individualized Family Support Plans: A Training Manual**
Brookline Books
34 University Road
Brookline, MA  02445

617-734-6772
800-666-2665
FAX: 617-734-3952
e-mail: milt@brooklinebooks.com
www.brooklinebooks.com

*William H Walters, Author*
*Esther Isabe Wilder, Author*

This manual provides in-service training coordinators, administrators, supervisors and university personnel with a compact package of functional and practical methods to train professionals about implementing family-centered individualized family support plans (IFSP'S). Also, case studies provide concrete examples to aid in learning to write IFSP's. *$24.95*

*ISBN 0-914797-69-7*

**2745  Developing Staff Competencies for Supporting People with Disabilities**
Brookes Publishing
PO Box 10624
Baltimore, MD  21285

410-337-9580
800-638-3775
FAX: 410-337-8539
e-mail: custserv@brookespublishing.com
www.brookespublishing.com

*Clary Creighton, Exhibits Coordinator*
*Tracy Gray, Educational Sales Manager*
*Paul Brooks, Owner*

This timely second edition, now in a new easier to read format, gives service providers helpful strategies for increasing effectiveness and maintaining well-being while working in the rewarding yet challenging field of human services. *$34.00*
*480 pages Paperback*
*ISBN 1-55766 -07-3*

**2746  Development of Language**
McGraw-Hill, School Publishing
220 East Danieldale Road
Desoto, TX  75115

972-224-1111
800-442-9685
FAX: 972-228-1982
e-mail: mcgrawhill.com
www.mhschool.com

*Cheri Scott, Director*
*Joseph Gavigan, President*

An organizational book based on the developmental stages of language.
*464 pages*

**2747  Developmental Diagnosis Treatment**
Books on Special Children
PO Box 3378
Amherst, MA  01004

413-256-8164
FAX: 413-256-8896
e-mail: irene@boscbooks.com

Account of diagnosis and treatment of severely handicapped people of Japan. *$30.50*

*209 pages Hardcover*

**2748 Developmental Disabilities of Learning**
Gallery Bookshop
PO Box 270
Mendocino, CA 95460
707-937-2665
FAX: 707-937-3737
e-mail: info@gallerybooks.com
www.gallerybooks.com

*Linda Pack, Manager*
*Tony Miksak, Owner*

Manual for professionals on developmental and learning disabilities in the growing child. *$25.00*
*224 pages Illustrated*

**2749 Developmental Disabilities: A Handbook for Occupational Therapists**
Haworth Press
10 Alice Street
Binghamton, NY 13904
607-722-5857
800-429-6784
FAX: 607-722-6362
e-mail: orders@haworthpress.com
www.haworthpress.com

*Sandy Sickels, Vice President*
*Becky Millerbaum, Advertising Manager*
*William Cohen, Owner*

Provides broad coverage of the spectrum of problems confronted by patients with developmental disabilities and the many kinds of occupational therapy services these individuals need. Experts identify exemplary institutional and community service programs for treating patients with autism, cerebral palsy, epilepsy, and mental retardation. *$74.95*
*268 pages Hardcover*
*ISBN 0-866569-59-6*

**2750 Developmental Disabilities: A Handbook for Interdisciplinary Practice**
Brookline Books
39 University Road
Brookline, MA 02445
617-734-6772
800-666-BOOK
FAX: 617-734-3952
e-mail: brooklinebooks@brooklinebooks.com
www.brooklinebooks.com

*William H Walters, Author*
*Esther Isabe Wilder, Author*

Successful interdisciplinary team practice for persons with developmental disabilities that require each team member to understand and respect the contributions of the others. This handbook explains the professions most often represented on interdisciplinary teams: their natures, concerns and roles in the interdisciplinary context. *$29.95*
*256 pages*
*ISBN 1-571290-03-6*

**2751 Developmental Variation and Learning Disorders**
Educators Publishing Service
625 Mount Auburn Street
Suite 3
Cambridge, MA 02138
617-547-6706
800-225-5750
FAX: 617-440-2665
e-mail: feedback@epsbooks.com
www.epsbooks.com

*Charles H Heinle, Vice President*
*Alexandra S Bigelow, Author*
*Gunnar Voltz, President*

Discusses seven major areas of development and four major areas of academic proficiency and then ties this information together by examining factors that predispose a child to dysfunction and disability, offering guidelines to assessment and management, and analyzing long-range outcomes and factors that promote resiliency for parents, educators and clinicians. *$69.00*

*640 pages Cloth*
*ISBN 0-838819-92-3*

**2752 Diagnosis and Treatment of Old Age**
S Karger Publishers
26 W Avon Road
# 529
Unionville, CT 06085
860-675-7834
FAX: 860-675-7302

*Monica Brendel, President*

These papers furnish a concise update on the diagnosis and treatment of Alzheimer's disease. *$57.75*
*112 pages Hardcover*
*ISBN 3-80554 -44-3*

**2753 Digest of Neurology and Psychiatry**
Institute of Living: Hartford Hospital
200 Retreat Avenue
Hartford, CT 06106
860-545-7841
800-673-2411
FAX: 860-545-2351
e-mail: fishe@harthosp.org
www.instituteofliving.org

*Harold I Schwartz MD, Vice President*
*John Meehan, President*

Abstracts and reviews of selected current literature in psychiatry, neurology and related fields.

**2754 Disability Funding News**
C D Publications
8204 Fenton Street
Silver Spring, MD 20910
301-588-6380
800-666-6380
FAX: 301-588-0591
e-mail: subscription@cdpublications.com
www.cdpublications.com

*Jim Rogers, Editor*
*Michael Gerecht, President*

Grantseeking tips and strategies for nonprofit, government administrators, plus proved fundraising ideas. Includes grant application critiques, ho-to advice, and private and public funding updates. *$ 199.00*
*8 pages Weekly*

**2755 Disability and Rehabilitation**
Taylor & Francis
7625 Empire Drive
Florence, KY 41042
859-371-9571
800-634-7064
FAX: 800-248-4724
www.taylorandfrancis.com

*Mike Hunninghake, Journals Representative*
*Jeff Taylor, Owner*

An international, multidisciplinary journal seeking to encourage a better understanding of all aspects of disability, and to promote the rehabilitation process. *$395.00*
*Monthly*
*ISSN 0963-82 8*

**2756 Divided Legacy: A History of the Schism in Medical Thought, The Bacteriological Era**
North Atlantic Books
1435 4th Street
Berkeley, CA 94710
510-559-8277
800-337-2665
FAX: 510-559-8279
e-mail: orders@northatlanticbooks.com
www.northatlanticbooks.com

*Richard Grossinger, Publisher*
*Lindy Hough, Publisher*

Concluding volume of Coulter's history of medical philosophy, from ancient times to today. Covers the orgins of bacteriology and immunology in world medicine; describes the clash between orthodox and alternative medicine.

*1993*

**2757  Dual Relationships in Counseling**
American Counseling Association
5999 Stevenson Avenue
Alexandria, VA  22304        703-823-9800
                            800-347-6647
                    FAX: 703-823-0252
        e-mail: webmaster@counseling.org
                www.counseling.org

*Sam Gladding, President*
*Debra Bass, Marketing Coordinator*
*Richard Yep, Executive Director*

Covers topics such as whether to accept a client, whether to reveal information, whether to refer a case, whether to consider
factors you might not otherwise consider, and how to deal with
gifts, invitations and social situations. *$23.95*
        *244 pages paperback 1992*
        *ISBN 1-556200-90-0*

**2758  Early Communication Skills For Children wi th Down
Syndrome**
Woodbine House
6510 Bells Mill Road
Bethesda, MD  20817          301-897-3570
                            800-843-7323
                    FAX: 301-897-5838
        e-mail: info@woodbinehouse.com
                www.woodbinehouse.com

*Irv Shapell, Owner*

An expert shares her knowledge of speech and language development in young children and adolescents with Down syndrome. Intelligibility, hearing loss, apraxia and other factors
that affect communications are discussed. It also covers
speech-language assessments and alternative communication
options and literacy. *$19.95*
        *368 pages 2003*
        *ISBN 1-890627-27-5*

**2759  Early Intervention, Implementing Child & Family Ser-
vices for At-Risk Infants**
Pro-Ed Publications
8700 Shoal Creek Boulevard
Austin, TX  78757            512-451-3246
                            800-897-3202
                    FAX: 800-397-7633
        e-mail: feedback@proedinc.com
                www.proedinc.com

*Donald Hammill, Owner*
*Courtney King, Marketing Coordinator*

New directions and recent legislation have produced a need for
this guide which is designed for professionals facing the challenge of program development for disabled and at-risk infants,
toddlers and their families. *$36.00*
        *394 pages*
        *ISBN 0-890796-21-1*

**2760  Ecology of Troubled Children**
Brookline Books
34 University Road
Brookline, MA  02445         800-666-2665
                            800-666-2665
                    FAX: 617-734-3952
        e-mail: milt@brooklinebooks.com
                www.brooklinebooks.com

*William H Walters, Author*
*Esther Isabe Wilder, Author*

Designed for frontline mental health clinicians working with
children with serious emotional disturbances; shows how to
make childrens' worlds more supportive by changing the places,
activities and people in their lives. *$15.95*

*256 pages*
*ISBN 1-571290-57-5*

**2761  Educating Children with Disabilities: A
Transdisciplinary Approach, 3rd Edition**
Brookes Publishing
PO Box 10624
Baltimore, MD  21285         410-337-9580
                            800-638-3775
                            800-638-3775
                    FAX: 410-337-8539
    e-mail: custserv@brookespublishing.com
                www.brookespublishing.com

*Clary Creighton, Exhibits Coordinator*
*Tracy Gray, Educational Sales Manager*
*Paul Brooks, Owner*

Widely respected textbook presents you with the strategies you
need for developing an inclusive curriculum, integrating health
care and educational programs and addressing needs and concerns. *$38.00*
        *512 pages 1996*
        *ISBN 1-557662-46-0*

**2762  Educating Children with Multiple Disabilities: A
Transdisciplinary Approach**
Brookes Publishing
PO Box 10624
Baltimore, MD  21285         410-337-9580
                            800-638-3775
                    FAX: 410-337-8539
    e-mail: custserv@brookespublishing.com
                www.brookespublishing.com

*Clary Creighton, Exhibits Coordinator*
*Tracy Gray, Educational Sales Manager*
*Paul Brooks, Owner*

Emphasizing transdisciplinary cooperation between teachers,
therapists, nurses and parents, this book describes a general
model and specific techniques for effectively educating children with multiple disabilities. *$29.00*
        *496 pages Paperback*
        *ISBN 1-557662-46-0*

**2763  Educating Students Who Have Visual Impairments
with Other Disabilities**
Brookes Publishing
PO Box 10624
Baltimore, MD  21285         410-337-9580
                            800-638-3775
                    FAX: 410-337-8539
    e-mail: custserv@brookespublishing.com
                www.brookespublishing.com

*Clary Creighton, Exhibits Coordinator*
*Tracy Gray, Educational Sales Manager*
*Paul Brooks, Owner*

This introductory text provides techniques for facilitating functional learning in students with a wide range of visual impairments and multiple disabilities. With a concentration on
educational needs and learning styles, the authors of this
multidisciplinary volume demonstrate functional assessment
and teaching adaptations that will improve students' inclusive
learning experiences. *$49.95*
        *552 pages Paperback*
        *ISBN 1-557662-80-0*

**2764  Educating all Students in the Mainstream**
Brookes Publishing Company
PO Box 10624
Baltimore, MD  21285         410-337-9580
                            800-638-3775
                    FAX: 410-337-8539
    e-mail: custserv@brookespublishing.com
                www.brookespublishng.com

*Clary Creighton, Exhibits Coordinator*
*Tracy Gray, Educational Sales Manager*
*Paul Brooks, Owner*

Incorporating the research and viewpoints of both regular and special educators, this textbook provides an effective approach for modifying, expanding, and adjusting regular education to meet the needs of all students. *$34.00*
*304 pages 1989*
*ISBN 1-557660-22-0*

**2765  Education and Deafness**
Longman Publishing Group
10 Bank St
9th Floor
White Plains, NY  10606                    212-782-3330

www.ablongman.com

*Thomas Longman, Founder*

Provides coverage of the interrelated issues that affect the teaching of deaf students. Concentrates on the severely to profoundly hearing impaired and includes an entire chapter devoted to students whose impairments are less severe (hard-of-hearing students).
*320 pages Paperback 1990*
*ISBN 0-801300-26-6*

**2766  Education and Training in Mental Retardation and Developmental Disabilities**
Council for Exceptional Children
1110 Northbe Road
Suite 300
Arlington, VA  22201                    703-245-0600
FAX: 703-264-9494
e-mail: service@cec.sped.org
www.cec.sped.org

*Trudy Kerr, Executive Director*
*Jim Mccormick, President*
*Bruce Ramirez, Manager*

A medium for continuing education for teachers and practitioners by providing timely information about the direction, management and accountability of special education programs for individuals with mental retardation and developmental disabilities. Individual, $30; Institution, $75.
*Quarterly*

**2767  Educational Audiology for the Limited Hearing Infant and Preschooler, 3rd Edition**
Charles C Thomas
2600 South 1st Street
Springfield, IL  62704                    217-789-8980
800-258-8980
FAX: 217-789-9130
e-mail: books@ccthomas.com
www.ccthomas.com

*Micheal Thomas, President*
*Donald Goldberg, Author*
*Nancy Coleffe-Schenck, Author*

Offers information on current concepts and practices in audio-logic screening and evaluation, development of the listening function, development of speech, development of language, the role of parents, parent education, mainstreaming of the limited-hearing child, and program modifications for the severely learning disabled child. Also includes information on auditory assessment, sensory aides, cochlear implants, acoupedics and auditory verbal programs. *$69.95*
*430 pages paperback 1997*
*ISBN 0-39806 -28-1*

**2768  Educational Care**
Educators Publishing Service
625 Mount Auburn Street
Suite 3
Cambridge, MA  02138                    617-547-6706
800-225-5750
FAX: 888-440-2665
e-mail: feedback@epsbooks.com
www.epsbooks.com

*Charles H Heinle, Vice President*
*Alexandra S Bigelow*
*Gunnar Voltz, President*

This book, written for both parents and teachers, is based on the view that education should be a system of care that is able to look after the specific needs of individual students. Using case studies, it analyzes various types of learning disorders and then suggests ways to help students with these problems. *$31.50*
*325 pages*
*ISBN 0-838819-87-7*

**2769  Educational Dimensions of Acquired Brain Injury**
Pro-Ed Publications
8700 Shoal Creek Boulevard
Austin, TX  78757                    512-451-3246
800-897-3202
FAX: 800-397-7633
e-mail: feedback@proedinc.com
www.proedinc.com

*Donald Hammill, Owner*
*Courtney King, Marketing Coordinator*

This book is a compilation of the working experiences of the professionals concerned about the educational dimensions of acquired brain injury. *$43.00*
*574 pages Hardcover*

**2770  Educational Intervention for the Student with Multiple Disabilities**
Charles C Thomas
2600 South 1st Street
Springfield, IL  62704                    217-789-8980
800-258-8980
FAX: 217-789-9130
e-mail: books@ccthomas.com
www.ccthomas.com

*Donna Irons-Reavis, Author*
*Michael Thomas, Presidentm*

This text will assist those who want to teach severely, multiply disabled students by providing information on general principles of education and classroom organization and managing the behavior of students. Also available in cloth $34.95 (ISBN# 0-398-05793-1) *$24.95*
*140 pages Softcover*
*ISBN 0-398061-73-4*

**2771  Educational Prescriptions**
Educators Publishing Service
625 Mount Auburn Street
Suite 3
Cambridge, MA  02138                    617-547-6706
800-225-5750
FAX: 888-440-2665
e-mail: feedback@epsbooks.com
www.epsbooks.com

*Charles H Heinle, Vice President*
*Alexandra S Bigelow, Author*
*Gunnar Voltz, President*

This book provides specific recommendations for the classroom management of students who are experiencing subtle developmental and/or learning difficulties. Intended for regular classroom teachers, specific examples of accommodations teachers can make are provided for grades 1-3 and 4-6. *$13.50*
*64 pages*
*ISBN 0-838819-90-7*

**2772  Effective Instruction for Special Education, 2nd Edition**

Pro-Ed Publications
8700 Shoal Creek Boulevard
Austin, TX  78757                    512-451-3246
800-897-3202
FAX: 800-397-7633
e-mail: info@proedinc.com
www.proedinc.com

*Joshua Jeffrey, Marketing Custodian*
*Courtney King, Marketing Coordinator*
*Donald Hammill, Owner*

This exciting and wide-ranging book provides special educators with effective methods for teaching students with mild and moderate learning and behavioral problems, as well as for teaching remedial students in general. *$37.00*
*419 pages Paperback*

**2773    Effective Teaching Methods for Autistic Children**
Charles C Thomas
2600 South 1st Street
Springfield, IL  62704
217-789-8980
800-258-8980
FAX: 217-789-9130
e-mail: books@ccthomas.com
www.ccthomas.com

*Michael Thomas, President*
*$20.95*
*124 pages Paper*
*ISBN 0-398063-09-5*

**2774    Effectively Educating Handicapped Students**
Longman Publishing Group
10 Bank Street
9th Floor
White Plains, NY  10606
914-287-8000
FAX: 914-421-5598
www.pearsoned.com

*Kathryn Costello, President*
For educators and other professionals who work with deaf and hearing impaired students in preschool and elementary programs. A developmental approach provides the foundation for several intervention methods including preparation for instruction, language, speech, audition and speechreading.
*468 pages Paperback 1991*
*ISBN 0-801303-17-6*

**2775    Emotional Problems of Childhood and Adolescence**
McGraw-Hill School Publishing
220 East Danieldale Road
Desoto, TX  75115
972-224-1111
800-442-9685
FAX: 972-228-1982
mhschool.com

*Joseph Gavigan, President*
For future special educators, psychologists and others who work with emotionally disturbed children and adolescents.

**2776    Enabling & Empowering Families: Principles & Guidelines for Practice**
Brookline Books
39 University Road
Brookline, MA  02445
617-734-6772
800-666-2665
FAX: 617-734-3952
e-mail: brooklinebooks@brooklinebooks.com
www.brooklinebooks.com

*William H Walters, Author*
*Esther I Wilder, Author*
*Angela Deal MSW, Author*
This book was written for practioners who must work with families but who have insufficient training in family systems assessment and intervention. The authors' system enables professionals to help the family identify its needs, locate the formal and informal resources to meet these needs and develop the abilities to effectively access these resources. *$24.95*

*220 pages*
*ISBN 0-914797-59-X*

**2777    Enhancing Self-Concepts and Achievement of Mildly Handicapped Students**
Charles C Thomas
2600 South 1st Street
Springfield, IL  62704
217-789-8980
800-258-8980
FAX: 217-789-9130
e-mail: books@ccthomas.com
www.ccthomas.com

*Micheal Thomas, President*
*Carroll J Jones, Author*
This book is aimed towards students who are learning disabled, mildly mentally retarded, and who have behavior disorders. Individuals should be aware that unless they appreciate and understand themselves, it is difficult to relate to the world around them. This is no less true of exceptional than nonhandicapped learners. This book provides a wonderfully complete window of insight into the most tenuous of human aspects, the self-concept. Also available in cloth at $55.95 (ISBN# 0-398-05760-5)
*$39.95*
*294 pages Paperback*
*ISBN 0-398061-91-2*

**2778    Evaluation and Educational Programming of Deaf-Blind/Severly Multihandicapped Students**
Charles C Thomas
2600 South 1st Street
Springfield, IL  62704
217-789-8980
800-258-8980
FAX: 217-789-9130
e-mail: books@ccthomas.com
www.ccthomas.com

*Michael Thomas, President*
Offers information on the special education of deaf-blind students. *$41.95*
*314 pages Softcover*
*ISBN 0-398055-15-7*

**2779    Evaluation and Treatment of the Psychogeriatric Patient**
Haworth Press
10 Alice Street
Binghamton, NY  13904
607-722-5857
800-429-6784
FAX: 607-722-6362
e-mail: orders@haworthpress.com
www.haworthpress.com

*Sandy Sickels, Vice President*
*Becky Minerbaum, Advertising Manager*
*William Cohen, Owner*
This pertinent book assists occupational therapists and other health care providers in developing up-to-date psychogeriatric programs and understands details of treating the cognitively impaired elderly. *$74.95*
*111 pages Hardcover*
*ISBN 1-560240-52-0*

**2780    Exceptional Children in Focus**
McGraw-Hill School Publishing
220 East Danieldale Road
Desoto, TX  75115
972-224-1111
800-442-9685
FAX: 972-228-1982
www.mhschool.com

*Joseph Gavigan, President*
*Todd Painter, Assistant Director*
Combines a light, personal look at the problems of special educators experiences with the basic facts of exceptionality.

*288 pages*

**2781 Exceptional Lives: Special Education in Today's Schools, 4th Edition**
Pearson Education
1 Lake Street
Upper Saddle River, NJ 07458    201-236-7000
FAX: 201-236-3400
www.pearsoned.com

*John Fallon, Chief Executive Officer*
*Rod Bristow, President Of Higher Education*
*George Werner, Chief Financial Officer*

Comprehensive coverage is built upon six guiding principles: 1) high expectations for individuals with disabilities and their educators, 2) inclusion for all students, 3) relationships and friendships as essential outcomes of collaboration, 4) positive contributions by students with disabilities, 5) the importance of choice and self-advocacy for students with disabilities, and 6) full citizenship for all students with disabilities. Emphasizes the daily lives of students and educators. *$90.00*
*592 pages 2003*
*ISBN 0-131126-00-8*

**2782 Exercise Activities for the Elderly**
Springer Publishing Company
11 West 42nd Street
15th Floor
New York, NY 10036    212-431-4370
877-687-7476
FAX: 212-941-7842
e-mail: contactus@springerpub.com
www.springerpub.com

*Annette Imperati, Marketing/Sales Director*
*Sheri Sussman, Senior Vice President*
*Ursula Springer, President*

A variety of exercises geared to clients with such conditions as arthritis, diabetes and Parkinson's disease, and others which are designed to build up muscular strength and maintain flexibility. *$23.95*
*240 pages Softcover*
*ISBN 0-82615 -10-9*

**2783 Facilitating Self-Care Practices in the Elderly**
Haworth Press
10 Alice Street
Binghamton, NY 13904    607-722-5857
800-429-6784
FAX: 607-722-6362
e-mail: orders@haworthpress.com
www.haworthpress.com

*Sandy Sickels, Vice President*
*Becky Minerbaum, Advertising Manager*
*William Cohen, Owner*

This up-to-date book is a synthesis of current knowledge from published sources and expert consultants relating to three commonly occurring problems in home health care practice: self-administration of medications, family caregiving issues, and teaching the elderly. *$ 74.95*
*185 pages Hardcover*
*ISBN 1-560240-13-X*

**2784 Family Assessment in Early Intervention**
Books on Special Children
PO Box 3378
Amherst, MA 01004    413-256-8164
FAX: 413-256-8896
e-mail: irene@boscbooks.com
www.boscbooks.com
Includes sources and measure used for assessment, strengths and weaknesses of families and comparisons between typical families and handicapped families. *$37.95*

*280 pages Softcover*

**2785 Family-Centered Early Intervention with Infants and Toddlers**
Brookes Publishing
PO Box 10624
Baltimore, MD 21285    410-337-9580
800-638-3775
FAX: 410-337-8539
e-mail: cutserv@brookespublishing.com
www.brookespublishing.com

*Clary Creighton, Exhibits Coordinator*
*Tracy Gray, Educatrional Sales Manager*
*Paul Brooks, Owner*

This informative text provides professionals with insight and practical guidelines to help fulfill the federal requirements for provision of early intervention services. *$37.00*
*368 pages Hardcover 1993*
*ISBN 1-557661-24-3*

**2786 Feeding Children with Special Needs**
Arizona Department of Health Services
1740 West Adams Street
Phoenix, AZ 85007    602-542-1886
FAX: 602-542-1890
www.hs.state.az.us/cfhs/ons/

*Margaret Tate, Manager*

Guide designed to help develop a greater awareness of the special challenges involved in the nutrition and feeding concerns for children with special health care needs, and ways to approach the issues. *$5.00*

**2787 Focal Group Psychotherapy**
New Harbinger Publications
5674 Shattuck Avenue
Oakland, CA 94609    510-652-0215
800-748-6273
FAX: 510-652-5472
e-mail: customerservice@newharbinger.com
www.newharbinger.com

*Lorna Garano, Director*
*Matthew McKay, Owner*

Guide to leading brief, theme-based groups. This book offers an extensive week-by-week description of the basic concepts and interventions for 14 theme or focal groups for: codependency, rape victims, shyness, survivors of incest, agoraphobia, survivors of toxic parents, depression, child molesters, anger control, domestic violence offenders, assertiveness, alcohol and drug abuse, eating disorders, and parent training. *$59.95*
*544 pages Cloth*
*ISBN 1-879237-18-0*

**2788 Free Hand: Enfranchising the Education of Deaf Children**
TJ Publishers
2544 Tarpley Road
Suite 108
Carrollton, TX 75006    972-416-0800
800-999-1168
FAX: 301-585-5930
e-mail: TJPubinc@aol.com

*Angela K Thames, President*
*Jerald A Murphy, VP*

A select group of nationally prominent educators, linguists and researchers met at Hofstra University to consider the most vital and controversial question in education of the deaf: what role should ASL play in the classroom? Become part of that discussion with A Free Hand. *$16.95*

*204 pages Softcover 1990*
*ISBN 0-93266 -40-X*

**2789    Functional Assessment Inventory Manual**
Stout Vocational Rehab Institute
University of Wisconsin-Stout
Menomonie, WI  54751                              715-232-1411
                                        FAX: 715-232-2356
                    e-mail: botterbuschd@uwstout.edu

*Ronald R Fry, Manager*
*Darlene Botterbusch, Program Assistant*

The Functional Assessment is a systematic enumeration of a client's vocationally relevant strengths and limitations. *$12.00*
            *96 pages Paperback*
            *ISBN 0-916671-53-4*

**2790    Global Perspectives on Disability: A Curriculum**
Mobility International U SA
PO Box 10767
Eugene, OR  97440                              541-343-1284
                                        FAX: 541-343-6812
                         e-mail: info@miusa.org
                              www.miusa.org

*Susan Sygall, Executive Director*
*Melissa Mitchell, Public Relations Coordinator*
*Tracy Scharn, Project Assistant*

Designed for secondary and higher education instructors. Includes five lesson plans covering disability awareness, disability rights and international perspectives on disability. Available in alternative formats. *$40.00*

**2791    Glossary of Terminology for Vocational Assessment/Evaluation/Work**
Rehabilitation Resource University
University of Wisconsin-Stout
Menomonie, WI  54751                              715-232-1478
                                        FAX: 715-232-2356

*Ronald R Fry, Manager*
*Darlene Botterbusch, Program Assistant*

This glossary contains 254 terms and their definitions. Primary focus is on the terminology related to the practice and professionals of vocational assessment, vocational evaluation and work adjustment. *$9.50*
            *40 pages Softcover*

**2792    Graduate Technological Education and the Human Experience of Disability**
Haworth Press
10 Alice Street
Binghamton, NY  13904                          607-722-5857
                                          800-429-6784
                                        FAX: 607-722-6362
                    e-mail: orders@haworthpress.com
                         www.haworthpress.com

*Sandy Sickels, Vice President*
*Becky Minerbaum, Advertising Manger*
*William Cohen, Owner*

This book examines graduate schools of theology and their limited familiarity with the study of disability — and the presence of people with disabilities in particular — on their campuses. This text offers critical research and illuminates new pathways for theologia and practice in the community of faith. It offers suggestions for incorporating disability studies into theological education and religious life. *$34.95*

*115 pages Hardcover*
*ISBN 0-789060-08-6*

**2793    HIV Infection and Developmental Disabilities**
Brookes Publishing
PO Box 10624
Baltimore, MD  21285                            410-337-9580
                                          800-638-3775
                                        FAX: 410-337-8539
                e-mail: cstserv@brookespublishing.com
                         www.brookespublishing.com

*Tracy Gray, Educational Sales Manager*
*Clary Creighton, Exhibits Coordinator*
*Paul Brooks, Owner*

A resource for service providers pinpointing the most crucial medical, legal and educational issues to control HIV infection. *$47.00*
            *320 pages*
            *ISBN 1-557660-83-2*

**2794    Handbook for Implementing Workshops for Siblings of Special Children**
Special Needs Project
324 State Street
Suite H
Santa Barbara, CA  93101                        805-962-8087
                                          800-333-6867
                                        FAX: 805-962-5087
                              www.specialneeds.com

*Hod Gray, Founder*

Based on three years of professional experience, this handbook provides guidelines and techniques for those who wish to start and conduct workshops for siblings. *$40.00*

**2795    Handbook for Speech Therapy**
Psychological & Educational Publications
PO Box 520
Hydesville, CA  95547                          707-768-1807
                                          800-523-5775
                                        FAX: 800-447-0907
                e-mail: psych-edpublications@cck.net
                         www.psych-edpublications.com

*Morrison Gardner, President*

Basic handbook for beginning speech teachers, shows how speech sounds are made, what their individual characteristics are, how they relate to each other, what the most common errors are, and how to correct those errors.
            *143 pages paperback*

**2796    Handbook for the Special Education Administrator**
Edwin Mellen Press
PO Box 450
Lewiston, NY  14092                            716-754-4421
                                          800-753-2788
                                        FAX: 716-754-4056
                         e-mail: mellen@wzrd.com
Organization and procedures for special education. *$ 49.95*
            *96 pages Hardcover*
            *ISBN 0-88946 -22-9*

**2797    Handbook of Developmental Education**
Greenwood Publishing Group
88 Post Road West
Suite 5007
Westport, CT  06880                            203-226-3571
                                        FAX: 203-222-1502
                              www.greenwood.com

*Duane L Dobbert, Author*
*Wayne Smith, President*

This comprehensive handbook has brought together the leading practitioners and researchers in the field of developmental education to focus on the developmental learning agenda. Hardcover.

*400 pages $65 - $75*
*ISBN 0-275932-97-4*

**2798  Handbook on Supported Education for People with Mental Illness**
Brookes Publishing
PO Box 10624
Baltimore, MD  21285                    410-337-9580
                                        800-638-3775
                                   FAX: 410-337-8539
e-mail: custserv@brookespublishing.com
        www.brookespublishing.com

*Clary Creighton, Exhibits Coordinator*
*Tracy Gray, Educational Sales Manager*
*Paul Brooks, Owner*

Here you will find all necessary information that mental health professionals need in order to provide supported education services. There are specific suggestions on how to help people with mental illness return to or remain in college, trade school, or GED programs. Also addressed are funding and legal issues, accommodations, and specific interventions.
*208 pages Paperback 1998*
*ISBN 1-55766 -52-1*

**2799  Head Injury Rehabilitation: Children**
Taylor & Francis
47 Runway Drive
Suite G
Levittown, PA  19057
                                   FAX: 215-785-5515
Rehabilitation guide for the help of children or adolescents that have suffered brain injury.
*460 pages Cloth*
*ISBN 0-85066 -67-1*

**2800  Health Care Management in Physical Therapy**
Charles C Thomas
2600 South 1st Street
Springfield, IL  62704                  217-789-8980
                                        800-258-8980
                                   FAX: 217-789-9130
e-mail: books@ccthomas.com
        www.ccthomas.com

*Laura I Moriarty, Author*
*Joseph Antho Travers, Author*
*Michael Thomas, President*

The focus of this book is on physical therapists as supervisors in health care settings of hospitals, nursing homes, home health agencies and in private practice. *$62.95*
*328 pages Hardcover*
*ISBN 0-398056-42-0*

**2801  Health Care for Students with Disabilities**
Brookes Publishing Company
PO Box 10624
Baltimore, MD  21285                    410-337-9580
                                        800-638-3775
                                   FAX: 410-337-8539
e-mail: custserv@brookespublishing.com
        www.brookespublishing.com

*Clary Creighton, Exhibits Coordinator*
*Tracy Gray, Educational Sales Manager*
*Paul Brooks, Owner*

This practical guidebook provides detailed descriptions of the 16 health-related procedures most likely to be needed in the classroom by students with disabilities. *$25.00*

*304 pages Paperback 1990*
*ISBN 1-557660-37-9*

**2802  Helping Learning Disabled Gifted Children Learn Through Compensatory Play**
Charles C Thomas
2600 South 1st Street
Springfield, IL  62704                  217-789-8980
                                        800-258-8980
                                   FAX: 217-789-9130
e-mail: books@ccthomas.com
        www.ccthomas.com

*Micheal Thomas, President*
*James H Humphrey, Author*

About 3% of the school population is gifted and 5 to 8% of this number suffer from learning disabilities. These children experience a great deal more trauma than the normal child. *$24.95*
*164 pages Softcover*
*ISBN 0-398061-62-9*

**2803  Helping Students Grow**
American College Testing Program
PO Box 168
Iowa City, IA  52243                    319-337-1000

                                        www.act.org

*Richard Ferguson, Chief Executive Officer*

Designed to assist counselors in using the wealth of information generated by the ACT Assessment.

**2804  How to Teach Autistic & Severely Handicapped Children**
Autism Society of North Carolina Bookstore
505 Oberlin Road
Suite 230
Raleigh, NC  27605                      919-743-0204
                                        800-442-2762
                                   FAX: 919-743-0208
e-mail: info@autismsociety-nc.org
        www.autismsociety-nc.org

*Ann Palmer, President*
*Darla Coffey, Bookstore Manager*
*Jill Keel, Executive Director*

Book provides procedures for effectively assessing and teaching autistic and other severely handicapped children. *$8.00*

**2805  How to Teach Spelling/How to Spell**
Educators Publishing Service
625 Mount Auburn Street
Suite 3
Cambridge, MA  02138                    617-547-6706
                                        800-225-5750
                                   FAX: 888-440-2665
e-mail: feedback@epsbooks.com
        www.epsbooks.com

*Charles H Heinle, Vice President*
*Alexandra Bigelow, Author*
*Gunnar Voltz, President*

This is a comprehensive resource manual based on the Orton-Gillingham approach to reading and spelling. It recommends what and how much to teach at each grade level at the beginning of each lesson or section. There are four student manuals that accompany this. *$22.50*
*Teachers Manual*
*ISBN 0-838818-47-1*

**2806  Human Exceptionality: Society, School, and Family**
Allyn & Bacon
75 Arlington Street
Suite 300
Boston, MA  02116                       617-848-6000
                                        800-852-8024
                                   FAX: 617-848-7490
                                        www.ablongman.com

Examination of the definitions, classification, prevalence and characteristics of each category of exceptionality in relation to the major topics and issues of the field of special education.
*615 pages*
*ISBN 0-20528 -39-0*

**2807  I Heard That!**
3417 Volta Place NW
Washington, DC  20007
202-337-5220
866-337-5220
FAX: 202-337-8314
e-mail: info@agbell.org
www.agbell.org

*Todd Houston, Executive Director*

Provides a framework for teachers, clinicians and parents when writing objectives and designing activities to develop listening skills in children with hearing loss from newborn to 3 years.
*$7.95*
*36 pages*

**2808  I Heard That!2**
Alexander Graham Bell Association
3417 Volta Place NW
Washington, DC  20007
202-337-5220
FAX: 202-337-8314
e-mail: info@agbell.org
www.agbell.org

*Jessica Ripper, Senior Director*
*Todd Houston, Executive Director*

Provides a framework for teachers, clinicians and parents when writing objectives and designing activities to develop listening skills in children who are deaf or hard of hearing. *$7.95*
*36 pages*

**2809  Images of the Disabled, Disabling Images**
Greenwood Publishing Group
88 Post Road West
Suite 5007
Westport, CT  06880
203-226-3571
FAX: 203-222-1502
e-mail: hr@greenwood.com
www.greenwood.com

*Robert K Mueller, Author*
*Richard B Higgins, Author*
*Wayne Smith, President*

Combines an examination of the presentation of persons with disabilities in literature, film and the media with an analysis of the ways in which these images are expressed in public policy concerning the disabled. *$55.00*
*227 pages Hardcover*
*ISBN 0-275921-78-6*

**2810  Implementing Family-Centered Services in Early Intervention**
Brookline Books
PO Box 1047
Cambridge, MA  02139
617-868-0360
800-666-2665
FAX: 617-868-1772
e-mail: brooklinebks@delphi.com
www.brooklinebooks.com
This book describes a team-based decision-making workshop for implementing family-centered services in early interventions. Unlike a training curriculum, it focuses on the decisions that teams must make as they seek to become family-centered.
*$19.95*

*180 pages Paperback*
*ISBN 0-91479 -62-*

**2811  Including All of Us: An Early Childhood Curriculum About Disability**
Educational Equity Concepts
114 East 32nd Street
New York, NY  10016
212-725-1803
FAX: 212-725-0947
TTY:212-725-1803
e-mail: information@equity.org
www.edequity.org

*Barbara Sprung, Author*

The first nonsexist, multicultural, mainstreamed curriculum. Step-by-step activities incorporate disability into three curriculum areas: Same/Different (hearing impairment), Body Parts (visual impairment), and Transportation (mobility impairment).
*$14.95*
*144 pages*
*ISBN 0-93162 -00-4*

**2812  Including Students with Severe and Multiple Disabilites in Typical Classrooms**
Brookes Publishing
PO Box 10624
Baltimore, MD  21285
410-337-9580
800-638-3775
FAX: 410-337-8539
e-mail: custserv@brookespublishing.com
www.brookespublishing.com

*Clary Creighton, Exhibits Coordinator*
*Tracy Gray, Educational Sales Manager*
*Paul Brooks, Owner*

This straightforward and jargon free resource gives instructors the guidance needed to educate learners who have one or more sensory impairments in addition to cognitive and physical disabilities. *$32.95*
*224 pages Paperback*
*ISBN 1-55766 -39-8*

**2813  Including Students with Special Needs: A Practical Guide for Classroom Teachers**
Allyn & Bacon
75 Arlington Street
Suite 300
Boston, MA  02116
617-848-6000
800-852-8024
FAX: 617-848-7490
e-mail: ab_webmaster@abacon.com
www.ablongman.com
Focuses on educating students with special needs in inclusive settings based on substantive admisistrative backing, support for general education teachers, and an understanding that sometimes not all needs can be met in a single location.
*544 pages*
*ISBN 0-20528 -85-4*

**2814  Inclusive & Heterogeneous Schooling: Assessment, Curriculum, and Instruction**
Brookes Publishing
PO Box 10624
Baltimore, MD  21285
410-337-9580
800-638-3775
FAX: 410-337-8539
e-mail: custserv@brookespublishing.com
www.brookespublishing.com

*Clary Creighton, Exhibits Coordinator*
*Tracy Gray, Educational Sales Manager*
*Paul Brooks, Owner*

Presents methods for successfully restructuring classrooms to enable all students, particularly those with disabilities, to flourish. Provides specific strategies for assessment, collaboration, classroom management, and age-specific instruction. *$34.95*

# Education /Professional Texts

*448 pages Paperback*
*ISBN 1-55766 -02-9*

**2815 Independent Living Approach to Disability Policy Studies**
World Institute on Disability
510 16th Street
Suite 100
Oakland, CA 94612
510-763-4100
FAX: 510-763-4109
e-mail: wid@wid.org
www.wid.org

*Stanley Yarnell, Chairman*
*Martin Schulter, Vice Chairman*

This collection of essays and bibliographies attempts to build a framework for understanding how the relationship between public policy, disability studies and disability policy studies will impact us in the future. $17.50
*240 pages Paperback*

**2816 Information & Referral Center**
Mississippi State University
PO Box 6189
Mississippi State, MS 39762
662-325-2001
800-675-7782
FAX: 662-325-8989
www.blind.msstate.edu

*Kelly Schaefer, Publications Manager*
*Elton Moore, Executive Director*

A comprehensive website that includes information about client assistance programs, vocational rehabilitation agencies, low vision clinics and information about blindness and low vision. $25.00
*150 pages*

**2817 Instructional Methods for Students**
Allyn & Bacon
75 Arlington Street
Suite 300
Boston, MA 02116
617-848-6000
800-852-8024
FAX: 617-848-7490
www.ablongman.com
Instructional methods for students with learning and behavior problems.
*450 pages 1986*
*ISBN 0-205087-35-3*

**2818 Interactions: Collaboration Skills for School Professionals**
Longman Education/Addison Wesley
95 Church Street
White Plains, NY 10601
914-328-2090
800-322-1377
FAX: 800-333-3328
www.longman.awl.com

*Thomas Longman, Founder*

Shows school professionals how to develop and use the skills necessary for effective collaboration among teachers, school support staff, and parents of children with special needs. $35.00
*270 pages Paperback*
*ISBN 0-80131 -21-2*

**2819 International Journal of Arts Medicine**
MMB Music
3526 Washington Avenue
Saint Louis, MO 63103
314-531-9635
800-543-3771
FAX: 314-531-8384
e-mail: info@mmbmusic.com
www.mmbmusic.com

*Marcia Lee Goldberg, President*

Exploration of the creative arts and healing. Presents peer-reviewed articles clearly written by educators in the creative arts, as well as internationally prominent physicians, therapists and health care professionals.

**2820 Interpreting Disability: A Qualitative Reader**
Teachers College Press
Columbia University
New York, NY 10027
212-678-3929
800-575-6566
FAX: 212-678-4149
e-mail: Carol
www.tcpress.com

*Mary Lynch, Manager*

This book offers a collection of exemplary qualitative research affecting people with disabilities and their families. Instead of focusing upon methodological details, the chapters illustrate the variety of styles and formats that interpretive research can adopt in reporting its results. $24.95
*328 pages Paperback*
*ISBN 0-807731-21-8*

**2821 Intervention Research in Learning Disabilities**
Gallery Bookshop
PO Box 270
Mendocino, CA 95460
707-937-2665
FAX: 707-937-3737
e-mail: info@gallerybooks.com
www.gallerybooks.com

*Linda Pack, Manager*
*Tony Miksak, Owner*

Based on the Symposium on Intervention Research, this volume presents 12 papers addressing issues in intervention research, academic interventions, social and behavioral interventions, and postsecondary interventions. $30.00
*347 pages*

**2822 Introducing Students to Careers in Special Education and Related Services**
Council for Exceptional Children
1110 North Glebe Road
Suite 300
Arlington, VA 22201
703-245-0600
FAX: 703-264-9494
e-mail: service@cec.sped.org
www.cec.sped.org

*Jim Mccormick, President*
*Drew Allbritten, Executive Director*
*Bruce Ramirez, Manager*

Presents an array of activities appropriate for high school and college students to engage in to find out how it feels to be disabled. $5.00
*25 pages*

**2823 Introduction to Learning Disabilities, 2nd Edition**
Allyn & Bacon
75 Arlington Street
Suite 300
Boston, MA 02116
617-848-6000
800-852-8024
FAX: 617-848-7490
e-mail: ab_webmaster@abacon.com
vig.abacon.com
Presents the current state of research in the area of learning disabilities, as well as intervention ideas and programs. Includes updated material on the 1997 re-authorization of IDEA (Individuals with Disabilities Education Act) and expanded coverage of ADHD and its relationship to learning disabilities. Presents the latest information on the characteristics of persons with learning disabilities, causes, and educational interventions.
*608 pages*
*ISBN 0-20529 -43-4*

**2824 Introduction to Mental Retardation**
Allyn & Bacon
75 Arlington Street
Suite 300
Boston, MA 02116
617-848-6000
800-852-8024
FAX: 617-848-7490
e-mail: ab_webmaster@abacon.com
vig.abacon.com

A thorough overview of mental retardation with a level of knowledge suitable for an undergraduate or beginning graduate student.
*350 pages Casebound 1986*
*ISBN 0-134879-27-9*

**2825 Introduction to Special Education: Teaching in an Age of Challenge, 4th Edition**
Allyn & Bacon
75 Arlington Street
Suite 300
Boston, MA 02116     617-848-6000
800-852-8024
FAX: 617-848-7490
e-mail: ab_webmaster@abacon.com
vig.abacon.com
Provides an applied approach to children with disabilities through the use of specific research and suggestions to focus on how the educational practices impact the lives of children, their families, and their teachers.
*640 pages cloth*
*ISBN 0-20526 -94-4*

**2826 Introduction to the Nature and Needs of Students with Mild Disabilities**
Charles C Thomas
2600 South 1st Street
Springfield, IL 62704     217-789-8980
800-258-8980
FAX: 217-789-9130
e-mail: books@ccthomas.com
www.ccthomas.com

*Laura I Moriarty, Author*
*Joseph Antho Travers, Author*
*Michael Thomas, President*

Source of information for the special educator on the needs of students with mild disabilities. It has been designed as an introductory text for an undergraduate degree program in special education. The first chapter includes an overview of students who are at risk for academic failure. The remaining chapters are divided into three categorical units: students with mild mental retardation, behavior disorders, and learning disabilities.
*300 pages Paperback*
*ISBN 0-398067-12-0*

**2827 Introduction to the Profession of Counseling**
McGraw-Hill School Publishing
220 East Danieldale Road
Desoto, TX 75115     972-224-1111
800-442-9685
FAX: 972-228-1982
www.mhschool.com

*Joseph Gavigan, President*

Offers information, theories and techniques for counseling numerous cases from drug addiction to special populations.
*464 pages*

**2828 Issues and Practices in Special Education**
Longman Publishing Group
10 Bank Street
9th Floor
White Plains, NY 10606     914-993-5000
FAX: 914-421-5598
www.tearson.com

*Joanne Dresner, President*

Utilizes current literature, classic articles and case histories to examine such topics as: withholding treatment from severely defective newborns, plastic surgery for Down Syndrome, handicapped offenders, and AIDS.

*290 pages Paperback 1988*
*ISBN 0-582286-39-5*

**2829 Issues and Research in Special Education**
Teachers College Press
PO Box 20
Williston, VT 05495     800-575-6566
FAX: 802-664-7626
www.teacherscollegepress.com

*Marilen McConell, Director*

Provides up-to-date research and discourse on a wide range of topics affecting professionals in the field of special education.
*$38.00*
*264 pages Hardcover*
*ISBN 0-807731-95-1*

**2830 Kendall Demonstration Elementary School Curriculum Guides**
Gallaudet University Bookstore
800 Florida Avenue NE
Washington, DC 20002     202-651-5220
FAX: 202-651-5724
e-mail: bookstore.mailorder@gallaudet.edu
www.bookstore.gallaudet.edu

*Priscilla O'Donnell, Manager*

These guides provide detailed information to help teachers organize curriculums and education programs. Pre-school: $15.95, Health: $8.95, Language Arts: $13.75, Social Studies: $14.95, Math: $11.95, Science: $17.95, Auditory & Speech: $10.95.

**2831 Language Arts: Detecting Special Needs**
Allyn & Bacon
75 Arlington Street
Suite 300
Boston, MA 02116     617-848-6000
800-852-8024
FAX: 617-848-7490
www.ablongman.com
Describes special language arts needs of special learners.
*180 pages paperback 1989*
*ISBN 0-205116-36-1*

**2832 Language Disabilities in Children and Adolescents**
McGraw-Hill School Publishing
220 East Danieldale Road
Desoto, TX 75115     972-224-1111
800-442-9685
FAX: 972-228-1982
www.mhschool.com

*Joseph Gavigan, President*

A comprehensive review of research in language disabilities.

**2833 Language Learning Practices with Deaf Children**
Pro-Ed Publications
8700 Shoal Creek Boulevard
Austin, TX 78757     512-451-3246
800-897-3202
FAX: 800-397-7633
e-mail: feedback@proedinc.com
www.proedinc.com

*Donald Hammill, Owner*
*Courtney King, Marketing Coordinator*

This new edition describes the variety of language-development theories and practices used with deaf children without advocating anyone. *$38.00*

# Education /Professional Texts

*321 pages Hardcover*

**2834  Language and Communication Disorders in Children**
McGraw-Hill School Publishing
220 East Danieldale Road
Desoto, TX  75115                972-224-1111
                                800-442-9685
                         FAX: 972-228-1982
                         www.mhschool.com

*Joseph Gavigan, President*

Comprehensive coverage encompassing all aspects of children's language disorders.
*512 pages*

**2835  Learning Disabilities, Literacy, and Adult Education**
Brookes Publishing
PO Box 10624
Baltimore, MD  21285            410-337-9580
                                800-638-3775
                        FAX: 410-337-8539
             e-mail: custserv@brookespublishing.com
                    www.brookespublishing.com

*Clary Creighton, Exhibits Coordinator*
*Tracy Gray, Educational Sales Manager*
*Paul Brooks, Owner*

This book focuses on adults with severe learning disabilities and the educators who work with them. Described are the characteristics, demographics, and educational and employment status of adults with LD and the laws that protect them in the workplace and in educational settings.
*450 pages Paperback 1998*
*ISBN 1-55766-47-5*

**2836  Learning Disabilities: Concepts and Characteristics**
McGraw-Hill School Publishing
220 East Danieldale Road
Desoto, TX  75115                972-224-1111
                                800-442-9685
                         FAX: 972-228-1982
                         www.mhschool.com

*Cheri Scott, Director*
*Joseph Gavigan, President*

Covers the conceptual basis of learning disabilities, identification, etiology and diagnosis.
*448 pages*

**2837  Learning Disability: Social Class and the Cons of Inequality In American Education**
Greenwood Publishing Group
88 Post Road West
Suite 5007
Westport, CT  06880             203-226-3571
                         FAX: 203-222-1502
                         www.greenwood.com

*Wayne Smith, President*

Presents a detailed historical description of the social and educational assumptions integral to the idea of learning disability.
*167 pages $43.95 - $47.95*
*ISBN 0-313253-96-X*

**2838  Learning and Individual Differences**
National Association of School Psychologists
8455 Colesville Road
Suite 1000
Silver Spring, MD  20910         301-681-3223
                         FAX: 301-608-2514

A multidisciplinary journal in education.

**2839  Learning to See: American Sign Language as a Second Language**
Gallaudet University Press
11030 South Langley Avenue
Chicago, IL  60628              800-621-2736
                         FAX: 800-621-8476
                         TTY:800-621-9347
                         gupress.gallaudet.edu

*Sherman Wilcox, Co-Author*
*Phyliss Wilcox, Co-Author*

This important book has been updated to help teachers teach American Sign Language as a second language, including information on Deaf culture, the history and structure of ASL, teaching methods and issues facing educators. *$19.95*
*160 pages Softcover*

**2840  Legal-Ethical Considerations, Restrictions and Obligations for Clinicians**
Charles C Thomas
2600 South 1st Street
Springfield, IL  62704          217-789-8980
                                800-258-8980
                         FAX: 217-789-9130
                         e-mail: books@ccthomas.com
                         www.ccthomas.com

*Micheal Thomas, President*

Legal-Ethical Considerations, Restrictions and Obligations for Clinicians who Treat Communicative Disorders is a clinical functioning of speech-language pathologists and audiologists is determined not only by their clinical skills but by their awareness of the legal-ethical restrictions and obligations they are required by law to consider in their relationships with their clients and their families *$51.95*
*258 pages Softcover*
*ISBN 0-39806-29-6*

**2841  Library Manager's Guide to Hiring and Serving Disabled Persons**
Mc Farland & Company
PO Box 611
Jefferson, NC  28640            336-246-4460
                                800-253-2187
                         FAX: 336-246-5018
                         e-mail: infoinso@mcfarlandpub.com
                         www.mcfarlandpub.com

*Krall Heinz Roscman, Director*

Information for library staff on hiring and serving disabled persons. *$35.00*
*171 pages Illustrated*
*ISBN 0-89950-16-3*

**2842  Life Beyond the Classroom: Transition Strategies for Young People**
Brookes Publishing
PO Box 10624
Baltimore, MD  21285            410-337-9580
                                800-638-3775
                         FAX: 410-337-8539
             e-mail: custserv@brookespublishing.com
                    www.brookespublishing.com

*Clary Creighton, Exhibits Coordinator*
*Tracy Gray, Educational Sales Manager*
*Paul Brooks, Owner*

This textbook is an essential guide to planning, designing, and implementing successful transition programs for students with disabilities. *$44.00*

*496 pages*
*ISBN 1-55766 -05-7*

**2843 Life-Span Approach to Nursing Care for Individuals with Developmental Disabilities**
Brookes Publishing
PO Box 10624
Baltimore, MD 21285          410-337-9580
                             800-638-3775
                        FAX: 410-337-8539
e-mail: custserv@brookespublishing.com
www.brookespublishing.com

*Clary Creighton, Exhibits Coordinator*
*Tracy Gray, Educational Sales Manager*
*Paul Brooks, Owner*

This reference book was written by and for nurses. This guide addresses fundamental nursing issues such as health promotion, infection control, seizure management, adaptive and assistive technology, and sexuality. Also offered are in-depth case studies, helpful charts and tables, and problem-solving strategies. *$49.95*
*464 pages Hardcover*
*ISBN 1-557661-51-0*

**2844 Lipreading for Children**
Health Publishing Company
PO Box 3805
San Francisco, CA 94119          415-282-8585
                            FAX: 415-750-6550

*Jane Burrows, President*

Collection of games, activities and stories has been used for many years by teachers, educational therapists and language audiologists working with hearing impaired children. *$19.25*

**2845 Look, Now Hear This: Combined Auditory Training and Speech-Reading Instruction**
Charles C Thomas
2600 South 1st Street
Springfield, IL 62704          217-789-8980
                               800-258-8980
                          FAX: 217-789-9130
e-mail: books@ccthomas.com
www.ccthomas.com

*Micheal Thomas, President*

A manual on combined auditory training and speech reading instruction. Also available in cloth: $42.95 (ISBN# 0-398-03830-9) *$ 30.95*
*230 pages Softcover*
*ISBN 0-398061-81-5*

**2846 Mainstreaming Deaf and Hard of Hearing Students: Questions and Answers**
Gallaudet University Bookstore
800 Florida Avenue NE
Washington, DC 20002          202-651-5000
                             800-451-1073
                        FAX: 202-651-5489
www.gallaudet.edu

*Erving Jordan, President*

This booklet presents mainstreaming as one educational option and suggests some considerations for parents, teachers and administrators. *$6.00*
*40 pages*

**2847 Mainstreaming Exceptional Students: A Guide for Classroom Teachers, 4th Edition**
Allyn & Bacon
75 Arlington Street
Suite 300
Boston, MA 02116          617-848-6000
                     FAX: 617-848-7490
e-mail: ab_webmaster@abacon.com
vig.abacon.com
Covers the various categories of exceptional students and discusses educational strategies and classroom management.

*464 pages paperback*
*ISBN 0-20515 -24-6*

**2848 Mainstreaming: A Practical Approach for Teachers**
McGraw-Hill School Publishing
220 East Danieldale Road
Desoto, TX 75115          972-224-1111
                          800-442-9685
                     FAX: 972-228-1982
e-mail: custserv@mcgraw-hill.com
www.mhschool.com

*Joseph Gavigan, President*

Provides teachers, administrators and school psychologists with the background, techniques and strategies they need to offer appropriate services for mildly handicapped students in the mainstream classroom.

**2849 Management of Autistic Behavior**
Pro-Ed Publications
8700 Shoal Creek Boulevard
Austin, TX 78757          512-451-3246
                          800-897-3202
                     FAX: 800-397-7633
e-mail: feedback@proedinc.com
www.proedinc.com

*Donald Hammill, Owner*
*Courtney King, Marketing Coordinator*

This excellent reference is a comprehensive and practical book that tells what works best with specific problems. *$41.00*
*450 pages*

**2850 Managing Diagnostic Tool of Visual Perception**
Gallery Bookshop
PO Box 270
Mendocino, CA 95460          707-937-2665
                        FAX: 707-937-3737
e-mail: info@gallerybooks.com
www.gallerybooks.com

*Linda Pack, Manager*
*Tony Miksak, Owner*

For diagnosing specific perceptual learning abilities and disabilities. *$14.00*

*ISBN 0-80580 -83-4*

**2851 Medical Rehabilitation**
Lippincott, Williams & Wilkins
227 East Washington Square
Philadelphia, PA 19106          215-521-8300
                                800-777-2295
                           FAX: 301-824-7390
www.lpub.com

*J Lippincott, Chief Executive Officer*

Information for the professional on new techniques and treatments in the medical rehabilitation fields. *$80.50*
*368 pages Illustrated*
*ISBN 0-88167 -85-5*

**2852 Mental & Physical Disability Law Digest**
A BA Commission on Mental and Physical Disability
740 15th Street NW
9th Floor
Washington, DC 20005          202-662-1570
                              800-285-2221
                         FAX: 202-662-1032
e-mail: cmpdl@abanet.org
www.abanet.org/disability

*John Parry, Executive Director*
*Amy Allbright, Managing Editor*

Provides comprehensive, summary and analysis of federal and state disability and state disability laws from mental disability law and disability discrimination law perspectives. *$60.00*

*376 pages*
*ISBN 1-590310-05-5*

**2853 Mental Health Concepts and Techniques for the Occupational Therapy Assistant**
Lippincott, Williams & Wilkins
227 East Washington Square
Philadelphia, PA 19106

215-521-8300
800-777-2295
FAX: 301-824-7390
www.lpub.com

*J Lippincott, Chief Executive Officer*

This text offers clear and easily understood explanations of the various theoretical and practiced health models. *$36.00*
*344 pages*
*ISBN 0-88167 -53-X*

**2854 Mental Health and Mental Illness**
Lippincott, Williams & Wilkins
227 East Washington Square
Philadelphia, PA 19106

215-521-8300
800-777-2295
FAX: 301-824-7390
www.lpub.com

*J Lippincott, Chief Executive Officer*

Concise, comprehensive and completely up to date, this book presents the most current theory in mental health nursing for the student and the new practitioner. *$28.95*
*480 pages*
*ISBN 0-39755 -73-7*

**2855 Mentally Ill Individuals**
Mainstream
3 Bethesda Metro Center
Suite 830
Bethesda, MD 20814

301-961-9299
800-247-1380
FAX: 301-654-6714
e-mail: info@mainstreaminc.org

*Charles Moster*

Mainstreaming mentally ill individuals into the workplace. *$2.50*
*12 pages*

**2856 Mentally Retarded Individuals**
Mainstream
3 Bethesda Metro Center
Suite 830
Bethesda, MD 20814

301-961-9299
800-247-1380
FAX: 301-654-6714
e-mail: info@mainstreaminc.org

*Charles Moster*

Mainstreaming mentally retarded individuals into the workplace. *$2.50*
*12 pages*

**2857 Midland Treatment Furniture**
Sammons Preston Rolyan
W68 N158 Evergreen Boulevard
Cedarburg, WI 53012

800-228-3693
FAX: 262-387-8748
e-mail: customerservice@sammonspreston.com
www.sammonspreston.com

This catalog has the biggest selection of OT/PT products anywhere. Whether you deal with larger or smaller caseloads, you need treatment furniture you can count on. Midland Treatment Furniture from SPR is designed and built to stand up to the heaviest use. From tilt tables and traction packages to mat platforms and parallel bars, you'll find the complete line of Midland Treatment Furniture inside this brochure. All products are assembled from premium materials and carefully crafted.

*Free*

**2858 Multidisciplinary Assessment of Children With Learning Disabilities and Mental Retardation**
Gallery Bookshop
PO Box 270
Mendocino, CA 95460

707-937-2665
FAX: 707-937-3737
e-mail: info@gallerybooks.com
www.gallerybooks.com

*Linda Pack, Manager*
*Tony Miksak, Owner*

Assessment of children with learning disabilities and mental retardation. *$24.00*
*346 pages Illustrated*
*ISBN 0-93371 -62-1*

**2859 Multisensory Teaching of Basic Language Skills: Theory and Practice**
Brookes Publishing
PO Box 10624
Baltimore, MD 21285

410-337-9580
800-638-3775
FAX: 410-337-8539
e-mail: custserv@brookespublishing.com
www.brookespublishing.com

*Clary Creighton, Exhibits Coordinator*
*Tracy Gray, Educational Sales Manager*
*Paul Brooks, Owner*

This book presents specific multisensory methods for helping students who are having trouble learning to read due to dyslexia or other learning disabilities. Recommended techniques are offered for teaching alphabet skills, composition, comprehension, handwriting, math, organization and study skills, phonological awareness, reading and spelling. *$59.00*
*608 pages Hardcover 1999*
*ISBN 1-557663-49-1*

**2860 Negotiating the Special Education Maze: A Guide for Parents and Teachers**
Spina Bifida Association of America
4590 MacArthur Boulevard NW
Suite 250
Washington, DC 20007

202-944-3285
800-621-3141
FAX: 202-944-3295
e-mail: sbaa@sbaa.org
www.sbaa.org

*Douglas Soroco, Chairman*
*Joyce Jones, Vice Chairman*
*Cindy Brownstein, Chief Executive Officer*

An excellent aid for the development of an effective special education program. *$19.00*

**2861 No Longer Immune: A Counselor's Guide to AIDS**
American Counceling Association
5999 Stevenson Avenue
Alexandria, VA 22304

703-823-9800
800-473-2329
FAX: 703-823-0252
www.counseling.org

*Richard Yep, Executive Director*

Covers a broad range of issues such as working with specific populations, handling pre and post testing situations, coping with fear, grief and survivor guilt, struggling with spiritual issues and dealing with counter transference. *$26.95*

*295 pages*
*ISBN 1-55620 -64-1*

**2862  Occupational Therapy Across Cultural Boundaries**
Haworth Press
10 Alice Street
Binghamton, NY  13904　　　　　607-722-5857
　　　　　　　　　　　　　　　　800-429-6784
　　　　　　　　　　　　　　FAX: 607-722-6362
　　　　　　　　e-mail: orders@haworthpress.com
　　　　　　　　　　　www.haworthpress.com

*Sandy Sickels, Vice President*
*Becky Minerbaum, Advertising Manager*
*William Cohen, Owner*

Examines the concept of culture from a unique perspective, that of individual occupational therapists who have worked in environments very different from those in which they were educated or had worked previously. *$74.95*
　　　　　　*107 pages Hardcover*
　　　　　　*ISBN 1-560242-23-X*

**2863  Occupational Therapy Approaches to Traumatic Brain Injury**
Haworth Press
10 Alice Street
Binghamton, NY  13904　　　　　607-722-5857
　　　　　　　　　　　　　　　　800-429-6784
　　　　　　　　　　　　　　FAX: 607-722-6362
　　　　　　　　e-mail: orders@haworthpress.com
　　　　　　　　　　　www.haworthpress.com

*Sandy Sickels, Vice President*
*Becky Minerbaum, Advertising Manager*
*William Cohen, Owner*

Focuses on the disabled individual, the family, and the societal responses to the injured, this comprehensive book covers the spectrum of available services from intensive care to transitional and community living. *$74.95*
　　　　　　*137 pages Hardcover*
　　　　　　*ISBN 1-560240-64-4*

**2864  Overcoming Dyslexia in Children, Adolescents and Adults**
Pro-Ed Publications
8700 Shoal Creek Boulevard
Austin, TX  78757　　　　　　　512-451-3246
　　　　　　　　　　　　　　　　800-897-3202
　　　　　　　　　　　　　　FAX: 512-451-8542
　　　　　　　　e-mail: feedback@proedinc.com
　　　　　　　　　　　www.proedinc.com

*Donald Hammill, Owner*
*Courtney King, Marketing Coordinator*

This book describes some forms of dyslexia in detail and then relates those problems to the social, emotional and personal development of dyslexic individuals. *$34.00*
　　　　　　*350 pages Paperback*

**2865  Oxford Textbook of Geriatric Medicine**
Oxford University Press
198 Madison Avenue
New York, NY  10016　　　　　　212-726-6000
　　　　　　　　　　　　　　　　800-334-4249
　　　　　　　　　　　　　　FAX: 212-726-6440
　　　　　　　　　　　www.oup.com/us

*Laura Brown, Chief Executive Officer*
*Ellen Taus, Senior Vice President*

This comprehensive text brings together extensive experience in clinical geriatrics with a strong scientific base in research. *$125.00*

*784 pages*

**2866  PKU for Children: Learning to Measure**
University of Washington PKU Clinic
PO Box 357920
Seattle, WA  98195　　　　　　　206-685-3015
　　　　　　　　　　　　　　　　877-685-3015
　　　　　　　　　　　　　　FAX: 206-685-1286
　　　　　　e-mail: vam@u.washington.edu
　　　　　　www.depts.washington.edu/pku

*Ronald Scott, Medical Director*

Lesson format for parents and teachers.

**2867  Pain Centers: A Revolution in Health Care**
Lippincott Williams And Wilkins
227 East Washington Square
Philadelphia, PA  19106　　　　　215-521-8300
　　　　　　　　　　　　　　　　800-777-2295
　　　　　　　　　　　　　　FAX: 301-824-7390
　　　　　　　　　　　www.lpub.com

*J Lippincott, Chief Executive Officer*
*$103.00*
　　　　　*280 pages*

**2868  Parental Concerns in College Student Mental Health**
Haworth Press
10 Alice Street
Binghamton, NY  13904　　　　　607-722-5857
　　　　　　　　　　　　　　　　800-429-6784
　　　　　　　　　　　　　　FAX: 607-722-6362
　　　　　　　　e-mail: orders@haworthpress.com
　　　　　　　　　　　www.haworthpress.com

*Sandy Sickels, Vice President*
*Becky Minerbaum, Advertising Manager*
*William Cohen, Owner*

An instructive guide for parents and mental health professionals regarding the most important issues about psychological development in college students. *$74.95*
　　　　　　*204 pages Hardcover*
　　　　　　*ISBN 0-866567-20-8*

**2869  Parents and Teachers**
Alexander Graham Bell Association
3417 Volta Place NW
Washington, DC  20007　　　　　202-337-5220
　　　　　　　　　　　　　　　　866-337-5220
　　　　　　　　　　　　　　FAX: 202-337-8314
　　　　　　　　　　e-mail: info@agbell.org
　　　　　　　　　　　www.agbell.org

*Todd Houston, Executive Officer*

This excellent book offers in-depth guidance to parents and teachers whose partnership can foster language in school-aged children with hearing impairments. The first section examines roles of parents, teachers, professionals and children in language acquisition, residual hearing and audiological management, language development stages and readying children for preschool. The second portion of the book presents specific objectives and teaching strategies to use at school and at home. *$27.95*
　　　　　*386 pages*

**2870  Patient and Family Education**
Springer Publishing Company
11 West 42nd Street
15th Floor
New York, NY  10036　　　　　　212-431-4370
　　　　　　　　　　　　　　　　877-687-7476
　　　　　　　　　　　　　　FAX: 212-941-7842
　　　　　e-mail: contactus@springerpub.com
　　　　　　　www.springerpub.com

*Sheri Sussman, Vice President*
*Ursula Springer, President*

This guide outlines the actual clinical content needed to develop, implement and maintain patient education programs. Conveniently arranged in one-hour long lesson plans, each disease or condition is organized in an easy-to-follow format. *$26.95*
*272 pages Softcover*
*ISBN 0-82615 -41-7*

**2871  Peer Tutoring: A Guide for School Psychologists**
National Association of School Psychologists
8455 Colesville Road
Suite 1000
Silver Spring, MD  20910                    301-681-3223
FAX: 301-608-2514
In recent years the term peer tutoring has received more attention as an alternative to the traditional academic arrangements in the classroom for at-risk students. Remedial instruction is often needed by at-risk students and peer tutoring is an attractive alternative due to its use of available resources.
*36 pages*

**2872  Person to Person: Guide for Professionals Working with the Disabled, 2nd Edition**
Paul H Brookes Publishing Company
PO Box 10624
Baltimore, MD  21285                    410-337-9580
800-638-3775
FAX: 410-337-8539
e-mail: custserv@brookespublishing.com
www.brookespublishing.com

*Clary Creighton, Exhibits Coordinator*
*Tracy Gray, Educational Sales Manager*
*Paul Brooks, Owner*

This second edition of an already-popular book helps professionals approach interactions with a people-first, disability second attitude. *$29.00*
*288 pages Paperback 1992*
*ISBN 1-557661-00-6*

**2873  Personality and Emotional Disturbance**
Taylor & Francis
47 Runway Drive
Suite G
Levittown, PA  19057
FAX: 215-785-5515
The brain injured person has unique needs. Recent findings have highlighted that it is the personality, behavioral and emotional problems which most prohibit a return to work, create the greatest burden for the long-term care and rehabilitation of physical and cognitive functions. *$72.00*
*260 pages Cloth*
*ISBN 0-85066 -71-3*

**2874  Peterson's Guide to Colleges with Programs for Learning Disabled Students**
Special Needs Project
324 State Street
Suite H
Santa Barbara, CA  93101                    805-962-8087
800-333-6867
FAX: 805-962-5087
e-mail: books@specialneeds.com
www.specialneeds.com

*Hod Gray, Administrator/Owner*
*Laraine Gray, Coordinator*

The most complete and accurate guide to the more than 900 colleges with programs for the learning disabled. *$19.95*
*406 pages*

**2875  Phenomenology of Depressive Illness**
Human Sciences Press
233 Spring Street
New York, NY  10013                    212-229-2859
800-221-9369
FAX: 212-463-0742
Provides the reader with a detailed knowledge of the clinical characteristics of depressive disorders that will permit judgement of the general ability of the various theoretical models of depressive disorders. *$42.95*

*263 pages Cloth*
*ISBN 0-89885 -69-9*

**2876  Physical Disabilities and Health Impairments: An Introduction**
McGraw-Hill School Publishing
220 East Danieldale Road
Desoto, TX  75115                    972-224-1111
800-442-9685
FAX: 972-228-1982
www.mhschool.com

*Joseph Gavigan, President*

A comprehensive text which presents a wealth of up-to-date medical information for teachers.

**2877  Physical Education and Sports for Exceptional Students**

McGraw-Hill Company
2460 Kerper Boulevard
Dubuque, IA  52001                    563-588-1451
800-338-3987
FAX: 614-755-5654
www.mhhe.com/hper/physed

*Kurt Strand, Vice President*

Physical education for exceptional students and teaching students with learning and behavior exceptionalities.
*Cloth*

**2878  Physical Management of Multiple Handicaps: A Professional's Guide**
Brookes Publishing Company
PO Box 10624
Baltimore, MD  21285                    410-337-9580
800-638-3775
FAX: 410-337-8539
e-mail: custserv@brookespublishing.com
www.brookespublishing.com

*Clary Creighton, Exhibits Coordinator*
*Tracy Gray, Educational Sales Manager*
*Paul Brooks, Owner*

Comprehensive guide, takes a transdisciplinary approach to therapeutic/technological management of persons with multiple handicaps. *$36.00*
*352 pages Hardcover*
*ISBN 1-557660-47-6*

**2879  Physically Handicapped in Society**
Ayer Company Publishers
RR 1
Box 85-1
North Stratford, NH  03590                    603-669-9307
888-267-7323
FAX: 603-669-7945
e-mail: stg@ncia.net

*Kathy Train, Office Manager*
*Ellie Phipps, Customer Service*

A group of 39 books. Biographies that offer studies on attitudes, sociological and psychological. Please write or call for catalog. *$965.00*
*Hardcover*
*ISBN 0-40513 -00-3*

**2880  Practicing Rehabilitation with Geriatric Clients**
Springer Publishing Company
11 West 42nd Street
New York, NY  10036                    212-431-4370
877-687-7476
FAX: 212-941-7842
e-mail: marketing@springerpub.com
www.springerpub.com

*Annette Imperati, Marketing/Sales Director*
*Ursula Springer, President*

Physical therapy in the geriatric client, psychological and psychiatric considerations in the rehabilitation of the elderly. *$32.95*

*256 pages Hardcover*
*ISBN 0-82616 -80-5*

**2881  Pragmatic Approach**
Educators Publishing Service
625 Mount Auburn Street
Suite 3
Cambridge, MA  02138            617-547-6706
                               800-225-5750
                          FAX: 888-440-2665
                   e-mail: feedback@epsbooks.com
                          www.epsbooks.com

*Charles H Heinle, Vice President*
*Alexandra S Bigelow, Author*
*Gunnar Voltz, President*

Monograph on evaluation of children's performances on
Slingerland Pre-Reading Screening Procedures to Identify First
Grade Academic Needs. *$6.00*
*56 pages*
*ISBN 0-838816-85-1*

**2882  Preschoolers with Special Needs: Children At-Risk,
Children with Disabilities, 2nd Edition**
Allyn & Bacon
75 Arlington Street
Suite 300
Boston, MA  02116            617-848-6000
                             800-852-8024
                        FAX: 617-848-7490
                        www.ablongman.com
Explores ways of providing preschool children with special
needs and their families with a learning environment that will
help them develop and learn. Emphasizes the needs of preschoolers age three to six and provides information to teachers
and others who work with young children in all settings. Current
models of curricula, which incorporate new features from research and practical expreiences with children who have special
needs, are described and discussed. *$59.00*
*336 pages cloth*
*ISBN 0-205358-79-9*

**2883  Preventing Academic Failure**
Educators Publishing Service
625 Mount Auburn Street
Suite 3
Cambridge, MA  02138            617-547-6706
                               800-225-5750
                          FAX: 888-440-2665
                   e-mail: feedback@epsbooks.com
                          www.epsbooks.com

*Charles H Heinle, Vice President*
*Alexandra S Bigelow, Author*
*Gunnar Voltz, President*

Ungraded multisensory curriculum coordinating
Orton-Gillingham and Merrill Linguistic reading techniques for
language disabled students. Teaches phonics, spelling and reading to reinforce the development of language skills. A separate
handwriting program is available. *$42.00*
*284 pages Paperback*
*ISBN 0-838852-71-8*

**2884  Preventing School Dropouts**
Pro-Ed Publications
8700 Shoal Creek Boulevard
Austin, TX  78757            512-451-3246
                             800-897-3202
                        FAX: 800-397-7633
                   e-mail: feedback@proedinc.com
                          www.proedinc.com

*Donald Hammill, Owner*
*Courtney King, Marketing Coordinator*

For secondary teachers, special education and regular, who have
difficulty teaching youth in their classes. Presented are 120 tactics, specific instructional techniques, for helping adolescents to
stay in school. Each tactic is written in a format that includes five
sections. *$38.00*

*509 pages*

**2885  Prevocational Assessment**
Exceptional Education
PO Box 15308
Seattle, WA  98115            206-262-9538
                        FAX: 475-486-4510

*J E Stewart, Owner*

Use the PACG to assess your students in nine areas (attendance
and endurance, learning and behavior, communication skills,
social skills, grooming and eating and toileting) covering 46
specific workshop experiences. *$12.00*
*16 pages Complete Set*
*ISBN 1-87786 -23-7*

**2886  Progress Without Punishment: Approaches for
Learners with Behavior Problems**
Teachers College Press
Columbia University
New York, NY  10027            212-854-1754
                               800-575-6566
                          FAX: 212-678-4149
                   www.teacherscollegepress.com

*Carol Saltz, Director*
*Brian Ellerbeck, Executive Acquisitions Editor*
*Lee Bollinger, President*

In this volume, the authors argue against the use of punishment,
and instead advocate the use of alternative intervention procedures. *$17.95*
*184 pages Paperback*
*ISBN 0-807729-11-6*

**2887  Promoting Postsecondary Education for Students with
Learning Disabilities**
Pro-Ed Publications
8700 Shoal Creek Boulevard
Austin, TX  78757            512-451-3246
                             800-897-3202
                        FAX: 800-397-7633
                   e-mail: feedback@proedinc.com
                          www.proedinc.com

*Donald Hammill, Owner*
*Courtney King, Marketing Coordinator*

Primarily designed for postsecondary service providers who are
responsible for serving college students with learning disabilities. *$41.00*
*440 pages*

**2888  Promoting Special Education Career Awareness**
Council for Exceptional Children
1110 North Glebe Road
Suite 300
Arlington, VA  22201            703-245-0600
                          FAX: 703-264-9494
                   e-mail: service@cec.sped.org
                          www.cec.sped.org

*Drew Allbritten, Executive Director*
*Bruce Ramirez, Manager*

Written for use by individuals or groups interested in promoting
careers in special education. *$10.00*
*57 pages*

**2889  Psychiatric Mental Health Nursing**
Lippincott, Williams & Wilkins
227 East Washington Square
Philadelphia, PA  19106            215-521-8300
                                   800-777-2295
                          FAX: 301-824-7390
                          www.lpub.com

*J Lippincott, Chief Executive Officer*

This text emphasizes and contrasts the roles of the generalist
nurse and the psychiatric nurse specialist. *$52.00*

*1120 pages Illustrated*

**2890  Psychoeducational Assessment of Hearing-Impaired Students**
Pro-Ed Publications
8700 Shoal Creek Boulevard
Austin, TX 78757                           512-451-3246
                                           800-897-3202
                                   FAX: 800-397-7633
                       e-mail: feedback@proedinc.com
                                     www.proedinc.com

*Donald Hammill, Owner*
*Courtney King, Marketing Coordinator*

This book includes a comprehensive presentation of issues and procedures related to the assessment of hearing-impaired students. *$29.00*
            *251 pages Paperback*

**2891  Psychoeducational Assessment of Visually Impaired and Blind Students**
Pro-Ed
8700 Shoal Creek Boulevard
Austin, TX 78757                           512-451-3246
                                           800-897-3202
                                   FAX: 800-397-7633
                       e-mail: feedback@proedinc.com
                                     www.proedinc.com

*Joshua Jeffrey, Marketing Custodian*
*Courtney King, Marketing Coordinator*
*Donald Hammill, Owner*

Professional reference book that addresses the problems specific to assessment of visually impaired and blind children. Of particular value to the practitioner are the extensive reviews of available tests, including ways to adapt those not designed for use with the visually handicapped. *$29.00*
            *140 pages Paperback*
            *ISBN 0-890791-08-2*

**2892  Rational-Emotive Therapy with Alcoholics**
Pergamon Press
655 Avenue of the Americas
New York, NY 10010                         212-213-8310

*Jeff Sinaw, President*

Therapy text on alcoholism and substance abusers. *$ 15.95*
            *176 pages Softcover*
            *ISBN 0-08033 -74-3*

**2893  Reading and Deafness**
Pro-Ed Publications
8700 Shoal Creek Boulevard
Austin, TX 78757                           512-451-3246
                                           800-897-3202
                                   FAX: 800-397-7633
                       e-mail: feedback@proedinc.com
                                     www.proedinc.com

*Donald Hammill, Owner*
*Courtney King, Marketing Coordinator*

Three areas are looked at in this book: deaf children's prereading development of real-world knowledge, cognitive abilities and linguistic skills. *$39.00*
            *422 pages*

**2894  Reading and the Special Learner**
Ablex Publishing Corporation
PO Box 811
Stamford, CT 06904
                                   FAX: 203-661-0792
Explores the needs of the special learner: compensatory methods and adaptive means. *$73.25*

*272 pages*
*ISBN 0-89391 -95-9*

**2895  Readings on Research in Stuttering**
Longman Publishing Group
10 Bank Street
9th Floor
White Plains, NY 10606                     914-993-5000
                                   FAX: 914-421-5598
                                     www.ablongman.com

*Roth Wilkofsky, Systems Contact*
*Joanne Dresner, President*

Collection of the key journal articles published on stuttering over the past decade, addressing trends in recent research in the field.
            *231 pages Paperback 1991*
            *ISBN 0-801304-10-5*

**2896  Recreation Activities for the Elderly**
Springer Publishing Company
11 West 42nd Street
15th Floor
New York, NY 10036                         212-431-4370
                                           877-687-7476
                                   FAX: 212-941-7842
                   e-mail: marketing@springerpub.com
                                     www.springerpub.com

*Annette Imperati, Marketing/Sales Director*
*Joanne Dresner, President*

Included in this volume are simple crafts that utilize easily obtainable, inexpensive materials, hobbies focusing on collections, nature, and the arts' and games emphasizing both mental and physical activity. *$23.95*
            *240 pages Softcover*
            *ISBN 0-82616 -30-1*

**2897  Reference Manual for Communicative Sciences and Disorders**
Pro- Ed Publications
8700 Shoal Creek Boulevard
Austin, TX 78757                           512-451-3246
                                           800-897-3202
                                   FAX: 800-397-7633
                       e-mail: feedback@proedinc.com
                                     www.proedinc.com

*Donald Hammill, Owner*
*Courtney King, Marketing Coordinator*

An indispensable guide to standards and values essential in the assessment of communication disorders. *$54.00*
            *393 pages*

**2898  Rehabilitation Counseling and Services: Profession and Process**
Charles C Thomas
2600 South 1st Street
Springfield, IL 62704                      217-789-8980
                                           800-258-8980
                                   FAX: 217-789-9130
                       e-mail: books@ccthomas.com
                                     www.ccthomas.com

*Michael Thomas, President*

Gives information on the rehabilitation and counseling process, work evaluation, work adjustment and more. *$52.95*
            *376 pages Cloth*
            *ISBN 0-39052 -24-4*

**2899  Rehabilitation Interventions for the Institutionalized Elderly**
Haworth Press
10 Alice Street
Binghamton, NY 13904                       607-722-5857
                                           800-429-6784
                                   FAX: 607-771-0012
                   e-mail: orders@haworthpress.com
                                     www.haworthpress.com

*William Cohen, Owner/Publisher*

Gerontology professionals offer suggestions to enrich the quality of rehabilitation services offered to the institutionalized elderly. This volume examines up to the minute ideas, some that would have been unlikely even a few years ago, that focus exclusively on rehabilitation services for the institutionalized elderly. *$44.95*
*77 pages Hardcover*
*ISBN 0-866568-33-6*

**2900  Rehabilitation Nursing for the Neurological Patient**
Springer Publishing Company
536 Broadway
New York, NY  10012                    212-431-4370
877-687-7476
FAX: 212-941-7842
e-mail: marketing@springerpub.com
www.springerpub.com

*Annette Imperati, Marketing/sales Director*
*Ursula Springer, President*

A practical new reference written especially for practicing nurses who work with neurologically disabled persons. *$32.95*
*240 pages*

**2901  Rehabilitation Resource Manual: VISION**
Resources for Rehabilitation
33 Bedford Street
Suite 19A
Lexington, MA  02420                    781-890-6371
FAX: 781-867-7517

*Susan Greenblatt*

A desk reference that enables service providers, librarians and others to make effective referrals. Includes guidelines on establishing self-help groups, information on research and service organizations, and chapters on assistive technology, for special population groups and by eye condition. *$44.95*
*Biennial*

**2902  Rehabilitation Technology**
Haworth Press
10 Alice Street
Binghamton, NY  13904                    607-722-5857
800-429-6784
FAX: 607-722-6362
e-mail: orders@haworthpress.com
www.haworthpress.com

*Sandy Sickels, Vice President*
*Becky Minerbaum, Advertising Manager*
*William Cohen, Owner*

Learn how the use of technological devices can enhance the lives of disabled children. Informs physical therapists, occupational therapists, and rehabilitation technologists about the devices that are available today and provides important background information on these devices. *$74.95*
*173 pages Hardcover*
*ISBN 1-560240-33-4*

**2903  Report Writing in Assessment and Evaluation**
Stout Vocational Rehab Institute
University of Wisconsin-Stout
Menomonie, WI  54751                    715-232-1478
FAX: 715-232-2356

*Ronald R Fry, Manager*
*Darlene Botterbusch, Program Assistant*

This examines questions of who are you writing for and what does the referral source want. Defines characteristics of good reports, common problems, writing in different settings, types of reports, getting ready to write, and writing prescriptive recommendations. *$17.75*

*188 pages Softcover*

**2904  Resources for Rehabilitation**
33 Bedford Street
Suite 19A
Lexington, MA  02420                    781-862-6455
FAX: 781-368-9096

*R Frances Weisse, President*

Provides training and information to professionals and the public about disabilities and resources available to help. Publishes resource guides, professional publications and patient/client educational materials. Conducts custom designed training programs and workshops.

**2905  Restructuring High Schools for All Students: Taking Inclusion to the Next Level**
Brookes Publishing
PO Box 10624
Baltimore, MD  21285                    410-337-9580
800-638-3775
FAX: 410-337-8539
e-mail: custserv@brookespublishing.com
www.brookespublishing.com

*Clary Creighton, Exhibits Coordinator*
*Tracy Gray, Educational Sales Manager*
*Paul Brooks, Owner*

Details the process of creating an inclusive, collaborate community of learners and teachers at the secondary level. *$29.95*
*304 pages Paperback 1998*
*ISBN 1-557663-13-0*

**2906  Restructuring for Caring and Effective Education: Administrative Guide**
Brookes Publishing
PO Box 10624
Baltimore, MD  21285                    410-337-9580
800-638-3775
FAX: 410-337-8539
e-mail: custserv@brookespublishing.com
www.brookespublishing.com

*Clary Creighton, Exhibits Coordinator*
*Tracy Gray, Educational Sales Manager*
*Paul Brooks, Owner*

In this empowering book, leading general and special education schools reform experts synthesize the major school restructuring initiatives and describe the processes and rationale for changing the organizational structure and instructional practices of schools. *$29.00*
*384 pages Paperback*
*ISBN 1-55766 -91-3*

**2907  Scoffolding Student Learning**
Brookline Books
PO Box 1047
Cambridge, MA  02139                    617-495-3682
800-666-2665
FAX: 617-868-1772
e-mail: brooklinebks@delphi.com
www.brooklinebooks.com

*William Walters, Author*
*Esther Isabe Wilder, Author*

Collection of papers on the theory and practice of scoffolding—an interactive style of instructions that helps students develop more powerful thinking tools.. *$21.95*

*180 pages Paperback*
*ISBN 1-571290-36-2*

**2908 Screening in Chronic Disease**
Oxford University Press
2001 Evans Road
Cary, NC 27513

919-677-0977
800-451-7556
FAX: 919-677-2673
e-mail: humaneres@oup-usa.org
www.oup-usa.org

*Henry Reece, Chief Executive Officer*
*Thomas Carty, Senior Vice President*

Early detection, or screening, is a common strategy for controlling chronic disease, but little information has been available to help determine which screening procedures are worthwhile. *$42.50*
*256 pages*

**2909 Selective Nontreatment of Handicapped**
Oxford University Press
2001 Evans Road
Cary, NC 27513

919-677-0977
800-451-7556
FAX: 919-677-2673
e-mail: humanres@oup-usa.org
www.us.oup.com

*Thomas Carty, Senior Vice President*

Information on selective nontreatment of handicapped newborns, moral dilemmas in neonatal medicine. *$17.95*
*304 pages Paperback*

**2910 Service Coordination for Early Intervention: Parents and Friends**
Brookline Books
34 University Road
Brookline, MA 02445

800-666-2665
800-666-2665
FAX: 617-734-3952
e-mail: brooklinebks@delphi.com
www.brooklinebooks.com

*William H Walters, Author*
*Esther I Wilder, Author*

This book helps administrators and professionals to structure early intervention and ongoing services so that professionals work collaboratively with parents to promote the health, well being and development of children with special needs. *$19.95*
*110 pages Paperback*
*ISBN 0-91479-91-3*

**2911 Services for the Seriously Mentally Ill: A Survey of Mental Health Centers**
Nat'l Council for Community Behavioral Healthcare
12300 Twinbrook Parkway
Suite 320
Rockville, MD 20852

301-984-6200
FAX: 301-881-7159
www.nccbh.org

*Linda Rosenberg, President/CEO*
*Dale K Klatzker, Board Chair*

This ground-breaking report documents what administrators and practitioners have maintained for many years: community mental health organizations devote a significant percentage of the human and financial resources to serving the seriously mentally ill. *$30.00*

**2912 Shop Talk**
Research Press
PO Box 9177
Champaign, IL 61826

217-352-3273
800-519-2707
FAX: 217-352-1221
e-mail: rp@researchpress.com
www.researchpress.com

*Russell Pence, President*

A well-structured group training program that covers five crucial communication areas: social communication routines, identification information, basic language skills, language-related concepts and cognitive components. The authors emphasize direct cooperation between educators and parents by providing over 100 interesting activities that focus on the student's affective impact on others, unique identify as a person, self-care, grooming, leisure and ability to work independently. *$25.95*
*236 pages Paperback*
*ISBN 0-878222-29-4*

**2913 Signed English Schoolbook**
Gallaudet University Press
11030 South Langley Avenue
Chicago, IL 60628

800-621-2736
FAX: 800-621-8476
TTY:800-621-9347
www.gupress.gallaudet.edu

*Karen Hyzy, Customer Service Manager*

The Signed English Schoolbook provides vocabulary for teachers and others who serve school-age children and adolescents and covers the full range of school activities. *$13.95*
*184 pages Softcover*

**2914 Smart But Stuck: Emotional Aspects of Learning Disabilities and Imprisoned Intelligence**
Haworth Press
10 Alice Street
Binghamton, NY 13904

607-722-5857
800-429-6784
FAX: 607-722-6362
e-mail: orders@haworthpress.com
www.haworthpress.com

*Sandy Sickles, Vice President*
*Beck Minerbaum, Advertising Manager*
*William Cohen, Owner*

Elaborates on new research about imprisoned intelligence and the emotional consequences of learning disabilities. It is also for psychoterapists, educators, school social workers, medical personnel, people dealing with prisons, etc. It helps those who struggle with learning disabilities (and people who help them) build self esteem, face LD obstacles, bypass weaknesses, and enhance strenghts. *$34.95*
*228 pages Hardcover*
*ISBN 0-789014-66-1*

**2915 Social Studies: Detecting and Correcting Special Needs**
Allyn & Bacon
75 Arlington Street
Suite 300
Boston, MA 02116

617-848-6000
800-852-8024
FAX: 617-848-7490
www.ablongman.com

Describes social studies and special needs for special learners.
*180 pages 1990*
*ISBN 0-205121-51-9*

**2916 Social and Emotional Development of Exceptional Students: Handicapped**
Charles C Thomas
2600 South 1st Street
Springfield, IL 62704

217-789-8980
800-258-8980
FAX: 217-789-9130
e-mail: books@ccthomas.com
www.ccthomas.com

*Michael Thomas, President*

Sixteen years after the passage of P.L. 94-142, the dream of special educators to educate the handicapped and nonhandicapped children and youth together resulting in increased academic gains and age-appropriate school skills for handicapped children and youth has not yet materialized. This book helps eliminate an existing void by providing teachers with understandable information regarding the social and emotional development of exceptional students. Also in cloth at $41.95 (ISBN# 0-398-05781-8) *$29.95*

*218 pages Softcover*
*ISBN 0-398061-94-7*

**2917  Socialization Games for Persons with Disabilities**
Charles C Thomas
2600 South 1st Street
Springfield, IL  62704
217-789-8980
800-258-8980
FAX: 217-789-9130
e-mail: books@ccthomas.com
www.ccthomas.com

*Michael Thomas, President*

This text will assist those who want to teach severely multiple disabled students by providing information on: general principles of intervention and classroom organization; managing the behavior of students; physically managing students and using adaptive equipment; teaching eating skills; teaching toileting, dressing , and hygiene skills; teaching cognition, communication, and socialization skills; teaching independent living skills; and teaching infants and preschool students. *$24.95*
*140 pages Paperback*
*ISBN 0-39806 -73-4*

**2918  Special Education Today**
LifeWay Christian Resources Southern Baptist Conv.
127 9th Avenue N
Nashville, TN  37234
615-251-2089
800-458-2772
FAX: 651-251-5764
e-mail: specialed@lifeway.com
www.lifeway.com

*Ellen Beene, Editor*
*Wade Stapleton, Manager*

This unique quarterly publications ministers to people with special education needs and to their families, the church, and other caregivers. It offers a variety of helps and encouragement, including: What's working in churches, Suggestions for adapting teaching techniques, inspirational stories about people who have disabilities, Parenting and family issues, Ideas for reaching, witnessing, worship, and recreation. *$4.25*
*36 pages Quarterly*

**2919  Special Education for Today**
Allyn & Bacon
75 Arlington Street
Suite 300
Boston, MA  02116
617-848-6000
800-852-8024
FAX: 617-848-7490
www.ablongman.com

*Thomas Longman, Founder*
*Nancy Forfyth, President*

An undergraduate introduction to special education covering all major areas of exceptionality. Contains pedagogical features designed to make the book accessible to the undergraduate.
*576 pages hardcover 1984*
*ISBN 0-138264-53-8*

**2920  Speech and the Hearing-Impaired Child**
Alexander Graham Bell Association
3417 Volta Place NW
Washington, DC  20007
202-337-5220
866-337-5220
FAX: 202-337-8314
e-mail: info@agbell.org
www.agbell.org

*Todd Houston, Executive Director*

This textbook for professionals deals with basic theoretical issues in the acquisition of speech and the form of language (phonetics and phonology) in children with hearing losses. It provides a systematic framework to develop and evaluate speech target behaviors and their underlying subskills. *$29.95*

*402 pages Paperback*

**2921  Speech-Language Pathology and Audiology: An Introduction**
McGraw-Hill School Publishing
220 East Danieldale Road
Desoto, TX  75115
972-224-1111
800-442-9685
FAX: 972-228-1982
www.mhschool.com

*Joseph Gavigan, President*

Offers classroom-tested coverage of clinical objectives and functioning.
*301 pages*

**2922  Spinal Cord Dysfunction**
Oxford University Press
2001 Evans Road
Cary, NC  27513
919-677-0977
800-451-7556
FAX: 919-677-1303
e-mail: humanres@oup-usa.org
www.oup-usa.org

*Henry Reece, Chief Executive Director*
*Thomas Carty, Senior Vice President*

Offers information on restoration of function after spinal cord damage as seen from the point of view of identification of impaired or absent function in the nerve cells and processes which survive after the initial insult, intact but with impaired functions. *$95.00*
*368 pages*

**2923  Spotting Language Problems**
Los Amigos Research Associates
7035 Galewood Street
San Diego, CA  92120
619-286-3162
FAX: 619-286-3162

*Donald R Omark, Partner*

A screening tool for educators, clinicians, and paraprofessionals to help them identify students with language problems that may result in learing difficulties. Based on evaluating ordinary conversation. *$30.00*

**2924  Strategies for Teaching Learners with Special Needs**
McGraw-Hill School Publishing
220 East Danieldale Road
Desoto, TX  75115
972-224-1111
800-442-9685
FAX: 972-228-1982
www.mhschool.com

*Joseph Gavigan, President*

This is a text that helps special educators develop the full range of teaching competencies needed to be effective.
*560 pages*

**2925  Strategies for Teaching Students with Learning and Behavior Problems**
Allyn & Bacon
75 Arlington Street
Suite 300
Boston, MA  02116
617-848-6000
800-852-8024
FAX: 617-848-7490
www.ablongman.com

*Thomas Longman, Founder*

Provides descriptions of methods and strategies for teaching students with learning and behvior problems, managing professional roles, and collaborating with families, professionals, and paraprofessionals.

*544 pages*
*ISBN 0-205113-89-3*

**2926 Students with Acquired Brain Injury: The School's Response**
Brookes Publishing
PO Box 10624
Baltimore, MD 21285      410-337-9580
800-638-3775
FAX: 410-337-8539
e-mail: custserv@brookespublishing.com
www.brookespublishing.com

*Clary Creighton, Exhibits Coordinator*
*Tracy Gray, Educational Sales Manager*
*Paul Brooks, Owner*

This book is designed for school professionals and describes a range of issues that this population faces and presents proven means of addressing them in ways that benefit all students. Included topics are hospital-to-school transitions, effective assessment strategies, model programs in public schools, interventions to assist classroom teachers, and ways to involve family members in the educational program. *$29.95*
*424 pages Paperback 1997*
*ISBN 1-55766 -85-1*

**2927 Students with Mild Disabilities in the Secondary School**
Longman Group
1185 Avenue of the Americas
New York, NY 10036      212-782-3300

www.ablongman.com

*Roth Wilkofsky, Chief Executive Officer*

Provides methods and strategies for curriculum delivery to students with mild disabilities at the secondary school level.
*2313G pages Paperback 1991*
*ISBN 0-801301-66-1*

**2928 Support Groups for Practicing Special Education Professionals**
Council for Exceptional Children
1110 North Glebe Road
Suite 300
Arlington, VA 22201      703-245-0600
FAX: 703-264-9494
www.cec.sped.org

*Jim McCormick, President*
*Trudy Kerr, Executive Director*
*Bruce Ramirez, Manager*

The demands and logistics of teaching make it difficult for teachers to form and maintain professional support networks as part of their working day. *$10.00*
*56 pages*

**2929 Supporting and Strengthening Families**
Brookline Books
34 University Road
Brookline, MA 02445      617-734-6772
800-666-2665
FAX: 617-734-3952
e-mail: brooklinebks@delphi.com
www.brooklinebooks.com

*William Walters, Author*
*Esther Isabe Wilder, Author*

A collection of papers addressing the theory, methods, strategies, and practices involved in adopting an empowerment and family-centered resources approach to supporting families and strengthening individual and family functioning. *$30.00*

*252 pages Paperback*
*ISBN 0-91479 -94-8*

**2930 Survival Guide for the First-Year Special Education Teacher**
Council for Exceptional Children
1110 North Glebe Road
Suite 300
Arlington, VA 22201      703-245-0600
866-915-5000
FAX: 703-264-9494
e-mail: service@cec.sped.org
www.cec.sped.org

*Drew Allbritten, Executive Director*
*Bruce Ramirez, Manager*

Help for teachers. This survival guide was developed to help teachers be prepared for and enjoy the challenges of a new career. *$12.00*
*47 pages*

**2931 TESTS**
Slosson Educational Publications
PO Box 280
East Aurora, NY 14052      716-652-0930
800-828-4800
FAX: 800-665-3840
e-mail: slosson@slosson.com
www.slosson.com

*Leslie Foote, Office Personnel*
*Peggy Meyer, Office Personnel*
*Steven Slosson, President*

Slosson Educational Publications, Inc. offers educators an extensive selection of testing products, along with books on autism. ADED and other special needs materials. Our catalog includes 30 pages of speech-language testing and language rehabilitation products. The behavioral conduct. Special needs section includes checklist and scales on aberrant/disruptive behavior, tapes on ADD, as well as products for dyslexia and remediation of reversals.

**2932 Teacher's Guide to Including Students with Disabilities in Regular Physical Education**
Brookes Publishing
PO Box 10624
Baltimore, MD 21285      410-337-9580
800-638-3775
FAX: 410-337-8539
e-mail: custserv@brookespublishing.com
www.brookespublishing.com

*Clary Creighton, Exhibits Coordinator*
*Tracy Gray, Educational Sales Manager*
*Paul Brooks, Owner*

Provides simple and creative strategies for meaningfully including children with disabilities in regular physical education programs. *$39.00*
*288 pages Paperback*
*ISBN 1-557661-56-1*

**2933 Teachers Working Together**
Brookline Books
34 University Road
Brookline, MA 02445      617-734-6772
800-666-2665
FAX: 617-734-3952
e-mail: brooklinebks@delphi.com
www.brooklinebooks.com

*Hon Deshier, Author*
*Jean Schumaker, Author*
*Karen Harris, Author*

This collection of papers describes collaboraborative efforts for such classroom settings as preschools, elementary, middle and high schools, for content area teaching and into the transition to work. Each chapter describes actual practice and analyzes what is required to accomplish this collaboration. *$19.95*

Paperback 1998
ISBN 1-57139 -66-4

**2934 Teaching Adults with Learning Disabilities**
Krieger Publishing Company
PO Box 9542
Melbourne, FL 32902

321-724-9542
800-724-0025
FAX: 321-951-3671
e-mail: info@krieger-publishing.com
www.krieger-publishing.com

James Gardner, Editor
Peter Lapaglia, Editor
R Krieger, Owner

Designed to teach literacy providers and classroom instructors how to recognize specific learning disability (LD) patterns and block reading, spelling, writing and arithmetic skills in students of all ages. One of the major problems faced by literary providers is keeping low-skill adults involved in basic education programs long enough to increase their literacy skills to the level of success. Shows instructors in adult education how to modify teaching strategies. $25.50
160 pages
ISBN 0-894649-10-8

**2935 Teaching Children with Autism: Strategies for Initiating Positive Interactions**
Brookes Publishing
PO Box 10624
Baltimore, MD 21285

410-337-9580
800-638-3775
FAX: 410-337-8539
e-mail: custserv@brookespublishing.com
www.brookespublishing.com

Clary Creighton, Exhibits Coordinator
Tracy Gray, Educational Sales Manager
Paul Brooks, Owner

Stategies for initiating positive interactions and improving learning opportunities. This guide begins with an overview of characteristics and long-term strategies and proceeds through discussions that detail specific techniques for normalizing environments, reducing disruptive behavior, improving language and social skills, and enhancing generalization. $32.95
256 pages Paperback
ISBN 1-55766 -80-4

**2936 Teaching Disturbed and Disturbing Students: An Integrative Approach**
Pro-Ed Publications
8700 Shoal Creek Boulevard
Austin, TX 78757

512-451-3246
800-897-3202
FAX: 800-397-7633
e-mail: feedback@proedinc.com
www.proedinc.com

Donald Hammil, Owner
Courtney King, Author

Using an integrative approach, this text provides teachers with step-by-step details of how to implement and use the methods and theories discussed in each chapter. $37.00
465 pages

**2937 Teaching Every Child Every Day: Integrated Learning in Diverse Classrooms**
Brookline Books
34 University Road
Brookline, MA 02445

617-734-6772
800-666-2665
FAX: 617-734-3952
e-mail: brooklinebks@delphi.com
www.brooklinebooks.com

William H Walters, Author
Esther Isabe Wilder, Author

Collection of articles addressing various issues in teaching to diverse classrooms—varied in need for special educational services, English proficiency, and socioeconomic and racial backgrounds. $19.95
224 pages Paperback
ISBN 0-57129 -40-0

**2938 Teaching Infants and Preschoolers with Handicaps**
Mc Graw- Hill, School Publishing
220 East Danieldale Road
Desoto, TX 75115

972-224-1111
800-442-9685
FAX: 972-228-1982
www.mhschool.com

Joseph Gavigan, President

Builds a solid background in early childhood special education.
380 pages

**2939 Teaching Language-Disabled Children: A Communication/Games Intervention**
Brookline Books
34 University Road
Brookline, MA 02445

617-734-6772
800-666-2665
FAX: 617-734-3954
e-mail: brooklinebks@delphi.com
www.brooklinebooks.com

William Walters, Author
Esther Isabe Wilder, Author
Barbara Hecht, Author

Describes exactly how to play the communication games. It does not simply exhort practitioners to give topic-relevant responses and take advantage of opportunities. It provides specific teaching methods and not simply a new perspective on language remediation. $22.95
Hardcover
ISBN 0-91479 -38-7

**2940 Teaching Learners with Mild Disabilities: Integrating Research and Practice**
Brooke Publishing
PO Box 10624
Baltimore, MD 21285

410-337-9580
800-638-9580
FAX: 431-033-7853
e-mail: bc-info@brookscole.com
www.brookespublishing.com

Clary Creigthon, Exhibits Coordinator
Paul Brooks, Owner

The authors illustrate interactions among regular teachers, special education teachers and students with mild disabilities through the use of hypothetical case studies of students and teachers.
496 pages Paperbound
ISBN 0-53421 -02-0

**2941 Teaching Mathematics to Students with Learning Disabilities**
Pro-Ed Publications
8700 Shoal Creek Boulevard
Austin, TX 78757

512-451-3246
800-897-3202
FAX: 800-397-7633
e-mail: feedback@proedinc.com
www.proedinc.com

Donald Hammill, Owner
Courtney King, Marketing Coordinator

New trends in school mathematics have surfaced in the teaching world. Problem-solving, estimation and the use of computers are receiving considerably greater emphasis than in the past and these areas are included in the new text. $38.00

*486 pages Paperback*

## 2942 Teaching Mildly and Moderately Handicapped Students

Allyn & Bacon
75 Arlington Street
Suite 300
Boston, MA 02116               617-848-6000
                               800-852-8024
                               FAX: 617-848-7490
                               www.ablongman.com

A cross-categorical text providing teaching ideas and techniques. Focuses on the theme of learning as a constructive process in which the learner interacts with the environment, constructing new systems of knowledge, Behavioral techniques and research are also presented.
*hardcover 1986*
*ISBN 0-138939-00-4*

## 2943 Teaching Reading to Children with Down Syndrome: A Guide for Parents and Teachers

Woodbine House
6510 Bells Mill Road
Bethesda, MD 20817             301-897-3570
                               800-843-7323
                               FAX: 301-897-5838
                               www.woodbinehouse.com

*Alison Oelwein, Illustrator*
*Irv Shapell, Owner*

Guide includes lessons customized to meet the unique interests and learning style of each child. *$16.95*
*371 pages Paperback*
*ISBN 0-933149-55-7*

## 2944 Teaching Reading to Disabled and Handicapped Learners

Charles C Thomas
2600 South 1st Street
Springfield, IL 62704          217-789-8980
                               800-258-8980
                               FAX: 217-789-9130
                               e-mail: books@ccthomas.com
                               www.ccthomas.com

*Michael Thomas, President*

Designed as a text for undergraduate and graduate students, it's aim is to help the many children, adolescents, and adults who encounter difficulty with reading. It guides prospective and present special education teachers in assisting and teaching handicapped learners to read. The text integrates traditional methods with newer perspectives to provide and effective reading program in special education. *$37.95*
*260 pages Paperback*
*ISBN 0-398062-48-X*

## 2945 Teaching Reading to Handicapped Children

Love Publishing Company
9101 East Kenyon Avenue
Suite 2200
Denver, CO 80237               303-221-7333
                               FAX: 303-221-7444
                               e-mail: lpc@lovepublishing.com
                               www.lovepublishing.com

*Stan Love, Owner*

The author covers skills teaching through letter sound association, word identification, synthetic and analytic methods and others, plus testing and assessment. *$24.95*

*ISBN 0-89108 -13-5*

## 2946 Teaching Self-Determination to Students with Disabilities

Brookes Publishing
PO Box 10624
Baltimore, MD 21285            410-337-9580
                               800-638-3775
                               FAX: 410-337-8539
                               e-mail: custserv@brookespublishing.com
                               www.brookespublishing.com

*Clary Creighton, Exhibits Coordinator*
*Tracy Gray, Educational Sales Manager*
*Paul Brooks, Owner*

Basic skills for successful transition. This teacher-friendly source will help educators prepare students with disabilities with the specific skills they need for a satisfactory, self-directed life once they leave school. *$34.95*
*384 pages Paperback 1997*
*ISBN 1-55766 -02-5*

## 2947 Teaching Students with Learning Problems

McGraw-Hill School Publishing
220 East Danieldale Road
Desoto, TX 75115               972-224-1111
                               800-442-9685
                               FAX: 972-228-1982
                               mhschool.com

*Joseph Gavigan, President*

Expanded coverage of learning strategies, generalization training, self-monitoring techniques, and techniques for increasing the time students spend on academic tasks.
*608 pages*

## 2948 Teaching Students with Learning and Behavior Problems

Pro-Ed Publications
8700 Shoal Creek Boulevard
Austin, TX 78757               512-451-3246
                               800-897-3202
                               FAX: 512-397-7633
                               e-mail: feedback@proedinc.com
                               www.proedinc.com

*Donald Hammill, Owner*
*Courtney King, Marketing Coordinator*

Popular, classic text with a comprehensive overview of best practices in assessing and instructing students with mild-to-moderate learning and behavior problems. *$44.00*
*520 pages Paperback*

## 2949 Teaching Students with Mild and Moderate Learning Problems

Allyn & Bacon Longman College Faculty
75 Arlington Street
Suite 300
Boston, MA 02116

                               800-852-8024
                               FAX: 617-848-7490
                               e-mail: info@ablongman.com
                               www.ablongman.com

*Tom Smith, Author*
*Ed Polloway, Author*

Provides teachers with skills for assisting students with mild to moderate handicaps in making successful transitions in school and community environments.

*496 pages 1990*
*ISBN 0-205123-62-7*

**2950   Teaching Students with Moderate/Severe Disabilities, Including Autism**
Charles C Thomas
2600 South 1st Street
Springfield, IL  62704                    217-789-8980
                                          800-258-8980
                                  FAX: 217-789-9130
                        e-mail: books@ccthomas.com
                                     www.ccthomas.com

*Micheal Thomas, President*

This resource and guide was written to help teachers, parents, and other caregivers provide the best educational opportunities for their students with moderate and severe disabilities. The author addresses functional language and other language intervention strategies, vocational training, community based instruction, transition and postsecondary programming, the adolescent student with autism, students with multiple disabilities, parent and family issues, and legal concerns. *$58.95*
*416 pages Paperback*
*ISBN 0-398067-01-5*

**2951   Teaching Students with Special Needs in Inclusive Settings**
Allyn & Bacon
75 Arlington Street
Suite 300
Boston, MA  02116                         617-848-6000
                                          800-852-8024
                                  FAX: 617-848-7490
                                     www.ablongman.com

*Nancy Forfyth, President*
*Thomas Longman, Founder*
*James Patton, Author*

This text is intended to be a survey text providing practical guidance to general education teachers. It will help them to meet the diverse needs of students with disabilities.
*544 pages*
*ISBN 0-20527-16-6*

**2952   Teaching Young Children to Read**
Brookline Books
PO Box 1047
Brookline, MA  02446                      617-868-0360
                                          800-666-2665
                                  FAX: 617-868-1772
                     e-mail: brooklinebks@delphi.com
                                 www.brooklinebooks.com

*Milt Budoff, Publisher*

Detailed instructions on teaching reading to preschoolers. Gradually develops full fluency. *$16.95*
*192 pages Paperback*
*ISBN 0-57129-48-6*

**2953   Teaching and Mainstreaming Autistic Children**
Love Publishing Company
9101 East Kenyon Avenue
Suite 2200
Denver, CO  80237                         303-221-7333
                                  FAX: 303-221-7444
                    e-mail: lpc@lovepublishing.com
                                  www.lovepublishing.com

*Stan Love, Owner*

Dr. Knoblock advocates a highly organized, structured environment for autistic children, with teachers and parents working together. His premise is that the learning and social needs of autistic children must be analyzed and a daily program designed with interventions that respond to this functional analysis of their behavior. *$24.95*

*ISBN 0-89108-11-9*

**2954   Teaching the Bilingual Special Education Student**
Ablex Publishing Corporation
PO Box 811
Stamford, CT  06904
                                  FAX: 201-767-6717
This book focuses on teaching those students who are bilingual, handicapped and in need of special instruction. It responds to the complex and practical issues of teaching these students in an effective way.

*ISBN 0-89391-23-4*

**2955   Teaching the Learning Disabled Adolescent**
Love Publishing Company
9101 East Kenyon Avenue
Denver, CO  80237                         303-221-7333
                                  FAX: 303-221-7444
                  e-mail: lovepublishing@compuserve.com

*Stan Lover, Owner*

This book gives expert strategies and methods for teaching learning disabled adolescents how, rather than what, to learn. *$34.95*

*ISBN 0-89108-94-5*

**2956   Teaching the Mentally Retarded Student: Curriculum, Methods, and Strategies**
Allyn & Bacon
75 Arlington Street
Suite 300
Boston, MA  02116                         617-848-6000
                                          800-852-8024
                                  FAX: 617-848-7490
                                     www.ablongman.com

*Tom Smith, Author*
*Ed Polloway, Author*

Represents a comprehensive approach to curriculum, methods and strategies for teaching the mildly mentally retarded student.
*640 pages hardcover 1987*
*ISBN 0-205102-62-X*

**2957   Technology and Handicapped People**
Springer Publishing Company
11 West 42nd Street
15th Floor
New York, NY  10036                       212-431-4370
                                          877-687-7476
                                  FAX: 212-941-7842
                     e-mail: contactus@springerpub.com
                                     www.springerpub.com

*Sheri Sussman, Vice President*
*Ursula Springer, President*

Important information for concerned professionals about new rehabilitation techniques and treatments for handicapped people. *$29.95*
*224 pages Hardcover*
*ISBN 0-82614-10-8*

**2958   Textbooks and the Student Who Can't Read Them: A Guide for Teaching Content**
Brookline Books
PO Box 1046
Cambridge, MA  02139                      617-868-0360
                                          800-666-2665
                                  FAX: 617-868-1772
                     e-mail: brooklinebks@delphi.com
                                 www.brooklinebooks.com
Based on a careful analysis of 10 textbook programs, the author concisely and sensibly indicates the procedures that facilitate teachers' use of regular grade level textbooks with low-reading students. *$21.95*

*Paperback*
*ISBN 0-91479 -57-3*

**2959  There's a Hearing Impaired Child in My Class**
Gallaudet University Bookstore
800 Florida Avenue NE
Washington, DC  20002                    202-651-5000
                                         800-451-1073
                               FAX: 202-651-5489
                          www.bookstore.gallaudette.edu

*Joseph Cachie*
*Erving Jordan, President*

This complete package provides basic facts about deafness,
practical strategies for teaching hearing impaired children, and
the question-and-answer information for all students. *$16.95*
*44 pages*

**2960  To Teach a Dyslexic**
AVKO Educational Research Foundation
3084 West Willard Road
Clio, MI  48420                          810-686-9283
                                         866-285-6612
                               FAX: 810-686-1101
                               e-mail: info@abko.org
                                    www.abko.org

*Don McCabe, Executive Research Director*

A dyslexic tells how luck enabled him to learn to read and how
his blissful ignorance and stubbornness enabled him to discover
how to teach other dyslexics to read and write. *$14.95*
*288 pages Paperback*

**2961  Toward Effective Public School Program for Deaf Students**
Teachers College Press
Columbia University
New York, NY  10027                      212-678-3929
                                         800-575-6566
                               FAX: 212-678-4149
                                  www.tc.columbia.edu

*Mary Lynch, Manager*

This book translates research and data into useable recommendations and possible courses of action for organizing effective
public school programs for deaf students. *$22.95*
*272 pages Paperback*
*ISBN 0-807731-59-5*

**2962  Traumatic Brain Injury: Mechanisms of Damage, Assessment & Intervention**
Pro-Ed Publications
8700 Shoal Creek Boulevard
Austin, TX  78757                        512-451-3246
                                         800-897-3202
                               FAX: 800-397-7633
                          e-mail: feedback@proedinc.com
                                    www.proedinc.com

*Donald Hammill, Owner*
*Courtney King, Marketing Coordinator*

Traumatic Brain Injury ranks as one of the most prevalent disorders with estimates ranging in hundreds of thousands of new
cases each year. This book focuses on the mechanisms of acquired brain injury and the methods of assessment, along with
treatment and outcome variables. *$41.00*
*458 pages Hardcover*

**2963  Treating Cerebral Palsy for Clinicians by Clinicians**
Pro-Ed Publications
8700 Shoal Creek Boulevard
Austin, TX  78757                        512-451-3246
                                         800-897-3202
                               FAX: 800-397-7633
                          e-mail: feedback@proedinc.com
                                    www.proedinc.com

*Donald Hammill, Owner*
*Courtney King, Marketing Coordinator*

A clinical manual for professionals beginning to work with persons who have cerebral palsy. *$31.00*
*312 pages*

**2964  Treating Disordered Speech Motor Control**
Pro-Ed Publications
8700 Shoal Creek Boulevard
Austin, TX  78757                        512-451-3246
                                         800-897-3202
                               FAX: 512-451-8542
                          e-mail: feedback@proedinc.com
                                    www.proedinc.com

*Donald Hammill, Owner*
*Courtney King, Marketing Coordinator*

This book about neuromotor disturbances of speech production
is aimed at practicing professionals and advanced graduate students interested in the neuropathologies of communication.
*$36.00*
*410 pages*

**2965  Treating Families of Brain Injury Survivors**
Springer Publishing Company
11 West 42nd Street
15th Floor
New York, NY  10036                      212-431-4370
                                         877-687-7476
                               FAX: 212-941-7842
                     e-mail: contactus@springerpub.com
                                   www.springerpub.com

*Annette Imperati, Marketing/Sales Director*
*Sheri Sussman, Vice President*
*Ursula Springer, President*

Provides the mental health practitioner with a comprehensive
program for helping families of head injury survivors cope with
the change in their lives. Includes background on medical aspects of head injury, family structure functioning and special
needs of various family members.
*220 pages*
*ISBN 0-82616 -20-1*

**2966  Understanding and Teaching Emotionally Disturbed Children & Adolescents**
Pro-Ed Publications
8700 Shoal Creek Boulevard
Austin, TX  78757                        512-451-3246
                                         800-897-3202
                               FAX: 800-397-7633
                          e-mail: feedback@proedinc.com
                                    www.proedinc.com

*Donald Hammill, Owner*
*Courtney King, Marketing Coordinator*

The teacher's handbook provides information that will change
misconceptions about children who are frequently labeled as
emotionally disturbed. It also gives information about a wide
variety of intervention methods and approaches for use in educational settings. *$41.00*
*620 pages Hardover*

**2967  Using the Dictionary of Occupational Titles in Career Decision Making**
Stout Vocational Rehab Institute
University of Wisconsin Stout
Menomonie, WI  54751                     715-232-2470
                               FAX: 715-232-5008
                               e-mail: luij@uwstout.edu
                                   www.svri.uwstout.edu

*John Lui, Contact Person*

This is a self-study manual for learning how to use the 1991 U.S.
Department of Labor's Dictionary of Occupational Titles. It
gives the DOT user a tool to understand the DOT and then put its
information to work. Shows how to quickly obtain information
about the work performed in 12,741 occupations listed and described in the DOT and the worker requirements for those occupations. *$24.00*

*142 pages Softcover*

**2968 VBS Special Education Teaching Guide**
Life Way Christian Resources Southern Baptist Conv
1 Lifeway Plaza
Nashville, TN 37234     615-251-2000

e-mail: specialed@lifeway.com
www.lifeway.com

*Mike Harland, Director*
*James Draper Jr, President*

This book contains teaching plans for five bible study sessions with reproducible handouts for learners. The plans use multisensory, experiential-based learning activities designed for adults and older youth who have mental retardation. Suggestions for Bible learning, crafts, recreation, snacks and theme interpretation are included. Designed primarily for Vacation Bible School, but may be used in camp/retreat settings. *$9.95*
*56 pages Yearly*

**2969 Vermont Interdependent Services Team Approach (VISTA)**
Brookes Publishing
PO Box 10624
Baltimore, MD 21285     410-337-9580
800-638-3775
FAX: 410-337-8539
e-mail: custserv@brookespublishing.com
www.brookespublishing.com

*Clary Creighton, Exhibits Coordinator*
*Tracy Gray, Educational Sales Manager*
*Paul Brooks, Owner*

A guide to coordinating educational support services. This manual enables IEP team members to fulfill the related services provisions of IDEA as they make effective support services decisions using a collaborative team approach. *$27.95*
*176 pages Spiral bound*
*ISBN 1-55766-30-4*

**2970 Vocational Rehabilitation and Employment**
Books on Special Children
PO Box 305
Congers, NY 10920     845-638-1236
FAX: 845-638-0847
e-mail: irene@boscbooks.com
Defines kinds of work, expectations, goals and programs. Contributions in general issues of supported employment, training and management and community based programs. *$47.00*
*372 pages Hardcover*

**2971 We Can Speak for Ourselves: Self Advocacy by Mentally Handicapped People**
Brookline Books
39 University Road
Brookline, MA 02445     617-734-6772
800-666-BOOK
FAX: 617-734-3952
www.brooklinebooks.com

*William H Walters, Author*
*Esther Isabe Wilder, Author*

The fundamental right of speaking for oneself has long been denied people with developmental disabilities. This book offers practical advice and support for parents, group home residence workers, day activity workers, citizens and professionals interested in developing self-advocacy for mentally handicapped people. *$17.95*

*Paperback*
*ISBN 0-253363-65-9*

**2972 When You Have a Visually Impaired Student in Your Classroom: A Guide for Teachers**
American Foundation for the Blind
11 Penn Plaza
Suite 300
New York, NY 10001     212-502-7600
800-232-5463
FAX: 212-502-7777
e-mail: afbinfo@afb.net
www.afb.org/store

*Carl R Augusto, President/CEO*

This guide provides information on students' abilities and needs, resources and educational team members, federal special education requirements, and technology materials used by students. *$9.95*
*84 pages 2001*
*ISBN 0-891283-93-5*

**2973 Wintergreen Orchard House**
Wintergreen Orchard House
PO Box 15899
New Orleans, LA 70175     504-866-8658
800-321-9479
FAX: 504-866-8710

*Allan B Corderman, Publisher*

*$25.95*
*320 pages Annual*

**2974 Working Bibliography on Behavioral and Emotional Disorders**
Natl. Clearinghouse for Alcohol & Drug Information
PO Box 2345
Rockville, MD 20847     301-468-2600
800-729-6686
FAX: 301-468-6433
e-mail: info@health.org
www.health.org

*Lizabeth J Foster, Librarian/Info. Resource Manager*

NCADI is a service of the U.S. Substance Abuse and Mental Health Services Administration. As the national focal point for information on alcohol and other drugs, NCADI collects, prepares, classifies, and distributes information about alcohol, tobacco and other drugs, prevention strategies and materials, research, treatment, etc.
*40 pages*

**2975 Working Together with Children and Families: Case Studies**
Brookes Publishing Company
PO Box 10624
Baltimore, MD 21285     410-337-9580
800-638-3775
FAX: 410-337-8539
e-mail: custerv@brookespublishing.com
www.brookespublishing.com

*Clary Creighton, Exhibits Coordinator*
*Tracy Gray, Educational Sales Manager*
*Paul Brooks, Owner*

Early interventionists will be able to bridge the gap between theory and practice with this edited collection of case studies. *$23.00*

*336 pages 1993*
*ISBN 1-557661-23-5*

**2976 Working with Visually Impaired Young Students: A Curriculum Guide**
Charles C Thomas
2600 South 1st Street
Springfield, IL 62704
217-789-8980
800-258-8980
FAX: 217-789-9130
e-mail: books@ccthomas.com
www.ccthomas.com

*Micheal Thomas, President*

The first step in the education process of a visually impaired child is the early identification and treatment by an eye care specialist. This book is geared to the age of birth through 3-years. Available in cloth, paperback and hardcover. *$36.95*
*208 pages Paperback*
*ISBN 0-398068-75-5*

# Testing Resources

**2977 AEPS Child Progress Report: For Children Ages Birth to Three**
Brookes Publishing
PO Box 10624
Baltimore, MD 21285
410-337-9580
800-638-3775
FAX: 410-337-8539
e-mail: custserv@brookespublishing.com
www.brookespublishing.com

*Clary Creighton, Exhibits Coordinator*
*Tracy Gray, Educational Sales Manager*
*Paul Brooks, Owner*

This chart helps monitor change by visually displaying current abilities, intervention targets, and child progress. In packages of 30. *$18.00*
*6 pages Gate-fold*
*ISBN 1-55766 -65-0*

**2978 AEPS Data Recording Forms: For Children Ages Birth to Three**
Brookes Publishing
PO Box 10624
Baltimore, MD 21285
410-337-9580
800-638-3775
FAX: 410-337-8539
e-mail: custserv@brookespublishing.com
www.brookespublishing.com

*Paul Brooks, Owner*

These forms can be used by child development professionals on four separate occasions to pinpoint and then monitor a child's strengths and needs in the six key areas of skill development measured by the AEPS Test. Packages of 10. *$23.00*
*36 pages Saddle-stiched*
*ISBN 1-55766 -97-2*

**2979 AEPS Measurement for Birth to Three Years**
Brookes Publishing
PO Box 10624
Baltimore, MD 21285
410-337-9580
800-638-3775
FAX: 410-337-8539
e-mail: custserv@brookespublishing.com
www.brookespublishing.com

*Clary Creighton, Exhibits Coordinator*
*Tracy Gray, Educational Sales Manager*
*Paul Brooks, Owner*

This dynamic volume explains the Assessment, Evaluation and Programming System, provides the complete AEPS Test and parallel assessment/evaluation tools for families and includes the forms and plans needed for implementation. *$39.00*

*352 pages*

**2980 AEPS Measurement for Three to Six Years**
Brookes Publishing
PO Box 10624
Baltimore, MD 21285
410-337-9580
800-638-3775
FAX: 410-337-8539
e-mail: custserv@brookespublishing.com
www.brookespublishing.com

*Clary Creighton, Exhibits Coordinator*
*Tracy Gray, Educational Sales Manager*
*Paul Brooks, Owner*

*$57.00*
*400 pages Spiral-bound*
*ISBN 1-55766 -87-1*

**2981 AIR: Assessment of Interpersonal Relations**
Pro-Ed Publications
8700 Shoal Creek Boulevard
Austin, TX 78757
512-451-3246
800-897-3202
FAX: 512-451-8542
e-mail: feedback@proedinc.com
www.proedinc.com

*Donald Hammill, Owner*
*Courtney King, Marketing Coordinator*

A thoroughly researched and standardized clinical instrument assessing the quality of adolescents' interpersonal relationships in a hierarchical fashion, including global relationship quality and relationship quality with three domains: Family, Social and Academic. *$89.00*

**2982 ALST: Adolescent Language Screening Test**
Pro-Ed Publications
8700 Shoal Creek Boulevard
Austin, TX 78757
512-451-3246
800-897-3202
FAX: 800-397-7633
e-mail: feedback@proedinc.com
www.proedinc.com

*Joshua Jeffrey, Marketing Custodian*
*Courtney King, Marketing Coordinator*
*Donald Hammill, Owner*

Provides speech/language pathologists and other interested professionals with a rapid thorough method for screening adolescents (ages 11-17). *$119.00*

**2983 Academic Skills Problems**
National Association of School Psychologists
8455 Colesville Road
Suite 100
Silver Spring, MD 20910
301-657-0270
FAX: 301-657-0275
Offers direct assessment and intervention information for professionals.
*232 pages*

**2984 Adaptive Mainstreaming: A Primer for Teachers and Principals, 3rd Edition**
Longman Publishing Group
1185 Avenue of the Americas
New York, NY 10036
212-782-3300
www.ablongman.com
An introduction to education for handicapped and gifted students. Presents research-based rationales for teaching exceptional students in the least restrictive environment. Provides historical perspectives, offers realistic descriptions of prevailing practices in the field, and reviews trends and new directions.

*366 pages Paperback 1988*
*ISBN 0-582285-04-6*

**2985**  **Ages & Stages Questionnaires**
Brookes Publishing
PO Box 10624
Baltimore, MD  21285                                          410-337-9580
                                                              800-638-3775
                                               FAX: 410-337-8539
e-mail: custserv@brookespublishing.com
www.brookespublishing.com

*Clary Creighton, Exhibits Coordinator*
*Tracy Gray, Educational Sales Manager*
*Paul Brooks, Owner*

ASQ is an economical and field-tested system for identifying whether infants and young children may require further developmental evaluation and offers a screening and tracking program that helps early intervention professionals, service coordinators, and administrators maximize financial resources while promoting the health and growth of the children they serve. Set includes 11 color-coded, reproducible questionnaires, 11 reproducible, age appropriate scoring sheets. *$135.00*

**2986**  **American College Testing Program**
PO Box 168
Iowa City, IA  52243                                          319-537-1028
                                               FAX: 319-537-1014
www.act.org

*Richard L Ferguson, Chief Executive Officer*
*Michael Eisenstein, President/COO*

An independent, nonprofit organization that provides a variety of educational services to students and their parents, to high schools and colleges, and to professional associations and government agencies.

**2987**  **Assessing Students with Special Needs**
Longman Publishing Group
10 Bank Street
9th Floor
White Plains, NY  10606                                       914-993-5000

www.ablongman.com

*Thomas Longman, Founder*
*Joanne Dresner, President*

Step-by-step guide to informal, classroom assessment of students with special needs.
*174 pages Paperback 1990*
*ISBN 0-801301-77-7*

**2988**  **Assessing Young Children**
National Association of School Psychologists
8455 Colesville Road
Suite 1000
Silver Spring, MD  20910                                      301-681-3223
                                               FAX: 301-608-2514
Assessment is the key topic in this manual which discusses why and how assessment is unique for the early childhood population.
*63 pages*

**2989**  **Assessing and Screening Preschoolers**
National Association of School Psychologists
4340 East West Highway
Suite 402
Bethesda, MD  20814                                           301-657-0270
                                               FAX: 301-657-0275
e-mail: webmaster@naspweb.org
www.nasponline.org

*Susan Gorin, Executive Director*
*Ted Feinberg, Assistant Executive Director*

A comprehensive and practical source to help professionals in counseling, school, and clinical psychology, special education, and human development become more competent in assessing preschoolers with special needs.

*484 pages*

**2990**  **Assessment Log & Developmental Progress Charts for the CCPSN**
Brookes Publishing
PO Box 10624
Baltimore, MD  21285                                          410-337-9580
                                                              800-638-3775
                                               FAX: 410-337-8539
e-mail: custserv@brookespublishing.com
www.brookespublishing.com

*Clary Creighton, Exhibits Coordinator*
*Tracy Gray, Educational Sales Manager*
*Paul Brooks, Owner*

This 28-page booklet allows readers to actually chart the ongoing progress of each preschool child. Available in packages of 10. *$22.00*
*28 pages Saddle-stiched*
*ISBN 1-55766 -39-5*

**2991**  **Assessment of Learners with Special Needs**
Allyn & Bacon
75 Arlington Street
Suite 300
Boston, MA  02116                                             617-848-6000
                                                              800-852-8024
                                               FAX: 617-848-7490
www.ablongman.com

*Nancy Forfyth, President*
*Thomas Longman, Founder*

The central goal of this book is to help teachers become sophisticated, informed test consumers in terms of choosing, using and interpreting commercially prepared tests for their special needs students.
*508 pages Casebound 1989*
*ISBN 0-205227-33-3*

**2992**  **Benchmark Measures**
Educators Publishing Service
625 Mount Auburn Street
Suite 3
Cambridge, MA  02138                                          617-547-6706
                                                              800-225-5750
                                               FAX: 888-440-2665
e-mail: feedback@epsbooks.com
www.epsbooks.com

*Charles H Heinle, Vice President*
*Alexandra S Bigelow, Author*
*Gunnar Voltz, President*

Ungraded test containing three sequential levels that assess alphabet and dictionary skills, reading, handwriting and spelling, and correspond to the first three schedules of the Alphabetic Phonics curriculum. The tests can be used at any level to measure a student's general knowledge of phonics. *$64.40*
*Kit*

**2993**  **CREVT: Comprehensive Receptive and Expressive Vocabulary Test**
Pro-Ed Publications
8700 Shoal Creek Boulevard
Austin, TX  78757                                             512-451-3246
                                                              800-897-3202
                                               FAX: 800-397-7633
e-mail: feedback@proedinc.com
www.proedinc.com

*Donald Hammill, Owner*
*Courtney King, Marketing Coordinator*

A new, innovative, efficient measure of both receptive and expressive oral vocabulary. The CREVT has two subtests and is based on the most current theories of vocabulary development, suitable for ages 4 through 17. *$174.00*

# Education /Testing Resources

*Complete Kit*

**2994  Carolina Curriculum for Preschoolers with Special Needs**
Brookes Publishing
PO Box 10624
Baltimore, MD 21285
410-337-9580
800-638-3775
FAX: 410-337-8539
e-mail: custserv@brookespublishing.com
www.brookespublishing.com

*Clary Creighton, Exhibits Coordinator*
*Tracy Gray, Educational Sales Manager*
*Paul Brooks, Owner*

This curriculum provides detailed teaching and assessment techniques, plus a sample 28-page Assessment Log that shows readers how to chart a child's individual progress. This guide is for children between 2 and 5 in their developmental stages who are considered at risk for developmental delay or who exhibit special needs. *$35.95*
*352 pages Spiral-bound*
*ISBN 1-557660-32-8*

**2995  DAYS: Depression and Anxiety in Youth Scale**
Pro-Ed Publications
8700 Shoal Creek Boulevard
Austin, TX 78757
512-451-3246
800-897-3202
FAX: 512-451-8542
e-mail: feedback@proedinc.com
www.proedinc.com

*Donald Hammill, Owner*
*Courtney King, Marketing Coordinator*

A unique battery of three norm-references scales useful in identifying major depressive disorder and overanxious disorders in children and adolescents. *$129.00*
*Complete Kit*

**2996  DOCS: Developmental Observation Checklist System**
Pro- Ed Publications
8700 Shoal Creek Boulevard
Austin, TX 78757
512-451-3246
800-897-3202
FAX: 800-397-7633
e-mail: feedback@proedinc.com
www.proedinc.com

*Donald Hammill, Owner*
*Courtney King, Marketing Coordinator*

A three-part system for the assessment of very young children with respect to general development, adjustment behavior and parent stress and support. *$124.00*

**2997  Daytime Development Center**
Joseph Willard Health Center
3750 Old Lee Highway
Fairfax, VA 22030
703-246-7100
FAX: 703-246-7307

*Susan Delauter, Program Coordinator*
*Allan Phillips, Director Early Intervention*
*Cheryl Clatterbuck, Manager*

Offers assessments, evaluations and educational/therapeutic infant programs for parents and their children.
*Sliding Scale*

**2998  Developmental Services Center**
Therapeutic Nursery Program
4525 Lee Street NE
Washington, DC 20019
202-388-3216
FAX: 202-576-8799

*Alice Anderson*

Offers assessment information and evaluation for developmentally delayed students.

**2999  Frames of Reference for the Assessment of Learning Disabilities**
Brookes Publishing
PO Box 10624
Baltimore, MD 21285
410-337-9580
800-638-3775
FAX: 410-337-8539
e-mail: custserv@brookespublishing.com
www.brookespublishing.com

*Clary Creighton, Exhibits Coordinator*
*Tracy Gray, Educational Sales Manager*
*Paul Brooks, Owner*

New views on measurement issues. Here you'll find an in=depth look at the fundamental concerns facing those who work with children with learning disabilities - assessment and identification. *$55.00*
*672 pages Hardcover*
*ISBN 1-55766 -38-3*

**3000  How to Conduct an Assessment**
FSSI
3905 Huntington Drive
Amarillo, TX 79109
806-853-1114
FAX: 806-353-1114
e-mail: webamster@winfssi.com
www.winfssi.com

*Ed Hammer, Director*

**3001  Inclusive & Heterogeneous Schooling: Assessment, Curriculum, and Instruction**
Brookes Publishing
PO Box 10624
Baltimore, MD 21285
410-337-9580
800-638-3775
FAX: 410-337-8539
e-mail: custserv@brookespublishing.com
www.brookespublishing.com

*Clary Creighton, Exhibits Coordinator*
*Tracy Gray, Educational Sales Manager*
*Paul Brooks, Owner*

Presents methods for successfully restructuring classrooms to enable all students, particularly those with disabilities, to flourish. Provides specific strategies for assessment, collaboration, classroom management, and age-specific instruction. *$34.95*
*448 pages Paperback*
*ISBN 1-557662-02-9*

**3002  K-BIT: Kaufman Brief Intelligence Test**
AGS
PO Box 99
Circle Pines, MN 55014
800-328-2560
FAX: 800-471-8457
e-mail: agsmail@agsnet.com
www.agsnet.com

*Kevin Brueggeman, President*
*Robert Zaske, Market Manager*

Quick and easy-to-use, KBIT assesses verbal and non-verbal abilities through two reliable subtests - vocabulary and matricies. *$124.95*
*Ages 4-90*

**3003  K-FAST: Kaufman Functional Academic Skills Test**
AGS
PO Box 99
Circle Pines, MN 55014
800-328-2560
FAX: 800-471-8457
e-mail: agsmail@agsnet.com
www.agsnet.com

*Robert Zaske, Market Manager*

Helps assess a person's capacity to function effectively in society regarding functional reading and math skills. *$99.95*

*Ages 15-85+*

**3004   K-SEALS: Kaufman Survey of Early Academic and Language Skills**
AGS
PO Box 99
Circle Pines, MN  55014

800-328-2560
FAX: 800-471-8457
e-mail: agsmail@agsnet.com
www.agsnet.com

*Kevin Brueggeman, President*
*Robert Zaske, Market Manager*

An individually administered test of children's of both expressive and receptive skills, pre-academic skills and articulation. K-SEALS offers reliable scores usually in less than 25 minutes. *$ 179.95*
*Ages 3-0; 6-11*

**3005   KLST-2: Kindergarten Language Screening Test Edition, 2nd Edition**
Pro-Ed
8700 Shoal Creek Boulevard
Austin, TX  78757

512-451-3246
800-897-3202
FAX: 800-397-7633
e-mail: feedback@proedinc.com
www.proedinc.com

*Donald Hammill, Owner*
*Courtney King, Marketing Coordinator*

Identifies children who need further diagnostic testing to determine whether or not they have language deficits that will accelerate academic failure. *$94.00*

**3006   Kaufman Test of Educational Achievement (K-TEA)**
AGS
PO Box 99
Circle Pines, MN  55014

800-328-2560
FAX: 800-471-8457
e-mail: agsmail@agsnet.com
www.agsnet.com

*Robert Zaske, Marketing Manager*
*Kevin Brueggeman, President*

K-TEA is an individually administered diagnostic battery that measures reading, mathematics, and spelling skills. Setting the standards in achievement testing today, K-TEA Comprehensive provides the complete diagnostic information you need for educational assessment and program planning. The Brief Forum is indispensable for school and clinical psychologists, special education teachers when a quick a measure of achievement is needed. *$249.95*

**3007   Life Centered Career Education: A Contemporary Based Approach, 4th Edition**
Council for Exceptional Children
1110 N Glebe Road
Suite 300
Arlington, VA  22201

703-245-0600
888-232-7733
FAX: 703-264-9494
e-mail: president@cec.sped.org
www.cec.sped.org

*Janice Burdick, President*
*Bruce Ramirez, Manager*

Provides a framework for building 97 functional skill competencies appropriate for preparing for adult life and special education students. *$28.00*
*175 pages*

**3008   Managing Attention Disorders in Children**
National Association of School Psychologists
8455 Colesville Road
Suite 1000
Silver Spring, MD  20910

301-681-3223
FAX: 301-608-2514

A guide for practitioners offering information on treating Attention Deficit Disorders.

**3009   Measure of Cognitive-Linguistic Abilities (MCLA)**
Speech Bin
1965 25th Avenue
Vero Beach, FL  32960

772-770-0007
800-477-3324
FAX: 772-770-0006
e-mail: info@speechbin.com
www.speechbin.com

*Jan J Binney, Senior Editor*

A diagnostic test of cognitive-linguistic abilities of adolescents and adults with traumatically induced brain injuries. High level. Normed. *$89.00*
*100 pages*
*ISBN 0-93785 -72-*

**3010   ONLINE**
West Virginia Research and Training Center
PO Box 1004
Institute, WV  25112

304-766-9495
800-624-8284
FAX: 304-766-2689
e-mail: info@icdi.wvu.edu
www.icdi.wvu.edu

*Clifford Lantz, President*

A quarterly newsletter offering information about hardware technology, software (commercial and home grown); applications that work and bonuses such as an exchange program for copyright-free software. *$25.00*
*Quarterly*

**3011   OWLS: Oral and Written Language Scales LC/OE & WE**
AGS
PO Box 99
Circle Pines, MN  55014

800-328-2560
FAX: 800-471-8457
e-mail: agsmail@agsnet.com
www.agsnet.com

*Kevin Brueggeman, President*
*Robert Zaske, Market Manager*

One kit provides an assessment of listening comprehension while the other assesses oral expression tasks: semantic, syntactic, pragmatic, and supralinguistic aspects of language. Written Expression may be administered individually or in small groups. *$249.95*

**3012   PAT-3: Photo Articulation Test**
Pro-Ed Publications
8700 Shoal Creek Boulevard
Austin, TX  78757

512-451-3246
800-897-3202
FAX: 800-397-7633
e-mail: feedback@proedinc.com
www.proedinc.com

*Joshua Jeffrey, Marketing Custodian*
*Courtney King, Marketing Coordinator*
*Barbara Lippke, Author*

This test consists of 72 color photographs. The first 69 photos test consonants and all but one vowel and one diphthong. The remaining pictures test connected speech and the remaining vowel and diphthong. *$144.00*

*Complete Kit*

## 3013 Peabody Early Experiences Kit (PEEK)
AGS
PO Box 99
Circle Pines, MN 55014

800-328-2560
FAX: 800-471-8457
e-mail: agsmail@agsnet.com
www.agsnet.com

*Kevin Brueggeman, President*
*Robert Zaske, Market Manager*

1,000 activities and all the materials you need to build youngsters' cognitive, social and language skills. Manuals, puppets, manipulatives, picture card deck, picture mini decks and more to teach early development concepts. *$789.95*

## 3014 Peabody Individual Achievement Test-Revised Normative Update (PIAT-R-NU)
AGS
PO Box 99
Circle Pines, MN 55014

800-328-2560
FAX: 800-471-8457
e-mail: agsmail@agsnet.com
www.agsnet.com

*Kevin Brueggeman, President*
*Robert Zaske, Market Manager*

PIAT-R-NU is an efficient individual measure of academic achievement. Reading, mathematics, and spelling are assessed in a simple, non-threatening format that requires only a pointing response for most items. This multiple choice format makes the PIAT-R ideal for assessing individuals who hesitate to give a spoken response, or have limited expressive abilities. *$289.98*

## 3015 Peabody Language Development Kits (PLDK)
AGS
PO Box 99
Circle Pines, MN 55014

800-328-2560
FAX: 800-471-8457
e-mail: agsmail@agsnet.com
www.agsnet.com

*Kevin Brueggeman, President*
*Robert Zaske, Market Manager*

The main goals of the Peabody Kit language program are to stimulate overall language skills in Standard English and, for each level of the program, advance children's cognitive skills about a year. *$ 649.95*
*Level P*
*ISBN 0-88671 -25-1*

## 3016 Pediatric Early Elementary (PEEX II) Examination
Educators Publishing Service
625 Mount Auburn Street
Suite 3
Cambridge, MA 02138

617-547-6706
800-225-5750
FAX: 888-440-2665
e-mail: feedback@epsbooks.com
www.epsbooks.com

*Charles H Heinle, Vice President*
*Alexandra S Bigelow, Author*
*Gunnar Voltz, President*

Assesses the second-fourth grade child's performance on thirty-two tasks in six specific areas of development: fine-motor function, language, gross-motor function, memory, visual processing, and delayed recall. At three points during the exam, the child is rated on selective attention and behavior and effect.

*$15.40 - $93*
*ISBN 0-83888 -80-6*

## 3017 Pediatric Exam of Educational-PEERAMID Readiness at Middle Childhood
Educators Publishing Service
625 Mount Auburn Street
Suite 3
Cambridge, MA 02138

617-547-6706
800-225-5750
FAX: 888-440-2665
e-mail: feedback@epsbooks.com
www.epsbooks.com

*Charles H Heinle, Vice President*
*Alexandra S Bigelow, Author*
*Gunnar Voltz, President*

Assesses the 4th-10th grade child's performance on thirty-one tasks in six specific areas: minor neurological indicators, fine-motor function, language, gross-motor function, temporal-sequential organization, and visual processing. Complete set.
*$15.40 - $109*
*ISBN 0-83888 -99-3*

## 3018 Pediatric Examination of Educational Readiness
Educators Publishing Service
PO Box 9031
Cambridge, MA 02139

617-547-6706
800-225-5750
FAX: 888-440-2665
e-mail: feedback@epsbooks.com
www.epsbooks.com

*Charles H Heinle, Vice President*
*Alexandra S Bigelow, Author*
*Gunnar Voltz, President*

Assesses the Pre-1st grade child's performance on twenty-nine tasks in six specific areas of development: orientation, gross-motor, visual-fine motor, sequential, linguistic and preacademic learning. The child is rated on ten dimensions of selective attention/activity processing efficiency and adaptation. Complete set.
*$12.85 - $86.40*
*ISBN 0-83888 -80-1*

## 3019 Pediatric Extended Examination at-PEET Three
Educators Publishing Service
625 Mount Auburn Street
Suite 3
Cambridge, MA 02138

617-547-6706
800-225-5750
FAX: 888-440-2665
e-mail: feedback@epsbooks.com
www.epsbooks.com

*Charles H Heinle, Vice President*
*Alexandra S Bigelow, Author*
*Gunnar Volta, President*

Assesses the preschool-age child's performance on twenty-eight tasks in five basic areas of development: gross-motor, language, visual-fine motor, memory, and intersensory integration. Complete set.
*$13.75 - $126*
*ISBN 0-83888 -79-4*

## 3020 Pre-Reading Screening Procedures
Educators Publishing Service
625 Mount Auburn Street
Suite 3
Cambridge, MA 02138

617-547-6706
800-225-5750
FAX: 888-440-2665
e-mail: feedback@epsbooks.com
www.epsbooks.com

*Charles H Heinle, Vice President*
*Alexandra S Bigelow, Author*
*Gunnar Voltz, President*

This revised group test, for grades K-1, evaluates auditory, visual and kinesthetic strengths in order to identify children who may have some form of dyslexia or specific language disability.
*$ 18.00*
*Grades K-1*
*ISBN 0-83885 -23-4*

**3021   Preparing for ACT Assessment**
American College Testing Program
PO Box 168
Iowa City, IA  52243                    319-337-1000

www.act.org

*Richard L Ferguson, Chief Executive Officer*

Designed to help high school students ready themselves for the ACT Assessment's subject area tests, explains the purposes of the four tests, describes their content and format, provides tips and exercises to improve student's test-taking skills and includes a complete sample text with scoring key.

**3022   Psycho-Educational Assessment of Preschool Children**
National Association of School Psychologists
8455 Colesville Road
Suite 1000
Silver Spring, MD  20910               301-681-3223
                                       FAX: 301-608-2514
This is a contributed text on assessing specific skills of preschool children.
*592 pages*

**3023   RULES: Revised**
Speech Bin
1965 25th Avenue
Vero Beach, FL  32960                  772-770-0007
                                       800-477-3324
                                       FAX: 772-770-0006
                                       e-mail: info@speechbin.com
                                       www.speechbin.com

*Jan J Binney, Senior Editor*

Treatment program for young children who have phonological disorders. *$43.95*
*280 pages*
*ISBN 0-93785 -51-3*

**3024   Receptive-Expressive Emergent-REEL-2 Language Test, 2nd Edition**
Pro-Ed Publications
8700 Shoal Creek Boulevard
Austin, TX  78757                      512-451-3246
                                       800-897-3202
                                       FAX: 800-397-7633
                                       e-mail: feedback@proedinc.com
                                       www.proedinc.com

*Donald Hammill, Owner*
*Courtney King, Marketing Coordinator*

A revision of the popular scale used for the multidimensional analysis of emergent language. The REEL-2 is specifically designed for use with a broad range of at risk infants and toddlers in the new multidisciplinary programs developing under P.L. 99-457. *$79.00*

**3025   Slingerland High School/College Screening**
Educators Publishing Service
625 Mount Auburn Street
Suite 3
Cambridge, MA  02138                   617-547-6706
                                       800-225-5750
                                       FAX: 888-440-2665
                                       e-mail: feedback@epsbooks.com
                                       www.epsbooks.com

*Charles H Heinle, Vice President*
*Alexandra S Bigelow, Author*
*Gunnar Voltz, President*

Assessments of high school and college level students to determine specific language disability and predict academic strengths as well as difficulties.

*$17 - $23.95*
*ISBN 0-83882 -78-2*

**3026   Slingerland Screening Tests**
Educators Publishing Service
625 Mount Auburn Street
Suite 3
Cambridge, MA  02138                   617-547-6706
                                       800-225-5750
                                       FAX: 888-440-2665
                                       e-mail: feedback@epsbooks.com
                                       www.epsbooks.com

*Charles H Heinle, Vice President*
*Alexandra S Bigelow, Author*
*Gunnar Voltz, President*

These tests, by Beth Slingerland, for individuals or groups of children, grades 1-6, identify children who show indications of having specific language disability in reading, handwriting, spelling or speaking. Form D evaluates personal orientation in time and space as well as the ability to express ideas in writing.
*$14.80 - $27.45*
*ISBN 0-83882 -02-2*

**3027   Spatial Orientation and Sequencing Development Remedial Activities**
Psychological & Educational Publications
PO Box 520
Hydesville, CA  95547                  800-523-5775
                                       FAX: 800-447-0907
                                       e-mail: psych-edpublications@cox.net
                                       www.psych-edpublications.com

*Morrison Gardner, President*

Designed to be used to remediate those children who perform poorly on any one or more activities of the Test of Pictures test.
*$59.95*

**3028   Specific Language Disability Test**
Educators Publishing Service
625 Mount Auburn Street
Suite 3
Cambridge, MA  02138                   617-547-6706
                                       800-225-5750
                                       FAX: 888-440-2665
                                       e-mail: feedback@epsbooks.com
                                       www.epsbooks.com

*Charles H Heinle, Vice President*
*Gunnar Voltz, President*

Tests for individuals or groups to evaluate students in grades 6-8. Sub-tests I-V evaluate perception in visual discrimination, visual memory, visual motor-coordination. Sub-tests VI-X evaluate auditory discrimination, auditory-visual coordination, auditory-motor coordination and comprehension. Teacher's manual, test booklet, charts and cards are also available.
*$2.85 - $21.15*
*ISSN 0838-84 0*

**3029   Speech Bin**
1965 25th Avenue
Vero Beach, FL  32960                  772-770-0007
                                       800-477-3324
                                       FAX: 772-770-0006
                                       e-mail: info@speechbin.com
                                       www.speechbin.com

*Jan J Binney, Senior Editor*

Catalog offering test materials, assessment information, books and special education resources for speech-language pathologists, occupational and physical therapists, audiologists, and other rehabilitation professionals in schools, hospitals, clinics and private practices.

*ISSN 4773-324*

**3030    Stocker Probe: Revised**
Speech Bin
1965 25th Avenue
Vero Beach, FL 32960

772-770-0007
800-477-3324
FAX: 772-770-0006
e-mail: info@speechbin.com
www.speechbin.com

*Jan J Binney, Senior Editor*

Diagnostic and treatment program for stuttering and language impairment in children and adults. *$75.00*
*144 pages*
*ISBN 0-93785 -58-0*

**3031    Stuttering Severity Instrument for Children and Adults**
Psychological & Educational Publications
PO Box 520
Hydesville, CA 95547

707-768-1807
800-523-5775
FAX: 800-447-0907
e-mail: psych-edpublications@cox.net
www.psych-edpublications.com

*Morrison Gardner, President*

With this tool teachers can determine whether to schedule a child for therapy or to evaluate the effects of treatment.

**3032    Survey of Educational Skills and the Survey of Problem-Solving Skills**
Educators Publishing Service
625 Mount Auburn Street
Suite 3
Cambridge, MA 02138

617-547-6706
800-225-5750
FAX: 888-440-2665
e-mail: feedback@epsbooks.com
www.epsbooks.com

*Charles H Heinle, Vice President*
*Alexander Bigelow, Author*
*Gunnar Voltz, President*

Both surveys are process measures designed to characterize the problem-solving and learning strategies of students in middle childhood. A detailed rating system enables educators and psychologists to observe each child's performance, to analyze error patterns and to guide the assessment procedure. *$10.00*
*96 pages $10.65 - $37.90*
*ISBN 0-83881 -56-*

**3033    Taking Part: Introducing Social Skills to Young Children**
AGS
PO Box 99
Circle Pines, MN 55014

800-328-2560
FAX: 800-471-8457
e-mail: agsmail@agsnet.com
www.agsnet.com

*Kevin Brueggeman, President*
*Robert Zaske, Market Manager*

The first social skills curriculum to be linked directly to an assessment tool. More than 30 lessons correlate with the skills assessed by the Social Skills Rating System, a multirater approach to assessing prosocial and problem behaviors. *$149.95*

**3034    Teaching Resources & Assessment of Critical Skills**
Becoming Independent
1425 Corporate Center Parkway
Santa Rosa, CA 95407

707-524-6600

www.becomingindependent.org

*John McCue, Chief Executive Officer*
*Tom Richardson, Chief Operating Officer*

An independent living assessment tool consisting of four booklets and master forms and a cassette tape. The tool was developed by Becoming Independent/TRACE, incorporating over 15 years of experience in providing independent living services. *$129.00*

**3035    Test Accommodations for Students with Disabilities**
Charles C Thomas
2600 S 1st Street
Springfield, IL 62704

217-789-8980
800-258-8980
FAX: 217-789-9130
e-mail: books@ccthomas.com
www.ccthomas.com

*Michael Thomas, President*

Considers legal questions, theoretical issues, and practical methods for meeting the assessment needs of students with diabilities. The book is comprised of ten chapters and includes test accommodations topics relating to federal and state regulations (including the IDEA Amendments Act of 1997), problems concerning reliability and validity, and practical strategies for planning test accomodations and adapting and modifying tests. *$51.95*
*340 pages Paperback 1998*
*ISBN 0-398068-45-3*

**3036    Test Critiques: Volumes I-X**
Pro-Ed Publications
8700 Shoal Creek Boulevard
Austin, TX 78757

512-451-3246
800-897-3202
FAX: 800-397-7633
e-mail: feedback@proedinc.com
www.proedinc.com

*Donald Hammill, Owner*
*Courtney King, Marketing Coordinator*

Provides the professional and nonprofessional with in-depth, evaluative studies of more than 800 of the most widely used of these assessment instruments. *$649.00*

**3037    Test of Early Reading Ability Deaf or Hard of Hearing**
Pro- Ed Publications
8700 Shoal Creek Boulevard
Austin, TX 78757

512-451-3246
800-897-3202
FAX: 800-397-7633
e-mail: feedback@proedinc.com
www.proedinc.com

*Donald Hammill, Author/Owner*
*Courtney King, Marketing Coordinator*

This adaptation of the TERA-2 for simultaneous communication of American Sign Language is the ONLY individually administered test of reading designed for children with moderate to profound sensory hearing loss. *$169.00*
*Complete Kit*

**3038    Test of Language Development: Primary**
Pro-Ed Publications
8700 Shoal Creek Boulevard
Austin, TX 78757

512-451-3246
800-897-3202
FAX: 800-397-7633
e-mail: feedback@proedinc.com
www.proedinc.com

*Donald Hammill, Owner*
*Coutney King, Marketing Coordinator*

TOLD P:2 and TOLD 1:2 are the most popular tests of spoken language used by clinicians today. They are used to identify children who have language disorders and to isolate the particular types of disorders they have. Primary Edition for ages 1-4 to 8-11: Intermediate Edition for ages 8-6 to 12-11.

**3039    Test of Mathematical Abilities, 2nd Editio n**
Pro-Ed Publications
8700 Shoal Creek Boulevard
Austin, TX  78757                                    512-451-3246
                                                     800-897-3202
                                                FAX: 512-451-8542
                                  e-mail: feedback@proedinc.com
                                              www.proedinc.com

*Donald Hammill, Owner*
*Courtney King, Marketing Coordinator*
*Elizabeth McEntire, Author*

The latest version was developed for use in grades 3 through 12.
It measures math performance on the two traditional major skill
areas in math as well as attitude, vocabulary and general application of math concepts in real life. *$84.00*

**3040    Test of Nonverbal Intelligence, 3rd Editio n**
Pro-Ed Publications
8700 Shoal Creek Boulevard
Austin, TX  78757                                    512-451-3246
                                                     800-897-3202
                                                FAX: 800-397-7633
                                  e-mail: feedback@proedinc.com
                                              www.proedinc.com

*Donald Hammill, Owner*
*Courtney King, Marketing Coordinator*
*Susan K Johnson, Author*

A language-free measure of intelligence, aptitude and reasoning. The administration of the test requires no reading, writing,
speaking or listening on the part of the test subject. The items included in this test are problem-solving tasks that increase in difficulty. Each item presents a set of figures in which one or more
components is missing. The test items include one or more of the
characteristics of shape, position, direction, rotation, contigu-
ity, shading, size, movement or pattern. *$229.00*
                                  *Complete Kit*

**3041    Test of Phonological Awareness**
Pro-Ed Publications
8700 Shoal Creek Boulevard
Austin, TX  78757                                    512-451-3246
                                                     800-897-3202
                                                FAX: 800-397-7633
                                  e-mail: feedback@proedinc.com
                                              www.proedinc.com

*Donald Hammill, Owner*
*Courtney King, Marketing Coordinator*

Measures young children's awareness of the individual sounds
in words. Children who are sensitive to the phonological structure of words in oral language have a much easier time learning
to read than children who are not. *$143.00*

**3042    Test of Pictures/Forms/Letters/Numbers Spatial Orien-
tation Skills**
Psychological & Educational Publications
PO Box 520
Hydesville, CA  95547                                 707-768-1807
                                                     800-523-5775

*Morrison Gardner, President*

Developed to aid professionals in determining a child's ability
to visually perceive forms and letters in the correct direction.
*$35.00*

                        *ISBN 0-93142 -09-8*

**3043    Test of Visual-Motor Skills: Upper Level**
Psychological & Educational Publications
PO Box 520
Hydesville, CA  95547                                 707-768-1807
                                                     800-523-5775

*Morrison Gardner, President*
Measures eye-hand coordination. *$59.00*

*ISBN 0-93142 -72-1*

**3044    Test of Written Spelling, 3rd Edition**
Pro- Ed Publications
8700 Shoal Creek Boulevard
Austin, TX  78757                                    512-451-3246
                                                     800-897-3202
                                                FAX: 800-397-7633
                                  e-mail: feedback@proedinc.com
                                              www.proedinc.com

*Donald Hammill, Owner*
*Courtney King, Marketing Coordinator*

This revised edition assesses the student's ability to spell words
whose spellings are readily predictable in sound-letter patterns,
words whose spellings are less predictable and both types of
words considered together. *$74.00*

**3045    Welcoming Students who are Deaf-Blind into Typical
Classrooms**
Brookes Publishing
PO Box 10624
Baltimore, MD  21285                                 410-337-9580
                                                     800-638-3775
                                                FAX: 410-337-8539
                          e-mail: custserv@brookespublishing.com
                                       www.brookespublishing.com

*Clary Creighton, Exhibits Coordinator*
*Tracy Gray, Educational Sales Manager*
*Paul Brooks, Owner*

Facilitating School Participation, Learning, and Friendships.
Examines successful inclusive educational practices that encourage the participation of students who are deaf-blind. *$37.00*
                        *480 pages Paperback*
                        *ISBN 1-55766 -44-8*

**3046    Woodcock Reading Mastery Tests**
A GS
PO Box 99
Circle Pines, MN  55014
                                                     800-627-7271
                                                FAX: 800-632-9011
                                   e-mail: agsmail@agsnet.com
                                              www.agsnet.com

*Kevin Brueggeman, President*
*Robert Zaske, Market Manager*

The Woodcock Reading Mastery Tests - Revised provides an interpretive system and age range to help you assess reading skills
of children and adults. Two forms, G and II, make it easy to test
and retest, or you can combine the results of both forms for a
more comprehensive assessment. Revised with recent updates.
*$329.95*

**3047    Young Children with Special Needs: A Developmentally
Appropriate Approach**
Allyn & Bacon
75 Arlington Street
Suite 300
Boston, MA  02116                                    617-848-6000
                                                     800-852-8024
                                                FAX: 617-848-7490
                                              www.ablongman.com

*Nancy Forfyth, President*
*Thomas Longman, Founder*

This book is designed to prepare students in making curriculum
decisions in order to care for and foster the development of
young children with special needs in normal early childhood settings.

*270 pages*
*ISBN 0-20518 -94-X*

## Treatment & Training

**3048    22LE Program MCC-Longview**
500 SW Longview Road
Lees Summit, MO  64081
816-672-2366
FAX: 816-672-2719
TTY:816-672-2144
e-mail: MaryEllen.Jenison@mcclcc.edu
mcclcc.edu/

*Mary Ellen Jenison, Director*
*Kay Owens, Administrative Assistant*

Intensive support services program for post secondary students with neurological disabilities. The ABLE Program can be reached at http://mcclcc.edu/home.asp?qlinks=ABLE+Program+at+Longview+C=Z

**3049    Academy for Guided Imagery**
30765 Pacific Coast Highway
Suite 369
Malibu, CA  90265
800-726-2070
FAX: 800-727-2070
www.academyofguidedimagery.com

*David E Bresler, President*

Aims to teach people to access and use the power of the mind/body connection for healing and to further understanding of the imagery process in human life and development. Also to provide systematic training and guidance to health professionals who are interested in the use of Guided Imagery in their practice.

**3050    Asthma & Allergy Education for Worksite Clinicians**
Asthma and Allergy Foundation of America
1233 20th Street NW
Suite 402
Washington, DC  20036
202-466-7643
800-727-8462
FAX: 202-466-8940
e-mail: info@aafa.org
www.aafa.org

*Bill McLin, Executive Director*
*Eileen Marcus, VP Marketing/Communications*

Developed to teach health professionals in the worksite about asthma and allergies and ultimately improve the health of the employees who have theses de\iseases. The program gives worksite clinicians the knowledge and tools they need to give employees guidance on how to control environmental factors both in the home and in the workplace, self-manage thier asthma and/or allergies and to determaine if ti is necessary for employees to see an allergist if symptoms persist.

**3051    Asthma & Allergy Essentials for Children's Care Provider**
Asthma and Allergy Foundation of America
1233 20th Street NW
Suite 402
Washington, DC  20036
202-466-7643
800-727-8462
FAX: 202-466-8940
e-mail: info@aafa.org
www.aafa.org

*Bill McLin, Executive Director*

Course gives child care providers the tools and knowledge they need to care for children with asthma and allergies. During the interactive, three hour program, a trained health professional teaches providers how to recognize the signs and symptoms of an asthma or allergy episode, how to institute environmental control measures to prevent these episodes, and how to properly use medication and the tools for asthma management. In areas of the country serviced by AAFA's 14 chapters.

**3052    Asthma Care Training for Kids (ACT)**
Asthma and Allergy Foundation of America
1125 15th Street NW
Suite 502
Washington, DC  20005
202-466-7643
FAX: 202-466-8940
e-mail: info@aafa.org
www.aafa.org

*Bill McLin, Executive Director*

Interactive program for children ages seven to 12 and their families. Children and their families attend three group sessions seperately to learn their own unique styles and then come together at the end of each session to share their knowledge.

**3053    Autism Treatment Center of America**
2080 South Undermountain Road
Sheffield, MA  01257
413-229-2100
877-760-7473
FAX: 413-229-3220
e-mail: information@son-rise.org
www.son-rise.org

Since 1983, the Autism Treatment Center of America has provided innovative training programs for parents and professionals caring for children challenged by Autism, Autism Spectrum Disorders, Pervasive Developmental Disorders (PDD) and other development difficulties. The Son-Rise Program teaches a specific yet comprehensive system of treatment and education designed to help families and caregivers enable their children to dramatically improve in all areas of learning.

**3054    Ayurvedic Institute**
11311 Menaul Boulevard NE
Suite A
Albuquerque, NM  87112
505-291-9698
800-863-7721
FAX: 505-294-7572
e-mail: registrar@ayurveds.com
www.ayurveda.com

*Vasant Lad, President/Chairman of the Board*
*Wynn Werner, Administrator*

Directed by Dr. Vasant Lad, trains people in Ayurveda.

**3055    East Brunswick Adult and Community Education Program**
Adult Life Skills
380 Cranbury Road
E Brunswick, NJ  08816
732-613-6984
FAX: 732-390-6432
e-mail: bmethven@ebnet.org
www.ebnet.org

*Bernadette Methven LSW, Project Coordinator*
*Wayne Dyer, Adult Education Administrator*

Offers education, training, and social programs for adults with developmental disabilities in an integrated adult/evening school environment. Residents of Middlesex County, New Jersey, ages 18 and over are eligible to register. Limited transportation is also available. Annual enrollment fee $40.00.

**3056    Harriet & Robert Heilbrunn Guild School**
JGB Audio Library for the Blind
15 West 65th Street
New York, NY  10023
212-769-6331
FAX: 212-769-6266
e-mail: info@JGB.org
www.JGB.org

*Peter Williamson, Executive Director*
*Ken Stanley, Manager*

**3057 Howard School**

1246 Ponce De Leon Aveune NE
Atlanta, GA 30306         404-377-7436
FAX: 404-377-0884
e-mail: kschuller@yahoo.com
www.howardschool.org

*Keren Schuller, Director Of Admissions*
*Marifred Cilella, Head Of School*
*Sandra Kleinman, Executive Director*

Enrolls students whose language-learning disabilities and differences hinder their learning to their fullest potential. Goal is to help students simultaneously build basic academi skills, maximize academic progress, develop higher level thinking skills, gain self-advocacy strategies and become independent life-long learners. Average class size is less than 12 students.

**3058 Lake Michigan Academy**

West Michigan Learning Disabilities Foundation
2428 Burton Street SE
Grand Rapids, MI 49546       616-464-3330
FAX: 616-285-1935
e-mail: exd@iserv.net
www.wmldf.org

*Linda Chaffee, Executive Director*

Is a private day school for children with learning disabilities.

**3059 Mad Hatters: Theatre That Makes a World of Difference**

PO Box 50002
Kalamazoo, MI 49005
FAX: 269-385-5868

*Bobbe A Luce, Executive Director*

A nationally-known theater which has presented effective and innovative programs to more than 175,000 people in over 1,150 performances in the past 15 years. Our presentations and training programs are a proven method of changing attitudes and behaviors. The Mad Hatters is a leader in the field of sensitivity training to build community and foster the inclusion of all people in society. Fees: $500-$4000 per program, depending on topic and audience.

**3060 Riverview School**

551 Route 6a
East Sandwich, MA 02537      508-888-0489
FAX: 508-833-7001
e-mail: admissions@riverviewschool.org
www.riverviewschool.org

*Jeanne M Pacheco, Director Admissions/Placement*
*Maureen B Brenner, Principal*

An independent residential school of interntional reputation services enrolling 183 male and female students in its secondary and post secondary programs. Students share a common history of lifelong difficulty with academic achievement and the development of friendships. On measures of intellectual ability, most studets score within the 70-100 range have a primary diagnosis of a learning disability and/or a complex language or learning disorder.

**3061 Sandhills Academy**

1500 Hallbrook Drive
Columbia, SC 29209       803-695-1400
FAX: 803-695-1214
e-mail: info@sandhillsacademy.com
www.sandhillsacademy.com

*Anne Vickers, Executive Director*
*Thrace Mears, Admissions Director*
*John W Weaver, Advancement Director*

Exists to provide educational programs and intellectual development for average to above average students, six to 15, who learn differently and to promote the development of self-awareness, joy in learning and a vision of themselves as life-long learners.

**3062 Senior Program for Teens and Young Adults with Special Needs**

Camp J CC
6125 Montrose Road
Rockville, MD 20852       301-230-3759
FAX: 301-881-6549
e-mail: jcccamp@jccgw.org
www.jccgw.org

The senior Program is a transitional program for teens and young adults with mental retardation, severe learning disabilities and multiple disabilities. Socialization, recreation and independent living skills are enhanced ina fun enviroment. Activities include art, music, recreational swim and more.

**3063 Shema V'Ezer**

Camp J CC
6125 Montrose Road
Rockville, MD 20852       301-881-0100
FAX: 301-881-6549
e-mail: jcccamp@jccgw.org
www.jccgw.org

*Arnie Sohinki, Chief Executive Officer*
*Sarah Milner, Director*

The Shema V'Ezer Religious School program offers Judaic education to children and teens with disabilities, ages 6 to 21, who may not benefit from a traditional religious school setting. Children with mental retardation, svere learning disabilities, visual or auditory impairment, mobility impairment, behavioral disorders and or multiple disabilities particpate in Sunday morning classes at the JCC.

**3064 Vanguard School**

Valley Forge Specialized Educational Services
PO Box 730
Paoli, PA 19301       610-296-6700
FAX: 610-640-0132
www.vanguardschool-pa.org

*Ernest Brattstrom, Principal*
*James Kirkpatrick, Chief Financial Officer*
*Donna Annechino, Admissions Director*

An Approved Private School (APS) for students aged 2.7-21 years with traumatic brain injury (TBI), social/emotional disturbance (SED) and/or autism/pervasive developmental disorder.

**3065 Worthmore Academy**

1301 North Riley Avenue
Indianapolis, IN 46201      317-253-5367
FAX: 317-253-5824
www.familyeducation.com/IN/worthmore_academy

*Brenda Jackson, Director*
*Sandy Foster, Assistant Director*

A center for learning disabilities providing educational assessments, alternative educational programs, academic guidance and public awareness services available as follows: full-time day school, K-8th, 1 to 1 teacher student ratio; six week summer school, K-12th, 1 to 1 teacher student ratio; after school tutoring; adult tutoring, educational assessments, counseling and educational seminars.
*1988*

## General

**3066  American Institute for Foreign Study**
9 W Broad Street
Stamford, CT  06902                203-399-5000
                                   800-727-2437
                              FAX: 203-399-5590
                         e-mail: info@aifs.com
                                   www.aifs.org

*Anthony Cook, Executive Director*
*William Gertz, President*

Organizes cultural exchange programs throughout the world for more than 50,000 students each year and arranges insurance coverage for our own participants as well as participants of other organizations. Also provides summer travel programs overseas and in the US ranging from one week to a full academic year.

**3067  American Universities International Programs**
307 S College Avenue
Fort Collins, CO  80524            970-495-0869
                                   888-730-2847
                              FAX: 970-484-6997
                         e-mail: info@auip.com
                                   www.auip.com

*Linda Detling, Program Coordinator AUIP*

Study abroad organization sending students to universities in Australia and New Zealand.

**3068  American-Scandinavian Foundation**
58 Park Avenue
New York, NY  10016                212-879-9779
                              FAX: 212-879-2301
                         e-mail: info@amscan.org
                                   www.amscan.org

*Jean Prahl, Director Training*
*E Gallagher, President*

Promotes international understanding through educational and cultural exchange between the United States and Denmark, Finland, Iceland, Norway and Sweden.

**3069  Antioch College**
795 Livermore Street
Yellow Springs, OH  45387          937-769-1000
                              FAX: 937-767-6429
                  e-mail: aea@antioch-college.edu
                         www.antioch-college.edu

*Robert Whyte, Executive Director*
*Sally Frye, Executive Asst to the President*
*Richard Jurasek, President*

Education abroad offers numerous programs which can be included in undergraduate and graduate study programs.

**3070  Army and Air Force Exchange Services**
PO Box 660202
Dallas, TX  75266                  214-312-2011
                              FAX: 214-312-3429
                                   www.aafes.com

*Management Recruiter, Contact*

Brings a tradition of value, service, and support to its 11.5 million authorized customers at military installations in the United States, Europe and in the Pacific.

**3071  Association for International Practical Training**
10400 Little Patuxent Parkway
Suite 250
Columbia, MD 21044                 410-997-2200

                         e-mail: aipt@aipt.org
                                   www.aipt.org

*Karl Compton, President*
*Elizabeth Chazottes, Chief Executive Officer*

Nonprofit organization dedicated to encouraging and facilitating the exchange of qualified individuals between the US and other countries so they may gain practical work experience and improve international understanding.

**3072  Basic Facts on Study Abroad**
International Education
809 United Nations Plaza
New York, NY  10017                212-883-8200
                              FAX: 212-963-3489
                         e-mail: publications@un.org

*Allen Goodman, Chief Executive Officer*

Information book including foreign study planning, educational choices, finances and study abroad programs. *$35.00*
            *30 pages*

**3073  Beaver College**
Arcadia University
450 S Easton Road
Glenside, PA  19038                215-572-2900
                                   888-232-8379
                              FAX: 215-572-2174
                         e-mail: cea@beaver.edu
                                   www.beaver.edu/cea

*Lorna Stern, Deputy Director*
*Jerry Greiner, President*

One of the largest college-based study abroad programs in the country. Prices from $8000.00 semester to $22000.00 a year.

**3074  Buffalo State (SUNY)**
University College at Buffalo State
1300 Elmwood Avenue, SW 140
Buffalo, NY  14222                 716-878-4620
                              FAX: 716-878-3054
                e-mail: intleduc@buffalostate.edu
                www.buffalostate.edu/studyabroad

*Lee Ann Grace, Asst Dean, Intl/Exchange Program*

Provides international educational exchange opportunities for students of university age and older through its Office of International Education.

**3075  Building Bridges: Including People with Disabilities in International Programs**
Mobility International USA
PO Box 10767
Eugene, OR  97440                  541-343-1284
                              FAX: 541-343-6812
                         e-mail: info@miusa.org
                                   www.miusa.org

*Susan Sygall, CEO/Executive Director*
*Cindy Lewis, Director of Programs*

Empowers people with disabilities around the world through international exhange and international development to achieve their human rights. The international exchange programs usually last two-four weeks and are held throughout the year in the US and abroad. Activities include living with homestay families, leadership seminars, disability rights workshops, cross cultural learning and teambuilding activities such as river rafting and challenging courses.

**3076  Davidson College, Office of Study Abroad**
PO Box 1719
Davidson, NC 28036                704-892-2351
                                 FAX: 704-892-2120
e-mail: caortmayer@davidson.edu
www.davidson.edu/academic/sasian/application.

*Carolyn Ortmayer, Coordinator Study Abroad*

Recognizes the value of study abroad for both the devlopment of
worl understanding and the development of the student as a
broadminded, objective and mature individual.

**3077  High School Students Guide to Study, Travel, and Adventure Abroad**
205 E 42nd Street
New York, NY 10017
                                 888-COU-NCIL
                                 FAX: 212-822-2649
                                 www.councilexchanges.org

*Priscilla Tovey, Information Services*
*Cheryl Jeffries, Administrative Assistant*

This guide provides high school students with all the information they need for a successful trip abroad. Included are sections
to help students find out if they're ready for a trip abroad, make
the necessary preparations and get the most from their experience. Over 200 programs are described including language
study, summer camps, homestays, study tours and work camps.
The program descriptions include information for people with
disabilities. *$13.95*
                    *308 pages Biennial*
                    *ISBN 0-31211 -22-8*

**3078  Higher Education Consortium for Urban Affairs (HECUA)**
Wright Building
2233 University Avenue W
Suite 210
Saint Paul, MN 55114             651-644-6300
                                 800-554-1089
                                 FAX: 651-659-9421
                                 e-mail: info@hecua.org
                                 www.hecua.org

*Maryy Delorie, Marketing & Recruitment*
*Dan Hartnett, Manager*

HECUA offers college-level off-campus study programs in
Latin America, Asia, Europe and the U.S. Internships, field projects and other forms of experimental learning are combined
with academic study. Programs focus on issues of inequality and
ways to bring about positive social change. HECUA has thirty
years of experience and a national reputation for the best in
teaching and learning that engages students in meaningful study
and action. Students with disabilities welcome to apply.

**3079  International Christian Youth Exchange**
134 W 26th Street
New York, NY 10001               212-206-7307
                                 FAX: 212-633-9085

*Ed Gragert*

Offers participants a unique experience to learn about another
culture and make friends from different countries.

**3080  International Partnership for Service-Learning and Leadership**
815 2nd Avenue
Room 315
New York, NY 10017               212-986-0989
                                 FAX: 212-986-5039
                                 e-mail: info@ipsl.org
                                 www.ipsl.org

*Nevin Brown, President*

A not for profit educational organization incorporated in New
York State serving students, colleges, universities, service
agenices and related organizations around the world by fostering programs that link volunteer service to the community and
academic study.
            *1982*

**3081  International University Partnerships**
University of Pennsylvania
1011 South Drive
Indiana, PA 15705                724-357-2295
                                 FAX: 724-357-2514

*Dr. Robert Morris*

Offers a variety of international educational exchange programs
to students who wish to study overseas.

**3082  Lake Erie College**
Academic Programs Abroad
Painesville, OH 44077            440-352-3361
                                 FAX: 440-352-3533

*Catherine Shaw*
*Harold Laydon, President*

Sends students abroad for a term or longer to develop intellectual awareness and individual maturity.

**3083  Lane Community College**
4000 E 30th Avenue
Eugene, OR 97405                 541-463-3000

                                 www.lanecc.edu

*Mary Spilde, President*

To be a learning centered community college that provides affordable, quality, lifelong educational opportunities that include: professional technical and lower division college transfer
programs, employess skill upgrading, business development
and career enhancement, foundational academic, language and
life skills development, lifelong personal development and enrichment, and cultural and community services.

**3084  Lions Clubs International**
300 W 22nd Street
Oak Brook, IL 60523              630-571-5466
                                 FAX: 630-571-8890
                                 e-mail: info@lionsclubs.org
                                 www.lionsclubs.org

*Ashok Mehta, International President*
*Jimmy Ross, 1st Vice President*
*Gary Lapetina, Chief Executive Officer*

Over 46,000 individual clubs in over 194 countries and geographical areas which provide community service and promote
better international relations. Clubs work with local communities to provide needed and useful programs for sight, diabetes
and hearing.

**3085  Lisle**
900 County Road 269
Leander, TX 78641                512-259-7621
                                 FAX: 512-259-0392
                                 e-mail: mkinney@utnet.utoledo.edu
                                 www.lisle.utoledo.edu

*Barbara Bratton, Executive Director*

Educational organization which works toward world peace and
better quality of human life through increased understanding between persons of similar and different cultures.

**3086 National 4-H Council**
7100 Connecticut Avenue
Chevy Chase, MD 20815          301-961-2800
FAX: 301-961-2894
www.fourhcouncil.edu

*Donald T Floyd Jr, President/CEO/Asst Secretary*
*Denise W Streeter, CFO/Assistant Treasurer*

National, private sector non profit partner of 4-H and the Cooperative Extenisive System. Also manages the National 4-H Conference Center, which is a full service conference facility, and the National 4-H Supply Service which is the authorized agent for items bearing the 4-H name and emblem. Partners with 4-H at all levels national,state and local and provides training and support, curriculum development, fostering innovative programming and facilitating meetings and connections.

**3087 New Directions for People with Disabilities**
5276 Hollister Avenue
Suite 207
Santa Barbara, CA 93111          805-967-2841
888-967-2841
FAX: 805-964-7344
e-mail: info@newdirectiontravel.org
www.newdirectionstravel.org

*Dee Duncan, Executive Director/Founder*

Provides high quality local, national, and international travel vacations and holiday programs for people with mild to moderate developmental disabilities. Through these programs, people with disabilities are increasingly understood, appreciated and more accepted as important and contributing members of our world.

**3088 People to People International**
501 E Armour Boulevard
Kansas City, MO 64109          816-531-7231
800-676-7874
FAX: 816-561-7502
e-mail: ptpi@ptpi.org
www.ptpi.org

*Mary Eisenhowser, President/CEO*
*Marc L Bright, Deputy CEO/Executive VP*
*Tracy Geise, Executive Assistant*

Exchanges international understanding and friendship through educational, cultural and humantarian activities involving the exchange of ideas and experiences directly among people of different countries and diverse cultures. Is also dedicated to enhancing cross cultural communication within each communityand across communities and nations.

**3089 Rotary Youth Exchange**
Rotary International
1560 Sherman Avenue
Evanston, IL 60201          847-866-3000
FAX: 847-328-8554
www.rotary.org

*Carl Wilhelm Stenhammar, International President*
*Jonathan Magiyagbe, President*

Rotary a worlwide organization of business and professional leaders that provides humanitarian service, encourages high ethical standards in all vocations, and helps build goodwill and peace in the world. Approximately 1.2 million Rotarians belong to more than 31,000 Rotary clubs located in 167 countries.

**3090 Scandinavian Seminar**
24 Dickinson Street
Amherst, MA 01002          413-253-9736
FAX: 413-253-5282
e-mail: study@scandinavianseminar.org
www.scandinavianseminar.org

*Jacqueline D Waldman, Manager*
Student exchange program founded in 1949.

**3091 Sister Cities International**
1301 Pennsylvania Avenue NW
Suite 850
Washington, DC 20004          202-347-8630
FAX: 202-393-6524
e-mail: info@sister-cities.org
www.sister-cities.org

*Steven Honey, Executive Director*
*Cynthia M Maka, Assistant Executive Director*
*Ami Neiberger-Miller, Communications Director*

A non profit citizen diplomacy netowrk creating and strengthening partnerships between US and international communities in an effort to increase global cooperation at the municipal level, to promote cultural understnading and to stimulate economic development. Also leads the movement for local community development and volunteer action by motivating and empowering private citizens, municipal officials and business leaders to conduct long term programs of mutual benefits.

**3092 Southern Illinois University at Carbondale**
NW Anx
Room B220
Carbondale, IL 62901          618-453-5348
FAX: 618-453-7647
e-mail: studyabr@siu.edu
www.siu.edu

*James E Walker, President*
*Arron Stearn, Manager*

Main emphasis in international programs abroad is school-to-school direct exchanges and exchanges through organizations such as the International Student Exchange Program.

**3093 State University of New York**
1400 Washington Avenue
Albany, NY 12222          518-442-3300
FAX: 518-442-3235
www.albany.edu

*Kermit L Hall, President*

Offers over 150 international educational exchange programs in 37 different countries. Broad mission of excellence in undergraduate and graduate education, research and public service engages 17,000 diverse students in nine schools and colleges across three campuses.

**3094 University of Minnesota at Crookston**
2900 University Avenue
Crookston, MN 56716          218-281-6510
800-862-6466
FAX: 218-281-8050
e-mail: mprada@mail.crk.umn.edu
www.crk.umn.edu

*Joe Massey, CEO*
*Mario Prada, Program Director*

A four-year college with innovative educational programs for the acquisition of technical skills and a liberal arts education.

**3095 University of Oregon International Service**
5209 University of Oregon
Eugene, OR 97403          541-346-3206
FAX: 541-346-1232
www.uoregon.edu

*Dave Frohmayer, President*

International programs offered through the University of Oregon offer participants the opportunity to gain academic, cultural, and personal experience.

**3096  University of Portland**
5000 N Willamette Boulevard
Portland, OR  97203
　　　　　　　　　503-943-8000
　　　　　　FAX: 503-943-7178
　　　　e-mail: webmaster@up.edu
　　　　　　　　　www.up.edu

*E William Beauchamp, President*

Study/cultural experience is available in Tokyo and other Japanese cities as part of the Japan Studies Program at the University.

**3097  Western Washington University**
516 High Street
Bellingham, WA  98225
　　　　　　　　　360-650-3000
　　　　　　FAX: 360-650-9046
　　　　e-mail: president@wwu.edu
　　　　　　　　　www.wwu.edu

*Karen Morse, President*
*Elizabeth Schoenfeld, Executive Asst to the President*

Nurtures the intellectual, ethical, social, physical and emotional development of each student. It aims to teach learning skills useful in a rapidly changing and highly technical world to develop a consciousness of the challenges and responsibilities of living in a diverse and pluralistic society.

**3098  World Experience**
2440 S Hacienda Boulevard
Suite 116
Hacienda Heights, CA  91745
　　　　　　　　　626-330-5719
　　　　　　　　　800-633-6653
　　　　　　FAX: 626-333-4914
　　e-mail: weworld@worldexperience.org
　　　　　　www.worldexperience.org

*Bobby Fraker, President*

Offers a quality and affordable program for over two decades and continues to provide students and host families a youth exchange program based on individual attention, with the help of an international network of overseas directors and USA coordinators

**3099  World of Options**
Mobility International USA
PO Box 10767
Eugene, OR  97440
　　　　　　　　　541-343-1284
　　　　　　FAX: 541-343-6812
　　　　e-mail: info@miusa.org
　　　　　　　　　www.miusa.org

*Susan Sygall, Executive Director*

Empowering people with disabilities around the world through international exchange and international development to achieve their human rights. *$16.00*
　　*338 pages*
　　*ISBN 1-880034-01-8*

**3100  World of Options: A Guide to International Educational Exchange**
Mobility International USA
PO Box 10767
Eugene, OR  97440
　　　　　　　　　541-343-1284
　　　　　　FAX: 541-343-6812
　　　　e-mail: info@miusa.org
　　　　　　　　　www.miusa.org

*Susan Sygall, Executive Director*

A Guide to International Educational Exchange, Community Service and Travel for People with Disabilities includes information travel and international programs, as well as personal experience stories from people with disabilities who have had successful international experiences. *$45.00*

*600 pages 1997*
*ISBN 1-880034-24-7*

**3101  Youth for Understanding International Exchange**
6400 Goldsboro Road
Suite 100
Bethesda, MD  20817
　　　　　　　　　240-235-2100
　　　　　　　　　800-833-6243
　　　　　　FAX: 240-352-2104
　　　　e-mail: admissions@yfu.org
　　　　www.youthforunderstanding.org

*Rachel Andreson, Founder*

Youth for Understanding (YFU) International Exchange, an educational, nonprofit organization, prepares young people for the opportunities and responsabilities in a changing, independent world. With YFU, students can choose a year, semenster, or summer program in one or more than 35 countries worldwide. More than 200,000 young people from more than 50 nations in Asia, Europe, North and South America, Africa and the Pacific have participated in YFU exchanges.

## Alabama

**3102 Alabama Power Foundation**
600 18th Street N
17th Floor
Birmingham, AL 35203      205-326-8002
800-245-2244
FAX: 205-226-1441

*Charles McCrary, Chief Executive Officer*

Giving is limited to Alabama. No support is given for religious or political organizations, individuals or for operating funds that duplicate the United Way support.

**3103 Andalusia Health Services**
PO Box 667
Andalusia, AL 36420      334-222-2030
FAX: 334-222-7844
e-mail: gwen@andalusiachamber.com
www.andalusiachamber.com

*George Proctor Sr, President*
*Dawn Reeves, Executive Vice President*

Only offers grants to the residents of Covington County in Alabama who are pursuing a degree in a medical field.

**3104 Arc of Alabama**
Arc of United States
300 S Hull Street
Montgomery, AL 36104      334-262-7688
FAX: 334-834-9737
e-mail: info@thearcofalabama.com
www.thearcalabama.com

*Mike Sullivan, President*
*Leland Conner, Director*
*Tom Holmes, Executive Director*

The Arc of Alabama is committed to securing for all people with mental retardation the opportunity to choose and realize their goals in regard to where and how they learn, live, work and play.

**3105 Blount Foundation**
4520 Executive Park Drive
Montgomery, AL 36116      334-244-4000

*D Joseph McInnes*

Established in 1970, the Foundation was created to serve as the voice with which the Blount Companies address the need to provide financial assistance to a variety of activities and programs concerned with the general welfare of our country and its citizens. The Foundation has a strong commitment to corporate citizenship and endorses the concept that companies, as well as individuals, must contribute to the well-being of society.

## Alaska

**3106 Arc of Alaska**
2211 Arca Drive
Anchorage, AK 99508      907-277-6677
FAX: 907-272-2161
www.arc-anchorage.org

*Gwen Lee, Chief Executive Officer*
*Lisa Anderson, Executive Assistant*

**3107 Rasmuson Foundation**
301 W Northern Lights Boulevard
Suite 400
Anchorage, AK 99503      907-297-2700
FAX: 907-297-2770
e-mail: rasmusonfdn@rasmuson.org
www.rasmuson.org

*Diane Kaplan, President*

Grants for Alaska 501C3 nonprofits only.

## Arizona

**3108 Arc of Arizona**
5610 S Central Avenue
Phoenix, AZ 85040      602-268-6101
800-252-9054
FAX: 602-268-7483
e-mail: Arcofarizona@aol.com
www.arcofarizona.org

*Jim Hailey, Executive Director*
*Cindy Waymire, Manager*

The Arc, a national organization on mental retardaion, is committed to securing for all people with developmental disabilities the opportunity to choose and realize their goals in regard to where they live, learn, work and play.

**3109 Arizona Community Foundation**
2201 E Camelback Road
Suite 202
Phoenix, AZ 85016      602-381-1400
800-222-8221
FAX: 602-381-1575
e-mail: sdoubleday@azfoundation.com
www.azfoundation.org

*Stephen Mittenthal, Chief Executive Officer*

**3110 JW Kieckhefer Foundation**
PO Box 1151
Prescott, AZ 86302      928-445-4010

*John Kieckhefer, Trustee/Owner*

**3111 Margaret T Morris Foundation**
PO Box 592
Prescott, AZ 86302      928-445-6633
FAX: 928-445-5368

*Eugene P Polk, Contact*

## Arkansas

**3112 Arc of Arkansas**
2004 Main Street
Little Rock, AR 72206      501-375-7770
FAX: 501-372-4621
www.arcark.org

*Steve Hitt, Executive Director*

**3113 Roy and Christine Sturgis Charitable Trust**
PO Box 7599
Little Rock, AR 72217      501-337-5109

Physically disabled, hospitals, child welfare and visually impaired are priorities of giving for this foundation.

**3114 Winthrop Rockefeller Foundation**

308 E 8th Street
Little Rock, AR 72202                    501-376-6854
                                         FAX: 501-374-4797

*Mahlon Martin*
*Sybil Hampton, President*

Mission is to improve the quality of life in Arkansas. It focuses its grantmaking efforts in three areas: education, economic development and civic affairs. Education projects funded in the past have included grants to schools that are working to involve teachers and parents in making decisions about what happens at their schools, projects that work to remove prejudice from the educational process and more. Major grants are made to support the development of new programs.

# California

**3115 Ahmanson Foundation**

9215 Wilshire Boulevard
Beverly Hills, CA 90210                  310-278-0770

*Lee Walcott, Managing Director*
*Robert Ahmanson, President*

The Foundation primarily gives in Southern California with major emphasis in Los Angeles County. The Foundation focuses on the arts and humanities, education, mental health and support for a broad range of social welfare programs.

**3116 Alice Tweed Touhy Foundation**

205 E Carrillo Street
Suite 219
Santa Barbara, CA 93101                  805-962-6430

*Harris Seed, President*
*Eleanor Van Cott, Executive VP*

Rehabilitation, recreation and building funds are given to organizations only within the Santa Barbara area.

**3117 Alternating Hemiplegia of Childhood Foundation**

239 Nevada Street
Redwood City, CA 94062                    650-365-5798
                                          800-225-3353
                                          FAX: 650-365-5798
                                          e-mail: laegan6@sbcglobal.net
                                          www.ahckids.org

*Lynn Egan, Vice President*
*Carol Presunka, Secretary*

Voluntary not-for-profit organizations dedicated to promoting professional and public awareness of Alternating Hemiplegia of Childhood (AHC) and providing current information to affected individuals and their families. Supports ongoing medical research into the cause, treatment and potential cure of AHC. Disseminates information about this disorder to promote proper diagnosis and maintains a registry of families, affected children and physicians who are familiar with AHC.

**3118 Amateur Athletic Foundation of Los Angeles**

2141 W Adams Boulevard
Los Angeles, CA 90018                     323-730-4600
                                          FAX: 323-730-9637
                                          e-mail: info@aafla.org
                                          www.aafla.org

*Anita Defrantz, President*

Enables AAF to serve as an educational and research center for sport— a leading forum for the advancement of coaching, the exchange of ideas and exploration of important issues in sport.

**3119 Annuziata Sanguinetti Foundation**

420 Montgomery Street
5th Floor
San Francisco, CA 94104                   415-477-1000

*Eugene Ranghiasci*

Hard-of-hearing, speech impaired and recreation. Serves only the San Francisco Bay area.

**3120 Apple Computer**

Worldwide Disability Solutions Group
2851 Park Avenue
Santa Clara, CA 95050                     408-996-1010
                                          800-692-7753
                                          TTY:800-755-0601

*Steven Jobs, Chief Executive Officer*

Offers grants in the areas of education, health and in areas of company operations.

**3121 Arc of California**

1225 8th Street
Suite 210
Sacramento, CA 95814                      916-552-6619
                                          FAX: 916-441-3494
                                          e-mail: tanderson@arccalifornia.org
                                          www.arccalifornia.org

*Shirley Dove, President*
*Pat Heineke, VP*
*John Foley, Executive Director*

**3122 Atkinson Foundation**

1720 S Amphlett Boulevard
Suite 100
San Mateo, CA 94402                       650-357-1101
                                          FAX: 650-357-1101
                                          e-mail: atkinfdn@aol.com

*Elizabeth Curtis, Administrator*
*Linda Lanier, President of the Board*

The Foundation focuses and awards grants to community service and civic organizations serving the residents of San Mateo County, California through programs that benefit children, youth, seniors, the disadvantaged and those in need of rehabilitation. Grants are also made to local churches and schools, and overseas for sustainable development, health education and family planning. No grants to individuals or for research, travel, special events, annual campaigns, media and publications.

**3123 Baker Commodities Corporate Giving Program**

4020 Bandini Boulevard
Los Angeles, CA 90023                     323-268-2883
                                          800-427-0696
                                          FAX: 323-268-5166
                                          www.bakercommodities.com

*James Andreoli, President*
*Maxine Taylor, Executive Secretary*

**3124 Bank of America Foundation**

315 Montgomery Street
8th Floor
San Francisco, CA 94104                   415-622-3456
                                          888-488-9802
                                          FAX: 704-386-6444
                                          www.bankamerica.com/foundation

*Caroline Boitano*

The Foundation will consider grants in four categories including: Health & Human Services, which provides support to health & human service organizations primarily through grants to the United Way campaigns; Education, with the focus on preparing people to become productive employees and participating citizens; Conservation & Environment, the improvement of California communities for the benefit of their citizens; and Culture & The Arts, supporting the leading performing and visual arts groups.

**3125 Bergen Brunswig Corporation Contributions Program**

4000 W Metropolitan Drive
Orange, CA 92868      714-385-1077
800-442-3040
FAX: 714-385-6948
www.amerisourceburgen.com

*Jeanne Fisher, Executive Vice President*

**3126 Blind Babies Foundation**

1200 Gough Street
San Francisco, CA 94109      415-922-9185
FAX: 415-771-9026

*Dennak Murphy, Executive Director*
*Ken Gardner, Owner*

Founded in 1949, provides services and programs that enable and empower families, professionals and the broader community to meet the unique needs of infants and preschool children who are blind or visually impaired. *$5.00*

**3127 Bothin Foundation**

1660 Bush Street
# 300
San Francisco, CA 94109      415-561-6540
FAX: 415-771-4064

*Lyman J Casey, Executive Director*
*Eric Sloan, Manager*

The broad purpose of this foundation is to support public charities located in the five counties of San Francisco, Marin, Sonoma, San Mateo and Santa Barbara. Bothin elects to support charitable organizations that promote youth, elderly, disabled, health care, minorities, community social services and the environment. Grants for the arts are made mainly to those groups predominantly serving youth or with heavy emphasis on youth participation.

**3128 Briggs Foundation**

PO Box 1510
Rancho Santa Fe, CA 92067      858-756-4875

*Blaine A Briggs*

**3129 Burns-Dunphy Foundation**

5 3rd Street
Suite 1200
San Francisco, CA 94103      415-421-6995
FAX: 415-882-7774

*Walter Gleason*
*Cressey Nakagawa*

Grants are given to promote wellness for the visually impaired, physically and mentally disabled and to promote research in these areas.

**3130 CNF Transportation Corporate Giving Program**

3240 Hillview Avenue
Palo Alto, CA 94304      650-494-2900
FAX: 650-493-0360
e-mail: info@cnf.com
www.cnf.com

*Doug Stotlar, President*
*Jim Allen, Vice President*

**3131 California Community Foundation**

445 S Figueroa Street
Suite 3400
Los Angeles, CA 90071      213-413-4130
FAX: 213-622-2979
www.calfund.org

*Jack Shakely, President*

Areas of funding priority include grants for the disabled, child welfare, rehabilitation, developmentally disabled, employment projects, research and computer projects. Giving is limited to the greater Los Angeles area.

**3132 California Endowment**

1000 N Alameda Street
Los Angeles, CA 90012      800-449-4149
FAX: 213-928-8801
e-mail: questions@calendow.org
www.calendow.org

*Robert K Ross, President/CEO*
*Irene M Ibarra, Executive VP*

California Endowment's mission is to expand access to affordable, quality health care for underserved individuals and communities, and to promote fundamental improvements in the health status of all Californians.

**3133 Carrie Estelle Doheny Foundation**

707 Wilshire Boulevard
Suite 4960
Los Angeles, CA 90017      213-488-1122
FAX: 413-488-1544
e-mail: doheny@earthlink.net
dohenyfoundation.org

*Robert A Smith III, President*

**3134 Clorox Company Foundation**

PO Box 24305
Oakland, CA 94623      510-271-7000

e-mail: community.relations@clorox.com
www.clorox.com/company/foundation

*Patricia Marino, President*
*Robert Matschullat, Chief Executive Officer*

Community Support Programs are offered to make the communities in which we live and work stronger, while providing measurable benefits to the Company and its shareholders. The Foundation's primary concern continues to be youth and K-12 education. The Foundation is helping our young people to improve their educational and job skills and develop their leadership potential.

**3135 Coeta and Donald Barker Foundation**

PO Box 936
Rancho Mirage, CA 92270      760-321-2345
FAX: 760-321-8662

*Coeta Barker, Owner*

It is an independent organization that gives its attention to organizations that are charitable or nonprofit under the laws of the state of Oregon or California.

**3136 Community Foundation of Santa Clara County**

111 W Saint John Street
Suite 230
San Jose, CA 95113      408-264-2437

*Peter Hero*

Visually impaired, mentally and physically disabled, hard-of-hearing, special education, mental health and employment projects are areas of priority. Giving is limited to Santa Clara and surrounding counties.

**3137 Crescent Porter Hale Foundation**
220 Bush Street
Suite 1069
San Francisco, CA 94104
FAX: 415-986-5197

*Ulla Davis, Executive Director*

Serves organizations in the San Francisco Bay Area who are involved in the following areas of concern: education in the fields of art and music; private elementary, high school and university education; capital funding; and other worthwhile programs which can be demonstrated as serving broad community purposes, leading toward the improvement of the quality of life.

**3138 Darrow Foundation**
1000 4th Street
Suite 570
San Rafael, CA 94901
415-453-0534
FAX: 415-453-0441

*Dewitt K Macdonald, Director*
*Peter Mitchell, Partner*

Grants are given in the areas of child welfare, visually impaired, projects involving independence, mentally and physically disabled.

**3139 David and Lucile Packard Foundation**
300 2nd Street
Suite 200
Los Altos Hills, CA 94022
650-948-7658

www.packfound.org

*Richard Schlesburg, President*
*Carol Larson, Chief Executive Officer*

This foundation provides grants to nonprofit organizations in the following areas: conservation; population; science; children, familes, and communities; arts and organizational effectiveness; and philanthropy. It provides national and international grants and also has a special focus on the Northern California Counties.

**3140 Deutsch Foundation**
5454 Beethoven Street
Los Angeles, CA 90066
310-862-3000
877-340-7700
FAX: 310-862-3100
www.deutschinc.com

*Mike Sheldon, Manager*

Learning disabled, visually impaired, mental health, eye research, child welfare, speech and hearing impaired, physically disabled and independence projects are funded through this Foundation. Giving is limited to California.

**3141 East Bay Community Foundation**
200 Frank H Ogawa Plaza
Oakland, CA 94612
510-836-3223
FAX: 510-836-3287
e-mail: admin@eastbaycp.org
www.eastbaycf.org

*Kate Wealty, Program Director*
*Mike Howe, President*

A collection of funds created by many people, organizations and businesses, the Foundation helps those people and groups to support effective nonprofit organizations to the East Bay and beyond.

**3142 Evelyn and Walter Hans Jr**
1 Lombard Street
Suite 305
San Francisco, CA 94111
415-398-4474
FAX: 415-986-4779

*Ira Hirschfield, President*
*Pamela David, Executive Director*

A private foundation interested in programs which assist people who are hungry, homeless, or at risk of homelessness; enable older adults to maintain independent lives in the community and support Hispanic community development in San Francisco's Mission District. The Foundation also encourages proposals for corporate social responsibility efforts within the business community.

**3143 Financial Aid for Study and Training Abroad**
Reference Service Press
5000 Windplay Drive
Suite 4
El Dorado Hills, CA 95762
916-939-9620
FAX: 916-939-9626
e-mail: findaid@aol.com
www.rspfunding.com

*Gail Ann Schlachter, Author/Owner*
*R David Weber, Editor*

This directory, which Children's Bookwatch calls invaluable describes more than 1,100 financial aid opportunities available to support study abroad. Updated every 2 years. *$39.50*
300 pages
ISBN 1-588410-31-5

**3144 Fireman's Fund Foundation**
Firemans Fund Insurance Companies
777 San Marin Drive
Novato, CA 94998
415-899-2000
800-227-1700
FAX: 415-899-2012
www.ffic.com

*Phyllis Secosky, Executive Director*
*Charles Kavitsky, Chief Executive Officer*

Provides discretionary grants to the disabled only in Marin and Sonoma counties in the San Francisco Bay area.

**3145 Fred Gellert Foundation**
1 Embarcadero Center
Suite 2480
San Francisco, CA 94111
415-433-6147
FAX: 415-433-7952

*Fred Gellert Jr, Chairman*

Focuses on organizations and programs serving residents of San Mateo and San Francisco and Marin counties in California, with the exception of environmentally concerned organizations.

**3146 Gallo Foundation**
PO Box 1130
Modesto, CA 95353
209-341-3111
FAX: 209-341-3307

*John Gallo, Senior VP Operations*
*Joseph Gallo, Chief Executive Officer*

Physically and mentally disabled, child welfare, Special Olympics, United Cerebral Palsy and Easter Seal Society are among the grants provided by this foundation.

**3147 Glaucoma Research Foundation**
251 Post Street
Suite 600
San Francisco, CA 94108
415-986-3162
800-826-6693
FAX: 415-986-3763
e-mail: info@glaucoma.org
www.glaucoma.org

*Thomas Brunner, President/CEO*

A national organization dedicated to protecting the sight of people with glaucoma through research and education. The Foundation conducts and supports research that contributes to improved patient care and a better understanding of the disease process. Provides education, advocacy and emotional support to patients and their families.

**3148  Harden Foundation**
PO Box 779
Salinas, CA  93902                          831-442-3005
                                       FAX: 831-443-1429
                                   www.hardenfoundation.org

*Joseph C Grainger, Executive Director*

**3149  Harry and Grace Steele Foundation**
441 N Newport Boulevard
Suite 30
Newport Beach, CA  92663                    949-631-0418
                                       FAX: 949-631-1255

*Marie Kowert, Manager*

Gives grants to qualified tax-exempt charitable organizations
which are not private foundations. Tax-supported organizations
of any kind, and applications from individuals are not accepted.
Grants are made for altruistic purposes, charitable, benevolent
or educational, primarily local giving.

**3150  Henry J Kaiser Family Foundation**
2400 Sand Hill Road
Menlo Park, CA  94025                       650-854-9400
                                       FAX: 650-854-4800
                                             www.kff.org

*Drew Altman, President/CEO*
*Dawn B Teall, Administrator*

**3151  Henry W Bull Foundation**
Santa Barbara Bank & Trust
PO Box 2340
Santa Barbara, CA  93120                    805-898-8878
                                       FAX: 805-884-1404

*Janice Gibbons, VP/Senior Trust Officer*
*Sharon McGinness, Sr Trust Admin Assistant*
*Brandee Hostler, Manager*

Grant given to a wide range of organizations that include those
which provide services for the disabled; arts, education, services
for elderly and youth grants awarded two times a year. Grant size
ranges from $500 to $5,000. Proposal deadlines April 1, Sept 1.

**3152  Irvine Health Foundation**
18301 Von Karman Avenue
Irvine, CA  92612                           949-253-2959
                                       FAX: 949-253-2962
                                       e-mail: info@ihf.org
                                             www.ihf.org

*Edward B Kacic, President*

**3153  Joseph Drown Foundation**
1999 Avenue of the Stars
Suite 1930
Los Angeles, CA 90067                       310-277-4488
                                       FAX: 310-277-4573
                                           www.jdrown.org

*Norman Obrow, President*

Giving is focused primarily in California. No support for religious purposes or to individuals.

**3154  Junior Blind of America**
5300 Angeles Vista Boulevard
Los Angeles, CA  90043                      323-295-4555
                                            800-352-2290
                                       FAX: 323-296-0424
                                   e-mail: info@juniorblind.org
                                         www.juniorblind.org

*Miki Jordan, President*

Junior Blind provides programs and services for children and
adults who are blind or visually impaired and their families to
achieve independence and self-esteem. Progrmas include;
Camp Bloomfield, Visions: Adventures in Learning, In-
fant-Family Program, Special Education School, Children's
Residential Program, Davidson Program for Independence, and
Student Transition and Enrichment Program.

**3155  Kenneth T and Eileen L Norris Foundation**
11 Golden Shr
Suite 450
Long Beach, CA  90802                       562-435-8444
                                       FAX: 562-436-0584
                                       e-mail: grants@ktn.org
                                       www.norrisfoundation.org

*Ronald Barnes, Executive Director*
*Savannah Gerringer, Grants Assistant*

The Foundation is primarily focused on medicine and education.
To a lesser extent the foundation contributes to community programs including visually impaired, autism, mentally and physically disabled, deaf and mental health in the Southern California
area. Average grant size in this area is $5,000-$10,000. Grants
are also given in the area of culture and youth.

**3156  Koret Foundation**
33 New Montgomery Street
Suite 1090
San Francisco, CA 94105                     415-882-7740
                                       FAX: 415-882-7775
                                   e-mail: info@koretfoundation.org
                                       www.koretfoundation.org

*Rosemary Peterson*
*Jeff Farber, Executive Director*

**3157  LJ Skaggs and Mary C Skaggs Foundation**
1221 Broadway
Suite 21
Oakland, CA  94612                          510-451-3300
                                       FAX: 510-451-1527

*James Soper, Manager*

The Foundation presently makes grants under four program categories: performing arts, social concerns, projects of historic interest and special projects.

**3158  LK Whittier Foundation**
625 Fair Oaks Avenue
Suite 360
S Pasadena, CA  91030                       626-441-5188
                                       FAX: 626-441-3672

*Linda Blinkenberg, Foundations Director*

Giving is primarily offered to preselected organizations. No
grants are given to individuals.

**3159  Lawrence Welk Foundation**
2700 Pennsylvania Avenue
Santa Monica, CA  90404                     310-829-9355
                                       FAX: 310-451-4268

*Lisa Parker, Executive Director*
*Larry Walk, President*

Awards grants in the range of $500 to $10,000. They are given to
private, nonprofit organizations in Southern California whose
focus is social services agencies working in inner cities with
families to alleviate the effects of poverty. Fund is unable to al-
locate funds to individuals, pass-through organizations, arts or
environmental organizations, or to those requesting planning
grants and prefers to fund capital improvements and seed or special projects rather than operating budgets.

# Foundations & Funding Resources /California

**3160 Legler Benbough Foundation**
2550 5th Avenue
Suite 132
San Diego, CA 92103    619-235-8099
FAX: 619-235-8077
www.benboughfoundation.org

*Peter K Elsworth, President*

**3161 Levi Strauss Foundation**
1155 Battery Street
7th Floor
San Francisco, CA 94111    415-501-7208
FAX: 415-501-3939
www.levistrauss.com/responsibility/foundation

*Judy Belk, Executive Director*

Has a funding initiative to support organizations which provide services for people with AIDS, and/or educational programs which help prevent the further spread of the HIV virus. The Foundation will assist in the development and enhancement of such services only in those communities where Levi Strauss & Co. has plants and distribution centers.

**3162 Louis R Lurie Foundation**
Louis R Lurie Foundation
555 California Street
Suite 5100
San Francisco, CA 94104    415-392-2470
FAX: 415-286-9
hhttp://www.stncenter.com

*Robert Lurie, Director*
*Gloria Kemp, Manager*

Visually impaired, hard-of-hearing and physically disabled in the San Francisco Bay Area and Metropolitan Chicago areas only.

**3163 Luke B Hancock Foundation**
360 Bryant Street
Palo Alto, CA 94301    650-321-5536
FAX: 650-321-0697

*Kimberly Hancock, Trustee*
*Thomas Hancock, Trustee*

Has concentrated its resources over the past year on programs which provide job training and employment for at-risk youth. Consortium funding with other foundations in areas where there is unmet need; emergency and transitional funding; and selected funding for music education.

**3164 Marin Community Foundation**
5 Hamilton Lane
Suite 200
Novato, CA 94949    415-461-3333
FAX: 415-464-2555
e-mail: mcf@marincf.org
www.marincf.org

*Aileen Sweeney, Director*
*Thomas Peters, Chief Executive Officer*

**3165 Mary A Crocker Trust**
233 Post Street
Floor 2
San Francisco, CA 94108    415-982-0138
FAX: 415-982-0141
e-mail: mact@best.com
www.mactrust.org

*Barbaree Jernigan, Administrator*

Established in 1889, the Foundation is interested in Bay Area programs such as environment, education and community relations.

**3166 National Foundation of Wheelchair Tennis**
940 Calle Amanecer
Suite B
San Clemente, CA 92673    949-366-2410
FAX: 949-361-6822

*Bradley Parks, President*

Founded in January of 1980, the intention of this foundation is to assist the newly physically disabled individual to realize his full potential in society by enhancing his esteem, independence productivity and physical capabilities regardless of age, sex, creed or disability extent.

**3167 Optometric Extension Program Foundation**
1921 Carnegie Avenue
Suite 31
Santa Ana, CA 92705    949-250-8070
FAX: 949-250-8157
e-mail: oep@oep.org
www.oep.org

*Robert Williams, Executive Director*

Offers continuing education in behavioral optometry for consumers and optometrists.

**3168 Parker Foundation**
4365 Executive Drive
Suite 1100
San Diego, CA 92121    858-677-1431
FAX: 858-677-1477

*Robbin Powell, Assistant Secretary*
*William Beamer, President*

The assets are directed to projects which will contribute to the betterment of any aspect of the people of San Diego County, California and solely to entities which, among other things, are organized exclusively for charitable purposes and are operating in San Diego County, California.

**3169 Pasadena Foundation**
260 S Los Robles Avenue
Suite 119
Pasadena, CA 91101    626-796-2097
FAX: 626-583-4738
e-mail: pfstaff@pasadenafoundation.org
www.pasadenacf.org

*Jennifer Devoll, Executive Director*

The mission of the Pasadena Foundation is to improve the quality of life for citizens of the Pasadena area through support of nonprofit organizations that provide services beneficial to the community.

**3170 Peninsula Community Foundation**
1700 S El Camino Real
Suite 300
San Mateo, CA 94402    650-358-9369
FAX: 650-358-9817

*Sterling Speirn, President*
*Ellen Clear, VP Community Programs*

For more than 36 years, Peninsula Community Foundation has built involvement and investment in the community. Develops resources and imaginative programs that make it easy for Peninsula and Silicon Valley residents— from Daly City to San Jose, from the Pacific Ocean to the San Francisco Bay— to support the common good and connect with causes they care about.

**3171 RC Baker Foundation**
PO Box 6150
Orange, CA 92863    714-750-8987

*F Scott, Manager*

327

Established in 1952, for general philanthropic purposes. The bulk of assistance and support has been to religious, scientific, educational institutions and youth organizations.

**3172 Ralph M Parsons Foundation**

1055 Wilshire Boulevard
Suite 1701
Los Angeles, CA 90017
213-482-3185
FAX: 213-482-8878
www.parsonsfoundation.org

*Joseph Hurley, President*
*Wendy Hoppe, Executive Director*

The Foundation is concerned with the encouragement and support of projects and programs deemed beneficial to mankind in several major areas of interest such as: education; social impact; civic and cultural; health and special products. Only funds in Los Angeles County.

**3173 Robert Ellis Simon Foundation**

152 S Lousky Drive
Beverly Hills, CA 90212
310-275-7335

*Joan Willens*

Mental health and visually impaired grants are the main concerns of this organization.

**3174 San Francisco Foundation**

225 Bush Street
500
San Francisco, CA 94104
415-733-8500
FAX: 415-477-2783
www.sff.org

*Robert Fisher, Director*
*Sandra Hernandez, Chief Executive Officer*

The Foundation's purpose is to improve life, promote greater equality of opportunity and assist those in need or at risk in the San Francisco Bay Area. The Foundation strives to protect and enhance the unique resources of the Bay Area, committed to equality of opportunity for all and the elimination of any injustice, seeks to enhance human dignity and seeks to establish mutual trust, respect and communication among the Foundation.

**3175 Santa Barbara Foundation**

15 E Carrillo Street
Santa Barbara, CA 93101
805-963-1873
FAX: 805-966-2345

*Charles Slosser, President/CEO*
*Suzanne Farwell, Communications Associate*
*James Rivera, VP Administration*

Giving is limited to Santa Barbara County, California with no support given to individuals (except sutdent aid) or religious organizations. We do n not make grants to individuals but only to non-profit organizations with 501(c)3 tax status.

**3176 Sidney Stern Memorial Trust**

PO Box 893
Pacific Palisades, CA 90272
310-459-2117

*Peter Hooffers, Chair*
*Marvin Hoffenberg, Advisor*

A Southern California-based foundation providing grants to nonprofit organizations for various projects. The foundation gives priority to the following areas of interest: education, health and science, community service projects, youth, services to the mentally and emotionally disabled, the arts, organizations and activities serving California. The Board prefers to make contributions to organizations that use the funds directly in the furtherance of their charitable and public purposes.

**3177 Sierra Health Foundation**

2525 Natomas Park Drive
Suite 200
Sacramento, CA 95833
916-447-4617
FAX: 916-635-3362

*Dorothy Beaumont, VP*
*Jose Sierra, Owner*

The Foundation strives to establish a collaborative relationship with its grantees, and with other funders and foundations, through an open dialogue. The Foundation approaches each grant as a partnership, with opportunities for the grantee and grantor to work cooperatively to enhance the effectiveness of the grant project.

**3178 Sonora Area Foundation**

PO Box 577
Sonora, CA 95370
209-533-2596
FAX: 209-533-2412
e-mail: acorn@sonora-area.org
www.sonora-area.org

*Mick Grimes, Executive Director*

**3179 Stella B Gross Charitable Trust**

Bank of the West
PO Box 1121
San Jose, CA 95108
408-947-5005
800-232-2430
FAX: 408-971-0933
e-mail: fmendoza@bankofthewest.com

*Lori C Stetzenmyer, Managing Director*
*Fatima Mendoza, Trust Associate*
*Henry Chow, Manager*

Organization must be federal and state tax-exempt and reside within the bounds of Santa Clara County, California to be eligible.

**3180 Teichert Foundation**

3500 American River Drive
Sacramento, CA 95864
916-484-3280
FAX: 916-480-5559
e-mail: info@teichertfoundation.org
www.teichert.com

*Frederick A Teichert, Executive Director*
*Jud Riggs, President*

**3181 Times Mirror Foundation**

202 W 1st Street
Los Angeles, CA 90012
213-237-3700
FAX: 213-237-2116
www.timesmirrorfoundation.org

*Michelle Williams, Executive Director*
*Vanessa Briseno, Contributions Coordinator*

**3182 WM Keck Foundation**

550 S Hope Street
Suite 2500
Los Angeles, CA 90071
213-680-3833
FAX: 213-614-0934
www.wmkeck.org

*Dr. Dorothy Fleisher, Program Director*
*Robert Day, Chief Executive Officer*

Created to support accredited colleges and universities with particular emphasis on the sciences, engineering and medical research. The Foundation also maintains a Southern California Grant Program that provides support for non-profit organizations in the field of civic and community services, health care, precollegiate education and the arts.

**3183  Willam G Gilmore Foundation**
120 Montgomery Street
San Francisco, CA 94104               415-546-1400
                                 FAX: 415-391-8732

*Robert C Harris, President*
*Faye Wilson, Executive Director*

## Colorado

**3184  Adolph Coors Foundation**
4100 E Mississippi Avenue
Suite 1850
Denver, CO 80246                     303-388-1636
                                 FAX: 303-388-1684
                              www.coorsfoundation.org

*Sally Rippey, Executive Director*

Applicant organizations must be classified as 501 and must operate within the United States. The areas covered by the Foundation are health, education, youth, community services, civic and cultural and public affairs.

**3185  Anschutz Family Foundation**
555 17th Street
Denver, CO 80202                     303-293-2338
                                 FAX: 303-298-8881

*Sue Anschutz Rodgers, President*

The Foundation's interests are to support efforts helping the elderly, the young and the economically disadvantaged. The Foundation has supported over 600 public and private charities sharing in the concern for neighborhood strengthening and community cooperation.

**3186  Arc of Colorado**
8000 E Prentice Avenue
Suite D1
Greenwood Village, CO 80111          303-864-9334
                                     800-333-7690
                                 FAX: 303-864-9330
                     e-mail: bbaesman@thearcfco.org
                              www.thearcofco.org

*Bill Baesman, Executive Director*

**3187  Bonfils-Stanton Foundation**
1601 Arapahoe Street
Floor 5
Denver, CO 80202                     303-825-3774

               www.bonfils-stantonfoundation.org

*Dorothy Horrell, President*
*Johnston Livingston, Manager*

Grants limited to Colorado 501 (c) (3) organizations. Grants are for general, charitable philanthropic activities within the State. Major categories include education, scientific (including hospital and health services), civic and cultural, community and human services. Organizations should request foundation guidelines before submitting a proposal.

**3188  Comprecare Foundation**
PO Box 740610
Arvada, CO 80006                     303-629-8661

*JR Gilsdorf, Executive Director*

**3189  Denver Foundation**
950 S Cherry Street
Suite 200
Denver, CO 80246                     303-300-1790
                                 FAX: 303-300-6547
                   e-mail: information@denverfoundation.org
                              www.denverfoundation.org

*David Miller, President*

Neighbors helping neighbors, that's what the foundation is for. As Denver's only community foundation we've been accepting charitable donations since 1925. Those funds have been given back to the community in ongoing grants to nonprofit organizations - organizations that touch nearly every meaningful artistic, cultural, civic, health and human services interest of metro Denver's citizens.

**3190  El Pomar Foundation**
10 Lake Circle
Colorado Springs, CO 80906           719-633-7733
                                     800-554-7711
                                 FAX: 719-577-5702
                                     www.elpomar.org

*William J Hybl, Chairman/President/CEO*

**3191  Gates Family Foundation**
3200 Cherry Creek South Drive
Suite 630
Denver, CO 80209                     303-778-9227
                                 FAX: 303-698-9031
                          e-mail: Gatesfdn@aol.com

*Charles Cannon, Executive Director*
*Joe Gates, Owner*

Purpose is to aid, encourage, initiate or carry on activities that will promote the health, well-being, security and education of all people. Because of a deep concern for and confidence in the future of Colorado, the foundation will invest primarily in institutions, projects and programs that will enhance the quality of life of those who live and work in the state, especially the Denver metropolitan area. Also finds ways to encourage greater cooperation between public and private sectors.

**3192  Helen K and Arthur E Johnson Foundation**
1700 Broadway
Suite 1100
Denver, CO 80290                     303-861-4127
                                     800-232-9931
                                 FAX: 303-861-0607
                   e-mail: info@johnsonfoundation.org
                              www.johnsonfoundation.org

*John Alexander Jr, President*
*Brigit Davis, VP Program Officer*

A nonprofit, grantmaking private foundation incorporated under the laws of the State of Colorado in 1948. The Foundation is a general purpose foundation whose grant program consists of a wide variety of creative efforts to solve problems and to enrich the quality of life. The areas of interest are: education, youth, health, community services, civic and culture and senior citizens. Grants limited to the state of Colorado.

**3193  Herbert F Parker Foundation**
First Interstate Bank of Denver
PO Box 5825
Denver, CO 80217

Cancer research, care and education of mentally retarded children and promoting sporting programs for youths.

**3194  Hill Foundation**
First Interstate Bank of Denver
PO Box 5825
Denver, CO 80217

*Robert Lorentz, Vice President*

Offers grants primarily for higher education (private), health and human services, cultural projects.

**3195 JM McDonald Foundation**
PO Box 3219
Evergreen, CO 80437
303-674-9215
FAX: 303-674-9216

*Donald R McJunkin, Manager*

**3196 Kitzmiller-Bales Trust**
PO Box 96
Wray, CO 80758
970-332-3484

*Robert U Hansen*

**3197 V Hunter Trust**
650 S Cherry Street
Suite 535
Denver, CO 80246
303-399-5450
FAX: 303-399-5499

*Sharon Siddons, Executive Director*

# Connecticut

**3198 Aetna Foundation**
151 Farmington Avenue
Hartford, CT 06156
860-273-6382

www.aetna.com/foundation

*Diana Kinosh, Consultant*

**3199 Arc of Connecticut**
Arc of Usa
1030 New Britain Avenue
Suite 102b
West Hartford, CT 06110
860-953-8335
FAX: 860-953-8343
e-mail: arcct@aol.com
www.arcct.com

*Margaret Dignoti, Executive Director*

**3200 Clipper Ship Foundation**
Hartford Insurance Group
Hartford Plaza
Hartford, CT 06115
860-547-5000

*Richard M Madden, Director*

The purpose of this Foundation is to offer financial help to federally, nonprofit operating organizations serving the poor and the sick of the greater Boston area in order to assist them in fulfilling their goals and broadening the scope of their activities. Priority will be given to organizations devoted to helping the homeless, destitute, handicapped, children and the aged, or supplying the special needs of minority, low-income families and individuals.

**3201 Community Foundation of Southeastern Connecticut**
PO Box 769
New London, CT 06320
860-442-3572
FAX: 860-442-0582
e-mail: jenno@cfsect.org
www.cfsect.org

*Alice F Fitzpatrick, Executive Director*

**3202 Connecticut Mutual Life Foundation**
140 Garden Street
Hartford, CT 06154
860-727-3000

*Astrida Olds, Executive Director*

Distinguished throughout its long history by unusual commitment to high principles of corporate purpose and business ethics. That commitment has been reflected not only in the firm belief that normal business functions must be carried out with a sense of responsibility beyond that required by the marketplace. Maintains an ongoing program of corporate contributions, a nationwide matching gifts plan for all employees on behalf of private and public education, skills training programs, and more.

**3203 Cornelia de Lange Syndrome Foundation**
302 W Main Street
Suite 100
Avon, CT 06001
860-676-8166
800-223-8355
FAX: 860-676-8337
e-mail: info@cdlsusa.org
www.cdlsusa.org

*Rob Rodriguez, Vice President*
*Gayle Binney, President*
*Julie Mairano, Executive Director*

Provides information about birth defects caused by Cornelia de Lange Syndrome.

**3204 Fidelco Guide Dog Foundation**
PO Box 142
Bloomfield, CT 06002
860-243-5200
FAX: 860-243-7215
e-mail: training@fidelco.org
www.fidelco.org

*Roberta C Kaman, Chairman*
*George J Salpietro, Vice Chairman*
*Nancy Levin, Vice President*

Purpose is to breed, train and place Fidelco German Shepherd guide dogs with persons who are visually impaired throughout the Northeast. Provides in community training services to persons receiving guide dogs, reviews performance of the guide dog teams to see that satisfactory level of achievement is maintained, utilizes genetic processes and clinical methods to improve and refine the breed and maintains an ongoing program for development and improvement of training methods.

**3205 GE Foundation**
General Electric Company
3135 Easton Tpke
Fairfield, CT 06828
203-373-2211
FAX: 203-373-3029
e-mail: gefoundation@ge.com
www.gefoundation.com

*Robert Corcoran, President*
*Roger Nozaki, Executive Director*
*Jeffrey Immelt, Chief Executive Officer*

Believes that our greatest national resource is the work force. If we are to successfully compete in the global arena, then we become involved in improving the education of all of our citizens. The Foundation sets examples for others to emulate helping people with their international grant program to higher education and to health care for children in developing countries.

**3206 General Electric Foundation**
3135 Easton Tpke
Fairfield, CT 06828
203-373-2211
FAX: 203-373-3029
e-mail: gefoundation@ge.com
www.ge.com/foundation

*Robert Corcoran, President*
*Roger Nozaki, Executive Director*
*Jeffrey Immelt, Chief Executive Officer*

Blind, physically and mentally disabled and rehabilitation grants are among the priorities of the company.

**3207  Hartford Foundation for Public Giving**
550 Main Street
Hartford, CT 06103                  860-548-1888
                                FAX: 860-722-6014
                        e-mail: hfpg2@ursa.hartnet.org
                                www.hartnet.org

*D Anwar Al Ghani, Chairman*
*Michael Bangser, Executive Director*

Developmentally disabled, housing, deaf, recreation and education grants.

**3208  Hartford Insurance Group**
690 Asylum Avenue
Hartford, CT 06105                  860-547-5000

                                www.thehartford.com

*Ramani Ayer, President/CEO*
*Thomas Marra, Executive Vice President*

Giving is primarily in the Hartford, CT area and in communities where the company has a regional office. No support is available for political or religious purposes. Grants are given in the areas of education, health and United Way organizations.

**3209  Henry Nias Foundation**
2 Batterson Park Road
Milford, CT 06460                   203-874-2787

*Charles D Fleischman, VP*

**3210  Heublein Foundation**
PO Box 778
Hartford, CT 06142                  860-702-4000

*Moira E Burke, Treasurer*

The Foundation awards grants to class organizations in communities where there is a high concentration of employees, or in which the company has a major operating facility. The areas of interest are charitable, civic and health and social care.

**3211  Jane Coffin Childs Memorial Fund for Medical Research**
Jane Coffin Childs Memorial Fund
333 Cedar Street
LW300-SHM
New Haven, CT 06510                 203-785-4612
                                FAX: 203-785-3301
                        e-mail: info@jjcfund.org
                                www.jccfund.org

*Kim Roberts, Administrative Director*

The Fund awards fellowships to suitably qualified individuals for full time postdoctoral studies in the medical and related sciences bearing on cancer.

**3212  John H and Ethel G Nobel Charitable Trust**
Bankers Trust Company
1 Fawcett Place
Greenwich, CT 06830                 203-629-7120
                                FAX: 203-629-7170

*Paul J Bisset, Vice President*

**3213  Scheuer Associates Foundation**
Robert Scheuer
960 Lake Avenue
Greenwich, CT 06831                 203-861-6525
                                FAX: 203-622-5002

*Thomas Scheuer, President*
*Robert Scheuer, Treasurer*
*B Scharbach, Owner*

**3214  Swindells Charitable Foundation Trust**
Shawmut Bank
777 Main Street
242
Hartford, CT 06115                  860-728-4900
                                FAX: 860-240-1210

*Maggie Willard, Vice President*
*Joseph Giangreco, Personal Trust Association*
*Paul Spinella, Manager*

Grants made to charitable organizations or societies incorporated for the relief of sick and suffering poor children and/or the relief of sick suffering and indigent aged men and women and/or the support of public charitable hospitals. Geographic area includes Hartford, CT area primarily. Application is required, deadlines are Feb. 1 and Aug. 1.

## Delaware

**3215  Arc of Delaware**
1016 Centre Road
Suite 1
Wilmington, DE 19805                302-996-9400

                                www.arcde.org

*Timothy F Brooks, President*
*Wesley E Perkins, Executive Vice President*

**3216  Laffey-McHugh Foundation**
PO Box 2207
Wilmington, DE 19899                202-654-1880
                                FAX: 302-654-1681

*Arthor G Connolly Jr, Junior President*

**3217  Longwood Foundation**
100 W 10th Street
Suite 1109
Wilmington, DE 19801                302-654-2477
                                FAX: 302-654-2323

*David D Wakefield, Executive Secretary*
*H Sharp III, President*

Offers grants to the mentally and physically disabled - capital, program, education and housing grants in the state of Delaware.

## District of Columbia

**3218  Albert L and Elizabeth T Tucker Foundation**
1120 20th Street NW
Suite 300
Washington, DC 20036                202-457-1600
                                FAX: 202-457-1678

*Nicholas S McConnell*
*James Schaller, President*

**3219 Alexander and Margaret Stewart Trust**

888 17th Street NW
Suite 610
Washington, DC 20006                    202-669-4052
                              FAX: 202-785-0918
                 e-mail: dlustine@stewart-trust.org

*Doris Lustine, Executive Secretary*
*Wiliam Bierbower, Manager*

Grants are given only to the Washington, DC area organizations providing care or treatment to cancer patients or those with childhood afflictions.

**3220 Arc of the District of Columbia**

817 Varnum Street NE
Washington, DC 20017                    202-636-2950
                              FAX: 202-636-2996
                      e-mail: arcdc@juno.com
                              www.arcdc.net

*Mary Durso, Social Worker*
*Tasha Kluseman, Manager Employment Services*
*Monita Short-Ellis, Manger Commerical Services*

Advocating for and providing services to persons with mental retardation.

**3221 Charles Delmar Foundation**

1918 16th Street NW
Washington, DC 20009                    202-293-2494
                              FAX: 202-293-1788

*Mareen D Hughes, President*

**3222 Eugene and Agnes E Meyer Foundation**

1400 16th Street NW
Suite 360
Washington, DC 20036                    202-483-8294
                              FAX: 202-328-6850
                      www.meyerfoundation.org

*Julie Rogers, President*

Awards grants to projects dealing with the learning disabled, blind, mental health and vocational training in the Washington metropolitan area.

**3223 Federal Student Aid Information Center**

U S Department of Education
400 Maryland Avenue SW
Washington, DC 20202                    202-401-2000
                                        800-433-3243
                              FAX: 202-401-0689
               www.ed.gov/prog_info/SFA/StudentGuide

*William Ryan, Acting Director*
*Margaret Spellings, Chief Executive Officer*

Answers questions about Federal student aid from students, parents and Members of Congress, as well as financial aid administrators.

**3224 GEICO Philanthropic Foundation**

1 Geico Plaza
Washington, DC 20076                    301-986-3000
                                        877-206-0215
                              TTY:800-833-8255
                              www.geico.com

*Olza Nicely, Chief Executive Officer*
*Karen Watson, Marketing Director*

Hospitals, physically disabled and Special Olympics.

*1980*

**3225 Giant Food Foundation**

PO Box 1804
Washington, DC 20013                    202-331-0200
                                        888-4MY-GIAN
                              FAX: 301-618-4667
                              www.giantfood.com

*Barry F Scher, VP Public Relations*
*Luis Guinot, Partner*

Offers grants in the areas of mental health, recreation, community and cultural programs, art, and educational programs for the health and prosperity of the greater Washington area.

**3226 Jacob and Charlotte Lehrman Foundation**

1027 33rd Street NW
2nd Floor
Washington, DC 20007                    202-338-8400
                              FAX: 202-338-8405
                      www.lehrmanfoundation.org

*Samuel Lehrman, President*

**3227 John Edward Fowler Memorial Foundation**

1725 K Street NW
Suite 1201
Washington, DC 20006                    202-728-9080
                              FAX: 202-728-9082

*Richard Lee, President*

Although not a program priority, the foundation does offer grants to the physically disabled in the Washington, DC area only.

**3228 Joseph P Kennedy Jr Foundation**

1325 G Street NW
Suite 500
Washington, DC 20005                    202-637-3440
                              FAX: 202-824-0351
                      e-mail: info@jpkf.org
                              www.jpkf.org

*Eunice Shriver, Executive Vice President*
*Virginia Knowlton, Executive Director*
*Michael Maibach, Chief Executive Director*

Has two firm objectives: to seek the prevention of mental retardation, and to improve the way society deals with its citizens who are already mentally retarded. The Foundation uses its funds in areas where a multiplier effect can be achieved through development of innovative models for the prevention and amelioration of mental retardation, through provision of seed money that encourages new researchers, and thorough use of the Foundation's influence to promote public awareness.

**3229 Kiplinger Foundation**

1729 H Street NW
Washington, DC 20006                    202-887-6400
                              FAX: 202-778-8976

*Andrea Wilkes, Secretary*
*Knight Kiplinger, President*

Limited to the greater Washington, DC area, the grants focus primarily on education, social welfare, cultural activities and community programs. Matching grants to eligible secondary or higher education institutions are provided on behalf of employees and retirees of Kiplinger Washington Editors, Inc. The Foundation does not fund scholarships.

**3230 Morris and Gwendolyn Cafritz Foundation**
1825 K Street NW
14th Floor
Washington, DC 20006          202-232-3000
FAX: 202-296-7567
e-mail: info@cafritzfoundation.com
www.cafritzfoundation.org

*Kathleen Zeifang, Executive Director*

Grants are awarded to only 501(c)(3) organizations that are in the DC area. Grants are not awarded for capitol purposes, special events, endowments, or to individuals.

**3231 Paul and Annetta Himmelfarb Foundation**
4545 42nd Street NW
Suite 203
Washington, DC 20016          202-966-3796

*Michael Preston, Executive Director*

**3232 Public Welfare Foundation**
1200 U Street NW
Washington, DC 20009          202-965-1800
FAX: 202-265-8851
e-mail: reviewcommittee@publicwelfare.org
www.publicwelfare.org

*Thomas J Scanlon, Chair*
*Robert H Haskell, Vice Chair*
*Larry Kressly, Executive Director*

The foundation's funding is specifically targeted to economically disadvantaged populations. Proposals must fall within one of the following categories: criminal justice, disadvantaged elderly, disadvantaged youth, environment, health and population and reproductive health, human rights and global security, and community economic developmental and participation. Proposals should be addressed to the Review Committee.

# Florida

**3233 Able Trust**
Florida Endowment Foundation for Vocational Rehab
106 E College Avenue
Suite 820
Tallahassee, FL 32301          850-224-4493
888-838-2253
888-838-2253
FAX: 850-224-4496
e-mail: info@abletrust.org
www.abletrust.org

*Sharon Griffith, President*
*Kristen Knapp, Vice President*
*Guenevere Crum, Director Grants Program*

Provides grant funds to further employment for people with disabilities and employment-related programs for non-profit agencies in Florida. Assists agencies through educational conferences, and youth training programs. Provides businesses free resources for hiring people with disabilities.

**3234 Arc of Florida**
2898 Mahan Drive
Suite 1
Tallahassee, FL 32308          850-921-0460
800-637-2316
FAX: 850-921-0418
e-mail: arcofflorida@comcast.net
www.arcflorida.org

*John C Hall, Executive Director*
*Deborah Linton, Assistant Director*

Promotes, for all people with mental retardation and other developmental disablilities, through education, awareness, research, advocacy and the support of families, friends and community.

**3235 BCR Foundation**
PO Box 13307
Pensacola, FL 32591          850-438-2509

*Betty Rainwater, Director*

**3236 Bank of America Client Foundation**
1800 2nd Street
Suite 750
Sarasota, FL 34236          941-957-0442
FAX: 941-957-3135
www.selbyfdn.org

*Debra Jacobs, President/CEO*

**3237 Baron de Hirschmeyer Foundation**
407 Lincoln Road
Suite 6j
Miami Beach, FL 33139          305-672-0934

*Polly Lux de Hirshmeyer, President*

**3238 Barron Collier Jr Foundation**
2600 Golden Gate Parkway
Suite 200
Naples, FL 34105          239-262-2600
FAX: 239-262-1840

*Lamar Gabel, Director*
*Paul Marinelli, President*

Giving to the Special Olympics is a top priority of the Foundation.

**3239 Camiccia-Arnautou Charitable Foundation**
Bill T Smith Jr
980 N Federal Highway
Suite 402
Boca Raton, FL 33432          561-368-5757
FAX: 561-368-8505

*Bill Smith Jr, Owner*

**3240 Chatlos Foundation**
PO Box 915048
Longwood, FL 32791          407-862-5077

e-mail: cj@chatlos.org
www.chatlos.org

*William J Chatlos, President*
*Joy D'Arata, Vice President*

Funds nonprofit organizations in the USA and around the globe. Funding is provided in the following areas of giving: Bible Colleges/Seminaries, Religious Causes, Medical Concerns, Liberal Arts Colleges and Social Concerns. Category of placement is determined by the organizations overall mission rather than the project under consideration. The Foundation does not make scholarship grants directly to individuals but rather to educational institutions which in turn select recipients.
*1953*

**3241 Dade Community Foundation**
200 S Biscayne Boulevard
Suite 2780
Miami, FL 33131          305-371-2711
FAX: 305-371-5342
e-mail: dadecomfdn@aol.com

*Ruth Shack, President*

**3242 Dr. Jack Widrich Foundation**
400 W Rivo Alto Drive
Miami Beach, FL 33139          305-673-5050

*Jack Widrich, Owner*

**3243 EIS Foundation**
550 SE Mizner Boulevard
Apt 507
Boca Raton, FL 33432          561-852-6854
FAX: 561-852-6884

*Maurice L Schwarz, President*

**3244 Edyth Bush Charitable Foundation**
PO Box 1967
Winter Park, FL 32790          407-647-4322
888-647-4322
FAX: 407-647-7716
www.edythbush.org

*David A Odahowski, President/CEO*
*Mary Gretche Belloff, Vice Chairman*

Funding is resricted to 501c3 nonprofit organizations located
and operating in Orange, Osceola, Seminole and Lake Counties,
Florida. Visit www.edythbush.org for a list of funding policies.

**3245 FPL Group Foundation**
700 Universe Boulevard
Juno Beach, FL 33408          561-694-4000
800-222-4511
FAX: 561-694-4620

*John L Kitchens*
*James Robo, President*

**3246 Florida Rock Industries Foundation**
155 E 21st Street
Jacksonville, FL 32206          904-355-1781
FAX: 904-791-1810

*HB Horner, Secretary*
*John Baker II, Chief Executive Officer*

**3247 Frank Stanley Beveridge Foundation**
1340 US Highway One
Suite 102
Jupiter, FL 33469
800-600-3723
FAX: 561-748-0644
e-mail: administrator@beveridge.org
www.beveridge.org

*Philip Caswell, President*
*Carole S Lenhart, CPA, VP/Treasurer*

The mission of The Frank Stanley Beveridge Foundation, Inc. is
to preserve and enhance the quality of life by embracing and per-
petuating Frank Stanley Beveridge's philanthropic vision
through grantmaking initiatives in support of The Stanley Park
of Westfield, Inc. and programs in youth development, health,
education, religion, art and environment primarily in Hampden
and Hampshire Counties, Massachusetts.

**3248 Jack Eckerd Corporation Foundation**
PO Box 4689
Clearwater, FL 33758          727-395-6000
FAX: 727-395-7934
e-mail: serve@eckerd.com
www.eckard.com

*Tamz Alderman, MCR, PR*
*Robert Sloan, Plant Manager*

The foundation limits its giving to nonprofit, tax-exempt organizations located in Eckerd Drug Company's 13-state marketing
area. The majority of our funds are committed to national health
organizations, the United Way campaigns, and scholarship
funding at various colleges of pharmacy.

**3249 Jefferson Lee Ford III Memorial Foundation**
9600 Collins Avenue
546487
Bal Harbour, FL 33154          305-885-5447
FAX: 305-868-2646

*Herbert Kurras, Trustee*
*Suzanne Kingsbury, Trustee*

Disabled children, hearing and speech center. Grants are only
given to tax exempt organizations, no individual grants are offered.

**3250 Jessie Ball duPont Fund**
1 Independent Drive
Suite 1400
Jacksonville, FL 32202          904-353-0890
800-252-3452
FAX: 904-353-3870
e-mail: contactus@dupontfund.org
www.dupontfund.org

*Sherry P Magill PhD, President*
*Davena Sawyer, Executive Assistant*

Established under the terms of the will of the late Jessie Ball
duPont. The fund is a national foundation having a special
though not exclusive interest in issues affecting the South. The
Fund works with the approximately 325 individual institutions
to which Mrs. duPont personally contributed during the
five-year period, 1960 through 1964.

**3251 Joe and Emily Lowe Foundation**
249 Royal Palm Way
Palm Beach, FL 33480          561-659-1203
FAX: 561-655-7130

*Bernard Sterm, President*

Emphasis is on Jewish welfare funds, the arts, museums, higher
education including medical education, hospitals, medical research, aid to the handicapped, underprivileged children's organizations and women's projects. The funding is limited to the
New York Metropolitan Area including New Jersey and Palm
Beach County, Florida. No grants are made to individuals.

**3252 John E & Nellie J Bastien Memorial Foundation**
440 E Sample Road
Suite 209
Pompano Beach, FL 33064          954-942-3203

*Carol Kearns, Manager*

**3253 Lost Tree Village Charitable Foundation**
11555 Lost Tree Way
North Palm Beach, FL 33408          561-622-3780
FAX: 561-622-7558
e-mail: losttreefoundation@adelphia.net
www.losttreefoundation.org

*Pamela M Rue, Executive Director*

**3254 Publix Super Markets Charities**
Publix Super Market Corporation Office
PO Box 407
Lakeland, FL 33802          863-688-1188
800-242-1227
FAX: 863-499-8536
www.publix.com

*Charles Jenkins Jr, Chief Executive Officer*

**3255 Richard W Higgins Charitable Foundation Trust**
Marshall & Ilsley Trust of Florida
800 Laurel Oak Drive
Suite 101
Naples, FL 34108
239-597-2440
800-874-2427
FAX: 239-592-2454
www.micorp.com

William Wade, Manager
Donna Graziuso, Assistant

## Georgia

**3256 Community Foundation for Greater Atlanta**
50 Hurt Plaza
Suite 449
Atlanta, GA 30303
404-688-5525
FAX: 404-688-3060
www.atlcf.org

Alicia Philipp, President
Jeremy Arkin, Vice President

**3257 Florence C and Harry L English Memorial Fund**
Sun Trust Bank Atlanta
PO Box 4418-Mail
Atlanta, GA 30302
404-870-3120
FAX: 404-724-3082
e-mail: raymond.king@suntrust.com
www.suntrustatlantafoundation.org

Raymond B King, Senior VP
Renee P Barnett, Foundation Administrator
Eduardo Andrade, Manager

Grants only made to Metro Atlanta non-profit organizations; no grants to churches or individuals.

**3258 Georgia Arc Network**
1996 Cliff Valley Way NE
Suite 102
Atlanta, GA 30329
404-982-1099
e-mail: gaarcnetwork@earthlink.net
www.arcga.org

Scott Walker, Owner

Provides unified advocacy so that individuals with mental retardation or developmental disabilities and their families achieve valued lives throuh full, productive and dignified participation in their communities.

**3259 Georgia Power Company Contributions Program**
Southern Company
241 Ralph McGill Boulevard NE
Atlanta, GA 30308
404-506-5000
FAX: 404-506-1485
e-mail: gpfoundation@southernco.com
www.georgiapower.com

Susan Carter, Executive Director
Valerie Huff, Assistant Director
David Ratcliffe, Chief Executive Officer

**3260 Grayson Foundation**
PO Box 515
Grayson, GA 30017
770-554-1000
FAX: 770-554-1003
e-mail: graysonfoundation@yahoo.com
www.graysonfoundation.org

Sam B Grayson, President
Dan Hicks, Principal

Grayson Foundation enhances the quality of public educationfor the students of the Grayson cluster of schools by providing funds which enrich and extend educational oppurtunities.

**3261 Harriet McDaniel Marshall Trust in Memory of Sanders McDaniel**
Sun Trust Bank Atlanta
PO Box 4418-Mail
Atlanta, GA 30302
404-870-3120
FAX: 404-724-3082
e-mail: raymond.king@suntrust.com
www.suntrustatlantafoundation.org

Raymond B King, Senior Vice President
Renee P Barnett, Foundation Administrator
Eduardo Andrade, Manager

Grants only made to Metro Atlanta non-profit organizations, no grants to churches or individuals.

**3262 IBM Corporation**
4111 Northside Parkway NW
Atlanta, GA 30327
404-238-5200
FAX: 404-238-3409

Manages disability programs (which leverage IBM resources through partnerships) designed to train persons with disabilities and assist them in gaining employment. Also, disseminates information regarding products and resources for persons with disabilities with those of other companies and organizations.

**3263 John H and Wilhelmina D Harland Charitable Foundation**
3565 Piedmont Road NE
Atlanta, GA 30305
404-264-9912
e-mail: harland@randomc.com

John A Conant, Secretary
Margeret Dixon, Manager
Margaret Reiser, President

**3264 Lettie Pate Whitehead Foundation**
50 Hurt Plaza
Suite 1200
Atlanta, GA 30303
404-522-6755
FAX: 404-522-7026
e-mail: fdns@woodruff.org
www.lpwhitehead.org

Charles H McTier, President

Non-profit organization dedicated to the support of needy women in nine southeastern states.

**3265 Patterson-Barclay Memorial Foundation**
6487 Peachtree Industrial Boulevard
Suite A
Atlanta, GA 30360
770-458-9888
FAX: 770-452-7704

Hugh R Powell Jr, Secretary

**3266 Perkins-Ponder Foundation**
Bank of America
PO Box 4007
Macon, GA 31213
478-744-6488

**3267 Rich Foundation**
11 Piedmont Center NE
Suite 204
Atlanta, GA 30305
404-262-2266
FAX: 404-262-4123

Anne Poland-Berg, Grant Consultant

**3268 Savannah Widows Society**
3025 Bull Street
Savannah, GA 31405
912-232-6312

Martha Peeples

# Foundations & Funding Resources /Hawaii

**3269  SunTrust Bank, Atlanta Foundation**
Sun Trust Bank Atlanta
PO Box 4418
Atlanta, GA 30302
404-870-3120
FAX: 404-724-3082
e-mail: raymond.king@suntrust.com
www.suntrustatlantafoundation.org

*Raymond B King, Senior VP*
*Eduardo Andrade, Manager*

## Hawaii

**3270  Arc of Hawaii**
3989 Diamond Head Road
Honolulu, HI 96816
808-737-7995
FAX: 808-732-9531
e-mail: collenk@thearcinhawaii.org
www.thearcinhawaii.org/

*Colleen Kojima, Executive Director*

**3271  Atherton Family Foundation**
222 Merchant Street
Honolulu, HI 96813
808-537-6333

*Jane Smith*
*Kelvin Taketa, Chief Executive Officer*

Supports educational projects, programs and institutions as the highest priority, with the enterprises of a religious nature and those concerned with health and social services given careful attention. The Foundation is one of the largest private resources in the State devoted exclusively to the support of activities of a charitable nature.

**3272  Clarence TC Ching Foundation**
PO Box 4107
Honolulu, HI 96812
808-521-8841
FAX: 808-521-8835

*Lawrence SL Ching, Chairperson*

**3273  GN Wilcox Trust**
Pacific Century Trust
PO Box 3170
Honolulu, HI 96802
808-538-4580

*Peter Ho, Executive Vice President*

**3274  Hawaii Community Foundation**
900 Fort Street Mall Pioneer Plaza
Suite 1300
Honolulu, HI 96813
808-537-6333
888-731-6286
FAX: 808-521-6286
e-mail: info@hcf-hawaii.org
www.hcf-hawaii.org

*Kelvin Taketa, Chief Executive Officer*

**3275  McInerny Foundation**
Pacific Century Trust
130 Merchant Street
Honolulu, HI 96813
808-538-4580

*Lois C Loomis, VP*
*Peter Ho, Executive Vice President*

**3276  Sophie Russell Testamentary Trust**
PO Box 2390
Honolulu, HI 96804
808-524-4488
FAX: 808-523-2195

*Lois Loomis, Secretary*
*Jo Byrne, Owner*

Supports qualified tax-exempt charitable organizations, in the State of Hawaii only. Offers grants to the Humane Society and institutions giving nursing care and serving the physically and mentally handicapped.

## Illinois

**3277  Abbott Laboratories Fund**
Contributions Committee
100 Abbott Park Road
Abbott Park, IL 60064
847-937-6100
FAX: 847-938-6511

*Margaret Norman, Executive Director*

An Illinois, nonprofit, philanthropic organization that makes a significant contribution to human welfare through the development and worldwide distribution of technologically advanced health care products.

**3278  Alfred Bersted Foundation**
231 S Lasalle Street
Chicago, IL 60604
312-251-8850

*M Catherine Ryan*
*Gregory Rothman, Owner*

Grants are given to programs serving the mentally and physically disabled, and organizations included in the broader focus of the foundation. Grants are restricted to organizations in four Illinois counties: DuPage, Kane, McHenry and DeKalb.

**3279  Alzheimer's Association**
Medical and Scientific Affairs
225 N Michigan Avenue
Floor 17
Chicago, IL 60601
312-355-8700
800-272-3900
FAX: 312-335-1110
e-mail: info@alz.org
www.alz.org

*Lawrence Varnes, Chairman*
*Marilyn S Albert, Vice Chaiman*

**3280  American Foundation for the Blind-Midwest**
401 N Michigan Avenue
Suite 350
Chicago, IL 60611
312-396-4420
800-232-5463
FAX: 312-527-4660
e-mail: chicago@afb.net
www.afb.org

*Jay Stiteley, Director*

**3281  American National Bank and Trust Company**
33 N La Salle Street
Chicago, IL 60602
312-661-6000
FAX: 815-961-7745

*Joan M Klaus, Foundation Director*

Supports the endeavors of organizations working to meet the critical needs of the city and its surrounding communities. Success is greatly affected by the well-being of the communities the company serves, thus the foundation seeks to fulfill the social obligations both through financial funding and human resources. The Foundation funding categories include organizations and programs involved in economic development, education, community and social services, healthcare and culture and the arts.

**3282  Ameritech Corporation Contributions Program**

30 S Wacker Drive
34th Floor
Chicago, IL  60606
312-263-2805
FAX: 312-727-1496
www.ameritech.com

*Michael E Kuhlin, Senior Director*

**3283  Amerock Corporation**

PO Box 7018
Rockford, IL  61125
815-963-9631
800-618-9559
FAX: 815-969-6029
www.amerock.com

*Robert Bailey, President*

Grants are given to organizations promoting wellness, health and rehabilitation of the visually impaired and physically disabled.

**3284  Arc of Illinois**

Arc of Illinois
18207 Dixie Highway
Suite A
Homewood, IL  60430
708-206-1930
800-588-7002
FAX: 708-206-1171
e-mail: tony@thearcofil.org
www.illinoislifespan.org

*Mike Kaminsky, Director*
*Mike Paulauski, Executive Director*

The Arc of Illinois is committed to empowering persons with disabilities to achieve full participation in community life thru informed choices.

**3285  Benjamin Benedict Green-Field Foundation**

18313 Greenleaf Court Tinley Park
Chicago, IL  60477
708-444-4241
FAX: 708-444-4241
www.greenfieldfoundation.org

*Sheldon Rachman, VP*
*Colin Fisher, President*

A privately endowed grantmaking organization trying to improve the qaulity of life for children and the elderly in the city of chicago.

**3286  Blowitz-Ridgeway Foundation**

1701 E Woodfield Road
Suite 201
Schaumburg, IL  60173
847-446-1010
FAX: 847-446-6318

*Tina M Erickson, Administrator*

Provides limited program, capital and research grants to organizations aiding the physically and mentally disabled, and agencies serving children and youth. Grants generally limited to Illinois.

**3287  Burlington Northern Santa Fe Foundation**

5601 W 26th Street
Cicero, IL  60804
630-222-4815
FAX: 630-222-4857

*Dick Russack, President*

**3288  Chicago Community Trust and Affiliates**

111 E Wacker Drive
Suite 1400
Chicago, IL  60601
312-616-8000
FAX: 312-580-7411
TTY:312-853-0394
e-mail: info@cct.org
www.cct.org

*Sandy Chears, Grants Manager*
*Donald Stewart, Chief Executive Officerl*

**3289  Community Foundation of Champaign County**

404 W Church Street
Champaign, IL  61820
217-359-0125
FAX: 217-352-6494

*Joan Dixon, Executive Director*

**3290  Dr. Scholl Foundation**

1033 Skokie Boulevard
Suite 230
Northbrook, IL  60062
847-559-7430

www.drschollfoundation.com

*Pamela Scholl, President*

**3291  Duchossois Foundation**

845 N Larch Avenue
Elmhurst, IL  60126
630-279-3600
800-282-6225
FAX: 630-993-6911
www.chamberlain.com

*Kimberly Duchossois Lenczuk, President*
*Craig Duchossois, Chief Executive Officer*

Established in 1984, the foundation returns dollars to the communities supporting its facilities and employees. Within these following areas, organizations are carefully selected on the basis of community needs and the organization's value and performance. Areas aimed at include: medical research, children/youth programs and cultural institutions.

**3292  Evenston Community Foundation**

1007 Church Street
Suite 108
Evanston, IL  60201
847-492-0990
FAX: 847-492-0904
e-mail: info@evcommfdn.org
www.evcommfdn.org

*Sara Schastok, Executive Director*
*Julie Durham, Assistant Director*

**3293  Field Foundation of Illinois**

200 S Wacker Drive
Suite 3860
Chicago, IL  60606
312-831-0910

*Aurie Pennick, Executive Director*

The Foundation awards grants to institutions and agencies in the fields of health, welfare, education, cultural and conservation activities, and urban and community affairs, primarily serving the people of the Chicago metropolitan area.

**3294  Francis Beidler Charitable Trust**

53 W Jackson Boulevard
Suite 530
Chicago, IL  60604
312-922-3792
FAX: 312-922-3799

*Thomas B Dorris, Director*
*Francis Beidler, Partner*

**3295  Fred J Brunner Foundation**
9300 King Street
Franklin Park, IL  60131            847-678-3232
                                    FAX: 847-678-0642

*Pam Sthwegal, Director*
*Fred Brunner, Chief Executive Officer*
General disability grants.

**3296  George M Eisenberg Foundation for Charities**
2340 S Arlington Heights Road
Suite 480
Arlington Heights, IL  60005        847-981-0545
                                    FAX: 847-941-0548

*James Marousis, Manager*

**3297  George Zoltan Lefton Family Foundation**
George Zoltan Lefton Company
3622 S Morgan Street
Chicago, IL  60609                  773-254-4344

*Magda Lefton, Secretary*

**3298  Green Bay Foundation**
Goldman, Sachs & Company
71 S Wacker Drive
Suite 1
Chicago, IL  60606                  312-655-4600

General disability grants.

**3299  Grover Hermann Foundation**
Paul K Rhoads
233 S Wacker Drive
Chicago, IL  60606                  312-876-1000
                                    FAX: 312-258-6600
                                    www.schiffhardin.com

*Lauralyn Bengel*

Provides funds for educational, health, public policy, community and religious organizations throughout the United States. Its major interests are in higher education and health.

**3300  Harry F and Elaine Chaddick Foundation**
The Chaddick Institute for Metropolitan Developmen
243 S Wabash Avenue
Suite 9000
Chicago, IL  60604                  312-362-5731
                                    FAX: 312-362-5506
                                    e-mail: chaddick@depaul.edu
                                    www.condor.depaul.edu

*Joseph P Scwieterman, Director*
*Gloria Simo, Assistant Director*

**3301  Helen Brach Foundation**
55 W Wacker Drive
Suite 701
Chicago, IL  60601                  312-372-4417
                                    FAX: 312-372-0290

*Raymond F Simon, President*

**3302  John D and Catherine T MacArthur Foundation**
140 S Dearborn Street
Suite 1200
Chicago, IL  60603                  312-726-8000
                                    800-662-8004
                                    FAX: 312-920-6258
                                    e-mail: 4answers@macfnd.org
                                    www.macfound.org

*Richard Kaplan, Director*
*Rebecca Koman, Manager*

**3303  LaSalle Chicago Community Trust**
222 N Lasalle Street
Suite 1400
Chicago, IL  60601                  312-372-3356
                                    FAX: 312-580-7411
                                    www.cct.org

*Sandy Chears, Grants Manager*

A community foundation established in 1915, which receives gifts and bequests from individuals, families or organizations interested in providing through the community foundation, financial support for the charitable agencies or institutions which serve the residents of metropolitan Chicago.

**3304  Les Turne Amyotrophic Laterial Sclerosis Foundation**
3325 Main Street
Skokie, IL  60076                   847-679-3311
                                    FAX: 847-679-9103
                                    e-mail: info@lturner-als.org
                                    www.lturner-als.org

*Harvey Gaffen, President*
*Wendy Abrams, Executive Director*

Voluntary health organization dedicated to raising funds for ALS research, patient services and public awareness. Provides educational materials for affected individuals and family members, health care professionals, and the general public. Program services include referrals and counseling; audio-visual aids and periodic newsletters. Offers support groups and patient networking to affected individuals, family members, and caregivers.

**3305  Little City Foundation**
1760 W Algonquin Road
Palatine, IL  60067                 847-358-5510
                                    FAX: 847-358-3291
                                    www.littlecity.org

*Alex Alexandrou, President*
*Alex Gianaras, Vice President*
*Mary Ann Scott, Director Adult Services*

Provides progressive community-based services and service coordination for children and adults with mental retardation or other developmental, emotional and behavioral challenges. Services include direct care with up to 24-hour per day support for children and adults, Foster Care, Families One, adoption opportunities, respite care, supported employment, studio and multidisciplinary fine arts, public education, and advocacy.

**3306  MAGIC Foundation for Children's Growth**
6645 North Avenue
Oak Park, IL  60302                 708-383-0808
                                    800-362-4423
                                    FAX: 708-383-0899
                                    e-mail: mary@magicfoundation.org
                                    www.magicfoundation.org

*Dianne Tamburrino, Executive Director*

This is a national nonprofit organization providing support and education regarding growth disorders in children and related adult disorders, including adult GHD. Dedicated to helping children whose physical growth is affected by a medical problem by assisting families of afflicted children through local support groups, public education/awareness, newsletters, specialty divisions and programs for the children.

**3307  McDonald's Corporation Contributions Program**
Mc Donalds Plaza
Oak Brook, IL  60521                630-623-3000

www.mcdonalds.com/countries/usa/community/ind

*Jackie Meara, Supervisor Contributions*
*James Skinner, Chief Executive Officer*

**3308    Michael Reese Health Trust**
20 N Wacker Drive
Suite 760
Chicago, IL  60606                           312-726-1008
                              FAX: 312-726-2797
                    e-mail: info@healthtrust.net
            www.gih.org/usr_doc/may21,%202001.pdf

*Dorothy H Gardner, President*

**3309    Moen Foundation**
First National Bank of Chicago
1 S Northwest Highway
Park Ridge, IL  60068                        815-729-1850
                              FAX: 815-729-5047

**3310    National Eye Research Foundation (NERF)**
910 Skokie Boulevard
Suite 207a
Northbrook, IL  60062                         847-205-0002
                                             800-621-2258
                              FAX: 847-564-0807
                    e-mail: nerfl955@aol.com
                         www.eyemac.com/nerf

*Elliot Silber, Owner*

Dedicated to improving eye care for the public and meeting the professional needs of eye care practitioners; sponsors eye research projects on contact lens applications and eye care problems. Special study sections in such fields as orthokertology, primary eyecare, pediatrics, and through continuing education programs. Provides eye care information for the public and professionals. Educational materials including pamphlets. Program activities include education and referrals.

**3311    National Headache Foundation**
820 N Orleans Street
Suite 217
Chicago, IL  60610                            312-274-2650
                                             800-843-2256
                              FAX: 773-525-7357
                         www.headache.org

*Suzanne Simons, Executive Director*
Headache physicians.

**3312    OMRON Foundation**
O MR ON Systems
1 Commerce Drive
Schaumburg, IL  60173                         847-843-7900
                              FAX: 847-240-5362

*Nicholas Hahn, Director*
*Craig Bauer, President*

**3313    Oris B Hastings Charitable Foundation**
PO Box 186
Cairo, IL  62914                              618-734-2800

*John G Holland, Owner*

**3314    Parkinson's Disease Foundation**
833 W Washington Boulevard
Chicago, IL  60607                            312-733-1893
                                             800-457-6676
                              FAX: 312-733-1896
                    e-mail: pdfchgo@rcn.com
                              www.pdf.org

*Jeanne Rosner, Executive Director*

International voluntary not-for-profit organization dedicated to patient services; education of affected individuals, family members, and healthcare professionals; and promotion and support of research for Parkinson's Disease and related disorders. Offers an extensive referral service to guide affected individuals to proper diagnosis and clinical care. Provides referrals to genetic counseling and support groups; promotes patient advocacy; and offers a variety of educational and support materials
                              *Quarterly*

**3315    Peoria Area Community Foundation**
124 SW Adams Street
Suite 1
Peoria, IL  61602                             309-674-7256
                              FAX: 309-674-8754
                    e-mail: PACF@worldnet.att.net

*George H Kreiss, Executive Director*

**3316    Polk Brothers Foundation**
20 W Kinzie Street
Suite 1110
Chicago, IL  60610                            312-527-4684
                              FAX: 312-527-4681
                    e-mail: info@polkborsfdn.org
                         www.polkborsfdn.org

*Nikki W Stein, Executive Director*
*Sandra Guthman, Chief Executive Officer*

**3317    Retirement Research Foundation**
8765 W Higgins Road
Suite 430
Chicago, IL  60631                            773-714-8080
                              FAX: 773-714-8089
                         e-mail: info@rrf.org
                              www.rrf.org

*Marilyn Hennessy, President*
*Julie Kaufman PhD, Senior Program Officer*

A private philanthropy with primary interest in improving the quality of life of older persons in the United States.

**3318    Rush Hayward Masonic Fund**
14 Bel Air Court
Champaign, IL  61820                          217-352-7528

*Ruth Hayword*

**3319    Sears-Roebuck Foundation**
3333 Beverly Road
Chicago, IL                                   847-286-2500

                              www.sears.com

*Alan Lacy, Chief Executive Officer*

**3320    Siragusa Foundation**
875 N Michigan Avenue
Chicago, IL  60611                            312-280-0833
                              FAX: 312-943-4489
                              www.siragusa.org

*Irene S Phelps, Executive Director*
*John Siragusa, President*

**3321    Square D Foundation**
1415 S Roselle Road
Palatine, IL  60067                           847-397-2600
                              FAX: 847-397-8814

*Chris Richardson, Chief Executive Officer*

Makes donations for operating support, capital development needs, and special projects to nonprofit organizations that have been granted exemption from the Federal Income Tax. The Foundation has a strong commitment to the following areas: health and welfare, education, civic and community affairs, and culture and the arts. Support of higher education is also made for scholarships, endowments for facility and acquisition or expansion of equipment or facilities, through Matching Gift Program.

## 3322 WP and HB White Foundation
540 W Frontage Road
Suite 33240
Northfield, IL 60093          847-446-1441

*Margaret Blandford, Executive Director*

The Foundation's funds are allocated on a continuing basis within the metropolitan area of Chicago where our founder's business prospered. The Foundation helps organizations specializing in the visually impaired, mental health, youth and recreation.

## 3323 Washington Square Health Foundation
875 N Michigan Avenue
Suite 3516
Chicago, IL 60611
312-664-6488
FAX: 312-664-7787
e-mail: washington@wshf.org
www.wshf.org

*Howard Nochumson, Executive Director*
*Angelo P Creticos, President*
*Authur Wirtz, VP*

## 3324 Wheat Ridge Ministries
1 Pierce Place
Suite 250
Itasca, IL 60143
630-766-9066
800-762-6748
FAX: 630-766-9622
e-mail: wrmin@aol.com
www.wheatridge.org

*Richard Bimler, President*

# Indiana

## 3325 Arc of Indiana
107 N Pennsylvania Street
Suite 300
Indianapolis, IN 46204
317-977-2375
800-382-9100
FAX: 317-977-2385
e-mail: arcin@in.net
ww.arcind.org

*George Rowlas, President*
*Judy Abbott, Senior Vice President*
*John Dickerson, Executive Director*

Arc of Indiana is commited to people with mental retardation and othe developmental disabilities realizing their goals of learning, living, working, and playing in the community.

## 3326 Ball Brothers Foundation
222 S Mulberry Street
1408
Muncie, IN 47305
765-741-5500
FAX: 765-741-5518

*Douglas Bakken, Executive Director*
*Doug Foy, Manager*

Mentally and physically disabled, only serving Indiana area.

## 3327 Central Indiana Community Foundation
615 N Alabama Street
Suite 119
Indianapolis, IN 46204
317-634-2423
FAX: 317-684-0943
e-mail: program@cicf.org
www.cicf.org

*Kenneth L Gladish, Executive Director*
*Brian Payne, President*

## 3328 Community Foundation of Boone County
Boone County Community Network
PO Box 451
Zionsville, IN 46077
317-873-0210
FAX: 317-873-0219
www.bccn.boone.in.us

*John Wallace, President*
*Terry Mccain, Vice President*
*Lisa John, Executive Director*

## 3329 Crown Point Community Foundation
PO Box 522
Crown Point, IN 46308
219-662-7252
FAX: 219-662-9493
e-mail: cpcf@urisp.com

*Patricia Huber-Salach, Executive Director*
*John Barney, President*
*Steve Leurck, First VP*

Crown Point Community Foundation is a not for profit organization that serves as a facilitataor for the community good, builds endowments, allocates grants and awards scholarships to better serve Crown Point and South Lake county area of Indiana.

## 3330 Eli Lilly & Co Corporate Contributions Pro gram
Lilly Corporate Center
Indianapolis, IN 46285          317-276-2000

www.lilly.com/about/overview/access/foundatio

*Kendy S Smith, Secretary*

## 3331 Indianapolis Foundation
615 N Alabama Street
Suite 119
Indianapolis, IN 46204
317-634-2423
FAX: 317-684-0943
www.indyfund.org

*Kenneth L Gladish, Executive Director*
*Brian Payne, President*
*David Kleiman, Trustee Attorney*

## 3332 John W Anderson Foundation
402 Wall Street
Valparaiso, IN 46383          219-462-4611

*Wilfred Wilkins, Chairman*
*Willam N Vinovich, Vice Chairman*

Physically and mentally disabled, recreation and youth agencies in Northwest Indiana area.

## 3333 Trabant North Knox
Bank One, Trust Group
111 Monument Circle
Suite 1501
Indianapolis, IN 46277          317-321-8030

**3334 William H Willennar Foundation**
Fort Wayne National Bank
PO Box 110
Fort Wayne, IN 46801          260-426-0555

*MC Haggarty, Secretary*

# Iowa

**3335 Arc of Iowa**
715 E Locust Street
Des Moines, IA 50309          515-283-2358
                              800-362-2927
                    e-mail: arciowa@aol.com

*Patricia Kramer, Manager*

**3336 Hall-Perrine Foundation**
115 3rd Street SE
Suite 803
Cedar Rapids, IA 52401        319-362-9079

*Jack B Evans, President*
This foundation is dedicated tio improving the quality of life for
peole in Linn County, IA by responding to the changing social,
economic, and cultural needs of the community.

**3337 Homer G Barr Trust**
PO Box 370
Webster City, IA 50595        515-832-1133
                              877-611-1754
                         FAX: 515-832-1708
                    www.firstamericanbankia.com

*Scott Bargfrede, President*

**3338 Kinney-Lindstrom Foundation**
PO Box 520
Mason City, IA 50402          641-896-3888

*Lowell Hall, Secretary*
Offers grants only to the area of Iowa for projects to help; Special Olympics, physically disabled and art and cultural affairs.

**3339 Mid-Iowa Health Foundation**
553 39th Street
Suite 104
Des Moines, IA 50312          515-277-6411
                         FAX: 515-271-7579

*Kathryn Bradley, Director*

**3340 Principal Financial Group Foundation**
711 High Street
Des Moines, IA 50392          515-247-5111
                         FAX: 515-246-5475
              e-mail: bassett.kendra@principal.con
                    www.principal.com/about/giving

*Kendra Bassett, Contributions Assistant*
*J Griswell, Chief Executive Officer*

**3341 Siouxland Community Foundation**
505 5th Street
Suite 412
Sioux City, IA 51101          712-293-3303

               e-mail: sxlfdn@aol.com
      www.siouxlandcommunityfoundation.org

*Debbie Hubbard, Executive Director*

# Kansas

**3342 Arc of Kansas**
3601 SW 29th Street
Topeka, KS 66614              785-271-8783
                         FAX: 785-272-4645
                e-mail: thearcks@thearcks.org
                           www.thearcks.org

**3343 Cessna Foundation**
PO Box 7706
Wichita, KS 67277             316-660-1200
                         FAX: 316-517-7812

*Marilyn Richwine, Secretary Treasurer*
*Leon Metzinger, President*
Some grants are available to organizations which meet the
guidelines for serving the physically disabled. Grants are restricted to communities where Cessna has manufacturing facilities.

**3344 Hutchinson Community Foundation**
PO Box 298
Hutchinson, KS 67504          620-663-5293
                         FAX: 620-663-9277
                           www.hutchcf.org

*Lynette Lacy, President*

# Kentucky

**3345 Arc of Kentucky**
833 E Main Street
Frankfort, KY 40601           502-875-5225
                              800-281-1272
                         FAX: 502-875-5226
                e-mail: arcofky@aol.com
                           www.arcofky.org

*Patty Dempsey, Executive Director*
The Arc of Kentucky helps in securing a positive future for individuals with mental retardation. The Arc values services and
supports that enhance the quality of life through independence,
friendship, choice and respect for individuals with mental retardation.

**3346 Kentucky Social Welfare Foundation**
P NC Bank N A
500 W Jefferson Street
Louisville, KY 40296          502-581-2157

*W Michael Hanks, Vice President*

**3347 Omnicare Foundation**
1717 Dixie Highway
Suite 800
Ft Wright, KY 41011           859-426-3000
                         FAX: 859-426-3118

*Cheryl D Hodges, Secretary*
*D Laney, Vice President*

## Louisiana

**3348  Arc of Louisiana**
365 N 4th Street
Baton Rouge, LA 70801
                         225-383-1033
                    FAX: 225-383-1092
                        www.thearcla.org

*Julia Kenny, Executive Director*

**3349  Baton Rouge Area Foundation**
402 N 4th Street
Baton Rouge, LA 70802
                         225-387-6126
                    FAX: 225-387-6153
                        www.braf,org

*John G Davies, President*
*John Stain, Vice President*

**3350  Booth-Bricker Fund**
826 Union Street
Suite 300
New Orleans, LA 70112        504-581-2430

*Gray S Parker, President*

**3351  Community Foundation of Shreveport-Bossier**
401 Edwards Street
Suite 105
Shreveport, LA 71101
                         318-221-0582
                    FAX: 318-221-7463
                        www.comfoundsb.org

*Thomas McElroy, Chairman*
*Carolyn Nelson, Vice Chairman*
*Paula Hickman, Executive Director*

Public Foundation that makes grants only to 501C3 organizations.

## Maine

**3352  UNUM Charitable Foundation**
2211 Congress Street
Portland, ME 04122
                         207-770-6800
                    FAX: 800-447-2498

*Janine Manning, Manager*

The Foundation encourages projects that: stimulate others in the private or public sector to participate in problem solving; advance innovative and cost-effective approaches for addressing defined, recognized needs; and demonstrate ability to obtain future project funding, if needed. The foundation generally limits its consideration of capital campaign requests to the Greater Portland, Maine area.

## Maryland

**3353  American Health Assistance Foundation**
22512 Gateway Center Drive
Clarksburg, MD 20871
                         301-948-3244
                         800-437-2423
                    FAX: 301-258-9454
                        www.ahaf.org

*Isabel Quiroz, Information Specialist*
*Pam Senda, Grants Manager*
*Kathy Honaker, Executive Director*

**3354  American Occupational Therapy Foundation**
PO Box 31220
Bethesda, MD 20824
                         301-652-7590
                    FAX: 301-652-7711
                        www.aotf.org

*Martha Kirkland, Executive Director*
*M Baum, President*

**3355  Arc of Maryland**
49 Old Solomons Island Road
Suite 205
Annapolis, MD 21401
                         410-974-6139
                    FAX: 410-974-6021
                    e-mail: info@thearcmd.org
                        www.thearcmd.org

*Christine Marchand, Manager*

**3356  Baltimore Community Foundation**
2 E Read Street
Baltimore, MD 21202
                         410-332-4173
                    FAX: 410-837-4701

*Thomas Wilcox, President*

**3357  Candlelighters Childhood Cancer Foundation**
PO Box 498
Kensington, MD 20895
                         301-962-3520
                         800-366-2223
                    e-mail: info@candlelighters.org
                        www.candlelighters.org

*Ruth Hoffman, Executive Director/Owner*

An international organization providing information and support, and advocacy to parents of children with cancer and survivors of childhood cancer.Health and Education professionals also welcome as members.Network of local support groups. Information on disabilities related to treatment of childhood cancer. Publications.

**3358  Children's Fresh Air Society Fund**
Baltimore Community Foundation
2 E Read Street
Baltimore, MD 21202
                         410-332-4173
                    FAX: 410-837-4701
                    e-mail: khoeller@bcf.org
                        www.bcf.org

*Anne Knoeller, Grants Administrator*
*Thomas Wilcox, President*

Makes grants to nonprofit camps to provide tuition for disadvantaged and disabled Maryland children to attend summer camp.

**3359  Clark-Winchcole Foundation**
3 Bethesda Metro Center
Suite 550
Bethesda, MD 20814
                         301-654-3607
                    FAX: 301-654-3140

*Laura Phillips*

Supported tax-exempt charitable organizations operating in the metropolitan area of Washington, DC in the following areas: deaf, higher education and physically disabled.

**3360  Columbia Foundation**
10221 Wincopin Circle
Columbia, MD 21044
                         410-730-7840
                    FAX: 410-715-3043

*Barbara K Lawson, Executive Director*

**3361 Cystic Fibrosis Foundation**
6931 Arlington Road
Bethesda, MD 20814
301-951-4422
800-FIG-HTCF
FAX: 301-951-6378
e-mail: info@cff.org
www.cff.org/research.htm

*Robert Dressing, President*
*Robert Beall, Chief Executive Officer*

**3362 Foundation Fighting Blindness**
11435 Cronhill Drive
Owings Mills, MD 21117
410-568-0150
800-683-5555
888-394-3937
FAX: 410-363-2393
TTY:800-683-5551
e-mail: info@blindness.org
www.fightblindness.org

*Mitsy Palmer, Constituent Service Coordinator*
*William T Schmidt, CEO*
*Randy Hove, Manager*

The urgent mission of The Foundation Fighting Blindness is to fund the research with will discover the causes, treatments, preventive methods and cures for Retinitis Pigmentosa, Macular Degeneration, Usher Syndrome, Stargart disease, and the entire spectrum of retinal degenerative diseases.

**3363 George Wasserman Family Foundation**
Grossberg Company
6707 Democracy Boulevard
Suite 300
Bethesda, MD 20817
301-571-1900
FAX: 301-571-1932

*Janice W Goldsten, President*
*Anthony Cpa, Partner*

**3364 Harry and Jeanette Weinberg Foundation**
7 Park Center Court
Owings Mills, MD 21117
410-654-8500
FAX: 410-654-4900
hjweinbergfoundation.org

*Alfred L Castle, Executive Director/Treasurer*
*Lester M Salamon, Director*
*Bernard Siegel, President*

**3365 Miracle-Ear Children's Foundation**
PO Box 59261
Minneapolis, MN 55459
612-378-0794
800-234-5422
FAX: 612-520-9793
TTY: 612-520-9791
www.miracle-ear.com

*Jerry Krbec, President*
*Richard C Brandt, Executive Director*
*Arlan Mercil, Manager*

Nonprofit organization that provides hearing aids to children whose families to not qualify for public assistance. Provides hearing aid fittings and follow-up care and services free of charge through Miracle-Ear Hearing Centers. Provides information on alternative communication. Offers educational materials and brochures.

**3366 National Federation of the Blind**
1800 Johnson Street
Baltimore, MD 21230
410-659-9314
FAX: 410-685-5653
e-mail: nfb@access.digex.net
www.nfb.org

*Marc Maurer, President*

The largest consumer membership organization of the blind, founded in 1940, it has 50,000 members nationwide in 52 affiliates and over 700 local chapters. Provides public education about blindness, support services to the newly blinded, scholarships, publications about blindness, adaptive equipment for the blind, advocacy services, Newsline for the Blind, assistive technology information and Job Opportunities for the Blind.

**3367 National Retinitis Pigmentosa Foundation Fighting Blindness**
11435 Cronhill Drive
Owings Mills, MD 21117
410-568-0150
800-683-5555
FAX: 410-363-2393
www.fightblindness.org

*William Schmidt, Executive Director*
*Randy Hove, Manager*

The Foundation provides information and referral services, support networks. The main focus of the Foundation is to fund research on causes, cures and prevention of RP and related retinal degenerations. Volunteer affiliates throughout the United States are offered to promote public awareness, raise funds and provide opportunity for those who have RP to interact.

**3368 Ryland Group Corporate Giving Program**
11000 Broken Land Parkway
Columbia, MD 21044
800-267-0998
FAX: 443-367-3500

*Maurice M Simpkins, Vice President*

**3369 Sjogren's Syndrome Foundation**
8120 Woodmont Avenue
Suite 530
Bethesda, MD 20814
301-718-0300
800-475-6473
FAX: 301-718-0322
e-mail: ssf@sjorgrens.org
www.sjogrens.org

*Edna Scott, Office Manager*
*Steven Taylor, Executive Director*

Provides patients practical information and coping strategies that minimize the effects of Sjogren's syndrome. In addition, the Foundation is the clearinghouse for medical information and is the recognized national advocate for Sjogren's syndrome.
$25.00
*Monthly*

## Massachusetts

**3370 Abbot and Dorothy H Stevens Foundation**
PO Box 111
North Andover, MA 01845
978-688-7211
FAX: 978-686-1620
e-mail: 74722.637@compuserve.com

**3371 Arc Massachusetts**
217 South Street
Waltham, MA 02453
781-891-6270
FAX: 781-891-6271
e-mail: arcmass@arcmass.org
www.arcmass.org

*Leo Sarkissian, Executive Director*

**3372 Bank of Boston Corporation Charitable Foundation**
100 Federal Street
Boston, MA 02110
617-434-2659

Giving primarily to New England.

**3373    Boston Foundation**
1 Boston Place
24th Floor
Boston, MA  02108                              617-338-1700
                                          FAX: 617-723-7415
                                       e-mail: alk@tbf.ork
                                               www.tbf.org

*Ann Kurk, Director Public Relations*
*Paul Grogan, President*

**3374    Boston Globe Foundation**
135 Morrissey Boulevard
Dorchester, MA  02125                          617-929-2000
                                          FAX: 617-929-2041
                                   e-mail: foundation@globe.com
                                     www.bostonglobe.com/foundation

*Renee Loth, Editor*
*Mary Jacobus, President*

Seeks to empower low income families and children in the
Boston area plus youth frequently excluded from equal participation in our society. The Foundation hopes their funding will
have a special impact on children in communities of color. Focus
areas are on: community services; education; culture; health
care and environment.

**3375    Bushrod H Campbell and Ada F Hall Charity Fund**
Palmer & Dodge
111 Huntington Avenue
Boston, MA  02199                              617-239-0540
                                          FAX: 617-227-4420

*Brenda Taylor, Foundation Administrator*
*Marsha Anderegg*

The fund's areas of interest include organizations and/or their
projects supporting aid to the elderly, healthcare and population
control. Medical research grants are administered through the
Medical Foundation. No grants are awarded to individuals and
the geographical area of support is limited to organizations located in Massachusetts within the area of Boston and Route 128.

**3376    Clipper Ship Foundation**
Grants Management Associates
77 Summer Street
8th Floor
Boston, MA  02110                              617-426-7080
                                          FAX: 617-426-5441
                                   www.agmconnect.org/clipper1.html

*Raymond C Woodring, Foundation Assistant*
*Newell Flather, President*

**3377    Community Foundation of Western Massachusetts**
PO Box 15769
Springfield, MA  01115                         413-732-2858
                                          FAX: 413-733-8565
                            e-mail: wmass@communityfoundation.org
                                     www.communityfoundation.org

*Kent W Faerber, President*

Provides a simple way to achieve the charitable objectives of do-
nors most effectively; supports nonprofit organizations that offer programs in the arts, education, human services, healthcare,
housing, and the environment; and works to improve the quality
of life in our region.

**3378    Frank R and Elizabeth Simoni Foundation**
434 Providence Highway
Norwood, MA  02062                             781-762-3449
                                          FAX: 781-769-6166

*Victor F Coletti, Vice President*
*Robert Donald, Manager*

**3379    Friendly Ice Cream Corp Contributions Prog ram**
Public Affairs Department
1855 Boston Road
Wilbraham, MA  01095                           413-543-2400
                                          FAX: 413-543-9355
                                               www.friendlys.com

*Barbara Miller, Director*
*Lurie Thompson, Assistant Director*
*John Cutter, Chief Executive Officer*

**3380    Greater Worcester Community Foundation**
370 Main Street
Suite 650
Worcester, MA  01608                           508-755-0980
                                          FAX: 508-755-3406
                            e-mail: gwcf@greaterworcester.org
                                     www.greaterworcester.org

*Ann T Lisi, Executive Director*

**3381    Hyams Foundation**
175 Federal Street
14th Floor
Boston, MA  02110                              617-426-5600
                                          FAX: 617-426-5696
                            e-mail: info@hyamsfoundation.org
                                     www.hyamsfoundation.org

*Elizabeth B Smith, Executive Director*

**3382    Nathaniel and Elizabeth P Stevens Foundation**
PO Box 111
North Andover, MA  01845                       978-688-7211
                                          FAX: 978-686-1620

*Elizabeth A Beland, Administrator*

**3383    Raytheon Company Contributions Program**
870 Winter Street
Waltham, MA  02451                             781-522-3000
                                          FAX: 781-860-2172
                                   raytheon.com/about/contributions

*Janet C Taylor, Manager*
*William Swanson, Chief Executive Officer*

Industry leader in defense and government electronics, space,
information technology, technical services, and business aviation and special mission aircraft.

**3384    Spero Charitable Foundation**
Shirley Spero
79 Florence Street
Suite 200
Chestnut Hill, MA  02467                       617-244-3174
                                          FAX: 617-244-3174

**3385    TJX Foundation**
T JX Companies
770 Cochituate Road
Framingham, MA  01701                          508-390-1000
                                          FAX: 508-390-2091

*Christine A Strickland, Foundation Manager*
*Bernard Cammarata, Chief Executive Officer*

**3386    Vision Foundation**
818 Mount Auburn Street
Watertown, MA  02472                           781-926-4232
                                               800-852-3029
                                          FAX: 781-926-1412

*Barbara Kibler, Executive Director*

Offers counseling, support groups, seminars and transportation
for the blind providing 600 members.

## Michigan

**3387 Ann Arbor Area Community Foundation**
201 S Main Street
Suite 501
Ann Arbor, MI 48104
734-663-0401
FAX: 734-663-3514
e-mail: info@aaacf.org
www.aaacf.org

*Cheryl Elliott, President/CEO*
*Martha L Bloom, Vice President*

Interested in funding projects which will improve the quality of life for citizens of the Ann Arbor area. Eligible projects generally fall within these categories: education, culture, social service, community development, environmental awareness and health and wellness. The Foundation aims to support creative approaches to community needs and problems by making grants which will benefit the widest possible range of people.

**3388 Arc of Michigan**
State of Michigan
1325 S Washington Avenue
Lansing, MI 48910
517-487-5426
800-292-7851
FAX: 517-487-0303
e-mail: dhoyle@arcmi.org
www.arcmi.org

*Dohn Hoyle, Director*

**3389 Berrien Community Foundation**
2900 S State Street
Suite 2e
Saint Joseph, MI 49085
269-983-3304
FAX: 269-983-4939
e-mail: bcf@gtm.net

*Margaret Poole, Executive Director*

**3390 Blind Children's Fund**
311 W Broadway Street
Suite 1
Mt Pleasant, MI 48858
989-779-9966
FAX: 989-779-0015
e-mail: bcf@blindchildrensfund.org
www.blindchildrensfund.org

*Karla Storrer, Executive Director*
*Didi Duncan, Outreach Director*

Provides parents and profesionsals informaion materials and resources that help them scuccesfullly teach and nurture blind, visually and multi-impaired infants and preschoolers.

**3391 Clarence & Grace Chamberlin Foundation**
600 Woodbridge Street
Detroit, MI 48226
313-567-1000
FAX: 313-567-1001
e-mail: jking@berrymoorman.com

*John L King, President*

**3392 Community Foundation of Monroe County**
PO Box 627
Monroe, MI 48161
734-242-1976
FAX: 734-242-1234
e-mail: info@cfmonroe.org
www.cfmonroe.org

*Kristyn Thesen, Executive Director*
*Michelle Sandiefer, Administrative Assistant*

**3393 Cowan Slavin Foundation**
7881 Dell Road
Saline, MI 48176
734-944-0469
FAX: 734-944-3529

*Marjorie Bovee, Executive Director*

**3394 Daimler Chrysler**
Automobility Program
PO Box 5080
Troy, MI 48007
800-255-9877
FAX: 248-925-3062
TTY:800-922-3826
www.dc-automobility.com

*Jennifer Rossbach, Account Supervisor*

Provides a cash reimbursement to assist in reducing the cost of adaptive driving equipment and conversion aids installed on new model Daimler Chrysler LLC vehicles. Up to a maximum of $1000 on Dodge Caravan, Grand Caravan, and Chrysler Town and Country vans and up to $750 on all other vehicles.

**3395 Frank & Mollie S VanDervoort Memorial Foun dation**
4646 Okemos Road
Okemos, MI 48864
517-349-7232

*Ann L Gessert, Secretary*

**3396 Fremont Area Foundation**
PO Box B
Fremont, MI 49412
231-924-5350
FAX: 231-924-5391
e-mail: gzerlaut@tfaf.org
www.tfaf.org

*Elizabeth Cherin, Executive Director*

**3397 Grand Rapids Foundation**
161 Ottawa Avenue NW
Suite 209c
Grand Rapids, MI 49503
616-454-1751
FAX: 616-454-6455
e-mail: grfound@grfoundation.org
www.grfoundation.org

*Marcia Rapp, Vice President Programs*
*Diana Sieger, President*

**3398 Granger Foundation**
PO Box 22187
Lansing, MI 48909
517-393-1670
FAX: 517-393-0901
e-mail: tfate@grangerconstruction.com
www.grangerfoundation.org

*Al Granger, President*
*Janice Granger, Trustee*

**3399 Harvey Randall Wickes Foundation**
4800 Fashion Square Boulevard
Saginaw, MI 48604
989-799-1850
FAX: 989-799-3327

*James Finkbeiner*
Grants for rehabilitation.

**3400 Havirmill Foundation**
3503 Greenleaf Boulevard
Suite 203
Kalamazoo, MI 49008
269-375-1800
FAX: 269-375-1346

*Jerry L Miller, President*
*Kenneth Miller, Owner*

**3401 Kelly Services Foundation**
999 W Big Beaver Road
Troy, MI 48084
248-362-4444
FAX: 248-244-5518

*Kelly Sylvested, Corporate Manager*
*Carl Camden, Chief Executive Officer*

**3402 Kresge Foundation**
3215 W Big Beaver Road
Troy, MI 48084
248-643-9630
FAX: 248-643-0588
www.kresge.org

*John E Marshall III, Chief Executive Officer*

This foundation offers challenge grants for capital projects, most often for construction or renovation of buildings, but also for the purchase of major equipment and real estate. As challenge grants, they are intended to stimulate new, private gifts in the midst of an organized fund raising effort. Offers special opportunities to build capacity, both in providing enhanced facilities in which to present programs and in generating private support. Only charitable organizations may apply.

**3403 Lanting Foundation**
1575 S Shore Drive
Holland, MI 49423
616-355-2740

*Arlyn Lanting, Partner*

**3404 Ransom Fidelity Company Foundation**
702 Michigan National Tower
Lansing, MI 48933
517-482-1538
FAX: 517-482-1539
Grants for the schools, Native Americans, minorities, environmnt, youth and physically disabled.

**3405 Rollin M Gerstacker Foundation**
PO Box 1945
Midland, MI 48641
989-631-6097

*E N Brandt, Vice President*

**3406 Steelcase Foundation**
PO Box 1967
Grand Rapids, MI 49501
616-246-4695
FAX: 616-475-2200
e-mail: sbroman@steelcase.com

*Susan Broman, Executive Director*

## Minnesota

**3407 Arc of Minnesota**
The Arc of Minnesota
770 Transfer Road
Suite 26
Saint Paul, MN 55114
651-523-0823
800-582-5256
FAX: 651-523-0829
e-mail: mail@arcmn.org
www.thearcofminnesota.org

*Steve Larson, Executive Director*
*Mike Gude, Communications Associate*

The Arc of Minnesota provides advocacy and support to persons with developmental disabilities and their families as they choose to live, learn, work and play.

**3408 Deluxe Corporation Foundation**
Deluxe Corporation
PO Box 64235
Saint Paul, MN 55164
651-483-7842
FAX: 651-481-4371
www.deluxe.com

*Jennifer A Anderson, Director Foundations*

**3409 General Mills Foundation**
PO Box 9452
Minneapolis, MN 55440
800-248-7310
FAX: 763-764-8330
e-mail: mills999@mail.genmills.com
www.generalmills.com/corporate/about

**3410 Hugh J Andersen Foundation**
PO Box 204
Bayport, MN 55003
651-439-1557
888-439-9508
FAX: 681-439-9480
www.workinggroup.org/lgbtfunders/FD/dstate.ht

*Sarah J Andersen, President/Owner*
*Christine E Andersen, VP*
*William H Rubenstein, Secretary*

Established in 1962, this fund is a nonprofit charitable corporation classified as a private foundation. The Foundation was established as a general charitable fund, but now identifies projects that build individual and community capacity to be a priority. Giving is focused primarily in the counties of Washington, Minnesota, & St. Croix, Polk and Pierce of Wl. Grants are given in the areas of human services, health, education, arts and culture, community services and the environment.

**3411 James R Thorpe Foundation**
5201 Eden Circle
Suite 202
Minneapolis, MN 55436
952-944-7650
FAX: 651-291-0969
www.mnprivatecolleges.com

*Edith D Thorpe, President*
*Greg Barron, Director*
*Gary Thorp, Owner*

**3412 Jay and Rose Phillips Family Foundation**
10 2nd Street NE
Suite 200
Minneapolis, MN 55413
612-623-0752
FAX: 612-623-1653
e-mail: phillipsfnd@phillipsfnd.org

*Amy Crawford, Executive Director*

**3413 Minneapolis Foundation**
821 Marquette Avenue
Minneapolis, MN 55402
612-672-3878
FAX: 612-672-3870
www.mplsfoundation.org

*Emmett D Carson, President*

**3414 Ordean Foundation**
424 W Superior Street
Duluth, MN 55802
218-726-4785

*Stephen A Mangan, Executive Director*

Grants are given for a variety of purposes including: treatment and rehabilitation for persons who are chronically or temporarily mentally ill, persons whose physical capacity is impaired by injury or illness, promotes mental and physical health of the elderly, provides for youth guidance programs designed to avoid delinquency, and provides relief, aid and charity to people with no or low incomes. Grants are only offered to certain cities and townships near and around St. Louis County/Duluth.

**3415 Otto Bremer Foundation**
445 Minnesota Street
Suite 2000
Saint Paul, MN 55101
651-227-8036
FAX: 651-227-2522
e-mail: obf@bremer.com
www.ottobremer.org

*John Kostishack, Executive Director*
*Twana Williams, Administrative Assistant*

**3416 Rochester Area Foundation**
2200 2nd Street SW
Suite 300
Rochester, MN 55902
507-285-3111
FAX: 507-282-4938
e-mail: info@rochesterarea.org
www.rochesterarea.org

*Steve Thornton, Executive Director*
*Sean Allen, Assistant Director*

## Mississippi

**3417 Arc of Mississippi**
7 Lakeland Circle
Suite 600
Jackson, MS 39216
601-982-1180
800-717-1180
FAX: 601-982-5792
e-mail: arcms@arcms.org
www.arcms.org

*Matt Nalker, Manager*

## Missouri

**3418 Allen P & Josephine B Green Foundation**
PO Box 523
Mexico, MO 65265
573-581-5568
FAX: 573-581-1714
e-mail: wstaley@greenfdn.org
www.greenfdn.org

*Walter G Staley Jr, Secretary/Treasurer/Manager*
While the Foundation makes grants in a variety of fields, in the past its major support was in the field of medical research. During a 20-year period, 1951-71, it contributed over $900,000 to research in Parkinson's and related diseases of the nervous system; $600,000 for research in pediatric neurology and lesser amounts in other areas of medical research, but the board is now trending in other directions. Grants are limited to Missouri and none are offered to individuals.

**3419 Anheuser-Busch Foundation**
1 Busch Place
Saint Louis, MO 63118
314-577-0671
800-342-5288
FAX: 314-577-3251

*Stephen Burrows, Chief Executive Officer*
Giving in areas of company operation.

**3420 Greater Kansas City Community Foundation and Affiliated Trusts**
1055 Broadway Street
Kansas City, MO 64105
816-842-0944
FAX: 816-842-8079
www.gkccf.org

*Janice C Kreamer, President/CEO*

**3421 Greater St. Louis Community Foundation**
319 N 4th Street
Suite 300
Saint Louis, MO 63102
314-588-8200
FAX: 314-588-8088
e-mail: info@gstlcf.org
www.stlcf.org

*David R Lickes, President/CEO*
To improve the quality of life across the region by helping individuals, families and businesses make a difference through charitable giving.

**3422 H&R Block Foundation**
4410 Main Street
Kansas City, MO 64111
816-753-6900
FAX: 816-931-7486

*Barbara Allmon, President*
*Mark Ernst, Chief Executive Officer*

A charitable organization under the not-for-profit corporation law of the state of Missouri. Grants are made only to organizations which are tax exempt from Federal Income taxation and which are not classified as private foundations. Major emphasis is placed in the metropolitan areas of Kansas City, Missouri: and Columbus, Ohio. The goal is to provide proportionately significant support of relatively few activities, as opposed to minor support for a great many.

**3423 James S McDonnell Foundation**
1034 S Brentwood Boulevard
Suite 1850
Saint Louis, MO 63117
314-721-1532
FAX: 314-721-7421
www.jsmf.org

*John T Bruer Md, President*
*Susan M Fitzpatrick, Vice President*

**3424 Lutheran Charities Foundation of St. Louis**
211 N Broadway
Suite 1290
Saint Louis, MO 63102
314-231-2244

e-mail: info@lutheranfoundation.org
www.lutheranfoundation.org

*Fred A Bleeke, President/CEO*

**3425 Mary's Call**
504 W Highway 24
Salisbury, MO 65281
660-388-5308
FAX: 660-388-5453

*Ray Goffinet, President*
*Rick Monnig, Manager*

**3426 Oppenstein Brothers Foundation**
PO Box 13095
Kansas City, MO 64199
816-234-8671

*Sheila K Rice, Program Officer*

**3427 RA Bloch Cancer Foundation**
4400 Main Street
Kansas City, MO 64111
816-932-8453
800-433-0464
FAX: 816-931-7486
e-mail: hotline@hrblock.com
www.blochcancer.org

*Vangie Rich, Administrator*
*Ann Hron, Co-Director Bloch Cancer Hotline*

Provides a hotline that matches newly diagnosed cancer patients with someone who has survived the same kind of cancer. Offers free infomration, resources and support groups, and distributes lists of multidisciplinary second opnion centers. Also supplies three books at no charge: Fighting Cancer; Cancer... There's Hope; and A Guide for Cancer Supporters. All services and books are free of charge.

**3428 Victor E Speas Foundation**
PO Box 419119
Kansas City, MO 64141          816-979-7481

*David P Ross, Senior VP Bank of America*

## Nebraska

**3429 Arc of Nebraska**
1672 Van Dorn Street
Lincoln, NE 68502          402-475-4407
e-mail: arcneb@inetnebr.com
www.arc-nebraska.org

*Richard Klein, President*
*Debra Weston, Executive Director*

Arc of Nebraska is commited to helping children and adults with disabilities secure the oppurtunity to choose and realize their goals of where and how they learn, live, work, and play.

**3430 Cooper Foundation**
304 Cooper Plaza
Lincoln, NE 68508          402-476-7571
FAX: 402-476-2356
www.cooperfoundation.com

*Elwood Thompson, President*

Serves only Nebraska with the primary interest in education, arts and humanities and the human services area.

**3431 Hazel R Keene Trust**
152 E 6th Street
Fremont, NE 68025          402-753-2246
FAX: 402-753-2204

*Joe Twidwell, Contact*
*Steve Wade, President*

**3432 Slosburg Family Charitable Trust**
10040 Regency Circle
Suite 200
Omaha, NE 68114          402-391-7900
FAX: 402-391-6615

*D David Slosburg, Treasurer/Owner*

**3433 Union Pacific Foundation**
1400 Douglas Street
Omaha, NE 68179          402-544-5000
FAX: 402-271-5477
e-mail: union_pacific_foundation@notes.up.com
www.up.com

*Darlynn Herweg, Director*
*Richard Davidson, Chief Executive Officer*

## Nevada

**3434 Conrad N Hilton Foundation**
100 W Liberty Street
Suite 840
Reno, NV 89501          775-323-4221
FAX: 775-323-4150

*Steven M Hilton, President*
*Marcia Penman, Manager*

Our grant-making style is to initiate and develop major long-term projects and then seek out the organizations to implement them. As a consequence of this proactive approach, the Foundation does not generally consider unsolicited proposals. Our major projects currently include: blindness prevention and treatment, support the work of the Catholic Sisters, drug abuse prevention among youth, support of the Conrad N. Hilton College of Hotel and Restaurant Management, and much more.

**3435 EL Wiegand Foundation**
165 W Liberty Street
Reno, NV 89501          775-333-0300
FAX: 775-333-0314

*Kristen A Avansino, President*
*Raymond Avansino Jr, Manager*

**3436 Mark B Wallner Foundation**
1105 Cambria Way
El Dorado Hills, CA 95762          775-856-1166

*Kimberly England, President*

**3437 Nell J Redfield Foundation**
PO Box 61
Reno, NV 89504          775-323-1373
FAX: 775-323-4476

*Gerald C Smith, Director*

**3438 William N and Myriam Pennington Foundation**
441 W Plumb Lane
Reno, NV 89509          775-333-9100
FAX: 775-333-9111

*Kent Green, Manager*
*William Pennington, Owner*

## New Hampshire

**3439 Agnes M Lindsay Trust**
660 Chestnut Street
Manchester, NH 03104          603-669-1366
866-669-1366
FAX: 603-665-8114
e-mail: admin@lindsaytrust.org
www.lindsaytrust.org

*Robert Chiesa, Managing Trustee*
*Susan Bouchard, Administrative Director*
*Ernest Dion, Trustee*

Funding for health and wefare organizations, special needs, mental health, blind, deaf and cultural programs to organizations, specifically for capital needs, not operating funds, located in the New England states of Maine, Massachusetts, New Hampshire and Vermont. We highly recommend you visit our web site.

**3440  Foundation for Seacoast Health**

100 Campus Drive
Suite 1
Portsmouth, NH  03801                     603-422-8200
                                    FAX: 603-422-8207
                          e-mail: ffsh@communitycampus.org
                                         www.ffsh.org

*Susan R Bunting EdD, President/CEO*

Giving limited to Portsmouth, Rye, New Castle, Greenland, Newington, North Hampton, NH; and Kittery, Eliot, and York, ME.

## New Jersey

**3441  American Express Foundation**

200 Vesey Street
New York, NY  10285                       212-640-2000
                                    FAX: 201-209-4303

*Kenneth Chenault, Chief Executive Officer*

Giving primarily in Arizona, California, Colorado, Florida, Georgia, Illinois, Minnesota, North Carolina, Nebraska, New York, Texas, Utah, Massachusetts and Pennsylvania. Also include international committees.

**3442  Arc of New Jersey**

985 Livingston Avenue
N Brunswick, NJ  08902                     732-246-2525
                                    FAX: 732-214-1834
                             e-mail: info@arcnj.org
                                        www.arcnj.org

*Thomas Baffuto, Executive Director*
*Celine Fortin, Assistant Director*

**3443  Arnold A Schwartz Foundation**

15 Mountain Boulevard
Warren, NJ  07059                          908-757-7800
                                    FAX: 908-757-8039
                                        www.dbnjlaw.org

*Edwin D Kunzman, President*

**3444  Campbell Soup Foundation**

PO Box 60f
Camden, NJ  08101                          856-342-4800
                                    FAX: 856-342-3878

*John M Coleman, Chairman*
*James J Baldwin, Vice Chairman*
*Douglas Conant, Chief Executive Officer*

Goal of this foundation is to match the company's assets with community needs in order to help forge solutions to community challenges. The Foundation believes that involvement at the community level can play a catalytic role in improving the quality of life. Giving is located in the areas of education, nutrition and health, cultural and youth related programs. The major focus of the foundation is on nutrition and health related matters, and places a high priority on Camden, New Jersey areas.

**3445  Children's Hopes & Dreams Wish Fulfillment Foundation**

280 Us Highway 46
Dover, NJ  07801                           973-361-7348
                                         800-IDR-EAM2
                                    FAX: 973-361-6627
                          e-mail: info@chdfdover.org
                                    www.childrenswishes.org

*Victor Franklin Jr, President*
*Mariann Oswald, Executive Director*

Provides continual support for children and their families through the International Pen-Pal Program and the Kid's Kare Packages program. All services are free. Fulfills the last dreams of children with life threatening illnesses.

**3446  Community Foundation of New Jersey**

PO Box 338
Morristown, NJ  07963                      973-267-5533
                                         800-659-5533
                                    FAX: 973-257-2903
                                        www.cfnj.org

*Hans Dekker, President*
Giving limited to the state of New Jersey.

**3447  Cowles Charitable Trust**

PO Box 219
Rumson, NJ  07760                          732-936-9826

*Gardner Cowles III, President*

**3448  F Mason Perkins Trust**

210 Main Street
Hackensack, NJ  07601                      201-646-5225
                                    FAX: 201-646-9881

**3449  FM Kirby Foundation**

PO Box 151
Morristown, NJ  07963                      973-538-4800
                                    FAX: 973-538-4801
                          fdncenter.org/grantmaker/kirby/

*F Kirby, President*

**3450  Fannie E Rippel Foundation**

180 Mount Airy Road
Suite 200
Basking Ridge, NJ  07920                   908-766-0404

                                    e-mail: rippel@gti.net
                          www.mharc.com/fundpri-rz.htm

*Edward W Probert, President/CEO*

**3451  Fund for New Jersey**

94 Church Street
Suite 303
New Brunswick, NJ  08901                   732-220-8656
                                    FAX: 732-220-8654
                             e-mail: info@fundformj.org
                                        www.fundfornj.org

*Candace McKee-Ashmun, Vice Chairman*
*Mark Murphy, Executive Director*

**3452  Merck Company Foundation**

PO Box 100
Whitehouse Station, NJ  08889              908-423-1000
                                    FAX: 908-423-1987
                                        www.merck.com

*David A Ruth, Executive Vice President*
*Richard Clark, Chief Executive Officer*

**3453  Merrill Lynch & Company Foundation**

2 World Financial Center
New York, NY  10281                        212-236-5065

*Eddy Bayardelle, Vice President*

# Foundations & Funding Resources /New Mexico

**3454 Milton Schamach Foundation**
411 Hackensack Avenue
Hackensack, NJ 07601      973-423-9494
                          FAX: 973-423-2376

*Andrew Er Frommel Jr, Secretary/Treasurer*

**3455 Nabisco Foundation**
7 Campus Drive
Parsippany, NJ 07054      973-682-5000
                          FAX: 973-503-3018

**3456 Ostberg Foundation**
PO Box 1098
Alpine, NJ 07620          201-569-6800
                          FAX: 201-569-6606

*Charles Borhan*

**3457 Prudential Foundation**
Prudential Financial
751 Broad Street
15th Floor
Newark, NJ 07102          973-802-6000
                          FAX: 973-802-3345
e-mail: community.resources@prudential.com
www.prudential.com

*Gabriella Morris, President*
*Arthur Ryan, Chief Executive Officer*

Gives priority to national programs that further our objectives and programs serving areas where The Prudential has a substantial employee presence. Places special emphasis on the home state of New Jersey and the headquarters city, Newark.

**3458 Robert Wood Johnson Foundation**
PO Box 2316
Princeton, NJ 08543       609-452-8701
                          FAX: 888-727-1966
e-mail: mail@rwjf.org
www.rwjf.org

*Richard J Toth, Director Office/Proposal*
*Risa Lavizzo-Mourey, Chief Executive Officer*

Our mission is to assure that all Americans have access to basic health care at reasonable cost, improve care and support for people with chronic health conditions, promote healthy communities and lifestyles and also, reduce the personal, social and economic harm caused by substance abuse.

**3459 Victoria Foundation**
946 Bloomfield Avenue
Glen Ridge, NJ 07028      973-748-5300
                          FAX: 973-748-0016
e-mail: CMCFFarvic@aol.com
www.victoriafoundation.org

*Catherine M McFarland, Executive Officer*

Desire is to help individuals in need reach their potential remains. Provides emergency coal for needy families and treated rheumatic fever in children.

**3460 Walking Tomorrow**
Christopher & Dana Reeve Paralysis Resource Center
636 Morris Tpke
Suite 3a
Short Hills, NJ 07078     800-539-7309
                          FAX: 973-912-9433
e-mail: info@paralysis.org
www.paralysis.org

*Christopher Reeve, Founder*
*Dana Reeve, Founder*

## New Mexico

**3461 Arc of New Mexico**
3655 Carlisle Boulevard NE
Albuquerque, NM 87110     505-883-4630
                          800-358-6493
                          FAX: 505-883-5564
e-mail: arcnm@arcnm.org
www.arcnm.org

*Simon Chavez, President*
*Rebecca Schuman, Executive Director*

Our mission is to improve the quality of life for individuals with developmental disabilities of all ages by advocating for equal opportunities and choices in where and how they learn, live, work, play and socialize. The Arc of New Mexico promotes self-determination, healthy families, effective community support systems and partnerships.

**3462 Frost Foundation**
511 Armijo Street
Apt A
Santa Fe, NM 87501        505-986-0208
                          FAX: 505-986-0430
www.frostfound.org

*Mary Whited-Howell, President*

**3463 McCune Charitable Foundation**
345 E Alameda Street
Santa Fe, NM 87501        505-983-8300
                          FAX: 505-983-7887
e-mail: info@nmmccune.com
www.nmmccune.org

*Frances R Sowers, Associate Director*
*Sarah M Losinger, Chairman*
*Owen Lopez, Executive Director*

**3464 Santa Fe Community Foundation**
PO Box 1827
Santa Fe, NM 87504        505-988-9715
                          FAX: 505-988-1829
e-mail: foundation@santafecf.org
www.santafecf.org

*Amy S Duggan, Program Officer*
*Billie Blair, President*

## New York

**3465 AT&T Foundation**
32 Avenue of the Americas
24th Floor
New York, NY 10013        212-387-5400
                          FAX: 212-387-5097
e-mail: rdabney@att.com
www.att.com/foundation/

*Ronald Dabney, Communications Manager*
*Edward Whitacre, Chief Executive Officer*

**3466 Achelis Foundation**
Morris & Mc Veigh
767 3rd Avenue
Floor 4
New York, NY 10017        212-418-0500
                          FAX: 212-759-6510
e-mail: main@achelis-bodman-fnds.org
www.fdncenter.org/grantmaker/achelis-bodman

*John N Irwin III, Chairman*
*Russell P Pennoyer, President*
*Mary S Phipps, Second VP*

Follows donor intent with distribution of funds for charitable, benevolent, educational and religious uses and purposes. Primarily funds in the New York City area.

*1940*

**3467  Alavi Foundation of New York**

500 5th Avenue
Floor 34
New York, NY  10110          212-944-8333
                             FAX: 212-921-0325
                        www.alavifoundation.org/index.html

*M Geramian, President*

Purposes are charitable and philanthropic with an emphasis on education and civic concerns.

*1973*

**3468  Altman Foundation**

521 5th Avenue
Floor 35
New York, NY  10175          212-682-0970

                        e-mail: cia@fdncenter.org
                   www.foundationcenter.org/grantmaker/altman

*Jane B O'Connell, President*
*Karen L Rosa, VP/Executive Director*
*John W Townsend, VP*

For the benefit of such charitable and educational institutions in the City of New York as said directors shall approve. Foundation grants support programs and institutions that enrich the quality of life in the city, with a particular focus on initiatives that help individuals, families and communities benefit from the services and opportunities that will enable them to achieve their full potential.

*1913*

**3469  Ambrose Monell Foundation**

1 Rockefeller Plaza
Room 301
New York, NY  10020          212-586-0700
                             FAX: 212-245-1863
                   e-mail: mailto:mjmorello@fultonrowe.com
                   www.monellvetlesen.org/monell/default.ht m

*George Rowe Jr, Partner*

Voluntary aiding and contributing to religious, charitable, scientific, literary, and educational uses and purposes, in New York, elsewhere in the US and throughout the world.

**3470  American Chai Trust**

41 Madison Avenue
40th Floor
New York, NY  10010          212-889-0575
                             FAX: 212-743-8120
                        www.perlmanandperlman.com

*Clifford Perlman, Director/Owner*

**3471  American Foundation for the Blind**

11 Penn Plaza
Suite 300
New York, NY  10001          212-502-7600
                             200-232-5463
                             FAX: 212-502-7777
                        e-mail: afbinfo@afb.org
                             www.afb.org

*Carl R Augusto, President/CEO*
*Richard J O'Brien, Chairman*

Dedicated to addressing issues of literacy, independent living, employment, and access through technology for the ten million Americans who are blind or visually impaired.

**3472  Arthur Ross Foundation**

20 E 74th Street
Suite 4c
New York, NY  10021          212-737-7311
                             FAX: 212-650-0332

*Arthur Ross, President*

**3473  Artists Fellowship**

47 5th Avenue
New York, NY  10003          646-230-9833

*Richard Pionk, Treasurer*

**3474  Bell Atlantic Foundation**

1095 Avenue of the Americas
Room 3200
New York, NY  10036
                             800-360-7955
                             FAX: 212-398-0951
                        www.horizon.com/foundation

*Suzanne A Du Bose, President*

**3475  Bodman Foundation**

767 3rd Avenue
Floor 4
New York, NY  10017          212-644-0322
                             FAX: 212-759-6510
                   e-mail: main@achelis-bodman-fmds.org
                   www.fdncenter.org/grantmaker/bodman

*Joseph Dolan, Executive Director*

**3476  Booth Ferris Foundation**

60 Wall Street
46th Floor
New York, NY  10260          212-809-1630

Giving limited to the New York metropolitan area.

**3477  Brooklyn Home for Aged Men**

PO Box 280062
Brooklyn, NY  11228          718-745-1638

*Nancy K Munson, President*

**3478  Cancer Care**

1180 Avenue of the Americas
New York, NY  10036          212-221-3300
                             800-813-HOPE
                             FAX: 212-719-0263
                        e-mail: info@cancercareinc.org
                   celebratinglife.org/Organization_Support.htm

*Diane Blum, Executive Director*

**3479  Charles A Dana Foundation**

745 5th Avenue
Suite 900
New York, NY  10151          212-223-4040
                             FAX: 212-593-7623
                        e-mail: danainfo@dana.org
                             www.dana.org

*Edward F Rover, President*
*William Safire, Chairman*
*Josephine Donahue, Manager*

**3480  Clark Foundation**

1 Rockefeller Plaza
New York, NY  10020          212-977-6900

*Kevin Moore, President*

Giving in New York and New York City.

**3481** **Commonwealth Fund**

1 E 75th Street
New York, NY 10021

212-535-0400
FAX: 212-606-3500
e-mail: cmwf@cmwf.org
www.cmwf.org

*Samuel O Thier, Chairman*
*Karen David, President*

A private foundation with the broad charge to enhance the common good. Carries out this mandate by supporting efforts that help people live healthy and productive lives, and by assisting certain groups with serious and neglected problems. Supports independent research on health and social issues and makes grants to improve heathcare practice and policy.
*1918*

**3482** **Community Foundation for Greater Buffalo**

712 Main Street
Buffalo, NY 14202

716-852-2857
FAX: 716-852-2861
e-mail: cfgb@buffnet.net
www.cfgb.org

*Jean M Brun, Program Officer*
*Gail Johnstone, Executive Director*

**3483** **Community Foundation of Herkimer & Oneida Counties**

1222 State Street
Utica, NY 13502

315-735-8212
FAX: 315-735-9363
e-mail: commfdn@borg.com

*Susan D Smith, Senior Program Officer*

**3484** **Community Foundation of the Capitol Region**

6 Tower Place
Albany, NY 12203

518-446-9638
FAX: 518-446-9708
e-mail: info@cfcr.org
www.cfcr.org

*Judith Lyons, Executive Director*
*Maureen Yee, Grant Director*
*Kristen Frederick, President*

**3485** **Comsearch: Broad Topics**

Foundation Center
79 5th Avenue
New York, NY 10003

212-620-4230
800-424-9836
FAX: 212-807-3677
www.fdncenter.org

*Sara Engelhardt, President*
*Maureen Mackey, Executive Vice President*

Subset publications of The Foundation Grants Index, are printouts of actual foundation grants, covering 26 key areas of grantmaking. This tool is designed for fundraisers who wish to examine grantmaking activities in a broad field of interest.
*$55.00*

**3486** **DE French Foundation**

120 Genesee Street
Suite 503
Auburn, NY 13021

315-253-9321

*J Douglas Pedley, President*

**3487** **David J Green Foundation**

599 Lexington Avenue
Suite 12
New York, NY 10022

212-371-4200
FAX: 212-371-5099

*Barbara A McBride, Secretary*
*Michael Greene, Manager*

**3488** **Easter Seals New York**

230 Washington Avenue Ext
Albany, NY 12203

518-456-4880
800-727-8785
ny.easter-seals.org

*Christine McMahon, Chief Operating Officer*
*Candi Tercenti, Manager*

Offers resources and expertise that allow children and adults with disabilities to live with dignity and independence. A long standing commitment to serve those for whom no other resources exist. Statewide, provides innovative solutions that enhance the lives of people with disabilities, while heightening community awareness and acceptance.

**3489** **Edward John Noble Foundation**

32 E 57th Street
Floor 19
New York, NY 10022

212-759-4212

*Noble Smith, Executive Director*
*June Larkin, Owner*

**3490** **Epilepsy Foundation of Long Island**

506 Stewart Avenue
Garden City, NY 11530

516-739-7733
888-672-7154
e-mail: rdaly@epil.org
www.epilepsyfoundation.org/longisland

*Richard E Daly, Executive Director*
*Henry Hertl, Associate Executive Director*
*Elaine Lubelsky, Controller*

Provides education, counseling and residential care to Long Island residents with epilepsy and related conditions.
*1953*

**3491** **Epilepsy Society of New York**

305 7th Avenue
12th Floor
New York, NY 10001

212-633-2930
FAX: 212-633-2991
www.epilepsynyc.org

*George H Smith, Executive Director*
*Tara Powers, President*

**3492** **Episcopal Charities**

1047 Amsterdam Avenue
New York, NY 10025

212-316-7426
FAX: 212-316-7431
e-mail: EPCHARNY@aol.com

*David P Shover, Executive Director*

**3493** **Esther A & Joseph Klingenstein Fund**

787 7th Avenue
Floor 6
New York, NY 10019

212-492-6181
FAX: 212-492-7007

*John Klingenstein, President*

**3494  Fay J Lindner Foundation**
1161 Meadowbrook Road
Merrick, NY  11566                516-292-1331

*Ruth Torito, Director*
*Robert Goldberg, President*

**3495  Florence V Burden Foundation**
630 5th Avenue
Suite 2900
New York, NY  10111              212-332-1100

*Edward P H Burden, President*
Publishes an annual or periodic report.

**3496  Ford Foundation**
320 E 43rd Street
New York, NY  10017              212-983-6234
                                 FAX: 212-351-3677
                                 e-mail: jdassin@fordfound.org
                                 www.fordfound.org

*Joan Dassin, Director*
*Susan Berresford, Chief Executive Officer*
*Barry D Gaberman, Senior VP*

A resource for innovative people and institutions worldwide. Goals are to: strenghthen democratic values; reduce poverty and injustice; promote international cooperation; and advance human achievement.

**3497  Fortis Foundation**
1 Chase Manhattan Plaza
New York, NY  10005              212-859-7000
                                 FAX: 212-859-7058
                                 www.assurant.com

*Christy Hall, Director*

Grants are offered in healthcare fields, especially in medical research ($500-$5,000). New York City social, educational organizations also receive funds ($250-$5,000).

**3498  Foundation Center**
79 5th Avenue
New York, NY  10003              212-620-4230
                                 800-424-9836
                                 FAX: 212-807-3677
                                 e-mail: communications@fdncenter.org
                                 www.fdncenter.org

*Sara Engelhardt, President*
*Macy Morin, Executive Vice President*
*Laura Cascio, Fulfillment Manager*

The center disseminates current information on foundation and corporate giving through our national collections in New York City and Washington D.C., our field offices in San Francisco and our network of over 180 cooperating libraries in all 50 states and abroad.

**3499  Foundation Center Library Services**
Foundation Center
79 5th Avenue
New York, NY  10003              212-620-4230
                                 800-424-9836
                                 FAX: 212-807-3677
                                 www.fdncenter.org

*Sara Engelhardt, President*
*Macy Morin, Executive Vice President*

The Center disseminates current information on foundation and corporate giving through our national collections in New York City and Washington D.C., our field offices in San Francisco and our network of over 180 cooperating libraries in all 50 states and abroad.

**3500  Foundation for Advancement in Cancer Therapy**
PO Box 1242
New York, NY  10113              212-741-2790
                                 www.fact-ltd.org

*Ruth Sackman, President*

A clearinghouse for information regarding alternative cancer therapies, emphasizing nutritional and metabolic approaches.

**3501  Foundation for the Advancement of Innovative Medicine**
2 Executive Boulevard
Ofc 206
Suffern, NY  10901               877-634-3246
                                 e-mail: faim@healthlobby.com
                                 www.faim.org

*Howard G Hindin, Treasurer*
*Diane D Udzinki, President*
*Alan Lambert MD JD, Legal Counsel*

A voice for innovative medicine's professionals, patients, and suppliers. Defines innovative medicine as a treatment or therapy of empirical clinical benefit that is yet outside the mainstream of conventional medicine. Complementary to conventional medicine, offering alternatives as an individual situation may warrant.
    *1989*

**3502  Gebbie Foundation**
111 W 2nd Street
Suite 1100
Jamestown, NY  14701             716-487-1062
                                 FAX: 716-484-6401
                                 www.gebbie.org

*John Mernio, Executive Director*

Giving in Chautauqua County, and secondly, in neighboring areas of western New York. Giving is offered in other areas only when the project is consonant with program objectives that cannot be developed locally.

**3503  Gladys Brooks Foundation**
1055 Franklin Avenue
Garden City, NY  11530           516-746-6103

*Harman Hawkins, Chairman*
*James J Daly, Board of Governors*
*Jessica Rutledge, Manager*

The purpose of this Foundation is to provide for the intellectual, moral and physical welfare of the people of this country by establishing and supporting nonprofit libraries, educational institutions, hospitals and clinics. The Foundation will make grants only to private, publicly supported, nonprofit, tax-exempt organizations.

**3504  Glickenhaus Foundation**
6 E 43rd Street
New York, NY  10017              212-953-7867

*Maddy Wehle*

**3505  Graphic Controls Corporate Giving Program**
PO Box 1271
Buffalo, NY  14240               716-853-7500

*Phyllis Rudz*
*John Bellotti, Plant Manager*

**3506  Guide Dog Foundation for the Blind**
371 E Jericho Tpke
Smithtown, NY  11787                           631-265-2121
                                               800-548-4337
                                         FAX: 516-361-5192
                                    e-mail: info@guidedog.org
                                            www.guidedog.org

*Wells B Jones, Chief Executive Officer*
*Pam Vitale, Executive Assistant*

Established in 1946, the Foundation provides rehabilitation for
the blind by breeding and training guide dogs. A fully trained
guide dog is given to blind applicants from all over the United
States and some foreign countries. They train together as a team
for 25 days on campus. All of these programs, including the cost
of transportation and after-care programs, are given without cost
to the blind recipients. Quarterly newsletter, video cassette, audio cassette.

**3507  Hearst Foundation**
888 7th Avenue
45th Floor
New York, NY  10106                            212-586-5404
                                               800-375-5283
                                         FAX: 212-586-1917
                                            www.hearstfdn.org

*Robert M Frehse Jr, Executive Director*

**3508  Henry and Lucy Moses Fund**
Moses and Singer
405 Lexington Avenue
Floor 12
New York, NY  10174                            212-554-7800
                                         FAX: 212-554-7700
                                          www.mosessinger.com

*Erica Busch, Associate*
*Declan Butvick, Associates*
*Jay Fialkoff, Partner*

**3509  Herman Goldman Foundation**
61 Broadway
Floor 18
New York, NY  10006                            212-797-9090

                                 e-mail: goldfound@aol.com

*Richard K Baron, Executive Director*

**3510  Horace W Goldsmith Foundation**
375 Park Avenue
Suite 1602
New York, NY  10152                            212-319-8700

*James C Slaughter, CEO/Executive Director*

**3511  International Paper Company Foundation**
2 Manhattanville Road
Purchase, NY  10577                            914-397-4057
                                         FAX: 914-397-1500
                                  www.internationalpaper.com

*Robert Amen, President*
*Martha Brooks, Chief Operation Officer*

**3512  JM Foundation**
654 Madison Avenue
Room 1605
New York, NY  10021                            212-687-7735
                                         FAX: 212-697-5495

*Carl O Helstrom, Executive Director*

**3513  Jedra Charitable Foundation**
11011 Queens Boulevard
Apt 208
Forest Hills, NY  11375                        718-263-4956

*David Shechet, President*

**3514  Joseph Alexander Foundation**
400 Madison Avenue
Room 906
New York, NY  10017                            212-355-3688

**3515  Kenneth & Evelyn Lipper Foundation**
101 Park Avenue
6th Floor
New York, NY  10178                            212-883-6333

*Kenneth Lipper, Treasurer*

**3516  Louis and Anne Abrons Foundation**
First Manhattan Company
437 Madison Avenue
New York, NY  10022                            212-756-3300
                                         FAX: 212-832-6698

*David Manischewitz, Chief Executive Officer*

**3517  Margaret L Wendt Foundation**
40 Fountain Plaza
Suite 277
Buffalo, NY  14202                             716-855-2146
                                         FAX: 716-855-2149

*Robert J Kresse, Secretary/Treasurer/Manager*

**3518  Marquis George MacDonald Foundation**
270 Park Avenue
New York, NY  10017                            212-270-6000

*Donna M Bowers, Administrator*
*William Harrison Jr, Chief Executive Officer*

**3519  MetLife Foundation**
1 Madison Avenue
New York, NY  10010                            212-578-8552
                                         FAX: 212-685-1435
                                e-mail: sjacobson@metlife.com
                                            www.metlife.org

*Bill Toppeta, President*
*Lisa Weber, Senior Executive VP*

**3520  Metzger-Price Fund**
230 Park Avenue
Suite 2300
New York, NY  10169                            212-867-9500
                                         FAX: 212-599-1759

*Isaac A Saufer, Secretary/Treasurer*
*Charles Palella*

**3521  Morgan Stanley Foundation**
1221 Avenue of the Americas
Floor 27
New York, NY  10020                            212-899-3400
                                         FAX: 212-762-7790

*John Mack, Chairman*
*Jeffrey Walker, Chief Executive Officer*

**3522  Mount Sinai Medical Center**
1 Gustve L Levy Place 1190 5th Ave
New York, NY 10029          212-241-7699
                    FAX: 212-987-1763
                    e-mail: giving@mountsinai.org
                    www.mountsinai.org

*Evdokia Anagnastou, Clinical Director Seaver Center*
*Janice Kelly, Manager*

Autism Research

**3523  National Foundation for Facial Reconstruction**
317 E 34th Street
Room 901
New York, NY 10016          212-263-6656
                    FAX: 212-263-7534
                    www.nffr.org

*Whitney Burnett, Executive Director*
*Michele Golombuski, Associate Executive Director*

A nonprofit organization whose major purposes are to provide facilities for the treatment and assistance of individuals who are unable to afford private reconstructive surgical care, to train and educate professionals in this surgery, to encourage research in the field and to carry on public education.

**3524  National Hemophilia Foundation**
Soho Building
110 Greene Street
Suite 406
New York, NY 10012          212-226-3100

*Tony Goldman, President*

**3525  National Neurofibromatosis Foundation**
95 Pine Street
16th Floor
New York, NY 10005          212-344-6633
                    800-323-7938
                    FAX: 212-747-0004
                    e-mail: info@ctf.org
                    www.nf.org

*John Risner, President*
*Jacqueline Medina, Director Programs*

A nonprofit 501 (c)(3) medical foundation, dedicated to improving the health and well-being of individuals and families affected by neurofibromatosis. The Foundation sponsors medical research, clinical services, public education programs and patient support services. It is the central source for up-to-date and accurate information about NF. It also assists patients and families with referrals to NF clinics and healthcare professionals specializing in NF. The goal is to find a cure for NF.

**3526  Neisloss Family Foundation**
1737 Veterans Highway
Suite 7
Central Islip, NY 11749          631-234-1600
                    FAX: 631-234-1066

*Stanley Neisloss, President/Owner*

**3527  New York Community Trust**
909 3rd Avenue
New York, NY 10022          212-686-0010
                    FAX: 212-532-8528
                    www.nycommunitytrust.org

*Lorie A Slutsky, President*

**3528  New York Foundation**
350 5th Avenue
Suite 2901
New York, NY 10118          212-594-8009

                    www.nyf.org

*Maria Mottola, Executive Director*

**3529  Northern New York Community Foundation**
120 Washington Street
Watertown, NY 13601          315-782-7110
                    FAX: 315-782-0047
                    e-mail: info@nnycf.org
                    www.nnycf.org

*Alex C Velto, Executive Director*

Raises, manages and administers an endowment and collection of funds for the benefit of the community

**3530  Parkinson's Disease Foundation**
1359 Broadway
Suite 1509
New York, NY 10018          212-923-4700
                    800-457-6676
                    FAX: 212-923-4778
                    e-mail: info@pdf.org
                    www.pdf.org

*Robin Elliott, Executive Director*

National not-for-profit organization dedicated to funding scientific research to investigate the cause and cure of Parkinson's disease and related disorders. The Foundation has a post-doctoral training program, Interntional Research Grant Program, and makes referrals to physicians who treat PD. Other services include supporting advocacy efforts, making referrals to self-help groups, conducting educational symposiums for patients and professionals.

**3531  Reader's Digest Foundation**
Readers Digest Association
Readers Digest Road
Pleasantville, NY 10570          914-238-1000
                    FAX: 914-238-4559
                    www.readersdigest.com

*Claudia L Edwards, Executive Director*
*Thomas Ryder, Chief Executive Officer*

**3532  Research to Prevent Blindness**
645 Madison Avenue
Floor 21
New York, NY 10022          212-421-1970
                    800-621-0026
                    FAX: 212-688-6231
                    e-mail: inforequest@rpbusa.org
                    www.rpbusa.org

*James V Romano, COO*
*Matthew Levine, Communications Director*

National voluntary health foundation supported by foundations, corporations and voluntary gifts and bequests from individuals. Established to stimulate basic and applied research into the causes, prevention and treatment of blinding eye diseases.

**3533  Rita J and Stanley H Kaplan Foundation**
866 United Nations Plaza
Room 306
New York, NY 10017          212-688-1047
                    FAX: 212-688-6907

*Rita J Kaplan, Director*
*Stanley Kaplan, President*

**3534  Robert Sterling Clark Foundation**
135 E 64th Street
New York, NY  10021
212-288-8900
FAX: 212-288-1033

*Margaret Ayers, Executive Director*
Giving primarily in New York with emphasis on advocacy, research, and public education aimed at informing New York City of state policies.

**3535  Skadden Fellowship Foundation**
4 Times Square
Room 40/228
New York, NY  10036
212-735-2550
FAX: 917-777-2956
www.skadden.com

*Susan Plum, Director*
*Jonathan Lerner, Director*

**3536  St. George's Society of New York**
175 9th Avenue
New York, NY  10011
212-924-1434
FAX: 212-727-1566

*John Shannon, Executive Director*

**3537  Stanley W Metcalf Foundation**
120 Genesee Street
Suite 503
Auburn, NY  13021
315-253-9321

*J Douglas Pedley, President*

**3538  Stonewall Community Foundation**
119 W 24th Street
9th Floor
New York, NY  10011
212-367-1155
FAX: 212-367-1157
e-mail: stnwlcmfd@aol.com

*William P Epke, Executive Director*

**3539  Surdna Foundation**
330 Madison Avenue
Floor 30
New York, NY  10017
212-557-0010
FAX: 212-557-0003
e-mail: request@surdna.org
www.surdna.org

*Elizabeth H Andrus, Director*
*Peter B Benedict, Director*

**3540  Sydney & Helen Jacoff Foundation**
120 W 45th Street
New York, NY  10036
212-704-0100
FAX: 212-704-0196

*Steve Wasserman, Manager*

**3541  Tisch Foundation**
655 Madison Avenue
Floor 8
New York, NY  10021
212-521-2930
FAX: 212-521-2983

*Mark J Krinsky, Vice President*

**3542  Van Ameringen Foundation**
509 Madison Avenue
New York, NY  10022
212-758-6221

www.vanamfound.org

*Henry P Van Ameringen, President*
*George Rowe Jr, Vice President*

**3543  Western New York Foundation**
237 Main Street
Buffalo, NY  14203
716-852-1002
FAX: 716-847-6440

*Welles V Moo Jr, President*
*Joseph Arcara, Owner*

**3544  William T Grant Foundation**
570 Lexington Avenue
18th Floor
New York, NY  10022
212-752-0071
FAX: 212-752-1398
e-mail: info@wtgrantfdn.org
www.wtgrantfoundation.org

*Robert Granger, President*
*Sharon Brewster, Director*

## North Carolina

**3545  Arc of North Carolina**
4200 Six Forks Road
Suite 100
Raleigh, NC  27609
919-782-4632
800-662-8706
FAX: 919-782-4634
e-mail: arcofnc@arcnc.org
www.arcnc.org

*Dave Richard, Executive Director*

**3546  Bob & Kay Timberlake Foundation**
1660 E Center Street Ext
Lexington, NC  27292
336-243-7777

*Daniel Timberlake, President*

**3547  Broyhill Family Foundation**
PO Box 500
Lenoir, NC  28645
828-758-6100
FAX: 828-754-7335

*Hunt Broyhill, President*

**3548  Duke Endowment**
100 North Tryon Street
Suite 3500
Charlotte, NC  28202
704-376-0291
FAX: 704-376-9336
e-mail: info@tde.org
www.dukeendowment.org

*Teme Cochrane, President*
*Elizabeth Locke, Chief Executive Officer*

**3549  First Union Foundation**
301 S College Street
Charlotte, NC  28288
704-383-0525
FAX: 704-374-2484

*Judy Allison, Director*

**3550 Foundation for the Carolinas**
1043 E Morehead Street
Suite 100
Charlotte, NC 28204
704-973-4500
FAX: 704-376-1243
www.fftc.org

*Michael Marsicano, Chief Executive Officer*

Giving primarily to organizations serving the citizens of North and South Carolina.

**3551 John H Wellons Foundation**
PO Box 1254
Dunn, NC 28335
910-892-0887
FAX: 910-892-4888

*John H Wellons, Senior President/Owner*

**3552 Kate B Reynolds Charitable Trust**
The Kate B Reynolds Charitable Trust
128 Reynolda Vlg
Winston Salem, NC 27106
336-723-1456
e-mail: www.webmaster@kbr.org
www.kbr.org

*Jan Johnson Yopp, Author*
*Karen Yoak Lewis, Office Manager*
*E Cope, President*

Grants resricted to the state of North Carolina only.

**3553 Kathleen Price and Joseph M Bryan Family Foundation**
220 S Eugene Street
Greensboro, NC 27401
336-273-0080
FAX: 336-288-5458

*Nancy H Poteet, Interim Director*
*Joseph M Bryan Jr, President*

Only organizations or projects demonstrating direct benefits to North Carolina are eligible for consideration with emphasis on Greensboro and Guilford County and rural communities in North Carolina with financial need. The Foundation does not consider support for annual campaigns, conferences, video production, individuals, research, travel for band and sports teams. There are no discretionary or emergency funds.

**3554 Mary Reynolds Babcock Foundation**
102 Reynolda Vlg
Winston Salem, NC 27106
336-748-9222
FAX: 919-777-0095
e-mail: info@mrbf.org

*Gayle W Williams, Executive Director*

For 1994, this foundation is committed to an extensive educational and planning process to better understand the Southeast and to articulate the role the foundation seeks to play in the region into the twenty-first century.

**3555 Triangle Community Foundation**
4813 Emperor Boulevard
Durham, NC 27703
919-474-8370
FAX: 919-941-9208
e-mail: info@trianglecf.org
www.trianglecf.org

*Fred Stang, Director of Development*
*Shannon John, President*

## North Dakota

**3556 Alex Stern Family Foundation**
609 1/2 1st Avenue N
Fargo, ND 58102
701-237-0170
FAX: 701-234-9724

*Don Scott, Executive Director*

**3557 Arc of North Dakota**
PO Box 12420
Grand Forks, ND 58208
701-772-6191
877-250-2022
FAX: 701-772-2195
e-mail: thearc@arcuv.com
www.thearcuppervalley.com

*Dianne Sheppard, Executive Director*

**3558 North Dakota Community Foundation**
1025 N 3rd Street
PO Box 387
Bismarck, ND 58502
701-222-8349
www.ndcf.net

*Kevin J Dvorak, President*
*Valerie Bren, Executive Assistant*

## Ohio

**3559 Akron Community Foundation**
345 W Cedar Street
Akron, OH 44307
330-376-8522
FAX: 330-376-0202
www.akroncommunityfdn.org/financialadvisor/

*Jody Bacon, President*
*Steven Schloenvach, VP Finance*

**3560 Albert G and Olive H Schlink Foundation**
49 Benedict Avenue
Suite C
Norwalk, OH 44857
419-668-8211
FAX: 419-668-2813

*Robert A Wiedemann, Partner*

**3561 American Foundation Corporation**
720 National City Bank Building
Cleveland, OH 44114
216-241-6664

*William Murphy, President*
*Barbara Lattner, Manager*

**3562 Arc of Ohio**
1335 Dublin Road
Suite 205c
Columbus, OH 43215
614-487-4720
800-875-2723
FAX: 614-487-4720
e-mail: thearcohio@aol.com
www.thearcofohio.org

*Gary Tonks, Executive Director*
*Joan Arnold, Assistant Director*

357

**3563  Cleveland Foundation**
1422 Euclid Avenue
Suite 1300
Cleveland, OH  44115                216-861-3810
                                FAX: 216-861-1729
                            www.clevelandfoundation.org

John Sherwin Jr, Chairman
Jacqueline F Woods, Vice Chairperson
Ronald Richard, President

**3564  Columbus Foundation and Affiliated Organizations**
1234 E Broad Street
Columbus, OH  43205                614-251-4000
                                FAX: 614-251-4009
                        e-mail: info@columbusfoundation.org
                            www.columbusfoundation.org

Doug Krilder, President

**3565  Eleanora CU Alms Trust**
Fifth Third Bank
9990 Montgomery Road
Dept 00864
Cincinnati, OH  45263              513-793-2200

Bryan Webb, Manager
Giving limited to Cincinnati, OH.

**3566  Emma Leah and Laura Bell Bahmann Foundation**
8041 Hosbrook Road
Suite 210
Cincinnati, OH  45236              513-891-3799
                                FAX: 513-891-3722

John T Gatch, Executive Director

**3567  Eva L and Joseph M Bruening Foundation**
1422 Euclid Avenue
Cleveland, OH  44115               216-621-2632
                                FAX: 216-621-8198
                        e-mail: fmscleveland.com/bruening
                            www.fmscleveland.com/bruening

Janet E Narten, Executive Director

Charitable foundation providing grants to noprofit organizations located inCuyahoga county Ohio. No grant are awarded to inviduals.

**3568  Fred & Lillian Deeks Memorial Foundation**
PO Box 1118
Cincinnati, OH  45201              937-339-2329
                                FAX: 937-339-1861

**3569  GAR Foundation**
PO Box 1500
Akron, OH  44309                   330-643-0201
                                FAX: 330-252-5584
                        e-mail: rob_briggs@akron.BDBLaw.com
                            www.garfdn.org

Robert W Briggs, Executive Director
Margaret Canzonetta, Administrative Director

**3570  George Gund Foundation**
45 W Prospect Avenue
Cleveland, OH  44115               216-241-3114
                                FAX: 216-241-6560
                        e-mail: info@gundfoundation.org
                            www.gundfdn.org

David Abbott, Executive Director
Marcia Egbert, Senior Program Officer

**3571  Greater Cincinnati Foundation**
300 W 4th Street
Suite 200
Cincinnati, OH  45202              513-621-2142
                                FAX: 513-852-6886
                            www.greatercincinnatifdn.org

Myrtis H Powell, Chief Executive Officer
Nancy K Swanson, Vice President
Alan Welch, President

**3572  HCR Manor Care Foundation**
PO Box 10086
Toledo, OH  43699                  419-252-5989
                                FAX: 419-252-5221
                        e-mail: foundation@hcr-manorcare.com
                            www.hcr-manorcare.com

Susan J Harless, President
Jennifer Steiner, Executive Director

**3573  Harry C Moores Foundation**
100 S 3rd Street
Columbus, OH  43215                614-227-8884

Mary B Cummins, Administrator

**3574  Helen Steiner Rice Foundation**
221 E 4th Street
Cincinnati, OH  45202              513-451-9241
                                    800-877-2665
                            e-mail: hsrice@fuse.net
                            www.helensteinerrice.com

Willis Gradison Jr, Director
Andrea Cornett, Administrator/Grant Coordinator
Virginia Ruehlmann, Executive Director

**3575  Herbert W Hoover Foundation**
220 Market Avenue
Canton, OH  44702                  330-454-1010

Harry Nealy, Owner

**3576  John P Murphy Foundation**
50 Public Square
Suite 924
Cleveland, OH  44113               216-623-4770
                                FAX: 216-623-4773
                        www.fdncenter.org/grantmaker/jpmurphy/

Nancy W McCann, President
Robert R Broadbent, Vice President

**3577  Nationwide Foundation**
1 Nationwide Plaza
Columbus, OH  43215                614-249-6226

                            www.nationwide.com

Stephan A Rish, President
Paula Edwards, Chief Executive Officer

**3578  Nordson Corporate Giving Program**
28601 Clemens Road
Westlake, OH  44145                440-892-1580

                        e-mail: kladiner@nordson.com
                            www.nordson.com

Constance T Haqq, Executive Director
Cecilia Render, Manager

**3579  Parker-Hannifin Foundation**
6035 Parkland Boulevard
Cleveland, OH  44124               216-896-3000
                              FAX: 216-896-4057
                                   www.parker.com

*Tom Mackie, President*

**3580  Reinberger Foundation**
27600 Chagrin Boulevard
Cleveland, OH  44122               216-292-2790

*Robert N Reinberger, Executive Director*

**3581  Robert Campeau Family Foundation**
7 W 7th Street
Cincinnati, OH  45202              513-579-7000
                              FAX: 513-579-7555

*Terry Lundgren, Chief Executive Officer*

**3582  Sisler McFawn Foundation**
PO Box 149
Akron, OH  44309                   330-849-8887
                              FAX: 330-996-6215

*Charlotte M Stanley, Grants Manager*

Our trust restricts giving to certain programs and types of organizations. You can see recent giving has been by referring to the list of grants approved and paid during the past year. Call foundation office to request a guidelines brochure and list.

**3583  Stark Community Foundation**
Unizan Plaza 220 Market Avenu
Suite 920
Canton, OH  44702                  330-454-5800
                              FAX: 330-454-5855
                     www.starkcommunityfoundation.org

*Vicki Conley, Executive Director*

**3584  Stocker Foundation**
559 Broadway
2noord Floor
Lorain, OH  44052                  440-246-5719
                              FAX: 440-246-5720
               e-mail: pobrien@stockerfoundation.org
                          www.stockerfoundation.org

*Patricia O'Brien, Executive Director*

**3585  Toledo Community Foundation**
608 Madison Avenue
Toledo, OH  43604                  419-241-5049
                              FAX: 419-242-5549

*Keith Burwell, President*

**3586  William J and Dorothy K O'Neill Foundation**
30195 Chagrin Boulevard
Suite 310
Cleveland, OH  44124               216-831-9667
                              FAX: 216-831-3779
                    e-mail: oneillfdn@aol.com
                          www.oneillfdn.org

*Catherine T Abbott, Director*
*William O'Neill, Owner*

**3587  Youngstown Foundation**
Dollar Savings & Trust Company
PO Box 450
Youngstown, OH  44501              330-744-0320
                              FAX: 330-744-0344

*Jerry Walsh, Executive Director*

## Oklahoma

**3588  Anne and Henry Zarrow Foundation**
401 S Boston Avenue
Suite 900
Tulsa, OK  74103                   918-295-8000
                              FAX: 918-295-8049
                     e-mail: ZFFound@aol.com

*Jeanne Gillert, Grants Manager*
*Scott Zarrow, Manager*

**3589  International Bio-Oxidative Medicine Foundation (IBOM)**
1015 Waterwood Parkway
Suite G
Edmond, OK  73034                  405-478-4266

Offers educational programs, referrals and a newsletter.

**3590  Sarkeys Foundation**
530 E Main Street
Norman, OK  73071                  405-364-3703
                              FAX: 405-364-8191
                                   www.sarkeys.org

*Cheri D Cartwright, Executive Director*
*Susan C Frantz, Sr Program Officer*
*Ann M Way, Sr Program Officer*

Improves the quality of life in Oklahoma. Offers contributions in the areas of social services, arts and cultural programs, educational funding and health care and medical research. Funding only in agencies in the state of Oklahoma.

**3591  William K Warren Foundation**
PO Box 470372
Tulsa, OK  74147                   918-492-8100

*W Warren Jr, President*

## Oregon

**3592  Arc of Oregon**
1745 State Street
Salem, OR  97301                   503-581-2726
                                   877-581-2726
                                   877-581-2726
                              FAX: 503-363-7168
                     e-mail: info@arcoregon.org
                          www.arcoregon.org

*Marcie Ingledue, Executive Director*

Guardianship, Advocacy and Planning Services. Oregon special needs trust; information and referral.

**3593  Chiles Foundation**
111 SW 5th Avenue
Suite 4050
Portland, OR  97204                503-222-2143

Giving in Oregon, with emphasis on Portland, and the Pacific Northwest.

**3594  Jackson Foundation**
PO Box 3168
Portland, OR  97208                503-275-6564

*Robert H Depew, Vice President*

**3595  Leslie G Ehmann Trust**
PO Box 3168
Portland, OR  97208          503-275-5929
                            800-522-9100
                        FAX: 503-275-4117
            e-mail: william.dollan@usbank.com

*William Dolan, Trustee*

**3596  Samuel S Johnson Foundation**
PO Box 356
Redmond, OR  97756          541-548-8104
                        FAX: 541-548-2014
            e-mail: ssjohnson@empnet.com

*Becky Johnson, President*

## Pennsylvania

**3597  Acorn Alcinda Foundation**
Rr 4
Box 710
Mifflintown, PA  17059          717-436-6597

*Robert J Kennedy, President/Treasurer*

**3598  Air Products Foundation**
7201 Hamilton Boulevard
Allentown, PA  18195          610-481-4911
                         FAX: 610-481-5900
                          www.airproducts.com

*John Jones III, Chief Executive Officer*

Giving primarily in areas of company operations throughout the US.

**3599  Arc of Pennsylvania**
Arc of United States
101 S 2nd Street
Suite 8
Harrisburg, PA  17101          717-234-2621
                            800-692-7258
                        FAX: 717-234-7615
                          www.thearcpa.org

*Stephen Suroviec, Executive Director*
*Wendy Kramer, Administrative Assistant/Finance*

**3600  Arcadia Foundation**
105 E Logan Street
Norristown, PA  19401          610-275-8460

*Marilyn L Steinbright, President*

**3601  Brachial Plexus Palsy Foundation**
210 Springhaven Circle
Royersford, PA  19468          610-792-0974
                         FAX: 610-792-0974
                       e-mail: brachial@aol.com
                        www.membrane.com/bpp

*Thomas J Cirino, President*
*Michael F Cirino, Executive Director*

Nonprofit organization dedicated to raising funds for support of families who hae children with brachial plexus injuries. Supports medical facilities that research and treat such injuries, holds fund-raising events to support further research, has support groups, and produces educational materials including a newsletter, Outreach, and brochures.

**3602  Claude Washington Benedum Foundation**
1400 Benedum
Pittsburgh, PA  15222          412-288-0360
                         FAX: 412-288-0366
                        e-mail: info@benedum.org
                www.fdncenter.org/grantmaker/benedum

*William Getty, President*
*Dwight Keating, Vice President*

Giving limited to West Virginia and southwestern Pennsylvania.

**3603  Columbia Gas of Pennsylvania Corporate Giv ing**
650 Washington Road
Pittsburgh, PA  15228          412-572-7104
                         FAX: 412-572-7140
            e-mail: mmarti@columbiaenergygroup.com
                www.columbiagaspamd.com/html/

*Rosemary Martinelli, Manager Corporation*

**3604  Connelly Foundation**
1 Tower Brg
Suite 1450
West Conshohocken, PA  19428          610-834-3222
                                 FAX: 610-834-0866
                            e-mail: info@connellyfdn.org
                              www.connellyfdn.org

*Josephine C Mandeville, Chief Executive Officer*
*Emily C Riley, Executive Vice President*

**3605  Dolfinger-McMahon Foundation**
1 Liberty Place
Philadelphia, PA  19103          215-979-1768

*Sharon Renz, Contact Person*

**3606  Harry C Trexler Trust**
33 S 7th Street
Suite 205
Allentown, PA  18101          484-664-3500

*Thomas Christman, Secretary Trustees*
*Thomas Gaughan, Executive Director*

Giving limited to Lehigh County, Pennsylvania.

**3607  Henry L Hillman Foundation**
2000 Grant Building
Pittsburgh, PA  15219          412-338-3466
                         FAX: 412-338-3463
               e-mail: foundation@hillmanfo.com

*Ronald W Wertz, President*

**3608  Howard Heinz Endowment**
625 Liberty Avenue
Pittsburgh, PA  15222          412-281-5777

*Maxwell King, President*

**3609  Hoxie Harrison Smith Foundation**
350 Pond View Road
Devon, PA  19333          610-688-0143
                     FAX: 610-688-0143

*Bruce M Brown, Secretary/Treasurer*

**3610  Jewish Healthcare Foundation of Pittsburgh**
Centre City Tower 650 Smithfi
Suite 2400
Pittsburgh, PA 15222                    412-594-2550
                                   FAX: 412-232-6240
                                    e-mail: info@jhf.org
                                          www.jhf.org

*Karen W Feinstein, President*

**3611  Juliet L Hillman Simonds Foundation**
330 Grant Street
Suite 2000
Pittsburgh, PA 15219                    412-338-3466
                                   FAX: 412-338-3463
                       e-mail: foundation@hillmanfo.com

*Ronald W Wertz, President*
*David Rager, Program Manager*

**3612  Oberkotter Foundation**
1600 Market Street
Suite 3600
Philadelphia, PA 19103                  215-751-2601
                                   FAX: 215-751-2678
                       e-mail: george_nofer@shsl.com

*George H Nofer, Executive Director*

**3613  PECO Energy Company Contributions Program**
2301 Market Street
7toorh Floor
Philadelphia, PA 19103                  215-841-4000
                                   FAX: 215-841-4040

*Anne Baker, Manager*
*Denis O'Brien, President*

**3614  PNC Bank Foundation**
249 5th Avenue
Pittsburgh, PA 15222                    412-762-2000
                                   FAX: 412-768-3779
                                       www.pncbank.com

*Bill Kosis, Chief Executive Officer*

**3615  Philadelphia Foundation**
1234 Market Street
Suite 1800
Philadelphia, PA 19107                  215-563-6417
                                   FAX: 215-563-6882
                           e-mail: parkow@philafound.org
                                    www.philafound.org

*R Andrew Swinney, President*
*Jeffery W Perkins, VP Finance/Administrator*

**3616  Pittsburgh Foundation**
1 Ppg Place
30th Floor
Pittsburgh, PA 15222                    412-391-5122
                                   FAX: 421-391-7259
                       e-mail: trueheartw@pghfdn.org
                            www.pittsburghfoundation.org

*William E Trueheart, President/CEO*
*Richard W Reed, Executive Vice President*

**3617  Shenango Valley Foundation**
33 Chestnut Avenue
Sharon, PA 16146                        724-347-3767
                                   FAX: 724-983-9044
                                    www.sv-foundation.org

*Larry Haynes, Executive Director*
*Tony Bianco, Owner*
Pooled Income Trust

**3618  Snee-Reinhardt Charitable Foundation**
500 Grant Street
Pittsburgh, PA 15219                    412-390-2677
                                   FAX: 412-390-2686

*Joan E Szymanski, Foundation Manager*
*James Wilharm, Manager*

**3619  Staunton Farm Foundation**
650 Smithfield Street
Pittsburgh, PA 15222                    412-281-8020
                                   FAX: 412-232-3115
                         e-mail: info@stauntonfarm.org
                                  www.stauntonfarm.org

*Joani Schwager, Executive Director*

**3620  Stewart Huston Charitable Trust**
Will of Stewart Huston
50 S 1st Avenue
Coatesville, PA 19320                   610-384-2666
                                   FAX: 610-384-3396
                         e-mail: admin@stewarthuston.org
                                  www.stewarthuston.org

*Scott G Huston, Executive Director*

**3621  Teleflex Foundation**
630 W Germantown Pike
Suite 461
Plymouth Meeting, PA 19462              610-834-6378
                                   FAX: 610-834-0248

*Thelma A Fretz, Executive Director*

**3622  USX Foundation**
600 Grant Street
Suite 685
Pittsburgh, PA 15219                    412-433-5238
                                   FAX: 412-433-6847

*CD Mallick, General Manager*
*Patricia Funaro, Program Manager*
Giving primarily in areas of company operations located within
the United States.

**3623  WW Smith Charitable Trust**
3515 W Chester Pike
Suite E
Newtown Square, PA 19073                610-359-1811
                                   FAX: 610-359-9717

*Frances R Pemberton, Trust Administrator*

**3624  William B Dietrich Foundation**
Duane Morrs Llt
1 Liberty Place 1650 Market Street
Philadelphia, PA 19103                  215-979-1919
                                   FAX: 215-979-1020
                                       www.duanemorrs.com

*William B Dietrich, President*

**3625  William Talbott Hillman Foundation**
2000 Grant Building
Pittsburgh, PA 15219                    412-338-3466
                                   FAX: 412-338-3463
                       e-mail: foundation@hillmanfo.com

*Ronald W Wertz, President*

**3626  William V and Catherine A McKinney Charitable
Foundation**
20 Stanwix Street
Pittsburgh, PA 15222                    412-644-8332
                                   FAX: 412-644-6058

*William M Schmidt, Senior Vice President*

## Rhode Island

**3627  Arc South County Chapter**
24 Salt Pond Road
Suite G3
Wakefield, RI  02879          401-789-4386
                              FAX: 401-789-4394

**3628  Arc of Northern Rhode Island**
320 Main Street
Woonsocket, RI  02895         401-765-3700
                              FAX: 401-766-0910
                              e-mail: info@arcofnri.org
                              www.arcofnri.org

*Robert Carl Jr, Executive Director*

**3629  Arc-Down Syndrome Society of Rhode Island**
99 Bald Hill Road
Cranston, RI  02920           401-463-5751

**3630  Blackstone Valley Chapter RI Arc**
115 Manton Street
Pawtucket, RI  02861          401-727-0150
                              FAX: 401-727-0153
                              e-mail: contact@bvcriarc.org
                              www.bvcriarc.org

*Peter Holden, Executive Director*
*Barbara Lindsay, Development Director*
*Kathy Hunt, Manager*

A private nonprofut organization providing residential developmental employment and recreational programs and services to more than 400 individuals with mental retardation and realted disabilities.

**3631  Bristol County Chapter Arc**
PO Box 711
Bristol, RI  02809            401-846-0340
                              FAX: 401-253-7880

*John Maher, Executive Director*

**3632  Champlin Foundations**
300 Centerville Road
Suite 300s
Warwick, RI  02886            401-736-0370
                              FAX: 401-736-7248

*David King, Director*
*Keith Lang, Executive Director*
Giving in the Rhode Island area.

**3633  Cranston Arc**
111 Comstock Parkway
Cranston, RI  02921           401-941-1112
                              FAX: 401-941-2516
                              e-mail: sharon@cranstocarc.org
                              www.cranstonarc.org

*Sharon Stewart, VP Program Services*
*Thomas Kane, Executive Director*

**3634  Greater Providence Arc**
220 Woonasquatucket Avenue
North Providence, RI  02911   401-353-7000

*Theodore Polak, Executive Director*

**3635  Horace A Kimball and S Ella Kimball Foundation**
23 Broad Street
Westerly, RI  02891           401-364-7799

                              www.hkimballfoundation.org

*Thomas F Black III, President*
Makes grants almost exclusively to Rhode Island operatives (charities) or those benefitting Rhode Island residents ans causes.

**3636  Kent County Arc**
3445 Post Road
Warwick, RI  02886            401-739-2700
                              FAX: 401-737-8907
                              www.kentcountyarc.org

*Mary Madden, Executive Director*
Providing individuals with disabilties meaningful opportunities throughout their communities.

**3637  Newport County Arc**
PO Box 4390
Middletown, RI  02842         401-846-4600
                              FAX: 401-849-4267

*Jack Maher, Executive Director*

**3638  Rhode Island Arc**
99 Bald Hill Road
Cranston, RI  02920           401-463-9191
                              FAX: 401-463-9244
                              e-mail: riarc@compuserve.com
                              riarc@compuserve.com

*James Healey, Executive Director*

**3639  Rhode Island Foundation**
1 Union Station
Providence, RI  02903         401-274-4564
                              FAX: 401-331-8085
                              www.rifoundation.org

*Pablo Rodriguez, Chairman*
*Ronald Gallo, President*

**3640  Westerly Chariho Arc**
93 Airport Road
Westerly, RI  02891           401-596-2091
                              FAX: 401-596-3945
                              www.oleancenter.org/website/index.html

*Anthony Vellucci, Executive Director*
*Tina Chernzia, Manager*

A non-profit organization representing and providing services and supports to persons with developmental disabilities and their families throughout Southern Rhode Island and Southeastern Connecticut.

## South Carolina

**3641  Arc of South Carolina**
Arc of United States
1823 Gadsden Street
Columbia, SC  29201           803-748-5020
                              FAX: 803-779-0017
                              e-mail: thearcsc@arcsc.org
                              www.arcsc.org

*Ron Kuebler, Vice President*
*Britnie Hasty, Executive Director*

**3642 Center for Developmental Disabilities**
University of South Carolina
8301 Farrow Road
Columbia, SC 29208
803-935-5231
FAX: 803-935-5059
e-mail: scsis@dccisc.edu
www.scsis.org

*Denise Rivers, Project Coordinator*
*Donald Wuori, MD*

A University Affiliated Program which develops model programs designed to serve persons with disabilities and to train students in fields related to disabilities.

**3643 Colonial Life and Accident Insurance Company Contributions Program**
1200 Colonial Life Boulevard W
Columbia, SC 29210
803-798-7000
FAX: 803-213-7245

*Edwina Carns, Public/Community Relations*
*Donna Northam, Plant Manager*

**3644 Pickens County Arc**
PO Box 1308
Easley, SC 29641
864-859-5416
FAX: 864-859-1157

*Elaine Thena, Executive Director*
*Kaye Golden, Assistant Executive Director*

## Tennessee

**3645 Arc Putnam County**
453 Gould Drive
Cookeville, TN 38506
931-432-5981
FAX: 931-432-5987

**3646 Arc of Anderson County**
PO Box 4823
Oak Ridge, TN 37831
865-481-0550

*Melanie Davis, Executive Director*

**3647 Arc of Davidson County**
Arc of Tennessee
111 N Wilson Boulevard
Nashville, TN 37205
615-321-5699
FAX: 615-322-9184
www.thearctn.org

*Norman Tenenbaum, Executive Director*
*Mary Hildedrand, Assistant Director*

**3648 Arc of Hamilton County**
4613 Brainerd Road
Chattanooga, TN 37411
423-624-6887
800-624-6887
FAX: 423-624-3974
e-mail: arcofhamilton@aol.com

*Shawn Ellis, Executive Director*
*Constance Tiller, Deputy Director*
*Richard Burke, Board President*

Provides assistance to individuals and families with mental retardation and related disabilities, in the form of advocacy, information, and support coordination

**3649 Arc of Tennessee**
44 Vantage Way
Suite 550
Nashville, TN 37228
615-248-5878
800-835-7077
FAX: 615-248-5879
e-mail: pcooper@thearctn.org
www.thearctn.org

*Walter Rogers, Executive Director*
*Peggy Cooper, Operations Manager*

Advocacy, information and support for people with developmental disabilities and their families.

**3650 Arc of Washington County**
2700 S Roan Street
Suite 300b
Johnson City, TN 37601
423-928-9362
FAX: 423-928-7431
e-mail: bill@arcwc.org
www.arcec.org

*Bill Schiers, Executive Director*

Is a non-profit organization that serves individuals with disabilities and their families. They have an independent support coordination service, as well as, early intervention, family support and respite services.

**3651 Arc of Williamson County**
129 W Fowlkes Street
Suite 151
Franklin, TN 37064
615-790-5787
FAX: 615-790-5891
www.thearcofwilliamsoncounty.org

*Sharon Bottoros, President*

**3652 Benwood Foundation**
736 Market Street
Suite 1600
Chattanooga, TN 37402
423-267-4311
FAX: 423-267-9049

*Corinne A Allen, Executive Director*

Giving primarily in the Chattanooga area.

**3653 Community Foundation of Greater Chattanooga**
1270 Market Street
Chattanooga, TN 37402
423-265-0586
FAX: 423-265-0586
e-mail: pcooper@cfgc.org
www.cfgc.org

*Peter T Cooper, President*

**3654 Education and Auditory Research Foundation**
PO Box 330867
Nashville, TN 37203
615-627-2724
800-545-4327
FAX: 615-627-2728
e-mail: info@earfoundation.org
www.earfoundation.org

*Sam Hook, Executive Director*

Provides the general public support services promoting the integration of the hearing and balance impaired into mainstream society; to provide practicing ear specialists continuing medical education courses and related programs specifically regarding rehabilitation and hearing preservation; to educate young people and adults about hearing preservation and early detection of hearing loss, enabling them to prevent at an early age hearing and balance disorders.

**3655 Montgomery County Arc**
PO Box 2145rive
Clarksville, TN 37042
931-905-0900
FAX: 931-905-0900

*Joann Wilson, President*

# Texas

**3656 Abell-Hangar Foundation**
PO Box 430
Midland, TX 79702
432-684-6655
FAX: 423-684-4474
e-mail: ahf@abell-hanger.org

*David L Smith, Chief Executive Officer*
Giving limited to Texas, preferably within the Permian Basin.

**3657 Albert & Bessie Mae Kronkosky Charitable Foundation**

112 E Pecan Street
Suite 830
San Antonio, TX 78205
210-475-9000
888-309-9001
FAX: 210-354-2204
e-mail: kronfdn@kronkosky.org
www.kronkosky.org

*Palmer Moe, Executive Director*
*Janet Clissord, Executive Assistant*

**3658 American Foundation for the Blind: Southwest**
260 Treadway Plaza
Dallas, TX 75235
214-352-7222
FAX: 903-352-3214
e-mail: dallas@afb.net
www.afb.org

*Mary Ann Siller, National Education Consultant*
*Judy Scott, Executive Director*

**3659 Arc of Texas**
Arc of United States
8001 Centre Park Drive
Austin, TX 78754
512-454-6694
800-252-9729
FAX: 512-454-4956
e-mail: secretary@thearcoftexas.org
www.thearcoftexas.com

*Mike Bright, Executive Director*
*Beverly Main, Chief Financial Officer*

**3660 Arch and Stella Rowan Foundation**
307 W 7th Street
Fort Worth, TX 76102
817-336-2679
FAX: 817-336-2679

*Alice B Myatt, Secretary*

**3661 BA and Elinor Steinhagen Benevolent Trust**
Chase Bank of Texas
PO Box 3928
Beaumont, TX 77704
FAX: 409-880-1437

*Jean Monica, Vice President*

**3662 Brown Foundation**
PO Box 130646
Houston, TX 77219
713-523-6867
FAX: 713-523-2917
e-mail: bfi@brownfoundation.org
www.brownfoundation.org

*Nancy Pittman, Executive Director*
*Pam Prasseux, Grants Director*
Giving primarily in Texas, with emphasis on Houston.

**3663 Burlington Northern Foundation**
777 Main Street
Fort Worth, TX 76102
817-878-2000
FAX: 800-677-4816

*Beverly Edwards, President*
*Becky Blankenship, Administrator*
Giving primarily in the areas of company operations, included, but not limited to the areas of civic service, culture and the arts, education, federated, human service and youth.

**3664 Burnett Foundation**
801 Cherry Street
Suite 1585
Fort Worth, TX 76102
817-877-3344

*Thomas F Beech, Executive VP*
*V Agather, Executive Director*

**3665 CH Foundation**
PO Box 94038
Lubbock, TX 79493
806-792-0448
FAX: 806-792-7824

*Nelda Thompson, Secretary*

**3666 Cockrell Foundation**
1000 Main Street
Suite 3250
Houston, TX 77002
713-209-7300
e-mail: foundation@cockrell.com
www.cockrell.com

*Jennifer Delaney, Assistant to the Board*
*M Nancy Williams, Executive VP*
Purpose is for giving for higher education at the University of Texas at Austin; support also for cultural programs, social services, youth services and health care. Limitations are giving in Houston, Texas and no grants are awarded to individuals.

**3667 Communities Foundation of Texas**
5500 Caruth Haven Lane
Dallas, TX 75225
214-750-4222
FAX: 214-750-4210
e-mail: jsmith@cftexas.org
www.cftexas.org

*Michael J Redfearn, VP Finance*
*Marcia Williams-Godwin, VP Administration*
*Brent Christopher, Manager*
Giving in the Dallas area.

**3668 Community Foundation of the Metropolitan Tarrant County**
306 W 7th Street
Suite 306
Fort Worth, TX 76102
817-877-0702
FAX: 817-877-1215
e-mail: hdowd@cfmtx.org
www.cfmtx.org

*Homer M Dowd, President*
*Melissa Saniuk, Director of Finance*

**3669  Cullen Foundation**
601 Jefferson Street
40th Floor
Houston, TX  77002                              713-651-8837
                                           FAX: 713-651-2374

*Alan M Stewart, Executive Director*

Grants are restricted to Texas-based organizations for programs
in Texas, primarily in the Houston area.

**3670  Curtis & Doris K Hankamer Foundation**
9039 Katy Fwy
Suite 530
Houston, TX  77024                           713-461-8140

*Gregory A Herbst, Manager*

**3671  Dallas Foundation**
900 Jackson Street
Dallas, TX  75202                               214-741-9898
                                           FAX: 214-741-9848
                              e-mail: info@dallasfoundation.org
                                       www.dallasfoundation.org

*Mary M Jalonick, Executive Director*
*Cathy McNally, Program Manager*

**3672  David D & Nona S Payne Foundation**
436 Hughes Street
Pampa, TX  79065                             806-665-7281

*Adelaide S Colwell, Secretary*
*Mark Buzzard, Partner*

**3673  El Paso Natural Gas Foundation**
PO Box 2511
Houston, TX  77252                              713-420-2878
                                           FAX: 713-420-5312
                                e-mail: foundation@elpaso.com
                                              www.elpaso.com

*Douglas Foshee, President/CEO*
*Bill Baerg, Manager And Investor Relations*

**3674  Epilepsy Foundation of Greater North Texas**
2906 Swiss Avenue
Dallas, TX  75204                               214-823-8809
                                                800-447-7778
                               e-mail: contactus@efgnt.org
                                              www.efgnt.org

*Robert Miller, President*
*Kathlyn Hampton, Vice President*

**3675  Epilepsy Foundation of Southeast Texas**
2630 Fountain View Drive
Suite 3210
Houston, TX  77057                              713-789-6295
                                                888-548-9716
                                           FAX: 713-789-5628
                                e-mail: dstahlhut@efset.org
                                              www.efset.org

*Donna Stahlhut, Executive Director*

**3676  Epilepsy Foundation: Central and South Texas**
10615 Perrin Beitel Road
Suite 602
San Antonio, TX  78217                          210-653-5353
                                                888-606-5353
                                              www.efcst.org

*Judy Allen, President*
*Neal Shaver, Vice President*
*Sindi Rosales, Executive Director*

**3677  Gil and Dody Weaver Foundation**
500 W 7th Street
Suite 1714
Fort Worth, TX  76102                        817-877-1712

*William R Weaver*

**3678  Harris and Eliza Kempner Fund**
2201 Market Street
Suite 601
Galveston, TX  77550                            409-762-1603
                                           FAX: 409-762-5435
                                          www.kempnerfund.org

*Barbara K Crews, Executive Director*

**3679  Henry & Tommy Lehmann Charitable Foundation**
PO Box 223
Giddings, TX  78942                          979-542-3636

*Jake Jacobson, Chairperson*

**3680  Hesta Stuart Christian Charitable Trust**
Bank One Texas N A
PO Box 2050
Fort Worth, TX  76113                        817-884-4151

                                             www.bankone.com

*Robert Lansford, Trust Officer*

**3681  Hillcrest Foundation**
Bank of America
PO Box 830241
Dallas, TX  75283                            214-740-1728

*Daniel Kelly, Vice President*
*Shannon James, Manager*

**3682  Hoblitzelle Foundation**
5956 Sherry Lane
Suite 901
Dallas, TX  75225                            214-373-0462

                                            www.hoblitzelle.org

*Paul W Harris, Executive Vice President*

**3683  Houston Endowment**
600 Travis Street
Suite 6400
Houston, TX  77002                              713-238-8100
                                           FAX: 713-238-8101
                                       www.houstonendowment.org

*H Nelson III, President*

**3684  John G & Marie S Kennedy Memorial Foundati on**
1700 First City Tower i I
Corpus Christi, TX  78478

**3685  John S Dunn Research Foundation**
3355 W Alabama Street
Suite 702
Houston, TX  77098                           713-626-0368

*Lloyd J Gregory Jr MD, Executive VP*
*John Dunn, President*

**3686  Kent Waldrep National Paralysis Foundation**
16415 Addison Road
Suite 550
Addison, TX  75001                    972-248-7100
                                      877-724-2873
                              FAX: 972-248-7313
                   e-mail: lkoen@spinalvictory.org
                              www.spinalvictory.org

*Lisa Koen, Office Manager/Media Coordinator*

Not-for-profit organization dedicated to raising funds for research to find a cure for paralysis caused by brain injury, spinal cord injury, or stroke. Educational materials include brochures and a quarterly newsletter.

**3687  Lola Wright Foundation**
PO Box 1138
Georgetown, TX  78627                  512-869-2574

*Wilford Flowers, President*
*Paul Hilgers, Vice President*
*Sandra Donnell, Manager*

**3688  Marcia & Otto Koehler Foundation**
Bank of America
PO Box 121
San Antonio, TX  78291                 210-637-8800

*Gregg Muenster, Senior Vice President*
*Jesse Ramos, Manager*

**3689  Meadows Foundation**
3003 Swiss Avenue
Dallas, TX  75204                      214-826-9431
                                       800-826-9431
                              e-mail: grants@mfi.org
                                      www.mfi.org

*Robert A Meadows, Chairman*
*John W Broadfoot, Director*
*Linda Evans, Chief Executive Officer*

**3690  Moody Foundation**
2302 Post Office Street
Suite 704
Galveston, TX  77550                   409-763-5333
                              FAX: 409-763-5564
                                      www.moody.org

*Peter M Moore, Grants Director*
*Francis Moody Dahlberg, Executive Director*
*Harold MacDonald, Chief Executive Officer*

**3691  Pearle Vision Foundation**
2534 Royal Lane
Dallas, TX  75229                      214-821-7770

*Trina Parasiliti, Secretary*
*Leo Priolo, Owner*

**3692  Rockwell Foundation**
1360 S Post Oak Road
Suite 780
Houston, TX  77056                     713-629-9022
                              FAX: 713-629-7702

*R Terry Bell, President*

**3693  San Antonio Area Foundation**
110 Broadway Street
Suite 230
San Antonio, TX  78205                 210-225-2243
                              FAX: 210-225-1980
                      e-mail: info@saafdn.org
                                      www.saafdn.org

*Raymond Carvajal, President*
*Pat Wilson, Vice President*
*Clarence Williams, Chief Executive Officer*

**3694  Shell Oil Company Foundation**
PO Box 2099
Houston, TX  77252                     281-544-7171
                              FAX: 713-241-3329
             e-mail: socfoundation@shellus.com
                              www.countonshell.com

*Ah Myresty, Vice President*
*BL McHam, Executive Director*

A not-for-profit foundation funded by donations from Shell Oil Company and other participating Shell companies and subsidiaries.

**3695  South Texas Charitable Foundation**
PO Box 2459
Victoria, TX  77902                    512-573-4383

*Rayford L Keller, Secretary*

**3696  Sterling-Turner Foundation**
815 Walker Street
Suite 1543
Houston, TX  77002                     713-237-1117
                              FAX: 713-223-4638
             e-mail: patricia@turnerfoundation.org
                      www.sterlingturnerfoundation.org

*Eyvonne Moser, Executive Director*
*Patricia Turner, Assistant Director*

**3697  Swalm Foundation**
PO Box 1248
New Ulm, TX  78950                     281-497-5280
                              FAX: 281-497-7340

*Miriam Minkoff, Secretary*

**3698  TLL Temple Foundation**
109 Temple Boulevard
Lufkin, TX  75901                      936-639-5197

                      e-mail: wcorley@tlltf.com

*A Wayne Corley, Executive Director*
*Buddy Zeagler, Assistant Executive Director*

**3699  Vale-Asche Foundation**
2001 Kirby Drive
Suite 1010
Houston, TX  77019                     713-520-7334
                              FAX: 713-520-6208

*Vale-asche Russell, President*

**3700  William Stamps Farish Fund**
1100 Louisiana Street
Suite 1250
Houston, TX  77002                     713-757-7300

*Terry Ward, Manager*
Primary giving in Texas.

## Utah

**3701  Arc of Utah**
155 S 300 W
Suite 201
Salt Lake City, UT  84101
801-364-5060
800-371-3060
FAX: 801-364-6030
e-mail: thearc@arcutah.com
www.arcutah.com

*Douglas Hathaway, Executive Director*
*Melba Gibson, Donor Services Manager*

**3702  Ben B and Iris M Margolis Foundation**
First Security Bank of Utah
PO Box 628
Salt Lake City, UT  84110
801-350-5583

*Julie Webster*

**3703  Marriner S Eccles Foundation**
79 S Main Street
Salt Lake City, UT  84111
801-532-0934

*Shannon K Toronto*

**3704  Questar Corporation Contributions Program**
PO Box 45433
Salt Lake City, UT  84145
801-324-5000
FAX: 801-324-5483
www.questar.com

*Janice Bates, Director Community Affairs*
*Keith Rattie, Chief Executive Officer*

## Vermont

**3705  Vermont Community Foundation**
PO Box 30
Middlebury, VT  05753
802-388-3355
FAX: 802-388-3398
e-mail: info@vermontcf.org
www.vermontcf.org

*Vicky Young, Chairman*
*Kathy Hoyt, Vice President*
*David Rahr, President*

## Virginia

**3706  Arc of Virginia**
2025 E Main Street
Suite 120
Richmond, VA  23223
804-649-8481
FAX: 804-649-3585
e-mail: thearc@arcofva.org
www.arcofva.org

*Nita Grignol, President*
*Jeannie Cummins, Vice President*
*Clarissa Riely, Executive Director*

**3707  Bell Atlantic Foundation**
1310 N Court House Road
Arlington, VA  22201
703-524-9761
FAX: 703-974-0131
www.foundation.verizon.com/04014.shtml

Concentrates efforts on programs that support its vision to produce more scientifically and technically literate population effecting measurable improvements in the way pre-collegiate science, math and technology education is delivered to and understood by students.

**3708  Camp Foundation**
PO Box 813
Franklin, VA  23851
757-562-3439

*Bobby B Worrell, Chief Executive Officer*

**3709  Community Foundation of Richmond & Central Virginia**
7325 Beaufont Springs Drive
Suite 210
Richmond, VA  23225
804-330-7400
FAX: 804-330-5992
www.tcfrichmond.org

*Darcy S Oman, President*

**3710  Gannett Foundation**
1100 Wilson Boulevard
30th Floor
Arlington, VA  22234
703-271-8330
FAX: 703-558-3819
e-mail: isimpson@gcil.gannett.com
www.gannett.com

*Irma Simpson, Manager*

**3711  Greater Lynchburg Community Trust**
Federal Fidelity
PO Box 714
Lynchburg, VA  24505
434-845-6500
FAX: 434-845-6530
e-mail: glct@inmind.com

*Stuart J Turille, Executive Director*
*George Murphy, President*

**3712  John Randolph Foundation**
PO Box 1606
Hopewell, VA  23860
804-458-2239
FAX: 804-458-3754
e-mail: jrf@covad.net
www.johnrandolphfoundation.org

*Lisa Sharpe, Executive Director*
*Diane Lowder, Assistant Director*

**3713  Norfolk Foundation**
1 Commercial Place
Suite 1410
Norfolk, VA  23510
757-622-7951
FAX: 757-622-1751
e-mail: Info@norfolkf.org
www.norfolk.org

*Angelica Light, Executive Director*
*Man Edgerton, VP Development*

**3714  Robey W Estes Family Foundation**
Robey W Estes Jr
PO Box 25612
Richmond, VA  23260
804-353-1900

*Robey Estes Jr, Chief Executive Officer*

**3715  Virginia Beach Foundation**
PO Box 4329
Virginia Beach, VA  23454
757-422-5249
FAX: 757-422-1849
fdncenter.org/grantmaker/vbf

*Ted Clarkson, Executive Director*

**3716  W Alton Jones Foundation**
232 E High Street
Charlottesville, VA  22902

434-245-5838
FAX: 434-295-1648
www.whn.org

# Washington

**3717  Arc of Washington State**
2600 Martin Way E
Suite B
Olympia, WA  98506

360-357-5596
888-754-8798
FAX: 360-357-3279
e-mail: info@arcwa.org
www.arcwa.org

*Sue Elliott, Executive Director*
*Jackie Thomason, Assistant Director*

**3718  Ben B Cheney Foundation**
3110 Ruston Way
Suite A
Tacoma, WA  98402

253-572-2442
FAX: 253-572-2902
e-mail: Info@benbcheneyfoundation.org
www.bebncheneyfoundation.org

*Brad Cheney, President*

**3719  Foundation Northwest**
221 N Wall Street
Suite 624
Spokane, WA  99201

509-624-2606
888-267-5606
FAX: 509-624-2608
e-mail: admin@foundationnw.org
www.foundationnw.org

*Mark Hurtubise, President*

**3720  Glaser Foundation**
2601 Elliott Avenue
Seattle, WA  98121

206-728-1050
FAX: 206-728-1123

*Martin Collier, Executive Director*
*Leslie Donald, Manager*

**3721  Greater Tacoma Community Foundation**
PO Box 1995
Tacoma, WA  98401

253-383-5622
FAX: 253-272-8099
e-mail: margy@gtcf.org

*Margy McGroarty*
*Rose Lincoln, President*

**3722  Greater Wenatchee Community Foundation**
PO Box 3332
Wenatchee, WA  98807

509-662-8580
FAX: 509-664-9569

*Raymond Taylor, President/CEO*

**3723  Medina Foundation**
801 2nd Avenue
Suite 1300
Seattle, WA  98104

206-652-8783

e-mail: info@medinafoundation.org
www.medinafoundation.org

*Tricia Mckay, Executive Director*
*Katie Heinrich, Programs/Operations Officer*
*Nick MacPhee, Programs Officer*

A family foundation that works to foster positive change in the Greater Puget Sound area. The Foundation strives to improve the human condition by supporting organizations that provide critical services to those in need.

**3724  Norcliffe Foundation**
999 3rd Avenue
Suite 1006
Seattle, WA  98104

206-682-4820
FAX: 206-682-4821
e-mail: arline@thenorcliffefoundation.com
www.thenorcliffefoundation.com

*Arline Hefferline, Foundation Manager*

Geographic area of funding limited to the Puget Sound Region in and around Seattle, Washington.

**3725  Stewardship Foundation**
PO Box 1278
Tacoma, WA  98401

253-620-1340
FAX: 253-572-2721
e-mail: info@stewardshipfdn.org
www.stewardshipfdn.org

*Cary A Paine, Executive Director*
*William T Weyerhaeuser, Chairman*

Christian, evangelical organizations - national or international impact.

**3726  Weyerhaeuser Company Foundation**
PO Box Ch1132
Tacoma, WA  98477

253-474-8888
FAX: 253-924-3658

*Karen Veitenhans, Finance Manager*
*Scott Gardner, Manager*

Although the foundation does fund programs for disabled persons from time to time, it is not a specific priority for the foundation. Since it was formed in 1948, the foundation has given more than $81.1 million to nonprofit organizations and is one of the oldest funds for corporate philanthropy in the country. Nearly all of its contributions have been made within the communities where Weyerhaeuser employees live and work and awards approximately 600 grants annually.

# West Virginia

**3727  Bernard McDonough Foundation**
311 4th Street
Parkersburg, WV  26101

304-424-6280
FAX: 304-424-6281

*James Wakley, President*
*Bob Stephen, Executive Vice President*

# Wisconsin

**3728  Arc of Dane County**
1320 Mendota Street
Suite 111a
Madison, WI  53714

608-257-9738

e-mail: arcdane@chorus.net

*Ken Hobbes, Executive Director*

**3729 Arc of Dunn County**
Arc Of United States
538 Woodridge Court
Menomonie, WI 54751
715-235-7373
FAX: 715-233-3565
e-mail: thearc@wwt.net

*Kathy Lausted, Executive Director*
*Joann Knutson, Residential Director*
Advocating for the rights of citizens with disabilities.

**3730 Arc of Eau Claire**
515 S Barstow Street
Eau Claire, WI 54701
715-834-7204
FAX: 715-834-7416
e-mail: thearcec@execpc.com

*Babara Shafer, Executive Director*

**3731 Arc of Outagamie County**
633 W Wisconsin Avenue
Appleton, WI 54911
920-731-9831
FAX: 920-731-9850

*Barb Vanharen, Executive Director*

**3732 Arc of Racine County**
1220 Mound Avenue
Suite 319
Racine, WI 53404
262-634-6303
FAX: 262-635-2640

*Sandra Engel, Executive Director*

**3733 Arc of Wisconsin Disability Association**
600 Williamson Street
Suite J
Madison, WI 53703
608-251-9272
877-272-8400
FAX: 608-251-1403
e-mail: arcw@itis.com
www.arc-wisconsin.org

*Jim Hoegmeier, Executive Director*
*Ginny Lukken, Administrative Coordinator*

The Arc-Wisconsin strives to be a major force in advocating and promoting self-determined quality of life opportunities for poeple with developmental and related disabilities and their families.

**3734 Faye McBeath Foundation**
1020 N Broadway
Milwaukee, WI 53202
414-272-2626
FAX: 414-272-6235
e-mail: mcbeath@execpc.com

*Sarah M Dean, Executive Director*

**3735 Helen Bader Foundation**
233 N Water Street
Milwaukee, WI 53202
414-224-6464
FAX: 414-244-1441
e-mail: info@hbf.org
www.hbf.org

*Daniel J Bader, President*

**3736 Johnson Controls Foundation**
PO Box 591
Milwaukee, WI 53201
414-476-2341
800-333-2222
FAX: 414-228-3200
e-mail: webmaster@jci.com
www.johnsoncontrols.com

*John Barth, Chairman/Chief Executive Officer*
*John Fiori, Executive Vice President*
*John Jensen, President*

Organized and directed to be operated for charitable purposes which include the distribution and application of financial support to soundly managed and operated organizations or causes which are fundamentally philanthropic.

**3737 Lynde and Harry Bradley Foundation**
1241 N Franklin Place
Milwaukee, WI 53202
414-291-9915
FAX: 414-291-9991
www.bradleyfdn.org

*Michael W Grebe, President/CEO*
*Daniel Schmidt, Executive Vice President*

The Foundation's programs support limited, competent government; a dynamic marketplace for economic, intellectual and cultural activity; a vigorus defense at home and abroad, of American ideas and institutions; and scholarly studies and academic achievement.

**3738 Milwaukee Foundation**
1020 N Broadway
Milwaukee, WI 53202
414-272-5805
FAX: 414-272-6235
e-mail: milwfdn@execpc.com
www.greatermilwaukeefoundation.org

*Douglas M Jansson, Executive Director*

**3739 Northwestern Mutual Life Foundation**
720 E Wisconsin Avenue
Milwaukee, WI 53202
414-665-1800
800-388-8123
FAX: 414-665-2199
www.northwesternmutual.com

*Edward Zore, Chief Executive Officer*
*Fredric H Sweet, Executive Vice President*

**3740 Patrick and Anna M Cudahy Fund**
PO Box 11978
Milwaukee, WI 53211
414-271-6020
FAX: 847-475-0679
e-mail: jborcher@ix.netcom.com
www.cudahyfund.org

*Judith L Borchers, Executive Director*

**3741 SB Waterman & E Blade Charitable Foundation**
Marshall & Ilsley Trust Company
PO Box 2980
Milwaukee, WI 53201
414-287-8700
FAX: 414-298-8097

*Thomas C Boettcher*
*Kenneth Krei, Chief Executive Officer*

# Wyoming

**3742 Arc of Wyoming**
PO Box 393
Casper, WY 82602
307-577-4913
FAX: 307-577-4014

*Festi Moon, President*
*Toni Hutchison, Executive Director*

## Funding Directories

**3743 AIDS Funding**
Foundation Center
79 5th Avenue
New York, NY 10003

212-620-4230
800-424-9836
FAX: 212-807-3677
e-mail: ajt@fdncenter.org
www.fdncenter.org

*Sara Engelhardt, President*
*Cheryl Loe, Director of Communications*

Gives vital information on over 450 foundations, corporate giving programs, and public charities; more than twice the number of grantmakers appeared in the last edition. All the grantmakers listed have proven their commitment by funding projects such as direct relief, medical research, legal aid and other programs to empower AIDS victims and combat the disease. *$60.00*

*ISBN 0-87954-82-5*

**3744 Chronicle Guide to Grants**
Chronicle Guide to Grants
1255 23rd Street NW
Washington, DC 20037

202-331-4267
800-287-6072
FAX: 202-659-2236

*Edward R Weidlein, Publisher*

A computerized research tool, on floppy disks or a CD-ROM, for immediate use on any IBM compatible personal computer. Offers electronic listings of 10,000 grants from hundreds of foundations, with a subscription that offers 1,000 plus new listings every two months. Each listing offers grant information as well as names, addresses and phone numbers of the grant-making organizations. *$295.00*

**3745 College Student's Guide to Merit and Other No-Need Funding**
Reference Service Press
5000 Windplay Drive
Suite 4
El Dorado Hills, CA 95762

916-939-9620
FAX: 916-939-9626
e-mail: findaid@aol.com
www.rspfunding.com

*Gail Schlachter, Director/Owner*

More than 1,200 funding opportunities for currently-enrolled or returning college students are described in this directory. *$32.00*

*450 pages*
*ISBN 1-588410-41-2*

**3746 Community Health Funding Report**
C D Publications
8204 Fenton Street
Silver Spring, MD 20910

301-588-6380
800-666-6380
FAX: 301-588-0591
e-mail: chf@cdpublications.com
www.cdpublications.com

*Michael Gerecht, Publisher/President*

Gives the widest range of funding information available anywhere, including public and private grant announcements, reports on successful health programs nationwide, interviews with grant officials, plus national news on health policy topics affecting various organizations. *$339.00*

*18 pages BiWeekly*

**3747 Corporate Foundation Files**
Foundation Center
79 5th Avenue
Department Ze
New York, NY 10003

212-620-4230
800-424-9836
FAX: 212-807-3677
www.fdncenter.org

*Sara Engelhardt, President*

Provides an even more updated in-depth examination of over 250 of America's top corporate foundations, grantmakers with assets of $1 million plus or annual giving of $100,000 or more. This book supplements information presented on leading corporate foundations and provides 4-6 page reports with full background data on each Corporation and foundation structure plus a complete grants analysis and listing of sample grants awarded to nonprofit organizations. *$125.00*

*ISBN 0-87954-36-1*

**3748 Corporate Foundation Profiles**
Foundation Center
79 5th Avenue
Department Ze
New York, NY 10003

212-620-4230
800-424-9836
FAX: 212-807-3677
www.fdncenter.org

*Sara Engelhardt, President*

Offers foundation portraits, grants analysis and grants list. *$135.00*

**3749 Crime and Justice**
Foundation Center
79 5th Avenue
New York, NY 10003

212-620-4230
800-424-9836
FAX: 212-807-3677
e-mail: ajt@fdncenter.org
www.fdncenter.org

*Sara Engelhardt, President*
*Cheryl Loe, Director of Communications*

This comprehensive work examines foundation funding for programs involved with crime prevention, juvenile justice, law enforcement, correction facilities, rehabilitation and victim assistance. This book looks at significant developments in the criminal justice field, changing public perceptions of crime and cuts in governmental expenditures. *$35.00*

*ISBN 0-87954-90-6*

**3750 Directory of Financial Aids for Women**
Reference Service Press
5000 Windplay Drive
Suite 4
El Dorado Hills, CA 95762

916-939-9620
FAX: 916-939-9626
e-mail: findaid@aol.com
www.rspfunding.com

*Gail Ann Schlachter, Author/Owner*
*David R Weber, Author*

Funding programs listed support study, research, travel, training, career development, or innovative effort at any level; descriptions of more than 1,700 funding programs - representing billions of dollars in financial aid set aside for women; also an annotated bibliography of 60 key directories that identify even more financial aid opportunities and a set of indexes that let you search the directory by title, sponser, researching, tenability, subject, and deadline. *$45.00*

*578 pages Biennial 1999*
*ISBN 1-588410-00-5*

**3751  Directory of Japanese Giving**
79 Fifth Avenue 16th Street
New York, NY  10003

212-620-4230
800-424-9836
FAX: 212-807-3677
e-mail: orders@fdncenter.org
www.fdncenter.org

*Laura Cascio, Fulfillment Manager*
*Cheryl Lee, Director of Communications*
*Sara Engelhardt, President*

Offers crucial information on the fastest growing sector of corporate philanthropy. *$190.00*

**3752  Directory of New and Emerging Foundations**
Foundation Center
79 5th Avenue
Department Ze
New York, NY  10003

212-620-4230
800-424-9836
FAX: 212-807-3677
e-mail: aj@fdncenter.org
www.fdncenter.org

*Sara Engelhardt, President*

Provides information on over 3,000 foundations that have incorporated as grantmaking institutions in the United States. *$95.00*

**3753  Directory of Venture Capital Firms**
Grey House Publishing
PO Box 860
Millerton, NY  12546

518-789-8700
800-562-2139
FAX: 518-789-0556
e-mail: books@greyhouse.com
www.greyhouse.com

*Leslie Mackenzie, Publisher*
*Richard Gottlieb, President*

This annual directory includes more than 2,000 active venture capital and private equity firms in both the US and overseas. Each detailed profile includes fund size, portfolio companies, investment criteria and key executives.
*Annual*

**3754  Disability Funding News**
C D Publications
8204 Fenton Street
Silver Spring, MD  20910

301-588-6380
800-666-6380
FAX: 301-588-6385
e-mail: info@cdpublications.com
www.cdpublications.com

*Jim Rogers, Editor*
*Michael Gerecht, President*

Offers comprehensive listings on federal grants, detailed listings of foundations, legal news, grant-seeking techniques and more. *$249.00*
*18 pages SemiWeekly*
*ISSN 1069-13 9*

**3755  Federal Funding to Fight AIDS**
Government Information Services
4301 Fairfax Drive
Suite 875
Arlington, VA  22203

703-465-9100
800-876-0226
FAX: 800-926-2012

Describes all the federal government grants and financial aid programs to fight the AIDS epidemic. Includes agency-by-agency description of $1.9 billion in available grants, including the name, address and telephone number of the federal official responsible for each program. *$57.00*

*74 pages Special Report*

**3756  Federal Grants & Contracts Weekly**
Capitol Publications
1333 H Street NW
Suite 100e
Washington, DC  20005

202-223-3000
800-655-5597
FAX: 703-736-6501

*Pam Moore, Editor*
*Claudia Moran, Marketing Manager*
*Merle Morgan, President*

The latest funding announcements of federal grants for project opportunities in research, training and services. Provides profiles of key programs, tips on seeking grants, updates on legislation and regulations, budget developments and early alerts to upcoming funding opportunities. *$369.00*
*Weekly*

**3757  Financial Aid for Asian Americans**
Reference Service Press
5000 Windplay Drive
Suite 4
El Dorado Hills, CA  95762

916-939-9620
FAX: 916-939-9626
e-mail: findaid@aol.com
www.rspfunding.com

*Gail Ann Schlachter, President/Owner*
*R David Weber, Editor-in-Chief*

This is the source to use if you are looking for financial aid for Asian Americans; nearly 1,000 funding opportunities are described. *$35.00*
*336 pages 1999*
*ISBN 1-588410-02-1*

**3758  Financial Aid for Hispanic Americans**
Reference Service Press
5000 Windplay Drive
Suite 4
El Dorado Hills, CA  95762

916-939-9620
FAX: 916-939-9626
e-mail: findaid@aol.com
www.rspfunding.com

*Gail Ann Schlachter, Author/Owner*
*R David Weber, Author*

Nearly 1,300 funding programs open to Americans of Mexican, Puerto Rican, Central American, or other Latin American heritage are described here. *$37.50*
*472 pages 1999*
*ISBN 1-588410-03-X*

**3759  Financial Aid for Native Americans**
Reference Service Press
5000 Windplay Drive
Suite 4
El Dorado Hills, CA  95762

916-939-9620
FAX: 916-939-9626
e-mail: findaid@aol.com
www.rspfunding.com

*Gail Ann Schlachter, Author/Owner*
*R David Weber, Author*

Detailed information is provided on 1,500 funding opportunities open to American Indians, Native Alaskans, and Native Pacific Islanders. *$37.50*

*546 pages*
*ISBN 1-588410-04-8*

**3760  Financial Aid for Research and Creative Ac tivities
Abroad**
Reference Service Press
5000 Windplay Drive
Suite 4
El Dorado Hills, CA  95762                    916-939-9620
                                        FAX: 916-939-9626
                                   e-mail: findaid@aol.com
                                        www.rspfunding.com

*Gail Ann Schlachter, Author/Owner*

Described here are 1,200 funding programs (scholarships, fellowships, grants, etc.) available to support research, professional, or creative activities abroad. *$45.00*
                *378 pages*
                *ISBN 1-588410-82-5*

**3761  Financial Aid for Veterans, Military Personnel and
their Dependents**
Reference Service Press
5000 Windplay Drive
Suite 4
El Dorado Hills, CA  95762                    916-939-9620
                                        FAX: 916-939-9626
                                   e-mail: findaid@aol.com
                                        www.rspfunding.com

*Gail Ann Schlachter, Author/Owner*
*David R Weber, Author*

According to Reference Book Review, this directory (with its
1,100 entries) is the most comprehensive guide available on the
subject. *$40.00*
                *392 pages*
                *ISBN 1-588410-43-9*

**3762  Financial Aid for the Disabled and their Families**
Reference Service Press
5000 Windplay Drive
Suite 4
El Dorado Hills, CA  95762                    916-939-9620
                                        FAX: 916-939-9626
                                  e-mail: info@rspfunding.com
                                        www.rspfunding.com

*Gail Ann Schlachter, Author/Owner*
*R David Weber, Author*

Organized to easily identify funding opportunities not only by
type, but by specific subject coverage, sponsoring organization,
program title, residency requirements, where the money can be
spent, and even deadline date; includes detailed program descriptions. Program profiles indicate purpose, eligibility, financial data, duration, special features, limitations, number
awarded, and application. Complete contact information is also
provided including fax numbers, toll-free, and email/website.
*$37.50*
                *508 pages Every other yr. 1999*
                *ISBN 1-588410-01-3*

**3763  Foundation & Corporate Grants Alert**
Capitol Publications
1333 H Street NW
Suite 100e
Washington, DC  20005                         202-223-3000
                                               800-655-5597
                                        FAX: 703-736-6501

*Patricia Hagmann, Editor*
*Claudia Moran, Marketing Manager*
*Merle Morgan, President*

A complete guide to foundation and corporate grant opportunities for nonprofit organizations. Tracks developments and
trends in funding and provides notification of changes in foundations' funding priorities. *$245.00*

*Monthly*
*ISSN 1062-46 6*

**3764  Foundation 1000**
Foundation Center
79 5th Avenue
Department Ze
New York, NY  10003                           212-620-4230
                                               800-424-9836
                                        FAX: 212-691-1828
                                           www.fdncenter.org

*Jeffrey Fulkenstein, Editor*
*Sara Engelhardt, President*

Full profiles of all 1,000 grantmakers across the United States.
*$195.00*

**3765  Foundation Center's User-Friendly Guide**
Foundation Center
79 5th Avenue
Department Ze
New York, NY  10003                           212-620-4230
                                               800-424-9836
                                        FAX: 212-807-3677
                                           www.fdncenter.org

*Sara Engelhardt, President*

This helpful book answers the most commonly asked questions
about fundraising in an upbeat, easy-to-read style. Specifically
designed for novice grantseekers, this publication will lead you
through the maze of unfamiliar jargon and the wide range of research guides used successfully by professional grantseekers
everyday. *$9.95*

                *ISBN 0-87954 -42-6*

**3766  Foundation Directory**
Foundation Center
79 5th Avenue
Department Ze
New York, NY  10003                           212-620-4230
                                               800-424-9836
                                        FAX: 212-807-3677
                                           www.fdncenter.org

*Sara Engelhardt, President*

An expanded, updated version of the fundraising research classic, offers a chance to bolster your prospect files with newly
gathered data on these influential funders: over 7,500 foundation entries and over 1,100 foundations covered for the very first
time in a Foundation Directory. *$140.00*

                *ISBN 0-87954 -45-0*

**3767  Foundation Grants to Individuals**
Foundation Center
79 5th Avenue
Department Ze
New York, NY  10003                           212-620-4230
                                               800-424-9836
                                        FAX: 212-807-3677
                                           www.fdncenter.org

*Sara Engelhardt, President*

The only publication that provides extensive coverage of foundation funding prospects for individual grantseekers. *$40.00*
                *Biennially*

**3768  From the State Capitals: Public Health**
Wakeman/ Walworth
PO Box 7376
Alexandria, VA  22307                         703-768-9600
                                        FAX: 703-768-9690
                              e-mail: newsletters@statecapitals.com
                                        www.statecapitals.com

*Keyes Walworth, Publisher*
*Christine Ryan, Marketing Manager*

Digest of state and municipal health care financing and cost containment measures, includes medical legislation, disease control, etc. *$245.00*
*6 pages*

**3769 Guide to Federal Funding for Child Care and Early Childhood Development**
Government Information Services
4301 Fairfax Drive
Suite 875
Arlington, VA 22203      703-465-9100
800-225-5750
FAX: 703-528-6060

*James J Marshall, Publisher*
*Joel M Drucker, Associate Publisher*

Describes more than 60 federal grant, loan and tax credit programs to assist child care and early childhood development programs. The guide describes more than $25 billion in federal aid for traditional day care, developmental programs such as Head Start and school-based early childhood education programs such as Even Start. *$169.00*
*372 pages 3-Ring Binder*

**3770 Guide to Federal Funding for Hospitals and Health Centers**
The Foundation Center
79 5th Avenue 16th Street
New York, NY 10003      212-620-4230
800-424-9836
FAX: 212-807-3677
www.fdncenter.org

*Laura Cascio, Fulfillment Manager*
*Maggie Morth, Director of Communications*

Describes approximately 150 federal grant and loan programs for hospitals, health centers, and other agencies involved in administering health services. *$297.00*
*958 pages 3-Ring Binder*

**3771 Guide to Federal Funding for Volunteer Programs & Community Service**
Government Information Services
4301 Fairfax Drive
Suite 875
Arlington, VA 22203      703-465-9100
800-225-5750
FAX: 703-528-6060

*James J Marshall, Publisher*
*Joel M Drucker, Associate Publisher*

Guide describes in detail roughly 60 federal programs that provide aid to establish and operate volunteer programs. *$85.00*
*3-Ring Binder*

**3772 High School Senior's Guide to Merit and Ot her No-Need Funding**
Reference Service Press
5000 Windplay Drive
Suite 4
El Dorado Hills, CA 95762      916-939-9620
FAX: 916-939-9626
e-mail: findaid@aol.com
www.rspfunding.com

*Gail Schlachter, Director/Owner*

Here's your guide to 1,100 funding programs that never look at income level when making awards to college bound high school seniors. *$29.95*

*400 pages*
*ISBN 1-588410-44-X*

**3773 How to Pay for Your Degree in Business & Related Fields**
Reference Service Press
5000 Windplay Drive
Suite 4
El Dorado Hills, CA 95762      916-939-9620
FAX: 916-939-9626
e-mail: findaid@aol.com
www.rspfunding.com

*Gail Schlachter, Director/Owner*

If you need funding for an undergraduate or graduate degree in business or related fields, this is the directory to use (500+ funding programs described). *$30.00*
*290 pages*
*ISBN 1-588410-49-8*

**3774 How to Pay for Your Degree in Education & Related Fields**
Reference Service Press
5000 Windplay Drive
Suite 4
El Dorado Hills, CA 95762      916-939-9620
FAX: 916-939-9626
e-mail: findaid@aol.com
www.rspfunding.com

*Gail Schlachter, Director/Owner*

Here's hundreds of funding opportunities available to support undergraduate and graduate students preparing for a career in education, guidance etc. *$30.00*
*250 pages*
*ISBN 1-588410-63-3*

**3775 International Encyclopedia of Foundations**
Foundation Center
79 5th Avenue
New York, NY 10003      212-620-4230
800-424-9836
FAX: 212-807-3677
e-mail: ajt@fdncenter.org
www.fdncenter.org

*Sara Engelhardt, President*
*Cheryl Loe, Director of Communications*

Compiled volume of useful and often hard-to-find information on the history and operation of major foundations located outside the U.S. One of the very few book-length accounts of international foundations in English, the book is made up of 146 historical sketches of the most significant foundations in 31 countries. *$75.00*

*ISBN 0-31325 -83-6*

**3776 Japanese Corporate Connection: A Guide for Fundraisers**
Foundation Center
79 5th Avenue
New York, NY 10003      212-620-4230
800-424-9836
FAX: 212-807-3677
e-mail: ajt@fdncenter.org
www.fdncenter.org

*Sara Engelhardt, President*
*Cheryl Loe, Director of Communications*

Shows how certain U.S. nonprofits have successfully approached major Japanese philanthropics. *$90.00*

**3777 National Data Book of Foundations**
Foundation Center
79 5th Avenue
Department Ze
New York, NY 10003
212-620-4230
800-424-9836
FAX: 212-807-3677
e-mail: fdnonline@fdncenter.org
www.fdncenter.org

*Sara Engelhardt, President*
*Allyson Tuffs, Vice President*

Gives fast access to vital information on 32,000 U.S. foundations, the most complete listing of grantmakers ever published. It reflects the broad scope of this important foundation locator. It can help you quickly develop a list of initial funding prospects from the largest national to the smallest local foundations. *$125.00*

*ISBN 0-87954-85-0*

**3778 National Directory of Corporate Giving**
Foundation Center
79 5th Avenue
New York, NY 10003
212-620-4230
800-424-9836
FAX: 212-807-3677
e-mail: ajt@fdncenter.org
www.fdncenter.org

*Sara Engelhardt, President*
*Cheryl Loe, Director of Communications*

Offers over 2,000 corporate funders, current giving reviews and profiles of sponsoring companies. *$195.00*

**3779 National Guide to Funding Religion**
Foundation Center
79 5th Avenue
New York, NY 10003
212-620-4230
800-424-9836
FAX: 212-807-3677
www.fdncenter.org

*Sara Engelhardt, President*
*Macy Morin, Executive Vice President*

This book gives access to a fundraising guide designed specifically for them. This new subject directory brings together a group of 2,800 foundations and corporate direct giving programs, all of which have a history of funding churches, religious welfare and religious education programs. *$125.00*

*ISBN 0-87954-80-9*

**3780 National Guide to Funding for Children, Youth & Families**
Foundation Center
79 Fifth Avenue 16th Street
New York, NY 10003
212-620-4230
800-424-9836
FAX: 212-807-3677
e-mail: orders@fdncenter.org
www.fdncenter.org

*Sara Engelhardt, President*
*Cheryl Lee, Director of Communications*

Caters specifically to development professionals for organizations serving the needs of children, youth and families. With over 2,400 listings of funding sources, both foundations and direct giving programs and over 8,000 sample grants. *$125.00*

*ISBN 0-87954-91-5*

**3781 National Guide to Funding for Elementary & Secondary Education**
Foundation Center
79 5th Avenue
Department Ze
New York, NY 10003
212-620-4230
800-424-9836
FAX: 212-807-3677
www.fdncenter.org

*Sara Engelhardt, President*

This guide gathers together, in one convenient source, a list of grantmakers committed to improving pre-college education. This book provides full profiles for over 1,400 foundations and corporate direct giving programs. *$125.00*

*ISBN 0-87954-94-9*

**3782 National Guide to Funding for Libraries and Information Services**
Foundation Center
79 5th Avenue
New York, NY 10003
212-620-4230
800-424-9836
FAX: 212-807-3677
e-mail: ajt@fdncenter.org
www.fdncenter.org

*Sara Engelhardt, President*
*Cheryl Loe, Director of Communications*

This guide features a long list of grantmakers that support facilities. This directory provides essential data on over 400 foundations and corporate direct giving programs. In addition, many of these grantmaker entries include grant lists. *$75.00*

*ISBN 0-87954-95-7*

**3783 National Guide to Funding for Women and Girls**
Foundation Center
79 5th Avenue
New York, NY 10003
212-620-4230
800-424-9836
FAX: 212-807-3677
e-mail: ajt@fdncenter.org
www.fdncenter.org

*Sara Engelhardt, President*
*Cheryl Loe, Director of Communications*

Fundraisers who seek support for nonprofits that provide services and advocate women and girls can now turn to this new subject directory. This book offers grantseekers the benefit of over 700 foundations and corporate direct giving program entries. *$95.00*

*ISBN 0-87954-93-0*

**3784 National Guide to Funding in Aging**
Foundation Center
79 5th Avenue
Department Ze
New York, NY 10003
212-620-4230
800-424-9836
FAX: 212-807-3677
www.fdncenter.org

*Sara Engelhardt, President*

Professional fundraisers recognize this book as the premier source of information on the agencies and foundations that support aging projects. This volume covers federal and state programs as well as foundations and other voluntary organizations. *$75.00*

*ISBN 0-87954 -33-7*

**3785  National Guide to Funding in Arts and Culture**
Foundation Center
79 5th Avenue
New York, NY  10003
212-620-4230
800-424-9836
FAX: 212-807-3677
e-mail: ajt@fdncenter.org
www.fdncenter.org

*Sara Engelhardt, President*
*Cheryl Loe, Director of Communications*

Designed specifically to meet the needs of development professionals in the field of arts and culture, this guide thoroughly prepares you for an informed grant search. With over 3,300 listings of foundations and corporate direct giving programs, the volume offers fundraisers in the field an excellent opportunity to increase their funding base. *$125.00*

*ISBN 0-87954 -48-9*

**3786  National Guide to Funding in Health**
Foundation Center
79 5th Avenue
New York, NY  10003
212-620-4230
800-424-9836
FAX: 212-807-3677
www.fdncenter.org

*Sara Engelhardt, President*
*Macy Morin, Executive Vice President*

Contains essential facts on more than 2,500 foundations and corporate direct giving programs, each with a history of awarding grant dollars to hospitals, universities, research centers, community-based facilities, rural health-care projects and a range of other health-related programs and projects. *$125.00*

*ISBN 0-87954 -79-5*

**3787  National Guide to Funding in Higher Education**
Foundation Center
79 5th Avenue
New York, NY  10003
212-620-4230
800-424-9836
FAX: 212-807-3677
e-mail: ajt@fdncenter.org
www.fdncenter.org

*Sara Engelhardt, President*
*Cheryl Loe, Director of Communications*

Designed for those seeking foundation support for higher education, this National Guide allows researchers to immediately find information on top funders in the field. This directory covers nearly 3,000 foundations, all with a history of awarding grants to colleges, universities, graduate programs and research institutes. *$125.00*

*ISBN 0-87954 -90-1*

**3788  New York State Foundations**
Foundation Center
79 5th Avenue
New York, NY  10003
212-620-4230
800-424-9836
FAX: 212-807-3677
www.fdncenter.org

*Sara Engelhardt, President*
*Macy Morin, Executive Vice President*

Provides a complete list of every grantmaking foundation in the state. *$150.00*

**3789  Report on Disability Programs**
Business Publishers
2601 University Boulevard W
Suite 200
Silver Spring, MD 20902
301-587-6300
800-274-6737
FAX: 301-589-8493
e-mail: custserv@bpinews.com
www.bpinews.com

*Leonard Eiser, Publisher*
*Adam Goldstein, President*
*Melissa Reid, Marketing Manager*

Follows all programs and funding sources in education, housing, job training, therapy, Social Security Supplemental Security Income, Medicare, Medicaid and more of importance to persons with disabilities. Also covers the latest on the Americans with Disabilities Act. Publishes a newsletter. *$327.00*
*25x Year*

**3790  Source Book Profiles**
Foundation Center
79 5th Avenue
New York, NY  10003
212-620-4230
800-424-9836
FAX: 212-807-3677
www.fdncenter.org

*Sara Engelhardt, President*
*Macy Morin, Executive Vice President*

Now the fundraising resource that publishes comprehensive portraits of the country's most influential foundations over a two-year cycle offers even more for your research dollars. A database publication which means that it is now more flexible and efficient than ever before, an even more essential part of your philanthropic library. *$350.00*

*ISBN 0-87954 -83-3*

**3791  Student Guide**
US Department of Education
400 Maryland Avenue SW
Washington, DC  20202
202-401-2000
800-872-5376
FAX: 202-401-0689
TTY: 800-437-0833
e-mail: customerservice@inet.ed.gov
www.ed.gov/prog_info/SFA/studentguide

*William J Ryan, Acting Director*
*Margaret Spellings, Chief Executive Officer*

Describes the major student aid programs the US Department of Education administers and gives detailed information about program procedures.
*74 pages Annual*

**3792  Substance Abuse Funding News**
C D Publications
8204 Fenton Street
Silver Spring, MD  20910
301-588-6380
800-666-6380
FAX: 301-588-6385
e-mail: info@cdpublications.com
www.cdpublications.com

*Jim Rogers, Editor*
*Michael Gerecht, Publisher/President*

Newsletter covers private and federal funding opportunities for alcohol, tobacco and drug abuse programs. Plus advice on grantseeking and proposal writing, tips from funding officials and reports on the latest federal and state initives to address substance abuse and related concerns.
*18 pages 2x Month*

## Federal

**3793 Administration on Children, Youth and Families**
U S Department of Health and Human Services
370 L Enfant Promenade
Washington, DC 20201 202-690-7650

www.acf.dhhs.gov
Responsible for federal programs that promote the economic and social well-being of families, children, individuals and communities.

**3794 Administration on Developmental Disabilities**
U S Department of Health and Human Services
370 L Enfant Promenade SW
Mail Stop: HHH 405-D
Washington, DC 20447 202-690-6590
FAX: 202-205-8037
www.acf.hhs.gov/programs/add

*Patricia Morrissey PhD, Commissioner*
*Faith McCormick, Director*

Ensures that individuals with developmental disabilities and their families participate in the design of and have access to culturally competent services, supports, and other assistance and opportunities that promote independence, productivity, and integration and inclusion into the community.

**3795 Administration on the Aging**
U S Department of Health and Human Services
3330 Independence Avenue SW
Washington, DC 20201 202-690-7650
FAX: 202-357-3556
e-mail: AoAInfo@aoa.gov
www.aoa.gov

*Josefina Carbonell, Commissioner*

Administers the Older Americans Act of 1965 to assist states and local communities to develop programs for older persons.

**3796 Americans with Disabilities Act Informatio n**
US Department of Justice
950 Pennsylvania Avenue NW
Washington, DC 20530 202-646-5095
800-574-0301
FAX: 202-307-1197
www.ada.gov
In cooperation with many federal agencies, the ADA assures that Americans with disabilities have the same opportunities as all Americans. To this end, the Justice Department produces publications, sponsors programs and continually reviews the needs of individuals with disabilities.

**3797 Clearinghouse on Disability Information: Office of Special Education & Rehab**
U S Department of Education
330 C Street SW
Room 3132
Washington, DC 20202 202-208-5815
FAX: 202-401-2608
www.ed.gov/OFFICE/OSERS

*Carolyn Corlett, Director*
*John Sherrod, Executive Director*

Provides information to people with disabilities or anyone requesting information, by doing research and providing documents in response to inquiries. The information provided includes areas of federal funding for disability-related programs. Information provided may be useful to disabled individuals and their families, schools and universities, teacher's and/or school administrators, and organizations who have persons with disabilities as clients.

**3798 Committee for Purchase from People Who Are Blind or Severely Disabled**
1421 Jefferson Davis Highway
Suite 10800
Arlington, VA 22202 703-603-7740
FAX: 703-603-0655
e-mail: info@jwod.gov
www.jwod.gov

*Leon A Wilson Jr, Executive Director*
*Patrick Rowe, Deputy Executive Director*
*Robert M Hartt, Manager Legislative Affairs*

A federal agency that administers the Javits-Wagner-O'Day Program, directing federal agencies to purchase products and services from nonprofit agencies that employ people who are blind or have other severe disabilities. Provides a wide range of vocational options to individuals with severe disabilities.

**3799 Equal Opportunity Employment Commission**
1801 L Street NW
Washington, DC 20036 202-663-4900
800-669-4000
e-mail: info@ask.eeoc.gov
www.eeoc.gov

*Carim Dominguez, Chairman*
*Naomi C Earp, Vice Chairman*
*Ida Castro, Manager*

This agency is responsible for drafting and implementing the regulations of Title I of the ADA.

**3800 Federal Communications Commission**
445 12th Street SW
Washington, DC 20554 202-418-0450
888-835-5322
888-225-5322
FAX: 866-418-0232
e-mail: fccinfo@fcc.gov
www.fcc.gov

*Jennifer Simpson, Specialist*
*Gloria Thomas, Manager*

Enforces ADA telecommunications provisions which require that companies offering telephone service to the general public must offer telephone relay services to individuals who use text telephones or similar devices. Also enforces closed captioning rules, hearing compatibility and access to equipment and services for people with disabilities.

**3801 Health Care Financing Administration**
200 Independence Avenue SW
Washington, DC 20201 202-690-6726
FAX: 202-690-6262

*William Roper, Administrator*
*Thomas Scully, President*

Through the Social Security administration, it administers the Medicare program under Title XVIII of the Social Security Act. Administers grants to the states for Medicaid under Title XIX of the Social Security Act for individuals who are medically indigent.

**3802 National Coalition of Federal Aviation Employees with Disabilities**
Federal Aviation Administration
6500 S Mac Authur Street
Oklahoma City, OK 73169 405-954-4709
FAX: 405-954-4490
TTY:405-954-4587
www.faa.gov/acr/ncfaed.htm

*Becky Pritchett, Treasurer*
*Alan Jones, President of Aeronautical Center*

NCFAED is working on: 1) improvement of work conditions for employees; 2) expansion on National Coalition to serve all FAA employees; 3) promote equal opportunity for people with disabilities in the FAA workplace; 4) assist the FAA in its commitment to remove physical and attudinal barriers which inhibit opportunities for people with disabilities; 5) align with internal and external organizations to attract future generations of people with disabilities to the FAA as employees.

**3803    National Council on Disability**
1331 F Street NW
Suite 850
Washington, DC  20004
202-272-2004
FAX: 202-272-2022
e-mail: info@ncd.gov
www.ncd.gov

*Mark Quigley, Communications Director*
*Ethel Briggs, Executive Director*

Federal agency led by 15 members appointed by the President of the United States and confirmed by the United States Senate. The overall purpose of the National Council is to promote policies, programs, practices and procedures that guarantee equal opportunity for all people with disabilities, regardless of the nature of severity of the disability; and to empower people with disabilities to achieve economic self-sufficiency, independent living and integration into all aspects of society.

**3804    National Division of the Blind and Visually Impaired**
330 C Street NW
Washington, DC  20001
202-205-8520

*Chester Avery, Director*

Develops methods, standards and procedures to assist state agencies in the rehabilitation of blind persons. Administers the Randolph-Sheppard Act, which assures priority for blind persons in the operation of vending facilities on federal property and serves as a program manager for the Helen Keller National Center for Youth who are deaf-blind.

**3805    National Institutes of Health: National Eye Institute**
31 Center Drive
Bethesda, MD  20892
301-496-5751
FAX: 301-496-9970
e-mail: kcl@nei.nih.gov
www.nei.nih.gov

*Paul A Sieving, Director*
*Audrey Penn, Executive Director*

Finances intramural and extramural research on eye diseases and vision disorders. Supports training of eye researchers.

**3806    Office of Policy**
Social Security Administration
2100 M Street NW
Washington, DC  20037
202-523-0412
800-772-1213
TTY:800-325-0778
e-mail: concepcion.mcneace@ssa.gov
www.ssa.gov/policy

*Laurence Love, Acting Deputy Commissioner*
*Edward Demarco, Assitant Deputy Commissioner*
*Serge Harrison, Executive Officer*

Administers grants to the states for social services under Title XX of the Social Security Act to welfare recipients and others likely to become them.

**3807    Office of Special Education Programs: Department of Education**
400 Maryland Avenue, SW
Washington, DC  20202
202-245-7468
e-mail: gblumenthal@acs.dhhs.gov
www.ed.gov/osers/osep

*Alexa Posny, Director*
*Patty Guard, Deputy Director*

The Office of Special Education Programs (OSEP) is dedicated to improving results for infants, toddlers, children and youth with disabilities ages birth through 21 by providing leadership and financial support to assist states and local districts.

**3808    President's Committee on People with Intellecutual Disabilities**
U S Department of Health and Human Services
370 L Enfant Promenade SW
Washington, DC  20447
202-619-0364
FAX: 202-205-9519
e-mail: gblumenthal@acf.dhhs.gov
www.acf.dhhs.gov/programs/pcmr

*Dalls Rob Sweezy, Chairperson*
*Sally Atwater, Executive Director*

Formerly the President's Committee on Mental Retardation, a federal advisory committee, estalished by the presidential executive order to adivse the President of the United States and the Secretary of the Department of Health and Human Services on issues concerning citizens with intellectual disabilities, coordinate activities between different federal agencies and assess the impact of their policies upon the lives of citizens with intellectual disabilities and their families.

**3809    Rehabilitative Services Administration**
U S Department of Education
400 Maryland Avenue, SW
Washington, DC  20202
202-245-7468
FAX: 202-205-9874
www.ed.gov

The Rehabilitation Services Administration (RSA) oversees formula and discretionary grant programs that help individuals with physical or mental disabilities to obtain employment and live more independently through the provision of such supports as counseling, medical and psychological services, job training and other individualized services.

**3810    Social Security Administration**
6401 Security Boulevard
Baltimore, MD  21235
410-965-6114
800-772-1213
www.socialsecurity.gov

*Martha Mcsteen, Acting Commissioner*
*Bill Vitek, Manager*

Administers old age, survivors, and disability insurance programs under Title II of the Social Security Act. Also administers the federal income maintenance program under Title XVI of the Social Security Act. Maintains network of local/regional offices nationwide.

**3811    US Department of Education: Office of Civil Rights**
300 C Street NW
Room 5414
Washington, DC  20202
202-208-5815
800-421-3481

*John Sherrod, Executive Director*

Prohibits discrimination on the basis of disability in programs and activities funded by the Department of Education. Investigates complaints and provides technical assistance to individuals and entities with rights and responsibilities under Section 504.

**3812 US Department of Education: Office of Civil Rights**
U S Department of Education
400 Maryland Avenue SW
Washington, DC 20202
202-401-2000
FAX: 202-401-0689
www.ed.gov

*Margaret Spellings, Chief Executive Officer*

Prohibits discrimination on the basis of disability in programs and activities funded by the Department of Education. Investigates complaints and provides technical assistance to individuals and entities with rights and responsibilities under Section 504.

**3813 US Department of Justice**
Civil Rights Division/ Disability Rights Section
950 Pennsylvania Avenue NW
Washington, DC 20530
202-514-3301
800-514-0301
FAX: 202-307-1197
www.ada.gov

*John Wodatch, Chief*

The US Department of Justice answers questions about the American Disabilities Act (ADA) and provides free publications by mail and fax through its ADA Information Line.

**3814 US Department of Labor: Office of Federal Contract Programs**
200 Constitution Avenue NW
Washington, DC 20210
202-693-5000
888-376-3227
FAX: 202-693-1304

*Elaine Chao, Chief Executive Officer*

Prohibits discrimination on the basis of disability and requires federal contractors and sub-contractors with contracts of $2,500 or more to take affirmative action to employ and advance individuals with disabilities.

**3815 US Department of Transportation**
400 7th Street SW
Washington, DC 20590
202-366-4000
FAX: 202-366-7149
www.dot.gov

*Norman Mineta, Chief Executive Officer*

Enforces ADA provisions that require nondiscrimination in public and private mass transportation systems and services.

**3816 US Office of Personnel Management**
1900 E Street NW
Washington, DC 20415
202-606-1381
FAX: 202-606-2532
e-mail: GENERAL@opm.gov
www.opm.gov

*Linda M Springer, Director*
*Claudio Benedi, Manager*

Establishes policies for employment of the handicapped within the federal service. Administers a merit system for the federal employment that includes recruiting, examining, training, and promoting people on the basis of knowledge and skills, regardless of sex, race, religion or other factors.

## Alabama

**3817 Alabama Council For Developmental Disabilities**
RSA Union Building
100 N Union Street
PO Box 301410
Montgomery, AL 36130
334-242-3973
800-232-2158
FAX: 334-242-0797
e-mail: mjones@mh.state.al.us
www.acdd.org

*Elmyra Jones, Executive Director*
*Joyce Carvana, Administrative Assistant*

Serves as an advocate for Alabama's citizens with developmental disabilities and their families; to empower them with the knowledge and opportunity to make informed choices and exercise control over their own lives; and to create a climate for positive socialchange to enable them to be respected, independent and productive integrated members of society.

**3818 Alabama Department of Public Health**
20 Monroe Street
Suite 1552
Montgomery, AL 36104
334-206-5200
FAX: 334-206-5520
www.adph.org

*William Son, State Health Officer*
*Donald Williamson, Administrator*

Provides professional services for the improvement and protection of the public's health through disease prevention and the assurance of public health services to resident and transient populations of the state regardless of social circumstances or the ability to pay.

**3819 Alabama Department of Rehabilitation Services**
2129 E S Boulevrad
Montgomery, AL 36116
334-281-8780
800-441-7607
FAX: 334-281-1973
e-mail: sshiver@rehab.state.al.us
www.rehab.state.al.us

*Steve Shivers, Commissioner/President*
*Jim Harris III, Assistant Commissioner*

**3820 Alabama Department of Senior Services**
770 Washington Avenue
Montgomery, AL 36130
334-242-4363
877-425-2243
FAX: 334-242-5594
e-mail: ageline@adss.state.al.us
www.adss.state.al.us

*Irene B Collins, Executive Director*

**3821 Alabama Disabilities Advocacy Program**
University of Alabama
PO Box 870395
Tuscaloosa, AL 35487
205-348-4928
800-826-1675
FAX: 205-348-3909
e-mail: adap@adap.ua.edu
www.adap.net

*Ellen Gillespie, Executive Director*
*Robin Lunceford, Marketing Coordinator*

The federally mandate statewide protection and advocacy system serving eligible individuals with disabilities in Alabama. ADAP has five program components: Protection and Advocacy for persons with developmental disabilities (PADD), Protection and Advocacy for Individuals with Mental Illness (PAIMT), Protection and Advocacy of Individual Rights (PAIR), Protection and Advocacy for Assistive Technology (PAAT) and Protection & Advocacy For Beneficiaries of Social Security (PABSS).

**3822 Alabama Division of Rehabilitation and Crippled Children**
2129 E South Boulevard
Montgomery, AL 36116        334-281-8780
800-441-7607
FAX: 334-281-1973
e-mail: sshiver@rehab.state.al.us
www.rehab.state.al.us

*Steve Shivers, President*
*Jim Harris III, Assistant Commissioner*

**3823 Alabama State Department of Human Resources**
PO Box 250380
Montgomery, AL 36125        334-293-3100
FAX: 334-293-3453
e-mail: ogapi@dhr.state.al.us
www.dhr.state.al.us/fsd/Child_Care.asp

*Terry Benton, Executive Director*

Partners with communities to promtoe family stability and provide for the safety and self-sufficiency of vulnerable Alabamians.

**3824 Client Assistance Program: Alabama**
2129 E South Boulevard
Montgomery, AL 36116        334-281-8780
FAX: 334-281-1973
www.rehab.state.al.us

*Lamona Lucas, Director*
*Steve Shivers, President*

**3825 Disability Determination Service: Birmingham**
PO Box 830300
Birmingham, AL 35283        205-870-1205
FAX: 256-773-2296

*Tammy Warren, Director*
*Janet Cox, Owner*

**3826 Governor's Committee on Employment of Persons with Disabilities**
Division of Rehabilitation Service
PO Box 11586
Montgomery, AL 36111        334-281-8780
FAX: 334-613-3893

*Lamona Lucas, Director*
*Steve Shivers, Manager*

**3827 Protection & Advocacy for Persons with Disabilities: Alabama**
PO Box 870395
Tuscaloosa, AL 35487        205-348-4920
800-826-1675
FAX: 205-348-3909
e-mail: adap@ban.ua.edu
www.adap.net

*Ellen Gillespie, Director*
*Denise Smith, Interim Associate Director*
*Robin Lunceford, Marketing Coordinator*

ADAP provides quality, legally-based advocacy services to Alabamians with disabilities in order to protect, promote and expand their rights.

**3828 Social Security: Mobile Disability Determination Services**
Disability Determination Services
PO Box 2371
Mobile, AL 36652        251-433-2820
800-292-6743
FAX: 251-436-0599
www.ssa.gov

*Tommy Warren, Executive Director*
*Jack Miller, Office Manager*

**3829 Workers Compensation Board Alabama**
Alabama Dept of Industrial Relation
649 Monroe Street
Montgomery, AL 36131        205-362-9040
FAX: 334-261-3143
e-mail: director@dir.alabama.gov
dir.alabama.gov/contacts

*Phyllis Kennedy, Director, DIR*
*Scottie Spates, Worker's Compensation Director*

## Alaska

**3830 ATLA**
2217 E Tudor Road
Suite 4
Anchorage, AK 99507        907-563-2599
800-723-2852
FAX: 907-563-0699
e-mail: atla@atla.biz
www.atla.biz

*Kathy Privratsky, Executive Director*
*Rich Sanders, Program Manager*
*Mystie Rail, PR/Marketing*

Assistive Technology sales and services. ATLA is Alaska's only assistive technology resource center.

**3831 Alaska Commission on Aging**
PO Box C
Juneau, AK 99811        907-465-3250
FAX: 970-465-1398
TTY:970-465-2205
www.alaskaaging.org

*Linda Gohl, Director*

**3832 Alaska Department of Handicapped Children**
1231 Gambell Street
Room 314
Anchorage, AK 99501        907-269-3400

*Rita Schmidt, Chief*

**3833 Alaska Division of Mental Health and Developmental Disabilities**
350 Main Street
110620
Juneau, AK 99801        907-465-3562
FAX: 907-465-2668
www.state.ak.us

*Julie Neyhart, Director*

The division plans for and provides appropriate prevention, treatment and support for families impacted by mental disorders or developmental disabilities while maximizing self-determination. Community based services are provided by grantees. Inpatient services are provided in two division operated facilities.

**3834 Alaska Division of Vocational Rehabilitation**
801 W 10th Street
Suite A
Juneau, AK 99801        907-465-2814
800-478-2815
FAX: 907-465-2856
www.labor.state.ak.us/ddr/home

*Gale Finnott, Executive Director*
*Russ Cusack, Chief Rehabilitation Therapist*

Provides comprehensive services to people with disabilities to assist in achieving an employment outcome.

**3835 Alaska Welcomes You**
PO Box 91333
Anchorage, AK 99509
907-349-6301
800-349-6301
FAX: 907-344-3259
e-mail: akwy@customcpu.com
www.accessiblealaska.com

*Paul Sandhofer, President*

Corporation that researches, inspects and assesses accommodations, restaurants, parks, fishing, cruises, trails, trains, tours and other Alaskan activities for travelers with disabilities. Additionally, they assess trails and design map for hikers with special needs.

**3836 Client Assistance Program: Alaska**
A SI ST
2900 Boniface Parkway
Suite 100
Anchorage, AK 99504
907-333-2211
800-478-0047
FAX: 907-333-1186
e-mail: akcap@alaska.com
www.home.gci.net/~alaskacap

*Gale Sinnott, Director*
*Pam Stratton, Executive Director*

We provide informatory referral to other programs in Alaska that are funded under the rehabilitation Act of 1973 as a amended; Individual assistance or advocacy, if an individual with disability has applied for or received services from an agency funded under the rehabilitation act and has concerns or questions we will work with them to help resolve their concerns with the agency.

**3837 Governor's Committee on Employment and Rehabilitation of People with Disabilities: Alaska**
801 W 10th Street
Suite A
Juneau, AK 99801
907-465-2814
800-478-2815
FAX: 907-465-2856
e-mail: Velja_Elstad@labor.state.ak.us
www.labor.state.ak.us/dvr

*Velja Elstad, Staff Liaison*
*Gale Finnott, Executive Director*

Carries on a continuing program to promote the employment and rehabilitation of citizens with disabilities in the State of Alaska. Advocates for a comprehensive statewide system for access to assistive technology. Obtains and maintains cooperation with public and private groups and individuals in this field.

**3838 Governor's Council on Disabilities and Special Education**
3601 C Street, Suite 740
PO Box 240249
Anchorage, AK 99524
907-269-8990
888-269-8990
FAX: 907-269-8995
e-mail: millie_ryan@health.state.ak.us
www.hss.state.ak.us/gcdse/

*Millie Ryan, Executive Director*
*Kathy Allely, Planner III*

**3839 Protection & Advocacy System: Alaska**
Disability Law Center of Alaska
3330 Arctic Boulevard
Suite 103
Anchorage, AK 99503
907-565-1002
800-478-1234
FAX: 907-565-1000
e-mail: akpa@dlcak.org
www.dlcak.org

*David Fleurant, Executive Director*
*Cynthia Hite, Business Manager*

Deals with rights of the disabled. Works in conjunction with agencies, law offices and family members.

**3840 Protection & Advocacy for Persons with Developmental Disabilities: Alaska**
Advocacy Services of Alaska
615 E 82nd Avenue
Suite 101
Anchorage, AK 99518
FAX: 907-349-1002
e-mail: rtessardore@dlcakelcak.org

*Rick Tessardore, Director*

**3841 Workers Compensation Board Alaska**
Department of Labor
PO Box 25512
Juneau, AK 99802
907-465-2790
FAX: 907-465-2797
www.labor.state.ak.us

*Greg O'Clary, Commissioner*
*Guy Bell, Assistant Commissioner*

---

# Arizona

**3842 Arizona Department of Children's Rehabilitative Services**
1740 W Adams Street
Suite 205
Phoenix, AZ 85007
602-271-0945

*W Sundin Applegate*
*Robert Plummer, Manager*

**3843 Arizona Department of Economic Security**
1717 W Jefferson Street
Phoenix, AZ 85007
602-542-5678

*Linda J Blessing, Director*
*Lynne Smith, Chief Exeuctive Officer*

The Department of Economic Security is a human service agency providing services in six areas: Aging and Community Services, Benefits and Medical Eligibility, Child Support Enforcement, Children and Family Services, Developmental Disabilities and Employment and Rehabilitation Services.

**3844 Arizona Department of Family Health Services**
1740 W Adams Street
Phoenix, AZ 85007
602-271-0945
FAX: 602-542-1235
e-mail: piowebmaster@azdhs.gov
www.azdhs.gov

*Susan Gerard, Director*
*Robert Plummer, Manager*

**3845 Arizona Department of Handicapped Children**
1740 W Adams Street
Room 205
Phoenix, AZ 85007
602-271-0945
FAX: 602-542-2589

*W Sundin Applegate, Chief*
*Robert Plummer, Manager*

**3846 Arizona Division of Aging and Adult Services**
1789 W Jefferson Street
Phoenix, AZ 85007
602-542-4446
FAX: 602-542-6575
www.azdcs.gov/aaa

*Rex Critchfield, Program Administrator*

**3847 Arizona Rehabilitation State Services for the Blind and Visually Impaired**
4620 N 16th Street
Suite 100
Phoenix, AZ 85016 602-938-2422

*Kenneth House, State Manager*
*Erik Markoff, Manager*

Offers clients a conservation program, eye examinations, treatments, counseling, social work, psychological testing and evaluation, professional training, computer training and more for the visually impaired. The staff includes 56 full time employees.

**3848 Developmental Disability Council: Arizona**
1717 W Jefferson Street
Phoenix, AZ 85007 602-542-4049
800-352-8168
FAX: 602-547-5320

*David Berns, Director*
*Nebal Chavez, Executive Director*
*Susan Madison, Manager*

**3849 Governor's Council on Developmental Disabilities**
3839 N 3rd Street
Phoenix, AZ 85012 602-863-0484
866-771-9378
FAX: 602-277-4454
e-mail: jsnyder@azdes.gov
www.azgcdd.org

*Crystal Snyder, Executive Director*

The purpose of the council is to advocate for and assure that individuals with developmental disabilities and their families participate in the design of and have access to culturally competent services, supports and provides opportunities to become integrated and included in the community.

**3850 International Dyslexia Association: Arizona Branch**
PO Box 6284
Scottsdale, AZ 85261 480-941-0308
800-222-3123
e-mail: info@interdys.org
www.dyslexia-az.org

*Kay Byrd, President*

Provides free information and referral services for diagnosis and tutoring for parents, educators, physicians, and individuals with dyslexia. The voice of our membership is heard in 48 countries. Membership includes yearly journal and quarterly newsletter. Call for conference dates.

**3851 Protection & Advocacy for Persons with with Disabilities: Arizona**
Arizona Center for Disability Law
3839 N 3rd Street
Suite 209
Phoenix, AZ 85012 602-274-6287
800-927-2260
FAX: 602-274-6779
e-mail: center@azdisabilitylaw.or
www.azdisabilitylaw.org

*Peri Jude Radecic, Director of Public Advocacy*
*Henry G Watkins, Executive Director*
*Judy Fox, Manager*

**3852 Social Security: Phoenix Disability Determination Services**
Social Security Admission
1122 N 7th Street
Suite 100
Phoenix, AZ 85006
800-772-1213
TTY:800-325-0778
www.ssa.gov

**3853 Social Security: Tucson Disability Determination Services**
3500 N Campbell Avenue
Tucson, AZ 85719
800-772-1213
TTY:800-325-0778
www.socialsecurity.gov

# Arkansas

**3854 Arkansas Assistive Technology Projects**
Increasing Capabilities Access
2201 Brookwood Drive
Suite 117
Little Rock, AR 72202 501-666-8868
800-828-2799
FAX: 501-666-5319
e-mail: aehurst@ars.state.ar.us
www.arkansas-ican.org

*Barbara Gullett, Executive Director*
*Barry Vuletich, Supervisor*
*Linda Morgan, Occupational Therapist*

A consumer responsive ,statewide program promoting assistive technology devices and sources for persons of all ages with all disabilities. Referral and information services provide information about devices, where to obtain them and their cost.

**3855 Arkansas Division of Aging & Adult Services**
Department of Human Services
PO Box 1437
Little Rock, AR 72203 501-682-2441
FAX: 501-682-8155
e-mail: ron.tatus@mail.state.ar.us
www.state.ar.us/dhs/aging

*Herb Sanderson, Director*
*Coney Parker, Assistant Director*
*Sandra Barrett, Assistant Director*

The division provides services geared for adults and the elderly including supervised living, home delivered meals, adult day care, senior centers, personal care, household chores, and adult protective services.

**3856 Arkansas Division of Developmental Disabilities Services**
PO Box 1437
Little Rock, AR 72203 501-682-8665
FAX: 501-682-8380

*Mike McCreight, Director*
*Charlie Green, Manager*

State agency to assist persons with developmental disabilities and their family in obtaining appropriate assistance and services.

**3857 Arkansas Division of Services for the Blind**
Department Of Health and Human Services
700 Main Street
Little Rock, AR 72201 501-682-5463
800-960-9270
FAX: 501-682-0366
e-mail: donnabirdwell@arkansas.gov
www.state.ar.us/dhs/dsd/newdsb/index.html

*James Hudson, Executive Director*
*Katy Morris, Assistant Director*

State program which offers services in the areas of health, counseling, social work, self help and education for the visually and multihandicapped. The staff includes 4 full time and 13 part time members including mobility specialists and rehabilitation teachers.

**3858    Baptist Health Rehabilitation Institute**
Baptist Heath
9601 Interstate 630 Exit 7
Little Rock, AR  72205                          501-202-7011
                                          FAX: 501-202-7259
                                          www.baptist-health.com

*Doug Weeks, Senior Vice President/Administra*
*Greg Craine, Vice President*
*Russell Harrington, President*

Acute rehab facility serving patients with ortho, spinal cord injury, brain injury, CVA, arthritis, cardiac and generalized weakness; JCAHO and CARF accredited; 17 outpatient therapy centers throughout central Arkansas.

**3859    Children's Medical Services**
PO Box 1437
Little Rock, AR  72203                          501-682-8224
                                               800-482-5850
                                          FAX: 501-682-8247

*Gilbert Buchanan, Medical Director*
*Nancy Holder, Program Director*
*Iris Fehr, Nursing Director*

**3860    Developmental Disability Council: Arkansas**
4815 W Markham Street
Little Rock, AR  72205                          501-661-2262
                                          FAX: 501-661-2399

*Wilma Stewart, Director*
*David Taylor, Manager*

**3861    President's Committee on People with Disabilities: Arkansas**
7th & Main Street
Little Rock, AR  72203

**3862    Social Security: Arkansas Disability Determination Services**
701 S Pulaski Street
Little Rock, AR  72201                          501-682-3030
                                               800-772-1213
                                          FAX: 501-682-7553
                                          www.socialsecurity.gov

*Arthur Boutiette, Executive Director*

# California

**3863    California Department of Aging**
1300 National Drive
Suite 200
Sacramento, CA  95834                          916-324-4244
                                          FAX: 916-327-3902
                                          www.aging.ca.gov

*Lora Connoly, Chief Deputy Director*
*David Supkofl, Manager*

**3864    California Department of Handicapped Children**
714 P Street
Room 323
Sacramento, CA  95814                          916-445-4171

*Maridee Gregory*
*Diana Bonta, Chief Executive Officer*

**3865    California Department of Rehabilitation**
830 K Street
Sacramento, CA  95814                          916-324-4244
                                          TTY:916-445-3971
                            e-mail: doroa.bpremo@hwl.cahwnet.gov

*Brenda Premo, Director*
*David Supkofl, Manager*

Assists people with disabilities, particularly those with severe disabilities, in obtaining and retaining meaningful employment and living independently in their communities. The department develops, purchases, provides and advocates for programs and services in vocational rehabilitation, habilitation and independent living with a priority on serving persons with all disabilities, especially those with the most severe disabilities.

**3866    California Governor's Committee on Employment of People with Disabilities**
800 Capitol Mall
MIC 41
Sacramento, CA  95814                          916-654-8055
                                               800-695-0350
                                          FAX: 916-654-9821
                                          TTY: 916-654-9820
                                     www.disabilityemployment.org
GCEPD works to eliminate the barriers that preclude equal consideration for employment opportunities for people with disabilities. The Governor's Committee is responsible for providing leadership to increase the numbers of people with disabilities in the California workforce.

**3867    California Protection & Advocacy: (PAI) A Nonprofit Organization**
Protection and Advocacy ( PA I)
100 Howe Avenue
Suite 235n
Sacramento, CA  95825                          916-488-9950
                                               800-776-5746
                                          FAX: 916-488-9960
                                     e-mail: legalmail@pai-ca.org
                                          www.pai-ca.org

*Catherine Blakemore, Executive Director*
*Barbara Silda, Deputy Director*
*Eric Gelber, Manager*

Advancing the human and legal rights of people with disabilities.

**3868    California State Council on Developmental Disabilities**
1507 21st Street
Suite 210
Sacramento, CA  95814                          916-322-8481
                                          FAX: 916-443-4957
                                     e-mail: council@scdd.ca.gov
                                          www.scdd.ca.gov

*Alan Kerzin, Executive Director*

**3869    Client Assistance Program: California**
CA Health and Human Services Agency, Dept of Rehab
2000 Evergreen Street
Sacramento, CA  95815                          916-263-7367
                                               800-952-5544
                                          TTY:866-712-1085
                                     e-mail: capinfo@dor.ca.gov
                                          www.dor.ca.gov

*Catherine Campisi, PhD, Director*

**3870    Governor's Committee for Employment of the Disabled: California**
PO Box 826880
Sacramento, CA  94280                          916-654-9072

**3871 International Dyslexia Association: Central California Branch**

4594 E Michigan Avenue
Fresno, CA 93703
559-251-9385
800-222-3123
FAX: 599-252-1216
e-mail: dyslexias@attbi.com
www.interdys.org

*Joy Moody, President*

Provides free information and referral services for diagnosis and tutoring for parents, educators, physicians, and individuals with dyslexia. The voice of our membership is heard in 48 countries. Membership includes yearly journal and quarterly newsletter. Call for conference dates. Other locations also available in California.

**3872 Long Beach Department of Health and Human Services**

2525 Grand Avenue
Long Beach, CA 90815
562-570-4000
FAX: 562-570-4049
e-mail: info@ci.long-beach.ca.us/health
www.ci.long-beach.ca.us/health

*Ronald Aries, Director*
*Michael Johnson, Manager*

**3873 Los Angeles County Department of Health Services**

313 N Figueroa Street
Los Angeles, CA 90012
800-427-8700
e-mail: webmaster@adhs.org
www.ladhs.org

*Bridget A Ward, Director*
*Jennifer Cayanan, Staff Development Specialist*

**3874 Social Security: California Disability Determination Services**

3164 Garrity Way
Richmond, CA 94806
800-772-1213
TTY:800-325-0778
www.ssa.gov

*Sally Keen, San Francisco Regional PDF Coord*

**3875 Social Security: Fresno Disability Determination Services**

Social Security
1052 C Street
Fresno, CA 93706
559-487-5391
800-772-1213
FAX: 510-970-2947
e-mail: sally.keen@ssa.gov
www.ssa.gov

*Sally Keen, Regional PDF Coordinator*

**3876 Social Security: Oakland Disability Determination Services**

238 11th Street
Oakland, CA 94607
800-772-1213
TTY:800-325-0778
www.ssa.gov

**3877 Social Security: Sacramento Disability Determination Services**

8351 Folsom Boulevard
Sacramento, CA 95826
916-381-9410
800-772-1213
FAX: 916-263-5310
TTY: 916-381-9445
www.ssa.gov

**3878 Social Security: San Diego Disability Determination Services**

1333 Front Street
San Diego, CA 92101
800-772-1213
FAX: 619-278-4303
TTY:800-325-0778
e-mail: josesanbria@ssa.gov
www.ssa.gov

---

## Colorado

**3879 Colorado Department of Aging & Adult Servi ces**

1575 Sherman Street
10th Floor
Denver, CO 80203
303-866-3851
FAX: 303-620-2696
www.cdhs.state.co.us/ADRS/AAS

*Jeanette Hensley, Director*

A department providing services to the elderly.

**3880 Colorado Developmental Disabilities Council**

3401 Quebec Street
Suite 6009
Denver, CO 80207
720-941-0176
FAX: 720-941-8490
e-mail: cdppc.email@state.co.us
www.coddc.org

*Marcia Tewell, Manager*

The mission is to advocate in collaboration with and on behalf of people with developmental disabilities for the establishment and implementation of public policy which will further their independence, productivity and integration.

**3881 Colorado Division of Mental Health**

3520 W Oxford Avenue
Denver, CO 80236
303-866-7066
FAX: 303-762-4373

*George Kawamura, Director*
*Keith Lagrenade, Chief Executive Officer*

**3882 Colorado Health Care Program for Children with Special Needs**

4300 Cherry Creek South Drive
Denver, CO 80246
303-861-8228
800-886-7689
FAX: 303-753-9249
www.state.cdphe.co.us

*Kathy Watters, Director*
*Arlene Miles, President*

Provides information and state aid to children with disabilities.

**3883 Eastern Colorado Services for the Disabled**

211 W Main Street
Sterling, CO 80751
970-842-2413
FAX: 970-522-7121

*Charles W Hayes, Executive Director*
*Marylu Walton, Administrative Assistant*

Case coordination, infant stimulation, family support, residential and vocational programs.

**3884 International Dyslexia Association: Rocky Mountain Branch**
PO Box 461010
Glendale, CO 80246
303-721-9425
800-222-3123
e-mail: info@interdys.org
www.interdys.org

*Lynn Kuhn, President*

Provides free information and referral services for diagnosis and tutoring for parents, educators, physicians, and individuals with dyslexia in Utah, Colorado and Wyoming. The voice of our membership is heard in 48 countries. Membership includes yearly journal and quarterly newsletter. Call for conference dates.

**3885 Legal Center for People with Disabilities & Older People**
455 Sherman Street
Suite 130
Denver, CO 80203
303-722-0300
800-288-1376
FAX: 303-722-0720
e-mail: tlcmail@thelegalcenter.org
www.thelegalcenter.org

*Mary Anne Harvey, Executive Director*
*Mark Ivandick, Manager*

Uses the legal system to protect and promote the rights of people with disabilities and older people in Colorado through direct legal representation, advocacy, education and legislative analysis. The Legal Center is Colorado's Protection and Advocacy System. We are also the State Ombudsman for nursing homes and assisted living facilities. Call for a free publications and products list.

**3886 Workers Compensation Board Colorado**
Division of Labor
1515 Arapahoe Street
14th Floor
Denver, CO 80202
303-318-8441
888-390-7936
FAX: 303-318-8710
www.coworkforce.com/dwc/

## Connecticut

**3887 Connecticut Board of Education and Service for the Blind**
184 Windsor Avenue
Windsor, CT 06095
860-602-4000
FAX: 860-602-4020
TTY:860-602-4002
e-mail: besb@po.state.ct.us
www.besb.state.ct.us

*Patricia Wilson, Commissioner*
*Alan Sylvestre, Chairman*
*Keith Maynard, Plant Manager*

Offers rehabilitative services and information for persons with legal blindness and childrenwhonare visually impaired that are residents of Connecticut.

**3888 Connecticut Commission on Aging**
210 Capitol Avenue
# 509
Hartford, CT 06106
860-240-5200
FAX: 860-240-5204
e-mail: coa@cga.ct.gov
www.cga.ct.gov/coa

*Julie Evans Starr, Executive Director*
*Robert J Norton, Communications Director*

Advocates on beha;f of elderly persons in Connecticut by regularly monitoring their status, assessing the impact of current and prosped initiatives, and conducting activities which promote the interests of these individuals and report to the Governor and the Legislature.

**3889 Connecticut Department of Children and Youth Services**
505 Hudson Street
Hartford, CT 06106
860-247-2732
FAX: 860-566-7947

*Linda D Amario Rossi, Commissioner*
*Bruce Douglas, Executive Director*

**3890 Connecticut Developmental Disabilities Council**
460 Capitol Avenue
Hartford, CT 06106
860-418-6160
800-653-1134
FAX: 860-418-6003
TTY: 860-418-6172
www.state.ct.us/ctcdd/

*Edward T Preneta, Executive Director*

**3891 Connecticut Office of Protection and Advocacy for Persons with Disabilities**
60 Weston Street
Suite B
Hartford, CT 06120
860-297-4300
800-842-7303
FAX: 860-566-8714
TTY: 860-566-2102
e-mail: OPA-Information@po.state.ct.us
www.ct.gov/opapd

*James McGaughey, Executive Director*
*Gretchen Knaff, Assistant Director*
*Linda Mizzi, CI Director*

Seeks to protect the rights of and to advocate for people with disabilities. The Consumer Information Section provides information, referral services and short-term advocacy assistance. The Case Services unit staff advocates for individuals who have been discriminated against based on disability or who have been denied needed services to which they are entitled to under state or federal law. Offers training & technical assistance to individuals and groups to promote self-advocacy.

**3892 Social Security: Hartford Area Office**
960 Main Street
2nd Floor
Hartford, CT 06103
860-493-1857
800-772-1213
FAX: 860-566-1795
TTY: 860-525-4967
www.ssa.gov

*Jan Gilbert, Professional Relations Coord.*

## Delaware

**3893 Delaware Assistive Technology Initiative Center for Applied Science & Engineering**
Univ. of DE/Alfred I duPont Hospital for Children
1600 Rockland Road
PO Box 269
Wilmington, DE 19899
302-651-6790
800-870-3284
FAX: 302-651-6793
TTY: 302-651-6794
e-mail: dati@asel.udel.edu
www.dati.org

*Beth Mineo-Mollica, Project Director*

The Delaware Assistive Technology Initiative (DATI) connects Delawareans who have disabilities with the tools they need in order to learn, work, play and participate in community life safely and independently. The Delaware Assistive Technology Initiative's (DATI) endeavors to improve access to assistive technology for all Delawareans with disabilities.

**3894** **Delaware Client Assistance Program**
United Cerebral Palsy Association
254 E Camden Wyoming Avenue
Camden, DE 19934                    302-698-9336
                                    800-640-9336
                              FAX: 302-698-9338
                    e-mail: capdir@magpage.com

*Melissa Shahan, Executive Director*

Provides advocacy services for persons involved with programs covered under the Rehabilitation Act of 1973 as amended, information and referrals on ADA, Title I.

**3895** **Delaware Department of Health and Social Services**
Administration Building D HS S Campus
1901 N Dupont Highway
New Castle, DE 19720                302-577-4500
                                    800-464-HELP
                              FAX: 302-577-4510
                  e-mail: dhssinfo@state.de.us
                    www.dhss.delaware.gov/dhss

*Vincent Meconi, Secretary*

**3896** **Delaware Department of Public Instructing**
PO Box 1402
Dover, DE 19903                     302-739-4686
                                    800-433-5292
                              FAX: 302-739-3092

*Dr. Pascal D Forgione Jr, Superintendent*

A publicly funded, state agency that gives information about local facilities and administers supplemental funds for visually handicapped students in local schools. It also maintains special teachers of sight conservation and braille programs for both children and adults.

**3897** **Delaware Developmental Disability Council**
410 Federal Street
Suite 2
Dover, DE 19901                     302-739-3613
                              FAX: 302-739-2015
                    e-mail: arose@state.de.us

*Christine O'Connor, Executive Director*
*Alexander Rose, Director of Social Services*
*Patricia Maichle, Manager*

**3898** **Delaware Division for the Visually Impaired**
1901 N Du Pont Highway
New Castle, DE 19720                302-577-4730
                              FAX: 302-255-4441
                  e-mail: dhssinfo@state.de.us
                              www.state.de.us

*Debra Wallace, Executive Director*
*Ken Sutton, Program Spec/Staff Dev Officer*

State agency serving the visually impaired persons from birth, with or without other handicaps. Services offered include educational, computer training, employment and pre-vocational training.

**3899** **Delaware Industries for the Blind**
1901 N Dupont Highway
New Castle, DE 19720                302-255-9855
                              FAX: 302-255-4442
                  e-mail: awingrove@state.de.us
                        www.promoplace.com/dib

*Alan B Wingrove, General Manager*

Provides jobs for blind and visually impaired via sales of products and services.

**3900** **Delaware Protection & Advocacy for Persons with Disabilities**
Arc of Delaware
144 E Market Street
Georgetown, DE 19947                302-856-6019
                              FAX: 302-856-6133
                    e-mail: challdover@aol.com

*Becky Allen, Executive Director*

**3901** **Delaware Workers Compensation Board**
Industrial Accident Board de dept
4425 N Market Street
Wilmington, DE 19802                302-761-8200

                              www.delawareworks.com

*James Cagle, Manager*

**3902** **Social Security: Wilmington Disability Determination**
U S Department of Health and Human Services
321 N Front Street
Wilmington, NC 28401                910-254-3456
                                    800-453-9851
                              FAX: 910-254-3444
                              www.socialsecurity.gov

*Allen J Murphy, Founder*
*Vickie O'Brien, Manager*

# District of Columbia

**3903** **District of Columbia Department of Handicapped Children**
D C General Hospital
1900 Massachusetts Avenue SE
Building 10
Washington, DC 20003                202-675-5000
                              FAX: 202-675-7694

*Jacqueline Mcmorris, Acting Chief*
*Nayab Ali, MD*

**3904** **District of Columbia Office on Aging**
441 4th Street NW
9th Floor
Washington, DC 20001                202-504-3400
                              FAX: 202-724-4979

*Francis Smith, Executive Director*

Serves the District of Columbia residents 60 years of age and older. Contact the Information and Assistance Unit for more information about innovative programs and services offered by the Office.

**3905** **Information, Protection & Advocacy for Persons with Disabilities**
IPACHI
4455 Connecticut Avenue NW
Suite B
Washington, DC 20008

                              FAX: 202-966-6313

*Vivianne Hardy-Townes, Executive Director*
*Ronald Tyson, Information/Referral*

Offers services and support for persons with disabilities in the Washington, DC area.

**3906 Information, Protection and Advocacy Center for Handicapped Individuals**
4455 Connecticut Avenue NW
Suite B100
Washington, DC 20008          202-659-0215
                              FAX: 202-966-6313

*Vivianne Hardy-Townes, Executive Director*
*Darell Hammond, Owner*

Serves all persons with disabilities in the DC, Maryland and Virginia areas offering them legal representation and advocacy, information and referrals and several publications.

**3907 International Dyslexia Association of DC**
5914 Reservoir Heights Avenue
Alexandria, VA 22311          703-827-9019
                              800-222-3123
                     e-mail: info@interdys.org
                              www.interdys.org

*Ruth R Tifford LCSW, President*

The DC Capital Area Branch, provides support for individuals with dyslexia and their families in the Washington, DC metropolitan area, including parts of Maryland, Virginia and West Virginia. Our conferences, book sales and online information resources are designed to further the understanding of dyslexia and encourage the use of systematic, multisensory teaching methods enabling children and adults to reach their educational potential.

**3908 Wage and Hour Division of the Employment Standards Administration**
US Department of Labor
200 Constitution Avenue NW
Washington, DC 20210          202-693-5000
                              FAX: 202-693-1406
                              www.dol.gov

*Elaine Chao, Chief Executive Officer*

Administers regulations governing the employment of individuals with disabilities in sheltered workshops and the disabled workers industries.

**3909 Washington Hearing and Speech Society**
1934 Calvert Street NW
Washington, DC 20009          202-537-4010

                   e-mail: support@dcsha.org

*Judyth Tinsley*
*Dianne Carthy, Manager*

Offers individuals with hearing or speech impairments, in the DC area, speech, reading classes, audiological services and new aids.

**3910 Well Mind Association of Greater Washington**
18606 New Hampshire Avenue
Ashton, MD 20861              301-774-6617
                              FAX: 301-946-1402
Holistic mental health information and publications, public lectures in the Washington D.C. area, and nationwide referrals.

**3911 Workers Compensation Board: District of Columbia**
1200 Upshur Street NW
Washington, DC 20011

## Florida

**3912 ARC Gateway**
3932 N 10th Avenue
Pensacola, FL 32503           850-434-2638
                              FAX: 850-438-2180
                              e-mail: aresc@aol.com
                              www.arc-gateway.org

*Donna Fassett, Executive Director*

To secure for all people with developmental disabilities the opportunity to choose and realize their goals of where and how they learn, live, work and play. ARC Gateway is committed to increasing the opportunities for all persons with, or at risk of, development disabilities the opportunity to choose where, how and with whom they live, learn, work and play.

**3913 Advocacy Center for Persons with Disabilities**
2671 W Executive Center Circle
Suite 100
Tallahassee, FL 32301         850-488-9071
                              800-342-0823
                              FAX: 850-488-8640
                              e-mail: info@advocacy.org
                              www.advocacycenter.org

*Gary Weston, Executive Director*
*Hubert Grisson, President*

**3914 Assistive Technology Educational Network of Florida**
1207 S Mellonville Avenue
Sanford, FL 32771             800-328-3678
                              FAX: 407-688-4593
                e-mail: diane_penn@scps.k12.fl.us
                              www.aten.scps.k12.fl.us

*Dee Wright, Executive Secretary*
*Diane Penn, MA, Technology Specialist*

Provides state-wide information, awareness and training for students, family members, teachers and other professionals in the area of assisted technology; a quarterly newsletter and a network of specialists (Local Assistive Technology Specialists) trained by ATEN to provide support at the district level.

**3915 Bureau of Education for Exceptional Children**
Turlington Building
Tallahassee, FL 32399         850-245-0477
                              FAX: 850-245-0987

*Shan Goff, Bureau Chief*

Provides consultative services for the establishment and operation of school programs for visually impaired students. Provides assistance for in-service teacher training through state or regional workshops or technical assistance to individual programs.

**3916 Department of Health & Rehabilitative Services**
1317 Winewood Boulevard
Tallahassee, FL 32399         850-488-8304
                              FAX: 850-921-5830

*Roderick Hall, Director*
*Beth Carter, Administrative Assistant*
*John Bryant, Manager*

Offers counseling and referrals on rehabilitation facilities.

**3917 Division of Workers Compensation**
2012 Capital Circle SE
Tallahassee, FL 32399         850-413-1600
                              800-342-1741
                              FAX: 850-922-6779
                              www.fldfs.com

*Tanner Hollaman, Manager*

**3918  Florida Adult Services**
1317 Winewood Boulevard
Tallahassee, FL  32399        850-488-8922
                         FAX: 850-922-4193
                 www.myglorida.com/adultservices

*Chris Schummacher, Director*
*Nancy Fulton, Executive Director*

**3919  Florida Department of Handicapped Children**
4030 Esplanade Way
Suite 380
Tallahassee, FL  32399        850-488-8304
                         FAX: 850-488-3813
                    www.apd.myflorida.com

*Shelly Branetley, Director*
*John Bryant, Manager*

**3920  Florida Department of Mental Health and Rehabilitative Services**
1317 Winewood Boulevard
Tallahassee, FL  32399        850-488-8304
                         FAX: 850-487-2239

*Rod Hall, Executive Director*
*John Bryant, Manager*

**3921  Florida Developmental Disabilities Council**
124 Marriott Drive
Suite 203
Tallahassee, FL  32301        850-488-4180
                              800-580-7801
                         FAX: 850-922-6702
                    e-mail: admin@fddc.org
                            www.fddc.org

*Debra Dowds, Executive Director*

**3922  Florida Division of Vocational Rehabilitation**
2002 Old Saint Augustine Road
Building A
Tallahassee, FL  32301        850-488-6210
                              800-451-4327
                         FAX: 850-921-7215
                         TTY: 850-488-2867
                e-mail: costin@vr.doe.state.fl.us

*Bill Palmer, Director*
*Linda Parnell, Manager*

State agency serving individuals with physical or mental disabilities that interfere with them keeping or maintaining employment.

**3923  Florida's Protection and Advocacy Programs for Persons with Disabilities**
2671 Executive Center Circle W
Suite 100
Tallahassee, FL  32301        850-488-9071
                              800-342-0823
                         FAX: 850-488-8640
                         TTY: 800-346-4127
                    www.advocacycenter.org
The Center is a non-profit organization providing protection and advocacy services in the State of Florida. The Center's mission is to advance the dignity, equality, self-determination and expressed choices of individuals with disabilities.

**3924  International Dyslexia Association: Florida Branch**
5005 W Laurel Street
Suite 100
Tampa, FL  33607          305-252-3474
                          800-222-3123
                 e-mail: jewasc@aol.com
                      www.interdys.org

*Jean Schmidt, President*

The Florida Branch is a non-p;rofit, scientific, educational organization committed to the study, prevention and treatment of language-based learning disabilities (dyslexia) for those in Florida and Puerto Rico. It is specifically concerned with the many children and adults with average or superior intelligence who experience difficulty in learning skills such as speaking, reading, writing, spelling and math.

**3925  Social Security Administration**
2002 Old Saint Augustine Road
Suite B12
Tallahassee, FL  32301        850-224-9337
                              800-772-1213
                         FAX: 850-942-8980
                      www.socialsecurity.gov

*Carrie Tucker, Operations Supervisor*
*Sheila Lee, Management Support Specialist*

Administers the Title II and Title XVII disability programs. To be insured for Title II benefits, applicants must have worked in covered employment for at least five of the last ten years prior to becoming disabled. To be eligible for Title XVII disability benefits, applicants must meet an income and resource test.

**3926  Social Security: Miami Disability Determination**
Social Security
11401 W Flagler Street
Miami, FL  33174              800-772-1213
                         FAX: 800-325-0778
                            www.ssa.gov

*Robert L Meekins, Deputy General for Executive Ope*

**3927  Social Security: Orlando Disability Determination**
Social Security
80 N Hughey Avenue
Federal Building, Room 159
Orlando, FL 32801             407-648-6673
                              800-342-2065
                         TTY:407-245-7057
                            www.ssa.gov

*John C Massolio Jr, Founder*
*Neil Bush, President*

**3928  Social Security: Tampa Disability Determination**
Social Security Administration
PO Box 340572
Tampa, FL  33694              813-878-2906
                              800-772-1213
                 e-mail: info@dbstampabay.org
                     www.dbsatampabay.org

*Neil Bush, President*
*John C Massolio Jr, Founder*

## Georgia

**3929  ADA Technical Assistance Program**
Southeast Disability & Business Technical Assist.
490 10th Street NW
Atlanta, GA  30318            404-385-0636
                              800-949-4232
                         FAX: 404-385-0641
            e-mail: sedbtacproject@coa.gatech.edu
                         www.sedbtac.org

*Amy Oliveras, Administrative Assistant*
*Shelley Kaplan, Director*
*Pam Williamson, Assistant Director*

One of ten regional centers funded by NIDRR, to provide information and technical assistance to assist in voluntary compliance with the Americans with Disabilities Act, and accessible education-based information technology.

**3930  Division of Birth Defects and Developmental Disabilities**

12 Executive Park Drive NE
Atlanta, GA  30329                404-498-3800

**3931  Georgia Advocacy Office**

150 E Ponce De Leon Avenue
Suite 430
Decatur, GA  30030                404-885-1234
                                  800-537-2329
                             FAX: 770-414-2948
                        e-mail: info@thegao.org
                                  www.thegao.org

*Ruby Moore, Executive Director*

Protection and advocacy services for Georgians with disabilities.

**3932  Georgia Client Assistance Program**

Division of Rehabilitation Services
2 Peachtree Street NW
Room 23-307
Atlanta, GA  30303                404-605-1986
                                  800-822-9727

*Gail Greene, Executive Director*

Helps eligible persons with complaints, appeals and understanding available benefits under the 1992 Rehabilitation Act Amendments and Title I of the Americans with Disabilities Act. CAP investigates complaints, mediates conflict, represents complainants in appeals, provides legal services if warranted, advocates for due process, identifies and recommends solutions to system problems, advises of benefits available under the 1992 Rehab Act Amendments and Americans with Disabilities Act.

**3933  Georgia Department of Aging**

878 Peachtree Street NE
Apt 318
Atlanta, GA  30309                404-656-4374
                             FAX: 404-730-7950

*Fred McGinnis, Director*
*Andrea Fuller-Ruffin, Administrator*

**3934  Georgia Department of Handicapped Children**

2600 Skyland Drive NE
Atlanta, GA  30319                770-980-5100

*Linnette Jackson-Hunt, Manager*
*Frank Koues, Auditor*

**3935  Georgia Division of Mental Health, Developmental Disabilities & Addictive Diseases**

2 Peachtree Street NW
22nd Floor
Atlanta, GA  30303                404-657-5737
                             FAX: 404-657-1137
                  e-mail: glwilson@dhr.state.ga.us
                             mhddad.dhr.georgia.gov

*Gwendolyn B Skinner, Director*
*Stuqrt Brown, Acting Director Division of Publ*

MHDDAD provides treatment and support services to people with mental illnesses and addictive diseases, and support to people with mental retardation and related developmental disabilities. MHDDAD serves people of all ages with the most severe and likely to be long-term conditions.

**3936  Georgia State Board of Workers' Compensation**

270 Peachtree Street NW
Atlanta, GA  30303                404-656-3875
                                  800-533-0682
                             FAX: 404-657-1767
                                  www.ganet.org/sbwc

*Ron Simpson, Executive Director*

**3937  Governor's Council on Developmental Disabilities**

Govenors Coucil on Development Disabilities
2 Peachtree Street NW
Atlanta, GA  30303                404-657-2126
                                  888-275-4233
                                  888-275-4233
                             FAX: 404-657-2132
                             TTY:404-657-3000
              e-mail: eejacobson@dhr.state.ga.us
                                  www.gcdd.org

*Eric E Jacobson, Executive Director*
*Daniel Doughman, Program Director*
*Yao Seidu, Public Information Officer*

Advocacy and support organization focusd on improving the lives of people with disabilities and their families.
        *Quartlery*

**3938  International Dyslexia Association: Georgia Branch**

1951 Greystone Road NW
Atlanta, GA  30318                404-256-1232
                                  800-222-3123
        e-mail: jennifer@syllablesreadingcenter.com
                                  www.interdys.org

*Jennifer Hasser, President*

The Georgi Branch was formed to increase public awareness about dyslexia in the State of Georgia. In addition, the Branch encourages teachers to train in multisensory language instruction. The Branch also provides a network for individuals with dyslexia, their families and professionals in the educational and medical fields.

**3939  Social Security: Atlanta Disability Determination**

401 W Peachtree Street
Suite 2860
Atlanta, GA  30308
                                  800-772-1213
                             TTY:800-325-0778
                             www.socialsecurity.gov

**3940  Social Security: Decatur Disability Determination**

2853 Candler Road
Suite 8
Decatur, GA  30034
                                  800-772-1213
                             TTY:800-325-0778
                             www.socialsecurity.gov

# Hawaii

**3941  Assistive Technology Resource Centers of Hawaii**

414 Kuwili Street
Suite 104
Honolulu, HI  96817                800-532-7110
                                   800-645-3007
                              FAX: 808-532-7120
                         e-mail: atrc-info@atrc.org
                                   www.atrc.org

*Barbara Fischlowitz-Leong, Executive Director*

Provides information and referral to anyone interested in assistive technology devices and services. Operates equipment loan. Provides training to consumer and professional groups including self-advocacy skills for consumers and family members. Works to ensure that schools, vocational rehabilitation agencies and health insurers provide assessments, funding and training in the use of assistive technology devices and services for their clients. Low-interest loan programs available.

**3942  Diabetes Network of East Hawaii**
1221 Kilauea Avenue
Suite 70
Hilo, HI 96720                    808-935-8658

*Martha Ahyee, Executive Director*

**3943  Disability and Communication Access Board**
919 Ala Moana Boulevard
Suite 101
Honolulu, HI 96814                808-586-8121
                        FAX: 808-586-8129
                    e-mail: dcab@doh.hawaii.gov
                    www.hawaii.gov/health/dcab

*Francine Wai, Executive Director*
*Debbra Jackson, Planner*

Clearinghouse of information related to disability issues, lead agency in the community for dissemination of ADA information, systems advocacy provided through the introduction and lobbying of bills at the state legislation, review of blueprints for state and county renovation and new construction to make recommendations for physical accessibility; establishment of guidelines for communication access, including sign language interpreters and conducts state test to credential interpreters.

**3944  Hawaii Assistive Technology Training and**
414 Kuwili Street
Suite 104
Honolulu, HI 96817                808-532-7110

*Barbara Fischlowitz'le, Executive Director*

**3945  Hawaii Department for Children With Special Needs**
Department of Health
741a Sunset Avenue
Honolulu, HI 96816                808-733-9030
                        FAX: 808-733-8355
                www.state.hi.us/doh/resource/family

*Dr Patricia Hue, Chief Medical Officer*
*Karen Mak, Manager*

**3946  Hawaii Department of Health, Adult Mental Health Division**
PO Box 3378
Honolulu, HI 96801                808-941-3894
                        FAX: 808-586-4745
                        www.amhd.org

*Thomas W Hester MD, Chief*

**3947  Hawaii Department of Human Services**
Hawaii Department of Human Serv
1901 Bachelot Street
Honolulu, HI 96817                808-941-3894
                        FAX: 808-586-4143
                        www.hoopono.com

*Linda Lingel, Governor*
*Lillian Koller, Director*

Provides services to blind and visually impaired persons in adjustment to blindness, vocational rehabilitation, low vision evaluation and assistance. Work Evaluation, operates Work Activities Center, Vending training and the Ho'opono Workshop, a sheltered workshop program for the blind and visually impaired persons.

**3948  Hawaii Disability Compensation Division Department Labor and Industrial Relations**
830 Punchbowl Street
Room 211
Honolulu, HI 96813                808-586-9174
                        FAX: 808-586-9219

*Gary Hamada, Administrator*
*Clyde Imada, Workers Comp Chief*

Administers Hawaii's Workers' Compensation Program.

**3949  Hawaii Disability Rights Center**
900 Fort Street Mall
Suite 1040
Honolulu, HI 96813                808-949-2922
                        800-882-1052
                        FAX: 808-949-2928
            e-mail: info@hawaiidisabilityrights.org
                    www.hawaiidisabilityrights.org

*Henry Smith, President*
*Ann Collins, Vice President*

**3950  Hawaii Executive Office on Aging**
250 S Hotel Street
Suite 406
Honolulu, HI 96813                808-586-0100
                        800-468-4644
                        FAX: 808-586-0185
            e-mail: eoa@mail.health.state.hi.us
                    www2.hawaii.gov/eoa

*Pat Sasaki, Executive Director*

State unit on aging responsible for policy formulation, program development, planning, information dissemination, advocacy and other activities, for persons age 60 and over.

**3951  Hawaii State Council on Developmental Disabilities**
919 Ala Moana Boulevard
Honolulu, HI 96814                808-586-8100
                        FAX: 808-586-7543
                    e-mail: council@hiddc.org
                        www.hiddc.org

*Waynette K Y Cabral, Executive Administrator*

The mission of the council is to support people with developmental disabilities to control their own destiny and determine the quality of life they desire.

**3952  International Dyslexia Association: Hawaii Branch**
PO Box 61610
Honolulu, HI 96839                808-538-7007
                        FAX: 808-566-6837
                e-mail: hida@dyslexia-hawaii.org
                    www.dyslexia-hawaii.org

*Sue Voit, Co-president*
*Margaret Higa, Manager*

Provides free information and referral services for diagnosis and tutoring for parents, educators, physicians, and individuals with dyslexia. The voice of our membership is heard in 48 countries. Membership includes yearly journal and quarterly newsletter. Call for conference dates.

**3953  Social Security: Honolulu Disability Determination**
Social Security
300 Ala Moana Boulevard
Honolulu, HI 96850                808-541-3600
                        800-772-1213
                        FAX: 800-825-0778
                e-mail: hivrsbd@kestrok.com
                        www.ssa.gov

*Neil Shim, Administrator*

**3954  State Planning Council on Developmental Disabilities**
919 Ala Moana Boulevard
Suite 113
Honolulu, HI  96814                 808-586-8121
                              FAX: 808-586-8129
                    e-mail: tiza100w@wonder.cm.cdc.gov

*Francine Wai, Executive Director*

Consists of 25 Hawaii residents appointed by the governor. The council addresses the needs of the people with developmental disabilities: specifically, develops a state plan that sets the priorities for persons with developmental disabilities.

## Idaho

**3955  Idaho Commission on Aging**
3380 Americana Ter
Suite 120
Boise, ID  83720                    208-334-3833
                                    877-471-2777
                              FAX: 208-334-3033
                              www.idahoaging.com

*Lois S Bauer, Administrator*
*Gioia M Frahm, Planner/Statistician*
*Cathy Hart, State Ombudsman*

**3956  Idaho Council on Developmental Disabilities**
Health and Wellfare
802 W Bannock Street
Suite 308
Boise, ID  83702                    208-334-6800
                                    800-544-2433
                              FAX: 208-334-3417
                        e-mail: icdd@icdd.state.id.us
                              www.state.id.us/icdd

*Marilyn B Sword, Executive Director*

**3957  Idaho Department of Handicapped Children**
Statehouse
Boise, ID  83720                    208-334-8000

*Thomas Bruck, Chief*
*Sandy Frazier, Manager*

**3958  Idaho Disability Determinations Service**
PO Box 21
Boise, ID  83707                    208-327-7333
                                    800-626-2681
                              FAX: 208-373-7287
                              www.accessidaho.org

*Barbara Bauer, Director*
*Rogelio Valdez, Executive Director*

Under contract with the Social Security Administration, makes determinations of medical eligibility for disability benefits.

**3959  Idaho Industrial Commission**
PO Box 83720
Boise, ID  83720                    208-334-6000
                                    800-950-2110
                              FAX: 208-334-2321
                              www.state.id.us

*Mindy Montgomery, Director*
*Nancy Bedson, Administrative Assistant*

Free rehabilitation services to workers' who have suffered on the job injuries in Idaho. Field offices throughout the state.

**3960  Idaho Mental Health Center**
1720 Westgate Drive
Boise, ID  83704                    208-334-0800
                              FAX: 208-334-0828

*Dr. Gary Payne, Director*
*Pat Fitzpatrick, Manager*

## Illinois

**3961  Attorney General's Office: Disability Rights Bureau & Health Care Bureau**
100 W Randolph Street
Chicago, IL  60601                  312-814-3000
                              FAX: 312-814-3212
                       www.illinoisattorneygeneral.gov

*Lisa Madigan, Manager*
*Raymond Throlkeld, Chief Health Care Bureau*

Information on Illinois' Comprehensive Health Insurance Plan and architectural accessibility. Enforcement of Illinois' access law and standards and other disability rights laws. Information on initiatives such as: Opening the Courthouse Doors to People with Disabilities; the abuse, neglect or financial exploitation of people with disabilities and voter accessibility. Other information and referrals.

**3962  Client Assistance Program (CAP)**
Illinois State Board of Education
100 N 1st Street
1st Floor
Springfield, IL  62777              866-262-6663
                                    800-641-3929
                              FAX: 217-524-1790
                              TTY: 217-782-1900
                              www.isbe.state.il.us/

*Brenda J Holmes, Interim State Superintendent*

**3963  Equip for Equality**
20 N Michigan Avenue
Suite 300
Chicago, IL  60602                  312-341-0022
                                    800-537-2632
                              FAX: 312-341-0295
                              TTY: 800-610-2779
                    e-mail: contactus@equipforequality.org
                              www.equipforequality.org

*Zena Naiditch, President/CEO*
*Barry C Taylor, Legal Advocacy Director*

The mission of Equip for Equality is to advance the human and civil rights of children and adults with physical and mental disabilities in Illinois. It is the only statewide, cross-disability, comprehensive advocacy organization providing self-advocacy assistance, legal services, and disability rights education while also engaging in public policy and legislative advocacy and conducting abuse investigations and other oversight activities.

**3964  Illinois Assistive Technology Project**
1 W Old State Capitol Plaza
Springfield, IL  62701              217-522-7985
                                    800-852-5110
                              FAX: 217-522-8067
                              TTY: 217-522-9966
                              e-mail: iatp@iltech.org
                              www.iltech.org

*Wilhelmina Gunther, Executive Director*
*Sue Castles, Info/Assistance Funding Advoc.*

Directed by and for people with disabilities and their family members. As a federally mandated program, IATP strives to break down barriers and change policies that make getting and using technology difficult. IATP offers solutions to help people find what is available in products and services that will best meet their needs, where to find it, and how to get it.

**3965 Illinois Council on Developmental Disability**
State of Illinois Center
100 W Randolph Street
Chicago, IL 60601
312-814-2700
800-843-6154
FAX: 312-814-7441
e-mail: drs@dhs.state.il.us
www.dhs.state.il.us/ors

*Robert Kilbury, Executive Director*
*Dennis Sienko, Manager*

**3966 Illinois Department of Mental Health and Developmental Disabilities**
314 E Madison
Suite 3b
Springfield, IL 62701
217-782-2000
FAX: 217-785-3066

*Carol Adams Phd, Secretary*
*Lori Stone, Director*

**3967 Illinois Department of Rehabilitation**
622 E Washington Street
Springfield, IL 62701
217-782-7820
FAX: 217-557-0142

*Susan Suter, Director*
*Timothy Martin, Manager*

**3968 Illinois Department on Aging**
421 E Capitol Avenue
Suite 100
Springfield, IL 62701
217-785-2870
800-252-8966
FAX: 217-785-4477
e-mail: ilsenior@age084r1.state.il.us
www.state.il.us/aging

*Charles D Johnson, Executive Director*
*Nikki Smith, Communications Director*

**3969 International Dyslexia Association: Illinois Branch**
751 Roosevelt Road
Building 7
Glen Ellyn, IL 60137
630-469-6900
800-222-3123
FAX: 808-538-7007
e-mail: slonghall@aol.com
www.interdys.org

*Susan Hall, President*
*Maria Leibold, Executive Director*
*Gail Oliphant, Manager*

Provides free information and referral services for diagnosis and tutoring for parents, educators, physicians, and individuals with dyslexia in Illinois and Missouri. The voice of our membership is heard in 48 countries. Membership includes yearly journal and quarterly newsletter. Call for conference dates.

**3970 Social Security: Springfield Disability Determination**
2715 W Monroe Street
Springfield, IL 62704
217-862-6651
800-772-1213
TTY:217-862-6681
www.ssa.gov

**3971 Workers Compensation Board Illinois**
100 W Randolph Street
Suite 8-200
Chicago, IL 60601
FAX: 312-814-6523

*John Hallock Jr, Director*

## Indiana

**3972 Indiana Client Assistance Program**
850 N Meridian Street
Suite 2c
Indianapolis, IN 46204
317-888-8366
800-622-4845

*Richard Gordon, Owner*

**3973 Indiana Developmental Disability Council**
143 W Market Street
Suite 404
Indianapolis, IN 46204
317-231-7100

*Dan Parker, Executive Director*

**3974 Indiana Protection & Advocacy Services**
4701 N Keystone Avenue
Suite 222
Indianapolis, IN 46205
317-722-5555
800-622-4845
FAX: 317-722-5564
e-mail: info@ipas.in.gov
www.in.gov/ipas

*Thomas Gallagher, Executive Director*
*Milo Gray, Client & Legal Services Director*
*Gary Richter, Support Services Director*

An independent state agency established to protect and promote the rights of individuals with disabilities through empowerment and advocacy.

**3975 Indiana State Commission for the Handicapped**
PO Box 1964
Indianapolis, IN 46206
317-233-1292

**3976 International Dyslexia Association: Indiana Branch**
2511 E 46th Street
Suite O2
Indianapolis, IN 46205
317-926-1450
800-222-3123
FAX: 317-705-2067
e-mail: inbofida@hotmail.com
www.inbofida.org

*Mary Ian McAtter, President*

The Indiana Branch was formed to help the members of the learning disabilities community in Indiana. Promotes understanding and facilitate treatment of the Specific Language Disability (Dyslexia) in children and adults, promotes teacher training and educational intervention strategies for dyslexic students and to foster effective teaching, supports research in the field and early identification of dyslexia, serves as a clearinghouse for information and to actively disseminate knowledge.

## Iowa

**3977 Governor's Developmental Disability Council**
617 E 2nd Street
Des Moines, IA 50309
515-281-9082
800-452-1936
FAX: 515-281-9087
e-mail: jshoema@dhs.state.ia.us
www.state.ia.us/ddcouncil

*Becky Maddy Harker, Executive Director*
*Rik Shannon, Public Policy Manager*
*Janet Shoeman, Program Planner/Contract Manager*

The Council identifies, develops and promotes public policy and support practices through capacity building, advocacy, and systems change activities. The purpose is to ensure that people with developmental disabilities and their families are included in planning, decision making, and development of policy related to services and supports that affect their quality of life and full participation in communities of their choice.

**3978  International Dyslexia Association: Iowa Branch**
PO Box 11188
Cedar Rapids, IA  52410                    319-551-2851
                                           800-222-3123
                        e-mail: info@interdys.org
                                www.interdys.org

*Terri Peterson, President*

The purpose of the Iowa Branch of IDA (IDA-IA) is to increase awareness of dyslexia and promote services that address the importance of diagnosis and remediation for those not meeting their reading potential. Our goal is to provide services and assistance in a way that promotes unity, support, and cooperation among those who work with these individuals so that all communities in Iowa benefit from the skills and talents of its citizens.

**3979  Iowa Child Health Specialty Clinics**
100 Hawkins Drive
Room 247
Iowa City, IA  52242                       319-356-1469
                                           866-219-9119
                        FAX: 319-356-3715
                        www.uihealthcare.com/chsc

*Jeffrey Lobas, Director*
*Brian Wilkes, Director Of Operations*

Child Health Specialty Clinics has a mission to improve the health, development, and well-being of Iowa's children and youth with special health care needs in partnership with families, service providers, and communities.

**3980  Iowa Commission of Persons with Disabilities**
Department of Human Rights
321 E 12th Street
Des Moines, IA  50319                      515-242-6171
                                           888-219-0471
                        FAX: 515-242-6119
                e-mail: dhr.disabilities@dhr.state.ia.us
                        www.state.ia.us/dhr/pd

*Jill Abery, Administrator*

**3981  Iowa Compass**
Center for Disabilities and Development
100 Hawkins Drive
Iowa City, IA  52242                       319-353-6900
                                           877-686-0032
                        FAX: 319-356-1343
                        TTY: 877-686-0032
                e-mail: iowacompass@uiowa.edu
                        www.medicine.uiowa.edu/cdd

*Jane Gay, Project Director*
*David Sorton, President*
*Mark Moser, Administrator*

A statewide program provides free information and referral about disability related services and resources: advocacy, assistive technology, community services, early intervention, education, financial support, healthcare, legal aid, residential services and transportation.

*BiMonthly*

**3982  Iowa Department for the Blind**
524 4th Street
Des Moines, IA  50309                      515-281-1333
                                           800-362-2587
                        FAX: 515-281-1263
                        TTY: 515-281-1355
                e-mail: harrisallen@blind.state.ia.us
                        www.blind.state.ia.us

*Allen C Harris, Executive Director*

Mission is to be the means for persons who are blind to obtain univeral access and full participation as citizens in whatever roles they may choose.

**3983  Iowa Department of Elder Affairs**
510 E 12th Street
Room 2
Des Moines, IA  50319                      515-725-3333
                                           800-532-3213
                        FAX: 515-725-3300
                        www.state.ia.us/elderaffairs

*Mark Haverland, Executive Director*
*Sherry James, Executive Secretary*

**3984  Iowa Department of Human Services**
1305 E Walnut Street
Des Moines, IA  50319                      515-281-3974
                                           800-972-2017
                        FAX: 515-242-6036
                e-mail: joverla@dhs.state.ia.us
                        www.dhs.state.ia.us

*Jim Overland, Bureau Chief*

**3985  Iowa Protection & Advocacy for the Disabled**
950 Office Park Road
Suite 221w
W Des Moines, IA  50265                    515-278-2502
                                           800-779-2502
                        FAX: 515-278-0539
                e-mail: info@ipna.org
                        www.ipna.org

*Sylvia Piper, Executive Director*

**3986  Social Security: Des Moines Disability Determination**
Social Security Administration
210 Walnut Street
Federal Building, Room 293
Des Moines, IA  50309                      800-532-1223
                        TTY:515-281-1333
                        www.ssa.gov

*Karen Brown, President*

**3987  Workers Compensation Board Iowa**
1000 E Grand Avenue
Des Moines, IA  50319                      515-281-5387

# Kansas

**3988  Beach Center on Families and Disability**
University of Kansas
1200 Sunnyside Avenue
Lawrence, KS  66045                        785-864-2700
                        FAX: 785-864-7605
                e-mail: beachcenter@ku.edu
                        www.beachcenter.org

*HR Turnbull, Director*
*Ann Turnbull, Co-Director*
*Robert Hemenway, Chief Executive Officer*

A federally funded center that conducts research and training in the factors that contribute to the successful functioning of families with members who have disabilities.

**3989  International Dyslexia Association: Kansas/West Missouri Branch**
430 E Blue Ridge Boulevard
Kansas City, MO  64145                816-838-7323

www.interdys.org

*Billie Calvery, President*
*Arden Murilo, VP*

IDA members in Kansas and Missouri work to establish and maintain a presence for IDA with parents, schools, and teachers in order to help individuals with dyslexia. We maintain a list of individuals in Kansas and Missouri who have specialized training and who are available for diagnosis and remediation of reading, writing, and spelling problems, information for parents, information for teachers, an annual spring conference, newsletter dealing with state and local issues.

**3990  Kansas Advocacy and Protective Services**
3745 SW Wanamaker Road
Topeka, KS  66610                785-273-9661
                                877-776-1541
                        FAX: 785-776-5783
                    e-mail: michelle@ksadv.org
                        www.ksadv.org

*Rocky Nichols, Executive Director*
*Tim Voth, Attorney*
*Michelle Rola, Director Operations*

Protection and advocacy for persons with disabilities.

**3991  Kansas Client Assistance Program**
300 SW Oakley Avenue
Topeka, KS  66606                785-296-4454

**3992  Kansas Commission on Disability Concerns**
1430 SW Topeka Boulevard
Topeka, KS  66612                785-296-1722
                                800-295-5232
                        FAX: 785-296-0466
                        www.kcdcinfo.com

*Martha Gabehart, Executive Director*
*Randy Fisher, Employment/Training Liaison*
*Kerrie Bacon, Legislative Liasion*

KCDC believes that all people with disabilities are entitled to be equal citizens and partners in Kansas society. The purpose is to involve all segments of the Kansas Community through legislative advocacy, education and resource networking to ensure full and equal citizenship for all Kansans with disabilities.

**3993  Kansas Department on Aging**
503 S Kansas Avenue
Topeka, KS  66603                785-296-4986
                                800-432-3535
                        FAX: 785-296-0256
                e-mail: wwwmail@aging.state.ks.us
                        www.agingKansas.org

*Wilda Davison, Information And Referral*
*Barbara Conant, Public Information Officer*

Services and information for Kansas seniors.

**3994  Kansas Developmental Disability Council**
Disability Rights Center of Kansas
635 SW Harrison Street
Suite 100
Topeka, KS  66603                785-273-9661
                                877-776-1541
                        TTY:877-335-3725
                e-mail: info@drckansas.org
                srskansas.org/rehab/text/CAP.html
To protect children and promote adult self-sufficiency.

## Kentucky

**3995  Kentucky Council on Developmental Disability**
100 Fair Oakes Lane
Suite 4E-F
Frankfort, KY  40601
                                877-367-5332
                        FAX: 502-564-9826
                e-mail: shelley.runkle@ky.gov
                        www.kcdd.ky.gov

*Pat Seybold, Executive Director*

Implementation of Developmental Disabilities Planning Council responsible under P.L. 101-496.

**3996  Kentucky Department for Mental Health and Mental Retardation Services**
100 Fair Oaks Lane
Suite 4E-B
Frankfort, KY  40621                502-564-4527
                                FAX: 502-564-5478
                        www.dmhmrs.chr.state.ky.us

*John M Burt, Commissioner*
*Deborah Anderson, Staff Assistant*

The Department for Mental Health and Mental Retardation Services contracts with fourteen regional community mental health and mental broads to provide an array of community based mental health services; operates three psychiatric hospitals and contracts with two additional hospitals; operates or contracts for 10 ICFs/MR; also operates two nursing facilities.

**3997  Kentucky Department for Mental Health:**
100 Fair Oaks Lane
Suite 4e-B
Frankfort, KY  40621                502-564-4527

**3998  Kentucky Department for the Blind**
PO Box 757
Frankfort, KY  40602                502-564-4754
                                800-321-6668
                        TTY:502-564-2929
                e-mail: Wayne.Thompson@ky.gov
                www.state.ky.us/agencies/wforce

*Stephen Johnson, Executive Director*

Provides career services and assistance to adults with severe visual handicaps who want to become productive in the home or work force. Also provides the Client Assistance Program established to provide advice, assistance and information available from rehabilitation programs to persons with handicaps.

**3999  Kentucky Office of Aging Services**
Cabinet for Health Services
275 E Main Street
5w-A
Frankfort, KY  40621                502-564-6930
                                FAX: 502-564-4595
                        www.chfs.ky.gov

*Jerry Whitley, Manager*

The Kentucky Office of Aging Services is the state agency directly responsible for programs and services for people with disabilities. Efforts are made to fully integrate the service response information that considers broad farmiliar implications.

**4000 Kentucky Protection & Advocacy Division**
100 Fair Oaks Lane
3rd Floor
Frankfort, KY 40601                     502-564-2967
                                        800-372-2988
                                   FAX: 502-564-0848
                       e-mail: info@mail.pa.state.ky.us
                                        www.kypa.net

*Maureen Fitzgerald, Executive Director*

Protecting the rights of persons with disabilities in Kentucky
with a disability-related rights violation, providing information
and referral, training and technical assistance.

**4001 Social Security: Frankfort Disability Determination**
Social Security
PO Box 1000
Frankfort, KY 40602                     502-875-2232
                                        800-928-8050
                                   FAX: 502-226-4519
                                   TTY: 502-226-4519
                                        www.ssa.gov

*Stephen Jones, Director*
*Burton Sisk, Manager*

**4002 Social Security: Louisville Disability Determination**
Social Security
601 W Broadway
Suite 101
Louisville, KY 40202                    502-582-6690
                                        800-772-1213
                                   www.socialsecurity.gov

# Louisiana

**4003 Louisiana Assistive Technology Access Network**
PO Box 3455
Baton Rouge, LA 70821                   225-342-6804
                                        800-922-3452
                                   FAX: 225-342-8823

*Jill Revers, Project Director*
*Sandee Winchell, Executive Director*

An information and training resource on Assistive Technology
for the State of Louisiana. LATAN operates three regional centers to provide better access for consumers.

**4004 Louisiana Center for Dyslexia and Related Learning
Disorders**
PO Box 2050
Thibodaux, LA 70310                     985-448-4214
                                   FAX: 985-448-4423
                    e-mail: karen.chauvin@nicholls.edu
                              www.nicholls.edu/dyslexia

*Karen Chauvin, Director*

Provides free information and referral services for diagnosis and
tutoring for parents, educators, physicians and individuals with
dyslexia. The voice of our membership is heard in 48 countries.
Membership includes yearly journal and quarterly newsletter.
Call for conference dates.

**4005 Louisiana Client Assistance Program**
225 Baronne Street
Suite 2112
New Orleans, LA 70112
                                        800-960-7705
                                   FAX: 504-522-5507
                e-mail: advocacycenter@advocacyla.org
                                   www.advocacyla.org

*Diane Mirvis, CAP Director*

Assistance to persons seeking, receiving or who have been denied rehabilitation services from Louisiana Rehabilitaton Services (LRS) or other projects, programs or facilities funded
under the Rehabilitation Act (such as Vocational Rehabilitation, Independent Living or Supported Living). Must be a Louisiana resident and have a physical or mental disability.

**4006 Louisiana Department of Aging**
Office of Elderly Affairs
412 N 4th Street, 3rd Floor
PO Box 61
Baton Rouge, LA 70802                   225-342-7100
                                   FAX: 225-342-7133

*Godfrey White, Executive Director*

Serves as a focal point for Louisiana's senior citizens and administers a broad range of home and community based services
through a network of 37 Area Agencies on Aging. Serve as the
focal point for the development, implementation, and administration of the public policy for the state of Louisiana, and address the needs of the state's elderly citizens.

**4007 Louisiana Developmental Disability Council**
PO Box 3455
Baton Rouge, LA 70821                   225-342-6804
                                        800-922-DIAL
                                   FAX: 225-342-1970
                                        www.laddc.org

*Sandee Winchell, Executive Officer*

**4008 Louisiana Division of Mental Health**
PO Box 4049
Baton Rouge, LA 70821                   225-342-2540
                                   FAX: 225-342-5066

*Cheryll Bowers-Scephens, Director*
*William Payne, Manager*

**4009 Louisiana Learning Resources System**
2525 Wyandotte Street
Baton Rouge, LA 70805                   225-355-6197
                                   FAX: 225-357-3508

*Dr. Charlene Bishop, Director*
*Bobbie Robertson, Administrator*

Provides consultation on educational services for local schools,
offers psychological testing and evaluation, maintains resource
rooms in district schools and more for the blind and handicapped
throughout the state.

**4010 Louisiana Protection & Advocacy for Persons with De-
velopmental Disabilities**
225 Baronne Street
Suite 2112
New Orleans, LA 70112                   504-566-1600
                                        800-960-7705
                                   FAX: 504-522-5507
                        e-mail: adce@advocacyla.org

*Lois Simpson, Executive Director*
*Loretta Topey, Manager*

Legal and advocacy services and training to persons whose legal
issue is directly related to their disablity and has been designated an AC priority issue. Provides legal representation, counseling, information and referral, outreach, technical assistance,
special subject speakers, and staff/professional training.

**4011** **Protection & Advocacy of Individual Rights**
Advocate for Developmentally Disabled
225 Baronne Street
Suite 2112
New Orleans, LA 70112          504-522-2337
                              800-960-7705
                         FAX: 504-522-5507
          e-mail: webmaster@advocacyla.org
                         www.advocacyla.org

*Freddie Pincus, Vice President*

Legal services and training to people whose legal issue is directly related to their disability and has been designated an AC priority issue. Provides legal representation, counseling, information and referral, outreach, technical assistance, special subject speakers, and staff/professional training.

**4012** **Social Security: Baton Rouge Disability Determination**
Department of Social Services
755 N 3rd Street
Room 328
Baton Rouge, LA 70802          225-342-0286
                              800-772-1213
                         FAX: 225-219-9399
          e-mail: adren.wilson@dss.state.la.us
                              www.ssa.gov

*Shirley Williams, Director*
*Ann Williamson, Manager*

**4013** **Workers Compensation Board Louisiana**
PO Box 94040
Baton Rouge, LA 70804          225-342-7561
                              800-201-2494
                         FAX: 504-342-6555
                              www.laworks.net

*Karen Winfrey, Executive Director*

# Maine

**4014** **Maine Assistive Technology Projects**
University of Maine at Augusta
University Hts
Augusta, ME 04330          207-621-3000
                      FAX: 207-772-1302

*Kathleen Powers, Project Director*
*Pat Lynch, Manager*

A statewide program promoting assistive technology devices and services for persons of all ages with all disabilities.

**4015** **Maine Bureau of Elder and Adult Services**
State of Maine
11 State House Station
Augusta, ME 04333          207-287-9200
                      FAX: 207-287-9229
                           www.maine.gov

*Catherine Cobb, Director*
*Christine Gianopoulos, Executive Director*

**4016** **Maine Department of Health and Human Services**
221 State Street
Augusta, ME 04333          207-287-3707
                      FAX: 207-287-3005
          e-mail: brenda.harvey@maine.gov
                           www.maine.gov

*Brenda Harvey, Commissioner*
*Katherine Veilleux, Administrative Assistant*

Provision of services to people with nental illness, mental retardation, substance abuse issues, children with special needs and people with developmental disabilities.

**4017** **Maine Developmental Disability Council**
45 Memorial Circle
Suite 302
Augusta, ME 04330          207-622-6345
                      FAX: 207-622-6346
                       e-mail: mdf@mdf.org
                              www.mdf.org

*Laurie Lachance, President/CEO*

**4018** **Maine Division for the Blind and Visually Impaired**
2 Anthony Avenue
Augusta, ME 04333          207-624-5120
                              800-760-1573
                         FAX: 207-624-5133
                         TTY: 800-698-4440
          e-mail: harold.j.lewis@state.me.us
                         www.state.me.us/rehab

*Harold Lewis, Director*
*Sandra Cavanaugh, Manager*

Works to bring about full access to employment, independence and community integration for people with disabilities in Maine.

**4019** **Maine Workers' Compensation Board**
27 State House Station
Augusta, ME 04333          207-287-3751
                              888-801-9087
                         FAX: 207-287-7198
                         www.state.me.us/wcb

*Paul Dionne, Executive Director*

**4020** **Social Security: Maine Disability Determination**
40 Western Avenue
Augusta, ME 04330          207-622-1451
                              800-772-1213
                         TTY:207-623-4190
                              www.ssa.gov

*Louis Tepin, Manager*

# Maryland

**4021** **Health Resources & Services Administration : State Bureau of Health**
Federal Government
5600 Fishers Lane
Rockville, MD 20857          301-443-2216
                              888-275-4772
                         FAX: 301-443-1246
                              www.hrsa.gov

*Elizabeth M Duke, Administrator*

Through appropriated funds, supports education programs, credentialing analysis, and development of human resources needed to staff the U.S. health care system.

**4022** **International Dyslexia Association: Maryland Branch**
International Dyslexia Association
8600 La Salle Road
Suite 382
Baltimore, MD 21286          410-296-0232
                              800-222-3123
                         FAX: 410-321-5069
                       e-mail: info@interdys.org
                              www.interdys.org

*Nancy Hennessy, President*
*Guinevere Eden, Vice President*
*Megan Cohen, Executive Director*

Nonprofit organization providing free information and referral services for diagnosis and tutoring for parents, educators, physicians, and individuals with dyslexia. The voice of our membership is heard in 48 countries. Membership includes yearly journal and quarterly newsletter. Call for conference dates.

**4023 Maryland Client Assistance Program Division of Rehabilitation Services**
2301 Argonne Drive
Baltimore, MD 21218
410-554-9361
888-554-0334
FAX: 410-554-9412
TTY: 800-735-2258
e-mail: dors@dors.state.md.us
www.dors.state.md.us

*Beth Lash, Manager*

Helps individuals with disabilities understand the rehabilitation process and receives appropriate and quality services from the Division of Rehabilitation Services and other programs and facilities providing services under the Rehabilitation Act of 1973.

**4024 Maryland Department of Aging**
State Office Building
301 W Preston Street
Suite 1007
Baltimore, MD 21201
410-767-1100
800-243-3425
FAX: 410-333-7943
e-mail: drb@mail.ooa.state.md.us
www.mdoa.state.md.us/

*Dakota Burgess, Senior Information Program Manag*
*Jean Roesser, Manager*

**4025 Maryland Department of Handicapped Children**
201 W Preston Street
Unit 50
Baltimore, MD 21201
410-396-4476

*Judson Force, Director*

Children's Medical Services is a joint federal/state/local program which assists in obtaining specialized medical, surgical and related habilitative/rehabilitative evaluation and treatment services for children with special health care needs and their families. To be eligible for the program's services, an individual must be a resident of Maryland, younger than 22 years, have or be suspected of having an eligible medical condition and meet both medical and financial criteria.

**4026 Maryland Developmental Disabilities Council**
217 E Redwood Street
Suite 1300
Baltimore, MD 21202
410-767-3670
800-305-6441
FAX: 410-333-3686
e-mail: brianc@md-council.org
www.md-council.org

*Brian Cox, Executive Director*
*Catherine Lyle, Deputy Director*

A public policy organization comprised of people with disabilities and family members who are joined by state officials, service providers and other designated partners. The Council is an independent, self-governing organization that represents the interests of people with developmental disabilities and their families.

**4027 Maryland Disability Law Center**
1800 N Charles Street
Suite 400
Baltimore, MD 21201
410-727-6352
800-233-7201
FAX: 410-727-6389
TTY: 410-727-6387
www.mdlcbalto.org

*Virginia Knowlton, Manager*

Legal assistance provided to Maryland residents with any mental and or physical disability and to their families for disability related problems. Due to limited resources, not all cases are accepted, no criminal, domestic or employment cases.

**4028 Maryland Division of Mental Health**
2301 Argonne Drive
Baltimore, MD 21218
410-243-7495
FAX: 410-333-7482

*Norma Pinette, Executive Director*

**4029 Social Security: Baltimore Disability Determination**
711 W 40th Street
Rotunda Mall, Suite 415
Baltimore, MD 21211
800-772-1213
TTY:800-325-0778
www.socialsecurity.gov

**4030 Workers Compensation Board Maryland**
10 E Baltimore Street
Baltimore, MD 21202
410-864-5100
800-492-0479
e-mail: wcc@state.md.us
www.wcc.state.md.us

*Sheldon Press, Vice Chairman*
*Mary Ahearn, Director*

# Massachusetts

**4031 Center for Public Representation PAIMI Program for MA**
22 Green Street
Northampton, MA 01060
413-584-7773
FAX: 413-586-5711
e-mail: info@cpr-ma.org
www.centerforpublicrep.org

*Steven Chwertz, Executive Director*
*Robert Fleischner, Assistant Director*
*Howard Kantor DDS*

**4032 International Dyslexia Association of New England**
8600 La Salle Road
Suite 382
Baltimore, MD 21286
410-296-0232
800-222-3123
FAX: 410-321-5069
e-mail: info@interdys.org
www.interdys.org

*Nancy Hennessy, President*
*Guinevere Eden, Vice President*

Provides free information and referral services for diagnosis and tutoring for parents, educators, physicians, and individuals with dyslexia in Connecticut, Maine, New Hampshire, Rhode Island, and Vermont. The voice of our membership is heard in 48 countries. Membership includes yearly journal and quarterly newsletter. Call for conference dates.

**4033 Massachusetts Assistive Technology Partnership**
Children s Hospital Boston
1295 Boylston Street
Suite 310
Boston, MA 02215
617-267-9397
800-848-8867
FAX: 617-355-6345
e-mail: info@matp.org
www.matp.org

*Marylyn Howe, Project Director*
*Pat Hill, Training Coordinator*

A statewide program promoting assistive technology devices and services for persons with all disabilities.

**4034   Massachusetts Client Assistance Program**
Massachusetts Office on Disability
1 Ashburton Place
Room 1305
Boston, MA  02108                           617-727-7440
                                            800-322-2020
                                       FAX: 617-727-0965
                   e-mail: barbara.lybarger@state.ma.us
                                        www.state.ma.us

*Barbara Lybarger, Assistant Director*
*Myra Berloff, Executive Director*

Provides advocacy and information services.

**4035   Massachusetts Department of Mental Health**

25 Staniford Street
Boston, MA  02114                           617-626-8000
                                       FAX: 617-727-4350

*Eileen Elias, Commissioner*
*Michele Anzaldi, Manager*

**4036   Massachusetts Developmental Disabilities Council**

1150 Hancock Street
Quincy, MA  02169                           617-770-7676
                                       FAX: 617-770-1987
                e-mail: adelia.deltrecco@state.ma.us
                                   www.state.ma.us/mddc/

*Adelia Deltrecco, Executive Assistant*
*Harold Lieberman, Administrative Assistant*
*Dan Shannon, Executive Director*

Group of citizens which analyzes needs of people with severe, lifelong disabilities and works to improve public policy. MDDC produces several publications and has committees and a grants program to study and advocate for changes in the service system.

**4037   Social Security: Boston Disability Determination**

10 Causeway Street
Room 148, 1st Floor
Boston, MA  02222
                                            800-772-1213
                                        TTY:800-325-0778
                                    www.socialsecurity.gov

*Manuel J Vaz, Commissioner*

**4038   Workers Compensation Board Massachusetts**

1 Ashburton Place
Room 211
Boston, MA  02108                           617-727-2720
                                       FAX: 617-727-3285
                                     www.state.ma.us/dia

*James J Campbell, Director*
*Russell Gilfus, Manager*

# Michigan

**4039   Bureau of Workers' & Unemployment Compensation**
PO Box 30016
Lansing, MI  48909                          888-396-5041
                                       FAX: 517-322-1808
                     e-mail: bwdcinfo@cis.state.mi.us
                                       www.michigan.gov

*Craig Petersen, Executive Director*
*Bruno Czyrka, Deputy Director*

**4040   Department of Blind Rehabilitation**
Western Michigan University
1903 W Michigan Avenue
Kalamazoo, MI  49008                        269-387-3248

                            e-mail: bldrehab@wmich.edu

*Dr. William Wiener, Chairperson*
*Daniel Litynski, President*

**4041   Michigan Association for Deaf and Hard of Hearing**
2929 Covington Court
Unit 200
Lansing, MI  48912                          517-487-0066
                                            800-968-7327
                                       FAX: 517-487-0202
                                       TTY: 517-487-2586
                         e-mail: yourear@madhh.org
                                         www.madhh.org

*Nancy Asher, Executive Director*
*L'Tonya Felder, Program Coordinator*
*SaDonna White, Interpreter/Project Coordinator*

Substance abuse and anti violence prevention videos for deaf and hard of hearing students (alcohol, marijuana, inhalants) acted in sign language, voicing and captioning. HIV/AIDS prevention and information for the deaf and hard of hearing. Lending library books, videos and audio tapes. Accessibility to courts video and information. TTY distribution program.

**4042   Michigan Association for Deaf, Hearing and Speech Services**
2929 Covington Court
Unit 200
Lansing, MI  48912                          517-487-0066
                                            800-968-7327
                                       FAX: 517-487-2586
                         e-mail: yourear@madhs.org
                                         www.madhs.org

*Nancy Asher, Executive Director*

Substance abuse prevention for deaf and hard of hearing students (alcohol, marijuana, inhalants) acted in sign language, voicing and captioning. HIV/AIDS prevention and information for the deaf and hard of hearing. Lending library books, videos and audio tapes. Accessibility in Courts video and information. TTY distribution Program.

**4043   Michigan Client Assistance Program**
PO Box 30008
Lansing, MI  48909                          517-487-1755

*Elmer Cerano, Executive Director*

**4044   Michigan Coalition for Staff Development and School Improvement**
530 W Ionia Street
Suite C
Lansing, MI  48933                          734-513-9080
                                            800-444-2014
                                       FAX: 517-371-1170

**4045   Michigan Commission for the Blind: Lansing**
Michigan Department Labor & Econmic Goverment
201 N Washington Square
Floor 2
Lansing, MI  48933                          517-373-2062
                                            800-292-4200
                                       FAX: 517-335-5140
                                     www.michigan.gov/mcb

*Patrick Cannon, Executive Director*

**4046 Michigan Commission for the Blind - Gaylord**
209 W 1st Street
Suite 102
Gaylord, MI 49735
989-732-2448
800-292-4200
FAX: 989-731-3587
www.michigan.gov

*Judy Terwilliger, Manager*

**4047 Michigan Commission for the Blind**
Michigan Department of Labor and Economic Growth
PO Box 30652
Lansing, MI 48909
517-373-2062
800-292-4200
FAX: 517-335-5140
TTY: 517-373-4025
e-mail: cannonp@mi.gov
www.michigan.gov/mcb

*Patrick Cannon, Executive Director*
*Bob Robertson, Administrative Services Director*

The Commission for the Blind serves as the vocational rehabilitation agency for the blind. The Commission also operates a residential training center in kalamazoo, provides independent living services for Michigan's older blind population, low-vision services for the state's youth, a deaf/blind program, and entrepreneurial opportunities for blind persons through its Business Enterprise Program.

**4048 Michigan Commission for the Blind Training Center**
1541 Oakland Drive
Kalamazoo, MI 49008
269-337-3875
800-292-4200
FAX: 269-337-3872
e-mail: mossc@michigan.gov
www.michigan.gov/mcb

*Melody Lindsey, Director*
*Roger Yake, Councilor*

Residential facility that provides instruction to legally blind adults in braille, computers, handwriting, keyboarding, cane travel, adaptive kitchen skills, daily living, industrial arts and also crafts. Clients may also learn to use a variety of adaptive devices such as raised dot timers and watches, hand tools, talking calculators, tape recorders, reading machines and computers. Special training is also offered in vending stand operation, college preparation and job seeking skills.

**4049 Michigan Commission for the Blind: Escanaba**
305 Ludington Street
Escanaba, MI 49829
906-786-8602
800-323-2535
FAX: 906-786-4638
michigan.gov/dhs

*Bernie Kramer, Manager*

**4050 Michigan Commission for the Blind: Flint**
125 E Union Street
Floor 7
Flint, MI 48502
810-760-2030
FAX: 810-760-2032
www.mfia.state.mi.us

*Elizabeth White, Manager*

**4051 Michigan Commission for the Blind: Grand Rapids**
350 Ottawa Avenue NW
Grand Rapids, MI 49503
616-356-0180
800-292-4200
FAX: 616-356-0199
www.mcp1.org

*Patrick Cannon, Director*
*Bernie Kramer, Manager*

**4052 Michigan Council of the Blind and Visually Impaired (MCBVI)**
Neal Freeling
1037 Winchester Avenue
Lincoln Park, MI 48146
313-381-7844
888-956-2284
e-mail: freeling@concentric.net

*Neal Freeling, Information/Referral Specialist*
Advocate for blind and visually impaired people throughout the state of Michigan.

**4053 Michigan Department of Community Health**
320 S Walnut
Lansing, MI 48913
517-373-3654
FAX: 517-335-3090
e-mail: mccullochs@michigan.gov
www.michigan.gov/mdch

*Janet Olszewski, Director*
*A Edwin Dore, Chief Deputy Director*
*Bobbie Butler, Manager*

**4054 Michigan Department of Handicapped Children**
3423 N Logan Street
Lansing, MI 48906
517-373-3654
FAX: 517-335-9222

*Karen Schrock*
*Bobbie Butler, Manager*

**4055 Michigan Developmental Disability Council**
1033 S Washington Avenue
Lansing, MI 48910
517-334-6123
FAX: 517-334-7353
TTY:517-334-7354
www.michigan.gov/ddcouncil

*Vendella Collins, Executive Director*
*Todd Koopmans, Council Chairmain*
*Mitzi Allen, Administrative*

The Michigan DD Council is a group of citizens from across the state. Its membership is made up of: people with developmental disabilities; people from families who have, among their members, people with developmental disabilities; and professionals from state and local agencies charged with assisting people with developmental disabilities.

**4056 Michigan Office of Services to the Aging**
PO Box 30026
Lansing, MI 48909
517-373-0219
FAX: 517-373-4092

*Diane K Braunstein, Director*
*Tom Fogle, Executive Director*

State unit on aging; allocates and monitors state and federal funds for the Older American Act services: nutrition, community services, administers home and community based waiver, develops programs through Area Agencies on Aging, advocates on behalf of seniors with legislature, governor, state departments, federal government, responsible for state planning of aging services, develops formula for distribution of state and federal funds.

**4057 Michigan Protection & Advocacy Service**
4005 Legacy Parkway
Suite 500
Lansing, MI 48911
517-487-1755
800-288-5923
FAX: 517-487-0827
e-mail: molsen@mpas.org
www.mpas.org

**4058 Michigan Rehabilitation Services**
PO Box 30010
Lansing, MI 48909
517-373-3390
800-605-6722
FAX: 517-373-0565
TTY: 517-373-4035
www.michigan.org

*Jaye Balthazar, Manager*

A state and federally funded program that helps persons with disabilities prepare for and fund a job that matches their interests and abilities. Assistance is also available to workers with disabilities who are having difficulty keeping a job. A person is eligible for MRS services if he or she has a disability, is unemployed and needs vocational rehabilitation services to prepare for and find a job or independent living services.

**4059 Social Security Administration**
5210 Perry Robinson Circle
Lansing, MI 48911
517-393-3876
800-772-1213
FAX: 517-393-4686
TTY: 800-366-3404
e-mail: mi.fo.lansing@ssa.gov
www.ssa.gov

*Julie McCarthy, District Manager*

**4060 State of Michigan/Bureau of Workers' Disability Compensation**
PO Box 30016
Lansing, MI 48909
888-396-5014
FAX: 517-322-1808
www.cis.state.mi.us/wkrcomp

## Minnesota

**4061 International Dyslexia Association: Minnesota Branch**
International Dyslexia Association
5021 Vernon Avenue
PMB 159
Minneapolis, MN 55436
651-450-7589
800-222-3123
e-mail: info@interdys.org
www.interdys.org

*Claire Eckley, President*

UMBIDA-the Upper Midwest Branch of the International Dyslexia Association (IDA-serves the residents of Minnesota, North Dakota, South Dakota, and Winnipeg, Canada and offers: local educational conferences about dyslexia and related subjects, Orton-Gillingham training for teachers, tutors, and parents, Quarterly speaker series, member discounts on conferences, information line, and tutor referral.

**4062 Minnesota Assistive Technology Project**
STAR
50 Sherburne Avenue
Suite 309
Saint Paul, MN 55155
651-296-7138
800-657-3862
FAX: 651-282-6671
e-mail: star.program@state.mn.us
www.admin.state.mn.us/assistivetechnology

*Chuck Rassbach, Executive Director*
*Nancy Stark, Manager*

A statewide program promoting assistive technology devices and services for persons of all ages with all disabilities.

**4063 Minnesota Board on Aging**
444 Lafayette Road N
Saint Paul, MN 55155
651-296-2770
800-627-3529
FAX: 651-297-7855
e-mail: mba@sate.mn.us
www.mnaging.org

*Jim Varpness, Director*
*Maria Gomez, Board Member*

A state unit on aging for the state of Minnesota. Funds 14 area agencies on aging throughout the state that provide services at the local level. The mission is to keep older people in the homes or places of residence for as long as possible.

**4064 Minnesota Children with Special Needs, Minnesota Department of Health**
85 E 7th Place
PO Box 64882
Saint Paul, MN 55164
651-201-3650
800-728-5420
FAX: 651-201-3655
e-mail: mcshnweb@health.state.mn.us
www.health.state.mn.us/mcshn

Minnesota Children with Special Health Needs (MCSHN) provides leadership through partnerships with families and other key stakeholders to improve the access and quality of all systems impacting children and youth with special health care needs and their families.

**4065 Minnesota Department of Labor & Industry Workers Compensation Division**
443 Lafayette Road N
Saint Paul, MN 55155
651-284-5005
800-342-5354
FAX: 651-284-5727
e-mail: dli.workcomp@state.mn.us
www.doli.state.mn.us

*Scott Brener, Manager*

To reduce the impact of work related injuries for employees and employers. Advice is given and questions answered on the toll-free number.

**4066 Minnesota Disability Law Center**
430 1st Avenue N
Suite 300
Minneapolis, MN 55401
612-332-1441
800-292-4150
FAX: 612-334-5755
www.mndlc.org

*Pamela Hoopes, Manager*

Provides free, civil, legal assistance to Minnesotans with disabilities on issues related to their disability.

**4067 Minnesota Governor's Council on Developmental Disabilities GCDD**
370 Centennial Office Building
658 Cedar Street
Saint Paul, MN 55155
651-296-4018
877-348-0505
FAX: 651-297-7200
e-mail: admin.dd@state.mn.us
www.mncdd.org

*Colleen Wieck PhD, Executive Director*

The mission of the Minnesota Governor's Council on Developmental Disabilities is to provide information, education, and training to build knowledge, develop skills, and change attitudes that will lead to increased independence, productivity, self determination, integration and inclusion (IPSII) for people with developmental disabilities and their families.

**4068  Minnesota Mental Health Division**
Human Services Building
444 Lafayette Road N
Saint Paul, MN 55155                651-296-6117
e-mail: dhs.info@state.mn.us
www.dhs.state.mn.us/Provider/faqs/mental_heal

*Edwin Swenson, Director*
*Kevin Goodno, Manager*

Oversees the provision of services to people with mental illness
in the state of Minnesota. Services are provided on the local level
through a network of 87 county social service departments.

**4069  Minnesota Protection & Advocacy for Persons with Disabilities**
Minnesota Disability Law Center
430 1st Avenue N
Suite 300
Minneapolis, MN 55401              612-334-5784
800-292-4150
FAX: 612-334-5755
www.mnlegalservices.org/mdlc

*Lisa Cohen, Administrator*
*Pamela Hoopes, Manager*

**4070  Minnesota State Council on Disability (MSCOD)**
121 7th Place E
Suite 107
Saint Paul, MN 55101               651-296-6785
800-945-8913
FAX: 651-296-5935
e-mail: joanwillshire@state.mn.us
www.disability.state.mn.us

*Joan Willshire, Executive Director*

The MSCOD collaborates, advocates, advises and provides information to expant opportunities, increase the quality of life
and empower all persons with disabilities. This mission is accomplished by: providing information, referral and technical assistance to thousands of individuals every year via email, letter
or telephone; through trainings on a variety of disability related
topics; through publications and its web site; and through its advocacy and advisory work.

**4071  Minnesota State Services for the Blind**
2200 University Avenue W
Suite 240
Saint Paul, MN 55114               651-642-0500
800-652-9000
FAX: 651-649-5927
www.mnssb.org

*Lyle Lundquist, Senior Services Supervisor*
*Chuck Hamilton, Executive Director*
*Pam Brown, Workforce Development Director*

State agency serving blind and visually impaired persons with
rehabilitation, information access, assistive technology, training and job placement services. Extensive older blind program.

**4072  Social Security: St. Paul Disability Determination**
190 5th Street E
Sibley Building, Suite 800
Saint Paul, MN 55101
800-772-1213
TTY:800-325-0778
www.ssa.gov

*Noreen Hale, Director*

# Mississippi

**4073  International Dyslexia Association: Mississippi Branch**
1604 Bistineau
Ruston, LA 71270                   985-414-2575
800-222-3123
e-mail: info@interdys.org
www.interdys.org

*Alice Higginbotham, President*

It is the mission of the Louisiana Branch to provide information
and resources to parents, educators, students and the community
in a way that creates a clear and positive understanding of dyslexia and related language learning needs so that every individual has the opportunity to lead a productive and fulfilling life for
the benefit of society.

**4074  Mississippi Assistive Technology Division**
PO Box 1698
Jackson, MS 39215                  601-853-5100
FAX: 601-853-5158
www.mdrs.state.ms.us

*Chris Geroux, Coordinator*
*Marie Gaddis, Administrative Assistant*
*Bob Richards, Manager*

A statewide program promoting assistive technology devices
and services for persons of all ages with all disabilities.

**4075  Mississippi Bureau of Mental Retardation**
1101 Robert E Lee Bldg
Jackson, MS 39201                  601-359-1288
FAX: 601-359-6295

*Ed LeGrand, Chief*
*Herb Loving, Executive Director*

**4076  Mississippi Client Assistance Program**
Mississippi Department of Rehabilitation Services
PO Box 39110
Jackson, MS 39215                  601-362-2585
FAX: 601-982-1951

*Presley Posey, Executive Director*

Advocacy program for clients/client applicants for state of MS
vocational services.

**4077  Mississippi Department of Mental Health**
1101 Robert E Lee Bldg
Jackson, MS 39201                  601-359-1288
FAX: 601-359-6295
www.dmh.state.ms.us

*Herb Loving, Executive Director*
*Edwin Legrand, Assistant Director*

Administers Mississippi's public programs of serving persons
with mental illness, mental retardation, alcohol and substance
abuse problems, and alzheimer's disease and related dementia.

**4078  Mississippi Division of Aging and Adult Services**
Mississippi Department Of Human Services
750 N State Street
Jackson, MS 39202                  601-359-4500
800-345-6347
FAX: 601-359-3664
e-mail: webspinner@mdhs.state.ms.us
www.mdhs.state.ms.us/

*Donald Taylor, Director*

Protects the rights of older citizens while expanding their opportunities and access to quality services.

**4079  Mississippi State Department of Health**
Children s Medical Program
PO Box 1700
Jackson, MS 39215
601-987-3965
800-844-0898
FAX: 601-987-5560

*Larry Clark, Director*
*Denise Faith, State Nursing Coordinator*
*Virginia Green MD, Medical Director*

Financial assistance to families of children with physical handicaps. Rehabilitative in nature and has as its goal the correction or reduction of physical handicaps. Eligibility determined by diagnosis and provided to children from birth to age twenty-one. Financial eligibility is determined by factors of family income, family size, estimated cost of treatment and family liabilities. Categories include, but are not limited to: orthopedic, congenital heart defects, cerebral palsy, etc.

**4080  Mississippi: Workers Compensation Commission**
1428 Lakeland Drive
Jackson, MS 39216
601-987-4200
FAX: 601-987-4233
www.mwcc.state.ms.us

*Ray Minor, Executive Director*
*Carla Clark, Division Director*

## Missouri

**4081  Institute for Human Development**
University of Missouri-Kansas City
2220 Holmes Street
Kansas City, MO 64108
816-235-1700
800-444-0821
FAX: 816-235-1762
e-mail: ellerbuschk@umkc.edu
www.ihd.umkc.edu

*Carl Calkins, Director*
*Lora Lacey-Haun, Administrator*

A statewide program promoting person-centered planning and services for persons of all ages with all disabilities.

**4082  Missouri Division of Mental Retardation & Developmental Disabilities**
Department of Mental Health
PO Box 687
Jefferson City, MO 65102
573-751-4054
FAX: 573-751-9207
e-mail: dmhmail@dmh.mo.gov
www.dmh.mo.gov

*Bernard Simons, Division Director*
*Ron Diettemore Ed,D, Department Director*
*Kent Stalder, Manager*

**4083  Missouri Protection & Advocacy Services**
925 S Country Club Drive
Jefferson City, MO 65109
573-893-3333
800-392-8667
FAX: 573-893-4231
e-mail: mopasjc@earthlink.net
www.moadvocacy.org

*Shawn T Loyola, Executive Director*
*Linda Snider, Information Specialist*
*Connie Wright, Information Specialist*

MO P&A provides protection of the rights of persons with disabilities in Missouri and assistance to clients who have disabilities through information, referral, advocacy or legal counsel. Informational brochures, Alliance newsletter, Client Assistance Program (CAP) Manual available upon request.

**4084  Missouri Rehabilitation Services for the Blind**
PO Box 88
Jefferson City, MO 65103
573-751-4249
800-592-6004
FAX: 573-751-4984
e-mail: mmerrick@mail.state.mo.us
www.dss.state.mo.us/dfs/rehab/rehab.htm

*Mike Fester, Executive Director*
*Mike Merrick, Policy Development Coordinator*

Offers services for the totally blind, legally blind, visually impaired, including counseling, educational, recreational, rehabilitation, computer training and professional training services.

**4085  Social Security: Jefferson City Disability Determination**
2401 E McCarty Street
Jefferson City, MO 65101
800-772-1213
www.ssa.gov

*Dr. Don Gann, Director*

**4086  Workers Compensation Board Missouri**
Department of Labor and Industrial Realtions
3315 W Truman Boulevard
Jefferson City, MO 65109
573-751-4231
FAX: 573-751-2012
e-mail: workerscomp@dolir.mo.gov
www.dolir.state.mo.us

*Patricia Secrest, Director*

## Montana

**4087  Addictive & Mental Disorders Division**
555 Fuller Avenue
Helena, MT 59601
406-444-3964
FAX: 406-444-4435
www.dphhs.state.mt.us

*Joyce Decunzo, Administrator*
*Joan Cassidy, Bureau Chief*
*Lou Thompson, MH Bureau Chief*

**4088  Montana Advocacy Program**
PO Box 1680
Helena, MT 59624
406-449-3266
800-245-4743
FAX: 406-449-2418
TTY: 800-245-4743
e-mail: advocate@mtadv.org
www.mtadv.org

*Bernadette Franks-ongoy, Executive Director*

Protects and advocates the human and legal rights of Montanans with mental and physical disabilities while advancing dignity, equality, and self-determination. Designated federal P&A, with AT, CAP, PADD, PAIMI and PAIR programs. Advocacy and legal services for abuse, neglect, rights violations, access, discrimination in employment, accommodations and housing, and assistance with vocational rehabilitation/visual services.

**4089  Montana Blind & Low Vision Services**
PO Box 4210
Helena, MT 59604
406-444-2590
FAX: 406-444-0230
www.dphhs.state.mt.us/dsd

*Joe Mathews, Manager*

Mission: promoting work and independence for Montanans with disabilities.

**4090  Montana Council on Developmental Disabilit ies**
PO Box 526
Helena, MT 59624
406-443-4332
FAX: 406-443-4192
e-mail: deborah@mtcdd.org
www.mtcdd.org

*Deborah Swingley, Executive Director*

**4091  Montana Department of Aging**
Capitol Station
Room 219
Helena, MT 59620
406-225-4411
FAX: 406-444-5529

*Hank Hudson, Aging Coordinator*
*Jeff Sturm, President*

**4092  Montana Department of Handicapped Children**
Cogswell Building
Helena, MT 59620
406-225-4411

*Jeff Sturm, President*

**4093  Montana Protection & Advocacy for Persons with Disabilities**
400 N Park Avenue
Helena, MT 59601
406-449-2344
800-245-4743
FAX: 406-449-2418
e-mail: advocate@mtav.org
www.mtadv.org

*Bernadette Franks-Ongoy, Executive Director*

**4094  Montana State Fund**
5 S Last Chance Gulch
PO Box 4759
Helena, MT 59601
406-444-6500
800-332-6102
FAX: 406-444-5963
e-mail: msfwebmaster@montanastatefund.com
www.montanastatefund.com

*Ed Henrich, Chairman*

Montana State Fund is committed to the health and economic prosperity of Montana through superior service, leadership and caring individuals, working in an environment of teamwork, creativity and trust.

**4095  Montech Rural Institute on Disabilities**
634 Eddy Avenue
Missoula, MT 59812
406-243-5511
877-243-5511
FAX: 406-243-4730
e-mail: montech@ruralinstitute.umt.edu
www.montech.ruralinstitute.umt.edu

*Kathleen Laurin, Program Director*
*Mary Swan, Equipment Loan Manager*

Montana's comprehensive resource center for assistive technology (AT) devices, information, training, evaluations and other AT related supports.

**4096  Social Security: Helena Disability Determination**
10 W 15th Street
Suite 1600
Helena, MT 59601
406-411-1270
800-772-1213
TTY:406-441-1278
www.socialsecurity.gov

## Nebraska

**4097  International Dyslexia Association: Nebraska Branch**
5921 Sunrise Road
Lincoln, NE 68510
402-488-7920
800-222-3123
e-mail: carolyn.brandle@ne-ida.com
www.interdys.org

*Carolyn Brandle, President*

The Nebraska Branch of the International Dyslexia Association is a 501(c)(3), non-profit organization dedicated to the study and treatment of dyslexia and related learning differences. This Branch was formed in 1981 to increase public awareness of dyslexia throughout Nebraska, and to serve individuals with dyslexia and their families. The organization includes professionals in the area of learning disabilities education, counseling and medicine as well as dylexics and their families and friends.

**4098  Nebraska Advocacy Services**
134 S 13th Street
Suite 600
Lincoln, NE 68508
402-474-3183
800-422-6691
FAX: 402-474-3274
e-mail: nas@nas-pa.org
www.nebraskaadvocacyservices.org

*Timothy Shaw, Executive Director*
*Eric Evans, Deputy Director*

Offers protection and advocacy services to people with developmental disabilities or mental illness. Direct assistance provided if issue within broad case priorities. Sliding scale fee. Information and referral at no cost.

**4099  Nebraska Client Assistance Program**
PO Box 94987
Lincoln, NE 68509
402-471-3656
800-742-7594
FAX: 402-471-0117
e-mail: victoria@cap.state.ne.us
www.cap.state.ne.us/

*Victoria Rasmussen, Director*
*Frank Lloyd, Executive Director*

**4100  Nebraska Commission for the Blind & Visually Impaired**
4600 Valley Road
Suite 100
Lincoln, NE 68510
402-471-2891
877-809-2419
FAX: 402-471-3009
e-mail: pearl.vanzandt@ncbvi.ne.gov
www.ncbvi.ne.gov

*Pearl Van Zandt PhD, Executive Director*
*Carlos Servan, Deputy Director*
*Bob Deaton, Deputy Director*

Offers services for the totally blind, legally blind, visually impaired, mentally retarded blind and more with health, counseling, educational, recreational, rehabilitation, computer training and professional training services.

**4101  Nebraska Department of Health & Human Services of Medically Handicapped Children's Prgm**
301 Centennial Mall S
5th Floor
Lincoln, NE 68508
402-471-5185
FAX: 402-471-6352
e-mail: roger.hillman@hhss.state.ne.us

*Jeanne Garvin MD, Medical Director*
*Harlow Hyde, Program Specialist*
*Roland Snuttjer, Program Manager*

Maternal and child health, Title V, children with special health care needs; community based, statewide programs to facilitate diagnoses and care of children with disabilities and chronic medical conditions.

**4102  Nebraska Department of Health and Human Services, Division of Aging Services**
PO Box 95044
Lincoln, NE  68509
402-471-5185
800-942-7830
FAX: 402-471-4619
www.hhss.ne.gov

*Joan Weis, Director*
*Arti Cover, Manager*

**4103  Nebraska Department of Mental Health**
301 Centennial Mall S
Lincoln, NE  68508
402-471-5185
FAX: 402-423-7045
www.nmhc-clinics.com

*Arti Cover, Manager*

**4104  Nebraska Planning Council on Developmental Disabilities**
Department of Health and Human Services
301 Centennial Mall S
PO Box 95044
Lincoln, NE  68509
402-471-2330
FAX: 402-471-0183
TTY:402-471-9570
e-mail: mary.gordon@hhss.ne.gov
www.hhs.state.ne.us/ddplanning

*Mary Gorden, Director*

The Council focuses on persons who experience a severe disability that occurs before the individual attains the age of 22, which includes persons with physical disabilities, mental/behavioral health conditions and persons that are served by the current state developmental disabilities system.

**4105  Nebraska Workers' Compensation Court**
State of Nebraska
PO Box 98908
Lincoln, NE  68509
402-471-6468
800-599-5155
FAX: 402-471-2700
e-mail: newcc@wcc.ne.gov
www.wcc.ne.gov/

*Glenn Morton, Administrator*
*Su Davis, Public Information Manager*

**4106  Social Security: Lincoln Disability Determination**
Department of Education
PO Box 94987
Lincoln, NE  68509
402-471-2295
800-772-1213
FAX: 471-362-
TTY: 402-471-3659
e-mail: flloyd@nde4.nde.state.ne.us
www.socialsecurity.gov

*Frank Lloyd, Assistant Commissioner*
*Doug Christensen, Manager*

## Nevada

**4107  Assistive Technology Center at NCEP: Nevada Community Enrichment Program**
2820 W Charleston Boulevard
Las Vegas, NV  89102
702-259-1903
FAX: 702-259-1907

*Terry Sjoberg Otr/l, Manager*
*Robert Hogan, Executive Director*
*Reggie Bennett, Independent Living Coordinator*

Provides information, demonstration and training to adults and children with disabilities in the use of microcomputers and other assistive technology product systems and devices. ATC offers peer screening, pre-service financial and resource planning, low interest loan program, technology matching, rehabilitation engineering, outreach training, and maintains a product information database.

**4108  Nevada Assistive Technology Project**
3656 Research Way
Suite 32
Carson City, NV  89706
775-687-4452
888-337-3839
FAX: 775-687-3292
www.hr.state.nv.us

*Kelleen Preston, Project Manager*
*Todd Butterworth, Chief*

Serves all ages and all disabilities through partnerships with community organizations. The NATP provides training, advocacy, funding, information and referral services, a newsletter and weekly television show.

**4109  Nevada Bureau of Services to the Blind and Visually Impaired**
505 E King Street
Suite 501
Carson City, NV  89701
775-684-4244
FAX: 775-684-4186

*Gayle Sherman, Chief*

Offers services for the totally blind, legally blind, visually impaired, mentally retarded blind and more with health, counseling, educational, recreational, rehabilitation, computer training and professional training services.

**4110  Nevada Department of Mental Health: Neuro Clinic**
505 E King Street
Suite 602
Carson City, NV  89701
775-684-5943
FAX: 775-684-5964
e-mail: mhds@govmail.state.nv.us
www.mdhs.state.nv.us

*Braden Burg, Director*
*Carlos Brandenberg, Administrator*

Offers treatment, prevention, education, habitation and rehabilitation for mental disorders. Works with advocacy groups, families, agencies and the community.

**4111  Nevada Developmental Disability Council**
3656 Research Way
Suite 32
Carson City, NV  89706
775-687-4452

e-mail: rweathermon@dhr.state.nv.us
www.nevadaddcouncil.org

*Richard Weathermon, Executive Director*
*Mary Bryant, Acting Council Chair*

The mission of the Nevada Developmental Disabilities Council is to provide resources at the community level which promote equal opportunity and life choices for people with disabilities through which they may positively contribute to Nevada society.

**4112 Nevada Disability Advocacy and Law Center -Sparks/Reno Office**

1311 N McCarran Boulevard
Suite 106
Sparks, NV 89431

775-333-7878
800-992-5715
FAX: 775-788-7825
TTY: 702-788-7824
e-mail: reno@ndalc.org
www.ndalc.org

*Anna Maria Carini, Office Coordinator*
*Jack Mayes, Executive Director*

Nevada's protection and advocacy system for the human legal and service rights of individuals with disabilities. NDALC has offices in Reno/Sparks and Las Vegas, with services provided statewide.

**4113 Nevada Division for Aging: Carson City**

3416 Goni Road
Building D
Carson City, NV 89706

775-687-4210
800-992-0900
FAX: 775-687-4264
e-mail: dascc@aging.state.nv.us
www.aging.nv.state.us

*Carol Fala, Administrator*

Provides services for seniors in Nevada including community based care. advocacy and volunteer programs. Call write or e-mail for more information.

**4114 Nevada Division for Aging: Las Vegas**

3100 W Sahara Avenue
Suite 103
Las Vegas, NV 89102

702-486-3545
FAX: 702-486-3572
e-mail: dasvegas@aging.nv.gov
www.nvaging.net

*Carol Sala, Administrator*
*Marilyn Wills, Deputy Administrator*
*Bruce Annany, Manager*

Develops, coordinates and delivers a comprehensive support service system in order for Nevada' senior citizens to lead independent, meaningful and dignified lives.

**4115 Social Security: Carson City Disability Determination**

1170 Harvard Way
Reno, NV 89502

800-352-1605
800-772-1213
TTY:800-325-0778
www.socialsecurity.gov

*Dan Mooney, Director*

**4116 State of Nevada Client Assistance Program**

2450 Wrondel Way
Suite E
Reno, NV 89502

775-688-1440
800-633-9879
FAX: 775-688-1627

**4117 Workers Compensation Board Nevada**

6515 E Musser Street
Carson City, NV 89714

775-687-6492
FAX: 775-687-5786

## New Hampshire

**4118 New Hampshire Workers Compensation Board**

46 Donovan Street
Concord, NH 03301

603-224-9222
FAX: 603-226-6903
www.nhprimex.org

*Paul Genevose, Chief Executive Officer*
*Kathy Fortin, Manager*

**4119 New Hampshire Assistive Technology Partnership Project**

Department of Education
State of New Hampshire
Concord, NH 03824

603-862-2260
FAX: 603-228-2468

*Jan Nisbet, Director*
*Mary Schuh, Associate Director*
*Eve Fralick, Associate Director*

The goal of the New Hampshire Assistive Technology Partnership Project is to increase access to assistive technology through the creation and support of consumer driven systems for the provision of state-of-the-art assistive technology products and services for citizens with disabilities in the state of New Hampshire.

**4120 New Hampshire Client Assistance Program**

57 Regional Drive
Concord, NH 03301

603-271-4175
FAX: 603-271-2837
www.state.nh.us/disability/caphomepage.html

*Bill Hagy, Director*

**4121 New Hampshire Commission for Human Rights**

2 Chenell Drive
Concord, NH 03301

603-271-2767
800-735-2964
FAX: 603-271-6339
e-mail: humanrights@nhsa.state.nh.us
www.state.nh.us

*Katharine A Daly, Executive Director*

Enforces New Hampshire law against discrimination in housing, employment or public accomodations. Disability discrimination is prohibited under New Hampshire law. Takes formal charges and investigates them.

**4122 New Hampshire Department of Mental Health**

State Office Park S
Concord, NH 03301

603-226-0111
FAX: 603-271-5058

*Donald Shumway, Director*
*Paul Garmon*
*Tim Rourke, Religious Leader*

**4123 New Hampshire Developmental Disabilities Council**

21 S Sruit Street
Suite 22
Concord, NH 03301

603-271-3236
800-852-3345
FAX: 271-115-
e-mail: NHDDCNCL@aol.com
www.nhddc.org

*Gordon Allen, Executive Director*
*Leslie Nelson, Director of Policy/Planning*
*Jennifer Daniels, Administrative Assistant*

Offers information, referral and support services to disabled persons. A federally funded state agency.

**4124  New Hampshire Division of Developmental Services**
Department of Health and Human Services
105 Pleasant Street
Concord, NH  03301                             603-271-5034
                                          FAX: 603-271-5166
                          e-mail: dpowers@dhhs.state.nh.us
                                      www.dhas.srare.nh.us.

*Matthew Ertas, Director*
*Michelle Rosado, Administrative Assistant*

Developmental Services promotes opportunities for normal life experiences for persons with developmental disabilities and aquired brain disorders in all areas of community life: employment, housing, recreation, social relationships and community association. Services and supports are organized throught a central state office and twelve private nonprofit community area agencies. Family support is provided to families of children with chronic health conditions or are developmentally disabled.

**4125  New Hampshire Division of Elderly and Adult Services**
Bureau of Elderly & Adult Services
129 Pleasant Street
Concord, NH  03301                             603-271-4680
                                               800-351-1888
                                          FAX: 603-271-4643
                                        www.dhhs.state.nh.us

*Douglas McNutt, Acting Bureau Chief*
*Mary Maggioncaida, Manager Program Development*

The Bureau of Elderly and Adult Services provides a variety of social and long-term supports to adults age 60 and older and to adults between the ages of 18 and 60 who have a chronic illness or disability. These services range from home care, meals on wheels, care management, transportation assistance and assisted living to nursing home care.

**4126  New Hampshire Governor's Commission on Disability**
57 Regional Drive
Suite 5
Concord, NH  03301                             603-271-2773
                                               800-852-3405
                                          FAX: 603-271-2837
                                        www.nh.gov/disability

*Carol Nadeau, Executive Director*

**4127  New Hampshire Protection & Advocacy for Persons
with Disabilities**
18 Low Avenue
Concord, NH  03301                             603-224-4394
                                               800-834-1721
                                          FAX: 603-225-2077
                             e-mail: advocacy@drcnh.org
                                           www.drcnh.org

*Richard Cohen, Executive Director*
*Ron Lospennato, Legal Director*

Legal services for individuals with disabilities; I & R.

**4128  Social Security: Concord Disability Determination**
70 Commercial Street
Suite 100
Concord, NH  03301                             603-224-1939
                                               800-772-1213
                                          TTY:603-225-8475
                                               www.ssa.gov

**4129  Workers Compensation Board New Hampshire**
95 Pleasant Street
Concord, NH  03301                             603-271-3176
                                               800-272-4353
                                          FAX: 603-271-6149
                       e-mail: workerscomp@labor.state.nh.us
                                       www.labor.state.nh.us

*Kathryn Barger, Executive Director*

---

## New Jersey

**4130  Division of Developmental Disabilities**
PO Box 726
Trenton, NJ  08625                             609-292-3742
                                               800-932-9173
                                          FAX: 609-292-6610
                              e-mail: advoca@njpanda.org
                                          www.njpanda.org

*James W Smith Jr, Extecutive Director*

New Jersey's designated protection and advocacy system for poeple with disabilities and provides legal, nonlegal individual and systems advocacy.

**4131  International Dyslexia Association: New Jersey Branch**
NJIDA
PO Box 32
Long Valley, NJ  07853                         908-879-1179

                                    e-mail: riegpainting@msn.com
                                          www.interdys.org

*Francie M Matthews PhD, President*

The New Jersey Branch of The International Dyslexia Association is a 501(c)(3) non-profit, scientific and educational organization which was formed to increase public awareness of dyslexia in New Jersey. We have been serving individuals with dyslexia, their families, and professionals in the field in this community for more than 25 years.

**4132  New Jersey Commission for the Blind and Visually Impaired**
153 Halsey Street
6th Floor, PO Box 47017
Newark, NJ  07101                              973-648-2324
                                               877-685-8878
                                          FAX: 973-648-7364
                         e-mail: Vito.DeSantis@dhs.state.nj.us
                          www.state.nj.us/humanservices/cbvi

*Vito J DeSantis, Executive Director*
*James W Smith, Jr, Acting Commissioner*
*Jose Morales, Manager*

The mission of the New Jersey Commission for the Blind and Visually Impaired is to promote and provide services in the areas of education, employment, independence and eye health through informed choice and partnership with persons who are blind or visually impaired, their families and the community. Serves Bergen, Essex, Hudson, Morris, Passaic, Sussex and Warren Counties.

**4133  New Jersey Department of Aging**
S Broad and Front Street
Trenton, NJ  08608                             609-292-3766

*Ruth Leader, Director*

**4134  New Jersey Department of Health/Special Child Health
Services**
New Jersey Department of Health and Senior Service
PO Box 364
Trenton, NJ  08625                             609-777-7778
                                          FAX: 609-292-3580
                           e-mail: plisciotto@doh.state.nj.us

*Gloria Rodriguez, Director*
*Pauline Lisciotto, Program Manager*

Provides services for New Jersey children that will prevent or reduce the effects of a developmental delay, chronic illness or behavioral disorder.

**4135 New Jersey Division of Mental Health Services**
Department Human Services
50 E State Street
Trenton, NJ 08608
609-292-3717
800-382-6717
FAX: 609-341-3333
www.state.nj.us/humanservices

*Lyn Gates, Bureau Chief*
*James Davy, Commissioner*

Oversees the public mental health system for the state of New Jersey. Operates six regional and specialty psychiatric hospitals, and contracts with over 125 not-for-profit agencies to provide a comprehensive system of community mental health services throughout all counties in the state.

**4136 New Jersey Governor's Liaison to the Office of Disability Employment Policy**
PO Box 52
Trenton, NJ 08625
609-292-2323
FAX: 609-633-9271
e-mail: cmycoff@dol.state.nj.us
www.state.nj.us/labor

*Mark B Boyd, Commissioner*
*Al Kirk, Assistant Director*
*Rick Shanberg, Program Assistant*

The Division of Vocational Rehabilitation Services provides vocational rehabilitation services to prepare and place in employment eligilbe individuals with disabilities who, because of their disabling conditions, would otherwise be unable to secure and/or mantain employment

**4137 New Jersey Protection & Advocacy for Persons with Disabilities**
Trenton, NJ 08625
609-530-5200
FAX: 609-292-6610

*Robert Nickolas, Director*
*Ida Castro, President*

**4138 Regional ADA Technical Assistance Center**
United Cerebral Palsy Associations of New Jersey
354 S Broad Street
Trenton, NJ 08608
609-392-4004
800-949-4232
FAX: 609-392-7044
TTY: 609-392-7044
e-mail: BTACUPNJ@aol.com
home.earthlink.net/~dawwn/dbtac.htm

*Richard Dodds, Contact Person*
*Jack Mudge, Executive Director*

**4139 Social Security Administration**
635 S Clinton Avenue
Trenton, NJ 08611
800-772-1213
TTY:800-325-0778
www.ssa.gov

Social Security disability is a social insurance program that workers and employers pay for with their Social Security taxes. Eligibility is based on your work history, and the amount of your benefit is based on your earnings. Social Security also has a disability program for people with limited income and resources-the Supplemental Security Income (SSI) program. For more information on these federal programs, please call our nationwide toll-free number.

## New Mexico

**4140 New Mexico Aging and Long-Term Services Department**
2550 Cerrillos Road
Santa Fe, NM 87505
505-827-7640
866-451-2901
FAX: 505-476-4836
www.nmaging.state.nm.us

*Debbie Armstrong, Executive Director*
*Patsy Trujillo-Knaver, Deputy Secretary*
*Michael Spanier, Deputy Secretary*

Information and services for seniors, people with disabilities and their families.

**4141 New Mexico Client Assistance Program**
1720 Louisiana Boulevard NE
Suite 204
Albuquerque, NM 87110
505-256-3100
800-432-4682
FAX: 505-256-3184
e-mail: info@nmpanda.org
www.nmpanda.org

*James Jackson, Exeuctive Director*

**4142 New Mexico Commission for the Blind**
2905 Rodeo Park Drive E
Building 4
Santa Fe, NM 87505
505-820-6860
FAX: 505-476-4475
e-mail: greg.trapp@state.nm.us
www.state.nm.us/cftb

*Robert Stark, Executive Director*

Offers services for the totally blind, legally blind, visually impaired, mentally retarded blind and more with health, counseling, educational, recreational, rehabilitation, computer training and professional training services.

**4143 New Mexico Department of Health: Children's Medical Services**
1190 S Saint Francis Drive
Santa Fe, NM 87505
505-827-2548
FAX: 505-827-1697
e-mail: lchristiansen@doh.state.nm

*Lynn Christiansen, Program Manager*

Title V MCH Program for children with special health care needs from birth to age 21 years. Services provided include: diagnosis, medical intervention, clinics and service coordination.

**4144 New Mexico Governor's Committee on Concerns of the Handicapped**
491 Old Santa Fe Trail
Santa Fe, NM 87501
505-986-4589
FAX: 505-827-6328

*Paula Tackett, Executive Director*

**4145 New Mexico Protection & Advocacy for Persons with Disabilities**
1720 Louisiana Boulevard NE
Suite 204
Albuquerque, NM 87110
505-256-3100
800-432-4682
FAX: 505-256-3184
e-mail: info@nmpanda.org
www.nmpanda.org

*James Jackson, Executive Director*

**4146  New Mexico Technology Assistance Program**
NMDVR/NMTAP
435 Saint Michaels Drive
Building D
Santa Fe, NM  87505

800-866-2253
FAX: 505-954-8608
TTY:800-659-4915
e-mail: andy.winnegar@state.mn.us
www.nmtap.com

*Andy Winnegar, Director*
*Yvonne Hart, Planner Director*

The New Mexico Technology Assistance Program (NMTAP)
offers free services to New Mexicans with disabilities to help
them get the assistive technology (AT)services they need. Our
mission is to help persons with disabilities enhance their quality
of life through the use of assistive technology.

**4147  New Mexico Workers Compensation Administration**
PO Box 27198
Albuquerque, NM  87125

505-841-6000
866-WOR-KOMP
FAX: 505-841-6866
www.state.nm.us/wca

*Alan Varela, Director*

Regulates workers' compensation in New Mexico.

**4148  Social Security: Santa Fe Disability Determination**
604 W San Mateo Road
Santa Fe, NM  87505

505-473-3707
800-772-1213
FAX: 505-827-3512
e-mail: terryb@oscar.state.nm.us
www.socialsecurity.gov

*Terry Brigance, Director*

**4149  Southwest Branch of the International Dyslexia Association**
International Dyslexia Association
PO Box 25891
Albuquerque, NM  87125

505-255-8234
800-222-3123
FAX: 505-262-8547
e-mail: swida@southwestida.com
southwestida.com

*Linda Curry, President*

Provides free information and referral services for diagnosis and
tutoring for parents, educators, physicians, and individuals with
dyslexia. The voice of our membership is heard in 48 countries.
Membership includes yearly journal and quarterly newsletter.
Call for conference dates.

**4150  Workers Compensation Board New Mexico**
PO Box 27198
Albuquerque, NM  87125

505-841-6000
FAX: 841-606-0

*Steven Kennedy, Director*
*Alan Varela, Manager*

## New York

**4151  Albany County Department for Aging**
162 Washington Avenue
Albany, NY  12210

518-447-7198
FAX: 518-447-7188
e-mail: aging@albanycounty.com
www.albanycounty.com

*Vincent Colonno, Director*

**4152  International Dyslexia Association of NY: Buffalo Branch**
c/o Gow School
2491 Emery Road
South Wales, NY  14139

716-687-2030
800-222-3123
e-mail: bufida@gow.org
www.interdys.org

*Timothy Madigan PhD, President*

**4153  Jawonio Vocational Center**
Jawonio Vocational Center
260 N Little Tor Road
New City, NY  10956

845-634-4648
FAX: 845-634-7731
www.jawonio.org

*Esther White, Associate Director Employment*
*Paul Tendler, Administrator*

Offers vocational evaluation, training, counseling and job
placement services.

**4154  NYS Commission on Quality of Care & Advocacy for Persons with Disabilities**
1 Empire State Plaza
Suite 1001
Albany, NY  12223

518-449-2825
800-522-4369
FAX: 518-473-6005
e-mail: webmaster@cqcapd.state.ny.us
www.cqcapd.state.ny.us

*Gary O'Brien, Commissioner*
*RoseMary Lamb, Associate Advocate*
*Mark Keegan, Director QA/Investigations*

**4155  NYSARC**
393 Delaware Avenue
Delmar, NY  12054

518-439-8311
800-724-2094
FAX: 518-439-1893
e-mail: info@nysarc.org
www.nysarc.org

*Marc Brandt, Executive Director*

**4156  National Alliance for the Mentally Ill of NY State**
260 Washington Avenue
Albany, NY  12210

518-462-2000
800-950-3228
FAX: 518-462-3811
e-mail: info@naminys.org
www.naminys.org

*Ione Christian, President*
*J David Seay, Executive Director*

**4157  New State Office of Mental Health Agency**
Office of Mental Health
44 Holland Avenue
Albany, NY  12229

518-473-6579
800-597-8481
FAX: 518-474-2149
www.omh.state.ny.us

*Sharon Carpinello, Commissioner*

Promoting the mental health of all New Yorkers with a particular focus on providing hope and recovery for adults with serious
mental illness and children with serious emotional disturbances.

**4158  New York Client Assistance Program**
99 Washington Avenue
Suite 1002
Albany, NY  12210

518-869-1543
FAX: 518-474-2652
www.nls.org/caplist.htm

**4159    New York Department of Handicapped Children**
Department of Heath Education
PO Box 678
Albany, NY 12201                              518-447-4691
                                        FAX: 518-447-4573
                        e-mail: jcrucetti@albanycounty.com
                                     www.health.state.ny.us

*Thomas Blake, Acting Bureau Chief*
*James Crucetti, Commisioner*

**4160    New York State Commission for the Blind**
52 Washington Street
Rensselaer, NY 12144                          518-473-8072
                                        FAX: 518-486-5819

*Thomas Robertson, Associate Commissioner*
*Madeline Raciti, Manager*

Offers services for the totally blind, legally blind, visually impaired, mentally retarded blind and more with health, counseling, educational, recreational, rehabilitation, computer training and professional training services.

**4161    New York State Commission on Quality of Care**
401 State Street
Schenectady, NY 12305                         518-388-2892
                                        FAX: 518-388-2890
                          e-mail: marcelc@cqc.state.ny.us
                                       www.cqc.state.ny.us

*Marcel Chaine, Director Advocacy Services*
*Gary O'Brien, Manager*

**4162    New York State Congress of Parents and Teachers**
1 Wembley Court
Albany, NY 12205                              518-452-8808
                                        FAX: 518-452-8105
                               e-mail: office@nypta.com
                                         www.nyspta.org

*Penny Leask, President*
*Maria Dewald, First Vice President*

**4163    New York State Office of Advocates for Persons with Disabilities**
1 Empire State Plaza
Suite 1001
Albany, NY 12223                              518-449-7860
                                              800-522-4369
                                        FAX: 518-473-6005
                           e-mail: oapwdinfo@oapwd.org
                                         www.oapwd.org

*Gary O'Brien, Chair Commissioner*

Provides information and referral services; administers NYS Tech Art Project; promotes implementation of disability-related laws.

**4164    New York State Office of Mental Health**
44 Holland Avenue
Albany, NY 12229                              518-474-2568
                                              800-597-8481
                                        FAX: 518-474-1846
                                     www.omh.state.ny.us

*Sharon E Carpinello RN PhD, Commissioner*

Promoting the mental health of all New Yorkers with a particular focus on providing hope and recovery for adults with serious mental illness and children with serious emotional disturbances.

**4165    New York State TRAID Project**
New York State Commisionon Qualityof Careand Advoc
1 Empire State Plaza
Suite 1001
Albany, NY 12223                              518-449-7860
                                              800-522-4369
                                        FAX: 518-473-6005
                                         www.oatwd.org

*Lisa Rosano, Project Director*

**4166    Parent to Parent of New York State**
500 Balltown Road
Schenectady, NY 12304                         518-381-4350
                                              800-305-8817
                                        FAX: 518-393-9607
                             e-mail: par2parent@aol.com
                                  www.parenttoparentnys.org

*Janice Fitzgerald, Executive Director*
*Mary Hebert, Manager*

**4167    Protection and Advocacy Agency of NY**
401 State Street
Schenectady, NY 12305                         518-388-2892
                                              800-624-4143
                                        FAX: 518-388-2890
                          e-mail: marcelc@cqc.state.ny.us
                                       www.cqc.state.ny.us

*Marcel Chaine, Director Advocacy Services*
*Gary O'Brien, Manager*

**4168    Regional Early Childhood Director Center**
875 E Main Street
Suite 240
Rochester, NY 14605                           585-399-4617
                                              800-462-4344
                                        FAX: 585-271-4228
                       e-mail: amy_campbell@boces.monroe.edu
                                     www.vesid.nysed.gov

*Amy Campbell, Director*
*Michael Reif, Executive Director*
*Jill Jensen, Family Information Specialist*

Provides information, support and referral assistance to parents and professionals who are concerned with chilren with special needs or handicapping condition between the ages of birth to five.

**4169    Resources for Children with Special Needs**
116 E 16th Street
Floor 5
New York, NY 10003                            212-677-4650
                                        FAX: 212-254-4070
                            e-mail: info@resourcesnyc.org
                                     www.resourcesnyc.org

*Karen Schlesinger, Executive Director*
*Dianne Littwin, Publishing Director*

An independent, nonprofit organization that provides information, referral, advocacy, training and support for parents and professionals in the New York City metropolitan area who are looking for programs and services for children from birth to 21 with learning, developmental, emotional or physical disabilities.

**4170    Singeria/Metropolitan Parent Center**
15 W 65th Street
6th Floor
New York, NY 10023                            212-496-1300
                                        FAX: 212-496-5608
                             e-mail: intake@sinergiany.org
                                       www.sinergiany.org

*Harminia Mendez, Human Resources Executive*

**4171 Social Security: Albany Disability Determination**
1 Clinton Avenue
Room 430, Federal Building
Albany, NY 12207                        518-431-4051
                                        800-772-1213
                                        TTY:518-431-4050
                                        www.ssa.gov

*Thomas A Robertson, Assistant Commissioner*

**4172 State Agency for the Blind and Visually Impaired**
52 Washington Street
Rensselaer, NY 12144                    518-474-6812
                                        866-871-3000
                                        FAX: 518-486-5819
                                        e-mail: info@ocfs.state.ny.us
                                        www.ocfs.state.ny.us

*Thomas Robertson, Associate Commissioner*
*Brian Daniels, Manager*

**4173 State Education Agency Rural Representative**
Education Building Anx
Room 876
Albany, NY 12234                        518-474-3936
                                        FAX: 518-473-2860
                                        e-mail: sspear@mail.nysed.gov
                                        www.nysed.gov

*Suzanne Spear, Supervisor*

**4174 State Mental Health Representative for Children and Youth**
44 Holland Avenue
Albany, NY 12229                        518-473-6328

                                        e-mail: cocompz@omh.state.ny.us

*David Woodlock, Deputy Commissioner*

**4175 State Mental Retardation Program**
44 Holland Avenue
Albany, NY 12229                        518-473-1997
                                        FAX: 518-473-1271
                                        www.omr.state.ny.us

*Thomas Maul, Commissioner*

**4176 United We Stand of New York**
594 Bushwick Avenue
Brooklyn, NY 11206                       718-748-1461
                                        FAX: 718-302-4315
                                        e-mail: uwsofny@aol.com
                                        www.uwsofny.org

*Lourdes Rivera-Putz, Program Director*
*George Likourezos, President*
*Amanda Putz, Child Advocate*
Assists families with improving the quality of life for all individuals with disabilities.

**4177 University Afiliated Program/Rose F Kennedy Center**
1971
Parkway South
Suite 10
Bronx, NY 10461

                                        430-850-
                                        www.aecom.yu.edu/cerc

*Hebert J Cohen, Director*

**4178 University of Rochester Medical Center**
601 Elmwood Avenue
Rochester, NY 14642                     585-275-6772
                                        FAX: 585-275-3366
                                        e-mail: phil_davidson@urmc.rochester.edu
                                        www.urmc.rochester.edu/strong/scdd

*Philp W Davidson, Director*
*Susan Edwards, Manager*

**4179 VESID**
New York State Education Department
1606 One Commerce Plaza
Room 1606
Albany, NY 12234                        518-474-2714
                                        FAX: 518-474-8802
                                        www.vesid.nysed.gov

*Dr Rebecca Cort, Deputy Commissioner*
Vocational and educational services for individuals with disabilities.

**4180 VSA Arts of New York City**
18-05 215 Street
Suite 15N
Bayside, NY 11360                       718-225-6305
                                        FAX: 717-225-6305
                                        e-mail: bbvsanyc@msn.com
                                        www.vsarts.org

*Dr Bebe Berenstein, Executive Director*
Provides art, educational and creative expression experiences to thousands of children, youth, and adults with disabilities who reside in the five boroughs of New York City. It provides opportunities for people with disabilities to demonstrate their accomplishments in the arts and foster increased understanding and acceptance.

**4181 Westchester Institute for Human Development**
Cedarwood Hall
Valhalla, NY 10595                      914-493-8150

                                        e-mail: wihd@wihd.org
                                        www.wihd.org

*Ansley Bacon PhD, President/CEO*
*Alison Bailey MSEd, Administrative Operations*
*Maritza Molina MD, Medical Director*
WIHD advances policies and practices that foster the healthy development and ensure the safety of all children, strengthen families and communities, and promote health and well-being among people of all ages with disabilities and special health care needs.

**4182 Workers Compensation Board New York**
20 Park Street
Albany, NY 12207                        800-877-1373
                                        877-632-4996
                                        FAX: 718-802-6642
                                        www.wcb.state.ny.us

*Linda Spano, District Administrator*
*Pat Wright, District Manager*

# North Carolina

**4183 Developmental Disability Services Section**
Albemarle
Building 325n
Raleigh, NC 27699                       919-733-7011
                                        FAX: 919-733-9455
                                        www.dhhs.state.nc.us/mhddsas/

*Michael Moseley, Director*
*Sylvia Prumpler, Human Resource Manager*

Makes policies and monitors public services and supports to people with mental illness, developmental disabilities and substance abuse throughout North Carolina.

**4184 International Dyslexia Association: North Carolina Branch**
1829 E Franklin Street
Franklin Square, Suite 1200 K
Chapel Hill, NC 27514
919-933-8880
800-222-3123
FAX: 828-963-1883
e-mail: edutherapy@earthlink.net
www.interdys.org

*Susan Lowell MA BCET, President*

The North Carolina Branch of The International Dyslexia Association (NCIDA) is a 501 (c)(3) non-profit, scientific and organization dedicated to educating the public about the learning disability, dyslexia. The North Carolina Branch has four objectives: to increase awareness in the dyslexic and general community; to network with other learning disability groups and legislators in education;to increase membership and provide services that will strengthen members presence in their communities

**4185 North Carolina Workers Compensation Board**
430 N Salisbury Street
Raleigh, NC 27603
919-676-2288
FAX: 919-715-0282
www.comp.state.nc.us/

*J Bunn Jr, Director*

**4186 North Carolina Assistive Technology Project**
1110 Navaho Drive
Suite 101
Raleigh, NC 27609
919-872-2298
FAX: 919-850-2792
e-mail: ncatp@minespring.com
www.ncatp.org

*Ricki Cook, Project Director*
*Annette Lauber, Funding Specialist*
*Jacquelyne Gordon, Consumer Resource Specialist*

The North Carolina Assistive Technology Project exists to create a statewide, consumer-responsive system of assistive technology services for all North Carolinians with disabilities. The project's activities impact children and adults with disabilities across all aspects of their lives.

**4187 North Carolina Children & Youth Branch**
North Carolina Publc of Health
1928 Mail Service Center
Raleigh, NC 27699
919-832-2839
FAX: 919-715-3187
e-mail: cathy.kluttz@nemail.net
www.nchealthychilderen.com

*Carol Tant, Head Children/Youth Branch*
*Cathy Kluttz, Unit Manager Special Service*
*Dianne Tyson, Help Line Manager*

**4188 North Carolina Client Assistance Program**
2806 Mail Service Center
Raleigh, NC 27699
919-855-3600
800-215-7227
FAX: 919-715-2456
e-mail: nccap@ncmail.net
cap.state.nc.us

*Kathy Brack, Director*
*Frank Ashfield, Client Advocate*

A federally funded program designed to assist individuals with disabilities in understanding and using rehabilitation services.

**4189 North Carolina Developmental Disabilities**
1001 Navaho Drive
Suite Gl103
Raleigh, NC 27609
919-850-2833
800-357-6916
FAX: 919-850-2895
e-mail: Holly.Riddle@ncmail.net
www.nc-ddc.org

*Holly Riddle*

A planning council established to assure that individuals with developmental disabilities and their families participate in the planning of and have access to culturally competent services, supports, and other assistance and opportunities that promote independence, productivity, and integration and inclusion into the community; and to promote, through systemic change, capacity building and advocacy activities, a consumer and family-centered comprehensive system.

**4190 North Carolina Division of Aging**
2101 Mail Service Center
Raleigh, NC 27699
919-733-3983
FAX: 919-733-0443
www.dhhs.state.nc.us/aging/home.htm

*Karen Gottivi, Director*

**4191 North Carolina Industrial Commission**
430 N Salisbury Street
Raleigh, NC 27603
919-733-3484
FAX: 919-715-0282
www.comp.state.nc.us

*J Howard Bunn Jr, Chairman*
*Peg Dorer, Executive Director*

**4192 Social Security: Raleigh Disability Determination**
4701 Old Wake Forest Road
Raleigh, NC 27609
919-790-2782
800-772-1213
FAX: 919-790-2773
TTY: 919-790-2773
e-mail: www.socialsecurity.gov
www.ssa.gov

Provides information on how to obtain social security through a disability.

## North Dakota

**4193 Division of Mental Health and Substance Abuse**
1237 W Divide Avenue
Suite 1C
Bismarck, ND 58501
701-328-8920
800-755-2719
FAX: 701-328-8969
e-mail: dhsmhsas@nd.gov
www.nd.gov/humanservices

*Jo Anne Hoesel, Director*
*Don Wright, Ass't. Director Substance Abuse*

The Department of Human Services' Mental Health and Substance Abuse Services Division provides leadership for the planning, development, and oversight of a system of care for children, adults, and families with severe emotional disorders, mental illness, and/or substance abuse issues.

**4194 North Dakota Workers Compensation Board**
50 E Front Avenue
Bismarck, ND 58504
701-328-3800
800-777-5033
FAX: 701-329-9911
TTY: 701-328-3786
www.ndworkerscomp.com

*Brent Edison, Director*

**4195  North Dakota Client Assistance Program**
1237 W Divide Avenue
Suite 3
Bismarck, ND  58501                  701-328-8947
                                     800-207-6122
                                 TTY:701-328-8968
                             e-mail: cap@state.nd.us
                                    www.nd.gov/cap

*Dennis Lyon, Chief Executive Officer*

CAP assists clients and client applicants of North Dakota Vocational Rehabilitation services, Tribal Vocational Rehabilitation, or Independent Living services.

**4196  North Dakota Department of Aging**
600 E Boulevard Avenue
Dept 325
Bismarck, ND  58505                  701-328-2455
                                     800-451-8693
                                 FAX: 701-328-4061
                         e-mail: dhsaging@state.nd.us
                         www.state.nd.us/humanservices/

*Linda Wright, Director*
*Bryan Klipfel, Manager*

**4197  North Dakota Department of Human Services**
600 E Boulevard Avenue
Dept 325
Bismarck, ND  58505                  701-328-2310
                                     800-472-2622
                                 FAX: 701-328-3480
                             e-mail: dhseo@nd.gov
                           www.nd.gov/humanservices

*Tamara Gallud-millner, Deputy Director*

Provides services that help vulnerable North Dakotans of all ages to maintain or enhance their quality of life, which may be threatened by lack of financial resources, emotional crises, disabling conditions, or an inability to protect themselves. Also supports the provision of services and care as close to home as possible to maximize each person's independence while preserving the dignity of all individuals and respecting their constitutional and civil rights.

**4198  Protection & Advocacy Project**
1984
400 E Broadway Avenue
Suite 409
Bismarck, ND  58501                  701-328-2950
                                     800-472-2670
                                 FAX: 701-328-3934
                           e-mail: panda@state.nd.us
                                  www.ndpanda.org

*Teresa Larsen, Executive Director*

The Protection and Advocacy is a state agency whose purpose is to advocate for and protect the rights of people with disabilities. The Protection and Advocacy Project has programs to serve people with developmental disabilities, mental illnesses and other types of disabilities. The projects programs and services are free to eligible individuals.

**4199  Social Security: Bismarck Disability Determination**
1680 E Capitol Avenue
Bismarck, ND  58501                  701-250-4200
                                     800-772-1213
                                 TTY:701-250-4620
                                      www.ssa.gov

**4200  Workers Compensation Board North Dakota**
4007 State Street
Bismarck, ND  58503                  701-328-3800

## Ohio

**4201  Epilepsy Council of Greater Cincinnati**
895 Central Avenue
Suite 550
Cincinnati, OH  45202                513-721-2905
                                     877-804-2241
                                 FAX: 531-721-0799
                             e-mail: ecgc@fuse.net
                   www.epilespsyfoundation.org/cincinatti

*Margie Frommeyer, Executive Director*

**4202  International Dyslexia Association: Central Ohio Branch**
PO Box 16216
Columbus, OH  43216                  614-899-5711
                                     800-222-3123
                    e-mail: cybdischultz@columbus.rr.com
                                    www.interdys.org

*Cyndi Schultz, President*

Provides free information and referral services for diagnosis and tutoring for parents, educators, physicians, and individuals with dyslexia. The voice of our membership is heard in 48 countries. Membership includes yearly journal and quarterly newsletter. Call for conference dates. Other locations available in Ohio state.

**4203  Ohio Bureau for Children with Medical Hand icaps**
Ohio Department of Health
PO Box 1603
Columbus, OH  43216                  614-466-2115
                                     800-755-4769
                                 FAX: 614-728-3616
                          e-mail: bcmb@.odh.ohio.gov
                                   www.odh.ohio.gov

*James Bryant Md, Bureau Chief*
*Nick Baird, Director*
*Steven Kelley, Manager*

Provides funding for the diagnosis, treatment and coordination of services for eligible Ohio children, under age 21, with medical handicaps; conducts quality assurance activities to establish standards of care and determine unmet needs of children with handicaps and their families; collaborates with public health nurses to increase access to care; and assists families to access and use third party resources. Conducts a separate program for adults with cystic fibrosis.

**4204  Ohio Bureau of Worker's Compensation**
30 W Spring Street
Columbus, OH  43215
                                     800-644-6292
                                 FAX: 877-520-6446
                                 TTY:800-292-4833
                   e-mail: ombudsperson@bwc.state.oh.us
                                   www.ohiobwc.com

*William E Mabe, Administrator/CEO*

To provide a quality, customer-focused workers' compensation insurance system for Ohio's employers and employees.

**4205  Ohio Client Assistance Program**
30 E Broad Street
Room 120
Columbus, OH  43215                  614-466-6920
                                 FAX: 614-752-4197

*Donald Bishop, Executive Director*

**4206  Ohio Department of Aging**
1982
50 W Broad Street
Floor 9
Columbus, OH  43215                      614-466-5500
                                         866-243-5678
                                         888-243-5678
                                   FAX: 614-466-5741
                                  www.goldenbuckeye.org

*Merle Grace Kearns, Director*
*John Ratliff, Public Information Officer*
*John Lawrence, Executive Director*

The department serves and represents about 2 million Ohioans age 60 & older. They advocate for the needs of all older citizens with emphasis on improving the quality of life, helping senior citizens live active, healthy, & independent lives, & promoting positive attitudes toward aging & older people. Committed to helping the frail elderly who choose to remain at home by providing home & community based services, their goal is to promote the level of choice, independence & self-care.

**4207  Ohio Department of Mental Health**
30 E Broad Street
Floor 8
Columbus, OH  43215                      614-466-4775
                                         877-275-6364
                                   FAX: 614-466-1571
                         e-mail: uhricks@mh.state.oh.us
                                     www.mh.state.oh.us

*Michael Hogan, Director*
*Christine Vincenty, Manager*

**4208  Ohio Developmental Disability Council**
8 E Long Street
12th Floor
Columbus, OH  43215                      614-466-5205
                                         800-766-7426
                                   FAX: 614-466-0298
                   e-mail: david.zwyer@dmr.state.oh.us
                                      www.ddc.ohio.gov

*David Zwyer, Director*

The Ohio Developmental Disabilities Council is one of 55 councils found in all states and territories which provides funding for systems change grant projects. The DD Council is a planning and advocacy agency that seeks to improve the lives of Ohioans with disabilities.

**4209  Ohio Governor's Council on People with Disabilities**
400 E Campus View Boulevard
Columbus, OH  43235                      614-438-1393
                                         800-282-4536
                                   FAX: 614-438-1274
                                       gcpd.ohio.gov

*Robin Moore Cooper, Executive Committee Chair*
*Marcella Eblin, Secretary*

The Governor's Council on People with Disabilities exists to: Advise the Governor and General Assembly on statewide disability issues, promote the value of diversity, dignity and the quality of life for people with disabilities, be a catalyst to create systemic change promoting awareness of disability-related issues that will ultimately benefit all citizens of Ohio, Educate and advocate for: partnerships at the local, state and national level, promotion of equality, access and independence.

**4210  Ohio Legal Rights Service**
8 E Long Street
5th Floor
Columbus, OH  43215                      614-466-9956
                                         800-282-9181
                                   FAX: 614-448-8
                                  www.state.oh.us/OLRS/

*Carolyn Knight, Administrator*

**4211  Ohio Rehabilitation Services Commission**
400 E Campus View Boulevard
Columbus, OH  43235                      614-438-1200
                                         800-282-4536
                                   FAX: 614-438-1257
                                     www.state.oh.us/rsc

*John M Connelly, Executive Director*

RSC is Ohio's state agency that provides vocational rehabilitation (VR) services to help people with disabilities become employed and independent. We also offer a variety of services to Ohio businesses, resulting in quality jobs for individuals who have disabilities.

**4212  Social Security: Columbus Disability Determination**
90 E Washington Bridge Road
Suite 160
Worthington, OH 43085                    614-888-5339
                                         800-772-1213
                                   TTY:614-288-0226
                                  www.socialsecurity.gov

*Jo Anne B Barnhart, Commissioner*
*Mary B Chatel, Executive Director of Disability*

**4213  Workers Compensation Board Ohio**
246 N High Street
Columbus, OH  43215                      614-466-4110

*Michele Frizzell, Manager*

# Oklahoma

**4214  Oklahoma Workers Compensation Board**
Department of Labor
400 N Lincon Boulevard
Oklahoma City, OK  73105                 405-528-1500
                                         888-269-5353
                                   FAX: 405-528-5751
                                  www.okdol.state.ok.us

*Trey Davis, Chief of Staff*
*Brenda Reneau, Commissioner*

**4215  Oklahoma Client Assistance Program**
2401 NW 23rd Street
Suite 90
Oklahoma City, OK  73107                 405-521-3756
                                   FAX: 405-522-6695
                                  www.ohc.state.ok.us

*James Sirmans, Director*
*Steve Stokes, Executive Director*

**4216  Oklahoma Department of Children with Disabilities**
4001 N Lincoln Boulevard
4th Floor
Oklahoma City, OK 73105                  405-521-2255
                                         888-269-5353
                                   FAX: 405-528-5751
                                  www.okdol.state.ok.us

*Trey Davis, Chief of Staff*
*Patrick McGuigun, Deputy Commissioner*

**4217  Oklahoma Department of Human Services Aging Services Division**
PO Box 25352
Oklahoma City, OK  73125                 405-521-2255
                                   FAX: 405-521-2086
                                       www.okdhs.org

*Karey Garland, Director*

**4218 Oklahoma Department of Mental Health & Substance Abuse Services**
PO Box 53277
Oklahoma City, OK 73152 405-522-3908
800-522-9054
FAX: 405-522-3650
www.odmhsas.org

*Terry Cline PhD, Executive Director/Commissioner*

State agency providing mental helath , substance abuse and domestic violence services.

**4219 Oklahoma Department of Rehabilitation Services**
3535 NW 58th Street
Suite 500
Oklahoma City, OK 73112 405-951-3400
800-845-8476
FAX: 405-951-3529
e-mail: jharlan@drs.state.ok.us
www.okrehab.org

*Linda Parker, Executive Director*
*Jody Harlan, Public Information Administrator*

Provides vocational rehabilitation, employment, education, independent living assistance and special services, and determines eligibility for disability benefits.

**4220 Workers Compensation Board Oklahoma**
1915 N Stiles Avenue
Oklahoma City, OK 73105 405-522-8600

*Marcia Davis, Administrator*

# Oregon

**4221 International Dyslexia Association: Oregon Branch**
International Dyslexia Association
PO Box 3677
Portland, OR 97208 503-228-4455
800-530-2234
FAX: 503-228-3152
e-mail: info@orbida.org
www.orbida.org

*Karen Brown, President*
*Charles Weswig, Vice President*

Provides free information and referral services for diagnosis and tutoring for parents, educators, physicians, and individuals with dyslexia. The voice of our membership is heard in 48 countries. Membership includes yearly journal and quarterly newsletter. Call for conference dates.

**4222 Office of Vocational Rehabilitation Servic es (OVRS)**
500 Summer Street NE
E-87
Salem, OR 97301 503-945-5880
877-277-0513
FAX: 503-947-5025
TTY: 503-378-3933
www.oregon.gov/dhs/index.shtml

*Stephaine Taylor, Administrator*
*Travis Wall, Planning and Program Manager*

The mission of OVRS to assist Oregonians with disabilities to achieve and maintain employment and independence.

**4223 Oregon Advocacy Center**
620 SW 5th Avenue
5th Floor
Portland, OR 97204 503-243-2081
800-452-6094
FAX: 503-243-1738
e-mail: welcome@oradvocacy.org
www.oradvocacy.org

*Robert Joondeph, Executive Director*
*Barbara Herget, Operations Director*

The protection and advocacy system for Oregon.

**4224 Oregon Client Assistance Program**
620 SW 5th Avenue
Suite 500
Portland, OR 97204 503-243-2081
FAX: 503-243-1738
www.oradvocacy.org

*Robert Joondeph, Executive Director*

**4225 Oregon Commission for the Blind**
535 SE 12th Avenue
Portland, OR 97214 503-731-3221
888-202-5463
FAX: 503-731-3230
e-mail: linda.mock@state.or.us
www.cfb.state.or.us

*Linda Mock, Administrator*
*Frank Armstrong, Representative of Blind Oregonia*
*Pat Donell, Executive Director*

**4226 Oregon Department of Mental Health**
500 Summer Street NE
E86
Salem, OR 97301 503-945-5944
FAX: 503-945-5895
www.oregon.gov/DHS

*Bob Nikkel, Assistant Director*
*Bruce Goldberg, Executive Director*

Sets out the purpose and guides the activities of our large, complex organization. Vision is for better outcomes for clients and communities through collaboration, integration and shared responsibility.

**4227 Oregon Technology Access for Life**
3070 Lancaster Drive NE
Salem, OR 97305 503-361-1201
FAX: 503-370-4530
e-mail: info@accesstechnologiesinnc.com
www.accesstechnologiesinc.org

*Laurie Brooks, Project Director*

A statewide program promoting assistive technology devices and services for persons of all ages with all disabilities.

**4228 Social Security: Salem Disability Determination**
530 Center Street NE
Suite 30
Salem, OR 97301 800-722-1213
TTY:800-325-0778
www.socialsecurity.gov

*Patrick P O'Caroll Jr, Inspector General*

**4229 Washington County Disability, Aging and Veteran Services**
133 S East Second Avenue
Hillsboro, OR 97123 503-640-3489
FAX: 503-693-6124
www.co.washington.or.us/aging

*Mary Lou Ritter, Director*

## Pennsylvania

**4230 International Dyslexia Association: Pennsylvania Branch**
PO Box 251
Bryn Mawr, PA 19010
610-527-1548
800-ABC-D123
FAX: 610-527-5011
e-mail: dyslexia@pbida.org
www.pbida.org

Jack Rogers, President
Mary Ellen Trent, Office Manager
Amy Ress, Manager

Provides free information and referral services for diagnosis and tutoring for parents, educators, physicians, and individuals with dyslexia. The voice of membership is heard in 48 countries. Membership includes yearly journal and quarterly newsletter, and Pennsylvania newsletter; discounts to conferences and events.

**4231 Mental Health Association in Pennsylvania**
1414 N Cameron Street
Harrisburg, PA 17103
717-236-8110
800-692-7443
FAX: 717-236-0192
e-mail: swalther@paonline.com
www.ttpinc.org

Ilene Shane, Executive Director

**4232 Pennsylvania Workers Compensation Board**
1171 S Cameron Street
Room 103
Harrisburg, PA 17104
717-939-9551
FAX: 717-772-0342

Joseph Brimmeier, Chief Executive Officer

**4233 Pennsylvania Bureau of Blindness**
Department of Pennsylvania
1621 N 6th Street
Harrisburg, PA 17102
717-236-3610
800-622-2842
FAX: 717-787-3210
www.dli.state.pa.us

Pamela Shaw, Director
Alfred Baker, President

Offers services for the totally blind, legally blind, visually impaired, mentally retarded blind and more with health, counseling, educational, recreational, rehabilitation, computer training and professional training services.

**4234 Pennsylvania Client Assistance Program**
1617 JFK Boulevard
Suite 800
Philadelphia, PA 19103
215-557-7112
888-745-2357
FAX: 215-557-7602
e-mail: info@equalemployment.org
www.equalemployment.org

Stephen S Pennington, Executive Director
Jamie C Ray, Assistant Director

The Pennsylvania Client Assistance Program is dedicated to ensuring that the rehabilitation system in Pennsylvania is open and responsive to your needs. CAP help is provided to you at no charge, regardless of income. CAP helps people who are seeking services from the Office of Vocational Rehabilitation, Blindness and Visual Services, Centers for Independent Living and other programs funded under federal law.

**4235 Pennsylvania Department of Aging**
555 Walnut Street
5th Floor
Harrisburg, PA 17101
717-783-1550
FAX: 717-783-6842
e-mail: aging@state.pa.us
www.aging.state.pa.us

Nora Dowd Eisenhower, Secretary

**4236 Pennsylvania Department of Children with Disabilities**
PO Box 90
Harrisburg, PA 17108
717-783-1289
FAX: 717-772-0323

Donna Wenger, Acting Director
Frank Maisano, Manager

**4237 Pennsylvania Developmental Disabilities Council**
569 Forum Building
Harrisburg, PA 17120
717-939-9551
FAX: 717-772-0738
e-mail: paddpc@aol.com

Graham Mulholland, Executive Director
Joseph Brimmeier, Chief Executive Officer

**4238 Pennsylvania Protection & Advocacy for Persons with Disabilities**
1414 N Cameron Street
Harrisburg, PA 17103
717-236-8110
800-692-7443
FAX: 717-236-0192
e-mail: ppa@ppaninc.org
www.ppainc.org

Ilene Shane, Executive Director

Provide advocacy, information and referral for persons with disabilities and mental illness issues.

**4239 Public Interest Law Center of Philadelphia**
125 S 9th Street
Suite 700
Philadelphia, PA 19107
215-627-7100
FAX: 215-627-3183
e-mail: pobint@aol.com

Michael Churchill, Chief Counsel
Judith Gramd, Director

A non-profit, public interest law firm with a Disabilities Project specializing in class action suits brought by individuals and organizations.

**4240 Social Security: Harrisburg Disability Determination**
555 Walnut Street
Harrisburg, PA 17101
717-782-3400
800-722-1213
TTY:717-783-8917
e-mail: ovr@dli.state.pa.us
www.ssa.gov

Susan Aldrete, Executive Director

**4241 Workers Compensation Board Pennsylvania**
1171 S Cameron Street
Room 103
Harrisburg, PA 17104
717-783-5421
800-482-2383
FAX: 717-772-0342
e-mail: ra-li-bwc-helpline@state.pa.us
www.dli.state.pa.us

John J Kupchinsky, Director

## Rhode Island

**4242 Department of Mental Health, Retardation and Hospitals of Rhode Island**
Goverment of Rhode Isalnd
14 Harrington Road
Cranston, RI 02920 401-462-3201
FAX: 401-462-3204
www.mhrh.state.ri.us www.nhirh.ri.gov

*Cathleen M Stanglei, Acting Director*
*Kathleen Spangler, Manager*

State department responsible for creating and administering systems of care for individuals with disabilities, specifically focused on mental health and mental illness; developmental disabilities, substance abuse and long term hospital care.

**4243 Rhode Island Department Health**
3 Capitol Hl
Providence, RI 02908 401-222-2231
FAX: 401-222-6548
e-mail: library@doh.state.ri.us
www.health.state.ri.us

*David R Gifford, Director*
*Patricia Nolan, Executive Director*
*Pamela Corcoran, Disability Health Program*

**4244 Rhode Island Department of Elderly Affairs**
35 Howard Avenue
Cranston, RI 02920 401-462-3000
FAX: 401-222-3389
e-mail: larry@dea.state.ri.us
www.dea.state.ri.us

*Corinne Cali Russo, Director*

**4245 Rhode Island Department of Mental Health**
Cottage 405 Court B
Cranston, RI 02920 401-467-9200
FAX: 401-464-2005

*Reed Cosper, Director*
*Robert Emerson, President*

**4246 Rhode Island Developmental Disabilities Council**
400 Bald Hill Road
Suite 515
Warwick, RI 02886 401-732-3240
FAX: 401-737-3395
e-mail: riddc@riddc.org
www.riddc.org

*Marie Citrone, Executive Director*
*Don Ouelette, Manager*

The Rhode Island Developmental Disabilities Council works to make Rhode Island a better place for people with developmental disabilities to live, work, go to school, and be part of their community.

**4247 Rhode Island Governor's Commission on Disabilities**
John O Pastore Center
41 Cherrydale Court
Cranston, RI 02920 401-462-0100
FAX: 401-462-0106
e-mail: disabilities@gcd.state.ri.us
www.disabilities.ri.gov

*Paul Chouquette, Chairperson*
*Bob Cooper, Executive Secretary*

Assures the rights of persons with disabilities, deals with state and federal regulations, building codes. Assists in the employment and education of disabled persons.

**4248 Rhode Island Parent Information Network**
175 Main Street
Unit 1
Pawtucket, RI 02860 401-727-4040
800-464-3399
FAX: 401-727-4040
e-mail: ripin@ripin.org
www.ripin.org

*Vivian Weisman, Executive Director*
*Matthew Cox, Associate Exeutive Director*

A nonprofit organization established by parents and concerned professionals providing culturally appropriate information, training and support for families and professionals designed to improve educational and life outcomes for all children. Serving the State of Rhode Island.

**4249 Rhode Island Protection & Advocacy for Persons with Disabilities**
Rhode Island Disability Law Center
349 Eddy Street
Providence, RI 02903 401-831-3150
FAX: 401-274-5568
e-mail: info@ridlc.org
www.ridlc.org

*Raymond Bandusky, Executive Director*

**4250 Rhode Island Services for the Blind and Visually Impaired**
40 Fountain Street
Providence, RI 02903 401-222-2300
800-752-8088
FAX: 401-222-1328
TTY: 401-277-3010
e-mail: thompson@ors.state.ri.us
www.ors.ri.gov

*Raymond Carroll, Administrator*
*Stephen Brunero, Deputy Administrator*

Offers services for the totally blind, legally blind, visually impaired, mentally retarded blind and more with health, counseling, educational, recreational, rehabilitation, computer training and professional training services.

**4251 Services for the Blind and Visually Impaired**
40 Fountain Street
Providence, RI 02903 401-222-2300
FAX: 401-222-1328
www.ors.ri.gov

*Gary Wier, Deputy Administrator*
*Raymond Carroll, Administrator*

Offers services for the blind and visually impaired.

**4252 Social Security: Providence Disability Determination**
Social Security
380 Westminster Street
3rd Floor
Providence, RI 02903 401-528-4501
800-772-1213
FAX: 401-273-6648
TTY: 401-273-6648
www.ssa.gov

*John J Corson, Director*

**4253 Workers Compensation Board Rhode Island**
1 Dorrance Plaza
Providence, RI 02903 401-458-5000
FAX: 401-421-3123

*John Sabatini, Administrator*
*George Healy Jr, Manager*

## South Carolina

### 4254 Protection & Advocacy for People with Disabilities
3710 Landmark Drive
Suite 208
Columbia, SC 29204      803-782-0639
866-275-7273
FAX: 803-790-1946
e-mail: info@protectionandadvocacy-sc.org

*Anne Trice, Director Administration*
*Gloria Prevost, Executive Director*

An independent, nonprofit organization responsible for safe guarding rights of South Carolinians with disabilities and other handicapped individuals without regard to age, income, severity of disability, sex, race, or religion.

### 4255 Social Security: West Columbia Disability Determination
1835 Assembly Street
Columbia, SC 29201      803-929-7635
800-772-1213
TTY:800-325-0078
www.socialsecurity.gov

### 4256 South Carolina Assistive Technology Project
University of South Carolina
Columbia, SC 29208      803-779-0343
FAX: 803-935-5342
TTY:803-935-5263
e-mail: jjendron@usit.net
www.sc.edu/scatp/

*Evelyn Evans, Project Director*
*Marie Queen, Executive Director*
*Mary Alice Bechtler, Program Coordinator*

A statewide program promoting assistive technology devices and services for persons of all ages with all disabilities. Recently a statewide AT resource, demonstrations and equipment loan center and lab annual expo and training and workshops on a variety of disabilities and technology topics.

### 4257 South Carolina Client Assistance Program
Governor's Office oe Executive Policy & Programs
1205 Pendleton Street
Columbia, SC 29201      803-734-0285
FAX: 803-734-0546
TTY:803-734-1147
e-mail: lbarker@govpoepp.state.ce.us
www.govoepp.state.sc.us/cap

*Larry Barker PhD, Director*

The Client Assistance Program (CAP) helps citizens of the State by acting as advocates regarding services provided by the Vocational Rehabilitation Department (VR), Commission for the Blind, and all Independent Living programs and projects funded under the Rehabilitation Act of 1973. As advocates, CAP staff can investigate, negotiate, mediate, and pursue administrative, and other remedies to ensure that clients' rights are protected.

### 4258 South Carolina Commission for the Blind
PO Box 79
Columbia, SC 29202      803-733-8100
800-922-2222
FAX: 803-898-8852
www.sccb.state.sc.us

*Nell Carney Md, Commissioner*
*Linda Johnston, Secretary*
*Clente Flemming, President*

Offers services for the totally blind, legally blind, visually impaired, mentally retarded blind and more with health, counseling, educational, recreational, rehabilitation, computer training and professional training services.

### 4259 South Carolina Department of Children with Disabilities
2600 Bull Street
Columbia, SC 29201      803-898-2038

*Ann Lee, Director*
*Peter Getz, Administrator*

### 4260 South Carolina Department of Mental Health and Mental Retardation
PO Box 485
Columbia, SC 29202      803-898-8581
FAX: 803-898-8316
www.state.sc.us/dmh

*Maureen Donnelly, Director*
*John J Connery, State Director*

### 4261 South Carolina Developmental Disabilities Council
Office of the Governor
1205 Pendleton Street
Suite 450
Columbia, SC 29201      803-734-0465
FAX: 803-734-0465
TTY:803-734-1147
e-mail: jjennings@oepp.sc.gov
www.scddc.state.sc.us

*Charles Lang, Executive Director*
*Jennifer Jennings, Program Information Coordinator*

The mission of the South Carolina Developmental Disabilities Council is to provide leadership in advocating, funding and implementing initiatives which recognize the inherent dignity of each individual, and promote independence, productivity, respect and inclusion for all persons with disabilities and their families.

### 4262 South Carolina Services Information System
University of South Carolina
Columbia, SC 29208      803-935-5300
800-922-1107
FAX: 803-935-5342
e-mail: ddsnweb@ddsn.sc.gov
www.state.sc.us/ddsn/pubs/scsis/scsis.htm

*Denise Rivers, Program Director*

SCSIS provides information on aging and disability services in the State of South Carolina. Also, has a used equipment referral exchange where buyers and sellers are matched.

### 4263 Workers Compensation Board: South Carolina
PO Box 1715
Columbia, SC 29202      803-737-5700
FAX: 803-737-5764
e-mail: Gary
www.state.sc.us/wcc

*Gary Thibault, Executive Director*

## South Dakota

### 4264 South Dakota Advocacy Services
221 S Central Avenue
Pierre, SD 57501      605-224-8294
800-658-4782
FAX: 605-224-5125
e-mail: sdas@sdadvocacy.com
www.sdadvocacy.com

*Robert J Kean, Executive Director*

Designated protection and advocacy progam for South Dakota providing legal, administrative, mediation and other services to elgible persons with disabilities in the state.

**4265 South Dakota Department of Aging**
700 Governors Drive
Pierre, SD 57501
605-773-3656
866-854-5465
FAX: 605-773-6834
www.state.sd.us/social/asa

*Gail Ferris, Executive Director*

**4266 South Dakota Department of Children's Special Health Services**
South Dakota State Department of Health
615 E 4th Street
Pierre, SD 57501
605-773-3011
800-305-3064
FAX: 605-773-5942
e-mail: barb.hemmelman@state.sd.us
www.state.sd.us/boh

*Kayla Tinker, Office Director*
*Barb Hemmelman, Director*
*Laurie Gill, Manager*

**4267 South Dakota Department of Human Services Division of Mental Health**
South Dakota of Human Services
500 E Capitol Avenue
Pierre, SD 57501
605-000-1111
800-265-9684
FAX: 605-773-7076
e-mail: infomh@dhs.state.sd.us
www.state.sd.us/dhs/dmh

*Jeff Peirce, Manager*
*Amy Iversen-Pollreisz, Director*
*Jennifer Fahey-Seale, Adult Svcs Program Specialist*

**4268 South Dakota Developmental Disability Council**
Hillsview Plaza E Highway 34
Pierre, SD 57501
605-000-1111
FAX: 605-773-5483
e-mail: info@ddc
www.state.sd.us/dhs/ddc

*Arlene Poncelet, Director*
*Jeff Pierce, Manager*

To assist individuals with developmental disabilities to control their own destiny and to achieve the quality of life they desire.

**4269 South Dakota Division of Rehabilitation**
700 Governors Drive
Pierre, SD 57501
605-773-3423
FAX: 605-773-5483

*David Miller, Director*
*Patrick Keating, Manager*

Offers diagnosis, evaluation and physical restoration services, counseling, social work, educational and professional training, employment and rehabilitation services for the disabled.

**4270 Workers Compensation Board: South Dakota**
700 Governors Drive
Pierre, SD 57501
605-773-3681
FAX: 605-773-4211
e-mail: jamesmarsh@state.sd.us
www.sdjobs.org

*James Marsh, Executive Director*

# Tennessee

**4271 International Dyslexia Association: Tennessee Branch**
3508 Hackworth Road
Knoxville, TN 37931
877-836-6432
800-222-3123
FAX: 865-693-3653
e-mail: tennessee_IDA@hotmail.com
www.tn-interdys.org

*Martie Wood, President*

The Tennessee Branch of the International Dyslexia Association (TN-IDA) was formed to increase awareness about Dyslexia in the state of Tennessee. TN-IDA supports efforts to provide information regarding appropriate language arts instruction to those involved with language-based learning differences and to encourage the identity of these individuals at-risk for such disorders as soon as possible.

**4272 Social Security: Nashville Disability Determination**
Social Security
4527 Nolensville Pike
Nashville, TN 37211
615-781-5800
800-772-1213
FAX: 615-781-5836
www.ssa.gov

**4273 Tennessee Assistive Technology Projects**
Doctor S Building
300
Nashville, TN 37243
615-322-1210

*Eh Buddy White*
*Julie Oden, Manager*

A statewide program promoting assistive technology devices and services for persons of all ages with all disabilities.

**4274 Tennessee Client Assistance Program**
Tennessee Protection and Advocacy
PO Box 121257
Nashville, TN 37212
615-298-1080
800-342-1660
FAX: 615-298-2046
e-mail: gethelp@tpainc.org
www.tpainc.org

*Shirley Shea, Executive Director*
*Doris Lopez, Assistant Executive Director*

**4275 Tennessee Commission on Aging and Disability**
500 Deaderick Street
8th Floor
Nashville, TN 37243
615-741-2056
FAX: 615-741-3309
e-mail: tnaging.tnaging@state.tn.us
www.state.tn.us/comaging

*Nancy Teace, Executive Director*
*Charles Hewgley, Assistant Director*

**4276 Tennessee Council on Developmental Disabilities**
500 Deaderick Street
13th Floor
Nashville, TN 37243
615-313-9980
FAX: 615-532-6964
e-mail: tnddc@state.tn.us
www.state.tn.us/cdd

*Linda Moynihan, Executive Director*

Provides leadership to ensure independence, productivity, integration and inclusion of individuals with disabilities in the community through promotion of systems change. The council works with members of the community, including public and private aencies, business, legislators and policymakers, to create a future in which; people with disabilities are full included in the community and experience no barriers related to attitudes about their disabilities as they persue their goals.

**4277 Tennessee Department of Children with Disabilities**
436 6th Avenue N
Room 525
Nashville, TN 37243      615-741-0466

*Judy Womack, Director*
*Haticile Buchanan, Manager*

**4278 Tennessee Department of Mental Health and Developmental Disabilities**
425 5th Avenue N
Nashville, TN 37243      615-741-7213
FAX: 615-532-6514
e-mail: kay.horner@state.tn.us
www.state.tn.us/mental

*Virginia Trotter Betts, Commissioner*
*Jill Hudson, Press Officer*
*Suzanne Hubbard, Executive Director*

**4279 Tennessee Division of Rehabilitation**
400 Deaderick Street
Nashville, TN 37243      615-248-4996

*Patsy Matthews, Commissioner*
*Randall Beasley, Manager*

Offers rehabilitation, medical and therapeutic information and referrals to the disabled.

**4280 Workers Compensation Board Tennessee**
710 James Robertson Parkway
Nashville, TN 37243      615-741-2395
FAX: 615-532-5929
www.state.tn.us/labor-wfd/wcomp.html

*Sueanne Head, Administrator*

# Texas

**4281 Disability Policy Consortium**
7800 Shoal Creek Boulevard
Suite 171e
Austin, TX 78757      512-454-4816
FAX: 512-458-9202
e-mail: dpctexas@advocacyinc.org
www.dpctexas.org

*Mary Faithfull, Executive Director*
*Jonas Schwartz, Manager*

An independent group of statewide advocacy organizations that strives to achieve the development and full implementation of public policy that promotes and supports the rights, inclusion, integration and independence of Texans with disabilities.

**4282 Division of Special Education**
1701 Congress Avenue
Austin, TX 78701      512-463-9414
FAX: 512-463-9560
e-mail: spedfrontdesk@tea.state.tx.us
www.tea.state.tx.us

*Gene Lenz, Deputy Associate Commissioner*
*Kathy Clayton, Senior Director*

**4283 Easter Seal of Greater Dallas, TX**
4443 N Josey Lane
Carrollton, TX 75010      972-394-8900
800-580-4718
www.easterseals.com

*Elizabeth Hart, President/CEO*
*Bob Painter, Vice President*
*Nancy Hitzfelder, MD*

**4284 Easter Seals Greater NW Texas**
2100 Circle Drive
Fort Worth, TX 76119      817-536-8693
888-288-8324
e-mail: info@easterseals.fw.org

*Monica Crather, Chief Executive Officer*

**4285 El Valle Community Parent Resource Center**
530 S Texas Boulevard
Suite J
Weslaco, TX 78596      956-969-3611
800-680-0255
e-mail: texasfiestaedu.org
www.tfepodder.org

*Laura Reagan, Project Coordinator*

**4286 Grassroots Consortium**
Greenroots Consortium
6202 Belmark Street
Houston, TX 77087      713-643-9576
FAX: 713-643-6291
Speckids@aol.com

*Agnes A Johnson, Director*

**4287 International Dyslexia Association: Austin Branch**
PO Box 92604
Austin, TX 78709      512-452-7658
800-222-3123
e-mail: info@interdys.org
www.interdys.org

*Sharon McMichael, President*

The Austin Area Branch of the International Dyslexia Association is a 501(c)(3) non profit organization dedicated to promoting reading excellence for all children through early identification of dyslexia, effective literacy education for adults and children with dyslexia, and teacher training.

**4288 NAMI Texas**
2800 S i H 35
Suite 140
Austin, TX 78704      512-693-2000
800-633-3760
FAX: 512-693-8000
e-mail: namitexas@texami.org
www.tx.nami.org

*Joe Lovelace, Executive Director*

NAMI Texas has a variety of programs directed to mental health consumers, family members, friends, professionals, other stake holders and the community at large to address the mental health needs of Texans. NAMI Texas works to inform the public about mental illness by distributing information about mental illness through every means of communication. Interviews are produced on television, stories are featured in newspapers, brochures are distributed, referrals are provided and more.

**4289 Parent Connection**
1020 Riverwood Court
Conroe, TX 77304      936-756-8321
800-839-8876
ParentCNCT@aol.com

**4290  Parents Supporting Parents Network**
601 N Texas Boulevard
Suite C
Weslaco, TX 78596                              956-447-8408
                                               888-857-8668
                                          FAX: 956-973-9503
                                   e-mail: cbtjr1@aol.com
                                      www.thearcoftexas.org

*Mike Bright, Executive Director*
*Rona Statman, Assistant Director*
*Leticia Padilla, Manager*

**4291  Partners Resource Network**
1090 Longfellow Drive
Suite B
Beaumont, TX 77706                             409-898-4684
                                               800-866-4726
                                  e-mail: path@partnerstx.org
                                       www.PartnersTx.org

*Leslie Vasquez, Program Director*
*Mary Ellen Peterson, Chief Executive Director*
*Janice Meyer, Executive Director*

**4292  Social Security: Austin Disability Determination**
903 San Jacinto Boulevard
Austin, TX 78701                               512-916-5404
                                               800-772-1213
                                          TTY:512-916-5958
                                             www.ssa.gov

**4293  Statewide Information at Texas School for the Deaf**
1102 S Congress Avenue
Austin, TX 78704                               512-462-5329
                                               800-DEA-FTSD
                                          FAX: 512-462-5663
                                  e-mail: ercod@tsd.state.tx.us
                                       www.tsd.state.tx.us

*Betty Bounds, Director of Instructions*
*Claire Bugen, Superintendent*

**4294  Texas Advocates Supporting Kids with Disabilities**
PO Box 162685
Austin, TX 78716                               512-310-2102
                                          FAX: 512-310-2102
                                  e-mail: ASKTASK@aol.com
                                       www.main.org/task/

**4295  Texas Commission for the Blind**
PO Box 12866
Austin, TX 78711                               512-459-2500
                                               800-252-5204
                                          FAX: 512-459-2685

*Terrell I Murphy, Executive Director*

Offers services for the totally blind, legally blind, and visually
impaired, with counseling, educational, recreational, rehabilitation, computer training and professional training services.

**4296  Texas Commission for the Deaf and Hard of Hearing**
D AR S
PO Box 12904
Austin, TX 78711                               512-407-3250
                                          FAX: 512-407-3299
                                          TTY:512-407-3251
                            e-mail: david.meyers@tcdhh.state.tx.us
                                       www.dars.state.tx.us

*David Meyers, Assistant Director*

**4297  Texas Council for Developmental Disabilities**
6201 E Oltorf Street
Suite 600
Austin, TX 78741                               512-437-5432
                                               800-262-0334
                                          FAX: 512-437-5434
                                          TTY: 512-437-5431
                                  e-mail: tcdd@tcdd.state.tx.us
                                       www.txddc.state.tx.us

*Roger Webb, Executive Director*
*Carl Risinger, Operations Director*

The Texas Council for Developmental Disabilities is a 27-mem-
ber board dedicated to ensuring that all Texans with developmental disabilities, about 411,479 individuals, have the
opportunity to be independent, productive and valued members
of their communities. The mission of the Texas Council for Developmental Disabilities is to create change so that all people
with disabilities are fully included in their communities and exercise control over their own lives.

**4298  Texas Department of Human Services**
701 W 51st Street
Austin, TX 78751                               512-438-3011
                                               888-834-7406
                                          TTY:888-425-6889
                                  e-mail: mail@dads.state.tx.us
                                       www.dads.state.tx.us

*Jim Hine, Division Director*
*Carlela Vogel, Vice Chair*

**4299  Texas Department of Mental Health & Mental Retarda-
tion**
PO Box 12668
Austin, TX 78711                               512-438-3011
                                          FAX: 512-206-4560
                                       www.mhmr.state.tx.us

*Eduardo J Sanchez, Commissioner*
*Randy Fritz, Chief Operating Officer*
Offers information and referrals.

**4300  Texas Department on Aging**
701 W 51st Street
Austin, TX 78751                               512-438-3200
                                               800-252-9240
                                  e-mail: mail@tdoa.state.tx.us
                                       www.dadds.state.tx.us

*James Hine, Executive Director*
*John Willis, Director Ombudsman*
*Karl Urban, Deputy Director*

The state's visible advocate and steward for a full range of services and opportunities that allow older Texans to live healthy,
dignified and independent lives.

**4301  Texas Federation of Families for Children's Mental
Health**
7701 N Lamar Boulevard
Suite 505
Austin, TX 78752                               512-407-8844
                                               866-893-3264
                                          FAX: 512-407-8266
                                  e-mail: info@txffcmh.org
                                       www.txffcmh.org

*Patti Derr, Executive Director*
*Pat Calley, Chairperson*
*S Barron, Director Operations*

Texas Federation of Families for Children's Mental Health is an
organization comprised of family members of with emotional,
behavioral and mental health needs; supporting families and
youth through advocacy, links to resources and training.

**4302  Texas Governor's Committee on People with Disabilities**
1100 San Jacinto Boulevard
Austin, TX 78701
512-463-5739
FAX: 513-463-5745
e-mail: ppound@governor.state.tx.us
www.governor.state.tx.us/disabilities

*Pat Pound, Executive Director*

**4303  Texas Protection & Advocacy Services for Disabled Persons**
Advocacy
7800 Shoal Creek Boulevard
Suite 171e
Austin, TX 78757
512-454-4816
800-252-9108
FAX: 512-323-0902
e-mail: infoai@advocacyinc.org
www.advocacyinc.org

*Mary Faithfull, Executive Director*
*Shirley R DeBerry, Executive Assistant*
*Jonas Schwartz, Manager*

A federally funded, independent, nonprofit agency that advocates for the legal, human and service rights of persons with disabilities. Publishes "Special Edition" newsletter, at a small fee and "It's a Good Idea!" a parent manual for $10, plus many other handouts free of charge.

**4304  Texas Respite Resource Network**
Station A
PO Box 7330
San Antonio, TX 78207
512-228-2794

e-mail: elizabethnewhouse@srhcc.org

*Jennifer Cernoch, Director*
*Liz Newhouse, Assistant Director*

A state clearinghouse and technical assistance network for respite in Texas. TRRN identifies, initiates and improves respite options for families caring for individuals with disabilities on the local, state and national levels. TRRN provides training/technical assistance to programs/groups wanting to establish respite services.

**4305  Texas Technology Access Project**
Center for Disabilities Studies
4030 W Braker Lane
Building 2
Austin, TX 78759
512-482-8682
800-828-7839
FAX: 512-232-0761
TTY: 512-232-0762
e-mail: john.moore@mail.utexas.edu
tatp.edb.utexas.edu/

*John Moore, Project Director*

Provides information, conducts training and technical assistance and works with policy makers to support children and adults with disabilities.

**4306  Texas UAP for Developmental Disabilities**
University of Texas
430 W Braker Lane
Building 2
Austin, TX 78753
512-471-4822
800-828-7839
FAX: 512-232-0761
e-mail: pseay@mail.utexas.edu
www.utexas.edu

*Penny Seay, Executive Director*
*Bob Harkins, Manager*

**4307  Texas Workers Compensation Commission**
4000 S Ih 35
Austin, TX 78704
512-804-4000
FAX: 512-440-3547

*Robert Shipe, Executive Director*

**4308  United Cerebral Palsy of Texas**
National Cerebral Palsy of American
5555 N Lamar Boulevard
Suite L139
Austin, TX 78751
512-472-8696
800-798-1492
FAX: 512-472-8026
e-mail: info@ucpa.org
www.ucpa.org

*Jean Langendorf, Executive Director*

# Utah

**4309  Access Utah Network**
155 S 300 W
Suite 100
Salt Lake City, UT 84101
801-533-4636
800-333-8824
FAX: 801-533-3968
e-mail: access@utah.gov
www.accessut.org

*Cecilia Giron, Information Specialist*
*Mark Smtih, Information Specialist I/Manager*

**4310  Social Security: Salt Lake City Disability Determination**

Social Security
202 W 400 S
Salt Lake City, UT 84101
801-524-4115
800-772-1213
TTY:801-524-5047
www.ssa.gov

*Wilkes R Barre, Program Director*

**4311  Utah Assistive Technology Projects**
Utah State University
6855 Old Main Hl
Logan, UT 84322
435-797-0037

e-mail: garthe@coe.usu.edu

*Marvin Fifield, Director*
*Dan Peterson, Manager*

A statewide program promoting assistive technology devices and services for persons of all ages with all disabilities.

**4312  Utah Client Assistance Program**
205205 N 400 W
Salt Lake City, UT 84103
801-363-1347
800-662-9080
FAX: 801-363-1437
e-mail: info@disabilitieslawcenter
www.disabilitylawcenter.org

*Nancy Friel, Chief of Client Assistance Progr*
*Fraser Nelson, Executive Director*

**4313  Utah Department of Aging**
120 N 200 W
Salt Lake City, UT 84103
801-538-3910
877-424-4640
FAX: 801-538-4395
e-mail: dirdhs@utah.gov
www.hsdaas.utah.gov

*Alan Ormsby, Director*
*Terri Ruesch, Assistant Director*

**4314 Utah Department of Human Services: Division of Services for People with Disabilities**
Utah Department of Human Services
120 N 200 W
Room 411
Salt Lake City, UT 84103          801-538-4200
                                 800-837-6811
                          FAX: 801-538-4279
                 e-mail: dirdhs@utah.gov
                        www.hsdspd.utah.gov

*George Kelner, Executive Director*
*Paul Day, Associate Director*

Information and referral services for people with disabilities, including DD/MR, brain injury and physical disabilities throughout the state of Utah.

**4315 Utah Department of Mental Health**
Utah Department of Human Services
120 N 200 W
Room 209
Salt Lake City, UT 84103          801-538-3939
                          FAX: 801-538-9892
                        www.hsmh.state.ut.us

*James Ashworth, Chairman*
*Michael Crookston, Vice Chairman*
*Mark Payne, Manager*

**4316 Utah Division of Services for the Disabled**
660 S 200 E
Suite 400
Salt Lake City, UT 84111          801-238-4560
                                 800-284-1823
                          FAX: 801-359-5627

*Wayne Peterson, Director*
*Don Uchida, Assistant Director*
*Bonnie Williams, Executive Director*

Offers services for the totally blind, legally blind, visually impaired, mentally retarded blind and more with health, counseling, educational, recreational, rehabilitation, computer training and professional training services.

**4317 Utah Governor's Council for People with Disabilities**
155 S 300 W
Suite 100
Salt Lake City, UT 84101          801-533-4636
                          FAX: 801-533-3968
                 e-mail: alozano@utah.gov
                        www.gcpd.org/

*Allison Lozano, Executive Director*
*Angela Allen, Administrative Secretary*
*Mark Smith, Manager*

**4318 Utah Labor Commission**
PO Box 146630
Salt Lake City, UT 84114          801-530-6801
                                 800-222-1238
                          FAX: 801-530-7609
                 e-mail: sdanielson@utah.gov
                        www.laborcommission.utah.gov

*R Lee Ellerston, Labor Commissioner*
*Alan Hennebold, Deputy Commisioner*
*Sherrie Hayashi, Director, Anti-Discrimination*

**4319 Utah Protection & Advocacy Services for Persons with Disabilities**
Disability Law Center
205 N 400 W
Salt Lake City, UT 84103          801-363-1347
                                 800-662-9080
                          FAX: 801-363-1437
                 e-mail: info@disabilitylawcenter.org
                        www.disabilitylawcenter.org

*Fraser Nelson, Executive Director*
*Rob Denton Esq, Senior Attorney*
*Eric Dmitchell, Advocacy Director*

# Vermont

**4320 Disability Law Project**
57 N Main Street
Rutland, VT 05701          802-775-0021
                                 800-769-7459
                          FAX: 802-775-0022
                 e-mail: nbreiden@vtlegalaid.org
                        www.vtlegalaid.org

*Tom Garrett, Executive Director*
*Rachel Corey, Office Manager*
*Robert Clark, Manager*

Legal services (protection and advocacy) for people with disabilities on legal issues arising from disability. Statewide. Adults and children. Employment, education, discrimination, housing, public benefits, health care.

**4321 Social Security: Vermont Disability Determination Services**
93 Pilgrim Park Road
Suite 6
Waterbury, VT 05676          802-241-2463
                                 800-734-2463
                          FAX: 802-241-2492
                        www.ssa.gov

*Trudy Lyon-Hart, Executive Director*

**4322 Vermont Assistive Technology Projects**
103 S Main Street
Weeks Building
Waterbury, VT 05671          802-241-2620
                                 800-750-6355
                          FAX: 802-241-2174
                          TTY: 802-241-1464
                 e-mail: atinfo@dail.state.vt.us
                        www.dad.state.vt.us/atp

*Julie L Tucker, Project Director*
*Betsy Ross, Administrative Assistant*

Increase awareness and change policies to insure assistive technology (AT) is available to all Vermonters with disabilities. Our Commitment is to enable Vermonters with disabilities to have greater independence, productivity, and confidence. To provide them with a clear and direct avenue toward integration and inclusion within the work force and community.

**4323 Vermont Client Assistance Program**
57 N Main Street
Rutland, VT 05701          802-775-0021
                                 800-769-7459
                 www.vocrehabvermont.org/html/clientassistance

*Patrick Flood, Commissioner*

The Client Assistance Program (CAP) is an independent advocacy program to help if you are applying for or receiving services from one of the following sources: Division of Vocational Rehabilitation (VR); Vermont Center for Independent Living (VCIL); Division for the Blind and Visually Impaired (DBVI); Vermont Association of Business, Industry & Rehabilitation (VABIR); Vermont Association for the Blind and Visually Impaired (VABVI); Supported Employment Programs; Transition Programs.

**4324  Vermont Department of Aging**
103 S Main Street
Waterbury, VT  05671          802-241-2400

*Patrick Flood, Manager*

**4325  Vermont Department of Developmental and**
103 S Main Street
Waterbury, VT  05671          802-241-2614

*Theresa Wood, Manager*

**4326  Vermont Department of Disabilities, Aging and Independent Living**
Aging and Disabilities
103 S Main Street
Waterbury, VT  05671          802-241-2401
                              FAX: 802-241-2325
                              www.dad.state.vt.us

*Patrick Flood, Commissioner*

**4327  Vermont Department of Health: Children with Special Health Needs**
Vermont Department Of Health
PO Box 70
Burlington, VT  05402          802-863-7338
                               FAX: 802-863-7635
                               www.healthy.vermonters.org

*Carol Hassler MD, Director*
*Steve Brooks, Administrator*

Multidisciplinary clinics and family support for children with chronic conditions, birth to age 21 years.

**4328  Vermont Developmental Disabilities Council**
103 S Main Street
Waterbury, VT  05671          082-241-2220

                              e-mail: vtddc@upgate1.ahs.state.vt.us
                              www.ahs.state.vt.us/vtddc

*Cynthia D LaWare, Secretary*

The mission of VTDDC is to facilitate connections and to promote supports that bring people with developmental disabilities into the heart of Vermont Communities.

**4329  Vermont Division for the Blind and Visually Impaired**
103 S Main Street
Waterbury, VT  05671          802-241-2210
                              888-405-5005
                              FAX: 802-241-2128
                              e-mail: vtblind_request@lists.dad.state.vt.us
                              www.dad.state.vt.us/dbvi

*Fred Jones, Director*
*Scott Langley, Program Service Chief*

Offers services for the totally blind, legally blind, visually impaired, mentally retarded blind and more with health, counseling, educational, recreational, rehabilitation, computer training and professional training services.

**4330  Vermont Division of Disability & Aging Services**
103 S Main Street
Waterbury, VT  05671          802-241-2614
                              FAX: 802-241-4224
                              www.dail.state.vt.us

*Theresa Wood, Deputy Commissioner*

**4331  Vermont Protection and Advocacy**
141 Main Street
Suite 7
Montpelier, VT  05602          802-229-1355
                               800-834-7890
                               FAX: 802-229-1359
                               TTY: 800-889-2047
                               e-mail: info@vtpa.org
                               www.vtpa.org

*Ed Paquin, Executive Director*
*AJ Ruben, Supervising Attorney*

Advocacy and legal services for people with mental illness on legal issues arising, out of disabilities. Children and adults.

**4332  Workers Compensation Board Vermont**
Department of Labor
PO Box 20
Montpelier, VT  05620          802-828-2286
                               FAX: 802-828-2195
                               www.state.vt.us/ladind

*Laura Collins, Commissioner*

# Virginia

**4333  International Dyslexia Association: Virginia Branch**
PO Box 17605
Richmond, VA  23226          804-285-1946
                             800-988-8336
                             FAX: 804-285-1946
                             e-mail: vbida@hotmail.com
                             www.interdys.org

*Debra Farr, President*
*Carolyn Russ, Executive Assistant*

The Virginia Branch of The International Dyslexia Association (VBIDA) is a 501(c)(3) non-profit, scientific and educational organization dedicated to the study and treatment of the learning disability, dyslexia. This Branch was formed to increase public awareness of dyslexia in the State of Virginia. We serve the entire state, with the exception of Northern Virginia, which is part of the DC-Capital Branch in Washington, DC. We have been serving individuals with dyslexia, their families.

**4334  Virginia Department for the Blind and Vision Impaired**
397 Azalea Avenue
Richmond, VA  23227          804-371-3140
                             FAX: 804-371-3351
                             e-mail: bowmanja@dbvi.virginia.gov
                             www.vdbvi.org

*Joseph A Bowman, Commissioner*
*James Taylor, Chief Deputy Commissioner*

Offers services for the totally blind, legally blind, visually impaired, mentally retarded blind and more with health, counseling, educational, recreational, rehabilitation, computer training and professional training services.

**4335  Virginia Department of Mental Health**
PO Box 1797
Richmond, VA  23218          804-340-0072
                             FAX: 804-786-3827

*Joe Damico, Director Administrative Services*

**4336** **Virginia Developmental Disability Council**
101 N 14th Street
Floor 17
Richmond, VA 23219
FAX: 804-225-3144
FAX: 804-225-3221

*Sandra Reen, Director*

**4337** **Virginia Office Protection and Advocacy for People with Disabilities**
1910 Byrd Avenue
Suite 5
Richmond, VA 23230
804-225-2042
800-552-3962
FAX: 804-662-7057
e-mail: general.vopa@vopa.virginia.gov
www.vopa.state.va.us
Through zealous and effective advocacy and legal representation to: protect and advance legal, human, and civil rights of persons with disabilities; combat and prevent abuse, neglect, and discrimination; and promote independence, choice, and self-determination by persons with disabilities.

**4338** **Virginia Office for Protection & Advocacy**
1910 Byrd Avenue
Suite 5
Richmond, VA 23230
804-225-2042
800-552-3962
FAX: 804-662-7077
www.vopa.state.va.us

*V Collen Miller, Executive Director*

An independent state agency that helps ensure that the rights of persons with disabiltiies in the Commonwealth are protected. The mission of DRVD is to provide zealous and effective advocacy and legal representation to protect and advance legal, human and civil rights of persons with disabilities, combat and prevent abuse, neglect and discrimination, and promote independence, choice and self-determination by persons with disabilities.

**4339** **Virginia Office for Protection and Advocacy**
1910 Byrd Avenue
Suite 5
Richmond, VA 23230
804-225-2042
800-552-3962
FAX: 804-662-7057
e-mail: general.vopa@vopa.virginia.gov
www.vopa.state.va.us

*V Colleen Miller, Executive Director*
*Annette Sannuti, Business Manager*

**4340** **Virginia's Developmental Disabilities Plan ning Council**
Stae Agency
202 N 9th Street
9th Floor
Richmond, VA 23219
804-786-0016
800-846-4464
FAX: 804-786-1118
e-mail: lindlekv@vbpd.state.va.us
www.vaboard.org

*Barbara Ettner, Director Policy & Program*
*Heidi Lawyer, Director*
*Nan Pembeston, Administrator*

**4341** **DSHS/Aging & Adult Disability Services Administration**
PO Box 45600
Olympia, WA 98504
800-422-3263
TTY:800-737-7931
www.adsa.dshs.wa.gov

*Kathy Leitch, Assistant Director*

The Aging and Disability Services Administration assists children and adults with developmental delays or disabilities, cognitive impairment, chronic illness and related functional disabilities to gain access to needed services and supports by managing a system of long-term care and supportive services that are high quality, cost effective, and responsive to individual needs and preferences.

**4342** **International Dyslexia Association: Washington State Branch**
PO Box 1247
Mercer Island, WA 98040
206-382-1020
800-222-3123
e-mail: wabida@drizzlw.com
www.wabita.org

*Stacy Turner, President*

Provides free information and referral services for diagnosis and tutoring for parents, educators, physicians, and individuals with dyslexia in Arkansas, Idaho, Montana and Washington state. The voice of our membership is heard in 48 countries. Membership includes yearly journal and quarterly newsletter. Call for conference dates.

**4343** **Social Security: Olympia Disability Determination**
Social Security
402 Yauger Way SW
Olympia, WA 98502
800-772-1213
TTY:800-325-0778
www.ssa.gov

*Laurie Watkins, Commissioner*

**4344** **WA Department of Services for the Blind**
402 Legion Way
Suite 100
Olympia, WA 98504
360-586-1224
800-552-7103
FAX: 360-586-7627
www.dsb.wa.gov

*Luoana Durand, Executive Director*
*Erin Larson, Assistant Director*
Vocational rehabilitation for the blind.

**4345** **Washington Client Assistance Program**
2531 Rainier Avenue S
Seattle, WA 98144
206-721-5999
888-721-6072
FAX: 206-721-5980
www.capseattle.org

*Jerry Johnson, Executive Director*

Advocacy and information assistance for persons of disability seeking services through vocational rehabilitation or other program under the 1973 Rehabilitation Act as commented. We provide counseling.

**4346  Washington Department of Mental Health**
Department of Social and Health Services
1115 Washington Street
PO Box 45320
Olympia, WA  98504                    360-902-8070
                                      FAX: 360-902-7691
                                      www.dshs.wa.gov

*Richard E Kellogg, MHD Director*

**4347  Washington Developmental Disability**
2600 Martin Way E
Suite F
Olympia, WA  98504                    360-586-3560

**4348  Washington Governor's Committee on Disability Issues & Employment**
605 Woodland Square Loop SE
Lacey, WA  98503                      360-438-3168
                                     FAX: 360-438-3208
                                     www.gcde.org

*Toby Olson, Director*

**4349  Washington Office of Superintendent of Public Instruction**
Old Capitol Building
PO Box 47200
Olympia, WA  98504                    360-725-6000
                                      TTY:360-644-3631
                         e-mail: webmaster@ospi.wednet.edu
                                      www.k12.wa.us

*Dr Terry Bergeson, State Superintendent*

The Office of Superintendent of Public Instruction (OSPI) is the primary agency charged with overseeing K-12 education in Washington state. OSPI works with the state's 296 school districts to administer basic education programs and implement education reform on behalf of more than one million public school students.

**4350  Washington Protection & Advocacy System**
315 5th Avenue S
Suite 850
Seattle, WA  98104                    206-324-1521
                                      800-562-2702
                                      FAX: 425-776-0601
                         e-mail: wpas@wpas-rights.org

*Mark Stroh, Executive Director*

WPAS is a private, non-profit right protection agency for persons with disabilities residin in Washington state. Our advocacy services include information referral, technical assistance, training, publications and systemic advocacy.

**4351  Washington State Developmental Disabilities Council**
2600 Martin Way East Suite F
PO Box 48314
Olympia, WA  98504                    360-586-3560
                                      800-634-4473
                                      FAX: 360-586-2424
                         e-mail: edh@cted.wa.gov
                                      www.ddc.wa.gov

*Ed Holen, Executive Director*

**4352  Workers Compensation Board Washington**
State of Washington
7273 Linderson Way SW
Tumwater, WA  98501                   360-236-4018
                                      800-547-8367
                                      www.lni.wa.gov

*Gary K Weeks, Director*
*Maxine Hayes, MD*

# West Virginia

**4353  Bureau of Employment Programs Division of Workers' Compensation**
State of West Virginia
409 Virginia Street E
Charleston, WV  25301                 304-357-0130
                                      800-628-4265
                                 FAX: 304-357-0585
                         e-mail: pgrinste@wvbep.org
                                      www.state.wv.us

*Kent W Carper, Commissioner*
*Vern Cormick, Manager*

**4354  Disability Determination Section**
500 Quarrier Street
Suite 500
Charleston, WV  25301                 304-343-5055
                                      800-344-5033
                                 FAX: 304-353-4212

*Jane Johnstone, Executive Director*

**4355  Social Security: Charleston Disability Determination**
Social Security
500 Quarrier Street
Suite 300
Charleston, WV  25301                 304-347-5217
                                      800-772-1213
                                 FAX: 304-353-4212
                                      www.socialsecurity.gov

**4356  West Virginia Advocates**
1207 Quarrier Street
4th Floor
Charleston, WV  25301                 304-346-0847
                                      800-950-5250
                                 FAX: 304-346-0867
                                      www.wvadvocates.org

*Clarice Hausth, Executive Director*

**4357  West Virginia Client Assistance Program**
West Virginia Advocates
1900 Kanawha Boulevard E
Room 6
Charleston, WV  25305                 304-346-0847
                                 FAX: 304-346-0867
                      e-mail: vhuffman@access.k12.wv.us
                                      wvde.state.wv.us/

*Clarice Hausch, Executive Director*

**4358  West Virginia Department of Aging**
PO Box 1100
Charleston, WV  25324                 304-345-7303
                                      888-825-7303
                         e-mail: hollygrove@juno.com

*Patricia Bedford, Director*

**4359  West Virginia Department of Children with Disabilities**
1116 Quarrier Street
Charleston, WV  25301                 304-755-5700

*Pat Kent, Administrative Director*

**4360  West Virginia Department of Health**
1900 Capital Complex
Building 3
Charleston, WV  25305                 304-558-0549
                                 FAX: 304-558-1008

*Taunja Willis-Miller, Secretary*
*Sarah Hamrick, Executive Director*

**4361 West Virginia Developmental Disabilities Council**
110 Stockton Street
Charleston, WV 25312 304-558-0416
FAX: 304-558-0941
e-mail: jchankins@wvdhhr.org
www.wvddc.org

*Steven Wiseman, Executive Director*
*Jonathan Hankins, Office Manager*
*6-8 pages Quarterly Newsl*

**4362 West Virginia Division of Rehabilitation Services**
PO Box 547
Institute, WV 25112 304-766-2634

www.wvdrs.org

*Deborah Lovely, Acting Director*
DRS' mission is to enable and empower individuals with disabilities to work and to live independently.

# Wisconsin

**4363 Disability Rights Wisconsin: Milwaukee Office**
6737 W Washington Street
Suite 3230
Milwaukee, WI 53214 414-733-4646
888-758-6049
FAX: 414-773-4647
TTY:414-342-8700
The protection and advocacy agency for people with disabilities in Wisconsin. WCA provides guidance, advice, investigation, negotiation and in some cases legal representation to people with disabilities and their families. Local and state level systems advocacy and training are also provided.

**4364 International Dyslexia Association: Wisconsin Branch**
WIBIDA
PO Box 284
Baraboo, WI 53913 608-355-0911
800-222-3123
FAX: 608-355-0911
e-mail: loral@centurytel.net
www.wis-dys.org

*Lorinda L Clary, President*
The International Dyslexia Association actively promotes effective teaching approaches and related clinical educational intervention strategies for dyslexics. We support and encourage interdisciplinary study and research. We facilitate the exploration of the causes and early identification of dyslexia and are committed to the responsible and wide dissemination of research-based knowledge.

**4365 Social Security: Madison Disability Determination**
6011 Odana Road
Madison, WI 53719 608-270-1141
800-772-1213
TTY:800-325-0778
www.ssa.gov

**4366 Wisconsin Bureau of Aging**
State Office of Wisconsin
PO Box 7851
Madison, WI 53707 608-266-2536
FAX: 608-267-3203
e-mail: mcdowdb@dhfs.state.wi.us
www.dhfs.state.wi.us/aging

*Donna Mcdowell, Executive Director*
*Gail Schwersenska, Section Chief*

Keeps and updates information and printed materials on senior housing directories, nursing home listings, and home care agencies.

**4367 Wisconsin Coalition for Advocacy: Madison Office**
16 N Carroll Street
Suite 400
Madison, WI 53703 608-267-0214
800-928-8778
FAX: 608-267-0368

*Kim Hogan, Intake Specialist*
*Mr Lynn Breedlove, Executive Director*

The protection and advocacy agency for people with disabilities in Wisconsin. WCA provides guidance, advice, investigation, negotiation and in some cases legal representation to people with disabilities and their families. Local and state level systems advocacy and training are also provided.

**4368 Wisconsin Council on Developmental Disabilities (WCDD)**
201 W Washington Avenue
Suite 110
Madison, WI 53703 608-266-7826
FAX: 608-267-3906
TTY:608-266-6660
e-mail: hfswiscwcdd@dhfs.state.wi.us
www.wcdd.org

*Jennifer Ondrejka, Executive Director*
*Helen Hartman, Office Manager*

Statewide systems advocacy group for people with developmental disabilities in Wisconsin.

**4369 Wisconsin Department of Health and Family Services**
Program for Children w/ Special Health Care Needs
PO Box 2659
Madison, WI 53701 608-266-3726
800-441-4576
FAX: 608-267-3824
e-mail: helmqp@dhfs.state.wi.us
www.dhfs.state.wi.us

*Peggy Helm-Quest, Health Promotion Consultant*

The Department of Health and Family Services operates the federal Title V Maternal and Child Health Block Grant Program for Children with Special Health Care Needs. The program provides program monitoring, consultation and technical assistance to five regional CSHCN centers throughout Wisconsin; a Birth Defects Monitoring and Surveillance Program and a Universal Newborn Hearing Screening Program.

**4370 Wisconsin Governor's Committee for People with Disabilities**
1 W Wilson Street, Room 1150
PO Box 7851
Madison, WI 53707 608-266-7974
FAX: 608-266-3386
TTY:608-267-9880
www.dhfs.state.wi.us
To advise the Governor and state agencies on problems faced by people with disabilities; to review legislation affecting people with disabilities; to promote effective operation of publicly-administered or supported programs serving people with disabilities; to promote the collection, dissemination and incorporation of adequate information about persons with disabilities for purposes of public planning at all levels of government.

**4371 Workers Compensation Board Wisconsin**
PO Box 7901
Madison, WI 53707 608-266-1340
FAX: 608-267-0394

*Frances Huntley-Cooper, Administrator*

## Wyoming

**4372  Social Security: Cheyenne Disability Determination**
Social Security
821 W Pershing Boulevard
Cheyenne, WY  82002                          307-777-7341
                                             800-438-5788
                                        FAX: 800-972-2372
            www.ssa.gov/disability/professional/procontac

*Vicky Johnson, Director*
*Jeff Graham, Manager*

**4373  WY Department of Health: Mental Health Division**
6101 Yellowstone Road
Suite 220
Cheyenne, WY  82002                          307-777-7094
                                        FAX: 307-777-5580
                                        TTY:307-777-5581
                                 e-mail: wdh@state.wy.us
                              www.mentalhealth.state.wy.us

*Charles Hayes, Administrator*

State office responsible for purchase of service and program development policy.

**4374  Workers Compensation Board Wyoming**
122 W 25th Street
2nd Floor
Cheyenne, WY  82001                          307-777-7159
                                        FAX: 307-777-5946

**4375  Wyoming Client Assistance Program**
Protection and Advocacy System
320 W 25th Street
2nd Floor
Cheyenne, WY  82001                          307-632-3496
                                             877-854-5041
                                        FAX: 307-638-0815
                              e-mail: wypanda@vcn.com
                                        wypanda.vcn.com

*Lee Beidlemam, Client Assistant*
*Jeanne A Thobro, Executive Director*

**4376  Wyoming Department of Aging**
State Department of Wyoming
6101 Yellowstone Road
Room 259b
Cheyenne, WY  82002                          307-777-7986
                                             800-442-2766
                                        FAX: 307-777-5340
            www.httt://wdhss.state.wi.us/aging/index.htm

*Beverly Morrow, Administrator*
*Ruth Davis, Excutive Secretary*

**4377  Wyoming Developmental Disability Council**
122 W 25th Street
Cheyenne, WY  82001                          307-777-7230
                                        FAX: 307-777-5690

*Lynn Achter, Director*
*Brenda Oswald, Manager*

**4378  Wyoming Protection & Advocacy for Persons with Disabilities**
320 W 25th Street
2nd Floor
Cheyenne, WY  82001                          307-632-3497
                                        FAX: 307-638-0815

*Jeanne Thobro, Manager*

## Alabama

**4379  Birdie Thornton Center**
M RA NC A
2305 Hine Street S
Athens, AL  35611                          256-232-0366
                                    FAX: 256-230-9398

*Edward Orum, Program Director*

**4380  Birmingham Independent Living Center**
206 13th Street S
Birmingham, AL  35233                      205-251-2223
                                    FAX: 205-251-0605
                                    TTY:205-254-7333
                              e-mail: bilc@bellsouth.net
                                 www.birminghamilc.org

*Daniel Kessler, Executive Director*
*Carolyn Agee, Programs Coordinator*
*Bobbie Austin, Fiscal Manager*

The mission of this Independent Living Center is to empower people with disabilities to fully participate in the community.

**4381  Independent Living Center**
206 13th Street S
Birmingham, AL  35233                      205-251-2223
                                    FAX: 205-251-0605
                                    TTY:205-254-7333
                              e-mail: bilc@bellsouth.net
                                 www.birminghamilc.org

*Carolyn Agee, Program Coordinator*
*Daniel Kessley, Executive Director*

Independent living center.

**4382  Independent Living Center of Alabaster**
120 Plaza Circle
Suite B
Alabaster, AL  35007                       205-685-0570
                                    FAX: 205-251-0605
                                    TTY:205-685-0605
                           e-mail: alabasterilc@bellsouth.net

*Dan Kessler, Director*

**4383  Independent Living Center of Jasper**
300 Birmingham Avenue
PO Box 434
Jasper, AL  35002                          205-387-0159
                                    FAX: 205-387-0162
                                    TTY:205-387-1594
                            e-mail: ilcwalker@bellsouth.net

*Dan Kessler, Director*

**4384  Independent Living Center of Mobile**
5304 Overlook Road
- B
Mobile, AL  36618                          251-460-0301
                                    FAX: 251-341-1267
                               e-mail: ilc@ilcmobile.org
                                     www.ilcmobile.org

*Michael Davis, Executive Director*
*Ann Robertson, Assistant Director/Interpreter*

The mission of the Independent Living Center of Mobile is to foster and promote programs which empower persons with disabilities to attain their maximum degree of independence.

**4385  Montgomery Independent Living Center**
600 S Court Street
Montgomery, AL  36104                      334-240-2520
                                    FAX: 334-240-6869
                              e-mail: mcil@bellsouth.net

*Scott Renner, Director*

## Alaska

**4386  Access Alaska: ADA Partners Project**
121 W Fireweed Lane
Suite 105
Anchorage, AK  99503                       907-222-6166
                                          888-462-1444
                                    FAX: 907-222-6166
                            e-mail: monam@adapartners.org
                                   www.adapartners.org

*Jim Beck, Executive Director*
*Mona McAleese, Coordinator*

The Partner's Project provides expert in-depth advise for implementing the Americans witht he Disabilities Act. The Project also maintains a statewide network of community based experts, most of whom experience disabilities, to provide interpretive guidance and training for business and local government.

**4387  Access Alaska: Fairbanks**
3550 Airport Way
Suite 3
Fairbanks, AK  99709                       907-479-7940
                                          800-770-7940
                                    FAX: 907-474-4052
                                    TTY: 907-474-8619
                               e-mail: sloudon@alaska.net
                          www.fairnet.org/agencies/accessak

*David Jacobson, Executive Director*

A local non profit agency using its resources to actively promote a society where persons with disabilities can live and work independently in the community of their choice.
*1983*

**4388  Access Alaska: Mat-Suvalley**
897 Commercial Drive
Wasilla, AK  99654                         907-357-2588
                                          800-770-0228
                                    FAX: 907-357-5585
                                    www.accessalaska.org

*Jim Beck, Care Services Supervisor*
*Maxie Smith, Administration/Owner*
*Cheryl Unthicum, Service Coordinator*

Provides independent living services to persons with significant disabilities. Mission is to encourage and promote the total integration of persons with disabilities into the community of their choice. Services include independent living skills training, information and referral, advocacy, peer support, case management services, care coordination, interim accessible transportation and at home modifications.

**4389  Alaska SILC**
1057 W Fireweed Lane
Suite 206
Anchorage, AK  99503                       907-263-2009
                                          888-294-7452
                                    FAX: 907-263-2012
                            e-mail: preinhart.silc@gci.net
                                    www.alaskasilc.org

*Patrick Reinhart, Executive Director*
*Runika Rollins, Office Manager*

The Alaska Statewide Independent Living is committed to promoting a philosophy of consumer control, peer support, self help, self determination, equal access, and individual and systems advocacy, in order to maximize leadership, empowerment, independence, productivity, and to support full inclusion and integration of individuals with disabilities into the mainstream of American society.

**4390 Arctic Access**
Independent Living Center
PO Box 930
Kotzebue, AK 99752
907-442-2393
877-442-2393
FAX: 907-442-2393
TTY: 907-442-2393
e-mail: arcticac@otz.net
www.arcticaccess.org

*Roger Wright Jr, Executive Director*
*Audrey Aanes, Member of the Board*

The Arctic Access Independent Living Center provides services and opportunities for elders and others with disabilities so they may remain in their village and be as active as possible with their families and commuities in the North West Arctic and Bering Straits Regions of Alaska.
*1993*

**4391 Hope Community Resources**
540 W International Airport Road
Anchorage, AK 99518
907-561-5335
800-478-0078
FAX: 907-564-7429
e-mail: kjez@hopealaska.org
www.hopealaska.org

*Stephen Lesko, Executive Director*
*Kris Jez, Deputy Director Public Relations*
*Tonja Rambow, Deputy Director Programs*

Independent living centers offer peer counseling, disability education and awareness, attendant care registry and other services to the community.

**4392 Kenai Peninsula IL Center**
PO Box 2474
Homer, AK 99603
907-235-7911
800-770-7911
FAX: 907-235-6236
e-mail: ilc@xyz.net
www.peninsulailc.org

*Joyanna Geisler, Executive Director*

Offers peer counseling, disability education and awareness, attendant care registry and information on accessible housing.

**4393 Kenai Peninsula IL Center: Seward**
PO Box 3523
Seward, AK 99664
907-224-8711
FAX: 907-224-7793
e-mail: sewardilc@qci.net
www.peninsulailc.org

*Joyanna Geisler, Executive Director*
*Lynn Hohl, Manager*

**4394 Kenai Peninsula IL Center: Soldotna**
PO Box 1907
Soldotna, AK 99669
907-262-6333
FAX: 907-260-4495
e-mail: nadine@peninsulailc.org
www.peninsulailc.org

*Joyanna Geisler, Executive Director*

**4395 SE Alaska ILC: Ketchikan**
602 Dock Street
Suite 107
Ketchikan, AK 99901
907-225-4735
888-452-7245
FAX: 907-225-4753
e-mail: ketchikan@sailinc.org
www.sailinc.org

*Joan Keese, Director*
*Kara Lunde, Manager*

**4396 SE Alaska Independent Living Center (SAIL)**
3225 Hospital Drive
Unit 300
Juneau, AK 99801
907-586-4920
800-478-7245
FAX: 907-586-4980
e-mail: info@sailinc.org
www.sailinc.org

*Joan O Keefe, Executive Director*
*Jerry Kainulainen, Independent Living Coordinator*
*Sierra Kaden, ORCA Director*

SAIL's purpose is to empower consumers with disabilities by providing services and information to support them in making choices that will positively affect their independence and productivity. SAIL also serves all people with physical and mental disabilities regardless of race, ancestry, color, religion, age, marital status, sexual preference, gender and/or income.

**4397 SE Alaska Independent Living Center**
SAIL/ORCA
3225 Hospital Drive
Suite 300
Juneau, AK 99801
907-586-4920
800-478-7245
FAX: 907-586-4980
www.sailnc.org

*Paul Douglas, President*
*Clark Gruening, Vice President*

SAIL is private, nonprofit organization that provides consumer-directed independent living services to people with disabilities throughout Southeast Alaska.
*1992*

**4398 SE Alaska Independent Living: Sitka**
210 Lake Street
Suite A
Sitka, AK 99835
907-747-6859
800-478-7245
FAX: 907-747-6783
e-mail: sitka@sailinc.org
www.sailinc.org

*Joan O'Keese, Executive Director*

**4399 Seward Independent Learning Center**
201 3rd Avenue
Suite 1
Seward, AK 99664
907-224-8711
FAX: 907-224-7793
e-mail: ilc@arctic.net
www.peninsulailc.org

*Joyanna Geisler, Director*
*Lynn Hohl, Manager*

**4400 Seward Independent Living Center**
PO Box 3523
Seward, AK 99664
907-224-8711
FAX: 907-224-7793
TTY:907-224-8711
e-mail: ilc@xyc.net

*Joyanna Geisler, Director*

## Arizona

Independent living centers offering peer counseling, disability education and awareness, advocacy and other services to the community.
*1973*

**4401 ASSIST! to Independence**
PO Box 4133
Tuba City, AZ 86045          928-283-6261
                             888-848-1449
                        FAX: 928-283-6284
                e-mail: assist01@frontiernet.net
                www.ASSISTtoIndependence.org

*Michael Blatchford, Executive Director*
*ElizaBeth Pifer, Director Rehab Technology Svcs.*
*Elizabeth Fowler, Administrative Assistant*

Native American owned and operated non-profit located on the Navagjo Nation. Programs: Center for Independent Living, Regional Resource Center for Assistive Technology, Functional Assessment Clinic, Sensory Integration Program, Special Needs Toy Lending Library.

**4402 Arizona Bridge to Independent Living**
1229 E Washington Street
Phoenix, AZ 85034          602-256-2245
                          800-280-2245
                     FAX: 602-254-6407
             e-mail: boardofdirectors@abil.org
                          www.abil.org

*Phil Pangrazio, Executive Director*
*Ann Pasco, Operations Director*
*Feng Chiou, Financial Director*

ABIL offers and promotes programs designed to empower people with disabilities to take personal responsibility so they may achieve or continue independent lifestyles within the community.
*1977*

**4403 Arizona Bridge to Independent Living: Phoenix**
10000 N 31st Avenue
Suite D-405
Phoenix, AZ 85051          602-424-4100
                     FAX: 602-424-4118
                     TTY: 602-296-0591
             e-mail: azbridgeQ@abil.org
                          www.abil.org

*Phil Pangrazio, Director*

**4404 Arizona Bridge to Independent Living: Mesa**
2150 S County Club Drive
Suite 10
Mesa, AZ 85210          480-655-9750
                        800-280-2245
                   FAX: 480-655-9751
                   TTY: 480-655-9750
           e-mail: azbridge@abil.org
                        www.abil.org

*Phil Pangrazio, Director*

**4405 Casa Del Rey**
PO Box W
Parker, AZ 85344          928-669-9695
                     FAX: 928-669-5280

*Shane Hall, President*

**4406 Community Outreach Program for the Deaf**
268 W Adams Street
Tucson, AZ 85705          520-792-1906
                          800-234-0344
                     FAX: 520-770-8544
                     TTY: 520-792-1906
             e-mail: annel@ccs-ddp.org
                          www.copdaz.org

*Anne Levy, Executive Director*
*Sue Henning-Mitchell, Deputy Director*

**4407 Direct Center for Independence**
1023 N Tyndall Avenue
Tucson, AZ 85719          520-624-6452
                          800-342-1853
                     FAX: 520-792-1438
                     TTY: 520-624-6452
             e-mail: annm@directilc.org
                          www.directilc.org

*Ann Meyer, Executive Director*
*Bennie Wik, Administrative Assistant*

A consumer directed, community based advocacy organization that promotes independent living and offers a variety of programs for all people with disabilities. Through DIRECT's programs, people are encouraged to achieve their full potential and to participate in the community.
*1980*

**4408 New Horizons Independent Living Center**
8085 E Manley Drive
Prescott Valley, AZ 86314          928-772-1266
                                   800-406-2377
                              FAX: 928-772-3808
                      e-mail: zen@cableone.net
                      www.newhorizonsilc.org

*Ken Edwards, Executive Director*
*Zena Taylor, Financial Manager*
*Jean Lasher, Community Info Coordinator*

**4409 New Horizons Independent Living Center:**
8085 E Manley
Suite 1
Prescott Valley, AZ 86314          928-772-1266
                                   800-428-5505
                              FAX: 928-772-3808
                      e-mail: horizons@bayou.com

*Harry Miley, Executive Director*

Advocacy, information and referrals, support groups, attendant services and loan closet.

**4410 Services Maximizing Independent Living and Empowerment (SMILE)**
1929 S Arizona Avenue
Suite 12
Yuma, AZ 85364          928-329-6681
                   FAX: 928-329-6715
           e-mail: smile1929@adelphia.net
           www.neiaw.com/smile/smileindex.org

*Cathryn Robins, Executive Director*
*Suzanne Canole, Chairman*

Independent Living Center.
*1998*

**4411 Sterling Ranch: Residence for Special Women**
Sterling Ranch
PO Box 36
Skull Valley, AZ 86338          928-442-3289
                           FAX: 928-442-9272
                e-mail: director@sterlingranch.info

*Russell Dryer, Executive Director*
*Trent Nichel, Manager*

A nonprofit residence for women with developmental disabilities which has been in operation since 1947. As a small facility (19 residents) the orientation is personal and family-like. Offers activities that range from gardening, quilting, academics, sign-language, crafts and a myriad of field trips and excursions. Private rooms and spacious living on 4 1/2 acres.

# Independent Living Centers /Arkansas

## Arkansas

**4412  Arkansas SILC**
8500 W Markham Street
Suite 215
Little Rock, AR  72205
501-372-0607
800-772-0607
FAX: 501-372-0598
TTY: 501-372-0607
e-mail: 105344.1767@kcompuserve.com
www.ailc@alltel.net

*Rebecca Riggs, Executive Director*
*Elizabeth Virden-Simmons, Assistant Director*
*Richard Royal, Chair*

The mission of the Arkansas Independent Living Council is to promote independence, including freedom of choice and full inclusion into the mainstream of society, for all Arkansans with disabilities.
*Quarterly*

**4413  Delta Resource Center for Independent Living**
1514 S Poplar
Pine Bluff, AR  71601
870-535-2222
FAX: 870-534-8191
TTY: 870-535-2222
e-mail: billyaltom@comcast.net

*Billy Altom, Executive Director*

Independent living center providing information and referrals, advocacy, peer counseling and independent living skills training to the Southeast region of Arkansas.

**4414  Mainstream**
300 S Rodney Parham Road
Suite 5
Little Rock, AR  72205
501-280-0012
FAX: 501-280-9267
TTY: 501-280-9262
e-mail: mainstreamlrc@earthlink.net
www.mainstreamilrc.com

*Rita Byers, Director*

A non residential, consumer driven independent living resource center for persons with disabilities. Mainstream operates with conviction that people with disabilities have the right and responsibility to make choices, to control their lives and to participate fully and equally in the community.

**4415  Our Way**
10434 W 36th Street
Little Rock, AR  72204
501-225-5030
FAX: 501-225-5190

*Wendy Harris, Project Manager*
*Carla Mithchell, Manager*

Advocacy and information services. One bedroom apartments for mobility impaired and elderly 62 years or older persons.
*Based on income*

**4416  Sources for Community IL Services**
1918 N Birch Avenue
Fayetteville, AR  72703
479-442-5600
888-284-7521
888-284-7521
e-mail: sources@arsources.org
www.arsources.org

*Richard Royal, Executive Director*

Sources provides services, supports, and advocacy for persons with disabilities, their families, and the communities at large. We serve persons with all types of disabilities.

**4417  Spa Area Independent Living Services**
600 Main Street
Suite O
Hot Springs, AR  71913
501-624-7710
FAX: 501-624-7003
www.arsales.org

*Brenda Stinebuck, Executive Director*

## California

**4418  Access Center of San Diego**
1295 University Avenue
Suite 10
San Diego, CA  92103
619-293-3500
FAX: 619-293-3508
TTY: 619-293-7757
e-mail: louisf@accesscentersd.org
www.accesscentersd.org

*Louis Frick, Executive Director*
*Sharon McCabe, Operations Manager*
*Roberto Frias, Program Director*

The Access Center, through advocacy, education, and opportunity, promotes full inclusion by empowering and challenging people with disabilities to achieve their greatest potential.

**4419  Access Center of San Diego N Branch**
209 E Broadway
Suite A
Vista, CA  92084
760-435-9205
FAX: 760-435-9206
TTY: 760-435-9213
e-mail: info@accesscentersd.org
www.accesscentersd.org

*Christina Mill, Program Manager*

**4420  CAPH Independent Living Center**
3475 W Shaw Avenue
Suite 101
Fresno, CA  93711
559-276-6777
FAX: 559-276-6778
TTY: 559-276-6779
e-mail: k_pendleton@cil-fresno.org
www.cil-fresno.org

*Karen Pendleton, Director*
*Robert Hand, Executive Director*

**4421  CIL: Fresno**
3475 W Shaw Avenue
Suite 101
Fresno, CA  93711
559-276-6777
800-204-2274
FAX: 559-276-6778
TTY: 209-276-6779
e-mail: exactdirector@cil-fresno.org
www.cil-fresno.org

*Robert Hand, Executive Director*
*Olivia Dwithe, Acting Director*

**4422  California Foundation for Independent Living Centers**
1029 J Street
Suite 120
Sacramento, CA  95814
916-325-1690
FAX: 916-325-1699
TTY: 916-325-1695
e-mail: cfilc@cfilc.org
www.cfilc.org

*Patricia Yeager, Executive Director*

CFILC's mission is to support independent living centers in their local communities through advocating for systems change and promoting access and integration for people with disabilities.

**4423  California State Independent Living Council (SILC)**
1600 K Street
Suite 100
Sacramento, CA  95814

916-445-0142
866-866-7452
FAX: 916-445-5973
TTY: 916-445-5627
e-mail: pporteous@calsilc.org
www.calsilc.org

*Michael C Collins, Director*

To maximize options for independence for persons with disabilities

**4424  Center for Independence**
355 Gellert Boulevard
Suite 256
Daly City, CA  94015

650-991-5122
FAX: 650-757-2075
TTY:650-991-5182
e-mail: cidcrewQ@aol.com

*Kent Mickelson, Director*

**4425  Center for Independence of the Disabled**
875 Oneill Street
Belmont, CA  94002

650-595-0783
FAX: 650-595-0261
TTY:650-595-0743
e-mail: info@cidbelmont.org
www.cidbelmont.org

*Kent Mickelson, Executive Director*
*Ray Pittsinger, Program Manager*
*Arsie Tuquero-Zacarias, Administrative Assistant*

Increase the social, educational, and economic participation of persons with disabilities in San Mateo County, and to encourage, support, and provide options for self determination, equal access and freedom of choice.

**4426  Center for Independent Living**
2539 Telegraph Avenue
Berkeley, CA  94704

510-841-4776
FAX: 510-841-6168
TTY:510-848-3101
e-mail: info@cilberkeley.org
www.cilberkeley.org

*Jan Garrett, Executive Director*

The Center for Independent Living, Inc (CIL) is a national leader in helping people with disabilities live independently and become productive members of society. Founded in 1972, CIL is a pioneer advocating for greater accessibility in communities, designing techniques in independent living and providing direct services to people with disabilities. A partial list of services includes Information and Referral, Personal Assistance Services, Independent Living Skills Training and Peer Counseling.

**4427  Center for Independent Living: Oakland**
610 16th Street
Suite 419
Oakland, CA  94612

510-763-9999
FAX: 510-763-4910
TTY:510-444-1837
e-mail: ddaviscil@yahoo.com

*Jan Garrett, Director*

**4428  Center for Independent Living:Fresno**
3475 Wesy Shaw Avenue
Suite 101
Fresno, CA  93711

559-276-6777
FAX: 559-276-6778
TTY:559-276-6779
e-mail: execdirector@cil-fresno.org
www.cil-fresno.org

*Robert Hand, Executive Director*

**4429  Center for Independent Living; East Oakland**
7200 Bancroft Avenue
Suite 9A
Oakland, CA  94612

510-635-4920
FAX: 510-635-4261
e-mail: cwood@cilberkeley.org

*Jan Garrett, Director*

**4430  Center for Independent Living; Oakland**
1470 Fruitvale Avenue
Oakland, CA  94601

510-536-2271
FAX: 510-261-2968
e-mail: ediazalvarezcil@yahoo.org

*Jan Garrett, Director*

**4431  Center of Independent Living: Visalia**
208 W Main Street
Suite N
Visalia, CA  93291

559-622-9276
FAX: 559-622-9638
e-mail: r_libbee@cil-fresno.org
www.cil-fresno.org

*Robin Libbee, Southern Valley Program Manager*
*Renee Ezelle, Manager*

**4432  Central Coast Center for IL: San Benito**
1029 J Street
Suite 120
Sacramento, CA  95814

916-325-1690
FAX: 916-325-1699
e-mail: cfile@cfilc.org
www.cfilc.org

*Cheryl Bergan, Director*
*Kim Cantrell, Director*
*Patricia Yeager, Executive Director*

**4433  Central Coast Center for Independent Living**
234 Capitol Street
Salinas, CA  93901

831-757-2968
FAX: 831-757-5549
TTY:831-757-3949
e-mail: cccil@cccil.org
www.cccil.org

*Elsa Quezada, Executive Director*

CCCIL promotes the independence of people with disabilities by supporting their equal and full participation in community life. CCCIL provides advocacy, education and support to all people with disabilities, their families and the community.

**4434  Central Coast Center: Independent Living - Santa Cruz Office**
1395 41st Avenue
Suite B
Capitola, CA  95010

831-462-8720
FAX: 831-462-8727
TTY:831-462-8729
e-mail: cccilcap@cccil.org
www.cccil.org

*Elsa Quezada, Director*

**4435  Central Coast for Independent Living**
1111 San Felipe Road
Suite 107
Hollister, CA  95023

831-636-5196
FAX: 831-637-0478
TTY:831-638-0826
e-mail: cccilQ@cccil.org
www.cccil.org

*Elsa Quezada, Director*

CCCIL promotes the independence of people with disabilities by supporting their equal and full particpation in community life. CCCIL provides advocacy, education and support to all people with disabilities, their families and the community.

**4436 Central Coast for Independent Living: Watsonville**

521 Main Street
Suite Y
Watsonville, CA 95076          831-786-0915
                              TTY:831-786-0915

*Elsa Quezada, Director*

**4437 Communities Actively Living Independent and Free**

634 S Spring Street
Suite 2
Los Angeles, CA 90014          213-627-0477
                              FAX: 213-627-0535
                    e-mail: lnavarro@calif-ilc.org
                              www.calif-ilc.org

*Lilibeth Navarro, Founder/Executive Director*

CALIF looks to achieve greater input, participation and control of over policies and services especially those for people with disabilities, including those that exclude them; addresses discrimination wherever it exists; encourages the meaningful participation of persons with disabilities in mainstream activities that enhance the positive image and experience disability; empowers people with disabilities by encouraging ongoing education and a broad knowledge of the history and heritage.

**4438 Community Access Center**

6848 Magnolia Avenue
Suite 150
Riverside, CA 92506          951-274-0358
                            FAX: 951-274-0833
                            TTY:951-274-0834
                    e-mail: execdir@ilcac.org
                    www.communityaccesscenter.org

*Laurie Hoirup, Executive Director*

**4439 Community Access Center: Beaumont**

550 E 6th Street
Beaumont, CA 92223          909-769-8539
                            FAX: 909-769-2794
                            TTY:909-769-2794
                    e-mail: pmgr1@ilcac.org

*Laurie Hoirup, Director*

**4440 Community Access Center: Indio Branch**

83233 Indio Boulevard
Suite 5
Indio, CA 92201          760-347-4888
                        FAX: 760-347-0722
                        TTY:760-347-6802
                e-mail: pmgr2@ilcac.org
                        www.ilcac.org

*Raymond Martin, Program Manager*
*Velma Pacrem, Manager*

**4441 Community Access Center: Perris**

371 Wilkerson Avenue
Suite L
Perris, CA 92570          951-443-1158
                         FAX: 951-940-1964
                         TTY:951-443-1158
                 e-mail: spmgr@ilcac.org
Community Access Center empowers persons with disabilities to control their own lives, create an accessible community and advocate to achieve complete social, economic, and political integration. CAC also implements this vision by providing information, suportive services and independent living skills training.

**4442 Community Rehabilitation Services**

844 E Mission Road
Suite A&B
San Gabriel, CA 91776          626-614-1570
                              FAX: 626-614-1590

*Geneva Soloman, Manager*

Services that includes physical therapy, occupational therapy, and speech therapy. Treating a wide variety of patients including those that have neurologic or orthopedic diagnosis.

**4443 Community Rehabilitation Services**

4716 E Cesar E Chavez Avenue
Building A
Los Angeles, CA 90022          323-266-0453
                              FAX: 323-266-7992
                              TTY:323-266-3016
                      e-mail: evasquez@covad.net
                              www.cfilc.org

*Eric Vasquez, Director*
*Frances Fontenelle, Manager*

Community Rehabilitation Services, Inc. (CRS) is a private, non-profit agency established in 1974 to assist persons with disabilities within the East/North East areas of Los Angeles County to enhance their options for living independently. Any person who is 18 yrs of age or more with physical, sensory, mental/emotional or developmental disabilities can work with us to become more self-sufficient. Our intake procedures provide an orientation to the staff, facilities and services at CRS.

**4444 Community Rehabilitation Services (CRS) Pasadena Office**

980 N Fair Oaks Avenue
Pasadena, CA 91103          626-794-9860
                           FAX: 626-794-9884

**4445 Community Rehabilitation Services for Independent Living**

4716 E Cesar E Chavez Avenue
Los Angeles, CA 90022          323-266-0453
                              FAX: 323-266-7992
                      e-mail: evasquez@covad.net
                              www.cfilc.org

*Eric Vasquez, Director*
*Frances Fontenelle, Manager*

Offer people with disabilities transportation, housing assistance, advocacy, attendant referral, peer counseling and information services. New programs include job club and independent living skills training and deaf services.

**4446 Community Rehabilitation Services: Downtown Office**

4716 E Cesar E Chavez Avenue
Los Angeles, CA 90022          323-266-0453
                              TTY:213-427-0173

*Eric Vasquez, Director*
*Eric Fontenelle, Manager*

Non-profit agency designed to assist people with disabilities to enhance their options of staying in their own home.

**4447 Community Resources for Independence**

980 Hopper Avenue
Santa Rosa, CA 95403          707-528-2745
                              800-528-7703
                              FAX: 707-528-9477
                              TTY: 707-528-2151
                      e-mail: shobart@sonic.net
                              www.cri-dove.org

*Sandy Hobart, Executive Director*
*Inga Lizdenyte-Phillips, Program Assistant*

Non profit organization that offers a wide variety of ways that enable individuals or corporations to contribute to our efforts to advocate for people and serve people with disabilities in Sonoma, Napa, Mendocino and Lake counties.

**4448 Community Resources for Independence: Mendocino/Lake Branch**
415 Talmage Road
Suite B
Ukiah, CA 95482
707-463-8875
FAX: 707-463-8878
TTY:707-463-4498
e-mail: cfilc@cfilc.org
www.cfilc.org

*Joyce Larson, Certified Benefits Advocate*
*Tammy Rogers, Independent Living Advocate*
*Tanner Silva, Rural Outreach Director/Manager*
*1995*

**4449 Community Resources for Independence: Fort Bragg Office**
980 Hopper Avenue
Santa Rosa, CA 95403
707-528-2745
FAX: 707-528-9477
www.cri-dove.org

*Adam Brown, Legal Services Director*
*Jeanette Chapman, Housing Staff Assistant*
*Sandy Hobart, Executive Director*

**4450 Community Resources for Independence: Napa Office**
1040 Main Street
Suite 208
Napa, CA 94559
707-258-0270
FAX: 707-258-0275
TTY:707-257-0274
e-mail: cfilc@cfilc.org
www.cfilc.org

*Vaughn Heldlas, Assistive Technology*
*Tyler Stanley, Independent Living Advocate*
*Sheila Oreilly, Manager*

**4451 Community Resources for Independent Living Hayward**
439 a Street
Hayward, CA 94541
510-881-5743
FAX: 510-881-1593
TTY:510-881-0218
e-mail: info@cril-online.org
www.cril-online.org

*Elizabeth Pazdral, Executive Director*
*John Quinn, Interim Program Director*
*Wayland Wong, Independent Living Coordinator*

CRIL offers independent living services at no charge to persons with disabilities living in southern and eastern Alameda county. CRIL is also a resource for disability awareness education and training, advocacy and technical advice.

**4452 Community Resources for Independent Living**
39155 Liberty Street
Suite A100
Fremont, CA 94538
510-794-5735
FAX: 510-794-5562
TTY:510-794-5562
e-mail: info@cril-online.org

**4453 Community Resources for Independence**
1040 Main Street
Suite 208
Napa, CA 94559
707-258-0270
FAX: 707-258-0275
TTY:707-258-0274
e-mail: crinapa@sonic.net

*Sandy Hobart, Director*

**4454 DRAIL (Disability Resource Agency for Independent Living)**
4555 Precissi Lane
Suite 2
Stockton, CA 95207
209-477-8143
FAX: 209-477-7730
TTY:209-477-7734
e-mail: jeff@drail.org
www.drail.org

*Jeff Vierra, Center Coordinator*
*George Lewis, Executive Director*

Provides services to meet the diverse needs of people who have a variety of disabilities in all age groups.

**4455 Dayle McIntosh Center for the Disabled**
13272 Garden Grove Boulevard
Garden Grove, CA 92843
714-621-3300
800-972-8285
FAX: 714-663-2094
TTY: 714-663-2087
e-mail: rdevylde@pacbell.net
www.daylemccenter.org

*Jose Alsaro, Information/Referrals*
*Bill Chrisener, Director*
*Tulynn Smylie, Executive Director*

Offers advocacy, counseling, attendant registry, information and referral, independent living skills training, communications, commend (medical emergency network for the deaf and children's services), housing, assistive technology, and emergency services.

**4456 Dayle McIntosh Center: Laguna Niguel**
24012 Calle De La Plata
Suite 210
Laguna Hills, CA 92653
949-460-7784
FAX: 949-855-8742
TTY:949-855-6749
dayle.org

*Tu Lynn Smylie, Director*
*Myvan Mguyen, Office Manager*
*Kyle Minnis, Field Coordinator*

DMC advances empowerment and inclusion of all persons with disabilities. DMC is the largest Independent Living Center in California, and was named in memory of a young woman with a severe physical disability who worked to found the center.
*1977*

**4457 Disability Resource Agency for Independent Living: Modesto**
221 McHenry Avenue
Modesto, CA 95354
209-521-7260
FAX: 209-521-4763
TTY:209-521-1425
e-mail: dwight@drail.org
www.drail.org

*Dwight Bateman, Executive Director*
*Fred Dickinson, Director of Services*

DRAIL provides services to persons with disabilities that lead to increased self-sufficiency and independent living. DRAIL's mission is to empower persons with disabilities to achieve their goals and dreams, increase their independence and increase their advocacy skills to become self-advocates.

**4458 Disability Resources Agency for IL (DRAIL)**
221 McHenry Avenue
Modesto, CA 95354
209-521-7260
FAX: 209-521-4763
TTY:209-521-1425
e-mail: dwight@drail.org

*Dwight Bateman, Executive Director*

**4459 Disabled Resources Center**
2750 E Spring Street
Suite 100
Long Beach, CA 90806                    562-427-1000
                                   FAX: 562-427-2027
                                   TTY:562-427-1366
                                   e-mail: info@drcinc.org
                                        www.drcinc.org

*Jeanette Nishikawa, Executive Director*
*Dolores Nathan, Assistant Director*

DRC provides services to all people with disabilities, regardless of their age, gender, ethnicity, sexual preference or disability type. DRC looks to empower people with disabilities to live independtly in the community, to make their own decisions about their lives and to advocate on their own behalf.
*1976*

**4460 FREED**
508 J Street
Marysville, CA 95901                    530-742-4474
                                   FAX: 530-742-4476
                                   TTY:530-742-4474
                                   e-mail: webmaster@freed.org
                                        www.freed.org

*Ann Guerra, Executive Director*
*Claudia Hidek, Program Manager*

A non profit Independent Living Resource Center, the goal is to empower people with disabilities to exercise their civil rights in becoming active, productive members of the community. FREED's Mission is to eliminate barriers to full equality for people with disabilities through programs which promote independent living and effect systems change, while honoring dignity and self determination.

**4461 FREED Center for Independent Living**
900 E Main Street
Suite 201
Grass Valley, CA 95945                  530-272-1732
                                   FAX: 530-272-7793
                                   TTY:530-272-1732
                                   e-mail: contact-04@Freed.org
                                        www.freed.org

*Ann Guerra, Executive Director*

A non profit Independent Living Resource Center, the goal is to empower people with disabilities to exercise their civil rights in becoming active, productive members of the community. FREED's Mission is to eliminate barriers to full equality for people with disabilities through programs which promote independent living and effect systems change, while honoring dignity and self determination.

**4462 First Step Independent Living**
1174 Nevada Street
Redlands, CA 92374
                                        800-362-0312
                                   e-mail: cvsfs@deltanet.com

**4463 IL Resource Cemter: San Luis Obispo**
1150 Laurel Lane
Suite 148, PO Box 4310
San Luis Obispo, CA 93401               805-593-0667
                                   FAX: 805-549-7423
                                   TTY:805-593-0667
                                   e-mail: jblack@ilrc-trico.org

*Josephine Black, Director*

**4464 IL Resource Center: Ventura**
1802 Eastman Avenue
Suite 112
Venutra, CA 93003                       805-650-5993
                                   FAX: 805-650-9278
                                   TTY:805-650-5993
                                   e-mail: jblack@ilrc-trico.org

*Josephine Black, Director*

**4465 ILC Southern CA**
14407 Gilmore Street
Van Nuys, CA 91401                      818-785-6934
                                   FAX: 818-785-0330
                                   TTY:818-785-6934
                                   e-mail: ilcsc@ilcsc.org
                                        www.ilcsc.org

*Norma Jean Vescovo, Executive Director*

**4466 ILRC: Richmond**
101 Broadway
Building #2A
Richmond, CA 94806                      510-232-4942

                                   e-mail: info@ilrccc.org

*Bryan Balch*

**4467 Imperial Valley ILC**
584 Main Street
Suite C
El Centro, CA 92243                     760-353-4191
                                   FAX: 760-353-4474
                                   TTY:760-353-2802
                                   e-mail: louisf@accesscentersd.org
                                        www.accesscentersd.org

*Louis Frick, Program Director*
*Denise Donaho-Smith, Manager*

**4468 Independence Center**
3640 S Sepulveda Boulevard
Apt 102
Los Angeles, CA 90034                   310-202-7102
                                   FAX: 310-202-7180
                          e-mail: judym@independencecenter.com
                               www.independencecenter.com

*Sandy Driver-gordon, President*
*Judith Maizlish, Executive Director*

A mainstreamed residential program teaching independent living to young adults (18-30+) with learning disabilities.

**4469 Independent Living Center of Southern California**
14407 Gilmore Street
Van Nuys, CA 91401                      818-785-6934
                                   FAX: 818-785-0330
                                   TTY:818-785-6934
                                   e-mail: ilcsc@ilcsc.org
                                        www.ilcsc.org

*Norma Jean Vescovo, Executive Director*

**4470 Independent Living Center of Kern County**
1631 30th Street
Bakersfield, CA 93301                   661-325-1063
                                        800-529-9541
                                   FAX: 661-325-6702
                                   TTY: 661-325-6702
                          e-mail: bonita@ilcofkerncounty.org
                               www.ilcofkerncounty.org

*Bonita Coyle, Executive Director*

**4471 Independent Living Center of Lancaster**
43805 Division
Suite A
Lancaster, CA 93535                     661-945-6602
                                   FAX: 661-945-5690
                                   TTY:661-945-6604
                                   e-mail: ilcsc@ilcsc.org
                                        www.ilcsc.org

*Norma J Vescovo, Executive Director*

ILCSC is a non-profit, consumer based, non-residential agency providing a wide range of services to a growing population of people with disabilities. ILCSC is dedicated to empowering persons with disabilities to exercise indpendence-pofessionally, personally and creatively-while striving to educate the community on their needs.

## 4472 Independent Living Center of Southern California

14407 Gilmore Street
Van Nuys, CA 91401

818-785-6934
FAX: 818-785-0330
TTY:818-988-3533
e-mail: ilcsc@ilcsc.org
www.ilcsc.org

*Norma Jean Vescovo, Executive Director*

Housing, advocacy, benefits counseling and independent living skills.

## 4473 Independent Living Center: San Gabriel Valley

109 Spring Street
PO Box 549
Claremont, CA 91711

909-621-6722
FAX: 909-445-0727
TTY:949-445-0729
e-mail: carol@ilc-car.org
www.ilc-clar.org

*Carol Lane, CEO*

Dedicated to expanding access to information and resources to help increase independence and enhance the quality of life for the East San Gabriel Valley residents with disabilities.

## 4474 Independent Living Resource Center

423 W Victoria Street
Santa Barbara, CA 93101

805-963-0595
FAX: 805-963-1350
TTY:8059630595
e-mail: jblack@ilcr-trico.org
www.ilrc-trico.org

*Josephine Black, Executive Director*
*Kathleen Riel, Program Manager*

A private, nonprofit organization founded by and for persons with disabilities to assist individuals to achieve optimal levels of self-sufficiency. Services include personal assistant referrals, peer and benefits counseling, advocacy, sign language interpreter/communication services, independent living skills training, information and referrals, community education and systems advocacy, housing and employment assistance.

## 4475 Independent Living Resource Center: San Francisco

649 Mission Street
3rd Floor
San Francisco, CA 94105

415-543-6222
FAX: 415-543-6318
TTY:415-543-6698
e-mail: info@ilrcsf.org
www.ilrcsf.org

*Herb Levine, Executive Director*

The ILRC Enables persons with persons with diabilites to take resposiblity for and control of their own lives to make decisions to reduce their dependence on people around them the ILRC Provides persons with disabilities the oppurtunties to develop the skills necessary to live their own lives. The ILRC Facilities independent living by making available on going support services thereby empowering persons with physical visual and or hearing disabilities to acheive self sufficiency.

## 4476 Independent Living Resource Center: Santa Maria Office

327 E Plaza Drive
Suite 3a
Santa Maria, CA 93454

805-925-0015
FAX: 805-349-2416
TTY:805-925-5892
e-mail: cridenour@ilrc-trico.org
www.ilrc-trico.org

*Josephine Black, Executive Director*
*Laurie Colson Young, Assistance/Outreach Specialist*
*Jennie Morales, Interpreter Registry Coordinator*

Peern and Benefit counseling, Independent living skills, Attendentr Recruitment/referral, American Sign language interpreting, Advocacy, housing and employment assistance information and referrals, Social Security benefit planning.

## 4477 Independent Living Resource Coast Country: Branch Office

1545 Webster Street
Suite C
Fairfield, CA 94533

707-435-8174
FAX: 707-435-8177
e-mail: robert@ilrccc.org
www.ilrccc.org

*Paul Demange, Program Director*
*Rich Broaddus, Manager*

## 4478 Independent Living Resource of Contra Coas t

3200 Clayton Road
Concord, CA 94519

925-363-7293

*Bryan Balch, Manager*

## 4479 Independent Living Resource of Fairfield

1545 Webster Street
Suite C
Fairfield, CA 94533

707-435-8174
FAX: 707-435-8177
e-mail: brchmgr@ilrccc.org
www.ilrccc.org

*Rich Broaddaus, Program Manager*

To empower people with disabilities to: control their own lives, provide advocacy and support for individuals with disabilities to live independently, create an accessible community free of physical and attitudinal barriers.

## 4480 Independent Living Resource: Antioch

310 West 10th Street
Antioch, CA 94509

707-435-8174

www.ilrccc.org

*Bryan M Balch, Executive Director*
*Paul Demange, Program Director*

## 4481 Independent Living Resource: Concord

3200 Clayton Road
Concord, CA 94519

925-363-7293
FAX: 925-363-7296
e-mail: bryanb@ilrccc.org
www.ilrcty.org

*Bryan Balch, Executive Director*

To empower people with disabilities to: control their own lives, provide advocacy and support for individuals with disabilities to live independently, create an accessible community free of physical and attitudinized barriers.

**4482 Independent Living Service Northern California: Redding Office**
1411 Yuba Street
Redding, CA 96001
530-242-8550
FAX: 530-241-1454
e-mail: evan.levang@ilsnc.org
www.ilsnc.org

Evan Le Vang, Executive Director
Jerry Towne, Manager

Independent Living Services of Northern California is a private non profit organization that provides support services to help empower community members with disabilities.

**4483 Independent Living Services of Northern California**
1161 East Avenue
Chico, CA 95926
530-893-8527
800-464-8527
FAX: 530-893-8574
e-mail: evan.levang@ilsnc.org
www.ilsnc.org

Evan LeVang, Executive Director

Independent Living Services of Northern California is a private, non profit organization that provides support services to help empower community members with disabilities.
1980

**4484 Marin Center for Independent Living**
710 4th Street
San Rafael, CA 94901
415-257-8555
FAX: 415-459-7047
e-mail: mcilbob@earthlink.net
www.marincil.org

Amy Reisch, Executive Director

A one stop resource center for seniors and people with disabilities, whose mission is to assist people with all types of disabilities to achieve their maximum level of sustainable independence as contributing, responsible and equal participants in society.

**4485 Mother Lode Independent Living Center**
67 Linoberg Street
Suite A
Sonora, CA 95370
209-532-0963
FAX: 209-532-1591
TTY:209-532-1591
e-mail: barry@drail.org

Dwight Bateman, Director

**4486 Placer Independent Resource Services**
11768 Atwood Road
Suite 29
Auburn, CA 95603
530-885-6100
800-833-3453
FAX: 530-885-3032
e-mail: administrator@pirs.org
www.pirs.org

Susan Miller, Executive Director

A non profit independent living center whose mission is to advocate, empower, educate and provide services for people with disabilities enabling them to control their alternatives for independent living.

**4487 Resources for Independent Living**
420 Ice Street
Sacramento, CA 95814
916-446-3074
FAX: 916-446-2443
e-mail: monicag@ril-sacramento.org
www.ril-sacramento.org

Frances Gracechild, Executive Director

The only organization in Sacramento providing services to people with all forms of disability. RIL is dedicated to providing services and support to disabled people, so they can live happy and productive lives.

**4488 Rolling Start**
570 W 4th Street
Suite 103
San Bernardino, CA 92401
909-884-2129
FAX: 909-386-7446
TTY:909-884-7396
e-mail: rs.inc@verizon.net
www.rollingstart.com

Frances Bates, Executive Director

Rolling Start looks to empower and educate people with disabilities to achieve the independent life of their choice.

**4489 Rolling Start: Victorville**
15647 Village Drive
Suite A
Victorville, CA 92392
760-843-7959
FAX: 760-241-8787
TTY:760-843-7959
e-mail: calimom394@aol.com

Frances Bates, Director

**4490 San Gabriel/Pomona Valley Center for Independent Living**
109 Spring Street
Claremont, CA 91711
909-621-6722
800-491-6722
FAX: 909-445-0727
TTY: 909-445-0726
e-mail: carol@ilc-clar.org
www.ilc-clar.org

Carol Lane, President/CEO

Independent Living Center is dedicated to expanding access to information and resources to help increase independence and enhance the quality of life for the East San Gabriel Valley residents with disabilities.

**4491 Service Center for Independent Living: Covina Office**
Claremont
109 Spring Street
Claremont, CA 91711
909-621-6722
800-491-6722
FAX: 909-445-0727
TTY: 626-967-4401
e-mail: carol@ilc-calr.org
www.ilc-clar.org

Carol Lane, Executive Director/CEO

**4492 Service Center for Independent Living**
PO Box 549
Claremont, CA 91711
909-621-6722
FAX: 909-445-0727
TTY:909-445-0726
e-mail: scilcovn@tstonramp.com
www.ilusa.com

Carol Lane, Chief Executive Officer

**4493 Silicon Valley Independent Living Center: Gilroy Office**

7415 Eigleberry Street
Suite C
Gilroy, CA 95020
408-847-1805
FAX: 408-842-2321
TTY:408-842-2591
e-mail: info@svilc.org
www.svilc.org

Cheryl L Cairns, Executive Director
Sheri Burns, Deputy Executive Director
Shobha Srinivasan, Development Services Director

SVILC strives to eliminate attitudinal, physical, and communication barriers faced by people with disabilities as they work towards independence and full integration in their communities. The programs and services available at SVILC meet a variety of independent living needs. In addition, SVILC offers classes, workshops, support groups, and recreational activities.

**4494 Silicon Valley Independent Living Center**

2306 Zanker Road
San Jose, CA 95131

408-894-9041
FAX: 408-894-9050
TTY:408-894-9012
e-mail: info@svilc.org
www.svilc.org

*Cheryl Cairnes, Executive Director*
*Sheri Burns, Deputy Executive Director*
*Shobha Srinivasan, Development Services Director*

SVILC strives to eliminate attitudinal, physical, and communication barriers faced by people with disabilities as they work towards independence and full integration in their communities. The programs and services available at SVILC meet a variety of independent living needs. In addition, SVILC offers classes, workshops, support groups, and recreational activities.

**4495 Southeast Center for Independent Living**

Merrill Street
Building 66
Fall River, MA 02720

508-679-9210
FAX: 508-677-2377
TTY:508-679-9210
e-mail: scil@cntn.net
www.secil.org

*Lisa M Titta, Executive Director*
*Liz Harbison, Program Coordinator*

The Philosophy of Independent Living, maintains that individuals with disabilities have the right to choose services and make decisions for themselves. This belief is the foundation and guiding principle of all of SCIL's policies and operations. SCIL provides training, information and support to help consumers achieve individual goals, experience personal growth and participate fully in community life.

**4496 Southern California Rehabilitation Services**

7830 Quill Drive
Suite D
Downey, CA 90242

562-862-6531
FAX: 562-923-5274
TTY:562-869-0931
e-mail: scrs@scrs-ilc.org
www.scrs-ilc.org

*Tim Whittier, Executive Director*
*Steve Brandt, Program Director*

Southern California Rehabilitation Services empowers persons with disabilities to achieve their personalized goals through community education and individualized services that provide the knowledge, skills, and confidence building to maximize their quality of life. SCRS develops comprehensive programs, responding to the needs of the disability community, enabling them to lead healthy, independent, and productive lives. Most services are provided free of charge to all persons with disabilities.
*1979*

**4497 Through the Looking Glass**

2198 6th Street
Suite 100
Berkeley, CA 94710

510-848-1112
800-644-2666
FAX: 510-848-4445
TTY: 800-804-1616
e-mail: tlg@lookingglass.org
www.lookingglass.org

*Megan Kirshbaum, Executive Director*
*Tina Evoyne Washington, Office Manager/Publications Dept*

**4498 Tri-County Independent Living Center**

955 Myrtle Avenue
Eureka, CA 95501

707-445-8404
877-756-5000
FAX: 707-445-9751
TTY: 707-445-8405
e-mail: chrisjones@tilinet.org
www.tilinet.org

*Chris Jones, Executive Director*
*Mari Dorenstreich, Independent Living Specialist*

Promotes the philosophy of independent living, to connect individuals to services, and to create and accessible community, so that people with disabilities can have control over their lives and full access to the communities in which they live.

**4499 Westside Center for Independent Living**

11201 S La Cienega Boulevard
Los Angeles, CA 90045

310-568-0107
888-851-9245
FAX: 310-390-4906
e-mail: wcil@wcil.org
www.wcil.org

*Mary Ann Jones, Executive Director*

A non-residential, public-benefit corporation to enable people with disabilities and seniors in the Los Angeles community to live more independent, self supporting and satisfying lives.
*1976*

## Colorado

**4500 Atlantis Community**

201 S Cherokee Street
Denver, CO 80223

303-733-7719
FAX: 303-733-9324
TTY:303-733-0047
e-mail: adaptbabs@earthlink.net
www.atlantiscommunity.net

*Tim Thornton, Co-Director*
*Terrance Turner, Co-Director*
*Babs Johnsona, Co-Administrator*

Provide direct services, and to empower people with disabilities integrating, with full and equal rights, into all parts of society including employment, affordable, accessible, housing, transportation, recreation, communication, education, and public places while exercising and exerting choice and self determination.
*1975*

**4501 Center for Independence**

1600 Ute Avenue
Suite 100
Grand Junction, CO 81501

970-241-0315
800-613-2271
FAX: 970-245-3341
TTY: 970-245-3341
e-mail: info@cfigj.org
www.cfigj.org

*Linda Taylor, Director*
*Kat Emmons, Executive Director*

**4502 Center for People with Disabilities**

615 Main Streetreet
Longmont, CO 80501

303-772-3250
FAX: 303-772-5125
TTY:303-772-3250
e-mail: davuid@cpwd-ilc.org

*David Bolin, Director*

CPWD provides resources, information, and advocacy to assist people with disabilities in overcoming barriers to independent living.

**4503  Center for People with Disabilities (CPWD)**

1675 Range Street
Boulder, CO 80301

303-442-8662
FAX: 303-442-0502
e-mail: info@cpwd-ilc.org
www.cpwd-ilc.org

*Andrew J Imparato, CEO and President*
*Lowel Aird, Executive Director*

Provides resources, information, and advocacy to assist people
with disabilities in overcoming barriers to independent living.
CPWD's goal is an integrated community that equally welcomes
all members.

**4504  Center for People with Disabilities: Pueblo**

1304 Berkley Avenue
Pueblo, CO 81004

719-546-1271
800-659-3656
FAX: 719-546-1374
e-mail: .htmeneamidei@yahoo.com
www.du.edu/~bfox2/ilcpueblo

*Larry Williams, Executive Director*

**4505  Center on Deafness**

3444 Dundee Road
Northbrook, IL 60062

847-559-0110
FAX: 847-559-8199
TTY:847-559-9493
e-mail: cod@centerondeafness.org
www.centerondeafness.org

*Patrick Palbicke, Technical Coordinator*
*Donna Gomez, Residential Services*
*Robert Dkye, Executive Director*

COD is dedicated to providing quality services for persons who
are deaf or hard of hearing and their families, through educational, vocational, and residential services in a therapuetic, community-based environment

**4506  Colorado Springs Independence Center**

21 E Las Animas Street
Colorado Springs, CO 80903

719-471-8181
FAX: 719-471-7829
TTY:719-471-2076
e-mail: info@csicindliving.org
www.csicindliving.org

*Vicki Skoog, Executive Director*

To empower persons with disabilities to maximize their independence within the community and to remove barriers which
impact their quality of life, while encouraging them to live independently in their community.

**4507  Connections for Independent Living**

1024 9th Avenue
Suite E
Greeley, CO 80631

970-352-8682
FAX: 970-353-8058
TTY:970-352-8682
e-mail: connectionsil@viawest.net

*Beth Danielson, Executive Director*

Certified IL Center, I and R advocacy, peer support, skills training, sign language interpretations, reader services, housing.
Cross-disability, all ages.

**4508  Deaf Counseling Services at Mental Health Corporation
of Denver**

1555 Humboldt Street
Denver, CO 80218

303-504-1650
FAX: 303-504-1660
TTY:303-322-6190
e-mail: contactmhcd@mhcd.org
www.mhcd.org

*Carl Clark MD, Chief Executive Officer*
*Cheryl Clark MD, Medical Director*
*Sam Radke MBA, CFO*

Provides conseling to deaf and hard of hearing persons who reside in Metro Denver. Our goal is to provide therapeutic service
that respects the dignity, privacy, and unique needs of the person.
    *1989*

**4509  Denver CIL**

455 Sherman Street
Suite 140
Denver, CO 80203

303-698-1900

*Greg Beran, Owner*

**4510  Disability Center for Independent Living**

5900 E 39th Avenue
Suite 4
Denver, CO 80207

303-320-1345
FAX: 303-320-1355
TTY:303-320-1345
e-mail: crlrynlds@aol.com

*Carol Reynolds, Executive Director*

**4511  Disabled Resource Services**

424 Pine Street
Suite 101
Fort Collins, CO 80524

970-482-2700
FAX: 970-407-7072
TTY:970-407-7060
e-mail: drs@fortnet.org
www.fortnet.org/drs

*Nancy Jackson, Executive Director*
*Marge Grell, Assistant Director*

To empower individuals with disabilities to achieve their maximum level of independence and to gain personal dignity within
society. Disabled Resource Services, as a private non-profit
state certified center for independent living, is dedicated to
working with individuals with all types of disabilities in Larimer
County to promote their independence and equality through services which support advocacy, awareness and access to their
community.

**4512  Disbled Resource Services**

620 E Eisenhower Boulevard
Loveland, CO 80537

970-667-0816
FAX: 970-663-9526
e-mail: drs@jymis.com

*Don Maroney, Director*

**4513  Greeley Center for Independence**

2780 28th Avenue
Greeley, CO 80634

970-339-2444
800-748-1012
FAX: 970-339-0033
e-mail: gciinc@gci.org
www.gci.org

*Hope Cassidy, Executive Director*
*Rob Rabe, Outpatient Services Director*
*Leslie Vail, Human Resources Director*

Provides places of growth, transition and encouragement, where people with temporary and permanent disabilities can reach toward their maximum potential of personal independence and wellness.

**4514  Independent Life Center**

PO Box 612
Craig, CO  81626                          970-826-0833
                                    FAX: 970-826-0832
                                    TTY:970-826-0833
                          e-mail: indlife@earthlink.net

*Evelyn Tileston, Director*

**4515  Martin Luther Home of Colorado**

1500 Casa Grande Boulevard
Fort Collins, CO  80526                   970-206-1645

*Cecelia Camp, Administrator*
*Fred Naumann III, Communications*

Providing a wide array of services to assist individuals and families in achieving positive life goals. Services to persons with disabilities and other special needs include community living options, training and employment options, spiritual growth and development options, training and counseling support.

**4516  Martin Luther Homes: Fort Collins**

109 Cameron Drive
Building A
Fort Collins, CO  80525                   970-223-1751
                                    FAX: 970-223-1781

*Molly Kennif, Executive Director*

Providing a wide array of services to assist individuals and families in achieving positive life goals. Services to persons with disabilities and other special needs include community living options, training and employment options, spiritual growth and development options, training and counseling support.

**4517  Pueblo Goodwill Center for Independent**

250 S Santa Fe Avenue
Pueblo, CO  81003                         719-543-4483

**4518  Pueblo Goodwill Industries**

1020 Constitution Road
Pueblo, CO  81001                         719-543-4483
                                    FAX: 719-545-5134
                                    TTY:719-543-4483
                  e-mail: customerservice@pueblogoodwill.com
                               www.pueblogoodwill.com

*Debbie Mill, Director*

Pueblo Goodwill Industries, Inc. is a community resource dedicated to assisting individuals with disabling and/or disadvantaging conditions in achieving their fullest potential by offering them, through networking and collaboration, enriching opportunities and choices geared toward wage earning and productive living. These opportunities and choices are provided through rehabilitative services, counseling, educational training, and employement.

**4519  Southwest Center for Independence**

835 E 2nd Avenue
Suite 200
Durango, CO  81301                        970-259-1672
                                    FAX: 970-259-0947
                                    TTY:970-259-1672
                          e-mail: isabel@swcidur.org
                                    swcidurango.org

*Isabel Viana, Executive Director*
*Larry Wales, Housing Coordinator*
*Gail Swinderman, OIB Coordinator*

Empowering individuals with disabilities and their families to achieve their maximum level of independence in work, play and other areas of life.

**4520  Southwest Center for Independence: Cortez**

6900 Cr Road 24.2
Cortez, CO  81321                         970-565-7169
                                    FAX: 970-565-9182
                          e-mail: swcidur@frontier.net

*Isabel Viana, Executive Director*
*Maxine Carton, Independent Living Coordinator*

Empowers indiviuals with disabilities and their families to achieve their maximum level of independence in work, play and other areas of life.

## Connecticut

**4521  Center for Disability Rights**

764 Campbell Avenue
Suite A
W Haven, CT  06516                        203-934-7077
                                    FAX: 203-934-7078
                                    TTY:203-934-7079
                          e-mail: cdr7077@aol.com

*Marc A Gallucci, Executive Director*

**4522  Center for Independent Living SC**

26 Palmer's Hill Road
Stamford, CT  06902                       203-353-8550
                                    FAX: 203-353-1423
                                    TTY:203-353-8550

*Dana Canevari, Director*

**4523  Chapel Haven**

1040 Whalley Avenue
New Haven, CT  06515                      203-397-1714
                                    FAX: 203-392-3698
                                    www.chapelhaven.org

*Betsey Parlato, President/CEO*
*Thayer Quoos, VP Residential Programs*
*Frank Hughes, VP Finance/Operations*

Chapel Haven is committed to providing a lifelong program of individualized support services for adults with cognitive disabilities, enabling them to live independent and productive lives.

**4524  Co-Op Initiatives**

20-28 Sargeant Street
Suite 102
Hartford, CT  06105                       860-724-4940
                                    FAX: 860-724-7102
                          e-mail: info@coopinit.org
                                    www.coopinit.org

*Lisa Caron, Independent Living Coordinator*
*Therese Nadeau, Program Director*

Provides community based oppputunities for people with disabilities in Connecticut.

**4525  Disabilities Network of Eastern Connecticut**

238 W Town Street
Norwich, CT  06360                        860-823-1898
                                    FAX: 860-886-2316
                          e-mail: dnec@snet.net
                                    www.disability-dnec.org

*Carolyn Newcombe, Executive Director*

The mission of the Disabilities Network is to empower persons with disabilities in Eastern Connecticut to live as independently as they choose, and to improve the quality of their lives, as well as to effect positive change that promotes the inclusion of all persons with disabilities within society.

**4526  Disability Resource Center of Fairfield County: Stratford Office**

80 Ferry Boulevard
Suite 210
Stratford, CT  06615
203-378-6977
FAX: 203-375-2748
TTY:203-378-3248
e-mail: info@drcfc.org
www.drcfc.org

*Anthony Lacava, Executive Director*
*Stephanie Mastrolillo, Executive Assistant*

The Disability Resource Center of Fairfield County DRCFC provides a comprehensive array of services both to the individuals and the communities of Fairfield County, Connecticut. These services embody the Independent Living philosophy...a philosophy that challenges the social attitudes and the physical barriers that stigmatize and exclude persons with disabilities from the community.
*1981*

**4527  Independence Northwest Center for Independent Living**

1183 New Haven Road
Suite 200
Naugatuck, CT  06770
203-729-3299
TTY:203-729-1281
members.aol.com/indnw

*Eileen Healy, Executive Director*
Offers peer counseling, disability education and awareness.

**4528  Independence Unlimited**

151 New Park Avenue
Suite D
Hartford, CT  06106
860-523-5021
FAX: 860-523-5603
e-mail: clowindunl@aol.com

*Eileen Healey, Contact*
*Candace Low, Executive Director*

**4529  New Horizons**

37 Bliss Road
Unionville, CT
203-675-4711
FAX: 203-675-4369

*Michael Shaw, Director*
Services offered Housing and other support systems for the physically disabled

# Delaware

**4530  Easter Seal Independent Living Center**

24 Reads Way
New Castle, DE  19720
302-324-4482
FAX: 302-324-4481
e-mail: rbrouill@inet.net

*Ray Brouillette, Contact*

**4531  Freedom Center for Independent Living**

3 E Main Street
Middletown, DE  19709
302-376-4399
866-687-3245
FAX: 302-376-4395
TTY: 302-376-4397
e-mail: info@fcilde.org
www.fcilde.org

*Catherine McKelvey, Executive Director*
*Margaret Owens, Independent Living Specialist*

FCILDE protects the Civil rights and promotes the empowerment of persons with disabilities and their families through the independent living philosophy.

**4532  Independent Living**

1800 N Broom Street
Apt 210
Wilmington, DE  19802
302-429-6693
FAX: 302-429-8031
TTY:302-429-8034

*Susan Cycyk, Executive Director*

Providing skilled support and caring guidance to adults with disabilities. Our case management services include: daily living skills training, medical coordination, transportation assistance, financial management, housing assistance, and vocational/educational planning.

**4533  Independent Resource Georgetown**

410 S Bedford Street
Suite 37
Georgetown, DE  19947
302-854-9330
FAX: 302-854-9408
TTY:302-854-9340
e-mail: pboyd@independentresource.org

*Larry Henderson, Director*
*Pat Boyd, Manager*

**4534  Independent Resources**

52 Reads Way
New Castle, DE  19720
302-328-6704
FAX: 302-328-6705

**4535  Independent Resources Wilmington**

6 Denny Road
Suite 205
Wilmington, DE  19809
302-765-0191

*Larry Henderson, Executive Director*

**4536  Independent Resources: Dover**

32 W Loockerman Street
Suite 104
Dover, DE  19904
302-735-4599
FAX: 302-735-5623
TTY:302-735-5629
e-mail: lhenderson@independentresources.org

*Larry Henderson, Director*

**4537  Independent Resources: Wilmington**

6 Denny Road
Suite 205
Wilmington, DE  19809
302-765-0191
FAX: 302-765-0195
e-mail: fox205007@aol.com

*Larry Henderson, Executive Director*

**4538  Martin Luther Homes of Delaware**
260 Chapman Road
Suite 104a
Newark, DE  19702

302-456-5995
877-366-7242
FAX: 302-456-5998
e-mail: info@mosaic.org
www.mosaicinfo.org

*Terry Olson, Program Director*

Provides services to adults with developmental disabilities who reside in homes and apartments. Services are designed to provide them with opportunities for choices and participation in the life of their communities. Supports are geared to assist each individual in becoming more independent in activities of daily living, vocational skills, community mobility and transportation, and recreation and leisure activities.

## District of Columbia

**4539  Centers for Independent Living Program Rehabilitation Services Department**
Mary E Switzer Building
330 C Street SW
Washington, DC  20237

202-619-3482

Approximately 400 Independent Living Centers, most funded by this program, provide local services and programs to enable individuals with severe disabilities to live and function independently.

**4540  DC Center for Independent Living**
1400 Florida Ave NE
Washington, DC  20002

202-388-0033

*Richard Simms, Executive Director*

**4541  Disability Rights Center**
2500 G Street NW
Washington, DC  20007

202-986-0375
FAX: 202-337-4939
e-mail: crippower@aol.com

*Susan Ferris, Contact*

**4542  District of Columbia Center for Independent Living**
1400 Florida Ave NE
Suite 3
Washington, DC  20002

202-388-0033
FAX: 202-398-3018
TTY:202-388-0277
e-mail: info@dccil.org
www.dccil.org

*Richard A Simms, Executive Director*

**4543  National Council on Independent Living**
1710 Rhode Island Avenue NW
# 5
Washington, DC  20036

202-895-2784
877-525-3400
FAX: 703-525-3409
TTY: 703-525-4153
e-mail: ncil@ncil.org
www.ncil.org

*John Lancaster, Executive Director*

## Florida

**4544  Ability 1st**
1823 Buford Court
Tallahassee, FL  32308

850-575-9621
FAX: 850-575-5740
TTY:850-576-5245
e-mail: ability1st@ability1st.info
www.ability1st.info

*Judith Barrett, Executive Director*

Formerly the Center for Independent Living of North Florida, empowers persons with disabilities to live indepdently and participate actively in their community.

**4545  Adult Day Training**
Goodwill Industries- Suncoast
10596 Gandy Boulevard N
St Petersburg, FL  33702

727-523-1512
888-279-1988
FAX: 727-563-9300
TTY:727-579-1068
e-mail: gw.marketing@goodwill-suncoast.com
www.goodwill-suncoast.org

*Cathy Roegiers, Program Manager*
*Lee Waits, President*

An innovative program which uses job skills to teach self-help, daily living, communication, mobility, travel, decision-making, behavioral and social skills. This focus provides concrete, transferable experiences to help prepare individuals for greater community inclusion by achieving the highest possible degree of independence in their daily life, increasing their confidence and supporting their successful transitions to less structured, self-sufficient environments.

**4546  CIL Options-One Stop Career Center: Royal Palm Beach**
1030 Royal Plam Beach Boulevard
Royal Palm Beach, FL  33411

561-798-7997

Promotes independence for people with disabilities.

**4547  CIL of Central Florida**
720 N Denning Drive
Winter Park, FL  32789

407-623-1070
FAX: 407-623-1390
e-mail: jgassie@cilorlando.org
www.cilorlando.org

*Elizabeth Howe, Executive Director*

A private non-profit organization that was founded in 1976 by Central Floridians dedicated to helping people with disabilities achieve their self-determined goals for independent living. CIL of Central Florida serves individuals with any type of disability of any age residing in Orange, Seminole, Osceola and Polk counties.

**4548  CIL of Florida Keys**
88005 Overseas Highway
Suite 17
Islamorada, FL  33036

305-852-0177
877-335-0187
FAX: 305-453-3488
e-mail: bpierce@cilkeys.org
www.cilkeys.org

*Brenda Pierce, Executive Director*
*Aleisa McGuirl, Consumer Advocate*

Offers assistance to persons with disabilities in acquiring independent living and self advocacy skills in order to obtain and maintain independence and self-sufficiency.

**4549  CIL of Florida Keys-Key West**

300 Southard Street
Suite 105
Key West, FL  33040                          305-295-7945
                                        FAX: 305-295-7945
                          e-mail: cilkeys@cilkeys.org
                                        www.cilkeys.org

*Brenda Pierce, Director*

Offers assistance to persons with disabilities in acquiring independent living and self-advocacy skills in order to obtain and maintain independence and self-sufficiency.

**4550  CIL of North Central Florida**

222 SW 36th Terrace
Gainesville, FL  32607                       352-378-7474
                                             800-265-5724
                                        FAX: 352-378-5582
                                        TTY: 352-375-8448
                              e-mail: admin@cilncf.org

*William Kennedy, Director*

Empowering people with disabilities to exert their individual rights to live as independently as possible, make personal life choices and achieve full community inclusion.

**4551  Caring and Sharing Center for Independent Living**

12552 Belcher Road S
Largo, FL  33773                             727-539-7550
                                             866-539-7550
                                        FAX: 727-539-7588
                                        TTY: 727-577-0065
                             e-mail: cascil@cascil.org
                                          www.cascil.org

*Michael Cook, Executive Director*
*Mary Jensen, Office Manager*

Assist persons with all type of disabilities and their families, to achieve the greatest degree of self-determination in accessibility, advocacy, education, employment, and place of residence in keeping with the consumer's freedom of choice

**4552  Caring and Sharing: Gulf Port**

5730 Shore Boulevard
Gulfport, FL  33707                          727-384-6346

                             e-mail: cascil@cascil.org
                                          www.cascil.org

*Michael Cook, Executive Director*

CASCIL assists persons with all types of disabilities and their families, to achieve the greatest degree of self-determination in accessibility, advocacy, education, employment and place of residence in keeping with the consumer's freedom of choice.

**4553  Caring and Sharing: Holiday**

24356 US Highway 19 N
Suite 300
Holidayt, FL  34691                          727-945-8933
                                             877-422-7245
                                        FAX: 727-945-8944
                                        TTY: 727-945-8933
                             e-mail: cascil@cascil.org
                                          www.cascil.org

*Michael Cook, Executive Director*

CASCIL assists persons with all types of disabilities and their families, to achieve the greatest degree of self-determination in accessibility, advocacy, education, employment and place of residence in keeping with the consumer's freedom of choice.

**4554  Cathedral Center for Independent Living**

3599 University Boulevard S
Jacksonville, FL  32216                      904-399-4185

*Susan Hughes, Administrator*
*Reza Taba, MD*

Offers comprehensive rehabilitation.

**4555  Center for Independent Living Options - One Stop Career Center: Stuart**

900 SE Central Parkway
Stuart, FL  34994                            772-223-2653
                                        FAX: 772-223-5041
                                             www.cilo.org

Promotes independence for people with disabilities.

**4556  Center for Independent Living in Central Florida - Advocacy Living Skills Peer Support**

720 N Denning Drive
Winter Park, FL  32789                       407-623-1070
                                             877-891-6448
                                        FAX: 407-623-1390
                                        TTY: 407-623-1885
                                        www.cilorlando.org

*Gassie Jeanneatte, Program Director*
*Elizabeth Howe, Executive Director*

Information and referral services, advocacy, living skills, peer support, employment.

**4557  Center for Independent Living of Broward**

4800 N State Road 7
Suite 102
Lauderdale Lakes, FL  33319                  954-722-6400
                                             888-722-6400
                                        FAX: 954-722-9801
                          e-mail: cilb@cilbroward.org
                                       www.cilbroward.org

*Karen Dickerhoof, Executive Director*
*William Knight, Deputy Director*

A non-profit organization whose mission is to offer assistance to people with disabilities in fulfilling the goals of independence and self sufficiency.

**4558  Center for Independent Living of Florida Keys**

103400 Overseas Highway
Suite 243
Key Largo, FL  33037                         305-453-3491
                                             877-335-0187
                                        FAX: 305-453-3488
                                        TTY: 305-453-3491
                          e-mail: cilkeys@cilkeys.org
                                        www.cilkeys.org

*Brenda Pierce, Director*

Offers assistance to persons with disabilities in acquiring independent living and self-advocacy skills in order to obtain and maintain independence and self-sufficiency.

**4559  Center for Independent Living of N Central Florida**

3445 NE 24th Street
Ocala, FL  34470                             352-368-3788
                                        FAX: 352-629-0098
                             e-mail: cilncf@cilncf.org
                                          www.cilncf.org

*Carol Terrillion, Site Coordinator*

CILNCF empowers people with disabilities to exert our individuals rights to live as independently as possible, make personal life choices and achieve full community inclusion.

**4560  Center for Independent Living of N Florida**

1823 Buford Court
Tallahassee, FL  32308                       850-575-9621

**4561    Center for Independent Living of NW Florida**
3600 N Pace Boulevard
Pensacola, FL 32505                              850-595-5566
                                                 877-245-2457
                                            FAX: 850-595-5560
                                            TTY: 850-595-5566
                                    e-mail: cilnwf@cilnwf.org
                                                www.cilnwf.org

*Frank Cherry, Executive Director*

We provide resources and services for people with disabilities in
Escambia, Santa Rosa, Okaloosa and Walton Counties. Equipment loan, home modifications, ramps, art class and many other
services.

**4562    Center for Independent Living of North Central Florida**

3774 W Gulf to Lake Highway
Lecanto, FL 34461                                352-527-8399
                                                 800-265-5724
                                            FAX: 352-527-9511
                                            TTY: 352-527-8399
                                  e-mail: jackson@cilncf.org
                                                www.cilncf.org

*Cathy Jackson, Site Coordinator*

Empowers people with disabilities to exert their individual
rights to live as independently as possible, make personal life
choices and achieve full community inclusion.

**4563    Center for Independent Living of S Florida**
6660 Biscayne Boulevard
Miami, FL 33138                                  305-751-8025
                                                 800-854-7551
                                            FAX: 305-751-8944
                                            TTY: 305-751-8025
                                    e-mail: info@soflacil.org
                                                www.soflacil.org

*Kelly Greene, Executive Director*
*Ubaldo Alvarez, Program Manager*
*Jackie , Information and Referral Special*

A community based non for profit, independent living center
serving people of all ages with any type of disability. Services:
Basic education, GED preperation, American sign language advocacy, peer support, information and referral, independent living skills training, housing assistance, transportation assistance,
home modiifications, transition from nursing facility to the community assisatnace filing ADA complaints, accessibility surveys, diability awareness traing.

**4564    Center for Independent Living of SW Florida**
3626 Evans Avenue
Fort Myers, FL 33901                             239-277-1447
                                                 888-343-6991
                                            FAX: 239-277-1647
                                            TTY: 239-277-3964
                                 e-mail: cilfl@neosmart.com
                                                www.cilfl.org

*Linda Hendricks, Director*
*Ronald Muschonge, President*

**4565    Center for Independent Technology and Education
(CITE)**
215 E New Hampshire Street
Orlando, FL 32804                                407-841-1500
                                            FAX: 407-895-5255
                                e-mail: lvaneepoel@lcf-fl.org
                              www.lighthousecentralflorida.org

*Lee Nasehi, Executive Director*
*Joyce Hildreth, CVRT, Associate Executive Director*
*Ori Kantor, Owner*

Lighthouse Central Florida promotes the independence of children and adults with blindness, low vision and other disabilities
through technology, education, support and advocacy.

**4566    Coalition for Independent Living Option**
6800 Forest Hill Boulevard
Greenacres, FL 33413                             561-966-4288
                                                 800-683-7337
                                            FAX: 561-641-6619
                                            TTY: 561-641-6538
                              e-mail: cilo2000@bellsouth.net
                                                www.cilo.org

*Shelley Gottsagen, Executive Director*

Independent living centers offer peer counseling, advocacy, information and referral and independent living skills development. CILO offers teen programs, an adaptive equipment loan
closet, disability sensitivity training and accessibility studies
and services for people who are crime victims, transition services for high school students and meal delivery programs.

**4567    Coalition for Independent Living Options- One Stop
Career Center**
209 SW Park Street
Okeechobee, FL 34974                             863-462-5350
                                            FAX: 863-462-5355
                                                www.cilo.org
Promotes independence for people with disabilities.

**4568    Disability Resource Center**
625 Highway 231
Suite 10B
Panama City, FL 32405                            850-769-6890
                                            FAX: 850-769-6891
                                            TTY:850-769-1513
                          e-mail: drcpanamacity@knology.net

*Jane Flower, Director*

**4569    Independent Living Resource Center of Northeast
Florida**
2709 Art Museum Drive
Jacksonville, FL 32207                           904-399-8484
                                            FAX: 904-399-0448
                                            TTY:904-398-6322
                                    e-mail: mattm@cilj.com
                                                www.cilj.com

*Matt Motko, Executive Director*
*Wanda Graham, Program/Services Director*
*John Hancock, Development Director*

Empowers all people with a disability to live independent and
self empowered lives.

**4570    Independent Living for Adult Blind**
101 W State Street
Jacksonville, FL 32202                           904-399-8484
                                            FAX: 904-632-5107
                                 e-mail: bsimpson@fccj.edu

*Becky Simpsons, Director*

Offers services for the totally blind, legally blind and visually
impaired. Services include independent living skills, training
and guidance toward rehabilitation. Also provides vocational
training in computers. Supported by government grants and private donations.

**4571    Miami-Dade County Disability Services and Independ-
ent Living (DSAIL)**
1335 NW 14th Street
Miami, FL 33125                                  305-547-5445
                                            FAX: 305-547-7355

*Edeline B Clermont, Director*

Offers information and referral services serving all types of disabilities with the goal of assisting the disabled acquiring independence and control over their lives. Teaches independent
living skills, job readiness and placement, home health care,
sensitivity training, training in ASL and Braille, counsel people
with disabilities or wide range of problems.

**4572 North Central Florida Citrus County**
1675 S Suncoast Boulevard
Homosassa, FL 34448
352-795-3144
800-476-5373
FAX: 352-628-3600
e-mail: sellfaster@eraamericanrealty.com
www.eraamericanrealty.com

*Alma Warren, Executive Director*
*Dennis Pilon, Manager*

**4573 Northern Florida Center for Independent Living**
572 Appleyard Drive
Suite C
Tallahassee, FL 32304
850-592-
FAX: 850-575-5740
e-mail: janetkahn@nettally.com
www.cilnf.org

*Janet Kahn, Contact*

**4574 SCCIL at Titusville**
725 S Deleon Avenue
Titusville, FL 32780
407-268-2244
FAX: 706-724-6729
TTY:706-724-6324
e-mail: kswoil@csranet.com
www.virtualcil.net

*Gerri Martin, Executive Director*

**4575 Self Reliance**
8901 North Armenia Avenue
Tampa, FL 33604
813-375-3965
FAX: 813-375-3970
TTY:813-375-3972
e-mail: jdidomencio@self-reliance.org
www.self-reliance.org

*Joseph DiDomenico, Director*

A cross disability agency providing services to both children and adults with disabilities to identify and overcome barriers to independence in their lives. Self Reliance also promotes independence through empowering persons with disabilities and improving the communities in which they live.

**4576 Self-Reliance Center for Independent Living**
8901 N Armenia Avenue
Tampa, FL 33604
813-375-3965
FAX: 813-375-3970
TTY:813-375-3972
e-mail: bruehl@self-reliance.org
www.self-reliance.org

*Joseph Domenico, Executive Director*

Prmotes independence through empowering persons with disabilities and improving the communities in which they live. Also a cross disability agency providing services to both children and adults with disabilities to identify and overcome barriers to independence in their lives.

**4577 Space Coast Center for Independent Living**
331 Ramp Road
Cocoa Beach, FL 32931
321-784-9008
FAX: 321-784-3702
e-mail: sccil@bellsouth.net

*Donna Taylor, Executive Director*

Provides overall services for individuals with al types of disabilities. Offers peer support, advocacy, skills training, accessibility surveys, support groups, transportation, specialized equipment and sign language interpreter coordination services.

**4578 Suncoast Center for Independent Living**
2989 Fruitville Road
Sarasota, FL 34237
941-351-9545
FAX: 941-351-9875
e-mail: admin@scil4u.com
www.scil4u.org

*Thomas Lawson, Executive Director*
*Dave Caufield, Program Manager*

A non-profit organizatio that assists persons with significant disabilities to live successfully in their communities. Also helps the disabled achieve their full potential with independent living services & advocating for the elimination of social and physical barriers that hinder integration in the community.

**4579 Suncoast Center for Independent Living: Arcadia**
14 East Oak Street
Arcadia, FL 34266
863-993-4142
FAX: 863-993-4142

**4580 Tampa Lighthouse for the Blind**
1106 W Platt St
Tampa, FL 33606
813-251-2407
FAX: 813-254-4305
e-mail: tlh@tampalighthouse.org
www.tampalighthouse.org

*Clifford Olstrom, Executive Director*

Provides comprehensive rehabilitation programs for persons who are blind or visually imapired in two locations in Florida.

**4581 Victory Lane Center for Independent Living**
475 South Nova Road
Ormond Beach, FL 32174
386-671-1960
FAX: 386-671-1961
TTY:386-671-1960
e-mail: allysounQ@victorylanecil.org
www.victorylanecil.org

*Allysoun Gallup, Director*

Victory Lane CIL assists in providing educational opportunities for individuals with disabilities and our community regardng disability rights and personal responsibilities via: networking, collaboration, and grassroots advocacty efforts to enhance self-empowered individual living.

# Georgia

**4582 Access Center for Independent Living**
430 Prior Street SE
Room 120
Gainesville, GA 30501
770-534-6656
FAX: 770-534-6626
TTY:770-534-6626
e-mail: remcgarry@earthlink.net

*Bob McGarry, Executive Director*

**4583 Bain**
PO Box 1674
Bainbridge, GA 39818
229-246-0150
888-830-1530
FAX: 229-246-1715
TTY: 800-255-0135
e-mail: bain@surfsouth.com
www.baincil.org

*Neil Griffin, Board President*
*Virginia Harris, Executive Director*

Established in 1995, a grass roots non profit advocacy organization founded by two disabled persons.

**4584  DisABILITY LINK NW**
477 Broad Street
Rome, GA  30501
770-534-6656
FAX: 770-534-6626
TTY:770-534-6656
e-mail: rrtuttle@disabilitylink.org

*Donna Baxley, Director*

disABILITY LINK NW is committed to promoting the rights of all people with disabilites.

**4585  Disability Action Center for Georgia**
755 Commerce Drive
Suite 415
Decatur, GA  30030
404-687-8890
800-239-2507
FAX: 404-687-8298
TTY: 404-687-9175
e-mail: info@disabilitylink.org
www.disabilitylink.org

*Rebecca Ramag-Tuttle, President/CEO*
*Hilary Elliott, Assistant Director*
*Diana Allen, Program Manager*

**4586  Disability Connections**
170 College Street
Macon, GA  31201
478-741-1425
800-743-2117
FAX: 478-755-1571
e-mail: dcinfo@disabilityconnections.com
www.disabilityconnections.com

*Jerilyn Leverett, Director*

A private non-profit organization that looks to enable all people with disabilities to attain and have access to all opportunities in life.

**4587  Disability LINK**
755 Commerce Drive
Suite 415
Decatur, GA  30030
404-687-8890
800-239-2507
FAX: 404-687-8298
TTY: 404-687-9175
e-mail: info@disabilitylink.org
www.disabilitylink.org

*Rebecca Ramag-Tuttle, President/CEO*
*Hilary Elliot, Assistant Director*
*Diana Allen, Program Manager*

**4588  Division of Rehabilitation Services**
Georgia Department of Labor
410 Mall Boulevard
Suite B
Savannah, GA  31406
912-356-2537
FAX: 912-691-6816
TTY:912-356-2940
e-mail: www.dol.state.ga.us

*Allen Beall, Regional Director*
*George Foley, Manager*
Vocational rehabilitation services.

**4589  Georgia's SILC**
1431 McLendon Drive
Suite C
Decatur, GA  30033
770-270-6860
888-288-9780
FAX: 770-270-5957
TTY:770-270-5671
e-mail: ppuckett@silcga.org
www.silcga.org

*Patricia Puckett, Executive Director*
*Colleen Caffrey, Executive Assistant*

**4590  Living Independence for Everyone (LIFE)**
17 Travis Street
Savannah, GA  31406
912-920-2414
800-948-4824
FAX: 912-920-0007
TTY: 912-920-2419
e-mail: info@lifecil.com
www.lifecil.com

*Frances Todd, Director*

**4591  Multiple Choices Center for Independent Living**
999 Gaines School Road
Athens, GA  30605
706-549-1020
877-549-1020
FAX: 706-549-1060
e-mail: info@multiplechoices.org
www.multiplechoices.org

*Peggy Chavis, Director*

Mutliple Choices is dedicated to the empowerment of people of all ages and with all types of disabilities to live independently and to control their lives as much as possible. Serves people in Barrow, Clark, Elbert, Green, Jackson, Madison, Morgan, Oconee, Oglethorpe and Walton counties.

**4592  North District Independent Living Program**
311 Green St NW
Suite 209
Gainesville, GA  30501
770-535-5930

*Sharon McCurry, Coordinator*
*Cindy Hanna, Executive Director*

Information and referral, advocacy, peer counseling, service co-ordination and ADA consultation.

**4593  Open Arms**
871 Forest Path
Stone Mountain, GA  30088
770-413-2241
FAX: 770-498-2778
e-mail: hmkennet@Qaol.com

*Ken Morris, Director*

**4594  Roosevelt Warm Springs Institute for Rehabilitation**
PO Box 1000
Warm Springs, GA  31830
770-655-5000
FAX: 706-655-5011
TTY:706-655-5176
e-mail: rwsir.webmaster@dol.state.ga.us
www.rooseveltrehab.org

*Carolyn Moreland, Director Education*
*Frank Ruzycki, Executive Director*

A comprehensive rehabilitation facility that encompasses medical and vocational rehabilitation services as well as long term acute care and nationally recognized outpatient services.

**4595  Southeastern PVA**
4010 Deans Bridge Road
Hephzibah, GA  30815
706-796-6301
800-292-9335
FAX: 706-796-0363
e-mail: paravet@comcast.net
www.pva.org

*David Vaughn, President*

**4596  Southwest District Independent Living Program**
PO Box 1606
Albany, GA  31702
229-430-4170
FAX: 229-430-4466

*Bill Layton, Director*
*Diane Davis, Executive Director*

Independent Living Centers /Hawaii

Offers peer counseling, disability education and awareness, attendant care registry, and information on accessible home for the disabled.

**4597 Walton Option for Independent Living**

PO Box 519
Augusta, GA 30903        706-724-6262
FAX: 706-724-6729
TTY: 706-724-6262
e-mail: tjohnston@walteroptions.org
www.waltonoptions.org

*Tiffany Johnston, Executive Director*

Services include advocacy, assistive technology services, braille instruction, community education, home modifications, orientation and mobility services, peer support, and return to work services

**4598 Walton Options**

928 E 1 Warrenton Highway
Warrenton, GA 30828        706-465-1148
FAX: 706-465-1168
TTY: 706-465-1148
e-mail: tjohnston@waltonoptions.org
www.waltonoptions.org

*Tiffany Johnston, Director*

Empowers persons of all ages with all types of disabilities to reach their highest level of independence, including community inclusion and employment. Walton OPtions covers 30 counties in north eastern Georgia, and 10 counties in western South Carolina.

## Hawaii

**4599 Center for Independent Living: E Hawaii**

400 Hualani Street
Suite 16d
Hilo, HI 96720        808-935-3777
FAX: 808-961-6737
e-mail: cileh@interpac.net

*Laura Tobosa, Contact*

Provides an array of support services for people with all types of disabilities of any age.

**4600 H.C.I.L. - Kauai**

PO Box 3529
Lihue, HI 96766        808-245-4034
FAX: 808-245-7218
e-mail: kcil@aloha.net

*Humberto Blanco, Administrator*
*Teri Yamashiro, IL Specialist*

Offers peer counseling, disability education, attendant care registry, outreach services and advocacy.

**4601 Hawaii Centers for Independent Living**

414 Kuwili Street
Suite 102
Honolulu, HI 96817        808-522-5400
FAX: 808-522-5427
TTY: 808-522-5415
e-mail: patl@pacificil.org
www.hcil.org

*Patricia Lockwood, Executive Director*

Living arrangements, personal care, assistive technology, mobility, accessibility, income, transportation, vacation, recreation, and interpersonal relationships are all parts of independent living In essence, the vast majority of HCIL consumers are able to make the transition to increase personal choices and a higher quality of life

**4602 Kailua Kona Center for Independent Living: West Hawaii**

81-6627 Mamalahoa Highway
Kealakekua, HI 96750        808-323-2221
FAX: 808-323-2383
TTY: 808-323-2262
e-mail: cilwh@ilhawaii.net
www.hcil.org

*Merle Martin, Contact*

A nonprofit organization run by and for persons with disabilities. Information on housing referrals, financial benefits, advocacy, personal care attendants, services for elderly blind, and independent living skills counseling. Services are free to all disabled persons.

**4603 Kauai Center for Independent Living**

PO Box 3529
Lihue, HI 96766        808-245-4034
FAX: 808-245-7218
e-mail: kcil@mail.aloha.net

*Laurao Tobosa, Program Coordinator*

Provides a variety of support services for people with all types of disabilities.

**4604 Maui Center for Independent Living**

220 Imi Kala Street
Suite 103
Wailuku, HI 96793        808-242-4966
FAX: 808-244-6978
TTY: 808-242-4968
e-mail: mcilogg@gte.net

*Pat Lockwood, Contact*
*Laura Tabosa, Administrator*

Offers disability education and awareness, advocacy and counseling.

## Idaho

**4605 American Falls Office: Living Independently for Everyone (LIFE)**

2110 Rollandet Street
Idaho Falls, ID 83402        208-529-8610
FAX: 208-529-6804
e-mail: deann@idlife.org
www.idlife.org

*Dean Nielson, Executive Director*
*Tina Noreen, Programs Coordinator*

Enables people with disabilities to manage their own lives, make their own choices, and give information and knowledge to assist in living with dignity and bravado.

**4606 Dawn Enterprises**

PO Box 388
Blackfoot, ID 83221        208-785-5890
FAX: 208-785-3095
e-mail: dawnent2@if.rmci.net
www.orgsites.com

*Teresa Oakes, Director*
*Donna Butler, Assistant Director*

**4607  Disability Action Center**
1323 E Sherman Avenue
Suite 7
Coeur D Alene, ID  83814
208-664-9896
800-854-9500
FAX: 208-666-1362
e-mail: cda@dacnw.org
www.dacnw.org

*Amy Dreps, Site Coordinator*
*Cindy Nelson, Independent Living Advocate*
*Mark Leeper, Executive Director*

Provides advocacy, peer counseling, information, referral, independent living skills and personal assistant services.

**4608  Disability Action Center NW**
124 E 3rd Street
Moscow, ID  83843
208-746-9033
800-475-0070
FAX: 208-883-0524
e-mail: moscow@dacnw.org
www.dacnw.org

*Mark Leeper, Organization Director*
*Gina Morris, Independent Living Advocate*

Information and referrals, accessibility consultant, advocacy, personal care attendant registry, peer support groups, counseling and recreation opportunities and skills training. Also provides assistive technology services and information. *$45.00*

**4609  Disability Action Center, NW**
307 19th Street
Suite A-1
Lewiston, ID  83501
208-746-9033
FAX: 208-746-1004
TTY:208-746-9033
e-mail: lewiston@dacnw.org
www.dacnw.org

*Mark Leeper, Director*
*Melissa Painter, Independent Living Advocate*

Information and referrals, accessibility consultant, advocacy, personal care attendent registry, peer support groups, counseling and recreation opportunities and skills training. Also provides assistive technology services and information.

**4610  Idaho Commission for the Blind and Visually Impaired**
PO Box 83720
Boise, ID  83720
208-334-3220
800-542-8688
FAX: 208-334-2963
e-mail: mblackal@icbvi.state.id.us
www.icbvi.state.id.us

*Mike Blackaller, Vocational Rehabilitation*
*Brian Jain, Independent Living*
*Nancy Wise, Sight Restoration*

Empowers persons who are blind or visually impaired by providing vocational rehabilitation training, skills training and educational opportunities to achieve self fulfillment through quality employment and independent living; to serve as a resource to families and employers and to expand public awareness regarding the potential of all persons who are blind or visually impaired.

**4611  Idaho Falls Office: Living Independently for Everyone (LIFE)**
640 Pershing Avenue
Suite A
Pocatello, ID  83201
208-529-8610
800-631-2747
FAX: 208-232-2753
e-mail: deann@idlife.org
www.idlife.org

*Dean Nielson, Executive Director*
*Tina Noreen, Programs Coordinator*

Enables people with disabilities to manage their own lives, make their own choices, and give information and knowledge to assist in living with dignity and bravado.

**4612  LIFE: Fort Hall**
PO Box 4185
Fort Hall, ID  83203
208-478-3952

e-mail: wparker@if.rmci.net

*Wnedy Parker, Director*

**4613  LINC Canyon County**
317 Happy Day Boulevard
Suite 130
Caldwell, ID  83607
208-454-5511
FAX: 208-454-5515
e-mail: linccc3info@aol.com
www2.state.id.us/silc/cils.htm

*Lonora Barney, Executive Director*

A non-profit organization, empowers people with disabilities to achieve their desired level of independence. LINC promotes personal growth and freedom of choice through advocacy, networking, public awareness and modification of environments.

**4614  LINC-Satellite Office**
132 Main Avenue S
Twin Falls, ID  83301
208-733-1712
FAX: 208-733-7711
e-mail: mheinrich@lincidaho.org
www.lincinc.org

*Melva Heinrich, Executive Director*

A non-profit organization empowering people with disabilities to achieve their desired level of independence. LINC promotes personal growth and freedom of choice through advocacy, networking, public awareness and modification of environments.

**4615  Life**
640 Pershing Avenue
Suite A
Pocatello, ID  83201
208-232-2747
FAX: 208-232-2753
TTY:208-232-2747
e-mail: eici@ida.net
www.idalife.org

*Dean Nielson, President*

Provides peer counseling, disability education, attendant care registry and information and referral services to the disabled.

**4616  Living Independence Network Corporation: Twin Falls Satellite**
132 Main Avenue S
Twin Falls, ID  83301
208-733-1712
FAX: 208-733-7711
TTY:208-733-1712
e-mail: info@lincidaho.org
www.lincidaho.org

*Melva Heinrich, Executive Director*

A non-profit organizaition, empowers people with disabilities to achieve their desired level of independence.

**4617  Living Independence Network Corporation**
2500 Kootenai Street
Boise, ID  83705
208-336-3335
FAX: 208-384-5037
e-mail: info@lincidaho.org
www.lincidaho.org

*Roger Howard, Executive Director*

A non-profit organization empowering people with disabilities to achieve their desired level of independence. LINC promotes personal growth and freedom of choice through advocacy, networking, public awareness and modification of environments.

**4618 Living Independence Network Corporation: Canyon County Satelite**

2922 Cleveland Boulevard
Suite 800
Caldwell, ID  83605
208-454-5511
FAX: 208-454-5515
TTY:208-454-5511
e-mail: info@lincidaho.org
www.lincidaho.org

*Lonora Barney, Executive Director*

A non-profit organizaition, empowers people with disabilities to achieve their desired level of independence.

**4619 Living Independent for Everyone (LIFE): Pocatello Office**

640 Pershing Avenue
Pocatello, ID  83201
208-232-2747
FAX: 208-232-2753
TTY:208-232-2747
e-mail: dean@if.rmci.net
www.idaholifecenter.org

*Dean Nielson, Executive Director*

**4620 Living Independently for Everyone (LIFE): Blackfoot Office**

Living Independently for Everyone (LIFE): Pocate
PO Box 86
Blackfoot, ID  83221
208-785-9648
FAX: 208-785-2398
e-mail: bfoot@ida.net
www.idaholifecenter.org

*Dean Nielson, Executive Director*
*Lucy Navo, Manager*
*Lori Galvan, Independent Living Advisor*

Enable people with disabilities to manage their own lives, make their own choices, and give information and knowledge to assist in living with dignity and bravado.

**4621 Living Independently for Everyone: Burley**

2311 Park Avenue
Suite 7
Burley, ID  83318
208-678-7705
FAX: 208-678-7771
e-mail: lifetoni@pmt.org
www2.state.id.us/silc/Life.htm

*Ruth Gneiting, President*
*Dean Nielson, Executive Director*
*Sandra Dressel, Program Coordinator/Manager*

**4622 Southwestern Idaho Housing Authority**

1108 W Finch Drive
Nampa, ID  83651
208-467-7461
FAX: 208-463-1772

*David W Patten, Executive Director*

---

# Illinois

**4623 Access Living of Metropolitan Chicago**

614 W Roosevelt Road
Chicago, IL  60607
312-253-7000
800-613-8549
FAX: 312-253-7001
TTY: 312-253-7002
e-mail: generalinfo@accessliving.org
www.accessliving.org

*Henry Chandler, Chairman*
*Marca Bristo, President/CEO*
*Joanne Crown, Life Director*

Access Living is a cross disability organization governed and staffed by a majority of people with disabilities. Access Living fosters the dignity, pride, and self esteem of people with disabilities and enhances the options available to them so they may choose and maintain individualized and satisfying lifestyles.

**4624 Center for Comprehensive Services**

Mentor A BI Network
PO Box 2825
Carbondale, IL  62902
618-529-3060
800-582-4227
FAX: 618-457-5372
e-mail: info@ccs-rehab.com
www.ccs-rehab.com

*Robin Ray, President*

Post-acute rehabilitation services for adults and adolescents with acquired brain injuries. Residential, day-treatment and out-patient services tailored to individual needs.

**4625 Central Illinois Center for Independent Living**

614 W Glen Avenue
Peoria, IL  61614
309-682-3500
877-501-9808
FAX: 309-682-3989
TTY: 309-682-3567
www.cicil.org

*Henry Salter, President*
*Doris Bowlby, VP*
*Melody Reynolds, Executive Director*

Dedicated to empowering persons with disabilities to achieve a higher quality of life through comprehensive programs that promote individual growth. CICIL provides services combined with advocacy for social change to allow greater integration of persons with disabilities into the mainstream of community life.

**4626 Community Residential Alternative**

Coleman Tri- County Services
835 W Lincoln Street
Harrisburg, IL  62946
618-252-3204
TTY:618-269-4211
e-mail: cracts6@shawneelink.net
www.colemantricounty.com

*Samantha Austin, Director*

Six bed group home that provides a residential alternative for the developmentally disabled adult. This program is designed to promote independence in daily living skills, economic self-sufficiency, and integration into the community.

**4627 Cornerstone Services**

777 Joyce Road
Joliet, IL  60436
815-727-6666
FAX: 815-723-1177
e-mail: jhogan@cornerstoneservices.org
www.cornerstoneservices.org

*James Hogan, President/CEO*

Cornerstone Services provides progressive, comprehensive services for people with disabilities, promoting choice, dignity and the opportunity to live and work in the community. Established in 1969, the agency provides developmental, vocational, residential and behavior health services.

**4628 Division of Rehabilitation Services**

Department of Human Services
400 W Lawrence Avenue
Springfield, IL  62704
217-557-1601
800-843-6154
e-mail: ors@dhs.state.il.us
www.dhs.state.il.us

*Rob Kilbury, Director*
*Carol Adams, Manager*

Provides medical, therapeutic and counseling services for the disabled, as well as employment services. TTY #: 800-447-6404

**4629  DuPage Center for Independent Living**
739 Roosevelt Road
Building 8
Glen Ellyn, IL  60137
630-469-2300
FAX: 630-469-2606
TTY:630-469-2300
e-mail: dcil@mcs.com
www.glen-ellyn.com/dcil

*Leigh Ann Heenan, Executive Director*

A non residential, community based, not for profit agency wich provides advocacy and services to persons with disabilities in DuPage County.

**4630  Fox River Valley Center for Independent Living**
730 W Chicago Street
Elgin, IL  60123
847-695-5818
FAX: 847-695-5892
e-mail: frvcil@mindspring.com
www.frvcil.net

*Mary Griffith, Executive Director*

Provides services to people with disabilities in Kane, Kendall and McHenry counties. Our non-residential agency provides independent living skills training, advocacy, information and referral and housing services. Also provides technical assistance to businesses and agencies to work with people with disabilities.

**4631  Gaining Access to IL**
PO Box 486
Effingham, IL  62401
217-342-7110
FAX: 217-347-2562
TTY:217-342-7110
e-mail: gailcil@consolidated.net
www.silcofillinois.org

*Debbie Beard, Executive Director*

Dedicated to assisting persons with disabilities to achieve their own independent lifestyle.

**4632  Illinois Department of Rehab Services**
Department of Human Services
400 W Laurence 100
2nd Floor
Springfield, IL  62762
217-557-1601
800-843-6154
FAX: 217-558-4207
ww.ths.state.il.us/ors/

*Rob Kilbury, Executive Director*
*Carol Adams, Manager*

**4633  Illinois Valley Center for Independent Living**
18 Gunia Drive
La Salle, IL  61301
815-224-3126
800-822-3246
FAX: 815-224-3576
TTY: 815-224-8271
e-mail: ivcil@ivcil.com
www.ivcil.com

*Donna Joerger, Executive Director*
*Brian M Szuda, Associate Director*

A community-based, non-residential center for independent living dedicated to enhancing options available to persons with disabilities so they may choose and maintain individualized and satisfying lifestyles.

**4634  Illinois and Iowa Center for Independent Living**
PO Box 6156
Rock Island, IL  61204
309-793-0090
877-541-2505
FAX: 309-283-0097
e-mail: iicil@iicil.com
www.iicil.com

*Liz Sherwin, Executive Director*

IICIl creates and maintains independence options for people with disabilities by advocating for civil rights, providing services, and promoting full participation of disabled individuals in all aspects of the community.

**4635  Impact Center for Independent Living**
2735 E Broadway
Alton, IL  62002
618-462-1411
FAX: 618-474-5309
e-mail: contarino@impactcil.org
www.impactcil.org

*Cathy Contarino, Executive Director*

IMPACT promotes pride and respect for people with disabilities by sharing the tools that are necessary to take control of one's own life. IMPACT advocates full community participation, with supports, of all citizens.

**4636  Jacksonville Area CIL: Havana**
220 W Main
Havana, IL  62644
309-543-6680
FAX: 309-543-6711
TTY:309-543-6680

*Becky McGinnis, Director*

**4637  Jacksonville Area Center for Independent Living**
60 E Central Park Plaza
Jacksonville, IL  62650
217-245-8371
888-317-3287
FAX: 217-245-1872
TTY:217-245-8371
e-mail: info@jacil.org
www.jacil.org

*Becky Mcginnis, Executive Director*

JACIL is organized to serve people with disabilities in Morgan, Scott, Cass and Mason counties. JACIl is committed to enabling persons with disabilities to gain effective control and direction of their lives in the home, in the workplace and in the comunity.

**4638  LIFE Center for Independent Living**
2201 Eastland Drive
Suite 1
Bloomington, IL  61704
309-663-5433
888-543-3245
FAX: 309-663-7024
TTY:309-663-0054
e-mail: gail@lifcil.org
www.lifecil.org

*Gail Kear, Executive Director*
*Marianne Cavanaugh-Wozniak, Admin Services Coordinator*

Disability advocacy, information & referral, independent living skills training, peer counseling, sign language interpreter referrals, braille & alternate formats, equipment loan. Services people with disabilities and their families and friends in DeWitt, Ford, Livingston, and McLean Counties in Illinois.

**4639  LINC-Monroe Randolph Center**
1514 S Main Street
Suite 4
Red Bud, IL  62278
618-282-3700
FAX: 618-282-2740
TTY:618-282-3700

*Violette Nast, Director*

**4640  Lake County Center for Independent Living**
377 N Seymour Avenue
Mundelein, IL  60060
847-949-4440
FAX: 847-949-4445
TTY:847-949-0641
e-mail: lccil@dls.org
www.lccil.org

*Anita Gorski, Executive Director*

Lake County Center for Independent Living is a disability rights organization governed and staffed by a majority of people with disabilities. LCCIL offers services and advocacy that promote a fully accessible society, which expects participation by persons with disabilities.

## 4641 Life Center for Independent Living

741 W Washington
Suite 3
Pontiac, IL 61764 815-844-1132
FAX: 815-844-1148

*Dana Craig, Director*

## 4642 Living Independently Now Center (LINC)

120 E a Street
Belleville, IL 62220 618-235-9988
FAX: 618-233-3729
TTY:618-235-9988
e-mail: info@lincinc.org
www.lincinc.org

*John Laker, Executive Director*
*Carolyn Durham, Assistant Director*

Empowering persons with disabilities to live independently in the St. Clair, Monroe and Randolph counties.

## 4643 Mosaic-Pontiac

725 W Madison Street
Pontiac, IL 61764 815-842-4166
FAX: 815-842-4053
www.mosaicinfo.org

*Rod Patterson, Executive Director*

Providing a wide array of services to assist individuals and families in achieving positive life goals. Services to persons with disabilities and other special needs include community living options, training and employment options, spiritual growth and development options, training and counseling support.

## 4644 Northwestern Illinois Center for Independent Living

229 1st Avenue
Suite 2
Rock Falls, IL 61071 815-625-7860
888-886-4245
FAX: 815-625-7876
e-mail: kathy@nicil.org
www.incil.org

*Kathy Fischer, Executive Director*

Northwestern Illinois center for Independent Living is a community based, non-profit residential, center for independent living dedicated to enhancing the options available to people with disabilities so they may choose and maintain individualized and satisfying lifestyles. NICIL combines direct services to individuals with advocacy for social change to allow greater integration of persons with disabilities into the mainstream of life.

## 4645 Opportunities for Access: A Center for Independent Living

4206 Williamson Place
Suite 3
Mount Vernon, IL 62864 618-244-9212
FAX: 618-244-9310
TTY:618-244-9575
e-mail: info@ofacil.org
www.ofacil.org

*Michael Egbert, Executive Director*

Serves, trains and provides information to persons with disabilities, family members and significant others and service providers. Services include: advocacy, information and referral, peer support, skills training, volunteer programs and other related services. Services are free. A cross disability community based, nonresidential, nonprofit organization serving Clay, Clinton, Edwards, Effingham, Fayette, Hamilton, Jasper, Jefferson, Marion, Wabash, Washington, Wayne and White Counties.

## 4646 Options CIL

22 Heritage Drive
Suite 107
Bourbonnais, IL 60914 815-936-0100
FAX: 815-936-0117
TTY:815-936-0132
e-mail: optionscil@optionscil.com
www.optionscil.com

*Kathy Jackson, Director*

Options CIL believes that persons with disabilities have the right to make choices about their own lives and to experience life as active participants in society.

## 4647 Options Center for Independent Living: Watseka

130 Laird Lane
Suite 103
Watseka, IL 60970 815-432-1332
FAX: 815-432-1360
TTY:815-432-4361
e-mail: options@daily-journal.com
www.optioncil.com

*Kathy Petersen, Executive Director*
*Dorei Schoolman, Operations Manager*

Promotes independent living for people with disabilities in Kankakee and Iroquis counties in Illinois. Offered free of charge are: advocacy information and referral, peer support, independent living skills training, personal assistant training and referral, community reintergration, elderly blind program, youth advocacy, free equipment/assistive technology loan, TTY training and distribution, and sign language interpreter referral.

## 4648 Options Center for Independent Living: Bourbonnais

22 Heritage Drive
Suite 107
Bourbonnais, IL 60914 815-936-0100
FAX: 815-936-0117
TTY:815-936-0132
e-mail: reception@options.com
www.optionscil.com

*Katheryn Petersen, Executive Director*

Options Center for Independent Living is a non residential, not for profit organization that promotes independent living for persons of all ages who have disabilities. Community based, the service area encompasses Kankakee and Iroquis Counties.

## 4649 PACE Center for Independent Living

1317 E Florida Avenue
Urbana, IL 61801 217-344-5433
FAX: 217-344-2414
TTY:217-344-5024
e-mail: paceurbana@aol.com
www.incil.org

*Nancy Hickey, Executive Director*
*Robin Arbiter, Program Director*

PACE is a Center for Independent Living serving people with disabilities, their families, ad service providers. PACE also offers disability awareness and information to the community at large. PACE covers Champaign, Douglas, Vermilion, Edgar and Piatt counties.

## 4650 Progress Center South

400 Forest Boulevard
Park Forest, IL 60466 708-748-5156
FAX: 708-748-1630
TTY:708-748-5156
e-mail: info@progresscil.org
www.progresscil.org

*Diane Coleman, Executive Director*
*John Jansa, Program Director*

Progress Center is a community-based, non-profit, non rsidential, service and advocacy organization, operated for people with disabilities, by people with disabilities.

**4651 Progress Center for Independent Living**
7521 Madison Street
Forest Park, IL 60130
708-209-1500
FAX: 708-209-1735
TTY:708-209-1826
e-mail: info@progresscil.org
www.progresscil.org

*Diane Coleman, Executive Director*
*John Jansa, Program Director*

Offers peer counseling, attendant registry, information and referral services, advocacy, independent living skills, paid internships, housing assistance, national headquarters of Not Dead Yet.

**4652 RAMP Regional Access and Mobility Project**
202 Market Street
Rockford, IL 61107
815-968-7467
FAX: 815-968-7612
TTY:815-968-2401
e-mail: jrouse@rampcil.org
www.rampcil.org

*Willie Wierman, President*
*Arles Hendershott Love, Vice President*
*Julie Bosma, Executive Director*

Provides services and advocacy for people with disabilities. Services include information and referral, personal assistant services, sign language interpreters, 24 hour emergency sign language service, bus training, peer counseling, independent living skills training, accessibility assessments and information on the Americans with Disabilities Act (ADA) serving Boone, DeKalb, Stephenson and Winnebago counties in north central Illinois.

**4653 Regional Access & Mobilization Project**
202 Market Street
Rockford, IL 61107
815-968-7467
FAX: 815-968-7612
TTY:815-968-2401
e-mail: jbosma@rampcil.org
www.rampcil.org

*Julie Bosma, Director*

RAMP promotes an accessible society that allows and expects full participation by people with disabilities.

**4654 Regional Access and Mobilization Project (RAMP)**
530 S State Street
Suite 103
Belviderer, IL 61008
815-544-8404
FAX: 815-544-1896
TTY:815-544-8404
e-mail: myerk@rampcil.org
www.rampcil.org

*Julie Bosma, Director*

RAMP promotes an accessible society that allows and expects full participation by people with disabilities.

**4655 Regional Access and Mobilization Project: DeKalb**
1022 W Lincoln Highway
DeKalb, IL 60115
815-756-3202
FAX: 815-756-3556
TTY:815-756-2058
e-mail: myerk@rampcil.org
www.rampcil.org
RAMP promotes an accessible society that allows and expects full participation by people with disabilities.

**4656 Southern Illinois Center for Independent Living**
2135 W Ramada Lane
Carbondale, IL 62901
618-457-3318
FAX: 618-549-0132
TTY:618-457-3318
e-mail: sicilccc@mychoice.net

*Bonnie Vaughn, Executive Director*

Services include: advocacy, skills training, peer counseling, information and referral, elderly blind, deaf services, personal attendant screening, community reintegration programs, limited transportation services and supported employment services.

**4657 Soyland Access**
1810 W South 3rd
Shelbyville, IL 62565
217-774-4322
866-415-0058
FAX: 217-774-4368
TTY: 217-774-4322
e-mail: sailsullQ@one-eleven.net
www.decatursail.org

*William Kienzle, Director*

A community-baes, non residential Center for Independent Living, is to promote and practice independent living for all persons with disabilities.

**4658 Soyland Access to IL**
18 W Harrison Street
Sullivan, IL 61951
217-523-2587
FAX: 217-523-0427
TTY:217-523-6304
e-mail: sailsull@one-eleven.net

*Bill Kienzle, Director*

**4659 Soyland Access to Independent Living (SAIL)**
2449 E Federal Drive
Decatur, IL 62526
217-876-8888
800-358-8080
FAX: 217-876-7245
e-mail: jwooters@decatursail.com
www.decatursail.com

*Jeri Wooters, Executive Director*

A community-based, non-residential Center for Independent Living, is to promote and practice independent living for all persons with disabilities. SAIL also strives to encourage and assist persons with disabilities to gain effective control of their lives by participation in all aspects of society to their fullest extent possible, especially in performing routine daily activities.

**4660 Soyland Access to Independent Living: Charleston**
757 Windsor Road
Charleston, IL 61920
217-345-7245
FAX: 217-345-7226
TTY:217-345-7245
e-mail: triplec@consolidated.net

*Brendt Ramsey, Director*

**4661 Springfield Center for Independent Living**
330 South Grand Avenue W
Springfield, IL 62704
217-535-2587
FAX: 217-523-0427
TTY:217-523-6304
e-mail: scil@scil.org
www.scil.org

*Pete Roberts, Director*

**4662 Stone-Hayes Center for Independent Living**
39 N Prairie Street
Galesburg, IL 61401
309-344-1306
888-347-4245
FAX: 309-344-1305
TTY:309-344-1306
e-mail: stonehayes@misslink.net
www.incil.org

*Catherine Holland, Executive Director*

**4663 West Central Illinois Center for Independent Living**
Illinois Network of Centers for Independent Living
131 N 4th Street
Quincy, IL 62301
217-223-0400
FAX: 217-223-0479
TTY:217-223-0475
e-mail: wcicil@adams.net
www.quincynet.com

*Julie Irvine, Director*
*Terry Solter, Contact*

A not for profit organization providing services to people with disabilities to promote, increase and improve opportunities within the community. WCICIL's four core services are advocacy, Independent Living Skills Training, Information and Referral, and Peer Counseling. The counties served are: Adams, Brown, Hancock, Pike, McDonough and Schuyler.

**4664 Will Grundy Center for Independent Living**
2415 W Jefferson Street
Suite A
Joliet, IL 60435
815-729-0162
FAX: 815-729-3697
TTY:815-729-2085
e-mail: wgcil@sbcglobal.net
www.will-grundycil.org

*Pam Heavens, Executive Director*
*Festus Fabilola, Program Manager*

The Will Grundy Center for Indpendent Living strives for equality and empowerment of persons with disabilities in the Will and Grundy County areas. The Center is a cross disability, community based organization.

# Indiana

**4665 Assistive Technology Training and Information Center (ATTIC)**
1721 Washington Avenue
Vincennes, IN 47591
812-886-0575
877-962-8842
FAX: 812-886-1128
e-mail: inattic1@aol.com
www.theattic.org

*Ruth Kimberly, Executive Director*
*Patricia Stewart, Executive Director*

ATTIC provides support, information and education for individuals with disabilities and for families of children with special needs, and the professionals who assist these families.

**4666 Damar Homes**
PO Box 41
Camby, IN 46113
317-856-5201

*Jim Dalton, Executive Director*

**4667 Damar Services**
6324 Kentucky Avenue
PO Box 41
Indianapolis, IN 46221
317-856-5201
FAX: 317-856-2333
e-mail: info@damar.org
www.damar.org

*Greg Johnson, CEO*
*Jim Dalton, COO*
*Carla Bill, Admissions Director*

Damar is Indiana's oldest private not for profit provider of residential services to children with disabilities and today serve hundreds of individuals and their families.

**4668 Everybody Counts Center for Independent Living**
9111 Broadway
Suite A
Merrillville, IN 46410
219-769-5055
FAX: 219-769-5325
TTY:219-756-3323
e-mail: ecount@netnitco.net
www.nitco.net

*Teresa Torres, Executive Director*

**4669 Four Rivers Resource Services**
PO Box 249
Linton, IN 47441
812-847-2231
FAX: 812-847-8836
e-mail: fourrivers@frrs.org
www.frrs.org

*Stephen Sacksteder, Executive Director*

FRRS is established to enable individuals with disabilities and other challenges to attain self independence and natural interdependence, inclusion in normal life experiences and opportunities, and general life enrichment, by working in partnership with them, their families and the communities in and around Greene, Sullivan, Daviess, and Martin Counties.

**4670 Future Choices Independent Living Center**
209 N High Street
Muncie, IN 47305
765-741-8332
866-741-3444
FAX: 765-741-8333
e-mail: futurechoicesinc@aol.com
www.futurechoices.org

*Beth Quarles, Director*

Provides unlimited options for minorities, youth, and hoosiers with disabilities.

**4671 Independent Living Center of Eastern Indiana (ILCEIN)**
201 S 5th Street
Richmond, IN 47374
765-939-9226
877-939-9226
FAX: 765-935-2215
TTY: 765-939-1309
e-mail: info@ilcein.org
www.ilcein.org

*Tom Cooney, Executive Director*
*Christi Gigliotti, Administrative Director*
*Thomas B Glen, Jr, Program Director*

Serving Fayette, Franklin, Henry, Decatur, Rush, Union and Wayne Counties.

**4672 Indianapolis Resource CIL (IRCIL)**
1426 W 29th Street
Suite 207
Indianapolis, IN 46208
317-926-1660
800-860-7181
FAX: 317-936-1687
TTY: 317-926-1660
e-mail: ircil@ircil.org
www.ircil.org

*Melissa Madill, Director*

ICIL provides services, support and information to people with disabilities to help insure equal access to all aspects of community life. IRCIL also provides educatiom amd advocacy to all members of the community to help increase awareness and break down barriers that impede inclusion.

**4673  Indianapolis Resource Center for Independent Living**
2110 N Capitol Avenue
Indianapolis, IN  46202
317-596-6440
800-860-7181
FAX: 319-926-1687
e-mail: ircil@ircil.org
www.ircil.org

*Melissa Madill, Executive Director*
*Marianna Kalli, Assistant Director*

Offers advocacy, information and referral services, independent living skills training, peer counseling, supported employment services and information on the Americans with Disabilities Act.

**4674  League for the Blind and Disabled**
5821 S Anthony Boulevard
Fort Wayne, IN  46816
260-441-0551
800-889-3443
FAX: 260-441-7760
TTY: 800-889-3443
e-mail: the.league@verizon.net
www.the-league.org

*David Nelson, President*
*Nancy Gasparini, Assistant Director*
*David Callister, Chief Executive Officer*

Peer counseling, education, advocacy services training and support, independent living skills training, assistive equipment loaner program, youth services, orientation and mobility training, information and referral, disability awareness, Braille transcription, Center for Independent living, and public education.

**4675  Martin Luther Homes of Indiana**
Mosaic
26 N Brown Avenue
Terre Haute, IN  47803
812-235-3399
FAX: 812-235-1590
e-mail: abean@mlhs.com
www.mlhs.com

*Sally Montgomery, Chief Executive Officer*
*Anita Bean, Program Director*

Providing a wide array of services to assist individuals and families in achieving positive life goals. Services to persons with disabilities and other special needs include community living options, training and employment options, spiritual growth and development options, training and counseling support.

**4676  Ruben Center for Independent Living**
4522 Indianapolis Boulevard
Suite 3
East Chicago, IN  46312
219-397-6496
FAX: 219-397-6496
TTY:219-397-6496

**4677  SILC, Indiana Council on Independent Living (ICOIL)**
PO Box 7083
Indianapolis, IN  46207
317-232-1303
800-545-7763
FAX: 317-232-6478
TTY: 317-232-1427
e-mail: nancy.young@fssa.in.gov

*Nancy Young, Program Director*
*Jodi James, Silc Chairperson*

**4678  Southern Indiana Center for Independent Living**
651 X Street
Bedford, IN  47421
812-277-9626
800-845-6914
FAX: 812-277-9628
e-mail: bsrimst@kiva.net

*Albert Tolbert, Executive Director*
*Darlene Webster, Director*

SICIL is a consumer controlled, community based, cross-disability, non-residential and not for profit organization that promotes and practices the philosophy of independent living: consumer control, peer support, self-help, self-determination, equal access, and individual and community advocacy. SICIL also promotes accesible and affordable housing, recreation and transportation.

**4679  Wabash Independent Living Center & Learning Center (WILL)**
4312 S 7th Street
Terre Haute, IN  47802
812-298-9455
877-915-9455
FAX: 812-299-9061
e-mail: info@thewillcenter.org
www.thewillcenter.org

*Teresa A Mager, Executive Director*
*Darlena Gentry, Program Director/Business Mgr*
*Danny Wayne Beemer, Services Program Manager*

The WILL Center is a nonprofit community based, nonresidential organization that is run by and for people with disabilities The WILL Center provides Systems Advocacy Information and Referral Independent Living Skills Training, Assistance in fionding anf obtaining affordable housing, Infromation on the Americans with Disabilities Act, and Assistive Technology Infromation

# Iowa

**4680  Black Hawk Center for Independent Living**
312 Jefferson Street
Waterloo, IA  50701
319-291-7755
888-291-7754
FAX: 319-291-7781
e-mail: bhcil@blackhawkcenter.org
www.blackhawkcenter.org

*Dave Schumaker, Executive Director*

BHCIL is a consumer controlled, private, non-residential, non-profit corporation. Provides services in the community when people with disabilities are unable to locate those services through existing agencies.

**4681  Central Iowa Center for Independent Living**
655 Walnut Street
Suite 131
Des Moines, IA  50309
515-243-1742
888-503-2287
FAX: 515-243-5385
e-mail: cicil@centraliowacil.com
www.centraliowacil.com

*Robert Jepson, Manager*

CICIL is a community based, non-profit, non-residential program serving persons with disabilities. CICIL is dedicated to assisting all persons, regardless of disability in making choices about their own lives and in experiencing success as active participants in society.

**4682  Evert Conner Rights & Resources CIL**
730 S Dubuque Street
Iowa City, IA  52240
319-338-3870
800-982-0272
FAX: 319-338-8385
TTY: 319-338-3870
e-mail: info@ownersvoices.com

*Chris O'Hanlon, Director*

**4683    Hope Haven**

1800 19th Street
Rock Valley, IA  51247                    712-476-2737
                                     FAX: 712-476-3110
                      e-mail: vbrummel@hopehaven.org
                                     www.hopehaven.org

*David Vanningen, Executive Director/CEO*
*Calvin Helmus, Associate Director*

Purpose is to assist persons with mental/physical/emotional disabilities to reach their potential based on Biblical convictions.
Services group homes, supervised apartments, and vocational
employment services.

**4684    Independent Living: Iowa Everett Conner Center**

730 S Dubuque Street
Iowa City, IA  52240                      319-338-3870
                                     FAX: 319-338-8385
                        e-mail: connerctr@aol.com

*Chris O' Hanlon, Executive Director*

An independent living center, non-profit, nonresidential, consumer run, community based. The center assists individuals with
disabilities to maintain control over day to day activities and to
advocate for themselves in order to achieve greater independence and full participation in an integrated society.

**4685    League of Human Dignity**

1520 Avenue M
Council Bluffs, IA  51501                  712-323-6863
                                     FAX: 712-323-6811
           e-mail: cinfo@leagueofhumandignity.com
                          www.leagueofhumandignity.com

*Michael Schafer, Contact*
*Christine Solomon, Manager*

League of Human Dignity actively promotes the full integration
of individuals with disabilities into society. To this end, the
League will advocate their needs and rights, and provide quality
services to involve these persons in becoming and remaining independent citizens.

**4686    Martin Luther Homes of Iowa**

445 7th Avenue SE
Waukon, IA  52172                         563-568-3992
                                     FAX: 563-568-3992

*Mary Lynn ReVoir, Administrator*
*Fred Naumann III, Communications*
*Richard Wicks, Executive Director*

Providing a wide array of services to assist individuals and families in achieving positive life goals. Services to persons with disabilities and other special needs include community living
options, training and employment options, spiritual growth and
development options, training and counseling support.

**4687    South Central Iowa Center for Independent Living**

1907 7th Avenue SE
Suite 301
Oskaloosa, IA  52577                      641-672-1867
                                         800-651-7911
                                     FAX: 641-672-1867
                     e-mail: nika.naylor@mahaska.org

*Nika Naylor, Executive Director*

**4688    Three Rivers Center for Independent Living**

505 6th Street
Sioux City, IA  51101                     712-255-1065
                                         866-253-3043
                                     FAX: 712-255-1065
                           e-mail: bjdenny@aol.com

*Brenda Denney, Director*
*Jeannie Theis, Program Coordinator*
*Jimmy Weber, Manager*

## Kansas

**4689    Center for Independent Living for SW Kansas**

2601 Central Avenue
Dodge City, KS  67801                     620-227-6660
                                     FAX: 620-227-8185
                                     TTY:620-227-6660
                        e-mail: cilswks@gcnet.com
                                     www.cilswks.org

*Bonnie Ray, Independent Living Coordinator*
*Mary Jane Sandoval, Independent Living Advocate*

Dedicated to helping people achieve full participation in society. Advocates for the choices, independence, and civil rights of
people with disabilities

**4690    Coalition for Independence**

3738 State Avenue 4911 State Avenue
Kansas City, KS  66102                    913-321-5140
                                     FAX: 913-321-5140
                                     TTY:913-321-5216
                          e-mail: mail@cfi-kc.org
                                     www.cfi-kc.org

*Clark Byron, Executive Director*
*Deborah L Wilmarth, Executive Assistant*

Coalition for Independence looks to facilitate positive and responsible independence for all people with disabilities by acting
as an advocate for individuals with disabilities, providing services, and promoting accessibility and acceptance.

**4691    Coalition for Independence Leavenworth**

4911 State Avenue
Kansas City, KS  66102                    913-321-5140

*Clark Byron, Executive Director*

**4692    Cowley County Developmental Services**

Strother Fiel
Arkansas City, KS  67005                  620-442-5270
                                     FAX: 316-442-6438

*Martha Crane, Director*
*Bill Brooks, Executive Director*

Offers peer counseling, attendant care registry and other services to the community.

**4693    Independence**

2001 Haskell Avenue
Lawrence, KS  66046                       785-841-0333
                                         888-824-7277
                                     FAX: 785-841-1094
                                     TTY:785-841-1046
              e-mail: webmaster@independenceinc.org
                                     www.independenceinc.org

*Tanya Dorf, Executive Director*
*Carol Hartmsn, Administrative Assistant*

Services include individual and systems advocacy, assistance
obtaining benefits, technical assistance, housing, assistance
with modifications for accessibility, counseling, peer support,
microcomputer training, transportation, community outreach
and education, business management services for persons using
attendants, a resource library, independent living skills training,
assistive technology, information and referral, human diversity
workshops and volunteer involvement.

**4694  Independent Connection**
1710 W Schilling Road
Salina, KS  67401
785-827-9383
800-526-9731
FAX: 785-823-2015
TTY: 785-827-7051
e-mail: occk@occk.com
www.occk.com

*Shiela Nelson-Stout, Contact*
*Carolee Miner, Chief Executive Officer*

Independent Connection believes that all people have the right to make their own decisions and exercise control over their own lives. People have the right to pursue success and take risks.

**4695  Independent Connection: Beloit**
501 W 7th
Beloit, KS  67420
785-827-4081
FAX: 785-738-3320
TTY:785-827-4081
e-mail: occk@occk.com

**4696  Independent Living Center of Northeast Kan sas**
521 Commercial Street
Suite C
Atchison, KS  66002
913-367-1830
888-845-2879
FAX: 913-367-1430
e-mail: ilcnek@sbcglobal.net
www.ilcnek.org

*Ken Gifford, Executive Director*

A not for profit agency providing services within the State of Kansas. ILCNEK looks to assist people with disabilities to live an integrated, quality life with dignity, respect, and independence.

**4697  Independent Living Resource Center**
3033 W 2nd Street N
Wichita, KS  67203
316-942-6300
800-479-6861
FAX: 316-942-2078
e-mail: jclifton@ilrcks.org
www.ilrcks.org

*Judy Weigel, Executive Director*

Empowers people with disabilities to lead independent lives by providing advocacy, community education and direct services.

**4698  Kansas Services for the Blind & Visually Impaired**
2601 SW East Circle Drive N
Topeka, KS  66606
785-296-3311
800-547-5789
FAX: 785-291-3138
e-mail: rehab@srskansas.org
www.srskansas.org

*Dianne Hemphill, Administrator*
*Dale Barnum, Director*

Helps persons who are blind or visually to improve their quality of life. KSBVI provides people with an array of services and experiences aimed at overcoming not only the physical difficulties brought on by the loss of vision, but also the fear of change associated with vision loss. KSBVI can also help with job search and retention activities; life skills training; access to medical services; and technical assistance.

**4699  LINK: Colby**
505G N Franklin Avenue
Colby, KS  67701
785-462-7600
FAX: 785-462-7679
TTY:785-462-7600
e-mail: scarver@st-tel.net

*Scot Carver, Director*

**4700  LINK: Hays**
2401 E 13th Street
Hays, KS  67601
785-625-6942

*Brian Atwell, Manager*

**4701  Living Independently in Northwest Kansas**
2401 E 13th Street
Hays, KS  67601
785-625-6942
800-569-5926
e-mail: brainatwell@eaglecom.net
www.linkinc.org

*Brian Atwell, Executive Director*

LINK promotes and supports the civil rights of people with disabilities and empowers them to achieve a life of independence and equality.

**4702  Osage City Resource Center for Independent Living**
PO Box 257
Osage City, KS  66523
785-528-3105
800-580-7245
FAX: 785-528-3665
TTY: 785-528-3106
e-mail: rcil@rcilinc.org
www.rcilinc.org

*Chad Wilkins, Contact*
*Mary Holloway, Chief Executive Officer*

RCIL is committed to working with individuals, families, and communities to promote independent living and individual choice to persons with disabilities.

**4703  Prairie IL Resource Center**
802 S Main
PO Box 8588
Pratt, KS  67124
620-672-6470
e-mail: info@pilr.org
www.pilr.org

*Chris Owens, Executive Director*
*Glenda Lickteig, Independent Living Specialist*

The Center is directed by and serves people with disabilities. The Center also provides servies designed to empower an individual to participate in community life to the greatest extent possible, and tp experience a productive, dignified life.

**4704  Prairie Independent Living Resource Center**
17th S Main Street
Hutchinson, KS  67501
620-663-9920
888-715-6818
FAX: 620-663-4711
TTY:620-663-9920
e-mail: info@pilr.org
www.pilr.org

*Chris Owens, Executive Director*
*Christi Ireland, Administrative Assistant*

The center is directed by and serves people with disabilities. The center provides services designed to empower an individual to participate in community life to the greatest extent possible, and to experience a productive, dignified life.

**4705  Resource Center for Independent Living: Emporia**
625 Merchant Street
Suite 238
Emporia, KS  66801
620-342-1648
888-261-4024
FAX: 316-342-1821
e-mail: chad@rcilinc.org
www.rcilinc.org

*Chad Wikins, Director*

RCIL is committed to working with individuals, families, and communities to promote independent living and individual choice to persons with disabilities.

# Independent Living Centers /Kansas

**4706 Resource Center for Independent Living: Bu rlington**
410 Cumberland Street
Burlington, KS  66839
316-364-2263
FAX: 620-364-2700
e-mail: chad@rcilinc.org
www.rcilinc.org

*Chad Wilkins, Director*

RCIL is committed to working with individuals, families, and communities to promote independent living and individual choice to persons with disabilities.

**4707 Resource Center for Independent Living: El Dorado**
615 N Main Street
El Dorado, KS  67042
316-322-7853
800-960-7853
FAX: 316-322-7888
e-mail: chad@rcilinc.org
www.rcilinc.org

*Chad Wilkins, Director*
*Doris Hammon, Manager*

RCIL is committed to working with individuals, families, and communities to promote independent living and individual choice to persons with disabilities.

**4708 Resource Center for Independent Living: Fo rt Scott**
Resource Center for Independent Living of Osage
602 Southdale
Kiowa, KS  67070
620-365-8144
877-944-8144
FAX: 620-365-7726
e-mail: chad@rcilinc.org
www.rcilinc.org

*Chad Wilkins, Director*

RCIL is committed to working with individuals, families, and communities to promote independent living and individual choice to persons with disabilities.

**4709 Resource Center for Independent Living: Ot tawa**
1302 S Main Street
Suite 8
Ottawa, KS  66067
785-242-1805
800-995-1805
FAX: 785-242-1448
e-mail: chad@rcilinc.org
www.rcilinc.org

*Chad Wilkins, Director*

RCIL is committed to working with individuals, families and communities to promote independent living anf individual choice to persons with disabilities.

**4710 Resource Center for Independent Living: Ov erland Park**
9948 W 87th Street
Suite G-1
Overland Park, KS  66212
913-385-9088
FAX: 913-385-1665
www.rcilinc.org

**4711 Southeast Kansas Independent Living: Yates Center**
119 W Butler Street
Yates Center, KS  66783
620-625-2818
866-927-2818
FAX: 620-625-2585
e-mail: skilyc@skilonline.com
www.skilonline.com

*Shari Coatney, Director*
*Gary Bates, Manager*

A private not for profit corporation devoted to meeting the needs of individuals with disabilities and to serving them, their families and communities.

**4712 Southeast Kansas Independent Living**
PO Box 957
Parsons, KS  67357
620-421-5502
800-688-5616
FAX: 620-421-3705
TTY: 620-421-0983
e-mail: sharic@skilonline.com
www.skilonline.com

*Shari Coatney, Chief Executive Officer*

A private not for profit coporation devoted to meeting the needs of individuals with disabilities and to serving them, their families and communities.

**4713 Southeast Kansas Independent Living: Pittsburg**
104 W 6th Street
Pittsburg, KS  66762
620-231-6780
866-927-6780
FAX: 620-231-5920
TTY: 620-231-6780
e-mail: skilpittsburg@skilonline.com
www.skilonline.com

*Shari Coatney, Director*

A private not for profit corporation devoted to meeting the needs of individuals with disabilities and to serving them, their families and communities.

**4714 Southeast Kansas Independent Living: Colum bus**
125 E Maple Street
PO Box 645
Columbus, KS  66725
620-429-3600
866-927-3600
FAX: 620-429-3695
e-mail: skilcolumbus@skilonline.com
www.skilonline.com

*Shari Coatney, President*

SKIL is a private, not-for-profit corporation devoted to meeting the needs of individuals with disabilities and to serving them, their families and communities.

**4715 Southeast Kansas: Chanute**
222 W Main Street
Suite D
Chanute, KS  66720
620-431-0757
866-927-0757
FAX: 620-431-7174
e-mail: skilchanute@skilonline.com
www.skilonline.com

*Shari Coatney, Director*

A private not for profit corporation devoted to meeting the needs of individuals with disabilities and to serving them, their families and comunities.

**4716 Southeast Kansas: Fredonia**
PO Box 448
Fredonia, KS  66736
620-378-4881
866-927-4881
FAX: 620-378-4851
TTY: 620-378-4881
e-mail: skilfredonia@skilonline.com
www.skilonline.com

*Shari Coatney, Director*
*Steffen Blevins, Manager*

A private not-for-profit corporation devoted to meeting the needs of individuals with disabilities and to serving them, their families and communities.

**4717 Southwest Kansas Center for Independent Living**
111 W Grant Avenue
Garden City, KS 67846
620-276-1900
800-736-9443
FAX: 620-271-0200
e-mail: thorton@cilswks.org
www.cilswks.org

*Troy Horton, Executive Director*

The Center for Independent Living in Southwest Kansas is dedicated to helping people achieve full participation in society.

**4718 Three Rivers IL Center**
408 Lincoln
PO Box 408
Wamego, KS 66547
785-456-9915
800-555-3994
FAX: 785-456-9923
TTY: 785-456-9915
e-mail: reception@threerivervsinc.org
www.threeriversinc.org

*Audrey Schremmer-Philip, Director*

Three Rivers is a nonprofit organization promoting the self reliance of individuals with disabilities through education, advocacy, training and support.

**4719 Three Rivers Independent Living Center: Centralia**
PO Box 236
Centralia, KS 66415
785-857-3521
FAX: 785-857-3521
e-mail: reception@threeriversinc.org
www.threeriversinc.org

*Audrey Schremmer-Philip, Director*

Three Rivers is a non-profit organization promoting the self reliance of individuals with disabilities through, education, advocacy, training and support.

**4720 Three Rivers Independent Resource Center**
323 Poyntz Avenue
Suite 202
Manhattan, KS 66502
785-537-8985
FAX: 785-537-3435
TTY:785-537-8985
e-mail: reception@threeriversinc.org
www.threeriversinc.org

*Audrey Phillips, Executive Director*

Three Rivers is a non profit organization promoting the self reliance of individuals with disabilities through education, advocacy, training and support.

**4721 Topeka Independent Living Resource Center**
501 SW Jackson Street
Suite 100
Topeka, KS 66603
785-233-4572
FAX: 785-233-1561
TTY:785-233-4572
e-mail: tilrc@tilrc.org
www.tilrc.org

*Michael Oxford, President*

A civil and human rights organization that advocates for justice, equality and essential services for a fully integrated and accessible society for all people with disabilities.

**4722 Whole Person: Nortonville**
PO Box 117
Nortonville, KS 66060
913-886-2738
FAX: 913-886-2739
e-mail: info@thewholeperson.org
www.thewholeperson.org

*Lon Swearingen, President*
*Grady Banker, VP*

**4723 Whole Person: Olathe**
114 W Gregory Boulevard
Floor 1
Kansas City, MO 64114
816-561-0304
800-878-3037
FAX: 816-753-8163
TTY: 816-627-2201
e-mail: info@thewholeperson.org
www.thewholeperson.org

*Lon Swearingen, President*
*Joseph Marvil, Vice President*
*David Robinson, Executive Director*

**4724 Whole Person: Prairie Village**
7301 Mission Road
Suite 135
Prairie Village, KS 67124
913-393-9805
877-767-8896
FAX: 913-393-4869
TTY: 913-393-9805
e-mail: ksdirector@thewholeperson.org
www.thewholeperson.org

*Evelyn Harden, Director*

The Whole Person assists people with disabilities to live independently and encourages change within the community to expand opportunities for independent living.

**4725 Whole Person: Tonganoxie**
10200 W Schilling Road
Salina, KS 67402
785-827-9383
FAX: 785-823-2015
TTY:785-827-7051
e-mail: ksdirector@thewholeperson.org
www.thewholeperson.org

*Evelyn Harden, Director*

The Whole Person assists people with disabilities to live independently and encourages change within the community to expand opportunities for independent living.

# Kentucky

**4726 Best Center for Independent Living**
624a Eastwood Avenue
Bowling Green, KY 42103
270-796-5992
866-286-3608
e-mail: bestcil@bestcil.org
www.bestcil.org

*Sharli Rogers, Executive Director*

BCIL provides needed services to persons with all disabilities in South Central Kentucky.

**4727 Center for Accessible Living**
305 W Broadway
Suite 200
Louisville, KY 40202
502-589-6620
888-813-8497
FAX: 502-589-3980
TTY:502-589-6690
e-mail: info@calky.org
www.calky.org

*Jan Day, Executive Director*
Independent living center.

**4728** **Center for Accessible Living: Murray**
1051 N 16th Street
Suite C
Murray, KY 42071
    270-753-7676
    888-261-6194
    FAX: 270-753-7729
    TTY: 270-767-0549
    e-mail: jgallimore@calky.org
    www.calky.org

*Jeanne Gallimore, Executive Director*

**4729** **Center for Community Alternatives**
115 E Jefferson Street
Suite 300
Syracuse, NY 13202
    315-422-5638
    FAX: 315-471-4924
    www.communityalternatives.org

*Marsha Weissman, Executive Director*

A private, not for profit agency whose primary mission is to develop effective alternatives to incarceration and to foster a more responsive juvenile and criminal justice system in order to help youth and adults live more productive and safe lives.

**4730** **Center for Independent Living Options**
3031 Dixie Highway
Suite 103
Edgewood, KY 41017
    859-341-4346
    FAX: 859-341-1252
    e-mail: ciloky@cilo.net
    www.cilo.net

*Lin Laing, Director*
*Steve Bradford, Executive Director*

Independent Living Center

**4731** **Center for Independent Living: Kentucky Department for the Blind**
Independent Living Office
409 N Miles Street
Rear
Elizabethtown, KY 42701
    270-766-5126

    e-mail: buel.stalls@mail.state.ky.us

*Buel E Stalls Jr, Office Manager and IL Specialist*
*Nancy Bachuss, Manager*

Offers peer counseling, attendant care registry and other services to the community as they relate to the blind community. The Murray office is an independent living regional office which covers 20 far western counties of Kentucky.

**4732** **Community Alternatives**
115 E Jefferson Street
Suite 300
Syracuse, NY 13202
    315-422-5638

*Marsha Weissman, Executive Director*

**4733** **Disability Coalition of Northern Kentucky**
1032 Madison Avenue
1st Floor
Covington, KY 41011
    859-431-7668
    TTY: 800-648-6057
    e-mail: grader@fuse.net

*Sarah Todvine, Executive Director*
*Kit Heea, Administrative Assistant*

Groups working together on legislation issues concerning the people in Kentucky.

**4734** **Independence Place**
824 E Euclid Avenue
Suite 101
Lexington, KY 40502
    859-266-2807
    877-266-2807
    FAX: 859-335-0627
    e-mail: info@independenceplaceky.org
    www.independenceplaceky.org

*Barry Hamilton, Executive Director*
*Amber D Haag, Consumer Services Director*

The mission of Independence Place, is to educate and inform all persons regarding the Independent Living Philosophy for those with disabilities and for those living with disabilities. Our services include information and referral to resources, peer counseling, independent living skills training and public advocacy.

**4735** **Pathfinders for Independent Living**
105 E Mound Street
Harlan, KY 40831
    606-573-5777
    FAX: 606-573-5739
    e-mail: pathfinderil@kin.net

*Sandra Goodwyn, Executive Director*

They publish a newsletter called LifeLine 6-10 times a year. Most articles are written by Sandra Goodwyn. Editor is F.E. Goodwyn.

**4736** **SILC Department of Vocational Rehabilitation**
209 Saint Clair Street
Frankfort, KY 40601
    502-564-4440
    FAX: 502-564-6745
    e-mail: sarahf.richardson@ky.gov

*Sarah Richardson, SILC Liaison*

**4737** **SILC Department of Vocational Rehabilitati**
209 Saint Clair Street
Frankfort, KY 40601
    502-564-4440

*Beth Smith, Manager*

## Louisiana

**4738** **New Horizons: Alexandria**
3400 Jackson Street
Suite A
Alexandria, LA 71301
    318-484-3596
    888-361-3596
    FAX: 318-484-3640
    e-mail: nhilc@nhilc.org
    www.nhilc.org

*Gale M McLean, Executive Director*
*Dimple Hughes, Manager*

An association of adults with disabilities working to improve the quality of life for all who have disabilities.

**4739** **New Horizons: Monroe**
2406 Ferrand
Suite 18
Monroe, LA 71201
    318-323-4374
    800-428-5505
    FAX: 318-323-5445
    e-mail: dholloway@nhilc.org
    www.nhilc.org

*Gale Dean, Director*

New Horizons is a non-residential independent living center that offers a variety of programs and services for persons with disabilities.

**4740    New Horizons: Prescott Valley**
8085 E Manley Drive
Suite 1
Prescott Valley, AZ  86314                  928-772-1266

*Ken Edwards, Executive Director*

**4741    New Horizons: Shreveport**
6670 Saint Vincent Avenue
Shreveport, LA  71106                       860-675-4711
                                            877-219-7327
                                       FAX: 318-688-7823
                                      e-mail: nhilc@nhilc.org
                                            www.nhilc.org

*Gale M Dean, Executive Director*

New Horizons is an association of adults with disabilities working to improve the quality of life for all who have disabilities.

**4742    Resources for Independent Living: Baton Rouge**
New Orleans Resources for Independent Living
11931 Industriplex Boulevard
Suite 200
Baton Rouge, LA 70809                       225-753-4772
                                            800-505-2260
                                       FAX: 225-753-4831
                                       TTY: 225-753-4831
                                   e-mail: contact@noril.org
                                            www.noril.org

*Yazonka Archaga, Executive Director*

RIL provides quality services to individuals with disabilities to
assist with living independent. RIL also offers services to
inculde information and referral, advocacy, peer support and independent living skills training.

**4743    Resources for Independent Living: Baton Ro ge**
5700 Florida Boulevard
Baton Rouge, LA 70806                       225-216-3844
                                       FAX: 225-753-4831
                                   e-mail: contact@noril.org

*Yavnoka Archaga, Executive Director*

RIL provides quality services to individuals with disabilities to
assist with living independently; also offer a wide array of services to include information and referral, advocacy, peer support and independent living skills training.

**4744    Resources for Independent Living: Metairie**
3616 S I-10 Service Road W
Suite 111
Metairie, LA 70001                          504-522-1955
                                            877-505-2260
                                       FAX: 504-522-1954
                                       TTY: 504-522-1956
                                   e-mail: contact@noril.org
                                            www.noril.org

*Yavonka Archaga, Executive Director*

RIL provides quality services to individuals with disabilities to
assist with living independently. RIL also offers an array of services to include information and referral, advocacy, peer support and independent living skills training.

**4745    Southwest Louisiana Independence Center: L ake
          Charles**
1202 Kirkman Street
Suite C
Lake Charles, LA  70601                     337-477-7194
                                            888-403-1062
                                       FAX: 337-477-7198
                                       TTY:337-477-7196
                                            www.slic-la.org

*Mitch Granger, Executive Director*

SILC provides Information and Referral, Advocacy, Peer Counseling and other Independent Living Services, to develop community options for persons with significant disabilities in
Southwest and Central Louisiana, and to assist them in achieving and maintaining self-sufficient, productive lives.

**4746    Southwest Louisians Independence Center: Lafayette**
409 West St Mary Boulevard
Suite D1-04
Layfayette, LA 70506                        337-269-0027
                                       FAX: 337-233-7660
                                       TTY:337-233-7660
                                   e-mail: lafslic@catel.net
                                            www.slic-la.org

*Mitch Granger, Executive Director*

SILC provides Information and Referral, Advocacy, Peer Counseling and other Independent Living Services, to develop community options for persons with significant disabilities in
Southwest and South Central Louisiana, and to assist them in
achieving and maintaining self-sufficient, productive lives.

**4747    Southwest Lousiana Independence Center: La fayette**
850 Kaliste Saloom Road
Suite 118
Lafayette, LA  70508                        337-269-0027

*Chinelle Thorton, Manager*

**4748    Volunteers of America Supported Living Program**
3939 N Causeway Boulevard
Suite 3200
Metairie, LA  70002                         504-836-8702
                                       FAX: 504-835-0409

*Carrie Reinecke, Executive Director*

Provides supported living services including pca, respite, skills
traning, day, night, and behavior companion.

**4749    W Troy Cole Independent Living Specialist**
1900 Lamy Lane
Suite H
Monroe, LA  71201                           318-323-4374

*Katherine Carnell, Manager*

## Maine

**4750    Alpha One: Aroostook**
Alpha One: South Portland
PO Box 560
Mapleton, ME  04757                         207-764-6466
                                            800-974-6466
                                       FAX: 207-764-5396
                              e-mail: aroostook@alphaonenow.com
                                          www.alphaonenow.com

*Darlene Stewart, Independent Living Specialist*
*Ketra S Crosson, Aroostook County Coordinator*
*Kelley Teague, Manager*

Committed to being a leading enterprise providing the community with information, services and products that create opportunities for people with disabilities to live independently. Offers
adaptive equipment loan program, independent living skills instruction, adapted driver evaluation and training, information
and referral services, peer support, advocacy, access design
consultation, and more.

**4751 Alpha One: Augusta**

242 Western Avenue
Augusta, ME 04330
207-623-1115
800-499-2357
FAX: 207-623-1369
www.alphaonenow.com

*Steven Tremblay, Director*

Works throughout the state of Maine. The Board of Directors, staff and a network of personal and professional connections assist people with disabilities to gain access to and achieve their own independent living goals. Wherever persons are in Maine, this network creates improved and increased opportunities for people with disabilities.

**4752 Alpha One: Brewer**

1048 Union Street
Suite 2
Bangor, ME 04401
207-989-4968
800-300-6016
FAX: 207-941-6410
e-mail: dfitzgibbons@alphaonenow.com
www.alpha-one.org

*Dennis Fitzgibbons, Executive Director*
*Wally Qualia, Owner*

Committed to being a leading enterprise providing the community with information, services and products that create opportunities for people with disabilities to live independently. Provides many services including adaptive and mobility equipment selection, peer support, advocacy, information and referral services, adapted drive evaluation and training, and consumer directed personal assistance.

**4753 Alpha One: Main Office**

127 Main Street
South Portland, ME 04106
207-767-5690
800-640-7200
FAX: 207-799-8346
e-mail: dfitzgibbons@alphaonenow.com
www.alpha-one.org

*Dennis Fitzgibbons, Director*
*Steven Tremblay, Owner*

Alpha One, directed by people with disabilities, is committed to being a leading enterprise providing the community with information, services and products that create opportunities for people with disabilities to live independently. Offer a variety of services including access design consultation, information and referrals, attendant services, independent living skills instruction and more.

**4754 Maine Mental Health Connections**

150 Union Street
Bangor, ME 04401
207-941-2907
FAX: 207-941-2996
e-mail: mmhc@gwi.net
www.mmhc.us

*Robert J Mathien, Executive Director*
*Shelley Smith, Community Connections Manager*

MMHC offers a variety of social, recreational, residential, vocational, and personal growth opportunities for adult consumers of mental health and/or mental retardation services.

**4755 Motivational Services**

PO Box 229
Augusta, ME 04332
207-626-7002
FAX: 207-626-3469
TTY:2076212542
e-mail: rweiss@mocomaine.com
www.mocomaine.com

*Richard Weiss PhD, Executive Director*

Motivational Services has assisted adults recovering from significant mental illness living in the cities and towns of Kennebec County in Central Maine.

**4756 Shalom House**

PO Box 560
Portland, ME 04112
207-874-1080
FAX: 207-874-1077
TTY:207-842-6888
e-mail: generalmail@shalomhouseinc
www.shalomhouseinc.org

*Joe Prannigan, Executive Director*
*David Bronson, President*

Shalom House offers hope for adults living with severe mental illness by providing a choice of quality housing and support services that help people lead stab;e and fulfilling lives in the community.

# Maryland

**4757 Broadmead**

13801 York Road
Cockeysville, MD 21030
410-527-1900
800-201-7165
TTY:800-201-7165
e-mail: hr@broadmead.org
www.broadmead.org

*James E B Felter, Chairman*
*Rich Compton, Executive Director*

A accredited not for profit continuing care retirement community, provides continuing care services to a diverse group of seniors in a warm, congenial community founded and operated in the spirit of the Religious Society of Friends.

**4758 Eastern Shore Center for Independent Living**

9 Sunburst Center
Cambridge, MD 21613
410-221-7701
FAX: 410-221-7714
TTY:410-221-7701
e-mail: escil@comcast.net
www.escil.org

*Shirley Tarbox, Executive Director*

ESCIL provides services to people with all disabilities regardless of age, religion, gender, ethnicity, race or national origin. In addition to the core services of information and referral, skills training, peer support and advocacy, ESCIL also offers assistance with accessibility modifications, Americans with Disabilities Act education and training, housing referrals and counseling, transportation referral and information, Brailling capabilities, Personal Attendent Services referral, and more.

**4759 Freedom Center**

1560 Opossumtown Pike
Frederick, MD 21702
301-846-7811
FAX: 301-846-9070
TTY:301-846-7811
e-mail: advocate@thefreedomcenter-md.org
www.thefreedomcenter-md.org

*Jamey George, Executive Director*

A walk in center for independent living, provides services and supports to empower individuals with disabilities to lead self-directed, independent, and productive lives in a barrier-free community.

**4760 Housing Unlimited**

1398 Lamberton Drive
Suite G1
Silver Spring, MD 20902
301-230-2825
FAX: 301-592-9318
e-mail: information@housingunlimited.org
www.housingunlimited.org

To address the housing crisis for adults with psychiatric disabilities who reside in Montgomery County, Maryland.

**4761 Human Resources Management**
American Association of Childrens Residential Cent
11700 W Lake Park Drive
Milwaukee, WI 53224

877-332-2272
FAX: 877-362-2272
e-mail: mskarich@alliance1.org
www.aacrc-dc.org

*Brian Carroll MSW LICSW, President*
*Steven Elson PhD, Presient-Elect*
*Maggie Skarich, National Coordinator*

One-day seminar addresses the Management of Human Resources standards in the Comprehensive Accreditation Manual for Hospitals, Behavioral Health, Long Term Care, Ambulatory and Home Care, plus standards on orientation and education, staffing and managing staff requests.

**4762 Independence Now: Riverdale**
6811 Kenilworth Avenue
Suite 504
Riverdale, MD 20737

301-277-2839
TTY:301-277-2839
e-mail: info@innow.org
www.innow.org

*Patricia Laird, President*
*Catherine Raggio, Executive Director*

Center for Independent Living serving Montgomery and Prine George's Counties in Maryland.

**4763 Independence Now: Silver Spring**
1400 Spring Street
Suite 400
Silver Spring, MD 20910

301-587-4162
FAX: 301-588-3951
e-mail: info@InNow.org
www.InNow.org

*Catherine Raggio, Director*

A nonprofit organization created by people with disabilities. Provides services that promote independence and the inclusion of people with disabilities in their communities. Serves Montgomery and Prince George's counties.

**4764 Making Choices for Independent Living**
3011 Montebello Ter
Baltimore, MD 21214

410-444-1400
FAX: 410-444-0825
TTY:800-735-2258
e-mail: mcil@mcil-md.org
www.mcil-md.org

*Andrea Buonincontro, Executive Director*

**4765 Resources for Independence**
708 Fayette Street
Cumberland, MD 21503

301-784-1774
FAX: 301-784-1776
e-mail: phcil2hereintown.net

*Lori Magruder, Director*

**4766 Resources for Independent Living**
420 i Street
Suite 3
Sacramento, CA 95814

916-446-3074
FAX: 916-446-2443
e-mail: monicag@ril-sacramento.org
www.ril-sacramento.org

*Monica Gracechild, Office Manager*

The only organization in Sacramento providing services to peopl with all forms of disabilities. RIL is dedicated to providing services and support to disabled people so they can live happy and productive lives.

**4767 Southern Maryland Center for LIFE**
PO Box 657
Charlotte Hall, MD 20622

301-884-4498
FAX: 301-884-6099
e-mail: cflife@eartlink.net

*Gene Potts, Executive Director*
*Carrie Lanthier, Administrative Assistant*

# Massachusetts

**4768 AD-LIB**
215 North Street
Pittsfield, MA 01201

413-442-7047
FAX: 413-443-4338
TTY:413-442-7158
e-mail: jcastellani@adlibcil.org

*Joseph Castelani, Executive Director*

Offers information and referral services, independent living skills training, peer counseling, individual and group advocacy services available to all people with disabilities. Access consultation provided to businesses, agencies and institutions in accordance to the Americans with Disabilities Act.

**4769 ARC: Gateway**
PO Box 428
Hyannis, MA 02601

508-790-3667
888-593-8062
FAX: 508-775-5233
e-mail: arcofcapecod@hotmail.com
www.arcofcapecod.org

*Robert Spongberg, Executive Director*

Provides adults with developmental disabilities a full range of individual supports to assist them in becoming valued members of their community.

**4770 American Red Cross of Cape Cod**
American Red Cross in Washington DC
286 South Street
Hyannis, MA 02601

508-775-1540
FAX: 508-771-2209
e-mail: capecod@cape.com
www.capecodredcross.org

*Glen Beasley, Executive Director*

Handicapped accessible motor service to Boston Area Hospitals from Cape Cod with pick-up for Nantucket residents.

**4771 Boston Center for Independent Living**
95 Berkeley Street
Suite 206
Boston, MA 02116

617-338-6666
866-338-8085
888-338-8085
FAX: 617-338-6661
TTY:617-338-6662
e-mail: info@bostoncil.org
www.bostoncil.org

*Bill Henning, Executive Director*

Offers skills training, peer mentoring, advocacy training and information services to help persons with disabilities of all ages assume full control over their own life choices. Works with youth in schools to promote effective transition into adult independence. Empowers people by providing information in all aspects of daily living, including the statewide housing registry, personal care assistant program and ongoing assistance. Works with others to address social concerns effecting disabled.

**4772 Cape Organization for Rights of the Disabled (CORD)**
1019 Iyannough Road
Suite 4
Hyannis, MA 02601
508-775-8300
800-541-0282
FAX: 508-775-7022
e-mail: pburkley@cape.com
www.cordonline.org

*Pam Burkley, Executive Director*

CORD works to advance the independence, productivity, and integration of people with disabilities, inluding deaf and hard of hearing people, into mainstream society.

**4773 Center for Living & Working: Fitchburg**
76 Summer Street
Fitchburg, MA 01420
978-345-1568
TTY:978-345-1568
e-mail: centerlwA@centerlw.org
www.centerlw.org
The Center for Living and Working is a non-profit Independent Living Center which takes its direction from persons with disabilities. The Center advocates to empower persons with disabilities to take active roles in their lives and in their community in which they live. Also provides comprehensive amd innovative programs and services in order to maximize individual independence and opportunities.

**4774 Center for Living & Working: Milford**
100 Medway Road
Milford, MA 01757
508-473-2271
TTY:508-473-2271
e-mail: centerlw@centerlw.org
www.centerlw.org

*Mike Kennedy, President*
*Ann Ruder, VP*

The Center advocates to empower persons with disabilities to take active roles in their lives and in the community in which they live. Provides comprehensive and innovavtive programs and services in order to maximize individual independence and opportunities.

**4775 Center for Living & Working: Worcester**
67 Millbrook Street
Worcester, MA 01606
508-363-1226
FAX: 508-363-1254
TTY:508-363-1226
e-mail: centerlw@centerlw.org
www.centerlw.org

*Mike Kennedy, President*
*Jamie Ross, Executive Director*

The Center advocates to empower persons with disabilities to take active roles in their lives and in the community in which they live. We provide comprehensive and innovative programs and services in order to maximize individual independence and opportunities.

**4776 DEAF**
215 Brighton Avenue
Allston, MA 02134
617-254-4041
800-886-5195
FAX: 617-254-7091
TTY: 617-254-4041
e-mail: info@deafinconline.org
www.deafinconline.org

*Sharon Applegate, Executive Director*

DEAF encourages and empowers Deaf and Hard of Hearing individuals to lead independent and productive lives.

**4777 Independence Associates**
141 Main Street
Brockton, MA 02301
508-880-5325
FAX: 508-583-2165
e-mail: indasspc@iacil.org
www.iacil.org

*Constance Gallant, Executive Director*

Provides comprehensive services which wll enhance the range of acceptable options available to the consumer and improve the quality of life of persons with disabilities; to work on behalf of the objective of the disablility rights and independent living movement.

**4778 Independence Associates: Brockton**
141 Main Street
1st Floor
Brockton, MA 02301
508-583-2166
FAX: 508-583-2165
e-mail: indassoc@iacil.org

*Constance Gallant, Director*

**4779 Independent Living Center of the North Shore and Cape Ann**
27 Congress Street
Suite 107
Salem, MA 01970
978-741-0077
888-751-0077
FAX: 978-741-1133
TTY:978-745-1735
e-mail: smcduff@ilcnsca.org
www.ilcnsca.org

*Mary Margaret Moore, Executive Director*
*Kathy O'Brien, Associate Director*

ILNSCA is a service and advocacy center run by and for people with disabilities. Offered services include independent living skills training, peer counseling, information and referral, and advocacy; home modification, vehicle modifications and assistive equipment limited funding; ADA technical assistance.

**4780 Independent Living Center of Starvos: Spri ngfield**
262 Cottage Street
Springfield, MA 01104
413-781-5555
FAX: 413-733-5473
TTY:413-781-5555
e-mail: ebrancewicz@stavros.org
www.starvos.org

*James Kruidenier, Director*

Promoting independence and access in the communities for persons with disabilities and Deaf people.

**4781 Independent Living Center of Stavros: Amhe rst**
691 S East Street
Amherst, MA 01002
413-256-0473
800-804-1899
FAX: 413-256-0190
e-mail: info@stavros.org
www.stavros.org

*James Kruidenier, Executive Director*

Stavros promotes independence and access in the communities for persons with disabilities and Deaf people.

**4782 Independent Living Center of Stavros: Gree nfield**
55 Federal Street
Suite 210
Greenfield, MA 01301
413-774-3001
FAX: 413-772-2556
TTY:413-772-2556
e-mail: jkruidenier@starvos.org
www.starvos.org

*James Kruidenier, Director*

Promoting independence and access in the communities for persons with disabilities and Deaf people.

**4783 Independent Living Center of the North Shore and Cape Ann**

27 Congress Street
Suite 107
Salem, MA 01970

978-741-0077
888-751-0077
FAX: 978-741-1133
TTY: 978-745-1735
e-mail: smcduff@ilcnsca.org
www.ilcnsca.org

*Mary Moore, Excutive Director*
*Shawn McDuff, Director*

ILCNSCA works to address individual, community-wide and broad systemic issues that affect the ability of people with disabilities to live independently in the community. The staff provides peer counseling, independent living skills training, individual advocacy, information and referral to people with disabilities, and more. These services are offered to empower individuals with disabilities and assist them in gaining the control and skills needed to live independent lives.

**4784 Independent Living Center of the Southeast**

Merrill Street
Building 66
Fall River, MA 02720

508-679-9210
FAX: 508-677-2377
TTY:508-679-9210
e-mail: scil@secil.org
www.secil.org

*Lisa M Titta, Executive Director*
*Liz Harbison, Program Coordinator*

SCIL provides training, information and support to help consumers achieve individual goals, experience personal growth and participate fully in community life.

**4785 Independent Living Center: Massachusetts**

48 Boylston Street
Boston, MA 02116

617-727-5550

*Dave Govostes, Manager*

**4786 Independent Living Center: Multi-Culural Center of Boston**

22 Beechwood Street
#1
Dorchester, MA 02121

617-288-9431
FAX: 617-288-2597
TTY:617-288-2707
e-mail: dunn@milcb.org
www.milcb.org

*Suzeth Dunn, Executive Director*

MCILCB strives to empower the consumers by providing critical information that enhances their ability to live independently and function productively within their households and their communities.

**4787 Massachusetts Commission for the Blind**

48 Boylston Street
Boston, MA 02116

617-727-5550
800-392-6450
FAX: 617-626-7685
www.mass.gov/mcb

*Joseph Weisse, Director of Outreach/Info Svcs*

Provides social and rehabilitative services to all legally blind residents of the Commonwealth of Massachusetts.

**4788 MetroWest Center for Independent Living**

280 Irving Street
Framingham, MA 01702

508-875-7853
FAX: 508-875-8359
e-mail: pspooner@m2wcil.org
www.mwcil.org

*Paul Spooner, Executive Director*

A community-based, consumer-controlled, cross disability center for independent living, serving the MetroWest area of Massachusetts. MWCIL is dedicated to working on behalf of the objectives of the disability rights and independent living movements, through the provision of comprehensive services to enhance the range of options available to, and improve the quality of life of persons with disabilities.

**4789 Northeast Independent Living Program**

20 Ballard Road
Lawrence, MA 01843

978-687-4288
FAX: 978-689-4488
TTY:978-687-4288
e-mail: info@nilp.org
www.nilp.org

*Charles Carr, Executive Director*

A consumer controlled Independent Living Center providing Advocacy and Services to people with all disabilities in the greater Merrimack Valley who wish to live as independently as possible in the commuity.

**4790 Renaissance Clubhouse**

176 Walker Street
Lowell, MA 01854

978-454-7944
FAX: 978-937-7867
e-mail: renclub@channel1.com
www.tricitymentalhealth.org

*Elaine Walker, Director*
*Pammy Sadoie, Assistant Director*

Offers daily structure, assistance wtih jobs, retirement, and housing.

**4791 Student Independent Living Experience**

3 Randolph Street
Canton, MA 02021

781-830-8724
FAX: 781-830-8742
www.enable.com

Offers young adults with disabilities an opportunity to participate in a group learning situation, where they will develop independent and transitional living skills through a residential or non-residential model.

**4792 Vivienne S Thomson Independent Living Cent er**

555 Armory Street
Jamaica Plain, MA 02130

617-522-9840
FAX: 617-522-9839

It is a full service Independent Living Center serving the needs of people in the Jamaica Plain, Roslindale, West Roxbury area. In addition the Thomson Center is prepared to lend assistance to individuals from any part of Massachusetts who find that being a member of minority group impacts upon dealing with a disability.

## Michigan

**4793 Ann Arbor Center for Independent Living**
2568 Packard Street
Ann Arbor, MI 48104
734-662-5599
FAX: 734-971-0826
TTY:734-971-0310
e-mail: cilstaff@aacil.org
www.aacil.org

*Jim Magyar, President/CEOector*
*Tom Hoatlin, Development Director*
*Phil Zepeda, Manager*

AACIL assists people with disabilities and their families in living full and productive lives. AACIL assures the equality of opportunity, full participation, independent living and economic self-sufficiency of people with disabilities in the community.

**4794 Arc Detroit**
51 W Hancock Street
Detroit, MI 48201
313-831-0202
FAX: 313-831-7974
e-mail: thearcdetroit@aol.com
www.arcmi.org

*Tom Lerchen, President*
*Norm DeLisle, Vice President*
*Henry Johnson, Administrator*

Exists to empower local chapters of The Arc to asure that citizens with developmental disabilities are valued and that they and their families csn participate fully in and contribute to the life of their community

**4795 Association for Retarded Citizens of Muskegon County**
1145 Wesley Avenue
Muskegon, MI 49442
231-777-2006
FAX: 231-777-3507
www.arcmuskegon.org

*Margaret O'Toole, Executive Director*
*Denee Card, Administrative Assistant*

Offers information and referral, advocacy services and peer counseling.

**4796 Bad Axe Center for Independent Living**
610 Woodworth
Bad Axe, MI 48413
989-269-5421
888-772-0442
FAX: 989-269-5422
e-mail: huron@bwcil.org
www.bwcil.org

*Angela Hoff, Director*

BWCIL is a consumer based organization designed to serve persons with disabilities who have physical, psychiatric, sensory, cognitive, and multiple disabilities through the provision of advocacy, information and referral, service provision, and the promotion of needed services so to maximize the individual's optimal level of independence.

**4797 Bay Area Coalition for Independent Living**
701 South Elmwood
Suite 17
Traverse City, MI 49684
231-929-4865
FAX: 231-929-4896
e-mail: steve@bacil.org

*Steve Wade, Director*

**4798 Blue Water CIL: Lapeer**
392 Nepessing Street
Lapeer, MI 48446
810-664-9098
FAX: 810-664-9037
e-mail: lapeer@bwcil.org
www.bwcil.org

*Angela Hoff, Director*

A consumer based organization that is designed to serve persons with disabilities who have physical, psychiatric, sensory, cognitive and multiple disabilities through the provision of advocacy, information and referral, service provision and the promotion of needed services so to maximize the individual's optimal level of independence.

**4799 Blue Water CIL: Port Huron**
310 Watrer Street
Port Huron, MI 48060
810-987-9337
800-527-5167
FAX: 810-987-9548
TTY: 810-987-9337
e-mail: stclair@bwcil.org

*Angela Hoff, Executive Director*

Offers disability education, peer counseling, advocacy, transpotation, employment, substance abuse counseling, support groups and information on accessible housing.

**4800 CIL of Mid-Michigan**
201 Mulholland
#302B
Bay City, MI 48708
989-895-2359

e-mail: davert@cilmm.org
www.cilmm.org

*Melissa Davert, Director*

CILMM exists to assist people with disabilities in learning skills and giving guidance in order for them to make choices and decisions for themselves. CILMM also promotes and encourages independence for all people with disabilities. Serves Bay, Midland, Saginaw, Arenac, Clare, Gladwin, Gratiot and Isabella counties.

**4801 Capital Area Center for Independent Living**
1048 Pierpont Drive
Suite 9-10
Lansing, MI 48911
517-241-0393
FAX: 517-241-0438
e-mail: cacil@cacil.org
www.cacil.org

*Ellen Weaver, Executive Director*

CACIL empowers people with disabilities to take control of their lives.

**4802 Caro Center for Independent Living**
1184 Cleaver Road
Suite 1000
Caro, MI 48723
989-673-3678
888-673-8006
FAX: 989-673-3678
e-mail: tuscola@bwcil.org
www.bwcil.org

*Ralph Moore, IL Specialist/Manager*

**4803 Center for Community Access**
4750 Woodward Avenue
Suite 213
Detroit, MI 48201
313-832-4783
FAX: 313-832-4793
e-mail: infor@centerforcommunityaccess.org
www.centerforcommunityaccess.org

*Michael Paul, Director*

The Center for Community Access assists individuals with disabilities in the metropolitan Detroit area in maintaining their independence and gaining acess to the greater community through education, advocacy and celebrating the differences.

**4804   Center for Handicapped Affairs**
3815 W Saint Joseph Street
Suite D
Lansing, MI  48917                    517-373-1837
                                      FAX: 517-334-8000

**4805   Center for Independent Living of Mid-Michigan**
2568 Packard Street
Ann Arbor, MI  48104                  734-971-0277
                                      FAX: 734-971-0826
                                      www.aacil.org

*James Magyar, Executive Director*

Comprised of over 51 percent of people with disabilities, and advocates for the rights of people with disabilities in the Mid-Michigan area. Call for information on disability issues or for assistance in obtaining services, within your community..

**4806   Community Connections**
133 E Napier
Suite 2
Benton Harbor, MI  49022              269-925-6422
                                      FAX: 269-925-7141
                                      e-mail: kellis@match.org

*Kathy Ellis, Director*

**4807   Cristo Rey Handicappers Program**
1717 N High Street
Lansing, MI  48906                    517-372-4700
                                      FAX: 517-372-8499
                                      e-mail: jobs@cristo-rey.com
                                      www.cristo-rey.com

*John Roy Castillo, Executive Director*
*Cindi Benavides, Program Coordinator*

Social/recreational program, outreach, support and self sufficiency services, drop in area.

**4808   Detroit Center for Independent Living**
5555 Conner
Suite 2075
Detroit, MI  48201                    313-923-1655
                                      FAX: 313-923-1404
                                      TTY:313-923-1404
                                      e-mail: wayne@bwcil.org
                                      www.bwcil.org

*Richard Sides, Director*

BWCIL is a consumer-based organization designed to serve persons with disabilities who have physical, psychiatric, sendory, cognitive, and multiple disabilities through the provision of advocacy, information and referral, service provision, and the promotion of needed services so to maximize the individual's optimal level of independence.

**4809   DisAbility Connections**
409 Linden Avenue
Jackson, MI  49203                    517-782-6054
                                      FAX: 517-782-3118
                                      e-mail: monicas@disabilityconnect.org

*Monica Salgat, Director*

**4810   Disability Advocates of Kent County**
3600 Camelot Drive SE
Grand Rapids, MI  49546               616-949-1100
                                      FAX: 616-949-7865
                                      TTY:616-949-1100
                                      e-mail: contact@dakc.us
                                      www.dakc.us

*David Bulkowski, Executive Director*

DAKC exists to advocate, assist, educate and inform on independent living options for persons with disabilities and to create a barrier free society for all.

**4811   Disability Connection**
1871 Peck
Muskegon, MI  49441                   231-722-0088
                                      FAX: 231-722-0066
                                      TTY:231-722-0088
                                      e-mail: annal@dcimi.org

*Susan Cloutier-Myers, Executive Director*

An organization that supports a diverse range of people with disabilities through empowerment, advocacy, information and referral, and peer support.

**4812   Disability Network**
3600 S Dort Highway
Suite 54
Flint, MI  48507                      810-742-1800
                                      FAX: 810-742-2400
                                      TTY:810-742-7647
                                      e-mail: tdn@disnetwork.org
                                      www.disnetwork.org

*Mike Zelley, President/CEO*

The Disability Network's mission is to realize consumer empowerment, self determination, full inclusion and participation of all people in the communities through independent living philosophy and the unequivocal implementation of the Americans with Disabilities Act

**4813   Disability Network, Oakland/Macomb**
13213 E 14 Mile Road
Sterling Heights, MI  48312           586-268-4160
                                      FAX: 586-268-4720
                                      e-mail: info@omcil.org
                                      www.omcil.org

*Kelley Wilson, Executive Director*

Disability Network provides information and referral services, advocacy, independent living skills training and peer support to anyone with a disability

**4814   Disability Resource Center of SW Michigan**
104 Calhoun Street
Battle Creek, MI  49017               269-345-1516
                                      FAX: 269-345-0229
                                      TTY:269-288-0047
                                      e-mail: jcooper@drccil.org
                                      www.drccil.org

*Joel Cooper, President/CEO*
*Molly Dollahan, Independent Living Specialist*

DRCCIL educates and empowers people with disabilities to create change in their ow lives, and advocates for social change to create inclusive communities. Serving Barry, Branch, Calhoun, Kalamazoo, St. Joseph and Van buren Counties.

**4815   Disability Resource Center of Southwest Michigan**
517 E Crosstown Parkway
Kalamazoo, MI  49001                  269-345-1516
                                      800-394-7450
                                      FAX: 269-345-0229
                                      TTY: 269-345-5925
                                      e-mail: tveld@drccil.org
                                      www.drccil.org

*Joel Cooper, President*
*Karen Halsted, Associate Director*

A Center for Independent Living offering core services in the areas of advocacy, peer support, independent living skills training, and information and referral to persons with disabilities living in the following southwestern Michigan counties: Barry, Calhoun, Kalamazoo, St. Joseph and Van Buren. Specialized services available through DRC include: occupational therapy assessments; accessibility assessments, driver evaluation and training.

**4816  Grand Traverse Area Community Living Center**
2301 Garfield
Suite A
Traverse City, MI  49686                 231-922-0903
                                  FAX: 231-941-3421
                        e-mail: jimmoore@chartermi.net

*Jim Moore, Director*
*Mary Macy, Executive Director*

We are a training home for individuals with developmental disabilities over the age of 18

**4817  Great Lakes Center for Independent Living**
3850 2nd Street
Wayne, MI  48184                        734-727-0901
                                  FAX: 313-832-3850
                          e-mail: jmeece@glcil.org
                      www.misilc.org/partnerships.htm

*Jeannie Meece, Executive Director*
*Issac Hood, Owner*

Independent living skills training, de-institutionalization and empowerment training for persons with disabilities.

**4818  Great Lakes/Macomb Rehabilitation Group**
4 E Alexandrine Street
Apt 104
Detroit, MI  48201                      313-832-3371
                                  FAX: 313-832-3850
                        e-mail: jlcil@home.msen.com

*Jeannie Meece-Brooks, Contact*

**4819  Hope Network Independent Living Program**
1550 E Beltline Avenue SE
Suite 125
Grand Rapids, MI  49506                 616-831-2000
                                  FAX: 616-940-8151

*Kathryn Mullarkey, Manager*
*Samuel Roth PhD*

Postacute rehabilitation program serving adults with physical disabilities, especially spinal cord injuries, blindness, MS, brain injuries and stroke. Home adaptation, independent living skills and vocational services are highlighted. Program focus is independent living and return to work.

**4820  JARC**
30301 Northwestern Highway
Suite 100
Farmington Hills, MI  48334             248-538-6611
                                  FAX: 248-538-6615
                          e-mail: jarc@jarc.org
                                  www.jarc.org

*Joyce Keller, Executive Director*

Non-profit organization providing residential care and support services to adults with developmental disabilities. Operates 13 licensed homes and 5 unlicensed transition homes, and supports over 60 people who live on their own. JARC also offers an array of services to families of children and adults with any disability still living at home, including respite care, life planning, educational and social programming.

**4821  Jackson Center for Independent Living**
409 Linden Avenue
Jackson, MI  49203                      517-784-1723
                                  FAX: 517-784-9921
                       e-mail: jcil@modempool.com

*Jim Cyphers, Director*
*Perry Stahl, PR/Independent Living Specialist*
*Jim Cyphers, I&R/Human Resources/IL Advocate*

**4822  Kalamazoo Center for Independent Living**
4026 S Westnedge Avenue
Kalamazoo, MI  49008                    616-345-1516
                                  FAX: 616-345-0229

**4823  Lakeshore Center for Independent Living**
426 Century Lane
Holland, MI  49423                      616-396-5326
                                        800-656-5245
                                  FAX: 616-396-3220
                                  TTY: 616-396-5326
                          e-mail: ruth@lcil.org
                                  www.lcil.org

*Ruth Stegeman, Executive Director*
*Rick Diamond, Program Coordinator*

A cross-disability, community-based organization providing advocacy, education, and information and referral to persons with disabilities in Ottawa and Allegan counties.

**4824  Life Skills Services**
1608 Lake Street
Kalamazoo, MI  49001
                                  FAX: 269-344-0285

*Don Vanderkooy, Director*

Offers skill development and monitoring for children and supported living and respite services for adults with developmental disabilities and/or mental illnesses.

**4825  Livingston Center for Independent Living**
3075 E Grand River Avenue
Suite 108
Howell, MI  48843                       517-548-1741
                                  FAX: 517-548-1751
                        e-mail: dianaus1@yahoo.com

*Dan Durci, Director*

**4826  Michigan Commission for the Blind: Independent Living Rehabilitation Program**
411 E Genesee Avenue
Saginaw, MI  48607                      989-758-1765
                                        800-292-4200
                                  FAX: 989-758-1405
                                  www.mfia.state.mi.us

*Leaman Jones, Supervisor*
*Patrick Cannon, Manager*

Rehabilitation teaching, independent living skills for persons over 55 with severe vision loss.

**4827  Michigan Commission for the Blind: Detroit**
Cadillac Place
3038 W Grand Boulevard, Suite 4-450
Detroit, MI  48202                      313-456-1646

*Gwen McNeal, Supervisor*

**4828  Midland Center for Independent Living**
1160 James Savage Road
Midland, MI  48640                      989-835-4041
                                        800-782-4162
                                  FAX: 989-835-8121
                          e-mail: info@cilmm.org
                                  www.cilmm.org

*Sara Kristol-Brando, Executive Director*

**4829 Midland Center for Independent Living of Mid-Michigan**
1160 James Savage Road
Suite C
Midland, MI 48640
989-835-4041
800-782-4160
FAX: 989-835-8121
e-mail: info@cil.org
www.cilmm.org

*Sara Kristol-Brando, Executive Director*

**4830 Monroe Center for Independent Living**
40 N Roessler Street
Monroe, MI 48162
734-242-5919
FAX: 734-242-7129
e-mail: lmaier@aacil.org
www.aacil.org

*Linda Maier, Director*

Assists people with disabilities and their families in living full and productive lives. Assures the equality and opportunity, full participation, independent living and economic self-sufficency of people with disabilities in the community.

**4831 Southeastern Michigan Commission for the Blind**
4450 Grandy Street
Detroit, MI 48207
313-456-0334
800-292-4200
FAX: 313-456-1645
www.michigan.gov

*Patrick Cannon, Executive Director*
*Pat Bragg, Manager*

Vocational rehabilitation agency. Personal adjustment vocational assessment and training, job placement and follow-up services.

**4832 Superior Alliance for Independent Living (SAIL)**
129 W Baraga Avenue
Suite H
Marquette, MI 49855
906-228-5744
800-379-7245
FAX: 906-228-5573
e-mail: judyv@upsail.com
www.upsail.com

*Stoney Polman, Executive Director*
*David Carl, Independent Living Coordinator*

SAIL promotes the inclusion of people with disbilities into our communities on a full and equal basis through empowerment, education, participation and choice.

---

# Minnesota

---

**4833 Accessibility Home Fund**
400 Sibley Street
Suite 300
Saint Paul, MN 55101
651-296-7608
800-657-3769
FAX: 651-296-8139
TTY: 651-297-2361
e-mail: mhfa@state.mn.us
www.mhfa.state.mn.us

*Barb Collins, Program Manager*
*Rochelle Rubins, Director of Communications*

Offers peer counseling, education and referral services.

**4834 Accessible Space**
2550 University Avenue w
Suite 330n
Saint Paul, MN 55114
651-645-7271
800-466-7722
FAX: 651-645-0541
e-mail: info@accessiblespace.org
www.accessiblespace.org

*Stephen Schaaf, President/CEO*
*Steven F Wiggins, Founder*

Provides accessible, affordable community-based housing with support services at residential and apartment sites in 20 states. Support services offered in Minnesota, Montana, Nevada and North Dakota.

**4835 Accessnorth CIL of Northeastern MN: Aitkin**
105 4th Street, NW
Aitkin, MN 56431
218-927-3748
800-390-3681
FAX: 218-927-3749
TTY: 218-927-3748
e-mail: parson@accessnorth.net

*Kim Tyler, Director*

Assists individuals to live independently, pursue meaningful goals, and have equal opportunities and choices.

**4836 Accessnorth CIL of Northeastern MN: Duluth**
2016 W Superior Street
Duluth, MN 55806
218-625-1400
888-625-1401
FAX: 218-625-1401
TTY:218-625-1400
e-mail: roberta@accessnorth.net
www.accessnorth.net

*Kim Tyler, Director*

Assisting individuals with disabilities to live independently, puruse meaningful goals, and have equal opportunities and choices.

**4837 Center for Independent Living**
16090 U Te Avenue 1600
Suite 100
Grand Junction, CO 81501
970-241-0315
800-613-2271
FAX: 970-245-3341
e-mail: jshook@cfigj.org
www.cfigj.org

*Rochelle Larson, Director*
*Kat Emmons, Executive Director*

**4838 Center for Independent Living of NE Minnesota**
Mesabi Mall
Suite 25
Hibbing, MN 55746
218-262-6675
800-390-3681
FAX: 218-262-6677
TTY: 218-262-6675
e-mail: kim@accessnorth.net
www.accessnorth.net

*Kimberly Tyler, Executive Director*

Assisting individuals with disabilities to live independently, pursue meaningful goals, and have an equal opportunities and choices

**4839  Courage Center**
3915 Golden Valley Road
Minneapolis, MN 55422
763-520-0312
888-846-8253
FAX: 763-520-0577
TTY:763-520-0245
e-mail: courageinfo@courage.org
www.courage.org

*Jan Malcolm, CEO*
*Pete Berridge, VP, Human Resources*
*Mary Jensen Manager*

A not for profit rehabilitation organization, empowers people with physical disabilities to reach for their full potential in every aspect of life.

**4840  Freedom Resource Center for Independent Living: Fargo**
2701 9th Avenue SW
Fargo, ND 58103
701-478-0459
800-450-0459
FAX: 701-478-0510
TTY: 218-236-0459
e-mail: freedom@freedomrc.org
www.freedomrc.org

*Nate Aalgaard, Executive Director*

**4841  Freedom Resource Center for Independent Living: Fergus Falls**
125 W Lincoln Avenue
Suite 17
Fergus Falls, MN 56537
218-998-1799
FAX: 218-998-1798
e-mail: joycew@freedomrc.org
www.freedomrc.org

*Nathan Aalgaard, Executive Director*

Freedom Resource Center assists people in working towards goals they establish for themselves.

**4842  Independence Crossroads**
8932 Old Cedar Avenue S
Bloomington, MN 55425
952-854-8004
800-603-7760
FAX: 952-854-7842
e-mail: info@independencecrossroads.org
www.aplushomecare.org

*Leah Welch, Founder*

Offers free information and referral, advocacy, mental health, counseling services, support groups and public education.

**4843  Metropolitan Center for Independent Living**
1600 University Avenue W
Suite 16
Saint Paul, MN 55104
651-646-8342
FAX: 651-603-2006
TTY:651-603-2001
e-mail: margotsk@mcil-mn.org
www.mcil-mn.org

*David Hancox, Executive Director*
*Carol Streasick, Manager of Personal Care Program*

MCIL is dedicated to the full promotion of independent living philosophy by supporting individuals with disabilities in their personal efforts to pursue self-directed lives.

**4844  Minnesota Association of Centers for Independent Living**
519 2nd Street N
Saint Cloud, MN 56303
320-529-9000
888-529-0743
FAX: 320-529-0747
TTY:320-529-9000
e-mail: ilicil@independentlifestyles.org
www.macil.org

*Cara Ruff, President*

A non profit organization whose purpose is to advocate for the independent living needs of people with disabilities who are citizens of the State of Minnesota, to develop new resources, identify and provide access to existing resources which provide the services needed by persons with disabilities so that they may live independently in the situation and community of their choice.

**4845  OPTIONS**
123 S Main Street
Suite B
Crookston, MN 56716
218-281-5722
FAX: 218-281-5722
TTY:218-281-5722
e-mail: options3@rrv.net

*Gordie Haug, Director*

**4846  Options Interstate Resource Center for Independent Living**
318 3rd Street NW
E Grand Forks, MN 56721
218-773-6100
800-726-3692
FAX: 218-773-7119
TTY: 218-773-6100
e-mail: options@myoptions.info
www.macil.org/options

*Randy Sorensen, Executive Director*
Located in Minnesota, but also serves North Dakota.

**4847  Perry River Home Care**
330 High Way Pen S
Saint Cloud, MN 56304
320-255-1882
FAX: 320-255-5137

*Berna Florentine, CEO*
*Ken Figge, President*
*Courtney Salzi, Administrator*

Offers skilled nursing services RN, LPN, TV Therapy, Pediatrics, Rehabilitation Services, PT, OT, ST, Paraprofessional staff, Home Health Aides, Homemakers, Personal Care Attendents, Companions, Live-ins, Sleep overs, Respite care, Extended hours.

**4848  SMILES**
820 Winnebago Avenue
Suite 1
Fairmont, MN 56031
507-235-3488
FAX: 507-235-3488
e-mail: smiles@smilescil.org

*Alan Augustin, Director*

A non profit organization committed to providing a wide array of services that assists indivduals with disabilities that live independently, pursue meaningful goals, and enjoy the same opportunities and choices as all persons.

**4849  Southeastern Minnesota Center for Independent Living: Red Wing**
201 E 7th Street
Red Wing, MN 55066
651-388-0466
FAX: 651-385-0643
e-mail: semcil@pressenter.com
www.virtualcil.net

*Sharon Taft, Contact*

**4850 Southeastern Minnesota Center for Independent Living: Rochester**
2720 N Broadway
Rochester, MN 55906
507-285-1815
888-460-1815
FAX: 507-288-8070
e-mail: semcil@semcil.org
www.semcil.org

*Vicki Molle, Executive Director*

A non profit organization that assists people with disabilities to become independent and productive community members.

**4851 Southern Minnesota Independent Living Enterprises and Services**
709 S Front Street
Mankato, MN 56001
507-345-7139
888-676-6498
FAX: 507-345-8429
e-mail: smiles@smilescil.org
www.smilescil.org

*Alan Augustin, Executive Director*
*Julie Birkemeyer, IL Skills Specialist*

A nonprofit organization committed to providing a wide array of services that assist individuals with disabilities that live independently, puruse meaningful goals, and enjoy the same oportunities and choices as all persons.

**4852 Southwestern Center for Independent Living**
109 S 5th Street
Suite 700
Marshall, MN 56258
507-532-2221
800-422-1485
FAX: 507-532-2222
TTY: 507-532-2221
e-mail: swcil@swcil.com
www.swcil.com

*Steve Thovson, Executive Director*

SWCIL is dedicated to the ever changing needs of persons wih disabilities in southwestern Minnesota. SWCIL strives to provide services, supports, and resources, as defined necessary by consumers, that will lead to the creation or enhancement of independent living options. SWCIL is also committed to providing education and awareness to promote society acceptance, inculsion, and equal access for all persons with disabilities.

**4853 Vinland Center Lake Independence**
PO Box 308
Loretto, MN 55357
763-479-3555
FAX: 763-479-2605
e-mail: vinland@vinlandcenter.org
www.vinlandcenter.org

*Carol Jackson, Executive Director*
*Duane Reynolds, Associate Director*
*Mary Roehl, Operations Director*

A Minnesota based rehabilitation center which offers services in three distinct service areas: vocational rehabilitation; inclusive community programs; and for people with cognitive disabilities, specially adapted chemical dependency treatment.

## Mississippi

**4854 Alpha Home Royal Maid Association for the Blind**
PO Box 30
Hazlehurst, MS 39083
FAX: 601-894-2993
e-mail: sigworks@teclink.net

*Howard Becker, Director*

Offers attendant care registry, information on accessible housing and referrals.

**4855 Gulf Coast Independent Living Center**
18 J M Tatum Industrial Drive
Hattiesburg, MS 39401
601-544-4860
FAX: 601-582-2544

*Albert Holifield, Executive Director*

**4856 Jackson Independent Living Center**
300 Capers Avenue
Building 4
Jackson, MS 39203
601-968-5194
FAX: 601-351-1587
TTY:601-351-1585
e-mail: odhh@odhh.org
www.odhh.org

*Denea Smith, Director*
*Timothy Jackson*

Provides services to consumers with severe disabilities.

**4857 LIFE of Central Mississippi**
754 N President Street
Suite 1
Jackson, MS 39202
601-969-4009
800-748-9398
FAX: 601-969-1662
TTY: 800-748-9398
e-mail: lifecen@meta3.net
www.lifeofms.com

*Christy Dunaway, Executive Director*

The purpose of Living Independence For Everyone is to empower people with significant disabilities to be as independent and as fully involved in their communities as they can and want to be.

**4858 LIFE of South Mississippi**
710 Katie Avenue
Hattiesburg, MS 39401
601-583-2108
800-898-8477
FAX: 601-583-1814
e-mail: lifeofms@aol.com
www.lifeofms.com

*Susan Hanks, Executive Coordinator*

The purpose of Living Indepdence For Everyone is to empower people with significant disabilities to be as independent and as fully involved in their communities as they can and want to be.

**4859 Life of North Mississippi: Greenville**
638 Main Street
Apt 111
Greenville, MS 38701
601-332-2220
FAX: 601-332-2261

**4860 Life of North Mississippi: Tupelo**
201 Jefferson Street 1051 Cliff B
Suite D
Tupelo, MS 38801
662-844-6633
FAX: 662-844-6803
TTY:662-844-6633
e-mail: lifetup@netdoor.com

*Michael Sullivan, IL Specialist/Manager*

The purpose of Living Independence For Everyone is to empower people with significant disabilities to be as independent and as fully involved in their communities as they can and want to be.

**4861 Life of South Mississippi: Biloxi**
188c Main Street
Biloxi, MS 39530
228-435-5433
FAX: 228-435-1338
e-mail: lifebil@netdoor.com
www.lifeofms.com

*Christy Dunaway, Executive Director*
*Terri Redding, Independent Living Specialist*

The purpose of Living Independence For Everyone is to empower people with significant disabilities to be as independent and as fully involved in their communities as they can and want to be.

**4862  Mississippi State Independent Living Center**

300 Capers Avenue
Building 1
Jackson, MS  39203                    601-351-1525
                                     FAX: 601-351-1460
                                     www.mdrs.state.ms.us

*Sheila Browning, Director*

Offers peer counseling and disability education.

## Missouri

**4863  Access II Independent Living Center**

611 W Johnson Street
Gallatin, MO  64640                   660-663-2423
                                     FAX: 660-663-2517
                                     TTY:660-663-2663
                                     e-mail: access@accessii.org
                                     www.accessii.org

*Debra Hawman, Executive Director*

The mission of Access II is to remove architectural and attitudinal barriers that limit the independence of persons with disabilities, promote a positive change in attitudes about disability and persons with disabilities, and encourage greater independence for persons with disabilities within our communities. As a Center for Independent Living, Access II is comitted to the provision of a full range of independent living services.

**4864  Bootheel Area Independent Living Services**

PO Box 326
Kennett, MO  63857                    573-888-0002
                                     FAX: 573-888-0708
                                     TTY:573-888-0002
                                     e-mail: tshaw@bails.org
                                     www.bails.org

*Tim Shaw, Executive Director*

BAILS goal is to foster an open, barrier free society flor all people regardless of their disability. BAILS service area is predominantly rural and includes the Southeast Missouri counties of: Dunklin, New Madrid, Pemiscot and Stoddard.

**4865  Coalition for Independence: Missouri Branch Office**

6724 Troost Avenue
Suite408
Kansas City, MO  64131                816-231-7166
                                     FAX: 816-231-7899
                                     e-mail: kolson@cfikc.org
                                     www.cfi-kc.org

*Clark Byron, Executive Director*
*Deborah L Wilmarth, Executive Assistant*

Coalition For Independence (CFI) is to facilitate positive and responsible independence for all people with disabilities by acting as an advocate for individuals with disabilities, providing services, and promoting accessibility and acceptance.

**4866  Council for Extended Care of Mentally Retarded Citizens**

5257 Shaw Avenue
Suite 305
Saint Louis, MO  63110                314-781-4950
                                     FAX: 314-788-0
                                     e-mail: cec@stl.org

*Cynthia Compton, Executive Director*
*Marge Lindhorst, Supporting Living Director*

Services are provided to individuals with mental retardation. Supported living arrangements are located in St. Louis. Group homes and camping services are located in Dittmer, MO.

**4867  Delta Center for Independent Living**

5933 S Highway 94
Suite 107
Weldon Spring, MO  63304              636-926-8761
                                     866-727-3245
                                     FAX: 636-447-0341
                                     e-mail: info@dcil.org
                                     www.dcil.org

*Nancy Murphy, Executive Director*

A non profit corporation which assists people with significant disabilities who want to live more independently.

**4868  Disability Resource Association**

420 S Truman Boulevard
B
Crystal City, MO  63019               636-931-7696
                                     FAX: 636-937-9019
                                     TTY:636-937-9016
          e-mail: dra@disabilityresourcesassociation.org
          www.dissabilityresourceassociatio n.org

*Craig Henning, Executive Director*

**4869  Disabled Citizens Alliance for Independence**

PO Box 675
Viburnum, MO  65566                   573-244-5402
                                     FAX: 573-244-5609
                                     TTY:573-244-5402
                                     e-mail: dcitizen@misn.com

*Richard Blakley, Contact*

**4870  Independent Living Center of Southeast Missouri**

511 Cedar Street
Poplar Bluff, MO  63901               573-686-2333
                                     888-890-2333
                                     888-890-2333
                                     FAX: 573-686-0733
                                     TTY:573-686-2333

*Bruce Lynch, Director*

**4871  Life Skills Foundation**

10176 Corporate Square Drive
Suite 100
Saint Louis, MO 63132                 314-567-7705
                                     FAX: 314-567-6539
                                     TTY:314-802-5299
                                     e-mail: info@lifeskills-stl.org
                                     www.lifeskills-stl.org

*Wendy Buehler, President*
*Katie Smallen, VP, Programs*
*Jocelyn Jones, VP, Operations*

Supports people with developmental and other disabilities to live and work with dignity in the community.

**4872  Midland Empire Resources (MERIL)**

4420 S 40th Street
Building D
Saint Joseph, MO  64503               816-279-8558

*Debbie Merritt, Executive Director*

**4873 Midland Empire Resources for Independent Living (MERIL)**
4420 S 40th Street
St Joseph, MO 64503

816-279-8558
800-242-9326
FAX: 816-279-1550
TTY: 816-279-4943
e-mail: meril@meril.org
www.meril.org

Debra Merritt, Executive Director
Marilyn Finney, Assistant Director
Ian Gewin, PAS Program Director

MERIL is a community based, non residential program, designed to promote independent living and to enhance the quality of life for persons with disabilities by empowering them to control and direct their lives and thus participate actively and independently in society.

**4874 Northeast Independent Living Services**
109 Virginia Street
Hannibal, MO 63401

573-221-8282
877-713-7900
FAX: 573-221-9445
e-mail: neils@neilscenter.org
www.neilscenter.org

Stepahnie O'Bryan, Executive Director

NEILS offers afull range of programs for individuals with a disability and any family members, employers, and/or co-workers with disability concerns.

**4875 On My Own**
111 N Elm Street
Nevada, MO 64772

417-667-7007
FAX: 417-667-6262
e-mail: onmyown@softnet.net

John Klingaman, Executive Director

**4876 Ozark Independent Living**
109 Aid Avenue
West Plains, MO 65775

417-256-8714
888-440-7500
FAX: 417-257-2380
TTY:888-440-7500
e-mail: ozark@townsqr.com
www.ozarkcil.com

Cynthia Moore, Executive Director

OILÆwas created to provide independent living services to persons with disabilities who reside in the following counties in Missouri: Oregon Ozark, Shannon, Wright, Howell, Texas, and Douglas. OIL is non-profit, on-residential supported by grants, donations, and volunteers

**4877 Paraquad**
5240 Oakland Avenue
Saint Louis, MO 63110

314-567-1558
FAX: 314-289-4252
TTY:314-289-4201
e-mail: paraquad@paraquad.org
www.paraquad.org

Robert J Funk, Executive Director

Paraquad looks to empower people with disabilities to increase their independence through choice and opportunity.

**4878 Places for People**
4130 Lindell Boulevard
Saint Louis, MO 63108

314-535-7460
FAX: 314-535-6037
e-mail: contact@placesforpeople.org
www.placesforpeople.org

Mary Broderick, Executive Director

Places for People provides individualized, high quality and effective services to adults with serious and persistent mental disorders to assist them in living, working and socializing responsibility to serve those individuals who rely on public funding.

**4879 RAIL**
1100 Jamison Street
Kirksville, MO 63501

660-627-7245
888-295-6461
FAX: 660-665-9849
e-mail: center@cableone.net

Theresa Myers, Director
Terry Minnix, Executive Director

**4880 Rehabilitation Institute, Kansas City**
3011 Baltimore Avenue
Kansas City, MO 64108

816-751-7900
FAX: 816-751-7982
e-mail: webmaster@rehabkc.org
www.rehabkc.org

Don Harkins, President/CEO
Greg Gille, Chairman
Dick Jarmen, Vice Chairman

The Rehabilitation Institute, is a licensed, non-profit medical and vocational facility, established for the sole purpose of serving children, youth and adults with disabilities. The Institute offers comprehensive inpatient and outpatient medical services for general rehabilitation, spinal cord injuries, head injuries and other disabling conditions. It is also one of the largest vocational rehabilitation centers in Missouri with extensive work evaluation, counseling and placement programs.
*1947*

**4881 Services for Independent Living**
1401 Hathman Place
Columbia, MO 65201

573-874-1646
800-766-1968
TTY:573-874-4121
e-mail: sil@computerland.net
www.silcolumbia.org

Mark Stone, Executive Director
Tarzie Hart, Administrative Director

A non-residential, community-based center for independent living. Provides individualized and group services to persons with severe disabilities in the Mid-Missouri area; works to help people with disabilities achieve their highest potential in independent living and community life.

**4882 Southeastern Missouri Alliance for Independence (SEMO Alliance)**
121 S Broadview Street
Suite 12
Cape Girardeau, MO 63703

573-651-6464
FAX: 573-651-6565
TTY:573-651-6464
e-mail: miki@mail.sadi.org
www.sadi.org

Maryann Gudermuth, Executive Director

SADI is comitted to persons with disabilities to enable them to remain in their own home and community, and not in an institution.

**4883 Southwest Center for Independent Living (SWCIL)**
2864 S Nettleton Avenue
Springfield, MO 65807

417-886-1188
FAX: 417-886-3619
TTY:417-886-1188
e-mail: scil@swcil.org
www.swcil.org

Ann Morris, Executive Director

Provides services, advocacy, and resources for people with any disability in Southwest Missouri.

**4884   Tri-County Center for Independent Living**
1420 Highway 72 E
Rolla, MO  65401
573-368-5933
FAX: 573-368-5991
TTY:573-368-5933
e-mail: vevans@fidnet.com
www.tricountycenter.org

*Victoria Evans-Heitzler, Executive Director*

**4885   West Central Independent Living Solutions**
710d N College Avenue
Warrensburg, MO  64093
660-422-7883
800-236-5175
FAX: 660-422-7895
TTY: 660-422-7894
e-mail: wils@iland.net

*Leanne Weakley, Executive Director*

Works to empower people with disabilities to become more independent by providing independent living skills training, peer support, information and referral and advocacy.

**4886   Whole Person**
114 W Gregory Boulevard
Floor 1
Kansas City, MO  64114
816-561-0304
800-878-3037
FAX: 816-753-8163
TTY: 816-627-2201
e-mail: info@thewholeperson.org
www.thewholeperson.org

*David Robinson, Executive Director*

The Whole Person, assists people with disabilities to live independently and encourages change within the community to expand opportunities for independent living.

---

# Montana

**4887   Living Independently for Today and Tomorrow: Glendrive**
PO Box 621
Glendrive, MT  59330
406-365-4062
888-502-9700
FAX: 406-365-4064
TTY:406-365-4062
e-mail: liftt@midrivers.org
www.liftt.org

*Dave Swanson, Program Director*
*Sue Davidson, IL Specialist*

LIFTT's Independent living program workswith people with disabilities so they can live independently and have access to the community. LIFTT staff, most of whom havge disabilities, serves as mentors to people as they wotk to achieve the goals they have set for themselves.

**4888   Living Independently for Today and Tomorrow**
914 Wyoming Avenue
Billings, MT  59101
406-259-5181
800-669-6319
FAX: 406-259-5259
e-mail: daves@liftt.org
www.liftt.org

*David Swanson, Executive Director*
*Sue Davidson, IL Specialist*

LIFTT's Independent living program works with people with disabilities so they can live independently and have access to the community. LIFTT staff, most of whom have disabilities, serve as mentors to people as they work to achieve the goals they have set for themselves.

**4889   Montana Independent Living Project**
1820 11th Avenue
Helena, MT  59601
406-442-5755
800-735-6457
FAX: 406-442-1612
TTY: 406-442-5755
e-mail: milbob@qwest.net
www.dphhs.mt.gov

*Bob Maffit, Executive Director*

Montana Independent Living Center is located in Helena and provides services to southwestern Montana.

**4890   North Central Independent Living Services**
1120 25th Avenue NE
Black Eagle, MT  59414
406-452-9834
800-823-6245
FAX: 406-453-3940
e-mail: ncils.osborn@sofast.net
www.dphhs.mt.gov

*Tom Osborn, Exective Director*

North Central Independent Living Services is located in Great Falls and provides services from Glacier County across the Hi-Line to the North Dakota border. A satellite office is set up in Glasgow.

**4891   Summit Independent Living Center: Kalipsell**
275 Corporate Drive
Suite 901
Kalispell, MT  59901
406-257-0048
FAX: 406-257-0634
e-mail: fkiewel@summitilc.org
www.summitilc.org

*Mike Mayer, Director*
*Flo Kiewel, County Coordinator/Manager*

Advocacy for people with disabilities.

**4892   Summit Independent Living Center: Hamilton**
316 N 3rd Street
Suite 113
Hamilton, MT  59840
406-363-5242
800-398-9013
FAX: 406-375-9035
e-mail: jperkins@summitilc.org
www.summitilc.org

*Joanne Perkins, Program Coordinator*
*Dawn Gauthier, Program Specialist*

**4893   Summit Independent Living Center: Missoula**
700 SW Higgins Avenue
Suite 101
Missoula, MT  59803
406-728-1630
800-398-9002
FAX: 406-829-3309
e-mail: sbushell@summitilc.org
www.summitilc.org

*John Gabe Skibsrude, President*
*Becky Burke, Peer Advocate Coordinator*
*Jude Monson, Education Coordinator*

Summit ILC helps its consumers continue to live independently in the community through a variety of individual and community services.

## Nebraska

**4894  Center for Independent Living of Central Nebraska**
3204 College Street
Grand Island, NE 68803          308-382-9255
877-400-1004
FAX: 308-384-7832
TTY: 308-382-9255
e-mail: cleach@cilne.org
www.cilne.org

*Chuck Leach, Program Manager*
*Sid Cook, Executive Director*

Offers independent living skills training, peer sharing, information and referral, housing counseling and referral, accessibility and barrier removal consultation including ADA training and technical assistance, driver education and training, assistive technology services including demonstration and equipment loan, and a free lending library of adapted toys and ability switches for children with severe disabilities. Serves all diabilities and all ages.

**4895  League of Human Dignity: Lincoln**
1701 P Street
Lincoln, NE 68508          402-441-7871
888-508-4758
FAX: 402-441-7650
TTY:402-441-7871
e-mail: info@leagueofhumandignity.com
www.leagueofhumandignity.com

*Mike Schafer, CEO*

The mission of the League of Human Dignity is to actively promote the full integration of individuals with disabilities into society. To this end, we will advocate their needs and rights, and provide quality services to involve these persons in becoming and remaining independent citizens.

**4896  League of Human Dignity: Norfolk**
400 Elm Street
Norfolk, NE 68701          402-371-4475
800-843-5785
FAX: 402-371-4625
TTY: 402-371-4475
e-mail: ninfo@leagueofhumandignity.com
www.leagueofhumandignity.com

*Mike Schafer, CEO*
*Linda Carey, Executive Director*

The mission of the League of Human Dignity is to actively promote the full integration of individuals with disabilities into society. To this end, we will advocate their needs and rights, and provide quality services to involve these persons in becoming and remaining independent citizens.

**4897  League of Human Dignity: Omaha**
5513 Center Street
Omaha, NE 68106          402-595-1256
800-843-5784
FAX: 402-595-1410
e-mail: oinfo@leagueofhumandignity.com
www.leagueofhumandignity.com

*Mike Schafer, CEO*
*Bob Gomez, Executive Director*

The mission of the League of Human Dignity is to actively promote the full integration of individuals with disabilities into society. To this end, we will advocate their needs and rights, and provide quality services to involve these persons in becoming and remaining independent citizens.

**4898  Martin Luther Homes of Beatrice**
722 S 12th Street
607
Beatrice, NE 68310          402-223-4066
FAX: 402-223-4951
e-mail: jcampbell@mlhs.com
www.mlhs.com

*Alan Blakestad, Chief Operating Officer*
*Jerry Campbell, Program Director*

Providing a wide array of services to assist individuals and families in achieving positive life goals. Services to persons with disabilities and other special needs include community living options, training and employment options, spiritual growth and development options, training and counseling support.

**4899  Martin Luther Homes of Nebraska**
220 W S 21st Street
York, NE 68467          402-362-2180
FAX: 402-362-2961
www.mosaicinfo.org

*Jobey King, Executive Director*
*Jessica Schoepf, Coordinator*

Providing a wide array of services to assist individuals and families in achieving positive life goals. Services to persons with disabilities and other special needs include community living options, training and employment options, spiritual growth and development options, training and counseling support.

**4900  Panhandle Independent Living Services**
PO Box 2454
Scottsbluff, NE 69363          308-635-7901
FAX: 308-635-7676
e-mail: pils@bbc.net

*Carolyn Foged, Executive Director*

## Nevada

**4901  Carson City Center for Independent Living**
PO Box 3177
Carson City, NV 89702          775-841-2580

*Sandra Coyle, Owner*

**4902  Endeavor**
900 Broadway
Suite 600
New York, NY 10003          212-352-3200
FAX: 212-352-1892
e-mail: louise@endeavor.org
www.endeavor.org

*Louise Hulme, Director*
*Edgar Bronfman, Chairman*
*Linda Rottenburg, Chief Executive Officer*

A community based agency providing training, advocacy, support to persons with disabilities, regardless of age or type or degree of disability, developmental child care, employment services, family respite, and supported living.

**4903  Northern Nevada Center for Independent Living: Fallon**
1919 Grimes Street
Suite B
Fallon, NV 89406          775-423-4900
FAX: 775-423-1399
TTY:775-423-4900
e-mail: nncilf@cccomm.net

*Lisa Erquiaga, Director*

**4904  Northern Nevada Center for Independent Living: Reno**
205 Brinkby Avenue
Reno, NV  89509
775-826-2022
800-633-8324
FAX: 775-826-6040
e-mail: info@medtech-services.com
www.medtech-services.com

*Paul Gowins, Executive Director*
*Rick Graver, Owner*

Community based, not for profit organizaiton providing quality support services that include: independent living skills training, information and referral, peer counseling, and aggressive advocacy for all people with disabilites and disability issues.

**4905  Rural Center for Independent Living**
900 Mallory Way
Suite 112
Carson City, NV  89701
775-841-2580
FAX: 775-267-3969

*Dee Dee Foremaster, Executive Director*

**4906  Southern Nevada Center for Independent Living: North Las Vegas**
3100 E Lake Mead Boulevard
Suite 4A
North Las Vegas, NV 89030
702-649-3822
FAX: 702-649-5022
TTY:702-649-3822
e-mail: sncilnv@aol.com
www.sncil.org

*Mary Evilsizer, Director*
*Rosemarie Meza, Manager*

SNCIL is committed to removing barriers preventing indpendent living by providing services designed to empower people with disabilities.

**4907  Southern Nevada Center for Independent Living: Las Vegas**
6039 Eldora Avenue
Suite H-8
Las Vegas, NV  89146
702-889-4216
800-870-7003
FAX: 702-889-4574
e-mail: info@sncil.org
www.sncil.org

*Mary Evilsizer, Executive Director*
*Alicia Santiago, Administration Assistant*

SNCIL is committed to removing barriers preventing Independent Living by providing services designed to empower people with disabilities.

## New Hampshire

**4908  Granite State Independent Living Foundation**
267 Main Street
Suite 400
Littleton, NH  03561
603-444-0904
800-588-5772
FAX: 603-444-3128
e-mail: clyde.terry@gsil.org
www.gsil.org

*John Irwin, President*
*Ken Maillous, Second Vice President*

GSIL is a statewide non-profit that recognizes the fact that all of us will need some type of support in the course of the lives. GSIL offers tools and resources so that individuals can participate as fully as the choose in their lives, families and communities. Contact the Independent Living Foundation for referrals to living situations.

## New Jersey

**4909  Assistive Technology Advocacy Center (ATAC)**
New Jersey Protection and Advocacy
210 S Broad Street
3rd Floor
Trenton, NJ  08608
609-292-9742
800-922-7233
FAX: 609-777-0187
TTY: 609-633-7106
e-mail: advocate@njpanda.org
www.njpanda.org

*Ellen Catanese, Executive Director*
*Sarah Mitchell, Manager*

Consumer-driven program whose mission is to increase awareness of and improve access to assistive technology for all people with disabilities in the state. Provides information and referral through its 800 telephone number and Web site regarding all aspects of assistive technology.Also provides advocacy saervices.

**4910  Center for Independent Living: Camden**
2600 Mount Ephraim Avenue
Suite 413
Camden, NJ  08104
856-966-0800
FAX: 856-966-0832
TTY:609-966-0830
e-mail: lorraineccilc@aol.com
www.ilusa.com

*Lorraine Culbertson, Executive Director*

**4911  Center for Independent Living: Edison**
Alliance for Disabled in Action
629 Amboy Avenue
Lower Level
Edison, NJ  08837
732-738-4388
FAX: 732-738-4416
TTY:732-738-9644
e-mail: adacil@adacil.org
www.adacil.org

*Richard Ringhof, Executive Director*

Alliance for Disabled in Action is a private, not-for-profit center for independent living serving people in Middlesex, Somerset and Union Counties of New Jersey. ADA's mission is to support and promote choice, self-direction and independent living in the lives of people with disabilities, with the right of individuals to inclusion in the community as the primary goal.

**4912  Center for Independent Living: Long Branch**
279 Broadway
Suite 2
Long Branch, NJ  07740
732-571-4884
FAX: 732-571-4003
TTY:732-571-4878
e-mail: moceans@moceans.org
www.moceans.org

*Richard Garnger, Chairman*
*Pat McShane, Executive Director*
*Stan Soden, Dirirector IL Services*

Offers peer support, disability education and personal assistant services. Serving Monmouth and Ocean Counties with information and referrals, advocacy, peer support and independent living instructions.

**4913    Center for Independent Living: South Jersey**

1200 Delsea Drive
Plaza 47, Suite 6
Westville, NJ 08093

856-853-6490
800-413-3791
FAX: 856-853-1466
TTY: 856-853-7602
e-mail: cilsj@aol.com
cilsj@verizon.net

*Hazel Lee-Briggs, Executive Director*
*Danuta Debicki, Administrator*

Dedicated to providing people with disabilities in Gloucester and Camden counties the opportunity to actively participate in society, to provide freedom of choice, to work, to own a home, raise a family and in general, to participate to the fullest extent in day-to-day activities. The center provides information and referrals, advocacy, peer support, and independent living skills training.

**4914    Center for Independent Living: Tri-County**

955 Myrtle Avenue
Eureka, CA 95501

707-445-8404
877-576-5000
FAX: 707-445-9751
TTY: 707-445-8405
www.tilnet.org

*Chris Jones, Manager*

**4915    Community Action for Independent Living**

One Cornell Parkway
Springfield, NJ 07081

973-564-7557
FAX: 973-467-4255
e-mail: cailnj@aol.com

*Dawn Caris, Program Coordinator*
*Stanley John, Executive Director*

CAIL is dedicated to proiding uality services to individuals with developmental disabilities throughout the state of New Jersey. The programs are designed to develop the person's fullest social capabilities and personal self-realization through the provision of professional services and resources. Serves individuals in New Providence, South Orange, Maplewood, Hackensack and Totowa, NJ.

**4916    Dial: Disabled Information Awareness & Liv ing**

66 Mount Prospect Avenue
Building C-1
Clifton, NJ 07013

973-470-8090
FAX: 973-470-8171
TTY:973-470-2521
e-mail: info@dial-cil.org
www.dial-cil.org

*John Petix Jr, Executive Director*
*Ann Anderson Hunt, Administrative Assistant*

DIAL is a Center for Independent Living, which is part of a statewide network of non-residential centers designed and operated to provide service to individuals with significant disabilities. Services include information adn referral, advocacy, peer support, and independent living skills training. DIAL serves individuals in Passaic and Essex Counties.

**4917    Disabled Advocates Working for Northwest (DAWN)**

400 S Main Street
Suite 3
Wharton, NJ 07885

973-361-5666
888-383-3296
FAX: 973-361-7086
TTY:973-361-6032
e-mail: info@dawncil.org
www.dawncil.org

*Carmela Slivinski, Executive Director*
*Wanda Kasmedo, Program Assistant*

DAWN is the Center for Independent Living serving Morris, Sussex and Warren counties. DAWN empowers people with disabilities to strive for equality and to take control of their own lives by providing the tools that encourage independence and self-advocacy, promoting public awareness of the needs, desires and rights to individuals living with disabilities, and offering community activities that create new experiences and opportunities.

**4918    Family Resource Associates**

35 Haddon Avenue
Shrewsbury, NJ 07702

732-747-5310
FAX: 732-747-1896
e-mail: info@frainc.org
www.frainc.org

*Nancy Phalanukorn, Executive Director*
*Linda Magill, Development Director*

FRA is dedicated to helping children, adolescents and people of all ages with disabilities to reach their fullest potential. FRA also connects individuals to independence through modern therapies and advanced technology. FRA provides direct services to those in the greater Nonmouth/Ocean County area.

**4919    Heightened Independence and Progress: Hack ensack**

131 Main Street
Suite 120
Hackensack, NJ 07601

201-996-9100
FAX: 201-996-9422
TTY:201-966-9424
e-mail: ber@hipcil.org
www.hipcil.org

*Eileen Goff, Executive Director*
*Trish Carney, Finance/Development Director*

HIP empowers people with disabilities to achieve independent living through outreach, advocacy and education.

**4920    Heightened Independence and Progress: Jers ey City**

Hudson County CIL
26 Journal Square
Suite 602
Jersey City, NJ 07306

201-533-4407
FAX: 201-533-4421
TTY:201-413-0521
e-mail: hud@hipcil.org
www.hipcil.org

*Patricia Reilly, Executive Director*
*Trish Carney, Finance/Development Diretor*

Empowering People with Disabilities to Achieve Independent Living through Outreach, Advocacy, and Education.

**4921    Progressive Center for Independent Living**

1262 Whitehorse-Hamilton Road
Building A, Suite 2
Hamilton, NJ 08690

609-581-4500
877-917-4500
FAX: 609-581-4555
TTY: 609-581-4550
e-mail: info@pcil.org
www.pcil.org

*Scott Elliot, Executive Director*

PCIL advocates for the rights of people with disabilities to achieve and maintain independent lifestyles. Through promotion of choice, self-direction and inclusion, PCIL works with people with disabilities and their families to ensure the same freedoms and civil liberties as everyone else.

**4922    Project Freedom**

223 Hutchinson Road
Robbinsville, NJ 08691

609-448-2998
FAX: 609-448-5821
e-mail: projectfreedom1@aol.com
www.projectfreedom.org

*Norman Smith, Director*

Project Freedom is a non-profit organization that develops and operates barrier-free housing to enable individuals with disabilities to live independently. Supportive services such as recreation, training and advocacy are provided. In addition to being a developer of accessible, affordable housing, Project Freedom also provides supportive services, whereby self-directed people with disabilities can live independently in a non-medical environment.

**4923   Resources for Independent Living**

420 i Street
Sacramento, CA  95814
916-446-3074
FAX: 916-446-2443
TTY:856-461-3482
e-mail: monicag@ril-sacramento.org
www.ril-sacramento.org

*Monica Gracechild, Office Manager*

**4924   Total Living Center**

707 White Horse Pike
The Courtyard, Suite B-8
Absecon, NJ 08201
609-645-9547
FAX: 609-813-2318
TTY:609-645-9593
e-mail: info@tlcenter.org
www.tlcenter.org

*Julia T Bonelli, Executive Director*

Total Living Center is a non-profit organization whose mission is to empower individuals with significant disabilities to maximize their potential for independence and productivity, to live as fully as possible within the community, taking responsibility for themselves, and sharing this commitment with others.

# New Mexico

**4925   Ability Center**

715 E Idaho Avenue
Building 3, Suite E
Las Cruces, NM 88001
505-526-5016
800-376-4372
FAX: 505-526-1202
TTY: 505-526-5016
e-mail: freesom@theabilitycenter.org

*Nufie Hernandez, Executive Director*

**4926   CASA**

PO Box 36916
Albuquerque, NM  87176
505-298-7609

*Francis Nye, Director*

Offers peer counseling and information and referral services.

**4927   CHOICES Center for Independent Living**

720 E College Boulevard
Suite 15
Roswell, NM  88201
505-627-6727
800-387-4572
FAX: 505-627-6754
TTY: 505-627-6727
e-mail: lorechamberlin@yahoo.com

*Charles Bailey, Executive Director*

**4928   Independent Living Resource Center**

3033 W 2nd Street N
Wichita, KS  67203
316-942-6300
800-479-6861
FAX: 316-942-2078
e-mail: jweigel@ilrcks.org
www.ilrcks.org

*Judy Weigel, Executive Director*
*La Rae Santiagao, IL Services Manager*

Using a self-help peer approach model, ILRC staff provides services, such as, independent living skills training, peer counseling, individual and systems advocacy, information and referral and service coordination to more than 400 people with disabilities annually in the counties of Bernalillo, Valencia, Cibola, Sandoval, Torrance, Guadalupe and DeBaca. Also provides funding for home modifications, vehicle modifications, assistive technology, adaptive devices, and professional counseling.

**4929   New Mexico Technology Assistance Program**

New Mexico State Department Of Education
435 Saint Michaels Drive
Suite D
Santa Fe, NM 87505
505-954-8533
800-866-2253
FAX: 505-954-8608
TTY: 800-659-4915
e-mail: awinnegar@state.nm.us
www.nmtap.com

*Andy Winnegar, Director*
*Caroll Cadena, Public Contact*

Examines and works to eliminate barriers to obtaining assistive technology in New Mexico. Has established a statewide program for coordinating assistive technology services; is designed to assist people with disabilities to locate, secure, and maintain assistive technology.

**4930   New Vistas**

1121 Alto Street
Santa Fe, NM 87501
505-988-3803
FAX: 505-989-8740
e-mail: rgarcia@newvistas.org
www.newvistas.org

*Ronald Garcia, Executive Director*

The mission of New Vistas is to work in collaboration with individuals with disabilities and families of children with special needs on northern New Mexico to create access to opportunities and to enhance quality of life.

**4931   San Juan Center for Independence**

3535 E 30th Street
Suite 101
Farmington, NM  87402
505-566-5827
877-484-4500
FAX: 505-566-5842
e-mail: swatson@sjci.org
www.sjci.org

*Sherry Watson, Executive Director*
*Tim Carver, CFO*

SJCI is a New Mexico private residential, nonprofit corporation that serves people with disabilities. The purpose of SJCI is to provide a variety of community based, consumer driven service to people with disablties to promote independence, self-residence and intergration into the community.

## New York

**4932  AIM Independent Living Center: Corning**

271 E 1st Street
Corning, NY  14830                    607-962-8225
                                      FAX: 607-937-5125
                                      www.aimcil.org

*Diane Dimuse, Director*
*Diane Muth, Executive Director*

AIM's goal to enable the consumer to live an independent and comfortable lifestyle in the security of their home environment so they may feel dignity and pride in their achievements while controlig their own care.

**4933  AIM Independent Living Center: Elmira**

650 Baldwin Avenue
Suite 125-7
Elmira, NY  14901                     607-733-3718
                                      FAX: 607-733-0180
                                      TTY:607-733-7764
                                      e-mail: eaimoffice@aimcil.com
                                      www.aimcil.com

*Diane Demuth, Executive Director*
*Jill Durkin, Manager*

AIM's goal is to enable the consumer to live an independent and comfortable lifestyle in the security of their home environment so they may feel dignity and pride in their achievements while controling their own care.

**4934  ARISE: Center for Independent Living: Oswe go**

253 E Tenth Street
Oswego, NY  13126                     315-342-4088
                                      FAX: 315-342-4107
                                      TTY:315-342-8689
                                      e-mail: advocate@ariseinc.org
                                      www.ariseinc.org

*Tom McKeown, Executive Director*

ARISE's mission is to work with people of all abilities to create a fair and just community in which everyone can fully participate. It embrace the guiding principles of independent living-that individuals with disabilities have a right to dignity, personal responsibility, and self-determination. ARISE also offers advocacy and support serivces to people of all ages with all types of disabilities.

**4935  ARISE: Center for Independent Living: Syra cuse**

635 James Street
Syracuse, NY  13203                   315-472-3171
                                      FAX: 315-472-9252
                                      TTY:315-479-6363
                                      e-mail: advocate@ariseinc.org
                                      www.ariseinc.org

*Thomas McKeown, Executive Director*
*Ali Stieglitz, Development Director*

Offers peer counseling, attendant care registry, referrals and advocacy services, computer recycling, supported employment, career ladders transition program, universal design center.

**4936  Access to Independence of Cortland County**

26 N Main Street
Cortland, NY  13045                   607-753-7363
                                      FAX: 607-756-4884
                                      e-mail: maryew@odyssey.net
                                      www.cilcortland.org

*Mary Ewing, Executive Director*

An independent living center providing resources and advocacy for all people with disabilities. Services include: peer counseling, individual and systems advocacy, independent living skills training, information and referral.

**4937  Action Toward Independence: Middletown**

130 Dolson Avenue
Suite 35
Middletown, NY  10940                 845-343-4284
                                      FAX: 845-343-5269
                                      TTY:845-343-4282
                                      e-mail: ati@warwick.net
                                      www.actiontowardindependence.org

*Rachel Bartlow-Pappas, Executive Director*
*Joann Seligman-Hargabus, Orange County Director*
*Sarita Castillo-Cuevas, Program Coordinator*

**4938  Action Toward Independence: Monticello**

33 Lakewood Avenue
Monticello, NY  12701                 845-794-4228
                                      FAX: 845-794-4475
                                      e-mail: atisc@warwick.net
                                      web1.in4web.com

*Gilles Malkine, Manager*

**4939  Bergeron Health Care**

15 S 2nd Street
Dolgeville, NY  13329                 585-454-5030
                                      800-371-2778
                                      FAX: 315-429-8862
                                      e-mail: info@adaptivemall.com
                                      www.adaptivemall.com

*Katie Bergeron PT MS, President/COO*

The services at Adaptivemall.com help families find the best equipment to support their children at their highest functioning level. The primary goal is to empower the people with resources that allow you and your child's primary caregivers to make the best decisions to meet your child's unique needs.

**4940  Bronx Independent Living Services**

3525 Decatur Avenue
Bronx, NY  10467                      718-515-2800
                                      FAX: 718-515-2844
                                      e-mail: webmaster@bils.org
                                      www.bils.org

*Susan Attzs-Mendoza, Executive Director*

BILS is a not-for-profit community agency serving people with all kinds of disabilities. The mission is to empower people with disabilities toward living independent lives. BILS assists individuals by providing advocacy, peer counseling, housing information, and independent living training/counseling.

**4941  Brooklyn Center for Independence of the Disabled**

2044 Ocean Avenue
Suite B-3
Brooklyn, NY  11230                   718-998-3000
                                      FAX: 718-998-3743
                                      TTY:718-998-7406
                                      e-mail: advocate@bcid.org
                                      www.bcid.org

*Zainab Jama, Director*
*Maureen Alexander, Executive Director*

Operated by a majority of people with disabilities, BCID is dedicated to guaranteeing the civil rights of people with disabilities. BCID exists to improve the quality of life of brooklyn residents with disabilities thgouh programs that empower them to gain greater control of their lives and achieve full and equal integration into society.

**4942  Buffalo Independent Living Project**

3108 Main Street
Buffalo, NY  14214                    716-836-0822
                                      FAX: 716-835-3967
                                      TTY:716-836-0822
                                      e-mail: info@wnyilp.org
                                      www.wnyilp.org

*Douglas Usiak, President*

A nonprofit, cross-disability, consumer/citizen directed services and advocacy organization for persons with disabilities in Western New York. Its main purpose is to assist and educate persons with disabilities to take control of the events and processes that influence their daily lives. Services include: transportation, peer counseling, interpreters of the deaf, blind/deaf instruction, housing and architectural consultation.

### 4943 Capital District Center for Independence

855 Central Avenue
Suite 110
Albany, NY 12206

518-459-6422
FAX: 518-459-7847
TTY:518-459-6422
e-mail: cdci@nobleharbor.com
www.cdciweb.com

*Laurel Kelley, Executive Director*

One of 37 Independent Living Centers in New York State, the Center is a non-residential, community based organization, which primarily serves Albany and Schenetady Counties. The Center's mission is to assist people with disabilities to acquire self-advocacy skills and by teaching through example, consumers achieve greater control over the direction of their lives.

### 4944 Catskill Center for Independence

6104 State Highway 23
Oneonta, NY 13802

607-432-8000
FAX: 607-432-6907
TTY:607-432-8000
e-mail: ccfi@ccfi.us
www.ccfi.us

*Chris Zachmeyer, Executive Director*
*Edward Lynch, Operations Manager*

One of 37 community-based independent living centers located throughout the state of New York. As an advocacy agency, we provide a vareity of services to people with disabilities, their friends and family members. In addition, we provide advocacy, training, and technical assistance to our community members, organizations, businesses and state and local governments in a variety of disability related areas. Serves Otsego, Delaware and Schoharie counties.

### 4945 Center for Independence of the Disabled of New York

841 Broadway
Suite 301
New York, NY 10003

212-674-2300
FAX: 212-254-5953
TTY:212-674-5619
e-mail: info@cidny.org
www.cidny.org

*Susan Dooha, Executive Director*

CIDNY speaks for everyone who lives with a disability, whether it came at birth, by injury, disease, or during the process of aging. Together, CIDNY works to educate the public, and also advocate for our civil rights and a strong safety net of benefits and services. The staff at CIDNY is also ethnically diverse, with language capacity to assist customers in Spanish, Cantonese, Mandarin, Hindi, Russian, and American Sign Language.

### 4946 Center for Independent Living: Action Towards Independence

2927 Route 6
Slate Hill, NY 10973

914-355-2030
FAX: 845-355-2060
e-mail: ati@warwick.net

*Nancy Horton, Co-Director*
*Margaret Jeffries, Co-Director*

Information, referral, case management, transportation and system and individual advocacy, architectural barrier removal consultations, peer support, independent living skills development and parenting classes.

### 4947 Center for Independent Living: Amsterdam

2540 Riverfront Center
Amsterdam, NY 12010

518-842-3561
FAX: 518-842-0905
TTY:518-842-3593
e-mail: rcil@link.net
www.icil.com

*Ramon Rodriguez, Program Director*

Peer counseling, advocacy, independent living skills training, information and referral services, self-advocacy training, ADA consultation, home and community based services, community education, disability benefits, advisement and more. All programs and services are available in English and Spanish.

### 4948 Center for Independent Living: Queens

140-40 Queens Boulevard
Jamaica, NY 11435

718-658-2526
FAX: 718-658-5295
e-mail: contact@qilc.org
www.qilc.org

*Daniel Aliberti, Executive Director*

QILC is a consumer directed organization whose mission is to empower people with disabilities to take control of their own lives. QILC provides information and refferal to resources within the community, which persons with disabilities can utilize to achieve their social, vocational, and personal goals. QILC also provides direct assistance to individuals with disabilities in the areas of housing, employment, benefits counseling, group and peer counseling, and voter registration.

### 4949 Center for Independent Living: Rochester

1641 East Avenue
Rochester, NY 14610

585-442-6470
FAX: 585-271-8558
TTY:585-442-6470
e-mail: bdarling@rcil.org
www.rcil.org

*Todd Eggert, Executive Director*
*Mary Willy, Administrative Assistant*

RCIL looks to empower people with disabilities to self-advocate, to live independently and to enhance the quality of community life. The services and programsare primarily of an advocacy nature (both individual and systems). RCIL seeks to overcome the barriers faced by people with disabilities who choose to live independently.

### 4950 DD Center/St Lukes: Roosevelt Hospital Center

St Lukes Roosevelt
1000 10th Avenue
New York, NY 10019

212-523-3179
FAX: 212-523-6241

*Steven Wolf, Director*
*Farooq Chaudry, MD*

### 4951 Directions in Independent Living

512 W State Street
Olean, NY 14760

716-373-4602
FAX: 716-373-4604
TTY:716-373-4602
e-mail: oleanilc@yahoo.com
www.nysilc.org

*Leonard Liguori, Executive Director*

### 4952 Finger Lakes Independence Center

215 Fifth Street
Ithaca, NY 14850

607-272-2433
FAX: 607-272-0902
TTY:607-272-2433
e-mail: flic@clarityconnect.com
www.fliconline.org

*Lenore Schwager, Executive Director*

FLIC assists all people with disabilities, their families and friends to promote independence and make informed decisions in pursuit of their goals. The servides provided are free of charge, and services are primarily served to residents of Topkins, Cortland and Schuley counties.

**4953    Freedom House**
Barrier Free Living
270 E 2nd Street
New York, NY 10009                    212-677-6668
                                  FAX: 212-539-1526
                                  TTY:212-677-6668
                            e-mail: paulf@bflnyc.org
                                      www.bflnyc.org

*Daniel O Connor, Chairman*
*Paul B Feuerstein, President/CEO*

Services to disabled adults include: shelter for homeless disabled men and women; non-residential domestic violence intervention counseling; homeless outreach; mental health counseling. House location kept confidential.

**4954    Genesee Region Independent Living Center**
61 Swan Street
Batavia, NY 14020                     585-343-4524
                                  FAX: 585-343-6656
                                  TTY:716-343-4524
                                e-mail: grilc@bfn.org
                                      grilc.bfn.org

*Ann Bell, Executive Director*

GRILC offers a caring environment. GRILC assists in peer counseling, advocacy, benefits advisement, support groups, transportation, architectural barrier consultation, independent living skills instruction, and many other services.

**4955    Glens Falls Independent Living Center**
71 Glenwood Avenue
Queensbury, NY 12804                  518-792-3537
                                  FAX: 518-792-0979
                                  TTY:518-792-0505
                            e-mail: gfilc@adelphia.net
                                      www.gfilc.com

*Karen Thayer, Executive Director*
*Anna Livingston, Assistant Director*

The focus at the Glens Falls Independent Living Center is to assist individuals with disabilities to beconme independent empowered self-advocates. GFILC works within the community to remove physical and attitudinal barriers that stand in the way of independence. The Center will promote the comcepts of self-determination and person centered planning for work, leisure and life.

**4956    Harlem Independent Living Center**
289 Saint Nicholas Avenue
21
New York, NY 10027                    212-369-2371
                                      800-673-2371
                                  FAX: 212-222-7199
                            e-mail: harlemilc@aol.com

*Christina Curry, Executive Director*
*Edward Randolph, Intake Coordinator*

A non-profit agency that advocates for people with disabilities by assisting with the application process of housing, benefits, etc. Our services are free of charge.
            *Monthly*

**4957    Herkimer Center for Independent Living**
Steuben Center
401 E German Street, 2nd Floor
Herkimer, NY 13350                    315-866-7245
                                  FAX: 315-866-7280
                                  TTY:315-866-7246
                                      www.rcil.com

*Burt Danovitz, Executive Director*

RCIL's varied services are consumer-driected. With expertise in law and services assistance is available not only to persons with disabilities, but the community at large. Advocacy, independent living skills training, peer counseling information and referral, benefits advisement and a coalition of support services to persons with Alzheimer's disease and related dementias and to the families, caregivers and professionals involved with them.

**4958    Hudson Valley Center for Independent Livin g**
49 4th Street
Troy, NY 12180                        518-274-0701
                                      518-828-6293
                                  FAX: 518-274-7944
                                  TTY:518-828-6293
                              e-mail: admin@ilchv.org
                                      www.ilchv.org

*Denise Figueroa, Executive Director*
*Karen Garofallou, Director Programs/Services*

**4959    Long Island Center for Independent Living**
3601 Hempstead Turnpike
Suites 208 & 500
Levittown, NY                         516-796-0144
                                  FAX: 516-520-1247
                                  TTY:516-796-0135
                               e-mail: licil@aol.com
                                      www.licil.net

*Patricia Moore, Director*
*Michael Dc, Owner*

LICIL is committed to the empowerment of consumers with disabilities. LICIL staff functions as ambassadors to the belief that individuals with disabilities have a responsibility to take an active role in their own lives and self determined view of their futures.

**4960    Massena Center for Independent Living**
156 Center Street
Massena, NY 13662                     315-764-9442
                                  FAX: 315-764-9464
                                  TTY:315-764-9442
                              e-mail: milc@northnet.org

*Jeff Reifensnyder, Executive Director*

Provides a variety of non-residential direct services as well as educating the public through community awareness campaigns. Also seeks to address the current appropriate unmet needs of persons experiencing a disability - primarily in St Lawrence and Franklin Counties.

**4961    Minority Outreach Project**
200 Hamilton Avenue
White Plains, NY 10601                914-682-3926
                                  FAX: 914-682-8518
                                      www.wilc.org

*Joseph Drazo, Executive Director*

**4962    Nassau County Office for the Physically Challenged**
1550 Franklin Avenue
Mineola, NY 11501                     516-571-3972
                                  FAX: 516-571-6150

*Don Dreyer, Director*

This agency serves as the ADA compliance coordinating office for all Nassau County governmental facilities, programs and services. It also serves in an advisory capacity to local, regional and national policy-making organizations, planning committees and legislative bodies and conducts advocacy as well as direct programs and services to enhance inclusion by people with disabilities to employment, consumerism and transportation.

**4963  Newburgh Center for Independent Living**
5 Washington Terrace
Newburgh, NY  12550                845-565-1162
                                   FAX: 845-565-0567
                                   TTY:845-565-0337
               e-mail: vflorio@myindependentliving.org
                       www.myindependentliving.org

*Robert Browning, Bresident*
*Douglas J Ewvey, Executive Director*
*Arnie Abrams, Assoc Director, Development*

A consumer directed, cross-disability organization dedicated to
enhancing the quality of life for persons with disabilities

**4964  Niagara Frontier Center for Independent Living**
1522 Main Street
Niagara Falls, NY  14305           716-284-2452
                                   FAX: 716-284-0829
                                   TTY:716-284-2452
                      e-mail: kpautler@nfcil.org

*Kathleen Pautler, Executive Director*

Offers peer counseling, referrals and disability education.

**4965  North Country Center for Independent Livin g**
102 Sharron Avenue
Plattsburgh, NY  12901             518-563-9058
                                   FAX: 518-563-0292
                                   TTY:518-563-0292
                e-mail: andrew@ncci-online.com
                        www.ncci-online.com

*Andrew Pulrang, Executive Director*
*Mike Gagnier, Assistant Director*

Center for Independent Living serving Clinton and Essex counties, New York. Services include: Information and Referral, Independent Living Skills Training, Advocacy, and Peer
Counseling

**4966  Northern Regional Center for Independent Living:
Lowville**
7396 Turin Road
Lowville, NY  13367                315-376-8696
                                   800-585-8703
                                   FAX: 315-376-3404
                                   TTY: 315-785-8704
                    e-mail: aileeng@nrcil.net
                            www.nrcil.org

*Aileen Martin, Executive Director*
*Karenbolive Martin, Manager*

**4967  Northern Regional Center for Independent Living:
Watertown**
210 Court Street
Suite 107
Watertown, NY  13601               315-785-8703
                                   800-585-8703
                                   FAX: 315-785-8612
                                   TTY: 315-785-8704
                   e-mail: michaelg@nrcil.net
                           www.nrcil.net

*Brenda Canpany, Executive Director*

**4968  Options for Independence: Auburn**
75 Genesee Street
Auburn, NY  13021                  315-255-3447
                                   FAX: 315-255-0836
                                   TTY:315-255-3447
            e-mail: options@optionsforindependence.org
                    www.optionsforindependence.org

*Guy Thomas Cosentino, Executive Director*
*Crystal Purcell, Program Director*

Options for Independence is and Independent Living Center
which assists people with disabilities to gain opportunities,
make their own decision, pursue activities and become part of
comunity life. also provided is a variety of services to all people
with disabilities, their families and friends in Cayuga and Seneca Counties.

**4969  Options for Independence: Seneca Falls**
55 Fall Street
Seneca Falls, NY  13148            315-568-2724
                                   FAX: 315-568-1844
                       www.optionsforindependence.org

*Guy Thomas Constentino, Executive Director*
*Crystal Purcell, Program Director*

Options for Independence is an independent Living Center
which assists people with disabilities to gain opportunities,
make their own decisions, pursue activities and become part of
community life. Also provided is a variety of services to all people with disabilities, their families and friends in Cayuga and
Seneca Counti8es.

**4970  Resource Center for Accessible Living**
592 Ulster Avenue
Kingston, NY  12401                845-331-0541
                                   FAX: 845-331-2076
                                   TTY:845-331-8680
                      e-mail: rcal@hvc.rr.com
                              www.rcal.org

*Susan J Hoger, Executive Director*
*Suzanne de Beaumont, Assistant Executive Director*

RCAL is a non-profit, community based service and advocacy
run by and for people with any type of disability. RCAL is
dedicatd to assisting and empowering individuals, of all ages, to
live independently and participate in all aspects of community
life.

**4971  Rockland Independent Living Center**
230 N Main Street
Spring Valley, NY  10977           845-426-0707
                                   FAX: 845-426-0989
                                   TTY:845-426 1180
                        e-mail: mail@rilc.org
                                www.rilc.org

*Cathrine Oca, Executive Director*
*Jill Nizen, Vice President*

RILC provides services, programs and advocacy for all people
in Rockland County, New York who have disabilities so that
they may pursue lifestyles of their choice.

**4972  SILO: Cental Islip**
3180 Express Drive S
Central Islip, NY  11749           516-348-0207
                                   FAX: 516-348-0262

**4973  SILO: Hauppauge**
140 Fell Court
Suite 116
Hauppauge, NY  11788               631-348-0207
                                   FAX: 631-348-0262
                                   TTY:631-348-7655
                   e-mail: eahern@suffolkilc.org

*Edward Ahern, Director*

**4974  Saratoga County Options for Independent Living**
418 Geyser Road
Suite 2
Ballston Spa, NY  12020            518-884-4055
                                   FAX: 518-584-1195
                                   TTY:518-584-4752

*Teena Willard, Advocate*
*Dawn Lincoln, Advocate*
*Karen Thayer, Executive Director*

**4975 Southern Tier Independence Center**

24 Prospect Avenue
Binghamton, NY 13901

607-724-2111
FAX: 607-772-3600
TTY:607-724-2111
e-mail: stic@stic-cil.org
www.stic-cil.org

Maria Dibble, Executive Director
Frank Pennisi, Accessibility Services

STIC provides assistance and services to all people with disabilities of all ages to increase their independence in all aspects of integrated community life. STIC also serves their families and friends, and businesses, agencies, and goverments to enable them to better meet the needs of people with disabilities, and finally STIC educates and influences the community in pursuit of full inclusion of people with disabilities.

**4976 Southwestern Independent Living Center**

843 N Main Street
Jamestown, NY 14701

716-661-3010
FAX: 716-661-3011
TTY:716-661-3012
e-mail: marie@ilc-jamestown-ny.org
www.ilc-jamestown-ny.org

Marie T Carrubba, Executive Director
Linda Rumbaugh, Independent Living Specialist

Offers disability education, advocacy and information on accessible housing, wheelchair or acessible transportation, interpreting services, brulling, IL skills training, peer support.

**4977 Staten Island Center for Independent Living**

470 Castleton Ave
Staten Island, NY 10301

718-720-9016
FAX: 718-720-9664
e-mail: dorothy.doran@verizon.net

Dorothy Doran, Executive Director

**4978 Suffolk Independent Living Organization (SILO)**

745 Waverly Avenue
Holtsville, NY 11742

631-654-8007
FAX: 631-654-8077
TTY:631-654-8076
e-mail: eahern@suffolkilc.org
www.suffolkilc.org

Edward Ahern, Executive Director

**4979 Taconic Resources for Independence**

82 Washington Street
Suite 214
Poughkeepsie, NY 12601

845-452-3913
FAX: 845-485-3196
TTY:845-485-8110
e-mail: trionline@taconicresources.net
www.taconicresources.net

Cynthia Siore, Executive Director
Stephanie Jaczko, Assistant Director

A center for independent living, benefits advisement information, and referral, advocacy, independent living skills, peer counseling, parent advocacy, sign language interpreters.

**4980 Visions/Services for the Blind & Visually Impaired**

500 Greenwich Street
New York, NY 10013

212-625-1616
888-245-8333
FAX: 212-219-4078
e-mail: info@visionsvcb.org
www.visionsvcb.org

Nancy Miller, Executive Director
Betsy Fabricant, Dir Rec/Residential Programs
Diane Weiss, Dir Rehab/Community Outreach

A vision rehabilitation and social service agency promoting the independence of people of all ages who are blind or visually impaired. Free community center, vision rehabilitation, and camp programs.

**4981 Westchester County Independent Living Center**

200 Hamilton Avenue
White Plains, NY 10601

914-682-3926
FAX: 914-682-8518
TTY:914-682-0926
www.wilc.org

Joseph Bravo, Executive Director
Mildred Caballero-Ho, Deputy Executive Director

One of the Independent Living Centers in New York States, the WILC has a long hisotry of providing services designed, directed, and in most cases delivered by individuals with a wide range of disabilities.

**4982 Westchester Disabled on the Move**

984 N Broadway
Suite L-01
Yonkers, NY 10701

914-968-4717
FAX: 914-968-6137
e-mail: info@wdom.org
www.wdom.org

Melvyn R Tanzman CSW, Executive Director
Scott Smith, Program Director

WDOM empowers people with disabilities to control their own lives; advocates for civil rights and a barrier free society; encourages people with disabilities to participate in the political process; educates government, business, other entities, and a society as a whole to understand, accept, and accommodate people with disabilities; creates an environment that inspires self-respect

**4983 Wiswall Center for Independent Living**

71 Glenwood Avenue
Queensbury, NY 12804

518-793-5863
FAX: 518-745-7389
e-mail: info@crandalllibrary.org
www.crandalllibrary.org

Christine McDonald, Library Director
Lynn Osterberg, Manager

## North Carolina

**4984 Center for Accessible Housing**

North Carolina State University
PO Box 8613
Raleigh, NC 27695

919-515-2011
FAX: 919-515-3023
e-mail: cahd@ncsu.edu
www.ncsu.edu

James Oblinger, Manager

Established in 1989, the Center improves the quality and availability of housing for people with disabilities. The center provides assistance and information to individuals and industry through research, collaborative efforts with manufacturers, training and information services.

**4985 Disability Awareness Network**

609 Country Club Drive
Suite C
Greenville, NC 27834

252-355-5272
FAX: 252-353-5160
e-mail: DAWNpittco@aol.com

Marty Silverthorne, Contact

Information and referral for diabled persons; peer counseling for diabled persons; advocacy on ADA issues; independent living skills and training.

**4986  Disability Rights & Resources**
5801 Executive Center Drive
Suite 101
Charlotte, NC 28212
704-537-0550
FAX: 704-566-0507
www.disability-rights.org

*Niki Stamps, Peer Advocate*
*Julie Sain, Executive Director*
*Steve McCallum, Peer Advocate*

Offers information and referrals, peer counseling for people with disabilities, advocacy and independent living skills classes. DR&R helps people with disabilities achieve and maintain their independence in the community.

**4987  Joy: A Shabazz Center for Independent Living**
235 N Greene Street
Greensboro, NC  27401
336-272-0501
FAX: 336-272-0575
TTY:336-272-0501
e-mail: aaron.shabazz@shabazzcenter.org
www.shabazzcenter.org
Benita Williams, Deputy Director

**4988  Live Independently Networking Center**
PO Box 1135
Newton, NC  28658
828-464-0331
FAX: 828-464-7375
TTY:828-464-2838
e-mail: linc@twave.net
www.linconline.org

*Donavon Kirby, Deputy Director*

Private, nonprofit, federally funded center for independent living located in Western North Carolina.

**4989  Live Independently Networking Center: Hickory**
2830 16th Street NE
Hickory, NC  28601
828-464-0331
FAX: 828-464-7375

**4990  Pathways for the Future**
525 Mineral Springs Drive
Sylva, NC  28779
828-631-1167
FAX: 828-631-1169
e-mail: pathways@dnet.net
www.pathwayscil.org

*Barbara Davis, Executive Director*
*Gale Anglin, Assistant Director*

Pathways covers the counties of Jackson, Swain, Haywood, Cherokee, Graham, Clay, and Macon. Pathways is dedicated to increasing independence, changing attitudes, promoting equal acess and building a peer support network through the use of community education, independent living services and advocacy.

**4991  Western Alliance Center for Independent Living**
30-B London Road
Asheville, NC  28803
828-274-0444
FAX: 828-274-4461
e-mail: ashcilnc@bellsouth.net
www.westernalliance.org

*Bart Floyd, Site Coordinator*
*Barbara Davis, Executive Director*

Core: Information and Referral, Peer Counseling, Independent Living Skills Training and Advocacy. Counties served: Buncombe, Henderson, Madison, McDowell, Polk, Rutherford and Transylvania.

## North Dakota

**4992  Center for Independent Living: Fargo**
2701 9th Avenue SW
Fargo, ND  58103
701-478-0459
FAX: 701-478-0510
TTY:701-478-0459
e-mail: donenes@freedomrc.org
www.freedomrc.org

*Nate Aalgaard, Executive Director*

Freedom Resource Center is an independent non-profit organization, serving people of all ages and all disabilities. The mission of Freedom Resource Center is to work toward equality and inclusion for people with disabilities through programs of empowerment, community education and systems change.

**4993  Dakota Center for Independent Living: Dickinson**
40 1st Avenue W
Dickinson, ND  58601
701-483-4363
800-489-5013
FAX: 701-483-4361
TTY: 701-483-4363
e-mail: wendydcil@ndsupernet.com
www.dakotacil.org

*Wendy Sundheim, Program Coordinator*

**4994  Dakota Center for Independent Living: Bism arck**
3111 E Braodway Avenue
Bismarck, ND  58501
701-222-3636
800-489-5013
FAX: 701-222-0511
TTY: 701-222-3636
www.dakotacil.org

*Royce Schultze, Executive Director*
*Diana Medicine Stone, Sr Independent Living Counselor*

DCIL advocates for community based services and training opportunities that assist people with disabilities to live more independently. Outrech services are provided in eighteen south west and south central N.D. counties, and on the Standing Rock and the southern part of the Fort Berthold Native American reservations

**4995  Dakota Center for Independent Living: Mino t**
300 3rd Avenue SW
Suite F
Minot, ND  58701
701-839-4724
800-377-5114
FAX: 701-838-1677
TTY: 800-839-6561
e-mail: agency@independencecil.org
www.independencecil.org

*Stephen Repnow, Executive Director*

A resource center for independent living.

**4996  Fraser**
2902 University Drive S
Fargo, ND  58103
701-232-3301
FAX: 701-237-5775
e-mail: fraser@fraserltd.org
www.fraserltd.org

*Sandra Layland, Executive Director*
*David Laske, Treasurer*

## Ohio

**4997 Ability Center of Defiance**
1935 East Secomd Street
Suite C
Defiance, OH 43512
419-782-5441
FAX: 419-782-9231
TTY:419-782-5441
e-mail: knoe@abilitycenter.org
www.abilitycenter.org

*Kristina Noe, Executive Director*

**4998 Ability Center of Greater Toledo**
5605 Monroe Street
Sylvania, OH 43560
419-885-5733
866-885-5733
FAX: 419-882-4813
TTY: 419-885-5733
e-mail: sitemail@abilitycenter.org
www.abilitycenter.org

*Tim Harrington, Executive Director*
Ability Center is a non-profit independent living center in Northwest Ohio. The Center serves Defiance, Fulton, Henry, Lucas, Ottawa, Williams and Wood, with Satelitte offices in Defiance and Otawa counties. The mission is to assist people with disabilities to live their lives as idependently as possible. Services provided are: advocacy, community living and information, recreation inclusion, and youth and independent living skills.

**4999 Access Center for Independent Living**
35 S Jefferson Street
Dayton, OH 45402
937-341-5202
FAX: 937-341-5217
TTY:937-341-5218
e-mail: webmaster@acils.com
www.acils.com

*Alan Cochrun, Executive Director*
Offers peer counseling, disability education and other services to the community.

**5000 Fairfield Center for Disabilities and Cerebral Palsy**
South Eastern Ohio Center for Independent Living
681 E Sixth Avenue
Lancaster, OH 43130
740-653-5501
FAX: 740-653-6046
e-mail: fcdcp@spcglobal.net
www.fcdcp.org

*Edwin Payne, Board Secretary/Manager*
Adult Day Program and Transportation.

**5001 Help Foundation**
3622 Prospect Avenue E
Cleveland, OH 44115
216-432-4810
FAX: 216-361-2608
e-mail: dwillis@helpfoundationinc.org
www.helpfoundationinc.org

*Daniel J Rice, Executive Director*
*Patricia Schwartz, Chief Program Officer*
Help Foundation is a social service agency, serving people with mental retardation and developmental disabilities. Provides services to people in northeast Ohio including Cuyahoga, Geauga, Lake and Summit Counties.

**5002 Independent Living Center of Central Ohio**
670 Morrison Road
Suite 200
Gahanna, OH 43230
614-892-0390
800-566-7788
FAX: 614-861-0392
e-mail: info@ohiosilc.org
www.ohiosilc.org

*Brenda Curtiss, Executive Director*
*Kay Grier, Office Manager*
Committed to promoting a philosophy of consumer control, peer support, self-help, self-determination, equal acess, and individual and systems advocacy, in order to maximize leadership, empowerment, independence, productivity and to support full inclusion and integration of individuals with disabilities into the mainstream of American society.

**5003 Linking Employment Ability Potential: Independent Living Center**
2100 N Ridge Road
Elyria, OH 44035
440-324-3444
FAX: 440-324-2112
TTY:440-324-3444
e-mail: edanevich@leapinfo.org
www.leapinfo.org

*Elsie Danevich, Program Director*
LEAP is consumer directed to ensure a society of equal opportunity for all persons, regardless of disability

**5004 Mid-Ohio Board for an Independent Living Environment (MOBILE)**
690 S High Street
Columbus, OH 43206
614-443-5936
FAX: 614-443-5954
TTY:614-443-5957
e-mail: bev@mobileonline.org
www.mobileonline.org

*Beverly Rackett, Executive Director*
A non-profit Center for Independent Living directed by persons with disabilities. MOBILE was founded on principles that affirm the right of persons with disabilities to live their lives with a full measure of liberty and human dignity.

**5005 Rehabilitation Service of North Central Ohio**
270 Sterkel Bouleard
Mansfield, OH 44907
419-756-1133
800-589-1133
FAX: 419-756-6544
e-mail: info@therehabcenter.org
www.therehabcenter.org

*James Schaum, President/CEO*
*Linda Williams, VP Medical Rehab*
*Dan Loguda, VP Vocational Rehab*
Private nonprofit organization providing coordinated, team-oriented comprehensive outpatient rehabilitation services to children and adults of all ages. Serves 8 counties in N/C Ohio. Four umbrella areas of service include medical rehabilitation services, vocational rehabilitation services, behavioral health service and drug and alcohol addiction services. Medical rehabilitation services include physical therapy, occupational therapy, speech therapy and audiology.

**5006 Samuel W Bell Home for Sightless**
3775 Muddy Creek Road
Cincinnati, OH 45238
513-241-0720
FAX: 513-241-1481
e-mail: swbellhome@fuse.net
www.samuelbell.org

*Miles Hoff, Executive Director*
*Holly Hoeffer, Director of Residents*
Offers a residential home for the totally blind and legally blind adults, male and female.

**5007 Services for Independent Living**
25100 Euclid Avenue
Suite 105
Cleveland, OH 44117          216-731-1529
                            FAX: 216-731-3083
                            TTY:216-731-1529
                            e-mail: sil@sil-oh.org
                            www.silcolumbia.org

*Linda Hildebrand, Executive Director*
*Lynn Hildebrand, Manager*

Offers support ADA, consultation and education, advocacy, transitional education services, independent living skills training, information and referrals.

**5008 Society for Equal Access: Independent Living Center**
801 Anola Avenue
Suite B
Dover, OH 44622          330-343-3668
                        888-213-4452
                        FAX: 330-343-3721
                        TTY:330-602-2557
                        e-mail: ilc@tusco.net
                        www.seailc.org

*Dianne Rennicker, Executive Director*

The Society works with individuals to become more independent. Our agency assists with peer support, advocacy, information and referral, independent living skills and transportation. Our goal is to move those with challenges in the direction ofn independence.

**5009 Tri-County Independent Living Center**
955 Myrtle Avenue
Eureka, CA 95501          707-445-8404
                         877-576-5000
                         FAX: 707-445-9751
                         TTY: 707-445-8405
        www.rehab.cahwnet.gov/pulic/contacts/htm

*Chris Jones, Manager*

**5010 United Cerebral Palsy of Central Ohio**
440 Industrail Mile Road
Columbus, OH 43228          614-279-0109
                           FAX: 614-279-2527
                           www.ucpofcentralohio.org

*Charles Curley, President/Executive Committee*
*Kathy Streblo, Executive Director*

A private, non-profit agency whose mission is to provide an enviroment where people with disabilities and aging conditions recieve individualized programs and support services.

## Oklahoma

**5011 Ability Resources**
823 S Detroit Avenue
Suite 110
Tulsa, OK 74120          918-592-1235
                        FAX: 918-592-5651
                        www.ability-resources.org

*Carla Lawson, Executive Director*
*Debby Newman, Office Manager*

Offers disability education, peer counseling and referrals, assistive technology lending library, job readiness training, employment placement, nursing home outreach, ADA training, technical assistance, and benefits counseling.

**5012 Green County Independent Living Resource Center**
4100 SE Adams Road
Suite C106
Bartlesville, OK 74006          918-335-1314
                               800-559-0567
                               FAX: 918-333-1814
                               TTY: 800-559-0567
                        e-mail: vilesjudy@cableone.net

*Teresa Newton, IL Skills Specialist*
*Judy Biles, Executive Director*
*Carla Potts, IL Skills Specialist/Bookkeeper*

Independent living skills training, information and referrals, advocacy, a loan library of adaptive equipment and books. Services available to all individuals with disabilities and their family members who reside in Northeastern Oklahoma.

**5013 Oklahomans for Independent Living**
321 South 3rd
Suite 2
McAlester, OK 74501          918-426-6220
                            FAX: 918-426-3245
                            TTY:800-568-6821
                        e-mail: mikew@tulsaconnect.com
                            www.oil.cwis.net

*Mike Ward, Executive Director*

OIL encourages individuals of all ages, with all types of disabilities to increase: personal dependence; empowerment and self determiation; and ful integration and participation in their work, community, school and home activities.

**5014 Progressive Independence**
121 N Porter Road
Norman, OK 73071          405-321-3203
                         FAX: 405-321-7601
                         TTY:405-321-2942
                         e-mail: heathera@progind.org
                            www.progind.org

*Jeff Hughes, Executive Director*

Preovides four cores services of Information & Referral, Individaul& Systems Advocacy, Peer Counseling, and Skills Training; in addition, offers accessible computer lab, short term DME loans, ande benefits counseling for SSI/SSDI.

**5015 Sandra Beasley Independent Living Center**
705 S Oakwood Road
Enid, OK 73703          580-237-8508
                       FAX: 580-233-6403
                       TTY:508-237-8508
                       e-mail: sbilcenter@coxinet.net
                       www.members.tripod.com/lew_3

*Frieda Kliewer, Executive Director*

An independent living center which offers independent living skills training, peer counseling, attendant care registry, ADA consultation, advocacy services and an equipment Loan Closet.

## Oregon

**5016 Central Oregon Resources for Independent Living**
20436 Clay Pigeon Court
PO Box 9425
Bend, OR 97708          541-388-8103
                       FAX: 541-388-1226
                       TTY:541-388-8103
                       e-mail: coril@coril.org
                            www.coril.org

*Glenn VanCise, Executive Director*

CORIL empowers people with disabilities to maximize their independence, productivity and inclusio in community life. CORIL envisions a society where all people have the opportunity to develop their full capabilities with independence, productivity and more meaningful involvment in local community events and activities.

### 5017 Columbia Gorge Center

2940 Thomsen Road
Hood River, OR 97031
541-386-3520
866-424-2669
FAX: 541-386-7788
e-mail: cgc@gorge.net
www.cgc-direct.com

*Patty Elkins, Executive Director*
*C J Webb, Client Services Coordinator*

CGC assists people with disabilities or other barriers to employment or community living to: achieve control of their lives; attain competence in community and employment; an participate in satisfying lifestyles based on the same aspirations as well as citizens.

### 5018 Eastern Oregon Center for Independent Living

1021 SW 5th Avenue
Ontario, OR 97914
541-889-3119
866-248-8369
FAX: 541-889-4647
e-mail: eocil@eocil.org
www.eocil.org

*Kirt Toombs, Chief Executive Officer*

EOCIL is a nonprofit community based resource and advocacy center that promotes independent living and equal access for all persons with disabilities. EOCIL serves consumers in the counties of: Baker, Gilliam, Grant, harney, Malheur, Morrow, Umatilla, Union, Wallowa and Wheeler.

### 5019 HASL Independent Abilities Center

1252 Redwood Avenue
Grants Pass, OR 97527
541-479-4275
800-758-4275
FAX: 541-479-7261
TTY: 541-479-3588
e-mail: haslstaff@yahoo.com
www.haslonline.org

*Randy Samuelson, Executive Director*

To promote public awareness of the special needs and legal rights of individuals with cross-disabilities; to facilitate their integration into society and provide support through advocacy, peer counseling, skills training and information and referral to encourage independence.

### 5020 Independent Living Resources

2410 SE 11th Avenue
Portland, OR 97214
503-232-7411
FAX: 503-232-7480
TTY:503-232-8404
e-mail: ilrpdx@qwest.net
www.ilr.org

*Barry Quamee, Executive Director*

ILR looks to promote the philosophy of Independent Living by creating opportunities, encouraging choices, advancing equal access, and furthering the level of independence for all people with disabilities

### 5021 Laurel Hill Center Independent Living Program

2145 Centennial Plaza
Eugene, OR 97401
541-485-6340
FAX: 541-345-9218
e-mail: info@laurel.org
www.laurel.org

*Liz Cawood, Member of the Board*
*Mary Alice Brown, Executive Director*
*Dee Wirak, Director of Rehabilitation*

Laurel Hill Center provides nationally recognized rehabilitation services in Lane County, Oregon for people with severe and persistent mental illness. The Center is committed to providing individuals with mental illness hope and recovery process in rebuilding their lives, developing skills and increasing independence.

### 5022 Oregon Commission for the Blind

535 SE 12th Avenue
Portland, OR 97214
971-673-1588
888-202-5463
FAX: 971-673-1570
TTY:971-673-1577
e-mail: ocbmail@state.or.us
www.cfb.state.or.us

*Frank Armstrong, President*
*Pat Donell, Executive Director*

Oregon Commission for the Blind's mission is to assist blind Oregonians in making informed choices and decisions to achieve full inclusion and integration in society through employment, independent living, and socila self-sufficiency.

### 5023 Progressive Options

657 SW Coast Highway
Newport, OR 97365
541-574-0384
FAX: 541-574-1927
TTY:541-574-1927
e-mail: progop541@yahoo.com
www.progressive-options.org

Progressive Options seeks to provide free services and support to people with disabilities of all kinds to help them achieve and maintain maximum independence and self-sufficiency in Lincoln County and surrounding areas in Oregon.

### 5024 SPOKES Unlimited

415 Main Street
Klamath Falls, OR 97601
541-883-7547
FAX: 541-885-2469
TTY:541-883-7547
e-mail: info@spokesunlimited.org
www.spokesunlimited.org

*Tami Martin, Director*
*Wendy Howard, Executive Director*

Mission is to enhance the ability of people with disabilities to live more independently.

### 5025 Umpqua Valley Disabilities Network

419 NE Winchester Street
Roseburg, OR 97470
541-672-6336
FAX: 541-672-8606
TTY:541-440-2882
e-mail: uvdn@uvdn.org
www.uvdn.org

*Scott Cohan, Executive Director*
*Heather Allen, Office Manager*

UVDN's mission is to promote independent living and community inclusion for people with disabilities.

# Pennsylvania

### 5026 Abilities in Motion

416 Blair Aveue
Reading, PA 19601
610-376-0010
888-376-0021
FAX: 610-376-0021
TTY:610-228-2301
e-mail: staff@abilitiesinmotion.org
www.abilitiesinmotion.org

*Ralph Trainer, Executive Director*
*Michelle Charowsky, Independent Living Specialist*

Dedicated to advancing the rights of persons with disabilities in orer to promote a full life in the community through the prevention and elimination of physical, psychological, social and attitudinal barriers which serve to deny them the rights and privileges common to the general public.

**5027 Anthracite Region Center for Independent Living**
Pennsylvania Council on Independent Living
44 W Broad Street
Hazleton, PA 18201
570-455-9800
800-777-9906
FAX: 570-455-1731
TTY: 570-455-9800
e-mail: arcil@intergrafix.net
www.pcil.net

*Shirley Ray, Executive Director*

**5028 Brian's House**
1300 South Concord Road
West Chester, PA 19382
610-399-1175
FAX: 610-399-1828
www.brianshouse.org

*Lori Plunkett, Executive Director*
*Nancy Nelson, Director Development*

Residential care in a variety of homes and apartments for people with a range of development disabilities. Cost varies with needs. Also year-round recreation programs, vocational training and employment programs.

**5029 Community Resources for Independence**
2222 Filmore Avenue
Erie, PA 16506
814-838-7222
800-530-5541
FAX: 814-838-8491
TTY: 814-838-8115
e-mail: info@crinet.org
www.crinet.org

*Timothy Finegan, Executive Director*

CRI is committed to preserve, enhance, and enrich the quality of life for all people with disabilities.

**5030 Freedom Valley Disability Center**
3607 Chapel Road
Suite B
Newtown Square, PA 19073
610-353-6640
800-427-4754
FAX: 610-353-6753
TTY: 610-353-8900
www.fvdc.info

*Ann Cope, Executive Director*

Provides services to people with disabilities in Bucks, Chester, Delaware and Montgomery Counties. Also provided are Independent Living Services of Information and Referral, Peer-Support, Advocacy and Independent Living Skills Training.

**5031 Lehigh Valley Center for Independent Living**
435 Allentown Drive
Allentown, PA 18109
610-770-9781
800-495-8245
FAX: 610-770-9801
TTY: 610-770-9789
e-mail: info@lvcil.org
www.lvcil.org

*Amy Beck, Executive Director*
*Mark Piedmonte, Assistant Director*

LVCIL facilitates the empowerment of people with disabilities to reach their full potential, and enhacnes the community's awareness of the assets of its citizens with disabilities through: advocacy, life skills training, information and referral, peer support, housing services, and supported community services.

**5032 Liberty Resources**
1341 N Delaware Avenue
Suite 105
Philadelphia, PA 19125
215-634-2000
888-634-2155
FAX: 215-634-6628
TTY: 215-634-6630
e-mail: lrinc@libertyresources.org
www.libertyresources.org

*Thomas Earl, Executive Director/Owner*

A non-profit, consumer driven organization that advocates and promotes Independent Living for persons with disabilities.

**5033 Life and Independence for Today**
503 E Arch Street
Saint Marys, PA 15857
814-781-3050
800-341-5438
FAX: 814-781-1917
TTY: 814-781-3050
e-mail: lift@liftcil.org
www.liftcil.org

*Robert Mecca, Executive Director*

A Center for Independent Living athat provides services to people with disabilities in Cameron, Clearfield, Elk, Jefferson, McKean and Potter counties. The mission is to establish, develop, sponsorm promote or conduct educational programs, research, housing opportunities, human service programs and other charitable activities devoted to improving the health and welfare of individuals with disabilities.

**5034 North Central Pennsylvania Center for Inde pendent Living**
3600 N Pace Boulevard
Pensacola, FL 32505
850-595-5566
877-245-2457
FAX: 850-595-5560
TTY: 570-327-5254
e-mail: clinwf@clinwf.org
www.cilnwf.org

*Rajiv Rajah, President*
*Susan Patterson, Vice President*
*Frank Cherry, Executive Director*

**5035 Northeastern Pennsylvania Center for Independent Living**
431 Wyoming Avenue
Scranton, PA 18503
570-344-7211
800-344-7211
FAX: 570-344-7218
e-mail: nepacilinfo@nepacil.org
www.nepacil.org

*Daniel P Loftus, Executive Director*

Offers information, referral services, financial management, waiver service coordinator and ASL interpreter referral service.

**5036 Pennsylvania's Initiative on Assistive Technology**
Temple University
423 Ritter Anx
Philadelphia, PA 19122
215-204-5966
800-204-7428
FAX: 215-204-9371
TTY: 215-204-1356
e-mail: piat@astro.ocis.temple.edu
disabilities.temple.edu

*Amy S Goldman, Director*

Focuses on the creation of a consumer responsive system, supported by combined public and private resources, through which Pennsylvanians with disabilities have access to the assistive technology services and supports.

**5037  South Central Pennsylvania Center for Inde pendence Living**

1513 9th Avenue
Altoona, PA  16602

814-949-1905
800-237-9009
FAX: 814-949-1909
TTY: 814-949-1912
e-mail: cilscpa@cilscpa.org
4ww.cilscpa.org

*Susan Estep, Executive Director*

The missio of the Center for Independent Living of South Central PA is to empower people with disabilities to lead independent lives in their commnuitites. The Center covers Bedford, Blair, cambria, Fulton, Huntingdon, Indiana and Somerset counties.

**5038  Three Rivers Center for Independent Living**

900 Rebecca Avenue
Pittsburgh, PA  15221

412-371-7700
800-633-4585
FAX: 412-371-9430
e-mail: sholbrook@trcil.org
www.trcil.org

*Stanley Holbrook, President/CEO*
*Coleen Vuono, Deputy Director*

Offers peer counseling, information and referral services, housing data and referral service, assistive technology program, deinstitutionalization program, consumer-controlled personal assistance program, independent living skills training, advocacy and accessibility consultants.
*Sliding Fee*

**5039  Tri-County Patriots for Independent Living**

69 E Beau Street
Washington, PA  15301

724-223-5115
FAX: 724-223-5119
TTY:724-228-4028
e-mail: kathleen@tripil.com
www.tripil.com

*Kathleen Kleinmann, Executive Director*

TRIPIL promotes independent living in Southwestern Pennsylvania for and by individuals with disabilities; to enable them to take control of their lives; to make decisions about themselves and their future; to ensure tgat the necessary support services are available to enable them to be active participants in their communities; and to prevent unncessary institutionalization

**5040  Voices for Independence**

3711 W 12th Street
Suite 3
Erie, PA  16505

814-838-9890
FAX: 814-838-9779
TTY:814-838-3702
e-mail: vfi@voicesforindependence.org
www.voicesforindependence.org

*Shona Eakin, Executive Director*

A non-profit advocacy and service organization of and for individuals with disabilities. Voices for Independence was formed by individuals with disabilitites who felt that some of the primary disability service providers/organizations in Northwestern Pennsylvania were too paternalistic, laked true consumer direction and consumer control, and thus were not satisfactorily meeting the needs and concerns of individuals with disabilities in our region.

# Rhode Island

**5041  Blackstone Valley Center**

115 Manton Street
Pawtucket, RI  02861

401-727-0150
FAX: 401-727-0153
e-mail: contact@bvcriarc.org
www.bvcriarc.org

*Peter Holden, Executive Director*
*Kathy Hunt, Manager*
*John Padien, President*

**5042  Franklin Court Assisted Living**

180 Franklin Street
Bristol, RI  02809

401-253-3679
FAX: 401-253-5855
e-mail: jpierce@ebcdc.org
www.seniorlivingresidences.com

*Jean Pierce, Administrator*

Offers local seniors an affordable assisted living option with first-rate services and gracious accommodations.

**5043  IN-SIGHT Independent Living**

43 Jefferson Boulevard
Warwick, RI  02888

401-941-3322
FAX: 401-941-3356
e-mail: cbutler@in-sight.org
www.in-sight.org

*Judith Smith, President*

IN-SIGHT inspires confidence, builds skills, and empowers people who are blind and visually impaired to become fully integrated, equally valued members of society by providing diverse services that produce opportunities and choices.

**5044  Ocean State Center for Independent Living**

1944 Warwick Avenue
Warwick, RI  02889

401-738-1013
866-857-1161
FAX: 401-738-1083
TTY: 401-738-1015
e-mail: oscil@oscil.org
www.oscil.org

*Lorna Ricci, Executive Director*

OSCIL is a consumer controlled, community based, nonprofit organization established to provide a range of independent living services to enhance, through self direction, the quality of life of Rhode Islander with significant disability and to promote integration into the community.

**5045  PARI Independent Living Center**

500 Prospet Street
Pawtucket, RI  02860

401-725-1966
FAX: 401-725-2104
TTY:401-725-1966
e-mail: info@pari-ilc.org
www.pari-ilc.org

*Leo Canuel, Executive Director*
*Sue Bilodau, Program Director*

Offers information and referral services, personal care attendant services, home modifications, advocacy services and peer counseling, independent living skills training, and recycled equipment.

**5046 Rhode Island Assistive Technology Access Partnership**
Rhode Island Department of Human Services
40 Fountain Street
Providence, RI 02903
401-421-7005
800-916-8324
FAX: 401-222-3574
TTY: 401-421-7016
e-mail: reginac@ors.ri.gov
www.atap.state.ri.us

*Regina Connor, Project Director*
*Raymond Carroll, Administrator*

A statewide partnership of organizations and agencies, each with a targeted assistive technology focus, working together providing information and improving access to assistive technology for individuals with disabilities.

## South Carolina

**5047 Coastal Disability Access**
1021 3rd Avenue
Conway, SC 29526
843-488-1309
FAX: 843-488-0994
e-mail: cdaspecial1@aol.com

*Barbara Cole, IL Specialist*

Promotes independent living throughout Horry, Georgetown, and Marion Counties.

**5048 Columbia Disability Action Center**
1115 Belleview Street
Columbia, SC 29201
803-779-3944
800-681-6805
TTY:803-779-0949
www.dacsc.org

*Stephen Maglione, Executive Director*
*Neyoka Fisher, VP Budget Finance*

**5049 Graham Street Community Resources**
306 Graham Street
Florence, SC 29501
843-665-6674
FAX: 843-665-6675

*Faye Thompson, Manager*

**5050 Greenville Disability Action Center**
712 Laurens Road
Greenville, SC 29607
864-235-1421
800-681-7715
FAX: 864-235-2056
TTY: 864-235-8798
e-mail: amayne@dacsc.org
www.dacsc.org

*Stephen J Maglione, Executive Director*
*Carl Ennis, Manager*

Empowers people with disabilities to reach their highest level of independence.

**5051 SC Independent Living Council**
810 Dutch Square Boulevard
Suite 214
Columbia, SC 29210
803-731-1607
877-217-2331
FAX: 803-731-1439
e-mail: natalie@scilconline.org
www.scilconline.org

*Maris Burton, Executive Director*
*Natalie Derrick, Executive Assistant*

The SC Independent Living Council's mission is to jointly (with the DSUs) develop uses for Part B funding throughout the state. These monies can be used to: develop Centers for Independent Living; outreach to unserved and underserved populations; conduct needs assessments and research; make recommendation to policy makers regarding the delivery of IL services and provide resources for direct services.

## South Dakota

**5052 Adjustment Training Center**
607 N 4th Street
Aberdeen, SD 57401
605-229-0263
FAX: 605-225-3455

*Rob Wanouf, Superintendent/VP*
*Donna Howard, Business Official*
*Arlette Keller, Special Education Director*

Offers peer counseling, attendant care registry and referrals.

**5053 Black Hills Workshop & Training Center**
Black Hills Workshop
PO Box 2104
Rapid City, SD 57709
605-343-4550
FAX: 605-343-0879
e-mail: wadmin@bhws.com
www.bhws.com

*Dennis Popp, Chief Executive Officer*
*Dince Braun, VP Agency Operations*

Offers job placement, housing options, case coordination, supported employment and supported living for all disability groups, as well as specialized services for head trauma victims.

**5054 Communication Service for the Deaf: Yankton**
231 Broadway Avenue
Suite C6
Yankton, SD 57078
605-668-9759
FAX: 605-668-6712
TTY:605-668-9759
e-mail: kmerril@iw.net

**5055 Communication Service for the Deaf: Rapid City**
150 Knollwood Drive
Rapid City, SD 57701
605-394-6864
FAX: 605-394-6609
TTY:605-394-6864
www.c-s-d.org

*Benjamin J Soukup, President/CEO*
*Scot Atkins, Senior VP, Human Resources*
*Kevin Barber, Senior VP, Facilities/Technology*

A private, nonprofit organization dedicated to providing broad-based services, ensuring public accessibility and increasing public awareness of issues affecting deaf and hard of hearing inividuals.

**5056 Communication Services for the Deaf (CSD)**
102 N Krohn Place
Sioux Falls, SD 57103
605-367-5760
800-642-6410
FAX: 605-367-5958
TTY: 605-367-5761
e-mail: rnorris@c-s-d.org
www.c-s-d.org

*Benjamin J Soukup, President/CEO*
*Scott Atkins, Senior VP, Human Resources*
*Kevin Barber, Senior VP, Facilities/Technology*

A private, nonprofit organization dedicated to providing braod-based services, ensuring public accessibility and increasing public awareness of issues affecting deaf and hard of eharing individuals.

**5057** **Native American Advocacy Program for Perso ns with Disabilities**
208 S Main Street
PO Box 527
Winner, SD 57580

605-842-3977
800-303-3975
FAX: 605-842-3983
TTY: 605-842-3977
e-mail: admin@sdnaap.org
www.sdnaap.org

*Marla Bear, Executive Director*
*Diane Zephier, Business Manager*
*Beth Montour, Program Manager*

The mission is to encourage a healthy organization that assists Native Americans with disabilities, by providing prevention, education and training, advocacy, support, independent living skills and referrals.

**5058** **Native American Advocacy Project**
208 S Main Street
PO Box 527
Winner, SD 57580

605-842-3977
800-303-3975
FAX: 605-842-3983
TTY: 605-842-3977
e-mail: admin@sdnaap.org
www.sdnaap.org

*Marla Bear, Executive Director*
*Diane Zephier, Business Manager*
*Beth Montour, Program Manager*

NAAP is a statewide, non-profit, consumer and family membership organization for persons residing on and off the lands of the nine tribal nations in South Dakota. NAAP is also committed to providing support to the developing role of Native American consumers and their family members in system planning, decision-making, networking, advocacy, and service development for these populations.

**5059** **Opportunities for Independent Living**
1200 S Main Street
Suite A
Aberdeen, SD 57401

605-626-2976
800-406-2649
FAX: 605-626-2652
TTY: 605-626-2977
e-mail: gary.oil@midconetwork.com
www.oil.org

*Gary Wald, Executive Director*

Empowers individuals with disabilities who choose to live independently in their own homes and communities.

**5060** **Prairie Freedom Center for Independent Living of Yankton**
413 W 15th Street
Suite 106
Yankton, SD 57078

605-668-2940
800-947-3770
FAX: 605-668-3060
TTY: 605-668-2940
e-mail: p-f-c!@pfcil.org
www.pfcil.org

*Joyce Buechler, Manager*

Empowers individuals with disabilities who choose to live independently in the communities of their choice and to eliminate barriers of attitude, architecture and communication from the environment. Serves Beadle, Brown, Campbell, Clark, Codington, Day, Deuel, Edmunds, Faulk, Grant, Hamlin, Hand, Hyde, Marshall, McPherson, Roberts, Spink, Sully and Walworth counties.

**5061** **Prairie Freedom Center for Independent Living**
PO Box 282
Madison, SD 57042

605-256-5070
FAX: 605-256-5071
e-mail: freedom1@hcpd.com

*Patty Nelson, Program Coordinator*

**5062** **Prairie Freedom Center for Independent Living**
301 S Garfiled Avenue
Suite 9
Sioux Falls, SD 57104

605-367-5630
800-947-3770
FAX: 605-367-5639
TTY: 605-367-5630
e-mail: p-f-c@pfcil.org
www.state.sd.us

*Charles Anderson, Director*
*Char Crisp, Executive Director*

Empowers individuals with disabilities who choose to live independently in the communities of their choice and to eliminate barriers of attitude, architecture and communication from the environment. Serves Lincoln, McCook, Moody, Minnehaha and Turner counties.

**5063** **South Dakota Assistive Technology Project**
21 S Central
Pierre, SD 57501

605-224-5336
800-244-5336
FAX: 605-224-8320
e-mail: rfl@sd.easter-seals.org
dakotalink.tie.net

*Dave Vogel, Project Manager*

DakotaLink is a statewide program of resources and supports that enable individuals in South Dakota greater access to assistive technology devices and services, to maintain independence, to explore funding options, and to become educated about assistive technology issues.

**5064** **Western Resources for dis-ABLED Independence**
405 E Omaha Street
Suite A
Rapid City, SD 57701

605-718-1930
FAX: 605-718-1933
TTY:605-718-1930
e-mail: wrdi@wrdi.org

*Ann Van Loan, Executive Director*

WRDI advocates for the rights of equal inclusion of people with disabilities in all aspects of community life. WRDI also strives to identify and promote access to existing resources and to advocate for the development of new resources, which may enable people with disabilities to live more independently.

## Tennessee

**5065** **Center for Independent Living of Middle Tennessee**
480 Craighead Street
Suite 200
Nashville, TN 37204

615-292-5803
866-992-4568
FAX: 615-383-1176
TTY: 615-292-7790
e-mail: cilmt@tndisability.org
www.cil-mt.org

*Tom Hopton, Executive Director*

CILMT provides persons with disabilities opportunities to be self advocates and make their own decisions regarding living arrangements, means of transportation, employment, social and recreational activities, as well as other aspects of everyday life. Serves Davidson, Cheatham, Wilson, Robertson, Rutherford, Sumner and Williamson Counties.

**5066 DisAbility Resource Center: Knoxville**

900 E Hill Avenue
Suite 120
Knoxville, TN 37915        865-637-3666
       FAX: 865-637-5616
       TTY:865-637-6976
       e-mail: drc@drctn.org
       www.drctn.org

*Lillian Burch, Executive Director*
*Nicole Craig, Service Coordinator*
*Thomas Kahler, Independent Living Specialist*

DRC empowers people with disabilities to fully integrate and participate in the community.

**5067 Disability Resource Center**

900 E Hill Avenue
Suite 120
Knoxville, TN 37915        865-637-3666
       FAX: 865-637-5616
       TTY:865-637-6976
       e-mail: drc@drctn.org
       www.drctn.org

*Lillian Burch, Executive Director*
*Nicole Craig, Service Coordinator*
*Thomas Kahler, Independent Living Specialist*

DRCTN mission is to empower people with disabilities to fully integrate and participate in the community. DRC is a community-based non-residential program of services designed to assist people with disabilities to gain independence and to assist the commuity in eliminating barriers to independence.

**5068 Jackson Center for Independent Living**

1981 Hollywood Drive
Suite 200
Jackson, TN 38305        731-668-2211
       FAX: 731-668-0406
       TTY:731-664-3970
       e-mail: jcil05-06@yahoo.com
       www.jcilnow.net

*Glen Barr, Executive Director*

JCIL works with people with significant disabilities and the Deaf Community in achieving their Independent Living Goals while assisting the community in eliminating barriers to Independent Living.

**5069 Memphis Center for Independent Living**

1633 Madison Avenue
Memphis, TN 38104        901-726-6404
       FAX: 901-726-6521
       TTY:901-726-6404
       e-mail: mcil@mcil.org
       www.mcil.org

*Deborah Cunningham, Executive Director*
*Sandi Klink, Assistant Director*

MCIL is a community based non-profit organization whose primary mission is to facilitate the full integration of persons with disabilities into all aspects of community life.

**5070 Nashville Center for Independent Living**

Publications
480 Craighead Street
Suite 200
Nashville, TN 37204        615-292-5803
       866-992-4568
       FAX: 615-383-1176
       TTY: 615.292.7790
       e-mail: cilmt@tndisability.org
       www.cil-mt.org

*Floyd Stewart, Councilor*
*Tom Hopton, Executive Director*

**5071 Tennessee Technology Access Project (TTAP)**

Citizens Plaza State Office Buildin
400 Deadrick Street, 14th Floor
Nashville, TN 37248        615-313-5183
       800-732-5059
       FAX: 615-532-4685
       TTY: 615-313-5695
       e-mail: tn.ttap@state.tn.us
       www.state.tn.us/mental/ttap.html

*J D Hickey, Director*

TTAP's mission is to maintain a statewide program of technology-rated assistance that is timely, comprehensive and consumer driven to ensure that all Tennesseans with disabilities have the information, services and deices that they need to make choices about where and how they spend their time as independently as possible.

**5072 Tri-State Resource and Advocacy Corporation**

5708 Uptain Road
Suite 350
Chattanooga, TN 37411        423-892-4774
       800-868-8724
       FAX: 423-892-9866
       TTY: 423-892-4774
       e-mail: 4trac@bellsouth.net
       www.4trac.org

*Mark Woofall, Executive Director*

TRAC is dedicated to improving opportunities for individuals wuth disabilities.

# Texas

**5073 ABLE Center for Independent Living**

3641 N Dixie Boulevard
Odessa, TX 79762        432-580-3439
       FAX: 915-580-0280
       TTY:915-580-3439
       e-mail: abledcil@ablecenter.org
       www.able-cil.org

*Melvin White, Executive Director*
*Jacki Campbell, IL Specialist Director*

Non-residential, nonprofit organization, guided by the philosophy of consumer choice, to assist people with disabilities achieve and maintain independent lifestyle.

**5074 Austin Resource Center for Independent Living**

825 E Rundberg Lane
Suite A-1
Austin, TX 78753        512-832-6349
       FAX: 512-832-1869
       TTY:512-832-6349
       e-mail: arcil@arcil.com
       www.arcil.com

*Ronald Roacha, Executive Director*

ARCIL of Texas provides independent living services to persons with disabilities, their families and communities throughout Travis and surrounding counties. ARCIL also provides services throughout Hays, Caldwell, Comal and Blanco counties at ARCIL San Marcos, and Williamson, Bell, Burnett and Milan counties at ARCIL Round Rock.

**5075 Austin Resource Center: Round Rock**

525 Round Rock West
Suite A-120
Round Rock, TX 78681        512-828-4624
       FAX: 512-828-4625
       TTY:512-828-4624
       e-mail: roundrock@arcil.com
       www.arcil.com

*Ronald Rocha, Executive Director*

**5076  Austin Resource Center: San Marcos**

618 S Guadalupe Street
Suite 103
San Marcos, TX  78666

512-396-5790
FAX: 512-396-5794
TTY:512-396-5790
e-mail: sanmarcos@arcil.com
www.arcil.com

*Ronald Rocha, Executive Director*
*Jack Stratton, Manager*

Provides advocacy services, info and refferal, independent living skills and life skills classes. Other services include peer support and social and leisure activities and some community services.

**5077  Brazoria County Center for Independent Living**

1101 Division East Mulberry
Angleton, TX  77515

979-849-7060
888-872-7957
TTY:979-849-7060
e-mail: bccil@neosoft.com
www.coalitionforbarrierfreeliving.com

**5078  Center Serving Persons with Mental Retardation**

3550 West Dallas
PO Box 130564
Houston, TX  77019

713-525-8400
FAX: 713-525-8444
www.cri-usa.org

*C Wayne Johnson, President*
*Jim Aycock, Vice President*

Provides services for more than 600 children and adults with mental retardation and other developmental disabilities. The Center also offers a wide array of programs including education, vocational training and job placement services, three different residential options representing both urban and rural living environments, special programs designed to meet the needs of older adults, and a variety of therapeutic support services.

**5079  Coalition for Barrier Free Living/Houston Center for Independent Living**

7000 Regency Square Boulevard
Suite 160
Houston, TX 77036

713-974-4621
FAX: 713-974-6927
TTY:713-974-4621
e-mail: hcil@neosoft.com

*Sandra Bookman, Executive Director*

**5080  Crockett Resource Center for Independent Living**

1020 Loop 304 E
Crockett, TX 75835

936-544-2811
FAX: 936-544-7315
TTY:936-544-2811
e-mail: crcil@consolidated.net

*Cynthia Cook, Executive Director*

Provides independent living services to cross-disability groups to increase their personal self-determination and minimize dependence on others. Maintain comprehensive information on availability of resources and provides referrals to such resources. Provides instruction to assist people with disabilities to gain skills that would empower them to live independently. Peer counseling, advocacy - both individual and community by assisting to obtain support services to make changes in society.

**5081  Houston Center for Independent Living**

7000 Regency Square Boulevard
Suite 160
Houston, TX

713-974-4621
FAX: 713-974-6927
TTY:713-974-2703
e-mail: hcil@neosoft.com
www.coalitionforbarrierfreeliving.com

*Sandra Bookman, Executive Director*

HCIL promotes the full inclusion, equal opportunity and participation of persons with disabilities in every aspect of community life. HCIL also believes that people with disabilities have the right to make choices affecting their lives, a right to take risks, ad right to fail, and a right to succeed.

**5082  Independent Life Styles**

PO Box 571874
Houston, TX  77257

713-861-4266

www.independentlifestyles.org

*Peter Simmons, Director*

Offers peer counseling, advocacy and other services to the community.

**5083  Independent Living Research Utilization Project**

Institute For Rehabilitation & Research
2323 S Shepherd Drive
Suite 1000
Houston, TX  77019

713-520-0232
FAX: 713-520-5785
TTY:713-520-0232
e-mail: ilru@ilru.org
www.ilru.org

*Lex Frieden, Director*
*Laurie Redd, Executive Director*

ILRU is a national center for information, training, research and technical assistance in independent living. Its goal is to expand the body of knowledge in independent living and to improve utilization of results of research programs and demonstration projects in this field. ILRU is a program of The Institute for Rehabilitation and Research, a nationally recognized medical rehabilitation facility for persons with disabilities. TTY phone number: (713) 520-5136.

**5084  LIFE Independent Living Center**

4902 34th Stree
Suite 5
Lubbock, TX  79410

806-795-5433
FAX: 806-795-5607
TTY:806-795-5433
e-mail: wilmacrain@yahoo.com

*Michelle Crain, Executive Director*

**5085  LIFE/ Run Centers for Independent Living**

4902 34th Street
Suite 5
Lubbock, TX  79410

806-795-5433
FAX: 806-795-5607
TTY:806-795-5433
e-mail: wilmacrain@yahoo.com

*Michelle Crain, Executive Director*

**5086  Martin Luther Homes of Texas**

520 E Donagun Street
Suite 2
Seguin, TX  78155

830-372-3075
FAX: 830-303-3075

*Jerome Boeck, Manager*

Providing a wide array of services to assist individuals and families in achieving positive life goals. Services to persons with disabilities and other special needs include community living options, training and employment options, spiritual growth and development options, training and counseling support.

## 5087 Office for Students with Disabilities, University of Texas at Arlington

PO Box 19510
Arlington, TX 76019

817-272-3364
FAX: 817-272-1447
TTY:817.272.1520
e-mail: dianne@uta.edu
www.uta.edu/disability

*Dianne Hengst, Director*
*Penny Acrey, Assistant Director*
*Amber Mitchell, Interpreter Coordinator*

Offers disability counseling and academic accomodation for UTA community.

## 5088 Palestine Resource Center for Independent Living

421 Avenue A
Palestine, TX 75801

903-729-7505
888-326-5166
FAX: 903-729-7540
TTY:903-729-7505
e-mail: prcil@earthlink.net

*Cynthia Cook, Executive Director*
*Sara Manton, Manager*

Provides independent living services to cross-disability groups to increase their personal self-determination and minimize dependence on others. Maintain comprehensive information on availability of resources and provides referrals to such resources. Provides instruction to assist people with disabilities to gain skills that would empower them to live independently. Peer counseling, advocacy - both individual and community by assisting to obtain support services to make changes in society.

## 5089 Panhandle Action Center for Independent Living Skills

1118 S Taylor Street
Amarillo, TX 79101

806-374-1400
FAX: 806-374-4550
TTY:806-374-2774
e-mail: advocacy@nts-online.net
www.panhandleilc.org

*Carl McMillen, Director*
*Kevin Oliphant, Manager*

PILC is a non profit organization dedicated to the advancement of full participation in all aspects of life. PILC services are developed, directed, delivered, and governed primarily by individuals with disabilities.

## 5090 REACH of Dallas Resource Center on Independent Living

8625 King George Drive
Suite 210
Dallas, TX 75235

214-630-4796
FAX: 214-630-6390
TTY:214-630-5995
e-mail: reachdallas@reachcils.org
www.reachcils.org

*Charlotte Stewart, Executive Director*
*Susie Reukema, Assistant Director*

Information and referral services, peer counseling, independent living skills training, loaner adaptive equipment, advocacy assistance, social, recreational activities and ADA technical assistance.

## 5091 REACH of Denton Resource Center on Independent Living

405 S Elm Street
Suite 202
Denton, TX 76201

940-383-1062
FAX: 940-383-2742
e-mail: reachden@reachcils.org
www.reachcils.org

*Charlotte Stewart, Executive Director*
*Becky Teal, Manager*

REACH is a North Texas based nonprofit organization that provides services to people with disabilities and education to the community on disability-relatd topics.

## 5092 REACH/Resource Center on Independent Living

1205 Lake Street
Fort Worth, TX 76102

817-870-9082
FAX: 817-877-1622
TTY:817-870-9086
e-mail: reachftw@reachcils.org
www.reachcils.org

*Charlotte Stewart, Executive Director*
*Robin Laffiter, Manager*

Information and referral services, peer counseling, independent living skills training, loaner equipment, advocacy assistance, ADA technical assistance and social/recreational activities.

## 5093 RISE-Resource: Information, Support and Empowerment

755 S 11th Street
Suite 101
Beaumont, TX 77701

409-832-2599
FAX: 409-838-4499
e-mail: cherylbass@risecil.org

*Cheryl Bass, Executive Director*

Provide core services of Individual & Systems Advocacy, Information & Referral, IL Skills, Training, and Peer Support. Also Community Education regarding disability issues.

## 5094 SAILS

1028 S Alamo
San Antonio, TX 78210

210-281-1878
800-474-0295
FAX: 210-281-1759
TTY: 210-281-1878
e-mail: kbrietzke@sailstx.org
www.sailstx.org

*Kitty Brietzke JD, Executive Director*
*Gloria Banik, Assistant Executive Director*

SAILS advocates for the rights and empowerment of people with disabilities in San Antonio; as well as surrounding areas. Services are provided to people with disabilities in the following counties: Atacosa, Bandera, Bexar, Calhoun, Comal, DeWitt, Dimmit, Edwards, Frio, Gillespie, Goliad, Gonzalez, Guadalupe, Jackson, Karnes, La Salle, Kendall, Kerr, Kinney, Lavaca, Maverick, Medina, Real, Uvalde, Val Verde, Victoria, Wilson and Zavala.

## 5095 San Antonio Independent Living Services

1028 S Alamo Street
San Antonio, TX 78210

210-281-1878

*Kitty Brietzke, Executive Director*

Serves adults with disabilities through referrals, training and support.

**5096 Texas Rehabilitation Commission Independent Living Services**

4900 N Lamar Boulevard
Austin, TX 78751
512-424-4000
800-628-5115
FAX: 512-424-4283
e-mail: drswebfeedback@dars.state.tx.us
www.rehab.state.tx.us

*Tony Lawrence, Director*
*Max Arrell, Manager*

Provides technical assistance and other support services to the state's Independent Living Council, Independent Living Centers and Independent Living Counseling programs.

**5097 VOLAR Center for Independent Living**

8929 Viscount
Suite 101
El Paso, TX 79925
915-591-0800
FAX: 915-591-3506
TTY:915-591-0800
e-mail: volar@volarcil.org
www.volarcil.org

*Luis Enrique Chew, Executive Director*
*Dan Monroe, Chief Executive Officer*

VOLAR is committed to providing independent living ervices and information and referral, and to developing community options for persons with cross disabilities to empower them to live the kind of lives they choose. VOLAR is an organization of and for people with disabilities, advocating human and civil rights, community options and empowering people to live the lives they choose. Newsletter available.

**5098 Valley Association for Independent Living (VAIL)**

3012 N McColl Road
Suute B
McAllen, TX 78501
956-668-8245
FAX: 956-319-4
e-mail: wjohnston@valleyassociation.org
www.valleyassociation.org

*Woodie Johnston, Executive Director*

**5099 Valley Association for Independent Living: Brownsville**

880 Ridgewood Street
Suite 1
Brownsville, TX 78520
950-544-0468
FAX: 956-541-6036
e-mail: tstem@valleyassociation.org

*Teresa Stem, Independent Living Specialist*

# Utah

**5100 Active Re-Entry**

10 S Fairgrounds Road
Price, UT 84501
435-637-4950
FAX: 435-637-4952
TTY:435-637-4950
e-mail: active@arecil.org
www.arecil.org

*Nancy Bentley, Executive Director*

Active Re-Entry is a community based program which assists individuals with disabilities to acheive or maintain self-sufficient and productive live in their own communities. Active Re-Entry is committed to promoting the rights, dignity, and quality of life for all persons with disabilities.

**5101 Active Re-Entry: Vernal**

510 E Main Street
Suite 3
Vernal, UT 84078
435-789-4021
FAX: 435-789-1031
TTY:435-789-4021
www.arecil.org

*Nancy Bentley, Executive Director*

Active Re-Entry is a community based program which assists individuals with disabilities to achieve or maintain self-sufficient and productive lives in their own communities. We are committed to promoting the rights, dignity, and quality of life for all persons with disabilities.

**5102 Central Utah Independent Living Center**

491 N Freedon Boulevard
Provo, UT 84601
801-373-5044
877-421-4500
FAX: 801-373-5094
TTY: 801-373-5044
e-mail: sandra@cucil.org
www.cucil.org

*Sandra Curcio, Executive Director*
*Bill Peterson, Independent Living Specialist*

Central Utah Center for Independent Living (CUCIL) empowers people with disabilities to reach their full potential in community settings through peer support, advocacy, and education.

**5103 OPTIONS for Independence**

Northern Utah Center for Independent Living
1095 N Main Street
Logan, UT 84341
435-753-5353
FAX: 435-753-5390
TTY:435-753-5353
e-mail: jbiggs@optionind.org
www.optionsind.org

*Cheryl Atwood, Executive Director*

OPTIONS is a nonresidential Independent Living Center where people with disabilities can learn skills to gain more control and independence over their lives. OPTIONS raises the vision and capability of the comunity at large to the point where people of all abilities will have equal access.

**5104 Options for Independence: Brigham**

862 S Main Street
Suite 9
Brigham City, UT 84302
435-723-2171
FAX: 435-723-9618
TTY:435-723-2171
e-mail: paulab@brigham.net
www.optionsind.org

*Cheryl Atwood, Executive Director*
*Paula Bartholomew, Manager*

OPTIONS is a nonresidential Independent Living Center where people with disabilities can learn skills to gain more control and independence over their lives. OPTIONS raises the vision and capability of the community at large to the point where people of all abilities will have equal access.

**5105 Red Rock Center for Independence**

515 W 300 N
Suite A
Saint George, UT 84770
435-673-7501
800-649-2340
FAX: 435-673-8808
e-mail: rrci@rrci.org
www.rrci.org

*Garry Owens, Executive Director*
*Mary Light, Assistant Director*
*Mark Johnson, Independent Living Specialist*

Red Rock Center for Independence assists people with disabilities to live and participate independently.

**5106   Red Rock Center for Independence: Fillmore**

PO Box 531
Fillmore, UT  84631

435-619-7724
FAX: 435-619-8808
TTY:435-619-7501
e-mail: rrci@rrci.org
www.rrci.org

*Garry Owens, Executive Director*

Red Rock Center for Independence assists people with disabilities to live and participate independently.

**5107   Tri-County Independent Living Center**

2726 Washington Boulevard
PO Box 428
Ogden, UT  84401

801-612-3215
866-734-5678
FAX: 801-612-3732
TTY: 801-612-3215
e-mail: vickie@tri-county-ilc.com
www.tri-county-ilc.com

*Vickie Brenchley, Deputy Director/Office Manager*
*Andy Curry, Executive Director*

The mission of the Tri-County ILC is to enhance independence for all people with disabilities. Serves Davis, Weber and Morgan Counties.

**5108   Utah Assistive Technology Program (UTAP) Utah State University**

6855 Old Main Hill
Logan, UT  84322

435-797-3824
800-524-5152
FAX: 435-797-2355
e-mail: curtis@cpd2.usu.edu
www.uatpat.org

*Martin Blair, Assistant Director*
*Dan Peterson, Manager*

Provides expertise, resources, and a structure to enhance and expand AT services provided by private and public agencies in Utah. Occurs through monitoring, coordination, information dissemination, empowering individuals, the identification and removal of barriers, and expanding state resources.

**5109   Utah Independent Living Center**

3445 S Main Street
Salt Lake City, UT  84115

801-466-5565
800-355-2195
e-mail: uilc@xmission.com
www.uilc.org

*Debra A Mair, Executive Director*
*Kim Meichle, Program Director*
*Julie Beckstead, Program Coordinator*

Offers information and referral services.

**5110   Utah Independent Living Center: Minersville**

Minersville, UT  84752

435-691-7724

www.uilcxmission.net

**5111   Utah Independent Living Center: Tooele**

33 S Main Street
Tooele, UT  84074

435-843-7353
FAX: 435-843-7359
TTY:435-843-7353
e-mail: uilc@trilobyte.com
www.ilru.org

*Angie Slater, Director*

## Vermont

**5112   Vermont Assistive Technology Project: Department of Aging & Disabilities**

Department of Aging and Independent Living
103 S Main Street
Waterbury, VT  05671

802-241-2400
800-750-6355
FAX: 802-241-2174
TTY: 802-241-1464
e-mail: jtucker@dad.state.vt.us
www.dad.state.vt.us/atp

*Julie Tucker, Project Director*
*David Tunia, Information/Education Specialist*
*Patrick Flood, Manager*

Encompasses a state coordinating council for assistive technology issues, regional centers for demonstration, trial and technical support with computer and augmentative communication equipment and regional seating and positioning centers.

**5113   Vermont Center for Independent Living: Brattleboro**

59 Pearl Street
63-
Burlington, VT  05401

802-862-0234
800-539-1522
FAX: 802-258-2651
e-mail: vcil@vcil.org
www.vcil.org

*Candace Stouman, Peer Advocate Counselor*
*Missy Boothroyd, Deaf Peer Counselor*

**5114   Vermont Center for Independent Living: Brattleboro**

28 Vernon Street
Suite 401
Brattleboro, VT  05301

802-254-6851
FAX: 802-258-2651
TTY:802-254-6851
e-mail: bratvcil@vcil.org
www.vcil.org

*Deborah Lisi-Baker, Executive Director*

VCIL believes that individuals with disabilities have the right to live with dignity and with appropriate support in their own homes, fully participate in their communities, and to control and make decisions about their lives.

**5115   Vermont Center for Independent Living**

11 E State Street
Montpelier, VT  05602

802-229-0501
800-639-1522
FAX: 802-229-0503
TTY: 800-639-1522
e-mail: vcil@vcil.org
www.vcil.org

*Deborah Lisi-Baker, Executive Director*

VCIL believes that individuals with disabilities have the right to live with dignity and with appropriate support in their own homes, fully participate in their communities, and to control and make decisions about their lives.

**5116   Vermont Center for Independent Living: Bennington**

532 Main Street
Suite 1
Bennington, VT  05201

802-447-0574
FAX: 802-442-4052
TTY:802-447-0574
e-mail: vcilbenn@vcil.org
www.vcil.com

*Deborah Lisi-Baker, Executive Director*
*Rose Rahilly, Manager*

VCIL believes that individuals with disabilities have the right to live with dignity and with appropriate support in their own homes, fully participate in their communities, and to control and make decisions about their lives.

# Virginia

### 5117 Access Independence

403-b S Loudoun Street
Winchester, VA 22601
540-662-4452
FAX: 540-662-4474
TTY:540-722-9693
e-mail: askai@accessindependence.org
www.accessindependence.org

*Kim Shick, Executive Director*
*Diane Starkey, Programs Manager*
*Joan Davis, Manager*

Offers support services to persons with disabilities to assist in maintaining or increasing their independence and self-determination. Includes housing assistance, independent living skills training, information, referral services, assistance and representative payee and advocacy.

### 5118 Appalachian Independence Center

230 Charwood Drive
Abingdon, VA 24210
276-628-2979
FAX: 276-628-4931
TTY:276-676-0920
e-mail: aicadmin@ntelos.net
wwww.aicadvocates.org

*Greg Morrell, Executive Director*
*Donna Buckland, Assistant Director*
*Steve Halley, Independent Living Advocate*

AIC's mission is to foster a community environment in which people with disabilities will be able to achieve their maximum level of independence. It creates this environment by educating the public and promoting the needs and rights of people with disabilities while working with them to meet their personal potential for independence.

### 5119 Blue Ridge Independent Living Center - Troutville

US Route 11, N Lee Highway
Room 103
Troutville, VA 24175
540-966-4951
FAX: 540-342-9505
TTY:540-966-4951
e-mail: kmichbrilc@aol.com

*Leigh Taylor, Executive Director*

### 5120 Blue Ridge Independent Living Center

1502 Williamson Road NE
Roanoke, VA 24012
540-342-1231
FAX: 540-342-9505
TTY:540-342-1231
e-mail: kmichalski@brilc.org
www.brilc.org

*Karen Michalski, Executive Director*
*Sara Ingram, Program Services Director*
*Ava Coles, Independent Living Coordinator*

BRILC assists people with disabilities to live independently. The Center also serves the community at large by helping to create an environment that is accessible to all. BRILC offers a variety of servies ranging from referrals to community resources, support services, and direct services. These include peer counseling, support groups, training and seminars, advocacy, education, support services, awareness, aid in obtaining specialized equipment, and much more.

### 5121 Blue Ridge Independent Living Center: Christianburg

210 Pepper Street
Suite D
Christiansburg, VA 24073
540-381-8829
FAX: 540-381-8829
TTY:540-381-8829
e-mail: tlavinder@brilc.org
www.brilc.org

*Karen Michalski-Karney, Executive Director*
*Sara Ingram, Program Services Coordinator*
*Ava Coles, Independent Living Specialist*

### 5122 Blue Ridge Independent Living Center: Low Moor

PO Box 7
Low Moor, VA 24457
540-862-0252
FAX: 540-862-0252
TTY:540-862-0252

### 5123 Clinch Independent Living Services

PO Box 2741
Grundy, VA 24614
276-935-6088
FAX: 276-935-6342
TTY:276-935-6088
e-mail: cils@netscope.net

*Betty Bevins, Executive Director*

Nonprofit organization providing information and referral, peer counseling, advocacy and independent living skills training to persons with disabilities.

### 5124 Disability Resource Center

409 Progress Street
Fredericksburg, VA 22401
540-373-2559
FAX: 540-373-8126
TTY:540-373-5890
e-mail: rob@drc-fredericksburg.org

*Debe Fulps, Executive Director*

### 5125 ENDependence Center of Northern Virginia

3100 Clarendon Boulevard
Arlington, VA 22201
703-525-3268
FAX: 703-525-3585
TTY:703-525-3553
e-mail: info@ecnv.org
www.ecnv.org

*Michael J Cooper, Executive Director*

ECNV is a community-based resource and advocacy enter which is managed by and for people with disabilities. ENCV promotes independent living philosophy and equal access for all persons with disabilities and, like the nearly 400 centers for independent living across the country, ECNV grew from local disability rights and self-help movements.

### 5126 Equal Access Center for Independence

4031 University Drive
Suite 301
Fairfax, VA 22030
703-934-2020
FAX: 703-277-7730
e-mail: drc@patriot.net

*David Sharp, Executive Director*

### 5127 Independence Empowerment Center

9001 Digges Road
Suite 103
Manassas, VA 20110
703-257-5400
877-409-8165
FAX: 703-257-5043
TTY: 703-257-5400
e-mail: indempctr@comcast.net

*Bill Ward, Executive Director*

**5128 Independence Resource Center**
815 Cherry Avenue
Charlottesville, VA 22903
434-971-9629
FAX: 434-497-8242
TTY:434-497-9634
e-mail: tvandever@ntelos.net

*Thomas Vandever, Executive Director*
Information and referral services.

**5129 Independent Living Center Network: Department of the Visually Handicapped**
1809 Staples Mill Road
Suite 300
Richmond, VA 23230
804-355-7900
FAX: 804-355-9297

*Bob Burton, Director*
*Robert Kastenbaum, Partner*
Information and referral services.

**5130 Junction Center for Independent Living**
PO Box 1210
Norton, VA 24273
276-679-5988
FAX: 276-679-6569
TTY:276-679-5988
e-mail: jcil1@junctioncenter.org
www.juctioncenter.org

*Dennis Horton, Executive Director*
JCIL is a non-profit, non-residential program which provides services to persons with disabilities, their families, and their community. JCIL's mission is to assist people who have significant disabilities to live indpeneedntly in the least restrictive and most integrated environment possible.

**5131 Junction Center for Independent Living**
4907 Boone Trail Road
PO Box 408
Duffield, VA 24244
276-431-1195
FAX: 276-431-1196
TTY:276-431-1196
e-mail: jcil1@junctioncenter.org
www.junctioncenter.org

*Dennis Horton, Executive Director*
JCIL is a non-profit, non-residential program which provides services to persons with disabilities, their families, and their community. JCIL's mission is to assist people who have significant disabilities to live independently in the least restrictive and most integrated environment possible.

**5132 Lynchburg Area Center for Independent Living**
500 Alleghany Avenue
Lynchburg, VA 24501
434-528-4971
FAX: 434-528-4976
TTY:434-528-4972
e-mail: lacil@lacil.org
www.lacil.org

*Walter Sabin, Executive Director*
LACIL is a private non-profit, non-residential consumer driven organization that promotes the efforts of persons with disabilities to live independently in the community and supports the efforts of the community to be open and accessible to all citizens.

**5133 National Council on Independent Living**
1916 Wilson Boulevard
Suite 209
Arlington, VA 22201
703-525-3406
877-525-3400
FAX: 703-525-3409
TTY: 703-525-4153
e-mail: ncil@ncil.org
www.ncil.org

*Anne Marie Hughey, Executive Director*
*June Sutherland, Project Assistant*

Advances the independent living philosophy and advocates for the human rights of and services for people with disabilities to further their full integration and participation in society. The National Council on Independent Living (NCIL) is the oldest cross disability, grassroots organization run by and for people with disabilities.

**5134 Peidmont Independent Living Center**
Piedmont Living Center
1045 Main Street
Suite 2
Danville, VA 24541
434-797-2530
FAX: 434-797-2568
TTY:434-797-2530
e-mail: pilc@gamewood.com
www.vhda.com

*Clarence Dickerson, Executive Director*
*Jeanette King, ILS Coordinator/BPAD*
*Lori Penn, Office Manager*

Empowering indiviuals with disabilities to become self-sufficient and independent within their communities.

**5135 Peninsula Center for Independent Living**
2021-A Cunningham Drive
Suite 2
Hampton, VA 23666
757-827-0275
FAX: 757-827-0655
TTY:757-827-8800
e-mail: iepcil@iepcil.org
www.iepcil.org

*Ralph Shelman, Executive Director*
IEPCIL is a private non-profit non-residential Agency established to provide services to people with disabilities. The Centers Philosophy is that people with a disability should play a major role in deciding their future.The center provides services to people with disabilities in the cities of Hampton, Newport News, Poquoson, Williamsburg, and counties of James City, York, and Gloucester.

**5136 Resources for Independent Living**
4009 Fitzhugh Avenue
Suite 100
Richmond, VA 23230
804-353-6503
FAX: 804-358-5606
TTY:804-353-6583
e-mail: woodsonf@cavtel.net
www.ril-va.org

*Sandra Wagener, Executive Director*
Information and referral services.

**5137 Valley Associates for Independent Living (VAIL)**
Shenandoah Valley Workforce Investment Board
1909 A E Market Street
PO Box 869
Harrisonburg, VA 22803
540-442-7134
FAX: 540-434-0803
e-mail: satterwhite@valleyworkforce.com
www.valleyworkforce.com

*Taylor Howell, Manager*
*Bob Satterwhite, Executive Director*

VAIL is a not-for-profit, private Center for Independent Living providing advocacy, information and referral, independent living skills training, supported employment, and peer counseling to individuals with disabilities in our planning district.

**5138 Valley Associates for Independent Living: Lexington**
7 W McDowell Street
Suite A
Lexington, VA 24450
540-464-5454
FAX: 540-464-5454
e-mail: vail@govail.org
www.govail.org

*Marcia DuBois, Director*

Promoting self-direction among people with disabilities and removing barriers to independence in the community.

**5139   Woodrow Wilson Rehabilitation Center Training Program**
PO Box 1500
Fishersville, VA  22939
540-332-7000
800-345-9972
FAX: 540-332-7132
TTY: 800-811-7893
e-mail: colemawl@wwrc.state.va.us
www.wwrc.net

*Richard S Luck EdD, Director*

Information & referral services. Six week Virginia residential programs and evaluation services.

# Washington

**5140   Alliance for People with Disabilities: Sea ttle**
4649 Sunnyside Avenue N
Suite 100
Seattle, WA  98103
206-545-7055
866-545-7055
FAX: 206-545-7059
TTY: 206-632-3456
e-mail: info@disabilitypride.org
www.disabilitypride.org

*Jeanette Murphy, Executive Director*

The Alliance promotes equality and choice for people with disabilities. They provide advocacy, peer support, idependent living skills training, information and referral, transition assistance for youth and civil rights legal aid.

**5141   Alliance of People with Disabilities: Redmond**
East King County Office
16315 NE 87th Street
Suite B-3
Redmond, WA  98052
425-558-0993
800-216-3335
FAX: 425-558-4773
TTY: 425-861-4773
e-mail: information@disabilitypride.org
www.disabilitypride.org

*Robert Blumenfeld, Manager*
*Michelle Klekota, Independent Living Program*
*Charity Ranger, Independent Living Program*

Services include: information and referral, independent living skills training, peer groups, disAbility law project (DLP), access reviews, health insurance advising, and systems advocacy.

**5142   Central Washington Disability Resources**
422 N Pine Street
Ellensburg, WA  98926
509-962-9620
FAX: 509-933-1571
TTY:509-962-9620
e-mail: marianne@cwdrinfo.org
www.cwdrinfo.org

*Von Elison, Executive Director*

CWDR is a non-profit organization, created to assist those with disabilities with knowledge, support, and education. To provide the ability and assistance necessary to help them obtain independent living status, and further support to help them maintain that in their life.

**5143   Coalition of Responsible Disabled**
612 N Maple Street
Spokane, WA  99201
509-326-6355
877-606-2680
FAX: 509-327-2420
TTY: 509-326-6355
www.cordwa.info

*Linda McClain MSW, Executive Director*
*Laura Coston, REACH Independent Living Service*
*Linda Schappals, Executive Director*

CORD strives to enhance independent living opportunities and self-determination through advocacy, promoting civil rights, and empowerment. Improves the self-determination and self-reliance of people with disabilities through community and individual advocacy, education and provisions of independent living.

**5144   Community Service Center for the Deaf and Hard of Hearing**
1609 19th Avenue
Seattle, WA  98122
206-322-4996
877-301-0006
FAX: 206-720-3251
TTY: 206-322-4996
e-mail: cscdhh@cscdhh.org
www.cscdhh.org

*Susan Bernick, Interim Executive Director*
*Angelia Theriault, Advocate Specialist*

Community information and referral services; interpreter referral services such as sign language interpreting, real time captioning, relay interpreting, oral interpreting; 9-1-1/TTY eduction program; communication access advocacy; and community education.

**5145   Community Services for the Blind and Partially Sighted**
9709 3rd Avenue NE
Suite 100
Seattle, WA  98115
206-525-5556
800-458-4888
FAX: 206-525-0422
e-mail: csbps@csbps.com
www.csbps.com

*June Mansfield, President/CEO*

Founded in 1965 as an independent nonprofit, CSBPS works to restore, maintain, and enhance the independence and well-being of people with impaired vision. Programs include professional counseling and support; safe travel and orientation training; instruction in independent living skills; low vision clinic and low vision rehavilitation; one-on-one volunteer services, education, information and referral, assistive technology center; and an adaptive aids retail, and online store.

**5146   Designs for Independent Living**
819 S Hatch Street
Spokane, WA  99202
509-456-6955
www.privatedoor.com

*Gloria Caryl, Contact*

**5147   DisAbility Resource Center: Everett**
607 SE Everett Mall Way
Suite 6C
Everett, WA  98208
425-347-5768
800-315-3583
FAX: 425-710-0767
TTY: 425-347-5768
e-mail: drcnet@drconline.net
www.drc-online.net

*Sean Barrett, Executive Director*

disAbility Resource Connection is all about living your life as you choose. The staff is committed to assisting every individual to connect resources, connect to skills, connect to life.

**5148 Disability Resources of Southwest Washington**
5501 NE 109th Court
Suite N
Vancouver, WA 98662
360-694-6790
800-735-2900
FAX: 360-882-1324
TTY: 360-694-6790
e-mail: disabilityresources@darsw.com
www.darsw.com

*Jim Baker, Executive Director*

DARSW empowers individuals with disabilities by creating opportunities, promoting choice, advancing equal access, educating, and furthering independent living.

**5149 Epilepsy Foundation of Washington**
National Epilepsy Foundation
3800 Aurora Avenue N
Suite 370
Seattle, WA 98103
206-547-4551
800-752-3509
FAX: 206-547-4557
e-mail: info@epilepsynw.org
www.epilepsynw.org

*Joel Neier, President/CEO*
*Malanie Redman, Associate Director*
*Alta C Hancock, Director*

Epilepsy Foundation Washington works to ensure that people with sizures are able to particiapte in all life expirences. This is supported through education, advocacy and direct services.

**5150 Greater Lakes Mental Healthcare**
9330 59th Avenue SW
Lakewood, WA 98499
253-581-7020

e-mail: annettea@glmhc.org
www.glmhc.org

*Richard Towell, President/CEO*

GLMH is dedicated to prodiving behavioral healthcare to imporve the quality of individual, family and community life.

**5151 Independent Living Center of SW Washington**
PO Box 2129
Vancouver, WA 98668
FAX: 253-848-0798

*Morris Gielser, Director*

Offers peer counseling, referral and advocacy services.

**5152 Independent Living Service Center**
Disability Resouce Connection
607 SE Everett Mall Way
Suite 6C
Everett, WA 98208
425-347-5768
FAX: 425-710-0767
TTY:425-347-5768
e-mail: drcservices@drconline.net
www.drconline.net

*Sean Barrett, Executive Director*

disAbility Resource Connection is all about living your life as you choose. The staff is committed to assisting every individual to connect to resources, connect to skills, connect to life.

**5153 Kitsap Community Resources**
802 7th Street
Bremerton, WA 98337
360-478-2301
FAX: 360-415-2706
e-mail: info@kcr.org
www.kcr.org

*Teri Washburn, President*
*Heidi Gunter, Vice President*
*Larry Eyer, Executive Director*

Kitsap Community Resources is a local, non-profit organization dedicated to helping people in need. KCR creates hope and opportunity for low-income Kitsap County Residents by providing resources that promote self-sufficiency.

**5154 Lilac Blind Foundation**
1212 N Howard Street
Spokane, WA 99201
509-328-9116
800-422-7893
FAX: 509-328-8965
e-mail: info@lilacblindfoundation.org
www.lilacblindfoundation.org

*Colleen Stevens, President*
*Al Rubens, Vice President*
*Cheryl Martin, Executive Director*

Lilac Blind Foundation provides adaptive training and equiptment that enables blind and partially sighted individuals to live satisfying lives and pursue vocational or educational opportunities.

**5155 Resource Center for the Handicapped**
20150 45th Avenue NE
Lake Forest Park, WA 98155
206-364-8179
FAX: 425-271-1096

*Jeff Sykes, Director*

Information and referral services.

**5156 Tacoma Area Coalition of Individuals with Disabilities**
6315 S 19th Street
Tacoma, WA 98466
253-565-9000
877-538-2243
FAX: 253-565-5578
TTY: 253-565-5445
e-mail: tacid@tacid.org
www.tacid.org

*Christopher Ensor, Executive Director*

Promotes the independence of individuals with disabilities.

# West Virginia

**5157 Appalachian Center for Independent Living**
4710 Chimney Drive
Suite C
Charleston, WV 25302
304-965-0376
800-642-3003
FAX: 304-965-0377
TTY: 304-965-0377
e-mail: acil@westco.net

*Larry E Paxton, Executive Director*
*Scott Dc, Owner*

Provides services and formation to handicapped persons including professional and peer counseling, advocacy, referral, housing, transportation, support groups, build wheelchair ramps, mobility equipment loan, attendant care, older blind services and skills training.

**5158 Mountain State Center for Independent Living**
329 Prince Street
Beckley, WV 25801
304-255-0122
FAX: 304-255-0157
TTY:304-255-0122
e-mail: kmaynus@mtstcil.org
www.mtstcil.org

*Kevin Maynus, Director*
*Anne Weeks, Chief Executive Officer*

This office provides individual and systems advocacy, independent living skills development, information and referral, peer support, personal assistance services, housing referral and training, transportation. Serves Raleigh counties.

**5159 Mountain State Center for Independent Living**
821 4th Avenue
Huntington, WV 25701
304-525-3324
866-687-8245
FAX: 304-525-3360
TTY: 304-525-3324
e-mail: mtstcil@mtstcil.org
www.mtstcil.org

*Anne Weeks, President/CEO*
*John Gallaher, Manager*

Services provided are: individual and systems advocacy, independent living skills development, information and referral, peer support, personal assistance services, supported employment, community integration program, housing referral and training, transportation. Serves Cabell and Wayne counties.

**5160 Northern West Virginia Center for Independent Living**
601-3 E Brockway Avenue
Suite A&B
Morgantown, WV 26501
304-296-6091
FAX: 304-292-5217
e-mail: nwvcil@nwvcil.org
www.nwvcil.org

*Jan Derry, Director*

NWVCIL is committed to the philosophy that all persons have equal access and unconditional value, that all individuals shall be respected for their uniqueness and shall have the right to live within the community of their choice, having equal access to participate in and contribute to that community.

# Wisconsin

**5161 Access to Independence**
2345 Atwood Avenue
Madison, WI 53704
608-242-8484
800-362-9877
FAX: 608-242-0383
TTY: 608-242-8485
www.accesstoind.org

*James Powell, President*
*Ann Smith, VP*
*Neal Ewers, Director*

An Independent Living Center serving people with disabilities. Services include: information and referral, housing counseling, advocacy, deaf services, assistive technology, peer support, independent living skills training, and volunteer opportunities, among others.

**5162 Center for Independent Living of Western Wisconsin**
2920 Schneider Avenue SE
Menomonie, WI 54751
715-233-1070
800-228-3287
FAX: 715-233-1083
TTY: 715-233-1070
e-mail: info@cilww.com
www.cilww.com

*Tim Sheehan, Executive Director*
*Kay Sommerfeld, Assistant Director*

**5163 Great Rivers Independent Living Services**
4439 Mormon Coulee Road
La Crosse, WI 54601
608-787-1111
888-474-5745
FAX: 608-787-1114
TTY:888-378-2198
e-mail: advocacy@ilresources.org
www.ilresources.org

*Kathie Knoble-Iverson, Director*
*Michelle Olson, Assistant Director*
*Alicia Oliver, Independent Living Coordinator*

ILR will provide services to persons with any disability of any age within our service area. ILR is committed to community diversity through advocacy, choice and education resulting in empowerment for individuals with disabilities. Serves people in Buffalo, Crawford, Grant, Iowa, Jackson Juneau, La Crosse, La-Fayette, Monroe, Richland, Sauk, Trepealeau and Vernon counties.

**5164 Independence First First**
2001 Haskell Avenue
Lawrence, KS 66046
785-841-0333
888-824-7277
FAX: 414-291-7525
TTY: 785-841-1046
e-mail: bobm@independenceinc.org
www.independenceinc.org

*Tanya Dorf, Executive Director*

**5165 Independence First**
600 W Virginia Street
Suite 300
Milwaukee, WI 53204
414-291-7520
FAX: 414-291-7525
e-mail: kavery@independencefirst.org
www.independencefirst.org

*Lee Schulz, Executive Director*

Serves individuals with disabilities in the metro-Milwaukee four county area. Services include advocacy, independent living skills training, information/referral, peer counseling, youth camp and personal assistance services.

**5166 Independence First: West Bend**
735 S Main Stret
West Bend, WI 53095
262-306-6717
TTY:262-306-6717
e-mail: lee@independencefirst.org
www.west-bend.k12.wi.us

**5167 Independent Living Resources**
2410 SE 11th Avenue
Portland, OR 97214
503-232-7411
FAX: 503-232-7480
TTY:503-232-8404
e-mail: ilrpdx@qwest.net
www.irl.org

*Barry Quamee, Executive Director*

**5168 Inspiration Ministries**
PO Box 948
Walworth, WI 53184
262-275-5753
FAX: 262-275-3355
e-mail: tschnake@inspirationministries.org
www.inspirationministries.org

*David Rowland, President*
*Tim Schnake, VP Resident Services*

Formerly known as Christian League for the Handicapped.The ministry is a caring Christian community who enable and encourage people with disabilities. We address physical, mental and spiritual needs through accessible residential accommodations, work opportunities and integration into the local community and its churches. 160 acre campus including residential apartments, a work center, and a retreat center/summer camp (Inspiration Center).

**5169 Mid-state Independent Living Consultants**
10101 Market Street
Suite B20
Mosinee, WI 54455
715-241-6927
877-711-6452
FAX: 715-241-8168
TTY: 877-711-6452
e-mail: milc@dwave.net
www.tznet.com/comn/firstcall/database/

**5170 Mid-state Independent Living Consultants: Stevens Point**
3262 Church Street
Suite 1
Stevens Point, WI 54481
715-344-4210
800-382-8484
FAX: 715-344-4414
TTY: 800-382-8484
e-mail: milc@milc-inc.org
www.milc-inc.org

*Jennifer Fasula, Executive Director*

**5171 North Country Independent Living**
2231 Catlin Avenue
Suite 16
Superior, WI 54880
715-392-9118
800-924-1220
FAX: 715-392-4636
e-mail: ncil@superior-nfp.org
www.northcountryil.com

*John Nousaine, Executive Director*

**5172 North Country Independent Living: Ashland**
422 3rd Street
Suite B114
Ashland, WI 54806
715-682-5676
800-499-5676
FAX: 715-682-3144
TTY: 715-682-5676
e-mail: ncilstew@charterinternet.com
www.northcountryil.com

*John Nousaine, Director*

**5173 Options for Independent Living**
PO Box 11967
Green Bay, WI 54307
920-490-0500
888-485-1515
888-465-1515
FAX: 920-490-0700
TTY:920-490-0600
e-mail: tomd@optionsil.org
www.optionsil.com

*Thomas J Diedrick, Executive Director*

Provides independent living core services including: peer counseling, information and referral, IL skills training, advocacy - individual and systems, and housing referrals. Rehabilitation technology services provided include: home evaluations, vehicle evaluations, computer evaluations, deaf/hard of hearing equipment evaluations and ADA Title III Technical Assistance and benefits counseling.

**5174 Options for Independent Living:**
555 Country Club Road
PO Box 11967
Green Bay, WI 54307
920-490-0500
888-465-1515
FAX: 920-490-0700
TTY: 920-490-0600
e-mail: info@optionsil.com
www.optionsil.com

*Thomas Diedrick, Director*
*Kathryn Barry, Assistant Director*

**5175 Options for Independent Living: Fond du Lac**
555 Country Club Road
PO Box 11967
Green Bay, WI 54307
920-490-0500
888-465-1515
FAX: 920-490-0700
TTY:920-490-0600
e-mail: info@optionsil.com
www.options.com

*Thomas Diedrick, Executive Director*

Options for Independent Living, Inc. is a non-profit organization committed to empowering people with disabilities to lead independent and productive lives in their community through advocacy, the provision of information, education, technology and related services.

**5176 Society's Assets: Elkhorn**
615 E Geneva Street
Elkhorn, WI 53121
262-723-8181
FAX: 262-723-8184
TTY:262-723-8181
e-mail: info@sai-inc.org
www.sai-inc.org

*Bruce Nelson, Director*
*Jill Vigueres, Manager*

To ensure the rights of all persons with disabilities to live and function as independently as possible in the community of their choice, through supporting individual's efforts to achieve control over their lives and become integrated into community life.

**5177 Society's Assets: Kenosha**
5727 6th Avenue
Kenosha, WI 53140
262-657-3999
888-317-3999
FAX: 262-657-1672
TTY: 262-657-3999
e-mail: info@sai-inc.org
www.sai-inc.org

*Joanie May, Manager*
*Bruce Nelsen, Executive Director*

**5178 Society's Assets: Racine**
5200 Washington Avenue
Suite 225
Racine, WI 53406
262-637-9128
FAX: 262-637-8646
e-mail: info@sai-inc.org
www.sai-inc.org

*Bruce Nelsen, Executive Director*
*Karen Olufs, Director Independent Living*
*Jean Rumachik, Director Home Care Services*

Society's Assets assists people with disabilities to live as independently as possible. A non-profit human services agency, Society's Assets provides information and referal, independent living skills training, peer support, advocacy, and supportive home care. Home health care is provided by SAI Home Health Care. The agency serves 5 counties in southeastern Wisconsin and also provides information about interpreters, employment, benefits, home modifications, assistive equipment and accessibility.

*Fees vary*

# Wyoming

**5179 LifeQuest: Interdisciplinary Rehabilitation**
339 W Loucks Street
Sheridan, WY 82801
307-674-4462
800-684-2289
FAX: 307-674-4552
e-mail: mlr@renew-wyo.com
www.renew-wyo.com

*Theresa Faulkner*

Multi-disciplines organization dedicated to the highest possible economic and social independence for persons with disabilities. Extensive referral service, specialized employment placement, occupational therapy, psychological services, evaluation services, and coordination of external services as needed to meet client plans and objectives.

**5180** **Rehabilitation Enterprises of North Eastern Wyoming: Sheridan**
1969 S Sheridan Avenue
Sheridan, WY  82801
    307-672-7481
    888-309-2020
    FAX: 307-674-5117
    e-mail: ceo@renew-wyo.com
    www.renew-wyo.com

*Larry Samson, President/CEO*
*Sandy Theil, Vice President*

Committed to enhancing personal and community relationships, providing opportunities for growth, and helping people with varying abilities achieve their personal goals.

**5181** **Rehabilitation Enterprises of North Easter n Wyoming: Newcastle**
35 Fairgrounds Road
Newcastle, WY  82701
    307-746-4733
    888-693-9245
    FAX: 307-746-9071
    e-mail: ceo@renew-wyo.com
    www.renew-wyo.com

*Larry Samson, President*
*Sandy Theil, Vice President*

Committed to enhancing personal and community relationships, providing opportunities for growth, and helping people with varying abilities achieve their personal goals.

**5182** **Wyoming Independent Living Rehabilitation**
305 W 1st Street
Casper, WY  82601
    307-266-6956
    800-735-8322
    FAX: 307-266-6957
    TTY: 307-266-6956
    e-mail: dpotter@trib.org
    www.wilr.org

*Kenneth Hoff, Executive Director*

Creates opportunities for severly disabled individuals to live more independently, direct services, advocacy, home modifications and independent living skills.

**5183** **Wyoming Services for Independent Living**
1156 S 2nd Street
Lander, WY  82520
    307-332-4889
    FAX: 307-332-2491
    TTY:307-332-7582
    e-mail: wsil@wyoming.com

*Carol Fontaine, Executive Director*

## Associations & Referral Agencies

**5184 AIDS Legal Council of Chicago**
188 W Randolph Street
Suite 2400
Chicago, IL 60601
312-427-8990
FAX: 312-427-8419
e-mail: info@aidslegal.com
www.aidslegal.com

*Robert D Lo Prete, President*
*Robert F Harris, Vice President*
*Ann Fisher, Executive Director*

Legal advice and services for persons who are HIV positive or
have AIDS, and their companions, families, etc., regarding
HIV-related legal matters.

**5185 AIDSLAW of Louisiana**
Greater New Orleans Foundation
2515 Canal Street
New Orleans, LA 70119
504-598-4663
FAX: 504-821-8326

*Gregory Ben Johnson, President*

Second year of funding for new legal agency serving persons affected by HIV/AIDS.

**5186 Advocacy**
7800 Shoal Creek Boulevard
Suite 171-East
Austin, TX 78757
512-454-4816
800-252-9108
FAX: 202-777-7577
e-mail: info@advocacy.org
www.advocacyinc.org

*Kathleen D Sheekey, President/CEO*
*Sharvell Becton, Program Director*
*Jonas Schwartz, Manager*

Advocacy, Inc advocates for, protects and advances the legal,
human and service rights of people with disabilities throughout
the state of Texas.

**5187 Center for Disability and Elder Law**
710 N Lake Shore Drive
Chicago, IL 60611
312-908-4463
FAX: 312-908-0866

*Jan Dragovich, Executive Director*
*Miriam Seitz, Executive Manager*

Provides legal services at no cost to low income persons with
disabilities in Cook County. LCD staff screen applicants to determine if they meet the financial, disability and geographical
eligibility requirements for service.

**5188 Chicago Lawyers' Committee for Civil Rights Under
Law**
100 N La Salle Street
Suite 600
Chicago, IL 60602
312-630-9744
FAX: 312-630-1127
e-mail: clccrul@clccrul.com
www.clccrul.org

*Clyde Murphy, Executive Director*
*Alesha Jackson, Office Manager*

Provides legal services to individuals and groups with civil
rights problems through class action and law reform cases. Also
provides technical assistance to community groups. Spanish-speaking staff available. Individual cases and walk-ins are
not accepted. Wheelchair accessible.

**5189 DNA People's Legal Services**
Central Office D NA People Civil Services
PO Box 987
Shiprock, NM 87420
505-368-3200
FAX: 505-368-3212
www.dnalegalservices.org/dnalegalservices

*Loretta Danzuka, Manager*
*Elsie Shorthair, Office Manager*

Offers legal assistance to Native Americans.

**5190 Disability Rights Education and Defense Fund**
2212 6th Street
Berkeley, CA 94710
510-644-2555
800-348-4232
FAX: 510-841-8645
e-mail: dredf@dredf.org
www.dredf.org

*Susan Henderson, Managing Director*

Nonprofit organization dedicated to advancing the civil rights
of individuals with disabilities through legislation, litigation,
informal and formal advocacy and education and training of
lawyers, advocates and clients with respect to disability issues.
DREDF also provides training, advocacy, technical assistance
and referrals for parents of disabled children.

**5191 Equal Employment Advisory Council**
1015 15th Street NW
Suite 1200
Washington, DC 20005
202-789-8650
FAX: 202-789-2291

*Jeffrey Norris, President*

A nonprofit association for the purpose of monitoring federal
equal employment litigation and filing amicus curiae briefs in
precedent-setting cases. Also file comments on equal opportunity employment and affirmative action regulatory proposals
and monitors judicial developments.

**5192 Guardianship Services Associates**
41 South Boulevard
A
Oak Park, IL 60302
708-386-5398
FAX: 708-386-5970
e-mail: GSAoakpark@aol.com

*Robert R Wohlgemuth, Director/Owner*

Information and counseling on guardianship issues. Can provide direct assistance in obtaining guardianship for disabled
adults. Also provides information and direct assistance on durable powers of attorney. Can assume appointment as guardian in
selected cases.

**5193 Judge David L Bazelon Center for Mental Health Law**
1101 15th Street NW
Suite 1212
Washington, DC 20005
202-467-5730
FAX: 202-223-0409
e-mail: info@bazelon.org
www.bazelon.org

*Robert Bernstein, Executive Director*
*Lee Carty, Communications Director*

National litigation and technical assistance center for advocates
for people with mental disabilities. Offers a website with advocacy resources and a variety of publications, handbooks, issue
papers and manuals to help advocate for, implement, enforce
and comply with federal laws and court orders on involuntary
outpatient commitment, discrimination based on a label of mental disability, fair housing, criminalization, custody relinquish-
ment for access to children's mental health care.

**5194  Legal Action Center**

236 Massachusetts Avenue NE
Suite 505
Washington, DC 20002                202-544-5478
                                FAX: 202-544-5712
                            e-mail: lacdc@lac-dc.org

*Ellen Weber, Senior VP*
*Willery Murray, Manager*

Provides technical assistance and education programs on ADA
issues related to individuals with drug and alcohol abuse and
HIV disease and legal assistance to individuals who have faced
discrimination on the basis of these disabilities.

**5195  Legal Center**

455 Sherman Street
Suite 130
Denver, CO 80203                    303-722-0300
                                    800-288-1376
                                FAX: 303-722-0720
                        e-mail: tlcmail@thelegalcenter.org
                            www.thelegalcenter.org

*Mary Anne Harvey, Executive Director*
*Mark Ivandick, Manager*

The Legal center uses the legal system to protect and promote the
rights of people with disabilities and older people in Colorado
through direct legal representation, advocacy, education and
legislative analysis. We are also the State Ombudsman for nursing homes and assisted living facilities. Call for a free publications and products list.

**5196  Legal Center for the Elderly and Disabled**

2862 Arden Way
Suite 200
Sacramento, CA 95825                916-488-5298
                                FAX: 916-973-3199
                        e-mail: jonellison@sbcglobal.net
                                www.iced.org

*Jonathan Ellison, Executive Director*

Free civil legal services for low-income people over sixty and
permanently disabled persons under sixty, specializing in social
security, medical benefits elder law, disability rights and housing in North Central California.

**5197  NHeLP**

National Health Law Program
2639 S La Cienega Boulevard
Los Angeles, CA 90034               310-204-6010
                                FAX: 310-204-0891
                        e-mail: nhelp@healthlaw.org
                                www.healthlaw.org

Helps ensure equity and non-discrimination in federal, state, local and private health care programs by assisting local legal service attorneys, paralegal and non-LSC attorneys representing
LSC-eligible clients. NHeLP provides advice, co-counsel and
other litigation assistance and trainings. *$85.00*
                *30-32 pages Quarterly*

**5198  National Center for State Courts**

300 Newport Avenue
Williamsburg, VA 23185              757-259-7575
                                    800-616-6164
                                FAX: 757-564-2022
                        e-mail: webmaster@ncsc.dni.us
                                www.ncsconline.org

*Deborah White, HR Director*
*Toni Engle, Administrative Manager*

Develops a national clearinghouse and resource center for local
and state courts to focus on requirements and methods of
compliances with ADA.

**5199  National Center for Youth Law**

405 14th Street
15th Floor
Oakland, CA 94612                   510-835-8098
                                FAX: 510-835-8099
                        e-mail: info@youthlaw.org
                                www.youthlaw.org

*Peter B Edelman, President*
*Terrence Lee Hancock, Vice President*
*John O'Toole, Executive Director*

Support services to legal services attorneys and child advocates
on SSI (Supplemental Security Income) disability benefits for
children.

**5200  National Legal Center for the Medically Dependent and
Disabled**

50 S Meridian Street
Suite 605
Indianapolis, IN 46204              317-638-1700
                                FAX: 812-232-0620
                        e-mail: nlcmdd@juno.com
                            www.tmarzon@aol.com

*Howard Howe*

Litigation and support center for the disabled specializing in
medical treatment lights/attendant care issues. *$49.00*

**5201  National Right to Work Legal Defense and Education
Foundation**

8001 Braddock Road
Suite 600
Springfield, VA 22160               703-321-8510
                                    800-336-3600
                            e-mail: info@nrtw.org
                                www.nrtw.org

*Reed Larson, President*
*Stefan Gleason, Vice President*

Provides free legal aid to employees whose human and civil
rights are being violated by compulsory unionism abuses.

**5202  REACH/Resource Center on Independent Living**

1205 Lake Street
Fort Worth, TX 76102                817-870-9082
                                FAX: 817-877-1622
                        e-mail: reachdal@fiberramp.net
                            www.reachcil.org/rchftw.php4

*Charlotte Stewart, Director*
*Anne Ancy, Case Manager*
*Robin Laffiter, Manaager*

Information and referral services, peer counseling, independent
living skills training, loaner equipment, advocacy assistance,
ADA technical assistance and social/recreational activities.

**5203  TASH Connections**

29 W Susquehanna Avenue
Suite 210
Baltimore, MD 21204                 410-828-8274
                                    800-482-8274
                                FAX: 410-828-6706
                            e-mail: info@tash.org
                                www.tash.org

*Nancy Weiss, Executive Director*
*Priscilla Newton, Director Marketing/Communication*

International association of people with disabilities, their family members, other advocates and professionals fighting for a
society in which inclusion of all people in all aspects of society
is the norm.

*November*

**5204  Winifred Law Opportunity Center**
106 E 2nd Avenue
Indianola, IA  50125
           515-961-5341
           FAX: 515-961-5002

*Diane M Griffith MS, Executive Director*

---

# Resources for the Disabled

**5205  AACD Legal Series**
American Counseling Association
5999 Stevenson Avenue
Alexandria, VA  22304
           703-823-9800
           800-347-6647
           FAX: 703-823-0252
      e-mail: webmaster@counseling.org
           www.counseling.org

*Sam Gladding, Ace President*
*Richard Yep, Executive Director*

Offering three volumes: Preparing for Court Appearances; Documentation in Counseling Records; and The Counselor and The Law.
    *3 Volumes*

**5206  ABDA/ABMPP Workshop: The Art of Courtroom Testifying**
American Board of Disability Analysts
342 24th Avenue N
Suite 200
Nashville, TN  37203
           615-327-2984
           FAX: 615-327-9235
      e-mail: americanbd@aol.com

*Kenneth Anchor, President*

February workshop. Workshop leader: Dr. William Tsushima.

**5207  ADA Mandate for Social Change**
Paul H Brookes Publishing Company
PO Box 10624
Baltimore, MD  21285
           410-337-9580
           800-638-3775
           FAX: 410-337-8539

*Paul Brooks, Owner*

This timely book moves a large step beyond detailing the legislative requirements of the ADA by focusing on the changes the ADA is generating for persons with disabilities. *$32.00*
    *320 pages Paperback 1993*
    *ISBN 1-557661-17-0*

**5208  Americans with Disabilities Act Manual**
American Bar Association
740 15th Street NW
9th Floor
Washington, DC  20005
           202-662-1011
           800-285-2221
           FAX: 202-662-1032
    e-mail: hammillj@staff.abanet.org
           www.abanet.org/disability

*Robert J Grey Jr, President*
*Robert A Stein, Executive Director*
*Nancy Scholnick, Manager*

An in-depth analysis of the legal and practical implications of the ADA using non-technical language. *$20.00*

**5209  Americans with Disabilities Act: Selected Resources for Deaf**
Gallaudet University Bookstore
800 Florida Avenue NE
Washington, DC  20002
           202-651-5271
           800-621-2736
           FAX: 202-651-5477
  e-mail: infotech.services@gallaudet.edu
           www.gallaudet.edu

*Priscilla O'Donnell, Bookstore Manager*
*Iva Williams, Bookstore Secretary*
*Elaine Vance, Human Resources Director*

This resource identifies programs and publications specific to the ADA and deafness and also lists ADA materials and programs for people with any disability.

**5210  Approaching Equality**
T J Publishers
2544 Tarpley Road
Suite 108
Carrollton, TX  75006
           972-416-0800
           800-999-1168
           FAX: 301-585-5930
      e-mail: TJPubinc@aol.com

*Angela K Thames, President*
*Jerald A Murphy, Vice President*

Public education laws guarantee special education for all deaf children, but may find the special education system confusing, or are unsure of their rights under current laws. For anyone with an interest in education, advocacy and the deaf community, this book reviews dramatic developments in education of deaf children, youth and adults since COED's 1988 report, Toward Equality. *$12.95*
    *112 pages*
    *ISBN 0-93266 -39-6*

**5211  Assessment of the Feasibility of Contracting with a Nominee Agency**
Mississippi State University
PO Box 6189
Mississippi State, MS  39762
           662-325-2001
           800-675-7782
           FAX: 662-325-8989
           www.blind.msstate.edu

*Kelly Schaefer, Publications Manager*
*Elton Moore, Executive Director*

Only five State Licensing Agencies currently utilize nominee agreements. This study compared the Pennsylvania program with four states that utilize nominee agencies and four states that do not. Results and recommendations compared state and national data from Federal FY 1991-1993. *$20.00*
    *152 pages Paperback*

**5212  Bluebook: Explanation of the Contents of the ADA**
Disability Rights Education and Defense Fund
2212 6th Street
Berkeley, CA  94710
           510-644-2555
           FAX: 510-841-8645
        e-mail: dredf@dredf.org
           www.dredf.org

*Susan Henderson, Managing Director*

Written in narrative form for both professionals and lay people, DREDF's bluebook offers detailed, thorough analysis of all of the law's provisions, encompassing ADA legislative history, the statute and regulations. Available in alternative formats. *$100.00*

*214 pages*

**5213  Can America Afford to Grow Old?**
Brookings Institution
1775 Massachusetts Avenue NW
Washington, DC  20036          202-797-6000
                               FAX: 202-797-6004
                    e-mail: bibooks@brookings.edu
                               www.brookings.edu

*Strobe Talbott, President*

Social security laws and regulations. *$8.95*
        *144 pages Paperback*
        *ISBN 0-815700-43-1*

**5214  Childcare and the ADA**
Eastern Washington University
705 W 1st Avenue
Room 223
Spokane, WA  99201             509-623-4200
                               FAX: 509-623-4230
              e-mail: susan.vanmeter@mail.ewu.edu

*Nancy Ashworth, Director Child Development*
*Allen Barrom, Manager*

Provides information on how childcare providers must comply
with the ADA. Eight videotapes plus an instructional manual
with examples of situations and problems. *$85.00*
        *Set*

**5215  Complying with the Americans with Disabilities Act**
Greenwood Publishing Group
88 Post Road W
Suite 5007
Westport, CT  06880            203-226-3571
                               FAX: 203-222-1502
                               www.greenwood.com

*Wayne Smith, President*

A guidebook for management and people with disabilities.
Hardcover.
        *280 pages $52.95 - $57.95*
        *ISBN 0-899307-14-0*

**5216  Convicting the Innocent**
Brookline Books
39 University Road
Brookline, MA  02445           617-734-6772
                               800-666-BOOK
                               FAX: 617-734-3952
                 e-mail: brooklinebks@delphi.com
                               www.brooklinebooks.com

*William H Walters, Author*
*Esther Isabe Wilder, Author*

Exposes the dirtiest secret of American Law Enforcement: the
process of subjecting innocent citizens- often poor or mentally
impaired- to inquisitions to elicit confessions which often result
in wrongful convictions. These thoughtful and compassionate
essays analyze scandals nationwide, spotlighting the Richard
Lapointe case featured on 60 minutes. Contributions include Pu-
litzer Prize winners William Styron, Arthur Miller, and Richard
Ofshe. *$16.95*
        *220 pages Paperback*
        *ISBN 1-57129 -21-4*

**5217  Council for Disability Rights**
30 E Adams Street
Suite 1130
Chicago, IL  60603             312-444-9484
                               FAX: 312-444-1977
                               TTY:312-444-1967
                 e-mail: cdr@disabilityrights.org
                               www.disabilityrights.org

*Jo Holzer, Executive Director*

Promotes human rights of persons with disabilities and their
families. Offers legal referrals, information services and disability awareness training.

**5218  Court-Related Needs of the Elderly and Persons with Disabilities**
Mental Health Commission
2700 Martin Luther King Jr Ave SE
Washington, DC  20032          202-282-0027
                               FAX: 202-373-7982

This book features the ground-breaking recommendations from
the national Conference on the Court-Related Needs of the Elderly and Persons with Disabilities, funded by the States Justice
Institute and co-sponsored by the American Bar Association and
National Judicial College. Accompanying the recommendations are detailed commentaries and extensive background research papers organized around issues. *$20.00*
        *276 pages*

**5219  Criminal Law Handbook on Psychiatric & Psychological Evidence & Testimony**
ABA Commission on Mental & Physical Disability Law
740 15th Street NW
9th Floor
Washington, DC  20005          202-662-1011
                               800-285-2221
                               FAX: 202-662-1032
                e-mail: hammillj@staff.abanet.org
                               www.abanet.org/disability

*John Hammill, Publications Coordinator*
*Amy Allbright, Managing Editor*
*Nancy Scholnick, Manager*

Examines the admissibility of psychiatric and psychological evidence and testimony pertaining to key civil mental health standards. *$45.00*
        *376 pages*
        *ISBN 1-570738-49-1*

**5220  Critical Issues in the Lives of People with Severe Disabilities**
Paul H Brookes Publishing Company
PO Box 10624
Baltimore, MD  21285           410-337-9580
                               800-638-3775
                               FAX: 410-337-8539

*Paul Brooks, Owner*

This comprehensive book explores the values, practices and empirical research that have guided legal and practical decisions
concerning the lives of people with severe disabilities in the
past. *$90.00*
        *704 pages Hardcover 1991*
        *ISBN 1-557660-48-4*

**5221  Dealing with Mental Incapacity**
Center for Public Representation
PO Box 260049
Madison, WI  53726             608-251-4008
                               800-369-0388
                               FAX: 606-251-1263
                e-mail: cpr@lawmail.law.wisc.edu
                               www.law.wisc.edu/pal

This manual contains a comprehensive introduction to the problem of guardianship as well as chapters of financial and health
care planning tools, guardianship under Wisconsin law, protective placement and Watts reviews. *$19.95*

**5222  Dimensions of State Mental Health Policy**
Greenwood Publishing Group
88 Post Road W
Suite 5007
Westport, CT  06880            203-226-3571
                               FAX: 203-222-1502
                               www.greenwood.com

*Wayne Smith, President*

Introduces students to the emerging field of state mental health
policy. Hardcover.

*320 pages $59.95 - $65*
*ISBN 0-275932-52-4*

**5223 Disability Compliance Bulletin**
L RP Publications
360 Hiatt Drive
Palm Beach Gardens, FL 33418           561-622-6520
                                        800-341-7874
                                  FAX: 561-622-0757
                          e-mail: custserve@lrp.com
                                        www.lrp.com

*Kenneth Kahn, Founder/CEO*
*Honora McDowell, Product Group Manager*

This biweekly newsletter gives you timely coverage and insightful analyses of the latest developments in disability law. You'll learn the most recent case law dealing with the Americans with Disabilities Act, the Family and Medical Leave Act and more. Disability Compliance Bulletin will help you understand the laws' obligations and show you emerging legal trends. *$165.00*
*24 pages BiWeekly*

**5224 Disability Law in the United States**
William Hein & Company
1285 Main Street
Buffalo, NY 14209                      716-882-2600
                                        800-828-7571
                                  FAX: 716-883-8100
                          e-mail: mail@wshein.com
                                        www.wshein.com

*Customer Service Department*
*Kevin Marmion, President*

Offers thousands of pages of information on the laws and legislation affecting the disabled in the United States. Its purpose is to provide a clear and comprehensive mandate to end discrimination against individuals with disabilities and to bring disabled persons into the economic and social midstream of American Life. *$650.00*
*5750 pages*
*ISBN 0-899417-97-3*

**5225 Disability Rights Now**
Disability Rights Education and Defense Fund
2212 6th Street
Berkeley, CA 94710                     510-644-2555
                                  FAX: 510-841-8645
                          e-mail: dredf@dredf.org
                                        www.dredf.org

*Susan Henderson, Managing Director*

Free quarterly publication describing the activities of the Disability Rights Education and Defense Fund, available in alternative formats.
*Quarterly*

**5226 Education of the Handicapped: Laws, Legislative Histories and Administrative Documents**
William Hein & Company
1285 Main Street
Buffalo, NY 14209                      716-882-2600
                                        800-828-7571
                                  FAX: 716-883-8100
                          e-mail: mail@wshein.com
                                        www.wshein.com

*Kevin Marmion, President*
*Brian Joblonski, Director Marketing/Publications*

Focuses upon elementary and secondary Education Act of 1965 and its amendment, Education For All Handicapped Children Act of 1975 and its amendments and acts providing services for the blind, deaf, mentally retarded, etc. Hardcover. *$2850.00*

*55 Volume set*
*ISBN 0-899411-57-6*

**5227 ElderLawAnswers.com**
535 Boylston Street
8th Floor
Boston, MA 02116
                                        866-267-0947
                  e-mail: support@elderlawanswers.com
                                  www.elderlawanswers.com

*Harry Margolis, Founder/President*
*Mark Miller, Operations Director*
*Ken Coughlin, Managing Editor*

Provides information about legal issues facing senior citizens and a searchable directory of attorneys.

**5228 Ethical and Legal Issues in School Counseling**
American Counseling Association
5999 Stevenson Avenue
Alexandria, VA 22304                   703-823-9800
                                        800-473-2329
                                  FAX: 703-823-0252
                  e-mail: webmaster@counseling.org
                                        www.counseling.org

*Sam Gladding, Ace President*
*Richard Yep, Executive Director*

This comprehensive text is filled with answers to many of the most controversial and challenging questions faced by the professional every day. This text helps avoid ethical violations and provides thorough information on: confidentiality, privacy, privileged communication, access to school records, using group techniques ethically, computerized record keeping and reporting unethical practices. *$24.95*
*341 pages paperback 1988*
*ISBN 1-556200-55-2*

**5229 Families Forward: Health Care Resource Guide for Children with Special Care Needs**
Center for Public Representation
PO Box 260049
Madison, WI 53726                      608-251-4008
                                        800-369-0388
                                  FAX: 606-251-1263
                  e-mail: cpr@lawmail.law.wisc.edu
                          www.law.wisc.edu/pal/famfrwd.htm
Extensive resource material: health insurance, HMOs, dealing with medical debt, services to keep your child at home and more. *$10.00*

*ISBN 0-932622-54-2*

**5230 Federal Laws of the Mentally Handicapped: Laws, Legislative Histories and Admin. Documents**
William Hein & Company
1285 Main Street
Buffalo, NY 14209                      716-882-2600
                                        800-828-7571
                                  FAX: 716-883-8100
                          e-mail: mail@wshein.com
                                        www.wshein.com

*Kevin Marmion, President*
*Scott Fiddler, Vice President of Production*

Chronological compilation of all relevant federal laws dealing with the mentally handicapped along with supporting documentation necessary to create a complete legislative history. *$2200.00*

*42 Volume/Set*
*ISBN 0-899411-06-1*

**5231    Formed Families: Adoption of Children with Handicaps**

Haworth Press
10 Alice Street
Binghamton, NY  13904                    607-722-5857
                                         800-429-6784
                                    FAX: 607-722-6362
                        e-mail: orders@haworthpress.com
                                    www.haworthpress.com

*Laraine Masters Glidden Phd, Editor*
*William Cohen, Owner*

Provides broad coverage of the issues relating to the adoption of
children with handicaps. Concerned professionals can find here
all the answers about clinical programs, legal issues, estimates
of frequency, and important factors related to positive and negative outcomes of these adoptions. *$74.95*
                    *242 pages Hardcover 1990*
                    *ISBN 0-866569-14-6*

**5232    Free Appropriate Public Education**

Love Publishing Company
9101 E Kenyon Avenue
Denver, CO  80237                         303-221-7333
                                         877-240-6396
                                    FAX: 303-221-7444
                    e-mail: lovepublishing@compuserve.com
                                    www.lovepublishing.com

*Laura Banks, Administrative Officer*
*Stan Love, Owner*

Information on significant legislation regarding the handicapped. Laws are discussed with attention to their impact on the
child, the parents, the public schools and higher education.
*$44.95*

                    *ISBN 0-89108 -11-5*

**5233    Handbook on Mental Disability Law**

A BA Commission on Mental & Physical Disability La
740 15th Street NW
9th Floor
Washington, DC  20005                    202-662-1570
                                         800-285-2221
                                    FAX: 202-662-1032
                        www.abanet.org/disability

*Letty Brown, Publications Coordinator*
*Amy Allbright, Managing Editor*
*John Parry, Executive Director*

Provides a comprehensive analysis of federal and state statues
and case law with a disability discrimination focus. *$45.00*
                    *313 pages*

**5234    Health Care Quality Improvement Act of 1986**

William Hein & Company
1285 Main Street
Buffalo, NY  14209                        716-882-2600
                                         800-828-7571
                                    FAX: 716-883-8100
                            e-mail: mail@wshein.com
                                    www.wshein.com

*Kevin Marmion, President*
*Daniel P Rosati, Senior Vice President*

In order to encourage more stringent peer review by doctors and
hospitals, and to protect reporting physicians and institutions
from retaliatory lawsuits, Congress enacted The Health Care
Quality Improvement Act. The Act was also intended to address
the increasing incidence of medical malpractice and to prevent
the ease with which incompetent practitioners moved from state
to state. Hardcover. *$75.00*

*730 pages*
*ISBN 0-899416-93-4*

**5235    Housing and Transportation of the Handicapped**

William Hein & Company
1285 Main Street
Buffalo, NY  14209                        716-882-2600
                                         800-828-7571
                                    FAX: 716-883-8100
                            e-mail: mail@wshein.com
                                    www.wshein.com

*Kevin Marmion, President*

National laws, recognizing the problems encountered by the
handicapped in the areas of housing and transportation and providing assistance in an effort to surmount those problems. Hardcover or microfilm. *$1850.00*
                    *250 documents*
                    *ISBN 0-899412-47-5*

**5236    Human Resource Management and the Americans with
Disabilities Act**

Greenwood Publishing Group
88 Post Road W
Suite 5007
Westport, CT  06880                       203-226-3571
                                    FAX: 203-222-1502
                                    www.greenwood.com

*John G Veres Iii, Editor*
*Ronald R Sims, Editor*
*Wayne Smith, President*

Concrete advice for human resource professionals on how to
cope with the vague, often obscure provisions of the Americans
with Disabilities Act.
                    *232 pages $59.95 - $62.95*
                    *ISBN 0-899308-57-0*

**5237    International Handbook on Mental Health Policy**

Greenwood Publishing Group
88 Post Road W
Suite 5007
Westport, CT  06880                       203-226-3571
                                         800-225-5800
                                    FAX: 203-222-1502
                        e-mail: webmaster@greenwood.com
                                    www.greenwood.com

*John G Veres, Author*
*Ronald R Sims, Author*
*Wayne Smith, President*

The first major reference book for academics and practitioners
that provides a systematic survey and analysis of mental health
policies in twenty representative countries.
                    *512 pages $110 - $125*
                    *ISBN 0-313275-67-X*

**5238    Knowing Your Rights**

A AR P Fulfillment
601 E Street NW
Washington, DC  20049                     202-434-2277
                                         800-424-3410
                                    FAX: 202-434-3443
                            e-mail: member@aarp.org
                                    www.aarp.org

*William Novelli, Chief Executive Officer*
*Lynn Smith, Director of Human Resources*

Describes how changes in Medicare's reimbursement policies
are designed to reduce health care costs and suggests steps that
Medicare beneficiaries, their families and friends can take to assure that they continue to receive quality care under the Prospective Payment System.

*19 pages*

**5239  Law Center Newsletter**
Public Interest Law Center of Philadelphia
125 S 9th Street
Philadelphia, PA  19107                215-627-7100

*Michael Churchill, Manager*

Information on mental health, foster care and public education.
Provides all updates concerning the law in these areas.

**5240  Legal Center**
455 Sherman Street
Suite 130
Denver, CO  80203                       303-722-0300
                                        800-288-1376
                                   FAX: 303-722-0720
               e-mail: tlcmail@thelegalcenter.org
                            www.thelegalcenter.org

*Mary Anne Harvey, Executive Director*
*Mark Ivandick, Manager*

The Legal center uses the legal system to protect and promote the
rights of people with disabilities and older people in Colorado
through direct legal representation, advocacy, education and
legislative analysis. We are also the State Ombudsman for nursing homes and assisted living facilities. Call for a free publications and products list.

**5241  Legal Right: The Guide for Deaf and Hard of Hearing
People**
Gallaudet University Press
800 Florida Avenue NE
Washington, DC  20002                   202-651-5488
                                        800-621-2736
                                   FAX: 202-651-5489
                                   TTY: 800-621-9347
                  e-mail: gupress@gallaudet.edu
                            www.gupress.gallaudet.edu

*Sy Dubrow, Author*
*Sarah Geer, Author*
*Karen Peltz Strauss, Author*

This revised fifth edition is in easy-to-understand language, offering the latest state and federal statues and administrative procedures that prohibit discrimination against the deaf, hard of
hearing and other physically challenged people. *$24.95*
        *282 pages Paperback*
        *ISBN 1-563680-00-9*

**5242  Legal Rights of Persons with Disabilities: An Analysis of
Federal Law**
L RP Publications
360 Hiatt Drive
Palm Beach Gardens, FL  33418           561-622-6520
                                        800-341-7874
                                   FAX: 561-622-6520
                       e-mail: custserve@lrp.com
                                   www.lrp.com

*Kenneth Khan, Founder/CEO*
*Gary Bagin, Director of Communications*

A comprehensive analysis of the rights accorded individuals
with disabilities under federal law covering such issues as: Definitions of individuals with disabilities, reasonable
accomidations, architectural barriers, access to transportation
and communication services, education and newborns. *$185.00*

*1536 pages*
*ISBN 0-934753-46-6*

**5243  Legislative Network for Nurses**
Business Publishers
2601 University Boulevard W
Suite 200
Silver Spring, MD  20902                301-587-6300
                                        800-274-6737
                  e-mail: bpinews@bpinews.com
                                   www.bpinews.com

*Sarah Spencer, Editor*
*Adam Goldstein, President*

Provides up-to-date information on the nursing shortage, nurse
training programs, AIDS and Hepatitis B, unionization, registered care technologies, compensation, child care, home health
care staffing and much more. *$286.00*
        *8 pages Newsl./BiMonth*

**5244  Making News: How to Get News Coverage of Disability
Rights Issues**
Advocado Press
PO Box 145
Louisville, KY  40201                   888-739-1920
                                   FAX: 502-899-9562
               e-mail: office@advocadopress.org
                            www.advocadopress.org

*Mary Johnson, Author*
*Tari Susan Hartman, Author*

This book gives examples and tips on how to fight back and get
on the front pages, lead the newscasts and influence public debate. *$10.95*
        *165 pages Paperback*
        *ISBN 0-96270 -43-4*

**5245  Medicare and Medicaid Patient and Program Protec-
tion Act of 1987**
William Hein & Company
1285 Main Street
Buffalo, NY  14209                      716-882-2600
                                        800-828-7571
                                   FAX: 716-883-8100
                       e-mail: mail@wshein.com
                                   www.wshein.com

*Kevin Marmion, President*

This act enables the Department of Health and Human Services
to protect Medicare and Medicaid patients and federal health
care programs from censured practitioners. Hardcover. *$185.00*
        *3 Volumes*
        *ISBN 0-899416-95-0*

**5246  Mental & Physical Disability Law Reporter**
American Bar Association
740 15th Street NW
9th Floor
Washington, DC  20005                   202-662-1011
                                        800-285-2221
                                   FAX: 202-662-1032
               e-mail: hammillj@staff.abanet.org
                            www.abanet.org/disability

*John Hammill, Publications Coordinator*
*John Parry, Managing Editor*
*Nancy Scholnick, Manager*

Contains over 2,000 summanes per year of federal and state
court decisions and legislation that affect persons with mental
and physical disabilities. Includes bylined articles by experts in
the field regarding disability law developments and trends.
*$384.00*

*350+ pages BiMonthly*

*8 pages Monthly*

**5247   Mental Disabilities and the Americans with Disabilities Act**
Greenwood Publishing Group
88 Post Road W
Suite 5007
Westport, CT  06880                     203-226-3571
                                        800-225-5800
                                   FAX: 203-222-1502
                        e-mail: webmaster@greenwood.com
                                   www.greenwood.com

*John G Veres III, Author*
*Ronald R Sims, Author*
*Wayne Smith, President*

A clear, practical compliance guide, written by a psychologist, to help organizations conform to provisions on mental disabilities in the Americans with Disabilities Act. Hardcover.
    *216 pages $45 - $49.95 1997*
    *ISBN 0-899308-26-0*

**5248   Mental Disabilities and the Americans with Disabilities Act**
A BA Commission on Mental & Physical Disability La
740 15th Street NW
9th Floor
Washington, DC  20005                   202-662-1570
                                   FAX: 202-662-1032
                          e-mail: cmpdl@abanet.org
                               www.abanet.org/disability

*Robert Burgdorf, Director*
*John Durocher, Director*
*John Parry, Executive Director*

Written for lawyers, advocates, teachers, consumers, employers, and employees, this ADA handbook examines the ADA from the legal and non-legal practitioner's point of view. In six parts, the handbook covers ADA Titles I, II, and III provides case law summaries of ADA court decisions affecting individuals with mental disabilities including mental illness, developmental disabilities, learning disabilities, substance abuse, and organic brain injuries. *$40.00*

**5249   Mental Health Law News**
Interwood Publications
3 Interwood Place
20241
Cincinnati, OH  45220                   513-221-3715

*Frank Bardack, Marketing Director/Editor*

Mental health case law summaries — malpractice, patient rights, discrimination, alcoholism, guardianship, negligence, professional liability, commitment, drug dependency and conservatorship. *$99.00*
    *6 pages Monthly Nwslttr*
    *ISSN 0889-01 0*

**5250   Mental Health Law Reporter**
Business Publishers
2601 University Boulevard W
Suite 200
Silver Spring, MD 20902                  301-587-6300
                                        800-274-6737
                                   FAX: 301-587-1081
                          e-mail: custserv@bpinews.com
                                   www.bpinews.com

*Leonard A Eiserer, Publisher*
*Jeremy Bond, Editor MHLR*
*Bob Grupe, Editor MHLR*

MHLR brings you the most timely, focused and thorough information on the legal issues that concern mental health practitioners in mental health litigation. Topics include: malpractice litigation, patient-therapist confidentiality, sexual victimization of patients, the insanity defense, social security administrative case law and much more. *$286.00*

**5251   Mentally Disabled and the Law**
William Hein & Company
1285 Main Street
Buffalo, NY  14209                       716-882-2600
                                        800-828-7571
                                   FAX: 716-883-8100
                            e-mail: mail@wshein.com
                                   www.wshein.com

*Kevin Marmion, President*
*Daniel P Rosati, Senior Vice President*

Offers information on treatment rights, the provider-patient relationship, and the rights of the mentally disabled persons in the community. *$85.00*
    *867 pages*
    *ISBN 0-910059-05-5*

**5252   NAD Broadcaster**
National Association of the Deaf
8630 Fenton Street
Suite 820
Silver Spring, MD  20910                 301-587-1788
                                   FAX: 301-587-1791
                                   TTY:301-587-1789
                            e-mail: NADinfo@nad.org
                                   www.nad.org

*Andrew J Lange, President*
*Mark D Apodaca, Vice President*

National newspaper published 11 times a year by the nation's largest organization safeguarding the accessbility and civil rights of 28 million deaf and hard of hearing Americans in education, employment, health care, and telecommunications. Membership: individual $30 per year. *$7.00*

**5253   National Focus**
PO Box 37485
Phoenix, AZ  85069                       602-943-6044
                                   FAX: 602-866-9206
Offers information on disabilities issues and legal information for the disabled.

**5254   No Longer Disabled: The Federal Courts**
Greenwood Publishing Group
88 Post Road W
Suite 5007
Westport, CT  06880                      203-226-3571
                                        800-225-5800
                                   FAX: 203-222-1502
                        e-mail: webmaster@greenwood.com
                                   www.greenwood.com

*John G Veres III, Author*
*Ronald R Sims, Author*
*Wayne Smith, President*

This book is a case study of judicial policy making. It focuses on the role of adjudication in the making and refining of federal policy.
    *208 pages $45 - $55*
    *ISBN 0-313254-24-9*

**5255   Opening the Courthouse Door: An ADA Access Guide for State Courts**
American Bar Association
740 15th Street NW
9th Floor
Washington, DC  20005                    202-662-1000
                                        800-285-2221
                                   FAX: 202-662-1032
                         e-mail: hammillj@staff.abanet.org
                               www.abanet.org/disability

*Scott Labarre, Chair*
*John Hammill, Publications Coordinator*
*Robert Evans, Executive Director*

Practical, step-by-step guide explains how to comply with the public access provisions of the ADA in the courthouse. The centerpiece of the guide is a series of action steps. *$12.00*

**5256  Operation Help: A Mental Health Advocate's Guide to Medicaid**
Nat l Council for Community Behavioral Healthcare
12300 Twinbrook Parkway
Suite 320
Rockville, MD  20852                                301-984-6200
                                              FAX: 301-881-7159
                                                  www.nccbh.org

*Linda Rosenberg, President/Chief Executive Office*
*Jennie Campbell, Vice President*

This book explains the Medicaid entitlement program in easy-to-read language and focuses on the needs of your clients. *$17.00*

**5257  PAL News**
Parent Professional Advocacy League
56 Temple Place
Suite 664
Boston, MA  02111                                  617-542-7860
                                                   800-537-0446
                                              FAX: 617-542-7832
                                              e-mail: pal@fcsn.org
                                                  www.ppal.net

*Donna Welles, Executive Director*
*Lisa Lambert, Assistant Director*

Offers information on medical and technological updates in the area of research on birth defects, support groups and family resources for persons with disabled children.
        *Quarterly*

**5258  Power of Attorney for Health Care**
Center for Public Representation
PO Box 260049
Madison, WI  53726                                 608-251-4008
                                                   800-369-0388
                                              FAX: 606-251-1263
Discusses Wisconsin law regarding medical decisions, the Cruzan case and ethical considerations in addition to legal implications and advantages of this document. Book tells how to create a personalized Power of Attorney document, including language for the special provisions portion. *$49.95*
        *132 pages*
        *ISBN 0-93262 -38-0*

**5259  Title II & III Regulation Amendment Regarding Detectable Warnings**
U S Department of Justice
950 Pennsylvania Avenue NW
Washington, DC  20530                              202-646-5095
                                                   800-574-0301
                                              FAX: 202-514-5331
                                                  www.ada.gov
This document suspends the requirements for detectable warnings at curb ramps, hazardous vehicular areas, and reflecting pools.

**5260  Title II Complaint Form**
U S Department of Justice
950 Pennsylvania Avenue NW
Washington, DC  20530                              202-646-5095
                                                   800-514-0301
                                              FAX: 202-307-1197
                                                  www.ada.gov

*John Wodatch, Chief*

Standard form for filing a complaint under Title II of the ADA or Section 504 of the Rehabilitation Act of 1973.

**5261  Title II Highlights**
U S Department of Justice
950 Pennsylvania Avenue NW
Washington, DC  20530                              202-646-5095
                                                   800-514-0383
                                              FAX: 202-307-1198
                                                  www.ada.gov

*John L Wodatch, Chief*
*Allison J Nichol, Deputy Chief*

An 8-page outline of the key requirements of the ADA for state and local governments.

**5262  Title III Technical Assistance Manual and Supplement**
U S Department of Justice
950 Pennsylvania Avenue NW
Washington, DC  20530                              202-646-5095
                                                   800-574-0301
                                              FAX: 202-307-1197
                                                  www.ada.gov
A 12-page outline of the key requirements of the ADA for businesses and nonprofit service agencies.

**5263  Toward Independence**
National Council on Disability
1331 F Street NW
Suite 850
Washington, DC  20004                             202-272-2004
                                              FAX: 202-272-2022
                                              TTY:202-272-2074
                                                  www.ncb.gov

*Mark Quigley, Communications Director*
*Ethel Briggs, Executive Director*

A 1986 report to the U.S. Congress on the federal laws and programs serving people with disabilities, and recommendations for legislation.

**5264  US Department of Health and Human Services Office for Civil Rights**
200 Independence Avenue SW
Washington, DC  20201                             202-690-7650
                                                   800-368-1019
                                              FAX: 202-619-3818
                                                  www.hhs.gov

*Mike Levitt, Secretary*

Enforces the Rehabilitation Act of 1973, which prohibits discrimination against handicapped persons by recipients of federal funding.

**5265  US Department of Labor**
200 Constitution Avenue NW
Washington, DC  20210                             202-693-5000
                                                   866-487-2635
                                              FAX: 202-219-7312

*Elaine Chao, Chief Executive Officer*

Offers publications to assist employers in determining and achieving workplace accessibility.

**5266  US Department of Labor Office of Federal Contract Compliance Programs**
Kluczynski Federal Building
230 S Dearborn Street, Room 570
Chicago, IL  60604                                312-596-7010
                                              FAX: 312-596-7037
                                  e-mail: OFCCP-MW-PreAward@dol.gov
                                                  www.dol.gov/esa

*Sandra Zeigler, Regional Director*
*Margaret Kraak, District Director*

Administers and enforces three legal authorities that require equal employment opportunity: Executive Order 11246, as amended; Section 503 of the Rehabilitation Act of 1973, as amended; and the Vietnam Era Veterans' Readjustment Assistance Act of 1974, as amended, 38 U.S.C. 4212. These authorities prohibit Federal contractors and subcontractors from discriminating on the basis of race, color, religion, sex, national origin, disability, and protected veteran status.

**5267    University Legal Services AT Program**
220 i Street NE
Suite 130
Washington, DC  20002            202-547-4747
                                 877-221-4638
                            FAX: 202-547-2662
                            TTY: 202-547-2657
                    e-mail: atpdc@uls-dc.org
                            www.atpdc.org

*Jane Brown, Executive Director*
*Alicia Johns, Program Manager*

Designed to empower individuals with disabilities; to promote
consumer involvement and advocacy, and provide information,
referral and training as they relate to accessing assistive technology services and devices; and to identify and improve access to
funding resources.

**5268    Washington Watch**
United Cerebral Palsy Association
3135 8th Street NE
Washington, DC  20017            202-269-1500
                            FAX: 202-526-0519
                            TTY:202-973-7197
                  e-mail: webmaster@ucpdc.org
                            www.ucpa.org

*Ted Bertoron, Director*

Dependable, timely information on national legislative and regulatory issues affecting people with disabilities and their families. *$25.00*
        *4 pages BiWeekly*

**5269    William S Hein & Company**
1285 Main Street
Buffalo, NY  14209               716-882-2600
                                 800-828-7571
                            FAX: 716-883-8100
                    e-mail: mail@wshein.com
                            www.wshein.com

*Kevin Marmion, President*
*Daniel P Rosati, Senior Vice President*

Offers a catalog of periodicals, publications and reprints, micro-
forms and government publications on medical, handicapped
and health law.

**5270    Word from Washington**
United Cerebral Palsy
3135 8th Street NE
Washington, DC  20017            202-269-1500
                                 800-USA-5UCP
                            FAX: 202-526-0519
                            TTY: 202-973-7197
                  e-mail: webmaster@ucpdc.org
                            www.ucpa.org

*Stephen Bennett, President/CEO*
*Duncan Wyeth, Vice Chair*

Provides information on national legislation and regulatory affairs, updates on disability and social service fields. *$25.00*
        *24-36 pages Quarterly*

## Alabama

**5271 Alabama Institute for Deaf and Blind Library and Resource Center**
295 E South Street
PO Box 698
Talladega, AL 35161
256-761-3237
800-848-4722
FAX: 256-761-3344
e-mail: lacy.teresa@aidb.aidb.state.al.us
www.aidb.org

*Dr Terry Graham, President*
*Teresa Lacy, Director*

Book collection includes discs, cassettes, braille and large print. Also closed-circuit TV and magnifiers. Offers braille production and binding.

**5272 Alabama Radio Reading Service Network (ARRS)**
650 11th Street S
Birmingham, AL 35294
205-934-2606
800-444-9246
FAX: 205-934-5075
e-mail: info@wbhm.org
www.wbhm.org

*Mike Morgan, General Manager*
*Phillip Habmeeb, ARRS Program Manager*

Services and readings are broadcast over a subcarrier service of public radio WBHM. This is a statewide service devoted to Alabama's blind and handicapped community.

**5273 Alabama Regional Library for the Blind and Physically Handicapped**
Alabama Public Library Service
6030 Monticello Drive
Montgomery, AL 36130
334-213-3906
800-392-5671
FAX: 334-213-3993
e-mail: fzaleski@apls.state.al.us
www.apls.state.al.us

*Fara Zaleski, Executive Director/Librarian*

Recreational reading in special format for persons unable to use standard print. Reference materials offered include materials on blindness and other handicaps, films, local subjects and authors.

**5274 Houston-Love Memorial Library**
PO Box 1369
Dothan, AL 36302
334-793-9767
FAX: 334-793-6645

*Bettye Forbus, Executive Director*

Offers magnifiers, summer reading programs and more for the blind and physically handicapped. Scanner, software, jaws for Windows.

**5275 Huntsville Subregional Library for the Blind & Physically Handicapped**
915 Monroe Street SW
Huntsville, AL 35801
256-532-5940
FAX: 256-532-5994
e-mail: askus@hpl.lib.al.us
www.hpl.lib.al.us

*Regina Cooper, Executive Director*

Talking books for people who are blind or disabled offering reference materials on the blind and other disabilities, large-print photocopier, thermaform duplicator and more.

**5276 Library for the Blind & Handicapped Public Library: Anniston/Calhoun Counties**
PO Box 308
Anniston, AL 36202
256-237-8501
FAX: 256-238-0474
e-mail: bandph@anniston.lib.al.us

*Bonnie Seymour, Executive Director*

Reference materials on blindness, cassettes, large print books and discs.

**5277 Research for Rett Foundation**
PO Box 50347
Mobile, AL 36605
251-479-8293
800-422-7388
FAX: 251-479-8293

*Jack Tillman, Chief Executive Officer*
*Anna Luce, Executive Director*

National, not-for-profit, voluntary organization dedicated to raising funds for critical ongoing medical research into Rett Syndrome, hosting medical research symposia, and funding grant applications. Committed to expanding public awareness of and encouraging Rett Syndrome research within the National Institute of Child Health and Human Development. Provides a variety of educational mateials including brochures and fact sheets.

**5278 Technology Assistance for Special Consumers**
2075 Max Luther Drive
Huntsville, AL 35810
256-852-5600
FAX: 256-532-2355
TTY:205-532-5996
e-mail: tasc@hiwaay.net
www.tasc.ataccess.org

*Lisa Synader, Director*

Provide individuals with disabilities, their families and/or advocates, and associated professionals access to assistive technology devices and services to increase independence at home, school, and work.

**5279 Tuscaloosa Subregional Library for the Blind & Physically Handicapped**
1801 River Road Jack Warner Parkway
Tuscaloosa, AL 35401
205-345-3994
800-548-2547
FAX: 205-752-8300
TTY: 800-548-2546
e-mail: bjordan@tuscaloosa-library.org
www.tuscaloosa-library.org

*Barbara Jordan, Executive Director/Librarian*

Provide talking books to patrons who are unable to use standard print because of a visual or physical limitation. Deliver playback equipment to qualified patrons. Provides reference and referral service to this special population also.

## Alaska

**5280 Alaska State Library Talking Book Center**
344 W 3rd Avenue
Suite 125
Anchorage, AK 99501
907-269-6575
800-776-6566
FAX: 907-269-6580
e-mail: patience_frederiksen@eed.state.ak.us
www.library.state.ak.us/dev/tbc.htm l

*Patience Frederiksen, Librarian*
*Beverly Griffin, Library Assistant II/Manager*

The Talking Book Center circulates fiction and nonfiction books on tape to patrons who are visually handicapped or whose physical handicaps prevent them from reading standard print. The center also has a small collector of large print books available to library patrons statewide.

## Arizona

**5281 Arizona Braille and Talking Book Library**
1030 N 32nd Street
Phoenix, AZ 85008
602-255-5578
800-255-5578
FAX: 602-255-4312
e-mail: btbl@lib.az.us
www.lib.az.us/braille

*Linda Montgomery, Executive/Director*

Audio and braille books and magazines, summer reading program, volunteer-produced cassette books, braille writer, films, large-print photocopier and more.

**5282 Books for the Blind of Arizona**
6120 E 5th Street
Unit A107
Tucson, AZ 85711
602-792-9153
FAX: 520-886-9839

*Betty Evans, Chairperson*

Offers large print photocopier, textbooks, recreational, career, vocational, braille books, talking books, cassettes, large print books and more for the visually impaired K-12, college students and adults.

**5283 Children's Center for Neurodevelopmental Studies**
5430 W Glenn Drive
Glendale, AZ 85301
623-915-0345
FAX: 623-937-5425
e-mail: info@thechildrenscenteraz.org
www.thechildrenscenteraz.org

*Kelli Sullivan, Director*
*Windy Farr, Special Education Coordinator*
*Kay King, Executive Director*

The Center is a non-profit school and therapy center for children with autism and other developmental delays specializing in the use of sensory integration.

**5284 Flagstaff City-Coconino County Public Library**
300 W Aspen Avenue
Flagstaff, AZ 86001
928-779-7670
FAX: 928-774-9573
TTY:928-214-2417
e-mail: colguin@fpl.lib.az.us
www.flagstaffpubliclibrary.org

*Christina Olguin, Librarian*
*Kay Whitaker, Executive Director*

Reference materials on blindness and other handicaps, braille writer, magnifiers and large-print photocopier. Large-type books, closed captioned videos, adapters and books on tape.

**5285 Fountain Hills Lioness Braille Service**
PO Box 18332
Fountain Hills, AZ 85269
480-837-3961

*Jean Hauck, Chairperson*

Braille and large print books on the subjects of recreation, career and vocations, religion, novels and cookbooks for the visually impaired.

**5286 Prescott Public Library**
215 E Goodwin Street
Prescott, AZ 86303
928-777-1500
FAX: 928-445-1851
www.prescottlibrary.info.com

*Toni Kaus, Director*
*Roger Faft, Assistant Director*

Large print, braille and audio books; magnifiers; text to voice scanner; talking book machine application; toy library for children with special needs; special needs product catalogs; home book delivery; descriptive videos; 43 point PC monitor.

**5287 Special Needs Center/Phoenix Public Library**
1221 N Central Avenue
Phoenix, AZ 85004
602-262-4636
TTY:602-254-8205
e-mail: specialneeds@phxlib.org
www.phoenixpubliclibrary.org

*Mimi Mccain, Supervisor*
*Toni Grbey, Executive Director*

Offers large print books and magazines, print/braille books, amd braille magazines, Descriptive video services videotapes, several video print enlargers and computer workplace for persons with disabilities.

**5288 WAHEC Medical Library Consortium**
Bullhead Community Hospital
2735 Silver Creek Road
Bullhead City, AZ 86442
928-763-1505
FAX: 928-704-6759

*Kathleen Stanley, Medical Library Co.*

Medical library management.

**5289 World Research Foundation**
41 Bell Rock Plaza
Sedona, AZ 86351
928-284-3300
FAX: 928-284-3530
e-mail: info@wrf.org
www.wrf.org

*Steven Ross, President/Co-Founder*
*LaVerne Boeckmann, Co-Founder*

Large research library of alternative medicine; offers a computer search and printout of specific health issues for a nominal fee.

## Arkansas

**5290 Arkansas Regional Library for the Blind and Physically Handicapped**
1 Capitol Mall
Little Rock, AR 72201
501-682-1155
866-660-0885
FAX: 501-682-1529
TTY: 501-682-1002
e-mail: nlsbooks@asl.lib.ar.us
www.asl.lib.ar.us

*John D Hall, Director*

Public library books in recorded or braille format. Popular fiction and nonfiction books for all ages, books and players are on free loan, sent to patrons by mail and may be returned postage free. Anyone who cannot see well enough to read regular print with glasses on or who has a disability that makes it difficult to hold a book or turn the pages is eligible.

**5291  Arkansas School for the Blind**
PO Box 668
Little Rock, AR  72203                      501-296-1810
                                            800-362-4451
                                        TTY:501-296-1813
                        www.arkansasschoolfortheblind.com

*Jim Hill, Director*
*Sharon Berry, Principal*

**5292  Educational Services for the Visually Impaired**
PO Box 668
Little Rock, AR  72203                      501-296-1815

*David Beavers, Director*
Offers textbooks, braille books and more to the visually impaired grades K-12 in the Arizona area.

**5293  Library for the Blind and Physically Handicapped SW Region of Arkansas**
PO Box 668
Magnolia, AR  71754                         870-234-0399
                                            866-234-8273
                                        FAX: 870-234-5077
                            e-mail: lbph@hotmail.com
                                       colcnty.lib.ar.us

*Sharon Irons, Assistant Director*
*Sandra Grissom, Manager*
A free library service that serves adults and children who meet the eligiblity requirements, offers free loan of cassette machine and recorded books, which meet the reading preferences of a highly diverse clientele.

**5294  Northwest Ozarks Regional Library for the Blind and Handicapped**
217 E Dickson Street
Fayetteville, AR  72701                     501-442-6253
                                        FAX: 501-442-6254
                        e-mail: arachel@orl.lib.ar.us
                                            www.uark.edu

*Rachel Anne Ames, Librarian*
Offers a summer reading program, closed-circuit TV, magnifiers, braille writers and large print books.

# California

**5295  Association of Visual Science Librarians**
School of Optometry
Berkeley, CA  94720                         501-642-1020

*Bette Anton, President*
Promotes information services in ophthalmology and optometry. Conducts institutes, workshops, and training courses for professional personnel and provides legislative consultation.

**5296  Autism Research Institute**
4182 Adams Avenue
San Diego, CA  92116                        619-281-7165
                                        FAX: 619-563-6840
                        www.autismresearchinstitute.com

*Bernard Rimland Phd, Executive Director*
*Matt Kabler, Assistant Director*
Conducts research on the causes, diagnosis, and treatment of autism and publishes a quarterly newsletter that reviews worldwide research. Literature on causes and treatment available. Refers patients and families to health care professionals and clinics. Request publication list and sample newsletter, Autism Research Review.

**5297  Braille Institute Library**
741 N Vermont Avenue
Los Angeles, CA  90029                      323-660-3880
                                            800-808-2555
                                        FAX: 323-663-0867
                        e-mail: dls@braillelibrary.org
                                     www.braillelibrary.org

*Henry Chang, Director*
*Leslie E Stocker, President*
Cassettes, braille, reference materials on blindness and other disabilities. Reading lab area with closed-circuit TV, Kurzweil Personal Reader (scanner), and typewriters, field visits and interlibrary loans of books on cassettes, braille or other medium.

**5298  Braille Institute Library**
741 N Vermont Avenue
Los Angeles, CA  90029                      323-663-1111
                                            800-808-2555
                        e-mail: bils@braillelibrary.org
                                     www.brailleinstitute.org

*Leslie Stocker, President*
*Sally Jameson, Programs/Services VP*
Braille Institute provides an environment of hope and encouragement for people who are blind and visually impaired through integrated educational, social and recreational programs and services.

**5299  Braille Institute Orange County Center**
Braille Institute of Los Angeles
527 N Dale Avenue
Anaheim, CA  92801                          714-821-5000
                                            800-272-4553
                                        FAX: 714-527-7621
                        e-mail: info@brailleinstitute.org
                                     www.brailleinstitute.org

*Thomas Burton, Chairman*
*Richard Larson, Vice Chairman*
*Sheila Daily, Executive Director*
Offers services, publications, information and programs free of charge to blind and visually impaired persons of all ages.

**5300  Braille Institute Santa Barbara Center**
2031 De La Vina Street
Santa Barbara, CA  93105                    805-682-6222
                                            800-BRA-ILLE
                                        FAX: 805-962-6331
                        e-mail: info@brailleinstitute.org
                                     www.brailleinstitute.org

*Leslie E Stocker, President*
*Thomas Burton, Chairman*
*Michael Larzarovits, Manager*
Offers programs, services and information for persons with visual impairments.

**5301  Braille Institute Sight Center**
741 N Vermont Avenue
Los Angeles, CA  90029                      323-660-3880
                                            800-272-4553
                                        FAX: 323-663-0867
                        e-mail: info@brailleinstitute.org
                                     www.brailleinstitute.org

*Thomas W Burton, Chairman*
*Leslie E Stocker, President*
Offers help, programs, services and information to the blind and visually impaired children and adults.

**5302** **Braille and Talking Book Library**
900 N Street
Sacramento, CA 95814       916-654-0640
800-952-5666
FAX: 916-654-1119
e-mail: btbl.library.ca.gov
www.library.ca.gov

*Aimee Sgourakis, Librarian/Manager*

**5303** **Braille and Talking Book Library: Californ ia State Library**
PO Box 942837
Sacramento, CA 94237       916-654-0640
800-952-5666
FAX: 916-654-1119
e-mail: btbl@library.ca.gov
www.library.ca.gov

*Cameron Robertson, Deputy State Librarian*
*Diane Matsuda, Executive Officer*
*Aimee Sgourakis, Manager*

Provides library services to people in Northern California who are unable to read standard print books because of visual or physical disabilities. Braille and talking books, magazines, machines, catalogs and postage are provided free to qualified appicants. The service is conducted by mail.

**5304** **Broadcast Services for the Blind**
214 Van Ness Avenue
San Francisco, CA 94102       415-431-1481
FAX: 415-863-7568
TTY:415-431-4572
e-mail: dpickering@lighthouse-sf.org
www.lighthouse-sf.org

*Chuck Godwin, Executive Support*
*Anita Aaron, Executive Director*

Offers radio broadcasting, braille books, cassettes, records, and more for the visually handicapped in the nine San Francisco Bay Area major cities.

**5305** **Clearinghouse for Specialized Media and Technology**
California Department of Education
1430 N Street
Room 3207
Sacramento, CA 95814       916-324-4244
FAX: 916-323-9732
e-mail: rbrawley@cde.ca.gov
www.cde.ca.gov/re/pn/sm

*David Supkofl, Manager*

Assists schools and students in the identification and acquisition of textbooks, reference books and study materials in aural media, Braille, large print and electronic media access technology.

**5306** **Fresno County Free Library Blind and Handicapped Services**
770 N San Pablo Avenue
Fresno, CA 93728       559-488-3217
800-742-1011
FAX: 559-488-1971
TTY: 559-488-1642
e-mail: wendy.eisenberg@fresnolibrary.org
www.fresnolibrary.org/tblb

*Wendy Eisenberg, Librarian/Manager*

Magnifiers, home visits, volunteer-produced cassette books, discs and cassettes.

**5307** **Glaucoma Research Foundation**
251 Post Street
Suite 600
San Francisco, CA 94108       415-986-3162
800-826-6693
FAX: 415-986-3763
e-mail: info@glaucoma.org
www.glaucoma.org

*Thomas M Brunner, President/CEO*

Clinical and laboratory studies of glaucoma.

**5308** **Herrick Health Sciences Library**
Alta Bates Medical Center
2001 Dwight Way
Berkeley, CA 94704       510-204-4444
FAX: 510-204-4091
e-mail: sutterhealth.org
www.altabates.com

*Laurie Bagley, Librarian*
*Carol Hirsch-Butler, Administrator*

Information on rehabilitation, psychiatry and psychoanalysis.

**5309** **Kuzell Institute for Arthritis and Infectious Diseases**
Medical Research Institute Of San Francisco
2200 Webster Street
San Francisco, CA 94115       415-441-6249
FAX: 415-441-8548

*Lowell Young, Director*
*Edward Byrd, Owner*

One of seven units comprising the Medical Research Institute of San Francisco that offers basic and applied research in arthritis and related diseases.

**5310** **New Beginnings: The Blind Children's Center**
4120 Marathon Street
Los Angeles, CA 90029       323-664-2153
800-222-3566
FAX: 323-665-3228
www.blindchildrenscenter.org

*Midge Horton, Executive Director*
*Muriel Scharf, Director of Development*

The purpose of the Center is to turn initial fears into hope. Helps children and their families become independent by creating a climate of safety and trust. Children learn to develop self confidence and to master a wide range of skills. Services include an infant stimulation program, educational preschool, interdisciplinary assessment services, family services, correspondence program, toll free national hotline and a publication and research service.

**5311** **Research & Training Center on Mental Health for Hard of Hearing Persons**
California School of Professional Psychology
6215 Ferris Square
Suite 140
San Diego, CA 92121       619-282-4443
800-HEA-R619
FAX: 800-642-0266

*Raymond J Trybus, Director*
*Thomas J Goulder, Associate Director*

Funded by the National Institute on Disability and Rehabilitation Research, this training center aims to address issues of psychological relevance to persons who are hard of hearing or late deafened (as distinct from prelingually, culturally deaf persons). Also serves as information clearinghouse on this topic.

**5312  Rosalind Russell Medical Research Center for Arthritis**
350 Parnassus Avenue
Suite 607
San Francisco, CA  94143                    415-476-1192
                                       FAX: 415-476-3526
                          e-mail: ephraim@itsa.ucsf.edu
                                     www.oarg.ucsf.edu

*Ephraim P Engelman, Executive Director*
*Arthur Weiss, Associate Director*
*Paula Gambs, Chairman*

Arthritis research and its probable causes.

**5313  San Francisco Public Library for the Blind and Print Handicapped**
100 Larkin Street
San Francisco, CA  94102                    415-557-4400
                                       FAX: 415-557-4375
                          e-mail: lbphmgr@sfpl.lib.ca.us
                                          www.sfpl.org

*Kathy Lawhun, Chief*
*Martin Maqid, Librarian*
*Luis Herrera, Manager*

Foreign-language books on cassette, children's books on cassettes and more.

**5314  San Jose State University Library**
150 E San Fernando Street
San Jose, CA  95112                         408-808-2000
                                       FAX: 408-924-2476
                          e-mail: office@wahoo.sjsu.edu
                                      www.sjlibrary.org

*Patricia Sen Breivik, Dean*
*Jane Light, Library/Executive Director*

Information on physical disabilities, accessibility and learning disabilities.

## Colorado

**5315  AMC Cancer Research Center**
1600 Pierce Street
Lakewood, CO  80214                         303-239-3422
                                            800-321-1557
                                       FAX: 303-239-3400
                          e-mail: silverbergb@amc.org
                                          www.amc.org

*David Silverberg, President*
*Carolyn Draper, Executive Assistant*
*Beth Bochniak, Accounting Manager*

Provides trained counselors who provide understanding and support for cancer patients; information and referral services; and screening programs.

**5316  Boulder Public Library**
1000 Canyon Boulevard
Boulder, CO  80302                          303-441-3100

                          e-mail: feedback@boulder.lib.co.us
                                     www.boulder.lib.co.us

*Liz Abbott, Director*
*Priscilla Hudson, Manager*

Offers braille books, cassettes, talking books, large print photocopier, large print books and more for the visually impaired.

**5317  Colorado Library for the Blind and Physically Handicapped**
Colorado Talking Book Library
180 Sheridan Boulevard
Denver, CO  80226                           303-727-9277
                                            800-685-2136
                                       FAX: 303-727-9281
                          e-mail: ctbl.info@cde.state.co.us
                                 www.cde.state.co.us/ctbl

*Debbie MacLeod, Director*

Offers reference materials on blindness and other handicaps, children's print/braille books, cassettes, large print books, and volunteer-produced cassette books and magazines.

**5318  National Jewish Medical & Research Center**
1400 Jackson Street
Denver, CO  80206                           303-388-4461
                                            800-222-5864
                          e-mail: allstetterw@njc.org
                                          www.njc.org

*Lynn Taussig, President/CEO*
*Nancy Hafer, Fellowship Coordinator*

The only medical center in the country whose research and patient care resources are dedicated to respiratory and immunologic diseases.

## Connecticut

**5319  Connecticut Braille Association**
107 Vanderbilt Avenue
West Hartford, CT  06110                    203-227-5243
                                       FAX: 860-953-9692

*Yolanda Rossi, Manager*

Offers textbooks, cassettes, large print books, braille books and more.

**5320  Connecticut State Library**
Connecticut State Government
231 Capitol Avenue
Hartford, CT  06106                         860-757-6500
                                       FAX: 860-757-6677
                          e-mail: isref@cslib.org
                                        www.cslib.org

*Kendall Wiggin, State Librarian/Manager*
*Mollie Keller, Chairman*

Discs, cassettes, braille, reference materials on blindness and other handicaps, closed-circuit TV and large-print photocopier.

**5321  Connecticut Tech Act Project: Connecticut Department of Social Services**
Bureau of Rehabilitations Services
25 Sigourney Street
Hartford, CT  06106                         860-424-4881
                                            800-842-4510
                                       FAX: 860-424-4850
                                       TTY: 860-602-4002
                          e-mail: jficarro@aol.com
                                  www.techactproject.com

*John Ficarro, Project Director*

Single point of entry, advocacy, information and referral, peer counseling, and access to objective expert advice and consultation for people with disabilities.

**5322   Library for the Blind and Physically Handicapped**
198 W Street
Rocky Hill, CT  06067                                860-566-2151
                                                     800-842-4516
                                                FAX: 860-354-5534
                                             e-mail: ctaylor@cslib.org
                                                     www.cslib.org

*Carol Taylor, Executive Director*

Braille writer, magnifiers, closed-circuit TV, cassette books and
magazines, children's books on cassette, home visits and other
reference materials on blindness and other handicaps.

**5323   Prevent Blindness Connecticut**
984 Southford Road
Middlebury, CT  06762                                203-598-0529
                                                     800-850-2020
                                                FAX: 860-347-0613
                                      e-mail: info@preventblindnessct.org
                                             www.preventblindnessct.org

*Steven Peterson, President and CEO*
*Paul Armor, VP*
*Maria Giarratana, Program Director*

The mission of Prevent Blindness Connecticut is to save sight
and prevent blindness through eye screenings, education, safety
activities and research.

**5324   Yale University: Vision Research Center**
330 Cedar Street
New Haven, CT  06510                                 203-785-2020
                                                     800-395-7949
                                                FAX: 203-785-6123
                                      e-mail: pamela.berkheiser@yale.edu
                                                     info.med.yale.edu

*Bruce Shields, Chairman*
*Pam Burkheiser, Manager*

Vision including studies on growth and development.

# Delaware

**5325   Delaware Assistive Technology Initiative Center for Applied Science and Engineering**
Univ. of Delaware/duPont Hospital for Children
1600 Rockland Road
PO Box 269
Wilmington, DE  19899                                302-651-6790
                                                     800-870-3284
                                                FAX: 302-651-6793
                                                TTY: 302-651-6794
                                           e-mail: dati@asel.udel.edu
                                                     www.dati.org

*Beth Mineo Mollica, Director*
*Sonja Rathel, Project Coordinator*

Connects Delawareans who have disabilities with the tools they
need in order to learn, work, play and participate in community
life safely and independently.

**5326   Delaware Library for the Blind and Physically Handicapped**
Government
43 S Dupont Highway
Dover, DE  19901                                     302-739-4748
                                                     800-282-8676
                                                FAX: 302-739-6787
                                             e-mail: debph@lib.de.us
                                                     www.state.lib.de.us

*Anne Norman, Director/State Librarian*

Books on cassette and playback equipment are provided to patrons who are unable to read regular printed books.

**5327   Elwyn Delaware**
321 E 11th Street
Wilmington, DE  19801                                302-658-8860
                                                FAX: 302-657-5658
                                         e-mail: eve.austin@elwyn.org
                                                     www.elwyn.org

*Evangeline E Austin, Director Governmental Relations*
*Carol Chapin, Executive Director*

Provides work training, job placement and supported employment, and elder care services.

# District of Columbia

**5328   District of Columbia Public Library: Services to the Deaf Community**
District of Columbia Public Library
901 G Street NW
Room 215
Washington, DC  20001                                202-727-2142
                                                FAX: 202-727-1129
                                      e-mail: library_deaf_dc@yahoo.com
                                                     www.dclibrary.org

*Marie H Aldridge, President*
*James Lewis, Vice President*
*Phillip Long-Cross, Manager*

Offers reference services through TTY, signers for library programs, sign language classes, information about deafness, print
and non-print materials for persons who have hearing disabilities. Book talks on deaf culture are held once a month

**5329   District of Columbia Regional Library for the Blind and Physically Handicapped**
901 G Street NW
Room 215
Washington, DC  20001                                202-727-2142
                                                FAX: 202-727-1129
                                                TTY: 202-727-2145
                                        e-mail: lbphb_2000@yahoo.com
                                                     www.dclibrary.org

*Marie H Aldridge, President*
*James Lewis, Vice President*
*Phillip Long-Cross, Manager*

Regional library/RPH is network library in the Library of Congress, National Library Services for the Blind and Physically
Handicapped.

**5330   Georgetown University Center for Child and Human Development**
PO Box 571485
Washington, DC  20057                                202-687-5000
                                                FAX: 202-687-8899
                                                TTY: 202-687-5000
                                        e-mail: gucdc@georgetown.edu
                                                     gucchd.georgetown.edu

*Phillis Magrab, Director*
*John J De Goia, President*

Established over four decades ago to improve the quality of life
for all children and youth, especially those with, or at risk for,
special needs and their families. Located in the nation's capital,
this center both directly serves vulnerable children and their
families, as well as influences local, state, national and international programs and policy.

**5331 National Institute on Disability and Rehabilitation Research**
U S Department of Education
400 Maryland Avenue SW
Washington, DC 20202
202-401-2000
800-437-0833
FAX: 202-401-0689
TTY: 800-437-0833
e-mail: customerservice@inet.ed.gov
www.ed.gov

*Theresa S Shaw, Chief Operating Officer*
*Grover J Whitehurst, Director Institute of Education*
*Margaret Spellings, Chief Executive Officer*

A national leader in sponsoring research. Mission is to generate, disseminate and promote new knowledge to improve the options available to disabled persons.
*1978*

# Florida

**5332 Brevard County Talking Books Library**
Brevard County Libraries
308 Forrest Avenue
Cocoa, FL 32922
321-635-7845
FAX: 321-633-1838
e-mail: kbriley@brev.org
www.brev.org

*Kay Briley, Librarian*
*Camille Johnson, Executive Director*
*Catherine J Schweinsburg, Library Services Director*

Subregional library for the blind and physically handicapped, assistive reading devices collection, reference materials on blindness and other handicaps, descriptive videos, CCTV, phonic ear, reading edge and LOUD-R assistive listening devices available.

**5333 Broward County Talking Book Library**
100 S Andrews Avenue
Fort Lauderdale, FL 33301
954-357-7444
FAX: 954-357-7399
www.browardlibrary.org

*Robert Cannon, Director*
*Carolyn Kayne, Manager*

Reference materials on blindness and other handicaps, films, closed-circuit TV, discs, cassettes and a book discussion group is offered.

**5334 Dade County Talking Book Library**
Miami Dade Public Library System
2455 NW 183rd Street
Miami Gardens, FL 33056
305-625-6429
800-451-9544
FAX: 305-757-8401
e-mail: talkingbooks@mdpls.org
www.mdpls.org

*Raymond Sanpiago, Executive Director*
Library services for people with disabilities.

**5335 Florida Division of Blind Services**
Regional Library
420 Platt Street
Daytona Beach, FL 32114
386-239-6000
FAX: 386-239-6069
TTY:800-226-6075
e-mail: mike-gunde@dbs.doe.state.fl.us
www.state.fl.us

*Linda Hill, Manager*

Discs, cassettes, closed-circuit TV, large-print photocopier, films, children's books on cassettes and more.

**5336 Florida Instructional Materials Center for the Visually Handicapped**
5002 N Lois Avenue
Tampa, FL 33614
813-872-5281
800-282-9193
FAX: 813-872-5284
e-mail: sdalton@fimcvi.org
www.fimcvi.org

*Suzanne Dalton, Supervisor*
*Jeffery Fitterman, Coordinator*
*John F Cardinale, Coordinator*

Operates a clearinghouse depository and production center for braille, large print and recorded texts. Provides assistance in assessment of materials and specialized apparatus, organizes volunteers for material production and more for the visually handicapped.

**5337 Hillsborough County Talking Book Library**
**Tampa-Hillsborough County Public Library**
900 N Ashley Drive
Tampa, FL 33602
813-671-7638
FAX: 813-272-5640
TTY:813-273-3610
www.hcplc.org

*John F Germany, Public Library*
*Joe Stines, Executive Director*

**5338 Lee County Library System: Talking Books Library**
13240 N Cleveland Avenue
5-6
North Fort Myers, FL 33903
239-995-2665
800-854-8195
FAX: 239-995-1681
TTY: 239-995-2665
www.lee-county.com/library

*Cynthia N Cobb, Director*
*Terri Crawford, Deputy Director*
*Debbie Parrott, Manager*

Provides free books and magazines to Lee County residents of all ages who have any disability that prevents them from reading printed material. Books are played on special players provided free by the National Library Service. Circulates low tech assistive aids and devices for temporary loan to Lee County Library card holders. Directs people to assistive technology and disability related resources.

**5339 Louis de la Parte Florida Mental Health Institute Research Library**
University of South Florida
13301 Bruce B Downs Boulevard
Tampa, FL 33612
813-974-4565
FAX: 813-974-7242
e-mail: library@fmhi.usf.edu
www.fmhi.usf.edu

*Judy Genshaft, President*
*David L Shern, Dean*

Information offered on mental illness, autism and pervasive developmental disabilities mental health research and archives management.

**5340 Orange County Library System: Audio-Visual Department**
101 E Central Boulevard
Orlando, FL 32801
407-835-7323
FAX: 407-835-7646
TTY:407-835-7641
www.ocls.info

*Maryann Hodel, Manager*

**5341  Pearlman Biomedical Research Institute**
Mt Sinai Medical Center
1600 NW 10th Avenue
Miami Beach, FL  33140                     305-674-2121
                                     FAX: 305-674-2198
                    e-mail: william-abraham@msmc.com

*William Abraham, Director*

Pulmonary medicine, arthritis, sleep disorders and gynecology
departments of research.

**5342  Pinellas Talking Book Library for the Blind and
Physically Handicapped**
1330 Cleveland Street
Clearwater, FL  33755                      727-441-8408
                                     FAX: 727-441-9068
                                     TTY:727-441-3168
                    e-mail: mstevenson@pplc.us
                                   www.pplc.us/tbl

*Marilyn Stevenson, Talking Book Librarian*
*Harriet Thompson, Assistant Librarian*
*Marianne Morawetz, Reader Advisor*

**5343  Subregional Talking Book Library**
Jacksonville Public Library
1755 Edgewood Avenue W
Suite 1
Jacksonville, FL  32208                    904-786-6633
                                     FAX: 904-768-7404
                                     TTY:904-924-5387
                        e-mail: jerryr@coj.net

*Jerry Reynoods, Department Head*
*Anthony Jackson, Manager*

Offers cassettes, reference materials on blindness and other
handicaps, children's braille books, descriptive videos, and
some assistive devices.

**5344  Talking Book Service: Mantatee County Central Library**
6081 26th Street W
Bradenton, FL  34207                       941-742-5914
                                     FAX: 941-751-7098

*Patricia Schobert, Librarian/Manager*

Offers children's books on disc and cassette and more reference
materials for the blind and physically handicapped.

**5345  Talking Books Library for the Blind and Physically
Handicapped**
Palm Beach County Library
3650 Summit Boulevard
West Palm Beach, FL  33406                 561-233-2600
                                            888-780-4962
                                     FAX: 561-233-2627
                    e-mail: webmaster@pbclibrary.org
                                   www.pbclibrary.org

*Jerry Brownlee, Librarian Director*

Library services for people with disabilities.

**5346  Talking Books/Homebound Services**
Brevard County Library System
308 Forrest Avenue
Cocoa, FL  32922                           321-635-7845
                                     FAX: 321-633-1838
                    e-mail: kbriley@brev.org
                                   www.brev.org

*Kay Briley, Librarian*
*Camille Johnson, Executive Director*

Offers reference materials on blindness and other handicaps.
Subregional library for the blind and physically handicapped,
assistive reading devices collection, reference materials on
blindness and other handicaps; CCTV, phonic ear, reading edge
and LOUD-R assistive listening devices available.

**5347  University of Miami: Bascom Palmer Eye Institute**
Department Of Ophthalmalogy
17t800h Street
Miami, FL  33136                           305-326-6000
                                            800-329-7000
                                     FAX: 305-326-7000
                                   www.bascompalmer.org

*Carmen Puliafito, Chairman*
*Teresa Spaulding, Manager*

Clinical and basic research into blindness and visual impairments.

**5348  University of Miami: Mailman Center for Child Development**
1601 NW 12th Avenue
Miami, FL  33136                           305-243-3985
                                     FAX: 305-326-7594
                    e-mail: ruben@miami.edu
                                   pediatrics.med.miami.edu

*Anna Matias, Staff Associate*
*Ruben Garcia, Associate Director*
*Dennis Harris, Manager*

Focuses on birth defects and children's illnesses.

**5349  West Florida Regional Library**
200 W Gregory Street
Pensacola, FL  32502                       850-436-5060
                                     FAX: 850-436-5039
                                     TTY:850-436-5063
                    e-mail: hhudson@ci.pensacola.fl.us
                                   www.wfrl.lib.fl.us

*Gene Fischer, Library Director*
*Helen Hudson, Outreach Librarian*
*Eugene Fischer, Manager*

Offers children's print/braille books.

# Georgia

**5350  Albany Talking Book Center**
Dougherty County Public Library
300 Pine Avenue
Albany, GA  31701                          229-420-3200
                                            800-337-6251
                                     FAX: 229-420-3215
                                     TTY: 912-430-1911
                    e-mail: katy@docolib.org
                                   www.docolib.org

*Michael Dugan, Director*
*Teresa Cole, Assistant Director*

Offers discs, cassettes, reference materials on blindness and
other handicaps, large-print photocopiers, summer reading programs, cassette books and more.

**5351  Athens Regional Library Talking Book Center**
2025 Baxter Street
Athens, GA  30606                          706-613-3655
                                            800-531-2063
                                     FAX: 706-613-3660
                                   www.specialneeds@library.org

*Stacey Chandler, Manager*

Discs, cassettes, large print books, reference materials on blindness, descriptive videos, films, closed-circuit TV, magnifiers,
braille writer, summer reading programs, cassette books and
magazines and more.

**5352  Augusta Talking Book Center**
425 9th Street
Augusta, GA  30901                     706-821-2625
                                   FAX: 706-724-5403
                            e-mail: talkbook@ecgrl.org
                            www.ecgrl.public.lib.ga.us

*Gary Swint, Director*
*Audrey Bell, Manager*

Discs, cassettes, braille writer, films, large print books, summer
reading program, magnifiers and reference materials on blindness and other handicaps.

**5353  Bainbridge Subregional Library for the Blind &
Physically Handicapped**
S W Georgia Regional Library
301 S Monroe Street
Bainbridge, GA  39819                  229-248-2665
                                       800-795-2680
                                   FAX: 229-248-2670
                              e-mail: lbph@swgrl.org
                                       www.swgrl.org

*Susan Whittle, Librarian/Manager*
*Kathy Hutchins, Supervisor*

Cassettes, large print books, summer reading programs,
closed-circuit TV, magnifiers and more.

**5354  Emory Autism Resource Center**
Emory University
151 Shout Ct
Atlanta, GA  30322                     404-727-5150
                                   FAX: 404-727-3969
                         e-mail: tohannon@emory.edu
              www.phsychiatry.emory.edu./program./autism

*Charles Nemeroff, Manager*
Offers on-line bulletin boards which are relevant to autism.

**5355  Emory University Laboratory for Ophthalmic Research**

1365b Clifton Road NE
Atlanta, GA  30322                     404-778-3381
                                   FAX: 404-778-4143
                          e-mail: pbennet@emory.edu
                                       www.emory.edu

*Henry F Edelhauser, Director*
*Larry Hagan, Manager*
Various studies into the aspects of blindness.

**5356  Georgia Library for the Blind and Physically Handi-
capped**
Georgia Public Library
1150 Murphy Avenue SW
Atlanta, GA  30310                     404-756-4619
                                       800-248-6701
                                   FAX: 404-756-4618
                    e-mail: dscott@georgialibraries.org
                              www.georgialibraries.org

*Linda Stetson, Director*
*Deborah Scott, Business Manager*
*Stella Cone, Executive Director*

Discs, cassettes, braille, films, closed-circuit TV, braille writer,
large-print photocopier, cassette books and magazines.

**5357  Hall County Library: East Hall Branch and Special
Needs Library**
2434 Old Cornelia Highway
Gainesville, GA  30507                 770-532-3311
                                   FAX: 770-531-2502
                                   TTY:770-531-2520
                   e-mail: ehcirc@hallcountylibrary.org
                              www.hallcountylibrary.org

*Barbara Perry, Branch Manager*
*Adrian Mixson, Manager*

Summer reading programs, braille writer, magnifiers, scanners
and readers, audio described videos, closed captioned videos,
closed-circuit TV, large-print photocopier, cassette books and
magazines, large print books, children's books on cassette,
home visits and other reference materials on blindness and other
handicaps.

**5358  Macon Library for the Blind and Physically Handi-
capped**
Washington Memorial Library
1180 Washington Avenue
Macon, GA  31201                       478-744-0800
                                       800-805-7613
                                   FAX: 478-742-3161

*Charles Schmidt, Director*
*Hoyt Cannon, Finance Officer*
*Joan Anderson, Executive Director*

Summer reading programs, braille writer, magnifiers,
closed-circuit TV, large-print photocopier, cassette books and
magazines, children's books on cassette, home visits and other
reference materials on blindness and other handicaps.

**5359  National Center on Birth Defects and Developmental
Disabilities**
Centers for Disease Control and Prevention
1600 Clifton Road
Mail Stop E-86
Atlanta, GA  30331                     404-498-3800
                                   FAX: 404-498-3070
                                www.cdc.gov/ncbddd/

*Jose Cordero, Director*
Promotes child development, prevents birth defects and developmental disabilities.

**5360  North Georgia Talking Book Center**
LaFayette-Walker Public Library
305 S Duke Street
La Fayette, GA  30728                  706-638-1958
                                       888-506-0509
                                       888-506-0509
                                   FAX: 706-638-4913
                        e-mail: cstubblefield@chrl.org
                                       www.chrl.org

*Charles H Stubblefield, Manager*
*June DeLong, Assistant Manager*
We offer books on cassette for the visual and physically disabled
induvidual, books in braille, magazines on cassette, zoom text
screen magnifier, computer voice program, large-print photocopier, summer reading program, home visits na dother reference materials on blindness and other disabilities.

**5361  Oconee Regional Library**
PO Box 100
Dublin, GA  31040                      478-272-5710
                                   FAX: 478-275-0524
                          www.laurens.public.lib.ga.us

*Leard Daughety, Director*
*April Warren, Special Service Manager*

Summer reading programs, braille writer, magnifiers,
closed-circuit TV, large-print photocopier, cassette books and
magazines, children's books on cassette, home visits and other
reference materials on blindness and other handicaps.

**5362  Rome Subregional Library for the Blind and Physically
Handicapped**
205 Riverside Parkway
Rome, GA  30161                        706-236-4618
                                       888-263-0769
                                   FAX: 706-236-4631
                                   TTY: 706-236-4618
              e-mail: dianam@mail.floyd.public.lib.ga.us
                              www.floyd.public.lib.ga.us

*Diana Mills, Librarian*
*Delana Hickman, Manager*

**5363 South Georgia Regional Library-Valdosta Talking Book Center**
300 Woodrow Wilson Drive
Valdosta, GA 31602
229-333-0086
FAX: 229-333-7669
e-mail: suggestions@sgrl.org
www.sgrl.org

*Liza Newsome, Director*

Summer reading programs, Braille writer, magnifiers, closed-circuit TV, large print photocopier, cassette books and magazines, children's books on cassette, home visits and other reference materials on blindness and other handicaps.

**5364 Subregional Library for the Blind and Physically Handicapped**
1120 Bradley Drive
Columbus, GA 31906
706-649-0780
FAX: 706-649-1914
TTY: 706-649-0974
e-mail: slpbh@mail.muscogee.public.lib.ga.us

*Dorothy Bowen, Librarian*

Braille writer, magnifiers, closed-circuit TV, large-print photocopier, cassette books and magazines, children's books on cassette, home visits and other reference materials on blindness and other handicaps.

**5365 Talking Book Center Brunswick-Glynn County Regional Library**
208 Gloucester Street
Brunswick, GA 31520
912-267-1212
FAX: 912-267-9597
e-mail: bransom@trll.org

*Betty Ransom, Librarian*
*Joe Shinnick, Executive Director*

## Hawaii

**5366 Assistive Technology Resource Centers of Hawaii (ATRC)**
414 Kuwili Street
Suite 104
Honolulu, HI 96817
808-532-7110
800-645-3007
FAX: 808-532-7120
TTY: 808-532-7110
e-mail: atrc@atrc.org
www.atrc.org

*Barbara Fischlowitz'le, Executive Director*

Provides information and training on assistive technology devices, services, and funding resources. Conducts presentations and demonstrations in the community to increase AT awareness and promote self-advocacy among people with disabilities.

**5367 Hawaii State Library for the Blind and Physically Handicapped**
402 Kapahulu Avenue
Honolulu, HI 96815
808-733-8444
800-559-4096
FAX: 808-733-8449
www.hcc.hawaii.edu

*Fusako Miyashiro, Manager*

Supported by the Hawaii State Public Library System and the National Library Service for the Blind and Physically Handicapped, Library of Congress. Staff with knowledge of sign language; Special interest periodicals; Books on deafness and sign language; captioned media; Special Services: Radio Reading Service, Talking Books Reader's Club, educational and cultural programs, machine lending agency. Braille, cassette and large type. Regional and National service, quarterly newsletter.

## Idaho

**5368 Idaho Assistive Technology Project**
University of Idaho
129 W 3rd Street
Moscow, ID 83843
208-885-6466
800-432-8324
FAX: 208-885-3628
TTY: 208-885-3573
e-mail: ywright@uidaho.edu
www.educ.uidaho.edu/idatech

*Ron Seiler, Director*
*Bob Hieronymus, Executive Director*

Project engages in systems change activities, training, materials development, information dissemination and advocacy activities directed at increasing the availability of assistive devices and services to Idahoans who have disabilities.

**5369 Idaho State Library: Talking Book Library**
325 W State Street
Boise, ID 83702
208-334-2117
800-458-3271
FAX: 208-334-4016
e-mail: lili@isl.state.id.us
www.lili.org/isl

*Sheila Winther, Volunteer Coordinator*
*Sue Walker, Manager*

Offers talking books and magazines, large print materials, braille, equipment and accessories. Available to all residents of Idaho who are visually impaired and/or have disabilities which disallows the use of print material.

## Illinois

**5370 Catholic Guild for the Blind**
180 N Michigan Avenue
Suite 1700
Chicago, IL 60601
312-243-8569
FAX: 312-236-8128
e-mail: info@guildfortheblind.org
www.guildfortheblind.org

*David Tabak, Executive Director*
*Kathy Firak, Operations Manager*

Offers assistive devices for sale, provides computer assistive traing. Offers audio and braille transcription, sponsers seminars on a wide arrange of topics and provides weekly sales information via telephone.

**5371 Chicago Public Library Talking Book Center**
400 S State Street
Chicago, IL 60605
312-747-4999
800-757-4654
e-mail: dtaylor@chipublib.org
www.chipublib.org

*Deborah Taylor, Director*
*Mary Dempsey, Manager*

Summer reading programs, braille writer, closed-circuit TV, large print photocopier, cassette books and magazines, children's books on cassette, home visits and other reference materials on blindness and other handicaps. Three assistive technology centers designed and equipped for the blind and visually impaired, funded by the National Library Service for the Blind and Handicapped, a division of the Library of Congress. All services FREE!

**5372  Department of Ophthalmology and Visual Science**
1855 W Taylor Street
Banner Dept: 2-539000
Chicago, IL 60612                                  312-996-8938
                                                   800-786-3937
                                              FAX: 312-996-7770
                                      e-mail: adriadel@uic.edu
                                                   www.uic.edu

Dimitri Azar, Professor/Director
Maria Myrianthopolus, Administrator
Adrienne Adelman, Administrative Secretary

Offers help, support, information and research for persons with
vision problems, including Retinitis Pigmentosa.

**5373  Horizons for the Blind**
2 N Williams Street
Crystal Lake, IL 60014                             815-444-8800
                                              FAX: 815-444-8830
                                  e-mail: mail@horizons-blind.org
                                          www.horizons-blind.org
Mission is to improve the quality of life for people who are blind
or visually impaired by increasing accessibility to culture, education, recreation and consumer information on a national basis.
                                                          1977

**5374  Illinois Early Childhood Intervention Clearinghouse**
830 S Spring Street
Springfield, IL 62704                              217-522-4340
                                                   800-852-4302
                                              FAX: 217-522-4670
                        e-mail: clearinghouse@eiclearinghouse.com
                                          www.eiclearinghouse.org

Chet Brandt, Project Director
Patricia Traylor, Project Associate

Free lending library of materials related to early childhood and
disability. Books, audiovisuals and articles available. Computerized database with more than 31,000 items available to Illinois
residents.

**5375  Illinois Regional Library for the Blind and Physically
Handicapped**
1055 W Roosevelt Road
Chicago, IL 60608                                  312-746-9210
                                                   800-331-2351
                                              FAX: 312-746-9192

Shawn Thomas, Reference Librarian
Barbara Perkins, Acting Director

Summer reading programs, braille writer, magnifiers,
closed-circuit TV, large-print photocopier, cassette books and
magazines, descriptive videos, children's books on cassette,
home visits and other reference materials on blindness and other
handicaps.

**5376  Mid-Illinois Talking Book Center**
600 High Point Lane
Peoria, IL 61611
                                                   800-426-0709
                                        e-mail: info@mitbc.org
                                                   www.mitbc.org

Karen Bersche, Director
Valerie Brandon, PR/Outreach Coordinator

Providing a free library service to anyone unable to read regular
print because of a visual or physical disability. There are books
and magazines on tape and playback equipment; and also in
Braille. Books and magazines are mailed free to and from library
patrons, wherever they reside.

**5377  National Eye Research Foundation (NERF)**
910 Skokie Boulevard
Suite 207a
Northbrook, IL 60062                               847-205-0002
                                                   800-621-2258
                                              FAX: 847-564-0807
                                       e-mail: info@nerf.org
                                                   www.nerf.org

Elliot Silber, Owner

Dedicated to improving eye care for the public and meeting the
professional nees of eye care practitioners; sponsors eye research projects on contact lens applications and eye care problems. Special study sections in such fields as orthokertology,
primary eyecare, pediatrics, and through continuing education
programs. Provides eye care information for the public and professionals. Educational materials including pamphlets. Program activities include education and referrals.

**5378  National Lekotek Center**
3204 W Armitage Avenue
Chicago, IL 60647                                  773-276-5164
                                                   800-366-PLAY
                                              FAX: 773-276-8644
                                    e-mail: lekotek@lekotek.org
                                                   www.lekotek.org

Diana Nielander, Executive Director
Helene Levine, Director

Toy library and play-centered programs for children with special needs and their families with branches in 17 states. Sliding
fee scale. Lekotek also has a Toy Resource Helpline that provides individualized assistances in the selection of toys and play
materials and general resources for families with children with
disabilities.

**5379  Northwestern University Multipurpose Arthritis &
Musculoskeletal Center**
303 E Chicago Avenue
Chicago, IL 60611                                  312-503-8186
                                              FAX: 312-503-1204
                             e-mail: ghsl-ref@northwestern.edu

James Shedlock, Director
Lewis Landsberg, Administrator

Conducts biomedical, educational and health services research
into musculoskeletal diseases.

**5380  Rehabilitation Institute of Chicago Learning Resource
Center**
345 E Superior Street
Chicago, IL 60611                                  312-238-1000
                                                   800-354-7342
                                              FAX: 312-908-1369
                                     e-mail: education@ric.org
                                                   www.ric.org

Wayne M Lerner, President/Chief Executive Office
Laura Ferrio, Vice President
Henry Betts, Chairman

Offers information on rehabilitation and physical disabilities.

**5381  Skokie Accessible Library Services**
Skokie Public Library
5215 Oakton Street
Skokie, IL 60077                                   847-673-7774
                                              FAX: 847-673-7797
                             e-mail: askref@skokie.libbrary.info
                                          www.skokielibrary.info

Carolyn A Anthony, Executive Director
John J Graham, President

Library services for people with disabilities, including electronic aids, materials in special formats, programs and special
services, and access to the North Suburban Library System.

**5382 Southern Illinois Talking Book Center**
607 S Greenbriar Road
Carterville, IL 62918
618-985-8375
800-455-2665
FAX: 618-985-4211
e-mail: bphdept@shawls.lib.il.us
www.shawls.lib.il.us/talkingbooks

*Diana Sussman, Director*

Library service, recorded books & magazines for people with
difficulty reading print due to visual or physical limitations or
reading disability (all ages), reference/referral, descriptive videos, newsline newspaper service, presentations/in-service.
Free. Part of the Library of Congress NLS program.

**5383 University of Illinois at Chicago: Lions of Illinois Eye
Research Institute**
University of Illinois at Chicago
957 Lieri
Chicago, IL 60612
312-996-6590
FAX: 312-996-9005
www.uic.edu

*John J Denardo, Executive Director*
*Jingtao Guo, MD*

Visual impairments and blindness research, including glaucoma
studies.

**5384 Voices of Vision Talking Book Center at DuPage Li-
brary System**
127 S 1st Street
Geneva, IL 60134
630-208-0398
800-227-0625
FAX: 630-208-0399
e-mail: kodean@dupagels.lib.il.us
www.dupagels.lib.il.us

*Karen O'Dean, Director*

Provides library service to persons who are unable to use standard printed material because of visual or physical disabilities.
Part of the Illinois network of Talking Book Libraries. The service is free to those who are eligable. Provides books and magazines on audio-cassettes. Special playback equipment needed to
use the books is also loaned. Braille books and magazines are
also available. The collection includes popular books, classics
and magazines.

# Indiana

**5385 Allen County Public Library**
PO Box 2270
Fort Wayne, IN 46801
260-482-8523
FAX: 260-241-1386
TTY:260-421-1302
e-mail: ncompton@acpl.lib.in.us
fuji.acpl.lib.in.us

*Jeffrey Krull, Director*
*Steven Fortriede, Associate Director*
*Mark Allen, Vice President*

Summer reading programs, braille writer, magnifiers,
closed-circuit TV, large-print photocopier, cassette books and
magazines, children's books on cassette, home visits and other
reference materials on blindness and other handicaps.

**5386 Bartholomew County Public Library**
536 5th Street
Columbus, IN 47201
812-379-1255
FAX: 812-379-1275
e-mail: library@barth.lib.in.us
www.barth.lib.in.us

*Wilma Perry, Librarian*
*Beth Poor, Executive Director*

Summer reading programs, braille writer, magnifiers,
closed-circuit TV, large-print photocopier, cassette books and
magazines, children's books on cassette, home visits and other
reference materials on blindness and other handicaps.

**5387 Elkhart Public Library for the Blind and Physiclly
Handicapp**
300 S 2nd Street
Elkhart, IN 46516
574-522-2665
800-622-4970
FAX: 574-293-9213
www.elkhartpubliclibrary.com

*Pat Ciancio, Librarian/Department Supervisor*
*Connie Ozinga, Executive Director*

Summer reading programs, braille writer, magnifiers,
closed-circuit TV, large-print photocopier, cassette books and
magazines, children's books on cassette, home visits and other
reference materials on blindness and other handicaps.

**5388 Indiana Resource Center for Autism**
Indiana Institute on Disability and Community
2853 E 10th Street
Bloomington, IN 47408
812-855-9396
800-825-4733
FAX: 812-855-9630
e-mail: prattc@indiana.edu
www.iidc.indiana.edu/irca

*Cathy Pratt, Director*
*Stott Bellini, Assistant Director*
*Marilyn Irwin, Executive Director*

The Indiana Resource Center for Autism staff conduct outreach
training and consultations, engage in research and develop and
disseminate information focused on building the capicity of local communities, organizations, agencies and families to support children and adults across the autism spectrum in typical
work, school, home and community settings. Please check our
website for a complete list of publications.

**5389 Indiana University: Multipurpose Arthritis Center**
School Of Medicine, Rheumatology Division
1110 W Michigan Street
LO 545
Bloomington, IN 47405
317-274-4225
FAX: 317-274-7792
e-mail: dbrandt@iupui.edu
www.research.iu.edu/centers/mamdc.html

*Dr. Kenneth Brandt MD, Director*

The mission of the center is to pursue major biomedical research
interests relevant to the rheumatic diseases. Current areas of emphasis include; articular cartilage biology, pathogenesis of articular cartilage breakdown in osteoarthritis, causes of pain and
disability in QA, the pathogenesis and treatment of various
forms of amyloidosis, the pathogenesis of dermatomyositis, and
immunologic and biochemical markers of cartilage breakdown
and repair.

**5390 Lake County Public Library Talking Books Service**
1919 W 81st Avenue
Merrillville, IN 46410
219-769-3541
FAX: 219-756-9358
e-mail: webmaster@lakeco.lib.in.us
www.lakeco.lib.in.us

*Larry Acheff, Manager*

Large-print books, descriptive videos, braille writer, magnifiers, closed-circuit TV, large-print photocopier, cassette books
and magazines, children's books on cassette, and other reference materials on blindness and other handicaps.

**5391  Northwest Indiana Subregional Library for Blind and Physically Handicapped**
1919 W 81st Avenue
Merrillville, IN  46410           219-769-3541
                                 FAX: 219-769-0690
            e-mail: webmastr@lakeco.lib.in.us
                             www.lakeco.lib.in.us

*Sally Benson, PR Manager*
*Larry Acheff, Manager*

Summer reading programs, braille writer, magnifiers, closed-circuit TV, large-print photocopier, cassette books and magazines, children's books on cassette, home visits and other reference materials on blindness and other handicaps.

**5392  Special Services Division: Indiana State Library**
140 N Senate Avenue
Indianapolis, IN  46204           317-232-3675
                                  800-622-4970
                             FAX: 317-232-3728
                             TTY: 317-232-7763
              e-mail: lbph@statelib.lib.in.us
                             www.statelib.lib.in.us

*Lissa Shanahan, Librarian*
*Barbara Maxwell, State Librarian*
*C Ewick, Manager*

Circulates a collection of braille, recorded, and large print books and magazines and the special equipment needed to play the recorded materials to anyone in Indiana who cannot read regular print due to a visual or physical disability.

**5393  St. Joseph Hospital Rehabilitation Center**
700 Broadway
Fort Wayne, IN  46802             260-425-3606
                             FAX: 260-425-3741

*Roberta Archer, Case Manager*
*Bob Hailes, Vice President*

Information offered on rehabilitation.

**5394  Talking Books Service Evansville Vanderburgh County Public Library**
200 SE Martin Luther King Jr Blvd
Evansville, IN  47713             812-428-8200
                             FAX: 812-428-8397
                                     www.evpl.org

*Brenda Scheidler, President*
*Connie Davis, Vice President*
*Marcia Au, Executive Director*

# Iowa

**5395  Iowa Department for the Blind Library**
524 4th Street
Des Moines, IA  50309             515-281-1333
                                  800-362-2587
                             FAX: 515-281-1378
                             TTY: 515-281-1355
       e-mail: keninger.karen@blind.state.ia.us
                             www.blind.state.ia.us

*Allen Harris, Executive Director*
*Karen Keninger, Program Manager/Librarian*

Summer reading programs, large print, disc, Braille and cassette books and magazines, descriptive videos and reference materials on blindness and other handicaps.

**5396  Iowa Registry for Congenital and Inherited Disorders**
University of Iowa
Department of Epidemiology
M107 Oakdale Hill
Iowa City, IA 52242               319-335-4107
                                  866-274-4237
                             FAX: 319-335-4030
                 e-mail: ircid@uiowa.edu
        www.public-health.uiowa.edu/ircid/

*Paul Romitti, Ph.D, Director*
*Bradley McDowell, Ph.D, Deputy Director*

The mission of the Iowa Registry for Congenital and Inherited Disorders is; maintain statewide surveillance for collecting information on selected congenital and inherited disorders in Iowa, monitor annual trends in occurrence and mortality of these disorders, provide data for research studies and educational activities for the prevention and treatment of these disorders.

**5397  Library Commission for the Blind**
524 4th Street
Des Moines, IA  50309             515-281-1333
                                  800-362-2587
                             FAX: 515-281-1263
                             TTY: 515-281-1355
         e-mail: library@blind.state.ia.us
                             www.blind.state.ia.us

*Allen Harris, Executive Director*
*Karen Keninger, Program Director*

Summer reading programs, Braille writer, magnifiers, closed-circuit TV, large print photocopier, cassette books and magazines, children's books on cassette and other reference materials on blindness and other handicaps.

# Kansas

**5398  CKLS Headquarters**
1409 Williams Street
Great Bend, KS  67530             620-792-2393
                                  800-362-2642
                             FAX: 620-792-5495
                 e-mail: jmasden@ckls.org
                                     www.ckls.org

*Joaniea Doll-Masden, Dept Head/Consultant*
*James Swan, Administrator*

Summer reading programs, braille writer, magnifiers, closed-circuit TV, large-print photocopier, cassette books and magazines, children's books on cassette, home visits and other reference materials on blindness and other handicaps. Assistive technology available.

**5399  Center for the Improvement of Human Functioning**
3100 N Hillside Street
Wichita, KS  67219                316-682-3100
                             FAX: 316-682-5054
            e-mail: docron@brightspot.org
                             www.brightspot.org

*Hugh D Riordan, President*
*Olive W Garvey, Chief Medical Officer*

Medical, research, and educational facility specializing in the treatment of chronic illness.

**5400 Kansas State Library**
Esu Memorial Union
1200 Commercial Street
Emporia, KS 66801 620-341-6778
800-362-0699
FAX: 620-343-7124
e-mail: tonih@kslib.info
www.kslib.info

*Toni Herrel, Director*
*Jo Kord, Manager*

Summer reading programs, braille writer, magnifiers, closed-circuit TV, large-print photocopier, cassette books and magazines, children's books on cassette, home visits and other reference materials on blindness and other handicaps.

**5401 Manhattan Public Library**
629 Poyntz Avenue
Manhattan, KS 66502 785-776-4741
800-432-2796
FAX: 785-776-1545
e-mail: annp@manhattan.lib.ks.us
www.manhattan.lib.ks.us

*Ann Pearce, Department Head*
*Sue Colley, Reader Advisor*
*Fred Atchison, Manager*

Summer reading programs, Braille writer, magnifiers, closed-circuit TV, large-print photocopier, cassette books and magazines, children's books on cassette, home visits and other reference materials on blindness and other disabilities.

**5402 Northwest Kansas Library System Talking Books**
PO Box 446
Norton, KS 67654 785-877-5148
800-432-2858
FAX: 785-877-5697
e-mail: tbook@ruraltel.net
skyways.lib.ks.us

*Clarice Howard, Librarian*
*Leslie Bell, Director*
*Kimberly Gallentine, Business Manager*

Offers books on disc and cassette. Library of Congress talking book and program for qualified individuals. Also offers descriptive videos to eligible persons.

**5403 South Central Kansas Library System**
Talking Bookz/ Sckls
901 N Main Street
Hutchinson, KS 67501 620-663-5441
800-234-0529
FAX: 620-663-1215
e-mail: ksocha@sckls.org
www.skyways.lib.ks.us

*Karen Socha, Librarian*
*Leroy Gattin, Manager*

Summer reading programs, Braille writer, closed-circuit TV, large-print photocopier, cassette books and magazines, children's books on cassette, home visits and other reference materials on blindness and other handicaps.

**5404 Topeka & Shawnee County Public Library Talking Book Service**
1515 SW 10th Avenue
Topeka, KS 66604 785-580-4400
800-432-2925
FAX: 785-231-0579
e-mail: tbooks@tscpl.lib.ks.us
www.tscpl.org

*Gina Millsap, Executive Director*
*Nancy Watkins, Director of Finance*

Summer reading programs, braille writer, magnifiers, closed-circuit TV, large-print photocopier, cassette books and magazines, children's books on cassette, home visits and other reference materials on blindness and other handicaps.

**5405 Wichita Public Library**
223 S Main Street
Wichita, KS 67202 316-261-8500
FAX: 316-262-4540
e-mail: friends@wichita.lib.ks.us
www.wichita.lib.ks.us

*Donna Aldrich, Director*
*Barbara Baker, Director*
*Cynthia Berner-Harris, Executive Director*

Summer reading programs, braille writer, magnifiers, closed-circuit TV, large-print photocopier, cassette books and magazines, children's books on cassette, home visits and other reference materials on blindness and other handicaps.

**5406 Wichita Public Library/Talking Book Service**
Wichita Public Library
223 S Main Street
Wichita, KS 67202 316-261-8500
FAX: 316-262-4540
TTY:316-262-3972
e-mail: cnazar@wichita.lib.ks.us
www.wichita.lib.ks.us

*Sarah Bagby, Member of the Board*
*Cynthia Berner-Harris, Executive Director*
*Eric J Larson, Member of the Board*

Furnish recorded reading material (books and magazines) for visually and physically challenged citizens.

# Kentucky

**5407 EnTech: Enabling Technologies of Kentuckiana**
Spaulding University
851 S 4th Street
Administration Bldg, Room 011
Louisville, KY 40203 502-585-9911
800-896-8941
FAX: 502-585-7104
e-mail: Entech@iglou.com
www.spalding.edu

*Joy Vessels, Information Contact*
*Mary Kaye Steinmietz, Outreach Coordinator*

Assistive technology resource and demonstration center, serving persons of all ages and disabilities in Kentucky and Southern Indiana. Services include: assistive technology information, demonstration, evaluation, training, technical support and short-term loan of equipment.

**5408 Kentucky Talking Book Library**
PO Box 537
Frankfort, KY 40602 502-564-8300
800-372-2968
FAX: 502-564-5773
e-mail: ktbl.mail@ky.gov
www.kdla.ky.gov/collectionsktbl

*Barbara Penegor, Regional Librarian*
*James Nelson, Manager*

Provides library service to those who are physically unable to read print. Cassete and braille books and magazines, descriptive videos, web-braille.

**5409 Louisville Free Public Library**
301 York Street
Louisville, KY 40203 502-574-1611
FAX: 502-574-1657
e-mail: webteam@lfpl.org
www.lfpl.org

*Craig Buthod, Director*

Summer reading programs, braille writer, magnifiers, closed-circuit TV, large-print photocopier, cassette books and magazines, children's books on cassette, home visits and other reference materials on blindness and other handicaps.

## Louisiana

**5410  Central Louisiana State Hospital Medical and Professional Library**
PO Box 5031
Pineville, LA  71361                     318-484-6363
                                    FAX: 318-484-6284
                                www.state.lib.la.us/libdir

*Elizabeth Hecker Perkins, Membership Coordinator*
*Carol Gee, Manager*

Information offered on psychiatry, psychology and mental
health.

**5411  Louisiana State Library**
701 N 4th Street
Baton Rouge, LA  70802                   225-342-4913
                                         800-543-4702
                                    FAX: 225-342-4923
                            e-mail: admin@state.lib.la.us
                                    www.state.lib.la.us

*Rebecca Hamilton, State Librarian/Manager*
*Diane Brown, Deputy State Librarian*

Summer reading programs, braille writer, magnifiers,
closed-circuit TV, large-print photocopier, cassette books and
magazines, children's books on cassette. Descriptive videoss
and other reference materials on blindness and other handicaps.

**5412  Louisiana State Library: Section for the**
701 N 4th Street
Baton Rouge, LA  70802                   225-342-4913

*Rebecca Hamilton, Manager*

**5413  Louisiana State University Genetics Section of Pediatrics**
533 Bolivar Street
New Orleans, LA  70112                   504-568-6148
                                    FAX: 504-568-4008
                            www.medschool.lsuhsc.edu/genetics

*Janis Gissel Letourneau, Medical Director*

**5414  State Library of Louisiana: Services for the Blind and Physically Handicapped**
701 N 4th Street
Baton Rouge, LA  70802                   225-342-0035
                                         800-543-4702
                                    FAX: 225-342-6817
                            e-mail: sbph@state.lib.la.us
                                    www.state.lib.la.us

*Margaret C Harrison, Head Svcs For Blind/Handicapped*
*Emma Schroth, Children's Librarian*
*Angela Cinquemario, Studio Manager*

Summer reading programs, braille publications, cassette books
and magazines, children's books on cassette and other reference
materials on blindness and other handicaps. Louisiana Hotlines -
quarterly newsletter. Affiliated with National Library Service
for the Blind and Physically Handicapped, Washington, DC.
Louisiana Voices recording program uses volunteers to record
books for the blind.

## Maine

**5415  Bangor Public Library**
145 Harlow Street
Bangor, ME  04401                        207-947-8336
                                    FAX: 207-945-6694
                            e-mail: bpill@bpl.lib.me.us
                                    www.bpl.lib.me.us

*Tanian Erickson, Acquisitions*
*Anne Murdy, Children's Department Head*
*Barbara Dade, Manager*

Summer reading programs, braille writer, magnifiers,
closed-circuit TV, large-print photocopier, cassette books and
magazines, children's books on cassette, home visits and other
reference materials on blindness and other handicaps.

**5416  Cary Library**
107 Main Street
Houlton, ME  04730                       207-532-1302
                                    FAX: 207-532-4350
                            e-mail: bettyf@cary.lib.me.us
                                    www.cary.lib.me.us

*Betty Fraser, Librarian/Manager*
*Linda Faucher, Assistant Librarian*

Summer reading programs, braille writer, magnifiers,
closed-circuit TV, large-print photocopier, cassette books and
magazines, children's books on cassette, home visits and other
reference materials on blindness and other handicaps.

**5417  Lewiston Public Library**
200 Lisbon Street
Lewiston, ME  04240                      207-784-0135
                                    FAX: 207-784-3011
                                    TTY:207-784-3123
                            e-mail: lplweb@lplonline.org
                                    www.lplonline.org

*Richard Speer, Director*

Summer reading programs, braille writer, magnifiers,
closed-circuit T.V., large-print photocopier, cassette books and
magazines, children's books on cassette, home visits and other
reference materials on blindness and other handicaps.

**5418  Maine State Library**
Maine State
64 State House Station
Augusta, ME  04333                       207-287-5650
                                         800-762-7106
                                    FAX: 207-287-5654
                                    TTY: 207-287-5622
                    e-mail: benitad@ursus3.ursus.maine.edu
                                    www.state.me.us

*Linda H Lord, Director Library*
*J Gary Nichols, State Librarian*
*Melora Norman, Manager*

Summer reading programs, cassette books and magazines, children's books on cassette, home visits and other reference materials on blindness and other handicaps.
*Newsl./BiAnnual*

**5419  New England Regional Genetics Group**
PO Box 920288
Needham, MA  02492                       781-444-0126
                                    FAX: 781-444-0127
                            e-mail: mfgnergg@verizon.net
                                    www.nergg.org

*Mary Frances Garber, Executive Director*
*Leslie Ciarleglio, Co-Director*

Human genetic services and educational planning pertaining to
birth defects.

**5420  Portland Public Library**
5 Monument Square
Portland, ME  04101                          207-871-1700
                                            FAX: 207-871-1715
                    e-mail: reference@portland.lib.me.us
                              www.portlandlibrary.com

*Sheldon Kaye, Director*
*Claire Hannan, Business Manager*

Summer reading programs, braille writer, magnifiers, closed-circuit T.V., large-print photocopier, cassette books and magazines, children's books on cassette, home visits and other reference materials on blindness and other handicaps.

**5421  Waterville Public Library**
73 Elm Street
Waterville, ME  04901                        207-872-5433
                                            FAX: 207-873-4779
                    e-mail: wplhelpdesk@waterville.lib.me.us
                              www.waterville.lib.me.us

*Sarah Sugden, Executive Director*
*Lee-Anne Folsom, Circulation Coordinator*

Summer reading programs, braille writer, magnifiers, closed-circuit T.V., large-print photocopier, cassette books and magazines, children's books on cassette, home visits and other reference materials on blindness and other handicaps.

# Maryland

**5422  Johns Hopkins University Dana Center for Preventive Ophthalmology**
Wilmer Ophthalmology Institute
600 N Wolfe Street
Baltimore, MD  21287                         410-955-5080
                                            FAX: 410-955-2542
                              e-mail: hquigley@jhmi.edu

*Harry A Quigley, Director*
*Barbara Lake, Manager*

**5423  Johns Hopkins University: Asthma and Allergy Center**
5501 Hopkins Bayview Circle
Baltimore, MD  21224                         410-550-0545
                                            FAX: 410-550-1733
                              e-mail: jhuallergy@jhmi.edu
                                    www.hopkinsmedicine.org

*Lawrence Lichtenstein, Director*

Studies of allergic diseases and individuals with allergic disease, pulmonary diseases and diseases involving inflammation and immunological processes.

**5424  Maryland State Library for the Blind and Physically Handicapped**
Maryland State Department of Education
415 Park Avenue
Baltimore, MD  21201                         410-230-2446
                                             800-964-9209
                                            FAX: 410-333-2095
                    e-mail: referenc@lbph.lib.md.us
                              www.lbph.lib.md.us

*Gillian Lewis, Branch Chief*
*Diana Jarvis, Administrative Specialist*
*LaTarsha Wilson, Secretary*

Provide comprehensive library services to the eligible blind and physically handicapped residents of the State of Maryland. The vision is to provide innovative and quality services to meet the needs and expectations of the patrons of Maryland.

**5425  Montgomery County Department of Public Libraries/Special Needs Library**
6400 Democracy Boulevard
Bethesda, MD  20817                          301-469-7601
                                            TTY:301-897-2217

*Susan F Cohen, Assistant Head Librarian*
*James Montgomery, Owner*

Serves the library information and reading needs of people with disabilities, family members, students and service providers. Some of its services include books, periodicals, and videos on disability issues, adaptive technology, community information; the National Library for the Blind and Physically Handicapped Talking Book program; large print books; and computer room with adaptive technology.

**5426  National Epilepsy Library (NEL)**
Epilepsy Foundation
4351 Garden City Drive
Landover, MD  20785                          301-459-3700
                                             800-332-4050
                                            FAX: 301-577-4941
                              e-mail: nel@efa.org
                                    www.epilepsyfoundation.org

*William E Braulinch, Chairman*
*Eric Hargis, President*

Contains information about epilepsy and seizure disorders and serves physicians and other health professionals. Provides in-house bibliographic database (ESDI), searches and documents delivery and interlibrary loans. Maintains the Albert and Ellen Grass Archives.

**5427  National Rehabilitation Information Center**
4200 Forbes Boulevard
Suite 202
Lanham, MD  20706                            301-459-5900
                                             800-346-2742
                                            FAX: 301-459-4263
                    e-mail: naricinfo@heitechservices.com
                              www.naric.com

*Mark Odum, Director*

A national disability and rehabilitation library and information center that collects and disseminates the results of NIDRR-funded research projects. The collection, which also includes commercially published books, journals, articles and audiovisuals, grows at a rate of 300 documents a month. NARIC currently has more than 50,000 documents on all aspects of disability and rehabilitation. Searchable web page includes 5 databases and a calendar of events.

**5428  Red Notebook**
Friends of Libraries for Deaf Action
2930 Craiglawn Road
Silver Spring, MD  20904                     301-572-5168
                                            FAX: 301-572-5168
                                            TTY:301-572-5168
                              e-mail: folda@aol.com
                                    www.folda.net

*Alice L Hagemeyer, Founder/President*
*Merrie Davidson, Webmaster*

A binder containing fact sheets, library reprints, announcements and other printed informational materials that are related to both deaf and library issues. It is designed to help build communication among individuals and groups within the deaf community. The focus is on assisting libraries in providing cost-effective and efficient library and information services to these consumers in a unbiased fashion.

**5429  Social Security Library**
U S Social Security Administration
6401 Security Boulevard
Baltimore, MD  21235

410-965-1234
800-772-1213
TTY:800-325-0778
www.socialsecurity.gov

*Leo Hollenbeack, Reference Librarian*
*Jo B Barnhart, Chief Executive Officer*

Information on social security and disability insurance.

**5430  Warren Grant Magnuson Clinical Center**
National Institue Health
9000 Rockville Pike
Building 10-Room
Bethesda, MD  20892

301-496-2447
866-411-1010
FAX: 301-480-9793
TTY: 866-411-1010
e-mail: occc@cc.nih.gov
www.cc.nih.gov

*John Gallin, Director*

Established in 1953 as the research hospital of the National Institutes of Health. Designed so that patient care facilities are close to research laboratories so new findings of basic and clinical scientists can be quickly applied to the treatment of patients. Upon referral by physicians, patients are admitted to NIH clinical studies.

## Massachusetts

**5431  Boston University Arthritis Center**
Boston University
715 Albany Street
Boston, MA  02118

617-638-5300
FAX: 617-638-5226
www.bumc.bu.edu

*David Felson, Director*
*Vanesa Vliura, Manager*

**5432  Boston University Center for Human Genetics**
715 Albany Street
4th Floor
Boston, MA  02118

617-638-4620
FAX: 617-638-7092
e-mail: amilunsk@bu.edu

*Aubrey Milunsky, Director*
*Jeff Milunsky, Associate Director*
*Ilga Wohlrab, Manager*

Offers research into genetic disorders and growth disorders.

**5433  Boston University Robert Dawson Evans Memorial Dept. of Clinical Research**
75 East Newton Street
Boston, MA  02118

617-638-7250
FAX: 617-638-8728

*Norman Levinsky, Director*
*Jack Ansel, MD*

Integral unit of the University Hospital specializing in arthritis and connective tissue studies.

**5434  Braille and Talking Book Library, Perkins School for the Blind**
175 N Beacon Street
Watertown, MA  02472

617-924-3434
800-852-3133
FAX: 617-926-2027
e-mail: library@perkins.org
www.perkinslibrary.org

*Kim Johnston, President*
*Kim Charlson, Executive Director*

Provides free books on tape and Braille to persons who cannot read printed material because of a physical disability such as blindness, visual impairment, physical impairment or learning disability. Serves Massachusetts. For Braille, also serves New Hampshire, Rhode Island, Maine and Vermont.

**5435  Brigham and Women's Hospital: Asthma and Allergic Disease Research Center**
75 Francis Street
Boston, MA  02115

617-732-6816
FAX: 617-730-2858
e-mail: arc@partners.org

*K Frank Austen MD, Director*
*Judith Kennedy, Manager*

Integral unit of the hospital focusing research attention on asthma and allergy related disorders.

**5436  Brigham and Women's Hospital: Robert B Brigham Multipurpose Arthritis Center**
Brigham and Women s Hospital
75 Francis Street
Boston, MA  02115

617-732-5500
FAX: 617-432-0979

*Matthew Liang MD, Director*
*Gary Gottlieb, Chief Executive Officer*

Research studies into arthritis and rheumatic diseases.

**5437  Caption Center**
125 Western Avenue
Boston, MA  02134

617-927-9225
FAX: 617-300-1020
TTY:617-300-3600
e-mail: access@wgbh.org
www.wgbh.org/caption

*Tom Apone, Director*
*Larry Goldberg, Director*

Has been pioneering and delivering accessible media to disabled adults, students and their families, teachers and friends for over 30 years. Each year, the Center captions more than 10,000 hours worth of broadcast and cable programs, feature films, large-format and IMAX films, home videos, music videos, DVDs, teleconferences and CD-Roms.

**5438  Center for Interdisciplinary Research on Immunologic Diseases**
Childrens Hospital Medical Center
300 Longwood Avenue
Boston, MA  02115

617-355-6000
FAX: 617-355-0443
TTY:617-355-0443
e-mail: webteam@tch.harvard.edu
www.tch.harvard.edu

*James Mandell, Chief Executive Officer*
*Sandra Fenwick, Chief Operating Officer*
*Lynda Scheider, MD*

Organizational research unit of the Children's Hospital that focuses on the causes, prevention and treatments of asthma, infections and allergies.

**5439 Harvard University Howe Laboratory of Ophthalmology**
Massachusetts Eye & Ear Infirmary
243 Charles Street
Boston, MA 02114                    617-573-3285
                              TTY:617-523-5498
                e-mail: inetwebmaster@meei.harvard.edu
                              www.meei.harvard.edu

*George Rabstejnek, Chairman*
*Joseph W Haley, Vice Chairman*
*Maryellen Doyle, Manager*

Development ophthalmology and eye research.

**5440 Laboure College Library**
2120 Dorchester Avenue
Dorchester Center, MA 02124            617-296-8300
                              FAX: 617-296-7947
                        e-mail: admit@laboure.edu
                              www.laboure.edu

*Mark Ostrem, Director Medical Unit*
*Andrew Callo, Manager*

Offers information on physical disabilities, independent living, peer counseling and advocacy.

**5441 Massachusetts Rehabilitation Commission Library**
27 Wormwood Street Fort Point Pl
Suite 600
Boston, MA 02210                    617-727-2183
                                    800-245-6543
                              FAX: 617-727-1354
                              TTY: 800-245-6543
                              www.mass.gov/mrc

*Elmer C Bartels, Commissioner/Manager*
*Mitt Romney, Governor*
*Kerry Healey, Lieutenant Governor*

Library and information science, rehabilitation and the handicapped.

**5442 Schepens Eye Research Institute**
20 Staniford Street
Boston, MA 02114                    617-912-0100
                              FAX: 617-912-0110
                e-mail: geninfo@vision.eri.harvard.edu
                              www.theschepens.org

*Michael Gilmore, President*
*Kennett Burnes, Chairman*

Prominent center for research on eye, vision, and blinding diseases; dedicated to research that improves the understanding, management, and prevention of eye diseases and visual deficiencies; fosters collaboration among its faculty members; trains young scientists and clinicians from around the world; promotes communication with scientists in allied fields; leader in the worldwide dispersion of basic scientific knowledge of vision.

**5443 Talking Book Library at Worcester Public Library**
3 Salem Square
Worcester, MA 01608                  508-799-1730
                                    800-762-0085
                              FAX: 508-799-1676
                e-mail: talkbook@cwmars.org
                www.worcpublib.org/talkingbook

*James Izatt, Manager*

Braille embosser, magnifiers, closed-circuit TV, adapted computers, cassette books and magazines, children's books on cassette, reference materials on blindness and other disabilities.

# Michigan

**5444 Artificial Language Laboratory**
Michigan State University
405 Computer Center
East Lansing, MI 48824              517-355-7474
                              FAX: 517-353-4766
                e-mail: artlang@pilot.msu.edu
                        www.artlang@pilot.msu.edu

*John B Eulenberg, Director*
*Stephen Blosser, Technical Director*
*Shawn Miller, Laboratory Manager*

Multidisciplinary research center in the Audiology & Speech Science department, Michigan State University. Its basic research program includes speech analysis and synthesis. Applied research is carried out on computer-based systems for persons who are blind and for persons with cerebral palsy and head injury. The laboratory develops physical, cognitive and linguistic assessment technology.

**5445 Burger School for the Autistic**
30922 Beechwood Street
Garden City, MI 48135               734-762-8420
                              FAX: 734-793-1831
                              garden-city.lib.mi.us

*Joan Elmouchi, Director*
*Jan Smith, Assistant Director*
*Judy Gapp, Director Childrens Unit*

Burger school for students with autism is the largest public school in the United States that specializes in the education of students with autism.

**5446 Chi Medical Library**
Ingham Regional Medical Center
401 W Greenlawn
Lansing, MI 48910                   517-334-2121
                              FAX: 517-334-2939
                              www.irmc.org

*Judith Barnes, Information Resources Coordinato*

Consumer health and patient education collection in books, videotapes, pamphlets. Open to the public.

**5447 Glaucoma Laser Trial**
Sinai Hospital of Detroit: Dept. of Opthalmology
29275 Northwestern Highway
Southfield, MI 48034                248-493-5157

                              www.nei.nih.gov/neitrials

*Hugh Beckman, MD, Chairman*

The purpose of the trial is to compare the safety and long-term efficacy of argon laser treatment of the trabecular meshwork with standard medical treatment for primary open-angle glaucoma.

**5448 Grand Traverse Area Library for the Blind and Physically Handicapped**
610 Woodmere Avenue
Traverse City, MI 49686             231-932-8500
                                    877-931-8558
                              FAX: 231-932-8578
                e-mail: webmaster@tadl.tcnet.org
                              www.tadl.org

*Gay Travis, President*
*Beth Bynum, Vice President*
*Michael Guire, Executive Director*

**5449  Kent District Library for the Blind and Physically Handicapped**
775 Ball Avenue NE
Grand Rapids, MI 49503

616-336-3265
FAX: 616-336-3256
e-mail: kdlsc@lakeland.lib.mi.us
www.nlc.lib.mi.us

*Claudya Muller, Director*

Summer reading programs, braille writer, magnifiers, large-print photocopier, cassette books and magazines, children's books on cassette, and other reference materials on blindness and other handicaps.

**5450  Library of Michigan Service for the Blind**
PO Box 30007
Lansing, MI 48909

517-373-1580

e-mail: librarian@michigan.gov
www.michigan.gov/hal

*Mase Sheryl, Director*
*Christie Brandau, Manager*

Braille writer, magnifiers, closed-circuit T.V., large-print photocopier, cassette books and magazines, children's books on cassette, and other reference materials on blindness and other handicaps.

**5451  Macomb Library for the Blind and Physically Handicapped**
16480 Hall Road
Clinton Township, MI 48038

586-286-1580
800-649-3777
FAX: 586-286-0634
e-mail: macbld@libcoop.net
www.libcoop.net/macspe

*Beverlee Babcock, Executive Director*

Summer reading programs, braille writer, closed-circuit T.V., large-print books, cassette books and magazines, children's books on cassette, other reference materials on blindness and other handicaps, descriptive videos and bifokal kits. Assistive technology including JAWS, Zoomtext, OpenBook, and Duxbury.

**5452  Michigan's Assistive Technology Resource**
Physically Impaired Association of Michigan
1023 S US 27
St. Johns, MI 48879

989-224-0333
800-274-7426
FAX: 989-224-0330
e-mail: matr@edzone.net
www.cenmi.org

*Jeffrey Diedrich, Director*
*Maryann Jones, Coordinator*
*Barbara Warren, Information Specialist*

Provides information services, support materials, technical assistance, and training to local and intermediate school districts in michigan to increase their capacity to address the needs of students with disabilities for assistive technology.

**5453  Michigan's Assistive Technology Resources**
1023 S Us 27
Saint Johns, MI 48879

989-224-0333
800-274-7426
FAX: 989-224-0330
e-mail: matr@edzone.net
www.cenmi.org/mater

*Jeff Diedrich, Executive Director*

Michigan's Assistive Technology Resource (MATR) is a comprehensive support center located in St Johns, Michigan. The overall purpose of MATR is to provide information services, support materials, technical assistance and training to local and intermediate school districts in Michigan to increase their capacity to address the needs of students with disabilities for assistive technology.

**5454  Mideastern Michigan Library Co-op**
503 S Saginaw Street
Suite 839
Flint, MI 48502

810-232-7119
800-641-6639
FAX: 810-232-6639
e-mail: rmendel@flint.org
www.mideastern.lib.mi.us

*Roger Mendel, Director*

Summer reading programs, braille writer, magnifiers, closed-circuit T.V., large-print photocopier, cassette books and magazines, children's books on cassette, home visits and other reference materials on blindness and other handicaps.

**5455  Muskegon County Library for the Blind**
97 E Apple Avenue
Muskegon, MI 49442

231-724-6248
877-569-4801
FAX: 231-724-6675
TTY: 231-722-4103
e-mail: mclsm@llcoop.org
www.muskcolib.org

*Elizabeth Winsche, Chief Executive Officer*
*Sheila Miller, Librarian*
*Karla Bates, Assistant Director*

Braille typewriter, magnifiers, closed-circuit TV, large-print photocopier, cassette books and magazines, children's books on cassette, home visits and other reference materials on blindness and other handicaps, The Reading Edge, and large print books.

**5456  Northland Library Cooperative**
Library Cooperative/ Library for the blind
316 E Chisholm Street
Alpena, MI 49707

989-356-1622
800-446-1580
FAX: 989-354-3939
e-mail: nlcref@northland.lib.mi.us
www.nlc.lib.mi.us

*Jennifer Dean, Director*
*Christine Johnston, Executive Director*

Summer reading programs, Braille writer, magnifiers, closed-circuit TV, large-print photocopier, cassette books and magazines, children's books on cassette and other reference materials on blindness and other handicaps.

**5457  Oakland County Library for the Visually & Physically Impaired**
1200 N Telegraph Road
Dept 482
Pontiac, MI 48341

248-858-5050
800-774-4542
FAX: 248-858-9313
TTY: 248-452-2247
e-mail: lvpi@co.oakland.mi.us
www.co.oakland.mi.us

*David Conklin, Librarian/Supervisor*

**5458  St. Clair County Library Special Technologies Alternative Resources (S.T.A.R.)**
210 McMorran Boulevard
Port Huron, MI 48060

810-987-7323
800-272-8570
FAX: 810-987-6768
TTY: 810-455-0200
e-mail: star@sccl.lib.mi.us
www.sccl.lib.mi.us/star.html

*Mary Jo Koch, Subregional Librarian*
*James Warwick, Executive Director*

Offers library services to the blind, deaf and blind, visually disabled, phsyically disabled, and reading disabled.

**5459 University of Michigan: Orthopaedic Research Laboratories**
University of Michigan
400 N Ingalls Street
Ann Arbor, MI 48109
734-936-5216
FAX: 734-647-0003
e-mail: svaassen@umich.edu
www.orl.med.umich.edu/orl

*Steve Goldstein, Lab Director*
*Laurence McMahon Jr, MD*

Develops and studies the causes and treatments for arthritis including new devices and assistive aids.

**5460 Upper Peninsula Library for the Blind**
1615 Presque Isle Avenue
Marquette, MI 49855
906-228-7697
800-562-8985
FAX: 906-228-5627
TTY: 906-228-7697
e-mail: rruff@uproc.lib.mi.us
www.uproc.lib.mi.us

*Ruth Ruff, Librarian*
*Suzanne Dees, Executive Director*

Summer reading programs, braille writer, magnifiers, closed-circuit T.V., large-print photocopier, cassette books and magazines, children's books on cassette, home visits and other reference materials on blindness and other handicaps.

**5461 Washtenaw County Library for the Blind & Physically Handicapped**
4135 Washtenaw Avenue
Ann Arbor, MI 48108
734-971-6056
FAX: 734-971-6059
www.ewashtenaw.org

*Mary Udoji, Director*

Michigan Subregional Library, Library of Congress National Library Service network. General library service for persons unable to use standard print materials for various physical reasons. Lends audio books and listening equipment, large type books, descriptive videos. Provides reference information and programs. Kurzweil scanner with components which convert standard print to Braille, large type or audio and closed circuit TV magnifier on site.

**5462 Wayne County Regional Library for the Blind**
30555 Michigan Avenue
Westland, MI 48186
734-727-7300
888-968-2737
888-968-2737
FAX: 734-727-7333
TTY:734-727-7330
e-mail: wcrlbph@wayneregional.lib.mi.us
www.wayneregional.lib.mi.us

*Reginald Williams, Director*
*Frederick Howkins, Manager*

Summer reading programs, braille writer, magnifiers, closed-circuit T.V., large-print photocopier, cassette books and magazines, children's books on cassette, and other reference materials on blindness and other handicaps.

**5463 Wayne State University: CS Mott Center for Human Genetics and Development**
275 E Hancock Street
Detroit, MI 48201
313-577-1485
FAX: 313-577-8554
e-mail: c.yurkovich@wayne.edu
www.media.wayne.edu

*Cheryl Yurkovich, Director Public Relations*
Human growth and development disorders.

# Minnesota

**5464 Century College**
3300 Century Avenue N
White Bear Lake, MN 55110
651-779-3300
800-228-1978
FAX: 651-779-5779
TTY: 651-773-1715
www.century.cc.mn.us

*Larry Litecky, President*
*Nancy Levingston, Director*

Programs of study - Orthotic Practitioner, Orthotic Technician, Prosethetic Practitioner, Prosthetic Technician. In addition, Century College offers more than 50 other programs in liberal arts, career and occupational programs.

**5465 Communication Center/Minnesota State Services for the Blind**
Services for the Blind
2200 University Avenue W
Suite 240
Saint Paul, MN 55114
651-642-0500
800-652-9000
FAX: 651-649-5927
e-mail: chamilto@ssb.state.mn.us

*Chuck Hamilton, Director*

Special library service for the blind and physically handicapped providing tape and Braille transcription of textbooks and vocational materials; Minnesota Radio Talking Book providing current newspaper, magazines and best selling books; Dial-in-News, a touch tone phone accessed newspaper service; Library of Congress cassette and phonograph talking book equipment; repair services for special audio reading equipment, with most services free to Minnesota Residents.

**5466 Duluth Public Library**
520 W Superior Street
Duluth, MN 55802
218-723-3800
FAX: 218-723-3822
e-mail: webmail@duluth.lib.mn.us
www.duluth.lib.mn.us

*Elizabeth Kelly, Library/Executive Director*

Adapted access to Apple computer, adapted toys and adapted library equipment.

**5467 Minnesota Library for the Blind and Physically Handicapped**
Department of Education
388 6th Avenue SE
Faribault, MN 55021
507-333-4828
800-722-0550
FAX: 507-333-4832
e-mail: mn.lbph@sate.mn.us
education.state.mn.us

*Catherine Durivage, Program Director*
*Rene Perrance, Librarian*

Provides books and magazines in Braille, large print, records, and cassettes to qualified residents of Minnesota who have a visual or physical impairment, including reading disabilities due to an organic cause certified by a medical doctor, that prevents residents from reading standard print or physically handling a book. Equipment for in-house use include magnifiers, braillers, listening equipment, and CCTV. Reference collection for in-house use only on visual impairment topics.

**5468 Special U**
University of Minnesota
PO Box 721-Umhc
Minneapolis, MN 55455
612-625-3846
800-276-8642
FAX: 612-624-0997
e-mail: kdwb-var@umn.edu
www.peds.umn.edu/peds-adol/

Brings together comprehensive sources of information related to youth with chronic or disabling conditions and their families. Topics include psychosocial issues, disability awareness, developmental processes, family, sexuality, education, employment, independent living, cultural issues, gender issues, service delivery, professional issues, advocacy and legal issues, and health issues. Special focus on transition from childhood to adolesecence to adulthood.

## Mississippi

**5469  Mississippi Library Commission**
1221 Ellis Avenue
Jackson, MS  39209

601-352-3917
800-446-0892
FAX: 601-354-7007
TTY: 601-354-6411
e-mail: mslib@mlc.lib.ms.us
www.mlc.lib.ms.us

*Sharman B Smith, Executive Director*
*Ewing Ethel, Executive Support Director*
*Mary Anderson, Manager*

Summer reading programs, braille writer, magnifiers, closed-circuit T.V., large-print photocopier, cassette books and magazines, children's books on cassette, home visits and other reference materials on blindness and other handicaps.

**5470  Mississippi Library Commission\Talking Book and Braille Services**
1221 Ellis Avenue
Jackson, MS  39209

601-961-4111
800-446-0892
FAX: 601-354-7007
e-mail: mslib@mlc.lib.ms.us
www.mlc.lib.ms.us

*Sharman B Smith, Executive Director*
*Rey Tuchett, Director for the Blind/Handicapp*

Library service for the print handicapped braille, cassette and disc materials (books & periodicals) for children and adults. Large print RG production (copier & printer), braille embosser and other handicaps.

## Missouri

**5471  Assemblies of God National Center for the Blind: Adriene Resource Center for Blind Children**
Assemblies of God Headquarters
1445 N Boonville Avenue
Springfield, MO  65802

417-862-2781
FAX: 417-862-5120
e-mail: blind@ag.org
www.blind.ag.org

*Paul Weingartner, Director*
*Caryl Weingartner, Administrative Assistant*
*Juleen Turnage, Religious Leader*

Offers braille and cassette lending library, braille and cassette Sunday School materials for all ages, braille and cassette periodicals, resource assistance, and resources for blind children and children of blind parents.

**5472  Church of the Nazarene**
Nazarene Publishing House
2923 Troost Avenue
Kansas City, MO  64109

816-931-1900
800-877-0700
FAX: 800-849-9827
e-mail: it@nazarene.org
www.nazarene.org

*Hardy Weathers, President*

Offers braille and large print books. Also offers a lending library and cassettes for the blind.

**5473  Judevine Center for Autism**
1101 Olivette Executive Parkway
Saint Louis, MO  63132

314-432-6200
FAX: 314-849-2721
e-mail: judevine@judevine.org
www.judevine.org

*Becky Blackwell, President*

Evaluations and assessments, parent and professional training programs, consultations, workshops, seminars, family support, clinical therapies, adult programs and support, residential services.

**5474  Lutheran Library for the Blind**
1333 S Kirkwood Road
Saint Louis, MO  63122

314-965-9000
888-215-2455
FAX: 314-963-0738
e-mail: blind.mission@blindmission.org
www.blindmission.org

*Lynne Borchelt, Manager*
*Gerald Kieschnick, President*

Offers Christian books in braille and large print books and cassettes for the blind and visually impaired, on loan, as well as Christian periodicals in braille, large print and cassette tape.

**5475  University of Missouri: Columbia Arthritis Center**
University of Missouri
1 Hospital Drive
Columbia, MO  65212

573-882-4991
FAX: 573-884-3996
e-mail: webeditor@missouri.edu
www.muhealth.org

*Jerry C Parker, Director*
*David Cravens, MD*

Research into arthritis and rheumatic diseases.

**5476  Wolfner Library for the Blind**
Secretary State Office
PO Box 387
Jefferson City, MO  65102

573-751-8720
800-392-2614
TTY:800-347-1379
e-mail: wolfner@sos.mo.gov
www.sos.mo.gov

*Richard J Smith, Division Director*

Free library service in alternate formats, braille, recorded, large print. For any Missouri resident who cannot read standard print, due to a physical disability. Summer reading programs, braille writer, magnifiers, closed-circuit T.V., large-print photocopier, cassette books and magazines, children's books on cassette, home visits and other reference materials on blindness and other handicaps.

## Montana

**5477  MonTECH**
University of Montana
634 Eddy Avenue
Missoula, MT  59812

406-243-5751
877-243-5511
FAX: 406-243-4730
TTY: 406-243-5676
e-mail: montech@ruralinstitute.umt.edu
www.montech.ruralinstitute.umt.edu

*Kathy Laurin, Ph.D, Director*
*Leslie Mullete, Clinical Coordinator*
*Mary Swan, Community Relations/Info Liaison*

Specializing in Assistive Technology and oversee a variety of AT related grants and contracts. The overall goal is to develop a comprehensive, statewide system of assistive technology related assistance. Striving to ensure that all people in Montana with disabilities have equitable access to assistive technology devices and services in order to enhance their independence, productivity, and quality of life.

**5478  Montana State Library**
PO Box 201800
Helena, MT  59620

406-444-3115
800-332-3400
FAX: 406-444-8266
e-mail: cbriggs@state.mt.us
www.msl.state.mt.us/tbl

*Christie Briggs, Supervisor*
*Darlene Staffeldt, Manager*

Over 50,000 titles on 4-track cassette, WebBraille, Web0pac, WebBlud, summer reading programs, braille writer, magnifiers, closed-circuit T.V., large-print photocopier, cassette books and magazines, children's books on cassette, home visits and other reference materials on blindness and other handicaps. Large print and Braille services to blind, low vision, physically handicapped and reading disabled citizens of Montana.

**5479  Montana State Library\Talking Book Library**
PO Box 201800
Helena, MT  59620

406-444-3115
800-338-5087
FAX: 406-444-0266
e-mail: msl@state.mt.us
www.msl@.mt.gov

*Christie Briggs, Librarian*
*Darlene Staffeldt, Manager*

Summer reading programs, braille writer, magnifiers, large-print photocopier, cassette books and magazines, children's books on cassette, and other reference materials on blindness and other handicaps.

## Nebraska

**5480  Martin Luther Home Society Resource Center**
804 J Street
Suite 305
Lincoln, NE  68508

402-486-3848
800-443-4899
FAX: 402-434-3253
e-mail: mlhs_MEINTS@compuserve.com
www.mlhs.com

*Alice Meints, Resource Center Director*
*Fred Naumann III, Communications Director*

Provides materials and opportunities for consultation with individuals and communities assisting persons with special needs.

**5481  Nebraska Assistive Technology Partnership Nebraska Department of Education**
5143 S 48th Street
Suite C
Lincoln, NE  68516

402-471-0734
888-806-6287
888-806-6287
FAX: 402-471-6052
TTY:402-471-0734
e-mail: atp@atp.state.ne.us
www.nde.state.ne.us/ATP

*Mark Schultz, Executive Director*
*Lilly Blase, Program Coordinator*

Provides statewide assistive technology and home modification services for Nebraskans of all ages and disabilities.

**5482  Nebraska Library Commission: Talking Book and Braille Service**
Talking Book and Braille Service
1200 N Street
Suite 120
Lincoln, NE  68508

402-471-4038
800-742-7691
FAX: 402-471-2083
TTY: 402-471-4083
e-mail: talkingbook@nlc.state.ne.us
www.nlc.state.ne.us

*Dave Oertli, Executive Director*
*Kay Goehring, Reader Services Coordinator*
*Bill Ainsley, Audio Production Studio Manager*

Summer reading programs, braille writer, magnifiers, closed-circuit T.V., large-print photocopier, cassette books and magazines, children's books on cassette, home visits and other reference materials on blindness and other handicaps.

## Nevada

**5483  Las Vegas-Clark County Library District**
833 Las Vegas Boulevard
Las Vegas, NV  89101

702-734-7323
FAX: 702-733-1567
www.lvccld.lib.nv.us

*Elaine Sanchez, Chairman*
*Verlia Davis, Vice Chair*
*Laura Golod, Manager*

Summer reading programs, braille writer, magnifiers, closed-circuit T.V., large-print photocopier, cassette books and magazines, children's books on cassette, home visits and other reference materials on blindness and other handicaps.

**5484  Nevada State Library and Archives**
Capitol Complex
Carson City, NV  89710

775-687-5469
FAX: 775-687-8311
TTY:702-687-8338
e-mail: putnam@equinox.unr.edu

*Kevin E Putnam, Librarian*
*Kenneth Rohrs, Manager*

Summer reading programs, braille writer, magnifiers, closed-circuit T.V., large-print photocopier, cassette books and magazines, children's books on cassette, home visits and other reference materials on blindness and other handicaps.

## New Hampshire

**5485  New Hampshire State Library: Library Services to Persons with Disabilities**
117 Pleasant Street
Concord, NH  03301

603-271-3429
FAX: 603-271-8370
www.state.nh.us/nhsl/talkbks/index.html

*Donna Gilbreth, Librarian*
*John Barrett, Executive Director*

Regional Library for National Library Service for the Blind & Physically Handicapped offers cassette books and magazines, children's books on cassette, home visits, descriptive videos, large print books, and other reference materials on blindness and other handicaps.

## New Jersey

**5486  Children's Specialized Hospital Medical Library - Parent Resource Center**
150 New Providence Road
Mountainside, NJ 07092          908-233-3720
                                FAX: 908-301-5569
          e-mail: Lungin@childrensspecialized.org

*Mila Lungin, Medical Librarian*
*Amy Mansue, Chief Executive Officer*

Contains some 3,000 books, and journals specializing in nursing, pediatrics, child neurology, and rehabilitation. Also provides a Parent Resource Center, a special collection of books, videos and pamphlets designed to meet the information needs of parents and families, as well as the local community.

**5487  Christopher & Dana Reeve Paralysis Resource Center**
636 Morris Tpke
Suite 3a
Short Hills, NJ 07078          973-467-8270
                               800-539-7309
                          FAX: 973-467-9845
                     e-mail: info@paralysis.org
                               www.paralysis.org

*Joe Canose, VP Quality Of Life*
*Angela Carter, Associate Director Operations*

A national clearinghouse for information, referral and educational materials on paralysis. Offers a free book "Paralysis Resource Guide" in English or Spanish. Free lending library.

**5488  Eye Institute of New Jersey**
New Jersey Medical School
90 Bergen Street
Newark, NJ 07103          973-972-2111
                          FAX: 973-972-2068
                     www.umdnj.edu/eyeweb

*Marco Zarbin, Chairman*

Ophthamology, including research into cornea, retina and neuro-ophthamalogy.

**5489  Mycoclonus Research Foundation**
200 Old Palisade Road
Apt 17d
Fort Lee, NJ 07024          201-585-0770
                             FAX: 201-585-0770
            e-mail: research@myoclonus.com
                         www.myoclonus.com

*Mark Seiden, VP*

Supports clinical and basic research into the cause and treatment of myoclonus; four international workshops facilitated the sharing of information by physicians, scientists, and investigators active in the field, resulted in three publications; supports promising research projects, clinical neurological fellows, with special emphasis on posthypoxic myoclonus and encourages all who are interested in futhering the understanding, treatment, and cure of myoclonus.

**5490  New Jersey Center for Outreach and Services for the Autism Community (COSAC)**
1450 Parkside Avenue
Suite 22
Ewing, NJ 08638          609-883-8100
                          800-428-8476
                     FAX: 609-883-5509
         e-mail: information@njcosac.org
                     www.njcosac.org

*Paul A Potito, Executive Director*

Purpose is to assist families, individuals and agencies concerned with the welfare and education of children and adults with autism and other pervasive development disorders.

**5491  New Jersey Library for the Blind and Handicapped**
PO Box 501
Trenton, NJ 08625          609-530-4000
                             800-792-8322
                        FAX: 609-530-6384
                        TTY: 609-530-4000
              e-mail: njlbh@njstatelib.org
                         www.njstatelib.org

*Anne McArthur, Outreach & Public Education*
*Faith Lundgren, Assistant Director*
*Venetia Demson, Executive Director*

Summer reading programs, braille writer, magnifiers, closed-circuit T.V., large-print, cassette, braille books and magazines, children's books on cassette, and other reference materials on blindness and other handicaps. Provides reading material on audio, cassette, large print and braille to eligible NJ residents.

## New Mexico

**5492  New Mexico State Library for the Blind and Physically Handicapped**
325 Don Gaspar Avenue
Santa Fe, NM 87501          505-986-4550
                             800-456-5515
                        FAX: 505-827-3888
                        TTY: 800-659-4915
        e-mail: jbrewstr@stlib.state.nm.us
                     www.stlib.state.nm.us

*Glee Wenzel, Librarian*
*David Abbey, Executive Director*

Summer reading programs, braille writer, magnifiers, closed-circuit T.V., large-print photocopier, cassette books and magazines, children's books on cassette, home visits and other reference materials on blindness and other handicaps.

## New York

**5493  Braille Book Bank**
National Braille Association
3 Townline Circle
Rochester, NY 14623          585-427-8260
                              FAX: 585-427-0263
          e-mail: nbaoffice@national.org
                     www.nationalbraille.org

*Louis Braille, Inventor*
*Angela Coffaro, Executive Director*

Contains over 1800 Braille titles and Braille music scores. Copies produced on demand and sold below cost. Catalog available on request.

**5494  Center on Human Policy: School of Educatio n**
Syracuse University
805 S Crouse Avenue
Syracuse, NY 13244          315-443-3851
                             800-894-0826
                        FAX: 315-443-4338
                 e-mail: thechp@syr.edu
                     www.thechp.syr.edu

*Steve Taylor, Director*
*Rachael Zubal-Ruggieri, Information Coordinator*
*Raymond Colton, Manager*

The Center on Human Policy is a Syracuse University-based policy, research and advocacy organization involved in the national movement to ensure the rights of people with disabilities.

**5495   DREAMMS for Kids**

273 Ringwood Road
Freeville, NY 13068                     607-539-3027
                                   FAX: 607-539-9930
                              e-mail: janet@dreamms.org
                                       www.dreamms.org

*Janet Hosmer, Executive Director*

DREAMMS is committed to increasing the use of computers, high quality instructional technology, and assistive technologies for students with special needs in schools, homes and the workplace.

**5496   Eastern Paralyzed Veterans Association**

7520 Astoria Boulevard
East Elmhurst, NY 11370                 718-803-3782
                                        800-444-0120
                                   FAX: 718-803-0414
                              e-mail: info@unitedspinal.org
                                       www.unitedspinal.org

*Gerard Kelly, Director*
*Peter Addesso, President*

Library offering information on physical disabilities, spinal cord injury and rehabilitation. Also provides literature searches on specific topics. Association news and free publications on architecture and barrier-free designs, legislation and other current events affecting Americans with Disabilities.

**5497   Ehrman Medical Library**

New York University Medical Center
550 1st Avenue
New York, NY 10016                      212-263-5341
                                   FAX: 212-263-6534
                                   library.med.nyu.edu

*Karen Brewer, Director*

Statistics, reports and evaluation.

**5498   Helen Keller International**

352 Park Avenue S
Floor 12
New York, NY 10010                      212-532-0544
                                        877-535-5374
                                   FAX: 212-532-6014
                                   e-mail: info@hki.org
                                       www.hki.org

*Kathy Spahn, President/CEO*
*Jennifer Klopp, Dir Development/Communications*

Nonprofit international organization whose mission is to combat the causes and consequences of blindness and malnutrition.

**5499   Helen Keller National Center for Deaf-Blin d Youths
and Adults**

141 Middle Neck Road
Sands Point, NY 11050                   516-944-8900
                                   FAX: 516-944-7302
                              e-mail: hkncinfo@hknc.org
                                       www.HKNC.org

*Nancy O'Donnell, Information Services*
*Joseph McNulty, Executive Director*

Provides evaluation and training in vocational skills, adaptive technology and computer skills, orientation and mobility, independent living, communication, speech-language skills, creative arts, fitness and leisure activities.

**5500   Institute for Basic Research in Developmental Disabilities**

1050 Forest Hill Road
Staten Island, NY 10314                 718-494-0600
                                   FAX: 718-494-0833

*W Ted Brown, Director*
*Peter Piotrkozlowski, Executive Director*

Conducts research into neurodegenerative diseases, alzheimer's disease, developmental disabilities, fragile X syndrome, Down's Syndrome, autism, epilepsy and basic science issues underlying all developmental disabilities.

**5501   Institute for Visual Sciences**

1 E 71st Street
New York, NY 10021                      212-249-1140
                                   FAX: 212-472-0295

*Francis Lesperance, Chairman*

Ophthalmology with emphasis on the development of care for the eye.

**5502   JGB Cassette Library International**

15 W 65th Street
New York, NY 10023                      212-769-6331
                                   FAX: 212-769-6266
                                   e-mail: bemass@aol.com

*Peter Williamson, Executive Director*

Summer reading programs, braille writer, magnifiers, closed-circuit T.V., large-print photocopier, cassette books and magazines, children's books on cassette, home visits and other reference materials on blindness and other handicaps.

**5503   Monroe Developmental Center**

620 Westfall Road
Rochester, NY 14620                     585-461-8500
                                   FAX: 585-461-8952
                              e-mail: folwelbe@nysomr.emi.com
                                       www.cs.state.newyork.us

*Sue Mann, Director*
*Carolyn Bassett, Manager*

Information on mental retardation and developmental disabilities.

**5504   Nassau Library System**

900 Jerusalem Avenue
Uniondale, NY 11553                     516-292-8920
                                   FAX: 516-481-4777
                              e-mail: outreach@nassaulibrary.org
                                       www.nassaulibrary.org

*Elizabeth Olesh, Manager Outreach Services*
*Francine Siegel, Sr Connections Project Director*
*Jackie Thresher, Executive Director*

Information about public library services in Nassau County, including services for people with disabilities and the Senior Connections volunteer project (information and referral for seniors and their families).

**5505   New York Public Library: Andrew Heiskell Library for
the Blind and Physically Handicapped**

New York Public Library
40 W 20th Street
New York, NY 10011                      212-206-5400
                                   FAX: 212-206-5418
                                   TTY:212-206-5458
                              e-mail: ahlbph@nypl.org
                                       www.nypl.org/branch/lb

*Robert McBrian, Regional Librarian/Manager*

By mail and on-site offers talking books and braille books to eligible patrons in New York City and Long Island. Additional on-site services include large-print books, books on tape, descriptive videos, class visits, programs, and assistive devices such as closed circuit televisions and Karzweil Personal Readers

**5506  New York State Talking Book & Braille Library**
Empire State Plaza
Albany, NY  12230

518-474-5935
800-342-3688
FAX: 518-486-1957
TTY: 518-474-5935
e-mail: tbbl@mail.nysed.gov
www.nysl.nysed.gov

*Jane Somers, Director*

Books on audio cassette, cassette players, braille books, summer reading programs, braille writer, magnifiers, closed-circuit T.V., large-print photocopier, cassette books and magazines, children's books on cassette, reference materials on blindness and other handicaps.

**5507  Postgraduate Center for Mental Health**
124 E 28th Street
New York, NY  10016

212-576-4100
FAX: 212-696-1679
www.dvguide.com/newyork/postgrad.html

*Marge Slobetz, Assistant Director*
*Marie Serrano, Manager*

Information on mental health.

**5508  Rehabilitation Research Library**
Human Resources Center
Albertson, NY  11507

516-741-2010
FAX: 516-746-3298

*Amnon Tishler, Research Librarian*
*Susan Feifer, Manager*

Information on rehabilitation and occupational rehabilitation.

**5509  State University of New York Health Sciences Center**
PO Box 32
Brooklyn, NY  11203

718-270-1934
FAX: 718-778-5397

*Adolf Christ, Director*
*James Cottrell, MD*

Child psychiatry research programs.

**5510  Suffolk Cooperative Library System: Long Island Talking Book Library**
Long Island Talking Book Library System
PO Box 9000
Bellport, NY  11713

631-286-1600
866-833-1122
FAX: 631-286-1647
TTY: 631-286-4546
e-mail: lbph@suffolk.lib.ny.us
www.litbl.org

*Valerie Lewis, Librarian*
*Gerald Nichols, Executive Director*

Offers a variety of support services to its 55 member libraries and other patrons including, an extensive talking book program, assistive technology and other services for people with disabilities.

**5511  Wallace Memorial Library**
Rochester Institute Of Technology
1 Lomb Memorial Drive
Rochester, NY  14623

585-475-2411
FAX: 585-475-7007
TTY:585-475-2760
e-mail: circwml@rit.edu
wally.rit.edu

*Chandra McKenzie, Director*
*Albert Simone, President*

Information on physical disabilities and deafness.

**5512  Xavier Society for the Blind**
154 E 23rd Street
New York, NY  10010

212-473-7800

*Alfred E Ceruana, Director*
*Kathleen Lynch, Manager*

Provides spiritual and inspirational reading material to visually impaired persons in suitable format: braille, large print and cassette, throughout U.S. and Canada. Services are provided both by way of regular periodical publications sent through the mail and non-returnable; and by means of a lending library where books are returned. All services are provided free.

## North Carolina

**5513  Autism Society of North Carolina**
Autism Society Of North Carolina Bookstore
505 Oberlin Road
Suite 230
Raleigh, NC  27605

919-743-0204
800-442-2762
FAX: 919-743-0208
e-mail: jhkeel@autismsociety-nc.org
www.autismsociety-nc.org

*Jill Keel, Executive Director*
*Tracey Sheriff, Director Operations*
*David Laxton, Director Communications*

One of the largest autism-specific bookstores in the US. All proceeds are used to provide services to people with autism and their families.

**5514  Great Smokies Diagnostic Laboratory**
63 Zillicoa Street
Asheville, NC  28801

828-285-2223
800-522-4762
FAX: 828-252-9303
www.gsdl.com

*Ted Hull, President/CEO*
*Patrick J Hanaway, VP/ Chief Medical Officer*

Functional testing assesses the dynamic inter-relationshp of physiological systems.
*1986*

**5515  North Carolina Library for the Blind and Physically Handicapped**
State Library Of N Orth Carolina
1811 Capital Boulevard
Raleigh, NC  27604

919-733-4376
888-388-2460
FAX: 919-733-6910
TTY: 919-733-1462
e-mail: nclbph@ncmail.net
statelibrary.dcr.state.nc.us

*Francine Martin, Librarian/Manager*
*Laurie Williams, Assistant Librarian*

Free loan of large print, braille, and cassette tape books and magazines and specialized playback equipment to registered eligible North Carolinians. Call for an application form. Collection contains general fiction and nonfiction titles. Registered borrowers may subscribe to receive descriptive videos for a one time fee.

**5516  Pediatric Rheumatology Clinic**
Duke Medical Center
PO Box 3212
Durham, NC  27710

919-477-9292
FAX: 919-684-6575
e-mail: rabin001@mc.duke.edu
www.duke.edu

*Egla Rabinovich, Medical Director*
*Michael Duke, Owner*

Clinical and laboratory pediatric rheumatoid studies.

**5517 University of North Carolina at Chapel Hill: Brain Research Center**
Cb 7250
Chapel Hill, NC 27599
919-966-2405
FAX: 919-966-1844

*Kunihiko Suzuki, Director*

## North Dakota

**5518 North Dakota State Library Talking Book Services**
604 E Boulevard Avenue
Dept 250
Bismarck, ND 58505
701-328-2000
800-472-2104
FAX: 701-328-2040
TTY: 800-892-8622
e-mail: sbchneider@nd.gov
ndsl.lib.state.nd.us

*Wayne G Sanstead, Superintendent*
*Doris Ott, State Librarian*
*Stella B Cone, Talking Manager*

## Ohio

**5519 Case Western Reserve University**
10900 Euclid Avenue
Cleveland, OH 44106
216-368-3200
e-mail: president@case.edu
www.case.edu

*Eric Cottington, Associate VP for Research*
*Paula Baughn, Director*
*Edward Hundert, President*

Programs which encompass the arts and sciences, engineering, health sciences, law, management, and social work.

**5520 Case Western Reserve University Northeast Ohio Multipurpose Arthritis Center**
11100 Euclid Avenue
Cleveland, OH 44106
216-844-3952
www.uhhs.com

*Fred Rothstein, Executive Director*

Basic and clinical research into the causes, diagnosis and treatment of arthritis.

**5521 Cleveland FES Center**
11000 Cedar Avenue
Cleveland, OH 44106
216-231-3257
FAX: 216-231-3258
TTY:216-231-3257
e-mail: info@fesc.org
http//:fescenter.case.edu

*John Chae, Director Stroke Rehab*
*Peckham P Hunter, Director*

Research and development center on functional electrical stimulation. Houses the FES Information Center, a resource center with a library. Publications, newsletters and videotapes for persons with disabilities and others interested in electrical stimulation are offered.

**5522 Cleveland Public Library**
325 Superior Avenue E
Cleveland, OH 44114
216-623-2999
FAX: 216-623-7015
e-mail: info@library.cpl.org
www.cpl.org

*Andrew Venable, Director*
*Joan Clark, Manager*

Summer reading programs, braille writer, magnifiers, closed-circuit T.V., large-print photocopier, cassette books and magazines, children's books on cassette, and other reference materials on blindness and other handicaps.

**5523 Clovernook Center for the Blind and Visually Impaired**
7000 Hamilton Avenue
Cincinnati, OH 45231
513-522-3860
888-234-7156
TTY:513-522-3860
e-mail: eweaver@clovernook.org
www.clovernook.org

*Jeffrey Brasie, President*
*Jacqueline Conner, VP Multi-State Center*
*Murali Muraleetharan, VP Finance*

Clovernook promotes independence and fosters the highest quality of life for people with visual impairments, including those with multiple disabilities. The Center provides comprehensive rehabilitation services including training and support for independent living, orientation and mobility instruction, vocational training, job placement, counseling, low vision assessment, computer training, recreation, and youth services. Headquarters located in Cincinatti, Ohio.

**5524 Ohio Regional Library for the Blind and Physically Handicapped**
National Library Office
800 Vine Street Library Square
Cincinnati, OH 45202
513-369-6999
800-582-0335
FAX: 513-369-3111
TTY: 513-369-6072
e-mail: lb@cincinnatilibrary.org
www.klas.com/talkingbooks/ohio

*Donna Sousg, Director*

Summer reading programs, braille writer, magnifiers, closed-circuit T.V., large-print photocopier, cassette books and magazines, children's books on cassette, and other reference materials on blindness and other handicaps.

**5525 State Library of Ohio: Talking Book Program**
National Library Service in Washington
274 E 1st Avenue
Suite 100
Columbus, OH 43201
614-644-6895
FAX: 614-995-2186
e-mail: jbudler@sloma.state.oh.us
winslo.state.oh.us

*Jo Budler, State Librarian*
*Jim Buchman, Dir Patron & Catalog Services*
*Peter Bates, Deputy Director*

A machine-lending agency for the visually impaired.

**5526 University Affiliated Cincinnati Center for Developmental Disabilities**
University Of Cincinnati Uap
3333 Burnet Avenue
Cincinnati, OH 45229
513-636-4688
800-344-2462
FAX: 513-636-2837
TTY: 513-636-4900
e-mail: oopes0@chmcc.org
www.cincinattichildren.org

*Lee A Carter, Chairman*
*James M Anderson, Chief Executive Officer*
*David Schonfeld, Executive Director*

## Oklahoma

**5527 Oklahoma Library for the Blind & Physically Handicapped**
300 NE 18th Street
Oklahoma City, OK 73105
405-521-3514
800-523-0288
FAX: 405-521-4582
TTY: 405-521-4672
e-mail: library@drs.state.ok.us
www.library.state.ok.us

*Vicky Golightly, PR Coordinator*
*Geraldine Adams, Executive Director*

Braille writer, magnifiers, closed-circuit T.V., large-print photocopier, cassette books and magazines, children's books on cassette, home visits and other reference materials on blindness and other handicaps.

**5528 Oklahoma Medical Research Foundation**
825 NE 13th Street
Oklahoma City, OK 73104
405-271-6673
800-522-0211
FAX: 405-271-3980
www.omrf.org

*Len Cason, Chairman*
*James Bass, Chairman/Executive Committee*
*J Capra, Chief Executive Officer*

Focuses on arthritis and muscoloskeletal disease research.

**5529 Tulsa City-County Library System: Outreach Services**
Tulsa City- County Library System
400 Civic Center
1st Floor
Tulsa, OK 74103
918-596-7977
FAX: 918-596-7941
e-mail: os@tulsalibrary.org
www.tulsalibrary.org

*Amy Stephens, Program Manager*
*Linda Saferite, Director*

Homebound delivery of library services for the physically disabled.

## Oregon

**5530 Oregon Health Sciences University, Elks' Children's Eye Clinic**
Casey Eye Institute
3375 SW Terwilliger Boulevard
Portland, OR 97239
503-494-3000
e-mail: Roystere@ohsu.edu
www.oregonelks.org/ECEC.htm

*Earl A Palmer MD, Director*
*Eleen Reyster, Clinic Manager*
*James Rosenbaum, Manager*

The elks children's eye clinic is the major charitable project of the Oregon State Elks association. The clinic would not be possible without the organization's dedication and commitment to providing eye care for babies and children.

**5531 Oregon Talking Book & Braille Services**
250 Winter Street NE
Salem, OR 97301
503-378-3849
800-452-0292
FAX: 503-588-7119
TTY: 503-378-4276
e-mail: tbabs@oslmac.osl.state.or.us
www.tbabs.org

*Evelyn Kimbrell, Quality Coordinator*
*Eugene Newbill, Machine Program Coordinator*

We serve the blind and physically disabled. Cassette books and magazines, Braille books-magazines, for children and adults. Descriptive videos. Audiocassette machines are provided free of charge. Call us for an application.

**5532 Talking Book & Braille Services Oregon State Library**
250 Winter Street NE
Salem, OR 97310
503-378-4243
800-452-0292
FAX: 503-378-4276
e-mail: tbabs@sparkie.osl.state.or.us
www.osl.state.or.us/home/tbabs

*Keith Adams, Business Manager*
*Denise Davis, Program Manager*
*Jim Scheppke, Manager*

Braille writer, magnifiers, large-print photocopier, cassette books and magazines, children's books on cassette and braille books.

## Pennsylvania

**5533 Carnegie Library of Pittsburgh Library for the Blind & Physically Handicapped**
4724 Baum Boulevard
Pittsburgh, PA 15213
412-687-2440
800-242-0586
FAX: 412-687-2442
e-mail: lbph@carnegielibrary.org
www.clpgh.org

*Herb Elish, Director*
*Sue Murdock, Manager*
*Jane Dayton, Assistant Director*

Loans recorded books/magazines and playback equipment, large print books and described videos to western PA residents unable to use standard printed materials due to a visual, physical, or physically-based reading disability.

**5534 Free Library of Philadelphia: Library for the Blind and Physically Handicapped**
919 Walnut Street
Philadelphia, PA 19107
215-683-3213
800-222-1754
FAX: 215-683-3211
e-mail: flpblind@library.phila.gov
www.library.phila.gov

*Renee Snowten, Public Services Manager*
*Vickie L Collins, Director*
*Pat Shotzbarger, Technical Services Manager*

Summer reading programs for children and teens. Closed-circuit T.V.for enlarging print for low vision; computers with screen readers and large print; cassette books and magazines; braille books and magazines; and descriptive videos for the blind and visually impaired.

**5535  Pennsylvania College of Optometry Eye Institute**
8360 Old York Road
Lkins Park
PA  19027                                   215-780-1260

www.pco.edu

**5536  Reading Rehabilitation Hospital**
Rr 1
Box 250
Reading, PA  19607                          610-926-4017
                                            FAX: 610-796-6303

*Margaret Hsieh, Librarian*
*Doug Mehrkam, Owner*

Information on physical disabilities, stroke, head injuries, aging
and spinal cord injuries.

**5537  Recorded Periodicals**
Associated Services For The Blind
919 Walnut Street
Philadelphia, PA  19107                     215-627-0600
                                            FAX: 215-922-0692
                                            www.asb.org

*Patricia C Johnson, Chief Executive Officer*

A service of Associated Services for the Blind. 26 magazines are
available on cassette through this subscription service. A magazine list can be sent, in both large print and on audio cassette.
*$18.00*

## Rhode Island

**5538  Rhode Island Department of State Library for the Blind
and Physically Handicapped**
82 Smith Street
Providence, RI  02903                       401-222-6905
                                            FAX: 401-222-4195
                                 e-mail: webmaster@lori.state.ri.us
                                            www.lori.ri.gov

*Anne Parent, Chief Library Services*
*William J Allen, Member of the Board*
*Deborah Barchi, Member of the Board*

Offers information and services for the visually impaired including reference materials, braille printers, braille writers,
large-print books and more.

**5539  Talking Books Plus**
Library for the Blind & Physically Handicapped
1 Capitol Hill
Providence, RI  02908                       401-222-5800
                                            FAX: 401-222-4195
                                 e-mail: tbplus@lori.state.ri.us
                                            www.lori.state.ri.us/tbp

*Andrew Egan, Regional Library Supervisor*
*Beth Perry, Program Manager*

Offers talking book services for the blind and physically handicapped. Collection includes reference materials, braille printer,
braille writer, large-print books, adaptive computer
workstations and referrals to appropriate agencies/programs for
other services.

## South Carolina

**5540  Medical University of South Carolina Arthritis Clini-
cal/Research Center**
171 Ashley Avenue
Charleston, SC  29425                       843-792-1414
                                            800-424-MUSC
                                            FAX: 843-792-7121
                                            www.muschealth.com

*Paula Harper Bethea, Chairman*
*Morris Kalinsky, Vice Chairman*

Offers patient care services and basic and clinical research on
various types of arthritis and connective tissue diseases.

**5541  South Carolina State Library**
PO Box 11469
Columbia, SC  29211                         803-734-8666
                                            FAX: 803-734-8676
                                            TTY:711-734-4611
                                            www.statelibrary.sc.gov

*Patti Butcher, Director*
*James Johnson Jr, Executive Director*

Summer reading programs, braille writer, magnifiers,
closed-circuit T.V., large-print photocopier, cassette books and
magazines, children's books on cassette, home visits and other
reference materials on blindness and other handicaps.

## South Dakota

**5542  South Dakota State Library**
800 Governors Drive
Pierre, SD  57501                           605-773-3131
                                            800-423-6665
                                            FAX: 605-773-4950
                                            TTY: 605-773-4950
                                 e-mail: library@state.sd.us
                                            www.sdstatelibrary.com

*Dorothy Liegl, Program Manager Outreach*

Summer reading programs, braille writer, magnifiers,
closed-circuit T.V., large-print photocopier, cassette books and
magazines, children's books on cassette, home visits and other
reference materials on blindness and other handicaps.

## Tennessee

**5543  Tennessee Library for the Blind and Physically Handi-
capped**
403 7th Avenue N
Nashville, TN  37243                        615-741-3915
                                            800-342-3308
                                            FAX: 615-532-8856
                                 e-mail: tlbph.tsla@state.tn.us
                                            www.tennessee.gov/tsla/lbph

*Ruth Hemphill, Director*
*Janie Murphree, Assistant Director*

Offers free public library services to those unable to hold, read
or turn the pages of pritnt books and magazines due to physical
or visual impairment or reading disabilities. Special library materials are provided by the Library of Congress, and free mailing
privileges for these materials is provided through the US Post
Office. Playback equipment is provided along with books and
magazines on cassette, in Braille and in large print.

## Texas

**5544  Baylor College of Medicine Birth Defects Center**
6621 Fannin Street
Houston, TX  77030                                    832-824-3750
                                                 FAX: 713-770-4294

*Frank Greenberg, Director*

**5545  Baylor College of Medicine: Cullen Eye Institute**
Baylor College of Medicine
6550 Fannin Street
Suite 1501
Houston, TX  77030                                    713-798-6100
                                                      888-562-3937
                                                 FAX: 713-798-1521
                                             www.baylorvision.com

*M Bowes Hamill, Director*
*Al Vaughan, Manager*
*Michael Cassidy, Plant Manager*

Research activities focus on restoring vision and preventing blindness through a better understanding of the disease.

**5546  Brown-Heatly Library**
4900 N Lamar Boulevard
3rd Floor
Austin, TX  78751                                     800-252-5204
                                                      800-628-5115
                         e-mail: webmaster@dars.state.tx.us
                                              www.dars.state.tx.us

Houses a collection of books, audio and video tapes and periodicals focusing on rehabilitation, disabilities, employment skills and practices and management for the Texas Rehabilitation Commission. Houses materials on developmental and other disabilities, assessment and evaluation for the Texas Interagency on Early Childhood Intervention.

**5547  Center for Research on Women with Disabilities**
Baylor College of Medicine
1 Baylor Plaza
Suite B
Houston, TX  77046                                    713-798-5782
                                                      800-443-7693
                                                 FAX: 713-798-4688
                              e-mail: crowd@bcm.tmc.edu
                                              www.bcm.edu/crowd

*Margaret Nosek, Executive Director*
*Rosemary Hughes, Director*
*Kathy Fire, Administrator*

Research organization dedicated to conducting research and promoting, developeing, and disseminating information to expand the life choices of women with disabilities. Conducts research and training activities on issues related to the health, independence and community integration of women and men with physical disabilities. The center has a database of psychosocial behaviors of women with disabilities.

**5548  Christian Education for the Blind**
4200 S Freeway Drive 3702
Fort Worth, TX  76115                                 817-920-0444
                                                 FAX: 817-920-0777
                                        e-mail: bceb@ev1.net
                                             www.bcebonline.tom

*Roger Dyer, Director*

Offers braille and large print books and cassettes for the visually impaired.

**5549  Houston Public Library: Access Center**
500 McKinney Street
1st Floor
Houston, TX  77002                                    713-236-1313
                                              TTY:832-393-1539
                              e-mail: website@hpl.lib.tx.us
                                                 www.hpl.lib.tx.us

*Toni Lambert, Director*
*Jack S, Member of the Board*

Offers full library services to the visually and hearing impaired in Houston, TX at no charge. Houses unique and critical services for its users including online access to the Internet in a private and secure area.

**5550  Talking Book Program/Texas State Library**
Talking Book Program
PO Box 12927
Austin, TX  78711                                     512-463-5458
                                                      800-252-9605
                                                 FAX: 512-936-0685
                         e-mail: tbp.services@tsl.state.tx.us
                                          www.texastalkingbooks.org

*Ava M Smith, Director*

Provides reading materials in special formats to Texas residents who cannot read conventional printed matter because of visual or physical limitations, whether permanent or temporary. The service is free and materials are sent through the mail free. Books and magazines are available in cassette, braille, recorded disk and large print formats. A Disabilities Reference Center can answer questions on topics related to disabilities.

**5551  University of Texas Southwestern Medical Center/Allergy & Immunology**
5323 Harry Hines Boulevard
Dallas, TX  75390                                     214-648-3111

                   e-mail: philip.schoch@utsouthwestern.edu
                                             www.utsouthwestern.edu

*Philip Schoch, Director*
*Gail Alexander, MD*

**5552  University of Texas at Austin Library**
1 University Station
Austin, TX  78712                                     512-471-3434
                                                 FAX: 512-495-4347
                              e-mail: webform@lib.utexas.edu
                                                www.lib.utexas.edu

*Curtis Ohlendorf, Director*
*Sheldon Ekland-Olson, Chief Executive Officer*

Provides access to information for all users, including those with disabilities, in accordance with the overall mission of the General Libraries of the University of Texas at Austin.

## Utah

**5553  Family Resource Library/Center for Persons with Disabilities**
6845 Old Main Hl
North Logan, UT  84341                                435-797-0348
                                                 FAX: 435-797-2044
                                              TTY:801-753-9750
                                        e-mail: frl@cpd2.usu.edu
                                               www.cpd.usa.edu/frl

*Marilyn Hammond, Director*

Not-for-profit service organization dedicated to collecting and loaningg materials containing practical information for families of persons with disabilities. Serves persons with disabilities and their famlies in the United States. Educational materials include books, booklets, videotapes and audiotapes.

**5554** **Utah State Library Division: Program for the Blind and Disabled**
250 N 1950 W
Suite A
Salt Lake City, UT  84116
801-715-6777
800-662-5540
FAX: 801-715-6767
e-mail: blind@utah.gov
www.blindlibrary.utah.gov

*Bessie Oakes, Librarian*
*Donna Morris, Manager*

Summer reading programs, Braille embosser, cassette books and magazines, children's books on cassette and other reference materials on blindness and other handicaps, descriptive videos, Braille books, large print books and radio reading service.

## Vermont

**5555** **Vermont Department of Libraries/Special Services Unit**
578 Paine Tpke N
Berlin, VT  05602
802-828-3273
800-479-1711
FAX: 802-828-2199
e-mail: marianne.kotch@dol.state.vt.us
dol.state.vt.us

*Marianne Kotch, Director*
*Grace W Greene, Program Coordinator*
*Francis Woods, Manager*

Service consists of reading material in large print and in talking book formats. The book collection consists of cassettes and large print. Special collections include: childrens print/braille books, reference materials on blindness, and descriptive videos.

## Virginia

**5556** **Alexandria Library Talking Book Service**
5005 Duke Street
Alexandria, VA  22304
703-838-4555
FAX: 703-519-5916
TTY:703-519-5911
e-mail: emccaffrey@alexandria.lib.va.us
www.alexandria.lib.va.us

*Loni McCaffrey, Supervisor*
*Luis Labra, Manager*

Summer reading programs, braille writer, magnifiers, closed-circuit T.V., large-print photocopier, cassette books and magazines, children's books on cassette, home visits and other reference materials on blindness and other handicaps.

**5557** **Arlington County Department of Libraries**
Arlington County Library
1015 N Quincy Street
Arlington, VA  22201
703-228-5990
FAX: 703-228-5962
TTY:703-228-6320
e-mail: libraries@arlingtonva.us
www.arlingtonva.us

*Chang Liu, Branch Manager*

Summer reading programs, braille writer, magnifiers, closed-circuit T.V., large-print photocopier, cassette books and magazines, children's books on cassette, home visits and other reference materials on blindness and other handicaps.

**5558** **Braille Circulating Library for the Blind**
2700 Stuart Avenue
Richmond, VA  23220
804-359-3743
FAX: 804-359-4777

*Brian Barton, Executive Director*

Offers library materials for the blind and visually impaired on a free-loan basis. Serves the entire USA and 41 foreign countries with cassette tapes, reel to reel tapes, braille books, large print books along with talking book records.

**5559** **Central Rappahannock Regional Library**
1201 Caroline Street
Fredericksburg, VA  22401
540-372-1144
FAX: 540-373-9411
TTY:540-371-9165
www.librarypoint.org

*Donna Cote, Director*
*Alison Heartwell, Librarian*

Offers reference materials on blindness and other disabilities.

**5560** **Council for Exceptional Children**
1110 N Glebe Road
Suite 300
Arlington, VA  22201
703-245-0600
888-232-7733
FAX: 703-264-9494
e-mail: president@cec.sped.org
www.cec.sped.org

*Janice Burdick, President*
*Suzanne Martin, Immediate Past President*
*Bruce Ramirez, Manager*

Members are teachers, college faculty members, administrators, supervisors and others concerned with the education and welfare of visually handicapped and blind children and youth. This is a division of the Council For Exceptional Children.

**5561** **Hampton Subregional Library for the Blind**
Hampton Public Library
1 S Mallory Street
Hampton, VA  23663
757-727-1900
800-552-7015
FAX: 757-727-1047

*Douglas Peroy, Director*
*Marsha Knox, Department Head*
*Merry Woolard, Manager*

Summer reading programs, braille writer, magnifiers, closed-circuit T.V., large-print photocopier, cassette books and magazines, children's books on cassette, home visits and other reference materials on blindness and other handicaps.

**5562** **James Branch Cabell Library**
Virginia Commonwealth University
PO Box 842033
Richmond, VA  23284
804-827-0556
866-828-2665
866-828-2665
FAX: 804-828-0151
www.library.vcu.edu

*James Branch Cabell, Founder*
*Gregory Rentz, Manager*

Provides individualized orientations and assistance with library research and equipment.

**5563** **Newport News Public Library System**
700 Town Center Drive
Suite 300
Newport News, VA  23606
757-247-8875
FAX: 757-926-1365
e-mail: icieszyn@ci.newport-news.va.us
www.newport-news.va.us/library

*Izabela M Cieszynski, Executive Director Libraries*

Summer reading programs, braille writer, magnifiers, closed-circuit T.V., large-print photocopier, cassette books and magazines, children's books on cassette, home visits and other reference materials on blindness and other handicaps.

**5564 Northern Virginia Resource Center for Deaf and Hard of Hearing Persons**
3951 Pender Drive
Suite 130
Fairfax, VA 22030
703-352-9056
FAX: 703-352-9058
TTY:703-352-9056
e-mail: info@nvrc.org
www.nvrc.org

*Cheryl Heppner, Executive Director*

Empowering deaf and hard of hearing individuals and their families through education, advocacy and community involvement.

**5565 Roanoke City Public Library System**
706 S Jefferson Street
Roanoke, VA 24016
540-853-2473
FAX: 540-853-1781
www.roanokegov.com/library

*Sheila Umberger, Executive Director*

Summer reading programs, braille writer, magnifiers, closed-circuit T.V., large-print photocopier, cassette books and magazines, children's books on cassette, home visits and other reference materials on blindness and other handicaps.

**5566 Special Services/Talking Books**
Fairfax County Public Library
12000 Government Center Parkway
Suite 123
Fairfax, VA 22035
703-324-3185
FAX: 703-324-8386
TTY:703-324-8365
e-mail: access@fairfaxcounty.gov
www.fairfax.gov/library

*E S Clay, Director*
*Lindsey Culin, Manager*

Offers talking books, TDD access, assistive devices such as decoders for three-week loans, support groups for people who are visually impaired, library program interpreters available with four weeks advance notice, adapted computer work station with braille printer and assistive listening devices.

**5567 Staunton Public Library Talking Book Center**
1 Churchville Avenue
Staunton, VA 24401
540-332-3902
800-995-6215
FAX: 540-332-3906
e-mail: library@ci.staunton.va.us

*Oakley Pearson, Librarian*

Offers free library service by circulating recorded books, magazines, and playback equipment to individuals unable to use standard print materials because of visual or physical impairment.

**5568 University of Virginia Health System General Clinical Research Group**
PO Box 800787
Charlottesville, VA 22908
434-924-5204
FAX: 434-924-9960
e-mail: gcrc@virginia.edu
gcrc.med.virginia.edu

*Eugene J Barrett, Program Director*
*Mary Vance, Associate Director*
*Cassie Bourne, Manager*

Provides investigators with the specialized resources necessary to conduct advanced clinical research. The facility includes ten inpatient beds, skilled research nurses, a core assay laboratory, a metabolic kitchen, outpatient facilities, computing and statistical consultants and facilities, and sleep and exercise physiology laboratories.

*1968*

**5569 Virginia Autism Resource Center**
4100 Price Club Boulevard
Midlothian, VA 23112
804-674-8888
877-667-7771
877- -
FAX: 804-276-3970
e-mail: info@varc.org
www.grafton.org

*Carol Schall, Director*
*Florence McLeod, Administrative Assistant*
*Janee Sprinkle, Manager*

Provides training, individual case consultation, materials and information to families and professionals working with individuals with autism in Virginia.
*1983*

**5570 Virginia Beach Public Library Special Services Library**
936 Independence Boulevard
Virginia Beach, VA 23455
757-464-9175
FAX: 757-464-6741
www.vpgov.com/library

*Carolyn Caywood, Director*
*Allenne Wicher, Manager*

A public library for people with visual and physical disabilities, braille writer, magnifiers, closed-circuit T.V., large-print photocopier, cassette books and magazines, children's books on cassette, and other reference materials on blindness and other disabilities.

**5571 Virginia Chapter of the Arthtitis Foundation**
3805 Cutshaw Avenue
Suite 200
Richmond, VA 23230
804-359-1700
800-456-4687
FAX: 804-359-4900
e-mail: info.va@arthritis.org
www.arthritis.org

*W Robert Irby, Medical Director*

Provides free information, services and counseling to the public. Services include assistance in locating and accessing government and other health care programs for persons with arthritis, referral to doctors specializing in the treatment of arthritis, free literature about the different types of arthritis and counseling for people with arthritis and their families.

**5572 Virginia State Library for the Visually and Physically Handicapped**
395 Azalea Avenue
Richmond, VA 23227
804-266-2477
800-552-7015
FAX: 804-371-3508
e-mail: barbara.mccarthy@dbvi.virginia.gov

*Nicholas Morgan, Executive Director*
*Laura Rhodes, Office Manager*

Summer reading programs, braille writer, magnifiers, closed-circuit T.V., large-print photocopier, cassette books and magazines, children's books on cassette, home visits and other reference materials on blindness and other handicaps.

## Washington

**5573 Meridian Valley Clinical Laboratory**
801 SW 16th Street
Suite 126
Renton, WA 98057                    425-271-8689
                              FAX: 425-271-8674
e-mail: meridian@meridianvalleylab.com
                www.meridianvalleylab.com

*Jonathan Wright, Medical Director*
*Holly Han, Owner*

A clinical test facility dedicated to providing the most accurate and informative data for patient diagnosis and therapeutic monitoring. With our current research and up-to-date information and various aspects of clinical nutritional medicine, our methodologies and capabilities include areas of analytical chemistry, heavy metal determination, microbiology, and immunology.

**5574 Ophthalmic Research Laboratory Eye Institute**
747 Broadway
Seattle, WA 98122                    206-386-6000
                                     800-793-3474
                                     www.swedish.org

*Richard Peterson, Chief Executive Officer*

Color vision physiology, vision disorders and blindness research.

**5575 Washington Talking Book and Braille Library**
2021 9th Avenue
Seattle, WA 98121                    206-615-0400
                                     800-542-0866
                              FAX: 206-464-0247
                              TTY: 206-615-0418
                          e-mail: wtbbl@wtbbl.org
                                  www.wtbbl.org

*Gloria Leonard, Director*

Summer reading programs, braille writer, magnifiers, closed-circuit T.V., large-print photocopier, cassette books and magazines, children's books, and other reference materials on blindness and other handicaps, online catalog, reference station with assistive devices and a radio reading service.

## West Virginia

**5576 Autism Services Center**
PO Box 507
Huntington, WV 25710                 304-525-8014
                              FAX: 304-525-8026
                      e-mail: candy@autismwv.org
                          www.autismservicescenter.org

*Ruth C Sullivan, Executive Director*
*Mark Gravy, Director*

Provides developmental disabilities services with a specialty in autism. Services include case management, residential, personal care, assessments and evaluations, supported employment, independent living and family support.
        *1979*

**5577 Cabell County Public Library/Talking Book Department/Subregional Library for the Blind**
455 9th Street
Huntington, WV 25701                 304-528-5700
                              FAX: 304-528-5701
                  e-mail: library@cabell.lib.wv.us
                              www.cabell.lib.wv.us

*Lottie Simms, President*
*Judy Rule, Manager*

Summer reading programs, Braille writer, magnifiers, closed-circuit TV, cassette books and magazines, children's books on cassette reference materials on blindness and other handicaps, enlargers and Arkenstone Reader.

**5578 Division of Rehabilitation Services: Staff Library**
PO Box 1004
Institute, WV 25112                  304-766-4644
                                     800-642-8207
                  e-mail: carolc@mail.drs.state.wv.us

*Carol R Johnson, Librarian/Manager*

Specialized library with information on disabilities and the rehabilitation there of special collections: deaf and hard of hearing, visually impaired/blind, wellness center, literacy and career. The library has assistive devices such as CCTV, scanner and enhancement software. Also braille magazines, large print, talking books, magazines on cassette, descriptive videos, captioned media program, newspapers, magazines/journals, video, computers with internet access, fax, and a copier.

**5579 Kanawha County Public Library**
123 Capitol Street
Charleston, WV 25301                 304-343-4646
                              FAX: 304-348-6530
          e-mail: webmaster@kanawha.lib.wv.us
                              /kanawha.lib.wv.us

*Pamela D Tarr, President*
*Linda Wright, Manager*

Summer reading programs, large print PC option, magnifiers, large type books, cassette books, and magazines, children's books on cassette, home visits and other reference materials on blindness and other handicaps

**5580 Ohio County Public Library Services for the Blind and Physically Handicapped**
52 16th Street
Wheeling, WV 26003                   304-232-0244
                              FAX: 304-232-6848
          e-mail: ocplweb@weirton.lib.wv.us
                      wheeling.weirton.lib.wv.us

*Lester Hess, Chairman*
*Dorothy Thomas, Manager*

**5581 Talking Book Department, Parkersburg and Wood County Public Library**
3100 Emerson Avenue
Parkersburg, WV 26104                304-420-4587
                                     800-642-8674
                              FAX: 304-420-4589
          e-mail: hickmanm@hp9k.park.lib.wv.us

*Michael Hickman, Coordinator Services*
*Brian Raitz, Manager*

Services for the bind and physically handicapped. Library of Congress Talking Book Program.

**5582 West Virginia Autism Training Center**
Marshall University College Of Educational & Human
400 Hal Greer Boulevard
Suite 316
Huntington, WV 25755                 304-696-2772
                                     800-344-5115
                          www.marshall.edu/coe/atc

Provides education, training, and treatment programs for W Virginians who have autism, pervasive devolopmental disorders or Asperger's disease and have formally been registered with the center.

**5583 West Virginia Library Commission**
1900 Kanawha Boulevard E
Charleston, WV 25305 304-558-0549
800-642-9021
FAX: 304-558-2044
e-mail: web_one@wvlc.lib.wv.us
www.librarycommision.lib.wv.us

*Denise Ash, Director*
*Joe Manchin, Governor*
*Sarah Hamrick, Executive Director*

Summer reading programs, braille writer, magnifiers, closed-circuit T.V., large-print photocopier, cassette books and magazines, children's books on cassette, home visits and other reference materials on blindness and other handicaps.

**5584 West Virginia School for the Blind Library**
301 E Main Street
Romney, WV 26757 304-822-4801
FAX: 304-822-4896
e-mail: cjohn@access.mountain.net

*Jane McBride, Director*
*Cynthia Johnson, Librarian*

Summer reading programs, braille writer, magnifiers, closed-circuit T.V., large-print photocopier, cassette books and magazines, children's books on cassette, home visits and other reference materials on blindness and other handicaps.

# Wisconsin

**5585 Brown County Library**
Central Library Downtown
2255 Main Street
Green Bay, WI 54302 920-391-4600
FAX: 920-391-4601
TTY:920-448-4400
e-mail: bc_library@co.brown.wi.us
www.co.brown.wi.us/library

*Bob Bush, President*
*Mike Aubinger, Vice President*
*Louanne Crowder, Manager*

Summer reading programs, braille writer, magnifiers, closed-circuit TV, large-print photocopier, cassette books and magazines, children's books on cassette, home visits and other reference materials on blindness and other handicaps.

**5586 Eye Institute of the Medical College of Wisconsin and Froedtert Clinic**
925 N 87th Street
Milwaukee, WI 53226 414-456-2020

e-mail: eyecare@mcw.edu

*Mary Blackwelder, Director*
*Richard Schultz, MD*

A full service academic ophthalmology program.
*1976*

**5587 Trace Research and Development Center**
University of Wisconsin-Madison
1550 Engineering Drive
2107 ECB
Madison, WI 53706 608-262-6966
FAX: 608-262-8848
TTY:608-263-5408
e-mail: info@trace.wisc.edu
www.trace.wisc.edu

*Gregg Vanderheiden, Center Director*

The mission is to prevent the barriers and capitalize on the opportunities presented by current and emerging information and telecommunication technologies, in order to create a world that is as accessible and usable as possible. Currently the center is working on ways to make standard information technologies and telecommunications systems more accessible and usable by people with disabilities.

**5588 Wisconsin Regional Library for the Blind & Physically Handicapped**
813 W Wells Street
Milwaukee, WI 53233 414-286-3040
800-242-8822
FAX: 414-286-3102
TTY: 414-286-3548
e-mail: lbph@mpl.org
www.regionallibrary.wi.gov

*Marsha Valance, Regional Librarian/Manager*

Circulates recorded materials, playback equipment and braille materials to print-handicapped Wisconsin residents.

# Wyoming

**5589 Wyoming Services for the Visually Impaired**
Wyoming Department of Education
2300 Capitol Avenue
Cheyenne, WY 82002 307-777-7690
FAX: 307-777-6234
e-mail: golson@educ.state.wy.us
www.k12.wy.us/SE/svi.asp

*Gary Olson, Supervisor*

Services for the Visually Impaired assists people of all ages who have low vision or are blind. The goal is to provide information, education, and support to individuals with low vision in order that they may lead enjoyable and productive lives with maximum degree of independence.

**5590 Wyoming's New Options in Technology (WYNOT) - University of Wyoming**
1465 N 4th Street
Suite 111
Laramie, WY 82072 307-766-2084
800-861-4312
FAX: 307-721-2084
e-mail: wynot.uw@uwyo.edu
wind.uwyo.edu/wind/community/wynotinfo.htm

*Kathy Laurin, Executive Director*
*Britney Alspach, PR Coordinator*

Designed to develop and implement a consumer oriented statewide system of technology-related assistance for people with disabilities of all ages.

# AIDS

### 5591 A Woman's Guide To Living With HIV Infecti on
Johns Hopkins University Press

A resource for women with HIV that discusses coping with the diagnosis, finding a physician, recognizing symptoms, and preventing complications. Explains the latest treatment options and advice on coping with gynecologic infections. *$15.95*
*288 pages 2004*
*ISBN 0-801879-14-0*

### 5592 AIDS 2nd Edition
JB Lippincott
227 E Washington Square
Philadelphia, PA 19106        215-521-8300
800-777-2295
FAX: 301-824-7390

*J Lippincott, Chief Executive Officer*

Gives the latest information on AIDS covering basic science considerations, clinical aspects and public health issues. *$55.00*
*474 pages*

### 5593 AIDS Alert
American Health Consultants
3525 Piedmont Road
Building 6
Atlanta, GA 30305        404-262-7436
800-688-2421
FAX: 800-850-1232
e-mail: customerservice@ahcpub.com
www.ahcpub.com

*Glen Harris, Managing Editor*
*Jeff MacDonald, Executive Vice Presidet*

Source of AIDS news and advice for health care professionals. Covers up-to-the-minute developments and guidance on the entire spectrum of AIDS challenges, including treatment, education, precautions, screening, diagnosis and policy. *$467.00*
*12 pages Monthly*
*ISSN 0887-02 2*

### 5594 AIDS Disease State Management Resource
PO Box 740056
Atlanta, GA 30374        404-262-7436
FAX: 800-284-3291
e-mail: customerservices@ahcpub.com
www.ahcpub.com

*Milo Falcon, Managing Editor*
*Jeff MacDonald, Executive Vice President*

Provides staff and patient education materials on HIV/AIDS. *$299.00*
*Paperback*

### 5595 AIDS and Other Manifestations of HIV Infec tion
Academic Press

A comprehensive overview of the biological properties of this etiologic viral agent, its clinicopathological manifestations, the epidemiology of its infection, and present and future therapeutic options. *$249.95*
*1000 pages 2004*
*ISBN 0-127640-51-7*

### 5596 AIDS in the Twenty-First Century: Disease and Global-ization
Palgrav Macmillan

The authors — exprets in the field for over 15 years — argue that it is vital to not only look at AIDS in terms of prevention and treatment, but to also consider consequences which affect households, communities, companies, governments, and countries. This is a major contribution toward understanding the global public health crisis, as well as the relationship between poverty, inequality, and infectious diseases. *$19.95*
*432 pages 2003*
*ISBN 1-403900-06-X*

### 5597 AIDS, What Does it Mean to You?
Walker Publishing Company
104 5th Avenue
New York, NY 10011        212-727-8300
800-289-2553
FAX: 212-727-0984
e-mail: orders@walkerbooks.com

*Ramsey Walker, Vice President*

Researchers have been working frantically to solve the puzzle of AIDS - a disease that has taken the lives of thousands of men and women during the past ten years. *$13.95*
*128 pages Cloth/Hardcover*
*ISBN 0-802782-02-7*

### 5598 AIDS: The HIV Myth
St. Martin's Press
175 5th Avenue
New York, NY 10010        212-674-5151
www.stmartins.com

*John Sargent, Chief Executive Officer*

Challenges the theory that AIDS is caused by a virus called HIV. Puts forward the view that in the rush to identify the cause of an apparently new disease, a harmless passenger virus was leapt upon as the sole culprit.
*1989*
*ISBN 0-333489-30-6*

### 5599 AIDS: The Official Journal of the Internat ional AIDS Society
Lippincott Williams & Wilkins
590 Walnut Street
Philadelphia, PA 19106        215-521-8300
www.aidsonline.com

*J Lippincott, Chief Executive Officer*

The latest groundbreaking research on HIV and AIDS. *$433.00*
*18 per year*

### 5600 APLA Update
AIDS Project Los Angeles
550 N Larchmont Boulevard
Suite 202
Los Angeles, CA 90004        323-993-1600
FAX: 323-993-1392
Presents news about AIDS and programs of AIDS Project Los Angeles to people affected by the disease.
*20 pages*

### 5601 Encyclopedia of AIDS: Social, Political, C ultural, and Scientific Record of the HIV Epidemic
Penguin Books

A reference on Autoimmune Deficiency Syndrome as a historical phenomenon, focusing on the period from 1981 when the first cases began to be identified among gay men in the US and 1996 with the introduction of the class of potent antiviral medications called protease inhibitors. *$25.00*
*782 pages 2001*
*ISBN 0-140514-86-4*

### 5602 Guide to Living With HIV Infection: Develo ped at the Johns Hopkins AIDS Clinic
Johns Hopkins Press Health Book

A handbook and reference for people living with HIV infection and their families, friends, and caregivers. *$18.95*
*428 pages 2001*
*ISBN 0-801867-44-4*

**5603 HIV Drug Book Revised**
Pocket

From a community-based AIDS treatment information and advocacy organization comes a comprehensive guide to the drugs and experimental treatments most used by those who are HIV-positive or suffering from AIDS. *$30.95*
*704 pages 1998*
*ISBN 0-671014-90-0*

**5604 Healing HIV: How To Rebuild Your Immune Sy stem**
Healthfirst Press

Practical advice that focuses on overall health for HIV sufferers. *$19.95*
*362 pages 1998*
*ISBN 0-966637-30-5*

**5605 I Just Found Out I Have HIV... Now What?**
1stBooks Library

Issues surrounding living with HIV. *$15.50*
*144 pages 2002*
*ISBN 1-403321-65-5*

**5606 Invisible People: How the US Has Slept Thr ough the Global AIDS Pandemic**
Free Press

Presents many of the reasons for the languishing American response to gloabl AIDS in the 1990's, including Congressional antagonism to foreign aid spending, passive racism, and disarray among United Nations health officials, who failed to offer plausibe global figures on HIV prevalence until 1998. The author also points to the early silence of domestic AIDS activists, African-American leaders and heads of countries being ravaged by the disease.
*304 pages 2004*
*ISBN 0-743257-55-3*

**5607 Living Well With HIV and AIDS**
Bull Publishing

New drugs and drug combinations have turned HIV/AIDS into a long-term illness rather than a death sentence. Practical advice on mental adjustments and physical vigilance is outlined. *$18.95*
*245 pages 2000*
*ISBN 0-923521-52-6*

**5608 POZ Magazine**
Smart + Strong
1 Little West 12th Street
6th Floor
New York, NY 10014          212-242-2163

www.poz.com

*Sean Strub, Owner*

A health title written for individuals who are HIV+, their friends and families. POZ provides the latest treatment information, investigative journalism and survivor profiles.

**5609 Penitent, With Poses: An HIV+ Mother Refle cts**
Middlebury College Press

Peterson, a married, middle-class, Jewish mother, was diagnosed with full-blown AIDS four years into her marriage and 11 months after her son was born. In seven poignant autobiographical essays and a collection of letters to her uninfected, four-year-old son, the author maintains an upbeat tone and describes her unsuccessful attempts to find the source of her infection (her husband tested negative), her relationships with her doctors, and her work as an HIV activist. *$ 26.95*
*256 pages 2001*
*ISBN 1-584651-28-8*

**5610 Questions and Answers: The ADA and Persons with HIV/AIDS**
US Department of Justice
950 Pennsylvania Avenue NW Drs
- Nyav
Washington, DC 20530          202-586-5000
                              800-574-0301
                         FAX: 202-307-1197
                              www.ada.gov

*Joanne Graham, Manager*

A 16-page publication explaining the requirements for employers, businesses and nonprofit agencies that serve the public, and state and local governments to avoid discriminating against persons with HIV/AIDS.

**5611 Rights of People Who Are HIV Positive**
America Civil Liberites Union

The authors tackle the subject in four parts: the disease itself and the related testing, public health, and confidentiality issues; day-to-day issues involving insurance, family law, and healthcare decision-making; discrimination in housing and work; and AIDS in prisons, schools, as a factor in immigration, and among IV drug users. The topics are broached using a question-and-answer format, and each chapter is documented with citations to source material. *$19.95*
*448 pages 1996*
*ISBN 0-809319-92-6*

**5612 The River: A Journey to the Source of HIV and AIDS**
Back Bay Books

The author's thesis, that HIV made the jump from simians to humans via the administration of oral polio vaccine in Africa in the 1950s, is still controversial, all that is lacking is conclusive proof. *$24.95*
*1168 pages 2000*
*ISBN 0-316371-67-8*

**5613 What's a Virus, Anyway? The Kid's Book About AIDS**
Waterfront Books
85 Crescent Road
Burlington, VT 05401          802-658-7477

A simple introduction to help adults talk with children about the subject of AIDS. Includes children's drawings and questions and provides basic information in a manner appropriate for 4-10 years old. *$8.95*
*67 pages*

**5614 World Without AIDS: The Controvertial Holistic Health**
HarperCollins
1350 Avenue of the Americas
New York, NY 10019          212-261-6500

*Erin Gorman, Sales Executive*

A convincing argument that conventional medicine approaches do not 'cure' disease, which outlines how AIDS can be treated using methods of naturopathic medicine. Also includes an appendix outlining 21 ways to strengthen the immune system.

*288 pages Paperback 1988*
*ISBN 0-722516-32-0*

---

## Children & Young Adults

**5615  ABCD Newsletter Volume Reprints**
Birth Defect Research for Children
930 Woodcock Road
Suite 225
Orlando, FL  32803                     407-895-0802
                                  FAX: 407-895-0824
                      e-mail: staff@birthdefects.org
                              www.birthdefects.org

*Betty Mekdeci, Executive Director*

Offers a variety of reprints from the ABCD newsletter on birth
defects
*Monthly*

**5616  ACPOC News**
6300 N River Road
Suite 727
Rosemont, IL  60018                    847-698-1637
                                  FAX: 847-823-0536
                       e-mail: raymond@aaos.org
                                   www.acpoc.org

*Sheril King, Executive Director*

Quarterly publication from the Association of Children's Pros-
thetic/Orthotic Clinics. Included with membership.
*35-40 pages Quarterly*

**5617  ADHD with Comorbid Disorders: Clinical Assessment
and Management**
Guilford Press
72 Spring Street
New York, NY  10012                    212-431-9800
                                       800-365-7006
                                  FAX: 212-966-6708
                                   www.guilford.com

*James M Swanson, Author*
*Bob Matloff, President*
*$44.00*
*Cloth*
*ISBN 1-572304-78-2*

**5618  AT for Infants and Toddlers with Disabilities**
Idaho Assistive Technology Project
129 W 3rd Street
Moscow, ID  83843                      208-885-3559
                                       800-432-8324
                                  FAX: 208-885-3628
                          e-mail: rseiler@uidaho.edu
                         www.educ.uidaho.edu/idatech
*$5.00*
        *68 pages*

**5619  Adolescent in Family Therapy: Breaking the Cycle of
Conflict and Control**
Guilford Press
72 Spring Street
New York, NY  10012                    212-431-9800
                                       800-365-7006
                                  FAX: 212-966-6708
                                   www.guilford.com

*Bob Matloff, President*

Presenting a developmentally grounded approach, Joseph
Micucci shows how troubled teenagers and their parents can be
helped to use family relationships as catalysts for growth and
change. Filled with case examples and clinical advice, the book
describes specific family intervention strategies for eating disorders, depression, underachievement, stress caused by psy-
chotic symptoms and other conditions. Also in cloth at $40.00
(ISBN# 1-57230-389-1) *$23.00*

*336 pages Paper 2000*
*ISBN 1-572305-88-6*

**5620  Assistive Technology for School Age**
Idaho Assistive Technology Project
129 W 3rd Street
Moscow, ID  83843                      208-885-3559
                                       800-432-8324
                                  FAX: 208-885-3628
                          e-mail: rseiler@uidaho.edu
                         www.educ.uidaho.edu/idatech
*$5.00*
        *84 pages*

**5621  Autism Research Review International**
Autism Research Institute
4182 Adams Avenue
San Diego, CA  92116                   619-281-7165
                                  FAX: 619-563-6840
                 e-mail: br@autismresearchinstitute.com
                       www.autismresearchinstitute.com

*Bernard Rimland PhD, Director*
*$18.00*
        *8 pages Quarterly*

**5622  Belonging**
Dial Books
375 Hudson Street
New York, NY  10014                    212-366-2000
                                  FAX: 212-414-3394
Meg attended special schools for the blind until she was ready
for high school. She decided that she wanted to go to a regular
high school. She and her mother practiced her walks to school
and studied the layout of the building prior to school starting,
but Meg was unprepared for the trip when there were 1,500 students. She adjusted quickly to the crowds and the pace of the
new school.
        *200 pages Hardcover*
        *ISBN 0-80370 -30-1*

**5623  Best Toys, Books, Videos & Software for Kids:
Kid-Tested Classic and New Products**
Exceptional Parent Library
PO Box 1807
Englewood Cliffs, NJ  07632            201-947-6000
                                       800-535-1910
                                  FAX: 201-947-9376
                          e-mail: eplibrary@aol.com
                                   www.eplibrary.com

*Ron Richards, Executive Director*

Aims to take the guesswork out of finding the best products for
kids from infancy to age ten. Reviews over one-thousand products that have been tested by kids and evaluated by experts. *$
12.00*

**5624  Birth Defect News**
Birth Defect Research for Children
930 Woodcock Road
Suite 225
Orlando, FL  32803                     407-895-0802
                                  FAX: 407-895-0824
                      e-mail: staff@birthdefects.org
                              www.birthdefects.org

*Betty Mekdeci, Executive Director*

Offers updated information on the association activities, events
and updates regarding birth defects and environmental exposures.
        *Monthly*

**5625  Burnish Me Bright**
Pantheon Books
1540 Broadway
New York, NY  10036                    212-782-9000
                                       800-638-6460
                                  FAX: 212-302-7985
                          www.randomhouse.com/pantheon/

*Carol Schneider, Marketing Executive*

Hilaire, a famous mime, had retired to a small village to live out his life. He met frail Auguste, who was unable to speak, and immediately he saw the potential for this agile and physically expressive youth to become a mime.
*80 pages Hardcover 1970*

**5626   Bus Girl: Selected Poems**
Brookline Books
34 University Road
Brookline, MA  02445                           617-558-8010
                                               800-666-2665
                                          FAX: 617-558-8011
                                  e-mail: brbooks@yahoo.com
                                    www.brooklinebooks.com
Poems written over several decades by a young woman with Down Syndrome. *$14.95*
*144 pages Paperback*
*ISBN 1-57129 -41-9*

**5627   But I'm Ready to Go**
Bradbury Press
8306 Aurora Avenue N
Seattle, WA  98103                             206-524-4910
                                               800-257-5755

*Jack Bradbury, Owner*

Judy always had a problem learning math and performing skills that required good motor control.
*230 pages Hardcover*
*ISBN 0-87888 -07-7*

**5628   Camping Magazine**
5000 State Road 67 N
Martinsville, IN  46151                        765-342-8456
                                               800-428-2267
                                          FAX: 765-342-2065
                                            www.acacamps.org

*Kim Bruno, Communications/Development Spec*
*Peg Smith, Executive Director*
*Terri Nicodemus, Manager*

Bi-monthly periodical published by the American Camping Association. *$24.95*
*45-76 pages Bi-monthly*

**5629   Camps 2004: A Directory of Camps & Summer Programs for Children and Youth with Disablities**
Resources for Children with Special Needs
116 E 16th Street
Floor 5
New York, NY  10003                            212-677-4650
                                          FAX: 212-254-4070
                              e-mail: info@resourcesnyc.org
                                       www.resourcesnyc.org

*Karen Schlesinger, Executive Director*
*Dianne Littwin, Director Publications*

Yearly publication from Resources for Children with Special Needs, Inc. *$22.00*
*308 pages Yearly*
*ISBN 0-967836-57-3*

**5630   Caring for Children with Chronic Illness**
Springer Publishing Company
536 Broadway
New York, NY  10012                            212-431-4370
                                               877-687-7476
                                          FAX: 212-941-7842
                            e-mail: marketing@springerpub.com
                                       www.springerpub.com

*Annette Imperati, Marketing/Sales Director*
*Ursula Springer, President*

A critical look at the current medical, social, and psychological framework for providing care to children with chronic illnesses. Emphasizing the need to create integrated, interdisciplinary approaches, it discusses issues such as the roles of families, professionals, and institutions in providing health care, the impact of a child's illness on various family structures, financing care, the special problems of chronically ill children as they become adolescents and more. *$36.95*
*320 pages Hardcover*
*ISBN 0-82615 -00-1*

**5631   Child Who Never Grew Up**
Exceptional Parent Library
PO Box 1807
Englewood Cliffs, NJ  07632                    201-947-6000
                                               800-535-1910
                                          FAX: 201-947-9376
                                 e-mail: eplibrary@aol.com
                                       www.eplibrary.com
Offers Pearl Buck's inspiring account of her struggle to understand and help her daughter with mental retardation. *$14.95*
*112 pages 1992*
*ISBN 0-933149-49-2*

**5632   Child and Adolescent Therapy: Cognitive-Be havioral Procedures, Second Edition**
Guilford Press
72 Spring Street
New York, NY  10012                            212-431-9800
                                               800-365-7006
                                          FAX: 212-966-6708
                                          www.guilford.com

*Bob Matloff, President*

Incorporating significant developments in treatment procedures, theory and clinical research, new chapters in this second edition examine the current status of empirically supported interventions and developmental issues specific to work with adolescents. *$45.00*
*432 pages Cloth 2000*
*ISBN 1-572305-56-8*

**5633   Children Who Vary from the Normal Type: Special Education in Boston, 1838-1930**
Gallaudet University Press
11030 S Langley Avenue
Chicago, IL  60628
                                               800-621-2736
                                          FAX: 800-621-8476
                                          TTY:800-621-9347
                                      gupress.gallaudet.edu
Identifies Boston as both typical of and a national leader in Special Education programs, tracing its history with an eye towards the future. *$49.95*
*220 pages Hardcover*

**5634   Commonly Asked Questions About Child Care Centers and the Americans with Disabilities Act**
US Department of Justice
950 Pennsylvania Avenue NW Drs
- Nyav
Washington, DC 20530                           202-586-5000
                                               800-574-0301
                                          FAX: 202-307-1197
                                               www.ada.gov

*Joanne Graham, Manager*

A 13-page publication explaining how the requirements of the ADA apply to Child Care Centers. The document also describes some of the Department of Justice's ongoing enforcement efforts in the child care area and it provides a resource list on sources of information on the ADA.

**5635  Communication Coloring Book**
Speech Bin
1965 25th Avenue
Vero Beach, FL  32960
772-770-0007
800-477-3324
FAX: 772-770-0006
www.speechbin.com

*Jan J Binney, VP*

Publisher and distributor of books and materials for professionals in rehabilitation, speech-language pathology, special education and related fields and persons interested in communication disorders and related disabilities. Major product lines include professional and children's books, computer software, diagnostic tests, instructional games and materials for children and adults and specialty items. *$14.95*
    *48 pages*
    *ISBN 0-93785 -53-0*

**5636  Complete IEP Guide: How to Advocate for Yo ur Special Ed Child**
Spina Bifida Association of America
4590 Macarthur Boulevard NW
Suite 250
Washington, DC 20007
202-944-3285
800-621-3141
FAX: 202-944-3295
e-mail: sbaa@sbaa.org
www.sbaa.org

*Cindy Brownstein, Chief Executive Officer*

This all-in-one guide will help you understand special education law, identify your child's needs, prepare for meetings, develop the IEP and resolve disputes. *$28.95*

**5637  Coping When a Parent Has Multiple Sclerosis**
Rosen Publishing Group
29 E 21st Street
New York, NY  10010
212-777-3017
800-237-9932
FAX: 888-436-4643
e-mail: triciab@rosenpub.com
www.rosenpub.com

*Tricia Bauer, Director Special Markets*
*Roger Rosen, President*

Explains to young people how living with a parent who has Multiple Sclerosis will affect their lives. Hardcover. *$19.95*
    *128 pages*
    *ISBN 0-823914-06-2*

**5638  Coping for Kids Who Stutter**
Speech Bin
1965 25th Avenue
Vero Beach, FL  32960
772-770-0007
800-477-3324
FAX: 772-770-0006
www.speechbin.com

*Jan J Binney, Senior Editor*

Informative book for children and adults about stuttering and how to manage it. *$15.95*
    *32 pages*
    *ISBN 0-93785 -43-2*

**5639  Coping with Being Physically Challenged**
Rosen Publishing Group
29 E 21st Street
New York, NY  10010
212-777-3017
FAX: 888-436-4643
e-mail: rosenpub@tribeca.ios.com

*Roger Rosen, President*

Ratto deals with strong emotions, such as general anger and depression, which affect these young adults and their families. The author shows them how to deal and cope on a day-to-day basis. *$15.95*

*ISBN 0-82391 -44-9*

**5640  Coping with Special Needs Classmates**
Rosen Publishing Group
29 E 21st Street
New York, NY  10010
212-777-3017
800-237-9932
FAX: 888-436-4643
e-mail: rosenpub@tribeca.ios.com

*Tricia Bauer, Director Special Markets*
*Roger Rosen, President*

Special needs classmates include people who are physically different, disfigured or challenged, emotionally disturbed, or those who have learning disabilities. The author offers guidance on how to get past discomfort or fear of confrontation with someone who seems very different, but is, in reality, not so different after all. Hardcover. *$17.95*
    *128 pages*
    *ISBN 0-823915-98-0*

**5641  Coping with a Learning Disability**
Rosen Publishing Group
29 E 21st Street
New York, NY  10010
212-777-3017
800-237-9932
FAX: 888-436-4643
e-mail: rosenpub@tribeca.ios.com

*Tricia Bauer, Director Special Markets*
*Roger Rosen, President*

Being a teen with a learning disorder does not have to be a devastating experience. The authors discuss family, personal, and peer emotional reactions. Biographies of famous people with learning disorders provide positive role models and special education is discussed. Hardcover. *$17.95*
    *128 pages*
    *ISBN 0-823928-87-X*

**5642  Coping with a Physically Challenged Brother or Sister**
Rosen Publishing Group
29 E 21st Street
New York, NY  10010
212-777-3017
800-237-9932
FAX: 888-436-4643
e-mail: rosenpub@tribeca.ios.com

*Tricia Bauer, Director Special Needs*
*Roger Rosen, President*

Dealing with a relative who is born physically challenged or who suffers a personal tragedy is one of the biggest adjustments in life. This book shows step-by-step methods of coping with these emotions so the reader may learn how to have a happy life once again. Hardcover. *$17.95*

*ISBN 0-823914-92-5*

**5643  Deenie**
Bradbury Press
135 S Mount Zion Road
Lebanon, IN  46052
800-257-5755
FAX: 800-882-8583

Deenie, a beautiful thirteen-year-old girl, had a mother who was pushing her to become a model. The agency representatives told Deenie she had the looks but walked differently. Deenie's main wish was to become a cheerleader. Her close friend, Janet, made the cheerleading squad but Deenie didn't make the final list. After this her gym teacher noticed her posture and called her family. After seeing therapists, the diagnosis of adolescent idiopathic scoliosis was made.

*159 pages Hardcover*
*ISBN 0-02711 -20-6*

**5644 Delicate Threads**
Woodbine House
6510 Bells Mill Road
Bethesda, MD 20817
301-897-3570
800-843-7323
FAX: 301-897-5838
www.woodbinehouse.com

*Irv Shapell, Owner*

How do friendships between children with and without disabilities develop? How do they compare to friendships between typically developing children? What happens to these friendships over time? In Delicate Threads, author Debbie staub helps to answer these questions through careful observations of friendships between seven pairs of children - each including a child with a moderate to severe disability - who are classmates in an inclusive Pacific Northwest elementary school. *$16.95*
*250 pages Paperback*
*ISBN 0-933149-90-5*

**5645 Determined to Win: Children Living with Allergies and Asthma**
Gareth Stevens
1555 N Rivercenter Drive
Milwaukee, WI 53212
414-332-3520
800-542-2595
FAX: 414-332-3567
www.gsinc.com

*Claire Messier, Marketing Associate*
*Bob Famighetti, Publisher*

Isabell, a six year old girl, has been living with allergies and asthma almost her entire life. With proper medical care and a determined attitude, she leads an active life. *$15.95*
*48 pages*
*ISBN 0-83681 -75-9*

**5646 Don't Call Me Special: A First Look at Dis ability**
Barron's Educational Series

This picture book explores questions and concerns about physical disabilities in a simple and reassuring way. Youger children can find out about individual disabilities, special equipment that is available to help the disabled, and how people of all ages can deal with disabilities and live happy and full lives. *$6.95*
*32 pages Paperback 2002*
*ISBN 0-764121-18-9*

**5647 Don't Feel Sorry for Paul**
JB Lippincott
E Washington Square
Philadelphia, PA 19105
215-521-8300
FAX: 215-824-7390

*J Lippincott, Chief Executive Officer*

Paul is seven but was born with deformities of both hands and feet. Paul must wear a prosthesis on both feet so that he can walk. He has a third prosthesis for his right hand. The third prosthesis has a pair of hooks Paul uses as fingers.
*94 pages Hardcover*
*ISBN 0-39731 -88-0*

**5648 Enabling Romance: A Guide to Love, Sex & Relationships for the Disabled**
Spina Bifida Association of America
4590 Macarthur Boulevard NW
Suite 250
Washington, DC 20007
202-944-3285
800-621-3141
FAX: 202-944-3295
e-mail: sbaa@sbaa.org
www.sbaa.org

*Cindy Brownstein, Chief Executive Officer*

An uncensored, illustrated guide to intimacy and sexual expression for persons with physical disabilities. *$15.95*

**5649 Family Therapy for ADHD: Treating Children , Adolescents and Adults**
Guilford Press
72 Spring Street
New York, NY 10012
212-431-9800
800-365-7006
FAX: 212-966-6708
www.guilford.com

*Bob Matloff, President*
*$40.00*
*Cloth*
*ISBN 1-572304-38-3*

**5650 For Siblings Only**
Family Resource Associates
35 Haddon Avenue
Shrewsbury, NJ 07702
732-747-5310
FAX: 732-747-1896

*Sue Levine, Social Worker*
*Nancy Phalanukorn, Manager*

A newsletter for brothers and sisters, aged 4 through 10, whose sibling has a disablilty. Includes stories, library resources, activities and discussion of feelings. $12/year for families, $20/year for professionals. *$12.00*
*12 pages Quarterly*

**5651 Funology Fables: Stories for Phonology Learning**
Speech Bin
1965 25th Avenue
Vero Beach, FL 32960
772-770-0007
800-477-3324
FAX: 772-770-0006
www.speechbin.com

Talking Tales develop children's language skills and enhance their phonological competence. *$45.00*
*264 pages*
*ISBN 0-93785 -59-9*

**5652 Getting a Grip on ADD: A Kid's Guide to Understanding & Coping with ADD**
Educational Media Corporation
PO Box 21311
Minneapolis, MN 55421
763-781-0088
800-966-3382
FAX: 763-781-7753
educationalmedia.com

*Earl Sorenson, President/Owner*

Free catalog of resources.
*64 pages Yearly*

**5653 Goldilocks and the Three Bears in Signed English**
Gallaudet University Press
11030 S Langley Avenue
Chicago, IL 60628
800-621-2736
FAX: 800-621-8476
TTY:800-621-9347
gupress.gallaudet.edu

*Harry Bornstein, Co-Author*
*Karen L Saulnier, Co-Author*

The classic story is told again but with a twist. Full color illustrations show the Bears, Goldilocks and the text. Includes line drawings that show the story in Signed English. *$15.95*
*48 pages Hardcover*

**5654 Guide to ACA Accredited Camps**
American Camping Association
5000 State Road 67 N
Martinsville, IN 46151
765-342-8456
800-428-2267
FAX: 765-349-6357
e-mail: bookstore@ACAcamps.org
www.acacamps.org

*Melody Snider, Director Bookstore/Distribution*
*Peg Smith, Chief Executive Officer*

A national listing of accredited camping programs. Listed by: special clientele, specific disabilities, camp name, activities. *$10.95*
*Quarterly*

**5655    Handbook of Infant Mental Health**
Guilford Press
72 Spring Street
New York, NY  10012                        212-431-9800
                                           800-365-7006
                                      FAX: 212-966-6708
                                       www.guilford.com

*Bob Matloff, President*

*$65.00*
*Cloth*
*ISBN 1-572305-15-0*

**5656    Helping Children Understand Disabilities**
Brookline Books
PO Box 1046
Cambridge, MA  02139                       617-868-0360
                                           800-666-2665
                                      FAX: 617-868-1772
                         e-mail: brooklinebks@delphi.com
                                   www.brooklinebooks.com
Examines children's literature as a vehicle to help children, parents and teachers understand important issues relating to the effects of disability on children. Using the child as narrator, the author demonstrates how to use popular children's fiction to explore taboo areas and stimulate discussion by children and adults. *$10.95*
*Hardcover*
*ISBN 0-91479 -09-3*

**5657    Ideas for Kids on the Go**
Accent Books & Products
PO Box 700
Bloomington, IL  61702                     309-378-2961
                                           800-787-8444
                                      FAX: 309-378-4420
                           e-mail: acmtlvng@aol.com

*Raymond C Cheever, Publisher*
*Betty Garee, Editor*

This guide shows kids with physical disabilities how to go for it! Lists products and where to get them, and includes tips from others for having fun and getting ahead. Ages 1-18. *$6.95*
*69 pages Paperback*
*ISBN 0-91570 -17-5*

**5658    Infant & Toddler Health Sourcebook**
Omnigraphics
615 Griswold Street
Detroit, MI  48226                         313-961-1340
                                           800-234-1340
                                      FAX: 800-875-1340
                                     www.omnigraphics.com

*Paul Rogers, Publicity Associate*
*Georgiann Lauginger, Customer Service Manager*
*Peters Ruffner, President*

Includes information on the mental and physical development of infants, including nutrition and common pediatric disorders. *$78.00*
*600 pages 2000*

**5659    It isn't Fair!: Siblings of Children with Disabilities**
Greenwood Publishing Group
88 Post Road W
Suite 5007
Westport, CT  06880                        203-226-3571
                                      FAX: 203-222-1502
                                       www.greenwood.com

*Wayne Smith, President*

This book presents a wide range of perspectives on the relationship of siblings to children with disabilities. These perspectives are written in the first person by parents, young adult siblings, younger siblings, and professionals.

*200 pages $39.95 - $45*
*ISBN 0-897893-32-8*

**5660    JRA and Me**
American Juvenile Arthritis Organization
PO Box 7669
Atlanta, GA  30357                         404-872-7100
                                           800-283-7800
                                      FAX: 404-872-9559
                              e-mail: help@arthritis.org
                                       www.arthritis.org

*John Klippel, Chief Executive Officer*

A workbook for school-aged children who have juvenile arthritis. This book offers a variety of educational games, puzzles and worksheets to teach children about their illness and how to take care of themselves. *$7.85*
*57 pages*

**5661    Jason & Nordic Publishers**
PO Box 441
Hollidaysburg, PA  16648                   814-696-2920
                                      FAX: 814-696-4250
                                e-mail: turtlbks@nb.net
                                  www.jasonandnordic.com

*Richard S McPhee, Director*
*Norma Phee, Owner*

Turtle Books for children with disabilities present heroes who look like them, have problems like theirs, have similar doubts and feelings in non-threatening, fun stories. They are motivational, bridge the gap and promote understanding among peers and siblings. 16 children's books (grades preK-3) plus Sensitivity and Awareness Guide containing lesson plans, activities, background information keyed to the series. Disabilities include: Down syndrome, cerebral palsy, blindness, deafness and more.

**5662    Jazz Man**
Atheneum
135 S Mount Zion Road
Lebanon, IN  46052
                                      FAX: 800-882-8583
Zeke and his family moved to Harlem from the South and lived in a walk-up tenement. He didn't go to school; instead, he watched out the window all day, especially at the yellow room. The yellow room came to be inhabited by the Jazz Man, who played all day and night to the whole family's delight.
*42 pages Paperback*

**5663    Jumpin' Johnny Get Back to Work, A Child's Guide to ADHD/Hyperactivity**
25 Van Zant Street
Suite 15-5
Norwalk, CT  06855                         203-838-5010
                                      FAX: 203-866-6108
                           e-mail: CACLD@optonline.net
                                       www.CACLD.org

*Beryl Kaufman, Executive Director*

Written primarily for elementary age youngsters with ADHD to help them understand their disability. Also valuable as an educational tool for parents, siblings, friends and classmates. Includes two pages on medication. *$12.50*
*24 pages*

**5664    Keeping Childhood**
Alliance for Parental Involvement in Education
PO Box 59
East Chatham, NY  12060                    518-392-6900
                                      FAX: 518-392-6900
Understanding the anthropological views of child development. *$12.00*

**5665  Kid Kare News**
3101 SW Sam Jackson Park Road
Portland, OR  97239
FAX: 503-241-5090
www.shrinershq.org

*Barbara Flaherty, New Patient Coordinator*
*Sonia Bouchard, Rehabilitation Services Manager*
*Kerry Grindeland, Care Coordination Manager*

Bi-annual publication from the Shriners Hospital for Children in
Portland, Oregon. Free. Produced by the medical staff.

**5666  Kid-Friendly Parenting with Deaf and Hard of Hearing
Children: A Treasury of Fun Activities**
Gallaudet University Press
11030 S Langley Avenue
Chicago, IL  60628
800-621-2736
FAX: 800-621-8476
TTY:800-621-9347
gupress.gallaudet.edu

*Denise Chapman, Co-Author*
*Daria Medwid, Co-Author*

Scores of activities, parenting techniques and insights by experts, both hearing and deaf, to help parents of deaf and hard of
hearing children. Activities are designed to promote better behavior and educate. *$24.95*
*382 pages Softcover*

**5667  Kidz Korner**
Children's Hopes & Dreams Wish Foundation
280 Us Highway 46
Dover, NJ  07801
973-361-7348
800-437-3262
FAX: 973-361-6627
e-mail: chdfdover@juno.com
www.childrenswishes.org

*Mariann Oswald, Manager*
*6 pages Monthly*

**5668  Kitten Who Couldn't Purr**
William Morrow & Company
1350 Avenue of the Americas
New York, NY  10019
212-261-6500
FAX: 212-261-6925
Jonathan the kitten doesn't know how to purr to say thank you, so
he sets off to find someone to teach him. *$12.95*
*32 pages*

**5669  Language and the Developing Child**
International Dyslexia Association
382 S Chester Street
Baltimore, MD  21231
800-ABC-D123
FAX: 410-296-0232
www.interdys.org
This collection of papers introduces a new generation of teachers, clinicians and parents to the work of one of the key figures in
the search for the causes and treatment of dyslexia. *$15.00*

**5670  Let's Talk About Having Asthma**
Rosen Publishing Group's PowerKids Press
29 E 21st Street
New York, NY  10010
212-777-3017
800-237-9932
FAX: 888-436-4643
e-mail: rosenpub@tribeca.ios.com

*Roger Rosen, President*

This book talks about the cause and treatments for asthma as
well as the precautions sufferers should take. Recommended for
grades K-4. *$13.95*

ISBN 0-823950-32-8

**5671  Lollipop Lunch**
Speech Bin
1965 25th Avenue
Vero Beach, FL  32960
772-770-0007
800-477-3324
FAX: 772-770-0006
www.speechbin.com
Cleverly illustrated stories and activities for phonological and
language development. *$19.95*
*128 pages*
*ISBN 0-93785 -54-8*

**5672  Loop the Loop**
William Morrow & Company
1350 Avenue of the Americas
New York, NY  10019
212-974-3100
FAX: 212-974-3188
www.williammorrow.com
Anne has never met anyone like Mrs. Simpson. She travels in a
wheelchair and performs fabulous yo-yo tricks. *$14.00*
*32 pages*

**5673  Mandy**
William Morrow & Company
1350 Avenue of the Americas
New York, NY  10019
212-974-3100
FAX: 212-261-6595
www.williammorrow.com
Told from the point of view of a deaf child, this warm picture
book is neither saccharine nor preachy. Mandy has never heard
anyone speak or sing. It is from her close relationship with her
grandmother that the small girl learns about the world through
lip-reading, facial expression, gesture, touch and sign. *$14.95*
*32 pages*

**5674  Me, Too**
JB Lippincott
227 E Washington Square
Philadelphia, PA  19106
215-521-8300
800-777-2295
FAX: 215-824-7390

*J Lippincott, Chief Executive Officer*

Lydia and Lornie were twins. Lydia was a bright twelve year old
who vowed to spend her summer vacation teaching her retarded
sister, Lornie, how to be normal.
*158 pages Hardcover*
*ISBN 0-39731 -85-X*

**5675  My Buddy**
Exceptional Parent Library
PO Box 1807
Englewood Cliffs, NJ  07632
201-947-6000
800-535-1910
FAX: 201-947-9376
e-mail: eplibrary@aol.com
www.eplibrary.com
Story focuses on the friendship between a boy with a disability
and his loyal golden retriever. *$5.95*
*Library Binding 1999*
*ISBN 0-785799-24-9*

**5676  My Signing Book of Numbers**
Gallaudet University Press
800 Florida Avenue NE
Washington, DC  20002
202-651-5000
800-621-2736
FAX: 202-651-5489
TTY: 888-630-9347

*Dan Wallace, Marketing Manager*
*Erving Jordan, President*

This full-color book helps children learn their numbers in sign
language. Each two-page spread of this delightfully illustrated
book has the appropriate number of things or creatures for the
numbers 0 through 20. *$14.95*

*56 pages Hardcover*
*ISBN 0-93032 -37-8*

**5677   Natural Child Care: A Complete Guide to Safe Holistic Remedies for Infants and Children**
Crown Publishing Group
1540 Broadway
New York, NY  10036                 212-782-9000
                                    FAX: 212-302-7985
Devoted to raising children by natural, holistic, drug-free methods, this comprehensive guide includes charts showing the uses of sixty readily available medicinal herbs.
*Paperback 1989*
*ISBN 0-517568-31-4*

**5678   Negotiating the Special Education Maze: A Guide for Parents and Teachers**
Spina Bifida Association of America
4590 Macarthur Boulevard NW
Suite 250
Washington, DC 20007                202-944-3285
                                    800-621-3141
                                    FAX: 202-944-3295
                                    e-mail: sbaa@sbaa.org
                                    www.sbaa.org

*Cindy Brownstein, Chief Executive Officer*

An excellent aid for the development of an effective special education program. *$19.00*

**5679   New Language of Toys: Teaching Communicati on Skills to Children with Special Needs**
Spina Bifida Association of America
4590 Macarthur Boulevard NW
Suite 250
Washington, DC 20007                202-944-3285
                                    800-621-3141
                                    FAX: 202-944-3295
                                    e-mail: sbaa@sbaa.org
                                    www.sbaa.org

*Cindy Brownstein, Chief Executive Officer*

A guide for parents and teachers and a reader-friendly resource guide that provides a wealth of information on how play activities affect a child's language development and where to get the toys and materials to use in these activities. *$19.00*

**5680   New York Families for Autistic Children**
9516 Pitkin Avenue
Ozone Park, NY  11417               718-641-3441
                                    FAX: 718-641-4452
                                    e-mail: help@nyfac.org
                                    www.nufac.org

*Andrew Baumann, Chief Executive Officer*

Education, recreations and support services for families and children with developmental disabilities.

**5681   Nick Joins In**
Spina Bifida Association of America
4590 Macarthur Boulevard NW
Suite 250
Washington, DC 20007                202-944-3285
                                    800-621-3141
                                    FAX: 202-944-3295
                                    e-mail: sbaa@sbaa.org
                                    www.sbaa.org

*Cindy Brownstein, Chief Executive Officer*

When Nick, who is in a wheelchair, enters a regular classroom for the first time, he realizes that he has much to contribute. *$17.00*

**5682   Nursery Rhymes from Mother Goose**
Gallaudet University Press
800 Florida Avenue NE
Washington, DC  20002               202-651-5000
                                    FAX: 202-651-5704
                                    TTY:888-630-8347

*Dan Wallace, Marketing Manager*
*Erving Jordan, President*

Each complete nursery rhyme is presented in Signed English and delightfully illustrated in full color. *$14.95*
*64 pages*
*ISBN 0-93032 -99-8*

**5683   On Our Own Terms: Children Living with Physical Disabilities**
Gareth Stevens
1555 N River Center Drive
Milwaukee, WI 53212                 414-332-3520
                                    800-542-2595
                                    FAX: 414-225-0377

*Bob Famighetti, Publisher*

Meet Kicki, a three-year-old with Spina Bifida, battling to walk for the first time. Meet Annelie, nine years old, learning to walk again after a bad car accident. Face the physical challenges with her. *$13.95*
*48 pages*
*ISBN 1-555329-42-X*

**5684   One Day at a Time: Children Living with Leukemia**
Gareth Stevens
1555 N Rivercenter Drive
Milwaukee, WI  53212                414-332-3520
                                    800-542-2595
                                    FAX: 414-225-0377
                            beta.healthlinkusa.com/bookpage/184_27.html

*Claire Messier, Marketing Associate*
*Bob Famighetti, Publisher*

Focus on Hanna, two years old, and 3 year old Frederick. Both diagnosed with Leukemia and follows them as they are treated for their illness. Includes such daily routines as eating breakfast, washing and playing. *$16.95*
*56 pages Hardcover*
*ISBN 1-55532 -13-6*

**5685   Out of the Corner of My Eye**
American Foundation for the Blind/AFB Press
PO Box 1020
Sewickley, PA  15143                412-741-1142
                                    800-232-3044
                                    FAX: 412-741-0609
                                    e-mail: afborders@abdintl.com
                                    www.afb.org
A personal account of students' vision loss and subsequent adjustment that is full of practical advice and cheerful encouragement, told by an 87 year old retired college teacher who has maintained her independence and zest for life. *$14.95*

*ISBN 0-891281-93-2*

**5686   Parent Teacher Packet**
Spina Bifida Association of America
4590 Macarthur Boulevard NW
Suite 250
Washington, DC 20007                202-944-3285
                                    800-621-3141
                                    FAX: 202-944-3295
                                    e-mail: sbaa@sbaa.org
                                    www.sbaa.org

*Cindy Brownstein, Chief Executive Officer*

Includes educational material, learning disabilities literature, children's book, social development and the person with spina bifida and one copy of each fact sheet. *$14.00*

**5687  Please Don't Say Hello**
Human Sciences Press
233 Spring Street
New York, NY 10013

212-229-2859
800-221-9369
FAX: 212-463-0742

Paul and his family moved into a new neighborhood. Paul's brother was autistic. The children thought that Eddie was retarded until they learned that there were skills that he could do better than they could. *$10.95*
*47 pages Paperback*
*ISBN 0-89885 -99-8*

**5688  Quad City Deaf & Hard of Hearing Youth Group: Tomorrow's Leaders for our Community**
Independent Living Research Utilization ILRU
2323 S Shepherd Drive
Suite 1000
Houston, TX 77019

713-520-0232
FAX: 713-520-5785
www.ilru.org

*Laurie Redd, Executive Director*

IICIL staff see this program as a way to develop young leaders for the movement. Emphasis is given to providing oppportunities for members of the youth group to develop skills in planning and organizing activities.
*10 pages*

**5689  Rajesh**
Atheneum
135 S Mount Zion Road
Lebanon, IN 46052

FAX: 800-882-8583

Rajesh, a student in a headstart program, was born without complete legs and must wear two prostheses to walk. When Rajesh first attended school he found that older children teased him. After he explained about his legs to the class, his classmates began to accept him.
*32 pages Hardcover*
*ISBN 0-68931 -74-9*

**5690  Reading, Writing and Speech Problems in Children**
International Dyslexia Association
382 S Chester Street
Baltimore, MD 21231

800-ABC-D123
FAX: 410-296-0232
www.interdys.org

A tribute to the man who more than any other aroused the attention of the scientific community and who provided the sound educational principles on which much teaching of dyslexics today is based. *$27.00*

*ISBN 0-89079 -79-1*

**5691  Reflections on Growing Up Disabled**
Council for Exceptional Children
1110 N Glebe Road
Suite 300
Arlington, VA 22201

703-245-0600
FAX: 703-264-9494
www.cec.sped.org

*Janice Burdick, President*
*Bruce Ramirez, Manager*

Understand how it feels to be a disabled person in school by tuning in to the first-hand accounts of people who have disabilities. *$10.00*
*112 pages*

**5692  Rehab Update**
New England Medical Center
750 Washington Street
Suite 75k-R
Boston, MA 02111

617-636-5000
FAX: 617-636-4269

*Vincent Licenziato, Training Coordinator*
*Mohammed Ahmed, MD*

Reports on causes and consequences of injuries among children and adolescents. Focus on rehabilitation research, family adjustment, special education, and violence prevention. Special attention on brain injury among youth.
*8 pages BiAnnual*

**5693  Ride the Red Cycle**
Houghton Mifflin
222 Berkeley Street
Boston, MA 02116

617-351-5000
800-225-3362
www.hmco.com

*Tony Lucki, Chief Executive Officer*

Jerome Johnson is nine, but due to brain damage he can't walk and his speech is hard to understand. Jerome gets around in a wheelchair, but he knows that if he could get a tricycle he could go where and when he wanted. His parents not only agreed to buy him the cycle, but his dad built up the pedals and added a seat with a back and a seatbelt to hold Jerome.
*34 pages Hardcover*
*ISBN 0-39529 -83-6*

**5694  Rolling Along with Goldilocks and the Thre e Bears**
Spina Bifida Association of America
4590 Macarthur Boulevard NW
Suite 250
Washington, DC 20007

202-944-3285
800-621-3141
FAX: 202-944-3295
e-mail: sbaa@sbaa.org
www.sbaa.org

*Cindy Brownstein, Chief Executive Officer*

The familiar fairytale with a special needs twist. Ages 3-7. *$17.00*

**5695  Rose-Colored Glasses**
Human Sciences Press
233 Spring Street
New York, NY 10013

212-229-2859
800-221-9369
FAX: 212-463-0742

After a vacation, Deborah was excited about going back to school. Renewing old friendships, she met a classmate who seemed stuck up. Deborah learned that Melanie was in a recent accident resulting in impaired vision. She did not wish to wear her glasses, which were rose-colored and very funny looking. With Deborah's help, Miss Davis, the teacher showed a blurry film and then had Melanie speak about her impaired vision. When Melanie began to participate in the class they accepted her. *$16.95*
*30 pages Hardcover*
*ISBN 0-87705 -08-8*

**5696  Seeing-Children Living with Blindness**
Gareth Stevens
1555 N Rivercenter Drive
Milwaukee, WI 53212

414-332-3520
800-341-3569
FAX: 414-225-0377

*Bob Famighetti, Publisher*

Go with Thomas to a special school for children who can't see, where you will meet Andrew, Kate, Jordan, Katherine, Peter and Kent. Read what they told Thomas about being blind, about daily life, their feelings, the funny things, and the sad. *$10.95*

*ISBN 1-555329-15-2*

**5697  Self-Control Games & Workbook**
Western Psychological Services
12031 Wilshire Boulevard
Los Angeles, CA 90025

310-478-2061
800-648-8857
FAX: 310-478-7838
www.wpspublish.com

*Gregg Gillmar, Vice President*

This game is designed to teach self-control in academic and social situations. Addresses a total of 24 impulsive, inattentive and hyperactive behaviors. The companion workbook reinforces the use of positive self-statements, and problem-solving techniques, instead of expressing anger. *$62.50*
*Game TCGS*

**5698  Sibling Forum**
Family Resource Associates
35 Haddon Avenue
Shrewsbury, NJ  07702                        732-747-5310
                                        FAX: 732-747-1896

*Susan Levine, Social Worker*
*Nancy Phalanukorn, Manager*

A newsletter for brothers and sisters, aged 10 through teen, whose sibling has a disablilty. Includes input from readers, library resources and discussion of feelings. $12/year for families, $20/year for professionals. *$12.00*
*8-12 pages Quarterly*

**5699  Sibshops: Workshops for Siblings of Children with Special Needs**
Brookes Publishing
PO Box 10624
Baltimore, MD  21285                        410-337-9580
                                            800-638-3775
                                        FAX: 410-337-8539
                e-mail: custserv@brookespublishing.com
                            www.brookespublishing.com

*Paul Brooks, Owner*

Sibshops is a program that brings together 8-to 13-year-old brothers and sisters of children with special needs. The siblings receive support and information in a recreational setting, so they have fun while they learn. *$32.00*
*256 pages Paperback*
*ISBN 1-55766-69-3*

**5700  Sleeping Beauty**
Gallaudet University Press
800 Florida Avenue NE
Washington, DC  20002                        202-651-5000
                                            800-621-2736
                                        FAX: 800-660-8476
                                        TTY: 888-630-9347

*Dan Wallace, Marketing Manager*
*Erving Jordan, President*

The popular fairytale of the princess put to sleep for a hundred years is presented with beautiful full color illustrations and selected sentences in American Sign Language. *$14.95*
*64 pages*
*ISBN 0-93032-97-1*

**5701  Somebody Called Me a Retard Today...and My Heart Felt Sad**
Walker Publishing Company
104 5th Avenue
New York, NY  10011                        212-727-8300
                                            800-289-2553
                                        FAX: 212-727-0984
                e-mail: orders@walkerbooks.com
                            www.walkerbooks.com

*David Garner, Illustrator*
*Ramsey Walker, Vice President*

A simple, moving story that empowers mentally challenged children and sensitizes everyone to the need to celebrate the differences in all of us. *$14.85*
*24 pages Cloth/Hardcover*
*ISBN 0-802781-97-7*

**5702  Son-Rise: The Miracle Continues**
2080 S Undermountain Road
Sheffield, MA  01257                        413-229-2100
                                            800-562-7171
                                        FAX: 413-229-3202
                e-mail: sonrise@option.org
                            www.son-rise.org

Part One is the astonishing record of Raun Kaufman's development from an autistic and retarded child into a loving, brilliant youngster who shows no traces of his former condition. Part Two follows Raun's development after the age of four, teaching the limitless possibilities of the Son-Rise Program. Part Three shares moving accounts of five other ordinary families who became extraordinary when they used the Son-Rise Program to reach their own unreachable children. *$12.95*
*343 pages*
*ISBN 0-915811-53-7*

**5703  Sorrow's Song**
Atlantic-Little Brown
34 Beacon Street
Boston, MA  02108
                                            800-343-9204
                                        FAX: 800-286-9471
                                        www.twbookmark.com
Sorrow never learned to talk. Her parents had taken her to all the specialists to find out why she couldn't talk, but no reason was ever found.
*150 pages Hardcover*
*ISBN 0-31612-97-4*

**5704  Sound Connections for the Adolescent**
Speech Bin
1965 25th Avenue
Vero Beach, FL  32960                        772-770-0007
                                            800-477-3324
                                        FAX: 772-770-0006
                                        www.speechbin.com
A resource to help older elementary and secondary students understand their sound systems an how it functions. It targets skills critical for academic achievement: phonological awareness, phonemic relationships, phonemic processing, listening and memory and teaches linguistic rules they need to succeed. *$19.95*
*Paperback*

**5705  Special Education Report**
Aspen Publishers
7201 McKinney Circle
Frederick, MD  21704                        301-698-7100
                                            800-638-8437
                                        FAX: 301-695-7931
                e-mail: customer.service@aspenpubl.com
                            www.aspenpublishers.com

*Judith Ree, Manager*

Published biweekly, Special Education Report is the independent news service on law, policy and funding of programs for disabled children. *$16.00*
*8-12 pages Newsletter*

**5706  Special Format Books for Children and Youth Ages 3-19**
Cultural Education Center
Albany, NY  12230                        518-474-5935
                                            800-342-3688
                            www.nysl.nysed.gov/tbbl/index.html

*Jane Somers, Director*

**5707  Special Format Books for Children and Youth: Ages 3-19.Serving New York City/Long Island**
476 5th Avenue
New York, NY  10018                        212-206-5400

                e-mail: pleclerc@nypl.org
                            www.nypl.org

*Paul LeClerc, President*
*Robert Brian, Manager*

**5708 Spinabilities: A Young Person's Guide to Spina Bifida**
Woodbine House
6510 Bells Mill Road
Bethesda, MD 20817
301-897-3570
800-843-7323
FAX: 301-897-5838
e-mail: info@woodbinehouse.com
www.woodbinehouse.com

*Irv Shapell, Owner*

Advice for teenagers on managing daily and long-term healthcare, tips on sex and relationships, and strategies for success at school and on the job. *$16.95*
*138 pages 1997*
*ISBN 0-933149-86-7*

**5709 Steps to Independence: Teaching Everyday S kills to Children with Special Needs**
Spina Bifida Association of America
4590 Macarthur Boulevard NW
Suite 250
Washington, DC 20007
202-944-3285
800-621-3141
FAX: 202-944-3295
e-mail: sbaa@sbaa.org
www.sbaa.org

*Cindy Brownstein, Chief Executive Officer*

A guide to help parents teach life skills to their disabled child. *$28.00*

**5710 Straight Talk About Psychiatric Medications for Kids**
Guilford Press
72 Spring Street
New York, NY 10012
212-431-9800
FAX: 212-966-6708
www.guilford.com

*Bob Matloff, President*

Also in cloth at $29.95 (ISBN# 1-57230-404-9 *$35.00*
*280 pages Paperback 1998*
*ISBN 1-572302-04-6*

**5711 Students with Learning Disabilities**
McGraw-Hill, School Publishing
220 E Danieldale Road
Desoto, TX 75115
972-224-1111
800-442-9685
FAX: 972-228-1982
mhschool.com

*Joseph Gavigan, President*

A comprehensive text which introduces students to the entire field of learning disabilities.
*512 pages*

**5712 Superkids**
Superkids
60 Clyde Street
Newton, MA 02460

www.super-kids.org
Non-profit organization and newsletter for families and friends of children with limb differences. It is published twice a year and is free to interested families and professionals. Offers timely information and support to those affected by limb differences.

**5713 Taking Charge**
Spina Bifida Association of America
4590 Macarthur Boulevard NW
Suite 250
Washington, DC 20007
202-944-3285
800-621-3141
FAX: 202-944-3295
e-mail: sbaa@sbaa.org
www.sbaa.org

*Cindy Brownstein, Chief Executive Officer*

Teenagers talk about life and physical disabilities. *$7.95*

**5714 Talkable Tales**
Speech Bin
1965 25th Avenue
Vero Beach, FL 32960
772-770-0007
800-477-3324
FAX: 772-770-0006
www.speechbin.com

*Jan J Binney, Senior Editor*

Read-a-rebus stories and pictures targeting most consonant phonemes for K-5 children. *$25.95*
*128 pages*
*ISBN 0-93783 -44-0*

**5715 Teenagers with ADD**
Woodbine House
6510 Bells Mill Road
Bethesda, MD 20817
301-897-3570
800-843-7323
FAX: 301-897-5838
www.woodbinehouse.com

*Irv Shapell, Owner*

This best selling guide to understanding and coping with teenagers with attention deficit disorder (ADD) provides complete coverage of the special issues and challenges faced by these teens. Based on current diagnostic criteria and the latest literature and research in the field, the book discusses diagnosis, medical treatment, family and school life, intervention, advocacy, legal rights, and options after high school. Parents find strategies for dealing with their teen's difficult behaviors. *$18.95*
*370 pages Paperback*
*ISBN 0-933149-69-7*

**5716 Tempered Wind**
Atheneum
135 S Mount Zion Road
Lebanon, IN 46052
FAX: 800-882-8583
Gabrielle was a dwarf and was never out of her house until her parents died and she was sent from one aunt to the next. At age thirteen she was enrolled in school for the first time. The children teased her about being a dwarf, and although she excelled academically, she failed socially. After three years in school an illness forced her aunt to take Gabrielle to the doctor. The doctor's prognosis was grim and led Gabrielle's aunt to tell her that she would have to find a job.
*210 pages Hardcover*
*ISBN 0-68931 -39-X*

**5717 Texas Families**
7701 N Lamar Boulevard
Suite 505
Austin, TX 78752
512-407-8844
866-893-3264
FAX: 512-407-8266
e-mail: info@txffcmh.org
www.txffcmh.org

*Patti Derr, Executive Director*
*Pat Calley, Board Chair*
*SG Barron, Director of Operations*

A quarterly publication from Texas Federation of Families for Children's Mental Health. Free.
*8 pages Quarterly*

**5718 Thinking Big**
William Morrow & Company
1350 Avenue of the Americas
New York, NY 10019
212-974-3100
FAX: 212-261-6595
www.williammorrow.com

Eight-year-old Jaime's lively personality shines through in this perceptive photo essay which explains what being a dwarf means physically and then presents Jaime's world at home and at school from her viewpoint. *$15.95*

*48 pages*

**5719  Tourette Syndrome Association Children's Newsletter**
4240 Bell Boulevard
Bayside, NY  11361

718-224-2999
800-237-0717
FAX: 718-279-9596
e-mail: ts@tsa-usa.org
www.tsa-usa.org

*Fred Cook, Chair*
*Judit Ungar, President*

National, nonprofit membership organization. Mission is to identify the cause of, find the cure for, and control the effects of this disorder. A growing number of local chapters nationwide provide educational materials, seminars, conferences and support groups for over 35,000 members.

**5720  Transition Matters: from School to Independence**
Resources for Children with Special Needs
116 E 16th Street
Floor 5
New York, NY  10003

212-677-4650
FAX: 212-254-4070
e-mail: info@resourcesnyc.org
www.resourcesnyc.org

*Karen Schlesinger, Executive Director*
*Dianne Littwin, Director Publications*

Published every 24-36 months. *$35.00*
*496 pages*
*ISBN 0-967836-56-5*

**5721  Trouble with Explosives**
Bradbury Press
135 S Mount Zion Road
Lebanon, IN  46052

800-257-5755
FAX: 800-882-8583

Polly moved regularly with her family, changing schools almost every year. This was especially difficult as she couldn't pronounce her explosive name, Polly Banks, without stuttering.
*117 pages Hardcover*
*ISBN 0-87888 -94-1*

**5722  Understanding Cub Scouts with Disabilities**
Boy Scouts of America
1325 W Walnut Hill Lane
Irving, TX  75038

972-580-2000
800-323-0732

*Roy Williams, Chief Executive Officer*

Manual on how to teach and understand boy scouts with handicaps.
*10 pages*

**5723  Views from Our Shoes**
Spina Bifida Association of America
4590 Macarthur Boulevard NW
Washington, DC  20007

202-944-3285
800-621-3141
FAX: 202-944-3295
e-mail: sbaa@sbaa.org
www.sbaa.org

*Cindy Brownstein, Chief Executive Officer*

Siblings share what it is like to have a brother or sister with a disability. Age 9 and up. *$17.00*
*106 pages Paperback*

**5724  We Laugh, We Love, We Cry: Children Living with Mental Retardation**
Gareth Stevens
1555 N River Center Drive
Milwaukee, WI  53212

414-332-3520
800-524-2595
FAX: 414-225-0377

*Bob Famighetti, Publisher*

Two sisters, Asa and Anna Karin, are mentally retarded. They find it hard to understand things quickly, so learning to walk and talk has been slow work for them. With help from their parents, friends and teachers and their doctors, they are both learning to do the things that most of us are not lucky enough to learn easily. *$13.95*
*48 pages*
*ISBN 1-555329-14-4*

**5725  What About Me? Growing Up with a Developme ntally Disabled Sibling**
Perseus Publishing

Silverstein, a physician, gives a first-person account of his experiences as the older brother of an autistic sibling. Siegel, a developmental psychologist, presents discussion of family approaches to handicaps based on clinical interviews with some 1,000 families of various ethnic, social, and educational backgrounds. *$24.00*
*316 pages Paperback 2001*
*ISBN 0-738206-30-X*

**5726  What Happens Next?**
Exceptional Parent Library- Star Bright Books
PO Box 1807
Englewood Cliffs, NJ  07632

201-947-6000
800-535-1910
FAX: 201-947-9376
e-mail: eplibrary@aol.com
www.eplibrary.com

Photo-flap book where babies lift the sturdy flap, page by page, to find out what happens next. *$4.95*
*14 pages Hardcover 1996*
*ISBN 1-887734-10-4*

**5727  What It's Like to be Me**
Friendship Press
PO Box 37844
Cincinnati, OH  45222

513-948-8733
FAX: 513-761-3722
www.ncccusa.org

*Nancy Kennedy, Customer Service*
*Robert Bray, Manager*

This was written and illustrated entirely by children with handicapped conditions. These contributions invite the reader to set aside any pity or prejudices and listen. Black and white, and color drawings and photographs make this book visually appealing, enjoyable for all ages. *$10.95*

**5728  You Seem Like a Regular Kid to Me**
American Foundation for the Blind/AFB Press
PO Box 1020
Sewickley, PA  15143

412-741-1142
800-232-3044
FAX: 412-741-0609
e-mail: afborders@abdintl.com
www.afb.org

An interview with Jane, a blind child, tells other children what it's like to be blind. Jane explains how she gets around, takes care of herself, does her school work, spends her leisure time and even pays for things when she can't see money.
*16 pages*
*ISBN 0-891289-21-6*

## Community

**5729  A Commitment to Inclusion: Outreach to Un-served/Underserved Populations**
Independent Living Research Utilization ILRU
2323 S Shepherd Drive
Suite 1000
Houston, TX  77019

713-520-0232
FAX: 713-520-5785
www.ilru.org

*Laurie Redd, Executive Director*

Carol Bradley describes Independent Living Resource Center San Francisco's community organizing/outreach approach to serving under-represented consumers. This organization successfully reaches persons with pychiatric disabilities, environmental illness/multiple chemical sensitivities, chronic fatigue immune deficiency syndrome, learning disabilities, institutionalized persons, Chinese, Latinos, deaf/hard of hearing, and lesbian/bisexual populations.
*10 pages*

**5730 A World Awaits You**
Mobility International USA
PO Box 10767
Eugene, OR 97440

541-343-1284
FAX: 541-343-6812
e-mail: info@miusa.org
www.miusa.org

*Misty Gren, Information Services Coordinator*
*Pamela Houston, Public Relations Coordinator*
*Susan Sygall, Executive Director*

A yearly publication from Mobility International USA. Free.
*44 pages Yearly*

**5731 Advocacy-Oriented Peer Support: Moving from Talk to Action**
Independent Living Research Utilization ILRU
2323 S Shepherd Drive
Suite 1000
Houston, TX 77019

713-520-0232
FAX: 713-520-5785
www.ilru.org

*Laurie Redd, Executive Director*

This month's Readings examines how staff at centers for independent living can identify and support potential leaders who will move beyond talking about their problems to making changes in their communities.
*10 pages*

**5732 Annual Community Awards Booklet**
National Organization on Disability
910 16th Street NW
Suite 600
Washington, DC 20006

202-293-5960
FAX: 202-293-7999
e-mail: ability@nod.org
www.nod.org

*Michael Deland, President*
*Brewster Thackeray, VP Communications*
*John Hershey, Advice and Resource Manager*

Information on disability programs in communities across the nation.

**5733 Arc Connection Newsletter**
Arc of Tennessee
44 Vantage Way
Suite 550
Nashville, TN 37228

615-248-5878
800-835-7077
FAX: 615-248-5879
e-mail: pcooper@thearctn.org
www.thearctn.org

*Walter Rogers, Executive Director*

Quarterly publication from the ARC of Tennessee. *$ 10.00*
*12 pages Quarterly*

**5734 Asthma and Allergy Answers: A Patient Education Library**
Asthma and Allergy Foundation of America
1125 15th Street NW
Suite 502
Washington, DC 20005

202-466-7643
FAX: 202-466-8940
e-mail: info@aafa.org
www.aafa.org

*Bill Lin, Executive Director*

A resource tool has information on more than 40 topics of interest to patients. These reproducible camera ready Answers are written in a patient friendly questions and answer format. There is space to personalize these handy patient education materials with your practice or facility information. *$50.00*

**5735 California Community Care News California Residential Care Association of CA**
Charles W Skoien Jr
PO Box 163270
Sacramento, CA 95816

916-455-0723
FAX: 916-455-7201
e-mail: sncnews@aol.com

*Charles W Skoien Jr, Editor/Publisher*

Forum for the exchange of ideas, information and opinions among clients, families and service providers. Information regarding services and assisted living programs for the elderly, mentally ill and disabled. *$45.00*
*24 pages Monthly*

**5736 Community Recreation and People with Disabilities: Strategies for Inclusion**
Brookes Publishing
PO Box 10624
Baltimore, MD 21285

410-337-9580
800-638-3775
FAX: 410-337-8539
e-mail: custserv@brookespublishing.com
www.brookespublishing.com

*Paul Brooks, Owner*

Offers creative ideas and new techniques for including people with disabilities in community recreation programs. *$39.00*
*368 pages Paperback 1997*
*ISBN 1-55766 -59-2*

**5737 Crossing the River: Creating a Conceptual Revolution in Community & Disability**
Brookline Books
PO Box 1047
Cambridge, MA 02139

617-868-0360
800-666-2665
FAX: 617-868-1772
e-mail: brooklinebks@delphi.com
www.brooklinebooks.com

For persons with disabilities, a new conception of care is beginning to emerge—a conception seeking to embed these persons in a web of personal relationships, and to involve them in the dynamics of their community. Schwartz explores the promise, potential, and limits of this new direction. *$24.95*
*238 pages Paperback*
*ISBN 0-91479 -82-4*

**5738 Culture and the Restructuring of Community Mental Health**
Greenwood Publishing Group
88 Post Road W
Suite 5007
Westport, CT 06880

203-226-3571
FAX: 203-222-1502
www.greenwood.com

*Wayne Smith, President*

Examines treatment, organizational planning and research issues and offers a critique of the theoretical and programmatic aspects of providing mental health services to traditionally underserved populations. $45.00-$52.95.
*168 pages Hardcover*
*ISBN 0-313268-87-8*

**5739 Disablement in the Community**
Oxford University Press
2001 Evans Road
Cary, NC 27513

919-677-0977
800-451-7556
FAX: 919-677-1303
www.oup-usa.org

*Thomas Carty, Senior Vice President*

This book shows how the knowledge of the epidemiology of disablement can help planners, service providers, patients and voluntary organizations choose strategies for community care. *$39.95*
*248 pages Illustrated*

**5740 Empowering Youth**
Independent Living Research Utilization ILRU
2323 S Shepherd Drive
Suite 1000
Houston, TX 77019
713-520-0232
FAX: 713-520-5785
www.ilru.org

*Laurie Redd, Executive Director*

ILRU's innovative program demonstrates how combined peer support and hands-on advocacy projects empower teens to become leaders.
*10 pages*

**5741 HealthViews**
New Orleans VA Medical Center
1601 Perdido Street
New Orleans, LA 70112
504-568-0811
800-935-8387
FAX: 504-589-5210
e-mail: Stacie.Rivera@med.va.gov
www.va.gov

*John D Church Jr, President*
*Fernando Rivera, Assoc Medical Center Director*
*Sam Lucero, Special Assistant to Director*

Publication of a teaching hospital, providing a full range of patient care services, with state-of-the-art technology as well as education and research. Comprehensive health care is provided through primary care, tertiary care, and long-term care in areas of medicine, surgery, psychiatry, physical medicine and rehabilitation, neurology, oncology, dentistry, geriatrics, and extended care.
*quarterly*

**5742 Home and Community Care for Chronically Ill Children**
Oxford University Press
2001 Evans Road
Cary, NC 27513
919-677-0977
800-451-7556
FAX: 919-677-1303
www.oup-usa.org

*Thomas Carty, Senior Vice President*

This book lays common ground for all who have reason and responsibility to enhance the capability of families to care for their ill children over the long term at home. *$32.95*
*192 pages*

**5743 Housing, Support, and Community**
Brookes Publishing
PO Box 10624
Baltimore, MD 21285
410-337-9580
800-638-3775
FAX: 410-337-8539
e-mail: custserv@brookespublishing.com
www.brookespublishing.com

*Paul Brooks, Owner*

Choices and strategies for adults with disabilities. *$32.00*

*416 pages Paperback*
*ISBN 1-55766 -90-5*

**5744 Inclusive Child Care for Infants and Toddlers: Meeting Individual and Special Needs**
Brookes Publishing
PO Box 10624
Baltimore, MD 21285
410-337-9580
800-638-3775
FAX: 410-337-8539
e-mail: custserv@brookespublishing.com
www.brookespublishing.com

*Paul Brooks, Owner*

This book gives child care providers the practical guidance they need to serve infants and toddlers with and without disabilities in inclusive settings. It offers information and helpful advice on handling daily care tasks, teaching responsively, meeting individual needs, developing rapport with parents, understanding toddlers' behavior, working with IFSPs, and maintaining high standards of care. *$34.95*
*400 pages Paperback 1997*
*ISBN 1-55766 -96-7*

**5745 Independence & Transition to Community Living: The Role of Independent Living Centers**
Independent Living Research Utilization ILRU
2323 S Shepherd Drive
Suite 1000
Houston, TX 77019
713-520-0232
FAX: 713-520-5785
www.ilru.org

*Laurie Redd, Executive Director*

This publication covers important information on why we all should make assistance to people living in nursing homes a priority. Just as important, this is an excellent summary of all the facts - quality of life, health, and costs - which support deinstitutionalization.
*10 pages*

**5746 Independent Living Matters**
DisAbility Resources of Southwest Washington
5501 NE 109th Court
Suite N
Vancouver, WA 98662
360-694-6790
FAX: 360-694-6910
e-mail: ilrswwa@lqwest.net

*Jim Baker, Executive Director*
*Angela Hartford, Editor/Administrative Technician*
*Scott Anfinson, Independent Living Specialist*

To promote the philosophy of independent living by creating opportunities, encouraging choices, advancing equal access and furthering the level of independence for all people with disabilities.
*8-10 pages Quarterly*

**5747 JCIL Advocate Times**
Jackson Center for Independent Living
409 Linden Avenue
Jackson, MI 49203
517-784-1723
FAX: 517-784-9921

*Perry Stahl, author*
*Quarterly*

**5748 Lifelong Leisure Skills and Lifestyles for Persons with Developmental Disabilities**
Brookes Publishing
PO Box 10624
Baltimore, MD 21285
410-337-9580
800-638-3775
FAX: 410-337-8539
e-mail: custserv@brookespublishing.com
www.brookespublishing.com

*Paul Brooks, Owner*

This instructional manual offers ideas and detailed examples that describe how to guide individuals of all ages through popular activities using adaptations that foster skill acquisition and inclusion. Some of the concepts explored are home-school-community collaboration, choice making and the dignity of risk, and leisure skill acquisition for the life span. *$35.00*
> *352 pages Paperback*
> *ISBN 1-55766 -47-2*

**5749  Living in the Community**
Independent Living Research Utilization ILRU
2323 S Shepherd Drive
Suite 1000
Houston, TX  77019                          713-520-0232
                                      FAX: 713-520-5785
                                          www.ilru.org

*Laurie Redd, Executive Director*

James, Lori, and Jamey describe the elements of their successful program to move people out of nursing homes and into the community: providing funding for deposits, first month's rent and other neccessities, including assistive technology; providing training and the other core services before and after consumers leave the nursing home; developing relationships with housing and other service providers.
> *10 pages*

**5750  Loud, Proud and Passionate**
Mobility International USA
PO Box 10767
Eugene, OR  97440                          541-343-1284
                                      FAX: 541-343-6812
                                   e-mail: info@miusa.org
                                         www.miusa.org

*Susan Sygall, Executive Director*
*Pamela Houston, Public Relations Coordinator*
*Tracy Scharn, Project Assistant*

A resource book for international development and women's organization about including women with disabilities in projects in the community. Informs women sith disabilities about the efforts and successes of their peers worldwide. *$30.00*

**5751  NSEE Quarterly**
9001 Braddock Road
Suite 380
Springfield, VA  22151                     703-426-4268
                                           800-803-4170
                                      FAX: 703-426-8400
                                   e-mail: info@nsee.org
                                          www.nsee.org

*Charles Walker, Executive Director*

Quarterly publication from the National Society for Experiential Education.
> *16 pages Quarterly*

**5752  National Registry of Community Mental Health Services**
Nat'l Council for Community Behavioral Healthcare
12300 Twinbrook Parkway
Suite 320
Rockville, MD  20852                       301-984-6200
                                      FAX: 301-881-7159
                                          www.nccbh.org

*Linda Rosenberg, Chief Executive Officer*

Lists more than 1,900 agencies in all 50 states giving names, addresses and phones. *$59.00*

**5753  Northwest Media**
326 W 12th Avenue
Eugene, OR  97401                          541-343-6636
                                           800-777-6636
                                      FAX: 541-343-0177
                          e-mail: nwm@northwestmedia.com
                                    www.sociallearning.com

*Lee White, President*

Northwest Media is an independent publishing company that focuses on independent living and foster care products.

**5754  Parc Views**
PO Box 3418
Peoria, IL  61612                          309-691-3800
                                      FAX: 309-689-3613
                                        www.peoriaarc.org

*Anne Follis, Editor*
*Roy Rickettes, President*

Quarterly publication from Peoria ARC, free with donation.

**5755  Part Two: A Preview of Independence and Transition to Community Living**
Independent Living Research Utilization ILRU
2323 S Shepherd Drive
Suite 1000
Houston, TX  77019                          713-520-0232
                                      FAX: 713-520-5785
                                          www.ilru.org

*Laurie Redd, Executive Director*

This publication covers important strategies for helping people leave nursing homes. It includes several important recommendations which CIL leaders and staffs will find useful in organizing transition activities.
> *10 pages*

**5756  Perspective**
900 Varnum Street NE
Washington, DC  20017                      202-636-2950
                                      FAX: 202-636-2996
                                  e-mail: arcdc@juno.com
                                          www.arcdc.net

*Mary Durso, Social Worker*
*Tasha Kluseman, Manager Employment Services*
*Monita Short-Ellis, Manger Commerical Services*

Bi-annual publication from the Arc of the District of Columbia.
> *4 pages Bi-annual*

**5757  Positive Behavioral Support: Including People with Difficult Behavior in the Community**
Brookes Publishing
PO Box 10624
Baltimore, MD  21285                       410-337-9580
                                           800-638-3775
                                      FAX: 410-337-8539
                        e-mail: custserv@brookespublishing.com
                                  www.brookespublishing.com

*Paul Brooks, Owner*

This text demonstrates how people with challenging behavior can be fully included at home, at school, and in the community. Offers intervention techniques and explores the planning and assistance needed to implement nonaversive inclusion strategies. *$37.95*
> *528 pages Paperback*
> *ISBN 1-55766 -28-2*

**5758  Prevention in Community Mental Health**
Brookline Books
PO Box 1046
Cambridge, MA  02139                       617-868-0360
                                           800-666-2665
                                      FAX: 617-868-1772
                          e-mail: brooklinebks@delphi.com
                                    www.brooklinebooks.com

Describes prevention programs written through a collaborative effort between university researchers and community practitioners. The result is theoretical and practical perspectives in each chapter which provide explicit examples of how prevention focused community mental health networks operate and evaluate efforts. *$27.95*

*ISBN 0-91479 -70-0*

**5759   Resourceful Woman**
Rehabilitation Institute of Chicago
345 E Superior Street
Chicago, IL  60611                                          312-238-1000
                                                        FAX: 312-238-1205
                                                        TTY:312-908-8523
                                          e-mail: hrcwd@rehabchicago.org
                                                        rehabchicago.org

*Judy Panko Reis, Director*
*Kristi Kirchner, MD, Medical Director*
*Linda E Miller, Domestic Violence Coordinator*

National, not-for-profit, general health and service center providing accessible medical services for women with disabilities.
Conducts research into health issues concerning disabled
women and offers educational resources for healthcare professionals and women with disabilities. Provides materials and educational opportunities through its library and resource center,
newsletter, information sheets, brochures, videos and free seminars for women and their healthcare providers.
                                                                *yearly*

**5760   Strengthening the Roles of Independent Living Centers
            Through Implementing Legal Services**
Independent Living Research Utilization ILRU
2323 S Shepherd Drive
Suite 1000
Houston, TX  77019                                         713-520-0232
                                                        FAX: 713-520-5785
                                                             www.ilru.org

*Laurie Redd, Executive Director*

Featuring the Disability Law Clinic at Community Resources
for Independence (CRI) in Northern California.
                                                              *10 pages*

**5761   Supporting Young Adults Who are Deaf-Blind in Their
            Communities**
Brookes Publishing
PO Box 10624
Baltimore, MD  21285                                       410-337-9580
                                                           800-638-3775
                                                        FAX: 410-337-8539
                                   e-mail: custserv@brookespublishing.com
                                             www.brookespublishing.com

*Paul Brooks, Owner*

A Transition Planning Guide for Service Providers, Families,
and Friends. This handbook stresses the importance of person-centered planning in helping individuals who are deaf-blind
make the transition from school to adult life. *$39.95*
                                          *384 pages Paperback*
                                          *ISBN 1-55766 -61-8*

**5762   Transitioning Exceptional Children and Youth Into the
            Community**
Haworth Press
10 Alice Street
Binghamton, NY  13904                                      607-722-5857
                                                           800-429-6784
                                                        FAX: 607-722-6362
                                       e-mail: orders@haworthpress.com
                                             www.haworthpress.com

*William Cohen, Owner*

Focusing on the dynamic process of mainstreaming exceptional
children and youth into the community, experts examine some of
the exciting technological advances made to accompany the social changes enacted over the years. *$44.95*

*202 pages Hardcover*
*ISBN 0-866567-33-X*

**5763   Transitions to Adult Life**
Books on Special Children
PO Box 305
Congers, NY  10920                                         845-638-1236
                                                        FAX: 845-638-0847
                                          e-mail: irene@boscbooks.com
Transition programs that can help severely handicapped people
become participating, contributing members of the community.
*$ 37.00*
                                          *385 pages Softcover*

# Elderly

**5764   Abstracts in Social Gerontology: Current Literature on
            Aging**
National Council on the Aging
600 Maryland Avenue SW
Washington, DC  20024                                      202-479-1200
                                                        FAX: 202-479-0735

*James Firman, Chief Executive Officer*

Detailed abstracts are provided for recent major journal articles,
books, reports and other materials on many facets of aging, including: adult education, demography, family relations, institutional care and work attitudes.

**5765   Activities in Action**
Haworth Press
10 Alice Street
Binghamton, NY  13904                                      607-722-5857
                                                           800-429-6784
                                                        FAX: 607-722-6362
                                       e-mail: orders@haworthpress.com
                                             www.haworthpress.com

*William Cohen, Owner*

An invaluable resource which serves as a catalyst for professional and personal growth and provides a national forum on geriatric and activity issues. *$74.95*
                                          *98 pages Hardcover*
                                          *ISBN 1-560241-32-2*

**5766   Activities with Developmentally Disabled Elderly and
            Older Adults**
Haworth Press
10 Alice Street
Binghamton, NY  13904                                      607-722-5857
                                                           800-429-6784
                                                        FAX: 607-722-6362
                                       e-mail: orders@haworthpress.com
                                             www.haworthpress.com

*William Cohen, Owner*

Learn how to effectively plan and deliver activities for a growing number of older people with developmental disabilities. It
aims to stimulate interest and continued support for recreation
program development and implementation among developmental disability and aging service systems. *$59.95*
                                          *156 pages Hardcover*
                                          *ISBN 1-560240-92-X*

**5767   Aging & Vision News**
Lighthouse International
111 E 59th Street
New York, NY  10022                                        212-821-9200
                                                           800-829-0500
                                                        FAX: 212-821-9706
                                          e-mail: info@lighthouse.org
                                             www.lighthouse.org

*Joanna Mellor, VP Information Services*
*Tara Cortes, President*

Intended for professionals engaged in research, education or
service delivery in the field of vision and aging.

*6-12 pages BiAnnually*

**5768  Aging Eye and Low Vision**
Lighthouse International
111 E 59th Street
New York, NY 10022
212-821-9200
800-829-0500
FAX: 212-821-9706
e-mail: info@lighthouse.org

*Joanna Mellor, VP Information Services*
*Tara Cortes, President*

A study guide for physicians on common age-related vision disorders.

**5769  Aging News Alert**
CD Publications
8204 Fenton Street
Silver Spring, MD 20910
301-588-2280
800-666-6380
FAX: 301-588-6385
e-mail: cdpubs@clark.net
www.cdpublications.com/seniors/ana.htm
Publishes short articles on legislation and other federal action affecting elderly people. *$237.00*
*16-18 pages Weekly*
*ISSN 1050-31 8*

**5770  Aging Process: Therapeutic Implications**
Lippincott, Williams & Wilkins
227 E Washington Square
Philadelphia, PA 19106
215-521-8300
800-777-2295
FAX: 301-824-7390
www.lpub.com

*J Lippincott, Chief Executive Officer*

Experts examine the physiological and biological aspects of aging that impinge upon drug disposition and medical therapeutics.
*352 pages*

**5771  Aging Research & Training News**
Business Publishers
2601 University Boulevard W
Suite 200
Silver Spring, MD 20902
301-587-6300
800-274-6737
FAX: 301-587-4530
e-mail: bpinews@bpinews.com
www.bpinews.com

*Leonard A Eiserer, Publisher*
*Nancy Aldrich, Editor*
*Katie Johnson, Marketing Manager*

Essential information on aging education and staff training, funding and grant oppurtunities, the National Institute on Aging, medical and scientific research, ans statistical measures in geveontology and genetics. *$282.00*
*10 pages Monthly*

**5772  Aging and Family Therapy: Practitioner Perspectives on Golden Pond**
Haworth Press
10 Alice Street
Binghamton, NY 13904
607-722-5857
800-429-6784
FAX: 607-722-6362
e-mail: orders@haworthpress.com
www.haworthpress.com

*William Cohen, Owner*

Here are creative strategies for use in therapy with older adults and their families. This significant new book provides practitioners with information, insight, reference tools, and other sources that will contribute to more effective intervention with the elderly and their families. *$74.95*

*244 pages Hardcover*
*ISBN 0-866567-78-X*

**5773  Aging and Our Families**
Human Sciences Press
233 Spring Street
New York, NY 10013
212-229-2859
800-221-9369
FAX: 212-463-0742

Handbook for family caregivers. *$18.95*
*132 pages Paperback*
*ISBN 0-89885 -41-5*

**5774  Aging and Vision News**
National Center for Vision and Aging
111 E 59th Street
New York, NY 10022
212-821-9200
800-829-0500
FAX: 212-821-9707
TTY: 212-821-9713

*Tara Cortes, President*
*3x Year*

**5775  Aging in Stride**
CAREsource Program Development
2200 6th Avenue
Suite 833
Seattle, WA 98121
206-625-9128
800-448-5213
FAX: 206-682-2901
e-mail: service@caresource.com
www.caresource.com

*Connie Parsons, VP Marketing*
*Dennis Kenny, Owner*

Guide to aging, the special needs of older adults, and the demands of providing care and support. Experts explain potential conflicts, planning opportunities and strategies for success. Six guides. *$49.95*
*475 pages Paperback*
*ISBN 1-87886 -12-5*

**5776  Aging in the Designed Environment**
Haworth Press
10 Alice Street
Binghamton, NY 13904
607-722-5857
800-429-6784
FAX: 607-722-6362
e-mail: orders@haworthpress.com
www.haworthpress.com

*William Cohen, Owner*

The key sourcebook for physical and occupational therapists developing and implementing environmental designs for the aging. *$74.95*
*133 pages*
*ISBN 1-560240-31-8*

**5777  Aging with a Disability**
Special Needs Project
324 State Street
Suite H
Santa Barbara, CA 93101
805-962-8087
800-333-6867
FAX: 805-962-5087
www.specialneeds.com
This unique and recent book discusses the role of family, financial resources and the American health care system in the life of aging adults with developmental disabilities. *$32.95*

**5778  Assistive Technology for Older Persons**
Idaho Assistive Technology Project
129 W 3rd Street
Moscow, ID 83843
208-885-3559
800-432-8324
FAX: 208-885-3628
e-mail: rseiler@uidaho.edu
www.educ.uidaho.edu/idatech

*$5.00*

*60 pages*

**5779 California Financial Power of Attorney**
NOLO
950 Parker Street
Berkeley, CA 94710        510-549-1976
       800-955-4775
       FAX: 510-548-5902
       www.nolo.com

*Maira Dizgalvis, Trade Customer Service Manager*
*Susan McConnell, Director Sales*
*Natasha Kaluza, Sales Assistant*

A plain-English book packed with forms and instructions to give a trusted person the legal authority to handle your financial affairs.
       *paperback*

**5780 Caring for Alzheimer's Patients**
Plenum Publishing Corporation
233 Spring Street
New York, NY 10013        212-242-1490
       800-221-9369
       FAX: 212-463-0742
       e-mail: info@plenum.com
This handbook is designed for families, friends, and health-care professionals coping with the myriad of problems encountered by those afflicted with Alzheimer's disease. *$22.95*
       *308 pages Cloth*
       *ISBN 3-06431 -98-*

**5781 Caring for Those You Love: A Guide to Compassionate Care for the Aged**
Horizon Publishers
191 N 650 E
Bountiful, UT 84010        801-295-9451
       800-453-0812
       FAX: 801-295-0196

*Duane Crowther, Owner*

This book is a practical guide to coping with special problems of the aged and infirm, and examines the many challenges of caring for the elderly on a personal and family level. *$12.98*

       *ISBN 0-88290 -70-9*

**5782 Caring for the Disabled Elderly**
Brookings Institution
1775 Massachusetts Avenue NW
Washington, DC 20036        202-797-6000
       FAX: 202-797-6004
       e-mail: bibooks@brookings.edu
       www.brookings.edu

*Strobe Talbott, President*

Financial information for the elderly. *$31.95*
       *318 pages Cloth*
       *ISBN 0-815774-97-4*

**5783 Choose the Right Long Term Care: Home Care Assisted Living and Nursing Homes**
NOLO
950 Parker Street
Berkeley, CA 94710        510-549-1976
       800-955-4775
       FAX: 510-548-5902
       www.nolo.com

*Maira Dizgalvis, Trade Customer Service Manager*
*Susan McConnell, Director Sales*
*Natasha Kaluza, Sales Assistant*

Don't guess. Use this book to figure out how to choose a nursing home, or find a viable alternative. Covers how to get the most out of Medicare and other benefit programs. *$21.95*

*336 pages paperback*
*ISBN 0-873375-15-7*

**5784 Chronically Disabled Elderly in Society**
Greenwood Publishing Group
88 Post Road W
Suite 5007
Westport, CT 06880        203-226-3571
       FAX: 203-222-1502
       www.greenwood.com

*Wayne Smith, President*

This timely work increases awareness of and knowledge about problems of societal living among the chronically disabled elderly, with implications for policy makers, educational institutions, advocacy groups, families and individuals. Hardcover.
       *160 pages $52.95 - $55*
       *ISBN 0-313291-09-8*

**5785 Communication Disorders in Aging**
Gallaudet University Press
800 Florida Avenue NE
Washington, DC 20002        202-651-5000
       800-451-1073
       FAX: 202-651-5489

*Erving Jordan, President*

This text presents contemporary practices in the medical and clinical assessment of the aged, reviews clinical evaluation techniques, and provides a comprehensive discussion of neurological imaging techniques. *$39.95*
       *528 pages Hardcover*

**5786 Coping and Caring: Living with Alzheimer's Disease**
AARP Fulfillment
601 E Street NW
Washington, DC 20049        202-434-2277
       800-424-3410
       FAX: 202-434-3443
       e-mail: member@aarp.org
       www.aarp.org

*William Novelli, Chief Executive Officer*

Addresses the questions: What is Alzheimer's? How does the disease progress? How long does it last? How can families cope?

       *24 pages*

**5787 Directory of Self-Help/Mutual Aid Support Groups for Older People**
Lighthouse International
111 E 59th Street
New York, NY 10022        212-821-9200
       800-829-0500
       FAX: 212-821-9706
       e-mail: info@lighthouse.org

*Joanna Mellor, VP Information Services*
*Tara Cortes, President*

State-by-state listings of over 650 support groups for older people with impaired vision, plus listings of state commissions for the blind, self-help clearinghouses, vision rehabilitation agencies, and national resource organizations. *$10.00*

**5788 Domestic Mistreatment of the Elderly: Towards Prevention**
AARP Fulfillment
601 E Street NW
Washington, DC 20049        202-434-2277
       800-424-3410
       FAX: 202-434-3443
       e-mail: member@aarp.org
       www.aarp.org

*William Novelli, Chief Executive Officer*

This comprehensive publication addresses the problem of mistreatment or neglect in the home.

*39 pages*

**5789  Early Story of Alzheimer's Disease**
Lippincott, Williams & Wilkins
227 E Washington Square
Philadelphia, PA 19106
215-521-8300
800-777-2295
FAX: 301-824-7390
www.lpub.com

*J Lipppincott, Chief Executive Officer*

Translation of the historical papers by Alos Alzheimer. *$58.50*
*160 pages Illustrated*
*ISBN 0-88167-68-4*

**5790  Elder Abuse**
Human Sciences Press
233 Spring Street
New York, NY 10013
212-229-2859
800-221-9369
FAX: 212-463-0742

Practice, policy and laws for abuse on the aging.
*232 pages Cloth*
*ISBN 0-89885-15-6*

**5791  Elder Care**
Center for Public Representation
PO Box 260049
Madison, WI 53726
608-251-4008
800-369-0388
FAX: 608-251-1263
www.law.wisc.edu/pal

A compendium of alternatives for providing and financing long-term care. This practical guide provides the most comprehensive and comforting information to help navigate a number of consumer mine fields. *$16.95*
*224 pages*
*ISBN 0-87337-13-5*

**5792  Enabling News**
Access II Independent Living Centers
611 W Johnson Street
Gallatin, MO 64640
660-663-2423
FAX: 660-663-2517
e-mail: access@accessii.org
www.accessii.org

*Debra Hawman, Executive Director*
*Charlotte Hamilton, Program Manager*
*8 pages Quarterly*

**5793  Exercise and the Older Adult**
Kendall/Hunt Publishing Company
1900 Association Drive
Reston, VA 20191
703-476-3400
800-213-7193
FAX: 703-476-9527
e-mail: aaalf@aahperd.org
www.aahperd.org

*Jan A Seaman MBA PED, Executive Director*
*Michael Davis, Manager*

The latest information on physical activity for the older adults is in this textbook. Biomechanics, exercise physiology, health issues, sensory-motor function and measurement are covered by leading experts in the field. Other topics addressed include low-impact aerobics, strength development, exercise and activities for the frail elderly. *$35.00*

*202 pages*
*ISBN 0-787210-04-8*

**5794  Falling in Old Age**
Springer Publishing Company
536 Broadway
New York, NY 10012
212-431-4370
877-687-7476
FAX: 212-941-7842
e-mail: marketing@springerpub.com
www.springerpub.com

*Annette Imperati, Marketing/Sales Director*
*Ursula Springer, President*

Presented are practical techniques for the prevention of falls and for determining and correcting the causes.

**5795  Functional Fitness Assessment for Adults**
American Alliance for Health, Phys. Ed. & Dance
1900 Association Drive
Reston, VA 20191
703-476-3400
FAX: 703-476-9527
e-mail: aaalf@aahperd.org

*Michael Davis, Manager*

This field test assesses the functional fitness of adults over 60 years of age. It is designed to serve the larger population through field based measurement techniques that can be used in a facility where older persons live and can be conducted by personnel not necessarily trained for clinical responsibilities. *$7.50*
*24 pages*
*ISBN 0-88314-47-6*

**5796  Handbook of Assistive Devices for the Handicapped Elderly**
Haworth Press
10 Alice Street
Binghamton, NY 13904
607-722-5857
800-429-6784
FAX: 607-722-6362
e-mail: orders@haworthpress.com
www.haworthpress.com

*William Cohen, Owner*

Concise yet comprehensive reference of assistive devices for handicapped elders. *$34.95*
*77 pages Hardcover*
*ISBN 0-866561-52-8*

**5797  Handbook on Ethnicity, Aging and Mental Health**
Greenwood Publishing Group
88 Post Road W
Suite 5007
Westport, CT 06880
203-226-3571
FAX: 203-222-1502
www.greenwood.com

*Wayne Smith, President*

State-of-the-art reference by leading experts and first book-length appraisal of research, practices and policies concerning mental health needs of the ethnic elderly in America. *$95-$99.50.*
*376 pages Hardcover*
*ISBN 0-313282-04-8*

**5798  Health Care of the Aged**
Haworth Press
10 Alice Street
Binghamton, NY 13904
607-722-5857
800-429-6784
FAX: 607-722-6362
e-mail: orders@haworthpress.com
www.haworthpress.com

*William Cohen, Owner*

Focusing on the need for developing new service delivery models for the aged, this book examines fiscal, political, and social criteria influencing this challenge of the 1990's. The aged are caught in the sweeping changes currently occurring in the financing, organizing and delivery of human health care services. *$74.95*
*183 pages Hardcover*
*ISBN 1-560240-65-2*

**5799    Health Promotion and Disease Prevention**
Lippincott, Williams & Wilkins
227 E Washington Square
Philadelphia, PA  19106                    215-521-8300
                                          800-777-2295
                                     FAX: 301-824-7390
                                          www.lpub.com

*J Lippincott, Chief Executive Officer*
Professional directory offering information on health care and rehabilitation for the elderly. *$87.00*
*218 pages*
*ISBN 0-88167-90-0*

**5800    International Health Guide for Senior Citizen Travelers**

Pilot Books
PO Box 2102
Greenport, NY  11944                       631-477-1094
                                     FAX: 631-477-0978
Covers essential pre-departure health planning; advice on specific health concerns; disease prevention and more. *$4.95*

**5801    Managing Aging and Human Services Agencies**
Springer Publishing Company
536 Broadway
New York, NY  10012                        212-431-4370
                                          877-687-7476
                                     FAX: 212-941-7842
                        e-mail: marketing@springerpub.com
                                       www.springerpub.com

*Annette Imperati, Marketing/Sales Director*
*Ursula Springer, President*
Offers specialized information for the human resources professional who works with the elderly. *$27.95*
*160 pages*

**5802    Mastering the Medicare Maze**
Center for Public Representation
PO Box 260049
Madison, WI  53726                         608-251-4008
                                          800-369-0388
                                     FAX: 606-251-1263
This book provides simple explanations of how to appeal denied Medicare claims. Less than 3% of Medicare claims are ever appealed. But of those that are, over 60% are successful in returning dollars to beneficiaries. With simple instructions, this book tells you how to do it and includes all the necessary forms. *$9.95*
*128 pages*
*ISBN 0-93262-40-2*

**5803    Medicare Maximization**
Center for Public Representation
PO Box 260049
Madison, WI  53726                         608-251-4008
                                          800-369-0388
                                     FAX: 606-251-1263
                        e-mail: cpr@lawmail.law.wisc.edu
                                    www.law.wisc.edu/pal
This manual for nursing homes provides information on Medicare billing procedures, Medicare coverage guidelines - Part A and Part B as well as Medicare Bed Certification for nursing homes. Chapters with examples and exercises give you the knowledge to maximize Medicare reimbursements. *$39.95*

*150 pages*
*ISBN 0-93262-34-8*

**5804    Mentally Impaired Elderly: Strategies and Interventions to Maintain Function**
Haworth Press
10 Alice Street
Binghamton, NY  13904                      607-722-5857
                                          800-429-6784
                                     FAX: 607-722-6362
                        e-mail: orders@haworthpress.com
                                     www.haworthpress.com

*S Harrington-Miller, Advertising*
*William Cohen, Owner*
Provides effective support and sensitive care for the most vulnerable segment of the elderly population, those with mental impairment. *$74.95*
*171 pages Hardcover*
*ISBN 1-560241-68-3*

**5805    Mirrored Lives: Aging Children and Elderly Parents**
Greenwood Publishing Group
88 Post Road W
Suite 5007
Westport, CT  06880                        203-226-3571
                                     FAX: 203-222-1502
                                       www.greenwood.com

*Wayne Smith, President*
Discusses geriatric decline connected to nonterminal illness in old age. Koch takes a sensitive but thorough look at the declining years of his father. *$19.95-$21.95.*
*240 pages Hardcover*
*ISBN 0-275936-71-6*

**5806    Now Where Did I Put My Keys?**
AARP Fulfillment
601 E Street NW
Washington, DC  20049                      202-434-2277
                                          800-424-3410
                                     FAX: 202-434-3443
                             e-mail: member@aarp.org
                                          www.aarp.org

*William Novelli, Chief Executive Officer*
Your copies of this brochure won't last long on your information counter.

**5807    Older & Wiser: A Workbook for Coping with Aging**
New Harbinger Publications
5674 Shattuck Avenue
Oakland, CA  94609                         510-652-0215
                                          800-748-6273
                                     FAX: 510-652-5472
                   e-mail: customerservice@newharbinger.com

*Matthew McKay, Owner*
This compassion guide teaches the practical skills and elicits personal insight necessary to meet the demands of aging in our society. *$12.95*
*300 pages*
*ISBN 1-87923-10-5*

**5808    Older Adults with Developmental Disabilities: Optimizing Choice and Change**
Brookes Publishing
PO Box 10624
Baltimore, MD  21285                       410-337-9580
                                          800-638-3775
                                     FAX: 410-337-8539
                   e-mail: custserv@brookespublishing.com
                                   www.brookespublishing.com

*Paul Brooks, Owner*
*$37.00*

*416 pages Paperback*
*ISBN 1-55766 -20-0*

**5809   On Your Behalf**
CAREsource Program Development
505 Seattle Tower
Seattle, WA  98101                          206-625-9128
                                            800-448-5213
                                       FAX: 206-682-2901
                            e-mail: service@caresource.com
                                       www.caresource.com

*Dennis Kenny, Owner*

This book takes the mystery out of very important sets of legal options. It gives lay people as well as advisors, service providers, and caregivers the information they need to understand their options and the importance of individual choice.
*16 pages Books & Video*
*ISBN 1-87886 -14-1*

**5810   Operation Help: A Mental Health Advocate Guide to Medicaid**
Nat'l Council for Community Behavioral Healthcare
12300 Twinbrook Parkway
Suite 320
Rockville, MD  20852                        301-984-6200
                                       FAX: 301-881-7159
                                            www.nccbh.org

*Linda Rosenberg, Chief Executive Officer*

Explains the Medicaid entitlement program in easy-to-understand language and focuses on the needs of adults with serious mental illness, children with serious emotional disturbance and elderly persons who need mental health care. *$17.00*

**5811   Perspective on Aging**
National Council on the Aging
600 Maryland Avenue SW
Washington, DC  20024                       202-479-1200
                                       FAX: 202-479-0735

*James Firman, Chief Executive Officer*

Explores significant developments in the field of aging, including disabilities, through opinion articles, profiles and book reviews. *$4.00*

**5812   Perspectives on Prevention and Treatment of Cancer in the Elderly**
Lippincott, Williams & Wilkins
227 E Washington Square
Philadelphia, PA  19106                     215-521-8300
                                            800-777-2295
                                       FAX: 301-824-7390
                                            www.lpub.com

*J Lippincott, Chief Executive Officer*

This book presents an exchange of ideas and information on the complexities of cancer and aging. Clinicians and investigators from a wide range of pertinent disciplines highlight the issues unique to the elderly patient in cancer prevention, diagnosis and treatment. *$113.00*
*360 pages*

**5813   Prescriptions for Independence**
American Foundation for the Blind/AFB Press
PO Box 1020
Sewickley, PA  15143                        412-741-1142
                                            800-232-3044
                                       FAX: 412-741-0609
                           e-mail: afborders@abdintl.com
                                            www.afb.org
Easy-to-read manual on how older visually impaired persons can pursue their interests and activities in community residences, senior centers, long-term care facilities and other community settings. Paperback. *$29.95*

*ISBN 0-891282-44-0*

**5814   Rehabilitation in the Aging**
Lippincott, Williams & Wilkins
227 E Washington Square
Philadelphia, PA  19106                     215-521-8300
                                            800-777-2295
                                       FAX: 301-824-7390
                                            www.lpub.com

*J Lippincott, Chief Executive Officer*

This volume provides the physician with a comprehensive approach to the medical and rehabilitative management of geriatric patients. *$82.50*
*390 pages*

**5815   Senior Citizens and the Law**
Center for Public Representation
PO Box 260049
Madison, WI  53726                          608-251-4008
                                            800-369-0388
                                       FAX: 606-251-1263
                         e-mail: cpr@lawmail.law.wisc.edu
                                         www.law.wisc.edu
An introduction to legal problems facing the elderly in Wisconsin. This edition discusses legal problems associated with Social Security, Medicare, SSI, guardianship and its alternatives, community-based services, probate, taxes, private health insurance and consumer protection. *$5.00*

*ISBN 0-936226-15-1*

**5816   Sharing Solutions: A Newsletter for Support Groups**
Lighthouse International
111 E 59th Street
New York, NY  10022                         212-821-9200
                                            800-829-0500
                                       FAX: 212-821-9706
                              e-mail: info@lighthouse.org
                                        www.lighthouse.org

*Joanna Mellor, VP Information Services*
*Tara Cortes, President*

A newsletter for members and leaders of support groups for older adults with impaired vision. The letter provides a forum for support groups members to network and share information, printed in a very large type format.

**5817   So Many of My Friends Have Moved Away or Died**
AARP Fulfillment
601 E Street NW
Washington, DC  20049                       202-434-2277
                                            800-424-3410
                                       FAX: 202-434-3443
                                e-mail: member@aarp.org
                                            www.aarp.org

*William Novelli, Chief Executive Officer*

A typical problem faced by older persons, discussion focuses on coping with the loss of old friends and finding new ones.

**5818   Social Security Bulletin**
US Social Security Administration
4301 Connecticut Avenue NW
Room 209
Washington, DC  20008                       202-523-0588
                                            800-772-1213
                                       FAX: 202-282-7219
                                       www.ssa.gov/policy
Reports on results of research and analysis pertinent to the Social Security and SSI programs. *$16.00*

*Monthly*

**5819 Social Security, Medicare, and Pensions**
NOLO
950 Parker Street
Berkeley, CA 94710
510-549-1976
800-955-4775
FAX: 510-548-5902
www.nolo.com

*Maira Dizgalvis, Trade Customer Service Manager*
*Susan McConnell, Director Sales*
*Natasha Kaluza, Sales Assistant*

A plain-speaking guide explaining the ins and outs of the Social Security system; retirement, disability and benefits for dependents and survivors. *$24.95*
*320 pages paperback*
*ISBN 0-873374-87-8*

**5820 Successful Models of Community Long Term Care Services for the Elderly**
Haworth Press
10 Alice Street
Binghamton, NY 13904
607-722-5857
800-429-6784
FAX: 607-722-6362
e-mail: orders@haworthpress.com
www.haworthpress.com

*S Harroington-Miller, Advertising*
*William Cohen, Owner*

Experienced practitioners provide examples of successful community-based long term care service programs for the elderly. *$74.95*
*174 pages*
*ISBN 0-866569-87-1*

**5821 Therapeutic Interventions in Alzheimer's**
Aspen Publishers
200 Orchard Ridge Drive
Gaithersburg, MD 20878
301-698-7100
800-234-1660
FAX: 301-695-7931
www.aspenpublishers.com
A program of functional skills for activities of daily living.
Hardcover. *$65.00*
*256 pages*
*ISBN 0-834209-30-6*

**5822 Topics in Geriatric Rehabilitation**
Aspen Publishers
200 Orchard Ridge Drive
Gaithersburg, MD 20878
301-698-7100
800-638-8437
FAX: 301-695-7931
www.aspenpublishers.com
Peer-review journal presenting clinical, basic and applied research as well as theoretical information. Published quarterly. *$86.00*
*90 pages*

**5823 Unloving Care**
Harper Collins Publishers/Basic Books
10 E 53rd Street
New York, NY 10022
212-207-7000
800-242-7737
FAX: 212-207-7203

*Jane Friedman, Chief Executive Officer*

A leading public health expert gives a definitive account of what nursing homes are really like. *$9.95*

*305 pages*
*ISBN 0-46508 -81-3*

**5824 Vision and Aging: Issues in Social Work Practice**
Haworth Press
10 Alice Street
Binghamton, NY 13904
607-722-5857
800-429-6784
FAX: 607-722-6362
e-mail: orders@haworthpress.com
www.haworthpress.com

*S Harrington-Miller, Advertising*
*William Cohen, Owner*

Responds to the needs of the growing population of blind or severely disabled elderly. *$74.95*
*196 pages Hardcover*
*ISBN 1-560241-99-3*

**5825 Visually Impaired Seniors as Senior Companions: A Reference Guide**
American Foundation for the Blind/AFB Press
PO Box 1020
Sewickley, PA 15143
412-741-1142
800-232-3044
FAX: 412-741-0609
e-mail: afborders@abdintl.com
www.afb.org
This useful guide describes the Senior Companion Program that is intended to broaden opportunities for older persons with disabilities. Appendix includes training materials, evaluation forms, recruitment and public relations information. *$15.00*
*108 pages Paperback*
*ISBN 0-891282-38-6*

**5826 Work, Health and Income Among the Elderly**
Brookings Institution
1775 Massachusetts Avenue NW
Washington, DC 20036
202-797-6000
FAX: 202-797-6004
e-mail: bibooks@brookings.edu
www.brookings.edu

*Strobe Talbott, President*

Employment, health and financial information for the elderly. *$26.95*
*318 pages Cloth*
*ISBN 0-815774-97-4*

# Employment

**5827 A Guide for People with Disabilities Seeking Employment**
US Department of Justice
950 Pennsylvania Avenue NW Drs
- Nyav
Washington, DC 20530
202-586-5000
800-574-0301
FAX: 202-307-1197
www.ada.gov

*Joanne Graham, Manager*

A 2-page pamplet for people with disabilities providing a general explanation of the employment provisions of the ADA and how to file a complaint with the Equal Employment Opportunity Commission.

**5828 ADA Questions and Answers**
US Department of Justice
950 Pennsylvania Avenue NW Drs
- Nyav
Washington, DC 20530
202-586-5000
800-574-0301
FAX: 202-307-1197
www.ada.gov

*Joanne Graham, Manager*

A 31-page booklet giving an overview of the ADA's requirements affecting employers, businesses, nonprofit service agencies, and state and local governments programs, including public transportation.

**5829    ANCOR Wage and Hour Handbook**
American Network of Community Options & Resources
1101 King Street
Suite 380
Alexandria, VA  22314                          703-535-7850
                                          FAX: 703-535-7860
                                    e-mail: ancor@ancor.org
                                               www.ancor.org

*Renee L Pietrangelo, CEO*
*Suellen Galbraith, Director Public Policy*

This useful publication contains the latest rules and interpretations from the U.S. Department of Labor relative to employment in residential support services for people with disabilities, including copies of enforcement policies and letters of interpretation. It outlines in detail when exemptions from miniimum wage and overtime rules can be applied,a nd when and how employees may be paid on a salary basis. Sample staffing patterns are provided.
*121 pages*

**5830    Americans with Disabilities**
Federal Consumer Information Center
Department 513j
Pueblo, CO  81009                              719-948-3334
                                               888-878-3256
                                          FAX: 719-948-9724
                                 e-mail: catalog.pueblo@gsa.gov
                                            www.pueblo.gsa.gov

*Alfred Pino, Manager*

Explains how civil rights of persons with disabilities are protected at work and in public places.

**5831    Americans with Disabilities Act: Questions and Answers**

Federal Consumer Information Center
Department 513j
Pueblo, CO  81009

                                               888-878-3256
                                          FAX: 719-948-9724
                                 e-mail: catalog.pueblo@gsa.gov
                                            www.pueblo.gsa.gov

*Judi Mahaney, Public Affairs*

Explains how the Civil Rights of Persons with disabilities are protected at work and in public places. Free.

**5832    Career Education for Handicapped Individuals**
McGraw-Hill, School Publishing
220 E Danieldale Road
Desoto, TX  75115                              972-224-1111
                                               800-442-9685
                                          FAX: 972-228-1982
                                               mhschool.com

*Joseph Gavigan, President*

Based on a life-centered career education program that goes beyond elementary school level to include handicapped people of all ages.
*454 pages*

**5833    Disability Under the Fair Employment & Housing Act: What You Should Know About the Law**
California Department of Fair Employment & Housing
2014 T Street
Suite 210
Sacramento, CA  95814                          916-324-4244
                                               800-884-1684
                                          FAX: 916-227-2870
                                               www.dfeh.ca.gov

*Dia S Poole, Deputy Director Public Affairs*
*David Supkofl, Manager*

*$12.90*

ISSN 9311-5126

**5834    Discrimination is Against the Law**
California Department of Fair Employment & Housing
2014 T Street
Suite 210
Sacramento, CA  95814                          916-324-4244
                                               800-884-1684
                                          FAX: 916-227-2870
                                               www.dfeh.ca.gov

*Dia S Poole, Deputy Director Public Affairs*
*David Supkofl, Manager*

*$12.90*

ISSN 9311-5114

**5835    Earning a Living**
Accent Books & Products
PO Box 700
Bloomington, IL  61702                         309-378-2961
                                               800-787-8444
                                          FAX: 309-378-4420
                                  e-mail: acmtlvng@aol.com

*Raymond C Cheever, Publisher*
*Betty Garee, Editor*

Discusses how to prepare a person for a career, what to say in an interview, and gives examples of both home businesses and jobs away from home. Tells how to modify a worksite and how to be successful on the job. *$9.50*
*88 pages Paperback*
*ISBN 0-91570 -23-0*

**5836    Employee Complaint Handling: Tested Techniques for Human Resource Managers**
Greenwood Publishing Group
88 Post Road W
Suite 5007
Westport, CT  06880                            203-226-3571
                                          FAX: 203-222-1502
                                               www.greenwood.com

*Wayne Smith, President*

Examines issues of human relations and communications as well as those of legal and ethical concerns. *$59.95*
*208 pages Hardcover*
*ISBN 0-899304-33-8*

**5837    Employment Discrimination Based on Disability**
California Department of Fair Employment & Housing
2014 T Street
Suite 210
Sacramento, CA  95814                          916-324-4244
                                               800-884-1684
                                          FAX: 916-227-2870
                                               www.dfeh.ca.gov

*Dia S Poole, Deputy Director Public Affairs*
*David Supkofl, Manager*

*$12.90*

ISSN 9311-8413

**5838    Employment in the Mainstream**
Mainstream
3 Bethesda Metro Center
Suite 830
Bethesda, MD  20814                            301-961-9299
                                               800-247-1380
                                          FAX: 301-891-8778
                                 e-mail: info@mainstreaminc.org
                                            www.mainstreaminc.org

*David Pichette, Executive Director*
*Fritz Rumpel, Editor*
*Charles Moster*

Reports on issues, ideas, problems and solutions in employing persons with any kind of physical or mental disability. Quarterly magazine. *$25.00*
*32 pages*

**5839    Encyclopedia of Basic Employment and Daily Living Skills**
PO Box 130
Indian Rocks Beach, FL  33785                727-593-2700
                                             800-255-9085
                                        FAX: 727-595-2685

*Ruth Bragman PhD, President*
*Phillip Roy, Manager*
*$450.00*
*1200 pages*
*ISBN 1-568182-25-2*

**5840    Good Employee Is Capable, Conscientious, Productive**
American Foundation for the Blind/AFB Press
PO Box 1020
Sewickley, PA  15143                         412-741-1142
                                             800-232-3044
                                        FAX: 412-741-0609
                              e-mail: afborders@abdintl.com
                                           www.afb.org
Answers employers' questions about the blind and visually handicapped and provides assurance to employees with visual impairments can get to work, perform their jobs safely and require little in the way of special training.

*ISBN 0-891289-19-4*

**5841    Guide to Successful Employment for Individuals with Autism**
Brookes Publishing
PO Box 10624
Baltimore, MD  21285                         410-337-9585
                                             800-638-3775
                                        FAX: 410-337-8539
                    e-mail: custserv@brookespublishing.com
                               www.brookespublishing.com

*Melissa Behm, President*
Describing all aspects of job placement, this book details strategies for assessing workers, networking for job opportunities, and tailoring job supports to each individual. Also illustrates how to help individuals with autism become productive workers, and with detailed descriptions of specific jobs help provide ideas for employment. *$ 32.95*
*336 pages Paperback*
*ISBN 1-55766 -71-5*

**5842    Handbook of Career Planning for Special Needs Students**
Pro-Ed Publications
8700 Shoal Creek Boulevard
Austin, TX  78757                            512-451-3246
                                             800-897-3202
                                        FAX: 512-451-8542
                               e-mail: info@proedinc.com
                                        www.proedinc.com

*Donald Hammill, Owner*
The practitioner's guide will show you how to help special needs adolescents and young adults overcome barriers to employment by identifying goals and problems, assessing interests and aptitudes, involving client families and developing communication skills. *$46.00*

*358 pages Hardcover*
*ISBN 0-890797-06-4*

**5843    Job Hunting Tips for the So-Called Handicapped**
Special Needs Project
324 State Street
Suite H
Santa Barbara, CA  93101                     805-962-8087
                                             800-333-6867
                                        FAX: 805-962-5087
                                        www.specialneeds.com

*Richard Bolles*
This nifty booklet from the guru of job hunting himself is sincere, useful and brief. *$4.95*

**5844    Job Search Handbook for People with Disabi lities**
JIST Publishing
8902 Otis Avenue
Indianapolis, IN  46216                      317-613-4200
                                             800-648-5478
                                        FAX: 800-547-8329
                                     e-mail: info@jist.com
                                           www.jist.com

*Mike Farr, President*
Provides a complete career planning and job search guide identifying the job hunter's strengths and abilities. Explore career options, locate job openings in the hidden job market, when and how to tell a potential employer about a disability, write powerful resumes, cover letters, and follow up correspondence. *$35.00*
*288 pages 2003*
*ISBN 1-557666-52-0*

**5845    Learning a Living: A Guide to Planning Yo ur Career and Finding a Job for People with ADD**
Woodbine House
6510 Bells Mill Road
Bethesda, MD  20817                          301-897-3570
                                             800-843-7323
                                        FAX: 301-897-5838
                            e-mail: info@woodbinehouse.com
                                     www.woodbinehouse.com

*Irv Shapell, Owner*
Focuses on helping people with learning disabilities, dyslexia, and ADD. The author has worked with thousands of people with these disabilities and shares her personal experiences. Provides a wide array of vital information, tips, insights, and advice for anyone seeking to overcome learning disabilities and pursue a successful career. *$ 18.95*
*340 pages 2000*
*ISBN 0-933149-87-5*

**5846    Let Community Employment be the Goal for Individuals with Autism**
Autism Society of North Carolina Bookstore
505 Oberlin Road
Suite 230
Raleigh, NC  27605                           919-743-0204
                                             800-442-2762
                                        FAX: 919-743-0208
                       e-mail: dcoffey@autismsociety-nc.org
                                     www.autismsociety-nc.org

*Darla Coffey, Bookstore Manager*
*Jill Keel, Executive Director*
A guide designed for people who are responsible for preparing individuals with autism to enter the work force. *$7.00*

**5847 Making Self-Employment Work for People wit h Disabilities**
Brookes Publishing
PO Box 10624
Baltimore, MD 21285                410-337-9580
                                   800-638-3775
                         FAX: 410-337-8539
        e-mail: custserv@brookespublishing.com
                www.brookespublishing.com

*Paul Brooks, Owner*

Practical support for individuals with significant disabilities in starting and maintaining a small business. Covers building a business plan; pinpointing interests, strengths, and goals; and finding helpful information and support *$35.00*
        *288 pages 2003*
        *ISBN 1-557666-52-0*

**5848 Making the Workplace Accessible: Guidelines, Costs and Resources**
Spina Bifida Association of America
4590 Macarthur Boulevard NW
Suite 250
Washington, DC 20007              202-944-3285
                                  800-621-3141
                         FAX: 202-944-3295
                e-mail: sbaa@sbaa.org
                        www.sbaa.org

*Fritz Rumpel, Editor*
*Cindy Brownstein, Chief Executive Officer*

A 20 page reference guide on how to provide physical access to persons with disabilities in a cost effective manner. *$9.00*

**5849 Marketing Your Abilities: A Guide for the Disabled Job-Seeker**
Mainstream
3 Bethesda Metro Center
Suite 830
Bethesda, MD 20814               301-961-9299
                         FAX: 301-654-6714
                e-mail: info@mainstreaminc.org

*Charles Moster*

A publication designed to assist the individual with a disability in conducting a successful job search. Major topics include how to write an effective resume and how to give a good interview. *$4.95*
        *24 pages*

**5850 Meeting the Needs of Employees with Disabilities**
Resources for Rehabilitation
33 Bedford Street
Suite 19a
Lexington, MA 02420              781-368-9094
                         FAX: 781-368-9096

*Susan Greenblatt*

Provides information to help people with disabilities retain or obtain employment. Information on government programs and laws, supported employment, training programs, environmental adaptations and the transition from school to work are included. Chapters on mobility impairment, vision impairment and hearing and speech impairments. *$ 47.95*
        *167 pages Biennial*
        *ISBN 0-92971 -13-5*

**5851 Mental Health in the Workplace: An Employer's & Manager's Guide**
Greenwood Publishing Group
88 Post Road W
Suite 5007
Westport, CT 06880               203-226-3571
                         FAX: 203-222-1502
                www.greenwood.com

*Wayne Smith, President*

A guide to the impact of mental health issues on the workplace, with special attention to complying with provisions of the Americas with Disabilities Act. *$59.95*

*296 pages $59.95 - $67.95*
*ISBN 0-899307-03-5*

**5852 Model Program Operation Manual: Business Enterprise Program Supervisors**
Mississippi State University
PO Box 6189
Mississippi State, MS 39762      662-325-2001
                                 800-675-7782
                         FAX: 662-325-8989
                www.blind.msstate.edu

*Kelly Schaefer, Publications Manager*
*Elton Moore, Executive Director*

This monograph serves as a Model Program Operation Manual for Business Enterprise Program Supervisors who administer Randolph-Sheppard vending facilities under the Randolph-Sheppard Act. A wide variety of topics are covered including the role of the State Committee of Blind Venders, the role and responsibilities of the Vending Facility Operator, model qualification, for potential Facility Managers, guidelines for location of vending facilities and policies for closing vending facilities. *$20.00*
        *199 pages Paperback*

**5853 More Than a Job: Securing Satisfying Careers for People with Disabilities**
Brookes Publishing
PO Box 10624
Baltimore, MD 21285              410-337-9585
                                 800-638-3775
                         FAX: 410-337-8539
        e-mail: custserv@brookespublishing.com
                www.brookespublishing.com

*Melissa Behm, President*

This text shows employment professionals how to transform job placement into career counseling for people with physical and developmental disabilities. Issues such as transition from school to adult life, transportation, social relationships, and community access are also discussed. *$34.95*
        *368 pages Paperback 1998*
        *ISBN 1-55766 -28-9*

**5854 No More Job Interviews!: Self-Employment Strategies for People with Disabilities**
Training Resource Network

Offers self-employment strategies targeted to people with disabilities, the largest unemployed minority group in the US today. The book reflects recent charges in business, offering Internet tips and business training trends. Also includes four business plans and profiles of individuals with disabilities. *$29.95*
        *183 pages 2000*
        *ISBN 1-883302-36-6*

**5855 Paraplegics and Quadriplegics**
Mainstream
3 Bethesda Metro Center
Suite 830
Bethesda, MD 20814               301-961-9299
                                 800-247-1380
                         FAX: 301-654-6714
                e-mail: info@mainstreaminc.org

*Charles Moster*

Mainstreaming paraplegics and quadriplegics into the workplace. *$2.50*

*12 pages*

**5856 People with Hearing Loss and the Workplace Guide for Employers/ADA Compliances**
Self Help for Hard of Hearing People
7910 Woodmont Avenue
Suite 1200
Bethesda, MD 20814
301-657-2248
FAX: 301-913-9413
e-mail: national@shhh.org

*Nancy Macklin, Business Manager*
*Terry Portis, Executive Director*

A guide for both people with hearing loss and their employers to learn about accommodations under the law. Includes employment guidelines, resource list of manufacturers and case studies. *$15.00*
*40 pages Paperback*

**5857 Planning Reasonable Accommodations: A Cost Effective Guide in a Legal Framework**
Spina Bifida Association of America
4590 Macarthur Boulevard NW
Suite 250
Washington, DC 20007
202-944-3285
800-621-3141
FAX: 202-944-3295
e-mail: sbaa@sbaa.org
www.sbaa.org

*Fritz Rumpel, Editor*
*Cindy Brownstein, Chief Executive Officer*

A 24 page reference guide on the reasonable accomodations process under the ADA. *$9.00*

**5858 Project LINK Guidebook**
Mainstream
3 Bethesda Metro Center
Suite 830
Bethesda, MD 20814
301-961-9299
800-247-1380
FAX: 301-654-6714
e-mail: info@mainstreaminc.org

*Charles Moster*

A manual for operating an employment services program for persons with disabilities. *$49.95*
*78 pages*

**5859 Providing Employment Support for People with Long-Term Mental Illness**
Brookes Publishing
PO Box 10624
Baltimore, MD 21285
410-337-9585
800-638-3775
FAX: 410-337-8539
e-mail: custserv@brookespublishing.com
www.brookespublishing.com

*Melissa Behm, President*

Choices, resources, and practical strategies. Topics covered include natural supports, behavior management, Social Security issues, vocational barriers to productive employment, and workers' rights under the Americans with Disabilities Act. Also includes detailed discussions of specific psychiatric diagnoses vocational assessment and career development, crisis intervention, interdisciplinary support models, and more. *$30.95*

*352 pages Paperback*
*ISBN 1-55766 -90-1*

**5860 Questions and Answers: The ADA and Hiring Police Officers**
US Department of Justice
950 Pennsylvania Avenue NW Drs
- Nyav
Washington, DC 20530
202-586-5000
800-574-0301
FAX: 202-307-1197
www.ada.gov

*Joanne Graham, Manager*

A 5-page publication providing information on ADA requirements for interviewing and hiring police officers.

**5861 Road Ahead: Transition to Adult Life for Persons with Disabilities**
Training Resource Network

Explores transition planning, assessment, instructional strategies, career development and support, social life, quality of life, supported living, and post-secondary education. *$32.95*
*223 pages 2002*
*ISBN 1-883302-46-3*

**5862 Supported Employment for Disabled People**
Human Sciences Press
233 Spring Street
New York, NY 10013
212-229-2859
800-221-9369
FAX: 212-463-0742

Highlights the major features of supported employment. Contributions offer service providers in social work, education and mental health much-needed information. *$38.95*
*288 pages Cloth*
*ISBN 0-89885 -46-6*

**5863 Survey of Direct Labor Workers Who Are Blind & Employed by NIB**
Mississippi State University
PO Box 6189
Mississippi State, MS 39762
662-325-2001
800-675-7782
FAX: 662-325-8989
www.blind.msstate.edu

*Kelly Schaefer, Publications Manager*
*Elton Moore, Executive Director*

This report is a follow-up to surveys by National Industries for the Blind in 1983 and 1987 and summarizes the results of a national survey of approximately 500 legally blind direct labor workers. *$10.00*
*101 pages Paperback*

**5864 Vocational Counseling for Special Populations**
Chrisann Schire-Geist
2600 S 1st Street
Springfield, IL 62704
217-789-8980
800-258-8980
FAX: 217-789-9130
e-mail: books@ccthomas.com
www.ccthomas.com

*Michael Thomas, President*
*$36.95*

*172 pages Paperback*
*ISBN 0-398056-50-1*

**5865  Vocational Training and Employment of the Autistic Adolescent**
Charles C Thomas
2600 S 1st Street
Springfield, IL  62704                    217-789-8980
                                          800-258-8980
                                     FAX: 217-789-9130
                              e-mail: books@ccthomas.com
                                        www.ccthomas.com

*Michael Thomas, President*

Professionals and parents are now advocating, demanding and arranging that persons receive vocational training and equal rights for the disabled. Also available in paper edition. *$41.95*
*182 pages Cloth*
*ISBN 0-398058-01-6*

**5866  WORK**
64511 Via Real
Suite 9
Carpinteria, CA  93013                    805-566-9000
                                     FAX: 805-566-9070

*Kathy Webb, Executive Director*

Vocational and residential training and support services for adults with developmental disabilities.

**5867  Work and Disability: Issues and Strategie s in Career Development and Job Placement**
PRO-ED

Textbook. *$60.00*
*480 pages 2003*
*ISBN 0-890799-10-5*

**5868  Working Together: Workplace Culture, Employment and Disabilities**
Brookline Books
PO Box 1046
Cambridge, MA  02139                      617-868-0360
                                          800-666-2665
                                     FAX: 617-868-1772
                           e-mail: brooklinebks@delphi.com
                                    www.brooklinebooks.com
Presents a new approach to assisting individuals with significant disabilities achieve meaningful careers, the book stresses partnerships between work, service providers and natural support systems to achieve positive employment outcomes. *$27.95*
*Paperback*
*ISBN 0-91479 -88-3*

---

## General Disabilities

**5869  A Christian Approach to Overcoming Disability: A Doctor's Story**
Haworth Press
10 Alice Street
Binghamton, NY  13904                     607-722-5857
                                          800-429-6784
                                     FAX: 607-722-6362
                          e-mail: orders@haworthpress.com
                                     www.haworthpress.com

*S Harrington-Miller, Advertising*
*William Cohen, Owner*

This is the personal account of a Christian physician who changed her career specialty from obstetrics and gynecology when she was diagnosed with a genetic disease that would cause her to become blind. Dr. Elaine Eng offers faith-based and psychological techniques for coping with disability. *$29.95*

*174 pages Hardcover*
*ISBN 0-789022-57-5*

**5870  A Guide to Disability Rights Law**
US Department of Justice
950 Pennsylvania Avenue NW Drs
- Nyav
Washington, DC 20530                       202-586-5000
                                          800-574-0301
                                     FAX: 202-307-1197
                                           www.ada.gov

*Joanne Graham, Manager*

A 21-page booklet providing a brief description of the ADA, the Telecommunications Act, Fair Housing Act, Air Carrier Access Act, Voting Accessibility for the Elderly and Handicapped Act, National Voter Registration Act, Civil Rights of Institutionalized Persons Act, Individuals with Disabilities in Education Act, Rehabilitation Act, Architectural Barriers Act, and the federal agencies to contact for more information.

**5871  A Guidebook on Consumer-Controlled Housing for Minnesotans with Disabilities**
Arc Minnesota
770 Transfer Road
Suite 26
Saint Paul, MN  55114                     651-523-0823
                                          800-582-5256
                                     FAX: 651-523-0829
                          e-mail: mail@arcminnesota.com
                                     www.arcminnesota.com

*Mike Gude, Administrative Assistant*
*Steve Larson, Executive Director*

*$10.00*
*8 pages*
*ISBN 0-965040-41-0*

**5872  A World Awaits You**
Mobility International USA
PO Box 10767
Eugene, OR  97440                         541-343-1284
                                     FAX: 541-343-6812
                              e-mail: info@miusa.org
                                        www.miusa.org

*Pamala Houston, Public Relations Coordinator*
*Tracy Scharn, Project Assstant*
*Susan Sygall, Executive Director*

Free publication from Mobility International USA.
*44 pages Yearly*

**5873  AAPD News**
American Association of People with Disabilities
1629 K Street NW
Suite 503
Washington, DC  20006                     202-457-0046
                                          800-840-8844
                                     FAX: 202-457-0473
                                 e-mail: aapd@aol.com
                                        www.aapd-dc.org

*Anelie Bush, Editor*
*Quarterly*

**5874  ADA Guide for Small Businesses**
US Department of Justice
950 Pennsylvania Avenue NW Drs
- Nyav
Washington, DC 20530                       202-586-5000
                                          800-574-0301
                                     FAX: 202-307-1197
                                           www.ada.gov

*Joanne Graham, Manager*

A 15-page booklet for businesses that provide goods and services to the public. This publication explains basic ADA requirements, illustrates ways to make facilities accessible, and provides information about tax credits and deductions.

**5875**   **ADA Guide for Small Towns**
US Department of Justice
950 Pennsylvania Avenue NW Drs
- Nyav
Washington, DC 20530                    202-586-5000
                                        800-574-0301
                                   FAX: 202-307-1197
                                        www.ada.gov

*Joanne Graham, Manager*

A 21-page guide that presents an informal overview of some basic ADA requirements and provides cost-effective tips on how small towns can comply with the ADA.

**5876**   **ADA Information Services**
US Department of Justice
950 Pennsylvania Avenue NW Drs
- Nyav
Washington, DC 20530                    202-586-5000
                                        800-574-0301
                                   FAX: 202-307-1197
                                        www.ada.gov

*Joanne Graham, Manager*

A 2-page list with the telephone numbers and internet addresses of federal agencies and other organizations that provide information and technical assistance to the public about the ADA.

**5877**   **ADA Pipeline**
ADA Technical Assistance Program
490 10th Street NW
Atlanta, GA  30318                      404-605-0515
                                        800-949-4232
                                   FAX: 404-385-0641
                             e-mail: sedbtac@catea.org
                                        www.sedbtac.org

*Amy Oliveras, Administrative Assistant*
*Mary Morder, Alternative Format Coordinator*
*Shelley Kaplan, Director*
        *16 pages Quarterly*

**5878**   **ADA Questions and Answers**
US Department of Justice
950 Pennsylvania Avenue NW Drs
- Nyav
Washington, DC 20530                    202-586-5000
                                        800-574-0301
                                   FAX: 202-307-1197
                                        www.ada.gov

*Joanne Graham, Manager*

A 31-page booklet giving an overview of the ADA's requirements affecting employers, businesses, nonprofit service agencies, and state and local governments programs, including public transportation.

**5879**   **ADA Tax Incentive Packet for Business**
US Department of Justice
950 Pennsylvania Avenue NW Drs
- Nyav
Washington, DC 20530                    202-586-5000
                                        800-574-0301
                                   FAX: 202-307-1197
                                        www.ada.gov

*Joanne Graham, Manager*

A 13-page packet of information to help businesses understand and take advantage of the tax credit and deduction available for complying with the ADA.

**5880**   **ADA and City Governments: Common Problems**
US Department of Justice
950 Pennsylvania Avenue NW Drs
- Nyav
Washington, DC 20530                    202-586-5000
                                        800-574-0301
                                   FAX: 202-307-1197
                                        www.ada.gov

*Joanne Graham, Manager*

A 9-page document that contains a sampling of common problems shared by city governments of all sizes, provides examples of common deficiencies and explains how these problems affect persons with disabilities.

**5881**   **ADA-TA: A Technical Assistance Update from the Department of Justice**
US Department of Justice
950 Pennsylvania Avenue NW Drs
- Nyav
Washington, DC 20530                    202-586-5000
                                        800-574-0301
                                   FAX: 202-307-1197
                                        www.ada.gov

*Joanne Graham, Manager*

A serial publication that answers Common Questions about ADA requirements and provides Design Details illustrating particular design requirements. The first edition addresses Readily Achievable Barrier Removal and Van Accessible Packing Spaces.

**5882**   **AID Bulletin**
Project AID Resource Center
PO Box 5190
Kent, OH  44242                         330-672-2672
                                   FAX: 330-672-4724

*Alex Boros PhD, Director AID*
*J Sue Adams, Senior Counselor*
*Peter Mueller, Executive Director*

Has the latest news on upcoming conferences, literature, developments in programs and/or services for disabled persons who are substance abusers. Offers articles on their experiences, ideas and questions of others in this field which includes providers and consumers. *$7.50*

**5883**   **ARC's Government Report**
Arc of the District of Columbia
817 Varnum Street NE
Washington, DC  20017                   202-636-2950
                                   FAX: 202-636-2996
                             e-mail: arcdc@juno.com
                                        www.arcdc.net
Reports on government activities related to individuals with disabilities with a focus on persons with mental retardation. *$50.00*

**5884**   **ARCA Newsletter**
ARCA - Dakota County Technical College
1300 145th Street E
Rosemount, MN  55068                    651-423-8000
                                        800-548-5502

*Ron Thomas, President*

Offers information on support groups, conventions, books, manuscripts and programs for the rehabilitation professional and the disabled.
        *Monthly*

**5885**   **Accent on Living Magazine**
Cheever Publishing
PO Box 700
Bloomington, IL  61702                  309-378-2961
                                        800-787-8444
                                   FAX: 309-378-4420

*Julie Cheever, Marketing Manager*

A magazine published for forty four years, serves physically disabled people, with general interest, travel, and home modification features. *$12.00*
*112 pages Quarterly*

**5886  Access Design Services: CILs as Experts**
Independent Living Research Utilization ILRU
2323 S Shepherd Drive
Suite 1000
Houston, TX 77019                          713-520-0232
                                      FAX: 713-520-5785
                                           www.ilru.org

*Laurie Redd, Executive Director*

Featuring the Access Design Services of Alpha One in Maine, this month's Readings is another of the winners of the recent competition for innovative CIL programs.
*10 pages*

**5887  Access Info**
Access to Independence
2345 Atwood Avenue
Madison, WI 53704                          608-242-8484
                                           800-362-9877
                                      FAX: 608-242-0383
                                      TTY: 608-242-8485

*Tracy Miller, Editor*

Covers news, features and resources for people with disabilities living in the Madison, Wisconsin area.
*24 pages Semi-Annual*

**5888  Access for 911 and Telephone Emergency Services**
US Department of Justice
950 Pennsylvania Avenue NW Drs
- Nyav
Washington, DC 20530                       202-586-5000
                                           800-574-0301
                                      FAX: 202-307-1197
                                           www.ada.gov

*Joanne Graham, Manager*

A 10-page publication explaining the requirements for direct, equal access to 911 for persons who use teletypewritters (TTYs).

**5889  Achieving Diversity and Independence**
Independent Living Research Utilization ILRU
2323 S Shepherd Drive
Suite 1000
Houston, TX 77019                          713-520-0232
                                      FAX: 713-520-5785
                                           www.ilru.org

*Laurie Redd, Executive Director*
*10 pages*

**5890  Ad Lib Drop-In Center: Consumer Management, Ownership and Empowerment**
Independent Living Research Utilization ILRU
2323 S Shepherd Drive
Suite 1000
Houston, TX 77019                          713-520-0232
                                      FAX: 713-520-5785
                                           www.ilru.org

*Laurie Redd, Executive Director*

Joe describes how Ad Lib ensured consumer control in their Drop-In Center: the DIC came about because of consumer input, and consumers are involved in planning the program; members can choose to become volunteers or paid staff members. All of the staff at the DIC are consumers; and active consumer advisory board helps develop policies and programs and provides input to the Ad Lib board.

*10 pages*

**5891  Adaptive Tracks**
Adaptive Sports Center
PO Box 1639
Crested Butte, CO 81224                    970-349-2296
                                           866-349-2296
                                      FAX: 970-349-4950
                             e-mail: info@adaptivesports.org
                                   www.adaptivesports.org

*Christopher Hensley, Executive Director*
*6 pages Quarterly*

**5892  Adobe News**
Santa Barbara Foundation
15 E Carrillo Street
Santa Barbara, CA 93101                    805-963-1873
                                           805-966-2345

*Charles Slosser, Chief Executive Officer*
*8 pages Bi-Annually*

**5893  Advocate**
Arc Massachusetts
217 S Street
Waltham, MA 02453                          781-891-6270
                                      FAX: 781-891-6271
                            e-mail: arcmass@arcmass.org
                                        www.arcmass.org

*Leo Sarkissian, Executive Director*
*$20.00*
*8-12 pages Quarterly*

**5894  Alcoholism Sourcebook**
Omnigraphics
615 Griswold Street
Detroit, MI 48226                          313-961-1340
                                           800-234-1340
                                      FAX: 800-875-1340
                                   www.omnigraphics.com

*Karen Bellenir, Editor*
*Georgiann Lauginiger, Customer Service Manager*
*Peter Ruffner, President*

Provides information on the disorders which may result from alcohol abuse. *$78.00*
*650 pages 2000*
*ISBN 0-780803-25-6*

**5895  Alerter**
San Diego Area Chapter of the Arthritis Foundation
9089 Clairemont Mesa Boulevard
Suite 104
San Diego, CA 92123                        858-492-1090
                                           800-422-8885
                                      FAX: 858-492-9248
                             e-mail: cchase@arthritis.org
                                        www.arthritis.org

*Chris Chase, Programs & Services Coordinator*
*Veronica Braun, President*

Offers chapter updates, information on activities and events, resources and medical research for members.

**5896  American Herb Association Newsletter**
PO Box 353
Nevada City, CA 95959                      530-265-9552
                                      FAX: 530-274-3140
                                           www.ahaherb.com
Information on many different herbs and herb usues. *$ 20.00*

**5897** **Americans with Disabilities Act Checklist for New Lodging Facilities**
US Department of Justice
950 Pennsylvania Avenue NW Drs
- Nyav
Washington, DC 20530          202-586-5000
                             800-574-0301
                        FAX: 202-307-1197
                             www.ada.gov

*Joanne Graham, Manager*

This 34-page checklist is a self-help survey that owners, franchisors, and managers of lodging facilities can use to identify ADA mistakes at their facilities.

**5898** **Americans with Disabilities Act Guide for Places of Lodging: Serving Guests Who Are Blind**
US Department of Justice
950 Pennsylvania Avenue NW Drs
- Nyav
Washington, DC 20530          202-586-5000
                             800-574-0301
                        FAX: 202-307-1197
                             www.ada.gov

*Joanne Graham, Manager*

A 12-page publication explaining what hotels, motels, and other places of transient lodging can do to accommodate guests who are blind or have low vision.

**5899** **An Interdisciplinary Journal for the Socia l Study of Health, Illness and Medicine**
Sage Publications
2455 Teller Road
Thousand Oaks, CA 91320          805-499-0721
                                800-818-7243
                           FAX: 805-499-0871
                                hea.sagepub.com

*Alan Radley, Editor*
*Blaise Simqu, Chief Executive Officer*
        *Quarterly*

**5900** **Anesthesia**
Advocado Press
PO Box 145
Louisville, KY 40201          502-894-9492
                         FAX: 502-899-9562
              e-mail: office@advocadopress.org
                     www.advocadopress.org
*$14.95*
        *96 pages*
        *ISBN 0-962706-46-9*

**5901** **Annual Report Sarkeys Foundation**
530 E Main Street
Norman, OK 73071          405-364-3703
                     FAX: 405-364-8191

*Cheri Cartwright, Manager*
        *Yearly*

**5902** **Applied Kinesiology: Muscle Response in Diagnosis, Therapy and Preventive Medicine**
Inner Traditions
1 Park Street
Rochester, VT 05767          802-767-3174
                            800-246-8648
                       FAX: 802-767-3726
            e-mail: orders@innertraditions.com
                    www.InnerTraditions.com

*Jessica Dudley, Sales Associate*
*Ehud Sperling, Owner*
*$12.95*

*144 pages*
*ISBN 0-892813-28-8*

**5903** **Arc Connection Newsletter**
Arc of Tennessee
44 Vantage Way
Suite 550
Nashville, TN 37228          615-248-5878
                            800-835-7077
                       FAX: 615-248-5879
           e-mail: pcooper@thearctn.org
                   www.thearctn.org

*Walter Rogers, Executive Director*
*Peggy Cooper, Associate Director*

The Arc of Tennessee is a nonprofit organization that offers advocacy, information, referral and support to people with mental retardation or a related developmental disability and their families. This is their publication. It is free to members. *$10.00*
        *12 pages Quarterly*

**5904** **Arc Light**
Arc of Arizona
5610 S Central Avenue
Phoenix, AZ 85040          602-268-6101
                          800-252-9054
                     FAX: 602-268-7483
          e-mail: Arcofarizona@aol.com
                  www.arcofarizona.org

*Cindy Waymire, Manager*
        *Quarterly*

**5905** **Aromatherapy Book: Applications and Inhalations**
North Atlantic Books
1435a 4th Street
Berkeley, CA 94710          510-559-8277
                       FAX: 510-559-8279
          e-mail: info@northatlanticbooks.com
                  www.northatlanticbooks.com
Considered a bible for those interested in aromatherapy. *$18.95*
        *1992*
        *ISBN 1-556430-73-6*

**5906** **Aromatherapy for Common Ailments**
Simon & Schuster
100 Front Street
Delran, NJ 08075
                           800-323-7445
                      FAX: 800-943-9831
                           www.simonsays.com
Explains aromatherapy with emphasis on medicinal uses.
        *96 pages 1991*
        *ISBN 0-671731-34-3*

**5907** **Assistive Technology News**
South Carolina Assistive Technology Project
University of South Carolina
Columbia, SC 29208          803-779-0343
                       FAX: 803-935-5342
           e-mail: jjendron@usit.net
                   www.sc.edu/scatp/

*Evelyn Evans, Editor*
*Janet Jendron, Editor*
*Mary Alice Bechtler, Editor*
        *7-8 pages Bi-annually*

**5908** **Attending to America: Personal Assistance for Independent Living**
World Institute on Disability
510 16th Street
Suite 100
Oakland, CA 94612          510-763-4100
                      FAX: 510-763-4109
           e-mail: wid@wid.org
                   www.wid.org

This unique 1987 report explores the then-current publicly provided personal assistance system in the US. It contains policy recommendations and action steps, a definition of terms, a directory of attendant service programs in the US and a bibliography. $20.00
*190 pages Paperback*

## 5909 Attitudes Toward Persons with Disabilities
Springer Publishing Company
536 Broadway
New York, NY 10012 212-431-4370
877-687-7476
FAX: 212-941-7842
e-mail: marketing@springerpub.com
www.springerpub.com

*Annette Imperati, Marketing/Sales Director*
*Ursula Springer, President*

This volume examines what is known of people's complex and multifaceted attitudes toward persons with disabilities. Divided into five areas of concern: theory, origin of attitudes, attitude measurement, attitudes of specific groups and attitude change. $38.95
*352 pages Hardcover*
*ISBN 0-82616-90-1*

## 5910 Augmentative and Alternative Communication
Brookes Publishing
Suite 308
Toronto, Ontario, Canada, M3C-3 416-385-0351
800-638-3775
FAX: 416-385-0352
e-mail: secretariat@issac-online.org
www.jadea.dk/baggrund.htm

*Nancy Christie, Executive Director*

This 2nd edition contains the most recent information available on implementing augmentative and alternative communication (AAC), explaining principles and procedures of AAC assessment and offering intervention techniques. $59.95
*592 pages Hardcover 1998*
*ISBN 1-55766-33-5*

## 5911 Authoritative Guide to Self- Help Resource in Mental Health
Guilford Press
72 Spring Street
New York, NY 10012 212-431-9800
800-365-7006
FAX: 212-966-6708
www.guilford.com

*Linda F Campbell PhD, Author*
*Thomas P Smith PsyD, Author*
*Robert Sommer PhD, Author*

Reviews and rates 600+ self-help books, autobiographies, and popular films, and evaluates hundreds of Internet sites. Addresses 28 of the most prevalent clinical disorders and life challenges- from ADHD, Alzheimer's, and anxiety disorders, to marital problems, mood disorders and weight management. Also in cloth at $45.00 (ISBN# 1-57230-506-1) $25.00
*377 pages Paperback 2000*
*ISBN 1-572305-80-0*

## 5912 AwareNews
Services for Independent Living
25100 Euclid Avenue
Suite 105
Cleveland, OH 44117 216-731-1529
FAX: 216-731-3083
e-mail: sil@stratos.net

*Molly Thomas, Services Coordinator*
*Lynn Hilderbrand, Manager*

*12 pages Quarterly*

## 5913 Bach Flower Therapy: Theory and Practice
Inner Traditions
1 Park Street
Rochester, VT 05767 802-767-3174

*Ehud Sperling, Owner*

Contemporary study of Bach's techniques, intended for practitioners and lay readers alike. Includes lists of symptoms to facilitate diagnosis, ans aims to provide an understanding of psychosomatic elements in relation to physical complaints.
*1988*
*ISBN 0-892812-39-7*

## 5914 Balancing Act
Vestibular Disorders Association
PO Box 4467
Portland, OR 97208 503-229-7705
800-837-8428
FAX: 503-229-8064
e-mail: veda@vestibular.org
www.vestibular.org

*Lisa Haven, Editor*
*Connie Pilcher, Editor*

$15.00
*2001*
*ISBN 0-963261-15-0*

## 5915 Beliefs, Values, and Principles of Self Advocacy
Brookline Books
PO Box 1047
Cambridge, MA 02139 617-868-0360
800-666-2665
FAX: 617-868-1772
e-mail: brooklinebks@delphi.com
www.brooklinebooks.com

Written by self-advocates around the world, they tell about the beliefs, values, and principles important to them, and the empowerment and personal growth they experience through self-advocacy. $7.00
*48 pages Paperback*
*ISBN 0-57129-22-2*

## 5916 Beliefs: Pathways to Health and Well Being
Metamorphous Press
PO Box 10616
Portland, OR 97296 503-228-4972
FAX: 503-223-9117
www.metamodels.com/meta/bks/hea1.htm

*David Balding, Publisher*

Explores behavioral technologies and belief change strategies that can alter beliefs that support unhealthy habbits such as smoking, overeating, and drug use. Also covers the changing of thinking processes that create phobias and unreasonable fears, retraining the immune system to eliminate allergies and to deal optinally with cancer, AIDS, and other diseases. Includes strategies to transform unhealthy beliefs into lifelong constructs of wellness.

## 5917 Bench Marks
Govennor's Council on Developmental Disabilities
1717 W Jefferson Street
Phoenix, AZ 85007 602-542-4049
800-889-5893
FAX: 602-542-5320
e-mail: mward@mail.dc.state.us

*Micheal Ward, Executive Director*
*Susan Madison, Manager*

*Quarterly*

**5918  Beyond Antibiotics: Healthier Options for Families**
North Atlantic Books
1435a 4th Street
Berkeley, CA  94710                              510-559-8277
                                            FAX: 510-559-8279
e-mail: info@northatlanticbooks.com
www.northatlanticbooks.com
An overview of ways to boost immunity and avoid antibiotics.
Provides a range of alternative health measures, including vita-
mins and herbal medicines. *$16.95*
        *Paperback 1992*
        *ISBN 1-556431-34-1*

**5919  Beyond Gentle Teaching**
Autism Society of North Carolina Bookstore
505 Oberlin Road
Suite 230
Raleigh, NC  27605                            919-743-0204
                                              800-442-2762
                                         FAX: 919-743-0208
e-mail: dcoffey@autismsociety-nc.org
www.autismsociety-nc.org

*Darla Coffey, Bookstore Manager*
*Jill Keel, Executive Director*

A nonaversive approach to helping those in need, caregivers.
*$35.00*

**5920  Body Reflexology: Healing at Your Fingertips**
Parker Publishing Company
1501 Broadway
Suite 2605
New York, NY  10036                        212-354-7100

*Valerie Porter*

Features step-by-step instructions of how to send healing flows
of energy through the body to relieve back pain, headaches, arthritis, and other afflictions. Illustrated.
        *343 pages Hardcover 1995*
        *ISBN 0-132997-36-3*

**5921  Body Silent: The Different World of the Disabled**
WW Norton & Company
324 State Street
Santa Barbara, CA  93101
                                            800-333-6867
                                       FAX: 805-962-5087
www.specialneeds.com/store/
The author's personal account of his progressive and terminal
loss of muscle function caused by a spinal tumor, resulting in
quadripilegia. Includes society's fears, myths, and misunder-
standings about disability and the damage they inflict. *$9.95*
        *256 pages 2001*
        *ISBN 0-393320-42-1*

**5922  Body of Knowledge/Hellerwork**
406 Berry Street
Mount Shasta, CA  96067                   530-926-2500

*Joseph Heller, Owner*

Information, referral directory, training and certification.

**5923  Breaking Ground**
Tennessee Council on Developmental Disabilities
500 Deaderick Street
13th Floor
Nashville, TN  37243                         615-313-9980
                                         FAX: 615-532-6964
e-mail: tnddc@state.tn.us
www.state.tn.us/cdd

*Linda Moynihan, Executive Director*

*20 pages 6 A Year*

**5924  Breaking New Ground News Note**
Purdue University
1146 Abe Building
W Lafayette, IN  47907                        765-494-4600
                                              800-825-4264
                                         FAX: 765-496-1356
e-mail: bng@ecn.purdue.edu
engineering.purdue.edu/CEM/News/2002/cem_news

*Paul Jones, Coordinator*
*Martin Jischke, Chief Executive Officer*

News, practical ideas and success stories of and for farmers with
physical disabilities.
        *12-16 pages Quarterly*

**5925  Breaking New Ground Resource Center**
Purdue University
1146 Abe Building
W Lafayette, IN  47907                        765-494-4600
                                              800-825-4264
                                         FAX: 765-496-1356
e-mail: bng@ecn.purdue.edu
www.agrability.org

*William Field, Director*
*Paul Jones, Information Specialist*
*Martin Jischke, Chief Executive Officer*

A resource center devoted to helping farmers and ranchers with
physical disabilities. Several resource materials and a free
newsletter are available to anyone.

**5926  Breathe Free**
Lotus Press
PO Box 325
Twin Lakes, WI  53181                         262-889-8561
                                              800-824-6396
                                         FAX: 262-889-2461
e-mail: lotuspress@lotuspress.com
www.lotuspress.com

*Santosh Krinsky, President*

A nutritional and herbal medicine self-help guide to treating a
full range of respiratory conditions, including colds and flu.
        *179 pages 1998*
        *ISBN 0-914955-07-1*

**5927  Bridge Newsletter**
Arizona Bridge to Independent Living
1229 E Washington Street
Phoenix, AZ  85034                            602-256-2245
                                              800-280-2245
                                         FAX: 602-254-6407
e-mail: azbridge@abil.org
www.abil.org

*Phil Pangrazio, Executive Director*
        *12 pages Monthly*

**5928  Bulletin of the Association on the Handicapped**
Assoc. on Handicapped Student Service Program
PO Box 21192
Columbus, OH  43221                           614-365-5216
                                         FAX: 614-365-6718
Membership journal including Association news, articles and
sections such as Literature in Review and Speak Out. *$16.00*

**5929  Bush Fellows News**
Bush Foundation
332 Minnesota Street
Saint Paul, MN  55101                         651-227-0891
                                         FAX: 651-297-6485
e-mail: kkleppe@bushfoundation.org
www.bushfoundation.org

*Kelly Kleppe, Editor*
*Anita Pampusch, Chief Executive Officer*

*24-32 pages Quarterly*

**5930    CDR Reports**
Council for Disability Rights
20 N Wacker Drive
Suite 1540
Chicago, IL  60606                    312-444-9484
                                 FAX: 312-444-1977
                     e-mail: cdrights@interaccess.com
                             www.disabilityrights.org

*Jo Holzer, Executive Director/Editor*
*Bruce Moore, Employment Specialist*

*$15.00*
            *8 pages Monthly*

**5931    California Financial Power of Attorney**
NOLO
950 Parker Street
Berkeley, CA  94710                   510-549-1976
                                      800-955-4775
                                 FAX: 510-548-5902
                                      www.nolo.com

*Maira Dizgalvis, Trade Customer Service Manager*
*Susan McConnell, Director Sales*
*Natasha Kaluza, Sales Assistant*

A plain-English book packed with forms and instructions to give
a trusted person the legal authority to handle your financial affairs.
            *paperback*

**5932    Caring for America's Heroes**
Oklahoma City VA Medical Center
921 NE 13th Street
Oklahoma City, OK  73104              405-270-0501
                                 FAX: 405-270-1560
                                      www.va.gov

*Steven J Gentling, Director*
*Kathleen Fogarty, Associate Director*
*D Robert McCaffree MD, Chief of Staff*

**5933    Center for Libraries and Educational Improvement**
400 Maryland Avenue SW
Washington, DC  20202                 202-260-2226
                                 FAX: 202-401-0689

*Malcolm Davis, Acting Director*

Administers the Library Services Construction Act, which au-
thorizes grants to the states for library services to the physically
handicapped.

**5934    Centers for Disease Control Public Health Service**
US Department of Health and Human Services
Ms C09 1600 Clifton Road NE
Atlanta, GA  30333                    404-639-3311

Publishes an annually updated list of infectious and communica-
ble diseases transmitted through the handling of food in accordance with Section 103 of Title I.

**5935    Centurion**
Delaware Commision of Veterans Affairs
802 Silver Lake Boulevard
Suite 100
Dover, DE  19904                      302-739-2792
                                      800-344-9900
                                 FAX: 302-739-2794
                     e-mail: adavila@state.de.us
                                   www.state.de.us

*Antonio Davila, Executive Director*

*Quarterly*

**5936    Charting a Hero's Journey**
International Partnership for Service-Learning
815 2nd Avenue
Room 315
New York, NY  10017                   212-986-0989
                                 FAX: 212-986-5039
                             e-mail: info@ipsl.org
                                      www.ipsl.org

*Nevin Brown, President*
*Sarah Callahan, Coordinator Special Projects*

A guide to the writing of a journal for college students engaged
in study abroad, off-campus study. and/or service-learning. *$
23.95*
            *328 pages*
            *ISBN 0-970198-42-6*

**5937    Chinese Herbal Medicine**
Shambhala Publications
PO Box 308
Boston, MA  02117                     617-424-0030
                                 FAX: 617-236-1563
                     e-mail: editors@shambhala.com
                                 www.shambhala.com

*Peter Turner, President*

Gives an in-depth look into herbal medicine.
            *176 pages*
            *ISBN 0-877733-98-8*

**5938    Christian Approach to Overcoming Disabilit y: A Doc-
tor's Story**
Haworth Press
10 Alice Street
Binghamton, NY  13904                 607-722-5857
                                      800-429-6784
                                 FAX: 607-722-6362
                     e-mail: orders@haworthpress.com
                                 www.haworthpress.com

*William Cohen, Owner*

*$29.95*
            *128 pages 2003*
            *ISBN 0-789022-57-5*

**5939    Civil Law Handbook on Psychiatric and Psyc hological
Evidence and Testimony**
ABA Commission on Mental & Physical Disability Law
740 15th Street NW
9th Floor
Washington, DC  20005                 202-662-1011
                                      800-285-2221
                                 FAX: 202-662-1032
                             www.abanet.org/disability

*Nanchy Scholnick, Manager*

**5940    Closing the Gap**
PO Box 68
Henderson, MN  56044                  507-248-3294
                                 FAX: 507-248-3810
                     e-mail: info@closingthegap.com
                                 www.closingthegap.com

*Megan Turek, Editor*
*Delores Hagen, President*

Explores use of microcomputers as personal and educational
tools for persons with disabilities.
            *36+ pages BiMonthly*

**5941    Color Therapy**
Aurora Press
300 Catron Street
Suite B
Santa Fe, NM  87501                   505-989-9804

Guide to daily uses.

**5942 Commonly Asked Questions About the ADA and Law Enforcement**
US Department of Justice
950 Pennsylvania Avenue NW Drs
- Nyav
Washington, DC 20530
202-586-5000
800-574-0301
FAX: 202-307-1197
www.ada.gov

*Joann Graham, Manager*

A 13-page publication explaining ADA requirements for ensuring that people with disabilities receive the same law enforcement services and protections as provided to others.

**5943 Commuique/Newspaper**
National Association of School Psychologist
4340 Ew Highway
Suite 402
Bethesda, MD 20814
301-657-0270
FAX: 301-657-0275
e-mail: inealis@naspweb.org
www.nasponline.org

*Susan Gorin, Executive Director*
*$45.00*
*50 pages Monthly*

**5944 Communicating at the End of the Twentieth Century: Innovative Computer Programs**
Independent Living Research Utilization ILRU
2323 S Shepherd Drive
Suite 1000
Houston, TX 77019
713-520-0232
FAX: 713-520-5785
www.ilru.org

*Laurie Redd, Executive Director*

This month's readings features two more of the winners in last year's Innovative CIL competitions. Steve Brown of the Institute on Disability Culture has combined the submissions of MetroWest Center for Independent Living and Pathways for the future, Inc. into an article that looks at how centers can use their independence.
*10 pages*

**5945 Communication Outlook**
Artificial Language Laboratory
405 Computer Center
East Lansing, MI 48824
517-353-0870
FAX: 517-353-4766
e-mail: artling@msu.edu
www.msu.edu/~artlang

*Caroline Watt, Editor*
*Katie Smith, Editor*

Communication Outlook (CO) is an international quarterly magazine, which focuses on the techniques and technology of augmentative and alternative communication. CO provides information on technological developments for persons experiencing communication handicaps due to neurological, sensory or neuromuscular conditions. *$18.00*
*32 pages Quarterly*

**5946 Community Connections Newsletter**
Mental Health Association of NY State
194 Washington Avenue
Suite 415
Albany, NY 12210
518-434-0439
800-766-6177
FAX: 518-427-8676
e-mail: infocenter@mhanys.org
www.mhany.org

*Quarterly*

**5947 Community Services Reporter**
National Assoc. of State Directors of DD Services
113 Oronoco Street
Alexandria, VA 22314
703-683-4202
FAX: 703-683-8773
e-mail: lsarigoi@nasddds.org
www.nasddds.org/index.shtml

*Leyla Sarigor, State Policy Analyst*
*Robert Gettings, Executive Director*

Reports exclusively on state and local policy and programmatic initiatives affecting people with developmental disabilities, including; person-centered planning models, quality assurance activities, managed care initiatives, state reorganizations, waiting list reduction initiatives, community-living options, and key state legislation, including an annual nationwide summary of newly enacted state laws. *$ 95.00*
*8 pages Yearly*

**5948 Complete Aromatherapy Handbook: Essential Oils for Radiant Health**
Sterling Press
420 W 1700 S
Salt Lake City, UT 84115
801-486-4641
FAX: 801-467-2221

*Dale Parks, Owner*

Describes the history of aromatherapy.
*1991*

**5949 Complete Guide To Mercury Toxicity from De ntal Fillings**
Environmental Dental Association
285 N El Camino Real
Suite 102
Encinitas, CA 92024
858-586-1208
800-388-2184
FAX: 858-756-7843
e-mail: info@enviormentaldental.com
www.enviormentaldental.com
*191 pages*
*ISBN 0-944796-36-2*

**5950 Complete Guide to Health and Nutrition**
Delacorte Press
1540 Broadway
New York, NY 10036
212-782-9000
FAX: 212-302-7985

*Carol Schneider, Marketing Executive*

Explores the nurtitional field.

**5951 Comprehensive Directory of Programs and Services**
Resources for Children with Special Needs
116 E 16th Street
Floor 5
New York, NY 10003
212-677-4650
FAX: 212-254-4070
e-mail: info@resourcesnyc.org
www.resourcesnyc.org

*Karen Schlesinger, Executive Director*
*Dianne Littwin, Director Publications*

Published every 24-36 months. *$55.00*
*1096 pages*
*ISBN 0-976836-51-4*

**5952 Constellations**
Minnesota STAR Program
50 Sherburne Avenue
Suite 309
Saint Paul, MN 55155
651-296-2771
800-657-3862
FAX: 651-282-6671
e-mail: star.program@state.mn.us
www.admin.state.mn.us/assistivetechnology

*Chuck Rassbach, Executive Director*

Free quarterly publication from the Minnesota STAR Program.
*8 pages Quarterly*

**5953 Consumer Buyer's Guide for Independent Living**
American Occupational Therapy Association (AOTA)
4720 Montgomery Lane
Bethesda, MD 20814                    301-652-7590
                                   800-OHE-LP4U
                               FAX: 301-652-7711

*Cheryl Hager, Marketing Director*
*M Baum, President*

A buyer's directory of products and publications for the general
public listing suppliers' names, addresses and telephone numbers. This directory lists AOTA publications on numerous topics (back pain, Alzheimers, Carpal Tunnel Syndrome, etc.) and
suppliers of equipment to assist in activities of daily living for
individuals with disabilities.
*60 pages Annual*

**5954 Consumer Information Catalog**
Consumer Information Center
Pueblo, CO 81009
                                    888-878-8256
                               FAX: 719-948-9724
                    e-mail: catalog.pueblo@gsa.gov
                               www.pueblo.gsa.gov

*Judi Mahaney, Media Specialist*

The Consumer Information Center publishes the free, quarterly
Consumer Information Catalog. The catalog lists over 200 selected booklets of consumer interest published by more than 40
agencies of the federal government. Topics covered includes
employment and education, children, cars, small business, housing, health, nutrition, money management, federal programs and
more. Nearly half of the publications listed are available for
free; the remainder are moderately priced.

**5955 Coping+Plus: Dimensions of Disability**
Greenwood Publishing Group
88 Post Road W
Suite 5007
Westport, CT 06880                   203-226-3571
                               FAX: 203-222-1502
                               www.greenwood.com

*Wayne Smith, President*

Everyone can learn new or more effective coping skills and strategies to deal with times of loss, crisis and disability. $55-$59.95
*280 pages Hardcover*
*ISBN 0-275945-44-8*

**5956 Council News**
Northern Nevada Center for Independent Living
999 Pyramid Way
Sparks, NV 89431                     775-353-3599
                               FAX: 775-353-3588
                     e-mail: nncil@sbcglobal.net

*Lee Erquiaga, Executive Director*
*12 pages Quarterly*

**5957 Cox-2 Connection**
Healing Arts Press
1 Park Street
Rochester, VT 05767                  802-767-3174
                                    800-246-8648
                               FAX: 802-767-3726
             e-mail: orders@innertraditions.com
                               www.InnerTraditions.com

*Jessica Dudley, Sales Associate*
*Ehud Sperling, Owner*
*$12.95*

*176 pages*
*ISBN 0-892819-84-7*

**5958 Creating Wholeness: Self-Healing Workbook Using Dy-
namic Relaxation, Images and Thoughts**
Plenum Publishing Corporation
233 Spring Street
Floor 7
New York, NY 10013                   212-242-1490
                               FAX: 212-463-0742

*232 pages*
*ISBN 0-306441-72-1*

**5959 Creative Care Package Catalog**
Centering Corporation
1531 N Saddle Creek Road
Omaha, NE 68104                      402-553-1200
                               FAX: 402-533-0507
                          e-mail: j1200@aol.com
                               www.centering.org

*Janet Sieff, Editor*
*Joy Johnson, Executive Director*

A full catalog of all our available bereavement resources. We are
a small, non-profit organization providing help to families in
crisis situations.
*32 pages BiAnnually*

**5960 DAV Magazine**
DAV Magazine
807 Maine Avenue SW
Washington, DC 20024                 202-554-3501
                               FAX: 202-554-3581
                  e-mail: feedback@davmail.org
                               www.dav.org

*David Autry, Editor*
*David Gorman, Executive Director*

Reports the news, activities and programs of the organization
and its members.

**5961 DRS Connection**
Disabled Resource Services
424 Pine Street
Suite 101
Fort Collins, CO 80524               970-482-2700
                               FAX: 970-407-7072
                          e-mail: drs@lymis.com
                               www.drs@fortnet.org

*Nancy Jackson, Executive Director*
*4 pages Quaterly*

**5962 Dayspring Associates**
2111 Foley Road
Havre De Grace, MD 21078             410-939-5900
                               FAX: 410-939-6252

*Benedict Schwartz, Manager*

This publisher provides a directory of 1,000 rehabilitation aids.

**5963 Demand Response Transportation Through a Rural
ILC**
Independent Living Research Utilization ILRU
2323 S Shepherd Drive
Suite 1000
Houston, TX 77019                    713-520-0232
                               FAX: 713-520-5785
                               www.ilru.org

*Laurie Redd, Executive Director*

Oklahomans for Independent Living's transportation program
was selected as exemplary becuase they marketed it by emphasizing people with disabilities as economic constituency.

*10 pages*

**5964  Dental Amalgam Syndrome (DAMS) Newsletter**
725-9 Tramway Lane NE
Albuquerque, NM 87122          505-291-8239
                               FAX: 505-294-3339
Dedicated to informing the public about the potential risks of mercury in dental amalgam fillings.

**5965  Determined to Win The Inspirational Story of Paradymic Athlete Jean Driscoll**
Spina Bifida Association of America
4590 Macarthur Boulevard NW
Suite 250
Washington, DC 20007          202-944-3285
                              800-621-3141
                              FAX: 202-944-3295
                              e-mail: sbaa@sbaa.org
                              www.sbaa.org

*Cindy Brownstein, Chief Executive Officer*
*$21.00*

**5966  Developing Organized Coalitions and Strategic Plans**
Independent Living Research Utilization ILRU
2323 S Shepherd Drive
Suite 1000
Houston, TX 77019            713-520-0232
                             FAX: 713-520-5785
                             www.ilru.org

*Laurie Redd, Executive Director*
*10 pages*

**5967  Dictionary of Developmental Disabilities Terminology**
Brookes Publishing
PO Box 10624
Baltimore, MD 21285          410-337-9580
                             800-638-3775
                             FAX: 410-337-8539
             e-mail: custserv@brookesopublishing.com
                     www.brookespublishing.com

*Barbara Y Whitman MSW PhD, Editor*
*Carla Laszewski MSW*
*Paul Brooks, Owner*

With more than 3,000 easy-to-understand entries, this dictionary provides thorough explanations of terms associated with developmental disabilities and disorders. *$55.95*
        *368 pages Hardcover 1996*
        *ISBN 1-557662-45-2*

**5968  Directory of Members**
American Network of Community Options & Resources
1101 King Street
Suite 380
Alexandria, VA 22314         703-535-7850
                             FAX: 703-535-7860
                             e-mail: ancor@ancor.org
                             www.ancor.org

*Renee L Pietrangelo, CEO*
*Suellen Galbraith, Director Public Policy*
*Renee Pietrangelo, Chief Executive Officer*

The Directory lists over 600 agencies that provide residential services and supports in 48 states and the District of Columbia. The listings include the name of the Executive Directors, the name, address, and phone number of the agency, describe the types of services that are provided and how many individuals receive services from that agency. *$25.00*

*189 pages*

**5969  Disabilities Sourcebook**
Omnigraphics
615 Griswold Street
Detroit, MI 48226            313-961-1340
                             800-234-1340
                             FAX: 800-875-1340
                             www.omnigraphics.com

*Paul Rogers, Publicity Associate*
*Georgiann Lauginger, Customer Service Manager*
*Peter Ruffner, President*
*$78.00*
        *616 pages 2000*
        *ISBN 0-780803-89-2*

**5970  Disability Awareness Guide**
Central Iowa Center for Independent Living
655 Walnut Street
Suite 131
Des Moines, IA 50309         515-243-1742
                             FAX: 515-243-5385
                             e-mail: cicil@raccoon.com
                             www.raccoon.com/-cicil

*Robert Jeppesen, Director*
*Frank Strong, Assistant Director Programs*
*Bob Jepson, Manager*

The Disability Awareness Guide contains information about our center; who we are and what we do. It also contains the telephone numbers of local and national agencies and resources available for people with disabilities.

**5971  Disability Bookshop Catalog**
PO Box 129
Vancouver, WA 98666          360-694-2462
                             800-637-2256
                             FAX: 360-696-3210
             e-mail: twinpeak@pacifier.com
                     disabilitybookshop.virtualave.net/
Offers more than 400 hard-to-find titles covering a wide range of health topics for the general public, and matters of interest to people with disabilities. Catalog. *$4.00*
        *40 pages*

**5972  Disability Rights Movement**
Children's Press
Sherman Tpke
Danbury, CT 06813
                             800-621-1115
                             FAX: 800-374-4329

*Elena Rockman, Marketing Manager*

Author Deborah Kent illuminates both the history of the National Disability Rights Movement and the inspiring personal stories of individuals with various disabilities. *$18.00*
        *32 pages Hardcover*
        *ISBN 0-53106 -32-3*

**5973  Disabled People's International Fifth World Assembly as Reported by Two US Participants**
Independent Living Research Utilization ILRU
2323 S Shepherd Drive
Suite 1000
Houston, TX 77019            713-520-0232
                             FAX: 713-520-5785
                             www.ilru.org

*Laurie Redd, Executive Director*

This report describes the international conference on independent living held in Mexico City in December 1998 as experienced by staff members from two U.S. centers. Kaye Beneke interviewed Luis Chew and Marco Antonio Coronado for this edition of Readings in Independent Living.

*10 pages*

**5974 Disabled We Stand**
Brookline Books
PO Box 1046
Cambridge, MA 02139       617-868-0360
800-666-2665
FAX: 617-868-1772
e-mail: brooklinebks@delphi.com
www.brooklinebooks.com
This book is impassioned, often angry, but also hopeful and practical, suggesting a series of actions that will lead to constructive change. It is imbued with spirit and energy of disabled people who are determined to take their lives into their own hands. *$ 10.95*
*Paperback*
*ISBN 0-25331 -80-0*

**5975 Disabled, the Media, and the Information Age**
Greenwood Publishing Group
88 Post Road W
Suite 5007
Westport, CT 06880       203-226-3571
FAX: 203-222-1502
www.greenwood.com

*Wayne Smith, President*

A short and easy-to-read overview of how disabled Americans have been portrayed by the media and how images and the role of the handicapped are changing. *$55.00*
*264 pages Hardcover*
*ISBN 0-313284-72-5*

**5976 Discovery Newsletter**
North Dakota State Library Talking Book Services
604 E Boulevard Avenue
Dept 250
Bismarck, ND 58505       701-328-2000
800-843-9948
FAX: 701-328-2040
e-mail: sbschneider@nd.gov
ndsl.lib.state.nd.us/DisabilityServices.html

*Susan Hammer-Schneider, Manager Talking Books*
*6 pages Bi-Annually*

**5977 Diverse Abilities: An Outcome of Organizat ional Collaboration & Operative Integration**
Independent Living Research Utilization ILRU
2323 S Shepherd Drive
Suite 1000
Houston, TX 77019       713-520-0232
FAX: 713-520-5785
www.ilru.org

*Laurie Redd, Executive Director*

Hawaii Centers for Independent Living collaborated with other non-profit agencies to reduce costs and expand services. Although the resulting platform organization, DiverseAbilities, is still in its infancy, Mark Obatake, executive director of HCIL and one of this months authors, believes that the processthey went through in developing the collaboration has value for centers and SILCs.
*10 pages*

**5978 Dressing Tips and Clothing Resources for Making Life Easier**
Attainment Company
PO Box 930160
Verona, WI 53593       608-848-2640
800-327-4269
FAX: 608-845-8040
e-mail: info@attainmentcompany.com
www.attainmentcompany.com

*Don Bastian, President*
*Brent Denu, Marketing Manager*

Learn hundreds of simple tips and techniques to make dressing easier. Learn how to adapt/modify ready-to-wear garments to accommodate your special dressing needs. Find out how to locate more than 100 resources offering specially designed or easy-on/easy-off clothing for men, women, children and/or wheelchair users. You'll find everything you need to look your best. An invaluable resource for people with special dressing needs, people with disabilities, caregivers and healthcare professionals. *$19.00*
*144 pages 2000*
*ISBN 1-578611-19-9*

**5979 EP Resource Guide**
Exceptional Parent Library
PO Box 1807
Englewood Cliffs, NJ 07632       201-947-6000
800-535-1910
FAX: 201-947-9376
e-mail: eplibrary@aol.com
www.eplibrary.com
Lists directories of national organizations, associations, products and services. *$9.95*

**5980 ESCIL Update Newsletter**
Eastern Shore Center for Independent Living
9 Sunburst Center
Cambridge, MD 21613       410-221-7701
800-705-7944
FAX: 410-221-7714
e-mail: escil@comcast.net
www.escil.org

*Shirley Tarbox, Executive Director*
*Jean Reed, Administrative Assistant*
*Lisa Morgan, Director IL Services*
*6 pages Quarterly*

**5981 Easy Things to Make Things Simple: Do It Yourself Modifications for Disabled Persons**
Brookline Books
PO Box 1047
Cambridge, MA 02139       617-495-3682
800-666-2665
FAX: 617-868-1772
e-mail: brooklinebks@delphi.com
www.brooklinebooks.com
This book aims at older adults and others with physical limitations who require adaptations for safer and easier living in the kitchen, bathroom, bedroom, yard, and garden. The adaptations can be done inexpensively, from common materials. Large print format and detailed diagrams, plus special sections with advice caregivers . *$15.95*
*160 pages Paperback*
*ISBN 1-571290-24-9*

**5982 Eating Out: Your Guide to More Enjoyable Dining**
Plume
375 Hudson Street
New York, NY 10014       212-366-2000

In this book, a nationally recognized expert on diabetes nutrition, shows you how eating out can be fun, without fear of weight gain or an uncontrolled rise in blood sugar. *$4.95*
*272 pages Paperback 2000*
*ISBN 0-452279-76-3*

**5983 Edge Effect: Achieve Total Health and Long evity with the Balanced Brain Advantage**
Sterling Press
420 W 1700 S
Salt Lake City, UT 84115       801-486-4641
FAX: 801-467-2221

*Dale Parks, Owner*

Dr Eric Braverman reveaks the impact that proper brain nourishment can have on the quality of life. He sketches out a program to achieve logevity and well-being by balancing the brain's four important neurotransmitters. *$19.95*

*304 pages Hardcover 2004*
*ISBN 1-402712-05-7*

**5984   Effective Strategies for Interacting with Policy-Makers**
Independent Living Research Utilization ILRU
2323 S Shepherd Drive
Suite 1000
Houston, TX  77019                713-520-0232
                                 FAX: 713-520-5785
                                 www.ilru.org

*Laurie Redd, Executive Director*
     *10 pages*

**5985   Embracing the Monster: Overcoming the Cha llenges of Hidden Disabilities**
Paul H Brookes Publishing Company
PO Box 10624
Baltimore, MD  21285             410-337-9580
                                 800-638-3775
                                 FAX: 410-337-8539
         e-mail: custserv@brokespublishing.com
                 www.brookespublishing.com

*Paul Brooks, Owner*
The author shares her experience of living with LD, ADHD and bipolar disorder to give readers an awareness of the challenges of living with hidden disabilities and what can be done to help
*$21.95*
     *192 pages 2002*
     *ISBN 1-557665-22-2*

**5986   Encyclopedia of Disability**
Sage Publications
2455 Teller Road
Thousand Oaks, CA  91320         805-499-0721

                 e-mail: info@sagepub.com
                         www.sagepub.com

*Gary L Albrecht, Editor*
*Blaise Simqu, Chief Executive Officer*
A five volume set that covers disabilities A-Z *$850.00*
     *2500 pages 1905*
     *ISBN 0-761925-65-1*

**5987   Enforcing the ADA: A Status Report from th e Department of Justice**
US Department of Justice
950 Pennsylvania Avenue NW Drs
- Nyav
Washington, DC 20530             202-586-5000
                                 800-574-0301
                                 FAX: 202-307-1197
                                 www.ada.gov

*Joanne Graham, Manager*
A quarterly report providing timely information about ADA cases and settlements, building codes that meet ADA accessibility standards, and ADA technical assistance activities. The most current issue of the Status Report is available by Fax.

**5988   EveryBody's Different: Understanding and Changing Our Reactions to Disabilities**
Brookes Publishing
PO Box 10624
Baltimore, MD  21285             410-337-9580
                                 800-638-3775
                                 FAX: 410-337-8539
         e-mail: custserv@brookespublishing.com
                 www.brookespublishing.com

*Paul Brooks, Owner*

This book discusses the emotions, questions, fears, and stereotypes that people without disabilities sometimes experience when they interact with people who do have disabilities. The author teaches readers to become more at ease with the concept of disability and to communicate more effectively with each other. Features activities and exercises that encourage self-examination, helping people to create more enriching personal relationships and work toward a fully inclusive society.
     *Paperback 1998*
     *ISBN 1-55766 -59-9*

**5989   Everybody's Guide to Homeopathic Medicines**
Jeremy P Tarcher
375 Hudson Street
New York, NY  10014              212-366-2000

Covers alternative treatments in homeopathic medicines.
     *375 pages 1997*
     *ISBN 0-874778-43-3*

**5990   Everyday Social Interaction: A Program for People with Disabilities, 2nd Edition**
Brookes Publishing
PO Box 10624
Baltimore, MD  21285             410-337-9580
                                 800-638-3775
                                 FAX: 410-337-8539
         e-mail: custserv@brookespublishing.com
                 www.brookespublishing.com

*Paul Brooks, Owner*

This source guides teachers and human services professionals in helping people with disabilities acquire social interaction skills and develop satisfying relationships. Included is a checklist and task analyses that shows how complex skills can be broken down into major components for easy performance monitoring accompanied by tips on social courtesies, rewards, praise, and criticism. *$41.95*
     *342 pages Paperback*
     *ISBN 1-55766 -58-4*

**5991   Explore Your Options**
Kansas Department on Aging
503 S Kansas Avenue
Topeka, KS  66603                785-296-4986
                                 800-432-3535
                                 FAX: 785-296-0256
                                 www.agingKansas.org
     *Yearly*

**5992   Farmington Valley ARC**
10 Tower Lane
Avon, CT  06001                  860-693-6662
                                 FAX: 860-693-8662

*Lynn Flerri, President*
*Tom Thompson, Executive Director*
The official newsletter containing information, new ideas, progress and more on the Farmington Valley Association for Retarded and Handicapped Citizens.

**5993   Fast Forward**
627 Sunrise Service Road N
Bellport, NY  11713              631-286-1600
                                 631-286-1647
                                 www.soffollk.llb.us/abp

*Gerald Nichols, Executive Director*
*Flo Denny, Assistant Director*
*Julie Klauber, Outreach Services*

*bi-annually*

**5994 Fedcap News**
Fedcap Rehabilitation Services
211 W 14th Street
New York, NY 10011          212-727-4200
FAX: 212-727-4374
e-mail: info@fedcap.org
www.fedcap.org

*Susan Jourad, Director Community Relations*
*Susan Fonsa, Executive Director*

A publication from Fedcap Rehabilitation Services.
*12 pages*

**5995 Focus Newsletter**
Arc Minnesota
770 Transfer Road
Suite 26
Saint Paul, MN 55114          651-523-0823
800-582-5256
FAX: 651-523-0829
e-mail: mail@arcminnesota.com
www.arcminnesota.com

*Mike Gude, Editor*
*Steve Larosn, Executive Director*
*8 pages 3 times a year*

**5996 Force A Miracle**
Writer's Showcase Press

A testament to the inner human strength to overcome extreme
adversity, to triumph and continue a worthwhile and self-re-
warding life. *$14.95*
*244 pages 2002*
*ISBN 0-595226-88-4*

**5997 Forum**
Coalition for the Education of Disabled Children
165 W Center Street
Marion, OH 43302          740-382-5452
800-374-2806
FAX: 740-383-6421
e-mail: oceed@gte.net
www.oceed.org

*Margret Burley, Executive Director*
*Leeann Derugen, Manager*

Forum is a newsletter reporting on legislative and other developments affecting persons with disabilities.
*Quarterly*

**5998 Fosters Botanical and Herb Reviews**
B&H Reviews
PO Box 106
Eureka Springs, AR 72632
FAX: 479-253-7442

**5999 Four-Ingredient Cookbook**
Laurel Designs
1805 Mar West Street
Apt A
Belvedere Tiburon, CA 94920
FAX: 415-435-1451
e-mail: laureld@ncal.verio.com

*Janet Sawyer, Owner*
*Lynn Montoya, Owner*

Simple, easy to follow recipes, each containing four ingredients.
Particularly suited to persons with limited physical ability. Includes 400 recipes, appetizers to desserts. *$9.00*

**6000 Freedom Press**
Freedom Resource Center for Independent Living
2701 9th Avenue SW
Fargo, ND 58103          701-478-0459
800-450-0459
FAX: 701-478-0510
e-mail: freedom@fargocity.com
www.macil.org/freedom

*Nate Aalgaard, Executive Director*
*Bobbi Franks, Information Specialist*
*Quarterly*

**6001 Freedom of Movement: IL History and Philosophy**
Independent Living Research Utilization ILRU
2323 S Shepherd Drive
Suite 1000
Houston, TX 77019          713-520-0232
FAX: 713-520-5785
www.ilru.org

*Laurie Redd, Executive Director*
*10 pages*

**6002 Frequently Asked Questions About Multiple Chemical Sensitivity**
Independent Living Research Utilization ILRU
2323 S Shepherd Drive
Suite 1000
Houston, TX 77019          713-520-0232
FAX: 713-520-5785
www.ilru.org

*Laurie Redd, Executive Director*

This FAQ covers important information about multiple chemical sensitivity and environmental illness. The FAQ describes
the conditions, recommends strategies for improving access,
and lists resources for CILs and other organizations. As the fact
sheet states, centers must set an example in assuring that all people can enter their offices.
*10 pages*

**6003 General Guidelines for Disability Policy Change Agents**
Independent Living Research Utilization ILRU
2323 S Shepherd Drive
Suite 1000
Houston, TX 77019          713-520-0232
FAX: 713-520-5785
www.ilru.org

*Laurie Redd, Executive Director*
*10 pages*

**6004 Genetic Disorders Sourcebook**
Omnigraphics
615 Griswold Street
Detroit, MI 48226          313-961-1340
800-234-1340
FAX: 800-875-1340
www.omnigraphics.com

*Kathy Massimini, Editor*
*Peter Ruffner, President*

Provides information on hereditary diseases and disorders.
*$7800.00*
*650 pages 2000*
*ISBN 0-789892-41-1*

**6005 Genetic Nutritioneering**
McGraw-Hill Company
2460 Kerper Boulevard
Dubuque, IA 52001          563-588-1451
800-338-3987
FAX: 614-755-5654
www.mhhe.com/hper/physed

*Kurt Strand, Vice President*

Describes how to modify the expression of genetic traits, potentially preventing heart disease, cancer, arthritis, and hormone-related problems. Features how to slow biological aging and reduce the risk of age-related diseases. *$16.95*
*288 pages 1999*
*ISBN 0-879839-21-X*

**6006    Getting Better**
Vestibular Disorders Association
PO Box 4467
Portland, OR  97208
503-229-7705
800-837-8428
FAX: 503-229-8064
e-mail: veda@vestibular.org
www.vestibular.org

*Dr. Lisa Haven, Executive Director*
*Connie Pilcher, Outreach Coordinator*

A non-profit organization dedicated to providing education and support to people with inner ear balance/dizziness disorder and their families and people who help them. *$25.00*
*Quarterly*
*ISBN 0-963261-17-7*

**6007    Getting Life**
Avacado Press
PO Box 145
Louisville, KY  40201
502-894-9492
FAX: 502-899-9562
e-mail: office@avocadopress.org
www.advocadopress.org

*$16.00*
*304 pages*
*ISBN 0-962706-48-5*

**6008    Grief: What it is and What You Can Do**
Centering Corporation
1531 N Saddle Creek Road
Omaha, NE  68104
402-553-1200
FAX: 402-533-0507
e-mail: j1200@aol.com
www.centering.org

*Joy Johnson, Executive Director*

General grief information for all grief issues. *$3.50*
*32 pages Paperback*

**6009    Guidelines on Disability**
US Department of Housing & Urban Development
451 7th Street SW
Washington, DC  20410
202-708-1112
TTY:202-708-1455
Contains information on housing and accessibility for persons with disabilities.

**6010    Handbook of Mental Disorders Among Black Americans**
Greenwood Publishing Group
88 Post Road W
Suite 5007
Westport, CT  06880
203-226-3571
FAX: 203-222-1502
www.greenwood.com

*Wayne Smith, President*

In addition to providing a wealth of new data on the mental health status of black communities, this handbook presents analyses of specific social, structural, and cultural conditions that affect the lives of individual Black Americans. $55-$65.
*352 pages Hardcover*
*ISBN 0-313263-30-2*

**6011    Handbook of Services for the Handicapped**
Greenwood Publishing Group
88 Post Road W
Suite 5007
Westport, CT  06880
203-226-3571
FAX: 203-222-1502
www.greenwood.com

*Wayne Smith, President*

A handy reference book offering information and services for disabled individuals. $59.95-$65.00.
*291 pages Hardcover*
*ISBN 0-313213-85-2*

**6012    Handbook on Diability Discrimination Law**
ABA Commission on Mental & Physical Disability Law
740 15th Street NW
9th Floor
Washington, DC  20005
202-662-1011
800-285-2221
FAX: 202-662-1032
www.abanet.org/disability

*Nancy Scholnick, Manager*

**6013    Handbook on Mental Health Policy in the United States**
Greenwood Publishing Group
88 Post Road W
Suite 5007
Westport, CT  06880
203-226-3571
FAX: 203-222-1502
www.greenwood.com

*Wayne Smith, President*

Covers the historical, policy and administrative aspects of public mental health care. *$95.00*
*563 pages $95 - $99.50*
*ISBN 0-313250-09-0*

**6014    Headache Newsletter**
19 Mantua Road
Mount Royal, NJ  08061
856-423-0043
800-255-2243
FAX: 856-423-0082
e-mail: achehq@talley.com
www.achenet.org

*Linda Gillicuddy, Executive Director*

*$20.00*
*Quarterly*

**6015    Healing Herbs**
Rodale Press
33 E Minor Street
Emmaus, PA  18098
610-967-5171
FAX: 610-967-8963
www.rodale.com

*Steven Murphy, Chief Executive Officer*

Covers everything from growing the herbs to home remedies.

**6016    Healing Without Fear**
Healing Arts Press
1 Park Street
Rochester, VT  05767
802-767-3174
800-246-8648
FAX: 802-767-3726
e-mail: orders@innertraditions.com
www.InnerTraditions.com

*Jessica Dudley, Sales Associate*
*Ehud Sperling, Owner*

How to overcome your fear of doctors, hospitals and the health care system and find your way to true healing. *$14.95*
*192 pages*
*ISBN 0-892819-92-8*

**6017    Healing Yourself: a Step-by-Step Program for Better Health Through Imagery**
Pocket Books
100 Front Street
Delran, NJ  08075
800-323-7445
FAX: 800-943-9831
www.simonsays.com

**6018 Health Insurance Resource Manual**
Demos Medical Publishing
386 Park Avenue S
Suite 301
New York, NY 10016
212-683-0072
800-532-8663
FAX: 212-683-0118
e-mail: orderdept@demosmedpub.com
www.demosmedpub.com

*Phyllis D Gold, President*
Information about a wide variety of options for individuals who are uninsured, underinsured, or who have questions about insurance and don't know where to begin. *$24.95*
*208- pages 2003*
*ISBN 1-888799-69-2*

**6019 Heart of the Mind**
Real People Press
PO Box F
Moab, UT 84532
435-259-7578
FAX: 435-259-4042
e-mail: realpoep@lasal.net
www.realpeoplepress.com

*Susan Ossana, Office Manager*
Provides common NLP problems and several new techniques.

**6020 Herbs for the Mind: What Science Tells Us about Nature's Remedies for Depression, Stress...**
Guilford Press
72 Spring Street
New York, NY 10012
212-431-9800
800-365-7006
FAX: 212-966-6708
e-mail: info@guilford.com
www.guilford.com

*Bob Matloff, President*
Translates hard data into the accessible answers consumers need to make informed decisions on taking St. John's wort for depression, kava for stress or anxiety, valerian for insomnia or ginko for memory loss. *$14.95*
*278 pages Paperback 2000*
*ISBN 1-572304-76-6*

**6021 Homeopathic Medicines at Home: Natural Remedies for Everyday Ailments and Minor Injuries**
Jeremy P Tarcher
375 Hudson Street
New York, NY 10014
212-366-2000

book.realbuy.ws/0874771951.html
Guide for common ailments and their cures.

**6022 Hospice Alternative**
Harper Collins Publishers/Basic Books
10 E 53rd Street
New York, NY 10022
212-207-7000
800-242-7737
FAX: 212-207-7203

*Jane Friedman, Chief Executive Officer*
An account of the hospice experience. An innovative and humane way of caring for the terminally ill. *$8.95*
*256 pages*
*ISBN 0-46503 -61-0*

**6023 Housing and Independence: How Innovative CILs are Assisting Housing for Disabled People**
Independent Living Research Utilization ILRU
2323 S Shepherd Drive
Suite 1000
Houston, TX 77019
713-520-0232
FAX: 713-520-5785
www.ilru.org

*Laurie Redd, Executive Director*

This month's Readings is the first of many publications which will feature the winners of the Innovative CILs competition. This article is a compilation of the four winning essays as well as telephone interviews with the key staff members at each of the centers.
*10 pages*

**6024 How to File a Title III Complaint**
US Department of Justice
950 Pennsylvania Avenue NW Drs
- Nyav
Washington, DC 20530
202-586-5000
800-574-0301
FAX: 202-307-1197
www.ada.gov

*Joanne Graham, Manager*
This publication details the procedure for filing a complaint under Title III of the ADA.

**6025 How to Live Longer with a Disability**
Accent Books & Products
PO Box 700
Bloomington, IL 61702
309-378-2961
800-787-8444
FAX: 309-378-4420
e-mail: acmtlvng@aol.com

*Raymond C Cheever, Publisher*
*Betty Garee, Editor*
Eleven chapters to help you enjoy every aspect of your life, and live easier and happier. Includes sexuality and disability, getting more from the medical community and benefit programs. Co-authored by Robert Mauro, sociologist and Elle Becker, counselor and psychologist, both disabled. *$11.50*
*266 pages Paperback*
*ISBN 0-19570 -38-8*

**6026 How to Outsmart Your Allergies**
Asthma and Allergy Foundation of America
1125 15th Street NW
Suite 502
Washington, DC 20005
202-466-7643
FAX: 202-466-8940
e-mail: info@aafa.org
www.aafa.org

*Bill Lin, Executive Director*
Colorful poster that will enhance any office or waiting room while educating patients. Contains innovative and factual tips for avoiding allergens and reducing or eliminating allergic symptoms. The poster depicts common allergens in an appealing format. *$1.00*

**6027 If I Only Knew What to Say or Do**
AARP Fulfillment
601 E Street NW
Washington, DC 20049
202-434-2277
800-424-3410
FAX: 202-434-3443
e-mail: member@aarp.org
www.aarp.org

*William Novelli, Chief Executive Officer*
Provides a concise discussion of how to help a friend in crisis. Learn what to say and what not to say.

**6028 If it Weren't for the Honor: I'd Rather Have Walked**
Accent Books & Products
PO Box 700
Bloomington, IL 61702
309-378-2961
800-787-8444
FAX: 309-378-4420
e-mail: acmtlvng@aol.com

*Raymond C Cheever, Publisher*
*Betty Garee, Editor*

Revealing, often humorous, highly interesting and important reading. This book offers an account told by the author who was on the scene and actually saw and participated in many events that paved the way for progress for all those with disabilities. *$14.50*
> *262 pages Paperback*
> *ISBN 0-91570 -41-8*

**6029    Imagery in Healing Shamanism and Modern Medicine**
Shambhala Publications
PO Box 308
Boston, MA  02117                    617-424-0030
                                FAX: 617-236-1563
                        e-mail: editors@shambhala.com
                            www.shambhala.com

*Peter Turner, President*

Patients use self imagery to fight sickness and pain throughout their lives. *$15.95*
> *272 pages 2002*
> *ISBN 1-570629-34-x*

**6030    Imagine!**
Imagine!
1400 Dixon Avenue
Lafayette, CO  80026                 303-665-7789
                                FAX: 303-665-2648
                    e-mail: gstebick@imaginecolorado.org
                            www.imaginecolorado.org

*Gary Stebick, Communication Coordinator*
*Fred Hobbs, Director Marketing*

For people of all ages with cognitive, developmental, physical & health related needs, so they may live lives of independence & quality in their homes and communities.
> *12-16 pages quarterly*

**6031    InTouch Networks: National Radio Reading Service**
JGB Audio Library for the Blind
15 W 65th Street
New York, NY  10023                  212-769-6331
                                     800-284-4422
                                FAX: 212-769-6266
                            e-mail: info@JGB.org
                                 www.JGB.org

*Peter Williamson, Director*
*Ken Stanley, Manager*

**6032    Independence**
Easter Seals
1219 Dunn Avenue
Daytona Beach, FL  32114             386-255-4568
                                     877-255-4568
                                FAX: 386-258-7677
                        e-mail: info@eseals-vf.org
                        www.easterseals-volusiaflagler.org

*Penny Young, Communications Director*
*Lynn Sinnot, President*
> *4-6 pages Quarterly*

**6033    Independent Living Centers and Managed Care: Results of an ILRU Study on Involvement**
Independent Living Research Utilization ILRU
2323 S Shepherd Drive
Suite 1000
Houston, TX  77019                   713-520-0232
                                FAX: 713-520-5785
                                    www.ilru.org

*Laurie Redd, Executive Director*

This month's Readings presents findings from an ILRU study of roles centers are taking vis-a-vis managed care. Initiated in spring 1998, we asked Drew Batavia to take the lead in conducting this study for us. We were interested in collecting data on frequency with which centers are contacted by consumers with managed care problems. This is a study that will need to be repeated periodically as our experiences with managed care evolves. Meanwhile, here are the initial findings.

*10 pages*

**6034    Independent Living Challenges the Blues**
Independent Living Research Utilization ILRU
2323 S Shepherd Drive
Suite 1000
Houston, TX  77019                   713-520-0232
                                FAX: 713-520-5785
                                    www.ilru.org

*Laurie Redd, Executive Director*

Patricia's article highlights the Georgia SILC's health care advocacy efforts: the Georgia legislature passed a bill enabling Georgia Bleu to convert to for-profit status without a distribution of assets to similar nonprofit corporations; the Georgia SILC joined other health care advocates in filing a class action law suit to challenge the legality of the conversion; the Georgia SILC continues advocacy efforts to involve people with disabilities in developing and monitoring health care policy.
> *10 pages*

**6035    Independent Living Office**
Department of Housing & Urban Development (HUD)
451 7th Street SW
Washington, DC  20410                202-863-2800

This office within HUD is charged with encouraging the construction of housing that is accessible to handicapped persons. The Office of Independent Living encourages modifications of apartments and other dwellings so that handicapped persons can enter without assistance.

**6036    Independent Newsletter**
Easter Seals Nebraska
638 N 109th Plaza
Omaha, NE  68154                     402-345-2200
                                     800-650-9880
                                FAX: 402-345-2500
                    e-mail: kginder@ne.easterseals.com
                            www.ne.easterseals.com

*Ingra Winkler Anderson, author*
> *4 pages Quarterly*

**6037    Information Services for People with Developmental Disabilities**
Greenwood Publishing Group
88 Post Road W
Suite 5007
Westport, CT  06880                  203-226-3571
                                FAX: 203-222-1502
                                www.greenwood.com

*Linda Lucas Walling, Editor*
*Marilyn M Irwin, Editor*
*Wayne Smith, President*

Overviews the information needs of people with developmental disabilities and tells librarians how to meet them. $65.oo-$75.00.
> *368 pages Hardcover*
> *ISBN 0-313287-80-5*

**6038    Informed Touch**
Healing Arts Press
1 Park Street
Rochester, VT  05767                 802-767-3174
                                     800-246-8648
                                FAX: 802-767-3726
                    e-mail: orders@innertraditions.com
                            www.InnerTraditions.com

*Jessica Dudley, Sales Associate*
*Ehud Sperling, Owner*

A Clinician's guide to the evaluation and treatment of myofascial disorders. *$30.00*

*224 pages*
*ISBN 0-892817-40-2*

**6039   Innovative Programs: An Example of How CILs Can Put Their Work in Context**
Culture
2323 S Shepherd Drive
Suite 1000
Houston, TX  77019                    713-535-2200
                                      FAX: 713-520-5785
                                      www.ilru.org

*Jim Alister Sr, President*

Another winner in the innovative CIL competition- Steve Brown describes the Talking Books Program of Southeast Alaska Independent Living, discussing their efforts to record the oral history and life experiences of people with disabilities in the larger context of disability culture.
*10 pages*

**6040   Innovative Resources for Cognitive & Physi**
1400 Dixon Street
Lafayette, CO  80026                  303-665-7789

*John Taylor, President*

**6041   Inside The Halo and Beyond: The Anatomy o f a Recovery**
WW Norton & Company
324 State Street
Santa Barbara, CA  93101
                                      800-333-6867
                                      FAX: 805-962-5087
                                      www.specialneeds.com/store/
A skilled horsewoman and lifelong athlete, poet Kumin was 73 when a riding accident left her with two broken vertebrae in her neck. Kumin survived in the face of overwhelming odds that she would be paralyzed for the rest of her life. Miraculously, however, she was walking again within weeks of the accident; now, though one hand and an arm remain partially immobilized, her life has largely resumed its normal course. Here is the journal of her first nine months of recovery. *$ 13.95*
*208 pages 2001*
*ISBN 0-393322-61-0*

**6042   Insurance Solutions: Plan Well, Live Better**
Demos Medical Publishing
386 Park Avenue S
Suite 201
New York, NY  10016                   212-683-0072
                                      800-532-8663
                                      FAX: 212-683-0118
                                      e-mail: orderdep@demospub.com
                                      www.demosmedpub.com

*Diana Schneider PhD, President*
*Phyllis Gold, Owner*

Learn how to look at various insurance options from a new perspective — including life, disability, health, and long-term care. Concrete information for dealing with potential problems in your coverage, to secure your financial future. *$24.95*
*192 pages 2002*
*ISBN 1-888799-55-2*

**6043   International Ventilator Users Network**
Gazette International Networking Institute
4207 Lindell Boulevard
Suite 110
Saint Louis, MO  63108                314-534-0475
                                      FAX: 314-534-5070
                                      e-mail: gini_intl@msn.com
                                      www.post-polio.org/ivun

*Joan L Headley, Executive Director*
*Judith R Fischer, Editor*

IVUN is a worldwide network of ventilator users and health professionals experienced in and committed to home care and long term mechanical ventilation. IVUN News, a quarterly newsletter, offers articles on family adjustments, equipment, techniques, travel, ethical issues, medical topics, and resources. Also publishes the annual iVUN resource directory, listing ventilator users, health professionals, equipment manufacturers and vendors, as well as other related organizations. *$ 17.00*
*8 pages Quarterly*

**6044   It Feels Good to be in Control**
Accent Books & Products
PO Box 700
Bloomington, IL  61702               309-378-2961
                                     800-787-8444
                                     FAX: 309-378-4420
                                     e-mail: acmtlvng@aol.com

*Raymond C Cheever, Publisher*
*Betty Garee, Editor*

Understanding yourself can make almost anything work better, your health, your personal relationships, your happiness, you name it. This small book could be the best medicine and the most inexpensive a person could ever have. *$4.50*
*18 pages Paperback*
*ISBN 0-91570 -39-6*

**6045   Journal of Rehabilitation**
National Rehabilitation Association (NRA)
633 S Washington Street
Alexandria, VA  22314                703-836-0850
                                     FAX: 703-836-0848
                                     e-mail: info@nationalrehab.org
                                     www.nationalrehab.org

*Carol Jaafar, Director Program Services*
*Linda Winslow, Executive Director*

Articles are written by professionals in the fields of rehabilitation and are peer reviewed. Editorial content reflects the broad perspectives of the association's memberhsip.

**6046   Just Like Everyone Else**
World Institute on Disability
510 16th Street
Suite 100
Oakland, CA  94612                   510-763-4100
                                     FAX: 510-763-4109
                                     e-mail: wid@wid.org
                                     www.wid.org
The oversize-format publication, intended for general audiences, provides perspective, inspiration and information about the Independent Living Movement and the Americans with Disabilities Act. *$5.00*
*16 pages*

**6047   Kaleidoscope: Exploring the Experience of Disability Through Literature & the Fine Arts**
United Disability Services
701 S Main Street
Akron, OH  44311                     330-762-9755
                                     FAX: 330-762-0912
                                     TTY:330-379-3349
                                     e-mail: mshiplett@udsakron.org
                                     www.udsakron.org

*Mildred Shiplett, Editorial Coordinator*
*Gail Willmott, Senior Editor*
*Phyllis Boerner, Publication Director*

This magazine explores the experiences of disability through the lens of creative arts. Unlike rehabilitation, advocacy or independent living journals, this journal challenges and transcends stereotypical, patronizing and sentimental attitudes about disability. Offers a variety of articles, fiction, art and poetry relating to issues of disability, literature and the fine arts. *$10.00*

*64 pages BiAnnually*

**6048 Keep the Promise: Managed Care and People with Disabilities**
American Network of Community Options & Resource
1101 King Street
Suite 380
Alexandria, VA 22314 703-535-7850
FAX: 703-535-7860
e-mail: ancor@ancor.org
www.ancor.org

*Renee L Pietrangelo, CEO*
*Suellen Galbraith, Director Public Policy*

This publication presents a detailed review of the process and the lessons learned. Details a way for all stake holders to work together for a state or local system.
*119 pages $18 - $22*

**6049 Keeping Our Families Together**
Through the Looking Glass
2198 6th Street
Suite 100
Berkeley, CA 94710 510-848-1112
800-644-2666
FAX: 510-848-4445
e-mail: TLG@lookingglass.org
www.lookingglass.org

*Megan Kirshbaum, Executive Director*
*Tina Evoyne, Office Manager*

Report of the National Task Force on parents with disabilities and their families. Available in braille, large print or cassette. *$2.00*
*12 pages*

**6050 Keys to Independence**
Coalition for Independence
1281 Eisenhower Road
Leavenworth, KS 66048 913-250-0287
FAX: 913-250-0167
e-mail: kolson@cfikc.org
www.cfikc.org

*Kathy Cooper, Manager*
*Bi-Monthly*

**6051 Kids Get Arthiritis Too!**
American Juvenile Athritis Organization (AJAO)
PO Box 7669
Atlanta, GA 30357 404-872-7100
800-283-7800
FAX: 404-872-9559
e-mail: help@arthritis.org
www.arthritis.org

*John Klippel, Chief Executive Officer*
*8 pages Quarterly*

**6052 LDA Newsbriefs**
Learning Disabilities Association of America
4156 Library Road
Pittsburgh, PA 15234 412-341-1515
FAX: 412-344-0224
e-mail: info@ldaamerica.org
www.ldaamerica.org

*Jane Browning, National Executive Director*
*Barb Lefler, Director Affiliate Services*

Articles of interest to all persons concerned with learning disabilities. *$15.00*

*24 pages BiMonthly*

**6053 Laugh with Accent, #3**
Accent Books & Products
PO Box 700
Bloomington, IL 61702 309-378-2961
800-787-8444
FAX: 309-378-4420
e-mail: acmtlvng@aol.com

*Raymond C Cheever, Publisher*
*Betty Garee, Editor*

These special cartoons prove laughter is the best medicine of all. It's when the laughter stops that we become truly disabled, say readers. *$3.50*
*89 pages Paperback*
*ISBN 0-91570-16-7*

**6054 Learn About the ADA in Your Local Library**
US Department of Justice
950 Pennsylvania Avenue NW Drs
- Nyav
Washington, DC 20530 202-586-5000
800-574-0301
FAX: 202-307-1197
www.ada.gov

*Joanne Graham, Manager*

A 10-page annotated list of 95 ADA publications and one videotape that are available in 15,000 public libraries throughout the country.

**6055 Learning to Listen: Positive Approaches & People with Difficult Behavior**
Brookes Publishing
PO Box 10624
Baltimore, MD 21285 410-337-9580
800-638-3775
FAX: 410-337-8539
e-mail: custserv@brookespublishing.com
www.brookespublishing.com

*Paul Brooks, Owner*

This book describes how the interactive process of learning to listen provides practical alternatives to overly controlling behavior modification techniques. Includes compelling and detailed case studies that illustrate possible positive approaches and reveal how people with disabilities can take control of their lives. *$27.00*
*288 pages Paperback*
*ISBN 1-55766-64-2*

**6056 Life After Trauma: A Workbook for Healing**
Guilford Press
72 Spring Street
New York, NY 10012 212-431-9800
800-365-7006
FAX: 212-966-6708
www.guilford.com

*Bob Matloff, President*

*$18.95*
*352 pages Paperback 1999*
*ISBN 1-572302-39-9*

**6057 LifeLines**
Disabled & Alone/Life Services for the Handicapped
352 Park Avenue S
11th Floor
New York, NY 10010 212-532-6740
800-995-0066
FAX: 212-532-3588
e-mail: info@disabledandalone.org
www.disabledandalone.org

*Roslyn Brilliant, Executive Director*

Newsletter providing current and valuable information about lifetime care and planning for persons with disabilities and their families and the organizations serving them. Free upon request.

*4-10 pages BiAnnual*

**6058  Livin'**
Lehigh Valley Center for Independent Living
435 Allentown Drive
Allentown, PA  18109                    610-770-9781
                                        FAX: 610-770-9801

*Amy C Beck, Executive Director*
*4 pages Quarterly*

**6059  Living in a State of Stuck**
Brookline Books
PO Box 1046
Cambridge, MA  02139                    617-868-0360
                                        800-666-2665
                                        FAX: 617-868-1772
                             e-mail: brooklinebks@delphi.com
                                        www.brooklinebooks.com
Offers explanations on how adaptive technologies affect the
lives of people with disabilities. *$24.95*
*3rd ed., paper*
*ISBN 1-571290-27-3*

**6060  Love: Where to Find It, How to Keep It**
Accent Books & Products
PO Box 700
Bloomington, IL  61702                  309-378-2961
                                        800-787-8444
                                        FAX: 309-378-4420
                                  e-mail: acmtlvng@aol.com

*Raymond C Cheever, Publisher*
*Betty Garee, Editor*

Offers ideas such as how to meet other single people, avoid the
wrong type; communications skills and much more for the disabled person wanting to date. *$6.95*
*104 pages Paperback*
*ISBN 0-91570 -31-0*

**6061  MAGIC Touch**
MAGIC Foundation for Children's Growth
6645 North Avenue
Oak Park, IL  60302                     708-383-0808
                                        800-362-4423
                                        FAX: 708-383-0899
                             e-mail: mary@magicfoundation.org
                                        www.magicfoundation.org

*Dianne Andrews, Executive Director*

Provides support and education regarding growth disorders in
children and related adult disorders, including adult GHD. Dedicated to helping children whose physical growth is affected be a
medical problem by assisting families of afflicted children
through local support groups, public education/awareness,
newsletters, specialty divisions and programs for the children.
*36-40 pages Quarterly*

**6062  MOOSE: A Very Special Person**
Brookline Books
PO Box 1046
Cambridge, MA  02139                    617-868-0360
                                        800-666-2665
                                        FAX: 617-868-1772
                             e-mail: brooklinebks@delphi.com
                                        www.brooklinebooks.com
Moose, which in very human terms, teaches us that each of us is
different and that we have our own unique capacity for loving,
sharing, enjoying and learning. *$10.95*
*Paperback*
*ISBN 0-91479 -73-5*

**6063  Mainstream Magazine**
2973 Beech Street
San Diego, CA  92102                    619-234-3138
                                        FAX: 619-234-3155
                             e-mail: editor@mainstream.mag.com
                                        www.mainstream-mag.com

*Cyndi Jones, Publisher/President*

The authoritative, national voice of people with disabilities,
publishes in-depth reports on employment, education, new
products and technology, legislation and disability rights advocacy, recreation and travel, disability arts and culture, plus personality profiles and challenging commentary. *$24.00*
*Monthly*

**6064  Making Informed Medical Decisions: Where to Look
and How to Use What You Find**
Patient-Centered Guides
101 Morris Street
Sebastopol, CA  95472                   707-829-0515
                                        800-998-9938
                                        FAX: 707-829-0104
                                        www.patientcenters.com

*Tim O'Reilly, Chief Executive Officer*

Making Informed Medical Decisions acts like a friendly reference librarian, explaining: tips for researching for someone
else; medical journal articles; statistics and risk; standard treatment options; clinical trial; making an ally of your doctor; and
determining your own best course. Authors Oster, Thomas, and
Joseff-a patient advocate, medical librarian, and medical doc-
tor-also share examples and stories. *$17.95*
*280 pages Paperback*
*ISBN 1-565924-59-2*

**6065  Making News**
Avacado Press
PO Box 145
Louisville, KY  40201                   502-894-9492
                                        FAX: 502-899-9562
                             e-mail: office@advocadopress.org
                                        www.advocadopress.org
*$8.00*
*165 pages*
*ISBN 0-962706-43-4*

**6066  Making Wise Decisions for Long-Term Care**
AARP Fulfillment
601 E Street NW
Washington, DC  20049                   202-434-2277
                                        800-424-3410
                                        FAX: 202-434-3443
                                  e-mail: member@aarp.org
                                        www.aarp.org

*William Novelli, Chief Executive Officer*

Here's a comprehensive consumer education effort in the area of
long-term care.
*28 pages*

**6067  Management of Genetic Syndromes**
Wiley-Liss

Clinical information on 30 of the most common genetic syndromes. *$157.00*
*554 pages 2001*
*ISBN 0-471312-86-X*

**6068  Managing Your Symptoms**
Vestibular Disorders Association
PO Box 4467
Portland, OR  97208                     503-229-7705
                                        800-837-8428
                                        FAX: 503-229-8064
                                  e-mail: veda@vestibular.org
                                        www.vestibular.org
*$25.00*

ISBN 0-963261-16-9

**6069    Marriage & Disability**
Accent Books & Products
PO Box 700
Bloomington, IL  61702

309-378-2961
800-787-8444
FAX: 309-378-4420
e-mail: acmtlvng@aol.com

*Raymond C Cheever, Publisher*
*Betty Garee, Editor*

This guide can help you make the right decision and it can help smooth the way to a happier life. *$7.95*
*Paperback*
*ISBN 0-91570 -34-5*

**6070    Massage Magazine**
NOAH Publishing Company
638 2nd Street
Kenyon, MN  55946

507-789-6161

*Doug Noah, President*

Covers the art and science of massage, bodywork and related healing arts.
*BiMonthly*

**6071    Matheny Matters**
Matheny School and Hospital
PO Box 339
Peapack, NJ  07977

908-234-0011
FAX: 908-719-2137
e-mail: info@matheny.org
www.matheny.org

*Steven Proctor, President*
*Gabor Barabas MD, Medical Director*
*Gary E Eddey MD, Director of Medicine & Dentistry*

A publication from the Matheny School and Hospital.
*3 times a year*

**6072    Medical Aspects of Disability: A Handbook For The Rehabilitation Professional**
Springer Publishing Company
536 Broadway
New York, NY  10012

212-431-4370
877-687-7476
877-687-7976
FAX: 212-941-7842
e-mail: marketing@springerpub.com
www.springerpub.com

*Annette Imperati, Marketing/Sales Director*
*Ursula Springer, President*

*$62.92*
*744 pages*
*ISBN 0-826179-71-1*

**6073    Medical Herbalism**
Bergner Communications
PO Box 20512
Boulder, CO  80308

303-541-9552

e-mail: bergner@concentric.com
www.medherb.com

*Paul Bergner, Editor*

Newsletter written by physicians and published six times a year.

**6074    Mending the Body, Mending the Mind**
Bantam
1540 Broadway
New York, NY  10036

212-782-9000
FAX: 212-302-7985

**6075    Meniere's Disease: What You Need To Know**
Vestibular Disorders Association
PO Box 4467
Portland, OR  97208

503-229-7705
800-837-8428
FAX: 503-229-8064

*$34.95*
*Quarterly*
*ISBN 0-963261-11-8*

**6076    Menopause without Medicine**
Hunter House
PO Box 2914
Alameda, CA  94501

510-865-5282
800-266-5592
FAX: 510-865-4295
e-mail: sales@hunterhouse.com
www.hunterhouse.com

*JoAnne Retzlaff, Sales/Marketing Associate*
*Christina Sverdrup, Customer Service Manager*
*Kiran Rana, Publisher*

Research on nutrition, exercise, and osteoporosis, including good news about the body's ability to rebuild bone later in life; describes how women can best prepare their minds and bodies for the transition of menopause, and explains how women can prevent osteoporosis and control the disturbing symptoms of hot flashes, insomnia, fatigue, and weight gain. *$15.95*
*368 pages*
*ISBN 0-897932-81-1*

**6077    Mental Retardation, Third Edition**
McGraw-Hill, School Publishing
220 E Danieldale Road
Desoto, TX  75115

972-224-1111
800-442-9685
FAX: 972-228-1982
mhschool.com

*Joseph Gavigan, President*

Combines significant findings from the most current research, focusing on a unique relationship between the special educator and the learner with mental retardation.
*656 pages Casebound*

**6078    Mental Retardation: A Life-Cycle Approach**
McGraw-Hill, School Publishing
220 E Danieldale Road
Desoto, TX  75115

972-224-1111
800-442-9685
FAX: 972-228-1982
mhschool.com

*Joseph Gavigan, President*

This text considers the needs of the retarded individual at every stage of life.
*512 pages*

**6079    Mental and Physical Disability Law Reporter**
ABA Commission on Mental & Physical Disability Law
740 15th Street NW
9th Floor
Washington, DC  20005

202-662-1011
FAX: 202-662-1032
e-mail: hammillj@staff.abanet.org
www.abanet.org/disability

*John Hammill, Publications Coordinator*
*Amy Allbright, Managing Editor*
*Nancy Scholnick, Manager*

Contains over 2,000 summaries of federal and state court decisions and legislation that affect persons with mental and physical disabilities. Includes bylined articles by experts in the field regarding disability law developments and trends. *$374.00*

*150+ pages Bimonthly*

**6080 Midtown Sweep: Grassroots Advocacy at its Best**
Independent Living Research Utilization ILRU
2323 S Shepherd Drive
Suite 1000
Houston, TX 77019          713-520-0232
FAX: 713-520-5785
www.ilru.org

*Laurie Redd, Executive Director*

Josie, Janetta, and Linda describe the steps their center's advocacy group have taken to ensure enforcement of the ADA: target one neighborhood; survey and collect information on businesses that are inaccessible; send letters offering to work with the businesses to help them become accessible and providing information on tax incentives; file lawsuits against businesses that do not respond; involve the media.
    *10 pages*

**6081 Miles Away and Still Caring: A Guide for Long Distance Caregivers**
AARP Fulfillment
601 E Street NW
Washington, DC 20049        202-434-2277
800-424-3410
FAX: 202-434-3443
e-mail: member@aarp.org
www.aarp.org

*William Novelli, Chief Executive Officer*

This is one of the most helpful and frequently requested publications. Helps people who must coordinate the care of a loved one from a long distance.
    *18 pages*

**6082 Mind Over Mood: Change How You Feel By Changing the Way You Think**
Guilford Press
72 Spring Street
New York, NY 10012        212-431-9800
800-365-7006
FAX: 212-966-6708
www.guilford.com

*Bob Matloff, President*
*$21.00*
    *243 pages Paperback 1995*
    *ISBN 0-898621-28-3*

**6083 Mississippi Message**
Arc of Mississippi
7 Lakeland Circle
Suite 600
Jackson, MS 39216        601-982-1180
800-717-1180
FAX: 601-982-5792
e-mail: arcms@arcms.org
www.arcms.org

*Cindy Dittis, Community Outreach*
*Matt Nalker, Manager*
    *Quarterly*

**6084 Mother to Be**
Through the Looking Glass
2198 6th Street
Suite 100
Berkeley, CA 94710        510-848-1112
800-644-2666
FAX: 510-848-4445
e-mail: TLG@lookingglass.org
www.lookingglass.org

*J Rogers*
*M Matsumura*
*Megan Kirshbaum, Executive Director*

Guide to pregnancy and birth for women with disabilities.
*$34.00*

*410 pages*

**6085 Multiple Sclerosis and Having A Baby**
Healing Arts Press
1 Park Street
Rochester, VT 05767        802-767-3174
800-246-8648
FAX: 802-767-3726
e-mail: orders@innertraditions.com
www.InnerTraditions.com

*Jessica Dudley, Sales Associate*
*Ehud Sperling, Owner*

Everything you need to know about conception, pregnancy and parenthood. *$12.95*
    *160 pages*
    *ISBN 0-892817-88-7*

**6086 Myotherapy**
Ballantine Books
1540 Broadway
New York, NY 10036        212-751-2600
FAX: 212-572-4949

Myotherapy explained as a technique.
    *1985*

**6087 NBA Bulletin**
National Braille Association
3 Townline Circle
Rochester, NY 14623        585-427-8260
FAX: 585-427-0263
e-mail: nbaoffice@compuserve.com
www.nationalbraille.org

*Joanna E Venneri, Editor*
*Angela Coffaro, Executive Director*

Quarterly publication from the National Braille Association. *$50.00*
    *28-32 pages Quarterly*

**6088 NCD Bulletin**
National Council on Disability
1331 F Street NW
Suite 850
Washington, DC 20004        202-272-2004
FAX: 202-272-2022
www.ncd.gov

*Mark Quigley, Communication Director*
*Ethel Briggs, Executive Director*

Reports on the latest issues and news affecting people with disabilities.
    *2 pages Monthly*

**6089 NCDE Survival Strategies for Oversease Liv ing for People with Disabilities**
National Clearinghouse on Disability and Exchange
PO Box 10767
Eugene, OR 97440        541-373-1284
FAX: 541-343-6812
e-mail: info@miusa.org
www.miusa.org

*Pamela Houston, Public Relations Coordinator*

This book will provide individuals with disablilities information, resources and guidance on pursuing international exchange opportunities. It addresses disability-related aspects of the international exchange process such as choosing a program, applying, preparing for the trip, adjusting to a new country and returning home.

**6090  NOD E-Newsletter**
National Organization on Disability
910 16th Street NW
Suite 600
Washington, DC  20006                    202-293-5960
                                    FAX: 202-293-7999
                              e-mail: ability@nod.org
                                          www.nod.org

*Michael Deland, President*
*Brewster Thackeray, VP Communications*
*John Hershey, Advice and Resource Manager*

Monthly E-Newsletter from the National Organization on Disability. Free.
                        *3 pages Monthly*

**6091  NORD Resource Guide**
National Organization for Rare Disorders
PO Box 1968
Danbury, CT  06813                       203-744-0100
                                         800-999-6673
                                    FAX: 203-798-2291
                                    TTY: 203-746-6927
                        e-mail: orphan@rarediseases.org
                                    www.rarediseases.org

*Mary Dunkle, Vice President/Communications*
*Abbey Meyers, President*

Book providing information on more than 1,200 organizations, support groups and government agencies offering help to people with rare diseases.

**6092  Nat-Cent News**
Helen Keller National Center
141 Middle Neck Road
Sands Point, NY  11050                   516-944-8900
                                    FAX: 516-944-7302
                              e-mail: hkcinfo@rcn.com
                                          www.hknc.org

*Nancy O'Donnell, Information Services*
*Joseph Nulty, Executive Director*

**6093  National Hookup**
ISC
16 Liberty Street
Larkspur, CA  94939                      415-924-3549
                                    FAX: 415-927-9556
                        e-mail: russab@earthlink.net

*Russ Bohlke, Executive Secretary*

Newsletter published by ISC, a national organization of people with physical disabilities. *$6.00*
                        *12-16 pages Quarterly*

**6094  National Network of Learning Disabled Adults**
808 N 82nd Street
Apt F2
Scottsdale, AZ  85257                    480-941-5112

*Bill Butler, VP*

Offers general information, software, articles and products for the learning disabled.

**6095  Natural Health Bulletin**
Princeton Educational Publishers
117 Cuttermill Road
Great Neck, NY  11021                    516-482-3800

*Carlson Wade, Editor*

Diet and nutrition, physical fitness lifestyle, attitude, developments in natural and preventive medicine.

                        *4 pages Monthly*

**6096  Negotiating the Disability Maze**
Charles C Thomas
2600 S 1st Street
Springfield, IL  62704                   217-789-8980
                                         800-258-8980
                                    FAX: 217-789-9130
                              e-mail: books@ccthomas.com
                                          www.ccthomas.com

*Michael Thomas, President*

This book has been designed and written to furnish people from diverse backgrounds with important information regarding education of children with disabilities. The authors are as thorough as they are explicit. They analyze the concepts, translate the jargon, and outline the characteristics of various disabilities. Also avalable in cloth edition. *$36.95*
                        *206 pages Paperback*
                        *ISBN 0-398066-64-7*

**6097  New Horizons in Sexuality**
Accent Books & Products
PO Box 700
Bloomington, IL  61702                   309-378-2961
                                         800-787-8444
                                    FAX: 309-378-4420
                              e-mail: acmtlvng@aol.com

*Raymond C Cheever, Publisher*
*Betty Garee, Editor*

This manual helps both males and females progress toward a satisfying post-injury relationship. *$7.95*
                        *50 pages Paperback*
                        *ISBN 0-91570 -42-6*

**6098  New Mobility**
23815 Stuart Ranch Road
Malibu, CA  90265                        310-317-4522
                                         800-543-4116
                                    FAX: 310-317-9644
                                          www.newmobility.com

*Sam Maddox, Publisher*
*Barry Corbet, Editor*

The full-service, full-color lifestyle magazine for the disability community. The award-winning magazine is contemporary, witty and candid. Produced by professional journalists and visual artists, the magazine's voice is uncompromising and unsentimental, yet practical, knowing and friendly. The magazine covers issues that matter to readers: medical news, and cure research; jobs, benefits and civil rights; sports, recreation and travel; product news, technology and innovation.

                        *ISSN 1065-21 4*

**6099  New Voices: Self Advocacy By People with Disabilities**
Brookline Books
PO Box 1047
Cambridge, MA  02139                     617-868-0360
                                         800-666-2665
                                    FAX: 617-868-1772
                        e-mail: brooklinebks@delphi.com
                                    www.brooklinebooks.com

A collection of original papers, many by self advocates, that vividly illustrate the dynamic, ever-growing self-advocacy movement — persons with disabilities speaking out and seeking better non-institutional living situations, social and political equality and decent jobs at reasonable pay. *$29.95*
                        *274 pages Paperback*
                        *ISBN 1-57129 -04-4*

**6100  Nine Nineteen News**
Free Library of Philadelphia Library
919 Walnut Street
Philadelphia, PA  19107                  215-683-3213
                                         800-222-1754
                                    FAX: 215-683-3211
                        e-mail: flpblind@library.phila.gov

*Vickie Collins, Manager*

*4 pages Quarterly*

**6101  Nolo's Guide to Social Security Disability**
NOLO
950 Parker Street
Berkeley, CA 94710
510-549-1976
800-955-4775
FAX: 510-548-5902
www.nolo.com

*Maira Dizgalvis, Trade Customer Service Manager*
*Susan McConnell, Director Sales*
*Natasha Kaluza, Sales Assistant*

Not many bureaucratic programs are as large- and as confusing-as Social Security disability. This book shows you the ins and outs of the system. *$29.95*
*350 pages paperback*
*ISBN 0-873375-74-2*

**6102  North Star Community Services**
3420 University Avenue
Waterloo, IA 50701
319-236-0901
FAX: 319-236-3701
e-mail: info@northstarcs.org
www.northstarcs.org

*Mark Witmer, Executive Director*
*Donna Davis, Dir Development/Public Relations*

North Star Community Services is a rehabilitative services organization with home office in Waterloo, IA and several branch offices in Northeast, Northern and Central Iowa. North Star helps indiviuals with disabilities live and work in their communities. Services include: adult day services, supported community living services, employment services, and case management/service coordination.

**6103  North Star Community Services Annual Report For Fiscal Year 2005**
3420 University Avenue
Waterloo, IA 50701
319-236-0901
888-879-1365
FAX: 319-236-3701
e-mail: info@aincservices.org
www.aincservices.org

*Donna Davis, Editor*
*Mark Witmer, Editor*

Free upon request. Is also online or our website.
*12 pages Yearly*

**6104  Nothing is Impossible: Reflections on a N ew Life**
Ballantine Books
4958 Main Street
Downers Grove, IL 60515
630-663-1472

www.randomhouse.com/BB/
Reeve offers a uniquely powerful message of hope on topics ranging from the controversial stem cell debate to the mind-body connection he credits with his recent physical improvements. *$6.99*
*224 pages 2004*
*ISBN 0-345470-73-7*

**6105  Nutritional Action Health Letter: Center for Science in the Public Interest**
1875 Connecticut Avenue NW
Suite 300
Washington, DC 20009
202-332-9110
FAX: 202-265-4954
e-mail: cspi@cspinet.org
www.cspinet.org

*Michael Jacobson, Executive Director*

**6106  Nutritional Desk Reference**
Keats Publishing
PO Box 876
New Canaan, CT 06840
203-966-8721
800-323-4900

**6107  Nutritional Influences on Illness: 2nd Edition**
Third Line Press
4751 Viviana Drive
Tarzana, CA 91356
818-996-0076

tlp@third-line.com

*Melvyn Werbach, Owner*

A comprehensive summary of the world's knowledge concerning the relationship between dietary and nutrtional factors and illness. This book does not try to promote any particular school of thought. Instead of the author telling readers his opinion as to what research says, he makes it easy for them to see data for themselves and then form their own opinions.
*504 pages*
*ISBN 0-879835-31-1*

**6108  Obesity Sourcebook**
Omnigraphics
615 Griswold Street
Detroit, MI 48226
313-961-1340
800-234-1340
FAX: 800-875-1340
www.omnigraphics.com

*Wilma Caldwell, Editor*
*Peter Ruffner, President*

Discusses diseases and other problems associated with obesity. *$48.00*
*400 pages 2000*
*ISBN 0-780803-33-7*

**6109  Occupational Therapy Strategies and Adaptations for Independent Daily Living**
Haworth Press
10 Alice Street
Binghamton, NY 13904
607-722-5857
800-429-6784
FAX: 607-722-6362
e-mail: orders@haworthpress.com
www.haworthpress.com

*S Harrington-Miller, Advertising*
*William Cohen, Owner*

This contains clinical expertise of some fourteen authors or author teams addressing the issue of occupational therapy to assist in independent daily living. Also available as hardcover. *$74.95*
*186 pages Softcover*
*ISBN 0-866563-50-4*

**6110  One in Five**
PO Box 560
Mapleton, ME 04757
207-764-6466
800-974-6466
FAX: 207-764-5396

*Kelly Teague, Manager*
*Quarterly*

**6111  Options**
People Against Cancer
PO Box 10
Otho, IA 50569
515-972-4444
FAX: 515-972-4415
e-mail: info@PeopleAgainstCAncer.com
www.peopleagainstcancer.com

*Frank Wiewel, Executive Director*

*8 pages Quarterly*

**6112  Oregon Clarion**
Oregon Developmental Disability Council
540 24th Pl NE
Salem, OR  97301                     503-945-9941
                                     800-292-4154
                                FAX: 503-945-9947
                                e-mail: ocdd@ocdd.org
                                     www.ocdd.org

*Michael T Bailey, Editor*
*Bill Lynch, Acting Executive Director*

A quarterly publication from the Oregon Developmental Disability Council.

**6113  Organ Transplants: Making the Most of Your Gift of Life**
Patient-Centered Guides
101 Morris Street
Sebastopol, CA  95472                707-829-0515
                                     800-998-9938
                                FAX: 707-829-0104
                                www.patientcenters.com

*Linda Lamb, Editor*
*Shawnde Paull, Marketing*
*Tim O'Reilly, Chief Executive Officer*

Over 64,000 people in the US are awaiting an organ transplant. Although transplant surgeries are now fairly routine and can give their recipients the gift of new life, the road to getting a transplant can be long and harrowing. Living with immunosuppressive drugs and strong emotional responses can also be more challenging than families imagine. Medical journalist Robert Finn answers the concerns of these families, with the latest facts about transplantation - as well as the stories behind them. *$19.95*
*326 pages Paperback*
*ISBN 1-565926-34-X*

**6114  Orphan Disease Update**
NORD
PO Box 1968
Danbury, CT  06813                   203-744-0100
                                     800-999-6673
                                FAX: 203-798-2291
                                TTY: 203-797-9590
                          e-mail: orphan@rarediseases.org
                                www.rarediseases.org

*James Broatch, Chair*
*Carolyn Asbury PhD, Vice Chair*
*Abbey Meyers, President*

Publication of NORD, a unique federation of voluntary health organizations dedicated to helping people with rare orphan diseases and assisting the organizations that serve them. NORD is committed to the identification, treatment and cure of rare disorders through programs of education, advocacy, research and service.

**6115  Our Bodies, Ourselves for the New Century: A Book by and for Women**
Simon & Schuster
100 Front Street
Delran, NJ  08075                    800-323-7445
                                FAX: 800-943-9831
Health refernce for women of all ages and ethnic groups, covering such issues as managed care and the insurance industry, breast cancer treatment options, and recent developments in contraception. Includes 150 photographs and charts and graphs throughout.

*780 pages Hardcover 1998*
*ISBN 0-684842-31-9*

**6116  PALAESTRA**
Challenge Publications, Limited
PO Box 508
Macomb, IL  61455                    309-833-1902
                                FAX: 309-833-1902
                          e-mail: challpub@macomb.com
                                www.palaestra.com

*Julian Stein, Associate Editor*
*David Beaver, Editor-in-Chief/Owner*

A quarterly publication from PALAESTRA. *$19.95*
*64 pages Quarterly*

**6117  PIRS Hotsheet**
Placer Independent Resource Services
11768 Atwood Road
Suite 29
Auburn, CA  95603                    530-885-6100
                                FAX: 530-885-3032
                          e-mail: tmiller@pirs.org
                                www.pirs.org

*Susan Miller, author*
*Susan Miller, Executive Director*

Monthly publication from Placer Independent Resource Services that is provided free of charge to constituents.
*6 pages Monthly*

**6118  Pacing Yourself**
Accent Books & Products
PO Box 700
Bloomington, IL  61702               309-378-2961
                                     800-787-8444
                                FAX: 309-378-4420
                          e-mail: acmtlvng@aol.com

*Raymond C Cheever, Publisher*
*Betty Garee, Editor*

A guide loaded with ideas and tips on starting the day, housekeeping, meal preparation, parenting and socializing. Also includes information on how to group errands and manage household chores, improve posture to make movement easier, and much more. *$10.95*
*141 pages Paperback*
*ISBN 0-91570 -31-0*

**6119  Partnering with Public Health: Funding & Advocacy Opportunities for CILs and SILCs**
Independent Living Research Utilization ILRU
2323 S Shepherd Drive
Suite 1000
Houston, TX  77019                   713-520-0232
                                FAX: 713-520-5785
                                www.ilru.org

*Laurie Redd, Executive Director*

Laura Rauscher discusses how CILs and SCILs can use funding from the Centers for Disease Control and partnerships with public health agencies to provide innovative programs promoting the health of people with disabilities.
*10 pages*

**6120  Peer Counseling: Advocacy-Oriented Peer Support —Part One**
Independent Living Research Utilization ILRU
2323 S Shepherd Drive
Suite 1000
Houston, TX  77019                   713-520-0232
                                FAX: 713-520-5785
                                www.ilru.org

*Laurie Redd, Executive Director*

This month's Readings examines how peer support from the point of view of how in talking to each other and sharing life experiences, we help to form groups that are making changes around the world.

*10 pages*

**6121 Peer Counseling: Roles, Functions, Boundaries**
Independent Living Research Utilization ILRU
2323 S Shepherd Drive
Suite 1000
Houston, TX 77019                713-520-0232
                                FAX: 713-520-5785
                                www.ilru.org

*Laurie Redd, Executive Director*

In this article, the following points were discussed: describing peer support as counseling suggests safeguards and expectations which cannot be provided by nonprofessionals; the purpose of peer counseling is to promote the independent living philosophy and encourage consumers to embrace it; peer counseling cannot and is not intended to help individuals deal with intense emotional stress, whether it is related to their disability or to something else.
*10 pages*

**6122 Peer Mentor Volunteers: Empowering People for Change**
Independent Living Research Utilization ILRU
2323 S Shepherd Drive
Suite 1000
Houston, TX 77019                713-520-0232
                                FAX: 713-520-5785
                                www.ilru.org

*Laurie Redd, Executive Director*

Arizona Bridge to Independent Living (ABIL) in Phoenix, featured in this issue, is another winner in the innovative CIL program competition.
*10 pages*

**6123 People with Disabilities & Abuse: Implications for Center for Independent Living**
Independent Living Research Utilization ILRU
2323 S Shepherd Drive
Suite 1000
Houston, TX 77019                713-520-0232
                                FAX: 713-520-5785
                                www.ilru.org

*Laurie Redd, Executive Director*
*10 pages*

**6124 People with Disabilities Magazine**
New Jersey Devlopmental Disabilities Council
PO Box 700
Trenton, NJ 08625                609-292-3745
                                800-216-1199
                                FAX: 609-292-7114
                                TTY: 609-777-3238
                                e-mail: njddc@njddc.org
                                www.njddc.org

*Ethan Ellis, Director/Editor*
*Susan Richmond, Assistant Director*
*Norman Reim, Communications*

A free magazine for people with disabilities, their families and the public about disability topics such as personal assistance, deinstitutionalization, health care and community living. Published by the New Jersey Developmental Disabilities council, a federally funded advocacy and policy advisory body. The council has 30 members - 15 consumer/product volunteers and 15 professionals.
*48 pages Quarterly*

**6125 People with Disabilities Who Challenge the System**
Brookes Publishing
PO Box 10624
Baltimore, MD 21285              410-337-9580
                                800-638-3775
                                FAX: 410-337-8539
                                e-mail: custserv@brookespublishing.com
                                www.brookespublishing.com

*Paul Brooks, Owner*

Helpful forms, tables, and case studies plus an emphasis on self-determination point the way to the development of supports so that people who are deaf-blind, have severe to profound physical and cognitive disabilities, or have serious behavior problems can be fully included in the classroom, workplace, and community. *$34.00*
*464 pages Paperback*
*ISBN 1-55766 -29-0*

**6126 People's Voice**
Independence CIL
300 3rd Avenue SW
Suite F
Minot, ND 58701                 701-839-4724
                                800-377-5114
                                FAX: 701-838-1677

*Stephen Repnow, Executive Director*
*8 pages Quarterly*

**6127 Personal Perspectives on Personal Assistance Services**
World Institute on Disability
510 16th Street
Suite 100
Oakland, CA 94612               510-763-4100
                                FAX: 510-763-4109
                                e-mail: wid@wid.org
                                www.wid.org

This collection of personal essays explores a wide range of perspectives on Personal Assistance Services. Family issues and PAS concerns for people with various different disabilities, of different ages and as members of minority groups are addressed. *$5.00*
*80 pages Paperback*

**6128 Perspectives**
National Assoc. of State Directors of DD Services
113 Oronoco Street
Alexandria, VA 22314            703-683-4202
                                FAX: 703-683-8773

*Robert Gettings, Executive Director*

Provides a concise summary of national policy developments and initiatives affecting persons with devlopmental disabilities and the programs that serve them. From bills pending before Congress, to the growth in Medicaid-funded services, to changes in federal-state Medicaid policies and the shift of responsibility from Washington to the states, keeps readers in tune with the latest national issues shaping publically funded disability services. *$95.00*
*Monthly*

**6129 Place to Live**
Accent Books & Products
PO Box 700
Bloomington, IL 61702           309-378-2961
                                800-787-8444
                                FAX: 309-378-4420
                                e-mail: acmtlvng@aol.com

*Raymond C Cheever, Publisher*
*Betty Garee, Editor*

Many disabled people have found that group housing or accessible apartments are the best alternative to living in a nursing home. These articles tell about some of the alternatives people have found so they can live independently. Just one idea might be the answer for better living for you. *$4.95*
*64 pages Paperback*
*ISBN 0-91570 -30-2*

**6130 Practice of Aromatherapy**
Inner Traditions
1 Park Street
Rochester, VT 05767             802-767-3174
                                800-246-8648
                                FAX: 802-767-3726
                                e-mail: orders@innertraditions.com
                                www.InnerTraditions.com

*Ehud Sperling, Owner*

The classic manual provides detailed evidence for the efficacy of plant medicine. *$16.95*
  *280 pages*
  *ISBN 0-892813-98-9*

**6131 Proceedings**
AHEAD
PO Box 21192
Columbus, OH 43221          617-287-3880
                           FAX: 617-287-3881
                           TTY:617-287-3882
    e-mail: aagad@postbox.acs.ohio-state.edu
                           www.ahead.org

National conferences, innovative programs, research, evaluation services, auxiliary aids, career information and other vital information.

**6132 Protecting Against Latex Allergy**
Spina Bifida Association of America
4590 Macarthur Boulevard NW
Suite 250
Washington, DC 20007          202-944-3285
                              800-621-3141
                         FAX: 202-944-3295
                         e-mail: sbaa@sbaa.org
                              www.sbaa.org

*Cindy Brownstein, Chief Executive Officer*

Because awareness and proper action may help prevent an allergic reation, learning about latex allergy is especially important for parents, health care workers and anyone who is exposed to latex regulary. *$20.00*

**6133 Psychological & Social Impact of Disabilit y**
Springer Publishing Company
536 Broadway
New York, NY 10012          212-431-4370
                           877-687-7476
                      FAX: 212-941-7842
        e-mail: marketing@springerpub.com
                      www.springerpub.com

*Annette Imperati, Marketing/Sales Director*
*Ursula Springer, President*

*$49.95*
  *488 pages*
  *ISBN 0-826122-13-2*

**6134 Psychology and Health**
Springer Publishing Company
536 Broadway
New York, NY 10012          212-431-4370
                           877-687-7476
                      FAX: 212-941-7842
        e-mail: marketing@springerpub.com
                      www.springerpub.com

*Annette Imperati, Marketing/Sales Director*
*Ursula Springer, President*

Content of this book spans a wide range of clinical conditions, including somatization disorders, chronic pain, migraine, anxiety and cancer. *$29.95*
  *256 pages*

**6135 Psychology of Disability**
Springer Publishing Company
536 Broadway
New York, NY 10012          212-431-4370
                           877-687-7476
                      FAX: 212-941-7842
        e-mail: marketing@springerpub.com
                      www.springerpub.com

*Annette Imperati, Marketing/Sales Director*
*Ursula Springer, President*

Reactions to the disabled. *$27.95*

*288 pages*
*ISBN 0-82613 -40-1*

**6136 Quality Care Newsletter**
National Association for Continence
PO Box 1019
Charleston, SC 29402          843-377-0900
                              800-252-3337
                         FAX: 843-377-0905
        e-mail: memberservices@nafc.org
                              www.nafc.org

*Rachel Coker, Editor*
*Nancy Muller, Executive Director*

Newsletter from NAFC. *$25.00*
  *14-16 pages Quarterly*

**6137 Quality of Life for Persons with Disabilities**
Brookline Books
PO Box 1046
Cambridge, MA 02139          617-868-0360
                             800-666-2665
                        FAX: 617-868-1772
       e-mail: brooklinebks@delphi.com
                        www.brooklinebooks.com

Quality of life generally refers to a person's subjective experience of his or her life and focuses attention on how the individual with a disabling condition experiences the world. This book presents a comprehensive and international view of this concept as applied to a broad range of settings in which persons with disabilities live, work and play. *$35.00*
  *Paperback*
  *ISBN 0-91479 -92-1*

**6138 REACHing Out Newsletter**
REACH of Dallas Resource on Independent Living
8625 King George Drive
Suite 210
Dallas, TX 75235          214-630-4796
                     FAX: 214-630-6390
       e-mail: reachdallas@reachcils.org
                          www.reachcils.org

*Charlotte Stewart, Executive Director/Owner*
*Susie Reukema, Assistant Director*
*Becky Teal, Editor*

Quarterly newsletter from REACH of Dallas Resource Center on Independent Living.
  *16 pages*

**6139 RTC Connection**
Research and Training Center
University of Wisconsin Stout
Menomonie, WI 54751          715-232-2236
                        FAX: 715-232-2251
        e-mail: menz@uwstout.edu
                        www.rtc.uwstout.edu

*Julie Larson, Program Assistant*

Bi-annual reports on disability and rehabilitation research and policy topics.
  *Newsletter*

**6140 Ragged Edge**
Advocado Press
Pox 145
Louisville, KY 40201          502-894-9492
                         FAX: 502-899-9562
       e-mail: office@advocadopress.org
                         www.advocadopress.org

*$18.95*

*38 pages*
*ISBN 0-962706-45-0*

**6141    Ragged Edge: The Disability Experience**
Advocado Press
PO Box 145
Louisville, KY  40201                                   502-894-9492
                                          FAX: 502-899-9562
                          e-mail: office@advocadopress.orgom
                                      www.advocadopress.org

*Barrett Shaw, Editor*

Anthology of writing from the pages of the first 15 years of The
Disability Rag. *$18.95*
          *245 pages*
          *ISBN 0-96270 -45-0*

**6142    Reaching Out**
REACH of Denton Resource Center
405 S Elm Street
Suite 202
Denton, TX  76201                                   940-383-1062
                                          FAX: 940-383-2742
                          e-mail: reachdes@reachcils.org
                                      www.reachcils.org

*Charlotte Stuart, Owner*
          *Quarterly*

**6143    Reachout**
405 S Elm Street
Suite 202
Denton, TX  76201                                   940-383-1062
                                          FAX: 940-383-2742

*Becky S Teal, Office Manager*
          *12 pages Quarterly*

**6144    Referral Directory of Social Services in Metropolitan
           Washington**
Prevent Child Abuse of Metropolitan Washington
7404 Salford Ct
Alexandria, VA  22315                               202-223-0020
                                          FAX: 202-296-4046
                          e-mail: pcamw@juno.com
                                      www.pcamw.org

*Kendra Dunn, Executive Director*
*$60.00*
          *630 pages Bi-Annually*

**6145    Rehabilitation Gazette**
Gazette International Networking Institute
4207 Lindell Boulevard
Suite 110
Saint Louis, MO  63108                              314-534-0475
                                          FAX: 314-534-5070
                          e-mail: gini_intl@msn.com
                                      www.post-polio.org
International journal of independent living for people with dis-
abilities. *$12.00*
          *8 pages Bi-Annually*

**6146    Relaxation: A Comprehensive Manual for Adults and
           Children with Special Needs**
Research Press
2612 N Mattis Avenue
Champaign, IL  61822                                217-352-3273
                                          800-519-2707
                                          FAX: 217-352-1221
                          e-mail: rp@researchpress.com
                                      www.researchpress.com

*Gail Salyards, Marketing Services Manager*
*Russell Pence, President*

This unique contribution to the field of relaxation training presents: self relaxation techniques designed for adults, methods for
teaching relaxation to adults and older children, and procedures
for teaching relaxation to young children and children with developmental disabilities. The clear, concise text is supplemented by over 100 helpful illustrations. *$16.95*
          *108 pages Paperback*
          *ISBN 0-878221-86-7*

**6147    Resources for People with Disabilities and Chronic
           Conditions**
Resources for Rehabilitation
33 Bedford Street
Suite 19a
Lexington, MA  02420                                781-890-6371
                                          FAX: 781-861-7517

*Susan Greenblatt*

A comprehensive resource directory that helps people with disabilities and chronic conditions achieve their maximum level of
independence. Chapters on spinal cord injuries, low back pain,
diabetes, hearing and speech impairments, epilepsy, multiple
sclerosis. Describes organizations, products and publications.
*$49.95*
          *215 pages Biennial*
          *ISBN 0-92971 -12-7*

**6148    Role Portrayal and Stereotyping on Television**
Greenwood Publishing Group
88 Post Road W
Suite 5007
Westport, CT  06880                                 203-226-3571
                                          FAX: 203-222-1502
                                      www.greenwood.com

*Nancy Signorielli, Author*
*Wayne Smith, President*

An annotated bibliography of studies relating to women, minorities, aging, health and handicaps.
          *214 pages $55 - $59.95*
          *ISBN 0-313248-55-9*

**6149    Rolling Start News**
570 W 4th Street
Suite 103
San Bernardino, CA  92401                           909-884-2129
                                          FAX: 909-386-7446
                          e-mail: fran.ed@verizon.net
                                      www.rollingstart.com

*Frances Bates, Executive Director*
          *6 pages Quarterly*

**6150    Screening in Chronic Disease**
Oxford University Press
2001 Evans Road
Cary, NC  27513                                     919-677-0977
                                          800-451-7556
                                          FAX: 919-677-1303
                                      www.oup-usa.org

*Thomas Carty, Senior Vice President*

Early detection, or screening, is a common strategy for controlling chronic disease, but little information has been available to
help determine which screening procedures are worthwhile, until this textbook. *$42.50*
          *256 pages*

**6151    See A Bone**
Facts on File
132 W 31st Street
Floor 17
New York, NY  10001                                 212-967-8800
                                          800-322-8755
                                          FAX: 212-967-9196
                          e-mail: jchambers@factsonfile.com
                                      www.factsonfile.com

*Mark Donnell, President*
*$65.00*

*352 pages*
*ISBN 0-816042-80-2*

**6152 Serving Adults with Cognitive Disabilities**
Independent Living Research Utilization ILRU
2323 S Shepherd Drive
Suite 1000
Houston, TX 77019          713-520-0232
                          FAX: 713-520-5785
                          www.ilru.org

*Laurie Redd, Executive Director*

Darrel, Tyrone and Susan of Arizona Bridge to Independent Living (ABIL) describe the success of their Community Living Options Program for adults with developmental disabilities in this months readings.
*10 pages*

**6153 Setebaid Sentinel**
Setebaid Services
PO Box 196
Winfield, PA 17889          570-524-9090
                          FAX: 570-523-0769
                          e-mail: info@setebaidservices.org
                          www.setebaidservices.org

*Mark Moyer, Executive Director*
*Diane Facer, Office Assistant*
*4-8 pages Bi-Annually*

**6154 Sexual Adjustment**
Accent Books & Products
PO Box 700
Bloomington, IL 61702          309-378-2961
                          800-787-8444
                          FAX: 309-378-4420
                          e-mail: acmtlvng@aol.com

*Raymond C Cheever, Publisher*
*Betty Garee, Editor*

Essential information concerning sexual adjustment for the paraplegic male. *$4.95*
*73 pages Paperback*
*ISBN 0-19570 -00-0*

**6155 Sexuality and Disabilities: A Guide for Human Service Practitioners**
Haworth Press
10 Alice Street
Binghamton, NY 13904          607-722-5857
                          800-429-6784
                          FAX: 607-722-6362
                          e-mail: orders@haworthpress.com
                          www.haworthpress.com

*Jackie Blakeslee, Advertising*
*Romel W Mackelpranf DSW, Editor*
*Deborah Valentine, Editor*

This book addresses persons with physical, sensory, intellectual and cognitive disabilities and their concerns in the areas of intimacy, family issues, sexuality and sexual functioning. *$74.95*
*159 pages Hardcover*
*ISBN 1-560243-75-9*

**6156 Sickened: The Memoir of a Muchausen by Pro xy Childhood**
Bantam Books
1540 Broadway
New York, NY 10036          212-782-9000
                          FAX: 212-302-7985
                          www.randomhouse.com
From early childhood, Julie Gregory was continually X-rayed, medicated, and operated on — in the vain pursuit of an illness that was created in her mother's mind. Munchausen by prozy (MBP) in which the caretaker — almost always the mother — invents or induces symptoms in her child because she craves the attention of medical professionals. *$24.95*

*256 pages Hardcover 2003*
*ISBN 0-553803-07-7*

**6157 Sixty Days of Low-Fat, Low-Cost Meals in Minutes**
John Wiley and Son
111 River Street
Suite 2000
Hoboken, NJ 07030          201-748-6000
                          FAX: 212-850-6088

*Leigh Anne Godfreg, Sales Coordinator*
*William Pesce, Chief Executive Officer*

A great way to get patients on the road to healthy eating. It contains 150 recipes complete with facts on lowering calories, fat, salt and cholesterol. It contains complete menu plans for 60 days and recipes that use ingredients you can find anywhere. *$12.95*
*294 pages Paperback*
*ISBN 1-56561 -10-5*

**6158 Socialization Games for Persons with Disabilities**
Nevalyn F Nevil, Marna L Beatty & David Moxley
2600 S 1st Street
Springfield, IL 62704          217-789-8980
                          800-258-8980
                          FAX: 217-789-9130
                          e-mail: books@ccthomas.com
                          www.ccthomas.com

*Michael Thomas, President*

This book is a compilation of practical suggestions and games with easy-to-follow guide lines that provide a solid foundation for the encouragement of positive social behavior. *$47.95*
*176 pages Paperback 1997*
*ISBN 0-398067-46-5*

**6159 Sometimes You Just Want to Feel Like a Human Being**
Brookes Publishing
PO Box 10624
Baltimore, MD 21285          410-337-9580
                          800-638-3775
                          FAX: 410-337-8539
                          e-mail: custserv@brookespublishing.com
                          www.brookespublishing.com

*Paul Brooks, Owner*

Case studies of empowering psychotherapy with people with disabilities. This text reveals how counseling can be beneficial to individuals with disabilities of all kinds, including autism, mental retardation, sensory impairment, cerebral palsy, or HIV infection. *$ 26.95*
*272 pages Paperback*
*ISBN 1-55766 -96-0*

**6160 Source of Help and Hope Newsletter**
Arthritis Foundation
3544 N Progress Avenue
Suite 204
Harrisburg, PA 17110          717-763-0900
                          800-776-0746
                          FAX: 717-763-0903
                          www.arthritis.org

*Catherine Penrod, President*

Offers information on activities and events of the Chapter.
*3x Year*

**6161 Space Coast CIL News**
Space Coast Center for Independent Living
331 Ramp Road
Cocoa Beach, FL 32931          321-784-9008
                          FAX: 321-784-3702
                          TTY:321-784-9008
                          e-mail: agrau@bellsouth.net

*Anna Grau, Ind. Living Services Coordinator*
*Donna Taylor, Executive Director*

Non-profit organization that provides services which enable people with disabilities to live as independently as possible.

*12 pages Quarterly*

**6162  Special Care in Dentistry**
Academy of Dentistry for Persons with Disabilities
211 E Chicago Avenue
Floor 5
Chicago, IL 60611
312-337-2169
FAX: 312-440-2824
e-mail: fosccdzz@worldnet.att.net
www.specialdentistry.org

*John Rutkauskaf, Executive Director*
*$125.00*
*48 pages BiMonthly*

**6163  Special Siblings: Growing Up With Someone with A Disability**
Brookes Publishing
PO Box 10624
Baltimore, MD 21285
410-337-9580
800-638-3775
FAX: 410-337-8539
e-mail: custserv@brookespublishing.com
www.brookespublishing.com

*Paul Brooks, Owner*

The author reveals what she experienced as the sister of a man with cerebral palsy and mental retardation — and shares what others have learned about being and having a special sibling. Weaving a lifetime of memories and reflections with relevant research and interviews with more than 100 other siblings and experts, McHugh explores a spectrum of feelings — from anger and guilt to love and pride — and helps readers understand the issues siblings may encounter. *$21.95*
*256 pages Paperback 2002*
*ISBN 1-557666-07-5*

**6164  Spectrum Aquatics Catalog**
Spectrum Aquatics
7100 Spectrum Lane
Missoula, MT 59808
406-543-5309
800-776-5309
FAX: 406-728-7143
e-mail: info@spectrumaquatics.com
www.spectrumaquatics.com

*Dave Murray, President*
*Yearly*

**6165  Spud Tech Notes**
Idaho Assistive Technology Project
129 W 3rd Street
Moscow, ID 83843
208-885-3559
800-432-8324
FAX: 208-885-3628
e-mail: rseiler@uidaho.edu
www.educ.uidaho.edu/idatech
*Bi-annually*

**6166  Still Me**
Ballantine Books
4958 Main Street
Downers Grove, IL 60515
630-663-1472

www.randomhouse.com/BB/
The man who was Superman begins with his debilitating riding accident, then weaves back and forth between past and present, creating a thorough biography of Reeve's life. *$7.99*

*324 pages 1999*
*ISBN 0-345432-41-X*

**6167  Sweet Charity**
Good Shepherd Rehabilitation Network
543 Saint John Street
Allentown, PA 18103
610-776-3559
877-734-2747
FAX: 610-776-3552
e-mail: emcdonald@gsrh.org
www.goodshepherdrehab.org

*Kelly Spiece, Editor*
*Maryellen Dickey, Vice President*

**6168  TECH Watch**
Tech Connection
35 Hudson Avenue
Red Bank, NJ 07701
732-747-5310
732-747-1896
e-mail: tecconn@aol.com
www.techconnection.org
*8 pages Quarterly*

**6169  The Guiding Hand**
Home of the Guiding Hands
1825 Gillespie Way
Suite 200
El Cajon, CA 92020
619-448-3700
FAX: 619-448-7208
www.guidinghands.org

*Carol Fitzgibbons, Executive Director*
*Quarterly*

**6170  To Live with Grace and Dignity**
World Institute on Disability
510 16th Street
Suite 100
Oakland, CA 94612
510-763-4100
FAX: 510-763-4109
e-mail: wid@wid.org
www.wid.org

This unique book combines photographs and essays to allow the reader to enter some of the real day to day relationships that develop between individuals with disabilities and their personal assistants. Looking at and listening to what these relationships are all about is what motivated and inspired this book, says author Lydia Gans. The individuals included in this book represent a wide range of ages, disabilities and cultural backgrounds. *$26.00*
*72 pages Paperback*

**6171  Touch/Ability Connects People with Disabilities & Alternative Health Care Pract.**
Independent Living Research Utilization ILRU
2323 S Shepherd Drive
Suite 1000
Houston, TX 77019
713-520-0232
FAX: 713-520-5785
www.ilru.org

*Laurie Redd, Executive Director*

The people at DIRECT center for Independence and Touch/Ability in Tuscon, Arizona, have collaborated to develop a wellness program that makes alternative health care choices available to people with disabilities. The Touch/Ability Wellness program was selected as one of last year's winners in the Innovative CILs competition because of this outcome of increased options open to people with disabilities.
*10 pages*

**6172  US Role in International Disability Activities: A History**

World Institute on Disability
510 16th Street
Suite 100
Oakland, CA 94612
510-763-4100
FAX: 510-763-4109
e-mail: wid@wid.org
www.wid.org

This study was undertaken to present an initial introduction to US involvement in the field of international rehabilitation and disability. *$12.00*
*169 pages Paperback*

**6173  Understanding and Accommodating Physical Disabilities: Desk Reference**
Greenwood Publishing Group
88 Post Road W
Suite 5007
Westport, CT  06880
203-226-3571
FAX: 203-222-1502
www.greenwood.com

*Wayne Smith, President*

Medical conditions that qualify as disabilities under the American's with Disabilities Act are explained in non-medical terminology. Hardcover.
*200 pages $52.95 - $55*
*ISBN 0-899308-14-7*

**6174  Vaccines: Are They Really Safe and Effective?**
New Atlantean Press
PO Box 9638
Santa Fe, NM  87504
505-983-1856

*Nathan Wright, Publisher*

Evaluates 'mandated' and many newer vaccines to determine their safety and both short- and long-term effects.
*2002*
*ISBN 1-881217-30-2*

**6175  Vibrational Medicine**
Bear & Company
1 Park Street
Rochester, VT  05767
802-767-3174
800-246-8648
FAX: 802-767-3726
e-mail: orders@innertraditions.com
www.InnerTraditions.com

*Ehud Sperling, Owner*
*608 pages*
*ISBN 1-879181-58-4*

**6176  Vision, Values & Vitality: Bringing IL Principles to Mental Health Peer Support**
Independent Living Research Utilization ILRU
2323 S Shepherd Drive
Suite 1000
Houston, TX  77019
713-520-0232
FAX: 713-520-5785
www.ilru.org

*Frederick Moe*
*Cindy Perkins*
*Pat Spiller*

Frederick, Cindy, and Pat describe the technical assistance GSIL provides to drop-in centers to enable them to become consumer-controlled peer support centers.
*10 pages*

**6177  Visions & Values**
Idaho Council on Developmental Disabilities
802 W Bannock Street
Suite 308
Boise, ID  83702
208-336-8508
800-544-2433
FAX: 208-334-3417
e-mail: msword@icdd.state.id.us
www.state.id.us/icdd

*Marilyn B Sword, Executive Director/Editor*
*Pat Barclay, Manager*

A quarterly publication from the Idaho Council on Developmental Disabilities.

**6178  WA & NEWS**
Wheelchair Access
PO Box 12
Glenmoore, PA  19343
610-942-3266
FAX: 610-942-0282
e-mail: info@waccess.org
www.waccess.org

*Frank Gomez, Publisher*

Features wheelchair accessible houses and apartments for rent or for sale. Currently the newsletter includes ads from all states. Ads received from any State will be accepted free of charge. Featured also are ads of wheelchairs, vans, equipment, etc., for sale. Complete ad information and more is listed in the Web site. A free copy of WA & NEWS sent upon request. *$12.00*
*20 pages Monthly*

**6179  Walking Tomorrow**
Christopher Reeve Paralysis Foundation
636 Morris Tpke
Suite 3a
Short Hills, NJ  07078
973-379-2690
800-252-0292
FAX: 973-912-9433
e-mail: paralysis@aol.com
www.paralysis.com

*Kathy Lewis, President*

A newsletter offering medical and technological updates for people with physical disabilities, including paralysis.
*Quarterly*

**6180  Walton Independent**
Walton Rehabilitation Health System
PO Box 2223
Augusta, GA  30903
706-823-8504
866-492-5866
FAX: 706-823-5292
e-mail: postmaster@wrh.org
www.wrh.org

*Oleana Scarboro, Marketing Coordinator*

A publication from the Walton Rehabilitation Health System. Published two times a year, and it is free.
*40 pages 2 times yearly*

**6181  Weiner's Herbal**
Quantum Books
4 Cambridge Center
Cambridge, MA  02142
617-494-5042
FAX: 617-577-7282
e-mail: orders@quantumbk.com
www.quantumbooks.com

*William Szabo, Owner*

A-Z index covering all aspects of herbs.
*Paperback 1980*
*ISBN 0-812825-86-1*

**6182  What You Need To Know**
Vestibular Disorders Association
PO Box 4467
Portland, OR  97208
503-229-7705
800-837-8428
FAX: 503-229-8064

*$24.95*
*Quarterly*
*ISBN 0-963261-13-4*

**6183  What's Line**
Alabama Public Library Service
6030 Monticello Drive
Montgomery, AL  36130
334-213-3906
800-392-5671
FAX: 334-213-3993
e-mail: fzaleski@apls.state.al.us
www.apls.state.al.us

*Fara Zaleski, Executive Director*

*4 pages Quarterly*

**6184  Wheelchair Batteries**
Accent Books & Products
PO Box 700
Bloomington, IL  61702
309-378-2961
800-787-8444
FAX: 309-378-4420
e-mail: acmtlvng@aol.com

*Raymond C Cheever, Publisher*
*Betty Garee, Editor*

Offers valuable tips for trouble-free travel at minimum cost: selecting the right battery the first time and how to use and re-charge your battery to make it last longer. *$3.50*
*32 pages Paperback*
*ISBN 0-91570 -22-1*

**6185  Wheelin' Around**
6614 W Sweetwater Avenue
Glendale, AZ  85304
623-776-8830
800-456-1371
FAX: 623-412-9920
e-mail: info@wheelerscanrentals.com
www.wheelersvanrentals.com

*Tammy Smith, Manager*

A quarterly publication. Free.
*Quarterly*

**6186  Women with Physical Disabilities: Achievin g & Maintaining Health & Well-Being**
Spina Bifida Association of America
4590 Macarthur Boulevard NW
Suite 250
Washington, DC 20007
202-944-3285
800-621-3141
FAX: 202-944-3295
e-mail: sbaa@sbaa.org
www.sbaa.org

*Cindy Brownstein, Chief Executive Officer*

Introduces the critical concept of womens health in the context of physical disabilities. *$42.00*

**6187  Women's Health Alert**
Addison-Wesley Publishing Company
75 Arlington Street
Suite 300
Boston, MA  02116
617-848-6000
FAX: 617-848-6034
www.awprofessional.com

*William Barke, President*

This book provides up-to-date information on the practice of female medicine with data and statistics that can help a woman make wise decisions about her health. Information on hormone-replacement therapy and osteoporosis are detailed.
*1991*

**6188  Work in the Context of Disability Culture**
Independent Living Research Utilization ILRU
2323 S Shepherd Drive
Suite 1000
Houston, TX  77019
713-520-0232
FAX: 713-520-5785
www.ilru.org

*Laurie Redd, Executive Director*

Another winner in the innovative CIL competition-Steve Brown describes the Talking Books Program of Southeast Alaska Independent Living, discussing their efforts to record the oral history and life experiences of people with disabilities in the larger context of the disability culture.

*10 pages*

**6189  Working with Your Doctor: Getting the Healthcare You Deserve**
Patient-Centered Guides
101 Morris Street
Sebastopol, CA  95472
707-829-0515
800-998-9938
FAX: 707-829-0104
e-mail: health@oreilly.com
www.patientcenters.com

*Linda Lamb, Editor*
*Shawnde Paull, Marketing*
*Tim O'Reilly, Chief Executive Officer*

Working with Your Doctor shows how to form a satisfying partnership with your doctor in a rapidly changing healthcare environment. It contains in-depth and practical information on how to find the right doctor, communicate clearly, ask about tests and treatments, seek opinions, take action when wronged, and deal effectively with managed care. This book is a great primer for patient empowerment. *$15.95*
*377 pages Paperback*
*ISBN 1-565922-73-5*

**6190  Your Body's Many Cries for Water**
Global Health Solutions
PO Box 3189
Falls Church, VA  22043
703-848-2333
800-759-3999
FAX: 703-848-0028
e-mail: info@watercure.com
www.watercure.com

*Kristin Swan, Office Administrator*
*Joy Barber, Secretary*
*Xiaopo Batmanghelidj, President*

Global Health Solutions provides materials by Dr F Batmanghelidj. He writes about dehydration and traces many illnesses to the fact that we do not drink enough water. The ability of the body to heal itself is greatly impaired by inadequate water consumption. *$ 14.95*
*182 pages*
*ISBN 0-962994-23-5*

**6191  Your Inner Physician and You: CranioSacral Therapy SomatoEmotional Release**
North Atlantic Books
1456 Forth Street
Berkeley, CA  94710
510-559-8277
FAX: 510-559-8279
www.northatlanticbooks.com
*163 pages 1997*
*ISBN 1-556432-46-1*

## Hearing Impaired

**6192  ASHA Leader**
American Speech-Language-Hearing Association
10801 Rockville Pike
Rockville, MD  20852
301-897-5700
800-638-8255
FAX: 301-897-7348
e-mail: actioncenter@asha.org
www.asha.org

*Joanne K Jessen, Publications Director*
*John E Bernthal, President*
*Arlene Pietranton, Executive Director*

Association publication containing news, notices of events and activities and information for members on issues facing the profession of audiology and speech-language pathology. *$80.00*

*35 pages 2 x month*

**6193  Adult Bible Lessons for the Deaf**
LifeWay Christian Resources Southern Baptist Conv.
127 9th Avenue N
Nashville, TN  37234                          615-251-2089
                                              800-458-2772
                                       FAX: 651-251-5764
                            e-mail: specialed@lifeway.com
                                              www.lifeway.com

*Wade Stapleton, Manager*

Bible study lessons for every three months written by and for
persons who are deaf. Based on the Family Bible Series (International Sunday School Lessons).
*Quarterly*

**6194  Advanced Sign Language Vocabulary: A Resource Text
for Educators**
2600 S 1st Street
Springfield, IL  62704                        217-789-8980
                                              800-258-8980
                                       FAX: 217-789-9130
                         e-mail: books@ccthomas.com
                                              www.ccthomas.com

*Michael Thomas, President*

A resource text for educators, interpreters, parents and sign language instructors. *$46.95*
    *202 pages Paperback*
    *ISBN 0-398057-22-2*

**6195  American Annals of the Deaf**
PO Box 1778
St Augustine, FL  32085                       904-810-5200
                                       FAX: 904-810-5525
                            e-mail: email@ceasd.org
                                              www.ceasd.org

*Joe Finnegan, Executive Director*
*Barbara Raimondo, Government Relations Liaison*
*Mike Bello, Treasurer*

Quarterly publication from the Conference of Educational Administrators Serving the Deaf.
*Quarterly*

**6196  American Journal of Audiology**
American Speech-Language-Hearing Association
10801 Rockville Pike
Rockville, MD  20852                          301-897-5700
                                              800-638-8255
                                       FAX: 301-897-7348
                               e-mail: info@asha.org
                                              www.asha.org

*John E Bernthal, President*
*Arlene Peitranton, Executive Director*
*Joanne Jessen, Publications Director*

Articles concern screening, assesment, and treatment techniques; prevention; professional issues; supervision; administration. Includes clinical forums, clinical reviews, letters to the editor, or research reports that emphasize clinical practice.

**6197  American Journal of Speech-Language Pathology**
American Speech-Language-Hearing Association
10801 Rockville Pike
Rockville, MD  20852                          301-897-5700
                                              800-638-8255
                                       FAX: 301-897-7348
                               e-mail: info@asha.org
                                              www.asha.org

*John E Bernthal, President*
*Arlene Pietranton, Executive Director*
*Joanne Jessen, Publications Director*

**6198  American Sign Language (ASL): Quick Facts**
Federal Government
31 Center Drive Msc2320
Bethesda, MD  20892
                                              800-241-1044
                                       FAX: 301-402-0018
                   e-mail: nidcdinfo@nidcd.nih.gov
                                              www.nidcd.nih.gov

Ouick facts on what is ASL, where did it orginate, how it compares with spoken language, and why has ASL become a first language for many deaf people.

**6199  American Sign Language Handshape Dictionary**
Gallaudet University Press
11030 S Langley Avenue
Chicago, IL  60628
                                              800-621-2736
                                       FAX: 800-621-8476
                                       TTY:800-621-9347
                                       gupress.gallaudet.edu

*Richard A Tennant, Co-Author*
*Marianne Gluszak Brown, Co-Author*

More than 1,600 sign illustrations arranged by handshape for easy identification. Allows readers to look up signs they have seen without needing to know their English meaning beforehand, complemented by a complete English index cross-referenced to every sign. *$35.00*
    *408 pages Hardcover*

**6200  American Sign Language Phrase Book**
TJ Publishers
2544 Tarpley Road
Suite 108
Carrollton, TX  75006                         972-416-0800
                                              800-999-1168
                                       FAX: 301-585-5930
                               e-mail: TJPubinc@aol.com

*Angela K Thames, President*
*Jerald A Murphy, VP*

The author provides interesting, realistic and meaningful situations. Sign language is learned through novel remarks cleverly organized around everyday topics. *$18.95*
    *362 pages Softcover*
    *ISBN 0-80923 -00-5*

**6201  American Sign Language: A Look at Its Structure &
Community**
TJ Publishers
2544 Tarpley Road
Suite 108
Carrollton, TX  75006                         972-416-0800
                                              800-999-1168
                                       FAX: 301-585-5930
                               e-mail: TJPubinc@aol.com

*Angela K Thames, President*
*Jerald A Murphy, VP*

Answers basic questions about American Sign Language. What is it? What is its history? Who uses it? What is the deaf community? *$3.95*
    *22 pages Softcover*
    *ISBN 0-93266 -01-9*

**6202  Anna's Silent World**
JB Lippincott
227 E Washington Square
Philadelphia, PA  19106                       215-521-8300
                                              800-777-2295
                                       FAX: 215-824-7390

*J Lippincott, Chief Executive Officer*

Anna was a hearing impaired child who lived in New York City with her family. The text followed Anna through a hearing evaluation, speech therapy, and her participation in a class for hearing impaired children.

*48 pages Hardcover*
*ISBN 0-39731 -39-5*

**6203   At Home Among Strangers**
TJ Publishers
2544 Tarpley Road
Suite 108
Carrollton, TX  75006                  972-416-0800
                                       800-999-1168
                                  FAX: 301-585-5930
                              e-mail: TJPubinc@aol.com

*Angela K Thames, President*
*Jerald A Murphy, Executive Assistant*

Discusses deaf culture and its uniqueness in two sections: the
first describes the deaf community - its development, structure
and culture; the second explains Schein's theory of deaf community development. *$24.95*
            *254 pages Hardcover*
            *ISBN 0-930323-51-3*

**6204   Auditory Processing Disorders in Children: What Does
         It Mean?**
Federal Government
31 Center Drive Msc2320
Bethesda, MD  20892
                                       800-241-1044
                                  FAX: 301-402-0018
                       e-mail: nidcdinfo@nidcd.nih.gov
                                       www.nidcd.nih.gov
This fact sheet describes what is auditory processing disorder,
what causes APD diffculty, what are the symtoms, how is it diagnosed, what treatments are available, and current research into
the rehabilitation of child language disorders which will help us
better understand the nature of auditory processing disorders.

**6205   Auricle**
Auditory-Verbal International
1390 Chain Bridge Road
# 100
Mc Lean, VA  22101                     703-739-1049
                                  FAX: 703-739-0395
                                  TTY:703-739-0874
                          e-mail: audiverb@aol.com
                                www.auditory-verbal.org

*Sara Blair Lake, Executive Director/CEO*
*Tom Lucches, President*

To provide the choice of listening and speaking as the way of life
for children and adults who are deaf or hard of hearing.
            *Quarterly*

**6206   BPPV**
Vestibular Disorder Association
PO Box 4467
Portland, OR  97208                    503-229-7705
                                       800-837-8428
                                  FAX: 503-229-8064
                           e-mail: veda@vestibular.org
                                  www.vestibular.org

*Lisa Haven, Editor*
*Connie Pilcher, Outreach Coordinator*
            *2000*

**6207   Basic Course in Manual Communication**
Gallaudet University Bookstore
11030 S Langley Avenue
Chicago, IL  60628                     202-651-5488
                                       800-621-2736
                                  FAX: 202-651-5489
Teach your students manual communication - that living, chang-
ing, growing language of signs. *$11.95*

*158 pages Softcover*

**6208   Basic Vocabulary: ASL for Parents and Children**
TJ Publishers
2544 Tarpley Road
Suite 108
Carrollton, TX  75006                  972-416-0800
                                       800-999-1168
                                  FAX: 301-585-5930
                              e-mail: TJPubinc@aol.com

*Angela K Thames, President*
*Jerald A Murphy, VP*

Carefully selected words and signs include those that children
use every day. Alphabetically organized vocabulary incorporates developmental lists helpful to both deaf and hearing children and over 1000 clear sign language illustrations. *$8.95*
            *240 pages Softcover*
            *ISBN 0-93266 -00-0*

**6209   Ben's Story: A Deaf Child's Right to Sign**
TJ Publishers
2544 Tarpley Road
Suite 108
Carrollton, TX  75006                  972-416-0800
                                       800-999-1168
                                  FAX: 301-585-5930
                              e-mail: TJPubinc@aol.com

*Angela K Thames, President*
*Jerald A Murphy, Executive Assistant*

This is a mother's story of how she responded to the diagnosis of
her son's deafness and how she struggled to have her son educated using sign language. *$7.95*
            *267 pages Softcover*
            *ISBN 0-930323-47-5*

**6210   Between Friends**
Beltone Electronics Corporation
4201 W Victoria Street
Chicago, IL  60646                     773-583-3600
                                  FAX: 773-583-1361

*Renee Rockoff, Editor*
*Dave McKissack*

For hearing aid wearers: quizzes, jokes, health, recipes and financial items.
            *6 pages*

**6211   Book of Name Signs**
Gallaudet University Bookstore
11030 S Langley Avenue
Chicago, IL  60628                     202-651-5488
                                       800-621-2736
                                  FAX: 202-651-5489
Discusses the rules for American Sign Language name sign for-
mation and their appropriate use. *$12.95*
            *112 pages*

**6212   Bridges Beyond Sound**
Brookes Publishing
PO Box 10624
Baltimore, MD  21285                   410-337-9580
                                       800-638-3775
                                  FAX: 410-337-8539
                 e-mail: custserv@brookespublishing.com
                              www.brookespublishing.com

*Paul Brooks, Owner*

An instructional workbook on understanding and including students with a hearing loss. Supplement to the Bridges Beyond
Sound videotape. Besides the videotape script, background information on hearing loss, discussion questions, activities, and
reproducible worksheets are included. *$33.00*

*176 pages Spiral-bound*
*ISBN 1-55766 -26-6*

**6213  Bulletin Newsletter**
806 W Adams Boulevard
Los Angeles, CA  90007
213-748-5481
800-522-4582
FAX: 213-749-1651
e-mail: mmartindale@jtc.org
www.jtc.org

*Barbara F Hecht PhD, Executive Director*
*Mary Ann Bell, VP Development & Communications*
*Jack Cooper, Editor*

Bi-annual publication from the John Tracy Clinic.
*8 pages Bi-annually*

**6214  CSD Spectrum**
Communication Service for the Deaf (CSD)
102 N Krohn Place
Sioux Falls, SD  57103
605-367-5760
800-642-6410
FAX: 605-367-5958
e-mail: info@c-s-d.org
www.c-s-d.org

*Marvin Miller, Author/Editor*

A free quarterly publication from CSD.
*Quarterly*

**6215  Captions for Deaf and Hard-of-Hearing View ers**
Federal Government
31 Center Drive Msc2320
Bethesda, MD  20892
800-241-1044
FAX: 301-402-0018
e-mail: nidcdinfo@nidcdnih.gov
www.nidcd.nih.gov
This fact sheet explains what are the captions, current research studying caption features, speeds, and the effects od visula impairments on reading captions, ans offers additional resources.

**6216  Changing the Rules**
TJ Publishers
2544 Tarpley Road
Suite 108
Carrollton, TX  75006
972-416-0800
800-999-1168
FAX: 301-585-5930
e-mail: TJPubinc@aol.com

*Angela K Thames, President*
*Jerald A Murphy, VP*

Like many deaf adults, Frank Bowe was mainstreamed in the small Pennsylvania town where he was raised. This is a humorous and poignant account of the obstacles that shaped this leading disability rights activist. Bowe's account of coming of age and personal growth, the discovery of signed language and an insider's view of the equal rights movement is a compelling record of one man's struggle with the challenges of profound deafness. *$8.95*
*204 pages Hardcover*
*ISBN 0-93266 -31-0*

**6217  Chelsea: The Story of a Signal Dog**
Gallaudet University Bookstore
800 Florida Avenue NE
Washington, DC  20002
202-651-5000
800-451-1073
FAX: 202-651-5489

*Erving Jordan, President*

This is a story of a young deaf couple and their Belgian sheepdog, who acts as their ears. It explains how these dogs are trained and paired with their new owners. *$18.95*

*169 pages*

**6218  Children of a Lesser God**
Gallaudet University Bookstore
11030 S Langley Avenue
Chicago, IL  60628
202-651-5488
800-621-2736
FAX: 202-651-5489
The movie that won the hearts of thousands. This is a story of a deaf woman who refuses to succumb to the hearing people's image of what a deaf person should be. *$4.50*
*91 pages Softcover*

**6219  Choices in Deafness**
Woodbine House
6510 Bells Mill Road
Bethesda, MD  20817
301-897-3570
800-843-7323
FAX: 301-897-5838
www.woodbinehouse.com

*Irv Shapell, Owner*

A useful aid in choosing the appropriate communication option for a child with a hearing loss. Experts present the following communication options: Auditory-Verbal Approach, Bilingual-Bicultural Approach, Cued Speech, Oral Approach, and Total Communication. This new edition explains medical causes of hearing loss, the diagnostic process, audiological assessment, and cochlear implants. Children and parents also offer their personal experiences. *$16.95*
*275 pages Paperback*
*ISBN 0-933149-85-9*

**6220  Clerc: The Story of His Early Years**
TJ Publishers
2544 Tarpley Road
Suite 108
Carrollton, TX  75006
972-416-0800
800-999-1168
FAX: 301-585-5930
e-mail: TJPubinc@aol.com

*Angela K Thames, President*
*Jerald A Murphy, VP*

This imaginative tale recounts the youthful history of Laurent Clerc, the deaf teacher who helped Thomas Gallaudet establish schools for the deaf in the 19th century. Early experiences influenced the teaching methods Clerc developed in later life and young adults will relish identifying with the hero of this entertaining story. *$9.95*
*208 pages Softcover*
*ISBN 0-93032 -23-8*

**6221  Client Assistance Program: Arizona**
3839 N 3rd Street
Suite 209
Phoenix, AZ  85012
602-274-6287
FAX: 602-274-6779

*John Guiterrez, Director*
*Judy Fox, Manager*

**6222  Cochlear Implants**
Federal Government
31 Center Dirve Msc2320
Bethesda, MD  20892
800-241-1044
FAX: 301-402-0018
e-mail: nidcdinfo@nidcd.nih.gov
www.nidcd.nih.gov
This fact sheet explains what is a cochlear implant, how it works, who gets cochlear implants, how someone receives a cochlear impant and what the future holds for cochlear impants.

**6223 Cochlear Implants and Children**
Alexander Graham Bell Association
3417 Volta Place NW
Washington, DC 20007
202-337-5220
FAX: 202-337-8314
e-mail: info@agbell.org
www.agbell.org

*Todd Houston, Executive Director*

Designed to educate readers about cochlear implants, including surgery, the importance of rehabilitation and the significance of parents' and professionals' roles. *$42.95*
*189 pages Paperback*

**6224 Cochlear Implants for Kids**
Alexander Graham Bell Association
3417 Volta Place NW
Washington, DC 20007
202-337-5220
FAX: 202-337-8314
e-mail: info@agbell.org
www.agbell.org

*Todd Houston, Executive Director*

Designed to educate readers about cochlear implants, including surgery, the importance of rehabilitation and the significance of parents' and professionals' roles. *$42.95*
*404 pages Paperback*

**6225 Cognition, Education and Deafness**
Gallaudet University Press
800 Florida Avenue NE
Washington, DC 20002
202-651-5000
800-451-1073
FAX: 202-651-5489

*Erving Jordan, President*

The work of 54 authors is gathered in this definitive collection of current research on deafness and cognition. The articles are grouped into seven sections: cognition, problem solving, thinking processes, language development, reading methodologies, measurement of potential, and intervention programs. *$21.95*
*260 pages Hardcover*

**6226 College and Career Programs for the Deaf**
Gallaudet University Bookstore
11030 S Langley Avenue
Chicago, IL 60628
202-651-5488
800-621-2736
FAX: 202-651-5489

Which college is the right one for you? This is a guide to colleges in the United States and Canada that offer special programs for deaf students. *$12.95*
*108 pages Softcover*

**6227 Come Sign with Us**
Gallaudet University Press
11030 S Langley Avenue
Chicago, IL 60628
800-621-2736
FAX: 800-621-8476
TTY:800-621-9347
gupress.gallaudet.edu

*Jan C Hafer, Co-Author*
*Robert M Wilson, Co-Author*

This fun guide for parents and educators on teaching hearing children how to sign has been thoroughly revised with completely new activities that provide contexts for practice. *$29.95*

*160 pages Softcover*

**6228 Come Sign with Us: Sign Language Activities for Children**
TJ Publishers
2544 Tarpley Road
Suite 108
Carrollton, TX 75006
972-416-0800
800-999-1168
FAX: 301-585-5930
e-mail: TJPubinc@aol.com

*Angela K Thames, President*
*Jerald A Murphy, VP*

Illustrated activities manual contains more than 300 line drawings of adults and children signing familiar words, phrases and sentences using ASL in English word order. *$29.95*
*144 pages Softcover*
*ISBN 0-930321-56-3*

**6229 Communicating with Deaf People: An Introduction**
Gallaudet University Bookstore
800 Florida Avenue NE
Washington, DC 20002
202-651-5000
800-451-1073
FAX: 202-651-5489

*Erving Jordan, President*

This illustrated publication introduces the various ways deaf people can communicate, including gesture and facial expression, speech-reading, fingerspelling and other manual communication systems. *$2.00*
*20 pages*

**6230 Communication Options for Children Who are Deaf or Hard-of-Hearing**
Federal Government
31 Center Drive McS2320
Bethesda, MD 20892
800-241-1044
FAX: 301-402-0018
e-mail: midcdinfo@nidcd.nih.gov
www.nidcd.nih.gov

Explains how hearing loss or deafness is identified in newborns, how later onset of hearing loss is identified in young children, what causes hearing loss or deafness in newborns, what communication options are available to deaf and har-of-hearing children, and how your family can particiapte in research related hereditary deafness, hearing impairment, or intervention strategies.

**6231 Communique**
Michigan Association for Deaf Hard Of Hearing
2929 Covington Court
Unit 200
Lansing, MI 48912
517-487-0066
800-968-7327
FAX: 517-487-2586
e-mail: yourear@madhh.org
www.madhh.org

*Nancy Asher, Executive Director*
*4-8 pages Bi-annually*

**6232 Comprehensive Reference Manual for Signers and Interpreters**
Charles C Thomas
2600 S 1st Street
Springfield, IL 62704
217-789-8980
800-258-8980
FAX: 217-789-9130
e-mail: books@ccthomas.com
www.ccthomas.com

*Michael Thomas, President*
Manual for signers. *$47.95*

*314 pages Paperback*
*ISBN 0-398059-19-5*

**6233   Comprehensive Signed English Dictionary**
Gallaudet University Press
11030 S Langley Avenue
Chicago, IL  60628

800-621-2736
FAX: 800-621-8476
TTY:800-621-9347
gupress.gallaudet.edu

*Harry Bornstein, Co-Author*
*Karen L Saulnier, Co-Author*
*Lillian B Hamilton, Co-Author*

This complete dictionary has over 3,100 signs, including signs reflecting lively and contemporary vocabulary. *$35.00*
*464 pages Hardcover*

**6234   Connect**
Hearing, Speech & Deafness Center (HSDC)
1625 19th Avenue
Seattle, WA  98122

206-323-5770
FAX: 206-328-6871
e-mail: hsdc@hsdc.org
www.hsdc.org

*David Delmar, Editor*
*Susie Burdick, Executive Director*

A not-for-profit United Way Agency building community through communications since 1937. Call V/TTY. The mission of HSDC is to strengthen community by promoting effective communication
*8 pages Quarterly*

**6235   Connect Newsletter**
Hearing, Speech & Deafness Center (HSDC)
1625 19th Avenue
Seattle, WA  98122

206-323-5770
FAX: 206-328-6871
e-mail: hsdc@hsdc.org
www.hsdc.org

*Susie Burdick, Executive Director*
*8 pages Bi-annually*

**6236   Conversational Sign Language II**
Harris Communications
15155 Technology Drive
Eden Prairie, MN  55344

952-906-1180
800-825-6758
FAX: 952-906-1099
e-mail: mail@harriscomm.com
www.harriscomm.com

*Bill Williams, National Sales Manager*
*Robert Harris, Owner*

This book presents English words and their American Sign Language equivalents. *$12.95*
*218 pages Paperback*
*ISBN 0-913580-00-7*

**6237   Coping with the Multi-Handicapped Hearing Impaired: A Practical Approach**
Charles C Thomas
2600 S 1st Street
Springfield, IL  62704

217-789-8980
800-258-8980
FAX: 217-789-9130
e-mail: books@ccthomas.com
www.ccthomas.com

*Michael Thomas, President*

Professional text offers suggestions on how to deal with the multi-handicapped deaf person. Also available in cloth.

*90 pages $20.95*
*ISBN 0-398063-33-8*

**6238   Deaf Catholic**
International Catholic Deaf Association
1030 S La Grange Road
Suite 9
La Grange, IL  60525

FAX: 708-579-5847
TTY:708-579-5817
e-mail: icdaus@ameritech.com

*Richard Kush, Editor*

Quarterly publication from the International Catholic Deaf Association. *$15.00*
*16 pages Quarterly*

**6239   Deaf Empowerment: Emergence, Struggle and Rhetoric**

Gallaudet University Press
11030 S Langley Avenue
Chicago, IL  60628

800-621-2736
FAX: 800-621-8476
TTY:800-621-9347
gupress.gallaudet.edu

The story of the Deaf social movement, from its beginnings in the mid 1800s through its growth and strengthening in the late 20th century, much of it due to rhetoric and tactics adopted from other social movements. *$34.95*
*192 pages Hardcover*

**6240   Deaf Heritage: A Narrative History**
Gallaudet University Bookstore
11030 S Langley Avenue
Chicago, IL  60628

202-651-5488
800-621-2736
FAX: 202-651-5489

This in-depth history of deaf America contains pictures, illustrations, vignettes, and biographical profiles. *$21.95*
*500 pages Paperback*

**6241   Deaf History Unveiled: Interpretations from the New Scholarship**
Gallaudet University Press
11030 S Langley Avenue
Chicago, IL  60628

800-621-2736
FAX: 800-621-8476
TTY:800-621-9347
gupress.gallaudet.edu

*John Vickrey Van Cleve, Editor*

An all-star cast of historians explores the new themes driving Deaf History, including comparisons with other minority cultures and the social paternalism that affects deaf communities around the globe. *$27.50*
*316 pages Softcover*

**6242   Deaf Like Me**
Gallaudet University Press
800 Florida Avenue NE
Washington, DC  20002

202-651-5000
800-451-1073
FAX: 202-651-5489

*Erving Jordan, President*

Written by the uncle and father of a deaf girl, this is an account of parents coming to terms with deafness. This paperback edition contains a special epilogue by Lynn Spradley, grown and in her twenties, as she reflects on her growing-up years with the advantage of hindsight. *$10.95*

*292 pages Softcover*

**6243 Deaf in America: Voices from a Culture**
TJ Publishers
2544 Tarpley Road
Suite 108
Carrollton, TX 75006                    972-416-0800
                                         800-999-1168
                                   FAX: 301-585-5930
                              e-mail: TJPubinc@aol.com

*Angela K Thames, President*
*Jerald A Murphy, VP*

Now available in paperback, this book opens deaf culture to outsiders, inviting readers to imagine and understand a world of silence. This book shares the joy and satisfaction many people
have with their lives and shows that deafness may not be the
handicap most hearing people think. *$12.95*
      *134 pages Softcover*
      *ISBN 0-67419 -24-1*

**6244 Deaf-Blind Perspective**
Teaching Research
345 Monmouth Avenue
Monmouth, OR 97361                      503-838-8391
                                        800-438-9376
                                   FAX: 503-838-8150
                              e-mail: dblink@tr.wou.edu
                                   www.tr.wou.edu/dblink

*John Reiman PhD, Director*
*Meredith Brodsky, Executive Director*

**6245 Discovering Sign Language**
Gallaudet University Press
800 Florida Avenue NE
Washington, DC 20002                    202-651-5000
                                        800-451-1073
                                   FAX: 202-651-5489

*Erving Jordan, President*

Here is a book of information about deaf people and sign communication. *$6.95*
      *104 pages Softcover*

**6246 EASE**
Telecommunications for the Deaf (TDI)
8630 Fenton Street
Suite 604
Silver Spring, MD 20910                 301-589-3786
                                   FAX: 301-589-3797
                              e-mail: info@tdi-online.org
                                   www.tdi-online.org

*Claude L Stout, Executive Director*
*James D House, Member Service/Public Rel. Dir.*

Training package for 911 professionals.
      *48 pages*

**6247 Effectiveness of Cochlear Implants and Tactile Aids for
Deaf Children**
Alexander Graham Bell Association
3417 Volta Place NW
Washington, DC 20007                    202-337-5220
                                   FAX: 202-337-8314
                              e-mail: info@agbell.org
                                   www.agbell.org

*Todd Houston, Executive Director*

This monograph presents a fascinating study to evaluate differences in the rate of change in speech perception, speech production and spoken language skills among children using the
Nucleus 22-channel cochlear implant, tactile aids and conventional hearing aids. This monograph also offers teaching strategies in perception, lipreading and spoken language. *$13.95*

*232 pages Paperback*

**6248 Encyclopedia of Deafness and Hearing Disorders**
Gallaudet University Bookstore
800 Florida Avenue NE
Washington, DC 20002                    202-651-5000
                                        800-451-1073
                                   FAX: 202-651-5489

*Erving Jordan, President*

Presents the most current information on deafness and hearing
disorders in an authoritative A-to-Z compendium. *$45.00*
      *278 pages*

**6249 Exploring the Bible: Bible Studies for the DEAF**
Lifeway Church Resources
127 9th Avenue N
Nashville, TN 37234                     615-251-2089
                                        800-458-2772
                                   FAX: 615-251-2710
                              e-mail: lifewaynews@lifeway.com
                                   www.lifeway.com/lwc

*Rob Phillips, Director*
*Wade Stapleton, Manager*

Bible study lessons for every three months written by and for
persons who are deaf. Based on the Family Bible Series (International Sunday School Lessons).

**6250 Expressive and Receptive Fingerspelling**
Gallaudet University Bookstore
800 Florida Avenue NE
Washington, DC 20002                    202-651-5000
                                        800-451-1073
                                   FAX: 202-651-5489

*Erving Jordan, President*

Here is a new and meaningful way for adults to increase their
comfort with fingerspelling. The system is based on the principles of phonetics rather than letters of the English alphabet.
*$2.50*
      *42 pages Softcover*

**6251 Flute Song Magic**
TJ Publishers
2544 Tarpley Road
Suite 108
Carrollton, TX 75006                    972-416-0800
                                        800-999-1168
                                   FAX: 301-585-5930
                              e-mail: TJPubinc@aol.com

*Angela K Thames, President*
*Jerald A Murphy, Executive Assistant*

Gallaudet student Andrea Shettle created a memorable fantasy
world, Nevlin, where it is forbidden to talk with people below
one's class. An improbable friendship leads the High Noble
Flutir to discover that friendship and individuality defy class
limitations. *$ 2.95*
      *218 pages Softcover*
      *ISBN 0-380762-25-0*

**6252 For Hearing People Only**
Harris Communications
15155 Technology Drive
Eden Prairie, MN 55344                  952-906-1180
                                        800-825-6758
                                   FAX: 952-906-1099
                              e-mail: mail@harriscomm.com
                                   www.harriscomm.com

*Bill Williams, National Sales Manager*
*Robert Harris, Owner*

A book that answers some of the questions hearing people ask
about deaf culture. Also availible in hardcover. *$19.95*

*336 pages Paperback*
*ISBN 0-963401-61-0*

**6253 From Gesture to Language in Hearing and Deaf Children**
Gallaudet University Press
11030 S Langley Avenue
Chicago, IL 60628

800-621-2736
FAX: 800-621-8476
TTY:800-621-9347
gupress.gallaudet.edu

*Virginia Volterra, Editor*
*Carol J Erting, Editor*

In 21 essays on communicative gesturing in the first two years of life, this vital collection demonstrates the importance of gesture in a child's transition to a linguistic system. *$34.95*
*358 pages Softcover*

**6254 GA and SK Etiquette**
Gallaudet University Bookstore
800 Florida Avenue NE
Washington, DC 20002

202-651-5000
800-451-1073
FAX: 202-651-5489

*Erving Jordan, President*

This booklet presents guidelines for proper usage of the TDD. It includes everything you wanted to know about sending and receiving TDD calls. *$8.95*
*53 pages*

**6255 GA-SK**
Telecommunications for the Deaf
8630 Fenton Street
Suite 604
Silver Spring, MD 20910

301-589-3786
FAX: 301-589-3797
e-mail: info@tdi-online.org
www.tdi-online.org

*Claude L Stout, Executive Director*
*James D House, Member Service/Public Rel. Dir.*

Promoting equal access to telecommunications and media for people who are deaf, late-deafened, hard-of-hearing or deaf-blind through consumer education and involvement; technical assistance and consulting; applications of exisiting and emerging technologies; networking and collaboration; uniformity of standards; and national policy development and advocacy.
*48 pages Quarterly*

**6256 Gallaudet Survival Guide to Signing**
Harris Communications
15155 Technology Drive
Eden Prairie, MN 55344

952-906-1180
800-825-6758
FAX: 952-906-1099
e-mail: mail@harriscomm.com
www.harriscomm.com

*Bill Williams, National Sales Manager*
*Robert Harris, Owner*

Features 500 of the most frequently used signs with clear illustrations and descriptions for each one. *$6.95*
*203 pages Paperback*
*ISBN 0-930323-67-x*

**6257 Growing Together: Information for Parents of Deaf Children**
Gallaudet University Bookstore
800 Florida Avenue NE
Washington, DC 20002

202-651-5000
800-451-1073
FAX: 202-651-5489

*Erving Jordan, President*

This publication answers questions often asked by parents of children with a hearing loss. *$8.00*

*92 pages*

**6258 Handtalk Zoo**
MacMillan Publishing Company
135 S Mount Zion Road
Lebanon, IN 46052

800-257-5755
FAX: 800-882-8583

Wonderful photographs are used to show children at the zoo communicating with sign language.
*28 pages Hardcover*
*ISBN 0-02700 -01-0*

**6259 Hearing Aids**
Federal Government
31 Center Drive Msc2320
Bethesda, MD 20892

800-241-1044
FAX: 301-402-0018
e-mail: nidcdinfo@nidcd.nih.gov
www.nidcd.nih.gov

Explains what is a hearing aid, how can hearing aids help, what to expect from hearing aids, what questions to ask before buying hearing aids, tips for taking care of hearing aids, and what research is being done on hearing aids.

**6260 Hearing Impaired Employee**
Allyn & Bacon
75 Arlington Street
Suite 300
Boston, MA 02116

617-848-6000
FAX: 617-848-7490
www.ablongman.com

An invaluable aid for both large and small firms for employment agencies and counselors and for all firms, schools and associations providing equipment or services for the hearing impaired.
*1991*
*ISBN 0-887441-08-4*

**6261 Hearing Loss: The Journal of Self Help for Hard of Hearing People**
Self Help for Hard of Hearing People
7910 Woodmont Avenue
Suite 1200
Bethesda, MD 20814

301-657-2248
FAX: 301-913-9413
TTY:301-657-2249
e-mail: national@shhh.org
www.shhh.org

*Bonnie Sporren, Business Manager*
*Terry Portis, Executive Director*

SHHH, a non-profit, educational organization is dedicated to the well-being of people of all ages and communication styles who do not hear well. SHHH is the largest international consumer organization of its kind. SHHH offers a nationwide support network of chapters and groups, a bi-monthly magazine, discounted publications and resource materials for members, an annual convention, state and regional conferences and more. *$25.00*
*40 pages BiMonthly*

**6262 Hearing, Speech & Deafness Center (HSDC)**
1625 19th Avenue
Seattle, WA 98122

206-323-5770
FAX: 206-328-6871
e-mail: hsdc@hsdc.org
www.hsdc.org

*Susie Burdick, Development/Marketing Director*
*David Stoner, Editor*

Mission is to enrich the lives of all adults and children who experience hearing loss, speech and language impairments, or who are deaf, by providing professional services and technology, and by promoting community awareness and accessibility. A not-for-profit United Way Agency.

*16 pages Yearly 1937*

**6263 Hearing-Impaired Children and Youth with Developmental Disabilities**
Gallaudet University Bookstore
800 Florida Avenue NE
Washington, DC 20002
202-651-5000
800-451-1073
FAX: 202-651-5489

*Erving Jordan, President*

The insights of 24 experts help clarify relationships between hearing impairment and developmental difficulties and propose interdisciplinary cooperation as an approach to the problems created. *$29.95*
*416 pages*

**6264 Hollywood Speaks**
Gallaudet University Bookstore
800 Florida Avenue NE
Washington, DC 20002
202-651-5000
800-451-1073
FAX: 202-651-5489

*Erving Jordan, President*

How deafness has been treated in movies and how it provides yet another window onto social history in addition to a fresh angle from which to view Hollywood. *$24.95*
*167 pages Hardcover*

**6265 How You Gonna Get to Heaven if You Can't Talk with Jesus?**
TJ Publishers
2544 Tarpley Road
Suite 108
Carrollton, TX 75006
972-416-0800
800-999-1168
FAX: 301-585-5930
e-mail: TJPubinc@aol.com

*Angela K Thames, President*
*Jerald A Murphy, VP*

This collection of articles examines deaf culture and its relationship, profiling sociolinguistic and anthropological perspectives in research on American deaf society and culture. *$4.50*
*78 pages Softcover*
*ISBN 0-93266-15-9*

**6266 I Have a Sister, My Sister is Deaf**
TJ Publishers
2544 Tarpley Road
Suite 108
Carrollton, TX 75006
972-416-0800
800-999-1168
FAX: 301-585-5930
e-mail: TJPubinc@aol.com

*Angela K Thames, President*
*Jerald A Murphy, VP*

An emphatic, affirmative look at the relationship between siblings, as a young deaf child is affectionately described by her older sister. This Coretta Scott King Honor Award winner helps young children develop an understanding that deaf children share the same interests as hearing children. *$5.95*
*32 pages Softcover*
*ISBN 0-06443-59-6*

**6267 I Was #87: A Deaf Woman's Ordeal of Misdiagnosis, Institutionalization and Abuse**
Gallaudet University Press
11030 S Langley Avenue
Chicago, IL 60628
800-621-2736
FAX: 800-621-8476
TTY:800-621-9347
gupress.gallaudet.edu

*Anne M Bolander, Co-Author*
*Adair N Renning, Co-Author*

Misdiagnosed as mentally retarded, a deaf woman emerges from six torturous years at an institution for unwanted children and a lifetime of abuse and neglect to tell her remarkable, sobering story. *$24.95*
*232 pages Hardcover*

**6268 In This Sign**
Gallaudet University Bookstore
800 Florida Avenue NE
Washington, DC 20002
202-651-5000
800-451-1073
FAX: 202-651-5489

*Erving Jordan, President*

This modern classic follows a family of deaf parents and their hearing child through several decades of growth and pain, tragedy and triumph. *$10.95*
*275 pages Softcover*

**6269 Innovative Practices for Teaching Sign Language Interpreters**
Gallaudet University Press
11030 S Langley Avenue
Chicago, IL 60628
800-621-2736
FAX: 800-621-8476
TTY:800-621-9347
gupress.gallaudet.edu

*Cynthia B Roy, Editor*

Six experts draw upon the new understanding of sign language interpreting as a discourse between two languages and cultures. Develops bold, original techniques for training interpreters. *$34.95*
*200 pages Hardcover*

**6270 Intermediate Conversational Sign Language**
TJ Publishers
2544 Tarpley Road
Suite 108
Carrollton, TX 75006
972-416-0800
800-999-1168
FAX: 301-585-5930
e-mail: TJPubinc@aol.com

*Angela K Thames, President*
*Jerald A Murphy, VP*

Unique approach to using American Sign Language and English in a bilingual setting. Each of the 25 lessons includes an introductory paragraph, glossed vocabulary review, translation exercises, grammatical notes, substitution drills and activities. *$21.95*
*400 pages Softcover*
*ISBN 7-91358-79-1*

**6271 International Directory of Periodicals Related to Deafness**
Gallaudet University Bookstore
800 Florida Avenue NE
Washington, DC 20002
202-651-5000
800-451-1073
FAX: 202-651-5489

*Erving Jordan, President*

This one-of-a-kind directory has useful information on more than 500 magazines and journals related to deafness. The entries come from all over the world. *$10.00*
*150 pages*

**6272 International Telephone Directory**
Gallaudet University Bookstore
800 Florida Avenue NE
Washington, DC 20002
202-651-5000
800-451-1073
FAX: 202-651-5489

*Erving Jordan, President*

Almost 12,000 TDD numbers for Telecommunications for the Deaf, members and organizations serving deaf people. *$20.00*

*190 pages Softcover*

**6273    Interpretation: A Sociolinguistic Model**
Gallaudet University Bookstore
800 Florida Avenue NE
Washington, DC  20002                    202-651-5000
                                         800-451-1073
                                    FAX: 202-651-5489

*Erving Jordan, President*

This text presents a sociolinguistically sensitive model of the interpretation process. The model applies to interpretation in any two languages although this one focuses on ASL and English. *$16.95*
        *199 pages*

**6274    Interpreting: An Introduction, Revised Edition**
TJ Publishers
2544 Tarpley Road
Suite 108
Carrollton, TX  75006                    972-416-0800
                                         800-999-1168
                                    FAX: 301-585-5930
                               e-mail: TJPubinc@aol.com

*Angela K Thames, President*
*Jerald A Murphy, VP*

This text is written by a practicing interpreter and includes information on history, terminology, research, competence, setting and a comprehensive bibliography. *$22.50*
        *244 pages Softcover*
        *ISBN 0-91688 -01-9*

**6275    Journal**
Academy of Rehabilitative Audiology
PO Box 26532
Minneapolis, MN  55426                    952-920-0484
                                     FAX: 952-920-6098
                               e-mail: ara@incnet.com
                                     www.audrehab.org

*Frances Laven, Assistant Director*

Yearly publication from the Academy of Rehabilitative Audiology.
        *Yearly*

**6276    Journal of Speech, Language and Hearing Re search**
American Speech-Language-Hearing Association
10801 Rockville Pike
Rockville, MD  20852                      301-897-5700
                                         800-638-8255
                                    FAX: 301-897-7348
                                  e-mail: irc@asha.org
                                       www.asha.org

*John E Berntah;, President*
*Arlene Pietranton, Executive Director*
*Joanne Jessen, Publications Director*

Pertains broadly to studies of the processess and disorders of hearing, language, and speech diagnosis and treatment of such disorders.

**6277    Journal of the American Deafness and Rehabilitation Association**
JADARA
6212 Ferris Square
San Diego, CA  92121                      619-558-7444

Articles of interest to professionals providing services to deaf people, with special emphasis on research-practice interactions and on mental health issues. *$46.00*

**6278    Joy of Signing**
Gallaudet University Bookstore
800 Florida Avenue NE
Washington, DC  20002                    202-651-5000
                                         800-451-1073
                                    FAX: 202-651-5489

*Erving Jordan, President*

This manual on signing includes illustrations, information on sign origins, practice sentences, and step-by-step descriptions of hand positions and movements. *$16.95*
        *336 pages Hardcover*

**6279    Joy of Signing Puzzle Book**
Harris Communications
15155 Technology Drive
Eden Prairie, MN  55344                   952-906-1180
                                         800-825-6758
                                    FAX: 952-906-1099
                            e-mail: mail@harriscomm.com
                                    www.harriscomm.com

*Bill Williams, National Sales Manager*
*Robert Harris, Owner*

Whether you are learning sign language to communicate with a family member, co-worker, student or friend, this puzzle book makes the learning fun and interesting. *$3.95*
        *57 pages Paperback*
        *ISBN 0-882435-38-8*

**6280    Keys to Raising a Deaf Child**
Barron's Educational Series
250 Wireless Boulevard
Hauppauge, NY  11788                      631-434-3311
                                         800-645-3476
                                    FAX: 631-434-3723
                          e-mail: info@barronseduc.com
                                    www.barronseduc.com

*Lonny Stein , Director Marketing*
*Manuel Barron, Chief Executive Officer*

Two educators offer positive advice and encouragement on helping children adapt to deafness. They show how problems related to deafness can be overcome so that the child interacts as a social and intellectual equal with children who can hear. The authors recommend bimodal communication - having the child, parents and other non-deaf family members combine sign language and speech as a first step in normal communication. *$6.95*
        *208 pages Paperback*
        *ISBN 0-764107-23-2*

**6281    LSDC News**
DC Public Library, Services to the Deaf
901 G Street NW
Room 215
Washington, DC  20001                     202-727-1101
                                     FAX: 202-727-1129
                      e-mail: library_deaf_dc@yahoo.com
                                      www.dclibrary.org

*Janice Rosen, Librarian*
*Francis Buckley Jr, Manager*

Newsletter
        *5-6 pages Quarterly*

**6282    Linguistics of ASL: An Introduction**
Gallaudet University Press
11030 S Langley Avenue
Chicago, IL  60628
                                         800-621-2736
                                    FAX: 800-621-8476
                                    TTY:800-621-9347
                                 gupress.gallaudet.edu

*Clayton Valli, Co-Author*
*Ceil Lucas, Co-Author*

An introduction to the struture of American Sign Language, featuring all the linguistic disciplines plus practice exercises. *$60.00*
        *460 pages Hardcover*

**6283    Lisa and Her Soundless World**
Human Sciences Press
233 Spring Street
New York, NY  10013                       212-229-2859
                                         800-221-9369
                                    FAX: 212-463-0742

Describes the impact deafness has on communication and functioning in a hearing world. Lisa, born with a severe hearing loss, was not diagnosed as hearing impaired until her parents were worried about her lack of speech and other children had rejected her. *$18.95*
*30 pages Hardcover*
*ISBN 0-87705 -04-6*

**6284   Listen to Me**
Alexander Graham Bell Association
3417 Volta Place NW
Washington, DC  20007                    202-337-5220
                                    FAX: 202-337-8314
                                    e-mail: info@agbell.org
                                    www.agbell.org

*Todd Houston, Executive Director*

Entertaining wookbook contains exercises that help adults who are hard of hearing learn to listen and concentrate. *$9.95*
*65 pages Paperback*

**6285   Listening and Talking**
Alexander Graham Bell Association
3417 Volta Place NW
Washington, DC  20007                    202-337-5220
                                    FAX: 202-337-8314
                                    e-mail: info@agbell.org
                                    www.agbell.org

*Todd Houston, Executive Director*

This research-based text for professionals promotes communication by developing language, audition and speech in early intervention programs for young children with hearing loss. *$25.95*
*191 pages Paperback*

**6286   Literacy & Your Deaf Child: What Every Pa rent Should Know**
Gallaudet University Press
11030 S Langley Avenue
Chicago, IL  60628                       202-651-5488
                                    800-621-2736
                                    FAX: 202-651-5489
                                    www.gallaudet.edu
*David A Stewart, Bryan R Clarke, author*

An instructional guide specifically appropriate for parents of deaf and hard-of-hearing children who want to do everything they can to insure their hearing-impaired child learns to read and write with fluency and competence. *$21.95*
*208 pages 2003*
*ISBN 1-563681-36-6*

**6287   Literature Journal**
Gallaudet University Bookstore
800 Florida Avenue NE
Washington, DC  20002                    202-651-5000
                                    800-451-1073
                                    FAX: 202-651-5489

*Erving Jordan, President*

This book includes extensive examples of student and teacher entries taken from actual journals of deaf high school students. *$7.95*
*44 pages*

**6288   Loss for Words**
Gallaudet University Bookstore
11030 S Langley Avenue
Chicago, IL  60628                       202-651-5488
                                    800-621-2736
                                    FAX: 202-651-5489
She was an interpreter for her parents at four, a virtual head of household at eight, teacher and helper for her little sisters, buffer between her family and the world. Here is a daughter's account of growing up with loving parents, both of whom are deaf. *$11.00*

*208 pages Paperback*

**6289   Mask of Benevolence: Disabling the Deaf Community**
Gallaudet University Bookstore
800 Florida Avenue NE
Washington, DC  20002                    202-651-5000
                                    800-451-1073
                                    FAX: 202-651-5489

*Erving Jordan, President*

Dr. Harlan Lane does not view deafness as a handicap but rather a different state from hearing. Deaf people are a societal minority and should be treasured, not eradicated. *$23.00*
*310 pages*

**6290   Matthew Pinkowski's Special Summer**
TJ Publishers
2544 Tarpley Road
Suite 108
Carrollton, TX  75006                    972-416-0800
                                    800-999-1168
                                    FAX: 301-585-5930
                                    e-mail: TJPubinc@aol.com

*Angela K Thames, President*
*Jerald A Murphy, Executive Assistant*

Matthew Pinkowski meets an unlikely crew of friends - Sandy, the acrobat; Tommy, her brother who moves and learns slowly; and Laura, a deaf girl visiting an overprotective aunt and uncle. In solving a mystery together, the friends learn to expect the best of people. It is a funny, genuine story about a memorable summer. *$5.95*
*150 pages Softcover*
*ISBN 0-930323-82-3*

**6291   Mother Father Deaf: Living between Sound and Silence**

Through the Looking Glass
2198 6th Street
Suite 100
Berkeley, CA  94710                      510-848-1112
                                    800-644-2666
                                    FAX: 510-848-4445
                                    e-mail: TLG@lookingglass.org
                                    www.lookingglass.org

*P Preston*
*Megan Kirshbaum, Executive Director*
*$18.00*
*278 pages*

**6292   My First Book of Sign**
TJ Publishers
2544 Tarpley Road
Suite 108
Carrollton, TX  75006                    972-416-0800
                                    800-999-1168
                                    FAX: 301-585-5930
                                    e-mail: TJPubinc@aol.com

*Angela K Thames, President*
*Jerald A Murphy, VP*

Full-color book gives alphabetically grouped signs for 150 words most frequently used by young children. *$14.95*
*76 pages Hardcover*
*ISBN 0-93032 -20-3*

**6293   Newsletter of American Hearing Research Foundation**
American Hearing Research Foundation
8 S Michigan Avenue
Suite 814
Chicago, IL  60603                       312-726-9670
                                    FAX: 312-726-9695
                                    e-mail: blederer@american-hearing.org
                                    www.american-hearing.org

*William Lederer, Executive Director*
*Lorraine L Koch, Assistant Director*

Concerned with hearing research and education. Only if one can afford to pay, a suggested appropriate donation of $15 for cover postage and printing.
*6-8 pages TriAnnual*

**6294  Outsiders in a Hearing World**
Gallaudet University Bookstore
800 Florida Avenue NE
Washington, DC  20002

202-651-5000
800-451-1073
FAX: 202-651-5489

*Erving Jordan, President*

An introduction to the social world of deaf people. The author gives a sociologists view of what it's like to be deaf. *$19.95*
*240 pages Softcover*

**6295  Paws for Silence**
International Hearing Dog
5901 E 89th Avenue
Henderson, CO  80640

303-287-3277
FAX: 303-287-3425
e-mail: ihdi@aol.com
www.ihdi.org

*Valerie Foss-Brugger, President/Director*

Publication from International hearing dog.
*4-8 pages Quarterly*

**6296  Perigee Visual Dictionary of Signing**
Harris Communications
15155 Technology Drive
Eden Prairie, MN  55344

952-906-1180
800-825-6758
FAX: 952-906-1099
e-mail: mail@harriscomm.com
www.harriscomm.com

*Bill Williams, National Sales Manager*
*Robert Harris, Owner*

An A-to-Z guide to American Sign Language vocabulary. *$15.95*
*450 pages Paperback*
*ISBN 0-399519-52-1*

**6297  Perspective: Parent-Child Folio**
Gallaudet University Bookstore
800 Florida Avenue NE
Washington, DC  20002

202-651-5000
800-451-1073
FAX: 202-651-5489

*Erving Jordan, President*

Ranging from table conversation to bedtime reading, the seven articles collected here emphasize family communications while providing important information for parents about deafness and deaf culture. *$5.95*
*29 pages*

**6298  Perspectives: Whole Language Folio**
Gallaudet University Bookstore
800 Florida Avenue NE
Washington, DC  20002

202-651-5000
800-451-1073
FAX: 202-651-5489

*Erving Jordan, President*

The 19 articles in this collection offer practical help to teachers seeking to emphasize whole language strategies in their classroom. *$9.95*

*64 pages*

**6299  Phone of Our Own: The Deaf Insurrection Against Ma Bell**
Gallaudet University Press
11030 S Langley Avenue
Chicago, IL  60628

202-651-5488
800-621-2736
FAX: 202-651-5489
TTY: 800-621-9347
gupress.gallaudet.edu

A recount of the history of the teletypewriter, from the three deaf engineers who developed the acoustic coupler that made mass communication on TTY's feasible, through the deaf community's twenty-year struggle against the government and AT&T to have TTY's produced and distributed. *$29.95*
*304 pages Hardcover*

**6300  Place of Their Own: Creating the Deaf Community in America**
TJ Publishers
2544 Tarpley Road
Suite 108
Carrollton, TX  75006

972-416-0800
800-999-1168
FAX: 301-585-5930
e-mail: TJPubinc@aol.com

*Angela K Thames, President*
*Jerald A Murphy, VP*

Traces development of American deaf society to show how deaf people developed a common language and sense of community. Views deafness as the distinguishing characteristic of a distinct culture. *$16.95*
*212 pages Paperback*
*ISBN 0-930324-91-*

**6301  PreReading Strategies**
Gallaudet University Bookstore
800 Florida Avenue NE
Washington, DC  20002

202-651-5000
800-451-1073
FAX: 202-651-5489

*Erving Jordan, President*

Here is a wealth of good advice for preparing students to understand what they read, building comprehension and enjoyment. *$8.95*
*65 pages*

**6302  Psychology of Deafness**
Longman Publishing Group
10 Bank Street
9th Floor
White Plains, NY  10606

914-993-5000
FAX: 914-421-5598

*Roth Wilkofsky, Systems Contact*
*Joanne Dresner, President*

Portrays hearing impairments as a psychological variable causing life experiences of the deaf to consistently differ from those of the non-deaf. Covers all levels of hearing loss, from prelingual and profound deafness to partial and mild hearing loss. Demonstrates how and why a hearing loss creates psychological stress no matter what its degree.
*292 pages Hardcover*
*ISBN 0-801303-22-2*

**6303  Registry of Interpreters for the Deaf**
8630 Fenton Street
Suite 324
Silver Spring, MD  20910

301-608-0050
FAX: 301-608-0508
e-mail: pr@rid.org
www.rid.org

Membership association for sign language interpreters; promoting national certification, professional development and training, and quality assurance through ethical practices system.

*Monthly*

**6304  Religious Signing: A Comprehensive Guide for All Faiths**
TJ Publishers
2544 Tarpley Road
Suite 108
Carrollton, TX  75006        972-416-0800
                             800-999-1168
                         FAX: 301-585-5930
               e-mail: TJPubinc@aol.com
                             www.agbell.org

*Angela K Thames, President*
*Jerald A Murphy, VP*

Contains over 500 religious signs for all denominations and their meanings illustrated by clear upper torso illustrations that show movements of hand, body and face. Includes a section on signing favorite verses, prayers and blessings. *$17.95*
        *219 pages Paperback*
        *ISBN 0-553344-44-*

**6305  Seeing Voices: A Journey into the World of the Deaf**
TJ Publishers
2544 Tarpley Road
Suite 108
Carrollton, TX  75006        972-416-0800
                             800-999-1168
                         FAX: 301-585-5930
               e-mail: TJPubinc@aol.com

*Angela K Thames, President*
*Jerald A Murphy, VP*

Well known for his exploration of how people respond to neurological impairments, Dr Sacks explores the world of the deaf and discovers how deaf people respond to their loss of hearing and how they develop language. A highly readable introduction to deaf people, deaf culture and American Sign Language. *$11.00*
        *186 pages Softcover*
        *ISBN 0-06097 -47-1*

**6306  Sign Language Coloring Books**
Gallaudet University Bookstore
800 Florida Avenue NE
Washington, DC  20002        202-651-5000
                             800-451-1073
                         FAX: 202-651-5489

*Erving Jordan, President*

A mischievous mouse and a spinning top, a doll on the sofa, a hobo clown with this friend the elephant: these coloring books are a FUNtastic way for children to learn to sign, fingerspell, read and write. *$4.50*

**6307  Sign Language Feelings**
Gallaudet University Bookstore
800 Florida Avenue NE
Washington, DC  20002        202-651-5000
                             800-451-1073
                         FAX: 202-651-5489

*Erving Jordan, President*

Worksheets teach signs for happy, sad and all of the feelings in between. *$4.50*

**6308  Sign Language Interpreters and Interpreting**
Gallaudet University Bookstore
800 Florida Avenue NE
Washington, DC  20002        202-651-5000
                             800-451-1073
                         FAX: 202-651-5489

*Erving Jordan, President*

This monograph presents articles about personal characteristics and abilities of interpreters, the effects of lag time on interpreter errors, and the interpretation of register. *$15.95*

*161 pages*

**6309  Sign with Me Books**
Gallaudet University Bookstore
11030 S Langley Avenue
Chicago, IL  60628           202-651-5488
                             800-621-2736
                         FAX: 202-651-5489
Bold, colorful pictures and accurate diagrams make it fun for beginners to learn everyday signs. Titles in this series include ABC Sign With Me; Colors Sign With Me; Weather Sign With Me; and 1,2,3 Sign With Me. *$3.95*
        *Per Title*

**6310  Signed English Starter**
Harris Communications
15155 Technology Drive
Eden Prairie, MN  55344      952-906-1180
                             800-825-6758
                         FAX: 952-906-1099
               e-mail: mail@harriscomm.com
                             www.harriscomm.com

*Bill Williams, National Sales Manager*
*Robert Harris, Owner*

The first book to use when learning Signed English. *$ 13.95*
        *208 pages Paperback*
        *ISBN 0-913580-82-1*

**6311  Signing for Reading Success**
Gallaudet University Bookstore
800 Florida Avenue NE
Washington, DC  20002        202-651-5000
                             800-451-1073
                         FAX: 202-651-5489

*Erving Jordan, President*

This booklet provides summaries of four research students on the usefulness of signing for reading achievement. *$3.95*
        *24 pages Softcover*

**6312  Signing: How to Speak with Your Hands**
TJ Publishers
2544 Tarpley Road
Suite 108
Carrollton, TX  75006        972-416-0800
                             800-999-1168
                         FAX: 301-585-5930
               e-mail: TJPubinc@aol.com

*Angela K Thames, President*
*Jerald A Murphy, VP*

Presents 1,200 basic signs with clear illustrations in logical topical groupings. Linguistic principles are described at the beginning of each chapter, giving insight into the rules which govern American Sign Language. *$17.95*
        *248 pages Paperback*
        *ISBN 0-553375-39-3*

**6313  Signs Across America**
TJ Publishers
2544 Tarpley Road
Suite 108
Carrollton, TX  75006        972-416-0800
                             800-999-1168
                         FAX: 301-585-5930
               e-mail: TJPubinc@aol.com

*Angela K Thames, President*
*Jerald A Murphy, VP*

A look at regional variations in ASL. Signs for selected words collected from 25 different states. More than 1,200 signs illustrated in the text. *$19.95*

*285 pages Paperback*
*ISBN 0-913589-61-*

**6314 Signs Everywhere**
Harris Communications
15155 Technology Drive
Eden Prairie, MN 55344

952-906-1180
800-825-6758
FAX: 952-906-1099
e-mail: mail@harriscomm.com
www.harriscomm.com

*Bill Williams, National Sales Manager*
*Robert Harris, Owner*

This books includes signs for towns, cities, states and provinces.
*$14.95*
*254 pages Paperback*
*ISBN 0-916708-05-5*

**6315 Signs for Computing Terminology**
Gallaudet University Bookstore
11030 S Langley Avenue
Chicago, IL 60628

202-651-5488
800-621-2736
FAX: 202-651-5489

This sign reference will facilitate communication among deaf persons involved with computers by providing a significant vocabulary base for the computing field of today and tomorrow.
*$12.95*
*182 pages Softcover*

**6316 Signs for Me: Basic Sign Vocabulary for Children, Parents & Teachers**
TJ Publishers
2544 Tarpley Road
Suite 108
Carrollton, TX 75006

972-416-0800
800-999-1168
FAX: 301-585-5930
e-mail: TJPubinc@aol.com

*Angela K Thames, President*
*Jerald A Murphy, VP*

Sign language vocabulary for preschool and elementary school children introduces household items, animals, family members, actions, emotions, safety concerns and other concepts. *$12.95*
*112 pages Softcover*
*ISBN 0-91503 -27-8*

**6317 Signs for Sexuality: A Resource Manual**
Gallaudet University Bookstore
800 Florida Avenue NE
Washington, DC 20002

202-651-5000
800-451-1073
FAX: 202-651-5489

*Erving Jordan, President*

An important book for those who want to listen to and talk with other people about feelings, loving and caring. *$24.95*
*122 pages Softcover*

**6318 Signs of the Times**
Gallaudet University Press
11030 S Langley Avenue
Chicago, IL 60628

800-621-2736
FAX: 800-621-8476
TTY:800-621-9347
gupress.gallaudet.edu

An excellent beginner's contact signing book that fills the gap between sign language dictionaries and American Sign Language text. Designed for use as a classroom text. *$24.95*

*448 pages Softcover*

**6319 Silent Garden: Raising Your Deaf Child**
Gallaudet University Press
11030 S Langley Avenue
Chicago, IL 60628

202-651-5488
800-621-2736
FAX: 202-651-5489
www.gallaudet.edu

*Paul W Ogden, author*

The author explain the broad range of hearing loss types, from minor to profound. Parents also are advised about what type of school their child should attend and what kinds of professional help will be best for the entire family. The book describes all forms of communication, including choices in signing from American Sign Language to the various manual systems based upon English. Technological alternatives are presented also, including when and when not to consider cochler implants. *$34.95*

*313 pages 1996*
*ISBN 1-563680-58-0*

**6320 Simultaneous Communication, ASL, and Other Communication Modes**
Gallaudet University Bookstore
800 Florida Avenue NE
Washington, DC 20002

202-651-5000
800-451-1073
FAX: 202-651-5489

*Erving Jordan, President*

This monograph presents four major articles that examine issues surrounding communications in an educational environment. *$15.95*
*236 pages*

**6321 Sing Praise Hymnal**
Broadman and Holman
127 9th Avenue S
Nashville, TN 37203

615-251-5005
800-458-2772
FAX: 651-251-5764
www.bssb.com/lwc

*Ken Stephens, President*
A song book for the deaf. *$6.95*

**6322 Spring Dell Center**
6040 Radio Station Road
La Plata, MD 20646

301-870-2474

*Melissa Tyner, Transportation Director*
*Donna Retzlaff, Executive Director*

Since 1967, Spring Dell center has been, bridging the gap to enhance the lives of developmentally disabled people. Spring Dell's goal is to empower people in every aspect of their lives through the implementation of two programs, employment/vocational services and residential services including transportation. Spring Dell offers transportation door-to-door for persons with developmental disabilities, including day care programs, supportive environment, residential and any other transportation.

**6323 Store @ HDSC Product Catalog**
Hearing, Speech & Deafness Center (HDSC)
1625 19th Avenue
Seattle, WA 98122

206-323-5770
FAX: 206-328-6871
e-mail: hsdc@hsdc.org
www.hsdc.org

*Susie Burdick, Executive Director*

*32 pages Yearly*

**6324 TDI National Directory & Resource Guide: Blue Book**
Telecommunications for the Deaf
8630 Fenton Street
Suite 604
Silver Spring, MD 20910

301-589-3786
FAX: 301-589-3797
e-mail: info@tdi-online.org
www.tdi-online.org

*Claude L Stout, Executive Director*
*James D House, Member Service/Public Rel. Dir.*

*$27.00*
*639 pages Annual*

**6325 Talk with Me**
Alexander Graham Bell Association
3417 Volta Place NW
Washington, DC 20007

202-337-5220
FAX: 202-337-8314
e-mail: info@agbell.org
www.agbell.org

*Todd Houston, Executive Director*

This book addresses the urgent need to enlighten parents and professionals responsible for the crucial early decisions that affect the speech, language, social, emotional and intellectual development of children who are deaf and hard of hearing. *$22.95*
*222 pages Paperback*

**6326 Teaching Social Skills to Hearing-Impaired Students**
Alexander Graham Bell Association
3417 Volta Place NW
Washington, DC 20007

202-337-5220
FAX: 202-337-8314
e-mail: info@agbell.org
www.agbell.org

*Todd Houston, Executive Director*

This book provides teachers and parents with a comprehensive, clearly presented hands-on program to develop social skills in children and young adults who are deaf or hard of hearing. *$21.95*
*203 pages*

**6327 Telecommunication Relay Services**
Ferderal Government
31 Center Drive Msc2320
Bethesda, MD 20832

800-241-1044
FAX: 301-402-0018
e-mail: nidcdinfo@nidcd.nih.gov
www.nidcd.nih.org

This telecommunication relay services fact sheet explains what the service is, how the relay service allows people who are deaf, har-of-hearing or speech impaired to communicate through a communications assiatnt with people who use a standard telephone.

**6328 Telephone Communication and Hearing Impaired**
Taylor & Francis
47 Runway Drive
Suite G
Levittown, PA 19057

215-625-8900
FAX: 215-625-2940

This is a practical book containing valuable information for audiologists, teachers and others concerned with rehabilitation of the hearing impaired.
*200 pages Illustrated*
*ISBN 0-85066-18-3*

**6329 The Mask of Benevolence: Disabling the De af Community**
Dawnsign Press

A look at the gulf that seperates the deaf minority from the hearing world, this book sheds light on the mistreatment of the deaf community by a hearing establishment that resists understanding and awareness. *$11.95*
*334 pages 1999*
*ISBN 1-581210-09-4*

**6330 Theoretical Issues in Sign Language Research**
Gallaudet University Bookstore
11030 S Langley Avenue
Chicago, IL 60628

202-651-5488
800-621-2736
FAX: 202-651-5489

These volumes are an outgrowth of a conference held at the University of Rochester in 1986, dealing with the four traditional core areas of phonology, morphology, syntax and semantics. *$29.95*
*338 pages*

**6331 They Grow in Silence**
Taylor & Francis
47 Runway Drive
Suite G
Levittown, PA 19057

FAX: 215-785-5515

Gives a comprehensive picture of the deaf child in society, not only looking at the individual but also, at the related problems for the family, community and the professional. Only by the examination of such a broad perspective can questions on the position and circumstances of the deaf child be fully considered.
*223 pages Paper*
*ISBN 0-85066 -54-6*

**6332 Tinnitus Today**
American Tinnitus Association
PO Box 5
Portland, OR 97207

503-248-9985
800-634-8978
FAX: 503-248-0024
e-mail: tinnitus@ata.org
www.ata.org

*Cherly McGinnis MBA, Executive Director*
*Barbara Sanders, Editor*

Published quarterly by the American Tinnitus Association. Also available online. Online ISSN# is 1530-6569. *$25.00*
*28 pages Quarterly*

**6333 US Government TTY Directory**
Consumer Information Center
Department 627f
Pueblo, CO 81009

e-mail: catalog.pueblo@gsa.gov

*Judi Mahoney, Public Affairs*

Gives details on how to use the Federal Relay Service and which agencies and congressional offices have text telephone devices.

**6334 Understanding Deafness Socially**
Charles C Thomas
2600 S 1st Street
Springfield, IL 62704

217-789-8980
800-258-8980
FAX: 217-789-9130
e-mail: books@ccthomas.com
www.ccthomas.com

*Michael Thomas, President*

A look at the social difficulties of being hearing impaired in a hearing society. Also available in cloth. *$29.95*

*168 pages Softcover*
*ISBN 0-398065-70-5*

**6335** **Very Special Friend**
TJ Publishers
2544 Tarpley Road
Suite 108
Carrollton, TX 75006                   972-416-0800
                                         800-999-1168
                                    FAX: 301-585-5930
                              e-mail: TJPubinc@aol.com

*Angela K Thames, President*
*Jerald A Murphy, VP*

Six year old Frannie finds a very special friend who talks in sign
language. She learns to sign and the two become best friends.
*$9.95*
*32 pages Hardcover*
*ISBN 0-93032 -55-6*

**6336** **Vision**
National Catholic Office of the Deaf
7202 Buchanan Street
Landover Hills, MD 20784              301-577-1684
                                    FAX: 301-577-1690
                              e-mail: ncod@erols.com

*Arvilla Rank, Executive Director/Editor*

Published as a pastoral service for the deaf and hard of hearing.
Provides information to members and others working in ministry. Prepares an annual gathering called Pastoral Week meeting
in January. Price: $15.00 per year, $25 for 2 years; Foreign: $17
per year; $27 for 2 years. *$15.00*
*16 pages quarterly*

**6337** **Volta Review**
Alexander Graham Bell Association
3417 Volta Place NW
Washington, DC 20007                 202-337-5220
                                    FAX: 202-337-8314
                              e-mail: info@agbell.org
                                         www.agbell.org

*Todd Houston, Executive Director*

Professionally refereed journal that publishes articles and research on education, rehabilitation and communicative development of people who have hearing impairments. Also includes
subscription to Valta Voices, up-to-date magazine, bimonthly.
*$62.00*
*Quarterly*

**6338** **Volta Voices**
Alexander Graham Bell Association
3417 Volta Place NW
Washington, DC 20007                 202-337-5220
                                    FAX: 202-337-8314
                              e-mail: info@agbell.org
                                         www.agbell.org

*Todd Houston, Executive Director*

Contains Association news and educates readers on the abilities
and needs of children and adults who are deaf or hard of hearing.
Includes subscription to The Valta Review, published four times
a year. *$62.00*

**6339** **We CAN Hear and Speak**
Alexander Graham Bell Association
3417 Volta Place NW
Washington, DC 20007                 202-337-5220
                                    FAX: 202-337-8314
                              e-mail: info@agbell.org
                                         www.agbell.org

*Todd Houston, Executive Director*

Written by parents for families of children who are deaf or hard
of hearing, this work describes auditory-verbal terminology and
approaches and contains personal narratives written by parents
and their children who are deaf or hard of hearing. *$24.95*

*171 pages Paperback*

**6340** **Week the World Heard Gallaudet**
Gallaudet University Press
800 Florida Avenue NE
Washington, DC 20002                 202-651-5220
                                         800-451-1073
                                    FAX: 202-651-5489
                        e-mail: gupress@gallaudet.edu
                    gupress.gallaudet.edu/homeSLSorder.html
This day-to-day description of the events surrounding the Deaf
President Now movement at Gallaudet University includes full
color and black and white photographs and interviews with people involved in the events of that week.
*192 pages*

**6341** **When the Mind Hears**
Gallaudet University Bookstore
800 Florida Avenue NE
Washington, DC 20002                 202-651-5000
                                         800-451-1073
                                    FAX: 202-651-5489

*Erving Jordan, President*

Comprehensive history of the deaf and their relationship with
hearing academic communities. *$19.95*
*414 pages Paperback*

**6342** **You and Your Hearing Impaired Child: A Self-Instruc-**
**tional Parents Guide**
TJ Publishers
2544 Tarpley Road
Suite 108
Carrollton, TX 75006                   972-416-0800
                                         800-999-1168
                                    FAX: 301-585-5930
                              e-mail: TJPubinc@aol.com

*Angela K Thames, President*
*Jerald A Murphy, VP*

Designed specifically for parents who have children newly diagnosed as hearing impaired. Provides vital information on hearing impairment, setting limits, behavior management,
nonverbal behavior and much more. *$17.95*
*142 pages Softcover*
*ISBN 0-93032 -40-8*

# Music

**6343** **A Comprehensive Guide to Music Therapy: T heory,**
**Clinical Practice, Research and Training**
Jessica Kingsley Publishers

A guide to accessing and understanding the ideas, theory, research results and clinical outcomes that are the foundations of
this field. *$39.95*
*286 pages 2002*
*ISBN 1-843100-83-5*

**6344** **Art Therapy SourceBook**
McGraw-Hill Company
2460 Kerper Boulevard
Dubuque, IA 52001                    563-588-1451
                                         800-338-3987
                                    FAX: 614-755-5654
                              www.mhhe.com/hper/physed

*Kurt Strand, Vice President*

An overview of the uses of art as a mentally therapeutic tool.
*$18.00*

272 pages 1998
ISBN 1-565658-84-1

## 6345 Art and Healing: Using Expressive Art to Heal Your Body, Mind, and Soul
Three Rivers Press

The author believes creating a visual image through any medium can produce physical and emotional benefits for both the creator as well as those who view it. $17.00
256 pages 1999
ISBN 0-609803-16-6

## 6346 Braille Book Bank, Music Catalog
National Braille Association
3 Townline Circle
Rochester, NY 14623          585-427-8260

e-mail: nbaoffice@compuserve.com
www.nationalbraille.org

Angela Coffaro, Executive Director
Offers hundreds of musical titles in print form, braille and on cassette.
62 pages

## 6347 Clinical Applications of Music Therapy in Developmental Disability, Pediatrics and Neurology
Taylor & Francis
47 Runway Drive
Suite G
Levittown, PA 19057          215-269-0400
FAX: 215-625-2940

Harold Stecker, President
Music therapists from Brooklyn to Belgium reflect on how music one plays or listens to has the ability to penetrate the anguish of grief, pain, and even the cognitive distortions of schizophrenia and Alzheimer's disease. $34.95
312 pages 1999
ISBN 1-853027-34-0

## 6348 Contemporary Art Therapy with Adolescents
Taylor & Francis
47 Runway Drive
Suite G
Levittown, PA 19057          215-269-0400
FAX: 215-625-2940

Harold Stecker, President
Reviews contemporary theories on adolescent development and therapy and offers solutions to the treatment of young people. $26.95
285 pages 1999
ISBN 1-853026-37-9

## 6349 Creative Arts Resources Catalog
MMB Music
3526 Washington Avenue
Saint Louis, MO 63103          314-531-9635
800-343-3771
FAX: 314-531-8384
e-mail: mlg@mmbmusic.com
www.mmbmusic.com

Marcie Lee Goldberg, VP Sales/Marketing
Publisher and distributor of creative arts therapy materials in the areas of music, dance, art, drama, and poetry. Free catalog contains hundreds of books, recordings, and videos.

## 6350 Guide to the Selection of Musical Instruments
MMB Music
3526 Washington Avenue
Saint Louis, MO 63103          314-531-9635
800-543-3771
FAX: 314-531-8384
e-mail: info@mmbmusic.com

Marcia Goldberg, President

A marvelous resource book to aid therapists teaching disabled to play musical instruments. $7.75

## 6351 Instrumental Music for Dyslexics: A Teaching Handbook
Whurr Publishers

Describes dyslexia in layman's terms and explains how the various problems that a dyslexic may have can affect all aspects of learning to play a musical instrument. It alerts the music teacher with a problem pupil to the possibilities of that pupil having some form of dyslexia. It offers suggestions as to how to teach dyslexics, with particular reference to piano teaching, and it suggests ways in which the music teacher may contribute to the welfare of a dyslexic pupil. $ 34.95
200 pages 2002
ISBN 1-861562-91-8

## 6352 Mozart Effect: Tapping the Power of Music to Heal the Body, Strengthen the Mind
Perennial Currents

Offers dramatic accounts of how doctors, shamans, musicians, and others use music to deal with everything from anxiety to cancer and chronic pain, from dyslexia to mental illness. $14.00
352 pages 2001
ISBN 0-060937-20-3

## 6353 Music Therapy
Future Horizons

Provides an overview of music therapy as it applies to cognitive, communication, and social goals for children with autism. $19.95
123 pages 2000
ISBN 1-885477-53-8

## 6354 Music Therapy and Leisure for Persons with Disabilities
Sagamore Publishing

Explores the use of musical therapy in order to enhance the development of independent leisure skills with a variety of special populations. Suggestions are provided for alternative avenues through musical experiences enabling individuals to achieve their greatest potential for independence and a high quality of life. $19.95
2002
ISBN 1-571675-11-6

## 6355 Music Therapy for the Developmentally Disabled
Pro-Ed Publications
8700 Shoal Creek Boulevard
Austin, TX 78757          512-451-3246
800-897-3202
FAX: 512-451-8542
e-mail: info@proedinc.com
www.proedinc.com

Donald Hammill, Owner
Included are practical guidelines, case samples and step-by-step instructions that enable a music therapist to bring about dramatic improvements in developmentally disabled adults and children. $40.00
269 pages Hardcover
ISBN 0-890791-90-2

## 6356 Music Therapy in Dementia Care
Jessica Kingsley Publishers

A comprehensive look at music therapy as a means of improving memory, health, and identity in those suffering from dementia, particularly Alzheimer's. For music therapists and those involved in psychogeriatry. $29.95

*256 pages 2000*
*ISBN 1-853027-76-6*

**6357 Music Therapy, Sensory Integration and the Autistic Child**
Jessica Kingsley Publishers

Examines the human physiologic function, the brain, information processing, functional adaption, and how that might be affected by music interventions in persons with sensory integration difficulties. *$23.95*
*256 pages 2001*
*ISBN 1-843107-00-7*

**6358 Music and Dyslexia: Opening New Doors**
Whurr Publishers

Dyslexic musicians can succeed provided only that they are given sufficient encouragement and understanding *$34.95*
*200 pages 2001*
*ISBN 1-861562-05-5*

**6359 Music for the Hearing Impaired**
MMB Music
3526 Washington Avenue
Saint Louis, MO 63103          314-531-9635
                              800-543-3771
                         FAX: 314-531-8384
              e-mail: info@mmbmusic.com

*Marcia Goldberg, President*
A resource manual and curriculum guide. It is the product of a four-year developmental music program, placing emphasis on the needs of those with severe and profound losses. *$29.95*

**6360 Music: Physician for Times to Come**
Quest Books
306 West Geneva Road
Wheaton, IL 60187             630-665-0130
                              800-669-9425
                         FAX: 630-665-8791
              e-mail: orders@questbooks.net
                         www.questbooks.net

*Elisabeth Trumpler, Manager*
A resource guide for various types of music and their theraputic oputcome.
*365 pages 2000*
*ISBN 0-835607-88-7*

**6361 New Music Therapist's Handbook**
Berklee Press Publications

New developments in the field of music therapy. Includes an introduction to the profession, guidelines for setting up a practice, new clinical applications, and helpful case studies. *$29.95*
*256 pages 2000*
*ISBN 0-634006-45-2*

**6362 Open Road**
102 Brook Lane
Boulder Creek, CA 95006       510-222-6662
                         FAX: 831-338-3210
*Staff, author*
*Teresa Tucker, Manager*

Arts, Music, Sports, and Field Trips.
*2 pages Monthly*

**6363 Pied Piper: Musical Activities to Develop Basic Skills**
Jessica Kingsley Publishers

Describes 78 enjoyable music activities for groups of children or adults who may have learning difficulties. The emphasis is on using music, rather than learning songs or rhythms, so group members do not need any special skills to be able to participate. Full details are given about any equipment required for the games, as well as suggestions for variations or modifications. *$21.95*
*96 pages 2001*
*ISBN 1-853029-94-*

**6364 Power of Sound: How to Manage Your Persona l Soundscape for a Vital, Productive, Healthy Life**
Healing Arts Press
1 Park Street
Rochester, VT 05767           802-767-3174
                              800-246-8648
                         FAX: 802-767-3726
        e-mail: orders@innertraditions.com
                      www.InnerTraditions.com

*Ehud Sperling, Owner*
Describes how harmonics can be used as sonic yoga for meditation and deep relaxation to enhance energy. *$16.95*
*192 pages 2002*
*ISBN 0-892819-93-6*

**6365 Teaching Basic Guitar Skills to Special Learners**
MMB Music
3526 Washington Avenue
Saint Louis, MO 63103          314-531-9635
                              800-543-3771
                         FAX: 314-531-8384
              e-mail: info@mmbmusic.com

*Marcia Goldberg, President*
The first-of-its-kind guitar book for use with persons who have difficulty learning to play via traditional methods. *$16.00*

# Parenting: General

**6366 AEPS Family Report: For Children Ages Three to Six**
Brookes Publishing
PO Box 10624
Baltimore, MD 21285           410-337-9580
                              800-638-3775
                         FAX: 410-337-8539
     e-mail: custserv@brookespublishing.com
                      www.brookespublishing.com

*Paul Brooks, Owner*
This is a 64-item questionnaire that asks parents to rank their child's abilities on specific skills. In packages of 10 paperback. *$23.00*
*28 pages Saddle-stiched*
*ISBN 1-557662-50-9*

**6367 AT for Parents with Disabilities**
Idaho Assistive Technology Project
129 W 3rd Street
Moscow, ID 83843              208-885-3559
                              800-432-8324
                         FAX: 208-885-3628
             e-mail: rseiler@uidaho.edu
              www.educ.uidaho.edu/idatech
*$5.00*
*80 pages*

**6368 Alex: The Life of a Child**
Rutledge Hill Press

Alexandra Deford was just eight years old when she died in 1980 following a battle against cystic fibrosis. In a new Introduction, her father summarizes some of the developments made in combating the disease and tells how the family has come to terms with her loss. *$ 13.98*

*228 pages 1997*
*ISBN 1-558535-52-7*

**6369 Alternative Approach to Allergies**
Harper Perennial
10 E 53rd Street
New York, NY 10022      212-207-7000
FAX: 212-207-7145
www.harpercollins.com

*Abigail Kunath, Marketing Executive*

A comprehensive guide to staying well and allergy-free by a pioneer in the field of environmental medicine.

**6370 Baby Book for the Developmentally Challenged Child**
Exceptional Parent Library
PO Box 1807
Englewood Cliffs, NJ 07632     201-947-6000
800-535-1910
FAX: 201-947-9376
e-mail: eplibrary@aol.com
www.eplibrary.com
This baby book is for parents to write milestones for their developmentally challenged child. It incorporates the usual baby book features with very special sections covering any special needs child. *$25.00*
*48 pages Hardcover*

**6371 Babycare Assistive Technology**
Through the Looking Glass
2198 6th Street
Suite 100
Berkeley, CA 94710     510-848-1112
800-644-2666
FAX: 510-848-4445
e-mail: TLG@lookingglass.org
www.lookingglass.org

*C Tuleja*
*A DeMoss*
*Megan Kirshbaum, Executive Director*

Available in braille, large print or cassette. *$2.00*
*8 pages*

**6372 Babycare Assistive Technology for Parents with Physical Disabilties**
Through the Looking Glass
2198 6th Street
Suite 100
Berkeley, CA 94710     510-848-1112
800-644-2666
FAX: 510-848-4445
e-mail: TLG@lookingglass.org
www.lookingglass.org

*Megan Kirshbaum, Executive Director*

Relational, systems and Cultural perspectives. Available in braille, large print or cassette. *$2.00*
*7 pages*

**6373 Babyface: A Story of Heart and Bones**
Spina Bifida Association of America
4590 Macarthur Boulevard NW
Suite 250
Washington, DC 20007     202-944-3285
800-621-3141
FAX: 202-944-3295
e-mail: sbaa@sbaa.org
www.sbaa.org

*Cindy Brownstein, Chief Executive Officer*

A must read for families that seek insight into coping with a chronic condition. Many useful resources provided. *$32.90*

**6374 Backyards and Butterflies**
Brookline Books
PO Box 1047
Cambridge, MA 02139     617-868-0360
800-666-2665
FAX: 617-868-1772
e-mail: brooklinebks@delphi.com
www.brooklinebooks.com
Backyards And Butterflies: Ways to Include Children with Disabilities In Out Door Activites is an illustrated book with dozens of imaginative ways parents can include children with physical disabilities in outdoor activities. Offers clear concise, how-to directions for constructing homemaode toys, utensils, and other items that can be enjoyed outside safely and comfortably *$14.95*
*72 pages Paperback*
*ISBN 1-57129 -11-7*

**6375 Behavior Problems**
Research Press
PO Box 9177
Champaign, IL 61826     217-352-3273
800-519-2707
FAX: 217-352-1221
e-mail: rp@researchpress.com
www.researchpress.com

*Russell Pence, President*

A practical book that provides effective techniques for solving behavior problems that are characteristic of children with developmental disabilities. Numerous charts and examples accompanied by helpful illustrations make this book an invaluable resource for parents, special education teachers and residential staff. *$12.95*
*80 pages Paperback*
*ISBN 0-878221-70-0*

**6376 Beyond Baby Talk: From Sounds to Sentence s, a Parent's Guide to Language Development**
Prima Publishing
PO Box 1260
Rocklin, CA 95677     916-787-7000
800-632-8676
FAX: 916-787-7001
e-mail: websupportlife@primapub.com
www.primapublishing.com
The authors discuss the best ways to help your child develop the all-important skill of communication and to recognize the signs of language development problems. *$15.00*
*224 pages 2001*
*ISBN 0-761526-47-1*

**6377 Books on Special Children**
BOSC
PO Box 305
Congers, NY 10920     845-638-1236
FAX: 845-638-0847
e-mail: irene@boscbooks.com
www.boscbooks.com

*Irene Slovak, Owner*

Distributes books by mail to professionals and parents of handicapped children. The BOSC Directory contains facilities for people with learning disabilities (all disabilities, published annually)
*300+ pages Hardcover*
*ISBN O-G61386-08-8*

**6378 Brain Allergies: The Psychonutrient**
Keats Publishing
PO Box 876
New Canaan, CT 06840     203-966-8721
800-323-4900
A comprehensive look at the role nutrition and orthomolecular medicine can play in treating brain allergies, including a self-help protocol and a special appendix for physicians.

**6379 Brothers, Sisters, and Special Needs**
Brookes Publishing
PO Box 10624
Baltimore, MD 21285
410-337-9580
800-638-3775
FAX: 410-337-8539
e-mail: custserv@brookespublishing.com
www.brookespublishing.com

*Paul Brooks, Owner*

Information and activities for helping young siblings of children with chronic illnesses and developmental disabilities. *$30.00*
*224 pages Paperback*
*ISBN 1-55766 -43-3*

**6380 Building the Healing Partnership: Parents, Professionals and Children**
Brookline Books
PO Box 1046
Cambridge, MA 02139
617-868-0360
800-666-2665
FAX: 617-868-1772
e-mail: brooklinebks@delphi.com
www.brooklinebooks.com
Successful programs understand that the disabled child's needs must be considered in the context of a family. This book was specifically written for practitioner's who must work with families but who have insufficient training in family systems assessment and intervention. It is a valuable blend of theory and practice with pointers for applying the principles. *$24.95*
*Paperback*
*ISBN 0-91479 -63-8*

**6381 Child With Special Needs: Encouraging Inte llectual and Emotional Growth**
Addison-Wesley Publishing Company
75 Arlington Street
Suite 300
Boston, MA 02116
617-848-6000
800-238-9682
FAX: 617-848-6034
www.awprofessional.com

*William Barke, President*

Covering all kinds of disabilities — including cerebral palsy, autism, retardation, ADD, and language problems — this guide offers parents specific ways of helping all special needs chidren reach their full intellectual and emotional potential. *$32.00*
*496 pages 1998*
*ISBN 0-201407-26-4*

**6382 Children with Disabilities**
Brookes Publishing
PO Box 10624
Baltimore, MD 21285
410-337-9580
800-638-3775
FAX: 410-337-8539
e-mail: custserv@brookespublishing.com
www.brookespublishing.com

*Mark L Batshaw MD, Editor*
*Paul Brooks, Owner*

Extensive coverage of genetics, heredity, pre- and postnatal development, specific disabilities, family roles, and intervention. Features chapters on substance abuse, HIV and AIDS, Down syndrome, fragile X syndrome, behavior management, transitions to adulthood, and health care in the 21st century. Also reveals the causes of many conditions that can lead to developmental disabilities. *$69.95*
*912 pages Hardcover*
*ISBN 1-557665-81-8*

**6383 Children with Mental Retardation**
Woodbine House
6510 Bells Mill Road
Bethesda, MD 20817
301-897-3570
800-843-7323
FAX: 301-897-5838
www.woodbinehouse.com

*Irv Shapell, Owner*

A book for parents of children with mild to moderate mental retardation, whether or not they have a diagnosed syndrome or condition. It provides a complete and compassionate introduction to their child's medical, therapeutic, and educational needs, and discusses the emotional impact on the family. New parents can rely on Children with Mental Retardation to provide that solid foundation and confidence they need to help their child reach his or her highest potential. *$14.95*
*437 pages Paperback*
*ISBN 0-933149-39-5*

**6384 Conditional Love: Parents' Attitudes Toward Handicapped Children**
Greenwood Publishing Group
88 Post Road W
Suite 5007
Westport, CT 06880
203-226-3571
FAX: 203-222-1502
www.greenwood.com

*Wayne Smith, President*

Offers parents information on understanding disabled children and mainstreaming them into their normal family life. *$49.95*
*312 pages*
*ISBN 0-89789 -24-7*

**6385 Coordinacion De Servicios Centrado En La Familia**
Brookline Books
PO Box 1047
Cambridge, MA 02139
617-868-0360
800-666-2665
FAX: 617-868-1772
e-mail: brooklinebks@delphi.com
www.brooklinebooks.com
This book, translated into Spanish from the English original, is designed to orient and educate parents about issues of service coordination, to assist families in caring for an infant or toddler with developmental delays or disabilities. *$7.00*
*34 pages Paperback*
*ISBN 0-91479 -90-5*

**6386 Creative Play Activities for Children with Disabilities**
Human Kinetics
PO Box 5076
Champaign, IL 61825
800-747-4457
FAX: 217-351-2674
e-mail: orders@hkusa.com
www.humankinetics.com
Contains 250 games and activities designed to help children with all types of disabilities grow through play. Each chapter focuses on a particular world or activity theme. Themes include exploring the world of the senses, active games, building and creating, imaginative outdoor fun and water play, and group games and activities. *$16.95*
*232 pages*
*ISBN 0-873229-33-9*

**6387 Detecting Your Hidden Allergies**
Professional Books/Future Health
211 N Sycamore Street
Newtown, PA 18940
215-504-1700
FAX: 215-860-5374
Gives specific instructions on how to use an elimination diet to determine food allergies.

**6388 Developing Personal Safety Skills in Children with Disabilities**
Brookes Publishing
PO Box 10624
Baltimore, MD 21285
410-337-9580
800-638-3775
FAX: 410-337-8539
e-mail: custserv@brookespublishing.com
www.brookespublishing.com

*Paul Brooks, Owner*

A guide for teachers, parents, and caregivers, this volume explores the issue of personal safety for children with disabilities and offers strategies for empowering and protecting them at home and in school. Recognizing that children with disabilities are vulnerable to abuse, this work explores why children with disabilities need personal safety skills, offers, curriculum ideas and exercises, and advocates the development of self-esteem and assertiveness so that children can protect themselves. *$34.00*

*220 pages Paperback*
*ISBN 1-557661-84-7*

**6389 Developmental Disabilities in Infancy and Childhood, 2nd Edition**
Brookes Publishing
PO Box 10624
Baltimore, MD 21285

410-337-9580
800-638-3775
FAX: 410-337-8539
e-mail: custserv@brookespublishing.com
www.brookespublishing.com

*Paul Brooks, Owner*

This two volume set explores advances in assessment and treatment, retains a clinical focus, and incorporates recent developments in research and theory. Can be purchased individually or as a set (Vol. 1: Neurodevelopmental Diagnosis and Treatment Vol. 2: The Spectrum of Developmental Disabilities). *$210.00* Hardcover
*ISBN 1-55766O-CA-P*

**6390 Dictionary of Developmental Disabilities Terminology**
Brookes Publishing
PO Box 10624
Baltimore, MD 21285

410-337-9580
800-638-3775
FAX: 410-337-8539
e-mail: custserv@brookespublishing.com
www.brookespublishing.com

*Paul Brooks, Owner*

Answers thousands of questions for medical or human services professionals, parents or advocates of children with disabilities, or students preparing for their careers. Provides thorough explanations of the most common terms associated with disabilities. *$55.95*

*368 pages Hardcover*
*ISBN 1-557662-45-2*

**6391 Difficult Child**
Bantam Books
1540 Broadway
New York, NY 10036

212-782-9000
FAX: 212-302-7985
www.randomhouse.com

The classic and definitive work on parenting hard-to-raise children with new sections on ADHD and the latest medications for childhood disorders. *$15.95*

*302 pages Paperback 2000*
*ISBN 0-553380-36-2*

**6392 Disability Culture Perspective on Early Intervention**
Through the Looking Glass
2198 6th Street
Suite 100
Berkeley, CA 94710

510-848-1112
800-644-2666
FAX: 510-848-4445
e-mail: TLG@lookingglass.org
www.lookingglass.org

*Megan Kirshbaum*

For parents with physical or cognitive disabilities and their families. Available in braille, large print or cassette. *$2.00*

*12 pages*

**6393 Encyclopedia of Genetic Disorders & Birth Defects**
Facts on File
132 W 31st Street
Floor 17
New York, NY 10001

212-967-8800
800-322-8755
FAX: 212-967-9196
e-mail: jchambers@factsonfile.com
www.factsonfile.com

*Mark Donnell, President*

Layperson-accessible entries on genetic terminology and genetically-influenced conditions. *$71.50*

*474 pages 2000*
*ISBN 0-816038-09-0*

**6394 Equal Treatment for People With Mental Ret ardation: Having and Raising Children**
Harvard University Press

A Harvard law professor and civil liberties practitioner provide a comprehensive examination of the reproductive and parental rights of mentally retarded citizens. *$19.95*

*464 pages Paperback 2001*
*ISBN 0-674006-97-6*

**6395 Everday Social Interaction**
Brookes Publishing
PO Box 10624
Baltimore, MD 21285

410-337-9580
800-638-3775
FAX: 410-337-8539
e-mail: custserv@brookespublishing.com
www.brookespublishing.com

*Paul Brooks, Owner*

Useful strategies for assessing needs and setting objectives, along with helpful teaching techniques, are accompanied by tips on social courtesies, rewards, praise, and criticism. Checklists and task analyses that show how complex skills can be broken down into major components for easy performance monitoring are also included. *$41.95*

*342 pages Paperback*
*ISBN 1-55766 -58-4*

**6396 Exceptional Parent Magazine**
Psy-Ed Corp
551 Main Street
Johnstown, PA 15901

877-372-7368
FAX: 740-389-5574
e-mail: EPAR@kable.com
www.eparent.com

*Joseph Valenzano Jr, President/CEO*
*Bob Salluzzo, COO*
*Kendra Kelly, Ad Traffic Manager*

Addresses concerns of raising, treating or teaching children or young adults with disabilities, for parents and professionals. *$4.95*

*100 pages Monthly*
*ISSN 0046-91 7*

**6397 Explosive Child**
Perennial Currents

An explosive child frequently exhibits severe noncompliance, temper outbursts, and verbal or physical aggression. Greene offers help for frustrted, guilt-ridden parents and their child at school and at home. *$14.00*

*366 pages 2001*
*ISBN 0-060931-02-7*

**6398    Face of Inclusion**
Special Needs Project
324 State Street
Suite H
Santa Barbara, CA  93101                      805-962-8087
                                               800-333-6867
                                        FAX: 805-962-5087
                              e-mail: eplibrary@aol.com
                                         www.eplibrary.com
A unique and moving parents' perspective of inclusion for administrators, teachers, and parents of children with disabilities.
*$99.00*

**6399    Families Magazine**
New Jersey Developmental Disabilities Council
PO Box 700
Trenton, NJ  08625                            609-292-3745
                                               800-216-1199
                                        FAX: 609-292-7114
                                        TTY: 609-777-3238
                              e-mail: njddc@njddc.org
                                              www.njddc.org

*Ethan Ellis, Executive Director/Editor*
*Norman Reim, Managing Editor*

Quarterly magazine for people with disabilities, their families and the public, features family profiles, news, columns and the New Jersey Family support councils newsletter.
*Quarterly*

**6400    Families, Illness & Disability**
Through the Looking Glass
2198 6th Street
Suite 100
Berkeley, CA  94710                           510-848-1112
                                               800-644-2666
                                        FAX: 510-848-4445
                              e-mail: TLG@lookingglass.org
                                         www.lookingglass.org

*J Rolland*
*Megan Kirshbaum, Executive Director*

*$35.00*
              *320 pages*

**6401    Family Context and Disability Culture Reframing: Through the Looking Glass**
Through the Looking Glass
2198 6th Street
Suite 100
Berkeley, CA  94710                           510-848-1112
                                               800-644-2666
                                        FAX: 510-848-4445
                              e-mail: TLG@lookingglass.org
                                         www.lookingglass.org

*Mega Kirshbaum, Executive Director*
Available in braille, large print or cassette. *$2.00*
              *5 pages*

**6402    Family Interventions Throughout Disability**
Springer Publishing Company
536 Broadway
New York, NY  10012                           212-431-4370
                                               877-687-7476
                                        FAX: 212-941-7842
                              e-mail: marketing@springerpub.com
                                         www.springerpub.com

*Annette Imperati, Marketing/Sales Director*
*Ursula Springer, President*

Family attitudes throughout chronic illness and disability.
*$31.95*

*320 pages*
*ISBN 0-82615 -80-4*

**6403    Family-Centered Service Coordination: A Manual for Parents**
Brookline Books
PO Box 1047
Cambridge, MA  02139                          617-868-0360
                                               800-666-2665
                                        FAX: 617-868-1772
                              e-mail: brooklinebks@delphi.com
                                         www.brooklinebooks.com
A manual designed to orient and educate parents about issues of service coordination, to assist families in caring for an infant or toddler with developmental delays or disabilities. *$7.00*
              *34 pages Paperback*
              *ISBN 0-91479 -90-5*

**6404    Growing Up Gifted**
McGraw-Hill, School Publishing
220 E Danieldale Road
Desoto, TX  75115                             972-224-1111
                                               800-442-9685
                                        FAX: 972-228-1982
                                              mhschool.com

*Joseph Gavigan, President*

A book that develops the potential of children at home and at school.
              *512 pages*

**6405    Handbook About Care in the Home**
AARP Fulfillment
601 E Street NW
Washington, DC  20049                         202-434-2277
                                               800-424-3410
                                        FAX: 202-434-3443
                              e-mail: member@aarp.org
                                              www.aarp.org

*William Novelli, Chief Executive Officer*

Offers valuable information for the disabled.
              *24 pages*

**6406    How to Deal with Back Pain and Rheumatoid Joint Pain**
Global Health Solutions
2146 Kings Garden Way
Falls Church, VA  22043                       703-848-2333
                                               800-759-3999
                                        FAX: 703-848-0028
                              e-mail: shipping@watercure.com
                                         www.watercure.com

*Kristin Swan, Secretary*
*Joy Barber, Secretary*
*Xiaopo Batmanghelidj, President*

The physiology of pain production and its direct relationship to chronic regional dehydration of some joint spaces is explained: Special movements that would create vacuum in the disc spaces and draw water and the displaced discs into the vertebral joints are demonstrated.

**6407    Human Kinetics**
PO Box 5076
Champaign, IL  61825                          217-351-5076
                                        FAX: 217-351-2674
                                         www.humankinetics.com

*Rainer Martens, President*

**6408    It's All in Your Head**
Avery Publishing Group
375 Hudson Street
New York, NY  10014                           212-366-2000

Dr. Higgins's critique of the use of mercury, a toxic element and environmental hazard, in dentistry. For those suffering mercury poisoning, the book examines a number of conventional and alternative treatments.

**6409  Keys to Parenting a Child with a Learning Disability**
Barron's Educational Series
250 Wireless Boulevard
Hauppauge, NY  11788

631-434-3311
800-645-3476
FAX: 631-434-3723
e-mail: info@barronseduc.com
www.barronseduc.com

*Lonny Stein, Director Marketing*
*Manuel Barron, Chief Executive Officer*

The authors discuss the diagnosis and treatment of learning disabilities. They provide a practical course of action for parents who suspect a learning disability is present in their child. They also describe methods of special education, dealing with learning disabled children at home, and integrating them into community activities. *$6.95*
    *208 pages Paperback*
    *ISBN 0-812016-79-3*

**6410  Kids to the Rescue**
Alliance for Parental Involvement in Education
PO Box 59
East Chatham, NY  12060

518-392-6900
FAX: 518-392-6900

Parents and children should read this book together. The author offers children the information they need for fourteen emergency situations. *$7.95*

**6411  Life Planning Workbook**
Exceptional Parent Library
PO Box 1807
Englewood Cliffs, NJ  07632

201-947-6000
800-535-1910
FAX: 201-947-9376
e-mail: eplibrary@aol.com
www.eplibrary.com

A hands-on guide to help parents provide for the future security and happiness of their child with a disability after their death. *$24.95*

**6412  LifeLines**
Disabled and Alone
352 Park Avenue S
11th Floor
New York, NY  10010

212-532-6740
800-995-0066
FAX: 212-532-3588
e-mail: info@disabledandalone.org
www.disabledandalone.org

*Rosyln Brilliant, Executive Director*

Disabled and Alone is a national, nonprofit organization whose sole purpose is to assure the well being of disabled individuals, particularly those whose families have died and have engaged Disabled and Alone to provide advocacy and oversight for the lifetime of their disabled children. This newsletter provides information about "future planning" for a person with a disability.
    *8-16 pages Bi-annual*

**6413  Making Changes: Family Voices on Living Disabilities**
Brookline Books
PO Box 1047
Cambridge, MA  02139

800-666-2665
FAX: 617-868-1772
e-mail: brooklinebks@delphi.com
www.brooklinebooks.com

What are the day to day impacts on the family when a disabled child is born? Or when a child who grows up without a disability becomes disabled through accident or disease? This provocative set of reports illuminates the conditions of those peoples lives, and the way they and those around them adjust to the disabilities. *$16.95*

    *216 pages Paperback*
    *ISBN 0-91479 -93-*

**6414  Mobility Training for People with Disabilities**
Charles C Thomas
2600 S 1st Street
Springfield, IL  62704

217-789-8980
800-258-8980
FAX: 217-789-9130
e-mail: books@ccthomas.com
www.ccthomas.com

*Michael Thomas, President*

Children and adults with mental, visual, physical and hearing impairments can learn to travel. Also available in cloth. *$28.95*
    *144 pages Paper*
    *ISBN 0-398063-56-7*

**6415  Mothers Talk About Learning Disabilities**
Gallery Bookshop
PO Box 270
Mendocino, CA  95460

707-937-2665
FAX: 707-937-3737
e-mail: info@gallerybooks.com
www.gallerybooks.com

*Tony Miksak, Owner*

In this work, the mother of two learning disabled boys seeks to give mothers in similar circumstances encouragement, support and everyday advice. *$17.95*
    *157 pages*
    *ISBN 0-13502 -70-1*

**6416  Muscular Dystrophy in Children: A Guide fo r Families**

Demos Medical Publishing
386 Park Avenue S
Suite 201
New York, NY  10016

212-683-0072
800-532-8663
FAX: 212-683-0118
e-mail: orderdep@demospub.com
www.demosmedpub.com

*Phyllis Gold, Owner*

Defines the available medical options at every stage of the disease and offers guidance even when it may seem that little or nothing can be done. Includes a glossary and suggestions for furhter reading. *$19.95*
    *130 pages Paperback 1999*
    *ISBN 1-888799-33-1*

**6417  New Language of Toys: Teaching Communicati on Skills to Children with Special Needs**
Spina Bifida Association of America
4590 Macarthur Boulevard NW
Suite 250
Washington, DC 20007

202-944-3285
800-621-3141
FAX: 202-944-3295
e-mail: sbaa@sbaa.org
www.sbaa.org

*Cindy Brownstein, Chief Executive Officer*

A guide for parents and teachers and a reader-friendly resource guide that provides a wealth of information on how play activities affect a child's language development and where to get the toys and materials to use in these activities. *$19.00*

**6418  NewsLine**
Federation for Children with Special Needs
56 Temple Place
Suite 664
Boston, MA  02111

617-542-7860
800-537-0446
FAX: 617-542-7832
e-mail: pal@fcsn.org
www.ppal.net

*Donna Welles, Executive Director*
*Lisa Lambert, Asistant Director*

Offers information for parents and families on resources, medical updates, activities, fund-raising events and association news for their disabled children.
*Quarterly*

**6419 No More Allergies**
Villiard Books
1540 Broadway
New York, NY 10036          212-782-9000
                            FAX: 212-302-7985

*Carol Schneider, Marketing Executive*

A detailed investigation into the causes of allergies related both to food and the environment, as well as their link to other illnesses, such as asthma, arthritis, chrinic fatigue syndrome, and diabetes. Also outlines testing methods, treatments, and a diet plan to restore immune function.

**6420 No One to Play with: The Social Side of Learning Disabilities**
Special Needs Project
324 State Street
Suite H
Santa Barbara, CA 93101          805-962-8087
                                 800-333-6867
                            FAX: 805-962-5087

*Betty Osman*

Your child suffers from a learning disability, and you have read reams on how to improve his or her academic skills and now want to address his or her social needs. *$10.00*
*188 pages*

**6421 No Time for Jello: One Family's Experience**
Brookline Books
PO Box 1046
Cambridge, MA 02139          617-868-0360
                             800-666-2665
                        FAX: 617-868-1772
                e-mail: brooklinebks@delphi.com
                        www.brooklinebooks.com
One family's story of their attempts to remediate and cure the effects of a cerebral palsied condition the oldest son was born with. The Bratts traveled traditional routes, through distinguished medical centers in Boston, and nontraditional routes in a search for treatments that would help their son. *$17.95*
*Softcover*
*ISBN 0-91479 -56-5*

**6422 On the Road to Autonomy: Promoting Self- Competence in Children & Youth with Disabilities**
Brookes Publishing
PO Box 10624
Baltimore, MD 21285          410-337-9580
                             800-638-3775
                        FAX: 410-337-8539
            e-mail: custserv@brookespublishing.com
                    www.brookespublishing.com

*Paul Brooks, Owner*

This book provides detailed conceptual, practical, and personal information regarding the promotion of self-esteem, self-determination, and coping skills among children and youth with and without disabilities. *$48.00*
*432 pages Paperback*
*ISBN 1-55766 -35-5*

**6423 One-Two-Three Magic: Effective Discipline for Children 2-12**
Child Management
800 Roosevelt Road
Glen Ellyn, IL 60137          630-469-0484
                              800-442-4453
                         FAX: 630-469-4571
                         www.parentmagic.com

*Nancy Roe, Office Manager*

Time tested program provides easy-to-follow steps for disciplining children ages 2-12 without arguing, yelling or spanking. Excellent for parents, grandparents and teachers. Available on video ($39.95) cd ($24.95), book ($14.95), and dvd (39.95). *$12.95*
*180 pages Paperback*
*ISBN 0-96338 -61-9*

**6424 Pain Erasure**
M Evans and Company
216 E 49th Street
New York, NY 10017          212-979-0880
                            FAX: 212-486-4544

*Mary Evans, Owner*

This book explains Bonnie Prudden's method for pain relief using myotherapy, a method hailed by doctors and patients.
*1985*
*ISBN 0-345331-02-8*

**6425 Parent Centers and Independent Living Centers: Collectively We're Stronger**
Independent Living Research Utilization ILRU
2323 S Shepherd Drive
Suite 1000
Houston, TX 77019          713-520-0232
                           FAX: 713-520-5785
                           www.ilru.org

*Laurie Redd, Executive Director*

This article describes several examples of effective working relationships of PTIs and CILs. The examples highlight how parent and consumer organizations have identified complimentary strengths and formed partnerships to better support children with disabilities and their families. These partnerships can also be a very important way of involving youth in the disability movement so they may become leaders of tomorrow.
*10 pages*

**6426 Parent Survival Manual**
Exceptional Parent Library
PO Box 1807
Englewood Cliffs, NJ 07632          201-947-6000
                                    800-535-1910
                               FAX: 201-947-9376
                        e-mail: eplibrary@aol.com
                                www.eplibrary.com
A guide to crises resolution in autism and related developmental disorders. *$39.95*

**6427 Parent-Child Interaction and Developmental Disabilities**
Greenwood Publishing Group
88 Post Road W
Suite 5007
Westport, CT 06880          203-226-3571
                            FAX: 203-222-1502
                            www.greenwood.com

*Wayne Smith, President*

This volume brings together the original papers by international scholars and practitioners on the question of the effects of parent interaction with developmentally disabled children. $65.00-$69.50.
*395 pages Hardcover*
*ISBN 0-275928-35-7*

**6428 Parenting**
Accent Books & Products
PO Box 700
Bloomington, IL 61702          309-378-2961
                               800-787-8444
                          FAX: 309-378-4420
                       e-mail: acmtlvng@aol.com

*Raymond C Cheever, Publisher*
*Betty Garee, Editor*

Experienced parents (who are disabled) discuss: raising children from infant to teens, balancing career and motherhood, discipline methods and more when both parents are disabled. *$7.95*

*83 pages*
*ISBN 0-91570 -26-4*

**6429  Parenting with a Disability**
Through the Looking Glass
2198 6th Street
Suite 100
Berkeley, CA  94710                          510-848-1112
                                             800-644-2666
                                     FAX: 510-848-4445
                           e-mail: TLG@lookingglass.org
                                     www.lookingglass.org

*Megan Kirshbaum, Executive Director*
International newsletter. Available in braille, large print or cassette.
                    *3 per year*

**6430  Parents and Young Mentally Handicapped Children**
Brookline Books
PO Box 1046
Cambridge, MA  02139                          617-868-0360
                                              800-666-2665
                                      FAX: 617-868-1772
                         e-mail: brooklinebks@delphi.com
                                     www.brooklinebooks.com
Critically reviews and analyzes the effects of having a developmentally delayed child on the daily life of the family. Examined are the parents' crucial role in their child's development, the part played by other extended family members, parents' attitudes and parents' styles of interaction with their disabled and non-disabled child. *$ 29.95*
                    *Hardcover*
                    *ISBN 0-91479 -28-X*

**6431  Perspectives on a Parent Movement**
Brookline Books
PO Box 1046
Cambridge, MA  02139                          617-868-0360
                                              800-666-2665
                                      FAX: 617-868-1772
                         e-mail: brooklinebks@delphi.com
                                     www.brooklinebooks.com
This book captures Rosemary Dybwad's truly innovative wisdom and pioneering for people with intellectual limitations in these previously unpublished essays and speeches. *$17.95*
                    *Paperback*
                    *ISBN 0-91479 -74-3*

**6432  Plan Ahead: Do What You Can**
Spina Bifida Association of America
4590 Macarthur Boulevard NW
Suite 250
Washington, DC 20007                          202-944-3285
                                              800-621-3141
                                      FAX: 202-944-3295
                            e-mail: sbaa@sbaa.org
                                     www.sbaa.org

*Cindy Brownstein, Chief Executive Officer*
Folic aciid information for women at risk for recurrence. *$15.00*

**6433  Power Dialogues**
Option Indigo Press
2080 S Undermountain Road
Sheffield, MA  01257                          413-229-8727
                                              800-562-7171
                                      FAX: 413-229-8727
                          e-mail: indigo@option.org
                                     www.optionindigo.com

*Kate Wilde*
Learn our core system for helping others. This key program teaches participants the simple, yet profound principles and practical skills involved in using the Option Process Dialogue. This process consists of a system of nonjudgmental, non-directive questions that enables people to uncover the beliefs that underlie their feelings and behaviors. *$49.95*

*301 pages Paperback*
*ISBN 1-88725 -06-4*

**6434  Promoting Communication in Infants and Young Children: 500 Ways to Succeed**
Speech Bin
1965 25th Avenue
Vero Beach, FL  32960                         772-770-0007
                                              800-477-3324
                                      FAX: 772-770-0006
                                     www.speechbin.com
This practical reference for parents, caregivers and professional service providers how to promote communication development in infants and yourn children. Gives down-to-earth information and activities to help your youngest children succeed. It provides step-by-step suggestions for stimulationg children's speech and language skills. Paperback. *$14.95*

**6435  Raising Your Child to be Gifted**
Brookline Books
PO Box 1047
Cambridge, MA  02139                          617-868-0360
                                              800-666-2665
                                      FAX: 617-868-1772
                         e-mail: brooklinebks@delphi.com
                                     www.brooklinebooks.com
Dr. Campbell studied more than 10,000 gifted children in four countries, and found that what they shared most was not IQ, but parents who nurtured their ability and supported their efforts in school. This book explains the underlying principles and strategies these parents used in nurturing their childrens' abilities. *$15.95*
                    *196 pages Paperback*
                    *ISBN 1-57129 -00-1*

**6436  Risk, Resilience, & Prevention: Promoting the Well-Being of All Children**
Brookes Publishing
PO Box 10624
Baltimore, MD  21285                          410-337-9580
                                              800-638-3775
                                      FAX: 410-337-8539
                         e-mail: custserv@brookespublishing.com
                                     www.brookespublishing.com

*Paul Brooks, Owner*
This book investigates the implications of a primary prevention agenda for policy, practice, and research. Provides an in-depth examination of the increase in teenage pregnancy, school dropout, neglect and abuse, unintentional injury, depression and mental illness, behavior disorders, sexually transmitted disease, and illiteracy. An essential for health care professionals, educators, and administrators, psychologists, school counselors, policy makers, and child services providers. *$34.00*
                    *384 pages Paperback*
                    *ISBN 1-55766 -66-9*

**6437  Sexuality and the Developmentally Handicapped**
Edwin Mellen Press
PO Box 450
Lewiston, NY  14092                           716-754-2266
                                      FAX: 716-754-4056
                           e-mail: mellen@wzrd.com

*Herbert Richardson, Owner*
Presents the knowledge, attitudes, and skills pertinent to responding to the sexual problems of developmentally handicapped persons, their families and communities. Details fully documented cases, issues concerning the law, and resource materials available. *$89.95*

*245 pages Hardcover*
*ISBN 0-88946 -32-5*

**6438   Shattered Dreams-Lonely Choices: Birth Parents of Babies with Disabilities**
Greenwood Publishing Group
88 Post Road W
Suite 5007
Westport, CT  06880                           203-226-3571
                                         FAX: 203-222-1502
                                         www.greenwood.com

*Wayne Smith, President*

Written by a mother who, without warning, gave birth to a boy with Down Syndrome, this book is meant to help parents through the initial shock and the realization that they are not able to care for their child. $29.95-$35.00. *$29.95*
*208 pages Hardcover*
*ISBN 0-897892-86-0*

**6439   Since Owen, A Parent-to-Parent Guide for Care of the Disabled Child**
Special Needs Project
324 State Street
Suite H
Santa Barbara, CA  93101                      805-962-8087
                                              800-333-6867
                                         FAX: 805-962-5087
                                         www.specialneeds.com

*Charles Callahan, Editor*

Against the background of his experience as the parent of a severely disabled young man, Callahan writes conscientiously to other parents. *$16.95*
*486 pages*

**6440   Sleep Better! A Guide to Improving Sleep for Children with Special Needs**
Brookes Publishing
PO Box 10624
Baltimore, MD  21285                          410-337-9580
                                              800-638-3775
                                         FAX: 410-337-8539
                           e-mail: custserv@brookespublishing.com
                                    www.brookespublishing.com

*Paul Brooks, Owner*

This book offers step-by-step, how to instructions for helping children with disabilities get the rest they need. For problems ranging from bedtime tantrums to night waking, parents and caregivers will find a variety of widely tested and easy-to-implement techniques that have already helped hundreds of children with special needs. *$21.95*
*288 pages Paperback 1997*
*ISBN 1-55766 -15-7*

**6441   Something's Wrong with My Child**
Charles C Thomas
2600 S 1st Street
Springfield, IL  62704                        217-789-8980
                                              800-258-8980
                                         FAX: 217-789-9130
                              e-mail: books@ccthomas.com
                                         www.ccthomas.com

*Michael Thomas, President*

A straight forward presentation to help professionals and parents to better understand themselves in dealing with the emotionally charged subject of disabled children. Also available in cloth. *$26.95*
*210 pages Paperback*
*ISBN 0-398068-99-2*

**6442   Sometimes I Get All Scribbly**
Exceptional Parent Library
PO Box 1807
Englewood Cliffs, NJ  07632                   201-947-6000
                                              800-535-1910
                                         FAX: 201-947-9376
                               e-mail: eplibrary@aol.com
                                         www.eplibrary.com

Clinical, educational and emotional information from the point of view of a parent. *$16.00*

**6443   Son-Rise: The Miracle Continues**
2080 S Undermountain Road
Sheffield, MA  01257                          413-229-2100
                                              800-714-2779
                                         FAX: 413-229-3202
                               e-mail: sonrise@option.org
                                         www.son-rise.org

Documents Raun Kaufman's astonishing development from a lifeless, autistic, retarded child into a highly verbal, lovable youngster with no traces of his former condition. Details Raun's extraordinary progress from the age of four into young adulthood, also shares moving accounts of five families that successfully used the Son-Rise Program to reach their own special children.
*372 pages 1994*
*ISBN 0-915811-53-7*

**6444   Special Kids Need Special Parents: A Resou rce for Parents of Children With Special Needs**
Berkley Publishing Group

The author, herself the parent of a child with special needs, draws on interviews with health care professionals, nationally recognized authorities, and other partens to give readers the answers, advice, and comfort they crave. *$13.95*
*319 pages Paperback 2001*
*ISBN 0-425176-62-2*

**6445   Special Parent, Special Child**
Exceptional Parent Library
PO Box 1807
Englewood Cliffs, NJ  07632                   201-947-6000
                                              800-535-1910
                                         FAX: 201-947-9376
                               e-mail: eplibrary@aol.com
                                         www.eplibrary.com

Offers information for facing the challenges of being a special parent. *$21.95*
*Hardcover*

**6446   Spoiling Childhood: How Well-Meaning Parents Are Giving Children Too Much...**
Guilford Press
72 Spring Street
New York, NY  10012                           212-431-9800
                                              800-365-7006
                                         FAX: 212-966-6708
                                         www.guilford.com

*Bob Matloff, President*

*$15.95*
*263 pages Paperback 1999*
*ISBN 1-572304-50-2*

**6447   Steps to Independence: Teaching Everyday Skills to Children with Special Needs**
Spina Bifida Association of America
4590 Macarthur Boulevard NW
Suite 250
Washington, DC 20007                          202-944-3285
                                              800-621-3141
                                         FAX: 202-944-3295
                                  e-mail: sbaa@sbaa.org
                                         www.sbaa.org

*Cindy Brownstein, Chief Executive Officer*

A guide to help parents teach life skills to their disabled child. *$28.00*

**6448    Strategies for Working with Families of Young Children with Disabilities**
Brookes Publishing
PO Box 10624
Baltimore, MD  21285
410-337-9580
800-638-3775
FAX: 410-337-8539
e-mail: custserv@brookespublishing.com
www.brookespublishing.com

*Paul Brooks, Owner*

This text offers useful techniques for collaborating with and supporting families whose youngest members either have a disability or are at risk for developing a disability. The authors address specific issues such as cultural diversity, transitions to new programs, and disagreements between families and professionals. *$33.00*

> *272 pages Paperback*
> *ISBN 1-55766 -57-6*

**6449    Summeries of Legal Precedents and Law Review Articles concern Parents with Disabilities**
Through the Looking Glass
2198 6th Street
Suite 100
Berkeley, CA  94710
510-848-1112
800-644-2666
FAX: 510-848-4445
e-mail: TLG@lookingglass.org
www.lookingglass.org

*L Baer*
*D Taube*
*Megan Kirshbaum, Executive Director*

Available in braille, large print or cassette. *$25.00*
> *24 pages*

**6450    That's My Child**
Exceptional Parent Library
PO Box 1807
Englewood Cliffs, NJ  07632
201-947-6000
800-535-1910
FAX: 201-947-9376
e-mail: eplibrary@aol.com
www.eplibrary.com

Offers information to help parent successfully navigate the maze of resources and services available for children with special needs. *$12.95*

**6451    Tips for Teaching Infants & Toddlers**
Speech Bin
1965 25th Avenue
Vero Beach, FL  32960
772-770-0007
800-477-3324
FAX: 772-770-0006
www.speechbin.com

A pratical multisensory approach to Early Intervention including a whole year's worth of weekly thematic lessons which give children abundant opportunities to see, hear, feel, manipulate, smell and taste. Lessons cover: early concepts, prespeech and language, body image, directionality, fine and gross motor, categories, early acitons, activities just for fun and attributes. Paperback. *$39.95*

**6452    To a Different Drumbeat**
Alliance for Parental Involvement in Education
PO Box 59
East Chatham, NY  12060
518-392-6900
FAX: 518-392-6900

Parents of special needs children contributed to this book. *$16.95*

**6453    Training Module: Adaptive Baby Care Equipment**
Through the Looking Glass
2198 6th Street
Suite 100
Berkeley, CA  94710
510-848-1112
800-644-2666
FAX: 510-848-4445
e-mail: TLG@lookingglass.org
www.lookingglass.org

*Megan Kirshbaum, Executive Director*

Curriculum for OT programs includes Adaptive Baby Care Equipment Video and Book. *$250.00*

**6454    Uncommon Fathers**
Woodbine House
6510 Bells Mill Road
Bethesda, MD  20817
301-897-3570
800-843-7323
FAX: 301-897-5838
www.woodbinehouse.com

*Irv Shapell, Owner*

Nineteen fathers talk about the life-altering experience of having a child with special needs and offer a welcome, seldom-heard perspective on raising kids with disabilities, including autism, cerebral palsy, and Down syndrome. Uncommon Fathers is the first book for fathers by fathers, but it is also helpful to partners, family, friends, and service providers. *$14.95*

> *206 pages Paperback*
> *ISBN 0-933149-68-9*

**6455    We Can Speak for Ourselves: Self Advocacy by Mentally Handicapped People**
Brookline Books
PO Box 1047
Cambridge, MA  02139
617-868-0360
800-666-2665
FAX: 617-868-1772
e-mail: brooklinebks@delphi.com
www.brooklinebooks.com

Practical advice and support for parents, group resident workers, and others interested in fostering self-advocacy for people with developmental disabilities. *$10.00*
> *246 pages Paperback*
> *ISBN 0-25336 -65-9*

**6456    What Works in Children's Mental Health Services? Uncovering Answers to Critical Questions**
Brookes Publishing
PO Box 10624
Baltimore, MD  21285
410-337-9580
800-638-3775
FAX: 410-337-8539
e-mail: custserv@brookespublishing.com
www.brookespublishing.com

*Paul Brooks, Owner*

Provides a comprehensive overview of research on the effectiveness of eight mental health service components in systems of care for children with emotional and behavioral disabilities. *$30.00*

> *256 pages Paperback*
> *ISBN 1-55766 -54-1*

**6457    Why Can't My Child Behave?**
Feingold Association of the US
554 E Main Street
Suite 301
Riverhead, NY  11901
631-369-9340
800-321-3287
FAX: 631-369-2988
e-mail: help@feingold.org
www.feingold.org

*Debbie Lehner, Manager*
*$22.00*

*400 pages*

**6458 Yeast Connection**
Vintage Books
1540 Broadway
New York, NY 10036
212-782-9000
FAX: 212-302-7985
www.randomhouse.com

*Carol Schneider, Marketing Executive*

One of the first and best book giving practicle advice regarding what has come to be known as the candida or yeast problem.
*434 pages*
*ISBN 0-394747-00-3*

**6459 You May Be Able to Adopt**
Through the Looking Glass
2198 6th Street
Suite 100
Berkeley, CA 94710
510-848-1112
800-644-2666
FAX: 510-848-4445
e-mail: TLG@lookingglass.org
www.lookingglass.org

*L Toms Barker*
*Megan Kirshbaum, Executive Director*

A guide to the adoption process for prospective mothers with disabilities and their partners. Available in braille, large print or cassette. *$10.00*
*112 pages*

**6460 You Will Dream New Dreams**
Kensington Publishing

A parent's support group in print. The shared narratives come from those with newly diagnosed children, adult disabled children, and everything in between. *$13.00*
*278 pages Paperback 2001*
*ISBN 1-575665-60-3*

**6461 Your Child Has a Disability: A Complete So urcebook of Daily and Medical Care**
Brookes Publishing
PO Box 10624
Baltimore, MD 21285
410-337-9580
800-638-3775
FAX: 410-337-8539
e-mail: custserv@brookesopublishing.com
www.brookespublishing.com

*Paul Brooks, Owner*

Offers expert advice on a wide range of issues-from finding the right doctor and investigating the medical aspects of a child's condition to learning care techniques and fulfilling education requirements. *$24.95*
*368 pages Paperback 1998*
*ISBN 1-557663-74-2*

**6462 Your Defiant Child: Eight Steps to Better Behavior**
Guilford Press
72 Spring Street
New York, NY 10012
212-431-9800
800-365-7006
FAX: 212-966-6708
www.guilford.com

*Bob Matloff, President*

Also in cloth at $37.00 (ISBN# 1-57230-405-7) *$15.95*

*239 pages Paperback 1998*
*ISBN 1-572303-21-2*

---

# Parenting: Specific Disabilities

**6463 ADD: Helping Your Child**
Warner Books
1271 Avenue of the Americas
New York, NY 10020
212-522-7200
FAX: 212-522-7989

*Laurence Krishbaum, Chief Executive Officer*

*$12.95*
*224 pages Paperback*
*ISBN 0-446670-13-8*

**6464 ADHD Book of Lists: A Practical Guide for Helping Children and Teens with ADDs**
Jossey-Bass

Current information about Atention Deficit/Hyperactivity Disorder including strategies, supports, and interventions that have been found to be the most effective. For teachers, parents, and counselors. *$29.95*
*320 pages 2003*
*ISBN 0-787965-91-X*

**6465 AFB Directory of Services for Blind and Visually Impaired Persons in the US and Canada**
American Foundation for the Blind/AFB Press
PO Box 1020
Sewickley, PA 15143
412-741-1142
800-232-3044
FAX: 412-741-0609
e-mail: afborders@abdintl.com
www.afb.org

*Stephanie Biagioli, Marketing Coordinator*

Comprehensive CD-ROM and print resource containing more that 2,500 local, state, regional, and national services throughout the US and Canada for persons who are blind or visually impaired. *$74.95*
*624 pages Hardcover/CDROM*
*ISBN 0-89128 -00-5*

**6466 American Academy of Pediatrics Guide to Yo ur Child's Alleriges And Asthma**
Villard Books

Consumer resource for parents who need answers and information about their children's allergies and asthma. Current advice on identifying allergies and asthma, preventing attacks, minimizing triggers, understanding medications, explaining allergies to young children, and helping children manage symptoms. *$15.00*
*191 pages 2000*
*ISBN 0-679769-82-X*

**6467 Attention Deficit Disorder: Children**
Aquarius Health Care Videos
PO Box 1159
Sherborn, MA 01770
508-650-6905
888-440-2963
FAX: 508-650-4216
e-mail: aqvideos@tiac.net
www.aquariusproductions.com

*Leslie Kussmann, President/Producer*

Everyone has been impulsive or easily distracted for different periods of time, so these symptoms that are hallmarks of Attention Deficit Disorder (ADD) have also led to criticism that too many people are being diagnosed with this biochemical brain disorder. This program examines who is being diagnosed, and what treatments are working. An innovative private school specializing in alternative education is profiled, and tips on structuring the school and home environment are included. *$149.00 Video*

**6468  Attention-Deficit/Hyperactivity Disorder, What Every Parent Wants to Know**
Brookes Publishing
PO Box 10624
Baltimore, MD  21285                                  410-337-9580
                                                       800-638-3775
                                                  FAX: 410-337-8539
                             e-mail: custserv@brookespublishing.com
                                        www.brookespublishing.com

*Paul Brooks, Owner*

New easy-to-understand, non-technical edition helps teachers and parents get accessible answers to their ADHD. *$21.95*
        *304 pages Paperback 2000*
        *ISBN 1-557663-98-X*

**6469  Bipolar Child: The Definitive & Reassuring Guide to Childhood's Most Misunderstood Disorder**
Broadway

Drawing upon recent advances in the fields of neuroscience and genetics, the Papaloses convey what is known and not known about the illness. They detail the diagnosis, tell how to find good treatment and medications, and advise parents about ways to advocate effectively for their children at school. The book also offers critical information about the stages of adolescence, hospitalization, the world of insurance, and the psychological impact the illness has on the child. *$26.00*
        *480 pages 2002*
        *ISBN 0-767912-85-3*

**6470  Bipolar Disorders: A Guide to Helping Children & Adolescents**
Patient-Centered Guides
101 Morris Street
Sebastopol, CA  95472                                  707-829-0515
                                                       800-998-9938
                                                  FAX: 800-997-9901
                                    e-mail: order@oreilly.com
                                        www.patientcenters.com

*Linda Lamb, Editor*
*Shawnde Paull, Marketing*
*Tim O'Reilly, Chief Executive Officer*

A million children and adolescents in the U.S. may have childhood-onset bipolar disorder, including an estimated 23 percent of those currently diagnosed with ADHD. Bipolar Disorders helps parents and professionals recognize, treat, and cope with bipolar disorders in children and adolescents. It covers diagnosis, family life, medications, talk therapies, other interventions (improving sleep patterns, diet, preventing seasonal mood swings), insurance, and school. *$24.95*
        *458 pages Paperback*
        *ISBN 1-565926-56-0*

**6471  Bowel Continence & Spina Bifida**
Spina Bifida Association of America
4590 Macarthur Boulevard NW
Suite 250
Washington, DC 20007                                   202-944-3285
                                                       800-621-3141
                                                  FAX: 202-944-3295
                                    e-mail: sbaa@sbaa.org
                                        www.sbaa.org

*Cindy Brownstein, Chief Executive Officer*

An excellent book aimed at anyone trying to attain bowel continence with sample menus, bowel tracking charts and glossary of terms. *$8.00*

**6472  Cancer Clinical Trials: Experimental Treatments and How They Can Help You**
Patient-Centered Guides
101 Morris Street
Sebastopol, CA  95472                                  707-829-0515
                                                       800-998-9938
                                                  FAX: 707-829-0104
                                        www.patientcenters.com

*Linda Lamb, Editor*
*Shawnde Paull, Marketing*
*Tim O'Reilly, Chief Executive Officer*

Most cancer patients face treatment options that are less than ideal, whether because of a risk of recurrence or side effects. Finally, however, basic research on cell biology is leading to promising new treatments. If you are not evaluating potential experimental treatments alongside the standard treatment protocols, you aren't considering all the facts you need. Cancer Clinical Trials guide you through understanding your options and finding and considering experimental treatments. *$14.95*
        *222 pages Paperback*
        *ISBN 1-565925-66-1*

**6473  Caring for Children with Cerebral Palsy: A Team Approach**
Brookes Publishing
PO Box 10624
Baltimore, MD  21285                                  410-337-9580
                                                       800-638-3775
                                                  FAX: 410-337-8539
                             e-mail: custserv@brookespublishing.com
                                        www.brookespublishing.com

*Paul Brooks, Owner*

A guide to the interdisciplinary care of children with cerebral palsy. Delivers detailed information on a multitude of issues relevant to treatment and supports. *$38.95*
        *496 pages Paperback 1998*
        *ISBN 1-55766 -22-X*

**6474  Childhood Cancer Survivors: A Practical Guide to Your Future**
Patient-Centered Guides
101 Morris Street
Sebastopol, CA  95472                                  707-829-0515
                                                       800-998-9938
                                                  FAX: 707-829-0104
                                        www.patientcenters.com

*Linda Lamb, Editor*
*Shawnde Paull, Marketing*
*Tim O'Reilly, Chief Executive Officer*

More than 250,000 people have survived childhood cancer - a cause for celebration. Authors Keene, Hobbie, and Ruccione chart the territory of long-term survivorship: relationships; overcoming employment or insurance discrimination; maximizing health; follow-up schedules; medical late effects. The stories of over sixty survivors - their challenges and triumphs - are told. Includes medical history record-keeper. *$27.95*
        *510 pages Paperback*
        *ISBN 1-565924-60-6*

**6475  Childhood Cancer: A Parent's Guide to Solid Tumor Cancers**
Patient-Centered Guides
101 Morris Street
Sebastopol, CA  95472                                  707-829-0515
                                                       800-998-9938
                                                  FAX: 707-829-0104
                                        www.patientcenters.com

*Linda Lamb, Editor*
*Shawnde Paull, Marketing*
*Tim O'Reilly, Chief Executive Officer*

Childhood Cancer: A Parent's Guide to Solid Tumor Cancers features a wealth of resources for parents of children with solid tumor cancers, plus many stories of veteran parents. Parents will encounter medical facts simply explained, practical advice to ease their daily lives, and tools to be strong advocates for their child. Includes a passport to record patient's medical history. *$24.95*
    *537 pages Paperback*
    *ISBN 1-565925-31-9*

**6476   Childhood Leukemia: A Guide for Families, Friends & Caregivers: 2nd Edition**
Patient-Centered Guides
101 Morris Street
Sebastopol, CA  95472                      707-829-0515
                                           800-998-9938
                                   FAX: 707-829-0104
                                   www.patientcenters.com

*Linda Lamb, Editor*
*Shawnde Paull, Marketing*
*Tim O'Reilly, Chief Executive Officer*

The second edition of this comprehensive guide offers detailed and precise medical information for parents that includes day-to-day practical advice on how to cope with procedures, hospitalization, family and friends, school, and social, emotional, and financial issues. It features a wealth of tools for prents and contains significant updates on treatments and procedures. *$24.95*
    *513 pages Paperback*
    *ISBN 1-565926-32-3*

**6477   Children With Cerebral Palsy: A Parents' G uide**
Woodbine House

A classic primer for parents that provides a complete spetrum of information and compassionate advice about cerebral palsy and its effect on their child's development and education. *$16.95*
    *481 pages 1998*
    *ISBN 0-933149-82-4*

**6478   Children with Acquired Brain Injury: Education and Supporting Families**
Brookes Publishing
PO Box 10624
Baltimore, MD  21285                       410-337-9580
                                           800-638-3775
                                   FAX: 410-337-8539
                          e-mail: custserv@brookespublishing.com
                                   www.brookespublishing.com

*Ann Glang PhD, Editor*
*Janet M Williams MSW, Editor*
*Paul Brooks, Owner*

*$28.95*
    *288 pages Paperback 1996*
    *ISBN 1-557662-33-9*

**6479   Children with Asthma: A Manual for Parents**
Allergy Control Products
PO Box 793
Ridgefield, CT  06877                      203-438-9580
                                           800-422-3878
                                   FAX: 203-431-8963
                                   www.allergycontrol.com

*Edward Steube, President*

Known as the asthma bible, this second edition is sprinkled with anecdotes by patients and their parents. *$10.00*

*296 pages Paperback*

**6480   Children with Autism**
Woodbine House
6510 Bells Mill Road
Bethesda, MD  20817                        301-897-3570
                                           800-843-7323
                                   FAX: 301-897-5838
                                   www.woodbinehouse.com

*Irv Shapell, Owner*

Recommended as the first book parents should read, this volume offers information and a complete introduction to autism, while easing the family's fears and concerns as they adjust and cope with their child's disorder. *$17.95*
    *368 pages Paperback*
    *ISBN 0-933149-16-6*

**6481   Children with Facial Difference: A Parent' s Guide**
Woodbine House
6510 Bells Mill Road
Bethesda, MD  20817                        301-897-3570
                                           800-843-7323
                                   FAX: 301-897-5838
                                   www.woodbinehouse.com

*Irv Shapell, Owner*

The first guide for parents about their child's congenital craniofacial anomaly - a condition that affects the appearance and function of the head and face. This accessible book discusses conditions such as cleft lip, cleft palate, and Teacher Collins, Apert, and Crouzon syndromes, and more. Parents learn about the diagnostic process, interdisciplinary treatment approach, education, speech and language issues, and how to help their child and family adjust emotionally. *$ 16.95*
    *361 pages Paperback 1996*
    *ISBN 0-933149-61-1*

**6482   Children with Spina Bifida: A Parents Guide**
Spina Bifida Association of America
4590 Macarthur Boulevard NW
Suite 250
Washington, DC 20007                       202-944-3285
                                           800-621-3141
                                   FAX: 202-944-3295
                                   e-mail: sbaa@sbaa.org
                                   www.sbaa.org

*Cindy Brownstein, Chief Executive Officer*

Provides parents with information, guidance and support to help meet the child's needs through childhood. *$16.95*

**6483   Children with Tourette Syndrome**
Exceptional Parent Library
PO Box 1807
Englewood Cliffs, NJ  07632                201-947-6000
                                           800-535-1910
                                   FAX: 201-947-9376
                                   e-mail: eplibrary@aol.com
                                   www.eplibrary.com

Written by a team of professionals and parents, this book covers medical, educational, legal, family life, daily care, and emotional issues. *$14.95*

**6484   Complete Kid's Allergy and Asthma Guide: T he Parent's Handbook for Children of All Ages**
Robert Rose

For a child who has not yet received a medical diagnosis, The Complete Kid's Allergey & Asthma Guide provides parents with vital information on how to read the signs of allergy and asthma — from keeping a food diary, to monitoring asthma symptoms, to tracking allergic reactions. *$17.95*

*288 pages 2003*
*ISBN 0-778800-78-4*

**6485 Control Your Child's Asthma**
Owl Publishing

Offers parents of children with asthma ways to create an asthma-management plan geared specifically toward the child's needs, incorporating medical, social and emotional needs into one system. Includes a detailed resource section of organizations dealing with asthma management. *$14.00*
*256 pages 2001*
*ISBN 0-805064-55-9*

**6486 Controlling Asthma**
American Lung Association
61 Broadway
New York, NY 10006
212-315-8700
FAX: 212-315-8870
e-mail: info@lungusa.org
www.lungusa.org

*Cindy Kirkwood, Chief Executive Officer*

For parents of children with asthma, this news magazine tells how parents can help their child deal with the many problems presented by asthma.
*16 pages*

**6487 Cystic Fibrosis: A Guide for Patient and Family**
Lippincott Williams & Wilkins

Text is designed specifically for patients with cystic fibrosis and their families. Explains the disease process, outlines the fundamentals of diagnosing and screening, and addresses the challenges of treatment for those living with CF. Includes new material on carrier testing, infection control, and more. *$29.95*
*448 pages 2003*
*ISBN 0-781741-52-1*

**6488 Deaf Parents and Their Hearing Children**
Through the Looking Glass
2198 6th Street
Suite 100
Berkeley, CA 94710
510-848-1112
800-644-2666
FAX: 510-848-4445
e-mail: TLG@lookingglass.org
www.lookingglass.org

*J L Singleton*
*M D Tittle*
*Megan Kirshbaum, Executive Director*

*$2.00*
*8 pages*

**6489 Epilepsy: Patient and Family Guide**
FA Davis Company

A guide for adults with epilepsy and for parents of children with the disorder explains the nature and diversity of seizures, the risks and benefits of the various antiepileptic drugs, and medical and surgical therapies. *$26.95*
*434 pages 2001*
*ISBN 0-803604-98-X*

**6490 Final Report: Adapting Through the Looking Glass**
Through the Looking Glass
2198 6th Street
Suite 100
Berkeley, CA 94710
510-848-1112
800-644-2666
FAX: 510-848-4445
e-mail: TLG@lookingglass.org
www.lookingglass.org

*P Preston*
*M Lou*
*Megan Kirshbaum, Executive Director*

Adapting Through the Looking Glass intervention model for deaf parents and their children. Available in braille, large print or cassette. *$2.00*
*24 pages*

**6491 Final Report: Challenges and Strategies of Disabled Parents: Findings from a Survey**
Through the Looking Glass
2198 6th Street
Suite 100
Berkeley, CA 94710
510-848-1112
800-644-2666
FAX: 510-848-4445
e-mail: TLG@lookingglass.org
www.lookingglass.org

*L Toms Barker*
*V Maralani*
*Megan Kirshbaum, Executive Director*

Available in braille, large print or cassette. *$25.00*
*24 pages*

**6492 Going Places, Children Living with Cerebral Palsy**
Gareth Stevens
1555 N River Center Drive
Milwaukee, WI 53212
414-332-3520
800-542-2595
FAX: 414-225-0377

*Bob Famighetti, Publisher*

Mathias is a charming six-year-old with cerebral palsy. He needs special exercises to help him learn to control his muscles. He is also almost completely deaf. But with the love and encouragement of his family, Mathias is developing an interesting and busy life. Every morning finds him eager to start the day's activities. *$13.95*
*48 pages*
*ISBN 0-836801-99-7*

**6493 Growing Up with Epilepsy: A Pratical Guide for Parents**
Demos Medical Publishing
386 Park Avenue S
Suite 201
New York, NY 10016
212-683-0072
800-532-8663
FAX: 212-683-0118
e-mail: orderdep@demospub.com
www.demosmedpub.com

*Diana Schneider PhD, President*
*Phyllis Gold, Owner*

Developed to help parents with the uniques challenges that this disorder presents *$19.95*
*156 pages 2003*
*ISBN 1-888799-74-9*

**6494 Hand-Me-Down Blues: How to Stop Depression from Spreading in Families**
St. Martin's Press
175 5th Avenue
New York, NY 10010
212-674-5151

www.stmartins.com

*John Sargent, Chief Executive Officer*

Discusses the interrelationship of depression, parenting styles, and family dynamics, contending that inherited depression cannot be solely explained in terms of genetic inheritance or biochemical imbalance. *$12.95*

*256 pages 2000*
*ISBN 0-312263-32-5*

**6495    Helping Your Hyperactive: Attention Deficit Child**
Prima Publishing
PO Box 1260
Rocklin, CA  95677                    916-787-7000
                                      800-632-8676
                                 FAX: 916-787-7001
      e-mail: websupportlife@primapub.com
                www.primapublishing.com

*$19.95*

        *ISBN 1-559584-23-8*

**6496    If Your Child Has Diabetes: An Answer Book for Parents**
Putnam Publishing Group
200 Madison Avenue
New York, NY  10016                   212-889-6330

*Alex Luchars, Owner*

Provides information and recommendations for parents of children with diabetes on subjects such as school, recreation, medical and life insurance and employment as well as general information about diabetes. *$9.95*

**6497    If Your Child Stutters: A Guide for Parents**
Stuttering Foundation of America
PO Box 11749
Memphis, TN  38111                    901-452-7343
                                      800-992-9392
                                 FAX: 901-452-3931
          e-mail: stutter@vantek.net
                www.stutterhelp.org

*Jane Fraser, President*

A guide that enables parents to provide appropriate help to children who stutter. *$1.00*

**6498    Introduction to Spina Bifida**
Spina Bifida Association of America
4590 Macarthur Boulevard NW
Suite 250
Washington, DC 20007                  202-944-3285
                                      800-621-3141
                                 FAX: 202-944-3295
           e-mail: sbaa@sbaa.org
                  www.sbaa.org

*Cindy Brownstein, Chief Executive Officer*

An aid for parents, family and nonmedical people who care for a child with spina bifida. *$7.00*

**6499    Keys to Parenting a Child with Attention Deficit Disorder**
Barron's Educational Series
250 Wireless Boulevard
Hauppauge, NY  11788                  631-434-3311
                                      800-645-3476
                                 FAX: 631-434-3723
        e-mail: info@barronseduc.com
                www.barronseduc.com
*Lonny Stein , Director Marketing*
*Manuel Barron, Chief Executive Officer*

This book shows how to work with the child's school, effectively manage the child's behavior and act as the child's advocate. *$6.95*

*160 pages Paperback*
*ISBN 0-812014-59-6*

**6500    Keys to Parenting a Child with Cerebral Palsy**
Barron's Educational Series
250 Wireless Boulevard
Hauppauge, NY  11788                  631-434-3311
                                      800-645-3476
                                 FAX: 631-434-3723
        e-mail: info@barronsedu.com
                www.barronseduc.com

*Margaret E Myers, Author*
*Manuel Barron, Chief Executive Officer*

This volume helps parents adjust to the challenge of having a child with cerebral palsy. It stresses the child's potential and encourages independence. Facets of the child's total well-being are discussed, including common health problems, physical, mental and social development, therapy, and new trends in medical management. *$6.95*
        *Paperback*
        *ISBN 0-764100-91-2*

**6501    Keys to Parenting a Child with Downs Syndrome**
Barron's Educational Series
250 Wireless Boulevard
Hauppauge, NY  11788                  631-434-3311
                                      800-645-3476
                                 FAX: 631-434-3723
        e-mail: info@barronsedu.com
                www.barronseduc.com

*Lonny Stein, Director Marketing*
*Manuel Barron, Chief Executive Officer*

Down Syndrome poses many challenges for children and their families. This book prepares parents and guardians to raise a child with Down Syndrome by discussing adjustment, advocacy, health and behavior, education and planning for greater independence. *$5.95*
        *160 pages Paperback*
        *ISBN 0-812014-58-8*

**6502    Keys to Parenting the Child with Autism**
Barron's Educational Series
250 Wireless Boulevard
Hauppauge, NY  11788                  631-434-3311
                                      800-645-3476
                                 FAX: 631-434-3723
       e-mail: barrons@barronseduc.com
                www.barronseduc.com

*Manuel Barron, Chief Executive Officer*

Parents of children with autism will find a solid balance between home and practical information in this book. It explains what autism is and how it is diagnosed, then advises parents on how to adjust to their child and give the best care. *$6.95*
        *208 pages Paperback*
        *ISBN 0-812016-79-3*

**6503    Late Talker: What to Do If Your Child Isn' t Talking Yet**
St Martin's Griffin

This handbook offers advice on ways to identify the warning signs of a speech disorder, information on how to get the right kind of evaluations and therapy, ways to obtain appropriate services through the school system and health insurance, at-home activities that parents can do with their child to stimulate speech, benefits of nutritional supplementation, and advice from experienced parents who've been there on what to expect and what you can do to be your child's best advocate. *$13.95*

*256 pages Paperback 2004*
*ISBN 0-312309-24-4*

**6504 Learning Disabilities: A to Z Parent's Com plete Guide to Learning Disabilities**
Free Press
135 S Mount Zion Road
Lebanon, IN 46052

800-323-7445
FAX: 800-882-8583

This book is about helping youngsters with learning disabilities hold onto their dreams. It is also about helping their mothers and fathers negotiate the maze of challenges that so often leaves parents and students alike feeling overwhelmed and helpless. *$15.00*
*416 pages Paperback 1999*
*ISBN 0-684844-68-0*

**6505 Legislative Handbook for Parents**
NAPVI
PO Box 317
Watertown, MA 02471

617-972-7441
800-562-6265
FAX: 617-972-7444
e-mail: napvi@perkins.org
www.napvi.org

Written by parents for parents in dealing with Legislative Processes that ultimately affect their children's lives. *$5.50*
*24 pages Paperback*

**6506 Living with Brain Injury: A Guide for Fam ilies**
Delmar Learning

A consumer text to aid people living with brain-injured survivors, includes facts on neuroplasticity, experimental rehabilitation research, and the process of rehabilitation itself. *$16.95*
*225 pages 2001*
*ISBN 1-891525-09-3*

**6507 Living with Spina Bifida: A Guide for Fam ilies and Professionals**
University of North Carolina at Chapel Hill
Cb
Wing E # 7180
Chapel Hill, NC 27599

919-962-2211
FAX: 919-966-4127
www.teacch.com

*James Moeser, Chief Executive Officer*

A handbook that addresses patients' biopsychosocial and developmental needs from birth through adolescence and into adulthood. Sandler's holistic approach encourages families to focus more on the child and less on the disability while providing abundant information about this condition. *$19.95*
*296 pages 2004*
*ISBN 0-807855-47-2*

**6508 Multiple Sclerosis: A Guide for Patients and Their Families**
Lippincott, Williams & Wilkins
227 E Washington Square
Philadelphia, PA 19106

215-521-8300
800-777-2295
FAX: 301-824-7390
www.lpub.com

*J Lippincott, Chief Executive Officer*
*$16.00*
*288 pages*

**6509 My House Is Killing Me! The Home Guide for Families With Allergies and Asthma**
Johns Hopkins University Press

Chemical consultant May describes where and how the various parts of a residence can cause temporary or chronic illness for those with allergies or other sensitivities. *$17.95*

*338 pages 2001*
*ISBN 0-801867-30-4*

**6510 Nonverbal Learning Disabilities at Home: A Parent's Guide**
Taylor & Francis Group

Explores the variety of daily life problems children with NLD may face, and provides practical strategies for parents to help them cope and grow, from preschool age through their challenging adolescent years. *$21.95*
*267 pages Paperback 2001*
*ISBN 1-853029-40-8*

**6511 Not Deaf Enough: Raising a Child Who is Hard of Hearing**
Alexander Graham Bell Association
3417 Volta Place NW
Washington, DC 20007

202-337-5220
FAX: 202-337-8314
e-mail: info@agbell.org
www.agbell.org

*Todd Houston, Executive Director*

This sensitive book portrays a family's struggle to identify, accept and support their youngest child through his diagnosis of mild to moderate hearing loss. This book provides a much needed overview of this under-diagnosed and under-served disability. *$24.95*
*242 pages Paperback*

**6512 Obsessive-Compulsive Disorder: Help for Children and Adolescents**
Patient-Centered Guides
101 Morris Street
Sebastopol, CA 95472

707-829-0515
800-998-9938
FAX: 707-829-0104
www.patientcenters.com

*Linda Lamb, Editor*
*Shawnde Paull, Marketing*
*Tim O'Reilly, Chief Executive Officer*

Obsessive-compulsive disorders (OCD) is one of the most common psychiatric problems faced by children. Childhood OCD can be a truly debilitating disability, not just a minor problem or personality quirk. The good news is that it is very treatable. Obsessive-Compulsive Disorder helps parents secure a diagnosis, manage family life, understand medical interventions, explore therapeutic interventions, get care within their existing healthcare plan, and navigate the special education system. *$24.95*
*400 pages Paperback*
*ISBN 1-565927-58-3*

**6513 On the Edge of Deaf Culture: An Annotated Bibliography of Hearing Children/Deaf Parents**
Through the Looking Glass
2198 6th Street
Suite 100
Berkeley, CA 94710

510-848-1112
800-644-2666
FAX: 510-848-4445
e-mail: TLG@lookingglass.org
www.lookingglass.org

*Megan Kirshbaum, Executive Director*
*$35.00*
*360 pages*

**6514 Parent's Guide to Allergies and Asthma**
National Allergy and Asthma Network
3554 Chain Bridge Road
Suite 200
Fairfax, VA 22030

703-385-4403
FAX: 703-352-4354

A up-to-date, easy-to-read resource offering essential information on asthma and allergies.

**6515 Parent's Guide to Autism**
Autism Society of North Carolina Bookstore
505 Oberlin Road
Suite 230
Raleigh, NC 27605                            919-743-0204
                                             800-442-2762
                                        FAX: 919-743-0208
                      e-mail: dcoffey@autismsociety-nc.org
                                 www.autismsociety-nc.org

*Darla Coffey, Bookstore Manager*
*Jill Keel, Executive Director*

An essential handbook for anyone facing autism. *$14.00*

**6516 Parent's Guide to Down Syndrome: Toward a Brighter Future: 2nd Edition**
Brookes Publishing
PO Box 10624
Baltimore, MD 21285                          410-337-9580
                                             800-638-3775
                                        FAX: 410-337-8539
                   e-mail: custserv@brookespublishing.com
                                 www.brookespublishing.com

*Paul Brooks, Owner*

Highlights developmental stages and shows the advances that improve a child's quality of life. Includes discussions on easing the transition from home to school and choosing integration and curricular priorities, as well as guidelines for confronting adolescent and adult issues such as social and sexual needs and independent living and vocational options. *$21.95*
*352 pages 2000*
*ISBN 1-557664-52-8*

**6517 Parenting Preschoolers: Suggestions for Raising Young Blind Children**
American Foundation for the Blind/AFB Press
PO Box 1020
Sewickley, PA 15143                          412-741-1142
                                             800-232-3044
                                        FAX: 412-741-0609
                        e-mail: afborders@abdintl.com
                                         www.afb.org

Provides practical answers to questions most frequently asked by parents and gives advice on what to expect, how to adapt to a child's situation and what to look for in early education programs. $50.00/pack of 25.
*28 pages*
*ISBN 0-891289-98-4*

**6518 Parents Helping Parents: A Directory of Support Groups for ADD**
Novartis Pharmaceuticals Division
59 State Route 10
East Hanover, NJ 07936                       862-778-7500
                                             800-742-2422

*Paulo Costa, Chief Executive Officer*

**6519 Pervasive Developmental Disorders; Finding a Diagnosis and Getting Help**
Patient-Centered Guides
101 Morris Street
Sebastopol, CA 95472                         707-829-0515
                                             800-998-9938
                                        FAX: 707-829-0104
                                     www.patientcenters.com

*Linda Lamb, Editor*
*Shawnde Paull, Marketing*
*Tim O'Reilly, Chief Executive Officer*

This unique book encompasess both the practical aspects as well as ther personal stories and emotional facets of living with PDD-NOS, the most common pervasive developmental disorder. Parents of an undiagnosed child may suspect many things, from autism to servere allergies. Pervasive Developmental Disorders is for parents (or newly diagnosed adults) who struggle with this neurological condition that profoundly impacts the life of child and family. *$24.95*

*580 pages Paperback*
*ISBN 1-565925-30-0*

**6520 Preschool Learning Activities for the Visually Impaired Child**
NAPVI
PO Box 317
Watertown, MA 02471                          617-972-7441
                                             800-562-6265
                                        FAX: 617-972-7444
                           e-mail: napvi@perkins.org
                                         www.napvi.org

This guide for parents offers games and activities to keep visually impaired children active during the preschool years. *$8.00*
*91 pages Paperback*

**6521 Preventing Secondary Conditions Associated with Spina Bifida or Cerebral Palsy**
Spina Bifida Association of America
4590 Macarthur Boulevard NW
Suite 250
Washington, DC 20007                         202-944-3285
                                             800-621-3141
                                        FAX: 202-944-3295
                              e-mail: sbaa@sbaa.org
                                         www.sbaa.org

*Cindy Brownstein, Chief Executive Officer*

This report is for health professionals, parents and teachers. *$3.00*

**6522 Reaching the Autistic Child, 2nd Edition: A Parent Training Program**
Brookline Books/Lumen Editions
PO Box 1047
Cambridge, MA 02139                          617-868-0360
                                             800-666-2665
                                        FAX: 617-868-1772
                        e-mail: brooklinebks@delphi.com

Detailed case studies of social and behavioral change in autistic children and their families show parents how to implement the principles for improved socialization and behavior. *$15.95*
*Softcover*
*ISBN 1-571290-56-7*

**6523 Retarded Isn't Stupid, Mom!, Revised Edition**
Brookes Publishing
PO Box 10624
Baltimore, MD 21285                          410-337-9580
                                             800-638-3775
                                        FAX: 410-337-8539
                   e-mail: custserv@brookespublishing.com
                        www.pbrookescom/store/books/kaufman-3785

*Paul Brooks, Owner*

Sandra Kaufman reveals the feelings of denial, guilt, frustration and eventual acceptance that resulted in a determination to help her daughter, Nicole, live an independent life. This edition, revised on the 10th anniversary of the book's original publication, adds a progress report that updates readers on Nicole's adult years and reflects on the revolutionary changes in society's attitudes toward people with disabilities since Nicole's birth. *$22.95*

*272 pages Paperback 1999*
*ISBN 1-557663-78-5*

**6524 Seizures and Epilepsy in Childhood: A Guid e**
John Hopkins University Pres

A resources for parents of a child with epilepsy. Information allows parents to have informed discussions with physician and treatment teams. Also provides information for parents to become participants in treatment plans. *$19.95*

*360 pages 2002*
*ISBN 0-801870-51-8*

**6525  Show Me How: A Manual for Parents of Preschool Blind Children**
American Foundation for the Blind/AFB Press
PO Box 1020
Sewickley, PA  15143                 412-741-1142
                                      800-232-3044
                                  FAX: 412-741-0609
                          e-mail: afborders@abdintl.com
                                        www.afb.org

A practical guide for parents, teachers and others who help preschool children attain age-related goals. Covers issues on playing precautions, appropriate toys and facilitating relationships
with playmates. Paperback. *$12.95*
     *56 pages*
     *ISBN 0-891281-13-4*

**6526  Signing Family: What Every Parent Should Know About Sign Communication**
Gallaudet University Press
11030 S Langley Avenue
Chicago, IL  60628
                                      800-621-2736
                                  FAX: 800-621-8476
                                  TTY: 800-621-9347
                                 gupress.gallaudet.edu

*David A Stewart, Co-Author*
*Barbara Luetke-Stahlman, Co-Author*

This reader-friendly book shows parents how to create a set of
goals around the communication needs of their deaf child. Describes in even-handed terms the major signing options available, from American Sign Language to Signed English. *$24.95*
     *192 pages Softcover*

**6527  Social Development and the Person with Spina Bifida**
Spina Bifida Association of America
4590 Macarthur Boulevard NW
Suite 250
Washington, DC 20007               202-944-3285
                                   800-621-3141
                              FAX: 202-944-3295
                          e-mail: sbaa@sbaa.org
                                   www.sbaa.org

*Cindy Brownstein, Chief Executive Officer*

Examines how spina bifida and hydrocephalus may influence
development and learning social skills.

**6528  Strategies and Adaptations in Working with Parents with Intellectual Disabilities**
Through the Looking Glass
2198 6th Street
Suite 100
Berkeley, CA  94710                 510-848-1112
                                    800-644-2666
                               FAX: 510-848-4445
                       e-mail: TLG@lookingglass.org
                               www.lookingglass.org

*K Corbus*
*S Hansen*
*Megan Kirshbaum, Executive Director*

*$5.00*
     *11 pages*

**6529  Taking Charge of ADHD Complete Authoritative Guide for Parents**
Guilford Press
72 Spring Street
New York, NY  10012                 212-431-9800
                                    800-365-7006
                               FAX: 212-966-6708
                                    www.guilford.com

*Bob Matloff, President*

Revised and updated to incorporate the most current information on ADHD and its treatment. Provides parents with the
knowledge, guidance and confidence they need to ensure that
their child receives the best care possible. Also in cloth at $40.00
(ISBN# 1-57230-600-9 *$18.95*
     *321 pages Paperback 2000*
     *ISBN 1-572305-60-6*

**6530  Taking Charge of ADHD, Revised Edition: Th e Com-plete, Authoritative Guide for Parents**
Guilford Press

A step-by-step plan for behavior management that has helped
thousands of children with ADHD including hard data that clear
up current controversies about increased diagnosis and
stimuland use, new strategies that give children greater chances
of success at school and in social situations, advances in genetic
and neurological research that enhance out understanding of
what causes ADHD, practical advice for parents on managing
stress and keeping peace in the family. *$19.95*
     *321 pages 2000*
     *ISBN 1-572305-60-6*

**6531  Two Hundred Fifty Tips for Making Life with Arthritis Easier**
Arthritis Foundation Distribution Center
PO Box 6996
Alpharetta, GA  30023
                                      800-207-8633
                                  FAX: 770-442-9742
                                    www.arthritis.com

What do aerosol cooking spray and snow-shoveling have in
common? Learn the answer to this question, and other clever and
handy tips to make your life with-or without-arthritis easier.
Plus learn about helpful serviced you didn't know were available through you bank, post office, phone company, grocery
store, and other businesses you frequent. *$9.95*
     *88 pages*

**6532  Understanding Down Syndrome: An Introduction for Parents**
Brookline Books
PO Box 1046
Cambridge, MA  02139               617-868-0360
                                   800-666-2665
                              FAX: 617-868-1772
                     e-mail: brooklinebks@delphi.com
                           www.brooklinebooks.com

Using positive and readable language, this book helps parents
understand Down Syndrome. Medical details are explained in
lay terms, and advice is given on working with professionals,
obtaining services, and treatment techniques that help the child.
Cunningham alerts families to potential problems, the prospects
for the child in schooling and the passage to adulthood. Revised
1996. *$14.95*
     *Softcover*
     *ISBN 1-57129 -09-5*

**6533  What Your Doctor May Not Tell You About Ch ildren's Allergies and Asthma**
Warner Books

The authors explain to parents: why children with allergies are
sometimes misdiagnosed as having other ailments; how to use
alternative treatments and holistic remedies; simple methods to
allergy-proof their homes and pets; the 10 things parents do that
make their children's allergy symptoms worse. *$14.95*
     *336 pages 2003*
     *ISBN 0-446679-88-7*

**6534  Without Reason: A Family Copes with Autism**
Books on Special Children
PO Box 305
Congers, NY  10920                 845-638-1236
                               FAX: 845-638-0847
                      e-mail: irene@boscbooks.com

The author discovers his son has autism. He delves into problems of the autistic person and explains reasons for their actions.
*$20.95*

*292 pages Hardcover*

**6535** **You and Your ADD Child**
Nelson Publications
1 Gateway Plaza
Port Chester, NY 10573                914-937-8400
                                       FAX: 914-937-8950
*$12.99*
        *252 pages Paperback*
        *ISBN 0-785278-95-8*

**6536** **You and Your Deaf Child: A Self-Help Guide for Parents of Deaf and Hard of Hearing Children**
Gallaudet University Press
11030 S Langley Avenue
Chicago, IL 60628
                                       800-621-2736
                                       FAX: 800-621-8476
                                       TTY:800-621-9347
                                       gupress.gallaudet.edu
The classic self-instructional guide has been completely written with more information dealing with feelings, communication and other issues. Includes worksheets and practice exercises. *$19.95*
        *224 pages Softcover*

**6537** **Your Child in the Hospital: A Practical Guide for Parents**
Patient-Centered Guides
101 Morris Street
Sebastopol, CA 95472                707-829-0515
                                    800-998-9938
                                    FAX: 707-829-0104
                                    www.patientcenters.com

*Linda Lamb, Editor*
*Shawnde Paull, Marketing*
*Tim O'Reilly, Chief Executive Officer*

This book offers advice from dozens of veteran parents on how to cope with a child's hospitalization, relieving anxious parents so they can help dispel their child's fears and concerns. Parents will find easy-to-read tips on preparing their child, handling procedures without trauma, and preventing insurance snafus. The second edition features a journal to help open communication and give the child a measure of control over the experience. *$11.95*
        *166 pages Paperback*
        *ISBN 1-565925-73-4*

**6538** **Your Cleft-Affected Child**
Publishers Group West

Pocket-sized consumer text covers causes of cleft palate and how it can be fixed. Includes advice on feeding, dental and speech-related issues. *$15.95*
        *288 pages Paperback\ 2001*
        *ISBN 0-897931-85-8*

## Parenting: School

**6539** **ADHD in Schools: Assessment and Intervention Strategies**
Guilford Press
72 Spring Street
New York, NY 10012                212-431-9800
                                  800-365-7006
                                  FAX: 212-966-6708
                                  e-mail: info@guilford.com

*Bob Matloff, President*

This landmark volume emphasizes the need for a team effort among parents, community-based professionals, and educators. Provides practical information that is based on empirical findings. Chapters focus on: how to identify and assess students who might have ADHD; the relationship between ADHD and learning disabilities; how to develop and implement classroom-based programs; communication strategies to assist physicians; and the need for community-based treatments. *$36.00*
        *269 pages Hardcover*
        *ISBN 0-898622-45-X*

**6540** **Allergies & Asthma At School Kit**
Allergy and Asthma Network Mothers of Asthmatics
2751 Prosperity Avenue
Suite 150
Fairfax, VA 22031                703-641-9595
                                 800-878-4403
                                 FAX: 703-573-7794
                                 e-mail: memserv@aanma.org
                                 www.breatherville.org
Practical, medical, and legal information for school administrators and parents of students with asthma. *$7.00*

**6541** **Attention Deficit Disorders: Assessment & Teaching**
Brooks/Cole Publishing Company
511 Forest Lodge Road
Pacific Grove, CA 93950                831-333-1175
                                       FAX: 408-375-6414
                                       e-mail: bc-info@brookscole.com
                                       www.brookscole.com

*Theresa Brooks, President*

A handy resource that offers teachers, school psychologists, counselors, social workers, administrators, and parents practical advice for working with children who have attention deficit disorders. *$18.95*
        *258 pages Paperback*
        *ISBN 0-534250-44-0*

**6542** **Carolina Curriculum for Infants and Toddlers with Special Needs, 2nd Edition**
Brookes Publishing
PO Box 10624
Baltimore, MD 21285                410-337-9580
                                   800-638-3775
                                   FAX: 410-337-8539
                                   e-mail: custserv@brookespublishing.com
                                   www.brookespublishing.com

*Paul Brooks, Owner*

This book includes detailed assessment and intervention sequences, daily routine integration strategies, sensorimotor adaptations, and a sample 24-page Assessment Log that shows readers how to chart a child's individual progress. *$41.95*
        *384 pages Spiral-bound*
        *ISBN 1-557660-74-3*

**6543** **Children, Problems and Guidelines: A Resource Book For School & Parents**
Slosson Educational Publications
PO Box 280
East Aurora, NY 14052                716-652-0930
                                     888-756-7766
                                     FAX: 800-655-3840
                                     e-mail: slosson@slosson.com
                                     www.slosson.com

*Leslie Foote, Office Personnel*
*Peggy Meyer, Office Personnel*
*Steven Slosson, President*

Dr. Casey's book is a professional and responsible resource book which addresses many of the most common problems involving children and their homes or schools. Student achievement is very sensitive to home environments, family structure, emotional state, drugs and alcohol usage, and pressures from a great number of sources. Information relevant to answering questions or concerns is provided for dozens of common but devastating problems such as dicipline, study skills, and school behavior. *$43.00*

*99 pages*

**6544  Choosing Outcomes and Accommodations for Children (COACH), 2nd Edition**
Brookes Publishing
PO Box 10624
Baltimore, MD  21285                      410-337-9580
                                          800-638-3775
                                    FAX: 410-337-8539
            e-mail: custserv@brookespublishing.com
                        www.brookespublishing.com

*Paul Brooks, Owner*

A guide to educational planning for students with disabilities, second edition. Focuses on life outcomes such as social relationships and participation in typical home, school, and community activities. *$37.95*
        *400 pages Spiral bound 1997*
        *ISBN 1-55766 -23-8*

**6545  College Admissions: A Guide for Homeschoolers**
Alliance for Parental Involvement in Education
PO Box 59
East Chatham, NY  12060                   518-392-6900
                                    FAX: 518-392-6900
The author's son was educated at home through junior and senior high school without much imposed structure. *$7.50*

**6546  College and Career Success for Students wi th Learning Disabilities**
McGraw-Hill Company
2460 Kerper Boulevard
Dubuque, IA  52001                        563-588-1451
                                          800-338-3987
                                    FAX: 614-755-5654
                        www.mhhe.com/hper/physed

*Kurt Strand, Vice President*

Covers finding and gaining admission to the right college, preparing cover letters and resumes, exploring career options through networking and interviewing, and evaluating job offers. *$14.95*
        *224 pages 1996*
        *ISBN 0-844244-79-1*

**6547  Complete IEP Guide: How to Advocate for Yo ur Special Ed Child**
Spina Bifida Association of America
4590 Macarthur Boulevard NW
Suite 250
Washington, DC 20007                      202-944-3285
                                          800-621-3141
                                    FAX: 202-944-3295
                           e-mail: sbaa@sbaa.org
                                     www.sbaa.org

*Cindy Brownstein, Chief Executive Officer*

This all-in-one guide will help you understand special education law, identify your child's needs, prepare for meetings, develop the IEP and resolve disputes. *$28.95*

**6548  Exceptional Student in the Regular Classroom**
McGraw-Hill, School Publishing
220 E Danieldale Road
Desoto, TX  75115                         972-224-1111
                                          800-442-9685
                                    FAX: 972-228-1982
                                   mhschool.com

*Joseph Gavigan, President*

Offers good, solid information through a practical understandable presentation unencumbered by specialized jargon. Covers topics associated with special learners.
        *480 pages*

**6549  Families Writing**
Alliance for Parental Involvement in Education
PO Box 59
East Chatham, NY  12060                   518-392-6900
                                    FAX: 518-392-6900

This book is full of writing activities and examples of ways writing can be encouraged and enjoyed in the home. *$14.99*

**6550  Family Math**
Alliance for Parental Involvement in Education
PO Box 59
East Chatham, NY  12060                   518-392-6900
                                    FAX: 518-392-6900
Here are dozens of interesting activities to share with your children. *$18.00*

**6551  Getting the Best Bite of the Apple**
Alliance for Parental Involvement in Education
PO Box 59
East Chatham, NY  12060                   518-392-6900
                                    FAX: 518-392-6900
This book takes a hard critical look at public school. The author is a parent who is also a former public school classroom teacher, school psychologist and principal. *$11.95*

**6552  Home Education Resource Packet for New York State**
Longview Publishing
R9 Kinderhook Street
Chatham, NY  12037                        518-392-6900
                                    FAX: 518-392-6900
For those considering home education in New York State, a packet containing the complete NYS Home Instruction Regulation, the laws referred to in the regulation, how to comply, resource listings, curriculum providers, support groups and more. *$8.00*
        *Paperback*

**6553  Homeschooling for Excellence**
Alliance for Parental Involvement in Education
PO Box 59
East Chatham, NY  12060                   518-392-6900
                                    FAX: 518-392-6900
Children will learn if we recognize and respect their different interests and abilities and give them a chance to develop them. *$11.99*

**6554  In Their Own Way**
Alliance for Parental Involvement in Education
PO Box 59
East Chatham, NY  12060                   518-392-6900
                                    FAX: 518-392-6900
For the parents whose children are not thriving in school, Armstrong offers insight into individual learning styles. *$11.95*

**6555  LD Child and the ADHD Child: Ways Parents & Professionals Can Help**
1406 Plaza Drive
Winston Salem, NC  27103
                                          800-222-9796
                                    FAX: 336-768-9194
                           e-mail: blairpub@aol.com
                                    www.blairpub.com

*Carolyn Sakowski, President*
*John F Blair, Publisher*

Book about learning disabilities available to parents. Stevens cuts through the jargon and complex theories which usually characterize books on the subject to present effective and practical techniques that parents can employ to help their child succeed at home and at school. New edition adds information about ADHD children. *$12.95*
        *201 pages Paperback*
        *ISBN 0-895871-42-4*

**6556  Learning All the Time**
Alliance for Parental Involvement in Education
PO Box 59
East Chatham, NY  12060                   518-392-6900
                                    FAX: 518-392-6900
Writes about how to aid young children in learning and how to allow them to figure things out for themselves, with the same insight and love of children that was apparent in his book. *$12.00*

**6557 Magic Feather**
Alliance for Parental Involvement in Education
PO Box 59
East Chatham, NY 12060          518-392-6900
FAX: 518-392-6900
The Grangers were the victims of the special education system. Their son was mistested, mislabeled and more, but their story has a happy ending. *$9.95*

**6558 Making the Writing Process Work**
Brookline Books
PO Box 1047
Cambridge, MA 02139          617-868-0360
800-666-2665
FAX: 617-868-1772
e-mail: brooklinebks@delphi.com
www.brooklinebooks.com
Making the Writing Process Work: Strategies for Composition and Self-Regulation is geared toward students who have difficulty organizing their thoughts and developing their writing. The specific strategies teach students how to approach, organize, and produce a final written product. *$24.95*
*240 pages Paperback*
*ISBN 1-57129-10-9*

**6559 Negotiating the Special Education Maze: A Guide for Parents and Teachers**
Spina Bifida Association of America
4590 Macarthur Boulevard NW
Suite 250
Washington, DC 20007          202-944-3285
800-621-3141
FAX: 202-944-3295
e-mail: sbaa@sbaa.org
www.sbaa.org

*Cindy Brownstein, Chief Executive Officer*

An excellent aid for the development of an effective special education program. *$19.00*

**6560 Nurturing Independent Learners Brookline Press**
PO Box 1047
Cambridge, MA 02139          617-868-0360
800-666-2665
FAX: 617-868-1772
e-mail: brooklinebks@delphi.com
www.brooklinebooks.com
Presents programs that effectively improve students' independence—the ability to manage their own learning—and explain how to implement them in the classroom. *$24.95*
*256 pages Paperback*
*ISBN 1-57129-47-8*

**6561 One School at a Time: School Based Management**
Alliance for Parental Involvement in Education
PO Box 59
East Chatham, NY 12060          518-392-6900
FAX: 518-392-6900
School based management is a school-by-school approach to educational reform. Parents, students and other community members work with the principal, teachers and other members of the school staff to shape the schools the community wants. *$8.95*

**6562 Parent Teacher Packet**
Spina Bifida Association of America
4590 Macarthur Boulevard NW
Suite 250
Washington, DC 20007          202-944-3285
800-621-3141
FAX: 202-944-3295
e-mail: sbaa@sbaa.org
www.sbaa.org

*Cindy Brownstein, Chief Executive Officer*

Includes educational material, learning disabilities literature, children's book, social development and the person with spina bifida and one copy of each fact sheet. *$14.00*

**6563 Parent's Guide to the Montessori Classroom**
Alliance for Parental Involvement in Education
PO Box 59
East Chatham, NY 12060          518-392-6900
FAX: 518-392-6900
This guide gives a concise explanation of the meaning of Montessori. It describes in detail the Montessori program for children between the ages of three to six. *$5.95*

**6564 Rethinking Attention Deficit Disorder**
Brookline Books
PO Box 1047
Cambridge, MA 02139          617-868-0360
800-666-2665
FAX: 617-868-1772
e-mail: brooklinebks@delphi.com
www.brooklinebooks.com
In contrast to the common focus on behavioral symptoms of attention disorders, this book emphasizes internal factors that make attention regulation difficult. In-depth discussions of social, emotional, and academic consequences and appropriate interventions are provided. *$27.95*
*250 pages Paperback*
*ISBN 1-57129-37-0*

**6565 Schools for Children with Autism Spectrum Disorders**
Resources for Children with Special Needs
116 E 16th Street
Floor 5
New York, NY 10003          212-677-4650
FAX: 212-254-4070
e-mail: info@resourcesnyc.org
www.resourcesnyc.org

*Karen Schlesinger, Executive Director*
*Dianne Littwin, Director Publications*

Published every 24-36 months. *$20.00*
*160 pages*
*ISBN 0-967836-53-0*

**6566 Sharing Nature with Children**
Alliance for Parental Involvement in Education
PO Box 59
East Chatham, NY 12060          518-392-6900
FAX: 518-392-6900
A book of wonderful games for exploring nature in a natural, comfortable way. *$7.95*

**6567 So Your Child Has a Learning Problem?**
CPPC
605 3rd Avenue
New York, NY 10158          212-996-6967
800-433-8234
Designed for parents of children who are encountering learning problems in the classroom. *$19.95*
*160 pages*

**6568 Study Power: Study Skills to Improve Your Learning and Your Grades: A Workbook**
Brookline Books
PO Box 1047
Cambridge, MA 02139          617-868-0360
800-666-2665
FAX: 617-868-1772
e-mail: brooklinebks@delphi.com
www.brooklinebooks.com
The techniques in the easy-to-use, self-teaching manual have yielded remarkable success for students from elementary to medical school, at all levels of intelligence and achievement. Key skills covered include: listening, note taking, concentration, summarizing, reading comprehension, memorization, test taking, preparing papers and reports, time management, and more. These abilities are vital to success throughout every stage of learning; the benefits will last a lifetime. 1999.ISBN 157129067X *$15.95*

*Paperback 1998*
*ISBN 1-57129 -46-X*

**6569    Symptoms and Treatment of Child's Learning**
Health Publishing Company
PO Box 3805
San Francisco, CA  94119                     415-282-8585
                                        FAX: 415-826-1470

*Jane Burrows, President*
Handbook for parents who need to know the symptoms and treatments of a child's learning and academic disorders. *$4.95*

**6570    Taking Charge Through Homeschooling**
Alliance for Parental Involvement in Education
PO Box 59
East Chatham, NY  12060                      518-392-6900
                                        FAX: 518-392-6900
While this book offers solid information and suggestions for educating children without school, it also offers concrete suggestions on ways home schoolers can unite to protect their rights and freedoms. *$12.95*

**6571    Teaching Children Self-Discipline**
Alliance for Parental Involvement in Education
PO Box 59
East Chatham, NY  12060                      518-392-6900
                                        FAX: 518-392-6900
Mr. Gordon draws on research findings and his experience helping parents and teachers. *$17.95*

**6572    Teaching Young Children to Read Brookline Books**
PO Box 1047
Cambridge, MA  02139                         617-868-0360
                                             800-666-2665
                                        FAX: 617-868-1772
                       e-mail: brooklinebks@delphi.com
                                www.brooklinebooks.com
Detailed instructions on teaching reading to preschoolers. Gradually develops full fluency. *$16.95*
*192 pages Paperback*
*ISBN 0-57129 -48-6*

**6573    Unlocking Potenial: College and Other Choi ces for People with LD and AD/HD**
Spina Bifida Association of America
4590 Macarthur Boulevard NW
Suite 250
Washington, DC 20007                         202-944-3285
                                             800-621-3141
                                        FAX: 202-944-3295
                            e-mail: sbaa@sbaa.org
                                         www.sbaa.org

*Cindy Brownstein, Chief Executive Officer*
An indispensable look for high school students with learning disabilities and AD/HD. Includes comprehensive listing of resources. *$22.95*

**6574    You are Your Child's First Teacher**
Alliance for Parental Involvement in Education
PO Box 59
East Chatham, NY  12060                      518-392-6900
                                        FAX: 518-392-6900
Presents principles of Waldorf early education in the home from birth to age six. *$12.95*

**6575    You, Your Child, and Special Education: A Guide to Making the System Work**
Brookes Publishing
PO Box 10624
Baltimore, MD  21285                         410-337-9580
                                             800-638-3775
                                        FAX: 410-337-8539
                 e-mail: custserv@brookespublishing.com
                            www.brookespublishing.com

*Paul Brooks, Owner*

This book shows parents how to obtain the educational services their children rightfully deserve. It examines the internal workings of the education system, reveals the challenges that await, lists the services that are available, and discusses the rights that are federally guaranteed. Comes with a resource list, directions for filing a complaint, and explanations of relevant legislation and regulations. *$24.00*
*272 pages Paperback*
*ISBN 1-55766 -15-4*

# Parenting: Spiritual

**6576    A Miracle to Believe In**
Option Indigo Press
2080 S Undermountain Road
Sheffield, MA  01257                         413-229-8727
                                             800-562-7171
                                        FAX: 413-229-8727
                        e-mail: happiness@option.org
                                   www.optionindigo.com
A group of people from all walks of life come together and are transformed as they reach out, under the direction of the Kaufmans, to help a little boy the medical world has given up as hopeless. This heartwarming journey of loving a child back to life will inspire and presents a compelling new way to deal with life's traumas and difficulties. *$7.99*
*379 pages Paperback*
*ISBN 0-44920 -08-2*

**6577    After the Tears**
Centering Corporation
1531 N Saddle Creek Road
Omaha, NE  68104                             402-553-1200
                                        FAX: 402-533-0507
                            e-mail: j1200@aol.com
                                         www.centering.org

*Joy Johnson, Executive Director*
Offers talk, articles on raising a child with a disability. This one book combines feelings and emotions of parents on the subject of raising their disabled child. *$11.00*
*87 pages Paperback*
*ISBN 0-15602 -00-6*

**6578    Be Quiet, Marina!**
Star Bright Books

A noisy little girl with cerebral palsy and a quiet little girl with Down Syndrome learn to play together and eventually become best friends. *$16.95*
*40 pages Hardcover 2001*
*ISBN 1-887734-79-1*

**6579    Before and After Zachariah**
Special Needs Project
324 State Street
Suite H
Santa Barbara, CA  93101                     805-962-8087
                                             800-333-6867
                                        FAX: 805-962-5087
                                     www.specialneeds.com
This intimate chronicle of one family's life with a severely brain damaged child is recently back in print. *$7.95*
*241 pages*

**6580    Bethy and the Mouse: A Father Remembers His Children with Disabilities**
Brookline Books
PO Box 1047
Cambridge, MA  02139                         617-868-0360
                                             800-666-2665
                                        FAX: 617-868-1772
                       e-mail: brooklinebks@delphi.com
                                www.brooklinebooks.com
A moving collection of poetry, photographs, and prose following a father's experiences with two disabled children—one with Down Syndrome and one with an underdeveloped brain. *$16.95*

*184 pages Paperback*
*ISBN 0-57129 -35-4*

**6581** **Dimensions: Visually Impaired Persons with Multiple Disabilities**
American Foundation for the Blind/AFB Press
PO Box 1020
Sewickley, PA 15143      412-741-1142
800-232-3044
FAX: 412-741-0609
e-mail: afborders@abdintl.com
www.afb.org

*Stephanie Biagioli, Marketing Coordinator*

Twenty-one articles from the Journal of Visual Impairment and Blindness, present a wide range of approaches for working with persons with multiple disabilities. *$24.95*
*116 pages Paperback*
*ISBN 0-89128 -63-0*

**6582** **Disabled God: Toward a Liberatory Theology of Disability**
Abingdon Press
201 8th Avenue S
Nashville, TN 37203      615-749-6000
800-251-3320
FAX: 800-836-7802
www.abingdon.org

*Dr. Rex Matthews, Senior Editor*
*Neil Alexander, President*

Draws on themes of the disability rights movement to identify people with disabilities as members of a socially disadvantaged minority group rather than as individuals who need to adjust. Highlights the history of people with disabilities in the church and society. *$ 13.95*
*27 pages Paperback*
*ISBN 0-68710 -01-2*

**6583** **Dying and Disabled Children: Dealing with Loss and Grief**
Haworth Press
10 Alice Street
Binghamton, NY 13904      607-722-5857
800-429-6784
FAX: 607-722-6362
e-mail: orders@haworthpress.com
www.haworthpress.com

*Harold M Dick MD, Editor*
*S Harrington-Miller, Advertising*
*William Cohen, Owner*

In this sensitive and compassionate look at terminally ill and disabled children, professionals from the medical community examine the stresses faced by their parents and siblings. They address the crucial element of communication in dealing with a child's serious illness. Ethical decision making, learning to recognize the child's suffering, and talking to children about death are honestly and clearly discussed. *$ 59.95*
*153 pages Hardcover*
*ISBN 0-866567-59-3*

**6584** **Eye-Centered: A Study of Spirituality of Deaf People**
NCOD
7202 Buchanan Street
Landover Hills, MD 20784      301-577-1684
FAX: 301-577-1690
e-mail: ncod@erols.com
www.ncod.org
The findings of the five-year De Sales Project conducted by The National Catholic Office for the Deaf. *$12.00*

*167 pages*

**6585** **Giant Steps**
Option Indigo Press
2080 S Undermountain Road
Sheffield, MA 01257      413-229-8727
800-562-7171
FAX: 413-229-8727
e-mail: indigo@option.org
www.optionindigo.com

*Kate Wilde*

This book illustrates the powerful, life-changing Option Process Dialogue in action. Barry takes us on a very intimate journey presenting ten uplifting, in-depth portraits of young people engaged in transformative dialogues with him. The reader witnesses moments of extreme crisis involving rape, questions of sexuality, a dying parent, divorce, the prison of drugs as these people learn to break through their pain and triumph in the face of challenge and crisis. *$5.99*
*351 pages Paperback*
*ISBN 0-449215-69-5*

**6586** **Happiness is a Choice**
Ballantine Books
2080 S Undermountain Road
Sheffield, MA 01257      413-229-8737
800-562-7171
FAX: 413-229-8737
e-mail: indigo@option.org
www.optionindigo.com

*Kate Wilde*

Happiness is a Choice represents the cutting edge of Barry Neil Kaufman's evolving teaching, focusing on empowering our moment of change, the moment in which we can make self-acceptance, inner peace, joy and love immediately tangible with these easy-to-use tools. This book takes us step by step on a journey to increase personal power. A book to cherish and to share, a book that will ignite the healing process. *$ 10.95*
*284 pages Paperback*
*ISBN 0-449907-99-6*

**6587** **How to Thrive, Not Just Survive**
American Foundation for the Blind/AFB Press
PO Box 1020
Sewickley, PA 15143      412-741-1142
800-232-3044
FAX: 412-741-0609
e-mail: afborders@abdintl.com
www.afb.org

*Stephanie Biagioli, Marketing Coordinator*

Practical, hands-on guide for parents, teachers, and everyone involved in helping children develop the skills necessary for socialization, orientations and mobility, and leisure and recreational activities. Some of the subjects covered are eating, dressing, personal hygiene, self-esteem and etiquette. *$24.95*
*104 pages Paperback*
*ISBN 0-89128 -48-7*

**6588** **Hug Just Isn't Enough**
Gallaudet University Bookstore
11030 S Langley Avenue
Chicago, IL 60628      202-651-5488
800-621-2736
FAX: 202-651-5489
Offers valuable information for the disabled. *$15.95*
*94 pages Hardcover*

**6589** **In Time and with Love: Caring for the Special Needs Infant and Toddler, 2nd Edition**
Newmarket Press
18 E 48th Street
New York, NY 10017      212-832-3575
FAX: 212-832-3629
e-mail: sales@newmarketpress.com
www.newmarketpress.com

*Heidi Sachner, Sales Director*
*Esther Margolis, President*

For families and caregivers of preteen and handicapped children in their first three years - more than one hundred tips for adjusting and coping. *$15.95*
*208 pages*
*ISBN 1-557044-45-7*

**6590 Little Children, Big Needs**
Exceptional Parent Library
PO Box 1807
Englewood Cliffs, NJ 07632
201-947-6000
800-535-1910
FAX: 201-947-9376
e-mail: eplibrary@aol.com
www.eplibrary.com
Contains candid interviews with fifty families of children with a wide variety of disabilities. *$12.95*

**6591 Loving & Letting Go**
Centering Corporation
1531 N Saddle Creek Road
Omaha, NE 68104
402-553-1200
FAX: 402-533-0507
e-mail: j1200@aol.com
www.centering.org

*Joy Johnson, Executive Director*

For parents who decide to turn away from aggressive medical intervention for their critically ill newborn. *$5.95*
*48 pages Paperback*

**6592 Loving Justice**
Exceptional Parent Library
PO Box 1807
Englewood Cliffs, NJ 07632
201-947-6000
800-535-1910
FAX: 201-947-9376
e-mail: eplibrary@aol.com
www.eplibrary.com
How the Americans with Disabilities Act affects religious institutions, including congregations, hospitals, nursing homes, seminaries, universities and more. *$10.00*

**6593 Misunderstood Child**
Gallery Bookshop
PO Box 270
Mendocino, CA 95460
707-937-2665
FAX: 707-937-3737
e-mail: info@gallerybooks.com
www.gallerybooks.com

*Tony Miksak, Owner*

A guide for parents with learning disabled children. *$8.95*
*224 pages Paperback*
*ISBN 0-07057-89-5*

**6594 Nobody's Perfect: Living and Growing with Children Who Have Special Needs**
Brookes Publishing
PO Box 10624
Baltimore, MD 21285
410-337-9580
800-638-3775
FAX: 410-337-8539
e-mail: custserv@brookespublishing.com
www.brookespublishing.com

*Paul Brooks, Owner*

This book offers parents who have children with special needs a new and positive perspective on the challenges of family life. This book guides parents through the process of adaptation, describing specific strategies for success in balancing one's own life, developing a parenting partnership, and interacting with children, friends, relatives, professionals, and others. *$21.00*

*352 pages Paperback*
*ISBN 1-55766 -43-X*

**6595 Pastoral Care of the Mentally Disabled: Advancing Care of the Whole Person**
Haworth Press
10 Alice Street
Binghamton, NY 13904
607-722-5857
800-429-6784
FAX: 607-722-6362
e-mail: orders@haworthpress.com
www.haworthpress.com

*S Harrington-Miller, Advertising*
*William Cohen, Owner*

The beginning step to encourage a partnership for treating and evaluating patients with mental illness. It addresses the perceived roles of clergy and physicians for hearing the whole person which best occurs when medicine and ministry are linked. *$59.95*
*116 pages Hardcover*
*ISBN 1-560246-65-0*

**6596 Place for Everyone: A Guide for Special Education Bible Teaching**
Baptist Sunday School Board
127 9th Avenue N
Nashville, TN 37234
800-458-2772
FAX: 615-251-5933
www.bssb.com

*Ron Brown, Team Leader*
*Doug Merritt, Manager*

Begin a ministry for exceptional people in your church or strengthen an existing ministry. This resource helps pastors, ministers of education, and Sunday School directors understand educational and developmental issues in meeting special education needs. It will train leaders to minister in specific ways, emphasizing the need to reach disabled persons for Christ and for church membership through life-changing Bible study. *$19.95*

*ISBN 0-767318-98-6*

**6597 Special Education Bible Study**
LifeWay Christian Resources Southern Baptist Conv.
127 9th Avenue N
Nashville, TN 37234
615-251-2089
800-458-2772
FAX: 615-251-5017
e-mail: SpecialEd@lifeway.com
www.lifeway.com

*Ellen Beene, Editor*
*Wade Stapleton, Manager*

Easy to use Bible study helps for mentally handicapped adults and youth. Features full-color pictures plus an emphasis on applying biblical truth to real-life situations. *$1.50*
*48 pages Quarterly*

**6598 Special Education Teacher Packet**
LifeWay Christian Resources Southern Baptist Conv.
127 9th Avenue N
Nashville, TN 37234
615-251-2089
800-458-2772
FAX: 615-251-5017
e-mail: SpecialEd@lifeway.com
www.lifeway.com

*Ellen Beene, Editor*
*Wade Stapleton, Manager*

Resources to help teachers who lead Sunday School classes for adults and older youth with mental retardation. Includes teaching plans, posters, and one copy of Special Education Bible Study. *$10.00*

*Quarterly*

**6599    Special Kind of Parenting**
La Leche League International
PO Box 4079
Schaumburg, IL  60168                     847-519-7730
                                     FAX: 847-519-0035
                                     e-mail: LLLI@llli.org
                                     www.lalecheleague.org

*Schielany Bautista, Marketing Assistant*
*Judy Torgus, Publications Director*

Disabled children have special needs which challenge their parents' emotional and physical resources. This book guides parents through the problems and helps them discover their disabled child as an individual. The author covers both facts and feelings about handicaps, parents' reactions to the initial diagnosis, the grieving process, and effects on the marriage and the rest of the family. They also provide suggestions for choosing the programs and professionals best suited. *$7.50*
*172 pages Softcover*
*ISBN 0-912500-27-1*

**6600    Spirit of Lo: An Ordinary Family's Extraor dinary Journey**
Mind Matters

An ordinary family is faced with an extraordinary challenge, a child with cystic fibrosis. Their love, faith and commitment to each other carry them through battles with depression, anger, despair and the ravages of the disease as they join a race with death for a cure. *$14.95*
*280 pages 2000*
*ISBN 0-970193-40-8*

**6601    That All May Worship**
Exceptional Parent Library
PO Box 1807
Englewood Cliffs, NJ  07632               201-947-6000
                                          800-535-1910
                                     FAX: 201-947-9376
                                     e-mail: mailto:eplibrary@aol.com
                                          www.eplibrary.com
An interfaith handbook to assist congregations in welcoming people with disabilities to promote acceptance and full participation. *$10.00*

**6602    Why Mine?**
Centering Corporation
1531 N Saddle Creek Road
Omaha, NE  68104                          402-553-1200
                                     FAX: 402-533-0507
                                     e-mail: j1200@aol.com
                                          www.centering.org

*Joy Johnson, Executive Director*

Offers quotes from parents all across the country on their fears, feelings, marriage, the ill child and other children. *$3.25*
*32 pages Paperback*

**6603    Worst Loss: How Families Heal from the Death of a Child**
Exceptional Parent Library
PO Box 1807
Englewood Cliffs, NJ  07632               201-947-6000
                                          800-535-1910
                                     FAX: 201-947-9376
                                     e-mail: mailto:eplibrary@aol.com
                                          www.eplibrary.com
Combines anecdotal case histories and the latest research to help bereaved parents cope with the loss of a child, offering practical and comforting advice on how to overcome the disabling symptoms of grief. *$25.00*

*ISBN 0-805032-41-X*

## Professional

**6604    2003 Annual Report**
Jessie Ball duPont Fund
1 Independent Drive
Suite 1400
Jacksonville, FL  32202                   904-353-0890
                                          800-252-3452
                                     FAX: 904-353-3870

*Notes from the Field, author*
*Sherry Magill, President*
*Yearly*

**6605    A Practical Guide to Art Therapy Groups**
Haworth Press
10 Alice Street
Binghamton, NY  13904                     607-722-5857
                                          800-429-6784
                                     FAX: 607-722-6362
                                     e-mail: orders@haworthpress.com
                                          www.haworthpress.com

*S Harrington-Miller, Advertising*
*William Cohen, Owner*

Unique approaches, materials, and device will inspire you to tap into your own well of creativity to design your own treatment plans. It lays out the ingredients and the skills to get the results you want. *$64.95*
*115 pages Hardcover*
*ISBN 0-789001-36-5*

**6606    ADHD Report**
Guilford Press
72 Spring Street
New York, NY  10012                       212-431-9800
                                          800-365-7006
                                     FAX: 212-966-6708
                                     e-mail: info@guilford.com

*Bob Matloff, President*

Presents the most up-to-date information on the evaluation, diagnosis and management of ADHD in children, adolescents and adults. This important newsletter is an invaluable resource for all professionals interested in ADHD. *$49.95*
*BiMonthly*
*ISSN 1065-8025*

**6607    Aging and Developmental Disability: Current Research, Programming, and Practice**
Haworth Press
10 Alice Street
Binghamton, NY  13904                     607-722-5857
                                          800-429-6784
                                     FAX: 607-722-6362
                                     e-mail: orders@haworthpress.com
                                          www.haworthpress.com

*Joy Hammel PhD OTR/L, Co-Editor*
*Susan M Nochajski PhD OTR, Co-Editor*
*S Harrington-Miller, Advertising*

Explores research findings and their implications for practice in relation to normative and disability-related aging experiences and issues. It discusses the effectiveness of specific intervention targeted toward aging adults with developmental disabilities such as Down's Syndrome, cerebral palsy, autism, and epilepsy, and offers suggestions for practice and future research in this area. *$39.95*

*100 pages Hardcover*
*ISBN 0-789010-39-9*

**6608  American Association of Spinal Cord Injury Nurses**
American Association of Spinal Cord Injury Nurses
7520 Astoria Boulevard
East Elmhurst, NY  11370
718-397-4181
FAX: 718-803-0414
www.aascin.org

*Sara Lerman MPH, Program Manager*

Disseminates information to nurses and others caring for spinal cord injured individuals. Membership in AASCIN represents registered and licensed practical and vocational nurses in the US and Canada who practice in the diverse SCI settings such as intensive care, acute care and long-term care; rehabilitation; home care; and outpatient care. There is a Nursing Research Program which funds research in the area of spinal cord impairment. Annual educational conference.

**6609  American Forensic Association Journal**
American Forensic Association
University of Wisconsin River Fls
River Falls, WI  54022
715-425-3198
FAX: 715-425-9533
e-mail: james.wpratt@uwrf.edu

*James Pratt, Manager*
Communication disorders newsletter. *$25.00*

**6610  American Journal of Art Therapy**
Vermont College of Norwich University
Montpelier, VT  05602
802-828-8540
FAX: 802-828-8585
e-mail: mzimmerm@norwich.edu

*Gladys Agell PhD ATR-BC HLM, Editor*

Discusses the graphic and plastic arts as they contribute to human understanding, psycotherapy, rahabilitation and education. *$ 32.00*
*35-40 pages Quarterly*
*ISSN 0007-47 4*

**6611  American Journal of Orthopsychiatry**
American Orthopsychiatric Association
330 7th Avenue
18th Floor
New York, NY  10001
212-564-5930
FAX: 212-564-6180
e-mail: amerortho@aol.com

*Joan Adler, Managing Editor*
*Ellen L Bassuk, Editor*

Mental health issues from multidisciplinary and interprofessionals perspectives: clinical, research and expository approaches. *$45.00*
*160 pages Quarterly*

**6612  American Journal of Physical Medicine**
Lippincott, Williams & Wilkins
PO Box 1551
Hagerstown, MD  21741
800-638-3030
FAX: 301-824-7390
www.lww.com
Journal of the Association of Academic Psychiatrists. Articles covering research and clinical studies and applications of new equipment, procedures and therapeutic advances. *$45.00*

**6613  American Journal of Psychiatry**
American Psychiatric Publishing
1000 Wilson Boulevard
Suite 1825
Arlington, VA  22209
703-907-7300
800-368-5777
FAX: 202-789-2648
e-mail: mailto:accessnumber@psych.org
ajp.psychiatryonline.org

*Nancy C Andreasen MD PhD, Editor-in-Chief*
*James Scully, Manager*

Peer-reviewed articles focus on developments in biological psychiatry as well as on treatment innovations and forensic, ethical, economic, and social topics. *$56.00*
*Monthly*

**6614  American Journal of Public Health**
American Public Health Association
1015 15th Street NW
Washington, DC  20005
202-777-2742
FAX: 202-777-2534
e-mail: comments@msmail.apha.org
www.apna.org

*Dr. Mervyn Susser, Editor*
*Georges Benjamin, Executive Director*

Association journal containing professional articles and sections such as Notes from the Field and Association News. Single copies are $15.00. $50.00 per year for special consumer membership.
*Monthly*
*ISSN 0090-00 6*

**6615  American Journal on Mental Retardation**
American Association on Mental Retardation
444 N Capitol Street NW
Washington, DC  20001
202-387-1968
800-424-3688
FAX: 202-387-2193
e-mail: aamr@access.digex.net
www.aamr.org

*Bruce Appelgen, Director Publications*
*Doreen Croser, Executive Director*

Articles cover biological, behavioral, and educational research: theory papers; and reviews of research literature on specific aspects of mental retardation. *$142.00*
*112 pages BiMonthly*

**6616  American Rehabilitation**
Rehabilitation Services Administration
3033 Mes
Washington, DC  20202
202-205-8296
FAX: 202-205-9874
e-mail: frank.romano@ed.gov
www.ed.gov/pubs/AmericanRehab

*Frank Romano, Editor*

Covers medical, social and employment aspects of vocational rehabilitation. *$15.00*
*40 pages Quarterly*

**6617  Annals of Otology, Rhinology and Laryncology**
Annals Publishing Company
4507 Laclede Avenue
Saint Louis, MO  63108
314-367-4987
FAX: 314-367-4988
e-mail: manager@annals.com
www.annals.com

*Kenneth A Cooper Jr, Business Manager*
*Ken Cooper, Owner*

Original, peer-reviewed articles in the fields of otolaryngology - head and neck medicine and surgery, broncho-esophagology, audiology, speech, pathology, allery, and maxillofacial surgery. Official journal of the American Laryngological Association/American Broncho-Esophagological Association. *$170.00*

*112 pages Monthly*

**6618 Archives of Neurology**
American Medical Association
515 N State Street
Chicago, IL 60610
312-464-5000
FAX: 312-464-4184
e-mail: ama-subs@ama-assn.org
www.archneurol.com

*Roger Rosenberg MD, Editor*
*Nawn Gupta PhD, VP Publishing/Group Publisher*
*Michael Maves, Chief Executive Officer*

Mission is to publish scientific information primarily important to those physicians caring for people with neurologic disorders, but also for those interested in the structure and function of the normal and diseased nervous system. *$235.00*
*198 pages Monthly*

**6619 Art Therapy**
American Art Therapy Association
5999 Stevenson Avenue
Suite 200
Alexandria, VA 22304
847-949-6064
FAX: 847-556-4580

*Nancy Stygar*

Publishes articles on the uses of art in the education, enrichment, development and treatment of disabled people. *$10.00*
*76+ pages Quarterly*
*ISSN 0742-16 6*

**6620 Brown University Long Term Care Advisor**
Manisses Communications Group
208 Governor Street
Providence, RI 02906
401-831-6020
800-333-7771
FAX: 401-861-6370
e-mail: manisses@manisses.com
www.manisses.com

*Fraser Lang, Publisher*

Contains practical reports for health care professionals working in long-term care facilities. Published monthly. *$329.00*
*8 pages Newsletter*
*ISSN 1088-92 8*

**6621 CAREERS & the disABLED Magazine**
Equal Opportunity Publications
445 Broadhollow Road
Suite 425
Melville, NY 11747
631-421-9421
FAX: 631-421-0359
e-mail: jschneider@eop.com
www.eop.com

*John R Miller III, Publisher*
*James Schneider, Editorial Director*

A career magazine for professional career seekers who have disabilities. Profiles disabled people who have achieved successful careers. Features a career section in Braille, career guide. *$10.00*

*64 pages 3X*

**6622 Characteristics of Emotional and Behaviora l Disorders of Children and Youth**
Pearson Education

An introductory text in special education on the subject of children and youth with emotional and behavioral disorders, and a companion website with resources for the professor and the student. *$ 88.00*

*544 pages Hardcover 2004*
*ISBN 0-131118-17-X*

**6623 Clinician's Practical Guide to Attention-Deficit/Hyperactivity Disorder**
Brookes Publishing
PO Box 10624
Baltimore, MD 21285
410-337-9580
800-638-3775
FAX: 410-337-8539
www.brookespublishing.com

*Paul Brooks, Owner*

Quick reference volume with comprehensive data on psychoeducational and neuropsychological assessment, related symptoms, drug and counseling therapies and critical issues. *$39.95*
*368 pages 1999*
*ISBN 1-557663-58-0*

**6624 Colon Health: Key to a Vibrant Life**
Norwalk Press
Prescott, AZ
928-445-5567
FAX: 928-445-5567

Includes complete glossary of terms and index of referrals.

**6625 Counseling Parents of Children with Chronic Illness or Disability**
Brookes Publishing
PO Box 10624
Baltimore, MD 21285
410-337-9580
800-638-3775
FAX: 410-337-8539
e-mail: custserv@brookespublishing.com
www.brookespublishing.com

*Paul Brooks, Owner*

*$23.00*
*144 pages Paperback*
*ISBN 1-85433 -91-8*

**6626 Cystic Fibrosis: Medical Care**
Lippincott, Williams & Wilkins
227 E Washington Square
Philadelphia, PA 19106
215-521-8300
800-777-2295
FAX: 301-824-7390
www.lpub.com

*J Lippincott, Chief Executive Officer*

A guide to the medical community to the principles and practices of cystic fibrosis care. After chapters on the molecular and cellular bases of CF and its diagnosis, they cover the major organ systems affected by CF and deal with surgery for CF patients, transplantation (lung and liver), hospitalization, and terminal care. Also included are chapters on special populations, exercise, and laboratory testing. *$ 47.95*
*365 pages 2000*
*ISBN 0-781717-98-1*

**6627 Disability Analysis Handbook**
American Board of Disability Analysts
345 24th Avenue N
Suite 200
Nashville, TN 37203
615-327-2984
FAX: 615-327-9235
e-mail: americanbd@aol.com

*Alex Horwitz MD, Executive Officer*
*Kenneth Anchor, President*

Official newsletter of the American Board of Disability Analysts; features Healthnews Headlines, Meeting Calendar, Application Packet and much more. Free to members; $20 per year for non-members. *$60.00*

*396 pages*
*ISBN 0-787226-70-x*

**6628  Ethical Conflicts in Management of Home Care**
Springer Publishing Company
536 Broadway
New York, NY  10012                212-431-4370
                                   877-687-7476
                              FAX: 212-941-7842
          e-mail: marketing@springerpub.com
                       www.springerpub.com

*Annette Imperati, Marketing/Sales Director*
*Ursula Springer, President*

Offers answers to the questions what is case management and
why does it raise ethical issues. *$29.95*
          *288 pages*

**6629  Evaluation of the Association for Children with
Learning Disabilities**
National Center for State Courts
300 Newport Avenue
Williamsburg, VA  23185             757-259-7575
                                   800-877-1233
                              FAX: 757-564-2028
                       www.ncsconline.org
Final report on children with learning disabilities training insti-
tute. *$6.96*
          *116 pages*

**6630  Failure to Thrive and Pediatric Undernutrition: A
Transdisciplinary Approach**
Brookes Publishing
PO Box 10624
Baltimore, MD  21285                410-337-9580
                                   800-638-3775
                              FAX: 410-337-8539
          e-mail: custserv@brookespublishing.com
                       www.brookespublishing.com

*Paul Brooks, Owner*

Offers comprehensive coverage of pediatric undernutrition
complete with assessment and intervention techniques. Theoretical as well as practical concerns such as epidemiology, nutrition, medical issues, feeding, families, history, research, and
community programs are addressed. A family-centered approach shows practitioners how to enhance treatment by capital-
izing on family strengths and acknowledging the impact of
larger issues such as culture, social environment, and public policy. *$62.95*
          *592 pages Hardcover 1998*
          *ISBN 1-55766 -48-3*

**6631  Families in Recovery**
Brookes Publishing
PO Box 10624
Baltimore, MD  21285                410-337-9580
                                   800-638-3775
                              FAX: 410-337-8539
          e-mail: custserv@brookespublishing.com
                       www.brookespublishing.com

*Paul Brooks, Owner*

This book teaches professionals how to use each families
strengths to promote recovery. The authors demonstrate effective, family-focused intervention techniques developed in their
combined 35 years of practice. Motivational techniques and
stress reducers for counselors are also provided. *$34.00*
          *352 pages Paperback 1997*
          *ISBN 1-55766 -64-9*

**6632  Family and Community Health**
Aspen Publishers
7201 McKinney Circle
Frederick, MD  21704                301-698-7100
                                   800-234-1660
                              FAX: 301-695-7931
                       www.aspenpublishers.com

*Judith Ree, Manager*

Peer-view journal addressing the information needs of
health-care practitioners. *$124.00*
          *Quarterly*

**6633  Health Care Management Review**
Aspen Publishers
7201 McKinney Circle
Frederick, MD  21704                301-698-7100
                                   800-234-1660
                              FAX: 301-695-7931
                       www.aspenpublishers.com

*Judith Ree, Manager*

Provides health care administrators with useful information on
health care management. *$145.00*

**6634  Health Technology Trends**
Emergency Care Research Institute (ECRI)
5200 Butler Pike
Plymouth Meeting, PA  19462         610-825-6000
                              FAX: 610-834-1275
                         e-mail: info@ecri.org
                              www.ecri.org

*Damian Carlson, Associate Editor*
*Evelyn Kuserk, Manager*

Provides analysis and information about health care technology
to administrators and health care providers. *$275.00*
          *12 pages Monthly*

**6635  Home Health Care Services Quarterly**
Haworth Press
10 Alice Street
Binghamton, NY  13904               607-722-5857
                                   800-429-6784
                              FAX: 607-722-6362
          e-mail: orders@haworthpress.com
                       www.haworthpress.com

*W June Simmons, Editor*
*S Harrington-Miller, Advertising*
*William Cohen, Owner*

Professional journal in book format. *$75.00*
          *Quarterly*

**6636  Human Ecologist**
Human Ecology Action League (Heal)
PO Box 509
Stockbridge, GA  30281              404-248-1898
                              FAX: 404-248-0162
                     e-mail: healnatnl@aol.com
                              members.aol.com

*Diane Thomas, Editor*
*Katherine Collier, Manager*

*$26.00*
          *35 pages Quarterly*

**6637  Immune Deficiency Foundation Newsletter**
Immune Deficiency Foundation
40 W Chesapeake Avenue
Suite 308
Towson, MD  21204                   410-321-6647
                                   800-296-4433
                              FAX: 410-321-9165
              e-mail: idf@primaryimmune.org
                       www.primaryimmune.org

*Marcia Boyle, President/Founder/CEO*
*C Belser, Marketing*

Offers information on immune deficiencies. How to treat them,
what they are and more.

*4-6 pages*

**6638    Issues in Law and Medicine**
National Legal Center for the Medically Dependent
3 S 6th Street
Terre Haute, IN 47807                 812-232-0103
                                  FAX: 812-232-0103

*James Bopp Jr, Editor-in-Chief*
*Larry Ligget, Subscriptions*

A peer-reviewed journal providing technical and informational
assistance to attorneys, health care professionals, educators, and
administrators concerned with severely disabled persons of all
ages who may be subjected to discrimination in the delivery of
medical care. *$89.00*
           *124 pages 3x Year*
           *ISSN 8756-81 0*

**6639    JAMA: The Journal of the American Medical Association**
American Medical Association
515 N State Street
Chicago, IL 60610                      312-464-5000
                                  FAX: 312-464-2580
                                  e-mail: ama.jama
                                  jama.ama-assn.org

*Roger Rosenberg MD, Editor*
*Peter Payerli, Publisher*
*Michael Maves, Chief Executive Officer*

Articles cover all aspects of medical research and clinical medicine. *$66.00*

**6640    Journal of Addictions and Offender Counseling**
American Counseling Association
5999 Stevenson Avenue
Alexandria, VA 22304                   703-823-9800
                                       800-473-2329
                                  FAX: 703-823-6862
                                  www.counseling.org

*Jane Carroll, Editor*
*Carolyn Baker, Publications Director*
*Richard Yep, Executive Director*

Contains articles of interest to professionals in the field of addictions and offender counseling and focuses on descriptions of
prevention and treatment programs, theoretical and
philosophocal rationales for programs with juvenile and adult
offenders, and descriptions of research conducted on rehabilitation programs with offenders and public offender counselors. It
is also open to literature focusing on the attitudes and behaviors
of addictions and offender counselors *$30.00*
           *64 pages Bi-Annually*

**6641    Journal of Adolescent Health Care**
655 Avenue of the Americas
New York, NY 10010                     212-989-5800
                                  FAX: 212-633-3990
                                  www.elsevier.com/locate/jadohea

*Micheal Targwwsk, Advertising Representative*

Peer-reviewed publication for the multidisciplinary study of adolescent medicine and health care. *$7.00*

**6642    Journal of Applied Rehabilitation Counseling**
National Rehabilitation Counseling Association
PO Box 4480
Manassas, VA 20108                     703-361-2077
                                  FAX: 703-361-2489
                                  e-mail: nrcaoffice@aol.com
                                  www.nrca-net.org

*Debra Harley, Editor*
*Ellen Fabian, Associate Editor*
*Hal Cain, Book and Media Review Editor*

Articles on counseling history, research and practice of interest
in rehabilitation. $20.00 for individuals, $35.00 institutional.
*$20.00*

*Quarterly*

**6643    Journal of Children's Communication Development**
CEC Div for Childrens' Communication Development
1920 Association Drive
Reston, VA 20191                       703-620-3660
                                  FAX: 703-312-9193

*Alexander Brice, Editor*

Contains scholarly articles pertaining to the many aspects of
communication disorders in children, encompassing speech,
language, hearing and learning disabilities. *$16.00*
           *2x Year*

**6644    Journal of Cognitive Rehabilitation**
Neuroscience Publishers
6555 Carrollton Avenue
Indianapolis, IN 46220                 317-257-9672
                                  FAX: 317-257-9674
                                  e-mail: nsc@netdirect.net
                                  www.jofcr.com

*Odie L Bracy III PhD, Editor/Executive Director*
*Sandra Reichle, Production Manager*

Publication for therapists, family and patient, designed to provide information relevant to the rehabilitation of impairment resulting from brain injury. *$50.00*
           *36-48 pages Quarterly*

**6645    Journal of Employment Counseling**
American Counseling Association
5999 Stevenson Avenue
Alexandria, VA 22304                   703-823-9800
                                       800-473-2329
                                  FAX: 703-823-6862
                                  www.counseling.org

*Robert Drummond, Editor*
*Richard Yep, Executive Director*

*$20.00*
           *Quarterly*

**6646    Journal of Head Trauma Rehabilitation**
Aspen Publishers
200 Orchard Ridge Drive
Gaithersburg, MD 20878                 301-698-7100
                                       800-234-1660
                                  FAX: 301-695-7931
                                  www.aspenpublishers.com
Scholarly journal designed to provide information on clinical
management and rehabilitation of the head-injured for the practicing professional. Published bimonthly. *$119.00*
           *128 pages*

**6647    Journal of Humanistic Education and Development**
American Counseling Association
5999 Stevenson Avenue
Alexandria, VA 22304                   703-823-9800
                                       800-473-2329
                                  FAX: 703-823-6862
                                  www.counseling.org

*Richard J Hazler, Editor*
*Richard Yep, Executive Director*

*$12.00*
           *Quarterly*

**6648    Journal of Multicultural Counseling and Development**
American Counseling Association
5999 Stevenson Avenue
Alexandria, VA 22304                   703-823-9800
                                       800-473-2329
                                  FAX: 703-823-6862
                                  www.counseling.org

*Frederick D Harper, Editor*
*Richard Yep, Executive Director*

*$14.00*

*Quarterly*

**6649  Journal of Rehabilitation**
National Rehabilitation Association (NRA)
633 S Washington Street
Alexandria, VA  22314                703-836-0850
                              FAX: 703-836-0848
                              TTY:7038360849
              e-mail: info@nationalrehab.org
                  www.nationalrehab.org

*Paul Leung, Editor*
*Linda Winslow, Executive Director*

This journal offers information on rehabilitation services and
programs for the disabled and the professional. *$12.50*
            *100 pages Quarterly*

**6650  Journal of Religion, Disability & Health**
Haworth Press
10 Alice Street
Binghamton, NY  13904              607-722-5857
                                  800-429-6784
                              FAX: 607-722-6362
              e-mail: orders@haworthpress.com
                  www.haworthpress.com

*William Gaventa MD, Co-Editor*
*David Coulter MD, Co-Editor*
*S Harrington-Miller, Advertising/Journal Liaison*

This journal aims to inform religious professionals about developments in the field of disability and rehabilitation in order to facilitate greater contributions on the part of pastors, religious
educators and pastoral counselors. *$60.00*
            *Quarterly*

**6651  Journal of Social Work in Disabilty & Rehabilitation**
Haworth Press
10 Alice Street
Binghamton, NY  13904              607-722-5857
                                  800-429-6784
                              FAX: 607-722-6362
              e-mail: orders@haworthpress.com
                  www.haworthpress.com

*John T Oardeck PhD, Editor*
*S Harrington-Miller, Advertising*
*William Cohen, Owner*

Presents and explores issues related to disabilities and social
policy, practice, research, and theory. Reflecting the broad
scope of social work in disabilty practice, this interdisciplinary
journal examines vital issues aspects of the field — from innovative practice methods, legal issues, and literature reviews to program descriptions and cuttinf-edge practice research.
            *Quarterly*

**6652  Journal of the Association for Persons with Severe
Handicaps**
29 W Susquehanna Avenue
Suite 210
Baltimore, MD  21204               410-828-8274
                              FAX: 410-828-6706
              e-mail: info@tash.org
                  www.tash.org
Provides contemporary articles on specialized topics of interest
to TASH members and others in the field of development dis-
abilities. *$25.00*
            *Quarterly*

**6653  Modern Healthcare**
Crain Communications
360 N Michigan Avenue
Chicago, IL  60601                 312-649-5200
                              FAX: 312-397-5510
                  modernheatlhcare.com

*Brenda Stewart, Director Marketing*
*Gloria Scoby, Senior Vice President*

Business news magazine for healthcare professionals. *$7.00*

*Weekly*

**6654  Most Frequently Asked Questions About Lobbying and
CILs (Revised 3/98)**
Independent Living Research Utilization ILRU
2323 S Shepherd Drive
Suite 1000
Houston, TX  77019                 713-520-0232
                              FAX: 713-520-5785
                  www.ilru.org

*Laurie Redd, Executive Director*

This FAQ was written to provide an overview of the federal laws
and regulations about lobbying which apply to non-profit organizations. It also covers what constitutes advocacy and what dis-
tinguishes it from lobbying. This FAQ is not intended to be a
substitute for sound guidance from your organization's attorney
and accountant. Consult them before engaging in these activities.
            *10 pages*

**6655  National Clearinghouse of Rehabilitation Training Ma-
terials**
5202 N Richmond Hill Drive
Stillwater, OK  74078              405-624-7650
                                  800-223-5219
                              FAX: 405-624-0695
                  www.nchrtm.okstate.edu

*Judy Seefeld, Director*
*Carolyn Cash, Information Coordinator*

Newsletter produced quarterly to provide information and opportunities to learn more about related fields.
            *Quarterly*

**6656  Neuropsychiatry of Epilepsy**
Cambridge University Press

Covers the practical implications of ongoing research, and offers a diagnostic and management perspective. Topics include
cognitive aspects, nonepileptic attacks, and clinical aspects. For
professionals treating epileptic patients. *$70.00*
            *360 pages 2002*
            *ISBN 0-521005-16-7*

**6657  Occupational Therapy in Mental Health**
Haworth Press
10 Alice Street
Binghamton, NY  13904              607-722-5857
                                  800-429-6784
                              FAX: 607-722-6362
              e-mail: orders@haworthpress.com
                  www.haworthpress.com

*Marie Louise Blount AM BS, Co-Editor*
*Mary Donohue, Co-Editor*
*S Harrington-Miller, Advertising/Journal Liaison*

An essential journal for all OT's in mental health fields. Provides professionals with a forum in which to discuss challenges.
*$ 60.00*
            *Quarterly*

**6658  Orthotics and Prosthetics Almanac**
Orthotics and Prosthetics National Office
1650 King Street
Suite 500
Alexandria, VA  22314              703-836-7114
                              FAX: 703-836-0838
              e-mail: opalmanac@aol.com
                  www.aopanet.org

*Stacey L Bell, Editor-in-Chief*
*Kathy Carter, Executive Director*

Features articles covering current professional, patient care,
government, business and National Office activities affecting
the orthotics and prosthetics profession and industry. *$40.00*

*80 pages Monthly*
*ISSN 1061-46 1*

**6659 PDP Products**
14524 61st Street Court N
Stillwater, MN 55082
651-439-8865
FAX: 651-439-0421
e-mail: products@pdppro.com
www.pdppro.com

*Alexis Richter, Administrator*

PDP Products acquires books and therapy materials recommended or developed by therapists and makes those materials available at PDP courses and through mail order.

**6660 Parkinsons Report**
National Parkinson Foundation
1501 NW 9th Avenue
Miami, FL 33136
305-547-6666
800-327-4545
FAX: 305-243-4403
e-mail: mailbox@parkinson.org
www.parkinson.org

*Julian Pearson, Administrator*
*Jose Garcia-Pedrosa, Executive Director*

Articles, reports and news on Parkinson's disease and the activities of the National Parkinson Foundation.
*32 pages Qarterly*

**6661 Part B News**
United Communications Group
11300 Rockville Pike
Rockville, MD 20852
301-816-8950
FAX: 301-816-8945
www.ucg.com
Washington news practical strategies for maximizing Medicare Part B.

**6662 Partners in Everyday Communicative Exchanges**
Brookes Publishing
PO Box 10624
Baltimore, MD 21285
410-337-9580
800-638-3775
FAX: 410-337-8539
e-mail: custserv@brookespublishing.com
www.brookespublishing.com

*Paul Brooks, Owner*

A Guide to Promoting Intervention Involving people with Severe Intellectual Disability. This book helps improve communication with people with severe disabilities using practical forms, numerous examples, and illustrative case studies. *$43.00*
*192 pages Paperback*
*ISBN 1-55766 -41-X*

**6663 Physical & Occupational Therapy in Geriatrics...Current Trends in Geriatrics Rehab**
Haworth Press
10 Alice Street
Binghamton, NY 13904
607-722-5857
800-429-6784
FAX: 607-722-6362
e-mail: orders@haworthpress.com
www.haworthpress.com

*Ellen Dunievey Taira OTR/L, Editor*
*Jodi Carison MS, OTR/L, Assistant Editor*
*S Harrington-Miller, Advertising*

Focuses on current practices and emerging issues in the care of the older client, including long-term care in institutional and community settings, crisis intervention, and innovative programming; the entire range of problems experienced by the elderly; and the current skills needed for working with older clients.

*Quarterly*

**6664 Physical Therapy**
American Physical Therapy Association
1111 N Fairfax Street
Alexandria, VA 22314
703-684-2782
800-999-2782
FAX: 703-684-7343
TTY: 703-683-6748
www.apta.org

*Jan Reynolds, Managing Editor*
*Frank Mallon, Chief Executive Officer*

Contains articles on clinical and testing procedures. *$45.00*
*Monthly*

**6665 Professional Report**
National Rehabilitation Association (NRA)
633 S Washington Street
Alexandria, VA 22314
703-836-0850
FAX: 703-836-0848
TTY:703-836-0849
e-mail: info@nationalrehab.org
www.nationalrehab.org

*Linda Winslow, Executive Director*

Association newsletter containing news, programs and information of interest to the Association and its members.

**6666 Provider Magazine**
American Health Care Association
1201 L Street NW
Washington, DC 20005
202-842-4444
800-321-0343
FAX: 202-842-3860

*Dave Kyllo, Vice President*

Magazine for long-term healthcare professionals. *$ 48.00*
*72 pages Monthly*
*ISSN 0888-03 2*

**6667 Psychiatric Rehabilitation Journal**
Boston Unversity
940 Commonwealth Avenue
Boston, MA 02215
617-353-3549
FAX: 617-353-9209
e-mail: leroys@bu.edu
www.bu.edu/cpr/pjr

*Kathleen Furlong-Norman MEd MSW, Managing Editor*

Discusses issues, programs and research on psychiatric rehabilitation.
*112 pages Quarterly*

**6668 Public Health Reports**
Oxford Journals
Jfk Federal Building
Room 1855
Boston, MA 02203
513-636-0257
FAX: 617-565-4260
e-mail: robert.rinsky@chmcc.org
phr.oupjournals.org

*Robert Rinsky PhD, Editor*

Scholarly articles on issues that relate to public health and the healthcare system. *$13.00*
*BiMonthly*

**6669 Public Health/State Capitols**
Wakeman/Walworth
300 N Washington Street
Alexandria, VA 22314
703-768-9600
800-876-2545
FAX: 703-768-9690
e-mail: newsletters@statecapitals.com
www.statecapitals.com

*Keyes Walworth, Publisher*
*Christine Ryan, Editor*

Digest of state and municipal health care financing and legislation, including disease control, medicaid, AIDS, abortion, substance abuse programs, cancer prevention such as smoking restrictions, mental health and disability programs, regulation of hospitals & nursing homes, food safety, medical policies, health insurance for children, home regulation, managerial care, public health issues, pest control, and water quality. Issued weekly-52 issues/year. *$245.00*
*10 pages*

**6670 Public Law 101-336**
US Department of Justice
950 Pennsylvania Avenue NW Drs
- Nyav
Washington, DC 20530          202-586-5000
                              800-574-0301
                         FAX: 202-307-1197
                              www.ada.gov

*Joanne Graham, Manager*

Text of the Americans with Disabilities Act, as enacted on July 26, 1990.

**6671 Public Policy Report**
Nat'l Council for Community Behavioral Healthcare
12300 Twinbrook Parkway
Suite 320
Rockville, MD 20852          301-984-6200
                         FAX: 301-881-7159
                              www.nccbh.org

*Linda Rosenberg, Chief Executive Officer*

Information on promoting advocacy, action and association for people with mental disabilities.
*Monthly*

**6672 Public Technology**
US Department of Transportation
Urban Mass Transportation Adm
Washington, DC 20016          202-366-4000

*J Rutter, Chief Executive Officer*

One of a series of reports concerned with improving transportation for elderly and disabled persons.
*28 pages*

**6673 Ragged Edge Magazine**
Advocado Press
PO Box 145
Louisville, KY 40201          502-894-9492
                         FAX: 502-899-9562
          e-mail: circulation@raggededgemagazine.com
                    www.raggededgemagazine.com

*Mary Johnson, Editor*

Ragged Edge magazine is the successor to The Disability Rag, and covers disability in America today: rights, culture, ideas and controversy. Here you'll find new voices speaking out about disability culture and lives; you'll get the newest cutting-edge thinking on headlines in the news today on genetic discrimination, assisted suicide, healthcare policy. *$17.50*
*40 pages BiMonthly*
*ISSN 0749-95 6*

**6674 Rehabilitation Counseling Bulletin**
American Counseling Association
5999 Stevenson Avenue
Alexandria, VA 22304          703-823-9800
                              800-347-6647
                         FAX: 800-473-2329
                              TTY: 7038236862
                              www.counseling.org

*Randall M Parker, Editor*
*Richard Yep, Executive Director*

A research journal for professionals in rehabilitation counseling. *$18.00*

*64 pages Quarterly*

**6675 Rehabilitation Counseling: Profession & Pr actice**
Springer Publishing Company
536 Broadway
New York, NY 10012          212-431-4370
                              877-687-7476
                              877-687-7976
                         FAX: 212-941-7842
          e-mail: marketing@springerpub.com
                    www.springerpub.com

*Annette Imperati, Marketing/Sales Director*
*Ursula Springer, President*

*$49.95*
*392 pages*
*ISBN 0-826195-10-5*

**6676 Rehabilitation Psychology**
Springer Publishing Company
536 Broadway
New York, NY 10012          212-431-4370
                              877-687-7476
                         FAX: 212-941-7842
          e-mail: marketing@springerpub.com
                    www.springerpub.com

*Annette Imperati, Marketing/Sales Director*
*Ursula Springer, President*

Publishes articles addressing psychological and behavioral aspects of rehabilitation. *$28.00*

**6677 Saint Anthony's Healthcare Resources Alert**
Saint Anthony Publishing
11410 Isaac Newton Square S
Reston, VA 20190          703-904-3900
                              800-632-0123
                         FAX: 703-707-5700

*Suzanne Vel, Jr Product Manager*
*Mary Randell, Sales Executive*

News, resources and services for practicing healthcare professionals.

**6678 School Psychology Review**
National Association of School Psychologists
4340 Ew Highway
Suite 402
Bethesda, MD 20814          301-657-0270
                         FAX: 301-657-0275
          e-mail: inealis@naspweb.org
                    www.nasponline.org

*Susan Gorin, Executive Director*
*$75.00*
*2150 pages Quarterly*

**6679 Sexuality and Disability**
Human Sciences Press
233 Spring Street
New York, NY 10013          212-620-8000
                              800-221-9369
                         FAX: 212-463-0742
                              www.wkap.com

*Rudiger Gebauer, Owner*

A journal devoted to the psychological and medical aspects of sexuality in rehabilitation and community settings. The journal features original scholarly articles that address the psychological and medical aspects of sexuality in the field of rehabilitation, case studies, clinical practice reports, and guidelines for clinical practice. Plenum Publishers is now part of Kluner Academic Publishers. Journal fulfillment in the NYC office as before for HSP and Plenum Journals. *$160.00*

*64 pages Quarterly*
*ISSN 0146-10 4*

**6680 Smart But Stuck: Emotional Aspects of Learning Disabilities and Imprisoned Intelligence**
Haworth Press
10 Alice Street
Binghamton, NY 13904 607-722-5857
800-429-6784
FAX: 607-722-6362
e-mail: orders@haworthpress.com
www.haworthpress.com

*S Harrington-Miller, Advertising*
*William Cohen, Owner*

Elaborates on new research about imprisoned intelligence and the emotional consequences of learning disabilities. It is also for psychoterapists, educators, school social workers, medical personnel, people dealing with prisons, etc. It helps those who struggle with learning disabilities (and people who help them) build self esteem, face LD obstacles, bypass weaknesses, and enhance strenghts. *$34.95*
*228 pages Hardcover*
*ISBN 0-789014-66-1*

**6681 Social Perceptions of People with Disabilities in History**
Charles C Thomas
2600 S 1st Street
Springfield, IL 62704 217-789-8980
800-258-8980
FAX: 217-789-9130
e-mail: books@ccthomas.com
www.ccthomas.com

*Michael Thomas, President*

This book helps to develop a social history on disabilities by providing a multidisciplinary overview of images of people with disabilities in Western history; promotion the exchange of cross-disciplinary information on disabled people from art, literature, original data, and historical works. With the growing interest in people with disabilities and the recent passage of the American Disability Act, this book will be of interest to special educators, humanities students, and social scientists. *$49.95*
*324 pages Paperback 1998*
*ISBN 0-398068-38-0*

**6682 Special Talents, Special Needs: Drama for People With Learning Disabilities**
Tayylor & Francis Group

Handbook for educators and facilitators working with learning disabled people in creative expression through drama. Offers a step-by-step guide to operating a drama group. *$29.95*
*186 pages Paperback 1999*
*ISBN 1-853025-61-5*

**6683 Starting and Sustaining Genetic Support Gr oups**
Johns Hopkins University Press

Guide to the establishment and maintenance of genetic support groups for individuals with genetic disorders and their families. For therapists and group leaders. Discusses practical matters including finding a leader, fund-raising, organizing peer support training programs. *$21.95*
*152 pages 1996*
*ISBN 0-801852-64-1*

**6684 Sterilization of People with Mental Disabilities**
Greenwood Publishing Group
88 Post Road W
Suite 5007
Westport, CT 06880 203-226-3571
FAX: 203-222-1502
www.greenwood.com

*Wayne Smith, President*

An examination of the medical and legal trends in sterilization with an emphasis on people with disabilities. Hardcover.

*280 pages $59.95 - $65*
*ISBN 0-865692-25-4*

**6685 Strategic Health Care Marketing**
Health Care Communications
11 Heritage Lane
Rye, NY 10580 845-687-2328

*Michele Von Dambrowski, Editor*

Marketing strategies for hospitals, medical group practices, home health services, urgent care centers.
*12 pages Monthly*

**6686 Substance Abuse and Physical Disability**
Haworth Press
10 Alice Street
Binghamton, NY 13904 607-722-5857
800-429-6784
FAX: 607-722-6362
e-mail: orders@haworthpress.com
www.haworthpress.com

*William Cohen, Owner*

This book offers information on alcohol and drug abuse being a contributing factor in traumatic and disabling injuries. *$ 74.95*
*289 pages Hardcover*
*ISBN 1-560242-89-2*

**6687 Teaching Dressing Skills: Buttons, Bows and More**
Therapro
225 Arlington Street
Framingham, MA 01702 508-872-9494
800-257-5376
FAX: 508-875-2062
e-mail: info@theraproducts.com
www.theraproducts.com

*Karen Conrad, Owner*

Teaches us how to teach children and adults of varying abilities how to tie shoes, button buttons, use zippers and put on/remove clothing. Developed by an experienced occupational therapist, these methods have been successfully used with many children. Each task is broken down with each step clearly illustrated and specific verbal directions given to avoid confusion and to eliminate verbalization that can distract the learner. *$9.95*
*5 pages Pamphlets*

**6688 TeamRehab Report**
PO Box 8987
Malibu, CA 90265 310-317-4522
800-543-4116
FAX: 310-317-9644

*Andria Segedy, Publisher*
*Kim Pfaff, Managing Editor*

A magazine for rehab professionals who prescribe, purchase or recommend assistive technology and related services for clients who are permanently disabled. *$24.00*
*48 pages Monthly*

**6689 The Asha Leader**
10801 Rockville Pike
Rockville, MD 20852 301-897-5700
800-638-8255
FAX: 301-897-7348
e-mail: actioncenter@asha.org
www.asha.org

*Lawrence Higdon, President*
*Arlene A Pietranton, Executive Director*
*Joanne Jessen, Publications Director*

*$80.00*

*33 pages 2 Monthly*

**6690  What Psychotherapists Should Know about Disabilty**
Through the Looking Glass
2198 6th Street
Suite 100
Berkeley, CA  94710                    510-848-1112
                                       800-644-2666
                              FAX: 510-848-4445
                    e-mail: TLG@lookingglass.org
                                www.lookingglass.org

*R Olkin*
*Mega Kirshbaum, Executive Director*

*$24.00*
          *368 pages*

**6691  Women with Visible & Invisible Disabilitie es: Multiple Intersections, Issues, Therapies**
Haworth Press
10 Alice Street
Binghamton, NY  13904                  607-722-5857
                                       800-429-6784
                              FAX: 607-722-6362
               e-mail: orders@haworthpress.com
                                www.haworthpress.com

*Martha E Banks PhD, Co-Editor*
*Ellyn Kaschak PhD, Co-Editor*
*S Harrington-Miller, Advertising*

Addesses the issues faced by women with disabilities, examines the social construction of disability, and makes suggestions for the development and modification of culturally relevant therapy to meet the needs fo disabled women. *$69.95*
          *418 pages Hardcover*
          *ISBN 0-789019-36-1*

## Specific Disabilities

**6692  A Miracle to Believe In**
Option Indigo Press
2080 S Undermountain Road
Sheffield, MA  01257                    413-229-8727
                                        800-714-2779
                               FAX: 413-229-8727
                        e-mail: indigo@bcn.net
                         www.optionindigo.com
A group of people from all walks of life come together and are transformed as they reach out, under the direction of the Kaufmans, to help a little boy the medical world had given up as hopeless. This heartwarming journey of loving a child back to life will not only inspire you, the reader, but presents a compelling new way to deal with life's traumas and difficulties.
          *379 pages 1981*
          *ISBN 0-449201-08-2*

**6693  ABC of Asthma, Allergies & Lupus**
Global Health Solutions
2146 Kings Garden Way
Falls Church, VA  22043                 703-848-2333
                                        800-759-3999
                               FAX: 703-848-0028
               e-mail: shipping@watercure.com
                             www.watercure.com

*Kristin Swan, Secretary*
*Joy Barber, Secretary*
*Xiaopo Batmanghelidj, President*

*$17.00*
          *240 pages 2000*
          *ISBN 0-962994-26-x*

**6694  ADD/ADHD Behavior-Change Resource Kit**
Jossey-Bass

For teachers, couselors and parents, this resource offers information and practical strategies to help kids with attention deficits learn to control and change their own behaviors and build the academic, social, and personal skills necessary for success iun scholl and in life. The kit first explains ADD/ADHD behavior, its biological bases and basic characteristics and describes procedures used for diagnosis and various treatment options. *$29.95*
          *416 pages 2002*
          *ISBN 0-876281-44-7*

**6695  ADD/ADHD Checklist**
Jossey-Bass

This resource supplies up-to-date facts, findings, and proven strategies and techniques for understanding and helping children and adolescents with attention deficit problems and hyperactivity. *$ 12.95*
          *272 pages 2002*
          *ISBN 0-137623-95-X*

**6696  ADHD: Handbook for Diagnosis & Treatment**
Western Psychological Services
12031 Wilshire Boulevard
Los Angeles, CA  90025                  310-478-2061
                                        800-648-8857
                               FAX: 310-478-7838

*Gregg Gillmar, Vice President*

This second edition helps clinicians diagnose and treat Attention Deficit Hyperactivity Disorder. Written by an internationally recognized authority in the field, it covers the history of ADHD, its primary symptoms, associated conditions, developmental course and outcome, and family context. A workbook companion manual is also available. *$ 68.00*
          *700 pages*

**6697  AJAO Newsletter**
American Juvenile Arthritis Organization
PO Box 7669
Atlanta, GA  30357                      404-872-7100
                                        800-283-7800
                               FAX: 404-872-9559
                    e-mail: help@arthritis.org
                                www.arthritis.org

*Janet Austin MEd, Editor*
*John Klippel, Chief Executive Officer*

Offers information and updates about the organization's activities and events. Legislative information, medical updates, camp information and more for children living with arthritis.
          *Quarterly*

**6698  Adolescents with Down Syndrome: Toward a More Fulfilling Life**
Brookes Publishing
PO Box 10624
Baltimore, MD  21285                    410-337-9580
                                        800-638-3775
                               FAX: 410-337-8539
          e-mail: custserv@brookespublishing.com
                          www.brookespublishing.com

*Paul Brooks, Owner*

Written for health care professionals, psychologists, other developmental disabilities practitioners, educators, and parents, it covers biomedical concerns; behavioral, psychological, and psychiatric challenges; and education, employment, recreation, community, and legal concerns. *$35.95*

*416 pages Paperback 1997*
*ISBN 1-55766-81-9*

**6699    Adult ADD: The Complete Handbook: Everyt hing You Need to Know About How to Cope with ADD**
Prima Publishing
PO Box 1260
Rocklin, CA 95677                                    916-787-7000
                                                     800-632-8676
                                            FAX: 916-787-7001
                        e-mail: websupportlife@primapub.com
                                    www.primapublishing.com
In simple and friendly terms, the authors offer help to those leading frustrating lives. They provide coping mechanisms, both psychological and an up-to-date guide to the latest technology *$14.95*
            *272 pages 1997*
            *ISBN 0-761507-96-5*

**6700    Adult Leukemia: A Comprehensive Guide for Patients and Families**
Patients-Centered Guides
101 Morris Street
Sebastopol, CA 95472                                 707-829-0515
                                                     800-998-9938
                                            FAX: 707-829-0104
                                    www.patientcenters.com

*Linda Lamb, Editor*
*Shawnde Paull, Marketing*
*Tim O'Reilly, Chief Executive Officer*

For the tens of thousands of Americans with adult leukemia, Adult Leukemia: A Comprehensive Guide for Patients and Families addresses diagnosis, medical tests, finding a good oncologist, treatments, side effects, getting emotional and other support, resources for further study, and much more. The book includes real-life stories from those who have battled leukemia themselves. *$29.95*
            *536 pages Paperback*
            *ISBN 0-596500-01-7*

**6701    Advanced Breast Cancer: A Guide to Living with Metastic Disease**
Patients-Centered Guides
101 Morris Street
Sebastopol, CA 95472                                 707-829-0515
                                                     800-998-9938
                                            FAX: 707-829-0104
                                    www.patientcenters.com

*Linda Lamb, Editor*
*Shawnde Paull, Marketing*
*Tim O'Reilly, Chief Executive Officer*

This is the only book on breast cancer that deals honestly with the realities of living with metastic disease, yet offers hope and comfort. All aspects of facing the disease are covered, including: coping with the shock of recurrence, seeking information and making treatment decisions, communicating effectively with medical personnel finding support, and handling disease progression and end-of-life issues. A comprehensive guide, it also provides updated resources and treatment developments. *$24.95*
            *532 pages Paperback*
            *ISBN 1-565925-22-X*

**6702    Advanced Diagnosis and Treatment for Neck and Back Pain**
American Back Society
2647 International Boulevard
Suite 401
Oakland, CA 94601                                    510-536-9929
                                            FAX: 510-536-1812
                        e-mail: info@americanbacksoc.org
                                    www.americanbacksoc.org

*Nedra Swartz, Manager*

A membership organization dedicated to relieving the pain and impairment caused by back problems. Sponsors symposia for presenting research findings.

**6703    Adventures in Fast Forward: Life, Love, a nd Work for the ADD Adult**
Taylor & Francis
47 Runway Drive
Suite G
Levittown, PA 19057                                  215-269-0400
                                            FAX: 215-625-2940

*Harold Stecker, President*

The Q&A format provides access to the following queries: do I have ADD? What are the symptoms? Would I be taking medication? How can I manage the condition? How do I explain ADD to the significant people in my life? Why can't my spouse understand me? Is this the right job for me? Are there techniques to increase my memory? Can I go back to college and do well? Does ADD affect men and women differently? What should I consider when choosing a doctor or therapist? *$23.95*
            *210 pages 1996*
            *ISBN 0-876308-00-0*

**6704    After School and More**
Resources for Children with Special Needs
116 E 16th Street
Floor 5
New York, NY 10003                                   212-677-4650
                                            FAX: 212-254-4070
                        e-mail: info@resourcesnyc.org
                                    www.resourcesnyc.org

*Karen Schlesinger, Executive Director*
*Dianne Littwin, Director Publications*

Published every 24-36 months. *$25.00*
            *240 pages*
            *ISBN 0-967836-55-7*

**6705    Alive at 25: How I'm Beating Cystic Fibro sis**
Longstreet Press
325 N Milledge Avenue
Athens, GA 30601                                     706-543-5999
                                            FAX: 404-254-0016
                        e-mail: info@longstreetpress.com
                                    www.longstreetpress.com
The author's personal journey of dealing with a deadly disease. *$24.95*
            *256 pages*
            *ISBN 1-563526-81-6*

**6706    All About Attention Deficit Disorders, Revised**
Parent Magic
800 Roosevelt Road
Glen Ellyn, IL 60137                                 630-790-9600
                                            FAX: 630-469-4571
                                    www.parentmagic.com

*Nancy Roe, Office Manager*
*Thomas Phelan, Owner*

A psychologist and expert on ADD outlines the symptoms, diagnosis and treatment of this neurological disorder. *$12.95*
            *248 pages Paperback*
            *ISBN 1-889140-11-2*

**6707    Allergies Sourcebook, 2nd Edition**
Omnigraphics
615 Griswold Street
Detroit, MI 48226                                    313-961-1340
                                                     800-234-1340
                                            FAX: 800-875-1340
                                    www.omnigraphics.com

*Peter Ruffner, President*

Includes information on the causes of allergies, identification, treatments and statistics. *$78.00*

*650 pages 2000*
*ISBN 0-780803-76-0*

**6708  Alternative Medicine and Multiple Sclerosis**
Demos Medical Publishing
386 Park Avenue S
Suite 201
New York, NY  10016                    212-683-0072
                                       800-532-8663
                          FAX: 212-683-0118
                 e-mail: orderdep@demospub.com
                          www.demosmedpub.com

*Diana Schneider PhD, President*
*Phyllis Gold, Owner*

Offers reliable information on the relevance, safety, and effectiveness of various alternative therapies that are not typically considered in discussions of MS management, yet are in widespread use. *$24.95*
*272 pages 2001*
*ISBN 1-888799-52-8*

**6709  American Heart Association Guide to Stroke Treatment, Recovery & Prevention**
Random House
1540 Broadway
New York, NY  10036                    212-782-9000
                                       800-726-0600
                          FAX: 212-302-7985
          e-mail: customerservice@randonhouse.com
                          www.randomhouse.com

*Peter Olson, Chief Executive Officer*

From the nation's premier authority on heart disease and stroke, the definitive book on stroke prevention, treatment and recovery. *$29.00*
*304 pages*

**6710  Amputations and Prosthetics: A Case Study Approach**
FA Davis Company

Emphasizes the decision-making process of the physical therapist and the role of the physical therapy assistant. *$37.95*
*256 pages 2001*
*ISBN 0-803608-39-X*

**6711  Amyotrophic Lateral Sclerosis: A Guide for Patients and Families**
Demos Medical Publishing
386 Park Avenue S
Suite 201
New York, NY  10016                    212-683-0072
                                       800-532-8663
                          FAX: 212-683-0118
                 e-mail: orderdep@demospub.com
                          www.demosmedpub.com

*Diana Schneider PhD, President*
*Phyllis Gold, Owner*

This comprehensive guide covers every aspect of the management of ALS. Beginning with discussions of its clinical features of the disease, diagnosis, and an overview of symptom management, major sections deal with medical and rehabilitative management, living with ALS, managing advanced disease and end-of-life issues, and reources that can provide support and assistance. *$34.95*
*350 pages 2000*
*ISBN 1-888799-28-5*

**6712  Annals of Dyslexia**
International Dyslexia Association
382 S Chester Street
Baltimore, MD  21231
                                       800-ABC-D123
                          FAX: 410-296-0232
                          www.interdys.org
Offers information on auditory discrimination, dyslexia, attitudes, advocacy and more on people with learning disabilities. *$ 15.00*

*Paper*

**6713  Answering Your Questions About Spina Bifid a**
Spina Bifida Association of America
4590 Macarthur Boulevard NW
Suite 250
Washington, DC 20007                   202-944-3285
                                       800-621-3141
                          FAX: 202-944-3295
                     e-mail: sbaa@sbaa.org
                          www.sbaa.org

*Cindy Brownstein, Chief Executive Officer*

Provides information to help you understand the basic medical, educational and socail issues which commonly affect people with spina bifida. *$8.00*

**6714  Aphasia**
Federal Government
31 Center Drive Msc2320
Bethesda, MD  20892
                                       800-241-1044
                          FAX: 301-402-0018
             e-mail: nidcdinfo@nidcd.nih.gov
             www.aphasia.org/NAAfactsheet.html
This fact sheet explains who has aphasia, the causes of aphasia, how aphasia is diagnosed and treated, and what research is being conducted on aphasia.

**6715  Aphasia: What is It?**
Speech Bin
1965 25th Avenue
Vero Beach, FL  32960                  772-770-0007
                                       800-477-3324
                          FAX: 772-770-0006
                          www.speechbin.com
Brochures for families and caregivers of persons who have suffered aphasic language disorders secondary to strokes. Set of ten copies. *$14.95*
*16 pages Package of 10*
*ISBN 0-93785 -56-4*

**6716  Arthritis 101: Questions You Have Answers You Need**
Arthritis Foundation Distribution Center
PO Box 6996
Alpharetta, GA  30023
                                       800-207-8633
                          FAX: 770-442-9742
                          www.arthritis.com
Expert reviewers answer questions about basic arthritis facts, treatments, research, surgery and more. Also, specific information about six common conditions: rheumatoid arthritis, osteoarthritis, osteoporosis, fibromyalgia, lupus and gout. *$11.95*
*144 pages*

**6717  Arthritis Accent**
Arthritis Foundation Southern N.E. Chapter
35 Cold Spring Road
Suite 411
Rocky Hill, CT  06067                  860-563-1177
                                       800-541-8350
                          FAX: 860-563-6018
                e-mail: inpubne@arthritis.org
                          www.arthritis.org

*Susan Nesci, Program Director - CT*
*Stephen Evangelista, President*

Offers information on chapter events and activities.

# Media, Print /Specific Disabilities

*Quarterly*

## 6718 Arthritis Bible
Healing Arts Press
1 Park Street
Rochester, VT 05767
802-767-3174
800-246-8648
FAX: 802-767-3726
e-mail: orders@innertraditions.com
www.InnerTraditions.com

*Jessica Dudley, Sales Associate*
*Ehud Sperling, Owner*

A comprehensive guide to the alternative therapies and conventional treatments for Arthritic diseases including Osteoarthritis, Rheumatoid Arthritis, Gout, Fibromyalgia and more. *$14.95*
*272 pages*
*ISBN 0-892818-25-5*

## 6719 Arthritis Foundation of Illinois News
2621 N Knoxville Avenue
Peoria, IL 61604
309-682-6600
800-795-9115
FAX: 309-682-6732
e-mail: greaterillinois@arthritis.org

*Marilynn J Cason, Chairman*
*Gary Dutro, President*

A publication offering information about the activities of the chapter. Program news, legislative information, workshops and resources are also included.
*Quarterly*

## 6720 Arthritis Foundation: Greater Southwest Chapter
1313 E Osborn Road
Suite 200
Phoenix, AZ 85014
602-264-7679
800-477-7679
FAX: 602-264-0563
e-mail: info.caz@arthritis.org
www.arthritis.org

*Sherry Ladd, Administration*
*Vikki Scarafiotti, President*

Provides information, programs and services for people affected by arthritis.
*Quarterly*

## 6721 Arthritis Helpbook
Addison-Wesley Publishing Company
75 Arlington Street
Suite 300
Boston, MA 02116
617-848-6000
617-848-6034
www.awprofessional.com

*William Barke, President*

A self-care program for coping with arthritis that includes diet, nutrition, exercise, and mind/body techniques such as guided imagery and meditation.

## 6722 Arthritis Helpbook: A Tested Self-Management Program for Coping
Addison-Wesley Publishing Company
75 Arlington Street
Suite 300
Boston, MA 02116
617-848-6000
800-238-9682
FAX: 617-848-6034
www.awprofessional.com

*William Barke, President*
*$13.50*

*288 pages 4th Edition*
*ISBN 0-201409-63-1*

## 6723 Arthritis News
Wisconsin Chapter of the Arthritis Foundation
1650 S 108th Street
Milwaukee, WI 53214
414-321-3933
FAX: 262-872-0457
e-mail: info@wi.arthritis.org
www.arthritis.org

*Dana Motley, Public Relations Coordinator*
*Kim Wilbur, Administrator*

Offers information on activities, events, medical research, information and referrals to persons living in the Wisconsin area that are afflicted with arthritis.
*8 pages Quarterly*

## 6724 Arthritis Observer
Rocky Mountain Chapter of the Arthritis Foundation
2280 S Albion Street
Denver, CO 80222
303-756-8622
800-475-6647
e-mail: sturman@arthritis.org

*Susan Turman, VP Operations*
*James Goddard, President*

Offers chapter information and updates on fund-raising events and activities, resources and publications and medical updates for the arthritis community.
*Quarterly*

## 6725 Arthritis Relief at Your Fingertips
Warner Books
1271 Avenue of the Americas
New York, NY 10020
212-522-7200
FAX: 212-522-7989
www.twbookmark.com

*Laurence Kirshbaum, Chief Executive Officer*

A self-help guide for relieving arthritis pain through exercise and acupressure massage by a leader in the field.

## 6726 Arthritis Reporter
New York Chapter of the Arthritis Foundation
122 E 42nd Street
Floor 18
New York, NY 10168
212-984-8700
FAX: 212-878-5960
e-mail: info.ny@arthritis.org
www.arthritis.org

*Phyllis Geraghty, Editor*
*Theresa Davis, Program Director*
*Ross Alfieri, President*

Chapter newsletter offering information on upcoming events, activities and groups for the arthritis community.
*Quarterly*

## 6727 Arthritis Self Help Products
Aids for Arthritis
35 Wakefield Drive
Medford, NJ 08055
609-654-6918
800-654-0707
FAX: 609-654-8631
e-mail: aidsforar@aol.com
www.aidsforarthritis.com

More than 200 arthritis self-help products for kitchen, resting, dressing, bathroom, driving, therapy and foot care. Available online or through catalog. Low prices, quick shipping, since 1979.

655

*24 pages Quarterly*

**6728 Arthritis Self-Help Book**
Addison-Wesley Publishing Company
75 Arlington Street
Suite 300
Boston, MA 02116
617-848-6000
800-238-9682
FAX: 617-848-6034
www.awprofessional.com

*William Barke, President*

A useful and informative book used in conjunction with the Arthritis Foundation's Self-Help Course. *$12.00*

**6729 Arthritis Today**
Arthritis Foundation
1330 W Peachtree Street NW
Atlanta, GA 30309
404-872-7100
FAX: 404-872-9559
www.arthritis.org

*John Klippel, Chief Executive Officer*

Magazine for patients, physicians, public authorities and others with an interest in the field of arthritis. ( Price noted paid for yearly subscription ) *$20.00*

**6730 Arthritis: A Comprehensive Guide**
Addison-Wesley Publishing Company
75 Arlington Street
Suite 300
Boston, MA 02116
617-848-6000
800-238-9682
FAX: 617-848-6034
www.awprofessional.com

*William Barke, President*

Reviews types of arthritis, different aspects of treatment including exercise, medications, surgery, the role of diet and an extensive section on challenges of daily living. *$12.00*

**6731 Arthritis: Stop Suffering, Start Moving**
Walker Publishing Company
104 5th Avenue
New York, NY 10011
212-727-8300
800-289-2553
FAX: 212-727-0984
e-mail: orders@walkerbooks.com
www.walkerbooks.com

*Ramsey Walker, Vice President*

*$22.95*
*160 pages*
*ISBN 0-802713-08-4*

**6732 Arthritis: Taking Care of Yourself Health Guide for Understanding Your Arthritis**
Addison-Wesley Publishing Company
75 Arlington Street
Suite 300
Boston, MA 02116
617-848-6000
FAX: 617-848-6034
www.awprofessional.com

*William Barke, President*

*$13.50*
*4th Edition*
*ISBN 0-201409-17-8*

**6733 Arthritis: What Exercises Work**
St. Martin's Press
175 5th Avenue
New York, NY 10010
212-674-5151
800-221-7945
FAX: 212-420-9314

*John Sargent, Chief Executive Officer*
*$19.95*

*160 pages*
*ISBN 0-312097-43-3*

**6734 Arthritis: Your Complete Exercise Guide**
Human Kinetics Press
PO Box 5076
Champaign, IL 61825
217-351-5076
FAX: 217-351-2674
e-mail: orders@hkusa.com
www.humankinetics.com

*Rainer Martens, President*

The Cooper Clinic and Research Institute Fitness Series provides an exercise rehabilitation alternative for people with chronic medical conditions. *$13.95*
*152 pages Paperback*
*ISBN 0-873223-92-6*

**6735 Ask the Doctor: Asthma**
Andrews McMeel Publishing
4520 Main Street
Kansas City, MO 64111
816-932-6700
800-826-4216
FAX: 800-437-8683

*Kathleen Andrews, Chief Executive Officer*
*$8.95*
*128 pages Soft Cover*
*ISBN 0-836270-23-1*

**6736 Asperger's Syndrome: A Guide for Parents a nd Professionals**
Taylor & Francis Group

A guide to the most relevant and useful information on Asperger's Syndrome, incorporating case studies from the author's own practical experience as a Clinical Psychologist, with examples of, and numerous quotations from people with Asperger's. *$22.95*
*256 pages 2002*
*ISBN 1-843107-14-7*

**6737 Asthma & Allergy Advocate Newsletter**
Academy of Allergy, Asthma, Immunology
611 E Wells Street
Milwaukee, WI 53202
414-272-6071
800-822-2762
FAX: 414-272-6070
e-mail: info@aaaai.org
www.aaaai.org

*Kay Whalen, Executive Vice President*

Offers tips and medical information on allergies and asthmatic conditions including the newest treatments and public awareness news. *$6.00*
*4 pages Quarterly*

**6738 Asthma Challenge**
Asthma and Allergy Foundation of America
1125 15th Street NW
Suite 502
Washington, DC 20005
202-466-7643
FAX: 202-466-8940
e-mail: info@aafa.org
www.aafa.org

*Bill Lin, Executive Director*

Fun and engaging activity to assess asthma knowledge. This custom designed, full colored stand up board comes with two sets of pre-tested question cards and can be used with large or small groups. Players test their knowledge in categories like Sneezes and Wheezes, and Nuts and Bolts. *$50.00*

**6739 Asthma Resource Directory**
National Allergy and Asthma Network
3554 Chain Bridge Road
Suite 200
Fairfax, VA 22030
703-385-4403
FAX: 703-352-4354

Valuable reference tool with over 2,500 listings of resources and products nationwide including suppliers, camps, research centers and support groups.

**6740  Asthma Sourcebook**
Omnigraphics
615 Griswold Street
Detroit, MI  48226                     313-961-1340
                                        800-234-1340
                                   FAX: 800-875-1340
                                   www.omnigraphics.com

*Annemarie S Muth, Editor*
*Peter Ruffner, President*

Provides information about asthma, including symptoms, remedies and research updates. *$78.00*
*650 pages 2000*
*ISBN 0-780803-81-7*

**6741  Asthma and Exercise**
Henry Holt and Company
3554 Chain Bridge Road
Suite 200
Fairfax, VA  22030                     703-385-4403
                                   FAX: 703-352-4354
This book offers clear and detailed advice on how adults and children with asthma can participate in exercise and sports activities. *$10.00*

**6742  Asthma in the School: Improving Control with Peak Flow Monitoring**
National Allergy and Asthma Network
3554 Chain Bridge Road
Suite 200
Fairfax, VA  22030                     703-385-4403
                                   FAX: 703-352-4354
Comprehensive and practical guide to help the school nurse monitor and assist students with asthma. *$7.00*

**6743  Asthma in the Workplace**
John H Dekker & Sons
2941 Clydon Avenue SW
Grand Rapids, MI  49519                616-538-5160
                                   FAX: 616-538-0720

*John Dekker, President*
*$199.00*
*664 pages*
*ISBN 0-824787-99-4*

**6744  Attention**
Children & Adults with ADHD
8181 Professional Place
Suite 150
Landover, MD  20785                    301-306-7070
                                        800-233-4050
                                   FAX: 301-306-6788
                                   www.chadd.org

*Clarke Ross, CEO*
*Karen White, Director Natl Resource Center*
*Marsha Bokamn, Manager*

A bi-monthly publication from CHADD. Free with membership.

*bi-monthly*

**6745  Attention Deficit Disorder and Learning Disabilities**
Books on Special Children
PO Box 305
Congers, NY  10920                     845-638-1236
                                   FAX: 845-638-0847
                                   e-mail: irene@boscbooks.com
Introduces ADD and learning disabilities. This is an easy reading book. Gives definitions and discusses some effective and controverial medication, dietary, biofeedback, cognitive therapy, and many more issues. *$15.95*

*246 pages Softcover*
*ISBN 0-385469-31-4*

**6746  Attention Deficit Disorder in Adults Workbook**
Taylor Publishing Company
1550 W Mockingbird Lane
Dallas, TX  75235                      214-637-2800
                                   FAX: 214-819-8580

*Don Percenti, Chief Executive Officer*
*$17.99*
*192 pages Paperback*
*ISBN 0-878338-50-0*

**6747  Attention Deficit Disorder: A Different Perception**
Underwood-Miller
708 Westover Drive
Lancaster, PA  17601                   717-285-2255
                                   FAX: 717-285-2255
*$9.95*
*180 pages Paperback*
*ISBN 0-887331-56-4*

**6748  Attention-Deficit Hyperactivity Disorder: Symptoms and Suggestons for Treatment**
Slosson Educational Publications
PO Box 280
East Aurora, NY  14052                 716-652-0930
                                   FAX: 800-655-3840
                                   e-mail: slosson@slosson.com
                                   www.slosson.com

*Leslie Foote, Office Personnel*
*Peggy Meyer, Office Personnel*
*Steven Slosson, President*

An exhaustive review of current research and decades of experience as practicing school-based professionals, as well as being a parent of an ADHD child, have culminated in this brief, to-the-point, and yet informed ADHD package which has recieved tremendous reviews. Well-grounded answers and suggestions which would facillitate behavior, learning, social-emotional functioning, and other factors in preschool and adolesence are discussed. Answers most commonly asked questions about ADHD/ADD. *$60.00*
*61 pages*

**6749  Augmenting Basic Communcation in Natural Contexts**
Brookes Publishing
PO Box 10624
Baltimore, MD  21285                   410-337-9580
                                        800-638-3775
                                   FAX: 410-337-8539
                                   e-mail: custserv@brookespublishing.com
                                   www.brookespublishing.com

*Paul Brooks, Owner*

Here you will find the techniques needed to establish a basic communication system for people of all ages with cognitive disabilities or motor sensory impairments. *$41.95*
*304 pages Paperback*
*ISBN 1-55766-43-6*

**6750  Autism**
Autism Society of North Carolina Bookstore
505 Oberlin Road
Suite 230
Raleigh, NC  27605                     919-743-0204
                                        800-442-2762
                                   FAX: 919-743-0208
                                   e-mail: dcoffey@autismsociety-nc.org
                                   www.autismsociety-nc.org

*Darla Coffey, Bookstore Manager*
*Jill Keel, Executive Director*

Everything there is to know about autism research book. *$17.95*

**6751 Autism Handbook: Understanding & Treating Autism & Prevention Development**
Oxford University Press
2001 Evans Road
Cary, NC 27513
919-677-0977
800-451-7556
FAX: 919-677-1303
www.oup-usa.org

*Thomas Carty, Senior Vice President*

*$25.00*
*320 pages*
*ISBN 0-195076-67-2*

**6752 Autism Research Institute**
4182 Adams Avenue
San Diego, CA 92116
619-281-7165
FAX: 619-563-6840
www.autism.com/ari

*Bernard Rimland PhD, Executive Director*

Offers information and conducts research on autism and related disorders. Please write for info. *$18.00*
*8 pages Qtrly. nwsltr.*

**6753 Autism Treatment Guide**
Autism Society of North Carolina Bookstore
505 Oberlin Road
Suite 230
Raleigh, NC 27605
919-743-0204
800-442-2762
FAX: 919-743-0208
e-mail: dcoffey@autismsociety-nc.org
www.autismsociety-nc.org

*Darla Coffey, Bookstore Manager*
*Jill Keel, Executive Director*

A comprehensive book covering treatments and methods used to help individuals with autism. *$12.95*

**6754 Autism and Asperger Syndrome**
Autism Society of North Carolina Bookstore
505 Oberlin Road
Suite 230
Raleigh, NC 27605
919-743-0204
800-442-2762
FAX: 919-743-0208
e-mail: dcoffey@autismsociety-nc.org
www.autismsociety-nc.org

*Darla Coffey, Bookstore Manager*
*Jill Keel, Executive Director*

Chapters include topics such as the relationship of autism and asperger syndrome, living with the syndrome and asperger syndrome in adulthood. *$23.95*

**6755 Autism and Learning**
David Fulton Publishers
2 Barbon Close Great Ormond Street
London, WCIN
171-405-5606
FAX: 171-831-4840
This book is about how a cognitive perception on the way in which individuals with autism think and learn may be applied to particular curriculum areas.
*160 pages Paperback*
*ISBN 1-853464-21-X*

**6756 Autism in Adolescents and Adults**
Plenum Publishing Corporation
233 Spring Street
New York, NY 10013
212-242-1490
FAX: 212-463-0742
e-mail: info@plenum.com

*$63.00*

*456 pages*
*ISBN 0-306410-57-5*

**6757 Autism...Nature, Diagnosis and Treatment**
Autism Society of North Carolina Bookstore
505 Oberlin Road
Suite 230
Raleigh, NC 27605
919-743-0204
800-442-2762
FAX: 919-743-0208
e-mail: dcoffey@autismsociety-nc.org
www.autismsociety-nc.org

*Darla Coffey, Bookstore Manager*
*Jill Keel, Executive Director*

Covers perspectives, issues, neurobiological issues and new directions in diagnosis and treatment. *$49.00*

**6758 Autism: A Strange, Silent World**
Filmakers Library
124 E 40th Street
New York, NY 10016
212-808-4980
FAX: 212-808-4983
e-mail: info@filmakers.com
www.filmakers.com

*Sue Oscar, Co-President/Owner*

British educators and medical personnel offer insight into autism's characteristics and treatment approaches through the cameos of three children.

**6759 Autism: Explaining the Enigma**
Autism Society of North Carolina Bookstore
505 Oberlin Road
Suite 230
Raleigh, NC 27605
919-743-0204
800-442-2762
FAX: 919-743-0208
e-mail: dcoffey@autismsociety-nc.org
www.autismsociety-nc.org

*Darla Coffey, Bookstore Manager*
*Jill Keel, Executive Director*

Explains the nature of autism. *$27.95*

**6760 Autism: From Tragedy to Triumph**
Branden Publishing Company
17 Station Street
Brookline, MA 02445
617-734-2045
FAX: 781-790-1056
e-mail: branden@branden.com
www.branden.com
A new book that deals with the Lovaas method and includes a foreward by Dr. Ivar Lovaas. The book is broken down into two parts — the long road to diagnosis and then treatment. *$12.95*

**6761 Autism: Identification, Education and Treatment**
Autism Society of North Carolina Bookstore
505 Oberlin Road
Suite 230
Raleigh, NC 27605
919-743-0204
800-442-2762
FAX: 919-743-0208
e-mail: dcoffey@autismsociety-nc.org
www.autismsociety-nc.org

*Darla Coffey, Bookstore Manager*
*Jill Keel, Executive Director*

Chapters include medical treatments, early intervention and communication development in autism. *$36.00*

**6762 Autism: The Facts**
Oxford University Press
2001 Evans Road
Cary, NC 27513
919-677-0977
800-451-7556
FAX: 919-677-1303
www.oup-usa.org

*Thomas Carty, Senior Vice President*

$19.95
*128 pages*
*ISBN 0-192623-28-1*

**6763  Autistic Adults at Bittersweet Farms**
Haworth Press
10 Alice Street
Binghamton, NY  13904
607-722-5857
800-429-6784
FAX: 607-722-6362
e-mail: orders@haworthpress.com
www.haworthpress.com

*Norman Giddan PhD, Editor*
*Jane Giddan MA, Editor*
*William Cohen, Owner*

A touching view of an inspirational residential care program for autistic adolescents and adults. Also available in softcover. *$94.95*
*Hardcover*
*ISBN 1-560240-42-3*

**6764  Awareness Posters**
Spina Bifida Association of America
4590 Macarthur Boulevard NW
Suite 250
Washington, DC 20007
202-944-3285
800-621-3141
FAX: 202-944-3295
e-mail: sbaa@sbaa.org
www.sbaa.org

*Cindy Brownstein, Chief Executive Officer*

An aid for building community awareness of Spina Bifida and the need for adequate amounts of folic acid in pregnant women. *$7.00*

**6765  Away with Arthritis**
Vantage Press
516 W 34th Street
New York, NY  10001
212-736-1767
FAX: 212-736-2273

*Martin Kleinwald, President*
*$12.50*

*ISBN 0-533108-14-4*

**6766  Biology of the Autistic Syndromes, 2nd Edition**
Autism Society of North Carolina Bookstore
505 Oberlin Road
Suite 230
Raleigh, NC  27605
919-743-0204
800-442-2762
FAX: 919-743-0208
e-mail: dcoffey@autismsociety-nc.org
www.autismsociety-nc.org

*Darla Coffey, Bookstore Manager*
*Jill Keel, Executive Director*

A revision of the original classic text in the light of new developments and current knowledge. This book covers the epidemiological, genetic, biochemical, immunological and neuropsychological literature on autism. *$74.95*

**6767  Bittersweet Chances: A Personal Journey o f Living and Learning in the Face of Illness**
PublishAmerica

Recounts Doug and Dana Broehl's journey of growth through the darkness of cystic fibrosis and the renewed hope of a double lung transplant. *$19.95*

*192 pages 2004*
*ISBN 1-413713-24-6*

**6768  Blooming Where You're Planted**
Meeting Life's Challenges
9042 Aspen Grove Lane
Madison, WI  53717
608-824-0402
FAX: 608-824-0403
e-mail: help@MeetingLifesChallenges.com
www.MeetingLifesChallenges.com

Author Shelley Peterman Schwarz takes you on her journey of self-discovery and change following her diagnosis of multiple sclerosis in 1979. Her personal stories are warm and humorous, and insightful. This 138-page book will motivate and inspire you to rise above life's challenges and live life to its fullest. *$12.95*
*138 pages*
*ISBN 0-891854-01-1*

**6769  Bone Up on Arthritis**
Arthritis Foundation
PO Box 6996
Alpharetta, GA  30023
800-207-8633
FAX: 770-442-9742
www.arthritis.com

A self-help education packet designed for home-study use, this program can improve your pain and function levels by teaching proven self-help techniques. *$19.50*
*w/Audio Tapes*

**6770  Bowel Cancer**
Oxford University Press
2001 Evans Road
Cary, NC  27513
919-677-0977
800-451-7556
FAX: 919-677-1303
www.oup-usa.org

*Thomas Carty, Senior Vice President*

Offers information and public awareness on the disease of bowel cancer. *$18.95*
*152 pages*

**6771  Bowel Management: A Manual of Ideas and Techniques**

Accent Books & Products
PO Box 700
Bloomington, IL  61702
309-378-2961
800-787-8444
FAX: 309-378-4420
e-mail: acmtlvng@aol.com

*Raymond C Cheever, Publisher*
*Betty Garee, Editor*

Paras and quads can gain much greater freedom. Includes considerations as frequency, timing, water intake, exercise and successful programs from three rehab centers. *$3.50*
*25 pages Paperback*
*ISBN 0-91570 -02-7*

**6772  Breaking the Patterns of Depression**
Main Street Books

The author presents skills that enable readers to understand and ultimately avert depression's recurring cycles. Focusing on future prevention as well as initial treatment, the book includes over one hundred structured activities to help sufferers learn the skills necessary to become and remain depression-free. *$13.95*

*362 pages 1998*
*ISBN 0-385483-70-8*

**6773  Breaking the Speech Barrier: Language Develpment Through Augmented Means**
Brookes Publishing
PO Box 10624
Baltimore, MD  21285                     410-337-9580
                                          800-638-3775
                              FAX: 410-337-8539
            e-mail: custserv@brookespublishing.com
                         www.brookespublishing.com

*Paul Brooks, Owner*

This resource describes the creation of the System for Augmenting Language (SAL) for school-age youth with mental retardation and offers important insights into the language development of children who are not learning to communicate typically. *$37.00*
*224 pages Paperback*
*ISBN 1-557663-90-4*

**6774  Breast Cancer Sourcebook**
Omnigraphics
615 Griswold Street
Detroit, MI  48226                       313-961-1340
                                          800-234-1340
                              FAX: 800-875-1340
                         www.omnigraphics.com

*Edward J Prucha, Editor*
*Peter Ruffner, President*

Provides information on the prevention of Breast Cancer, self care, treatment options, alternative therapies and diagnostic methods. *$78.00*
*600 pages 2000*
*ISBN 0-780802-44-6*

**6775  Breathing Disorders: Your Complete Exercise Guide**
Human Kinetics
PO Box 5076
Champaign, IL  61825                     217-351-5076
                                          800-747-4457
                              FAX: 217-351-1549
                      e-mail: orders@hkusa.com
                         www.humankinetics.com

*Rainer Martens, President*

*$11.95*
*144 pages Paperback*
*ISBN 0-873224-26-4*

**6776  Bronchial Asthma: Principles of Diagnosis and Treatment**
Humana Press
999 Riverview Drive
Suite 208
Totowa, NJ  07512                        973-256-1699
                              FAX: 973-256-8341

*Thomas Lanigan, Owner*

*$125.00*
*784 pages*
*ISBN 0-896032-53-1*

**6777  Building Communicative Competence with Indiv. Who Use Augmentative & Alternative Commun.**
Brookes Publishing
PO Box 10624
Baltimore, MD  21285                     410-337-9580
                                          800-638-3775
                              FAX: 410-337-8539
            e-mail: custserv@brookespublishing.com
                         www.brookespublishing.com

*Paul Brooks, Owner*

This is a hands-on instructional program offering goal-setting, teaching, and coaching methods for improving the communicative skills of people who depend on AAC systems. Appropriate for children, adolescents, and adults at any state of communicative development. *$36.95*
*336 pages Spiral-bound 1997*
*ISBN 1-55766-24-6*

**6778  Cancer Sourcebook for Women, 2nd Edition**
Omnigraphics
615 Griswold Street
Detroit, MI  48226                       313-961-1340
                                          800-234-1340
                              FAX: 800-875-1340
                         www.omnigraphics.com

*Edward J Prucha, Editor*
*Peter Ruffner, President*

Provides information on the specific forms of cancer that affect women. *$78.00*
*600 pages 2000*
*ISBN 0-780802-26-8*

**6779  Cancer Sourcebook, 3rd Edition**
Omnigraphics
615 Griswold Street
Detroit, MI  48226                       313-961-1340
                                          800-234-1340
                              FAX: 800-875-1340
                         www.omnigraphics.com

*Edward J Prucha, Editor*
*Peter Ruffner, President*

Includes information on the major forms and stages of cancer. *$78.00*
*1100 pages 2000*
*ISBN 0-780802-27-6*

**6780  Cancer Victors Journal**
International Association for Cancer Victors
5336 Harwood Road
San Jose, CA  95124                      408-448-4094
                              FAX: 408-264-9659
                         www.cancervictors.org
Published by the volunteer community service organization to inform and support interested persons who want to learn more about natural, nontoxic remedies and practices.

**6781  Cerebral Palsy: A Complete Guide for Care giving**
Johns Hopkins University Press

A guide for parents and caregivers of children and adults with cerebral palsy, as well as for adolescents and adults with the condition. *$19.95*
*465 pages 1998*
*ISBN 0-801859-49-2*

**6782  Chadder**
Children & Adults with Attention Deficit Disorder
499 NW 70th Avenue
Suite 101
Plantation, FL  33317                    954-587-3700
                                          800-233-4050
                              FAX: 954-587-4599

*Quarterly*

**6783  Change Your Brain, Change Your Life: The Breakthrough Program for Conquering Depression**
Three Rivers Press

Clinical neuroscientist and psychiatrist Amen uses nuclear brain imaging to diagnose and treat behavioral problems. He explains how the brain works, what happens when things go wrong, and how to optimize brain function. Five sections of the brain are discussed, and case studies clearly illustrate possible problems. *$15.00*

*352 pages 2000*
*ISBN 0-812929-98-5*

**6784    Charting: The Systematic Approach to Achieving Control**
RA Rapaport Publishing
150 W 22nd Street
New York, NY  10011                    212-989-0200
                                       FAX: 212-989-4786

*Jim Moorehead, Manager*

One of America's leading diabetes educators shows you, in this book, how to analyze your body's responses to diet, exercises and medication, and how to create a personalized systematic program for total diabetes control. *$3.95*
*38 pages Paperback*
*ISBN 0-96317 -10-*

**6785    Chesity**
Spina Bifida Association of America
4590 Macarthur Boulevard NW
Suite 250
Washington, DC 20007                   202-944-3285
                                       800-621-3141
                                   FAX: 202-944-3295
                              e-mail: sbaa@sbaa.org
                                       www.sbaa.org

*Cindy Brownstein, Chief Executive Officer*

**6786    Childen with Cerebral Palsy**
Woodbine House
6510 Bells Mill Road
Bethesda, MD  20817                     301-897-3570
                                       800-843-7323
                                   FAX: 301-897-5838
                              www.woodbinehouse.com

*Irv Shapell, Owner*

It provides a complete spectrum of information and compassionate advice about cerebral palsy and its effect on their child's development and education. Covers these areas: diagnosis, medical issues, family life, legal rights, early intervention, coping, therapies, treatment, development, advocacy, special ed., and daily care. *$16.95*
*470 pages Paperback*
*ISBN 0-933149-82-4*

**6787    Childhood Speech, Language & Listening Pro blems**
Wiley Publishing
605 3rd Avenue
New York, NY  10158                     212-850-6000
                                       FAX: 212-850-6088
Language pathologist Hamaguchi employs her 15 years of experience to show parents how to recognize the most common speech, language, and listening problems. *$16.95*
*224 pages Paperback 2001*
*ISBN 0-471387-53-3*

**6788    Children With Cerebral Palsy: A Manual for Therapists, Parents and Community Workers**
ITDG Publishing

The book provides sets of principles by which to observe and analyze a child's problems and then plan treatment. *$24.95*
*204 pages 2003*
*ISBN 1-853395-65-X*

**6789    Chronic Fatigue Syndrome: Your Natural Gu ide To Healing with Diet, Herbs and Other Methods**
Prima Publishing
PO Box 1260
Rocklin, CA  95677                      916-787-7000
                                       800-632-8676
                                   FAX: 916-787-7001
                     e-mail: websupportlife@primapub.com
                                   www.primapublishing.com
Explains specific measures sufferers can take to improve stamina, mental energy, and physical abilities. *$12.95*

*196 pages 1994*
*ISBN 1-559584-90-4*

**6790    Cleft Palate-Craniofacial Journal**
1504 E Franklin Street
Suite 102
Chapel Hill, NC  27514                  919-933-9044
                                   FAX: 919-933-9604
                              e-mail: info@cleftline.org
                                       www.cleftline.org

*Michael P Karnell, President*
*A Michael Sadove, VP*
*Nancy Smythe, Executive Director*

Publication of the international nonprofit medical society of health care professionals who treat and/or perform research on birth defects of the head and face.

**6791    Clinical Care in Rheumatic Disease**
Arthritis Foundation Distribution Center
PO Box 6996
Alpharetta, GA  30023                   800-207-8633
                                   FAX: 770-442-9742
                                       www.arthritis.com

This book was written for all health professionals caring for people with rheumatic diseases and for students in these disciplines. *$35.00*
*224 pages*

**6792    Coffee in the Cereal: The First Year with Multiple Sclerosis**
Pathfinder Publishing

Moorehead recounts the experience of her first year with multiple sclerosis with a vitality unique in the often gloomy world of personal medical histories. *$14.95*
*96 pages 2003*
*ISBN 0-934793-07-7*

**6793    Colon & Rectal Cancer: A Comprehensive Guide for Patients & Families**
Patient-Centered Guides
101 Morris Street
Sebastopol, CA  95472                   707-829-0515
                                       800-998-9938
                                   FAX: 707-829-0104
                                   www.patientcenters.com

*Linda Lamb, Editor*
*Shawnde Paull, Marketing*
*Tim O'Reilly, Chief Executive Officer*

The fourth most common cancer, colon and rectal cancer is diagnosed in 130,000 new cases in the United States each year. Patients and families need uo-to-date and in-depth information to participate wisely in treatment decisions (e.g., knowing what sexual and fertility issues to discuss with the doctor before surgery). This book covers coping with tests and treatment side effects, caring for ostomies, finding supportt, and other practical issues. *$24.95*
*544 pages Paperback*
*ISBN 1-565926-33-1*

**6794    Communication Development and Disorders in African American Children**
Brookes Publishing
PO Box 10624
Baltimore, MD  21285                    410-337-9580
                                       800-638-3775
                                   FAX: 410-337-8539
                     e-mail: custserv@brookespublishing.com
                                   www.brookespublishing.com

*Paul Brooks, Owner*

Research, Assessment, and Intervention. This text presents research on communication disorders and language development in African American children. Also addresses multicultural aspects of service delivery and intervention and discusses issues in assessing, diagnosing, and treating communication disorders. *$39.00*
*400 pages Paperback*
*ISBN 1-55766 -53-3*

**6795 Communication Development in Children with Down Syndrome**
Brookes Publishing
PO Box 10624
Baltimore, MD 21285 410-337-9580
800-638-3775
FAX: 410-337-8539
e-mail: custserv@brookespublishing.com
www.brookespublishing.com

*Paul Brooks, Owner*

This book offers an extensive, detailed explanation of communication development in children with Down syndrome relative to their advancing cognitive skills. It introduces a critical framework for assessing and treating hearing, speech, and language problems and provides explicit intervention methods and tested clinical protocols.
*Paperback 1998*
*ISBN 1-55766 -50-5*

**6796 Communication in Autism**
Federal Government
31 Center Drive Msc2320
Bethesda, MD 20892 800-241-1044
FAX: 301-402-0018
e-mail: nidcdinfo@nidcd.nih.gov
www.nidcd.nih.org
Describes what is autism, who is affected by autism, the communication problems with autism, how are the speech and language problems of autism treated, and what research is being conducted to improve the communication of individuals with autism.

**6797 Communication-Based Intervention for Problem Behavior**
Brookes Publishing
PO Box 10624
Baltimore, MD 21285 410-337-9580
800-638-3775
FAX: 410-337-8539
e-mail: custserv@brookespublishing.com
www.brookespublishing.com

*Paul Brooks, Owner*

A user's guide for producing positive change. This manual details methods for conducting functional assessments, communication-based intervention strategies, procedures for facilitating generalization and maintenance, and crisis management tactics. Useful for handling intense behavior problems. Also included are case studies and checklists of things to do to ensure success. *$38.00*
*288 pages Paperback*
*ISBN 1-557662-46-0*

**6798 Comprehensive Guide to ADD in Adults: Research, Diagnosis & Treatment**
Taylor & Francis
7625 Empire Drive
Florence, KY 41042 859-371-9571
800-634-7064
FAX: 800-248-4724

*Jeff Taylor, Owner*
*$50.95*

*426 pages*
*ISBN 0-876307-60-8*

**6799 Concentration Cockpit: Explaining Attention Deficits**
Educators Publishing Service
PO Box 9031
Cambridge, MA 02139 617-367-2700
800-225-5750
FAX: 617-547-0412
www.epsbooks.com
This eight-page pamphlet explains the administration of The Concentration Cockpit, a newly revised poster that helps children with attention deficits gain insight into their problems and monitor their progress in grappling with these problems. *$64.50*

*ISBN 0-838820-59-X*

**6800 Confronting Traumatic Brain Injury: Devas tation, Hope, and Healing**
Yale University Press

Explains what traumatic brain injury is, how it is caused, and what can be done to treat, cope with, and prevent it. The book includes case studies, key ethical and legal issues, public policy proposals, and practical steps to take to protect ourselves from brain trauma. *$19.00*
*220 pages 1999*
*ISBN 0-300079-42-7*

**6801 Confronting the Challenges of Spina Bifida**
Spina Bifida Association of America
4590 Macarthur Boulevard NW
Suite 250
Washington, DC 20007 202-944-3285
800-621-3141
FAX: 202-944-3295
e-mail: sbaa@sbaa.org
www.sbaa.org

*Cindy Brownstein, Chief Executive Officer*

A group curriculum addressing self care, self esteem and social skills in eight to 13 year olds. *$19.00*

**6802 Connections Newsletter**
Kessler Institute for Rehabilitation
1199 Pleasant Valley Way
West Orange, NJ 07052 973-731-3600
888-KES-SLER
FAX: 973-243-6992

*Maura Bergen, Editor/Public Relations Coordin.*
*Maria Anan, Editor/N. NJSCI System Coord.*
*Karen Hwang, Editor*

Quarterly newsletter for individuals with a spinal cord injury. Funded by the Northern New Jersey Spinal Cord Injury System.
*Quarterly-Free*

**6803 Conquering Kids' Cancer: Triumphs and Trag edies of a Children's Cancer Doctor**
Emeral Ink Publishing

The author shares heartwarming stories about his road in the pediatric oncology world. *$19.95*
*240 pages 1999*
*ISBN 1-885373-22-8*

**6804 Conquering the Darkness: One Story of Reco vering from a Brain Injury**
Paragon House
1925 Oakcrest Avenue
Suite 7
Saint Paul, MN 55113 651-644-3087
800-447-3709
FAX: 800-494-0997
e-mail: info@paragonhouse.com
www.paragonhouse.com

*Rosemary Yokoi, Publicity Department*
*Gordon Anderson, Executive Director*

The course of recovery from a brain injury by a woman who lived through it. *$15.95*
*420 pages 1999*
*ISBN 1-557787-63-8*

**6805  Coping and Prevailing with Multipe Scleros is and Other Life Struggles**
J&T Corp

A journey of victorious self-discovery. *$14.95*
*102 pages 2002*
*ISBN 0-971761-40-X*

**6806  Coping with ADD/ADHD**
Rosen Publishing Group
29 E 21st Street
New York, NY  10010                   212-777-3017
                                       800-237-9932
                          FAX: 888-436-4643
                    e-mail: rosenpub@tribeca.ios.com

*Roger Rosen, President*

At least 3.5 million American youngsters suffer from attention deficit disorder. This book defines the syndrome and provides specific information about treatment and counseling. *$16.95*

*ISBN 0-823920-70-4*

**6807  Coping with Asthma**
Rosen Publishing Group
29 E 21st Street
New York, NY  10010                   212-777-3017
                                       800-237-9932
                          FAX: 888-436-4643
                    e-mail: rosenpub@tribeca.ios.com

*Roger Rosen, President*

This book prepares students by explaining to them the dangers of asthma, a condition which, when properly treated, is completely manageable. *$16.95*

*ISBN 0-823920-69-0*

**6808  Coping with Cerebral Palsy**
Pro-Ed Publications
8700 Shoal Creek Boulevard
Austin, TX  78757                     512-451-3246
                                       800-897-3202
                          FAX: 512-451-8542
                    e-mail: info@proedinc.com
                          www.proedinc.com

*Donald Hammill, Owner*

This second edition book provides parents of children and adults with cerebral palsy the answers to more than 300 questions that have been carefully researched. It represents 40 years of experience by the author and is presented in a highly readable, jargon-free manner. *$26.00*
*252 pages*

**6809  Coping with Mild Traumatic Brain Surgery**
Avery Publishing Group
375 Hudson Street
New York, NY  10014                   212-366-2000

Explains what is involved in the diagnosis, treatment, and rehabilitation of brain-injured people *$15.95*
*334 pages 1998*
*ISBN 0-895297-91-4*

**6810  Counseling People with Diabetes**
Brookes Publishing
PO Box 10624
Baltimore, MD  21285                  410-337-9580
                                       800-638-3775
                          FAX: 410-337-8539
                    e-mail: custserv@brookespublishing.com
                          www.brookespublishing.com

*Paul Brooks, Owner*

*$29.00*
*158 pages Paperback*
*ISBN 1-85433 -36-1*

**6811  Counseling for Heart Disease**
Brookes Publishing
PO Box 10624
Baltimore, MD  21285                  410-337-9580
                                       800-638-3775
                          FAX: 410-337-8539
                    e-mail: custserv@brookespublishing.com
                          www.brookespublishing.com

*Paul Brooks, Owner*

*$25.00*
*144 pages Paperback*
*ISBN 1-85433 -96-9*

**6812  Counseling in Terminal Care & Bereavement**
Brookes Publishing
PO Box 10624
Baltimore, MD  21285                  410-337-9580
                                       800-638-3775
                          FAX: 410-337-8539
                    e-mail: custserv@brookespublishing.com
                          www.brookespublishing.com

*Paul Brooks, Owner*

Provides practical suggestions for addressing the needs of patients and family members who are anticipating or currently dealing with grief and bereavement, such as hospice care, hospitals, or at home care. *$34.00*
*210 pages Paperback*
*ISBN 1-85433 -78-7*

**6813  Count Us In**
Exceptional Parent Library
PO Box 1807
Englewood Cliffs, NJ  07632           201-947-6000
                                       800-535-1910
                          FAX: 201-947-9376
                    e-mail: eplibrary@aol.com
                          www.eplibrary.com
Offers information on growing up with Downs Syndrome. *$9.95*

**6814  Curing MS: How Science is Solving the Mys teries of Multiple Sclerosis**
Crown Publishing Group
1540 Broadway
New York, NY  10036                   212-782-9000
                          FAX: 212-302-7985
Founder-director of the Multiple Sclerosis Center at Mass General Hospital discusses what ends up as a deconstruction of the last 30 years of his own and general MS research and of experience in treating patients with the puzzling disorder. Weiner summarizes what is currently known about treatments and the potential for a cure. *$24.95*
*320 pages 2004*
*ISBN 0-609609-00-9*

**6815  Cystic Fibrosis in the 20th Century: Peop le, Events, and Progress**
AM Publishing

A blend of science, clinical concerns, and personal accounts of those touched by Cystic Fibrosis. It tells the story of the efforts of investigators, clinicians, and members of the CF community, documenting the rapid progress of research and treatment and improvement in survival rates since the first description of the disease in 1938. *$35.95*

*417 pages 2002*
*ISBN 0-971706-40-9*

**6816  Darkness Visible: A Memoir of Madness**
Vintage Books
1540 Broadway
New York, NY  10036                                212-782-9000
                                              FAX: 212-302-7985
                                              www.randomhouse.com

*Carol Schneider, Marketing Executive*

A meditation on Styron's serious depression at the age of 60, this essay evokes with detachment and dignity the months-long turmoil whose symptoms included the novelists dank joylessness, insomnia, physical aversion to alcohol (previously an invaluable senior partner of my intellect) and his persistent fantasies of self-destruction leading to psychiatric treatment and hospitalization. *$11.00*
        *96 pages 1992*
        *ISBN 0-679736-39-5*

**6817  Depression in Adults (the Latest Assessmen ts and Treatment Strategies)**
Compact Clinicals

*$14.95*
        *104 pages 2001*
        *ISBN 1-887537-16-3*

**6818  Diabetes 101**
Chronimed Publishing
13911 Ridgedale Drive
Minnetonka, MN  55305                              612-916-2500
                                                   800-848-2793
                                              FAX: 952-513-6170

*Sandra A Hintz, Marketing Coordinator*

A pure and simple guide for people who use insulin. *$ 10.95*
        *208 pages Paperback*
        *ISBN 1-56561 -24-5*

**6819  Diabetes Self-Management**
RA Rapaport Publishing
150 W 22nd Street
New York, NY  10011                                212-989-0200
                                              FAX: 212-989-4786

*James Hazlett, Editor*
*Jim Moorehead, Manager*

Publishes practical how-to information, focusing on the day-to-day and long-term aspects of diabetes in a positive and upbeat style. Gives subscribers up-to-date news, facts and advice to help them maintain their wellness and make informed decisions regarding their health. *$18.00*
        *BiMonthly*

**6820  Diagnosis and Treatment of Autism**
Autism Society of North Carolina Bookstore
505 Oberlin Road
Suite 230
Raleigh, NC  27605                                 919-743-0204
                                                   800-442-2762
                                              FAX: 919-743-0208
                          e-mail: dcoffey@autismsociety-nc.org
                                   www.autismsociety-nc.org

*Darla Coffey, Bookstore Manager*
*Jill Keel, Executive Director*

Various chapters written by professionals working with autistic children and adults. *$150.00*

**6821  Dictionary of Congenital Malformations & Disorders**
Parthenon Publishing Group
120 Mill Road
Park Ridge, NJ  07656                              201-391-6796
                                                   800-272-7737
                                              FAX: 800-374-3401
                               e-mail: orders@crcpress.com
                                     www.crcpress.com

*$55.00*
        *193 pages*
        *ISBN 0-850705-77-1*

**6822  Directions**
Families of Spinal Muscular Dystrophy
PO Box 196
Libertyville, IL  60048                            847-367-7620
                                                   800-886-1762
                                              FAX: 847-367-7623
                                              e-mail: sma@fsma.org
                                                   www.fsma.org

*Audrey Lewis, Executive Director*
*Colleen McCarthy*
*Audrey Lewis, Manager*

*$35.00*
        *60-70 pages Quarterly*

**6823  Disorders of Motor Speech: Assessment, Treatment, and Clinical Characterization**
Brookes Publishing
PO Box 10624
Baltimore, MD  21285                               410-337-9580
                                                   800-638-3775
                                              FAX: 410-337-8539
                        e-mail: custserv@brookespublishing.com
                                 www.brookespublishing.com

*Paul Brooks, Owner*

This book provides a probing examination of normal, dysarthric, and apraxic speech. Great for speech-language pathologists, neurologists, physical or occupational therapists, and physiatrists. *$47.00*
        *400 pages Hardcover*
        *ISBN 1-55766 -23-1*

**6824  Driven to Distraction**
National Alliance for the Mentally Ill
2107 Wilson Boulevard
Suite 300
Arlington, VA  22201                               703-524-7600
                                                   800-950-6264

*Suzanne Vogel-Scibilia, President*

A practical book discussing adult as well as child attention deficit disorder (ADD). Non-technical, realistic and optimistic, it is an informative how-to manual for parents and consumers. *$23.00*

**6825  Duchenne Muscular Dystrophy**
Oxford University Press
198 Madison Avenue
New York, NY  10016                                212-726-6000
                                                   800-451-7556
                                              FAX: 919-677-1303
                                                   www.oup-usa.org

*Laura Brown, Chief Executive Officer*

Identification of the genetic defect responsible for Duchenne Muscular Dystrophy and isolation of the protein dystrophin have led to the development of new theories for the disease's pathogenesis. This title incorporates these advances from the field of molecular biology, and describes the resultant opportunities for screening, prenatal diagnosis, genetic counselling and management. *$125.00*
        *272 pages 2003*
        *ISBN 0-198515-31-6*

**6826  Dyslexia over the Lifespan**
Educators Publishing Service
PO Box 9031
Cambridge, MA  02139                               617-367-2700
                                                   800-225-5750
                                              FAX: 617-547-0412
                                                   www.epsbooks.com

Discusses the educational and career development of 56 dyslexic boys from a private school that was one of the first to have a program to detect and treat developmental language disabilities. *$ 18.00*

*224 pages*
*ISBN 0-838816-70-3*

**6827 Eating Disorders Sourcebook**
Omnigraphics
615 Griswold Street
Detroit, MI 48226
313-961-1340
800-234-1340
FAX: 800-875-1340
www.omnigraphics.com

*Dawn D Mattews, Editor*
*Peter Ruffner, President*

Provides general imformation, causes and treatments of eating
disorders. *$78.00*
*600 pages 2000*
*ISBN 0-780803-35-3*

**6828 Encounters with Autistic States**
Jason Aronson
400 Keystone Industrial Park
Dunmore, PA 18512
800-782-0015
FAX: 201-840-7242
www.aronson.com

*$50.00*
*Hardcover*
*ISBN 0-765700-62-*

**6829 Epilepsy, 199 Answers: A Doctor Responds t o His Patients' Questions**

An epilepsy specialist answers questions about the causes, diagnosis, and treatments, and how to live and work with this brain disorder. Includes an epilepsy history timeline, patient health record form, resources, and a glossary. *$19.95*

**6830 EpilepsyUSA**
Epilepsy Foundation
4351 Garden City Drive
Landover, MD 20785
301-459-3700
800-332-1000
FAX: 301-577-2684
e-mail: postmaster@efa.org
www.epilepsyfoundation.org

*Judith O'Toole, Editor*
*Eric Hargis, President*

Magazine reporting on issues of interest to people with epilepsy
and their families. *$15.00*
*22 pages Quartlery*

**6831 Fall Down, Laughing: How Squiggy Caught M ultiple Sclerosis and Didn't Tell Nobody**
Jeremy P Tarcher
375 Hudson Street
New York, NY 10014
212-366-2000

Diagnosed with the illness after filming the last episode of Laverne & Shirley, Lander continued to develop his film and television career while hiding his illness. His success was an astonishing testament to his physical and emotional strength and his determination to prove that those with MS can still enjoy fulfilling and challenging lives. *$22.95*
*200 pages 2000*
*ISBN 1-585420-52-2*

**6832 Family Urology**
American Foundation for Urologic Disease
1100 Corporate Boulevard
Linthicum, MD 21090
800-242-2383
FAX: 410-468-1808
e-mail: admin@afud.org
www.afud.org

*Jodi L Miller, Director Education*

Dedicated to the prevention of urologic diseases through the expansion of patient education, research, public awareness and advocacy. Available with annual membership dues.
*Quarterly*

**6833 Fighting for Darla: Challenges for Family Care & Professional Responsibility**
Baker & Taylor, International
1200 Us Highway 22
Bridgewater, NJ 08807
908-541-7000
FAX: 908-541-7862
e-mail: intsale@bakertaylor.com

*D Sopko, Manager*

Follows the story of Darla, a pregnant adolescent with autism.
*$18.95*
*176 pages*
*ISBN 0-807733-56-3*

**6834 Focus**
Arthritis Foundation
3740 Ridge Mill Drive
Hilliard, OH 43026
614-876-8200
888-382-4673
FAX: 614-876-8363
www.arthritis.org

*Irene Baird, President*

Offers updated information on arthritis as well as news of the
services and activities of the Chapter.
*Quarterly*

**6835 Focus Newsletter**
Attention Deficit Disorder Association
PO Box 543
Pottstown, PA 19464
847-432-2332
FAX: 847-432-5874
e-mail: michelenovotni@yahoo.com
www.add.org

*Michele Novotni PhD, President/Editor*

ADDA's mission is to help people with AD/HD lead happier, more successful lives through education, research and public advocacy. Whether you have AD/HD yourself, someone special in your life does, or you treat, counsel or teach those who do, ADDA is an organization for you. ADDA focuses especially on the needs of AD/HD adults and young adults with AD/HD. Parents of children with AD/HD are also welcome.

**6836 Folic Acid Counseling Pocket Card**
Spina Bifida Association of America
4590 Macarthur Boulevard NW
Suite 250
Washington, DC 20007
202-944-3285
800-621-3141
FAX: 202-944-3295
e-mail: sbaa@sbaa.org
www.sbaa.org

*Cindy Brownstein, Chief Executive Officer*

For health care professionals. Quick reference card that fits in
the white coat pocket. *$18.00*

**6837 Fourth and Long**
Kent Walderep National Paralysis Foundation
16415 Addison Road
Suite 550
Addison, TX 75001
972-248-7100
877-724-2873
FAX: 972-248-7313
e-mail: lkoen@spinalvictory.org
www.spinalvictory.org

*Lisa Koen, Office Manager/Media Coordinator*

*$19.95*

*207 pages*
*ISBN 0-824515-08-0*

**6838  Fragile Success: Nine Autistic Children, Childhood to Adulthood**
Autism Society of North Carolina Bookstore
505 Oberlin Road
Suite 230
Raleigh, NC  27605                        919-743-0204
                                          800-442-2762
                                      FAX: 919-743-0208
                        e-mail: dcoffey@autismsociety-nc.org
                                    www.autismsociety-nc.org

*Darla Coffey, Bookstore Manager*
*Jill Keel, Executive Director*

A book about the lives of autistic children, whom the author has followed from their early years at the Elizabeth Ives School in New Haven, CT, through to adulthood. *$27.50*

**6839  Freedom from Arthritis Through Nutrition & Help for Allergies, 6th Edition**
Tree of Life Publications
PO Box 126
Joshua Tree, CA  92252                     760-366-2395
                                      FAX: 760-228-9081

*Michael Tree, Manager*

*$14.95*
        *256 pages Paperback*
        *ISBN 0-930852-15-X*

**6840  From Fatigue to Fantastic!: A Proven Prog ram to Regain Vibrant Health**
Avery Publishing Group
375 Hudson Street
New York, NY  10014                        212-366-2000

Argues that a mixture of causes usually underlie SCFS, each of which can trigger additional problems. The approach is to breack the vicious cycle of overwhelming fatigue, infections, brain fog, achiness, poor sleep, allergies, anxiety and depression by treating them all simultaneously. Recommends encompassing prescriptions and over-the-counter drugs, dietary modifications, vitamin and mineral supplements, acupuncture, massage, chiropractic, herbs, simple home remedies and psychotherapy. *$13.95*
        *444 pages 2001*
        *ISBN 1-583330-97-6*

**6841  From Where I Sit: Making My Way wih Cereb ral Palsy**
Scholastic

An autobiographical account of a young woman explores how it feels to live with cerebral palsy while struggling to have a full life despite the challenges facing her every day. *$13.00*
        *136 pages 1999*
        *ISBN 0-590395-84-X*

**6842  Functional Electrical Stimulation for Ambulation by Paraplegics**
Krieger Publishing Company
PO Box 9542
Melbourne, FL  32902                       321-724-9542
                                          800-724-0025
                                      FAX: 321-951-3671
                     e-mail: info@krieger-publishing.com
                                www.krieger-publishing.com

*R Krieger, Owner*

FES is employed to enable spinal cord injury patients who are complete paraplegics to stand and ambulate without bracing. The text covers 12 years of amulation experience. Also available in hardcover, ISBN #0-89464-845-4, selling for $42.50. *$32.50*

*210 pages Paper*
*ISBN 1-575240-28-9*

**6843  Functional Restoration of Adults and Child ren with Upper Extremity Amputation**
Demos Medical Publishing
386 Park Avenue S
Suite 201
New York, NY  10016                        212-683-0072
                                          800-532-8663
                                      FAX: 212-683-0118
                        e-mail: orderdep@demospub.com
                                    www.demosmedpub.com

*Phyllis Gold, Owner*

Provides a comprehensive reference to the surgery, prosthetic fitting, and rehabilitation of individuals sustaining an arm amputation. Covers the recent advancements in prosthetics and rehabilitation. *$150.00*
        *384 pages 2004*
        *ISBN 1-888799-73-0*

**6844  Getting Our Heads Together**
Thoms Rehabilitation Hospital
68 Sweeten Creek Road
Asheville, NC  28803                       828-274-2400
                                      FAX: 828-274-9452

*Kathi Petersen, Director Planning/Communication*
*Edgardo Diez MD, Medical Director Brain Injury*
*Kathy Price, Director Admissions*

A handbook for families of head injured patients - available in Spanish as well as English. *$4.00*
        *40 pages Paperback*

**6845  Guide to Hydrocephalus**
Spina Bifida Association of America
4590 Macarthur Boulevard NW
Suite 250
Washington, DC 20007                       202-944-3285
                                          800-621-3141
                                      FAX: 202-944-3295
                                    e-mail: sbaa@sbaa.org
                                             www.sbaa.org

*Cindy Brownstein, Chief Executive Officer*

Information to help you understand the circumstances that surround you and facilitate job advocacy. *$8.00*

**6846  Guidlines for Spina Bifida & Health Care S ervices Throughout Life**
Spina Bifida Association of America
4590 Macarthur Boulevard NW
Suite 250
Washington, DC 20007                       202-944-3285
                                          800-621-3141
                                      FAX: 202-944-3295
                                    e-mail: sbaa@sbaa.org
                                             www.sbaa.org

*Cindy Brownstein, Chief Executive Officer*

These guidelines are designed to help people who have spina bifida expirence a greater sense of purpose and place in society. *$19.00*

**6847  Handbook of Autism and Pervasive Developmental Disorders**
Autism Society of North Carolina Bookstore
505 Oberlin Road
Suite 230
Raleigh, NC  27605                        919-743-0204
                                          800-442-2762
                                      FAX: 919-743-0208
                        e-mail: dcoffey@autismsociety-nc.org
                                    www.autismsociety-nc.org

*Darla Coffey, Bookstore Manager*
*Jill Keel, Executive Director*

A list of contributors address such topics as characteristics of autistic syndromes and interventions. *$125.00*

**6848 Handbook of Chronic Fatigue Syndrome**
Wiley Publishing
605 3rd Avenue
New York, NY 10158                    212-850-6000
                                 FAX: 212-850-6088
Discusses diagnosis and treatment as well as the history, phenomenology, symptomatology, assessment, and pediatric and community issues. Introduces phase-based therapy and nutritional approaches. $ 90.00
            794 pages 2003
            ISBN 0-471415-12-X

**6849 Handbook of Epilepsy**
Lippincott, Williams & Wilkins
227 E Washington Square
Philadelphia, PA 19106               215-521-8300
                                     800-777-2295
                                 FAX: 301-824-7390
                                     www.lpub.com

*J Lippincott, Chief Executive Officer*

Pocket-sized reference provides concise, up-to-date, clinically oriented reviews of each of the major areas of diagnosis and management of epilepsy. $42.95
            272 pages 2003
            ISBN 0-781743-52-4

**6850 Head Injury: The Facts: A Guide for Fami lies and Care-Givers**
Oxford University Press
198 Madison Avenue
New York, NY 10016                   212-726-6000
                                     800-451-7556
                                 FAX: 919-677-1303
                                     www.oup-usa.org

*Laura Brown, Chief Executive Officer*

A pocket-sized explanation of head injuries for patients. $19.95
            167 pages
            ISBN 0-192627-13-9

**6851 Healing Anxiety and Depression**
Berkley Publishing Group


Reveals the major anxiety and depression centers of the brain, offers guidelines and diagnostic tools to determine the specific type of anxiety and depression, and provides a comprehensive program for treating each type. $14.95
            352 pages 2004
            ISBN 0-425198-44-8

**6852 Healthcare Guidelines for Spina Bifida and Healthcare Services Throughout Life**
Spina Bifida Association of America
4590 Macarthur Boulevard NW
Suite 250
Washington, DC 20007                 202-944-3285
                                     800-621-3141
                                 FAX: 202-944-3295
                                 e-mail: sbaa@sbaa.org
                                     www.sbaa.org

*Cindy Brownstein, Chief Executive Officer*
    $19.00

**6853 Hearing, Speech and Deafness Center (HSDC)**
Hearing, Speech & Deafness Center (HSDC)
1625 19th Avenue
Seattle, WA 98122                    206-323-5770
                                 FAX: 206-328-6871
                                 e-mail: hsdc@hsdc.org
                                     www.hsdc.org

*Susie Burdick, Executive Director*

Our mission is to enrich lives of all adults and children who experience hearing loss, speech and language impairments or who are deaf, by providing professional services and by promoting community awareness and accessibility.

**6854 Heart Disease in Persons with Down Syndrome**
Brookes Publishing
PO Box 10624
Baltimore, MD 21285                  410-337-9580
                                     800-638-3775
                                 FAX: 410-337-8539
                         e-mail: custserv@brookespublishing.com
                                 www.brookespublishing.com

*Susie Burdick, Executive Director*

Offers access to findings from state-of-the-art research on congenital heart disease in children and adults with Down syndrome. Information on cardiac malformations and anomalies, heart and lung pathology, hemodynamic evaluations, and surgical intervention. $62.00
            240 pages Hardcover
            ISBN 1-55766 -24-X

**6855 Help Yourself Cookbook**
Arthritis Foundation
PO Box 6996
Alpharetta, GA 30023
                                     800-207-0633
                                 FAX: 770-442-9742
                                     www.arthritis.com
    $12.95
        158 pages

**6856 Help for the Learning Disabled Child: Symptoms and Solutions - Revised**
Slosson Educational Publications
PO Box 280
East Aurora, NY 14052                716-652-0930
                                     800-756-7766
                                 FAX: 800-655-3840
                                 e-mail: slosson@slosson.com
                                     www.slosson.com

*Leslie Foote, Office Personnel*
*Peggy Meyer, Office Personnel*
*Steven Slosson, President*

This easy-to-read text describes observable behaviors, offers remediation techniques, materials, and specific tests to assist teachers in further diagnosis. This revision has been updated to include specific information and techniques to use with children who appear to have attention deficit disorders. Teachers and parents gain a better understanding of their child's difficulties in school and at home. $ 36.00
            48 pages

**6857 Helping People with Autism Manage Their Behavior**
Autism Society of North Carolina Bookstore
505 Oberlin Road
Suite 230
Raleigh, NC 27605                    919-743-0204
                                     800-442-2762
                                 FAX: 919-743-0208
                         e-mail: dcoffey@autismsociety-nc.org
                                 www.autismsociety-nc.org

*Darla Coffey, Bookstore Manager*
*Jill Keel, Executive Director*

Covers the broad topic of helping people with autism manage their behavior. $7.00

**6858 Hidden Child: The Linwood Method for Reaching the Autistic Child**
Woodbine House
6510 Bells Mill Road
Bethesda, MD 20817                   301-897-3570
                                     800-843-7323
                                 FAX: 301-897-5838
                                 www.woodbinehouse.com

*Irv Shapell, Owner*

Chronicle of the Linwood Children's Center's successful treatment program for autistic children. $17.95

*286 pages Paperback*
*ISBN 0-933149-06-9*

**6859 How To Reach and Teach Children and Teens with Dyslexia**
Jossey-Bass

This practical resource gives educators at all levels essential information, techniques, and tolls for understanding dyslexia and adapting teaching methods in all subject areas to meet the learning style, social, and emotional needs of students who have dyslexia. *$ 22.95*
*340 pages 2002*
*ISBN 0-130320-18-8*

**6860 How to Live with a Spinal Cord Injury**
Accent Books & Products
PO Box 700
Bloomington, IL  61702                  309-378-2961
                                        800-787-8444
                                   FAX: 309-378-4420
                              e-mail: acmtlvng@aol.com

*Raymond C Cheever, Publisher*
*Betty Garee, Editor*

A guide packed with realistic information about how this disability affects your life and what you can do about it. Answers lots of questions and gives you positive information providing hope and plenty of encouragement. *$6.95*
*58 pages Paperback*
*ISBN 0-91570 -27-2*

**6861 Hydrocephalus: A Guide for Patients, Families & Friends**
Patient-Centered Guides
101 Morris Street
Sebastopol, CA  95472                    707-829-0515
                                        800-998-9938
                                   FAX: 707-829-0104
                              www.patientcenters.com

*Linda Lamb, Editor*
*Shawnde Paull, Marketing*
*Tim O'Reilly, Chief Executive Officer*

Hydrocephalus is a life-threatening condition often referred to as, water on the brain, that is treated by surgical placement of a shunt system. Hydrocephalus: A Guide for Patients, Families and Friends educates families so they can select a skilled neurosurgeon, understand treatments, participate in care, know what symptoms need attention, discover where to turn for support, keep records needed for follow-up treatments, and make wise lifestyle choices. *$19.95*
*379 pages Paperback*
*ISBN 1-565924-10-X*

**6862 Hyperactive Child, Adolescent, and Adult: ADD Through the Lifespan**
CACLD
25 Van Zant Street
Suite 15-5
Norwalk, CT  06855                       203-838-5010
                                   FAX: 203-866-6108
                              e-mail: CACLD@optonline.net
                                      www.CACLD.org

*Beryl Kaufman, Executive Director*

Comprehensive general review. Update on previous research by the author, offering a basic text. Published by Connecticut Association for Children & Adults with Learning Disabilities (CACLD). *$8.75*
*162 pages*

**6863 I'll Carry the Fork!: Recovering a Life A fter Brain Surgery**
Rising Star Press

The author provides a glimpse into the life of someone who has been changed by a head injury. By sharing her personal triumphs and challenges she gives us a new sensitivity for the countless people and families who focus each and every day on their recoveries. *$16.95*
*205 pages 1999*
*ISBN 0-933670-04-4*

**6864 IAL News**
International Association of Laryngectomees
8900 Thornton Road
Stockton, CA  95209                      209-472-0516
                                        866-425-3678
                                   FAX: 209-472-0516
                              e-mail: ial@larynxlink.com

*Jack Henslee, Executive Director*

Focuses on rehabilitation and well-being of persons who have had laryngectomy surgery.

**6865 In Control**
Arthritis Foundation
PO Box 7669
Atlanta, GA  30357                       404-872-7100
                                        800-283-7800
                                   FAX: 404-872-9559
                              e-mail: help@arthritis.org
                                      www.arthritis.org

*John Klippel, Chief Executive Officer*

An excellent at-home program which includes video, audio cassettes and the Arthritis Helpbook. Provides tools to help meet the challenges of arthritis.

**6866 In Search of Wings: A Journey Back from T raumatic Brain Injury**
Wings Press

The true story of one woman coping with traumatic brain injury after a car accident that affected her cognitive skills and memory *$14.95*
*233 pages 1992*
*ISBN 1-882332-00-8*

**6867 Increasing Behaviors of Persons with Severe Retardation and Autism**
Research Press
2612 N Mattis Avenue
Champaign, IL  61822                     217-352-3273
                                        800-519-2707
                                   FAX: 217-352-1221
                              e-mail: rp@researchpress.com
                                      www.researchpress.com

*Russell Pence, President*

Shows how to increase desirable behaviors by using techniques such as shaping, prompting, fading, modeling, backward chaining, and graduated guidance. Includes exercises, review questions, and numerous examples. *$15.95*
*230 pages Paperback*
*ISBN 0-878222-63-4*

**6868 Individuals with Arthritis**
Mainstream
3 Bethesda Metro Center
Suite 830
Bethesda, MD  20814                      301-961-9299
                                        800-247-1380
                                   FAX: 301-654-6714
                              e-mail: info@mainstreaminc.org

*Charles Moster*

Mainstreaming individuals with arthritis into the workplace. *$2.50*

*12 pages*

**6869  Individuals with Cerebral Palsy**
Mainstream
3 Bethesda Metro Center
Suite 830
Bethesda, MD  20814                     301-961-9299
                                        800-247-1380
                                   FAX: 301-654-6714
                          e-mail: info@mainstreaminc.org

*Charles Moster*

Mainstreaming individuals with cerebral palsy into the work-place. *$2.50*
*12 pages*

**6870  Informer**
Simon Foundation
PO Box 835
Wilmette, IL  60091                     847-864-3913
                                        800-237-4666
                                   FAX: 847-864-9758
                          www.simonfoundation.org

*Cheryle B Gartley, President*

Publishes items of interest to people with bladder or bowel incontinence, including medical articles, helpful devices, publications and a pen pal list. Quarterly newsletter.

**6871  Injured Mind, Shattered Dreams: Brian's Survival from a Severe Head Injury**
Brookline Books
PO Box 1046
Cambridge, MA  02139                    617-868-0360
                                        800-666-2665
                                   FAX: 617-868-1772
                     e-mail: brooklinebks@delphi.com
                          www.brooklinebooks.com
Brian, headed for normal adulthood, crashes his car and suffers a severe head injury. This book speaks to the issues in his recovery and the victory a family can achieve through caring advocacy and faith. *$17.95*
*Paperback*
*ISBN 0-91479-95-6*

**6872  Inside MS**
National Multiple Sclerosis Society
421 New Karner Road
Suite 6
Albany, NY  12205                       518-464-0630
                                        800-344-4867
                                   FAX: 518-464-1232
                     e-mail: chapter@msupstateny.org
                          www.nationalmssociety.org

*Jim Ahearn, President*

News and information on research progress, medical treatments, patient services, therapeutic claims and activities.

**6873  Interdisciplinary Clinical Assessment of Young Children with Developmental Disabilities**
Brookes Publishing
PO Box 10624
Baltimore, MD  21285                    410-337-9580
                                        800-638-3775
                                   FAX: 410-337-8539
                e-mail: custserv@brookespublishing.com
                          www.brookespublishing.com

*Paul Brooks, Owner*

Offers insight from veteran team members on interdisciplinary team assessments. Professionals organizing a team as well as students preparing for practice will find advice on how practitioners gather information, approach assessment, make decisions, and face the challenges of their individual fields. Includes case studies and appendix of photocopiable questionnaires for clinicians and parents. *$42.00*

*432 pages Hardcover 2000*
*ISBN 1-557664-50-1*

**6874  Is the Child Really Stuttering? Questions & Answers About Disfluency**
Speech Bin
1965 25th Avenue
Vero Beach, FL  32960                   772-770-0007
                                        800-477-3324
                                   FAX: 772-770-0006
                          www.speechbin.com
In a question and answer format concisely shows differences between normal developmental and abnorlam disfluency and motivates adult listeners to deal with problems speech behaviors in a positive way. Set of ten brochures. *$9.95*

**6875  Joslin Guide to Diabetes**
Joslin Diabetes Center
1 Joslin Place
Boston, MA  02215                       617-732-2400
                                   FAX: 617-732-2452
                          www.joslin.harvard.edu
Discusses the causes of diabetes, the role of diet and exercise, meal planning and complications. Also provide information on drawing blood, mixing and injecting insulin, special challenges, living with diabetes. *$20.00*
*352 pages*

**6876  Journey to Well: Learning to Live After S pinal Cord Injury**
Altarfire Publishing

The author's close-up view of what life is like during and after such an incident, including her experience with institutional medicine and insurance companies (for better and for worse), and her determined - and ultimately successful - effort to rehabilitate herself and reconstruct her life. *$15.95*
*251 pages 1997*
*ISBN 0-965555-82-8*

**6877  Ketogenic Diet: A Treatment for Epilepsy**
Demos Medical Publishing

Patient education reference on the use of the ketogenic diet to conrol epilepsy in children. *$24.95*
*224 pages Paperback 2000*
*ISBN 1-888799-39-0*

**6878  Key**
National Mental Health Consumers' Self-Help
1211 Chestnut Street
Suite 1207
Philadelphia, PA  19107                 215-751-1810
                                        800-553-4539
                                   FAX: 215-636-6312
                          e-mail: info@mhselfhelp.org
                          www.mhselfhelp.org

*Tom Leibfried, Editor*
*Shannon Flannagan, Manager*
*12 pages Quarterly*

**6879  Labeling the Mentally Retarded**
University of California Press
2120 Berkeley Way
Berkeley, CA  94720                     510-642-4247
                                   FAX: 510-643-7127
                          www.ucpress.edu

*Lynne Whity, Executive Director*

Clinical and social system perspectives on mental retardation. *$12.95*

*333 pages Paper*

**6880  Language Disabilities in Children and Adolescents**
McGraw-Hill, School Publishing
220 E Danieldale Road
Desoto, TX  75115                                    972-224-1111
                                                     800-442-9685
                                                FAX: 972-228-1982
                                                     mhschool.com

*Joseph Gavigan, President*
A comprehensive review of research in language disabilities.

**6881  Language-Related Learning Disabilities: Their Nature and Treatment**
Brookes Publishing
PO Box 10624
Baltimore, MD  21285                                 410-337-9580
                                                     800-638-3775
                                                FAX: 410-337-8539
               e-mail: custserv@brookespublishing.com
                      www.brookespublishing.com

*Paul Brooks, Owner*
*$47.00*
       *464 pages Paperback*
       *ISBN 1-55766 -53-0*

**6882  Lead Poisoning in Childhood**
Brookes Publishing
PO Box 10624
Baltimore, MD  21285                                 410-337-9580
                                                     800-638-3775
                                                FAX: 410-337-8539
               e-mail: custserv@brookespublishing.com
                      www.brookespublishing.com

*Paul Brooks, Owner*
This book examines the epidemiology, etiology, and pathophysiology of lead poisoning - the most prevalent preventable childhood health problem today. Also provides practical prevention strategies that are cost-effective and easy to implement. *$31.95*
       *256 pages Paperback*
       *ISBN 1-55766 -32-0*

**6883  Learning Disabilities: Lifelong Issues**
Brookes Publishing
PO Box 10624
Baltimore, MD  21285                                 410-337-9580
                                                     800-638-3775
                                                FAX: 410-337-8539
               e-mail: custserv@brookespublishing.com
                      www.brookespublishing.com

*Paul Brooks, Owner*
Sections of this book are devoted to education, labor, justice, and health and human services offering an overview of research and a critical appraisal of the status of learning disability practices. This book sets forth an agenda for improving the educational and ultimately, the social and economic futures of people with learning disabilities. *$36.00*
       *352 pages Paperback*
       *ISBN 1-55766 -40-1*

**6884  Life Line**
National Hydrocephalus Foundation
12413 Centralia Street
Lakewood, CA  90715                                  562-402-3523
                                                     888-857-3434
                                                     888-260-1789
                                                FAX: 562-924-6666
               e-mail: debbifields@nhfonline.org
                      www.nhfonline.org

*Debbi Fields, Executive Director*

A national and worldwide organization established in order to provide information and education on the conditions of hydrocephalus. We also offer video/DVD on the subject, offer contacts for peer support, quarterly meetings that help individuals state and maintain a support group in their area and offer a quarterly newsletter to our membership. *$35.00*
       *12 pages Quarterly*

**6885  Life on Wheels: For the Active Wheelchair User**
Patient-Centered Guides
101 Morris Street
Sebastopol, CA  95472                                707-829-0515
                                                     800-294-4747
                                                FAX: 800-997-9901
                      e-mail: order@oreilly.com
                      www.patientcenters.com

*Linda Lamb, Editor*
*Shawnde Paull, Marketing*
*Tim O'Reilly, Chief Executive Officer*

For 1.5 million Americans, life includes a wheelchair for mobility. Life on Wheels is for people who want to take charge of their life experience. Author Gary Karp describes medical issues (paralysis, circulation, rehab, cure research); day-to-day living (exercise, skin, bowel and bladder, sexuality, home access, maintaining a wheelchair); and social issues (self-image, adjustment, friends, family, cultural attitudes, activism). *$24.95*
       *573 pages Paperback*
       *ISBN 1-565922-53-0*

**6886  Living Beyond Multiple Sclerosis: A Woman 's Guide**
Hunter House Publishers
PO Box 2914
Alameda, CA  94501                                   510-865-5282
                                                     800-266-5592
                                                FAX: 510-865-4295
                      e-mail: sales@hunterhouse.com
                      www.hunterhouse.com

*Tim O'Reilly, Chief Executive Officer*
This collection of e-mail conversations provides anecdotal and personal information contributed by women with multiple sclerosis. *$14.95*
       *256 pages 2000*
       *ISBN 0-897932-93-5*

**6887  Living Well with Asthma**
Guilford Press
72 Spring Street
New York, NY  10012                                  212-431-9800
                                                     800-365-7006
                                                FAX: 212-966-6708
                      www.guilford.com

*Cynthia L Divino PhD, Author*
*Bob Matloff, President*
*$15.95*
       *213 pages Paperback 1998*
       *ISBN 1-572300-51-5*

**6888  Living Well with Chronic Fatigue Syndrome and Fibromyalgia**
HarperCollins
1350 Avenue of the Americas
New York, NY  10019                                  212-261-6500

                      virusmyth.net/aids/books/mcbsurv.htm

*Erin Gorman, Sales Executive*
A comprehensive guide to the diagnosis and treatment of chronic fatigue syndrome and fibromyalgia. *$14.95*
       *416 pages 2004*
       *ISBN 0-060521-25-2*

**6889  Living With Brain Injury: A Guide for Fam ilies and Caregivers**
University of Toronto Press

Healthcare and legal experts from Canada and the US guide the reader through the process of rehabilitation and explain how to live with brain injury. The advice of these professionals is complemented by the stories of two people who have survived injuries and are adjusting to their new lives. *$18.95*
*182 pages 1998*
*ISBN 0-802081-03-7*

**6890    Living with Rheumatoid Arthritis**
Johns Hopkins University Press
2715 North Charles Street
Baltimore, MD  21218                                    410-516-6900
                                                        800-537-5487
                                                   FAX: 410-516-6998
                                                   www.jhupbooks.com

*William Brody, President*

This book offers practical and usable answers to the questions of everyday life. The authors provide clear explanations of the causes, diagnosis, and treatment of the disease, and why medication, joint protection, physical activity, and good nutrition are essential components of care. *$18.95*
*312 pages Paperback*
*ISBN 0-801851-85-8*

**6891    Lung Cancer: Making Sense of Diagnosis, Treatment, & Option**
Patient-Centered Guides
101 Morris Street
Sebastopol, CA  95472                                  707-829-0515
                                                        800-998-9938
                                                   FAX: 707-829-0104
                                                   www.patientcenters.com

*Linda Lamb, Editor*
*Shawnde Paull, Marketing*
*Tim O'Reilly, Chief Executive Officer*

Straightforward language and the words of patients and their families are the hallmarks of this book on the number one cancer killer in the US. Written by a widely respected author and patient advocate, Lung Cancer: Making Sense of Diagnosis, Treatment, & Options has been meticulously reviewed by top medical experts and physicians. Readers will find medical facts simply explained, advice to ease their daily life, and tools to be strong advocates for themselves or a family member. *$ 27.95*
*530 pages Paperback*
*ISBN 0-596500-02-5*

**6892    Lupus: Alternative Therapies That Work**
Healing Arts Press
1 Park Street
Rochester, VT  05767                                   802-767-3174
                                                        800-246-8648
                                                   FAX: 802-767-3726
                                        e-mail: orders@innertraditions.com
                                                   www.InnerTraditions.com

*Jessica Dudley, Sales Associate*
*Ehud Sperling, Owner*

*$14.95*
*256 pages*
*ISBN 0-892818-89-1*

**6893    MSFOCUS Magazine**
Multiple Sclerosis Foundation
6350 N Andrews Avenue
Fort Lauderdale, FL  33309                             954-776-6805
                                                        888-673-6287
                                                   FAX: 954-351-0630
                                        e-mail: support@msfocus.org
                                                   www.msfocus.org

*Kathleen Truax, Case Worker*
*Jules Kuperberg, Administrator*

Contemporary national, nonprofit organization that provides free support services and public education for persons with Multiple Sclerosis, newsletters, toll-free phone support, information, referrals, home care, assitive technology and support groups.

*48 pages Quarterly*

**6894    Management of Autistic Behavior**
Pro-Ed
8700 Shoal Creek Boulevard
Austin, TX  78757                                      512-451-3246
                                                        800-897-3202
                                                   FAX: 512-451-8542
                                        e-mail: info@proedinc.com
                                                   www.proedinc.com

*Donald Hammill, Owner*

Comprehensive and practical book that tells what works best with specific problems. *$41.00*
*450 pages Paperback*
*ISBN 0-890791-96-1*

**6895    Managing Attention Disorders in Children: A Guide for Practitioners**
Books on Special Children
PO Box 305
Congers, NY  10920                                     845-638-1236
                                                   FAX: 845-638-0847
                                        e-mail: irene@boscbooks.com
Offers information about human personality, structure and dynamics, assessment and adjustment. *$27.50*
*214 pages*

**6896    Managing Post-Polio Syndrome**
Polio Connection of America
PO Box 182
Howard Beach, NY  11414                                718-835-5536
                                                   FAX: 718-738-1509
                                        e-mail: w1066@msn.com
                                                   www.geocities.com/w1066w

*240 pages*

**6897    Managing the Symptoms of Multiple Sclerosis**
Demos Medical Publishing
386 Park Avenue S
Suite 201
New York, NY  10016                                    212-683-0072
                                                        800-532-8663
                                                   FAX: 212-683-0118
                                        e-mail: orderdep@demospub.com
                                                   www.demosmedpub.com

*Diana Schneider PhD, President*
*Phyllis Gold, Owner*

Guide for the management of MS symptoms, providing both up-to-date pathophysiological explanation and carefully weighed clinical advice. *$19.95*
*192 pages 2003*
*ISBN 1-888799-78-1*

**6898    Meeting the Challenge of Progressive Multiple Sclerosis**

Demos Medical Publishing
386 Park Avenue S
Suite 201
New York, NY  10016                                    212-683-0072
                                                        800-532-8663
                                                   FAX: 212-683-0118
                                        e-mail: orderdep@demospub.com
                                                   www.demosmedpub.com

*Diana Schneider PhD, President*
*Phyllis Gold, Owner*

A concise, practical and useful overview of worsening MS and the dilemma faced when progression presents its challenges to patients and those who care about them. *$21.95*

*136 pages 2001*
*ISBN 1-888799-46-3*

**6899  Meniere's Disease**
Vestibular Disorders Association
PO Box 4467
Portland, OR  97208

503-229-7705
800-837-8428
FAX: 503-229-8064
e-mail: veda@vestibular.org
www.vestibular.org

*Lisa Haven, Editor*
*Connie Pilcher, Editor*
*1998*

**6900  Moisture Seekers**
Sjogren's Syndrome Foundation
366 N Broadway
Suite Ph
Jericho, NY  11753

301-718-0300
800-475-6473
FAX: 301-718-0322
e-mail: ssf@sjogrens.org
www.sjogrens.org

*Alexis Stegemann, Executive Director*

Newsletter of the organization for lay people and professionals interested in Sjogren's Syndrome. Contains medical news, current research, and essential tips for daily living. *$25.00*
*15-16 pages Monthly*

**6901  Moonrise: One Family, Genetic Identity, a nd Muscular Dystrophy**
St. Martin's Press
175 5th Avenue
New York, NY  10010

212-674-5151

www.stmartins.com

*John Sargent, Chief Executive Officer*

A first-person account of the author's family, her son Ansel, and his progressive disability, caused by genetic disease, Duchenne muscular dystrophy. The journey begins when he is born and deemed a particularly beautiful baby, continues with the alarming possibility, at the age of two, of wrongness, through the diagnosis of disease and prognosis of early death, and to his adolescence, where his parents are never sure if the moon is rising or setting over his life. *$23.95*
*256 pages 2003*
*ISBN 0-312289-08-*

**6902  Motor Speech Disorders**
WB Saunders Company
1810 Creekside Lane
Darien, IL  60561

630-910-0749
FAX: 630-910-5789
www.wbsaunders.com

Professional text on rehabilitation techniques for motor speech disorders. *$74.00*
*304 pages*
*ISBN 0-72162 -78-8*

**6903  Motor Speech Disorders: Advances in Assessment and Treatment**
Brookes Publishing
PO Box 10624
Baltimore, MD  21285

410-337-9580
800-638-3775
FAX: 410-337-8539
e-mail: custserv@brookespublishing.com
www.brookespublishing.com

*Paul Brooks, Owner*

*$38.00*

*288 pages Paperback*
*ISBN 1-55766 -37-5*

**6904  Multiple Sclerosis**
Demos Medical Publishing
386 Park Avenue S
Suite 201
New York, NY  10016

212-683-0072
800-532-8663
FAX: 212-683-0118
e-mail: orderdep@demospub.com
www.demosmedpub.com

*Diana Schneider PhD, President*
*Phyllis Gold, Owner*

Guide for living and coping with multiple sclerosis. *$39.95*
*615 pages 2000*
*ISBN 1-888799-43-9*

**6905  Multiple Sclerosis Q&A: Reassuring Answer s to Frequently Asked Questions**
Avery Publishing Group
375 Hudson Street
New York, NY  10014

212-366-2000

Answers to many questions that overwhelm those undergoing testing and treatment for multiple sclerosis. It discusses traditional and complementary therapies for MS; explains medical terminology and diagnostics; and compassionately addresses the lifestyle changes many patients face while learning to manage this chronic and potentially debilitating disorder. *$14.95*
*208 pages 2003*
*ISBN 1-583331-74-3*

**6906  Multiple Sclerosis: The Guide to Treatmen t and Management**
Demos Medical Publishing
386 Park Avenue S
Suite 201
New York, NY  10016

212-683-0072
800-532-8663
FAX: 212-683-0118
e-mail: orderdep@demospub.com
www.demosmedpub.com

*Phyllis Gold, Owner*

A current guide to modern therapies. *$24.95*
*152 pages 2001*
*ISBN 1-888799-54-4*

**6907  Multiple Sclerosis: A Guide for the Newly Diagnosed**
Demos Medical Publishing
386 Park Avenue S
Suite 201
New York, NY  10016

212-683-0072
800-532-8663
FAX: 212-683-0118
e-mail: orderdep@demospub.com
www.demosmedpub.com

*Diana Schneider PhD, President*
*Phyllis Gold, Owner*

A must-have title for anyone who has recently been diagnosed with MS and a good idea for family members and friends. *$ 21.95*
*160 pages 2002*
*ISBN 1-888799-60-9*

**6908  Muscular Dystrophies**
Oxford University Press
198 Madison Avenue
New York, NY  10016

212-726-6000
800-451-7556
FAX: 919-677-1303
www.oup-usa.org

*Laura Brown, Chief Executive Officer*

Describes the opportunities for management of more than 30 types of MD through respiratory care, physiotherapy and surgical correction of contractures, and examines the potential for effective treatment utilizing the new techniques of gene and cell therapy *$ 106.00*
*316 pages 2002*
*ISBN 0-192632-91-4*

**6909    Muscular Dystrophy and Other Neuromuscular Diseases**
Haworth Press
10 Alice Street
Binghamton, NY 13904
607-722-5857
800-429-6784
FAX: 607-722-6362
e-mail: orders@haworthpress.com
www.haworthpress.com

*S Harrington-Miller, Advertising*
*William Cohen, Owner*

A thoughtful new book from professionals who assist persons afflicted with neuromuscular disorders to help them and their families adapt to lifestyle changes accompanying the onset of these disorders. *$74.95*
*250 pages Hardcover*
*ISBN 1-560240-77-6*

**6910    Muscular Dystrophy: The Facts**
Oxford University Press
198 Madison Avenue
New York, NY 10016
212-726-6000
800-451-7556
FAX: 919-677-1303
www.oup-usa.org

*Laura Brown, Chief Executive Officer*

A good first book for individuals and families faced with the likelihood or reality of a muscular dystrophy diagnosis. *$19.95*
*166 pages 2000*
*ISBN 0-192632-17-5*

**6911    NADS News**
PO Box 4542
Oak Brook, IL 60522
630-325-9112
FAX: 630-325-8842
www.nads.org

*Kim Xidas, Family Support Coordinator*

A bi-monthly publication from the National Association for Down Syndrome. Subscription prices: $20 for parents; $25 for professionals.
*12 pages Bi-monthly*

**6912    NHIF Newsletter**
National Head Injury Foundation
1776 Massachusetts Ave NW
Washington, DC 20036
202-452-1999
800-444-6443
FAX: 202-466-4265
www.biausa.org

*Christopher Flavin, President*

Contains news and articles for families and professionals concerned with head injury. *$25.00*

**6913    National Council News**
Nat'l Council for Community Behavioral Healthcare
12300 Twinbrook Parkway
Suite 320
Rockville, MD 20852
301-984-6200
FAX: 301-881-7159

*Linda Rosenberg, Chief Executive Officer*
*$40.00*

*Monthly*

**6914    Nature of Melancholy: From Aristotle to K risteva**
Oxford University Press
198 Madison Avenue
New York, NY 10016
212-726-6000
800-451-7556
FAX: 919-677-1303
www.oup-usa.org

*Laura Brown, Chief Executive Officer*

This anthology collects over thirty selections of important Western writing about melancholy and its related conditions by philosophers, doctors, religious and literary figures, and modern psychologists. *$25.00*
*392 pages 2002*
*ISBN 0-195151-65-8*

**6915    Neurobiology of Autism**
Johns Hopkins University Press
2715 N Charles Street
Baltimore, MD 21218
410-516-6900
FAX: 410-516-6998

*William Brody, President*

This book discusses recent advances in scientific research that point to a neurobiological basis for autism and examines the clinical implications of this research. *$28.00*
*272 pages*
*ISBN 0-801856-80-9*

**6916    Neuromotor Speech Disorders: Nature, Assessment, and Management**
Brookes Publishing
PO Box 10624
Baltimore, MD 21285
410-337-9580
800-638-3775
FAX: 410-337-8539
e-mail: custserv@brookespublishing.com
www.brookespublishing.com

*Paul Brooks, Owner*

Topics included in this book are: motor-speech imaging, anatomical structure and function in dysarthria, physiological and acoustic analyses of dysarthria intelligibility, dysphonia, and linguistic considerations in apraxia of speech. *$44.95*
*320 pages Hardcover 1998*
*ISBN 1-55766 -26-2*

**6917    Non-Hodgkin's Lymphomas: Making Sense of Diagnosis, Treatment & Options**
O'Reilly
101 Morris Street
Sebastopol, CA 95472
707-829-0515
800-294-4747
FAX: 800-997-9901
e-mail: order@oreilly.com
www.patientcenters.com

*Tim O'Reilly, Chief Executive Officer*
*$24.95*
*580 pages Paperback*
*ISBN 1-565924-44-4*

**6918    Noonday Demon: An Atlas of Depression**
Scribner

Drawing on his own struggles with the illness and interviews with fellow sufferers, doctors and scientists, policy makers and politicians, drug designers and philosophers, Andrew Solomon confronts the challenge of defining the illness and describes the vast range of available medications, the efficacy of alternative treatments, and the impact the malady has on various demographic populations - around the world and throughout history. *$16.00*

*576 pages 2002*
*ISBN 0-684854-67-8*

**6919  Official Patient's Sourcebook on Cystic Fi brosis**
Icon Health

For parents who have decided to make education and research an integral part of the treatment process. Although it also gives information useful to doctors, caregivers and other health professionals, it tells paretns where and how to look for information covering virtually all topics related to cystic fibrosis (also fbrocystic disease of pancreas; mucosis; mucoviscidosis; pancreatic fibrosis), from the essentials to the most advanced areas of research. *$28.95*
*356 pages 2002*
*ISBN 0-597831-46-7*

**6920  Official Patient's Sourcebook on Muscular Dystrophy**
Icon Health

Created for patients who have decided to make education and research an integral part of the treatment process. Although it also gives information useful to doctors, caregivers and other health professionals, it tells patients where and how to look for information covering virtually all topics related to muscular dystrophy. *$24.95*
*268 pages 2002*
*ISBN 0-597832-10-2*

**6921  Official Patient's Sourcebook on Post-Poli o Syndrome: A Revised and Updated Directory**
Icon Health

A sourcebook created for patients who have decided to make education and Internet-based research an integral part of the treatment process. Although it gives information useful to doctors, caregivers and other health professionals, it also tells patients where and how to look for information covering virtually all topics related to post-polio syndrome, from the essentials to the most advanced areas of research. *$28.95*
*124 pages 2003*
*ISBN 0-597835-31-4*

**6922  Omega-3 Connection: The Groundbreaking An ti-Ddepression Diet and Brain Program**
Free Press
135 S Mount Zion Road
Lebanon, IN  46052

800-323-7445
FAX: 800-882-8583

Provides readers with the information they need to restore their natural balance of omega-3 fatty acids, including: which omega-3 foods to eat, the most effective over-the-counter supplements, how to integrate flaxseed and fish oils into diet and medication plans, and simple recipes, supplement doses and sources. *$14.00*
*304 pages 2002*
*ISBN 0-684871-39-4*

**6923  On the Level**
Vestibular Disorders Association
PO Box 4467
Portland, OR  97208

503-229-7705
800-837-8428
FAX: 503-229-8064
e-mail: veda@vestibular.org
www.vestibular.org

*Lisa Haven, Editor*
*Connie Pilcher, Outreach Coordinator*

*$25.00*

*12 pages Quarterly*

**6924  Options**
PO Box 106273
Washington, DC  20016

301-897-8180
FAX: 202-466-1911
www.polio.org/

*Ed Grebenstein, President*
*Jessica Scheer PhD, Executive Director*

Quarterly newsletter of the national, not-for-profit, voluntary organziation created to provide education resources and support group services to people who had polio and are now experiencing the late effects of polio. Activities include maintenance of a national membership database of polio survivors and health care professionals; sponsorship of major national UPDATE conferences about post-polio issues; and publication of Options, quarterly newsletter.

**6925  Options: Revolutionary Ideas in the War on Cancer**
People Against Cancer
PO Box 10
Otho, IA  50569

515-972-4444
FAX: 515-972-4415
e-mail: info@PeopleAgainstCancer.net
www.peopleagainstcancer.com

Publication of People Against Cancer, a nonprofit, grassroots public benefit organization dedicated to 'New Directions in the War on Cancer.' We are a democratic organization of people with cancer, their loved ones and citizens working together to protect and enhance medical freedom of choice.

**6926  Osteoporosis Sourcebook**
Omnigraphics
615 Griswold Street
Detroit, MI  48226

313-961-1340
800-234-1340
FAX: 800-875-1340
www.omnigraphics.com

*Allan R Cook, Editor*
*Peter Ruffner, President*

Discusses causes, risk factors, treatments and traditional and non-traditional pain management issues concerning osteoporosis. *$ 78.00*
*600 pages 2000*
*ISBN 0-780802-39-X*

**6927  Otitos Media in Young Children: Medical, Developmental, & Educational Considerations**
Brookes Publishing
PO Box 10624
Baltimore, MD  21285

410-337-9580
800-638-3775
FAX: 410-337-8539
e-mail: custserv@brookespublishing.com
www.brookespublishing.com

*Ina F Wallace PhD, Editor*
*Frederick W Henderson, Editor*
*Paul Brooks, Owner*

This book reviews the current literature on the epidemiology, diagnosis, and medical management of otitis media; its secondary audiologic and communicative effects; and its impact on children and families. *$48.95*
*352 pages Hardcover 1997*
*ISBN 1-557662-78-9*

**6928  Out of the Fog: Treatment Options and Cop ing Strategies for ADD**
Hyperion

Discusses the recent recognition of attention deficit disorder as a problem that is not outgrown in adolescence, and cogently summarizes the stumbling blocks this affliction creates in the pursuit of a career or attainment of a healthy family life *$14.95*

*300 pages 1995*
*ISBN 0-786880-87-2*

**6929 Out-Of-Sync Child: Recognizing and Coping With Sensory Integration Dysfunction**
Perigee Books

This guide explains how SI Dysfunction can be confused with ADD, learning disabilities, and other problems, tells how parents can recognize the problem and offers a drug-free treatment approach for children who need help. *$14.95*
*322 pages 1998*
*ISBN 0-399523-86-3*

**6930 Overcoming Dyslexia**
Vintage

Yale neuroscientist Shaywitz demystifies the roots of dyslexia (a neurologically based reading difficulty affecting one in five children) and offers parents and educators hope that children with reading problems can be helped. *$15.00*
*432 pages 1905*
*ISBN 0-679781-59-5*

**6931 PDF News**
Parkinson's Disease Foundation
833 W Washington Boulevard
Chicago, IL  60607

312-733-1893
FAX: 312-733-1896
e-mail: pdfchgo@enteract.com
PDF@info.org

*Lewis P Rowland MD, President*
*Jeanne Rosner, Executive Director*
*8-12 pages Quarterly*

**6932 PDF Newsletter**
Parkinson's Disease Foundation
710 W 168th Street
New York, NY  10032

212-923-4700
800-457-6676
FAX: 212-923-4778
e-mail: info@pdf.org
www.pdf.org

*Robin Elliott, Executive Director*
*Patricia Arroyo, Business Administrator*
*12-16 pages Quarterly*

**6933 PSP Advocate**
Society for Progressive Supranuclear Palsy
1838 Greene Tree Road
Baltimore, MD  21208

410-486-3330
800-457-4777
FAX: 410-486-4283
e-mail: spsp@psp.org
www.psp.org

*Elizabeth Brisson, President*
*Stephen Hamer, VP*
*Kelley Harrison PhD, Secretary*

Quarterly newsletter. The society's mission is to promote and fund research into finding the cause and cure for progressive supranuclear palsy (PSP). Provides information, support and advocacy to persons diagnosed with PSP, their families and caregivers. Educates physicians and allied health professionals on PSP and how to improve patient care.

**6934 Partial Seizure Disorders: Help for Patients and Families**
Patient-Centered Guides
101 Morris Street
Sebastopol, CA  95472

707-829-0515
800-998-9938
FAX: 707-829-0104
www.patientcenters.com

*Linda Lamb, Editor*
*Shawnde Paull, Marketing*
*Tim O'Reilly, Chief Executive Officer*

Partial Seizure Disorders helps patients and families get an accurate diagnosis of this condition, understand medications and their side effects, and learn coping skills and other adjuncts to medication. It walks readers through developmental and school issues for young children; adult issues such as employment and driving; working with an existing health plan; and getting further help through advocacy and support organizations, articles, and online resources. *$19.95*
*288 pages Paperback*
*ISBN 0-596500-03-3*

**6935 Personal Guide to Living Well with Fibromyalgia**
Arthritis Foundation Distribution Center
PO Box 6996
Alpharetta, GA  30023

800-207-8633
FAX: 770-442-9742
www.arthritis.com

With this guide you'll learn the latest information about fibromyalgia, what researchers have uncovered about its causes, and an overview of the best treatment options available. Helpful worksheets and tables allow you to manage your condition and document your progress. *$14.95*
*224 pages*

**6936 Peterson's Colleges With Programs for Students With Learning Disabilities or ADDs**
Peterson's

Lists over 1,000 two- and four-year colleges that welcome students with learning disabilities. Includes schools that offer services and comprehensive programs. CD-ROM and quick-reference chart provided. *$29.95*
*672 pages 2000*
*ISBN 0-768904-55-2*

**6937 Polio Network News**
Gazette International Networking Institute
4207 Lindell Boulevard
Suite 110
Saint Louis, MO  63108

314-534-0475
FAX: 314-534-5070
e-mail: gini_intl@msn.com
www.post-polio.org

International newsletter for polio survivors, support groups and health professionals concerned about the late effects of polio. *$20.00*
*12 pages Quarterly*

**6938 Post Polio**
Accent Books & Products
PO Box 700
Bloomington, IL  61702

309-378-2961
800-787-8444
FAX: 309-378-4420
e-mail: acmtlvng@aol.com

*Raymond C Cheever, Publisher*
*Betty Garee, Editor*

What does post-polio syndrome mean? What can make a difference in a persons future mobility? These questions and more are answered in this great guide. *$3.95*

*47 pages Paperback*
*ISBN 0-91570 -21-3*

**6939 Post-Polio Health**
Post-Polio Health International
4207 Lindell Boulevard
Suite 110
Saint Louis, MO 63108

314-534-0475
FAX: 314-534-5070
TTY:800-735-2966
e-mail: info@post-polio.org
www.post-polio.org

*John L Headly, Editor*

To enhance the lives and independence of polio survivors by promoting education, networking, and advocacy among these individuals and healthcare providers. Post-Polio Health supports Post-Polio Health International's educational, research, and advocacy efforts. Offers information about relevant events.
*12 pages quarterly*

**6940 Post-Polio Syndrome Information Book**
PO Box 182
Howard Beach, NY 11414

718-835-5536
FAX: 718-738-1509
e-mail: w1066@msn.com
www.geocities.com/w1066w

*100 pages*

**6941 Post-Polio Syndrome: A Guide for Polio Su rvivors and Their Families**
Yale University Press

A guide for polio survivors, their families, and their health care providers offers expert advice on all aspects of post-polio syndrome. Based on the author's experience treating post-polio patients, Silver discusses issues of critical importance, including how to find the best medical care, deal with symptoms, sustain mobility, manage pain, approach insurance issues, and arrange a safe living environment. *$ 16.95*
*304 pages 2002*
*ISBN 0-300088-08-6*

**6942 Prader-Willi Alliance of New York Monthly Newsletter**
267 Oxford Street
Rochester, NY 14607

585-442-1655
800-442-1655
FAX: 716-271-2782
e-mail: balleregballer@aol.com
www.prader-willi.org

*Elinor G Baller, Secretary*
*Volena How, Owner*

The Prader-Willi Foundation is a national, nonprofit public charity that works for the benefit of individuals with Prader-Willi syndrome and their families.

**6943 Prader-Willi Syndrome: Development and Ma nifestations**
Cambridge University Press

Seeks to identify and provide the latest findings about how best to manage the complex medical, nutritional, psychological, educational, social and therapeutic needs of people with PWS.
*$100.00*

*230 pages 2004*
*ISBN 0-521840-29-5*

**6944 Pressure Sores**
Accent Books & Products
PO Box 700
Bloomington, IL 61702

309-378-2961
800-787-8444
FAX: 309-378-4420
e-mail: acmtlvng@aol.com

*Raymond C Cheever, Publisher*
*Betty Garee, Editor*

All it takes is one to put a stop to all of your activities. This book offers ways to be able to be comfortable and worry-free by knowing how to treat, recognize and prevent pressure sores.
*$3.50*
*29 pages Paperback*
*ISBN 0-91570 -20-5*

**6945 Preventable Brain Damage**
Springer Publishing Company
536 Broadway
New York, NY 10012

212-431-4370
877-687-7476
FAX: 212-941-7842
e-mail: marketing@springerpub.com
www.springerpub.com

*Annette Imperati, Marketing/Sales Director*
*Ursula Springer, President*

Offers information on brain injuries from motor vehicle accidents, contact sports and injuries of children. *$35.95*
*256 pages*

**6946 Preventing Secondary Conditions Associated with Spina Bifida or Cerebral Palsy**
Spina Bifida Association of America
4590 Macarthur Boulevard NW
Suite 250
Washington, DC 20007

202-944-3285
800-621-3141
FAX: 202-944-3295
e-mail: sbaa@sbaa.org
www.sbaa.org

*Cindy Brownstein, Chief Executive Officer*

This report is for health professionals, parents and teachers. *$3.00*

**6947 Primer on Amputations and Artificial Limbs**
CC Thomas

Based on recommendations developed at the 1990 international conference on amputation surgery. Following a short history of prosthetics, chapters detail surgery involving each joint and limb, fitting of protheses, and in conclusion, special considerations in the management of child and elderly amputees. *$57.95*
*295 pages 1998*
*ISBN 0-398068-01-1*

**6948 Primer on the Rheumatic Diseases**
Arthritis Foundation
PO Box 6996
Alpharetta, GA 30023

800-207-8633
FAX: 404-872-0457
www.arthritis.com

Written to educate medical students and family physicians, this is the authoritative guide on the rheumatic diseases. *$39.95*

*513 pages*

**6949 Progress in Research**
Christopher Reeve Paralysis Foundation
636 Morris Tpke
Suite 3a
Short Hills, NJ 07078 973-379-2690
800-225-0292
FAX: 973-912-9433
e-mail: paralysis@aol.com
www.paralysis.org

*Kathy Lewis, President*

Summarizes research on paralysis and spinal cord injury, emphasizing neural regeneration.

**6950 Pure Facts**
Feingold Association of the US
554 E Main Street
Suite 301
Riverhead, NY 11901 631-369-9340
800-321-3287
FAX: 631-369-2988
e-mail: help@feingold.org
www.feingold.org

*Jane Hersey, Editor*
*Debbie Lehner, Manager*

Relationship between foods, food additives and behavior/learning problems, including Attention Deficit Disorder (ADD) and hyperactivity. *$38.00*
*10+ pages Monthly*

**6951 Rasmussen's Syndrome and Hemispherectomy Support Network Newsletter**
8235 Lethbridge Road
Millersville, MD 21108 410-987-5221
FAX: 410-987-521
e-mail: rssnlynn@aol.com

*Al & Lynn Miller, Founders*

National, not-for-profit organization dedicated to providing information and support to individuals affected by Rasmussen's Syndrome and hemispherectomy. Publishes a periodic newsletter and disseminates reprints of medical journal articles concerning Rasmussen's Syndrome and its treatments. Maintains a support network that provides encouragement and information to individuals affected by Rasmussen's Syndrome and their families.

**6952 Reality of Dyslexia**
Brookline Books
PO Box 1047
Cambridge, MA 02139 617-868-0360
800-666-2665
FAX: 617-868-1772
e-mail: brooklinebks@delphi.com
www.brooklinebooks.com
An informative and sensitive study of living with dyslexia which affects one in 25. He introduces the reader to the subject by sharing the difficulties of his dyslexic son. He then uses the personal accounts of other children and adult dyslexics, even entire dyslexic families, to illuminate the problems they encounter. *$14.95*
*150 pages Paperback*
*ISBN 1-57129-17-6*

**6953 Record Book for Individuals with Autism**
Autism Society of North Carolina Bookstore
505 Oberlin Road
Suite 230
Raleigh, NC 27605 919-743-0204
800-442-2762
FAX: 919-743-0208
e-mail: dcoffey@autismsociety-nc.org
www.autismsociety-nc.org

*Darla Coffey, Bookstore Manager*
*Jill Keel, Executive Director*

Developed with parent input to provide one place to keep information about an autistic child. *$7.00*

**6954 Relationship Development Intervention with Young Children**
Taylor & Francis Group

Social and emotional development activities for Asperger Syndrome, Autism, PDD and NLD. Comprehensive set of activities emphasizes foundation skills for younger children between the ages of two and eight. Covers skills such as social referencing, regulating behvior, conversational reciprocity, and synchronized actions. For use in therapeutic settings as well as schools and parents. *$22.95*
*256 pages 2002*
*ISBN 1-843107-14-7*

**6955 Riddle of Autism: A Psychological Analysis**
Jason Aronson
400 Keystone Industrial Park
Dunmore, PA 18512
800-782-0015
FAX: 201-840-7242
www.aronson.com
Dr. Victor examines the myths that cloud an understanding of this disorder and describes the meanings of its specific behavioral symptoms. *$30.00*
*356 pages Softcover*
*ISBN 1-568215-73-8*

**6956 SCI Psychosocial Process**
Amer. Assn. of Spinal Cord Injury Psych./Soc. Wks.
7520 Astoria Boulevard
East Elmhurst, NY 11370 718-803-3782
FAX: 718-803-0414
e-mail: ssofer@epua.org
www.aascipsw.org

*E Jason Mask LCSW, Editor*
*Peter Addesso, President*

Quarterly newsletter.

**6957 SCI/LIFE**
National Spinal Cord Injury Association
6701 Democracy Boulevard
Suite 300-9
Bethesda, MD 20817 301-214-4006
800-962-9629
FAX: 301-588-9414
e-mail: Info@spinalcord.org
www.spinalcord.org

*Charles W Haynes, Publisher*
*J Charles Haynes JD, Publisher*
*Thomas H Countee Jr, Esq, Editor-in-Chief*

SCI/LIFE is dedicated to the presentation of news concerning people with spinal cord injuries caused by trauma or disease. *$38.00*
*39 pages Quarterly*

**6958 SPINabilities: A Young Person's Guide to Spina Bifida**
Spina Bifida Association of America
4590 Macarthur Boulevard NW
Suite 250
Washington, DC 20007 202-944-3285
800-621-3141
FAX: 202-944-3295
e-mail: sbaa@sbaa.org
www.sbaa.org

*Cindy Brownstein, Chief Executive Officer*

A cool and practical book for young adults becoming independent. *$19.00*

**6959  School Based Assessment of Attention Deficit Disorders**
National Clearinghouse of Rehabilitation Materials
5202 N Richmond Hill Drive
Stillwater, OK  74078                   405-624-7650
                                        800-223-5219
                                    FAX: 405-624-0695
Presents an overview of current thoughts concerning ADD from an educational perspective, contrast traditional assessment strategies with an alternative model, and describe phases of evaluation.Paperback $6.10
*61 pages*

**6960  Self-Coaching: How to Heal Anxiety and De pression**
Wiley Publishing
605 3rd Avenue
New York, NY  10158                     212-850-6000
                                    FAX: 212-850-6088
For those who are uncomfortable with the thought of entering therapy or using medication, the self-coaching work here may be just the ticket to greater freedom from depression and anxiety. *$14.95*
*272 pages 2001*
*ISBN 0-471387-37-1*

**6961  Self-Therapy for the Stutterer**
Stuttering Foundation of America
PO Box 11749
Memphis, TN  38111                      901-452-7343
                                        800-992-9392
                                    FAX: 901-452-3931
                             e-mail: stutter@vantek.net
                                    www.stutterhelp.org

*Jane Fraser, President*

A guide to help adults who stutter overcome the problem on their own. *$3.00*
*191 pages Paperback*
*ISBN 0-933388-32-2*

**6962  Sexuality After Spinal Cord Injury: Answers to Your Questions**
Brookes Publishing
PO Box 10624
Baltimore, MD  21285                    410-337-9580
                                        800-638-3775
                                    FAX: 410-337-8539
                    e-mail: custserv@brookespublishing.com
                            www.brookespublishing.com

*Paul Brooks, Owner*

Anatomy, fertility, sexually transmitted diseases, self-esteem, sexual satisfaction, and parenting are among the many physical and emotional issues discussed in this guide. Question-and-answer format. *$24.95*
*272 pages Paperback 1997*
*ISBN 1-557662-65-7*

**6963  Sexuality and the Person with Spina Bifida**
Spina Bifida Association of America
4590 Macarthur Boulevard NW
Suite 250
Washington, DC 20007                    202-944-3285
                                        800-621-3141
                                    FAX: 202-944-3295
                               e-mail: sbaa@sbaa.org
                                    www.sbaa.org

*Cindy Brownstein, Chief Executive Officer*

Dr Sloan foucuses on sexual development, sexual activity and other important issues. *$11.00*

**6964  Shoebox Tasks: Work Activities**
Autism Society of North Carolina Bookstore
505 Oberlin Road
Suite 230
Raleigh, NC  27605                      919-743-0204
                                        800-442-2762
                                    FAX: 919-743-0208
                    e-mail: dcoffey@autismsociety-nc.org
                            www.autismsociety-nc.org

*Darla Coffey, Bookstore Manager*
*Jill Keel, Executive Director*

*$250.00*

**6965  Simon Foundation for Continence**
PO Box 815
Wilmette, IL  60091                     847-864-3913
                                        800-23S-IMON
                                    FAX: 847-864-9758
                                www.simonfoundation.org

*Cheryle B Gartley, President*

Publishes items of interest to people with bladder or bowel incontinence, including medical articles, helpful devices, publications and a pen pal list.

**6966  Single-Handed: A Book for Persons with the Use of Only One Hand**
Accent Books & Products
PO Box 700
Bloomington, IL  61702                  309-378-2961
                                        800-787-8444
                                    FAX: 309-378-4420
                              e-mail: acmtlvng@aol.com

*Raymond C Cheever, Publisher*
*Betty Garee, Editor*

Includes information on devices and aids; special techniques; tips on how-to; illustrations; other helpful publications and more. *$4.25*
*25 pages Paperback*
*ISBN 0-91570 -06-0*

**6967  Sinus Survival**
Jeremy P Tarcher
8552 E Dry Creek Place
Centennial, CO  80112
                                        888-434-0033
                                    FAX: 303-221-5320
Self-help manual for sufferers of bronchitis, sinusitis, allergies, and colds.

**6968  Smart But Stuck: Emotional Aspects of Learning Disabilities and Imprisoned Intelligence**
Haworth Press
10 Alice Street
Binghamton, NY  13904                   607-722-5857
                                        800-429-6784
                                    FAX: 607-722-6362
                    e-mail: orders@haworthpress.com
                            www.haworthpress.com

*S Harrington-Miller, Advertising*
*William Cohen, Owner*

Elaborates on new research about imprisoned intelligence and the emotional consequences of learning disabilities. It is also for psychotherapists, educators, school social workers, medical personnel, people dealing with prisons, etc. It helps those who struggle with learning disabilities (and people who help them) build self esteem, face LD obstacles, bypass weaknesses, and enhance strenghts. *$34.95*

*228 pages Hardcover*
*ISBN 0-789014-66-1*

**6969 Solving the Puzzle of Chronic Fatigue**
Life Sciences Press
1216 S 1580 W
Suite A
Orem, UT 84058                     801-224-6228
                                   800-336-6308
        e-mail: info@essentialscience.net
    www.insight-books.com/new/0943685117.html
Although primarily a book about CFS, this comprehensive study
also provides a detailed overview of candidiasis, including its
causes and best approaches for treatment. *$14.95*
        *190 pages 1992*
        *ISBN 0-943685-11-7*

**6970 Son-Rise: The Miracle Continues**
2080 S Undermountain Road
Sheffield, MA 01257                413-229-2100
                                   800-714-2779
        FAX: 413-229-3202
        e-mail: sonrise@option.org
            www.son-rise.org
Documents Raun Kaufman's astonishing development from a
lifeless, autistic, retarded child into a highly verbal, lovable
youngster with no traces of his former condition. Details Raun's
extraordinary progress from the age of four into young adulthood, also shares moving accounts of five families that successfully used the Son-Rise Program to reach their own special
children.
        *372 pages 1994*
        *ISBN 0-915811-53-7*

**6971 Soon Will Come the Light**
Autism Society of North Carolina Bookstore
505 Oberlin Road
Suite 230
Raleigh, NC 27605                  919-743-0204
                                   800-442-2762
        FAX: 919-743-0208
        e-mail: dcoffey@autismsociety-nc.org
            www.autismsociety-nc.org

*Darla Coffey, Bookstore Manager*
*Jill Keel, Executive Director*

Offers new perspectives on the perplexing disability of autism.
*$19.95*

**6972 Spectrum**
Autism Society of North Carolina
505 Oberlin Road
Suite 230
Raleigh, NC 27605                  919-743-0204
                                   800-442-2762
        FAX: 919-743-0208
        e-mail: dcoffey@autismsociety-nc.org
            www.autismsociety-nc.org

*David Laxton, Editor*
*Jill Keel, Executive Director*

Quarterly publication from the Autism Society of North
Carolina. *$30.00*
        *Quarterly*

**6973 Spinal Cord Injury Life**
National Spinal Cord Injury Association
8701 Georgia Avenue
Suite 500
Silver Spring, MD 20910            617-469-0004
                                   800-962-9629
        FAX: 301-588-9414
        e-mail: nscia2@aol.com
            www.spinalcord.org

*Thomas H Countee Jr, Executive Director*

Includes sections such as Legislative Action, Information Resources and Research Notes. *$30.00*

*45-60 pages Quarterly*

**6974 Spinal Network: The Total Wheelchair Reso urce Book**
Nine Lives Press

Nearly 600 pages of profiles, articles and resources on every
topic of interest to wheelchair users. Subjects include health,
coping, relationships, sexuality, parenthood, computers, sports,
recreation, travel, personal assistance services, legal rights, financial strategies, employment, and media images. *$39.95*
        *586 pages 2002*
        *ISBN 0-971522-30-8*

**6975 Spine**
JB Lippincott
E Washington Square
Philadelphia, PA 19105             215-521-8300
                                   FAX: 215-824-7390

*J Lippincott, Chief Executive Officer*

Publishes original papers on theoretical issues and research concerning the spine and spinal cord injuries. *$9.00*
        *Monthly*

**6976 Sports n' Spokes Magazine**
Paralyzed Veterans of America
801 18th Street NW
Washington, DC 20006               202-872-1300
                                   800-424-8200
                                   888-888-2201
        e-mail: info@pva.org
            www.pva.org

*Joseph L Fox Sr, National President*
*Tom Wheaton, Senior VP*
*Gene A Crayton, National VP*

Publication of the PVA, a congressionally chartered veterans
service organization, with unique expertise on a wide variety of
issues involving the special needs of our members— veterans of
the armed forces who have experienced spinal cord injury or
dysfunction.
        *1946*

**6977 Stricken: Voices from the Hidden Epidemic of Chronic
Fatigue Syndrome**
Haworth Press
10 Alice Street
Binghamton, NY 13904               607-722-5857
                                   800-429-6784
        FAX: 607-722-6362
        e-mail: orders@haworthpress.com
            www.haworthpress.com

*William Cohen, Owner*

A collection of personal accounts from sufferers of chronic fatigue immune dysfunction syndrome. The contributions come
from patients from all walks of life, from a former marathon run-
ner to a public health activist living in the margins of race and
gender. An exploration of the complex social and political dynamics surrounding the disorder. *$24.95*
        *270 pages 2000*
        *ISBN 0-789008-95-5*

**6978 Stroke Connection**
American Heart Association
7272 Greenville Avenue
Dallas, TX 75231                   214-373-6300
                                   800-553-6321
                                   FAX: 214-369-3685

*M Wheeler, Chief Executive Officer*

A forum for stroke survivors and their families to share information about coping with stroke. Provides information and referrals, and carries stroke related books, videos and literature
available for purchase.

**6979 Stuttering**
Federal Government
31 Center Drive Msc2320
Bethesda, MD 20892

800-241-1044
FAX: 301-402-0018
e-mail: nidcdinfo@nidcd.nih.gov
www.nidcd.nih.gov

*Marin P Allen PhD, Chief OHCPL*

Describes how speech is produced, treatments for stuttering and research supported by the federal government.

**6980 TBC Focus**
400 S State Street
5
Chicago, IL 60605

312-747-4001
800-757-4654
e-mail: mgrady@ch.publib.org

*Mamie Grady, Librarian*

Published quarterly by the Chicago Public Library Talking Book Center. Free of charge.
*4 pages Quarterly*

**6981 TSA Newsletter**
Tourette Syndrome Association
4240 Bell Boulevard
Bayside, NY 11361

718-224-2999
800-237-0717
FAX: 718-279-9596
e-mail: ts@tsa-usa.org
www.tsa-usa.org

*Fred Cook, Editor*
*Judit Ungar, Editor*
*Tracy Colletti-Flynn, Editor*
*Quarterly*

**6982 Teach and Reach Students with Attention Deficit Disorders**
MultiGrowth Resources
12345 Jones Road
Suite 101
Houston, TX 77070

281-890-5334
FAX: 281-894-8611

*Nancy Eisenberg, Owner*

Handbook adn resource guide for parents and educators of ADD students. *$19.95*
*200 pages*
*ISBN 0-963084-70-4*

**6983 Teaching Children with Autism: Strategies to Enhance Communication**
Autism Society of North Carolina Bookstore
505 Oberlin Road
Suite 230
Raleigh, NC 27605

919-743-0204
800-442-2762
FAX: 919-743-0208
e-mail: dcoffey@autismsociety-nc.org
www.autismsociety-nc.org

*Darla Coffey, Bookstore Manager*
*Jill Keel, Executive Director*

This valuable new book describes teaching strategies and instructional adaptations which promote communication and socialization in children with autism. *$38.95*

**6984 Teaching and Mainstreaming Autistic Children**
Love Publishing Company
1777 S Bellaire Street
Denver, CO 80222

303-221-7333
FAX: 303-221-7444
e-mail: lovepublishing@compuserve.com

*Stan Love, Owner*

Dr. Knoblock advocates a highly organized, structured environment for autistic children, with teachers and parents working together. His premise is that the learning and social needs of autistic children must be analyzed and a daily program be designed with interventions that respond to this functional analysis of their behavior. *$24.95*

*ISBN 0-891081-11-9*

**6985 Techniques for Aphasia Rehab: (TARGET) Generating Effective Treatment**
Speech Bin
1965 25th Avenue
Vero Beach, FL 32960

772-770-0007
800-477-3324
FAX: 772-770-0006
www.speechbin.com

Practical treatment manual for use by aphasia clinicians. *$45.00*
*384 pages*
*ISBN 0-93785 -50-5*

**6986 Ten Things I Learned from Bill Porter**
New World Library

Bill Porter worked for the Watkins Corp, selling household products door-to-door in one of Portland's worst neighborhoods. Afflicted with cerebral palsy and burdened with continual pain, Porter was determined not to live on government disability and went on to become Watkin's top-grossing salesman in Portland, the Northwest, and the US. This book was written by the woman who worked as Porter's typist and driver and later became his friend and cospeaker. *$20.00*
*160 pages 2002*
*ISBN 1-577312-03-1*

**6987 Three Hundred Tips for Making Life with Multiple Sclerosis Easier**
Demos Medical Publishing
386 Park Ave S
Suite 201
New York, NY 10016

212-683-0072
800-532-8663
FAX: 212-683-0118
e-mail: orderdep@demosmedpub.com
www.demosmedpub.com

*Diana Schneider PhD, President*
*Phyllis Gold, Owner*

This latest book in the Making Life Easier series features tip, techniques and shortcuts for conserving time and energy so you can do more of the things you want to do. These tips should help increase the number of good days you have while encouraging you to develop your own techniques for making life easier. *$18.95*
*109 pages 1999*
*ISBN 1-888799-23-4*

**6988 Tourette Syndrome Association Annual Medical Letter**
4240 Bell Boulevard
Bayside, NY 11361

718-224-2999
800-237-0717
FAX: 718-279-9596
e-mail: ts@tsa-usa.org
www.tsa-usa.org

*Fred Cook, Chair*
*Judit Ungar, President*

National, nonprofit membership organization. Mission is to identify the cause of, find the cure for, and control the effects of this disorder. A growing number of local chapters nationwide provide educational materials, seminars, conferences and support groups for over 35,000 members.

**6989 Tourette Syndrome Association Newsletter**
4240 Bell Boulevard
Bayside, NY 11361
718-224-2999
800-237-0717
FAX: 718-279-9596
e-mail: ts@tsa-usa.org
www.tsa-usa.org

*Fred Cook, Chair*
*Judit Ungar, President*

National, nonprofit membership organization. Mission is to identify the cause of, find the cure for, and control the effects of this disorder. A growing number of local chapters nationwide provide educational materials, seminars, conferences and support groups for over 35,000 members.
*Quarterly*

**6990 Tourette Syndrome: The Facts**
Oxford University Press
198 Madison Avenue
New York, NY 10016
212-726-6000
800-451-7556
FAX: 919-677-1303
www.oup-usa.org

*Laura Brown, Chief Executive Officer*

The causes of the syndrome, how it is diagnosed, and the ways in which it can be treated. *$19.95*
*110 pages 1998*
*ISBN 0-198523-98-X*

**6991 Tourette's Syndrome - Tics, Obsessions, Co mpulsions: Developmental Psychopathology**
Wiley Publishing
605 3rd Avenue
New York, NY 10158
212-850-6000
FAX: 212-850-6088
Contains 21 contributions compromising the work of researchers associated with the Yale Child Study Center, which has been at the forefront of research on Tourette's syndrome and associated disorders. *$65.00*
*600 pages 2001*
*ISBN 0-471113-75-1*

**6992 Tourette's Syndrome: Finding Answers and Getting Help**
Patient-Centered Guides
101 Morris Street
Sebastopol, CA 95472
707-829-0515
800-998-9938
FAX: 707-829-0104
www.patientcenters.com

*Linda Lamb, Editor*
*Shawnde Paull, Marketing*
*Tim O'Reilly, Chief Executive Officer*

Tourette's Syndrome is a neurological disorder usually diagnosed in childhood and characterized by tics, physical jerks, and involuntary vocalizations. Tourette's can be a devastating disability. The good news is that it's very treatable. Tourette's Syndrome helps you secure a diagnosis, understand medical interventions, get healthcare coverage, and manage Tourette's in family life, school, community, and workplace. *$24.95*
*356 pages Paperback*
*ISBN 0-596500-07-6*

**6993 Toward Healthy Living: A Wellness Journal**
Arthritis Foundation Distribution Center
PO Box 6996
Alpharetta, GA 30023
800-207-8633
FAX: 770-442-9742
www.arthritis.com
This spiral-bound journal has ample pages where you can unleach you thoughts, plus scales to monitor your mook and pain. Throught the book you will also find wisdom from a variety of famous and ordinary people - those who live with chronic ilness, and those whose life lessons can help you gain a more positive outlook on daily living. *$9.95*

*144 pages*

**6994 Traumatic Brain Injury: Cognitive & Communication Disorders**
Federal Government
31 Center Drive Msc2320
Bethesda, MD 20892
800-241-1044
FAX: 301-402-0018
e-mail: nidcdinfo@nidcd.nih.gov
www.nidcd.nih.org
Explains what is traumatic brain injury, who suffer from head trauma, what are the cognitive and communication problems that result from traumatic brain injury, how cognitive and communication probles assessed and how they are treated, and what research is being done for the cognitive and communication prblems caused by traumatic brain injury.

**6995 Treating Epilepsy Naturally: A Guide to A lternative and Adjunct Therapies**
McGraw-Hill Company
2460 Kerper Boulevard
Dubuque, IA 52001
563-588-1451
800-338-3987
FAX: 614-755-5654
www.mhhe.com/hper/physed

*Kurt Strand, Vice President*

Offers alternative treatments to replace and to complement traditional therapies and sound advice to find the right health practitioner. *$16.95*
*288 pages 2001*
*ISBN 0-658013-79-3*

**6996 Treatment for Chronic Depression**
Guilford Press
72 Spring Street
New York, NY 10012
212-431-9800
800-365-7006
FAX: 212-966-6708
www.guilford.com

*Bob Matloff, President*

*$39.00*
*Cloth*
*ISBN 1-572305-27-4*

**6997 Two Hundred Fifty Tips for Making Life with Arthritis Easier**
Longstreet Press
325 N Milledge Avenue
Athens, GA 30601
706-543-5999
FAX: 404-254-0016
e-mail: info@longstreetpress.com
www.longstreetpress.com

*Thomas Cogburn, Distribution Director*

Is it difficult for you to handle everyday chores because of pregnancy, back problems, or the general effects of aging? If so, you'll find tremendous help in the 250 tips in this book. Discover ways to do everything from adapting your home to completing chores and organizing household activities. Even if your limitations are only minimal, you'll find an abundance of suggestions to help you work smarter, faster and more efficiently. *$9.95*
*88 pages 1997*
*ISBN 1-563523-81-7*

**6998 Ultimate Stranger, The Autistic Child**
Academic Therapy Publications
20 Commercial Boulevard
Novato, CA 94949
415-883-3314
800-442-7249
FAX: 415-883-3720
www.bookfinder.com

*Anna M Arena, President*

Clinical background and theories of rehabilitation for the autistic child. *$15.00*

*240 pages Paperback*
*ISBN 0-878794-46-8*

**6999 Understanding & Controlling Stuttering: A Comprehensive New Approach Based on the Valsa Hypo**
National Stuttering Association

Demonstrates how physical and psychological factors may interact to stimulate and perpetuate stuttering through a Valsalva-Stuttering cycle. *$25.00*
*176 pages 2000*
*ISBN 7-929773-01-3*

**7000 Understanding Asthma: The Blueprint for Breathing**
National Allergy and Asthma Network
3554 Chain Bridge Road
Suite 200
Fairfax, VA 22030                          703-385-4403
                                     FAX: 703-352-4354
A layman's guide to asthma facts based on a presentation from the first national asthma patient conference.

**7001 Understanding Cystic Fibrosis**
University Press of Mississippi

A reference for CF patients and their families. *$12.00*
*133 pages 1998*
*ISBN 0-878059-67-9*

**7002 Understanding Juvenile Rheumatoid Arthritis**
American Juvenile Arthritis Organization
PO Box 7669
Atlanta, GA 30357                          404-872-7100
                                          800-283-7800
                                     FAX: 404-872-9559
                                e-mail: help@arthritis.org
                                     www.arthritis.org

*John Klippel, Chief Executive Officer*
A manual for health professionals to use in teaching children with JRA and their families about disease management and self-care. *$61.20*
*372 pages*

**7003 Understanding Multiple Sclerosis**
MacMillan Publishing Company
135 S Mount Zion Road
Lebanon, IN 46052
                                     FAX: 800-882-8583
Two psychologists discuss their roles with a member who has multiple sclerosis. Includes chapters on adolescents with multiple sclerosis, employment, and research.

**7004 Understanding and Managing Learning Disabilities in Adults**
Krieger Publishing Company
PO Box 9542
Melbourne, FL 32902                        321-724-9542
                                          800-724-0025
                                     FAX: 321-951-3671
                        e-mail: info@krieger-publishing.com
                             www.krieger-publishing.com

*R Krieger, Owner*
This book first explains how the brain functions in learning and remembering throughout one's life span. Individual chapters then describe the types of learning disabilities (LD) that exist throughout adulthood: dyslexia, attention deficit disorders, Scotopic Sensitivity syndrome, Nonverbal LD, Social-Emotional LD, and mental health factors that frequently accompany learning disabilities. The discussion is two-fold. First each type of LD is described and explained, then management strategies. *$24.50*

*150 pages Hardcover*
*ISBN 1-575241-08-0*

**7005 Understanding the Nature of Autism**
Autism Society of North Carolina Bookstore
505 Oberlin Road
Suite 230
Raleigh, NC 27605                          919-743-0204
                                          800-442-2762
                                     FAX: 919-743-0208
                        e-mail: dcoffey@autismsociety-nc.org
                             www.autismsociety-nc.org

*Darla Coffey, Bookstore Manager*
*Jill Keel, Executive Director*
*$54.00*

**7006 Undoing Depression: What Therapy Doesn't Teach You and Medication Can't Give You**
Berkley Publishing Group

Psychotherapist O'Conner explains how to undo depression, by replacing depressive patterns of thinking, relating, and behaving with a new and more effective set of skills *$14.00*
*358 pages 1999*
*ISBN 0-425166-79-1*

**7007 Until Tomorrow: A Family Lives with Autism**
Autism Society of North Carolina Bookstore
505 Oberlin Road
Suite 230
Raleigh, NC 27605                          919-743-0204
                                          800-442-2762
                                     FAX: 919-743-0208
                        e-mail: dcoffey@autismsociety-nc.org
                             www.autismsociety-nc.org

*Darla Coffey, Bookstore Manager*
*Jill Keel, Executive Director*
The central theme of this book is an effort to show what it is like to live with a child who cannot communicate. *$10.00*

**7008 Usher Syndrome**
Federal Government
31 Center Drive Msc2320
Bethesda, MD 20892
                                          800-241-1044
                                     FAX: 301-402-0018
                        e-mail: nidcdinfo@nidcd.nih.gov
                             www.nidcd.nih.gov
Explains what is Usher Syndrome, who is affected by Usher syndrome, what causes Usher syndrome, how is Usher syndrome treated, and what research is being conducted on Usher syndrome.

**7009 Ventilator-Assisted Living**
Post-Polio Health International
4207 Lindell Boulevard
Suite 110
Saint Louis, MO 63108                      314-534-0475
                                     FAX: 314-534-5070
                                     TTY:800-735-2966
                             e-mail: info@post-polio.org
                                  www.post-polio.org
To enhance the lives and independence of ventilator-assisted living by promoting education, networking, and advocacy among these individuals and healthcare providers. Ventilator-Assisted Living supports Post-Polio Health International's educational, research, and advocacy efforts. Offers information about relevant events.

*12 pages quarterly*

**7010 Victims of Dementia: Services, Support and Care**
Haworth Press
10 Alice Street
Binghamton, NY 13904      607-722-5857
800-429-6784
FAX: 607-722-6362
e-mail: orders@haworthpress.com
www.haworthpress.com

*S Harrington-Miller, Advertising*
*William Cohen, Owner*
Provides an in-depth look at the concept, construction and operation of Wesley Hall, a special living area at the Chelsea United Methodist retirement home in Michigan. *$74.95*
*155 pages Hardcover*
*ISBN 1-560242-64-7*

**7011 Visually Structured Tasks**
Autism Society of North Carolina Bookstore
505 Oberlin Road
Suite 230
Raleigh, NC 27605      919-743-0204
800-442-2762
FAX: 919-743-0208
e-mail: dcoffey@autismsociety-nc.org
www.autismsociety-nc.org

*Darla Coffey, Bookstore Manager*
*Jill Keel, Executive Director*
Independent activites for students with autism and other visual learners. *$24.95*

**7012 Voice of the Diabetic**
Diabetes Action Network of the NFB
1412 i 70 Drive SW
Suite C
Columbia, MO 65203      573-875-8911
FAX: 573-875-8902
e-mail: ebrnant@socvet.net
www.nfb.org/voice.htm

*Ed Bryant, Editor*
Newsletters containing personal stories and practical guidelines by blind diabetics and medical professionals, medical news, resource column and a recipe corner. We are a support and information network for all diabetics.
*28 pages Quarterly*

**7013 Volunteer Voice**
Kentucky Chapter of the Arthritis Foundation
2908 Brownsboro Road
Suite 100
Louisville, KY 40206      502-585-1866
FAX: 502-585-1657
www.kecc.org

*Barbara Perez, Chief Executive Officer*
Newsletter offering information and updates on chapter activities, events, camps, juvenile programs and government/legislative information.

**7014 What is Vocal Hoarseness?**
Speech Bin
1965 25th Avenue
Vero Beach, FL 32960      772-770-0007
800-477-3324
FAX: 772-770-0006
www.speechbin.com
Brochures to teach parents, teachers and individuals with voice disorders about chronic hoarseness and what to do about it. Set of ten copies. *$16.95*
*24 pages Package of 10*
*ISBN 0-93785 -55-6*

**7015 What to Do When Someone You Love is Depres sed**
Owl Publishing

Directed toward the caregiver of any of the more than seventeen million Americans who suffer from this common but often misunderstood affliction. Woven throughout are the personal experiences of Mitch Golant, who spent most of his childhood with a mother who was seriously depressed, an experience that not only catapulted him into his work as a clinical psychologist, but also informs this book with a tone of compassionate understanding. *$15.00*
*192 pages 1998*
*ISBN 0-805058-29-X*

**7016 When the Road Turns: Inspirational Storie s About People with MS**
Health Care Communications
11 Heritage Lane
Rye, NY 10580      845-687-2328

An inspiring collection of stories written by people living with multiple sclerosis. *$12.95*
*300 pages 2001*
*ISBN 1-558749-07-1*

**7017 Where is the Mango Princess**
Vintage Books
1540 Broadway
New York, NY 10036      212-782-9000
FAX: 212-302-7985
www.randomhouse.com

*Carol Schneider, Marketing Executive*
When her husband Alan is injured in a speedboat accident, Cathy Crimmins reluctantly assumes the role of caregiver and learns to cope with the person he has become. Crimmins' husband has emerged from the accident a childlike and unpredictable replica of his former self with a short attention span and a penchant for inane cartoons *$13.00*
*257 pages 2001*
*ISBN 0-375704-42-6*

**7018 Winter Blues: Seasonal Affective Disorder: What it is and How to Overcome It**
Guilford Press
72 Spring Street
New York, NY 10012      212-431-9800
800-365-7006
FAX: 212-966-6708
www.guilford.com

*Bob Matloff, President*
*$15.95*
*355 pages Paperback 1998*
*ISBN 1-572303-95-6*

**7019 Women with Attention Deficit Disorder: Em bracing Disorganization at Home and Work**
Underwood-Miller
708 Westover Drive
Lancaster, PA 17601      717-285-2255
FAX: 717-285-2255
Addresses the millions of withdrawn little girls and chronically overwhelmed women with ADD who go undiagnosed because they don't fit the stereotypical notion of people with ADD. *$11.95*
*288 pages 1995*
*ISBN 1-887424-05-9*

**7020 World's Best Books from the Diabetes Experts: Publications Catalog**
American Diabetes Association
1701 N Beauregard Street
Alexandria, VA 22311      703-549-1500
800-232-6733
FAX: 770-442-9742
e-mail: bookorders@diabetes.org
www.diabetes.org

*John Fedor, Associate Director*
*Janel Chrobot, Marketing Specialist*
*Lynn Nicholas, Chief Executive Officer*

A 24 page, full-color catalog of more than 80 books and products for people with diabetes. Titles of categories of books include: cookbooks, meal planning and nutrition, new books and self-care.

**7021 You Mean I'm Not Lazy, Stupid or Crazy?!: A Self-Help Book for Adults with ADD**
Scribner

Practical advice on controlling adult ADD, a straightforward guide explains how to get along in groups, become organized, improve memory, and pursue professional help. *$15.00*
*464 pages 1996*
*ISBN 0-684815-31-1*

**7022 Young Person's Guide to Spina Bifida**
Spina Bifida Association of America
4590 Macarthur Boulevard NW
Suite 250
Washington, DC 20007          202-944-3285
                              800-621-3141
                         FAX: 202-944-3295
                     e-mail: sbaa@sbaa.org
                              www.sbaa.org

*Cindy Brownstein, Chief Executive Officer*

Gives practical tips and suggestions for becoming independent and managing your health. *$19.00*

## Visually Impaired

**7023 ABC Sign with Me**
TJ Publishers
2544 Tarpley Road
Suite 108
Carrollton, TX  75006         972-416-0800
                              800-999-1168
                         FAX: 301-585-5930
                   e-mail: TJPubinc@aol.com

*Angela K Thames, President*
*Jerald A Murphy, VP*

Offers bright pictures of familiar objects, lower case alphabet and corresponding manual alphabet hand shapes. *$3.95*
*32 pages Softcover*
*ISBN 0-93984 -00-3*

**7024 AFB News**
American Foundation for the Blind/AFB Press
11 Penn Plaza
Suite 300
New York, NY  10001           212-502-7600
                              800-232-3044
                         FAX: 212-502-7777
                  e-mail: afborders@abdintl.com
                              www.afb.org

*Carl Augusto, President*

National newsletter for general readership about blindness and visual impairments featuring people, programs, services and activities.
*12 pages Quarterly*

**7025 Access to Art: A Museum Directory for Blind and Visually Impaired People**
American Foundation for the Blind/AFB Press
PO Box 1020
Sewickley, PA  15143          412-741-1142
                              800-232-3044
                         FAX: 412-741-0609
                  e-mail: afborders@abdintl.com
                              www.afb.org

Details the access facilities of over 300 museums, galleries and exhibits in the United States. Also included are organizations offering art-related resources such as, art classes, competitions and traveling exhibits. *$19.95*

*144 pages Large Print*
*ISBN 0-891281-56-8*

**7026 African Americans in the Profession of Blindness Services**
Mississippi State University
PO Box 6189
Mississippi State, MS  39762     662-325-2001
                                 800-675-7782
                            FAX: 662-325-8989
                         www.blind.msstate.edu

*Kelly Schaefer, Dissemination Specialist*
*Elton Moore, Executive Director*

This study investigated the level of participation by African Americans in vocational rehab. (VR) services to persons who are visually impaired. Using surveys and interviews with all state VR directors, national census data and national RSA data, it was found nationally that African Americans are substantially under-represented in the service provider ranks, yet over-represented as clients. *$20.00*
*61 pages Paperback*

**7027 Age-Related Macular Degeneration**
National Association for Visually Handicapped
22 W 21st Street
Floor 6
New York, NY  10010           212-889-3141
                         FAX: 212-727-2931
                     e-mail: staff@navh.org
                              www.navh.org

*Dr Lorraine H Marchi, Founder/CEO*
*Cesar Gomez, COO*

A large booklet offering information and up-to-date research on Macular Degeneration. Also available in Russian. Revised in 2002. *$4.00*

**7028 Aging and Vision: Declarations of Independence**
American Foundation for the Blind/AFB Press
PO Box 1020
Sewickley, PA  15143          412-741-1142
                              800-232-3044
                         FAX: 412-741-0609
                  e-mail: afborders@abdintl.com
                              www.afb.org

A very personal look at five older people who have successfully coped with visual impairmant and continue to lead active, satisfying lives. Their stories are not only inspirational, but also provide practical, down-to-earth suggestions for adapting to vision loss later in life. 18 minute video tape. Also available in PAL, $52.95, 0-89128-276-9. *$42.95*
*VHS*
*ISBN 0-891282-20-3*

**7029 American Printing House for the Blind**
PO Box 6085
Louisville, KY  40206         502-895-2405
                              800-223-1839
                         FAX: 502-899-2274
                      e-mail: info@aph.org
                              www.aph.org

*Fred Gissoni, Customer Support*
*Tuck Tinsley, President*

Devoted solely to producing products for people who are visually impaired. We manufacture books and magazines in braille, large type and recorded form from over 200 vendors across the U.S. We also make a wide range of educational and daily living aids, such as braille paper and styluses, talking book equipment, and synthetic speech computer products. APH also offers LOUIS, an electronic database that lists accessible books in all formats.

**7030  Annual Report/Newsletter**
National Accreditation Council for Agencies/Blind
15 E 40th Street
Room 1004
New York, NY  10016                      212-683-5068
                                    FAX: 212-683-4475

*Ruth Westman, Executive Director*

Provides standards and a program of accreditation for schools
and organizations which serve children and adults who are blind
or vision impaired.

**7031  Art and Science of Teaching Orientation and Mobility
to Persons with Visual Impairments**
American Foundation for the Blind/AFB Press
PO Box 1020
Sewickley, PA  15143                    412-741-1142
                                        800-232-3044
                                    FAX: 412-741-0609
                            e-mail: afborders@abdintl.com
                                          www.afb.org
Comprehensive decription of the techniques of teaching orientation and mobility, presented along with considerations and strategies for sensitive and effective teaching. Hardcover. Paperback
also available. *$48.00*
        *200 pages*
        *ISBN 0-891282-45-9*

**7032  Association for Macular Diseases Newsletter**
210 E 64th Street
8th Floor
New York, NY  10021                     212-605-3719
                                    FAX: 212-605-3795
                    e-mail: association@retinal-research.org
                                        www.macula.org

*Nikolai Stevenson, President*
*Walter Ross, Editor-in-Chief*
*Joan Daly, Treasurer*

Not-for-profit organization promotes education and research in
this scarcely explored field. Acts as a nationwide support group
for individuals and their families endeavoring to adjust to the restrictions and changes brought about by macular disease. Offers
hotline, educational materials, quarterly newsletter, support
groups, referrals and seminars for persons and families affected
by macular disease.
        *1978*

**7033  Awareness**
NAPVI
PO Box 317
Watertown, MA  02471                    617-972-7441
                                        800-562-6265
                                    FAX: 617-972-7444
                            e-mail: napvi@perkins.org
                                        www.napvi.org

*Susan LaVenture, Executive Director*

Newsletter offering regional news, sports and activities, conferences, camps, legislative updates, book reviews, audio reviews,
professional question and answer column and more for the visually impaired and their families.
        *Quarterly*

**7034  Basic Course in American Sign Language**
TJ Publishers
2544 Tarpley Road
Suite 108
Carrollton, TX  75006                   972-416-0800
                                        800-999-1168
                                    FAX: 301-585-5930
                                    TTY: 301-585-4440
                            e-mail: TJPubinc@aol.com

*Angela K Thames, President*
*Jerald A Murphy, VP*

Accompanying videotapes and textbooks include voice translations. Hearing students can analyze sound for initial instruction,
or opt to turn off the sound to sharpen visual acuity. Package includes the Basic Course in American Sign Language text, Student Study Guide, the original four 1-hour videotapes plus the
ABCASI Vocabulary videotape. *$139.95*
        *280 pages Video*

**7035  Beam**
1850 W Roosevelt Road
Chicago, IL  60608                      312-666-1331
                                    FAX: 312-243-8539
                            www.thechicagolighthouse.org

*James Kesteloot, Executive Director*
*Terrence Longo, Assistant Director*

Quarterly newsletter of the organization offering progressive
programs for the blind, visually impaired, deaf-blind and
multi-disabled children and adults, including vocational programs, computer and office skills training, job placement, independent living skills, orientation and mobility training,
counseling and a low vision clinic.

**7036  Behavioral Vision Approaches for Persons with Physi-
cal Disabilities**
Optometric Extension Program Foundation
2912 Daimler Street
Santa Ana, CA  92705                    949-250-0846

A discussion of the behavioral vision/neuro-motor approach to
providing directions for prescriptive and therapeutic services
for the visually handicapped child or adult. *$49.50*
        *197 pages*

**7037  Berthold Lowenfeld on Blindness and Blind People**
American Foundation for the Blind/AFB Press
PO Box 1020
Sewickley, PA  15143                    412-741-1142
                                        800-232-3044
                                    FAX: 412-741-0609
                            e-mail: afborders@abdintl.com
                                          www.afb.org
These writings of the pioneering educator, author and advocate
range over a forty-year period include various ground-breaking
papers for the blind educator, a remembrance of Helen Keller
and other essays on education, sociology and history. *$21.95*
        *254 pages Paperback*
        *ISBN 0-891281-01-0*

**7038  Blind Educator**
National Federation of the Blind
1800 Johnson Street
Baltimore, MD  21230                    410-659-9314
                                    FAX: 410-685-5653
                            e-mail: nfb@iamdigex.net
                                          www.nfb.org

*Marc Maurer, President*

Magazine specifically for blind educators.

**7039  Blind and Vision-Impaired Individuals**
Mainstream
3 Bethesda Metro Center
Suite 830
Bethesda, MD  20814                     301-961-9299
                                        800-247-1380
                                    FAX: 301-654-6714
                            e-mail: info@mainstreaminc.org

*Charles Moster*

Mainstreaming blind individuals into the workplace. *$ 2.50*

*12 pages*

**7040  Blindness and Early Childhood Development Second Edition**
American Foundation for the Blind/AFB Press
PO Box 1020
Sewickley, PA  15143                    412-741-1142
                                        800-232-3044
                                   FAX: 412-741-0609
                        e-mail: afborders@abdintl.com
                                        www.afb.org
A review of current knowledge on motor and locomotor development, perceptual development, language and cognitive processes, and social, emotional and personality development. Paperback. *$34.95*
        *384 pages*
        *ISBN 0-891281-23-1*

**7041  Blindness, A Family Matter**
American Foundation for the Blind/AFB Press
PO Box 1020
Sewickley, PA  15143                    412-741-1142
                                        800-232-3044
                                   FAX: 412-741-0609
                        e-mail: afborders@abdintl.com
                                        www.afb.org
A frank exploration of the effects of an individual's visual impairment on other members of the family and how those family members can play a positive role in the rehabilitation process. Features interviews with three families whose 'success stories' provide advice and encouragement, as well as interviews with newly blinded adults currently involved in a rehabilitation program. 23 minute video tape. Also available in PAL, $49.95, 0-89128-271-8. *$43.95*
        *VHS 1986*
        *ISBN 0-891282-22-X*

**7042  Blindness: What it is, What it Does and How to Live with it**
American Foundation for the Blind/AFB Press
PO Box 1020
Sewickley, PA  15143                    412-741-1142
                                        800-232-3044
                                   FAX: 412-741-0609
                        e-mail: afborders@abdintl.com
                                        www.afb.org
A classic work on how blindness affects self-perception and social interaction and what can be done to restore basic skills, mobility, daily living and an appreciation of life's pleasures. *$15.95*
        *396 pages Paperback*
        *ISBN 0-891282-05-*

**7043  Braille Book Review**
National Library Service for the Blind
1291 Taylor Street NW
Washington, DC  20542                   202-707-5100
                                   FAX: 202-707-0712
                                   TTY:202-707-0744
                            e-mail: nls@loc.gov
                                  www.loc.gov/nls

*Robert Fistick, Head Publications/Media Section*
*Frank Cylke, Executive Director*

New braille books and product news.
        *30 pages BiMonthly*

**7044  Braille Documents**
Metrolina Association for the Blind
704 Louise Avenue
Charlotte, NC  28204                    704-372-3870
                                        800-926-5460
                                   FAX: 704-372-3872

*Robert Scheffel, Manager*

This production shop creates Braille and large-print documents.

**7045  Braille Forum**
American Council of the Blind
1155 15th Street NW
Suite 1004
Washington, DC  20005                   202-467-5081
                                        800-424-8666
                                   FAX: 202-467-5085
                        e-mail: slovering@acb.org
                                        www.acb.org

*Penny Reeder, Editor*
*Melanie Brunson, Executive Director*

Offered in print, braille, cassette, IBM computer disk and e-mail. $25 per format per year for companies and non-US residents.
        *48 pages Magazine*

**7046  Braille Monitor**
National Federation of the Blind
1800 Johnson Street
Baltimore, MD  21230                    410-659-9314
                                   FAX: 410-685-5653
                        e-mail: nfb@iamdigex.net
                                        www.nfb.org

*Marc Maurer, President*

Leading publication in the blindness field, with a circulation of 30,000, this publication addresses issues of concern to the blind and the philosophy and activities of the National Federation of the Blind.
        *Monthly*

**7047  Building Blocks: Foundations for Learning for Young Blind and Visually Impaired Children**
American Foundation for the Blind/AFB Press
PO Box 1020
Sewickley, PA  15143                    412-741-1142
                                        800-232-3044
                                   FAX: 412-741-0609
                        e-mail: afborders@abdintl.com
                                        www.afb.org
Presents the essential components of a successful early intervnetion program, including collaboration with family members, positive relationships between parents and professionals, public education, and attention to important programming components such as space exploration, braille readiness, orientation and mobility, play, cooking and music. Includes interviews with parents. Available in English or Spanish. 10 minute video tape. Also available in PAL, $33.95, 0-89128-268-8. *$26.95*
        *VHS*
        *ISBN 0-891282-14-9*

**7048  Bulletin**
National Association for Visually Handicapped
22 W 21st Street
New York, NY  10010                     212-889-3141
                                   FAX: 212-727-2931
                        e-mail: staff@navh.org
                                        www.navh.org

*Lorianie Marchi, Chief Executive Officer*

Annual report offering information on Association activities and events, conferences, vision aids and resources for the visually impaired.

**7049  Burns Braille Transcription Dictionary**
American Foundation for the Blind/AFB Press
PO Box 1020
Sewickley, PA  15143                    412-741-1142
                                        800-232-3044
                                   FAX: 412-741-0609
                        e-mail: afborders@abdintl.com
                                        www.afb.org
A handy, portable guide that is a quick reference for anyone who needs to check print-to-braille and braille-to-print meanings and symbols. Paperback. *$19.95*

*96 pages*
*ISBN 0-891292-32-7*

**7050 Can't Your Child See? A Guide for Parents of Visually Impaired Children**
Pro-Ed Publications
8700 Shoal Creek Boulevard
Austin, TX 78757                        512-451-3246
                                        800-897-3202
                                   FAX: 512-451-8542
                          e-mail: info@proedinc.com
                                      www.proedinc.com

*Donald Hammill, Owner*

This second edition offers parents optimistic, practical guidelines for helping visually impaired children reach their full potential. *$26.00*
*279 pages Paperback*

**7051 Career Perspectives: Interviews with Blind and Visually Impaired Professionals**
American Foundation for the Blind/AFB Press
PO Box 1020
Sewickley, PA 15143                     412-741-1142
                                        800-232-3044
                                   FAX: 412-741-0609
                        e-mail: afborders@abdintl.com
                                          www.afb.org
Profiles of 20 successful archivers who describe in their own words what it takes to pursue and attain professional success in a sighted world. Available in large print, cassette and braille. *$16.95*
*96 pages Large Print*
*ISBN 0-891281-70-3*

**7052 Careers in Blindness Rehabilitation Services**
Mississippi State University
PO Box 6189
Mississippi State, MS 39762            662-325-2001
                                        800-675-7782
                                   FAX: 662-325-8989
                                   www.blind.msstate.edu

*Kelly Schaefer, Dissemination Specialist*
*Elton Moore, Executive Director*

In a follow-up study in a series examining the substantial under-representation of African Americans as professionals in blindness services, researchers questioned college students about their knowledge, opinions and interests in blindness services. *$15.00*
*54 pages Paperback*

**7053 Cataracts**
National Association for Visually Handicapped
22 W 21st Street
Floor 6
New York, NY 10010                      212-889-3141
                                   FAX: 212-727-2931
                           e-mail: staff@navh.org
                                        www.navh.org

*Lorianie Marchi, Chief Executive Officer*

A booklet offering information about Cataracts, diagnosis and treatment of this common condition. *$2.50*

**7054 Characteristics, Services, & Outcomes of Rehab. Consumers who are Blind/Visually Impaired**
Mississippi State University
PO Box 6189
Mississippi State, MS 39762            662-325-2001
                                        800-675-7782
                                   FAX: 662-325-8989
                                   www.blind.msstate.edu

*Brenda Cavenaugh, Principal Investigatorst*
*Steven J Pierce, Graduate Research Assistant*
*Kelly Schaefer, Dissemination Specialist*

Issues regarding the efficacy of separate state agencies providing specialized vocational rehabilitation (VR) services to consumers who are blind have generated spirited discussions within the rehabilitation community throughout the history of the state-federal program. In this monograph, RRTC researches report results of their investigation of services provided to blind consumers in separate and general (combined) rehabilitation agencies. *$20.00*
*45 pages Paperback*

**7055 Childhood Glaucoma: A Reference Guide for Families**
NAPVI
PO Box 317
Watertown, MA 02471                     617-972-7441
                                        800-562-6265
                                   FAX: 617-972-7444
                          e-mail: napvi@perkins.org
                                        www.napvi.org

**7056 Children with Visual Impairments Woodbine House**
American Foundation for the Blind/AFB Press
11 Penn Plaza
Suite 300
New York, NY 10001                      212-502-7600
                                        800-232-3044
                                   FAX: 301-897-5838
                         e-mail: afborder@abdintl.com
                                          www.afb.org

*Carl Augusto, President*

Written by parents and professional, this book presents a comprehensive overview of the issues that are crucial to the healthy development of children with mild to severe visual impairments. It also offers insight from parents about coping with the emotional aspects of raising a child with special needs. *$16.95*
*416 pages*
*ISBN 0-933149-36-0*

**7057 Choice Magazine Listening**
85 Channel Drive
Port Washington, NY 11050               516-883-8280
                                        888-724-6423
                                   FAX: 516-944-6849
                          e-mail: choicemag@aol.com
                          www.choicemagazinelistening.org

*Lois Miller, Office Manager*

A free audio anthology is available bi-monthly to visually impaired/physically disabled persons nationwide. Playable on the special free 4-track cassette playback equipment which is provided by the Library of Congress through the National Library Service. Each issue features eight hours of unabridged magazine articles, short stories, poetry and media selections from over 100 sources. College level and older. Bimonthly distribution.
*Bi-Monthly*

**7058 Communication Skills for Visually Impaired Learners**
Charles C Thomas
2600 S 1st Street
Springfield, IL 62704                   217-789-8980
                                        800-258-8980
                                   FAX: 217-789-9130
                          e-mail: books@ccthomas.com
                                      www.ccthomas.com

*Michael Thomas, President*

This book has been designed to provide a foundation for a better understanding of teaching reading, writing, and listening skills to students with visual impairments from preschool age through adult levels. The plan of the book incorporates the latest research findings with the practical experiences learned in the classroom. *$49.95*

*322 pages Paperback 1997*
*ISBN 0-39806 -93-0*

**7059 Comprehensive Examination of Barriers to Employment Among Persons who are Blind or Impaired**
Mississippi State University
PO Box 6189
Mississippi State, MS 39762
662-325-2001
800-675-7782
FAX: 662-325-8989
www.blind.msstate.edu

*J Elton Moore, Author/Executive Director*
*Kelly Shaefer, Dissemination Specialist*

A multi-phase research project designed to: identify barriers to employment; identify and develop innovative successful strategies to overcome these barriers; develop methods for others to utilize these strategies; disseminate this information to rehabilitation providers; replicate the use of selected strategies in other settings. *$20.00*
*90 pages Paperback*

**7060 Concept Development for Visually Handicapped Children: A Resource Guide**
American Foundation for the Blind/AFB Press
PO Box 1020
Sewickley, PA 15143
412-741-1142
800-232-3044
FAX: 412-741-0609
e-mail: afborders@abdintl.com
www.afb.org
A program for integrating such concepts as body imagery, gross motor movement, posture and tactile discrimination into the curriculum from kindergarten on. Paperback. *$16.95*
*80 pages*
*ISBN 0-891280-18-9*

**7061 Contrasting Characteristics of Blind and Visually Impaired Clients**
Mississippi State University
PO Box 6189
Mississippi State, MS 39762
662-325-2001
800-675-7782
FAX: 662-325-8989
www.blind.msstate.edu

*Kelly Schaefer, Publications Manager*
*Elton Moore, Executive Director*

This report examines cases in the National Blindness and Low Vision Employment Database to identify and profile environmental and personal characteristics of clients who are blind or visually impaired and who were achieving successful and unsuccessful retention of competitive jobs. A total of 787 cases were analyzed. *$15.00*
*44 pages Paperback*

**7062 DVH Quarterly**
University of Arkansas at Little Rock
2801 S University Avenue
Little Rock, AR 72204
501-569-3000

*Bob Brasher, Editor*
*Mary Boaz, Manager*

Offers information on upcoming events, conferences and workshops on and for visual disabilities. Book reviews, information on the newest resources and technology, educational programs, want ads and more.
*Quarterly*

**7063 Dancing Cheek to Cheek**
Blind Children's Center
4120 Marathon Street
Los Angeles, CA 90029
323-664-2153
800-222-3567
FAX: 323-665-3828
e-mail: info@blindchildrenscenter.org
www.blindchildrenscenter.org

*Midge Horton, Executive Director*

Beginning social, play and language interactions. *$ 10.00*
*23 pages*

**7064 Data on Blindness and Visual Impairment in the US: A Resource Manual**
American Foundation for the Blind/AFB Press
PO Box 1020
Sewickley, PA 15143
412-741-1142
800-232-3044
FAX: 412-741-0609
e-mail: afborders@abdintl.com
www.afb.org
Provides facts and figures for long-range planning, preparing grant proposals and legislative services. Paperback. *$47.00*
*412 pages*
*ISBN 0-891281-52-5*

**7065 Deaf-Blind Perspective**
Teaching Research
345 Monmouth Avenue
Monmouth, OR 97361
503-838-8391
800-438-9376
FAX: 503-838-8150
e-mail: dblink@tr.wou.edu
www.tr.wou.edu/dblink

*John Reiman PhD, Director*
*Meredith Brodsky, Executive Director*

**7066 Development of Social Skills by Blind and Visually Impaired Students**
American Foundation for the Blind/AFB Press
PO Box 1020
Sewickley, PA 15143
412-741-1142
800-232-3044
FAX: 412-741-0609
e-mail: afborders@abdintl.com
www.afb.org
Offers an examination of the social interactions of blind and visually impaired children in mainstreamed settings and the community that highlights the need to teach social interaction skills to children and provide them with support. Paperback. *$39.95*
*232 pages*
*ISBN 0-891282-17-3*

**7067 Diabetic Retinopathy**
National Association for Visually Handicapped
22 W 21st Street
Floor 6
New York, NY 10010
212-889-3141
FAX: 212-727-2931
e-mail: staff@navh.org
www.navh.org

*Lorianie Marchi, Chief Executive Officer*

A booklet offering information about Diabetic Retinopathy.

**7068 Dialogue Magazine**
Blindskills
PO Box 5181
Salem, OR 97304
503-581-4224
800-860-4224
FAX: 503-581-0178
e-mail: info@blindskills.com
www.blindskills.com

*Carol M McCarl, Executive Director*
*Karen Lynn Thomas, Editor*

Publishes quarterly magazine in braille, large-type, cassette, e-mail and disk of news items, technology and articles of special interest to visually impaired youth and adults. $40.00 for not blind/legally blind. *$28.00*

*Quarterly*

**7069    Directory of Camps for Blind and Visually Impaired Children & Adults**
American Foundation for the Blind/AFB Press
PO Box 1020
Sewickley, PA  15143                 412-741-1142
                                     800-232-3044
                                FAX: 412-741-0609
              e-mail: afborders@abdintl.com
                                  www.afb.org
A guide to 200 sleepaway camps and day camps in the United States. Descriptions cover types of campers, age ranges, special activities offered, length of seasons and contact names. *$15.95*
                *34 pages Papberack*
                *ISBN 0-891281-59-2*

**7070    Diversity and Visual Impairment: The Influ ence of Race, Gender, Religion and Ethnicity**
American Foundation for the Blind
11 Penn Plaza
Suite 300
New York, NY  10001                 212-502-7600
                                    800-232-5463
                               FAX: 212-502-7777
               e-mail: afbinfo@afb.net
                             www.afb.org/store

*Carl R Augusto, President/CEO*

Cultural, social, ethnic, gender, and religious issues can influence the way an individual perceives and copes with a visual impairment. *$45.95*
                *480 pages 2001*
                *ISBN 0-891283-83-8*

**7071    Do You Remember the Color Blue: And Other Questions Kids Ask About Blindness**
Viking Books

The author answers thirteen thought-provoking questions that children have asked her over the years about being blind.
                *78 pages 2000*
                *ISBN 0-670880-43-4*

**7072    Early Focus: Working with Young Blind and Visually Impaired Children**
American Foundation for the Blind/AFB Press
PO Box 1020
Sewickley, PA  15143                 412-741-1142
                                     800-232-3044
                                FAX: 412-741-0609
                                  www.afb.org
Describes early intervention techniques used with blind and visually impaired children and stresses the benefits of family involvement and transdisciplinary teamwork. Paperback. *$32.95*
                *176 pages*
                *ISBN 0-891282-15-7*

**7073    Encyclopedia of Blindness and Vision Impairment Second Edition**
Facts on File
132 W 31st Street
Floor 17
New York, NY  10001                 212-967-8800
                                    800-322-8755
                               FAX: 212-967-9196
            e-mail: jcchambers@factsonfile.com
                           www.factsonfile.com

*James Chamber, Editor-in-Chief Arts/Humanities*
*Mark Donnell, President*

Designed to provide both laymen and professionals with concise, practical information on the second most common disability in the U.S. *$65.00*

*340 pages Hardbound*
*ISBN 6-810021-53-8*

**7074    Equals in Partnership: Basic Rights for Families of Children with Blindness**
NAPVI
PO Box 317
Watertown, MA  02471                617-972-7441
                                    800-562-6265
                               FAX: 617-972-7444
               e-mail: napvi@perkins.org
                                 www.napvi.org

**7075    Eye Research News Briefs**
Research to Prevent Blindness
645 Madison Avenue
Floor 21
New York, NY  10022                 212-421-1970
                                    800-621-0026
                               FAX: 212-688-6231
               e-mail: info@rpbusa.org
                                 www.rpbusa.org

*James V Romano PhD, COO/Manager*
*Thomas Furlong, Director Public Information*

Yearly publication from Research to Prevent Blindness. Free.
                *4 pages Yearly*

**7076    Eye and Your Vision**
National Association for Visually Handicapped
22 W 21st Street
Floor 6
New York, NY  10010                 212-889-3141
                               FAX: 212-727-2931
               e-mail: staff@navh.org
                                 www.navh.org

*Lorianie Marchi, Chief Executive Officer*

A large booklet offering information, with illustrations, on the eye. Includes information on protection of eyesight, how the eye works and vision disorders. Available in Russian and Spanish also. *$ 2.75*

**7077    Fathers: A Common Ground**
Blind Children's Center
4120 Marathon Street
Los Angeles, CA  90029              323-664-2153
                                    800-222-3567
                               FAX: 323-665-3828
         e-mail: info@blindchildrenscenter.org
                    www.blindchildrenscenter.org

*Midge Horton, Executive Director*

Exploring the concerns and roles of fathers of children with visual impairments. *$10.00*
                *50 pages*

**7078    Fighting Blindness News**
RP Foundation Fighting Blindness
1401 W Mt Royal Avenue
4th Floor
Baltimore, MD  21217                410-225-9400
                                    800-683-5555
                               FAX: 410-225-3936
                               TTY: 410-225-9409

*Greg Vaughan, Manager*

Offers information on medical updates, donor programs, assistive devices, resources and clinical trial information for persons with visual impairments, blindness and retinal degenerative diseases.

# Media, Print /Visually Impaired

**7079 First Steps**
Blind Children's Center
4120 Marathon Street
Los Angeles, CA 90029
323-664-2153
800-222-3567
FAX: 323-665-3828
e-mail: info@blindchildrenscenter.org
www.blindchildrenscenter.org

*Midge Horton, Executive Director*

A handbook for teaching young children who are visually impaired. Designed to assist students, professionals and parents working with children who are visually impaired. Visit our website for many publications addressing training very young children who are blind or visually impaired. *$35.00*
*203 pages*

**7080 Focus**
Visually Impaired Center
1422 W Court Street
Flint, MI 48503
313-235-2544

*Laurie MacArthur, Executive Director*

Newsletter offering information for the visually impaired person in the forms of legislative and law updates, ADA information, support groups, hotlines, and articles on the newest technology in the field.
*Quarterly*

**7081 Foundations of Orientation and Mobility**
American Foundation for the Blind/AFB Press
PO Box 1020
Sewickley, PA 15143
412-741-1142
800-232-3044
FAX: 412-741-0609
e-mail: afborders@abdintl.com
www.afb.org

This text has been updated and revised and includes current research from a variety of disciplines, an international perspective, and expanded contents on low vision, aging, multiple disabilities, accessibility, program design and adaptive technology from more that 30 eminent subject experts. *$68.95*
*775 pages*
*ISBN 0-891289-46-1*

**7082 Foundations of Rehabilitation Counseling with Persons Who Are Blind**
American Foundation for the Blind/AFB Press
PO Box 1020
Sewickley, PA 15143
412-741-1142
800-232-3044
FAX: 412-741-0609
e-mail: afborders@abdintl.com
www.afb.org

Rehabilitation professionals have long recognized that the needs of people who are blind or visually impaired are unique and requie a special knowledge and expertise to provide and corrdinate rehabilitation services. *$59.95*
*477 pages*
*ISBN 0-891289-45-3*

**7083 Future Reflections**
Natl. Organization for Parents of Blind Children
1800 Johnson Street
Baltimore, MD 21230
410-659-9314
FAX: 410-685-5653
e-mail: nfb@iamdigex.net

*Marc Maurer, President*

National magazine written specifically for parents and educators of blind children. Each issue addresses various topics important to blind children, their families and to school personnel.

**7084 Get a Wiggle On**
American Alliance for Health, Phys. Ed. & Dance
1900 Association Drive
Reston, VA 20191
703-476-3400
FAX: 703-476-9527
e-mail: aaalf@aahperd.org

*Michael Davis, Manager*

Gives teachers and parents practical suggestions for helping blind and visually impaired infants grow and learn like other children. *$5.00*
*80 pages*
*ISBN 0-88314 -77-2*

**7085 Gleams Newsletter**
Glaucoma Research Foundation
251 Post Street
Suite 600
San Francisco, CA 94108
415-986-3162
800-826-6693
FAX: 415-986-3763
e-mail: info@glaucoma.org
www.glaucoma.org

*Yuko Madono, Outreach/Public Relations*
*Tom Brunner, Chief Executive Officer*

Offers updated medical & research information on glaucoma. Included are glaucoma treatmant and coping tips, legsilative information, professional articles and book reviews.
*6 pages Quarterly 1982*

**7086 Guidelines and Games for Teaching Efficient Braille Reading**
American Foundation for the Blind/AFB Press
PO Box 1020
Sewickley, PA 15143
412-741-1142
800-232-3044
FAX: 412-741-0609
e-mail: afborders@abdintl.com
www.afb.org

Based on research in the areas of rapid reading and precision teaching, these guidelines represent a unique adaptation of a general reading program to the needs of braille readers. Paperback. *$ 24.95*
*116 pages*
*ISBN 0-891281-05-3*

**7087 Guideway**
Guide Dog Foundation for the Blind
371 E Jericho Tpke
Smithtown, NY 11787
631-265-2121
800-548-4337
FAX: 516-361-5192

*Wells Jones, Executive Director*

Offers updates and information on the foundation's activities and guide dog programs. In print form but is also available on cassette.
*Monthly*

**7088 Guild Audio Library**
JGB Audio Library for the Blind
15 W 65th Street
New York, NY 10023
212-769-6331
800-284-4422
FAX: 212-769-6266
e-mail: info@JGB.org
www.JGB.org

*Peter Williamson, Executive Director*
*Ken Satnley, Manager*

**7089 Guild Briefs**
Catholic Guild for The Blind
180 N Michigan Avenue
Suite 1700
Chicago, IL 60601
312-243-8569
FAX: 312-236-8128
e-mail: guild@guildfortheblind.org
www.guildfortheblind.org

*David Tabak, Executive Director*
*Bi-Annually*

**7090 Handbook for Itinerant and Resource Teachers of Blind Students**
National Federation of the Blind
1800 Johnson Street
Baltimore, MD 21230
410-659-9314
e-mail: nfb@iamdigex.net

*Marc Maurer, President*
The Handbook provides help to teachers, school administrators or other school personnel that have experience with blind or visually impaired students. The Handbook devotes 45 pages to Braille and how to teach Braille for parents and teachers. There are other chapters offering information on the law, physical education, fitting in socially, testing and evaluation, home economics, daily living skills and more. *$23.00*
*533 pages Softcover*
*ISBN 0-962412-20-1*

**7091 Handbook of Information for Members of the Achromatopsia Network**
PO Box 214
Berkeley, CA 94701
510-540-4700
FAX: 510-540-4767
e-mail: futterman@achromat.org
www.achromat.org

**7092 Health Care Professionals Who Are Blind or Visually Impaired**
American Foundation for the Blind
11 Penn Plaza
Suite 300
New York, NY 10001
212-502-7600
800-232-5463
FAX: 212-502-7777
e-mail: afbinfo@afb.net
www.afb.org/store

*Carl R Augusto, President/CEO*
This resource is essential reading for older students and young adults who are blind or visually impaired, their families, and the professionals who work with them. *$21.95*
*160 pages 2001*
*ISBN 0-891283-88-9*

**7093 Hearsay**
Int'l Association of Audio Information Services
1102 W International Airport Road
Anchorage, AK 99518
412-434-6023
800-280-5325
e-mail: aiblink@ak.net
www.iaais.org
Newsletter for persons interested in radio reading services. *$7.00*
*Quarterly*

**7094 Heart to Heart**
Blind Children's Center
4120 Marathon Street
Los Angeles, CA 90029
323-664-2153
800-222-3567
FAX: 323-665-3828
e-mail: info@blindchildrenscenter.org
www.blindchildrenscenter.org

*Midge Horton, Executive Director*
Parents of children who are blind and partially sighted talk about their feelings. *$10.00*

*12 pages*

**7095 Helen Keller National Center Newsletter**
111 Middle Neck Road
Sands Point, NY 11050
516-944-8900
800-225-0411
FAX: 516-944-7302
e-mail: hkncdir@aol.com
www.helenkeller.org/national

*Joseph McNulty, Executive Director*
The center provides evaluation and training in vocational skills, adaptive technology and computer skills, orientation and mobility, independent living, communication, speech-language skills, creative arts, fitness and leisure activities.

**7096 Helen and Teacher: The Story of Helen & Anne Sullivan Macy**
American Foundation for the Blind/AFB Press
PO Box 1020
Sewickley, PA 15143
412-741-1142
800-232-3044
FAX: 412-741-0609
e-mail: afborders@abdintl.com
www.afb.org

*Stephanie Biagioli, Marketing Coordinator*
A pictorial biography emphasizing Hellen Keller's accomplishments in public life over a period of more than 60 years. Traces Anne Sullivan's early years and her meeting with Helen Keller, and goes on to recount the joint events of their lives. A definitive biography. $29.95.
*Paperback*
*ISBN 0-891282-89-0*

**7097 Helping the Visually Impaired Child with Developmental Problems**
Teachers College Press
Columbia University
New York, NY 10027
212-678-3929
800-575-6566
FAX: 212-678-4149

*Mary Lynch, Manager*
This book aims to explore the human consequences of severe visual problems combined with other handicaps. The application of child development research to educational interventions, the need for educational and rehabilitative services that serve the human and the special needs of children and their families and the promise of technology in helping to expand communicative possibilities are also discussed. *$18.95*
*216 pages Paperback*
*ISBN 0-807729-02-7*

**7098 Hub**
SPOKES Unlimited
415 Main Street
Klamath Falls, OR 97601
541-883-7547
FAX: 541-885-2469
e-mail: spokes@internetcds.com

*Wendy Howard, Program Coordinator*
*Celeste Wolf, Clerical Support Specialist II*
Newsletter on rehabilitation, peer counseling, blindness, visual impairments, information and referral.

**7099 If Blindness Comes**
National Federation of the Blind
1800 Johnson Street
Baltimore, MD 21230
410-659-9314
FAX: 410-685-5653
e-mail: nfb@iamdigex.net
www.nfb.org

*Marc Maurer, President*

An introduction to issues relating to vision loss and provides a positive, supportive philosophy about blindness. It is a general information book which includes answers to many common questions about blindness, information about services and programs for the blind and resource listings. Contact the Materials Center.

**7100  If Blindness Strikes Don't Strike Out**
Charles C Thomas
2600 S 1st Street
Springfield, IL  62704
217-789-8980
800-258-8980
FAX: 217-789-9130
e-mail: books@ccthomas.com
www.ccthomas.com

*Michael Thomas, President*

This book is a storehouse of information on daily life for the visually impaired and those around them. From opticons and laser canes to housekeeping to travel, the author describes how to successfully cope with the problems posed by visual impairment and blindness. Also available in cloth. *$36.95*
*316 pages Paperback*
*ISBN 0-398064-34-2*

**7101  Imagining the Possibilities: Creative Approaches to Orientation and Mobility Instruction**
American Foundation for the Blind
11 Penn Plaza
Suite 300
New York, NY  10001
212-502-7600
800-232-5463
FAX: 212-502-7777
e-mail: afbinfo@afb.net
www.afb.org/store

*Carl R Augusto, President/CEO*

Innovative and varied approaches to O&M techniques and teaching and dynamic suggestions on how to analyze learning styles are just some of the important topics included. *$49.95*
*378 pages 2001*
*ISBN 0-891283-82-X*

**7102  Increasing Literacy Levels: Final Report**
Mississippi State University
PO Box 6189
Mississippi State, MS  39762
662-325-2001
800-675-7782
FAX: 662-325-8989
www.blind.msstate.edu

*Kelly Schaefer, Dissemination Specialist*
*Elton Moore, Executive Director*

This study is composed of three research projects to identify and analyze the appropriate use of and instruction in Braille, optical devices and other technologies as they relate to literacy and employment of individuals who are blind or visually impaired. *$20.00*
*148 pages Paperback*

**7103  Independence Without Sight and Sound: Suggestions for Practitioners**
American Foundation for the Blind/AFB Press
PO Box 1020
Sewickley, PA  15143
412-741-1142
800-232-3044
FAX: 412-741-0609
e-mail: afborders@abdintl.com
www.afb.org
This practical guidebook covers the essential aspects of communicating and working with deaf-blind persons. Includes useful information on how to talk with deaf-blind people, and adapt orientation and mobility techniques for deaf-blind travelers. *$39.95*

*193 pages Paperback*
*ISBN 0-891282-46-7*

**7104  Information Access Project**
National Federation of the Blind
1800 Johnson Street
Baltimore, MD  21230
410-659-9314
FAX: 410-685-5653
e-mail: nfb@iamdigex.net
www.nfb.org

*Marc Maurer, President*

Assists entities covered by the ADA in finding methods for converting visually displayed information, such as flyers, brochures and pamphlets, to formats accessible to individuals who are visually impaired.

**7105  Inside the Beltway**
DC Regl Lib for the Blind & Physically Handicapped
901 G Street NW
Room 215
Washington, DC  20001
202-727-2142
FAX: 202-727-1129
TTY:202-727-2145
e-mail: lbphb_2000@yahoo.com
www.dclibrary.org

*Grace J Lyons, Librarian*
*Phillip Long-Cross, Manager*

Regional library/RPH is network library in the Library of Congress, National Library Services for the Blind and Physically Handicapped.
*8 pages Quarterly*

**7106  Insight**
United States Association of Blind Athletes
33 N Institute Street
Colorado Springs, CO  80903
719-630-0422
FAX: 719-630-0616
e-mail: media@usaba.org
www.usaba.org

*Mark Lucas, Executive Director*

Covers news, announcements and activities of the association.
*20 pages Quarterly*

**7107  International Directory of Libraries for the Disabled**
KG Saur/Division of RR Bowker
121 Chanlon Road
New Providence, NJ  07974
908-286-1090
800-521-8110

*Michael Cairns, Chief Executive Officer*

An essential resource for improving the quality and quantity of materials available to the print-handicapped audience. Featuring talking books, braille books, large print books as well as production centers for these materials. *$46.00*
*257 pages*
*ISBN 3-59821 -81-1*

**7108  Intervention Practices in the Retention of Competitive Employment**
Mississippi State University
PO Box 6189
Mississippi State, MS  39762
662-325-2001
800-675-7782
FAX: 662-325-8989
www.blind.msstate.edu

*Kelly Schaefer, Dissemination Specialist*
*Elton Moore, Executive Director*

This study investigated the methods by which an individual can retain competitive employment after the onset of a significant vision loss. Interviews were conducted with 89 rehabilitation counselors across the US Strategies that contribute to successful job retention were identified as well as best rehabilitation practices in job retention. *$15.00*

*60 pages Paperback*

**7109    Jewish Braille Review**
Jewish Braille Institute of America
110 E 30th Street
New York, NY  10016
212-889-2525
800-433-1531
FAX: 212-689-3692
e-mail: admin@jbilibrary.org
www.jbilibrary.org

*Ellen Isler MD, President*
*Israel A Taub, Associate Director*

The JBI seeks the integration of Jews who are blind, visually impaired and reading disabled into the Jewish community and society in general. More than 20,000 men, women and children in 50 countries receive a broad variety of JBI services.
*1931*

**7110    Jewish Heritage for the Blind**
1655 E 24th Street
Brooklyn, NY  11229
718-338-8200

Offers large print traditional prayer books for the High Holy days, festivals, fast days and daily rituals for those finding it difficult or impossible to read small print.

**7111    Journal of Visual Impairment and Blindness**
Sheridan Press, c/o FB
PO Box 465
Hanover, PA  17331
717-632-3535
800-352-2210
FAX: 717-633-8929
e-mail: pubsvc@tsp.sheridan.com
www.sheridanreprints.com

*Sharon Shively, Managing Editor*
*Jane Erin, Editor-in-Chief*
*Joan Weisman, President*

Published in braille, regular print and on ASC II disk and cassette, this journal contains a wide variety of subjects including rehabilitation, psychology, education, legislation, medicine, technology, employment, sensory aids and childhood development as they relate to visual impairments. $130 annual individual subscription, $180 annual institutional subscription.
*64 pages Monthly*
*ISSN 0145-48 x*

**7112    Kernal Book Series**
National Federation of the Blind
1800 Johnson Street
Baltimore, MD  21230
410-659-9314
FAX: 410-685-5653
e-mail: nfb@iamdigex.net
www.nfb.org

*Marc Maurer, President*

A series of books written by the blind themselves. Each book is a collection of articles and stories about the real life experiences of blind persons. These books help educate the blind and the sighted alike about a positive philosophy regarding blindness. Contact the materials center.
*$5 - $10 each*

**7113    King James Bible, Large Print**
Science Products
PO Box 888
Southeastern, PA  19399
610-296-2111
800-888-7400
FAX: 610-296-0488

*Mary Ann Case, Marketing Director*
*Lee Benham, Owner*

A hardcover book with 24 point type easily seen with 20/200 acuity. Makes bible reading for children easier too. New Testament ($69.95:

**7114    Large Print Loan Library**
National Association for Visually Handicapped
22 W 21st Street
New York, NY  10010
212-889-3141
FAX: 212-727-2931
e-mail: staff@navh.org
www.navh.org

*Lorianie Marchi, Chief Executive Officer*

A huge large print catalog of all the publications, fiction and non-fiction, cassette tapes, books-on-tape and videos available for the visually impaired from the loan library of the National Association for the Visually Handicapped.
*100 pages*

**7115    Large Print Recipies for a Healthy Life**
123601 Wilshire
Los Angeles, CA  90025
310-826-8280
800-481-EYES
FAX: 310-458-8179

*Judith Caditz, PhD, author*
*Dave Grill*

*$21.95*
*283 pages*
*ISBN 0-962236-82-9*

**7116    Learning to Play**
Blind Children's Center
4120 Marathon Street
Los Angeles, CA  90029
323-664-2153
800-222-3567
FAX: 323-665-3828
e-mail: info@blindchildrenscenter.org
www.blindchildrenscenter.org

*Midge Horton, Executive Director*

Presenting play activities to the pre-school child who is visually impaired. *$10.00*
*12 pages*

**7117    Let's Eat**
Blind Children's Center
4120 Marathon Street
Los Angeles, CA  90029
323-664-2153
800-222-3567
FAX: 323-665-3828
e-mail: info@blindchildrenscenter.org
www.blindchildrenscenter.org

*Midge Horton, Executive Director*

Feeding a child with visual impairment. *$10.00*
*28 pages*

**7118    Library Resources for the Blind and Physically Handicapped**
National Library Service for the Blind
1291 Taylor Street NW
Washington, DC  20542
202-707-5100
FAX: 202-707-0712
TTY:202-707-0744
e-mail: nls@loc.gov
www.loc.gov/nls

*Frank Cylke, Executive Director*

NLS administers a national library service that provides braille and recorded books and magazines on free loan to anyone who cannot read standard print because of visual or physical disabilities and who are eligible residents of the United States or American citizens living abroad. The directory describes the cooperating libaries. Online at www.loc.gov/reference/directories.html.

*83 pages*

**7119   Library Services for the Blind**
South Carolina State University
300 College Street NE
Orangeburg, SC  29117

803-536-7000
FAX: 803-536-8902
e-mail: bagingu@scsu.edu
library.scsu.edu

*Mary L Small Dean, Library/Information Services*
*Andrew Hugine, President*

News and information on developments in library services for
readers who are blind and physically disabled.

**7120   Library Users of America Newsletter**
American Council of the Blind
1155 15th Street NW
Suite 1004
Washington, DC  20005

202-467-5081
800-424-8666
FAX: 202-467-5085
e-mail: info@acb.org
www.acb.org

*Sharon Strzalkowski, President*
*Melanie Brunson, Executive Director*

Published twice yearly, the newsletter contains much information about library services of particular interest to blind and visually impaired patrons, and is available in the following
formats: Braille, audiocassette, large print and e-mail.

**7121   Lifestyles of Employed Legally Blind People**
Mississippi State University
PO Box 6189
Mississippi State, MS  39762

662-325-2001
800-675-7782
FAX: 662-325-8989
www.blind.msstate.edu

*Lynn W McBroom PhD, Senior Research Scientist*
*Elton Moore, Executive Director*

Results from a telephone survey show that visually impaired respondents are involved in a wide variety of activities with little
restrictions on their range of activities. Sighted respondents
tended to spend more time in child care, obtaining goods and services, attending to self-care activities and engaging in social activities, while visually impaired respondents spent more time in
education and passive activities. This report is a study of expenditures and time use. *$ 10.00*
*193 pages Paperback*

**7122   Light the Way**
Blind Children's Center
4120 Marathon Street
Los Angeles, CA  90029

323-664-2153
800-222-3567
FAX: 323-665-3828
e-mail: info@blindchildrenscenter.org
www.blindchildrenscenter.org

*Midge Horton, Executive Director*

Newsletter of the Blind Childrens Center, a family-centered
agency which serves children with visual impairments from
birth to school-age. The center-based and home-based services
help the children to acquire skills and build their independence.
The center utilizes its expertise and experience to serve families
and professionals worldwide through support services, education and research.

**7123   Lion**
Lion's Clubs International
300 W 22nd Street
Oak Brook, IL  60570

630-571-5466

*Gary Lapetina, Chief Executive Officer*
Publication for the blind.

**7124   Living with Achromatopsia**
PO Box 214
Berkeley, CA  94701

510-540-4700
FAX: 510-540-4767
e-mail: futterman@achromat.org
www.achromat.org

**7125   Long Cane News**
American Foundation for the Blind/AFB Press
PO Box 1020
Sewickley, PA  15143

412-741-1142
800-232-3044
FAX: 412-741-0609
e-mail: afborders@abdintl.com
www.afb.org

*Liz Greco*
*SemiAnnual*

**7126   Low Vision Questions and Answers: Definitions, De-
vices, Services**
American Foundation for the Blind/AFB Press
PO Box 1020
Sewickley, PA  15143

412-741-1142
800-232-3044
FAX: 412-741-0609
e-mail: afborders@abdintl.com
www.afb.org

What does low vision mean? What do low vision services cost?
What diseases cause low vision? Answers to these and other
questions are presented in a comprehensive format with accompanying photographs. $50.00/pack of 25.
*21 pages*
*ISBN 0-891281-96-7*

**7127   Low Vision: Reflections of the Past, Issues for the Fu-
ture**
American Foundation for the Blind/AFB Press
PO Box 1020
Sewickley, PA  15143

412-741-1142
800-232-3044
FAX: 412-741-0609
e-mail: afborders@abdintl.com
www.afb.org

Background papers and a strategies section are used to identify
the shifting needs of visually impaired persons and the resources
that may be needed to address them. Paperback. *$29.95*

*ISBN 0-891282-18-1*

**7128   Mainstreaming and the American Dream**
American Foundation for the Blind/AFB Press
PO Box 1020
Sewickley, PA  15143

412-741-1142
800-232-3044
FAX: 412-741-0609
e-mail: afborders@abdintl.com
www.afb.org

Based on in-depth interviews with parents and professionals,
this research monograph presents information on the needs and
aspirations of parents of blind and visually impaired children.
Paperback. *$34.95*
*256 pages*
*ISBN 0-891281-91-6*

**7129   Mainstreaming the Visually Impaired Child**
NAPVI
PO Box 317
Watertown, MA  02471

617-972-7441
800-562-6265
FAX: 617-972-7444
e-mail: napvi@perkins.org
www.napvi.org

A unique, informative guide for teachers and educational professionals that work with the visually impaired. *$10.00*

*121 pages Paper*

**7130   Making Life More Livable**
American Foundation for the Blind
11 Penn Plaza
Suite 300
New York, NY  10001
212-502-7600
800-232-5463
FAX: 212-502-7774
e-mail: afborder@abdintl.com
www.afb.org

*Carl Augusto, President*

Shows how simple adaptations in the home and environment can make a big difference in the lives of blind and visually impaired older persons. The suggestions offered are numerous and specific, ranging from how to mark food cans for greater visibility to how to get out of the shower safley. Large print. *$24.95*
*128 pages 2001*
*ISBN 0-891283-87-0*

**7131   Meeting the Needs of People with Vision Loss:**
**Multidisciplinary Perspective**
Resources for Rehabilitation
33 Bedford Street
Suite 19a
Lexington, MA  02420
781-890-6371
FAX: 781-867-7517

*Susan Greenblatt*

Written by rehabilitation professionals, physicians, and a sociologist, this book discusses how to provide appropriate information and how to serve special populations. Chapters on the role of the family, diabetes and vision loss, special needs of children and adolescents, adults with hearing and vision loss. *$29.95*

*ISBN 0-92971 -07-0*

**7132   More Alike Than Different: Blind and Visually Impaired Children**
American Foundation for the Blind/AFB Press
PO Box 1020
Sewickley, PA  15143
412-741-1142
800-232-3044
FAX: 412-741-0609
e-mail: afborders@abdintl.com
www.afb.org
Offers photographs of blind and visually impaired children around the world learning to read and write, travel independently and performing basic living skills. Covers the most recent technological advances and demonstrates the universality of educational needs and goals. Paperback. $100.00/pack of 25.

*ISBN 0-891281-69-0*

**7133   Mothers with Visual Impairments who are Raising Young Children**
Through the Looking Glass
2198 6th Street
Suite 100
Berkeley, CA  94710
510-848-1112
800-644-2666
FAX: 510-848-4445
e-mail: TLG@lookingglass.org
www.lookingglass.org

*C Conley-Jung*
*R Olkin*
*Megan Kirshbaum, Executive Director*

Available in braille, large print or cassette. *$2.00*

*16 pages*

**7134   Move With Me**
Blind Children's Center
4120 Marathon Street
Los Angeles, CA  90029
323-664-2153
800-222-3567
FAX: 323-665-3828
e-mail: info@blindchildrenscenter.org
www.blindchildrenscenter.org

*Midge Horton, Executive Director*

A parent's guide to movement development for babies who are visually impaired. *$10.00*
*12 pages*

**7135   Musical Mainstream**
National Library Service for the Blind
1291 Taylor Street NW
Washington, DC  20542
202-707-5100
FAX: 202-707-0712
e-mail: nls@loc.gov
www.loc.gov/nls

*Frank Cylke, Executive Director*

Articles selected from print music magazines.
*Quarterly*

**7136   NLS News**
National Library Service for the Blind
1291 Taylor Street NW
Washington, DC  20542
202-707-5100
FAX: 202-707-0712
e-mail: nls@loc.gov
www.loc.gov/nls

*Frank Cylke, Executive Director*

Newsletter on current program developments.
*Quarterly*

**7137   NLS Update**
National Library Service for the Blind
1291 Taylor Street NW
Washington, DC  20542
202-707-5100
FAX: 202-707-0712
e-mail: nls@loc.gov
www.loc.gov/nls

*Frank Cylke, Executive Director*

Newsletter on the service's volunteer activities.
*Quarterly*

**7138   News from Advocates for Deaf-Blind**
National Family Association for Deaf-Blind
111 Middle Neck Road
Sands Point, NY  11050
516-944-8900
800-225-0411
FAX: 516-944-7302
e-mail: NFADB@aol.com
www.NFADB.org

*Mary Fox, Administrative Assistant*
*Joseph Nulty, Executive Director*

A membership organization which provide resources, education, advocacy, referrals and support for families with children who are deaf-blind; professionals in the field; and individuals who are deaf-blind.
*20 pages TriAnnual*

**7139   Newsline for the Blind**
National Federation of the Blind
1800 Johnson Street
Baltimore, MD  21230
410-659-9314
FAX: 410-685-5653
e-mail: nfb@iamdigex.net
www.nfb.org

*Peggy Chong, Contact*
*Marc Maurer, President*

Nation's only digital talking newspaper service for the blind. Allows the blind to read the full text of leading national and local newspapers by using a touch-tone telephone. Service is free of charge and available 24 hours a day, 7 days per week.

**7140  Not Without Sight**
American Foundation for the Blind/AFB Press
PO Box 1020
Sewickley, PA  15143
412-741-1142
800-232-3044
FAX: 412-741-0609
e-mail: afborders@abdintl.com
www.afb.org

This video describes the major types of visual impairment and their causes and effects on vision, while camera simulations approximate what people with each impairmant actually see. Also demonstrates how people with low vision make the best use of the vision they have. 20 minute video tape. Also available in PAL, $52.95, 0-89128-272-6. *$42.95*
*VHS 1975*
*ISBN 0-891282-27-0*

**7141  One Two Three Sign with Me**
TJ Publishers
2544 Tarpley Road
Suite 108
Carrollton, TX  75006
972-416-0800
800-999-1168
FAX: 301-585-5930
e-mail: TJPubinc@aol.com

*Angela K Thames, President*
*Jerald A Murphy, VP*

Charming full color illustrations include basic shapes and counting. *$3.95*
*24 pages Softcover*

**7142  Open Windows, Audiocassette**
LifeWay Christian Resources Southern Baptist Conv.
127 9th Avenue N
Nashville, TN  37234
615-251-2089
800-458-2772
FAX: 651-251-5764
e-mail: specialed@lifeway.com
www.lifeway.com

*Judy Wooldridge, Product Development Specialist*
*Wade Stapleton, Manager*

Guide for personal devotions on audiocassette tape, using Bible references, devotional readings, and prayer calendar of popular Open Windows devotional guide. Available quarterly on three cassette tapes. *$10.70*
*Quarterly*

**7143  Opportunity**
National Industries for the Blind
1310 Braddock Place
Alexandria, VA  22314
703-998-0770
FAX: 703-998-8268
www.nib.org

*George J Mertz, President/CEO*

Offers information and articles on the newest technology, equipment, services and programs for blind and visually impaired persons.
*Quarterly*

**7144  Orientation and Mobility Primer for Families and Young Children**
American Foundation for the Blind/AFB Press
PO Box 1020
Sewickley, PA  15143
412-741-1142
800-232-3044
FAX: 412-741-0609
e-mail: afborders@abdintl.com
www.afb.org

Practical information for helping a child learn about his or her environment right from the start. Covers sensory training, concept development and orientation skills. Paperback. *$14.95*

*48 pages*
*ISBN 0-891281-57-6*

**7145  Out of Left Field**
American Foundation for the Blind/AFB Press
PO Box 1020
Sewickley, PA  15143
412-741-1142
800-232-3044
FAX: 412-741-0609
e-mail: afborders@abdintl.com
www.afb.org

Illustrates how youngsters who are blind or visually impaired integrated with their sighted peers in a variety of recreational and athletic activities. 17 minute video tape. Also available in PAL, $33.95, 0-89128-270-X. *$26.95*
*VHS 1975*
*ISBN 0-891282-28-9*

**7146  Out of the Corner of My Eye: Living with Vision Loss in Later Life**
American Foundation for the Blind/AFB Press
PO Box 1020
Sewickley, PA  15143
412-741-1142
800-232-3044
FAX: 412-741-0609
e-mail: afborders@abdintl.com
www.afb.org

*Stephanie Biagioli, Marketing Coordinator*

A personal account of students' vision loss and subsequent adjustment that is full of practical advice and cheerful encouragement, told by an 87 year old retired college teacher who has maintained her independence and zest for life. Available in paperback or on audio cassette. *$23.95*
*120 pages*
*ISBN 0-891281-82-1*

**7147  PB News**
Prevent Blindness America
500 E Remington Road
Schaumburg, IL  60173
847-843-2020
800-331-2020
FAX: 847-843-8458
e-mail: info@preventblindness.org
www.preventblindness.org

*Ken West, Director Marketing Comm.*

*$10.00*
*Quarterly*

**7148  PBA News**
Prevent Blindness America
500 E Remington Road
Schaumburg, IL  60173
847-843-8458
800-331-2020
FAX: 847-843-2020
e-mail: info@preventblindness.org
www.preventblindness.org

*Betsy van Die, Media Relations Director*
*Hugh R Parry, President/CEO*
*Daniel D Garrett, Senior VP*

Publication offered three times yearly.
*3 times yearly*

**7149  Pediatric Visual Diagnosis Fact Sheets**
Blind Children's Center
4120 Marathon Street
Los Angeles, CA  90029
323-664-2153
800-222-3567
FAX: 323-665-3828
e-mail: info@blindchildrenscenter.org
www.blindchildrenscenter.org

*Midge Horton, Executive Director*

Fact sheets addressing commonly encountered eye conditions, diagnostic tests and materials. *$10.00*

*10 pages*

**7150 Perkins Activity and Resource Guide: A Handbook for Teachers**
Perkins School for the Blind
175 N Beacon Street
Watertown, MA 02472
617-924-3434
FAX: 781-926-2027
www.perkins.org

*Steven Rothstein, President*

This is a comprehensive, two volume guide with over 1,000 pages of activities, resources and instructional strategies for teachers and parents of students with visual and multiple disabilities. *$65.00*

**7151 Personal Reader Update**
Personal Reader Department
9 Centennial Drive
Peabody, MA 01960
978-977-2000
800-343-0311
FAX: 978-977-2409
Offers information on new services, assistive devices and technology for the blind.

**7152 Perspective**
Clovernook Center for Blind & Visually Impaired
7000 Hamilton Avenue
Cincinnati, OH 45231
513-522-3860
888-234-7156
FAX: 513-728-3946
e-mail: clovernook@clovernook.org
www.clovernook.org

*Carol Friedman, Editor*
*Joshua Howard, Editor*
*8 pages Quarterly*

**7153 Picture is Worth a Thousand Words for Blind and Visually Impaired Persons Too!**
American Foundation for the Blind/AFB Press
PO Box 1020
Sewickley, PA 15143
412-741-1142
800-232-3044
FAX: 412-741-0609
e-mail: afborders@abdintl.com
www.afb.org
Audiodescription - the art of describing in words for visually impaired viewers the visual aspects seen in television, film, etc. - is highlighted in this book for the blind and visually impaired person. *$7.95*
*32 pages Large Print*
*ISBN 0-891282-12-2*

**7154 Popular Activities and Games for Blind, Visually Impaired & Disabled People**
American Foundation for the Blind/AFB Press
PO Box 1020
Sewickley, PA 15143
412-741-1142
800-232-3044
FAX: 412-741-0609
e-mail: afborders@abdintl.com
www.afb.org
A manual of easy-to-follow instructions for more than 50 games and activities for blind and visually impaired persons of all ages, their families, recreation leaders and health care professionals. Large print. *$19.95*
*64 pages*
*ISBN 0-959974-78-4*

**7155 Providing Services for People with Vision Loss: Multidisciplinary Perspective**
Resources for Rehabilitation
33 Bedford Street
Suite 19a
Lexington, MA 02420
781-862-6455
FAX: 781-861-7517
www.nfr.org

A collection of articles by ophthalmologists and rehabilitation professionals, including chapters on operating a low vision service, starting self-help programs, mental health services, aids and techniques that help people with vision loss. *$19.95*
*136 pages*
*ISBN 0-929718-02-0*

**7156 Psychoeducational Assessment of Visually Impaired and Blind Students**
Pro-Ed
8700 Shoal Creek Boulevard
Austin, TX 78757
512-451-3246
800-897-3202
FAX: 512-451-8542
e-mail: info@proedinc.com
www.proedinc.com

*Donald Hammill, Owner*

Professional reference book that addresses the problems specific to assessment of visually impaired and blind children. Of particular value to the practitioner are the extensive reviews of available tests, including ways to adapt those not designed for use with the visually handicapped. *$29.00*
*140 pages Paperback*
*ISBN 0-890791-08-2*

**7157 Quarterly Update**
National Association for Visually Handicapped
22 W 21st Street
Floor 6
New York, NY 10010
212-889-3141
FAX: 212-727-2931
e-mail: staff@navh.org
www.navh.org

*Lorianie Marchi*

Quarterly newsletter offering information on new products for the visually impaired, advances in medical treatments, new books available in the NAVH large print loan library and any new/updated booklets. Free. *$2.25*

**7158 RP Messenger**
Texas Association of Retinitis Pigmentosa
PO Box 8388
Corpus Christi, TX 78468
361-852-8515
FAX: 361-852-8515
e-mail: phstiefel@grande.com.nist
A bi-annual newsletter offering information on Retinitis Pigmentosa. *$15.00*
*BiAnnual*

**7159 Raised Dot Computing Newsletter**
Raised Dot Computing
408 S Baldwin Street
Madison, WI 53703
608-257-9595

e-mail: info@rdcbraille.com
Discusses braille computer techniques and devices for blind persons. *$7.00*

**7160 Reaching, Crawling, Walking....Let's Get Moving**
Blind Children's Center
4120 Marathon Street
Los Angeles, CA 90029
323-664-2153
800-222-3567
FAX: 323-665-3828
e-mail: info@blindchildrenscenter.org
www.blindchildrenscenter.org

*Midge Horton, Executive Director*

Orientation and mobility for preschool children who are visually imapired. *$10.00*

*24 pages*

**7161 Recording for the Blind News**
Recording for the Blind
20 Roszel Road
Princeton, NJ 08540

609-452-0606
800-221-4792
FAX: 609-987-8116

*John Kelly, Chief Executive Officer*

A nonprofit organization that provides recorded books free of charge to blind and print-handicapped individuals.
*3x Year*

**7162 Resources for Family Centered Intervention for Infants, Toddlers, and Preschoolers**
Hope
1856 N 1200 E
Logan, UT 84341

435-245-2888
FAX: 435-245-2888
e-mail: hope@hopepubl.com
www.hopepubl.com

*Susan Watkins, Owner*

Describes children with vision impairment in terms of characteristics, needs, and parent concerns. *$98.00*
*Two volumes*

**7163 SCENE**
Braille Institute
527 N Dale Avenue
Anaheim, CA 92801

714-821-5000
800-272-4553
FAX: 714-527-7621
www.brailleinstitute.org

*Sheila Daily, Executive Director*

Offers information on the organization, question and answer column, articles on the newest technology and more for visually impaired persons.

**7164 Seeing Eye Guide**
Seeing Eye
PO Box 375
Morristown, NJ 07963

973-539-4425
FAX: 973-539-0922
e-mail: info@seeingeye.org
www.seeingeye.org

*Kenneth Rosenthal, President*

A quarterly publication from Seeing Eye.
*Quarterly*

**7165 Selecting a Program**
Blind Children's Center
4120 Marathon Street
Los Angeles, CA 90029

323-664-2153
800-222-3567
FAX: 323-665-3828
e-mail: info@blindchildrenscenter.org
www.blindchildrenscenter.org

*Midge Horton, Executive Director*

A guide for parents of infants and preschoolers with visual impairments. *$10.00*
*28 pages*

**7166 Shared Visions**
Vista Center for the Blind & Visually Impaired
413 Laurel Street
Santa Cruz, CA 95060

831-458-9766
800-705-2970
FAX: 831-426-6233
www.vistacenter.org

*Pam Brandin, Executive Director*
*Alice McGrath, CR Coordinator*

A quarterly publication for Blind and Visually Impaired individuals from Vista Center for the Blind and Visually Impaired.

**7167 Sightings Newsletter**
Schepens Eye Research Institute
20 Staniford Street
Boston, MA 02114

617-912-0100
FAX: 617-912-0110
e-mail: geninfo@@vision.eri.harvard.edu
www.eri.harvard.edu/default/htm

*Michael Gilmore, President*

Prominent center for research on eye, vision, and blinding diseases; dedicated to research that improves the understanding, management, and prevention of eye diseases and visual deficiencies; fosters collaboration among its faculty members; trains young scientists and clinicians from around the world; promotes communication with scientists in allied fields; leader in the worldwide dispersion of basic scientific knowledge of vision.

**7168 Smith Kettlewell Rehabilitation Engineering Research Center**
Smith-Kettlewell Eye Research Institute
2318 Fillmore Street
San Francisco, CA 94115

415-345-2000
FAX: 415-345-8455
e-mail: rerc@ski.org
www.ski.org

*Ruth S Poole, COO*
*Henry Metz, President*

Reports on technology and devices for persons with visual impairments.

**7169 Social Maturity Scale for Blind Preschool Children: A Guide to Its Use**
American Foundation for the Blind/AFB Press
PO Box 1020
Sewickley, PA 15143

412-741-1142
800-232-3044
FAX: 412-741-0609
e-mail: afborders@abdintl.com
www.afb.org

An adaptation of the Vineland Social Maturity Scale for use with children from infancy to 6 years of age. *$9.95*
*57 pages Paperback*
*ISBN 0-891280-59-6*

**7170 Specifications for Selecting a Vocabulary and Teaching Method/Braille Readers**
American Foundation for the Blind/AFB Press
PO Box 1020
Sewickley, PA 15143

412-741-1142
800-232-3044
FAX: 412-741-0609
e-mail: afborders@abdintl.com
www.afb.org

Specifications for a reading series developing braille developed at the American Printing House For The Blind. Paperback. *$12.95*
*84 pages*
*ISBN 0-891280-69-3*

**7171 Standing On My Own Two Feet**
Blind Children's Center
4120 Marathon Street
Los Angeles, CA 90029

323-664-2153
800-222-3567
FAX: 323-665-3828
e-mail: info@blindchildrenscenter.org
www.blindchildrenscenter.org

*Midge Horton, Executive Director*

A guide to constructing mobility devices for children who are visually impaired. *$10.00*

*38 pages*

**7172  Starting Points**
Blind Children's Center
4120 Marathon Street
Los Angeles, CA  90029                     323-664-2153
                                           800-222-3567
                                      FAX: 323-665-3828
                  e-mail: info@blindchildrenscenter.org
                            www.blindchildrenscenter.org

*Midge Horton, Executive Director*

Basic information for the classroom teacher of 3 to 8 year olds
whose multiple disabilities include visual impairment. *$35.00*
               *157 pages*

**7173  Step-By-Step Guide to Personal Management for Blind
Persons**
American Foundation for the Blind/AFB Press
PO Box 1020
Sewickley, PA  15143                       412-741-1142
                                           800-232-3044
                                      FAX: 412-741-0609
                       e-mail: afborders@abdintl.com
                                           www.afb.org
A manual of techniques in the areas of hygiene, grooming, cloth-
ing, shopping and child care. *$19.95*
               *136 pages Spiralbound*
               *ISBN 0-891280-61-8*

**7174  Student Advocate**
National Alliance of Blind Students
1010 Vermont Avenue NW
Suite 1100
Washington, DC  20005                      202-783-2077
                                           800-424-8666

*Alan Kraut, Executive Director*

A communication forum covering issues of concern to
postsecondary students who are blind.

**7175  Student Teaching Guide for Blind and Visually Im-
paired College Students**
American Foundation for the Blind/AFB Press
PO Box 1020
Sewickley, PA  15143                       412-741-1142
                                           800-232-3044
                                      FAX: 412-741-0609
                       e-mail: afborders@abdintl.com
                                           www.afb.org
A comprehensive resource designed to enable the student to en-
ter the classroom of a university or college with confidence.
Large print. *$14.95*
               *52 pages*
               *ISBN 0-891281-42-8*

**7176  Syndicated Columnists Weekly**
National Braille Press
88 Saint Stephen Street
Boston, MA  02115                          617-266-6160
                                           800-548-7323
                                      FAX: 617-437-0456
                           e-mail: orders@nbp.org
                                           www.nhp.org

*William Kilimanjaro, President*

*$24.00*
               *Weekly*

**7177  Talk to Me**
Blind Children's Center
4120 Marathon Street
Los Angeles, CA  90029                     323-664-2153
                                           800-222-3567
                                      FAX: 323-665-3828
                  e-mail: info@blindchildrenscenter.org
                            www.blindchildrenscenter.org

*Midge Horton, Executive Director*

A language guide for parents of children who are visually impaired. *$10.00*

*11 pages*

**7178  Talk to Me II**
Blind Children's Center
4120 Marathon Street
Los Angeles, CA  90029                     323-664-2153
                                           800-222-3567
                                      FAX: 323-665-3828
                  e-mail: info@blindchildrenscenter.org
                            www.blindchildrenscenter.org

*Midge Horton, Executive Director*

*$10.00*
               *15 pages*

**7179  Talking Book Topics**
National Library Services for the Blind
1291 Taylor Street NW
Washington, DC  20542                      202-707-5100
                                      FAX: 202-707-0712
                              e-mail: nls@loc.gov
                                       www.loc.gov/nls

*Frank Cylke, Executive Director*

Offers hundreds of listings of books, fiction and nonfiction, for
adults and children on cassette. Also offers listings on foreign
language books on cassette, talking magazines and reviews.
               *BiMonthly*

**7180  Teaching Orientation and Mobility in the Schools: An
Instructor's Companion**
American Foundation for the Blind
11 Penn Plaza
Suite 300
New York, NY  10001                        212-502-7600
                                           800-232-5463
                                      FAX: 212-502-7777
                          e-mail: afbinfo@afb.net
                                       www.afb.org/store

*Carl R Augusto, President/CEO*

This book, with its useful forms, checklists, and tips, will help
O&M instructors and teachers of visually impaired students
master the arts of planning schedules, organizing equipment and
work routines, working with school personnel and educational
team members, and effectively providing instruction to children
with diverse needs. *$ 39.95*
               *176 pages 2002*
               *ISBN 0-891283-91-1*

**7181  Teaching Visually Impaired Children**
Charles C Thomas
2600 S 1st Street
Springfield, IL  62704                     217-789-8980
                                           800-258-8980
                                      FAX: 217-789-9130
                          e-mail: books@ccthomas.com
                                       www.ccthomas.com

*Michael Thomas, President*

A comprehensive resource for the classroom teacher who is
working with a visually impaired child for the first time, as well
as a systematic overview of education for the specialist in visual
disabilities. It approaches instructional challenges with clear
explanations and practical suggestions, and it addresses common concerns of teachers in a reassuring and positive manner.
Also available in cloth. *$35.95*
               *274 pages Paperback*
               *ISBN 0-398065-96-9*

**7182  Telephone Pioneer**
Telephone Pioneers of America
930 15th Street
12th Floor
Denver, CO  80202                          303-571-1200
                                      FAX: 303-571-9292
                                       www.telephonepioneers.org

*Marty Lee, President*

*Quarterly*

**7183  Textbook Catalog**
National Braille Association
3 Townline Circle
Rochester, NY  14623                        585-427-8260

e-mail: nbaoffice@compuserve.com
www.nationalbraille.org

*Angela Coffaro, Executive Director*

Lists hundreds of scholarly, college and professional textbooks
offered in large print, braille or on cassette for visually impaired
readers.
*80 pages*

**7184  The Deaf-Blind American**
American Association of the Deaf-Blind (AADB)
814 Thayer Avenue
Suite 320
Silver Spring, MD  20910                     301-495-4403
FAX: 301-495-4404
e-mail: info@aadb.org
www.aadb.org

*Elizabeth Spiers, author*
*Jamie McNamara Pope, Executive Director*

*$5.00*
*Quartlery*

**7185  Three Rivers News**
Carnegie Library of Pitts. Library for the Blind
4724 Baum Boulevard
Pittsburgh, PA  15213                         412-687-2440
800-242-0586
FAX: 412-687-2442
e-mail: clbph@clpgh.org
www.clpgh.org/clp/LBPH

*Sue Murdock, Director*
*Kathleen Kappel, Editor*

Loans recorded books/magazines and playback equipment,
large print books and described videos to western PA residents
unable to use standard printed materials due to a visual, physical, or physically-based reading disability.
*12 pages Quarterly*

**7186  To Love this Life: Quotations by Helen Keller**
American Foundation for the Blind/AFB Press
11 Penn Plaza
Suite 300
New York, NY  10001                          212-502-7600
800-232-5463
FAX: 212-502-7774
e-mail: afborder@abdintl.com
www.afb.org

*Carl Augusto, President*

Inspirational work that offers the penetrating observations of
Helen Keller, the beloved deaf-blind champion of the rights of
people with disabilities. Also available on cassette at $21.95
(ISBN# 0-89128-348-X) *$21.95*
*144 pages Hardcover 2000*
*ISBN 0-891283-47-1*

**7187  Touch the Baby: Blind & Visually Impaired Children
As Patients**
American Foundation for the Blind/AFB Press
PO Box 1020
Sewickley, PA  15143                          412-741-1142
800-232-3044
FAX: 412-741-0609
e-mail: afborders@abdintl.com
www.afb.org
A how-to manual for health care professionals working in hospitals, clinics and doctors' offices. Teaches the special communication and touch-related techniques needed to prevent blind and
visually impaired patients from withdrawing from the
healthcare workers and the outside world. $25.00/pack of 25.

*13 pages*
*ISBN 0-891281-97-5*

**7188  Transition Activity Calendar for Students with Visual
Impairments**
Mississippi State University
PO Box 6189
Mississippi State, MS  39762                  662-325-2001
800-675-7782
FAX: 662-325-8989
www.blind.msstate.edu

*Kelly Schaefer, Dissemination Specialist*
*Elton Moore, Executive Director*

The Transition Activity Calendar guides the student with a visual disability through the maze of college preparation. Beginning in junior high school, clearly written steps are listed for
each grade level. Students planning to enter college after high
school graduation can check-off their accomplishments each
step of the way. The calendar helps students focus on their goals
while providing reminders of tasks yet to be completed. It can be
used in a self-directed manner or in a group format. *$4.25*
*16 pages Paperback*

**7189  Transition to College for Students with Visual Impair-
ments: Report**
Mississippi State University
PO Box 6189
Mississippi State, MS  39762                  662-325-2001
800-675-7782
FAX: 662-325-8989
www.blind.msstate.edu

*Lynn McBroom PhD, Senior Research Scientist*
*Elton Moore, Executive Director*

A report offering results from telephone interviews of college
students with visual impairments and mail surveys of college officials which examines the transition experience of successful
college students. General domains in the study include demographics, educational history, computers, specialized and adaptive equipment, resources, college preparation, problems
adjusting to college and O&M skills. A literature review covers
preparing for college, task timelines,and classroom, labs and
tests. *$20.00*
*151 pages Paperback*

**7190  Understanding and Coping with Achromatopsia**
PO Box 214
Berkeley, CA  94701                           510-540-4700
FAX: 510-540-4767
e-mail: futterman@achromat.org
www.achromat.org

**7191  United States Association of Blind Athletes**
33 N Institute Street
Colorado Springs, CO  80903                   719-630-0422
FAX: 719-630-0616
e-mail: media@usaba.org
www.usaba.org

*Mark Lucas, Executive Director*

Covers news, announcements and activities of the association.
*20 pages Quarterly*

**7192  Unseen Minority: A Social History of Blindness in the
United States**
American Foundation for the Blind/AFB Press
PO Box 1020
Sewickley, PA  15143                          412-741-1142
800-232-3044
FAX: 412-741-0609
e-mail: afborders@abdintl.com
www.afb.org
A lively narrative, peppered with anecdotes, recounts how the
blind overcame discrimination to gain full participation in the
social, educational, economic and legislative spheres. Hardcover. *$ 40.00*

*573 pages*
*ISBN 0-679505-39-3*

**7193  Vision Enhancement**
UN Printing
5707 Brockton Drive
Apt 302
Indianapolis, IN 46220
317-254-1332
800-431-1739
FAX: 317-251-6588
e-mail: info@visionww.org
www.visionww.org

*Patricia L Price, President/Managing Editor*

Designed to encourage and support individuals with vision loss,
family members, and caregivers. *$25.00*
*72-78 pages Quarterly*

**7194  Visual Aids and Informational Material**
National Association for Visually Handicapped
22 W 21st Street
Floor 6
New York, NY 10010
212-889-3141
FAX: 212-727-2931
e-mail: staff@navh.org
www.navh.org

*Lorianie Marchi, Chief Executive Officer*

A complete listing of the visual aids NAVH carries such as magnifiers, talking clocks, large print playing cards, etc. *$2.50*
*65 pages*

**7195  Visual Handicaps and Learning**
Pro-Ed Publications
8700 Shoal Creek Boulevard
Austin, TX 78757
512-451-3246
800-897-3202
FAX: 512-451-8542
e-mail: info@proedinc.com
www.proedinc.com

*Donald Hammill, Owner*

The major focus of this new, third edition is to present a new way
of thinking about individuals with visual impairment so that they
are viewed as participating members of a seeing world despite
their reduced visual functioning. *$28.00*
*213 pages*

**7196  Visual Impairment: An Overview**
American Foundation for the Blind/AFB Press
PO Box 1020
Sewickley, PA 15143
412-741-1142
800-232-3044
FAX: 412-741-0609
e-mail: afborders@abdintl.com
www.afb.org
An overall look at the most common forms of vision loss and
their impact on the individual. Includes drawings as well as photographs that stimulate how people with vision loss see. Paperback. *$19.95*
*56 pages*
*ISBN 0-891281-74-6*

**7197  Visually Handicapped Child in Your Class**
Brookes Publishing
PO Box 10624
Baltimore, MD 21285
410-337-9580
800-638-3775
FAX: 410-337-8539
www.pbrookes.com

*Paul Brooks, Owner*

This book considers the theory and issues relating to the movement to integrate visually handicapped children into ordinary
schools and offers practical suggestions to teachers to help such
children participate fully in school life. *$21.50*

*192 pages Paper*
*ISBN 0-304314-00-5*

**7198  Viva Vital News**
5016 Silk Oak Drive
Sarasota, FL 34232

Membership service organization offering information for veterans and is an affiliate of the American Council of the Blind.

**7199  Voice of Vision**
GW Micro
725 Airport North Office Park
Fort Wayne, IN 46825
260-489-3671
FAX: 260-489-2608
e-mail: sales@gwmicro.com
www.gwmicro.com

*Dan Weirich, Owner*

Offers product reviews, product announcements, tips for making systems or applications more accessible, or explanations of
concepts of interest to any computer user or would-be computer
user. This association newsletter is available in braille, in large
print, on audio cassette and on 3.5 or 5.25 IBM format diskette.
*Quarterly*

**7200  Walking Alone and Marching Together**
National Federation of the Blind
1800 Johnson Street
Baltimore, MD 21230
410-659-9314
FAX: 410-685-5653
e-mail: nfb@iamdigex.net
www.nfb.org

*Marc Maurer, President*

The history of the organized blind movement, this book spans
more than 50 years of civil rights, social issues, attitudes and experiences of the blind. Published in 1990, it has been read by
thousands of blind and sighted persons and is used in colleges,
libraries and programs across the country as an important tool in
understanding blindness and it's impact on both personal lives
and the society at large. Braille $130, 2 track or 4 track cassette
$40, Print $33.00. Contact Materials Center.

**7201  We Can Do it Together!**
American Foundation for the Blind/AFB Press
PO Box 1020
Sewickley, PA 15143
412-741-1142
800-232-3044
FAX: 412-741-0609
e-mail: afborders@abdintl.com
www.afb.org
This video illustrates a transdisciplinary team orientation and
mobility program for students with severe visual and multiple
impairments, covering both adapted communication systems
used to teach mobility skills and basic indoor mobility in the
school. For mobility instructors, administrators, teachers of the
visually and severely handicapped, occupational, physical and
speech therapists and parents. Discussion guide included. 10
minute video tape. Also available in PAL, $33.95,
0-89128-267-X. *$26.95*
*VHS*
*ISBN 0-891282-13-0*

**7202  Webster Large Print Thesaurus**
Science Products
PO Box 888
Southeastern, PA 19399
610-296-2111
800-888-7400
FAX: 610-296-0488

*Mary Ann Case, Marketing Director*
*Lee Benham, Owner*

10 point type, more than 57,000 word entries and illustrations,
14 pt. body copy, 16 pt. heads and 20 pt. page headings. *$22.50*

**7203 What Museum Guides Need to Know: Access for the Blind and Visually Impaired**
American Foundation for the Blind/AFB Press
PO Box 1020
Sewickley, PA 15143
412-741-1142
800-232-3044
FAX: 412-741-0609
e-mail: afborders@abdintl.com
www.afb.org
Explains how blind and visually impaired museum-goers experience art and offers pointers on greeting people, asking if help is needed and teaching about a specific work of art. Contains information on access laws, resources, training guides and guidelines for preparing large print, cassette and braille materials. *$14.95*
*64 pages Paperback*
*ISBN 0-891281-58-4*

**7204 Witch's Daughter**
JB Lippincott
227 E Washington Square
Philadelphia, PA 19106
215-521-8300
800-777-2295
FAX: 215-824-7390

*J Lippincott, Chief Executive Officer*

Perdeta had been scorned by her peers on the small Scottish island where she lived. The island children believed her to be a witch and spent their time chasing and teasing her. When Tim and his blind sister Janey arrived for a vacation, Perdeta had her first opportunity to make friends. Janey and Perdeta enjoyed each other's company immediately, while Tim eventually accepted their new friend.
*181 pages Hardcover*

**7205 You Seem Like a Regular Kid to Me**
American Foundation for the Blind/AFB Press
PO Box 1020
Sewickley, PA 15143
412-741-1142
800-232-3044
FAX: 412-741-0609
e-mail: afborders@abdintl.com
www.afb.org
An interview with Jane, a blind child, tells other children what it's like to be blind. Jane explains how she gets around, takes care of herself, does her schoolwork, spends her leisure time and even pays for things when she can't see money. Paperback and pamphlet. $25.00/pack of 25. *$25.00*
*16 pages Pack of 25*
*ISBN 0-89128 -21-6*

## Vocations

**7206 ABC's of Starting a Private School**
Alliance for Parental Involvement in Education
PO Box 59
East Chatham, NY 12060
518-392-6900
FAX: 518-392-6900
Job placement programs, remunerative work services and work adjustment training programs. *$17.95*

**7207 Ability**
George J DePontis
PO Box 370788
Miami, FL 33137

Features articles on living, working, playing and entertainment for the disabled. *$12.00*

**7208 Ability Magazine**
Jobs Information Business Service
1682 Langley Avenue
Irvine, CA 92614
949-622-1040
800-453-JOBS
Provides an electronic classified system which allows employers to recruit qualified individuals with disabilities, and people with disabilities to locate employment opportunities.

**7209 Cambridge Career Products Catalog**
Cambridge Educational
PO Box 931
Monmouth Junction, NJ 08852
304-744-9323
800-468-4227
FAX: 800-329-6687
e-mail: lisa.schmuclei@films.com
www.cambridgeeducational.com

*Lisa Schmuclei, Marketing Director*

A full color catalog featuring hundreds of products designed to aid people in career exploration, selecting specific occupations and obtaining these jobs through resume and interview preparation.
*64 pages BiAnnual*

**7210 Career Development Quarterly**
American Counseling Association
5999 Stevenson Avenue
Alexandria, VA 22304
703-823-9800
800-473-2329
FAX: 703-823-6862
www.counseling.org

*Mark L Savickas, Editor*
*Richard Yep, Executive Director*

*$35.00*
*Quarterly*

**7211 Case Management in the Vocational Rehabilitation of Disabled Persons**
Berkeley Planning Associates
440 Grand Avenue
Suite 500
Oakland, CA 94610
510-465-7884
FAX: 510-465-7885

*Linda Toms Barker*
*Hans Bos, President*

Journal examining the effectiveness of case management services in the context of vocational rehabilitation for persons with psychiatric disabilities.

**7212 Closer Look: The English Program at the Model Secondary School for the Deaf**
Gallaudet University Bookstore
800 Florida Avenue NE
Washington, DC 20002
202-651-5000
800-451-1073
FAX: 202-651-5489

*Erving Jordan, President*

Job placement programs, remunerative work services and work adjustment training programs incorporating the whole language philosophy into classroom routines. *$8.50*
*67 pages*

**7213 College Guide for Students with Learning Disabilties**
Riverside Publishing/Wintergreen Orchard House
425 Spring Lake Drive
Itasca, IL 60143
630-467-7000
800-323-9540
FAX: 630-467-6194

*Tina Tripoli, Marketing/Account Manager*
*Lee Jones, President*

There is a role to play whether you are a teacher, counselor, administrator or parent and this guide explains them all. *$26.95*
*372 pages*

**7214 DEP, Disabled Employment Program**
Department of Health
PO Box 678
Albany, NY 12201
518-402-7090
FAX: 518-447-4573
e-mail: jcrucetti@albanycounty.com
www.health.state.ny.us

*Patricia Hess, Manager*

**7215 Demystifying Job Development: Field-Based Approaches to Job Development for the Disabled**
Training Resource Network

A guide to successful placement of individuals with severe disabilities in quality jobs in the community. *$29.95*
*105 pages 2000*
*ISBN 1-883302-37-4*

**7216 Economic Opportunity Report**
Business Publishers
2601 University Boulevard NW
Suite 200
Silver Spring, MD 20902        301-587-6300
800-274-6737
FAX: 301-587-4530
e-mail: bpinews@bpinews.com
www.bpinews.com

*Leonard A Eiserer, Publisher*
*Lan Wilhelm, Editor*
*Adam Goldstein, President*

Reports the latest on key poverty programs such as homelessness, housing, welfare reform, job training, early childhood education, health care, adult literacy, and more. *$417.00*
*10 pages Newsletter Wkly*

**7217 Economics, Industry and Disability**
Paul H Brookes Publishing Company
PO Box 10624
Baltimore, MD 21285        410-337-9580
800-638-3775
FAX: 410-337-8539

*Paul Brooks, Owner*

An analysis of the movement toward nonsheltered employment, this book addresses the expanding opportunities, future challenges and economic changes surrounding efforts to ensure the development of positive and constructive employment for persons with disabilities. *$42.00*
*Hardcover*

**7218 Employment Standards Administration Department of Labor**
200 Constitution Avenue NW
Washington, DC 20210        202-254-8628
877-889-5627
www.dol.gov

*Corlis Sellers, Branch Chief*
*Edie West, Executive Director*

Monitors compliance with sub-minimum wage requirements for handicapped workers in sheltered workshops, competitive industry and hospitals and institutions under Section 14 of the Fair Labor Standards Act of 1938.

**7219 Employment for Individuals with Asperger S yndrome or Non-Verbal Learning Disability**
Taylor & Francis
47 Runway Drive
Suite G
Levittown, PA 19057        215-269-0400
FAX: 215-625-2940

*Harold Stecker, President*

With practical and technical advice on everything from job-hunting to interview techniques, from fitting in the workplace to whether or not to disclose diagnosis, this book guides people with NLD or AS successfully through the employment field. *$22.95*

*272 pages 2004*
*ISBN 1-843107-66-X*

**7220 Guide to Developing Language Competence in Handicapped Preschool Children**
Charles C Thomas
2600 S 1st Street
Springfield, IL 62704        217-789-8980
800-258-8980
FAX: 217-789-9130
e-mail: books@ccthomas.com
www.ccthomas.com

*Ennio Cipani*
*Michael Thomas, President*

Job placement programs, remunerative work services and work adjustment training programs handicaps: teachers, administrators and parents. *$54.95*
*268 pages Cloth 1991*
*ISBN 0-398057-48-6*

**7221 Handbook for Counseling the Gifted and Talented**
American Counseling Association
5999 Stevenson Avenue
Alexandria, VA 22304        703-823-9800
800-473-2329
FAX: 703-823-6862
www.counseling.org

*Barbara A Kerr, Editor*
*Richard Yep, Executive Director*

Tells how to identify, inspire and nurture gifted and talented students. Effective techniques for making a qualitative and quantitative differentiation of gifted students, conducting a successful search for gifted students, nurturing underachievers and helping multipotential students make career choices. *$32.95*
*218 pages*
*ISBN 1-55620 -79-1*

**7222 Job Placement Digest**
National Rehabilitation Association (NRA)
613 S Washington Street
Alexandria, VA 22314        703-836-0850

e-mail: info@nationalrehab.org

*Linda Winslow, Executive Director*

Newsletter discussing employment options for persons with disabilities.

**7223 Job-Hunting for the So-Called Handicapped or People Who Have Disabilities**
Ten Speed Press

Guides readers through the often frustrating, but ultimately rewarding process of securing independence in their lives and personal satisfaction in their careers. Begins by demystifying the intricacies of the Americans with Disabilities Act, describing in clear terms what the act does and does not guarantee disabled job-hunters, and then moves on to job-hunting strategies tailored specifically to people with disabilities. *$12.95*
*160 pages 2000*
*ISBN 1-580081-95-9*

**7224 Life Beyond the Classroom: Transition Str ategies for Young People with Disabilities**
Paul H Brookes Publishing Company
PO Box 10624
Baltimore, MD 21285        410-337-9580
800-638-3775
FAX: 410-337-8539
e-mail: custserv@brookespublishing.com
www.brookespublishing.com

*Paul Brooks, Owner*

Specialists in a variety of disciplines use creative and practical techniques to ensure careful transition planning, to build young people's confidence and competence in work skills, and to foster support from businesses and community organizations for training and employment programs. *$64.95*
*543 pages 2001*
*ISBN 1-557664-76-5*

**7225 Life Skills for Vocational Success**
Workshops
4244 3rd Avenue S
Birmingham, AL 35222     205-592-9683
FAX: 205-592-9687

*Jim Crim, Executive Director*

*$35.00*
*250 pages*

**7226 Mentally Retarded Individuals**
Mainstream
3 Bethesda Metro Center
Suite 830
Bethesda, MD 20814     301-961-9299
800-247-1380
FAX: 301-654-6714
e-mail: info@mainstreaminc.org

*Charles Moster*

Mainstreaming mentally retarded individuals into the workplace. *$2.50*
*12 pages*

**7227 OT Practice**
American Occupational Therapy Association
164 Rollins Avenue
Suite 301
Rockville, MD 20852     301-951-9070
800-877-1383
FAX: 301-652-7711

*Jeanette Bair, Executive Director*

Offers information on conferences, books, resources, materials and information and referral services for persons with disabilities.

**7228 Occupational Outlook Quarterly**
US Department of Labor/Bureau of Labor Stats
2 Massachusetts Avenue NE
Washington, DC 20212     202-691-5200
FAX: 202-691-7890

*Kathleen Utgoff, Chief Executive Officer*

Information on new educational and training opportunities, emerging jobs, prospects for change in the work world, and occupational projections. *$9.50*
*40 pages Quarterly*

**7229 Options**
6610 N Clark Street
Chicago, IL 60626     773-973-7900
FAX: 773-973-5268
e-mail: AskAnixter@Anixter.org
www.anixter.org

*Allan Bergman, President*
*Robert Dolgan, Editor*

Anixter Center's quarterly publication. Free.
*Quarterly*

**7230 Preparation and Employment of Students**
Paul H Brookes Publishing Company
PO Box 10624
Baltimore, MD 21285     410-337-9580
800-638-3775
FAX: 410-337-8539

*Paul Brooks, Owner*

A practical guide on vocational training and employment issues for persons with severe multiple and physical disabilities. *$ 213.00*
*224 pages Paper*

**7231 Principles and a Philosophy for Vocational Education**
Center on Education and Training for Employment
1900 Kenny Road
Columbus, OH 43210     614-292-4353
800-848-4815
FAX: 614-292-1260
www.cete.org/products

Identifies and analyzes underlying principles of vocational education and uses them as a basis for coherent philosophical position for vocational education that reflects human and economic needs, a contemporary knowledge base, and the values inherent in our society. *$15.50*
*250 pages*

**7232 Retaining At-Risk Students: The Role of Career and Vocational Education**
Center on Education and Training for Employment
1900 Kenny Road
Columbus, OH 43210     614-292-4353
800-848-4815
FAX: 614-292-1260

Reviews the causes of at-risk students and their implications for the U.S. labor force. *$6.00*
*48 pages*

**7233 Social Competence for Workers with Developmental Disabilities**
Paul H Brookes Publishing Company
PO Box 10624
Baltimore, MD 21285     410-337-9580
800-638-3775
FAX: 410-337-8539

*Paul Brooks, Owner*

A guide to enhancing employment outcomes in integrated settings. *$35.00*
*128 pages Paper 1990*

**7234 Start with the Arts**
1300 Connecticut Avenue NW
Suite 700
Washington, DC 20036     202-628-2800
800-933-8721
FAX: 202-737-0725
e-mail: info@vsarts.org
www.vsarts.org

*Soula Antoniou, Executive Director*
*Tanya L Travers, Marketing Manager*

*$59.00*

**7235 Successful Job Accommodation Strategies**
LRP Publications
PO Box 24668
West Palm Beach, FL 33416     561-622-6520
800-341-7874
FAX: 215-784-9639
e-mail: custserve@lrp.com
www.lrp.com

*Honora McDowell, Product Group Manager*
*Kenneth Kahn, Chief Executive Officer*

This monthly newsletter provides you with quick tips, new accommodation ideas and innovative workplace solutions. You learn the outcomes of the latest cases involving workplace accommodations. *$ 140.00*
*12 pages Monthly*

**7236 Sucessful Job Search Strategies for the Di sabled: Understanding the ADA**
Wiley Publishing
605 3rd Avenue
New York, NY 10158     212-850-6000
FAX: 212-850-6088

Following a concise overview of the Americans with Disabilities Act (ADA), covers such topics as job identification, self-assessment, job leads, resumes, disability disclosure, interviewing, and accommodating specific disabilities. Includes dozen of relevant and instructive situation analyses, case examples, and answers to commonly asked questions. *$165.00*
*229 pages 1994*

**7237   Teaching Chemistry to Students with Disabilities**
American Chemical Society
1155 16th Street NW
Washington, DC  20036                        202-872-4600
800-227-5558
FAX: 202-776-8299
TTY: 202-872-6355
e-mail: cwd@acs.org
membership.acs.org/C/CWD

*Dorothy Miner, Editor*
*Judith Summers-Gates, Chair, CCD*
*Anne Swanson, Editor*

Promotes the full involvement of individuals with physical and learning disabilities in educational and career opportunities in the chemical and allied sciences. CWD members lead the American Chemical Society's efforts to help: individuals with disabilities who seek education or employment in chemical and allied sciences; employers and educators of persons with disabilities; other committees, offices and members of ACS who are interested in the full involvement of persons with disabilities.
*148 pages*
*ISBN 0-841238-16-2*

**7238   Transition from School to Work**
Paul H Brookes Publishing Company
PO Box 10624
Baltimore, MD  21285                        410-337-9580
800-638-3775
FAX: 410-337-8539

*Paul Brooks, Owner*

A hands-on guide to planning and implementing successful transition programs for adolescents with disabilities. *$25.00*
*336 pages Paper 1988*

**7239   Transition from School to Work for Persons with Disabilities**
Longman Publishing Group
10 Bank Street
9th Floor
White Plains, NY  10606                      914-993-5000
FAX: 914-421-5598

*Joanne Dresner, President*

Examines the multidimensional process needed to effectively prepare persons with disabilities for life beyond school and addresses the key issues in the transition process.
*251 pages Paper 1989*
*ISBN 0-801302-28-5*

**7240   Vocal Rehabilitation: A Practice Book for Voice Improvement**
Pro-Ed
8700 Shoal Creek Boulevard
Austin, TX  78757                            512-451-3246
800-897-3202
FAX: 512-451-8542
e-mail: info@proedinc.com
www.proedinc.com

*Donald Hammill, Owner*

A complete program that clinicians can use to help clients eliminate vocal misuses or abuse and gain a healthy, proficient voice.

**7241   Vocational Education for Multihandicapped Youth**
Paul H Brookes Publishing Company
PO Box 10624
Baltimore, MD  21285                        410-337-9580
800-638-3775
FAX: 410-337-8539

*Paul Brooks, Owner*

The first book with specific vocational teaching strategies, adaptations and rehabilitation guidelines for preteens and young adults with cerebral palsy. *$25.00*
*320 pages Paper 1988*

**7242   Vocational Evaluation and Traumatic Brain Injury: A Procedural Manual**
Stout Vocational Rehab Institute
University of Wisconsin-Stout
Menomonie, WI  54751
FAX: 715-232-2356

*Ronald R Fry, Manager*
*Darlene Botterbusch, Program Assistant*

This is a written guide for rehabilitation professionals interested in effectively developing new or modifying existing evaluation/assessment services for persons with traumatic brain injury. A practical manual for identifying local support services; creating specific processes, tools and techniques; and formulating meaningful outcome information to facilitate the provision or goal-directed services *$ 14.75*
*61 pages Softcover*

**7243   Vocational Rehabilitation and Employment**
Books on Special Children
PO Box 305
Congers, NY  10920                          845-638-1236
FAX: 845-638-0847
e-mail: irene@boscbooks.com
Defines kinds of work, expectations, goals and programs. Contributions in general issues of supported employment, training and management and community based programs. *$47.00*
*372 pages Hardcover*

**7244   Vocational Rehabilitation and Supported Employment**
Paul H Brookes Publishing Company
PO Box 10624
Baltimore, MD  21285                        410-337-9580
800-638-3775
FAX: 410-337-8539

*Paul Brooks, Owner*

A timely, comprehensive resource on how vocational rehabilitation can play a major role in facilitating and implementing supported employment programs. *$43.00*
*384 pages Paper 1988*

## Pamphlets

**7245   A Guide for People with Disabilities Seeking Employment**
US Department of Justice
950 Pennsylvania Avenue NW Drs
- Nyav
Washington, DC 20530                        202-586-5000
800-574-0301
FAX: 202-307-1197
www.ada.gov

*Joanne Graham, Manager*

A 2-page pamplet for people with disabilities providing a general explanation of the employment provisions of the ADA and how to file a complaint with the Equal Employment Opportunity Commission.

**7246  ABC's of Latex Allergy**
Asthma and Allergy Foundation of America
1125 15th Street NW
Suite 502
Washington, DC  20005                    202-466-7643
                                    FAX: 202-466-8940
                                    e-mail: info@aafa.org
                                    www.aafa.org

*Bill Lin, Executive Director*

Brochure provides excellent coverage of this topic including symptoms, diagnosis, causes, and treatments.

**7247  ADA Business Brief: Restriping Parking Lots**
US Department of Justice
950 Pennsylvania Avenue NW Drs
- Nyav
Washington, DC 20530                    202-586-5000
                                        800-574-0301
                                    FAX: 202-307-1197
                                        www.ada.gov

*Joanne Graham, Manager*

A 2-page illustrated design guide explaining the number of accessible parking spaces that are required and the restriping requirements for accessible parking spaces for cars and vans.

**7248  ADA Business Brief: Service Animals**
US Department of Justice
950 Pennsylvania Avenue NW Drs
- Nyav
Washington, DC 20530                    202-586-5000
                                        800-574-0301
                                    FAX: 202-307-1197
                                        www.ada.gov

*Joanne Graham, Manager*

A 1-page publication summarizing the ADA rules on service animals.

**7249  ADHD**
Learning Disabilities Association of America
4156 Library Road
Pittsburgh, PA 15234                    412-341-1515
                                    FAX: 412-344-0224
                                    e-mail: info@ldaamerica.org
                                        www.ldaamerica.org
A booklet for parents offering information on Attention Deficit-Hyperactivity Disorders and learning disabilities. *$3.00*

**7250  About Asthma**
American Lung Association
61 Broadway
New York, NY 10006                    212-315-8700
                                    FAX: 212-315-8870
                                    e-mail: info@lungusa.org
                                        www.lungusa.org

*John Kirkwood, Chief Executive Officer*

A popular style pamphlet explaining symptoms, treatment and more for persons with asthma.
                        *16 pages*

**7251  About Attention Disorder**
CACLD
25 Van Zant Street
Suite 15-5
Norwalk, CT  06855                    203-838-5010
                                    FAX: 203-866-6108
                                    e-mail: CACLD@optonline.net
                                        www.CACLD.org

*Beryl Kaufman, Executive Director*

Introduction to ADHD for the child with the disorder, parents, professionals, family and friends. Brief description as well as causes, challenges involved, treatment options, ways for parents and teachers to help and how children can help themselves. Published by Connecticut Association for Children & Adults with Learning Disabilities (CACLD). *$2.00*

*14 pages*

**7252  About Children's Eyes**
National Association for Visually Handicapped
22 W 21st Street
Floor 6
New York, NY  10010                    212-889-3141
                                    FAX: 212-727-2931
                                    e-mail: staff@navh.org
                                        www.navh.org

*Lorianie Marchi, Chief Executive Officer*

How to identify the child with a visual problem.

**7253  About Children's Vision: A Guide for Parents**
National Association for Visually Handicapped
22 W 21st Street
Floor 6
New York, NY  10010                    212-889-3141
                                    FAX: 212-727-2931
                                    e-mail: staff@navh.org
                                        www.navh.org

*Lorianie Marchi, Chief Executive Officer*

Offers a better understanding of the normal and possible abnormal development of a child's eyesight. *$.50*

**7254  Accessible Stadiums**
US Department of Justice
950 Pennsylvania Avenue NW Drs
- Nyav
Washington, DC 20530                    202-586-5000
                                        800-574-0301
                                    FAX: 202-307-1197
                                        www.ada.gov

*Joanne Graham, Manager*

A 4-page publication highlighting features that must be accessible in new stadiums including line of sight for wheelchair seating locations.

**7255  Agent Orange & Spina Bifida**
Spina Bifida Association of America
4590 Macarthur Boulevard NW
Suite 250
Washington, DC 20007                    202-944-3285
                                        800-321-6141
                                    FAX: 202-944-3295
                                    e-mail: sbaa@sbaa.org
                                        www.sbaa.org

*Cindy Brownstein, Chief Executive Officer*

**7256  Ankylosing Spondylitis**
Arthritis Foundation
PO Box 7669
Atlanta, GA  30357                    404-872-7100
                                        800-283-7800
                                    FAX: 404-872-9559
                                    e-mail: help@arthritis.org
                                        www.arthritis.org

*John Klippel, Chief Executive Officer*

**7257  Arthritis Answers: Basic Information About Arthritis**
Arthritis Foundation
PO Box 7669
Atlanta, GA  30357                    404-872-7100
                                        800-283-7800
                                    FAX: 404-872-9559
                                    e-mail: help@arthritis.org
                                        www.arthritis.org

*John Klippel, Chief Executive Officer*

**7258 Arthritis Information: Children**
Arthritis Foundation
PO Box 7669
Atlanta, GA 30357
404-872-7100
800-283-7800
FAX: 404-872-9559
e-mail: help@arthritis.org
www.arthritis.org

*John Klippel, Chief Executive Officer*

List of materials for children with arthritis, their families and the health professionals who care for them.

**7259 Arthritis and Diet**
National Institute of Arthritis
1 Ams Circle
Bethesda, MD 20892
301-495-4484
877-226-4267
FAX: 301-881-2731
e-mail: niamsinfo@mail.nih.gov
www.nih.gov/niams

*Kelly Collins, Manager*

Offers information on nutrition and diet pertaining to the arthritis community. *$2.00*
*16 pages*

**7260 Arthritis and Employment: You Can Get the Job You Want**
Arthritis Foundation
PO Box 7669
Atlanta, GA 30357
404-872-7100
800-283-7800
FAX: 404-872-9559
e-mail: help@arthritis.org
www.arthritis.org

*John Klippel, Chief Executive Officer*

**7261 Arthritis and Pregnancy**
Arthritis Foundation
PO Box 7669
Atlanta, GA 30357
404-872-7100
800-283-7800
FAX: 404-872-9559
e-mail: help@arthritis.org
www.arthritis.org

*John Klippel, Chief Executive Officer*

How arthritis affects pregnancy, managing pregnancy and a new baby.

**7262 Arthritis in Children**
National Institute of Arthritis
1 Ams Circle
Bethesda, MD 20892
301-495-4484
877-226-4267
FAX: 301-881-2731
e-mail: niamsinfo@mail.nih.gov
www.nih.gov/niams

*Kelly Collins, Manager*

**7263 Arthritis in Children and La Artritis Infantojuvenil**
American Juvenile Arthritis Organization
PO Box 7669
Atlanta, GA 30357
404-872-7100
800-283-7800
FAX: 404-872-9559
e-mail: help@arthritis.org
www.arthritis.org

*John Klippel, Chief Executive Officer*

A medical information booklet about juvenile rheumatoid arthritis. This booklet is written for parents or other adults and includes details about different forms of JRA, medications, therapies and coping issues.

**7264 Arthritis in Children: Resources for Children, Parents and Teachers**
National Institute of Arthritis
9000 Rockville Pike
Bethesda, MD 20892
301-495-4484
877-226-4267
FAX: 301-881-2731
e-mail: niamsinfo@mail.nih.gov
www.nih.gov/niams

*Kelly Collins, Manager*

A resource offering information on juvenile arthritis, causes, treatments and prevention.
*38 pages*

**7265 Arthritis on the Job: You Can Work with It**
Arthritis Foundation
PO Box 7669
Atlanta, GA 30357
404-872-7100
800-283-7800
FAX: 404-872-9559
e-mail: help@arthritis.org
www.arthritis.org

*John Klippel, Chief Executive Officer*

**7266 Arthritis, Rheumatic Diseases and Related Disorders**
National Institute of Arthritis
9000 Rockville Pike
Bethesda, MD 20892
301-495-4484
877-226-4267
FAX: 301-881-2731
e-mail: niamsinfo@mail.nih.gov
www.nih.gov/niams

*Kelly Collins, Manager*

This pamphlet offers information, technical articles and research on arthritis and related disorders. Also included are referral organizations to help patients uncover more information.

**7267 Arthritis: Do You Know?**
Arthritis Foundation
PO Box 7669
Atlanta, GA 30357
404-872-7100
800-283-7800
FAX: 404-872-9559
e-mail: help@arthritis.org
www.arthritis.org

*John Klippel, Chief Executive Officer*

A brief overview of arthritis and the services of the Arthritis Foundation.

**7268 Assistance at Self-Serve Gas Stations**
US Department of Justice
950 Pennsylvania Avenue NW Drs
- Nyav
Washington, DC 20530
202-586-5000
800-574-0301
FAX: 202-307-1197
www.ada.gov

*Joanne Graham, Manager*

A 1-page document providing guidance on the ADA and refueling assistance for customers with disabilities at self-serve gas stations.

**7269 Asthma & Allergy Medications**
Academy of Allergy, Asthma, Immunology
611 E Wells Street
Milwaukee, WI 53202
414-272-6071
800-822-2762
FAX: 414-272-6070
e-mail: info@aaaai.org
www.aaaai.org

*Kay Whalen, Executive Vice President*
*$.50*

*4 pages*

**7270 Asthma Alert**
American Lung Association
61 Broadway
New York, NY 10006

212-315-8700
FAX: 212-315-8870
e-mail: info@lungusa.org
www.lungusa.org

*John Kirkwood, Chief Executive Officer*

Quick reference folders with information on asthma, the symptoms and what to do in an emergency.

**7271 Asthma Handbook**
American Lung Association
61 Broadway
New York, NY 10006

212-315-8700
FAX: 212-315-8870
e-mail: info@lungusa.org
www.lungusa.org

*John Kirkwood, Chief Executive Officer*

Explains asthma, gives self-care methods for handling it and helps patients work more effectively with their doctor.
*28 pages*

**7272 Asthma Lifelines**
American Lung Association
61 Broadway
New York, NY 10006

212-315-8700
FAX: 212-315-8700
e-mail: info@lungusa.org
www.lungusa.org

*John Kirkwood, Chief Executive Officer*

Promotional brochure providing descriptions of ALA asthma education materials.
*12 pages*

**7273 Asthma and Pregnancy**
Academy of Allergy, Asthma, Immunology
611 E Wells Street
Milwaukee, WI 53202

414-272-6071
800-822-2762
FAX: 414-272-6070
e-mail: info@aaaai.org
www.aaaai.org

*Kay Whalen, Executive Vice President*
*$.50*

**7274 Attention Deficit-Hyperactivity Disorder: Is it a Learning Disability?**
Georgetown University, School of Medicine
3800 Reservoir Road NW
Washington, DC 20007

202-342-2400

*Joy Drass, Chief Executive Officer*

Offers information on learning disabilities and related disorders.

**7275 Avoiding Unfortunate Situations**
Autism Society of North Carolina Bookstore
505 Oberlin Road
Suite 230
Raleigh, NC 27605

919-743-0204
800-442-2762
FAX: 919-743-0208
e-mail: dcoffey@autismsociety-nc.org
www.autismsociety-nc.org

*Darla Coffey, Bookstore Manager*
*Jill Keel, Executive Director*

A collection of tips and information from and about people with autism and other developmental disabilities. *$5.00*

**7276 BVA Bulletin**
Blinded Veterans Association
477 H Street NW
Washington, DC 20001

202-371-8880
800-669-7079
FAX: 303-914-5832
e-mail: bva@bva.org
www.bva.org

*Thomas H Miller, Executive Director*
*John K Williams, Administrative Director*
*George E Brummell, Nat'l Dir. Field Service Program*
*Bi-Monthly*

**7277 Being Close**
National Jewish Center for Immunology
1400 Jackson Street
Denver, CO 80206

303-388-4461

e-mail: allstetterw@njc.org
www.njc.org

*William Allstetter, Media Relations Manager*
*Lynn Taussig, Chief Executive Officer*

A booklet offering information to patients suffering from a respiratory disorder such as emphysema, asthma or tuberculosis, that discusses sexual problems and feelings.

**7278 Blind and Vision-Impaired Individuals**
Mainstream
1030 5th Street NE
Washington, DC 20002

202-898-1400

e-mail: info@mainstreaminc.org
Mainstreaming blind individuals into the workplace. *$ 2.50*
*12 pages*

**7279 Books are Fun for Everyone**
National Library Service for the Blind
1291 Taylor Street NW
Washington, DC 20542

202-707-5100
FAX: 202-707-0712
e-mail: nls@loc.gov
www.loc.gov/nls

*Frank Cylke, Executive Director*

**7280 Braille: An Extraordinary Volunteer Opportunity**
National Library Service for the Blind
1291 Taylor Street NW
Washington, DC 20542

202-707-5100
FAX: 202-707-0712
e-mail: nls@loc.gov
www.loc.gov/nls

*Frank Cylke, Executive Director*

**7281 Bursitis, Tendonitis and Other Soft Tissue Rheumatic Syndromes**
Arthritis Foundation
PO Box 7669
Atlanta, GA 30357

404-872-7100
800-283-7800
FAX: 404-872-9559
e-mail: help@arthritis.org
www.arthritis.org

*John Klippel, Chief Executive Officer*

**7282 Carpal Tunnel Syndrome**
Arthritis Foundation
PO Box 7669
Atlanta, GA 30357

404-872-7100
800-283-7800
FAX: 404-872-9559
e-mail: help@arthritis.org
www.arthritis.org

*John Klippel, Chief Executive Officer*

Offers an introduction to Carpal Tunnel, causes, symptoms, diagnosis and resources.

**7283 Cataracts**
National Eye Institute
Building 31
Bethesda, MD 20892          301-496-0417
                           800-869-2020
                      FAX: 301-402-1065
                    e-mail: 2020@nei.nih.gov
                           www.nei.nih.gov
Provides information about this common condition and its treatment.

**7284 Childhood Asthma**
Academy of Allergy, Asthma, Immunology
611 E Wells Street
Milwaukee, WI 53202          414-272-6071
                           800-822-2762
                      FAX: 414-272-6070
                    e-mail: info@aaaai.org
                           www.aaaai.org

*Kay Whalen, Executive Vice President*
*$.50*
      *4 pages*

**7285 Childhood Asthma: A Matter of Control**
American Lung Association
61 Broadway
New York, NY 10006          212-315-8700
                      FAX: 212-315-8700
                    e-mail: info@lungusa.org
                           www.lungusa.org

*John Kirkwood, Chief Executive Officer*
A guide for parents of children with asthma, this booklet covers topics such as identifying asthma signs and symptoms as well as controlling the condition.
      *28 pages*

**7286 Classification of Impaired Vision**
National Association for Visually Handicapped
22 W 21st Street
Floor 6
New York, NY 10010          212-889-3141
                      FAX: 212-727-2931
                    e-mail: staff@navh.org
                           www.navh.org

*Lorianie Marchi, Chief Executive Officer*
Describes various degrees of impaired vision.

**7287 Club Foot & Other Foot Deformities Fact Sheet**
March of Dimes
1275 Mamaroneck Avenue
White Plains, NY 10605          914-949-7166
                      FAX: 914-997-4763
                    e-mail: askus@marchofdimes.com
                           www.marchofdimes.com
Provides information about pregnancy, birth defects, genetics, drug use, environmental hazzards and related topics. The Resource Center's health information specialists provide acccurate and up-to-date information via e-mail and Web site. One copy of this fact sheet can be obtained free of charge by visiting our website.

**7288 Cogrehab**
Life Science Associates
1 Fenimore Road
Bayport, NY 11705          631-472-2111

Divided into six groups for diagnosis and treatment of attention, memory and perceptual disorders to be used by and under the guidance of a professional. $95.-$1,950

**7289 Common ADA Errors and Omissions in New Construction and Alterations**
US Department of Justice
950 Pennsylvania Avenue NW Drs
- Nyav
Washington, DC 20530          202-586-5000
                           800-574-0301
                      FAX: 202-307-1197
                           www.ada.gov

*Joanne Graham, Manager*
This 13-page document lists a sampling of common accessibility errors or omissions that have been identified through the Department of Justice's ongoing enforcement efforts. The significance of the errors is discussed and references are provided to the requirements of the ADA Standards for Accessible Design.

**7290 Common ADA Problems at Newly Constructed Lodging Facilities**
US Department of Justice
950 Pennsylvania Avenue NW Drs
- Nyav
Washington, DC 20530          202-586-5000
                           800-574-0301
                      FAX: 202-307-1197
                           www.ada.gov

*Joanne Graham, Manager*
This 11-page document lists a sampling of common accessibility problems at newly constructed lodging facilities that have been identified through the Department of Justice's ongoing enforcement efforts.

**7291 Commonly Asked Questions About Service Animals in Places of Business**
US Department of Justice
950 Pennsylvania Avenue NW Drs
- Nyav
Washington, DC 20530          202-586-5000
                           800-574-0301
                      FAX: 202-307-1197
                           www.ada.gov

*Joanne Graham, Manager*
A 3-page publication providing information about service animals and ADA requirements.

**7292 Commonly Asked Questions About Title III of the ADA**

US Department of Justice
950 Pennsylvania Avenue NW Drs
- Nyav
Washington, DC 20530          202-586-5000
                           800-574-0301
                      FAX: 202-307-1197
                           www.ada.gov

*Joanne Graham, Manager*
A 6-page publication providing information for state and local governments about ADA requirements for ensuring that people with disabilities receive the same services and benefits as provided to others.

**7293 Communicating with People Who Have Trouble Hearing & Seeing: A Primer**
National Association for Visually Handicapped
22 W 21st Street
Floor 6
New York, NY 10010          212-889-3141
                      FAX: 212-727-2931
                    e-mail: staff@navh.org
                           www.navh.org

*Lorianie Marchi, Chief Executive Officer*
Line drawings that depict problems for those with both deficiencies. *$2.00*

**7294 Connect Information Service**
150 S Progress Avenue
Harrisburg, PA 17109 717-657-1798
800-692-7288
Pamphlet offering information on child development, special education programs, resources for parents and local contact persons.

**7295 Department of Justice ADA Mediation Program**
US Department of Justice
950 Pennsylvania Avenue NW Drs
- Nyav
Washington, DC 20530 202-586-5000
800-574-0301
FAX: 202-307-1197
www.ada.gov

*Joanne Graham, Manager*

A 6-page publication describing the Department's ADA mediation program and examples of successful mediation efforts.

**7296 Developing a Functional and Longitudinal Plan**
Autism Society of North Carolina Bookstore
505 Oberlin Road
Suite 230
Raleigh, NC 27605 919-743-0204
800-442-2762
FAX: 919-743-0208
e-mail: dcoffey@autismsociety-nc.org
www.autismsociety-nc.org

*Darla Coffey, Bookstore Manager*
*Jill Keel, Executive Director*

This booklet examines the importance of planning and possible goals in self-care. *$4.00*

**7297 Diet and Arthritis**
Arthritis Foundation
PO Box 7669
Atlanta, GA 30357 404-872-7100
800-283-7800
FAX: 404-872-9559
e-mail: help@arthritis.org
www.arthritis.org

*John Klippel, Chief Executive Officer*

**7298 Dog Sponsorship Program**
Guide Dog Foundation for the Blind
371 E Jericho Tpke
Smithtown, NY 11787 631-265-2121
800-548-4337
FAX: 516-361-5192

*Wells Jones, Executive Director*

Offers information to an individual or an organization that wishes to sponsor a guide dog.

**7299 Don't Lose Sight of Cataracts**
National Eye Institute
Building 31
Bethesda, MD 20892 301-496-0417
800-869-2020
FAX: 301-402-1065
e-mail: 2020@nei.nih.gov
www.nei.nih.gov

**7300 Don't Lose Sight of Glaucoma**
National Eye Institute
Building 31
Bethesda, MD 20892 301-496-0417
800-869-2020
FAX: 301-402-1065
e-mail: 2020@nei.nih.gov
www.nei.nih.gov

**7301 Easy Access Housing**
Easter Seals
230 W Monroe Street
Suite 1800
Chicago, IL 60606 312-726-6800
FAX: 312-726-1494

*Janet D Jamieson, Communications Manager*
*James Williams Jr, Chief Executive Officer*

Booklet with a checklist for finding homes that are already accessible or structurally adaptable to accommodate changes in physical abilities and needs. Includes suggestions for solving common accessibility problems such as narrow doors, high thresholds and round knob fixtures.
*12 pages*

**7302 Educational Issues Among Children with Spi na Bifida**
Spina Bifida Association of America
4590 Macarthur Boulevard NW
Suite 250
Washington, DC 20007 202-944-3285
800-321-6141
FAX: 202-944-3295
e-mail: sbaa@sbaa.org
www.sbaa.org

*Cindy Brownstein, Chief Executive Officer*

**7303 Efficacy of Asthma Education, Selected Abstracts**
American Lung Association
61 Broadway
New York, NY 10006 212-315-8700
FAX: 212-315-8700
e-mail: info@lungusa.org
www.lungusa.org

*John Kirkwood, Chief Executive Officer*

Abstracts documenting the efficacy of asthma education programs for physicians and other health professionals.

**7304 Enhancing Communication in Individuals with Autism Through Pictures/Words**
Autism Society of North Carolina Bookstore
505 Oberlin Road
Suite 230
Raleigh, NC 27605 919-743-0204
800-442-2762
FAX: 919-743-0208
e-mail: dcoffey@autismsociety-nc.org
www.autismsociety-nc.org

*Darla Coffey, Bookstore Manager*
*Jill Keel, Executive Director*

Booklet addressing the description and implementation of visually aided communication. *$4.00*

**7305 Exercise and Your Arthritis**
Arthritis Foundation
PO Box 7669
Atlanta, GA 30357 404-872-7100
800-283-7800
FAX: 404-872-9559
e-mail: help@arthritis.org
www.arthritis.org

*John Klippel, Chief Executive Officer*

Types of exercise for people with arthritis and how to do them.

**7306 Exercise-Induced Asthma**
Academy of Allergy, Asthma, Immunology
611 E Wells Street
Milwaukee, WI 53202 414-272-6071
800-822-2762
FAX: 414-272-6070
e-mail: info@aaaai.org
www.aaaai.org

*Kay Whalen, Executive Vice President*

This brochure covers testing, treatment, and other advice on how to deal with exercise-induced asthma. *$.50*

**7307  Eye-Q Test**
National Association for Visually Handicapped
22 W 21st Street
Floor 6
New York, NY  10010                    212-889-3141
                                   FAX: 212-727-2931
                               e-mail: staff@navh.org
                                        www.navh.org

*Lorianie Marchi, Chief Executive Officer*

Five questions and answers to assist in knowing more about vision. Also available in Spanish and Russian.

**7308  Fact Sheet: Attention Deficit-Hyperactivit y Disorder**
Learning Disabilities Association of America
4156 Library Road
Pittsburgh, PA  15234                  412-341-1515
                                   FAX: 412-344-0224
                             e-mail: info@ldaamerica.org
                                   www.ldaamerica.org
A pamphlet offering factual information on ADHD.

**7309  Fact Sheet: Autism Spectrum Disorders**
Autism Society of America
7910 Woodmont Avenue
Suite 300
Bethesda, MD  20814                    301-657-0881
                                        800-3AU-TISM
                                   FAX: 301-657-0869
                          e-mail: info@autism-society.org
                                 www.autism-society.org

*Ann Pulley, Manager*

Offers information on autism spectrum disorders. What it is, symptoms, causes, diagnosis, treatments and research. Also provides Autism Source, a free online referral database of autism services and support at www.autismsource.org.

**7310  Facts About Asthma**
American Lung Association
61 Broadway
New York, NY  10006                    212-315-8700
                                   FAX: 212-315-8700
                               e-mail: info@lungusa.org
                                      www.lungusa.org

*John Kirkwood, Chief Executive Officer*
Primary public information leaflet on asthma.
                    *12 pages*

**7311  Facts: Books for Blind and Physically Handicapped Individuals**
National Library Service for the Blind
1291 Taylor Street NW
Washington, DC  20542                  202-707-5100

                                 e-mail: nls@loc.gov
                                      www.loc.gov/nls

*Frank Cylke, Executive Director*
                    *Annual*

**7312  Facts: Music for Blind and Physically Handicapped Individuals**
National Library Service for the Blind
1291 Taylor Street NW
Washington, DC  20542                  202-707-5100

                                 e-mail: nls@loc.gov
                                      www.loc.gov/nls

*Frank Cylke, Executive Director*

                    *Annual*

**7313  Family Guide to Vision Care**
American Optometric Association
243 N Lindbergh Boulevard
Saint Louis, MO  63141                 314-991-4100
                                   FAX: 314-991-4101
                                        www.aoanet.org

*Michael Jones, Executive Director*

Offers information on the early developmental years of your vision, finding a family optometrist and how to take care of your eyesight through the learning years, the working years and the mature years.

**7314  Family Guide: Growth & Development of the Partially Seeing Child**
National Association for Visually Handicapped
22 W 21st Street
Floor 6
New York, NY  10010                    212-889-3141
                                   FAX: 212-727-2931
                               e-mail: staff@navh.org
                                        www.navh.org

*Lorianie Marchi, Chief Executive Officer*
Offers information for parents and guidelines in raising a partially seeing child. *$.60*

**7315  Free Information/Membership Kit**
National Association for Visually Handicapped
22 W 21st Street
New York, NY  10010                    212-889-3141
                                   FAX: 212-727-2931
                               e-mail: staff@navh.org
                                        www.navh.org

*Eva M Cohen, CEO Assistant*
*Lorianie H Marchi, Founder/CEO*

A free packet describing brochures, pamphlets, and flyers available addressing the needs of the partially seeing, their families, friends and professionals who serve them: large print, visual aids, self-help, referrals. Includes information regarding vision dysfunction and coping with vision loss.
                    *Quarterly*

**7316  General Facts and Figures on Blindness**
National Society to Prevent Blindness
500 E Remington Road
Schaumburg, IL  60173
                                        800-331-2020

**7317  General Interest Catalog**
National Braille Association
3 Townline Circle
Rochester, NY  14623                   585-427-8260

                        e-mail: nbaoffice@compuserve.com
                                   www.nationalbraille.org

*Angela Coffaro, Executive Director*
Lists hundreds of titles of fiction and nonfiction books offered in large print, braille or on cassette to visually impaired readers.
                    *19 pages*

**7318  Genetics and Spina Bifida**
Spina Bifida Association of America
4590 Macarthur Boulevard NW
Suite 250
Washington, DC 20007                   202-944-3285
                                        800-621-3141
                                   FAX: 202-944-3295
                                  e-mail: sbaa@sbaa.org
                                        www.sbaa.org

*Cindy Brownstein, Chief Executive Officer*

**7319 Gift of Sight**
RP Foundation Fighting Blindness
1401 W Mt Royal Avenue
Baltimore, MD 21217
410-225-9409
800-683-5555
FAX: 410-225-3936
A pamphlet offering information on the Retina Donor Program, which studies diseased, human retinal tissue in their search for a cure of retinal degenerative diseases.

**7320 Glaucoma**
Glaucoma Research Foundation
251 Post Street
Suite 600
San Francisco, CA 94108
415-986-3162
800-826-6693
FAX: 415-986-3763
e-mail: info@glaucoma.org
www.glaucoma.org

*Yuko Madono, Outreach/Public Relations*
*Tom Brunner, Chief Executive Officer*

Offers information on what glaucoma is, the causes, treatments, types of glaucoma, eye exams and prevention.

**7321 Glaucoma: The Sneak Thief of Sight**
National Association for Visually Handicapped
22 W 21st Street
Floor 6
New York, NY 10010
212-889-3141
FAX: 212-727-2931
e-mail: staff@navh.org
www.navh.org

*Lorianie Marchi, Chief Executive Officer*

A pamphlet describing the disease, treatment and medications. Also available in Russian and Spanish. Revised in 1999. *$3.50*

**7322 Guide Dog Foundation Flyer**
Guide Dog Foundation for the Blind
371 E Jericho Tpke
Smithtown, NY 11787
631-265-2121
800-548-4337
FAX: 516-361-5192

*Wells Jones, Executive Director*

Offers information on the programs and services provided by the Foundation.

**7323 Guidelines for Comprehensive Low Vision Care**
National Association for Visually Handicapped
22 W 21st Street
Floor 6
New York, NY 10010
212-889-3141
FAX: 212-727-2931
e-mail: staff@navh.org
www.navh.org

*Lorianie Marchi, Chief Executive Officer*

A description of the proper method to conduct a low vision evaluation. *$.50*

**7324 Guidelines for Helping Deaf-Blind Persons**
Helen Keller National Center
111 Middle Neck Road
Sands Point, NY 11050
516-944-8900
800-225-0411
FAX: 516-944-7302
e-mail: hkncdir@aol.com
www.helenkeller.org

*Joseph McNulty, Executive Director*

Pamphlet offering information on how persons should interact with deaf-blind individuals. Includes drawings of the one hand manual alphabet.

**7325 Healthy Breathing**
National Jewish Center for Immunology
1400 Jackson Street
Denver, CO 80206
303-388-4461
e-mail: allstetterw@njc.org
www.njc.org

*William Allstetter, Media Relations Manager*
*Lynn Taussig, Chief Executive Officer*

Offers patients with lung or respiratory disorders information on exercise and healthy breathing.

**7326 Heart to Heart**
Blind Children's Center
4120 Marathon Street
Los Angeles, CA 90029
323-664-2153
800-222-3567
FAX: 323-665-3828
e-mail: info@blindchildrenscenter.org
www.blindchildrenscenter.org

*Midge Horton, Executive Director*

Parents of blind and partially sighted children talk about their feelings. *$10.00*
        *12 pages*

**7327 Heartbreak of Being A Little Bit Blind**
National Association for Visually Handicapped
22 W 21st Street
Floor 6
New York, NY 10010
212-889-3141
FAX: 212-727-2931
e-mail: staff@navh.org
www.navh.org

*Lorianie Marchi, Chief Executive Officer*

Summary of what it means to have impaired vision; includes illustrations.

**7328 Helping Others Breathe Easier**
National Allergy and Asthma Network
3554 Chain Bridge Road
Suite 200
Fairfax, VA 22030
703-385-4403
FAX: 703-352-4354
Offers information on educational resources, support groups and the Network for persons afflicted with asthma or allergic disorders.

**7329 Helping Your Child with Attention-Deficit Hyperactivity Disorder**
Learning Disabilities Association of America
4156 Library Road
Pittsburgh, PA 15234
412-341-1515
FAX: 412-344-0224
e-mail: info@ldaamerica.org
www.ldaamerica.org

**7330 Hip Function & Ambulation**
Spina Bifida Association of America
4590 Macarthur Boulevard NW
Suite 250
Washington, DC 20007
202-944-3285
800-621-3141
FAX: 202-944-3295
e-mail: sbaa@sbaa.org
www.sbaa.org

*Cindy Brownstein, Chief Executive Officer*

**7331  History and Use of Braille**
American Council of the Blind
1155 15th Street NW
Suite 1004
Washington, DC  20005                    202-467-5081
                                         800-424-8666
                                    FAX: 202-467-5085
                               e-mail: info@acb.org
                                         www.acb.org

*Melanie Brunson, Executive Director*

**7332  Home Control of Allergies and Asthma**
American Lung Association
61 Broadway
New York, NY  10006                      212-315-8700
                                    FAX: 212-315-8700
                             e-mail: info@lungusa.org
                                      www.lungusa.org

*John Kirkwood, Chief Executive Officer*

Discusses substances in the home that may trigger asthma and allergy problems and offers suggestions for controlling them.
*12 pages*

**7333  How Does a Blind Person Get Around?**
American Foundation for the Blind/AFB Press
PO Box 1020
Sewickley, PA  15143                     412-741-1142
                                         800-232-3044
                                    FAX: 412-741-0609
                        e-mail: afborders@abdintl.com
                                         www.afb.org
Offers information on daily living as a blind person.

**7334  How to Choose an Air Ambulance**
National Air Ambulance
PO Box 22460
Fort Lauderdale, FL  33335               954-359-9900
                                         800-327-3710
                                    FAX: 954-359-9500
                    e-mail: inquiry@nationaljets.com
                         www.nationalairambulance.com

*Alan Altman MD, Medical Director*
*Thomas E Boy, President*
*George Martinez, Operations Manager*

This booklet was prepared to help inform persons about air ambulance operations and to assist if the need for air ambulance transportation should arise.
*15 pages*

**7335  How to Find More About Your Child's Birth Defect or Disability**
Birth Defect Research for Children
930 Woodcock Road
Suite 225
Orlando, FL  32803                       407-895-0802
                                    FAX: 407-895-0824
                       e-mail: abdc@birthdefects.org
                                  www.birthdefects.org

*Betty Mekdeci, Executive Director/Manager*

An informational fact sheet that encourages parents who have a child with a birth defect or disability to become the expert on the child's disability with some suggestions on how to educate themselves.

**7336  How to Own and Operate an Attention Deficit Disorder**
Learning Disabilities Association of America
4156 Library Road
Pittsburgh, PA  15234                    412-341-1515
                                    FAX: 412-344-0224
                       e-mail: info@ldaamerica.org
                                   www.ldaamerica.org
Clear, informative and sensitive introduction to ADHD. Packed with practical things to do at home and school, from a professional and mother of a son with ADHD. *$8.95*

*43 pages*

**7337  Hyperactivity, Attention Deficits, and School Failure: Better Ways**
Learning Disabilities Association of America
4156 Library Road
Pittsburgh, PA  15234                    412-341-1515
                                    FAX: 412-344-0224
                       e-mail: info@ldaamerica.org
                                   www.ldaamerica.org

**7338  Individuals with Arthritis**
Mainstream
1030 5th Street NE
Washington, DC  20002                    202-898-1400

                          e-mail: info@mainstreaminc.org
Mainstreaming individuals with arthritis into the workplace.
*$2.50*
*12 pages*

**7339  Indoor Allergens**
Academy of Allergy, Asthma, Immunology
611 E Wells Street
Milwaukee, WI  53202                     414-272-6071
                                         800-822-2762
                                    FAX: 414-272-6070
                              e-mail: info@aaaai.org
                                        www.aaaai.org

*Kay Whalen, Executive Vice President*

This brochure covers some good ideas on how to reduce dust in the home. *$.50*
*4 pages*

**7340  Information on Glaucoma**
Glaucoma Research Foundation
251 Post Street
Suite 600
San Francisco, CA  94108                 415-986-3162
                                         800-826-6693
                                    FAX: 415-986-3763
                           e-mail: info@glaucoma.org
                                     www.glaucoma.org

*Yuko Madono, Outreach/Public Releations*
*Tom Brunner, Chief Executive Officer*

**7341  Inhaled Medications for Asthma**
Academy of Allergy, Asthma, Immunology
611 E Wells Street
Milwaukee, WI  53202                     414-272-6071
                                         800-822-2762
                                    FAX: 414-272-6070
                              e-mail: info@aaaai.org
                                        www.aaaai.org

*Kay Whalen, Executive Vice President*

This brochure gives helpful information on classes of inhaled medication, types of inhalation devices, spacers and holding chambers, how proper training is necessary. *$.50*
*4 pages*

**7342  Issues in Independent Living**
Independent Living Research Utilization
2323 S Shepherd Drive
Suite 1000
Houston, TX  77019                       713-520-0232
                                    FAX: 713-520-5785

*Lex Frieden, Program Director*
*Laurie Redd, Executive Director*

This booklet is a report of the National Study Group on the Implications of Health Care Reform for Americans with Disabilities and Chronic Health Conditions.

*30 pages*

**7343 It's All Right to be Angry**
National Association for Visually Handicapped
22 W 21st Street
Floor 6
New York, NY 10010         212-889-3141
FAX: 212-727-2931
e-mail: staff@navh.org
www.navh.org

*Lorianie Marchi, Chief Executive Officer*

A helpful pamphlet describing reactions to learning to live with vision impairment. Also available in Russian. *$2.25*

**7344 Know Your Eye**
American Council of the Blind
1155 15th Street NW
Suite 1004
Washington, DC 20005      202-467-5081
800-424-8666
FAX: 202-467-5085
e-mail: info@acb.org
www.acb.org

*Melanie Brunson, Executive Director*

**7345 Large Print Loan Library Catalog**
National Association for Visually Handicapped
22 W 21st Street
Floor 6
New York, NY 10010         212-889-3141
FAX: 212-727-2931
e-mail: staff@navh.org
www.navh.org

*Lorianie Marchi, Chief Executive Officer*

Listing of over 7,000 commercially published and NAVH large print books available through NAVH on a loan basis. Includes a limited selection of titles available for purchase. *$5.00*

**7346 Latex Allergy in Spina Bifida Patients**
Spina Bifida Association of America
4590 Macarthur Boulevard NW
Suite 250
Washington, DC 20007      202-944-3285
800-621-3141
FAX: 202-944-3295
e-mail: sbaa@sbaa.org
www.sbaa.org

*Cindy Brownstein, Chief Executive Officer*

**7347 Learning Among Children with Spina Bifida**
Spina Bifida Association of America
4590 Macarthur Boulevard NW
Suite 250
Washington, DC 20007      202-944-3285
800-621-3141
FAX: 202-944-3295
e-mail: sbaa@sbaa.org
www.sbaa.org

*Cindy Brownstein, Chief Executive Officer*

**7348 Learning to Play**
Blind Children's Center
4120 Marathon Street
Los Angeles, CA 90029      323-664-2153
800-222-3567
FAX: 323-665-3828
e-mail: info@blindchildrenscenter.org
www.blindchildrenscenter.org

*Midge Horton, Executive Director*

Discusses how to present play activities to the visually impaired preschool child. *$10.00*

*12 pages*

**7349 Ledger**
Mental Health Risk Retention Group
PO Box 206
Cedar Grove, NJ 07009      973-239-9107

Information on the Mental Health Risk Retention Group, a liability insurance company.

**7350 Lipomas & Lipomyelomeningocele**
Spina Bifida Association of America
4590 Macarthur Boulevard NW
Suite 250
Washington, DC 20007      202-944-3285
800-621-3141
FAX: 202-944-3295
e-mail: sbaa@sbaa.org
www.sbaa.org

*Cindy Brownstein, Chief Executive Officer*

**7351 Living with Asthma and Allergies Brochure Series**
Asthma and Allergy Foundation of America
1125 15th Street NW
Suite 502
Washington, DC 20005      202-466-7643
FAX: 202-466-8940
e-mail: info@aafa.org
www.aafa.org

*Bill Lin, Executive Director*

Informative series was developed to provide up-to-date, accurate information on common topics. Written in easy to understand language, with helpful illustrations, cover some of the most commonly asked questions about asthma and allergies.

**7352 Mama: Your Guide to a Healthy Pregnancy**
March of Dimes
1275 Mamaroneck Avenue
White Plains, NY 10605      914-949-7166
FAX: 914-997-4763
e-mail: askus@marchofdimes.com
www.marchofdimes.com

The March of Dimes Resource Center provides information about pregnancy, birth defects, genetics, drug use, environmental hazards and related topics. The Resource Center's health information specialists provide accurate, up-to-date information via e-mail and Web site.

**7353 Management of Children and Adolescents with AD-HD**
Learning Disabilities Association of America
4156 Library Road
Pittsburgh, PA 15234      412-341-1515
FAX: 412-344-0224
e-mail: info@ldaamerica.org
www.ldaamerica.org

**7354 Managing Your Activities**
Arthritis Foundation
PO Box 7669
Atlanta, GA 30357      404-872-7100
800-283-7800
FAX: 404-872-9559
e-mail: help@arthritis.org
www.arthritis.org

*John Klippel, Chief Executive Officer*

**7355 Managing Your Fatigue**
Arthritis Foundation
PO Box 7669
Atlanta, GA 30357      404-872-7100
800-283-7800
FAX: 404-872-9559
e-mail: help@arthritis.org
www.arthritis.org

*John Klippel, Chief Executive Officer*

**7356 Managing Your Health Care**
Arthritis Foundation
PO Box 7669
Atlanta, GA 30357
404-872-7100
800-283-7800
FAX: 404-872-9559
e-mail: help@arthritis.org
www.arthritis.org

*John Klippel, Chief Executive Officer*

**7357 Managing Your Pain**
Arthritis Foundation
PO Box 7669
Atlanta, GA 30357
404-872-7100
800-283-7800
FAX: 404-872-9559
e-mail: help@arthritis.org
www.arthritis.org

*John Klippel, Chief Executive Officer*

**7358 Many Faces of Asthma**
American Lung Association
61 Broadway
New York, NY 10006
212-315-8700
FAX: 212-315-8700
e-mail: info@lungusa.org
www.lungusa.org

*John Kirkwood, Chief Executive Officer*

Provides an overview of asthma as a major public health problem, describes what happens during asthma attacks and explains how asthma is treated and managed.
*12 pages*

**7359 Marfan Syndrome Fact Sheet**
March of Dimes
1275 Mamaroneck Avenue
White Plains, NY 10605
914-949-7166
FAX: 914-997-4763
e-mail: askus@marchofdimes.com
www.marchofdimes.com

**7360 Mental Health Resource Guide**
1 Renaissance Boulevard
Oakbrook Terrace, IL 60181
630-792-5000

A small pamphlet listing education programs and publications for community mental health centers, child/adolescent services, adult mental health services and MR/DD services.

**7361 Move With Me**
Blind Children's Center
4120 Marathon Street
Los Angeles, CA 90029
323-664-2153
800-222-3567
FAX: 323-665-3828
e-mail: info@blindchildrenscenter.org
www.blindchildrenscenter.org

*Midge Horton, Executive Director*

A parent's guide to movement development for visually impaired babies. *$10.00*
*12 pages*

**7362 Myositis**
Arthritis Foundation
PO Box 7669
Atlanta, GA 30357
404-872-7100
800-283-7800
FAX: 404-872-9559
e-mail: help@arthritis.org
www.arthritis.org

*John Klippel, Chief Executive Officer*

**7363 Myths and Facts**
US Department of Justice
950 Pennsylvania Avenue NW Drs
- Nyav
Washington, DC 20530
202-586-5000
800-574-0301
FAX: 202-307-1197
www.ada.gov

*Joanne Graham, Manager*

A 3-page publication dispelling some common misconceptions about the ADA's requirements and implementation.

**7364 National Institute of Mental Health: Decade of the Brain**
6001 Executive Boulevard
Bethesda, MD 20892
301-443-4513
FAX: 301-443-4279
www.nimh.nih.gov

A consumer's pamphlet to services for persons with mental illness or retardation.

**7365 Newsletter of PA's AT Lending Library**
Temple University Institute on Disabilities
1301 Cecil B Moore Avenue
Philadelphia, PA 19122
215-204-7331
800-204-7428
FAX: 215-204-9371
TTY: 800-750-7428
e-mail: piat@temple.edu
disabilities.temple.edu

*Amy Goldman, Project Director*
*Sandra McNally, Editor*

Newsletter from the Assistive Technology Lending Library in Pennsylvania. It is published quarterly and is free of charge.
*4-8 pages Quarterly*

**7366 Nocturnal Asthma**
National Jewish Center for Immunology
1400 Jackson Street
Denver, CO 80206
303-388-4461
e-mail: allstetterw@njc.org
www.njc.org

*William Allstetter, Media Relations Manager*
*Lynn Taussig, Chief Executive Officer*

Offers information to patients about how to understand and manage asthma at night.

**7367 Obesity**
Spina Bifida Association of America
4590 Macarthur Boulevard NW
Suite 250
Washington, DC 20007
202-944-3285
800-621-3141
FAX: 202-944-3295
e-mail: sbaa@sbaa.org
www.sbaa.org

*Cindy Brownstein, Chief Executive Officer*
*$8.00*

**7368 Occulta**
Spina Bifida Association of America
4590 Macarthur Boulevard NW
Suite 250
Washington, DC 20007
202-944-3285
800-621-3141
FAX: 202-944-3295
e-mail: sbaa@sbaa.org
www.sbaa.org

*Cindy Brownstein, Chief Executive Officer*
*$8.00*

**7369 Occupational Asthma**
Academy of Allergy, Asthma, Immunology
611 E Wells Street
Milwaukee, WI 53202　　　　　414-272-6071
800-822-2762
FAX: 414-272-6070
e-mail: info@aaaai.org
www.aaaai.org

*Kay Whalen, Executive Vice President*

This brochure also contains a list of most common agents that
cause occupational asthma and who is at risk. *$.50*
*4 pages*

**7370 Occupational Asthma: Lung Hazards on the Job**
American Lung Association
61 Broadway
New York, NY 10006　　　　　212-315-8700
FAX: 212-315-8700
e-mail: info@lungusa.org
www.lungusa.org

*John Kirkwood, Chief Executive Officer*

Discusses occupational asthma, a form of asthma in which air-
ways overreact to various irritants in the workplace.

**7371 Oral/Facial Clefts Fact Sheet**
March of Dimes
1275 Mamaroneck Avenue
White Plains, NY 10605　　　　　914-949-7166
FAX: 914-997-4763
e-mail: askus@marchofdimes.com
www.marchofdimes.com
The March of Dimes Resource Center provides information
about pregnancy, drug use, environmental hazards and other related topics. The Resource Center's health information specialists provide accurate and up-to-date information via e-mail and
Web site.

**7372 Osteoarthritis**
Arthritis Foundation
PO Box 7669
Atlanta, GA 30357　　　　　404-872-7100
800-283-7800
FAX: 404-872-9559
e-mail: help@arthritis.org
www.arthritis.org

*John Klippel, Chief Executive Officer*

Offers introductions, examples, explanations and research pertaining to this type of arthritis.

**7373 Out of Darkness**
CACLD
25 Van Zant Street
Suite 15-5
Norwalk, CT 06855　　　　　203-838-5010
FAX: 203-866-6108
e-mail: CACLD@optonline.net
www.CACLD.org

*Beryl Kaufman, Executive Director*

Article by an adult who discovers at age 30 that he has ADD.
*$1.00*
*4 pages*

**7374 Overcoming Rheumatoid Arthritis**
Arthritis Foundation - Michigan Chapter
17117 W 9 Mile Road
Suite 960
Southfield, MI 48075　　　　　248-424-9001
800-968-3030
www.arthritis.org

*Anthony Zambraus, Owner*

Provides extensive information about the disease and treatment,
with an emphasis on what you can do for yourself. *$5.00*

**7375 Parenting Attention Deficit Disordered Teens**
CACLD
25 Van Zant Street
Suite 15-5
Norwalk, CT 06855　　　　　203-838-5010
FAX: 203-866-6108
e-mail: CACLD@optonline.net
www.CACLD.org

*Beryl Kaufman, Executive Director*

Detailed outline of the various problems of adolescents with
ADHD. Published by Connecticut Association for Children &
Adults with Learning Disabilities (CACLD). *$3.25*
*14 pages*

**7376 Patient's Guide to Visual Aids and Illumination**
National Association for Visually Handicapped
22 W 21st Street
New York, NY 10010　　　　　212-889-3141
FAX: 212-727-2931
e-mail: staff@navh.org
www.navh.org

*Lorianie Marchi, Chief Executive Officer*

A reference booklet offering information on aids for the visually
impaired.

**7377 Peak Flow Meter: A Thermometer for Asthma**
Academy of Allergy, Asthma, Immunology
611 E Wells Street
Milwaukee, WI 53202　　　　　414-272-6071
800-822-2762
FAX: 414-272-6070
e-mail: info@aaaai.org
www.aaaai.org

*Kay Whalen, Executive Vice President*
*$.50*
*4 pages*

**7378 People Against Cancer**
PO Box 10
Otho, IA 50569　　　　　515-972-4444
FAX: 515-972-4415
e-mail: info@PeopleAgainstCancer.net
www.peopleagainstcancer.com

*Frank Wiewel, Executive Director*

Publication of People Against Cancer, a nonprofit, grassroots,
public benefit organization dedicated to 'New Directions in the
War on Cancer.' We are a democratic organization of people
with cancer, their loved ones and citizens working together to
protect and enhance medical freedom of choice.
*8 pages*

**7379 Pocket Guide to the ADA: Accessibility Gu idelines for
Buildings and Facilities**
Wiley Publishing
605 3rd Avenue
New York, NY 10158　　　　　212-850-6000
FAX: 212-850-6088
Easy-access to the American's with Disabilities Act, which ex-
plains the network of federal civil rights laws with which busi-
nesses must comply. It includes the scope and technical
requirements for accessibility elements and spaces. *$24.95*
*144 pages 1997*
*ISBN 0-471181-37-4*

**7380 Pollen Calendar**
Asthma and Allergy Foundation of America
1125 15th Street NW
Suite 502
Washington, DC 20005　　　　　202-466-7643
FAX: 202-466-8940
e-mail: info@aafa.org
www.aafa.org

*Bill Lin, Executive Director*

Color poster of the US shows types of pollens and when they appear in each region. *$3.00*

**7381 Polymyalgia Rheumatica and Giant Cell Arthritis**
Arthritis Foundation
PO Box 7669
Atlanta, GA 30357
404-872-7100
800-283-7800
FAX: 404-872-9559
e-mail: help@arthritis.org
www.arthritis.org

*John Klippel, Chief Executive Officer*

**7382 Psoriatic Arthritis**
National Institute of Arthritis
1 Ams Circle
Bethesda, MD 20892
301-495-4484
877-226-4267
FAX: 301-881-2731
e-mail: niamsinfo@mail.nih.gov
www.nih.gov/niams/

*Kelly Collins, Manager*

**7383 Raynaud's Phenomenon**
Arthritis Foundation
PO Box 7669
Atlanta, GA 30357
404-872-7100
800-283-7800
FAX: 404-872-9559
e-mail: help@arthritis.org
www.arthritis.org

*John Klippel, Chief Executive Officer*

**7384 Reaching, Crawling, Walking....Let's Get Moving**
Blind Children's Center
4120 Marathon Street
Los Angeles, CA 90029
323-664-2153
800-222-3567
FAX: 323-665-3828
e-mail: info@blindchildrenscenter.org
www.blindchildrenscenter.org

*Midge Horton, Executive Director*

Orientation and mobility for preschool children who are visually imapired. *$10.00*
*24 pages*

**7385 Reading Is for Everyone**
National Library Service for the Blind
1291 Taylor Street NW
Washington, DC 20542
202-707-5100
FAX: 202-707-0712
e-mail: nls@loc.gov
www.loc.gov/nls

*Frank Cylke, Executive Director*

**7386 Reading with Low Vision**
National Library Service for the Blind
1291 Taylor Street NW
Washington, DC 20542
202-707-5100
FAX: 202-707-0712
e-mail: nls@loc.gov
www.loc.gov/nls

*Frank Cylke, Executive Director*

**7387 Reference and Information Services From NLS**
National Library Service for the Blind
1291 Taylor Street NW
Washington, DC 20542
202-707-5100
FAX: 202-707-0712
TTY:202-707-0744
e-mail: nls@loc.gov
www.loc.gov/nls

*Frank Cylke, Executive Director*

**7388 Referring Blind and Low Vision Patients for Rehabilitation Services**
American Foundation for the Blind/AFB Press
PO Box 1020
Sewickley, PA 15143
412-741-1142
800-232-3044
FAX: 412-741-0609
e-mail: afborders@abdintl.com
www.afb.org

Clear information on such basic topics as the objectives of low vision services, what's covered in the examinations, what rehabilitation services do and how to locate these services. Available in purchase of bulk quantity only.

*ISBN 0-891289-13-5*

**7389 Reiter's Syndrome**
Arthritis Foundation
PO Box 7669
Atlanta, GA 30357
404-872-7100
800-283-7800
FAX: 404-872-9559
e-mail: help@arthritis.org
www.arthritis.org

*John Klippel, Chief Executive Officer*

**7390 Resource List for Persons with Low Vision**
American Council of the Blind
1155 15th Street NW
Suite 1004
Washington, DC 20005
202-467-5081
800-424-8666
FAX: 202-467-5085
e-mail: info@acb.org
www.acb.org

*Melanie Brunson, Executive Director*

**7391 Rheumatoid Arthritis**
National Institute of Arthritis
1 Ams Circle
Bethesda, MD 20892
301-495-4484
877-226-4267
FAX: 301-881-2731
e-mail: niamsinfo@mail.nih.gov
www.nih.gov/niams/

*Kelly Collins, Manager*

Offers an introduction and definition of Rheumatoid Arthritis, treatments, causes, objectives, daily living, resources and medical information.

**7392 Selecting a Program**
Blind Children's Center
4120 Marathon Street
Los Angeles, CA 90029
323-664-2153
800-222-3567
FAX: 323-665-3828
e-mail: info@blindchildrenscenter.org
www.blindchildrenscenter.org

*Midge Horton, Executive Director*

A guide for parents of infants and preschoolers with visual impairments. *$10.00*
*28 pages*

**7393 Sex Education: Issues for the Person with Autism**
Autism Society of North Carolina Bookstore
505 Oberlin Road
Suite 230
Raleigh, NC 27605
919-743-0204
800-442-2762
FAX: 919-743-0208
e-mail: dcoffey@autismsociety-nc.org
www.autismsociety-nc.org

*Darla Coffey, Bookstore Manager*
*Jill Keel, Executive Director*

Discusses issues of sexuality and provides methods of instruction for people with autism. *$4.00*

**7394 Spina Bifida**
Spina Bifida Association of America
4590 Macarthur Boulevard NW
Suite 250
Washington, DC 20007
202-944-3285
800-621-3141
FAX: 202-944-3295
e-mail: sbaa@sbaa.org
www.sbaa.org

*Cindy Brownstein, Chief Executive Officer*

**7395 Standards for the Diagnosis and Care of Patients with Asthma**
American Lung Association
61 Broadway
New York, NY 10006
212-315-8700
FAX: 212-315-8700
e-mail: info@lungusa.org
www.lungusa.org

*John Kirkwood, Chief Executive Officer*
Standards developed by the American Thoracic Society, the medical section of the ALA. For physicians.
*24 pages*

**7396 Standing On My Own Two Feet**
Blind Children's Center
4120 Marathon Street
Los Angeles, CA 90029
323-664-2153
800-222-3567
FAX: 323-665-3828
e-mail: info@blindchildrenscenter.org
www.blindchildrenscenter.org

*Midge Horton, Executive Director*
A step-by-step guide to designing and constructing simple, individually tailored, adaptive mobility devices for preschool-age children who are visually impaired. *$10.00*
*36 pages*

**7397 Surgery: Information to Consider**
Arthritis Foundation
PO Box 7669
Atlanta, GA 30357
404-872-7100
800-283-7800
FAX: 404-872-9559
e-mail: help@arthritis.org
www.arthritis.org

*John Klippel, Chief Executive Officer*

**7398 Symptomatic Chiari Malformation**
Spina Bifida Association of America
4590 Macarthur Boulevard NW
Suite 250
Washington, DC 20007
202-944-3285
800-621-3141
FAX: 202-944-3295
e-mail: sbaa@sbaa.org
www.sbaa.org

*Cindy Brownstein, Chief Executive Officer*

**7399 Talk to Me**
Blind Children's Center
4120 Marathon Street
Los Angeles, CA 90029
323-664-2153
800-222-3567
FAX: 323-665-3828
e-mail: info@blindchildrenscenter.org
www.blindchildrenscenter.org

*Midge Horton, Executive Director*
A language guide for parents of deaf children. *$10.00*

*11 pages*

**7400 Talk to Me II**
Blind Children's Center
4120 Marathon Street
Los Angeles, CA 90029
323-664-2153
800-222-3567
FAX: 323-665-3828
e-mail: info@blindchildrenscenter.org
www.blindchildrenscenter.org

*Midge Horton, Executive Director*
A sequel to Talk To Me, available in English and Spanish. *$10.00*
*15 pages*

**7401 Teaching Social Skills to Youngsters with Disabilities**
Federation for Children with Special Needs
56 Temple Place
Suite 644
Boston, MA 02111
617-542-7860
800-537-0446
FAX: 617-542-7832
e-mail: pal@fcsn.org
www.ppal.net

*Donna Welles, Director*
*Lisa Lambert, Assistant Director*
Explains the importance of instruction and training to learn appropriate social behavior.

**7402 Teens Talk to Teens about Asthma**
Asthma and Allergy Foundation of America
1125 15th Street NW
Suite 502
Washington, DC 20005
202-466-7643
FAX: 202-466-8940
e-mail: info@aafa.org
www.aafa.org

*Bill Lin, Executive Director*
Brochure provides support to a teen you care about. Includes quotes and thoughts from teens that capture the essence of what it feels like to live with asthma.

**7403 Tethering Cord**
Spina Bifida Association of America
4590 Macarthur Boulevard NW
Suite 250
Washington, DC 20007
202-944-3285
800-621-3141
FAX: 202-944-3295
e-mail: sba@sbaa.org
www.sbaa.org

*Cindy Brownstein, Chief Executive Officer*

**7404 There are Solutions for the Student with Asthma**
American Lung Association
61 Broadway
New York, NY 10006
212-315-8700
FAX: 212-315-8700
e-mail: info@lungusa.org
www.lungusa.org

*John Kirkwood, Chief Executive Officer*
Leaflet telling how parents and school personnel can work together to make life easier for children with asthma.
*4 pages*

**7405 Thinking About Tomorrow: A Career Guide for Teens with Arthritis**
Arthritis Foundation
PO Box 7669
Atlanta, GA 30357
404-872-7100
800-283-7800
FAX: 404-872-9559
e-mail: help@arthritis.org
www.arthritis.org

*John Klippel, Chief Executive Officer*

**7406 Tips to Remember**
Academy of Allergy, Asthma, Immunology
611 E Wells Street
Milwaukee, WI 53202                    414-272-6071

e-mail: info@aaaai.org
www.aaaai.org

*Kay Whalen, Executive Vice President*

A set of 23 tip sheets offering information on various topics including allergy and asthma treatments, pregnancy and asthma, animal allergies, sinusitis and more.

**7407 Transition in Adolescence**
Spina Bifida Association of America
4590 Macarthur Boulevard NW
Suite 250
Washington, DC 20007                    202-944-3285
800-621-3141
FAX: 202-944-3295
e-mail: sbaa@sbaa.org
www.sbaa.org

*Cindy Brownstein, Chief Executive Officer*

**7408 Triggers Management of Asthma**
Academy of Allergy, Asthma, Immunology
611 E Wells Street
Milwaukee, WI 53202                    414-272-6071
800-822-2762
FAX: 414-272-6070
e-mail: info@aaaai.org
www.aaaai.org

*Kay Whalen, Executive Vice President*

This brochure gives helpful information on what will cause an asthma attack. *$.50*

**7409 Understanding**
Easter Seals
230 W Monroe Street
Suite 1800
Chicago, IL 60606                    312-726-6800
FAX: 312-726-1494

*Janet D Jamieson, Communications Manager*
*James Williams Jr, Chief Executive Officer*

A brochure series for use in patient, family and public education programs and in career recruitment and counseling.
*10 Brochures*

**7410 Understanding Asthma**
National Jewish Center for Immunology
1400 Astackson Street
Denver, CO 80206                    303-388-4461

e-mail: allstetterw@njc.org
www.njc.org

*William Allstetter, Media Relations Manager*
*Lynn Taussig, Chief Executive Officer*

Offers a brief introduction to asthma and then goes into the physiology of asthma, the triggers of asthma, and diagnosis and monitoring of asthma.
*27 pages*

**7411 Understanding Learning Disabilities: A Guide for Faculty**
CACLD
25 Van Zant Street
Suite 15-5
Norwalk, CT 06855                    203-838-5010
FAX: 203-866-6108
e-mail: CACLD@optonline.net
www.CACLD.org

*Beryl Kaufman, Executive Director*

Written for the faculty at Georgetown to help them identify, understand, teach and advise students in their classes who have learning disabilities. Ideal for any college offering special services to the learning disabled as well as high school guidance counselors and propective college students with LD and their parents. Published by Connecticut Association for Children & Adults with Learning Disabilities (CACLD). *$10.00*
*36 pages*

**7412 Urologic Care of the Child with Spina Bifida**
Spina Bifida Association of America
4590 Macarthur Boulevard NW
Suite 250
Washington, DC 20007                    202-944-3285
800-621-3141
FAX: 202-944-3295
e-mail: sbaa@sbaa.org
www.sbaa.org

*Cindy Brownstein, Chief Executive Officer*

**7413 What Do You Do When You See a Blind Person - and What Don't You Do?**
American Foundation for the Blind/AFB Press
PO Box 1020
Sewickley, PA 15143                    412-741-1142
800-232-3044
FAX: 412-741-0609
e-mail: afborders@abdintl.com
www.afb.org

Examples of real-life situations that teach sighted persons how to interact effectively with blind persons. Topics covered include how to help someone across the street, how not to distract a guide dog and how to take leave of a blind person.
*8 pages*
*ISBN 0-891281-95-9*

**7414 What Every Parent Should Know About Learning Diabilities**
CACLD
25 Van Zant Street
Suite 15-5
Norwalk, CT 06855                    203-838-5010
FAX: 203-866-6108
e-mail: CACLD@optonline.net
www.CACLD.org

*Beryl Kaufman, Executive Director*

Published by Connecticut Association for Children & Adults with Learning Disabilities (CACLD). *$2.00*

**7415 What Everyone Needs to Know About Asthma**
National Allergy and Asthma Network
3554 Chain Bridge Road
Suite 200
Fairfax, VA 22030                    703-385-4403
FAX: 703-352-4354

Offers information and facts on gaining control of asthma, asthma triggers and monitoring asthma disorders.

**7416 What is Auditory Processing?**
Speech Bin
1965 25th Avenue
Vero Beach, FL 32960                    772-770-0007
800-477-3324
FAX: 772-770-0006
www.speechbin.com

*Jan J Binney, Senior Editor*

Booklet for parents and teachers explaining children's difficulties in listening and auditory skills. Set of ten copies. *$14.95*

*16 pages*
*ISBN 0-93785 -45-9*

**7417 What to Do When a Friend is Depressed: Guide for Students**
National Institute of Mental Health
5600 Fishers Lane
Rockville, MD 20857               301-443-9094

*Barbara Vermillion, Manager*

This pamphlet provides students with valuable information about depression: how to overcome it and how to help others.

**7418 When Your Student Has Arthritis: A Guide for Teachers**
Arthritis Foundation
PO Box 7669
Atlanta, GA 30357               404-872-7100
                                 800-283-7800
                          FAX: 404-872-9559
                   e-mail: help@arthritis.org
                          www.arthritis.org

*John Klippel, Chief Executive Officer*

A medical information booklet written for teachers or other adults who have arthritis. The booklet describes different forms of juvenile arthritis, how arthritis might affect the child at school, and how to help the child work around these problems.

**7419 Without Sight and Sound**
Helen Keller National Center
111 Middle Neck Road
Sands Point, NY 11050               516-944-8900

                   e-mail: hkncdir@aol.com
                          www.helenkeller.org

*Joseph McNulty, Executive Director*

Pamphlet offering facts, causes, types and descriptions of deaf-blindness.

**7420 Your Child and Asthma**
National Jewish Center for Immunology
1400 Jackson Street
Denver, CO 80206               303-388-4461

                   e-mail: allstetterw@njc.org
                          www.njc.org

*William Allstetter, Media Relations Manager*
*Lynn Taussig, Chief Executive Officer*

A booklet offering information to parents and family about their child with asthma. Offers information on diagnosis, treatments, triggers and family concerns.

## Audio/Visual

**7421 A Place for Me**
Educational Productions
9000 SW Gemini Drive
Beaverton, OR 97008
503-644-7000
800-950-4949
FAX: 503-350-7000
e-mail: custserve@edpro.com
www.edpro.com

*Linda Freedman, President/Owner*
*Molly Krumm, Marketing Director*

In this video, parents discuss the issues they face in planning for their child's future. This program is designed to stimulate discussion of these issues and help increase awareness of the options available in your local community.

**7422 A Wheelchair for Petronilia**
Fanlight Productions
4196 Washington Street
Suite 2
Boston, MA 02131
617-469-4999
800-937-4113
FAX: 617-469-3379
e-mail: info@fanlight.com
www.fanlight.com

*Sandy St Louis, Distribution Director*
*Nicole Johnson, Publicity Coordinator*
*Ben Achtenberg, Owner*

Profiles a program, organized and run by Guatemalans with disabilities, which trains them to manufacture and repair cheap, sturdy wheelchairs designed for conditions in developing countries. 28 Minutes. *$199.00*

*ISBN 1-572953-98-5*

**7423 ADD, Stepping Out of the Dark**
ADD Videos
PO Box 622
New Paltz, NY 12561
845-255-3612
FAX: 845-883-6452

*Lenae Madonna, Producer*

A powerful, effective video, ideal for health professionals, educators and parents providing a visual montage designed to promote an understanding and awareness of attention deficit disorder. Based on actual accounts of those who have ADD, including a neurologist, an office worker, and parents of children with ADD. The video allows the viewer to feel the frustration and lack of attention that ADD brings to many. *$52.95*
*Video*

**7424 ADHD in Adults**
Guilford Press
72 Spring Street
New York, NY 10012
212-431-9800
800-365-7006
FAX: 212-966-6708
e-mail: info@guilford.com
www.guilford.com

*Bob Matloff, President*

This program integrates information on ADHD with the actual experiences of four adults who suffer from the disorder. Representing a range of professions, from a lawyer to a mother working at home, each candidly discusses the impact of ADHD on his or her daily life. These interviews are augmented by comments from family members and other clinicians who treat adults with ADHD. *$95.00*

*Video*
*ISBN 0-898629-86-1*

**7425 ADHD: What Can We Do?**
Guilford Press
72 Spring Street
New York, NY 10012
212-431-9800
800-365-7006
FAX: 212-966-6708
e-mail: info@guilford.com

*Bob Matloff, President*

A video program that introduces teachers and parents to a variety of the most effective technologies for managing ADHD in the classroom, at home, and on family outings. *$95.00*
*Video*
*ISBN 0-898629-72-1*

**7426 ADHD: What Do We Know?**
Guilford Press
72 Spring Street
New York, NY 10012
212-431-9800
800-365-7006
FAX: 212-966-6708
e-mail: info@guilford.com

*Bob Matloff, President*

An introduction for teachers and special education practitioners, school psychologists and parents of ADHD children. Topics outlined in this video include the causes and prevalence of ADHD, ways children with ADHD behave, other conditions that may accompany ADHD and long-term prospects for children with ADHD. *$95.00*
*Video*
*ISBN 0-898629-71-3*

**7427 Able to Laugh**
Fanlight Productions
4196 Washington Street
Suite 2
Boston, MA 02131
617-469-4999
800-937-4113
FAX: 617-469-3379
e-mail: fanlight@fanlight.com
www.fanlight.com

*Sandy St Louis, Marketing Director*
*Kelli English, Publicity Coordinator*
*Ben Achtenberg, Owner*

An exploration of the world of disability as interpreted by six professional comedians who happen to be disabled. It is also about the awkward ways disabled and able-bodied people relate to one another. *$195.00*

*ISBN 1-572951-05-2*

**7428 Access for All: Integrating Deaf, Hard of Hearing and Hearing Preschoolers**
Gallaudet University Bookstore
800 Florida Avenue NE
Washington, DC 20002
202-651-5000
800-451-1073
FAX: 202-651-5489

*Erving Jordan, President*

This exciting new 90 minute videotape and manual describes a model program for integrating deaf and hard of hearing children in early education. *$24.95*
*150 pages*

**7429 Activity-Based Intervention: 2nd Edition**
Brookes Publishing
PO Box 10624
Baltimore, MD 21285
410-337-9580
800-638-3775
FAX: 410-337-8539
e-mail: custserv@brookespublishing.com
www.brookespublishing.com

*Paul Brooks, Owner*

This 14 minute video illustrates how activity-based intervention can be used to turn everyday events and natural interactions into opportunities to promote learning in young children who are considered at risk for developmental delays or who have mild to significant disabilities. *$39.00*

*ISBN 1-55766 -86-3*

**7430  Adaptive Baby Care Equipment Video and Book**
Through the Looking Glass
2198 6th Street
Suite 100
Berkeley, CA  94710                     510-848-1112
                                        800-644-2666
                                   FAX: 510-848-4445
                            e-mail: TLG@lookingglass.org
                                   www.lookingglass.org

*Megan Kirshbaum, Executive Director*

Includes Adaptive Baby care Equipment: Guide Lines; Prototypes and Resources, plus a twelve minute video. Available in braille, large print or cassette. *$79.00*

**7431  All About Attention Deficit Disorders, Revised**
Parent Magic
800 Roosevelt Road
Glen Ellyn, IL  60137                   630-790-9600
                                   FAX: 630-469-4571
                                   www.parentmagic.com

*Nancy Roe, Office Manager*
*Thomas Phelan, Owner*

A psychologist and expert on ADD outlines the symptoms, diagnosis and treatment of this neurological disorder. Video ($49.95 - 2 parts) and audio cassette ($24.95).

**7432  All of Us: Talking Together, Sex Education for People with Developmental Disabilities**
Aquarius Health Care Videos
PO Box 1159
Sherborn, MA  01770                     508-650-6905
                                        888-440-2963
                                   FAX: 508-650-4216
                            e-mail: aqvideos@tiac.net
                              www.aquariusproductions.com

*Leslie Kussmann, President/Producer*

For parents, caregivers and young people with developmental disabilities often feel isolated and unsure when approaching sex education with their children. In this video, parents of children with developmental disabilities share their difficulties in talking to their children about the social/sexual arena. Real life conversations between parents and their children demonstrate their discomfort, concerns, thoughts and hopes. *$195.00*
*Video*

**7433  All the Way Up There**
Britannica Film Company
345 4th Street
San Francisco, CA  94107                415-777-9876

This is the story of Bruce Burgess who has Cerebral Palsy but wants to climb a mountain. Bruce makes his dreams come true with the help of Grame Dingle, a New Zealand mountain climber.
*Film*

**7434  Allergic Rhinitis**
Academy of Allergy, Asthma, Immunology
611 E Wells Street
Milwaukee, WI  53202                    414-272-6071
                                        800-822-2762
                                   FAX: 414-272-6070
                              e-mail: info@aaaai.org
                                   www.aaaai.org

*Kay Whalen, Executive Vice President*

Allergic rhinitis, often called hay fever, affects the quality of life of millions of Americans. This video covers the causes and symptoms of seasonal and chronic allergic rhinitis, as well as controls and treatments. *$25.00*
*10-13 Minutes*

**7435  Anaphylaxis**
Academy of Allergy, Asthma, Immunology
611 E Wells Street
Milwaukee, WI  53202                    414-272-6071
                                        800-822-2762
                                   FAX: 414-272-6070
                              e-mail: info@aaaai.org
                                   www.aaaai.org

*Kay Whalen, Executive Vice President*

For a few people, allergic reactions can be extremely serious-even life-threatening. This video provides vital information on the symptoms, causes and treatment of those anaphylactic reactions, and how your allergist can help you take precautions to ensure your safety. *$25.00*
*10-13 Minutes*

**7436  Around the Clock: Parenting the Delayed AD HD Child**

Guilford Press
72 Spring Street
New York, NY  10012                     212-431-9800
                                        800-365-7006
                                   FAX: 212-966-6708
                              e-mail: info@guilford.com

*Bob Matloff, President*

This videotape provides both professionals and parents a helpful look at how the difficulties facing parents of ADHD children can be handled. Video. *$150.00*

*ISBN 0-898629-68-3*

**7437  As I Am**
Fanlight Productions
4196 Washington Street
Suite 2
Boston, MA  02131                       617-469-4999
                                        800-937-4113
                                   FAX: 617-469-3379
                         e-mail: fanlight@fanlight.com
                                   www.fanlight.com

*Sandy St Louis, Marketing Director*
*Ben Achtenberg, Owner*

Three young people with developmental disabilities speak for themselves about their lives, the problems they face and their hopes and expectations for the future. *$99.00*

*ISBN 1-572950-58-7*

**7438  Asthma Handbook Slides**
American Lung Association
61 Broadway
New York, NY  10006                     212-315-8700
                                   FAX: 212-315-8700
                              e-mail: info@lungusa.org
                                   www.lungusa.org

*John Kirkwood, Chief Executive Officer*

Slides and script based on The Asthma Handbook for asthma patients and others.
*Film*

**7439  Asthma Management**
Academy of Allergy, Asthma, Immunology
611 E Wells Street
Milwaukee, WI  53202                    414-272-6071
                                        800-822-2762
                                   FAX: 414-272-6070
                              e-mail: info@aaaai.org
                                   www.aaaai.org

*Kay Whalen, Executive Vice President*

Although there is currently no cure for asthma, attacks can be controlled by appropriate asthma management. This video describes what happens during an asthma attack, how your allergists diagnoses asthma, and ways your allergist can help you to manage your condition. *$25.00*
*10-13 Minutes*

**7440  Asthma Triggers**
Academy of Allergy, Asthma, Immunology
611 E Wells Street
Milwaukee, WI  53202                     414-272-6071
                                         800-822-2762
                                    FAX: 414-272-6070
                                 e-mail: info@aaaai.org
                                         www.aaaai.org

*Kay Whalen, Executive Vice President*

In the U.S. alone, over 50 million people suffer from asthma, and the incidence is rising. This video relates how patients with asthma can reduce their risk of an attack by avoiding triggers and practicing appropriate asthma management. *$25.00*
*10-13 Minutes*

**7441  Asthma and the Athlete**
Academy of Allergy, Asthma, Immunology
611 E Wells Street
Milwaukee, WI  53202                     414-272-6071
                                         800-822-2762
                                    FAX: 414-272-6070
                                 e-mail: info@aaaai.org
                                         www.aaaai.org

*Kay Whalen, Executive Vice President*

In the past, people with asthma were sometimes discouraged from exercising. Today we know that everyone, including asthmatics, can benefit from physical activity. This video details which exercises are best for those with asthma, and how an allergist can help asthmatic athletes to properly manage and treat their disease. *$25.00*
*10-13 Minutes*

**7442  Attention Deficit Disorder**
Pro-Ed
8700 Shoal Creek Boulevard
Austin, TX  78757                        512-451-3246
                                         800-897-3202
                                    FAX: 512-451-8542
                              e-mail: info@proedinc.com
                                         www.proedinc.com

*Donald Hammill, Owner*

A book providing helpful suggestions for both home and classroom management of students with attention deficit disorder.

**7443  Attention Deficit Disorder: Adults**
Aquarius Health Care Videos
PO Box 1159
Sherborn, MA  01770                      508-650-6905
                                    FAX: 508-650-4216
                            e-mail: aqvideos@tiac.net
                              www.aquariusproductions.com
Adults with ADD talk about how the disorder that went undiagnosed for so many years has affected their choice of spouses and work, and what they have found to help them. Biofeedback, which is growing as a treatment, is explained and demonstrated by its founder, Dr. Joel Lubar. Medical treatments like antidepressants and stimulants are also discussed, along with behavioral changes that can help the person with ADD and his or her spouse and family. *$149.00*
*Video*

**7444  Autism**
Aquarius Health Care Videos
PO Box 1159
Sherborn, MA  01770                      508-650-6905
                                    FAX: 508-650-4216
                            e-mail: aqvideos@tiac.net
                              www.aquariusproductions.com

This video takes you into the lives of autistic people and their families to understand more about autism. What defines autism and how can we help those living with the disability? Children, teens, and adults are also profiled and we begin to see the varying levels of development and new technology to help these people communicate. Preview Available. *$149.00*
*Video*

**7445  Autism: A World Apart**
Fanlight Productions
4196 Washington Street
Suite 2
Boston, MA  02131                        617-469-4999
                                         800-937-4113
                                    FAX: 617-469-3379
                            e-mail: fanlight@fanlight.com
                                         www.fanlight.com

*Karen McMillen, Marketing Director*
*Ben Achtenberg, Owner*

Autism's cause is unknown. There is no cure, and it strikes each victim differently. In this documentary, three families show us what the textbooks and studies cannot - what it is like to live with autism day after day - to love and raise children who may be withdrawn and violent, and unable to make personal connections with their families. *$195.00*

**7446  Awareness Training**
Landmark Media
3450 Slade Run Drive
Falls Church, VA  22042                  703-241-2030
                                         800-342-4336
                                    FAX: 703-536-9540
                         e-mail: landmarkmed@aol.com
                                      www.landmarkmedia.com

*Michael Hartogs, President*

Covers disabilities of various types — vision, hearing, speech disorders, loss of limbs, loss of mobility, or mental/emotional limitations and how to integrate such individuals into various business and educational settings. It is a 4-part series designed to identify and enable others to interact effectively with those suffering such disabilities. *$495.00*
*Set of 4*

**7447  Basic Course in American Sign Language**
Harris Communications
15155 Technology Drive
Eden Prairie, MN  55344                  952-906-1180
                                         800-825-6758
                                    FAX: 952-906-1099
                         e-mail: mail@harriscomm.com
                                      www.harriscomm.com

*Bill Williams, National Sales Manager*
*Robert Harris, Owner*

This series of four one-hour tapes is designed to illustrate the various exercises and dialogues in the text. *$39.95*
*Video*

**7448  Beginning ASL Video Course**
Harris Communications
15155 Technology Drive
Eden Prairie, MN  55344                  952-906-1180
                                         800-825-6758
                                    FAX: 952-906-1099
                         e-mail: mail@harriscomm.com
                                      www.harriscomm.com

*Bill Williams, National Sales Manager*
*Robert Harris, Owner*

You'll watch a family teach you to learn American Sign Language during funny and touching family situations. A total of 15 tapes in the course. *$49.95*

*Video*

**7449 Beginning Reading and Sign Language**
Harris Communications
15155 Technology Drive
Eden Prairie, MN 55344
    952-906-1180
    800-825-6758
    FAX: 952-906-1099
    e-mail: mail@harriscomm.com
    www.harriscomm.com

*Bill Williams, National Sales Manager*
*Robert Harris, Owner*

Features a deaf performer signing more than 120 words while standing in front of the object she is signing. Appropriate for children eighteen months to eight years. *$21.95*
*Video*

**7450 Beyond the Barriers**
Aquarius Health Care Videos
PO Box 1159
Sherborn, MA 01770
    508-650-6905
    888-440-2963
    FAX: 508-650-4216
    e-mail: aqvideos@tiac.net
    www.aquariusproductions.com

*Leslie Kussmann, Presdient*

For too many years, paraplegics, amputees, quadraplegics and the blind have felt trapped by their disabilities. No more! Mark Wellman and other disabled adventurers, rock climb the deser towers of Utah, sail in British Columbia, body-board the big waves of Pipeline and Waimea Bay, scuba dive with sea lions in Mexico and hand glide the California coast. This film delivers the simple message: Don't give up, and never give in. If you can't ever lose, then you can't ever win. Preview option. *$90.00*
*Video*

**7451 Biology Concepts Through Discovery**
Educational Activities Software
PO Box 754
Baldwin, NY 11510
    516-867-7878
    800-645-2796
    FAX: 516-379-7429
    e-mail: achieve@ea-software.com

*Alan Stern, Manager*

These videos, available in English and Spanish versions, encourage learning by presenting interactive problem solving in an effective VISUAL/AUDITORY style. *$89.00*
*Video*

**7452 Blindness**
Landmark Media
3450 Slade Run Drive
Falls Church, VA 22042
    703-241-2030
    800-342-4336
    FAX: 703-536-9540

*Michael Hartogs, President*

Cataracts are the most common cause of blindness in the 42 million people worldwide defined as blind. 90% live in developing countries. Cataracts are the most common cause but now can be treated cheaply and safely. *$250.00*
*Video*

**7453 Braille Documents**
Metrolina Association for the Blind
704 Louise Avenue
Charlotte, NC 28204
    704-372-3870
    800-926-5460
    FAX: 704-372-3872

*Robert Scheffel, Manager*

This production shop creates Braille and large-print documents.

**7454 Breakthroughs: How to Reach Students with Autism**
Aquarius Health Care Videos
PO Box 1159
Sherborn, MA 01770
    508-650-6905
    FAX: 508-650-4216
    e-mail: aqvideos@tiac.net
    www.aquariusproductions.com

A hands-on, how-to program for reaching students with autism, featuring Karen Sewell, Autism Society of America's teacher of the year. Here Sewell demonstrates the successful techniques she's developed over a 20-year career. A separate 250 page manual ($59) is also available which covers math, reading, fine motor, self help, social adaptive, vocational and self help skills as well as providing numerous plan reproducibles and an exhaustive listing of equipment and materials resources. Video. *$99.00*

**7455 Breathe Easy Young People's Guide to Asthma**
Magination Press
2751 Prosperity Avenue
Suite 150
Fairfax, VA 22031
    703-385-4403
    800-878-4403
    FAX: 703-573-7794
    www.aanma.org

Practical, personal guide for those up to age 13 with asthma. They will learn how to control their asthma with techniques that will bring increased self-confidence. *$9.95*
*Video*

**7456 Breathing Lessons: The Life and Work of Mark O'Brien**
Fanlight Productions
4196 Washington Street
Suite 2
Boston, MA 02131
    617-469-4999
    800-937-4113
    FAX: 617-469-3379
    e-mail: fanlight@fanlight.com
    www.fanlight.com

*Ben Achtenberg, Owner*

A new documentary which focuses on poet-journalist Mark O'Brien. Crippled by polio in childhood, and later forced to rely on an iron lung as a result of post-polio syndrome, for more than forty years he has fought against illness and bureaucracy in his determination to lead an independent life. According to Mark O'Brien, the two mythologies of disabled people break down to one: we can't do anything or two; we can do everything. But the truth is we're just human. *$195.00*
*35 Minutes*

**7457 Bridging the Gap: A National Directory of Services for Women & Girls with Disabilities**
Educational Equity Concepts
114 E 32nd Street
New York, NY 10016
    212-725-1803
    FAX: 212-725-0947
    TTY: 212-725-1803
    e-mail: infomration@edequity.org
    www.edequity.org

*Ellen Rubin, Coordinator Disability Programs*
*Merle Froschl, Editor*

Contains a resource section of publications and videos geared specifically to women and girls with disabilities. Available in print, on cassette, and also in braille. *$24.95*

*ISBN 0-931629-16-0*

**7458 Bringing Out the Best**
Research Press
PO Box 9177
Champaign, IL 61826
    217-352-3273
    800-519-2707
    FAX: 217-352-1221
    e-mail: rp@researchpress.com
    www.researchpress.com

*Russell Pence, President*

This video training program introduces teachers, staff and parents to a variety of techniques for teaching expressive communication skills to children with multiple handicaps. The video illustrates how to assess a child's current levels of expressive ability, build on that ability, then gradually work toward more advanced communication. It shows how to use everyday situations to help children move beyond passive understanding to more active, intentional communication. *$150.00*
*Video*

**7459 Business Enterprise Service: Marketing the Randolph-Sheppard Program**
Mississippi State University
PO Box 6189
Mississippi State, MS 39762 662-325-2001
800-675-7782
FAX: 662-325-8989
www.blind.msstate.edu

*Kelly Schaefer, Publications Manager*
*Elton Moore, Executive Director*

This 10-minute videotape and Marketing Information Kit are for use by State Licensing Agencies throughout the country. They are designed for use in promoting the BEP with building managers, plant managers, building superintendents and others who might be interested in utilizing the services provided under the Randolph-Sheppard Act. *$ 30.00*

**7460 Business as Usual**
Fanlight Productions
4196 Washington Street
Suite 2
Boston, MA 02131 617-469-4999
800-917-4113
FAX: 617-469-3379
e-mail: fanlight@fanlight.com
www.fanlight.com

*Karen McMillen, Marketing Director*
*Ben Achtenberg, Owner*

An enlightening new documentary, brings a unique international perspective to this struggle. This film examines five innovative programs which create opportunities for people with mental and physical disabilities to own and operate their own businesses. *$145.00*

**7461 Buying Time: The Media Role in Health Care**
Fanlight Productions
4196 Washington Street
Suite 2
Boston, MA 02131 617-469-4999
800-937-4113
FAX: 617-469-3379
e-mail: fanlight@fanlight.com
www.fanlight.com

*Karen McMillen, Marketing Director*
*Ben Achtenberg, Owner*

This video program is a thoughtful and disturbing examination in the role of the media in determining the allocation of health care resources. This program is a powerful tool on ethics, policy, journalism, sociology, medicine and nursing as well as for professional workshops, and continuing education programs. *$99.00*

**7462 Caring for Persons with Developmental Disabilities**
Research Press
2612 N Mattis Avenue
Champaign, IL 61822 217-352-3273
800-519-2707
FAX: 217-352-1221
e-mail: rp@researchpress.com
www.researchpress.com

*Russell Pence, President*

A competency-baced video traning program that teaches the skills needed to care for individuals with a wide range of psysical and mental disabilities. Consists of six videotapes that feature demonstrations of respite care procedures. Provides quizzes in which viewers are asked to respond to on-screen situations. *$495.00*
*Video*

**7463 Center for Health Research: Eastern Washin gton University**
Showalter 209a
Cheney, WA 99004 509-359-2279
800-221-9369
FAX: 509-359-2778
e-mail: sharon.wilson@mail.ewu.edu
iceberg.ewu.edu

Produces eight videotapes, accompanying printed materials, and a videotaped public services announcement to serve as training and resource materials for use by daycare centers.

**7464 Challenge**
Spina Bifida Association of America
4590 Macarthur Boulevard NW
Suite 250
Washington, DC 20007 202-944-3285
800-621-3141
FAX: 202-944-3295
e-mail: sbaa@sbaa.org
www.sbaa.org

*Cindy Brownstein, Chief Executive Officer*

Fourteen minute video tape. An excellent introduction to the physical and social challenges faced by individuals with spina bifida. *$20.00*

**7465 Children's Classics Videotape Sets**
Gallaudet University Bookstore
11030 S Langley Avenue
Chicago, IL 60628 202-651-5488
800-621-2736
FAX: 202-651-5489

Tells fairytales from the Grimm Brothers and Hans Christian Anderson in American Sign Language. Includes The Little Mermaid, Emperor's New Clothes, Fisherman & His Wife, Hansel and Gretal and The Musician's of Bremmen. *$29.95*

**7466 Christmas Stories**
Gallaudet University Bookstore
11030 S Langley Avenue
Chicago, IL 60628 202-651-5488
800-621-2736
FAX: 202-651-5489

The unique talents of Bobby Giles and Doris Wilding present these great stories in American Sign Language. *$29.95*
*Video*

**7467 Clinicians View**
6007 Osuna Road NE
Albuquerque, NM 87109 505-880-0058
FAX: 505-880-0059

*Gary J Magrun, President*
*W Michael Magrun, VP*

A video and book publishing catalog dedicated to bringing clinicians (PTs; OTs; SLPs) and parents of children with special needs, the best educational and instructional information available. Paperback and videocassette.

**7468 Clockworks**
Learning Corporation of America
6493 Kaiser Drive
Fremont, CA 94555 510-490-7311

*Oonchia Chia, Owner*

Scotty, who has Down Syndrome, is fascinated by clocks. This film follows him on his adventures of employment in the clock shop.

*Film*

**7469 Close Encounters of the Disabling Kind**
Mainstream
6930 Carroll Avenue
Suite 204
Takoma Park, MD 20912                    301-891-8777
                                    FAX: 301-891-8778
                          e-mail: info@mainstreaminc.org
                                  www.mainstreaminc.org

*Lillie Harrison, Information Programs Clerk*
*Fritz Rumpel, Editor*

A training video that provides a hiring manager with information on how to learn the basics of disability etiquette and, by the end of the video, seems much better prepared and willing to interview qualified individuals with disabilities. Includes trainer and trainee guides. *$99.95*
*Video*

**7470 Come Back Jack: The Revealing Story of a Child Diagnosed with Autism**
Aquarius Health Care Videos
PO Box 1159
Sherborn, MA 01770                       508-650-6905
                                    FAX: 508-650-4216
                            e-mail: aqvideos@tiac.net
                          www.aquariusproductions.com
Persistent ear infections, medically misguided over-treatment with antibiotics, and other mysterious physiological factors sent Jack's mind spinning. By the time Jack reached the age of two, his intellectual and emothional development had come to a schreeching halt. Terrified by the prospect of losing their youngest son, Jack's parents began searching for answers. Chronicles the ups and downs. *$ 99.00*

**7471 Concentration Video**
Learning disAbilities Resources
PO Box 716
Bryn Mawr, PA 19010                      610-525-8336
                                         800-869-8336
                                    FAX: 610-525-8337
An instructional video which provides a perspective about attention problems, possible causes and solutions. *$19.95*
*Video*

**7472 Dancing from the Inside Out**
Fanlight Productions
4196 Washington Street
Suite 2
Boston, MA 02131                         617-469-4999
                                         800-937-4113
                                    FAX: 617-469-3379
                          e-mail: fanlight@fanlight.com
                                   www.fanlight.com

*Karen McMillen, Marketing Director*
*Ben Achtenberg, Owner*

This eloquent new video looks at the lives and work of three talented dancers who dance professionally with the acclaimed AXIS Dance Troupe, which includes both disabled and non-disabled dancers. They discuss the process they went through in adapting to their disability and how they came to re-discover physical expression through dance. *$ 195.00*

**7473 Deaf Children Signers**
Harris Communications
15155 Technology Drive
Eden Prairie, MN 55344                   952-906-1180
                                         800-825-6758
                                    FAX: 952-906-1099
                          e-mail: mail@harriscomm.com
                                   www.harriscomm.com

*Bill Williams, National Sales Manager*
*Robert Harris, Owner*

This three-part collection of children signers is great for children, teachers, parents and interpreters. *$39.95*

*Video*

**7474 Deaf Culture Series**
Harris Communications
15155 Technology Drive
Eden Prairie, MN 55344                   952-906-1180
                                         800-825-6758
                                    FAX: 952-906-1099
                          e-mail: mail@harriscomm.com
                                   www.harriscomm.com

*Bill Williams, National Sales Manager*
*Robert Harris, Owner*

Each video in this five-part series features a topic dealing with the unique culture of deaf people. It is an excellent resource for deaf studies programs, Interpreter Preparation programs and Sign Language programs. *$59.95*
*Video*

**7475 Deaf Mosaic Series**
Harris Communications
15155 Technology Drive
Eden Prairie, MN 55344                   952-906-1180
                                         800-825-6758
                                    FAX: 952-906-1099
                          e-mail: mail@harriscomm.com
                                   www.harriscomm.com

*Bill Williams, National Sales Manager*
*Robert Harris, Owner*

A national magazine show produced monthly by Gallaudet University, this show has been awarded nine Emmys. As the only nation-wide program about the deaf community, these videotapes are the best of the best from the shows programs. *$29.95*
*Video*

**7476 Descriptive Video Service**
WGBH Educational Foundation
125 Western Avenue
Boston, MA 02134                         617-300-2000
                                         800-333-1203
                                    FAX: 617-300-1011
                              e-mail: ncam@wgbh.org
                                      www.wgbh.org

*Sharon King, Outreach Director*
*Mary Ann Pack, Assistant Director*
*Henry Becton, Chief Executive Officer*

A national service that makes PBS television programs, Hollywood movies on video and other visual media accessible to people who are blind or visually impaired. DVS provides narrated descriptions of the key visual elements without interfering with the audio or dialogue of a program or movie. The narration describes visual elements such as actions, settings, body language and graphics.

**7477 Different Heart**
Fanlight Productions
4196 Washington Street
Suite 2
Boston, MA 02131                         617-469-4999
                                         800-937-4113
                                    FAX: 617-469-3379
                          e-mail: fanlight@fanlight.com

*Karen McMillen, Marketing Director*
*Ben Achtenberg, Owner*

Though hundreds of children are born each year with potentially fatal heart disease, their parents may feel isolated from those facing similar crises. This sensitive video profiles three such families. *$99.00*

**7478 Do You Hear That?**
Alexander Graham Bell Association
3417 Volta Place NW
Washington, DC 20007
202-337-5220
FAX: 202-337-8314
e-mail: info@agbell.org
www.agbell.org

*Todd Houston, Executive Director*

This video shows auditory-verbal therapy sessions of a therapist working individually with 11 children who range in age from 7 months to 7 years old and have hearing aids or cochlear implants.

*Video*

**7479 Doing Things Together**
Britannica Film Company
345 4th Street
San Francisco, CA 94107
415-777-9876

Steve went with his parents to an amusement park. He met another boy named Martin who at first was shocked by Steve's prosthetic hand.
*Film*

**7480 Down Syndrome**
Aquarius Health Care Videos
PO Box 1159
Sherborn, MA 01770
508-650-6905
FAX: 508-650-4216
e-mail: aqvideos@tiac.net
www.aquariusproductions.com
This is an excellent video for families who have just had a baby with Down Syndrome as well as professionals in the field of genetics and nursing. Through honest and open discussion, parents of children with Down Syndrome express the feelings and concerns they had during the early years of their child's life. Preview option available. *$150.00*
*Video*

**7481 Dream Catchers**
University of New Hampshire: Inst on Disability
7 Leavitt Lane
Suite 101
Durham, NC 03824
603-862-2110
FAX: 603-862-0555
e-mail: institutedisability@unh.edu
www.iod.unh.edu

*Jan Nisbet, Director*
*Janice Mutschler, Manager*

This video tells the stories of three young people with disabilities, and how they each pulled together a network of people called the circle of support.

**7482 Educating Inattentive Children**
Western Psychological Services
12031 Wilshire Boulevard
Los Angeles, CA 90025
310-478-2061
800-648-8857
FAX: 310-478-7838

*Gregg Gillmar, Vice President*

An excellent resources for teachers who encounter inattention and hyperactivity in the classroom. It helps teachers distinguish deliberate misbehavior from the incompetent, nonpurposeful behavior of the inattentive child. *$120.00*
*Video*

**7483 Effective Behavioral Programming**
Research Press
PO Box 9177
Champaign, IL 61826
217-352-3273
800-519-2707
FAX: 217-352-1221
e-mail: rp@researchpress.com
www.researchpress.com

*Russell Pence, President*

A comprehensive video-based training program for educators and residential staff who work with people with developmental disabilities. It is presented in clear, nontechnical language and does not require an extensive background in the use of behavioral procedures. The program includes eight instructional videotapes, a leader's guide and a set of five participant's manuals. It is suitable for group training or individual study and has no rigid time line. *$895.00*
*Video*

**7484 Effective Intervention for Self-Feeding Success**
Exceptional Parent Library
PO Box 1807
Englewood Cliffs, NJ 07632
201-947-6000
800-535-1910
FAX: 201-947-9376
e-mail: eplibrary@aol.com
www.eplibrary.com
An effective and easy to follow video program for parents, which provides the tools needed to be successful in moving your child toward independent self-feeding. *$39.95*

**7485 Einstein and Me: Talking About Learning Disabilities**
Fanlight Productions
4196 Washington Street
Suite 2
Boston, MA 02131
617-469-4999
800-937-4113
FAX: 617-469-3379
e-mail: fanlight@fanlight.com
www.fanlight.com

*Karen McMillen, Marketing Director*
*Ben Achtenberg, Owner*

In this straightforward and engaging video, panels of teens and younger students speak candidly with Schultz, a Clinical Psychologist, about how they found out about their learning disabilities, the policies and people who have made life difficult, the programs which have helped them cope, their strengths and talents, and their futures. *$99.00*

**7486 Emerging Leaders**
Mobility International USA
PO Box 10767
Eugene, OR 97440
541-343-1284
FAX: 541-343-6812
e-mail: info@miusa.org
www.miusa.org

*Susan Sygall, Executive Director*
*Pamela Houston, Public Relations Coordinator*
*Tracy Scharn, Project Assistant*

Looks at the emergence of people with disabilities as leaders in the world community this video discusses the value of internation exchange programs in fostering leadership skills. Available in English, Spanish and Russian. *$49.00*
*Video*

**7487 Emotional Intelligence, Lessons in Conflict and Anger**
Aquarius Health Care Videos
PO Box 1159
Sherborn, MA 01770
508-650-6905
FAX: 508-650-4216
e-mail: aqvideos@tiac.net
www.aquariusproductions.com
Up until recently, most of us expected to learn those kinds of skills, like listening, sharing, being kind, at home, and not find them in any organized class at school. Buth that is changing because of reserach shoing that school age children stay healthier, and learn better, when they know how to handle the ups and downs of growing up. this video profiles classes and programs in the New Haven, Connecticut school system and in Highland Park, New Jersey. — Videocassette. *$149.00*

**7488  Endurance & Body Sculpting Exercise Programs**
Seat-A-Robics
PO Box 1253
Jamestown, NC  27282

FAX: 336-454-4615
e-mail: seatarobics@hotmail.com
www.homelife.com/products/1093.asp

*Clarice Burns, President*

Safe, affordable and medically approved exercise videos developed by a health advisory board in conjunction with a licensed aerobics instructor and paraplegic. These videos are aimed at persons with temporary injuries, permanent disabilities, health professionals and educators. Both programs are available on one tape. *$36.95*
*56 Minutes*

**7489  Environmental Control Measures**
Academy of Allergy, Asthma, Immunology
611 E Wells Street
Milwaukee, WI  53202

414-272-6071
800-822-2762
FAX: 414-272-6070
e-mail: info@aaaai.org
www.aaaai.org

*Kay Whalen, Executive Vice President*

By conrtolling your environment, you can reduce your exposure to substances called allergens that trigger your allergic symptoms. This program depicts common outdoor and indoor allergens, methods an allergist uses to diagnose which substances you're allergic to, and how to reduce your exposure to allergic triggers. *$25.00*
*10-13 Minutes*

**7490  Explore the Bible: Adult Audiocassette**
LifeWay Christian Resources Southern Baptist Conv.
127 9th Avenue N
Nashville, TN  37234

615-251-2089
800-458-2772
FAX: 651-251-5764
e-mail: specialed@lifeway.com
www.lifeway.com

*Ben Garner, Editor*
*Wade Stapleton, Manager*

Full-length recorded bible study lessons as printed in Explore the Bible: Adults. *$12.00*

**7491  Face First**
Fanlight Productions
4196 Washington Street
Suite 2
Boston, MA  02131

617-469-4999
800-937-4113
FAX: 617-469-3379
e-mail: fanlight@fanlight.com
www.fanlight.com

*Karen McMillen, Marketing Director*
*Cynthia Conti, Publicity Coordinator*
*Mike Grundmann, Producer*

In this documentary, the stories told reflect the reality faced by all those who are seen as different. Despite their difficult experiences, the survival of the profiled individuals affords comic relief &, by adulthood, they possess unusual strengths that shape their careers in pediatrics, disability care, public speaking, and journalism. *$195.00*

**7492  Fairy Tales & Christmas Stories**
Harris Communications
15155 Technology Drive
Eden Prairie, MN  55344

952-906-1180
800-825-6758
FAX: 952-906-1099
e-mail: mail@harriscomm.com
www.harriscomm.com

*Bill Williams, National Sales Manager*
*Robert Harris, Owner*

A collection of videotapes featuring classic fairytales and Christmas stories signed by deaf storytellers. *$29.95*
*Video*

**7493  Family Challenges: Parenting with a Disability**
Aquarius Health Care Videos
PO Box 1159
Sherborn, MA  01770

508-650-6905
888-440-2963
FAX: 508-650-4216
e-mail: aqvideos@tiac.net
www.aquariusproductions.com

*Leslie Kussmann, President/Producer*

When a parent has a disability, everyone in the family is affected. For children, these experiences may profoundly influence their lives and views of the world. In this sensitive film, you will hear about different roles that all the family members take on at varying times. *$195.00*

**7494  Family-Guided Activity-Based Intervention for Toddlers & Infants**
Brookes Publishing
PO Box 10624
Baltimore, MD  21285

410-337-9580
800-638-3775
FAX: 410-337-8539
e-mail: custserv@brookespublishing.com
www.brookespublishing.com

*Paul Brooks, Owner*

Early childhood professionals will be able to teach parents and other caregivers how to use daily routines and activities to help young children with special needs gain vital skills. Included on the video are activity-based teaching methods that enhance children's development, accommodate families' daily schedules, address children's IFSP goals, and promote family interactions. *$37.00*
*20 Minutes*
*ISBN 1-55766-19-3*

**7495  Fantastic Series**
Harris Communications
15155 Technology Drive
Eden Prairie, MN  55344

952-906-1180
800-825-6758
FAX: 952-906-1099
e-mail: mail@harriscomm.com
www.harriscomm.com

*Bill Williams, National Sales Manager*
*Robert Harris, Owner*

These videotapes offer a blend of entertainment and information to both deaf and hearing children ages 6-10. A total of eight tapes in the series. *$29.95*

**7496  Fibromyalgia Interval Training**
Arthritis Foundation Distribution Center
PO Box 6996
Alpharetta, GA  30023

800-207-8633
FAX: 770-442-9742
www.arthritis.com

This video was designed for people with fibromyalgia. The video features warm water exercises in shallow and deep water, including warmup, stretching, upper and lower body exercises, aerobics, strengthing, cool-down and relaxation. Designed to help you manage the pain, stiffness and fatigue of fibromyalgia. *$29.99*

**7497  Filmakers Library**
124 E 40th Street
New York, NY  10016

212-808-4980
FAX: 212-808-4983
e-mail: info@filmakers.com
www.filmakers.com

*Sue Oscar, Owner*

A distributor of educational, award-winning videotapes and films on issues relating to disabilities for educators, counsellors and organizations. The films and tapes are available for rental or sale to institutions, schools, hospitals and organizations. Among the topics covered in the videotapes are autism, schizophrenia, and physical disabilities. *$100 - $300*

**7498 Films & Videos on Aging and Sensory Change**
Lighthouse International
111 E 59th Street
New York, NY 10022          212-821-9200
800-829-0500
FAX: 212-821-9706
e-mail: info@lighthouse.org

*Joanna Mellor, VP Information Services*
*Tara Cortes, President*

An annotated list of over 80 films and videos dealing with age-related sensory change, divided into sections on vision impairment, hearing impairment, and multiple sensory impairments. *$5.00*

**7499 Fingerspelling: Expressive and Receptive Fluency**
Gallaudet University Bookstore
11030 S Langley Avenue
Chicago, IL 60628          202-651-5488
800-621-2736
FAX: 202-651-5489
Improve your fingerspelling with this new video guide. A 24-page instructional booklet is included with fingerspelling practice suggestions. *$39.95*
*120 Minutes*

**7500 Foundation Fundamentals for Nonprofit Organizations**
Foundation Center
79 5th Avenue
Department Ze
New York, NY 10003          212-620-4230
800-424-9836
FAX: 212-807-3677
www.fdncenter.org

*Sara Engelhardt, President*

This video is designed to give fundraisers a general overview of the foundation funding process and to introduce them to the many resources available through our libraries and cooperating collections. The video gives clear, step-by-step instructions on how to build a fundraising program. *$24.00*
*Video*

**7501 Foundations: The People and the Money**
Foundation Center
79 5th Avenue
Department Ze
New York, NY 10003          212-620-4230
800-424-9836
FAX: 212-807-3677
www.fdncenter.org

*Sara Engelhardt, President*

This award-winning documentary film, introduced by Robert MacNeil, provides a fascinating introduction to the world of American philanthropic foundations. Through interviews with both grant-makers and grantees, this book offers a vivid and human perspective on the work of foundations today. *$5.00*
*Video*

**7502 Fragile X Family**
4196 Washington Street
Suite 2
Boston, MA 02131          617-469-4999
800-937-4113
FAX: 617-469-3379
e-mail: info@fanlight.com
www.fanlight.com

*Sandy St Louis, Distribution Director*
*Kelli English, Publicity Coordinator*
*Ben Achtenberg, Owner*

Fragile X Family takes viewers inside the lives of a developmentally disabled family who are affected by Fragile X Syndrome, an inherited chromosomal disorder which is the second most common cause of mental retardation. *$149.00*
*2004*
*ISBN 1-572954-14-0*

**7503 Fred's Story**
Aquarius Health Care Videos
PO Box 1159
Sherborn, MA 01770          508-650-6905
FAX: 508-650-4216
e-mail: aqvideos@tiac.net
www.aquariusproductions.com
Fred tells about the 40 years he spent inside Mansfield Training School, a Connecticut institution closed in 1990 by the Department of Mental Retardation. The film cuts between Fred's telling of the reality of the institution and black-and-white newsreel footage of state officials describing their visions of and goals for the institution in which Fred lived. Fred's indomitable, lyrical spirit shines throughout. Golden Chris Award, Columbus International Film Festival. Preview option available. *$90.00*
*Video*

**7504 Free to Breathe**
Allergy and Asthma Network/Mothers of Asthmatics
2751 Prosperity Avenue
Suite 150
Fairfax, VA 22031          703-641-9595
800-878-4403
FAX: 703-573-7794
www.aanma.org
Characters rap, joke, and learn different ways to use inhalers. Kids are encouraged to talk to their parents and doctor about their choices. 8 minutes. *$10.00*
*Video*

**7505 Freedom to Create**
National Institute of Art and Disabilities
551 23rd Street
Richmond, CA 94804          510-620-0290
FAX: 510-620-0326
e-mail: reddot@niadart.org
www.niadart.org

*Elias Katz, Author*
*Patricia Coleman, President*

Presents philosophy and practical experiences enabling teachers to stimulate creativity in the visual arts for students with and without disabilities. Videotape. *$35.00*

**7506 From Mime to Sign Package**
TJ Publishers
2544 Tarpley Road
Suite 108
Carrollton, TX 75006          972-416-0800
800-999-1168
FAX: 301-585-5930
e-mail: TJPubinc@aol.com

*Angela K Thames, President*
*Jerald A Murphy, VP*

As a drama professor, television personality, performer and storyteller, multiple Emmy winner Gil Eastman has developed a unique presentation style. Now, he shares his expressive communication approach in a highly illustrated American Sign Language text and videotape series. A text and three videotapes. *$139.95*
*183 pages*

**7507 Fundamentals of Reading Success**
Educators Publishing Service
PO Box 9031
Cambridge, MA 02139          617-367-2700
800-225-5750
FAX: 617-547-0412
www.epsbooks.com
This video series is designed to help teachers learn a phonics or code-emphasis approach to teaching reading, spelling and handwriting. There is one set for teaching children and one for teaching adults. *$480.00*

*Complete Set*
*ISBN 0-838872-52-2*

**7508  Getting Started with Facilitated Communication**
Syracuse University, Institute on Communication
805 S Krouse
Syracuse, NY  13244                          315-443-4485

*Raymond Colton, Manager*

Describes in detail how to help individuals with autism and/or severe communication difficulties to get started with facilitated communication.
*Video*

**7509  Getting Together: A Head Start/School District Collaboration**
Brookes Publishing
PO Box 10624
Baltimore, MD  21285                         410-337-9580
                                             800-638-3775
                                    FAX: 410-337-8539
                    e-mail: custserv@brookespublishing.com
                            www.brookespublishing.com

*Paul Brooks, Owner*

This video describes how to include children with disabilities in the Head Start classrooms. Addresses such issues as leadership, staff support, and policy development. Comes with a 24-page saddle-stitched booklet. *$34.95*
*25 Minutes*
*ISBN 1-55766 -97-5*

**7510  Getting in Touch**
Research Press
PO Box 9177
Champaign, IL  61826                         217-352-3273
                                             800-519-2707
                                    FAX: 217-352-1221
                        e-mail: rp@researchpress.com
                            www.researchpress.com

*Russell Pence, President*

When communicating with a child who is deaf/blind, there are certain basic procedures that can be used to help the child understand. This video introduces these procedures to teachers, staff, parents and others who work with children who have sensory impairments. The video demonstrates techniques that involve the use of two types of tactile cues - Touch Cues (signals made by actually touching the child) and Object Cues (signals made by presenting an object to the child). *$150.00*
*19 Minutes*

**7511  Going to School with Facilitated Communication**
Syracuse University, School of Education
230 Huntington Hall
Syracuse, NY  13244                          315-443-5550

*Nancy Mudrick, Manager*

A video in which students with autism and/or severe disabilities illustrate the use of facilitated communication focusing on basic principles fostering facilitated communication.
*Video*

**7512  Good Weather or Not**
Nat'l Council of Community Mental Health Center
12300 Twinbrook Parkway
Suite 320
Rockville, MD  20852

One of the few resources of its kind, this set will help clinicians present material about parents' mental illness that is generated to young children's levels of thinking. *$290.00*

**7513  Granny Good's Signs of Christmas**
Gallaudet University Bookstore
11030 S Langley Avenue
Chicago, IL  60628                           202-651-5488
                                             800-621-2736
                                    FAX: 202-651-5489
Come join the folks at Granny's cottage where Hans Signer, from the silent forest, interprets his favorite story, Twas The Night Before Christmas. *$29.95*
*Video*

**7514  Harry**
Research Press
PO Box 9177
Champaign, IL  61826                         217-352-3273
                                             800-519-2707
                                    FAX: 217-352-1221
                        e-mail: rp@researchpress.com
                            www.researchpress.com

*Russell Pence, President*

Harry is one of the most unforgettable documentaries ever produced. It is honest, dramatic, touching and REAL. None of the scenes were staged, actual treatment sessions, conducted by Dr. Richard M. Foxx, were videotaped through a one-way mirror. Harry is the subject of the remarkably successful treatment program. At the time of this taping he was 24 years old and had spent most of his life in institutions wearing various types of physical restraints. 38 minutes. *$495.00.*
*Video*

**7515  Hear to Listen & Learn: A Language Approach for Children with Ear Infections**
Brookes Publishing
PO Box 10624
Baltimore, MD  21285                         410-337-9580
                                             800-638-3775
                                    FAX: 410-337-8539
                    e-mail: custserv@brookespublishing.com
                            www.brookespublishing.com

*Paul Brooks, Owner*

This video describes the behavioral characteristics that signal when middle ear fluid is causing problems for a child. Also provides professionals with ideas for modifying classrooms and incorporating teaching practices that promote learning opportunities and language acquisition for children with middle ear fluid and associated hearing loss. *$42.00*
*20-min VHS*
*ISBN 1-55766 -99-5*

**7516  Heart to Heart**
Blind Children's Center
4120 Marathon Street
Los Angeles, CA  90029                       323-664-2153
                                             800-222-3567
                                    FAX: 323-665-3828
                    e-mail: info@blindchildrenscenter.org
                            www.blindchildrenscenter.org

*Midge Horton, Executive Director*

Parents of blind and partially sighted children talk about their feelings. *$35.00*
*Video*

**7517  Helping Hands**
Fanlight Productions
4196 Washington Street
Suite 2
Boston, MA  02131                            617-469-4999
                                             800-937-4113
                                    FAX: 617-469-3379
                        e-mail: fanlight@fanlight.com
                            www.fanlight.com

*Ben Achtenberg, Owner*

The ADA mandates equal access and opportunity for the 43 million people with disabilities in the United States. These individuals may have limited speech, sight or mobility; a developmental disability; or a medical condition which limits some life activities. Many, however, are ready, willing and very able to join the workforce. This video demonstrates that many modifications or adaptations can be made simply by using ingenuity or common sense — such as keeping the aisles clear, etc. *$145.00*
*37 Minutes*

**7518    Helping the Family Understand**
Vestibular Disorders Association
PO Box 4467
Portland, OR  97208                          503-229-7705
                                             800-837-8428
                                     FAX: 503-229-8064
                              e-mail: veda@vestibular.org
                                      www.vestibular.org

*Lisa Haven, Editor*
*Connie Pilcher, Editor*
*2002*

**7519    Home is in the Heart: Accommodating People with Disabilities in the Homestay Experience**
Mobility International USA
PO Box 10767
Eugene, OR  97440                            541-343-1284
                                     FAX: 541-343-6812
                                 e-mail: info@miusa.org
                                         www.miusa.org

*Susan Sygall, Executive Director*
*Pamela Houston, Public Relations Coordinator*
*Tracy Scharn, Project Assistant*

Provides information and ideas for exchange organizations. Discusses how to recruit homestay families, meet accessibility needs and accommodate international participants with disabilities. *$49.00*
*Video*

**7520    How Come You Walk Funny?**
4196 Washington Street
Suite 2
Boston, MA  02131                            617-469-4999
                                             800-937-4113
                                     FAX: 617-469-3379
                                e-mail: info@fanlight.com
                                        www.fanlight.com

*Sandy St Louis, Distribution Director*
*Kelli English, Publicity Coordinator*
*Ben Achtenberg, Owner*

Profiles a unique experiment in reverse integration: a school where non disabled kids attend a kindergarten designed for children with physical disabilities. The kids and families tackle their differences and discover common ground through finding a way that all can play. *$ 179.00*
*2004*
*ISBN 1-572954-18-3*

**7521    How Difficult Can This Be ? (Fat City)**
CACLD
25 Van Zant Street
Suite 15-5
Norwalk, CT  06855                           203-838-5010
                                     FAX: 203-866-6108
                              e-mail: cacld@optonline.net
                                         www.CACLD.org

*Beryl Kaufman, Executive Director*

This informative and entertaining video allows the viewer to see the world through the eyes of a learning disabled child. It features a unique workshop attended by teacher, psychologists, social workers, parents, siblings and a student with LD They participate in a series of classroom activiteis which cause frustration, anxiety and tension; emotions all too familiar to a student with a learning disability.

**7522    How We Play**
Fanlight Productions
4196 Washington Street
Suite 2
Boston, MA  02131                            617-469-4999
                                             800-937-4113
                                     FAX: 617-469-3379
                            e-mail: fanlight@fanlight.com
                                        www.fanlight.com

*Karen McMillen, Marketing Director*
*Ben Achtenberg, Owner*

Though most of the people in this new, short documentary are in wheelchairs, and one is blind, they are anything but handicapped. Playing tennis, snorkeling, whitewater canoeing, practicing karate - they are living proof that a disability can be a challenge, not an obstacle. *$99.00*

**7523    I Can Do It**
Britannica Film Company
345 4th Street
San Francisco, CA  94107                     415-777-9876

Tommy's parents took him shopping. Although he had trouble moving around with his braces he wanted to go shopping alone. In the pet shop he had some trouble moving around, but he was able to solve his problems and even help other customers. A teacher's guide is available with this video.
*Film*

**7524    I Want My Little Boy Back**
A Britsh Broadcasting Corporation Documentary
2080 S Undermountain Road
Sheffield, MA  01257                         413-229-2100
                                             800-714-2779
                                     FAX: 413-229-8931
                              e-mail: happiness@option.org
                                        www.option.org
A great video for parents and professionals caring for children with special needs. Join one British family and their autistic son before, during and after their journey to America to attend The Son-Rise Program at The Autism Treatment Center of America. This informative, inspirational and deeply moving story not only captures the joy, tears, challenges and triumps of this amazing little boy and his family, but also serves as a powerful introduction to the attitude and principles of the program. *$25.00*

**7525    I'm Not Disabled**
Landmark Media
3450 Slade Run Drive
Falls Church, VA  22042                      703-241-2030
                                             800-342-4336
                                     FAX: 703-536-9540

*Michael Hartogs, President*

Young people talk about their disabilities and the importance of sports in their lives. The afflictions range from blindness and missing limbs to paralysis. Through physical education and therapy they enjoy freedom of movement and participate in sports such as tennis, basketball, kayaking, skiing, and swimming. *$195.00*
*Video*

**7526    If I Can't Do It**
Fanlight Productions
4196 Washington Street
Suite 2
Boston, MA  02131                            617-469-4999
                                             800-937-4113
                                     FAX: 617-469-3379
                            e-mail: fanlight@fanlight.com
                                        www.fanlight.com

*Karen McMillen, Marketing Director*
*Cynthia Conti, Publicity Coordinator*
*Walter Brock, Producer*

Arthur Campbell, Jr. doesn't want your sympathy, he just wants what most people want: a living wage, a meaningful social life, a few good laughs and the means to get around. This outstanding documentary is an unflinching portrait of one cantankerous and courageous disabled man. *$245.00*

**7527 Imagery Procedures for People with Special Needs**
Research Press
PO Box 9177
Champaign, IL 61826    217-352-3273
    800-519-2707
FAX: 217-352-1221
e-mail: rp@researchpress.com
www.researchpress.com

*Russell Pence, President*

This video features numerous training sessions in which clinicians are shown leading individuals through imagery scenes that focus on controlling specific behaviors. *$195.00*
*32 Minutes*

**7528 In the Middle**
Fanlight Productions
4196 Washington Street
Suite 2
Boston, MA 02131    617-469-4999
    800-937-4113
FAX: 617-469-3379
e-mail: fanlight@fanlight.com
www.fanlight.com

*Karen McMillen, Marketing Director*
*Ben Achtenberg, Owner*

Documents the problems and joys shared by Ryanna, who has Spina Bifida, and her parents, teachers and classmates during her first year of being mainstreamed in a Head Start Program. *$99.00*

**7529 In the Mind of the Beholder.... a Video About Newly Blind Adults**
Aquarius Health Care Videos
PO Box 1159
Sherborn, MA 01770    508-650-6905
FAX: 508-650-4216
e-mail: aqvideos@tiac.net
Newly blind adults making the transition to using their non-visual senses. In a society in which most people are terrified of losing their vision- and yet know virtually nothing about vision loss- the blind are wrongly viewed as mysterious, pitiful or courageous. Produced by Karen Brown Davison, this film puts a human face and voice to blindness. By sharing the experience of losing their eyesight and relearning skills they once took for granted, the people in this film: nonvisual clues. *$195.00*

**7530 Include Us**
Exceptional Parent Library
PO Box 1807
Englewood Cliffs, NJ 07632    201-947-6000
    800-535-1910
FAX: 201-947-9376
e-mail: eplibrary@aol.com
www.eplibrary.com
First children's video to feature a proportionate number of children with disabilities. Inclusion works via eight songs. *$19.95*

**7531 Intensive Early Intervention and Beyond School-Based Inclusion Program**
Research Press
2612 N Mattis Avenue
Champaign, IL 61822    217-352-3273
    800-519-2707
FAX: 217-352-2707
e-mail: rp@researchpress.com
www.researchpress.com

*Russell Pence, President*

Shows the successful application of a school-based inclusion program. The video focuses on the lives of young children with autism who have shown remarkable progress in personal, social, and academic skills. 22 minutes. *$195.00*

*Video*

**7532 Interpretations**
Fanlight Productions
4196 Washington Street
Suite 2
Boston, MA 02131    617-469-4999
    800-937-4113
FAX: 617-469-3379
e-mail: fanlight@fanlight.com
www.fanlight.com

*Karen McMillen, Marketing Director*
*Ben Achtenberg, Owner*

This new film uses humor and drama to explore the interaction between the deaf and hearing communities. Janice, a freelance photographer who is deaf, has been given her first assignment by an advertising agency. She hires her hearing friend Maureen to interpret for her. When conflicts arise between Janice and the client, Maureen changes Janice words. The film looks at the interplay of dependence and responsibility in the relationship of communicator and interpreter. $145.00.

**7533 Invisible Children**
Learning Corporation of America
6493 Kaiser Drive
Fremont, CA 94555    510-490-7311

*Oonchia Chia, Owner*

Renaldo was blind, Mandy was deaf, and Mark had Cerebral Palsy and used a wheelchair. These child-size puppet characters interacted with non-handicapped puppets.
*Film*

**7534 Is This Abuse?**
YAI: Natl. Institute for People with Disabilities
460 W 34th Street
New York, NY 10001    212-273-6100
FAX: 212-947-7524
www.yai.org

*Philip Levy, Manager*

Video clarifies issues of abuse for professionals working with disabled adults. *$145.00*

**7535 It's Just Attention Disorder**
Western Psychological Services
12031 Wilshire Boulevard
Los Angeles, CA 90025    310-478-2061
    800-648-8857
FAX: 310-478-7838

*Gregg Gillmar, Vice President*

This ground-breaking videotape takes the critical first steps in treating attention-deficit disorder: it enlists the inattentive or hyperactive child as an active participant in his or her treatment. *$99.50*
*Video*

**7536 JBI Voice**
Jewish Braille Institute of America
110 E 30th Street
New York, NY 10016    212-889-2525
    800-433-1531
FAX: 212-689-3692
e-mail: admin@jbilibrary.org
www.jbilibrary.org

*Ellen Isler MD, President*
*Israel A Taub, Associate Director*

Monthly recorded magazine emphasizing Jewish current events and culture.

*1931*

**7537 Journey**
Landmark Media
3450 Slade Run Drive
Falls Church, VA 22042

703-241-2030
800-342-4336
FAX: 703-536-9540

*Michael Hartogs, President*

A moving portrayal of the extraordinary journey to Japan of 74-year-old Billie Sinclair, who is deaf, blind and mute. He funds his travels by weaving and selling baskets. In Japan he rides a roller coaster, tries judo and visits a deaf and blind acupuncturist. He demonstrates how it is possible to communicate by touch alone. *$195.00*
*Video*

**7538 Juggler**
Beacon Press
25 Beacon Street
Boston, MA 02108

617-742-2110
FAX: 617-743-3097

*Helen Atwan, Executive Director*

Andre was the young son of a wealthy, early Quebec fur trader. Because he was almost totally blind, he was overly protected by his family, and his movement outside his home was very limited.

*Film*

**7539 Just 4 Kids**
Seat-A-Robics
PO Box 1253
Jamestown, ND 58402

336-454-4615
FAX: 336-454-4615
e-mail: seatarobics@hotmail.com
www.seat-a-robics.com

*Clarice Burns, President*

Seated aerobic exercise program incorporates animation, props and musical themes that children five through adolescent can relate to. Adaptive instruction and safety tips are provided while demonstrating proper form. The warm-up and marching band sections include eight kid instructors as participants. Recommended for ages five through adolescent. *$39.95*
*Ages 5-14*
*ISBN 1-887479-03-1*

**7540 Keeping the Balance**
Fanlight Productions
4196 Washington Street
Suite 2
Boston, MA 02131

617-469-4999
800-937-4113
FAX: 617-469-3379
e-mail: fanlight@fanlight.com
www.fanlight.com

*Karen McMillen, Marketing Director*
*Ben Achtenberg, Owner*

Brothers and sisters of children with serious lung diseases share their experiences of being the normal child. Insightful and articulate, they explore the frequent conflict between their feelings of love and concern, and their resentment over the attention denied to them because of the sibling's illness. *$99.00*

**7541 Key Changes: A Portrait of Lisa Thorson**
Fanlight Productions
4196 Washington Street
Suite 2
Boston, MA 02131

617-469-4999
800-937-4113
FAX: 617-469-3379
e-mail: fanlight@fanlight.com
www.fanlight.com

*Karen McMillen, Marketing Director*
*Ben Achtenberg, Owner*

A documentary profiling Lisa Thorson, a gifted vocalist who uses a wheelchair. Ms. Thorson defines herself as a performer first, a person with a disability second, and this thoughtful portrait respects that distinction. Her work as a jazz singer is at the heart of the film, reflecting her philosophy that the biggest contribution that she can make to the struggle for the rights of people with disabilities is doing her art the best way she can. *$145.00*

**7542 Know Your Diabetes, Know Yourself**
Joslin Diabetes Center
1 Joslin Place
Boston, MA 02215

617-732-2400

An hour-long videotape in which Joslin patients talk about daily issues of diabetes management - meal planning, exercise, monitoring, injections, foot and eye care, and managing the disease when sick or traveling. *$3.00*

**7543 Landmark Media**
3450 Slade Run Drive
Falls Church, VA 22042

703-241-2030
800-342-4336
FAX: 703-536-9540
e-mail: landmrkmed@aol.com

*Michael Hartogs, President*

Supplier and distributor of educational videocassettes and CD's. $79-$280.00.

**7544 Learning Disabilities and Discipline**
CACLD
25 Van Zant Street
Suite 15-5
Norwalk, CT 06855

203-838-5010
FAX: 203-866-6108
e-mail: CACLD@optonline.net
www.CACLD.org

*Beryl Kaufman, Executive Director*

This video comes with a 16 page Program Guide containing information about specific aspects of the learing disabilities profile that can cause misbehavior. Some basic concepts which can be valuable as you develop your own behavior management plans are discussed. Included are dozens of field test techniques and strategies that can be used to monitor, evaluate and manage childrens behavior and more.

**7545 Learning Disabilities and Self Esteem**
CACLD
25 Van Zant Street
Suite 15-5
Norwalk, CT 06855

203-838-5010
FAX: 203-866-6108
e-mail: CACLD@optonline.net
www.CACLD.org

*Beryl Kaufman, Executive Director*

The 60 minute Teacher video contains program material for building self-esteem in the classroom. The 60 minute parent video contains program material for building self esteem in the home. A 16 page Program Guide accompanies each video.

**7546 Learning Disabilities and Social Skills**
CACLD
25 Van Zant Street
Suite 15-5
Norwalk, CT 06855

203-838-5010
FAX: 203-866-6108
e-mail: CACLD@optonline.net
www.CACLD.org

*Beryl Kaufman, Executive Director*

Noting that LD children do not have the cognitive skills to simply pick up socially correct behavior by watching their parents, like most children do, nationally recognized expert on learning disabilities, Richard Lavoie, gives parents and teachers examples on how to help their LD children succeed in everyday situations where they might normally fail. The program includes an explanation of social autopsies and the techniques Lavoie uses to correct them.

**7547 Let's Eat Video**
Blind Children's Center
4120 Marathon Street
Los Angeles, CA 90029          323-664-2153
                              800-222-3567
                        FAX: 323-665-3828
          e-mail: info@blindchildrenscenter.org
                www.blindchildrenscenter.org

*Midge Horton, Executive Director*
*$35.00*

**7548 Let's be Friends**
Britannica Film Company
345 4th Street
San Francisco, CA 94107          415-777-9876

The teacher left the room and asked Shelly, a hearing impaired child to be the mother. Margaret, an emotionally disturbed child, became frightened and verbally attacked Shelly. The teacher worked to get them to become friends and understand each other's problems.
*Film*

**7549 Look Out for Annie**
Lighthouse International
111 E 59th Street
New York, NY 10022          212-821-9200
                            800-829-0500
                      FAX: 212-821-9706
            e-mail: info@lighthouse.org

*Joanna Mellor, VP Information Services*
*Tara Cortes, President*

Depicts an older woman coping with her vision loss. It focuses on the emotional issues surrounding vision loss and conveys the idea that both the person with the vision disorder and their family and friends will need to make adjustments. *$25.00*
*Video*

**7550 Look Who's Laughing**
Aquarius Health Care Videos
PO Box 1159
Sherborn, MA 01770          508-650-6905
                      FAX: 508-650-4216
            e-mail: aqvideos@tiac.net
            www.aquariusproductions.com
This video is packed with laugh-out-loud comedic moments, but is also full of intelligent and inspiring messages. Look Who's Laughing introduces viewers to some of today's funniest comedians - who just happen to be physically disabled. We hear them talk openly and honestly about their limitations as well as their abilities and talents. Helpful for those who work with the disabled and motivational to both the disabled and able-bodied. Preview option available. *$95.00*
*Video*

**7551 Loud, Proud and Passionate**
Mobility International USA
PO Box 10767
Eugene, OR 97440          541-343-1284
                      FAX: 541-343-6812
            e-mail: info@miusa.org
                www.miusa.org

*Susan Sygall, Executive Director*
*Pamela Houston, Public Relations Coordinator*
*Tracy Scharn, Project Assistant*

Documents MIUSA's Women's Institute on Leadership and Disability. Interviews with participants highlight the vision, determination, challanges and recommendations of women with disabilities who are grassroots leaders in over 25 countries. MIUSA's unique model of international leadership training is illustrated as women with mobility, visual and hearing disabilities are shown in training workshop and team-building activities. Available in English, Spanish and Russian. *$49.00*
*Video*

**7552 Making a Difference**
Government Council on Developmental Disabilities
2 Peachtree Street NW
Atlanta, GA 30303          404-657-2126
                          888-275-4233
                    FAX: 404-657-2123
        e-mail: eejacobson@dhr.state.ga.us
                www.gcdd.org

*Eric E Johnson, Executive Director*
*Beth Spinning, Program Director*
*Yao Seidu, Public Information Officer*

**7553 Making a Difference: A Wise Approach**
Easter Seals
230 W Monroe Street
Chicago, IL 60606          312-726-0653
                    FAX: 312-726-1494

*Janet D Jamieson, Communication Manager*

The town of Wise, Virginia, and its leading citizen, Virgil Craft, personify what Making a Difference is all about when a community supports implementing the provisions of the Americans with Disabilities Act. Craft, a person with a disability, has spent his life giving back to the community. The community, in turn, has supported Craft's efforts to improve the environment, education, healthcare and access for disabled persons. A must buy for companies of all sizes, clubs and organizations. *$50.00*

**7554 Managed Mental Healthcare Video**
Nat'l Council for Community Behavioral Healthcare
12300 Twinbrook Parkway
Suite 320
Rockville, MD 20852          301-984-6200
                      FAX: 301-881-7159
                      www.nccbh.org

*Linda Rosenberg, Chief Executive Officer*

Get an overview of the managed healthcare climate with this premier strategic planning and training tool.

**7555 Manic Depression: Voices of an Illness**
Fanlight Productions
4196 Washington Street
Suite 2
Boston, MA 02131          617-469-4999
                          800-937-4113
                    FAX: 617-469-3379
        e-mail: fanlight@fanlight.com

*Karen McMillen, Marketing Director*
*Ben Achtenberg, Owner*

This audio cassette focuses on the lives of nine people and their families who are living with the pervasive illness. *$29.00*
*Audio*

**7556 Martin Luther Home Society**
650 J Street
Suite 305
Lincoln, NE 68508          402-486-3848
                          800-727-8317
                    FAX: 402-434-3253
        e-mail: info@mlhs.com
                www.mlhs.com

*Faye Colburn, Communications Specialist*
*David Frye, Communications Director*

Video production: public education and public relations programs. Staff training materials. Public Service announcements and script writing services.

**7557   Mayor of the West Side**
4196 Washington Street
Suite 2
Boston, MA  02131                    617-469-4999
                                      800-937-4113
                            FAX: 617-469-3379
                        e-mail: info@fanlight.com
                              www.fanlight.com

*Sandy St Louis, Distribution Director*
*Kelli English, Publicity Coordinator*
*Ben Achtenberg, Owner*

What happens when love gets in the way of letting go? As a teenager with multiple disabilities prepares for his Bar Mitzvah, his family and community consider what Mark's life will be like when they are no longer able to protect him. *$199.00*

   *ISBN 1-572953-95-0*

**7558   More Than Just a Job**
Institution on Disability
Morrill Hall
Room 312
Durham, NH  03824

Narrative case studies and interviews with persons with disabilities, their employers, families and experts in the field. *$ 20.00*

**7559   My Body is Not Who I Am**
Aquarius Health Care Videos
PO Box 1159
Sherborn, MA  01770                  508-650-6905
                                      888-440-2963
                            FAX: 508-650-4216
                        e-mail: aqvideos@tiac.net
                         www.aquariusproductions.com

*Leslie Kussman, President*

This thought-provoking video introduces viewers to people who openly discuss the struggles and triumphs they have experienced living in a body that is physically disabled. They talk honestly about the social stigma of their disability and the problems they face in terms of mobility, health care and family relationships, as well as the challenges of emotional and sexual intimacy. Preview option available. *$195.00*
            *Video*

**7560   My Country**
Aquarius Health Care Videos
PO Box 1159
Sherborn, MA  01770                  508-650-6905
                                      888-440-2963
                            FAX: 508-650-4216
                        e-mail: aqvideos@tiac.net
                         www.aquariusproductions.com

*Leslie Kussmann, President*

By telling the stories of three people with disabilities and their struggle for equal rights under the law, this film draws a powerful parallel between the efforts of disability rights activists and the civil rights struggle of the 1960s. Great for disability awareness programs, and for discussions of disability rights issues. Should be part of every college curriculum on disabilities. Awarded Best of Show Superfest 98. Preview option available. *$195.00*

*Video*

**7561   Nancy's Special Workout for the Physically Challenged**
Laurel Designs
1805 Mar West Street
Apt A
Belvedere Tiburon, CA  94920
                            FAX: 415-435-1451
                      e-mail: laureld@ncal.verio.com

*Janet Sawyer, Owner*
*Lynn Montoya, Owner*

Aerobic exercise video with syncopated music for seated people with disabilities from minimal to severe. *$42.00*
      *45 Minutes*

**7562   Narcolepsy**
Fanlight Productions
4196 Washington Street
Suite 2
Boston, MA  02131                    617-469-4999
                            FAX: 617-469-3379
                      e-mail: fanlight@fanlight.com
                              www.fanlight.com

*Ben Achtenberg, Owner*

Presents the experiences of three individuals who lives and relationships have been disrupted by narcolepsy. Rental $50/day. *$195.00*
      *25 Minutes*

**7563   No Barriers**
Aquarius Health Care Videos
PO Box 1159
Sherborn, MA  01770                  508-650-6905
                            FAX: 508-650-4216
                        e-mail: aqvideos@tiac.net
                         www.aquariusproductions.com
Everyone faces the world with different abilities and disabilities. But everyone has at least one goal in common...to break through their own barriers says Mark Wellman. Mark, a paraplegic, knows this well. No Barriers takes us into Mark's world where he defies the odds for most able bodied individuals by climbing Yosemite's Half Dome and El Capitan. This video is more than inspiring and fun to watch...it helps one make that paradigm shift from can't do to can do! Preview option available *$90.00*
            *Video*

**7564   NoBody's Perfect....Educating Children about Disabilities**
Aquarius Health Care Videos
PO Box 1159
Sherborn, MA  01770                  508-650-6905
                            FAX: 508-650-4216
                        e-mail: aqvideos@tiac.net
An upbeat, inclusion-friendly program for kids that profiles three children with disabilties. Viewers discover that accepting differences is an essential part of growing up. We learn how the kids cope and, in the process, are introduced to signing, prosthetics, and assistive technology and Braille. Videocassette, preview option is available. *$ 99.00*

**7565   Nobody is Burning Wheelchairs**
Easter Seals
230 W Monroe Street
Chicago, IL  60606                   312-726-0653
                            FAX: 312-726-1494

*Janet D Jamieson, Communications Manager*

Explains the employment, public accommodations, transportation and telecommunications provisions of the Americans with Disabilities Act and what this law means to people with disabilities and business and industry. The video can be used for training and information seminars, awareness training and for groups interested in learning more about people with disabilities. *$35.00*

*Video*

**7566 Observing Kassandra**
Brookes Publishing
PO Box 10624
Baltimore, MD 21285

410-337-9580
800-638-3775
FAX: 410-337-8539
e-mail: custserv@brookespublishing.com
www.brookespublishing.com

*Paul Brooks, Owner*

Provides professionals with a firsthand opportunity to practice taking notes during a TPBA. Comes with summary forms that can be completed for additional guidance in learning how to use TPBA. Also included is a 28-page saddle-stitched booklet. *$169.00*

    *50 Minutes*
    *ISBN 1-55766 -66-5*

**7567 Once Upon a Time...Children's Classics Retold in American Sign Language**
Harris Communications
15155 Technology Drive
Eden Prairie, MN 55344

952-906-1180
800-825-6758
FAX: 952-906-1099
e-mail: mail@harriscomm.com
www.harriscomm.com

*Bill Williams, National Sales Manager*
*Robert Harris, Owner*

Children's classics come alive on videotapes. Six tapes are available, each telling a favorite fairy tale. *$29.95*

**7568 One to Grow On**
Nat'l Council for Community Behavioral Healthcare
12300 Twinbrook Parkway
Suite 320
Rockville, MD 20852

301-984-6200
FAX: 301-881-7159
www.nccbh.org

*Linda Rosenberg, Chief Executive Officer*

Provides an important service to clinicians. This video will allow therapists to make in-depth observations of clients' treatment needs and reduce therapist-client mismatches. *$595.00*

**7569 Open for Business**
Disability Rights Education and Defense Fund
2212 6th Street
Berkeley, CA 94710

510-644-2555
FAX: 510-841-8645
e-mail: dredf@dredf.org
www.dredf.org

*Susan Henderson, Managing Director*

An award-winning film that depicts the disability and business communities working together in one small town to remove architectural barriers, when readily achievable, as required by the Americans with Disabilities Act. Package includes 15 and 30 minute closed-captioned versions and 15 to 30 minute versions with audio description. *$179.00*

**7570 Open to the Public**
Aquarius Health Care Videos
PO Box 1159
Sherborn, MA 01770

508-650-6905
FAX: 508-650-4216
e-mail: aqvideos@tiac.net
www.aquariusproductions.com

Provides an overview of the Americans with Disabilities Act as it applies to state and local governments. The ADA doesn't provide recommendations for solving common problems, but this film could provide enough information for governments to solve some common problems without turning to high-priced consultants. Preview option available. *$125.00*

*Video*

**7571 Our Own Road**
Aquarius Health Care Videos
PO Box 1159
Sherborn, MA 01770

508-650-6905
FAX: 508-650-4216
e-mail: aqvideos@tiac.net
www.aquariusproductions.com

*Leslie Kussmonn, President*

This video shows the disabled helping other people who are disabled and portrays the sense of pride they get from helping others. This multicultural program features many different healing techniques, and teaches the importance of helping those who are disabled become independent and productive. *$99.00*

**7572 PACE II**
Arthritis Foundation
PO Box 6996
Alpharetta, GA 30023

800-207-8633
FAX: 770-442-9742
www.arthritis.com

*$19.50*

**7573 Parallels in Time**
MN Governor's Council on Development Disabilities
658 Cedar Street
Saint Paul, MN 55155

651-296-4018
877-348-0505
FAX: 651-297-7200
e-mail: admin.dd@state.mn.us
www.mncdd.org

*Colleen Wieck PhD, Executive Director*

Parallels in Time traces present attitudes and the treatment of people with disabilities, and supplements the first weekend seesion of Partners in Policymaking. This CD-ROM includes the History of the Parent Movement and the History of the Independent Living Movement, as well as personal stories of self advocates, leaders in the self advocacy movement.

**7574 Part of the Team**
Easter Seals
230 W Monroe Street
Suite 1800
Chicago, IL 60606

312-726-6800
FAX: 312-726-1494

*Janet D Jamieson, Communications Manager*
*James Williams Jr, Chief Executive Officer*

Designed for employers of all sizes, rehabilitation organizations and all others concerned with the employment of people with disabilities. It addresses managers' concerns and questions about supervising persons with disabilities and can be used as a discussion/team-building tool for employees with and without disabilities. The video recognizes people with disabilities as strong contenders for almost any job. *$15.00*

**7575 Passion for Justice**
Fanlight Productions
4196 Washington Street
Suite 2
Boston, MA 02131

617-469-4999
800-937-4113
FAX: 617-469-3379
e-mail: fanlight@fanlight.com
www.fanlight.com

*Ben Achtenberg, Owner*

An engaging portrait of Bob Perske, the author of Unequal Justice and a crusader for the rights of people with developmental disabilities. The tape focuses on cases in which people with developmental disabilities have been convicted of crimes they didn't commit. The tape asks challenging questions about society's responsibility to this population, and about ways to protect their rights to equality and justice. *$99.00*

*29 Minutes*

**7576 Pathways to Better Living**
Arthritis Foundation
PO Box 6996
Alpharetta, GA 30023

800-207-8633
FAX: 770-442-9742
www.arthritis.com

*$29.95*

**7577 Paul**
Miriam Perrone
440 Park Avenue
Saint Simons Island, GA 31522

How a determined mother carved a semi-independent life for her
now-grown down syndrome child. *$63.20*

**7578 Pharmacologic Therapy of Pediatric Asthma**
American Lung Association
61 Broadway
New York, NY 10006

212-315-8700
FAX: 212-315-8700
e-mail: info@lungusa.org
www.lungusa.org

*John Kirkwood, Chief Executive Officer*

A Learning Resource Program developed by a joint committee
of the American Thoracic Society and the ALA.
*Film*

**7579 Pool Exercise Program**
Arthritis Foundation Distribution Center
PO Box 6996
Alpharetta, GA 30023

800-207-8633
FAX: 770-442-9742
www.arthritis.com

This video features water exercises that will help you increase
and maintain joint flexibility, strengthen and tone muscles, and
increase endurance. All exercises are performed in water at
chest level. No swimming skills are necessary. *$19.50*

**7580 Potty Learning for Children who Experience Delay**
Exceptional Parent Library
PO Box 1807
Englewood Cliffs, NJ 07632

201-947-6000
800-535-1910
FAX: 201-947-9376
e-mail: eplibrary@aol.com
www.eplibrary.com

This video presents a unique developmental approach to supporting the child in learning independence in the management of
bathroom skills. *$39.95*

**7581 Raising Kids with Special Needs**
Aquarius Health Care Videos
PO Box 1159
Sherborn, MA 01770

508-650-6905
FAX: 508-650-4216
e-mail: aqvideos@tiac.net
www.aquariusproductions.com

An intimate look into the lives of parents of three kids with very
different disabilities. The objective of this video is an understanding of paprenting a child with special nees. This outstanding program looks at safety concerns, issues of anger and grief,
the importance of a support network and other important issues.
Ultimately, this is a narrative about raising and educating a child
with disabilities. Preview option is available. *$89.00*

*Video*

**7582 Reasonable Accommodations of the Enabling Kind**
Mainstream
3 Bethesda Metro Center
Suite 830
Bethesda, MD 20814

301-961-9299

e-mail: info@mainstreaminc.org

*Lillie Harrison, Information Programs Clerk*
*Charles Moster*

In this training video a hiring manager demonstrates the basics
of doing a job analysis and is shown using the information in interview sessions to determine the reasonable accommodation
needs of three individuals with disabilities. Includes trainer and
trainee guide. *$59.95*

**7583 Recognizing Children with Special Needs**
Aquarius Health Care Videos
PO Box 1159
Sherborn, MA 01770

508-650-6905
FAX: 508-650-4216
e-mail: aqvideos@tiac.net
www.aquariusproductions.com

A great overview for caregivers of children on how to recognize
special needs. Often-times it is the little things children do everyday to compensate for, or express, a disability that can be ob-
served by their caregiver. All types of disabilities are addressed:
emotional, physical, psychological, and chronic illness. A wonderful tool for teachers, childcare staff, and students on how to
play a vital role in our children's development. Preview option
available. *$125.00*
*Video*

**7584 Regular Kid**
American Lung Association
61 Broadway
New York, NY 10006

212-315-8700
FAX: 212-315-8700
e-mail: info@lungusa.org
www.lungusa.org

*John Kirkwood, Chief Executive Officer*

This film shows how families and children cope with asthma
problems. Proven asthma management strategies are presented
through the experiences of four children with asthma, ranging in
age from toddler to teenager.
*Film*

**7585 Relaxation Techniques for People with Special Needs**
Research Press
2612 N Mattis Avenue
Champaign, IL 61822

217-352-3273
800-519-2707
FAX: 217-352-1221
e-mail: rp@researchpress.com
www.researchpress.com

*Gail Salyards, Marketing Services Manager*
*Russell Pence, President*

The developers discuss and demonstrate how to use special relaxation procedures with children and adolescents who have developmental disabilities. They emphasize the need for students
to learn relaxation as a means of coping with stress and developing self-control. During the scenes of Dr June Groden conducting relaxation training, viewers will see how to correctly use the
training procedures, how to use reinforcement during training
and how to use guided imagery. 23 minutes. Includes book.
*$195.00*
*Video*

**7586 Right at Home**
Aquarius Health Care Videos
PO Box 1159
Sherborn, MA 01770

508-650-6905
FAX: 508-650-4216
e-mail: aqvideos@tiac.net
www.aquariusproductions.com

Shows simple solutions for complying with the Fair Hoiusing Act amendments. Emphasizes low-cost, practical solutions, and working with people with disabilities to find the best applicable solution. Ideal for people with disabilities and their families, as well as housing providers, university courses, and disability awareness organizations. Preview option is available. *$99.00*
> *Video*

**7587  Say it with Sign Videotape**
Harris Communications
15155 Technology Drive
Eden Prairie, MN  55344

952-906-1180
800-825-6758
FAX: 952-906-1099
e-mail: mail@harriscomm.com
www.harriscomm.com

*Bill Williams, National Sales Manager*
*Robert Harris, Owner*

Contains both the serious and fun side of signing and provides the basic signs that might be needed in an emergency situation. *$39.95*
> *Video*

**7588  Science Accessed for All Students**
Center for Accessible Technology
2547 8th Street
Suite 12a
Berkeley, CA  94710

510-841-3224
FAX: 510-841-7956
e-mail: info@cfarat.org
www.cforat.org

*Lisa Wahl, Director*
*Dmitri Belser, Manager*

A 10 minute video that demonstrates inclusive in elementary school science two peer support, adaptation of notifices and assistance technology. *$15.00*
> *Video*

**7589  See What I Feel**
Britannica Film Company
345 4th Street
San Francisco, CA  94107

415-777-9876

A blind child tells her friends about her trip to the zoo. Each experience was explained as a blind child would experience it. A teacher's guide comes with this video.
> *Film*

**7590  See What I'm Saying**
Fanlight Productions
4196 Washington Street
Suite 2
Boston, MA  02131

617-469-4999
800-937-4113
FAX: 617-469-3379
e-mail: fanlight@fanlight.com
www.fanlight.com

*Karen McMillen, Marketing Director*
*Ben Achtenberg, Owner*

This program illustrates how the acquisition of communication skill, particularly sign language, enhances a child's self esteem and family and peer relationship. The documentary follows Patricia, who is deaf and from a Spanish-speaking family, through her first year at the Kendall Demonstration Elementary School of Gallaudet University. *$195.00*

**7591  See for Yourself**
Lighthouse International
111 E 59th Street
New York, NY  10022

212-821-9200
800-829-0500
FAX: 212-821-9706
e-mail: info@lighthouse.org

*Joanna Mellor, VP Information Services*
*Tara Cortes, President*

This video features older adults with impaired vision who have been helped by vision rehabilitation. *$50.00*

**7592  Shape Up 'n Sign**
Gallaudet University Bookstore
11030 S Langley Avenue
Chicago, IL  60628

202-651-5488
800-621-2736
FAX: 202-651-5489

An aerobic exercise tape introducing the basic sign language for deaf and hearing children ages six to ten. *$22.95*
> *30 Minutes*

**7593  Shining Bright: Head Start Inclusion**
Brookes Publishing
PO Box 10624
Baltimore, MD  21285

410-337-9580
800-638-3775
FAX: 410-337-8539
e-mail: custserv@brookespublishing.com
www.brookespublishing.com

*Paul Brooks, Owner*

This documentary depicts the collaborative efforts of a Head Start and a local education agency to include children with severe disabilities in a Head Start program. This video addresses issues such as support for children with severe health impairments, benefits of participating in Head Start, ability of teachers with a general education background to serve children with severe disabilities, and staff relations. Includes a 28-page saddle-stitched booklet. *$45.00*
> *23 Minutes*
> *ISBN 1-55766-95-9*

**7594  Sight by Touch**
Landmark Media
3450 Slade Run Drive
Falls Church, VA  22042

703-241-2030
800-342-4336
FAX: 703-536-9540

*Michael Hartogs, President*

This video features the life and importance of Louis Braille. Vision-impaired performers and teachers demonstrate how Braille has benefitted their lives, and how improvements are constantly being made. *$195.00*
> *Video*

**7595  Sign of the Times**
Fanlight Productions
4196 Washington Street
Suite 2
Boston, MA  02131

617-469-4999
800-937-4113
FAX: 617-469-3379
e-mail: fanlight@fanlight.com
www.fanlight.com

*Karen McMillen, Marketing Director*
*Ben Achtenberg, Owner*

Profiles a public school in the heart of Los Angeles - an American microcosm where over 300 languages are spoken, and where cultures and races collide. Fairfax High, publicized as the site of gang activity and murder, has long been a focus for bad press. But something very right is going on in this school. A Sign of the Times offers a positive example of how the American dream and American education are still alive *$154.00*

**7596  Sleeping Beauty Videotape**
Gallaudet University Bookstore
11030 S Langley Avenue
Chicago, IL  60628

202-651-5488
800-621-2736
FAX: 202-651-5489

Presents the entire story of Sleeping Beauty told in American Sign Language. Includes voice over. *$29.95*

*30 Minutes*

**7597  Small Differences**
Aquarius Health Care Videos
PO Box 1159
Sherborn, MA  01770
508-650-6905
FAX: 508-650-4216
e-mail: aqvideos@tiac.net
www.aquariusproductions.com
What happens when you give children with and without disabilities a camera and ask them to produce a video about disabilities? The result is an uplifting, award-winning disability video that both children and adults can relate to. The kids interviewed adults and children with physical and sensory disabilities. A top-quality production that increases understanding and awareness. Winner, Columbus International Film & Video Festival. Winner, National Education Media Network. Preview option availabe *$110.00*
*Video*

**7598  Social Skills on the Job**
AGS
PO Box 99
Circle Pines, MN  55014
800-328-2560
FAX: 763-786-9007
www.agsnet.com

*Robert Zaske, Market Manager*

Gives students a realistic picture of what's expected of them at work and models appropriate behavior on the job through a variety of videos and software. *$259.95*

**7599  Someday's Child**
Educational Productions
9000 SW Gemini Drive
Beaverton, OR  97008
503-644-7000
800-950-4949
FAX: 503-350-7000
e-mail: custserv@edpro.com
www.edpro.com

*Linda Freedman, President/Co-Owner*
*Molly Krumm, Marketing Director*

This video focuses on three families' search for help and information for their children with disabilities.

**7600  Something Magical**
Educational Productions
9000 SW Gemini Drive
Beaverton, OR  97008
503-644-7000
800-950-4949
FAX: 503-350-7000
e-mail: custserve@edpro.com
www.edpro.com

*Linda Freedman, President/Co-Owner*
*Molly Krumm, Marketing Director*

In 1984 two teachers and one music therapist decided that a collaboration between their two schools would be mutually beneficial. The result is recorded in this heart-warming documentary.

**7601  Sound & Fury**
Aquarius Health Care Videos
PO Box 1159
Sherborn, MA  01770
508-650-6905
888-440-2963
FAX: 508-650-4216
e-mail: aqvideos@tiac.net
www.aquariusproductions.com

*Leslie Kussmann, President/Producer*

This film takes viewers inside the seldom seen world of the deaf to witness a painful family struggle over a controversial medical technology called the cochlear implant. Some of the family members celebrate the implant as a long overdue cure for deafness while others fear it will destroy their language and way of life. This documentary explores this seemingly irreconcilable conflict as it illuminates the ongoing struggle for identity among deaf people today. *$195.00*

*Video*

**7602  Special Children/Special Solutions**
Option Indigo Press
2080 S Undermountain Road
Sheffield, MA  01257
413-229-8727
800-562-7171
FAX: 413-229-8727
e-mail: indigo@option.org
www.optionindigo.com

*Kate Wilde*

This four-tape audio series presents concrete, down-to-earth, no-nonsense alternatives which are full of love and acceptance for the special child while being wholly supportive of parents, professionals and helpers who want to reach out. The accepting (nonjudgmental) attitude presented is the basis of all Samahria's work and is the foundation for the nurturing teaching process that has encouraged and helped parents, children and others to accomplish more than most would have believed. *$55.00*
*Audio*

**7603  Special Education Cassette Recording**
LifeWay Christian Resources Southern Baptist Conv.
127 9th Avenue N
Nashville, TN  37234
615-251-2089
800-458-2772
FAX: 651-251-5764
e-mail: specialed@lifeway.com
www.lifeway.com

*Ellen Beene, Editor*
*Wade Stapleton, Manager*

This annual audiocassette features the 12 unit songs suggested for a special education Sunday school curriculum. *$15.00*

**7604  Spinal Cord Injury Series**
Fanlight Productions
4196 Washington Street
Suite 2
Boston, MA  02131
617-469-4999
800-937-4113
FAX: 617-469-3379
e-mail: fanlight@fanlight.com
www.fanlight.com

*Karen McMillen, Marketing Director*
*Ben Achtenberg, Owner*

A series of three videos produced by an individual who has experienced spinal cord injury himself. Changes: is about the consequences of spinal cord injury and the process of rehabilitation. Outside: emphasizes the life-long aspect of rehabilitation for people with spinal cord injury. Survivors: interviews 23 men and women who have lived at least 24 years with spinal cord injury. *$200.00*

**7605  Stay Tuned**
Fanlight Productions
4196 Washington Street
Suite 2
Boston, MA  02131
617-469-4999
800-937-4113
FAX: 617-469-3379
e-mail: fanlight@fanlight.com
www.fanlight.com

*Karen McMillen, Marketing Director*
*Ben Achtenberg, Owner*

This program looks at ways of coping with hearing loss. The program introduces us to one woman who, after suffering a mid-life hearing loss, confronts her situation and regains her ability to function and enjoy her life through taking advantage of hearing aids, speech reading instruction, assistive listening devices and the support of other hearing impaired people. *$99.00*

**7606  Stuttering & Your Child: A Videotape for Parents**
Stuttering Foundation of America
PO Box 11749
Memphis, TN  38111

901-452-7343
800-992-9392
FAX: 901-452-3931
e-mail: stutter@vantek.net
www.stutterhelp.org

*Anne Edwards, Coordinator*
*Jane Fraser, President*

Provides parents withup-to-date information on what stuttering is; what is thought to cause and worsen childhood stuttering; what parents can do to help their child. *$10.00*

**7607  TERI**
3225 Roymar Road
Oceanside, CA  92054

760-721-1706

*Cheryl Kilmer, Executive Director*

A private, nonprofit corporation which has been developing and operating programs for individuals with developmental disabilities since 1980. Offers staff training videos, staff training tools and technique manuals.

**7608  Teaching People with Developmental Disabilities**
Research Press
PO Box 9177
Champaign, IL  61826

217-352-3273
800-519-2707
FAX: 217-352-1221
e-mail: rp@researchpress.com
www.researchpress.com

*Russell Pence, President*

Hands-on video training series designed to help teachers, staff, volunteers, or family members master four behavioral techniques vital to teaching functional living skills. The videotapes which provide clear and simple teaching demonstrations, are designed to be stopped and started frequently to allow time for viewer response. Each tape includes numerous scenes of training sessions in which teachers and staff are shown working with individual students. *$595.00*
*Video*

**7609  Technology for the Disabled**
Landmark Media
3450 Slade Run Drive
Falls Church, VA  22042

703-241-2030
800-342-4336
FAX: 703-536-9540

*Michael Hartogs, President*

Physically disabled people cope with the frustrations of a body they cannot control. The computer age has made many disabled more self-reliant; armless feed themselves, the blind read newspapers and the voiceless speak through marvelous technological breakthroughs. *$195.00*
*Video*

**7610  Telling Stories**
Harris Communications
15155 Technology Drive
Eden Prairie, MN  55344

952-906-1180
800-825-6758
FAX: 952-906-1099
e-mail: mail@harriscomm.com
www.harriscomm.com

*Bill Williams, National Sales Manager*
*Robert Harris, Owner*

This international award winning play, now on video, uses the symbols and myths drawn from the struggles between the world of the deaf and the world of the hearing. *$59.95*

*Video*

**7611  Theatre Without Limits**
VSA Arts of Maine
PO Box 4002
Portland, ME  04101

207-761-3861
FAX: 207-761-4740
e-mail: me@vsarts.org
vsartsmaine.org

*Kippy Rudy, Executive Director*

Video demonstrates how to make theatrical performances accessible to people who are blind, deaf, or who have other disabilities.

**7612  They Don't Come with Manuals**
Fanlight Productions
4196 Washington Street
Suite 2
Boston, MA  02131

617-469-4999
800-937-4113
FAX: 617-469-3379
e-mail: fanlight@fanlight.com
www.fanlight.com

*Karen McMillen, Marketing Director*
*Ben Achtenberg, Owner*

The parents and adoptive parents in this video speak candidly of their day to day experiences caring for children with physical and mental disabilities. *$145.00*

**7613  They're Just Kids**
Aquarius Health Care Videos
PO Box 1159
Sherborn, MA  01770

508-650-6905
888-440-2963
FAX: 508-650-4216
e-mail: aqvideos@tiac.net
www.aquariusproductions.com

*Leslie Kussmann, President/Producer*

The importance and value of inclusion, excellent for anyone working with kids with disabilities. The documentary explores the advantages of the inclusion of disabled children in the classroom, cub scouts and other extracurricular activities. *$99.00*
*Video*

**7614  Three R's for Special Education: Rights, Resources, Results**
Brookes Publishing
PO Box 10624
Baltimore, MD  21285

410-337-9580
800-638-3775
FAX: 410-337-8539
e-mail: custserv@brookespublishing.com
www.brookespublishing.com

*Paul Brooks, Owner*

This is a guide for parents, and a tool for educators. Through this video parents learn how to work through the steps of the special education system and work toward securing the best education and services for their children. Reviews the laws to protect children with disabilities in easy to understand language. Also provides a list of national organizations that can offer resources, information and advice to parents. *$49.95*
*50 Minutes*
*ISBN 0-96461 -80-7*

**7615  Tools for Students**
Aquarius Health Care Videos
PO Box 1159
Sherborn, MA  01770

508-650-6905
FAX: 508-650-4216
e-mail: aqvideos@tiac.net
www.aquariusproductions.com

Provides a series of 26 fun occupational therapy sensory processing activities. Designed as an in-home, in-workshop, and in-class exercise leader with students. Activities include: Strenghten the muscles necessary for normal activities, provide the muscles necessary to enhance alertness and concentration, increase the ability to use good posture, help social skills and fitting in and increase coordination; concludes with emphasis on team collaboration between the student, teacher, and parents. *$99.00*
*Video*

**7616 Tools for Teachers: Practical Strategies f or Students with ADD & Learning Disabilities**
Aquarius Health Care Videos
PO Box 1159
Sherborn, MA 01770                    508-650-6905
                                       FAX: 508-650-4216
                                  e-mail: aqvideos@tiac.net
                                  www.aquariusproductions.com
Designed to provide a beneficial overview, Tools for Teachers is ideal for in-service programs, parent education, teacher familiarization, and group discussion. Useful for an adult audience, it explains why students rock in their chairs, why a student may have so much difficulty coordinating hand movements, why untreated sensory integration deficits can bring all kinds of problems in the classroom, how inclusion can be successful, and how OT techniques can help build successful education. *$99.00*
*Video*

**7617 Trackman: Y-Saves (Youth Substance Abuse Video Educational Series)**
Michigan Association for Deaf, Hearing and Speech
2929 Covington Court
Lansing, MI 48912                      517-487-0066
                                       800-YOU-HEAR
                                  e-mail: yourear@msu.edu
                                       www.madhs.org

*Nancy Asher, Executive Director*
*Jody Smith, Program Director*

A three part substance abuse, educational video program created by the Michigan Association for Deaf, Hearing and Speech services. The program provides a stimulating format for educating youth about drugs and alcohol. This video was written and produced especially for deaf middle and high school students, but is appropriate for all youth as it includes signing, open captioning and voice overs. An extensive guide provides guidance and plenty of ideas for activities and exercises.

**7618 Twitch and Shout**
Fanlight Productions
4196 Washington Street
Suite 2
Boston, MA 02131                       617-469-4999
                                       800-937-4113
                                       FAX: 617-469-3379
                                  e-mail: fanlight@fanlight.com
                                       www.fanlight.com

*Karen McMillen, Marketing Director*
*Cynthia Conti, Publicity Coordinator*
*Laurel Chiten, Producer*

This documentary provides an intimate journey into the startling world of Tourette Syndrome (TS), a genetic disorder that can cause a bizarre range of involuntary movements, vocalizations, and compulsions. Through the eyes of a photojournalist with TS, the film introduces viewers to others who have this puzzling disorder. This is an emotionally absorbing, sometimes, unsettling, and finally uplifting program about people who must contend with a society that often sees them as crazy or bad. *$275.00*

**7619 Understanding ADHD**
Aquarius Health Care Videos
PO Box 1159
Sherborn, MA 01770                     508-650-6905
                                       FAX: 508-650-4216
                                  e-mail: aqvideos@tiac.net
                                  www.aquariusproductions.com

A look at some of the controversies surrounding Attention Deficit Hyperactivity Disorder. This video shows how the disorder is diagnosed and presents strategies for living with a child with the disorder. Diverse and candid opinions from teachers, social workers, a behavior specialist, a pediatrician and a parent with ADHD twins. Recommended for child development students, social workers, and caregivers. Preview option available. *$120.00*
*Video*

**7620 Understanding Allergic Reactions**
Academy of Allergy, Asthma, Immunology
611 E Wells Street
Milwaukee, WI 53202                    414-272-6071
                                       800-822-2762
                                  FAX: 414-272-6070
                                  e-mail: info@aaaai.org
                                       www.aaaai.org

*Kay Whalen, Executive Vice President*

During an allergic reaction, your body responds to a substance generally considered harmless to most people. This video portrays what happens in you body's immune system during an allergic reaction, how to avoid allergic substances, and methods your allergist uses to treat your allergies. *$25.00*
*10-13 Minutes*

**7621 Understanding Attention Deficit Disorder**
CACLD
25 Van Zant Street
Suite 15-5
Norwalk, CT 06855                      203-838-5010
                                       FAX: 203-866-6108
                                  e-mail: CACLD@optonline.net
                                       www.CACLD.org

*Beryl Kaufman, Executive Director*

A video in an interview format for parents and professionals providing the history, symptoms, methods of diagnosis and three approaches used to ease the effects of attention deficit disorder. Published by Connecticut Association for Children & Adults with Learning Disabilities (CACLD). *$20.00*
*45 Minutes*

**7622 Understanding Autism**
Fanlight Productions
4196 Washington Street
Suite 2
Boston, MA 02131                       617-469-4999
                                       800-937-4113
                                       FAX: 617-469-3379
                                  e-mail: fanlight@fanlight.com
                                       www.fanlight.com

*Karen McMillen, Marketing Director*
*Ben Achtenberg, Owner*

This program explores some basic components of a behavioral analysis approach to educating individuals with autism. After giving an introduction to the disability, the program goes on to illustrate the principles of reinforcement, teaching methods and data collection and analysis, as well as outlining the philosophy behind using behavior modification techniques with children with autism. *$195.00*

**7623 Understanding Learning Disabilities**
Aquarius Health Care Videos
PO Box 1159
Sherborn, MA 01770                     508-650-6905
                                       FAX: 508-650-4216
                                  e-mail: aqvideos@tiac.net
                                  www.aquariusproductions.com
This video explains various learning disabilities that may effect many areas - language, reading, math skills, and behavior. Attention Deficit Disorder is gaining a lot of press these days and here we see the link between it and other disorders. Teaching children new ways to overcome their disability is shown in a how-to method. Preview option available. *$125.00*

*Video*

**7624  Upstate Update**
New York State Talking Book & Braille Library
Empire State Plaza Cec
Albany, NY  12230                              518-474-5935
                                          FAX: 518-486-1957
                                          TTY:518-474-7121
                                   e-mail: tbbl@mail.nysed.gov
                                      www.nysl.nysed.gov/tbbl

*Jane Somers, Regional Librarian/Manager*
*Peter Douglas, Editor*

Books on audio cassette, cassette players, braille books, summer
reading programs, braille writer, magnifiers, closed-circuit
T.V., large-print photocopier, cassette books and magazines,
children's books on cassette, reference materials on blindness
and other handicaps.
                    *4 pages Quarterly*

**7625  Video Guide to Disability Awareness**
Aquarius Health Care Videos
PO Box 1159
Sherborn, MA  01770                            508-650-6905
                                          FAX: 508-650-4216
                                       e-mail: aqvideos@tiac.net
                                    www.aquariusproductions.com
President Clinton opens and concludes this informative video
about disability awareness. A series of candid interviews with
people who have a wide range of disabilities provide personal insights into the issues surrounding visual, hearing, physical and
mental disabilities. Video comes with written reference guide
and is also available with open or closed captioning. Preview option available. *$195.00*
                    *Video*

**7626  Video Intensive Parenting**
Systems Unlimited/LIFE Skills
1556 S 1st Avenue
Iowa City, IA  52240                           319-338-9212

*Ginny Kirschling, Public Information Specialist*
*Geoffrey Lauer, Program Director*
*Bill Gorman, President*

Parents who have children with special needs share their reactions to their child's diagnosis and how they have learned to cope
with their feelings. *$69.95*

**7627  Vital Signs: Crip Culture Talks Back**
Fanlight Productions
4196 Washington Street
Suite 2
Boston, MA  02131                              617-469-4999
                                               800-937-4113
                                          FAX: 617-469-3379
                                   e-mail: fanlight@fanlight.com
                                          www.fanlight.com

*Karen McMillen, Marketing Director*
*Cynthia Conti, Publicity Coordinator*
*Ben Achtenberg, Owner*

This edgy, raw video documentary explores the politics of disability through the performances, debates and late-night conversations of artists at a recent national conference of disabilities
and the art's. Vital Signs conveys the intensity, variety and vitality of disability culture today. *$225.00*

*Video*

**7628  We Are PHAMALY**
4196 Washington Street
Suite 2
Boston, MA  02131                              617-469-4999
                                               800-937-4113
                                          FAX: 617-469-3379
                                    e-mail: info@fanlight.com
                                          www.fanlight.com

*Sandy St Louis, Distribution Director*
*Kelli English, Publicity Coordinator*
*Ben Achtenberg, Owner*

Stands for Physically Handicapped Musical Actors League.
This dynamic troupe doesn't cut any corners or make any
comprmises. The musicals they perform are chosen for their appeal to the audience, not because they are easy for the performers, who have a variety of sensory and mobility handicaps.
*$199.00*

                    *ISBN 1-572954-08-6*

**7629  We're Not Stupid**
Aquarius Health Care Videos
PO Box 1159
Sherborn, MA  01770                            508-650-6905
                                          FAX: 508-650-4216
                                       e-mail: aqvideos@tiac.net
                                    www.aquariusproductions.com
The U.S. Department of Education has estimated that up to five
percent of students have problems in school because of attention
deficit disorders. These kids often are impulsive and angry.
They hear throughout their schooling what not to do, but not
what to do. I know because I was diagnosed in high school with
mild dyslexia and ADD. This film is about people discussing
what their lives were like having learning problems. *$125.00*
                    *Video*

**7630  What About Me?**
Educational Productions
9000 SW Gemini Drive
Beaverton, OR  97008                           503-644-7000
                                               800-950-4949
                                          FAX: 503-350-7000
                                   e-mail: custserve@edpro.com
                                          www.edpro.com

*Linda Freedman, President/Co-Owner*
*Molly Krumm, Marketing Director*

This video focuses on two siblings of children with disabilities.
The siblings (Brian and Julie) share their perspectives, their
worries, concerns and victories about living with a sibling with a
disability.

**7631  What Can Baby Hear?: Auditory Tests and In
terventions for Infants with Multiple Disabilities**
Brookes Publishing
PO Box 10624
Baltimore, MD  21285                           410-337-9580
                                               800-638-3775
                                          FAX: 410-337-8539
                              e-mail: custserv@brookespublishing.com
                                    www.brookespublishing.com

*Paul Brooks, Owner*

This video and accompanying booklet explain the principles and
methods of various auditory tests designed for early detection
and teach viewers how to assess infants' auditory needs to begin
appropriate intervention. *$45.00*

*30 Minutes 1997*
*ISBN 1-557662-88-6*

**7632  What School Personnel Should Know About Asthma**
American Lung Association
61 Broadway
New York, NY 10006                    212-315-8700
                              FAX: 212-315-8700
                         e-mail: info@lungusa.org
                              www.lungusa.org

*John Kirkwood, Chief Executive Officer*

Professionally produced videotape discussing the triggers, symptoms and management of childhood asthma.
*Video*

**7633  When Billy Broke His Head...and Other Tales of Wonder**
Fanlight Productions
4196 Washington Street
Suite 2
Boston, MA 02131                     617-469-4999
                                   800-937-4113
                              FAX: 617-469-3379
                         e-mail: info@fanlight.com
                              www.fanlight.com

*Elena Cambio*
*Ben Achtenberg, Owner*

When Billy Golfus, an award-winning journalist, became brain damaged as the result of a motor scooter accident, he joined the ranks of the 43 million Americans with disabilities, this country's largest and most invisible minority. He helped create this video, which blends humor with politics and individual experience with a chorus of voices, to explain what it is really like to live with a disability in America. #136 *$195.00*

*ISBN 1-57295 -36-2*

**7634  When I Grow Up**
Britannica Film Company
345 4th Street
San Francisco, CA 94107              415-777-9876

At a costume party each child was to come as what they wanted to be when they grew up. Some of the children had handicaps, and they talked about why their handicaps would not prevent them from fulfilling their desires.
*Film*

**7635  When Parents Can't Fix It**
Fanlight Productions
4196 Washington Street
Suite 2
Boston, MA 02131                     617-469-4999
                                   800-937-4113
                              FAX: 617-469-3379
                       e-mail: fanlight@fanlight.com
                              www.fanlight.com

*Karen McMillen, Marketing Director*
*Cynthia Conti, Publicity Coordinator*
*Ben Achtenberg, Owner*

This documentary looks at the lives of five families who are raising children with disabilities - the problems they face, how they have learned to cope, and the rewards and stresses of adapting to their child's condition. It explores the medical complexities and financial pressures families encounter, the emotional and physical toll on parents and siblings, and the dangers of child abuse in this population. It offers a very realistic look at different family strengths and coping styles. *$245.00*

**7636  When the Brain Goes Wrong**
Fanlight Productions
4196 Washington Street
Suite 2
Boston, MA 02131                     617-469-4999
                                   800-937-4113
                              FAX: 617-469-3379
                         e-mail: info@fanlight.com
                              www.fanlight.com

*Elena Cambio, Contact*
*Ben Achtenberg, Owner*

An extraordinary and provocative series of seven short films which profile individuals with a range of brian dysfunctions. The seven brief segments focus on schizophrenia, manic depression, epilepsy, head injury, headaches and addiction. In addition to the personal stories, the segments include interviews with physicians who speak briefly about what is known about the disorders and treatment. #131 *$245.00*

*ISBN 1-572951-31-1*

**7637  Why My Child**
                                   800-313-ABDC
                              www.birthdefects.org
A 9 1/2 minute video that explores the feelings every parent has when their child is born with a birth defect. Emmy-award-winning producer, Karen Dorsett, has created a compelling video that begins with the parents' question, why my child? Follows through to concerns about links between birth defects and environmental exposures to drugs, pesticides, dioxin, radiation, hazardous wastes, etc. *$25.00*

**7638  Why Won't My Child Pay Attention?**
Western Psychological Services
12031 Wilshire Boulevard
Los Angeles, CA 90025                310-478-2061
                                   800-648-8857
                              FAX: 310-478-7838

*Gregg Gillman, Vice President*

Practical and reassuring videotape, noted child psychologist tells parents about two of the most common and complex problems of childhood: inattention and hyperactivity. *$49.50*
*Video*

**7639  With Standing Ovation**
Aquarius Health Care Videos
PO Box 1159
Sherborn, MA 01770                   508-650-6905
                              FAX: 508-650-4216
                         e-mail: aqvideos@tiac.net
                         www.aquariusproductions.com
Profiles two dynamic young people, Peaches and Daniel, who were born with severe congenital limb deformities; spent much of their time as children in hospitals learning to use mechanical prostheses to aid them in their daily activities. Despite the training however, both shed the devices and mastered active and creative lives with only a minimal reliance on their prostheses. Encourages health care providers to view their occupational therapy and rehabilitation patients as people with abilities. *$195.00*
*Video*

**7640  Without Pity**
Aquarius Health Care Videos
PO Box 1159
Sherborn, MA 01770                   508-650-6905
                              FAX: 508-650-4216
                         e-mail: aqvideos@tiac.net
                         www.aquariusproductions.com
This HBO documentary, narratd by Christopher Reeve, celebrates the efforts of the disabled to live full, productive lives. We meet a cross section of Americans. A young woman with cerebral palsy cares for her baby, while a man with cerebral palsy lives successfully on his own after forty years in an institution. We go to tschool with a remarkable 6-year-old without arms or legs, visit the workplace of a blind computer expert and meet a professor with polio. Preview option is available. *$129.00*

*Video*

**7641  Work Sight**
Lighthouse International
111 E 59th Street
New York, NY  10022

212-821-9200
800-829-0500
FAX: 212-821-9706
e-mail: info@lighthouse.org

*Joanna Mellor, VP Information Services*
*Tara Cortes, President*

Intended for employers and employees who have concerns about vision loss and job performance. *$25.00*

**7642  World Through Their Eyes**
Lighthouse International
111 E 59th Street
New York, NY  10022

212-821-9200
800-829-0500
FAX: 212-821-9706
e-mail: info@lighthouse.org

*Joanna Mellor, VP Information Services*
*Tara Cortes, President*

Intended to help nursing home staff understand how residents with impaired vision perceive the world. Concrete suggestions help staff provide better care to visually impaired residents. *$25.00*

---

# Web Sites

**7643  Abledata**

disabilities.about.com/health/disabili
Premier source for information on assistive technology.

**7644  Ablewear Aids for Daily Living**

www.ableware.com
Quality products to achieve independence in performing daily living activities.

**7645  Academy for Educational Development**

www.aed.org
Committed to addressing human development needs in the United States and throughout the world.

**7646  Access Unlimited**

accessunlimited.com
Adaptive transportation and mobility equipment for people with disabilities.

**7647  Ai Squared**

www.aisquared.com
Leaders in low vision software.

**7648  Alternatives in Education for the Hearing Impaired (AEHI)**

www.aehi.org
AEHI fosters literacy and empowers people with hearing impairments to achieve their full potential through unique educational options.

**7649  American Academy of Audiology**

www.audiology.org

**7650  American Association of People with Disabilities**

www.aapd.com
Non-profit, non-partisan, cross-disability, national membership organization whose goals are unity, leadership and impact. AAPD's mission is to advance the economic and political power of all people with disabilities.

**7651  American Botanical Council**

www.herbalgram.org
Conducts research and provides education on the safe, responsible and scientific uses of medicine herbs to the public, healthcare professionals, government, industry, and the media.

**7652  American College of Rheumatology Research and Education Foundation**

www.rheumatology.org
Arthritis afflictsone in every seven Americans. Your gift supports research, investigates the causes, improves treatment and works toward the prevention and cure of arthritis.

**7653  American Liver Foundation**

www.liverfoundation.org
Is the only national voluntary health organization dedicated to preventing, treating, and curing hepatitis and other liver and gall bladder diseases through research and education.

**7654  American Mobility: Personal Mobility Solutions**

www.americanmobility.com
Source of Pride Scooters, Jazzy Power Chairs, personal mobility vehicles, and lift and recline chairs.

**7655  American Speech-Language and Hearing Association**

www.asha.org
Exhibits by companies specializing in alternative and augmentative communications products, publishers, software and hardware compinies, and hearing aid testing equipment manufacturers.

**7656  Americans with Disabilities Act: ADA Home Page**

www.usdoj.gov
Provides facts on the Americans with Disabilities Act and other information relating to disability rights.

**7657  Appliance 411**

appliance411.com
A guide to remodeling and appliances for people with disabilities.

**7658  Arc of the United States**

www.thearc.org
National organization of and for people with mental retardation anad thier families.

**7659  Assist.com**

www.assist.com
Assistive technology web resource.

**7660  Assistive Technology Disabilities**

www.netins.net
Provides information on assistive technology.

**7661  Association for the Cure of Cancer of the Prostate**

www.capcure.org.il
CURE is a nonprofit public charity that is dedicated to supporting prostate cancer research and hastening the conversion of research into cures or controls.

**7662  Asthma and Allergy Foundation of America**

www.aafa.org
Supports research to cure asthma and allergies and helps sufferers through patient education, practical advice, and a nationwide chapter and support group network.

**7663  Audiology Foundation of America**

www.audfound.org
Commited to fostering the education and training of audiologists to meet the needs of the public, especially those with impaired hearing.

**7664  Auditory-Verbal International**

www.auditory-verbal.org

**7665  Beebe Center**

www.beebecenter.org
At the Beebe Center our mission is to help hearing-impaired children to listen and talk.

**7666  Cancer Biotherapy Research Group**

members.aol.com/cancerccsi
Cancer patients receive promising treatments in their communities through a nationwide research network of physicians and hospitals. All contributions are used to fund clinical research.

**7667  Cancer Immunology Research Foundation**

www.cancer-research.org
Immunology research will discover why the immune system fails and cancer develops. Herein lies the cure for cancer, AIDS, and other autoimmune diseases.

**7668  Cancer Immunotherapy and Gene Therapy Institute**

www.skcc.org
Researches effective, non-toxic therapies for cancer. Accelerates taking promising discoveries from the laboratories to clinics to treat people victimized by cancer. Treatments given at no charge.

**7669  Cancer Research Fund of Damon Runyon: Walter Winchell Foundation**

www.cancerresearchfund.org
Goal is to cure cancer. 100% of your gift funds research. With 49 Runyon-Winchell scientists who have won Nobel Prizes, chances are good.

**7670  Center on the Social & Emotional Foundations for Early Learning**

csefel.uiuc.edu
The center will: focus on promoting the social and emotional developmental of children as a means of preventing challenging behaviors; collaborate with existing T/TA providers for the purpose of ensuring the implementation and sustainability of practices at the local level; provide ongoing identification of training needs and preferred delivery formats of local programs and T/TA providers; disseminate evidence-based practices.

**7671  Disability Information and Resources**

www.eskimo.com

**7672  Disability Mall**

www.disabilityproducts.com
Online directory committed to featuring information on disability and medical products, resources and services, with over 2,500 links including over 400 companies for one-stop shopping convenence.

**7673  Disability Net**

www.bargione.co.uk/disabled.htm
The internet resource for disabled people that offers the latest news and events.

**7674  Disability Rights Activist**

www.disrights.org
Provides information to enable anyone intersted in the rights of disabled people to work for those rights.

**7675  DisabilityResources.org**

www.disabilityresources.org
Provides information on disability-related material on the Web.

**7676  Discover Technology**

discovertechnology.com
Provides links to websites that are specifically geared toward persons with disabilities who have special interest in adaptive technology.

**7677  Dynamic Living**

www.dynamic-living.com
Kitchen products, bathroom helpers, and unique daily living products that provide a convienient, comfortable, and safe environment for people with disabilities.

**7678  ElderLawAnswers.com**

www.elderlawanswers.com

Provides information about legal issues facing senior citizens and a searchable directory of attorneys.

**7679  Exploring Autism: A Look at the Genetics of Autism**

www.exploringautism.org

Dedicated to helping families who are living with the challenges of autism stay informed about the exciting breakthroughs involving the genetics of autism. Report and explain new genetic research findings. Explain genetic principles as they relate to autism, provide the latest research news, and seek your imput.

**7680  Federal Resource Center for Special Education**

www.dss.org

**7681  Foundation Fighting Blindness**

www.blindness.org

Largest voluntary, non-government sponsor to cure retinitis pigmentosa (RP), macular degeneration and related inherited disorders—leading causes of blindness and deaf-blindness.

**7682  Freedom Scientific**

www.hj.com

Assistive technology for blind and visually impaired computer users.

**7683  Gallaudet University Press**

www.gallaudet.edu

Source for titles on deafness and deaf related subjects.

**7684  Glaucoma Research Foundation**

www.glaucoma.org

Protecting both sight and independence for those with glaucoma, by providing improved treatments and education today and by leading research towards a cure for tomorrow.

**7685  Herb Research Foundation**

www.herbs.org

Research and public education on the health benefits of medicinal plants. Dedicated to world health through the informed use of herbs.

**7686  Hypokalemic Periodic Paralysis Resource Page**

www.periodicparalysis.org/PPRC/PP

Provides understandable information on HKPP, dynamia linkage to several additional sources of helpful information on the Internet, and offers several online networking opportunities.

**7687  Innovation Management Group**

www.imgpresents.com

US and international onscreen keyboards, Word Prediction, Switch Scanning, Hover and Dwell, Joystick emulation, and Magnification software programs.

**7688  Interstitial Cystitis Association**

www.ichelp.com

Providing information, support and assistance to the patients of Interstitial Cystitis, a highly debilitating bladder disease. We'll find a cure by funding and encouraging research.

**7689  LDOnLine**

www.ldonline.org

The interactive guide to learning disabilities for parents, teachers, and children.

**7690  Learning Disabilities Association of America (LDA)**

www.ldanatl.org

Our purpose is to advance the education and general welfare of children and adults of normal or potentially normal intelligence who manifest disabilities of a perceptual, conceptual, or coordinative nature.

**7691  Lyme Disease Foundation**

www.lyme.org

Provides critical information about tick-borne disease prevention, improves healthcare and funds research for solutions. 500,000 children, adults, and professionals assisted 25 countries.

**7692  Mainstream Online Magazine of the Able-Disabled**

www.mainstream-mag.com

The leading news, advocacy and lifestyle magazine for people with disabilities.

**7693  Med-Sell**

www.kansas.net/~cbaslock/classifi

Helps people buy and sell new and previously owned medical equipment and find accessible housing.

**7694  Medem Network Societies American Academy of Opthamology**

www.medem.com

Physician web site service empowered by the leading medical specialty societies.

**7695  Microsoft Accessibility Technology for Everyone**

microsoft.com/enable/

Information about accessibility features and options included in Microsoft products.

**7696  MossRehab ResourceNet**

www.mossresourcenet.org

Accessible travel, disability fact sheets, ADA, newsgroups, search tools.

**7697  Multiple Sclerosis National Research Institute**

www.ms-national-research.org

Conducts research for development of a vaccine to halt progression of mutiple sclerosis. Initial patient trials show promising results. Help us find a cure soon.

**7698 National Alliance of the Disabled (NAOTD)**

www.naotd.org
Premier source for information on assistive technology.

**7699 National Association for Visually Handicapped**

www.navh.org
Works with millions of people worldwide in dealing with the difficulties of vision impairment.

**7700 National Brain Tumor Foundation**

www.braintumor.org
Brain tumors strike children and adults in the prime of life. Your support gives help and gives hope by funding research and patient support services.

**7701 National Business & Disability Council**

www.business-disability.com
Works toward furthering the intersts of business and people with disabilities.

**7702 National Organization on Disability**

www.nod.org

**7703 National Rehabilitation Center**

www.naric.com
Serves both professionals and the general public intersted in disability and rehabilitation.

**7704 National Women's Health Information Center**

www.4women.gov
Provides information for women with disabilities, health professionals, researchers, and caretakers.

**7705 NeuroControl Corporation**

www.neurocontrol.com
Helps people with spinal cord injuries lead more independent lives.

**7706 Office of Juvenile Justice and Delinquency Prevention**

www.childrenwithdisabilities.ncjrs.org
Offers information and resources to disabled children, their families and service providers. This site is part of a joint effort by several federal agencies to promote a national agenda for children and foster positve youth development, and will provide informatin on learning disabilities, debilitating conditions and physical disabilities. It will include the latest research, programs and events designed specifically for children with disabilities.

**7707 Osteogenesis Imperfecta Foundation**

www.oif.org
Strives to improve the quality of life for indivduals with this brittle bone disorder through research, education, awareness, and mutual support.

**7708 Quantum Technology**

www.quantech.com
Provides access to information and tools for independence to serve the visually impaired and those with a learning disability.

**7709 Research!America**

www.researchamerica.org
Builds active public support for more government and private-industry research to find treatments and cures for both physical and mental disorders.

**7710 Skin and Dental Dysfunction Foundation**

www.nfed.org
Children left toothless from Ectodermal Dysplasia are provided dentures, support services and education. Established by National Foundation for Ectodermal Dysplasias which searches for a cure.

**7711 Social Security Online**

www.ssa.gov
Official website of the Social Secuirity Administration.

**7712 Special Clothes for Special Children**

www.special-clothes.com
A catalog of adaptive clothing for children with disabilities - helping boys and girls with special needs meet the world with pride and confidence since 1987.

**7713 Standard Search: Oral Health Care for People with Developmental Disabilities**

www.nohic.nidcr.hih.gov
Helps meet the information needs of special care patients and health care providers. Staff provides the custom or standardized services on special care topics in oral health, including developmental disabilities. Each record in the search contains a bibliographic citation and abstract including info for the user on how to obtain materials directly.

**7714 V Foundation for Cancer Research**

www.jimmyv.org
Named for basketball coach and broadcaster, Jim Valvano. The V Foundation funds critical stage research conducted by young researchers at NCI approved cancer research facilities.

**7715 ValueOptions**

www.valueoptions.com
Serves over 22 million people in behavioral healthcare through publicaly funded, federal, and commercial contracts.

**7716 Wardrobe Wagon: The Special Needs Clothing Store**

www.wardrobewagon.com
Wearing apparel for individuals with special clothing needs.

**7717 We Magazine**

www.icdri.org/NEWS/WEMagazine.htm
Lifestyle magazine for people with disabilities.

**7718  We Media**

www.wemedia.com
Online network for people with disabilities.

**7719  WebABLE**

www.hisoftware.com/press/webable.html
Provides disability-related internet resources.

**7720  WheelchairNet**

www.wheelchairnet.org

**7721  World Association of Persons with Disabilities**

www.wapd.org
Dedicated to improving the quality of life for those with disabilities.

## Associations

**7722  Access to Sailing**
6475 E Pacific Coast Highway
Long Beach, CA  90803                    562-433-0561

e-mail: info@accesstosailing.org
www.access2sailing.org

*Duncan Milne, Founder*
Sports association.

**7723  Achilles Track Club**
42 W 38th Street
4th Floor
New York, NY  10018                      212-354-0300
FAX: 212-354-3978
e-mail: achillestc@aol.com

*Mary Bryant, Executive Director*
Organization whose goal is to guide disabled athletes into the able-bodied community. Quarterly newsletter has affiliate chapters in various cities overseas.
*8 pages*

**7724  Adaptive Sports Center**
PO Box 1639
Crested Butte, CO  81224                  970-349-2296
866-349-2296
FAX: 970-349-4950
e-mail: info@adaptivesports.org
www.adaptivesports.org

*Christopher Hensley, Executive Director*
*Karen Render, Summer Program Director*
Year round adaptive, adventure recreation program located at the base of Crested Butte Mountain Resort, Crested Butte ,CO. The Adaptive Sports Centers provides adaptive downhill and cross country ski lessons, ski rentals and snowboarding lessons in the winter. Offers a variety of wilderness based programs in the summer including multi-day trips into the back country, extensive cycling programs, canoeing, and white water rafting.

**7725  American Blind Bowling Association**
315 N Main Street
Mercer, PA  16137                         724-662-5748

*Judy Refosco, President*
Promotes blind bowling throughout the US and Canada by sanctioning blind bowling leagues and conducting a National Tournament. Current membership exceeds 2,000 people in the United States and Canada.

**7726  American Hearing Impaired Hockey Association**
1143 W Lake Street
Chicago, IL  60607                        312-226-5880
FAX: 312-829-2098
e-mail: cheryl_hager@ahiha.org
www.ahiha.org

*Stan Mikita, Co Founder/President*
*Irv Tiahnybik, Manager*
Supports hockey for hearing-impaired youths.

**7727  American Wheelchair Bowling Association**
PO Box 69
Clover, VA  24534                         434-454-2269
FAX: 434-454-6276
TTY:954-630-2566
e-mail: bowlawba@aol.com
www.awba.org

*Dave Roberts, Executive Secretary*
Sports association.

**7728  Blind Outdoor Leisure Development**
PO Box M
Aspen, CO  81612                          970-923-0578
800-530-3907
FAX: 970-923-7338
e-mail: possibilities@challengeaspen.com
www.challengeaspen.com

*Houston Cowan, Executive Director*
Outdoor recreation for the blind. Winter program of skiing with guides plus numerous summer programs for the visually impaired.

**7729  Chesapeake Region Accessible Boating**
PO Box 6564
Annapolis, MD  21401                      410-974-2628
FAX: 410-263-1703
e-mail: info@crab-sailing.org
www.crab-sailing.org

*Donald Backe, Executive Director*
*Howard Baker, Program Director*
CRAB provides opportunities for the disabled and their friends to sail the Chesapeake Bay. Day sails, lessons, organized races. Call for charter information. Sail for free on the fourth Sunday of each month, May through October.

**7730  Disabled Sports USA**
451 Hungerford Drive
Suite 100
Rockville, MD  20850                      301-217-0960
FAX: 301-217-0968
e-mail: kbauer@dusa.org
www.dsusa.org

*Kirk Bauer, Executive Director*
*Cherly Collins, Administrative Services Manager*
*Patty Cornelius, Program Service Coordinator*
Provides year-round sports and recreation opportunities for people with physical disabilities, veterans and non-veterans alike, such as sanctioned regional and national events in alpine and Nordic skiing, cycling, shooting swimming, table tennis, track and field, volleyball, and weightlifting. The organization handles physical disabilities which restrict mobility, including amputations paraplegia, quadriplegia, cerebral palsy, head injury, mulitple sclerosis, muscular dystrophy, and more.

**7731  Disabled Watersports Program Mission Bay Aquatic Center**
1001 Santa Clara Place
San Diego, CA  92109                      619-488-1036
FAX: 619-488-9625
www.americanamputee.org

*Peter K Ballantyne, Program Manager*
*Marci Honstead, Program Coordinator*
A cooperative, collegiate waterfront facility which is intended and designed to provide water-oriented programs and equipment and to be a resource center for water oriented sports and activities of all types, instructional and recreational. Since 1980, the center has offered aquatic activities for disabled individuals. This program serves hundreds of people yearly throughout the southwest United States and particularly San Diego, and serves as a model for similar programs.

**7732  FORE! Future Opportunity for Recreation and Employment for the Handicapped**
Southern California Golf Association
3740 Cahuenga Boulevard
North Hollywood, CA 91604

818-980-3630
800-554-7242
e-mail: info@scga.org
www.scga.org

*Bill Cunnerty, President*
*Errol Shaw, Vice President*
*Tom Morgan, Executive Director*

Golfing association for the physically handicapped.

**7733  Handicapped Scuba Association International**
Handicapped Scuba Association
1104 El Prado
San Clemente, CA 92672

949-498-4540
FAX: 949-498-6128
e-mail: hsa@hsascuba.com
www.hsascuba.com

*Jim Gatacre, Founder*
*Patricia Derk, Vice President*

A nonprofit volunteer organization dedicated to improving the physical and social well being of those with special needs through the exhilarating sport of scuba diving. An educational program for able bodied scuba instructors to learn to teach and certify people with special needs. Accessible travel opportunities. Publishes quarterly newsletter.

**7734  ISC: National Organization of People with Physical Disabilities**
16 Liberty Street
Larkspur, CA 94939

415-924-3549
FAX: 415-927-9556
e-mail: russab@earthlink.net
www.localcommunities.org

*Ellen Lieber, President*

Providing opportunities for the handicapped to participate in accessible community activities is the objective of this service organization which has regional chapters in many states.

**7735  Lakeshore Foundation**
4000 Ridgeway Drive
Birmingham, AL 35209

205-313-7400
FAX: 205-313-7475
e-mail: information@lakeshore.org
www.lakeshore.org

*Norman B Davis Jr, Vice President*
*Jeffery Underwood, President*

Offers fitness, recreation and competitive sports programs for persons with physical disabilities.

**7736  Leaning Tower YMCA: Conquerors Gym and Swim Program**
Leaning Tower Y MC A
6300 W Touhy Avenue
Niles, IL 60714

708-647-8222
FAX: 708-647-7736
e-mail: leaningtower@ymcacommunity.net
www.campdepot.com

*Samantha Vircol, Director*
*Chris Bertana, Director*

Mission to support the spiritual, mental and physical well being of inviduals and families in order to improve their quality of life. Provides quality programs to meet the need of the individuals with and without disabilities.

**7737  National Deaf Bowling Association**
9244 E Mansfield Avenue
Denver, CO 80237

303-771-9018

*Van K Scheppach, President*
*Russell Stecker, VP*
*Keith Thompson, Publishing Director*

Holds world Deaf Bowling Torunament annually in July. Also holds Las Vegas Scratch Classic annually in October.

**7738  National Disability Sports Alliance**
25 W Independence Way
Kingston, RI 02881

401-792-7130
FAX: 401-792-7132
e-mail: info@ndsaonline.org
www.ndsaonline.org

*Jerry McCole, Executive Director*

Serves to present disabled athletes with the opportunity to perform in many different sports. Participants range from the beginning athlete to the elite, international caliber athlete.

**7739  National Skeet Shooting Association**
5931 Roft Road
San Antonio, TX 78253

210-688-3371
800-877-5338
FAX: 210-688-3014
e-mail: nssa@nssa-nsca.com
www.nssa-nsca.com

*Don Snyder, Executive Director*
*Carl Hensch, Director*

Offers information on sporting clay targets for the disabled hunter.

**7740  National Wheelchair Basketball Association**
6917 Grand Prairie Drive
Colorado Springs, CO 80923

719-266-4082

e-mail: toddhatfield@nwba.org
www.nwba.org

*Todd Hatfield, Program Manager*
*Dick Bryant, Commissioner*

Founded in 1949, engages in the interpretation and standardization of competitive regulations for all teams playing organized wheelchair basketball. Assists in the development of teams and educates the public in the sport.

**7741  National Wheelchair Poolplayers Association**
9651 Halekulani Drive
Garden Grove, CA 92841

866-636-3371
FAX: 714-636-3371
e-mail: KenForce@nwpainc.com
www.nwpainc.com

*Ken Force, CEO*

Works together with other groups, organizations, and tournaments to update rules to include wheelchair players.

**7742  Rehabilitation Institute of Chicago's Virginia Wadsworth Sports Program**
710 N Lake Shore Drive
Chicago, IL 60611

312-238-7767
FAX: 312-908-1051
e-mail: jjones02@rehabchicago.org
www.richealthfit.org

*Susan Barclay, President*
*Laura Davis, VP*
*Mitch Carr, Fitness Coordinator*

RIC's Center for Health and Fitness is a full service fitness center for individuals with disablilties and the administrative offices for RIC's Wirtz Sports Program. Eighteen different sport and recreation programs are offered free of charge. The facility is adjacent to RIC's main building and also is the location of a branch of The National Center for Physical Activity and Disability (NCPAD), a joint project operated by the University of Illinois-Chigcago.

**7743    Special Olympics**
1133 19th Street NW
# 11
Washington, DC  20036              202-628-3630
                                   800-700-8585
                              FAX: 202-824-0200
                  e-mail: info@specialolympics.org
                          www.specialolympics.org

*Mark Wagner, Director*
*Timothy Shriver, President*

A year-round worldwide program that promotes physical fitness, sports training and athletic competition for children and adults with intellectual disabilities.

**7744    Special Olympics International**
1133 19th Street NW
Washington, DC  20036              202-628-3630
                              FAX: 202-824-2200
                  e-mail: info@specialolympics.org
                          www.specialolympics.org

*Timothy Shriver, President/CEO*
*Nadia Comaneci, Chief Administrative Officer*
*Drake Turrentine, Chief Legal Officer/Secretary*

Provides year-round training and athletic competition in a variety of well-coached, Olympic-type sparts for persons with mental retardation. Offers opportunities to develop physical fitness, prepare for entry into school and community sports programs. Athletes express courage, experience joy and participate in gifts, skills and friendship with their families and other Special Olympics athletes. Local information can be provided by regional offices.

**7745    US Association of Blind Athletes**
33 N Institute Street
Colorado Springs, CO  80903        719-578-2206
                              FAX: 719-630-0616
                          e-mail: usa@usa.net
                                www.usaba.org

*Mark Lucas, Executive Director*
*Nicole Jomantas, Communications Director*
*Susan Weeks, Development Director*

Provides athletic opportunities and training in competitive sports for visually impaired and blind individuals throughout the US Competitions indlcude local, regional and national events, internation events, and the Winter and Summer Paralympic Games.

**7746    US Hang Gliding Association Jayne Defanfils**
PO Box 1330
Colorado Springs, CO  80901        719-632-8300
                                   800-616-6888
                              FAX: 719-632-6417
                     e-mail: ushga@ushga.org
                                www.ushga.org

*Jayne Depanfilif, Executive Director*

Offers information for the disabled about how they may discover to hang glide or paraglide in an tandem with a instructor.

**7747    US Paralympics**
1 Olympic Plaza
Colorado Springs, CO  80909        719-866-2030
                              FAX: 719-866-2029
                          www.usparalympics.org

A division of the US Olympic Committee focused on enhancing programs, funding and opportunities for persons with physical disabilities to participate in Paralymic sports.

**7748    USA Deaf Sports Federation**
102 N Krohn Place
Sioux Falls, SD  57103             605-367-5760
                              FAX: 605-367-4979
                              TTY:605-367-5761
               e-mail: homeoffice@usdeafsports.org
                          www.usdeafsports.org

Governing body for all deaf sports and recreation in the United States. 20 different national sports organizations and 20 member clubs are affiliates of USADSF. USADSF is an affiliate sponsor of US Olympic Committee.

**7749    United Foundation for Disabled Archers**
PO Box 251
Glenwood, MN  56334                320-634-3660

                     e-mail: dhendricks@hunting.net
                                www.uffdaclub.com

*Daniel Hendricks, President/Founder*

Promotes and provides access to the sport of archery for any physically challenged person. Arranges Archery hunts throughout the United States.

**7750    United States Blind Golf Association**
3094 Shamrock Street N
Tallahassee, FL  32309             615-885-2593

                     e-mail: usbga@blindgolf.com
                                www.blindgolf.com

*Jim Baker, President*
*Dick Pomo, VP*

Provides blind and vision impaired gold tournaments to members.

**7751    Wheelchair Motorcycle Association**
101 Torrey Street
Brockton, MA  02301                508-583-8614

*Eli Factor DDS, President*

Founded in 1975, after Scott Factor sustained injury resulting in paraplegia, this association offers information on all types of off-road vehicles for use by people with disabilities, also offers a newsletter.

**7752    Wheelchair Sports, USA**
PO Box 5266
Kendall Park, NJ  08824            515-833-2450
                              FAX: 515-833-2450
                          e-mail: wsusa@aol.com
                                www.wsusa.org

*Patricia Shepherd, Executive Director*

Initiates, stimulates and promotes the growth and development of wheelchair sports.

---

# Books

**7753    Adapted Physical Education National Standards**
Human Kinetics
PO Box 5076
Champaign, IL  61825               217-351-5076
                                   800-747-4457
                              FAX: 217-351-1549
                     e-mail: info@hkusa.com
                          www.humankinetics.com

*Rian Holding, Chief Executive Officer*
*Rainer Martens, President*

The book presents fifteen broad standards based on the responsibilities and perceived professional needs of practicing physical educators. Each standard is broken down into levels that include content that physical educators who work with individuals with disabilities should know, additional content for adapted physical educators, and sample applications that adapted physical educators should be able to demonstrate. *$28.00*
*224 pages Paperback*
*ISBN 0-873229-62-2*

**7754    Adapted Physical Education and Sport, 2nd Edition**
Human Kinetics
PO Box 5076
Champaign, IL  61825
800-747-4457
800-747-4457
FAX: 217-351-1549
e-mail: info@hkusa.com
www.humankinetics.com

*Colin Higgs, Director*

Designed as a resource for both present and future physical education leaders, this book is an exceptional book for teaching exceptional children. It emphasizes the physical education of young people with disabilities. *$47.00*
*472 pages*
*ISBN 0-873225-78-1*

**7755    Bold Tracks: Skiing for the Disabled**
Johnson Books: A Cordillera Press Guide
1880 57th Court S
Boulder, CO  80301
303-443-1576
800-258-5830
FAX: 303-443-1106
e-mail: books@jpcolorado.com

*Richard Croog, Sales/Promotion*
*Jerry Johnson, President*

The first complete teaching and learning guide to skiing for the disabled. The guide is essential for instructor and student alike. Beginning with the basic American Teaching System and continuing through three-track and four-track methods, the manual covers skiing for the visually and hearing impaired as well as the physically and developmentally disabled. It includes glossaries of skiing and medical terms and tips for skin program development. *$24.95*
*160 pages Paperback*
*ISBN 1-555661-14-9*

**7756    Conditioning with Physical Disabilities**
Human Kinetics
PO Box 5076
Champaign, IL  61825
800-747-4457
FAX: 217-351-2674
e-mail: info@hkusa.com
www.humankinetics.com
The first practical, authoritative exercise guide for people with all classifications and levels of physical disabilities. The authors share the successful strength and conditioning program they created at the highly regarded Rehabilitation Institute of Chicago - a pioneering program that is now the leading exercise approach for people with physical disabilities. *$22.95*
*288 pages*
*ISBN 0-873226-14-3*

**7757    Disability and Sport**
Human Kinetics
PO Box 5076
Champaign, IL  61825
800-747-4457
FAX: 217-351-1549
e-mail: info@hkusa.com
www.humankinetics.com

*Rainer Martens, President*

This new book, written by leading experts in adapted physical education and disability sport, is intended to serve as a comprehensive reference about the disability sport world. Topics include adapted equipment, event management, women and disability sport, medical management of disabled athletes and research highlights. This book should serve as a valuable reference for disabled individuals and their families interested in sport, physical educators and medical personnel who work with disabled. *$40.00*
*312 pages*
*ISBN 0-873228-48-0*

**7758    Exercise Activities for the Elderly**
Springer Publishing Company
11 W 42nd Street
15th Floor
New York, NY  10036
212-431-4370
877-687-7476
FAX: 212-941-7842
e-mail: contactus@springerpub.com
www.springerpub.com

*Sheri Sussman, Vice President*
*Annette Imperati, Marketing/Sales Director*
*Ursula Springer, President*

A variety of exercises geared to clients with such conditions as arthritis, diabetes and Parkinson's disease, and others which are designed to build up muscular strength and maintain flexibility. *$39.95*
*224 pages Softcover*
*ISBN 0-826187-03-X*

**7759    Fitness Programming for Physical Disabilities**
Human Kinetics
PO Box 5076
Champaign, IL  61825
217-351-2674
800-747-4457
FAX: 217-351-2674
e-mail: info@hkusa.com
www.humankinetics.com

*Rainer Martens, President*
*Julie Martens, Vice President*

A book offering information for developing and conducting exercise programs for groups that included people with physical disabilities. A dozen authorities in exercise science and adapted exercise programming explain how to effectively and safely modify existing programs for individuals with physical disabilities. *$32.00*
*208 pages*
*ISBN 0-873224-34-5*

**7760    Guide to Wheelchair Sports and Recreation**
Paralyzed Veterans of America
801 18th Street NW
Washington, DC  20006
202-872-1300
800-424-8200
888-860-7244
FAX: 202-416-7639
e-mail: info@pva.org
www.pva.org

*Randy Pleza, President*

PVA's new booklet has been produced in part through a generous grant from Everest & Jennings, Inc., to serve individuals as a resource guide to sports and recreation activities and equipment suppliers.
*28 pages*

**7761    Hang Gliding and Paragliding Mag**
U S Hang Gliding Association
PO Box 1330
Colorado Springs, CO  80901
719-632-8300
800-616-6888
719-632-6417
FAX: 719-632-6417
e-mail: ushga@ushga.org
www.ushga.org

*Jayne Depanfilif, Executive Director*

**7762  Inclusive Games**
Human Kinetics
PO Box 5076
Champaign, IL  61825                    217-351-2674
                                        800-747-4457
                                   FAX: 217-351-1549
                              e-mail: info@hkusa.com
                              www.humankinetics.com

*Rainer Martens, President*
*Julie Martens, Vice President*

Features more than 50 games, helpful illustrations, and hundreds of game variations. The book shows how to adapt games so that children of every ability level can practice, play and improve their movement skills together. The game finder makes it easy to locate an appropriate game according to its name, approximate grade level, difficulty within the grade level, skills required/developed, and number of players. *$14.95*
          *120 pages Paperback*
          *ISBN 0-873226-39-9*

**7763  Physical Activity for Individuals with Mental Retardation**
Human Kinetics
PO Box 5076
Champaign, IL  61825
                                        800-747-4457
                                   FAX: 217-351-2674
                              e-mail: info@hkusa.com
                              www.humankinetics.com

*Bryan Holding, Chief Executive Officer*

The first movement-oriented text to cover the life span of people with mental retardation. Readers will discover the characteristics and unique needs of individuals with mental retardation. They will also become familiar with methodologies for facilitating fitness and movement competencies. *$33.00*
          *480 pages*
          *ISBN 0-873223-61-6*

**7764  Physical Fitness Testing of the Disabled**
Human Kinetics
PO Box 5076
Champaign, IL  61825                    800-747-4457
                                        800-747-4457
                                   FAX: 217-351-1549
                              e-mail: info@hkusa.com
                              www.humankinetics.com

*Rainer Martens, President*

A physical fitness testing manual for selected disabled groups thanks to the research and professional teamwork of the authors. In this manual, they offer practitioners norm-referenced tests of physical fitness for youngsters with cerebral palsy, visual and auditory impairments, and spinoneuro-muscular conditions. *$25.00*
          *184 pages Spiral bound*
          *ISBN 0-931250-45-7*

**7765  Recreation & Sports**
Accent Books & Products
PO Box 700
Bloomington, IL  61702                  309-378-2961
                                        800-787-8444
                                   FAX: 309-378-4420
                              e-mail: acmtlvng@aol.com

*Raymond C Cheever, Publisher*
*Betty Garee, Editor*

A guide to fun, excitement and travel offering options for disabled persons. Includes photos and sources of some special products. *$4.95*

          *65 pages Paperback*
          *ISBN 0-91570 -18-3*

**7766  Sport Science Review: Adapted Physical Activity**
Human Kinetics
PO Box 5076
Champaign, IL  61825                    217-351-2674
                                        800-747-4457
                                   FAX: 217-351-1549
                              e-mail: info@hkusa.com
                              www.humankinetics.com

*Rainer Martens, President*
*Julie Martens, Vice President*

This special issue addresses disability and sport. Researchers from diverse academic backgrounds and parts of the world review the issues and controversies surrounding inclusion in physical education and sport. The papers explore inclusion in school settings, the history of disability sport, psychological and sociological aspects of adapted physical activity, and the need to identify reliable classification systems. *$15.00*
          *96 pages*
          *ISBN 0-736029-88-5*

**7767  Sports & Recreation for the Disabled**
Exceptional Parent Library
PO Box 1807
Englewood Cliffs, NJ  07632             201-947-6000
                                        800-535-1910
                                   FAX: 201-489-0074
                              e-mail: eplibrary@aol.com
                              www.eplibrary.com
A book designed to make dreams come true. *$32.00*

**7768  Sports Market Place Directory**
Grey House Publishing
185 Millerton Road
Millerton, NY  12546                    518-789-8700
                                        800-562-2139
                                   FAX: 518-789-0545
                              e-mail: books@greyhouse.com
                              www.greyhouse.com

*Leslie Mackenzie, Publisher*
*Richard Gottlieb, President*

This annual directory lists over 13,000 organizations and their key executives. This comprehensive directory has offered direct access to the Who, What, When & Where of the Sports Industry.

**7769  Sports and Exercise for Children with Chronic Health Conditions**
Human Kinetics
PO Box 5076
Champaign, IL  61825
                                        800-747-4457
                                   FAX: 217-351-1549
                              e-mail: info@hkusa.com
                              www.humankinetics.com

*Brian R Holding, Chief Executive Officer*
*Adrian C Hutber, Division Director*

Written by leading pediatric authorities, the practical guidelines in Sports and Exercise for Children with Chronic Health Conditions address these twenty common medical conditions: spina bifida, epilepsy, childhood progressive neuromuscular disease, cerebral palsy, childhood arthritis, asthma, cystic fibrosis, AIDS, hepatitis, hypertension, congenital heart disease-shunt lesions, congenital obstructive valvular heart disease, carditis, anemia, hemophilia and more. *$49.00*
          *392 pages Hardcover*

**7770  Tennis in a Wheelchair**
United States Tennis Association
707 Alexander Road
Princeton, NJ  08540                    609-987-2300
                                   FAX: 985-641-2267

*John Babcock, Manager*

A practical manual of tennis playing techniques for the wheelchair athlete. Included are sections on basic strokes from a wheelchair, wheelchair mobility, singles and doubles strategy, and more. Readers will discover how enjoyable and challenging the game of wheelchair tennis can be. *$3.75*
*40 pages Illustrated*

## Exercise Devices

**7771 Abilitations**
1 Sportime Way
Atlanta, GA  30340
770-449-5700
800-850-8603
FAX: 800-845-1535
e-mail: orders@sportime.com
www.abilitations.com

*Ilana Danneman PT, Catalog Director*
*Cecilia Cruse MS OTR/L, Education Director*
*Debbie Kissel, New Product Development*

Catalog provides products to patients, therapists and parents to assist in maximizing functional levels through movement, sensory integration, adapted play and positioning.
*240 pages Quarterly*

**7772 CC-M Productions**
7755 16th Street NW
Washington, DC  20012
202-882-7430
800-453-6280
FAX: 202-882-7432
e-mail: info@managementwisdom.com
www.armchairfitness.com

*Jon Abel, Marketing Manager*
*Robert Mason, Executive Director*

Armchair Fitness video series. 4 cassettes: Armchair Fitness Aerobic, Armchair Fitness Gentle, Armchair Fitness Strength and Armchair Fitness Yoga. $29.95-$39.95.
*$29.95 - $39.95*

**7773 Equalizer 1000 Series**
Helm Distributing
1516 Nicholas Road
Dayton, OH  45418
937-268-7415
FAX: 937-268-9525
e-mail: info@helmdistributing.com
www.helmdistributing.com

*Pruett B Helm, President and Owner*

Weight training equipment designed with the wheelchair user in mind. *$7050.00*

**7774 Equalizer 5000 Home Gym**
Helm Distributing
1516 Nicholas Road
Dayton, OH  45418
937-268-7415
FAX: 937-268-9525
e-mail: info@helmdistributing.com
www.helmdistributing.com

*Bob Helm, President*

Exercise machine for the able-bodied and the disabled, but specifically designed with a wheelchair user in mind. *$4250.00*

**7775 Freedom Ryder Handcycles**
Brike International
20589 SW Elk Horn Court
Tualatin, OR  97062
503-692-1029
800-800-5828

*Mike Lofgren, President*
*Brian Stewart, VP*

The finest handcycle in the world. The cycles incorporate body, lean steering and the finest bicycle components to make this a three-wheeled vehicle without equal. Suitable for both recreation and competition. *$1995.00*

**7776 Modular QuadDesk**
Gpk
535 Floyd Smith Drive
El Cajon, CA  92020
619-593-7381
800-468-8679
FAX: 619-593-7514
e-mail: info@gpk.com
www.gpk.com

*Rajesh Kanwar, President*

Worktable specially dsigned for people in wheelchairs who lack grip strength, or cannot learn or reach. Small or medium.

**7777 Pedal-in-Place Exerciser**
Thoele Manufacturing
849 U S Route 40
Montrose, IL  62445
217-924-4553
FAX: 217-924-4553

A great in-home exerciser that can benefit quadraplegics, paraplegics, stroke patients or anyone with limited use of their arms and legs.

**7778 Quad Commander**
Gpk
535 Floyd Smith Drive
El Cajon, CA  92020
619-593-7381
800-468-8679
FAX: 619-593-7514
e-mail: info@gpk.com
www.gpk.com-or-www.quadriplegia.com

*Rajesh Kanwar, President*

Joystick for people with quadriplegia.

**7779 Seat-A-Robics**
PO Box 630064
Little Neck, NY  11363
800-484-7046
FAX: EXT- 11-30

*Daria Alinovi, President*

Offers a variety of safe, affordable and medically approved video exercise programs that are listed in our video chapter. In addition the company offers two resources. The first Healthy Eating & Facts For Kids is geared specifically to health professionals and educators that work with disabled children ($39.95). The second is a recreational resource guide that stimulates children to be creative and get involved. It keeps them actively engaged while having fun and getting fit ($29.95).

**7780 Uppertone**
535 Floyd Smith Drive
El Cajon, CA  92020
619-593-7381
800-468-8679
FAX: 619-593-7514
e-mail: sales@gpk.com
www.gpk.com

*Rajesh Kanwar, President*

Unassisted muscle strengthening and conditioning system for quads. *$2495.00*

**7781 Versatrainer**
Pro- Max/ Division Of Bow- Flex Of America
2200 NE 65th Avenue
Vancouver, WA  98661
800-BOW-FLEX
FAX: 360-993-3610
www.boflex.com

One exercise system for the disabled person that does everything. Incorporates full body strength, muscle development, cardiovascular conditioning, gives full muscle movement and balanced muscle development.

## Periodicals

**7782 Access to Recreation**
8 Sandra Court
Newbury Park, CA 91320
805-498-7535
800-634-4351
FAX: 805-498-8186
e-mail: dkrebs@accesstr.com
www.accesstr.com

*Don Krebs, President*

The Access to Recreation catalog is full of recreation and exercise equipment. One can find items such as electric fishing reels and other fishing and hunting equipment for the disabled sportsman. There are also adapted golf clubs, swimming pool lifts, wheelchair gloves and cuffs and bowling equipment. There are devices to help with embroidery, knitting and card playing, videos, books and practical aides such as wheelchair ramps and book.
*64 pages Bi-Annually*

**7783 Adapted Aquatics: Swimming for Persons with Physical or Mental Impairments**
American Red Cross
2025 E Street NW
Washington, DC 20006
202-639-3685
800-435-7669
FAX: 202-303-0047
e-mail: ncctech@usa.redcross.org
www.redcross.org

*Jack McGuire, President/CEO*

Magazine for disabled swimmers.

**7784 National Sports Center for the Disabled**
PO Box 1290
Winter Park, CO 80482
970-726-1540
FAX: 970-726-4112
e-mail: info@nscd.org
www.nscd.org

*Craig Pollitt, President*
*Hal O'Leary, Founder*

Free newsletter with information and tips for adaptive skiing and other mountain sports for people with disabilities.
*6-8 pages Quarterly*

**7785 PALAESTRA: Forum of Sport/PE/Recreation for Those with Disabilities**
Challenge Publications Limited
PO Box 508
Macomb, IL 61455
309-833-1902
FAX: 309-833-1902
e-mail: challpub@macomb.com
www.palaestra.com

*Julian Stein, Associate Editor*
*David Beaver, Editor-in-Chief*
*David Beaver, Owner*

The most comprehensive resource on sport, physical education and recreation for individuals with disabilities, their parents and professionals in the field of adapted physical activity. Published in cooperation with US Paralympics and AAHPERD's Adapted Physical Activity Council. Informative yet entertaining and delivers valuable insights for consumers, families and professionals in the field. Published quarterly.

**7786 Strides Magazine**
North America Riding for the Handicapped Associati
PO Box 33150
Denver, CO 80233
303-452-1212
800-369-7433
FAX: 303-252-4610
e-mail: narha@narha.org
www.narha.org

*Sheila Kemperdietrich, Chief Executive Officer*
*Andrea Spridgen, Editor*

NARHA's monthly publication. *$35.00*
*42 pages Quarterly*

## Products & Programs

**7787 Aerospace Compadre**
Aerospace America
900 Truman Parkway
Suite 189
Bay City, MI 48706
989-684-4486
FAX: 989-684-4486

*Murray Sutherland, President*

Fully customized golf cart type vehicle for the physically impaired person. Fully equipped with hand controls, wheelchair rack, storage racks, head and tail lights and full safety belts. *$2500.00*

**7788 Basketball: Beeping Foam**
Maxi Aids
42 Executive Boulevard
Farmingdale, NY 11735
631-752-0521
800-522-6294
FAX: 631-752-0689
TTY: 516-752-0738
e-mail: sales@maxiaids.com
www.maxiaids.com

This sound making basketball enables the visually impaired to play basketball or other games. *$29.95*

**7789 Bounce Back**
Access To Recreation
8 Sandra Court
Newbury Park, CA 91320
805-498-7535
800-634-4351
FAX: 805-498-8186
e-mail: dkrebs@accesstr.com
www.accesstr.com

*Don Krebs, President*

**7790 Bowling: Ball Ramp**
Cleo Of New York
S Buckout Street
Irvington, NY 10533
914-591-4900
800-321-0595

*Elliott Goldberg, President*

Bowling devices for wheelchair occupants. *$109.00*

**7791 Center for Health and Fitness**
Rehabilitation Institute of Chicago
710 N Lake Shore Drive
Chicago, IL 60611
312-238-1149
FAX: 312-238-5017
e-mail: trichey@ric.org
www.richealthfit.org

*Tom Richey, Director*
*Pam Redding, Business Support Manager*
*Deborah Gaebler-Spira, MD*

Provides free sports and programs to individuals with physical disabilities in the greater Chicago area. Programs in 16 different sports including center for health and fitness which provides exercise opportunities seven days a week.

**7792  Challenge Golf**
Motivation Media
1245 Milwaukee Avenue
Glenview, IL  60025                     847-827-9057
                                   FAX: 847-297-6829

*Dorothy Bauer, Coordinator*

A plain-language video, Challenge Golf is packed with information for beginners or veterans. Peter Longo covers 5 handicaps (one-arm, one-leg, in a seated position, blind, and arthritis) clearly and concisely, on how to play golf with a physical disability. In color, complete with special effects, graphs and real handicapped golfers at play. *$38.95*
        *Home Edition*

**7793  Disabled Sports USA, Far West**
Tahoe Adaptive Ski School
PO Box 9780
Truckee, CA  96162                    530-581-4161
                                   FAX: 530-581-3127
                              e-mail: info@dsusafw.org
                                       www.dsusafw.org

*Katherine Rodriguez, Vice President*
*Doug Pringle, President*
*John Chase, Director*

Snow ski and snowboard lessons for people with disabilities. December through April. Two and a half hour lesson, adaptive equipment and beginner lift ticket: $50 midweek. Summer programs include: Water Skiing, Whitewater Rafting, Cycling, 4WD Backcountry Access and Kayaking.

**7794  EasyStand 6000 Glider**
Access To Recreation
8 Sandra Court
Newbury Park, CA  91320               805-498-7535
                                      800-634-4351
                                   FAX: 805-498-8186
                           e-mail: dkrebs@accesstr.com
                                       www.accesstr.com

*Don Krebs, President*

Provides dynamic leg motion for individuals who are unable to stand upright or walk on their own.

**7795  Fairway Spirit Adaptive Golf Car: Model 4852**
Fairway Golf Cars
3225 Gateway Road
Suite 300
Brookfield, WI  53045                 262-790-9363
                                      888-320-4850
                                      888-320-4850
                                   FAX: 262-790-9396
                               www.fairwaygolfcars.com

*John Perez, Sales and Marketing Director*
*Ed Gaffney, Owner*

Fairway Spirt is designed to allow access to all aspects of the game of golf- even greens and tee. Spirit 4850 features a 48 volt electronic system to provide unsurpassed power, range and speed. Couple the drive system performance with ergonomic features like an adjustable seat with flip up arm rests, 360 degree swivel and an adjustable tilter position.

**7796  Freedom Rider**
Freedom Rider
PO Box 4187
Manchester, NH  03108                 603-645-1811
                                      888-253-8811
                                   FAX: 603-645-1811
                            e-mail: info@freedomrider.com
                                     www.freedomrider.com

*Victoria Surr, President*

A catalog of equipment for people with disabilities who ride horses which includes instructional aids, vaulting equipment, and lots of hard to find items.

**7797  Golf Xpress**
Emotorsports
4275 County Line Road 214
Chalfont, PA  18914                   215-997-9555
                                      877-494-6532
                                   FAX: 215-997-9560
                            e-mail: mitch@golfxpress.com
                                      www.golfxpress.com

*Don Labowsky, President*

Patented single-rider adaptive golf cart allows you to play golf seated or supported. Hit woods, irons, and putt from the car. Drives onto tees and greens and into traps without damaging the course.

**7798  High Adventure Hang Gliding**
4231 Sepulveda Avenue
San Bernardino, CA  92404             909-882-1880
                                   FAX: 909-883-8488
                            e-mail: robndi@flytandem.com
                                      www.flytandem.com

*Rob McKenzie, Founder*
*Dianne McKenzie, Founder*
*Susan Haugh*

Tandem adventures.

**7799  National Sports Center for the Disabled**
PO Box 1290
Winter Park, CO  80482                970-726-1540
                                   FAX: 970-726-4112
                                 e-mail: info@nscd.org
                                         www.nscd.org

*Craig Politt, President/CEO*
*Hal O'Leary, Founder*
*Beth Fox, Operations Manager*

Innovative non-profit organization that provides year-round recreation for children and adults with disabilities. The world's largest adaptive ski program, teaching 25,000 lessons per winter at Winter Park Resort, Colorado. Also snowboarding, ski racing, showshoeing, cross-country skiing. Summer sports: rafting, sailing, camping, hiking, hand cycling, mountain biking, tandem biking, in-line skating, horseback riding, fishing, rock climbing. Sports symposium and clinics.

**7800  Rickshaw Exerciser**
Access To Recreation
8 Sandra Court
Newbury Park, CA  91320               805-498-7535
                                      800-634-4351
                                   FAX: 805-498-8186
                           e-mail: dkrebs@accesstr.com
                                       www.accesstr.com

*Don Krebs, President*
*Marie Krebs, Office Manager*

This Exerciser develops the muscle used most by those in wheelchairs. It develops the strength you need to lift yourself for pressure relief, doing transfers and pushing your wheelchair.

**7801  Sailing Fascination**
4010 Park Newport
Apt 224
Newport Beach, CA  92660              949-760-8650
                                      800-735-2922
                                   FAX: 949-760-8650
                                   TTY: 949-760-2646
                            e-mail: feedback@socalsail.com
                                      www.socalsail.com

*Jack W Hester, President*
*Tom Tolbert, Vice President*

Sailing Fascination provides sailing programs for anyone who is disabled. A non profit educational and charitable California State Corp. with an all volunteer staff, officers, and directors. Year round sailing classes are held on a 24 foot sailboat that is equipped to be accessible to the disabled student sailor.

**7802** **Slow Motion/Sea Legs**
Aquarius Health Care Videos
PO Box 1159
Sherborn, MA 01770
508-650-6905
FAX: 508-650-4216
e-mail: aqvideos@tiac.net
www.aquariusproductions.com

*Leslie Kussmonn, President*
Probably the last place you would expect to find a disabled person is flying down a mountain in a bucket...attached to a board. Mario Solis and Carla toll introduce a community where physical limitations need no longer stand in the way of strenuous physical performance... the community of disabled snow skiing. *$79.00*

**7803** **Wheelchair Roller**
Access To Recreation
8 Sandra Court
Newbury Park, CA 91320
805-498-7535
800-634-4351
FAX: 805-498-8186
e-mail: dkrebs@accesstr.com
www.accesstr.com

*Don Krebs, President*
The McClain Wheelchair Roller allows you to build strength and stamina in the comfort of your own home.

## General

**7804    AAN's Toll-Free Hotline**
Allergy and Asthma Network Mothers of Asthmatics
2751 Prosperity Avenue
Suite 150
Fairfax, VA  22031

703-641-9595
800-878-4403
FAX: 703-573-7794
www.aanma.org

*Grace Gerzian, Executive Director*

Offers answers to questions regarding allergies and asthma, provides referrals and support to assist the patient and his or her family.

**7805    American SIDS Institute**
509 Augusta Drive
Marietta, GA  30067

770-426-8746
800-232-7437
FAX: 770-426-1369
www.sids.org

*Betty McEntire PhD, Executive Director*

American SIDS Institute is a national nonprofit health care organization that is dedicated to the prevention of sudden infant death and the promotion of infant health through an aggressive, comprehensive nationwide program of: research, clinical services, education and family support.

**7806    American Speech-Language-Hearing Association**
10801 Rockville Pike
Rockville, MD  20852

301-897-5700
800-638-8255
FAX: 301-897-7348
e-mail: actioncenter@asha.org
www.asha.org

*Joanne Jessen, Publications Director*
*Arlene Pietranton, Executive Director*

Hotline for the speech and hearing impaired.

**7807    Anchor Houses**
1212 Monroe Street NW
Washington, DC  20010

202-832-5555
FAX: 202-832-8216

*Francis Palilkarambi*

Offers support groups and services such as: counseling, case management, advocacy for financial entitlements and more for individuals and families dealing with mental illness.

**7808    Arthritis Foundation Information Hotline**
PO Box 7669
Atlanta, GA  30357

404-872-7100
800-283-7800
FAX: 404-872-9559
e-mail: help@arthritis.org
www.arthritis.org

*John Klippel, Chief Executive Officer*

Offers information and referrals, counseling, physicians information and more to persons living with arthritis.

**7809    Aurora of Central New York**
518 James Street
Syracuse, NY  13203

315-422-7263
FAX: 315-422-4792
TTY:315422974692
e-mail: auroracny@auroracny.org
www.auroracny.org

*Debra Chaiken, Executive Director*

Professional counseling services to assist individuals and their families deal with the trauma of hearing or vision loss.

**7810    Autism Society of America**
7910 Woodmont Avenue
Suite 300
Bethesda, MD  20814

301-657-0881
800-3AU-TISM
www.autism-society.org

*Ann Pulley, Manager*

ASA is the largest and oldest grassroots organization within the autism community, with more than 200 chapters and over 20,000 members and supporters nationwide. ASA is the leading source of education, information and referral about autism and has been the leader in advocacy and legislative initiatives for more than three decades.

**7811    Braille Institute Orange County Center**
527 N Dale Avenue
Anaheim, CA  92801

714-821-5000
800-272-4553
FAX: 714-527-7621
e-mail: info@brailleinstitute.org
www.brailleinstitute.org

*Thomas Burton, Chairman*
*Leslie Stocker, President*
*Sheila Daily, Executive Director*

A toll free information and referral service where callers can obtain information about community programs and referrals to organizations serving the blind in their local areas.

**7812    Camp New Hope**
PO Box 764
Mattoon, IL  61938

217-895-2341
FAX: 217-895-3658
e-mail: cnhinc@rri.net
www.campnewhope.com

*Kim Carmack, Executive Director*
*Terri Taylor, Camp Director*

Offers advocacy services, social and recreational services and a summer camp for the disabled.

**7813    Cancer Information Service**
National Cancer Institute
6116 Executive Boulevard
Suite 3036a
Bethesda, MD  20892

301-496-2481
800-422-6237
www.nci.nih.gov

*Andrew C Von Eschenback, Director*
*Sallie Baird, Manager*

A nationwide network of 19 regional field offices supported by the National Cancer Institute which provides accurate, up-to-date information on cancer to patients and their families, health professionals and the general public. The CIS can provide specific information in understandable language about particular types of cancer, as well as information on second opinions and the availability of clinical trials.

**7814    Clearinghouse on Disability Information**
Office of Special Education & Rehabilitative Servi
330 C Street SW
Room 3132
Washington, DC  20202

202-205-8241
FAX: 202-401-2608
www.ed.gov/OFFICE/OSERS

*Carolyn Corlett, Director*

The Clearinghouse provides information to people with disabilities or anyone requesting information, by doing research and providing documents in response to inquiries. The information provided includes areas of federal funding for disability-related programs. Clearinghouse staff is trained to serve as experts in referring requests to other sources of disability-related information, if necessary.

## 7815  Community Connections
801 Pennsylvania Avenue SE
Suite 201
Washington, DC 20003
202-546-1512
FAX: 202-544-5365

*Helen Bergman, Chief Executive Officer*

Offers support groups and support systems for adults with mental and emotional disabilities.

## 7816  Community Support Center
13301 Bruce B Downs Boulevard
Tampa, FL 33612
813-228-6724
FAX: 813-250-0941

*Cecil Woodside, CSC Division Director*

Provides an alternative to institutionalization for persons 18 years to 55 years of age, with a mental disability. There are approximately 60 staff members and daily census for clients is about 600.

## 7817  Compassionate Friends
PO Box 3696
Oak Brook, IL 60522
630-990-0010
877-969-0010
FAX: 630-990-0246
e-mail: nationaloffice@compassionatefriends.org
www.compassionatefriends.org

*Patricia Loder, Executive Director*

Peer support for bereaved parents, grandparents and siblings, offering 600 chapters in the United States. The organization also offers a quarterly magazine, We Need Not Walk Alone, and TCF resources of booklets, tapes and brochures for the bereaved parent, grandparent and sibling.

## 7818  Consumer and Patient Information Hotline
Prevent Blindness America
211 W Wacker Drive
Chicago, IL 60606
312-363-6001
800-331-2020
FAX: 847-843-2020
e-mail: info@preventblindness.org
www.preventblindness.org

*Hugh Perry, Chief Executive Officer*
*Daniel Garrett, Senior VP*

A toll-free line offering free information on a broad range of vision, eye health and safety topics including sports eye safety, diabetic retinopathy, glaucoma, cataracts, children's eye disorders and more.

## 7819  Cornerstone Services
777 Joyce Road
Joliet, IL 60436
815-727-6666
FAX: 815-723-1177
e-mail: jhogan@cornerstoneservices.org
www.cornerstoneservices.org

*James A Hogan, President/CEO*
*Susan Murphy, Director Human Resources*

Cornerstone Services provides progressive, comprehensive services for people with disabilities, promoting choice, dignity and the opportunity to live and work in the community. Established in 1969, the agency provides developmental, vocational, employment, residential and mental health services at various community-based locations. The nonprofit social service agency helps approximately 750 people each day.

## 7820  Department of Ophthalmology Information Line
Eye & Ear Infirmary
1855 W Taylor Street
Chicago, IL 60612
773-487-2862

Offers eye clinic and physician referrals to persons suffering from vision disorders as well as offers emergency information.

## 7821  Dial-a-Hearing Screening Test
300 S Chester Road
Swarthmore, PA 19081
800-222-EARS
FAX: 610-543-2802
e-mail: dahst@aol.com

*George Biddle, Executive Director*

Hearing help information center. Provides toll free phone number for accurate telephone hearing screening test. Provides referral to audiologist or ear, nose and throat doctor. All services are free. Hours are 9 AM to 5 PM ET Monday to Friday.

## 7822  Disability Network
3600 S Dort Highway
Suite 54
Flint, MI 48507
810-742-1800
FAX: 810-742-2400
TTY:810-742-7647
e-mail: tdn@disnetowrk.org
www.disnetwork.org

*Mike Zelley, President/CEO*

The Disability Network is a private nonprofit organization that advcates for the rights of individuals with disabilities. The Disability Netowrk supports include technology and assistive technology training, issue action grops, information & referral of resources, peer support, Independent Living skills building, transition from school to work and Americans with Disabilities Act consultations.

## 7823  Disability and Health, National Center for Birth Defects and Developmental Disabilities
4770 Buford Highway
# F-35
Atlanta, GA 30341
770-488-7080
FAX: 770-488-7075
TTY:770-488-7083
e-mail: ncehinfo@cdc.gov
www.cdc.gov/ncbddd/dh

*Lisa Sinclair, Health Policy Analyst*

Located within the new CDC, National Center for Birth Defects and Developmental Disabilities, the Disability and Health section, operates a ralatively small program that primarily supports: data collection on the prevalence of people with disabilities & their health status and risk factors for poor health and well-being; research on measures of disability, functioning and health; health promotion intervention studies; and dissemination of health information.

## 7824  Easter Seals
230 W Monroe Street
Suite 1800
Chicago, IL 60606
312-726-6800
800-221-6827
FAX: 312-726-1494
TTY: 312-726-4258
e-mail: info@easterseals.com
www.easterseals.com

*Joan Fishman, Marketing Manager*
*Kristen Barnfield, Public Relations Manager*
*Rosemary Garza, Resource/Information Specialist*

Provides services that help children and adults with disabilities gain greater independence. Primary services medical rehabilitation, job training and employment, child care, adult day services, and camping and recreation benefit more than 1 million individuals and their families each year through one of 500 centers worldwide.

**7825 Epilepsy Foundation for the National Capitol Area**
4224 6th Street SE
Washington, DC 20032 202-561-6114

Offers information and referrals, support groups for dually diagnosed persons.

**7826 Family Support Project for the Developmentally Disabled**
3424 Kossuth Avenue
Room 15a10
Bronx, NY 10467 718-519-5000

*Monica Sanabria, Project Coordinator*

**7827 Green Door**
1623 16th Street NW
Washington, DC 20009 202-222-0232
FAX: 202-462-7562
e-mail: brenda.randall@greendoor.org
www.greendoor.org

*Judith Johnson, Executive Director*
*Brenda Randall, Deputy Director*

Green Door is a community program which prepares people with a severe and persistent mental illness to live and work independently. Since 1976, Green Door has provided comprehensive services to mentally ill people-members, including housing, job training, job placement, education, homeless outreach, case management, support for people with substance abuse problems, family support,and specialized help for people who have had repeated hospitalizations.

**7828 Head Injury Hotline**
PO Box 84151
Seattle, WA 98124 206-329-1371
FAX: 206-329-0912
e-mail: brain@headinjury.com
www.headinjury.com
Disseminates head injury information and provides referrals to facilitate adjustment to life following head injury. Organizes seminars for professionals, head injury survivors, and their families.

**7829 Headlines Support Group**
Center for Community Re-entry
313 N Main Street
Rockford, IL 61101 815-964-9555
FAX: 815-962-6113

*Pamela Solberg, Office Manager*

A local support group reaching northern Illinois and southern Wisconsin, for survivors and families of brain injury. The group helps survivors and families cope with awareness difficulties, social adjustment, and leisure awareness. The group shares information regarding head injuries and provides updates from the state and national associations. Headlines continually searches for new ideas, information and services which can help survivors fulfill their maximum potential.

**7830 Human Policy Press**
Center on Humany Policy
PO Box 35127
Syracuse, NY 13235 315-443-2761
800-894-0826
FAX: 315-443-4338
e-mail: thechp@sued.syr.edu
thechp.syr.edu/humanpolicypress/

*Rachael Zubal-Ruggieri, Information Coordinator*

Independent press started by the Center on Human Policy in 1974 to promote positive attitudes towards people with disabilities.

**7831 International Braille and Technology Center for the Blind**
National Federation of the Blind
1800 Johnson Street
Baltimore, MD 21230 410-659-9314
FAX: 410-685-5653
e-mail: nfb@nfb.org
www.nfb.org

*Marc Maurer, President*
*Joyce Scanlan, Program Director*

World's largest and most complete evaluation and demonstration center of all assistive technology used by the blind from around the world. Includes all braille, synthetic speech, print-to-speech scanning, internet and portable devices and programs. Available for tours by appointment to blind persons, employers, technology manufacturers, teachers, parents and those working in the assistive technology field.

**7832 Job Opportunities for the Blind**
National Federation of the Blind
1800 Johnson Street
Baltimore, MD 21230 410-659-9314
FAX: 410-685-5653
e-mail: nfb@iamdigex.net
www.nfb.org

*Marc Maurer, President*

A specialized service that provides free support, resources and information to blind persons seeking employment and to employers interested in hiring the blind. A partnership program with the US Department of Labor, this is the most successful program of its kind in helping blind persons find competitive work.

**7833 Kaleidoscope Network**
1777 NE Loop 410
Suite 300
San Antonio, TX 78217 210-436-2611
FAX: 210-829-1388
www.kALIVE.com

*Phyllis Nichols, Chief Operating Officer*
*Ron Dixon, President Programming Production*

KALEIDOSCOPE Network, inc. (KNI) is a broadband, multimedia health and lifestyle company which produces and distributes television and on-line programming and content emphasizing health and wellness. KNI airs its programming on PAX Television with a reach to 73% of the country or 74 million households. KNI's interactive web site provides authoritative health content, with links to its more than 240 health and disability-related National Advisory Board organizations.

**7834 Kids on the Block Arthritis Programs**
Arthritis Foundation
PO Box 7669
Atlanta, GA 30357 404-872-7100
800-283-7800
FAX: 404-872-9559
e-mail: help@arthritis.org
www.arthritis.org

*Dawnn Johnson, Employment Manager*
*John Klippel, Chief Executive Officer*

State and local programs that use puppetry to help children understand what it is like for children and adults who have arthritis.

**7835 Lighthouse International Information and Resource Service**
111 E 59th Street
New York, NY 10022 212-821-9200
800-829-0500
FAX: 212-821-9705
e-mail: info@lighthouse.org
www.lighthouse.org

*Tara A Cortes, President/CEO*

Provides information about eye diseases, low vision, age-related vision loss, adaptive technology, optical devices, large print and braille publishers, helps people find low vision services, vision rehabilitation services, and support groups across the U.S.; offers large selection of consumer products.

**7836  Lung Line Information Service**
National Jewish Center for Immunology
1400 Jackson Street
Denver, CO  80206
303-697-5095
800-222-LUNG
www.nationaljewish.org

*Lynn Taussig, President*
*Kris Frederickson, Owner*

A free information service answering questions, sending literature and giving advice to patients with immunologic or respiratory illnesses. The Line is an educational service and not a substitute for medical care. Diagnosis or suggested treatment will not be provided for a caller's specific condition.

**7837  Medic Alert Foundation, International**
2323 Colorado Avenue
Turlock, CA  95382
209-668-3333
800-432-5378
FAX: 209-669-2495
e-mail: customer_service@medicalert.org
www.medicalert.org

*Paul Kortschak, Chief Executive Officer*

Emergency medallions and bracelets containing emergency medical information and 24-hour emergency information telephone services.

**7838  Medicaid Information**
7500 Security Boulevard
Baltimore, MD  21244
410-786-3000
877-267-2323
www.cms.hhs.gov

*Michelle Snyder, Executive Director*

Information about eligibility and benefits for needy citizens who require health care is available by contacting the Health Care Financing administration or by contacting the local public welfare office.

**7839  Medicare Information**
200 Independence Avenue SE
Washington, DC  20201
202-690-6726
www.medicare.gov

*Thomas Scully, President*

Eligibility and benefits for the health care of the older american is available by contacting the health care financing office.

**7840  National AIDS Hotline**
Centers for Disease Control and Prevention
1600 Clifton Road NE
Atlanta, GA  30329
404-639-3533
800-342-2437
www.cdc.gov

*Julie Gerberding, Director*
*Elizabeth Unger PhD*

Offers free confidential information and publications on HIV infection and AIDS.

**7841  National Association for Home Care**
Val J Halomandaris
228 7th Street SE
Washington, DC  20003
202-547-7424
FAX: 202-547-3540
e-mail: webmaster@nahc.org
www.nahc.org

*Val J Halamandaris, President*
*Kristy Wright, Vice Chairman*

This is a non-profit trade association representing various home care, hospice and health aid organizations. Website contains a section with information on how to choose a home care provider and a zip code driven locator for home care and hospice. Publishes monthly newsletter.

**7842  National Association for Parents of Children with Visual Impairments (NAPVI)**
PO Box 317
Watertown, MA  02471
617-972-7441
800-562-6265
FAX: 617-972-7444
e-mail: napvi@perkins.org
www.napvi.org

*Susan LaVenture, Executive Director*
*Mary Zabelski, President*
*Lars Anderson, VP*

In 1979, a group of parents responding to their own needs founded NAPVI, the National Association for Parents of the Visually Impaired, Inc. Never before was there a self-help organization specific to the needs of families of children with visual impairments. Since that time, NAPVI has grown and helped families across the US and in other countries.

**7843  National Autism Hotline**
Autism Services Center
929 4th Avenue
Huntington, WV  25701
304-525-8014
FAX: 304-525-8026
www.autismservicescenter.com

*Ruth C Sullivan PhD, Executive Director*
*Jodi Fields, Director of Office Administratio*

Service agency for individuals with autism and developmental disabilities, and their families. Assists families and agencies attempting to meet the needs of individuals with autism and other developmental disabilities. Makes available technical assistance in designing treatment programs and more. The hotline provides informational packets to callers and assists via telephone when possible.

**7844  National Child Safety Council**
PO Box 1368
Jackson, MI  49204
517-764-6070
800-222-1464
FAX: 517-764-3068
Hotline.

**7845  National Depressive and Manic Depressive Association**
730 N Franklin Street
Suite 501
Chicago, IL  60610
312-642-0049
800-826-3632
FAX: 312-642-7243
e-mail: questions@ndmda.org
www.ndmda.org

*Lydia Lewis, Executive Director*
*April Robinson, Program Manager*

Mission is to educate patients, families, professionals and the public concerning the nature of depressive and manic-depressive illnesses as treatable medical diseases; to foster self-help for patients and families; to eliminate discrimination and stigma; to improve access to care; and to advocate for research toward the elimination of these illnesses; to improve access to care; and to advocate for research toward the elimination of these illnesses.

**7846  National Health Information Center**
U S Department of Health
PO Box 1133
Washington, DC  20013
301-565-4167
800-336-4797
301-468-7394
FAX: 301-984-4256
e-mail: info@nhic.org

Identifies health information resources, channels requests for information to these resources and develops publications available for small handling fees.

**7847 National Information Center for Health Related Services**
University of South Carolina
First Benson
Columbia, SC 29208                803-777-7000
                                 800-922-9236
                      e-mail: scsis@dccisc.edu
Hotline.

**7848 National Institute of Child Health and Human Development**
PO Box 3006
Rockville, MD 20847               301-496-7339
                                 800-370-2943
                            FAX: 301-984-1473
     e-mail: NICHDInformationResourceCenter@mail.nih.gov
                            www.nichd.nih.gov

*Duane Alexander, Director*
*Yvonne Thompson Maddox, Deputy Director*
*Sandra Ott, Manager*

Government agency that supports and conducts research on topics related to the health of children, adults, families and communities; offers free materials and information.

**7849 National Service Dog Center**
Delta Society
875 124th Avenue NE
Suite 101
Bellevue, WA 98005                425-226-7357
                            FAX: 425-235-1076
                      e-mail: info@deltasociety.org
                            www.deltasociety.org

*Robert T Franklin, Chairman*
*Alex Bolen, Chairman*
*Lawrence Norvell, Chief Executive Officer*

A service of the Delta Society, provides information about the selection, training, stewardship, and roles of service dogs; referral to service dog training programs and related resources; education to businesses and health care professionals regarding service dog issues; research assistance through a resource library and network of professional experts and advocacy on behalf of people with service dogs.

**7850 PALS Support Groups**
Parent Professional Advocacy League
56 Temple Place
Suite 664
Boston, MA 02111                  617-542-7860
                                 866-815-8122
                            FAX: 617-542-7832
                      e-mail: pal@fcsn.org
                            www.ppal.net

*Kenneth Davis, President*
*Patricia Freedman, Clerk*
*Donna Welles, Executive Director*

Offers emotional support to parents and families of disabled children.

**7851 PXE International**
4301 Connecticut Avenue NW
Suite 404
Washington, DC 20008              202-362-9599
                            FAX: 202-966-8553
                      e-mail: info@pxe.org
                            www.pxe.org

*Sharon Terry, Executive Director/Owner*

Offers vital services to those with pseudoxanthoma elasticum, a connective tissue disorder causing calcification of connective tissue in various places throughout the body, often affecting the membrane behind the eye.

**7852 Parent Assistance Network**
Good Samaritan Health Systems
PO Box 1810
Kearney, NE 68848                 308-865-2009
                            FAX: 308-865-2933
             e-mail: sheilameyer@catholichealth.net

*Sheila Meyer, Parent Assistance Service Coordi*
*Laura Meyer, Director*

Provides information and emotional support to all parents and especially to parents of children with disabilities in the central Nebraska area. Ongoing activities include parent support group meetings, parent-to-parent networking and referrals and Respite Care provider trainings.

**7853 Parent Support Network**
Independence Square
500 Prospect Street
Pawtucket, RI 02860               401-722-9540
                            FAX: 401-727-2810
                      e-mail: mmhra@aol.com

*Laure Turn, Director*
*John Padlen, Executive Director*

Offers support groups for parents of children and adolescents with emotional/behavioral disabilities.

**7854 Parent as Parnters in Education of Alabama**
P O Box 161274
Mobile, AL 36616                  251-478-1208
                                 800-222-7322
                            FAX: 251-473-7877
             e-mail: seacofmobile@seacpac.com
             www.parentsaspartnersineducation.com

*Dr Barbara Wheat, Director*

**7855 Physician Referral and Information Line**
Academy of Allergy, Asthma, Immunology
611 E Wells Street
Milwaukee, WI 53202
                                 800-822-2762
                            FAX: 414-272-6070
                      e-mail: info@aaaai.org
                            www.aaaai.org

Referral line offering information on allergy and asthma, referral to an allergy/immunology specialist.

**7856 Post-Polio Support Group**
Hinsdale Hospital
120 N Oak Street
Hinsdale, IL 60521                630-856-9000
                            FAX: 630-856-7524
                            www.ahsmidwest.org

*Todd Werner, Chief Executive Officer*

Information and support for polio patients and their families; meets the fourth Wednesday of each month.

**7857 Prevent Child Abuse of Metropolitan Washington**
7404 Salford Court
Alexandria, VA 22315              202-223-0020
                            FAX: 202-296-4046
                      e-mail: pcamw@juno.com
                            www.pcamw.org

*Kendra Dunn, Executive Director*

Through public education, community partnerships and support services, PCAMW helps everyone play a role in prevention. We share information on prevention stategies and effective parenting at community forums and events and advocate for polices and services that keep children safe. We operate PhoneFriend, a telephone support line for children at home without adult supervision and conduct personal safety workshops in schools, camps and libraries. PhoneFriend support line: 202-223-2244.

**7858 RET Project: (Rehabilitation Engineering Technology San Francisco State University**
1600 Holloway Avenue
San Francisco, CA 94132      415-338-1333
FAX: 415-338-1501
e-mail: rgrott@sfsu.edu

*Ray Grott, Director*

RET Training Project is designed as a one-year Graduate Certificate program for people interested in the field of assistive technology used by people with disabilities.

**7859 Recorded Periodicals**
Associated Services for the Blind
919 Walnut Street
Philadelphia, PA 19107      215-627-0600
FAX: 215-922-0692
www.ast.org

*John Corrigan, Manager*
*Patricia Johnson, Chief Executive Officer*

A subscription service of Associated Services for the Blind, these periodicals provide 21 magazines through this subscription service. A magazine list can be sent, in both large print and on audio cassette. *$18.00*

**7860 Son-Rise Program**
2080 S Undermountain Road
Sheffield, MA 01257      413-229-2100
800-714-2779
FAX: 413-229-3202
e-mail: sonrise@option.org
www.autismtreatmentcenter.org

*Glenna Klein, Publicist*

Internationally renowned and highly effective method for working with children challenged by autism, autism spectrum disorders, PDD and all other developmental difficulties. The program teaches parents, relatives, volunteers and professionals how to design and implement a child-centered, home-based educational program. Modality comprises an innovative and comprehensive system for learning and growth with specific impact in areas including eye contact, speech and communication and more.

**7861 Special Children**
1306 Wabash Avenue
Belleville, IL 62220      618-234-6876
FAX: 618-234-6150
e-mail: kcullan@peaknet.net
www.specialchildren.net

*Kathleen Cullen, Executive Director*
*John Hill, Assistant Director*

A nonprofit agency serving children with developmental disabilities ages birth to 21 years old.

**7862 Special Education Action Commette**
PO Box 161274
Mobile, AL 36616      251-478-1208

*Mavis Smith, Executive Director*

**7863 Stuttering Foundation of America**
3100 Walnut Grove Road
Memphis, TN 38111      901-452-7343
800-992-9392
FAX: 901-452-3931
e-mail: stutter@stetteringhelp.org
www.stutteringhelp.org

*Jane Fraser, President*
*Anne Edwards, Coordinator*

Toll-free hotline, brochures, books and videotapes on stuttering.

**7864 Support Works**
1018 East Boulevard
Suite 5
Charlotte, NC 28203      704-331-9500

www.supportworks.org

*Joel Fisher, Owner*

SupportWorks helps people find and form support groups. An 8 page publication Power Tools, clearly walks new group leaders through steps of putting together a healthy self-help group. SupportWorks also has a telephone conference program which allows people with similar diseases or other nonprofit issues to meet by phone conference for free or at very low cost.

**7865 Teratogen and Birth Defects Information Project**
University of South Dakota
414 E Clark Street
Vermillion, SD 57069      605-677-5306
FAX: 605-677-5778

*Jim Abbott, President*

For South Dakota residents only.

**7866 Toll-Free Information Line**
Asthma and Allergy Foundation of America
1125 15th Street NW
Suite 502
Washington, DC 20005      202-466-7643
800-7AS-THMA
FAX: 202-466-8940
e-mail: info@aafa.org
www.aafa.org

*Bill Lin, Executive Director*

Referral line for questions about asthma and allergies and how to get involved in your local chapter and support groups.

**7867 VUE: Vision Use in Employment**
Carroll Center for the Blind
770 Centre Street
Newton, MA 02458      617-969-6200
800-852-3131
FAX: 617-969-6204
www.carroll.org

*Rachel Rosenbaum, President*
*Robert Mcgilliuray, Low Vision Administration*

Provides engineering solutions plus training to help people keep jobs despite their vision loss.

**7868 Visiting Nurse Association of America**
99 Summer Street
Suite 1700
Boston, MA 02110      617-737-3200
FAX: 617-737-1144
e-mail: vnaa@vnaa.org
www.vnaa.org

*Carolyn Markey, President/CEO*

This agency represents independent VNA units across the United States. Each VNA unit may vary in their services, but most provide skilled nursing, physical therapy, occupational therapy, speech therapy, and home health aid services.

**7869 Washington Connection**
American Council of the Blind
1155 15th Street NW
Suite 1004
Washington, DC 20005      202-467-5081
800-424-8666
FAX: 202-467-5085
www.acb.org

*Day Al-Mohamed, Governmental Affairs Director*
*Melanie Brunson, Executive Director*

Coverage of issues affecting blind people via legislative information, participates in law-making, legislative training seminars and networking of support resources across the US.

# General

## 7870 Age Appropriate Puzzles
7756 Winding Way
Fair Oaks, CA 95628
916-961-3507
FAX: 916-961-0765
e-mail: miltcher@spcglobal.net

*Cheryl Meyers, President*

These unique puzzles teach numerous concepts: picture, name, color and shape recognition. Each of the two themes (holidays, and clothing) comes with self-adhesive stickers that name each picture in English, Hmong, Russian, Spanish and Vietnamese. A notch at each puzzle piece makes grasping and lifting the pieces easy to use., They are designed for children from 18 months and up. Special needs children, preschool through high school would also benefit. *$9.95*

## 7871 All-Turn-It Spinner
AbleNet
2808 Fairview Avenue N
Roseville, MN 55113
651-294-2200
800-322-0956
FAX: 651-294-2222
e-mail: customerservice@ablenetinc.com
www.ablenetinc.com

*Rick Osterhaus, Chief Executive Officer*

The All-Turn-It Spinner is a random spinner that comes with a dice overlay allowing user's to participate in any commercially-available game that require dice. Activate the spinner with its built-in switch or connect an external switch. Overlays are interchangeable with AbleNet designed spinner games or create your own overlay. A great inclusion tool!. *$89.00*

## 7872 Anthony Brothers Manufacturing
Convert-O-Bike
1945 South Rancho Santa Fe Road
San Marcos, CA 92069
760-744-4763
FAX: 760-744-2994
e-mail: kids@kidtrikes.com
www.kidtrikes.com

*Julia Anthony, President*
*Sue Coffin, Vice President*

Manufacture wheeled toys and goods for disabled children.

## 7873 Automatic Card Shuffler
Maxi Aids
42 Executive Boulevard
Suite 3209
Farmingdale, NY 11735
631-752-0521
800-522-6294
FAX: 631-752-0689
e-mail: sales@maxiaids.com
www.maxiaids.com

Simple to use, the cards are physically challenging for the player with limited hand dexterity. *$14.95*

## 7874 Backgammon Set: Deluxe
Maxi Aids
42 Executive Boulevard
Suite 3209
Farmingdale, NY 11735
631-752-0521
800-522-6294
FAX: 631-752-0689
e-mail: sales@maxiaids.com
www.maxiaids.com

Completely factual with a felt board, raised white dividers and white braille dice for the blind and visually impaired. *$29.95*

## 7875 Board Games: Snakes and Ladders
Maxi Aids
42 Executive Boulevard
Suite 3209
Farmingdale, NY 11735
631-752-0521
800-522-6294
FAX: 631-752-0689
e-mail: sales@maxiaids.com
www.maxiaids.com

A dice game for 2 to 6 players. This children's game is also fun for the whole family. Offers recreation, competition and eye/hand coordination skills. *$34.95*

## 7876 Board Games: Solitaire
Maxi Aids
42 Executive Boulevard
Suite 3209
Farmingdale, NY 11735
631-752-0521
800-522-6294
FAX: 631-752-0689
e-mail: sales@maxiaids.com
www.maxiaids.com

This popular solo board game lends itself to a number of less well-known variations. The board is accompanied by brightly colored pieces that are reversible for the visually impaired player. *$30.95*

## 7877 Braille Playing Cards: Plastic
Maxi Aids
42 Executive Boulevard
Suite 3209
Farmingdale, NY 11735
631-752-0521
800-522-6294
FAX: 631-752-0689
e-mail: sales@maxiaids.com
www.maxiaids.com

Playing cards that offer regular print and braille on plastic cards for the blind or visually impaired player. *$9.95*

## 7878 Braille: Bingo Cards, Boards and Call Numbers
Maxi Aids
42 Executive Boulevard
Suite 3209
Farmingdale, NY 11735
631-752-0521
800-522-6294
FAX: 631-752-0689
e-mail: sales@maxiaids.com
www.maxiaids.com

Bingo products for the visually impaired. Cards, boards and call numbers offer regular print and braille. *$4.99*

## 7879 Braille: Rook Cards
Maxi Aids
42 Executive Boulevard
Suite 3209
Farmingdale, NY 11735
631-752-0521
800-522-6294
FAX: 631-752-0689
e-mail: sales@maxiaids.com
www.maxiaids.com

This set of cards for Rook, the popular bidding card game with 23 variations, has regular size print and braille print for the blind/visually impaired player. *$13.75*

## 7880 Card Holder Deluxe
Maxi Aids
42 Executive Boulevard
Suite 3209
Farmingdale, NY 11735
631-752-0521
800-522-6294
FAX: 631-752-0689
e-mail: sales@maxiaids.com
www.maxiaids.com

A handsome-looking card holder takes the struggle out of holding playing cards in weak or arthritic hands. The two clear plastic tiers hold up to 18 cards. The wooden base has a non-skid bottom to prevent slipping, and is also great for holding recipe cards. *$19.75*

**7881 Cards: Musical**
Sense-Sations
919 Walnut Street
Philadelphia, PA 19107
215-627-0600
FAX: 215-922-0692
www.asb.org

*Patricia Johnson, Chief Executive Officer*

These cards, for all occasions, play music when they are opened,
for the visually impaired and blind persons. *$2.50*

**7882 Cards: UNO**
Maxi Aids
42 Executive Boulevard
Suite 3209
Farmingdale, NY 11735
631-752-0521
800-522-6294
FAX: 631-752-0689
e-mail: sales@maxiaids.com
www.maxiaids.com

Traditional card game in braille for the blind player recreation.
*$10.95*

**7883 Checker Set: Deluxe**
Maxi Aids
42 Executive Boulevard
Suite 3209
Farmingdale, NY 11735
631-752-0521
800-522-6294
FAX: 631-752-0689
e-mail: sales@maxiaids.com
www.maxiaids.com

A wooden board with sunken playing squares. The squares have
drilled holes for inserting the checker, offering help with
eye/hand coordination for the physically challenged. *$25.95*

**7884 Chess Set: Deluxe**
Maxi Aids
42 Executive Boulevard
Suite 3209
Farmingdale, NY 11735
631-752-0521
800-522-6294
FAX: 631-752-0689
e-mail: sales@maxiaids.com
www.maxiaids.com

Made out of wood material. Boards have raised dark squares and
all squares have drilled holes for inserting pegged chessmen, for
the physically challenged player with poor eye/hand coordination. *$43.95*

**7885 Dice: Jumbo Size**
New Vision Store
919 Walnut Street
Philadelphia, PA 19107
215-629-2990

The large white and black dice are over-sized and have grooved
dots to indicate the numbers, for easy reading for the visually
handicapped. *$4.95*

**7886 Enabling Devices**
385 Warburton Avenue
Hastings on Hudson, NY 10706
914-478-0960
800-832-8697
FAX: 914-479-1369
e-mail: info@enablingdevices.com
www.enablingdevices.com

*Elizabeth Bell, Marketing Manager*
*Karen O'Connor, Vice President Operations*
*Steven Kanor, Owner*

For more than 25 years, Enabling Devices has been dedicated to
providing affordable learning and assistive devices for the physically challenged. Products include augmentative communica-
tors, adapted toys, capability switches, training and sensory
devices and activity centers. Call for a free catalog.

**7887 Hands-Free Controller**
Nintendo
PO Box 957
Redmond, WA 98073
800-255-3700
www.nintendo.com

*Yoshio Tsuboike, Editor-in-Chief*

Nintendo controller for the physically disabled.

**7888 National Lekotek Center**
3204 West Armitage Avenue
Chicago, IL 60647
773-276-5164
800-366-PLAY
FAX: 773-276-8644
TTY: 800-573-4446
e-mail: lekotek@lekotek.org
www.lekotek.org

*Diana Nielander, Executive Director*
*Clarice Brown, Programs/Training Asst Director*

Maximizes the development of children with special needs
through play. Supports families through nationwide family play
centers, toy lending libraries and computer play programs. Publishes six-page newsletter three times per year.

**7889 One Hundred Board and Pegs**
Maxi Aids
42 Executive Boulevard
Suite 3209
Farmingdale, NY 11735
631-752-0521
800-522-6294
FAX: 631-752-0689
e-mail: sales@maxiaids.com
www.maxiaids.com

Cognitive skills and motor stimulation. *$34.95*

**7890 Puzzle Games: Cooking, Eating, Community and
Grooming**
PCI
PO Box 34270
San Antonio, TX 78265
210-670-3866
800-594-4263
FAX: 218-210-3771
www.pci.edu.com

*Janie Haugen, Program Director*
*Jeff McLane, President/CEO*
*Rebecca Phillips, Executive Director*

Each game has 63 pieces which are 2 inches in size. The completed full color puzzle is 19 inch x 15 inch. Step 1 - Work the
puzzle. Step 2 - Match picture or word cards to the correct space
on the puzzle. These puzzles teach basic life skills. *$19.95*

**7891 Single Switch Latch and Timer**
AbleNet
1081 10th Avenue SE
Minneapolis, MN 55414
800-322-0956
FAX: 612-379-9143
e-mail: customerservice@ablenetinc.com
www.ablenetinc.com

A Single Switch Latch and Timer allows a user to activate a battery-operated toy or appliance in the latch, timed seconds and
timed minutes modes of control. Choose for one user and one device at a time. *$63.00*

**7892 Take a Chance**
Speech Bin
1965 25th Avenue
Vero Beach, FL 32960
772-770-0007
800-477-3324
FAX: 772-770-0006
e-mail: info@speechbin.com
www.speechbin.com

*Jan J Binney, Senior Editor*

Card game for practice of commonly misarticulated speech
sounds. *$18.75*

*16 pages Book & Cards*
*ISBN 0-93785 -46-7*

**7893   Tic Tac Toe Plus**
Maxi Aids
42 Executive Boulevard
Suite 3209
Farmingdale, NY  11735                           631-752-0521
                                                 800-522-6294
                                            FAX: 631-752-0689
                                    e-mail: sales@maxiaids.com
                                             www.maxiaids.com
Offers the traditional tic-tac-toe game but with pieces that are
3/4 inch in diameter and 1/4 inch high in black and green, for the
visually impaired player. *$5.95*

**7894   Turnabout Game**
Maxi Aids
42 Executive Boulevard
Suite 3209
Farmingdale, NY  11735                           631-752-0521
                                                 800-522-6294
                                            FAX: 631-752-0689
                                    e-mail: sales@maxiaids.com
                                             www.maxiaids.com
A game of strategy for two, with large playing pieces and a
bright gameboard for the visually impaired player. *$7.70*

## Newsletters &amp; Books

**7895 A Guide for the Wheelchair Traveler**
Access For Disabled Americans
3685 Mount Diablo Boulevard
Suite 300
Lafayette, CA 94549                    925-284-6444
                                  FAX: 925-284-6448
                          e-mail: psmither@aol.com
                          www.accessfordisabled.com

*Neal Smither, President*
*Patricia Smither, Editor/Secretary*

All you need to know when traveling in a wheelchair. *$30.00*
*165 pages Paperback*
*ISBN 1-928616-00-3*

**7896 A World Awaits You**
Mobility International U SA
PO Box 10767
Eugene, OR 97440                       541-343-1284
                                  FAX: 541-343-6812
                             e-mail: info@miusa.org
                                      www.miusa.org

*Barb Cheshir, Information Services Coordinator*
*Susan Sygall, Executive Director*

A journal of success stories and tips of people with disabilities participating in international exchange programs.
*40 pages Yearly*

**7897 Access Travel: Airports**
Consumer Information Center
Department 575a
Pueblo, CO 81009                       719-948-3334

                      e-mail: catalog.pueblo@gsa.gov

*Michael Clark, Public Affairs*
*Alfred Pino, Manager*

Tips and suggestions for easier travel for persons with disabilities and the elderly. Lists designs, facilities, and services at 553 airport terminals worldwide.

**7898 Architectural Barriers Action League**
PO Box 57088
Tucson, AZ 85732                       520-628-8118

*Martin Floerchinger, Owner*

Offers guides to accessible hotels and motels across the country.

**7899 Directory of Accessible Van Rentals**
Disability Bookshop
PO Box 129
Vancouver, WA 98666                    360-694-2462

Designed to help people with disabilities locate rental vans that are accessible throughout the U.S. *$9.95*
*30+ pages*
*ISBN 0-93326-09-9*

**7900 Directory of Travel Agencies for the Disabled**
Twin Peaks Press
PO Box 129
Vancouver, WA 98666                    360-694-2462
                                       800-637-2256
                                  FAX: 360-696-3210
                        e-mail: twinpeak@pacifier.com
                                    home.pacifier.com

*David Lynch, Director*

Directory lists more than 360 travel agents specializing in arrangements for people with disabilities. Handbook provides information about accessibility. *$19.95*

*40 pages Paperback*
*ISBN 0-93326-04-8*

**7901 Elderly Guide to Budget Travel/Europe**
Pilot Books
PO Box 2102
Greenport, NY 11944                    631-477-1094
                                  FAX: 631-661-4379

Includes a list of over 250 inexpensive hotels in prime tourist areas. Covers special needs of senior citizens including inexpensive accommodations and fares. *$3.95*

**7902 Ideas for Easy Travel**
Accent Books &amp; Products
PO Box 700
Bloomington, IL 61702                  309-378-2961
                                       800-787-8444
                                  FAX: 309-378-4420
                          e-mail: acmtlvng@aol.com

*Raymond C Cheever, Publisher*
*Betty Garee, Editor*

Ideal for helping the new traveler get started having fun. Points out favorite accessible high-spots as reported by two travel experts (one is disabled), and offers basic ideas to help wherever you go. *$3.25*
*55 pages Paperback*
*ISBN 0-91570-36-1*

**7903 Survival Strategies for Going Abroad, A Guide for People with Disabilites**
PO Box 10767
Eugene, OR 97440                       541-343-1284
                                  FAX: 541-343-6812
                             e-mail: info@miusa.org
                                      www.miusa.org

*Susan Sygall, Executive Director*
*Melissa Mitchell, Public Relations*

*$16.95*
*225 pages*

**7904 Travel Information Service/Moss Rehab Hospital**
Moss Rehabilitation Hospital
1200 West Tabor Road
Philadelphia, PA 19141                 215-456-9900
                                       800-225-5667
                    e-mail: staff@mossresourcenet.org
                               www.mossresourcenet.org

*Joan Appel, Manager*
*Alberto Esquenazi, Plant Manager*

Offers information and resources, to telephone callers only, for persons with special traveling/accessibility needs.

**7905 United States Department of the Interior National Park Service**
Superintendent of Documents
1849 C Street NW
Washington, DC 20240                   202-208-3100
                                  FAX: 202-619-7302
                          e-mail: webteam@ios.doi.gov
                                       www.doi.gov

*Mainella, Director*
*Gale Norton, Chief Executive Officer*

Offers an informational packet containing books, guides and tours for the disabled and elderly.

**7906 Wheelin Around**
Wheelers Accessible Van Rentals
6614 West Sweetwater Avenue
Glendale, AZ 85304 623-776-8830
800-456-1371
FAX: 623-412-9920
e-mail: info@wheelersvanrentals.com
www.wheelersvanrentals.com

*Tammy Smith, President*
*Ron Smith, Corporate Treasurer*

**7907 Wheelin' Around**
Wheelers Accessible Van Rentals
710 N 55th Avenue
Glendale, AZ 85301

800-456-1371
FAX: 602-412-9920
e-mail: wheelens@primenet.com
www.wheelerz.com

*Tammy Smith, President*

A newsletter for persons with physical disabilities by Wheelers Accessible Van Rentals offering information on automotive assistive devices, van conversions and travel tips for the disabled.
*Quarterly*

**7908 Where to Stay USA**
Council On International Educational Exchange
633 3rd Avenue
New York, NY 10017 212-822-2600
888-COU-NCIL
FAX: 212-822-2649

*Priscilla Tovey, Information Services*
A guide to low-cost lodging throughout the United States including information on whether the establishment is accessible. *$15.95*
250 pages
ISBN 0-67179-49-5

## Associations & Programs

**7909 Access America**
Northern Cartographic
4050 Williston Road
Suite 131
South Burlington, VT 05403 802-860-2886
FAX: 802-865-4912
e-mail: info@ncarto.com
www.ncarto.com
Offers information on 36 national parks, providing detailed information on accessibility.

**7910 Access Yosemite National Park**
Special Needs Project
324 State Street
Suite H
Santa Barbara, CA 93101 805-962-8087
800-333-6867
FAX: 805-962-5087
e-mail: books@specialneeds.com
www.specialneeds.com

*Hod Gray, Executive Director*
*Laraine Gray, Coordinator*

Represents unprecedented combinations of intensive information survey data with high quality cartography. *$7.95*

*31 pages*

**7911 America West Airlines**
4000 East Sky Harbor Boulevard
Phoenix, AZ 85034 480-693-0800
800-327-7810
FAX: 480-693-3702
www.americawest.com

*Dan Berkey, Director*
*W Parket, Chief Executive Officer*

This airline trains employees to make sure that passengers with disabilities enjoy convenient, safe and comfortable travel.

**7912 American Hotel and Lodging Association**
1201 New York Avenue NW
Washington, DC 20005 202-289-3100
FAX: 202-289-3199
e-mail: comments@ahlaonline.org
www.ahma.com

*Joseph A McInerney, President/CEO*
*Pam Inman, Senior Vice President*

Will disseminate information, develop and conduct a series of seminars for the hotel and motel industry at state-level association conferences, and develop and distribute an ADA Compliance handbook for use by the lodging industry.

**7913 Amtrak**
60 Massachusetts Avenue NE
Washington, DC 20002 202-906-3000
800-872-7245
FAX: 202-906-4564
TTY: 202-906-2500
e-mail: access@w0.amtrak.com
www.amtrak.com

*David Gunn, President/CEO*
*David M Laney, Chairman of the Board*

Amtrak is committed to making travel for passengers with disabilities more accessible. Anyone interested should contact Amtrak's Special Services Desk at 1-800-USA-RAIL at least 24 hours in advance to arrange for special assistance. The type of equipment and accessibility vary from train to train and station to station.

**7914 Easter Seals Project ACTION**
700 13th Street NW
Suite 200
Washington, DC 20005 202-347-3066
800-659-6428
FAX: 202-737-7914
TTY: 202-347-7385
e-mail: project_action@easterseals.com
www.projectaction.org

*Alan Abeson, Director*
*Joseph Romer, Vice President*

A national technical assistance program designed to improve access to transportation services for people with disabilities and assist transit providers in implementing the Americans with Disabilities Act. Publishes quarterly newsletter.

**7915 Easy Access to National Parks: The Sierra Club Guide for the Disabled**
Sierra Club Books
85 2nd Street
Floor 2
San Francisco, CA 94105 415-977-5500
FAX: 415-977-5799
www.sierraclub.org

*Joan Hamilton, Editor In Chief*
*Martha Geering, Art Director*
*Carl Pope, Manager*

Includes practical information on planning safe trips to 50 national parks that are designated as best visits for their accessibility. *$16.00*

*432 pages*
*ISBN 0-87156 -20-6*

**7916 General Motors Mobility Program for Persons with Disabilities**
GM Mobility Program
PO Box 300
Detroit, MI 48265

313-665-0746
800-323-9935
www.gm.com

*Richard Wagoner, CEO And President*
*John M Devine, Vice Chairman*

GM Mobility Program provides up to $1000 reimbursement toward mobility adaptations for drivers or passengers and/or vehicle alerting devices for drivers who are deaf or hard of hearing. Provided on eligible new Chevrolet, Pontiac, Oldsmobile, Buick, Cadillac, and GMC vehicles. Complete GMC financing available. GM Mobility also offers free resource information, including list of area adaptive equipment installers, plus free resource video.

**7917 Kenny Foundation**
21700 Northwestern Highway
Suite 730
Southfield, MI 48075

248-552-0202
800-237-3422
FAX: 248-552-0275
e-mail: comnet@uwcs.org
www.comnet.org/kenny

*Susan Burstein, Executive Director*

Provides education, advocacy & direct services to people with mobility impairments throughout Michigan. Services include Equipment Connection, a database, available online, that connects buyers & sellers of used adaptive equipment; Attitudes is a disability awareness program for 1st & 2nd graders; Information & Referral services; and Accessbility, a program that uses volunteer labor and donated materials to buid ramps for people who can't afford them.

**7918 Melwood Access Adventures**
9035 Ironsides Road
Nanjemoy, MD 20662

301-934-3590
FAX: 301-870-2620
e-mail: accessadventures@melwood.com
www.melwood.com

*Earl Copus, CEO and President*
*Jane Greenweem, Program Manager*
*Heidi Aldous, Manager*

A year round recreation facility that serves mentally and physically disabled individuals, offers a variety of vacations, outdoor recreation, travel and respite care.

**7919 Nantahala Outdoor Center**
13077 Highway 19 West
Bryson City, NC 28713

828-488-2175
800-232-7238
FAX: 828-488-2498
e-mail: rafting@noc.com
www.noc.com

*Cathy Kennedy, Director*
*Payson Kennedy, Chief Executive Officer*

Nantahala Outdoor Center, the leader in outdoor recreation and education for more than 30 years, strongly encourages and supports participants with disabilities. We offer whitewater rafting adventures on six rivers in the Southeast for all skill and thrill levels for groups, also kayak and canoe adaptive instruction. NOC will tailor a whitewater program to your skill and ability level, modify the gear, and pace instruction for you. We also offer a Ropes Challenge Course and team building program

**7920 Paralysis Society of America**
Paralyzed Veterans Of America
801 18th Street NW
Washington, DC 20006

202-872-1300
888-772-1711
FAX: 202-973-8421
TTY: 202-973-8422
e-mail: info@psa.org
www.pva.org/psa

*Randy Pleza, President*
*Trish Armstrong, Membership Coordinator*

A national organization whose members are people with spinal cord injury or disease, their family members and caregivers, health-care professionals, and others with an interest in the disciplines of spinal cord medicine and paralsis. One year membership includes NewsWheels, a quarterly newsletter. *$10.00*

**7921 Respiratory Health Association**
301 Sicomac Avenue
Wyckoff, NJ 07481

201-447-8508

*Edward Duffie, President*

Offers eight-day cruises for people with respiratory conditions to Bermuda and Alaska at least twice a year.

**7922 Shilo Inns & Resorts**
11600 SW Shilo Lane
Portland, OR 97225

503-641-6565
800-222-2244
FAX: 503-644-0868
www.shiloinns.com

*Mark Hemstreet, President*
*Ivan McAffee, Director*
*John Kneeland, Chief Executive Officer*

Shilo Inns offers affordable excellence with special assist rooms at many of our locations throughout the western United States. These rooms include larger sized bathrooms equipped with assistance railings and wheelchair access. Special assist dogs are welcome free of charge ar most Shilo Inns. Call 1-800-222-2244 for details or make reservations or check out www.shiloinns.com

**7923 Special Assistance Services (SAS)**
3 High Street
Helmetta, NJ 08828

FAX: 732-521-9333

*James J Muzikowski, President*
*Steve Rosenel, Assistant Travel Coordinator*

The mission of this organization is to empower the quest to travel. They supply this by offering flexible plans and personal assistance. S.A.S. is dedicated to providing various types of assistance to persons with disabilities. The organization serves guests with a variety of special needs, including but not limited to persons with visual and hearing impairments, physical and development disabilities, and the mentally challenged.

**7924 Travelers Aid Society**
1612 K Street NW
Washington, DC 20006

202-546-1127
FAX: 202-546-9112
e-mail: tadcmichael@aol.com
www.travelersaid.org/ta

*Ray Flint, President*

Provides crisis intervention and casework services, limited financial assistance, protective travel assistance and information and referrals for travelers, transients and newcomers.

**7925  US Servas**

11 John Street
Room 505
New York, NY  10038

212-267-0252
FAX: 212-267-0292
e-mail: info@usservas.org
www.usservas.org

*Julie Schumacher, Program Director*
*Gilbert Sherr, Manager*

International network that links travelers with hosts in 130+ countries with the hope of building world peace through understanding and friendship.
*Quarterly*

**7926  Westin Hotels and Resorts**

PO Box 141609
Austin, TX  78714

FAX: 512-835-4417
www.westin.com

Westin Hotels include special parking stalls, wheelchair ramps, wide doors, wheelchairs, braille elevator buttons, recreational facilities for people with disabilities, restaurants and restrooms.

**7927  Wheelers Accessible Van Rentals**

Corporate Office
6614 W Sweetwater Avenue
Glendale, AZ  85304

623-776-8830
800-456-1371
FAX: 623-412-9920
e-mail: info@wheelersvanrentals.com
www.wheelersvanrentals.com

Rental wheelchairs and scooter accessible vans. Technically advanced engineering features bring a world of independence to the user. Locations throughout the U.S. call 800-456-1371 to make reservations at any of our locations nationwide.

**7928  Wilderness Inquiry**

808 14th Avenue SE
Minneapolis, MN  55414

612-676-9400
800-728-0179
FAX: 612-676-9401
TTY: 612-676-9475
e-mail: info@wildernessinquiry.org
www.wildernessinquiry.org

*Greg Lais, Executive Director*
*Steph Schmit, Administration Director*
*Terry Murtaugh, Program Director*

Allows people of all ages and abilities to share the adventure of wilderness travel. This nonprofit organization was formed in 1978 and conducts tours to some of the most beautiful and remote parts of the world.

# Tours

**7929  Accessible Journeys**

35 W Sellers Avenue
Ridley Park, PA  19078

610-521-0339
800-846-4537
FAX: 610-521-6959
e-mail: sales@disabilitytravel.com
www.disabilitytravel.com

*Henry Thoreau, President*
*Howard Coy, Owner*

Tour operator for slow walker and wheelchair travelers their families and their friends offering tours to culturally intriguing destinations like Europe, Canada, Alaksa, Great Britain and Hawaii.

**7930  Accesstotheplanet**

Accessible Journeys
35 W Sellers Avenue
Ridley Park, PA  19078

610-521-0339
800-846-4537
FAX: 610-521-6959
e-mail: sales@disabilitytravel.com
www.disabilitytravel.com

*Howard Coy, Owner*
*Kathy Pagliei, Vice President Cruise Operations*
*Monthly*

**7931  Anglo California Travel Service**

4250 Williams Road
San Jose, CA  95129

408-257-2257
FAX: 408-257-2664
www.webtravel.com

*Audrey Cooper, President*

Plans for one and two week accessible tours.

**7932  Bill Dvorak, Kayak and Rafting Expeditions**

17921 Us Highway 285
Nathrop, CO  81236

719-539-6851
800-824-3795
FAX: 719-539-3378
e-mail: dvorakex@amigo.net
www.dvorakexpeditions.com

*Bill Dvorak, President*
*Jaci Dvorak, Vice President*

This organization does river trips for people who are deaf, visually impaired, physically or mentally disabled. Rafting trips with groups and families and whitewater instruction.

**7933  Cunard Line**

6100 Blue Lagoon Drive
Miami, FL  33126

305-463-3000
800-528-6273
FAX: 305-463-3010
www.cunard.co.uk

*Debbie Nathanshoan, President*

Cunard Line, one of the world's most recognized brand names with a classic British heritage, operated by Cunard Line Limited, has provided the ultimate in deluxe ocean travel experience for the past 158 years. The fleet consists of famed liner Queen Elizabeth 2 and the Caronia, a classic ship formerly identified as Vistafjord. The Cunard Line brand, the epitome of British essence, focuses on recalling the golden age of sea travel for those who missed the first.

**7934  Dell Rapids Sportsmens Club**

PO Box 126
Dell Rapids, SD  57022

605-428-5501
FAX: 605-428-5502
e-mail: ezhealth@sd.cybernex.net
www.rodandgunclub.com

*Dan Anderson, Chief Executive Officer*

**7935  Diabetic Cruise Desk**

Hartford Holiday Travel
PO Box 536
Williston Park, NY  11596

516-746-6670
800-828-4813
FAX: 516-746-6690
e-mail: info@hartfordholidays.com
www.hartfordholidays.com

*Les Kertes, President*

Offers a seven-day cruise to Alaska for people with diabetes. Includes seminars on diabetes, self management, planning, special guidance for exercise classes and individual dietary advice.

**7936  Dialysis at Sea Cruises**
13555 Automobile Boulevard
Suite 220
Clearwater, FL 33762                        727-518-7311
                                             800-544-7604
                                         FAX: 727-573-1910
                                         www.dialysisatsea.com

*Steve Debroux, President*

Been in the business of providing travel opportunities for persons on hemodialysis and CAPD since 1977. Handle all aspects of their travel and medical requirements. Not Sold Through Travel Agents! Make all reservations and coordinates the total set-up and operation of an onboard ship mobile dialysis clinic. Cruises run from seven days to three weeks and have departures from cities around the world on a variety of cruise lines.

**7937  Directions Unlimited Acccessible Tours**
Empress Travel
123 Green Lane
Bedford Hills, NY  10507                    914-241-1700
                                             800-533-5343
                                         FAX: 914-241-0243

*Lois Bonanni, Director*
*Charles Digiacomo, Manager*

Arrange vacations throughout the world for all disabilities including accessible cruises, African safari, rafting and scuba diving, European and Caribbean vacations.

**7938  Environmental Traveling Companions**
Fort Mason Center
San Francisco, CA  94123                    415-474-7662
                                         FAX: 415-474-3919
                                         e-mail: info@etctrips.org
                                         www.etctrips.org

*Diane Poslosky, Executive Director*
*Davido Crow, River Program Manager*
*Greg Milano, Sea Kayak Program Manager*

Aids travelers regardless of physical or financial limitations to experience the beauty and challenge of the wilderness.

**7939  Flying Wheels Travel**
143 W Bridge Street
PO Box 382
Owatonna, MN  55060                         507-451-5005
                                         FAX: 507-451-1685
                                         e-mail: bjacobson@ll.net
                                         www.flyingwheelstravel.com

*Barbara Jacobson, President*

Arranges worldwide custom independent travel and cruises for the physically challenged.

**7940  Golden Eagle Passport**
U S Department of the Interior, National Park Serv
1849 C Street NW
Washington, DC  20240                       202-208-5815
                                         FAX: 202-208-6956
                                         e-mail: webteam@ios.doi.gov
                                         www.nps.gov

*Fran P Mainella, Director*
*John Sherrod, Executive Director*

A free lifetime passport to federally operated parks, monuments, historic sites, recreation areas and wildlife refuges for persons who are blind or permanently disabled.

**7941  Guide Service of Washington**
734 15th Street NW
Washington, DC  20005                       202-628-2842
                                         FAX: 202-638-2812

*Neil Amrine, President*
A guide service offering tours of Washington DC and vicinity.

**7942  Guided Tour for Persons 17 & Over with Developmental and Physical Challenges**
7900 Old York Road
Suite 111b
Elkins Park, PA  19027                      215-782-1370
                                             800-783-5841
                                         FAX: 215-635-2637
                                         e-mail: gtour400@aol.com
                                         www.guidedtour.com

*Irwin Segal DCSW/LSW, Director/Owner*
*Ari Segal MSW/LSW, Assistant Director*

Offers unique travel and vacation programs for individuals with mild to moderate developmental disabilities. We publish a free Rates & Dates brochure twice a year.

**7943  Hostelling North America Hostelling International: American Youth Hostels**
8401 Colesville Road
Suite 600
Silver Spring, MD  20910                    301-495-1240
                                         FAX: 301-495-6697
                                         e-mail: hostels@hiusa.org
                                         www.hiayh.org

*Demetria Trent, Executive Director*

Hostels are very inexpensive accommodations for travelers of all ages. They provide dorm-style sleeping rooms with separate quarters for males and females, fully equipped self-service kitchens, dining areas and common rooms for relaxing and socializing. HI-AYH has hostels in major cities, in national and state parks, near beaches and in the mountains. Send for a copy of Hostelling North America, a directory of hostels in U.S. and Canada, which lists hostels that are handicap accessible. *$ 3.00*
                                    *400 pages Yearly*

**7944  New Courier Travel**
532 Duane Street
Glen Ellyn, IL  60137                       630-469-0511
                                         FAX: 630-469-7390

*Janice Perkins, Travel Consultant*
*Ford Mueller, Owner*

Offers specialized assistance for independent travel or tours for persons with disabilities including cruises and travel in the USA and abroad. Fee charged for out-of-state clients, long-distance calls and clients who have free air.

**7945  New Directions**
5276 Hollister Avenue
Suite 207
Santa Barbara, CA  93111                    805-967-2841
                                             888-967-2841
                                         FAX: 805-964-7344
                                         e-mail: info@newdirectionstravel.com
                                         www.newdirectionstravel.com

*Dee Duncan, Executive Director*
*David McKean, Program Director*
*Jeanne Mohle, Sr Program Manager*

A non-profit organization providing high quality local, national, and international travel vacations and holiday programs for people with mild to moderate developmental disabilities. Each year New Directions serves over 600 teenagers, adults and seniors who have brain impairments such as mild to moderate developmental disabilities, mental retardation, cerebral palsy , Down Syndrome and autism.

**7946  Norwegian Cruise Line**
7665 NW 19th Street
Miami, FL  33126                            305-436-4000
                                         FAX: 305-436-4117
                                         www.ncl.com

*Colin Veitch, President/CEO*

Has accessible cabins but urges mobility impaired passengers to travel in the same cabin with a person who is not mobility impaired. Cruise fares vary.

**7947  People and Places**
3909 Genesee Street
Cheektowaga, NY 14225                    585-937-1813

*Joie Budington, Director*
*Patty Brown Schieder, Assistant Director*

Nonprofit organization that provides escorted small group vacation opportunities and outdoor experiences throughout the world for persons with developmental disabilities. Brochure available.

**7948  ROW Adventures**
P O Box 579- DI
Coeur D Alene, ID 83816              208-667-1835
                                     800-451-6034
                              FAX: 208-667-6506
                      e-mail: info@rowadventures.com
                              www.rowadventures.com

*Peter Grubb, Founder*

Offers one to six day rafting trips to physically disadvantaged people. Designs custom itineraries, or trips with a special focus for small groups. For those with special dietary needs, they prepare special meals. So come ride the rapids and enjoy life. They also offer canoe trips aboard 34' voyager canoes along the trail of Lewis and Clark on Montana's upper Missouri River. Free brochure upon request.

**7949  River Odysseys West: ROW**
PO Box 579
Coeur D Alene, ID 83816              208-667-1835

**7950  Search Beyond Adventures**
PO Box 68
Palmer, MA 01069                     612-721-2800
                                     800-800-9979
                              FAX: 866-721-3409
                      e-mail: travel@searchbeyond.com
                              www.searchbeyond.com

*Kilash Dhaksinamurdth, President/CEO/Owner*

Operates a wide variety of tours for adults with mental retardation. Programs vary from 2 to 16 days throughout North America, the Caribbean and Europe. Offices in Minneapolis, Boston, Orlando and Sacramento areas. Catalog of over 135 tours are available.

**7951  Sundial Special Vacations**
Sundial Special Vacations
2609 Highway 101 N
Suite 103
Seaside, OR 97138                    503-738-3324
                                     800-547-9198
                              FAX: 503-738-3369
                      e-mail: ssv@sundial-travel.com
                              www.sundialtour.com

*Bruce Conner, Tour Operations Director/Owner*
*Patsy Conner, Owner*
*Cathy Louden, Director of Operations*

Provides special vacations for developmentally disabled persons. Provides quality vacations for persons with developmental disabilities. Ratio is 1 for 7 or 1 for 5 depending on tour. Only two people to a room. Exciting destinations. 3 to 4 star properties. Great fun.

**7952  Ventures Travel**
10509 108th Street NW
Annandale, MN 55302                  952-852-0101
                                     866-692-7400
                              FAX: 952-852-0123
                      e-mail: vt@venturestravel.org
                              www.venturestravel.org

Ventures Travel a limited liability company is a service of Friendship Ventures-a nonprofit organization that has been enriching the lives of people with mental retardation and related developmental disabilities since 1985. Contact us to learn about our other programs, employment information, volunteer openings or donor opportunities.

**7953  Wheelchair Getaways**
4307 Crittenden Drive
Louisville, KY 40209                 502-363-4646
                                     800-458-1115
                              FAX: 502-363-9756
                      e-mail: sue@superiorvan.com
                              www.wheelchairgetaways.com

*Rebecca Heim, Manager*

Wheelchair Getaways, the largest wheelchair/scooter accessible van rental company in the US, has 50 franchise locations serving major cities and airports throughout the continental US and Hawaii. Rentals by the day, week, month or longer. Delivery/pickup available.

## Vehicle Rentals

**7954  ABC Union, ACE, ANLV, Vegas Western Cab**
5010 S Valley View Boulevard
Las Vegas, NV 89118                  702-736-8444
                              FAX: 702-736-5197

*George Rodriguez, Manager*
*Charles Frias, President*

Taxi service in Las Vegas that uses vans with wheelchair lifts at regular taxi rates.

**7955  Avis Rent-A-Car**
6 Sylvan Way
Suite 1
Parsippany, NJ 07054                 973-496-3500
                                     800-230-4898
                              FAX: 800-331-2323
                              www.avis.com

*F Salerno, Chief Executive Officer*

Requires 24-hour notice for hand control vehicles, available in any location across the US.

**7956  CEH**
4457 63rd Circle
Pinellas Park, FL 33781              727-522-0364
                                     800-677-0364
                              FAX: 727-522-9024

*Phillip G Faas, President/Owner*

New vans, used vans, rental vans; specializing in quad conversions, all types of handicap equipment. Celebrating 28 years in business.

**7957  Mobile Care**
6201 Riverdale Road
Suite 101
Riverdale, MD 20737                  301-649-0564
                              FAX: 301-699-1865
                      e-mail: jaklimo@aol.com

*Jeffery A Koch, President*

Specializing in non-emergency wheelchair service for the elderly and physically challenged.

**7958  National Car Rental System**
600 Terminal Drive
Suite 202
Fort Lauderdale, FL  33315          954-359-8303
                                    FAX: 954-359-8313
                                    www.nationalcar.com

*William Decker, Manager*

Accommodates special requests subject to availability. Offers hand controls, bench seats, extra mirrors and vans with lifts at many major locations.

**7959  Northwest Limousine Service**
9950 Lawrence Avenue
Schiller Park, IL  60176          847-671-5482
                                  800-376-5466
                                  FAX: 847-671-5482
                                  e-mail: chiohare@aol.com

*Kathleen Maloney, Manager*

Offers wheelchair accessible mini vans, sedans, stretch and super stretch limousines for hourly or daily rental.

**7960  Over the Rainbow Disabled Travel Services & Wheelers Accessible Van Rentals**
186 Mehani Circle
Kihei, HI  96753                  808-879-5521
                                  800-303-3750
                                  FAX: 808-871-7533

*David McKown, Vice President*

Offers the disabled traveler Hawaii airport arrangements and ticketing accessible accommodations, hotels and condos including roll-in showers, Wheelers' Accessible Van Rentals on Maui and Honolulu or cars with hand controls, personal care attendants, medical or recreational equipment rentals and activities such as: helicopter rides, luau's, whalewatching, boating and more. Airfare varies from departure points and time of the year.

**7961  Rehabiliation Engineering Center for Personal Licensed Transportation**
University Of Virginia School Of Engineering
PO Box 400246
Charlottesville, VA  22904          434-924-3072

*Tom Connors, Vice President*
*Mitch Rosen, Director*

**7962  Wheelchair Getaways Wheelchair/Scooter Accessible Van Rentals**
4307 Crittenden Drive
Louisville, KY  40209             502-363-4646
                                  800-458-1115
                                  FAX: 502-363-9756
                                  e-mail: corporate@wheelchairgetaways.com
                                  www.wheelchairgetaways.com

*Richard Gatewood, Owner*
*Moon Ko, Owner*
*Rebecca Heim, Manager*

Rents wheelchair/scooter accessible vans by the day, week, month or longer and offers delivery to major airports and other convenient locations in more than 200 cities in 42 states and Puerto Rico. Also offers full size and mini vans with automatic lifts and ramps. Some vans are equipped with hand controls, six-way power seats and remote controls for powered door operation and lifts.

**7963  Wheelers**
7101 N 55th Avenue
Glendale, AZ  85301
                                  800-456-1371
                                  FAX: 623-435-9989

Offers delivery to airports in 29 states and Washington, D.C. In about 40 cities, Wheelers works directly with Avis Rent-a-Car. Wheelers offers a variety of van configurations with capacity for up to three wheelchairs, automatic ramps or lifts and nylon tie-downs, hand controls or other modifications.

**7964  Wheelers Accessible Van Rentals**
6614 W Sweetwater Avenue
Glendale, AZ  85304
                                  800-456-1371
                                  FAX: 623-435-1518
                                  e-mail: info@wheelersvanrentals.com
                                  www.wheelersvanrentals.com

*Tammy Smith, President*
*Ron Smith, Corporate Treasurer*

## National Administrations

**7965  DAV National Service Headquarters**
807 Maine Avenue SW
Washington, DC  20024          202-554-3501
                               FAX: 202-554-3581
                               e-mail: feedback@davmail.org
                               www.dav.org

*Arthur H Wilson, National Adjutant*
*David W Gorman, Executive Director*

Serves America's disabled veterans and their families. Direct services include legislative advocacy; professional counseling about compensation, pension, educational and job training programs and VA health care; and assistance in applying for those entitlements.

**7966  Department of Medicine and Surgery Veterans Administration**
810 Vermont Avenue NW
Washington, DC  20420          202-273-8504
                               FAX: 202-273-9108

*Gerald MDdonald MD, Senior Consultant*

Provides hospital and outpatient treatment as well as nursing home care for eligible veterans in Veterans Administration facilities. Services elsewhere provided on a contract basis in the United States and its territories. Provides non-vocational inpatient residential rehabilitation services to eligible legally blinded veterans of the armed forces of the United States.

**7967  Department of Veterans Affairs Regional Office - Vocational Rehab Division**
380 Westminster Street
Providence, RI  02903          401-222-2488
                               800-827-1000
                               FAX: 401-254-3220
                               e-mail: dhs.state.ri.us/dhs/dvetsff.htm
                               www.va.gov

*Gerald E Allen, Counseling Officer*

Vocational rehabilitation is a program of services administered by the Department of Veterans Affairs for service members and veterans with service-connected physical or mental disabilities. If persons are compensibly disabled and are found in need of rehabilitation services because they have an employment handicap, this program can prepare them for a suitable job; get and keep that job; assist persons to become fully productive and independent.

**7968  Department of Veterans Benefits**
810 Vermont Avenue NW
Washington, DC  20420          202-273-6763
                               800-827-1000
                               www.va.gov

*Raymond Vogel, Chief Benefits*
*Joseph Thompson, Manager*

Furnishes compensation and pensions for disability and death to veterans and their dependents. Provides vocational rehabilitation services, including counseling, training, assistance and more towards employment, to blinded veterans disabled as a result of service in the armed forces during World War II, Korea and the Vietnam era; also provides rehabilitation services to certain peace-time veterans.

**7969  Disabled American Veterans**
PO Box 14301
Cincinnati, OH  45250          859-441-7300
                               FAX: 859-441-1416
                               www.dav.org

*James E Sursely, National Commander*

Advises veterans of their rights and employers of their obligations, under the Rehabilitation Act, the Americans with Disabilities Act, and legislation governing the employment and training of Vietnam era veterans with disabilities.

**7970  Federal Benefits for Veterans and Dependents**
Government Printing Office
Washington, DC  20402          202-512-1067
                               800-827-1000

*Bill Lewis, President*

Offers information on benefits for veterans and their families.
*93 pages*
*ISBN 0-16048 -58-*

**7971  Hospitalized Veterans Writing Project**
5920 Nall Avenue
Suite 105
Mission, KS  66202             913-432-1214

*Charlotte Black, Secretary*
*Priscilla Chansky, Administrator*

Individuals and organizations united to encourage hospitalized veterans to write for pleasure and rehabilitation during the hospital stay. Maintains speakers' bureau and audio tape version for the blind. Bestows numerous monetary awards in six areas: article; book review; cartoon and drawing; light verse; poetry and short story. *$ 15.00*
*64 pages Magazine*
*ISSN 0504-07 9*

**7972  US Department of Veterans Affairs National Headquarters**
1120 Vermont Avenue NW
Washington, DC  20420          202-273-5400
                               800-827-1000
                   e-mail: washingtondc.query@vba.va.gov
                               www.va.gov

*Togo D West Jr, Secretary Veterans Affairs*
*Hershel W Gober, Deputy Secretary Vet. Affairs*
*R Nicholson, Chief Executive Officer*

Administers the laws providing benefits and other services to veterans, their dependents, and their beneficiaries. Acts as their principal advocate in ensuring that they recieve medical care, benefits, social support, and lasting memorials promoting the health, welfare, and dignity of all veterans in recognition of their service to this nation. As the DVA heads into the 21st century, they will strive to meet the needs of the Nation's veterans today and tomorrow. Publishes a monthly magazine.
*80 pages*

**7973  US Veteran's Affairs**
810 Vermont Avenue NW
Washington, DC                 202-273-5400

                               www.va.gov

*Michael J Kussman, Deputy Under Secretary For Healt*

Provides a wide range of services for those who have been in the military and their dependents, as well as offering information on driver assessment and education programs.

## Alabama

**7974  Alabama VA Regional Office**
Veterans Benefits Administration, U S Dept. of V A
345 Perry Hill Road
Montgomery, AL 36109
800-827-1000
FAX: 334-213-3461
e-mail: montgomery.query@vba.va.gov
www.va.gov

*Joe Morris, Val Representative*
*William Rumph, Val Representative*

**7975  Alabama Veterans Facility**
809 Green Springs Highway
Homewood, AL 35209          205-916-2700

*Robert Herndon, Manager*
Veterans medical clinic offering disabled veterans medical treatments.

**7976  Birmingham VA Medical Center**
Veterans Health Administration U S Dept. of V A
700 19th Street S
Birmingham, AL 35233          205-933-8101
800-827-1000
e-mail: g.vhacss@forum.va.gov
www.va.gov

*Amos F Bailey, Director of Palliative Care*

**7977  Central Alabama Veterans Healthcare System**
Veterans Health Administration, US Dept. of VA
215 Perry Hill Road
Montgomery, AL 36109          334-272-4670
800-827-1000
e-mail: g.vhacss@forum.va.gov
www.va.gov

*Kenneth Ruyle, Executive Director*

**7978  Tuscaloosa VA Medical Center**
Veterans Health Administration, U S Dept. of V A
3701 Loop Road
Tuscaloosa, AL 35404          205-554-2000
FAX: 205-554-2845
www.va.gov

*Todd Hooper, Director*
*John Goldman, Executive Director*

## Alaska

**7979  Anchorage Regional Office**
Veterans Benefits Administration, U S Dept. of V A
2925 Debarr Road
Anchorage, AK 99508          907-257-4700
800-827-1000
e-mail: anchorage.query@vba.va.gov
www.va.gov

*Claude M Kicklighter, Chief Staff*
*Alex Spector, Executive Director*

**7980  DAV Department of Alaska**
2925 Debarr Road
Room 3101
Anchorage, AK 99508          907-257-4803
FAX: 907-258-9828

*George Hausermann, Treasurer*
*Ian Briggs, Manager*

## Arizona

**7981  Carl T Hayden VA Medical Center**
Veterans Health Administration, U S Dept. of V A
650 E Indian School Road
Phoenix, AZ 85012          602-277-5551
800-827-1000
e-mail: g.vhacss@forum.va.gov
www.va.gov

*D Gregg Gordon, President*
*Marva Greene, Vice President*
*John Fears, Chief Executive Officer*

**7982  Northern Arizona VA Health Center**
Veterans Health Administration, US Dept. of VA
500 N Us Highway 89
Prescott, AZ 86313          928-445-4860
800-827-1000
FAX: 928-768-6076
e-mail: g.vhacss@forum.va.gov
www.va.gov

*Deborah Thompson, Manager*

**7983  Phoenix Regional Office**
Veterans Benefits Administration U S Dept. of V A
3225 N Central Avenue
Phoenix, AZ 85012          800-827-1000
e-mail: phoenix.query@vba.va.gov
www.va.gov

*Neera Agrwal MD*

**7984  Southern Arizona VA Healthcare System**
Veterans Health Administration, U S Dept. of V A
3601 S 6th Avenue
Tucson, AZ 85723          520-792-1450
800-827-1000
FAX: 520-629-1818
e-mail: g.vhacss@forum.va.gov
www.va.gov

*Patrick F Chorpenning, State Director*
*Jerry Colye, Manager*

## Arkansas

**7985  Eugene J Towbin Healthcare Center**
Veterans Health Administration, U S Dept. of V A
2200 Fort Roots Drive
North Little Rock, AR 72114          501-396-4444
800-827-1000
e-mail: g.vhacss@forum.va.gov
www.va.gov

**7986  Fayetteville VA Medical Center**
Veterans Health Administration, US Dept. of VA
1100 N College Avenue
Fayetteville, AR 72703          479-444-4301
800-827-1000
e-mail: g.vhacss@forum.va.gov
www.va.gov

**7987  John L McClellan Memorial Hospital**
Veterans Health Administration, US Dept. of VA
4300 W 7th Street
Little Rock, AR 72205          501-257-1000
800-827-1000
e-mail: g.vhacss@forum.va.gov
www.va.gov

**7988  North Little Rock Regional Office**
Veterans Benefits Administration, U S Dept. of V A
2200 Fort Roots Drive
Building 65
N Little Rock, AR 72114

501-370-3820
800-827-1000
FAX: 501-370-3829
e-mail: littlerock.query@vba.va.gov
www.va.gov

*James Miller, Director*
*Herb Rummel, Deputy Director*

## California

**7989  Jerry L Pettis Memorial VA Medical Center**
Veterans Health Administration, U S Dept. of V A
11201 Benton Street
Loma Linda, CA  92357

909-825-7084
800-741-8387
e-mail: g.vhacss@forum.va.gov
www.lom.med.va.gov

*Kevin Dahl, Director*
*Dean Stordahl, President*

**7990  Long Beach VA Medical Center**
Veterans Health Administration, U S Dept. of V A
5901 E 7th Street
Long Beach, CA  90822

562-597-3592
800-827-1000
e-mail: g.vhacss@forum.va.gov
www.va.gov

*Stephen Davis, Director*
*Eric Yamaura, Director*
*Melinda Pettersen, Executive Director*

**7991  Los Angeles Regional Office**
Veterans Benefits Administration, U S Dept. of V A
11000 Wilshire Boulevard
Los Angeles, CA  90024

800-827-1000
e-mail: losangeles.query@vba.va.gov
www.va.gov

*Karl Lorenz, Work Group Leader*

**7992  Martinez Center for Rehab & Extended Care**
Veterans Health Administration, U S Dept. of V A
150 Muir Road
Martinez, CA  94553

925-372-2665
800-827-1000
e-mail: g.vhacss@forum.va.gov
www.va.gov

*John H Simms, Director*

**7993  Oakland VA Regional Office**
Veterans Benefits Administration U S Dept. of V A
1301 Clay Street
Room 1300
Oakland, CA  94612

800-827-1000
e-mail: oakland.query@vba.va.gov
www.va.gov

*Geri Spearman, Director*

**7994  Rehabilitation Research and Development Center**
Department of Veteran s Affairs
3801 Miranda Avenue
Palo Alto, CA  94304

650-493-5000
FAX: 650-493-4919
e-mail: jaffe@roses.stanford.edu
guide.stanford.edu

*Loretta V Barrow, Administrator*
*Louis Fajardo, MD*
*David L Jaffe MS, Research Biomedical Engineer*

The VA Center of Excellence on Mobility in Palo Alto, CA is dedicated to developing innovative clinical treatments and assistive devices for veterans with physical disabilities to increase their independence and improve their quality of life. The clinical emphasis of the center is to improve mobility, either ambulation or manipulation, in individuals with neurologic impairments or orthopaedic impairments. We do not publish any printed books, journals or periodicals.

**7995  Sacramento Medical Center**
Veterans Health Administration U S Department of V
10535 Hospital Way
Mather, CA  95655

916-366-5470
800-827-1000
e-mail: g.vhacss@forum.va.gov
www.va.gov

*Gail Crimmins-Wiggins, Director*

**7996  San Diego VA Regional Office**
Veterans Benefits Administration, U S Dept. of V A
8810 Rio San Diego Drive
San Diego, CA  92108

858-552-8585
800-827-1000
FAX: 858-552-7436
e-mail: oakland.query@vba.va.gov
www.va.gov

*Janet M Peyton, Administrative Officer*

**7997  San Francisco VA Medical Center**
Veterans Health Administration, US Dept. of VA
4150 Clement Street
San Francisco, CA  94121

415-221-4810
877-487-2838
FAX: 415-750-2185
www.sf.med.va.gov

*Gene Gibson, Public Affairs Officer*
*Sheila Cullen, Executive Director*

The San Francisco VA Medical Center (SFVAMC) serves as a major tertiary care referral center for veterans throughout Northern California. The facility has 124 acute care hospital beds. It is a high acuity medical center with over a third of bed days of care being in intensive care or monitored beds. Long term care programs include a 120 bed nursing home care unit at the San Francisco site and a home-based primary care program.

**7998  VA Central California Health Care Syste**
Veterans Health Administration, U S Dept. of V A
2615 E Clinton Avenue
Fresno, CA  93703

559-225-6100
888-826-2838
FAX: 559-268-6911
e-mail: g.vhacss@forum.va.gov
www.va.gov

*Ellen Perry, Director*
*Susan Shyshka, Associate Director*
*Alan Perry, Executive Director*

**7999 VA Greater Los Angeles Healthcare System**
Veterans Health Administration U S Deptartment of
11301 Wilshire Boulevard
Los Angeles, CA 90073 310-478-3711
800-827-1000
FAX: 310-268-4848
e-mail: g.vhacss@forum.va.gov
www.va.gov

*Charles Dorman, Chief Executive Officer*

**8000 VA Northern California Healthcare System**
Veterans Health Administration, U S Dept. of V A
150 Muir Road
Martinez, CA 94553 925-372-2000
800-827-1000
e-mail: g.vhacss@forum.va.gov
www.va.gov

*Lawrence Sander, Director*

**8001 VA San Diego Healthcare System**
Veterans Health Administration, U S Dept. of V A
3350 La Jolla Village Drive
San Diego, CA 92161 858-552-8585
800-827-1000
e-mail: g.vhacss@forum.va.gov
www.va.gov

*James R Nicholson, Secretary Veterans Affairs*
*Claude M Kicklighter, Chief of Staff*

## Colorado

**8002 Boulder Vet Center**
2336 Canyon Boulevard
Suite 103
Boulder, CO 80302 303-440-7306
FAX: 303-449-3907

*Stew Brown PhD, Team Leader*

Offers trauma and readjustment from military and civilian life counseling and assistance with disability claims, military benefits and employment are provided.

**8003 Colorado/Wyoming VA Medical Center**
Veterans Benefits Administration U S Dept. of V A
155 Van Gordon Street
Lakewood, CO 80228
800-827-1000
e-mail: denver.query@vba.va.gov
www.va.gov

*Forest Farley Jr, Medical Center Director*
*Thomas E Bowen, Chief of Staff*

**8004 Denver VA Medical Center**
Veterans Health Administration, U S Dept. of V A
1055 Clermont Street
Denver, CO 80220 303-399-8020
800-827-1000
e-mail: g.vhacss@forum.va.gov
www.va.gov

*Lisa A Brenner, Training Director*

**8005 Grand Junction VA Medical Center**
Veterans Health Administration, U S Dept. of V A
2121 North Avenue
Grand Junction, CO 81501 970-242-0731
800-827-1000
FAX: 970-244-1300
e-mail: g.vhacss@forum.va.gov
www.va.gov

*Claude M Kicklighter, Chief of Staff*
*Michael Murphy, Manager*

**8006 National Veterans Training Institute**
University of Colorado at Denver
1100 Stout Street
Suite 300
Denver, CO 80204 303-871-2000
800-331-0562
FAX: 303-825-0977

*Daniel Ritchie, Chief Executive Officer*

Training for specialists who serve veterans with disabilities.

## Connecticut

**8007 Disabled American Veterans: Connecticut**
35 Cold Spring Road
Suite 315
Rocky Hill, CT 06067 860-529-1759

www.davct.org

*Al Church, Manager*

**8008 Hartford Regional Office**
Veterans Benefits Administration U S Department of
450 Main Street
Hartford, CT 06103
800-827-1000
e-mail: hartford.query@vba.va.gov
www.va.gov

*Jeanette A Chirico Post, Network Director*

**8009 Hartford Vet Center**
30 Jordan Lane
Wethersfield, CT 06109 860-240-3543
FAX: 860-563-7246
e-mail: donna.hryb@med.va.gov

*Donna Hryb LCSW, Team Leader*
*Urania Petit BA, Office Manager*

A U.S. Department of Veterans Affairs counseling center offering counseling to Vietnam era and combat veterans. Sexual trauma/harassment counseling, medical screening and benefit referral is available to all veterans.

**8010 VA Connecticut Healthcare System: Newington Division**
Veterans Health Administration U S Department. of
555 Willard Avenue
Newington, CT 06111 860-666-6951
800-827-1000
FAX: 860-667-6764
e-mail: g.vhacss@forum.va.gov
www.va.gov

*Vincent Ng, Providence Director*

The mission of VA Connecticut Healthcare Systems is to fulfill a nation's commitment to its veterans by providing quality healthcare, promoting health through prevention and maintaining excellence in teaching and research. Provides primary, secondary and tertiary care in medicine, geriatrics, neurology, psychiatry and surgery with an operating capacity of 211 hospital beds.

**8011 VA Connecticut Healthcare System: West Haven**
Veterans Health Administration, U S Dept. of V A
950 Campbell Avenue
W Haven, CT 06516 203-932-5711
FAX: 203-937-3868
e-mail: g.vhacss@forum.va.gov
www.va.gov

*R James Nicholson, Secretary Veteran Affairs*
*Claude Kicklighter, Chief of Staff*
*Roger Johnson, Administrator*

## Delaware

**8012  Delaware Commission of Veterans Affairs**
802 Silver Lake Boulevard
Suite 100
Dover, DE  19904                        302-739-2792
                                        800-344-9900
                        FAX: 302-739-2794
                e-mail: adavila@state.de.us
                www.state.de.us/veteran/index.htm

*Antonio Davila, Executive Director*

To assist, advise, and represent Delaware's military veterans
and their families regarding programs and benefits available to
them under federal and state laws.

**8013  Delaware VA Regional Office**
Veterans Benefits Administration U S Dept. of V A
1601 Kirkwood Highway
Wilmington, DE  19805                    302-994-2511
                                        800-827-1000
                e-mail: wilmington.query@vba.va.gov
                                        www.va.gov

*Martin F Konwinski, Research/Development Coordinator*
*Dexter Dix, Executive Director*

**8014  Wilmington VA Medical**
Veterans Health Administration, US Dept. of VA
1601 Kirkwood Highway
Wilmington, DE  19805                    302-994-2511
                                        800-827-1000
                        FAX: 302-633-5516
                e-mail: g.vhacss@forum.va.gov
                                        www.va.gov

*Dexter Dix, Executive Director*

**8015  Wilmington Vet Center**
1601 Kirkwood Highway
Wilmington, DE  19805                    302-994-1660
                                        800-461-8262
                        FAX: 302-633-5250

*Mark A Kaufki EdD, Team Leader*

Veterans counseling program offering individual counseling
services, advocacy services and group counseling. The focus is
the counseling of all veterans coping with the aftermath of war,
sexual abuse/harassment in the military and all veterans of the
Vietnam era. The center also has an active outreach program to
seek veterans needing services. Hours of operation are between
8:00 AM - 4:30 PM, Monday - Friday and other times by appointment only. Services are free.

## District of Columbia

**8016  Disabled American Veterans, National Service & Legis-
lative Headquarters**
807 Maine Avenue SW
Washington, DC  20024                    202-554-3501

                                        www.dav.org

*Alan W Bowers, Chairman*
*Paul W Jackson, Vice Chairman*

**8017  PVA Sports and Recreation Program**
Paralyzed Veterans of America
801 18th Street NW
Washington, DC  20006                    202-872-1300
                                        800-424-8200
                        FAX: 202-416-7639
                        e-mail: info@pva.org
                                        www.pva.org

*Andy Krieger, Director Sports/Recreation*
*Randy Pleza, President*

**8018  VA Medical Center, Washington DC**
50 Irving Street NW
Washington, DC  20422                    202-745-8422
                                        888-553-0242
                www.washington.med.va.gov

*David J West, Associate Medical Center*
*Ross D Fletcher, Chief of Staff*

Acute general and specialized services in medicine, surgery,
neurology, and psychiatry.

**8019  Washington DC VA Medical Center**
Veterans Health Administration, U S Dept. of V A
50 Irving Street NW
Washington, DC  20422                    202-745-8000
                                        800-827-1000
                        FAX: 202-754-8530
                e-mail: g.vhacss@forum.va.gov
                                        www.va.gov

*James R Nicholson, Secretary of Veterans Affairs*
*Claude M Kicklighter, Chief of Staff*
*Bina Lakhanpal, MD*

## Florida

**8020  Bay Pines VA Medical Center**
Veterans Health Administration, U S Dept. of V A
10000 Bay Pines Boulevard
Bay Pines, FL  33744                    727-398-6661
                                        800-827-1000
                e-mail: g.vhacss@forum.va.gov
                                        www.va.gov

*Wallace M Hopkins, Medical Director*
*Kaye Green, Assistant Medical Director*
*Smith Jenkins, Chief Executive Officer*

**8021  Gainesville Division, North Florida/South Georgia Vet-
erans Healthcare System**
Veterans Health Administration, U S Dept. of V A
1601 SW Archer Road
Room 165a
Gainesville, FL  32608                    352-376-1611
                                        800-324-8387
                        FAX: 352-379-7445
                e-mail: g.vhacss@forum.va.gov
                                        www.va.gov

*Claude M Kicklighter, Chief of Staff*
*Frederick Malphurs, Chief Executive Officer*

**8022  James A Haley VA Medical Center**
Veterans Health Administration, U S Dept. of V A
13000 Bruce B Downs Boulevard
Tampa, FL  33612                        813-972-2000
                                        800-827-1000
                e-mail: g.vhacss@forum.va.gov
                                        www.va.gov

*James R Nicholson, Secretary of Veterans Affairs*
*Claude M Kicklighter, Chief of Staff*
*Edgar Bueno, MD*

**8023 Lake City Division, North Florida/South Georgia Veterans Healthcare System**
Veterans Health Administration, U S Dept. of V A
801 S Marion Street
Lake City, FL 32025
386-755-3016
800-827-1000
FAX: 386-758-3209
e-mail: g.vhacss@forum.va.gov
www.va.gov

*Claude M Kicklighter, Chief of Staff*

**8024 Miami VA Medical Center**
Veterans Health Administration, U S Dept. of V A
1201 NW 16th Street
Miami, FL 33125
305-575-7000
800-827-1000
FAX: 305-575-3266
e-mail: g.vhacss@forum.va.gov
www.va.gov

*Stephen M Lucas, Chief Executive Officer*

**8025 St. Petersburg Regional Office**
Veterans Benefits Administration, U S Dept. of V A
9500 Bay Pines Boulevard
St Petersburg, FL
727-319-7492
800-827-1000
e-mail: stpete.query@vba.va.gov
www.va.gov

*Warren McPherson, Executive Director*

**8026 West Palm Beach VA Medical Center**
Veterans Health Administration, U S Dept. of V A
7305 N Military Trail
Riviera Beach, FL 33410
561-882-8262
800-827-1000
FAX: 561-882-6707
e-mail: g.vhacss@forum.va.gov
www.va.gov

*Claude M Kicklighter, Chief of Staff*
*Andre Desgroseillers, MD*

## Georgia

**8027 Atlanta Regional Office**
Veterans Benefits Administration, U S Dept. of V A
730 Peachtree Street NE
Atlanta, GA 30308
800-827-1000
FAX: 606- -
e-mail: atlanta.query@vba.va.gov
www.va.gov

*William J Day*

**8028 Atlanta VA Medical Center**
Veterans Health Administration, U S Dept. of V A
1670 Clairmont Road
Decatur, GA 30033
404-321-6111
800-827-1000
FAX: 404-728-7734
e-mail: g.vhacss@forum.va.gov
www.va.gov

*James R Nicholson, Secretary of Veterans Affairs*
*Claude M Kicklighter, Chief of Staff*
*Thomas Cappello, Chief Executive Officer*

**8029 Augusta VA Medical Center**
Veterans Health Administration, U S Dept. of V A
1 Freedom Way
Augusta, GA 30904
706-733-0188
800-827-1000
FAX: 706-823-3934
e-mail: g.vhacss@forum.va.gov
www.va.gov

*R James Nicholson, Secretary of Veterans Affairs*
*Claude Kicklighter, Chief of Staff*
*James Trustley III, Chief Executive Officer*

**8030 Carl Vinson VA Medical Center**
Veterans Health Administration, U S Dept. of V A
1826 Veterans Boulevard
Dublin, GA 31021
478-272-1210
FAX: 478-277-2717
e-mail: dana.doles@med.va.gov
www.va.gov

*Claude M Kicklighter, Chief of Staff*
*Richard Fry, Chief Executive Officer*

**8031 Georgia Veterans Centers**
922 W Peachtree Street NW
Atlanta, GA 30309
FAX: 404-347-7274
Veterans medical clinic offering disabled veterans medical treatments.

## Hawaii

**8032 Hawaii Veterans Centers**
Hilo Veteran Center
201 Keawe Street
Hilo, HI 96720
808-969-3833
FAX: 808-969-2025
www.va.gov

*John Harlan, Director*
*Richard Talbott, Assistant Director*

Veterans medical clinic offering disabled veterans medical treatments, readjustment and PTSD counseling to combat veterans

**8033 Honolulu VBA Regional Office**
Veterans Benefits Administration, U S Dept. of V A
300 Ala Moana Boulevard
Room 1004
Honolulu, HI 96850
808-541-2570
800-827-1000
e-mail: honolulu.query@vba.va.gov
www.va.gov

*Claude M Kicklighter, Chief of Staff*
*Alan Furuno, Manager*

**8034 Pacific Islands Health Care System**
Veterans Health Administration, US Dept. of VA
459 Patterson Road
Honolulu, HI 96819
808-433-0600
800-827-1000
FAX: 808-433-0390
e-mail: g.vhacss@forum.va.gov
www.va.gov

## Idaho

**8035  Boise Regional Office**
Veterans Benefits Administration, U S Dept. of V A
805 W Franklin Street
Boise, ID  83702                  208-334-1245
                                  800-827-1000
                 e-mail: boise.query@vba.va.gov
                                      www.va.gov

*Jim Vance, Director*
*Pat Teague, Service Officer*
*Tom Ressler, Manager*

**8036  Boise VA Medical Center**
Veterans Health Administration, U S Dept. of V A
500 W Fort Street
Boise, ID  83702                  208-422-1000
                                  800-827-1000
                             FAX: 208-422-1326
                 e-mail: g.vhacss@forum.va.gov
                                      www.va.gov

*Claude M Kicklighter, Chief of Staff*

**8037  Idaho Division of Veterans' Services**
320 Collins Road
Boise, ID  83702                  208-334-3513
                             FAX: 208-334-2627
               e-mail: chaseo@veterans.idaho.gov
                              www.idvs.state.id.us

*Joe Bleymaier, Administrator*
*Oliver Chase, Management Assistant*

## Illinois

**8038  Chicago-Lakeside VA Medical Center**
Veterans Health Administration, U S Dept. of V A
333 E Huron Street
Chicago, IL  60611                312-943-6600
                                  800-827-1000
                             FAX: 312-640-2248
                 e-mail: g.vhacss@forum.va.gov
                                      www.va.gov

*James R Nicholson, Secretary of Veteran Affairs*
*Claude Kicklighter, Chief of Staff*

**8039  Chicago-West Side VA Medical Center**
Veterans Health Administration, U S Department of
820 S Damen Avenue
Chicago, IL  60612                312-666-6500
                                  800-827-1000
                 e-mail: g.vhacss@forum.va.gov
                                      www.va.gov

*Virginia C Fiedler, Professor Emeritus*

Interdisciplinary team of optometry, ophthalmology, low vision
training specialists, psychology, social work and audiology provide comprehensive low vision rehabilitation services for the
partially sighted.

**8040  Edward Hines Jr Hospital**
Veterans Health Administration, U S Dept. of V A
Fifth Avenue & Roosevelt Road
Hines, IL  60141                  708-202-5691
                                  800-827-1000
                             FAX: 708-202-2684
                 e-mail: g.vhacss@forum.va.gov
              www.va.gov/sta/guide/facility.asp?ID=58

*Nick Guzzi, Administrative Officer*

**8041  Illinois VA Regional Office Center**
Veterans Benefits Administration, U S Dept. of V A
536 S Clark Street
Chicago, IL  60605
                                  800-827-1000
               e-mail: chicago.query@vba.va.gov
                                      www.va.gov

*Kevin McCoy, Associate Director*

**8042  Marion VA Medical Center**
Veterans Health Administration U S Department of V
2401 W Main Street
Marion, IL  62959                 618-997-5311
                                  800-827-1000
                 e-mail: g.vhacss@forum.va.gov
                                      www.va.gov

**8043  North Chicago VA Medical Center**
Veterans Health Administration, U S Dept. of V A
3001 Green Bay Road
North Chicago, IL  60064          847-688-1900
                                  800-827-1000
                 e-mail: g.vhacss@forum.va.gov
                                      www.va.gov

*Claude M Kicklighter, Chief of Staff*
*John Avramidis, MD*

**8044  VA Illiana Health Care System**
Veterans Health Administration, U S Dept. of V A
1900 E Main Street
Danville, IL  61832
                                  800-827-1000
                             FAX: 217-554-4552
                 e-mail: g.vhacss@forum.va.gov
                                      www.va.gov

*Betsy Sleath, Chairman*

## Indiana

**8045  Indianapolis Regional Office**
Veterans Benefits Administration U S Department of
575 N Pennsylvania Street
Indianapolis, IN  46204           317-226-7860
                                  800-827-1000
             e-mail: indianapolis.query@vba.va.gov
                                      www.va.gov

**8046  Richard L Roudebush VA Medical Center**
Veterans Health Administration, U S Dept. of V A
1481 W 10th Street
Indianapolis, IN  46202           317-554-0000
                                  800-827-1000
                             FAX: 317-554-0127
                 e-mail: g.vhacss@forum.va.gov
                                      www.va.gov

*Claude M Kicklighter, Chief of Staff*
*Becky Hall, Manager*

**8047  VA North Indiana Health Care System: Fort Wayne
Campus**
Veterans Health Administration, U S Dept. of V A
2121 Lake Avenue
Fort Wayne, IN  46805             260-426-5431
                                  800-827-1000
                 e-mail: g.vhacss@forum.va.gov
                                      www.va.gov

*Michael W Murphy, Director*
*Cathi Spivey-Paul, Executive Director*

**8048**  **VA Northern Indiana Health Care System: Marion Campus**
Veterans Health Administration, U S Dept. of V A
1700 E 38th Street
Marion, IN 46953
765-674-3321
800-827-1000
e-mail: g.vhacss@forum.va.gov
www.va.gov

*Claude M Kicklighter, Chief of Staff*
*Cathi Spivey-Paul, Executive Director*

## Iowa

**8049**  **Des Moines VA Medical Center**
Veterans Health Administration, U S Dept. of V A
3600 30th Street
Des Moines, IA 50310
515-699-5850
800-827-1000
FAX: 515-699-5862
e-mail: g.vhacss@forum.va.gov
www.va.gov

*Claudia M Kicklighter, Chief of Staff*

**8050**  **Des Moines VA Regional Office**
Veterans Benefits Administration, U S Dept. of V A
210 Walnut Street
Room 1033a
Des Moines, IA 50309
515-323-7532
800-944-2039
FAX: 515-323-7405
e-mail: leander@vba.va.gov
www.va.gov

*Liz Erickson, Director*
*Rich Anderson, Service Director*

**8051**  **Iowa City VA Medical Center**
Veterans Health Administration, U S Dept. of V A
6 West
Iowa City, IA 52246
319-338-0581
800-827-1000
FAX: 319-339-7171
e-mail: g.vhacss@forum.va.gov
www.va.gov

*Kirt A Sickels, Public Affairs Officer*
*Gary Wilkinson, Administrator*

Tertiary care facility, affiliated teaching hospital, and research center seving an aging veteran populatiaon in eastern Iowa and western Illinois. Satellite clinics are located in Bettendord, Dubuque, and Waterloo, Iowa and in Quincy and Galesburg, Illinois.

**8052**  **Knoxville VA Medical Center**
Veterans Health Administration, U S Dept. of V A
1515 W Pleasant Street
Knoxville, IA 50138
641-828-5000
800-827-1000
FAX: 641-828-5124
e-mail: g.vhacss@forum.va.gov
www.va.gov

*Claudia M Kicklighter*

**8053**  **VA Central Iowa Health Care System**
3600 30th Street
Des Moines, IA 50310
515-699-5999
FAX: 515-699-5862
www.va.gov

*Elaine Brewster, Executive Program Manager*
*Donald Cooper, Executive Director*

Fulfilling the promise is our primary mission.

## Kansas

**8054**  **Colmery-O'Neil VA Medical Center**
Veterans Health Administration, U S Dept. of V A
2200 SW Gage Boulevard
Topeka, KS 66622
785-350-3111
800-827-1000
e-mail: g.vhacss@forum.va.gov
www.va.gov

*Jerry L Calhoun, Chairman*

**8055**  **Dwight D Eisenhower VA Medical Center**
Veterans Health Administration, U S Dept. of V A
4101 S 4th Street
Leavenworth, KS 66048
913-682-2000
800-827-1000
e-mail: g.vhacss@forum.va.gov
www.va.gov

*Donald L Courtney, Research/Development Coordinator*
*Deborah Fulk, Administrative Officer*
*Arnulfo Sulit, MD*

**8056**  **Kansas VA Regional Office**
Veterans Benefits Administration, U S Dept. of V A
5500 E Kellogg Drive
Wichita, KS 67218
800-827-1000
e-mail: wichita.query@vba.va.gov
www.va.gov

*Edgar L Tucker, Medical Center Director*

**8057**  **Wichita VA Medical Center**
Veterans Health Administration, U S Dept. of V A
5500 E Kellogg Drive
Wichita, KS 67218
316-685-2221
800-827-1000
FAX: 316-651-3666
e-mail: g.vhacss@forum.va.gov
www.va.gov

*Jack Perry, Research/Development Coordinator*
*Sheryl A Rodgers, Secretary*
*Kent Hill, Executive Director*

## Kentucky

**8058**  **Lexington VA Medical Center**
Veterans Health Administration, U S Dept. of V A
Lexington, KY 40511
859-233-4511
800-352-4000
e-mail: g.vhacss@forum.va.gov
www.va.gov/sta/guide/facility.asp?ID=72

**8059**  **Louisville VA Medical Center**
Veterans Health Administration, U S Dept. of V A
800 Zorn Avenue
Louisville, KY 40206
502-287-4000
800-827-1000
FAX: 502-287-6225
e-mail: g.vhacss@forum.va.gov
www.va.gov

*Leslie Beavers, Director*

**8060**  **Louisville VA Regional Office**
Veterans Benefits Administration, U S Dept. of V A
545 S 3rd Street
Louisville, KY 40202
502-582-5594
800-827-1000
e-mail: louisville.query@vba.va.gov
www.va.gov

*Gene Brainer, Regional Officer*

## Louisiana

**8061 Alexandria VA Medical Center**
Veterans Health Administration, U S Dept. of V A
2495 Highway 71 N
Alexandria, LA 71301          318-473-0010
          800-827-1000
          FAX: 318-483-5029
          e-mail: g.vhacss@forum.va.gov
          www.va.gov

*Claude M Kicklighter, Chief of Staff*
*Barbara Watkins, Executive Director*

**8062 New Orleans VA Medical Center**
Veterans Health Administration, U S Dept. of V A
1601 Perdido Street
New Orleans, LA 70112          504-568-0811
          800-935-8387
          FAX: 504-589-5210
          e-mail: Stacie.Rivera@med.va.gov
          www.va.gov

*John D Church Jr, Medical Director/President*
*Fernando Rivera, Association Medical Center Direc*
*Sam Lucero, Special Assistant to Director*

A teaching hospital, providing a full range of patient care services, with state-of-the-art technology as well as education and research. Comprehensive health care is provided through primary care, tetiary care, and long-term care in areas of medicine, surgery, psychiatry, physical medicine and rehabilitation, neurology, oncology, dentistry, geriatrics, and extended care.

**8063 Shreveport VA Medical Center**
Veterans Health Administration, U S Dept. of V A
510 E Stoner Avenue
Shreveport, LA 71101          318-221-8411
          800-827-1000
          FAX: 318-424-6156
          e-mail: g.vhacss@forum.va.gov
          www.va.gov

*Dorothy Jarzabek, Administrative Officer*
*Ali R Mansouri, Acting Acos/R&D*
*Gracie Specks, Chief Executive Officer*

## Maine

**8064 Chapter 15 Disabled American Veterans**
PO Box 544
Brunswick, ME 04011          207-677-6033

          e-mail: re.nee@verizon.net

*Cliff Workman, Commander*

**8065 Disabled American Veterans: Maine**
PO Box 3151
Augusta, ME 04330          207-623-5725

          e-mail: dav@mint.net
          www.dav.org

*Gary P Burns, President*
*Arthur H Wilson, Vice President*

**8066 Maine VA Regional Office**
Veterans Benefits Administration, U S Dept. of V A
1 Va Center
Augusta, ME 04330          800-827-1000
          FAX: 207-623-5737
          e-mail: togus.query@vba.va.gov
          www.va.gov

*Dale Demers, Director*
*Scott Karczewski, Manager*

**8067 Togus VA Medical Center**
Veterans Health Administration, U S Dept. of V A
1 Va Center
Augusta, ME 04330          207-623-8411
          800-827-1000
          e-mail: g.vhacss@forum.va.gov
          www.va.gov

*Jack Sims, Medical Center Director*
*John Sims, Executive Director*

## Maryland

**8068 Baltimore Regional Office**
Veterans Benefits Administration, U S Dept. of V A
31 Hopkins Plaza
Baltimore, MD 21201          800-827-1000
          e-mail: baltimore.query@vba.va.gov
          www.va.gov

*Jerry L Calhoun*

**8069 Baltimore VA Medical Center**
Veterans Health Administration, U S Dept. of V A
10 N Greene Street
Baltimore, MD 21201          410-605-7000
          800-463-6295
          FAX: 410-605-7901
          e-mail: g.vhacss@forum.va.gov
          www.va.gov

*David Johnson, Administrative Officer*
*Peggy Wess, Research Contact*
*Dennis Smith, Executive Director*

**8070 Fort Howard VA Medical Center**
Veterans Health Administration, U S Dept. of V A
9600 N Point Road
Fort Howard, MD 21052          410-778-0
          800-827-1000
          FAX: 410-477-7177
          e-mail: md.veterans@erols.com
          www.mdva.state.md.us

*Thomas Hutchins, Secretary*

**8071 Maryland Veterans Centers**
10 N Greene Street
Baltimore, MD 21201          410-605-7000
          FAX: 410-605-7901
          www.va.gov

*James Nocks, Director*
*Dennis H Smith, Executive Director*

Veterans medical clinic offering disabled veterans medical treatments.

**8072  Perry Point VA Medical Center**
Veterans Health Administration, U S Dept. of V A
Perry Point, MD  21902                          410-642-2411
                                                800-827-1000
                                      FAX: 410-642-1161
                              e-mail: g.vhacss@forum.va.gov
                                                www.va.gov

*Dennis H Smith, Executive Director*
*Allice Krupski, Assistant Director of Operations*

**8073  VA Maryland Health Care System**
10 N Greene Street
Baltimore, MD  21201                            410-605-7361
                                                800-827-1000
                                      FAX: 410-605-7900
                                      www.vamhcs.med.va.gov

*Christopher Bever, Director*
*Bruce Kaup, MD*

A dynamic and exciting health care organization that is dedicated to providing quality, compassionate and accessible care
and service to Maryland's veterans. As a part of one of the largest health care systems in the United States, the VAMHCS has a
reputation as a leader in veterans' health care, reserch and education. Provides comprehensive service to veterans including
medical, surgical, rehabilitative, nurological and mental health
care on both an inpatient and outpatient basis.

## Massachusetts

**8074  Boston VA Regional Office**
Veterans Benefits Administration, U S Dept. of V A
1400 Parkway
Boston, MA  02132                               617-232-9500
                                                800-827-1000
                              e-mail: boston.query@vba.va.gov
                                                www.va.gov

*Liza Catucci, Administrative Officer*
*Michael Lawson, President*

**8075  Edith Nourse Rogers Memorial Veterans Hospital**
Veterans Health Administration U S Deptartment of
200 Springs Road
Building 61
Bedford, MA  01730                              781-687-2926
                                                800-827-1000
                                      FAX: 781-687-3527
                              e-mail: g.vhacss@forum.va.gov
                                                www.va.gov

*Jeannette Chirico Post, Network Director*

**8076  Northampton VA Medical Center**
Veterans Health Administration, U S Dept. of V A
421 N Main Street
Leeds, MA  01053                                413-584-4040
                                                800-827-1000
                                      FAX: 413-582-3121
                              e-mail: g.vhacss@forum.va.gov
                                                www.va.gov

*Joanne Carney, Manager*

**8077  VA Boston Healthcare System: Brockton Division**
Veterans Health Administration, U S Dept. of V A
940 Belmont Street
Brockton, MA  02301                             508-583-4500
                                                800-827-1000
                                      FAX: 617-323-7700
                              e-mail: g.vhacss@forum.va.gov
                                                www.va.gov

*Tom Kelly, Commissioner*
*Richard Spicer, Director of Operations*
*Christine Croteau, Manager*

**8078  VA Boston Healthcare System: Jamaica Plain Campus**
Veterans Health Administration, U S Dept. of V A
150 S Huntington Avenue
Boston, MA  02130                               617-232-9500
                                                800-827-1000
                                      FAX: 617-278-4549
                              e-mail: g.vhacss@forum.va.gov
                                                www.va.gov

*Patricia Baker, Research Compliance Officer*
*Geraldine McGlynn, Director*
*Michael Lawson, President*

**8079  VA Boston Healthcare System: West Roxbury Division**
Veterans Health Administration, U S Dept. of V A
1400 Vfw Parkway
West Roxbury, MA  02132                         413-584-4040
                                                800-827-1000
                                      FAX: 413-582-3121
                              e-mail: g.vhacss@forum.va.gov
                                                www.va.gov

*Susan A Mac Kenzie, Associate Director*

## Michigan

**8080  Aleda E Lutz VA Medical Center**
Veterans Health Administration, U S Dept. of V A
1500 Weiss Street
Saginaw, MI  48602                              989-497-2500
                                                800-827-1000
                                      FAX: 989-791-2428
                              e-mail: g.vhacss@forum.va.gov
                                                www.va.gov

*Emily Houle, Research Contact*
*Menahem Lender, Research/Development Coordinator*
*Robert Sabin, Executive Director*

**8081  Battle Creek VA Medical Center**
Veterans Health Administration, U S Dept. of V A
5500 Armstrong Road
Battle Creek, MI  49015                         269-966-5600
                                                800-827-1000
                                      FAX: 269-966-5483
                              e-mail: g.vhacss@forum.va.gov
                                                www.va.gov

*Ronald W Kelley, Research/Development Coordinator*
*Elinor J Pettee, Research/Development Coordinator*
*Alice Wood, Manager*

**8082  Iron Mountain VA Medical Center**
Veterans Health Administration, U S Dept. of V A
325 E H Street
Iron Mountain, MI  49801                        906-774-3300
                                                800-827-1000
                                      FAX: 906-779-3114
                              e-mail: g.vhacss@forum.va.gov
                                                www.va.gov

*C L Holmes MD, Chief Of Staff*
*Janice Boss, Administrator*

**8083  John D Dingell VA Medical Center**
Veterans Health Administration, U S Dept. of V A
4646 John R Street
Detroit, MI  48201                              313-576-1000
                                                800-827-1000
                                      FAX: 313-576-1112
                              e-mail: g.vhacss@forum.va.gov
                                                www.va.gov

*Mary J Brady, Administrative Officer*

**8084  Michigan VA Regional Office**
Veterans Benefits Administration, U S Dept. of V A
477 Michigan Avenue
Room 1400
Detroit, MI  48226

800-827-1000
e-mail: detroit.query@vba.va.gov
www.va.gov

*Keith Thompson, Director*
*Dennis W Paradowski, Assistant Director*

**8085  VA Ann Arbor Healthcare System**
Veterans Health Administration, U S Dept. of V A
2215 Fuller Road
Ann Arbor, MI  48105

734-769-7100
FAX: 734-761-7870
e-mail: g.vhacss@forum.va.gov
www.va.gov

*Rodney A Hayward, Director*
*Susan A Zuk, Administrative Officer*
*James Roseborough, Executive Director*

Accepting eligible veterans.

**8086  Vet Center Readjustment Counseling Service**
1940 Eastern Ave SE
Grand Rapids, MI  49507

616-243-0385
FAX: 616-243-5390
www.va.gov

*William Busby PhD, Executive Director*
*Branden K Lyon, Counselor*
*Lynn Hall, Clinical Coordinator*

Providing a broad range of counseling outreach and referral services to eligible veterans in order to help make readjustments to cilvilian life.

## Minnesota

**8087  Minneapolis VA Medical Center**
Veterans Health Administration, U S Dept. of V A
1 Veterans Drive
Minneapolis, MN  55417

612-725-2000
800-827-1000
FAX: 612-725-2049
e-mail: g.vhacss@forum.va.gov
www.va.gov

*Hanna E Bloomfield, Director*
*Dana M Chesness, Project Coordinator*

**8088  St. Cloud VA Medical Center**
Veterans Health Administration, U S Dept. of V A
4801 Veterans Drive
Saint Cloud, MN  56303

320-252-6191
800-827-1000
FAX: 320-255-6472
e-mail: g.vhacss@forum.va.gov
www.va.gov

*Pat Sohler, Research/Development Coordinator*

**8089  St. Paul Regional Office**
Veterans Benefits Administration, U S Dept. of V A
1 Federal Drive
Fort Snelling, MN  55111

800-827-1000
e-mail: stpaul.query@vba.va.gov
www.va.gov

*Vincent Crawford, Director*

**8090  Vet Center**
405 E Superior Street
Duluth, MN  55802

218-722-8654
FAX: 218-723-8212

*Cynthia Macaulay MEd, Counselor*
*Rob Evanson, Counselor*
*Debbie Burt, Office Manager*

Counseling, social services and benefits assistance for combat veterans and those sexually traumatized in the military.

## Mississippi

**8091  Biloxi/Gulfport VA Medical Center**
Veterans Health Administration, U S Dept. of V A
400 Veterans Avenue
Biloxi, MS  39531

228-563-2472
800-827-1000
FAX: 228-563-2898
e-mail: g.vhacss@forum.va.gov
www.va.gov

*Kimberly Morgan, Administrative Officer*

**8092  Jackson Regional Office**
Veterans Benefits Administration, U S Dept. of V A
1600 E Woodrow Wilson Avenue
Jackson, MS  39216

601-364-7000
800-827-1000
FAX: 601-364-7007
e-mail: jackson.query@vba.va.gov
www.va.gov

*Neil Anthony Mcphie, Chairman*
*Barbara Sapin, Vice Chairman*

**8093  Jackson VA Medical Center**
Veterans Health Administration U S Department of V
PO Box 39288-5947
Pearl, MS  39288

601-576-4850
FAX: 601-576-4868
www.va.gov

*Adrian Grice, Executive Director*

## Missouri

**8094  Harry S Truman Memorial Veterans' Hospital**
Veterans Health Administration, U S Dept. of V A
800 Hospital Drive
Columbia, MO  65201

573-814-6552
800-349-8220
FAX: 573-814-6551
e-mail: g.vhacss@forum.va.gov
www.va.gov

*Larry L Propp, Executive Director*
*Lawrence Propp, Administrative Officer*

**8095  John J Pershing VA Medical Center**
Veterans Health Administration, U S Dept. of V A
1500 N Westwood Boulevard
Poplar Bluff, MO  63901

573-778-4697
800-827-1000
FAX: 573-778-4156
e-mail: g.vhacss@forum.va.gov
www.va.gov

*Dewayne Coleman, Research/Development Coordinator*
*Jo Nell Miller, Research Contact*

**8096  Kansas City VA Medical Center**
Veterans Health Administration, U S Dept. of V A
4801 E Linwood Boulevard
Kansas City, MO  64128                    816-861-4700
                                          800-827-1000
                                 e-mail: g.vhacss@forum.va.gov
                                                   www.va.gov

*Kenneth Grasing, Research/Development*
*Ram Sharma, Administrative Officer*
*Kent Hill, Executive Director*

The Kansas City VA Medical Center is a modern, well-equipped
teriary care inpatient and outpatient center. As the third largest
teaching hospital in the metropolitan area, it maintains educational affiliations with the University of Kansas School of Medicine.

**8097  Missouri Veterans Centers**
3931 Main Street
Kansas City, MO  64111                    816-753-1866
                                     FAX: 816-753-2328

*Bob Waechter, Manager*

Veterans medical clinic offering disabled veterans medical
treatments.

**8098  St. Louis Regional Office**
Veterans Benefits Administration, U S Dept. of V A
400 S 18th Street
Saint Louis, MO  63103
                                          800-827-1000
                                 e-mail: stlouis.query@vba.va.gov
                                                   www.va.gov

**8099  St. Louis VA Medical Center**
Veterans Health Administration, U S Dept. of V A
915 N Grand Boulevard
Saint Louis, MO  63106                    314-589-6333
                                          800-827-1000
                                     FAX: 314-289-7009
                                 e-mail: g.vhacss@forum.va.gov
                                                   www.va.gov

*Dolores Minor, Administrative Officer*

## Montana

**8100  Montana VA Regional Office**
Ft Harrison V Am Ro C
Fort Harrison, MT  59636                   406-442-7310

**8101  V A Montana Healthcare System**
U S Dept. of V A
1892 Williams Street
Fort Harrison, MT  59636                   406-442-6410
                                          800-827-1000
                                          877-468-8387
                                     FAX: 406-447-7916
                                 e-mail: ftharrison.query@vba.va.gov
                                                   www.va.gov

*Susanne Corbett, Pateint Representative*

**8102  VA Montana Healthcare System**
Veterans Health Administration, U S Dept. of V A
William Street
Fort Harrison, MT  59636                   406-442-6410
                                          800-827-1000
                                     FAX: 406-447-7965
                                 e-mail: g.vhacss@forum.va.gov
                                                   www.va.gov

*Anna Lithgoe, Research/Development Coordinator*
*Gregory Johnson, MD*

**8103  Vet Center**
Readjusment Counciling Service Western Mountain Re
1234 Avenue C
Billings, MT  59102                       406-657-6071
                                     FAX: 406-657-6603

*Robert Phillips MSW, Team Leader*
*Luanne Anderson, Office Manager*
*Barry Osgard MS, Counselor*

Readjustment counseling service for counseling veterans who
are having difficulty adjusting from military service especially
those diagnosed with PTSD.

## Nebraska

**8104  Grand Island VA Medical System**
Veterans Health Administration, U S Dept. of V A
2201 N Broadwell Avenue
Grand Island, NE  68803                   308-382-3660
                                          800-827-1000
                                 e-mail: g.vhacss@forum.va.gov
                                                   www.va.gov

*John Hilbert, Executive Director*
*Daniel L Parker, Deputy Director*

**8105  Lincoln Regional Office**
Veterans Benefits Administration, U S Dept. of V A
5631 S 48th Street
Lincoln, NE  68516
                                          800-827-1000
                                 e-mail: lincoln.query@vba.va.gov
                                                   www.va.gov

*John Hilgert, Executive Director*
*Daniel Parker, Deputy Director*

**8106  Lincoln VA Medical Center**
Veterans Health Administration, U S Dept. of V A
600 S 70th Street
Lincoln, NE  68510                        402-486-7825
                                          800-827-1000
                                     FAX: 402-486-7860
                                 e-mail: g.vhacss@forum.va.gov
                                                   www.va.gov

*Ryon L Adams, Research/Development Coordinator*

**8107  VA Nebraska-Western Iowa Health Care System**
Veterans Health Administration, U S Dept. of V A
4101 Woolworth Avenue
Omaha, NE  68105                          402-346-8800
                                     FAX: 402-449-0684
                                                   www.va.gov

*Al Washko, Director*
*Rowen Zetterman, Chief of Staff*

## Nevada

**8108  Las Vegas Veterans Center**
1919 S Jones Boulevard
Las Vegas, NV  89146                      702-251-7873
                                     FAX: 702-388-6664

*Daryl Harding, Resident Counselor LCSW*
*Matt Watson, Team Leader MSW*

Veterans clinical counseling center for veterans and their dependent individual and group counseling, marital and family
counseling, alcohol and drug assessment referral or treatment.
Community education and consultation, employment counseling.

**8109 Reno Regional Office**
Veterans Benefits Administration U S Deptartment o
1000 Locust Street
Reno, NV 89502
775-328-1486
800-827-1000
FAX: 775-328-1447
e-mail: reno.query@vba.va.gov
www.va.gov

*Joseph E Dardillo, Administrative Officer*

**8110 VA Sierra Nevada Healthcare System**
Veterans Health Administration, U S Dept. of V A
1000 Locust Street
Reno, NV 89502
775-786-7200
888-838-6256
FAX: 775-328-1816
www.va.gov

*Roy F Mackintosh, Acting Aces/Research/Development*
*Angela Fisher, Manager*

**8111 VA Southern Nevada Healthcare System**
Veterans Health Administration, U S Dept. of V A
901 Rancho Lane
Las Vegas, NV 89106
702-636-3000
800-827-1000
FAX: 707-636-3027
e-mail: g.vhacss@forum.va.gov
www.va.gov

*Chuck Fulkerson, Executive Director*
*Steve Long, Deputy Director*

## New Hampshire

**8112 Manchester Regional Office**
Veterans Benefits Administration, U S Dept. of V A
275 Chestnut Street
Manchester, NH 03101
800-827-1000
e-mail: manchester.query@vba.va.gov
www.va.gov

*Jerry Beale, Director*

**8113 Manchester VA Medical Center**
Veterans Health Administration, U S Dept. of V A
718 Smyth Road
Manchester, NH 03104
603-624-4366
800-892-8384
e-mail: g.vhacss@forum.va.gov
www.va.gov

*Marc Levenson, Executive Director*

**8114 New Hampshire Veterans Centers**
103 Liberty Street
Manchester, NH 03104
603-668-7060
800-562-3127
FAX: 603-666-7404

*Caryl Ahern Msw, Team Leader*
*Paulette Landry, Office Manager*
Veterans clinic offering combat veterans outpatient counseling

## New Jersey

**8115 Disabled American Veterans, New Jersey Northern Valley Chapter 32**
PO Box 505
Bergenfield, NJ 07621
201-384-0001

e-mail: DAV32GIN@aol.com
www.davnj.org

*Virginia McAleer-Hujber, Adjutant*
*Joseph Nulty, Manager*

**8116 Disabled American Veterans: Ocean County**
PO Box 1806
Toms River, NJ 08754
732-929-0907

e-mail: bvenga@thecore.com
community.nj.com/cc/dav24

*Mary Bencivenga, Contact*

**8117 East Orange Campus of the VA New Jersey Healthcare System**
Veterans Health Administration, US Dept. of VA
385 Tremont Avenue
East Orange, NJ 07018
973-676-1000
800-827-1000
FAX: 973-676-4226
e-mail: g.vhacss@forum.va.gov
www.va.gov

*Kenneth H Mizrach, Director*
*Samuel Greene, President*

**8118 Lyons Campus of the VA New Jersey Healthcare System**
Veterans Health Administration, U S Dept. of V A
151 Knollcroft Road
Lyons, NJ 07939
908-647-0180
800-827-1000
FAX: 908-647-3452
e-mail: g.vhacss@forum.va.gov
www.va.gov

*James J Farsetta, Director*
*Donna Henderson, Coordinator*

**8119 Newark Regional Office**
Veterans Benefits Administration, U S Dept. of V A
20 Washington Place
Newark, NJ 07102
800-827-1000
e-mail: newark.query@vba.va.gov
www.va.gov

*Stephen G Abel, Deputy Commissioner for Veterans*

## New Mexico

**8120 Albuquerque Regional Office**
Veterans Benefits Administration, U S Dept. of V A
PO Box 2324
Santa Fe, NM 87503
505-827-6312
800-827-1000
FAX: 505-827-6372
e-mail: nmvac@state.nm.us
www.state.nm.us/veterans/

*John Garcia, Director*

**8121  New Mexico VA Healthcare System**
Veterans Health Administration, US Dept. of VA
1501 San Pedro Drive SE
Albuquerque, NM  87108

505-265-1711
800-827-1000
FAX: 505-256-2855
e-mail: g.vhacss@forum.va.gov
www.va.gov

*Norman Brownel, Executive Director*

**8122  New Mexico Veterans Centers**
PO Box 927
Truth or Consequences, NM  87901

505-894-4200

e-mail: Lori

*Montgomery Administrator*

Veterans medical clinic offering disabled veterans medical treatments.

# New York

**8123  Albany VA Medical Center: Samuel S Stratton**
Veterans Health Administration, U S Dept. of V A
113 Holland Avenue
Albany, NY  12208

518-626-6711
800-823-9656
FAX: 518-626-5500
e-mail: g.vhacss@forum.va.gov
www.va.gov

*Linda Blumenstock, Marketing Director*
*Mary Ellen Piche, Director*

**8124  Albany Vet Center**
17 Computer Drive E
Suite 2
Albany, NY  12205

518-438-2505
FAX: 518-458-8613

*Maureen Chauvin, Office Manager*
*James Garrett, Executive Director*

Provides readjustment counseling for combat veterans and also provides benefits and job counseling for all veterans.

**8125  Bath VA Medical Center**
Veterans Health Administration U S Deptartment of
76 Veterans Medical Center
Bath, NY  14810

607-664-4000
800-827-1000
FAX: 607-664-4000
e-mail: g.vhacss@forum.va.gov
www.va.gov

*Barbara J Mahone, Chairman*

**8126  Bronx VA Medical Center**
Veterans Health Administration, U S Dept. of V A
130 W Kingsbridge Road
Bronx, NY  10468

718-584-9000
800-827-1000
FAX: 718-562-9120
e-mail: g.vhacss@forum.va.gov
www.va.gov

*Anthony Rotolo, Administrative Officer*
*Mary Sano, Research/Development Coordinator*
*Maryann Musumeci, Executive Director*

**8127  Brooklyn Campus of the VA NY Harbor Healthcare System**
Veterans Health Administration, U S Dept. of V A
295 Flatbush Avenue Ext
Brooklyn, NY  11201

718-836-6600
800-827-1000
e-mail: g.vhacss@forum.va.gov
www.va.gov

*George P Basher, Director*
*Irving Behr, MD*

**8128  Buffalo Regional Office**
Veterans Benefits Administration
3495 Bailey Avenue
Building 20
Buffalo, NY  14215

716-862-6527
800-827-1000
www.va.gov

**8129  Canandiagua VA Medical Center**
Veterans Health Administration, U S Dept. of V A
400 Fort Hill Avenue
Canandaigua, NY  14424

585-394-2000
800-827-1000
e-mail: g.vhacss@forum.va.gov
www.va.gov

*Robert W Ratliff, Interim Director*
*W Smith, Administrator*

**8130  Castle Point Campus of the VA Hudson Valley Healthcare System**
Veterans Health Administration, U S Dept. of V A
Castle Point Campus
Castle Point, NY  12511

914-737-4400
800-827-1000
FAX: 914-788-4244
e-mail: g.vhacss@forum.va.gov
www.va.gov

**8131  New York City Campus of the VA NY Harbor Healthcare System**
Veterans Health Administration, U S Dept. of V A
423 E 23rd Street
New York, NY  10010

212-951-7470
800-827-1000
FAX: 212-686-7470
e-mail: g.vhacss@forum.va.gov
www.va.gov

*Leslie Dowers, Administrative Officer*
*Camille R Varacchi, Administrative Officer*

**8132  New York Regional Office**
Veterans Benefits Administration, U S Dept. of V A
245 W Houston Street
New York, NY  10014

518-474-6114
800-827-1000
FAX: 518-473-0379
e-mail: newyork.query@vba.va.gov
www.va.gov

*George Basher, Director*

**8133  Northport VA Medical Center**
Veterans Health Administration, U S Dept. of V A
79 Middleville Road
Northport, NY  11768

631-261-4400
800-827-1000
e-mail: g.vhacss@forum.va.gov
www.va.gov

*Martina Parauda, Associate Director*

**8134 Syracuse VA Medical Center**
Veterans Health Administration, U S Dept. of V A
800 Irving Avenue
Syracuse, NY 13210                 315-476-7461
                                   800-827-1000
                        e-mail: g.vhacss@forum.va.gov
                                   www.va.gov

*George P Basher, Director*

**8135 Torah Alliance of Families of Kids with Disabilities**
T AF KI D
1433 Coney Island Avenue
Brooklyn, NY 11230                 718-252-2236
                              FAX: 718-252-2216
                     e-mail: tafkid@worldnet.att.net
                                   www.tafkid.org

*Juby Shapiro, President/Program Director*

Serves over 1k families whose children have a variety of disabilities and special needs. Many of these families are large families in the low socioeconomic level. Offers monthly meetings, guest lectures, parent matching, information of new developments in software, technology and techniques, sibling support groups, pen pal lists, audio and video library, alternative medicine and nutrition information and education on legal awareness and rights of disabled citizens.

**8136 VA Hudson Valley Health Care System**
Veterans Health Administration, U S Department of
PO Box 100
Montrose, NY 10548                 914-737-4400
                              FAX: 845-788-4244
                                   www.va.gov

*James J Farsette, Network Director*
*Michael Sabo, Executive Director*

**8137 VA Western NY Healthcare System, Batavia**
Veterans Health Administration, U S Dept. of V A
222 Richmond Avenue
Batavia, NY 14020                  585-343-7500
                                   800-827-1000
                        e-mail: g.vhacss@forum.va.gov
                                   www.va.gov

*Michael S Finegan, Medical Center Director*
*Timothy W Liezert, Assistant Director*
*Mary Olix, Manager*

**8138 VA Western NY Healthcare System, Buffalo**
Veterans Health Administration, U S Dept. of V A
3495 Bailey Avenue
Buffalo, NY 14215                  716-834-9200

                                   www.va.gov

*Michael S Finigan, Director*
*William Feeley, President*

---

## North Carolina

---

**8139 Asheville VA Medical Center**
Veterans Health Administration, U S Dept. of V A
1100 Tunnel Road
Asheville, NC 28805                828-298-7911
                                   800-827-1000
                              FAX: 828-299-2502
                        e-mail: g.vhacss@forum.va.gov
                                   www.va.gov

*Joseph Schimansky, Executive Director*
*Brian Peek, R&D Coordinator*

**8140 Charlotte Vet Center**
V A Department Veterans Affairs
223 S Brevard Street
Suite 103
Charlotte, NC 28202                704-333-6107
                              FAX: 704-344-6470
                                   www.va.gov

*Loretta Deaton, Team Leader*

Preadjustment Counseling for Combat Veterans with Post Traumatic Stress Disorder (PTSD).

**8141 Durham VA Medical Center**
Veterans Health Administration, U S Dept. of V A
508 Fulton Street
Durham, NC 27705                   919-286-0411
                                   800-827-1000
                              FAX: 919-286-5944
                     e-mail: leola.jenkins@med.va.gov
                                   www.va.gov

*Leola Jenkins, EED Manager*

**8142 Fayetteville VA Medical Center**
Veterans Health Administration, U S Dept. of V A
2300 Ramsey Street
Fayetteville, NC 28301             910-488-2120
                                   800-771-6106
                              FAX: 910-822-7926
                        e-mail: g.vhacss@forum.va.gov
                                   www.va.gov

*Janet Stout, Director*

**8143 Franklin Delano Roosevelt Campus of the VA Hudson Valley Healthcare System**
Veterans Health Administration, U S Dept. of V A
PO Box 100
Monroe, NC 28111                   845-737-4400
                                   800-887-2001
                              FAX: 914-788-4244
                        e-mail: g.vhacss@forum.va.gov
                                   www.va.gov

*James J Farsetta, Network Director*

**8144 WG Hefner VA Medical Center**
Vet Health Administration U S Department of VA
1601 Brenner Avenue
Salisbury, NC 28144                704-638-9000
                                   800-827-1000
                              FAX: 704-638-3395
                        e-mail: g.vhacss@forum.va.gov
                                   www.va.gov

*Nancy Stine, Manager*

**8145 Winston-Salem Regional Office**
Veterans Benefits Administration, U S Dept. of V A
251 N Main Street
Winston Salem, NC 27155            919-733-3851
                                   800-827-1000
                              FAX: 919-733-2834
                     e-mail: winsalem.query@vba.va.gov
                                   www.va.gov

*Charles F Smith, Assistant Secretary*

## North Dakota

**8146  Fargo VA Medical Center**
Veterans Health Administration, U S Dept. of V A
2101 Elm Street N
Fargo, ND  58102
701-239-7165
800-827-1000
FAX: 701-239-7166
e-mail: g.vhacss@forum.va.gov
www.va.gov

*Bob Hanson, Commissioner*
*Kathy Halgunseth, Manager*

**8147  North Dakota Department of Veterans' Affairs**
PO Box 9003
Fargo, ND  58106
701-239-7165
FAX: 701-239-7166
www.nasdva.com/northdakota.html

*Bob Hanson, Director*
*Kathy Halgunseth, Manager*

**8148  North Dakota VA Regional Office**
Veterans Benefits Administration, U S Dept. of V A
2101 Elm Street N
Fargo, ND  58102
701-239-3700
800-827-1000
FAX: 701-239-3790
e-mail: fargo.query@vba.va.gov
www.va.gov

*Thomas Santoro, Director Research Department*

## Ohio

**8149  Chillicothe VA Medical Center**
Veterans Health Administration, U S Dept. of V A
17273 State Route 104
Chillicothe, OH  45601
740-773-1141
800-827-1000
FAX: 740-772-7023
e-mail: g.vhacss@forum.va.gov
www.va.gov

*Douglas Moorman, Executive Director*

**8150  Cincinnati VA Medical Center**
Veterans Health Administration, U S Dept. of V A
3200 Vine Street
Cincinnati, OH  45220
513-861-3100
800-827-1000
FAX: 513-475-6500
e-mail: g.vhacss@forum.va.gov
www.va.gov

*Ronald D Edwards, Director*
*Gary Nugent, Executive Director*

**8151  Cincinnati Veterans Centers**
801b W 8th Street
Suite 126
Cincinnati, OH  45203
513-741-5600

Veterans medical clinic offering disabled veterans medical treatments.

**8152  Cleveland Regional Office**
Veterans Benefits Administration, U S Dept. of V A
1240 E 9th Street
Cleveland, OH  44199
800-827-1000
e-mail: cleveland.query@vba.va.gov
www.va.gov

*P Hunter Peckham, Director*
*Robert Ruff, Assistant Director*

**8153  Dayton VA Medical Center**
Veterans Health Administration U S Department of V
4100 W 3rd Street
Dayton, OH  45428
937-268-6511
800-827-1000
FAX: 937-262-2170
e-mail: g.vhacss@forum.va.gov
www.dayton.med.va.gov

*Charlene Ackerman, Director*
*Kathleen Mannix, Manager*

**8154  Louis Stokes VA Medical Center**
Veterans Health Administration, U S Dept. of V A
10701 East Boulevard
Cleveland, OH  44106
440-526-3030
800-827-1000
FAX: 440-838-6017
e-mail: g.vhacss@forum.va.gov
www.va.gov

*Anthony J Foster, Interim Director*

## Oklahoma

**8155  Muskogee VA Medical Center**
Veterans Benefits Administration, U S Dept. of V A
1011 Honor Heights Drive
Muskogee, OK  74401
918-683-3261
800-827-1000
e-mail: muskogee.query@vba.va.gov
www.va.gov

*Phillip L Driskill, Director*

**8156  Oklahoma City VA Medical Center**
Veterans Health Administration, U S Dept. of V A
921 NE 13th Street
Oklahoma City, OK  73104
405-270-0501
800-827-1000
FAX: 405-270-1560
www.va.gov

*Phillip L Driskill, Director*
*Tom Duchene, Plant Manager*
*D Robert McCaffree MD, Chief of Staff*

**8157  Oklahoma Veterans Centers Vet Center**
3033 N Walnut Avenue
Suite W101
Oklahoma City, OK  73105
405-528-5583
FAX: 405-270-5125

*Peter Sharp, Team Leader*
*Steve Kenzie, Owner*

PTSP counseling for all combat Veterans and victims of sexual trauma/sexual harassment.

## Oregon

**8158 Oregon Health Sciences University**
3181 SW Sam Jackson Park Road
Portland, OR 97239                     503-494-3460

*Thomas Talboe*
*James Morgan, Executive Director*

Offers services for the totally blind, legally blind, visually impaired, mentally retarded blind and more with health, counseling, educational, recreational, rehabilitation, computer training and professional training services.

**8159 Portland Regional Office**
Veterans Benefits Administration, U S Dept. of V A
1220 SW 3rd Avenue
Portland, OR 97204                     503-373-2388
                                       800-827-1000
e-mail: portland.query@vba.va.gov
                                       www.va.gov

**8160 Portland VA Medical Center**
Veterans Health Administration, U S Dept. of V A
PO Box 1034
Portland, OR 97207                     503-220-8262
                                       800-827-1000
                                FAX: 503-273-5319
e-mail: g.vhacss@forum.va.gov
                                       www.va.gov

*Mindy Aisen, Director Rehabilitation Research*
*Carolyn Tsai, Director of Neurology*
*Kim Winn, Manager*

**8161 Roseburg VA Medical Center**
Veterans Health Administration, U S Dept. of V A
913 NW Garden Valley Boulevard
Roseburg, OR 97470                     541-440-1000
                                       800-827-1000
                                FAX: 541-440-1225
e-mail: g.vhacss@forum.va.gov
                                       www.va.gov

*Jim Willis, Director*
*Mark Traines, MD*

**8162 White City VA Domiciliary**
Veterans Health Administration, U S Dept. of V A
8495 Crater Lake Highway
White City, OR 97503                   541-826-2111
                                       800-827-1000
                                FAX: 541-830-3500
e-mail: g.vhacss@forum.va.gov
                                       www.va.gov

*George Andries, Executive Director*

## Pennsylvania

**8163 Butler VA Medical Center**
Veterans Health Administration, U S Dept. of V A
325 New Castle Road
Butler, PA 16001                       724-287-4781
                                       800-827-1000
                                FAX: 724-282-4408
e-mail: g.vhacss@forum.va.gov
                                       www.va.gov

*David Wood, Executive Director*

**8164 Coatesville VA Medical Center**
Veterans Health Administration, U S Dept. of V A
1400 Blackhorse Hill Road
Coatesville, PA 19320                  610-384-7711
                                       800-827-1000
e-mail: g.vhacss@forum.va.gov
                                       www.va.gov

*Charlene Ackerman, Director*
*Gary Devansky, Chief Executive Officer*

**8165 Erie VA Medical Center**
Veterans Health Administration, U S Dept. of V A
135 E 38th Street
Erie, PA 16504                         814-868-8661
                                       800-274-8387
e-mail: g.vhacss@forum.va.gov
                                       www.va.gov

*Michael Adelman, Chief of Staff*
*Stephen Lucas, Executive Director*

**8166 James E Van Zandt VA Medical Center**
Veterans Health Administration, U S Dept. of V A
2907 Pleasant Valley Boulevard
Altoona, PA 16602                      814-943-8164
                                       800-827-1000
                                FAX: 814-940-7898
e-mail: g.vhacss@forum.va.gov
                                       www.va.gov

*Cecil B Hengeveld, Director*
*Gerald Williams, Executive Director*

**8167 Lebanon VA Medical Center**
Veterans Health Administration, U S Dept. of V A
1700 S Lincoln Avenue
Lebanon, PA 17042                      717-272-6621
                                       800-409-8771
                                FAX: 717-228-5907
e-mail: g.vhacss@forum.va.gov
                                       www.va.gov

*Steven W Young, Associate Director*

**8168 Pennsylvania Veterans Centers**
Veterans Health Administration, U S Department of
1000 State Street
Suite 2
Erie, PA 16501                         717-861-8901
                                       800-478-8
                                FAX: 717-861-8589
                                       www.va.gov

*Cecil B Hengeveld, Deputy Adjustant General*

Veterans medical clinic offering disabled veterans medical treatments.

**8169 Philadelphia Regional Office and Insurance Center**
Veterans Benefits Administration, U S Dept. of V A
5000 Wissahickon Avenue
Philadelphia, PA 19144
                                       800-827-1000
e-mail: phillyro.query@vba.va.gov
                                       www.va.gov

**8170 Philadelphia VA Medical Center**
Veterans Health Administration, U S Dept. of V A
University and Woodland Avenu
Philadelphia, PA 19104                 215-823-5800
                                       800-827-1000
e-mail: g.vhacss@forum.va.gov
                                       www.va.gov

*Cecil B Hengeveld, Director*

**8171   Pittsburgh Regional Office**
Veterans Benefits Administration U S Deparment of
University Drive C
Pittsburgh, PA  15240                      412-688-6100
                                           800-827-1000
                          FAX: 412-688-6121
             e-mail: pittsburgh.query@vba.va.gov
                                           www.va.gov

*Micahel E Moreland*

**8172   VA Pittsburgh Healthcare System, University Drive Division**
Veterans Health Administration, U S Dept. of V A
University Drive
Pittsburgh, PA  15240                      412-688-6000
                                           800-827-1000
                          FAX: 412-688-6901
             e-mail: g.vhacss@forum.va.gov
                                           www.va.gov

*Michael E Moreland, Chief Executive Officer*

**8173   VA Pittsburgh Healthcare System, Highland Drive Division**
Veterans Health Administration, U S Dept. of V A
7180 Highland Drive
Pittsburgh, PA  15206                      412-365-4900
                                           800-827-1000
                          FAX: 412-365-4213
             e-mail: g.vhacss@forum.va.gov
                                           www.va.gov

*Cecil Hengeveld, Deputy Adjutant General*
*Roger Sutton, MD*

**8174   Wilkes-Barre VA Medical Center**
Veterans Health Administration, U S Dept. of V A
1111 E End Boulevard
Wilkes Barre, PA  18711                    570-821-7207
                                           800-827-1000
                          FAX: 570-821-7278
             e-mail: g.vhacss@forum.va.gov
                                           www.va.gov

*William Grossman MD*

## Rhode Island

**8175   Providence Regional Office**
Veterans Benefits Administration, U S Dept. of V A
380 Westminster Street
Providence, RI  02903                      401-462-0324
                                           800-827-1000
                          FAX: 401-254-2320
             e-mail: providence.query@vba.va.gov
                                           www.va.gov

*Daniel Evangelista, Acting Associate Director*

**8176   Providence VA Medical Center**
Veterans Health Administration, U S Dept. of V A
830 Chalkstone Avenue
Providence, RI  02908                      401-273-7100
                          FAX: 401-457-3360
             e-mail: g.vhacss@forum.va.gov
                                           www.va.gov

*Vincent Ng, Executive Director*

**8177   Rhode Island Veterans Center**
789 Park Avenue
Cranston, RI  02910                        401-467-2046
                          FAX: 401-528-5253

*Berne Greene, Manager*
Veterans medical clinic offering disabled veterans medical
treatments.

## South Carolina

**8178   Columbia Regional Office**
Veterans Benefits Administration, U S Dept. of V A
1801 Assembly Street
Columbia, SC  29201                        803-734-0200
                                           800-827-1000
             e-mail: columbia.query@vba.va.gov
                                           www.va.gov

*Jimmie Ruff, Executive Director*

**8179   Ralph H Johnson VA Medical Center**
Veterans Health Administration, U S Dept. of V A
109 Bee Street
Charleston, SC  29401                      843-789-6710
                                           800-827-1000
                          FAX: 843-876-5384
             e-mail: g.vhacss@forum.va.gov
                                           www.va.gov

*Brenda M Synder, Administrative Officer*

**8180   William Jennings Bryan Dorn VA Medical Center**
Veterans Health Administration U S Department of V
6439 Garners Ferry Road
Columbia, SC  29209                        803-776-4000
                                           800-827-1000
                          FAX: 803-695-6739
             e-mail: g.vhacss@forum.va.gov
                                           www.va.gov

*Cynthia T Boris, Chief of Pharmacy*
*Julian H Bourn, Program Director*
*Brian Heckert, Executive Director*

## South Dakota

**8181   Sioux Falls VA Medical Center**
Veterans Health Administration, U S Dept. of V A
PO Box 5046
Sioux Falls, SD  57117                     605-336-3230
                                           800-827-1000
                          FAX: 605-333-6878
             e-mail: g.vhacss@forum.va.gov
                                           www.va.gov

*Joseph Dalpiaz, Director*
*Gary Million, Assistant Director*
*R Crawford, Executive Director*

**8182   South Dakota VA Regional Office**
Veterans Benefits Administration, U S Dept. of V A
PO Box 5046
Sioux Falls, SD  57117                     605-773-3269
                                           800-827-1000
                          FAX: 605-773-5380
             e-mail: siouxfalls.query@vba.va.gov
                                           www.va.gov

**8183   South Dakota Veterans Centers**
610 Kansas City Street
Rapid City, SD  57701                      605-348-0077
                                           800-743-1070
                          FAX: 605-348-0878

*Gary Johnson, Manager*
Veterans medical clinic offering disabled veterans medical
treatments.

## Tennessee

**8184 Alvin C York VA Medical Center**
Veterans Health Administration, U S Dept. of V A
3400 Lebanon Road
Murfreesboro, TN 37129
615-867-6000
800-827-1000
FAX: 615-867-5768
e-mail: g.vhacss@forum.va.gov
www.va.gov

*David Penninggon, Director*

**8185 Memphis VA Medical Center**
Veterans Health Administration, U S Dept. of V A
1030 Jefferson Avenue
Memphis, TN 38104
901-523-8990
800-636-8262
e-mail: g.vhacss@forum.va.gov
www.va.gov

*Peter St Arnold, Administrative Officer*
*John M Stuart, Research/Development Coordinator*
*Hardie Phipps, Manager*

**8186 Mountain Home VA Medical Center**
Veterans Health Administration, US Dept. of VA
Mountain Home, TN 37684
423-926-1171
800-827-1000
e-mail: g.vhacss@forum.va.gov
www.va.gov

*Nancy Doughtry, Manager*

**8187 Nasheville Regional Office**
Veterans Benefits Administration, U S Dept. of V A
110 9th Avenue S
Nashville, TN 37203
800-827-1000
e-mail: nashville.query@vba.va.gov
www.va.gov

*Michael R Walsh, Administrative Officer*
*Donald H Rubin, Research/Development Coordinator*

**8188 Nashville VA Medical Center**
Veterans Health Administration, US Dept. of VA
1310 24th Avenue S
Nashville, TN 37212
615-327-4751
800-827-1000
FAX: 615-321-6350
e-mail: g.vhacss@forum.va.gov
www.va.gov

*David Pennington, President*

## Texas

**8189 Amarillo VA Healthcare System**
Veterans Health Administration, U S Dept. of V A
6010 Emerald Boulevard W
Amarillo, TX 79106
806-355-9703
800-827-1000
FAX: 806-354-7869
e-mail: g.vhacss@forum.va.gov
www.va.gov

*Wallace N Hopkins, Director*

**8190 Amarillo Vet Center**
Department of Veterans Affairs
3414 Olsen Boulevard
Suite E
Amarillo, TX 79109
806-354-9779
FAX: 806-351-1104

*Pedro Garcia Jr, Team Leader*

Provides individual, group and family counseling to veterans who served in combat theaters of World War II and Korea, veterans of the Vietnam Era, and veterans of conflicts zones in Lebanon, Grenada, Panama, the Persian Guld and Somalia.

**8191 El Paso VA Healthcare Center**
Veterans Health Administration, U S Dept. of V A
5001 N Piedras Street
El Paso, TX 79930
915-564-6100
800-827-1000
FAX: 915-564-7920
e-mail: g.vhacss@forum.va.gov
www.va.gov

*Stephen Shapiro, R and D Coordinator*

**8192 Houston Regional Office**
Veterans Benefits Administration, U S Dept. of V A
6900 Almeda Road
Houston, TX 77030
713-791-1414
800-827-1000
e-mail: houston.query@vba.va.gov
www.va.gov

*Cecil Aultman, Executive Director*
*Edgar Tucker, Chief Executive Officer*

**8193 Houston VA Medical Center**
Veterans Health Administration, U S Dept. of V A
2002 Holcombe Boulevard
Houston, TX 77030
713-791-1414
800-827-1000
e-mail: g.vhacss@forum.va.gov
www.va.gov

*Edgar Tucker, Chief Executive Officer*

**8194 South Texas Veterans Healthcare System**
Veterans Health Administration, U S Dept. of V A
7400 Merton Minter Street
San Antonio, TX 78229
210-617-5300
800-827-1000
e-mail: g.vhacss@forum.va.gov
www.va.gov

*Pete Donahoe, Director*
*Charles Sepich, Chief Executive Officer*

**8195 VA North Texas Health Care System: Sam Rayburn Memorial Veterans Center**
Veterans Health Administration, U S Dept. of V A
1201 E 9th Street
Bonham, TX 75418
800-924-8387
FAX: 903-583-6688
e-mail: g.vhacss@forum.va.gov
www.va.gov

*James E Nier, Executive Director*

**8196 VA North Texas Health Veterans Affairs Car e System: Dallas VA Medical Center**
Veterans Health Administration, U S Dept. of V A
4500 S Lancaster Road
Dallas, TX 75216
214-742-8387
800-849-3597
FAX: 214-857-1171
www.va.gov

*Alan G Harper, Director*
*Jonnis Hamilton, Manager*
*Daniel K Heers, Assistant Director*

Health care system which serves veterans with medical care and rehabilitation services including spinal cord injury center. For VA benefit inquiries contact 1-800-827-1000. This system has locations in Bonham, Dallas, and Fort Worth.

**8197  Waco Regional Office**
Veterans Benefits Administration, U S Dept. of V A
701 Clay Avenue
Waco, TX  76799

800-827-1000
e-mail: waco.query@vba.va.gov
www.va.gov

*Keith Young, Research/Development Coordinator*

**8198  West Texas VA Healthcare System**
Veterans Health Administration, U S Dept. of V A
300 W Veterans Boulevard
Big Spring, TX  79720

432-264-4810
800-728-7000
FAX: 915-264-4834
e-mail: g.vhacss@forum.va.gov
www.va.gov

*Bruce A Gordon, Director*
*Robert W Ratliff, Deputy Director*
*Celsa Tiu, MD*

## Utah

**8199  Disabled American Veterans Department of Utah**
271 E 800 S
Salt Lake City, UT  84111

801-359-8168
FAX: 801-328-3443
e-mail: utdav.juno.com
www.utdav.org

*James Floyd, Director*
*Belinda Karabatso, Volunteer Service Director*
*John Maher, Manager*

**8200  Utah Division of Veterans Affairs**
Utah Division of Veterans Affairs
550 Foothill Drive
Suite 202
Salt Lake City, UT  84113

801-524-6048
800-894-9497
FAX: 801-326-2369
e-mail: tandrews@utah.gov
www.ut.ngb.army.mil/veterans

*Terry Schow, Director*
*Todd Andrews, Assistant to the Director*
*Lavonne Willis, Manager*

**8201  VA Salt Lake City Healthcare System**
Veterans Health Administration, U S Dept. of V A
500 Foothill Drive
Salt Lake City, UT  84148

801-582-1565
800-827-1000
FAX: 801-584-1289
e-mail: g.vhacss@forum.va.gov
www.va.gov

*Matthew H Samore, Director*
*Jonathan R Nebeker, Assistant Director*
*William Hodson, Administrator*

## Vermont

**8202  Vermont VA Regional Office Center**
Veterans Benefits Administration U S Department V
215 N Main Street
White River Junction, VT  05009

802-296-6339
800-827-1000
FAX: 802-290-6354
e-mail: whiteriver.query@vba.va.gov
www.va.gov

*Laura Miraldi, Executive Director*

**8203  Vermont Veterans Centers**
359 Dorset Street
South Burlington, VT  05403

802-862-1806

*Fred Forehand, Manager*

Veterans medical clinic offering disabled veterans medical treatments.

## Virginia

**8204  Hampton VA Medical Center**
Veterans Health Administration, U S Dept. of V A
100 Emancipation Drive
Hampton, VA  23667

757-722-9961
800-827-1000
FAX: 757-728-3135
e-mail: mike.eisenberg@med.va.gov
www.va.gov

*Myron Eisenberg, Aces/ Education & Research*
*Michelle Fronheiser, Research Contact*
*Joseph Williams, Executive Director*

**8205  Hunter Holmes McGuire VA Medical Center**
Veterans Health Administration, U S Dept. of V A
1201 Broad Rock Boulevard
Richmond, VA  23249

804-675-5151
800-827-1000
FAX: 804-675-5139
e-mail: g.vhacss@forum.va.gov
www.va.gov

*Robert C Dresch, Administrative Officer*
*Lauri A Weiler, Research Contact*

**8206  Roanoke Regional Office**
Veterans Benefits Administration, U S Dept. of V A
210 Franklin Road SW
Roanoke, VA  24011

540-857-7104
800-827-1000
e-mail: anne.atkins@vdvs.viginia.gov
www.vdvs.virginia.gov

*Vince M Burgess, Commissioner*
*Bert Boyd, COO/Executive Director*

**8207  Salem VA Medical Center**
Veterans Health Administration, U S Dept. of V A
1970 Roanoke Boulevard
Salem, VA  24153

540-982-2463
800-827-1000
FAX: 540-983-1096
e-mail: g.vhacss@forum.va.gov
www.va.gov

*Stephen L Lemons, Director*

**8208  Virginia Department of Veterans Services**
270 Franklin Road SW
Roanoke, VA  24011

540-857-7104
FAX: 540-857-7573
e-mail: pmigrand131@worldnet.att.net
www.vdva.vipnet.org

*Jon A Mangis, Commissioner of Veterans Service*
*Colbert Boyd, Chief Deputy Commissioner*
*Colbert Boyd, Executive Director*

## Washington

**8209  Jonathan M Wainwright Memorial VA Medical Center**
Veterans Health Administration, U S Dept. of V A
77 Wainwright Drive
Walla Walla, WA  99362                509-525-5200
                                      888-687-8863
                                 FAX: 509-946-3062
                                      www.va.gov

*Richard D Cornish, R and D Coordinator*

**8210  Seattle Regional Office**
Veterans Benefits Administration U S Department of
915 2nd Avenue
Seattle, WA  98174                    206-762-1010
                                      800-827-1000
                         e-mail: seattle.query@vba.va.gov
                                      www.va.gov

*Va Ad Harabanim, Executive Director*
*Timothy Williams, Chief Executive Officer*

**8211  Spokane VA Medical Center**
Veterans Health Administration, U S Dept. of V A
4815 N Assembly Street
Spokane, WA  99205                    509-434-7000
                                      800-827-1000
                                 FAX: 509-434-7119
                         e-mail: g.vhacss@forum.va.gov
                                      www.va.gov

*Alan Prentiss, Chief of Staff*
*Dirk Minatre, Coordinator*
*Joseph Manley, Executive Director*

**8212  VA Puget Sound Health Care System**
Veterans Health Administration, U S Dept. of V A
1660 S Columbian Way
Seattle, WA  98108                    206-762-1010
                                      800-827-1000
                         e-mail: g.vhacss@forum.va.gov
                                      www.va.gov

*John M King, Director*
*Timothy Williams, Chief Executive Officer*

## West Virginia

**8213  Beckley VA Medical Center**
Veterans Health Administration, U S Dept. of V A
200 Veterans Avenue
Beckley, WV  25801                    304-255-2121
                                      800-827-1000
                                 FAX: 304-255-2431
                         e-mail: g.vhacss@forum.va.gov
                                      www.va.gov

*Gerard Husson, Director*
*Karin McGraw, Assistant Director*
*Debbie Coloski, Manager*

**8214  Huntington Regional Office**
Veterans Benefits Administration, U S Dept. of V A
640 4th Avenue
Huntington, WV  25701                 304-558-3661
                                      800-827-1000
                                 FAX: 304-558-3662
                         e-mail: huntington.query@vba.va.gov
                                      www.va.gov

*Larry Linch, Director*

**8215  Huntington VA Medical Center**
Veterans Health Administration, U S Dept. of V A
1540 Spring Valley Drive
Huntington, WV  25704                 304-429-6755
                                 FAX: 304-429-6713
                                      www.va.gov

*Jack E Terry, R and D Coordinator*
*Richard Manis, MD*

**8216  Louis A Johnson VA Medical Center**
Veterans Health Administration, U S Dept. of V A
1 Med Center Drive
Clarksburg, WV  26301                 304-623-7640
                                      800-827-1000
                                 FAX: 304-626-7048
                         e-mail: g.vhacss@forum.va.gov
                                      www.va.gov

*William E Cox, Executive Director*
*Kathy Keener, Program Assistant*
*Leilani Sultan-Brown DDS*

**8217  Martinsburg VA Medical Center**
Veterans Health Administration, U S Dept. of V A
Rr 9
Martinsburg, WV  25404                304-263-0811
                                      800-827-1000
                                 FAX: 304-262-7433
                         e-mail: g.vhacss@forum.va.gov
                                      www.va.gov

*Marilyn LaFreniere, Science Coordinator*
*Fernando Rivera, Director*

**8218  US Department Veterans Affairs Beckley Vet Center**
101 Ellison Avenue
Beckley, WV  25801                    304-252-8220
                                 FAX: 304-254-8711
                                      www.va.gov

*Melody Friend, Director*
*Ron Johnson, Manager*

Vet Center services includes individual and group readjustment counseling, referral for benefits assistance, liason with community agencies, marital and family counseling, substance abuse counseling, job counseling and referral, sexual trauma counseling, and community education.

## Wisconsin

**8219  Clement J Zablocki VA Medical Center**
Veterans Health Administration U S Department of V
5000 W National Avenue
Milwaukee, WI  53295                  414-384-2000
                                      888-827-1000
                                 FAX: 414-382-5319
                                      www.va.gov

*Glen W Grippn, Director*
*Glen Grippen, Chief Executive Officer*

**8220  Tomah VA Medical Center**
Veterans Health Administration, U S Dept. of V A
500 E Veterans Street
Tomah, WI  54660                      608-372-3971
                                      800-827-1000
                                 FAX: 608-372-1224
                         e-mail: g.vhacss@forum.va.gov
                                      www.va.gov

*Ronald J Sweeney, R and D Coordinator*
*Stan Johnson, Executive Director*

**8221   William S Middleton Memorial VA Hospital Center**
Veterans Health Administration, U S Dept. of V A
2500 Overlook Ter
Madison, WI  53705                                        608-256-1901
                                                         800-827-1000
                                                    FAX: 608-280-7244
                                      e-mail: g.vhacss@forum.va.gov
                                                          www.va.gov

*Marvin G Rupp, Administrative Officer*
*Nathan Geraths, Executive Director*

**8222   Wisconsin VA Regional Office**
Veterans Benefits Administration, U S Dept. of V A
5000 W National Avenue
Building 6
Milwaukee, WI  53295                                      414-384-2000
                                                         800-827-1000
                                                    FAX: 414-382-5374
                                   e-mail: milwaukee.query@vba.va.gov
                                                          www.va.gov

*Philip L Cook, Executive Director*
*Neil S Mandel, Research/Development Coordinator*
*Glen Grippen, Chief Executive Officer*

# Wyoming

**8223   Cheyenne VA Medical Center**
Veterans Health Administration, U S Dept. of V A
2360 E Pershing Boulevard
Cheyenne, WY  82001                                       307-778-7322
                                                         800-827-1000
                                                    FAX: 307-778-7531
                                      e-mail: g.vhacss@forum.va.gov
                                                          www.va.gov

*William Mcintyre, Research/Development Coordinator*

**8224   Sheridan VA Medical Center**
Veterans Health Administration, U S Dept. of V A
1898 Fort Road
Sheridan, WY  82801                                       307-672-3473
                                                         800-827-1000
                                                    FAX: 307-672-1639
                                      e-mail: g.vhacss@forum.va.gov
                                                          www.va.gov

*Gary Morton, Executive Director*

**8225   Wyoming Veterans Centers**
111 S Jefferson Street
Casper, WY  82601                                         307-266-3633
                                                    FAX: 307-261-5439
Veterans medical clinic offering disabled veterans medical
treatments.

**8226   Wyoming/Colorado VA Regional Office**
Veterans Benefits Administration, U S Dept. of V A
155 Van Gordon Street
Lakewood, CO  80228                                       303-894-7474
                                                         800-827-1000
                                                    FAX: 303-894-7442
                                     e-mail: denver.query@vba.va.gov
                                                          www.va.gov

*E William Belz, Director*

## Alabama

**8227  Coffee County Training Center**
PO Box 311343
Enterprise, AL  36331                        334-393-1732
                                        FAX: 334-347-0252

*Vickie Florence, Director*

Clients 21 years and up receive training in Independent Living Skills, Self-Care, Language Skills, Learning, Self-Direction and Economic Self-Sufficiency. Transportation is also provided to clients of the center.

**8228  Easter Seal: Achievement Center**
Easter Seals of Alabama
510 W Thomason Circle
Opelika, AL  36801                           334-745-3501
                                        FAX: 334-749-5808
                          e-mail: info@achievement-center.org
                                   www.achievement-center.org

*Furrel Bailey, Interim Administrator*
*Elizabeth Griffin, Administratives Services*

Job placement programs, remunerative work services and work adjustment training programs. Clients must be at least 16 years old.

**8229  Easter Seal: Opportunity Center**
PO Box 2247
Anniston, AL  36202                          256-237-0381

Work adjustment and remunerative work programs.

**8230  Employment Service Division: Alabama**
Department of Industrial Relations
649 Monroe Street
Room 2813
Montgomery, AL  36131                        334-242-8990
                                        FAX: 334-242-3960
                          e-mail: director@dir.alabama.us
                                   www.dir.state.al.us/es

*Phyllis Kennedy, Director*
*Donald K Fisher, Assistant Director*
*Alice Kinney, Executive Director*

**8231  Fort Payne-Dekalb Rehab Center**
311 Gault Avenue N
Fort Payne, AL  35967                        256-845-5717
                                        FAX: 256-547-5761

*Sam Bishop, Director*
*Candy Shaffer, Manager*

Offers work adjustment, evaluation and job readiness skills for people with disabilities.

**8232  Lakeshore Rehabilitation Facility**
PO Box 59127
Birmingham, AL  35259                        205-870-5999
                                             800-441-7609
                                        FAX: 205-879-2685

*Paige Hebson, Administrator*

**8233  Montezuma Training Center**
Academy Drive
Andalusia, AL  36420                         334-222-8411

*Lillian Dixon, Director*
*W Underwood, Executive Director*

Individuals served in this program must be at least 21 years of age and have a primary diagnosis of mental retardation. Clients receive training in independent living skills, learning, self-direction and economic self-sufficiency. Special Olympic activities are also emphasized.

**8234  Thomasville Rehabilitation Center**
PO Box 1006
Thomasville, AL  36784                       334-636-5421
                                             800-335-3237
                                        FAX: 334-636-5421
                                   www.rehab.state.al.us

**8235  Vocational Rehabilitation Service Opelika**
520 W Thomason Circle
Opelika, AL  36801                           334-749-1259
                                             800-671-6835
                                        FAX: 334-749-8753
                                   www.rehab.state.al.us

*Patricia Floyd, Board Chairperson*
*James Myrick, Supervisor*

**8236  Vocational Rehabilitation Service: Scottsboro**
PO Box 296
Scottsboro, AL  35768                        256-574-5813
                                             800-888-3
                                        FAX: 256-574-6033
                                   www.rehab.state.al.us

*Steded Shiders, Director*
*Mark Williams, Manager*

**8237  Vocational Rehabilitation Service: Dothan**
795 Ross Clark Circle
Dothan, AL  36303                            334-792-0022
                                             800-275-0132
                                        FAX: 334-792-1783
                                   www.rehab.state.al.us

*Wyndal Adams, Director*

**8238  Vocational Rehabilitation Service: Gadsden**
State of Alama
1100 George Wallace Drive
Gadsden, AL  35903                           256-547-6974
                                             800-671-6839
                                        FAX: 256-543-1784
                                   www.rehab.state.al.us

*Connie Brechin, Supervisor*

**8239  Vocational Rehabilitation Service: Homewoo d**
PO Box 19888
Birmingham, AL  35219                        205-290-4400
                                             800-671-6837
                                        FAX: 205-290-0486
                                   www.rehab.state.al.us

*Milton Moats, Building Administrator*

**8240  Vocational Rehabilitation Service: Huntsvi lle**
2939 Johnson Road SW
Huntsville, AL  35805                        256-650-8219
                                             800-671-6840
                                   www.rehab.state.al.us

*James Odom, Unit Supervisor*
*Steve Shivers, Commissioner*

**8241  Vocational Rehabilitation Service: Jackson**
PO Box 1005
Jackson, AL  36545                           251-246-5708
                                             800-671-6836
                                        FAX: 251-246-5224
                                   www.rehab.state.al.us

*Jean Stewart, Manager*

**8242  Vocational Rehabilitation Service: Jasper**
301 N Walston Bridge Road
Suite 116
Jasper, AL  35504                              205-221-7840
                                               800-671-6841
                                          FAX: 205-221-1062
                                          www.rehab.state.al.us

*Steve Shivers, Commissioner*
*Angela Guire, Manager*

**8243  Vocational Rehabilitation Service: Mobile**
2419 Gordon Smith Drive
Mobile, AL  36617                              251-479-8611
                                               800-671-6842
                                          FAX: 251-478-2197
                                          www.rehab.state.al.us

*James Brewer, Manager*

**8244  Vocational Rehabilitation Service: Muscle Shoals**
1450 Avalon Avenue
Muscle Shoals, AL  35661                       256-381-1110
                                               800-275-0166
                                          FAX: 256-389-3149
                                          www.rehab.state.al.us

*Stece Butler, Director*

**8245  Vocational Rehabilitation Service: Selma**
2906 Citizens Parkway
Selma, AL  36701                               334-872-8422
                                               888-761-5995
                                          FAX: 334-877-3796
                                          www.rehab.state.al.us

*Richard Weishaupt, Manager*

**8246  Vocational Rehabilitation Service: Tallade ga**
4 Medical Park
Ofc
Talladega, AL  35160                           256-362-1300
                                               800-441-7592
                                          www.rehab.state.al.us

*Cayla Lackey, Manager*

**8247  Vocational Rehabilitation Service: Troy**
518 S Brundidge Street
Troy, AL  36081                                334-566-2491
                                               800-441-7608
                                          FAX: 334-566-9415
                                          www.rehab.state.al.us

*Wendell Adams, Manager*

**8248  Vocational Rehabilitation Service: Tuscalo osa**
PO Box 1610
Tuscaloosa, AL  35403                          205-554-1300
                                               800-331-5562
                                          FAX: 205-554-1369
                                          www.rehab.state.al.us

*Kathy Reeves, Supervisor*
*Henry Devasher, Supervisor*
*Hank Vasher, Manager*

**8249  Vocational Rehabilitation Services: Andalu sa**
1082 Village Square Drive
# 1
Andalusia, AL  36420                           334-222-4114
                                               800-671-6833
                                          FAX: 334-427-1216
                                          www.rehab.state.al.us

*Steve Shivers, Commissioner*
*Kathy Wyatt, Manager*

**8250  Vocational Rehabilitation Services: Annist on**
1105 Woodstock Avenue
Anniston, AL  36207                            256-238-9300
                                               800-671-6834
                                          FAX: 256-231-4852
                                          www.rehab.state.al.us

*Robert Watson, Manager*

**8251  Vocational and Rehabilitation Agency**
PO Box 11586
Montgomery, AL  36111                          334-281-8780
                                               800-441-7607
                                          FAX: 334-281-1973
                                          TTY: 888-737-2032
                                  e-mail: sshivers@rehab.state.al.us
                                          www.rehab.state.al.us

*Steve Shivers, President*

**8252  Vocational and Rehabilitation Service Columbiana**
PO Box 856
Columbiana, AL  35051                          205-669-3829
                                          FAX: 205-669-0605
                                          www.rehab.state.al.us

**8253  Vocational and Rehabilitation Service: Dec atur**
2129 E South Boulevard
Montgomery, AL  36116                          334-288-0220
                                               800-441-7607
                                          FAX: 256-281-1973
                                  e-mail: kate@rehab.state.al.us
                                          www.rehab.state.al.us

*Steve Shivers, Director*
*Jim Harris III, Assistant Director*

**8254  Wiregrass Rehabilitation Center**
795 Ross Clark Circle
Dothan, AL  36303                              334-792-0022
                                          FAX: 334-712-7632
                                          www.wrcjobs.com

*Hal Edwards, Chairman*
*Tom West, Vice Chairman*
*Susan Gilley, Manager*

Provides remunerative work.

**8255  Workshops**
4244 3rd Avenue S
Birmingham, AL  35222                          205-592-9683
                                          FAX: 205-592-9687
                                  e-mail: mail@workshopsinc.com
                                          www.workshopsinc.com

*Jim Crim, Executive Director*
*Shan Amerman, Director Client Services*

Provides vocational training, sheltered employment and other
support services to people with disabilities in central Alabama.

# Alaska

**8256  Anchorage Job Training Center**
235 E 8th Avenue
Anchorage, AK  99501                           907-334-2281
                                          FAX: 907-334-2286
                                          www.ci.anchorage.ak.us

**8257  Employment Service: Alaska**
Alaska Department of Labor
PO Box 25509
Juneau, AK  99802                              907-465-2723

*Dan Travis, Executive Director*

**8258 Fair Employment Practice Agency**
Alaska State Commission for Human Rights
800 a Street
Anchorage, AK 99501          907-276-6563

*Greg Maxwell, Manager*

**8259 Vocational and Rehabilitation Agency**
801 W 10th Street
Suite A
Juneau, AK 99801          907-465-2814
          800-478-2815
          FAX: 907-465-2856
          TTY: 907-465-2856
          e-mail: gale_sinnott@labor.state.ak.us
          www.labor.state.ak.us

*Gale Finnott, Executive Director*

## Arizona

**8260 Downtown Neighborhood Learning Center**
1001 W Jefferson Street
Phoenix, AZ 85007          602-256-0784
          800-869-8521
          FAX: 602-256-2524
          e-mail: marcian@first.inter.net

*Marcia R Newman, Executive Director*
*Mattie Johnson, Receptionist*
*Peg Osinski, El Mirage Learning Lab*

Adult education agency providing basic skills, GED, ESOL, life skills, computer skills, resume assistance and career testing.

**8261 Fair Employment Practice Agency: Arizona**
Arizona Civil Rights Division
1275 W Washington Street
Phoenix, AZ 85007          602-542-5263
          877-491-5742
          FAX: 602-542-8885
          www.azag.gov

*Virginia Gonzales, Director*
*Bruna Pedrini, Manager*

**8262 JOBS Administration Job Opportunities & Basic Skills**
1717 W Jefferson Street
Phoenix, AZ 85007          602-542-9596
          FAX: 602-542-5171

*Gretchen Evans, Program Administrator*

Assist applicants and recipients of temporary assistance to needy families to obtain job training and employment that will lead to economic independence.

**8263 TETRA Corporation**
308 W Glenn Street
Tucson, AZ 85705          520-622-4874

*Steven King, President*

Work hardening and disciplinary programs.

**8264 Vocational and Rehabilitation Agency Rehabilitation Services Administrations**
Division of Employment & Rehabilitation Services
1789 W Jefferson Street
Phoenix, AZ 85007          602-542-4910
          800-563-1221
          800-563-1221
          FAX: 602-542-3778
          TTY:602-542-6049
          e-mail: tazrsa@azdes.gov
          www.azdes.gov/rsa

*Jozef De Groot, Manager Program Services*
*Greg Warren, Administrator*
*Moises Gallegos, Manager*

This program serves individuals with disabilities seeking jobs and job training.

**8265 Yavapal Rehabilitation Center**
436 N Washington Avenue
Prescott, AZ 86301          928-445-0991
          FAX: 928-445-0994

*Bradley Newman, Executive Director*
Provides remunerative work.

## Arkansas

**8266 Arkansas Employment Service Agency and Job Training Program**
Arkansas Employment Security Department
PO Box 2981
Little Rock, AR 72203          501-682-2121
          FAX: 501-682-2273
          www.arstate.com

*Artee Williams, Director*

**8267 Easter Seal Work Center**
11801 Fairview Road
Little Rock, AR 72212          501-221-1063

          e-mail: mail@ar.easterseals.com
          www.ar.easterseals.com

*Lauren Zilk, Administrator*
Work hardening and disciplinary programs.

**8268 VCT/A Job Retention Skill Training Program**
Arkasas Rehab Services
PO Box 1358
Hot Springs, AR 71902          501-624-4411
          FAX: 501-624-0019
          www.state.ar.us/ars

*Barbara Lewis, Administrator*
*Mae Robinson, Assistant Administrator*

A training program designed for use in rehabilitation and educational settings. Using a social skill training strategy, VCT helps participants learn how to solve on-the-job problems and cope with common supervisory demands.

**8269 Vocational and Rehabilitation Agency Division of Services for the Blind**
700 Main Street
Little Rock, AR 72201          501-682-5463
          800-960-9270
          FAX: 501-682-0366
          TTY: 501-682-0093
          e-mail: jim.hudson@mail.state.ar.us
          www.state.ar.us

*Lyndel Lybarger, Field Adminstrator*
*James Hudson, Executive Director*

**8270    Vocational and Rehabilitation Agency for Persons Who Are Visually Impaired**
Arkansas Department of Human Services
PO Box 3237
Little Rock, AR  72203                501-682-5463
                                      800-960-9270
                                      TTY:501-324-9271
                                      e-mail: arkblind@edu.gte.net

*James C Hudson, Executive Director*

## California

**8271    ARC-Adult Vocational Program**
1500 Howard Street
San Francisco, CA  94103              415-255-7200
                                      FAX: 415-255-9488
                                      www.thearc.state.sanfrancisco.org

*Patricia Kemerling, Executive Director*

Job placement programs, remunerative work services and work adjustment training programs.

**8272    Ability First**
3770 E Willow Street
Long Beach, CA  90815                 562-426-6161
                                      FAX: 562-426-6148

*Michael Lande*
*Barbara Schlosser, Manager*

Job placement programs, remunerative work services and work adjustment training programs.

**8273    Bakersfield Association for Retarded Citizens**
B AR C
2240 S Union Avenue
Bakersfield, CA  93307                661-834-2272
                                      FAX: 661-834-9813
                                      e-mail: barc@barc-inc.org
                                      www.barc-inc.org

*Jim Baldwin, President*

Employment training & placement.

**8274    California Department of Fair Employment & Housing**
2000 O Street
Suite 120
Sacramento, CA  95814                 916-324-4244
                                      800-884-1684
                                      FAX: 916-323-6092
                                      www.dfeh.ca.gov

*Suzanne M Ambrose, Director*
*David Supkofl, Manager*

**8275    Career Connection Transition Program**
Whittier High School District
9401 Painter Avenue
Whittier, CA  90605                   562-698-8121
                                      FAX: 562-693-4414
                                      e-mail: Richard.Rosenberg@wuhsd.k12.ca.us
                                      www.wyouthhsd.k12.ca.us

*Richard L Rosenberg PhD, Vocational Coordinator*
*Bonnie Bolton, Transition Department Head*

Job placement programs, remunerative work services and work adjustment training programs. Transition services.

**8276    Career Development Program (CDP)**
260 W Grand Avenue
Escondido, CA  92025                  760-738-0277
                                      FAX: 760-741-9452

*Richard Brady MD*
*Wendy Hope, Supported Employment*
*Jill Hennessy, Independent Living*

Work hardening and disciplinary programs.

**8277    Community Outpatient Rehabilitation Center**
1925 E Dakota Avenue
Suite 120a
Fresno, CA  93726                     559-459-1842
                                      FAX: 559-459-1004
                                      www.communitymedical.org

*Andrew Robertson, Chief Medical Officer*
*Jan-Erik Paris, Manager*

Physical, occupational and speech therapy, neuropsychology services available for orthopedic and neurological diagnosis. Lymphedema program.

**8278    Cry-Rop: Colton-Redlands-Yucaipa Rop**
PO Box 8640
Redlands, CA  92375                   909-793-3115
                                      FAX: 909-793-6901
                                      www.cryrop.kla.ca.us

*Stephanie Houston, Manager Grants/Adult Service*
*Dalene Morris, Administrator*

Provides quality hands-on training programs in over 40 high demand career fields to assist high school students and adults in acquiring marketable job skills. Works in cooperation with local high schools, adult education colleges, and employers providing a collaborative team of academic and ROP occupational teachers who integrate academic and vocational competencies to provide sequenced paths within career majors. Support services, career guidance and services are provided to disabled people.

**8279    Desert Haven Training Center**
PO Box 2119
Lancaster, CA  93539                  661-948-8402

*Roy Williams*
*Jennie Moran, Manager*

Work adjustment and remunerative work programs.

**8280    Do-It-Leisure: Work Training Center**
3760 Morrow Lane
Suite S
Chico, CA  95928                      530-343-6055
                                      FAX: 530-343-4619
                                      e-mail: doitl@ewtc.org

*Carl Ochsner, Executive Director*
*Ken Steidley, President*

Therapeutic recreation programs providing a wide variety of services designed to meet individual needs with specialized, transitional or integrated activities.

**8281    ESS Work Center**
858 Stanton Road
Burlingame, CA  94010                 650-692-3377

*Jerry Martin, Executive Director*

**8282    Employment Service: California**
Employment Development Department
PO Box 826880
Sacramento, CA  94280                 916-653-0707

Provides job listings and unemployment listings for all.

**8283 Feather River Industries**
1811 Kusel Road
Oroville, CA 95966 530-534-1112
FAX: 530-534-3137

*Randy Guild, Rehabilitation Counselor*
*Dave Ennes, Manager*

Vocational training for persons with developmental disabilities provided through wood products fabrication and assembly tasks. Instructor to trainer rating ranging from 1 to 12, 1 to 8, 1 to 6, and 1 to 4 depending on individual needs and complexity of tasks.

**8284 Fit to Work**
3581 Palmer Drive
Suite 401
Cameron Park, CA 95682 530-676-7485
FAX: 530-676-9114

*Jennifer Roach*

Provides remunerative work.

**8285 Fresno City College: Disabled Students Programs and Services**
Fresno City College
1101 E University Avenue
Fresno, CA 93741 559-442-4600
FAX: 559-485-7304
e-mail: janice.emerzian@fresnocitycollege.edu
www.fresnocitycollege.com

*Ned Doffoney, President*
*Dr Janice Emerzian Ed D, District Director*

This program offers services to students with physical, learning and/or psychological disabilities beyond those provided by conventional Fresno City College Programs and enables students to successfully pursue their individual educational, vocational and personal goals.

**8286 Heartland Opportunity Center**
323 N E Street
Madera, CA 93638 559-674-8828
FAX: 559-674-8857

*Robert J Hand, Director*

Job placement programs, remunerative work services and work adjustment training programs.

**8287 Hollister Workshop**
Hope Rehabilitation Services
2300 Technology Parkway
Suite 7
Hollister, CA 95023 831-637-8283
FAX: 831-637-8726

*Kristi Alarid, Executive Director*

Work adjustment and remunerative work programs.

**8288 Job Training Program Liaison: California**
Employment Development Department
800 Capitol Mall
Sacramento, CA 95814 916-654-8210
800-300-5616
FAX: 916-654-9072
www.edd.ca.gov

*Patrick Henning, Director*

Provides information on filing an Unemployment Insurance or Disability Insurance claim, on-line job and resume bank which boasts thousands of job openings.

**8289 King's Rehabilitation Center**
PO Box 719
Hanford, CA 93232 559-582-9234
FAX: 559-582-1182
www.kingsrehab.com

*Carol A Rogers, Executive Director*
*Sherrie Martin, Director Human Resources*

**8290 Konocti Industries: People Services**
4195 Lakeshore Boulevard
Lakeport, CA 95453 707-263-3811
FAX: 707-263-0552

*Hank Montgomery*
*Ilene Dumont, Executive Director*

Work hardening and disciplinary programs.

**8291 Morongo Basin Work Activity Center**
74325 Joe Davis Drive
Twentynine Palms, CA 92277 760-366-8474

*Sheree Fraser*

Job placement programs, remunerative work services and work adjustment training programs.

**8292 Mother Lode Rehabilitation Enterprises**
399 Placerville Drive
Placerville, CA 95667 530-622-4848
FAX: 530-622-0204
www.morerehab.org

*Susie Davies, Executive Director*

Job placement programs, remunerative work services and work adjustment training programs.

**8293 NCI Affiliates**
1434 Chestnut Street
Paso Robles, CA 93446 805-238-6630
FAX: 805-239-9073
e-mail: info@nciaffiliates.org
www.nciaffiliates.org

*Crystal Nevosh, Executive Director*

Provides independent living skills and vocational training to people with disabilities.

**8294 Napa Valley PSI**
PO Box 600
Napa, CA 94559 707-255-0177
FAX: 707-255-0802

*Jeanne Fauquet, President*

Work adjustment, work training and educational services for developmentally disabled adults. Emphasis is on manufacture of quality wood products, primarily wooden office furniture.

**8295 New Opportunity Workshops**
PO Box 91476
Pasadena, CA 91109

*Ron Johnston, Rehabilitation Manager*

Offers a work services program, vocational rehabilitation, work activity programs and supported employment programs.

**8296 Oakland Work Activity Area**
6315 San Leandro Street
Oakland, CA 94621 510-639-9350

*Greg Whalley*
*Dennis Scharssenberg, Manager*

Job placement programs, remunerative work services and work adjustment training programs.

**8297  Opportunities for the Handicapped**
3340 Marysville Boulevard
Sacramento, CA  95838                 916-925-3522

*Kathy Dodd*
Work adjustment and remunerative work programs.

**8298  Orange County ARC**
225 W Carl Karcher Way
Anaheim, CA  92801                    714-744-5301
                                FAX: 714-744-5312

*Joyce Hearn, Chief Executive Officer*
Provides remunerative work through both site and community placements.

**8299  PRIDE Industries**
10030 Foothills Boulevard
Roseville, CA  95747                  916-783-5266
                                     800-550-6005
                                FAX: 916-788-2552
                        e-mail: info@prideindustries.com
                              www.prideindustries.com

*Michael Ziegler, President*
*Rosemary Elston, Services Manager*
*Roxanne Snyder, Employment Services Manager*

Vocational rehabilitation and employment services creating jobs for people with disabilites; services include career counseling, vocational assessment, work adjustment, work services, job seeking skills, job development, job placement, on-the-job support (coaching), mentoring, independent living skills, transition services and case management.

**8300  Pomona Valley Workshop**
4650 Brooks Street
Montclair, CA  91763                 909-624-3555
                                FAX: 909-624-5675
                                  www.tbwonline.org

*Karen Jones, Executive Director*
Assisting adults with disabilities reach their potential in vocational and socialization skills in order that they may achieve their highest level of employment and comminity integration in work program, supported employment Services, adult devopmental center and senior services.

**8301  Porterville Sheltered Workshop**
187 W Olive Avenue
Porterville, CA  93257               559-784-1399
                                FAX: 559-781-5651

*Nick Brown*
*Steve Tree, Executive Director*
Work adjustment and remunerative work programs.

**8302  Project Independence Supported Employment**
3505 Cadillac P 101
Costa Mesa, CA  92626                714-549-3464
                                FAX: 714-549-3559
                        e-mail: pop.mpowercom.net
                                       www.P-I.org

*Andrea Erickson, Executive Director*
*Tim Chervenak, Associate Director*
*Kristen Cook, Manager*
Provides remunerative work.

**8303  Sacramento Vocational Services**
6950 21st Avenue
Sacramento, CA  95820                 916-484-0550

*Diane De Rodeff, Director*
Work hardening and disciplinary programs.

**8304  Salinas Valley Training Center**
PO Box 453
Salinas, CA  93902                    831-758-8270

*Rosemary Anderson, Day Activity Manager*

**8305  San Francisco Vocational Services**
814 Mission Street
Suite 600
San Francisco, CA  94103             415-512-9500
                                FAX: 415-512-9507
                        e-mail: sfvs@sfvocational.org
                            www.sfvocationalservices.org

*Robert Campbell, Executive Director*
*Jeffrey Faircloth, Manager Case Management*

Comprehensive vocational rehabilitation center offering vocational evaluation, rehabilitative counseling, business office training, work experience, and job placement.

**8306  Shasta County Opportunity Center**
1265 Redwood Boulevard
Redding, CA  96003                    530-225-5781
                                FAX: 530-225-5751

*Jane Patterson, Program Manager*

**8307  Social Vocational Services**
350 Crenshaw Boulevard
Suite A104
Torrance, CA  90503                   310-783-0633
                                FAX: 310-944-3304
                             e-mail: nto@svsinc.org
                                      www.svsinc.org

*Dale Dutton Md, Executive Director*
*Dan Strohm, Manager*

**8308  South Bay Vocational Center**
1526 240th Street
Harbor City, CA  90710               310-784-2032
                                FAX: 310-539-6342
                                     www.sbvc1.com

*Corey Sylve, President/Chief Executive Office*
*Clare Grey, Vice President/COO*

**8309  Tri-County Independent Living Center**
955 Myrtle Avenue
Eureka, CA  95501                     707-445-8404
                                     877-576-5000
                                FAX: 707-445-9751
                                      www.tililig.org

*Chris Jones, Executive Director*
To provide programs, services and information for people with disabilities living in Humboldt, Del Norte and Trinity Counties in northern California in an effort to allow choices for individuals to optimize their independence.

**8310  Tulare County Training Center Able Industries**
2525 S K Street
Tulare, CA  93274                     559-686-8506

*Robert Stephenson*
Provides remunerative work.

**8311** **Tulare Workcenter Able Industries Able Industries**
2325 S K Street
Tulare, CA 93274

*Gary Horton, Executive Director*

**8312** **Unyeway**
2330 Main Street
Suite E
Ramona, CA 92065                    760-789-5960

*Hank Newman, Director*
*Kim Metli, Executive Director*

Job placement programs, remunerative work services and work adjustment training programs.

**8313** **V-Bar Enterprises**
720 Gordon Circle
Suisun City, CA 94585               707-864-1334

*Lu Brunet*

Job placement programs, remunerative work services and work adjustment training programs.

**8314** **Valley Light Industries**
822 N Grand Avenue
Covina, CA 91724                    626-331-9966

*Gary Miller*

Provides remunerative work.

**8315** **Visalia Workshop**
2544 E Valley Oaks Drive
Visalia, CA 93292                   559-734-1964

*Hortensia Venegas*

Work hardening and disciplinary programs.

**8316** **Vocational Services**
Parents & Friends
PO Box 656
Fort Bragg, CA 95437               707-964-4940
                              FAX: 707-964-8536
            e-mail: gjoy@parentsandfriends.org
                       www.parentsandfriends.org

*Guy Joy, Executive Director*
*Terry Scott, Controller*

Vocational Services provides opportunities for persons with developmental challenges and similar needs to participate fully in our community.

**8317** **Westside Opportunity Workshop**
9503 Jefferson Boulevard
Culver City, CA 90232              310-838-0521

*Edward Oritz*
*Anthony Vande Wydeven OD, Manager*

Job placement programs, remunerative work services and work adjustment training programs.

**8318** **Work Training Center for the Handicapped**
2255 Fair Street
Chico, CA 95928                    530-343-7994

*Barrie Dyer*
*Lee Laney, Manager*

Work hardening and disciplinary programs.

**8319** **Work Training Programs**
9430 Topanga Canyon Boulevard
Suite 103
Chatsworth, CA 91311               818-773-9570

*Stephen Miller*

Work hardening and disciplinary programs.

## Colorado

**8320** **Cheyenne Village**
6275 Lehman Drive
Colorado Springs, CO 80918         719-592-0200
                              FAX: 719-548-9947

*Ann Turner, Executive Director*
*Susan Watkins, President*

Residential and employment programs for adults with developmental disabilities.

**8321** **Colorado Civil Rights Divsion**
1560 Broadway
Suite 1050
Denver, CO 80202                   303-894-2997
                                   800-262-4845
                              FAX: 303-894-7830
                    e-mail: ccrd@dora.state.co.us
                              www.dora.state.co.us

*Wendell Pryer, Division Director*
*Virginia Butler, Commissioner*
*Nancy Snow, Housing Specialist*

Fair employment practices agency for Colorado. Accepts and investigates charges of discrimination. Does outreach, alternative dispute resolution and technical training in discrimination laws.

**8322** **Colorado Employment Service**
Department of Labor and Employment
600 Grant Street
Suite 900
Denver, CO 80203                   303-813-2800

**8323** **Developmental Training Services**
1401 Oak Creek Grade Road
Canon City, CO 81212               719-275-4504

*Roger Jensen, President*
*Linda Davis, Administrator*

**8324** **Dynamic Dimensions**
567th 18 Street
Burlington, CO 80807               719-346-5367
                              FAX: 719-346-6010

*Cheryl Reese, Executive Director*

Vocational, evaluation and assessment, training and placement for most disabilities.

**8325** **Gray Street Workcenter**
5685 Gray Street
Arvada, CO 80002                   303-422-1305
                              FAX: 303-467-2793

*Shelley Richardson, Executive Director*
*Tammy Drumright, Manager*

**8326   Hope Center**
3400 Elizabeth Street
Denver, CO  80205                303-388-4801
                        FAX: 303-388-0249
                e-mail: info@hopecenterhc.org
                        www.hopecenterlink.org

*George Brantley, Executive Director*

Work adjustment and remunerative work programs.

**8327   Imagine: Innovative Resources for Cognitive & Physical Challenges**
1400 Dixon Street
Lafayette, CO  80026             303-665-7789
                        FAX: 303-665-2648
        e-mail: caroline@imaginecolorado.org
                www.imaginecolorado.org

*John Taylor, Executive Director*
*Caroline Siegfried, Executive Assistant*

Creating and offering innovative supports to people of all ages with cognitive, developmental, physical and health related needs, so they may live lives of independence and quality in their homes and communities.

**8328   Las Animas County Rehabilitation Center**
1205 Congress Drive
Trinidad, CO  81082              719-846-3388
                        FAX: 719-846-4543
                        www.scdds.com

*Duane Roy, Executive Director*

Job placement programs, remunerative work services and work adjustment training programs.

**8329   NORESCO Workshop**
903 E Burlington Avenue
Fort Morgan, CO  80701           970-867-5702

*Robert Duffield*
*Nancy Study, Manager*

Provides remunerative work.

**8330   Regional Assessment and Training Center**
3520 W Oxford Avenue
Denver, CO  80236                303-866-7253

*Russell Porter, Executive Director*

**8331   Sedgwick County Workshop**
113 Elm Street
Julesburg, CO  80737             970-474-2446

*Robert Christiansen*
*Maria Contreras, Manager*

Provides remunerative work.

**8332   Valley Industries**
330 State Avenue
Alamosa, CO  81101               719-589-3123

*Tim Johnson, Executive Director*

Provides remunerative work.

**8333   Vocational and Rehabilitation Agency**
2211 W Evans Avenue
Unit B
Denver, CO  80223                303-866-4150
                        FAX: 720-884-1213
                        TTY:720-884-1234
        e-mail: diana.huerta@state.co.us
                www.cdhs.state.co.us

**8334   Yuma County Workshop**
710 E 2nd Avenue
Yuma, CO  80759                  970-848-3011

*Robert Stephens*
*Andrea Anderson, Manager*

Provides remunerative work.

## Connecticut

**8335   Area Cooperative Educational Services (ACES)**
350 State Street
North Haven, CT  06473           203-498-6881
                        FAX: 203-498-6890
                e-mail: acesinfo@aces.k12.ct.us
                        www.aces.k12.ct.us

*Craig W Edmondson, Executive Director*

Regional Educational Service Center providing high quality educational services in the south central Connecticut region.

**8336   CCARC**
950 Slater Road
New Britain, CT  06053           860-826-3898

*Julie Erickson, Day Service Director*
*Gina Palmieri, Manager*

Supported employment, work services, habilitation services, advocacy, recreation and residential services.

**8337   Cheshire Occupational and Career Center**
615 W Johnson Avenue
Suite 3
Cheshire, CT  06410              203-272-5607
                        FAX: 203-272-4284

*Peter Mason*
*Linda Fallon, Executive Director*

Work adjustment and remunerative work programs.

**8338   Community Enterprises**
PO Box 176
Windsor, CT  06095               860-683-2178
                        FAX: 860-688-5599
                www.communityenterprises.com

*Susan Cauley, VP Operations*
*Angela Daley, Executive Director*

Provide supported education services in a community college setting; supported employment including job training, placement and follow-up; transitional services from group homes and other settings to supported living within the community.

**8339   Connecticut Governor's Committee on Employment of Disabled Persons**
200 Folly Brook Boulevard
Wethersfield, CT  06109          860-566-5505

**8340   Constructive Workshops**
24 Willow Street
East Hartford, CT  06118         860-569-1410
                        FAX: 860-895-1168

*Sandie Lavoy, Coordinator*

**8341  Fotheringhay Farms**
84 Waterhole Road
Colchester, CT  06415                         860-267-4463
                                         FAX: 860-267-7628

*Wesley Martins, Executive/Medical Director*

Job placement programs, remunerative work services and work adjustment training programs.

**8342  George Hegyi Industrial Training Center**
5 Coon Hollow Road
Derby, CT  06418                              203-735-8727

*Joan Bucci, Executive Director*

Work adjustment and remunerative work programs.

**8343  Greater Enfield Association of Retarded Citizens**
3 Pearson Way
Enfield, CT  06082                            860-763-0192

*Dean Wem*

Work hardening and disciplinary programs.

**8344  Kennedy Center**
2440 Reservoir Avenue
Trumbull, CT  06611                           203-365-8522
                                         FAX: 203-365-8533
                      e-mail: mschwartz@kennedyctr.org
                              www.thekennedycenterinc.org

*Martin D Schwartz, President/CEO*

Provides vocational rehabilitation, job training and job placement services to 1,000 adults with disabilities including mental retardation, traumatic brain injury, psychiatric disabilities and more. Residential services, well integrated within the community, serve 97 individuals on a daily basis. Children's programs provide support to 85 children age birth to three, in addition to after hours and recreation programs to appromxately 100 school age children. Staff size is presently 450 employees.

**8345  Quaezar**
2480 Black Rock Tpke
Suite 8
Fairfield, CT  06825                          203-339-3476
                                         FAX: 203-377-6144

*William J Sedarweck, President*

Agency for adult mentally retarded/autistic people providing residential care in a group home or apartment setting. Also provides placement in community employment.

**8346  TEAM Vocational Program**
227 Elm Street
W Haven, CT  06516                            203-934-5221

*Peter Schwartz, Executive Director*
*Hannah Carlson, DD Director*

Provides remunerative work, vocational training, supported employment, and supportive services. Residential program including group living and supervised apartment, social club.

**8347  Valley Memorial Health Center**
435 E Main Street
Ansonia, CT  06401                            203-736-2905

*Marilyn Cormack, President*

Provides remunerative work.

**8348  Vocational and Rehabilitation Agency**
184 Windsor Avenue
Windsor, CT  06095                            860-602-4000
                                              800-842-4510
                                         FAX: 860-602-4020
                            e-mail: Besb@po.state.ct.us
                                    www.besb.state.ct.us

*Alan Sylvestre, Chairman*
*Eileen Akers, Requests Correspondence In Brail*
*Keith Maynard, Plant Manager*

**8349  Vocational and Rehabilitation Agency: State Department of Social Services**
Department of Social Services
25 Sigourney Street
Hartford, CT  06106                           860-424-4908
                                              800-537-2549
                                         FAX: 860-424-4850
                                         TTY: 8004244839
                         e-mail: brs.dss@po.state.ct.us
                                     www.dss.state.ct.us

*Brenda Moore, Executive Director*
*Patricia Wilson-Coker, Manager*

---

# Delaware

**8350  Delaware Division of Vocational Rehabilitation- Department of Labor**
PO Box 9969
Wilmington, DE  19809                         302-761-8275
                                         FAX: 302-761-6611
                  www.delawareworks.com/divisions/dvr/welcome.h

*Andrea Guest, Director*
*Cynthia Fairwell, Program Specialist*
*James Cagle, Manager*

Provides opportunities and resources to eligible individuals with disabilities leading to success in employment and independent living.

**8351  Delaware Fair Employment Practice Agency**
Delaware Department of Labor
820 N French Street
Suite 6
Wilmington, DE  19801                         302-575-7371

*Karen Gimbutas, Vice President*

**8352  Delaware Job Training Program Liaison**
Division of Employment & Training
PO Box 9828
Wilmington, DE  19809                         302-761-8085

*Harold Stafford, Manager*

**8353  Opportunity Center**
3030 Bowers Street
Wilmington, DE  19802                         302-762-0300
                                              800-738-1733
                                         FAX: 302-762-8797
                     e-mail: csterling@ourpeplework.com
                                  www.ourpeoplework.org

*Bob Lennon, Director Community Development*
*Cindy Sterling, Director Employment Services*
*Cathie Lloyd, Executive Director*

Work adjustment and remunerative work programs. Also offers career guidance, supported employment, work readiness and job placement.

## District of Columbia

**8354  Davis Memorial Goodwill Industries**
2200 S Dakota Avenue NE
Washington, DC  20018                    202-636-4225
                                         888-817-4323
                                    FAX: 202-526-3994
                                    www.tcgoodwill.org

*Catherine Melloy, President/CEO*

Offers vocational training, job training, sheltered employment
and work experience.

**8355  District of Columbia Department of Employment Services**
609 H Street NE
Washington, DC  20002                    202-724-7000
                                    FAX: 202-698-4817
                            www.does.ci.washington.dc.us

*Gottlieb Simon, Executive Director*
*Linda W Cropp, Chairperson*

To foster economic development and growth in the District of
Columbia by providing workforce training, bringing together
job seekers and employers, compensating unemployed and injured workers and promoting safe and healthy workplaces.

**8356  District of Columbia Dept. of Employment Services: Office of Workforce Development**
64 New York Ave NW
Washington, DC  20001                    202-393-5051
                                         877-319-7346
                                    FAX: 202-673-6774
                          e-mail: diana.johnson@dc.gov
                                    www.does.dc.gov

*Diana C Johnson, Public Information Officer*
*Marianna Lourenco, Specialist/ADA Coordinator*

To foster economic development and growth in the District of
Columbia by providing workforce training, bringing together
job seekers and employers, compensating unemployed and injured workers and promoting safe and healthy workplaces.

**8357  District of Columbia Fair Employment Practice Agencies**
D C Office of Human Rights
2000 14th Street NW
Suite 3
Washington, DC  20009                    202-727-3071

*Elizabeth Noel, Executive Director*

**8358  Green Door**
1623 16th Street NW
Washington, DC  20009                    202-222-0232
                                    FAX: 202-462-7562
                             e-mail: gdiadmin@aol.com
                                    www.greendoor.org

*Judith Johnson, Executive Director*
*Brenda Randall, Assistant Director*

Green Door is a community program which prepares people with
a severe and persistent mental illness to live and work independently. Since 1976, Green Door has provided comprehensive services to mentally ill people, including housing, job training, job
placement, education, homeless outreach, case management,
support for people with substance abuse problems, family support,and specialized help for people who have had repeated hospitalizations.

**8359  Operation Job Match**
National Multiple Sclerosis Society
2021 K Street NW
Suite 715
Washington, DC  20006                    202-296-5363
                                    FAX: 202-296-3425
                            www.operationjobmatch.org

*Steven Nissen, Program Director*
*Jeanne Angulo, Executive Director*

Job readiness program for individuals with adult-onset physical
disabilities.

**8360  Rehabilitation Services Administration**
810 1st Street NE
10th Floor
Washington, DC  20002                    202-442-8400
                                    FAX: 202-442-8742
                                         www.dc.gov

*Elizabeth Parker, Administrator*

State Rehabilitation Agency providing services to eligible persons with disabilities.

**8361  WAVE Work, Achievement, Value, & Education**
525 School Street SW
Suite 500
Washington, DC  20024                    202-484-0103
                                         800-274-2005
                                    FAX: 202-488-7595
                             e-mail: wave4kids@aol.com
                                    www.waveinc.org

*Larry Brown, President*
*J Taylor, Senior Vice President*

Job placement programs, remunerative work services and work
adjustment training programs for 18 and 21 years of age in many
cities across the country including Drop-Out Recovery Programs and Drop-Out Prevention Programs. Programs also available for youth ages 12-18. Youth Professionals Development
and Training and key aspects of WAVE services, as well.

## Florida

**8362  Abilities of Florida: An Affiliate of Service Source**
2735 Whitney Road
Clearwater, FL  33760                    727-538-7370
                                    FAX: 727-538-7387
                        e-mail: rabbott@ourpeoplework.org
                                    www.ourpeoplework.org

*Rhonda Abbott, VP Rehabilitation Services*
*Lori Simpson, Manager*

Provides a full range of employment services including work
evaulation, training, job coaching, job placement, advocacy and
education. Also provides housing assistance and specialized to
adults with cystic fibrosis.

**8363  Adult Day Training**
Goodwill Industries- Suncoast Incorporated
10596 Gandy Boulevard N
St Petersburg, FL  33702                  727-523-1512
                                          888-279-1988
                                          888-279-1988
                                     FAX: 727-563-9300
                    e-mail: michael_harvey@goodwill-suncoast.org
                                    www.goodwill-suncoast.org

*Michael Ann Harvey, Director Brand Marketing/Media R*
*Lee Waits, President*

An innovative program which uses job skills to teach self-help, daliy living, communication, mobility, travel, decision-making, behavioral and social skills. This focus provides concrete, transferable experiences to help prepare individuals for greater community inclusion by achieving the highest possible degree of independence in their daily life, increasing their confidence and supporting their successful transitions to less structured, self-sufficient environments.

**8364    Career Assessment & Planning Services**
Goodwill Industries- Suncoast Incorporated
10596 Gandy Boulevard N
St Petersburg, FL  33702                     727-523-1512
                                             888-279-1988
                                             888-279-1988
                                        FAX: 727-563-9300
        e-mail: gw.marketing@goodwillhisuncoast.com
                     www.goodwill-suncoast.org

*Lee Waits, President*

Provides comprehensive assessment, which can predict current and future employment and potential adjustment factors for physically, emotionally or developmentally disabled persons who may be unemployed or underemployed. Assessment evaluate interests, aptitudes, academic acheivements and physical abilities through coordinated testing, interviewing and behavioral observations.

**8365    Center for Independence, Training and Education**
215 E New Hampshire Street
Orlando, FL  32804                           407-841-1500
                                        FAX: 407-895-5255

*Mara Schlosser, Program Director*
*Jim Aldridge, Chairman of the Board*
*Ori Kantor, Owner*

Offers services for the totally blind, legally blind, visually impaired, mentally retarded blind and more with health, counseling, educational, recreational, rehabilitation, computer training and professional training services.

**8366    Choices for Work Program**
Goodwill Industries-Suncoast
10596 Gandy Boulevard N
St Petersburg, FL  33702                     727-523-1512
                                             888-279-1988
                                        FAX: 727-563-9300
                     www.goodwill-suncoast.org

*Lee Waits, President*

Assisting individuals currently eligible for Workman's Compensation, this program allows those recovering from injury on the job to prepare to return to independent employment, either through increasing ability and confidence in using adaptive behaviors and/or equipment to return to related employment, or adjusting to a more compatible employment environment.

**8367    Florida Division of Vocational Rehabilitation**
4221 N Himes Avenue
Tampa, FL  33607                             813-871-7300
                                        FAX: 813-873-4773

*Renee Dominic, Librarian*

Rehabilitation services are important when a physical or mental handicap interferes with your ability to work. Our purpose is to help prepare for, and return to, gainful employment.

**8368    Florida Fair Employment Practice Agency**
Florida Commission on Human Relations
325 John Knox Road
Building F
Tallahassee, FL  32303                       850-297-1386

**8369    Florida Vocational Rehabilitation for Persons Who Are Visually Impaired**
2540 W Executive Center Circle
Tallahassee, FL  32399

**8370    Florida's Governor's Alliance of Citizens with Disabilities**
106 E College Avenue
Suite 820
Tallahassee, FL  32301                       850-224-4493
                                             888-838-2253
                                             888-838-2253
                                        FAX: 850-224-4496
                     e-mail: info@abletrust.org
                            www.abletrust.org

*Sharon Griffith, President/CEO*
*Kristen Knapp, VP Public Relations*
*Guenevere Crum, Grants Director*

Provides grant funds purchasing equipment for current employment for people with disabilities and employment-related programs for nonprofit agencies in Florida. Assists families, individuals and agencies through educational conferences, and youth training programs. Provides businesses free resources for hiring people with disabilities.

**8371    Goodwill Temporary Services**
Goodwill Industries- Suncoast
10596 Gandy Boulevard N
St Petersburg, FL  33702                     727-523-1512
                                             888-279-1988
                                             888-279-1988
                                        FAX: 727-563-9300
               e-mail: gw.marketing@goodwill.com
                     www.goodwill-suncoast.org

*R Lee Waits, President/CEO*
*Martin W Gladysz, Chairman*

Provides employment links from potential employees, both disabled and non-disabled alike to employers with immediate employment opportunities seeking qualified candidates. Pre-screening on all applicants include: Employment history, personal references, law enforcement background checks and substance screening.

**8372    Impact: Ocala Vocational Services**
Goodwill Industries- Suncoast
10596 Gandy Boulevard N
St Petersburg, FL  33702                     727-523-1512
                                             888-279-1988
                                        FAX: 727-563-9300
                     www.goodwill-suncoast.org

*R Lee Waits, President/CEO*

Designed to enable individuals with disabilities to work in integrated settings in the community, receiving wages and benefits matching those of non-handicapped workers.

**8373    Job Works NISH Food Service**
Goodwill Industries- Suncoast
10596 Gandy Boulevard N
St Petersburg, FL  33702                     727-523-1512
                                             888-279-1988
                                        FAX: 727-563-9300
                     www.goodwill-suncoast.org

*R Lee Waits, President/Chief Executive Office*

An enclave style (or group) supported employment program designed to give consumers additional supports that allow and encourage increasingly independent employment opportunities within a food services environment.

**8374 Job Works NISH Postal Service**
Goodwill Industries- Suncoast
10596 Gandy Boulevard N
St Petersburg, FL 33702
727-523-1512
888-279-1988
FAX: 727-563-9300
www.goodwill-suncoast.org

*R Lee Waits, President/CEO*

An enclave style (or group) supported employment program designed to give consumers additional supports that allow and encourage increasingly independent employment opportunities within a mailroom environment.

**8375 MAClown Vocational Rehabilitation Workshop**
6390 NE 2nd Avenue
Miami, FL 33138
305-754-5015

*Pat Chavis*

Provides remunerative work.

**8376 One-Stop Service**
Goodwill Industries- Suncoast
10596 Gandy Boulevard N
St Petersburg, FL 33702
727-523-1512
888-279-1988
FAX: 727-563-9300
www.goodwill-suncoast.org

*R Lee Waits, President/Chief Executive Office*

Provides universal job search and placement related services are available to any person entering the service center. Each One-Stop Services Center provides on-site representation from a variety of employment-related service providers. All One-Stops host and/or facilitate local employment fairs and provides access to computerized job-postings.

**8377 Palm Beach Habilitation Center**
4522 S Congress Avenue
Lake Worth, FL 33461
561-965-8500

e-mail: postman@pbhab.com
www.pbhab.org

*Tina Philips, President/ Chief Executive Offic*

Providing work evaluation, work adjustment, job placement, employment, residential and retirement services for mentally, emotionally and physically disabled adults.

**8378 Primrose Supported Employment Programs**
2733 S Ferncreek Avenue
Orlando, FL 32806
407-898-7201
FAX: 407-898-2120

*Mary Van Buren, Executive Director*

Provides remunerative work.

**8379 SCARC**
213 W McCollum Avenue
Bushnell, FL 33513
352-793-5156
FAX: 352-793-6545
e-mail: marshaperkins@earthlink.net
www.sumtercountyarc.com

*Deborah Lord, President*
*Marsha Perkins, Executive Director*

Training and employment program for adults with disabilities. SCARC offers vocational evaluation, training, work services, transportation, supported independent living and community based training.

**8380 Seagull Industries for the Disabled**
3879 W Industrial Way
Riviera Beach, FL 33404
561-842-5814
FAX: 561-881-3554
e-mail: main@seagull.org
www.seagull.org

*Alfred Elsinger, Executive Director*

Dedicated to improving the quality of life of mentally, physically and emotionally challenged adults in Palm Beach County, Florida through advocacy and the provision of a variety of social service, vocational training and residential programs designed to encourage self reliance and independence.

**8381 Supported Employment Program**
Goodwill Industries- Suncoast
10596 Gandy Boulevard N
St Petersburg, FL 33702
727-523-1512
888-279-1988
FAX: 727-563-9300
www.goodwill-suncoast.org

*Lee R Waits, President/CEO*

Provides an employment option that enables individuals with severe disabilities to work in integrated settings in the community, receiving wages and benefits matching those of their non-disabled counterparts. The individual is provided with intensive, on-the-job training at job sites that have been carefully analyzed to be suitable for each individual.

**8382 Vocational and Rehabilitation Agency Department of Education**
2002 Old Saint Augustine Road
Building A
Tallahassee, FL 32301
850-488-6210
800-451-4327
FAX: 850-488-8062
TTY: 850-488-0867
www.2myflorida.com

*Linda Parnell, Manager*

**8383 Vocational and Rehabilitation Agency: Division of Blind Services**
2551 W Executive Center Circle
Tallahassee, FL 32301
850-488-1330
800-342-1828
FAX: 850-487-1804
e-mail: craig_kiser@dbe.doe.state.fl.us
www.state.fl.us/dbs

*Craig Kiser, Director*

**8384 Work Exploration Center**
3000 N West 83rd Street i 40
Gainesville, FL 32606
352-395-5265
FAX: 352-395-5271

*Patsy Frenchman, Coordinator*
*Karla Wooten, Vocational Evaluator*

The Work Exploration Center embraces a holistic approach to Comprehensive Vocational Evaluation and Community Employment services, encouraging individual understanding, hope and growth for a productive and fulfilling future.

# Georgia

**8385 Employment and Training Division, Region B**
Goodwill Industries of North Georgia
1123 Progress Road
Ellijay, GA 30540
706-276-4722
888-514-8112
FAX: 706-276-4732
e-mail: vti@ellijay.com

*Linda Rau, Director Programs/Services*

Employment training, assessment and job placement for people who have disabilities and/or are disadvantaged. Serving 15 counties in Northern Georgia.

**8386  Fair Housing and Fair Employment**
Georgia Commission on Equal Opportunity
710 Int Tower
Atlanta, GA  30303                          404-656-1736
                                      FAX: 404-656-4399
                        e-mail: gceo@gceo.state.ga.us
                                      www.gceo.state.ga.us

*Judith A Harris, Acting Fair Housing Manager*
*Stephanie Randolph, Intake Coordinator/Housing*
*Lisa Burroughs, Equal Employment Manager*

**8387  Griffin Area Resource Center Griffin Community Workshop Division**
511 Hamilton Boulevard
847
Griffin, GA  30223                          770-228-9919
                                      FAX: 770-228-3448
                        e-mail: griffincomwrkshp@aol.com

*Lynn H Leaptrot, Workshop Director*
*Charles Cary Grubbs, Garc Executive Director*

A CARF (The Rehabilitation Accreditation Commission) accredited Employment and Community Support organization providing daily services to participants with disabilities from 16 years of age and up in a 5 county area.

**8388  IBM National Support Center**
Special Needs Systems
PO Box 2150
Atlanta, GA  30301                          404-238-3000
                                            800-228-0752
                                      FAX: 561-982-6059
Serves to help health care leaders, agency directors, policy makers, employers, educators, public officials and individuals learn how computers can enhance the quality of life for the disabled person in the school, home and workplace. Also provide information and resource guides on disabilities affecting hearing, learning, speech and language, mobility and vision.

**8389  Kelley Diversified**
PO Box 967
Athens, GA  30603                          706-549-4398
                                      FAX: 706-549-4479

*Mary Patton, Executive Director*
*Sherry Burns, Rehabilitation Services Director*
*Jenny Taylor, Business Operations Manager*
Work adjustment and remunerative work programs.

**8390  New Ventures**
306 Fort Drive
Lagrange, GA  30240                          706-882-7723
                                      FAX: 706-882-5401
                        e-mail: customersvc@newventures.org
                                      www.newventures.org

*Dave Miller, Executive Director*

A rehabilitation and work training facility for individuals with barriers to employability. The program utilizes community based industrial work of varying levels of difficulty. A return to work conditioning program for the industrially injured is offered which features: first-day contact, workers compensation rehabilitation team management, and light-duty work conditioning. A training stipend is paid to defray costs associated with training.

## Hawaii

**8391  ASSETS School**
1 Ohana Nui Way
Honolulu, HI  96818                          808-423-1356
                                      FAX: 808-422-1920
                        e-mail: info@assets-school.net
                                      assets-school.net

*Lou Salza, Head of School*
*Ron Yoshmoto, Principal K-8*
*Patti Jenks, Principal, High School*

ASSETS is an independent school for gifted and or dyslexic children that provides an individualized, integrated learning enviroment. ASSETS' enviroment empowers these children to maximize their potential and to find their place as lifelong learners in school and society.

**8392  Hawaii Fair Employment Practice Agency**
888 Mililani Street
Ph 2
Honolulu, HI  96813                          808-599-5449
                                            800-586-8800

*Michael Yamamoto*

**8393  Hawaii Vocational Rehabilitation Division**
601 Kamokila Boulevard
Suite 515
Kapolei, HI  96707                          808-692-7715
                                      FAX: 808-692-7727
                                      www.state.hi.us/dhs

*John Nolan, Assistant Administrator*

**8394  Lanakila Rehabilitation Center**
1809 Bachelot Street
Honolulu, HI  96817                          808-834-2583
                                      FAX: 808-533-7264
                        e-mail: lanakila@lanakilahawaii.org
                                      www.lanakilahawaii.org

*Jim Wakafuji, President/CEO*

Lanakila is a private nonprofit organization whose mission is to provide services and supports that assist individuals with physical, mental, or age-related challenges to live as independently as possible within our community. A broad range of services are offered which include meal/senior services, community based adult day programming for individuals with disabilities, work training opportunities, and extended/supported employment for individuals with special needs.

**8395  Vocational and Rehabilitation Agency**
PO Box 339
Honolulu, HI  96809                          808-586-5162
                                      FAX: 808-692-7727
                        e-mail: nshim@dhs.state.hi.us

*Albert Perez, Manager*

**8396  Wahiawa Family**
330 Walker Avenue
Wahiawa, HI  96786                          808-621-7407

*Leslie Chinna*

Work adjustment and remunerative work programs.

## Idaho

**8397   High Reachers Employment and Training**
245 E 6th S
Mountain Home, ID 83647                 208-587-5804

*Joe McNeal, Executive Director*

**8398   Idaho Employment Service and Job Training Program Liaison**
Idaho Department of Employment
317 W Main Street
Boise, ID 83735                          208-332-3570

*Roger Madsen, Manager*

**8399   Idaho Fair Employment Practice Agency**
Idaho Human Rights Commission
450 W State Street
Boise, ID 83702                          208-334-5747

*David Rogers, Administrator*

**8400   Idaho Governor's Committee on Employment of People with Disabilities**
317 W Main Street
Boise, ID 83735

**8401   Idaho Vocational Rehabilitation Agency**
10200 W Emerald Street
Suite 101
Boise, ID 83704                          208-327-7411
                                    FAX: 208-327-7411
                                    www.vr.idaho.gov

*Darrell Quist, Regional Manager*
*Janet Thaldorf, Supervisor*

**8402   Vocational and Rehabilitation Agency**
Idaho Commission for the Blind & Visually Impaired
PO Box 83720
Boise, ID 83702                          208-334-3220
                                         800-542-8688
                                    FAX: 208-334-2963
                         e-mail: aroan@icbvi.state.id.us
                                    www.icbvi.state.id.us

*Angela Roan, Administrator*
*Jackie Bryan, Rehab Services Chief*
*Maggie Starkovich, Administrative Assistant*

Vocational rehabilitation, independent living training, medical intervention, adaptive technology and devices and employer advocacy.

## Illinois

**8403   Ada S McKinley Vocational Services**
725 S Wells Street
Chicago, IL 60607                        312-554-0600
                                    FAX: 312-554-0292
                                    TTY:312-697-9794
                       e-mail: ksmith@adasmckinley.org
                                    www.adasmckinley.org

*Aberra Zewdie, Division Director*
*George Jones, Executive Director*

**8404   Anixter Center**
6610 N Clark Street
Chicago, IL 60626                        773-973-7900
                                    FAX: 773-973-5268
                       e-mail: AskAnixter@anixter.org
                                    www.anixter.org

*Allan Bergman, President/CEO*

A Chicago-based human services agency that assists people with disabilities to live and work successfully in the community. Anixter Center provides vocational training, employment services, residences, special education, prevention programs, community services and health care. In addition, Anixter Center offers Illinois' only substance abuse treatment programs specifically for people with disabilities including Addiction Recovery of the Deaf.

**8405   C-4 Work Center**
5710 N Broadway Street
Chicago, IL 60660                        773-728-1000

                                    www.c4chicago.org

*Anthony A Kopera, Chief Executive Director*
*Mark T Hicks, Program Director*

Aftercare, case finding, information and referrals, vocational training and work activities offered to mentally ill persons.

**8406   Clearbrook**
1835 W Central Road
Arlington Heights, IL 60005              847-394-8539
                                    FAX: 847-870-7741
                         e-mail: info@clearbrook.org
                                    www.clearbrook.org

*Carl M La Mell, President*
*Tracy Martin, Admissions Director*

Offers educational, employment and residential services to the developmentally disabled children and adults.

**8407   Cornerstone Services**
777 Joyce Road
Joliet, IL 60436                         815-727-6666
                                    FAX: 815-723-1177
             e-mail: jhogan@cornerstoneservices.org
                                    www.cornerstoneservices.org

*James A Hogan, President/CEO*
*Susan Murphy, Coordinator Public Ralations*

Cornerstone Services provides progressive, comprehensive services for people with disabilities, promoting choice, dignity and the opportunity to live and work in the community. Established in 1969, the agency provides developmental, vocational, employment, residential and mental health services at various community-based locations. The nonprofit social service agency helps approximately 750 people each day.

**8408   Fulton County Rehab Center**
500 N Main Street
Canton, IL 61520                         309-647-5555
                                    FAX: 309-649-1047

*Rex Lewis, Executive Director*

Work adjustment and remunerative work programs.

**8409   Glenkirk**
3504 Commercial Avenue
Northbrook, IL 60062                     847-272-5111
                                    FAX: 847-272-7350
                                    www.glenkirk.org

*Allan Spector, Executive Director*

Helps infants, children and adults with developmental disabilities reach higher levels of independence. A non-profit organization serving people in north and northwest Chicago suburbs. Glenkirk's residential, vocational, educational and support programs include services which provide individual evaluation, therapeutic treatment and training.

**8410 Illinois Employment Service**
Department of Employment Security
401 S State Street
Room 615
Chicago, IL 60605                    312-353-5133

**8411 Jewish Vocational Services**
1 S Franklin Street
Chicago, IL 60606                    312-357-4500
                                FAX: 312-855-3282
Occupational training and job placement for handicapped persons of all religions.

**8412 JoDavies Workshop**
PO Box 6087
Galena, IL 61036                    815-777-2211
                                FAX: 815-777-3386
                            e-mail: jdwi@jdwi.org
                                    www.jdwi.org

*William Wubben, Treasurer*
*Tim Zueger, Chairperson*
*Dale Gereau, Plant Manager*

Intake and referral, early intervention for children only, vocational evaluation and work adjustment training services offered.

**8413 Kennedy Job Training Center**
7361 S Meade Avenue
Bedford Park, IL 60638                708-594-7155
                                FAX: 708-594-7156

*Robin Mertes, Placement Manager*
*Kandy Stamer, QMRP/Intake Coordinator*

Offers vocational evaluation, vocational training work adjustment training, and job placement services for developmentally disabled and hearing impaired persons.

**8414 Knox County Council for Developmental Disabilities**
2015 Windish Drive
Galesburg, IL 61401                  309-344-1700
                                FAX: 309-344-1754
                        e-mail: mccrittenden@grics.net
                                    www.kccdd.com

*Ned Hippensteel, Executive Director*

Developmental training, vocational evaluation, work adjustment training, extended training, placement, supported employment.

**8415 Kreider Services**
500 Anchor Road
Dixon, IL 61021                      815-288-6691
                                FAX: 815-288-1636

*Arlyn McClain, Executive Director*

Offers day service programs, vocational training programs, job placement, supported employment, respite care, residential and family support for ages birth to three years.

**8416 Lambs Farm**
PO Box 520
Libertyville, IL 60048               847-362-3343
                                FAX: 847-362-0742
                        e-mail: info@lambsfarm.org
                                    www.lambsfarm.org

*Dianne Yaconetti, President/CEO*
*Barbara Schwarz, Director of Development*
*Jim Hutson, Asst Dir Vocational Services*

Person-centered, comprehensive program of residential, vocational and social support service for adults with developmental disabilities.

**8417 Land of Lincoln Goodwill Industries**
PO Box 8528
Springfield, IL 62791                217-789-0400
                                FAX: 217-789-0540

*Sharon Durbin, Executive Director*

Offers a developmental training and community employment programs for persons with disabilities. Workforce development for adults with barriers to employment.

**8418 Orchard Village: Assoc for the Retarded**
7670 Marmora Avenue
Skokie, IL 60077                     847-967-1800
                                FAX: 847-967-9543
                                    www.orchardvillage.org

*Jim Vail, Executive Director*

Vocational program and counseling, respite services and community living facility for the retarded.

**8419 Owens Vocational Training Center**
2639 N Kildare Avenue
Chicago, IL 60639

*Janie Nelson, Executive Director*

**8420 President's Committee on Employment of Employment of the Disabled**
623 E Adams Street
Springfield, IL 62701                217-785-0218
                                    800-ASK-DORI
                                TTY:217-782-5734

*Audrey Mccrimon, Director*

**8421 Sertoma Centre**
4343 W 123rd Street
Alsip, IL 60803                      708-371-9700
                                FAX: 708-371-9747
                                    www.sertomacentre.org

*Gus Van Den Brink, Executive Director*
*Paula Phillips, Assistant Director*

Offers vocational services to promote independence and community integration; day training and residential services provided to individuals. Programs include: vocational evaluation, work adjustment training, janitorial training, job placement, sheltered work, supported employment, developmental training, respite care, residential services.

**8422 Shore Training Center**
Shore Community Services
8035 Austin Avenue
Morton Grove, IL 60053               847-581-0200
                                FAX: 847-581-0078
                                    www.sureinc.net

*Lisa Wright, Director*
*Michael Mack, Plant Manager*

Provides remunerative work.

**8423 Skills**
1122 5th Avenue
Moline, IL 61265                     309-797-3586
                                FAX: 309-797-4914
                                    www.skills-inc.org

*Stuart Olson, President*

Accredited through the Commission on Accreditation of Rehabilitation Facilities; offers job training partnership act and vocational evaluation services offered.

**8424 Thresholds AMISS**
12145 Western Avenue
Blue Island, IL 60406
708-597-7997
FAX: 708-597-8073

*Julia Rupp, Executive Director*
*Camille Rucks, Team Leader*

Services offered include psychosocial, vocational and residential programs for ages 18 or older with a primary diagnosis of mental illness. Facility is wheelchair accessible.

**8425 Vocational and Rehabilitation Agency**
214 Staehouse
Springfield, IL 62706
217-782-7884
800-843-6154
FAX: 217-524-6262
TTY: 217-782-5734
www.state.il.us

*Rod R Blavojevich, Governor*
*Pat Quinn, Manager*

**8426 Washington County Vocational Workshop**
PO Box 273
Nashville, IL 62263
618-327-4461

*Keith Curran, Executive Director*

**8427 Westside Parents Work Activity Center**
3765 W Ogden Avenue
Chicago, IL 60623
773-522-1200

Offers developmental training programs providing basic skills in self care for multiply and physically handicapped persons.

---

# Indiana

**8428 ADEC Resources for Independence**
19607 State Road 120
Bristol, IN 46507
574-848-7451

*Matt Leachman, Contact*
*Paula Shively, President*

Serves Elkhart County and surrounding area.

**8429 ARC of Allen County**
Arc of U S
2542 Thompson Avenue
Fort Wayne, IN 46807
260-456-4534
800-234-7811
FAX: 260-745-5200
www.easterseals.com

*F Gil Perry, Chairperson*
*Nikki Holm, Senior Vice Chairperson*
*Steven Hinkle, President*

**8430 BI-County Services**
425 E Harrison Road
Bluffton, IN 46714
260-824-1253
FAX: 260-824-1892
e-mail: jbussard@adifferentlight.com

*Joyce Bussard, Program Director*
*John Whicker, President*

Serves Wells and Adam Counties. Infant services, Medicaid waivers, music therapy, ICF, MR, group homes, sheltered employment, pay program and supported employment services available.

**8431 Balance Centers of America**
2538 Patricia Street
Portage, IN 46368
219-736-2930

*Jane Labar, Contact*

**8432 Bridge Pointe Services**
Goodwill International
PO Box 2117
Clarksville, IN 47131
812-283-7908
800-660-3355
FAX: 812-283-6248
e-mail: cmarshall@bridepointe.org
www.bridgepionte.org

*Caren Marshall, Executive Director*
*Terry Richards, Director*

Career assesment, job readiness and placement, office skills training

**8433 Carey Services**
2724 S Carey Street
Marion, IN 46953
765-668-8961
FAX: 765-664-6747

*Grant Black, Contact*
*Mark Draves, Chief Executive Officer*

**8434 Evansville Association for the Blind**
PO Box 6445
Evansville, IN 47719
812-422-1181
FAX: 812-424-3154
e-mail: eadcdc@evansville.net
www2.evansville.edu/ebaweb

*Karla Horrell, Director Rehabilitation*
*Diane Hagler, Vocational Specialist*
*Krysti Kite, Orientation/Mobility*

An community rehabilitation facility untilizing individual goals to assist persons with disabilities achieve or maintain potenial

**8435 Four Rivers Resource Services**
PO Box 249
Linton, IN 47441
812-847-2231
FAX: 812-847-8836
e-mail: fourrivers@frrs.org
www.frrs.org

*Stephen Sacksteder, Executive Director*
*Lyna Landis, Marketing Coordinator*

Employment, community living, connections, follow-along, early intervention, preschool, healthy families, child care resource and referral and child care voucher program, impact, and transpotation services.

**8436 Gateway Services/JCARC**
PO Box 216
Franklin, IN 46131
317-738-5500
888-494-8069
FAX: 317-738-5522

*Karen Luehmann, Executive Director*

**8437 Goodwill Industries of Central Indiana**
1635 W Michigan Street
Indianapolis, IN 46222
317-524-4313
FAX: 317-264-1336

*Irene Mcclesky, Contact*
*Jim Clelland, President*

**8438 Indiana Employment Services and Job Training Program Liaison**
10 N Senate Avenue
Indianapolis, IN 46204
317-232-6702
FAX: 317-233-5499

**8439 Indiana Fair Employment Practice Agency**
32 E Washington Street
Suite 900
Indianapolis, IN 46204          317-872-9991

**8440 LCAR**
2650 W 35th Avenue
Gary, IN 46408          219-884-1138

*Brian Davis, Contact*
*Kris Prohl, Executive Director*

**8441 Michigan Resources**
4315 E Michigan Boulevard
Michigan City, IN 46360          219-874-4288
FAX: 219-874-2689
e-mail: michiana@michianaresources.org
www.michianaresources.org

*Michael Horton, CEO*
Vocational training center for persons 16 and older with disabilities.

**8442 New Hope Services**
725 Wall Street
Jeffersonville, IN 47130          812-288-8248
800-237-6604
FAX: 812-288-8248
e-mail: info@newhopeservices.org
www.newhopeservices.org

*Pat Daily, Chairperson*
*Charles E Reisert, Vice Chairperson*
*James Bosley, President*

**8443 New Horizons Rehabilitation**
PO Box 98
Batesville, IN 47006          812-934-4528

*Greg Tow, Contact*
*Marie Dausch, Executive Director*
Serves Ripley, Franklin, Ohio, Switzerland Dearborn, and Decatur.

**8444 Noble Centers**
2400 N Tibbs Avenue
Indianapolis, IN 46222          317-929-3002
FAX: 317-264-5300

*Tom Cain, Contact*

**8445 Office of State Coordinator of Vocational Education for Students with Disability**
10 N Senate Avenue
Room 212
Indianapolis, IN 46204          317-232-1829

e-mail: tfields@dwd.state.in.us
www.state.in.us/dwd/techd

**8446 Putnam County Comprehensive Services**
630 Tennessee Street
Greencastle, IN 46135          765-653-4362
FAX: 765-653-3646
www.pccsinc.org

*Tammy Amore*
*Diana Huff, Manager*

**8447 Southern Indiana Resource Solutions**
1579 S Folsomville Road
Boonville, IN 47601          812-897-4840
FAX: 812-897-0123
e-mail: kelly@sirs.org
www.sirs.org

*Kelly Mitchell, CEO/President*
*Christal Moskos, Chairman of the Board*

**8448 Sycamore Rehabilitation Services**
PO Box 369
Danville, IN 46122          317-745-4715
888-298-6617
FAX: 317-745-8271

*Bob Gootee, President*
*Patrick Cockrum, Executive Director*

**8449 Vocational and Rehabilitation Agency**
PO Box 7083
Indianapolis, IN 46207          317-232-1401
800-545-7763
FAX: 317-232-1240
e-mail: peter.bispecos@sssa.in.gov
www.ssa.in.gov

*Peter Bispecos, Director*
*Mike Hedden, Executive Director*

**8450 Wabash/Employability Center**
S C6395 Earl Avenue
Suite 2
Lafayette, IN 47903          765-447-0300
FAX: 765-447-6456

*Bill Carmichael, Contact*
Serves Tippecanoe County.

# Iowa

**8451 ACT Assessment Test Preparation Reference Manual**
American College Testing Program
2201 Dodge
168
Iowa City, IA 52243          319-337-1000

www.act.org

*Richard L Ferguson, President/CEO*
*Tom Goedkem, Senior Vice President*

This reference manual was developed as a resource for high school teachers and counselors in assisting students with test preparation.

**8452 ACT Asset Technical Manual**
American College Testing Program
2201 Dodge
Suite 168
Iowa City, IA 52243          319-337-1000

www.act.org

*Richard Ferguson, Chief Executive Officer*
Provides a technical description of the ASSET program to guide users in working with the program and interpreting test results.

**8453 Franklin County Work Activity Center**
20 5th Street NW
Hampton, IA 50441          641-456-5293

*Steven Paul Woods, Executive Director*
*Jim Koenen, Owner*

Nonprofit organization providing residential and vocational services in Franklin and Hardin counties in the state of Iowa. Residential Services include RCF/MR services, Supported Community Living Services and Community Supervised Apartment Living Arrangement Services. Vocational Services include Work Services and Supported Employment Services. Accredited by the Commission on Accreditation of rehabilitation Facilities since 1984, and serves individuals with a wide range of needs.

**8454 Innovative Industries**
405 E Madison Street
Winterset, IA 50273
515-462-2926
FAX: 515-462-2870
e-mail: winnind@iowalink.com

*Sandi Smith, Secretary*
*Connie Bailey, Program Manager*

**8455 Iowa Civil Rights Commission**
400 E Street 14
Des Moines, IA 50319
515-281-4121
800-457-4516
FAX: 515-242-5840
www.state.ia.us/government/crc

*Ralph Rosenberg, Director*
*Ron Pothast, Executive Director*

**8456 Iowa Employment Service**
1000 E Grand Avenue
Des Moines, IA 50319
515-281-6647

**8457 Iowa Job Training Program Liaison**
Iowa Department of Economic Development
200 E Grand Avenue
Des Moines, IA 50309
515-242-4700

*David Lyons, Executive Director*

**8458 Iowa Valley Community College**
3702 S Center Street
Marshalltown, IA 50158
641-752-4643
FAX: 641-752-5909
www.iavalley.edu

*Marge Good, Career Development*
*Tim Wynes, President*

Offers two levels of specialized vocational preparatory programming for adults with disabilities. The Career Development Center serves dependent adults. The goal of the program is to maintain or improve skills to enable persons served to enter sheltered or supported employment. The IRP/CBVT programs are non-credit specialized vocational programs for independent adults served by Vocational Rehabilitation and our programs. The goals are for competitive placements in jobs. CARF accredited.

**8459 New Focus**
102 W Washington Street
Centerville, IA 52544
641-437-1722
FAX: 641-437-1028

*Susan Wright, Director Employment Services*
*Peggy Oden, Executive Director*

Provides vocational services for adults with disabilities. Includes work activity, supported employment and supported community living.

**8460 Second Time Around**
110 W Jackson Street
Centerville, IA 52544
641-437-7355

*Keith Lindley, Executive Director*
*Debbie Steen, Store Supervisor*
*Deana Edwards, Manager*

Work training site for adults with disabilities.

**8461 Vocational and Rehabilitation Agency: Iowa**
510 E 12th Street
Des Moines, IA 50319
515-281-4311
FAX: 515-281-7645
TTY:515-281-4311
www.ivrs.iowa.gov

*Stephen Wooderson, Executive Director*
*Charles Levine, Assistant Chief*

## Kansas

**8462 Clay Center Adult Training Center**
701 4th Street
Clay Center, KS 67432
785-632-5357
FAX: 785-632-5371

*Gail Habluetzel, Executive Director*

**8463 Kansas Fair Employment Practice Agency**
900 SW Jackson Street
Topeka, KS 66612
785-296-1500

*Mostafa Kamal, Manager*

**8464 Kansas Vocational Rehabilitation Agency**
300 SW Oakley Avenue
Topeka, KS 66606
785-296-3911
TTY:913-296-7029
e-mail: jac@srkspo.wpo.state.ks.us

*Joyce Cussimanio, Director*

## Kentucky

**8465 Kentucky Committee on Employment of People with Disabilities**
600 W Cedar Street
Louisville, KY 40202
502-595-4165
FAX: 954-59 -
www.oet.ky.gov

*Dennis Derman, Manager*

**8466 Kentucky Department for Employment Service and Job Training Program Liaison**
275 E Main Street 2-W
Frankfort, KY 40621
502-564-2367
FAX: 502-564-7799
www.desky.org

**8467** **Kentucky Department for the Blind**
PO Box 757
Frankfort, KY 40602
502-564-4754
877-592-5463
FAX: 502-564-2951
TTY: 502-564-2929
e-mail: dbohannon@state.ky.us.dfblind
www.blind.ky.gov

*Stephen Johnson, Executive Director*
*Marcia Egbert, Executive Secretary*

Provides career services and assistance to adults with severe visual handicaps who want to become productive in the home or work force. Also provides the Client Assistance Program established to provide advice, assistance and information available from rehabilitation programs to persons with handicaps.

**8468** **Kentucky Vocational Rehabilitation Agency**
500 Mero Street
Frankfort, KY 40601
502-564-3775

*Rodney Kelly, Executive Director*

**8469** **Pioneer Vocational/Industrial Services**
590 Stanford Avenue
Danville, KY 40422
859-236-8413

*Jack Goodbey II, Executive Director*

**8470** **Vocational and Rehabilitation Agency**
209 Saint Clair Street
Frankfort, KY 40601
502-564-4440
800-372-7172
FAX: 502-564-6745
TTY: 502-564-6817
e-mail: wfd.vocrehab@mail.state.ky.us
www.ovr.gov

*Beth Smith, Executive Director*

**8471** **Work Enhancement Center of Western Kentucky**
803 Poplar Street
Murray, KY 42071
270-762-1100
FAX: 502-767-3600

*Steve Passmore, Director*
*John O'Shaughnessy, Chief Executive Officer*

The center has been established in order to service industry in the three state area surrounding Kentucky. This service includes job/skill evaluation, job design consultation, pre-employment employee evaluations and economic evaluation.

## Louisiana

**8472** **Community Opportunities of East Ascension**
1122 E Ascension Complex Boulevard
Gonzales, LA 70737
225-621-2000
FAX: 225-621-2022

*Mark Thomas, Director*

Committed to affording individuals the opportunities that reflect and support choices, dignity, individuality, self-determination, community, coherency and commen sense. Programs incloude Respite, Personal Care Attendant, Support Living, Support Environment, Adult Day Training, and Elderly/Adult Waiver Services.

**8473** **Louisiana Employment Service and Job Training Program Liaison**
PO Box 94094
Baton Rouge, LA 70804
225-342-3111
FAX: 225-342-3030
www.laworks.net

*John Smith, Director*
*Warner Smith, Manager*

**8474** **Louisiana Vocational Rehabilitation Agency**
4051 Veterans Boulevard6620 Rivers
Suite 101
Metairie, LA 70003
504-838-5180
800-737-2957
FAX: 504-838-5413

*Irby Hornsey, Regional Manager*
*Ed Barras, Manager*

**8475** **St. James Association for Retarded Citizens**
29150 Health Unit Street
Vacherie, LA 70090
225-265-7910

*Jamie Chenier, Executive Director*

A private sheltered work program for mentally retarded and developmentally disabled adults.

**8476** **Westbank Sheltered Workshop**
1728 Hermosa Street
New Orleans, LA 70114
504-362-1311

A private non-residential facility serving severely disabled individuals referred through Louisiana Rehabilitation Services.

## Maine

**8477** **Addison Point Specialized Services**
PO Box 207
Addison, ME 04606
207-483-6500
FAX: 207-483-2817

*Paula Chartrand, Executive Officer*

Provides services to individuals who are deaf/blind, mentally retarded, autistic, behaviorally challenged and/or dual diagnosed. Training services to place these individuals in community employment.

**8478** **Bangor Veteran Center: Veterans Outreach Center**
352 Harlow Street
Bangor, ME 04401
207-947-3391
FAX: 207-941-8195
e-mail: bangorvc@aol.com
www.hud.gov/offices/cpd/about/hudvet/

*Joseph A Degrasse, Team Leader*
*Robert L Daisey MSW, Clinical Coordinator*

Readjustment counseling services for veterans of Vietnam, Vietnam Era, Persian Gulf, Panama, Grenada, Lebanon, Somalia, WWII and Korean conflicts.

**8479** **Creative Work Systems**
443 Congress Street
Portland, ME 04101
207-879-1140
FAX: 207-879-1146
e-mail: kraye@creativeworks.com
www.creativeworksystems.com

*Susan Percy, Executive Director*

Provides residential, day habilitation and supported emploment in Central and Southern Maine.

**8480 Maine Employment Service**
20 Union Street
Augusta, ME 04330                    207-287-3788

*Valerie Landry, Manager*

**8481 Maine Fair Employment Practice Agency**
Maine Human Rights Commission
51 State House Station
Augusta, ME 04333                    207-624-6050
                                     FAX: 207-624-6063
                                     www.state.me.us/mhrc

*Patricia Ryan, Director*

State agency with the responsibility of enforcing Maine's anti-discrimination laws. The commission investigates complaints of unlawful discrimination in employment, housing, education, access to public accommodations, extension of credit and offensive names.

**8482 Maine Governor's Committee on Employment of the Disabled**
35 Anthony Avenue
Augusta, ME 04330                    207-624-5335

**8483 Northeast Occupational Exchange**
248 Center Street
Bangor, ME 04401                     207-942-3816

*Dr. Charles Tingley Jr, Executive Director*

**8484 Vocational and Rehabilitation Agency**
Division for the Blind and Visually Impaired
2 Anthony Avenue 150
S
Augusta, ME 04333                    207-624-5959
                                     800-698-4440
                                     FAX: 207-624-5980
                                     TTY: 207-624-5955
                                     e-mail: paul.e.cote@maine .gov

*Jill Busond, Bureau Director*

## Maryland

**8485 Ardmore Developmental Center**
3000 Lottsford Vista Road
Bowie, MD 20721
                                     FAX: 301-731-4551

*Donalda Lovelace, CEO*

Offers supported employment programs and vocational education for persons who are mentally retarded as well as residential services and Emergency Respite Care.

**8486 Job Opportunities for the Blind**
National Federation of the Blind
1800 Johnson Street
Baltimore, MD 21230                  410-659-9314
                                     FAX: 410-685-5653
                                     e-mail: nfb@iamdigex.net
                                     www.nfb.org

*James Geshel, Director Governmental Affairs*
*Anthony Cobb, Director Job Opportunities*
*Marc Maurer, President*

This free service allows individuals touch-tone telephone access to the thousands of jobs listed in America's Job Bank, and internet service run by the Department of Labor. Any person registered with either a state rehabilitation agency or a state employment service can search across the country for jobs by either type of work or location.

**8487 Mainstream**
3 Bethesda Metro Center
Suite 830
Bethesda, MD 20814                   301-961-9299
                                     FAX: 301-891-8778
                                     e-mail: mainstrm@aol.com

*Patricia M Jackson, Executive Director*
*Charles Moster*

Nonprofit organization dedicated to improving competitive employment opportunities for persons with disabilities. Provides specialized services and acts as a bridge that links service providers, employers and persons with disabilties. Provides training, educational publications, and videos on disablityemployment issues. Educationa materials include a magazine, brochures, and audio-visual aids.

**8488 Maryland Employment Services and Job Training Program Liaison**
1100 N Eutaw Street
Room 600
Baltimore, MD 21201                  410-767-2173

**8489 Maryland Fair Employment Practice Agency**
400 Washington Avenue
Room 124
Towson, MD 21204                     410-887-5557
                                     FAX: 410-769-8914

*Adrienne Jones, Executive Director*

**8490 Maryland State Department of Education**
Division of Rehabilitation Services ( DI RS)
2301 Argonne Drive
Baltimore, MD 21218                  410-554-9100

*Robert Burns, Assistant State Supervisor*

The Vocational Rehabilitation Program delivers to eligible individuals with physical and/or mental disabilities to enable them to become employed. The Independent Living Program's goal is to assist people in remaining in their homes and communities. The Division operates the Maryland Rehabilitation Center, a comprehensive evaluation and training center that has dormitory space. There are field offices located statewide with counselors to advise and manage the provision of services offered.

**8491 PWI Profile**
Projects W Industry Goodwill Industries of America
9200 Wisconsin Avenue
Bethesda, MD 20814

Newsletter on employment of persons with disabilities.

**8492 Project LINK**
Mainstream
3 Bethesda Metro Center
Suite 830
Bethesda, MD 20814                   301-961-9299
                                     800-247-1380
                                     FAX: 301-891-8778
                                     e-mail: info@mainstreaminc.org
                                     www.mainstreaminc.org

*Charles Moster*

Provides job development and placement in services to dislocated workers with disabilities in the Washington, DC and Dallas, TX areas.

**8493 Treatment and Learning Centers (TLC)**
9975 Medical Center Drive
Rockville, MD 20850                   301-424-5200

*Richard Pavlin, Executive Director*

Helps parents, children and teachers understand and overcome educational difficulties. They offer interdisciplinary diagnostic testing individually tailored to pinpoint the specific strengths and needs of students who may have learning disabilities, Dyslexia or other learning problems.

## Massachusetts

**8494** **Division of Employment & Training**
State of Massachusetts
19 Staniford Street
3rd Floor
Boston, MA  02114                    617-626-6560

**8495** **Gateway Arts Program, Crafts Store & Gallery**
Vinsen Corporation
62 Harvard Street
Brookline, MA  02445                 617-734-1577
                                     FAX: 617-734-3199
                                     e-mail: gateway@vinfen.org
                                     www.gatewayarts.org

*Rae T Edelson, Program Director*
*Ted Lampe, Assistant Program Director*
*Mona Thaler, Marketing Director*

An arts-based vocational service for adults with developmental and other disabilities including mental illness, autism and head injury who can pursue paid work in fine art and crafts with the aid of professional artists/teachers, a professional marketer and a Crafts Store and Gallery. A service of Vinfen.

**8496** **Massachusetts Fair Employment Practice Agency**
1 Ashburton Place
Room 601
Boston, MA  02108                    617-727-8900

**8497** **Massachusetts Governor's Commission on Employment of Disabled Persons**
19 Staniford Street
3rd Floor
Boston, MA  02114                    617-864-2000

*Theodore Schipani, Owner*

**8498** **Vocational Rehabilitation Agency**
27-43 Wormwood Street
Boston, MA  02210                    617-204-3600
                                     800-642-0249
                                     FAX: 617-727-1354
                                     TTY: 800-764-0200
                                     e-mail: elmer.bartels@mrc.state.ma.us
                                     www.state.ma.us

*Elmer Bartels, Director*

**8499** **Vocational and Rehabilitation Agency Massachusetts Commission for the Blind**
48 Boyle Street
Boston, MA  02129                    617-727-5550
                                     800-392-6450
                                     FAX: 617-727-7685
                                     TTY: 800-392-6556
                                     e-mail: poliver@state.ma.us
                                     www.state.ma.us

*David Govostes, Commissioner*

**8500** **Work**
3 Arlington Street
North Quincy, MA  02171              617-691-1500

                                     www.workinc.org

*James Cassetta, President*

## Michigan

**8501** **Disability Community Small Business Development Center**
Ann Arbor Center for Independent Living
2568 Packard Street
Ann Arbor, MI  48104                 734-662-5599
                                     FAX: 734-971-0826

*Roseanne Herzog, Director*
*Phil Zepeda, Manager*

Offers small business counseling and training to individuals with disabilities in the state of Michigan.

**8502** **Lamplighter's Work Center**
1320 W State Street
Cheboygan, MI  49721                 906-274-5456

*Robert Spinella, Executive Director*

**8503** **Michigan Employment Service**
7310 Woodward Avenue
Detroit, MI  48202                   313-876-5217

**8504** **Michigan Fair Employment Practice Agency**
Michigan Department of Civil Rights
1200 6th Street
6th Floor
Detroit, MI  48226                   313-256-2663
                                     FAX: 313-256-6167
                                     e-mail: MDCR-INFO@michigan.gov
                                     www.michigan.gov/mdcr

**8505** **Michigan Rehabilitation Services: Dept of Labor And Economic Development**
PO Box 30010
Lansing, MI  48909                   517-373-3390
                                     800-605-6722
                                     FAX: 517-335-7277
                                     e-mail: shamsiddeenj@michigan.gov
                                     www.michigan.gov/mdcd

*Jaye Balthazar, Manager*

State vocational rehabilitation agency.

**8506** **Vocational and Rehabilitation Agency**
PO Box 30652
Lansing, MI  48909                   517-373-2062
                                     800-292-4200
                                     FAX: 517-335-5140
                                     TTY: 5173734025
                                     e-mail: kreinerc@state.mi.us
                                     www.mfia.state.mi.us

*Patrick Cannon, Director*

## Minnesota

**8507 Jewish Vocational Service of Jewish Family and Children's Services**
1500 Lilac Drive S
Suite 311
Minneapolis, MN 55416
612-546-0616
FAX: 612-593-1778

*Jeremy Waldman, Executive Director*

**8508 Minnesota Employment Practice Agency**
190 5th Street E
Suite 700
Saint Paul, MN 55101
651-296-5663

www.humanrights.state.mn.us

*Velma Korbel, Commissioner*
*James Kirkpatrick, Deputy Commissioner*
*Janeen Rosas, Manager*

**8509 Minnesota Rehabilitation Services**
332 Minnesota Street
Suite E200
Saint Paul, MN 55101
651-296-5616
800-328-9095
FAX: 651-297-5159
TTY: 800-657-3973
e-mail: Paul.Bridges@state.mn.us
www.deed.date.men.us

*Kimberly Pack, Director*
*Paul Bridges, Manager*

**8510 PWI Forum**
Multi Resource Centers
1900 Chicago Avenue
Minneapolis, MN 55404
612-752-8138

Newsletter for business, community and government leaders. Focuses on employment of persons with disabilities.

**8511 Vocational and Rehabilitation Agency**
21200 University Ave W
Suite 240
Saint Paul, MN 55114
651-642-0500
800-652-9000
FAX: 651-284-3307
TTY: 612-642-0506
e-mail: info@ngwmail.des.state.mn.us
www.mnwfc.org

*Chuck Hamilton, Executive Director*

## Mississippi

**8512 Allied Enterprises of Tupelo**
Ability Works Incorporated
2701 C R 402
Corinth, MS 38834
662-287-6964
FAX: 662-287-1463

*Michael Byrd, Facility Manager*
Vocational evaluation, work adjustment and job placement of disabled persons in a rehabilitation workshop.

**8513 Mississippi Department of Rehabilitation Services**
PO Box 1698
Jackson, MS 39215
601-853-5100
800-443-1000
FAX: 601-853-5158
TTY: 800-443-1000
e-mail: bmcmillan@mdrs.state.ms.us
www.mdrs.state.ms.us

*Hs Mcmillan, Director*
*Bob Richards, Manager*
Offers low vision aids and appliances, counseling, social work, educational and professional training, residential services, recreational services, computer training and employment opportunities for the handicapped.

**8514 Mississippi Employment Secutity Commission**
PO Box 1669
Jackson, MS 39215
601-961-7501
FAX: 601-961-7405
www.mesc.state.ms.us

**8515 Worksight**
Mississippi State University
PO Box 6189
Mississippi State, MS 39762
662-325-2001
800-675-7782
FAX: 662-325-8989
e-mail: rrtc@ra.msstate.edu
www.blind.msstate.edu

*Elton Moore, Director*
Discusses news, activities, research projects and training programs of the Center.

## Missouri

**8516 Missouri Fair Employment Practice Agency**
Missouri Fair Employment Practice Agency
3315 W Truman Boulevard
Jefferson City, MO 65109
573-751-4091
877-781-4236
FAX: 573-751-2905
e-mail: mchr@dolir.mo.gov
www.dolir.state.mo.us

*Renell Wynn, Director*
*Catherine Leapheart, Executive Director*

**8517 Missouri Governor's Council on Disability**
PO Box 1668
Jefferson City, MO 65102
573-751-2600
800-877-8249
FAX: 573-526-4109
TTY: 573-751-2600
e-mail: gcd@oa.mo.gov
www.gcd.oa.mo.gov

*Robert Honan, Executive Director*
Advocate training, civil rights, community education services, community resource referral, conferences, consumer education, disability awareness program, educational information and resources, information and education services, information and referral, newsletter, policy issues and services, publications, resource directory, seminars, technical assistance, training and seminars.

**8518 Missouri Job Training Program Liaison**
221 Metro Drive
Jefferson City, MO 65109
573-634-2321

*Joe Jerkins, Manager*

**8519  Missouri Vocational Rehabilitation Agency**
3024 W Truman Boulevard
Jefferson Cty, MO  65109                     573-751-3251
                                        FAX: 573-741-1441
                                        TTY:573-751-3251

*Don Glann, Assistant Commissioner*
*Jeanne Loyd, Manager*

**8520  Vocational and Rehabilitation Agency**
3024 Dupont Circle
Jefferson City, MO  65109                    573-751-3251
                                             877-222-8963
                                        TTY:573-751-0881
                                        www.vr.dese.state.mo.us

*Jeanne Loyd, Assistant Commissioner*

**8521  WX: Work Capacities**
17331 E 40th Highway
Suite 103
Independence, MO  64055                      816-478-2333

*Carol Lett, Executive Director*
*Mike Heinz, Manager*

## Montana

**8522  Montana Employment Services and Job Training Programs Liaison**
PO Box 1728
Helena, MT  59624                            406-444-3697

**8523  Montana Fair Employment Practice Agency**
PO Box 1728
Helena, MT  59624                            406-444-3697
                                             800-542-0807

**8524  Montana Governor's Committee on Employment of Disabled People**
Mitchell Building
Room 130
Helena, MT  59620

## Nebraska

**8525  Nebraska Employment Services**
Department of Labor
550 S 16th Street
Lincoln, NE  68508                           402-471-9000

**8526  Nebraska Fair Employment Practice Agency**
301 Centennial Mall S
Lincoln, NE  68508                           402-471-4997

**8527  Nebraska Vocational Rehabilitation Agency**
301 Centennial Mall S
Lincoln, NE  68508                           402-471-3644
                                             877-637-3422
                                        FAX: 402-471-0788
                        e-mail: vr_stateoffice@vocrehab.state.ne.us

*Cheryl Ferree, Manager*
Services for individuals with disabilities who want to become employed. Services are free to those who qualify.

**8528  Nebraska Work Force Development**
550 S 16th Street
Lincoln, NE  68508                           402-471-9000
                                        FAX: 402-471-2318

*Fernando Lecuona III, Commissioner*
*Joan Modrell, Executive Director*

**8529  Vocational and Rehabilitation Agency**
PO Box 94987
Lincoln, NE  68509                           402-471-3644
                                             877-637-3422
                                        FAX: 402-471-0788
                                        TTY: 402-471-3659
                    e-mail: vr_stateoffice@vocrehab.state.ne.us
                                        www.vocrehab.state.ne.us

*Frank Lloyd, Director*
*Margie Hossmann, Assistant Director*
*Cheryl Ferree, Manager*

## Nevada

**8530  Nevada Fair Employment Practice Agency**
1515 E Tropicana Avenue
Suite 590
Las Vegas, NV  89119

**8531  Nevada Governor's Committee on Employment of Persons with Disabilities**
3100 Mill Street
Suite 115
Reno, NV  89502

**8532  Nevada Job Training Program Liaison**
400 Capitol
Carson City, NV  89710

**8533  Vocational and Rehabilitation Agency**
State of Nevada
505 E King Street
Suite 502
Carson City, NV  89701                       775-684-4040
                                        FAX: 775-684-4184
                                    e-mail: mryasmer@nvdetr.org
                                        detr.state.nv.us

*Michael Coleman, Administrator*
*Peter Singleton, Rehabilitation Program Superviso*
*Bob Nichols, Rehabilitation Manager*

The Rehabilitation Division is comprised of four bureaus and the community-based services unit to address prevention, assessment, training, treatment and job placement for Nevadans with functional disabilities. The division places primary emphasis on providing necessary services to help clients work and live independently and substance-free. The division administrator, based in Carson City, oversees programs offered in offices throughout the state.

## New Hampshire

**8534  Fit for Work at Exeter Hospital**
10 Buzell Avenue
Exeter, NH  03833                            603-778-7311
                                        FAX: 603-778-6671

*Kevin Callahan, President*

Staffed by a team of allied health professionals, our outpatient rehabilitation program offers functional restoration, work therapy, diagnostic testing and physical therapy.

**8535  New Hampshire Employment Security**
32 S Main Street
Concord, NH 03301
603-224-3311
800-852-3400
FAX: 603-228-4145
TTY: 800-735-2964
e-mail: webmaster@nhes.state.nh.us
www.nhes.state.nh.us

*Richard S Brothers, Commissioner*

Operates a free public employment service and provides assisted and self directed employment and career related services and labor market information for employers and the general public.

**8536  New Hampshire Fair Employment Practice Agency**
2 Chenell Drive
Concord, NH 03301
603-225-3699
FAX: 603-271-6339

**8537  New Hampshire Job Training Program Liaison**
64 Old Suncook Road
Concord, NH 03301
603-228-3349

**8538  Vocational and Rehabilitation Agency**
Department of Education
21 S Fruit Street
Suite 20
Concord, NH 03301
603-271-3471
TTY:603-271-3471
www.ed.state.nh.us

*Paul Leather, Director*

Offers services for the totally blind, legally blind, visually impaired, mentally retarded blind and more with health, counseling, educational, recreational, rehabilitation, computer training and professional training services.

# New Jersey

**8539  ARC of Gloucester County**
1555 Gateway Boulevard
Woodbury, NJ 08096
856-848-8648
FAX: 856-848-7753
e-mail: webmaster@thearcgloucester.org
www.thearcgloucester.org

*Ana Rivera, Executive Director*

**8540  ARC of Hunterdon County**
1322 State Route 31
Suite 5
Annandale, NJ 08801
908-735-7775
FAX: 980-730-7726

*Barbara Gustassen, Contact*
*Robin Horne, Manager*

Serves Hunterdon County.

**8541  ARC of Mercer County**
180 Ewingville Road
Ewing, NJ 08638
609-406-0181
FAX: 609-406-9258
e-mail: arc@arcmercer.org
www.arcmercer.org

*Steven Cook, President*
*Geoffrey Morris, First Vice President*
*Dennis Micai, Manager*

**8542  ARC of Monmouth**
1158 Wayside Road
Tinton Falls, NJ 07712
732-493-1919
FAX: 732-493-3604
e-mail: info@arcofmonmouth.org
www.arcofmonmouth.org

*Rhona L Levy, President*
*Jacqueline Moskowitz, Director Social Services*
*Mary Scott, Executive Director*

**8543  Abilities Center of New Jersey**
1208 Delsea Drive
Westville, NJ 08093
856-848-1025
FAX: 856-848-8429
e-mail: info@abilities2worl.com
www.abilities2work.com

*Sharon Knubuehl, President*

**8544  Abilities of Northwest New Jersey**
PO Box 251
Washington, NJ 07882
908-689-1118
FAX: 908-689-6363

*Richard Lowe, President*

Serves northwestern New Jersey.

**8545  Alliance for Disabled in Action New Jersey**
629 Amboy Avenue
Suite Ll
Edison, NJ 08837
732-738-4388
FAX: 732-738-4416
TTY:732-738-9644
e-mail: adacil@adacil.org
www.adacil.org

*Richard Ringhof, Executive Director*

Serves Somerset, Union and Middlesex Counties in New Jersey.

**8546  Alternatives for Growth: New Jersey**
16-00 208 S
Fair Lawn, NJ 07410
201-797-8330
FAX: 201-797-3586

*Donna Flannery, Contact*

Serves all New Jersey.

**8547  Arc of Bergen and Passaic Counties**
223 Moore Street
Hackensack, NJ 07601
201-343-0322
FAX: 201-343-0401
e-mail: arcbp@aol.com
www.arcbergenpassaic.org

*James E Seath, President/CEO*
*Leonard F Nicolosi, Vice President*
*Olga Podolsig, Family Support*

Serving persons with disabilities and their families in Bergen and Passaic Counties, NJ.

**8548  Career Opportunity Development of New Jersey**
901 Atlantic Avenue
Egg Harbor City, NJ 08215
609-965-6871

*Jenine Emil, Contact*
*Linda Carney, President*

Serves Bergen and Passaic Counties.

**8549  Center for Educational Advancement New Jersey**
11 Minneakoning Road
Flemington, NJ  08822
908-782-1480
FAX: 908-782-5370
e-mail: jkunz@ceaemployment.com
www.ceaemployment.com

*Joanne Kunz, Vice President*
*Michael Skoczek, President*
Serves Somerset and Hunterdon Counties. Skills training in office technology and food service. Job placement and job coaching services are available. Employer Network for Ticket to Work.

**8550  Cerebral Palsy Association of Middlesex County**
Oak Drive
Edison, NJ  08837
732-549-5580
FAX: 201-603-0284

*Dominic Ursino, President*
Serves Central New Jersey.

**8551  Easter Seal Hackensack**
171 Atlantic Street
Hackensack, NJ  07601
201-342-5739
FAX: 201-342-4480

*Denise Sredeen, Contact*
Serves Hackensack.

**8552  Easter Seal Society of New Jersey Highlands Workshop**
Easter Seals
133 Main Street
Franklin, NJ  07416
973-827-9066
FAX: 973-827-3828

*Dave Shickle, Contact*
*Peggy Skipp, Manager*
Serves all New Jersey.

**8553  Easter Seal of Ocean County**
150 Oberlin Avenue N
Lakewood, NJ  08701
732-363-8990
FAX: 732-363-7540

*Greg Makely, Contact*

**8554  Easter Seals New Jersey**
1 Kimberly Road
E Brunswick, NJ  08816
732-257-6662

www.eastersealsnj.org

*Brian Fitzgerald, Chief Executive Officer*
Serves all New Jersey.

**8555  Eden Acres Administrative Services**
1 Eden Way
Princeton, NJ  08540
609-987-0099
FAX: 609-734-0069

*Tom Cool, President*
Provides services for the disabilitated.

**8556  Edison Sheltered Workshop**
328 Plainfield Avenue
Edison, NJ  08817
732-985-8834
FAX: 732-985-2216

*Ann Marie Stone, Vocational Rehab. Counselor*
*Veronica Valez, Executive Director*
Serves Middlesex County. Vocational training and job placement services.

**8557  First Occupational Center of New Jersey**
391 Lakeside Avenue
Orange, NJ  07050
973-672-5800
800-894-6265
FAX: 973-672-0065
e-mail: ocnj@idt.net
www.ocnj.org

*Rocco J Neola, President/CEO*
*Doreen Speller, Manager Rehabilitation Services*
A private, nonprofit multi-service community rehabilitation program. Services are offered to all people, such as developmentally disabled, visually impaired, hearing impaired and welfare recipients. Services include vocational evaluation and training, respite care, basic and remedial education and job placement and community support services.

**8558  Goodwill Industries of Southern New Jersey**
2835 Route 735
Maple Shade, NJ  08052
856-439-0174

*Mike Shaw, Vice President*

**8559  Hausmann Industries**
130 Union Street
Northvale, NJ  07647
201-767-1369
888-428-7626
FAX: 201-767-1369
e-mail: info@hausmann.com
www.hausmann.com

*George Batchelor, Director Sales/Marketing*
*Werner Hausmann, Manager*
Wheelchair acessible exam tables, treatment tables and mat platforms.

**8560  Jersey Cape Diagnostic Training & Opportunity Center**
152 Crest Haven Road
Cape May Court House, NJ  08210
609-465-4117
FAX: 609-465-3899

*Steve Madzelski, Director*
*George Plewa, Executive Director*
Serves Cape May County.

**8561  New Jersey Commission for the Blind and Visually Impaired**
Department of Human Services
PO Box 47017
Newark, NJ  07101
973-648-3333
877-685-8878
FAX: 973-648-7364
e-mail: Vito.DeSantis@cbvi.nj.us
www.cbvi.nj.gov

*Vito J Desantis, Executive Director*
*Pamela Gaston, Executive Assistant*
*Khmbrly Howard PhD, Deputy Executive Director*
Offers services for the totally blind, legally blind, visually impaired, deaf blind and more with eye health, counseling, educational, recreational, rehabilitation, computer training and vocational services.

**8562  New Jersey Employment Service and Job Training Program Services**
Department of Labor
Trenton, NJ  08625
609-292-1040

*Roland Machold, Manager*

**8563  Occupational Center of Hudson County**
780 Montgomery Street
Jersey City, NJ  07306
201-432-5959
FAX: 201-432-6227

*Christine Remler, Executive Director*
Serves Hudson County.

**8564  Occupational Center of Union County**
301 Cox Street
Roselle, NJ  07203
908-241-7200
FAX: 908-241-2025
e-mail: ocuc@OCUCNJ.com

*Michele Ford, VP*
Provides vocational rehabilitation and mental health service.

**8565  Occupational Training Center of Burlington County**
130 Hancock Lane
Westampton, NJ  08060
609-267-6677
FAX: 609-265-8418

*Joseph Bender, President*

**8566  Occupational Training Center of Camden County, New Jersey**
215 W White Horse Pike
Berlin, NJ  08009
856-768-0845
FAX: 856-767-1378

*Matt Treihart, President*
Serves Camden County.

**8567  Pathways to Independence**
60 Kingsland Avenue
Kearny, NJ  07032
201-997-6155
FAX: 201-991-7530
e-mail: PTI450@aol.com
www.pathwaystoindependencenj.org

*Alvin Cox, Executive Director*
*Tessa Farrell, Program Director*

Serves Hudson, South Bergen and Essex counties, providing vocational and pre-vocational services to adults with disabilities.

**8568  Somerset Training and Employment Program**
36 4th Street
Somerville, NJ  08876
732-846-2734

*Laurie Falka, Executive Director*
*Courtney Throckmorton, Owner*

**8569  St. John of God Community Services Vocational Rehabilitation**
1145 Delsea Drive
Westville, NJ  08093
856-848-4700
FAX: 856-848-1512

*Muncie Buckalew, Executive Director*
Serves Gloucester and Camden Counties.

**8570  United Cerebral Palsy Associations of New Jersey**
354 S Broad Street
Trenton, NJ  08608
609-392-4004
888-322-1918
FAX: 609-392-3505
www.cpofnj.org

*Jacqueline Stroman, Director of Education*
*Jack Mudge, Executive Director*

**8571  Vocational and Rehabilitation Agency**
PO Box 398
Trenton, NJ  08625
609-292-5987
FAX: 609-292-8347
TTY:609-292-2919
e-mail: tjennings@dol.state.nj.us
www.state.nj.us

*Thomas G Jennings, Director*

**8572  West Essex Rehab Center**
83 Walnut Street
Montclair, NJ  07042
973-744-7733
FAX: 201-744-3744

*Ben Viearisi, Contact*
*Shannon Williams, Contact*
*Eugene Stefanelli, Executive Director*

---

# New Mexico

**8573  Adelante Development Center**
3900 Osterna NE
Albuquerque, NM  87109
505-341-2000
FAX: 505-341-2001
www.go.adelante.org

*Mike Kivitze, Executive Director*
Serves Albuquerque and Belin.

**8574  Goodwill Industries of New Mexico**
5000 San Mateo Boulevard NE
Albuquerque, NM  87109
505-881-6612
FAX: 505-884-3157
www.goodwillnm.org

*Fred Calkins, President*
*Richard Thorne, Vice President*
*Patrick Michaels, Chief Executive Officer*
Serves Albuquerque, Santa Fe and Rio Rancho.

**8575  New Mexico Employment Services and Job Training Liaison**
PO Box 1928
Albuquerque, NM  87103
505-827-6827
FAX: 505-827-6812
e-mail: djones2@state.nm.us

*Reese Suliten, Director*

**8576  Opportunity Center: New Mexico**
873 Wright Avenue
Alamogordo, NM  88310
505-437-0919
FAX: 505-437-1135

*Meron Wilson, Executive Director*
Serves Alamogorda area.

**8577  RCI**
1023 Stanford Drive NE
Albuquerque, NM  87106
505-247-4936
FAX: 505-255-9971
www.rci-nm.org

*Greg Racca, Owner*
Serves Bernalillo County.

**8578 Tohatchi Area of Opportunity & Services**
PO Box 49
Tohatchi, NM 87325
505-733-2200
FAX: 505-733-2678

*Patrick Keptner, Executive Director*
*Marcella Franklin, Program Director*
*Daric Kalleco, Community Living Coordinator*

Serves McKinley County, San Jose County and the Havanjo Nation.

**8579 Vocational Rehabilitation Agency**
435 Saint Michaels Drive
Suite D
Santa Fe, NM 87505
505-954-8500
800-224-7005
FAX: 505-954-8556
TTY: 8779548583
e-mail: dvris@state.nm.us
www.dvrgetsjobs.com

*Catherine Cross-Maple, Manager*

**8580 Vocational and Rehabilitation Agency**
2905 Rodeo Park Drive E
Building 4
Santa Fe, NM 87505
505-954-8500
888-513-7968
FAX: 505-476-4475
e-mail: greg.trapp@state.nm.us
www.state.nm.us/cftb

*Greg Trapp, Executive Director*
*James Salas, Deputy Director*
*Adelmo Vigil, Deputy Director-IL/OB*

# New York

**8581 JOBS VI and SAGE**
P ES CO International
21 Paulding Street
Pleasantville, NY 10570
914-769-4266
800-431-2016
FAX: 914-769-2970
e-mail: pesco@pesco.org
www.pesco.org

*Charles Kass, Vice President*
*Joseph Kass, President*

A computerized matching system matching people to occupations, training, local jobs, local employers and giving job outlooks for the year 2005. Computerized Sage is online computerized testing with the ability for system to read all questions, and job descriptions. Manual Sage is a hands on-computer scored test battery with various adaptation. Braille, large print, bi-lingual and special devices.

**8582 Just One Break (JOBS)**
120 Wall Street
Fl 20
New York, NY 10005
212-785-7300
FAX: 212-785-4513
e-mail: jobs@justonebreak.com
www.justonebreak.com

*Susan S Odiseos, Executive Director*
*C Jeffrey Knittel, President*

**8583 New York State Department of Labor**
State Office Campus
Building 12
Albany, NY 12240
518-485-6800

e-mail: nysdol@labor.state.ny.us
www.labor.state.ny.us

*James J Mcgowan, Commissioner*
*Fredda Peritz, Employment Service Division Dire*
*Thomas Malone, Unemployment Insur. Div. Dir.*

The missin of the New York State Department of Labor is to help New York work by preparing individuals for the jobs of today and tomorrow. Provides direct job search and counseling services to job seekers, and can refer people who have disabilities for training opportunities. Provides unemployment insurance for those out of work through no fault of their own.

**8584 Rational Effectiveness Training Systems**
IRET Corporate Services Division
45 E 65th Street
New York, NY 10021
212-570-2868

*Dr. Dominic DiMattie, Director*

Offers advanced training for employee assistance professionals, full service outpatient counseling, consulting services and on-site workshops for the disabled.

**8585 Special Education and Vocational Rehabilitation Agency: New York**
1 Commerce Plaza
Room 1606
Albany, NY 12234
518-474-2714
800-222-5662
FAX: 518-474-8802
TTY: 518-474-5652
www.vesid.nysed.gov

*Rebecca Cort, Director*

# North Carolina

**8586 Division of Employment & Training**
4111 N Harrington Street
Raleigh, NC 27603
919-715-6500

*Gary Hunt, Executive Director*

**8587 Iredell Vocational Workshop**
200 Clanton Road
Charlotte, NC 28217
704-944-5100
FAX: 704-871-9881
www.lifespanservices.org

*Stacey Draison, Director*

**8588 North Carolina Division of Services for the Blind**
Department of Health and Human Services
2601 Mail Service Center
Raleigh, NC 27699
919-733-9822
FAX: 919-733-9769
TTY:919-733-9700
e-mail: debbie.jackson@ncmail.net
www.dhhs.state.nc.us/dsb

*Debbie Jackson, Director*
*Mary Flanagan, Assistant Director*

**8589 Rowan County Vocational Workshop**
2728 Old Concord Road
Salisbury, NC 28146
704-633-6223
FAX: 704-633-6224

*Carl Rapsher, Executive Director*

Offers vocational assessment and training, adult developmental activities.

**8590  Rutherford Vocational Workshop**
200 Fairground Road
Spindale, NC  28160  828-286-4352

*Larry Brown, Executive Director*

**8591  Transylvania Vocational Services**
PO Box 1115
Brevard, NC  28712  828-884-3195
FAX: 828-884-3102

*Nancy Stricker, Executive Director*

**8592  Vocational and Rehabilitation Agency**
2601 Mail Service Center
Raleigh, NC  27699  919-855-3500
FAX: 919-715-7905
TTY:919-733-9700
e-mail: John.DeLuca@ncmail.net
www.dhhs.state.nc.us

*Linda Harrington, Manager*
Offers services for the totally blind, legally blind, visually impaired, mentally retarded blind and more with health, counseling, educational, recreational, rehabilitation, computer training and professional training services.

**8593  Vocational and Rehabilitation Agency: Department of Health and Human Services**
2801 Mail Service Center
Raleigh, NC  27699  919-855-3500
FAX: 919-733-7968
TTY:919-733-5924
e-mail: bob.philbeck@ncmail.net
dvr.dhhs.state.nc.us

*Linda Harrington, Manager*

**8594  Webster Enterprises of Jackson County**
PO Box 220
Webster, NC  28788  828-586-8981
800-978-2681
FAX: 828-586-8125
www.websterenterprises.org

*Darrell Fox, Executive Director*
A community based employment and training program for people with disabilities. A full service program which includes a youth transitional program for life beyond high school, job coaching, vocational assessment and job placement.

**8595  Western Regional Vocational Rehabilitation Facility Clifford File, Jr.**
PO Box 1443
Morganton, NC  28680

*Clifford File Jr, Executive Director*
Vocational Evaluation, Work Adjustment, Job Placement, On-site Work Services Program. Serves most disability groups including CMI, DD, Deaf and Physically impaired.

## North Dakota

**8596  North Dakota Department of Labor, Equal Employment Opportunity Division**
600 E Boulevard Avenue
Dept 406
Bismarck, ND  58505  701-328-2455
800-582-8032
FAX: 701-328-2031
e-mail: labor@state.nd.us
www.state.nd.us/labor

*Bryan Klipfel, Manager*
Through a work-sharing agreement with the Equal Employment Opportunity Commission (EEOC), the North Dakota Department of Labor enforces the Americans with Disabilities Act (ADA) as related to employment discrimination.

**8597  North Dakota Employment Service and Job Training Program Liaison**
Job Service North Dakota
PO Box 1537
Bismarck, ND  58502  701-258-6353

*Leslie Weiss, Manager*

**8598  North Dakota Governor's Committee on Employment of Disabled Persons**
600 S 2nd Street
Suite 1b
Bismarck, ND  58504  701-328-8989
FAX: 701-328-8969

**8599  North Dakota Vocational Rehabilitation Agency**
Trarie Chills Plaza 1237 W
Suite B1
Bismarck, ND  58501  701-328-8950
800-755-2745
FAX: 701-328-8969
TTY: 701-328-8968

*Wanda Dier, Interim Director*
Offers services for the totally blind, legally blind, visually impaired, mentally retarded blind and more with health, counseling, educational, recreational, rehabilitation, computer training and professional training services.

## Ohio

**8600  Cornucopia**
18120 Sloane Avenue
Lakewood, OH  44107  216-521-4600
FAX: 216-521-9460
www.lkwdpl.org/paths/healingarts/ Nature s

*Chris Yurick, Program Manager*
*Scott Duennes, Executive Director*
Provides work adjustment training for people with and developmental disabilities in a unique community based setting; Nature's Bin, a natural fresh foods market. Consumers learn through participation in retail operations in produce, grocery, bakery, deli, maintenance and customer service areas. Retail revenues help offset the cost of the program. Job search skills training and placement assistance available to program graduates.

**8601 Great Oaks Joint Vocational School**
3254 E Kemper Road
Cincinnati, OH 45241     513-772-4603

*Harold Carr, Medical Director*
*Deb Graw, Manager*

**8602 Hearth Day Treatment and Vocational Services**
8301 Detroit Avenue
Cleveland, OH 44102     216-281-2660

*Ralph Fee, Executive Director*

**8603 Highland Unlimited Business Enterprises of CRI**
1322 E McMillan Street
Cincinnati, OH 45206     513-569-4730
FAX: 513-751-2938
e-mail: ddutton@cricincy.com
www.cricincy.com

*Tony Datillo, Executive Director*
*Debbie Dutton Lambert, Director Employment Programs*

**8604 Ohio Civil Rights Commission**
1111 E Broad Street
Suite 301
Columbus, OH 43205     614-466-2785
FAX: 614-644-8776

*G Payton, Manager*

**8605 Ohio Employment Services and Job Training**
145 S Front Street
Columbus, OH 43215     614-466-4000
FAX: 614-752-9049

*Cheryl Boyce, Executive Director*

**8606 Vocational and Rehabilitation Agency**
400 E Campus View Boulevard
Columbus, OH 43235     614-466-9364
800-282-4536
FAX: 614-785-5012
TTY: 614-438-1334
e-mail: john.connellyu@rsc.state.oh.us
www.state.oh.us

*John Connelly, Director*
*Rose Reed, Manager*

## Oklahoma

**8607 Oklahoma Department of Rehabilitation Services (DRS)**

3535 NW 58th Street
Suite 500
Oklahoma City, OK 73112     405-951-3400
800-845-8476
FAX: 405-951-3529
e-mail: jprice@drs.state.ok.us
www.okrehab.org

*Jody Harlem, Public Information Administrator*
*Linda Parker, Executive Director*

**8608 Oklahoma Employment Services and Job Training Program Liaison**
2401 N Lincoln Boulevard
Oklahoma City, OK 73105     405-557-7211
FAX: 405-557-5368

**8609 Oklahoma Governor's Committee on Employment of People with Disabilities**
2712 Villa Prom
Oklahoma City, OK 73107     405-424-8378
FAX: 405-943-7550

*Tom Kelly, President*

## Oregon

**8610 Bend Work Activity Center**
275 NE 2nd Street
Bend, OR 97701     541-389-0129
FAX: 541-389-2084
e-mail: info@ofco.org
www.ofco.org

*James Booth, Chairperson*
*Bill Schertzinger, Vice Chairperson*
*Cam Chambers, Manager*

**8611 Oregon Fair Employment Practice Agency**
Oregon Bureau of Labor & Industry
PO Box 800
Portland, OR 97207     503-229-6601

**8612 State of Oregon Office of Vocational Rehabilitation Service**
3165 10th Street
# 500
Baker City, OR 97814     541-523-8441
866-752-5235
FAX: 541-524-0441
e-mail: wendy.m.wall@state.or.us

*Wendy Wall, Counselor Assistant*
*Allan McCandless, Voc Rehab Counselor*
*Samantha McConnell, Voc Rahab Counselor*

**8613 Vocational and Rehabilitation Agency**
500 Summer Street NE
E-87
Salem, OR 97301     503-945-5880
877-277-0513
FAX: 503-947-5025
TTY: 503-945-5894
e-mail: bobby.c.simpson@state.or.us
www.oregon.gov/dhs/vr/index.shtml

*Stephanie Taylor, Administrator*

**8614 Vocational and Rehabilitation Agency: Commision for the Blind**
535 SE 12th Avenue
Portland, OR 97214     503-731-3221
FAX: 503-731-3230
e-mail: linda.mock@state.or.us
www.cfb.state.or.us

*Linda Mock, Administrator*
*Pat Donell, Executive Director*

## Pennsylvania

**8615 AC-ACLD/An Association for Children and Adults with Learning Disabilities**
4900 Girard Road
Pittsburgh, PA 15227
412-881-2253
FAX: 412-881-2263
e-mail: info@acldonline.org
www.acldonline.org

*Thomas Fogarty, President*

Offers services to children, adolescents and adults with specific learning disabilities.

**8616 Office of Vocational Rehabilitation**
7th and Forester Street
Harrisburg, PA 17120
717-787-4746
FAX: 717-783-5221

*Barry Brandt, Rehabilitation Specialist*

Information in vocational counseling and the governor's committee on Employment of People with Disabilities. Also serves persons with disabilities that present a substantial handicap to employment and independence. Services are provided when there is a reasonable expectation that employment is possible as a result of those services.

**8617 Pennsylvania Employment Services and Job Training**
P A Department of Labor and Industry
7th and Forster Street
Room 1700
Harrisburg, PA 17120
717-787-5279
FAX: 717-787-8826
www.dli.state.pa.us

*Edward Rendell, Governor*
*Stephen Schmerin, Manager*

**8618 Pennsylvania Governor's Committee on Employment of Disabled Persons**
7th and Forester Street
Harrisburg, PA 17120
717-787-4746

**8619 Pennsylvania Human Relations Commission Agency**
301 Chestnut Street
Suite 300
Harrisburg, PA 17101
717-787-4410
FAX: 717-214-0584
www.phrc.state.pa.us

*Homer Floyd, Executive Director*

**8620 US Healthworks**
1114 Commons Boulevard
Reading, PA 19605
610-926-0960
FAX: 610-926-6225

*Beverly Shaeff, Manager*

Helps injured workers overcome injuries or disabilities and return to their jobs.

**8621 Vocational and Rehabilitation Agency**
1521 N 6th Street
Harrisburg, PA 17102
717-787-5244
800-442-6351
FAX: 717-787-3210
TTY: 717-787-5244
e-mail: ovr@dli.state.pa.us
www.dli.state.pa.us

*William Gannon, Director*
*Thomas Washic, Manager*

**8622 Vocational and Rehabilitation Agency: Department of Labor and Industry**
909 Green Street
Harrisburg, PA 17102
717-236-6211
800-622-2842
FAX: 717-787-3210
TTY: 717-787-6176
e-mail: cboone@state.pa.us

*Thomas Carlock, Chief Executive Officer*

## Rhode Island

**8623 Goodwill Industries of RI**
100 Houghton Street
Providence, RI 02904
401-861-2080
FAX: 401-454-0889

*Laurie Norris, President/CEO*
*Jeff Machado, Cheif Deputy Officer*

**8624 Groden Center**
86 Mount Hope Avenue
Providence, RI 02906
401-274-6310

*Michael Smith, Administration*
*June Groden, Chief Executive Officer*

**8625 Newport County Chapter of Retarded Citizens**
PO Box 4390
Middletown, RI 02842
401-846-0340
FAX: 401-847-9459

*John Maher, Executive Director*

**8626 Office of Rehabilitation Services**
40 Fountain Street
Providence, RI 02903
401-421-7005
FAX: 401-222-3574
TTY: 401-421-7016
www.ors.ri.gov

*Raymond A Caroll, Administrator*
*Gary Wier, Deputy Administrator for Service*

Their goal is to help individuals with physical and mental disabilities prepare for and obtain appropriate employment.

**8627 Rhode Island Employment Services and Job Training**
101 Friendship Street
Providence, RI 02903
401-222-3732
FAX: 401-462-8798

**8628 Vocational and Rehabilitation Agency: Department of Human Services**
RI Services for the Blind and Visually Impaired
40 Fountain Street
Providence, RI 02903
401-222-2300
FAX: 401-222-1328
TTY: 401-222-3010
e-mail: garyw@ors.ri.gov
www.ors.ri.gov

*Raymond Carroll, Administrator*

Their goal is to help individuals with physical and mental disabilities prepare for and obtain appropriate employment.

## South Carolina

**8629** **South Carolina Employment Security Commission**
**South Carolina Center**
PO Box 567
Columbia, SC 29202
803-737-9935
800-436-8190
FAX: 803-737-2756
www.sces.org

*Camille Fallow, Disability Program Navigator*
*Regina Ratterros, Program Coordinator/State Office*

Public agency taht offers job search assistance. Unemployment Benefits and WIA program. Also offered is Disability Program Navigator who helps persons with disabilities to find needed resources

**8630** **South Carolina Governor's Committee on Employment of the Handicapped**
1330 Boston Street
Columbia, SC 29203
803-896-1208
FAX: 803-896-6373

*Gayle Brazell, Executive Director*

**8631** **South Carolina Vocational Rehabilitation Department**
1410 Boston Avenue
PO Box 15
West Columbia, SC 29171
803-896-6500
800-832-7526
TTY:803-896-6553
e-mail: info@scvrd.state.sc.us
www.scvrd.net

*Larry C Bryant, Commissioner*

The SCVRD's mission is to enable eligible South Carolinians with disabilities to prepare for, achieve and maintain competitive employment.

**8632** **Vocational and Rehabilitation Agency: Vocational Rehabilitation Department**
PO Box 15
West Columbia, SC 29171
803-896-6700
800-832-7526
FAX: 803-896-6510
e-mail: kmandeville@scvrd.state.sc.us
www.scvrd.net

*Kerry Mandeville, Director Case Services*
*Dan Parlor, Manager*

**8633** **Vocational and Rehabilitation Agency: Commission for the Blind**
Vocational and Rehabilitation Agency
PO Box 79
Columbia, SC 29202
803-737-5700
800-922-2222
FAX: 803-898-8852
e-mail: publicinfo@sccb.sc.gov
www.sccbc.sc.us

*Nell Carney, Director*

## South Dakota

**8634** **South Dakota Governor's Advisory Committee on Employment of the Disabled**
700 Governors Drive
Pierre, SD 57501
605-773-3423
FAX: 605-773-4236

*Patrick Keating, Manager*

**8635** **South Dakota State Vocational Rehabilitati on**
Department of Human Services
3800 E Highway 34 Hillview Plaza
Pierre, SD 57501
605-773-5990
265-865-9684
FAX: 605-773-5483
TTY: 605-773-3195
e-mail: eric.weiss@state.sd.us
www.state.sd.us

*Eric Weiss, Assistant Director*
*Berrie Grimme, Assistant Director Div of Rehab*
*Betty Oldenkamp, Manager*

South Dakota State Vocational Rehabilitation consists of five agencies; Rehab Services and service to the Blind and Visually Impaired. There mission is the same to provide individualized rehabilitation services that result in optimal employment and independent living outcomes for individuals with disabilities.

**8636** **South Dakota Workforce Investment Act Training Programs**
700 Governors Drive
Pierre, SD 57501
605-773-3423
800-952-3216
FAX: 605-773-4211
www.sdjobs.org

*Michael Ryan, Director*
*Patrick Keating, Manager*

**8637** **Vocational and Rehabilitation Agency: Divi sion of Services to the Blind/Visually Impaired**
3800 E Highway 34 Hillview Plaza
Pierre, SD 57501
605-773-4644
800-265-9684
FAX: 605-773-5483
TTY: 605-773-4644
e-mail: gaye.mattke@state.sd.us
www.state.sd.us

*Gaye Mattke, Director*

## Tennessee

**8638** **Tennessee Department of Labor: Job Training Program Liaison**
501 Union Street
Nashville, TN 37219
615-741-6642

*James Neeley, Manager*

**8639** **Tennessee Fair Employment Practice Agency**
Human Rights Commission
226 Capitol Boulevard
Suite 602
Nashville, TN 37219
615-741-5825

*Tricia Crawford, Manager*

**8640** **Vocational and Rehabilitation Agency**
Tennessee Department Human Services
400 Deaderick Street
15th Floor
Nashville, TN 37248
615-313-4700
FAX: 615-741-4165
e-mail: karen.a.wayson@state.tn.us
www.state.tn.us/humanserv/rehabilitation.htm

*Andrea Cooper, Assistant Commissioner*
*Gina Lodge, Manager*

## Texas

**8641 C-CAD Center of United Cerebral Palsy of Metropolitan Dallas**
1950 N Stemmons Freeway
Dallas, TX 75207
214-746-4217
FAX: 214-800-2224
e-mail: info@ucpdallas.org
www.ucp.dallas.org

*Debi Jobin, Director Assistive Tech Services*
*Susan Black, Special Products Coordinator*

Offers a wide range of technology opportunities for persons with all types of disabilities, their families and the professionals who serve them. Services include assesments, traiing, technology access showroom, and workshops for rehabilitation and educational personnel.

**8642 Handbook of Career Planning for Students with Special Needs**
Pro- Ed Publications
8700 Shoal Creek Boulevard
Austin, TX 78757
512-451-3246
800-897-3202
FAX: 800-397-7633
e-mail: feedback@proedinc.com
www.proedinc.com

*Donald Hammill, Owner*
*Courtney King, Marketing Coordinator*

The practitioner's guide will show you how to help special needs adolescents and young adults overcome barriers to employment by identifying goals and problems, assessing interests and aptitudes, involving client families and developing communication skills. *$42.00*
*358 pages*

**8643 Texas Employment Services and Job Training Program Liaison**
Texas Workforce Commission
101 E 15th Street
Austin, TX 78778
512-444-7763
800-735-2988
TTY:700-735-2989
www.tec.state.tx.us

**8644 Vocational and Rehabilitation Agency: State Rehabilitation Commission**
Vocational and Rehabilitation Agency
4800 N Lamar Boulevard
Austin, TX 78756
512-926-1446
800-628-5115
FAX: 512-424-4730
TTY: 800-628-5115
e-mail: dars.inquiries@dars.state.tx.us
www.dars.state.tx.us

*Sylvia Stacy, Inquiries Specialist*
*Tim Spong, Manager*

## Utah

**8645 Utah Employment Services**
720 S 200 E
Salt Lake City, UT 84111
801-536-7401
FAX: 801-536-7011

**8646 Utah Governor's Committee on Employment of the Handicapped**
PO Box 45500
Salt Lake City, UT 84145
801-538-4200
FAX: 801-538-4446
www.hsdspd.utah.gov

*George Kelner, Executive Director*

**8647 Utah Veterans Centers**
750 N 200 W
Suite 105
Provo, UT 84601
801-377-1117
800-246-1197
FAX: 801-377-0227

*Dennis Stevens, Executive Director*
*Brent Price, Manager*

Readjustment counseling services to veterans.

**8648 Utah Vocational Rehabilitation Agency**
Utah State Office of Rehabilitation
PO Box 144200
Salt Lake City, UT 84114
801-538-7530
800-473-7530
FAX: 801-538-7522
e-mail: duchida@utah.gov
www.usor.utah.gov

*Donald R Uchida, Executive Director*
*Russell Thelin, Director*
*Blaine Petersen, Manager*

Vocational Rehabilitation Services for individuals with disabilities.

**8649 Vocational and Rehabilitation Agency: Division of Services for the Blind/Visually Imp.**
250 N 1950 W
Suite B
Salt Lake City, UT 84116
801-323-4343
800-284-1823
FAX: 801-323-4396
e-mail: wgibson@utah.gov
www.usor.utah.gov

*Bill Gibson, Director*
*Melanie Showell, Assistant Director*

## Vermont

**8650 State of Vermont Department of Aging and Disabilities**
103 S Main Street
Waterbury, VT 05671
802-241-2210
888-405-5005
FAX: 802-241-2128
e-mail: fredj@dad.state.vt.us
www.dad.state.vt.us/dbvi

*Fred Jones, Director*

**8651 Vermont Employment Services and Job Training**
5 Green Mountain Drive
PO Box 488
Montpelier, VT 05601
802-828-4000
FAX: 802-828-4022
TTY:802-828-4203
e-mail: tdouse@labor.state.vt.us
www.labor.vermont.gov

*Tom Douse, Acting/Deputy Commissioner*
*Jill Greenwood, Workforce Development Director*

**8652 Vermont Governor's Committee on Employment of People with Disabilities**
103 S Main Street
Waterbury, VT 05671
802-241-2186
866-879-6757
FAX: 802-241-3359
www.vocrehad.vermont.org

*Diane Dalmasse, Director*

**8653 Vocational and Rehabilitation Agency**
103 S Main Street
Waterbury, VT 05671
802-241-2186
866-879-6757
FAX: 802-241-3359
TTY: 802-241-2186
e-mail: diane@dail.state.vt.us
www.vocrehabvermont.org

*Diane Dalmasse, Director*

## Virginia

**8654 Alexandria Community Y Head Start**
418 South Washington Street
Alexandria, VA 22314
703-329-2050
FAX: 703-998-5707

*Yvonne Walker*

Offers social services, on-the-job-training for parents, play therapy, physical therapy, speech therapy and any other specialized services.

**8655 Didlake**
8641 Breeden Avenue
Manassas, VA 20110
703-361-4195
FAX: 703-369-7141

*Rexford Parr Jr, President/CEO*
*John S Craig, VP Rehabilitation Services*

Offers situational assessments, work training, employment and job placement services to people with disabilities.

**8656 Learning Services: Shenandoah**
9524 Fairview Avenue
Manassas, VA 20110
703-335-9771
FAX: 703-335-1064

*Peter Patrick, Administrator*

Postacute rehabilitation program.

**8657 NISH**
2235 Cedar Lane
Vienna, VA 22182
703-560-6800
FAX: 703-560-9345
www.nish.org

*E Robert Chamberlin, President/CEO*
*Mary Jame Williamson*

A nonprofit agency desigated by the Committee for Purchase from People Who Are Blind or Severely Disabled to provide technical assistance to rehabilitation programs interested in obtaining federal contracts under Public Law 92-28, the Javits-Wagner-O'Day Act. NISH's primary objective is to assist community rehabilitation programs in providing jobs for people with severe disabilities.

**8658 Richmond Research Training Center**
PO Box 842011
Richmond, VA 23284
804-828-1222

*Paul Wehman MD, Director*
*Dolores Taylor, Executive Director*

Research and training center report on the supported employment of persons with developmental and other disabilities.

**8659 ServiceSource**
6295 Edsall Road
Suite 175
Alexandria, VA 22312
703-461-6000
800-244-0817
FAX: 703-461-3906
www.ourpeoplework.org

*Janet Samuelson, President*
*Edie Castner, Assistant Director*

Provides training, job placement and employment services in private sector and government contract employment.

**8660 Sheltered Occupational Center of Virginia**
750 23rd Street S
Arlington, VA 22202
703-521-4441
FAX: 703-521-3443
www.socent.org

*Charles Richman, President*
*Virgro Newkirk, Director of Operation*

Assists, empowers and supports people with disabilities to achieve employment, independence and integration in the workplace and community. Our services include: printing, copying, hand work, mail shop, fulfillment and distribution.

**8661 Vocational and Rehabilitation Agency**
PO Box K300
Richmond, VA 23288
804-662-7000
800-552-5019
FAX: 804-662-9532
TTY: 800-464-9950
e-mail: drs@drs.state.va.us
www.vadrs.org

*James Rothrock, Commissioner*

**8662 Vocational and Rehabilitation Agency: Department for the Blind/Visually Impaired**
397 Azalea Avenue
Richmond, VA 23227
804-371-3140
800-622-2155
FAX: 804-371-3351
e-mail: webmaster@drs.virginia.gov
www.vdbvi.org

*Joseph A Bowman, Commissioner*
*James A Taylor, Chief Deputy*

## Washington

**8663 Career Connections**
421 N Mullan Road
Spokane Valley, WA 99206
509-928-0423
866-404-5867
FAX: 509-928-0441
e-mail: carconn@mindspring.com
www.peoplelinking.com

*Susan Warwick, Executive Director*
*Teresa Antosyn, Program Coordinator*
*Dan Moody, CFO*

**8664 Department of Services for the Blind National Business & Disability Council**
Department of Services for the Blind
PO Box 40933
Olympia, WA 98504
360-586-1224
800-552-7103
FAX: 360-586-7627
www.dsb.wa.gov

*Louana Durand, Executive Director*

**8665 Department of Social & Health Services National Business & Disability Council**
Department of Social & Health Services
PO Box 45340
Lacey, WA
360-725-3413
FAX: 360-407-0955
e-mail: dddcoreception@dshs.wa.gov
www1.dshs.wa.gov

*Paul Strand, Co-Chair*

**8666 SL Stuart and Associates**
25 W Nora Avenue
Spokane, WA 99205
509-328-2740
FAX: 509-326-9207
e-mail: info@slstart.com
www.slstart.com

*Ray White, Director Employment Services*
*Stephen Start, Owner*

**8667 School of Piano Technology for the Blind**
2510 E Evergreen Boulevard
Vancouver, WA 98661
360-693-1511
FAX: 360-693-6891
e-mail: info@pianotuningschool.org
www.pianotuningschool.org

*Len Leger, Executive Director*
*Donald Mitchell, Director Instruction*
*Sharon Mitchell, Registar*

Teaches piano tuning and repair to blind and visually impaired menand women, leading to employment and/or self-employment in the piano service industry. Licensed by Washington State and accredited by the Accrediting Commission of Career Schools and Colleges of Technology (ACCSCT). 20-month course.

**8668 Vocational and Rehabilitation Agency: Division of Vocational Rehabilitation**
Department of Social and Health
PO Box 45340
Olympia, WA 98504
360-438-8000
800-637-5627
FAX: 360-438-8007
TTY: 360-438-8000
e-mail: krullk@dshs.wa.gov
www1.dshs.wa.gov/dvr

## West Virginia

**8669 West Virginia Division of Rehabilitation Services**
PO Box 50890
Charleston, WV 25305
304-766-4600
800-642-8207
FAX: 304-766-4905
TTY: 304-766-4965
www.wvdrs.org

*Deborah Lovely, Acting Director*
*Donna Ashworth, Assistant Director*

Vocational rehabilitation agency.

**8670 West Virginia Employment Services and Job Training Programs Liaison**
112 California Avenue
Charleston, WV 25305
304-558-0342
FAX: 304-558-0349
www.wvbep.org

*Valerie Comer, Director*
*Allan Galloway, Manager*

**8671 West Virginia Vocational Rehabilitation**
PO Box 1004
Institute, WV 25112
304-342-9952

*Earl Wolfe, Director*

Offers services for the totally blind, legally blind, visually impaired, mentally retarded blind and more with health, counseling, educational, recreational, rehabilitation, computer training and professional training services.

## Wisconsin

**8672 Vocational and Rehabilitation: Division of Wisconsin**
201 E Washington Avenue
Madison, WI 53702
608-261-0050
FAX: 608-266-1784
TTY:6082435601
www.dwd.state.wi.us/dvr

*Roberta Gassman, Secretary*
*Larry Studesville, Administrator*
*Charlene Dwyer, Manager*

Offers services for the totally blind, legally blind, visually impaired, mentally retarded blind and more with health, counseling, educational, recreational, rehabilitation, computer training and professional training services.

**8673 Wisconsin Vocational Rehabilitation Agency**
201 E Washington Avenue
Room A100
Madison, WI 53707
608-243-5600
800-442-3477
FAX: 608-243-5680
TTY: 888-877-5939
e-mail: dwddvr@dwd.state.wi.us
www.dwd.state.wi.us/dvr

*Charlene Dwyer, Administrator*

Wisconsin's Vocational Rehabilitation is a federal/state program designed to obtain, maintain, and improve employment for people with disabilities by working with VR consumers, employers, and other partners.

## Wyoming

**8674 Division of Vocational Rehabilitation of Wyoming**
Wyoming Department of Workforce Services
1100 Herschler Buiding
Cheyenne, WY 82002
307-777-7389
FAX: 307-777-5939
wyomingworkforce.org/how/vr.aspx

*Jim Mcintosh, Administrator*
*Kathy Emmones, Director Workforce Services*

Provides only those services which are necessary for eligible individuals to reach the employment goal agreed to in the Individualized Plan for Employment.

**8675 Vocational Rehabilitation, Division of Department of Workforce Services**
1160 Herschler Building
Suite 1e
Cheyenne, WY 82002
307-777-7385
FAX: 307-777-7155
TTY:307-777-7386
e-mail: jmcint@state.wy.us
www.wyomingworkforce.org

*Jim McIntosh, Administrator*

**8676** **Wyoming Department of Employment Unemployment Insurance**
PO Box 2760
Casper, WY 82602

307-235-3288
FAX: 307-235-3278
doe.state.wy.us

*Randy Hopper, Administrator*

**8677** **Wyoming Governor's Committee on Employment of the Handicapped**
Herschler
Room 1102
Cheyenne, WY 82002

307-777-7230
FAX: 307-777-5690

*Brenda Oswald, Manager*

## Alabama

**8678  HealthSouth Rehabilitation Hospital of North Alabama**
107 Governors Drive SW
Huntsville, AL 35801
256-535-2300
FAX: 256-535-2402
www.healthsouth.com
A comprehensive 50 bed rehabilitation hospital serving the need of patients in the North Alabama area. Guides patients with physically disabling conditions along an individualized treatment pathway so they can reach their highest level of physical, social and emotional well-being.

**8679  Lakeshore Rehabilitation Hospital**
3800 Ridgeway Drive
Birmingham, AL 35209
205-868-2000
FAX: 205-868-2007

*Terry Brown, Administrator*

**8680  Mobile Infirmary Medical Center: Rotary Rehabilitation Division**
5 Mobile Infirmary Circle
Mobile, AL 36607
251-435-2400
800-826-2085
FAX: 251-435-3403
e-mail: resource@mobileinfirmary.org
www.mobileinfirmary.org

*E Bramlett, Chief Executive Officer*

**8681  Montgomery Rehabilitation Hospital**
4465 Narrow Lane Road
Montgomery, AL 36116
334-262-5945
FAX: 334-288-3789

**8682  UAB Spain Rehabilitation Center**
1717 6th Avenue S
Birmingham, AL 35233
205-934-4816
800-822-8816
FAX: 205-934-5584

*Sonia A Arledge, Marketing Director*
*Cheryl Kennedy, Manager*

Spain offers a comprehensive approach to healing for persons challenged by stroke, spinal cord injury, arthritis, head injury, chronic pain or other disabilities resulting from illness or accident. In addition to a model facility, dedicated physicians and staff, and efficient programs tailored to meet the diverse needs of the physically challenged Spain has a wealth of resources found at the UAB Hospital, the number three health care facility in the United States.

## Arkansas

**8683  Central Arkansas Rehab Hospital**
2201 Wildwood Avenue
Sherwood, AR 72120
501-835-9919
FAX: 501-834-2227

*Randy Harris, Admissions*

**8684  HealthSouth Rehabilitation Hospital**
1401 S J Street
Fort Smith, AR 72901
479-785-3300
FAX: 479-785-5203
www.healthsouth.com

*Julie Stec, Administrator*

**8685  HealthSouth Rehabilitation Hospital of Jonesboro**
1201 Fleming Avenue
Jonesboro, AR 72401
870-932-0440
FAX: 870-933-5157

*Donna Bloodworth, Administrator*

Comprehensive physical rehabilitation hospital. Services include inpatient and outpatient services in Jonesboro, Newport, Paragould, Blytheville, and Pocahontas. Programs include stroke, amputee, brain injury, multiple trauma, joint replacement, spinal injury, arthritis, aquatic, pediatric, sports medicine, incontinence and balance.

**8686  Northwest Arkansas Rehabilitation Hospital**
153 E Monte Painter Drive
Fayetteville, AR 72703
479-444-2207
FAX: 479-444-2390

*K Hurlbut MD*

**8687  Rebsamen Rehabilitation Center**
1400 Braden Street
Jacksonville, AR 72076
501-985-7000
FAX: 501-985-7384

*Kurt Meer, Chief Executive Officer*

**8688  St. Michael Hospital: RehabCare Unit**
6th & Hazel Street
Texarkana, AR 71854
903-792-7380

## Arizona

**8689  Barrow Neurological Institute Rehab Center**
350 W Thomas Road
Phoenix, AZ 85013
602-406-3000
FAX: 602-406-4104

*Irwin Altman*
*Linda Hunt, President*

**8690  HealthSouth Hospital**
9630 E Shea Boulevard
Scottsdale, AZ 85260
480-860-0671
FAX: 480-551-5376
www.healthsouth.com

*Kathleen Cahill, Admissions*

**8691  HealthSouth Rehabilitation Center**
1151 S La Canada Drive
Suite 100
Green Valley, AZ 85614
520-625-4625
FAX: 520-648-5272

*Shaunna Schelin, Administrator*
*Greta Bame Otr/l, Director Marketing*
*Carol Altschuler, Front Office Group Coordinator*

Outpatient rehabilitation services, focus on orthopedic, sports and hand rehabilitation. Heavy industrial rehab focus. Accept all major insurances except Cigna and Pacfica.

**8692  HealthSouth Rehabilitation Center of Tucson**
75 N Wilmot Road
Tucson, AZ 85711
520-790-0900
800-476-2036
FAX: 520-745-0974

*Kristi Carrier, Administrator*
*Margo Stra, Director Marketing*
*Carol Altschuler, Front Office Group Coordinator*

Outpatient rehabilitation services, focus on orthopedic, sports and hand rehabilitation. Heavy industrial rehab focus. Accept all major insurances except Cigna and Pacfica.

**8693 HealthSouth Rehabilitation Centers of Tuscon**
7400 N Oracle Road
Suite 142
Tucson, AZ 85704 520-742-4822
FAX: 520-742-6711

*Shaunna Schelin, Administrator*
*Greta Bame, Director Marketing*
*Carol Altschuler, Front Office Group Coordinator*

Outpatient rehabilitation services, focus on orthopedic, sports and hand rehabilitation. Heavy industrial rehab focus. Accept all major insurances except Cigna and Pacfica.

**8694 HealthSouth Sports Medicine Center**
5111 N Scottsdale Road
Suite 100
Scottsdale, AZ 85250 480-941-9232
FAX: 928-772-1276
e-mail: chamine@wiley@healthsouth.com
www.healthsouth.com

*Chamine Wiley, Administrator*

**8695 Healthsouth Rehab Institute of Tucson**
2650 N Wyatt Drive
Tucson, AZ 85712 520-325-1300
800-333-8628
FAX: 520-327-4045
www.healthsouth.com

*Mark Tellier, CEO*
*Dave Tupper, COO*
*Joan Nelson, Administrator*

**8696 St. Joseph Hospital and Medical Center**
350 W Thomas Road
Phoenix, AZ 85013 602-406-3410
FAX: 602-406-4190

*Linda Hunt, Manager*

Rehabilitation programs offered by the clinic assists clients with rehabilitation health needs in the comfort of their own home. The home care rehabilitation team of professionals focuses on correcting deficiencies in self-care, mobility skills and communication. Services offered include physical therapy, occupational therapy, speech pathology, rehabilitative nursing and restorative nursing assistants.

## California

**8697 Bakersfield Regional Rehabilitation Hospital**
5001 Commerce Drive
Bakersfield, CA 93309 661-323-5500
800-288-9829
FAX: 661-323-5521

*Susan Golino, Admissions*
*Ann Feaver, Chief Executive Officer*

**8698 Brotman Medical Center: RehabCare Unit**
3828 Delmas Ter
Culver City, CA 90232 310-836-7000
FAX: 310-202-4105

*Ellen Graham, Program Manager*

**8699 Casa Colinas Centers for Rehabilitation**
255 E Bonita Avenue
Pomona, CA 91767 909-596-7733
FAX: 909-593-0153
e-mail: rehab@casacolina.org
www.casacolina.org

*Stephanie Bradhurst, Director Marketing*
*Felice Loverso, Chief Executive Officer*

**8700 Cedars-Sinai Medical Center and Inpatient Rehabilitation Center**
8700 Beverly Boulevard
West Hollywood, CA 90048 310-423-3751
800-233-2771
FAX: 310-659-0235
e-mail: jurt.vaillancourt@cshs.com
www.csmc.edu

*Kurt Vaillancourt, Intake Coordinator*
*Jeanne Flores, Senior Vice President*
*Jan Hobbs, Manager*

A comprehensive team approach with the primary goal of helping patients achieve optimal physical functioning in their daily activities. The Center also strives to educate both the patient and the patient's family and to help them adjust emotionally and socially. The Center offers various inpatient and outpatient programs including brain injury, spinal cord injury, stroke, orthopedic and a chronic pain management program.

**8701 Community Hospital of Los Gatos Rehabilitation Services**
355 Dardanelli Lane
Los Gatos, CA 95032 408-866-4020
FAX: 408-866-3875
e-mail: CHLG.ask@renethealth.com
www.communityhospitalLG.com

*Modestine Sain, Executive Director*

Rehabilitation Services provide individualized treatment programs for inpatient/outpatient care. The team is supervised by a Physiatrist and may include Nurses, Physical Therapists, Occupational Therapists, Speech/Language Therapists, Psychologists, Case Managers, Dietitians, Respiratory Therapists, Recreation Therapists and/or Prosthetists/Orthotists.

**8702 Daniel Freeman Hospitals: Center for Diagnostic and Rehab Medicine**
333 N Prairie Avenue
Inglewood, CA 90301 310-674-7050

www.centinelafreeman.com

*Mike Rembis, Chief Executive Officer*
*Von Crockette, Chief Operation Officer*

Provides a full spectrum of rehabilitation services from sub-acute, skilled nursing, acute rehabilitation, post-acute day program for brain injury, comprehensive outpatient, home health and home/community services. Also offer pediatric rehabilitation and accept ventilator patients. The facility is CARF and JCAHO accredited and have specialized teams for each program such as brain injury, spinal cord injury, stroke/neuro and pain management. Specialized support groups are also offered.

**8703 Garfield Medical Center**
525 N Garfield Avenue
Monterey Park, CA 91754 626-573-2222
FAX: 626-307-2077

*Shelly Hansen, Referrals*
*Philip Cohen, Chief Executive Officer*

**8704**  **Grossmont Hospital Rehabilition Center**
PO Box 158
La Mesa, CA 91944                        619-644-4100
                                     FAX: 619-644-4159

*Clair Jonesn, Contact*

**8705**  **Holy Cross Comprehensive Rehabilitation Center**
15031 Rinaldi Street
Mission Hills, CA 91345                  818-898-4502
                                     FAX: 818-898-4472

*Jorilyn Lima, Director*
*Cindy Damboise, Manager*

**8706**  **Kentfield Rehabilitation Hospital & Outpatient Center**
1125 Sir Francis Drake Boulevard
Kentfield, CA 94904                      415-456-9680
                                     FAX: 415-485-3613
                                     www.kentfieldrehab.com

*Susan Jensen, Liaison*
*Ann Gors, Chief Executive Officer*

**8707**  **Laurel Grove Hospital: Rehab Care Unit**
19933 Lake Chabot Road
Castro Valley, CA 94546                  510-727-2755
                                     FAX: 510-727-2778

*Judith Mather, Program Manager*
*Sue Nissim, Manager*

**8708**  **Lodi Memorial Hospital West**
Lodi Memorial Hospital
800 S Lower Sacramento Road
Lodi, CA 95242                           209-333-3136
                                         800-323-3360
                                     FAX: 209-368-3745
                                     www.lodihealth.org

*Michael Mericle, Director of Rehabilitation Unit*
*Joseph Harrington, Chief Executive Officer*

**8709**  **Long Beach Memorial Medical Center Memorial Rehabilitation Hospital**
2801 Atlantic Avenue
Long Beach, CA 90806                     562-933-2800
                                     FAX: 562-933-9018

*Trish Baeseman, Administrator*

The hospital offers rehabilitation after catastrophic injury of disabling disease to give patients the opportunity for maximum recovery. The Hospital offers many of the area's finest rehabilitation specialists and most advanced technology, making it one of Southern California's most respected rehabilitation centers.

**8710**  **Meadowbrook Neurologic Center**
340 Northlake Drive
San Jose, CA 95117                       408-249-0344
                                         800-826-9152

*Mary Ligetti, Marketing*

**8711**  **Mercy American River Hospital**
4747 Engle Road
Carmichael, CA 95608                     916-484-2222
                                     FAX: 916-482-4203

*Christine Shipman, Rehab Director*

**8712**  **North Coast Rehabilitation Center**
151 Sotoyome Street
Santa Rosa, CA 95405                     707-433-9600
                                     FAX: 707-525-8413

*Joyce Cavagnaro, Admissions*

**8713**  **North Valley Rehabilitation Hospital**
340 W East Avenue
Chico, CA 95926                          530-345-9592
                                     FAX: 530-894-4139

*Karen Geissinger, Admissions*

**8714**  **Northridge Hospital Medical Center**
18300 Roscoe Boulevard
Northridge, CA 91325                     818-885-8500
                                     FAX: 818-885-5435

*Debra Flaherty, Director Rehab Services*
*Mike Wall, Chief Executive Officer*

**8715**  **PEERS Program**
8912 W Olympic Boulevard
Beverly Hills, CA 90211                  310-553-9322
                                     FAX: 310-858-8008

*Paul Berns, Medical Director*

Offers a new approach for wheelchair users. PEERS uses a combination of modern physical therapy, the DOUGLAS Reciprocating Gait System and when necessary, functional electrical stimulation to assist selected individuals to walk with recently patented specially made lightweight braces.

**8716**  **Pacifica Nursing and Rehab Center**
385 Esplanade
Pacifica, CA 94044                       650-993-5576
                                     FAX: 650-359-9388

*Brian Ramos, Administrator*
*Lana Ronin, Director Admissions*

68 beds offering skilled nursing and complete rehabilitation services, PT, OT, Speech and respiratory therapy, social services, nutritional services, and restorative nursing care.

**8717**  **Providence Holy Cross Medical Center**
Providence Health System
15031 Rinaldi Street
Mission Hills, CA 91345                  818-898-4529
                                         888-432-5464
                                     FAX: 818-898-4472
                                     www.providence.org

*Derek Brez, Director of Case Management*
*Kerry Carmody, Chief Executive Officer*

**8718**  **Queen of Angels/Hollywood Presbyterian Medical Center**
1300 N Vermont Avenue
Los Angeles, CA 90027                    323-913-4934
                                     FAX: 323-660-0446
                             e-mail: maurine.cate@tenethealth.com
                                     www.qahpmc.com

*Lu Hallam, Program Manager*

**8719**  **Queen of the Valley Hospital**
1000 Trancas Street
Napa, CA 94558                           707-252-4411

www.thequeen.org/

*Dennis Sisto, President/Chief Executive Office*
*Jane Willemsen, Executive Vice President*

**8720  Rancho Los Amigos National Rehabilitation Center**
7601 Imperial Highway
Downey, CA 90242
562-401-7111
888-RAN-CHO
FAX: 562-401-6690
www.rancho.org

*Valerie Orange, Chief Executive Officer*
*Chris Thomas, Public Relations Director*
*Anne Potter, Director Business Development*

Specialty programs: APR, AMP, CIR, COR, DYS, HI, MT, NPT, OT, ORT, PED, PT, RN, SS, SLP, ST, TR, VR. Credentials include: JCAHO, CARF, SCI/BI/CARF approved. Prices vary, please call for information.

**8721  San Diego Rehabilitation Institute**
6645 Alvarado Road
San Diego, CA 92120
619-286-7374
FAX: 619-229-4590
www.alvaradohospital.com

*Lance Stone Do*

Provides acute and subacute level physical rehab programs specializing in brain injuries, spinal cord injuries and pulmonary/ventilator management. Outpatient programs include brain injury day treatment, pain management, visual rehabilitation and work reconditioning.

**8722  San Joaquin Valley Rehabilitation Hospital**
7173 N Sharon Avenue
Fresno, CA 93720
559-436-3600
FAX: 559-436-3688
www.sjvrehab.com

*James A Page, Director Marketing*
*Edward Palacios, Chief Executive Officer*

Complete comprehensive rehabilitation services from acute rehab, outpatient and community fitness services.

**8723  Santa Clara Valley Medical Center**
County of Santa Clara
751 S Bascom Avenue
San Jose, CA 95128
408-885-5000

www.scvmed.org

*Susan Murphy, Director*

**8724  Scripps Memorial Hospital**
354 Santa Fe Drive
Encinitas, CA 92024
760-633-7708
FAX: 760-633-7348
www.scrippshealth.org

*Chris D Van Gorder, President/CEO*
*Peter Pieslor, MD*

**8725  Scripps Memorial Hospital at La Jolla**
9888 Genesee Avenue
La Jolla, CA 92037
858-457-4123
800-727-4777
FAX: 858-626-6122
www.scrippshealth.org

*Chris D Van Gorder, President/CEO*
*Gary Fybel, Executive Director/Administrator*

**8726  Sierra Vista Regional Medical Center: Reha bilitation Center**
1010 Murray Street
San Luis Obispo, CA 93405
805-546-7600
FAX: 805-546-7871

*Emily Lipscomb PT MBA, Director*
*Jeanette Petrus PT, Community Liaison*
*Gary Stokes, Chief Executive Officer*

Acute inpatient rehabilitation center provides a seven day comprehensive inpatient treatment program for individuals suffering a disabling injury or illness and outpatient rehabilitation center providing an interdisciplinary treatment approach to rehab patients and the community.

**8727  South Coast Medical Center**
31872 Coast Highway
Laguna Beach, CA 92651
949-499-1311
FAX: 949-499-8644
e-mail: info@southcoastmedcenter.com
www.southcoastmedcenter.com

*Martha A Farrington, VP/Executive Director*
*Timothy Mcmahon, Chairman*
*Bruce Christian, President*

A 208 bed acute care hospital. Services include maternity, surgical, subacute care, psychiatric program, eating disorder treatment, chemical dependency treatment, radiology, ICU/CCU, comprehensive rehabilitation services, bariatric surgery and movement disorders program..

**8728  St. Joseph Rehabilitation Center**
St. Joseph Health System
2200 Harrison Avenue
Eureka, CA 95501
707-445-5111
FAX: 707-441-4429

*Michael Purvis, Chief Executive Officer*
*Sam Fallon, Rehabilitation Director*

Comprehensive inpatient and outpatient rehabilitation services.

**8729  St. Jude Brain Injury Network**
St. Jude Hospital
251 Imperial Highway
Suite 440
Fullerton, CA 92835
714-449-4848
866-785-8332
FAX: 714-447-0987
e-mail: jgable@sif.stjoe.org
www.pdioc.org

*Jana Gable, Program Coordinator*
*David Bogdan, Service Coordinator*
*Lina Marroquin, Servicer Coordinator*

Provides comprehensive planning, program referral, assists with funding possibilities, and interagency coordination of services. Areas of emphasis include day treatment, vocational and housing options, and the requirements are adults who have suffered a brain injury from an external force.

**8730  St. Jude Medical Center**
101 E Valencia Mesa Drive
Fullerton, CA 92835
714-871-3280

www.stjudemedicalcenter.org

*Robert Fraschetti, President/CEO*

A 331 bed full-service regional medical center that serves as a major referral hospital attracting rehabilitation patients throughout southern California for over twenty years.

**8731  St. Mary Medical Center**
1050 Linden Avenue
Long Beach, CA 90813
562-491-9000
FAX: 562-436-6378
www.smmc.com

*Joel Yuhas, Chief Executive Officer*

A 556-bed hospital owned by the Sisters of Charity of the Incarnate World Healthcare Systems, one of the nation's largest Catholic healthcare networks. Services include a trauma unit, a comprehensive Cancer Care Center, complete older adult services, a Low Vision Center, a Rehabilitation Institute, an outpatient Surgi/Center and the only kidney transplant program in Long Beach. St. Mary's is a teaching hospital affiliated with the UCLA School of Medicine.

**8732  Sunnyside Nursing Center**
22617 S Vermont Avenue
Torrance, CA  90502                    310-320-4130
                                  FAX: 310-320-8602

*John Macarthur, Director*
*Judy Marolda, Administrator*

**8733  Tustin Rehabilitation Hospital**
14851 Yorba Street
Tustin, CA  92780                     714-832-9200
                                  FAX: 714-508-4550
                                  www.healthsouth.com

*Linda McCaskill, Chief Executive Officer*
*Scott Rifken, President*

**8734  UCLA Medical Center: Department of Anesthesiology,**
**Acute Pain Services**
U CL A Medical Center
1245 16th Street Medical Plaza
Suite 225
Santa Monica, CA  90404               310-319-4000
                                  FAX: 310-794-1511
                                  www.medcnt.ucla.edu

*Michael Ferrante, Clinical Director*
*William Parente, MD*

**8735  White Memorial Medical Center Rehabilitation**
Adventist Healthcare
1720 E Cesar E Chavez Avenue
Los Angeles, CA  90033                323-260-4622
                                       800-995-4389
                                  FAX: 323-881-8736
                                  e-mail: riveras1@ah.org
                                  www.whitememorial.com

*Samantha Rivera, Admission Coordinator*
*Sherry Foldvary, Director*
*Mona Marin, Manager*

Strokes/neurological disorders, brain injury, musculoskeletal
injuries, pulmonary disorders, developmental disorders (arthritis, cardiac rehabilitation), cleft palate, fractures, amputations,
joint replacement, burns, swallowing disorders, pain and more.

# Colorado

**8736  Children's Hospital Rehabilitation Center**
University of Colorado Health Sciences Center
1056 E 19th Avenue
Denver, CO  80218                     303-315-3297
                                       800-629-6553
                                  e-mail: webmaster@tchden.org
                                  www.thechildrenshospital.org

*Doris J Biester, Chief Executive Officer*
*Michael J Farrell, Chief Operating Officer*
*Helen Martinez, Manager*

**8737  Craig Hospital**
3425 S Clarkson Street
Englewood, CO  80113                  303-789-8000
                                  FAX: 303-789-8219
                                  e-mail: administration@craighospital.org
                                  www.craighospital.org

*Mary Hewitt, Director Health Information Serv*
*Dennis O'Malley, President*

Offers the following rehabilitation services: Traumatic Brain
Injury Rehab, Spinal Cord Injury Rehab

**8738  Mapleton Center**
Boulder Community Hospital
311 Mapleton Avenue
Boulder, CO  80304                    303-440-2273
                                  FAX: 303-440-2435
                                  www.bch.org

*David Gehant, President*

Comprehensive inpatient and outpatient rehabilitation services
for all age groups. Treatment provided by interdisciplinary
teams and staff physicians. CARF accredited in brain injury rehabilitation, pediatric rehabilitation, pain management, work
hardening and inpatient rehabilitation.

**8739  Mediplex Rehab: Denver**
Vibra Health Care
8451 Pearl Street
Thornton, CO  80229                   303-288-3000
                                  FAX: 303-286-1253
                                  www.northvalleyrehab.com

*Walter Sacckett, Chief Executive Officer*

**8740  Rehabilitation Hospital of Colorado Springs**
325 Parkside Drive
Colorado Springs, CO  80910           719-630-2313
                                  FAX: 719-636-3772

**8741  Spalding Rehabilitation Hospital**
Healthone
900 Potomac Street
Aurora, CO  80011                     303-367-1166
                                  FAX: 303-360-8208
         e-mail: Syntax error: , lookahead: , current char: 0
                                  www.spaldingrehab.com

*Rose Reinhardt, Marketing/Business Development*
*Cindy Kreutz, Chief Executive Officer*

Rebuilding Lives, Renewing Hope is the mission at Spalding
Rehabilitation Hospital. We offer acute inpatient and outpatient
rehabilitation services at 3 convenient locations in the Denver
metro area. Spalding specializes in treating the neurologically
injured patient, including stroke and traumatic brain injury.

# Connecticut

**8742  Mariner Health Care: Connecticut**
125 Eugene Oneill Drive
New London, CT  06320                 860-701-2000

# District of Columbia

**8743  National Rehabilitation Hospital**
102 Irving Street MW
Washington, DC  20010                 202-877-1000
                                  TTY:202-877-1450

*Edward A Eckenhoff, President/CEO*
*Robert S Hartmann, VP Communications*

A private facility dedicated solely to medical rehabilitation. The
hospital offers intensive inpatient programs and full-service
outpatient programs.

## Florida

**8744 Brooks Rehabilitation**
Brooks Health Foundation
3599 University Boulevard S
Jacksonville, FL 32216
904-858-7600
800-487-7342
FAX: 904-858-7610
e-mail: rehab@brookshealth.org
www.brookshealth.org

*Douglas M Baer, President/CEO*
*Joanna Buzar, Public Relations*

A 127 bed rehabilitation hospital focused on treatment of brain and spinal cord injuries, orthopedic and neurological impairment. Treating adults and pediatrics in our hospital and outpatient network.

**8745 Florida Hospital Rehabilitation Center**
601 E Rollins Street
Orlando, FL 32803
407-893-8055
FAX: 407-893-9459

*Diane Lowder, Admissions Director*

**8746 HealthSouth Regional Rehab Center/Florida**
20601 Old Cutler Road
Miami, FL 33189
305-251-3800
FAX: 305-251-0498
www.healthsouth.com

*Murray Rolnic, Medical Director*
*Jackie Arocho, Chief Executive Officer*

**8747 HealthSouth Rehab Hospital: Largo**
901 Clearwater Largo Road N
Largo, FL 33770
727-586-2999
FAX: 727-588-3404

*Sherri Beasley, Director Marketing Operations*
*Vicki Yasoua, Manager*

Inpatient acute rehabilitation 70 beds.

**8748 HealthSouth Sports Medicine and Rehabilitation Center**

2141 a S
Lt A1
Jupiter, FL 33477
561-743-8890
FAX: 561-840-8637

*Curtis Becker PT, Administrator*
*Diane Reiley, Manager*

Outpatient orthopedic and sports medicine/physical therapy.

**8749 HealthSouth Sunrise Rehabilitation Hospital**
4399 N Nob Hill Road
Sunrise, FL 33351
954-746-1501
800-648-9111
FAX: 954-746-1300

*Fran Warm Hundley RN, CEO*
*Dave Rafter, PR Representative*
*Matthew Deutscher, MD*

A 108-bed, JCAHO-accredited, comprehensive medical rehabilitation hospital treating patients from throughout South Florida, the Caribbean and Latin America. HEALTHSOUTH Sunrise Rehabilitation Hospital is known for its CARF-accredited specialty programs, including brain injury, spinal cord, pain management, traumatic burns, and pediatrics. Services available on inpatient and outpatient basis.

**8750 HealthSouth Treasure Coast Rehabilitation Hospital**
Health South Corporation of Alabama
1600 37th Street
Vero Beach, FL 32960
772-778-2100
FAX: 772-567-6916
www.healthsouth.com

*Jason Roebach, Chief Executive Officer*
*Teresa Hilton, Director Marketing Operations*

HealthSouth Treasure Coast Rehabilitation Hospital is a 90-bed inpatient comprehensive rehabilitation hospital serving Indian River, St. Lucie, Martin and Okeechobee counties. Outpatient services are available at the hospital and at four other clinics. Therapies include physical, occupational, speech and psychology services.

**8751 Infusion Therapies**
7901 SW 36th Street
Suite 206
Davie, FL 33328
800-342-3777
FAX: 954-452-4262

Specializes in fully managed enteral and parenteral therapies. Offers pharmaceuticals, supplies, pumps, equipment and delivery. Infusion cares for pediatrics to geriatrics, patients at home, in extended care facilities, clinics, physician offices, adult congregate living facilities are on site. Provides IV hydration, chemotherapy, gastric/tube feedings, lab/blood work and medical equipment and supplies.

**8752 Manatee Springs Care & Rehabilitation Center**
5627 9th Street E
Bradenton, FL 34203
941-753-8941
FAX: 941-756-7563
e-mail: cbrooks@seniorcaregroup.com

*Cynthia Brooks, Director Adimissions*
*Donna Steiermann, Administrator*

Skilled rehabilitation facility specializing in PT, OT, speech therapy, aquatic therapy and an indoor pool. Piped oxygen bed for specialized respiratory care. Compassionate end of life care. Some Medicare, private insurance, and Medicaid.

**8753 Miami Rehabilitation Institute**
3280 Ponce De Leon Boulevard
Coral Gables, FL 33134
305-444-0909
FAX: 305-444-5760
www.healthsouth.com

*Jay Greeney, President*
*Ray Jaffet, Administrator*

**8754 Perry Health Facility**
207 Forest Drive
Perry, FL 32347
850-584-6334
FAX: 850-838-2370

*Jo Ann Gnewuch, Facility Administrator*
*Michael Brust, Director Rehabilitation*

Full rehabilitation team available, Physiatrist, DOR, Psychiatrist, Psychologist, RD, Geriatric Nursing, PT/OT/ST/RT, Orthotiet/Prosthetist. Provider for PPO's & HMO's as well as medicare, private insurance and medicare/medicaid.

**8755 Pinecrest Rehabilitation Hospital and Outpatient Centers**
Tenet South Florida
5360 Linton Boulevard
Delray Beach, FL 33484
561-495-0400
800-686-7632
FAX: 561-499-6812
www.pinecrestrehab.com

*Ruth Stewart, Chief Operating Officer*
*Migtiala Hernandez, Human Resources Executive*

Pinecrest Rehabilitation Hospital is a 90 bed, accredited hospital and is comprised of a Specialty Unit, a Neuro Trauma Unit and Joint Replacement Unit. Additional services at Pincrest include six outpatient rehab centers throughout Palm Beach County. The Outpatient Centers each focus on various specialties such as orthopedic and neurological rehab, pain management, cardiac and pulmonary rehab, occupational medicine, Hearing Institute, dizziness and balance and wellness.

**8756 Rehabilitation Institute of Sarasota**

3251 Proctor Road
Sarasota, FL 34231 941-923-4625
FAX: 941-922-6228

**8757 Sea Pines Rehabilitation Hospital**

101 E Florida Avenue
Melbourne, FL 32901 321-984-4600
FAX: 321-727-7440

*Denise Grath, Chief Executive Officer*

**8758 Shriners Hospitals for Children**

Shriners International Headquarters
2900 N Rocky Point Drive
Tampa, FL 33607 813-281-0300
800-237-5055
FAX: 813-281-8496
www.shrinershq.org

*Alicia Argiz Lyons, PR Director*
*Jessica Kappaz, Projects Manager*
*Brad Nease, Corporate Website Manager*

Provide specialized acute and reconstructive burn care, orthopaedic care and spinal cord injury rehabilitation to children under 18 at absolutely no cost to the child or family. No insurance monies or government funds are sought or received. Call for application or visit our website.

**8759 Shriners Hospitals for Children: Tampa**

12502 Pine Drive
Tampa, FL 33612 813-972-2250
813-281-0300
FAX: 813-978-9442
www.shrinershq.org

*Alice Lanford, Chief Executive Oficer*
*Alicia Argiz-Lyons, Director Public Relations*

Pediatric orthopedic.

**8760 South Miami Hospital**

6200 SW 73rd Street
South Miami, FL 33143 305-661-4611

www.baptisthealth.net

*Hubert Alan Aronson, Medical Director*
*Wayne Brackin, Chief Executive Officer*

**8761 St. Anthony's Hospital**

1200 7th Avenue N
St Petersburg, FL 33705 727-825-1100

www.stanthonys.com

*Ian Payne, Director*
*Ford Kyes, Chief Executive Officer*

Offers the following rehabilitation services: Sub-Acute rehabilitation, Occupational Therapy, Speech/Language Pathology services, Physical Therapy.

**8762 Tampa General Rehabilitation Center**

PO Box 1289
Tampa, FL 33601 813-844-7000
FAX: 813-253-4283
www.tgh.org

*Ron Hytoff, Chief Executive Officer*
*Annie Sod, Admission Nurse*
*Sandra Taylor, Admission Nurse*

Offers a full range of inpatient and outpatient programs all aimed at helping patients achieve their full potentials. JCAHO and CARF accredited and V.R. designated center. A wide range of inpatient and outpatient programs are available such as Brain and Spinal Cord Injury Programs, Comprehensive Medical Rehabilitation, Pain Management, Cardiac Rehab, Pediatric Therapy Service, Sleep Disorders, Epilepsy, and Wheelchair Seating.Hosts the Florida Alliance for Assistive Services and Technolgy.

**8763 University of Miami: Jackson Memorial Rehabilitation Center**

University of Miami
1611 NW 12th Avenue
Miami, FL 33136 305-585-7275
FAX: 305-585-6092

*Mark Brown, Manager*

**8764 West Gables Rehabilitation Hospital and Healthcare Center**

2525 SW 75th Avenue
Miami, FL 33155 305-262-6800
FAX: 305-264-9031

*Charlotte Raymor, Chief Executive Officer*

Offers case management services, patient services, a neurological rehabilitation program, cancer rehabilitation, spinal cord injury rehabilitation, orthopedic program, functional restoration and pain management programs, as well as outpatient programs.

**8765 Winter Park Memorial Hospital**

200 N Lakemont Avenue
Winter Park, FL 32792 407-646-7001
FAX: 407-646-7639
e-mail: healthcare@winterparkhospital.com
www.winterparkhospital.com

*Ken Bradley, Chief Executive Officer*
*Ben Everidge, Developmental Office*

Offers Acute Rehabilitation.

## Georgia

**8766 Candler General Hospital: Rehabilitation Unit**

5353 Reynolds Street
Savannah, GA 31405 912-819-6000
FAX: 912-692-2039

*Virginia Donaldson, Admissions Director*

**8767 Children's Healthcare of Atlanta at Egleston**

1405 Clifton Road NE
Atlanta, GA 30322 404-315-3070
FAX: 404-315-2158

*Tricia Easley, Satellite Manager*

Rehabilitation Center at Egleston accepts children from birth to age 18 with acute or chronic problems. The length of rehab stay varies for each child according to the determined program of care. The center offers inpatient, outpatient & day rehab programs for comprehensive evaluation & treatment. The program emphasizes the development of the child's abilities & concentrates on helping the family & child compensate for any long-term disabilities. Short term stays require one or two weeks.

**8768    Cobb Hospital and Medical Center: Rehab Ca re Center**
3950 Austell Road
Austell, GA  30106                           770-732-4000

e-mail: Web.Master@WellStar.org
www.wellstar.org

*Gerald W Bortolazzo, Medical Director*
*Donald Campbell, Medical Director*
*Randy Cook, Administrator*

**8769    Emory Healthcare Center for Rehabilitation Medicine**
1441 Clifton Road NE
Atlanta, GA  30322                           404-778-5000
800-753-6679
FAX: 404-712-4746
e-mail: sheryl_hope@emoryhealthcare.org
www.emoryhealthcare.org

*Sheryl Hope, Manager Admissions/Referrals*
*Sara Swanson, Intake Nurse Coordinator*
*Devera Brown, Outpatient Services Manager*

Dedicated to restoring wholeness to a patient after experiencing a stroke, brain injury, spinal cord injury or other disabling injury or illness. Offers an entire interdisciplinary team who work with patients to help them regain or compensate for lost abilities and to adapt to the many changes in their lives. Services provide a continuum of care by offering a wide variety of inpatient/outpatient programs.

**8770    HealthSouth Central Georgia Rehabilitation Hospital**
3351 Northside Drive
Macon, GA  31210                            478-471-3500
FAX: 478-474-6601

*Vernona L Moseley, Director Market Operations*
*Beverly Owens, Controller*

HealthSouth Central Georgia rehabilitation hospital is a 55 bed comprehensive medical rehabilitation hospital meeting the medical patients and famloity members in Central Georgia.

**8771    Shepherd Center**
Shepherd Center
2020 Peachtree Road NW
Atlanta, GA  30309                           404-350-7355
FAX: 404-350-7773

*Gary R Ulicny PhD, President/CEO*
*James Shepherd, Chairman*

A private hospital specializing in treatment of people with spinal cord and acquired brain injury, multiple sclerosis and other neuromuscular diseases, and urological diseases. Houses the largest model spinal cord injury program in the country and the Southeastern Multiple Sclerosis Center, designated by the National Multiple Sclerosis Society. Serving the Southeast since 1975, the 100-bed specialty hospital offers a continuum of services from intensive care through rehabilitation.

**8772    Specialty Hospital**
Floyd Healthcare Resources
PO Box 233
Rome, GA  30162                             706-802-4100
FAX: 706-802-4175

*Mark Fall, Chief Executive Officer*
*Susan Stovall, Chief Operations Officer*
*Jon Dixon, Administrator*

Offers acute rehabilitation.

# Hawaii

**8773    Shriners Hospital for Children: Honolulu**
1310 Punahou Street
Honolulu, HI  96826                          808-941-4466
888-888-6314
FAX: 808-942-8573
www.shrinershq.org

*Susan Yammoto, Assistant Coordinator*
*Iwalani Deyton, Public Relations Director*
*Thomas Schneider, Administrator*

One of 22 hospitals across North America that provide excellent, no-cost medical care to children with orthopedic problems and burn industries.

# Idaho

**8774    Eastern Idaho Regional Medical Center Rehabilitation Program**
3100 Channing Way
Idaho Falls, ID  83404                       208-529-6111
800-575-8426
FAX: 208-529-7075

*Doug Crabtree, Chief Executive Officer*

CARF certified rehabilitation program in Eastern Idaho, providing acute medical rehabilitation services to patients recovering from strokes, spinal cord injury, head trauma, amputation, fractures, arthritis, multiple trauma, neurological disorders, burns, congenital deformity, generalized deconditioning, etc. The rehabilitation team consists of three psychiatrists, physical therapists, occupational therapists, speech pathologists, etc.

**8775    Pocatello Regional Medical Center**
777 Hospital Way
Pocatello, ID  83201                         208-236-6920
FAX: 208-239-3719

*Edward Shafer, Manager*

# Illinois

**8776    Builders of Skills**
9021 N Clifton Avenue
Niles, IL  60714                             847-296-6783
FAX: 847-824-6539
www.avenuestoindependence.org

*Bob Okavaki, Director*
*Jay Patel, Manager*

Residential setting for hearing-impaired, developmentally disabled adults who are assisted with daily living skills.

**8777    Center for Learning**
National-Louis University
2840 Sheridan Road
Evanston, IL  60201                          847-475-1100

*Jerry Dachs, Manager*

Psychoeducational evaluations for children, adolescents, and adults.

**8778 Illinois Center for Rehabilitation and Education (ICRE-Wood)**
U IC Interdisciplinary Phd Program and dissabiliti
1640 W Rosenburg Road
Chicago, IL 60608
312-996-1508
FAX: 312-996-0885
www.ahs.uic.edu/ahs/php/intex.php?sightname=t

*Carol Gill, Director*

Residential rehabilitation center for adults who are blind or visually impaired.

**8779 Institute of Physical Medicine and Rehabilitation**
6501 North Sheridan Road
Peoria, IL 61614
309-692-8110
800-957-4767
FAX: 309-692-8673
www.ipmr.org

*Richard Erickson, President*
*Sue Paul, Manager*

Comprehensive CARF accredited programs in outpatient medical rehabilitation services. Eight outpatient locations, specialty programs include adult day services, driving evaluations, balance and visual rehabilitation board certified physiatrists.

**8780 LaRabida Children's Hospital and Research Center**
E 65th and Lake Michigan
Chicago, IL 60649
773-753-8646
FAX: 773-363-9554

*Paula Jaudas, Executive Director*

Counseling, educational services, medical and nursing services for children through age 18.

**8781 Marianjoy Rehabilitation Hospital and Clinics**
26 W 171 Roosevelt Road
Wheaton, IL 60187
630-462-4000
800-462-2366
FAX: 630-462-4440
www.marianjoy.org

*Kathleen Yosko, President/CEO*
*Debbie Gambino, Manager*

**8782 Regional ADA Technical Assitance Agency**
1640 W Roosevelt Road
Chicago, IL 60608
312-413-1407
800-949-4232
FAX: 312-413-1856
e-mail: gldbtac@uic.edu
www.adagreatlakes.org

*Robin Jones, Project Director*

provides training, technical assistance and consultation on the rights and resposibilities of indiviualsand entities covered by the ADA. Toll free number for technical assistance and materials provided electronically or via mail at no cost.

**8783 Rehabilitation Institute of Chicago**
345 E Superior Street
Chicago, IL 60611
312-238-1000
800-354-REHA
www.ric.org

*Wayne Lerner, President & CEO*
*Henry Betts, Chairman*

Each year more than 14,000 children and adults benefit from the full range of inpatient, outpatient, day treatment and subacute services offered by the Rehabilitation Institute of Chicago (RIC) at its 18 sites of care. Specialized treatment programs include: amputee, arthritis, brain injury, burn, general rehab, pain management and more. RIC is an academic affiliate of Northwestern University Medical School and houses the nation's largest residency program in physical medicine.

**8784 Rush Copley Medical Center-Rehab Neuro Physical Unit**
2000 Ogden Avenue
Aurora, IL 60504
630-978-6250
866-426-7539
FAX: 630-218-3504
e-mail: ckovarik@rsh.net
www.rushcopley.com

*Richard Edelman, President*
*Barry C Finn, President/CEO*
*Rush Copley, MD*

**8785 Shriners Hospitals for Children: Chicago**
2211 N Oak Park Avenue
Chicago, IL 60707
773-622-5400
800-237-5055
FAX: 773-385-5453
e-mail: vlwalter@earthlink.net
www.shrinerschicago.org

*Shana Jones, Chief Executive Officer*
*Beth Mikalauskas, Manager for Outpatient Clinic*
*Vickie Walter, Director Public Relations*

A leading Midwest children's hospital providing high quality orthopedic treatments, plastic and reconstructive surgery, and spinal cord injury care with innovative education and research, the hospital is one of 22 operated by the Shrine fraternity, the only health care system in the US funded totally through philanthropy. Any child under 18 is eligable for treatment, as long as there is a reasonable possibility that there will benefit the child.

**8786 Wood River Township Hospital: RehabCare Unit**
Edwardsville Road
Wood River, IL 62095
618-254-3134
FAX: 618-251-4307

*Jo Anne Baker, Clinical Coordinator*
*Richard Wilson, Owner*

---

# Indiana

**8787 ATTAIN**
U S Department of Education/ NI DR R
32 E Washington Street
Suite 1400
Indianapolis, IN 46204
317-486-8808
FAX: 317-486-8809
e-mail: attain@attaininc.org
www.attaininc.org

*Gary Hand, Executive Director*
*Mary Duff, Executive Assistant*

**8788 Clark Memorial Hospital: RehabCare Unit**
1220 Missouri Avenue
Jeffersonville, IN 47130
812-282-6631
FAX: 812-283-2656

*Jan Goldhammer, Program Manager*
*Carter Brown, MD*

**8789 Developmental Disabilities Planning Council**
140 W Market Street
Suite 628
Indianapolis, IN 46204
317-232-7770
FAX: 317-233-3712
www.state.in.us/gpcpd

*Suellen Jackson-Boner, Director*

**8790 Down Syndrome Association of North East Indiana**
PO Box 80141
Fort Wayne, IN 46898
260-471-9964
877-713-7264
www.indianadsf.org

Steve Simpson, President
Sherri O'Keefe, Vice President

**8791 Easter Seals Wayne/Union Counties**
5632 US Highway 40 E
PO Box 86
Centerville, IN 47330
765-855-2482
FAX: 756-855-2482
e-mail: easterseals@juno.com
eastersealswu.tripod.com

Pat Bowers, Executive Director

Helps people discover nature and much more at camps equipped to offer physcial, social and emotional support and fun for campers with physical and/or developmental disabilities.

**8792 IN Speechl Language-Hearing Association**
1829 Cunningham Road
PO Box 24167
Indianapolis, IN 46224
317-916-4146
FAX: 317-481-1825
e-mail: ann@centraloffice1.com
www.islha.org

Michael Flahive, President

ISHA is to support its members in the provision of quality services through advocacy, professional development, and public awareness.

**8793 IN-SOURCE**
Indiana Resource Center for Families with Special
809 Nosth Michigan Street
South Bend, IN 46601
574-234-7101
800-332-4433
FAX: 574-234-7294
e-mail: insource@insource.org
www.insource.org

Richard Burden, Executive Director
Scott Carson, Assistant Director

**8794 Indiana Congress of Parent and Teachers**
2525 N Shadeland Avenue
Indianapolis, IN 46219
317-357-5881
FAX: 317-357-3751
e-mail: pta@indianapta.org
www.indianapta.org

Marilyn Jones, President
Tina Hartman, Vice President

**8795 Indiana Parent Information Association**
4755 Kingsway Drive
Suite 105-A
Indianapolis, IN 46205
317-257-8683
800-964-4746
FAX: 317-251-7488
e-mail: FamilyNetw@ipin.org
www.ipin.org

Rebecca Kirby, Executive Director

**8796 Indiana Resource Center for Autism**
Indiana Institute on Disability and Community
2853 E 10th Street
Bloomington, IN 47408
812-855-9396
FAX: 812-855-9630
e-mail: prattc@indiana.edu
www.iidc.indiana.edu/irca

Cathy Pratt, Director
Marilyn Irwin, Executive Director

The Indiana Resource Center for Autism staff conduct outreach training and consultations, engage in research and develop and disseminate information focused on building the capicity of local communities, organizations, agencies and families to support children and adults across the autism spectrum in typical work, school, home and community settings. Please check our website for a complete list of publications.

**8797 Kokomo Rehabilitation Hospital**
829 N Dixon Road
Kokomo, IN 46901
FAX: 765-868-8108

Brenda Harry, Admissions Director

**8798 Learning Disabilities Association of IN**
1508 E 86th Street
#275
Indianapolis, IN 46240
800-284-2519
www.lda-in.org

Dawn Lytle, IN State President

Committed to promoting awareness, knowledge and acceptance of individuals with LD and AD/HD by encouraging early detection, appropriate educational services, accommodations and programs at all educational levels, vocational and career opportunities, and by offering information, advocacy training and support through the annual state conference, newsletter, chapters and contact persons located across Indiana.

**8799 Memorial Regional Rehabilitation Center**
615 N Michigan Street
South Bend, IN 46601
574-647-7312
FAX: 574-647-3195
www.qualityoflife.org

Phil Newbold, Chief Executive Officer
Carl Ellison, Vice President
Sue Wright, Manager

20-bed CARF accredited inpatient rehabilitation, outpatient orthopedic clinic and work performance program, head injury clinic. Outpatient neuro rehab and a driver education and training program are provided.

**8800 Mental Health Association in Indiana**
1431 N Delaware Street
Indianapolis, IN 46202
317-685-8497
800-555-6424
e-mail: mhai@mentalhealthassociation.com
www.mentalhealthassociation.com

Stephen McCaffrey, President/CEO
Marjorie Mansfield, Executive Vice President/COO

**8801 Methodist Hospital Rehabilitation Institute**
8701 Broadway
Merrillville, IN 46410
219-738-5500
FAX: 219-738-6636

James Berg, Chief Executive Officer

**8802 NAMI Indiana**
PO Box 22697
Indianapolis, IN 46222
317-925-9399
800-677-6442
FAX: 317-925-9398
e-mail: nami-in@nami.org
www.namiindiana.org

Pamela McConey, Executive Director

**8803  Parkview Regional Rehabilitation Center**
2200 Randallia Drive
Fort Wayne, IN  46805                    260-373-4280

*Elizabeth Williamson, Admissions Coordinator*
*Sheryl Scott, Executive Director*

**8804  Programs for Children with Disabilities: Ages 3 through 5**
Department of Education
229 State House
Indianapolis, IN  46204                  317-232-0506
                                         877-851-4106
                                    FAX: 317-232-0589
                        e-mail: scochran@doe.state.in.us
                           www.doe.state.in.us/exceptional

*Robert A Marra, Assistant Superintendent*
*Sheron Cochran, Preschool Coordinator*
*Suellen Reed, Chief Executive Officer*

**8805  Programs for Children with Special Health Care Needs**
2 N Meridian Street
Indianapolis, IN  46204                  317-233-5578

                        e-mail: wgettelf@isdh.state.in.us

*Wendy Gettelfinger, Director*

**8806  Programs for Infants and Toddlers with Disabilities: Ages Birth through 2**
402 W Washington Street
Room W386
Indianapolis, IN  46204                  317-233-9292

                         e-mail: mgreer@fssa.state.in.us

**8807  Protection and Advocacy Agency of Indiana**
4701 N Keystone Avenue
Suite 222
Indianapolis, IN  46205                  317-722-5555
                                         800-838-1131
                                    FAX: 317-722-5564
                          e-mail: info@ipas.state.in.us
                                    www.state.in.us

*Thomas Gallagher, Executive Director*

**8808  Riley Child Development Center**
702 Barnhill Drive
Room 5837
Indianapolis, IN  46202                  317-274-8168

                          e-mail: jdrau@child-dev.com

*Steven Viehweg, Manager*

**8809  Saint Vincent Pediatric Rehabilitation Center**
PO Box 40407
Indianapolis, IN  46240                  317-415-5500
                                    FAX: 317-415-5595

*Ann Coon, Referral Coordinator*
*Diane Reeder, Case Manager*
*Lori Leach, Manager*

A free-standing pediatric facility providing children with the opportunity to grow physically and emotionally. SVPRC offers
specialty programs in burn treatment, Cerebral Palsy, feeding
disorders, juvenile rheumatoid arthritis, neuromuscular disorders, orthopedic conditions, spinal cord injuries, traumatic brain
injuries, and children who require pulmonary rehab. Patients are
involved with a professional interdisciplinary team, nurses, respiratory therapists, social workers and others.

**8810  Spina Bifida Association of Northern IN**
PO Box 1935
South Bend, IN  46634                    574-234-6260

*Carla Beres, Director*

**8811  St. Anthony Memorial Hospital: Rehab Unit**
301 W Homer Street
Michigan City, IN  46360                 219-879-8511
                                    FAX: 219-877-1838

*Doran Lounsbury, Program Manager*
*Bruce Rampage, President*

**8812  State Blind and Visually Impaired Services Agency**
PO Box 7083
Indianapolis, IN  46207                  317-232-1143
                                         800-962-8408
                                    FAX: 317-233-1566
                                    www.in.gov/fssa/dhhs

*James Van Mannen, Interim Deputy Director*

**8813  State Developmental Disability Agency**
PO Box 7083
Indianapolis, IN  46207                  317-323-7842

*Steven C Cook, Director*

**8814  State Division of Vocational Rehabilitation**
PO Box 7083
Indianapolis, IN  46207                  317-232-1401
                                         800-545-7763
                         e-mail: martin@fssa.state.in.us
                                    www.state.in.us/fssa

*Rita Martin, Deputy Director*
*Mike Hedden, Executive Director*

**8815  State Mental Health Agency**
402 W Washington Street
Room W353
Indianapolis, IN  46204                  317-232-7845
                                    FAX: 317-233-3472
                                    www.IN.gov/fssa

*Cathy Boggs, Director*

**8816  State Mental Health Representative for Children**
Division of Mental Health and Addiction
402 W Washington Street
Room W353
Indianapolis, IN  46204                  317-232-7824
                                    FAX: 317-233-3472
                        e-mail: cheryl.shearer@fssa.in.gov
                                    www.in.gov/sa

*Cheryl Shearer, Chief Executive Officers*

**8817  VSA Arts of Indiana**
Harrison Center for the Arts
1505 N Delaware Street
Suite 100
Indianapolis, IN  46202                  317-974-4123
                                    FAX: 317-974-4124
                              e-mail: gholtman@vsai.org
                                    www.vsai.org

*Gayle Holtman, Director*
*James Nulty, Executive Director*

**8818  Wabash Valley Spina Bifida Support Group**
PO Box 21
Farmersburg, IN 47850                812-696-2288

e-mail: sbawareness@hoymail.com
www.homestead.com/planetzachary/main.html

*Kim Zink, Coordinator*

## Iowa

**8819  Younker Rehabilitation Center of Iowa Methodist Medical Center**
1200 Pleasant Street
Des Moines, IA 50309                515-241-6741
FAX: 515-241-5872

*Fran Wendling, Admissions Coordinator*
*Sue Knapp, Manager*

## Kansas

**8820  Kansas Rehabilitation Hospital**
1504 SW 8th Avenue
Topeka, KS 66606                785-235-6600
FAX: 785-232-8556

*Julie DeJean, Administrator*
*Paul Livingston, Chief Executive Officer*

**8821  Mid-America Rehabilitation Hospital HealthSouth**
Health South Corporation
5701 W 110th Street
Overland Park, KS 66211                913-491-2400
FAX: 913-491-1097
e-mail: tiffany.kiehl@healthsouth.com
www.healthsouth.com

*Kristen DeHart, Chief Executive Officer*
*Tiffany Kiehl, Director Marketing/Operations*
*Melissa Higgins, Director Clinical Services*

80 bed Acute Rehab hospital offering full continuum from in-patient, day treatment and outpatient services for individuals with physical limitations due to CVA, TBI, SCI, other traumas, joint replacement, etc.

## Kentucky

**8822  Cardinal Hill Rehabilitation Hospital**
2050 Versailles Road
Lexington, KY 40504                859-254-5701
800-888-5377
FAX: 859-255-9303
e-mail: webmaster@cardinalhill.org
www.cardinalhill.org

*Sandy Shill CRRN, Manager Referral Relations*
*Beth A Monarch, COO*
*Kerry Gillihan, Chief Executive Officer*

CARF-accredited rehab center provides comprehensive inpatient and outpatient services in two locations to people with physical and cognitive disabilities. We provide diagnosis-specific programs to 100 inpatients, outpatient clinics, outpatient therapies, pain management and therapeutic pool services. The Pediatric Center serves children from birth to age 18 years of age.

**8823  HealthSouth Rehabilitation of Louisville**
1227 Goss Avenue
Louisville, KY 40217                502-636-1200
FAX: 502-636-0351
www.healthsouth.com

*Michele McCoy, Marketing Representative*
*Regina Durbin, Administrator*

**8824  Humana Hospital: Lake Cumberland Rehab Uni t**
305 Langdon Street
Somerset, KY 42503                606-679-7441
FAX: 606-679-5739

*Chris Lovelace, Program Manager*
*Jeff Seraphine, Chief Executive Officer*

**8825  Lakeview Rehabilitation Hospital**
134 Heartland Drive
Elizabethtown, KY 42701                270-769-3100
FAX: 270-769-6870

*Diane Stephens, Assistant Director Marketing*
*Lorrie Young, Marketing Executive*

40-beds, comprehensive physical rehabilitation.

**8826  Shriners Hospitals for Children, Lexington**
1900 Richmond Road
Lexington, KY 40502                859-266-2101
800-444-8314
FAX: 859-268-5636
www.shrinershq.org

*Joan Snowden, Director Family/Cmmty Service*
*Tony Lewgood, Administrator*

A 50-bed, pediatric orthopedic hospital providing FREE, expert orthopedic medical care to children and adolescents in Kentucky, Tennessee, West Virginia, Ohio, and Indiana.

## Louisiana

**8827  HealthSouth Specialty Hospital Of North Louisiana**
1401 Ezelle Street
Ruston, LA 71270                318-251-5427
800-548-9157
FAX: 318-251-5491
www.healthsouth.com

*Mark Rice, Executive Director*

Specialty hospital offering both inpatient and outpatient services.

**8828  Our Lady of Lourdes Rehabilitation Center**
611 Saint Landry Street
Lafayette, LA 70506                337-289-2000
FAX: 318-289-2681

*William Barrow, Chief Executive Officer*

**8829  Rehabilitation Center of Lake Charles Memorial Hospital**
Lake Charles Memorial Hospital
1701 Oak Park Boulevard
Lake Charles, LA 70601                337-494-3000
FAX: 337-494-2656
www.lcmh.com

*Candy Marks, Director*
*Elton Williams Jr, Chief Executive Officer*

Rehabilitation center offering intensive physical, occupational, speech, neuropsychology, recreational therapies along with rehabilitation nursing.

**8830  Shriners Hospital for Children-Shreveport**
3100 Samford Avenue
Shreveport, LA  71103            318-222-5704
                                FAX: 318-424-7610
                                www.shrinershc.org

*Kim Green, Administrator*
*Gail Rains, Director of Patient Services*

**8831  South Louisiana Rehabilitation Hospital**
715 W Worthy Street
Gonzales, LA  70737            225-647-8277

e-mail: soberup@powerhouseprograms.com
www.powerhouseprograms.com

*Tonja S Randolph, President*
*Mark Broussard, Executive Director*
Rehabilitation center for substance abuse.

**8832  St. Frances Cabrini Hospital: Rehab Unit**
St Frances Cabrini Hospital
3330 Masonic Drive
Alexandria, LA  71301            318-487-1122
                                FAX: 318-448-6822

*Stephen Wright, President/CEO*

**8833  St. Patrick Hospital: Rehab Unit**
524 S Ryan Street
Lake Charles, LA  70601            337-436-2511
                                   FAX: 337-491-7157
                                   www.christushealth.org

*Ellen Jones, Chief Executive Officer*

**8834  Thibodaux Hospital: Regional Rehabilitatio n Center**
602 N Acadia Road
Thibodaux, LA  70301            985-493-4438

## Maine

**8835  Head Injury Treatment Program at Brewer**
74 South Road
Brewer, ME  04412

*Mary Goyoi, Program Rep*

**8836  New England Rehabilitation Hospital of Portland**
335 Brighton Avenue
Portland, ME  04102            207-775-4000
                               FAX: 207-879-8168

*Amy Morse, Chief Executive Officer*

## Maryland

**8837  Mt. Washington Pediatric Hospital**
1708 W Rogers Avenue
Baltimore, MD  21209            419-578-8600
                                FAX: 410-542-8717

*Winne Sherman RN, Admissions Center Manager*
*Violet Ebbesen RN, Admissions Nurse*

**8838  Sinai Rehabilitation Center**
2401 W Belvedere Avenue
Baltimore, MD  21215            410-601-5530
                                FAX: 410-601-8284

*Bonnie Hartley, Senior Field Service Nurse*
*Marcie Weinberg, Manager*

Provides comprehensive inpatient and outpatient medical rehabilitation services to individuals disabled by head injury, stroke, musculoskeletal/orthopedic disorders, neurologic conditions and other medical diagnoses that impact on their functional capacity. Recognizing that many individuals have special needs, SRC has developed the following specialty programs: driver evaluation and training, electrodiagnostics, oncology, prosthetic/orthotic services, acute and post-acute brain injury services.

## Massachusetts

**8839  Braintree Hospital**
250 Pond Street
Braintree, MA  02184            781-848-5353
                                800-99R-EHAB
                                FAX: 781-849-9949

*Elizabeth Glenn RN BSN CRRN, Patient Access*
*Erik Purins, MD*

Since Braintree Hospital's founding in 1975, we have gained recognition as a world class health care provider. Today the Braintree Rehabilitation Network serves as the flagship hospital of Horizon Health Care, the largest independent provider of comprehensive medical rehabilitation in the world. The network consists of a growing number of rehabilitation facilities which provide both inpatient and outpatient services Programs include: amputee, general rehab, neuro rehab and stroke.

**8840  Greenery Extended Care Center**
59 Acton Street
Worcester, MA  01604            508-791-3147
                                FAX: 508-757-0423

*Tom Johnsrud, Admissions*
*Joel Stevens, Administrator*

**8841  Greenery Rehab Center Massachusetts**
99 Chestnut Hill Avenue
Boston, MA  02135            617-787-3390
                             FAX: 617-787-9169

*William Garvin, Medical Director*

**8842  Mediplex Rehabilitation Hospital**
4499 Acushnet Avenue
New Bedford, MA  02745            508-995-6900
                                  FAX: 508-998-8131

*Albert Loerinc MD*

**8843  New England Home for the Deaf**
154 Walter Street
Danvers, MA  01923            978-774-0445
                              FAX: 781-337-6742

*Eddy Laird, Executive Director*
*Judith Good, President*

Offers services for the deaf, totally blind, legally blind, visually impaired, mentally retarded blind and more with health, counseling, educational, recreational, rehabilitation, computer training and professional training services.

**8844  New England Rehabilitation Hospital: Massachusetts**
2 Rehabilitation Way
Woburn, MA  01801
781-935-5050
FAX: 781-932-8152
www.healthsouth.com

*Dianne Landy, Marketing Coordinator*
*Eileen Gibbons, Chief Executive Officer*

**8845  Shriners Burns Hospital: Boston**
51 Blossom Street
Boston, MA  02114
617-726-8807
800-255-1916
FAX: 617-523-1684
www.shrinershq.org

*Ralph Pino, Chairman*
*Jeevendra Martyn, MD*

Provides treatment for children to their 18th birthday with acute, fresh burns, plastic reconstructive surgery for patients with healed burns, severe scarring and facial deformity. Some non-burn conditions such as Scalded Skin Syndrome, Cleft Lip, Cleft Palate and purpura fulminians are also treated. Call the Hospital for information. All medical treatment is without cost to the patient, parents, or any third party.

**8846  Shriners Hospital Springfield Unit Springfield Unit for Crippled Children**
516 Carew Street
Springfield, MA  01104
413-787-2000
800-237-5055
FAX: 413-787-2009
www.shrinershq.org

*Charles H Weaver, Chairman Board of Governors*
*Mark Niederpruem, Chief Executive Officer*

# Michigan

**8847  Community Rehabilitation Center**
Community Hospital
400 Medical Park Drive
Watervliet, MI  49098
269-463-9009
800-463-1164
FAX: 269-463-6729

*Sandra L Dugal, Community Relations Coordinator*
*Linda Beushausen, Program Administrator*

Comprehensive medical rehabilitation program in a community hospital setting, providing inpatient and outpatient services to individuals who have become physically challenged by stroke, spinal cord injuries, traumatic brain injuries, major multiple trauma, orthopedic conditions, neurologic disorders, amputation, arthritis conditions and other diagnoses.

**8848  Covenant Healthcare Rehabilitation Program**
515 N Michigan Avenue
Saginaw, MI  48602
989-583-0000
FAX: 989-583-2843

*Spence Maidlow, President*

**8849  Farmington Health Care Center**
34225 Grand River Avenue
Farmington, MI  48335
248-477-7373
FAX: 248-477-2888

*Michael Mithen, Administrator*

**8850  Flint Osteopathic Hospital: RehabCare Unit**
3921 Beecher Road
Flint, MI  48532
810-762-4682

*Susan Malone, Program Manager*
*Joy Finkenbiner, Executive Director*

**8851  Integrated Health Services of Michigan at Clarkston**
4800 Clintonville Road
Clarkston, MI  48346
248-674-0903
FAX: 248-674-3359

*Carol Doll, Admissions Director*
*Margaret Canny, Administrator*
*Rose Berg, Admission*

**8852  Mecosta County General Hospital Rehabilitation Center**
Mecosta County General Hospital
605 Oak Street
Big Rapids, MI  49307
231-796-8691
FAX: 231-592-4456
e-mail: info@mcghhospital.com
www.mcghhospital.com

*Eugene A Riegle, Program Director*
*Samuel Daugherty, Chief Executive Officer*

Comprehensive medical rehabilitation program in a hospital setting, providing inpatient and outpatient services to individuals who have become physically challenged by stroke, spinal cord injuries, brain injuries, traumatic multiple traumas, arthritis conditions and other diagnoses.

**8853  Rehabilitation Institute of Michigan**
261 Mack Avenue
Detroit, MI  48201
313-745-1160
FAX: 313-745-1175
e-mail: cangelel@dmc.org
www.rimrehab.org

*Terry Reiley, President*
*Cheryl Angelelli, Marketing & Public Relations*
*Mildred Matlock, Manager*

Rehabilitation Institute of Michigan is a national leader in the delivery of physical medicine and rehabilitation and one of the country's largest freestanding rehabilitation hospitals. A comprehensive spectrum of both inpatient and outpatient services and programs are available for spinal cord injuries, brain injuries, stroke, cerebral palsy, musculoskeletal disorders, low back problems, amputations, sports injuries, work-related injuries and other medical conditions requiring physical rehab.

**8854  St. John Hospital: North Shore**
Ascension Health
26755 Ballard Street
Harrison Township, MI  48045
586-465-5501
FAX: 586-466-5397
www.stjohn.org

*David Sessions, Chief Executive Officer*
*Dave Denny, Director for Rehabilitation*

**8855  Three Rivers Rehabilitation Pavilion**
Three Rivers Area Hospital
1111 W Broadway Street
Three Rivers, MI  49093
269-279-5224
FAX: 269-279-7375

*Christine M Strom RN CRRN, Program Director*
*Sandra L Cooper, Community Relations*
*Diana Graaf, Owner*

Comprehensive medical rehabilitation program in a community hospital setting, providing inpatient and outpatient services to individuals who have become physically challenged by stroke, spinal cord injuries, traumatic brain injuries, major multiple trauma, orthopedic conditions, neurologic disorders, amputation, arthritis conditions and other diagnoses.

## Minnesota

**8856  North Memorial Medical Center: Rehabilitat ion Services**
3300 Oakdale Avenue N
Robbinsdale, MN  55422          763-520-2770
                               FAX: 763-520-1772
                               www.northmemorial.com

*Pete Pytlak, Director*
*Susan Keeney RN, Inpatient Unit Nurse Manager*
*Deb Christian, Evaluator*

Inpatient unit primarily serves adults and young adults that have a physical disability as a result of TBI, SCI, CVA, multiple trauma, spinal cord dysfunction or tumors and amputation. The interdisciplinary team approach includes the patient and family, as well as representatives from all rehab related disciplines. The program is CARF and JCAHO accredited, consisting of 18 beds.

**8857  Sister Kenny Institute**
800 E 28th Street
Minneapolis, MN  55407          612-863-4495
                                FAX: 612-863-8942

*Helen Kettner, Nurse-Liaison*

## Missouri

**8858  Columbia Regional Hospital: RehabCare Unit**
404 Keene Street
Columbia, MO  65201          573-875-9454
                             FAX: 573-875-4417
                             www.columbiaregional.org

*George Gumbert, Program Manager*

A medical and physical rehabilitation program serving patients throughout Mid-Missouri with functional deficits due to neurologic, orthopaedic or other medical conditions.

**8859  Jewish Hospital of St. Louis: Department of Rehabilitation**
216 N Kings Highway
Saint Louis, MO  63108          314-454-7390
                                FAX: 314-454-5277

*Mary Mitchell, Admitting Clerk*

**8860  PremierCare Neurohabilitation Program of Bethesda General Hospital**
3655 Vista Avenue
Saint Louis, MO  63110          314-772-9200
                                FAX: 314-772-1819

*Tim Imhoff, Program Director*

**8861  Rusk Rehabilitation Center**
315 Business Loop 70 W
Columbia, MO  65203          573-882-3101
                             FAX: 573-817-4690

*Tracy Rimki, Marketing Coordinator*
*Patrick Lee, Hospital Administrator*

A 60-bed comprehensive rehabilitation hospital. This CARF-accredited facility utilizes a multidisciplinary approach to provide inpatient and outpatient services with specialized programming in head injury, spinal cord injury and chronic pain.

**8862  St. Mary's Regional Rehabilitation Center**
201 NW R D Mize Road
Blue Springs, MO  64014          816-228-5900

                                 www.carondeletehealth.org

*Gordon Docking, Chief Executive Officer*
*Susan Bottmker, Assessment Coordinator*
*Robin Velaer, Manager*

A 17-bed inpatient physical rehabilitation unit offering PT, OT, ST, recreational therapy, psychiatry and all other ancillary services of a full-service hospital. Specialize in orthopedic and neurologic disabilities.

**8863  Three Rivers Health Care**
2620 N Westwood Boulevard
Poplar Bluff, MO  63901          573-785-1331

*Lori Norton, Manager*

## Montana

**8864  St. Vincent Hospital and Health Center**
1233 N 30th Street
Billings, MT  59101          406-237-4116
                             FAX: 406-657-8817

*John Brewer, Admission*
*Mike Bush, MD*

## Nebraska

**8865  Madonna Rehabilitation Hospital**
5401 South Street
Lincoln, NE  68506          402-483-9531
                            800-676-5448
                            FAX: 402-483-9406
                            e-mail: information@madonna.org
                            www.madonna.org

*Marsha Lommel, President/CEO*
*Lori Warner, Marketing/PR Manager*
*Kiranmayi Chilappa, MD*

Provides a complete range of inpatient and outpatient rehabilitation for patients of all ages and abilities. Through highly specialized programs and services, Madona offers individualized treatment and support to help every patient.

## Nevada

**8866  University Medical Center**
1800 W Charleston Boulevard
Las Vegas, NV  89102          702-383-2000
                              FAX: 702-383-2536

*Debbie Gulo, Rehab Evaluator*
*Lacy Thomas, Chief Executive Officer*

## New Hampshire

**8867  Head Injury Treatment Program at Dover**
307 Plaza Drive
Dover, NH  03820
603-742-2676
FAX: 603-749-5375

*Sue Mills, Program Rep*
*Jill Bosa, Administrator*

**8868  Lakeview NeuroRehabilitation Center**
101 High Watch Road
Center Ossipee, NH  03814
603-539-7451
800-4R3-H221
FAX: 603-539-8888
www.lakeviewsystem.com

*Susan Bartlett Msw Crc, Director Admissions*
*Tina Trudel PhD, VP Clinical Services*
*Edward C Morton Jr, Executive Director*

Residential treatment center serving individuals with neuro-logic/behavioral disorders. Lakeview serves both children and adults in functionally based program environment. Transistional programs in various group homes also available to clients as they progress in their treatment.

**8869  Northeast Rehabilitation Hospital**
70 Butler Street
Salem, NH  03079
603-893-2900
800-825-7292
FAX: 603-893-1628
www.northeastrehad.com

*John Prochilo, President/CEO*

**8870  St. Joseph Hospital Rehabilitation**
172 Kinsley Street
Nashua, NH  03060
603-595-3175
FAX: 603-595-3192

*Patti Montyha, Program Director*

A 24-bed acute rehabilitation unit offering general and special-ized programs. Located within St. Joseph acute care hospital and associated with Spaulding Rehabilitation Hospital

## New Jersey

**8871  Betty Bacharach Rehabilitation Hospital**
Jim Leeds Road
Pomona, NJ  08240
609-652-9057
FAX: 609-748-3586

*Virginia Wells, Admissions*
*Pat Nalepka, Manager*

**8872  Children's Specialized Hospital**
150 New Providence Road
Mountainside, NJ  07092
908-233-3720
888-244-5373
FAX: 908-301-5509
www.Childrens-specialized.org

*Jeannie Brooks RN, Director*
*Amy Mansue, President/CEO*

New Jersey's largest comprehensive pediatric rehabilitation hospital, treats children and adolescents from birth through 21 years of age. Programs include spinal dysfunction, brain injury, respiratory, burn, Day Hospital, early intervention, preschool, and cognitive rehabilitation. Locations in Fairwood, Roselle Park, Newark, Toms River and Hamilton

**8873  Garden State Rehabilitation Hospital**
14 Hospital Drive
Toms River, NJ  08755
732-244-3100
FAX: 732-244-2542

*Dave Coluzzie, Intake Coordinator*
*Tatty Scewski, Chief Executive Officer*

**8874  JFK Johnson Rehab Institute**
65 James Street
Edison, NJ  08820
732-321-7056
FAX: 732-321-0994
e-mail: webmaster@solarishs.org
www.solarishs.org

*Norman Batra, Physicians*
*David Brown, Physicians*

**8875  Kessler Institute for Rehabilitation, Welkind Facility**
201 Pleasant Hill Road
Chester, NJ  07930
908-879-9733
800-KES-SLER
FAX: 973-252-6343
e-mail: jkment@kessler-rehab.com
www.kessler-rehab.com

*Samuel P Grissom, Associate Medical Director*
*Steven Kessler*

Set in the rolling hills of Morris County, this 72 bed facility pro-vides specialized services to brain injury patients, including our unique Cognitive Redmediation Program, as well as a full range of stroke, amputee and orthopedic services. Kessler's team of dedicated rehabilitation professionals, including physicians, nurses and therapists, work with each patient to build physical strength, optimize movement, maximize independence, in-crease cognitive skills and address any other issues.

**8876  Mediplex Rehab: Camden**
2 Cooper Plaza
Camden, NJ  08103
856-342-7600
FAX: 856-342-7979

*Beth Crawford, Admissions*
*Celeste Johnson, Administrator*

## New Mexico

**8877  HealthSouth Rehabilitation Center: New Mexico**
7000 Jefferson Street NE
Albuquerque, NM  87109
505-344-9478
FAX: 505-344-2851

*Sylia Kelley, Administrator*

**8878  St. Joseph Rehabilitation Hospital and Outpatient Center**
Ardence
505 Elm Street NE
Albuquerque, NM  87102
505-727-4700
FAX: 505-727-4793
www.sjhs.org

*Janelle Raborn, Administrator/CEO*
*Sherrie Peterson, Director*

A member of the four hospital, St. Joseph healthcare system, this facility provides inpatient and outpatient care for those re-quiring physical medicine and rehabilitation. Specialty pro-grams include brain injury, stroke, spinal cord, orthopedics, occupational and physical therapies, clinical psychology, speech/language pathology, hand clinic and functional capacity evaluations. The only facility in New Mexico accredited in four areas by the commission on accreditation of rehab facilities.

## New York

**8879 Burke Rehabilitation Hospital**
785 Mamaroneck Avenue
White Plains, NY 10605
914-597-2500
888-99B-URKE
FAX: 914-946-0866
e-mail: web@burke.org
www.burke.org

Ann Herring, Marketing Coordinator
Mary Walsh, Manager

A 150 bed rehabilitation hospital providing both in and out patient physical rehabilitation to people with stroke, spinal cord injury, head injury, pulmonary, cardiac, amputee, orthopedic arthritis and other related diagnoses.

**8880 Rusk Institute of Rehabilitation Medicine**
400 E 34th Street
New York, NY 10016
212-263-6028
FAX: 212-263-8510
www.med.nyu.edu/rusk

Howard A Rusk, Founder
Jung Hwan, Clinical Professor
Eric Rackow, President

**8881 Silvercrest Center for Nursing and Rehabil itation**
14445 87th Avenue
Briarwood, NY 11435
718-480-4000
800-645-9806
FAX: 718-658-2367
e-mail: admissions@silvercrest.org
www.silvercrest.org

Stephen S Mills, President/CEO
Susan Barnett, Director Admissions
Cosmo Costa, Senior Vice President

The Silvercrest Center for Nursing and Rehabilitation has earned a wide-spread reputatiopn for combing the best in clinical care with the best in nursing care and for making available to its communities the broadest menu of services to ease a patients' path to recovery from hospital to home. The Center is for the treatment of medically complex patients beginning their recovery, for the rehabilitation of patients who need restorative therapy before going home and much more.

## North Carolina

**8882 Horizon Rehabilitation Center**
Trans Health Incorporated
3100 Erwin Road
Durham, NC 27705
919-383-1546
800-541-7750
FAX: 919-383-0862
e-mail: michelle.ayers@thicare.com
www.thicare.com./durham

John Dugan, Administrator

A 125-bed rehabilitation, subacute and long term care facility. HRC is JCAHO and CARF accredited with a physician-directed rehabilitation program, internal case management and a therapy department composed of physical, occupational, speech, recreational and respiratory therapists - pulmonary rehabilitation/ventilator unit.

**8883 Integrated Health Services of Durham**
Duke University Medical Center
3100 Erwin Road
Durham, NC 27705
919-684-8111
FAX: 919-383-0862
e-mail: webmaster@mcduke.edu
www.mc.duke.edu

Steve Rum, Vice Chancellor for Development
Dottie Williams, Assistant Vice Chancellor for De
Thomas Pafford, Manager

**8884 Learning Services Corporation**
Corporate Office
10 Speen Street
4th Floor
Framingham, MA 01701
888-419-9955
FAX: 919-419-9966
www.learningservices.com

A licensed postacute rehabilitation program for adults who have an acquired brain injury. Individuals who are enrolled in the program participate in active, intensive rehabilitation carried out by a team of neuropsychology, speech/language therapy, physical therapy, occupational therapy, vocational services, family services and life skills training. Services include residential rehabilitation, home based treatment, day treatment, subacute rehabilitation and supported living.

## Ohio

**8885 Arbors at Columbus**
44 S Souder Avenue
Columbus, OH 43222
614-228-5900
FAX: 614-228-3989

Kelly Fligor, Administrator
Postacute rehabilitation program.

**8886 Franciscan Rehabilitation Center**
601 S Edwin C Moses Boulevard
Dayton, OH 45408
937-229-6081
800-272-8042
FAX: 937-229-6074

Linda Didas, Case Manager

Acute, inpatient rehabilitation, 77 beds. Twenty-plus years serving the Dayton community. Vocational and assistive technology services are available. Extensive outpatient services include: hand therapy, back school, drivers' training. Accredited by JCAHO and CARF. Liaison with community support groups: SCI, BI, stroke, amputee, ALS, chronic pain. On-site clinics: SCI, MDA, amputee and wheelchair/seating.

**8887 Great Lakes Regional Rehabilitation Center**
3700 Kolbe Road
Lorain, OH 44053
440-282-4368
FAX: 440-960-4636

Roberta Yehman, Admissions Director
Klaus Grm, Owner

**8888 HCR Health Care Services**
1 Seagate
Toledo, OH 43604
419-321-5470
800-736-4427
FAX: 419-252-5543

Charles Norman, CPA

Specialty transitional care and intensive rehabilitation services. Specialized services are focused on patients with catastrophic conditions or whose length of stay at an acute care or rehabilitation hospital can be dramatically reduced by transferring to a subacute level of care.

**8889 Heather Hill Rehabilitation Hospital**
Heather Hill
12340 Bass Lake Road
Chardon, OH 44024 440-285-4040
800-423-2972

*Robert Harr, President*

Individualized treatment programs for adults and adolescents can participate in and benefit from three-plus hours a day of active therapy.

**8890 Parma Community General Hospital Acute Rehabilitation Center**
7007 Powers Boulevard
Parma, OH 44129 440-743-3000
FAX: 440-743-4036
www.parmahospital.org

*Joseph Coleman, Chairman*
*Patricia A Ruflin, President/CEO*

The mission of this CARF accredited unit is to provide the most comprehensive, cost-effective, acute rehabilitation program possible in order for every patient and family to adjust to his/her disability and to achieve the maximum potential of independent functioning when returning to community living.

**8891 Rehabilitation Hospital at Heather Hill**
12340 Bass Lake Road
Chardon, OH 44024 440-285-4040
FAX: 440-285-0946
e-mail: info@heatherhill.org
www.heatherhill.org

*Jacques Leverette, Executive Director*
*Sheila Larosa, Admissions Director*

250-bed, non-profit, multi-level care facility serving the frail elderly and physiclaly disabled.

**8892 Rehabilitation Institute of Ohio at Miami Valley Hospital**
1 Wyoming Street
Dayton, OH 45409 937-208-8000

www.miamivalleyhospital.com

*Sharyl Kuhnen RN, Rehab Coordinator*

A regional center designed for the treatment of those with disabling conditions. RIO offers physcial, occupational, speech, recreational and pool therapies, as well as the use of a transitional apartment to perpare patients for a return to independent living.

**8893 Shriners Burn Institute: Cincinnati Unit**
Shriners Hospitals for Children Cincinnati
3229 Burnet Avenue
Cincinnati, OH 45229 513-872-6000
800-875-8580
FAX: 513-872-6999
www.shinnershq.org

*Ronald Hitzler, Administrator*

**8894 St. Francis Health Care Centre**
401 N Broadway Street
Green Springs, OH 44836 419-639-2626
800-248-2552
FAX: 419-639-6222
e-mail: jholmer@sfhcc.org
www.sfhcc.org

*Greg Raubenolt, Director Marketing*
*Jane Holmer, Admissions Coordinator*
*Joy Kinnear CRRN, Dir Admissions/Care Coordinator*

**8895 St. Rita's Medical Center Rehabilitation Services**
730 W Market Street
Lima, OH 45801 419-226-9332
FAX: 419-226-9705

*Kelly Recker, Administrative Physical Medicine*
*Sharon Bilopavlovich, Manager*

**8896 University of Cincinnati Hospital**
Health Alliance
234 Goodman Street
Cincinnati, OH 45219 513-585-1000
FAX: 513-584-7712
www.healthall.com

*James Kingsbury, Executive Director*

**8897 Upper Valley Medical/Rehab Services**
3130 N Dixie Highway
Troy, OH 45373 937-440-4000
FAX: 937-440-7337
e-mail: info@uvmc.com
www.uvmc.com

*Pam Cornett, Director Rehab Services*

## Oklahoma

**8898 HealthSouth Rehab Center: Oklahoma**
700 NW 7th Street
Oklahoma City, OK 73102 405-236-3131
FAX: 405-553-1153
www.healthsouth.com

*Susan Nelson, Director Business Development*
*Stacey Smith, Chief Executive Officer*

Inpatient Rehab Facility including all therapy services serving people who have been injured and had an illness resulting in a decreased level of independence.

**8899 Hilcrest Medical Center: Kaiser Rehab Cent er**
1125 S Trenton Avenue
Tulsa, OK 74120 918-579-7100
FAX: 918-579-7110

*Kevin Gross, Chief Executive Officer*

**8900 Jane Phillips Episcopal Memorial Medical Center: RehabCare Unit**
Jane Phillips Episcopal Memorial Medical Center
3500 E Frank Phillips Boulevard
Bartlesville, OK 74006 918-331-1857
FAX: 918-331-1360

*Joy Sandborn, Manager*

**8901 Jim Thorpe Rehabilitation Center at Southwest Medical Center**
Southwest Medical Center
4401 S Western Avenue
Oklahoma City, OK 73109 405-636-7000
800-677-1238
FAX: 405-636-7501

*Gary Zook, Unit Director*
*Denise Uvino, Marketing Director*
*Stanley Hupfeld, Chief Executive Officer*

Provides inpatient rehabilitation for people with head injuries, spinal cord injuries, orthopedic conditions, pain management, neurological diseases, strokes and a variety of diagnoses that stop individuals from being able to take care of themselves independently. Services available include medical direction, physical therapy, social work, occupational therapy, speech therapy, recreational therapy, and aftercare follow-up.

**8902   Mercy Memorial Health Center-Rehab Center**
1011 14th Avenue NW
Ardmore, OK  73401

580-223-5400
800-572-1182
FAX: 580-220-6681
www.mercyok.net

*Bob Thompson, President*

**8903   St. Anthony Hospital: Rehabilitation Unit**
St. Anthony Hospital
1000 N Lee Avenue
Oklahoma City, OK  73102

405-272-7000
FAX: 405-271-7563
www.saint.ok.com

*Joe Hodges, President*

# Oregon

**8904   Shriners Hospitals for Children: Portland**
3101 SW Sam Jackson Park Road
Portland, OR  97239

503-241-5090
800-237-5055
FAX: 503-221-3475
www.shrinershq.org

*Bill Millan, Chief Executive Officer*
*William A Horton, Director of Research*
*Kerry Grindeland, Care Coordination Manager*

Pediatric orthopedic and plastic surgery; inpatient and outpatient services. No charge for any services provided at the Hospital. Diagnosis, rehabilitation, surgery, sports and recreation for ages 0-18 for people with physical disabilities involving bones, muscles or joints or in need of plastic surgery for burn scars or cleft lip/palate.

# Pennsylvania

**8905   Allied Services John Heinz Institute of Rehabilitation Medicine**
150 Mundy Street
Wilkes Barre, PA  18702

570-826-3900
FAX: 570-826-3898
www.allied-services.org

*Thomas E Pugh, VP/CEO*
*Gregory Basting MD, VP Medical Affairs*
*Karen Kearney, AVP Inpatient Services*

A 94-bed hospital offering comprehensive inpatient and outpatient rehabilitation services. The Institute specializes in rehabilitation programs in the areas of head trauma, injured worker recovery and outpatient.

**8906   Allied Services Rehabilitation Hospital**
475 Morgan Highway
Scranton, PA  18508

570-348-2211
FAX: 570-348-1281
e-mail: alliedcom@aol.com

*Donna Esken, Director Admissions*
*Susan Lantner, Assistant Director*
*James Paddock, Executive Director*

**8907   Brighten Place**
131 N Main Street
Chalfont, PA  18914

215-997-7746
FAX: 215-997-0403
e-mail: brightenplace@enter.net
members.aol.com/vmoc3

*Suzann Ditzel, Program Director*
*William Koffros, Chief Executive Officer*

A residential brain injury program with the mission to encourage growth and foster independence on an individual level for each resident. We are CARF accredited and provide additional services which include a day program and respite care.

**8908   Chestnut Hill Rehabilitation Hospital**
8601 Stenton Avenue
Wyndmoor, PA  19038

215-233-6200
FAX: 215-233-6879

*James Caslin, Administrator*

**8909   Doylestown Hospital Rehabilitation Center**
595 W State Street
Doylestown, PA  18901

215-345-2230
FAX: 215-345-2512
e-mail: dseif@dh.org
www.dh.org

*Donna Seif, Outpatient Rehab Case Manager*
*Gloria Peterson, Inpatient Rehab Services*
*Theophila Cemanoff, MD, Owner*

**8910   Health Care Solutions**
500 Abbott Drive
Suite B
Broomall, PA  19008

610-583-3500
800-451-1671
FAX: 610-583-3550
www.lincare.com

*John P Byrnes, Chief Executive Officer*
*Shawn Schabel, Chief Operation Officer*
*Patty Vitvlli, Manager*

Develops unique containment programs, offers equipment set-up, patient instruction, patient assessment and equipment usage. Offers clinical services that include oxygen systems, ventilators, aerosol therapy, suction equipment, T.E.N.S. programs, compression pumps, custom orthotics, enteral feeding.

**8911   HealthSouth**
143 E 2nd Street
Erie, PA  16507

814-878-1200
800-234-4574
FAX: 814-878-1448
www.healthsouth.com

*Kathy Lamb, Admissions*
*Louis Condrasky, Chief Executive Officer*

**8912   HealthSouth Harmarville Rehabilitation Hospital**
PO Box 11460
Pittsburgh, PA  15238

412-828-1300
FAX: 412-828-7705
www.healthsouth.com

*Sharon Noro, Chief Executive Officer*

A 202-bed facility providing inpatient and outpatient physical medicine and rehabilitation to adults and adolescents in Pennsylvania, West Virginia, Ohio and Maryland.

**8913   HealthSouth Nittany Valley Rehabilitation Hospital**
Health South of Nittany Valley
550 W College Avenue
Pleasant Gap, PA  16823

814-359-3421
800-842-6026
FAX: 814-359-5898
www.healthsouth.com

*Connnie Poisant, Program Director*
*Susan Hartman, Chief Executive Officer*

Comprehensive inpatient and outpatient facilities. Treatment for symptoms relating to: stroke, head injury, pulmonary disease, orthopedic conditions, neurological disorders, cardiac illnesses and spinal cord injuries. Healthsouth Nittany Valley Rehabilitation Hospital is a part of Healthsouth's national network of more than 2,000 facilities in 50 states.

# Rehabilitation Facilities, Acute /South Carolina

**8914  HealthSouth Rehabilitation Hospital of Altoona**
2005 Valley View Boulevard
Altoona, PA  16602  814-944-3535
FAX: 814-944-6160

*Scott Filler, Administrator/CEO*

**8915  Healthsouth Rehabilitation Hospital of Greater Pittsburgh**
2380 McGinley Road
Monroeville, PA  15146  412-856-2400
FAX: 412-856-2437

*Sharon Noro, Administrator*

**8916  Healthsouth Rehabilitation Hospital of Mechanicsburg**
175 Lancaster Boulevard
Mechanicsburg, PA  17055  717-691-3700
FAX: 717-697-6524

*Roberta Weaver, Director Admissions*
*Gregory Toot, Chief Executive Officer*

**8917  Healthsouth Rehabilitation Hospital of York**
1850 Normandie Drive
York, PA  17408  717-767-6941
FAX: 717-764-1341

*Cheryl Fleming, CEO*
*Susan Hartman, Business Development*
*Brent Burger, Controller*

A 120-bed rehabilitation hospital dedicated to providing advanced, comprehensive services to patients who have suffered head injury, spinal cord injury, stroke, burns, amputation, chronic pain and other neurological and musculoskeletal disorders. HRH of York provides outpatient services in seven locations. Healthsouth is located in York, Pennsylvania, approximately 50 miles north of Baltimore and 25 miles south of Harrisburg.

**8918  Lake Erie Institute of Rehabilitation**
137 W 2nd Street
Erie, PA  16507  814-838-7555
FAX: 814-878-1448

*Jeff Ondrey, Program Director*
*Arnold Thompson, Owner*

**8919  Magee Rehabilitation Hospital**
1513 Race Street
Philadelphia, PA  19102  215-587-3000
800-96M-AGEE
FAX: 215-568-3736
e-mail: magee@mageerehab.org
www.mageerehab.org

*David Brodar, Director Human Resources*
*William E Staas, President/CEO*

**8920  Moss Rehabilitation Hospital**
1200 W Tabor Road
Philadelphia, PA  19141  215-456-9900
FAX: 215-456-9646

*Mary Stears, Intake Coordinator*
*Alberto Ezquenazi, Plant Manager*

The Philadelphia region's major resource for medical rehabilitation since 1959. This 152 bed facility offers comprehensive care to people with broad ranges of conditions, diagnostic laboratories and a multidisciplinary team of rehabilitation professionals.

**8921  Shriners Hospitals for Children, Philadelphia**
Shrinners Hospitals for Children
3551 N Broad Street
Philadelphia, PA  19140  215-430-4000
800-281-4051
FAX: 215-430-4126
www.shrinershq.org/shc/philadelphia

*Sharon Rajnic, Administrator*

The Shriners Hospital in Philadelphia is a 59-bed pediatric orthopaedic hospital providing a complete range of specialized medical and rehabilitation services at no charge to children with orthopaedic problems or spinal injuries. The hospital is one of 22 Shriners Hospitals for Children throughout North america. In addition to treating children with routine and complex orthopaedic problems, the Philadelphia Hospital provides a comprehensive and individualized rehabilitation program.

**8922  Shriners Hospitals for Children, Erie**
1645 W 8th Street
Erie, PA  16505  814-875-8700
FAX: 814-875-8756
www.shrinershq.org/shc/erie/index.html

*Richard W Brzuz, Administrator*
*James O Sander MD, Chief of Staff*
*Bridget Hines, Applications/Admissions Coord.*

The Shriners Hospitals for Children, Erie, is a 30-bed pediatric orthopaedic hospital providing comprehensive orthopaedic care to children at no charge. The hospital is one of 22 Shriners Hospitals throughout North America. The Erie Hospital accepts and treats children with routine and complex orthopaedic and neuromuscular problems, utilizing the latest treatments and technology available in pediatric orthopaedics, resulting in early ambulation and reduced length of stay.

**8923  Shriners Hospitals, Philadelphia Unit, for Crippled Children**
3551 N Broad Street
Philadelphia, PA  19140  215-430-4000
FAX: 215-430-4126
www.shrinershq.org/hospitals/index.html

*Sharon Rajnic, Administrator*

## South Carolina

**8924  Colleton Regional Hospital: RehabCare Unit**
501 Robertson Boulevard
Walterboro, SC  29488  843-549-2000

*Johnnie Benson, Program Manager*
*Rebecca Brewer, Chief Executive Officer*

**8925  HealthSouth Rehab Hospital: South Carolina**
2935 Colonial Drive
Columbia, SC  29203  803-254-7777
FAX: 803-414-1414

*Candace Knox, Administrator*

**8926  Rebound Head Injury Recovery Services of the Carolinas**
800 W Meeting Street
Lancaster, SC  29720  803-286-1418
FAX: 803-286-1824

851

**8927  Shriners Hospitals for Children, Greenville**
Shrinners Hospital sfor Children
950 W Faris Road
Greenville, SC  29605                864-271-3444
                                     866-459-0013
                              FAX: 864-271-4471
                              www.shrinershp.org

*Gary Fraley, Administrator*

## Tennessee

**8928  Health South Cane Creek Rehabilitation Center**
Health South Corporation
180 Mount Pelia Road
Martin, TN  38237                    731-587-4231
                              FAX: 731-587-6716

*Dayle Unger RN NHN, Administrator*
*Martha Stephenson RN, Rehab Liaison*
*Ray Ann Dudley LPN, Rehab Liaison*

**8929  HealthSouth Chattanooga Rehabilitation Hospital**
2412 McCallie Avenue
Chattanooga, TN  37404               423-698-0221
                                     800-763-5189
                              FAX: 423-697-9124

*Donna L Bourdon, Administrator/CEO*
*Scooter Brunson, Marketing Coordinator*

Offers orthopaedic rehabilitation, stroke rehabilitation, amputee rehabilitation, brain injury program, pain management, ventilator weaning, carpal tunnel screening, low intensity program, oncology program, aquatic therapy, day treatment, burn program and outpatient services.

**8930  HealthSouth Rehabilitation Cntr/Tennessee**
6100 Primacy Parkway
Suite 115
Memphis, TN  38119                   901-682-3730
                              FAX: 901-685-1968

**8931  Healthsouth Rehabilitation at Sumner**
555 Hartsville Pike
Gallatin, TN  37066                  615-230-3900
                              FAX: 615-230-3903

*Andrea Sanders, Program Director*
*Doug Danforth, Director Nurses*

Inpatient general rehabilitation programs for orthopedic injury, joint replacements, head injury, arthritis, general weakness and cardio/pulmonary diseases.

**8932  James H And Cecile C Quillen Rehabilitation Hospital**
2511 Wesley Street
Johnson City, TN  37601              423-952-1700
                                     800-235-1994
                              FAX: 423-283-0153
                              www.msha.com

*John Turner, Chief Executive Officer*

A 60-bed, freestanding comprehensive medical rehabilitation hospital. Full range of outpatient and day treatment, 14-bed traumatic brain injury unit, in ground therapeutic pool, transitional living apartment, outdoor ambulation course. All inpatient and outpatient programs utilize an interdisciplinary team approach designed to improve a patient's physical and cognitive functioning.

**8933  Nashville Rehabilitation Hospital**
610 Gallatin Road
Nashville, TN  37206                 615-226-4330
                                     800-227-3108
                              FAX: 615-650-2562

*Anne Jacobs RN, Director CM/UR*
*Sherry Lawlwer LCSW, Social Services*
*Jane Andrews, Chief Executive Officer*

A free-standing physical rehabilitation facility offering services to patients on an inpatient and outpatient basis. Programs include CVA, orthopedic, neuromuscular, traumatic brain injury, spinal cord injury, general rehabilitation and Bridges - geriatric psychiatric unit. Intra-disciplinary team approach is utilized to assist patients in obtaining their maximum fuctional level.

**8934  Patricia Neal Rehab Center : Ft. Sanders R egional Medical Center**
Covenant Health
1901 W Clinch Avenue
Knoxville, TN  37916                 865-374-1000
                                     800-728- 632
                              FAX: 865-541-2247
                              www.patneal.com

*David McReynolds, Chief Executive Officer*
*Keith Altshuler, Administrator*

**8935  Rebound Comprehensive Rehabilitation Center at Cane Creek**
180 Mount Pelia Road
Martin, TN  38237
                              FAX: 731-587-6716

**8936  Rehabilitation Center Baptist Hospital**
137 E Blount Avenue
Knoxville, TN  37920                 865-632-5360

                              www.baptist.org

**8937  Rehabilitation Center at McFarland Hospital**
University Medical Center
1411 Baddour Parkway
Lebanon, TN  37087                   615-444-8262
                              FAX: 615-444-7901
                              www.universitymedicalcenter.com

*Vincent T Cherry Jr, Chief Executive Director*

**8938  St. Mary's Medical Center: RehabCare Center**
Oak Hill Avenue
Knoxville, TN  37917                 865-545-8000
                              FAX: 865-545-8133

*Debra London, Chief Executive Officer*

## Texas

**8939  Bayshore Medical Center: Rehab**
4000 Spencer Highway
Pasadena, TX  77504                  713-359-2000
                              FAX: 713-359-1121

*Bill Brady, Program Manager*
*Phillip Robinson, Chief Executive Officer*

**8940  Cecil R Bomhr Rehabilitation Center of Nacogdoches Memorial Hospital**
1204 N Mound Street
Nacogdoches, TX  75961               936-568-8547
                              FAX: 936-569-4616

*Bette M Guzman, Director Rehabilitation Services*

The only JCAHO and CARF, ASHA/PSB certified acute inpatient physical rehab center in East Texas.

**8941    Dallas Rehabilitation Institute**

9713 Harry Hines Boulevard
Dallas, TX 75220

FAX: 214-904-6119

*Judi McCann, Intake Coordinator*

A 126-bed facility offering comprehensive and outpatient programs for brain injury, spinal cord injury, chronic pain, amputation, orthopedic and work-related injuries. Houses a full-service ICU and two surgical suites, a 14,000 square foot physical therapy gym, hydrotherapy pool and an on-site orthotics and prosthetics lab. The Institute is also accredited by CARF, JCAHO and Texas Rehabilitation Commission; certified by Medicare and is an affiliate of the University of Texas Medical School.

**8942    Del Oro Institute for Rehabilitation**

8081 Greenbriar Street
Houston, TX 77054

800-388-1422

*Cece Matthews, Admissions*

Del Oro offers an interdisciplinary team approach to care, meeting the needs of rehabilitation patients with a wide spectrum of services, including immediate access to surgery, intensive care or other medical treatment which may be required in an emergency.

**8943    Ft. Worth Rehabilitation Hospital**

6701 Oakmont Boulevard
Fort Worth, TX 76132

817-370-4727
FAX: 817-370-4977

*Gala Lewis, Admissions*
*Felipe Garcia, MD*

**8944    Gonzales Warm Springs Rehabilitation Hospital**

200 Memorial Drive
Luling, TX 78648

830-875-8400
FAX: 830-672-8102

*Brenda Miles, Administrator*

**8945    Good Shepherd Medical Center: RehabCare Unit**

621 N 5th Street
Longview, TX 75601

903-236-3937
FAX: 541-667-3443

*Retta Crim, Program Manager*

**8946    Harris Methodist Fort Worth Hospital Mabee Rehabilitation Center**

1301 Pennsylvania Avenue
Fort Worth, TX 76104

814-250-2000

**8947    HealthSouth Plano Rehabilitation Hospital**

2800 W 15th Street
Plano, TX 75075

972-612-9000
FAX: 972-423-4293
www.healthsouth.com

*Chester Crouch, Administrator*
*Mary Alexander, Executive Director*

**8948    HealthSouth Rehabilitation Center of Humble Texas**

18903 S Memorial Drive
Humble, TX 77338

936-760-3443
FAX: 281-446-8022

*Katherine Schutz, Administrator*

**8949    HealthSouth Rehabilitation Hospital of Bea umont**

3340 Plaza 10 Drive
Beaumont, TX 77707

409-835-0835
FAX: 409-835-0649
www.healthsouth.com

*Bale Clamfoth, Administrator*
*Sam Coco, Manager*

**8950    Hillcrest Baptist Medical Center: Rehab Care Unit**

3000 Herring Avenue
Waco, TX 76708

254-202-8525
FAX: 254-202-8975
e-mail: listening@hillcrest.net
www.hbmc.org

*J M Dawson, President*
*Debbie Meurer, Manager*

**8951    Institute for Rehabilitation & Research**

Tirr System
1333 Moursund Street
Houston, TX 77030

713-799-5000
FAX: 713-797-5289
www.tirr.org

*Jean Herzog, President*
*Karen Hart, Vice President Education*

A national center for information, training, research, and technical assistance in independent living. The goal is to extend the body of knowledge in independent living and to improve the utilization of results of research programs and demonstration projects in this field. It has developed a variety of strategies for collecting, synthesizing, and disseminating information related to the field of independent living.

**8952    Memorial Hospital and Medical Center**

PO Box H
Midland, TX 79701

432-586-5864

*Judene Wilhelm, Administrator*

**8953    Methodist Hospital Rehabilitation Institute**

3615 19th Street
Lubbock, TX 79410

806-793-4251
FAX: 806-793-4037

**8954    Navarro Regional Hospital: RehabCare Unit**

Navarro Hospital
3201 W Highway 22
Corsicana, TX 75110

903-654-6800
FAX: 903-872-4627
www.navarrohospital.com

*Nancy Byrnes, Chief Executive Officer*
*Glenda Teri, Chief Nursing Officer*

**8955    Pocatello Rehabilitation Center**

777 Hospital Way
Pocatello, ID 83201

208-234-1984
FAX: 208-239-3795
www.ihc.com

*R Eric Goodwin, Director Rehab*
*Susan Proctor, Manager*

Provides the full spectrum of medical rehabilitation services including acute inpatient rehab, subacute rehab, home health and comprehensive outpatient services. Accredited by CARF and JCAHO.

**8956    Rebound: San Antonio**

12412 Judson Road
Live Oak, TX 78233

210-614-7474

*Joe Hernandez, Manager*

**8957  Rehabilitation Hospital of Austin**
1215 Red River Street
Austin, TX 78701                 512-474-5700
                            FAX: 512-474-2720
                            www.healthsouth.com
A comprehensive 83 bed medical rehabilitation hospital serving
the needs of patients in the Central Texas area. The mission is to
promote recovery for persons with disabling conditions by providing individualized treatment so they can reach the highest
level of physical, social and emotional well-being.

**8958  Rehabilitation Hospital of North Texas**
3200 Matlock Road
Arlington, TX 76015              817-419-0866
                            FAX: 817-468-3055

**8959  Rehabilitation Institute of San Antonio Healthsouth**
9119 Cinnamon Hl
San Antonio, TX 78240            210-691-0737
                            FAX: 210-558-1297
                            www.healthsouth.com

*Aleen Arabit, CEO/Administrator*
*Larry Spriggs, CFO*

**8960  Rio Vista Rehabilitation Hospital**
1740 Curie Drive
El Paso, TX 79902                915-544-3399
                                800-999-8392
                            FAX: 915-544-4838

*Gene Miller, Administrator*

**8961  San Antonio Warm Springs Rehabilitation Hospital**
5101 Medical Drive
San Antonio, TX 78229            210-616-0100
                            FAX: 210-592-5452
                            www.warmsprings.org

*Linda Simpson, Administrator*

**8962  Shannon Medical Center: RehabCare Unit**
120 E Harris Avenue
San Angelo, TX 76903             325-653-6741
                            FAX: 915-653-8261

*Bryan Horner, President*

**8963  Shriners Burn Institute: Galveston Unit**
815 Market Street
Galveston, TX 77550              409-761-2516

                            www.shrinersHQ.org

*John Swartwout, Administrator*

Providing expert, no-cost orthopaedic and burn care to children
under 18.

**8964  Shriners Hospitals for Children, Houston**
6977 Main Street
Houston, TX 77030                713-797-1616
                                800-853-1240
                            FAX: 713-793-3770
                            e-mail: shriners@argolink.net

*Steven Reiter, Administrator*

Shriners Hospitals provides at no charge quality pediatric orthopedic serivces to children ages newborn to 18 years old. These
services include both outpatient and inpatient needs. Specialties
include cerebrel palsy, spina bifida, scoliosis, hand, hip and feet
problems. An application is required and may be completed by
phone.

**8965  South Arlington Medical Center: Rehab Care Unit**
3301 Matlock Road
Arlington, TX 76015              817-472-4903
                            FAX: 817-472-4963
                            www.medicaclcenterarlington.com

*Patrice Oliver, Manaager*

A medical center providing a variety of services to every individual.

**8966  South Texas Rehabilitation Hospital**
Ernest Health
425 E Alton Gloor Boulevard
Brownsville, TX 78526            956-554-6000
                            FAX: 956-350-6150
                            strh.ernesthealth.com
STRH was designed for the provision of specialized rehabilitative care, in the only freestanding acute rehabilitation hospital
serving Brownsville and the Rio Grande Valley. The hospital
provides rehabilitative services for patients with functional deficits as a result of debilitating illnesses or injuries.

**8967  St. David's Rehabilitation Center**
St. David s Medical Center
98 San Jacinto Boulevard
Suite 1800
Austin, TX 78701                 512-708-9700
                            FAX: 512-370-4439
                            www.stdavids.com

*Jon M Foster, Chief Executive Officer*

**8968  Texas NeuroRehab Center**
1106 W Dittmar Road
Austin, TX 78745                 512-444-4835
                                800-252-5151
                            FAX: 512-462-6636
                            www.texasneurorehab.com

*Nancy Childs, Medical Director*
*Edgar Prettyman, Administrator*

Internationally recognized provider in brain in-
jury/neurobehavioral treatment for children, adolescents, and
adults with complex medical, physical and/or behavioral issues.
Medical rehabilitation, neurobehavioral, and neuropsychiatric
programs combine traditional therapies with education, vocational, substance abuse, and sensory integration services.

**8969  Texas Specialty Hospital at Dallas**
7955 Harry Hines Boulevard
Dallas, TX 75235                 214-637-0000

*Waylon Maynard, Director Clinical Services*
*Cathy Campbell, Chief Executive Officer*

66 beds offering active/acute rehabilitation, brain injury day
treatment, cognitive rehabilitation, complex care, extended rehabilitation and short term evaluation.

**8970  Touchstone Neurorecovery Center**
Nexus Health Systems
9297 Wahrenberger Road
Conroe, TX 77304                 936-788-7770
                                800-414-4824
                            FAX: 936-788-7885
                            www.nhsltd.com

*John Cassidy, Executive Director*

Provides leading edge neurobehavioral rehabilitation. Develops
and provides state-of-the-art transitional, residential and vocational rehabilitation services for indivduals with traumatic brain
injuries, and other long term ilnesses.

**8971 Valley Regional Medical Center: RehabCare Unit**
100 E Alton Gloor Boulevard
Brownsville, TX 78526
956-350-7000
FAX: 956-350-7796

*David Handley, Chief Executive Officer*

## Utah

**8972 LDS Hospital Rehabilitation Center**
Eighth Avenue & C Street
Salt Lake City, UT 84143
801-408-5429
888-301-3880
FAX: 801-408-5610
e-mail: jeanette.kucharski@intermountainmail.org
www.intermountainhealthcare.org

*Jeanette Kucharski CRRN, Rehab Liaison*
*Brad Zollinger, Administrator*

Located within a Trauma I Center, this facility provides comprehensive inpatient and outpatient rehabilitation to people with physical disabilities. CARF/JCAHO accredited. Low cost family housing is available and Medicaid/Medicare is accepted.

**8973 Primary Children's Medical Center**
100 N Medical Drive
Salt Lake City, UT 84113
801-588-2000
FAX: 801-588-2318
www.ihc.com

*Joseph Horton, CEO*
*Scott S Parker, President*

**8974 Rehabilitation Services**
University Health Care
50 N Medical Drive
Salt Lake City, UT 84132
801-581-2897
FAX: 801-585-3778

*Sunny Vance-Lauritzen, Director*
*Trish Jensen, Program Coordinator*
*Joseph Webster, Executive Director*

Provides quality, comprehensive, rehabilitation services to persons with complex rehabilitation needs, including spinal cord injuries, head trauma, stroke, and other disabling conditions. Rehabilitation Services has been serving physicians, their patients, and the community since 1965. Rehabilitation Services has been an established leader in comprehensive inpatient, outpatient and home/community rehabilitation programs. Accredited by CARF and JCAHO.

**8975 Shriners Hospitals for Children: Intermountain**
Fairfax Avenue Road @ Virgini
Salt Lake City, UT 84103
801-536-3500
800-841-0204
FAX: 801-536-3852
www.shrinershq.org

*James C Davis, Chairman*
*John Patchin, Administrator*

One of nineteen hospitals in North America specializing in pediatric orthopedics (plus four hospitals providing pediatric burn treatment). This hospital serves the Intermountain region. All services provided in the hospital are at no cost to family, insurance company, nor state/federal agency regardless of ability to pay.

**8976 Stewart Rehabilitation Center: McKay Dee Hospital**
4335 Harrison Boulevard
Suite D
Ogden, UT 84403
801-387-2080
FAX: 801-387-7720

*Bob Martin, Nurse Coordinator*
*Judy Grover, Manager*

**8977 Western Rehabilitation Institute**
8074 S 1300 E
Sandy, UT 84094
801-565-6500
FAX: 801-565-6576

*Vauna Allison, Admissions*
*Arina Merrill, MD*

## Vermont

**8978 Vermont Achievement Center**
88 Park Street
Rutland, VT 05701
802-775-2395
FAX: 802-773-9656

*Joanne Mattsson, Executive Director*

## Virginia

**8979 Inova Mount Vernon Hospital Rehabilitation Program**
Inova Rehabilitation Center
2501 Parkers Lane
Alexandria, VA 22306
703-664-7190
FAX: 703-664-7128
www.inova.com

*Toni Jones, Rehab Admissions*
*Ann Vennell, Executive Director*

Inova Rehabilitation Center at Inova Mount Vernon Hospital provides comprehensive inpatient and outpatient programs for patients with brain injuries, stroke and spinal cord, neurological and orthopedic injuries.

**8980 Kluge Children's Rehabilitation Center**
University of Virginia
2270 Ivy Road
Charlottesville, VA 22903
434-924-5567
800-627-8596
FAX: 434-924-5559
www.universityvirginia.edu

*James Blackman, Medical Director*

**8981 Portsmouth General Hospital: RehabCare Unit**
850 Crawford Parkway
Portsmouth, VA 23704
757-465-7772

*Anne Fisher, Program Manager*

## Washington

**8982 Good Samaritan Healthcare Physical Medicine and Rehabilitation**
Good Samaritan Hospital
8012 112th Street Court E
Puyallup, WA 98373
253-864-2703
FAX: 253-286-2719
www.goodsamhealth.org

*Lynn Siedenstrang, Interim Director*
*Paul Nutter, MD*

**8983 Northwest Hospital Center for Medical Rehabilitation**
1550 N 115th Street
Seattle, WA 98133
206-364-0500
FAX: 206-368-1399

*C Schneider, Chief Executive Officer*

**8984 Providence Medical Center**
500 17th Avenue
Seattle, WA 98122 206-000-1111
FAX: 206-320-3387

*Paul Casey MD*

**8985 Providence Rehabilitation Services**
Providence Rehabilitation Services
Pacific and Nassau
Everett, WA 98206 425-258-7953

*Elaine Thayer PT, Clinical Director*
*Leslie Baumgarten, Manager*

Continuum of care available: Acute Care, Inpatient Rehabilitation Unit, Transitional Care, Outpatient therapies, and In-home services.

**8986 Shriners Hospitals for Children: Spokane**
Shriners Hospitals
PO Box 2472
Spokane, WA 99210 509-455-7844
FAX: 509-623-0474
www.shrinershq.org

*Chuck Young, Administrator*
*Cheri Hollenback, Director Nursing*
*Ron L Ferguson MD, Chief of Staff*

Provides pediatric orthopedic services plus burn scar revision to children birth to 18. All services at no charge to the family.

## West Virginia

**8987 MountainView Regional Rehabilitation Hospital**
1160 Van Voorhis Road
Morgantown, WV 26505 304-598-1100
800-388-2451
FAX: 304-598-1103

*Carla Stadelman, Assistant Administrator*
*John Forester, Chief Executive Officer*

An 80-bed freestanding rehabilitation hospital serving central WV, southwestern PA, western MD and northwestern VA. Offers specialized programs to serve the patient population. Brain injury, spinal cord injury, stroke, neuromuscular, pulmonary disorders, pediatrics, ventilator dependence, orthopedics, amputee, case management and pain management.

**8988 Western Hills Rehabilitation Hospital**
3 Western Hills Drive
Parkersburg, WV 26105 304-420-1300
FAX: 304-420-1374

*Dean Hatcher, Chief Executive Officer*

## Wisconsin

**8989 Extendicare**
111 W Michigan Street
Milwaukee, WI 53203 414-908-8000
800-395-5000
FAX: 414-908-8143
www.extendicare.com

*Mel Rhinelander, Chief Executive Officer*

**8990 Midwest Neurological Rehabilitation Center**
1701 Sharp Road
Waterford, WI 53185
800-697-5380
FAX: 262-534-8505

A comprehensive, integrated neurological rehabilitation center located only 25 minutes from Milwaukee. The Center provides seven comprehensive programs: acute hospital rehabilitation, pediatric acute rehabilitation, pediatric postacute rehabilitation, rehabilitation and skilled nursing, community-based rehabilitation and vocational rehabilitation.

**8991 St. Catherine's Hospital**
3556 7th Avenue
Kenosha, WI 53140
FAX: 262-653-5795

*Rick Schultz, Program Manager*

**8992 St. Joseph Hospital**
611 Saint Joseph Avenue
Marshfield, WI 54449 715-387-1713
FAX: 715-389-3939
www.ministryhealth.org

*Raymond Carroll, Head Nurse*
*Catherine Olson, Director*
*Michael Schmidt, Chief Executive Officer*

A values-driven healthcare delivery network of aligned hospitals, clinics, long-term care facilities, home care agencies, dialysis centers and many other programs and services in Wisconsin and Minnesota.

## Wyoming

**8993 Spalding Rehabilitation Hospital at Memorial Hospital of Laramie**
300 E 23rd Street
Cheyenne, WY 82001 307-635-4141

*Michael Spaulding MD*

## Alabama

**8994    Alabama Department of Rehabilitation Services**
2129 E South Boulevard
Montgomery, AL  36116                    334-281-8780
                                        800-441-7607
                                   FAX: 334-281-1973
                                   www.rehab.state.al.us

*Steve Shivers, President*

State agency which provides services and assistance to Alabama's children and adults with disabilities.

**8995    Alabama Goodwill Industries**
2350 Green Springs Highway S
Birmingham, AL  35205                    205-323-6331
                                   FAX: 205-324-9059

*Don Smith, Director*

Work adjustment and remunerative work programs.

**8996    American Rehab Center Neuro Care Unit Mobile Infirmary**
5 Mobile Infirmary Circle
Mobile, AL  36607                        251-431-5559
                                   FAX: 251-431-5222

*Robert Berg, President*

Postacute rehabilitation program.

**8997    Arc of Jefferson County**
300 S Hull Street
Montgomery, AL  36104                    334-262-7688
                                        866-243-9557
                                   FAX: 334-834-9737
                       e-mail: info@thearcofalabama.com
                                   www.thearcofalabama.com

*Thomas B Holmes, Executive Director*

The Arc of Jefferson County serves children and adults with mental retardation and/or other developmental disabilities. Services are provided through the following programs: the HOPE (Helping Others through Parent Education) Early Intervention Program; Adult Day Services; Residential Services; and Arc-Way Industries, a sheltered and supported employment program.

**8998    Association for Retarded Citizens of Jefferson County (The Arc)**
215 21st Avenue S
Birmingham, AL  35205                    205-323-6383
                                   FAX: 205-323-0085

*William F Hoehle II, Executive Director*

The ARC has four primary components. The HOPE Program provides early intervention therapy services to developmentally delayed infants and toddlers up to the age of three years. The ARC also provides services to adults ages 21 and over with mental retardation. Adult services provides education, pre-vocational screening, and socialization skills training. Employment services provides vocational training, a sheltered workshop, off-site job skills training, job coach services and more. Residential s

**8999    Briarcliff Nursing Home & Rehab Facility**
850 9th Street NW
Alabaster, AL  35007                     205-663-3859
                                   FAX: 205-663-9791

*Michelle Bonner, Director Nursing*
*Jody McMichen, Administrator*

Postacute rehabilitation program.

**9000    Butler Adult Training Center**
680 Hardscramble Road
Greenville, AL  36037                    334-382-2353
                                   FAX: 334-382-9518

*Nikitin Tayne, Director*

Clients 21 years of age and older who are mentally retarded. School age clients are also served at the center and must also be mentally retarded. Clients receive training in Independent Living Skills, Self-Care, Language Skills, Learning, Self Direction and Economic Self-Sufficiency. The clients also participate in Special Olympics activities.

**9001    Cheaha Mental Health**
PO Box 1248
Sylacauga, AL  35150                     256-245-1340
                                   FAX: 256-245-1343

*Larry Morris, President*
*Michelle Houston, Business Manager*

Offers mental health rehabilitation, respite care, residential facilities and more for the mentally disabled. Serves Talladega, Coosa, Clay and Randolph counties.

**9002    Children's Rehabilitation Service**
2121 E South Boulevard
Montgomery, AL  36116                    334-288-0220
                                        800-441-7607
                                   FAX: 334-281-1388
                       e-mail: alabama@rehab.state.al.us

*Steve Shivers, Commissioner*

**9003    Chilton-Shelby Mental Health Center/ The Mitchell Center**
PO Box 689
Calera, AL  35040                        205-668-1327
                                   FAX: 205-685-0900
                                   www.chiltonshelby.org/

*Melodie Crawford, Executive Director*
*Kathryn T Crouthers, Assistant Clinical Director*
*Kim Akridge, Manager*

Offers mental health rehabilitation services and more for the recovery of mentally disabled adults. Serves Chilton and Shelby counties.

**9004    EL Darden Rehabilitation Center**
1001 E Broad Street
Gadsden, AL  35903                       256-547-5751
                                   FAX: 256-547-5761

*Tom Strother*

Work hardening and disciplinary programs.

**9005    Easter Seals Central Alabama**
2125 E South Boulevard
Montgomery, AL  36116                    334-288-0240
                                   FAX: 334-288-7171
                       e-mail: easterseals@worldnet.att.net

*Larry Johnson, Executive Director*

A private, nonprofit organization offering services audiology, physical, occupational, lymphedemia and speech therapy, psychological counseling, vocational evaluation and assessment, person, social and work adjustment training, GED preparation, computer service training, job placement and follow-up, and special learning disabilities service and supported employment service.

**9006 Easter Seals West Alabama**
1110 6th Avenue E
Tuscaloosa, AL 35401          205-759-1211
                             800-726-1216
                        FAX: 205-349-1162
                   e-mail: eswa@dbtech.net
                www.alabama.easter-seals.org

*Loie Sears Robinson, Administrator*

Leading organization in helping children and adults with disabilities to live with equality, dignity and independence. Rehabilitation services are provided in two divisions: outpatient rehabilitation division (physical therapy, occupational therapy, speech therapy, hearing evaluation, sell and service hearind aids) and vocational division (vocational evaluation and vocational development). Services are rendered regardless of age, race, sex, color, creed, national origin, veteran's status.

**9007 Geer Adult Training Center**
PO Box 419
Carrollton, AL 35447          205-367-8032
                        FAX: 205-367-8032

*Yvonne Williams, Program Coordinator*

**9008 Goodwill Easter Seals of the Gulf Coast**
2448 Gordon Smith Drive
Mobile, AL 36617              251-471-1581
                             800-411-0068
                        FAX: 251-476-4303
                 e-mail: stephanie@gesgc.org
                    alabama.easterseals.com

*John McCain, Chief Executive Officer*
*Stephanie Constantine, VP Marketing*

Vocational, medical, pre-school education, day care, recreation and other support services.

**9009 Indian Rivers**
1915 6th Street
2190
Tuscaloosa, AL 35401          205-345-1600
                        FAX: 205-391-0106

*Laurie Prentice-dunn, Director*
*Jim Moore, Executive Director*

Services are available to adults who have serious mental illness resulting in personal, family or work-related problems. Counseling may take place in either individual or group settings, identification, evaluation and treatment services are available to persons who experience problems related to alcohol and drug abuse and counseling services are available for children and adolescents who have a severe emotional disturbance causing discipline problems at home and school.

**9010 Lighthouse**
PO Box 218
Brent, AL 35034              205-926-4681
                        FAX: 205-926-6016

*Gwen Langley, Program Coordinator*
*Gwen Pow, Manager*

**9011 Low Vision Clinic/UAB School of Optometry**
1716 University Boulevard
Birmingham, AL 35294          205-956-3276
                        FAX: 205-934-0911
                   www.main.uab.edu/optometry

*RW Nowakowski, Chief of Staff*
*Dr. Marsha Swanson, Chief Low Vision Patient Care*
*Brenda Watkins, Optometric Technician*

Multidisciplinary clinic in a major medical center which provides a comprehensive vision evaluation and prescription of low vision aids for those who are visually impaired. Fees are charged for all examination procedures, special diagnostic tests and materials with most insurance plans accepted. Cost depends on services rendered.

**9012 MARC Enterprises**
759 Congress Street
Mobile, AL 36603              251-470-0821
                        FAX: 251-470-0824

*Andrew Acklen, Executive Director*

Serving the mentally retarded of Mobile County both locally and through its state and national affiliations. Their united efforts through this voluntary association assure the availability of services and provide the opportunity for achievement.

**9013 North Central Alabama Mental Retardation Authority**
PO Box 597
Decatur, AL 35602             256-355-7315
                        FAX: 256-355-7317

*Earl E Brightwell, Executive Director*

NCA, MRA, Inc. functions as an entrance to the service delivery system for the Alabama Department of Mental Health and Mental Retardation and is responsible for planning, development, implementation of programs, sanction, monitoring, referral, and case management for persons with mental retardation/developmental disabilities in Morgan, Lawrence and Limestone Counties.

**9014 Northwest Alabama Easter Seals Children's Clinic Rehabilitation Center**
1450 E Avalon Avenue
Muscle Shoals, AL 35661       256-381-1110

*Robert H Nelson, Administrator*

**9015 Southeastern Blind Rehabilitation Center**
Department of Veterans Affairs Medical Center
700 19th Street S
Birmingham, AL 35233          205-933-4512
                        FAX: 205-933-4484

*Frank D Wilkes, Director*
*Y Parris, Administrator*

The Center is a 32-bed inpatient blind rehabilitation program which serves the southeastern region. The majority of client services are for basic adjustment and management to sight loss. Basic services include: low vision, orientation and mobility, manual skills, ADL and communications. Training on electronic mobility aids and adapted computers is also available on a restricted basis. The program maintains graduate education affiliations and an active applied research program.

**9016 Tennessee Valley Rehabilitation**
PO Box 1926
Decatur, AL 35602             256-350-2041
                             866-350-2041
                        FAX: 256-350-2806
                     www.tvrcdecatur.com

*Kathy Cagle, Director*

Work hardening and disciplinary programs.

**9017 Vaughn-Blumberg Services**
PO Box 8646
Dothan, AL 36304              334-793-3102
                        FAX: 334-793-7740

*Ed Dorsey, Executive Director*

**9018 West Central Alabama Easter Seals Rehabilitation Center**
PO Box 750
Selma, AL 36702 334-872-8421
800-801-4776
FAX: 334-872-3907
e-mail: wcarcdw@tomnet.com
www.al.easter-seals.org/selma

*Larry F Lewis, Administrator*
*David White, Program Coordinator*

Vocational evaluation, job development, employment development, job coaching, counseling, medical services, audiology, pre-school development programs.

## Alaska

**9019 Alaska Center for the Blind and Visually Impaired**
3903 Taft Drive
Anchorage, AK 99517 907-248-7770
800-770-7517
e-mail: info@alaskabvi.org
www.alaskabvi.org

*Karla Jutzi, Executive Director*
*Karen Coady, Program Manager*
*Arlee Cada, Finance Manager*

Services to help the adult residential or community-based student become independent and self-sufficient by offering independent travel, Braille reading and writing, use of assiative technology such as talking computers, manual skills and personal, as well as home management. There is a special program for those 55 years of age and older who are experiencing a vision loss and another program for rural Alaska Native youth who are visually impaired.

**9020 Alaska Veterans Facility**
4201 Tudor Centre Drive
Suite 115
Anchorage, AK 99508 907-277-3224

*David Law DVM, Owner*
Veterans medical clinic offering disabled veterans medical treatments.

## Arizona

**9021 Arizona Center for the Blind and Visually Impaired**
3100 E Roosevelt Street
Phoenix, AZ 85008 602-273-7411
FAX: 602-273-7410
e-mail: jlamay@acbi.org
www.acbvi.org

*James May, Executive Director*
*Frank Vance, Director*
*Diana Miladin, Communication/Development Coord.*

A private, nonprofit organization that provides comprehensive rehabilitation services and more for the blind and visually handicapped. The staff includes 20 instructional and adminstrative professionals.

**9022 Arizona Industries for the Blind**
3013 W Lincoln Street
Phoenix, AZ 85009 602-269-5131
FAX: 602-269-9462
www.azdes.gov/aib

*Richard Monaco, General Manager*

Offers rehabilitation services, vocational/pre-vocational evaluation and training, work adjustment, job development and employment and training opportunties for individuals who are blind.

**9023 Beacon Foundation for the Mentally Retarded**
25 E Drachman Street
Tucson, AZ 85705 520-623-3454
FAX: 520-623-3494

*Paul Wagler, Chief Executive Director*
*Wendy Toth, Manager*

Committed to effectively assisting adults with disabilities to maximize their personal, social, vocational and educational skills in order to attain a successful and meaningful independence within the Tucson community.

**9024 Carondelet Brain Injury Programs and Services (Bridges Now)**
350 N Wilmot Road
Tucson, AZ 85711 520-873-3761
FAX: 520-873-3743
e-mail: sascher@carondelet.org

*Sarah Ascher, Rehab Coordinator*
*Wes Colvin, Chief Executive Officer*

Comprehensive outpatient rehabilitation program. PT, OT, ST, Psychology and Rehab Counseling Services.

**9025 Casa Grande Rehabilitation Programs**
208 W Main Street
Casa Grande, AZ 85222 602-254-0754
FAX: 520-426-9471

*James Musick, Executive Director*

**9026 Community Rehabilitation Services: Tucson**
1789 W Jefferson Street
Phoenix, AZ 85007 602-542-3332
800-563-1221
FAX: 602-542-3778
TTY: 602-542-6049
www.azdes.gov

*Craig Warren, Administrator*
Postacute rehabilitation program.

**9027 Desert Life Health Care Center**
1919 W Medical Street
Tucson, AZ 85704 520-297-8311
FAX: 520-544-0930

*Carolyn Blasi, Executive Director*
Postacute rehabilitation program.

**9028 Freestone Rehabilitation Center**
10617 E Oasis Drive
Apache Junction, AZ 85220 480-986-1531
FAX: 480-986-1538

*Randy Gray, Executive Director*
*Cherie Vance, Manager*

**9029 Institute for Human Development**
Northern Arizona University
PO Box 5630
Flagstaff, AZ 86011 928-523-7319
FAX: 928-523-9127
www.nau.edu/ihd

*Levi Esguerra, Director*

The Institute values and supports the independence, productivity and inclusion of Arizona's citizens with disabilities. Based on the values and beliefs, the Institute conducts training, research and services that further these goals.

**9030 John C Lincoln Hospital North Mountain**
250 E Dunlap Avenue
Phoenix, AZ 85020
602-943-2381
FAX: 602-944-8062
e-mail: webmaster@jcl.com
www.jcl.com

*Daniel Coleman, President/CEO*

Mission is to assist each person entrusted to our care to enjoy the fullest gift of health possible, and work with others to build a community where a helping hand is available for our most vulnerable members.

**9031 La Frontera Center**
502 W 29th Street
Tucson, AZ 85713
520-884-9920

*Floyd Martinez MD*
*Daniel Ranieri, Chief Executive Officer*

Provides remunerative work.

**9032 Manor Care Nursing and Rehab Center: Tucson**
3705 N Swan Road
Tucson, AZ 85704
520-229-7088
FAX: 520-529-0038

*Mark Bedinger, Administrator*
*Sheila Powell, Director Admissions/Marketing*

Postacute rehabilitation program.

**9033 Nova Care**
1010 E McDowell Road
Suite 102
Phoenix, AZ 85006
602-256-7232
FAX: 602-256-7292

*Jeff Sullvin, Manager*

Work hardening and disciplinary programs.

**9034 Perry Rehabilitation Center**
3146 E Windsor Avenue
Phoenix, AZ 85008
602-956-0400
FAX: 602-957-7610
e-mail: perrycenteratuswest.com

*Robin Ratcliff, Director*
*Jim Musick, President*

Provides services for people with disabilities, cognitive disabilities including residential services, day treatment, job training and job placement.

**9035 Phoenix Veterans Center**
141 E Palm Lane
Suite 100
Phoenix, AZ 85004
602-379-4769
FAX: 602-379-4139

*John Dooley, Contact Person*
*Ken Benckwitz, Manager*

Veterans medical clinic offering disabled veterans medical treatments.

**9036 Progress Valley: Phoenix**
10830 N 71st Place
Suite 203
Scottsdale, AZ 85254
602-274-5424
FAX: 602-274-5473
e-mail: jlarson@progressvalley.org

*Julie Larsson, Associate Director*
*Joe Brugh, Senior Counselor*

Residential aftercare for alcoholism and chemical dependency. Certified chemical dependency counselors provide individual treatment.

**9037 Samaritan Rehabilitation Institute**
1111 E McDowell Road
Phoenix, AZ 85006
602-239-2296
FAX: 602-239-5868

*Ronald Herrick, Associate Administrator*
*Annette Bowen, Manager*

**9038 Toyei Industries**
PO Box 55
Ganado, AZ 86505
928-736-2417
888-45T-OYEI
FAX: 928-736-2495

*Anita Hildreth, Social Services Manager*
*Russell Morgan, Executive Director*
*Donna Alesandro, Assistant Clinical Director*

Serves the needs of developmentally disabled and the severely mentally impaired adult citizens of the Navajo Nation and other Indian Nations. Staff of 60+ serves the needs of all the Navajo adults. Services include day treatment programs, home community-based services and residential and group home services.

**9039 Tucson Association for the Blind and Visually Imparied**

3767 E Grant Road
Tucson, AZ 85716
520-881-4313
FAX: 520-795-1336
e-mail: mgordon@saddi.us
www.saadi.us

*Michael Gordon, Executive Director*

Offers health services, counseling, social work, home and personal management, computer training, low vision aids and more for the visually handicapped 18 years or older.

**9040 Valley of the Sun Rehabilitation Hospital**
13460 N 67th Avenue
Glendale, AZ 85304
623-878-8800
FAX: 623-878-5254
www.healthsouth.com

*Beth Bacher, Administrator*

A 60-bed free-standing hospital that offers acute physical rehabilitation, outpatient therapy services and day hospital treatment.

**9041 Yuma Center for the Visually Impaired**
2770 S Avenue B
Yuma, AZ 85364
928-726-1310
FAX: 928-783-3261

*Calvin Roberts, Executive Director*

A private nonprofit agency offering services for totally blind and legally blind children and adults in the Arizona area.

## Arkansas

**9042 Arkansas Lighthouse for the Blind**
PO Box 192666
Little Rock, AR 72219
501-562-2222
FAX: 501-568-5275
e-mail: ALB49799@aol.com

*Bill Johnson, Executive Vice President*

Offers educational industrial evaluation and training to the legally blind and multihandicapped. Funded by workshop sales and contributions, the staff includes ten full time employees

**9043   Beverly Enterprises Network**
1200 S Waldron Road
Fort Smith, AR  72903                     479-201-2000
                                          800-666-9996
                                   FAX: 479-452-5131

*Randy Churchey, Chief Executive Officer*

Offers a progressive approach to subacute care. The goal of this organization is to assist injured and disabled individuals regain the level of independence to which they have been accustomed. Provides support and training programs, patient and family services and specialty programs for patients.

**9044   Easter Seals: Arkansas**
3920 Woodland Heights Road
Little Rock, AR  72212                     501-227-3602
                                          877-533-3600
                                   FAX: 501-227-3658
                             e-mail: infol@easterseals.com
                                   www.ar.easter-seals.org

*Sharon Moone-Jochums, President/CEO*
*Linda Rogers, VP Programs*
*Stephanie Smith, VP Finance/Administration*

**9045   HEALTHSOUTH Rehabilitation Hospital Fort Smith**
Health South
1401 S J Street
Fort Smith, AR  72901                     479-785-3300
                                   FAX: 479-785-8599
                                   www.healthsouth.com

*Julie Stec, Chief Executive Officer*
*Holli Baker, Director Business Development*

A free-standing 80-bed comprehensive physical medicine and rehabilitation hospital offering inpatient and outpatient services. Provides specialized medical and therapy services, designed to assist physically challenged persons to reach their highest level of independent function.

**9046   Lions World Services for the Blind**
2811 Fair Park Boulevard
Little Rock, AR  72204                     501-664-7100
                                          800-248-0754
                                   FAX: 501-664-2743
                              e-mail: training@lwsb.org
                                          www.lwsb.org

*Ramona Sangalli, Chief Executive Officer*

Offers services in the areas of health education, recreation, rehabilitation, counseling, employment, computer training and more for all legally blind residents of the U.S. The staff includes 56 full time employees.

**9047   Little Rock Vet Center #0713**
Department of Veterans Affairs of Washington DC
201 W Broadway Street
Suite A
North Little Rock, AR 72114                501-324-6395

*Jeffrey Geye, Director*

Vet Center provides PTSD counseling to veterans of a combat zone. No medical care provided.

**9048   New Medico Rehabilitation Center at Timber Ridge Ranch**
PO Box 208
Benton, AR  72018                         501-594-5211
                                   FAX: 501-594-5211

*Rob Daniels, Executive Director*

## California

**9049   ARC-VC Magic Muffin Cafe**
1661 Pacific Avenue
Oxnard, CA  93033                         805-483-0341
                                   FAX: 805-483-2594

*Shirley Dove*

Provides remunerative work.

**9050   ARC: VC Community Connections West**
295 Arcade Drive
Ventura, CA  93001                        805-652-0541
                                   FAX: 805-652-0542

*Mary Kay, Program Manager*

**9051   ARC: VC Ventura**
295 Arcade Drive
Ventura, CA  93003                        805-652-0541

*Mary Kay, Manager*

**9052   Accentcare**
135 Technology Drive
Suite 150
Irvine, CA  92618                         949-623-1500
                                          800-834-3059
                                   FAX: 949-623-1499
                              e-mail: info@accentcare.com
                                          www.accentcare.com

*William Comte, Chief Executive Officer*

Postacute rehabilitation program: home care aides follow through with rehabilitation instructions given by physical, occupational and speech therapists. Other home care services are available, serving special needs for Alzheimer's, blind, brain injury, MS, ostomies, parkinsonism, spinal injury and stroke.

**9053   American Rehab Centers Neuro Care Unit**
2776 Pacific Avenue
Long Beach, CA  90806                     562-426-4561
                                   FAX: 562-427-0149
Postacute rehabilitation program.

**9054   Arrow Center**
3035 G Street
San Diego, CA  92102                      619-233-8855
                                   FAX: 619-233-4932

*Dorothy Cummings*
*Melanie Coy, Manager*
Work hardening and disciplinary programs.

**9055   Association for Retarded Citizens: Alameda County**
575 Independent Road
Oakland, CA  94621                        510-639-4680
                                   FAX: 510-639-4684

*Ram Sirck, Director*

Offers the Right Track program in which selected workers are grouped together on a contract basis to maximize work productivity. Provides a full benefit package, as well as a permanent supervisor. A worker is matched to a job of at least 20 hours per week and then trained by the staff of The Right Track.

**9056  Azure Acres Chemical Dependency Recovery Center**
C RC Health
2264 Green Hill Road
Sebastopol, CA 95472                    707-823-3385
                                        800-222-7292
                                   FAX: 707-823-8972
                                   www.azureacres.com

*Shannon Clay, Executive Director*

Offers rehabilitation services and residential care for the person
with an alcohol or drug abuse related problems.

**9057  Back in the Saddle**
9775 Mockingbird Avenue
Apple Valley, CA 92308                  760-240-3217
                                   FAX: 760-240-3274

*Richard Smith PhD, Owner*
*Erika Reed, Co-Director*

A long term community residential facility for head injured
adults. House parents live on-site; and oversee a variety of programs which are individually designed and might include
classes in community college, placement in a workshop or on a
workstation, volunteer positions and home skills assignments.
Recreational outing range from horseback riding to weekend
camping. Apartment programs available as set-up. Price:
$2800-$3000 per month.

**9058  Ballard Rehabilitation Hospital**
Sun Health Sun Bridge Sun Dance
1760 W 16th Street
San Bernardino, CA 92411                909-473-1200
                                        800-761-1226
                                   FAX: 909-473-1276
                                   www.ballardrehab.org

*Robert Herrick, Chief Executive Officer*
*Mary Hunt, Chief Operating Officer*
*Patty Meinhardt, Director Marketing/Admissions*

Ballard Rehab Hospital is a free standing specialty hospital and
provides the complete continuum of acute, subacute and outpatient rehabilitation, dedicated to providing rehab seminars to
adults and children. The following inpatient and outpatient programs are available: CNA (Stroke) Rehab; Spinal Cord Injury
Rehab; Brain Injury Rehab; Pain Management Rehab; Injured
Worker Programs; and Post Amputation Rehab.

**9059  Bayview Nursing and Rehabilitation**
516 Willow Street
Alameda, CA 94501                       510-521-5600
                                   FAX: 510-337-0698
                                                www.

*Mary Webster, Administrator*
Postacute rehabilitation program.

**9060  Belden Center**
606 Humboldt Street
Santa Rosa, CA 95404                    707-579-2735
                                   FAX: 707-579-4145

*Wes Killian, Program Director*
*Pamela Fadden, Owner*

Postacute rehabilitation program.

**9061  Brotman Medical Center: RehabCare Unit**
Brotman Medical Center
3828 Delmas Ter
Culver City, CA 90232                   310-836-7000
                                        800-677-1238
                                   FAX: 310-202-4105
                                   www.brotmanmedicalcenter.com

*Jennifer Cortez, Program Manager*

Culver City is centrally located within the city of Los Angeles.
These are two programs offering inpatient rehabilitation. The
acute rehab program is designed for patients who need physical
rehabilitation due to injury or medical disability. This program
requires patients to participate in 3 hours therapy per day. The
sub-acute program is designed especially for patients who need
rehab but cannot tolerate the intensity of the acute rehab program.

**9062  Build Rehabilitation Industries**
1323 Truman Street
San Fernando, CA 91340                  818-898-0020
                                   FAX: 818-898-1949

*Matthew Lynch, President/CEO*
*Michele A Utley, Vice President*
*Isabel Boniface, Human Resources Executive*

Comprehensive C.A.R.F. Accredited vocational rehabilitation
services for adults with disabilities or other barriers to employment. Programs include: Sheltered Workshops, Work Evaluation, Work Hardening and Adjustment, Supported Employment,
Job Placement, Independent Living Skills, Behavior Management, Adult Development Center, On-the-Job Training, and
One-Stop Workforce Development Career Center.

**9063  California Elwyn**
18325 Mount Baldy Circle
Fountain Valley, CA 92708               714-557-6313
                                   FAX: 714-963-2961
                                   e-mail: info@caelwyn.org
                                              www.elwyn.org

*Joan McKinney, Executive Director*

Provides opportunities for people challenged by physical and
mental disabilities who are 18 or older. California Elwyn develops an Individual Rehabilitation Plan for all consumers. Contract work, shrinkwrap, janitorial are just some of the types of
jobs done. Supported Employment Services are available and
over 100 consumers currently are employed. Funded by the
State Department of Rehabilitation and Vocational Rehabilitation.

**9064  California Eye Institute**
1360 E Turdan Avenue
Fresno, CA 93720                        559-449-5000
                                   FAX: 559-499-5090

*Virgil Snow*
*Denise Haar, Manager*

A private, nonprofit agency offering services such as health, educational, recreational, rehabilitation and employment counseling to the totally blind, legally blind and visually impaired. The
staff includes two full time workers.

**9065  California Veterans Center**
859 S Harbor Boulevard
Anaheim, CA 92805                       714-776-0161

*Robert Key, Manager*

Veterans medical clinic offering disabled veterans medical
treatments.

**9066  Camp Recovery Center**
3192 Glen Canyon Road
Scotts Valley, CA 95066                 831-438-1868
                                        800-924-2879
                                   FAX: 831-438-5833
                                   www.camprecovery.com

*Paige Bottom, Executive Director*

A free-standing social model recovery center for chemical dependency located on 25 wooded acres in the Santa Cruz Mountains. The services include: medical detoxification, complete medical evaluation, psychiatric evaluation and counseling, psychological testing, individual counseling and more. Helps the recovery from chemical dependency in a easier, warm and caring environment.

**9067 Campobello Chemical Dependency Recovery Center**
3250 Guerneville Road
Santa Rosa, CA 95401
707-579-4066
800-805-1833
FAX: 707-579-1603
e-mail: campocdrc@aol.com
www.campobello.org

*James Cody, Executive Director*

**9068 Casa Colina Centers for Rehabilitation**
PO Box 6001
Pomona, CA 91769
909-596-7733
800-926-5462
FAX: 909-593-0153
e-mail: rehab@casacolina.org
www.casacolina.org

*Fred Ardnow, Associate Director*
*Felice Loverso, Chief Executive Officer*

Casa Colina, has pioneered effective programs to create opportunity for health, productivity and self-esteem for persons with disability since 1936. Through medical rehabilitation, transitional living, residential, community, and prevention and wellness programs. Casa Colina serves more than 7,000 persons annually. Casa Colina, a non-profit organization, offers a unique spectrum of opportunities, achievement and results to patients and their families.

**9069 Casa Colina Paova Village**
PO Box 6001
Pomona, CA 91769
909-596-7733
800-926-5462
FAX: 909-593-0153
e-mail: rehab@casacolina.org
www.casacolina.org

*Chandrahas Agarwal, Medical Director*
*Felice Loverso, Chief Executive Officer*

Long term residential services for adults with developmental disability. Residences include Malmquist House, Woodbend House, and Hillsdale House, all located in Claremont, California.

**9070 Casa Colina Residential Services: Rancho Pino Verde**
Casa Colina Center for Rehabilitation
11981 Midway Avenue
Lucerne Valley, CA 92356
760-248-6245
FAX: 760-248-2245
e-mail: rehab@casacolina.org
www.casacolina.org

*Rodney Peek, Director*
*Chris Schlanser, Program Director*

Long term residential services in rural environment for adults with brain injury.

**9071 Casa Colina Transitional Living Center**
255 E Bonita Avenue
Pomona, CA 91767
909-596-7733
FAX: 909-593-7541
www.casacolina.org

*Barbara Urabe, Program Administrator*
*Felice Loverso, Chief Executive Officer*

Postacute rehabilitation program.

**9072 Casa Colina Transitional Living Center: Pomona**
PO Box 6001
Pomona, CA 91769
909-596-7733
800-926-5462
FAX: 909-593-0153
e-mail: rehab@casacolina.org
www.casacolina.org

*Felice L Loverso, President/CEO*
*Robert E Duncan, Chairman*

Post acute short term residential program for persons with brain injury. In a home-like setting, therapy promotes successful re-entry to home and community living.

**9073 Cedars of Marin**
PO Box 947
Ross, CA 94957
415-454-5310
FAX: 415-454-0573
www.thecedarsofmarin.org

*Brenda McIvor, Executive Director*
*Alexa Witter, Executive Assistant*
*Martin Williamson, Administrator*

Provides residential and day programs for adults with developmental disabilities.

**9074 Center for Neuro Skills**
2658 Mount Vernon Avenue
Bakersfield, CA 93306
661-872-3408
800-843-2943
FAX: 661-872-5150
e-mail: cns@neuroskills.com
www.neuroskills.com/cns

*John Schultz, Vice President*
*Mark J Ashley, President/Owner*

A comprehensive, post-acute, community based head-injury rehabilitation program serving over 100 clients per year. Since 1980, CNS has effectively treated the entire spectrum of head-injured clients, including those with severe behavioral disorders, cognitive/perceptual impairments, speech/language problems, physical disabilities and post-concussion syndrome.

**9075 Center for the Partially Sighted**
12301 Wilshire Boulevard
Suite 600
Los Angeles, CA 90025
310-458-3501
800-481-EYES
FAX: 310-458-8179
e-mail: info@low-vision.org
www.low-vision.org

*LaDonna Ringering PhD, Executive Director*
*Pat Jordan, Public Information Manager*
*Phyllis Amarai PhD, Clinical Director*

Services for partially sighted and legally blind people include low vision evaluations, the design and prescription of low vision devices and adaptive technology, as well as counseling and rehabilitation training (independent living skills and orientation/mobility training). Special programs include children's program, diabetes and vision loss program, Technology demonstrations. Store carries low vision aids. Catalog available.

**9076 Central Coast Neurobehavioral Center OPTIONS**
OPTIONS
800 Quintana Road, Suite 2C
PO Box 877
Morro Bay, CA 93443
805-772-6066
FAX: 805-772-6067
e-mail: info@optionsccnbc.org
www.optionsccnbc.org

*Michael Mamot, CEO*
*Ole von Frausing-Borch, COO*

Serves adults with developmental disabilities, traumatic head injuries, or other neurological impairments. OPTIONS operates two transitional living centers, eight licensed residential facilities, two licensed community integration day programs and a licensed short term stabilization center. Services offered include: supported and independent living services, group and individual vocational services, neuropsychological assessment, occupational therapy, cognitive therapy, speech therapy and more.

**9077 Cerebral Palsy: North County Center**
San Diego Center
205 W Mission Avenue
Suite G
Escondido, CA 92025       760-743-1050
888-827-0771
FAX: 760-746-0172
www.ucpsd.org

*Gill Hennessey, Director*
*Georgia Baskin, Manager*

Provides remunerative work.

**9078 Children's Hospital Central California Reh abilitation Center**
9300 Valley Childrens Place
Madera, CA 93636       559-353-7290
FAX: 559-353-8060
www.valleychildrens.org

*Shirleen Fowler, Manager*
*David Meagher, MD*

We provide rehabilitation services for those birth through 21 years in both inpatient and outpatient settings.

**9079 Children's Hospital Los Angeles Rehabilitation Program**
4650 W Sunset Boulevard
6
Los Angeles, CA 90027       323-669-2231
FAX: 323-665-4118

*Luis Montes, Director*

A comprehensive program specializing in the treatment of patients with brain injury.

**9080 Children's Therapy Center**
770 Paseo Camarillo
Suite 120
Camarillo, CA 93010       805-383-1501
FAX: 805-383-1504
e-mail: ctcinc@paragon.net
www.ctcinc@paragon.net

*Jo Murphy Hyland, Administrative Director*

Provides individual occupational therapy, speech/language therapy, family/child consulting, education services and physical therapy consultation for children. Evaluations and treatment are on an individual basis and special emphasis is placed on a multidisciplinary approach with information sharing, and often team treatment.

**9081 Clausen House**
88 Vernon Street
Oakland, CA 94610       510-839-0050
FAX: 510-444-5790
e-mail: info@clausenhouse.org
www.clausenhouse.org

*Nan Butterworth, Executive Director*
*Megan Hornbecker, Development Associate*

A private nonprofit organization which emphasizes greater independence for developmentally disabled adults. Programs encompass residential services, adult education, day program training, recreational opportunities, supported employment services, independent living, supported living training and assistance.

**9082 Coastline Enterprises**
PO Box 1025
Crescent City, CA 95531       707-464-8338

*Nancy L Borge, Executive Director*

Services people with special needs, and their families.

**9083 Community Access Program: Hilltop**
2801 Robert Miller Drive
Richmond, CA 94806       510-222-8266
FAX: 510-222-8290
e-mail: carolmcap@aol.com
www.ContraCostaARC.com

*Carol Anne McCrary, Executive Director*
*Naomi Santos, Program Coordinator*

A private nonprofit membership-based organization dedicated to enhancing the quality of life of individuals with mental retardation and other developmental disabilities.

**9084 Community Hospital and Rehabilitation Center of Los Gatos-Saratoga**
355 Dardanelli Lane
Los Gatos, CA 95032       408-866-4020
FAX: 408-866-4077
e-mail: CHLG.ask@renethealth.com
www.communityhospitalLG.com

*Modestine Sain, Director Rehab Services*

Offers rehabilitation services, inpatient and outpatient care, physical therapy, occupational therapy and more for the physically challenged adult.

**9085 Critical Air Medicine**
Montgomery Field
4141 Kearny Villa Road
San Diego, CA 92123       858-514-6060
800-247-8326
FAX: 619-571-0835

Offers emergency medical care by air medical transport carriers. These carriers are fully equipped with medical equipment and supplies for cardiovascular emergencies, respiratory supplies, orthopedic supplies and medications.

**9086 Crutcher's Serenity House**
50 Hillcrest Road
Saint Helena, CA 94574       877-274-4968
FAX: 707-963-2309
e-mail: crutcherssh@earthlink.net
www.crutcherssh.com

*Robert Crutcher, Owner/CEO*
*Lu Crutcher, Executive Director*

A privately owned and operated facility that introduces to residents a new lifestyle free of all chemicals, and a new awareness of their total being. The length of the program is four weeks and is within five minutes of an acute care hospital. The Center is licensed for 19 beds, male and female located in a home-like setting with an emphasis on maintaining a family atmosphere.

**9087 Daniel Freeman Rehabilitation Centers**
333 N Prairie Avenue
Inglewood, CA 90301       310-674-7050
FAX: 310-419-8232

*Louis Ceppi, Associate Administrator*

Comprehensive rehabilitation services which address needs and issues of the physically diabled and their families. We offer accute input rehabilitation, outpatient and short term skilled nursing rehabilitaion. Specialty areas include: brain injury, stroke, spinal chord injury, chronic pain, arthritis.

**9088 Delano Regional Medical Center**
1401 Garces Highway
Delano, CA 93215
661-725-4800
FAX: 661-721-5211
www.drmc.com

*Allan Komarek, Chief Executive Officer*
Postacute rehabilitation program.

**9089 Devereux Santa Barbara**
PO Box 6784
Santa Barbara, CA 93160
805-968-2525
FAX: 805-968-3247
e-mail: amcniff@devereux.org
www.devereux.org

*Anne McNiff, Director Agency Relations*
*Anna Martinez, Admissions Coordinator*
*Janis Johnson, Public Relations Coordinator*

Serves ages 8-88, who have developmental disabilities, emotional disturbances, neurological impairments, brain injuries, schizophrenia, autism, and dual diagnosis. The Center has a licensed capacity of 188 served in a continuum of services including residential, vocational, educational and more.

**9090 Division of Physical Medicine and Rehabilitation**
San Joaquin General Hospital
500 W Hospital Road
French Camp, CA 95231
209-334-6599
FAX: 209-468-6281
www.sjphysicalmedicine.com

*Carolyn Genschmer, Rehabilitation Coordinator*
*Ken Cohen, Manager*

Offers rehabilitation services, inpatient and outpatient care, speech therapy, physical therapy, occupational therapy and more for the physically challenged individual.

**9091 Dr. Karen H Chao Developmental Optometry Karen H. Chao. O.D.**
121 S Del Mar Avenue
Suite A
San Gabriel, CA 91776
626-287-0401
FAX: 626-287-1457
e-mail: drkhchao@yahoo.com
www.BeacoNet.com/Dr.Chao

*James Young, Practice Manager*
*Karen Chao OD, Owner*

Developmental optometrist specializing in the testing and treatment of vision problems and the enhancement of visual performance. Performs visual perceptual testing and training for children and adults. Undetected vision problems interfere with the ability to achieve and are highly correlated with learning difficulties and developmental problems. Provides the opportunity to overcome vision and visual-perceptual dysfunctions.

**9092 Early Childhood Services**
Desert Area Resources & Training
216 N Gold Canyon Street
Ridgecrest, CA 93555
760-375-8494
FAX: 760-375-1288
e-mail: dlukens@dartontarget.org
www.dartontarget.org

*Deanna Lukens, Coordinator*

Provides early intervention services to children who have disabilities or are experiencing delays in development. Provides developmental activities to promote the attainment of developmental milestones so that each child may reach his/her maximum potential. The program also provides therapeutic and educational intervention and offers support and guidance to families.

**9093 East County Training Center**
1855 John Towers Avenue
1865
El Cajon, CA 92020
619-444-9417
FAX: 619-449-7853

*Val Swan*
*Mike Wasyliw, Executive Director*
Work adjustment and remunerative work programs.

**9094 East Los Angeles Doctors Hospital**
4060 Whittier Boulevard
Los Angeles, CA 90023
323-721-2244
FAX: 323-980-9824

*Sergio Castilla, Owner*
Postacute rehabilitation program.

**9095 Easter Seals Disability Svcs: Bay Area**
230 W Monroe Street
Suite 1800
Chicago, IL 60606
312-726-6800
800-221-6827
FAX: 312-726-1494
www.easter-seals.org

*James Williams Jr, Chief Executive Officer*
*Johnny Jones, VP*

**9096 Easter Seals Superior California**
Sacramento Center & Regional Offices
3205 Hurley Way
Sacramento, CA 95864
916-485-6711
888-877-3257
FAX: 916-485-2653
e-mail: info@easterseals-superiorca.org
www.easterseals-superiorca.org

*Gary Kasai, President/CEO*
*Terry Colborn, VP Programs/Government Affairs*
*Jessica Cone, VP Marketing/Development*

Provides outpatient rehabilitation services including day training programs for adults with disabilities and traumatic brain injuries, warm water therapy, non-public agency services to children including pediatric OT and PT services, work training/employment services, medical equipment loans, early intervention services for infants and toddlers. Serving the counties of Alpine, Calaveras, El Dorado, Sacramento, San Joaquin, Sutter, Tuolumne, Yolo, Yuba, Amador, Stanislaus, Nevada and Placer, CA.

**9097 El Mirador Rehabilitation Center at Desert Hospital**
1156 N Indian Canyon Drive
Suite W214
Palm Springs, CA 92262
760-416-4550
FAX: 760-416-4555
www.desertmedctr.com

*Patricia Sandoval, Manager*
Offers occupational, physical and speech therapy.

**9098 Exceed: A Division of Valley Resource Cent er**
PO Box 1773
Perris, CA 92572
951-657-0609
800-423-1227
FAX: 909-657-2277
e-mail: prsings@earthlink.net
www.exceed-aws.com

*Pattie Robert, Business Development Specialist*
*Mary Morse, Marketing Director*
*Kathy Cooke, Manager*

**9099    Eye Medical Clinic of Fresno**
Eye Medical Center
1122 S Street
Fresno, CA  93721                              559-486-5000
                                              800-606-3937
                                         FAX: 559-439-7854

*Rachel Moring-Garcia, Assistant Administrator*
*Denise Haar, Administrator*
*Donald Crumb, Manager*

A private, nonprofit agency offering services such as health, educational, recreational, rehabilitation, employment and counseling to the totally blind, legally blind and visually impaired.
The staff includes hundreds of full time workers.

**9100    Fontana Rehabilitation Workshop**
Industrial Support Systems
130 N Lilac Avenue
Rialto, CA  92376                              909-820-0230

*Carole Holt, Executive Director*
*Antonio Diaz, Owner*

**9101    Foothill Vocational Opportunities**
789 N Fair Oaks Avenue
Pasadena, CA  91103                            323-684-0797
                                         FAX: 626-449-4802

*James Hall, Executive Director/Owner*

**9102    Fred Finch Youth Center**
3800 Coolidge Avenue
Oakland, CA  94602                             510-482-2244
                                         FAX: 510-530-2047
                                e-mail: adamchase@fredfinch.org
                                         www.fredfinch.org

*John Steinfirst MSW, Executive Director*

A structured, psychiatric (JCAH accredited) residential treatment center for emotionally disturbed girls and boys between
the ages of 12 and 18. Our treatment incorporates an on-site,
non-public, special education school, an extensive activities and
recreational program, a strong professional psychotherapy component (providing individual, group, and family therapy) and a
parent support group. We provide 24-hour awake staff.

**9103    Gateway Center of Monterey County**
850 Congress Avenue
Pacific Grove, CA  93950                       831-372-8002
                                         FAX: 831-372-2411
                                e-mail: info@gateway.org
                                         www.gatewaycenter.org

*Kathleen Adamson, Chief Executive Officer*

Provides residential and day programs for developmentally disabled adults.

**9104    Gateway Industries: Castroville**
1663 Catalina Street
Sand City, CA  93955                           831-393-1575

*Mike Sweeney, Executive Director*
*Anna Foglia, Manager*

**9105    Gilroy Workshop**
8855 Murray Avenue
Gilroy, CA  95020                              408-842-0334
                                         FAX: 408-842-6770

*Cathy Andrade*
*Sally French, Manager*

Work adjustment and remunerative work programs.

**9106    Glendale Memorial Hospital and Health Center Reha-
bilitation Unit**
Glendale Memorial Hospital and Health Center
1420 S Central Avenue
Glendale, CA  91204                            818-502-2356
                                         FAX: 818-409-7688

*Charles Barrett, President*

Offers rehabilitation services, occupational therapy, physical
therapy, residential services and more for the disabled.

**9107    Goleta Valley Cottage Hospital**
Cottage Health System
351 S Patterson Avenue
Santa Barbara, CA  93111                       805-681-6435
                                              800-782-2288
                                         FAX: 805-681-6437
                                              www.sbch.org

*Diane Wisby, VP Operations*
*Ron Wreft, Chief Executive Officer*
*Rob Manchester, Manager*
Postacute rehabilitation program.

**9108    Goose Hill**
PO Box 1101
Santa Ynez, CA  93460

*Else Wolff, Owner/Operator*

A small facility licensed for three developmentally disabled
children. Provides residential services for the children currently
residing there. The Center is located in a small Danish community of Solvang 45 miles north of Santa Barbara.

**9109    Greenery Rehabilitation Center: Pacifica**
385 Esplanade
Pacifica, CA  94044
                                              800-356-5959
                                         FAX: 650-359-9388
68 beds offering active/acute rehabilitation, brain injury day
treatment, complex care and short-term evaluation.

**9110    Hacienda La Puente Adult Education**
14101 Nelson Avenue
La Puente, CA  91746                           626-934-2800
                                         FAX: 626-934-2900
                                e-mail: info@hlpusd.k12.ca.us
                                         www.hlpusd.k12.ca.us

*Donald Carmack, Director*
*Rachelle Wilson, Counselor*
*Jerry Fenning, Counselor*

**9111    Hi-Desert Continuing Care Center**
6722 White Feather Road
Joshua Tree, CA  92252                         760-366-1500
                                              800-782-2288

*Larry Kelley, Manager*
Postacute rehabilitation program.

**9112    Hillhaven Extended Care**
1115 Capitola Road
Santa Cruz, CA  95062
                                         FAX: 831-462-9812
Postacute rehabilitation program.

**9113    Home of the Guiding Hands**
1825 Gillespie Way
Suite 200
El Cajon, CA  92020                            619-448-3700
                                         FAX: 619-448-7208
                                e-mail: sara@guidinghands.org
                                         www.guidinghands.org

*Carol Fitzgibbons, Executive Director*

Residential and training services; In home respite and communitu living programs

**9114 Hospital of the Good Samaritan Acute Rehabilitation Unit**
616 Witmer Street
Los Angeles, CA 90017
213-977-2121
FAX: 213-482-2770
www.goodsam.org

*Andrew B Leeks, President/CEO*
*David N Shaw MD, Medical Director Acute Rehab*

Physicians, researchers and staff are united by a common mission: to foster growth into one of the most comprehensive medical centers in the West. Services offered include: cardiology and cardiovascular services, neurosciences, movement disorders and Parkinsons disorder, wound care center and transfusion-medicine and surgery center.

**9115 Industrial Therapy Center**
St. John s Regional Medical Center
295 E Hueneme Road
Port Hueneme, CA 93041
805-988-2737
FAX: 805-986-3535

*Mark Whitman PT, Manager*

A non-profit health care facility offering multi-disciplinary programs for pain management and work hardening, as well as physical and occupational therapy.

**9116 Janus of Santa Cruz**
200 7th Avenue
Suite 150
Santa Cruz, CA 95062
831-462-1060
FAX: 831-462-4970
www.janussc.org

*Jan Tice, Executive Director*
*Kay Owsley, Business Manager*

**9117 John Muir Medical Center Rehabilitation Services, Therapy Center**
1601 Ygnacio Valley Road
Walnut Creek, CA 94598
925-947-5231
FAX: 925-947-3262
e-mail: human.resouces@jmmdsh.com
www.jmmdhs.com

*Sandra Reese, Vice President*
*Patty Haggen, Director*
*Helen Doughty, Manager*

**9118 Kelso Activity Center**
4567 N Marty Avenue
Suite 101
Fresno, CA 93722
559-237-5101
FAX: 559-237-5326

*Tami Grinstead*
*Heather Harrison*
*Kathleene Moorhead, Manager*

Serves DTAC and ADP consumers.

**9119 King's View Work Experience Center**
PO Box 774
Atwater, CA 95301
209-357-0321
FAX: 209-357-0398

*Samuel Kalember, Executive Director*

**9120 King-Drew Medical Center**
12021 Wilmington Avenue
Los Angeles, CA 90059
310-668-4321
FAX: 310-632-6965

*Elliot Cohen, Chief Executive Officer*

A private, nonprofit agency offering services such as health, educational, recreational, rehabilitation, employment and counseling to the totally blind, legally blind and visually impaired. The staff includes many full time workers.

**9121 LaPalma Intercommunity Hospital**
7901 Walker Street
La Palma, CA 90623
714-670-7400
FAX: 714-670-6004

*Steven Dickson, President*
*Patricia Wolfram, Chief Executive Officer*

**9122 Lawrence L Frank Center Workshop**
2570 E Foothill Boulevard
Pasadena, CA 91107
626-449-5662
FAX: 626-449-0418
e-mail: otto@abilityfirst.org
www.abilityfirst.biz

*Marlene Otto, Director*

Provides remunerative work.

**9123 Lawrence L Frank Rehabilitation Workshop**
3812 S Grand Avenue
Los Angeles, CA 90037
213-748-7309
FAX: 213-748-7248
e-mail: imcdonald@abilityfirst.org
www.abilityfirst.org

*Isis McDonlad, Director*
*Lori Gangemi, Chief Executive Officer*

**9124 Learning Services of Northern California**
10855 De Bruin Way
Gilroy, CA 95020
408-848-4379

*Ann Kent, Marketing Manager*
*Kayree Shreeve, Administrator*

Graduates several hundred individuals each year from its community-integrated rehabilitation programs. These people accomplish renewed productivity in meeting the challenge of their disabling injury, and are more likely to avoid economic and human costs of unnecessary dependency.

**9125 Learning Services: Gilroy**
10855 De Bruin Way
Gilroy, CA 95020
408-848-4379
FAX: 408-848-6509

*Mike Howard, Program Director*
*Kayree Shreeve, Administrator*

Flexible sub and post acute rehabilitation for persons with acquired brain injury. Services include subacute long term care and rehab, residential post acute rehab, day treatment, outpatient and home-based rehab.

**9126 Learning Services: South Valley Ranch**
10855 De Bruin Way
Gilroy, CA 95020
408-848-4379
FAX: 408-848-6509

*Kayree Shreeve, Administrator*

**9127 Learning Services: Supported Living Programs**
10855 De Bruin Way
Gilroy, CA 95020
408-848-4379
800-466-4379
FAX: 408-848-6509

*Carol Hughes, Admissions Director*
*Steven P Johnson, Program Director*
*Kayree Shreeve, Administrator*

Long term living programs provided in normalized community settings. Programs include campus-based living for person in need of high levels of support and/or 24 hour nursing; supervised apartment living and assisted apartment living programs for persons with acquired brain injuries.

**9128 Leon S Peters Rehabilitation Center**

PO Box 1232
Fresno, CA 93715        559-459-3957
       800-628-9099
       FAX: 559-498-0261
e-mail: foundation@communitymedical.org
www.communitymedical.org

*Jeff Dimarco RN, Manager*
*Jenny Lau Rtc Ctrs, Community Liaision Rehab Serv.*
*Wes Qualls, Finance Executive*

**9129 Lion's Blind Center**

101 N Bascom Avenue
San Jose, CA 95128        408-295-4016
       FAX: 408-295-1398
e-mail: recetion@visionbeyondsight.com
www.visionbeyondsight.org

*Kenneth Frasse, Executive Director*
*Carolyne Haskin, Program Director*

The Santa Clara Valley BlindCenter, Inc. DBA The Lions Blind Center is a social/recreational training facility for any blind or sight impaired person in Santa Clara County over the age of 12. It provides an hospitable atmosphere that utilizes interactive socialization methods and classes to assist the blind and sight-impaired cope with their disability. Staff includes 2 sighted individuals in management positions.

**9130 Lion's Blind Center of Diablo Valley**

175 Alvarado Avenue
Pittsburg, CA 94565        925-432-3013

*Phil Sitzman, Director*
*Peggy Nichols, Executive Director*

A private, nonprofit agency offering services such as health, educational, recreational, rehabilitation, employment and counseling to the totally blind, legally blind and visually impaired. The staff includes two full time workers.

**9131 Lion's Blind Center of Oakland**

3834 Opal Street
Oakland, CA 94609        510-450-1580
       FAX: 510-654-3603

*Peggy Nichols, Executive Director*
*Cathy Manham, Manager*

A private nonprofit organization offering services for the totally blind, legally blind, deaf-blind and multihandicapped blind. Services include: professional training, rehabilitation, educational, counseling, social work, self help and more. The staff includes 17 full time and two part time workers.

**9132 Lions Center for the Blind of Oakland**

3834 Opal Street
Oakland, CA 94609        510-450-1580
       FAX: 510-654-3603
e-mail: info@lbcenter.org
www.lbcenter.org

*Anjelica Randall, Administrative Assistant*
*Kathyrine Brown, Program Manager*
*Cathy Manham, Manager*

Job placement service orientation and mobility services for cane users. Computer training for the blind or visually impaired. Work activity program for the developmentally disabled and the visually impaired. Life enrichment program.

**9133 Living Skills Center for the Visually Impaired**

2430 Road 20
Apt B112
San Pablo, CA 94806        510-234-4984
       FAX: 510-234-4986
e-mail: skillscr@flash.net
www.livingskillscenter.org

*Patricia Williams, Executive Director*

A private, nonprofit agency offering services such as independent living skills training, recreational, employment and accessible technology training to the totally blind, legally blind and visually impaired. The staff includes six full time teachers.

**9134 Loma Linda University Orthopedic and Rehabilitation Institute**

11234 Anderson Street
Loma Linda, CA 92354        909-558-8000
       FAX: 909-558-4133
www.llu.edu/lluhc/rehabilitation.index.htm

*Todd Nelson, Senior Intake Officer*

Offers a full range of clinical programs for both inpatients and outpatient. The specific diagnosis leading to patient admission includes stroke, spinal cord injury, traumatic or anoxic brain damage, amputation, post neurosurgery, chronic neurological disease, Guillain-Barre syndrome, arthritis, multiple trauma or other complex orthopedic problems. The facilities and professional services are comprehensive and ensure that the best care is provided to pediatric and adult patients.

**9135 Manor Care Nursing: Citrus Heights**

7807 Uplands Way
Citrus Heights, CA 95610        916-967-2929
       FAX: 916-965-8439

*Lisa Schuman, Manager*
Postacute rehabilitation program.

**9136 Manor Care Nursing: Fountain Valley**

11680 Warner Avenue
Fountain Valley, CA 92708        714-241-9800
       FAX: 714-966-1654

*Mark Schroepfer, Administrator*
Postacute rehabilitation program.

**9137 Manor Care Nursing: Hemet**

1717 W Stetson Avenue
Hemet, CA 92545        951-925-9171
       FAX: 909-925-8186

*Ronn Ellenich, Administrator*
Postacute rehabilitation program.

**9138 Manor Care Nursing: Palm Desert**

74350 Country Club Drive
Palm Desert, CA 92260        760-341-0261
       FAX: 760-779-1564

*Debbie Burger, Administrator*
Postacute rehabilitation program.

**9139 Manor Care Nursing: Sunnyvale**

1150 Tilton Drive
Sunnyvale, CA 94087        408-735-7200
       FAX: 408-736-8619
www.hcr-manorcare.com

*John Moreno, Director*
Postacute rehabilitation program.

**9140  Manor Care Nursing: Walnut Creek**
1226 Rossmoor Parkway
Walnut Creek, CA  94595
925-975-5000
FAX: 925-947-2149

*John Gallick, Executive Director*
Postacute rehabilitation program.

**9141  Maynord's Chemical Dependency Recovery Centers**
PO Box 1657
Tuolumne, CA  95379
209-928-3737
800-228-8208
FAX: 209-928-1152
e-mail: recovery@maynords.com
www.maynords.com

*Joan Maynord, Chief Executive Officer*
*Walter Reed MFT, Clinical Director*
*Ralph Rutherford MD, Medical Director*

Maynord's Recovery Centers has always been dedicated to the recovery of good people whose lives are being destroyed by alcohol and drugs. Since 1978, Maynord's residential program has helped thousands of people put their lives back together after addiction has taken its toll. Today, Maynord's offers a treatment system over much of the San Joaquin Valley and the San Francisco Bay Area.

**9142  Maynord's Ranch for Men**
PO Box 1657
Tuolumne, CA  95379
209-928-3737
800-228-8208
FAX: 209-928-1152
www.maynords.com

*Joan Maynord, Chief Executive Officer*
*Walter Reed MFT, Clinical Director*
*Daniel Meador MD, Medical Director*

Provides treatment for chemical dependency problems to men. The treatment addresses their recovery through a comprehensive plan created for their individual needs. Also offers a program for women called the Meadows.

**9143  Meadowbrook Los Angeles: Community Re-Entry Services**
4600 Woodley Avenue
Encino, CA  91436
818-994-4634

*Ayla Zejni, Manager*
Postacute rehabilitation program.

**9144  Meadows**
19227 South Court
Sonora, CA  95370
209-533-0935

*Ron Schoon, Administrator*
*Bea Schoon, Owner*

Provides treatment designed for women that is directed at every important facet of their lives - mentally, physically and spiritually. Clients receive a variety of treatment approaches to facilitate their recovery and a comprehensive treatment plan is created for their individual needs. Issues relating to the cause of addictions are addressed in lectures, one-on-one counseling sessions, group therapy and re entry groups. Also offers a male treatment programs called Maynord's Ranch.

**9145  Medical Center of La Mirada**
14900 Imperial Highway
La Mirada, CA  90638
562-944-1900

*John Edwards, Executive Director*
*Robin Wapp, Manager*

**9146  Memorial Hospital of Gardenia**
1145 W Redondo Beach Boulevard
Gardena, CA  90247
310-532-4200
800-782-2288
Postacute rehabilitation program.

**9147  Mercy Outpatient Rehab Center**
Mercy Hospital
406 1/2 Sunrise Avenue
Suite 300
Roseville, CA  95661
916-536-2425
FAX: 916-780-5770
e-mail: leaton@chw.edu

*Margareth Keeling, Director*
*Lynda Eaton, Client Services Liaison*

Postacute rehabilitation program for traumatic brain injury survivors.

**9148  Napa County Mental Health**
2344 Old Sonoma Road
Napa, CA  94559
707-253-4785
FAX: 707-253-4155

*Robin Payne, Manager*
Work hardening and disciplinary programs.

**9149  Napa Valley Support Systems**
650 Imperial Way
Suite 202
Napa, CA  94559
707-253-7490
FAX: 707-253-0115

*Beth Atton, Executive Director*
Work hardening and disciplinary programs.

**9150  North Valley Services #2**
1350 Vista Way
Red Bluff, CA  96080
530-529-2100
FAX: 530-529-4450

*Judy Ferrell, Director*

**9151  Northridge Hospital Medical Center: Center for Rehabilitation Medicine**
18300 Roscoe Boulevard
Northridge, CA  91325
818-885-8500
FAX: 818-701-7367
www.northridgehospital.com

*Debra Flaherty, Director Rehabilitation Services*
*Mike Wall, Chief Executive Officer*

**9152  Old Adobe Developmental Services**
235 Casa Grande Road
Petaluma, CA  94954
707-763-9807
FAX: 707-763-7708
e-mail: nickbobo@aol.com

*Dennis Orner, Executive Director*
Provides remunerative work.

**9153  PRIDE Industries**
10030 Foothills Boulevard
Roseville, CA  95747
916-783-5266
800-550-6005
FAX: 916-788-2560
e-mail: info@prideindustries.com
www.prideindustries.com

*Michael Ziegler, President/CEO*
*Cynthia Sommer, Vice President*
*Roxanne Snyder, Employment Services Manager*

To provide opportunities through employment, training, evaluation and placement maximizing community access, independence and quality of life for people with barriers to employment.

**9154    Pain Center**
9888 Genesee Avenue
La Jolla, CA  92037
                                        858-626-6952
                            FAX: 858-626-7213

*Corinna Nyquist, Outreach Coordinator*

Offers both inpatient and outpatient programs including: physical activity management, individual pain management, group therapy, medication adjustment, pain control classes, occupational therapy, biofeedback training, family counseling, vocational and leisure counseling and recreational therapy.

**9155    Parents and Friends**
PO Box 656
Fort Bragg, CA  95437
                                        707-964-4940
                                        800-222-0343
                            FAX: 707-964-2701
                    e-mail: friends1@mcn.org
                    www.parentsandfriends.org

*Linda Rosengarten, Executive Director*
*Teri Scott, Controller*
*Russ Pals, Vocational Director*

Parents and Friends provides opportunities for persons with developmental challenges and similar needs to participate fully in our community.

**9156    Peninsula Center for the Blind & Visually Impaired**
2470 El Camino Real
Suite 107
Palo Alto, CA  94306
                                        650-858-0202
                                        800-660-2009
                            FAX: 650-858-0214
                    e-mail: center@pcbvi.org
                            www.pcbvi.org

*Pam Brandin, Executive Director*
*Sharon Hudson, Director of Rehabilitation Servi*

Private nonprofit agency that serves the visually impaired in the San Mateo, Santa Clara and San Benito counties. Offers rehabilitation services, counseling, social work, self support groups, computer training, employment services, orientation and mobility.

**9157    Peninsula ReCare**
1764 Marco Polo Way
Burlingame, CA  94010
                                        650-259-8500
                            FAX: 650-697-5010

*Kirk F Cunningham, President/CEO*

Vocational, health and recreational services for individuals with disabilities.

**9158    People Services**
4195 Lakeshore Boulevard
Lakeport, CA  95453
                                        707-263-3810
                            FAX: 707-263-0552
            e-mail: peopleservices@mindspring.com
                    www.peopleservices.org

*Mike Adams, Vice President*
*Dennis Rollins, Special Education Teacher*
*Ilene Dumont, Executive Director*

Providing an array of services for adults with developmental disabilities and other people with disabilities. Services include supported employment, work services, supported living, personal, social and community training, transportation, specialized individual services and much more.

**9159    Petaluma Recycling Center**
Old Adobe Developmental Services
315 2nd Street
Petaluma, CA  94952
                                        707-763-4761
                            FAX: 707-763-4921
                                www.oadsinc.org

*David Donati, Supervisor*
*Dennis Orner, Director*

**9160    Pomerado Rehabilitation Outpatient Service**
15708 Pomerado Road
Suite N102
Poway, CA  92064
                                        858-613-4636
                            FAX: 858-613-4248
                                www.pmc.com

*Sheila Brown, Director Rehab Services*
*Jonathan Pee, Manager*

A modern outpatient rehabilitation facility featuring state-of-the-art therapies, techniques and equipment in the areas of physical therapy, occupational therapy and speech/language pathology.

**9161    Pride Industries: Grass Valley**
12451 Loma Rica Drive
Grass Valley, CA  95945
                                        530-477-1832
                                        800-550-6005
                            FAX: 530-477-8038
                            www.prideindustries.com

*Kimberly Jones, Site Manager*
*Dawn Horwath, Counselor*
*Craig Hays, Adult Day Program Coordinator*

Work adjustment and remunerative work programs. We offer an adult day program as well.

**9162    Rancho Adult Day Care Center**
Rancho Los Amigos Medical Center
7601 Imperial Highway
Downey, CA  90242
                                        562-401-7111

                    www,usc.edu/dept/gero/RRTConAging/

*Bryan Kemp, Center Director*
*Margaret L Campbell, Research Director*
*Valerie Orange, Chief Executive Officer*

Provides personal care, social services and a therapeutic program to older adults in order to improve their quality of life. Offers a Clinical Gerontology Service, an Alzheimer's Disease Diagnostic and Treatment Center and a Geriatric Assessment and Rehabilitation Unit.

**9163    Redlands Psychological and Psychiatric Group**
Maxine Mc Gowan Smith
440 Cajon Street
Redlands, CA  92373
                                        909-793-4475

*Marjorie Smith, Director*

**9164    Regional Center for Rehabilitation**
2288 Auburn Boulevard
Sacramento, CA  95821
                                        916-421-4167
                            FAX: 916-925-1586

Postacute rehabilitation program.

**9165    Regional Infant Center**
3010 W Harvard Street
Santa Ana, CA  92704

*Joan Hess, Public Health Nurse*

**9166    Rehabilitation Center at Corona Community Hospital**
800 S Main Street
Corona, CA  92882                     951-737-4343

*Michael Schultz, President*
*John Calderone, Chief Executive Officer*

Offers inpatient and outpatient rehabilitation services. The Center consists of an acute rehab unit, a subacute rehab unit containing modules for long-term ventilator care, respiratory rehab, coma intervention and orthopedics. In addition to inpatient therapies, the Center's outpatient programs include sports and industrial medicine.

**9167    Rehabilitation Institute Glendale Adventist Medical Center**
1509 Wilson Ter
Glendale, CA  91206                    818-409-8070
                                  FAX: 818-546-5609
                              www.glendaleadventist.com

*Jan Adduie, Rehabilitation Manager*

Complete inpatient and outpatient programs for orthopedic and neurological disabilities.

**9168    Rehabilitation Institute of Santa Barbara**
2415 De La Vina Street
Santa Barbara, CA  93105              805-569-8999
                                  FAX: 805-683-0381
                                     www.risb.org

*Melinda Stavely, CEO*

A regional rehabilitation system with an acute care hospital at the center, the Institute provides specialized inpatient and outpatient programs for brain injury, spinal cord injury, stroke, work-related injury, chronic pain, orthopedic problems and more. Offers a 46-bed acute-care rehabilitation hospital, a free-standing outpatient center, the brain injury continuum, chronic pain program.

**9169    Rehabilitation Institute of Southern California**
1800 E La Veta Avenue
Orange, CA  92866                     714-633-7400
                                  FAX: 714-633-4586
                              e-mail: rhayes@rio.rehab
                                   www.rio-rehab.com

*Raylene Hays, Director Programs*
*Praim Singh, Chief Executive Officer*

Outpatient rehabilitation serving physically and disabled children and adults. Child development programs, adult day care for disabled seniors, child care for disabled and non-disabled children, outpatient therapy, aquatics, adult day healthcare, independent living, vocational services, social services, and housing.

**9170    Rehabilitation Unit, Northridge Hospital Medical Center**
18300 Roscoe Boulevard
Northridge, CA  91325                  888-553-0
                                  FAX: 818-701-7367

*Debra Flaherty, Director Rehabilitation Services*

**9171    Rex Industries**
9575 Aero Drive
San Diego, CA  92123                  760-471-0250
                                      800-748-5575
                                  FAX: 858-715-3788

*Gary Luce, Operations Manager*

Offers many different programs including: North County Parent/Infant Program which is an educational program for children, birth to three years who are showing delays in development or who are at risk for developmental delays. The Adult Development Center is a program for adults, eighteen and over, with a developmental disability in the severe to profound range. The program focuses on self-help, communication, daily living and pre-vocational skills. Other programs are available.

**9172    Rohnert Park Services (Behavioral)**
6920 Commerce Boulevard
Suite 114
Rohnert Park, CA  94928               707-664-8019
                                  FAX: 707-664-8057
                          e-mail: webmaster@oadsinc.org
                                   www.oadsinc.org

*Dennis Orner, Executive Director*
*Helen Gunderson, Administrative Assistant*

The program services are designed to assist individuals who demonstrate basic work skills, to develop social skills and work habits necessary to succeed in supported or competitive employment. Most often individual program services involve working with the client to replace those behavioral excesses that have been a barrier to vocational placement.

**9173    Rubicon Programs**
2500 Bissell Avenue
Richmond, CA  94804                   510-231-3900
                                  FAX: 510-235-2025
                        e-mail: rubicon@rubiconpgms.org
                               www.rubiconprograms.org

*Lindy Hahn, Chairman*
*Constance Fraser, Vice-Chairman*
*Rick Aubry, Chief Executive Officer*

Provides remunerative work, placement and training.

**9174    San Bernardino Valley Lighthouse for the Blind**
762 N Sierra Way
San Bernardino, CA  92410             909-884-3121
                                  FAX: 909-884-2964

*Robert McBay, Executive Director*
*Sandra Wood, Administrative Assistant*

Provides training in independent living skills - cooking, mobility and orientation, sewing, Braille and typing. Also, we have classes in macrame, ceramics and basket weaving. Weekly support group and Bible study.

**9175    San Diego Center**
3821 Calle Fortunada
Suite C
San Diego, CA  92123                  619-263-7600
                                  FAX: 619-571-0919

*Nancy Oro*

Provides remunerative work.

**9176    Sharp Coronado Hospital**
250 Prospect Place
Coronado, CA  92118                   619-522-3600
                                  FAX: 619-522-3782
                                     www.sharp.com

*Marcia Hall, Chief Executive Officer*

Postacute rehabilitation program.

**9177**  **Shriners Hospitals for Children**
3160 Geneva Street
Los Angeles, CA 90020
213-388-3151
888-486-5437
888-486-KIDS
FAX: 213-387-7528
e-mail: edever@shrinenet.org
www.shrinershq.org

*Elizabeth Dever, Director Public Relations*
*Faviola Ramirez, Applications Coordinator*
*G Frank LaBonte, Hospital Administrator*

Treats children under the age of 18 with burn scars, orthopedic conditions and limb deficiencies. All medical care is provided completely free of charge for patients and their families. Conditions commonly treated include scoliosis, club feet, leg length discrepancies osteogenesis imperfecta (brittle bone disease), arthrogryposis, orthopedic problems related to cerebral palsy and spina bifida. Also treated are deformities due to burns, scar revision and reconstructive surgery.

**9178**  **Shriners Hospitals, San Francisco Unit, for Crippled Children**
2425 Stockton Boulevard
Sacramento, CA 95817
916-453-2000
FAX: 415-661-3615

*Maggie Bryan, Administrator*

**9179**  **Society for the Blind**
2750 24th Street
Sacramento, CA 95818
916-452-8271
FAX: 916-452-2622
e-mail: director@societyfortheblind.org
www.societyfortheblind.org

*Alan Frank, Assistant Director of Programs*

A private, local nonprofit organization providing blind and visually impaired people with the training supplies and support they need to live independent, productive and fulfilled lives with limited vision. Services include the Low Vision Clinic, Braille classes, computer training, support groups, living skills instruction, mobility training and the Products for Independence Store.

**9180**  **Solutions at Santa Barbara: Transitional Living Center**
1135 N Patterson Avenue
Santa Barbara, CA 93111
805-683-1995
FAX: 805-683-4793
e-mail: 5011135@aol.com
www.solutionsatsantabarbara.com

*Susan Hannigan, Executive Director*
*Brandi Fresh, Case Manager*

Postacute rehabilitation program. Short-term transitional living program for individuals with traumatic brain injury, stroke, aneurysm and other neurological disorders.

**9181**  **South Bay Rehabilitation Center at Paradise Valley Hospital**
2400 E 4th Street
National City, CA 91950
619-470-4300
FAX: 619-470-4126

*Fred Harder, President*
*Jay Flaherty, Executive Director*

**9182**  **Southeast Industries**
9501 Washburn Road
Downey, CA 90242
562-803-4606
FAX: 562-803-4080

*Kevin Donald, Executive Director*
Work hardening and disciplinary programs.

**9183**  **St. John's Pleasant Valley Hospital Neuro Care Unit**
2309 Antonio Avenue
Camarillo, CA 93010
805-389-5800
FAX: 805-389-5968

*Rosa Vasquez, Director*
*Maureen Malone, Administrator*

Subacute rehabilitation program; ventilator dependent.

**9184**  **Starlight Center**
Arc of San Diego
1280 Nolan Avenue
Chula Vista, CA 91911
619-427-7524
FAX: 619-427-4657
e-mail: info@arc-sd.com
www.arc-sd.com

*Skit Covell, President*
*Terri Phorn, Executive Director*

Provides remunerative work.

**9185**  **Sub-Acute Saratoga Hospital**
18611 Sousa Lane
Saratoga, CA 95070
408-378-8875
FAX: 408-866-8144

*Mike Zarcone, President*
Postacute rehabilitation program.

**9186**  **Synergos Neurological Center: Hayward**
27200 Calaroga Avenue
Hayward, CA 94545
510-264-4000

www.strosehospital.org

*Michael Mahoney, President/CEO*
Postacute rehabilitation program.

**9187**  **Synergos Neurological Center: Mission Hills**
15031 Rinaldi Street
Mission Hills, CA 91345
818-898-4412

Postacute rehabilitation program.

**9188**  **Tehama County Opportunity Center**
13315 Baker Road
Red Bluff, CA 96080
530-527-0407
FAX: 530-527-7091

*Delbert Brownfield, Executive Director*
*Lynn Freece, Chief Executive Officer*

**9189**  **Temple Community Hospital**
235 N Hoover Street
Los Angeles, CA 90004
213-382-7252
FAX: 213-389-4559

*Herbert Needman, Chief Executive Officer*
Postacute rehabilitation program.

**9190**  **Tunnell Center for Rehab**
1359 Pine Street
San Francisco, CA 94109
415-673-8405
FAX: 415-563-2174

*Jan Clements, Administrator*
Postacute rehabilitation program.

**9191 Ukiah Valley Association for Habilitation**
PO Box 689
Ukiah, CA 95482
707-468-8824
FAX: 707-468-9149
e-mail: pam@uvah.org
www.uvah.org

*Pamela Jensen, Executive Director*
*Kris Vipond, Business Manager*
*Crystal Anderson, Rural Adult Program Director*

Work adjustment and suppoted employment and social and community services.

**9192 Valley Center**
546 Brunken Avenue
Salinas, CA 93901
831-754-5509
FAX: 831-758-0250

*Anna Foglia, Executive Director*

**9193 Valley Center for the Blind**
1060 Fulton Mall
Suite 315
Fresno, CA 93721
559-222-4447
FAX: 559-222-4844
e-mail: info@valleycenterblind.org
www.valleycenterblind.org

*Russell Hoeltzer, Executive Director*
*Millie Marshall, Marriage Family Therapist*
*Roben Asher, Specialist*

A private, nonprofit organization that offers educational, health, recreational and professional training services to the totally blind, legally blind or severely visually impaired. Staff numbers one full- time and four part- time employees.

**9194 Valley Rehabilitation Industries**
2701 E Hammer Lane
Stockton, CA 95210
209-948-2065
FAX: 209-463-1511
e-mail: arcsj@gotnet.net

*Ronald Tognoli, Executive Director*
*Sandra Monroe, Director*

Vocational training, supported employment and job placement for persons with mental retardation and other developmental disabilities. Valley Rehabilitation Industries is a program of the Association for Retarded Citizens-San Joaquin.

**9195 Variety Club Blind Babies Foundation**
1200 Gough Street
San Francisco, CA 94109
415-771-9035
FAX: 415-771-9026

*Phillip Hatlen, Executive Director*

A private, nonprofit agency offering services in the areas of health, counseling, social work, self help and education to blind and visually impaired infants. The educated staff includes 8 full time and 3 part time employees.

**9196 Villa Esperanza Services**
2116 E Villa Street
Pasadena, CA 91107
626-449-2919
FAX: 626-449-2850
www.villaesperanzaservices.org

*Dottie Cebula Nelson, Chief Executive Officer*
*Kelly White, Chief Operation Officer*

Serving disabled infants to seniors in a school, adult day program, adult work program and residences and adult day health care program and care management program.

**9197 Village Square Nursing Center**
1586 W San Marcos Boulevard
San Marcos, CA 92078
760-471-2986
FAX: 760-471-5176

*Melanie Henderson, Director*
Postacute rehabilitation program.

**9198 Western Neuro Care Center**
Health South Corporation
14851 Yorba Street
Tustin, CA 92780
714-832-9200
FAX: 714-508-4550
www.healthsouth.com

*Scott Rifkin, Chief Executive Officer*
*Rosemary Vaizaidenberg, Manager*

**9199 Winways**
7732 E Santiago Canyon Road
Orange, CA 92869
714-771-5276
FAX: 714-771-1452
e-mail: helpdesk@winwaysrehab.com
www.winwaysrehab.com

*Pam Kauss, Executive Director*
Postacute rehabilitation program.

## Colorado

**9200 Capron Rehabilitation Center**
Penrose Hospital/ St. Francis Healthcare System
2215 N Cascade Avenue
Colorado Springs, CO 80907
719-776-5000
FAX: 719-776-2534

*James O'Connell, Chief Executive Officer*
Southern Colorado's most complete inpatient and outpatient rehabilitation center.

**9201 Cerebral Palsy of Colorado**
2200 S Jasmine Street
Denver, CO 80222
303-691-9339
FAX: 303-691-0846
e-mail: info@cpco.org
www.cpco.org

*Judith I Ham, President/CEO*
*Mark Welle, Chairman of the Board*

Provides services for children birth-5 years, employment services for adults, information and referral, donation pickup and cell phone/ink cartridge recycling services.

**9202 Cherry Hills Health Care Center**
Kindred
3575 S Washington Street
Englewood, CO 80113
303-789-2265
FAX: 303-781-8808

*Michael Speidel, Administrator*
*Judy Holmes, Director*
Postacute rehabilitation program.

**9203 Community Hospital Back and Conditioning Clinic**
1060 Orchard Avenue
Grand Junction, CO 81501
970-243-3400
800-621-0926
FAX: 970-856-6510

*Amy Hibberd, Executive Director*
*David Scherman, Manager*

**9204 Developmental Preschool**
1333 Elm Avenue
Canon City, CO 81212                    719-275-0550

*Paulette Bolton, Deputy Director*

**9205 Laradon Hall Society for Exceptional Children and Adults**
5100 Lincoln Street
Denver, CO 80216                       303-296-2400
                                  FAX: 303-296-0737
                                       www.laradon.org

*Timothy C Hall, Executive Director*

Laradon provides educational, vocational and residential services to children and adults with developmental disabilities and other special needs. Laradon was founded in 1948. It is among the largest and most comprehensive service providers in Colorado.

**9206 Learning Services: Bear Creek**
7201 W Hampden Avenue
Lakewood, CO 80227                     303-989-6660
                                  FAX: 303-989-2830
Supported living program for persons with acquired brain injury.

**9207 Manor Care Nursing and Rehabilitation Center: Boulder**
Manor Care Ohio
2800 Palo Parkway
Boulder, CO 80301                      303-440-9100
                                  FAX: 303-440-9251
                                       www.hcrmanorcare.com

*Amy Tarrell, Director*
*Morrine Wise, Administrator*

Postacute rehabilitation program. Inpatient and Outpatient programs.

**9208 Manor Care Nursing: Denver**
290 S Monaco Parkway
Denver, CO 80224                       303-355-2525
                                  FAX: 303-355-6960

*Rob Turner, Administrator*
*Rose Reinhardt, Admissions Director*

Postacute rehabilitation program.

**9209 Martin Luther Homes: Colorado Springs**
1785 N Academy Boulevard
Suite 127
Colorado Springs, CO 80909
                                  FAX: 719-531-0582

*Coleen Abeyta, Administrator*
*Fred Naumann III, Communications*

Providing a wide array of services to assist individuals and families in achieving positive life goals. Services to persons with disabilities and other special needs include community living options, training and employment options, spiritual growth and development options, training and counseling support.

**9210 Mediplex of Colorado**
8451 Pearl Street
Thornton, CO 80229                     303-288-3000
                                  FAX: 303-286-1253
                                       www.northvalleyrehab.com

*Ann Marie Zuccarelli, Marketing Director*
*Wally Sacckett, Chief Executive Officer*

Our programs and services help each patient along the road to recovery toward our ultimate aim; the greatest possible restoration of the individual's self-esteem, ability to set goals, and self-sufficiency. Also offer specialized acute inpatient rehabilitative services, including special programs in Trauma Rehabilitation.

**9211 Platte River Industries**
490 Bryant Street
Denver, CO 80204                       303-825-0041
                                  FAX: 303-825-0564

*Robert Smith, Executive Director*

**9212 Pueblo Diversified Industries**
2828 Granada Boulevard
Pueblo, CO 81005                       719-564-0000
                                       800-466-8393
                                  FAX: 719-564-3407
                                  e-mail: pdihs@qwest.net
                                       www.pdipueblo.net

*Karen Lillie, President/CEO*
*Toml Drolshagen, Director Operations*

A place where people can turn limitations into opportunities. People can experience the independence, pride and self worth of securing and maintaining a job.

**9213 SHALOM Denver**
2498 W 2nd Avenue
Denver, CO 80223                       303-623-0251
                                  FAX: 303-620-9584
                      e-mail: sgehrke@jewishfamilyservice.org
                                       www.shalomdenver.com

*Arnold Kover, Executive Director*

Work hardening and disciplinary programs.

**9214 Schaefer Rehabilitation Center**
500 26th Street
Greeley, CO 80631                      970-353-0662
                                  FAX: 970-353-2779

*Richard Kuhn*
*Valorie Randall, Executive Director*

Work hardening and disciplinary programs.

**9215 Spalding Rehab Hospital West Unit**
150 Spring Street
Morrison, CO 80465                     303-697-4334
                                  FAX: 303-697-0570
Postacute rehabilitation program.

## Connecticut

**9216 ACES/ACCESS Inclusion Program**
60 United Drive
North Haven, CT 06473                  203-234-2406
                                  FAX: 203-234-1369
                      e-mail: acesinfo@aces.k12.ct.us
                                       www.aces.k12.ct.us

*Cheryl Saloom, Director*

Provides a person centered planning approach for integrated employment, volunteer community based opportunities for adults who have developmental disabilities.

**9217 APT Residential Services**
PO Box 1587
Newtown, CT 06470                      203-781-4790
                                  FAX: 203-270-3729

*Sharon Sokolowski, Executive Director*

**9218 Apria Healthcare**
40 Sebethe Drive
Cromwell, CT 06416
860-613-4900
800-277-4288
e-mail: contact_us@apria.com
www.apria.com

*Mermisa Shaw, Manager*

Provides a broad range of high quality and cost effective specialty infusion therapies and related services to patients in their homes throughout the Northeastern United States. Offer home infusion antibiotic therapy, quality pharmacy services, skilled nursing services and related support services.

**9219 Arc of the Farmington Valley**
PO Box 1099
Canton, CT 06019
860-677-2971
FAX: 860-693-8662
e-mail: favarh@favarh.org
www.favarh.org

*John Woods, Director Clinical Services*

Serving over 300 mentally retarded adults through a comprehensive program of residential and support services. These include three group homes, three apartments, competitive and supported employment options, a day program for mentally retarded seniors, community experience day services for severe and profoundly disabled adults, recreation and leisure services, advocacy, transportation, case management, in-home respite and other support services.

**9220 Connecticut Subacute Corporation**
19 Tuttle Place
Middletown, CT 06457
860-347-6300
FAX: 860-347-2446
www.cpl-usa.com

*Evan K Lyle, Managed Care Director*
*Cheri Kauset, Corporate Rep.*

Specializes in subacute medical and rehabilitation programming. The strength of our system is in its' ability to service a broad range of clinical and psychosocial needs which enable each individual to attain his/her optimal potential. Programming includes neurological and orthopedic rehabilitation, post-surgical and wound care management, intravenous therapy, pulmonary rehabilitation including ventilator services, and long term care.

**9221 Datahr Rehabilitation Institute**
4 Berkshire Boulevard
Bethel, CT 06801
203-775-2418
888-8DA-TAHR
FAX: 203-740-7129
www.datahr.org

*Thomas Fanning, President*

Providers of comprehensive rehabilitation services with a history of nearly 5 decades of service. This institute is recognized as a leading resource in meeting the needs of those disabled by illness, injury or developmental disorders in Connecticut and New York. A team of rehabilitation and health care professionals offering career development, residential services, supported employment, volunteer services, occupational therapy, day activities and more.

**9222 Eastern Blind Rehabilitation Center**
950 Campbell Avenue
West Haven, CT 06516
203-937-4850
FAX: 203-937-3806
www1.va.gov/blindrehab

*Penny Schuckers, Chief of EBRC*
*Pamela Redmond, Executive Director Public Affair*

Provides residential rehabilitation services to eligible legally blind veterans in the Northeast and Middle Atlantic portions of the country. Referral applications by Veterans Administration Medical Centers and Outpatient Clinics in the geographical area served by the Blind Rehabilitation Center.

**9223 FAVRAH**
23 W Avon Road
Avon, CT 06001
860-674-8839
FAX: 860-676-0275

*Nancy Ralston, Manager*
Provides remunerative work.

**9224 Gaylord Hospital**
PO Box 400
Wallingford, CT 06492
203-284-2800
866-GAY-LORD
FAX: 203-284-2700
e-mail: pjohnson@gaylord.org
www.gaylord.org

*James Cullen, President*

Works to restore ability and build courage. Offers rehabilitation care with one goal in mind: to help patients return to their homes, communities and jobs.

**9225 Hockenum Greenhouse**
Hockenum Industry
Rr 44
Mansfield, CT 06251
860-429-6697

*Sarah Beardsley, Program Director*

**9226 Kuhn Employment Oppurtunities**
1630 N Colony Road
Meriden, CT 06450
203-235-2583
860-347-5843
FAX: 203-235-0827
e-mail: info@kuhngroup.org
www.kuhnemployment.com

*Robert L Stephens, Executive Director/Owner*

**9227 Meriden-Wallingford Society for the Handic**
226 Cook Avenue
Meriden, CT 06451
203-237-9975
FAX: 203-639-0946
e-mail: mwshinc@snet.net

*Pamela Smith, Chief Executive Officer*
*Diane Morra, Director Program Services*
*Pauline Bouffard, Director Employment Services*

Provides remunerative work, supported employment and job placement and recreation.

**9228 Rehabilitation Associates**
60 Katona Drive
Fairfield, CT 06824
203-384-8681
FAX: 203-384-0722
e-mail: rehabinc@concentric.net
www.rehabassociatesinc.com

*Carol Landsman, Director/Owner*
*Myra Watnick, Director*

A comprehensive outpatient rehabilitation facility offering physical therapy, occupational therapy, speech-language pathology, clinical social work services and nutritional services to all age groups. Facility locations in Fairfield, Stratford, Milford, Shelton and Westport. All facilities are CARF accredited.

**9229    Rehabilitation Center of Fairfield County**
226 Mill Hill Avenue
Bridgeport, CT 06610 203-378-0092
FAX: 203-336-5465

*Sally Gammon, President*
Medical services are provided by physicians who are specialists in physical medicine and rehabilitation. The physical therapy department provides a variety of services and utilizes sophisticated modalities to restore and reinforce physical abilities.

**9230    Reliance House**
40 Broadway
Norwich, CT 06360 860-887-6536
FAX: 860-885-1970

*David Burnett, Executive Director*
A residential vocational and recreational support network. An active and productive clubhouse where people with mental illness can gain skills, strength and self-esteem.

**9231    Section of Physical Medicine and Rehabilitation**
24 Stevens Street
Norwalk, CT 06850
FAX: 203-852-2027

*Dr. Claudio Petrillo, Director*

**9232    South Church Activity Program**
99 Main Street
New Britain, CT 06051 860-224-9480
FAX: 860-827-8681

*Margaret Stowell, Supervisor*

## Delaware

**9233    Alfred I DuPont Hospital for Children**
Division of Rehabilitation
1600 Rockland Road
Wilmington, DE 19803 302-651-4000
FAX: 302-651-4055
www.nemours.org

*Thomas Ferry, VP Hospital Operations/CEO*
Offers rehabilitative services for the physically challenged individual.

**9234    Community Systems**
3204 Drummond Plaza
Newark, DE 19711 302-322-5066
FAX: 302-456-5733

*George Baer, Executive Director*

**9235    Delaware Association for the Blind**
800 N West Street
Wilmington, DE 19801 302-655-2111
888-777-3925
FAX: 302-655-1442
www.dabdel.org

*Linda Lauria, Executive Director*
A private, nonprofit organization that offers adjustment to blindness counseling, recreation activities, summer camps and financial assistance for the legally blind. The staff includes five full time, nine part time and twelve seasonal. Operates a store selling items for the blind.

**9236    Delaware Elwyn**
321 E 11th Street
Wilmington, DE 19801 302-658-8860
FAX: 302-654-5815

*Carol Chapin, Executive Director*

**9237    Delaware Veterans Center**
1601 Kirkwood Highway
Wilmington, DE 19805 302-992-0539
FAX: 302-633-5250
Veterans medical clinic offering disabled veterans medical treatments.

**9238    Easter Seal Rehabilitation Center: New Castle County**
61 Corporate Circle
New Castle, DE 19720 302-324-4444
FAX: 302-324-4481

*Bill Adami, Executive Director*
*Sandy Tuttle, President*

**9239    Edgemoor Day Program**
500 Duncan Road
Ofc A
Wilmington, DE 19809 302-762-1391
FAX: 302-762-2416

*Shawn Stevens, Executive Director*
*Ann Kitchen, Assistant Executive Director*

**9240    First State Senior Center**
291 A Rehoboth Boulevard
Milford, DE 19963 302-422-1510
FAX: 302-422-1354

*Marcella Wilson, Supervisor*
Improves the quality of life for Delaware's citizens by promoting health and well-being, fostering self-sufficiency, and protecting vulnerable populations.

**9241    Georgetown Day Program**
5 Academy Street
Georgetown, DE 19947 302-856-5366
FAX: 302-856-5360

*Joyce Oliver, Supervisor*
*Linda Ragin, Manager*

**9242    Salvation Army Developmental Disabilities Program**
701 N Broad Street
Philadelphia, PA 19123 215-787-2804
www.developmentaldisabilities.org

*Michael Paoli, Executive Director*
Provides residential and employment supports in eastern Pennsylvania and Delaware.

**9243    Woodside Day Program**
941 Walnut Shade Road
Dover, DE 19901 302-739-4494
FAX: 302-697-4490

*Connie Grace, Supervisor*
*Joyce Oliver, Manager*

## District of Columbia

**9244 Barbara Chambers Children's Center**
1470 Irving Street NW
Washington, DC 20010 202-387-6755
FAX: 202-319-9066

*Francisca Torres*
*Reina Argueta, Administrator*

Offers special education, play and speech therapy services to children 2-5 years of age with developmental delays.

**9245 District of Columbia General Hospital Physical Medicine & Rehab Services**
19th and Mass Avenue
Room 1358
Washington, DC 20003 202-529-6211
FAX: 202-675-7819

*Dr. Maribel Bieberach, Chairperson PM&R*
*Dr. Raman Kapur, Staff Physiatrist*

Offers comprehensive physical medicine and rehabilitation services including in and outpatient consultations and electrodiagnostic testing; in and outpatient physical and occupational therapy; inpatient recreational therapy, and a multidisciplinary prosthetic clinic which meets once a month.

**9246 George Washington University Medical Center**
George Washington University Medical Center
2150 Pennsylvania Avenue NW
Washington, DC 20037 202-741-3000
FAX: 202-741-2427
www.gwdocs.com

*Steven Badger, Director*

Offers an Ambulatory Physical Therapy/Sports Medicine Center, a Medical Center Prosthetics/Orthotics Clinic and a Speech and Hearing Center to persons in the District of Columbia, Virginia and Maryland.

**9247 Hospital for Sick Children**
1731 Bunker Hill Road NE
Washington, DC 20017 202-832-4400
800-226-4444
FAX: 202-635-5780
hfscsite.org

*Deborah T Zients, COO*
*Dr Murry M Pollack, VP, Medical Affairs*

Provides the highest quality rehabilitative and transitional care for infants, children, adolescents, and young adults with special health care needs and their families in a supportive environment that respects their needs, strengths, vslues and priorities.

**9248 Howard University Child Development Center**
1911 5th Street NW
Washington, DC 20001 202-865-4620

Offers children with developmental problems diagnosis, treatment, evaluation and follow along visits.

**9249 Psychiatric Institute of Washington**
5225 Wisconsin Avenue NW
Suite 104
Washington, DC 20015 202-885-5600
FAX: 202-966-7374
www.psychinstitute.com

*Howard Hoffman, Director*
*Carol Desjuns, Chief Operations Officer*

Psychiatric intensive care, crisis intervention, adult day treatment, drug treatment and other services to children and adults who have psychiatric and chemical dependency problems.

**9250 Spina Bifida Program of DC Children's Hospital**
Department of Physical Medicine and Rehabilitation
111 Michigan Avenue NW
Washington, DC 20010 202-884-3080
FAX: 202-884-3422
www.cnmc.org

*Sarah Evans, Director*
*Leslie Phillips, Nurse Practitoner*

Offers neurosurgery, orthopedics,physical medicine, social work, urology and nursing.

## Florida

**9251 Back Technology of Miami**
545 San Esteban Avenue
Coral Gables, FL 33146

*Jerry Fogel*

Provides remunerative work.

**9252 Bayfront Rehabilitation Center**
Bayfront Medical Center
701 6th Street S
St Petersburg, FL 33701 727-893-6108
FAX: 727-893-6779
www.bayfront.org

*JoAnn W Gardner MA RPT, Director Rehab Services*
*Daniel Stone, MD*

Bayfront Medical Center has an Inpatient Rehabilitation Hospital and two outpatient rehabilitation clinics that each provide progressive, comprehensive, individualized treatment. Specialized care in Physiatry (physical medicine), rehab nursing, occupational therapy, speech language pathology, recreational therapy, patient/family services and psychology is tailored to each patient from admission to community and/or school reintegration.

**9253 Bon Secours Hospital**
1050 NE 125th Street
North Miami, FL 33161 305-891-8851
800-345-3885
FAX: 305-891-3361
www.catholichealthservices.org

*James Reece, Administrator*

Offers rehabilitation services, occupational therapy, physical therapy, inpatient and outpatient care and more for the physically challenged.

**9254 Brain Injury Rehabilitation Center Sand Lake Hospital**
Brain Injury Rehabilitation Center Sand Lake Hospi
9400 Turkey Lake Road
Orlando, FL 32819 407-351-8500

www.orhs.org

*Shannon Elswick, President*

Dedicated to restoring brain injured patients with rehabilitation potential to their highest level of functioning. This is accomplished through an interdisciplinary team demonstrating personal responsibility to the patient, their family and each other.

**9255 Center for Pain Control and Rehabilitation**
2780 Cleveland Avenue
Suite 607
Fort Myers, FL 33901 239-337-4332

*Dr. Harris Bonnette, Medical Director*

**9256 Comprehensive Rehabilitation Center at Lee Memorial Hospital**
2776 Cleveland Avenue
Fort Myers, FL 33901          239-334-5200

*Palma Fuson, Director*

Offers rehabilitation services, occupational therapy, physical therapy, respite services and more for the physically challenged individual.

**9257 Comprehensive Rehabilitation Center of Naples Community Hospital**
350 7th Street N
Naples, FL 34102          239-436-5177
                         FAX: 239-436-5250

*William Crone, President*
*Heather Baker, Administrative Director*
*Ken Schields, Marketing Coordinator*

Offers rehabilitation services, inpatient and outpatient care at 5 locations in the county and more for the benefit of the disabled.

**9258 Conklin Center for the Blind**
405 White Street
Daytona Beach, FL 32114          386-258-3441
                                 FAX: 386-258-1155
                    e-mail: robert@conklincenter.org
                              www.conklincenter.org

*Robert Kelly, Executive Director*

Offers services for the totally blind, legally blind, visually impaired, mentally retarded blind and more with health, counseling, educational, recreational, rehabilitation, through computer training and professional training services. Serves people who are blind and who are challenged by one or more additional disabling conditions. Functional skills training and employment services, including supported employment.

**9259 Davis Center for Rehabilitation Baptist Hospital of Miami**
8900 N Kendall Drive
Miami, FL 33176          786-596-6520
                         FAX: 305-270-3640

*Elizabeth Matalon, Administrative Director*
*Bradley Aiken, MD*

A full-service, nonprofit community hospital providing a full range of inpatient and outpatient rehabilitation services. The overall commitment to excellence has extended to this specialized field. Access to medical expertise and services ensures that the best in medical resources are available should an unforeseen medical problem arise.

**9260 Division of Blind Services**
2551 W Executive Center Circle
Tallahassee, FL 32301          850-488-1330
                               800-342-1828
                          FAX: 850-487-1804
              e-mail: randy_touchton@fdles.state.fl.us

*Randy Touchton, Director*
*Craig Kiser, Manager*

Serves the totally blind, legally blind, visually impaired, deaf-blind, learning disabled, mentally retarded and other multiply handicapped by offering health, counseling, educational, recreational and computer training services.

**9261 Easter Seal Society of Dade County**
1475 NW 14th Avenue
Miami, FL 33125          305-325-0470
                         888-325-0470
              e-mail: info@miami.easterseals.com
                        www.easterseal.com

*Joan L Bornstein PhD, Acting President*
*Hosie Howe, Social Worker*
*Ronnie Waldman, Principal*

**9262 Easter Seals Broward County**
6951 W Sunrise Boulevard
Plantation, FL 33313          954-792-8772
                         FAX: 954-791-8275
              e-mail: info@esbc-fl.easterseals.com
                        www.broward.easterseals.com

*Cathy Susskind, Clinic Director*
*Becky Dausman, Chief Executive Officer*

ESBC provides direct services to children and adults with physical, neurological and communications disabilities and their families.

**9263 Easter Seals Southwest Flordia**
350 Braden Avenue
Sarasota, FL 34243          941-355-7637
                            800-807-7899
                       FAX: 941-351-4997
              e-mail: info@easterseal.org
                        www.swfl.easterseals.org

*Mary Hitchcock, President/CEO*
*Mary Ann Zyla Smith, Director Adult Services*
*Amy Spears, Director Health/Children Srvcs*

Easter Seals Sothwest Florida provides educational and therapeutic services to disabled children and adults

**9264 Easter Seals: Volusia and Flagler Counties , FL**
Easter Seals National
1219 Dunn Avenue
Daytona Beach, FL 32114          386-255-4568
                                 877-255-4568
                            FAX: 386-258-7677
                    e-mail: info@eseals-vf.org
              www.easterseals-volusiaflagler.org

*Lynn Sinnot, President*
*Jane Bronkie, Operations Manager*

Provides early intervention services: inclusive pre-school, aquatherapy and sensory processing therapy, OT, PT, ST and parenting programs, audiology services, equipment loan program, assistive technology information and referral. Residential summer camp and respite.

**9265 FIRE**
1286 Cedar Center Drive
Tallahassee, FL 32301          850-942-3658
                          FAX: 850-942-4518
                    e-mail: ibskip@earthlink.net

*Barbara Ross, Executive Director*

Provides independent living and vocational rehabilitation services to Florida residents who are legally blind. Services include instruction in orientation and mobility, accessible technology, daily living skills and employability skills. Information, referral and counseling services are also offered. All services are provided without charge.

**9266 Florida CORF**
Columbia Medical Center: Peninsula
264 S Atlantic Avenue
Ormond Beach, FL 32176          386-676-4222

www.memorial-health.com

*John Feore, Executive VP*
*Sandra Trovato, Executive Director*

Offers Medicare authorized therapy programs for seniors, disabled and others who need rehabilitation. CORF can provide coordinated and extended services in the home after a hospital stay, or when physical status changes. Patients who are treated at CORF, include amputations, arthritis, chronic/acute pain, depression/anxiety, nerve injury, sports injury, stroke and swallowing problems.

**9267 Florida Community College at Jacksonville/ Services for Students with Disabilities**
101 W State Street
Jacksonville, FL 32202 904-633-8100
FAX: 904-633-8110

*Cecilia Sumner, Director*
*Edith Abdullah, President*

**9268 Florida Institute for Neurologic Rehabilitation, Inc**
PO Box 1348
Wauchula, FL 33873 863-773-2857
800-697-5390
FAX: 863-773-0867
e-mail: info@finr.net
www.finr.net

*Stephen C Freeley, Director Marketing*
*Joseph Brennick, President*

A residential rehabilitation facility providing a therapeutic environment in which children, adolescents and adults who have survived head-injury can develop the independence and skills necessary to re-enter the community.

**9269 Florida Veterans Centers**
713 NE 3rd Avenue
Fort Lauderdale, FL 33304 954-356-7926
FAX: 954-356-7609

*Robert White, Executive Director*
Veterans medical clinic offering disabled veterans medical treatments.

**9270 Goodwill Industries-Suncoast**
10596 Gandy Boulevard N
St Petersburg, FL 33702 727-523-1512
888-279-1988
FAX: 727-563-9300
www.goodwill-suncoast.org

*Deborah A Passerini, VP Operations*
*Jean-Marie Moore, Operations Director*
*Lee Waits, President*

A nonprofit community-based organization whose purpose is to improve the quality of life for people who are handicapped, disabled and/or disadvantaged or aged. This mission is accomplished through providing independent living skills, affordable housing, training and placement in useful employment. Annually, the organization serves more than 1,400 handicapped, disabled or disadvantaged people in various components within the Human Services Department. Staff consists of 120+ full time employees.

**9271 Halifax Hospital Medical Center Eye Clinic Professional Center**
306 N Clyde Morris Boulevard
Daytona Beach, FL 32114 386-254-4000
FAX: 386-274-5889

*James Clower*
*Ron Rees, Chief Executive Officer*

Offers services for the totally blind, legally blind, visually impaired, mentally retarded blind and more with health, counseling, educational, recreational, rehabilitation, computer training and professional training services.

**9272 HealthQuest Subacute and Rehabilitation Programs**
Regenta Park
7130 Southside Boulevard
Jacksonville, FL 32256
FAX: 904-641-7896

HealthQuest offers four centers within the state of Florida offering exceptional staff, comfortable surroundings and individually designed, closely monitored programs dedicated to enabling patients to achieve their goals. Each location offers a progressive and cost effective alternative to in-hospital subacute and rehabilitative care. Centers are offered in Jacksonville, Winter Park, Sarasota and Sunrise.

**9273 HealthSouth Regional Rehabilitation Center**
20601 Old Cutler Road
Miami, FL 33189 305-251-3800
FAX: 305-251-5978

*Les Alt, Administrator*
*Jackie Arocho, Chief Executive Officer*

A comprehensive source of medical rehabilitation services for Pinellas County, Florida area residents, their families and their physicians. Offers the people of Florida all the clinical, technical and professional resources of the nation's leading provider of comprehensive rehabilitation care.

**9274 HealthSouth Rehabilitation Hospital of Tallahassee**
Healthsouth Corporation
1675 Riggins Road
Tallahassee, FL 32308 850-656-4800
888-476-8849
FAX: 850-656-4809
www.healthsouth.com

*Lynn Streetman, Administrator*
*Paige Mitchell, Director Business Development*
*Donna Crawford, Director Clinical Services*

North Florida's sole acute rehabilitation hospital between Jacksonville \, Panama City, and Gainesville. With 250 employees providing a full continuum of care form its 70 bed facility, the hospital is accredited by JCAHO, CARF and state designated and certified by Vocational Rehabilitation for traumatic brain injury, as well as a wide variety of other diagnoses. With the addition of our outpatients, the facility has served the greater community by touching the lives of over 50,000 patients.

**9275 HealthSouth Rehabilitation Hospital of Sarasota**
Health South Corporation in Burmingham Alabama
3251 Proctor Road
Sarasota, FL 34231 941-921-8600
800-873-4222
FAX: 941-925-7526
www.healthsouth.com

*Margaret Holloway, Chief Executive Officer*

**9276 HealthSouth Sports Medicine & Rehabilitation Center/Worksite Program**
1710 Lisenby Avenue
Panama City, FL 32405 850-784-4878
FAX: 850-769-7566

*Jim McGonley MPT/ATC, Director Clinical Services*
*Michelle Miller, Manager*

Outpatient sports medicine and rehabilitation center providing physical therapy, occupational therapy, industrial rehab, work hardening/work simulation, worksite and ergonomic analysis, FCE's, work assessment and pre-employment goals of returning the clients back to work, and returning to all recreational, sports and functional activities safely.

**9277 Holy Cross Hospital**
Catholic Southwest
4725 N Federal Highway
Fort Lauderdale, FL 33308
954-771-8000
FAX: 954-351-5994
www.holy-cross.com

*John C Johnson, President/CEO*

A full-service, non-profit Catholic hospital sponsored by the Sister of Mercy.

**9278 Lee Memorial Hospital**
PO Box 2218
Fort Myers, FL 33902
239-418-0014

*Martica Pitt, Director*
*Catherine Lee, Owner*

Offers a complete inpatient program of intensive rehabilitation designed to restore a patient to a more independent level of functioning. The comprehensive care includes medical rehabilitation and training for spinal cord injury, brain injury, stroke and neurological disorders.

**9279 Lighthouse for the Blind of Palm Beach**
PO Box 17980
West Palm Beach, FL 33416
561-586-5600
FAX: 561-586-5630

*William S Thompson, President/CEO*
*Sandra L Lamb, VP Administration/HR*
*Dawn M Clemons, VP Development/Services*

A private, non-profit rehabilitation and education agency in its 55th year of service. Offers programs to assist persons who areblind or visually impaired, an on-site Industrial Center, a technology training center, an Aids and appliances Store, special equipment grant programs, outreach services for children and adults, Early Intervention and Preschool Services, and a variety of support groups. These programs provide services and education for blind children and their parents.

**9280 Lighthouse for the Visually Impaired and Blind**
8610 Galen Wilson Boulevard
Port Richey, FL 34668
727-815-0303
FAX: 727-815-0203
e-mail: dgriffin@lighthouse-pasco.org
www.lighthouse-pasco.org

*Don Griffin PhD, Executive Director*
*Nancy Terkeurst, Director Clinical Services*

The Lighthouse offers services for visually impaired or blind adults and children ages 0-5 years old. Counseling, educational services, recreational services, rehabilitation, computer training and support groups.

**9281 MacDonald Training Center**
5420 W Cypress Street
Tampa, FL 33607
813-870-1300
FAX: 813-872-6010
TTY:813-873-7631
www.macdonaldcenter.org

*James Freyvogel, President/CEO*
*Mara Brad, Director Services*

A private, non-profit, community-based human services organization serving adults with disabilities (since 1953). Persons are provided the opportunity to achieve their highest potential through the Center's various programs that include day training, employment, community living and various support services.

**9282 Medical Rehabilitation Center of Jacksonville**
836 Prudential Drive
Jacksonville, FL 32207
904-202-1611
FAX: 904-202-3147

*Mark Kosier, Executive Director*

**9283 Medicenter of Tampa**
4411 N Habana Avenue
Tampa, FL 33614
813-872-2271

*Robert Westhoff, Administrator*
Postacute rehabilitation program.

**9284 Memorial Hospital Rehabilitation Center**
3599 University Boulevard S
Jacksonville, FL 32216
904-858-7600
FAX: 904-858-7610

*Charles Schauer, President*
*Douglas Baer, Chief Executive Officer*

An entire care facility featuring five day inpatient evaluation, pre-operative evaluation programs, five week pain management program, referral criteria and treatment goals, therapy services, psychological services and more to the physically challenged.

**9285 Miami Heart Institute Adams Building**
4701 N Meridian Avenue
Suite 601
Miami Beach, FL 33140
305-674-5956

www.msmc.com

*David Lehrman MD*
*Lourdes Donikian, Manager*

Dr. Lehrman now works with Dr. Sher and Dr. Lozman in orthopaedic surgery

**9286 Miami Lighthouse for the Blind**
601 SW 8th Avenue
Miami, FL 33130
305-856-2288
FAX: 305-285-6967
e-mail: info@miamilighthouse.com
www.miamilighthouse.com

*Carol Brady-simmons, Director of Children's Program*
*Annely Rose, Rehabilitation Teacher*
*Virginia Jacko, Executive Director*

Offers services for the legally blind and severely visually impaired (including those who are developmentally delayed) of all ages in the areas of counseling and educational, recreational, rehabilitation, computer and vocational training services.

**9287 Mount Sinai Medical Center Rehabilitation Unit**
4300 Alton Road
Miami Beach, FL 33140
305-673-0646
FAX: 305-674-2606
e-mail: webmaster@msmc.com
www.msmc.com

*Anne Vale, President*

**9288 Neuropsychiatric Pain Rehabilitation Clinic**
5330 George Street
New Port Richey, FL 34652
727-849-2005
FAX: 727-849-2087

*Charlene Evina, Administrative Assistant*
*Vickie Penick, Administrator*
*Donna Taylor, Manager*

A multidisciplinary outpatient program for the evaluation and treatment of chronic pain. Consultation services for hospitalized patients are also provided upon request.

**9289 North Broward Rehab Unit**
North Broward Medical Center
201 E Sample Road
Pompano Beach, FL 33064
954-941-8300
FAX: 954-786-6476

*Wendy Burkholder, Regional Manager*
*Pauline Grant, Chief Executive Officer*

CARF accredited, 30-bed inpatient rehabilitation unit treating adults with brain injuries, spinal cord injuries, stroke, orthopedic and neurologic injuries.

**9290  Northwest Medical Center**
Health Care Corporation of America
2801 N State Road 7
Margate, FL  33063
954-974-0400
866-442-2362
FAX: 954-984-1463
www.northwestmed.com

*Mary Lynn Swartz, Chief Executive Officer*
*Michael Bass, Chief Operation Officer*

**9291  Pain Institute of Tampa**
4178 N Armenia Avenue
Tampa, FL  33607
813-875-5913
FAX: 813-872-6215

*Dave Braughton*
*Laszlo Szollas, MD*

Pain management.

**9292  Pain Treatment Center, Baptist Hospital of Miami**
8900 N Kendall Drive
Miami, FL  33176
305-000-1111
FAX: 305-273-2406

*Brian Keeley, President*

**9293  Pine Castle**
4911 Spring Park Road
Jacksonville, FL  32207
904-733-2650
FAX: 904-733-2681
e-mail: pcastle@ilnk.com
www.edcationcentral.org/fdlsr/Special%20Place

*Jonathan May, Executive Director*

Provides remunerative work, training, community employment and community living options for adults with developmental disabilities.

**9294  Polk County Association for Handicapped Citizens**
1038 Sunshine Drive E
Lakeland, FL  33801
863-665-3846
FAX: 863-665-2330

*Shirley Balogh, President*

Work adjustment and remunerative work programs.

**9295  Quest**
380 Semorian Commerce Place
Suite B-204
Apopka, FL  32703
407-889-4530
FAX: 407-889-5710
e-mail: WebAdmin@QuestInc.org
www.questinc.org

*Katie Forta, President/CEO*
*Laura Victoria, Administrator*
*Cheryl Lyng, Associate Exec Dir/Production*

A multi-faceted vocational rehabilitation facility. Programs offered are vocational evaluation and assessment, work adjustment, placement, supported employment, community employment, developmental training, long-term sheltered care and residential services.

**9296  Rehab of Melbourne**
Sea Pines Rehabilitation Hospital
101 E Florida Avenue
Melbourne, FL  32901
321-984-4600
FAX: 321-952-6532

*Mark Tellier, Administrator*
*Denise Grath, Chief Executive Officer*

**9297  Rehabilitation Center for Children and Adults**
300 Royal Palm Way
Palm Beach, FL  33480
561-655-7266
FAX: 561-655-3269
e-mail: info@rcca.org
www.rcca.org

*Pamela Henderson, Executive Director*
*Ellen O'Bannon, Manager*

A private, nonprofit organization whose purpose is to improve physical function, independence and communication of people with physical disabilities. Any child or adult with a physical or speech disability is eligible for services.

**9298  Renaissance Center**
PO Box 19249
Jacksonville, FL  32245
904-743-1883
FAX: 904-743-5109

*Robert Sommers MD, President*
*Gregory Sikora, Vice President*

**9299  Sarasota Memorial Hospital/Comprehensive Rehabilitation Unit**
1700 S Tamiami Trail
Sarasota, FL  34239
941-917-9000

*Phillip Beauchamp, President*
*G Finlay, Chief Executive Officer*

**9300  South Dade Nursing Home**
2525 SW 75th Avenue
Miami, FL  33155
305-262-6800

*Frank Jimenez, Executive Director*
*Charlotte Raymor, Chief Executive Officer*

**9301  Strive Physical Therapy Centers**
2620 SE Maricamp Road
Ocala, FL  34471
352-351-8883
FAX: 352-351-4219
www.striverehab.com

*Richard Shutes, President/Owner*
*Izivan Levinrad, Clinical Director*

**9302  Sunbridge Care and Rehabilitation**
5627 9th Street E
Bradenton, FL  34203
941-753-8941
FAX: 941-739-4409

*Donna Steiermann, Administrator*

A comprehensive medical rehabilitation facility that is committed to helping individuals with disabilities improve their quality of life. This is a 120-bed facility offering a full range of acute and sub-acute inpatient programs as well as community-based outpatient programs.

**9303  Tampa Bay Academy**
12012 Boyette Road
Riverview, FL  33569
813-677-6700
800-678-3838
FAX: 813-671-3145
e-mail: info@tampayfcs,com
www.tampabay-academy.com

*Ted Hoesle, Director*
*Kenneth Sladkin, Executive Director*

A psychiatric residential treatment center and partial hospitalization program for ages 7 to 17.

**9304 Tampa General Rehabilitation Center**
PO Box 1289
Tampa, FL 33601          813-251-7000
          FAX: 813-253-4283

*Cindy Leistner, Development Director*
*Irwin Browasiky, MD*

Offers a full range of programs all aimed at helping patients achieve their full potentials. It is one of three centers in the state that provides Driver Training and Evaluation Programs for persons with disabilities, and also an Assisted Reproduction Program for neurologically impaired males. A Community Re-entry Day Treatment Program is available for individuals who have recovered from a brain injury. A wide variety of inpatient and outpatient programs are available.

**9305 Tampa Lighthouse for the Blind**
1106 W Platt Street
Tampa, FL 33606          813-251-2407
          FAX: 813-254-4305
          e-mail: tlh@templelighthouse.org
          www.templelighthouse.org

*Clifford Olstrom, Executive Director*

Offers services for the totally blind, legally blind, visually impaired, mentally retarded blind and more with health, counseling, educational, recreational, rehabilitation, computer training and professional training services.

**9306 University of Miami Comprehensive Pain and Rehabilitation Center**
600 Alton Road
Miami Beach, FL 33139          305-532-7246
          FAX: 309-534-3974

*Renee Stelle-Rosomoff, Programs Director*
*Hubert Rossomoff, Owner*

**9307 UpReach Pavilion**
8900 NW 39th Avenue
Gainesville, FL 32606

*Cindy Toth, Administrator*

**9308 Upper Pinellas Association for Retarded Citizens**
1501 N Belcher Road
Clearwater, FL 33765          727-797-8712
          FAX: 727-799-4632
          e-mail: uparc@aol.com
          www.members.aol.com/uparc/index.htm

*Karen Crown, Executive Director*

Offers services to more than 500 persons with mental retardation and other developmental disabilities. Services include two early intervention pre-schools, physical, speech and occupational therapies, homebound education and family support for children, birth to five years and transitional, vocational, habilitation, employment and placement services for adolescents and adults. UPARC operates 31 group homes, a 22 unit apartment complex, and Supported Living options to provide for residential need

**9309 Visually Impaired Persons of Southwest Florida**
35 W Mariana Avenue
North Fort Myers, FL 33903          239-997-7797
          FAX: 239-997-8462
          www.vipcenter.org

*Marylou Tuckwiller, Executive Director*

Provides training in independent living skills, orientation and mobility, counseling, computer and other communication skills, family support groups, peer counseling, socialization and a low vision clinic. Second location in Charlotte County. Phone: 941-625-8501.

**9310 West Florida Hospital: The Rehabilitation Institute**
8383 N Davis Highway
Pensacola, FL 32514          850-494-4000
          FAX: 850-494-4881
          www.westfloridahospital.com

*Dennis A Taylor, President/CEO*
*Carol Saxton, Senior VP Patient Care Services*

A 58-bed comprehensive rehabilitation facility offering inpatient and outpatient services. JCAHO and CARF accredited and a State designed head and spinal cord injury center. CARF accredited programs include: comprehensive inpatient rehab, spinal cord injury, brain injury and work hardening.

**9311 Willough at Naples**
9001 Tamiami Trail E
Naples, FL 34113          239-775-4500
          800-722-0100
          FAX: 239-775-0534

*Milton Branham, Director*
*James O'Shea, President*

A licensed psychiatric hospital in Southwest Florida which provides quality management and treatment for eating disorders and chemical dependency in adults.

# Georgia

**9312 Annandale at Suwanee**
3500 Annandale Lane
Suwanee, GA 30024          770-945-8381
          FAX: 770-945-8693
          e-mail: administration@annandale.org
          www.annandale.org

*Adam Pomeranz, Executive Director*
*Melissa Burton, Business Office Manager*

Private nonprofit residential facility for adults with developmental disabilities. Located on 124 acres just north of Atlanta. Annandale provides full program and 24 hour residential services, pay program services, respite care and skilled nursing services.

**9313 Atlanta Institute of Medicine and Rehabilitation**
2915 Piedmont Road NE
Suite A
Atlanta, GA 30305          404-365-0160
          FAX: 404-365-0751

*Faina Vladi, Manager*

**9314 Bobby Dodd Institute (BDI)**
2120 Marietta Boulevard NW
Atlanta, GA 30318          678-365-0071
          FAX: 678-365-0098
          e-mail: wmcmillan@bdi-atl.org
          www.bobbydodd.org

*Wayne McMillan, President/CEO*
*David Turner, Director Finance*
*Barbara Massey, VP Operations/Marketing*

BDI annually serves approximately 400 clients in Atlanta, GA. BDI works primarily with people with developmental disabilities such as autism, down syndrome or mental retardation, but includes clients with physical or acquired disabilities. Client age varies from teenagers to adults.

**9315  Cave Spring Rehabilitation Center**
Georgia Department of Labor
7 Georgia Avenue
Cave Spring, GA  30124                706-777-2341
                                  FAX: 706-777-2366

*Joe Holcombe, Director*
*David Stevenson, Assistant Director*

**9316  Center for Assistive Technology and Environmental Access**
GA Institute of Technology
490 10th Street, NW
Atlanta, GA 30332                     404-894-4960
                                 FAX: 404-894-9320
                                     www.catea.org

*Barbara Christopher, Administrative Coordinator*
*Elizabeth Bryant, Project Director II*

The Center for Assistive Technology and Environmental Access (CATEA) promotes maximum function, activity and access of persons with disabilities through the use of technology. The foci of the Center includes the development, evaluation and utilization of Assistive Technology and the design and development of Accessible Environments.

**9317  Center for the Visually Impaired**
739 W Peachtree Street NW
Atlanta, GA  30308                    404-875-9011
                                 FAX: 404-607-0062
                        e-mail: info@cviatlanta.org
                                  www.cviatlanta.org

*Susan B Green, Director Development*
*La Della Holmes-Raddick, Director Client Services*
*Subie Green, Manager*

Offers services to people of all ages who are blind or visually impaired with training in orientation and mobility, computer technology, activities of daily living, communication skills and employment readiness. Aso offers two children's programs, a community-based rehabilitation program for senior citizens, and a low vision clinic.

**9318  Devereux Georgia Treatment Network**
PO Box 1688
Kennesaw, GA  30156                   770-427-0147
                                      800-342-3357
                                 FAX: 770-427-4030
                     e-mail: jzdencan@devereux.org
                                www.devereuxga.org

*Mario Bolivar, Executive Director*

Serves ages 10 to 17, males and females with a capacity for up to 187. Serves moderate to severe emotional, behavioral and/or learning disabilities. A specialized psychiatric hospital/intensive residential treatment program for below average to superior intelligence. Community programming that serves ages 3 to 21, males and females, providing wraparound, Therapeutic Foster Care and Independent Living Services.

**9319  Easter Seals East Georgia**
PO Box 2441
Augusta, GA  30903                    706-667-9695
                                 FAX: 706-667-8831
                     e-mail: sthomas@esega.org
                         www.ga-ea.easter-seals.org

*Sheila H Thomas, President/CEO*

**9320  Georgia Industries for the Blind**
PO Box 218
Bainbridge, GA  39818                 229-248-2666
                                 FAX: 229-248-2669

*James Hughes, Executive Director*

Offers services for the totally blind, legally blind, visually impaired, mentally retarded blind and more with health, counseling, educational, recreational, rehabilitation, computer training and professional training services.

**9321  Head Injury Treatment Program at Marietta**
26 Tower Road NE
Marietta, GA  30060                   770-422-8913
                                      800-526-5782

*Karen Erlinger, Program Director*
*Valerie Hamilton, Administrator*

Postacute rehabilitation program.

**9322  Hillhaven Rehabilitation**
26 Tower Road NE
Marietta, GA  30060                   770-422-8913
                                      800-526-5782
                                 FAX: 770-425-2085

*Leslie Ann Marie Parrish, Case Manager*
*Valerie Hamilton, Administrator*

Routine skilled and subacute medical and rehabilitation care including physical therapy, occupational therapy, speech pathology and therapeutic recreation. Programs include stroke and head injury rehab; orthopedic rehab; complex IV therapy; woundcare; cancer; total parental nutrition and dialysis.

**9323  In-Home Medical Care**
Care Master Medical Services
240 Odell Road
Griffin, GA  30224                    770-227-1264
                                      800-542-8889
                                 FAX: 770-412-0014
              e-mail: caremaster@accesunited.com
                             www.caremastermedical.com

*Nancy Frederick, VP*
*Eddie Grogan, Chief Executive Officer*

Offers the devoted attention of a professional nurse, the use of I.V. therapies, pain management and provision of medical equipment and supplies right where the patient wants to be.

**9324  Learning Services: Peachtree**
337 W Pike Street
Suite B
Lawrenceville, GA  30045              770-962-4828
                                 FAX: 770-995-1253
                               www.learningservices.com

*Greg Lang, Admissions*

Postacute rehabilitation program.

**9325  Pain Control & Rehabilitation Institute of Georgia**
2784 N Decatur Road
Suite 120
Decatur, GA  30033                    404-297-1400
                                 FAX: 404-297-1427

*Shulim Spektor MD, Chief Executive Officer*
*Anna Britman, Office Manager*

Provides pain management for chronic and acute pain resulted from injuries, diseases of muscles and nerve, Reflex Sympathetic Dystrophy, perform disabilities and impairment ratings.

**9326  Savannah Association for the Blind**
214 Drayton Street
Savannah, GA  31401                   912-236-4473
                                 FAX: 912-234-4156

*W Chandler Simmons, Executive Director*

Offers services for the totally blind, legally blind, visually impaired, mentally retarded blind and more with health, counseling, educational, recreational, rehabilitation, computer training and professional training services.

**9327  Shepherd Center for Treatment of Spinal Injuries**
2020 Peachtree Road NW
Atlanta, GA  30309

404-350-7743
FAX: 404-350-7479

*James Collins, Administrator*
*Charles Willingham, Manager*

Dedicated exclusively to the care of patients with spinal cord injuries and other paralyzing spinal disorders. It serves predominately residents of Georgia and neighboring states as one of the only 14 hospitals designated by the U.S. Department of Education as a Model Spinal Cord Injury System Program.

**9328  Transitional Hospitals Corporation**
7000 Central Parkway NE
Suite 1000
Atlanta, GA  30328

770-821-5328
800-683-6868
FAX: 770-913-0015

*Dean Rustin, Owner*

A national network of intensive care hospitals providing care for patients who suffer from a chronic illness and/or catastrophic accident. The mission is founded on providing quality health care to patients who require highly skilled nursing care and access to technologically advanced therapies.

**9329  Walton Rehabilitation Hospital**
PO Box 2223
Augusta, GA  30903

706-823-8511
866-492-5866
FAX: 706-724-5752
e-mail: postmaster@wrh.org
www.wrh.org

*Dennis Skelley, President*
*Frank Lewis, COO*
*Mike Harrell, CFO*

A 58-bed comprehensive physical rehabilitation hospital offering inpatient and outpatient services. Services offered include: stroke recovery, orthopedic injury, pediatrics, head injury, pain management for chronic pain syndrome, TMJ/Craniofacial pain and chronic headache disorders, spinal cord injury, driving instruction, work re-entry, independent living, assistive technology and ADA consulting.

## Hawaii

**9330  Rehabilitation Hospital of the Pacific**
226 N Kuakini Street
Honolulu, HI  96817

808-531-3511
FAX: 808-544-3335
www.rehabhospital.org

*Stuart Ho, President/CEO*
*Pauline Osborne, Vice President/CFO*
*Dr Thomas Au, VP Clinical Affairs/Medical Dir*

## Idaho

**9331  Ashton Memorial Nursing Home and Chemical Dependency Center**
700 N 2nd
Ashton, ID  83420

208-652-7461
FAX: 208-652-7252
e-mail: ashmem@frtel.com

*Sheila Kellogg, Administrator*

**9332  Easter Seal Society**
Easter Seals National
1465 S Vinnell Way
Boise, ID  83709

208-378-9924
800-374-1910
FAX: 208-378-9965
www.easterseals.org

*Donna Grummer, Executive Director*

**9333  Idaho Elks Rehabilitation Hospital**
PO Box 1100
Boise, ID  83701

208-489-4444
FAX: 208-489-4005
www.idahoelkrehab.org

*Joseph Caroselli, Administrator*

A nonprofit hospital serving Idaho and the Pacific Northwest. All inpatient and outpatient programs and services are supervised by the hospital's full-time medical directors whose specialty is psychiatry, the profession of physical rehabilitative medicine. Services include: occupational therapy, rehabilitative nursing, social skills, head injury program, physical therapy, speech pathology, audiology and cardiac rehabilitation.

**9334  Portneuf Medical Center Rehabilitation**
651 Memorial Drive
Pocatello, ID  83201

208-239-1836
FAX: 208-239-1838
www.portmed.org

*Robbie Oyler, Director*

## Illinois

**9335  Advocate Christ Medical Center & Advocate Hope Children's Hospital**
4440 West 95th Street
Oak Lawn, IL  60453

708-684-8000
800-323-8622
FAX: 708-684-4045
www.advocatehealth.com/christ

*Kenneth W Lukhard, President*
*Darcie Brazel, VP/Chief Nurse Executive*

**9336  Alexian Brothers Medical Center**
800 Biesterfield Road
Elk Grove Village, IL  60007

847-437-5500

e-mail: costellc@alexian .net
www.alexian.org

*Roger Johnson, President/CEO*
*Caroline Costello, Director/Communications*

A threefold mission: Works toward maximizing physical function, enhance independent social skills and optimize communication skills consistent with an individual's ability. The Center helps those disabled by accident or illness achieve a new personal best.

**9337  Back in the Saddle Hippotherapy Program**
Corcoran Physical Therapy
PO Box 597901
Chicago, IL  60659

312-541-0567
847-604-4145
FAX: 847-673-8895
e-mail: info@hippotherapychicago.com
www.hippotherapychicago.com

*Julie Naughton, Program Coordinator*
*Maureen Corcoran, Physical Therapist*
*Tom Corcoran, Owner*

A direct medical treatment used by licensed physical therapists who have a strong treatment background in posture and movement, neuromotor function and sensory processing. The benefits of Hippotherapy are available to individuals with just about any disability. Two locations: Glen Grove, IL and Morton Grove, IL. Accepts all insurance.

**9338  Barbara Olson Center of Hope**

3206 N Central Avenue
Rockford, IL 61101
815-964-9275
FAX: 815-964-9607
e-mail: wdovenport@b-olsoncenterofhope.org
www.b-olsoncenterofhope.org

*Carm Herman, Executive Director*
*Nancy Flanagan, President of the Board*
*Susan Nagy, Accoutant*

We provide vocational employment, educational and social opportunities for adults with developmental disabilities.

**9339  Baxter Healthcare Corporation**

1 Baxter Parkway
Deerfield, IL 60015
847-948-2000
800-422-9837
FAX: 847-948-3642
www.baxter.com

*John D Forsyth, Chairman*
*Gail D Fosler, Executive VP/Chief Economist*

**9340  Beacon Therapeutic Diagnostic and Treatment Center**

10650 S Longwood Drive
Chicago, IL 60643
773-881-1005
FAX: 773-881-1164
www.beacon-diabetic.org

*Susan Yna, Executive Director*
*Cheryl Thompson, Chief Administrator of Office Af*

Offers community day treatment, education, diagnostic services, family counseling, learning disabled, speech and hearing and psychiatric services.

**9341  Blind Service Association**

16 N Wabash Avenue
Chicago, IL 60602
312-782-8188

*Debbie Grossman, Executive Director*
*Louis Bellande Jr, Partner*

Offers services for the totally blind, legally blind and visually impaired with reading and recording low vision network, social services, referrals and support groups.

**9342  Brandecker Rehabilitation Center**

9455 S Hoyne Avenue
Chicago, IL 60620
773-239-2191
FAX: 773-239-6229
www.eastersealschicago.org

*Mary COOney, Program Director*
*Dolores Nickel, Manager*

We offer early intervention services for infants and toddlers with developmental delays and disabilities. Our outpatient Medical Rehabilitation Program offers direct therapy services for children from age birth-16.

**9343  Brentwood Subacute Healthcare Center**

T HI Brentwood
5400 W 87th Street
Burbank, IL 60459
708-423-1200
800-430-0098
FAX: 708-423-1266
www.thicare.com

*Audrey Protrowski, Director Business Development*
*Jill Sattersield, Administrator*
*John Walton, Chief Executive Officer*

Postacute rehabilitation program and ventilator weaning.

**9344  Caremark Healthcare Services**

2211 Sanders Road
Northbrook, IL 60062
847-559-4700
800-423-1411

*Mac Crawford, President*

An 80-service-center network providing services anywhere in the U.S. Offers 24 hour access to nursing and pharmacy services, case management resource centers, HIV/AIDS services, women's health services, transplant care services, nutrition support services, infectious disease management and other therapies and programs.

**9345  Center for Comprehensive Services**

Mentor Network
306 W Mill Street
Carbondale, IL 62901
618-529-3060
800-582-4227
FAX: 618-457-5372
e-mail: sandy.boston@thementornetwork.com
www.thementornetwork.com

*Sandra Boston, National Director of Admissions*
*Robin Ray, President*

Post-acute rehabilitation services for adults and adolescents with acquired brain injuries. Residential, day-treatment and out-patient services tailored to individual needs.

**9346  Center for Rehabilitation at Rush Presbyterian:**
**Johnston R Bowman Health Center**

710 S Paulina Street
Chicago, IL 60612
312-942-3600
FAX: 312-942-3601
e-mail: teri_sommerfeld@rush.edu
www.rush.edu

*Teri Sommerfeld, Administrator*

Postacute rehabilitation program.

**9347  Center for Spine, Sports & Occupational Rehabilitation**

1030 N Clark Street
Suite 500
Chicago, IL 60610
312-238-7767
FAX: 312-238-7709
www.rehabchicago.org

*Wayne Lerner, Executive Director*
*Sharon Seitz, Manager*

Offers evaluation and treatment of patients with acute and subacute musculoskeletal and sports injuries.

**9348  Children's Home and Aid Society of Illinois**

125 S Wacker Drive
14th Floor
Chicago, IL 60606
312-424-0071

www.chasi.org

*Nancy B Ronquillo, President/CEO*

Private state-wide. Multi-service, racially integrated staff and client populations. Provides educational, placement and community services for children-at-risk and their families. Advocacy, consultation and follow-up services provided according to our philosophy of continuum of care. No one, child or adult, is denied service because of disabilities, if the program services meet their needs. Higher quality in-service training for staff as well as parenting figures.

**9349  Christ Hospital and Medical Center**

4440 W 95th Street
Oak Lawn, IL 60453
708-684-8000

*Kenneth Lukhard, Chief Executive Officer*

**9350 Clinton County Rehabilitation Center d/b/a CCRC Community Link**
1665 N 4th Street
Breese, IL 62230
618-526-2252
FAX: 618-526-2021
e-mail: marla@commlink.org
www.commlink.org

*Julie Majezel, Service Coordinator*
*John Sedivy, Executive Director*

Provides Adult Day Programs (developmental training, work training, job readiness and job placements); Residentail Programs (CILA Intermittent Care, CILA 24 hour care); Infant Programs (early interventions, early head start); Community Services (specialized services and family support).

**9351 Continucare, A Service of the Rehab Institute of Chicago**
West Suburban Hospital Medical Center
3 Erie Court
Oak Park, IL 60302
708-383-6200
800-354-7342
FAX: 312-908-1369
www.westsuburban.reshealth.org

*Heidi Asbury MD*

Offers inpatient subacute rehabilitation program.

**9352 Delta Center**
1400 Commercial Avenue
Cairo, IL 62914
618-734-3626
800-471-7213
FAX: 618-734-1999
www.deltacenter.org

*Frederica Garnett, Executive Director*
*Lisa Tholbert, Assistant Executive Director*

**9353 Division of Rehabilitation-Education Services, University of Illinois**
1207 S Oak Street
Champaign, IL 61820
217-351-8473
FAX: 217-333-0248
www.disability.ui.uc.edu

*Brad Hedrick, Director*
*Patrick Davisson, Manager*

Offers services for the totally blind, legally blind, visually impaired, mentally retarded blind and more with health, counseling, educational, recreational, rehabilitation, computer training and professional training services.

**9354 Easter Seals**
Easter Seals in Chicago
212 Barney Drive
Joliet, IL 60435
815-725-2194
FAX: 815-725-5150
www.easterseals.com

*Debra Condotti, President*

Services for children and adults with disabilities and their families. Pediatric outpatient medical rehabilitation, inclusive childcare, fostercare, residential homes, clinics.

**9355 Easter Seals DuPage Dold Center for Children**
830 S Addison Avenue
Villa Park, IL 60181
630-620-4433
FAX: 630-620-1148

*Mary D'Arcy, Executive Director*
*Linda Matheson, Program Services*

Maximizes independence for infants, children and adults with disabilities by providing physical, occupational and speech therapy, audiology, social work, early intervention, assistive technology, toy lending, equipment loan and special needs day care.

**9356 Easter Seals Jayne Shover Center**
799 S McLean Boulevard
Elgin, IL 60123
847-742-3264
FAX: 847-742-9436
e-mail: il-ja.easter-seals.org
www.il-js.easter-seals.org

*Larry M Narum, President/CEO*
*Susan Dilley, Chief Executive Officer*

A free-standing, comprehensive outpatient rehabilitation center serving children and adults with physical and developmental disabilities.

**9357 El Valor Corporation**
Early Intervention Program
185 W 21th Street
Chicago, IL 60608
312-997-2021
FAX: 312-432-9849
www.elvalor.net

*Vincent Allocco, Director*

Mission is to challenge people with disabilities. It is a center for people with disabilities and their families and serves Chicago and surrounding areas, providing services in English and Spanish to individuals whose lives would be drastically impoverished without them.

**9358 Elgin Rehabilitation Center**
1485 Davis Road
Elgin, IL 60123
847-888-5540

*Robert Borchert, Vice President*

**9359 Family Counseling Center**
Washington & Market Street
Golconda, IL 62938
618-683-2461
FAX: 618-683-2066
e-mail: fccgolconda@shawneelink.com

*Larry Mizell, Executive Director*
*Beci Gates, Behavioral Health Division Dir.*
*Donna Perez, Housing Coordinator*

Provides counseling, developmental training, evaluations, assisted living services, referrals, psychosocial rehabilitation, and a variety of work services.

**9360 Family Matters**
A RC Community Support Systems
2502 S Veterans Drive
Effingham, IL 62401
217-347-0880
866-4FM-PTIC
FAX: 217-347-5119
e-mail: deinhorn@arc-css.org
www.fmptic.org

*Debbie Einhorn, Director Family Support*
*Nancy Mader, Office Manager*

Parent Training and Information Center and family support programs for families of children who have disabilities from the ages of birth through 21. Services include: Parent support and training, school advocacy, home visits, information and referral, parent-to-parent networking, special education rights workshops and other training sessions on special education topics for parents and school personnel throughout Illinois except in the Chicago area.

**9361 Five Star Industries**
PO Box 60
Du Quoin, IL 62832
618-542-5421
FAX: 618-542-5556

*Susan Engelhardt, Executive Director*

Incorporated as a private, non-profit corporation under the laws of the State of Illinois, is an equal opportunity employer and provides equal opportunity in compliance with the Civil Rights Act of 1964 and all other appropriate laws, rules and regulations referring to civil rights.

**9362 Gilchrist-Marchman Rehabilitation Center**
2345 W N Avenue
Chicago, IL 60647
FAX: 773-276-5653

*Therese O'Shea, Executive Director*

**9363 HSI Austin Center For Development**
1819 S Kedzie Avenue
Chicago, IL 60623
773-854-1676
FAX: 773-854-8300
Provides an educational program designed to enhance academic, behavioral and social performance of children 4-14 years of age experiencing emotional disorders that result in exclusion from the public school setting.

**9364 Hardin County Center**
580 Westport Road
Elizabethtown, KY 42701
270-765-6196

*Stefanie Goff, Manager*

**9365 Henry County Clinic**
117 S East Street
Cambridge, IL 61238
309-937-5391
FAX: 309-937-2023

*John DC, Owner*

Individual, group, marital and family therapy, psychological testing and evaluation services offered.

**9366 Hyde Park-Woodlawn**
950 E 61st Street
Chicago, IL 60637
773-288-8000
FAX: 773-493-2397

*William Cinwell, Executive Director*

**9367 ILC Enterprises**
6415 Stanley Avenue
Berwyn, IL 60402
630-789-0511
FAX: 708-788-0831

*Cindy Holbrook, Program Director*

A nonprofit tax exempt private social service agency serving suburban Chicago offering day treatment and vocational counseling to individuals who encountered a pattern of job loss due to emotional problems.

**9368 Illinois Center for Autism**
548 S Ruby Lane
Fairview Heights, IL 62208
618-398-7500
FAX: 618-397-9869

*Susan Szekely, Director*
*Sandra Rodenberg, Principal*

A community-based mental health/educational treatment center dedicated to serving autistic clients.

**9369 Illinois Masonic Medical Center**
836 W Wellington Avenue
Chicago, IL 60657
773-975-1600

www.advocatehealth.com

*Susan Lopez, Chief Executive Officer*
*Otto Aldana-Centeno, MD*

Consultation, education, family counseling, parent training in behavior modification techniques offered to developmentally disabled adults.

**9370 Infant Program**
409 W New Indian Trail Court
Aurora, IL 60506
630-879-9119

**9371 Julius and Betty Levinson Center**
332 Harrison Street
Oak Park, IL 60304
708-383-8887
FAX: 708-383-9025
e-mail: info@ucp.net.org
www.ucp.org

*Laurie Wisenski, Manager*

Houses one of its three adult developmental training programs for substantially physically disabled men and women.

**9372 Lake County Health Department**
3012 Grand Avenue
Waukegan, IL 60085
847-377-8170
FAX: 847-336-1517
www.co.lake.il.us

*Dale Valance, Administrator*
*Gale Galass, Manager*

Includes counseling, crisis intervention, emergency management, psychotherapy and chemotherapy management for individuals and families.

**9373 Little Friends**
140 N Wright Street
Naperville, IL 60540
630-355-6533
FAX: 630-355-3176
e-mail: tniemeyer@lilfriends.com
www.littlefriendsinc.com

*Tammy Niemeyer, Public Relations Director*
*Jack Ryan, President*

Nonprofit early intervention and special education programs with focus on children with autism or other developmental, emotional or behavioral disabilities. Vocational and residential services for adults with developmental disabilities.

**9374 MAP Training Center**
7th and Mc Kinley Street
Karnak, IL 62956
618-634-9401
FAX: 618-634-9090

*Larry Earnhart, President*
*Cindy Earnhart, Community Liaison*

Training, employment, residential and support services, targeted for adults with developmental disabilities.

**9375 Macon Resources**
PO Box 2760
Decatur, IL 62524
217-875-1910
FAX: 217-875-8899
TTY:217-875-8898
e-mail: kscrogin@maconresources.org
www.maconresources.org

*Kay Scrogin, Executive Director*
*Linda Clary, Administrative Assistant*
*Tommy Nelson, Deputy Director Clinical Svcs.*

The purpose is to provide a comprehensive array of habilitative/rehabilitative training programs and support services to assist individuals and/or family units of an individual with a developmental disability, mental illness, or other handicapping condition to live, attend school or day program, and/or work in the least restrictive, most normalized environment possible.

**9376  Mary Bryant Home for the Blind**

2960 Stanton Street
Springfield, IL 62703                217-529-1611
                                FAX: 217-529-6975
                        e-mail: MBHA@springnet1.com
                             www.marybryanthome.org

*Jerry Curry, Administrator*

Supportive living facility for blind or visually impaired adults over the age of 22.

**9377  Northern Illinois Medical Center**

4201 W Medical Center Drive
McHenry, IL 60050                    815-759-4300
                                     800-734-7342
                                FAX: 815-759-8062

*Kathryn Murauskas, Inpatient Rehabilitation Unit*
*Nora Connors, Director Rehabilitation Network*
*Lisa Forino, Marketing Coordinator*

Providing rehabilitation services in Lake and McHenry Counties, the Rehabilitation Unit is a complete living environment for up to 15 patients after a debilitating illness of trauma. Various locations offering a multitude of services: PT, OT, speech, HT, RT aquatics, work hardening, FCE's, vocational counseling, rehab nursing, physiatry, neuropsychology, case management. Comprehensive Inpatient Rehabilitation Unit, and many more services.

**9378  Northern Illinois Special Recreation Association**

820 E Terra Cotta Avenue
Suite 125
Crystal Lake, IL 60014               815-459-0737
                                FAX: 815-459-0388
                             e-mail: info@nisra.org
                                   www.NISRA.org

*Randy Reopelle, Director*
*Cindy McCauley, Director*
*Brian Shahinian, Executive Director*

Leisure and recreation services to those with disabilities who are unable to participate successfully in park district and city recreation programs.

**9379  Oak Forest Hospital of Cook County**

15900 Cicero Avenue
Oak Forest, IL 60452                 708-687-7200
                                FAX: 708-687-7979

*Cyntjia T Henderson, Interim Hospital Director*
*Joe Turner, Public Information*
*Dan Martin, Chief Executive Officer*

A 654 bed health care center devoted to the diagnosis, rehabilitation and long-term care of adults suffering from chronic illnesses, diseases and physical impairments.

**9380  Peoria Area Blind People's Center**

2905 W Garden Street
Peoria, IL 61605                     309-637-3693
                                FAX: 309-673-3699

*Mabel Vandeusen, Executive Director*

Offers services for the totally blind, legally blind, visually impaired, mentally retarded blind and more with health, counseling, educational, recreational, rehabilitation, computer training and professional training services.

**9381  Peoria Association for Retarded Citizens**

PO Box 3418
Peoria, IL 61612                     309-691-3800
                                FAX: 309-689-3613
                                   www.peoriaarc.org

*Kim Cornwell, VP Quality Improvement*
*Roy Ricketts, Interin President/CEO*
*Anne Follis, Executive Director*

Serves all ages that are diagnosed with mental retardation and other developmental and physical disabilities. Programs include early intervention, family support, respite care, vocational training, supported employment, adult day programs and residential services. Serves 1,000 clients with 400 staff members.

**9382  Phoenix I**

3075 Grand Avenue
Galesburg, IL 61401                  309-343-6126
                                FAX: 309-344-1754
                           e-mail: kccdd@galesburg.net

*Ned Hippensteel, Executive Director*

**9383  Pioneer Center of McHenry County**

4001 W Dayton Street
McHenry, IL 60050                    815-344-1230
                                FAX: 815-344-3815
                        e-mail: private@pioneercenter.org
                              www.pioneercenter.org

*Lorraine Kopczynski, President/CEO*
*Lenard J Duncan, Chairman of the Board*
*Dan Haligus, VP Programs*

Early intervention, sheltered employment, developmental training, employment services, residential services, mental health services, respite care and Voice: Sexual assault services.

**9384  Prosthetics and Orthotics Center in Blue Island**

2310 York Street
Blue Island, IL 60406                708-597-2611
                                     800-354-7342
                                FAX: 800-908-1932
                www.rehabchicago.org/about/blue_island.php
Provides orthotic and prosthetic fittings and follow-up services to adults and children in the south suburbs of Chicago.

**9385  RB King Counseling Center**

2300 N Edward Street
Decatur, IL 62526                    217-877-8121
                                FAX: 217-875-0966

*Gordon Cross MD*

Offers outpatient, individual, group, divorce and meditation, family and re-adjustment counseling.

**9386  REHAB Products and Services**

3715 N Vermilion Street
Danville, IL 61832                   217-446-1146
                                FAX: 217-446-1191

*Frank Drunacci, President*

**9387  RIC Northshore**

Rehabilitation Institute of Chicago
345 E Superior Street
Chicago, IL 60611                    312-238-1000
                                     800-354-7342
                            e-mail: webmaster@ric.org
                               www.rehabchicago.org

*Wayne Lerner, President/CEO*

Provides rehabilitation for sports-related injuries, musculoskeletal conditions, neurological conditions, stroke, arthritis, amputation, burns, and general deconditioning.

**9388  RIC Prosthetics and Orthotics Center**

1055 175th Street
Suite 101
Homewood, IL 60430                   708-597-2611
                                FAX: 708-957-8353
                        e-mail: webmaster@rehabchicago.org
                              www.rehabchicago.org

*Wayne Lerner, Executive Director*

Offers almost all the prosthetics and orthotics services provided at RIC's main hospital in downtown Chicago, including consultations, fittings and training.

**9389 RIC Windermere House**

5548 S Hyde Park Boulevard
Chicago, IL 60637
312-908-9554
800-354-7342
FAX: 773-256-5060
www.rehabchicago.org
Evaluation, therapeutic services and patient education are offered in the areas of arthritis, multiple sclerosis, musculoskeletal conditions, orthopedics, stroke, spinal cord injury, brain injury and sports medicine.

**9390 RIC and Swedish Covenant Hospital Rehabilitation Services**

5145 N California Avenue
Chicago, IL 60625
773-878-8200
FAX: 773-907-3032
www.schosp.org

*Claudia Moorehead, Executive Director*
*Ketki Modi, Medical Director*
*Mark Newton, Chief Executive Officer*

Provides acute rehabilitation services, subacute care and outpatient services for many types of disabling injuries and conditions, including amputation, arthritis, brain injury, general deconditioning, multiple sclerosis, musculoskeletal injuries, stroke, and joint replacements.

**9391 Ray Graham Association for People with Disabilities**

2801 Finley Road
Suite 3c
Downers Grove, IL 60515
630-620-2222
FAX: 630-628-2350
e-mail: cathyfickerterill@yahoo.com
www.ray-graham.org

*Cathy Terrill, President*

Provides developmental services at 15 sites to infants, children and adults with disabilities. Services range from 1 hr/wk respite to full-time residential.

**9392 Reach Rehabilitation Program: Americana Healthcare**

9401 S Kostner Avenue
Oak Lawn, IL 60453
708-423-1505

*Jean Roche, Owner*
Postacute rehabilitation program.

**9393 Rehabilitation Achievement Center**

5150 Capitol Drive
Wheeling, IL 60090
847-215-9977
FAX: 847-215-9376

*Richard Green, Program Director*
*Mary Helen Ekstam, Director Clinical Relations*

A post-acute head injury program designed specifically to help survivors and their families meet the challenge of community re-entry after discharge from acute care settings. RAC uses an integrated team approach to develop and implement a realistic program to suit each person's individual needs.

**9394 Rehabilitation Institute of Chicago: Alexian Brothers Medical Center**

800 Biesterfield Road
Elk Grove Village, IL 60007
847-956-5422
800-354-7342
FAX: 312-908-9561

*Christine Sommerfeldt, Executive Director*
A 32-bed rehabilitation unit under the medical direction and supervision of the Rehabilitation Institute of Chicago.

**9395 Riverside Medical Center**

Mental Health Unit
350 N Wall Street
Kankakee, IL 60901
815-933-1671
FAX: 815-935-7485
www.riversidehealthcare.org

*Rhonda Huber, VP Institutional Advancement*

Offers recreation, parenting therapy, emergency services, psychological testing and inpatient treatment programs.

**9396 Robert Young Mental Health Center Division of Trinity Regional Haelth System**

Trinity Health Foundation
2701 17th Street
Rock Island, IL 61201
309-779-2232
800-322-1431
FAX: 309-779-2027
www.trinityqc.com

*Berlinda Tyler-Jamison, President*

Services include comprehensive inpatient rehabilitation, chronic pain management programs, outpatient medical rehabilitation, work hardening programs, vocational evaluation, alcohol and other drug dependency rehabilitation programs, Burn Center, and mental health services for inpatient, partial hospitalization, residential treatment, case management, emergency/crisis intervention and outpatient therapy. Licensed for 443 beds, it is the largest health care institution in the Iowa/Illinois area.

**9397 Sampson-Katz Center**

2020 W Devon Avenue
Chicago, IL 60659
773-761-9000
FAX: 312-553-5523
TTY:773-761-6672
e-mail: jvsskc@jvschicago.org
www.jvschicago.org

*Alan Goldstein, Executive Director*

**9398 Shelby County Community Services**

1810 W South 3rd Street
Shelbyville, IL 62565
217-774-5587
FAX: 217-774-5120

*Richard Gloede, Executive Director*

**9399 St Elizabeth Hospital Physical Rehabilitation Unit In-Patient/CARFT Certified**

211 S 3rd Street
Belleville, IL 62220
618-234-2120
FAX: 618-222-4606

*Lucy Beaver, Rehab Services Director*
*Mike Mecurico, Executive Director*
*Tom Dibadj, Rehab Therapy Manager*

Comprehensive inpatient and outpatient physical rehab services that include the services of a psychiatrist, rehab nursing, OT, PT, Speech, RT, social service, neuro psychologist and other resource and support personnel that support the rehab program.

**9400 Streator Unlimited**

305 N Sterling Street
Streator, IL 61364
815-673-5574
FAX: 815-673-1714
www.streatorunlimited.com

*Jeffrey Dean, Executive Director*
*Lynn Fukar, Director of Day Services*
*Julie Caestens, Director Residential Services*

Vocational and personal skills training, residential services, client and family support, supported and computerized employment. Serves adults with intellectual disabilities.

**9401  TCRC Sight Center**
111 W Washington Street
Suite 410
East Peoria, IL  61611
309-698-4001
FAX: 309-698-9227

*Jeff Turnbull, Administrator/VP*
*Annecia Payne, Office Manager*

Offers services for persons who are totally blind, legally blind, partially sighted or visually impaired along with other disabilities. Have support group, rehabilitation classes, orientation and mobility services, counseling services, low vision clinic, Braille transcription services, technology services and specialized aids and appliances for sale.

**9402  Tazewell County Resource Center**
Rr 1
Box 12
Tremont, IL  61568
309-477-2272
FAX: 309-925-4241

*Gus Van Den Brink, Executive Director*
*Dale Claus, Administrator*

A private, nonprofit agency providing programs for the special needs of infants, adults, children and their families residing in Tazewell County. Services offered include: birth-three infant/parent program, adult day care services, family support, residential, vocational services, sheltered work and activity services programs.

**9403  Thresholds Bridge Deaf North**
Thresholds Psychiatric Rehabilitation Centers
4101 N Ravenswood Avenue
Chicago, IL  60613
773-880-6260
888-991-9488
FAX: 773-989-1075
TTY: 773-989-1875
www.thresholds.org

*Susan Bottum, President*
*Herminio Cardona Jr, Program Director*
*Mark Furlong, Administrator*

A private, nonprofit psychosocial rehabilitation center that serves the hearing impaired mental health consumers at the highest risk of hospitalization, those with serious and persistent mental illness. The program provides residential and assertive treatment case management services focused on rehabilitation.

**9404  Thresholds South Suburbs**
12145 Western Avenue
Blue Island, IL  60406
708-597-8073
FAX: 708-597-8053
www.tresholds.org

*Natalie Marsh, Program Director*
*Camille Rucks, Team Leader*

Services offered include psychosocial, vocational and residential programs for ages 18 or older with a primary diagnosis of mental illness. Facility is wheelchair accessible.

**9405  Tri-County Rehabilitation Center**
1650 S Kanner Highway
Stuart, FL  34994
772-221-4050
FAX: 772-286-4364
www.hpsfl.org

*Suzanne Hutcheson, President/CEO*
*Robert Beyo, Financial Director*

**9406  Trumbull Park**
10530 S Oglesby Avenue
Chicago, IL  60617
773-375-7022
FAX: 773-375-5528

*Gregory Terry, Director*
*Diana Moore, Site Supervisor*
*Ada McKinley, Manager*

Offers consultation, education, general counseling, recreation, self-help and social services for children and adults.

**9407  University of Illinois Medical Center**
1855 W Taylor Street
Chicago, IL  60612
312-355-4000
FAX: 312-996-7770

*Timothy McMahon, Chief*
*Marilyn Plomann, Manager*

Offers services for the totally blind, legally blind, visually impaired, mentally retarded blind and more with health, counseling, educational, recreational, rehabilitation, computer training and professional training services.

**9408  VanMatre Rehabilitation Center**
950 S Mulford Road
Rockford, IL  61108
815-381-8500
866-754-3347
FAX: 815-484-9953
www.healthsouth.com

*Dan Woloszyn, Administrator/CEO*
*Scott Craig, Medical Director*

A CARF-accredited comprehensive rehabilitation center based within the Rockford Memorial Hospital providing inpatient and outpatient services for physically and cognitively challenged persons with debilitating illness and injuries.

**9409  Warren Achievement Center**
1220 E 2nd Avenue
Monmouth, IL  61462
309-734-3131
FAX: 309-734-7114
e-mail: info@warrenachievement.com
www.warrenachievement.com

*Michael Lewis, President*
*James Keefe, VP*

For developmentally disabled children and adults. Parent-infant education programs are for parents of infants with disabilities or developmental delays; Children's Group Homes which serve children on a fulltime basis and can serve additional children on a respite basis; Vocational training and residential programs assist the handicapped adult and developmental training for adults; adult residential community living; manufacturing, capabilities in workshop includes packaging, and assembly.

# Indiana

**9410  Ball Memorial Hospital**
2401 W University Avenue
Muncie, IN  47303
765-747-3111
FAX: 765-747-3313
www.cardinalhealthsystem.org

*Brent L Batman, President*
*Robert Curtis, Chief Executive Officer*

Offers rehabilitation services, occupational therapy, physical therapy and more for the physically challenged child or adult.

**9411  Community Hospitals, Indianapolis**
1500 N Ritter Avenue
Indianapolis, IN  46219
317-355-5457
FAX: 317-351-7723

*Barbara Gebhardt, Executive Director*
*Anita Harden, President*

**9412  Crossroads Industrial Services**
4740 Kingsway Drive
Indianapolis, IN  46205
317-803-9614
FAX: 317-897-9763

*Pamela Leal, Executive Director*

**9413    Department of Veterans Affairs Vet Center #418**
311 N Weinbach Avenue
Evansville, IN  47711                              812-473-5993
                                          FAX: 812-473-4028
                     e-mail: vcen418@evansville.net

*Jack Weber, Manager*

Provides readjustment counseling to combat veterans of all eras. Onsite assistance for employment problems and Department of Veteran Affairs, Vocational Rehabilitation and Sexual Trauma Counsel.

**9414    Frasier Rehabilitation Center Division of Clark Memorial Hospital**
2201 Greentree N
Clarksville, IN  47129                            812-282-4257
                                          FAX: 812-288-1161

*Juanita Love, Manager*

Designed to help patients in their adjustment to a physically limiting condition, both psychologically and physically, by helping to maximize each patient's abilities so he or she can function as independently as possible. The program treats patients whose functional impairment may range from temporary to permanent, from partial to total disability.

**9415    HealthSouth Tri-State Rehabilitation Hospital**
4100 Covert Avenue
Evansville, IN  47714                             812-476-9983
                                                 800-677-3422
                                          FAX: 812-476-4270
                                          www.healthsouth.com

*Barbara Butler, President/CEO*
*Tina Densley, Opperations Director*
*Dick Ondrey, Clinical Services Director*

An 80-bed JCAHO accredited freestanding hospital specializing in comprehensive medical rehabilitation for Brain Injury, Spinal Cord Injury, Orthopedic, Pulmonary, Cardiac, Oncology and disabilities and general disabilities.

**9416    Healthwin Specialized Care**
20531 Darden Road
South Bend, IN  46637                             574-272-0100
                                          FAX: 574-277-3233

*Teresa Smucker, Administrator*

Postacute rehabilitation program.

**9417    Memorial Regional Rehabilitation Center**
221 W Wayne Street
South Bend, IN  46601                             574-232-4861
                                                 877-282-0964
                                          FAX: 574-232-1476

*Dave Haluta, Director*
*Judy Smith, Manager*

CARF accredited outpatient medical rehabilitation and post acute brain injury program. Serves neurologically impaired adults and young adults.

**9418    Saint Joseph Regional Medical Center- South Bend**
801 E La Salle Avenue
South Bend, IN  46617                             574-237-7111

                     e-mail: sgersp@sjrmc.com

*Phyllis Syers Msn Crrn, Director Inpatient Rehab*
*Nancy Hellyer, Chief Executive Officer*

Continuum of rehabilitation services offered. Included are: acute rehabilitation, a 26 bed CARF accredited comprehensive inpatient unit, a CARF certified inpatient brain injury program, a CARF outpatient day treatment brain injury program, comprehensive outpatient services, with available case management, and Driver's Training Program, a 30 bed state of the art subacute rehab unit, CARF accredited Industrial Rehabilitation Programs and CARF accredited Pain and Complimentary Medicine Program.

# Iowa

**9419    Crossroads of Western Iowa**
1 Crossroads Place
Missouri Valley, IA  51555                        712-642-4114
                                          FAX: 712-642-4115
                     e-mail: info@cwiowa.org
                                          www.cwiowa.org

*David Lobell, CEO*

CWI provides services in Missouri Valley, Onawa and Council Bluffs, Iowa. An array of services for people with mental illness, mental retardation and brain injury are provided in each location.

**9420    Easter Seals Iowa**
Easter Seals National
PO Box 4002
Des Moines, IA  50333                             515-289-1933
                                          FAX: 515-289-1281
                     e-mail: infi@eastersealsia.org
                                          www.eastersealsia.org

*Tracy Keninzer, Director Marketing*
*Donna Elbrecht, President*

Easter Seals is a leading nonprofit provider of services to Iowans with disabilities. Services include vocational and employment training, camping recreation and respite services, craft training and sales, home and farm adaptations, transportation, scholarships and a club for stroke survivors and their families.

**9421    Genesis Regional Rehabilitation Center**
Genesis Health System
2720 W Locust Street
Suite B2
Davenport, IA  52804                              563-421-3495
                                          FAX: 563-421-3499
                                          www.genesishealthsystem.com

*Janet King, Executive Director*
*Mike Shaw, Supervisor*

Serves persons of all ages experiencing a disability, whether acquired at birth or following a serious interdisciplinary service. Rehabilitation programs include acute rehabilitation; adult rehabilitation, pediatric rehabilitation, outpatient orthopaedics. LIFT, a community based, nontraditional approach to the treatment of adolescents and adults with brain injuries is also offered at Genesis. It is designed to facilitate re-entry into the community or return to appropriate employment.

**9422    Homelink**
Van G Miller & Associates
PO Box 2817
Waterloo, IA  50704                               319-235-7100
                                                 800-482-1993
                                          FAX: 319-235-7822
                                          www.edm.com

*Dave Kazynski, President*

A national network of home medical equipment, respiratory therapy, rehabilitation and infusion therapy service providers with over 2,500 locations serving all fifty states.

**9423 Iowa Central Industries**
127 Avenue M
Fort Dodge, IA 50501
515-576-2126
FAX: 515-576-2251

*Quentin Weidner, Director*
*Tom Eckman, Executive Director*

Services include evaluation and training in pre-vocational and vocational skills, personal behavior management, cognitive skills, communication skills, self-care skills and social skills. Services arranged include: independent living training, medical services, psychological services, therapeutic services and social services.

**9424 Iowa Veterans Centers**
2600 Harding Road
Des Moines, IA 50310
515-285-6701
FAX: 515-284-4901

Veterans medical clinic offering disabled veterans medical treatments.

**9425 Life Skills Laundry Division**
1510 Industrial Road SW
Le Mars, IA 51031
712-546-9554
FAX: 712-546-4985

*Don Nore, Executive Director*

**9426 MIW**
909 S 14th Avenue
Marshalltown, IA 50158
641-752-3697
FAX: 641-752-1614
e-mail: jstegmamann@miwi.org

*Janet Stegmann, Services Manager*
*Rich Byers, President*

Vocational services for adults with disabilities. Includes organizational employment services, supported employment, job placement.

**9427 Mercy Pain Center**
400 University Avenue
Des Moines, IA 50314
FAX: 515-248-8867

*Dianne Alber, Administrative Director*

An outpatient program dedicated to helping people with chronic pain live more productive, satisfying lives. The program is not designed for conditions that are surgically curable, but rather approaches the problem using a comprehensive, holistic treatment.

**9428 Mercy Physical Rehabilitation Unit**
Mercy Drive
Dubuque, IA 52001
563-589-9035
FAX: 563-589-8193

*Joan Hentges, Director*
*Bobbi Schell, Executive Director*

Provides services which open the door to improved communication, offering the opportunity to enrich the quality of life. Mercy offers many other branches of services including, rehabilitation services for children, pulmonary rehabilitation program, services for the head-injured patient, back to school, and the disabled driver program.

**9429 Nishna Productions**
PO Box 70
Shenandoah, IA 51601
712-246-1242
FAX: 712-246-1243
e-mail: nci@nishna.org
www.nishna.org

*Sherri Clark, Executive Director*

Shelter, workshop and job training for the disabled.

**9430 Northstar Community Services**
3420 University Avenue
Waterloo, IA 50701
319-236-0901
800-879-1365
FAX: 319-236-3701
e-mail: info@northdstarcs.org
www.northstarcs.org

*Mark Witmer, Executive Director*
*Denise Hinders, Director, Services*
*Donna Davis, Director Development/Public Rel*

Provides adult day services, employment services and supported community living so people with disabilities can live and work in the community. Populations served include, but are not limited to: senior adults with age-related disabilities, youth with disabilities (age 16+) or withing 2 years of leaving high school, adults with disabilities, including those with mental and physical disabilities. CARF accredited. Serves northeast, north and central Iowa. Head Injury Program serves the whole state

**9431 Options of Linn County**
1019 7th Street SE
Cedar Rapids, IA 52401
319-892-5800
FAX: 319-892-5849
e-mail: optons@linncounty.org
www.linncounty.org/options

*Jim Nagel, Director*
*Reggie Ancelet, Associate Director*
*Carter Baldwin, Associate Director*

Provides employment services to adults with disabilities. Options serves over 300 people annually in community based and facility based services.

**9432 RISE**
106 Rainbow Drive
Elkader, IA 52043
563-245-1868

*Edward Josten, Executive Director*

**9433 Ragtime Industries**
116 N 2nd Street
Albia, IA 52531
641-932-7813
FAX: 641-932-7814

*Diana Shehan, Executive Director*

A work-oriented rehabilitation organization which provides training for mentally and physically disabled adults in Monroe County. A variety of programs which help to develop each person's individual potential are offered so that the person may live as normal a life as possible.

**9434 Sunshine Services**
PO Box 225
Spencer, IA 51301
712-262-7805
FAX: 712-262-8369

*Ann Vandehar, Executive Director*

**9435 Tenco Industries**
710 Gateway Drive
1287
Ottumwa, IA 52501
641-682-8114
FAX: 641-684-4223
e-mail: luehlingtech@lisco.com
www.tenco.org

*Lorraine Uhling-Tecagl, Executive Director*

To advocate and provide opportunities for people with disabilities, or conditions that limit their abilities, to develop and maintain the skills necessary for personal dignity and independence in all areas of life. Provide a wide array of services to individuals with disabilities. By looking at each person as individuals, we are able to work with them to maximize their skills. Residentials services, including HCBS and CSALA are also provided in all communities.

## Kansas

**9436  Arrowhead West**

PO Box 1417
Dodge City, KS  67801

620-227-8803
FAX: 620-227-8812
e-mail: paul@arrowheadwest.org
www.arrowheadwest.org

*Paul Lehmkuhler, Public Relations Coordinator*
*Janet Heit, Admission Coordinator*
*Paul Lehmkuhler, Public Relations Coordinator*

Services and programs offered include: developmental and therapy services for children birth to age 3. Adult center-based work services and community integrated employment options; adult life skills and retirement programs; adult residential services including supervised living, supported living and independent living services. Staff includes over 200 employees. Services are provided over a 14 county area with service centers in Dodge City, Kinsley, Pratt, Medicine Lodge and Wichita.

**9437  Bethany Rehabilitation Center**

51 N 12th Street
Kansas City, KS  66102

913-281-8898
FAX: 913-281-7696

*Wayne Kutz, VP*

Offers rehabilitation services, inpatient and outpatient care, respite programs, psychiatric evaluations and more.

**9438  Big Lakes Developmental Center**

1416 Hayes Drive
Manhattan, KS  66502

785-776-9201
FAX: 785-776-9830
e-mail: biglakes@biglakes.org
www.biglakes.org

*James Shaver, President*
*Shawn Funk, Community Education Director*

Work services, community employment and residential services. Serving adults with developmental disabilities. Family support services also available.

**9439  Developmental Services of Northwest Kansas**

PO Box 1016
Hays, KS  67601

785-625-5678
800-637-2229
FAX: 785-625-8204
e-mail: comments@notes1dsnwk.org
www.dsnwk.org

*James W Blume, President*
*Ruth Lang, Administrative Assistant*

A private nonprofit organization serving both children and adults with disabilities. Offers services to children ages birth to three years, youth and adults through a network of community-based and outreach programs and inter-agency agreements with other service providers in the eighteen counties of Northwest Kansas.

**9440  ENVISION**

2301 S Water Street
Wichita, KS  67213

316-267-2244
FAX: 316-267-4312
e-mail: envision@envisionus.com
www.envisionus.com

*Linda Merrill, President*
*David Austin, Manager Public Relations*

Provides jobs, job training and vision rehabilitation services to people who are blind or low vision.

**9441  Heartspring**

8700 E 29th Street N
Wichita, KS  67226

316-634-8750
800-835-1043
FAX: 316-634-0555
www.heartspring.org

*Cara Rapp, Admissions Director*
*Cindy Chapman, Executive Director*
*Charlene Kuzma LMSW CLP, Life Care Planner*

Private, not-for-profit residential school for children from across the country ages five to twenty-one with multiple disabilities. Heartspring serves students with one or more of the following diagnosis: autism, cerebral palsy, maladaptive behaviors, seizures, or other disabilities. Services are provided by an interdisciplinary team of specialists. Assessments and therapies are provided in the areas of speech/language, physical, occupational learning and behavior

**9442  Indian Creek Nursing Center**

6515 W 103rd Street
Overland Park, KS  66212

913-642-5545
FAX: 913-642-3982

*Brad Baker, Administrator*

Postacute rehabilitation program.

**9443  Johnson County Developmental Supports**

10501 Lackman Road
Lenexa, KS  66219

913-492-6161
FAX: 913-492-5171

*Dennis Tucker, President*
*Shelly Toft, Executive Assistant*

**9444  Ketch Industries**

201 S Ida Street
Wichita, KS  67211

316-383-8770

*Kaye Herman, Executive Director*
*Ron Pasmore, Chief Executive Officer*

**9445  Lakemary Center**

100 Lakemary Drive
Paola, KS  66071

913-294-4361
FAX: 913-294-4361

*William R Craig PhD, President*
*Pauline Hintz, Principal*

A private, not-for-profit day and residential training facility which provides for the assessment, education, training, therapy and social development of children and adults, moderate and severe mental retardation. The Center is based 28 miles southwest of Kansas City in Paola, Kansas.

**9446  Northview Developmental Services**

700 E 14th Street
Newton, KS  67114

316-283-5170
FAX: 316-283-5196
e-mail: nds@northviewdsi.com
www.northviewdsi.org

*Stan Zienkewicz, President/CEO*

## Kentucky

**9447 Cardinal Hill Outpatient Center**
Cadinal Hill Medical Center
2050 Versailles Road
Lexington, KY 40504

859-254-5701
FAX: 859-254-4612
www.cardinalhill.org

*Martin Lautner, Manager Referral Relations*
*Elizabeth A Monarch, Viec President/coo*
*Kerry Gillihan, Chief Executive Officer*

Provides occupational health services, therapy services and urgent medical treatment of injured workers.

**9448 Frazier Rehab Institute**
220 Abraham Flexner Way
Louisville, KY 40202

502-582-7400
FAX: 502-582-7477
www.jewishhospital.org

*Joanne Berryman, Senior VP/CEO*
*Cheryl Fugate, VP Frasier Rehab/Neuroscience*
*Jean Russell, VP Rehab Operations*

Frazier Rehab Institute is a regional healthcare system dedicated entirely to rehabilitation. Through an expansive network of inpatient and outpatient facilites in Kentucky and southern Indiana, Frazier offers a wide array of services based on one common goal - helping people with disabilities reach their full potential.

**9449 HealthSouth Northern Kentucky Rehabilitation Hospital**
201 Medical Village Drive
Edgewood, KY 41017

859-341-2044
800-860-6004
www.healthsouth.com

*Brenda Gosney, Chief Executive Officer*
*Mary Pfeffer, Director Clinical Services*
*Lynn Bean, Director Nursing*

Offers all types of inpatient and outpatient rehabilitation services such as occupational therapy, physical therapy, speech therapy. Respiratory therpay, Psychology, Aquatics, Case Managemenet/Social Work and Nutritional Services.

**9450 King's Daughter's Medical Center's Rehab Unit/Work Hardening Program**
2201 Lexington Avenue
Ashland, KY 41101

606-327-4000
800-633-6388
FAX: 606-327-7542
www.komc.com

*Harry Bell, Medical Director*
*Sue Strehle, Service Line Manager*
*Fred Jackson, Chief Executive Officer*

Offers a 27-bed, inpatient rehabilitation services unit treating physical disabilities related to accident or illness. The program provides an interdisciplinary inpatient program designed to restore the individual to the highest level of independence. It is the goal of the staff to provide rehabilitative services that will enable the disabled or injured person to return home and re-enter the community at the maximum level of efficiency.

**9451 LifeSkills Industries**
PO Box 6499
Bowling Green, KY 42102

270-842-5509
FAX: 270-782-0058
www.lifeskills.com

*Joe Miller, Executive Director*
*Dale Bond, Chief Executive Officer*

**9452 Low Vision Services of Kentucky**
120 N Eagle Creek Drive
Suite 501
Lexington, KY 40509

859-977-1129
800-627-2020
FAX: 859-263-3757
e-mail: jwood@retinaky.com
www.lowvisionky.com

*William Wood Md, Clinical Director*
*Jennifer D Wood OD/FAAO, Low Vision Specialist*
*Helen Wade, Administrator*

Offers devices and services for the totally blind, legally blind, visually impaired educational, recreational and rehabilitation.

**9453 Muchlenberg County Opportunity Center**
615 Opportunity Way
Greenville, KY 42345

270-338-5970
FAX: 270-338-5977

*Michael Morgan, Executive Director*

**9454 New Vision Enterprises**
2200 Brownsboro Road
Louisville, KY 40206

502-893-0211
800-405-9135
FAX: 502-893-3885

*Robert Jarboe, Chief Executive Officer*

Offers employment training and services for the blind and legally blind.

**9455 Park DuValle Community Health Center**
3015 Wilson Avenue
Louisville, KY 40211

502-774-4401
FAX: 502-775-6195
e-mail: parkduvalle@pdchc.org
www.pdchc.org

*Richard Jones, Executive Director*

Offers services for the totally blind, legally blind, visually impaired, mentally retarded blind and more with health, counseling, educational, recreational, rehabilitation, computer training and professional training services.

## Louisiana

**9456 Alliance House**
2902 Florida Boulevard
Baton Rouge, LA 70802

225-343-5393
FAX: 225-346-0857

A non-residential facility serving male and female chronically mentally ill. Services include: social service, vocational evaluation, pre-vocational training and job placement.

**9457 Assumption Activity Center**
4201 Highway 1
Napoleonville, LA 70390

985-369-2907
FAX: 985-369-2657
e-mail: arcoa.catbl.net

*Warren Gonzales, Executive Director*
*Teal Stroud, Program Manager*

A community work center providing prevocational training and extended employment for adults with disabilities. Services include: social services, work activities, specialized training and supported employment.

**9458 Caddo-Bossier Association for Retarded Citizens**
4103 Lakeshore Drive
Shreveport, LA 71109

318-425-8888
FAX: 318-221-4262

*Janet Parker, Director*

A community operated workshop for male and female mentally retarded individuals. It provides work evaluation and transitional and extended employment.

**9459 Deaf Action Center of GNO**
1000 Howard Avenue
Suite 1200
New Orleans, LA 70113 504-525-0700
FAX: 504-525-6729
www.ccano.org

*Shari Bernius, Administrator*

This community service and resource center serves deaf, deaf-blind, hard of hearing and speech-impaired persons in the greater New Orleans area regardless of age, religion, race or secondary disability. DAC provides interpreting services, equipment distribution, sign language classes, case management and advocacy.

**9460 Donaldsville Association for Retarded Citizens**
1030 Clay Street
Donaldsonville, LA 70346 225-473-4516

*Marlene Domingue, Executive Director*

A private, nonprofit sheltered work program working with the mentally retarded and developmentally disabled adults.

**9461 East Jefferson General Hospital Rehab Center**
4200 Houma Boulevard
Metairie, LA 70006 505-454-4000

www.ejgh.org

*Cathy Brannon, Director*
*Tara Fitzpatrick, Supervisor*

Postacute rehabilitation program.

**9462 Family Service Society**
2515 Canal Street
Suite 201
New Orleans, LA 70119 504-822-0800
FAX: 504-822-0831

*Robert Quintana, Executive Director*
*Ronald Clain, President*

Offers services for the totally blind, legally blind, visually impaired, mentally retarded blind and more with health, counseling, educational, recreational, rehabilitation, computer training and professional training services.

**9463 Foundation Industries**
9995 Highway 64
Zachary, LA 70791 225-654-6283
FAX: 225-654-3988

*Jim Lambert-Oswald, President*

A private, nonprofit sheltered workshop providing extended employment and work activities for the mentally retarded and developmentally disabled clients.

**9464 Handi-Works Productions**
2700 Lee Street
Alexandria, LA 71301 318-442-3377
FAX: 318-473-0858
This is a nonprofit workshop for male and female clients who have vocational handicapping conditions. All types of handicapped persons are served in this non-residential workshop.

**9465 Iberville Association for Retarded Citizens**
PO Box 201
Plaquemine, LA 70765 225-687-4062
FAX: 225-687-3272
e-mail: arci@eatel.net

*Paul Rhorer, Executive Director*

A private sheltered work program operating out of one facility and providing transitional, extended employment and work activities for mentally and developmentally ill adults.

**9466 Lighthouse for the Blind in New Orleans**
123 State Street
New Orleans, LA 70118 504-899-4501
FAX: 504-895-4162

*Bill Price, Executive Director*

Offers services for the totally blind, legally blind, visually impaired, mentally retarded blind and more with health, counseling, educational, recreational, rehabilitation, computer training and professional training services.

**9467 Louisiana Center for the Blind**
101 S Trenton Street
Ruston, LA 71270 318-251-2891
800-234-4166
FAX: 318-251-0109
e-mail: pallen@lcb-ruston.com
www.lcb-ruston.com

*Pam Allen, Executive Director*
*Neita Ghrigsby, Office Manager*

A new kind of orientation and training center for blind persons. The center is privately operated and provides quality instruction in the skills of blindness. Offers employment assistance, computer literacy training, summer training and employment project, special seminars, outreach and referral services.

**9468 Louisiana State University Eye Center**
Lousiana State University
2020 Gravier Street
New Orleans, LA 70112 504-412-1200
FAX: 504-412-1315
www.lsuhsc.edu

*Bergs Sma, Director*
*Mark Graves, Manager*

**9469 New Orleans Speech and Hearing Center**
1636 Toledano Street
New Orleans, LA 70115 504-897-2606
FAX: 504-891-6048
e-mail: noshc@hotmail.com
www.noshc.org

*Lesley Jernigan, Executive Director*
*Patty Connolly, Coordinator Clinical Services*

This non-residential facility serves male and female clients for purposes of evaluating speech and hearing problems and providing speech therapy, hearing aids and other assistive technology for speech and hearing.

**9470 Port City Enterprises**
PO Box 113
Port Allen, LA 70767 225-344-1142
FAX: 225-344-1192

*Christine Dunlevy, Executive Director*

Offers supported employment, sheltered work and supervised programs for the mentally retarded, ages 22 and over.

**9471 Rehabilitation Center at Thibodeaux Regional**
Rehab Care
602 N Acadia Road
Thibodaux, LA 70301 985-447-5500
800-822-8442
FAX: 985-449-4600
e-mail: infoA@thibodaux.com
www.thibodaux.com/rehabilitation.html

*Jan Torres, Program Manager*
*Rose Pipes, Clinical Coordinator*

Designed to help patients in their adjustment to a physically limiting condition, both physically and psychologically, by helping to maximize each patients abilities so he or she can function as independently as possible.

**9472 Rehabilitation Hospital of Baton Rouge**

8595 United Plaza Boulevard
Baton Rouge, LA 70809      225-927-0567
                           800-264-0567
                  FAX: 225-926-2357

*Jill Root, Admissions Director*
*Amy Searles, Community Relations*
*Ken Alexander, Executive Director*

Dedicated to one field of medicine - physical rehabilitation medicine - and are committed to one goal, helping patients achieve the highest level of functioning possible after a debilitating injury or illness.

**9473 Rehabilitation Living Centers**

3434 Canal Street
New Orleans, LA 70119      225-482-3075
                  FAX: 504-483-2135

*Dr. Robert Voogt, Owner*

Postacute rehabilitation program.

**9474 St. Patrick RehabCare Unit**

RehabCare
524 S Ryan Street
Lake Charles, LA 70601      337-491-7789

*Annette Harlow, Program Manager*
*Ruth Thornton, Admissions*

Provides inpatient rehabilitation services in acute-care and sub-acute facilities. Treatment is provided for neurological and degenerative disorders.

**9475 Touro Rehabilitation Center**

1401 Foucher Street
New Orleans, LA 70115      504-897-8576
                  FAX: 504-897-8393
            e-mail: haunj@touro.com
                     www.touro.com

*Gary Glynn, Medical Director*
*Suzy Laborde, Director Inpatient Service*
*Keith Randazzo, Neuro Rehab Coordinator*

Located in New Orleans' Garden District, Touro Rehabilitation is a comprehensive rehabilitation facility dedicated to the restoration of function and independence for individuals with disabilities. The scope of rehabilitation services is broad, with 4 CARF accreditations for Brain Injury, Spinal Cord Injury, Chronic Pain and General Rehabilitation. TRC opened in 1984 and offers 69 rehab beds. TRC is part of Touro Infirmary which has a proud 150 year history as a nonprofit teaching hospital.

**9476 Training, Resource & Assistive-Technology**

Lakefront Campus
PO Box 1051
New Orleans, LA 70148      504-280-5700
                  FAX: 504-280-5707
            e-mail: ggaglian@uno.edu
                  www.uno.edu/trac

*Gayle Gagliano, Director*

Provides quality services to persons with disabilities, rehabilitation professionals, educators and employers.

**9477 University of New Orleans Training and Resource Center for the Blind**

Metro Campus Lakefront Campus
New Orleans, LA 70148      504-539-9560
                  FAX: 225-286-7294

*Timothy Ryan, Administrator*

This center offers a range of computer courses for the blind and visually impaired; maintains a resource lab with adaptive technology; conducts vocational evaluations for persons with disabilities; and provides information on the ADA.

# Maine

**9478 Charlotte White Center**

PO Box 380
Dover Foxcroft, ME 04426      207-564-2499
                      888-440-4158
                  FAX: 207-564-2404

*Pam Jacobson, Executive Director*
*Anthony Zambrono, Director Operations*

**9479 Iris Network for the Blind**

189 Park Avenue
Portland, ME 04102      207-774-6273
                  FAX: 207-774-0679
       e-mail: sobremski@theiris.org
                  www.theiris.org

*Steven Obremski, President/CEO*

Offers services to persons who are blind, visually impaired or multi-disabled blind with rehabilitation, counseling, educational, recreational, computer training and professional training services.

**9480 Limerick Adult Day Program**

Foss Road
Limerick, ME 04048

*Carol Snyder, Executive Director*

**9481 Roger Randall Center**

50 Green Street
Houlton, ME 04730      207-532-9196
                  FAX: 207-532-9494

*Dawn Ledger, Director Day Programs*

The Roger Randall Cneter is one of five Day Habilitation Programs adminsitered by Community Living Association, a private, non-profit agency. These programs may provide a supportive environment that allows the individual to achieve their maximum growth potential. Individualized services address but are not limtied to the following areas: fine/gross motor skills, communication, community awareness and involvement, appropriate social skills, and independent living skills.

**9482 Sebasticook Farms**

PO Box 65
Saint Albans, ME 04971      207-938-4615
                  FAX: 207-938-5670
            e-mail: pje@tdslelm.net

*Tom Davis, Executive Director*
*Pam Erskin, Program Coordinator*

Provides residential, educational and vocational services to adults who are developmentally disabled in order to maximize independent living and to provide assistance in obtaining an earned income.

**9483 Social Learning Center**

984 Sabattus Street
Lewiston, ME 04240      207-783-4672
                  FAX: 207-783-4673

*Deborah Beam, Unit Manager*

## Maryland

**9484  Blind Industries and Services of Maryland**
3345 Washington Boulevard
Halethorpe, MD 21227
410-737-2600
888-322-4567
FAX: 410-233-0544
www.bism.com

*Rosemary Lerdahl, Rehab Director*
*Fred Puente, President*

Offers a comprehensive residential rehabilitation training program for people who are blind. Areas of instruction: braille, cane travel, independent living, computer, adjustment and blindness seminars.

**9485  Center for Neuro-Rehabilitation**
2340238 N Cary Street
Annapolis, MD 21223
410-263-1704
410-462-4711
e-mail: cnrnhq@erols.com

*Jeanne Fryer*
*Laurent Pierre-Philippe*

Provide community-based inpatient and outpatient acute rehabilitation, vocational services and long-term care. Specializing in treating complex neurological conditions including spinal cord injuries, multiple sclerosis, strokes, and other brain injuries resulting from trauma, anoxia, tumors, genetic malformations and other related conditions. Locations in Annapolis, Bethesda, Frederick, Towson, MD and Fairfax, Va. CNR is licensed, a Medicare provider and CARF accredited.

**9486  Child Find/Early Childhood Disabilities Unit Montgomery County Public Schools**
10731 Saint Margarets Way
Suite A4
Kensington, MD 20895
301-929-2224
FAX: 301-929-2223

*Julie Bader, Supervisor*

Offers free developmental screening for children ages 3 years until eligible for kindergarten, evaluation and placement services.

**9487  Greenery Extended Care Center: Baltimore**
1300 S Ellwood Avenue
Baltimore, MD 21224
410-342-6644
FAX: 301-327-3949

*Shane Duffy, Administrator*

150 beds offering complex care treatment, extended rehabilitation and neurological restorative care.

**9488  James Lawrence Kerman Hospital**
2200 N Forest Park Avenue
Baltimore, MD 21207
410-285-6566
FAX: 410-448-6854

*Dennis Grote, Executive Director*
*James Lawrence III, MD*

**9489  Levindale Hebrew Geriatric Center**
2434 W Belvedere Avenue
Baltimore, MD 21215
410-466-8700
FAX: 410-367-9066
www.lifebridgehealth.org

*Ronald Rothstein, President/CEO*

**9490  Meridan Medical Center For Subacute Care**
770 York Road
Towson, MD 21204
410-821-5500
FAX: 410-337-7233

*Yvette Caldwell, Administrator*

Patients receive around-the-clock professional nursing care; physical and occupational, speech and respiratory therapists also assist patients. Each patient's individualized plan of care is reviewed and updated as patient needs change. Careful discharge planning prepares patients and their families for success at home by teaching them how to avoid complications that might lead to rehospitalization.

**9491  Rehabilitation Opportunities**
5100 Philadelphia Way
Suite A
Lanham Seabrook, MD 20706
301-731-4242
FAX: 301-322-5891

*Rory Brett, Executive Director*

Organization offering day programs, evaluation, work adjustments and sheltered workshops for persons who are mentally retarded or developmentally disabled.

**9492  Richard E Hoover Rehabilitation for Low Vision and Blindness**
6569 N Charles Street
Baltimore, MD 21204
443-849-2658
800-597-9142
FAX: 443-849-2631
www.gbmc.org/medicine/hoover

*Janet Sunness, Director Hoover Services*
*Trenitta Brady, Office Manager*

Offers services for the visually impaired and blind with low vision exams. Rehabilitation teaching and orientation and mobility in the home or workplace. Also offers a bimonthly newsletter for $12/yr for Hoover patients and monthly share group.

**9493  Rosewood Center**
200 Rosewood Lane
Owings Mills, MD 21117
410-951-5000
888-300-7071
FAX: 410-581-6157

*Leslie Smith, Program Director*
*James Anzalone, Director*

Offers a full range of habilitation services.

**9494  TLC: Treatment and Learning Centers**
9975 Medical Center Drive
Rockville, MD 20850
301-424-5200
FAX: 301-424-8063
e-mail: info@ttlc.org
www.ttlc.org

*Patricia A Ritter PhD, Assistant Executive Director*
*Richard Pavlin, Executive Director*

Provides audiological evaluations, testing and hearing aids, physical and occupational therapy and evaluation; speech-language evaluation and therapy, psycho-educational testing and tutoring services for learning disabled students, head injury services and infant and early childhood services including child care, summer therapeutic camp and a special education preschool-8th grade.

**9495   Workforce and Technology Center**
Division of Rehabilitation Services
2301 Argonne Drive
Baltimore, MD 21218                   410-554-9100
                                      888-200-7117
                                 FAX: 410-554-9112
                                 www.dors.state.md.us

*Jean Jackson, Program Director*
*Kathi Santora, Public Information/Planning*
*Robert Burns, Manager*

Is one of nine state operated comprehensive rehabilitation facilities in the country providing a wide range of services to individuals with disabilities. The Maryland Division of Rehabilitation Services operates the Workforce and Technology Program. Available services include medical functional evaluation, career training, mobility training, placement assistance, career assessment, rehab. technology assessments, driver's education and independent living skills training.

## Massachusetts

**9496   Baroco Corporation**
17 New South Street
Northampton, MA 01060                 413-584-9978
                                 FAX: 413-585-9010
                                 www.baroco.com

*Richard Barnard, President/Owner*
*Gail Rollins, Treasurer*

Provides training and therapeutic support for its recipients with developmental disabilities in order to aid them in securing and maintaining placement in a less-restrictive setting.

**9497   Berkshire Meadows**
249 N Plain Road
Housatonic, MA 01236                  413-528-2523
                                 FAX: 413-528-0293
                        e-mail: berkshiremeadows@jri.org
                                 www.berkshiremeadows.org

*Lisa Kelly, Program Director*
*Gail Charpentier, Administrator*

Private, non profit school for children, adolescents, young adults who are severely, developmentally disabled. approved special education learning center, work site program and foster care. Physical therapy, speech and language development, behavioral programming, occupational therapy, aquatic therapy, round-the-clock nursing. Also included is our state of the art equipment. *$8200.00*

**9498   Blueberry Hill Healthcare**
75 Brimbal Avenue
Beverly, MA 01915                     978-927-2020
                                 FAX: 978-922-4643

*Phil Sher, Administrator*
*Sharon Spittle, Executive Director*

Postacute rehabilitation program.

**9499   Boston University Hospital Vision Rehabilitation Services**
720 Harrison Avenue
Boston, MA 02118                      617-638-8340
                                 FAX: 617-638-8321

Offers services for the totally blind, legally blind, visually impaired, mentally retarded blind and more with health, counseling, educational, recreational, rehabilitation, computer training and professional training services.

**9500   Burbank Rehabilitation Center**
275 Nichols Road
Fitchburg, MA 01420                   978-343-5110
                                 FAX: 978-343-5342

*Diane O'Brien, Program Director*
*Jim Lillie, Manager*

The largest community hospital and regional referral center in the area. Offers the most extensive high quality, cost-effective healthcare services in the region. The hospital provides outstanding hospital-based services such as case management of high risk elderly and the region's only comprehensive geriatric evaluation service. Also offers patients access to a complete continuum of healthcare, skilled nursing homes, and adult day care. This range of services affords patients prompt care.

**9501   CPB/WGBH National Center for Access Media**
W GB H Educational Foundation
125 Western Avenue
Boston, MA 02134                      617-300-3400
                                 FAX: 617-300-1035
                                 TTY:617-300-2489
                                 e-mail: ncam@wgbh.org
                                 www.wgbh.org/ncam

*Larry Goldberg, Director*

Dedicated to the issues of media and information technology for people with disabilities in their homes, schools, workplaces, and communities. NCAM's mission is to expand access to present and future media for people with disabilities; explore how existing access technologies may benefit other populations; present its constituents in industry, policy and legislative circles; and to provide access to educational and media technologies for special needs students.

**9502   Carroll Center for the Blind**
770 Centre Street
Newton, MA 02458                      617-969-6200
                                      800-852-3131
                                 FAX: 617-969-6204
                        e-mail: rrosenbaum@carroll.org
                                 www.carroll.org

*Rachel Rosenbaum, President*
*Arthur O'Neill, Public Relations Director*

Offers services for the totally blind, legally blind, visually impaired, mentally retarded blind and more with health, counseling, educational, in dependent living, tronell skills, computer traing, recreational, rehabilitation, computer training and professional training services.

**9503   Center for Psychiatric Rehabilitation**
Boston University
940 Commonwealth Avenue
Boston, MA 02215                      617-414-6800
                                 FAX: 617-353-7700
                                 www.bu.edu/cpr

*William A Anthony PhD, Executive Director*
*Linda Getgen, Publications Manager*
*Kathy Furlong-Norman, Director Resource Information*

The mission of the Center is to increase knowledge, to train treatment personnel, to develop effective rehabilitation programs and to assist in organizing both personnel and programs into efficient and coordinated service delivery systems for people with mental illness.

**9504   Clark House of Fox Hill Village**
Kindred Healthcare
30 Longwood Drive
Westwood, MA 02090                    781-326-5652
                                 FAX: 781-326-4034

*Chris Wasel, Administrator*

Postacute rehabilitation program.

**9505  College Internship Program at the Berkshire Center**

PO Box 160
Lee, MA  01238

413-243-2576
FAX: 413-243-3351
e-mail: gshaw@berkshirecenter.org
www.berkshirecenter.org

*Gary Shaw, Program Director*
*Margaret Katz, Admissions Director*
*Michael McManmon, Executive Director*

A highly individualized postsecondary program for learning disabled young adults 18-30. Provides job placement services and follow-ups; college support; money management and social skills. Residential students share an apartment and have their own room. They learn independent living skills and leisure skills. Clinically, each student has individual and group therapy. Psychiatric consultation is available as well as medication supervision if necessary.

**9506  Eagle Pond**

PO Box 208
South Dennis, MA  02660

508-385-6034
FAX: 508-385-7064
eaglepond.com

*Paul Marchwat, Administrator*
*Ellen Reil, Marketing Director*
*Michael Gallagher, Executive Director*

Postacute rehabilitation program. Alzheimer's disorder and related dementia long-term care.

**9507  FOR Community Services**

75 Litwin Lane
Chicopee, MA  01020

413-592-6142
FAX: 413-598-0478
e-mail: ggolash1@aol.com

*Gina M Golash, Executive Director/President*

**9508  Fairlawn Rehabilitation Hospital**

189 May Street
Worcester, MA  01602

508-791-6351
FAX: 508-753-2087
www.fairlawnrehab.org

*Peter Mantegazza, President/CEO*
*Joyce Ellis, Director of Marketing Operations*

Offers comprehensive rehabilitation on both an inpatient and outpatient basis. Specialty programs include: head injury, spinal cord injury, young/senior stroke, oncology, geriatrics and orthopedics.

**9509  Greenery Extended Care Center: Worcester**

59 Acton Street
Worcester, MA  01604

508-791-3147
800-633-0887
FAX: 508-753-6267

*Joel Stevens, Administrator*

173 beds offering complex care, extended rehabilitation and neurobehavioral intervention.

**9510  Greenery Rehabilitation Center: Boston**

PO Box 1330
Middleboro, MA  02346

617-787-3390
FAX: 617-787-9169

201 beds offering programs of active/acute rehabilitation, cognitive rehabilitation, respiratory care and short-term evaluations.

**9511  Harrington House**

160 Main Street
Walpole, MA  02081

508-660-3080
FAX: 508-660-1634

*Anthony Lacke, Administrator*

Postacute rehabilitation program, sub-acute medical services and respiratory therapy program. Subacute accreditation by JCAHO.

**9512  Holiday Inn Boxborough Woods**

242 Adams Place
Boxborough, MA  01719

978-263-8701
800-465-4329
FAX: 978-263-0518
e-mail: box_sales@fine-hotels.com
www.holiday-inn.com

*Kathleen Kelly, Director Sales*
*Marcel Girard, Manager*

Located on 35 acres of wooded countryside just off I-495 at exit #28. Minutes from the Mass Turnpike, Route 2, 290 and 9. Conference center located on main level with 30,000 square feet of meeting space. Guest rooms feature two-line telephones, voice mail and dataports, irons and ironing boards, hair dryers and coffemakers. $129-$159.
*$129 - $159*

**9513  Kolburne School**

343 Nm Southfield Road
New Marlborough, MA  01230

413-229-8787
FAX: 413-229-7708
e-mail: info

*Jeane K Weinstein, Executive Director*
*Chris Eggo, Administrative Director*

A family owned residential treatment center offering psychiatric clinics and retirement therapeutic services, special education and vocational programs iwth campuses and community based group homes.

**9514  Lifeworks Employment Services**

588 Pleasant Street
Norwood, MA  02062

781-769-1212
FAX: 781-551-0045

*Ruth Antonucci, Director*

**9515  Mariner Health Care: Massachusetts**

45th Street
Peabody, MA  01960

508-229-0185

Postacute rehabilitation program.

**9516  Massachusetts Eye and Ear Infirmary & Vision Rehabilitation Center**

243 Charles Street
Boston, MA  02114

617-573-3285
FAX: 617-573-4178
www.meei.harvard.edu

*Joel Kraut MD FACS, Medical Director*
*Pat McCabe MPH, Director*
*Paulette Demors-Turco, Associate Director*

Visual rehabilitation encompasses a low vision rehabilitation evaluation, occupational therapy evaluation (with home visit if necessary), and social service evaluation.

**9517  New England Center for Children**

33 Turnpike Road
Southborough, MA  01772

508-481-1015
FAX: 508-485-3421
e-mail: cwelch@necc.org
www.necc.org

*Vincent Strully, Executive Director*
*Catherine Welch, Director Admissions*

A comprehensive year-round program for students with autism and PDD who require a highly specialized educational and behavior management program. Students are from all over the country and receive intensive, positive, behavioral counseling and social skills training free of aversive treatment and excessive medication.

**9518    New England Medical Center**
Vision Rehabilitation Service
750 Washington Street
Boston, MA  02111                                    617-636-5000
                                                     800-231-3316
                                                FAX: 617-636-4658
                              e-mail: eli@vision.eri.harvard.edu
                                                     www.nemc.org

*Eli Peli Od, Director Vision Rehabilitation*
*Maria Mercuri OD, Optometrist*

Offers services for the legally blind, visually impaired, mentally
retarded blind and more with health, counseling, educational,
recreational, rehabilitation, computer training and professional
training services.

**9519    New Medico Rehabilitation and Skilled Nursing Center
at Lewis Bay**
89 Lewis Bay Road
Hyannis, MA  02601                                   508-775-7601
                                                FAX: 508-790-4239

*Edmund Steinle, Executive Director*

**9520    Protestant Guild Learning Center**
411 Waverly Oaks Road
Waltham, MA  02452                                   781-893-6000
                                                FAX: 781-893-1171
                                e-mail: admin@protestantguild.org
                                            www.protestantguild.org

*Deborah Rossery, Executive Director*
*Marc De Chabert, Admissions Director*
*Pam Grath, Religious Leader*

Offers services for the diagnostically disabled children and adolescents with ages 6-22 years with health, counseling, educational, recreational, rehabilitation, computer training and
professional training services.

**9521    Rehabilitation Hospital of Western New England**
14 Chestnut Plaza
Ludlow, MA  01056                                    413-547-9063
                                                FAX: 413-547-6530

*Bonnie Breit, Outpatient Services*
Postacute rehabilitation program.

**9522    Shaughnessy-Kaplan Rehabilitation Hospital**
Dove Avenue
Salem, MA  01970                                     978-745-9000
                                                FAX: 978-740-4730
                                        www.shaughnessy-kaplan.org

*Anthony Sciola, President/CEO*
Rehabilitation for disabled and skilled nursing facility.

**9523    Son-Rise Program**
2080 S Undermountain Road
Sheffield, MA  01257                                 413-229-2100
                                                FAX: 413-229-3202
                                e-mail: correspondence@option.org
                                         www.autismtreatmentcenter.org

*Glenna Klein, Publicist*

THe Son-Rise Program is a powerful, effective and totally
unique treatment for children and adults challengedby Autism,
Autuism Spectrum Disorders, Pervasive Developmental Disorder (PDD), Asperger's Syndrome and other developmental difficulties.

**9524    Southern Worcester County Rehabilitation Center**
44 Morris Street
Webster, MA  01570                                   508-943-0700
                                                FAX: 508-949-6129
                                      e-mail: swcrc@swcrc.inc.org

*J Thomas Amick, Executive Director*

Provides day habilitation services, residential services, evaluation and personal adjustment training, sheltered employment,
supported employment services, supported work services for individuals with mental health problems. Serves the physically
disabled, developmentally disabled, mental health and mental
retardation. Vocational services and job placement programs
are available as well.

**9525    Vinfen Corporation**
950 Cambridge Street
Cambridge, MA  02141                                 617-441-1800
                                                     877-284-6336
                                                FAX: 617-441-1858
                                                     www.vinfen.org

*Gary W Lamson, President/CEO*

A private, nonprofit company, Vinfen Corporation is the largest
human services provider in Massachusetts. Vinfen offers clinical, educational, residential and support services to individuals
of all ages with mental illness and or mental retardation, who
also may have another disability (e.g. substance abuse, homelessness, AIDS). The company also trains professionals in the
mental health field and helps consumers to learn to live in community-based settings at the highest levels.

**9526    Visiting Nurse Association of North Shore**
5 Federal Street
Danvers, MA  01923                                   978-777-6100
                                                     800-457-8999
                                                FAX: 978-777-6517

*Susan Comparone, President*
*Elaine Kahigian, Manager*

Home health services including nurses, physical, occupational
and speech therapy, home health aides and more. Special programs include nutrition counseling, IV care, pediatric therapy,
HIV/AIDS services and wound management. Provides services
7 days a week, 365 days a year and we accept Medicare,
Medicaid and most HMO's and health insurers.

**9527    Weldon Center for Rehabilitation**
233 Carew Street
Springfield, MA  01104                               413-748-6840
                                                FAX: 413-748-6806

*Dr. James Lomastro, Vice President*

**9528    Westridge Healthcare Center**
121 Northboro Road E
Marlborough, MA  01752                               508-485-4040
                                                FAX: 508-481-5585

*Gina Querios, Administrator*
Postacute rehabilitation program.

**9529    Youville Hospital & Rehab Center**
1575 Cambridge Street
Cambridge, MA  02138                                 617-876-4344
                                                FAX: 617-547-5501

*T Richard Quigley, President*
*Daniel Leahey, Chief Executive Officer*

Meets the long and short term health care and rehabilitation
needs of patients who are physically disabled and chronically
ill. Strives to develop and maintain health as a human right on
physical, social, vocational and spiritual levels. The ultimate
goal of the hospital is to treat and assist each individual patient
in reaching his or her optimal level of living. Services include:
stroke, brain injury, spinal cord trauma, orthopedic disabilities
and more.

# Michigan

**9530** **Botsford General Hospital Inpatient Hospitalization Unit**
28050 Grand River Avenue
Farmington Hills, MI 48336          248-780-0
877-442-7900
FAX: 313-787-3
e-mail: info@botsfordsystem.org
www.botsfordsystem.org

*Allen Zieger, Executive Director*

A 20 bed inpatient physical rehabilitation unit, servicing individuals who have experienced a stroke, amputation, orthopedic fracture, or other neurological impairment.

**9531** **Chelsea Community Hospital Rehabilitation Unit**
775 S Main Street
Chelsea, MI 48118          734-475-0080
FAX: 734-475-4102
www.cch.org

*Sally Flack, Rehab Program Coordinator*
*Jackie Dalton, Neuro Rehab Services*

A private, non-profit, acute care facility that combines the best of small town values with national standards of healthcare excellence. The hospital has a 19-bed acute care inpatient rehabilitation unit with comprehensive outpatient programs, including a coordinated brain injury program.

**9532** **Clare Branch**
790 Industrial Drive
Clare, MI 48617          989-386-7707
FAX: 989-386-2199
www.mmionline.org

*Cris Zeigler, Executive Director*

**9533** **Eight CAP**
904 Oak Drive
Greenville, MI 48838          616-754-9315
FAX: 616-754-9310

*Ralph Loeschner, Executive Director*

**9534** **Greater Detroit Agency for the Blind and Visually Impaired**
16625 Grand River Avenue
Detroit, MI 48227          313-272-3900
FAX: 313-272-6893
e-mail: information@gdabvi.org
www.gdabvi.org

*Gail L McEntee, Executive Director*

Offers services for seniors 60 and over who are legally blind. Also provides eye health information, counseling, education and rehabilitation services.

**9535** **Greenery Healthcare Center: Clarkston**
4800 Clintonville Road
Clarkston, MI 48346          248-674-0903
800-837-1913
FAX: 313-674-3431

*Margaret Canny, Administrator*

120 beds offering active/acute rehabilitation, complex care, day treatment, extended rehabilitation, neurobehavioral intervention and short-term evaluation.

**9536** **Haggerty Center for Neurorehabilitation**
42005 W 12 Mile Road
Novi, MI 48377          248-305-7575
FAX: 248-347-4578

*Helene Rimer, Intake Coordinator*
*James Cole, Executive Director*

Postacute rehabilitation program.

**9537** **Hope Network Rehabilitation Services**
Hope Network
1490 E Beltline Avenue SE
Grand Rapids, MI 49506          616-940-0040
FAX: 616-940-8151
www.hopenetworkrehab.org

*Margaret Kroese, Executive Director*
*Mary Baily, Admissions Manager*
*Amanda Lake, Admissions Manager*

An office of Hope Network, one of the largest, private, nonprofit organizations of its kind in Michigan. The purpose is to assist people with brain injuries and/or physical disabilities in achieving an optimal level of self-determination, dignity, and independence as they develop and attain goals to overcome environmental barriers and mobilize adaptive skills.

**9538** **Lakeland Center**
26900 Franklin Road
Southfield, MI 48033          248-350-8070
FAX: 248-350-8078
www.thelakelandcenter.net

*Moira Donnelly-Kempf, Director Marketing*
*Kathy Powers, Marketing Associate*
*Irving Shapiro, Chief Executive Officer*

Subacute rehabilitation program directed toward those with severe neurologic diagnoses, ie: TBI, cerebral aneurysm, anoxic encephalopathy, CVA and cerebral hemorrhage, orthopedic injuries, and spinal cord injury. Subacute rehabilitation is provided for those who recover slowly and require individualized treatment plans. Residential program available as well.

**9539** **Mary Free Bed Rehabilitation Hospital**
235 Wealthy Street SE
Grand Rapids, MI 49503          616-242-0481
800-528-8989
FAX: 616-493-9666
e-mail: meg.derrer@maryfreebed.com
www.maryfreebed.com

*Meg Derrer, Marketing Director/Webmaster*
*Bill Blessing, President*

**9540** **Men-O-Mee Activity Center**
5522 W First Street
Hermansville, MI 49847
FAX: 906-498-7606

*Thomas Warren, Executive Director*

**9541** **Michigan Commission for the Blind Training Center**
1541 Oakland Drive
Kalamazoo, MI 49008          269-337-3875
FAX: 269-337-3872
www.mcb1.gov

*Melody Lindsey, Director*

Residential facility that provides instruction to legally blind adults in Braille, computers, handwriting, keyboarding, cane travel, adaptive kitchen skills, daily living, industrial arts and also crafts. Clients may also learn to use a variety of adaptive devices such as raised dot timers and watches, hand tools, talking calculators, tape recorders, reading machines and computers. Special training is also offered in vending stand operation, college preparation and job seeking skills.

**9542  Mid-Michigan Industries**

2426 Parkway Drive
Mt Pleasant, MI  48858

989-773-6918
888-773-7664
888-773-7664
FAX: 989-773-1317
e-mail: mail@mmionline.com
www.mmionline.com

*Alan Schilling, President*
*Andrea Christopher, Director Admissions*
*Chris Zeigler, VP Operations*

Providing jobs and training for persons with barriers to employment. Services include vocational evaluation, job placement, supported employment, work services, prevocational training and case management

**9543  New Medico Community Re-Entry Service**

216 St Marys Lake Road
Battle Creek, MI  49017

FAX: 269-962-2241

*James Rekshan, Executive Director*

**9544  Sanilac County Community Mental Health**

217 E Sanilac Road
Suite 1
Sandusky, MI  48471

810-648-0330
888-225-4447
888-225-4447
FAX: 810-648-0319
e-mail: scmh1@sanilacmentalhealth.org

*Roger Dean MD, Executive Director*

**9545  Special Tree Rehabilitation System**

1640 Axtell Drive
Troy, MI  48084

248-649-0101
800-649-5011
FAX: 248-649-5445
www.specialtree.com

*Joseph Richert, Founder*
*Margo Riza, Manager*

Postacute rehabilitation program.

**9546  State Technical Institute and Rehabilitation Center**

11611 Pine Lake Road
Plainwell, MI  49080

269-664-4461
FAX: 269-664-9850

*Dennis Hart, Executive Director*

**9547  Thumb Industries**

1263 Sand Beach Road
Bad Axe, MI  48413

989-269-9229
FAX: 989-269-9229

*Rhonda Wisenbaugh, Executive Director*

Provides job training and employment for disabled persons.

**9548  Visually Impaired Center**

1422 W Court Street
Flint, MI  48503

810-235-2544
FAX: 810-235-2597
e-mail: info@vicflint.org
www.vicflint.org

*Sharon Reigle, Executive Director*

Committed to developing resources and collaborative programs as well as providing services that enable independent life for people with vision loss. Services include: Information and referals, assessments of needs, peer support groups, training by a Rehabilitation teacher of the blind and visually impaired, independent living skills, computer skills, training by an Orientation and Mobility Specialist, safe traveling skills, Diabetes management/education.

*a pages*

**9549  Welcome Homes Retirement Community for the Visually Impaired**

1953 Monroe Avenue NW
Grand Rapids, MI  49505

616-363-9088
888-939-9292
888-939-9292
FAX: 616-363-3099
e-mail: info@welcomehomes.org
www.welcomehomes.org

*Kathy Higgins, CEO*

Offers services for the totally blind, legally blind, visually impaired, mentally retarded blind and more with health, counseling, educational, recreational, rehabilitation, computer training and professional training services.

**9550  William H Honor Rehabilitation Center Henry Ford Wyanclotte Hospital**

Henry Ford Health System
2333 Biddle Street
Wyandotte, MI  48192

734-284-4365
FAX: 734-246-6926
www.henryfordwyandotte.com

*Denise Dailing, Administration Leader/rehabilita*
*James Sexton, Chief Executive Officer*
*Henry Ford, Owner*

# Minnesota

**9551  Brown-Nichollet Industries**

21st North Street & Broadway
New Ulm, MN  56073

FAX: 507-345-4507

*Arne Berg, Executive Director*

**9552  Industries**

500 Walnut Street S
Mora, MN  55051

320-679-2354
FAX: 320-679-2355

*Lee Morrison, Executive Director*

Nonprofit organization that does vocational assessment and training for people with disabilities.

**9553  Shriners Hospitals for Children: Twin Cities**

2025 E River Parkway
Minneapolis, MN  55414

612-596-6100
888-293-2832
888-293-2832
FAX: 612-339-5954
www.shrinershq.org

*Lynn Shelander, Public Relations Specialist*
*Charles Lobeck, Director*

Shriners Hospital for Children-Twin Cities offers quality orthopedic medical care at no cost. Shriners Hospitals provide inpatient and outpatient services, surgery, casts, braces, artificial limbs, X-rays and physical and occupational therapy to any child under 18 who may benefit from treatment. To obtain an application, call toll free at (888)293-2832.

**9554  Vision Loss Resources**

1936 Lyndale Avenue S
Minneapolis, MN  55403

612-871-2222
FAX: 612-872-0189
www.visionlossresources.com

*Steven Fischer, Executive Director*
*Frank Alden, Low Vision Specialist*

Offers services for the totally blind, legally blind, visually impaired, and more with health, counseling, educational, recreational, rehabilitation, computer training and professional training services.

## Mississippi

**9555  Addie McBryde Rehabilitation Center for the Blind**
PO Box 5314
Jackson, MS  39296          601-364-2700
FAX: 601-364-2677
e-mail: kbrown@mdrs.ms.us
www.mdrs.ms.us

Karen Brown, Director
Karen Wallace, Assistant Director
Rosie Gibson, Assistant Director

Offers services for the totally blind, legally blind, visually impaired, mentally retarded blind and more with health, counseling, educational, recreational, rehabilitation, computer training services and orientation and mobility.

**9556  Mississippi Methodist Rehabilitation Center**
1350 E Woodrow Wilson Avenue
Jackson, MS  39216          601-981-2611
800-223-6672
FAX: 601-364-3465
www.mmrcrehab.org

Mark A Adams, President/CEO

Rebuild lives that have been broken by disabilities and impairments from serious illness or severe injury. The challenge is to help patients regain abilities, restore function and movement, and renew emotionally. It features personal rehabilitation treatment plans administered by specialized teams of health care professionals through a variety of outpatient programs, treatments and other services.

## Missouri

**9557  Alpine North Nursing and Rehabilitation Center**
4700 NW Cliff View Drive
Kansas City, MO  64150          816-741-5105
FAX: 816-746-1301

Sharon Garcia, Clinical Director
Bob Richard, Administrator
Postacute rehabilitation program.

**9558  Christian Hospital Northeast**
11133 Dunn Road
Saint Louis, MO  63136          314-653-5000
FAX: 314-653-4174
www.christianhospitalnortheast.org

Paul Macek, Chief Executive Officer

**9559  Integrated Health Services of St. Louis at Gravois**
10954 Kennerly Road
Saint Louis, MO  63128          314-843-4242
FAX: 314-843-4031

Lisa Niehaus, Administrator

Subacute, skilled and intermediate care; ventilator/tracheostomy management program; wound management program and complex rehabilitation program.

**9560  Joplin House Healthcare**
2502 S Moffet Avenue
Joplin, MO  64804          FAX: 417-623-0880

Jan Zacny, Administrator
Postacute rehabilitation program.

**9561  Metropolitan Employment & Rehabilitation Service**
M ER S Goodwill
1727 Locust Street
Saint Louis, MO  63103          314-241-3464
FAX: 314-241-9348
e-mail: info@mersgoodwill.org
www.mersgoodwill.org

Steve Roberts, Chairperson
Joan Newman, Vice Chairperson
Lewis Chartock, Chief Executive Officer

Vocational rehabilitation, primarily with the disabled, skills training and placement services.

**9562  Missouri Easter Seal Society: Southeast Region**
5025 Northrup Avenue
Saint Louis, MO  63110          314-664-6014
FAX: 314-664-4838
www.mo.easter-seals.org

The mission of the Easter Seal Society is to work with individuals, their families and the community to enhance the independence and quality of life for persons with disabilities.

**9563  Poplar Bluff RehabCare Program**
Lucy Lee Hospital
PO Box 88
Poplar Bluff, MO  63902          573-686-7320
FAX: 573-686-7307

Jim Martin, Program Manager
Chris Murray, Care Coordinator
Darlene Hill, Care Admissions Coordinator

Provides physical medicine and rehabilitation to individuals with a physically limiting condition. The program is designed to help individuals function as independently as possible by maximizing their strength and abilities.

**9564  Service Club for the Blind**
3719 Watson Road
Saint Louis, MO  63109          314-647-3306
FAX: 314-647-3306

Kathleen Demsky, President
Joann Hall, Office Assistant
Kathleen Demsky, Office Assistant

Offers services for the totally blind, legally blind, visually impaired, mentally retarded blind and more with health, counseling, educational, recreational, rehabilitation, computer training and professional training services.

**9565  Shriners Hospitals for Children St. Louis**
2001 S Lindbergh Boulevard
Saint Louis, MO  63131          314-432-3600
800-850-2960
FAX: 314-432-2930
www.shrinershq.org/SHC/STLOUIS

Carolyn P Golden, Administrator
Tammy M Dugan, Director Community Relations
Alice Woodruff, Executive Assistant

Medical care is provided free of charge for children 18 and under with orthopaedic conditions.

**9566** **St. Louis Society for the Blind and Visually Impaired**
8770 Manchester Road
Saint Louis, MO 63144
314-968-9000
FAX: 314-968-9003
e-mail: info@slsbvi.org
www.slsbvi.org

*David C Ekin, President*
*Brenda Dunn, Client Services Coordinator*

Offers vision rehabilitation services for the totally blind, legally blind, visually impaired, including counseling, educational, recreational, rehabilitation, computer training and professional training services. Low vision aids and appliance available through low vision clinic by appointment.

**9567** **TNC Community Truman Neurological Center**
15600 Woods Chapel Road
Kansas City, MO 64139
816-373-5060
FAX: 816-373-5787
e-mail: debbietnc@aol.com

*James Landrum, Executive Director*

A licensed habilitation center established for the purpose of assisting persons with developmental disabilities and/or mental retardation. The minimum age is 18. Residential care is provided in four group homes in the community licensed by the DMH and CARF accredited.

**9568** **Visual Independence Program**
Eye Foundation of Kansas City
2300 Holmes Street
Kansas City, MO 64108
816-404-1750
FAX: 816-881-6246

*Camille Matta MD, Medical Director*
*Brendan Smith OTR, Program Director*

Program offers in home rehabilitation services to older adults with visual impairments including training in use of magnifying devices for reading and other activities of daily living. Specialized rehabilitation program for persons with visual impairment secondary to stroke or head trauma.

## Montana

**9569** **Benefis Healthcare**
1101 26th Street S
Great Falls, MT 59405
406-455-5000
FAX: 406-455-2110
www.benefits.org

*John Goodnow, President/CEO*
*Laura Goldhahn-Konen, Chief Operation Officer*

**9570** **Disability Services Division**
Developmental Disability Program
PO Box 4210
Helena, MT 59604
406-444-2995
FAX: 406-444-0230
e-mail: dphhs@mt.gov
www.dphhs.state.mt.us/dsd

*Joe A Mathews, Administrator*
*Sandi Gory, Administrative Assistant*
*Janice Frisch, Chief Management Operations*

Responsible for coordinating, developing and implementing comprehensive programs to assist Montanans with disabilities with activities of daily living, community base services and coordinated programs of habilitation, rehabilitation and independent living.

**9571** **Montana Department of Developmental Disabilities Program**
PO Box 4210
Helena, MT 59604
406-444-2590
FAX: 406-444-0230
www.dphhs.state.mt.us/dsd

*Joe Mathews, Manager*

Information on developmental disabilities and automated systems.

## Nebraska

**9572** **Career Achievement Center**
PO Box 83589
Lincoln, NE 68501
402-483-5000
FAX: 402-483-1127

*Susie Feistner, Executive Director*
*Richard Peters, Owner*

**9573** **Las Vegas Convalescent Center**
2832 S Maryland Parkway
Las Vegas, NV 89109
702-796-3855
FAX: 702-735-6218

*Rick Eddins, Manager*

Postacute rehabilitation program.

**9574** **Sierra Pain Institute**
265 Golden Lane
Reno, NV 89502
775-323-7092
FAX: 775-323-5259

*Lyle Smith, Owner*

The program consists of a medically supervised outpatient program managed by an interdisciplinary team with input from specialties of Pain Medicine, Physical Therapy and Occupational Science. The format insures that each patient receives the full range of behavioral techniques in a well-integrated, individually tailored therapeutic regimen.

## New Hampshire

**9575** **Crotched Mountain Adult Brain Injury Center**
Crotched Mountain Foundation
1 Verney Drive
Greenfield, NH 03047
603-547-3311
FAX: 603-547-3232
e-mail: admissions@cmf.org
www.info@cmf.org

*Brant A Elkind, Director*
*Rita Phinney, Admissions Director*
*John Young, Registrar*

Adult Brain Injury Center provides sub-acute rehabilitative services and individualized care to survivors of acquired (including traumatic) brain injury. Ambulatory and non-ambulatory adults are served. Ages range from 18-59, the staff to client ratio is 3:1 and services are provided by experienced interdisciplinary clinical and therapeutic teams. Crotched Mountain is a licensed Special Hospital providing 24 hour medical coverage and skilled nursing. Clients reside in semi-private rooms w/superv

**9576  Department of Physical Medicine and Rehabilitation**
Exeter Hospital
10 Buzell Avenue
Exeter, NH  03833  603-778-7311
FAX: 603-778-6671
www.foreveryday.com

*Kevin Callahan, President*

Offers patient treatment, committed to enhancing the lives of individuals with short and long term physically disabling conditions.

**9577  Farnum Rehabilitation Center**
580 Court Street
Keene, NH  03431  603-354-6631
FAX: 603-355-2078

*Susan Loughrey, Program Director*
*Judy Bell, Manager*

Offers rehabilitation services, occupational therapy, physical therapy and more for the physically challenged individual.

**9578  Hackett Hill Nursing Center and Integrated Care**
191 Hackett Hill Road
Manchester, NH  03102  603-668-8161
FAX: 603-622-2584

*Claudia Gallo, Case Manager*
*Brett Lennerton, Administrator*

Postacute rehabilitation program.

**9579  New Hampshire Rehabilitation and Sports Medicine**
Catholic Medical Center
769 South Main Street
Suite 201
Manchester, NH  03102  603-641-6700
800-437-9666
FAX: 603-668-5348

*Heidi George, Director*
*Victor Carbone, Manager*

A specialized facility for comprehensive rehabilitation for individuals who have been injured or have a disability.

**9580  New Medico, Highwatch Rehabilitation Center**
Highwatch Road
Center Ossipee, NH  03814
FAX: 603-539-8888

*William Burke, Executive Director*

**9581  Northern New Hampshire Mental Health and Developmental Services**
87 Washington Street
Conway, NH  03818  603-447-3347
FAX: 603-447-8893
www.nnhmhds.org

*Stanley Marsden, Director*

Provides mental health and developmental services to northern New Hampshire, including early intervention, elderly services, residential program, outpatient services, employee assistance programs, inpatient services, etc.

**9582  The Mental Health Center: Northern Human S ervices**
312th Street
Berlin, NH  03570  603-752-7404
FAX: 603-752-5194

*Charles Cotton, Executive Director*

A center to help people that have mental disabilities.

## New Jersey

**9583  All Garden State Physical Therapy**
750 Broadway
Paterson, NJ  07514  973-345-1312
FAX: 973-742-0669
e-mail: agspt750@yahoo.com

*Carlos Chaparro, General Manager*
*Maria Maval, Manager*

Postacute rehabilitation program.

**9584  Bancroft NeuroHealth**
425 Kings Hwyighway
Haddonfield, NJ  08033  856-429-0010
800-774-5516
FAX: 856-429-1613
e-mail: inquiry@bancroft.org
www.bancroft.org

*Steve Bruce, Vice President*
*Robert Martin, Chief Executive Officer*
*Michelle Stewart, Director Communications*

Private, not-for-profit organization serving people with disabilities since 1883. Based in Haddonfield, New Jersey, help more than 1000 children and adults with autism, developmental disabilities, brain injuries, and other neurological impairments. Operates more than 140 sites throughout the U.S. and abroad.

**9585  Daughters of Miriam Center for the Aged**
155 Hazel Street
Clifton, NJ  07011  973-772-3700
FAX: 973-253-5389

*Fred Feinstein, Executive Director*

**9586  Devereux Center in New Jersey**
901 Mantua Pike
Woodbury, NJ  08096  856-384-9680
FAX: 856-384-6742
www.devereux.org

*Vincent Winterling, Director*
*Maureen Walsh, Executive Director*
*Carol Poirier, Admissions Assistant*

Serves emotionally disturbed females, ages 5-21, who have affective disorders, bi-polar disorders, adjustment reactions, behavioral disorders, specific developmental disorders, identity disorders, attention deficit disorders, schizoid disorders, anxiety disorders, enuresis, runaway behavior, substance abuse, in remission and personality disturbances. The center offers 95-100 full-time staff including, teachers, administrators, counselors, therapists, recreation staff and support services.

**9587  Integrated Health Services of New Jersey at Somerset Valley**
1621 Route 22 West
Bound Brook, NJ  08805  732-469-2000
FAX: 732-469-8917

*Carolyn Allen, Executive Director*
*Janice Vyzas, Social Work Director*

Subacute rehabilitation program, long term care, respite care.

**9588  Ladacain Network**
Schroth School & Technical Education Center
1701 Kneeley Boulevard
Ocean, NJ  07712  732-493-5900
FAX: 732-493-5980
www.ladcain.org

*Patricia Carlesimo, Executive Director*

Provides an array of services and programs specifically for children and adults with developmental and physical disabilities. Services include approved Department of Education school programs; adult education and training; vocational training, personal care assistance services, in-home and Saturday respite; child care programs, housing opportunities, and more.

**9589  Lourdes Regional Rehabilitation Center**
Our Lady of Lourdes Medical Center
1600 Haddon Avenue
Camden, NJ  08103                      856-757-3548
                                  FAX: 856-968-2522
                          e-mail: info@lourdesnet.org
                                  www.lourdesmed.org

*Mark T Bateman, Chief Administrative Officer*
*Susan Cleveland, Manager*
*Bernadette Summer, Outpatient Scheduling Coord.*

**9590  Mt. Carmel Guild**
494 Broad Street
Newark, NJ  07102              973-596-4100

*Edda Stewart, Coordinator*
*Anita Holland, Religious Leader*

Offers services for the totally blind, legally blind, visually impaired, mentally retarded blind and more with health, counseling, educational, recreational, rehabilitation, computer training and professional training services.

**9591  Pediatric Rehabilitation Department, JFK Medical Center**
2050 Oak Tree Road
Edison, NJ  08820                732-548-2956
                               FAX: 732-548-7751
                                  www.hssolaris.org

*Patricia Munday MD, Director Pediatric Rehab*

Comprehensive interdisciplinary, family focused outpatient pediatric rehabilitation services including evaluation and individual and group treatment programs for children birth-21.

**9592  REACH Rehabilitation Program: Leader Nursing and Rehabilitation Center**
550 Jessup Road
Paulsboro, NJ  08066           856-848-9551

*Karen Fattore, Case Manager*
*Anthony Stenson, Administrator*
Postacute rehabilitation program.

**9593  REACH Rehabilitation and Catastrophic Long-Term Care**
1180 Route 22
Mountainside, NJ  07092        908-654-0020

*Linda Sweeney, Program Director*
*Archie Ordana, Manager*
Postacute rehabilitation program.

**9594  Rehabilitation Specialists**
33 Sicomac Road
North Haledon, NJ  07508       973-636-9366
                               800-441-7488
                          FAX: 973-427-1463
                          www.rehab-specialist.com

*Carol Sloman, Admissions Coordinator*
*Dawn Thomas, Executive Director*

Rehabilitation Specialists, founded in 1983, is a quality, cost effective community re-entry center treating individuals with acquired brain injury. A non clinical environment based in the community is utilized that offers professional services enabling participants to learn skills they need to return to a productive life. Both our Day and Residential programming emphases focus on Functional Life Skills, Work Skills and Learning Skills. Each participant's program is tailored to meet their needs.

**9595  Summit Ridge Center**
20 Summit Street
West Orange, NJ  07052          973-736-2000
                               FAX: 973-731-4582
                                  www.ghv.com

*Charlene Harn, Admissions/Marketing Director*
*Chad Murin, Administrator*

Offers rehabilitation services, occupational therapy, physical therapy and more for the physically challenged.

# New Mexico

**9596  Lifecourse Rehabilitation Services**
525 S Schwartz Drive
Farmington, NM  87401           505-327-3422
                               FAX: 505-327-6562

*Bobi Logsdon RN, Case Manager*

Uses a team of professionals to provide a comprehensive rehabilitation program. Accomplishing the best possible physical and cognitive improvement is the aim of the following treatment members: nurses, physical therapists, physicians, speech and occupational therapists, therapeutic recreation specialist. Providing inpatient and out patient services.

**9597  Southwest Communication Resource**
PO Box 788
Bernalillo, NM  87004           505-867-3396
                               FAX: 505-867-3398
                          e-mail: info@abrazosnm.org
                                  www.abrazosnm.org

*Norman Segel, Executive Director*

Services for infants, children and adults with developmental disabilities in Sandoval County New Mexico.

# New York

**9598  Bronx Continuing Treatment Day Program**
1527 Southern Boulevard
Bronx, NY  10460                718-893-1414
                               FAX: 718-893-0707

*Hermina Torres, Executive Director*

**9599  Brooklyn Bureau of Community Service**
285 Schermerhorn Street
Brooklyn, NY  11217             718-310-5600
                               FAX: 718-855-1517

*Leslie Klein, Director Adult Rehabilitation*
*Maryclare Scerbo, Director Volunteer Services*
*Sonea Smith, Executive Director*

Offers independent living skills, counseling, work readiness, vocational trianing, job placement and job follow-up services to individuals with disabilities (to include individuals with psychiatric, physical, and developmental disabilities). Special programs to move disabled welfare recipients from welfare to work. Publishes a bi-annual newsletter.

**9600 Buffalo Hearing and Speech Center**
50 E North Street
Buffalo, NY 14203 716-885-8318
FAX: 716-885-4229
www.buffalohearingandspeech.org

*Janet Maher, President*

Assists individuals with speech, language and/or hearing impairments to achieve maximum communication potential.

**9601 Cora Hoffman Center**
2324 Forest Avenue
Staten Island, NY 10303 718-447-8205
FAX: 718-815-2182

*Kevin Kenney, Executive Director*

**9602 Elmhurst Hospital Center**
7901 Broadway
Elmhurst, NY 11373 718-334-4000

*Chris Constantino, Administrator*
*Benjamin Chu, Chief Executive Officer*

Offers rehabilitation services, occupational therapy, physical therapy and more for the physically challenged individual.

**9603 F-E-G-S**
315 Hudson Street
New York, NY 10013 212-366-8400
FAX: 212-366-8441
e-mail: execoffice@fegs.org
www.fegs.org

*Jill Colon-Regus, Rehabilitation Services Director*
*Loel Tayler, Treatment Programs Director*
*Rena Moore, Intensive Psychiatric Rehab Prgm*

**9604 Flushing Hospital**
4500 Parsons Boulevard
Flushing, NY 11355 718-670-5000
FAX: 718-670-3082

*David Karan MD, Director Clinic*
*David Rosen, Chief Executive Officer*

Offers services for the totally blind, legally blind, visually impaired, mentally retarded blind and more with health, counseling, educational, recreational, rehabilitation, computer training and professional training services.

**9605 Gateway Community Industries**
1 Amy Kay Parkway
Kingston, NY 12401 845-331-1261
800-454-9295
FAX: 845-331-2112
www.gatewaysindustries.org

*Francoise Dunalsky, President/CEO*
*Mary Anne Hildebrandt, Rehabilitation Services Director*
*Darcy McCourt, Residential Services Director*

**9606 Henkind Eye Institute Division of Montefiore Hospital**
3400 Bainbridge Avenue
Bronx, NY 10467 718-920-6244
FAX: 718-920-6244

*Lanny M Binstock*
*Jonathan Hoenig, MD*

Offers services for the totally blind, legally blind, visually impaired, mentally retarded blind and more with health, counseling, educational, recreational, rehabilitation, computer training and professional training services. Low vision services offered.

**9607 Industries for the Blind of New York State**
230 Washington Ave
Albany, NY 12210 518-456-8671
800-421-9010
FAX: 518-456-3587
www.ibnys.org

*Richard Healey, President/CEO*

Offers services for the totally blind, legally blind, visually impaired, mentally retarded blind and more with health, counseling, educational, recreational, rehabilitation, computer training and professional training services.

**9608 Inpatient Pain Rehabilitation Program**
301 E 17th Street
New York, NY 10003 212-598-6606
FAX: 212-598-6468
www.hjd.edu/hjd/hjd-home.jsp

*William Pinter Phd, Administrative Director*

The Inpatient Rehabilitation Program, established in 1983 specializes in the treatment of chronic pain. Our inpatient program is one of the oldest and well established pain programs in the country. It is the only interdisciplinary inpatient pain program in the tri-state area and one of only 20 pain programs in the entire US to have CARF accreditation. Upon completion of an extensive evaluation, patients are admitted for an 18-day inpatient stay.

**9609 Koicheff Health Care Center**
2324 Forest Avenue
Staten Island, NY 10303 718-447-0200
FAX: 718-981-1431

*Paul Castello, Clinic Director*

**9610 Marcus Pain Institute**
30 E 40th Street
New York, NY 10016 212-532-7999
FAX: 212-532-5957
e-mail: njm@nmpi.com
www.nmpi.com

*Norman Marcus MD, Medical Director*
*Brooke Johnson, Manager*

We focus on muscles as the cause of most common pains, i.e. back, neck, shoulders, and headaches. We make specific muscle diagnoses and have specific treatments that in many cases will eliminate the need for surgery or relieve the pain. Patients diagnosed with herniated disc, spinal stenosis, rotator cuff tear, impingement syndrome, sciatica, fibromyalgia and headache will generally find relief.

**9611 Pain Alleviation Center**
Comprehensive Pain Management Associates
125 S Service Road
Jericho, NY 11753 516-997-7246
FAX: 516-997-7281
www.paincenter.com

*Alex Weingarten, Director*
*Phillip Fyman, Director*
*Marisa French, Manager*

One of the first pain clinics to gain national accreditation from the Commission on Accreditation of Rehabilitation Facilities. This is due largely to a patient-centered program based on the latest research.

**9612 Pathfinder Village**
3 Chenango Road
Edmeston, NY 13335 607-965-8121
FAX: 607-965-8655
e-mail: info@pathfindervillage.org
www.pathfindervillage.org

*Edward Shafer, Chief Executive Officer*

Pathfinder Village is a warm, friendly community in the rolling hills of Central New York. Here children and adults with Down Syndrome gain independence, build lasting friendships, become partners in the world and take in all that life has to offer.

**9613 Pilot Industries: Ellenville**
845-331-4300
48 Canal Street
Ellenville, NY 12428
845-647-7711
FAX: 845-647-7711

*Peter Pierri, Executive Director*
*Betty Marks, Plant Manager*

**9614 Presbyterian Hospital in the City of New York**
622 W 168th Street
New York, NY 10032
212-305-2500
FAX: 212-305-1017

*Michael Bradley, Executive Director*
*Herbert Pardes, Chief Executive Officer*

**9615 Skills Unlimited**
405 Locust Avenue
Oakdale, NY 11769
631-567-3320
FAX: 516-567-3285

*Richard Kassnove, Executive Director*

**9616 United Cerebral Palsy of Western New York**
7 Community Drive
Buffalo, NY 14225
716-894-5399
FAX: 716-894-8257

*Virginia C Purcell, Executive Director*

Provides comprehensive services, to individuals with disabilities from infancy through adulthood. Also serves people with all types of developmental disabilities as well as providing clinical services to persons with other types of disabilities such as: spinal cord injury, multiple sclerosis, head trauma and others. The center employs over 750 people.

## North Carolina

**9617 Center for Vision Rehabilitation**
Academy Eye Associates
3115 Academy Road
Durham, NC 27707
919-493-7456
800-942-1499
FAX: 919-493-1718
e-mail: henry.greene@academyeye.com
www.academyeye.com

*Henry A Greene OD, President/Owner*

Vision rehabilitation and low-vision care for the visually impaired, post-stroke, head trauma and for neuro-oncology vision complications.

**9618 Diversified Opportunities**
610 Pender Street E
Wilson, NC 27893
252-291-0378
FAX: 252-291-1402

*Mike Petty, Executive Director*

**9619 Industries of the Blind**
920 W Lee Street
Greensboro, NC 27403
336-274-1591
800-909-7086
FAX: 336-274-9207
www.indusryotheblind.com

*Mark Durge, Director*
*Glenn Rainey, President*

Offers services for the totally blind, legally blind, visually impaired, mentally retarded blind and more with health, counseling, educational, recreational, rehabilitation, computer training and professional training services.

**9620 John C Whitaker Regional Rehabilitation**
Novant Health
3333 Silas Creek Parkway
Winston Salem, NC 27103
336-718-5780

www.novanthealth.org

*Mary Jo Weavil, Director*

**9621 Johnston County Industries**
912 N Brightleaf Boulevard
Smithfield, NC 27577
919-934-0677

*Vicki Shore, Executive Director*

**9622 Learning Services: Carolina**
707 Morehead Avenue
Durham, NC 27707
919-688-4444
FAX: 919-419-9951
www.learningservices.com

*Brian Preston, Executive Director*
Postacute rehabilitation program.

**9623 LifeSpan**
940 Beaumont Avenue
High Point, NC 27260
336-883-0111
FAX: 336-883-0031
www.lifespanservices.org

*Patti Huggins, Program Director*

Provide vocational and enrichment program for adults with developmental disabilities.

**9624 Lions Club Industries for the Blind**
1810 E Main Street
Durham, NC 27703
919-596-8277
FAX: 919-598-1179

*William Hudson, Executive Director*

Offers services for the totally blind, legally blind, visually impaired, mentally retarded blind and more with health, counseling, educational, recreational, rehabilitation, computer training and professional training services.

**9625 Lions Services**
4600 N Tryon Street
Charlotte, NC 28213
704-599-4760

*Charles Lamb, Administrator*
*Jimmy Cranford, President*

Offers services for the totally blind, legally blind, visually impaired, mentally retarded blind and more with health, counseling, educational, recreational, rehabilitation, computer training and professional training services.

**9626 McLeod Center West**
Old Highway 70
Black Mountain, NC 28711
FAX: 828-669-4164

*Steve Lee, Executive Director*

**9627 Regional Rehabilitation Center Pitt County Memorial Hospital**
2100 Stantonsburg Road
Greenville, NC 27834
252-847-4448
FAX: 252-816-7552
e-mail: mdixon@pcmh.com

*Martha M Dixon, VP General Services*

**9628 Rehab Home Care**
2660 Yonkers Road
Raleigh, NC 27604
800-447-8692
FAX: 919-831-2211

*Alan Silver, Chief Executive Officer*
*Janis Hansen, Chief Operating Officer*

A Medicare/Medicaid certified, state-licensed home health agency with emphasis on rehabilitation.

**9629 Thoms Rehabilitation Hospital**
Thoms Rehabilitation Hospital
68 Sweeten Creek Road
Asheville, NC 28803
828-274-2400
FAX: 828-274-9452
www.carepartners.org

*Kathi Petersen, Director Planning/Communications*
*Edgardo Diez MD, Medical Director of Brain Injury*
*Kathy Price, Director Admissions*

Freestanding physical rehabilitation hospital, founded 1938 - 100 beds, including 90 acute and 10 transitional - JCAHO accredited.

**9630 Winston-Salem Industries for the Blind**
7730 N Point Boulevard
Winston Salem, NC 27106
336-759-0551
800-242-7726
FAX: 336-759-0990
e-mail: info@wsifb.com
www.wsifb.com

*Daniel Boucher, President*
*John Googe, Chairman of the Board*

Offers services for the totally blind, legally blind, visually impaired, mentally retarded blind and more with health, counseling, educational, recreational, rehabilitation, computer training and professional training services.

---

# Ohio

**9631 Bellefaire Jewish Children's Bureau**
22001 Fairmount Boulevard
Shaker Heights, OH 44118
216-932-2800
800-879-2522
FAX: 216-932-8520
e-mail: yulishj@bellefairejcb.org
www.bellefairejcb.org

*Jill Yulish, Intake Coordinator*
*Adam Jacobs, Chief Executive Officer*

Residential treatment for ages 12 to 17 1/2 at time of admission offering individualized psychotherapy, special education, and group living for severaly emotionally disturbed children and adolescents. Also offers a variety of other programs including specialized and therapuetic foster care, partial hospitilization, outpatient counseling, home-based intensive counseling and adoption services.

**9632 Christ Hospital Rehabilitation Unit**
2139 Auburn Avenue
Cincinnati, OH 45219
513-585-2737
FAX: 513-585-3300

*Richard Seim, Senior VP*
*Regina Hartman, Manager*

**9633 Cleveland Society for the Blind**
Cleveland Sight Center
PO Box 1988
Cleveland, OH 44106
216-791-8118
FAX: 216-791-1101
e-mail: jdsidley@clevelandsightcenter.org
www.clevelandsightcenter.org

*John David Sidley, Manager Public Education*
*Michael E Grady, Executive Director*

Social, rehabilitation, education and support services for blind and visually impaired children and adults, early intervention program for children birth to age 6, low vision clinic, aid and appliance shop, Braille and taping transcription, training for rehabilitation, orientation, mobility and computer access, employment services and job placement, recreation program, resident camping, talking books, radio reading services, food service training and snack bar employment. Free screening.

**9634 Columbus Speech and Hearing Center**
510 E N Broadway Street
Columbus, OH 43214
614-263-5151
FAX: 614-263-5365
www.columbusspeech.org

*Dawn Gleason, President/CEO*
*Joanne Shannon, Director Vocational Services*

Serves persons who have speech-language and hearing challenges. Provides vocational rehabilitation services for individuals who are deaf, hard-of-hearing or deaf-blind.

**9635 CommuniCare of Clifton Nursing and Rehabilitation Center**
Communi Care Health Services
625 Probasco Street
Cincinnati, OH 45220
513-281-2464
FAX: 513-281-2559

*Lisa Renaker, Director of Nursing*
*Cindy Phillips*
*Sylvia Salvado, Owner*

A long term care facility which specializes in rehabilitation. Offers a full range of rehabilitative services including physical therapy, occupational therapy and speech therapy.

**9636 Doctors Hospital**
5100 W Broad Street
Columbus, OH 43228
614-544-1000
FAX: 614-870-9639

*Janet Hymiak, Executive Director*
*Kreg Gruber, Chief Executive Officer*

**9637 Dodd Hall at the Ohio State University Hospitals**
480 W 9th Street
Columbus, OH 43215
614-293-3300
800-293-5123
www.medicalcenter.osu.edu

*Fred Sanfilippo, Senior Vice President*
*Peter E Geier, Associate VP*
*Dennis Smith, Administrator*

Dodd Hall is a full service medical rehabilitation hospital offering comprehensive inpatient and outpatient rehabilitation.

**9638  Easter Seal Society of Mahoning**
National Easter Seals Chicago
299 Edwards Street
Youngstown, OH  44502
330-743-1168
FAX: 330-743-1616
www.mtc.easterseals.com

*Kenan J Sklenar, President/CEO*

Outpatient medical rehabilitation - physical therapy, speech therapy, occupational therapy, warm-water therapy and adult day services.

**9639  Four Oaks Center**
623 Dayton Xenia Road
Xenia, OH  45385
937-222-7474

*Margareth Conrad, School Administrator*

Starts children on the road to discovery by providing a learning environment rich in opportunities and encouragement. The program was designed to give children with delays or disabilities, or those at-risk the extra help needed to develop fully. Any child under the age of six who exhibits developmental delays, handicapping conditions, or is considered at risk may qualify to participate.

**9640  Genesis Healthcare System**
Rehabilitation Services
800 Forest Avenue
Zanesville, OH  43701
740-454-5000
800-322-4762
FAX: 740-455-7527
e-mail: llynn@genesishcs.org
www.genesishcs.org

*Keela Barker, Outpatient Manager*
*Kim Gates, Manager*
*Karen Eyberger, Rehab Development Manager*

A CARF and JACHO accredited 19-bed rehabilitation facility located within Genesis Healthcare System, a 732 bed, non-profit hospital system, located in Zanesville, Ohio. Freestanding outpatient services, including work hardening, pain management, vocational services, audiology, lymphedema, vestibular rehab, off-the-road driving evals, aquatic therpay, womens health and sports enhancement.

**9641  George A Martin Center**
3603 Washington Avenue
Cincinnati, OH  45229
513-961-0144
FAX: 513-221-3514

*William Poole, Administrator*

Offers services for the totally blind, legally blind, visually impaired, mentally retarded blind and more with health, counseling, educational, recreational, rehabilitation, computer training and professional training services.

**9642  Grady Memorial Hospital**
561 W Central Avenue
Delaware, OH  43015
740-369-8711
FAX: 740-363-3175

*Everett Weber, Executive Director*
*Steve Garlock, Chief Executive Officer*

**9643  Hamilton Center**
3400 Symmes Road
Hamilton, OH  45015
513-867-5970
FAX: 513-874-2977

*Donald Musnuff, Executive Director*

**9644  Holzer Clinic**
90 Jackson Pike
Gallipolis, OH  45631
740-446-5411
FAX: 740-446-5532
e-mail: webmaster@holzerclinic.com
www.holzerclinic.com

*Wayne Munro, President*
*John Sullivan, Vice President*

Serves medical needs of patients in an 8 county area, including counties in Ohio and West Virginia.

**9645  Holzer Medical Center RehabCare**
Holzer Medical Center
100 Jackson Pike
Gallipolis, OH  45631
740-446-5000
FAX: 740-446-5904
www.holzer.org

*Johanna Lampert, Program Manager*
*Lori Cremans, Director*
*Lamar Wyse, President*

Offers an individualized quality comprehensive rehabilitation program for people with disabilities by an interdisciplinary team including physical therapy, occupational, speech, nursing and social services to restore the patient to the highest degree of rehab outcomes attainable.

**9646  Human Resource Consultants**
1946 N 13th Street
Toledo, OH  43624

**9647  IKRON Institute for Rehabilitative and Psychological Services**
2347 Vine Street
Cincinnati, OH  45219
513-621-1117
FAX: 513-621-2350

*Randy E Strunk, Executive Director*
*Ken Carbonell, Fiscal Officer*
*Ann Webb, Program Director*

An accredited mental health facility and a certified rehabilitation center. Through a variety of creative treatment and rehabilitation services, IKRON assists adults with mental health and/or substance abuse problems to attain greater independence, to lead lives of sobriety, to obtain competitive work and live more satisfying lives. IKRON places a strong emphasis on respect and support for persons with problems of adjustment. Special contracts to persons desiring job placement.

**9648  Integrated Health Services at Waterford Commons**
955 Garden Lake Parkway
Toledo, OH  43614
419-382-2200
FAX: 419-381-0188

*Elaine Heatherwick, Administrator*

A subacute and rehabilitation program specializing in ventilator weaning and management, I.V. therapeutics and pain management, wound management and subacute rehabilitation.

**9649  Lake County Society for Rehabilitation**
9521 Lake Shore Boulevard
Mentor, OH  44060
440-352-8993

*Richard Kessler, Executive Director*

**9650  Lester H Higgins Adult Center**
2950 Whipple Avenue NW
Canton, OH  44708
330-484-4814

*Dr. Joseph James, Superintendent*
*Ed Allar, Manager*

**9651  Live Oaks Career Development Campus**
5956 Buckwheat Road
Milford, OH  45150                     513-575-1900
                                   FAX: 513-771-6575

*Harold Carr MD, Superintendent*
*Robin White, President/CEO*
*Jim Dixon, Principal*

**9652  Metro Health: St. Luke's Medical Center Pain Management Program**
2500 Metrohealth Drive
Cleveland, OH  44109                   216-778-4428
                                   FAX: 216-368-7140
                                   www.metrohealth.org

*Thomas McCafferty, Health Center Director*
*J Glen Smith, Health Center Director*
*Ceil Lewandowski, Manager*

CARF accredited comprehensive multidisciplinary pain management program.

**9653  MetroHealth Medical Center**
3395 Scranton Road
Cleveland, OH  44109                   216-778-4982
                                   FAX: 216-778-8376

*Henry Manning, Executive Director*

**9654  Middletown Regional Hospital: Inpatient Rehabilitation Unit**
105 McKnight Drive
Middletown, OH  45044                  513-424-2111
                                   FAX: 513-420-5718

*Bob Gauder, Program Manager*
*Douglas McNeill, Chief Executive Officer*

**9655  Newark Healthcare Center**
75 McMillen Drive
85
Newark, OH  43055                      740-344-0357
                                   FAX: 740-344-8615

*Joanne Whiteman, Administrator*
*Brian Newman, Executive Director*

Subacute rehabilitation program.

**9656  Parma Community General Hospital Acute Rehabilitation Center**
7007 Powers Boulevard
Parma, OH  44129                       440-743-3000
                                   FAX: 440-743-4036
                         e-mail: pat.ruflin@parmahospital
                                   www.parmahospital.org

*Dale Winsberg, Administrative Director*
*Patricia Ruflin, Chief Executive Officer*

The mission of this CARF accredited unit is to provide the most comprehensive, cost-effective, acute rehabilitation program possible in order for every patient and family to adjust to his/her disability and to achieve the maximum potential of independent functioning when returning to community living.

**9657  Peter A Towne Physical Therapy Center**
447 Nilles Road
Suite 10
Fairfield, OH  45014                   513-829-6100
                                   FAX: 513-829-7726

*Debbie Wilkerson, Office Manager*

Outpatient, private practice physical and occupational therapy. Three other offices in Hamilton, Monroe and West Chester.

**9658  Philomatheon Society of the Blind**
2701 Tuscarawas St W
Canton, OH  44708                      330-453-9157

*Gerald Dessecker, President*

Offers services for the totally blind, legally blind, visually impaired, mentally retarded blind and more with health, counseling, educational, recreational, rehabilitation, computer training and professional training services.

**9659  Providence Hospital Work**
2270 Banning Road
Cincinnati, OH  45239                  513-853-5261
                                   FAX: 513-853-5910

*Christopher West, Executive Director*

**9660  SCI: Six County**
2927 Bell Street
Zanesville, OH  43701                  740-452-9953
                                   FAX: 740-455-4134

*David O Wesner, Program Research*

**9661  Society for Rehabilitation**
9521 Lake Shore Boulevard
Mentor, OH  44060                      440-352-8993
                                       800-344-3159
                                   FAX: 440-352-6632
                         e-mail: info@societyhelps.org
                                   www.societyhelps.org

*Richard J Kessler, Executive Director*

**9662  Southeast Ohio Sight Center**
358 Lincoln Avenue
Suite A
Lancaster, OH  43130                   740-687-4785
                                       800-969-3490
                                   FAX: 740-689-9753
                     e-mail: sosc@seohiosightcenter.org
                     www.uwayfairfieldco.org/center.html

*John Sterba, Executive Director*

Offers services for the blind and visually impaired to include functional low vision evaluations, community rehabilitation trading, counseling, educational, recreational, rehabilitation and vocational services.

**9663  St. Francis Rehabilitation Hospital**
401 N Broadway Street
Green Springs, OH  44836               419-639-2626
                                   FAX: 419-639-6222

*Martha Stevens, Marketing Coordinator*
*Dan Schwanke, Chief Executive Officer*

Program offers specialized treatment for patients who have suffered a head injury, spinal cord injury, or stroke, or who have an orthopedic injury. The Head Injury Program provides a continuum of care from coma stimulation through transitional living. Their physicians, nurses, counselors and therapists are dedicated to helping our patients develop the motivation, strength and skills needed to overcome or adapt to their disability.

**9664  TAC I**
110 W Leffel Lane
Springfield, OH  45506                 937-328-5200
                                   FAX: 937-325-4623

*Mary Brandstetter, Executive Director*

**9665  TAC II**
110 W Leffel Lane
Springfield, OH  45506          937-328-5200
                                FAX: 937-325-4623

*Mary Brandstetter, Executive Director*

## Oklahoma

**9666  Dean A McGee Eye Institute**
608 Stanton L Young Boulevard
Oklahoma City, OK  73104          405-271-6060

*Dr. Amelia Miranda, Director*
*Selina Gee OD*

Offers services for the totally blind, legally blind, visually impaired, mentally retarded blind and more with health, counseling, educational, recreational, rehabilitation, computer training and professional training services.

**9667  Jane Phillips Rehab Services**
Rehab Care
3500 E Frank Phillips Boulevard
Bartlesville, OK  74006          918-333-7200
                                FAX: 918-333-7801
                                e-mail: webmaster@ipmc.org

*Jim Fram, President*
*Evan O Zorn, Executive Vice President*
*James Carver, MD*

Comprehensive inpatient rehabilitation services are provided to patients with orthopedic, neurologic, and other medical conditions of recent onset or regression, who have experienced a loss of function in activities of daily living, mobility, cognition and communication.

**9668  McAlester Regional Health Center RehabCare Unit**
1 E Clark Bass Boulevard
McAlester, OK  74501          918-426-1800
                              FAX: 918-421-6832

*Shawn Bedds, Administrator*
*Joel Tate, Chief Executive Officer*

A 19-bed inpatient physical rehabilitation unit serving the Southeast Oklahoma area. Offers physical therapy, occupational therapy, social work, speech and psychological services in an interdisciplinary framework.

**9669  Oklahoma League for the Blind**
PO Box 24020
Oklahoma City, OK  73124          405-232-4644
                                  FAX: 405-236-5438
                                  e-mail: ccampbell@olb.org
                                  www.olb.org

*Lauren White, President/CEO*
*Carol Campbell, Executive Assistant*
*Bob Allen, President*

Offers services for the blind and visually impaired, counseling, educational, recreational, rehabilitation, computer training and professional training services.

**9670  Valley View Regional Hospital RehabCare Unit**
430 N Monte Vista Street
Ada, OK  74820          580-332-2323
                        FAX: 580-421-1395
                        e-mail: valleyview@wrh.com
                        www.valleyviewregional.org

*Ronand Webb, Chief Executive Officer*

Comprehensive physical medicine and rehabilitation services designed to help patients in their adjustment to a physically limiting condition.

## Oregon

**9671  Emanuel Rehabilitation Center**
3025 N Vancouver Avenue
Portland, OR  97227          503-335-2000
                            FAX: 503-413-1501

*Gary Guidetta, Executive Director*
*Gail Weisgerber, Manager*

**9672  Garten Services**
3334 Industrial Way NE
Salem, OR  97301          503-581-4472
                          FAX: 503-581-4497
                          e-mail: garten@garten.org
                          www.garten.org

*Tim Rocak, Executive Director*

**9673  Oakcrest Care Center**
2933 Center Street NE
Salem, OR  97301
                          FAX: 503-588-5251

Postacute rehabilitation program.

**9674  Oakhill-Senior Program**
1190 Oakhill Avenue SE
Salem, OR  97302          503-364-9086
                          FAX: 503-365-2879

*Jan Dillon, Senior Services Manager*

Garten Senior Services provides an adult day service program to seniors with and without developmental disabilities. The program will provide community opportunities, college classes and a wide variety of leisure activities in group and individual settings.

**9675  Pacific Spine and Pain Center**
1801 Highway 99 N
Ashland, OR  97520          541-482-5515
                            866-482-5515
                            FAX: 541-482-2433

*Christine Gorrin, Manager*

**9676  Vision Northwest**
9225 Southwest Hall Boulevard
9225 SW Hall Boulevard
Tigard, OR  97223          503-684-8389
                          FAX: 503-243-2537

*Evelyn Maizels, Executive Director*

Offers services for the totally blind, legally blind, visually impaired, mentally retarded blind and more with health, counseling, educational, recreational, rehabilitation, computer training and professional training services.

**9677  Willamette Valley Rehabilitation Center**
1853 W Airway Road
Lebanon, OR  97355          541-258-8121
                            FAX: 541-451-1762
                            www.wvrc.org

*Martin Buckman, Executive Director*

Provides the best professional vocational services to those adults in the community who, by virtue of their physical or mental limitations, are negatively impacted by their ability to attain or maintain employment.

## Pennsylvania

**9678  Alcohol and Drug Abuse Services**
2 Main Street
Bradford, PA  16701　　　　　814-362-6517
　　　　　　　　　　　　　　FAX: 814-362-3202

*Carma Horner, Supervisor*
*Andrew Lehman, Executive Director*

Offers rehabilitation services to individuals with an alcohol or drug related problem.

**9679  Alpine Nursing and Rehabilitation Center of Hershey**
Pennstate
405 Marion Place
State College, PA  16801　　　　814-865-1710
　　　　　　　　　　　　　FAX: 814-863-9423
　　　　　　　　　　e-mail: geron@psu.edu
　　　　　　　　　　　　　　geron.psu.edu

*Melissa A Hardy, Director*
*Anna Shuey, Administrative Assistant*

Postacute rehabilitation program.

**9680  Alpine Ridge and Brandywood**
Devereux Foundation
600 Boot Road
Downingtown, PA  19335　　　　610-873-4900
　　　　　　　　　　　　　　800-345-1292
　　　　　　　　　　　FAX: 610-430-0567
　　　　　　　　　　　　www.devereus.org

*MaryAnn Fullam, Director*
*Sam Ewing, Owner*

Offers a continuum of services for residents requiring services ranging from minimal care and supervision to total physical and medical care.

**9681  Amity Lodge**
Devereux Foundation
600 Boot Road
Downingtown, PA  19335　　　　610-873-4900
　　　　　　　　　　　　　　800-345-1292
　　　　　　　　　　　FAX: 610-524-3000

*Kim Nash, Director*
*Sam Ewing, Owner*

Offers residents a continuum of services ranging from minimal care and supervision to total physical and medical care.

**9682  Beechwood Rehabilitation Services A Community Integrated Brain Injury Program**
469 E Maple Avenue
Langhorne, PA  19047　　　　　215-750-4299
　　　　　　　　　　　　　　800-782-3299
　　　　　　　　　　　FAX: 215-750-4327
　　　　　　　　　e-mail: dcerra-tyl@wood.org
　　　　　　　　　　www.beechwoodrehab.com

*Deborah Cerra-Tyl, Director Program Development*
*Thomas Felicetti, President*

Services include residential, day treatment and community based support services. Individuals with brain injury are served. The facility is Care Accredited.

**9683  Bryn Mawr Rehabilitation Hospital**
PO Box 3007
Malvern, PA  19355　　　　　610-251-5400
　　　　　　　　　　　　　　888-734-2241
　　　　　　　　　　　FAX: 610-647-3648
　　　　　　　　　　www.brynmawrrehab.org

*Donna Phillips, President*

**9684  Business & Computer Solutions Helping People Get Jobs**
923 Borough Road
Pembroke, NH  03275　　　　　603-230-9994
　　　　　　　　　　　　　　866-230-9994
　　　　　　　　　　　FAX: 603-230-9696
　　　　　　　　　e-mail: ljmader@bcsnh.com
　　　　　　　　　　　　www.bcsnh.com

*Lori Mader, President*

Computer and soft skill training and career development.

**9685  Clara Burke Nursing Home**
251 Stenton Avenue
Plymouth Meeting, PA  19462　　610-828-2272
　　　　　　　　　　　　　　FAX: 610-828-2519

*Terri Herd, Admissions*
*Jim Foulke, Administrator*

Postacute rehabilitation program.

**9686  Daman Villa**
Devereux Foundation
600 Boot Road
Downingtown, PA  19335　　　　610-873-4900
　　　　　　　　　　　　　　800-345-1292
　　　　　　　　　　　FAX: 610-430-0567
　　　　　　　　　　　　www.devereux.org

*Robert Kreider, President & CEO*
*Sam Ewing, Owner*

Offers residents a continuum of services ranging from minimal care and supervision to total physical and medical care.

**9687  Devereux**
444 Devereux Dr
Villanova, PA  19085　　　　　610-520-3000
　　　　　　　　　　　　　　800-345-1292
　　　　　　　　　　　FAX: 610-542-3100
　　　　　　　　　e-mail: knash@devereux.org
　　　　　　　　　　　　www.devereux.org

*Kimberleigh Nash, Director Corporate Communication*
*Robert Kreider, Chief Executive Officer*

Nationwide network of residential, day, and community-based services for children and adults who have special emotional and/or developmental needs.

**9688  Devereux Foundation Health Services Center**
600 Boot Road
Downingtown, PA  19335　　　　610-873-4900
　　　　　　　　　　　　　　800-345-1292
　　　　　　　　　　　FAX: 610-430-0567
　　　　　　　　　　　　www.devereux.org

*MaryAnn Fullam, Director*
*Sam Ewing, Owner*

Provides a continuum of residential services for adults with developmental disabilities. active treatment is offered in a safe and therapeutic environment which allows on-going assessment and individual growth that will enhance the quality of life for each of its residents. Candidates could have needs that range from minimal care and supervision to those requiring medical and behavioral assistance with an intensive support system. $145-$161.00 per day.

**9689  Devereux's Kanner Center**
620 E Boot Road
West Chester, PA  19380　　　　610-873-4930
　　　　　　　　　　　　　　FAX: 610-873-4969
　　　　　　　　　e-mail: kanner@devereux.org
　　　　　　　　　　www.devereuxcares.org

*Steve Silverman, Admissions Director*
*Kelly McCool, Admissions Coordinator*
*Carol Leeson, Director Network Relations*

A private nonprofit nationwide network of treatment services for individuals of all ages with emotional and/or developmental disabilities. Located in twelve states and the District of Columbia, Devereux's continuum includes inpatient and partial hospitalization, residential treatment, community based programs and outpatient services. Provides a continuum of care to children, adolescents and young adults who have developmental disabilities, mental retardation, autism and emotional disturbances.

**9690 Fox Subacute Center**
2644 Bristol Road
Warrington, PA 18976
215-343-2700
FAX: 215-343-8023

*Gerry Nevilln, Admissions*
*Joseph Murray, Administrator*
Postacute rehabilitation program.

**9691 Good Samaritan Hospital**
4th & Walnut Street
Lebanon, PA 17042
717-270-7500
866-276-3082
FAX: 215-238-0804
www.gshleb.org

*John Jeffers, Director*
*Frederick Davis, VP Clinical Services*
Offers services for the totally blind, legally blind, visually impaired, mentally retarded blind and more with health, counseling, educational, recreational, rehabilitation, computer training and professional training services.

**9692 Greater Pittsburgh Guild for the Blind**
311 Station Street
Bridgeville, PA 15017
724-224-8700
FAX: 412-257-8573

*Leroy Bectwy, Director*
*Linda Hill, Manager*
Offers services for the totally blind, legally blind, visually impaired, mentally retarded blind and more with health, counseling, educational, recreational, rehabilitation, computer training and professional training services.

**9693 IHS of Greater Pittsburgh**
890 Weatherwood Lane
Greensburg, PA 15601
724-837-8076
FAX: 724-837-7456
e-mail: pattim@tri-state-health.com

*Patti Mikosky RN CRRN, Provider Relations Specialist*
*Laurie Tamasy, Administrator*
*Marhsa Echard, Admissions Coordinator*
Subacate care, ventilator and pulmonary managment, comprehensive rehabilitation.

**9694 Pediatric Center at Plymouth Meeting Integrated Health Services**
491 Allendale Road
King of Prussia, PA 19406
610-265-9290
800-220-7337

*Fran Currick, Manager*
Subacute programs such as intensive respiratory care, stressing ventilator dependent children, pre and post transplant care, total parenteral nutrition, IV therapy, intensive/behavioral oral feeding programs. Provides extensive discharge planning including teaching or review for all the above programs with an emphasis on development and accessing community resources.

**9695 Pennsylvania Pain Rehabilitation Center**
252 W Swamp Road
Doylestown, PA 18901
215-348-5106
FAX: 215-348-5106

*Reza Azar MD*

**9696 Robert L Miller Rehab Center**
Good Samaritan Hospital
PO Box 1281
Lebanon, PA 17042
717-270-7500
FAX: 717-270-7840

*Joanne Ebert, Rehab Coordinator*
*Stuart Hartman, Medical Director*
Comprehensive inpatient rehab unit for adults regarding general physical rehabilitation. Specific programs include orthopedic, neurological, stroke, amputee, etc.

**9697 Therapy Services at Penn State Milton S Hershey Medical Center**
500 University Drive
Hershey, PA 17033
717-531-8070
FAX: 717-531-4558
www.hmc.psu.edu

*Lori Benner, Director*

## Rhode Island

**9698 In-Sight**
43 Jefferson Boulevard
Warwick, RI 02888
401-941-3322
FAX: 401-941-3356
e-mail: hqinsight@in-sight.org
www.in-sight.org

*Judith Smith, President*
Offers services for the totally blind, legally blind, visually impaired, mentally retarded blind and more with health, counseling, educational, recreational, rehabilitation, computer training and professional training services.

**9699 Vanderbilt Rehabilitation Center**
Newport Hospital
Friendship Street
Newport, RI 02840
401-846-6400
FAX: 401-845-1087
www.lifespan.org

*Robert Healey, Executive Director*
*Arthur Sampson, Chief Executive Officer*

## South Carolina

**9700 Association for the Blind**
1071 Morrison Drive
Charleston, SC 29403
843-723-6915
e-mail: aftb@aerolina.com

*Cornelia Pelzer, Executive Director*
Offers services for people who are blind, or are visually impaired with health, counseling, educational, recreational, rehabilitation, computer training and professional training services.

**9701    Hitchcock Rehabilitation Center**
690 Medical Park Drive
Aiken, SC  29801                               803-648-8344
                                               800-207-6924
                                          FAX: 803-649-4639
                    e-mail: mail@hitchcockhealthcare.org
                                     www.hitchcockrehab.com

*Pat Samuel, Executive Director*
*Dan Hillman, Case Manager*
*Carrie Morgan, Finance Director*

Comprehensive outpatient rehabilitation for adults, children, geriatrics, pediatric therapy, special needs preschool, sports medicine, home health and hospice.

**9702    Mentor of South Carolina**
3200 Devine Street
Columbia, SC  29205                            803-799-9025
                                          FAX: 803-931-8962
                                     www.thementornetwork.com

*Lynn Epps, Executive Director*

Mentor provides a full network of individually tailored services for people with development disabilities and their families. Individuals may be served in their homes, shared living home, or in a host home.

## Tennessee

**9703    Humana Hospital: Morristown RehabCare**
726 McFarland Street
Morristown, TN  37814                          423-586-2930
                                          FAX: 423-587-4417

*James Perry, Program Director*

Designed to help patients in their adjustment to a physically limiting condition by helping to maximize each patient's abilities so he or she can function as independently as possible.

**9704    Opportunity East Rehabilitation Services for the Blind**
PO Box 706
Morristown, TN  37815                          423-586-3998
                                               800-278-6274
                                          FAX: 423-586-2004
                               e-mail: vic@volblind.org
                                     www.opportunityeast.org

*Fred Overbay, Executive Director*
*Vic Mende, Director Rehabilitation Services*

Offers services for the totally blind, legally blind, visually impaired, mentally retarded blind and more with health, counseling, educational, recreational, rehabilitation, computer training and professional training services.

**9705    Patrick Rehab Wellness**
Lincoln County Health System
1001 Huntsville Highway
Fayetteville, TN  37334                        931-433-6505
                                          FAX: 931-438-0378

*Denning Harter, Director Rehab*
*Gloria Meadows, Administrator*
*Jim Stewart, Principal*

Provides rehabilitation services of physical, occupational, and speech therapy. Also, wellness memberships are available to the public.

**9706    PharmaThera**
1785 Nonconnah Boulevard
Memphis, TN  38132                             901-754-5485
                                               800-767-6714
                                          FAX: 901-348-8270

Offers 10 locations serving patients throughout the southern United States, each with an in-house, expertly trained staff. All locations use the latest technologies and techniques in infusion care to provide a broad range of individualized home infusion therapies.

**9707    Siskin Rehabilitation Hospital**
3 Siskin Plaza
Chattanooga, TN  37403                         423-267-4345

*Debby Barker, VP Development*
*Robert Siskin, Owner*

**9708    St. Mary's RehabCare Center**
Oak Hill Avenue
Knoxville, TN  37917                           865-545-7793
                                          FAX: 865-545-8133

*Debbie Keeton, Director*
*Beth Greco, Executive Director*

Provides comprehensive rehabilitation services for patients experiencing CVA, head trauma, orthopedic conditions, spinal cord injury or neurological impairment.

## Texas

**9709    Baylor Institute for Rehabilitation**
3505 Gaston Avenue
Dallas, TX  75246                              214-820-9300
                                               888-7BA-YLOR
                                          FAX: 214-841-2679

*Alice Douden, Admissions Manager*
*Luci Neumann, President*

A 92-bed specialty hospital offering comprehensive rehabilitation services for persons with spinal cord injury, traumatic brain injury, stroke, amputation, and other orthopedic and neurological disorders.

**9710    Brown-Karhan Health Care**
PO Box 419
Dripping Springs, TX  78620                    512-894-0801
                                          FAX: 512-858-4627
                               e-mail: info@brown-karhan.com
                                     www.brown-karhan.com

*James R Karhan, Chief Executive Officer*
*Eric Makowski, President*

Postacute rehabilitation program, long-term neuropsychiatric program, apartment living and full compliment of therapies, including cognitive rehabilitation. $225-$800/day.

**9711    Center for Neuro Skills**
3501 N Macarthur Boulevard
Suite 200
Irving, TX  75062                              972-580-8500
                                          FAX: 972-255-3162

*Rocky Brogdon, Admissions*
*John Schultz, Administrator*

Postacute rehabilitation program.

**9712    Center for Neuro Skills: Texas**
3501 N Macarthur Boulevard
Suite 200
Irving, TX  75062                              972-580-8500
                                          FAX: 972-255-3162
                               e-mail: cns@neuroskills.com
                                     www.neuroskills.com/~cns

*David Krych, Executive Director*
*Peter O'Neill, Admissions*
*Rocky Brogdon, Admissions*

A comprehensive, post-acute, community based head-injury rehabilitation program serving over 100 clients per year. Since 1985, CNS has effectively treated the entire spectrum of head-injured clients, including those with severe behavioral disorders, cognitive/perceptual impairments, speech/language problems, physical disabilities and post-concussion syndrome.

**9713 Comprehensive Rehabilitation**
Hillcrest Baptist Medical Center
3000 Herring Avenue
Waco, TX 76708
254-202-8525
FAX: 254-202-5105

*Carl Lutz MSW, Program Director*
*Ann Gammel, Nurse Manager*
*Debbie Meurer, Manager*

Designed to assist patients in adjustment to a physically limiting condition, utilizing interdisciplinary strategies to maximize each patient's ability and capability.

**9714 Dallas Services for Visually Impaired Children**
4242 Office Parkway
Dallas, TX 75204
214-828-9900
FAX: 214-828-9901

*Jim Gibson, Executive Director*

Offers services for the totally blind, legally blind, visually impaired, mentally retarded blind and more with health, counseling, educational, recreational, rehabilitation, computer training and professional training services.

**9715 Devereux Texas Treatment Network Adult Community**
PO Box 2666
Victoria, TX 77902
361-575-8271
800-383-5000
FAX: 361-575-6520
www.devereux.org

*Fred Williams, Executive Director*
*April Krus, Admissions Coordinator*

Provides a permanent home for individuals with chronic psychiatric and/or developmental disabilities who require long term or lifelong care, support or a transitional home for individuals who progress to a less structured setting. Located on a beautiful 400+ acre campus in sunny south Texas, the primary focus is to offer, in keeping with the philosophies of least restrictive alternatives and normalization, active treatment which will facilitate growth.

**9716 El Paso Lighthouse for the Blind**
200 Washington Street
El Paso, TX 79905
915-532-4495
FAX: 915-532-6338
www.lighthouse-elpaso.com

*Harry Tyler, President*
*Rusty Hooten, Chief Financial Officer*

Enables people of all ages to embody blindness and vision impairment through training, rehabilitation, employment opportunity, advocacy and research. Provides access to opportunities and quality of life so that the blind and visually impaired can reach their fullest potential for self-sufficiency and independence.

**9717 Harris Methodist Fort Worth/Mabee Rehabilitation Center**
1301 Pennsylvania Avenue
Fort Worth, TX 76104
817-882-2760
FAX: 817-882-2753

*Michelle Wilson, Speciality Program Manager*
*Peggyo Ehrlich, Rehab Manager*
*Karen Mallett, Executive Director*

A hospital based inpatient rehab program and outpatient day programs in chronic pain management, work hardening and brain injury transitional services.

**9718 Heights Hospital Rehab Unit**
1917 Ashland Street
Houston, TX 77008
713-861-6161
FAX: 713-802-8537
www.flectmedicalcorp.com

*Theresa Davis, Administrator*

This program is designed to assist patients with physical disabilities achieve their maximum functional abilities.

**9719 Houston Rehabilitation Institute**
17506 Red Oak Drive
Houston, TX 77090
713-774-3245
FAX: 281-580-6714

*Jerome Lengel, Executive Officer*
*Dewitt Hilton, Owner*

Offers an individualized approach to the process of rehabilitation for severely injured or disabled individuals. The process begins with a pre-admissions assessment of each referred patient. The Center combines state-of-the-art technology and equipment with multi-disciplinary therapy and education in a cheerful, secure environment.

**9720 Institute for Rehabilitation & Research**
1333 Moursund Street
Houston, TX 77030
713-799-5000
FAX: 713-797-5289
www.tirr.org

*John Kajander, Chief Executive Officer*
*Jean Herzog, President*

A national center for information, training, research, and technical assistance in independent living. The goal is to extend the body of knowledge in independent living and to improve the utilization of results of research programs and demonstration projects in this field. It has developed a variety of strategies for collecting, synthesizing, and disseminating information related to the field of independent living.

**9721 Integrated Health Services of Amarillo**
5601 Plum Creek Drive
Amarillo, TX 79124
806-351-1000
FAX: 806-355-9650

*Jayton McCoy, Case Manager*
*Neal Duncan, Executive Director*
*Roger Alexander, Administrator*

Postacute rehabilitation program including ventilator weening, complex wound program and interdisciplinary team case management.

**9722 Lighthouse of Houston**
3602 W Dallas Street
Houston, TX 77019
713-527-9561
FAX: 713-284-8451
e-mail: houstonlighthouse@houstonlighthouse.org
www.houstonlighthouse.org

*Gibson M Terroil, President*
*Shelagh Moran, VP/COO*
*Teresa Gaiza, Director Education*

Serves the blind, visually impaired, deaf-blind and multihandicapped blind. Provides workshops, vocational training and placement, low vision clinic, orientation and mobility, housing, Braille, volunteer services, senior center, visual aid sales, counseling and support, diabetic education and day health activity services and day summer camp, Summer Transition for Youth.

**9723 Mainland Center Hospital RehabCare Unit**
Highway 1764
Texas City, TX 77592
281-534-3522
FAX: 409-938-5501

*David Roberts, Program Manager*

The RehabCare program is designed and staffed to assist functionally impaired patients improve to their maximum potential. The opportunities for improvement and adjustments are provided in a pleasant, supportive inpatient environment by therapists from the occupational, physical, recreational and speech therapy disciplines.

**9724 North Texas Rehabilitation Center**
1005 Midwestern Parkway
Wichita Falls, TX 76302
940-322-0771
FAX: 940-766-4943
www.ntrehab.org

*Lesa Enlow, Director Programs*
*Cindy Duncan, Human Resource*
*Mike Castles, President*

Provides outpatient rehabilitation services to maximize independence or promote development to children and adults with disabilities. Programs include: physical, occupational, speech therapy, closed head injury, infant/child development, support groups, aquatics and wellness program and a child achievement program.

**9725 South Texas Lighthouse for the Blind**
PO Box 9697
Corpus Christi, TX 78469
361-883-6553
FAX: 361-883-1041

*Barbara Russell, Executive Director*
*Regis Barber, President*

Offers services for the totally blind, legally blind, visually impaired, mentally retarded blind and more with health, counseling, educational, recreational, rehabilitation, computer training and professional training services.

**9726 Texas Specialty Hospital at Dallas**
7955 Harry Hines Boulevard
Dallas, TX 75235
214-637-0000
FAX: 214-637-6512

*Waylon Maynard, Director Clinical Services*
*Cathy Campbell, Chief Executive Officer*

66 beds offering active/acute rehabilitation, brain injury day treatment, cognitive rehabilitation, complex care, extended rehabilitation and short term evaluation.

**9727 Transitional Learning Center at Galveston**
1528 Post Office Street
Galveston, TX 77550
409-762-6661
800-TLC-GROW
FAX: 409-763-3930

*Lee Kinard, Managed Care/Account Manager*
*Jim McCurdy, Director Business Development*

The Transitional Learning Center at Galveston has specialized in post-acute brain injury since 1982. TLC is a leader who offers comprehensive therapies in a residential setting, 24-hour monitoring, outcome focused pathways, superior staff credentials - including physician and nursing staff on-site to address medical issues, innovative clinical research integrated into treatment plans, discharge lifecare planning, and long-term living at Tideway Lodge.

**9728 Treemont**
5550 Harvest Hill Road
Dallas, TX 75230
972-661-1862
FAX: 972-715-5550

*Craig Hodges, Administrator*
Postacute rehabilitation program.

**9729 West Texas Lighthouse for the Blind**
2001 Austin Street
San Angelo, TX 76903
325-653-4231
FAX: 325-657-9367
e-mail: wtlb@wcc.net
www.lighthousefortheblind.org

*Robert Porter, Executive Director*
*Ron Beard, Operations Manager*
*Margene Hale, Office Manager*

Offers services for the totally blind, legally blind, visually impaired, mentally retarded blind and more with health, counseling, educational, recreational, rehabilitation, computer training and professional training services.

## Utah

**9730 Quincy Rehabilitation Institute of Holy Cross Hospital**
1050 E South Temple
Salt Lake City, UT 84102
801-350-8140
FAX: 801-350-4483

*Dave Jenson, President*
Postacute rehabilitation program.

**9731 Wasatch Villa**
849 E 400 S
Salt Lake City, UT 84102
801-328-2020
FAX: 801-486-0105

*Craig Kellar OD, Owner*
Postacute rehabilitation program.

## Vermont

**9732 Rutland Mental Health Services**
78 S Main Street
Rutland, VT 05701
802-775-2381
FAX: 802-747-7699

*Mark G Monson, President/CEO*

A private, non-profit comprehensive community mental health center. It provides services to individuals and families for mental health and substance abuse related problems and also to persons who are mentally retarded.

## Virginia

**9733 Bay Pine-Virginia Beach**
1148 First Colonial Road
Virginia Beach, VA 23454
757-481-3321
FAX: 757-481-4413

*David Vevoda, Administrator*
Postacute rehabilitation program.

**9734 Carilion Rehabilitation: New River Valley**
PO Box 5
Radford, VA 24143
540-731-2992
FAX: 540-731-2011
e-mail: info@carilion.com
www.carilion.com

*Jennie Smith, Clinical Team Leader*
*Rhonda Fanning, Department Secretary/Referrals*
*Robin Sutphin, Rehabilitation Assistant*

CARF-accredited pain management program, work hardening program and comprehensive outpatient therapy clinic, massage therapy, outpatient programs and more. Program emphasis is on interdisiplinary behavioral rehab based pain management and functional restoration in conjunction with medical treatment. Work hardening is a transdisciplinary work simulation program taylored to the individual. Comprehensive outpatient program is multi-disciplinary with emphasis on manual treatment.

**9735 Faith Mission Home**
3540 Mission Home Lane
Free Union, VA 22940
434-985-2294
FAX: 434-985-7633

*Merle Miller, Administrator*
*Reuben Yoder, Director*

A Christian residential center that serves 60 mentally retarded children, including individuals with Down Syndrome, Cerebral palsy and other similar conditions. Children may be admitted from the time they are ambulatory until they reach 15 years of age. He or she may stay as long as it is in the child's best interests. The training program stresses the following areas: self-care, social, academic, vocational, crafts, speech and physical development.

**9736 Pines Residential Treatment Center**
825 Crawford Parkway
Portsmouth, VA 23704
757-393-0061
FAX: 757-393-1029

*Dr. Leonard Lexier MD, Medical Director*
*Judy Kemp, Admissions Director*

A 310-bed residential treatment center in Portsmouth Virginia, providing a therapeutic environment for severely emotionally disturbed children and youth. Five unique programs meet behavioral, educational and emotional needs of males and females, five to twenty-two years of age. Multi-disciplinary teams devise individual service plans to enhance strengths and reverse self-defeating behavior. A highly effective positive reinforcement program with a proven track record.

**9737 Reach Rehabilitation Program: Manor Care**
H CR Manor Care Arlington
550 S Carlin Springs Road
Arlington, VA 22204
703-379-7200
FAX: 703-578-5524

*Marcia K Jarrell, Administrator*
*Ric Birch, Marketing Director*

Postacute rehabilitation program.

**9738 Resurrection Children's Center**
2280 N Beauregard Street
Alexandria, VA 22311
703-578-1314

*Kim Messinger, Administrative Director*

Offers children ages 2-5 with varying disabilities academic education, parent education, opportunities including classes, workshops, support groups and individual counseling.

**9739 Roanoke Memorial Hospital**
Carilion Health System
PO Box 13367
Roanoke, VA 24033
540-772-1736
FAX: 540-981-8233
e-mail: direct@carilion.com
www.carilion.com

*Beth Lindille, Director*
*Eric Carlen, President*

**9740 Southside Virginia Training Center**
PO Box 4110
Petersburg, VA 23803
804-524-7284
FAX: 804-524-7228

*Richard Buckley*
*Nirmala Vasa, MD*

Offers residential, vocational, occupational, physical, and speech therapies.

**9741 Woodrow Wilson Rehabilitation Center**
PO Box 1500
Fishersville, VA 22939
540-332-7000
800-345-9972
FAX: 540-332-7132
e-mail: colemawl@wwrc.state.va.lls
www.wwrc.net

*Greta Hodberg, Admissions Director*
*Wendell L Coleman, Volunteer Services Director*

Comprehensive residential rehabilitation center offering complete medical and vocational rehabilitation services including: vocation evaluation, vocational training, transition from school to work, occupational therapy, physical therapy, speech, language and audiology, assistive technology, rehabilitation engineering, counseling/case management, behavioral health services, nursing and physician services, etc.

# Washington

**9742 Arden Nursing Home**
16357 Aurora Avenue N
Shoreline, WA 98133
206-542-3103
FAX: 206-546-5480

*Gail Brockway, Administrator*
Postacute rehabilitation program.

**9743 Bellingham Care Center**
1200 Birchwood Avenue
Bellingham, WA 98225
360-734-9295
FAX: 360-671-4368

*Sheila Oberg, Administrator*
Postacute rehabilitation program.

**9744 Division of Vocational Rehabilitation Department of Social and Health Services**
PO Box 45340
Olympia, WA 98504
360-725-3636
800-637-5627
FAX: 360-438-8007
e-mail: krulik@dshs.wa.gov
www1.dshs.wa.gov/dvr

*Mike O Brien, Director*
*Lynnea Ruttledge, Manager*

Information on computers, supported employment, marketing rehabilitation facilities and transition.

**9745 First Hill Care Center**
21008 76th Avenue W
Edmonds, WA 98026
206-624-1484
FAX: 206-624-3090

Postacute rehabilitation program.

**9746 Harborview Medical Center, Low Vision Aid Clinic**
Harborview Medical Center
325 9th Avenue
Seattle, WA 98104
206-341-4446

*Thomas Gillette, Director*
*Susan Worden, Manager*

Offers services for the totally blind, legally blind, visually impaired, mentally retarded blind and more with health, counseling, educational, recreational, rehabilitation, computer training and professional training services.

**9747 Integrated Health Services of Seattle**

820 NW 95th Street
Seattle, WA 98117
206-783-7649
FAX: 206-781-1448

*Jerry Harvey, Administrator*
*Marlette Basada, Director Nursing*
*Flavia Lagrange, Director Admissions*

Postacute rehabilitation program. IHS provides 24 hour subacute and long-term care. We can handle vent/trach/hemo andritoneal dialysis and provide a full scope of rehabilitation services.

**9748 Intergrated Health Services**

820 NW 95th Street
Seattle, WA 98117
206-783-7649
FAX: 206-781-1448

Postacute rehabilitation program longterm acute care. Gero Psych.

**9749 Lakeside Recovery Centers**

535 Dock Street
Tacoma, WA 98402
253-272-2242
FAX: 253-272-0171

*Michael Kinder, Administrator*

**9750 Lakewood Health Care Center**

11411 Bridgeport Way SW
Tacoma, WA 98499
253-581-9002
FAX: 253-581-7016
www.kindredhealthcare.com

*Janice Olson, Admissions Coordinator*
*Patty Wood, Administrator*
*Linda Doll, Social Services*

Postacute rehabilitation program.

**9751 Manor Care Nursing: Tacoma**

5601 S Orchard Street
Tacoma, WA 98409
253-474-8421
FAX: 253-474-8172

*Robin Leitch, Administrator*

Postacute rehabilitation program.

**9752 ManorCare Health Services**

3701 188th Street SW
Lynnwood, WA 98037
425-775-9222
FAX: 425-744-1602

*Irene Dondo, Director*
*Liza Loyet, Administrator*

Postacute rehabilitation program.

**9753 ManorCare Health Services: Spokane**

6025 N Assembly Street
Spokane, WA 99205
509-326-8282
FAX: 509-326-4790

*Susan Cooper, Admissions Director*
*Sandra Hayes, Administrator*

Postacute rehabilitation program.

**9754 Northwest Continuum Care Center**
Kindred Health Care
128 Beacon Hill Drive
Longview, WA 98632
360-423-4060
FAX: 360-636-0958
www.kindred.com

*Steve Ross, Administrator*
*Tami Wilson, Director of Nursing*

Postacute rehabilitation program.

**9755 Park Manor Convalescent Center**

1710 Plaza Way
Walla Walla, WA 99362
509-529-4218
FAX: 509-522-1729

*Chris Bohnsack, Administrator*

Postacute rehabilitation program.

**9756 Queen Anne Health Care**
Queen Anne Health Care
2717 Dexter Avenue N
Seattle, WA 98109
206-284-7012
FAX: 206-283-3936

*Heather Eacker, Administrator*

Postacute rehabilitation program.

**9757 Rainier Vista Care Center**

920 12th Avenue SE
Puyallup, WA 98372
253-841-3422
FAX: 253-848-3937
www.nursing-homes.biz

*Debi Thompson, Administrator*

Postacute rehabilitation program.

**9758 Rehabilitation Enterprises of Washington**

430 E Lauridsen Boulevard
Port Angeles, WA 98362
360-452-9789
FAX: 360-452-9700
www.rewassociation.com

*Brett White, President*

REW is the professional trade association representing community rehabilitation programs before government and other publics. These organizations provide a wide array of employment and training services for people with disabilities. The goal is to assist member organizations to provide the highest quality rehabilitative and employment services to their customers.

**9759 Seattle Medical and Rehabilitation Center**
Evergreen Healthcare
12040 NE 128th Street
Kirkland, WA 98034
425-899-2267

e-mail: comment@evergreenhealthcare.org
www.evergreenhealthcare.org

*Steven E Brown, Chief Executive Officer*
*Louis Filhour, Senior Vice President*
*Matt Murray, Director Admissions*

103 beds offering subacute rehabilitation, complex care, subacute treatment and short-term evaluation. Pulmonary unit offering long and short term care for ventilator dependent patients.

**9760  Slingerland Institute for Literacy**
Educators Publishing Service
411 108th Avenue NE
Suite 2060
Bellevue, WA  98004
425-453-1190
FAX: 425-635-7762
e-mail: SlingInst@aol.com
www.slingerland.org

*Susan Heinz MD, Executive Director*
*Elyce Newton, Program Support*

A nonprofit public corporation founded in 1977 to carry on the work of Beth H. Slingerland in providing classroom teachers with the techniques, knowledge and understanding necessary for identifying and teaching children with Specific Language Disability. The main objective is to educate teachers in successful methods of identifying, diagnosing and instructing children and adults with SLD and to promote literacy through reading, writing and oral expression.

**9761  Timberland Opportunities Association**
T00 W Curtis Street
Aberdeen, WA  98520
360-533-5823
FAX: 360-533-5848

*Jim Eddy, Executive Director*

Provides training and employment for disabled people.

**9762  Vancouver Health and Rehabilitation Center**
400 E 33rd Street
Vancouver, WA  98663
360-696-2561
FAX: 360-750-0665

*Kevin Bowen, Manager*
Postacute rehabilitation program.

## West Virginia

**9763  West Virginia Rehabilitation Center**
Barron Drive
Institute, WV  25112
304-766-4600
800-642-8207
FAX: 304-766-4989
www.wvdrs.org

*Michael Meadows, Assistant Director Client*
*Bill Tanzey, Manager Center Services*
*Tracy Carr, Mgr State and Federal Relations*

The West Virginia Rehabilitation Center has been called West Virginia's best kept secret. Set on a 33-acre campus near Charleston, WV, the Center complex houses a school with 9 training areas, dormitories, a full-service rehabilitation hospital, a recreation program, a state-of-the-art assistive technology program and extension services statewide.

## Wisconsin

**9764  Colonial Manor of Wausau: Extended Rehab Services**
1010 E Wausau Avenue
Wausau, WI  54403
715-842-2028
FAX: 715-848-0510

*Terry Mantia, Administrator*
Postacute rehabilitation program.

**9765  Waushers Industries**
210 E Townline Road
Wautoma, WI  54982
920-787-4696
FAX: 920-787-4698

*Richard King, Executive Director*

**9766  Woodstock Health and Rehabilitation Center**
3415 Sheridan Road
Kenosha, WI  53140
262-657-6175
FAX: 262-657-5756
www.kindredhealthcare.com

*Steven Spencer, Executive Director*

Offers a full range of medical services to meet the individual needs of our residents, including short term rehabilitative services and long-tern skilled care.

## Alabama

**9767  Rehabilitation & Healthcare Center Of Birm ingham**
2728 10th Avenue S
Birmingham, AL  35205          205-933-7010
                              FAX: 205-933-8052

*Mary Edmonds, Administrator*

## Alaska

**9768  Fairbanks Memorial Hospital/Denali Center**
1650 Cowles Street
Fairbanks, AK  99701          907-452-8181
                              FAX: 907-458-5324

*Linda Smith, Assistant Administrator*
*Mike Powers, Chief Executive Officer*

Offers the following rehabilitation services: Physical Therapy,
Occupational Therapy, Speech Therapy, Sub-Acute Rehab.

## Arizona

**9769  Desert Life Rehabilitation & Care Center**
Kindred Healthcare
1919 W Medical Street
Tucson, AZ  85704          520-297-8311
                          FAX: 520-544-0930

*Susan Rice, Director*
*Jane Olmstead, Director of Nursing*
*Carolyn Blasi, Executive Director*

Offers the following rehabilitation services: Physical Therapy,
Occupational Therapy, Speech Therapy, Sub-Acute Rehab.

**9770  Hacienda Rehabilitation and Care Center**
660 S Coronado Drive
Sierra Vista, AZ  85635          520-459-4900

*Maria Ritter, Administrator*

Offers the following rehabilitation services: In-patient, Out-patient, Sub-Acute.

**9771  Kachina Point Health Care and Rehabilitati on Center**
505 Jacks Canyon Road
Sedona, AZ  86351          928-284-1000
                          FAX: 928-284-0626

*Christine Walker, Administrator*

Offers the following rehabilitation services: Occupational Therapy, Speech Therapy, Physical Therapy, Sub-Acute Rehab.

**9772  Mayo Clinic Scottsdale**
13400 E Shea Boulevard
Scottsdale, AZ  85259          480-301-8000
                              FAX: 480-301-4391

*Pasquale Palumbo MD*

**9773  Sonoran Rehabilitation and Care Center**
Kindred
4202 N 20th Avenue
Phoenix, AZ  85015          602-264-3824
                           FAX: 602-279-6234

*Jeffrey Barrett, Executive Director*

Offers the following rehabilitation services: Respiratory Therapy, Physical Therapy, Speech Therapy, Occupational Therapy,
Restorative Therapy, Sub-Acute Rehabilitation, Wound Care.

**9774  Valley Health Care and Rehabilitation Cent er**
Kindred Health Care Center
5545 E Lee Street
Tucson, AZ  85712          520-296-2306
                          FAX: 520-296-4072
                          www.dalleyhcr.com

*Stephanie Boatman, Executive Director*
*Sandra Lewis, Administrator*

Offers the following rehabilitation services: Physical Therapy,
Occupational Therapy, Speech Therapy, Sub-Acute Rehab.

## California

**9775  Alamitos-Belmont Rehab Hospital**
3901 E 4th Street
Long Beach, CA  90814          562-434-8421
                              FAX: 562-433-6732

*Darien Dahl, Administrator*

Offers the following rehabilitation services: Speech Therapy,
Occupational Therapy, Physical Therapy, Sub-Acute Rehab.

**9776  Bay View Nursing and Rehabilitation Center**
Kindred Health Care
516 Willow Street
Alameda, CA  94501          510-521-5600
                           FAX: 510-865-6441
                           www.kindredhealthcare.com

*Lauren Atkinson, Executive Director*
*Say Silva, Assistant Executive Director*
*Mary Webster, Administrator*

**9777  Canyonwood Nursing and Rehab Center**
2120 Benton Drive
Redding, CA  96003          530-243-6317
                           FAX: 530-243-4646

*Barbara Hutchinson, Administrator*

**9778  Foothill Nursing and Rehab Center**
People First Rehabilitation
401 W Ada Avenue
Glendora, CA  91741          626-335-9810
                            FAX: 626-914-4679
                            www.kindredhealthcare.com

*Yolanda Wilson, Chief Operating Officer*
*Marianne Schultz, Administrator*

Offers the following rehabilitation services: Physical Therapy,
Occupational Therapy, Speech Therapy, In and Out Patient
Rehab.

**9779  Long Beach Memorial Medical Center Memorial Reha-
bilitation Hospital**
2801 Atlantic Avenue
Long Beach, CA  90806          562-933-2800

*Trish Baeseman, Administrator*

The hospital offers rehabilitation after catastrophic injury of
disabling disease to give patients the opportunity for maximum
recovery. The Hospital offers many of the area's finest rehabilitation specialists and most advanced technology, making it one
of Southern California's most respected rehabilitation centers.

**9780  Mercy Medical Center Mt. Shasta**
914 Pine Street
Mount Shasta, CA  96067
530-926-6111
FAX: 530-926-0517
mtshasta.mercy.org

*Gary Blebins, Director*
*Susan Vrh, Manager*

**9781  Northridge Hospital Medical Center**
18300 Roscoe Boulevard
Northridge, CA  91325
818-885-8500

www.northridgehospital.org

*Debra Flaherty, Director Rehab Administration*
*Mike Wall, Chief Executive Officer*

Offers the following rehabilitation services: Physical Therapy, Occupational Therapy, Speech Therapy, Sub-Acute Rehab.

**9782  Riverside Community Hospital**
445 Magnolia Avenue
Riverside, CA  92501
951-788-3000
FAX: 909-788-3616
www.riversidecommunityhospital.org

*Jaime Wesolowski, Chief Executive Officer*

**9783  Saint Jude Medical Center**
101 E Valencia Mesa Drive
Fullerton, CA  92835
714-871-3280
FAX: 714-992-3029
www.stjudemedicalcenter.org

*Winkie Sonnefield, Director for Physical Therapy*
*Robert Fraschetti, Chief Executive Officer*

Offers the following rehabilitation services: Out-patient Rehab, Sub-Acute Rehab, Occupational Therapy, Physical Therapy, Speech and Audiology Therapy, Pain Management Program.

**9784  South Coast Medical Center**
31872 Coast Highway
Laguna Beach, CA  92651
949-499-1311
FAX: 949-499-8644
e-mail: info@southcoastmedcenter.com
www.southcoastmedcenter.com

*Nancy Boerner, Director*
*Bruce Christian, President*

Offers the following services: physical therapy, occupational therapy, speech therapy, cardica rehabilitation, incontinence program, sub-acute rehabilitation.

**9785  Valley Garden Health Care and Rehabilitati on Center**
1517 Knickerbocker Drive
Stockton, CA  95210
209-957-4539
FAX: 209-957-5831

*Keith Braley, Administrator*

## Colorado

**9786  Boulder Community Hospital Mapleton Center**
311 Mapleton Avenue
Boulder, CO  80304
303-443-0230

e-mail: publicinformation@bch.org
www.bch.org

*Ron Secrist, President*

Offers comprehensive rehabilitation services for individuals of all ages on both an inpatient and outpatient basis. Specialty programs include brain injury, chronic pain management, and pediatric rehabilitation.

**9787  Fairacres Manor**
1700 18th Avenue
Greeley, CO  80631
970-353-3370
FAX: 970-353-9347
www.fairacresmanor.com

*Kathy Mekelburg, Administrator*

Offers the following rehabilitation services: Physical Therapy, Occupational Therapy, Speech Therapy, Restorative Therapy, Skilled Nursing, and Sub-Acute Rehabilitation.

**9788  Rowan Community**
4601 E Asbury Circle
Denver, CO  80222
303-757-1228
FAX: 303-759-3390
www.pinonmgt.com

*Maxine Roby, Administrator*

Sixty bed skilled nursing facility in southwest Denver, serving younger residents with multiple sclerosis traumatic brain injury, chronic mental illness, 24 hour care need behavior.

## Connecticut

**9789  Hamilton Rehabilitation and Healthcare Cen ter**
89 Viets Street
New London, CT  06320
860-889-8358
FAX: 860-889-0395

*Jim Christofori, Administrator*

Offers the following rehabilitation services: Sub-Acute, Occupational Therapy, Speech Therapy, Physical Therapy.

**9790  Hospital For Special Care**
2150 Corbin Avenue
New Britain, CT  06053
860-223-2761
FAX: 860-832-6236
e-mail: info@hfsc.org
www.hfsc.org

*John Votto, President/CEO*

**9791  Masonic Healthcare Center**
MasoniCare Corporation
22 Masonic Avenue
Wallingford, CT  06492
203-284-8764
800-982-3919
FAX: 203-679-6427
www.masonicare.org

*William Piper, Vice President*
*Arthur Santilli, President*

**9792  Stamford Hospital**
30 Shelburne Road
Stamford, CT  06902
203-276-7595
FAX: 203-325-7905

*Dorothy Turnbull MD*

**9793  Windsor Rehabilitation and Healthcare Cent er**
581 Poquonock Avenue
Windsor, CT  06095
860-688-7211
FAX: 860-688-6715

*Laurie Tillestie, Director*
*Melissa Romano, Admissions*
*Jim Fidanza, Administrator*

Offers the following rehabilitation services: Physical Therapy, Occupational Therapy, Speech Therapy, Sub-Acute Rehabilitation

## Delaware

**9794   Arbors at New Castle Subacute and Rehab Ce nter**
32 Buena Vista Drive
New Castle, DE  19720
302-328-2580
FAX: 302-328-2036

*Leigh Weber, Administrator*

Offers the following rehabilitation services: Sub-Acute Rehab, Occupational Therapy, Physical Therapy, Speech Therapy.

## Florida

**9795   Boca Raton Rehabilitation Center**
755 Meadows Road
Boca Raton, FL  33486
561-391-5200
FAX: 561-391-0685
e-mail: dbuck@filtc.com

*Diana Buck LPN, Admissions Director*
*Tracey Dougherty, Administrator*

Offers the following rehabilitation services: Occupational Therapy, Speech Therapy, Physical Therapy, Sub-Acute Rehabilitation

**9796   Evergreen Woods Health and Rehabilitation Center**
7045 Evergreen Woods Trail
Spring Hill, FL  34608
352-596-8371
FAX: 352-596-8032

*Maria Seger, Administrator*

Offers the following rehabilitation services: Sub-Acute rehabilitation, Occupational therapy, Speech pathology therapy, Physical therapy.

**9797   Healthcare and Rehabilitation Center of Sanford**
950 S Mellonville Avenue
Sanford, FL  32771
407-322-8566
FAX: 407-322-0121

*David Hunt, Administrator*
*Vicky Smith, Director Admissions*

Offers the following rehabilitation services: Sub-Acute rehab, Stroke rehab, Cardiac rehab, Orthopedic rehab, Occupational therapy, Speech therapy, Physical therapy for long term care.

**9798   Highland Pines Rehabilitation Center**
1111 S Highland Avenue
Clearwater, FL  33756
727-446-0581
FAX: 727-442-9425

*Jena Carpenter, Administrator*

Offers the following rehabilitation services: Sub-Acute rehabilitation, Occupational Therapy, Speech Therapy, Physical Therapy.

**9799   Jupiter Medical Center-Pavilion**
1210 S Old Dixie Highway
Jupiter, FL  33458
561-747-2234
FAX: 561-743-5042

*Jay Mikosch, Administrator*
*R Barry, Chief Executive Officer*

Offers the following rehabilitation services: Sub-Acute Rehabilitation, Occupational Therapy, Speech Therapy, Physical Therapy.

**9800   Kindred Rehab**
Senior Health Management
401 E Sample Road
Pompano Beach, FL  33064
954-941-4100
FAX: 954-941-4233
www.slcare.com

*Jeff Naubaum, Administrator*

Offers the following rehabilitation services: Sub-Acute rehabilitation, Physical Therapy, Occupational Therapy, Speech Therapy, Respiratory Therapy.

**9801   Oaks at Avon Nursing and Rehabilitation Ce nter**
1010 Us 27 N
Avon Park, FL  33825
863-453-5200
FAX: 863-453-5308

*Juanita Ullman, Administrator*

Offers the following rehabilitation services: Sub-Acute rehabilitation, Occupational Therapy, Speech Therapy, Physical Therapy.

**9802   Pompano Rehabilitation and Nursing Center**
Senior Health Care Management
51 W Sample Road
Pompano Beach, FL  33064
954-941-5225
FAX: 954-942-0941

*Teggy Jarmolych, Administrator*
*Elaine Daniels, Director of Nursing*

Offers the following rehabilitation services: Sub-Acute Rehabilitation, Physical Therapy, Occupational Therapy, Speech Therapy

**9803   Rehabilitation Center of the Palm Beaches**
301 Northpoint Parkway
West Palm Beach, FL  33407
561-712-1717
FAX: 561-712-1118

*Amy Roberts, Administrator*

Offers the following rehabilitation services: Sub-Acute Rehabilitation, Physical Therapy, Occupational Therapy, Speech Therapy

**9804   Rehabilitation and Healthcare Center Of Ca pe Coral**
2629 Del Prado Boulevard S
Cape Coral, FL  33904
239-574-4434
FAX: 239-574-6968

*Joann Hodges, Administrator*

**9805   Rehabilitation and Healthcare Center of Ta mpa**
4411 N Habana Avenue
Tampa, FL  33614
813-872-2771
FAX: 813-871-2831

*Kate Hawk, Administrator*
*Melanie Cloud, Manager*

Offers the following rehabilitation services: Sub-Acute Rehabilitation, Physical Therapy, Occupational Therapy, Speech Therapy, Respiratory Therapy.

**9806   Shands Rehab Hospital**
8900 NW 39th Avenue
Gainesville, FL  32606
352-265-5491
FAX: 352-265-5430
org/find/service/rehab/

*Marina Cecchini, Director*
*Linda Brown, Director Marketing*

Offers the following rehabilitation services: Sub-acute rehabilitation, traumatic brain injury, spinal cord injury, stroke, degenerative neurological conditions, amputations, burns, organ transplantation.

**9807  St. Anthony's Hospital**
1200 7th Avenue N
St Petersburg, FL 33705          727-825-1040

www.stanthonys.com

*Angelo Cappelli, Chairman*
*Bill Kent, Director*

Offers the following rehabilitation services: Sub-Acute rehabilitation, Occupational Therapy, Speech/Language Pathology services, Physical Therapy.

**9808  Winkler Court**
3250 Winkler Avenue Ext
Fort Myers, FL 33916          239-939-4993
FAX: 239-939-1743

*Ed Shoman, Administrator*

Offers the following rehabilitation services: Sub-Acute Rehabilitation, Physical Therapy, Speech Therapy, Occupational Therapy.

**9809  Winter Park Memorial Hospital**
200 N Lakemont Avenue
Winter Park, FL 32792          407-646-7001
FAX: 407-646-7639
e-mail: healthcare@winterparkhospital.com
www.winterparkhospital.com

*Terry Barter, Director Rehabilitation*
*Ken Bradley, Chief Executive Officer*

Offers the following rehabilitation services: Sub-Acute Rehabilitation, Occupational Therapy, Speech Pathology, Physical Therapy.

## Georgia

**9810  Athena Rehab of Clayton**
2055 Rex Road
Lake City, GA 30260          404-361-1028
FAX: 404-363-6366
www.kindered.com

*Reginald Washington, Administrator*

Offers the following rehabilitation services: Sub-Acute rehabilitation, Occupational therapy, Speech therapy, Physical therapy, Restorative care.

**9811  Lafayette Nursing and Rehabilitation Cente r**
110 Brandywine Boulevard
Fayetteville, GA 30214          770-461-2928
FAX: 770-461-8507

*Jo Brooks, Executive Director*
*Virginia Tarr, Assistant Director*

Offers the following rehabilitation services: Sub-Acute rehabilitation, Physical Therapy, Occupational Therapy, Speech Therapy.

**9812  Savannah Rehabilitation and Nursing Center**
815 E 63rd Street
Savannah, GA 31405          912-352-8615
FAX: 912-355-4642

*Lettie Wilson, Administrator*

Offers the following rehabilitation services: Sub-Acute rehabilitation, Physical Therapy, Occupational Therapy, Speech Therapy

**9813  Specialty Hospital**
PO Box 233
Rome, GA 30162          706-802-2000
FAX: 706-802-2123

*Jon Dixon, Chief Executive Officer*
*Kurt Stuenkel, President*

Offers the following rehabilitation services: Sub-Acute rehabilitation, Physical Therapy, Occupational Therapy, Speech Therapy.

**9814  Walton Rehabilitation Hospital**
PO Box 2223
Augusta, GA 30903          706-823-8511
866-492-5866
FAX: 706-724-5752
e-mail: postmaster@wrh.org
www.wrh.org

*Dennis Skelley, President*
*Frank Lewis, Chief Operating Officer*
*Mike Harrell, CFO*

Has Centers of Excellence in Stroke Brain Injury, Complex Orthopedics, Spinal Cord Injury and Pain Management. 58-bed nonprofit facility.

**9815  Warner Robins Rehabilitation and Nursing C enter**
1601 Elberta Road
Warner Robins, GA 31093          478-922-2241
FAX: 478-328-1984
www.warnerrobinsrehab.com

*David Thorton, Administrator*

Offers the following rehabilitation services: Sub-Acute rehabilitation, Physical Therapy, Occupational Therapy, Speech Therapy.

## Hawaii

**9816  Aloha Nursing and Rehab Center**
45-545 Kamehameha Highway
Kaneohe, HI 96744          808-247-2220
FAX: 808-235-3676
www.alohanursing.com

*Charles Harris, Executive Director*
*Donna Wong, Administrator*

## Idaho

**9817  Eastern Idaho Regional Medical Center**
3100 Channing Way
Idaho Falls, ID 83404          208-529-6111
FAX: 208-529-7021
www.eirmc.com

*Doug Crabtree, Chief Executive Officer*

**9818  Emmett Rehabilitation and Healthcare**
Kindred Healthcare
714 N Butte Avenue
Emmett, ID 83617          208-365-4425
FAX: 208-365-6989

*John Schulikn, Executive Director*

Offers the following rehabilitation services: Sub-acute rehab, physical therapy, occupational therapy, speech therapy.

**9819 Hillcrest Rehabilitation and Care Center**
1001 S Hilton Street
Boise, ID 83705 208-345-4464
FAX: 208-345-2998
www.kindredhealthcare.com

*Nolan Hoffer, Administrator*

Offers the following rehabilitation services: Sub-acute rehabilitation, occupational therapy, speech therapy, physical therapy.

**9820 Lewiston Rehabilitation and Care Center**
3315 8th Street
Lewiston, ID 83501 208-743-9543
FAX: 208-743-3945

*Debbie Freeze, Director*

Offers the following rehabilitation services: Sub-acute rehabilitation, physical therapy, occupational therapy, speech therapy.

**9821 Mountain Valley Care and Rehabilitation Ce nter**
Kindred
601 W Cameron Avenue
Kellogg, ID 83837 208-784-1283

*Maryruth Butler, Administrator*

## Illinois

**9822 Chevy Chase Nursing and Rehabilitation Cen ter**
3400 S Indiana Avenue
Chicago, IL 60616 312-842-5000
FAX: 312-842-3790

*Barbara Casey, Administrator*

Offers the following rehabilitation services: Sub-acute rehabilitation, physical therapy, occupational therapy, speech therapy.

**9823 Glenview Terrace Nursing Center**
1511 Greenwood Road
Glenview, IL 60026 847-729-9090
FAX: 847-729-9135
www.glenviewterrace.com

*Amy Salzman, Administrator*

**9824 Halsted Terrace Nursing Center**
10935 S Halsted Street
Chicago, IL 60628 773-928-2000
FAX: 773-928-9154

*Bonnie Williams, Administrator*

Offers the following rehabilitation services: Sub-acute rehabilitation, physical therapy, occupational therapy, speech therapy, cardiac rehabilitation.

**9825 Harmony Nursing and Rehabilitation Center**
3919 W Foster Avenue
Chicago, IL 60625 773-588-9500
FAX: 773-588-9533

*John Sianghio, Administrator*

**9826 Imperial**
1366 W Fullerton Avenue
Chicago, IL 60614 773-248-9300
FAX: 773-935-0036

*David Hartman, Administrator*

Offers the following rehabilitation services: Sub-acute rehabilitation, physical therapy, occupational therapy, speech therapy.

**9827 Jackson Square Nursing and Rehabilitation Center**
5130 W Jackson Boulevard
Chicago, IL 60644 773-287-1429
FAX: 773-928-3980

*Farhat Sharif, Administrator*

Offers the following rehabilitation services: Sub-acute rehabilitation, physical therapy, occupational therapy, speech therapy.

**9828 Renaissance at 87th Street**
2940 W 87th Street
Chicago, IL 60652 773-434-8787
FAX: 773-434-8717

*Tom Smith, Administrator*

Offers the following rehabilitation services: Sub-acute rehabilitation, occupational therapy, physical therapy, speech therapy.

**9829 Renaissance at Hillside**
4600 Frontage Road
Hillside, IL 60162 708-544-9933
FAX: 708-544-9966

*Colleen Kamin, Administrator*

Offers the following rehabilitation services: Sub-acute rehabilitation, physical therapy, occupational therapy, speech therapy.

**9830 Renaissance at Midway**
4437 S Cicero Avenue
Chicago, IL 60632 773-884-0484
FAX: 773-884-0485

*Robin Harris, VP Marketing*
*Debra Kroner, Director Admissions*
*Mark Berger, Executive Director*

**9831 Renaissance at South Shore**
2425 E 71st Street
Chicago, IL 60649 773-721-5000
FAX: 773-721-6850

*David Schecter, Administrator*
*Benitta Harris, Human Resources Executive*

Offers the following rehabilitation services: Sub-acute rehabilitation, physical therapy, occupational therapy, speech therapy.

**9832 Schwab Rehabilitation Hospital**
Mt. Sinai
1401 S California Avenue
Chicago, IL 60608 773-522-2010

www.sinai.org/rehabilitation/

*Suzan Rayner MD, Medical Director*
*Judith Waterston, Chief Executive Officer*

Treats medically stable patients who require nursing and medical care that cannot be supplied at home, in an outpatient facility or in a nursing home. Treats stroke patients, amputees, individuals with brain injuries, burns, diabets and spinal cord injuries.

## Indiana

**9833 Angel River Health and Rehabilitation**
5233 Rosebud Lane
Newburgh, IN 47630 812-473-4761
FAX: 812-473-5190

*Kay Congleton, Administrator*

Offers the following rehabilitation services: Sub-acute rehabilitation, speech therapy, occupational therapy, physical therapy.

**9834 Chalet Village Health and Rehabilitation C enter**

1065 Parkway Street
Berne, IN 46711        260-589-2127
FAX: 260-589-3521

*Steven Schaaf, Administrator*

Offers the following rehabilitation services: Sub-acute rehabilitation, physical therapy, occupational therapy, speech therapy, respiratory therapy.

**9835 Columbus Health and Rehabilitation Center**

2100 Midway Street
Columbus, IN 47201        812-372-8447
FAX: 812-375-5117

*Mike Spencer, Executive Director*

**9836 Harrison Health and Rehabilitation Centre**

150 Beechmont Drive NE
Corydon, IN 47112        812-738-0550
FAX: 812-738-6273

*Inez Voyles, Administrator*

Offers the following rehabilitation services: Sub-Acute rehabilitation, speech therapy, physical therapy, occupational therapy.

**9837 Indian Creek Health and Rehabilitation Center**

240 Beechmont Drive NE
Corydon, IN 47112        812-738-8127
877-380-7211
FAX: 812-738-2917
e-mail: sherry.leclair@kindredhealthcare.com
www.indiancreekhealthcare.com

*Marianne Keller, Administrator*
*Sherry LeClair, Admissions Director*
*Bonnie Fallin, Executive Director*

140 bed facility offering the following rehabilitation services: Sub-Acute rehabilitation, Physical therapy, Occupational Therapy, Speech Therapy, pain management, Wound rehabilitation. Short and long term skilled nursing care certified for Medicare, Medicaid, Private Pay and Private Insurance. Hospice and respite care rated #1 in clinical care in southern Indiana district for 2002.

**9838 Meadowvale Health and Rehabilitation Cente r**

Kindred Health Care
1529 Lancaster Street
Bluffton, IN 46714        260-824-4320
FAX: 260-824-4689
e-mail: meadowvalehealth@kindredhealthcare.com
www.kindredhealthcare.com

*Sally Sharp, Executive Director*

Offers the following rehabilitation services: Sub-acute rehabilitation, physical therapy, occupational therapy, speech therapy.

**9839 Muncie Health Care and Rehabilitation**

4301 N Walnut Street
Muncie, IN 47303        765-282-0053
FAX: 765-282-3290
www.kindred.com

*Debbie Anderson, Administrator*

Offers the following rehabilitation services: Sub-Acute rehabilitation, physical therapy, occupational therapy, speech therapy.

**9840 Rehabilitation Hospital of Indiana**

4141 Shore Drive
Indianapolis, IN 46254        317-329-2000
FAX: 317-329-2104
www.rhin.com

*Dennis Armington, CEO*
*Nancy Stover, Director Operations*

Offers the following rehabilitation services: Sub-acute rehabilitation, brain injury, spinal cord injury programs.

**9841 Sellersburg Health and Rehabilitation Cent re**

7823 Old State Road 60
Sellersburg, IN 47172        812-246-4272
FAX: 812-246-8160

*Donna Thomas, Director of Nursing*
*Chris Hansen, Executive Director*

**9842 Westpark Rehabilitation Center**

25 S Boehne Camp Road
Evansville, IN 47712        812-423-7468
FAX: 812-423-7568

*Lara Beck, Administrator*

Offers the following rehabilitation services: Sub-acute rehabilitation, occupational therapy, physical therapy, speech therapy, respiratory therapy.

**9843 Westview Nursing and Rehabilitation Center**

1510 Clinic Drive
Bedford, IN 47421        812-279-4494
FAX: 812-275-8313

*Sandi Harpe*
*Mike Spencer, Executive Director*

Offers the following rehabilitation services: Sub-acute rehabilitation, physical therapy, occupational therapy, speech therapy.

**9844 Windsor Estates Health and Rehab Center**

429 W Lincoln Road
Kokomo, IN 46902        765-453-5600
FAX: 765-455-0110

*Jeff Hayne, Administrator*

---

# Iowa

---

**9845 Madison County Rehab Services**

Madison County Hospital
300 W Hutchings Street
Winterset, IA 50273        515-462-2373
FAX: 515-462-5108

*Marcia Jones, Utilization Review Nurse*
*Panndee Stebbins, Director*
*Andrea Miner, Manager*

Offers the following rehabilitation services: Sub-acute rehabilitation, occupational therapy, physical therapy, speech therapy, home health rehab, wellness programs.

**9846 Mercy Subacute Care**

603 E 12th Street
Des Moines, IA 50309        515-247-4400
FAX: 515-643-8871

*Bonnie McCoy, Administrator*
*Pam Nelson, Intake Coordinator*

Offers the following rehabilitation services: Sub-acute rehabilitation, physical therapy, speech therapy, occupational therapy.

# Rehabilitation Facilities, Sub-Acute /Kentucky

## Kentucky

**9847    Danville Centre for Health and Rehabilitat ion**
642 N 3rd Street
Danville, KY  40422                  859-236-3972
                                     FAX: 859-236-0033

*Jennifer Phillips, Administrator*
Offers the following rehabilitation services: Sub-acute rehabilitation, physical therapy, occupational therapy, speech therapy.

**9848    Lexington Center for Health and Rehabilita tion**
353 Waller Avenue
Lexington, KY  40504                 859-252-3558
                                     FAX: 859-233-0192

*Melissa Lammoore, Administrator*
Offers the following rehabilitation services: Sub-acute rehabilitation, speech therapy, occupational therapy, physical therapy.

**9849    Paducah Centre For Health and Rehabilitati on**
Wellsouth Health Systems
501 N 3rd Street
Paducah, KY  42001                   270-444-9661
                                     FAX: 270-443-9407

*Terri Humes, Director*

**9850    Pathways Brain Injury Program**
4200 Browns Lane
Louisville, KY  40220                502-459-8900
                                     FAX: 502-459-5026

*Pam Pearson, Program Director*
Offers the following rehabilitation services: Sub-acute rehabilitation, speech therapy, occupational therapy, physical therapy, recreational therapy.

**9851    Winchester Centre For Health and Rehabilit ation**
200 Glenway Road
Winchester, KY  40391                859-744-1800
                                     FAX: 859-744-0285

*Robert Hollins, Administrator*
Offers the following rehabilitation services: Sub-acute rehabilitation, speech therapy, physical therapy, occupational therapy.

## Louisiana

**9852    Guest House of Slidell Sub-Acute and Rehab Center**
1051 Robert Boulevard
Slidell, LA  70458                   985-643-5630
                                     800-303-9872
                                     FAX: 985-649-6065
                                     e-mail: jburch@ghslidell.com

*Linda Rogers, Administrator*
116 bed healthcare center offering the following subacute services within the skilled nursing setting: physical, occupational, and speech therapies, infusion therapy, respiratory care, wound care, neurological rehabilitation, cardiac reconditioning, pain management, post surgical recovery, orthopedic rehabilitation.

**9853    Irving Place Rehabilitation and Nursing Ce nter**
1736 Irving Place
Shreveport, LA  71101                318-221-1983
                                     FAX: 318-222-2095

*Linda Johnson, Administrator*

## Maine

**9854    Augusta Rehabilitation Center**
188 Eastern Avenue
Augusta, ME  04330                   207-622-3121
                                     FAX: 207-623-7666
                                     www.hospital.soup.com

*Carolyn Deblasi, Acting Administrator*
*Beth Whitcomb, Finance Executive*

**9855    Brentwood Rehabilitation and Nursing Cente r**
122 Portland Street
Yarmouth, ME  04096                  207-846-9021
                                     FAX: 207-846-1479

*Laurie Farren, Executive Director*

**9856    Den-Mar Rehabilitation and Nursing Center**
44 South Street
Rockport, MA  01966                  978-546-6311

*Tricia Shaw, Executive Director*

**9857    Eastside Rehabilitation and Living Center**
516 Mount Hope Avenue
Bangor, ME  04401                    207-947-6131
                                     FAX: 207-942-0884

*Michael Speidel, Executive Director*

**9858    Kennebunk Nursing and Rehabilitation Cente r**
158 Ross Road
Kennebunk, ME  04043                 207-985-7141
                                     FAX: 207-985-1946

*Thomas Foran, Administrator*

**9859    Norway Rehabilitation and Living Center**
29 Marion Avenue
Norway, ME  04268                    207-743-7075
                                     FAX: 207-743-9269

*Carolyn Farley, Administrator*

**9860    Shore Village Rehabilitation and Nursing C enter**
201 Camden Street
Rockland, ME  04841                  207-596-6423
                                     FAX: 207-596-7751

*Phyllis Nickerson, Administrator*

## Maryland

**9861    Greater Baltimore Medical Center**
6701 N Charles Street
Baltimore, MD  21204                 443-849-2000
                                     FAX: 443-849-3024

*Laurence Merlis, Chief Executive Officer*

927

## Massachusetts

**9862  Bolton Manor Nursing Home**
400 Bolton Street
Marlborough, MA  01752                508-481-6123
                                  FAX: 508-481-6130

*Scott Bullock, Administrator*

**9863  Brigham Manor Nursing and Rehabilitation C enter**
77 High Street
Newburyport, MA  01950               978-462-4221
                                  FAX: 978-463-3297

*Christine Rich, Administrator*

**9864  Country Gardens Skilled Nursing and Rehabilitation Center**
2045 Grand Army Highway
Swansea, MA  02777                   508-379-9700
                                  FAX: 508-379-0723
                          www.countrygardensnursing.com

*John Corliss, Administrator*

**9865  Country Manor Rehabilitation and Nursing C enter**
180 Low Street
Newburyport, MA  01950               978-465-5361
                                  FAX: 978-463-9366

*Shari Laroche, Administrator*

**9866  Franklin Skilled Nursing and Rehabilitation Center**
130 Chestnut Street
Franklin, MA  02038                  508-528-4600
                                  FAX: 508-528-7976

*Karen Wadlow, Administrator*

**9867  Great Barrington Rehabilitation and Nursing Center**
148 Maple Avenue
Great Barrington, MA  01230          413-528-3320
                                  FAX: 413-528-2302

*Carolyn Sammons, Executive Director*

**9868  Ledgewood Rehabilitation and Skilled Nursi ng Center**
87 Herrick Street
Beverly, MA  01915                   978-921-1392
                                  FAX: 978-927-8627

*Laurie Roberto, Administrator*

**9869  Leo P La Chance Center for Rehabilitation and Nursing**

59 Eastwood Circle
Gardner, MA  01440                   978-632-8776
                                  FAX: 978-632-5048

*Dennis Lopata, Administrator*

**9870  Oakwood Rehabilitation and Nursing Center**
11 Pontiac Avenue
Webster, MA  01570                   508-943-3889
                                  FAX: 508-949-6125

*Daniel O'Neil, Administrator*

**9871  Walden Rehabilitation and Nursing Center**
785 Main Street
Concord, MA  01742                   978-369-6889
                                  FAX: 978-369-8392

*Dan Burns, Administrator*

## Michigan

**9872  Boulder Park Terrace**
14676 W Upright Street
Charlevoix, MI  49720                231-547-1005
                                  FAX: 231-547-1039
                               www.northernhealth.org

*Saur Mackenzie, Director*
*Deb Saur-Macenzie, Administrator*

## Minnesota

**9873  Park Health And Rehabilitation Center**
4415 W 36 1/2 Street
St Louis Park, MN  55416             952-927-9717
                                  FAX: 952-927-7687

*Jennifer Kuhn, Administrator*

## Missouri

**9874  Barnes-Jewish Hospital Washington University Medical Center**
1 Barnes Jewish Hospital Plaza
Saint Louis, MO  63110               314-747-3000
                                  FAX: 314-286-0305
                               www.barnesjewish.org

*Steven Lipstein, President*

## Montana

**9875  Parkview Acres Care and Rehabilitation Cen ter**
200 N Oregon Street
Dillon, MT  59725                    406-683-5105
                                  FAX: 406-683-6388

*Jake Bowen, Administrator*

## Nebraska

**9876  Homestead Healthcare and Rehabilitation Ce nter**
4735 S 54th Street
Lincoln, NE  68516                   402-488-0977
                                  FAX: 402-488-4507
                            www.homesteadhealthcare.com

*Connie Crawford, Director*
*David Pettijohn, Administrator*

**9877  Madonna Rehabilitation Hospital**
5401 South Street
Lincoln, NE  68506                   402-483-9531
                                  FAX: 402-486-8285
                                  www.madonna.org

*Marsha Lommel, President/CEO*
*Kiranmayi Chilappa, MD*

Patients who need only one or two types of therapy for a specific condition are served in the subacute program. Patients who have a diagnosis suggesting a positive course of recovery are typical for the subacute level of care.

**9878 Mary Lanning Memorial Hospital**
715 N Saint Joseph Avenue
Hastings, NE 68901            402-463-4521
                             866-460-5884
                    e-mail: tanderson@mlmh.org
                             www.mlmh.org

*Michael Kearney, President*
*Mark Vincent, Vice President*
*W Kearney, Chief Executive Officer*

## Nevada

**9879 Las Vegas Healthcare and Rehabilitation Ce nter**
2832 S Maryland Parkway
Las Vegas, NV 89109          702-735-5848
                        FAX: 702-735-6218
                    www.lasvegaskindred.com

*Randall Fuller, Administrator*

## New Hampshire

**9880 Dover Rehabilitation and Living Center**
307 Plaza Drive
Dover, NH 03820              603-742-2676
                        FAX: 603-749-5375

*Jill Bosa, Administrator*

**9881 Northeast Rehabilitation Clinic**
70 Butler Street
Salem, NH 03079             603-893-2900
                            800-825-7292
                        FAX: 603-893-1628
                    www.northeastrehab.com

*John Prochilo, Executive Director*
*Tom Prince, Administrator Officer*

Subacute rehabilitation at NRH was designed for people who have experienced an acutely disabling orthopedic, medical, or neurologic condition but who either do not require or are unable to participate in a full acute inpatient program. Impairment groups pertinent to this level of care include brain injury, spinal cord injury (traumatic/non-traumatic), stroke, orthopedic injury, amputation, and neurologic disorder.

## New Jersey

**9882 Atlantic Coast Rehabilitation & Healthcare Center**
485 River Avenue
Lakewood, NJ 08701           732-364-7100
                        FAX: 732-364-2442
              e-mail: info@atlanticcoastrehab.com
                    www.atlanticcoastrehab.com

*Simon Shain, Administrator*
*Sharon Sckbower, Director of Nursing*

Offers the following rehabilitation services: Sub-acute rehab, physical therapy, occupational therapy, speech therapy.

**9883 Crestwood Nursing and Rehabilitation Cente r**
101 Whippany Road
Whippany, NJ 07981           973-887-0311
                        FAX: 973-887-8355

*Carol Shepard, Administrator*

**9884 Lakeview Subacute Care Center**
130 Terhune Drive
Wayne, NJ 07470              973-839-4501
                        FAX: 973-616-3409
                    www.lakeviewsubacute.com

*Richard Grosso, Executive Director*
*Susan R Ahlers, Director of Admission*

Offers physical therapy, occupational therapy, speech therapy, recreational therapy, respiratory therapy, aqua therapy. 68-bed subacute unit.

**9885 Merwick Rehabilitation and Sub-Acute Care**
79 Bayard Lane
Princeton, NJ 08540          609-497-3000
                        FAX: 609-497-3024
                             www.mcp.org

*Kathy Ales, Medical Director*
*Ryan Wismer, Administrator*

76-bed skilled nursing and residential center as well as a separate 17-bed comprehensive rehabilitation center. Offers rehabilitation, physiatry, occupational therapy, respite care, speech/hearing therapy, sub-acute care.

**9886 Seacrest Village Nursing Center**
1001 Center Street
Little Egg Harbor Twp, NJ 08087      609-296-9292
                            FAX: 609-296-0508
                 e-mail: info@seacrestvillagenj.com
                      www.seacrestvillagenj.com

*Brian T Holloway, Administrator*

**9887 St. Lawrence Rehabilitation Center**
2384 Lawrenceville Road
Lawrenceville, NJ 08648      609-896-9500
                        FAX: 609-895-0242

*Charles Brennan, Chief Executive Officer*

**9888 Summit Ridge Center Genesis Eldercare**
20 Summit Street
West Orange, NJ 07052        973-736-2000
                            800-699-1520
                        FAX: 973-731-4582
                             www.ghv.com

*Chad Murin, Administrator*
*Elizabeth Martin, Customer Relations Manager*

Skilled nursing facility with a total of 152 beds. 40 bed sub-acute unit and 24 bed secure dementia unit. Able to care for a wide variety of rehab and medical cases from orthopedics to TPN and tracheostomies.

## New York

**9889 Beth Abraham Health Services**
612 Allerton Avenue
Bronx, NY 10467              718-519-0152
                             888-238-4223
                        FAX: 718-519-4010
                    e-mail: info@bethabe.org
                             www.bethabe.org

*Michael Fassler, Chief Executive Officer*

Offers the following rehabilitation services: Sub-Acute rehabilitation, brain injury rehabilitation, pain management, post-operative recovery. Home visits and a network of community-based programs help patients and their families with a successful transition home.

**9890 Central Island Healthcare**
825 Old Country Road
Plainview, NY 11803      516-433-0600
FAX: 516-868-7251
www.centralislandhealthcare.net

*Scott Wheeler, Administrator*

**9891 Clove Lakes Health Care and Rehabilitation Center**
25 Fanning Street
Staten Island, NY 10314    718-289-7900
FAX: 718-761-8701

*Helen Demisay, Chief Executive Officer*
*M Gemisay, Executive Director*

**9892 Dr. William O Benenson Rehabilitation Pavi lion**
3617 Parsons Boulevard
Flushing, NY 11354    718-445-3539
FAX: 718-939-5032

*Richard Sherman, Administrator*

**9893 Flushing Manor Nursing and Rehab**
3515 Parsons Boulevard
Flushing, NY 11354    718-961-3500
FAX: 718-461-1784
e-mail: jenella.nh@flushingmanors.com
www.flushingmanors.com

*Jerry Enella, Administrator*
*Esther Benenson, Owner*
Skilled nursing facility and subacute rehabilitation.

**9894 Glengariff Health Care Center**
Dosoris Lane
Glen Cove, NY 11542    516-676-1100
FAX: 516-759-0216
e-mail: info@glenhaven.org
www.glenhaven.org

*Jean Campo, Director Admissions*
*Michael Miness, President*
Licensed skilled nursing and subacute medical and rehabilitation facility.

**9895 Haym Salomon Home for Nursing and Rehab**
2340 Cropsey Avenue
Brooklyn, NY 11214    718-373-1700
FAX: 718-449-9028

*Haym Lipschupv, Administrator*

**9896 Kings Harbor Multicare Center**
2000 E Gun Hill Road
Bronx, NY 10469    718-320-0400
FAX: 718-320-0557
e-mail: info@kingsharbor.com
www.kingsharbor.com

*Morris Tenenbaum, Owner*

**9897 Northwoods of Cortland**
28 Kellogg Road
Cortland, NY 13045    607-753-9631
FAX: 607-756-2968

*Amy Simrell, Yucca Executive Director*
*Dorothy Zegarelli, Administrator*

**9898 Port Jefferson Health Care Facility**
Dark Hollow Road
Port Jefferson, NY 11777    631-473-5400
FAX: 631-474-5362
e-mail: info@glenhaven.org
www.glenhaven.org

*Anne Kohlmann, Director Admissions*
*Kathy Peets, VP Corporate/External Affairs*
*Ellen Harte, Administrator*
Subacute medical and rehabilitative care and long term residential skilled nursing care.

**9899 Rehab Institute at Florence Nightingale He alth Center**
1760 3rd Avenue
New York, NY 10029    212-410-8760
800-786-8968
FAX: 212-410-8792
e-mail: info@rehabinstitute.org

**9900 Schnurmacher Center for Rehabilitation and Nursing**
Beth Abraham of Family Health Services
12 Tibbits Avenue
White Plains, NY 10606    914-287-7200
888-238-4223
FAX: 914-428-1216
e-mail: info@bethabe.org
www.bethabe.org

*Karen Nodiff, Director Admissions*
*Diane McKillop, Director Nursing*
*Karen Kaplan Blick, Director Social Services*

**9901 South Shore Healthcare**
275 W Merrick Road
Freeport, NY 11520    516-623-4000
FAX: 516-868-7251
www.southshorehealthcare.net

*Cathie Geraghty, Administrator*

**9902 St. Camillus Health and Rehabilitation Cen ter**
813 Fay Road
Syracuse, NY 13219    315-488-2951
FAX: 315-488-3255
www.st-camillus.org

*Aileen Balitz, President*

## North Carolina

**9903 Chapel Hill Rehabilitation and Healthcare Center**
1602 E Franklin Street
Chapel Hill, NC 27514    919-967-1418
FAX: 919-918-3811

*Robert Park, Administrator*

**9904 Cypress Pointe Rehabilitation and Healthca re Center**
2006 S 16th Street
Wilmington, NC 28401    910-763-6271
FAX: 910-351-9803

*Dan Daly, Administrator*

**9905 Pettigrew Rehabilitation and Healthcare Ce nter**
1551 W Pettigrew Street
Durham, NC 27705    919-286-0751
FAX: 919-286-7065

*Mark Anthony, Administrator*

**9906** **Raleigh Rehabilitation and Healthcare Cent er**
616 Wade Avenue
Raleigh, NC  27605     919-828-6251
FAX: 919-828-3294

*Steve Harrison, Administrator*

**9907** **Rehabilitation and Healthcare Center of Al manace**
779 Woody Drive
Graham, NC  27253     336-228-8394
FAX: 336-228-8170

*Cassandra Smith, Administrator*

**9908** **Rehabilitation and Healthcare Center of Mo nroe**
1212 E Sunset Drive
Monroe, NC  28112     704-283-8548
FAX: 704-283-4664
e-mail: Judy

*Judy Olson, Administrator*

**9909** **Winston-Salem Rehabilitation and Healthcar e Center**
1900 W 1st Street
Winston Salem, NC  27104     336-724-2821
FAX: 336-725-8314

*Leah Gage, Administrator*

## Ohio

**9910** **Arbors East Subacute and Rehabilitation Ce nter**
5500 E Broad Street
Columbus, OH  43213     614-501-1622
FAX: 614-575-9101

**9911** **Arbors at Canton Subacute And Rehabilitati on Center**
2714 13th Street NW
Canton, OH  44708     330-456-2842
FAX: 330-456-5343

*Kim Joye, Administrator*

**9912** **Arbors at Dayton**
320 Albany Street
Dayton, OH  45408     937-496-6200
FAX: 937-496-1990

*Ed Roberts, Administrator*

**9913** **Arbors at Marietta**
400 N 7th Street
Marietta, OH  45750     740-373-3597
FAX: 740-373-3597

**9914** **Arbors at Milford**
5900 Meadowcreek Drive
Milford, OH  45150     513-248-1655
FAX: 513-248-0466

*Jennifer Fehn, Administrator*
A nursing center hospital in search of giving the joy and fulfillment to the elderly.

**9915** **Arbors at Sylvania**
7120 Port Sylvania Drive
Toledo, OH  43617     419-841-2200
FAX: 419-841-2822

*Steve Arthur, Administrator*

**9916** **Arbors at Toledo Subacute and Rehab Centre**
2920 Cherry Street
Toledo, OH  43608     419-242-7458
FAX: 419-242-6514

*Michelle Hoff, Administrator*

**9917** **Bridgepark Center for Rehabilitation and N ursing Services**
145 Olive Street
Akron, OH  44310     330-762-0901
FAX: 330-762-0905

*Vesta Jones, Executive Director*

**9918** **Broadview Multi-Care Center**
5520 Broadview Road
Parma, OH  44134     216-749-4010
FAX: 440-748-6860
www.broadviewmulticare.com

*Debra Cerr, Administrator*
*Harold Shachter, Owner*

**9919** **Caprice Care Center**
9184 Market Street
North Lima, OH  44452     330-965-9200
FAX: 330-726-6097

*Alison Alvino, Manager*

**9920** **Cleveland Clinic**
9500 Euclid Avenue
Cleveland, OH  44195     216-444-2200
800-223-2273
FAX: 216-444-7021
www.ccf.com

*Floyd Loop, Chief Executive Officer*

**9921** **Columbus Rehabilitation And Subacute Insti tute**
44 S Souder Avenue
Columbus, OH  43222     614-228-5900
FAX: 614-228-3989

*Kelly Fligor, Administrator*

**9922** **LakeMed Nursing and Rehabilitation Center**
70 Normandy Drive
Painesville, OH  44077     440-357-1311
FAX: 440-352-9977

*Donstance L Ewmal, Executive Director*
*Chad Strong, Administrator*

**9923** **Oregon Nursing And Rehabilitation Center**
904 Isaac Streets Drive
Oregon, OH  43616     419-691-2483
FAX: 419-697-5401

*Jill Schlievert, Administrator*

**9924** **Sunset View Castle Nursing Homes Castle Nursing Homes**
434 N Washington Street
Millersburg, OH  44654     330-674-0015
FAX: 330-763-2215
e-mail: info@castlenursinghomes.com
www.castlenursinghomes.com

*Debra Lehr, Chief Executive Officer*

## Oregon

**9925  Care Center East Health & Specialty Care C enter**
Expendicare
11325 NE Weidler Street
Portland, OR  97220          503-253-1181
                            FAX: 503-253-1871

*Phyllis Radzom, Director*

**9926  Medford Rehabilitation and Healthcare Cent er**
Kindred Healthcare
625 Stevens Street
Medford, OR  97504          541-779-3551
                            FAX: 541-779-3658

*Grant Gloor, Executive Director*

## Pennsylvania

**9927  Dresher Hill Health and Rehabilitation Cen ter**
1390 Camp Hill Road
Fort Washington, PA  19034     215-643-0600
                               FAX: 215-641-0628

*Gary Heinrich, Administrator*

**9928  Good Shepherd**
543 Saint John Street
Allentown, PA  18103          610-776-3559
                              877-734-2247
                              FAX: 610-776-3552
                              www.goodshepherdrehab.org

*Sally Gammon, President/CEO*
*Maryellen Dickey, Vice President*

**9929  Statesman Health and Rehabilitation Center**
2629 Trenton Road
Levittown, PA  19056          215-943-7777
                              FAX: 215-943-1240

*Patricia Keyes, Administrator*

**9930  UPMC Braddock**
400 Holland Avenue
Braddock, PA  15104           412-636-5000
                              FAX: 412-636-5398
                              www.braddock.upmc.com

*Mark Sevco, President*
*Rodney Jones, Vice President*

Offers the following rehabilitation services: Sub-acute rehabilitation, speech therapy, occupational therapy.

**9931  UPMC McKeesport**
Presby
1500 Fifth Avenue
McKeesport, PA  15132         412-664-2000
                              FAX: 412-664-2318
                              mckeesport.upmc.com

*Ronald Ott, Chief Executive Officer*

Offers 56 beds for patients who need skilled nursing care. Offers ongoing rehabilitation and educational programs to patients with cardiac, neurologic, and orthopaedic diagnosis.

**9932  UPMC Passavant**
9100 Babcock Boulevard
Pittsburgh, PA  15237         412-367-6700
                              800-533-8762
                              e-mail: tomazichcw@ph.upmc.edu
                              www.upmc.edu/Passavant/

*Cynthia Tomazich, Dir Inpatient Physical Therapy*
*Teresa Petrick, Chief Executive Officer*

Patients who have had an acute illness, injury, or exacerbation of a disease and no longer need the intensity of services in the acute care setting, but still require some complex medical care or supervision and rehabilitation services, may be appropriate to be transferred into the Subacute Unit.

## Rhode Island

**9933  Health Havens Nursing and Rehabilitation C enter**
Kindred Healthcare
100 Wampanoag Trail
Riverside, RI  02915          401-438-4275
                              FAX: 401-438-8093
                              www.kindred.com

*Sandra Sarza, Administrator*
*Jean Aubin, Director*

**9934  Oak Hill Nursing and Rehabilitation Center**
Kindered Health Care
544 Pleasant Street
Pawtucket, RI  02860          401-725-8888
                              FAX: 401-727-6731
                              e-mail: scott_sanborn@kindredhealthcare.com
                              www.oakhillrehab.com

*Scott Sanborn, Administrator*
*Heidi Capela, Director Nursing*
*Amybeth Almeida, Director Admissions*

Subacute unit with Program Specific Medical Director (Pulmanologist). Complex pain and wound management. Long term beds and dedicated Alzheimers Unit.

**9935  Southern New England Rehab Center**
21 Peace Street
Providence, RI  02907         401-456-4177
                              FAX: 401-456-4019

*Sylvia Procaccini, Manager*

## South Carolina

**9936  Tuomey Healthcare System**
129 N Washington Street
Sumter, SC  29150             803-778-9000
                              FAX: 803-774-9489
                              www.tuomey.com

*Jay Cox, Chief Executive Officer*

Here to anticipte the needs of the communities we serve, responding with proactive healthcare initiatives, providing expert rehabilitative services and delivering life-saving acute care.

## Tennessee

**9937  Camden Healthcare and Rehabilitation Cente r**
197 Hospital Drive
Camden, TN  38320             731-584-3500
                              FAX: 731-584-2753

*Mark Walker, Administrator*

**9938  Centennial Medical Center Tri Star Health System**
2300 Patterson Street
Nashville, TN 37203      615-342-1000
      FAX: 615-342-1045

*Larry Kloess, Chief Executive Officer*

**9939  Cordova Rehabilitation and Nursing Center**
955 S Germantown Road
Cordova, TN 38018      901-754-1393
      FAX: 901-754-3332

*John Palmer, Administrator*

**9940  Erlanger Medical Center Baronness Campus**
975 E 3rd Street
Chattanooga, TN 37403      423-778-7287
      FAX: 423-778-7615
      www.orlando.org

*Jim Brexler, Chief Executive Officer*

**9941  Horizon Medical Center**
111 Highway 70 E
Dickson, TN 37055      615-446-0446
      FAX: 615-441-9695
      www.horizonmedctr.com

*Jeff Chain, Director*
*Robert Halliwel, Director Communications*
*B Smith, MD*

**9942  Huntington Health and Rehabilitation Cente r**
635 High Street
Huntingdon, TN 38344      731-986-8943
      FAX: 731-986-3188

*Anthony Mays, Administrator*

**9943  Madison Healthcare and Rehabilitation Cent er**
431 Larkin Springs Road
Madison, TN 37115      615-865-8520
      FAX: 615-868-4455

*Melissa Hansen, Administrator*

**9944  Mariner Health of Nashville**
3939 Hillsboro Circle
Nashville, TN 37215      615-297-2100
      FAX: 615-297-2197

*Molly Mitchell, Administrator*
*Amy Artrip, Director of Nursing*

**9945  Pine Meadows Healthcare and Rehabilitation Center**
700 Nuckolls Road
Bolivar, TN 38008      731-658-4707
      FAX: 731-658-4769

*Larry Shrader, Administrator*

**9946  Primacy Healthcare and Rehabilitation Cent er**
Kindred Health Care
6025 Primacy Parkway
Memphis, TN 38119      901-767-1040
      FAX: 901-685-7362

*George Munchow, Executive Director*
*Donni Dubert, Administrator*

**9947  Ripley Healthcare and Rehabilitation Cente r**
118 Halliburton Street
Ripley, TN 38063      731-635-5180
      FAX: 731-635-0663

*Jonathan Owens, Administrator*

**9948  Shelby Pines Rehabilitation and Healthcare Center**
3909 Covington Pike
Memphis, TN 38135      901-377-1011
      FAX: 901-377-0032

*Jeff Adams, Executive Director*

**9949  Siskin Hospital for Physical Rehabilitation**
1 Siskin Plaza
Chattanooga, TN 37403      423-634-1200
      FAX: 423-634-4538
      e-mail: info@siskinrehab.org
      www.siskinrehab.org

*Teresa Dinger, Director Marketing/Communication*

Dedicated exclusively to physical rehabilitation and offers specialized treatment programs in brain injury, amputation, stroke, spinal cord injury, orthopeadics, and major multiple trauma.

## Texas

**9950  North Hills Hospital**
4401 Booth Calloway Road
North Richland Hills, TX 76180      817-255-1000
      FAX: 817-255-1967
      www.northhillshospital.com

*Randy Moresi, Chief Executive Officer*

**9951  Valley Regional Medical Center**
100 E Alton Gloor Boulevard
Suite A
Brownsville, TX 78526      956-350-7000
      FAX: 956-350-7999
      www.valleyregionalmedicalcenter.com

*David Handley, Administrator*

## Utah

**9952  Crosslands Rehabilitation and Healthcare C enter**
575 E 11000 S
Sandy, UT 84070      801-571-7600
      FAX: 801-571-4875
      www.crosslandsrehab.com

*Wayne Barney, Administrator*
*Lyle Black, Manager*

**9953  Federal Heights Rehabilitation and Nursing Center**
Kindred
41 S 9th E
Salt Lake City, UT 84102      801-532-3539
      FAX: 801-553-0314

*Kelly Snowball, Administrator*

**9954  St. George Care and Rehabilitation Center**
Kindred Health Care
1032 E 100 S
Saint George, UT 84770      435-628-0488
      FAX: 435-628-7362
      www.kindredhealthcare.com

*Jeff Christensen, Executive Director*
*Erin Hammon, Director of Nursing*

**9955 St. Mark's Hospital**
1200 E 3900 S
Salt Lake City, UT 84124                    801-268-7111
                                       FAX: 801-270-3353
                                       www.stmarkshospital.com

*John Hanshaw, Chief Executive Officer*

**9956 Wasatch Valley Rehabilitation**
Kindred Center
2200 E 3300 S
Salt Lake City, UT 84109                    801-486-2096
                                       FAX: 801-484-3443
                                       www.wasatchvalleyrehabilitation.com

*Jamie Anderson, Admissions*
*Ric Toomer, Administrator*

## Virginia

**9957 Nansemond Pointe Rehabilitation and Health care Center**
200 Constance Road
Suffolk, VA 23434                    757-539-8744
                                       FAX: 757-539-6128
                                       www.nansemondhc.com

*David O'Brien, Executive Director*
Offers an entire contiuum of care from assisted living apartments to skilled nursing to long term care.

**9958 Rehabilitation and Research Center Virginia Commonwealth University**
PO Box 980661
Richmond, VA 23298                    804-828-2156
                                       FAX: 804-828-5074
                                       e-mail: beagle@hsc.vcu.edu
                                       www.rrc.pmr.vcu.edu

*Richard Sicemore, Executive Director*
Inpatient medical rehabilitation program.

**9959 Warren Memorial Hospital**
1000 N Shenandoah Avenue
Front Royal, VA 22630                    540-636-0300
                                       FAX: 540-636-0475

*Patrick Noland, Administrator*

**9960 Winchester Rehabilitation Center**
333 W Cork Street
Winchester, VA 22601                    540-536-5114
                                       800-382-0772
                                       FAX: 540-536-1122
                                       e-mail: wwilliam@valleyhealthlink.com
                                       www.valleyhealthlink.com

*Micheal J Halseth, President/CEO*
*Dena Kent, Executive Director*
Offers the following rehabilitation services: Sub-Acute inpatient rehabilitation, Speech therapy, Physical therapy, Occupational therapy, Disability evaluations. 30-bed inpatient center.

## Washington

**9961 Aldercrest Health and Rehabilitation Center**
21400 72nd Avenue W
Edmonds, WA 98026                    425-775-1961
                                       FAX: 425-771-0116
                                       www.healthgrades.com

*Sandy Wilkenson, Administrator*

**9962 Arden Rehabilitation and Healthcare Center**
16357 Aurora Avenue N
Shoreline, WA 98133                    206-542-3103
                                       FAX: 206-542-4562

*Gail Brockway, Administrator*

**9963 Bellingham Health Care and Rehabilitation Services**
1200 Birchwood Avenue
Bellingham, WA 98225                    360-734-9295
                                       FAX: 360-671-1583

*Sheila Oberg, Administrator*

**9964 Bremerton Convalescent and Rehabilitation Center**
2701 Clare Avenue
Bremerton, WA 98310                    360-377-3951
                                       FAX: 360-377-9756

*Stephanie Bonanzino, Administrator*

**9965 Edmonds Rehabilitation and Healthcare Cent er**
Kindred Healthcare
21008 76th Avenue W
Edmonds, WA 98026                    425-778-0107
                                       FAX: 425-776-9532
                                       www.kindred.com

*Jane Davis, Director*

**9966 Heritage Health and Rehabilitation Center**
Kindred Health Care
3605 Y Street
Vancouver, WA 98663                    360-693-5839
                                       FAX: 360-693-5515
                                       www.kindredhealthcare.com

*Jeremy Tolman, Executive Director*
*Su Patchett, Director of Nursing*

**9967 North Auburn Rehabilitation And Health Cen ter**
2830 i Street NE
Auburn, WA 98002                    253-854-4142
                                       800-395-5000
                                       FAX: 253-833-3743

*Terri Thornberg, Manager*

**9968 Northwoods Lodge**
2321 NW Schold Place
Silverdale, WA 98383                    360-698-3930
                                       FAX: 360-613-9520

*Leslie Krueger, Owner*

**9969 Pacific Specialty and Rehabilitation Cente r**
1015 N Garrison Road
Vancouver, WA 98664                    360-694-7501
                                       FAX: 360-694-8148

*Michael Coy, Manager*

**9970 Puget Sound Healthcare Center**
4001 Capitol Mall Drive SW
Olympia, WA 98502                    360-754-9792
                                       FAX: 360-754-2455

*Dan Murray, Administrator*

**9971 Vencor of Vancouver Healthcare and Rehabil itation Center**
400 E 33rd Street
Vancouver, WA 98663                    360-696-2561
                                       FAX: 360-750-0665

*Kevin Bowen, Manager*

## West Virginia

**9972  War Memorial Hospital**
109 War Memorial Drive
Berkeley Springs, WV  25411           304-258-1234

www.warmemorialhospital.com

*William C Locke, President*
*John H Borg, Administrator*

Offers physical therapy, occupational therapy, speech therapy, social services, and patient/family education for individuals who have experienced a recent physical disability due to disease, dysfunction, or general debilitation. Helps patients to maximize their abilities through activities of daily living, mobility, self-medication, and self-care and restore their ability to return to their previous lifestyle.

## Wisconsin

**9973  Brain Injury Rehabilitation Center at Mequ on Care Center**
10911 N Port Washington Road
Mequon, WI  53092                  262-241-2080
                                   FAX: 262-241-2090

**9974  Cedar Spring Health and Rehabilitation Cen ter**
N27w5707 Lincoln Boulevard
Cedarburg, WI  53012               262-376-7676
                                   FAX: 262-376-7808

*Mary Wirth, Executive Director*

**9975  Clearview-Brain Injury Center**
199 Home Road
Juneau, WI  53039                  920-386-3400
                                   877-386-3400
                                   FAX: 920-386-3800
                                   www.dodgecountywi.com

*Jane Goyer, Administrator*

**9976  Colonial Manor Medical and Rehabilitation Center**
1010 E Wausau Avenue
Wausau, WI  54403                  715-842-2028
                                   FAX: 715-845-5810

*Terry Mantia, Administrator*

**9977  Eastview Medical and Rehabilitation Center**
729 Park Street
Antigo, WI  54409                  715-623-2356
                                   FAX: 715-623-6345

*Wanda Hose, Administrator*

**9978  Family Heritage Medical and Rehabilitation Center**
130 Strawberry Lane
Wisconsin Rapids, WI  54494        715-424-1600
                                   FAX: 715-424-4817

*Art Schmitz, Administrator*

**9979  Hospitality Nursing and Rehabilitation Cen ter**
8633 32nd Avenue
Kenosha, WI  53142                 262-694-8300
                                   FAX: 262-694-3622
                                   www.extendedcare.com

*Georgette Miller, Administrator*

**9980  Kennedy Park Medical and Rehabilitation Ce nter**
Kindred Healthcare
6001 Alderson Street
Schofield, WI  54476               715-359-4257
                                   FAX: 715-355-4867

*Lori Kopdell, Administrator*
*Judy Kowalski, Plant Manager*

**9981  Lakeside Nursing and Rehabilitation Center**
Benedictine Health System
7490 156th Street
Chippewa Falls, WI  54729          715-723-9341
                                   FAX: 715-723-0454

*Beth Peterson, Director*
*Michelle Curry, Supervisor*
*Heather Rust, Supervisor*

Offers adult day service programs for people who may experience physical, emotional, memory and/or social limitations.

**9982  Middleton Village Nursing and Rehabilitati on Center**
Kindred
6201 Elmwood Avenue
Middleton, WI  53562               608-831-8300
                                   FAX: 608-831-4253

*Sheila Nelson, Administrator*

**9983  Mount Carmel Health and Rehabilitation Cen ter**
5700 W Layton Avenue
Milwaukee, WI  53220               414-281-7200
                                   FAX: 414-281-7183

*Mike Berry, Administrator*

**9984  Mount Carmel Medical and Rehabilitation Center**
677 E State Street
Burlington, WI  53105              262-763-9531
                                   FAX: 262-763-7579

*Kathlene Walker, Administrator*

**9985  North Ridge Medical and Rehabilitation Cen ter**
1445 N 7th Street
Manitowoc, WI  54220               920-682-0314
                                   FAX: 920-682-0553
                                                www.

*Jane Conway, Administrator*

**9986  Oshkosh Medical and Rehabilitation Center**
1580 Bowen Street
Oshkosh, WI  54901                 920-233-4011
                                   FAX: 920-233-5177

*Tom Wagner, Administrator*

**9987  San Luis Medical and Rehabilitation Center**
2305 San Luis Place
Green Bay, WI  54304               920-494-5231
                                   FAX: 920-494-1958

*Alisa Gerke, Administrator*

## Wyoming

**9988** **Mountain Towers Healthcare and Rehabilitat ion Center**
3128 Boxelder Drive
Cheyenne, WY 82001
307-634-7901
FAX: 307-634-7910
www.kindredhealthcare.com

*Licrecia Patterson, Administrator*
*Toni Wyenn, Director of Nursing*

**9989** **South Central Wyoming Healthcare and Rehab ilitation**

Kindred Healthcare
542 16th Street
Rawlins, WY 82301
307-324-2759
FAX: 307-324-7579

*Mickey Hanser, Administrator*

**9990** **Wind River Healthcare and Rehabilitation C enter**
Kindred Health Care
1002 Forest Drive
Riverton, WY 82501
307-856-9471
FAX: 307-856-1757
www.kindredhealthcare.com

*Bonnie Deyo, Administrator*
*Sandy Morton, Director*

# A

A-Solution, 544
A4 Tech (USA) Corporation, 2011
AACD Legal Series, 5205
AACRAO, 2592
AAN's Toll-Free Hotline, 7804
AAPD News, 5873
AARP, 2604
AARP Fulfillment, 5786, 5788, 5806, 5817, 6027, 6066, 6081, 6405
ABA Commission on Mental & Physical Disability Law, 5219, 5939, 6012, 6079
ABC Sign with Me, 7023
ABC Union, ACE, ANLV, Vegas Western Cab, 7954
ABC of Asthma, Allergies & Lupus, 6693
ABC's of Latex Allergy, 7246
ABC's of Starting a Private School, 7206
ABCD Newsletter Volume Reprints, 5615
ABDA/ABMPP Workshop: The Art of Courtroom Testifying, 5206
ABLE Center for Independent Living, 5073
ABLEDATA, 1950
AC-ACLD/An Association for Children and Adults with Learning Disabilities, 8615
ACB Government Employees, 1058
ACB Radio Amateurs, 1254
ACB Social Service Providers, 1059
ACES/ACCESS Inclusion Program, 9216
ACPOC News, 5616
ACS Federal Healthcare, 1060
ACS Wireless: Advanced Cyber Solutions, 147
ACT Assessment Test Preparation Reference Manual, 8451
ACT Asset Technical Manual, 8452
ACU Massage Cushion, 250
AD-LIB, 4768
ADA Business Brief: Restriping Parking Lots, 7247
ADA Business Brief: Service Animals, 7248
ADA Camp for Kids, 1603
ADA Guide for Small Businesses, 5874
ADA Guide for Small Towns, 5875
ADA Hotel Built-In Alerting System, 148
ADA Information Services, 5876
ADA Mandate for Social Change, 5207
ADA Pipeline, 5877
ADA Questions and Answers, 5828, 5878
ADA Tax Incentive Packet for Business, 5879
ADA Technical Assistance Program, 3929, 5877
ADA Teen Camp at Covenant Point, 1528
ADA Triangle D Camp, 1438
ADA and City Governments: Common Problems, 5880
ADA-TA: A Technical Assistance Update from the Department of Justice, 5881
ADD Challenge: A Practical Guide for Teachers, 2663
ADD Videos, 7423
ADD, Stepping Out of the Dark, 7423
ADD/ADHD Behavior-Change Resource Kit, 6694
ADD/ADHD Checklist, 6695
ADD: Helping Your Child, 6463
ADEC Resources for Independence, 8428
ADHD, 7249

ADHD Book of Lists: A Practical Guide for Helping Children and Teens with ADDs, 6464
ADHD Report, 6606
ADHD in Adults, 7424
ADHD in Schools: Assessment and Intervention Strategies, 6539
ADHD in the Classroom: Strategies for Teachers, 2664
ADHD in the Schools: Assessment and Intervention Strategies, 2665
ADHD with Comorbid Disorders: Clinical Assessment and Management, 5617
ADHD: Handbook for Diagnosis & Treatment, 6696
ADHD: What Can We Do?, 7425
ADHD: What Do We Know?, 7426
AEPS Child Progress Record: For Children Ages Three to Six, 2328
AEPS Child Progress Report: For Children Ages Birth to Three, 2977
AEPS Curriculum for Birth to Three Years, 2666
AEPS Curriculum for Three to Six Years, 2329
AEPS Data Recording Forms: For Children Ages Birth to Three, 2978
AEPS Data Recording Forms: For Children Ages Three to Six, 2330
AEPS Family Interest Survey, 2331
AEPS Family Report: For Children Ages Birth to Three, 2332
AEPS Family Report: For Children Ages Three to Six, 6366
AEPS Measurement for Birth to Three Years, 2979
AEPS Measurement for Three to Six Years, 2980
AFB Directory of Services for Blind and Visually Impaired Persons in the US and Canada, 6465
AFB News, 7024
AFB Press, 2508
AGS, 2356, 2379, 2411, 2432, 2451, 3002, 3003, 3004, 3006, 3011, 3013, 3014, 3015, 3033, 7598
AH! Asthma Camp, 1490
AHEAD, 2614, 6131
AHEAD Association, 1061
AI Squared, 2036
AID Bulletin, 5882
AIDS 2nd Edition, 5592
AIDS Alert, 5593
AIDS Disease State Management Resource, 5594
AIDS Funding, 3743
AIDS Legal Council of Chicago, 5184
AIDS Project Los Angeles, 5600
AIDS Treatment Data Network, 2655
AIDS and Other Manifestations of HIV Infection, 5595
AIDS in the Twenty-First Century: Disease and Globalization, 5596
AIDS, What Does it Mean to You?, 5597
AIDS: The HIV Myth, 5598
AIDS: The Official Journal of the International AIDS Society, 5599
AIDSLAW of Louisiana, 5185
AIM Independent Living Center: Corning, 4932
AIM Independent Living Center: Elmira, 4933
AIMS Multimedia, 2056

AIR: Assessment of Interpersonal Relations, 2981
AJ Pappanikou Center, 2649, 2650
AJAO Newsletter, 6697
ALST: Adolescent Language Screening Test, 2982
AM Publishing, 6815
AMC Cancer Research Center, 5315
AMI, 296
AMI: Accessories for Mobile Independence, 446, 1804
ANCOR Wage and Hour Handbook, 5829
APLA Update, 5600
APSE Conference: Revitalizing Supported Employment, Climbing to the Future, 2248
APT Residential Services, 9217
APT Technology, 197, 514, 674
A AR P Fulfillment, 2310, 5238
ARC, 808
ARC Gateway, 3912
ARC of Allen County, 8429
ARC of Gloucester County, 8539
ARC of Hunterdon County, 8540
ARC of Mercer County, 8541
ARC of Monmouth, 8542
ARC of Somerset County, 1590
ARC's Government Report, 5883
ARC-Adult Vocational Program, 8271
ARC-VC Magic Muffin Cafe, 9049
ARC: Gateway, 4769
ARC: VC Community Connections West, 9050
ARC: VC Ventura, 9051
ARCA - Dakota County Technical College, 5884
ARCA Newsletter, 5884
ARISE: Center for Independent Living: Oswe go, 4934
ARISE: Center for Independent Living: Syra cuse, 4935
ARJO, 97, 419
ARRISE, 1112
ASCCA, 1329
ASHA Leader, 6192
ASSETS School, 8391
ASSIST! to Independence, 4401
ASSISTECH, 131, 143, 144, 213
AT for Infants and Toddlers with Disabilities, 5618
AT for Parents with Disabilities, 6367
AT&T Foundation, 3465
ATLA, 3830
ATTAIN, 1951, 8787
ATV Solutions, 590, 599, 604
AU Kamp for Kids, 1510
AUCD, 840
AVKO Dyslexia Research Foundation, 2463, 2373
AVKO Educational Research Foundation, 2430, 2960
Abacus, 2012
Abbot and Dorothy H Stevens Foundation, 3370
Abbott Laboratories Fund, 3277
Abell-Hangar Foundation, 3656
Abilitations, 7771, 2436
Abilities Center of New Jersey, 8543
Abilities Expo, 2249
Abilities Unlimited, 1510
Abilities in Motion, 5026
Abilities of Florida: An Affiliate of Service Source, 8362
Abilities of Northwest New Jersey, 8544

Association on Higher Education and Disability (AHEAD), 841
Assumption Activity Center, 9457
Asthma & Allergy Advocate Newsletter, 6737
Asthma & Allergy Education for Worksite Clinicians, 3050
Asthma & Allergy Essentials for Children's Care Provider, 3051
Asthma & Allergy Medications, 7269
Asthma Action Cards: Child Care Asthma/Allergy Action Card, 2338
Asthma Action Cards: Student Asthma Action Card, 2339
Asthma Alert, 7270
Asthma Care Training for Kids (ACT), 3052
Asthma Challenge, 6738
Asthma Handbook, 7271
Asthma Handbook Slides, 7438
Asthma Lifelines, 7272
Asthma Management, 7439
Asthma Management and Education, 2693
Asthma Resource Directory, 6739
Asthma Sourcebook, 6740
Asthma Triggers, 7440
Asthma and Allergy Answers: A Patient Education Library, 5734
Asthma and Allergy Foundation of America, 1147, 7662, 2338, 2339, 2407, 2417, 2693, 3050, 3051, 3052, 5734, 6026, 6738, 7246, 7351, 7380, 7402, 7866
Asthma and Exercise, 6741
Asthma and Pregnancy, 7273
Asthma and the Athlete, 7441
Asthma in the School: Improving Control with Peak Flow Monitoring, 6742
Asthma in the Workplace, 6743
Aston-Patterning, 2694
At Home Among Strangers, 6203
At Home with Stickybear, 2084
Ataxia-Telangiectasia Children's Project (A-T Children's Project), 1148
Athena Rehab of Clayton, 9810
Atheneum, 5662, 5689, 5716
Athens Regional Library Talking Book Center, 5351
Atherton Family Foundation, 3271
Atkinson Foundation, 3122
Atlanta Institute of Medicine and Rehabilitation, 9313
Atlanta Regional Office, 8027
Atlanta VA Medical Center, 8028
Atlantic Coast Rehabilitation & Healthcare Center, 9882
Atlantic-Little Brown, 5703
Atlantis Community, 4500
Attainment Company, 2085, 5978
Attending to America: Personal Assistance for Independent Living, 5908
Attention, 6744
Attention Deficit Disorder, 7442
Attention Deficit Disorder Association, 1149, 6835
Attention Deficit Disorder and Learning Disabilities, 6745
Attention Deficit Disorder in Adults Workbook, 6746
Attention Deficit Disorder in Children and Adolescents, 2695
Attention Deficit Disorder: A Different Perception, 6747
Attention Deficit Disorder: Adults, 7443
Attention Deficit Disorder: Children, 6467

Attention Deficit Disorders Association, Southern Region: Annual Conference, 2264
Attention Deficit Disorders: Assessment & Teaching, 6541
Attention Deficit Information Network, 1150
Attention Deficit-Hyperactivity Disorder: Is it a Learning Disability?, 7274
Attention Getter, 2086
Attention Teens, 2087
Attention-Deficit Hyperactivity Disorder: Symptoms and Suggestons for Treatment, 6748
Attention-Deficit/Hyperactivity Disorder, What Every Parent Wants to Know, 6468
Attitudes Toward Persons with Disabilities, 5909
Attorney General's Office: Disability Rights Bureau & Health Care Bureau, 3961
Aud-A-Mometer, 299
Audapter Speech System, 2040
Audio Book Contractors, 624
Audiogram/Clinical Records Manager, 1953
Audiology Foundation of America, 7663
Auditech: Audioport Personal Amplifier, 545
Auditech: Classroom Amplification System Focus CFM802, 2340
Auditech: DirectEar Transmitter and Headset, 321
Auditech: Personal FM Educational System, 2341
Auditech: Personal PA Value Pack System, 322
Auditech: Pocketalker Pro, 323
Auditory Processing Disorders in Children: What Does It Mean?, 6204
Auditory-Verbal International, 992, 7664, 6205
Auditory-Verbal Therapy for Parents and Professionals, 2342
Augmentative Communication Consultants (ACCI), 2321
Augmentative Communication Systems (AAC), 1880
Augmentative and Alternative Communication, 5910
Augmenting Basic Communciation in Natural Contexts, 6749
Augusta Rehabilitation Center, 9854
Augusta Talking Book Center, 5352
Augusta VA Medical Center, 8029
Aural Habilitation, 2696
Auricle, 6205
Aurora Press, 5941
Aurora of Central New York, 7809
Austin Resource Center for Independent Living, 5074
Austin Resource Center: Round Rock, 5075
Austin Resource Center: San Marcos, 5076
Authoritative Guide to Self- Help Resource in Mental Health, 5911
Autism, 6750, 7444
Autism Handbook: Understanding & Treating Autism & Prevention Development, 6751
Autism Research Institute, 5296, 6752, 5621
Autism Research Review International, 5621
Autism Services Center, 1151, 5576, 7843
Autism Society Of North Carolina Bookstore, 5513
Autism Society of America, 1152, 7810, 7309
Autism Society of North Carolina, 5513, 1647, 6972

Autism Society of North Carolina Bookstore, 2542, 2804, 5846, 5919, 6515, 6750, 6753, 6754, 6757, 6759, 6761, 6766, 6820, 6838, 6847, 6857, 6953, 6964, 6971, 6983, 7005, 7007, 7011, 7275, 7296, 7304, 7393
Autism Treatment Center of America, 1153, 3053
Autism Treatment Guide, 6753
Autism and Asperger Syndrome, 6754
Autism and Learning, 6755
Autism in Adolescents and Adults, 6756
Autism...Nature, Diagnosis and Treatment, 6757
Autism: A Strange, Silent World, 6758
Autism: A World Apart, 7445
Autism: Explaining the Enigma, 6759
Autism: From Tragedy to Triumph, 6760
Autism: Identification, Education and Treatment, 6761
Autism: The Facts, 6762
Autistic Adults at Bittersweet Farms, 6763
Automated Functions, 2048
Automatic Card Shuffler, 7873
Automatic Wheelchair Anti-Rollback Device, 671
Automobile Lifts for Scooters, Wheelchairs and Powerchairs, 27
Automobility Program, 3394
Avacado Press, 6007, 6065
Avant Walker, 566
Avery Publishing Group, 6408, 6809, 6840, 6905
Avis Rent-A-Car, 7955
Avoid Eye Strain, Feel it T-Shirt, 1844
Avoiding Unfortunate Situations, 7275
AwareNews, 5912
Awareness, 7033
Awareness Posters, 6764
Awareness Training, 7446
Away We Ride, 2088
Away We Ride IntelliKeys Overlay, 1881
Away with Arthritis, 6765
Ayer Company Publishers, 2879
Ayurvedic Institute, 3054
Azure Acres Chemical Dependency Recovery Center, 9056

# B

B AR C, 8273
B&H Reviews, 5998
A BA Commission on Mental & Physical Disability La, 5233, 5248
A BA Commission on Mental and Physical Disability, 2852
BA and Elinor Steinhagen Benevolent Trust, 3661
BCR Foundation, 3235
BESTspeech, 165
BG Industries, 140
BI-County Services, 8430
BIGmack Communication Aid, 1882
BIPAP S/T Ventilatory Support System, 300
BIT Talking Scale Bathroom Scale, 102
BOSC, 6377
BOSC: Directory of Facilities for People with Learning Disabilities, 2494
BPPV, 6206
BVA Bulletin, 7276
Baby Book for the Developmentally Challenged Child, 6370

Braille Institute Library, 5298
Braille Institute Orange County Center, 5299, 7811
Braille Institute Santa Barbara Center, 5300
Braille Institute Sight Center, 5301
Braille Institute of America, 1271
Braille Institute of Los Angeles, 5299
Braille Keyboard Labels, 1938
Braille Monitor, 7046
Braille N' Speak, 1939
Braille Notebook, 614
Braille Plates for Elevator, 628
Braille Playing Cards: Plastic, 7877
Braille Revival League, 1272
Braille Touch-Time Watches, 629
Braille and Talking Book Library, 5302
Braille and Talking Book Library, Perkins School for the Blind, 5434
Braille and Talking Book Library: California State Library, 5303
Braille: An Extraordinary Volunteer Opportunity, 7280
Braille: Bingo Cards, Boards and Call Numbers, 7878
Braille: Greeting Cards, 615
Braille: Rook Cards, 7879
Brailled Desk Calendar, 616
Brailon Thermoform Duplicator, 1940
Brain Allergies: The Psychonutrient, 6378
Brain Injury Association of America, 1157
Brain Injury Association of New York State, 1158
Brain Injury Association of Texas, 1159
Brain Injury Rehabilitation Center Sand Lake Hospi, 9254, 9254
Brain Injury Rehabilitation Center at Mequon Care Center, 9973
Braintree Hospital, 8839
Brandecker Rehabilitation Center, 9342
Branden Publishing Company, 6760
Brandt Industries, 504
Braun Corporation, 30, 110, 38, 110, 436, 606
Bravo! + Three-Wheel Scooter, 567
Brazoria County Center for Independent Living, 5077
Breaking Barriers, 2704
Breaking Ground, 5923
Breaking New Ground News Note, 5924
Breaking New Ground Resource Center, 5925
Breaking the Patterns of Depression, 6772
Breaking the Speech Barrier: Language Develpment Through Augmented Means, 6773
Breakthroughs: How to Reach Students with Autism, 7454
Breast Cancer Action, 1160
Breast Cancer Sourcebook, 6774
Breathe Easy Young People's Guide to Asthma, 7455
Breathe Free, 5926
Breathing Disorders: Your Complete Exercise Guide, 6775
Breathing Lessons: The Life and Work of Mark O'Brien, 7456
Breckenridge Outdoor Education Center, 1395
Breezewood Acres United Way of Central Ohio, 1659
Breezy, 694
Bremerton Convalescent and Rehabilitation Center, 9964
Brentwood Rehabilitation and Nursing Center, 9855

Brentwood Subacute Healthcare Center, 9343
Brevard County Libraries, 5332
Brevard County Library System, 5346
Brevard County Talking Books Library, 5332
Brian's House, 5028
Briarcliff Nursing Home & Rehab Facility, 8999
Briarwood Day Camp, 1694
Bridge Newsletter, 5927
Bridge Pointe Services, 8432
Bridgepark Center for Rehabilitation and Nursing Services, 9917
Bridges Beyond Sound, 6212
Bridging the Gap: A National Directory of Services for Women & Girls with Disabilities, 7457
Briefs, 1868
Briggs Foundation, 3128
Brigham Manor Nursing and Rehabilitation Center, 9863
Brigham and Women s Hospital, 5436
Brigham and Women's Hospital: Asthma and Allergic Disease Research Center, 5435
Brigham and Women's Hospital: Robert B Brigham Multipurpose Arthritis Center, 5436
Bright Horizons Summer Camp, 1772
Brighten Place, 8907
Brike International, 7775
Bringing Out the Best, 7458
Bristol County Chapter Arc, 3631
Britannica Film Company, 7433, 7479, 7523, 7548, 7589, 7634
A British Broadcasting Corporation Documentary, 7524
Broadcast Services for the Blind, 5304
Broadman and Holman, 6321
Broadmead, 4757
Broadview Multi-Care Center, 9918
Broadway, 6469
Bronchial Asthma: Principles of Diagnosis and Treatment, 6776
Bronx Continuing Treatment Day Program, 9598
Bronx Independent Living Services, 4940
Bronx VA Medical Center, 8126
Brooke Publishing, 2940
Brookes Publishing, 2328, 2329, 2330, 2331, 2332, 2412, 2447, 2666, 2669, 2681, 2686, 2708, 2709, 2712, 2716, 2720, 2726, 2728, 2742, 2743, 2745, 2761, 2762, 2763, 2785, 2793, 2798, 2812, 2814, 2835, 2842, 2859, 2905, 2906, 2926, 2932, 2935, 2946, 2969, 2977, 2978, 2979, 2980, 2985, 2990, 2994, 2999, 3001, 3045, 5699, , 5736, 5743, 5744, 5748, 5757, 5761, 5808, 5841, 5847, 5853, 5859, 5910, 5967, 5988, 5990, 6055, 6125, 6159, 6163, 6212, 6366, 6379, 6382, 6388, 6389, 6390, 6395, 6422, 6436, 6440, 6448, 6456, 6461, 6461, 6468
Brookes Publishing Company, 2510, 2673, 2690, 2725, 2764, 2801, 2878, 2975
Brookings Institution, 5213, 5782, 5826
Brookline Books, 2511, 5, 10, 2374, 2396, 2399, 2400, 2446, 2449, 2450, 2688, 2705, 2724, 2740, 2744, 2750, 2760, 2776, 2810, 2907, 2910, 2929, 2933, 2937, 2939, 2952, 2958, 2971, 5216, 5626, 5656, 5758, 5868, 5915, 5974, 5981, 6059, 6062, 6099, 6137, 6374, 6380, 6385, 6403, 6413, 6421, 6430, 6431, 6435, 6455, , 6532, 6558, 6564, 6568, 6580, 6871, 6952
Brookline Books/Lumen Editions, 6522

Brooklyn Bureau of Community Service, 9599
Brooklyn Campus of the VA NY Harbor Healthcare System, 8127
Brooklyn Center for Independence of the Disabled, 4941
Brooklyn Home for Aged Men, 3477
Brooks / Cole Publishing Company, 2736
Brooks Health Foundation, 8744
Brooks Publishing Company, 2692, 2697
Brooks Rehabilitation, 8744
Brooks/Cole Publishing Company, 2512, 6541
Brothers, Sisters, and Special Needs, 6379
Brotman Medical Center, 9061
Brotman Medical Center: RehabCare Unit, 8698, 9061
Broward County Talking Book Library, 5333
Brown County Library, 5585
Brown Foundation, 3662
Brown University Long Term Care Advisor, 6620
Brown-Heatly Library, 5546
Brown-Karhan Health Care, 9710
Brown-Nicholet Industries, 9551
Broyhill Family Foundation, 3547
Bruno Independent Living Aids, 382, 27, 382, 387, 395, 396, 417, 432, 434, 438, 569, 588
Bryn Mawr Rehabilitation Hospital, 9683
Buck & Buck, 1780, 1781, 1782, 1783, 1784, 1786, 1787, 1788, 1789, 1792, 1793, 1796, 1797, 1798, 1799, 1800, 1814, 1820, 1823, 1825, 1830, 1835, 1837, 1838, 1840, 1841, 1842, 1845, 1846, 1847, 1848, 1850, 1851, 1858, 1859, 1860, 1870, 1871, 1872
Buck and Buck Clothing, 1811
Budget Cotton/Poly Open Back Gown, 1780
Budget Flannel Open Back Gown, 1781
Buffalo Hearing and Speech Center, 9600
Buffalo Independent Living Project, 4942
Buffalo Regional Office, 8128
Buffalo State (SUNY), 3074
Build Rehabilitation Industries, 9062
Builders of Skills, 8776
Building Blocks: Foundations for Learning for Young Blind and Visually Impaired Children, 7047
Building Bridges: Including People with Disabilities in International Programs, 3075
Building Communicative Competence with Indiv. Who Use Augmentative & Alternative Commun., 6777
Building Owners and Managers Association International, 2292
Building the Healing Partnership: Parents, Professionals and Children, 2705, 6380
Bull Publishing, 5607
Bulletin, 7048
Bulletin Newsletter, 6213
Bulletin of the Association on the Handicapped, 5928
Bullhead Community Hospital, 5288
Burbank Rehabilitation Center, 9500
Bureau of Education for Exceptional Children, 3915
Bureau of Elderly & Adult Services, 4125
Bureau of Employment Programs Division of Workers' Compensation, 4353
Bureau of Rehabilitations Services, 5321
Bureau of Workers' & Unemployment Compensation, 4039
Burger School for the Autistic, 5445

# I

# J

# N

National Institute of Arthritis and Musculoskeletal and Skin Diseases, 1218

National Institute of Child Health and Human Development, 7848

National Institute of Dental and Craniofac ial Research, 2644

National Institute of Health, 1956

National Institute of Mental Health, 7417

National Institute of Mental Health: Decade of the Brain, 7364

National Institute of Neurological Disorders and Stroke, 1219

National Institute on Deafness and Other Communication Disorders (NIDCD), 1040

National Institute on Disability and Rehabilitation Research, 933, 5331

National Institutes of Health: National Eye Institute, 3805

National Jewish Center for Immunology, 7277, 7325, 7366, 7410, 7420, 7836

National Jewish Medical & Research Center, 5318

National Kidney and Urologic Diseases Information Clearinghouse, 1220

National Legal Center for the Medically Dependent, 5200, 6638

National Lekotek Center, 5378, 7888

National Library Office, 5524

National Library Service for the Blind, 7043, 7118, 7135, 7136, 7137, 7279, 7280, 7311, 7312, 7385, 7386, 7387

National Library Service in Washington, 5525

National Library Services for the Blind, 7179

National Library Services for the Blind & Physically Handicapped, 1221, 1313

National Library of Medicine, 1970

National Managed Health Care Congress, 2279

National Manufacturing Company, 600

National Maternal and Child Health Bureau, 934

National Mental Health Association, 935, 1222, 1155

National Mental Health Consumers Self-Help Clearinghouse, 1223

National Mental Health Consumers' Self-Help, 6878

National Mobility Equipment Dealers Association, 1105

National Multiple Sclerosis Society, 1224, 6872, 8359

National Network of Learning Disabled Adults, 6094

National Neurofibromatosis Foundation, 3525

National Offices, 849

National Oral Health Information Clearinghouse, 2644

National Organization for Rare Disorders, 1225, 6091

National Organization of Parents of Blind Children, 1314

National Organization of the Senior Blind, 1315

National Organization on Disability, 936, 7702, 5732, 6090

National Parent Network on Disabilities, 937

National Parkinson Foundation, 1226, 2265, 2290, 6660

National Registry of Community Mental Health Services, 5752

National Rehabilitation Association (NRA), 938, 2275, 6045, 6649, 6665, 7222

National Rehabilitation Center, 7703

National Rehabilitation Counseling Association, 6642

National Rehabilitation Hospital, 8743, 1962

National Rehabilitation Information Center, 5427

National Rehabilitation Information Center (NARIC), 939, 1041

National Respite Locator Service, 940

National Retinitis Pigmentosa Foundation Fighting Blindness, 3367

National Right to Work Legal Defense and Education Foundation, 5201

National Service Dog Center, 7849

National Skeet Shooting Association, 7739

National Society for Experiential Education, 2488

National Society to Prevent Blindness, 7316

National Spinal Cord Injury Association, 6957, 6973

National Sports Center for the Disabled, 7784, 7799

National Stroke Association, 1227

National Stuttering Association, 6999

National Technical Institute For The Deaf (NTID), 997

National Technical Institute for the Deaf, 1042

National Technology Database, 1984

National Theatre Workshop of the Handicapped (NTWH), 18

National Theatre of the Deaf, 19, 1043

National Vaccine Information Center, 941

National Veterans Training Institute, 8006

National Voluntary Organizations for Independent Living for the Aging, 781

National Wheelchair Basketball Association, 7740

National Wheelchair Poolplayers Association, 7741

National Women's Health Information Center, 7704

National Women's Health Network, 942

National-Louis University, 8777

Nationwide Foundation, 3577

Native American Advocacy Program for Perso ns with Disabilities, 5057

Native American Advocacy Project, 5058

Native American Protection and Advocacy, 943

Natl. Clearinghouse for Alcohol & Drug Information, 2974

Natl. Organization for Parents of Blind Children, 7083

Natural Access, 717

Natural Child Care: A Complete Guide to Safe Holistic Remedies for Infants and Children, 5677

Natural Health Bulletin, 6095

Nature of Melancholy: From Aristotle to K risteva, 6914

Naval Home, 779

Navarro Hospital, 8954

Navarro Regional Hospital: RehabCare Unit, 8954

Nazarene Publishing House, 5472

NeSoDak Bible Camp/Klein Ranch, 1727

Neal Freeling, 4052

Nebraska Advocacy Services, 4098

Nebraska Assistive Technology Partnership Nebraska Department of Education, 5481

Nebraska Association of Homes for the Aging, 782

Nebraska Client Assistance Program, 4099

Nebraska Commission for the Blind & Visually Impaired, 4100

Nebraska Department of Education: Special Populations Office, 2560

Nebraska Department of Health & Human Services of Medically Handicapped Children's Prgm, 4101

Nebraska Department of Health and Human Services, Division of Aging Services, 4102

Nebraska Department of Mental Health, 4103

Nebraska Employment Services, 8525

Nebraska Fair Employment Practice Agency, 8526

Nebraska Library Commission: Talking Book and Braille Service, 5482

Nebraska Planning Council on Developmental Disabilities, 4104

Nebraska Vocational Rehabilitation Agency, 8527

Nebraska Work Force Development, 8528

Nebraska Workers' Compensation Court, 4105

NeckEase, 139

Needlepoint Daypoint, 1552

Negotiating the Disability Maze, 6096

Negotiating the Special Education Maze: A Guide for Parents and Teachers, 2860, 5678, 6559

Neisloss Family Foundation, 3526

Nejeda, 1598

Nek-Lo, Nek-Lo Hot and Cold Pillow-Perfect, Body Buddy, Hugg-L-O Pillow, 275

Nell J Redfield Foundation, 3437

Nelson Publications, 6535

NeuroControl Corporation, 7705

Neurobiology of Autism, 6915

Neuromotor Speech Disorders: Nature, Assessment, and Management, 6916

Neuropsychiatric Pain Rehabilitation Clinic, 9288

Neuropsychiatry of Epilepsy, 6656

Neuroscience Publishers, 6644

Nevada Assistive Technology Project, 4108

Nevada Bureau of Services to the Blind and Visually Impaired, 4109

Nevada Department of Education: Special Eduction Branch, 2565

Nevada Department of Mental Health: Neuro Clinic, 4110

Nevada Developmental Disability Council, 4111

Nevada Disability Advocacy and Law Center -Sparks/Reno Office, 4112

Nevada Division for Aging: Carson City, 4113

Nevada Division for Aging: Las Vegas, 4114

Nevada Fair Employment Practice Agency, 8530

Nevada Governor's Committee on Employment of Persons with Disabilities, 8531

Nevada Job Training Program Liaison, 8532

Nevada State Library and Archives, 5484

Nevalyn F Nevil, Marna L Beatty & David Moxley, 6158

New Atlantean Press, 6174

New Beginnings: The Blind Children's Center, 5310

New Courier Travel, 7944

New Directions, 7945

New Directions for People with Disabilities, 3087

New England Center for Children, 9517

# P

Pompano Rehabilitation and Nursing Center, 9802

Pond, 2141

Pool Exercise Program, 7579

Pool Lifts for In-Ground Pools, 420

Poplar Bluff RehabCare Program, 9563

Popular Activities and Games for Blind, Visually Impaired & Disabled People, 7154

Porch-Lift Vertical Platform Lift, 421

Port City Enterprises, 9470

Port Jefferson Health Care Facility, 9898

PortaPower Plus, 2026

Portable Hand Controls, 73

Portable Large Print Computer, 2037

Portable Shampoo Bowl, 121

Portable Vehicle Controls, 74

Porter Sargent Publishers, 2501

Porterville Sheltered Workshop, 8301

Portland Naturopathic Clinic: NCNM National Health Centers Eastside Clinic, 956

Portland Public Library, 5420

Portland Regional Office, 8159

Portland VA Medical Center, 8160

Portneuf Medical Center Rehabilitation, 9334

Portsmouth General Hospital: RehabCare Unit, 8981

Positive Behavioral Support: Including People with Difficult Behavior in the Community, 5757

Post Polio, 6938

Post-Polio Health, 6939

Post-Polio Health International, 1236, 6939, 7009

Post-Polio Support Group, 7856

Post-Polio Syndrome Information Book, 6940

Post-Polio Syndrome: A Guide for Polio Survivors and Their Families, 6941

Postgraduate Center for Mental Health, 5507

Posture-Glide Lounger, 719

Potomac Technology, 489

Potty Learning for Children who Experience Delay, 7580

Power Breathing Program, 2417

Power Dialogues, 6433

Power Door, 531

Power Seat Base (6-Way), 75

Power for Off-Pavement, 748

Power of Attorney for Health Care, 5258

Power of Sound: How to Manage Your Persona l Soundscape for a Vital, Productive, Healthy Life, 6364

PowerLink 2 Control Unit, 366

A Practical Guide to Art Therapy Groups, 6605

Practice of Aromatherapy, 6130

Practicing Rehabilitation with Geriatric Clients, 2880

Prader-Willi Alliance of New York, 1237

Prader-Willi Alliance of New York Annual Conference, 2280

Prader-Willi Alliance of New York Monthly Newsletter, 6942

Prader-Willi Syndrome Association USA, 1238

Prader-Willi Syndrome: Development and Ma nifestations, 6943

Pragmatic Approach, 2881

Prairie Cruiser, 720

Prairie Freedom Center for Independent Living, 5061, 5062

Prairie Freedom Center for Independent Living of Yankton, 5060

Prairie IL Resource Center, 4703

Prairie Independent Living Resource Center, 4704

Pre-Reading Screening Procedures, 3020

PreReading Strategies, 6301

Prelude, 122

PremierCare Neurohabilitation Program of Bethesda General Hospital, 8860

Prentke Romich Company, 192, 172, 176, 180, 219, 220, 224, 523, 2021, 2173

Prentke Romich Company Product Catalog, 490

Preparation and Employment of Students, 7230

Preparing for ACT Assessment, 3021

Presby, 9931

Presbyterian Center at Holmes, 1634

Presbyterian Hospital in the City of New York, 9614

Presbytery of Eastern Virginia, 1758, 1759

Preschool Learning Activities for the Visually Impaired Child, 6520

Preschoolers with Special Needs: Children At-Risk, Children with Disabilities, 2nd Edition, 2882

Prescott Public Library, 5286

Prescriptions for Independence, 5813

President's Committee for People with Intellectual Disabilities, 2489

President's Committee on Employment of Employment of the Disabled, 8420

President's Committee on People with Disabilities: Arkansas, 3861

President's Committee on People with Intellecutual Disabilities, 3808

Pressure Sores, 6944

Prevent Blindness America, 1317, 7147, 7148, 7818

Prevent Blindness Connecticut, 5323

Prevent Child Abuse of Metropolitan Washington, 7857, 6144

Preventable Brain Damage, 6945

Preventing Academic Failure, 2883

Preventing School Dropouts, 2884

Preventing Secondary Conditions Associated with Spina Bifida or Cerebral Palsy, 6521, 6946

Prevention in Community Mental Health, 5758

Prevocational Assessment, 2885

Pride Industries: Grass Valley, 9161

Prima Publishing, 6376, 6495, 6699, 6789

Primacy Healthcare and Rehabilitation Center, 9946

Primary Children's Medical Center, 8973

Primary Phonics, 2418

Prime Engineering, 243, 243

Primer on Amputations and Artificial Limbs, 6947

Primer on the Rheumatic Diseases, 6948

Primrose Supported Employment Programs, 8378

Princeton Educational Publishers, 6095

Principal Financial Group Foundation, 3340

Principles and a Philosophy for Vocational Education, 7231

Print, Play & Learn #1 Old Mac's Farm, 2142

Print, Play & Learn #7: Sampler, 2143

Printed Rear Closure Sweat Top, 1849

Priva, 141

Pro- Ed, 2346

Pro- Ed Publications, 2897, 2996, 3037, 3044, 8642

Pro- Max/ Division Of Bow- Flex Of America, 7781

Pro-Ed, 2522, 2611, 2618, 2891, 3005, 6894, 7156, 7240, 7442

Pro-Ed Publication, 2654

Pro-Ed Publications, 2367, 2414, 2415, 2600, 2606, 2610, 2626, 2685, 2714, 2722, 2723, 2735, 2759, 2769, 2772, 2833, 2849, 2864, 2884, 2887, 2890, 2893, 2936, 2941, 2948, 2962, 2963, 2964, 2966, 2981, 2982, 2995, 3012, 3024, 3036, 3038, 3039, 3040, 3041, 5842, 6355, 6808, 7050, 7195

Proceedings, 6131

Products for People with Disabilities, 491

Professional Books/Future Health, 6387

Professional Development Programs, 2554

Professional Fit Clothing, 1824

Professional Report, 6665

Profex Medical Products, 135

Program for Children w/ Special Health Care Needs, 4369

Programmed Phonics Books 1-2 & Cassettes, 2419

Programming Concepts, 2420, 2091, 2098, 2101, 2133, 2174, 2239

Programs for Aphasia and Cognitive Disorders, 2206

Programs for Children 3 to 5 with Disabilities, 1635

Programs for Children Birth to 2 with Disabilities, 1636

Programs for Children with Disabilities: Ages 3 through 5, 8804

Programs for Children with Special Health Care Needs, 1637, 8805

Programs for Infants and Toddlers with Disabilities: Ages Birth through 2, 8806

Progress Center South, 4650

Progress Center for Independent Living, 4651

Progress Valley: Phoenix, 9036

Progress Without Punishment: Approaches for Learners with Behavior Problems, 2886

Progress in Research, 6949

Progressive Center for Independent Living, 4921

Progressive Independence, 5014

Progressive Options, 5023

Project AID Resource Center, 5882

Project Freedom, 4922

Project Independence Supported Employment, 8302

Project LINK, 8492

Project LINK Guidebook, 5858

Project On Science, Technology and Disability, 818

Projects W Industry Goodwill Industries of America, 8491

Promoting Communication in Infants and Young Children: 500 Ways to Succeed, 6434

Promoting Postsecondary Education for Students with Learning Disabilities, 2887

Promoting Special Education Career Awareness, 2888

Prone Support Walker, 658

Prosthetics and Orthotics Center in Blue Island, 9384

ProtectaCap, ProtectaCap+PLUS, ProtectaChin Guard and ProtectaHip, 532

Protecting Against Latex Allergy, 6132

Protection & Advocacy Project, 4198

Protection & Advocacy System: Alaska, 3839

# Q

# R

# T

# U

# W

## Alabama

ASCCA, 1329
Adventure Program, 1330
Alabama Association of Homes and Services
  for the Aging, 756
Alabama Institute for Deaf and Blind Library
  and Resource Center, 5271
Alabama Power Foundation, 3102
Alabama Radio Reading Service Network
  (ARRS), 5272
Alabama Regional Library for the Blind and
  Physically Handicapped, 5273
Alabama VA Regional Office, 7974
Alabama Veterans Facility, 7975
Andalusia Health Services, 3103
Arc of Alabama, 3104
Basketball School, 1331
Birdie Thornton Center, 4379
Birmingham Independent Living Center,
  4380
Birmingham VA Medical Center, 7976
Blount Foundation, 3105
Camp Seale Harris Southeastern Diabetes
  Education Services, 1332
Camp Candlelight, 1333
Camp Rap-A-Hope Medical Society and the
  Alliance to the Medical, 1334
Camp Seale Harris, 1335
Camp Smile-A-Mile, 1336
Camp Wheezeaway American Lung
  Association of Alabama, 1337
Central Alabama Veterans Healthcare
  System, 7977
Coffee County Training Center, 8227
Easter Seal: Achievement Center, 8228
Easter Seal: Opportunity Center, 8229
Employment Service Division: Alabama,
  8230
Fort Payne-Dekalb Rehab Center, 8231
Houston-Love Memorial Library, 5274
Huntsville Subregional Library for the Blind
  & Physically Handicapped, 5275
Independent Living Center, 4381
Independent Living Center of Alabaster, 4382
Independent Living Center of Jasper, 4383
Independent Living Center of Mobile, 4384
Lakeshore Rehabilitation Facility, 8232
Library for the Blind & Handicapped Public
  Library: Anniston/Calhoun Counties, 5276
Liz Moore Low Vision Center, 1338
Montezuma Training Center, 8233
Montgomery Independent Living Center,
  4385
Parent as Partners in Education of Alabama,
  7854
Research for Rett Foundation, 5277
Special Education Action Commette, 7862
Summer Camp for Children with Muscular
  Dystrophy, 1339
Summer Enrichment Camp, 1340
Technology Assistance for Special
  Consumers, 5278
Thomasville Rehabilitation Center, 8234
Tuscaloosa Subregional Library for the Blind
  & Physically Handicapped, 5279
Tuscaloosa VA Medical Center, 7978
Vocational Rehabilitation Service Opelika,
  8235
Vocational Rehabilitation Service: Dothan,
  8237

Vocational Rehabilitation Service: Gadsden,
  8238
Vocational Rehabilitation Service: Homewoo
  d, 8239
Vocational Rehabilitation Service: Huntsvi
  lle, 8240
Vocational Rehabilitation Service: Jackson,
  8241
Vocational Rehabilitation Service: Jasper,
  8242
Vocational Rehabilitation Service: Mobile,
  8243
Vocational Rehabilitation Service: Muscle
  Shoals, 8244
Vocational Rehabilitation Service:
  Scottsboro, 8236
Vocational Rehabilitation Service: Selma,
  8245
Vocational Rehabilitation Service: Tallade
  ga, 8246
Vocational Rehabilitation Service: Troy, 8247
Vocational Rehabilitation Service: Tuscalo
  osa, 8248
Vocational Rehabilitation Services: Andalu
  sa, 8249
Vocational Rehabilitation Services: Annist
  on, 8250
Vocational and Rehabilitation Service
  Columbiana, 8252
Vocational and Rehabilitation Service: Dec
  atur, 8253
Wiregrass Rehabilitation Center, 8254
Workshops, 8255

## Alaska

Access Alaska: ADA Partners Project, 4386
Access Alaska: Fairbanks, 4387
Access Alaska: Mat-Suvalley, 4388
Alaska SILC, 4389
Alaska State Library Talking Book Center,
  5280
Anchorage Job Training Center, 8256
Anchorage Regional Office, 7979
Arc of Alaska, 3106
Arctic Access, 4390
Braille Revival League, 1272
Camp Alpine, 1342
Camp Birchwood, 1343
Camp Kushtaka American Diabetes Summer
  Camp, 1344
Camp Wheeze Away, 1345
DAV Department of Alaska, 7980
Employment Service: Alaska, 8257
Fair Employment Practice Agency, 8258
Hope Community Resources, 4391
International Association of Audio
  Information Services (IAAIS), 1291
Kenai Peninsula IL Center, 4392
Kenai Peninsula IL Center: Seward, 4393
Kenai Peninsula IL Center: Soldotna, 4394
Kushtaka, 1347
Muscular Dystrophy Association Free Camp,
  1348
Outdoor Recreation and Community
  Accesss, 1349
Rasmuson Foundation, 3107
SE Alaska ILC: Ketchikan, 4395
SE Alaska Independent Living Center, 4397
SE Alaska Independent Living Center
  (SAIL), 4396

SE Alaska Independent Living: Sitka, 4398
Seward Independent Learning Center, 4399
Seward Independent Living Center, 4400

## Arizona

ASSIST! to Independence, 4401
Arc of Arizona, 3108
Arizona Association of Homes and Housing
  for the Aging, 758
Arizona Braille and Talking Book Library,
  5281
Arizona Bridge to Independent Living, 4402
Arizona Bridge to Independent Living:
  Mesa, 4404
Arizona Bridge to Independent Living:
  Phoenix, 4403
Arizona Camp Sunrise, 1350
Arizona Community Foundation, 3109
Bonnie Prudden Myotherapy, 845
Books for the Blind of Arizona, 5282
CARF Rehabilitation Accreditation
  Commission, 847
Camp Civitan, 1351
Camp Honor, 1352
Camp Not-A-Wheeze American Lung
  Association, 1353
Camp Rainbow, 1354, 1372
Carl T Hayden VA Medical Center, 7981
Casa Del Rey, 4405
Children's Center for Neurodevelopmental
  Studies, 5283
Community Outreach Program for the Deaf,
  4406
Direct Center for Independence, 4407
Downtown Neighborhood Learning Center,
  8260
Easter Seals Arizona, 1355
Fair Employment Practice Agency: Arizona,
  8261
Flagstaff City-Coconino County Public
  Library, 5284
Fountain Hills Lioness Braille Service, 5285
International Association of Yoga Therapists,
  1088
International Ozone Association, 903
JOBS Administration Job Opportunities &
  Basic Skills, 8262
JW Kieckhefer Foundation, 3110
Lake Powell Summer Adventure Camp, 1356
Life Development Institute, 806
Lions Camp Tatiyee, 1357
Margaret T Morris Foundation, 3111
Muscular Dystrophy Association, 1198
New Horizons Independent Living Center,
  4408
New Horizons Independent Living Center:,
  4409
New Horizons: Prescott Valley, 4740
Northern Arizona VA Health Center, 7982
Phoenix Regional Office, 7983
Prescott Public Library, 5286
Services Maximizing Independent Living
  and Empowerment (SMILE), 4410
Sound, Listening, and Learning Center, 1051
Southern Arizona VA Healthcare System,
  7984
Special Needs Center/Phoenix Public
  Library, 5287
Sterling Ranch: Residence for Special
  Women, 4411

TETRA Corporation, 8263
Vocational and Rehabilitation Agency Rehabilitation Services Administrations, 8264
WAHEC Medical Library Consortium, 5288
Wheelers, 7963
Wheelers Accessible Van Rentals, 7964
World Chiropractic Alliance, 1111
World Research Foundation, 5289
Yavapal Rehabilitation Center, 8265

## Arkansas

American Amputee Foundation, 1118
Arc of Arkansas, 3112
Arkansas Employment Service Agency and Job Training Program, 8266
Arkansas Regional Library for the Blind and Physically Handicapped, 5290
Arkansas Rehabilitation Research and Training Center for the Deaf and Hard of Hearing, 990
Arkansas SILC, 4412
Arkansas School for the Blind, 5291
Breast Cancer Action, 1160
Case Management Society of America, 1082
Delta Resource Center for Independent Living, 4413
Easter Seal Work Center, 8267
Educational Services for the Visually Impaired, 5292
Eugene J Towbin Healthcare Center, 7985
John L McClellan Memorial Hospital, 7987
North Little Rock Regional Office, 7988
Northwest Ozarks Regional Library for the Blind and Handicapped, 5294
Our Way, 4415
Roy and Christine Sturgis Charitable Trust, 3113
Sources for Community IL Services, 4416
Spa Area Independent Living Services, 4417
VCT/A Job Retention Skill Training Program, 8268
Vocational and Rehabilitation Agency Division of Services for the Blind, 8269
Vocational and Rehabilitation Agency for Persons Who Are Visually Impaired, 8270
Winthrop Rockefeller Foundation, 3114

## California

ARC-Adult Vocational Program, 8271
Ability First, 8272
Access Center of San Diego, 4418
Access Center of San Diego N Branch, 4419
Achromatopsia Network, 1255
Acupressure Institute, 812
Ahmanson Foundation, 3115
Alice Tweed Touhy Foundation, 3116
Alliance for Technology Access, 816
Alternating Hemiplegia of Childhood Foundation, 3117
Amateur Athletic Foundation of Los Angeles, 3118
American Academy of Biological Dentistry, 1062
American Academy of Ophthalmology, 1256
American Academy of Ophthalmology Annual Meeting, 2252

American Association of Oriental Medicine, 983
American Back Society, 1123
American College of Advancement in Medicine, 1070
Amytrophic Lateral Sclerosis Association, 1140
Anglo California Travel Service, 7931
Annual Santa Barbara Sports Festival, 2262
Annuziata Sanguinetti Foundation, 3119
Apple Computer, 3120
Arc of California, 3121
Association of Visual Science Librarians, 5295
Atkinson Foundation, 3122
Autism Research Institute, 5296
Baker Commodities Corporate Giving Program, 3123
Bakersfield Association for Retarded Citizens, 8273
Bank of America Foundation, 3124
Bar 717 Ranch/Camp Trinity, 1358
Bergen Brunswig Corporation Contributions Program, 3125
Blind Babies Foundation, 3126
Blind Childrens Center, 1268
Blind Childrens Center Annual Meeting, 2266
Bothin Foundation, 3127
Braille Institute  Library, 5297
Braille Institute Library, 5298
Braille Institute Orange County Center, 5299, 7811
Braille Institute Santa Barbara Center, 5300
Braille Institute Sight Center, 5301
Braille Institute of America, 1271
Braille and Talking Book Library, 5302
Braille and Talking Book Library: Californ ia State Library, 5303
Briggs Foundation, 3128
Broadcast Services for the Blind, 5304
Burns-Dunphy Foundation, 3129
CAPH Independent Living Center, 4420
CIL: Fresno, 4421
CNF Transportation Corporate Giving Program, 3130
California Association of Homes and Services for the Aging, 760
California Community Foundation, 3131
California Department of Fair Employment & Housing, 8274
California Endowment, 3132
California Foundation for Independent Living Centers, 4422
California State Independent Living Council (SILC), 4423
California State Library Braille and Talki ng Book Library, 1273
California State Oriental Medical Association (CSOMA), 848
Camp  Paivika, 1359
Camp Bloomfield and Foundation for the Jun, 1360
Camp Bloomfield and the Junior Blind of Am erica Foundation, 1361
Camp Conrad Chinnock, 1362
Camp Del Corazon, 1363
Camp El Camino Pines, 1364
Camp Esperanza Arthritis Foundation, 1365
Camp Forrest, 1366
Camp Joan Mier, 1367
Camp Krem, 1368
Camp Okizu, 1370

Camp Paivika, 1371
Camp Ronald McDonald at Eagle Lake, 1373
Camp Ronald McDonald for Good Times, 1374
Camp-A-Lot, 1375
Camping Unlimited, 1376
Camps for Children & Teens with Diabetes, 1377
Cancer Control Society, 1162
Canine Companions for Independence, 849
Career Connection Transition Program, 8275
Career Development Program (CDP), 8276
Carrie Estelle Doheny Foundation, 3133
Center for Independence of the Disabled, 4425
Center for Independent Living: Oakland, 4427
Center for Independent Living: Tri-County, 4914
Center for Independent Living:Fresno, 4428
Center for Independent Living; East Oakland, 4429
Center for Independent Living; Oakland, 4430
Center of Independent Living: Visalia, 4431
Central Coast Center for IL: San Benito, 4432
Central Coast Center for Independent Living, 4433
Central Coast Center: Independent Living - Santa Cruz Office, 4434
Central Coast for Independent Living, 4435
Central Coast for Independent Living: Watsonville, 4436
Clearinghouse for Specialized Media and Technology, 5305
Clorox Company Foundation, 3134
Coeta and Donald Barker Foundation, 3135
College Student's Guide to Merit and Other No-Need Funding, 3745
Communities Actively Living Independent and Free, 4437
Community Access Center, 4438
Community Access Center: Beaumont, 4439
Community Access Center: Indio Branch, 4440
Community Access Center: Perris, 4441
Community Foundation of Santa Clara County, 3136
Community Outpatient Rehabilitation Center, 8277
Community Rehabilitation Services, 4442, 4443
Community Rehabilitation Services (CRS) Pasadena Office, 4444
Community Rehabilitation Services for Independent Living, 4445
Community Rehabilitation Services: Downtown Office, 4446
Community Resources for Independence: Fort Bragg Office, 4449
Community Resources for Independence: Mendocino/Lake Branch, 4448
Community Resources for Independence: Napa Office, 4450
Community Resources for Independent Living, 4452
Community Resources for Independent Living Hayward, 4451
Community Resoures for Independence, 4453
Costanoan, 1378
Crescent Porter Hale Foundation, 3137
Cry-Rop: Colton-Redlands-Yucaipa Rop, 8278

Santa Barbara Foundation, 3175
Santa Barbara Wheelchair Sports Conference, 2284
Service Center for Independent Living, 4492
Service Center for Independent Living: Covina Office, 4491
Shasta County Opportunity Center, 8306
Sidney Stern Memorial Trust, 3176
Sierra Health Foundation, 3177
Silicon Valley Independent Living Center, 4494
Silicon Valley Independent Living Center: Gilroy Office, 4493
Simonton Cancer Center, 1242
Social Vocational Services, 8307
Sonora Area Foundation, 3178
South Bay Vocational Center, 8308
Southern California Rehabilitation Services, 4496
Stella B Gross Charitable Trust, 3179
Summer Day Camp, 1394
Teichert Foundation, 3180
Through the Looking Glass, 4497
Times Mirror Foundation, 3181
Tri-County Independent Living Center, 4498, 5009, 5107, 5107, 8309
Tripod, 1054
Tulare County Training Center Able Industries, 8310
Tulare Workcenter Able Industries Able Industries, 8311
Unyeway, 8312
V-Bar Enterprises, 8313
VA Central California Health Care Syste, 7998
VA Greater Los Angeles Healthcare System, 7999
VA Northern California Healthcare System, 8000
VA San Diego Healthcare System, 8001
Valley Light Industries, 8314
Visalia Workshop, 8315
Visually Impaired Veterans of America, 1327
Vocational Services, 8316
WM Keck Foundation, 3182
WRAD, 1057
Westside Center for Independent Living, 4499
Westside Opportunity Workshop, 8317
Willam G Gilmore Foundation, 3183
Work Training Center for the Handicapped, 8318
Work Training Programs, 8319
World Experience, 3098
World Institute on Disability, 975

# Colorado

AMC Cancer Research Center, 5315
Adolph Coors Foundation, 3184
American Council of Blind Lions, 1259
American Society of Bariatric Physicians, 1076
American Universities International Programs, 3067
Anschutz Family Foundation, 3185
Arc of Colorado, 3186
Association for Applied Psychophysiology and Biofeedback, 835
Association for Network Care, 836
Atlantis Community, 4500

Bill Dvorak, Kayak and Rafting Expeditions, 7932
Bonfils-Stanton Foundation, 3187
Boulder Public Library, 5316
Boulder Vet Center, 8002
Breckenridge Outdoor Education Center, 1395
Camp Paha, 1396
Camp Shady Brook, 1397
Center for Independence, 4424, 4501
Center for Independent Living, 4426, 4837
Center for People with Disabilities, 4502
Center for People with Disabilities (CPWD), 4503
Center for People with Disabilities: Pueblo, 4504
Challenge Aspen, 1398
Cheyenne Village, 8320
Colorado Association of Homes and Services for the Aging (CAHSA), 763
Colorado Civil Rights Divsion, 8321
Colorado Employment Service, 8322
Colorado Library for the Blind and Physically Handicapped, 5317
Colorado Lions Camp, 1399
Colorado Springs Independence Center, 4506
Colorado/Wyoming VA Medical Center, 8003
Comprecare Foundation, 3188
Connections for Independent Living, 4507
Deaf Counseling Services at Mental Health Corporation of Denver, 4508
Denver CIL, 4509
Denver Foundation, 3189
Denver VA Medical Center, 8004
Developmental Training Services, 8323
Disability Center for Independent Living, 4510
Disabled Resource Services, 4511
Disbled Resource Services, 4512
Dynamic Dimensions, 8324
Easter Seals Colorado Rocky Mountain Villa, 1400
El Pomar Foundation, 3190
Estate Planning for the Disabled, 874
Gates Family Foundation, 3191
Glacier View Ranch, 1401
Grand Junction VA Medical Center, 8005
Gray Street Workcenter, 8325
Greeley Center for Independence, 4513
Hear Now, 1017
Helen K and Arthur E Johnson Foundation, 3192
Herbert F Parker Foundation, 3193
Hill Foundation, 3194
Hope Center, 8326
Imagine: Innovative Resources for Cognitive & Physical Challenges, 8327
Independent Life Center, 4514
Institute for Music, Health and Education, 892
International Hearing Dog, 1021
JM McDonald Foundation, 3195
Kitzmiller-Bales Trust, 3196
Las Animas County Rehabilitation Center, 8328
Lung Line Information Service, 7836
Magic of Music and Dance, 1402
Martin Luther Home of Colorado, 4515
Martin Luther Homes: Fort Collins, 4516
Mind/Body Health Services, 912
NLP Comprehensive, 914
NORESCO Workshop, 8329

National Jewish Medical & Research Center, 5318
National Stroke Association, 1227
National Veterans Training Institute, 8006
North America Riding for the Handicapped Association, 944
Pueblo Goodwill Center for Independent, 4517
Pueblo Goodwill Industries, 4518
Regional Assessment and Training Center, 8330
Rocky Mountain Resource & Training Institute, 961
Rocky Mountain Village, 1403
Rolf Institute, 1106
Scientific Health Solutions, 963
Sedgwick County Workshop, 8331
Sky Ranch Lutheran Camp, 1404
Southwest Center for Independence, 4519
Southwest Center for Independence: Cortez, 4520
United States Association of Blind Athletes, 1323
V Hunter Trust, 3197
Valley Industries, 8332
Wyoming/Colorado VA Regional Office, 8226
Yuma County Workshop, 8334

# Connecticut

Abilities Expo, 2249
Aetna Foundation, 3198
American Herbalists Guild, 826
American Institute for Foreign Study, 3066
Arc of Connecticut, 3199
Area Cooperative Educational Services (ACES), 8335
CCARC, 8336
Camp Harkness, 1405
Camp Horizons, 1406
Camp Isola Bella, 1407
Camp Jewell YMCA Outdoor Center, 1408
Center for Disability Rights, 4521
Center for Independent Living SC, 4522
Center for Understanding Aging, 761
Chapel Haven, 4523
Cheshire Occupational and Career Center, 8337
Co-Op Initiatives, 4524
Community Enterprises, 1084, 8338
Community Foundation of Southeastern Connecticut, 3201
Connecticut Association for Children and Adults with Learning Disabilities (CACLD), 1171
Connecticut Association of Not-for-Profit Providers for the Aging, 764
Connecticut Braille Association, 5319
Connecticut Governor's Committee on Employment of Disabled Persons, 8339
Connecticut Mutual Life Foundation, 3202
Connecticut State Library, 5320
Connecticut Tech Act Project: Connecticut Department of Social Services, 5321
Constructive Workshops, 8340
Cornelia de Lange Syndrome Foundation, 3203
Disabilities Network of Eastern Connecticut, 4525

Disability Resource Center of Fairfield County: Stratford Office, 4526
Disabled American Veterans: Connecticut, 8007
Easter Seal Camp Hemlocks, 1409
Favarh/Farmington Valley ARC, 877
Fidelco Guide Dog Foundation, 1281, 3204
Focus Alternative Learning Center, 879
Fotheringhay Farms, 8341
GE Foundation, 3205
General Electric Foundation, 3206
George Hegyi Industrial Training Center, 8342
Georgiana Institute, 1013
Greater Enfield Association of Retarded Citizens, 8343
Hartford Foundation for Public Giving, 3207
Hartford Insurance Group, 3208
Hartford Regional Office, 8008
Hartford Vet Center, 8009
Henry Nias Foundation, 3209
Heublein Foundation, 3210
Hole in the Wall Gang Camp, 1410
Independence Northwest Center for Independent Living, 4527
Independence Unlimited, 4528
Jane Coffin Childs Memorial Fund for Medical Research, 3211
John H and Ethel G Nobel Charitable Trust, 3212
Kennedy Center, 8344
Library for the Blind and Physically Handicapped, 5293, 5322
Mansfield's Holiday Hill Camp, 1411
Mansfields Holiday Hill, 1412
Marvelwood Summer, 1413
National Alliance of Blind Students NABS Liaison, 1297
National Federation of the Blind: Masonic Square Club, 1310
National Organization for Rare Disorders, 1225
National Theatre of the Deaf, 1043
New Horizons, 4529
Prevent Blindness Connecticut, 5323
Quaezar, 8345
Scheuer Associates Foundation, 3213
Shadybrook Learning Center, 1414
Swindells Charitable Foundation Trust, 3214
TEAM Vocational Program, 8346
TSA CT Kid's Summer Event, 1415
VA Connecticut Healthcare System: Newington Division, 8010
VA Connecticut Healthcare System: West Haven, 8011
Valley Memorial Health Center, 8347
Vocational and Rehabilitation Agency: State Department of Social Services, 8349
Yale University: Vision Research Center, 5324

## Delaware

Arc of Delaware, 3215
Childrens Beach House, 1416
Delaware Assistive Technology Initiative Center for Applied Science and Engineering, 5325
Delaware Association of Nonprofit Homes for the Aging, 765

Delaware Commission of Veterans Affairs, 8012
Delaware Division of Vocational Rehabilitation- Department of Labor, 8350
Delaware Fair Employment Practice Agency, 8351
Delaware Job Training Program Liaison, 8352
Delaware Library for the Blind and Physically Handicapped, 5326
Delaware VA Regional Office, 8013
Easter Seal Independent Living Center, 4530
Elwyn Delaware, 5327
Freedom Center for Independent Living, 4531
Independent Living, 4532
Independent Resource Georgetown, 4533
Independent Resources, 4534
Independent Resources Wilmington, 4535
Independent Resources: Dover, 4536
Independent Resources: Wilmington, 4537
Laffey-McHugh Foundation, 3216
Longwood Foundation, 3217
Martin Luther Homes of Delaware, 4538
Opportunity Center, 8353
Wilmington VA Medical, 8014
Wilmington Vet Center, 8015

## District of Columbia

ACB Government Employees, 1058
ACB Social Service Providers, 1059
Advocates for Hearing Impaired Youth, 979
Albert L and Elizabeth T Tucker Foundation, 3218
Alexander Graham Bell Association for the Deaf and Hard of Hearing Annual Conference, 980, 2250
Alexander and Margaret Stewart Trust, 3219
American Academy of Child and Adolescent Psychiatry, 1117
American Association for the Advancement of Science, 818
American Association of Homes and Services for the Aging, 757
American Association of Naturopathic Physicians, 1069, 1119, 1120, 1120
American Association of People with Disabilities, 820
American Association on Mental Retardation AAMR Annual Meeting, 2254
American Chemical Society Committee on Chemists with Disabilities, 1126
American Council of the Blind, 1260
American Council of the Blind Annual Convention, 2256
American Orthotic and Prosthetic Association, 1133
American Public Health Association, 830
American Red Cross: National Headquarters, 831
Anchor Houses, 7807
Arc of the District of Columbia, 3220
Asthma and Allergy Foundation of America, 1147
Blind Information Technology Specialists, 1081
Blinded Veterans Association, 1269
Blinded Veterans Association National Convention, 2267
Books for Blind and Physically Handicapped Individuals, 1270

Center for Mind/Body Studies, 855
Centers for Independent Living Program Rehabilitation Services Department, 4539
Change, 857
Charles Delmar Foundation, 3221
Children's National Medical Center, 859
Chronicle Guide to Grants, 3744
Clearinghouse on Disability Information, 7814
Cochlear Implant Club International, 998
Columbia Lighthouse for the Blind, 1277
Columbia Lighthouse for the Blind Summer Camp, 1417
Community Connections, 4806, 7815
DAV National Service Headquarters, 7965
DC Center for Independent Living, 4540
Davis Memorial Goodwill Industries, 8354
Deaf REACH, 1005
Deafness Research Foundation, 1007
Deafness and Communicative Disorders Branch of Rehab Services Administration Office, 1008
Department of Medicine and Surgery Veterans Administration, 7966
Department of Veterans Benefits, 7968
Disability Rights Center, 4541
Disabled American Veterans, National Service & Legislative Headquarters, 8016
Distance Education and Training Council, 865
District of Columbia Center for Independent Living, 4542
District of Columbia Department of Employment Services, 8355
District of Columbia Dept. of Employment Services: Office of Workforce Development, 8356
District of Columbia Fair Employment Practice Agencies, 8357
District of Columbia Public Library: Services to the Deaf Community, 5328
District of Columbia Regional Library for the Blind and Physically Handicapped, 5329
Epilepsy Foundation for the National Capitol Area, 7825
Eugene and Agnes E Meyer Foundation, 3222
Eye Bank Association of America, 1280
Eye Bank Association of America Annual Meeting, 2272
Federal Benefits for Veterans and Dependents, 7970
Federal Grants & Contracts Weekly, 3756
Federal Student Aid Information Center, 3223
Foundation & Corporate Grants Alert, 3763
GEICO Philanthropic Foundation, 3224
Gallaudet University Alumni Association, 1012
George Washington University Health Resource Center, 882
Georgetown University Center for Child and Human Development, 5330
Giant Food Foundation, 3225
Golden Eagle Passport, 7940
Green Door, 7827, 8358
Guide Service of Washington, 7941
Health Resource Center, 1016
Independent Visually Impaired Enterprisers, 803
Jacob and Charlotte Lehrman Foundation, 3226
John Edward Fowler Memorial Foundation, 3227

Joseph P Kennedy Jr Foundation, 3228
Judge David L Bazelon Center for Mental Health Law, 1187
Kiplinger Foundation, 3229
Lab School of Washington, 1418
Medicare Information, 7839
Morris and Gwendolyn Cafritz Foundation, 3230
Myositis Association, 1199
National AIDS Fund, 1201
National Association for Home Care, 7841
National Association of Blind Teachers, 1094
National Association of Protection and Advocacy Systems, 917, 1095
National Center for Education in Maternal and Child Health, 920
National Council on Disability, 924
National Council on the Aging Conference, 2278
National Deaf Education Network and Clearinghouse, 1035, 1098
National Dissemination Center for Children and Youth with Disabilities (NICHCY), 926
National Endowment for the Arts: Office for AccessAbility, 929
National Health Information Center, 7846
National Information Center for Children, 931
National Information Center for Children and Youth with Disabilities (NICHCY), 1038
National Institute on Disability and Rehabilitation Research, 933, 5331
National Library Services for the Blind & Physically Handicapped, 1221, 1313
National Organization on Disability, 936
National Parent Network on Disabilities, 937
National Voluntary Organizations for Independent Living for the Aging, 781
National Women's Health Network, 942
Operation Job Match, 8359
PVA Sports and Recreation Program, 8017
PXE International, 7851
Paralyzed Veterans of America, 1230
Paul and Annetta Himmelfarb Foundation, 3231
People-to-People Committee for the Handicapped, 952
Polio Society, 1235
Public Welfare Foundation, 3232
Rehabilitation Engineering Research Center on Hearing Enhancement and Assistive Devices, 1046
Rehabilitation Services Administration, 8360
Rehabilitation Services Administration of the District of Columbia, 960
Scottish Rite Center for Childhood Language Disorders, 1049
Shiloh Senior Citizens Center, 792
Sister Cities International, 3091
Spina Bifida Association of America, 1244
Student Guide, 3791
SubAcute Care: American SubAcute Care Association Annual Convention/Expo, 2285
Teacher Preparation and Special Education, 966
Tele-Consumer Hotline, 1052
Toll-Free Information Line, 7866
US Department of Veterans Affairs National Headquarters, 7972
US Veteran's Affairs, 7973
United Cerebral Palsy Association, 1249

United Cerebral Palsy Association Development Conference, 2287
VA Medical Center, Washington DC, 8018
WAVE Work, Achievement, Value, & Education, 8361
Washington Connection, 7869
Washington DC VA Medical Center, 8019

# Florida

Abilities of Florida: An Affiliate of Service Source, 8362
Ability 1st, 4544
Able Trust, 3233
Adult Day Training, 4545, 8363
Advocacy Center for Persons with Disabilities, 814
American Academy of Orthomolecular Medicine, 1064
American Society of Deaf Social Workers, 987
Arc of Florida, 3234
Arthritis Consulting Services, 1142
Association of Birth Defect Children, 1145
Ataxia-Telangiectasia Children's Project (A-T Children's Project), 1148
BCR Foundation, 3235
Bank of America Client Foundation, 3236
Baron de Hirschmeyer Foundation, 3237
Barron Collier Jr Foundation, 3238
Bay Pines VA Medical Center, 8020
Birth Defect Research for Children, 1156
Blazing Toward a Cure Annual Conference, 2265
Boggy Creek Gang Camp, 1419
Brevard County Talking Books Library, 5332
Broward County Talking Book Library, 5333
CEH, 7956
CIL Options-One Stop Career Center: Royal Palm Beach, 4546
CIL of Central Florida, 4547
CIL of Florida Keys, 4548
CIL of Florida Keys-Key West, 4549
CIL of North Central Florida, 4550
Camiccia-Arnautou Charitable Foundation, 3239
Camp Thunderbird, 1420
Camp World Light, 1421
Career Assessment & Planning Services, 8364
Caring and Sharing Center for Independent Living, 4551
Caring and Sharing: Gulf Port, 4552
Caring and Sharing: Holiday, 4553
Cathedral Center for Independent Living, 4554
Center Academy, 851
Center Academy at Pinellas Park, 1422
Center for Independence, Training and Education, 8365
Center for Independent Living Options - One Stop Career Center: Stuart, 4555
Center for Independent Living in Central Florida - Advocacy Living Skills Peer Support, 4556
Center for Independent Living of Broward, 4557
Center for Independent Living of Florida Keys, 4558
Center for Independent Living of N Central Florida, 4559

Center for Independent Living of N Florida, 4560
Center for Independent Living of NW Florida, 4561
Center for Independent Living of North Central Florida, 4562
Center for Independent Living of S Florida, 4563
Center for Independent Living of SW Florida, 4564
Center for Independent Technology and Education (CITE), 4565
Chatlos Foundation, 3240
Choices for Work Program, 8366
Coalition for Independent Living Option, 4566
Coalition for Independent Living Options-One Stop Career Center, 4567
Community Support Center, 7816
Conference of Educational Administrators Serving the Deaf, 1000
Cunard Line, 7933
Dade Community Foundation, 3241
Dade County Talking Book Library, 5334
Dialysis at Sea Cruises, 7936
Dr. Jack Widrich Foundation, 3242
EIS Foundation, 3243
Edyth Bush Charitable Foundation, 3244
FPL Group Foundation, 3245
Florida Camp for Children and Youth with Diabetes, 1423
Florida Diabetes Camp, 1424
Florida Division of Blind Services, 5335
Florida Division of Vocational Rehabilitation, 8367
Florida Fair Employment Practice Agency, 8368
Florida Instructional Materials Center for the Visually Handicapped, 5336
Florida Lions Camp, 1425
Florida Rock Industries Foundation, 3246
Florida School for the Deaf and Blind, 1426
Florida Sheriffs Caruth Camp, 1427
Florida Vocational Rehabilitation for Persons Who Are Visually Impaired, 8369
Florida's Governor's Alliance of Citizens with Disabilities, 8370
Frank Stanley Beveridge Foundation, 3247
Gainesville Division, North Florida/South Georgia Veterans Healthcare System, 8021
Goodwill Temporary Services, 8371
Hillsborough County Talking Book Library Tampa-Hillsborough County Public Library, 5337
Impact: Ocala Vocational Services, 8372
Independent Living Resource Center of Northeast Florida, 4569
Independent Living for Adult Blind, 4570
Indian Acres Camp for Boys, 1428
International Academy of Oral Medicine and Toxicology, 896
International Association of Professional Natural Hygienists, 897
International Institute of Reflexology, 901
Jack Eckerd Corporation Foundation, 3248
James A Haley VA Medical Center, 8022
Jefferson Lee Ford III Memorial Foundation, 3249
Jessie Ball duPont Fund, 3250
Job Works NISH Food Service, 8373
Job Works NISH Postal Service, 8374
Joe and Emily Lowe Foundation, 3251

John E & Nellie J Bastien Memorial Foundation, 3252

Lake City Division, North Florida/South Georgia Veterans Healthcare System, 8023

Lee County Library System: Talking Books Library, 5338

Lost Tree Village Charitable Foundation, 3253

Louis de la Parte Florida Mental Health Institute Research Library, 5339

MAClown Vocational Rehabilitation Workshop, 8375

Miami VA Medical Center, 8024

Miami-Dade County Disability Services and Independent Living (DSAIL), 4571

Multiple Sclerosis Foundation, 1197

National Car Rental System, 7958

National Mobility Equipment Dealers Association, 1105

National Parkinson Foundation, 1226

North Central Florida Citrus County, 4572

North Central Pennsylvania Center for Independent Living, 5034

Northern Florida Center for Independent Living, 4573

Norwegian Cruise Line, 7946

One-Stop Service, 8376

Orange County Library System: Audio-Visual Department, 5340

Palm Beach Habilitation Center, 8377

Pearlman Biomedical Research Institute, 5341

Pinellas Talking Book Library for the Blind and Physically Handicapped, 5342

Prader-Willi Syndrome Association USA, 1238

Primrose Supported Employment Programs, 8378

Publix Super Markets Charities, 3254

Richard W Higgins Charitable Foundation Trust, 3255

SCARC, 8379

SCCIL at Titusville, 4574

Seagull Industries for the Disabled, 8380

Self Reliance, 4575

Self-Reliance Center for Independent Living, 4576

Space Coast Center for Independent Living, 4577

St. Petersburg Regional Office, 8025

Subregional Talking Book Library, 5343

Suncoast Center for Independent Living, 4578

Suncoast Center for Independent Living: Arcadia, 4579

Supported Employment Program, 8381

Talking Book Service: Mantatee County Central Library, 5344

Talking Books Library for the Blind and Physically Handicapped, 5345

Talking Books/Homebound Services, 5346

Tampa Lighthouse for the Blind, 4580

University of Miami: Bascom Palmer Eye Institute, 5347

University of Miami: Mailman Center for Child Development, 5348

Upledger Institute, 970

VACC Camp, 1429

Victory Lane Center for Independent Living, 4581

Vocational and Rehabilitation Agency Department of Education, 8382

West Florida Regional Library, 5349

West Palm Beach VA Medical Center, 8026

Work Exploration Center, 8384

Young Onset Parkinson Conference, 2290

## Georgia

Albany Talking Book Center, 5350

American Cancer Society, 1125

American Juvenile Arthritis Organization (AJAO), 1130

American SIDS Institute, 7805

American Spinal Injury Association, 1137

American Spinal Injury Association Annual Scientific Meeting, 2261

Arthritis Foundation, 1143

Arthritis Foundation Information Hotline, 7808

Athens Regional Library Talking Book Center, 5351

Atlanta Regional Office, 8027

Atlanta VA Medical Center, 8028

Augusta Talking Book Center, 5352

Augusta VA Medical Center, 8029

Bain, 4583

Bainbridge Subregional Library for the Blind & Physically Handicapped, 5353

Camp Breathe Easy, 1430

Camp Independence, 1431

Camp Lookout, 1432

Camp Twin Lakes, 1433

Carl Vinson VA Medical Center, 8030

Center for Assistive Technology and Environmental Access, 853

Community Foundation for Greater Atlanta, 3256

DisABILITY LINK NW, 4584

Disability Action Center for Georgia, 4585

Disability Connections, 4586

Disability LINK, 4587

Disability and Health, National Center for Birth Defects and Developmental Disabilities, 7823

Emory Autism Resource Center, 5354

Emory University Laboratory for Ophthalmic Research, 5355

Employment and Training Division, Region B, 8385

Fair Housing and Fair Employment, 8386

Florence C and Harry L English Memorial Fund, 3257

Fragrance and Health, 880

Friends of Disabled Adults and Children, 881

Georgia Arc Network, 3258

Georgia Association of Homes and Services for the Aging, 766

Georgia Library for the Blind and Physically Handicapped, 5356

Georgia Power Company Contributions Program, 3259

Georgia Veterans Centers, 8031

Georgia's SILC, 4589

Grayson Foundation, 3260

Griffin Area Resource Center Griffin Community Workshop Division, 8387

Hall County Library: East Hall Branch and Special Needs Library, 5357

Harriet McDaniel Marshall Trust in Memory of Sanders McDaniel, 3261

Human Ecology Action League (HEAL), 888

IBM Corporation, 3262

IBM National Support Center, 8388

John H and Wilhelmina D Harland Charitable Foundation, 3263

Kelley Diversified, 8389

Kids on the Block Arthritis Programs, 7834

Lettie Pate Whitehead Foundation, 3264

Living Independence for Everyone (LIFE), 4590

Macon Library for the Blind and Physically Handicapped, 5358

MedTrade/Comtrade, FutureShow, 2277

Metametrix Clinical Laboratory, 910

Multiple Choices Center for Independent Living, 4591

National AIDS Hotline, 7840

National Center on Birth Defects and Developmental Disabilities, 5359

National Down Syndrome Congress, 1214

New Ventures, 8390

North District Independent Living Program, 4592

North Georgia Talking Book Center, 5360

Oconee Regional Library, 5361

Open Arms, 4593

Parent to Parent, 948

Patterson-Barclay Memorial Foundation, 3265

Perkins-Ponder Foundation, 3266

Rich Foundation, 3267

Rome Subregional Library for the Blind and Physically Handicapped, 5362

Roosevelt Warm Springs Institute for Rehabilitation, 4594

Savannah Widows Society, 3268

South Georgia Regional Library-Valdosta Talking Book Center, 5363

Southeastern PVA, 4595

Southwest District Independent Living Program, 4596

Squirrel Hollow Summer Camp, 1434

Subregional Library for the Blind and Physically Handicapped, 5364

SunTrust Bank, Atlanta Foundation, 3269

Talking Book Center Brunswick-Glynn County Regional Library, 5365

Walton Option for Independent Living, 4597

Walton Options, 4598

## Hawaii

ASSETS School, 8391

American Pacific University, 829

Arc of Hawaii, 3270

Assistive Technology Resource Centers of Hawaii (ATRC), 5366

Atherton Family Foundation, 3271

Camp Erdman YMCA, 1435

Camp Mokuleia, 1436

Center for Independent Living: E Hawaii, 4599

Clarence TC Ching Foundation, 3272

GN Wilcox Trust, 3273

H.C.I.L. - Kauai, 4600

Hawaii Centers for Independent Living, 4601

Hawaii Community Foundation, 3274

Hawaii Fair Employment Practice Agency, 8392

Hawaii State Library for the Blind and Physically Handicapped, 5367

Hawaii Veterans Centers, 8032

Hawaii Vocational Rehabilitation Division, 8393

Life Service Network of Illinois: Springfield, 771
Life Services Network of Illinois, 772
Lions Clubs International, 1296, 3084
Little City Foundation, 3305
Living Independently Now Center (LINC), 4642
MAGIC Foundation for Children's Growth, 3306
Marion VA Medical Center, 8042
McDonald's Corporation Contributions Program, 3307
Michael Reese Health Trust, 3308
Mid-Illinois Talking Book Center, 5376
Moen Foundation, 3309
Mosaic-Pontiac, 4643
National Association for Down Syndrome, 1205
National Depressive and Manic Depressive Association, 7845
National Easter Seal Society, 928
National Eye Research Foundation (NERF), 3310, 5377
National Fraternal Society of the Deaf, 1037
National Headache Foundation, 3311
National Lekotek Center, 5378
New Courier Travel, 7944
North Chicago VA Medical Center, 8043
Northwest Limousine Service, 7959
Northwestern Illinois Center for Independent Living, 4644
Northwestern University Multipurpose Arthritis & Musculoskeletal Center, 5379
OMRON Foundation, 3312
Olympia, 1447
Opportunities for Access: A Center for Independent Living, 4645
Options CIL, 4646
Options Center for Independent Living: Watseka, 4647
Options Center for Independent Living: Bourbonnais, 4648
Orchard Village: Assoc for the Retarded, 8418
Oris B Hastings Charitable Foundation, 3313
Owens Vocational Training Center, 8419
PACE Center for Independent Living, 4649
Peoria Area Community Foundation, 3315
Polk Brothers Foundation, 3316
Post-Polio Support Group, 7856
President's Committee on Employment of Employment of the Disabled, 8420
Prevent Blindness America, 1317
Progress Center South, 4650
Progress Center for Independent Living, 4651
RAMP Regional Access and Mobility Project, 4652
Regional Access & Mobilization Project, 4653
Regional Access and Mobilization Project (RAMP), 4654
Regional Access and Mobilization Project: DeKalb, 4655
Rehab Assist, 2326
Rehabilitation Institute of Chicago Learning Resource Center, 5380
Retirement Research Foundation, 3317
Rimland Services for Autistic Citizens, 1448
Rotary Youth Exchange, 3089
Rush Hayward Masonic Fund, 3318
Sears-Roebuck Foundation, 3319
Sertoma Centre, 8421
Shady Oaks Camp, 1449

Shore Training Center, 8422
Siragusa Foundation, 3320
Skills, 8423
Skokie Accessible Library Services, 5381
Southern Illinois Center for Independent Living, 4656
Southern Illinois Talking Book Center, 5382
Southern Illinois University at Carbondale, 3092
Soyland Access, 4657
Soyland Access to IL, 4658
Soyland Access to Independent Living (SAIL), 4659
Soyland Access to Independent Living: Charleston, 4660
Special Children, 7861
Springfield Center for Independent Living, 4661
Square D Foundation, 3321
Stone-Hayes Center for Independent Living, 4662
Summer Wheelchair Sports Camp, 1450
Thresholds AMISS, 8424
Thresholds Psychiatric Rehabilitation Centers, 968
Touch of Nature Environmental Center, 1451
Triangle D Camp for Children with Diabetes, 1452
University of Illinois at Chicago: Lions of Illinois Eye Research Institute, 5383
VA Illiana Health Care System, 8044
Voices of Vision Talking Book Center at DuPage Library System, 5384
WP and HB White Foundation, 3322
Washington County Vocational Workshop, 8426
Washington Square Health Foundation, 3323
West Central Illinois Center for Independent Living, 4663
Westside Parents Work Activity Center, 8427
Wheat Ridge Ministries, 3324
Will Grundy Center for Independent Living, 4664
YMCA Camp Duncan, 1453

# Indiana

ADEC Resources for Independence, 8428
ARC of Allen County, 8429
Allen County Public Library, 5385
American Academy of Osteopathy, 1065
American Camping Association, 823
Arc of Indiana, 3325
Assistive Technology Training and Information Center (ATTIC), 4665
BI-County Services, 8430
Balance Centers of America, 8431
Ball Brothers Foundation, 3326
Bartholomew County Public Library, 5386
Bradford Woods/Camp Riley, 1454
Bridge Pointe Services, 8432
CHAMP Camp, 1455
Camp Crosley YMCA, 1457
Camp John Warvel, 1458
Camp Millhouse, 1459
Carey Services, 8433
Central Indiana Community Foundation, 3327
Champ Camp American Lung Association of Alaska, 1346

Community Foundation of Boone County, 3328
Cranial Academy, 1172
Crown Point Community Foundation, 3329
Damar Homes, 4666
Damar Services, 4667
Easter Seal Crossroads Rehabilitation Center, 1460
Easter Seals ARC of Northeast Indiana, 1461
Easter Seals of Wayne & Union Counties, 1462
Eli Lilly & Co Corporate Contributions Program, 3330
Elkhart Public Library for the Blind and Physiclly Handicapp, 5387
Englishton Park Academic Remediation, 1463
Evansville Association for the Blind, 8434
Everybody Counts Center for Independent Living, 4668
Four Rivers Resource Services, 4669, 8435
Future Choices Independent Living Center, 4670
Gateway Services/JCARC, 8436
Goodwill Industries of Central Indiana, 8437
Happiness Bag, 1464
Happy Hollow Childrens Camp, 1465
Independent Living Center of Eastern Indiana (ILCEIN), 4671
Indiana Association of Homes for the Aging, 767
Indiana Employment Services and Job Training Program Liaison, 8438
Indiana Fair Employment Practice Agency, 8439
Indiana Resource Center for Autism, 5388
Indiana University: Multipurpose Arthritis Center, 5389
Indianapolis Foundation, 3331
Indianapolis Regional Office, 8045
Indianapolis Resource CIL (IRCIL), 4672
Indianapolis Resource Center for Independent Living, 4673
Isanogel Center, 1466
John W Anderson Foundation, 3332
LCAR, 8440
Lake County Public Library Talking Books Service, 5390
League for the Blind and Disabled, 4674
Martin Luther Homes of Indiana, 4675
Michigan Resources, 8441
New Hope Services, 8442
New Horizons Rehabilitation, 8443
Noble Centers, 8444
Northwest Indiana Subregional Library for Blind and Physically Handicapped, 5391
Office of State Coordinator of Vocational Education for Students with Disability, 8445
Putnam County Comprehensive Services, 8446
Richard L Roudebush VA Medical Center, 8046
Ruben Center for Independent Living, 4676
SILC, Indiana Council on Independent Living (ICOIL), 4677
Southern Indiana Center for Independent Living, 4678
Southern Indiana Resource Solutions, 8447
Special Services Division: Indiana State Library, 5392
St. Joseph Hospital Rehabilitation Center, 5393

Louisville VA Regional Office, 8060
Omnicare Foundation, 3347
Pathfinders for Independent Living, 4735
Pioneer Vocational/Industrial Services, 8469
SILC Department of Vocational Rehabilitati, 4737
SILC Department of Vocational Rehabilitation, 4736
Wheelchair Getaways, 7953
Wheelchair Getaways Wheelchair/Scooter Accessible Van Rentals, 7962
Work Enhancement Center of Western Kentucky, 8471

## Louisiana

Alexandria VA Medical Center, 8061
Arc of Louisiana, 3348
Baton Rouge Area Foundation, 3349
Booth-Bricker Fund, 3350
Camp Bon Coeur, 1485
Camp Challenge, 1456, 1486
Central Louisiana State Hospital Medical and Professional Library, 5410
Community Foundation of Shreveport-Bossier, 3351
Community Opportunities of East Ascension, 8472
LA Lions Camp for Disabled/Diabetic Youth, 1487
LA Lions LPDCI Camp Pelican, 1488
Louisiana Association of Homes and Service for the Aging, 774
Louisiana Employment Service and Job Training Program Liaison, 8473
Louisiana State Library, 5411
Louisiana State Library: Section for the, 5412
Louisiana State University Genetics Section of Pediatrics, 5413
Louisiana Vocational Rehabilitation Agency, 8474
Med-Camps of Louisiana, 1489
New Horizons: Alexandria, 4738
New Horizons: Monroe, 4739
New Horizons: Shreveport, 4741
New Orleans VA Medical Center, 8062
Resources for Independent Living: Baton Ro ge, 4743
Resources for Independent Living: Baton Rouge, 4742
Resources for Independent Living: Metairie, 4744
Shreveport VA Medical Center, 8063
Southwest Louisiana Independence Center: L ake Charles, 4745
Southwest Louisians Independence Center: Lafayette, 4746
Southwest Lousiana Independence Center: La fayette, 4747
St. James Association for Retarded Citizens, 8475
State Library of Louisiana: Services for the Blind and Physically Handicapped, 5414
Volunteers of America Supported Living Program, 4748
W Troy Cole Independent Living Specialist, 4749
Westbank Sheltered Workshop, 8476

## Maine

AH! Asthma Camp, 1490
Addison Point Specialized Services, 8477
Alpha One: Aroostook, 4750
Alpha One: Augusta, 4751
Alpha One: Brewer, 4752
Alpha One: Main Office, 4753
Bangor Public Library, 5415
Bangor Veteran Center: Veterans Outreach Center, 8478
Bishopswood, 1491
Camp Capella, 1492
Camp Lawroweld, 1493
Camp Waban, 1494
Cary Library, 5416
Chapter 15 Disabled American Veterans, 8064
Creative Work Systems, 8479
Disabled American Veterans: Maine, 8065
Lewiston Public Library, 5417
Maine Employment Service, 8480
Maine Fair Employment Practice Agency, 8481
Maine Governor's Committee on Employment of the Disabled, 8482
Maine Mental Health Connections, 4754
Maine State Library, 5418
Maine VA Regional Office, 8066
Motivational Services, 4755
Northeast Occupational Exchange, 8483
Northern New England Association of Homes and Services for the Aging, 786
Pine Tree Camp, 1495
Portland Public Library, 5420
Shalom House, 4756
St. John Valley Associates, 964
Togus VA Medical Center, 8067
UNUM Charitable Foundation, 3352
Waterville Public Library, 5421
Women to Women, 974

## Maryland

ARC, 808
Alzheimer's Disease Education and Referral Center (ADEAR), 1114
American Action Fund for Blind Children and Adults, 1257
American Association of Music Therapy, 819
American Association of the Deaf-Blind, 984, 1258
American Association of the Deaf-Blind National Conference, 2253
American College of Nurse Midwives, 1071
American Health Assistance Foundation, 3353
American Occupational Therapy Association, 1074
American Occupational Therapy Foundation, 3354
American Speech-Language-Hearing Association, 988, 2260, 7806, 7806
American Urological Association Foundation, 1139
Arc of Maryland, 3355
Ardmore Developmental Center, 8485
Association for International Practical Training, 3071

Association for Persons with Severe Handicaps (TASH), 839
Association of University Centers on Disabilities, 840
Autism Society of America, 1152, 7810
Baltimore Community Foundation, 3356
Baltimore Regional Office, 8068
Baltimore VA Medical Center, 8069
Behavior Service Consultants, 2322
Broadmead, 4757
Camp Glyndon, 1496
Camp Greentop, 1497
Camp JCC, 1498
Camp Merrick, 1499
Camp Sunrise, 1500
Camp Superkids, 1501
Cancer Information Service, 7813
Candlelighters Childhood Cancer Foundation, 3357
Capital Camps, 1502
Children and Adults with Attention Deficit Disorders (CHADD), 1165
Children's Fresh Air Society Fund, 3358
Clark-Winchcole Foundation, 3359
Columbia Foundation, 3360
Community Health Funding Report, 3746
Community Services for Autistic Adults and Children, 1170
Cystic Fibrosis Foundation, 3361
Deaf and Hard of Hearing Entrepreneurs Council, 1006
Deaf-Blind Division of the National Federation of the Blind, 1279
Department of Physical Medicine & Rehabilitation at Sinai Hospital, 862
Disability Funding News, 3754
Easter Seals Camp Fairlee Manor, 1503
Eastern Shore Center for Independent Living, 4758
Epilepsy Foundation, 1175
Fort Howard VA Medical Center, 8070
Foundation Fighting Blindness, 3362
Freedom Center, 4759
George Wasserman Family Foundation, 3363
Goodwill Industries International, 883
Guide Dog Users, 1283
Harry and Jeanette Weinberg Foundation, 3364
Hostelling North America Hostelling International: American Youth Hostels, 7943
Housing Unlimited, 4760
Independence Now: Riverdale, 4762
Independence Now: Silver Spring, 4763
Information Access Project: National Federation of the Blind, 1289
International Association of Machinists, 804
International Braille and Technology Center for the Blind, 7831
International Catholic Deaf Association, 1020
International Rett Syndrome Association, 1185
Job Opportunities for the Blind, 7832, 8486
Johns Hopkins University Dana Center for Preventive Ophthalmology, 5422
Johns Hopkins University: Asthma and Allergy Center, 5423
Junior National Association of the Deaf, 1025
Kamp A-Komp-Plish, 1504
Lions Camp Merrick, 1505
Mainstream, 907, 4414, 8487, 8487
Making Choices for Independent Living, 4764

Massachusetts Rehabilitation Commission Library, 5441

MetroWest Center for Independent Living, 4788

Mind-Body Clinic, 911

Nathaniel and Elizabeth P Stevens Foundation, 3382

National Association for Parents of Children with Visual Impairments (NAPVI), 1298, 7842

National Association of Guide Dog Users, 1301

National Braille Press, 1304

National Center for Accessible Media, 1033

National Council on Spinal Cord Injury, 1211

National Managed Health Care Congress, 2279

New England Regional Genetics Group, 5419

Northampton VA Medical Center, 8076

Northeast Independent Living Program, 4789

PALS Support Groups, 7850

Parent Professional Advocacy League, 947

Parents for Residential Reform, 950

Raytheon Company Contributions Program, 3383

Renaissance Clubhouse, 4790

Riverview School, 1525

Scandinavian Seminar, 3090

Schepens Eye Research Institute, 5442

Search Beyond Adventures, 1553, 7950

Son-Rise Program, 7860

Southeast Center for Independent Living, 4495

Spero Charitable Foundation, 3384

Student Independent Living Experience, 4791

TJX Foundation, 3385

Talking Book Library at Worcester Public Library, 5443

Tower Program at Regis College, 1526

VA Boston Healthcare System: Brockton Division, 8077

VA Boston Healthcare System: Jamaica Plain Campus, 8078

VA Boston Healthcare System: West Roxbury Division, 8079

VUE: Vision Use in Employment, 7867

Vision Foundation, 3386

Visiting Nurse Association of America, 971, 7868

Vivienne S Thomson Independent Living Cent er, 4792

Vocational and Rehabilitation Agency Massachusetts Commission for the Blind, 8499

Winnekeag, 1527

Work, 8500

# Michigan

Adventure Learning Center at Eagle Village, 1529

Aleda E Lutz VA Medical Center, 8080

Ann Arbor Area Community Foundation, 3387

Ann Arbor Center for Independent Living, 4793

Arc Detroit, 4794

Arc of Michigan, 3388

Artificial Language Laboratory, 5444

Association for Retarded Citizens of Muskegon County, 4795

Bad Axe Center for Independent Living, 4796

Battle Creek VA Medical Center, 8081

Bay Area Coalition for Independent Living, 4797

Berrien Community Foundation, 3389

Blind Children's Fund, 3390

Blue Water CIL: Lapeer, 4798

Blue Water CIL: Port Huron, 4799

Burger School for the Autistic, 5445

CIL of Mid-Michigan, 4800

Camp Barakel, 1530

Camp Catch-a-Rainbow, 1531

Camp Nissokone, 1532

Camp O'Fair Winds, 1533

Camp O'Fair Winds, 1534

Camp Roger, 1535

Camp Tall Turf, 1536

Capital Area Center for Independent Living, 4801

Caro Center for Independent Living, 4802

Center for Community Access, 4803

Center for Handicapped Affairs, 4804

Center for Independent Living of Mid-Michigan, 4805

Central Michigan University Summer Clinics, 1537

Chi Medical Library, 5446

Clarence & Grace Chamberlin Foundation, 3391

Community Foundation of Monroe County, 3392

Cowan Slavin Foundation, 3393

Cristo Rey Handicappers Program, 4807

Daimler Chrysler, 3394

Detroit Center for Independent Living, 4808

DisAbility Connections, 4809

Disability Advocates of Kent County, 4810

Disability Community Small Business Development Center, 801, 8501

Disability Connection, 4811

Disability Network, 4812, 7822

Disability Network, Oakland/Macomb, 4813

Disability Resource Center of SW Michigan, 4814

Disability Resource Center of Southwest Michigan, 4815

Echo Grove Camp, 1538

Educational Accessibility Services, 870

Fowler Center, 1539

Frank & Mollie S VanDervoort Memorial Foun dation, 3395

Fremont Area Foundation, 3396

Glaucoma Laser Trial, 5447

Grand Rapids Foundation, 3397

Grand Traverse Area Community Living Center, 4816

Grand Traverse Area Library for the Blind and Physically Handicapped, 5448

Granger Foundation, 3398

Great Lakes Center for Independent Living, 4817

Great Lakes/Macomb Rehabilitation Group, 4818

Harvey Randall Wickes Foundation, 3399

Havirmill Foundation, 3400

Hope Network Independent Living Program, 4819

Indian Trails Camp, 1540

Informed Birth and Parenting, 890

International Hearing Society, 1022

International Medical and Dental Hypnotherapy Association, 902

Iron Mountain VA Medical Center, 8082

JARC, 4820

John D Dingell VA Medical Center, 8083

Kalamazoo Center for Independent Living, 4822

Kelly Services Foundation, 3401

Kent District Library for the Blind and Physically Handicapped, 5449

Kresge Foundation, 3402

Lakeshore Center for Independent Living, 4823

Lamplighter's Work Center, 8502

Lanting Foundation, 3403

Library of Michigan Service for the Blind, 5450

Life Skills Services, 4824

Livingston Center for Independent Living, 4825

Macomb Library for the Blind and Physically Handicapped, 5451

Michigan Association for Deaf and Hard of Hearing, 1028

Michigan Association of Homes and Serivces for the Aging, 776

Michigan Commission for the Blind: Detroit, 4827

Michigan Commission for the Blind: Independent Living Rehabilitation Program, 4826

Michigan Employment Service, 8503

Michigan Fair Employment Practice Agency, 8504

Michigan Rehabilitation Services: Dept of Labor And Economic Development, 8505

Michigan VA Regional Office, 8084

Michigan's Assistive Technology Resource, 5452

Michigan's Assistive Technology Resources, 5453

Mideastern Michigan Library Co-op, 5454

Midland Center for Independent Living, 4828

Midland Center for Independent Living of Mid-Michigan, 4829

Monroe Center for Independent Living, 4830

Muskegon County Library for the Blind, 5455

National Child Safety Council, 7844

Northland Library Cooperative, 5456

Oakland County Library for the Visually & Physically Impaired, 5457

Ransom Fidelity Company Foundation, 3404

Rehabilitation Services, 959

Rollin M Gerstacker Foundation, 3405

Sherman Lake YMCA Outdoor Center, 1541

Southeastern Michigan Commission for the Blind, 4831

Special Technologies Alternative Resources, 1321

St. Clair County Library Special Technologies Alternative Resources (S.T.A.R.), 5458

Steelcase Foundation, 3406

Superior Alliance for Independent Living (SAIL), 4832

University of Michigan: Orthopaedic Research Laboratories, 5459

Upper Peninsula Library for the Blind, 5460

VA Ann Arbor Healthcare System, 8085

Vet Center Readjustment Counseling Serivce, 8086

Washtenaw County Library for the Blind & Physically Handicapped, 5461

Wayne County Regional Library for the Blind, 5462

Southwest Center for Independent Living (SWCIL), 4883
St. Louis Regional Office, 8098
St. Louis VA Medical Center, 8099
Sunnyhill Adventure Center, 1570
Tri-County Center for Independent Living, 4884
University of Missouri: Columbia Arthritis Center, 5475
Victor E Speas Foundation, 3428
WX: Work Capacities, 8521
West Central Independent Living Solutions, 4885
Whole Person, 4886
Whole Person: Olathe, 4723
Wolfner Library for the Blind, 5476
Wonderland Camp Foundation, 1571
YMCA Camp Lakewood, 1572

## Montana

Living Independently for Today and Tomorrow, 4888
Living Independently for Today and Tomorrow: Glendrive, 4887
MonTECH, 5477
Montana Employment Services and Job Training Programs Liaison, 8522
Montana Fair Employment Practice Agency, 8523
Montana Governor's Committee on Employment of Disabled People, 8524
Montana Independent Living Project, 4889
Montana State Library, 5478
Montana State Library\Talking Book Library, 5479
Montana VA Regional Office, 8100
North Central Independent Living Services, 4890
Summit Independent Living Center: Hamilton, 4892
Summit Independent Living Center: Kalipsell, 4891
Summit Independent Living Center: Missoula, 4893
V A Montana Healthcare System, 8101
VA Montana Healthcare System, 8102
Vet Center, 8090, 8103

## Nebraska

Arc of Nebraska, 3429
Boys Town National Research Hospital, 994
Camp Comeca, 1573
Camp Easter Seals, 1574
Camp Floyd Rogers, 1575
Center for Independent Living of Central Nebraska, 4894
Christian Record Services/National Camps for Blind Children, 1576
Cooper Foundation, 3430
Eastern Nebraska 4-H Camps and Centers, 1577
Grand Island VA Medical System, 8104
Hazel R Keene Trust, 3431
Kamp Kaleo, 1578
League of Human Dignity: Lincoln, 4895
League of Human Dignity: Norfolk, 4896
League of Human Dignity: Omaha, 4897

Lincoln Regional Office, 8105
Lincoln VA Medical Center, 8106
Martin Luther Home Society Resource Center, 5480
Martin Luther Homes of Beatrice, 4898
Martin Luther Homes of Nebraska, 4899
National Camps for Blind Children, 1579
Nebraska Assistive Technology Partnership Nebraska Department of Education, 5481
Nebraska Association of Homes for the Aging, 782
Nebraska Employment Services, 8525
Nebraska Fair Employment Practice Agency, 8526
Nebraska Library Commission: Talking Book and Braille Service, 5482
Nebraska Vocational Rehabilitation Agency, 8527
Nebraska Work Force Development, 8528
Panhandle Independent Living Services, 4900
Parent Assistance Network, 7852
Slosburg Family Charitable Trust, 3432
Union Pacific Foundation, 3433
VA Nebraska-Western Iowa Health Care System, 8107
YMCA Camp Kitaki, 1580

## Nevada

ABC Union, ACE, ANLV, Vegas Western Cab, 7954
Bio-Electro-Magnetics Institute, 844
Carson City Center for Independent Living, 4901
Conrad N Hilton Foundation, 3434
EL Wiegand Foundation, 3435
Las Vegas Veterans Center, 8108
Las Vegas-Clark County Library District, 5483
Nell J Redfield Foundation, 3437
Nevada Fair Employment Practice Agency, 8530
Nevada Governor's Committee on Employment of Persons with Disabilities, 8531
Nevada Job Training Program Liaison, 8532
Nevada State Library and Archives, 5484
Northern Nevada Center for Independent Living: Reno, 4903, 4904
Reno Regional Office, 8109
Rural Center for Independent Living, 4905
Southern Nevada Center for Independent Living: Las Vegas, 4906, 4907
VA Sierra Nevada Healthcare System, 8110
VA Southern Nevada Healthcare System, 8111
William N and Myriam Pennington Foundation, 3438

## New Hampshire

Agnes M Lindsay Trust, 3439
Camp Allen, 1581
Camp Dartmouth-Hitchcock, 1582
Camp Fatima, 1583
Camp Kaleidoscope, 1584
Easter Seal Camp: New Hampshire, 1585
Easter Seals NH Camp Sno-Mo, 1586
Fit for Work at Exeter Hospital, 8534

Foundation for Seacoast Health, 3440
Granite State Independent Living Foundation, 4908
Manchester Regional Office, 8112
Manchester VA Medical Center, 8113
National Guild of Hypnotists, 930
New Hampshire Employment Security, 8535
New Hampshire Fair Employment Practice Agency, 8536
New Hampshire Job Training Program Liaison, 8537
New Hampshire State Library: Library Services to Persons with Disabilities, 5485
New Hampshire Veterans Centers, 8114

## New Jersey

ARC of Gloucester County, 8539
ARC of Hunterdon County, 8540
ARC of Mercer County, 8541
ARC of Monmouth, 8542
Abilities Center of New Jersey, 8543
Abilities of Northwest New Jersey, 8544
Alliance for Disabled in Action New Jersey, 8545
Alternatives for Growth: New Jersey, 8546
American Organization for Bodywork Therapies of Asia, 828
American Self-Help Clearinghouse, 832
Arc of Bergen and Passaic Counties, 8547
Arc of New Jersey, 3442
Arnold A Schwartz Foundation, 3443
Assistive Technology Advocacy Center (ATAC), 4909
Association for the Care of Children's Health, 1079
Avis Rent-A-Car, 7955
Camp Chatterbox, 1589
Camp Jotoni, 1590
Camp Laurel, 1369
Camp Lou Henry Hoover, 1591
Camp Merry Heart, 1592
Camp Sun'N Fun, 1593
Camp Vacamas, 1594
Campbell Soup Foundation, 3444
Career Opportunity Development of New Jersey, 8548
Center for Educational Advancement New Jersey, 8549
Center for Independent Living: Camden, 4910
Center for Independent Living: Edison, 4911
Center for Independent Living: Long Branch, 4912
Center for Independent Living: South Jersey, 4913
Cerebral Palsy Association of Middlesex County, 8550
Cerebral Palsy Center Summer Program, 1595
Children's Hopes & Dreams Wish Fulfillment Foundation, 3445
Children's Specialized Hospital Medical Library - Parent Resource Center, 5486
Christopher & Dana Reeve Paralysis Resource Center, 5487
Christopher Reeve Paralysis Foundation, 1166
Community Action for Independent Living, 4915
Community Foundation of New Jersey, 3446

Cowles Charitable Trust, 3447
Cross Roads Outdoor Ministries, 1596
Davis Center for Hearing, Speech and Learning: Hearing Therapy, 1002
Dial: Disabled Information Awareness & Living, 4916
Disabled Advocates Working for Northwest (DAWN), 4917
Disabled American Veterans, New Jersey Northern Valley Chapter 32, 8115
Disabled American Veterans: Ocean County, 8116
East Orange Campus of the VA New Jersey Healthcare System, 8117
Easter Seal Hackensack, 8551
Easter Seal Society of New Jersey Highlands Workshop, 8552
Easter Seal of Ocean County, 8553
Easter Seals Camp Merry Heart, 1597
Easter Seals New Jersey, 8554
Eden Acres Administrative Services, 8555
Edison Sheltered Workshop, 8556
Eye Institute of New Jersey, 5488
F Mason Perkins Trust, 3448
FM Kirby Foundation, 3449
Family Resource Associates, 4918
Fannie E Rippel Foundation, 3450
First Occupational Center of New Jersey, 8557
Fund for New Jersey, 3451
Goodwill Industries of Southern New Jersey, 8558
Hausmann Industries, 8559
Heightened Independence and Progress: Hack ensack, 4919
Heightened Independence and Progress: Jersey City, 4920
Jersey Cape Diagnostic Training & Opportunity Center, 8560
Kessler Institute for Rehabilitation, 906
Lyons Campus of the VA New Jersey Healthcare System, 8118
Matheny School and Hospital, 908
Merck Company Foundation, 3452
Milton Schamach Foundation, 3454
Mycoclonus Research Foundation, 5489
Nabisco Foundation, 3455
National Association of Retired Volunteer Program Directors, 918
Nejeda, 1598
New Eyes for the Needy, 1316
New Jersey Association of Nonprofit Homes for the Aging, 783
New Jersey Camp Jaycee, 1599
New Jersey Center for Outreach and Services for the Autism Community (COSAC), 5490
New Jersey Commission for the Blind and Visually Impaired, 8561
New Jersey Employment Service and Job Training Program Services, 8562
New Jersey Library for the Blind and Handicapped, 5491
New Jersey YMHA/YWHA Camps Milford, 1600
Newark Regional Office, 8119
Oak Spring Program, 1601
Occupational Center of Hudson County, 8563
Occupational Center of Union County, 8564
Occupational Training Center of Burlington County, 8565
Occupational Training Center of Camden County, New Jersey, 8566

Ostberg Foundation, 3456
Pathways to Independence, 8567
Progressive Center for Independent Living, 4921
Project Freedom, 4922
Prudential Foundation, 3457
Recording for the Blind & Dyslexic, 1318
Robert Wood Johnson Foundation, 3458
Rolling Hills Country Day Camp, 1640
Round Lake Camp, 1602
Seeing Eye, 1319
Somerset Training and Employment Program, 8568
St. John of God Community Services Vocational Rehabilitation, 8569
Total Living Center, 4924
United Cerebral Palsy Associations of New Jersey, 8570
Universal Institute: Rehab & Fitness Center, 1108
Victoria Foundation, 3459
Walking Tomorrow, 3460
West Essex Rehab Center, 8572

# New Mexico

ADA Camp for Kids, 1603
Ability Center, 4925
Adelante Development Center, 8573
Albuquerque Regional Office, 8120
American Holistic Medical Association, 1073
Arc of New Mexico, 3461
CASA, 4926
CHOICES Center for Independent Living, 4927
Camp Enchantment, 1604
Family Voices, 876
Frost Foundation, 3462
Goodwill Industries of New Mexico, 8574
McCune Charitable Foundation, 3463
Native American Protection and Advocacy, 943
New Mexico Employment Services and Job Training Liaison, 8575
New Mexico State Library for the Blind and Physically Handicapped, 5492
New Mexico Technology Assistance Program, 4929
New Mexico VA Healthcare System, 8121
New Mexico Veterans Centers, 8122
New Vistas, 4930
Opportunity Center: New Mexico, 8576
Overeaters Anonymous World Service Office, 1228
RCI, 8577
San Juan Center for Independence, 4931
Santa Fe Community Foundation, 3464
Santa Fe Mountain Center, 1605
Tohatchi Area of Opportunity & Services, 8578
Vocational Rehabilitation Agency, 8498, 8579

# New York

AIDS Funding, 3743
AIM Independent Living Center: Corning, 4932

AIM Independent Living Center: Elmira, 4933
ARISE: Center for Independent Living: Oswe go, 4934
ARISE: Center for Independent Living: Syra cuse, 4935
AT&T Foundation, 3465
Abilities!, 799
Access Unlimited, 810
Access to Independence of Cortland County, 4936
Achelis Foundation, 3466
Action Toward Independence: Middletown, 4937
Action Toward Independence: Monticello, 4938
Advocacy Center, 813
Advocates for Children of New York, 815
Aging in America, 755
Alavi Foundation of New York, 3467
Albany VA Medical Center: Samuel S Stratton, 8123
Albany Vet Center, 8124
Altman Foundation, 3468
Ambrose Monell Foundation, 3469
American Association of Spinal Cord Injury Nurses, 1121
American Association of Spinal Cord Injury Psychologists & Social Workers, 1122
American Chai Trust, 3470
American Diabetes Association Summer Camp, 1606
American Express Foundation, 3441
American Foundation for the Blind, 1261, 3471
American Group Psychotherapy Association, 1072
American Lung Association, 1131
American Paraplegia Society, 1135
American-Scandinavian Foundation, 3068
Arthur Ross Foundation, 3472
Artists Fellowship, 3473
Associated Blind, 1264
Association for Children with Down Syndrome, 1144
Association for Macular Diseases, 1267
Association for Neurologically Impaired Brain Injured Children, 837
Aurora of Central New York, 7809
Basic Facts on Study Abroad, 3072
Bath VA Medical Center, 8125
Bergeron Health Care, 4939
Bodman Foundation, 3475
Booth Ferris Foundation, 3476
Braille Book Bank, 5493
Brain Injury Association of New York State, 1158
Bronx Independent Living Services, 4940
Bronx VA Medical Center, 8126
Brooklyn Campus of the VA NY Harbor Healthcare System, 8127
Brooklyn Center for Independence of the Disabled, 4941
Brooklyn Home for Aged Men, 3477
Buffalo Independent Living Project, 4942
Buffalo Regional Office, 8128
Buffalo State (SUNY), 3074
Camp Aldersgate, 1607
Camp Glengarra, 1608
Camp Huntington, 1609
Camp Jened, 1610
Camp Mark Seven, 1611
Camp Northwood, 1612

National Guide to Funding Religion, 3779
National Guide to Funding for Children, Youth & Families, 3780
National Guide to Funding for Elementary & Secondary Education, 3781
National Guide to Funding for Libraries and Information Services, 3782
National Guide to Funding for Women and Girls, 3783
National Guide to Funding in Aging, 3784
National Guide to Funding in Arts and Culture, 3785
National Guide to Funding in Health, 3786
National Guide to Funding in Higher Education, 3787
National Hemophilia Foundation, 1217, 3524
National Multiple Sclerosis Society, 1224
National Neurofibromatosis Foundation, 3525
National Technical Institute for the Deaf, 1042
Neisloss Family Foundation, 3526
New York Association of Homes and Services for the Aging, 784
New York City Campus of the VA NY Harbor Healthcare System, 8131
New York Community Trust, 3527
New York Foundation, 3528
New York Public Library: Andrew Heiskell Library for the Blind and Physically Handicapped, 5505
New York Regional Office, 8132
New York State Department of Labor, 8583
New York State Foundations, 3788
New York State Talking Book & Braille Library, 5506
Newburgh Center for Independent Living, 4963
Niagara Frontier Center for Independent Living, 4964
Ninety-Second Street Y Camps Nesher Program, 1633
North Country Center for Independent Living, 4965
Northern New York Community Foundation, 3529
Northern Regional Center for Independent Living: Watertown, 4966, 4967
Northport VA Medical Center, 8133
Nurse Healers: Professional Associates International, 945
Options for Independence: Auburn, 4968
Options for Independence: Seneca Falls, 4969
Parkinson's Disease Foundation, 3314, 3530
People and Places, 7947
Polarity Wellness Center, 955
Polio Connection of America, 1233
Postgraduate Center for Mental Health, 5507
Prader-Willi Alliance of New York, 1237
Prader-Willi Alliance of New York Annual Conference, 2280
Presbyterian Center at Holmes, 1634
Programs for Children 3 to 5 with Disabilities, 1635
Programs for Children Birth to 2 with Disabilities, 1636
Programs for Children with Special Health Care Needs, 1637
Radalbek, 1638
Rational Effectiveness Training Systems, 8584
Reader's Digest Foundation, 3531
RehabTech Associates, 2327
Rehabilitation International, 958, 2282

Rehabilitation Research Library, 5508
Research to Prevent Blindness, 3532
Resource Center for Accessible Living, 4970
Rita J and Stanley H Kaplan Foundation, 3533
Robert Sterling Clark Foundation, 3534
Rochester Rotary Sunshine Camp, 1639
Rockland Independent Living Center, 4971
SILO: Cental Islip, 4972
SILO: Hauppauge, 4973
Saratoga County Options for Independent Living, 4974
Skadden Fellowship Foundation, 3535
Source Book Profiles, 3790
Southern Tier Independence Center, 4975
Southwestern Independent Living Center, 4976
Special Education and Vocational Rehabilitation Agency: New York, 8585
St. George's Society of New York, 3536
Stanley W Metcalf Foundation, 3537
State University of New York, 3093
State University of New York Health Sciences Center, 5509
Staten Island Center for Independent Living, 4977
Stonewall Community Foundation, 3538
Suffolk Cooperative Library System: Long Island Talking Book Library, 5510
Suffolk Independent Living Organization (SILO), 4978
Summit Camp, 1641
Support Group for Brachial Plexus Injury, 1246
Surdna Foundation, 3539
Sydney & Helen Jacoff Foundation, 3540
Syracuse VA Medical Center, 8134
Taconic Resources for Independence, 4979
Tisch Foundation, 3541
Torah Alliance of Families of Kids with Disabilities, 8135
Tourette Syndrome Association, 1248
Tourette Syndrome Association Conference, 2286
United Cerebral Palsy Association of New York State Annual Conference, 1250, 2288
United Educational Services, 1107
VA Hudson Valley Health Care System, 8136
VA Western NY Healthcare System, Batavia, 8137
VA Western NY Healthcare System, Buffalo, 8138
VISIONS Vacation Camp for the Blind, 1642
Van Ameringen Foundation, 3542
Visions/Services for the Blind & Visually Impaired, 1326, 4980
Wagon Road Camp, 1643
Wallace Memorial Library, 5511
Westchester County Independent Living Center, 4981
Westchester Disabled on the Move, 4982
Western New York Foundation, 3543
William T Grant Foundation, 3544
Wiswall Center for Independent Living, 4983
Xavier Society for the Blind, 5512
YAI: National Institute for People with Disabilities, 1252
YMCA Camp Chingachgook on Lake George, 1644
YMCA Camp Weona, 1645

## North Carolina

American Cleft Palate/Craniofacial Association, 1127
American Social Health Association, 833
Arc of North Carolina, 3545
Asheville VA Medical Center, 8139
Autism Society of North Carolina, 5513
Bob & Kay Timberlake Foundation, 3546
Broyhill Family Foundation, 3547
Camp Royall, 1647
Camp Sky Ranch, 1648
Camp Tekoa UMC, 1649
Center for Accessible Housing, 4984
Center for Universal Design, 856
Charlotte Vet Center, 8140
Cleft Palate Foundation, 1168
Cullowhee Experience, 1650
Davidson College, Office of Study Abroad, 3076
Disability Awareness Network, 4985
Disability Rights & Resources, 4986
Division of Employment & Training, 8494, 8586
Duke Endowment, 3548
Durham VA Medical Center, 8141
Fayetteville VA Medical Center, 7986, 8142
First Union Foundation, 3549
Foundation for the Carolinas, 3550
Franklin Delano Roosevelt Campus of the VA Hudson Valley Healthcare System, 8143
Great Smokies Diagnostic Laboratory, 5514
Herpes Resource Center, 1182
Iredell Vocational Workshop, 8587
John H Wellons Foundation, 3551
Joy: A Shabazz Center for Independent Living, 4987
Kate B Reynolds Charitable Trust, 3552
Kathleen Price and Joseph M Bryan Family Foundation, 3553
Live Independently Networking Center, 4988
Live Independently Networking Center: Hickory, 4989
Mary Reynolds Babcock Foundation, 3554
Mount Shepherd Retreat Center, 1651
National Early Childhood Technical Assistance Center, 927
National Respite Locator Service, 940
North Carolina Association of Nonprofits for the Aging, 785
North Carolina Division of Services for the Blind, 8588
North Carolina Library for the Blind and Physically Handicapped, 5515
Opportunity Plus of NC, 807
Pathways for the Future, 4990
Pediatric Rheumatology Clinic, 5516
Rowan County Vocational Workshop, 8589
Rutherford Vocational Workshop, 8590
SOAR Summer Adventures, 1652
Stone Mountain School, 1653
Support Works, 7864
TEACCH, 965
Talisman Summer Camp, 1654
Transylvania Vocational Services, 8591
Triangle Community Foundation, 3555
University of North Carolina at Chapel Hill: Brain Research Center, 5517
WG Hefner VA Medical Center, 8144
Webster Enterprises of Jackson County, 8594

Western Alliance Center for Independent Living, 4991
Western Regional Vocational Rehabilitation Facility Clifford File, Jr., 8595
Winston-Salem Regional Office, 8145

## North Dakota

Alex Stern Family Foundation, 3556
American Diabetes Association, 1128, 1655
Arc of North Dakota, 3557
Camp Sioux, 1656
Center for Independent Living: Fargo, 4992
Dakota Center for Independent Living: Bismarck, 4994
Dakota Center for Independent Living: Dickinson, 4993
Dakota Center for Independent Living: Minot, 4995
Fargo VA Medical Center, 8146
Fraser, 4996
North Dakota Community Foundation, 3558
North Dakota Department of Labor, Equal Employment Opportunity Division, 8596
North Dakota Department of Veterans' Affairs, 8147
North Dakota Employment Service and Job Training Program Liaison, 8597
North Dakota Governor's Committee on Employment of Disabled Persons, 8598
North Dakota State Library Talking Book Services, 5518
North Dakota VA Regional Office, 8148
North Dakota Vocational Rehabilitation Agency, 8599

## Ohio

Ability Center of Defiance, 4997
Ability Center of Greater Toledo, 4998
Access Center for Independent Living, 4582, 4999
Akron Community Foundation, 3559
Akron Rotary Camp, 1657
Albert G and Olive H Schlink Foundation, 3560
American Foundation Corporation, 3561
Antioch College, 3069
Arc of Ohio, 3562
Association of Ohio Philanthropic Homes and Housing for Aging, 759
Batten Disease Support and Research Association, 1154
Beech Brook, 1658
Breezewood Acres United Way of Central Ohio, 1659
Camp Allyn, 1660
Camp Cheerful, 1661
Camp Courageous, 1662
Camp Emanuel, 1663
Camp Ho Mita Koda, 1664
Camp Libbey, 1665
Camp Nuhop, 1666
Camp Stepping Stone, 1667
Case Western Reserve University, 5519
Case Western Reserve University Northeast Ohio Multipurpose Arthritis Center, 5520
Chillicothe VA Medical Center, 8149
Cincinnati VA Medical Center, 8150

Cincinnati Veterans Centers, 8151
Cleveland FES Center, 5521
Cleveland Foundation, 3563
Cleveland Public Library, 5522
Cleveland Regional Office, 8152
Clovernook Center for the Blind and Visually Impaired, 5523
College of Optometrists in Vision Development, 1083
Columbus Foundation and Affiliated Organizations, 3564
Cornucopia, 8600
Day Happiness Camp, 1668
Dayton VA Medical Center, 8153
Disabled American Veterans, 7969
Echoing Hills, 1669
Eleanora CU Alms Trust, 3565
Emma Leah and Laura Bell Bahmann Foundation, 3566
Eva L and Joseph M Bruening Foundation, 3567
Fairfield Center for Disabilities and Cerebral Palsy, 5000
Fred & Lillian Deeks Memorial Foundation, 3568
GAR Foundation, 3569
George Gund Foundation, 3570
Great Oaks Joint Vocational School, 8601
Greater Cincinnati Foundation, 3571
HCR Manor Care Foundation, 3572
Handicapped Student Program Postsecondary Education Association, 2273
Happiness Day at Parmadale, 1670
Happiness Day at St. Augustine Academy, 1671
Happiness Day at the Center for Pastoral Leadership, 1672
Harry C Moores Foundation, 3573
Hearth Day Treatment and Vocational Services, 8602
Helen Steiner Rice Foundation, 3574
Help Foundation, 5001
Herbert W Hoover Foundation, 3575
Highbrook Lodge, 1673
Highland Unlimited Business Enterprises of CRI, 8603
Independent Living Center of Central Ohio, 5002
International Resource Center for Down Syndrome, 1184
John P Murphy Foundation, 3576
Ko-Man-She, 1674
Lake Erie College, 3082
Leo Yassenoff JCC Day Camps, 1675
Linking Employment Ability Potential: Independent Living Center, 5003
Louis Stokes VA Medical Center, 8154
Mid-Ohio Board for an Independent Living Environment (MOBILE), 5004
National Association of the Physically Handicapped, 919
National Cued Speech Association, 1034
Nationwide Foundation, 3577
Nordson Corporate Giving Program, 3578
Ohio Civil Rights Commission, 8604
Ohio Employment Services and Job Training, 8605
Ohio Regional Library for the Blind and Physically Handicapped, 5524
Parker-Hannifin Foundation, 3579
Recreation Unlimited, 1676

Rehabilitation Service of North Central Ohio, 5005
Reinberger Foundation, 3580
Robert Campeau Family Foundation, 3581
Samuel W Bell Home for Sightless, 5006
Services for Independent Living, 4881, 5007
Sisler McFawn Foundation, 3582
Society for Equal Access: Independent Living Center, 5008
Stark Community Foundation, 3583
State Library of Ohio: Talking Book Program, 5525
Stocker Foundation, 3584
Toledo Community Foundation, 3585
Trager International, 969
United Cerebral Palsy of Central Ohio, 5010
University Affiliated Cincinnati Center for Developmental Disabilities, 5526
William J and Dorothy K O'Neill Foundation, 3586
YMCA Camp Fitch, 1677
YMCA Outdoor Center Campbell Gard, 1678
Youngstown Foundation, 3587

## Oklahoma

Ability Resources, 5011
Anne and Henry Zarrow Foundation, 3588
Camp Classen YMCA, 1679
Easter Seals Oklahoma, 1680
Green County Independent Living Resource Center, 5012
International Bio-Oxidative Medicine Foundation (IBOM), 3589
Muskogee VA Medical Center, 8155
National Clearinghouse of Rehabilitation Training Materials, 1097
Oklahoma Association of Homes and Services for the Aging, 787
Oklahoma City VA Medical Center, 8156
Oklahoma Department of Rehabilitation Services (DRS), 8607
Oklahoma Employment Services and Job Training Program Liaison, 8608
Oklahoma Governor's Committee on Employment of People with Disabilities, 8609
Oklahoma Library for the Blind & Physically Handicapped, 5527
Oklahoma Medical Research Foundation, 5528
Oklahoma Veterans Centers Vet Center, 8157
Oklahomans for Independent Living, 5013
Progressive Independence, 5014
Sandra Beasley Independent Living Center, 5015
Sarkeys Foundation, 3590
Tulsa City-County Library System: Outreach Services, 5529
William K Warren Foundation, 3591

## Oregon

American Tinnitus Association, 989
Arc of Oregon, 3592
Bend Work Activity Center, 8610
Building Bridges: Including People with Disabilities in International Programs, 3075

Camp Christmas Seal, 1681
Camp Latgawa, 1682
Camp Magruder, 1683
Camp Taloali, 1684
Central Oregon Resources for Independent Living, 5016
Chiles Foundation, 3593
Columbia Gorge Center, 5017
DB-Link, 1173
Dogs for the Deaf, 1009
Easter Seals Oregon Camping Program, 1685
Eastern Oregon Center for Independent Living, 5018
Feldenkrais Guild of North America (FGNA), 1087
Gales Creek Diabetes Camp, 1686
HASL Independent Abilities Center, 5019
Independent Living Resources, 5020, 5167
Jackson Foundation, 3594
Lane Community College, 3083
Laurel Hill Center Independent Living Program, 5021
Leslie G Ehmann Trust, 3595
Little People of America, 1193
Meadowood Springs Speech and Hearing Camp, 1687
Mobility International USA, 913
Mt Hood Kiwanis Camp, 1688
Multiple Sclerosis Center of Oregon, 1196
National College of Naturopathic Medicine, 922
National Information Clearinghouse on Children who are Deaf-Blind, 1039
Oregon Association of Homes for the Aging, 788
Oregon Commission for the Blind, 5022
Oregon Fair Employment Practice Agency, 8611
Oregon Health Sciences University, 8158
Oregon Health Sciences University, Elks' Children's Eye Clinic, 5530
Oregon Talking Book & Braille Services, 5531
People First International, 951
Portland Naturopathic Clinic: NCNM National Health Centers Eastside Clinic, 956
Portland Regional Office, 8159
Portland VA Medical Center, 8160
Progressive Options, 5023
Roseburg VA Medical Center, 8161
SPOKES Unlimited, 5024
Samuel S Johnson Foundation, 3596
State of Oregon Office of Vocational Rehabilitation Service, 8612
Strength for the Journey, 1689
Sundial Special Vacations, 7951
Suttle Lake United Methodist Camp, 1690
Talking Book & Braille Services Oregon State Library, 5532
Umpqua Valley Disabilities Network, 5025
University of Oregon International Service, 3095
University of Portland, 3096
Upward Bound Camp: Evans Creek, 1691
Vestibular Disorders Association, 1056
Vocational and Rehabilitation Agency: Commision for the Blind, 8614
White City VA Domiciliary, 8162
World of Options, 3099
World of Options: A Guide to International Educational Exchange, 3100
YWCA Camp Westwind, 1692

# Pennsylvania

AC-ACLD/An Association for Children and Adults with Learning Disabilities, 8615
Abilities in Motion, 5026
Accessible Journeys, 7929
Accesstotheplanet, 7930
Achieva, 1693
Acorn Alcinda Foundation, 3597
Air Products Foundation, 3598
American Society for Deaf Children, 986
Anthracite Region Center for Independent Living, 5027
Arc of Pennsylvania, 3599
Arcadia Foundation, 3600
Associated Services for the Blind, 1265
Augmentative Communication Consultants (ACCI), 2321
Beaver College, 3073
Behavior Therapy and Research Society, 1080
Brachial Plexus Palsy Foundation, 3601
Brian's House, 5028
Briarwood Day Camp, 1694
Butler VA Medical Center, 8163
Camp AIM Lloyd Institute, 1695
Camp ARC Spencer, 1696
Camp Can Do, 1697
Camp Carefree, 1588, 1698
Camp Dunmore, 1699
Camp Joy, 1700
Camp Keystone, 1701
Camp Lee Mar, 1702
Camp Setebaid, 1703
Camp Surefoot, 1704
Carnegie Library of Pittsburgh Library for the Blind & Physically Handicapped, 5533
Children of Aging Parents, 762
Claude Washington Benedum Foundation, 3602
Coatesville VA Medical Center, 8164
Columbia Gas of Pennsylvania Corporate Giv ing, 3603
Community Resources for Independence, 4447, 5029
Connelly Foundation, 3604
Crestfield Camp, 1705
Dial-a-Hearing Screening Test, 7821
Dolfinger-McMahon Foundation, 3605
Elling Camps, 1706
Episcopal Conference of the Deaf, 1011
Erie VA Medical Center, 8165
Exceptional Cancer Patients, 1176
Free Library of Philadelphia: Library for the Blind and Physically Handicapped, 5534
Freedom Valley Disability Center, 5030
Guided Tour for Persons 17 & Over with Developmental and Physical Challenges, 7942
Handi Camp, 1707
Harry C Trexler Trust, 3606
Helping Hands, 1708
Henry L Hillman Foundation, 3607
Howard Heinz Endowment, 3608
Hoxie Harrison Smith Foundation, 3609
Innabah, 1709
International University Partnerships, 3081
James E Van Zandt VA Medical Center, 8166
Jewish Healthcare Foundation of Pittsburgh, 3610
Juliet L Hillman Simonds Foundation, 3611
Ken-Crest Services, 1710

Kweebec, 1711
Learning Disabilities Association of America (LDA), 1189
Lebanon VA Medical Center, 8167
Lehigh Valley Center for Independent Living, 5031
Liberty Resources, 5032
Life and Independence for Today, 5033
Living Waters, 1712
Make-a-Friend, 1713
MedEscort International, 909
National Mental Health Consumers Self-Help Clearinghouse, 1223
Northeastern Pennsylvania Center for Independent Living, 5035
Oberkotter Foundation, 3612
Office of Vocational Rehabilitation, 8616
Outside in School, 1714
PECO Energy Company Contributions Program, 3613
PNC Bank Foundation, 3614
Pennsylvania Association of Nonprofit Homes for the Aging, 789
Pennsylvania College of Optometry Eye Institute, 5535
Pennsylvania Employment Services and Job Training, 8617
Pennsylvania Governor's Committee on Employment of Disabled Persons, 8618
Pennsylvania Human Relations Commission Agency, 8619
Pennsylvania Veterans Centers, 8168
Pennsylvania's Initiative on Assistive Technology, 5036
Phelps School Summer School, 1715
Philadelphia Foundation, 3615
Philadelphia Regional Office and Insurance Center, 8169
Philadelphia VA Medical Center, 8170
Pittsburgh Foundation, 3616
Pittsburgh Regional Office, 8171
Ramah in the Poconos, 1716
Reading Rehabilitation Hospital, 5536
Recorded Periodicals, 5537, 7859
Sequanota, 1717
Shenango Valley Foundation, 3617
Snee-Reinhardt Charitable Foundation, 3618
Souderton Special Needs Day Camp, 1718
South Central Pennsylvania Center for Inde pendence Living, 5037
Staunton Farm Foundation, 3619
Stewart Huston Charitable Trust, 3620
Teleflex Foundation, 3621
Three Rivers Center for Independent Living, 4688, 5038
Tri-County Patriots for Independent Living, 5039
US Healthworks, 8620
USX Foundation, 3622
VA Pittsburgh Healthcare System, Highland Drive Division, 8173
VA Pittsburgh Healthcare System, University Drive Division, 8172
Variety Club Camp, 1719
Vocational Rehabilitation Center, 972
Voices for Independence, 5040
WW Smith Charitable Trust, 3623
Wesley Woods, 1720
Wheelchair Access, 973
Wilkes-Barre VA Medical Center, 8174
William B Dietrich Foundation, 3624
William Talbott Hillman Foundation, 3625

William V and Catherine A McKinney
Charitable Foundation, 3626
Woodlands, 1721

## Rhode Island

Aldersgate Center, 1587, 1722
Arc South County Chapter, 3627
Arc of Northern Rhode Island, 3628
Arc-Down Syndrome Society of Rhode
Island, 3629
Blackstone Valley Center, 5041
Blackstone Valley Chapter RI Arc, 3630
Bristol County Chapter Arc, 3631
Camp Ruggles, 1723
Canonicus Camp, 1724
Champlin Foundations, 3632
Cranston Arc, 3633
Department of Veterans Affairs Regional
Office - Vocational Rehab Division, 7967
Franklin Court Assisted Living, 5042
Goodwill Industries of RI, 8623
Greater Providence Arc, 3634
Groden Center, 8624
Horace A Kimball and S Ella Kimball
Foundation, 3635
IN-SIGHT Independent Living, 5043
Kent County Arc, 3636
Newport County Arc, 3637
Newport County Chapter of Retarded
Citizens, 8625
Ocean State Center for Independent Living,
5044
Office of Rehabilitation Services, 8626
PARI Independent Living Center, 5045
Parent Support Network, 7853
Providence Regional Office, 8175
Providence VA Medical Center, 8176
Rhode Island Arc, 3638
Rhode Island Assistive Technology Access
Partnership, 5046
Rhode Island Association of Facilities for the
Aging, 791
Rhode Island Department of State Library
for the Blind and Physically Handicapped,
5538
Rhode Island Employment Services and Job
Training, 8627
Rhode Island Foundation, 3639
Rhode Island Veterans Center, 8177
Shake-A-Leg, 1241
Talking Books Plus, 5539
Westerly Chariho Arc, 3640

## South Carolina

Arc of South Carolina, 3641
Burnt Gin Camp, 1725
Camp Gravatt, 1726
Captioned Media Program, 996
Center for Developmental Disabilities, 3642
Center for Disability Resources, 854
Coastal Disability Access, 5047
Colonial Life and Accident Insurance
Company Contributions Program, 3643
Columbia Disability Action Center, 5048
Columbia Regional Office, 8178
Graham Street Community Resources, 5049
Greenville Disability Action Center, 5050

Medical University of South Carolina
Arthritis Clinical/Research Center, 5540
National Association for Continence, 1204
National Information Center for Health
Related Services, 7847
Pickens County Arc, 3644
Ralph H Johnson VA Medical Center, 8179
SC Independent Living Council, 5051
South Carolina Association of Nonprofit
Homes for the Aging, 793
South Carolina Employment Security
Commission South Carolina Center, 8629
South Carolina Governor's Committee on
Employment of the Handicapped, 8630
South Carolina State Library, 5541
South Carolina Vocational Rehabilitation
Department, 8631
Vocational and Rehabilitation Agency:
Commission for the Blind, 8633
Vocational and Rehabilitation Agency:
Vocational Rehabilitation Department,
8632
William Jennings Bryan Dorn VA Medical
Center, 8180

## South Dakota

Adjustment Training Center, 5052
Black Hills Workshop & Training Center,
5053
Communication Service for the Deaf: Rapid
City, 5055
Communication Service for the Deaf: Sioux
Falls, 999
Communication Service for the Deaf:
Yankton, 5054
Communication Services for the Deaf
(CSD), 5056
Dell Rapids Sportsmens Club, 7934
Native American Advocacy Program for
Perso ns with Disabilities, 5057
Native American Advocacy Project, 5058
NeSoDak Bible Camp/Klein Ranch, 1727
Opportunities for Independent Living, 5059
Prairie Freedom Center for Independent
Living, 5060, 5061, 5062, 5062
Sioux Falls VA Medical Center, 8181
South Dakota Assistive Technology Project,
5063
South Dakota Governor's Advisory
Committee on Employment of the
Disabled, 8634
South Dakota State Library, 5542
South Dakota State Vocational Rehabilitati
on, 8635
South Dakota VA Regional Office, 8182
South Dakota Veterans Centers, 8183
South Dakota Workforce Investment Act
Training Programs, 8636
Teratogen and Birth Defects Information
Project, 7865
USA Deaf Sports Federation, 1055
Vocational and Rehabilitation Agency: Divi
sion of Services to the Blind/Visually
Impaired, 8637
Western Resources for dis-ABLED
Independence, 5064

## Tennessee

Alvin C York VA Medical Center, 8184
American Board of Disability Analysts, 2255
Arc Putnam County, 3645
Arc of Anderson County, 3646
Arc of Davidson County, 3647
Arc of Hamilton County, 3648
Arc of Tennessee, 3649
Arc of Washington County, 3650
Arc of Williamson County, 3651
Benwood Foundation, 3652
Camp Discovery, 1478, 1728
Center for Independent Living of Middle
Tennessee, 5065
Community Foundation of Greater
Chattanooga, 3653
DisAbility Resource Center: Knoxville, 5066
Ear Foundation, 1010
Easter Seals Camp, 1729
Education and Auditory Research
Foundation, 3654
Indian Creek Camp, 1730
Jackson Center for Independent Living,
4821, 5068
Joint Conference with ABMPP Annual
Conference, 2274
Memphis Center for Independent Living,
5069
Memphis VA Medical Center, 8185
Montgomery County Arc, 3655
Mountain Home VA Medical Center, 8186
Nasheville Regional Office, 8187
Nashville Center for Independent Living,
5070
Nashville VA Medical Center, 8188
Stuttering Foundation of America, 7863
Tennessee Association of Homes for the
Aging, 794
Tennessee Department of Labor: Job
Training Program Liaison, 8638
Tennessee Fair Employment Practice
Agency, 8639
Tennessee Library for the Blind and
Physically Handicapped, 5543
Tennessee Technology Access Project
(TTAP), 5071
Tri-State Resource and Advocacy
Corporation, 5072
Winter Conference, 2289

## Texas

ABLE Center for Independent Living, 5073
Abell-Hangar Foundation, 3656
Accessibility Consultants, 2319
Accu-Chem Laboratories, 811
Acid Maltase Deficiency Association
(AMDA), 1113
Albert & Bessie Mae Kronkosky Charitable
Foundation, 3657
Amarillo VA Healthcare System, 8189
Amarillo Vet Center, 8190
American Botanical Council, 822
American Foundation for the Blind:
Southwest, 3658
American Heart Association: National
Center, 1129
American Stroke Association, 1138
Arc of Texas, 3659

Vermont Center for Independent Living: Bennington, 5116
Vermont Center for Independent Living: Brattleboro, 5113, 5114
Vermont Community Foundation, 3705
Vermont Department of Libraries/Special Services Unit, 5555
Vermont Employment Services and Job Training, 8651
Vermont Governor's Committee on Employment of People with Disabilities, 8652
Vermont VA Regional Office Center, 8202
Vermont Veterans Centers, 8203

# Virginia

AAN's Toll-Free Hotline, 7804
ACS Federal Healthcare, 1060
APSE Conference: Revitalizing Supported Employment, Climbing to the Future, 2248
Access Independence, 5117
Adventure Day Camp, 1749
Alexandria Community Y Head Start, 8654
Alexandria Library Talking Book Service, 5556
American Academy of Otolaryngology: Head and Neck Surgery, 982
American Board for Certification in Orthotics & Prosthetics, 1124
American Board of Professional Disability Consultants, 2320
American Chiropractic Association, 824
American Counseling Association, 825
American Diabetes Association Annual Conference, 2257
American Diabetes Summer Camp, 1341, 1750
American Network of Community Options and Resources, 1132
American Physical Therapy Association Annual Conference & Exposition, 2258
American Psychiatric Association, 1075
American Rehabilitation Counseling Association, 2259
Appalachian Independence Center, 5118
Arc of Virginia, 3706
Arlington County Department of Libraries, 5557
Association for Education & Rehabilitation of the Blind & Visually Impaired Intl Conference, 1266, 2263
Association for Persons in Supported Employment, 838
Auditory-Verbal International, 992
Bell, 1155
Bell Atlantic Foundation, 3474, 3707
Better Hearing Institute, 993
Blue Ridge Independent Living Center, 5120
Blue Ridge Independent Living Center - Troutville, 5119
Blue Ridge Independent Living Center: Christianburg, 5121
Blue Ridge Independent Living Center: Low Moor, 5122
Braille Circulating Library for the Blind, 5558
Brain Injury Association of America, 1157
Camp Baker, 1751
Camp Carolina Trails for Children, 1646
Camp Dickenson, 1752

Camp Easter Seal: East/West, 1753
Camp Foundation, 3708
Camp Holiday Trails, 1754
Camp Virginia Jaycee, 1755
Central Rappahannock Regional Library, 5559
Child Neurology Service, 1164
Children and Adolescents with Emotional and Behavioral Disorders, 2268
Civitan Acres, 1756
Clinch Independent Living Services, 5123
Community Foundation of Richmond & Central Virginia, 3709
Council for Exceptional Children, 5560
Council for Exceptional Children Annual Convention and Expo, 2271
Council for Exceptional Children: Teacher Education Division, 1085
Council of Better Business Bureaus Foundation, 800
Didlake, 8655
Disability Resource Center, 4568, 5067, 5124, 5124
Division for Physical and Health Disabilities, 866
ENDependence Center of Northern Virginia, 5125
ERIC Clearinghouse on Disabilities and Special Education, 868
Equal Access Center for Independence, 5126
Federal Funding to Fight AIDS, 3755
Federation of Families for Children's Mental Health, 1179
From the State Capitals: Public Health, 3768
Gannett Foundation, 3710
Greater Lynchburg Community Trust, 3711
Guide to Federal Funding for Child Care and Early Childhood Development, 3769
Guide to Federal Funding for Volunteer Programs & Community Service, 3771
Hampton Subregional Library for the Blind, 5561
Hampton VA Medical Center, 8204
Hunter Holmes McGuire VA Medical Center, 8205
Independence Empowerment Center, 5127
Independence Resource Center, 5128
Independent Living Center Network: Department of the Visually Handicapped, 5129
International Chiropractors Association, 898
James Branch Cabell Library, 5562
John Randolph Foundation, 3712
Journal of Rehabilitation and Annual Conference, 2275
Junction Center for Independent Living, 5130, 5131
Learning Services: Shenandoah, 8656
Loudoun County Special Recreation Programs, 1757
Lynchburg Area Center for Independent Living, 5132
Makemie Woods Camp, 1758
Makemie Woods Camp/Conference Retreat, 1759
NISH, 8657
National Alliance on Mental Illness (NAMI), 1202
National Association of Developmental Disabilities Councils, 916
National Association of State Directors of Developmental Disabilities Services (NASDDDS), 1096
National Captioning Institute, 1031

National Council on Independent Living, 925, 4543, 5133, 5133
National Industries for the Blind, 1312
National Mental Health Association, 935, 1222
National Rehabilitation Association (NRA), 938
National Vaccine Information Center, 941
Newport News Public Library System, 5563
Norfolk Foundation, 3713
Northern Virginia Resource Center for Deaf and Hard of Hearing Persons, 5564
Oakland School & Camp, 1760
Oakland School and Camp, 1761
Okada Specialty Guide Dogs, 1044
Overlook Camp, 1762
Peidmont Independent Living Center, 5134
Peninsula Center for Independent Living, 5135
Prevent Child Abuse of Metropolitan Washington, 7857
RESNA Annual Conference, 2281
Registry of Interpreters for the Deaf, 1045
Rehabiliation Engineering Center for Personal Licensed Transportation, 7961
Resources for Independent Living, 4487, 4766, 4923, 4923, 5136
Richmond Research Training Center, 8658
Roanoke City Public Library System, 5565
Roanoke Regional Office, 8206
Robey W Estes Family Foundation, 3714
Salem VA Medical Center, 8207
ServiceSource, 8659
Sheltered Occupational Center of Virginia, 8660
Special Services/Talking Books, 5566
Staunton Public Library Talking Book Center, 5567
Technology and Media Division, 967
University of Virginia Health System General Clinical Research Group, 5568
Valley Associates for Independent Living (VAIL), 5137
Valley Associates for Independent Living: Lexington, 5138
Virginia Autism Resource Center, 5569
Virginia Beach Foundation, 3715
Virginia Beach Public Library Special Services Library, 5570
Virginia Chapter of the Arthtitis Foundation, 5571
Virginia Department of Veterans Services, 8208
Virginia State Library for the Visually and Physically Handicapped, 5572
Vocational and Rehabilitation Agency, 8251, 8259, 8333, 8333, 8348, 8395, 8402, 8425, 8449, 8470, 8484, 8506, 8511, 8520, 8529, 8533, 8538
Vocational and Rehabilitation Agency: Department for the Blind/Visually Impaired, 8593, 8622, 8628, 8628, 8662
W Alton Jones Foundation, 3716
Woodrow Wilson Rehabilitation Center Training Program, 5139

# Washington

Alliance for People with Disabilities: Seattle, 5140

## West Virginia

## Wisconsin

## Wyoming

LifeQuest: Interdisciplinary Rehabilitation, 5179

Quality Health Care Foundation of Wyoming, 790

Rehabilitation Enterprises of North Easter n Wyoming: Newcastle, 5181

Rehabilitation Enterprises of North Eastern Wyoming: Sheridan, 5180

Sheridan VA Medical Center, 8224

Vocational Rehabilitation, Division of Department of Workforce Services, 8675

Wyoming Department of Employment Unemployment Insurance, 8676

Wyoming Governor's Committee on Employment of the Handicapped, 8677

Wyoming Independent Living Rehabilitation, 5182

Wyoming Institute for Disabilities (WIND), 976

Wyoming Services for Independent Living, 5183

Wyoming Services for the Visually Impaired, 5589

Wyoming Veterans Centers, 8225

Wyoming's New Options in Technology (WYNOT) - University of Wyoming, 5590

## Alternative Therapies

## Amputation

## Amythrophic Lateral Sclerosis

## Art Therapies

## Arthritis

Rheumatoid Arthritis, 7391

Source of Help and Hope Newsletter, 6160

Surgery: Information to Consider, 7397

Thinking About Tomorrow: A Career Guide for Teens with Arthritis, 7405

Thumbs Up Cup, 372

Toward Healthy Living: A Wellness Journal, 6993

Understanding Juvenile Rheumatoid Arthritis, 7002

University of Michigan: Orthopaedic Research Laboratories, 5459

University of Missouri: Columbia Arthritis Center, 5475

Virginia Chapter of the Arthritis Foundation, 5571

When Your Student Has Arthritis: A Guide for Teachers, 7418

## Asthma

AAN's Toll-Free Hotline, 7804

ABC of Asthma, Allergies & Lupus, 6693

ABC's of Latex Allergy, 7246

About Asthma, 7250

Allergies & Asthma At School Kit, 6540

American Academy of Allergy, Asthma and Immunology, 1116

Ask the Doctor: Asthma, 6735

Asthma & Allergy Advocate Newsletter, 6737

Asthma & Allergy Education for Worksite Clinicians, 3050

Asthma & Allergy Essentials for Children's Care Provider, 3051

Asthma & Allergy Medications, 7269

Asthma Action Cards: Child Care Asthma/Allergy Action Card, 2338

Asthma Action Cards: Student Asthma Action Card, 2339

Asthma Alert, 7270

Asthma Care Training for Kids (ACT), 3052

Asthma Challenge, 6738

Asthma Handbook, 7271

Asthma Handbook Slides, 7438

Asthma Lifelines, 7272

Asthma Management, 7439

Asthma Management and Education, 2693

Asthma Resource Directory, 6739

Asthma Sourcebook, 6740

Asthma Triggers, 7440

Asthma and Allergy Answers: A Patient Education Library, 5734

Asthma and Allergy Foundation of America, 1147, 7662

Asthma and Exercise, 6741

Asthma and Pregnancy, 7273

Asthma and the Athlete, 7441

Asthma in the School: Improving Control with Peak Flow Monitoring, 6742

Asthma in the Workplace, 6743

Breathe Easy Young People's Guide to Asthma, 7455

Brigham and Women's Hospital: Asthma and Allergic Disease Research Center, 5435

Bronchial Asthma: Principles of Diagnosis and Treatment, 6776

Camp Vacamas, 1594

Camp Wheeze Away, 1345

Center for Interdisciplinary Research on Immunologic Diseases, 5438

Childhood Asthma, 7284

Childhood Asthma: A Matter of Control, 7285

Children with Asthma: A Manual for Parents, 6479

Controlling Asthma, 6486

Coping with Asthma, 6807

Determined to Win: Children Living with Allergies and Asthma, 5645

Efficacy of Asthma Education, Selected Abstracts, 7303

Exercise-Induced Asthma, 7306

Facts About Asthma, 7310

Free to Breathe, 7504

Helping Others Breathe Easier, 7328

Home Control of Allergies and Asthma, 7332

How to Outsmart Your Allergies, 6026

Inhaled Medications for Asthma, 7341

Johns Hopkins University: Asthma and Allergy Center, 5423

Let's Talk About Having Asthma, 5670

Living Well with Asthma, 6887

Living with Asthma and Allergies Brochure Series, 7351

MA Report, 2642

Many Faces of Asthma, 7358

Meeting-in-a-Box, 2407

Nocturnal Asthma, 7366

Occupational Asthma, 7369

Parent's Guide to Allergies and Asthma, 6514

Peak Flow Meter: A Thermometer for Asthma, 7377

Pharmacologic Therapy of Pediatric Asthma, 7578

Physician Referral and Information Line, 7855

Pollen Calendar, 7380

Power Breathing Program, 2417

Regular Kid, 7584

Standards for the Diagnosis and Care of Patients with Asthma, 7395

Teens Talk to Teens about Asthma, 7402

There are Solutions for the Student with Asthma, 7404

Tips to Remember, 7406

Toll-Free Information Line, 7866

Triggers Management of Asthma, 7408

Understanding Asthma, 7410

Understanding Asthma: The Blueprint for Breathing, 7000

University of Virginia Health System General Clinical Research Group, 5568

What Everyone Needs to Know About Asthma, 7415

What School Personnel Should Know About Asthma, 7632

Your Body's Many Cries for Water, 6190

Your Child and Asthma, 7420

## Attention Deficit Disorder

ADD Challenge: A Practical Guide for Teachers, 2663

ADD, Stepping Out of the Dark, 7423

ADD: Helping Your Child, 6463

ADHD Report, 6606

ADHD in Adults, 7424

ADHD in the Classroom: Strategies for Teachers, 2664

ADHD with Comorbid Disorders: Clinical Assessment and Management, 5617

ADHD: Handbook for Diagnosis & Treatment, 6696

ADHD: What Do We Know?, 7426

ALST: Adolescent Language Screening Test, 2982

ASHA Leader, 6192

About Attention Disorder, 7251

Adapted Physical Education for Students with Autism, 2670

Adventure Learning Center at Eagle Village, 1529

All About Attention Deficit Disorders, Revised, 6706, 7431

American Speech-Language-Hearing Association, 988, 2260, 7806

Around the Clock: Parenting the Delayed AD HD Child, 7436

Attention, 6744

Attention Deficit Disorder, 7442

Attention Deficit Disorder Association, 1149

Attention Deficit Disorder in Adults Workbook, 6746

Attention Deficit Disorder in Children and Adolescents, 2695

Attention Deficit Disorder: A Different Perception, 6747

Attention Deficit Disorder: Adults, 7443

Attention Deficit Disorder: Children, 6467

Attention Deficit Disorders Association, Southern Region: Annual Conference, 2264

Attention Deficit Disorders: Assessment & Teaching, 6541

Attention Deficit Information Network, 1150

Attention-Deficit Hyperactivity Disorder: Symptoms and Suggestons for Treatment, 6748

Attention-Deficit/Hyperactivity Disorder, What Every Parent Wants to Know, 6468

Augmentative Communication Consultants (ACCI), 2321

Braille Book Bank, Music Catalog, 6346

Burnish Me Bright, 5625

Camp Betsey Cox, 1745

Camp Buckskin, 1543

Camp Kaleidoscope, 1584

Camp Northwood, 1612

Camp Ruggles, 1723

Camp World Light, 1421

Casowasco Camp, Conference and Retreat Center, 1618

Chadder, 6782

Children and Adults with Attention Deficit Disorders (CHADD), 1165

Children with ADD: A Shared Responsibility, 2717

Clinical Connection, 2591

Clinical Management of Childhood Stuttering, 2nd Edition, 2722

Clinician's Practical Guide to Attention-Deficit/Hyperactivity Disorder, 6623

Cogrehab, 7288

Communication & Language Acquisition: Discoveries from Atypical Development, 2728

Community Signs, 2355

Comprehensive Assessment of Spoken Language (CASL), 2356

Comprehensive Guide to ADD in Adults: Research, Diagnosis & Treatment, 6798

Concentration Cockpit: Explaining Attention Deficits, 6799

Coping for Kids Who Stutter, 5638

Coping with ADD/ADHD, 6806

Counseling Persons with Communication Disorders and Their Families, 2735

## Autism

## Epilepsy

Aging and Developmental Disability: Current Research, Programming, and Practice, 6607
Camp Candlelight, 1333
Easter Seals Camp Harmon, 1381
Epilepsy Council of Greater Cincinnati, 4201
Epilepsy Foundation, 1175
Epilepsy Foundation for the National Capitol Area, 7825
Epilepsy Foundation of Greater North Texas, 3674
Epilepsy Foundation of Long Island, 3490
Epilepsy Foundation of Southeast Texas, 3675
Epilepsy Foundation of Washington, 5149
Epilepsy Foundation: Central and South Texas, 3676
Epilepsy Society of New York, 3491
EpilepsyUSA, 6830
Father Drumgoole Connelly Summer Camp, 1623
Growing Up with Epilepsy: A Pratical Guide for Parents, 6493
Institute for Basic Research in Developmental Disabilities, 5500
Narcolepsy, 7562
National Epilepsy Library (NEL), 5426
Phantom Lake YMCA Camp, 1775
Twin Lakes Camp, 1467
Vibration Watch/Countdown Timer, 145
When the Brain Goes Wrong, 7636
YMCA Camp Weona, 1645

## Head & Neck Injuries

Annals of Otology, Rhinology and Laryncology, 6617
Cervical Support Pillow, 134
Head Injury Hotline, 7828
Head Injury Rehabilitation: Children, 2799
Health and Rehabilitation Products, 474
IAL News, 6864
Injured Mind, Shattered Dreams: Brian's Survival from a Severe Head Injury, 6871
Jackson Cervipillo, 137
Journal of Head Trauma Rehabilitation, 6646
NeckEase, 139

## Hearing Impairments

ABC Sign with Me, 7023
ADA Hotel Built-In Alerting System, 148
ASSISTECH, 131
Academic Acceptance of ASL, 2585
Academy of Dispensing Audiologists, 977
Academy of Rehabilitative Audiology, 978
Access for All: Integrating Deaf, Hard of Hearing and Hearing Preschoolers, 7428
Access to Independence, 5161
Addison Point Specialized Services, 8477
Adult Bible Lessons for the Deaf, 6193
Advanced Sign Language Vocabulary: A Resource Text for Educators, 2674, 6194
Advocates for Hearing Impaired Youth, 979
Akron Resources, 156
Alexander Graham Bell Association for the Deaf and Hard of Hearing Annual Conference, 980, 2250
Alternatives in Education for the Hearing Impaired (AEHI), 7648
American Academy of Audiology, 7649

American Action Fund for Blind Children and Adults, 1257
American Annals of the Deaf, 6195
American Association of the Deaf-Blind, 984, 1258
American Association of the Deaf-Blind National Conference, 2253
American Council of the Blind Annual Convention, 2256
American Hearing Research Foundation, 985
American Sign Language (ASL): Quick Facts, 6198
American Sign Language Handshape Cards, 2336
American Sign Language Handshape Dictionary, 6199
American Sign Language Phrase Book, 6200
American Sign Language: A Look at Its Structure & Community, 6201
American Society for Deaf Children, 986
American Society of Deaf Social Workers, 987
American Speech-Language and Hearing Association, 7655
Americans with Disabilities Act: Selected Resources for Deaf, 5209
Ameriphone Hearing Assistance Telephone, 158
Amplified Handsets, 159
Amplified Phones, 160
Amplified Portable Phone, 161
Anna's Silent World, 6202
Answerall 100, 162
Approaching Equality, 5210
Arkansas Rehabilitation Research and Training Center for the Deaf and Hard of Hearing, 990
Assessment & Management of Mainstreamed Hearing-Impaired Children, 2685
Association of Late-Deafened Adults, 991
At Home Among Strangers, 6203
Audiology Foundation of America, 7663
Auditech: Audioport Personal Amplifier, 545
Auditech: Personal FM Educational System, 2341
Auditech: Personal PA Value Pack System, 322
Auditory-Verbal International, 992
Auditory-Verbal Therapy for Parents and Professionals, 2342
Aural Habilitation, 2696
Auricle, 6205
Aurora of Central New York, 7809
Basic Course in American Sign Language, 7034, 7447
Basic Course in American Sign Language Package, 2344
Basic Course in Manual Communication, 6207
Basic Vocabulary: ASL for Parents and Children, 6208
Bath and Shower Bench 3301B, 107
Battery Device Adapter, 324
Bed Rails, 301
Beebe Center, 7665
Beginning ASL Video Course, 7448
Beginning Reading and Sign Language, 7449
Belonging, 5622
Ben's Story: A Deaf Child's Right to Sign, 6209
Between Friends, 6210
Bishopswood, 1491

Book of Name Signs, 6211
Bridges Beyond Sound, 6212
Buffalo Independent Living Project, 4942
Bulletin Newsletter, 6213
CHAMP Camp, 1455
CSD Spectrum, 6214
Call Alarm/Switch Delay Unit, 506
Camp Courage, 1544
Camp El Camino Pines, 1364
Camp Emanuel, 1663
Camp Isola Bella, 1407
Camp Mark Seven, 1611
Camp Taloali, 1684
Caption Center, 995
Captioned Media Program, 996
Center on Employment, 997
Central Illinois Center for Independent Living, 4625
Challenge of Educating Together Deaf and Hearing Youth: Making Manistreaming Work, 2710
Changing the Rules, 6216
Chelsea: The Story of a Signal Dog, 6217
Children of a Lesser God, 6218
Children's Classics Videotape Sets, 7465
Choices in Deafness, 6219
Christmas Stories, 7466
Clark-Winchcole Foundation, 3359
Classroom GOAL: Guide for Optimizing Auditory Learning Skills, 2352
Classroom Notetaker: How to Organize a Program Serving Students with Hearing Impairments, 2353
Clerc: The Story of His Early Years, 6220
Closer Look: The English Program at the Model Secondary School for the Deaf, 7212
Cochlear Implant Club International, 998
Cochlear Implants and Children, 6223
Cochlear Implants for Kids, 6224
Cognition, Education and Deafness, 6225
College and Career Programs for the Deaf, 6226
Columbus Speech and Hearing Center, 9634
Come Sign with Us, 6227
Come Sign with Us: Sign Language Activities for Children, 6228
Communicating with Deaf People: An Introduction, 6229
Communication Options for Children Who are Deaf or Hard-of-Hearing, 6230
Communication Service for the Deaf: Sioux Falls, 999
Communique, 6231
Community Rehabilitation Services for Independent Living, 4445
Comprehensive Reference Manual for Signers and Interpreters, 6232
Comprehensive Signed English Dictionary, 6233
Conference of Educational Administrators Serving the Deaf, 1000
Connect, 6234
Conversational Sign Language II, 6236
Coping with the Multi-Handicapped Hearing Impaired: A Practical Approach, 6237
Crutches, 646
Custom Earmolds, 325
DB-Link, 1173
Davis Center, 168
Dayle McIntosh Center for the Disabled, 4455
Deaf Action Center of GNO, 9459

## Lung Disorders

Camp Breathe Easy, 1430
Camp Christmas Seal, 1681
Camp Crosley YMCA, 1457
Camp Glengarra, 1608
Camp Kushtaka American Diabetes Summer Camp, 1344
Camp L-Kee-Ta, 1470
Camp Libbey, 1665
Camp Tall Turf, 1536
Camp Tekoa UMC, 1649
Canonicus Camp, 1724
Chalet Village Health and Rehabilitation Center, 9834
Children's Specialized Hospital, 8872
Coast to Coast Home Medical, 302
Critical Air Medicine, 9085
Glacier View Ranch, 1401
Greenery Rehabilitation Center: Boston, 9510
Guest House of Slidell Sub-Acute and Rehab Center, 9852
Harrington House, 9511
Healthy Breathing, 7325
Heart Disease in Persons with Down Syndrome, 6854
Homelink, 9422
Horizon Rehabilitation Center, 8882
Hospital for Sick Children, 9247
Keeping the Balance, 7540
LA Lions LPDCI Camp Pelican, 1488
Lakeview Subacute Care Center, 9884
Lung Cancer: Making Sense of Diagnosis, Treatment, & Option, 6891
Lung Line Information Service, 7836
MedTrade/Comtrade, FutureShow, 2277
Meridan Medical Center For Subacute Care, 9490
National Jewish Medical & Research Center, 5318
Occupational Asthma: Lung Hazards on the Job, 7370
Pacifica Nursing and Rehab Center, 8716
Pediatric Center at Plymouth Meeting Integrated Health Services, 9694
Rehabilitation Center at Corona Community Hospital, 9166
Respiratory Health Association, 7921
Westpark Rehabilitation Center, 9842
YMCA Camp Ihduhapi, 1557
YMCA Camp Lakewood, 1572

### Mental Health Disorders

Addictive & Mental Disorders Division, 4087
Aging and Rehabilitation II, 2677
Agnes M Lindsay Trust, 3439
Ahmanson Foundation, 3115
Alaska Division of Mental Health and Developmental Disabilities, 3833
American Group Psychotherapy Association, 1072
American Journal of Art Therapy, 6610
American Lung Association, 1131
American Psychiatric Association, 1075
Anchor Houses, 7807
Authoritative Guide to Self- Help Resource in Mental Health, 5911
Beech Brook, 1658
Bell, 1155
Bennington School Summer Program, 1744
Central Louisiana State Hospital Medical and Professional Library, 5410
Cheaha Mental Health, 9001

Children and Adolescents with Emotional and Behavioral Disorders, 2268
Children's Needs Psychological Perspective, 2718
Chilton-Shelby Mental Health Center/ The Mitchell Center, 9003
Colorado Division of Mental Health, 3881
Community Action for Independent Living, 4915
Community Connections, 7815
Community Foundation of Santa Clara County, 3136
Community Support Center, 7816
Complete Mental Health Directory, 2498
Consulting Psychologists Press, 2734
Cornerstone Services, 4627, 7819, 8407
Counseling Psychologist, 2594
Criminal Law Handbook on Psychiatric & Psychological Evidence & Testimony, 5219
Culture and the Restructuring of Community Mental Health, 5738
Delta Center, 9352
Department of Mental Health, Retardation and Hospitals of Rhode Island, 4242
Developmental Disability Services Section, 4183
Dimensions of State Mental Health Policy, 5222
Division of Mental Health and Substance Abuse, 4193
Eating Disorders Sourcebook, 6827
Ecology of Troubled Children, 2760
Emotional Problems of Childhood and Adolescence, 2775
Eugene and Agnes E Meyer Foundation, 3222
Federation of Families for Children's Mental Health, 1179
Florida Department of Mental Health and Rehabilitative Services, 3920
Freedom House, 4953
Georgia Division of Mental Health, Developmental Disabilities & Addictive Diseases, 3935
Giant Food Foundation, 3225
Good Weather or Not, 7512
Greater Lakes Mental Healthcare, 5150
Green Door, 7827, 8358
Handbook of Infant Mental Health, 5655
Handbook of Mental Disorders Among Black Americans, 6010
Handbook on Ethnicity, Aging and Mental Health, 5797
Handbook on Mental Disability Law, 5233
Handbook on Mental Health Policy in the United States, 6013
Handbook on Supported Education for People with Mental Illness, 2798
Hawaii Department of Health, Adult Mental Health Division, 3946
IKRON Institute for Rehabilitative and Psychological Services, 9647
Idaho Mental Health Center, 3960
Illinois Center for Autism, 9368
Illinois Department of Mental Health and Developmental Disabilities, 3966
Independence Crossroads, 4842
Institute of Transpersonal Psychology, 894
International Handbook on Mental Health Policy, 5237
Jazz Man, 5662
Journal of Counseling & Development, 2609

Journal of the American Deafness and Rehabilitation Association, 6277
Judge David L Bazelon Center for Mental Health Law, 1187, 5193
Kentucky Department for Mental Health and Mental Retardation Services, 3996
Key, 6878
Lake County Health Department, 9372
Law Center Newsletter, 5239
Learning Disabilities: A to Z Parent's Complete Guide to Learning Disabilities, 6504
Louis de la Parte Florida Mental Health Institute Research Library, 5339
Louisiana Division of Mental Health, 4008
Louisiana Employment Service and Job Training Program Liaison, 8473
Maine Department of Health and Human Services, 4016
Maine Mental Health Connections, 4754
Managed Mental Healthcare Video, 7554
Maryland Division of Mental Health, 4028
Massachusetts Department of Mental Health, 4035
Mental & Physical Disability Law Digest, 2852
Mental Health Association in Indiana, 8800
Mental Health Association in Pennsylvania, 4231
The Mental Health Center: Northern Human Services, 9582
Mental Health Concepts and Techniques for the Occupational Therapy Assistant, 2853
Mental Health Law News, 5249
Mental Health Law Reporter, 5250
Mental Health Resource Guide, 7360
Mental Health and Mental Illness, 2854
Mental Health in the Workplace: An Employer's & Manager's Guide, 5851
Mentally Ill Individuals, 2855
Michigan Department of Community Health, 4053
Minnesota Mental Health Division, 4068
NAMI Texas, 4288
Napa County Mental Health, 9148
National Alliance on Mental Illness (NAMI), 1202
National Association of School Psychologists, 2520
National Council for Community Behavioral Healthcare, 923, 1210
National Institute of Mental Health: Decade of the Brain, 7364
National Maternal and Child Health Bureau, 934
National Mental Health Association, 935, 1222
National Mental Health Consumers Self-Help Clearinghouse, 1223
National Registry of Community Mental Health Services, 5752
Nebraska Department of Mental Health, 4103
Nevada Department of Mental Health: Neuro Clinic, 4110
New Hampshire Department of Mental Health, 4122
New Jersey Division of Mental Health Services, 4135
New State Office of Mental Health Agency, 4157
New York State Office of Mental Health, 4164
Northern New Hampshire Mental Health and Developmental Services, 9581
Occupational Center of Union County, 8564

## Mental Retardation

## Multiple Disabilities

Rochester Rotary Sunshine Camp, 1639
San Gabriel Valley Family YMCA Camping Ser vices, 1393
Senior Program for Teens and Young Adults with Special Needs, 3062
Shady Oaks Camp, 1449
Shadybrook Learning Center, 1414
Shema V'Ezer, 3063
Sidney R Baer Day Camp, 1569
Starting Points, 7172
Stepping Stones, 1770
Teaching Students with Moderate/Severe Disabilities, Including Autism, 2950
Texas Speech-Language-Hearing Association, 1247
Tik-A-Witha, 1558
Turnkey Computer Systems for the Visually, Physically, and Hearing Impaired, 2053
Upward Bound Camp: Evans Creek, 1691
Variety Club Camp, 1719
Vocational Education for Multihandicapped Youth, 7241
Volasuca Volunteers of America, 1767
Wagon Road Camp, 1643
What Can Baby Hear?: Auditory Tests and In terventions for Infants with Multiple Disabilities, 7631
Wilderness Canoe Base, 1556

## Multiple Sclerosis

Blooming Where You're Planted, 6768
Camp Discovery, 1478, 1728
Coping When a Parent Has Multiple Sclerosis, 5637
Dressing Tips and Clothing Resources for Making Life Easier, 5978
Inside MS, 6872
LiftUp, 410
MSFOCUS Magazine, 6893
Multiple Sclerosis, 6904
Multiple Sclerosis Center of Oregon, 1196
Multiple Sclerosis Foundation, 1197
Multiple Sclerosis National Research Institute, 7697
Multiple Sclerosis and Having A Baby, 6085
Multiple Sclerosis: A Guide for Patients and Their Families, 6508
Multiple Sclerosis: A Guide for the Newly Diagnosed, 6907
National Multiple Sclerosis Society, 1224
Rowan Community, 9788
Understanding Multiple Sclerosis, 7003

## Muscular Dystrophy

Camp Birchwood, 1343
MDA Newsmagazine, 2620
Muscular Dystrophy Association, 1198
Muscular Dystrophy and Other Neuromuscular Diseases, 6909
Summer Camp for Children with Muscular Dystrophy, 1339

## Neurological Impairments

Association for Neurologically Impaired Brain Injured Children, 837
Bancroft NeuroHealth, 9584
Central Coast Neurobehavioral Center OPTIONS, 9076
Child Neurology Service, 1164
Devereux Santa Barbara, 9089

Digest of Neurology and Psychiatry, 2753
National Institute of Neurological Disorders and Stroke, 1219
Seeing Voices: A Journey into the World of the Deaf, 6305

## Orthopedical Disabilities

American Journal of Orthopsychiatry, 6611
Doing Things Together, 7479
Orthotics and Prosthetics Almanac, 6658

## Pain Management

AMI, 296
Acrylic Leg Warmers, 1789
Foot Snugglers, 1793
TRU-Mold Shoes, 1795

## Parkinson Disease

Allen P & Josephine B Green Foundation, 3418
Blazing Toward a Cure Annual Conference, 2265
Exercise Activities for the Elderly, 2782, 7758
National Parkinson Foundation, 1226
PDF Newsletter, 6932
Parkinson's Disease Foundation, 3314, 3530
Parkinsons Report, 6660
Young Onset Parkinson Conference, 2290

## Pediatric Disorders

American Academy of Pediatrics, 817
American SIDS Institute, 7805
Assessment of Children and Youth, 2689
Association for the Care of Children's Health, 1079
Child with Disabling Illness, 2713
Children's Alliance, 858
Children's National Medical Center, 859
Choosing Options and Accommodations for Children, 2720
Cystic Fibrosis: Medical Care, 6626
Disabilities Sourcebook, 5969
Family Voices, 876
Federation for Children with Special Needs, 878
Handbook of Epilepsy, 6849
Inclusive Child Care for Infants and Toddlers: Meeting Individual and Special Needs, 5744
Infant & Toddler Health Sourcebook, 5658
It isn't Fair!: Siblings of Children with Disabilities, 5659
National Center for Education in Maternal and Child Health, 920
National Dissemination Center for Children and Youth with Disabilities (NICHCY), 926
National Early Childhood Technical Assistance Center, 927
National Information Clearinghouse, 932
National Parent Network on Disabilities, 937
Parent to Parent, 948
Parents Helping Parents (PHP), 949
Parents for Residential Reform, 950
Pediatric Early Elementary (PEEX II) Examination, 3016

Pediatric Exam of Educational-PEERAMID Readiness at Middle Childhood, 3017
Pediatric Examination of Educational Readiness, 3018
Pediatric Extended Examination at-PEET Three, 3019
Programs for Children Birth to 2 with Disa abilities, 1636
Ronald McDonald House, 962
Transitioning Exceptional Children and Youth Into the Community, 5762
Universal Pediatric Services, 1109

## Phenylketonuria

PKU for Children: Learning to Measure, 2866
A Teacher's Guide to PKU, 2661

## Physical Disabilities

ABC Union, ACE, ANLV, Vegas Western Cab, 7954
ACPOC News, 5616
ACS Wireless: Advanced Cyber Solutions, 147
ARJO, 97
Abilitations, 7771
Abilities Expo, 2249
Abilities!, 799
Ability Center, 22
Able-Phone 110, 149
Able-Phone 2500, 150
Able-Switch 300, 151
Able-Switch 500, 152
Able-Switch SW-1, 153
AbleNet, 447
Abledata, 7643
Ablewear Aids for Daily Living, 7644
Access America, 7909
Access Design Services: CILs as Experts, 5886
Access Info, 5887
Access Store Products for Barrier Free Environments, 448
Access Travel: Airports, 7897
Access Unlimited, 810, 7646
Access Yosemite National Park, 7910
Access to Sailing, 7722
Accessibility Consultants, 2319
Accessibility Lift, 377
Accessible Journeys, 7929
Achievement Products, 449
Achieving Diversity and Independence, 5889
Act Wheelchair, 690
Action Products, 251
Ad Lib Drop-In Center: Consumer Management, Ownership and Empowerment, 5890
Adapted Physical Activity Quarterly, 2586
Adapted Physical Education National Standards, 7753
Adapted Physical Education and Sport, 2nd Edition, 7754
Adaptive Design Shop, 98
Adaptive Sports Center, 7724
Adaptive Tracks, 5891
Address Book, 611
Adjustable Bath Seat, 99
Adjustable Bed, 132
Adjustable Chair, 226
Adjustable Clear Acrylic Tray, 227
Adjustable Incline Board, 378

## Polio

## Prader-Willi Syndrome

## Rare Disabilities

### Respiratory Disorders

### Severe Disabilites

### Sexual Abuse & Related Conditions

### Sjogren's Syndrome

### Speech Disorders

### Spina Bifida

# The Complete Directory for People with Disabilities

# Available Formats

## Online Database

*The Complete Directory for People with Disabilities* is available in Print and in an Online Database. Subscribers to the Online Database can access their subscription via the Internet and do customized searches that instantly locate needed resources of information. It's never been faster or easier to locate just the right resource. Whether you're searching for a Rehabilitation Center in your area or a particular Assistive Device, the information you need is only a click away with *The Complete Directory for People with Disabilities – Online Database.*

Online Database (annual subscription): $215.00
Online Database & Print Directory combo: $300.00

Visit www.greyhouse.com and explore the subscription site free of charge or call (800) 562-2139 for more information.

---

## Mailing List Information

This directory is available in mailing list form on mailing labels or diskettes. Call (800) 562-2139 to place an order or inquire about counts. There are a number of ways we can segment the database to meet your mailing list requirements.

---

## Licensable Database on Disk

The database of this directory is available on diskette in an ASCII text file, delimited or fixed fielded. Call (800) 562-2139 for more details.

# Call (800) 562-2139 for more information

To preview any of our Directories Risk-Free for 30 days, call (800) 562-2139 or fax to (518) 789-0556

# Sedgwick Press
## Health Directories

### The Complete Learning Disabilities Directory, 2007

*The Complete Learning Disabilities Directory* is the most comprehensive database of Programs, Services, Curriculum Materials, Professional Meetings & Resources, Camps, Newsletters and Support Groups for teachers, students and families concerned with learning disabilities. This information-packed directory includes information about Associations & Organizations, Schools, Colleges & Testing Materials, Government Agencies, Legal Resources and much more. For quick, easy access to information, this directory contains four indexes: Entry Name Index, Subject Index and Geographic Index. With every passing year, the field of learning disabilities attracts more attention and the network of caring, committed and knowledgeable professionals grows every day. This directory is an invaluable research tool for these parents, students and professionals.

*"Due to its wealth and depth of coverage, parents, teachers and others... should find this an invaluable resource." -Booklist*

900 pages; Softcover ISBN 1-59237-122-1, $145.00 ♦ Online Database $195.00 ♦ Online Database & Directory Combo $280.00

### The Complete Directory for People with Chronic Illness, 2005/06

Thousands of hours of research have gone into this completely updated 2005/06 edition – several new chapters have been added along with thousands of new entries and enhancements to existing entries. Plus, each chronic illness chapter has been reviewed by an medical expert in the field. This widely-hailed directory is structured around the 90 most prevalent chronic illnesses – from Asthma to Cancer to Wilson's Disease – and provides a comprehensive overview of the support services and information resources available for people diagnosed with a chronic illness. Each chronic illness has its own chapter and contains a brief description in layman's language, followed by important resources for National & Local Organizations, State Agencies, Newsletters, Books & Periodicals, Libraries & Research Centers, Support Groups & Hotlines, Web Sites and much more. This directory is an important resource for health care professionals, the collections of hospital and health care libraries, as well as an invaluable tool for people with a chronic illness and their support network.

*"A must purchase for all hospital and health care libraries and is strongly recommended for all public library reference departments." –ARBA*

1,200 pages; Softcover ISBN 1-59237-081-0, $165.00 ♦ Online Database $215.00 ♦ Online Database & Directory Combo $300.00

### The Grey House Rare Disorders Directory, 2006/07

This directory is the most comprehensive resource bringing together hard-to-find information on over 700 rare disorders, including rare cancers, muscular and genetic disorders, and more. This 2006/07 contains the most up-to-date information on each disorder. Written in layman's language, by physicians and faculty at Yale University School of Medicine and Yale New Haven Children's Hospital, the information in this directory is presented in a clear, understandable format, with helpful Cross-References running through the text. The Grey House Rare Disorders Directory is divided into five sections: Disorder Descriptions, Associations & Support Groups, Magazines, Journals & Periodicals, Government Agencies and Treatment Centers. Approximately 20 million, or 1 in every 12, Americans is affected with a rare disorder, so this directory serves a surprisingly wide range of the population. The Grey House Rare Disorders Directory will be an invaluable tool for the thousands of families that have been struck with a rare or "orphan" disease, who feel that they have no place to turn and will be a much-used addition to the reference collection of any public or academic library.

800 pages; Softcover ISBN 1-59237-123-X, $165.00

### The Complete Mental Health Directory, 2006/07

This is the most comprehensive resource covering the field of behavioral health, with critical information for both the layman and the mental health professional. For the layman, this directory offers understandable descriptions of 25 Mental Health Disorders as well as detailed information on Associations, Media, Support Groups and Mental Health Facilities. For the professional, *The Complete Mental Health Directory* offers critical and comprehensive information on Managed Care Organizations, Information Systems, Government Agencies and Provider Organizations. This comprehensive volume of needed information will be widely used in any reference collection.

*"... the strength of this directory is that it consolidates widely dispersed information into a single volume." –Booklist*

800 pages; Softcover ISBN 1-59237-124-8, $165.00 ♦ Online Database $215.00 ♦ Online & Directory Combo $300.00

To preview any of our Directories Risk-Free for 30 days, call (800) 562-2139 or fax to (518) 789-0556

## Older Americans Information Directory, 2006/07

Completely updated for 2006/07, this sixth edition has been completely revised and now contains 1,000 new listings, over 8,000 updates to existing listings and over 3,000 brand new e-mail addresses and web sites. You'll find important resources for Older Americans including National, Regional, State & Local Organizations, Government Agencies, Research Centers, Libraries & Information Centers, Legal Resources, Discount Travel Information, Continuing Education Programs, Disability Aids & Assistive Devices, Health, Print Media and Electronic Media. Three indexes: Entry Index, Subject Index and Geographic Index make it easy to find just the right source of information. This comprehensive guide to resources for Older Americans will be a welcome addition to any reference collection.

*"Highly recommended for academic, public, health science and consumer libraries…" –Choice*

1,200 pages; Softcover ISBN 1-59237-136-1, $165.00 ☐ Online Database $215.00 ☐ Online Database & Directory Combo $300.00

## The Complete Directory for Pediatric Disorders, 2007

This important directory provides parents and caregivers with information about Pediatric Conditions, Disorders, Diseases and Disabilities, including Blood Disorders, Bone & Spinal Disorders, Brain Defects & Abnormalities, Chromosomal Disorders, Congenital Heart Defects, Movement Disorders, Neuromuscular Disorders and Pediatric Tumors & Cancers. This carefully written directory offers: understandable Descriptions of 15 major bodily systems; Descriptions of more than 200 Disorders and a Resources Section, detailing National Agencies & Associations, State Associations, Online Services, Libraries & Resource Centers, Research Centers, Support Groups & Hotlines, Camps, Books and Periodicals. This resource will provide immediate access to information crucial to families and caregivers when coping with children's illnesses.

*"Recommended for public and consumer health libraries." –Library Journal*

1,200 pages; Softcover ISBN 1-59237-150-7 $165.00 ☐ Online Database $215.00 ☐ Online Database & Directory Combo $300.00

## The Directory of Drug & Alcohol Residential Rehabilitation Facilities

This brand new directory is the first-ever resource to bring together, all in one place, data on the thousands of drug and alcohol residential rehabilitation facilities in the United States. *The Directory of Drug & Alcohol Residential Rehabilitation Facilities* covers over 1,000 facilities, with detailed contact information for each one, including mailing address, phone and fax numbers, email addresses and web sites, mission statement, type of treatment programs, cost, average length of stay, numbers of residents and counselors, accreditation, insurance plans accepted, type of environment, religious affiliation, education components and much more. It also contains a helpful chapter on General Resources that provides contact information for Associations, Print & Electronic Media, Support Groups and Conferences. Multiple indexes allow the user to pinpoint the facilities that meet very specific criteria. This time-saving tool is what so many counselors, parents and medical professionals have been asking for. *The Directory of Drug & Alcohol Residential Rehabilitation Facilities* will be a helpful tool in locating the right source for treatment for a wide range of individuals. This comprehensive directory will be an important acquisition for all reference collections: public and academic libraries, case managers, social workers, state agencies and many more.

*"This is an excellent, much needed directory that fills an important gap…" –Booklist*

300 pages; Softcover ISBN 1-59237-031-4, $135.00

To preview any of our Directories Risk-Free for 30 days, call (800) 562-2139 or fax to (518) 789-0556

# Sedgwick Press
## Education Directories

## The Comparative Guide to American Elementary & Secondary Schools, 2006

The only guide of its kind, this award winning compilation offers a snapshot profile of every public school district in the United States serving 1,500 or more students – more than 5,900 districts are covered. Organized alphabetically by district within state, each chapter begins with a Statistical Overview of the state. Each district listing includes contact information (name, address, phone number and web site) plus Grades Served, the Numbers of Students and Teachers and the Number of Regular, Special Education, Alternative and Vocational Schools in the district along with statistics on Student/Classroom Teacher Ratios, Drop Out Rates, Ethnicity, the Numbers of Librarians and Guidance Counselors and District Expenditures per student. As an added bonus, *The Comparative Guide to American Elementary and Secondary Schools* provides important ranking tables, both by state and nationally, for each data element. For easy navigation through this wealth of information, this handbook contains a useful City Index that lists all districts that operate schools within a city. These important comparative statistics are necessary for anyone considering relocation or doing comparative research on their own district and would be a perfect acquisition for any public library or school district library.

*"This straightforward guide is an easy way to find general information. Valuable for academic and large public library collections." –ARBA*

2,400 pages; Softcover ISBN 1-59237-137-X, $125.00

## Educators Resource Directory, 2005/06

*Educators Resource Directory* is a comprehensive resource that provides the educational professional with thousands of resources and statistical data for professional development. This directory saves hours of research time by providing immediate access to Associations & Organizations, Conferences & Trade Shows, Educational Research Centers, Employment Opportunities & Teaching Abroad, School Library Services, Scholarships, Financial Resources, Professional Consultants, Computer Software & Testing Resources and much more. Plus, this comprehensive directory also includes a section on Statistics and Rankings with over 100 tables, including statistics on Average Teacher Salaries, SAT/ACT scores, Revenues & Expenditures and more. These important statistics will allow the user to see how their school rates among others, make relocation decisions and so much more. For quick access to information, this directory contains four indexes: Entry & Publisher Index, Geographic Index, a Subject & Grade Index and Web Sites Index. *Educators Resource Directory* will be a well-used addition to the reference collection of any school district, education department or public library.

*"Recommended for all collections that serve elementary and secondary school professionals." –Choice*

1,000 pages; Softcover ISBN 1-59237-080-2, $145.00 ☐ Online Database $195.00 ☐ Online Database & Directory Combo $280.00

To preview any of our Directories Risk-Free for 30 days, call (800) 562-2139 or fax to (518) 789-0556

# Sedgwick Press
## Hospital & Health Plan Directories

## The Comparative Guide to American Hospitals
This brand new title is the first ever resource to compare all of the nation's hospitals by 17 measures of quality in the treatment of heart attack, heart failure and pneumonia. This data is based on the recently announced Hospital Compare, produced by Medicare, and is available in print and in a unique and user-friendly format from Grey House Publishing, along with extra contact information from Grey House's *Directory of Hospital Personnel*. *The Comparative Guide to American Hospitals* provides a snapshot profile of each of the nations 6,000 hospitals. These informative profiles illustrate how the hospital rates in 17 important areas: Heart Attack Care (% who receive Aspirin at Arrival, Aspirin at Discharge, ACE Inhibitor for LVSD, Beta Blocker at Arrival, Beta Blocker at Discharge, Thrombolytic Agent Received, PTCA Received and Adult Smoking Cessation Advice); Heart Failure (% who receive LVF Assessment, ACE Inhibitor for LVSD, Discharge Instructions, Adult Smoking Cessation Advice); and Pneumonia (% who receive Initial Antibiotic Timing, Pneumococcal Vaccination, Oxygenation Assessment, Blood Culture Performed and Adult Smoking Cessation Advice). Each profile includes the raw percentage for that hospital, the state average, the US average and data on the top hospital. For easy access to contact information, each profile includes the hospitals address, phone and fax numbers, email and web addresses, type and accreditation along with 5 top key administrations. These profiles will allow the user to quickly identify the quality of the hospital and have the necessary information at their fingertips to make contact with that hospital. Most importantly, *The Comparative Guide to American Hospitals* provides an easy-to-use Ranking Table for each of the data elements to allow the user to quickly locate the hospitals with the best level of service. This brand new title will be a must for the reference collection at all public, medical and academic libraries.

2,500 pages; Softcover ISBN 1-59237-109-4 $175.00

## The Directory of Hospital Personnel, 2006
*The Directory of Hospital Personnel* is the best resource you can have at your fingertips when researching or marketing a product or service to the hospital market. A "Who's Who" of the hospital universe, this directory puts you in touch with over 150,000 key decision-makers. With 100% verification of data you can rest assured that you will reach the right person with just one call. Every hospital in the U.S. is profiled, listed alphabetically by city within state. Plus, three easy-to-use, cross-referenced indexes put the facts at your fingertips faster and more easily than any other directory: Hospital Name Index, Bed Size Index and Personnel Index. *The Directory of Hospital Personnel* is the only complete source for key hospital decision-makers by name. Whether you want to define or restructure sales territories… locate hospitals with the purchasing power to accept your proposals… keep track of important contacts or colleagues… or find information on which insurance plans are accepted, *The Directory of Hospital Personnel* gives you the information you need – easily, efficiently, effectively and accurately.

*"Recommended for college, university and medical libraries." -ARBA*

2,500 pages; Softcover ISBN 1-59237-107-8 $275.00 ☐ Online Database $545.00 ☐ Online Database & Directory Combo, $650.00

## The Directory of Health Care Group Purchasing Organizations, 2006
This comprehensive directory provides the important data you need to get in touch with over 800 Group Purchasing Organizations. By providing in-depth information on this growing market and its members, *The Directory of Health Care Group Purchasing Organizations* fills a major need for the most accurate and comprehensive information on over 800 GPOs – Mailing Address, Phone & Fax Numbers, E-mail Addresses, Key Contacts, Purchasing Agents, Group Descriptions, Membership Categorization, Standard Vendor Proposal Requirements, Membership Fees & Terms, Expanded Services, Total Member Beds & Outpatient Visits represented and more. Five Indexes provide a number of ways to locate the right GPO: Alphabetical Index, Expanded Services Index, Organization Type Index, Geographic Index and Member Institution Index. With its comprehensive and detailed information on each purchasing organization, *The Directory of Health Care Group Purchasing Organizations* is the go-to source for anyone looking to target this market.

*"The information is clearly arranged and easy to access…recommended for those needing this very specialized information." –ARBA*

1,000 pages; Softcover ISBN 1-59237-0091-8, $325.00 ☐ Online Database, $650.00 ☐ Online Database & Directory Combo, $750.00

To preview any of our Directories Risk-Free for 30 days, call (800) 562-2139 or fax to (518) 789-0556

## The HMO/PPO Directory, 2006

*The HMO/PPO Directory* is a comprehensive source that provides detailed information about Health Maintenance Organizations and Preferred Provider Organizations nationwide. This comprehensive directory details more information about more managed health care organizations than ever before. Over 1,100 HMOs, PPOs and affiliated companies are listed, arranged alphabetically by state. Detailed listings include Key Contact Information, Prescription Drug Benefits, Enrollment, Geographical Areas served, Affiliated Physicians & Hospitals, Federal Qualifications, Status, Year Founded, Managed Care Partners, Employer References, Fees & Payment Information and more. Plus, five years of historical information is included related to Revenues, Net Income, Medical Loss Ratios, Membership Enrollment and Number of Patient Complaints. Five easy-to-use, cross-referenced indexes will put this vast array of information at your fingertips immediately: HMO Index, PPO Index, Other Providers Index, Personnel Index and Enrollment Index. *The HMO/PPO Directory* provides the most comprehensive information on the most companies available on the market place today.

*"Helpful to individuals requesting certain HMO/PPO issues such as co-payment costs, subscription costs and patient complaints. Individuals concerned (or those with questions) about their insurance may find this text to be of use to them."* –ARBA

600 pages; Softcover ISBN 1-59237-100-0, $275.00 ▯ Online Database, $495.00 ▯ Online Database & Directory Combo, $600.00

## The Directory of Independent Ambulatory Care Centers

This first edition of *The Directory of Independent Ambulatory Care Centers* provides access to detailed information that, before now, could only be found scattered in hundreds of different sources. This comprehensive and up-to-date directory pulls together a vast array of contact information for over 7,200 Ambulatory Surgery Centers, Ambulatory General and Urgent Care Clinics, and Diagnostic Imaging Centers that are not affiliated with a hospital or major medical center. Detailed listings include Mailing Address, Phone & Fax Numbers, E-mail and Web Site addresses, Contact Name and Phone Numbers of the Medical Director and other Key Executives and Purchasing Agents, Specialties & Services Offered, Year Founded, Numbers of Employees and Surgeons, Number of Operating Rooms, Number of Cases seen per year, Overnight Options, Contracted Services and much more. Listings are arranged by State, by Center Category and then alphabetically by Organization Name. Two indexes provide quick and easy access to this wealth of information: Entry Name Index and Specialty/Service Index. *The Directory of Independent Ambulatory Care Centers* is a must-have resource for anyone marketing a product or service to this important industry and will be an invaluable tool for those searching for a local care center that will meet their specific needs.

*"Among the numerous hospital directories, no other provides information on independent ambulatory centers. A handy, well-organized resource that would be useful in medical center libraries and public libraries."* –Choice

986 pages; Softcover ISBN 1-930956-90-8, $185.00 ▯ Online Database, $365.00 ▯ Online Database & Directory Combo, $450.00

To preview any of our Directories Risk-Free for 30 days, call (800) 562-2139 or fax to (518) 789-0556

# Mackenzie & Harris
## General Reference Titles

## The Value of a Dollar 1600-1859, The Colonial Era to The Civil War

Following the format of the widely acclaimed, *The Value of a Dollar, 1860-2004*, *The Value of a Dollar 1600-1859, The Colonial Era to The Civil War* records the actual prices of thousands of items that consumers purchased from the Colonial Era to the Civil War. Our editorial department had been flooded with requests from users of our Value of a Dollar for the same type of information, just from an earlier time period. This new volume is just the answer – with pricing data from 1600 to 1859. Arranged into five-year chapters, each 5-year chapter includes a Historical Snapshot, Consumer Expenditures, Investments, Selected Income, Income/Standard Jobs, Food Basket, Standard Prices and Miscellany. There is also a section on Trends. This informative section charts the change in price over time and provides added detail on the reasons prices changed within the time period, including industry developments, changes in consumer attitudes and important historical facts. This fascinating survey will serve a wide range of research needs and will be useful in all high school, public and academic library reference collections.

600 pages; Hardcover ISBN 1-59237-094-2, $135.00

## The Value of a Dollar 1860-2004, Third Edition

A guide to practical economy, *The Value of a Dollar* records the actual prices of thousands of items that consumers purchased from the Civil War to the present, along with facts about investment options and income opportunities. This brand new Third Edition boasts a brand new addition to each five-year chapter, a section on Trends. This informative section charts the change in price over time and provides added detail on the reasons prices changed within the time period, including industry developments, changes in consumer attitudes and important historical facts. Plus, a brand new chapter for 2000-2004 has been added. Each 5-year chapter includes a Historical Snapshot, Consumer Expenditures, Investments, Selected Income, Income/Standard Jobs, Food Basket, Standard Prices and Miscellany. This interesting and useful publication will be widely used in any reference collection.

*"Recommended for high school, college and public libraries." –ARBA*

600 pages; Hardcover ISBN 1-59237-074-8, $135.00

## Working Americans 1880-1999
## Volume I: The Working Class, Volume II: The Middle Class, Volume III: The Upper Class

Each of the volumes in the *Working Americans 1880-1999* series focuses on a particular class of Americans, The Working Class, The Middle Class and The Upper Class over the last 120 years. Chapters in each volume focus on one decade and profile three to five families. Family Profiles include real data on Income & Job Descriptions, Selected Prices of the Times, Annual Income, Annual Budgets, Family Finances, Life at Work, Life at Home, Life in the Community, Working Conditions, Cost of Living, Amusements and much more. Each chapter also contains an Economic Profile with Average Wages of other Professions, a selection of Typical Pricing, Key Events & Inventions, News Profiles, Articles from Local Media and Illustrations. The *Working Americans* series captures the lifestyles of each of the classes from the last twelve decades, covers a vast array of occupations and ethnic backgrounds and travels the entire nation. These interesting and useful compilations of portraits of the American Working, Middle and Upper Classes during the last 120 years will be an important addition to any high school, public or academic library reference collection.

*"These interesting, unique compilations of economic and social facts, figures and graphs will support multiple research needs. They will engage and enlighten patrons in high school, public and academic library collections." –Booklist*

Volume I: The Working Class ☐ 558 pages; Hardcover ISBN 1-891482-81-5, $145.00 ☐ Volume II: The Middle Class ☐ 591 pages; Hardcover ISBN 1-891482-72-6; $145.00 ☐ Volume III: The Upper Class ☐ 567 pages; Hardcover ISBN 1-930956-38-X, $145.00

## Working Americans 1880-1999  Volume IV: Their Children

This Fourth Volume in the highly successful *Working Americans 1880-1999* series focuses on American children, decade by decade from 1880 to 1999. This interesting and useful volume introduces the reader to three children in each decade, one from each of the Working, Middle and Upper classes. Like the first three volumes in the series, the individual profiles are created from interviews, diaries, statistical studies, biographies and news reports. Profiles cover a broad range of ethnic backgrounds, geographic area and lifestyles – everything from an orphan in Memphis in 1882, following the Yellow Fever epidemic of 1878 to an eleven-year-old nephew of a beer baron and owner of the New York Yankees in New York City in 1921. Chapters also contain important supplementary materials including News Features as well as information on everything from Schools to Parks, Infectious Diseases to Childhood Fears along with Entertainment, Family Life and much more to provide an informative overview of the lifestyles of children from each decade. This interesting account of what life was like for Children in the Working, Middle and Upper Classes will be a welcome addition to the reference collection of any high school, public or academic library.

600 pages; Hardcover ISBN 1-930956-35-5, $145.00

To preview any of our Directories Risk-Free for 30 days, call (800) 562-2139 or fax to (518) 789-0556

## Working Americans 1880-2003 Volume V: Americans At War

*Working Americans 1880-2003 Volume V: Americans At War* is divided into 11 chapters, each covering a decade from 1880-2003 and examines the lives of Americans during the time of war, including declared conflicts, one-time military actions, protests, and preparations for war. Each decade includes several personal profiles, whether on the battlefield or on the homefront, that tell the stories of civilians, soldiers, and officers during the decade. The profiles examine: Life at Home; Life at Work; and Life in the Community. Each decade also includes an Economic Profile with statistical comparisons, a Historical Snapshot, News Profiles, local News Articles, and Illustrations that provide a solid historical background to the decade being examined. Profiles range widely not only geographically, but also emotionally, from that of a girl whose leg was torn off in a blast during WWI, to the boredom of being stationed in the Dakotas as the Indian Wars were drawing to a close. As in previous volumes of the *Working Americans* series, information is presented in narrative form, but hard facts and real-life situations back up each story. The basis of the profiles come from diaries, private print books, personal interviews, family histories, estate documents and magazine articles. For easy reference, *Working Americans 1880-2003 Volume V: Americans At War* includes an in-depth Subject Index. The *Working Americans* series has become an important reference for public libraries, academic libraries and high school libraries. This fifth volume will be a welcome addition to all of these types of reference collections.

600 pages; Hardcover ISBN 1-59237-024-1; $145.00
Five Volume Set (Volumes I-V), Hardcover ISBN 1-59237-034-9, $675.00

## Working Americans 1880-2005 Volume VI: Women at Work

Unlike any other volume in the *Working Americans* series, this Sixth Volume, is the first to focus on a particular gender of Americans. *Volume VI: Women at Work*, traces what life was like for working women from the 1860's to the present time. Beginning with the life of a maid in 1890 and a store clerk in 1900 and ending with the life and times of the modern working women, this text captures the struggle, strengths and changing perception of the American woman at work. Each chapter focuses on one decade and profiles three to five women with real data on Income & Job Descriptions, Selected Prices of the Times, Annual Income, Annual Budgets, Family Finances, Life at Work, Life at Home, Life in the Community, Working Conditions, Cost of Living, Amusements and much more. For even broader access to the events, economics and attitude towards women throughout the past 130 years, each chapter is supplemented with News Profiles, Articles from Local Media, Illustrations, Economic Profiles, Typical Pricing, Key Events, Inventions and more. This important volume illustrates what life was like for working women over time and allows the reader to develop an understanding of the changing role of women at work. These interesting and useful compilations of portraits of women at work will be an important addition to any high school, public or academic library reference collection.

600 pages; Hardcover ISBN 1-59237-063-2; $145.00

## Working Americans 1880-2005 Volume VII: Social Movements

The newest addition to the widely-successful *Working Americans* series, *Volume VII: Social Movements* explores how Americans sought and fought for change from the 1880s to the present time. Following the format of previous volumes in the Working Americans series, the text examines the lives of 34 individuals who have worked -- often behind the scenes — to bring about change. Issues include topics as diverse as the Anti-smoking movement of 1901 to efforts by Native Americans to reassert their long lost rights. Along the way, the book will profile individuals brave enough to demand suffrage for Kansas women in 1912 or demand an end to lynching during a March on Washington in 1923. Each profile is enriched with real data on Income & Job Descriptions, Selected Prices of the Times, Annual Incomes & Budgets, Life at Work, Life at Home, Life in the Community, along with News Features, Key Events, and Illustrations. The depth of information contained in each profile allow the user to explore the private, financial and public lives of these subjects, deepening our understanding of how calls for change took place in our society. A must-purchase for the reference collections of high school libraries, public libraries and academic libraries.

600 pages; Hardcover ISBN 1-59237-101-9; $145.00
Seven Volume Set (Volumes I-VII), Hardcover ISBN 1-59237-133-7, $945.00

## The Encyclopedia of Warrior Peoples & Fighting Groups

Many military groups throughout the world have excelled in their craft either by fortuitous circumstances, outstanding leadership, or intense training. This new second edition of The Encyclopedia of Warrior Peoples and Fighting Groups explores the origins and leadership of these outstanding combat forces, chronicles their conquests and accomplishments, examines the circumstances surrounding their decline or disbanding, and assesses their influence on the groups and methods of warfare that followed. This edition has been completely updated with information through 2005 and contains over 20 new entries. Readers will encounter ferocious tribes, charismatic leaders, and daring militias, from ancient times to the present, including Amazons, Buffalo Soldiers, Green Berets, Iron Brigade, Kamikazes, Peoples of the Sea, Polish Winged Hussars, Sacred Band of Thebes, Teutonic Knights, and Texas Rangers. With over 100 alphabetical entries, numerous cross-references and illustrations, a comprehensive bibliography, and index, the Encyclopedia of Warrior Peoples and Fighting Groups is a valuable resource for readers seeking insight into the bold history of distinguished fighting forces.

*"This work is especially useful for high school students, undergraduates, and general readers with an interest in military history." –Library Journal*

Pub. Date: May 2006; Hardcover ISBN 1-59237-116-7; $135.00

**To preview any of our Directories Risk-Free for 30 days, call (800) 562-2139 or fax to (518) 789-0556**

## The Encyclopedia of Invasions & Conquests, From the Ancient Times to the Present

Throughout history, invasions and conquests have played a remarkable role in shaping our world and defining our boundaries, both physically and culturally. This second edition of the popular Encyclopedia of Invasions & Conquests, a comprehensive guide to over 150 invasions, conquests, battles and occupations from ancient times to the present, takes readers on a journey that includes the Roman conquest of Britain, the Portuguese colonization of Brazil, and the Iraqi invasion of Kuwait, to name a few. New articles will explore the late 20th and 21st centuries, with a specific focus on recent conflicts in Afghanistan, Kuwait, Iraq, Yugoslavia, Grenada and Chechnya. Categories of entries include countries, invasions and conquests, and individuals. In addition to covering the military aspects of invasions and conquests, entries cover some of the political, economic, and cultural aspects, for example, the effects of a conquest on the invade country's political and monetary system and in its language and religion. The entries on leaders – among them Sargon, Alexander the Great, William the Conqueror, and Adolf Hitler – deal with the people who sought to gain control, expand power, or exert religious or political influence over others through military means. Revised and updated for this second edition, entries are arranged alphabetically within historical periods. Each chapter provides a map to help readers locate key areas and geographical features, and bibliographical references appear at the end of each entry. Other useful features include cross-references, a cumulative bibliography and a comprehensive subject index. This authoritative, well-organized, lucidly written volume will prove invaluable for a variety of readers, including high school students, military historians, members of the armed forces, history buffs and hobbyists.

*"Engaging writing, sensible organization, nice illustrations, interesting and obscure facts, and useful maps make this book a pleasure to read." –ARBA*

Pub. Date: March 2006; Hardcover ISBN 1-59237-114-0; $135.00

## Encyclopedia of Prisoners of War & Internment

This authoritative second edition provides a valuable overview of the history of prisoners of war and interned civilians, from earliest times to the present. Written by an international team of experts in the field of POW studies, this fascinating and thought-provoking volume includes entries on a wide range of subjects including the Crusades, Plains Indian Warfare, concentration camps, the two world wars, and famous POWs throughout history, as well as atrocities, escapes, and much more. Written in a clear and easily understandable style, this informative reference details over 350 entries, 30% larger than the first edition, that survey the history of prisoners of war and interned civilians from the earliest times to the present, with emphasis on the 19th and 20th centuries. Medical conditions, international law, exchanges of prisoners, organizations working on behalf of POWs, and trials associated with the treatment of captives are just some of the themes explored. Entries range from the Ardeatine Caves Massacre to Kurt Vonnegut. Entries are arranged alphabetically, plus illustrations and maps are provided for easy reference. The text also includes an introduction, bibliography, appendix of selected documents, and end-of-entry reading suggestions. This one-of-a-kind reference will be a helpful addition to the reference collections of all public libraries, high schools, and university libraries and will prove invaluable to historians and military enthusiasts.

*"Thorough and detailed yet accessible to the lay reader. Of special interest to subject specialists and historians; recommended for public and academic libraries." - Library Journal*

Pub. Date: March 2006; Hardcover ISBN 1-59237-120-5; $135.00

## The Religious Right, A Reference Handbook

Timely and unbiased, this third edition updates and expands its examination of the religious right and its influence on our government, citizens, society, and politics. From the fight to outlaw the teaching of Darwin's theory of evolution to the struggle to outlaw abortion, the religious right is continually exerting an influence on public policy. This text explores the influence of religion on legislation and society, while examining the alignment of the religious right with the political right. A historical survey of the movement highlights the shift to "hands-on" approach to politics and the struggle to present a unified front. The coverage offers a critical historical survey of the religious right movement, focusing on its increased involvement in the political arena, attempts to forge coalitions, and notable successes and failures. The text offers complete coverage of biographies of the men and women who have advanced the cause and an up to date chronology illuminate the movement's goals, including their accomplishments and failures. This edition offers an extensive update to all sections along with several brand new entries. Two new sections complement this third edition, a chapter on legal issues and court decisions and a chapter on demographic statistics and electoral patterns. To aid in further research, The Religious Right, offers an entire section of annotated listings of print and non-print resources, as well as of organizations affiliated with the religious right, and those opposing it. Comprehensive in its scope, this work offers easy-to-read, pertinent information for those seeking to understand the religious right and its evolving role in American society. A must for libraries of all sizes, university religion departments, activists, high schools and for those interested in the evolving role of the religious right.

*" Recommended for all public and academic libraries." - Library Journal*

Pub. Date: November 2006; Hardcover ISBN 1-59237-113-2; $135.00

**To preview any of our Directories Risk-Free for 30 days, call (800) 562-2139 or fax to (518) 789-0556**

## From Suffrage to the Senate, An Encyclopedia of American Women in Politics

From Suffrage to the Senate is a comprehensive and valuable compendium of biographies of leading women in U.S. politics, past and present, and an examination of the wide range of women's movements. Up to date through 2006, this dynamically illustrated reference work explores American women's path to political power and social equality from the struggle for the right to vote and the abolition of slavery to the first African American woman in the U.S. Senate and beyond. This new edition includes over 150 new entries and a brand new section on trends and demographics of women in politics. The in-depth coverage also traces the political heritage of the abolition, labor, suffrage, temperance, and reproductive rights movements. The alphabetically arranged entries include biographies of every woman from across the political spectrum who has served in the U.S. House and Senate, along with women in the Judiciary and the U.S. Cabinet and, new to this edition, biographies of activists and political consultants. Bibliographical references follow each entry. For easy reference, a handy chronology is provided detailing 150 years of women's history. This up-to-date reference will be a must-purchase for women's studies departments, high schools and public libraries and will be a handy resource for those researching the key players in women's politics, past and present.

*"An engaging tool that would be useful in high school, public, and academic libraries looking for an overview of the political history of women in the US." –Booklist*

Pub. Date: October 2006; Two Volume Set; Hardcover ISBN 1-59237-117-5; $195.00

## An African Biographical Dictionary

This landmark second edition is the only biographical dictionary to bring together, in one volume, cultural, social and political leaders – both historical and contemporary – of the sub-Saharan region. Over 800 biographical sketches of prominent Africans, as well as foreigners who have affected the continent's history, are featured, 150 more than the previous edition. The wide spectrum of leaders includes religious figures, writers, politicians, scientists, entertainers, sports personalities and more. Access to these fascinating individuals is provided in a user-friendly format. The biographies are arranged alphabetically, cross-referenced and indexed. Entries include the country or countries in which the person was significant and the commonly accepted dates of birth and death. Each biographical sketch is chronologically written; entries for cultural personalities add an evaluation of their work. This information is followed by a selection of references often found in university and public libraries, including autobiographies and principal biographical works. Appendixes list each individual by country and by field of accomplishment – rulers, musicians, explorers, missionaries, businessmen, physicists – nearly thirty categories in all. Another convenient appendix lists heads of state since independence by country. Up-to-date and representative of African societies as a whole, An African Biographical Dictionary provides a wealth of vital information for students of African culture and is an indispensable reference guide for anyone interested in African affairs.

*"An unquestionable convenience to have these concise, informative biographies gathered into one source, indexed, and analyzed by appendixes listing entrants by nation and occupational field." –Wilson Library Bulletin*

Pub. Date: July 2006; Hardcover ISBN 1-59237-112-4; $125.00

## American Environmental Leaders, From Colonial Times to the Present

A comprehensive and diverse award winning collection of biographies of the most important figures in American environmentalism. Few subjects arouse the passions the way the environment does. How will we feed an ever-increasing population and how can that food be made safe for consumption? Who decides how land is developed? How can environmental policies be made fair for everyone, including multiethnic groups, women, children, and the poor? American Environmental Leaders presents more than 350 biographies of men and women who have devoted their lives to studying, debating, and organizing these and other controversial issues over the last 200 years. In addition to the scientists who have analyzed how human actions affect nature, we are introduced to poets, landscape architects, presidents, painters, activists, even sanitation engineers, and others who have forever altered how we think about the environment. The easy to use A–Z format provides instant access to these fascinating individuals, and frequent cross references indicate others with whom individuals worked (and sometimes clashed). End of entry references provide users with a starting point for further research.

*"Highly recommended for high school, academic, and public libraries needing environmental biographical information." –Library Journal/Starred Review*

Two Volume Set; Hardcover ISBN 1-57607-385-8 $175.00

## World Cultural Leaders of the Twentieth Century

An expansive two volume set that covers 450 worldwide cultural icons, World Cultural Leaders of the Twentieth Century includes each person's works, achievements, and professional careers in a thorough essay. Who was the originator of the term "documentary"? Which poet married the daughter of the famed novelist Thomas Mann in order to help her escape Nazi Germany? Which British writer served as an agent in Russia against the Bolsheviks before the 1917 revolution? These and many more questions are answered in this illuminating text. A handy two volume set that makes it easy to look up 450 worldwide cultural icons: novelists, poets, playwrights, painters, sculptors, architects, dancers, choreographers, actors, directors, filmmakers, singers, composers, and musicians. World Cultural Leaders of the Twentieth Century provides entries (many of them illustrated) covering the person's works, achievements, and professional career in a thorough essay and offers interesting facts and statistics. Entries are fully cross-referenced so that readers can learn how various individuals influenced others. A thorough general index completes the coverage.

*"Fills a need for handy, concise information on a wide array of international cultural figures."–ARBA*

Two Volume Set; Hardcover ISBN 1-57607-038-7 $175.00

**To preview any of our Directories Risk-Free for 30 days, call (800) 562-2139 or fax to (518) 789-0556**

## Profiles of America: Facts, Figures & Statistics for Every Populated Place in the United States

*Profiles of America* is the only source that pulls together, in one place, statistical, historical and descriptive information about every place in the United States in an easy-to-use format. This award winning reference set, now in its second edition, compiles statistics and data from over 20 different sources – the latest census information has been included along with more than nine brand new statistical topics. This Four-Volume Set details over 40,000 places, from the biggest metropolis to the smallest unincorporated hamlet, and provides statistical details and information on over 50 different topics including Geography, Climate, Population, Vital Statistics, Economy, Income, Taxes, Education, Housing, Health & Environment, Public Safety, Newspapers, Transportation, Presidential Election Results and Information Contacts or Chambers of Commerce. Profiles are arranged, for ease-of-use, by state and then by county. Each county begins with a County-Wide Overview and is followed by information for each Community in that particular county. The Community Profiles within the county are arranged alphabetically. *Profiles of America* is a virtual snapshot of America at your fingertips and a unique compilation of information that will be widely used in any reference collection.

*A Library Journal Best Reference Book "An outstanding compilation." –Library Journal*

10,000 pages; Four Volume Set; Softcover ISBN 1-891482-80-7, $595.00

## The Comparative Guide to American Suburbs, 2005

*The Comparative Guide to American Suburbs* is a one-stop source for Statistics on the 2,000+ suburban communities surrounding the 50 largest metropolitan areas – their population characteristics, income levels, economy, school system and important data on how they compare to one another. Organized into 50 Metropolitan Area chapters, each chapter contains an overview of the Metropolitan Area, a detailed Map followed by a comprehensive Statistical Profile of each Suburban Community, including Contact Information, Physical Characteristics, Population Characteristics, Income, Economy, Unemployment Rate, Cost of Living, Education, Chambers of Commerce and more. Next, statistical data is sorted into Ranking Tables that rank the suburbs by twenty different criteria, including Population, Per Capita Income, Unemployment Rate, Crime Rate, Cost of Living and more. *The Comparative Guide to American Suburbs* is the best source for locating data on suburbs. Those looking to relocate, as well as those doing preliminary market research, will find this an invaluable timesaving resource.

*"Public and academic libraries will find this compilation useful…The work draws together figures from many sources and will be especially helpful for job relocation decisions." – Booklist*

1,700 pages; Softcover ISBN 1-59237-004-7, $130.00

## Weather America, A Thirty-Year Summary of Statistical Weather Data and Rankings

This valuable resource provides extensive climatological data for over 4,000 National and Cooperative Weather Stations throughout the United States. *Weather America* begins with a new Major Storms section that details major storm events of the nation and a National Rankings section that details rankings for several data elements, such as Maximum Temperature and Precipitation. The main body of *Weather America* is organized into 50 state sections. Each section provides a Data Table on each Weather Station, organized alphabetically, that provides statistics on Maximum and Minimum Temperatures, Precipitation, Snowfall, Extreme Temperatures, Foggy Days, Humidity and more. State sections contain two brand new features in this edition – a City Index and a narrative Description of the climatic conditions of the state. Each section also includes a revised Map of the State that includes not only weather stations, but cities and towns.

*"Best Reference Book of the Year." –Library Journal*

2,013 pages; Softcover ISBN 1-891482-29-7, $175.00

## The Asian Databook: Statistics for all US Counties & Cities with Over 10,000 Population

This is the first-ever resource that compiles statistics and rankings on the US Asian population. *The Asian Databook* presents over 20 statistical data points for each city and county, arranged alphabetically by state, then alphabetically by place name. Data reported for each place includes Population, Languages Spoken at Home, Foreign-Born, Educational Attainment, Income Figures, Poverty Status, Homeownership, Home Values & Rent, and more. Next, in the Rankings Section, the top 75 places are listed for each data element. These easy-to-access ranking tables allow the user to quickly determine trends and population characteristics. This kind of comparative data can not be found elsewhere, in print or on the web, in a format that's as easy-to-use or more concise. A useful resource for those searching for demographics data, career search and relocation information and also for market research. With data ranging from Ancestry to Education, *The Asian Databook* presents a useful compilation of information that will be a much-needed resource in the reference collection of any public or academic library along with the marketing collection of any company whose primary focus in on the Asian population.

1,000 pages; Softcover ISBN 1-59237-044-6 $150.00

To preview any of our Directories Risk-Free for 30 days, call (800) 562-2139 or fax to (518) 789-0556

## The Hispanic Databook: Statistics for all US Counties & Cities with Over 10,000 Population

Previously published by Toucan Valley Publications, this second edition has been completely updated with figures from the latest census and has been broadly expanded to include dozens of new data elements and a brand new Rankings section. The Hispanic population in the United States has increased over 42% in the last 10 years and accounts for 12.5% of the total US population. For ease-of-use, *The Hispanic Databook* presents over 20 statistical data points for each city and county, arranged alphabetically by state, then alphabetically by place name. Data reported for each place includes Population, Languages Spoken at Home, Foreign-Born, Educational Attainment, Income Figures, Poverty Status, Homeownership, Home Values & Rent, and more. Next, in the Rankings Section, the top 75 places are listed for each data element. These easy-to-access ranking tables allow the user to quickly determine trends and population characteristics. This kind of comparative data can not be found elsewhere, in print or on the web, in a format that's as easy-to-use or more concise. A useful resource for those searching for demographics data, career search and relocation information and also for market research. With data ranging from Ancestry to Education, *The Hispanic Databook* presents a useful compilation of information that will be a much-needed resource in the reference collection of any public or academic library along with the marketing collection of any company whose primary focus in on the Hispanic population.

*"This accurate, clearly presented volume of selected Hispanic demographics is recommended for large public libraries and research collections."-Library Journal*

1,000 pages; Softcover ISBN 1-59237-008-X, $150.00

## Ancestry in America: A Comparative Guide to Over 200 Ethnic Backgrounds

This brand new reference work pulls together thousands of comparative statistics on the Ethnic Backgrounds of all populated places in the United States with populations over 10,000. Never before has this kind of information been reported in a single volume. Section One, Statistics by Place, is made up of a list of over 200 ancestry and race categories arranged alphabetically by each of the 5,000 different places with populations over 10,000. The population number of the ancestry group in that city or town is provided along with the percent that group represents of the total population. This informative city-by-city section allows the user to quickly and easily explore the ethnic makeup of all major population bases in the United States. Section Two, Comparative Rankings, contains three tables for each ethnicity and race. In the first table, the top 150 populated places are ranked by population number for that particular ancestry group, regardless of population. In the second table, the top 150 populated places are ranked by the percent of the total population for that ancestry group. In the third table, those top 150 populated places with 10,000 population are ranked by population number for each ancestry group. These easy-to-navigate tables allow users to see ancestry population patterns and make city-by-city comparisons as well. Plus, as an added bonus with the purchase of *Ancestry in America*, a free companion CD-ROM is available that lists statistics and rankings for all of the 35,000 populated places in the United States. This brand new, information-packed resource will serve a wide-range or research requests for demographics, population characteristics, relocation information and much more. *Ancestry in America: A Comparative Guide to Over 200 Ethnic Backgrounds* will be an important acquisition to all reference collections.

*"This compilation will serve a wide range of research requests for population characteristics … it offers much more detail than other sources." —Booklist*

1,500 pages; Softcover ISBN 1-59237-029-2, $225.00

## The American Tally: Statistics & Comparative Rankings for U.S. Cities with Populations over 10,000

This important statistical handbook compiles, all in one place, comparative statistics on all U.S. cities and towns with a 10,000+ population. *The American Tally* provides statistical details on over 4,000 cities and towns and profiles how they compare with one another in Population Characteristics, Education, Language & Immigration, Income & Employment and Housing. Each section begins with an alphabetical listing of cities by state, allowing for quick access to both the statistics and relative rankings of any city. Next, the highest and lowest cities are listed in each statistic. These important, informative lists provide quick reference to which cities are at both extremes of the spectrum for each statistic. Unlike any other reference, *The American Tally* provides quick, easy access to comparative statistics – a must-have for any reference collection.

*"A solid library reference." –Bookwatch*

500 pages; Softcover ISBN 1-930956-29-0, $125.00

**To preview any of our Directories Risk-Free for 30 days, call (800) 562-2139 or fax to (518) 789-0556**

## The Grey House Handbook on Alternative Energy, 2006

This is the first ever resource to pull together information, resources and statistics for all types of Alternative Energy, including Hydro, Wind, Solar, Coal, Natural Gas and Atomic Energy sources. The Handbook begins with an informative Introduction to Alternative Energy Resources, including editorial on the history of energy, the necessity of using alternative energy, conservation and the economics of using alternative energy sources. Plus, handy charts are also included that cover uses of energy sources today; forecasts of energy sources and the availability of energy sources in the future. Next, readers will find chapters on each Type of Energy Source. Chapters begin with an Introduction to the specific energy source, History, Strengths & Drawbacks, Industrial & Residential Use and Trends. Several articles are also included for each energy source, followed by Resources, including Associations, Magazines, Trade Shows and Vendors. The Grey House Handbook on Alternative Energy also contains a informative, useful section on Statistics. These charts allow for easy location of very specific data. A handy Glossary and section on Public Energy Companies is also included for easy reference. Three indexes, Product Index, Subject Index and Entry Name Index allow the user to locate specific resources quickly and easily. As the need for alternative energy sources continues to grow, having access to these resources will become more and more important. This first edition will prove useful to the reference collections public and academic libraries.

800 pages; Softcover ISBN 1-59237-134-5; $165.00

## The Environmental Resource Handbook, 2005/06

*The Environmental Resource Handbook* is the most up-to-date and comprehensive source for Environmental Resources and Statistics. Section I: Resources provides detailed contact information for thousands of information sources, including Associations & Organizations, Awards & Honors, Conferences, Foundations & Grants, Environmental Health, Government Agencies, National Parks & Wildlife Refuges, Publications, Research Centers, Educational Programs, Green Product Catalogs, Consultants and much more. Section II: Statistics, provides statistics and rankings on hundreds of important topics, including Children's Environmental Index, Municipal Finances, Toxic Chemicals, Recycling, Climate, Air & Water Quality and more. This kind of up-to-date environmental data, all in one place, is not available anywhere else on the market place today. This vast compilation of resources and statistics is a must-have for all public and academic libraries as well as any organization with a primary focus on the environment.

> *"...the intrinsic value of the information make it worth consideration by libraries with environmental collections and environmentally concerned users."* –Booklist

1,000 pages; Softcover ISBN 1-59237-090-X, $155.00 ☐ Online Database $300.00

To preview any of our Directories Risk-Free for 30 days, call (800) 562-2139 or fax to (518) 789-0556

# Grey House Publishing
## Business Directories

## The Rauch Guide to the US Adhesives & Sealants, Cosmetics & Toiletries, Ink, Paint, Plastics, Pulp & Paper and Rubber Industries

*The Rauch Guides* are known worldwide for their comprehensive marketing information. Acquired by Grey House Publishing in 2005, new updated and revised editions will be published throughout 2005 and 2006. Each Guide provides market facts and figures in a highly organized format, ideal for today's busy personnel, serving as ready-references for top executives as well as the industry newcomer. *The Rauch Guides* save time and money by organizing widely scattered information and providing estimates for important business decisions, some of which are available nowhere else. Each Guide is organized into several information-packed chapters. After a brief introduction, the ECONOMICS section provides data on industry shipments; long-term growth and forecasts; prices; company performance; employment, expenditures, and productivity; transportation and geographical patterns; packaging; foreign trade; and government regulations. Next, TECHNOLOGY & RAW MATERIALS provide market, technical, and raw material information for chemicals, equipment and related materials, including market size and leading suppliers, prices, end uses, and trends. PRODUCTS & MARKETS provide information for each major industry product, including market size and historical trends, leading suppliers, five-year forecasts, industry structure, and major end uses. For easy access, each *Guide* contains a chapter on INDUSTRY ACTIVITIES, ORGANIZATIONS & SOURCES OF INFORMATION with detailed information on meetings, exhibits, and trade shows, sources of statistical information, trade associations, technical and professional societies, and trade and technical periodicals. Next, the COMPANY DIRECTORY profiles major industry companies, both public and private. Generally several hundred companies are analyzed. Information includes complete contact information, web address, estimated total and domestic sales, product description, and recent mergers and acquisitions. Each Guide also contains several APPENDICES that provide a cross-reference of suppliers, subsidiaries and divisions. The Rauch Guides will prove to be an invaluable source of market information, company data, trends and forecasts that anyone in these fast-paced industries.

The Rauch Guide to the U.S. Paint Industry Softcover ISBN 1-59237-127-2 $595 □ The Rauch Guide to the U.S. Plastics Industry Softcover ISBN 1-59237-128-0 $595 □ The Rauch Guide to the U.S. Adhesives and Sealants Industry Softcover ISBN 1-59237-129-9 $595 □ The Rauch Guide to the U.S. Ink Industry Softcover ISBN 1-59237-126-4 $595 □ The Rauch Guide to the U.S. Rubber Industry Softcover ISBN 1-59237-130-2 $595 □ The Rauch Guide to the U.S. Pulp and Paper Industry Softcover ISBN 1-59237-131-0 $595 □ The Rauch Guide to the U.S. Cosmetic and Toiletries Industry Softcover ISBN 1-59237-132-9 $895

## The Directory of Business Information Resources, 2007

With 100% verification, over 1,000 new listings and more than 12,000 updates, this 2007 edition of *The Directory of Business Information Resources* is the most up-to-date source for contacts in over 98 business areas – from advertising and agriculture to utilities and wholesalers. This carefully researched volume details: the Associations representing each industry; the Newsletters that keep members current; the Magazines and Journals - with their "Special Issues" - that are important to the trade, the Conventions that are "must attends," Databases, Directories and Industry Web Sites that provide access to must-have marketing resources. Includes contact names, phone & fax numbers, web sites and e-mail addresses. This one-volume resource is a gold mine of information and would be a welcome addition to any reference collection.

*"This is a most useful and easy-to-use addition to any researcher's library."* –The Information Professionals Institute

2,500 pages; Softcover ISBN 1-59237-146-9, $195.00 □ Online Database $495.00

## Nations of the World, 2006 A Political, Economic and Business Handbook

This completely revised edition covers all the nations of the world in an easy-to-use, single volume. Each nation is profiled in a single chapter that includes Key Facts, Political & Economic Issues, a Country Profile and Business Information. In this fast-changing world, it is extremely important to make sure that the most up-to-date information is included in your reference collection. This edition is just the answer. Each of the 200+ country chapters have been carefully reviewed by a political expert to make sure that the text reflects the most current information on Politics, Travel Advisories, Economics and more. You'll find such vital information as a Country Map, Population Characteristics, Inflation, Agricultural Production, Foreign Debt, Political History, Foreign Policy, Regional Insecurity, Economics, Trade & Tourism, Historical Profile, Political Systems, Ethnicity, Languages, Media, Climate, Hotels, Chambers of Commerce, Banking, Travel Information and more. Five Regional Chapters follow the main text and include a Regional Map, an Introductory Article, Key Indicators and Currencies for the Region. As an added bonus, an all-inclusive CD-ROM is available as a companion to the printed text. Noted for its sophisticated, up-to-date and reliable compilation of political, economic and business information, this brand new edition will be an important acquisition to any public, academic or special library reference collection.

*"A useful addition to both general reference collections and business collections."* –RUSQ

1,700 pages; Print Version Only Softcover ISBN 1-59237-0079-9, $155.00

## To preview any of our Directories Risk-Free for 30 days, call (800) 562-2139 or fax to (518) 789-0556

## The Directory of Venture Capital & Private Equity Firms, 2006

This edition has been extensively updated and broadly expanded to offer direct access to over 2,800 Domestic and International Venture Capital Firms, including address, phone & fax numbers, e-mail addresses and web sites for both primary and branch locations. Entries include details on the firm's Mission Statement, Industry Group Preferences, Geographic Preferences, Average and Minimum Investments and Investment Criteria. You'll also find details that are available nowhere else, including the Firm's Portfolio Companies and extensive information on each of the firm's Managing Partners, such as Education, Professional Background and Directorships held, along with the Partner's E-mail Address. *The Directory of Venture Capital & Private Equity Firms* offers five important indexes: Geographic Index, Executive Name Index, Portfolio Company Index, Industry Preference Index and College & University Index. With its comprehensive coverage and detailed, extensive information on each company, *The Directory of Venture Capital & Private Equity Firms* is an important addition to any finance collection.

*"The sheer number of listings, the descriptive information provided and the outstanding indexing make this directory a better value than its principal competitor, Pratt's Guide to Venture Capital Sources. Recommended for business collections in large public, academic and business libraries." –Choice*

1,300 pages; Softcover ISBN 1-59237-102-7, $450.00 ▢ Online Database (includes a free copy of the directory) $889.00

## The Directory of Mail Order Catalogs, 2006

Published since 1981, this updated edition features 100% verification of data and is the premier source of information on the mail order catalog industry. Details over 12,000 consumer catalog companies with 44 different product chapters from Animals to Toys & Games. Contains detailed contact information including e-mail addresses and web sites along with important business details such as employee size, years in business, sales volume, catalog size, number of catalogs mailed and more. Four indexes provide quick access to information: Catalog & Company Name Index, Geographic Index, Product Index and Web Sites Index.

*"This is a godsend for those looking for information." –Reference Book Review*

1,700 pages; Softcover ISBN 1-59237-103-5 $250.00 ▢ Online Database (includes a free copy of the directory) $495.00

## The Directory of Business to Business Catalogs, 2006

The completely updated *Directory of Business to Business Catalogs*, provides details on over 6,000 suppliers of everything from computers to laboratory supplies… office products to office design… marketing resources to safety equipment… landscaping to maintenance suppliers… building construction and much more. Detailed entries offer mailing address, phone & fax numbers, e-mail addresses, web sites, key contacts, sales volume, employee size, catalog printing information and more. Jut about every kind of product a business needs in its day-to-day operations is covered in this carefully-researched volume. Three indexes are provided for at-a-glance access to information: Catalog & Company Name Index, Geographic Index and Web Sites Index.

*"An excellent choice for libraries… wishing to supplement their business supplier resources." –Booklist*

800 pages; Softcover ISBN 1-59237-105-1, $165.00 ▢ Online Database (includes a free copy of the directory) $325.00

## Sports Market Place Directory, 2006

For over 20 years, this comprehensive, up-to-date directory has offered direct access to the Who, What, When & Where of the Sports Industry. With over 20,000 updates and enhancements, the *Sports Market Place Directory* is the most detailed, comprehensive and current sports business reference source available. In 1,800 information-packed pages, *Sports Market Place Directory* profiles contact information and key executives for: Single Sport Organizations, Professional Leagues, Multi-Sport Organizations, Disabled Sports, High School & Youth Sports, Military Sports, Olympic Organizations, Media, Sponsors, Sponsorship & Marketing Event Agencies, Event & Meeting Calendars, Professional Services, College Sports, Manufacturers & Retailers, Facilities and much more. *The Sports Market Place Directory* provides organization's contact information with detailed descriptions including: Key Contacts, physical, mailing, email and web addresses plus phone and fax numbers. Plus, nine important indexes make sure that you can find the information you're looking for quickly and easily: Entry Index, Single Sport Index, Media Index, Sponsor Index, Agency Index, Manufacturers Index, Brand Name Index, Facilities Index and Executive/Geographic Index. For over twenty years, *The Sports Market Place Directory* has assisted thousands of individuals in their pursuit of a career in the sports industry. Why not use "THE SOURCE" that top recruiters, headhunters and career placement centers use to find information on or about sports organizations and key hiring contacts.

1,800 pages; Softcover ISBN 1-59237-139-6, $225.00 ▢ Online Database $479.00

**To preview any of our Directories Risk-Free for 30 days, call (800) 562-2139 or fax to (518) 789-0556**

## Thomas Food and Beverage Market Place, 2006

*Thomas Food and Beverage Market Place* is bigger and better than ever with thousands of new companies, thousands of updates to existing companies and two revised and enhanced product category indexes. This comprehensive directory profiles over 18,000 Food & Beverage Manufacturers, 12,000 Equipment & Supply Companies, 2,200 Transportation & Warehouse Companies, 2,000 Brokers & Wholesalers, 8,000 Importers & Exporters, 900 Industry Resources and hundreds of Mail Order Catalogs. Listings include detailed Contact Information, Sales Volumes, Key Contacts, Brand & Product Information, Packaging Details and much more. *Thomas Food and Beverage Market Place* is available as a three-volume printed set, a subscription-based Online Database via the Internet, on CD-ROM, as well as mailing lists and a licensable database.

> *"An essential purchase for those in the food industry but will also be useful in public libraries where needed. Much of the information will be difficult and time consuming to locate without this handy three-volume ready-reference source."* –ARBA

8,500 pages, 3 Volume Set; Softcover ISBN 1-59237-096-9, $495.00 ◆ CD-ROM $695.00 ◆
CD-ROM & 3 Volume Set Combo $895.00 ◆ Online Database $695.00 ◆ Online Database & 3 Volume Set Combo, $895.00

## The Grey House Homeland Security Directory, 2006

This updated edition features the latest contact information for government and private organizations involved with Homeland Security along with the latest product information and provides detailed profiles of nearly 1,000 Federal & State Organizations & Agencies and over 3,000 Officials and Key Executives involved with Homeland Security. These listings are incredibly detailed and include Mailing Address, Phone & Fax Numbers, Email Addresses & Web Sites, a complete Description of the Agency and a complete list of the Officials and Key Executives associated with the Agency. Next, *The Grey House Homeland Security Directory* provides the go-to source for Homeland Security Products & Services. This section features over 2,000 Companies that provide Consulting, Products or Services. With this Buyer's Guide at their fingertips, users can locate suppliers of everything from Training Materials to Access Controls, from Perimeter Security to BioTerrorism Countermeasures and everything in between – complete with contact information and product descriptions. A handy Product Locator Index is provided to quickly and easily locate suppliers of a particular product. Lastly, an Information Resources Section provides immediate access to contact information for hundreds of Associations, Newsletters, Magazines, Trade Shows, Databases and Directories that focus on Homeland Security. This comprehensive, information-packed resource will be a welcome tool for any company or agency that is in need of Homeland Security information and will be a necessary acquisition for the reference collection of all public libraries and large school districts.

> *"Compiles this information in one place and is discerning in content. A useful purchase for public and academic libraries."* –Booklist

800 pages; Softcover ISBN 1-59237-084-5, $195.00 ◆ Online Database (includes a free copy of the directory) $385.00

## The Grey House Transportation Security Directory & Handbook

This brand new title is the only reference of its kind that brings together current data on Transportation Security. With information on everything from Regulatory Authorities to Security Equipment, this top-flight database brings together the relevant information necessary for creating and maintaining a security plan for a wide range of transportation facilities. With this current, comprehensive directory at the ready you'll have immediate access to: Regulatory Authorities & Legislation; Information Resources; Sample Security Plans & Checklists; Contact Data for Major Airports, Seaports, Railroads, Trucking Companies and Oil Pipelines; Security Service Providers; Recommended Equipment & Product Information and more. Using the *Grey House Transportation Security Directory & Handbook*, managers will be able to quickly and easily assess their current security plans; develop contacts to create and maintain new security procedures; and source the products and services necessary to adequately maintain a secure environment. This valuable resource is a must for all Security Managers at Airports, Seaports, Railroads, Trucking Companies and Oil Pipelines.

800 pages; Softcover ISBN 1-59237-075-6, $195

**To preview any of our Directories Risk-Free for 30 days, call (800) 562-2139 or fax to (518) 789-0556**

## The Grey House Safety & Security Directory, 2006

*The Grey House Safety & Security Directory* is the most comprehensive reference tool and buyer's guide for the safety and security industry. Arranged by safety topic, each chapter begins with OSHA regulations for the topic, followed by Training Articles written by top professionals in the field and Self-Inspection Checklists. Next, each topic contains Buyer's Guide sections that feature related products and services. Topics include Administration, Insurance, Loss Control & Consulting, Protective Equipment & Apparel, Noise & Vibration, Facilities Monitoring & Maintenance, Employee Health Maintenance & Ergonomics, Retail Food Services, Machine Guards, Process Guidelines & Tool Handling, Ordinary Materials Handling, Hazardous Materials Handling, Workplace Preparation & Maintenance, Electrical Lighting & Safety, Fire & Rescue and Security. The Buyer's Guide sections are carefully indexed within each topic area to ensure that you can find the supplies needed to meet OSHA's regulations. Six important indexes make finding information and product manufacturers quick and easy: Geographical Index of Manufacturers and Distributors, Company Profile Index, Brand Name Index, Product Index, Index of Web Sites and Index of Advertisers. This comprehensive, up-to-date reference will provide every tool necessary to make sure a business is in compliance with OSHA regulations and locate the products and services needed to meet those regulations.

*"Presents industrial safety information for engineers, plant managers, risk managers, and construction site supervisors..." –Choice*

1,500 pages, 2 Volume Set; Softcover ISBN 1-59237-104-3, $225.00

## The Grey House Biometric Information Directory, 2006

*The Biometric Information Directory* is the only comprehensive source for current biometric industry information. This 2006 edition is the first published by Grey House. With 100% updated information, this latest edition offers a complete, current look, in both print and online form, of biometric companies and products – one of the fastest growing industries in today's economy. Detailed profiles of manufacturers of the latest biometric technology, including Finger, Voice, Face, Hand, Signature, Iris, Vein and Palm Identification systems. Data on the companies include key executives, company size and a detailed, indexed description of their product line. Plus, the Directory also includes valuable business resources, and current editorial make this edition the easiest way for the business community and consumers alike to access the largest, most current compilation of biometric industry information available on the market today. The new edition boasts increased numbers of companies, contact names and company data, with over 700 manufacturers and service providers. Information in the directory includes: Editorial on Advancements in Biometrics; Profiles of 700+ companies listed with contact information; Organizations, Trade & Educational Associations, Publications, Conferences, Trade Shows and Expositions Worldwide; Web Site Index; Biometric & Vendors Services Index by Types of Biometrics; and a Glossary of Biometric Terms. This resource will be an important source for anyone who is considering the use of a biometric product, investing in the development of biometric technology, support existing marketing and sales efforts and will be an important acquisition for the business reference collection for large public and business libraries.

800 pages; Softcover ISBN 1-59237-121-3, $225

## The Grey House Performing Arts Directory, 2007

*The Grey House Performing Arts Directory* is the most comprehensive resource covering the Performing Arts. This important directory provides current information on over 8,500 Dance Companies, Instrumental Music Programs, Opera Companies, Choral Groups, Theater Companies, Performing Arts Series and Performing Arts Facilities. Plus, this edition now contains a brand new section on Artist Management Groups. In addition to mailing address, phone & fax numbers, e-mail addresses and web sites, dozens of other fields of available information include mission statement, key contacts, facilities, seating capacity, season, attendance and more. This directory also provides an important Information Resources section that covers hundreds of Performing Arts Associations, Magazines, Newsletters, Trade Shows, Directories, Databases and Industry Web Sites. Five indexes provide immediate access to this wealth of information: Entry Name, Executive Name, Performance Facilities, Geographic and Information Resources. *The Grey House Performing Arts Directory* pulls together thousands of Performing Arts Organizations, Facilities and Information Resources into an easy-to-use source – this kind of comprehensiveness and extensive detail is not available in any resource on the market place today.

*"Immensely useful and user-friendly ... recommended for public, academic and certain special library reference collections." –Booklist*

1,500 pages; Softcover ISBN 1-59237-138-8, $185.00 ◆ Online Database $335.00

To preview any of our Directories Risk-Free for 30 days, call (800) 562-2139 or fax to (518) 789-0556

## New York State Directory, 2006/07

*The New York State Directory*, published annually since 1983, is a comprehensive and easy-to-use guide to accessing public officials and private sector organizations and individuals who influence public policy in the state of New York. *The New York State Directory* includes important information on all New York state legislators and congressional representatives, including biographies and key committee assignments. It also includes staff rosters for all branches of New York state government and for federal agencies and departments that impact the state policy process. Following the state government section are 25 chapters covering policy areas from agriculture through veterans' affairs. Each chapter identifies the state, local and federal agencies and officials that formulate or implement policy. In addition, each chapter contains a roster of private sector experts and advocates who influence the policy process. The directory also offers appendices that include statewide party officials; chambers of commerce; lobbying organizations; public and private universities and colleges; television, radio and print media; and local government agencies and officials.

New York State Directory - 800 pages; Softcover ISBN 1-59237-145-0; $145.00
New York State Directory with Profiles of New York – 2 volumes; 1,600 pages; Softcover ISBN 1-59237-162-0; $225

## Research Services Directory: Commercial & Corporate Research Centers

This Ninth Edition provides access to well over 8,000 independent Commercial Research Firms, Corporate Research Centers and Laboratories offering contract services for hands-on, basic or applied research. *Research Services Directory* covers the thousands of types of research companies, including Biotechnology & Pharmaceutical Developers, Consumer Product Research, Defense Contractors, Electronics & Software Engineers, Think Tanks, Forensic Investigators, Independent Commercial Laboratories, Information Brokers, Market & Survey Research Companies, Medical Diagnostic Facilities, Product Research & Development Firms and more. Each entry provides the company's name, mailing address, phone & fax numbers, key contacts, web site, e-mail address, as well as a company description and research and technical fields served. Four indexes provide immediate access to this wealth of information: Research Firms Index, Geographic Index, Personnel Name Index and Subject Index.

*"An important source for organizations in need of information about laboratories, individuals and other facilities."* –ARBA

1,400 pages; Softcover ISBN 1-59237-003-9, $395.00 ▯ Online Database (includes a free copy of the directory) $850.00

## International Business and Trade Directories

Completely updated, the Third Edition of *International Business and Trade Directories* now contains more than 10,000 entries, over 2,000 more than the last edition, making this directory the most comprehensive resource of the worlds business and trade directories. Entries include content descriptions, price, publisher's name and address, web site and e-mail addresses, phone and fax numbers and editorial staff. Organized by industry group, and then by region, this resource puts over 10,000 industry-specific business and trade directories at the reader's fingertips. Three indexes are included for quick access to information: Geographic Index, Publisher Index and Title Index. Public, college and corporate libraries, as well as individuals and corporations seeking critical market information will want to add this directory to their marketing collection.

*"Reasonably priced for a work of this type, this directory should appeal to larger academic, public and corporate libraries with an international focus."* –Library Journal

1,800 pages; Softcover ISBN 1-930956-63-0, $225.00 ▯ Online Database (includes a free copy of the directory) $450.00

**To preview any of our Directories Risk-Free for 30 days, call (800) 562-2139 or fax to (518) 789-0556**